NEW CATHOLIC ENCYCLOPEDIA

An International Work of Reference on the Teachings, History, Organization, and Activities of the Catholic Church, and on All Institutions, Religions, Philosophies, and Scientific and Cultural Developments Affecting the Catholic Church from Its Beginning to the Present.

Prepared by an Editorial Staff at The Catholic University of America, Washington, District of Columbia.

McGRAW-HILL BOOK COMPANY NEW YORK ST LOUIS

Volume I

A to Azt

NEW CATHOLIC ENCYCLOPEDIA

SAN FRANCISCO TORONTO LONDON SYDNEY

Nihil Obstat:
John P. Whalen, M.A., S.T.D.
Censor Deputatus

Imprimatur:
✠ Patrick A. O'Boyle, D.D.
Archbishop of Washington
August 5, 1966

NEW CATHOLIC ENCYCLOPEDIA

Library of Congress Catalog Card Number: 66-22292

Pope Paul VI.

To His Holiness

Pope Paul VI

EDITORIAL STAFF, 1962 TO 1966

EDITOR IN CHIEF

MOST REV. WILLIAM J. MC DONALD, D.D., Ph.D., LL.D., *Rector, The Catholic University of America, Washington, D.C.; Auxiliary Bishop of Washington, D.C.; Chairman ex officio, NCE Executive Committee.*

ASSOCIATE EDITOR IN CHIEF

RT. REV. JAMES A. MAGNER, S.T.D., Ph.D., *Vice Rector for Business and Finance and Assistant Treasurer, The Catholic University of America, Washington, D.C.; Director, The Catholic University of America Press; member, NCE Executive Committee.*

SENIOR EDITOR

MARTIN R. P. MC GUIRE, Ph.D., L.H.D., *Professor of Greek and Latin and of Ancient History, The Catholic University of America, Washington, D.C.; Associate Editor, "Catholic Historical Review"; Chairman, Executive Committee of "Medieval and Renaissance Latin Translations and Commentaries"; member, NCE Executive Committee.*

MANAGING EDITOR

REV. JOHN P. WHALEN, M.A., S.T.D., *Associate Professor of Theology, School of Sacred Theology, The Catholic University of America, Washington, D.C.; Executive Secretary, NCE Executive Committee.*

STAFF EDITORS

DOGMATIC THEOLOGY

Editor: Earl A. Weis, SJ, M.A., Ph.L., S.T.D., Professor of Dogmatic Theology, Bellarmine School of Theology, North Aurora, Ill.

MORAL THEOLOGY

Editor: Paul K. Meagher, OP, S.T.L., S.T.M., Blackfriars, Cambridge, England; Coeditor in Chief, McGraw-Hill translation of St. Thomas Aquinas's *Summa theologiae.*

Assistant Editor: John Fearon, OP, S.T.Lr., S.T.L., S.T. Praes., Assistant Professor of Theology, Seattle University, Seattle, Wash.

LITURGY

Editor: John H. Miller, CSC, Ph.B., S.T.D., Associate Professor of Theology, University of Notre Dame, Notre Dame, Ind.; member, Board of Directors, North American Liturgical Conference.

SACRED SCRIPTURE

Editor: Louis F. Hartman, CSSR, S.S.L., Ling.Orient. Lic., Professor of Semitic Languages and Literatures, The Catholic University of America, Washington, D.C.; Executive Secretary, Catholic Biblical Association of America; Chairman, Editorial Board for the CCD Version of the Old Testament.

Assistant Editors: Joseph E. Fallon, OP, S.T.L., S.T.Lr., S.S.L., Professor of Scripture, Dominican House of Studies, Washington, D.C.

Joseph N. Jensen, OSB, S.T.L., Professor of Sacred Scripture, St. Anselm's Abbey, Washington, D.C.; Instructor in Sacred Scripture, Department of Religious Education, The Catholic University of America, Washington, D.C.

Charles H. Pickar, OSA, S.T.L., S.S.L., Assistant General, Generalate of the Augustinian Friars, Rome, Italy.

Robert G. Vincent, OMI, S.T.L., S.S.L., Professor of Sacred Scripture, Oblate College, Washington, D.C.

NON-CHRISTIAN RELIGIONS

Editor: Martin R. P. McGuire, Ph.D., L.H.D.

PHILOSOPHY AND PSYCHOLOGY

Editor: William A. Wallace, OP, B.E.E., M.Sc., S.T.L., Ph.D., S.T.D., S.T.Praes., Professor of Philosophy, St. Stephen's College, Dover, Mass.; Associate Editor, *The Thomist;* Director, Institute of Interdisciplinary Studies of the St. Thomas Aquinas Foundation.

Assistant Editor: James A. Weisheipl, OP, Ph.Lic., S.T.Lr., Ph.D., D.Phil. (Oxon.), Associate Professor of History of Medieval Science, Pontifical Institute of Mediaeval Studies, Toronto, Canada; Director, Leonine Commission, American Section.

EARLY CHURCH AND BYZANTINE HISTORY

Editor: Francis X. Murphy, CSSR, Ph.D., Professor of Patristic Moral Theology, Accademia Alfonsiana, Rome, Italy.

Assistant Editor: George A. Maloney, SJ, B.A., Ph.L., S.T.L., S.E.O.D., Scriptor, John XXIII Center for Oriental Studies, and Professor of Oriental Theology, Fordham University, New York, N.Y.

MEDIEVAL CHURCH HISTORY

Editor: Owen J. Blum, OFM, Ph.D., Professor of History, Quincy College, Quincy, Ill.

Associate Editor: Mary Jane Hamilton, Ph.D., Assistant Professor of History, Sacramento State College, Sacramento, Calif.

Assistant Editor: Sister Consuelo Maria Aherne, SSJ, Ph.D., Professor of History and Chairman of the Department, Chestnut Hill College, Philadelphia, Pa.

brarian, Marygrove College, Detroit, Mich.; Associate Editor, *The Pope Speaks;* President, Catholic Library Association.

STYLE

Editor: Sister Mary Francis Slattery, SC, Ph.D., Assistant Professor of English, College of Mt. St. Vincent-on-Hudson, New York, N.Y.
Assistant Editor: Barbara Foye, B.A.

LIBRARY CONSULTANT

Eugene P. Willging, A.B., A.B. in L.S., LL.D., Director of Libraries, The Catholic University of America, Washington, D.C. (deceased Sept. 20, 1965).

OFFICE MANAGER

Thomas R. Pollins, B.S.

ADMINISTRATIVE ASSISTANTS

Mary Alice Anderson, B.A.; Catherine Clarkson; Margaret C. Ready, LL.B.

EDITORIAL ASSISTANTS

Staff Assistants: Ellen Dale Carter, B.A.; Robert V. Devine, B.A., M.A.; Edward Foye, B.A., M.A.; Lucille Jimenez; Janet Marie Kearns, A.B.; William McCarthy, A.B., LL.B.; Mary Catherine McGarraghy, B.A.; Agnes McPadden, A.B., M.S.S.W.; Matthew Mullaney, B.A., LL.B.; Carroll McKelligott Shurney, B.A.; Joan Cunningham Zomberg, B.A.
Art and Illustrations: Naomi Vincent Butler, B.A.; Alice Ford, B.A., M.A.; Jean Hildreth, B.A.; Michael Iampieri, B.A.; Charles Kelly.

RESEARCH BIBLIOGRAPHERS

Norman Berube, S.T.B., M.A.; Barbara Dickinson, A.B.; Anthony Doherty, A.B.; Joan Domer, B.A.; Carolyn Drum, M.S.L.S.; Edward Heiss, A.B.; Livia Jansco, M.S.L.S.; Betty Kitsa, B.A.; Lawrence Moore, M.S.L.S.; Elizabeth Rowe, M.S.L.S.; William Rowe, B.A.; Sister Cora Maria Sakamoto, MM, M.S.L.S.

INDEXERS

Associates: Mary Hart, M.S.L.S.; Peter W. Hart, M.S.L.S.; Rachel M. Johnson, A.B.; Clara-Louise Kuehn, M.S.L.S.
Assistants: R. Gerard Callahan, B.A.; Mary Feldman, M.S.L.S.; Marjorie Fitzgibbon, A.B.; Dolores Larson, B.A.; Susanne Manovill; Marjorie Nash, A.B.; Elizabeth B. Zach, B.A.
Index Editorial Assistants: Alice Crozier, M.A.; Muriel Hass, A.B.L.S., M.A.; Joseph Placek, M.A., M.S.L.S.

Of the many devoted secretaries, typists, and clerks who assisted the editors, the following deserve special mention: Cecilia S. Balzer, Eleanor G. Brooke, Goldie I. Chaney, Kathleen H. Cox, Mary Elizabeth Cummings, Doreen M. Curties, Lillian Thomas Dent, Mary J. Donoghue, Patricia C. Elliott, Helen Fukasawa, Dorothy V. Giller, Jane G. Gilroy, Ruth Grayner, Annette M. Jensen, Jane Kenny, Elizabeth F. Malloy, Elaine H. Manss, Floridalma Mazariegos, Virginia Ozag, and Sheila Spillane.

McGraw-Hill Staff

Executive Editor

David I. Eggenberger

Director of Design and Production

Gerard G. Mayer

Assistant Art Director

David Ross-Robertson

Art Editor

Carl Vansag

Editing Managers

Margaret Lamb

William J. Redding

Catherine Yacker Winter

Assistant Editors

Richard H. Rosswurm

Paula A. Werk

Paul G. Zomberg

Foreword

The *Catholic Encyclopedia,* to which the present work acknowledges its lineage, issued its first volume in 1907, under the direction of a distinguished editorial board, representing the best in American scholarship and international collaboration. "As its name implies," the Preface stated, the *Encyclopedia* "proposes to give its readers full and authoritative information on the entire cycle of Catholic interests, action, and doctrine." The fifteenth, and last, volume of text was published in 1912, with an index volume following 2 years later.

From the outset, the work was hailed internationally as a major achievement of scholarship. It was immediately recognized and employed as an accurate and authoritative source of information on all matters pertaining to the history, teachings, and activities of the Catholic Church from its foundation to the early years of the 20th century. Yet it was inevitable that the great work should become inadequate. In view of the profound changes that have taken place in the world in general and in the life and work of the Church in particular, even the revisions undertaken in the form of *Supplements* could not keep the old work up to date. An entirely new work was badly needed. The purpose of the *NEW CATHOLIC ENCYCLOPEDIA* is to meet this need.

It would not be possible here to describe in detail the most interesting history of the project, although that history is important and should be published. However, a few salient matters may be mentioned. In 1958, Cardinal Samuel Stritch, Archbishop of Chicago, presented the project of a new encyclopedia for consideration by the Board of Trustees of The Catholic University of America. His proposal was received with enthusiasm. The Trustees subsequently approved plans for editing the new encyclopedia under the auspices of The Catholic University of America. Through the special offices of Cardinal Francis Spellman, Archbishop of New York, the University was able to acquire ownership of the existing sets and *Supplements* of the *Catholic Encyclopedia* owned by the Gilmary Society and full rights to use the original name. In the meantime, the McGraw-Hill Book Company, in a contact made with Eugene P. Willging, Director of The Catholic University of America Libraries, had expressed a willingness to publish a new Catholic encyclopedia. After negotiation, a contract was drawn up whereby the University assumed responsibility for the preparation of the *NEW CATHOLIC ENCYCLOPEDIA,* and the McGraw-Hill Book Company, the responsibility for the publication and distribution of the work, including the editorial and production costs. It was specified that the University would have full control of content.

The Trustees of the University approved the appointment of the Right Reverend Monsignor, later Most Reverend, William J. McDonald, Rector of the University, as editor in chief, and the establishment of an Editorial Committee. Subsequently they approved the appointment of an Executive Editorial Committee and a number of consultants. Much work remained to be done after these appointments were made. It became clear by early 1962 that a greatly expanded staff of editors, working on a full-time schedule, was necessary; and a thorough reorganization of the editorial work and personnel was completed by the end of September. The editing of the *NEW CATHOLIC ENCYCLOPEDIA* was finished 4 years later, at the beginning of September 1966.

While the *NEW CATHOLIC ENCYCLOPEDIA* has been prepared under the auspices of The Catholic University of America, and with the authorization of its Trustees, it should not be thought of as an exclusive Catholic University project in any sense. The majority of the staff editors were not members of the University faculty, but were released temporarily, and at great sacrifice, by their religious communities or dioceses, to engage in a work that was regarded by their superiors and ordinaries as of prime importance for the Church throughout the country.

It gives me special pleasure to state that the *NEW CATHOLIC ENCYCLOPEDIA*, thanks to careful planning and the competence of its dedicated editorial staff, not only maintains the high standard of the *Catholic Encyclopedia* but also exhibits many significant features of its own. It is considerably broader in scope than its title would suggest. Accordingly, it contains a large number of articles on literature, the arts, and the sciences, as well as on ecclesiastical disciplines and subjects. The treatment in these articles reflects a Catholic sense of values but is not partisan in tone. In keeping with the spirit of *aggiornamento* inaugurated by Pope John XXIII and continued so conspicuously by his successor, Pope Paul VI, the *NEW CATHOLIC ENCYCLOPEDIA* is ecumenical in its coverage, outlook, and approach. The Orthodox Churches, the various branches of Protestantism, Judaism, Islam, and all other religions have been treated at length and throughout with accuracy and understanding.

While emphasizing the Church, its life, and its history in the United States and in the English-speaking world in general, the *NEW CATHOLIC ENCYCLOPEDIA* is also international in scope. The Church in Latin America, for example, receives a much fuller treatment than it has received in any other religious encyclopedia. Some 4,800 individual contributors from all parts of the world have written articles with an authority that can come only from firsthand knowledge of subjects and regions. In regard to contributors, furthermore, it is a pleasure to note that numerous Jewish and other non-Catholic scholars have contributed articles in fields in which they are specialists. The value of the *NEW CATHOLIC ENCYCLOPEDIA* as an authoritative work of reference is further enhanced by some 7,500 illustrations, numerous maps, and an extensive and clearly arranged index.

The *NEW CATHOLIC ENCYCLOPEDIA,* in short, is a comprehensive, scholarly, authoritative, and readable work of reference dealing with every aspect of the Church, its teachings, its institutions, and its activities throughout the world. Above all, the Church is not treated in isolation, but always in relation to its whole environment.

As Archbishop of the jurisdiction and Chancellor of the University in which this great work has come to fruition, I wish to join with the editors in grateful appreciation to all who have shared in its preparation—the contributors, the consultants, the Press for many courtesies, the publishers, and the Most Reverend Hierarchy of the United States for their constant encouragement and support. It is our earnest hope that the encyclopedia's acceptance as a standard source of reference will justify the dedicated effort that has brought it into being.

Patrick A. O'Boyle
Archbishop of Washington
Chancellor, The Catholic University of America

Preface

The *NEW CATHOLIC ENCYCLOPEDIA* proposes to meet the need for an authoritative work of reference for the English-speaking world. It is not a revision of the *Catholic Encyclopedia* (1907-14), but a completely new work, abreast of the present state of knowledge and reflecting the outlook and interests of the second half of the 20th century.

SCOPE. In addition to providing full information on the doctrine, organization, and history of the Catholic Church through the close of Vatican Council II, the *ENCYCLOPEDIA* includes also within its scope the persons, institutions, religions, philosophies, scientific developments, and movements that have affected Catholicism in the past or are of particular concern at present. Accordingly, attention is given to Protestantism, Judaism, Islam, Buddhism, and other religions, as well as to the history of religion in general, worship as a universal phenomenon, mythology, comparative religion, and related subjects.

There is a total of about 17,000 separate articles in the *ENCYCLOPEDIA,* written by some 4,800 scholars, each qualified in his field. Nearly all the articles in the *ENCYCLOPEDIA* include a select bibliography of authoritative works for further reference. Every article appears over the name of its author. Full identification of a contributor, including his full name, name in religion, position, and titles of all his articles, may be found in the list of contributors (volume 15). These scholars are men and women, Catholic and non-Catholic, from all parts of the world.

SCRIPTURE, THEOLOGY, PATROLOGY, LITURGY. The advances made in Biblical scholarship are reflected in the up-to-date treatment of Sacred Scripture and its problems. Modern theological positions have been given full attention, without, however, neglecting the long history of theological development in the Church. The great advances in patrology during the preceding half century have been dealt with in detail. Liturgy is covered historically and descriptively and is given special emphasis in view of the contemporary reforms consequent upon the decisions of Vatican Council II.

CHURCH HISTORY, CANON AND CIVIL LAW. The history of the Church is presented in all its aspects and against the background of general political and cultural history. Comprehensive articles cover the Church history of each country in the world, as well as major periods and movements that cut across national boundaries, such as the Middle Ages, the Reformation, and the Enlightenment. The archdioceses of the world have separate articles. The Church in Latin America has been given a more extensive treatment than is to be found in any other religious encyclopedia. The Church in the United States receives even fuller coverage, with each state, archdiocese, and diocese treated in a separate article. Byzantine Church history also is given extensive treatment. Cities of importance in ecclesiastical history, significant monasteries and abbeys, and religious orders and congregations are given separate articles. The history of missionary efforts, both Catholic and Protestant, receives special attention, and a discussion of modern mission work and its problems is included. In the field of Canon Law, emphasis is placed on its historical development, and care has been taken to incorporate all new legislation. Particular attention has been given to civil law as it affects the Church; and the relations of Church and State have been dealt with fully and concretely. Legal questions related to Catholic education also are treated comprehensively.

PHILOSOPHY, PSYCHOLOGY, PSYCHIATRY. While Thomism and other scholastic systems receive full attention, all schools of ancient, medieval, modern, and contemporary philosophy are given detailed consideration. An attempt is made to treat systematically philosophy as it relates to philosophical and theological positions generally held within Catholicism. In addition, the thought and writings of all major and many lesser philosophers are examined in historical and biographical articles. The many branches of psychology and psychiatry, of increasing importance in the second half of the 20th century, likewise are given the full attention they deserve.

BIOGRAPHY. As a matter of policy, biographies of living persons, with the exception of the reigning Pope, have been excluded from the *ENCYCLOPEDIA;* however, the work of living persons is discussed in pertinent articles. The subjects of separate biographical articles were selected because of their significance for the Church. They include: Old and New Testament figures; the Fathers of the Church and ancient ecclesiastical writers; pagan and early Christian rulers; ancient pagan philosophers; heretics; leaders in the Reformation and Counter Reformation; medieval and modern kings, emperors, and other heads of state; popes; notable archbishops, bishops, priests, and religious; and theologians, philosophers, scholars, scientists, creative writers, composers, musicologists, painters, sculptors, and architects.

SOCIAL SCIENCES. The revolutionary progress made in the social sciences since 1900 is reflected in articles devoted to the fields of anthropology, economics, and sociology. Emphasis is placed on the important contributions made by Catholics in the fields of social welfare and social legislation. Particular attention is given to the development of Catholic charities, child welfare, and care of the sick. The teachings of the papal encyclicals that are applicable to the social sciences are dealt with systematically. The development of Catholic Action and the growth of the role of the laity in the work of the Church also receive thorough coverage.

LITERATURE. The *ENCYCLOPEDIA* does not confine itself strictly to Catholic literature or to Catholic writers but deals with literature on a universal basis from a Catholic point of view, while using literary standards of judgment and evaluation. Special attention has been given to the development of the Catholic press throughout the world and to other communications media, particularly radio, television, and motion pictures. Their application to Catholic education and missionary activity also has been considered.

EDUCATION. The development of education in the United States is covered systematically, and each Catholic college and university in the United States has been assigned a separate article. Education for the professions under Catholic auspices also is examined. The history of education from ancient times to the present receives close attention. Separate articles have been included on European universities that were founded under Catholic auspices. Educational psychology and many other aspects of educational theory, practice, and methodology also are treated.

PHYSICAL AND BIOLOGICAL SCIENCES. Science has achieved greater triumphs in the 20th century than ever before in history. Therefore, every effort has been made to indicate the present state of knowledge in the physical and biological sciences. In the articles on physics and its branches, on chemistry and its branches, on the biological sciences, and on medicine and the medical sciences, the scope and significance of each science in relation to Christian life are examined.

ART, MUSIC. Because of the importance of music and art in the liturgy of the Church, they have received comprehensive coverage from historical and descriptive points of view. The mutual influence of secular and ecclesiastical art, architecture, and music, as well as their relation to the liturgy, has been traced in detail.

ARRANGEMENT. The articles of the *ENCYCLOPEDIA* are arranged alphabetically by the first solid word; thus "New Zealand" precedes "Newman, John Henry," and "Old Testament Literature" precedes "Oldcastle, Sir John." In a series of articles with the same heading, the order is: persons, places, and things. Further details on this system of alphabetization may be found in volume 15.

MAPS, CHARTS, ILLUSTRATIONS. The *ENCYCLOPEDIA* contains more than 300 maps covering the geographical spread and organization of the Church; they furnish information on aspects of cultural history of direct concern to the Church. With few exceptions, these maps are newly drawn. Where useful, charts have been employed to enable the reader to visualize more clearly data that is difficult to present in words alone. The illustrations, totaling more than 7,500, are primarily functional in character. Emphasis has been placed on authentic pictorial representations of persons, historical buildings, and aspects of religious life in general.

ABBREVIATIONS. Abbreviations, like other matters of style in the *ENCYCLOPEDIA,* generally conform to conventions given in standard guides, e.g., *Webster's New International Dictionary* (2d edition) and *A Manual of Style* (Chicago 1949). The books of the Bible are abbreviated as in the Confraternity of Christian Doctrine (CCD) Version, except for Habacuc, which is designated Hab (not Hb). In Biblical citations, the chapter number is separated from the verse number by a period, e.g., Gn 3.4–11. The system of abbreviations used for the works of Plato, Aristotle, St. Augustine, and St. Thomas Aquinas is as follows: Plato is cited by book and Stephanus number only, e.g., *Phaedo* 79B; *Rep.* 480A. Aristotle is cited by book and Bekker number only, e.g., *Anal. post.* 72b 8–12; *Anim.* 430a 18. St. Augustine is cited as in the *Thesaurus Linguae Latinae,* e.g., *C. acad.* 3.20.45; *Conf.* 13.38.53; *Trin.* 15.28.51, but with capitalization of the first letter of the title. St. Thomas Aquinas is cited as in scholarly journals, but using Arabic numerals throughout, e.g., ST 1a2ae, 90.1 ad 2; *C. gent.* 3.21; *In Boeth. de Trin.* 5.2 ad 6; *In 2 phys.* 3.2. For ancient Latin authors, pagan and Christian, the abbreviations employed follow those in the *Thesaurus Linguae Latinae,* Index (1958); for Greek pagan authors, those in H. G. Liddell and R. Scott, comps., *A Greek-English Lexicon,* rev. H. S. Jones and R. McKenzie (9th ed. Oxford 1940); for Greek patristic authors, those in G. W. H. Lampe, *Patristic Greek Lexicon* (Oxford 1961–). For Canon Law, the *Codex Iuris Canonici* is abbreviated CIC, and the canons are cited as follows: CIC cc.1240.1n4; 1241 (i.e., canon 1240.1, n.4, and canon 1241). The system of abbreviations used for numerous other reference works and periodical publications will help make identification reasonably easy for the nonspecialist. A complete list of these abbreviations (sigla) and their full titles may be found in volume 15.

TRANSLITERATION. Throughout the *ENCYCLOPEDIA,* Greek words are printed in Porson type or transliterated according to the system used in the *Catholic Biblical Quarterly.* Words in Hebrew, Sanskrit, Russian, and other languages not using the Roman alphabet are printed in transliterated form. For Hebrew, transliteration again follows the practice of the *Catholic Biblical Quarterly.* For other languages, the Library of Congress transliteration system is used.

SPECIAL FEATURES. For a number of subjects, composite articles have been planned to provide a more thorough and systematic treatment than would otherwise have been possible. For example, under the general heading "Bible," the many subjects pertaining to the Bible are covered in numerous subdivisions, each written by a specialist. For the convenience and guidance of the reader, there are also brief articles outlining the scope of major fields: "Philosophy, Articles on," "Theology, Articles on," "Science, Articles on," etc.

The cross-reference system in the *ENCYCLOPEDIA* serves to direct the reader to related material in other articles. Cross references within an article are of two kinds. An asterisk before the name of a person or subject (e.g., Richard *Hooker) indicates that there is an article of that title. A *see* reference has the same function (e.g., *see* HOOKER, RICHARD). When a further aspect of the subject is treated under another title, a *see also* reference is placed at the end of the article. In addition to the cross-reference system, the analytical index of about 350,000 entries will greatly increase the reader's ability to get best use of the *ENCYCLOPEDIA.* Suggestions for the most effective use of the index are given in volume 15.

ACKNOWLEDGMENTS. The editors are pleased to express their grateful appreciation to all who have aided in the preparation of the *ENCYCLOPEDIA.* Thanks are owed first to the American Catholic Hierarchy for their sponsorship of the project, and to the many advisers and consultants who aided in its planning, and whose names appear in the list of consultants (volume 15). Special thanks are due also to those publishers who graciously gave permission to reproduce copyright material, as well as to curators of museums and directors of libraries for their kind cooperation. Finally, to the staff of McGraw-Hill, Inc., for their assistance in this large undertaking, and above all to the thousands of distinguished contributors, we acknowledge our heavy debt.

THE EDITORS

Colorplates

A CAPPELLA, a term referring to choral music without instrumental accompaniment. During the Renaissance the performances of the *Sistine Choir in Rome were considered exemplary; and since the use of instruments was forbidden by its statutes, the term came to be used for any performance in a manner similar to those in the Sistine chapel. The Sistine tradition of unaccompanied voices stems from the monophonic, purely vocal style of plainchant. Although musical historians of the 19th century believed that all music before 1600 was *a cappella,* they ignored the vast amount of evidence, especially that of paintings, to the contrary. Even in liturgical performance the older procedure was to double vocal lines with instruments of disparate tone colors, thus enhancing the individuality of the parts and accenting the music's polyphonic character. The *a cappella* practice is related to polyphony in what is called the "Palestrina style," a term referring not only to works of *Palestrina but also to imitations of his style, e.g., the *stile antico* of the baroque era. Though the *concertato* style with instruments became widespread during the 17th and 18th centuries, the Sistine Choir continued its *a cappella* tradition, thus furnishing a performance model for the revival of liturgical polyphony in the 19th century (*see* CAECILIAN MOVEMENT).

Bibliography: Fellerer CathChMus. J. HANDSCHIN, "Die Grundlagen des A-capella-Stils," *Hans Häusermann und der Häusermannsche Privatchor* (Zurich 1929). Láng MusWC. Reese MusR. Apel HDMus.

[L. J. WAGNER]

AACHEN

City in north Rhine-Westphalia, west central Germany. The scene of treaties ending the Wars of Devolution (1668) and of the Austrian Succession (1748), it was in great part destroyed in World War II (1944). The Diocese of Aachen (*Aquisgranensis*), suffragan to *Cologne since 1930, in 1963 had 950 secular and 324 religious priests, 583 men in 34 religious houses, 4,119 women in 242 convents, and 1,399,000 Catholics; it is 1,573 square miles in area. The name *Aquae Grani,* first mentioned at the time of Charlemagne, means water.

The earliest traces of Christianity appear in graves and in a chapel (5th century) at an ancient bath shrine, which King Pepin replaced with a small palace chapel. Charlemagne (786–814) had palace and chapel rebuilt (*c.* 786), and in the last part of his reign resided in Aachen, the center of the Carolingian Empire. Aachen's importance appears also in the many Carolingian synods held there, the Aachen rule for canons, and the influence of its court academy and palace school during the *Carolingian Renaissance. As a result of the tradition of Charlemagne, 30 German kings were crowned in the cathedral (936–1531), which rulers favored with gifts. Until 1802 Aachen belonged to the Diocese of *Liège. Under the French it became a diocese (1802–21), suffragan to *Mechelen; then it was suppressed and became part of the restored See of *Cologne (1821). Resurrected as a see by the Prussian Concordat (1929), Aachen was canonically erected in 1930.

The cathedral, a major monument, began with the octagonal building of Charlemagne, modeled after S. Vitale in *Ravenna and the Theodosian tomb chapel at Old St. Peter's in Rome; it was probably dedicated July 17, 800. Gothic side chapels were added in the 15th century; the hall choir was completed in 1414. Cathedral treasures include the throne of Charlemagne (with six steps modeled after Solomon's), Carolingian and Ottonian Gospels, the cross of Lothair, the golden table, the pulpit of Henry II, and the bronze corona chandelier of Frederick I Barbarossa.

From Pepin's time the palace chapel housed important relics, and the number increased under Charlemagne. Its Great Relics, apparently exhibited in Charlemagne's time, are the swaddling clothes of Christ, the loin cloth of the Lord, the cloth for John the Baptist's head, and the cloak of Mary. Veneration of these increased through the Middle Ages, with pilgrims coming from all central Europe. The 7-year cycle of the pilgrimage is known from the 14th century. At first kept in a Carolingian shrine, the Great Relics have been in a Gothic Marian shrine since 1239. The Shrine of Charlemagne (1215) houses his remains, exhumed in 1165 when a local cult of St. Charlemagne developed. The cathedral also has a 14th-century statue of Our Lady that is venerated as miraculous.

Many spiritual institutions have arisen in Aachen: St. Adalbert chapter, the Benedictine Burtscheid, smaller cloisters, hospitals, and a leprosarium outside

Aachen, interior of the octagonal portion of the cathedral, built between 792 and 805, view from the east.

the city. Charitable foundations include the 13th-century Alexian Brothers (Beghards) and the 17th-century Sisters of St. Elizabeth. Three pupils of the poetess Luise Hensel, a teacher at St. Leonhard (1827–32), founded orders: Clara *Fey (1815–94), Franziska *Schervier (1819–76), and Pauline von *Mallinckrodt (1818–81). Around Leonhard Nellessen (1783–1859), pastor of St. Nikolaus, arose the Aachen circle of priests, devoted to pastoral care and works of charity. Aachen was the origin of the May devotion in the 19th century. The Francis Xavier Mission Society (now part of the Society for the *Propagation of the Faith) and the Child Jesus Society (now part of the *Pontifical Association of the Holy Childhood) were founded there. Philipp Höver founded the Society of the Poor Brothers of St. Francis to care for school dropouts (1857). Recently the administration of Misereor, a work originated by the German episcopacy for spiritual and bodily needs in underdeveloped lands, has been in Aachen.

In 1964 the city's 177,000 inhabitants included 143,000 Catholics. There were 22 parishes, 140 secular priests, and 55 religious priests.

Bibliography: W. Henry, DACL 1.1:1039–42. L. Boiteux, DHGE 1:1245–70. J. Ramackers, "Werkstattheimat der Grabplatte Papst Hadrians I," RömQuartalsch 59 (1964) 36–78; "Das Grab Karls des Grossen und die Frage nach dem Ursprung des Aachener Oktogons," HistJb 75 (1956) 123–153; LexThK[2] 1: 1–3. H. Schiffers in *Lexikon der Marienkunde,* ed. K. Algermissen (Regensburg 1957–) 1:1–14; *Das katholische Aachen im Wandel der Jahrhunderte* (Aachen 1934). *Aus Aachens Vorzeit,* v.1–20 (Aachen 1888–1907). *Zeitschrift des Aachener Geschichtsvereins,* v.1–76 (Aachen 1879–1964). *Aachener Heimatgeschichte,* ed. A. Huyskens (Aachen 1924). *Handbuch des Bistums A.* (2d ed. Aachen 1962). J. Torsy, *Geschichte des Bistums A. während der französischen Zeit (1802–1814)* (Bonn 1940). C. Faymonville et al., eds., *Die Kunstdenkmäler der Stadt A.,* 3 v. (Die Kunstdenkmäler der Rheinprovinz, ed. P. Clemen, v.10; Düsseldorf 1916–24). *Aachener Kunstblätter,* v.16–29 (1957–64). W. Boeckelmann, "Von den Ursprüngen der Aachener Pfalzkapelle," *Wallraf-Richartz-Jahrbuch* 19 (1957) 9–38. W. Schöne, "Die künstlerische und liturgische Gestalt der Pfalzkapelle Karls des Grossen in A.," *Zeitschrift für Kunstwissenschaft* 15 (1961) 97–148. H. P. Hilger, *Der Skulpturenzyklus im Chor des Aachener Domes* (Die Kunstdenkmäler des Rheinlands, *op. cit.* Beiheft 8; Essen 1961). W. R. Köhler, *Die karolingischen Miniaturen,* 3 v. (Berlin 1930, 1958–60). J. Fleckenstein, *Die Hofkapelle der deutschen Könige,* v. 1 (Stuttgart 1959). **Illustration credit:** Marburg-Art Reference Bureau.

[J. RAMACKERS]

AARON, son of Amram and Jochabed; brother of *Moses and Mariam (Ex 6.20); and husband of Elisabe, who bore him Nadab, Abiu, Eleazar, and Ithamar (6.23). The actual role of Aaron has been obscured in the development of the *Pentateuch. Most scholars question whether Aaron appeared in the original *Yahwist tradition and suggest that a later editor was responsible for linking him with Moses. In the *Elohist tradition Aaron acts as Moses' deputy, holds up Moses' hands at Raphidim (Ex 17.10–12), goes up the mountain with Moses and sees the Lord (19. 24), and acts as leader with Hur in Moses' absence. He accedes to the wishes of the insecure Hebrews, casts the golden calf, and constructs an altar in its honor (32.1–24). He joins Mariam in a complaint against

Aaron, detail from a 3d-century fresco of the "Dedication of the Tabernacle," Synagogue at Dura-Europos.

Moses' marriage to a Chusite woman, although the text indicates their envy of Moses as the instrument of God's revelation (Nm 12.1–15). Later, the Pentateuchal *priestly writers cast Aaron in the role of religious leader who figured prominently in the liberation of Israel. When he and Moses appear before the Pharao, Aaron brings on the plagues (Ex 7.19–20; 8.1–2, 12–13). As coadjutor of Moses, he too suffers from the complaints of the people (16.2), is likewise consulted by them (Nm 9.6), is addressed by God (Ex 9.8–10), and is forbidden to enter the Promised Land because of the incident at Meriba, where he sinned against the Lord (Nm 20.1–13). The tragic fate of the followers of Core [*see* CORE (KORAH), DATHAN AND ABIRAM], the checking of the plague (Numbers ch. 16), as well as the event of the flowering rod are presented as the divine witness to the priesthood of Aaron with its exclusive rights and privileges (Nm 17.16–26). Tradition assigns Mt. Hor (Nm 20.22–29) and Moser (Dt 10.6) as the location of his death.

Bibliography: EncDictBibl 1–2. H. JUNKER, LexThK² 1:3–4. F. SOLE and K. RATHE, EncCatt 2:10–13. F. MAASS, RGG³ 1:2–3. F. S. NORTH, "Aaron's Rise in Prestige," ZATWiss 6 (1954) 191–199. **Illustration credit:** National Museum, Damascus.

[E. ROESSLER]

AARON, PIETRO, important music theorist (also Aron); b. Florence, Italy, *c.* 1480; d. Venice?, after 1545. His earliest recorded employment, with Pope Leo X to 1521, was followed by the post of choir-master in the Imola cathedral (1521) and canon in the Rimini cathedral (1523). In 1525 he was appointed *maestro di casa* to the Venetian prior of the Knights of Malta, Sebastiano Michele; he entered that order in 1529, and in 1536 the Order of the Cross-Bearers in Bergamo. He was thought to be still alive in Venice in 1545. His five treatises show him to be unusually concerned with contemporary problems of composition and performance. He demanded that composers notate all accidentals rather than leave them to the discretion of the performers. While many polyphonists still wrote each voice part separately, he suggested "vertical" composition with all voices conceived simultaneously. He was also the first to recommend "mean-tone" temperament with flattened fifths, thereby opening the way for the well-tempered tuning of the 18th century.

Frontispiece to Book I of Aaron's "Thoscanello de la musica" (Venice 1523). Subsequent editions had the title "Toscanello in musica."

See also MUSIC, SACRED, HISTORY OF, 4.

Bibliography: P. AARON, *Trattato della natura,* Strunk SourceR 205–218, an excerpt. Reese MusR 181–183. H. RIEMANN, *History of Music Theory,* ed. and tr. R. H. HAGGH (Lincoln, Nebr. 1962). C. F. POHL, Grove DMM 1:2. **Illustration credit:** Library of Congress.

[E. R. LERNER]

ABAD Y QUEIPO, MANUEL, ecclesiastical lawyer and bishop elect during the Spanish-American period of revolution; b. Villapedre, Asturias, Spain, Aug. 26, 1751; d. Sisla, Spain, Sept. 15, 1825. He studied law at the University of Salamanca. In 1779 he went to Comayagua, Guatemala, and was ordained. In 1784 he moved to Michoacán, Mexico, where for 24 years he held the office of ecclesiastical judge of wills, chaplaincies, ecclesiastical funds, and pious works. In 1805 he won, in open competition, the office of canon penitentiary of the cathedral of Michoacán. On the death of the bishop of Michoacán in 1809, the junta in Spain nominated Abad, but he was not confirmed by the Holy See. Abad was, however, authorized to exercise jurisdiction in the diocese. In the revolt of 1810 Bishop-elect Abad, a political moderate, lost favor with both sides: with the revolutionists, because he maintained they were traitors and excommunicated them; with the conservatives, because he held that many reforms were needed. In 1814 Ferdinand VII overrode Abad's appointment as bishop. Abad went to Spain to defend his right and finally won the appointment in 1818. The bull of confirmation, however, was not forthcoming, and he was not allowed to return to Mexico. In 1822 he was appointed bishop of Tortosa but again was not confirmed. He died as a political prisoner in Spain.

Bibliography: L. E. FISHER, *Champion of Reform: Manuel Abad y Queipo* (New York 1955).

[F. B. WARREN]

ABAD Y SÁNCHEZ, DIEGO JOSÉ, Jesuit educator, writer, and humanist of colonial Mexico; b. La Lagunita, near Jiquilpan, Michoacán, Mexico, June 1, 1727; d. Bologna, Italy, Sept. 30, 1779. After receiving his early education from tutors at home, he went to the Jesuit Colegio de San Ildefonso in Mexico City. Abad was an outstanding student, talented and hard working. On July 24, 1741, he entered the Society of Jesus at the novitiate in Tepotzoplán, and he was ordained Oct. 3, 1751, in Mexico City. Abad's reputation as a teacher of rhetoric, philosophy, theology, and of both canon and civil law at the Jesuit schools in Mexico City, Zacatecas, and Querétaro merited respect from his students and admiration from fellow scholars. No slave to tradition, Abad stressed a humanistic approach, especially in his classes of rhetoric, and introduced new methods of teaching and different authors. So intense was his dedication to work that before he was 40 his health was greatly impaired. When his doctors failed to help him, he studied medicine himself. The knowledge he gained is believed to have prolonged his life for another decade. Upon the expulsion of the Jesuits from the Spanish empire in 1767, Abad went to Ferrara, Italy, where he devoted his talents to writing. Both in Mexico and Italy he composed poems on various subjects. His most noted work in verse, *De deo deoque homine heroica,* is a praise of God's attributes. Intended for and dedicated to the youth of Mexico, the poem went through several editions and was highly regarded by Abad's European contemporaries. Besides his verse compositions, he wrote theological, philosophical, and mathematical treatises and a geographical description of the rivers of the world. He wrote in Latin, Spanish, and Italian and won a prominent place among Mexico's 18th-century men of letters.

Bibliography: V. LEEBER, *El Padre Diego José Abad, S.J., y su obra poética* (Madrid 1965). J. L. MANEIRO and M. FABRI, *Vidas de mexicanos ilustres del siglo XVIII,* ed. and tr. B. NAVARRO (Mexico City 1956).

[N. F. MARTIN]

ABADDON, synonym for *Sheol, the abode of the dead in OT Hebrew poetry [Jb 26.6; 28.22; 31.12; Ps 87(88).12; Prv 15.11]. Etymologically Abaddon (Heb. *'ăbaddōn,* from the verb *'ābad,* to perish) means the place of destruction. In rabbinical literature, Abaddon became the name of the lowest part of *Gehenna. In Ap 9.11 Abaddon (Ἀβαδδών) is not merely a poetic personification as in Jb 28.22, but it is made an actual person, "the angel of the abyss," who is "king" of the infernal demons and whose name in Greek is Apollyon (Ἀπολλύων, destroyer). There is no reason to connect this word with the name of the Greek god Apollo (Ἀπόλλων).

Bibliography: EncDictBibl 2. J. MICHL, LexThK[2] 1:4–5. A. ROMEO, EncCatt 1:7–8. J. JEREMIAS, Kittel ThW 1:4.

[I. H. GORSKI]

ABANDONMENT, SPIRITUAL. The term can be taken in either an active or a passive sense. In its active sense it refers to a person's self-abandonment to divine providence through the theological virtues. In its passive sense it refers to a condition in which the soul is really, because of sin, or only apparently, forsaken by God. This article refers to abandonment understood as that experience in which it seems to a spiritual person that God has forsaken him. This spiritual abandonment, then, is an interior trial in which the spiritually advanced soul, feeling the painful need of a clearer and stronger possession of God, has the keen impression that God has deserted it and no longer holds it in His favor.

In its less intense form this abandonment makes one feel that God is far away; in its more intense form it makes one feel rejected by God and destined to be lost. Such suffering is experienced only by persons who have reached a high degree of perfection. Although certain forms of abandonment may be experienced as a result of sin or of lukewarmness, the real suffering caused by the feeling of being forsaken by God is only conceivable in holy souls for whom God has become the sole object of an intense desire and love.

Christian hagiography from all ages offers examples of spiritual abandonment. The trial is described by such ancient writers as St. John Climacus and Cassian, but references to this suffering are much more abundant among the saints of modern times. This more recent testimony is undoubtedly attributable to the greater number of spiritual biographies and letters of spiritual direction; these manifest more clearly the interior secrets of souls and, notably, the painful aspects of their spiritual lives.

The experience of spiritual abandonment may arise from the purgative contemplation by which God effects the purification of the soul, especially in the passive night of the spirit; or it may be a means whereby already purified souls suffer as victims in union with Christ. In either case this trial enables the soul to share most intimately in the suffering of Christ's abandonment on the cross. This union with the crucified Christ in turn gives rise in the soul to the most sublime acts of self-abandonment.

See also SELF-ABANDONMENT, SPIRITUAL; PURIFICATION, SPIRITUAL.

Bibliography: JOHN OF THE CROSS, "The Dark Night," *Collected Works,* tr. K. KAVANAUGH and O. RODRIGUEZ (Garden City, N.Y. 1964) 295–389. A. POULAIN, *The Graces of Interior Prayer,* tr. L. L. YORKE SMITH, ed. J. V. BAINVEL (St. Louis 1950). L. CHARDON, *The Cross of Jesus,* tr. R. T. MURPHY and J. THORNTON, 2 v. (St. Louis 1957–59). H. MARTIN, DictSpirAscMyst 3:504–517, 631–645.

[K. KAVANAUGH]

ABBA. This is a transliteration of the Aramaic word *'abbā',* "father." At the time of Jesus, "Abba" was the common, familiar word used by Jewish children in addressing their fathers. It was also a title given to renowned teachers as a mark of honor (cf. Mt 23.9). In late Hebrew literature this Aramaic word almost completely replaced the Hebrew vocative *'ăbî,* "my father." Yet in reference to God, "Abba" is seldom found in Rabbinic literature. This may be due to the predominant use of Hebrew in liturgical prayers as evidenced by the Qumran literature (*see* DEAD SEA SCROLLS). When "Abba" is found in direct address to God, it is ordinarily followed by the phrase, "who art in heaven."

In the NT "Abba" is found only in Mk 14.36, Rom 8.15, and Gal 4.6. It is transliterated into Greek as ἀββά and is always followed by its Greek translation, ὁ πατήρ "father." In Mk 14.36 Jesus addressed His Father as "Abba" as He prayed in Gethsemane. In the Gospels this Aramaic term may also be behind the frequent and intimate reference of Jesus to His Father. This provoked His enemies' accusation that He made Himself equal to God, calling God His Father (Jn 5.18). The early Church in its liturgy treasured the memory of the very word that Jesus used in praying to His Father, for Christians could now pray in the same intimate way through the gift of the Spirit (Rom 8.15; Gal 4.6); *see* ADOPTION (IN THE BIBLE); SONS OF GOD. The tautology of ἀββά ὁ πατήρ has been variously explained: that ὁ πατήρ is a translation of the Aramaic *'abbā'* into Greek; or that "Abba" was taken to mean God Himself, since Jesus always used it in referring to Him. Thus the whole expression would mean, "O God, my (or, our) Father."

See also OUR FATHER, THE.

Bibliography: Kittel ThW 1:4–6. S. V. McCASLAND, "Abba, Father," JBiblLit 72 (1953) 79–91.

[J. A. GRASSI]

'ABBĀSIDS

Descendants of 'Abbās (d. A.D. 653), uncle of Mohammed the prophet of *Islam; in A.D. 750 they seized the office of *caliph earlier held by the *Umayyads, and reigned at Baghdad until 1258.

As Mohammed's surviving uncle and head of his clan, 'Abbās would have had a claim to succeed the Prophet after his death in 632, had not 'Abbās's delayed conversion to Islam counted against him. His son 'Abdallāh (d. 687), a prominent religious authority, was governor of Basra under *Ali ('Alī ibn Abī Ṭālib), but later was won to the cause of Mu'āwiya.

The family played no public role under Mu'āwiya's family, the Umayyads, but they were able by clandestine religious-political propaganda to turn to their advantage the social unrest of the early Arab Moslem Empire. Their message was egalitarian and messianic and seems to have incorporated certain Iranian religious ideas palatable to the newly converted. It was discreetly directed by agents in Kufa, the stronghold of Shī'ī sympathies in Iraq. Under the able Iranian propagandist Abū Muslim, 'Abbāsid propaganda found greatest response among the half-Islamized Iranian inhabitants of the old eastern marches of the Persian Empire, Khurasan, a frontier area where Zoroastrianism, Buddhism, Mazdakism, Manichaeism, and Nestorian Christianity had met and mixed. Here in 747 local revolts were raised that, by calling for "an Imām [religious leader] of the Prophet's family," grew by 749 into a general rebellion of all disaffected elements in the Umayyad Empire. Shī'īs participated enthusiastically in the belief that a descendant of 'Alī would come to power, but it was the head of the 'Abbāsid House, Abū al-'Abbās al-Saffāḥ (d. 754) who was acclaimed caliph in 749, and who rooted out the Umayyads in every province but Spain.

Like other revolutionary regimes, the 'Abbāsids had, when once in power, to reckon on conflicts with the differing groups and interests that had cooperated to give them the victory. Under al-Manṣūr, brother and successor of al-Saffāḥ, the new regime's power was consolidated. Abū Muslim was put to death and his closest followers crushed. The hostility of the Shī'īs pursued the dynasty through all its history, and succeeding 'Abbāsids were alternately led to employ repression or placation in dealing with them.

Al-Manṣūr's new capital on the Tigris, Madīnat al-Salam (popularly known as Baghdad, after an earlier village on that site), was built at the junction of several trade routes, and within 50 years had become one of the great centers of civilization.

With the 'Abbāsid accession, the transformation of the Islamic polity from an Arab kingdom to the Moslem Empire was completed. The economic base of the dynasty was Mesopotamia, seat of earlier multiracial Middle Eastern empires; it drew heavily on the skills and traditions of the conquered peoples, particularly of converted members of the Sassanian bureaucratic class, and it depended on the military support of the peoples of the eastern frontier. Islamic religion and the Arabic language gave their distinctive stamp to this richly syncretic civilization, but the Arabs had lost their exclusive right to the responsibilities and rewards of empire. Islam, not Arab origin, sufficed for full membership in the Empire, and advancement depended almost solely on the favor of the caliphs, who had now transformed the simplicity of the first caliphs into the elaborate and splendid court of Persian autocrats.

The rapidity with which the cultural brilliance of the 'Abbāsid prime was reached (under Harūn al-Rashīd, 786–809, and his son al-Ma'mūn, d. 833) led Prof. Arnold Toynbee to argue convincingly that in fact under the aegis of Islam the earlier civilization of Achaemenid times had come again into its own.

However, during the subsequent period (836–892) when the court resided at Samarra, a new royal city north of Baghdad, the caliphs became the virtual prisoners of the elite corps they had formed from Central Asian Turkish slaves. Local rulers asserted themselves in the provinces, the clash of new cultural ideas prepared the way for new heretical movements, and a slave uprising of Africans devastated lower Iraq. Caliphal authority was slowly reasserted after 870, but during the long reign of al-Muqtadir (908–932) the central administration of the empire began a period of self-strangulation through corruption and internal rivalries. In 909 the Isma'īlī Shī'īs established an anticaliphate "of the Children of Fāṭima" in Tunisia (capital at Cairo from 969–1171). From 945 to 1055 the 'Abbāsids at Baghdad were puppets of the Buwayhid dictators, Persian Shī'īs of the "Twelver" sect. From 1055 to *c.* 1194 they were under the patronage of sultans of the house of Seljuk, Turkish chiefs whom they invited to

Gold medallion from Fars with portrait of 'Aḍud-al-Dawlah (reigned 949–983), greatest ruler of the Iranian Buwayhid dynasty. In his empire, which included Iraq as well as Iran, the 'Abbāsid caliph of Baghdad was a mere figurehead.

rid them of the Buwayhids. The *Seljuks were at least orthodox in practice and led a Sunnī restoration.

In religious as well as imperial theory the caliph was still the sole fount of all validly exercised power, and most Sunnī Moslem monarchs found it advisable to secure a diploma of investiture from Baghdad. This has led to the caliphate's being rather inaccurately likened to the papacy.

A brief restoration of 'Abbāsid power, in Iraq at least, occurred with the passing of the Seljuks, under the Caliph al-Nāṣir (1180–1225). But in 1258 Hulagu, grandson of *Genghis Khan, destroyed Baghdad and put the Caliph al-Musta'ṣim to death.

Under the *Mamelukes of Cairo, a member of the 'Abbāsid family was established as caliph there in 1261. This shadow caliphate was continued by his descendants until the end of the sultanate in 1517, but it was only a legal device for the legitimization of Moslem rulers, and the Cairo 'Abbāsids were little more than court officials.

Bibliography: P. K. HITTI, *History of the Arabs* (6th ed. New York 1958). W. MUIR, *The Caliphate, Its Rise, Decline and Fall,* rev. T. H. WEIR (Edinburgh 1924). A. J. TOYNBEE, *A Study of History,* 12 v. (New York 1948–61). B. LEWIS, *The Arabs in History* (New York 1950); EncIslam² 1:15–23. **Illustration credit:** Photo courtesy of Société Encyclopédique Universelle, Paris.

[J. A. WILLIAMS]

ABBATINI, ANTONIO MARIA, baroque theorist and composer in the Roman tradition; b. Tiferno (Città di Castello), Italy, 1595?; d. Tiferno, *c.* 1679–80. He was a student of G. B. and G. M. *Nanino, and expanded their polychoral style in his church music, which consisted of several volumes of Masses, motets, psalms, *sacre canzoni,* and antiphons and Sequence for the feast of St. Dominic performed at S. Maria sopra Minerva in 1661. He was *maestro di cappella* at the Lateran (1626–28) and served in this capacity also at the Accademia degli Assorditi in Orvieto, and the Gesù, S. Lorenzo e Damaso, Notre Dame di Loreto, and St. Mary Major in Rome. Abbatini is noted primarily for his innovations in *opera buffa. Dal male il bene,* composed in collaboration with Marazzoli, contains a very early example of the ensemble finale, one of the most significant departures in operatic history. The opera's libretto was the work of G. Rospigliosi, later Pope Clement IX. Abbatini was said to have been commissioned by Urban VIII to edit *Inni della chiesa in canto gregoriano* in Palestrina style, but there is doubt that the work was completed (although some authorities give 1644 as its publication date). He is credited also with assisting A. Kircher (1602–80) with *Musurgia Universalis* (1650). His 14 discourses on music theory (*Discorsi e lezioni accademiche*, 1663–68) are preserved in a Bolognese edition.

Bibliography: F. CORADINI, *Antonio Maria Abbatini e d. Lorenzo Abbatini: Notizie biografiche* (Arezzo 1922). K. G. FELLERER, MusGG 1:15–16. Eitner QuellLex. Fellerer CathChMus. Buk MusB. Grout HistOp.

[M. CORDOVANA]

ABBELEN, PETER, controversialist; b. Germany, Aug. 8, 1843; d. Milwaukee, Wis., Aug. 24, 1917. He attended schools at Gaesdonk and Münster in Germany, and St. Francis Seminary, Milwaukee, Wis., where he was ordained Jan. 29, 1868. After teaching for a semester, he joined the La Crosse diocese, where he spent 8 years in pastorates at Chippewa Falls, La Crosse, and Prairie du Chien. In 1876 he became spiritual director of the *School Sisters of Notre Dame, Milwaukee, whose subsequent progress was credited to his zeal. Besides articles, he wrote a life of Mother Caroline Friess, first superior of the Milwaukee motherhouse. He was one of the theologians selected to do preliminary work for the Third Plenary Council of Baltimore. He was named vicar-general of the Milwaukee archdiocese in 1906, and a domestic prelate in 1907.

Acting for Abp. Michael Heiss and others, he became absorbed in the controversy between German- and English-speaking Catholics. The conflict involved questions concerning the selection of a coadjutor for Archbishop Henni, the juridical status of nationalistic parishes, the Bennett Law requiring the use of English in schools, Cahenslyism, and *Americanism. Among the items contained in his petition to Rome in 1886 were the recognition of parochial status for national churches and legislation assigning immigrants to national churches and their children to the schools thereof. The Congregation of the Propagation of the Faith delayed a decision; when rendered through Bps. John Ireland and John Keane, it was generally regarded as unfavorable to Abbelen. He constantly maintained that he had always been guided by moral objectives, and remarked that he thought Peter *Cahensly's program would serve the good of immigrants. The controversy was not fully resolved until the promulgation of the new Code of Canon Law and the end of World War I.

Bibliography: P. M. ABBELEN, "Memorial on the German Question . . .," in C. J. BARRY, *The Catholic Church and German Americans* (Milwaukee 1953) 289–296, with answers to the same, 296–312.

[P. L. JOHNSON]

ABBESS, term derived from *abbot (Aramaic *abba,* father), female superior of a community of 12 or more nuns, more properly *Benedictines, although the term is used also among *Poor Clares, Conceptionists, *Bridgettines, and *canonesses. Monastic communities of women spread from the East during the 4th century. Superiors were referred to as *mater monasterii, mater monacharum, praeposita;* the term "abbess" appeared for the first time in the West on the tomb of a certain "Serena, abbatissa" (d. *c.* 514) in the Roman church of St. Agnes-Outside-the-Walls. Growing Benedictine influence endowed the office of abbess with a liturgical character, making it elective by vote of the community, prescribing episcopal benediction, and granting the right to the ring, pectoral cross, and crosier. During the Middle Ages, abbesses of great monastic houses exercised practically all the temporal power of abbots and feudal lords, ranking among the nobles of the realm, sitting in parliament and in councils, and recognizing no ecclesiastical authority other than the pope. Many abbesses assumed spiritual power over their nuns also, to the point of incurring stern papal prohibitions against interference in the administration of penance, conferring the veil, and giving benedictions and even sacramental absolution. For such abuses *Innocent III rebuked abbesses of the royal monasteries in Burgos (*see* HUELGAS DE BURGOS, ABBEY OF) and Palencia,

St. Erentrude, abbess, with the crosier, symbol of her office, 15th-century statue in the Nonnberg, Salzburg.

Spain. The abbess of Conversano in Apulia, Italy, had the right to a quasi-episcopal authority over her clergy until 1810, when *Pius VII abolished her privileges. The abbess of *Fontevrault had jurisdiction over both monks and nuns of this monastic establishment, typical of other double *monasteries. With the breakdown of the feudal system, the temporal power of abbesses declined; their present status in Canon Law is simply that of major superior. Although formerly elected for life, abbesses are now restricted to 3 consecutive years in office and may not be immediately reelected without dispensation. They have complete temporal and spiritual authority over their nuns in matters pertaining to religious discipline and external affairs of the house, but no sacramental spiritual jurisdiction.

Bibliography: P. B. ALBERS, *Consuetudines monasticae,* 5 v. (Stuttgart 1900–12). K. H. SCHÄFER, *Die Kanonissenstifter im deutschen Mittelalter* (Stuttgart 1907); *Kanonissen und Diakonissen* (Freiburg 1910). M. SACHÉ, *Les Abbesses de Fontevraud: Influences et corruption* (Angers 1921). J. M. BESSE, DACL 1.1:42. E. C. BUTLER, *Benedictine Monachism* (2d ed. 1924; repr. New York 1961). S. HILPISCH, *Aus früh-mittelalterlichen Frauenklöstern* (Düsseldorf 1926); *Die Doppelklöster: Entstehung und Organisation* (Münster 1928). P. DE LANGOGNE, DTC 1.1:17–22. J. DE PUNIET, DictSpirAscMyst 1:57–61. J. M. ESCRIVÁ, *La abadesa de Las Huelgas* (Madrid 1944). T. J. BOWE, *Religious Superioresses: A Historical Synopsis and a Commentary* (Washington 1946). L. OLIGER, EncCatt 1:17–19. H. EMONDS, LexThK[2] 1:95. M. C. MCCARTHY, *The Rule for Nuns of St. Caesarius of Arles* (Washington 1960). **Illustration credit:** Austrian Information Service, New York City.

[M. F. LAUGHLIN]

ABBEVILLE, CLAUDE D', French Capuchin missionary and historian; b. place and date unknown; d. 1616 (not in 1622 or 1623, as some have stated). He entered the order in 1593. In 1611 he volunteered as a missionary in the French expedition to Brazil. He arrived in Maranhão in June 1612 and with six Indians returned to France to get aid in December of the same year. With 12 missionaries he returned to Maranhão in June of 1614, but they were expelled in December because of the war between the French and Portuguese. Abbeville's reputation is based on his literary work; he was a keen observer and an impartial historian, the first to write about the Brazilian lands conquered by the French. In August 1612 he was already writing interesting letters about the expedition and the Indians; these letters were edited six times in French and translated into German (Augsburg 1613) and Italian (Bérgamo-Treviso 1613). His principal work is the history of Maranhão Island and its first evangelization, *Histoire de la mission des Pères Capucins en l'isle de Maragnan et terres circonvoisines* (Paris 1614). It is valuable for its information on evangelization, colonization, ethnology, and linguistics.

Bibliography: *Histoire de la mission des pères capucins en l' isle de Maragnan et terres circonvoisines* (Paris 1614), Port. tr. S. MILLIET (São Paulo 1945). F. LEITE DE FARIA, *Os primeiros missionários do Maranhão* (Lisbon 1961).

[M. DE POBLADURA]

ABBO OF FLEURY, ST., abbot, writer; b. Orléans, *c.* 945–950; d. La Réole Abbey, Nov. 13, 1004 (feast, Nov. 13). Offered as an oblate in Fleury, he studied at Paris, Reims, and Orléans. He was ordained in England, where he had been called to preside over the school of *Ramsey (985–988). From 988 to 1004 he was abbot of *Saint-Benoît-sur-Loire (Fleury). One of the most remarkable teachers of his century, he was also a prolific writer and a staunch defender of papal authority against royal and episcopal power. When commissioned by King *Robert II to treat with the papacy in the royal interest, Abbo achieved harmony between the Church and the *Capetian dynasty. A zealous promoter of ecclesiastical reform and a champion of monastic independence, he obtained papal immunity for his own monastery and carried the principles of *Cluny into the monasteries of France and England. Abbo was fatally wounded during a quarrel that arose between his followers and the Gacons outside the Abbey of La Réole, where he was undertaking a reform. He is revered as a martyr and has received public veneration since 1031. The most notable of his writings (PL 139:463–582) are: *Apologeticus* to Hugh Capet and his son on the rights and duties of clergy, religious, and laity; *Liber de computo; Collectio canonum; Passio s. Eadmundi,* (ed. Arnold, *Memorials of St. Edmund's Abbey,* London, 1890–96).

Bibliography: *Epistola encyclica de caede A. abbatis,* PL 139: 417–418; ABBO OF FLEURY, *Epistolae,* Bouquet RGFS 10:434–442. AIMOIN, *Vita s. Abbonis,* PL 139:375–414. A. VAN DE VYVER, "Les Oeuvres inédites d'A.," RevBén 47 (1935) 125–169. P. Cousin, *A. de Fleury-sur-Loire* (Paris 1954). A. FLICHE, *La Réforme grégorienne,* 3 v. (Louvain 1924–37) 1:49–59. E. SACKUR, *Die Cluniacenser,* 2 v. (Halle 1892–94) 1:270–299. U. BERLIÈRE, DHGE 1:49–51. A. AMANIEU, DDC 1:71–76.

[P. J. MULLINS]

ABBO OF METZ, ST., bishop; b. Aquitaine; d. 647 (feast, Sept. 19). Abbo, or Goericus, was a member of the prominent family of Ansbertina. When St. *Arnulf of Metz, a kinsman, resigned from the See of *Metz in 629, Abbo succeeded him. The medieval *Vita Goerici* that gives other details of his life is wholly unreliable. Among the letters of St. *Desiderius of Cahors, there is a letter to Abbo and one from him (PL 87:253, 262). It is in the will of King Dagobert (d. 639) that he is called Abbo. He built St. Peter's in Metz.

Bibliography: ActSS Sept. 6:48–55. MGS 2:267–270. MGSrer Mer 2:417–425, 442. Butler Th Attw 3:597.

[B. L. MARTHALER]

ABBOT

Name and title of the superior of an autonomous *monastery of one of the old monastic orders such as the *Benedictines, *Camaldolese, *Vallombrosans, and *Cistercians. *Basilian monks sometimes employ the term hegumen (Greek ἡγούμενος), while Russian and other Oriental monasteries style their superior an archimandrite.

Origin. The term is derived from the Hebrew **abba*, meaning father, a word found in the Bible often with reference to God. It was employed in the early 4th century as descriptive of the role of some of the Egyptian hermits as guides and teachers of religious life for younger monks who came to live under their direction. The original idea of the abbot's spiritual fatherhood of his monks developed ultimately into the juridical office of abbot, vested with authority as set forth in the *Benedictine rule. In chapter 2 of the Rule St. *Benedict portrays the ideal abbot, and the traits of both father and officer are recognized in the double form of address the author dictates for him, *dominus et abbas*. As the representative of Christ the abbot is the father of the monastic community and exercises a father's jurisdiction over those under his care. He will be held accountable to God, Benedict points out, for the spiritual welfare of his charges. Chapter 64 of the Rule goes on to describe the authority of the abbot over his monks and emphasizes encouragement and understanding, as much as firmness and discipline, in the administration of his office. The monks, for their part, owe the abbot reverence and obedience because they should see in him Christ's deputy in their midst.

Election. The abbot is usually elected by the monks of the monastery, the constitutions of the various congregations setting forth the qualifications of electors, the time and manner of voting and the qualifications for the office itself (see also CIC c.504). It was originally intended that the abbot would hold office for life, although in modern times it is not unusual for his term to be limited to 6, 8, or 12 years (as with the English Benedictines). The election must be confirmed by proper authority, either the Holy See, frequently acting through the superior of the monastic congregation, or the local ordinary. The abbot must then seek episcopal benediction according to the rite prescribed in the Roman *Pontifical. Monastic founders who were religious often assumed the position of superior in their foundations and in the Middle Ages, as monasteries came to assume an increasingly important role in the economic and political life of their day, feudal lords often dictated the choice of abbots for houses within their territory. The Benedictine Rule envisioned an abbot ruling a single, independent community, but during certain periods, especially those of great monastic

Abbot Ramwold (d. 1000) of the Benedictine abbey of Sankt Emmeram, Regensburg, Germany; illumination in the Codex Aureus written at Reims c. 870 and given to Sankt Emmeram where it was restored by Ramwold (Munich Clm. 14,000).

reform, one man came to rule a number of widely scattered houses (*Benedict of Aniane, *John of Gorze, *Odo of Cluny) and later great monastic congregations came to develop (*Cluny in the 10th and 11th centuries, the *Maurists in the 17th century). The privilege of *exemption, granted since Merovingian times, gave the abbots more freedom from the control of local bishops and feudal lords and a number of houses established themselves as subject only to the Holy See. Among the Cistercians the father abbot and the abbots of the daughter houses have always had a strong influence on each other's abbatial elections while the modern Benedictines have formed themselves into national congregations. Certain privileges are attached to the office of abbot (see CIC cc.325, 625, 964) and he may be granted the right to the use of pontificals such as the ring, pectoral cross, miter, and crozier.

Types of Abbots. Canon Law distinguishes between the following types of abbots. The *abbas regularis de regimine* has *de jure* and *de facto* government of an abbey. Enjoying episcopal exemption, he has ordinary jurisdiction in the external and internal forum over all persons belonging to the abbey. An *abbas nullius* (*see* ABBOT NULLIUS) has actual episcopal jurisdiction over all clergy and laity in a specified territory subject directly to the abbey. *Archiabbas* (archabbot), *abbas praeses,* or *abbas generalis* is a designation for an abbot who is head of a monastic congregation. The *abbas primas* or abbot primate is the head of the modern Benedictine confederation. A titular abbot is one who has the rank, title, and insignia of an abbot but does not himself govern the abbey whose name he bears.

A commendatory abbot, or abbot *in commendam,* refers to a personage who was allotted the usufruct of a monastic benefice, and its revenues. Such an arrangement was much employed in the late Middle Ages but was forbidden by the Council of *Trent (*see* COMMENDATION).

See also ABBOT (CANON LAW); ABBESS.

Bibliography: F. CHAMARD, "Les Abbés au moyen-âge," Rev QuestHist 33 (1885) 71–108. J. M. BESSE, DACL 1.1:39–42. J. DE PUNIET, DictSpirAscMyst 1:49–57. F. CIMETIER, *Catholicisme* 1:19–22. C. BUTLER, *Benedictine Monachism* (2d ed. 1924; repr. New York 1961). J. BAUCHER, DDC 1:29–62. P. SCHMITZ, *Histoire de l'Ordre de Saint-Benoît,* 7 v. (Maredsous, Bel. 1942–56) 1:181–191, 259–262. H. EMONDS, LexThK² 1:90–93. B. HEGGLIN, *Der benediktinische Abt in rechtsgeschichtlicher Entwicklung und geltendem Kirchenrecht* (Kirchengeschichtliche Quellen und Studien 5; St. Ottilien 1961). P. SALMON, *L'Abbé dans la tradition monastique* (Paris 1962). *Handwörterbuch zur deutschen Rechtgeschichte,* ed. W. STAMMLER et al. (Berlin 1964–) 1:18–20, with bibliog. **Illustration credit:** Hirmer Verlag München.

[P. VOLK]

ABBOT (CANON LAW)

Abbot, the title applied to the religious superior of an abbey, derives from the earliest years of Oriental monasticism. The aspirant to holiness chose a suitable monk, whom he called his *abba* (father), to teach and guide him. Later, monastic rules, especially that of St. Benedict, introduced the term into Western Canon Law and liturgy. Since the mendicant orders and the more modern religious institutes adopted another nomenclature for their superiors, the title of abbot is found also among the Canons Regular and in the monastic orders, particularly those that follow the Benedictine Rule.

Election and Privileges. An abbot is usually selected by the secret vote of the community he will govern. The constitutions of each institute establish the specific requisites in the electorate, candidate, and election procedure. Generally there is required a majority vote of the solemnly professed religious taken by secret ballot for a priest who has been a professed member of the order for at least 10 years, is of legitimate birth, and is 30 years of age. Upon acceptance of his election and its confirmation by the competent ecclesiastical authority, the new abbot receives the abbatial blessing from the diocesan bishop. While this rite closely resembles an episcopal consecration, it confers no power of orders, but is a requisite for the use of some prelatial powers.

Though in some communities the term of office is limited, an abbot is elected for life. In the event of old age or other incapacity, he may request a coadjutor or he may even resign. Some resigned abbots are made titular abbots and hold in empty title an abbey no longer active. In very rare cases the title of abbot is directly granted by the Holy See as an honor.

Since the Middle Ages, abbots have received by papal privilege the use of insignia and ceremonial proper to bishops. These prelatial prerogatives are recognized in law (CIC c.625) and liturgy. An abbot is allowed the use of a ring, pectoral cross, and zucchetto. Vested for pontifical functions or assisting in formal choir, he wears the garb of a bishop, except that its color is proper to his religious order. Thus a Norbertine abbot wears white, a Benedictine abbot wears black. An abbot celebrates Holy Mass and performs other liturgical functions according to the ceremonial of a prelate. He uses a throne with a canopy, wears complete prelatial vesture, and observes the rubrics for a pontiff. While there remain no restrictions on the frequency of his use of these prerogatives, an abbot is normally allowed their use only in churches of his own order, though privilege and custom have modified this limitation. Unless the abbot is a bishop, however, he is not authorized to perform those consecrations that require episcopal power. Thus he does not ordinarily prepare the holy oils or ordain to major orders. He is allowed, after having received the abbatial blessing, to confer tonsure and minor orders on his own religious.

An abbot may be honored by being allowed to wear the Cappa Magna, a cloak and train, in processions. Less frequently the use of a violet zucchetto is permitted as a special distinction.

In formal address, an abbot is titled "right reverend abbot," but his religious would speak to him as "father abbot." In an assembly of their own institute, ruling abbots take precedence according to the time of their election after officers of the assembly, abbots *nullius,* and archabbots. The name of the abbot is not mentioned in the Canon of the Mass unless he is an abbot *nullius.* For his funeral, an abbot is vested in full pontifical garb, but the Mass is celebrated as for a priest.

Right to Govern. The abbot is, first of all, the religious superior of his community. His authority to instruct and command the religious is ideally a father's care for his sons. Monastic communities cherish their abbot not only as the superior or administrator, but also as the wise and solicitous parent who recognizes in each member of the family his particular talent and endowment, and by means best suited to the individual, develops that potential. Although the work of the apostolate and the care of temporalities demand consideration, the abbot is ever to be aware of spiritual goals as his first concern. The dominative power of the abbot arises from the religious profession of vows.

The authority of the abbot as a major superior in a clerical exempt institute is also jurisdictional (CIC c.501.1). As the ordinary for his religious, he grants faculties for the hearing of their confessions and he can dispense them from certain obligations of the common law, such as fasting. An abbot possesses exclusive authority and responsibility for his community and for each member of it. He chooses the several officials of the monastery, who are responsible to and remain dependent upon him. He has direct and immediate control of each member of the house, while these have the right to approach him directly. This relationship, while sometimes difficult in very large abbeys, is the significant characteristic of abbatial rule.

While each abbey is a separate and independent juridic entity, most are associated into monastic congregations. The authority of its abbot president is specified in the constitutions. Pope Leo XIII provided for the confederation of Benedictine monastic congregations with an abbot primate, whose authority is described in the *Lex propria* of 1952 (cf. CIC c.501.3).

If an abbey is to be specially distinguished, particularly as the motherhouse of many abbeys, it may be honored as an archabbey and its abbot called the archabbot. Unless the title is used for the head of a monastic congregation, an archabbot possesses almost no authority over other abbeys and their religious, but does enjoy some precedence. In the United States there are the Archabbeys of *St. Vincent (Latrobe, Pa.) and of *St. Meinrad (St. Meinrad, Ind.).

See also ABBOT NULLIUS.

Bibliography: M. DLOUHY, *The Ordination of Exempt Religious* (CUA CLS 271; Washington 1955) 68–87.

[M. J. DLOUHY]

ABBOT, BLESSING OF. In his own monastery and churches belonging to his monastery an abbot may celebrate the liturgy pontifically. To enjoy this privilege he must be blessed by the bishop of the place where the monastery is located or, in his absence, by a bishop of the abbot's own choice.

Mention of a special blessing for abbots is made in the 6th-century Rule of St. Benedict and also in the writings of St. Gregory the Great (d. 604). The nucleus of the present rite was already developed by the 8th century, but throughout the Middle Ages the ceremonial was embellished along the lines of an episcopal consecration.

The blessing takes place at Mass, usually a Pontifical Mass concelebrated by the bishop and the new abbot. Two other abbots assist in the ceremony. The rite begins with the presentation of the abbot, who is examined briefly by the bishop. Then the Mass begins and continues up to the Alleluia Verse or Tract following the Epistle. The abbot prostrates himself before the altar for the chanting of the Litany of the Saints. The bishop then recites two orations and sings the Consecratory Preface, in the course of which he imposes hands on the head of the abbot in blessing. The abbot is given a copy of the Holy Rule of St. Benedict, the crozier, and the ring.

The celebration of Mass is resumed and continues as usual until the Offertory, when the abbot presents the bishop with candles, bread, and wine. Following the last blessing, the abbot is given the miter and gloves and is enthroned by the bishop. During the singing of the *Te Deum,* the abbot goes through the church blessing the people. At his throne he receives the homage of his monks and then finally imparts his solemn blessing on all.

Bibliography: J. BAUDOT, DACL 2.1:723–727. P. RADÓ, *Enchiridion liturgicum,* 2 v. (Rome 1961) 2:1030–32.

[R. K. SEASOLTZ]

ABBOT NULLIUS

A religious prelate assigned to govern not only an abbey but also the clergy and laity of a territory that is separate from any diocese. The practice of subjecting an abbey, together with the surrounding territory and population, directly to the Holy See originated in about the 9th century and was a development of the exemption of monasteries from the authority of local bishops. Thus was derived the concept of an abbey *nullius diocesis* (of no diocese), or simply abbey *nullius,* its superior being an abbot *nullius.*

The chapter of the abbey, in electing its abbot, thereby chooses also the prelate of its territory. The religious constitutions specify the election procedure and can establish requirements beyond those stated in Canon Law. The candidate, who should have the qualities expected in a bishop, must receive at least an absolute majority of the votes cast. After the election is confirmed by the Holy See, the newly elected abbot receives the abbatial blessing from any bishop of his choice. By taking formal possession of his territory, he acquires quasi-episcopal powers of jurisdiction.

As the ruling superior of the religious community, he has all the duties and rights of an abbot toward his religious subjects. In addition to the dominative authority that is derived from their vows, he has jurisdictional power over them both as their religious ordinary and as the ordinary of the place in which they engage in the apostolate. This unity of command does much to foster harmony and obviate conflicts, and is effective especially in missionary work.

The jurisdictional powers of the abbot *nullius* over his clergy and people are the same as those of a prelate *nullius.* In the government of his territory, he has the aid of his abbey chapter, which functions after the manner of a bishop's cathedral chapter or diocesan consultors. For his vicar-general he may select a religious of his own institute (CIC c.367.2).

The abbot *nullius,* though usually solemnly blessed, is not necessarily consecrated a bishop; yet his priestly power of orders is extended, as in the case of the prelate *nullius.* He can ordain to tonsure and minor orders not only his own religious, but even his other subjects, as well as those who present dismissorial letters. He can administer the Sacrament of Confirmation and perform certain consecrations and reserved blessings within his territory.

Since an abbot is already allowed the use of pontifical vesture and ceremonial, the abbot *nullius* is distinguished principally by his violet zucchetto. He may pontificate anywhere within his territory as well as in churches of his own order. Except for cardinals, papal legates, and the metropolitan, the abbot *nullius* takes precedence over all when within his jurisdiction, though he may yield this preference outside of formal functions. Outside of his territory he ranks after bishops. In an assembly of his own institute, he would precede other abbots except officers of the monastic congregation and the abbot of the monastery. Those who celebrate Holy Mass within his territory mention his name in the Canon.

Unlike other religious, the abbot *nullius* is allowed to choose the church of his funeral (CIC c.1219.2) and may, if he so decides, be buried within the abbey church (CIC c.1205.2). Unless the religious constitutions provide otherwise, when the position of abbot is vacant the government of the abbey *nullius* devolves upon the chapter of the abbey, which is obligated to elect an administrator who holds power until, by abbatial election and approval of the Holy See, a new abbot *nullius* is installed.

An abbey *nullius* that consists of fewer than three parishes is governed by special legislation. About 20 abbeys *nullius,* most in the care of Benedictines, exist today. Belmont Abbey, Belmont, N.C., is the only abbey *nullius* in the U.S.

See also ABBOT (CANON LAW); PRELATE NULLIUS.

Bibliography: M. A. BENKO, *The Abbot Nullius* (CUA CLS 173; Washington 1943). Abbo 1:319–327. Woywod-Smith 319–327. Beste 319–327. Vermeersch-Creusen EpitCanIur 1:319–327.

[M. J. DLOUHY]

ABBOTT, LYMAN, Congregational clergyman and editor, whose writings offered a popular synthesis of Christianity and Darwinism; b. Roxbury, Mass., Dec.

13, 1835; d. Cornwall-on-Hudson, N.Y., Oct. 22, 1922. He was the son of Rev. Jacob Abbott, a popular writer, who moved to New York City in 1843. After graduating from New York University in 1853, Abbott was admitted to the bar, studied theology under his uncle Rev. John S. C. Abbott, and was ordained in 1860. An active abolitionist, he served as secretary of the American Freedmen's Union, which supported schools for freed slaves. In 1868 he became editor of the *Illustrated Christian Weekly* and literary editor of *Harper's,* resigning both posts in 1879. From 1876 to 1893 he edited the *Christian Union,* known later as the *Outlook* under his son's editorship. After the death of Henry Ward Beecher, Abbott succeeded to the pastorate of Plymouth Church, Brooklyn, N.Y., from which he resigned in 1898. He edited Beecher's collected works and wrote his official biography (1903). Abbott's other writings include the *Dictionary of Religious Knowledge* (1874), *The Spirit of Democracy* (1910), and autobiographical *Reminiscences* (1915). His Lowell Lectures, published as *The Evolution of Christianity* (1892), dealt with the development of theology and the church in Darwinian terms. *Christianity and Social Problems* (1896) called for reforms in the social organism. The *Theology of an Evolutionist* (1897) offered a synthesis of science and religion in Modernist terms.

Bibliography: I. V. BROWN, *Lyman Abbott: Christian Evolutionist* (Cambridge, Mass. 1953).

[R. K. MACMASTER]

ABBREVIATIONS

For saving space, abbreviations have been employed since Greek and Roman antiquity in writings on stone, metal, papyrus, and parchment, and in modern times on numerous other materials. Since the invention of printing, abbreviations have had a wider dissemination and are now in universal use. In the U.S. and Great Britain abbreviations of all kinds are employed to a much greater degree than in other countries. Abbreviations in general are confined to words and phrases that are frequently used in a given field and are, therefore, easily intelligible to those familiar with the field in question. The Romans, for example, employed abbreviations very frequently in inscriptions and documents dealing with public administration and law. In the Middle Ages abbreviations were utilized to an increasing extent in documents dealing with ecclesiastical and civil administration and in treatises on philosophy, theology, law, medicine, and science. They were much less common in works of a strictly literary character. Before the close of the medieval period, their use had spread also to the vernacular languages.

Classification of Abbreviations and Examples. Abbreviations may be classified under several categories; but among these suspension, contraction, and conventional symbols or signs are the most frequent and the most important. A given example, furthermore, may represent two or more kinds of shortening.

Suspension. This consists in the use of the first letter or of the first two, three, or even four letters of a word, with the omission of the remaining letters. It is the oldest form of abbreviation and the one that has had the longest and most flourishing life, for it is the type of current abbreviation familiar to all. In modern use, however, only the first letter of the word is normally employed. In ancient Greek, the letter abbreviations for certain numerals, such as Π for πέντε (5), Δ for δέκα (10), H for ἑκατόν (100), are in this category. The Greeks abbreviated the names of their cities in this way, especially on coins. The ancient Greeks, however, made somewhat sparing use of suspension in the strict sense.

The Romans, on the other hand, employed suspension in almost all phases of public and private life. Roman *praenomina* were almost always abbreviated: e.g., C. (Gaius), L. (Lucius), M. (Marcus), T. (Titus), and Ti. (Tiberius); likewise, the names of public offices: Q. (*quaestor*), Pr. (*praetor*), Cos. (*consul*), Praef. (*praefectus*), Imp. (*imperator*); and also religious offices: Aug. (*augur*), Pont. Max. (*Pontifex Maximus*). In dedications to divinities the name of the divinity was frequently abbreviated: e.g., IOM (*Iovi Optimo Maximo*). The titles of the emperors on monuments and coins appear regularly in abbreviated form, two *Augusti,* for instance, being indicated by the doubling of the last letter or of a single letter: Augg. NN. (*Augusti Nostri*). Official or private formulas of all kinds were expressed in suspensions: e.g., SPQR (*Senatus Populusque Romanus*), Q.F.P. D.E.R.I.C. (*Quid fieri placeret, de ea re ita censuere*), H.M.H.N.S. (*Hoc monumentum heredem non sequetur*), STTL (*Sit tibi terra levis*), and N.F.N.S.N.C. (*Non fui, non sum, non curo,* an Epicurean formula).

Tironian Notes. The term Tironian notes is employed to designate a Roman system of shorthand or tachygraphy, the invention of which was ascribed by tradition to Cicero's secretary M. Tullius Tiro. Its abbreviations or symbols were called *notae,* and its users were subsequently called *notarii* (first cited for Quintilian and Pliny the Younger). Unlike modern shorthand, the Tironian system was based essentially on letters or parts of letters, but conventional signs were also used for very common nouns and adjectives, for common verbs in the third person singular indicative, and for frequently recurring adverbs, prepositions, and conjunctions. A distinction was made between the main *nota* (*signum principale*) and the auxiliary *nota* (*signum auxiliare*). The auxiliary *notae* were used chiefly to indicate differences in declensional endings. Side by side with letter abbreviations and their modifications, the Tironian system made wide use also of strokes, in various positions or at various angles, and points, as differentiating signs for words and inflectional forms. In the course of time certain letter or syllabic abbreviations became merely conventional symbols.

The Tironian system passed on to the Middle Ages, when it acquired many accretions. In fact, it is difficult to separate the ancient inheritance from the medieval additions. It was especially popular among Irish scribes on the Continent between the 7th and the 10th centuries. Its use died out quickly, and it seems to have been practically forgotten before it was mentioned again by the abbot Johannes *Trithemius (1462–1516).

Contraction. In this form of abbreviation, the letters in the body of the word were omitted, with the letters at the beginning and the end being left. In inflected languages such as Greek and Latin, it was thus possible, through the retention of the ending of words, to indicate various grammatical constructions. L. Traube maintained that contraction was exclusively Jewish and Christian in origin, being based on the omission of the vowels in the Hebrew tetragram YHWH (Yaweh) and the omission of the central letters in the corresponding equivalents in Greek: $\overline{\Theta \mathrm{C}}$ (Θεός), $\overline{\mathrm{KC}}$ (Κύριος). Some later scholars have challenged Traube's view that the system is exclusively Judaeo-Christian, but the fact remains that it had no appreciable development before Christian times. The *nomina sacra,* as they are called, were abbreviated primarily out of a spirit of reverence and comprised a total of 15 words, among them, in addition to those given above: $\overline{\mathrm{IC}}$ (Ιησοῦς), $\overline{\mathrm{XC}}$ (Χριστός), $\overline{\mathrm{YC}}$ (Υἱός), $\overline{\Pi\mathrm{NA}}$ (Πνεῦμα), $\overline{\Pi\mathrm{HP}}$ (Πατήρ), $\overline{\mathrm{ANOC}}$ Ἄνθρωπος). A bar was invariably written above the contraction. In imitation of the Greek, this system passed easily into Latin: e.g., $\overline{\mathrm{DS}}$ (*Deus*), $\overline{\mathrm{DNS}}$ (*Dominus*), $\overline{\mathrm{SPS}}$ (*Spiritus*), $\overline{\mathrm{IHS}}$ $\overline{\mathrm{XPS}}$ (*Iesus Christus,* the Greek eta, chi, and rho being retained in Latin), $\overline{\mathrm{SCS}}$ (*Sanctus*).

In Greek, contraction was almost completely restricted to the sacred names, but in Latin the system had a phenomenal development. It was first extended to include the name of the Church itself and various ecclesiastical offices: e.g., $\overline{\mathrm{ECCLA}}$ (*ecclesia*), $\overline{\mathrm{EPS}}$ (*episcopus*), $\overline{\mathrm{PBR}}$ (*presbyter*), $\overline{\mathrm{MAR}}$ (*martyr*). Then it spread into general use, becoming especially common in documents of all kinds and in scholarly treatises in the later Middle Ages. Cappelli's *Lexicon abbreviaturarum* (Milan 1954) furnishes a wealth of examples. The retention of declensional endings was an important convenience and advantage of the system. Thus, the genitive of *episcopus* could be written $\overline{\mathrm{EPI}}$; of *Dominus,* $\overline{\mathrm{DNI}}$; and of *presbyter,* PBRI. In the Middle Ages contraction was often combined with other forms of abbreviation, especially with superimposed letters and conventional symbols or signs.

Abbreviation by Ligatures and Superposition of Letters. In the earlier form of ligature, which involved capital and uncial letters in Greek and Latin, two letters were combined in such a way that the right hasta of the first served at the same time as the left hasta of the second. A third letter could be included in the combination. For example, a "T" in Greek or Latin could be added by increasing the height of one hasta and capping it with a horizontal bar. In Greek minuscule writing ligatures became very common. They are employed in a wide variety of combinations, some of which are rather complex. Superimposed letters are common in the Greek and Latin minuscule scripts of the Middle Ages. In many cases superimposed letters form part of a suspension or contraction. For an example in Greek, see the accompanying list.

Conventional Signs or Symbols. The Greek papyri already exhibit a large number of signs or symbols as forms of abbreviation. Many of these are in part letter

Ↄ or 9	For	*con*—
ꝯ	For	*cum*
÷	For	*est*
=	For	*esse*
7	For	*et*

Conventional symbols as abbreviations.

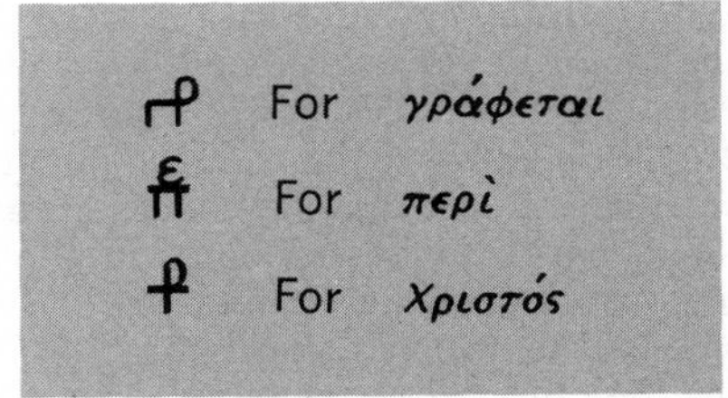

Greek superimposed letters as abbreviations.

suspensions, but many others are purely arbitrary conventional signs. As examples may be cited ὰ (ἀνά), μ- (μετά), σ́ (σύν), / (ἐστί), \ (εἶναι), \\ (εἰσί). Many conventional symbols were employed also to indicate weights and measures, the planets, etc. In the Greek minuscule MSS of the Middle Ages a large number of such conventional signs or symbols were in common use (see, for example, Thompson, 80–84).

The employment of similar abbreviations was frequent also in medieval Latin MSS, especially in those of a nonliterary character. The Tironian *notae* are in part represented in this form of abbreviation, and they contributed much to its further development. For examples of conventional symbols as abbreviations, see the accompanying list. The horizontal stroke was widely used to indicate the omission of letters. At first it was placed high in the line and to the right, as in AUTE— (*autem*), but later it was normally placed above the last letter: e.g., ENĪ (*enim*), NŌ (*non*), TENĒT (*tenent*). This symbol for an omitted "m" or "n" was retained by the early printers. As in Greek, there were numerous conventional signs for weights and measures, fractions, planets, stars, etc. (see, for example, Cappelli Lex, s.v. "Segni Convenzionali").

Ecclesiastical Abbreviations. In augmentation of the abbreviations and forms of abbreviation inherited from Christian antiquity, the Church in the Middle Ages and in early modern times created a large number of new abbreviations in the fields of ecclesiastical administration and institutions, theology, Canon Law, and liturgy. Pontifical documents for many centuries contained numerous abbreviations. However, Pope Leo XIII by his motu proprio of Dec. 29, 1878, not only introduced a modern style of writing in the papal chancery but also restricted the use of abbreviations. Lists of the abbreviations used in papal documents before 1878 and in ecclesiastical writings in general are available in the references given in the bibliography.

See also DIPLOMATICS, ECCLESIASTICAL; EPIGRAPHY, CHRISTIAN; PALEOGRAPHY, GREEK; PALEOGRAPHY, LATIN.

Bibliography: A. FERRUA et al., EncCatt 1:41–53, with excellent plates. H. LECLERCQ, DACL 1.1:155–183. E. MAGNIN, DDC 1:106–114, including a "Petit dictionnaire des abréviations autrefois en usage dans les documents canoniques." E. M. THOMPSON, *An Introduction to Greek and Latin Palaeography* (Oxford 1912) 71-92. B. A. VAN GRONINGEN, *Short Manual of Greek Palaeography* (3d ed. Leiden 1963) 43–47. R. DEVREESSE, *Introduction à l'étude des manuscrits grecs* (Paris 1954) 36–45. V. GARDTHAUSEN, *Griechische Paläographie,* 2 v. (2d ed. Leipzig 1911–13) 2:319–420, most comprehensive systematic treatment. G. BATTELLI, *Lezioni di paleografia latina* (3d ed. Vatican City 1949) 104–114, brief, but very good on Lat. abbrev. M. PROU, *Manuel de paléographie* (4th ed. Paris 1924) 109–165, with copious lists of Lat. and Fr. abbreviations, 311–474. L. C. HECTOR, *The Handwriting of English Documents* (London 1958). C. T. MARTIN, *The Record Interpreter: A Collection of Abbreviations, Latin Words and Names Used in English Historical*

Manuscripts and Records (2d ed. London 1910). L. TRAUBE, *Nomina Sacra: Versuch einer Geschichte der christlichen Kürzung* (Munich 1907). L. SCHIAPARELLI, *Avviamento allo studio delle abbreviature latine nel medioevo* (Florence 1926). W. M. LINDSAY, *Notae Latinae: An Account of Abbreviation in Latin MSS. of the Early Minuscule Period* (*c. 700–850*) (Cambridge, Eng. 1915); *Supplement* (*Abbreviations in Latin MSS. of 850 to 1050 A.D.*) by D. BAINS (Cambridge, Eng. 1936). M. H. LAURENT, *De abbreviationibus et signis scripturae Gothicae* (Rome 1939). P. LEHMANN, "Sammlungen und Erörterungen lateinischer Abkürzungen im Altertum und Mittelalter," AbhMünchAK Philos.-hist. Abt., NS 3 (1929). Cappelli Lex. J. L. WALTHER, *Lexicon diplomaticum, abbreviationes syllabarum et vocum in diplomatibus et codicibus a seculo VIII ad XVI usque occurrentes exponens* (Göttingen 1745–47; Ulm 1756). For official and popular abbreviations for religious orders and congregations, see esp. O. L. KAPSNER, *Catholic Religious Orders* (2d ed. Collegeville, Minn. 1957); the current issue of *The Official Catholic Directory,* under the headings "Statistics of Religious Orders," "Religious Orders," "Orders of Women."

[M. R. P. MC GUIRE]

ABBREVIATORS. This term was generically applied to one who drew up the first draft of a document, from which a good copy would be made to serve as the original. The ecclesiastical abbreviators were officials of the Apostolic Chancery, one of the oldest and most important offices in the Roman Curia. Their function was twofold: to compose the first, rather abbreviated, draft of papal letters, which were transcribed in proper form by copyists, and then to inspect the finished letter before it received the papal seal.

The origins of this office are uncertain. Mention is made of the existence of abbreviators in the Curia of Innocent III (1198–1216), but the first explicit use of the title abbreviator of apostolic letters occurs in the acts of John XXII (1316–34).

Whatever may be the date of the institution of the office of abbreviator, it is certain that it assumed greater importance upon its erection under Pius II (1458–64) into a college of prelates divided into a higher and a lower rank.

By decree of Leo X (1513–21) abbreviators were created nobles, counts palatine, and members of the papal household. They and their clerics and properties were exempt from all jurisdiction except the immediate jurisdiction of the pope. He also empowered them to confer the degree of doctor, to create notaries, to legitimize children, to ennoble three persons, and to make knights of the Order of St. Sylvester.

In the reforms of Pius VII (1800–23), the abbreviators of the lower rank were suppressed. The abolition of those of the higher rank in the reorganization of the papal chancery under Pius X (1903–14) brought to a close the long history of this institution.

Bibliography: E. FOURNIER, DDC 1:98–106. Pastor 4:38–39. M. LEGA, *Praelectiones in textum iuris canonici,* 4 v. (Rome 1896–1901) 2.1:289–290. G. CIAMPINI, *De abbreviatorum . . . statu . . .* (Rome 1691).

[L. A. VOEGTLE]

'ABDALLĀH ZĀḤIR, goldsmith, printer, lecturer, polemicist, deacon; b. Aleppo, Syria, 1680; d. monastery of Mar Ḥannā, Shuwair, Lebanon, Aug. 20, 1748. He was well educated in classical Arabic, philosophy, theology, and church history. Persecuted in Aleppo, he finally settled in the monastery of Mar Hannā (St. John) where he spent the rest of his life as a lay deacon, refusing priesthood out of humility. His greatest achievement was the construction of one of the very first printing presses for the Arabic language in the Orient, between 1723 and 1726. The first publication, however, dates from 1734. The purpose was to provide apologetic, instructional, and liturgical literature for Eastern Christians. He took an active part in the composition of the religious constitutions of the Basilian Shuwairite Order, vigorously opposed attempts by Patriarch Cyril Tānās to merge the Shuwairite monks and the Salvatorian missionaries into one order, and courageously denounced the efforts of Jesuit missionaries to Latinize the Melchite Church. The literary works of 'Abdallāh contain dissertations in reply to attacks of non-Catholic writers, an incomplete introduction to philosophy, a short manual of theology, several sermons, and a number of interesting letters. Also, many books on spiritual matters, edited and printed by him, bear the stamp of his character and zeal. He was buried in the church at St. John's Monastery, Shuwair.

Bibliography: Graf GeschChArabLit 3:191–201, contains good bibliog.

[L. MALOUF]

ABDIA (OBADIAH), BOOK OF, fourth of the *Minor Prophets. The "Vision of Abdia," which is its own title (v. 1), comprises only 21 verses and is thus the shortest book of the OT. It falls easily into two parts: (1) the punishment of Edom on the *day of the Lord because of its treachery against Juda when Jerusalem fell in 587 B.C. (1–15) and (2) Israel's victorious revenge (16–21). Verse 15b forms the closing sentence of the first part: the law of retaliation (Ex 21.23–25) will be applied to Edom. The passage in Jer 49.7–16, 22—with some differences of text and order of sentences—is similar to verses 1–14 of Abdia, and both pieces may be dependent on a common source. Edom, a long-standing enemy of Israel, will be the object of a day of vengeance described in Is 34.1–17; 63.1–6; Ez 25.12–14; 35.1–15; Jl 4.19; and Mal 1.2–5. In Abdia verses 11–14 vividly recall Edom's joy over Juda's calamity of 587 and its treachery on that occasion; these are the reasons for the downfall of Israel's ancient foe. The second part is eschatological; Edom's ruin is a sign of the Day of *Yahweh against all the pagan nations. Although the author was concerned primarily with Edom, the very mention of the Day of the Lord widened his horizon, and he saw the local event (judgment on Edom) as a symbol of the worldwide punishment of all Israel's enemies.

The Book of Abdia was composed probably in the early 5th century, though it may contain material that was somewhat earlier. Edom's predicted downfall occurred before 312 B.C. (when the *Nabataeans occupied Petra), and Edom was possibly already threatened *c.* 460. Thus, a reasonable date for "Abdia's Vision" would be after 587 and before 460 B.C. Faith in God's fidelity towards Israel is the main theme of the book. Abdia affirms that the day will come when oppressed Sion will become the place of salvation because of a catastrophic divine intervention ushering in a new and different order. The new order will recapture past glories, emerge in a new age beyond the divine *judgment, and bring about the fulfillment of God's purpose in history. Abdia is nationalistic in conceiving the day of Yahweh as a national restoration. The description of the new Israel (19–21) envisions the restoration of approximately the Davidic boundaries and is consistent with the aspirations of Abdia's contemporaries.

Bibliography: EncDictBibl 3–4. M. STENZEL, LexThK² 1:11. F. SALVONI and A. ROMEO, EncCatt 1:54–56. W. VOLLBORN, RGG³ 4:1547–48. S. BULLOUGH, CathCommHS 666–668.

[J. MORIARITY]

ABDIAS OF BABYLON, ST., according to legend, the first bishop of Babylon, appointed by the Apostles Simon and Jude. W. Lazius, in 1552, regarded Abdias as the author of a collection of legends about the Apostles, assuming that he had written them in Hebrew and that they had been translated into Greek by Eutropius, his disciple, and into Latin by *Julius Africanus. Actually the collection was drawn up by two anonymous authors in Gaul in the 6th century from earlier sources—one describing the martyrdoms of the Apostles and the other adding their virtues and miracles. It was used at the end of the 6th century in a revision at Auxerre of Jerome's martyrology and in a poem by Venantius *Fortunatus. The Abdias of a mutilated epitaph of the 5th century found at Henchir Djezza in Tunisia was probably a martyr under the *Vandals.

Bibliography: A. AUDOLLENT, DHGE 1:62–63; A. P. FRUTAZ, EncCatt 1:56.

[M. J. COSTELLOE]

ABDINGHOF, ABBEY OF, Paderborn, Westphalia, founded 1015 by *Meinwerk, Bishop of Paderborn, with the help of Benedictine monks from *Cluny. The abbatial church, dedicated to SS. Peter and Paul, was consecrated in 1031. The abbey was an important cultural center during the 11th and 12th centuries. The *Carmina Abdinhofensia* probably originated there toward the end of the 11th century, and during the 12th century the monks wrote the *Vita Meinwerci* (MGS 11:104–161), and the *Annales Patherbrunnenses.* However, in the 13th century a decline began to be apparent, and although various attempts at restoration were made, none produced any lasting improvement. After the plague of 1476, Abbot Henry of Peine (1477–91) united the abbey to the flourishing *Bursfeld Union, and it again became a center of discipline and religious life. But by the end of the 16th century signs of decline were again occurring, and once more restoration took place under Abbot Leonard Ruben (1598–1609); after that the abbey remained vigorous until its suppression in 1803.

Bibliography: U. BERLIÈRE, DHGE 1:64–65. *Westfälische Zeitschrift* 107 (1957). K. RATHE, EncCatt 1:57. K. HONSELMANN, LexThK² 1:12.

[C. FALK]

'ABDISHO IV (EBEDJESU), CHALDEAN PATRIARCH, 1555 to 1567. He was a monk and bishop of Gezirah, Mesopotamia (upper Tigris), when he succeeded the Patriarch John Sulaqa. He journeyed to Rome (1561), where he was recognized and given the pallium by Pope Pius IV (April 17, 1562). His profession of faith was read at the Council of Trent (Sept. 14, 1562). He consecrated many bishops. The Portuguese opposed his attempt to bring the Thomas Christians of India under his jurisdiction. He composed hymns in the honor of his predecessors who were martyred (*see* SYRIAN CHURCH IN INDIA).

Bibliography: J. M. VOSTÉ, "Trois poésies inédites," *Angelicum* 8 (1931) 187–234. G. BELTRAMI, *La chiesa Caldea nel secolo dell'Unione* (Orientalia Christiana 83; 1933). É. AMANN, DTC 11.1:229–230. E. TISSERANT, *ibid.* 14.2:3101–03. W. DE VRIES, LexThK² 3:626.

[F. X. MURPHY]

'ABDISHO, MARTYR, 4th-century Babylonian martyr (feast, May 16). According to the Syrian *Passio* 'Abdisho (Ebedjesu) was chorbishop of Kaskar, Babylonia. Accused of conspiracy with the Romans, he suffered martyrdom with Abdas and 38 Christians under the Sassanid King Shapur II in 374 or 375.

Bibliography: J. LABOURT, *Le Christianisme dans l'empire perse* (Paris 1904). A. CHRISTENSEN, *L'Iran sous les Sassanides* (Paris 1937). A. SCHALL, LexThK² 3:626. P. BEDJAN, ed., *Acta martyrum et sanctorum,* 7 v. (Paris 1890–97) 2:325–347.

[F. X. MURPHY]

'ABDISHO BAR BERĪKĀ, or Ebedjesu, Nestorian writer and metropolitan of Nisibis (Soba) and Armenia; d. November 1318. A monk (*c.* 1284) and bishop of Sīghar and Bet 'Arabājē, he became metropolitan of Nisibis in 1291. His voluminous writings in Syriac are listed at the end of his *Catalogue of Writers* (Badger, 361–379). *Commentaries* on the OT and NT, *Book of the Secrets of the Philosophy of the Greeks, Book on the Wonderful Economy of Salvation,* and many letters are lost. His *Book of the Pearl* and an *Introduction to the Trinity and Incarnation* are Nestorian dogmatic treatises; his *Symbolum, Canonical Collection, Table of Church Orders and Laws,* 50 spiritual poems called *Eden-Paradise, Book of Jewels,* and his *Book of the Foundations of Religion* are also preserved, some in Syriac and some in Arabic.

Bibliography: A. BAUMSTARK, *Geschichte der syrischen Literatur* (Bonn 1922) 323–325. J. PARISOT, DTC 1.1:24–27. B. KOTTER, LexThK² 3:625–626. S. P. RIDOLFINI, EncCatt 5:2. G. P. BADGER, *The Nestorians and their Rituals,* 2 v. (London 1852) 2:422. J. M. VOSTÉ, OrChrPer 7 (1941) 233–250, Ascension. Graf GeschChArabLit 1:165; 2:214–216. J. DAUVILLER, DDC 5:91–134.

[F. X. MURPHY]

ABDUCTION (IMPEDIMENT TO MARRIAGE)

Abduction as an impediment to marriage comes into being from the moment when a woman is forcibly carried off and violently retained in her abductor's power for the purpose of contracting marriage. While a definition of the impediment is not found in either the Latin or the Oriental code, it is described in identical phrasing in both codes (CIC c.1074; Creballat, c.64). Abduction is a diriment impediment since the law prescribes that there can be no valid marriage between the abductor and the woman abducted as long as she remains in the abductor's power or under his influence.

The impediment of abduction considered in itself and, excluding defect of consent that is frequently involved in it, is of ecclesiastical law and binds only baptized persons. Infidels, therefore, are not bound by this impediment when they intermarry unless the civil jurisdiction to which they are subject recognizes abduction as a diriment impediment. In the U.S. no civil jurisdiction considers abduction as an impediment to marriage, although most states punish abduction as a crime.

The abduction by an unbaptized person of a baptized person, or vice versa, brings the impediment into being because the impediment is intended not only as a protection for the abducted person, but also as a deterrent to the crime of abduction. The impediment of abduction will arise only if the abductor is a man and the one abducted is a woman, whether she is of good character or of loose morals. It will arise also even if she is otherwise impeded from marrying. Hence married women, close relatives of the abductors, and girls under marriageable age may all be objects of abduction.

The impediment arises whether the abductor acts personally or through agents, either men or women. If the woman is abducted by agents and detained by them up to the actual moment of the marriage, the impediment renders the marriage invalid between the man who ordered the abduction and the woman whom he ordered abducted.

Violent or forceful abduction must be for the sole purpose of contracting marriage. If the woman is taken away and retained for any other purpose, e.g., for extortion or turpitude, the impediment does not arise.

The impediment arises as soon as the abductor perpetrates his forceful act, and it continues to exist as long as the woman remains in his power. The impediment ceases to exist when the woman is separated from her abductor and has been restored to a safe and free place. Separation from the man entails a physical separation from him and from his agents. This has a special reference to the dwelling place. The woman must no longer be living in the same dwelling with the man but the length of time for which this separation must endure is not established in the law. A few days would certainly suffice if the woman enjoys perfect freedom and peace during that time. No change of place is absolutely required. If the woman has been detained by the man, the place can be said to become free and safe if the man departs and absolutely removes his influence and that of his agents over her. Hence a safe and free place is one in which the woman is able freely to dispose of her affairs as she will, and in which she can declare her own wishes without external constraint.

Since abduction is an impediment of the ecclesiastical law, the Church can dispense from it. In theory there is nothing to prevent this. In practice, however, it is not feasible, since abduction in itself implies an element of force and fear that further implies the presence of defective consent. Moreover, the Church has prescribed in her legislation that the impediment of abduction ceases to exist as soon as the woman is removed from the influence of her abductor or his agents. Hence in ordinary circumstances, dispensing from the impediment of abduction would be a superfluous and an unnecessary act.

Bibliography: B. F. FAIR, *The Impediment of Abduction* (CUA CLS 194; Washington 1944) 28–83. H. A. AYRINHAC, *Penal Legislation in the New Code of Canon Law* (New York 1920) 293–296. Ayrinhac-Lydon 145–150.

[W. A. O'MARA]

ABEL, FÉLIX MARIE, Biblical scholar and Palestinian geographer; b. Saint-Uze (Drôme), France, Dec. 29, 1878; d. Jerusalem, March 24, 1953. He entered the Dominican novitiate at Saint-Maximin, France, in 1897. Having pursued his philosophical and theological studies at the *studium generale,* which was then attached to the École Biblique in Jerusalem, he was ordained in 1902 and at once entered upon a teaching career that was to extend over half a century. He was a frequent contributor to the *Revue biblique, Journal of the Palestine Oriental Society, Dictionnaire de la Bible Suppl., Dictionnaire d'archéologie chrétienne et de liturgie.* His 2-volume *Géographie de la Palestine* (1933–38) established him as the outstanding authority on Palestinian geography. In 1952 he published the *Histoire de la Palestine depuis la conquête d'Alexandre jusqu'à l'invasion arabe.* For many decades the indefatigable director and guide of expeditions regularly conducted by the École Biblique to Sinai, Damascus, and sites of Biblical interest, he was chosen to write the section on Palestine in the *Guides bleus: Syrie et Palestine* (1932). His forte was a thorough, firsthand knowledge of the land and an extraordinary familiarity with all the pertinent literature. In collaboration with L. Vincent, he produced the following important works: *Jérusalem Nouvelle* (1914–22–24), *Bethléem: Le Sanctuaire de la Nativité* (1914), *Hébron: Le Haram el-Khalil* (1923), and *Emmaüs: Sa basilique et son histoire* (1932). He was president of the Palestine Oriental Society, a chevalier de la Légion d'Honneur, and in 1940 was named Consultor of the Pontifical Biblical Commission by Pius XII.

Félix Marie Abel.

Bibliography: R. DUSSAUD, *Syria* 30 (1953) 374–375. E. WEIDNER, ArchOr 16 (1953) 400–401.

[R. T. A. MURPHY]

ABELARD, PETER

Philosopher and theologian (Lat. *Abaelardus, Abeilardus*); b. Pallet, Brittany, 1079; d. Châlons-sur-Saône, April 21, 1142. One of the greatest philosophers of the 12th century, this peripatetic from Pallet, known as *Peripateticus palatinus* and *Doctor scholasticus,* is renowned for his solution of the problem of *universals. As a theologian, he outraged his contemporaries by his original use of *dialectics. As a man, he is known for his celebrated love affair with *Héloïse.

Life. Peter's father, Berengar, Lord of Pallet, planned a military career for him, but he chose learning instead. When he was about 15, he began the study of logic, probably under *Roscelin of Compiègne. In his autobiographical *Historia calamitatum,* he says that he traveled to any town where a teacher of logic could be found. Finally arriving in Paris, he studied under

*William of Champeaux, head of the cathedral school of Notre Dame. Prior to William's arrival, Paris had been considered intellectually inferior to the Benedictine Abbey of Bec and the cathedral schools of Laon and Chartres. Through William, Paris acquired great renown. While enrolled as a student, Abelard defeated William in public debate. On the strength of this victory, Abelard set up his own school in nearby Melun, and later in Corbeil. He was then only 25 years old. His youth and rashness in attacking men of established reputation in such a way that they were publicly disgraced, earned him celebrity, devoted followers, and persistent enemies. After about 2 years as a teacher in the region of Paris, he became ill and returned to his native Brittany. Returning to Paris in 1108, he studied rhetoric, under the same man against whom he had previously jousted, William of Champeaux. Public disputations had become a prominent feature of school life; during one of them Abelard forced the master to modify his extreme realist position, according to which there is a separately existent reality corresponding to each of the universal terms in one's vocabulary.

When he was 34, Abelard began to study theology under *Anselm of Laon. He found fault with Anselm's teaching methods, and to show that he could do better he gave a public lecture on the Book of Ezechiel after only one day's preparation. The novelty of his teaching consisted in the forthright raising of questions suggested by his dialectical studies; this was not the traditional method of communicating the patristic tradition with its heavy emphasis on questions that had affective implications. Once more Abelard earned the resentment of his teacher by arousing the interest of Anselm's students, thus showing that they preferred the work of a gifted amateur to Anselm's traditional mode of teaching.

Paris and Héloïse. When Abelard returned to Paris, he was allowed to teach both theology and dialectics first at the school of Mont Sainte-Geneviève and, in 1113, at the cathedral school of Notre Dame. Students flocked to him in such numbers that he acquired both wealth and honors. At this time he fell in love with Héloïse, the niece of Fulbert, a canon of Notre Dame. This unwitting man invited Abelard to live in his house and, ironically, to take charge of the further education of his niece. When Héloïse became pregnant, Abelard had her secretly conveyed to his home in Brittany. The whimsical name Astrolabe was given to their son. Later, to mollify Fulbert, Abelard secretly married Héloïse. This was possible since he had not received major orders at the time. When the marriage became known publicly and when students began to sing love songs and lyrics reputed to have been written by Abelard for Héloïse, Abelard tried to safeguard his position by having Héloïse enter the convent of Saint-Argenteuil, where she had been brought up. Fulbert regarded this as an evasion of responsibility and in anger hired men who, with the connivance of Abelard's servant, entered his room at night and emasculated him.

Abelard's personal fame as a man centers not so much on his philosophical and theological work as it does upon this love affair with Héloïse, told in such detail and with such frankness in letters that are still extant. He is the only philosopher in the Middle Ages who left an autobiography and personal letters, in which historians find details that are very illuminating for the study of social and intellectual life in the 12th century. The information supplied in these is invaluable for destroying false stereotypes set up by 19th-century historians, such as Jules Michelet, about intellectual freedom in the Middle Ages.

St. Bernard's Denunciation. After his downfall, Abelard entered the monastery at Saint-Denis to become a Benedictine monk. Characteristically, he aroused opposition by offering proof that the monastery's patron was not identical with Dionysius the Areopagite. He resumed teaching in Paris until 1121, when the Council of Soissons condemned his teaching on the Blessed Trinity. After spending some time in forced residence in a monastic house, he set up a school in what became the town of Nogent-sûr-Seine. In 1125 he was elected abbot of the Abbey of Saint-Gildas in his native Brittany. Finding his life as abbot difficult and complicated because of the monks of Saint-Gildas, he was back teaching in Paris in 1136. His teaching was denounced to St. *Bernard of Clairvaux by *William of Saint-Thierry, who accused him of a rationalist approach that attempted to empty even doctrines such as the Trinity of all mystery. Bernard wrote to Pope Innocent II and to numerous bishops against Abelard and his teaching. Under the illusion that he would have the opportunity of publicly disputing with Bernard, Abelard appeared before the Council of Sens in 1141 only to find that his role was to listen silently while a sentence of condemnation was read to him. He appealed to Pope Innocent, oblivious of the fact that Bernard's letters had closed all doors to him. On his way to Rome, he was received at the monastery of Cluny by *Peter the Venerable, who persuaded him to abandon the struggle, attempt reconciliation with Bernard, and accept a papal authorization to pass his remaining years under the protection of Cluny. He died at a Cluniac priory in 1142.

Writings. Abelard's more important extant works are those that treat of logic and theology. In addition, there are extant sermons, poems, and letters, one of which is an autobiography covering his life until about 1129.

Logic. His *Introductiones parvulorum* are short glosses on the logical treatises of Porphyry, Aristotle, and Boethius, probably representing the lessons he gave to beginners. *Logica ingredientibus* contained more elaborate glosses on Porphyry and on the *Categories* and *De interpretatione* of Aristotle. *Dialectica* is his most developed and complete work on logic; the beginning of this work, probably attacking the realist position, has not survived.

Theology. Tractatus de fide Trinitatis is the surviving record of his theological lectures prior to the Council of Soissons (1121). This work is notable for its lack of reference to the Church Fathers, and the substitution of personal and seemingly rationalistic attempts to explain the Blessed Trinity. The compilation *Sic et non* lists the opinions of the Fathers, often contradictory, on various theological topics raised in scholastic disputations. This is at the same time an answer to those who said that he was not concerned with the Fathers and a proof that some rational approach was needed to reconcile their differences. One version of this work seems to have been written about 1123, and another toward the end of his life in 1136. *Theologia Christiana* is a reworking of the *Tractatus de fide Trinitatis* with

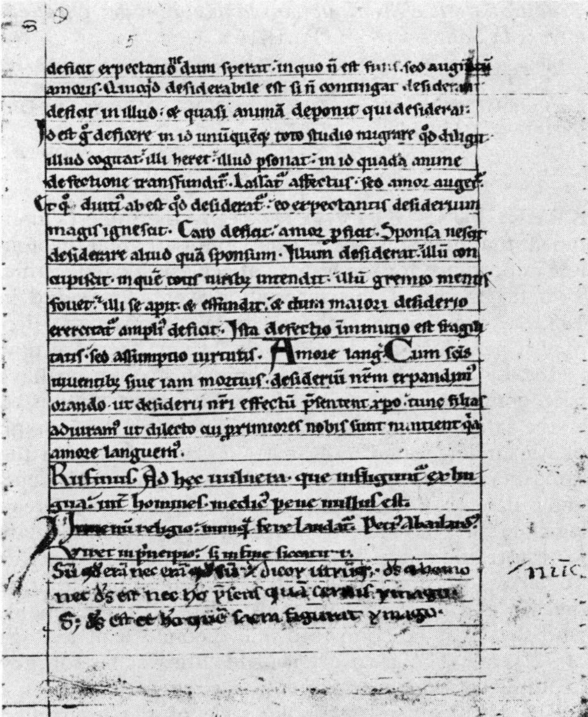

Folio of a fragment of a manuscript in verse and prose, 12th century, which contains quotations from Abelard, Ausonius, and Rufinus (Poole MSS, Indiana University).

many citations from the Church Fathers and the Scripture. It seems to have been written in 1124. Books 1 and 2 of *Introductio ad theologiam* are a reworking of his earlier books on theology. Book 3 represents an advanced form of his thought and was probably written in 1136. His *Ethics,* or *Scito teipsum,* probably written in 1137, deals with moral theology. *Dialogus inter philosophum, Judaeum et Christianum* was written during the last year of his life and gives his final thought on the problem of reason and faith.

Influence. The importance of Abelard in the history of philosophy rests mainly on his proposed solution to the problem of universals. He stood midway between the ultrarealist position of the Platonic tradition and the nominalist views of Roscelin, saying that universals as such exist only in the mind but that they signify the nature that individual things share in common. His place in theology depends mainly on his contribution toward the *scholastic method. Historically he stands close to the origin of the tradition, exemplified by Peter Lombard, that used varying opinions of the Fathers as the starting point for theological synthesis. His speculative pursuit of questions in theology without reference to their affective connotations seems to have outraged William of Saint-Thierry. In a letter to Bernard, the latter accuses Abelard of doing in theology what he had learned to do in dialectics, of being "a censor of the faith, not a disciple; an improver of it, not an imitator." Viewed from the vantage point of the great syntheses of faith and reason established by 13th-century *scholasticism, in which Abelardian methods had an important place, his work seems more defensible than it did to his contemporaries. As to the orthodoxy of Abelard's theological opinions there are, on the one hand, the condemnations of Soissons and Sens (the latter formally approved by Innocent II) and the firm, lasting hostility of Bernard. On the other hand, modern scholars such as Jean Cottiaux and J. Rozycki, after a careful study of the development of his doctrine on faith and reason and on the Trinity, have found it possible to give a much more benign interpretation. Two things are certain: (1) Abelard wished to reason in such a way as not to be separated from Christ, and (2) much that was condemned at Sens cannot be found, as such, in his writings. This does not mean that Bernard and the bishops were wrong in condemning what they thought his contemporaries would have drawn from his words. Extant MSS of some of Abelard's immediate disciples indicate that the sense of the errors condemned was the very sense defended by the school of Abelard.

Modern scholarship has shown the existence of a school of Abelard both in theology and in logic. Not all of his disciples, however, were like Adam, a canon of the Lateran, who taught the errors of his master concerning the Incarnation before 1135 and who, being attacked by *Gerhoh of Reichersberg, preferred apostasy to retraction. Direct disciples, such as *John of Salisbury and *Peter of Poitiers, were orthodox, while others, such as *William of Conches and *Gilbert de la Porrée, were accused of heresy. Bernard, William of Saint-Thierry, and John of Salisbury attest to the vast divulgation of Abelard's writings and influence, even after the condemnation of 1141. This is confirmed by the discovery of numerous MSS of *summae* of various *Sentences,* theological treatises, and logical works, many of them anonymous, belonging to the school of Abelard. Even after he was long dead, Peter Abelard was attacked by Walter of Saint-Victor as one of France's evils in *Contra quatuor labyrinthos Franciae*. By that time, Abelard's dialectics had taken firm hold in early scholasticism.

See also DIALECTICS IN THE MIDDLE AGES; SENTENCES AND SUMMAE; SCHOLASTICISM, 1; UNIVERSALS.

Bibliography: Works. *Opera omnia,* PL v.178; *Ouvrages inédits d'Abélard,* ed. V. COUSIN (Paris 1836); *Opera,* ed. V. COUSIN et al., 2 v. (Paris 1849–59); "Peter Abelards Philosophische Schriften," ed. B. GEYER, BeitrGeschPhilMA 21.1–4 (1919–33) 1–633; *Dialectica,* ed. L. M. DE RIJK (Assen 1956). Studies. Gilson HistChrPhil 153–163. J. G. SIKES, *Peter Abailard* (Cambridge, Eng. 1932). É. H. GILSON, *Héloise and Abelard,* tr. L. K. SHOOK (Chicago 1951). E. PORTALIÉ, DTC 1.1:36–55. P. GLORIEUX, DTC Tables générales 1:5–7. E. VACANDARD, DHGE 1:71–91. G. PARÉ et al., *La Renaissance du XIIe siècle: Les Écoles et l'enseignement* (Paris 1933). **Illustration credit:** Lilly Library, Indiana University, Bloomington, Ind.

[S. R. SMITH]

ABELL, ROBERT, missionary; b. Nelson County, Ky., Nov. 25, 1792; d. Louisville, Ky., June 28, 1873. He was one of seven sons and three daughters of Robert and Margaret (Mills) Abell. His father left Maryland for Kentucky in 1788, served in the first legislature of 1792, and was the only Catholic in the state constitutional convention of 1799. Robert was educated at St. Rose and entered St. Thomas Seminary, Bardstown, Ky., in 1812. He was ordained by Bp. B. J. Flaget on May 10?, 1818. He was noted for his height (6 feet 4 inches) and quickly became known for his native eloquence. His first mission was the vast area formerly served by the missionary Charles Nerinckx, with its center at St. Anthony in Breckinridge County, from which he traveled 800 miles. He opened a boarding school at Long Lick and in 1820 induced the Sisters of Charity of Nazareth to build Mt. Carmel convent and school. In 1824 he was moved to Louisville, where he built the second church of St. Louis. In 1834 he was transferred to Lebanon to build a new church, but hard times prevented the opening of St. Augustine until 1837. Three years later he was appointed vice president of St. Joseph College, Bardstown, where he had taught earlier. In 1844 he was sent to New Haven to build St. Catharine's, which was dedicated in 1848, and he remained there until 1860, when sciatica forced his retirement. The next 10 years he lived with relatives at Holy Mary, assisting pastors all over the state. In 1872 he became chaplain of St. Joseph Infirmary, Louisville, where he died suddenly. He was buried in St. Louis cemetery.

Bibliography: B. J. Webb, *The Centenary of Catholicity in Kentucky* (Louisville 1884). J. H. Schauinger, *Cathedrals in the Wilderness* (Milwaukee 1952).

[J. H. SCHAUINGER]

ABELL, THOMAS, BL., martyr; b. place unknown, toward the end of the 15th century; d. July 30, 1540. He was educated at Oxford (M.A., 1516), became a chaplain to Catherine of Aragon, and preached and wrote in her favor. When sent to Spain in 1529 at the time of the divorce question, he performed invaluable work on Queen Catherine's behalf. He was one of her counselors at the divorce trial and probably helped her in making her appeals against the jurisdiction of the Legatine Court. In 1531 he published his vigorous defense of Catherine's marriage, the *Invicta Veritas.* For this he was imprisoned, but was later released. In 1533 he was sent to the Tower because of his counsel to Catherine to persist in refusing the title of "Princess Dowager." His name was included in the attainder of 1534 against the Nun of Kent and others, but he had had no real association with the Nun. He remained in the Tower for more than 6 years, receiving appalling ill-treatment. He refused to acknowledge the royal supremacy and for this reason was attainted of treason in 1540. On July 30, 1540, he was hanged, drawn, and quartered at Smithfield. He was beatified on Dec. 29, 1886.

Bibliography: B. Camm, ed., *Lives of the English Martyrs Declared Blessed by Pope Leo XIII in 1886 and 1895,* 2 v. (London 1904–05).

[J. E. PAUL]

ABELLY, LOUIS, theologian; b. Paris, *c.* 1604; d. Paris, Oct. 4, 1691. He was educated at the Sorbonne and was closely associated with St. Vincent de Paul. In 1640 he was sent by the latter to Bayonne to help Bp. de Fouquet. When Bp. de Fouquet was transferred to Agde in 1644, Abelly returned to Paris, was pastor of Saint-Josse and then spiritual director of the Filles de la Croix. He devoted much of his time and energy to the Salpetrière Hospital. In 1662 he was named bishop of Rodez. In 1665 he was struck with paralysis; he returned to Paris and remained at the Saint-Lazare Home where he died. His most important work was *Vie du vénérable serviteur de Dieu, Vincent de Paul* (Paris 1664), the first life of St. Vincent and still of use to scholars today. *Medulla theologica* (Paris 1650) is a pastoral manual of probabilist doctrine. He adopts a positive method in his *Tradition de L'Église touchant la dévotion des chrétiens envers la Sainte Vierge* (Paris 1652).

Bibliography: P. Broutin, *La Réforme pastorale en France au XVII**e siècle,* 2 v. (Tournai 1956) 2:331–345. I. Cecchetti, EncCatt 1:68–69. A. Vogt, DHGE 1:97–103. A. Rastoul, Dict BiogFranc 1:130–140.

[P. BROUTIN]

ABERCIUS, EPITAPH OF, the oldest monument that mentions the Eucharist; it is of great theological importance for the history of ecclesiastical doctrine. Two fragments of this inscription were discovered in 1883 by the British archeologist W. Ramsay in Hieropolis, near Synnada, in Phrygia Minor; they are now in the Lateran Museum. The epitaph appears to have been composed at the end of the 2d century. It existed at the latest before the year 216, because the epitaph of Alexander, found by Ramsay a year before near the same place, quotes a part of the epitaph of Abercius and is dated 216. This epitaph of Alexander and a Greek legendary life of Abercius (4th century) enabled scholars to restore the entire text of the inscription. It contains 22 verses, a distichon, and 20 hexameters that describe the life and deeds of Abercius, Bishop of Hieropolis, who says that he composed and dictated it at the age of 72 years. The great event of his life was his journey to Rome, of which he gives an account.

The mystical and symbolic style of the inscription reflects the influence of the *discipline of the secret, and its metaphorical phraseology is responsible for the sharp controversy that followed the discovery. A number of scholars, among them G. Ficker, A. Dieterich,

Fragments of the epitaph of Abercius presented to Pope Leo XIII by W. Ramsay and Sultan Abdul-Hamid II, now preserved in Lateran Palace Museum.

and R. Reitzenstein, tried to demonstrate that Abercius was not a Christian, but a venerator of Cybele and Attis, the Phrygian divinities; A. von Harnack called him a syncretist. The majority of scholars, including W. Ramsay, G. de *Rossi, L. *Duchesne, and F. *Cumont, are convinced that the epitaph is of Christian origin. A thorough investigation of its language and style, its content and form by F. *Dölger has removed all doubt as to its Christian character. Abercius does not call himself a bishop, but "a disciple of the chaste shepherd," i.e., Christ, who "has great eyes that look on all sides." He taught him "faithful writings," i.e., the Holy Scriptures of the Christians and their doctrines. He sent him to Rome to see "the queen with golden robe and golden shoes," i.e., the Church of Christ, His Bride. Abercius saw there "a people bearing a splendid seal," i.e., the seal of Baptism. Faith was "his guide," and for this reason he met friends and fellow Christians everywhere who offered him as a meal the Lord's Supper of bread and wine. He calls Christ "the fish from the spring, mighty and pure," that "the spotless Virgin caught," i.e., whom the Virgin Mary conceived. The Christian teaching appears in the language of a mystery cult and explains why Abercius at the end says: "Let him who understands and believes this pray for Abercius," since only the initiated could comprehend the meaning of these words.

Bibliography: Quasten MonE 2–25, text and Lat. tr. F. J. DÖLGER, ΙΧΘΥΣ, v.1 (Rome 1910) 8–138; *ibid.* v.2 (Münster 1922) 454–507. A. ABEL, *Byzantion* 3 (1926) 321–411, complete bibliog. Quasten Patr 1:171–173, Eng. tr. A. FERRUA, Riv ArchCrist 20 (1943) 279–305; CivCatt (1943) 39–45. H. GRÉGOIRE, *Byzantion* 25–27 (1955–57) 363–368, and Bardesanes.
Illustration credit: Photographical Archives of the Pontifical Museum.

[J. QUASTEN]

ABERCROMBY, ROBERT

Scottish Jesuit, 19 years on the Scottish mission; b. Scotland, 1532; d. Braunsberg College, East Prussia, April 27, 1613. Robert, of a good Catholic family, was educated at St. Mary's College, Scotland. He was one of five young men who in 1562 went to the Continent to study for the priesthood in the company of the Papal Nuncio Nicholas de Gouda, SJ, who was then returning from an unsuccessful visit to the court of Queen Mary in order to bring Scottish bishops to the Council of Trent. All five became Jesuits and played a distinguished role in the Counter Reformation in Scotland: James Tyrie, William Crichton, John Hay, William Murdoch, and Abercromby. Father Tyrie, who died in Rome in 1597, was especially influential in gaining Abercromby for the mission to Scotland. Meanwhile Abercromby spent 23 years abroad assisting Catholics from England and Scotland and training Jesuit novices. He was a pupil of the celebrated Jesuit Diego *Laínez in the latter's last years and a friend of Cardinal Stanislaus *Hosius, who built a seminary for priests at Braunsberg, where many Scotsmen came to study and receive their training for the missions from the Jesuits.

In 1586 Elizabeth of England had concluded an alliance with James VI of Scotland that had as a condition the expulsion of the Jesuits from Scotland. But the execution of his mother, Mary Stuart, shortly after, disposed the King to show indulgence to his Catholic subjects. The Jesuit missionaries were not slow to take advantage; Abercromby and William Ogilvie arrived from Poland and went into hiding while administering to the Catholics. Abercromby converted a number of high-born Scots, among them James Lindsay, brother of the Earl of Crawford. His most notable convert was James VI's wife, Anne of Denmark, at Holyroodhouse in 1600. Abercromby's own account, in a letter from Braunsberg, September 1608, gives evidence of James's knowledge of this and tacit consent. "She [Anne] admitted [to the King] she had dealings with a Catholic priest and named me, an old cripple." James made no effort to reclaim Anne, but rather made it possible for her to have secret access to her Jesuit confessor by appointing Abercromby "Keeper of his Majesty's Hawks." In a report on the state of Scotland (1602), Abercromby, then superior of the Scottish mission, remarked that the Queen had received Holy Communion 9 or 10 times.

The *Gunpowder Plot of 1605 caused James, now King of England, to order a special search for Abercromby, offering a reward of 10,000 crowns for his capture, no mean proof of his worth to his enemies and his courage and skill in evading his pursuers. Forced finally to flee, Abercromby was one of the last priests to leave Scotland. He spent the remainder of his life at the Jesuit College at Braunsberg.

Bibliography: A. BELLESHEIM, *History of the Catholic Church of Scotland,* tr. D. O. HUNTER-BLAIR, 4 v. (Edinburgh 1887–90). W. FORBES-LEITH, ed., *Narratives of Scottish Catholics under Mary Stuart and James VI* (Edinburgh 1885). *Recusant History* 5 (1959–60) 205–206, for list of documents and bibliog. H. FOLEY, ed., *Records of the English Province of the Society of Jesus,* 7 v. in 15 (London 1877–82) v.7, pt. 2. G. OLIVER, *Collections towards Illustrating the Biography of the Scotch, English and Irish Members of the Society of Jesus* (London 1845). D. MCROBERTS, ed., *Essays on the Scottish Reformation, 1513–1625* (Glasgow 1962). T. COLLINS, *Martyr in Scotland . . .* (New York 1956).

[J. D. HANLON]

ABERDEEN, UNIVERSITY OF

Situated in northeast Scotland, the University derives its origin from two separate and at one time independent foundations: the 15th-century university founded at the instance of James IV and the 16th-century Marischal College, both reconstituted as the University of Aberdeen in 1860.

Origin and Development. The University honors as its founder the ambassador and statesman, William Elphinstone, Bishop of Aberdeen (1483–1514), who in 1495 obtained a bull from Alexander VI establishing in the cathedral city of old Aberdeen a *studium generale et universitas,* with authority to offer instruction in theology, Canon Law, civil law, medicine, and liberal arts. In 1505 Elphinstone created within this foundation a college dedicated to St. Mary *in nativitate,* with its own buildings and collegiate church, endowments, and exact regulations. The College enjoyed the patronage of James IV (1488–1513) and later came to be known as King's College. Elphinstone's charter of 1505 provided endowment for 36 members of the College including 6 masters, 5 students of theology who assisted with the teaching, and 13 students of arts holding scholarships or bursaries. The Elphinstone bursaries are still awarded.

The bishops of Aberdeen were chancellors of the University until the Scottish Reformation of 1560 sev-

Marischal College from the west, Aberdeen University.

ered the close links between the University and the Catholic Church. Thereafter Protestant bishops continued to hold office until the end of the episcopate within the reformed Church of Scotland in 1688. Following the Reformation, the Protestant authorities did not find King's College eager to introduce educational reforms that they considered desirable. In 1593 George Keith, hereditary Earl Marischal of Scotland and one of the foremost of the Protestant nobility, founded a new and separate university in Aberdeen named Marischal College. It was established in the Franciscan friary and endowed with the forfeited lands and revenues of the Aberdeen friars. The two Colleges remained as independent institutions for nearly 3 centuries until 1860, when they were united into one "University of Aberdeen." In the 20th century the University continues to occupy the sites of the historic colleges, and their names are still used to describe the main groups of teaching buildings: Marischal College near the center of the modern city and King's College in the northern outskirts. The existing buildings, however, are largely modern though at King's the original College chapel, with its crown tower and fine medieval woodwork, remains as one of the glories of the University.

The University Library, housing more than 400,000 volumes, and including a fine collection of 16th-century scientific treatises, is centered in King's College.

Expansion. In 1938 the University extended to a third important site with the opening of an extensive building for the clinical medical departments adjacent to the newly built Aberdeen Royal Infirmary in the western suburbs. Large extensions to the medical building are in the planning stage.

In 1900 the number of matriculated students was about 800; in 1939 it was more than 1,200. The number has risen rapidly since World War II and in 1964 reached 3,500. The University has undertaken to plan for 4,500 students (including 500 postgraduates) by 1967. To accomplish this, the University is largely dependent on government finance. In 1900 less than half its income came from government grants; by 1964 this had increased to more than 80 per cent.

The expansion in numbers has made necessary an extensive building program largely centered in Old Aberdeen. Chemistry and physics buildings with expanded facilities for research were opened in 1952 and 1963 respectively. In 1964 a new arts building was opened and a science library was in process of construction. The erection of buildings for agriculture, mathematics, and zoology was being planned.

Traditionally the University has drawn its students from its own hinterland. During the early 1960s, however, an increasing proportion have come from farther afield, particularly from England, thus necessitating the planning of additional residential accommodation. The first university residence, Crombie Hall, was opened in 1958 with provision for 46 men and 64 women. It was the first mixed university residence in Britain and the experiment has been wholly successful. More residences are planned.

Organization and Administration. The University is composed of five Faculties: Arts, Science, Medicine, Law, and Divinity, which confer respectively the following degrees: M.A., B.Sc., M.B., Ch.B., LL.B., and B.D. In 1964 the approximate enrollment within the various faculties was: 1,600, arts; 1,200, science; 550, medicine; 120, law; and 30, divinity. The ordinary degrees of M.A. and B.Sc. normally require 3 years' study, and the honors degrees, 4 years. The M.B. and Ch.B. course lasts 6 years and the LL.B., 3 years. The B.D. is awarded after 3 years' study and a previous degree in arts. Facilities for postgraduate study and research exist in all faculties. The teaching staff comprises approximately 450 members, holding appropriate doctoral, professional, and master's degrees.

Since Aberdeen stands in the midst of fishing and agricultural communities, particular emphasis in the faculty of science is placed on the biological sciences including agriculture and forestry. Close relations are maintained between the University and important local fishery, soil, and animal nutrition research institutions and with the North of Scotland College of Agriculture.

The governing bodies of the University are the University Court, which administers its finances, and the Senatus Academicus, which is responsible for teaching and discipline. The Court comprises 14 members including representatives of the Senatus, graduate body, and Aberdeen Town Council. The Senatus, which numbers more than 50, includes each professor and a certain number of other teachers. The resident head of the University is the principal, appointed by the Crown. He may or may not be chosen from among the professoriate.

Bibliography: R. S. Rait, *The Universities of Aberdeen* (Aberdeen 1895). J. M. Bulloch, *A History of the University Aberdeen, 1495–1895* (London 1895). P. J. Anderson, ed., *Studies in the History and Development of the University of Aberdeen* (Aberdeen 1900); *Record of the Celebration of the Quatercentenary of the University of Aberdeen . . . 1906* (Aberdeen 1907). W. D. Simpson, ed., *The Fusion of 1860: A Record of the Centenary Celebrations and a History of the United University of Aberdeen, 1860–1960* (London 1963).

[W. S. ANGUS; A. G. MITCHELL]

ABGAR, LEGENDS OF, two letters published by Eusebius of Caesarea as part of the *Acta Edessena* (*Hist. eccl.* 1.13), supposedly discovered in the archives of Edessa. They purport to be an exchange of correspondence between Jesus Christ and King Abgar V called Uchama (the "black" according to Tacitus), who reigned in Osrhoene from 4 B.C. to A.D. 7 and from 13 to 50. The first letter carried by an artist Ananias requests Christ to come to Osrhoene and cure the King. In His response Christ excuses Himself, but promises to send the Apostle Thaddeus (the Disciple Thomas the Younger, or Addai) after His Ascension. A version (*c.* 400) of the legend in the *Acts of Thaddeus* and the Syriac *Doctrina Addaei* or Thaddeus legend has Christ cure Abgar before sending Thaddeus who converts the King.

The legend is further elaborated with the story of the conversion of King Abgar IX (179–216) who became a Roman tributary in 195, and whose court was visited by *Julius Africanus and the gnostic Bardesanes [*Kestoi* 7, ed. J. Viellefond (Paris 1932) 49]. The so-called portrait of Christ at Edessa was supposedly painted by the messenger Ananias; and the words of Christ quoted in the second letter were used by Syrians and Eastern Egyptians as protective devices (Procopius, *Bell. Pers.* 2.12).

Recent investigation indicates that the Eusebian version that spread in the West through *Rufinus of Aquileia's translation of his Church History antedates the Thaddeus legend. Traces of Tatian's *Diatessaron* in the letters point to an early 3d-century composition. St. Augustine denied the existence of any letter written by Christ (*C. Faust.* 28.4) and the *Decretum Gelasianum* called this correspondence apocryphal. Considerable doubt now surrounds the conversion of King Abgar IX, which until recently was accepted as historical fact.

Bibliography: H. RAHNER, LexThK² 1:43. Quasten Patr 1:140–143. LABUBNĀ BAR SENNĀK, *The Doctrine of Addai,* ed. in Syriac and tr. G. PHILLIPS (London 1876). E. VON DOBSCHÜTZ, "Der Briefwechsel zwischen Abgar und Jesus," *Zeitschrift für wissenschaftliche Theologie* 43 (1900) 422–486; *Das Christusbild von Edessa* (TU 18, NS 3; 1899). A. VON HARNACK and E. VON DOBSCHÜTZ, eds., *Decretum Gelasianum* (TU 38; 1912). S. RUNCIMAN, CambHistJ 3 (1929–31) 238–252, portraits. H. C. YOUTIE, ". . . the Letter to Abgar," HarvThRev 23 (1930) 299–302; 24 (1931) 61–66. I. ORTIZ DE URBINA, "Le origini del cristianesimo in Edessa," Greg 15 (1934) 82–91; EncCatt 1:75.

[F. X. MURPHY]

ABIATHAR, son of the high priest Achimelech, of the Aaronic line of Ithamar, priest with *Sadoc during David's reign. When Doeg, the Edomite, at Saul's insistence slaughtered the priests at Nobe (1 Sm 22.18), Abiathar alone escaped, carrying the ephod with him (1 Sm 22.20–23; 23.6). He fled to David and served as his priest (1 Sm 23.6–12; 30.7–8). After the conquest of Jerusalem, Abiathar and Sadoc were David's priests; from the references it appears that Abiathar was subordinate to Sadoc since he is always listed after him (2 Sm 15.29, 35; 17.15; 19.11; 20.25; see also 1 Chr 18.16). A tradition lists Abiathar and Sadoc as priests also in Solomon's time (3 Kgs 4.4) but, since Abiathar in the struggle over the succession supported Adonia (3 Kgs 1.7, 19, 25; 2.22), he was exiled to Anathoth and escaped death only because of earlier services to David (3 Kgs 2.26). Abiathar's exile is interpreted as the fulfillment of the prophecy against *Heli (1 Sm 2.27–36). A son of Abiathar, Jonathan, is mentioned during Absalom's rebellion (2 Sm 15.36; 17.15–22). Abiathar is referred to in Mk 2.26, but it is obvious from context that his father Achimelech is meant. It is often assumed that Jeremia (1.1) was a descendant of the exiled Abiathar.

Bibliography: InterDictBibl 1:6–7. De Vaux AncIsr 372–374, 388–389. H. P. SMITH, *Samuel* (ICC; New York 1904) 209, 211, 246.

[F. BUCK]

ABIDING IN CHRIST, a New Testament concept. The verb μένειν, which in general means to remain or to abide, occurs about 117 times in the NT, and 67 of these are found in the Johannine writings. St. John favors this word to express his conviction that the new life of the last age, which the Christian believer possesses here and now, is in itself and in its fundamental orientation permanent and imperishable. This new life is everlasting, precisely because it joins the Christian in an abiding community of life with Christ and, through Christ, with the Father. Christ abides in His disciples, giving them a share in His own divine and everlasting life, which He holds from the Father (Jn 5.26; 6.56–57; 1 Jn 5.11–12). St. John uses with predilection the so-called reciprocal immanence formulas (e.g., "Abide in me, and I in you," Jn 15.4) to express this deep unchangeable community of life with Christ and, through Him, with the Father (Jn 6.56–57; 15.4–10; 1 Jn 3.24; 4.12–16). In St. John's view the Christian's union with the Father is an extension of his abiding union with the Son (Jn 14.20; 15.9–10; 17.21, 23, 26); and the communion among Christians grounded on their communion with the Son and Father, has as its exemplar the union between Father and Son (Jn 17.11, 21, 22).

The abiding new life in Christ is conferred by the Sacraments in *faith (Jn 3.5; 6.56–57), with the uncreated gift of the Spirit vouching for the fact that "we abide in God and He in us" (1 Jn 4.13; see 3.24b). Nevertheless the hostility of the world requires that Christians strive perseveringly to abide in faith, in love, and in the practice of the Commandments; see St. John's urgent imperatives: Jn 8.31; 15.4–27; 1 Jn 2.6, 24, 27, 28; 3.15, 17; 4.12, 16.

See also MYSTICAL BODY OF CHRIST; BROTHER IN CHRIST; INCORPORATION IN CHRIST; REBIRTH (IN THE BIBLE); REBIRTH (IN THEOLOGY); DIVINE NATURE, PARTAKER OF; GRACE, ARTICLES ON.

Bibliography: R. SCHNACKENBURG, LexThK² 2:528–529.

[F. X. LAWLOR]

ABIDJAN, ARCHDIOCESE OF (ABIDJANENSIS), metropolitan see since 1955, on the Atlantic in south *Ivory Coast, West Africa. In 1963 it had 28 parishes, 120 priests, 111 sisters, 550 catechists, 186,000 Catholics, and 25,000 catechumens in a population of 550,000; it is 14,480 square miles in area. Some 213,000 pagans, 80,000 Moslems, and 45,000 Protestants live in the see. The city of Abidjan, capital of Ivory Coast, was founded as a railroad terminus in 1903.

Systematic evangelization began in 1895, when the Prefecture Apostolic of the Ivory Coast was detached from that of the Gold Coast (*Cape Coast, *Ghana). The prefecture became a vicariate (1911), called Abidjan (1940). The following suffragan sees derive from the original territory: Abengourou (created in 1963), Bouaké (1955), Daloa (1955), Gagnoa (1956), and Katiola (1955). The Society of African Missions of Lyons is aided by French secular clergy, Franciscans, and Assumptionists (who have a high school with 400 pupils). Benedictines at Bouaké are associated with Toumliline in *Morocco. Sisters do hospital and school work; some 20,000 children are in mission schools. The major seminary at Anyama is under *Eudists; a minor seminary is in Bingerville. A novitiate for native sisters is at Moosou. The African Institute for Economic and Social Development (1962), affiliated with *Action Populaire (Paris) and directed by Jesuits, offers study and research in Abidjan and correspondence courses to all French-speaking Africa.

Bibliography: MissCattol 101–103. G. MONTICONE, EncCatt 1:77–78. AnnPont (1964) 14.

[J. HUCHET]

ABILENE, a mountainous region in the Anti-Lebanon range north of Palestine. Its capital, Abila (modern Sūq Wādī Baradā), lay on the banks of the Barada River, some 18 miles northeast of Damascus. In the only Biblical reference to this district, Luke (3.1), setting the stage for Christ's public ministry in the 15th year of Tiberius, mentions the area as a tetrarchy governed by Lysanias. Luke's reference has been corroborated by two rock inscriptions found at the site (CIG 3 4521). According to Josephus (AJ 19.5.1), Abilene came under the rule of Herod Agrippa I in A.D. 41. Herod Agrippa II governed the district from A.D. 44 until his death at the end of the century (AJ 20.7.1).

Bibliography: L. H. GROLLENBERG, *Atlas of the Bible*, tr. J. M. REID and H. H. ROWLEY (New York 1956) 116, 136. InterDict Bibl 1:9.

[E. MAY]

ABIMELECH, the son of *Gedeon and of his concubine from *Sichem (Jgs 8.31–9.57). Gedeon, a steadfast theocrat, had refused to institute a kingship in Israel (Jgs 8.22–23). When Gedeon died, Abimelech, supported by the priesthood of the Baal-Berith temple (*see* BAAL), killed his 70 brothers (with the exception of Joatham who escaped) and proclaimed himself king at Sichem, from where he ruled a considerable territory. The force of the famous curse of his brother Joatham (Jgs 9.7–15) eventually fell upon the ruthless tyrant, and he had to face a revolt of his subjects at Sichem. He devastated the city, but the rebellion spread. Finally, at the siege of Thebes, Abimelech met an untimely and humiliating death.

The Abimelech narrative reflects the growing awareness of the need for a strong central government, and probably recounts the first attempt to form a national hereditary kingship. However, in the context, it is difficult to see in the activity of Abimelech anything more than an imitation of the Canaanite city-state pattern.

Bibliography: J. VAN DER MEERSCH, "Problema de Expugnatione Sichem ab Abimlech (Jud IX, 22–49)," VerbDom 31 (1953) 335–343. E. SELLIN, *Wie wurde Sichem eine israelitische Stadt?* (Leipzig 1922). J. SIMONS, "Topographical and Archaeological Elements in the Story of Abimelech," *Oudtestamentische Studiën* 2 (1943) 35–78. H. CAZELLES, DBSuppl 4:1394–1414.

[J. MORIARITY]

ABINAL, ANTOINE, Jesuit missionary, author, and translator; b. Chanac, France, Jan. 10, 1829; d. Madagascar, Nov. 11, 1887. He published, with La Vaissière, *Vingt ans à Madagascar* (Paris 1881), and with Malzac, *Dictionnaire malgache français* (Tananariva 1888). He translated into Malagasy many books of the Old and New Testament as well as the *Imitation of Christ.*

Bibliography: Sommervogel 1.14; app. 1:1. E. M. RIVIÈRE, DHGE 1:123. B. GIOIA, EncCatt 1:81–82.

[B. CAVANAUGH]

ABINGDON, ABBEY OF, Benedictine house, Berkshire, England, founded *c.* 675, refounded *c.* 954, dissolved 1538. Its early history is doubtful, but according to its chronicler it was founded by a certain Cissa, King of Wessex. It was ruined by the Danes in the 9th

Interior view of one of the surviving medieval buildings of Abingdon Abbey. It probably served as the guesthouse.

century and left derelict until King Eadred gave it to St. *Ethelwold to restore *c.* 954. Regular Benedictine life was restored, and Abingdon became a powerhouse of the English monastic revival, sending colonies of monks to the new minster of *Winchester and to the Fenland abbeys of *Ely, *Peterborough, *Thorney, and *Crowland. After the Conquest, a Norman abbot from Jumièges was installed and the crown imposed a service of 30 knights on the abbey. It possessed extensive estates and church patronage in Berkshire, Oxford, Gloucester, and Warwick. The church and monastic buildings were rebuilt in the 12th century, but little of these remain. Its income in 1535 was £1,876. The last abbot, Thomas Rowland, formally surrendered the abbey to the crown on Feb. 9, 1538.

Bibliography: *Chronicon Monasterii de Abingdon*, ed. J. STEVENSON, 2 v. (RollsS 2; 1858). *The Victoria History of Berkshire*, ed. P. H. DITCHFIELD and W. PAGE, 4 v. (London 1906–24) v.2. F. M. STENTON, *The Early History of the Abbey of Abingdon* (Reading, Eng. 1913). Knowles MOE 31–56, *passim.* J. A. ROBINSON, *The Times of Saint Dunstan* (Oxford 1923).
Illustration credit: *Country Life*, London.

[C. H. LAWRENCE]

ABINGTON, THOMAS (HABINGTON), recusant and antiquarian; b. Thorpe, near Chertsey, Surrey, Aug. 23, 1560; d. Hindlip, near Worcester, Oct. 8, 1647. He was the son of John Abington, cofferer to Elizabeth I, and he attended Lincoln College, Oxford, and in 1579 went to the Continent to pursue his studies. At Rheims he was converted to the Catholic faith, and some time later he returned to England. The cause of the imprisoned Mary Queen of Scots elicited his devotion, and he became involved, along with his brother Edward, in the Babington Plot. Edward was executed (Sept. 30, 1586), but Thomas was committed to the Tower of London where he remained for 6 years. Released by order of Elizabeth (he was her godson), he retired to Hindlip Castle, the country seat his father had built in Worcestershire. For harboring priests (the house had 11 priest holes), Abington was arrested in January 1606, when four Jesuits—Fathers Garnet and Oldcorne, and Brothers Owen and Ashley—were found there. On the charge of complicity in the Gunpowder Plot, all four were executed; but Abington, who was tried with them, was released, on the intercession of Lord Monteagle, his brother-in-law. Forbidden to leave Worcestershire, he devoted his remaining years to local antiquarian researches.

Bibliography: DictEngCath 3:74–76. H. FOLEY, ed., *Records of the English Province of the Society of Jesus,* 7 v. (London 1877–82) 4.1:33–34. M. CREIGHTON, DNB 8:857–858.

[R. I. BRADLEY]

ABJURATION

The public act by which a non-Catholic Christian, or a Catholic (or Christian) who fell away from the faith, disavows his errors and professes to come (back) to the Catholic (or Christian) faith. This act is prescribed by Church law (CIC c.2314.2) as part of the ritual of reception of such converts into the Church, as a condition for absolution from *excommunication incurred by the delict of *apostasy, *heresy, or *schism. The exterior act naturally draws its meaning and genuineness from the interior and personally willed return to God.

The interior return to God is necessary because the return to the faith ought to be a free and personal act, undoing the free and guilty giving up of the faith. And because one's faith is the faith of the Church lived in the community of the *faithful, a *profession of that faith before the Church is the connatural and necessary completion of the inner return to God. A merely external abjuration would, of course, be a meaningless and deceitful hypocrisy. However, the disavowal of error, both interior and exterior, is but the negative side of an act whose positive aspect, namely, acceptance of the faith before God and the Church, gives it consistency and meaning. It is the negative side of conversion [*see* CONVERSION, III (THEOLOGY OF)].

The Church's ruling concerning abjuration supposes the delict of apostasy, heresy, or schism. Does it hold in the case of non-Catholic Christians in good faith who wish to be received into the Church but never committed the sin of heresy or schism? They happen to be separated from the Church through no fault of their own in spite of their Baptism and their faith in the gospel. The trend today is to stress the positive side of the abjuration, namely, the profession of faith, or the deliberate acceptance of the entire faith of the Church, without mentioning the specific errors at variance with the faith. Revisions of the formulae for abjuration have been made in that sense (see, for example, a formula approved for England by the Holy Office in 1945).

In fact, for separated brethren in good faith, the real meaning of their conversion and reception into the Church is a progress from a less complete profession and living of the Christian faith to a more complete one. This means that for them the inner act of abjuration is not possible in the sense of a disavowal of formal error. They need not disavow their faith but only its limitations and then express the desire of living that faith more fully within the Catholic fold. It would therefore be consistent with the present-day belief of the Church in the sincere good faith of the separated Christians that nothing more would be required of them at their reception into the Church than a profession of the faith of the Church. The corresponding inner act can be nothing more than the acknowledgment and disavowal of material error, the desire of correcting a mistake, not an act of repentance for sin. Such, then, is the real meaning of this abjuration.

The practice of abjuration is different for various classes of converts. Abjuration not being required from the unbaptized, in the case of a convert whose Baptism is found to be invalid no abjuration is necessary. In the case of doubtful Baptism, as also when the Baptism was certainly valid (as is the case of the Orthodox and the Lutherans), abjuration is needed in the sense just explained. It may be well to note that the Orthodox and some Protestants require a similar abjuration of converts to be received.

Abjuration is also understood to designate the "renouncement of the devil" that is part of the ritual of Baptism. The underlying idea is that of the "slavery of the devil" involved in the state of sin (cf. Denz 1511). Liberation from his captivity supposes a free renouncement of the prince of this world. Here, too, the positive side of the "abjuration" is dedication to Christ through the reception of Baptism.

Bibliography: F. DESHAYES and L. PETIT, DTC 1.1:74–90. A. STENZEL, LexThK² 1:69–70. Y. M. J. CONGAR, *Catholicisme* 1: 38–40.

[P. DE LETTER]

ABNER, son of Ner, cousin of Saul (1 Sm 14.50–51), commander in chief of his army (1 Sm 14.50), and later, the power behind the short rule of *Is-Baal. Held in high respect by Saul, Abner sat at his side at table (1 Sm 20.25). In keeping with the loyalty he had shown Saul during his struggles against David (1 Sm 26.5–16), Abner, upon Saul's death, installed Saul's son Is-Baal as king of Israel at *Mahanaim in Transjordan (2 Sm 2.8–10), while David became king of Juda (2 Sm 2.10–11). In the ensuing war, Abner was forced to kill Asael, *Joab's brother (2 Sm 2.12–3.1). Later, accused by Is-Baal of treasonable behavior, Abner transferred his allegiance to David (2 Sm 3.6–21). At the first opportunity Joab treacherously assassinated Abner in *blood vengeance for his brother's death (2 Sm 3.22–27), and, perhaps, with the added thought of securing for himself Abner's position as David's general. At the solemn funeral David lamented Abner's death (2 Sm 3.28–39) and explicitly instructed Solomon to punish Joab (3 Kgs 2.5, 28–34). The Chronicler records Abner's regard for the house of God (1 Chr 26.27–28) and mentions his son Jasiel as head of the tribe of Benjamin (1 Chr 27.21).

Bibliography: H. P. SMITH, *The Books of Samuel* (ICC; 1904). M. NOTH, *The History of Israel,* tr. P. R. ACKROYD (2d ed. New York 1960).

[F. BUCK]

ABNER OF BURGOS, a Jewish rabbi who practiced the medical profession until his conversion to Christianity, of which religion he then became a champion; b. Burgos, Spain, *c.* 1270; d. Valladolid, Spain, *c.* 1346. Rabbi Abner engaged in the medical profession at Valladolid in accordance with the custom of rabbis to support themselves by some trade or profession. His religious activity during this period before his conversion is evidenced by his composition of a commentary on the treatise of Abraham *ibn Ezra on the Ten Commandments.

Abner embraced Christianity at Valladolid in 1295. Subsequently he was in charge of the sacristy of the cathedral of that city. After his conversion he changed his name from Abner to Alfonso and was from then on known as Alfonso of Burgos or of Valladolid. In defense of Christianity he wrote, in Hebrew, a refutation of a work (*Milḥamot ha-Shem,* The Wars of the Lord) that Rabbi Ḳimchi had written against the Christians. It has been said that at Abner's urging Alfonso XI of Castile (1312–50) prohibited the recitation of certain Jewish prayers that were considered anti-Christian. Abner was the first to write theological (apologetical) treatises in Spanish, such as *El mostrador de la justicia* and *Libro de las tres gracias.* None of his works, however, have been printed; they are known from manuscript copies or from refutations made in Jewish writings.

Bibliography: P. Sicart, DHGE 2:696–697. F. Baer, Enc Judaica 1:339–340. F. de Sola Mendes, JewishEnc 1:72. G. Bartolocci, *Bibliotheca magna rabbinica,* 5 v. (Rome 1675–94) 1:366.

[S. M. POLAN]

ABNORMAL PSYCHOLOGY

Abnormal psychology is the branch of the science of psychology that studies marked deviations in human behavior. The study embraces the nature of abnormal behavior, its description, classification, and causes. This definition assumes that the principal goal is the understanding of abnormal behavior. Alteration of behavior, sometimes included in a consideration of abnormal psychology, properly belongs to general *psychology or to such specialized fields as *individual psychology, *psychiatry, and *psychotherapy. This presentation is concerned with abnormal behavior in the more restricted sense.

Historical Development. The early history of abnormal psychology is the history of psychiatry and *psychoanalysis. Physicians in ancient times attempted to explain abnormal behavior by recourse to biological or preternatural forces. *Hippocrates (460–377? B.C.) offered an organic explanation that was elaborated by *Galen (A.D. *c.* 130–*c.* 200) in his theories of humors. Earlier, *Heraclitus (*c.* 500 B.C.) seems to have taught that wet souls were mad souls. The treatment of disordered personalities in these times was characterized by both cruelty and kindness. Chains, starvation, thirst, and violence were used, along with musical harmony, baths, and swaying beds. In early Christianity the same extremes were found, reflecting various common understandings of abnormal behavior. Although men like *Agobard of Lyons (d. 841) protested against superstition, the pagan views of barbarians often prevailed. Substantial advances in the understanding of abnormal behavior date only from the time of Johann Weyer (1515–88), who is considered by G. *Zilboorg as the father of modern psychiatry.

Progress in the understanding and treatment of psychologically handicapped persons seems to have followed an exponential curve. It was still slow, when Philippe Pinel (1745–1826) in France, Benjamin Rush (1745–1813) in the U.S., and William Tuke (1732–1822) in England become concerned about the treatment of lunatics. With the establishment of hospitals and records, however, facts accumulated. Franz Mesmer (1734–1815) initiated the practice of mesmerism, which first met with opposition from physicians, but then gained respectability at the hands of the Englishman, James Braid (1795–1860). Under the term hypnosis, it returned to France to open the way for the study of neuroses. The term neuroses meant to imply that such psychological disorders had a foundation in physiology; yet lack of evidence and knowledge of the functions of the brain made it impossible to base this supposition upon anything more than analogy. A controversy concerning the treatment and nature of neuroses arose in Paris and Nancy. At Nancy, A. A. Liébault, H. Bernheim, and E. Coué supported a psychological theory based upon suggestion, while at Paris, J. M. Charcot, P. M. F. Janet, and briefly, S. Freud pursued neurological theories.

Out of these studies came the radical and far-reaching work of Sigmund *Freud (1856–1939). Heated controversy attended its evaluation for a number of reasons. Freud professed to be a materialist and wrote like an idealist. His dogmatic and authoritarian attitudes were offensive, especially his pronouncements in the field of religion, about which he obviously was ignorant. His unfortunate sexual analogies made it difficult to get to the center of his thought. To complicate these difficulties, Freud's ideas contained the double threat not only of being novel, but also of forcing a reevaluation of man, and hence of oneself. Most Catholics, and religious people generally, condemned his doctrine without even a hearing.

With the passage of time and the expansion of knowledge, much of Freud's work has become outdated. One contribution, however, cannot be denied him, nor can it be diminished in value. In offering what he supposed to be a psychological explanation of abnormal behavior, he jarred prevailing conceptions of the human personality in such a way as to provoke a new and critical appraisal of man in his culture. Again, rejection of Freudian thought, although formerly common among Catholics, was never universal among Catholic scholars. Men like Edward *Pace and T. V. Moore, of The Catholic University of America, and Agostino *Gemelli, of the Sacred Heart University of Milan, early saw in Freud's work a source of new ideas about man's psychic life. More recently other Catholic scholars, such as Noël Mailloux, Gregory Zilboorg, Karl Stern, and Josef Nuttin, have perceived the possibility of integrating Freud's contributions into Catholic thought.

Nature of Abnormal Behavior. To define abnormal behavior one must first know what is normal. Abnormality implies a departure from the norm. Unfortunately, no satisfactory criteria for *normality have been proposed. Criteria based on value, desirability, or morality are of no utility to the psychologist. Cross-cultural studies of anthropologists illustrate the inadequacy of value criteria, since what is valued in one culture may be taboo in another. Similarly, a moral criterion of goodness and badness is useless; the psychological condition, like the physical condition of a person, is in itself a matter of moral indifference. Merit and demerit assume importance only when a person considers his condition relative to God. The abnormally high intelligence, as well as abnormal impulses to violence, may be used either to the glory of God or in rebellion against Him.

In spite of criticism leveled at judging behavior relative to a scale of value, this is usually done, either implicitly or explicitly. Efficient and effective function is accepted as a partial criterion, but opinions differ regarding the measure of effectiveness. Should the person live according to the mores of his society or according to objective principles and ideals? A possible solution lies in the value of internal freedom: the person who can do what he ought is to that extent mature; and to the degree that he cannot do what he ought, because of internal constraints, he is suffering from pathology. This definition does not assume that the well person will do what he ought, but simply that he is internally free to do so. The man who does not do what he ought is a sinner, while the man who cannot do what he ought is suffering from a personality disorder. Besides avoiding the confusion of sin with personality defect, provision is here made for the fact that a psychotic and a saint may similarly behave in ways that are far from normal. (*See* PERSONALITY; PERSONALITY DISORDERS.)

Description and Classification. Classifications of abnormal behavior depend upon detailed theories of personality held by individual psychologists. Although frequently psychiatric classifications are followed, psychologists are tending to break from the concept of disease and to analyze abnormal behavior in relation to structure and function. Behind this tendency is the fact that behavior, motivation, and function cannot be correlated perfectly. A man may see visions, or hallucinate, for a variety of reasons, e.g., systemic disturbance arising from alcoholic intoxication or other drugs, brain injury, or the concept of self as a prophet. The psychological approach gives meaning and direction to research; it also forces a sharper differentiation among causes, dynamics, and resultant behavior.

In terms of such a classification, malfunction of a structure may be related to its development and its integration within the personality. The difficulty here lies in the confusion and diversity of theories concerning the complex process of personality organization. One theory, with much to commend it, sees the *ego, through a process of habit formation, integrating the basic structures of the personality into a hierarchy of structures, thus providing different levels of integration. The hierarchy of structures recognized in this theory are internal controls, *temperament, *habit, *character, and moral *consciousness, in ascending order. The basic structures thus far identified are the psychophysiological systems, *emotions, *will, and *intellect. Psychosis, according to this theory, is failure in differentiation or integration of the ego-systems: the ego-ideal, the self-image, the way others are thought to see the *self, and the way others are perceived. Neuroses are failures to integrate, or disintegrations at the level of internal controls; hence they are not so destructive of the total personality function. If the repercussions in the strivings of the person are reflected organically as in an ulcer, hypertension, etc., the disorder is classified by the clinical psychologist or psychiatrist as psychosomatic. In psychosomatic disease the chief systems affected are the digestive, neural, circulatory, excretory, reproductive, and probably the endocrine. (*See* PSYCHONEUROTIC DISORDERS; PSYCHOTIC DISORDERS; PSYCHOSOMATIC ILLNESS.)

Abnormal psychology is concerned also with the detailed understanding of the function of awareness, especially the phenomena of the *unconscious. Mechanisms, as they have been called by the psychoanalysts, are considered as ways, automatically set in operation without explicit *reflection, of solving problems of living. Psychologists accept the idea that there are processes by which the ego is protected from a loss of self-esteem. (*See* MENTAL MECHANISMS.)

Causes of Abnormality. One of the major tasks of abnormal psychology is to give a scientific account of causes of abnormality. Accordingly, psychologists have advanced numerous theories regarding their analysis and classification. In general, they distinguish material correlates, actual causes, goal determinants, and intentional causes.

Material correlates, such as life experience, or more precisely, *heredity and environment, provide the ingredients for a personality disorder. Frequently, material correlates are confused with actual causes, since it is possible to predict behavior with a high degree of accuracy if the home environment is known. War, slums, racial discrimination—all provide situations for abnormal behavior associated with the response of the person to the stresses within his personality.

Actual causes are those that vitalize the behavior. Broadly considered, the person is the actual cause. More precisely, it is the ego as it integrates or attempts to integrate the forces pulling the person in various directions. Among these internal forces may be distinguished goal determinants and intentional causes.

Goal determinants refer to the dynamic function of the person or structure, as sight is ordered to seeing. If the goal is selected by the person, it is intentional.

Intentional causes involve some kind of awareness. For instance, it may be said that the urge to walk is a goal-determined cause, since it is motivated by the possession of a perceptional motor system designed for walking. The awareness of the need for exercise may be the intentional causality that actually results in the walk.

Stress and Awareness. It is commonly admitted that every man in dealing with stress tends to become disorganized, this propensity depending on his degree of frustration tolerance. Under stress the person may no longer function with his accustomed effectiveness, a state known as decompensation, and may ultimately "break down." The stresses themselves are always relative to the individual personality, and are material correlates. A sudden increase in these can act as a precipitating factor; they may be psychological (e.g., combat, death, loss of a spouse, or a horrifying experience) or physical (e.g., malnutrition, high fever, severe pain, or brain damage). Under stress the person attempts to maintain his integrity. As long as he can identify the real threat and foresee some way of coping with it, his behavior is "reasonable" and oriented to the problem. Abnormal behavior is symptomatic of a failure to come to grips with a problem that is not clearly stated in awareness. It seems that the critical factor in the actual cause is the loss or narrowing of awareness of various aspects of the stressful situation on the part of the ego.

Four general reasons for this restriction in awareness are commonly advanced: (1) The person never formulated consciously his basic attitudes toward life and as a result cannot call them into awareness as organizing principles of behavior. In a vague way the person may sense that great things are demanded of him, or, on the contrary, that if he succeeds he will be punished with the consequent loss of love. The ways in which people arrive at such conclusions are called mechanisms, especially by psychoanalysts. (2) For a number of reasons a memory content may be isolated, so that it remains inaccessible to consciousness. An example would be some traumatic experience such as that of a child witnessing intercourse between his parents. Sometimes unreasonable fears arising from symbolic reminders of the experience may be traced to such events. The dynamic element would be a vague perception of losing face by being similarly attacked, or of suffering rejection for possessing secret knowledge. (3) Fragmentation of the memory content frequently takes place either because it is beyond the grasp of the individual as an organized unit, or because the unity in a series of experiences is not perceived. Again, only those acquisitions that touch the ego drives will cause trouble. Sometimes in a large, well-organized family one person has to spend some time in a mental hospital. It may be that on the surface, the family abounds in opportunity for good and realistic living. But investigation may reveal a whole series of events that led one of the children to the feeling of living in a chaotic world in which genuine recognition and acceptance for one's self is impossible. Such fragmentation of memory content may also be a symptom, as when a person attempts to escape an unpleasant situation by blotting out unwanted knowledge. (4) Finally, the person may remain unaware of the goals and real reasons for his behavior because, in some way or another, he feels that he will be subject to disgrace if he freely recognizes his goals and intentions, or motivations. A person who believes himself to be the Messiah may be hiding from himself his real motive, which is to avoid perceiving himself as worthless. (*See* DRIVES AND MOTIVES; MOTIVATION.)

Probably the principal difference between abnormal and normal behavior, from the point of view of causality, is in the way the person defines the goal of life and the means he employs to reach that goal. The determining condition is his awareness and insight into what he is about.

A Catholic View. A specific theory of abnormal behavior, as well as of normal behavior, that takes into account the Catholic attitude toward man is here presented briefly. The Catholic emphasis is on the unity of man; it sees the basic conflicts in him as unnecessary theoretically, but practically unavoidable because of the weakness of his intellect and will. By necessity man strives to appear in his own eyes and the eyes of others in the highest possible light. These two drives, conceived to be embedded in his ego as goal determinants, provide him with a basic problem to be solved. The reason for solving the problem, the dynamic element, is the need for psychological integrity. A philosophical correlate of this psychological integrity is the nature of the life principle, or human *soul, which reaches for completion and fruition. Maximum maturity is obtained only when a man lives as a man ought, that is, as a creature in perfect subjection to his Creator, absolutely and completely dependent upon his God. But man cringes at the thought of his dependency upon God and thereby becomes unrealistic in his thinking, to the extent that he may even consider himself to be God.

The Catholic psychologist is free to accept, or to improvise, any theory that does not violate his integrity as a scientist. But since psychology cannot develop in a vacuum, he must also take into account the teaching of the Church that man is a composite being, and not include in his theory, for example, anything that contradicts the fact of *original sin. Knowledge, especially when it is certain and revealed, does not limit freedom of thought but, on the contrary, frees the mind from the limitations of error.

See also CLINICAL PSYCHOLOGY; PSYCHOLOGY, HISTORY OF.

Bibliography: R. W. WHITE, *The Abnormal Personality* (2d ed. New York 1956). H. J. EYSENCK, ed., *Handbook of Abnormal Psychology* (New York 1961). T. V. MOORE, *The Driving Forces of Human Nature and Their Adjustment* (New York 1948). N. A. CAMERON, *Personality Development and Psychopathology* (Boston 1963). L. KANNER, *Child Psychiatry* (3d ed. Springfield, Ill. 1957). R. L. MUNROE, *Schools of Psychoanalytic Thought* (New York 1955). J. H. VAN DER VELDT and R. P. ODENWALD, *Psychiatry and Catholicism* (2d ed. New York 1957). H. MISIAK and V. M. STAUDT, *Catholics in Psychology: A Historical Survey* (New York 1954). G. ZILBOORG and G. W. HENRY, *A History of Medical Psychology* (New York 1941). R. A. HUNTER and I. MACALPINE, eds., *Three Hundred Years of Psychiatry, 1535–1860* (New York 1963).

[D. J. WACK]

ABOMINATION OF DESOLATION

This cryptic apocalyptic expression is employed contemptuously in Daniel to describe the profanation of the Temple by the King of Syria, *Antiochus IV Epiphanes, when he had the statue of Zeus Olympios placed in the Temple; in the NT the expression is used in the so-called "little apocalypse" of Christ's eschatological discourse to call attention to the blasphemous activity of the Antichrist (prefigured by Antiochus) that is to be expected prior to the Parousia.

In Daniel. The only OT usage of the now traditional expression "abomination of desolation" (Douay-Rheims Version) or "the horrible abomination" (Confraternity Version) is found in the Book of Daniel (9.27; 11.31; 12.11). Scholars now see in this mysterious expression [Heb. *šiqqûṣ (me)šōmēm*] a veiled description of the blasphemous actions of Antiochus IV, described with clearer detail in Machabees (1 Mc 1.57; 2 Mc 6.2). Thus chapter 11 of Daniel describes Antiochus's ruthless persecution climaxed by the erection of the abomination of desolation in the Temple; the texts of Machabees tell of the desecration of the Temple by the soldiers of Antiochus and the setting up of the idol Zeus Olympios on the altar. Since Baal Shamem (Aramaic, *ba'al šamēm,* lord of the heavens) is the Aramaic title of Zeus Olympios, scholars look on the abomination of desolation as a veiled and contemptuous reference to this idol. By replacing the name of Baal with *šiqqûṣ* (abomination, detested thing) and by eliminating the vowels of *šamēm* (heavens) and substituting those of *bōšet* (shame), the author obtained the Hebrew expression *šiqqûṣ šōmēm* (abomination of desolation). The entire expression would then refer to the statue of Baal Shamem (alias Zeus Olympios) that Antiochus IV erected in the Temple in 167 B.C.

In Christ's Eschatological Discourse. In Mt 24.15 and Mk 13.14 the abomination of desolation is linked with the fall of Jerusalem and the end of the world. Since the abomination of desolation is presented as "standing," with a grammatical switch from the neuter τὸ βδέλυγμα to the masculine participle ἑστηκότα (Mk 13.

14; see Taylor, 511–512), the text itself suggests that the abomination is really symbolic of a man. Noting the similarities between the eschatological discourse of Christ in the Synoptics (Mt 24.4–39; Mk 13.5–31) and St. Paul's description of the Antichrist (2 Thes 2.3–12), it is probable that the abomination of desolation is to be identified with the "man of sin," "the son of perdition," "the wicked one," who in the last days "sits in the temple of God and gives himself out as if he were God" (2 Thes 2.4). When Matthew cautions "let him who reads understand," his purpose is to recall the hideous desecration wrought by Antiochus (cf. 1 Mc 1.57) as a warning to his readers concerning the blasphemous activity of the Antichrist. According to earlier commentators, the prophecy was fulfilled when the Emperor Caligula attempted to have his statue erected in the Temple in A.D. 40, or when the fiery zealots turned the Temple into a fortress in A.D. 68, or at the actual destruction of the Holy City and the Temple by Titus in A.D. 70. Although the last opinion merits consideration, recent commentators hold that it is more likely that Matthew and Mark were not so much concerned with indicating a purely historical event but actualized a traditional expression by applying it to the godless and blasphemous activity of the Antichrist at the end of time.

Bibliography: EncDictBibl 10–12. InterDictBibl 1:13–14. W. FOERSTER, "Βδέλυγμα," Kittel ThW 1:598–600. R. H. CHARLES, *Commentary on Daniel* (Oxford 1929). J. A. MONTGOMERY, *Daniel* (ICC; New York 1927) 388–390. V. TAYLOR, ed., *The Gospel according to St. Mark* (London 1952) 511–515.

[F. J. MONTALBANO]

ABONDANCE, MONASTERY OF, former house of *Canons Regular of St. Augustine, and then of Cistercian Feuillants, more properly called the Abbey of Sainte-Marie d'Abondance (Latin, *Abundantia*), in the valley of the Drance, in Haute-Savoie, France, former Diocese of Geneva. Its origin is often attributed to St. *Columban, but none of his biographies mentions it. The ascription probably stems from a confusion of names between it and *Remiremont (original Latin, *Monasterium Habundense*). It is certain that in 1080 Louis of Féterne established canons regular at Abondance, and that the foundation was richly endowed by his family. Then in 1108, the canons of *Saint-Maurice gave the lands of Abondance to a group of Canons under Prior Herluin. In 1155 these canons were congratulated on their observance in a bull of Pope Adrian IV. Between 1128 and 1144 the monastery had achieved the status of an *abbey; Rudolph of Vauserier was made first abbot (1144). In 1156 and 1158 the Abbots of Abondance and Saint-Maurice signed agreements of association. But between mid-12th and early 13th century, Abondance founded or subordinated to itself five abbeys, Sixt, Entremont, Grandval, Goailles, and Filly, as well as 22 priories. Up to the 14th century, the monastery enjoyed great material prosperity; it held first place in the Diocese of Geneva. But excessive wealth and *commendation (1436) led to a relaxation of discipline. Decadence proceeded at a rapid pace in the 16th century, and the number of religious diminished to half. Though the commendatory Abbot Gaspard Provana opposed the reform attempted there by *Francis de Sales, the future bishop of Geneva, the latter finally won out in 1598. The new reform abbot, Vespasian Aiazza, come to an understanding with the

Cloister, 14th-century, Monastery of Abondance. On the back wall can be seen the Gothic frescoes.

Cistercian *Feuillants, and by a brief of Sept. 28, 1606, Pope Paul V sanctioned Abondance's concordat with the Feuillants, who, on May 7, 1607, installed Favre, vicar-general of Francis de Sales, as abbot. But these religious, isolated high up in the valley of the Drance, abandoned themselves in time to unhealthy distractions. Finally, Pope *Clement XIII's bull of May 9, 1761, granted King Charles-Emmanuel the right to suppress the Feuillants; another bull of May 4, 1762, allotted the goods of Abondance, with the exception of the benefices, to the Abbey of Sainte-Marie of Thonon. During the French Revolution the abbey was sold. Today the abbey church (14th and 17th centuries), the cloister (14th century with frescoes), and the rich treasury are all classified as historical monuments. The church serves the needs of the local parish.

Bibliography: L. CIBRARIO, ed., *Scriptorum*, 3 v. (Monumenta historiae patriae 3, 5, 11; Turin 1840–1863) 2:301–318, constitutions, 321–434, necrology. J. GARIN, DHGE 1:144–153. Cottineau 1:9–10. **Illustration credit:** Collection Viollet, Paris.

[J. DAOUST]

ABORTION, I

The deliberate destruction of a fetus before viability is induced abortion. Refinements in definition, common in Canon Law and medicine, are not generally known, but the distinction in civil law between legal and illegal abortion is of considerable social significance.

Sources of Knowledge. Knowledge of the extent, causation, motivation, and differential incidence, and also of the consequences of induced abortion is extremely limited. This is largely because in many societies abortion has been proscribed or discouraged, and has thus tended to be kept secret. The available reliable knowledge is derived principally from: (1) anthropological reports, primarily on preliterate societies, (2) data collected by physicians on clinical, hospital, or private patients, (3) social surveys using questionnaires or interview techniques, and (4) official government statistics. The last two sources have assumed increasing importance in recent years, as opposition to abortion, both in law and in public opinion, has tended to weaken.

Extent. Induced abortion is widespread in that there are few societies, past or present, in which it has not been known and used. Its antiquity is attested by a Chinese prescription for an abortifacient dating from approximately 2700 B.C. Ethnographic reports on preliterate societies point to it as common among such peoples. For more developed societies (whether of East or West, whether urban-industrial or rural-agricultural) there is evidence that abortion occurs with appreciable frequency.

Precise numerical data on its extent in any given society, however, are rare, and figures quoted on the point typically have little foundation in solid fact. In the U.S., for example, "estimates" of the annual number of abortions in recent years have ranged from 200,000 to 2,000,000. Estimates for many other nations are equally vague and unreliable. More reliable data have become available for nations where induced abortion for other than strictly medical reasons has been legalized, and where government facilities and subsidies have been provided for the operation. Soviet Russia, the nations of Eastern Europe, Scandinavia, and Japan are prime examples. The statistical confusion surrounding abortion has resulted in grossly false impressions about variations in its frequency among nations. With due allowance for these problems, an incomplete listing of some nations with almost certainly high incidence (more than 15 abortions per 100 live births) would include the U.S., Denmark, Norway, France, Hungary, Bulgaria, Poland, Czechoslovakia, Yugoslavia, Chile, Uruguay, and Japan.

Motivation and Differential Incidence. The generic motive for abortion is the prevention of a birth, so that the specific patterns of motivation and differential incidence are similar to those for any form of birth prevention. Abortion occurs in substantial numbers among married and unmarried, young and old, women with and without children, and at virtually all socioeconomic levels, and is not so confined to certain classes of women as is commonly supposed. In societies where the practice is widespread, probably the largest number of abortions can be accounted for among married women with several living children. In societies where abortion is effectively controlled by law or by community sentiment, it is presumably more likely to be the marginal members of the society or persons in extraordinary circumstances (for example, after premarital conception or pregnancy following rape) who account for the rates of occurrence.

The relation of induced abortion to other techniques of fertility control is extremely complex, and differs from one society to another. Among the preliterates, the alternatives were abortion and infanticide, with the latter often preferred because of the opportunity provided for selection of normal offspring or for those of the desired sex. In contemporary societies abortion is typically resorted to when no technique of preventing conception is known or utilized, or when attempts at prevention have been unsuccessful. In recent years much discussion has focused on the question whether the widespread promotion of contraception would tend to reduce substantially the incidence of abortion, as some have argued. Many reply that so long as no absolutely simple and effective contraceptive exists, increased motivation to regulate all births will invariably result in more frequent abortion. It is true that even where abortion is already widespread, intensive effort of sufficient duration can lead people to use preventive measures rather than abortion as the chosen means of fertility regulation; however, unless it is restrained by stringent legal and moral prohibitions, abortion tends to remain as a supplementary measure when contraception is unsuccessful. In general, there is no basis for expecting its disappearance from human society for the forseeable future.

See also ABORTION, II (MORAL ASPECT); ABORTION, III (CANON LAW); ABORTION, IV (U.S. LAW OF); BIRTH CONTROL MOVEMENT.

Bibliography: M. S. HANDMANN, EncSocSc 1:372–374. F. J. TAUSSIG, *Abortions, Spontaneous and Induced: Medical and Social Aspects* (St. Louis 1936). Planned Parenthood Federation of America, *Abortion in the United States*, ed. M. S. CALDERONE (New York 1958). S. DE LESTAPIS, "Birth Control as a Population Remedy: Contraception and Some of Its Effects on Society," *Christian Responsibility and World Poverty*, ed. A. MCCORMACK (Westminster, Md. 1963) 60–78.

[T. K. BURCH]

ABORTION, II (MORAL ASPECT)

While the civil law evaluates abortion in terms of a crime against the state and the canonist is concerned primarily with the ecclesiastical penalties for abortion, the moral theologian treats abortion in terms of the disorder it introduces into human nature itself and as a violation of the law of God.

Notion and Morality. The moral malice of abortion is found simply in the fact that it is a directly intended and totally indefensible destruction of innocent human life. Thus the moralist's definition of abortion is more generic than those used in civil or canon law or academic medicine and includes them all. The moral dimension is identified in the termination of any pregnancy before the fetus has attained viability, irrespective of the civil law of any particular jurisdiction or the canonical implications of the various surgical approaches; whether by separation of the living fetus from the uterus (abortion), or by the dismembering and evisceration of the fetus in the uterus (embryotomy), or by the destruction of the fetal head to facilitate the emptying of the uterus (craniotomy), or by the removal of a nonviable fetus from an extrauterine site of gestation (termination of ectopic pregnancy), or even by the prevention of implantation of the embryo, e.g., by the use of intrauterine coils and similar so-called contraceptive devices that are, from a moral viewpoint, rather abortifacients than contraceptives.

The medical distinctions pertinent to the moral aspects of the question include the distinction between induced abortion (an abortion that is brought about artificially and purposely, and sometimes called "therapeutic" if it is done in the interests of the maternal health) and spontaneous abortion, or one occurring naturally and not of set purpose. In moral terminology the former is called direct abortion and the latter is known as indirect abortion.

Fetal loss that is in no sense the purpose or intent of the physician, but occurs as a side effect of some very seriously indicated therapy or surgery demanded without delay for the sake of the mother, is indirect and can be justified under the principle of *double effect.

Direct abortion, however, as one that is intended as an end in itself or a means to an end, and is undertaken precisely and directly for the purpose of interrupting the pregnancy before viability, clearly includes the malice of a direct attack on innocent human life, even though this is done in the interest of the mother's health. If the abortionist fails to recognize any moral disorder in this, it is because he has erroneously judged that the rights of the innocent are not inviolable and that innocent human life can be directly destroyed if it is decided that some good will come of it. Such an error is opposed to the divine law. It likewise strikes at the roots of the democratic way of life and would, if generally admitted, make life in any society an insecure thing at best.

The only consideration that could make direct abortion tenable would be the supposition that the fetus is not human until after it has been delivered and has its existence completely separate from the mother. This is unacceptable legally, physiologically, philosophically, and theologically. After a certain stage of intrauterine development it is perfectly evident that fetal life is fully human. Although some might speculate as to when that stage is reached, there is no way of arriving at this knowledge by any known criterion; and as long as it is probable that embryonic life is human from the first moment of its existence, the purposeful termination of any pregnancy contains the moral malice of the violation of man's most fundamental human right—the right to life itself.

Although almost all the complications of pregnancy that were, in an earlier day, looked upon by some as so-called "medical indications for therapeutic abortion" have been solved by modern medical and surgical advances, more abortions came to be performed on the basis of psychiatric indications, as well as for the purpose of destroying an unborn infant when there is danger that the physical integrity of the fetus may be compromised to a greater or less degree because of some illness of the mother or exposure to drugs earlier in the pregnancy. The increasing number of medically normal pregnancies terminated in these circumstances reflects a spread of confusion in the moral thought underlying much obstetric policy.

From a purely medical viewpoint, abortion conflicts with the highest ideals and principles of the medical profession, which exists to protect life. The obstetrician should remember that in dealing with a pregnancy he has two patients—the mother and her unborn child—and he should not take the life of either.

The Catholic Church has always condemned the destruction of innocent human life. Pope Paul VI reviewed this doctrine, particularly in its application to direct abortion, for a group from the New England Obstetrical and Gynecological Society on Oct. 3, 1964 [*Pope Speaks* 10 (1964) 1] and at that time repeated the following words of Pius XII:

> Innocent human life, in whatever condition it is found, is to be secure from the very first moment of its existence from any direct deliberate attack. This is a fundamental right of the human person, which is of general value in the Christian concept of life; and hence as valid for the still hidden life within the womb of the mother as for the life of the already born and developing outside of her. . . . Whatever foundation there may be for the distinction between these various phases of the development of life that is born, or still unborn, in profane and ecclesiastical law, and as regards certain civil and penal consequences, all these cases involve a grave and unlawful attack upon the inviolability of human life. [Discourse of Nov. 26, 1951, *Discorsi e radio messagi di Sua Santità Pio XII* 13.415.]

Because of this profound respect for the life of the unborn child, the attitude of the Catholic Church has often been misinterpreted to be preference for the life of the child over that of the mother. Pius XII explained the error of this misinterpretation in the following words (*ibid.*):

> Never and in no case has the Church taught that the life of the child must be preferred to that of the mother. It is erroneous to put the question with this alternative: either the life of the child or that of the mother. No, neither the life of the mother nor that of the child can be subjected to an act of direct suppression.

Threatened and Inevitable Abortion. Threatened abortion is recognized, as a clinical entity, by early signs of possible spontaneous abortion, such as minor bleeding and minimal pain. The ordinary treatment is rest and medication designed to remedy the situation and save the pregnancy; and ordinary charity, reinforced by maternal love, dictates that the mother should do all that she reasonably can toward this end.

The moral problem may become acute for the obstetrician if threatened abortion deteriorates to the stage of inevitable abortion, in which the fetal attachments and environment have become so compromised that the spontaneous expulsion of the inviable fetus cannot be prevented. This is usually accompanied by spontaneous rupture of the membranes, dilation of the cervix, and severe bleeding and pain. In this situation the principles regarding direct abortion remain the same, and yet a critical point of danger may be reached at which the obstetrician rightfully judges that inevitable and advancing separation of the placenta has so irrevocably progressed that to empty the uterus, in the interest of the mother's welfare, could not be considered to be destructive of the fetus, even though some feeble fetal life might still possibly be present. The hastening of fetal death is neither sought nor intended nor, in these circumstances, is it likely to be materially influenced by the acceleration procedure (*Morals in Medicine* 168–173).

Bibliography: J. W. WILLIAMS, *Obstetrics,* ed. N. J. EASTMAN and L. M. HELLMAN (12th ed. New York 1961). G. A. KELLY, *Medico-Moral Problems* (St. Louis 1958). J. P. KENNY, *Principles of Medical Ethics* (2d ed. Westminster, Md. 1962). C. J. MCFADDEN, *Medical Ethics* (5th ed. Philadelphia 1961). T. J. O'DONNELL, *Morals in Medicine* (2d ed. Westminster, Md. 1959). R. J. HEFFERNAN and W. A. LYNCH, "What Is the Status of Therapeutic Abortion in Modern Obstetrics?" *American Journal of Obstetrics and Gynecology* 66 (1953) 335–345.

[T. J. O'DONNELL]

ABORTION, III (CANON LAW)

The law of the Church relative to the crime of abortion may be expressed as follows: Anyone who procures abortion incurs automatically the penalty of excommunication, reserved to the ordinary; a cleric, moreover, is liable also to the penalty of deposition. And, any guilty male automatically incurs an irregularity for Orders (CIC cc.2350.1, 985n4). These provisions go back to the legislation of Popes Sixtus V and Gregory XIV in the late 16th century. Formal ecclesiastical legislation punishing abortion was enacted in the West by the Council of Elvira *c.* 300, and in the East by the Council of Ancyra in 314.

Nature. Canon Law views abortion as a crime, that is, an external violation of a law that threatens penalties. Moral theology views it as a sin, that is, a violation of the law of God. Although not every sin of abortion is a crime, every crime of abortion does presuppose the abortion in question to be a mortal sin. For, in accordance with principles of ecclesiastical penal law, there can be no crime and no consequent liability to penalties unless serious moral guilt is involved (CIC cc.2195.1, 2218.2).

To procure an abortion implies (1) intent and (2) deliberate use of (3) effective means.

First, the abortion must be intended. It must be willed either as an end in itself, for example, simply to terminate the pregnancy, or as means to some other end, for example, to safeguard the health of the mother. Both of these are sometimes characterized as directly intended. If the abortion is merely permitted and not willed, the crime is not verified, for example, in the case of hysterectomy performed to remove a diseased uterus. This permitted abortion is sometimes designated as indirectly intended.

The second element in procuring an abortion is the deliberate and purposeful use of means. In addition to interiorly willing the abortion, the person must in his external actions designedly apply the cause of the abortion. If the cause were applied only accidentally or unknowingly, there would be no crime. For example, a woman wishes an abortion, but it is an accidental fall that causes it. This is not deliberate, and hence no crime results, despite the serious sin of interiorly willing the abortion.

Thirdly, the means employed must be efficacious in themselves. This signifies simply that the abortion must actually result from the means used for this specific purpose. Therefore, if some other cause is really responsible for the abortion, there is no crime.

From the aspect of physical causality, it is immaterial whether the means used affect the fetus directly and immediately, for example, curettage, or only indirectly and mediately, for example, hysterectomy.

Abortion is not defined in ecclesiastical law, and it is to be accepted for what it is in reality. As universally described in medical circles, abortion is the detachment and expulsion of the previable fetus. It is the interruption of pregnancy at any time before viability—while the fetus is still inherently incapable of extrauterine existence. Between the 26th and the 28th week is the generally accepted minimum age for viability.

The element of nonviability is required. Once the fetus is viable, the interruption of pregnancy before term is not abortion. This is true even though the interruption, for example, by craniotomy, involves serious sin. It may be murder, but it is not abortion, simply because the fetus is now inherently capable of an independent existence.

Penalty. The excommunication, which can be incurred by anyone, is a censure, i.e., a penalty whose purpose is to secure the repentance of the delinquent. Since this penalty is reserved to the ordinary, absolution from it must be sought from the diocesan bishop, or in communities of exempt male religious, from the major superior. (*See* EXCOMMUNICATION, CANONICAL.)

The irregularity, which is applicable only to males, is an impediment forbidding the reception and the exercise of Orders, for the purpose of safeguarding the sanctity and reputation of the sacred ministry. This irregularity can be removed only by dispensation from the Holy See, and understandably, it is not readily granted. (*See* HOLY ORDERS, IRREGULARITIES AFFECTING.)

In addition to the actual perpetrators of the abortion, others might incur criminal guilt due to their complicity in the crime. Thus, excommunication is incurred, in accordance with other provisions of law, by those who by threats, hire, etc. secure another to perform the abortion. They are called mandators. It is incurred also by those whose effective cooperation was necessary for the commission of a particular abortion. They are called necessary cooperators (CIC cc.2231, 2209.1, 3).

The irregularity is incurred by "all cooperators" also, by special provision of the canon establishing irregularity (CIC c.985n4). Hence included are not only necessary cooperators, but also those whose positive cooperation constitutes an objectively serious sin by reason of its relation to the abortion, for example, one whose advice induced another to commit the crime.

Bibliography: P. FELICI, "De delictis contra vitam," *Casus conscientiae*, ed. P. PALAZZINI (Rome 1954–) v.2, *De censuris* (1956) 57–64. J. DELMAILLE, DDC 1:1536–61. R. J. HUSER, *The Crime of Abortion in Canon Law* (CUA CLS 162; Washington 1942). Beste 2350.

[R. J. HUSER]

ABORTION, IV (U.S. LAW OF)

In the United States, except for the District of Columbia, abortion is matter for state or territorial legislation, and all have exercised this jurisdiction, as has Congress for the District of Columbia.

There is general agreement on the broad definition of induced abortion as the use of any means to destroy a child in the womb or to induce delivery before it is viable. Beyond this there is little agreement.

Jurisdictions differ on many issues: whether quickening is a prerequisite of abortion or if mere pregnancy is sufficient, whether the act is criminal if the woman is not pregnant, whether there is any justification for abortion, and whether the crime of abortion is a felony or a misdemeanor.

The 13 original states, during the colonial periods, were governed by the common law of England, as this was expounded by Coke and made better known by Blackstone. After our independence, Pennsylvania and North Carolina held and still hold that at common law either abortion or its attempt is a felony, at any stage of pregnancy. This is very close to the English statute of 1803. In most states legislation has established a rule close to that of Pennsylvania and North Carolina. In 1821 Connecticut enacted the first U.S. abortion statute making quickening an essential element and providing for no justifications. In 1827 however, Illinois declared abortion a crime at any stage of pregnancy and similarly declared no exceptions.

Justification. In the next year New York also, making abortion criminal at any stage, introduced the qualification that it should not apply where the abortion was necessary for preservation of the life of the mother. From then on almost all of our statutes have applied to abortion at any stage and have justified it when necessary for preservation of the life of the mother. There has been a sharp division, however, between statutes requiring proof of the danger to the mother as a fact and those which demand only the belief, or opinion of danger on the part of the operator, or a declaration of the purpose of the abortion. The common pattern has been to describe the operator as "any person," without reference to any medical or nursing training or experience. Only seven states require that the abortion be done by or on the advice of a physician.

Twenty-two states recognize the justification only if it be found as a fact that the abortion was necessary for preservation of the mother's life, and six others justify it to save the life of the mother or the unborn child. Seven other states require proof as a fact unless the operator was advised by medical men that the abortion was necessary.

In Hawaii, Virginia, and West Virginia, it is a good defense that preservation of the mother's life was the purpose of the abortion; five other states require only that the operator, whether lay or professional, has done the abortion "as necessary" in order to preserve the mother's life.

Four states provide no statutory exemption or justification in their penal codes. One, however, Massachusetts, confines its ban to "unlawful" abortion or attempts; and another, Louisiana, in its chapter on medical practice, makes abortion ground for revoking license unless "done for the relief of a woman whose life appears in peril, after due consultation with another licensed physician."

In 1901 the District of Columbia code was made to read "unless same were done as necessary for the preservation of the mother's life or health and under the direction of a competent licensed practitioner of medicine." More recently the Massachusetts Court declared that assumed danger to physical or mental health would justify abortion. The Oregon Court, in 1953, extended the justification to the case of "woman whose health appears in peril," with some safeguarding clauses. In 1956 the New Jersey Court held abortion to be "authorized when necessary for avoidance of death or permanent serious injury."

Similar changes were made by statute in Alabama, 1951 (to preserve her life or health); and in New Mexico, 1953 ("to preserve the life of the woman, or to prevent serious and permanent bodily injury").

Decisions to date are about equally divided on whether the state or the defendant has the burden of proof as to the necessity for an abortion. None of the successive English statutes (1803, 1828, 1837, and 1861) now in force have exempted abortion on any ground whatever.

Other Issues. Nineteen states and the District of Columbia make the attempt or intended purpose sufficient matter for violation of law, even though the woman was not actually pregnant.

Thirty-one states make actual pregnancy essential, and two (Alabama and Michigan) require quickening.

Sixteen states including New York, California, and Pennsylvania include the idea that self-abortion by the mother is a transgression, as does the English statute of 1861.

Abortion may be murder, manslaughter, or other heavily punished felony if it occurs after quickening (ten states), if it causes death of mother or child (eight states), or death of the unborn child (four states). It may be considered murder or manslaughter, whether committed before or after quickening, if it results in the death of the mother (17 states and District of Columbia), death of mother or child (six states), or death of the child (three states).

In three states it is not held to be abortion unless the child dies. In six states the crime is made complete by the death of either the child or the mother and is then classed as manslaughter.

Actions directed to cause abortion but which prove ineffective constitute criminal abortion, in most states a felony; in 22 states if the woman is actually pregnant (eight states contra), and apparently in 19 others whether she is actually pregnant or not (two states contra).

In several states even a fully completed abortion can be prosecuted only as a misdemeanor. Equally noteworthy is the fact that less than half of the states have any law against sale or advertising of abortifacients and abortionists.

Most of the states permit anyone, however ignorant and inept, to perform an abortion if he believes there is danger to the life of the mother.

No state makes any distinction between ethical and unethical licensed physicians and hospitals. Only one state makes any attempt to require the opinion of a disinterested physician. Several make consultation obligatory before the abortion but provide no control over the character of the consultants.

No state requires medical findings, unless the Oregon statute could be considered to have that effect. No state requires the opinion of any expert on the particular complication suggesting the necessity of abortion, although a few hospitals have voluntarily established such a rule.

Suggested Legislation. In considering American abortion laws at the end of 1963, it is necessary to take account of the widespread and well-organized drive for liberalization of these laws. The Model Penal Code, approved by the American Law Institute in 1961, contains the following on abortion (s.230.3):

> A licensed physician is justified in terminating a pregnancy if he believes there is substantial risk that continuance of the pregnancy would gravely impair the physical or mental health of the mother or that the child would be born with grave physical or mental defect, or that the pregnancy resulted from rape, incest, or other felonious intercourse. Justifiable abortions shall be performed only in a licensed hospital except in case of emergency when hospital facilities are unavailable.
>
> No abortion shall be performed unless two physicians, one of whom may be the person performing the abortion, shall have certified in writing the circumstances which they believe to justify the abortion. Such certificate shall be submitted before the abortion to the hospital where it is to be performed and, in the case of abortion following felonious intercourse, to the prosecuting attorney or the police.

Other subsections ban actual or attempted self-abortion after the 26th week; and actual pregnancy or opinion of the operator are considered immaterial.

Bibliography: E. QUAY, "Justifiable Abortion," *Georgetown Law Journal* 49 (1960–61) 173–256, 395–538. F. L. GOOD and O. F. KELLY, *Marriage, Morals, and Medical Ethics* (New York 1951). American Law Institute, *Model Penal Code: Tentative Draft[s]* (Philadelphia 1954–).

[E. QUAY]

ABRA DE RACONIS, CHARLES FRANÇOIS D', theologian; b. near Chartres, *c.* 1580; d. Paris, July 16, 1646. A convert from Calvinism, he taught philosophy and theology until he was appointed almoner and preacher to the French court. He first devoted himself to controversial writings against Protestantism and in 1637 was appointed bishop of Lavaur. He returned to Paris in 1643, where, encouraged by his friend Vincent de Paul, he spent the rest of his life writing against Jansenism [*Examen et jugement du livre De la fréquente communion fait contre la fréquente communion et publié sous le nom de sieur Arnauld* (Paris

1644)], and against the heresy of Martin de Barcos, who taught that SS. Peter and Paul were equally heads of the Church [*Primauté et souveraineté singulière de Pierre* (Paris 1644)]. He was accused by the bishop of Grasse before the General Assembly of the Clergy of denouncing French bishops to Rome for supporting Jansenism, a charge that he denied. He died a few months later.

Bibliography: Hurter Nomencl³ 3:992. V. OBLET, DTC 1.1:93–94. P. POURRAT, *Catholicisme* 1:51.

[A. ROCK]

ABRABANEL, ISAAC (ABRAVANEL)

Portuguese rabbi, Biblical scholar, and philosopher; b. Lisbon, 1437; d. Venice, 1508. Born in a rich Jewish family, Isaac ben-Judah Abrabanel received an excellent education and entered politics. He was the minister of finance, first of King Alfonso V of Portugal (1438–81), and then of King *Ferdinand V of Castile. The edict of 1492, which expelled all the Jews from Spain, drove him into exile. At first he was welcomed in Naples, where he held an important post at the court of Ferdinand I (1458–94) and Alfonso II (1494–95), but the French invasion forced him to take refuge in Sicily and later in Corfu. After a short stay in Apulia, he finally settled in Venice.

Despite these numerous changes of abode, Abrabanel wrote many works that are as varied as they are original. With his brilliant mind, encyclopedic knowledge, and noble and generous heart, he was an outstanding exception to the general decadence that marked the disastrous end of the Judeo-Spanish epoch. He once said of himself that he was "a descendant of Jesse of Bethlehem, a scion of the royal house of David"; and there was in fact something princely about him.

His numerous writings show him to have been well versed in Christian and Moslem, Greek and Hebrew literatures, a creative thinker, a careful and exact student of the Bible. While in Portugal, he wrote a commentary entitled *Merkebet Ha-Mishneh* (The Chariot of Deuteronomy); in Castile, he wrote commentaries on Josue, Judges, and Kings. In Naples, he composed a commentary on Daniel and a sort of ritual on the Passover sacrifice. In Corfu, he wrote a work on Isaia; in Venice, commentaries on the other Prophets and on the first four books of the Pentateuch. His dissertations on the Messiah influenced the messianic movements among the Jews of the 16th and 17th centuries (*see* SHABBATAÏSM).

Among his works are also the *Migdol Yeshu'ot* (Tower of Saving Deeds) on the evidence of God's grandeur as shown in His miraculous interventions, the *Lahaqat Nebi'im* (The Company of the Prophets), and the *'Aṭeret Zeqenim* (The Crown of the Ancients). As a philosopher, Abrabanel brought to a close the line of Jewish Aristotelian thinkers. He knew and respected Christian scholasticism, especially the works of St. Thomas Aquinas, whose treatise *De spiritualibus creaturis* he translated from Latin into Hebrew.

In his Biblical exegesis he followed in the footsteps of *Rashi and *Kimchi, avoiding both a mystical and a rationalistic interpretation of the text, in favor of a natural and simple explanation. He was regarded as an authority in learned matters among the Jews, who called him *Ḥakam* (the Sage) and *Nasi* (the Prince). His erudite introductions to the Scriptures rendered considerable service to Biblical criticism also among Christian scholars. Richard Simon did not hesitate to write emphatically: "We can gain more from him than from any other of the rabbinical scholars for a better understanding of the Scriptures . . .. His clarity and eloquence in Hebrew are not less than Cicero's in Latin." Yet this is tantamount to admitting that he was more of a rhetorician than an exegete. Besides, it must be conceded that his ideas were often oversubtle and his language too prolix, and that he indulged too much in violent diatribes against Christianity.

See also JEWISH PHILOSOPHY.

Bibliography: B. NETANYAHU, *Don Isaac Abravanel, Statesman and Philosopher* (Philadelphia 1953). J. SARACHEK, *Don Isaac Abravanel* (New York 1938). A. MELINEK, *Don Isaac Abrabanel: His Life and Times* (London 1952). J. B. TREND and H. M. J. LOEWE, eds., *Isaac Abravanel* (New York 1938). E. I. J. ROSENTHAL, "Don Isaac Abravanel: Financier, Statesman and Scholar, 1437–1937," BullJRylLibr 21 (1937) 445–478. J. BAER, "Don Isaac Abravanel and His Relation to Problems of History and Politics," *Tarbiz* 8 (1937) 241–259, in Heb. M. H. SEGAL, "R. Isaac Abravanel as Interpreter of the Bible," *ibid.* 260–299, in Heb. E. E. URBACH, "Die Staatsauffassung des Don Isaak Abrabanel," *Monatsschrift für Geschichte und Wissenschaft des Judentums* 81 (1937) 257–270. J. BERGMANN, "Abrabanels Stellung zur Agada," *ibid.* 270–280. H. FINKELSCHERER, "Quellen und Motive der Staats- und Gesellschaftsauffassung des Don Isaak Abravanel," *ibid.* 496–508. L. GINZBERG, JewishEnc 1: 126–128. I. LANDMAN, UnivJewishEnc 1:53–54. S. A. HORODEZKY, EncJudaica 1:588–596.

[A. BRUNOT]

ABRAHAM, PATRIARCH

Ancestor of the Israelites and neighboring peoples. One form of his name, Abram, regarded in Genesis as his earlier name is but a dialectic variant of the other form, Abraham, both meaning "Father [God] is exalted." However, by folk etymology, the form Abraham

Fig. 1. Abraham about to sacrifice Isaac, fresco of the end of the 3d century, tomb of the Giordani, Rome.

Fig. 2. Sculpture of the sacrifice of Isaac, detail of the sarcophagus of Junius Bassus (d. 359), in the Vatican.

Fig. 3. Mosaic, c. 432–440, Santa Maria Maggiore, Rome. Top: Abraham welcomes three heavenly visitors, the middle one represented, by a nimbus, as Our Lord; below: Sara prepares a meal for them, which Abraham serves.

ABRAHAM THE PATRIARCH

Fig. 4. Abraham and the three heavenly visitors. Oil, attributed to Antonello da Saliba (c. 1466–1535).

(Hebrew *'abrāhām*) is made to mean *'ab hămôn gôyīm,* "Father of a multitude of nations" (Gn 17.5).

Life. Although the formerly common identification of *Amraphel (Gn 14.1) with *Hammurabi is now regarded as very improbable, Abraham can nevertheless be considered roughly contemporaneous with this Babylonian king (18th century B.C.); the background of the Genesis stories of the Biblical *Patriarchs agrees very well with the known conditions of northern Mesopotamia in the first half of the 2d millennium B.C. Abraham was apparently one of the seminomads of *Amorrite stock who migrated from upper Mesopotamia into Syria and Canaan between 1900 and 1700 B.C. According to the traditions recorded by the *Yahwist and the *Elohist, his home was in Haran of Aram Naharaim (northern Mesopotamia). The later Pentateuchal *priestly writers locate his original home in "Ur of the Chaldees" in southern Mesopotamia (Gn 11.28, 31; 12.4–5; 15.7; 24.10; Jos 24.2; Neh 9.7). The motive for Abraham's migration was primarily religious, leaving Mesopotamia at Yahweh's command (Gn 12.1–4), to be free from its crass polytheism (Jdt 5.6–9), but political and economic reasons may also have influenced his decision to migrate. In Gn 14.13 Abraham is called "the Hebrew" (*hā'ibrî*), which later generations may have taken to mean "the descendant of Eber" (*'ēber*), (cf. Gn 11.14–26), but which more likely originally meant "the immigrant" (*see* HABIRU).

Biblical genealogies relate Abraham to many Near Eastern peoples: through his brother *Nahor to the *Aramaeans; through his son *Ismael (Ishmael) to the *Ismaelites (Ishmaelites; Gn 16; 21.9–21; 25.12–18); through his son Isaac and his grandson *Jacob (Israel) to the Israelites; through his other grandson *Esau to the *Edomites (Gn 36); through his second wife Cetura to several Arabic tribes (Gn 25.1–4); and through his nephew *Lot to the *Moabites and *Ammonites (Gn 19.30–38). Tradition associated Abraham with several places and sacred trees in Canaan: *Sichem (Shechem) and its sacred terebinth of More (Gn 12.6), *Bethel and its altar (12.8), *Hebron and its terebinths of Mamre (13.18), and *Bersabee (Beersheba) and its tamarisk (21.33). Besides his wanderings in Canaan, he also went to Gerar in the western *Negeb, according to the Elohist (Gn 20), and to Egypt, according to the Yahwist (Gn 12.10–20). According to Gn 25.7–11, Abraham died in his 175th year and was buried in the cave of Machphela, near Hebron.

Abraham in Salvation History. This Patriarch marks a significant point in the history of salvation. He is the first to worship the true God. Because of Yahweh's covenant with him, which included the promise that in him all the nations of the earth should be blessed and of which the sign was circumcision, descent from Abraham was considered a necessary condition for belonging to the people of God. Abraham's faith in God's promise of innumerable descendants survived a severe test when God commanded him to sacrifice his only son Isaac (Gn 22). "Abram believed the Lord, who credited the act to him as justice" (Gn 15.6). St. Paul cites these words (Rom 4.3, 9, 22; Gal 3.6) to show that it is not carnal descent or circumcision, but faith like that of Abraham that makes men the true descendants of Abraham (Rom 4; Heb 11.17–19). Because they are his offspring, the blessed after death recline at the messianic banquet "in *Abraham's bosom" (Lk 16.22–23).

Iconography. Perhaps the most frequently reproduced theme from the life of Abraham is that of his impending sacrifice of Isaac. This is found as early as the Synagogue of *Dura-Europos (*c.* A.D. 245) and in the Christian catacombs. As a type of the sacrifice of Christ, this scene became increasingly popular in the Middle Ages. It was also interpreted as a type of the Eucharist, as was likewise the frequently depicted encounter of Abraham with Melchisedec (Gn 14.18), e.g., in St. Mary Major in Rome. Another commonly portrayed scene was that of the visit to Abraham of three angels, sometimes represented as the Three Persons of the Blessed Trinity (Gn 18). Various motifs from Abraham's life were utilized by Titian, Tintoretto, Rembrandt, and Rubens.

Bibliography: L. PIROT, DBSuppl 1:7–28. V. HAMP and J. SCHMIDT, LexThK[2] 1:56–59. A. WEISER, RGG[3] 1:68–71. Enc DictBibl 12–15. **Illustration credits:** Fig. 1, Pontificia Commissione di Archaeologica Sacra. Fig. 2, Hirmer Verlag München. Fig. 3, Alinari-Art Reference Bureau. Fig. 4, Samuel H. Kress Collection, Denver Art Museum, Denver, Colo.

[E. MARTIN]

ABRAHAM OF CLERMONT, ST., hermit, abbot; d. between 474 and 481 (feast, June 15 in Diocese of Clermont). Abraham was of Persian origins. During the Sassanian persecution of Christians he was imprisoned, regained his freedom, and fled to the West. According to the *Vita patrum,* ch. 3, of *Gregory of Tours (MGSrerMer 1:672), who seems to have confused him with the Biblical patriarch, Abraham sojourned among the anchorites in Egypt before arriving in Auvergne. There he lived a hermit's life near Clermont. His reputation for sanctity attracted a number of disciples, and his hermitage became the nucleus of a monastery dedicated to St. Cyriacus with Abraham as abbot. *Sidonius Apollinaris composed his epitaph (*Epist.* 7.17; MGAucAnt 8:123). Abraham was invoked for the cure of fever.

Bibliography: ActSS June 3:534–536. R. AIGRAIN, *Catholicisme* 1:57. Baudot-Chaussin 6:251–252.

[B. L. MARTHALER]

ABRAHAM ECCHELLENSIS, Maronite scholar; b. Ḥāqil (Mt. Lebanon), Feb. 18, 1605; d. Rome, July 15, 1664. Ibrāhīm al-Ḥāqilānī studied at the Maronite Roman College, was ordained and remained a deacon, taught Syriac and Arabic at Pisa and in Rome, published a Syriac grammar (1628), and became the interpreter for the Propagation of Faith (1635), succeeding the Maronite bishop, Sergius Rezzee, on the project to revise the Arabic translation of the Bible. From 1640 he collaborated with C. *Le Jay on the Polyglot edition of the Bible, revised the work of *Gabriel Sionita, and published the Book of Ruth in Arabic and Syriac with a Latin translation, and Machabees 3 in Arabic and Latin. In 1645 he became professor of Syriac and Arabic at the Collège de France and in 1647 published three letters in defense of his book on Ruth. He was appointed by Pope *Alexander VII a scriptor for Arabic and Syriac at the Vatican Library (1660), and spent the rest of his life studying and publishing. His private library is conserved in the Vatican under *Fonds Ecchellensis.*

Bibliography: A. SCHALL, LexThK[2] 1:61–62. J. LAMY, DTC 1.1:116–118. L. PETIT, DHGE 1:169–171. Graf GeschChArabLit 3:354–359. Y. I. AD-DIBS, *Al-Ǧāmi' al-mufaṣṣal fī ta'rīḫ al-*

Mawārina al-mu'aṣṣal (Beirut 1905) 383–386, history of the Maronites. P. RAPHAËL, *Le Rôle du collège maronite romain dans l'orientalisme* (Beirut 1950) 88–92.

[E. EL-HAYEK]

ABRAHAM OF EPHESUS, ST., bishop; d. after 542 or 553 (feast, Oct. 28). He built a religious house in Constantinople and another in Jerusalem; the former was known as the monastery of the Abrahamites, the latter as that of the Byzantines. He succeeded to the See of *Ephesus as metropolitan of Asia, either in 542 after Hypatios, or in 553, after Andrew. Of his works, two homilies, important for the history of the liturgy are extant: one on the feast of the *Annunciation (*Euangelismos*) delivered on March 25, instead of the Sunday before Christmas according to earlier custom; the other, on the Presentation (*Hypapante*).

Bibliography: ActSS Oct. 12:757–769. M. JUGIE, "Abraham d'Éphèse et ses écrits," ByzZ 22 (1913) 37–59. Baudot-Chaussin 10:929. O. VOLK, LexThK² 1:62.

[B. L. MARTHALER]

ABRAHAM OF SANCTA CLARA

Discalced Augustinian friar, preacher, and author of popular devotional works; b. Kreenheinstetten near Baden, July 2, 1644; d. Vienna, Dec. 1, 1709. He was the son of Matthew Mergerle or Mergerlin, a tavern keeper in Kreenheinstetten, and received the name John Ulrich at baptism. His elementary education was gained at the village school and at Messkirch, and he entered the gymnasium of the Jesuits at Ingolstadt in 1656. Upon the death of his father he was adopted by an uncle, Abraham von Mergerlin, a canon of Altötting, who transferred him to the Benedictine school at Salzburg in 1659. After 3 years there John Ulrich entered the Discalced Augustinians, and at profession took the name of Abraham, doubtless out of courtesy to his uncle. He made his novitiate and completed his studies at Mariabrunn and was ordained in Vienna on June 8, 1668. After a brief assignment as preacher at the shrine in Taxa, near Augsburg, where he gained some fame for his dramatic sermons, Abraham went to Vienna, which was to be the chief center of his work. Leopold I named him preacher of the imperial court in 1677, and within the order he served as superior and prior of the convent in Vienna, as master of novices at Mariabrunn, and minister provincial of the Vienna province.

He gained a reputation as a forceful orator with unusual talent for presenting his themes in a graphic manner. Although accused by some of his contemporaries of being a buffoon in the pulpit, he seems in fact to have been a witty, cultivated, and learned man who utilized a varied store of knowledge and exceptional ability in such a manner as to be an effective preacher.

Abraham was a prolific author and his works include a vast mélange of both sacred and secular writings. He was a literary master of both prose and poetry. Schiller characterized him as a man of marvelous originality, worthy of respect, and not easy to surpass in wit or cleverness. Abraham regarded his writings as an apostolate and even in his most humorous works aimed at the moral elevation of his readers. The occasion that started Abraham's literary career was the plague that devastated Vienna in 1679. He wrote *Merk's Wien!* (Vienna 1680) as a dramatic description of the plague to show how death spares no one. He followed this with two lesser works, *Lösch Wien* (Vienna 1680) and *Die grosse Totenbruderschaft* (Vienna 1681), which exhorted the people to pray for the souls of those killed in the plague and listed personages of prominence who had succumbed. His next work, *Auff, auff, ihr Christen* (Vienna 1683) was an appeal to the Christian world to do battle against the Turks. This is chiefly remembered because Schiller used it as a model for the sermon of the Capuchin Friar in *Wallenstein's Lager*. A four-volume work, *Judas der Erzschelm* (Judas the Archknave) Salzburg, 1686–95, is usually considered Abraham's masterpiece. The fruit of a decade of labor, this work sets forth the apocryphal life of Judas with moral applications for the daily spiritual life of the reader. The remaining works, constituting a mixture of the most varied sort, can be found in a collective edition published at Passau in 1846. They range from the serious *Grammatica Religiosa* (Salzburg 1691), a compendium of moral teaching, to *Huy! und Pfuy der Welt* (Ho! and Phooey on the World), Würzburg, 1707, which shows the influence of Sebastian Brant's (*Narrenschiff,* Ship of Fools). Several volumes of literary works were published after his death, and various editions and collections have appeared down to the present century. These must be used with care since there are some doubtful and spurious entries.

Bibliography: T. G. VON KARAJAN, *Abraham a Sancta Clara* (Vienna 1867). K. BERTSCHE, *Die Werke Abrahams a Sancta Clara in ihren Frühdrucken* (Schwetzingen 1922). W. BRANDT, *Schwank und Fabel bei Abraham a Sancta Clara* (Münster 1923). L. BIANCHI, *Studien zur Beurteilung des Abraham a Santa Clara* (Heidelberg 1924). K. VANCSA, LexThK² 1:64–65.

[A. J. CLARK]

ABRAHAM THE SIMPLE, ST., called also Abraham the Child, 4th-century desert father (feast, Oct. 27). He is identified by John *Cassian as one of the great desert fathers known for his simplicity of manner and innocence and for miracles of healing. He was dead by the end of the 4th century. He may be the Abraham who relates Cassian's last *Conference,* a man of strictest austerity. He is not to be confused with the disciple of Pachomius and Theodore, but he may be the Abraham whose three maxims are given in the *Apophthegmata Patrum* PG 65:129–132.

Bibliography: J. CASSIAN, *Conlationes,* ed. M. PETSCHENIG (CSEL 13; 1886) 430–431, 672–711. S. SALAVILLE, DHGE 1: 171–172. B. KÖTTING, LexThK² 1:63. Tillemont 10:30–32.

[M. C. MC CARTHY]

ABRAHAMS, ISRAEL, Jewish scholar and author; b. London, Nov. 26, 1858; d. Cambridge, England, Oct. 6, 1925. He was the son of Barnett Abrahams, who was dayyan (rabbinical judge) of the Spanish and Portuguese congregation of London and principal of Jews' College, London, and he was trained in rabbinics by his father and educated formally at Jews' College and University College, where he graduated M.A. in 1881. He served as senior tutor of Jews' College, teaching homiletics and secular disciplines until 1902. He became reader in Talmudic and rabbinic literature at Cambridge. Active in both Jewish and non-Jewish learned circles, he was a close collaborator with Claude *Montefiore, who styled him "my dear and saintly friend" and the "greatest English-born Jewish scholar of his age." With Montefiore he founded and edited (1889–1908) the *Jewish Quarterly Review*. Especially noteworthy are his *Jewish Life in the Middle Ages* (London 1896; rev. ed. 1932) and his *Judaism* (London 1907). His literary production was also varied, including, for instance, *Campaigns in Palestine from Alexander the Great* (London 1927).

*Judaism for Abrahams meant the "later development of the religion of Israel which began with the reorganization after the Babylonian Exile [444 B.C.] and was crystallised by the Roman Exile [during the first centuries of the Christian Era]" (*Judaism* 2). He was deeply persuaded of its evolutionary character and freedom from all dogmas, and he insisted on the value of "inward" religion without denying all value to externals.

Bibliography: P. GOODMAN, UnivJewishEnc 1:47–48. Jewish Enc 1:123. EncJudaica 1:556–557. D. PHILIPSON, *The Reform Movement in Judaism* (rev. ed., New York 1931). J. A. KOHUT, ed., *Jewish Studies in Memory of Israel Abrahams* (New York 1928).

[E. A. SYNAN]

ABRAHAM'S BOSOM, the place, according to Jewish ideas at the time of Christ, where the just go after death. In the parable of the Rich Man and Lazarus (Lk 16.19–31), the reward of Lazarus after his death is described in terms of his being "borne away by angels into Abraham's bosom." The Greek κόλπος, like its Hebrew equivalent *hêq,* can mean either bosom or lap. Some exegetes understand the text in the sense that Abraham received Lazarus as a loving father would take his small son upon his lap or hold him close to his bosom (cf. Jn 1.18); others, that Lazarus was given a place of honor at the Messianic banquet, reclining at the right hand of Abraham (cf. Jn 13.23). The latter interpretation appears more probable, since the banquet image was used in Rabbinic literature (see KittelThW 3:824–826), and Jesus Himself describes the Kingdom of God in terms of the eschatological banquet prepared on top of the Mountain of God (Lk 13.22–29; Is 2.2; 49.12), where the elect will recline with Abraham, Isaac, and Jacob (Lk 13.28–29). At times, however, the repose in Abraham is unrelated to a banquet and signifies blissful happiness enjoyed with the Patriarch (4 Mc 13.17). The common notion of the Fathers of the Church that Abraham's bosom designates a place of happiness not only for Christians in heaven, but also for the just of the OT who there (in the *limbo of the fathers) await the coming of the Messiah, is foreign to Jewish thought.

Lazarus giving apples to the blessed in paradise as he sits in Abraham's Bosom, miniature from a 13th-century German Psalter. The artist has given Lazarus a cruciform halo of the type usually reserved for Our Lord.

Bibliography: EncDictBibl 15. E. W. SAUNDERS, InterDictBibl 1:21–22. J. SCHMID, LexThK² 1:58–59. W. STAERK, ReallexAnt Chr 1:27–28. **Illustration credit:** National Gallery of Art, Washington, D.C., Rosenwald Collection.

[J. PLASTARAS]

ABRANTOVIČ, FABIJAN, archimandrite of the Byzantine-Slavonic rite; b. Navahradak, Byelorussia, Sept. 14, 1884; d. Siberia?, 1940. He studied for the priesthood at the Catholic Academy of St. Petersburg (Leningrad) and later at the Catholic University of Louvain. Abrantovič, ordained Nov. 9, 1908, taught theology at the Catholic Academy, actively participated in the Byelorussian Christian Movement, and cooperated in the founding of the Byelorussian Christian Democracy, which did much to further the Byelorussian renaissance. After the proclamation of the independence of the Byelorussian Republic March 25, 1918, Abrantovič with Bp. Z. Losinski organized the Catholic Seminary in the capital city of Minsk. When the seminary was transferred in 1921 to Navahradak and then to Pinsk, Abrantovič continued to serve as rector, professor, and spiritual director. In 1926 he entered the Congregation of Marian Fathers and began his apostolate among his countrymen at Druja, the Marian's only Byelorussian house, whose purpose was to prepare workers for the apostolate among separated Christians, especially among Byelorussian Orthodox. In 1928 Abrantovič was sent by Pius XI to organize and, as exarch, to govern the first Byzantine-Slavonic diocese in the Far East at Harbin, Manchuria. In 1929 there were approximately one million inhabitants in Harbin of which 150,000 were of Slavic origin. There were 3 Orthodox bishops and 271 Orthodox priests, while Catholics of the Byzantine-Slavonic rite numbered only 18.

In spite of the poverty of the people, lack of organization, national and religious strife, Abrantovič in 10 years formed a diocese, built a Catholic church, founded a boarding school for boys, and eventually established a religious house of the Congregation of Marians. In 1938 he left Harbin for Rome where he attended the General Chapter of the Congregation and submitted a report on his diocese to the Holy See. From Rome, the following year, he went to his native Byelorussia. He was arrested by the Communists, brutally tortured as a Vatican spy, and finally either killed in prison or sent to Siberia where he perished.

Bibliography: *Podręczna encyklopedia Kościelna,* v. 43–44 (Warsaw-Cracow 1916) Suppl. 1:1. C. Sipovič, "Ajciec Archimandryt Fabijan Abrantovič," *Božym Šlacham* 76–81 (Paris 1957) 9–20.

[C. SIPOVIČ]

ABRAXAS, a magico-mystical word occurring in Hellenistic papyri and found also, along with other symbols, on ancient and medieval amulets. The numerical values of the Greek letters making up the word 'Αβράξας or its variant 'Αβράσαξ ('Α = 1, β = 2, ρ = 100, α = 1, ξ = 60, α = 1, ς = 200) give a sum of 365. This figure corresponds to the total number of days in the solar year. In the Gnostic system of Basilides the term is employed also to designate the First Principle or Supreme Being, the ultimate source of the 365 heavens. Some scholars consider that there is a connection between *Abraxas* and the magic word *abracadabra,* but the relationship is disputed.

Bibliography: H. Leclercq, DACL 1.1:127–155, with illustrations. N. Turchi, EncCatt 1:128–129. M. Hain, LexThK[2] 1:66.

[M. R. P. MC GUIRE]

ABREACTION

A term that, when used by psychiatrists and psychologists, refers to a process by which past emotional experiences that were forgotten (repressed) are reexperienced or discharged. Such a release may occur during *psychotherapy when unwanted feelings and attitudes originally felt during a person's early childhood are brought back to conscious awareness. Such recall results in a reliving of these previously repressed experiences, in the belief that such a combined intellectual and emotional discharge will assist self-understanding of emotional conflicts and thereby be of therapeutic benefit to an individual. The theoretical and clinical aspects of abreaction have undergone changes since the time of S. *Freud, who first regarded abreaction as essential to the cure of neurotic illness. Freud observed how emotionally charged repressed memories appeared during *hypnosis and noted how the expression of these emotions resulted in benefit to patients. He used this observation as one of the foundations for his theories of mental illness. Later he recognized that emotional discharge alone did not have permanent curative value. He then gave attention to reconstructing past traumatic events by focusing on the patient's ability to recall and understand them without the use of hypnosis but rather through his concept of free associations. The next step was the discovery of the *transference phenomenon that tended to shift the emphasis back to emotional experience and expression. Common to these changes in viewpoint was the theoretical belief that it was necessary to make repressed experiences available to conscious memory. In recent years the general principles pertaining to technique in psychotherapy were subjected to reconsideration by various authors. Associated with this was a gradual change in thinking as regards the necessity for achieving an emotional discharge during psychotherapy. There are those who believe emotional abreaction to be the most important of therapeutic factors and others who stress the importance of other factors, such as intellectual insight. However, as a superficial tool, abreaction has been found very useful in some of the amnesias, such as were seen during World War II in persons suffering acute emotional reactions to combat situations. In these instances barbiturates were used instead of hypnosis. It may also be of benefit in working out other emotional aspects arising from stressful experiences. However, it is not essential to achieving therapeutic benefit and may in certain individuals cause disruptive behavior. Another aspect of abreaction is its association with "talking things out" or confessing one's innermost problems, by means of which some relief of tension is realized. Although these two concepts are frequently equated, they are not the same. The difference is that confession in the religious sense pertains to rational guilt; abreaction pertains to those feelings or thoughts that are irrational in the sense that they are not volitional, as can be seen in the previously mentioned amnesic conditions.

Bibliography: A. P. Noyes and L. C. Kolb, *Modern Clinical Psychiatry* (6th ed. Philadelphia 1963). F. Alexander, *The Scope of Psychoanalysis* (New York 1961). F. Fromm-Reichmann, *Psychoanalysis and Psychotherapy,* ed. D. M. Bullard and E. V. Weigert (Chicago 1959). L. R. Wolberg, *The Technique of Psychotherapy* (New York 1954).

[R. T. KRAUS]

ABREACTION (MORAL ASPECT). Since the psychological explanation of abreaction is not yet developed to the point of general agreement, Catholic moralists are wary of making definitive statements about its morality. All the moralists grant that there is moral danger in the experience of abreaction, since the sudden access of sexual, hostile, or aggressive emotions can lead to sinful acts or at least to the danger of consenting to sinful thoughts and desires. Since, however, abreactions are not directly voluntary acts—by definition, they come on unexpectedly—the question of their morality is not a question of the morality of abreaction in itself but a question of whether or not a person can lawfully put himself in a situation in which an abreaction might take place. It is a question of an indirectly voluntary act (*see* DOUBLE EFFECT, PRINCIPLE OF).

The most common circumstances in which a person might place himself with some danger of experiencing abreaction is the occasion of some forms of psychiatric therapy. The mental probings involved in some forms of psychotherapy, whether or not drugs and hypnosis are used, not infrequently occasion an abreactive incident. The question of the morality of abreaction therefore is a question of whether the psychotherapeutic situation justifies the moral dangers of these sudden, intense, emotional outbursts.

Some moralists have judged that therapies that run the risk of abreaction are illicit. Others hold that they are licit because only material sin is involved, not formal sin. Some of these emphasize the special circumstances of the therapeutic situation that tend to insure a person against formal sin: e.g., the effects of drugs and hypnosis and the fact that the mental dynamics involved are operating below the level of conscious and deliberate engagement. The case might also be considered as a case of double effect. Abreaction in itself seems to be a morally neutral phenomenon: since its occurrence is secondary to the therapeutic process and intention, and since the circumstances that indicate the need for therapy are often sufficiently grave, it seems morally justifiable to undergo therapy even though abreaction might be occasioned. This is especially true since therapists themselves try to minimize the dangers involved in abreactive incidents. If, however, in any particular case it should be determined that a person could not experience abreaction without formal sin or harm to other individuals, therapy risking such abreaction would not be lawful.

Bibliography: H. GRATTON, "Le Problème de la responsabilité dans les abréactions surtout les abréactions psychoanalytiques," VieSpirit Suppl 41 (1957) 199–218. J. NUTTIN, *Psychoanalysis and Personality,* tr. G. LAMB (New York 1953) 148–153. A. SNOECK, "Moral Reflections on Psychiatric Abreaction," ThSt 13 (1952) 173–189. M. E. STOCK, "Some Moral Issues in Psychoanalysis," *Thomist* 23 (1960) 176–188.

[M. E. STOCK]

ABRUNCULUS OF TRIER, ST., bishop; d. *c.* 527 (feast, April 22). The only definite information about Abrunculus, or Apruncuculus, comes from *Gregory of Tours who says that upon his death Nicetius was elected bishop of Trier (*Vitae patrum,* 6.3, MGSrer Mer 1:682). In the 11th century his remains were translated from St. Symphorian to the church of St. Paulinus in Trier, and a century later, to the abbey church of Springiersbach.

Bibliography: ActSS April 3:30–31. BHL 5985. Baudot-Chaussin 4:556. A. HEINTZ, LexThK[2] 1:67.

[B. L. MARTHALER]

ABSALOM, David's third son, who was born at Hebron of Maacha, a Gessurite princess (2 Sm 3.3), and died ignominiously in his attempt to usurp the kingdom from his father. His recorded experiences begin with the story of the rape of his sister Thamar by their half brother Amnon, David's first-born son. In retaliation, Absalom successfully contrived to have Amnon assassinated; then, for safety he fled to his royal relatives in Gessur (2 Sm 13.1–38). After 3 years in exile and 2 further years of waiting in Jerusalem, Absalom was ultimately forgiven by David (2 Sm 14.1–33). Since Amnon and presumably Cheleab (or Daniel; cf. 2 Sm 3.3 with 1 Chr 3.1), David's second son, were dead, Absalom began a plot to seize the throne and had himself proclaimed king at Hebron (2 Sm 15.1–12). David, caught unaware, fled to the Transjordan town of *Mahanaim, where he found support (2 Sm 15.13–16.14; 17.27–29). After occupying Jerusalem, Absalom publicly violated the royal harem (2 Sm 16.20–23), a symbolic usurpation of his father's authority. Of David's two counselor's, the best, Achitophel, joined Absalom, but Chusai secretly remained loyal. Absalom listened to Chusai and foolishly dallied in Jerusalem (2 Sm 17.7–14). In the "Forest of Ephraim" Absalom was defeated in battle (2 Sm 18.6–8), met an ignominious death at the hand of Joab (2 Sm 18.14–15), and was buried under a great cairn of stones (2 Sm 18.17–18). David was inconsolable with grief (2 Sm 18.32–19.8). One tradition narrates that Absalom was the father of three sons and a daughter Thamar who possessed her father's beauty (2 Sm 14.25–27), while the tradition of the memorial pillar in the King's Valley states that Absalom had no sons, perhaps indicating that his sons died in infancy (2 Sm 18.18; however, the monument in the Cedron Valley, known as Absalom's Tomb, dates from the Hellenistic period). According to 2 Chr 11.20 King Roboam married Maacha, "the daughter of Absalom," but probably a granddaughter is meant.

Absalom caught by his long hair (2 Sm 14.26) on an oak in the Forest of Ephraim and pierced with three javelins by Joab (18.6–15). Detail from the Story of Absalom on the floor of the Siena cathedral by Pietro del Minella (1391–1458).

Bibliography: EncDictBibl 15–16. J. BRIGHT, *A History of Israel* (Philadelphia 1959). H. P. SMITH, *Samuel* (ICC; New York 1904) 329–360. **Illustration credit:** Alinari-Art Reference Bureau.

[F. BUCK]

ABSALON OF LUND, archbishop, founder of Copenhagen; b. Fjenneslev, Denmark, October 1128; d. Sorø, March 21, 1201. A member of one of the most powerful families on the island of Sjaelland, that of Skjalm the White, Absalon studied at Sainte-Geneviève-de-Paris. He was ordained there and enthusiastically adopted the Latin culture as well as the current ideology of Church reform. Upon his return to *Denmark, he became counselor to King Valdemar the Great, founded the monastery at Sorø, was elected bishop of Roskilde (1158), and in 1178 was appointed archbishop of *Lund (succeeding *Eskil of Lund), simultaneously retaining Roskilde up to 1191. He distinguished himself by the zeal with which he introduced into Denmark Western Church customs (e.g., tithing, clerical *celibacy) and Western monasticism (*Cistercians and *Carthusians). He proved to be an administrator and a statesman—even a warrior—as well as a builder and a patron of the arts. In fortifying his diocese against the invasion of the *Slavs (Wends), he built at Havn a castle-keep that became the nucleus of the city of Copenhagen. Multiplying the expeditions against these pagan Slavs on the southern coast of the Baltic, he took by storm the temple of Arkona (1169) on the island of Rügen, which was then annexed to Denmark. On the intellectual plane, Absalon dominated the Danish clergy of his time: a runic inscription at Nørre Aasum, Skåne, testifies to his interest in the traditional Scandinavian culture, but it is significant that he was the protector of the best Latin chronicler of his time, *Saxo Grammaticus, who dedicated his *Gesta Danorum* to Absalon. While remaining outside the *investiture struggle, Absalon was the faithful protector of royal power; this earned him the regency under the young King *Canute IV (*c.* 1187–90). He energetically upheld the interests of his family, promoted the career of his nephews Anders Sunesøn and Peder Sunesøn, like himself former students at Paris, who succeeded him at Lund and Roskilde respectively; Absalon also proclaimed the sanctity of his relative *Margaret of Roskilde. The city of Copenhagen venerates him as its founder; he can be considered the most brilliant Scandinavian prelate of the Middle Ages.

Bibliography: SAXO GRAMMATICUS, *Gesta Danorum*, ed. J. OLRIK and H. RAEDER, 2 v. (Copenhagen 1931–57). H. OLRIK, *Absalon*, 2 v. (Copenhagen 1908–09). H. KOCH and B. KORNERUP, eds. *Den danske kirkes historie* (Copenhagen 1950–) v.1. L. WEIBULL, *Nordisk Historia* 2 (1948) 526–538.

[L. MUSSET]

ABSOLUTE, THE

From the Latin *ab-solutus*, meaning separated, free from, or complete, that which is independent of conditions, relations, or impediments. In philosophical language the absolute may be said to function adverbially, adjectivally, and substantively. In an adverbial sense, a consideration is said to be absolute when something is discussed without reference to conditions that may *de facto* attach to it but are not essential to it. For example, in comparing intelligence and will, one may maintain that, absolutely speaking, the activity of intelligence is more perfect than that of will, although in man's present condition some objects are attained more perfectly by love than by knowledge. In an adjectival sense, the most important philosophical instance of the absolute is absolute truth. *Truth is the relation of a mental judgment to reality, and yet some truths are said to be eternal. Finally, in a substantive sense, the Absolute is that which is perfect and complete and preeminently the supreme principle of all things. Absolute truth and absolute being are the most important senses of the term for philosophy. This article summarizes the historical development of the concept from Augustine to Hegel and concludes with a brief evaluation of absolutism as compared to relativism.

Augustine. Although there are many historical precedents to his teaching in this matter, St. *Augustine is among the most notable examples of a thinker who moves from the necessity of eternal truth to a subsistent truth, an absolute being. *Platonism, through the intermediary of *Plotinus, is a major source of Augustinian doctrine, and yet the great African bishop had first to formulate a defense against the *skepticism of the Academy, Plato's old school. *Plato had held that the sensible world is incapable of grounding true knowledge but that there are other entities, the Forms or Ideas, that are objects commensurate with the demands of knowledge. The New Academy accepted Plato's teaching with respect to the inadequacy of the sensible world as a cause of knowledge, but it did not share his certitude in the existence of Ideas. In this way, the possibility of knowledge was called into question.

Augustine, in his attack on the new Academicians, appealed to the existence of the doubter as something that escapes doubt. Although this may seem an anticipation of the Cartesian *cogito,* it did not play the role of a truth from which all others are in some way derived. More positively, Augustine appealed to the truths of mathematics, which, being certain and independent of the sensible world, give strength to the belief that there is an intelligible world to respond to knowledge in the full sense—an intelligible world that is independent of the sensible world. Augustine employed the Platonic vocabulary to speak of the intelligible world, the realm of the Ideas. For him, the existence of Ideas is plain from the facts that this is a created world and that God must know what it is He creates. The Ideas are the patterns according to which God fashions creatures. The locus, as it were, of the Ideas is the Second Person of the Trinity; He is the wisdom philosophers are ever seeking. The supreme attribute of God, for Augustine, is truth; God is the truth who grounds all other truths. Thus the recognition of absolute truths, as in mathematics, led Augustine to the conclusion that there must be an absolute being who is subsistent truth.

Thomas Aquinas. In the teaching of St. *Thomas Aquinas there is an intimate connection between the notion of eternal or absolute truth and absolute being. This emerges quite clearly from his discussion of the question as to whether created truth is eternal. "Notice that the truth of statements is nothing other than the truth of intellect, for what is stated exists in the mind as well as in speech, and it is insofar as it is in the mind that it has truth properly speaking. As spoken it is said to be a true statement insofar as it expresses some truth in the mind, not because of any truth existing in the enunciation as in a subject. So, too, urine is said to be healthy, not from any health in it but from the health of the animal of which it is a sign. Similarly we have pointed out that things are called true with reference to the truth of understanding. Hence if no mind were eternal, no truth would be eternal. And, because only the divine mind is eternal, in it alone does truth have eternity. Nor does it follow from this that something besides God is eternal, because the truth of the divine mind is God Himself, as we argued earlier" (ST 1a, 16.7).

The ontology of Aquinas leads to a description of God as that being whose existence is His very nature. Any being other than God is such that it is possible for it not to exist; the cause of its existence must therefore be sought outside itself. God is His existence and His being is therefore absolute, utterly independent of every other being. It should not be thought that this involves something like the Anselmian *ontological argument; Aquinas dismisses somewhat curtly the suggestion that, since the term God signifies a being than which nothing greater can be thought, such a being must necessarily exist (ST 1a, 2.1 ad 2). St. Thomas holds that man's warrant for asserting that God exists and, indeed, *is* existence, must always be found in creatures. If man knew God directly, this would not be necessary; but the human mode of knowing, which has as its commensurate object the nature of sensible reality, precludes such a direct intuition. In short, man's knowledge of absolute being is relative to his knowledge of dependent or created being.

This analysis may seem to call into question the absoluteness of divine being since, if God is not somehow relative to creatures, it would seem to follow that knowledge of creatures could not lead to knowledge of God. Indeed, many of the names man applies to God seem to imply such a relation to creatures—names such as "Creator," "Savior," and even the word "God" itself insofar as its etymology refers to divine providence. And, of course, if God is related to the world, He cannot be absolute in the desired sense.

St. Thomas's solution to this difficulty involves a distinction between real relations and relations of reason. A real *relation is had when one thing is dependent on another for its being. Such a relation is often reciprocal. For example, a son is dependent on his father; but the father is dependent on his son as well since, if he had no child, he could not be a father. In the case of God and creatures, St. Thomas argues that while creatures are really related to God, the relation of God to creatures is one of reason alone (*De pot.* 7.11). Thus, in knowing that God's existence is absolute, man does not know Him absolutely, i.e., independently of his knowledge of things that are quite distinct from, and inessential to, God. That man comes to know God through His created effects is an indication of the imperfection of man's knowledge of God, since there is an infinite distance between created and divine perfection. "Perfect knowledge of a cause cannot be gained through effects that are not proportioned to the cause, but from any effect it can be clearly demonstrated to us that the cause exists, as we have argued. So it is that from the effects of God we demonstrate that God exists, although they do not permit us to know Him perfectly in His very essence" (ST 1a, 2.2 ad 3).

The position of St. Thomas, here as elsewhere, depends on the possibility of distinguishing what man knows from the way in which he knows it. If the human manner of knowing were a complete determinant of what man knows, he could not have knowledge even that an absolute exists. But, given the distinction, it can be maintained that, while the human manner of knowing absolute being necessarily entails relating absolute being to being other than itself—hence preventing man's knowing it absolutely—nevertheless what man knows is absolute being. In the case of God, however, one must quickly add that, since on the level of what is known creatures are the necessary bridge to knowledge of His existence, human knowledge of God is unavoidably imperfect and derived.

Spinoza. The absolute implies an opposite: the nonabsolute, or relative; given at least the definition of the absolute, the nonabsolute appears to have but a precarious hold on its claim to reality. For Aquinas, the distinction between the relative and the absolute could be expressed by the dualism of created and uncreated substance. This same dualism, though admittedly on quite another basis, was retained by R. *Descartes; but, in his wake, B. *Spinoza argued that the very concept of *substance leads to the conclusion that there can be but one substance and that substance is absolute. For him, thought and extension—one might simply say, the created—cannot be thought of as substances when compared to God. If they exist, they can exist only as attributes of the one substance. Thus Spinoza's insistence on absolute substance leads to a monism of substance; the only dualism remaining consists of parallel systems of attributes, mental and physical. Everything is reduced in pantheistic fashion to God (*see* PANTHEISM).

Fichte. The significance of the absolute ego in the thought of J. G. *Fichte has to be understood against the general background of his insistence on the *will, or ego, as a corrective of Kantian critical idealism. The upshot of the Kantian *Critiques* was that these provided man with a basis for a rational faith in the realm of freedom. The thing-in-itself, originally a postulated and surd element in the Kantian system, became the realm of morality and of God, which is inaccessible to critical reason. For Kant, the moral law within provides a ground for belief in, but not knowledge of, the existence of God, the spiritual order, and the immortality of the soul. In his view, while man cannot know any of these things by way of proof, he does have a warrant that will allow him to accept them on practical grounds.

Fichte refused to accept this relegation of freedom and self to the fringes of true knowledge; his own philosophy began with the assertion of the conception of *freedom, of the ego or *self, as the absolutely basic principle. From this principle must be derived the categories of experience. This was, in its own way, a Copernican revolution. The willing, free self became the source of all knowledge and experience. Freedom, the world order, and God were the basic realities; if anything else was to be admitted as real, it had to be deduced from these. The practical order was not merely saved as a realm unto itself, then; it became the fundamental and regulative order of reality. Fichte, in order to avoid the charge that he was deducing all reality from his own self, introduced a distinction between particular selves and the absolute self of which individual selves are manifestations. For this reason he would have denied that he had developed a system of subjective *idealism. He was able to account, to his own satisfaction, for the existence of the external world, since it did not depend in its entirety on his ego. The absolute ego that thus became the center of Fichte's philosophy is God, but God understood as a process, a self-determining spiritual evolution. This absolute self expresses and manifests itself in individual selves; it lives and acts in them as the law of their nature, the ultimate ground of both the phenomenal world and the necessary laws of thought.

Schelling. In Fichte nature is a product of the absolute ego; with reference to the individual ego, however, it is merely an obstacle. F. W. J. *Schelling attempted to go beneath this remaining dualism to find, in the concept of the absolute as nature or process, a completely monistic ground for reality. Nature, for him, is no longer a dead, mechanical process; it is unconscious intelligence just as man is conscious intelligence. There is therefore an affinity that permits knowledge. The common note of reality, for Schelling, is pure activity, self-determining energy; nature and mind are not parallel aspects but stages in the development of the absolute ego. The absolute is not something that exists, but something that evolves, unfolds, has a history; and nature and mind are moments in that history. Thus, Schelling maintains that individual selves, since they are the loci where blind intelligence becomes self-conscious, cannot be real except as rooted in the absolute. Schelling's nature is thus very much like the pre-Socratic *physis;* the ideal he sets for science is the ultimate identification of the laws of thought and the laws of nature. By such an identity, the whole of reality is reduced to intelligence.

Hegel. The identification of the laws of thought and the laws of reality, taught by Schelling, was accepted by G. W. F. *Hegel. Whether in knowledge or in the world, for Hegel one and the same process or development is taking place and the laws according to which it happens are the same. The real is the rational, the rational is the real. The absolute for Hegel is not something vague and amorphous, as he took Schelling's absolute to be, nor is it substance, as it was for Spinoza. The absolute is process that passes through unconscious moments but whose *telos* is total self-consciousness. The meaning of the process is had in that ultimate goal where the absolute has become completely conscious of itself and recognizes its identity with the ultimate purpose of the universe.

The Hegelian absolute is at once present in, and emerging from, every process. The business of philosophy is therefore to seek and find reason in every process, however apparently irrational and absurd. Hegel's interest in history is predictable: he urges man to seek the absolute in history. He provides religious motives for this search, saying that man is told not only to love God but to know Him as well. God reveals Himself to man in history, which is the theater of providence. One may think that things happen haphazardly and adventitiously in history, but this cannot be. Man must not think that there is any distinction between the way things are and the way they ought to be. In history everything happens necessarily and for the best, and it is the task of the philosopher to show this (*see* HISTORY, PHILOSOPHY OF).

The dialectical process and the claim that the principle of *contradiction rules all are both revealing of Hegel's identification of thought and reality. Just as one might think of thought as a process that moves from global confusion to determination and distinction, so Hegel views reality as progressing from the homogenous and undifferentiated abstract to concrete distinction. Each step of the process looks backward and forward. What is is not what it was or what it will be: a present state is the contradictory of a previous state and drives toward the contradictory of what it now is. Contradiction is the law of life and movement. In the whole, opposites and contradictories are swallowed up and reconciled. World development on the natural plane is unconscious, but the thinker must, so to speak, relive the process by thinking it. The dialectical method of thought begins with an abstract notion that gives rise to its contradiction, and these two are reconciled in a third concept: thesis, antithesis, and synthesis. The movement is from the abstract to the concrete universal. Thus Hegel's description of the progress of thought and the evolution of reality are the same.

Hegel's absolute is the evolutionary process of reality and the goal of that process. God does not exist prior to the world, which Hegel holds is eternally created; God is the logos, the reason, the law of the universe; the evolutionary process is the absolute's progressive consciousness of self. Hegel's absolute, accordingly, is unintelligible without the world.

Absolutism. The opposition between absolutism and *relativism is best understood as indicating epistemological options, even though these are based on ontological judgments. In the discussion of Aquinas, a distinction he would wish to make between absolute being and man's manner of knowing it was indicated. An absolute being is by definition one that exists in utter independence of all else. However, as known by someone other than itself, absolute being is relative to that knower, and it would seem to be doubly relative in a doctrine according to which it can be known only relative to another object of knowledge. Unless one can distinguish a thing's manner of being known from its manner of being, such considerations would effectively do away with the absolute. The relatedness to a knower implicit in all knowledge has been a source both of absolutism and relativism. Thus the observation that sense qualities are relative to sense organs leads to a questioning of their *objectivity. Some thinkers go on to insist on the existence of other absolute aspects of reality, while others conclude that whatever one knows is relative to his mode of knowing. These latter may then seek to ground the laws of knowing in an absolute subject. A thinker who maintains both that what one knows is essentially colored by his way of knowing and that his way of knowing is simply contingent may be called a relativist. Whether the relativist can ever successfully explain the relativity of knowledge without appeal to at least an ideal of absoluteness must, of course, be asked.

Summary. The Absolute is preeminently a changeless, eternal being, independent of all else. As applied to knowledge, absolute knowledge bears on objects whose being is independent of the knower, even though as known they are related to a knower. Whether in reality or in thought, an absolute is required; but it is not necessary to identify, as Hegel did, what is absolute in knowledge and what is absolute in reality.

See also PANENTHEISM; IMMANENCE; EVOLUTIONISM; HEGELIANISM AND NEO-HEGELIANISM; PRAGMATISM; VALUE, PHILOSOPHY OF.

Bibliography: Copleston v.7. M. C. CAHILL, *The Absolute and the Relative in St. Thomas and in Modern Philosophy* (Washington 1939). Eisler 1:3–6. J. MÖLLER, LexThK[2] 1:70–71. J. KLEIN, RGG[3] 1:74–76. A. CHOLLET, DTC 1.1:134–135. C. BOYER, EncCatt 2:190–192. A. CARLINI, EncFil 1:406–415.

[R. M. MC INERNY]

ABSOLUTION, SACRAMENTAL, the forgiveness of sins in the Sacrament of Penance. Absolution may be considered in either a passive or an active sense. In its passive sense, it is the forgiveness that is effected by the Sacrament; actively, it is the granting of a judicial pardon for sins, in the name of Christ and the Church, by the priest who administers the Sacrament. Absolution, considered passively, supposes (1) the priest's exercise of his power to forgive sins and (2) the sinner's own repentance, manifested by acts of contrition, confession, and satisfaction. Popularly, sacramental absolution is understood in its active sense, and it is so taken here. It is clear, however, that sacramental and sacerdotal absolution are not perfectly synonymous terms. The tendency to identify them neglects or minimizes the importance of the sinner's own repentance in the sacramental forgiveness of sins and leads to a concept of sacramental causality that lowers the Christian mysteries to the level of mere magic.

Historically, absolution in its active sense has taken various forms. In the early Church it was imparted by the bishop when he granted peace and communion to sinners after the performance of public penance. Fixed verbal forms of absolution were unknown. During the medieval period, deprecatory formulas came into use. These were regarded as intercessory prayers said by the priest in virtue of his power to loose from sins.

Priestly and episcopal absolutions were not always sacramental, but in the context of confession and the exercise of the power of the keys, deprecatory absolution formulas were thought of as having an essential part in the forgiveness of sins *ex opere operato. In the Thomistic view, sacerdotal absolution was the form of the Sacrament of Penance, effecting forgiveness only in conjunction with other essential elements of the sacramental sign, namely, the sinner's acts of contrition, confession, and satisfaction. Scotus and his followers looked upon absolution as the total sacramental sign and regarded the sinner's penitential acts as necessary dispositions for the reception of the Sacrament rather than intrinsic constituents of the Sacrament itself. These conflicting viewpoints have never been reconciled, and the exact relationship between sacerdotal absolution and the sacramental sign is still a matter of open discussion.

As sacramental theory developed during the scholastic period, the declaratory formula of absolution, substantially as it is today, gradually replaced the older deprecatory forms. The essentials of the declaratory formula are found in the words "I absolve you from your sins." No doubt this formula, especially in the private administration of the Sacrament of Penance, tended to obscure the earlier view that the direct and immediate effect of sacerdotal absolution is the reconciliation of the sinner with the Church. Modern research on the history and structure of the Sacrament of Penance, particularly the studies of B. Xiberta and B. Poschmann, has brought back into focus the ecclesial dimension of the Sacrament, and theologians today are in general agreement that the words of absolution are the words of a judicial sentence in which the priest, exercising the power of the keys for the remission of sins, directly and immediately reconciles the sinner to the living body of Christ, which is the Church, and thus restores him to friendship with God Himself.

For bibliography, *see* PENANCE, SACRAMENT OF, 1.

[W. P. LE SAINT]

ABSOLUTISM, both a theory of the nature of political authority and a practice that prevailed throughout the 17th and 18th centuries. According to its principles, the ruler possessed an authority that was unconditional and unlimited. He was subject only to his own will and was not restrained in his actions by the laws of God or those of nature or by any other legal limitations.

Essential to the theory of absolutism was the ruler's and the state's relation to law. In the medieval period, the ruler was considered subject to the laws of God and nature. The laws of the state were laws only so far as they were in harmony with the natural law. In the early modern period, law became a thing not of reason but of the will of the ruler. Instead of the state being based upon law, law became solely a command of the state, depending for its efficacy upon the authority of the one who commanded. This concept served the cause of the rising nation-states. It entailed the death of the idea of empire, the rise of the independent sovereign state, the secular state's independence of the Church, and the centralization of authority against existing customs and privileges of cities and of the nobility.

The theory of absolutism can be traced from *Machiavelli's justification of the separation of morality and politics, through the development of sovereignty in Jean *Bodin, to a full-blown absolutism in the legal theory of Thomas *Hobbes. The result was the justification of the monarchical absolutism of the dynastic nation-state. During the 18th-century Enlightenment, in writers like Jean Jacques *Rousseau, the source of absolute authority was transferred from the monarch to the people, or the "general will," to form a "democratic" absolutism.

Catholic theologians such as *Bellarmine and *Suárez upheld the concept of a limited authority. The moral theologians of the 17th century held that the ruler was subject to divine and natural law, but that he was the sole judge of that limitation. Further, a great number of them taught that will was the source of law, that the ruler was above his own law, that the people could not resist a law of the sovereign, and that law was valid without the consent of the people. To that extent they taught a legal theory identical with absolutism and necessary to the rise of the absolute state.

See also MONARCHY; DIVINE RIGHT OF KINGS.

Bibliography: M. BELOFF, *Age of Absolutism, 1660–1815* (New York 1954), bibliography 181–182. J. W. ALLEN, *A History of Political Thought in the Sixteenth Century* (3d rev. ed. New York 1957). A. D. LINDSAY, EncSocSc 1:380–382. J. N. FIGGIS, CModH 3:736–769. S. SKALWEIT, CModH^2 5:96–121.

[D. WOLF]

ABSTRACT ART

The term generally used to describe a type of art, derived from impressionism, the work of Cézanne, and cubism, and characterized by forms that are either separated from nature by the artist through a process of generalization on observation or wholly invented by him without reference to the external appearance of nature. Abstract ornamentation with or without figurative reference was utilized by artists in many of the early cultures; however, a series of visual experiments led, in the 20th century, to a new concept of art content in abstract art.

The impressionist paint stroke, placed so that its color mixed in the eye of the viewer with adjacent strokes of color, tended to dematerialize the solidity of subject matter through the dominance of the stroke pattern; this, by its emphasis on materials and techniques, minimized the importance of the subject. Paul *Cézanne's experiments in nonperspective spatial illusion resulted in a system whereby planar brushstrokes related foreground to background in a new plastic unity. His emphasis on the flatness of the painting surface became a precept for many later artists. Cézanne's advice to "seek in nature the sphere, cone and cylinder" also has been regarded as an important influence on the development of *cubism. Early protocubist works by Pablo Picasso and Georges *Braque show their reliance upon Cézanne's postimpressionist discoveries. Later cubist works abstracted the analysis of subject matter until its recognizability was lost in the emerging conventions of cubist art.

Wassily *Kandinsky is most often credited with being, in 1910, the first artist to make a totally nonreferential painting. For a period he continued to work in three modes. "(1) a direct impression of outward nature; (2) a largely unconscious and spontaneous expression of inner feeling (an improvisation); (3) an expression of a slowly formed inner feeling, which comes to utterance only after long maturing (a composition)." Kandinsky's improvisations began as variations on landscape themes with recognizable content.

Wassily Kandinsky, "Composition (4)," oil on canvas, 64 *by* 31½ *inches,* 1914.

Later works (1911–15) became progressively more free and finally took on an independent form exclusive of any need for the process of abstracting from visible nature. His compositions are inventions without reference to representation.

During the 1930s there was an effort to clarify the use of "abstract" by substituting "nonobjective" to describe works totally without references to visible nature or natural phenomena. In common usage "nonobjective" is used interchangeably with "abstract," though some authorities continue the distinction.

Robert *Delaunay (1885–1941), a French painter whose style was derived from cubism, began color studies in 1910 that influenced his own cubist precursors as well as the German expressionist artists. Delaunay was the only cubist to move unequivocally into a totally nonreferential art in those years. With his clear spectrum colors, organized in geometric patterns suggestive of prismatic refractions, he introduced full color into cubism, which had been monochromatic.

Piet *Mondrian (1872–1941), a classically trained Dutch painter influenced by cubism from 1912 to 1914 in Paris, painted his first abstract work in 1913. In Holland (1914) he founded the de *Stijl group and its magazine with Theo van Doesburg. De Stijl tried to establish a collaboration between painters and sculptors, architects, and designers. Mondrian's own work proceeded from still life and landscape to abstraction and eventually excluded any such reference to nature as local color or organic form and any content other than the right angle, primary colors, and black and white.

Kasimir *Malevitch (1878–1935), a Russian painter who led Russian cubist artists before founding the *Suprematist* movement in 1913, opposed any combination of art with utility and any imitation of nature. His aim was a pure art, and he asserted that the feelings that generate art were more basic and meaningful than political or religious belief. His own art took a severely geometric direction, ultimately to be reduced to a white square on a square white canvas. The Russian constructivist movement took encouragement from the example and leadership of Malevitch.

Abstract expressionism is a movement that developed in the U.S. in the years of World War II, under the influence of abstract art and *surrealism. It exerted worldwide influence between 1948 and 1960, under the leadership of Jackson *Pollock, Arshile Gorky, Hans Hofmann (d. 1966), Willem de Kooning, and Franz Kline. Abstract expressionism's organic form, emphasis on improvisation, spontaneity, and revitalized oil painting technique, has also been referred to as "action painting."

A new development in abstract art in the late 1950s and 1960s has been called "perceptual abstraction." This development renounces painterly handling, impasto surfaces, and broken color in favor of clear color, vivid contrasts, and geometric clarity of shapes. "Color imagists" such as Morris Louis and the "Washington school" work in thinly applied paint films on bare can-

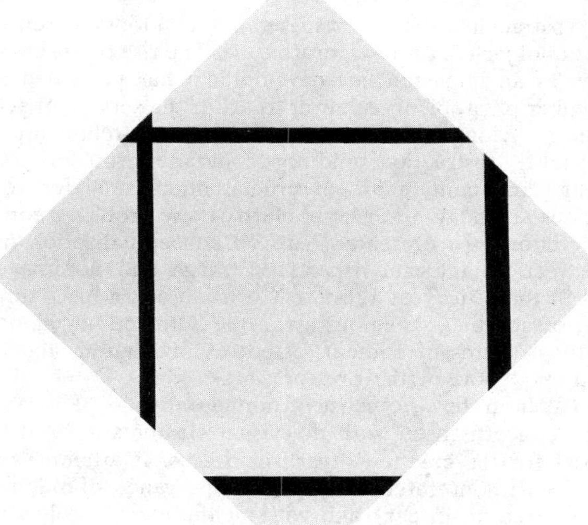

Piet Mondrian, "Painting I," oil on canvas, diagonal measurement 44¾ *by* 44 *inches,* 1926.

vas to achieve a sensuous tactility and openness unique in contemporary painting. A related group of "optical" painters utilizes repetitive geometric forms, often with complementary colors, to achieve an effect of visual shock through striking afterimages.

See also ABSTRACT EXPRESSIONISM; AMERICAN ART; ART, MODERN EUROPEAN, 3.

Bibliography: Seuphor DictAbstPaint. M. SEUPHOR [F. L. BERCKELAERS], *L'Art abstrait: Ses origines, ses premiers maîtres* (Paris 1950). M. BRION, *Art abstrait* (Paris 1956). *Art since 1945,* text by M. BRION et al. (New York 1958). Barr Cubism. C. GIEDION-WELCKER, *Contemporary Sculpture: An Evolution in Volume and Space* (3d ed. New York 1961). Haftmann Paint TwentCent. P. MONDRIAN, *Plastic Art and Pure Plastic Art, 1937, and Other Essays, 1941–43* (DocModArt 2; 1945). A. RITCHIE, *Abstract Painting and Sculpture in America* (New York 1951). M. SEUPHOR, *Piet Mondrian: Life and Work* (New York 1956). W. KANDINSKY, *Concerning the Spiritual in Art* (DocModArt; 1947). W. GROHMANN, *Wassily Kandinsky: Life and Work,* tr. N. GUTERMAN (New York 1958). K. S. MALEVICH, *The Non-objective World,* tr. H. DEARSTYNE (Chicago 1959). Rosenblum Cubism. W. SEITZ, *The Responsive Eye* (New York 1965). **Illustration credits:** Fig. 1, The Museum of Modern Art, New York. Mrs. Simon Guggenheim Fund. Fig. 2, The Museum of Modern Art, New York. Katherine S. Dreier Bequest.

[G. NORDLAND]

ABSTRACT ART AND THE CHURCH

Since the first totally nonfigurative painting (attributed to Kandinsky, 1910) abstract art has followed many directions with its theoreticians having great influence on architecture, industrial design, and modern man's artistic sensibility in general. International styles have developed and have received, since World War II, an increased private patronage in addition to the patronage of museums in the major art centers. Although with little success, modern renewal efforts within the Catholic Church worked since the latter half of the 19th century to overcome the separation from the Church of major artistic accomplishment. These efforts increased considerably in Europe between the wars; following World War II nonfigurative art has been employed within churches both in the U.S. and in Europe, though notably more so in Europe, where a number of clerics have taken active interest in the problem (especially the Dominicans led by the late Father Régamey; *see* LITURGICAL ART, 2).

Abstract art here is considered in the more strict sense of nonobjective or nonfigurative art. The rise of abstraction as an important art development has presented a number of problems relevant to art in the service of religion. Along with developments in architectural thought, abstraction and concomitant problems of image and content are of crucial importance for religious art today. In order to clarify these problems considerations are presented here on conceptualization in abstraction, relevant aspects of image and nonimage art in the history of Western Christian art, a brief survey of nonimage religious art in the 20th century along with problems of content, extent of realization, and a summary note of the present status.

Taken in the strict sense of nonfigurative art, abstraction concerns itself with the visual elements at its disposal for the creation of artistic forms. It attempts to do so without reference to the appearance of nature (e.g., tree, man, car) and without the use of arbitrary signs and symbols (e.g., cross, key, anchor).

The abstract artist does not attempt to structure a two-dimensional illusion of three-dimensional space nor does he offer a representation somehow styled to communicate events, persons, objects, or some relationship of identifiable signs and images. From this nonrepresentative aspect, abstract art is like the abstract ornamentation one sees often in mosaic floor patterns, ornamental book illumination (Fig. 1), and nonfigurative sculptural ornamentation in medieval architecture. Abstract art differs from ornament by the degree of its intention and experience. Ornamentation is the conception and technical repetition (often dispassionate) of a motif executed for the enrichment of objects and the pleasure in their contemplation. Modern abstract art, however, goes further, attempting to engage the expressive potential of visual form to achieve correspondence with realities of experience, the processes of life, the structure of reality, etc., depending on the sources of inspiration and intention of the artist. The sources and intentions (or nonintentions) of artists vary considerably. Some engage direct inner experience or the experience of action or process itself in various degrees of expressionism (*see* ABSTRACT EXPRESSIONISM; KANDINSKY, WASSILY; POLLOCK, JACKSON). Others search for pure form or supreme equilibrium in the structure of visual or spatial elements resulting in various degrees of constructivism (*see* STIJL, DE; MONDRIAN, PIET; MALEVICH, KAZIMIR SEVERINOVICH). Still others seek the key to reality in the magic, the fantastic, and the symbol hidden under the surface of consciousness; their efforts are manifest in various kinds of automatism and surrealism, which are less often pure abstraction since they do make use of symbols and figures that emerge from the world of dreams and the unconscious (*see* SURREALISM; DADA). Thus it is that abstract art in its strict sense is a "nonimage" art if visual image is understood in the sense of an image of nature as it appears to the naked eye. This does not mean, however, that it is unrelated to nature, man, and the structure of reality itself, as indeed it is part of this reality. On the basis of its self-contained logic some have argued that it is the least abstract of the visual art styles since it presents no illusion and is in itself an object of contemplation.

THE ICONIC AND ANICONIC IN RELIGIOUS ART

The problem presented by abstract art in the service of religion is one that centers on appropriateness or feasibility of use. Resistance to abstract art by ecclesiastics has stemmed mostly from the conviction that art in the service of religion must be an image for veneration or a conceptual representation of a mystery of the faith or a Biblical event. This conviction derives from centuries of experience of representational forms employed in churches and privately for devotional and didactic purposes.

The Iconic. In regard to the veneration of images and to their use, the position of the Church was clarified in 787 by the Council of Nicaea II, which condemned the iconoclasts and affirmed the legitimacy of the use of appropriate images (Mansi 13:377–380). Veneration of the image was to be understood as veneration of the reality or model depicted. The Council of Constantinople IV (869–870) added the understanding that what language and preaching does with syllables is accomplished also with that "writing" that is in colors: ". . . quae enim in syllabis sermo, haec et scriptura, quae in coloribus est, praedicat et commendat . . ." (Mansi 16: 161). Thus, as Gilson suggests, the Church understood the image also as a sort of audio-visual aid to the teaching of Christian dogma (*Les Arts du Beaux,* 188). The Council of Trent later reaffirmed the position of the Council of Nicaea II and stressed the responsibility of the bishops to exercise prudent judgment in keeping the churches free of the profane (Denz 1821–25). It is clear that image art, ranging from masterpieces of inestimable greatness to the often proliferated cheap and vulgar devotional card, has had an important role in the worship life of Christianity.

In addition to its cultic and didactic function image art served to enhance both the places of worship and liturgical objects. When this enrichment was achieved with superlative sensitivity and skill, great masterpieces emerged such as the grand medieval tympanum, the Byzantine mosaic, and the Renaissance fresco. Where image art in the service of religion achieved this greatness it served and continues to serve, in addition to cultic and didactic functions, to fulfill the aesthetic needs of man, which elevate him and prepare him for a more complete worship experience.

The Aniconic. Although the icon or image has played an important role in the worship life of the Church, there have been times when the aniconic (nonimage) tendency was strong; image art has not had prominent and universal endorsement as a most suitable servant of devotion throughout the history of Christianity. The legislation and instructions of the councils have concerned themselves with declaring the legitimacy of the use of images; these pronouncements (cited above) were aimed against the iconoclasts, who denied the usefulness of images for devotional purpose. The distinction between the iconoclastic position and aniconic position must be clearly drawn. The Church holds that the use of images for devotional purposes is acceptable and condemns the iconoclast who denies the image any place in worship life. However, the Church, in the Latin liturgy, does not require the veneration of images (with the single exception of the crucifix, which is required for veneration in the Good Friday services). The aniconic tendency does not deny the usefulness of images, but simply refrains from their use for either pastoral or aesthetic reasons. The aniconic has been manifest in religious art and architecture within the Church at various times and is in accord with traditional Catholic usage. The choice of image or nonimage in religious art is not a matter of dogma but rather a matter of pastoral judgment, e.g., helpful or harmful in a specific time and place. Thus the early 4th-century Synod of Elvira in Spain issued the decision that pictures of what is reverenced and adored must not be painted on the walls of the church: "Placuit, picturas in ecclesia esse non debere; ne quod colitur; et adoratur, in parietibus depingatur" (Mansi 2:11, can. 36; see also notes on the canon, 33, 46). This decision was made to meet the needs of the faithful who might easily have fallen into idolatry or confused the "holy" with the "material." For similar reasons the Greek fathers of the 4th century displayed a marked reserve for the growing practice of using holy images in the churches (see V. Grumel, DTC 7:768–774). In Romanesque times the austere reform measures of St. Bernard demanded a purified aniconic art and architecture to counteract the distractions of pretentious imagery that crept into monastic churches. The resulting *Cistercian art and architecture of the latter part of the 12th century stands witness to the spiritualizing force obtained without image (Figs. 2 and 3).

Nonimage art has not only been realized as a restraint against idolatrous tendencies and as a reaction against extravagances of imagery that threaten the wholesome balance of Christian worship; it has also appeared naturally as an artistic tendency quite sufficient in itself without reference to the dangers of superstition and idolatry that might accompany image art. This may be seen especially in the abstract ornament of Celtic illumination of the late 7th and early 8th centuries. Such abstract ornamentation gradually blended with Roman and Byzantine influences that reached the northern countries through Charlemagne's court and the later Ottos to produce the Romanesque amalgamation of abstraction and figuration. A nonimage sculptural ornamentation often derived from plant and animal configurations was employed in the stave churches of Norway and generally in the ornamentation of liturgical objects throughout the north in early Romanesque times.

A unique aniconic art appeared in Italy in the marble mosaic work of the *Cosmati (Fig. 4) that was dominant in and around Rome during the 12th and 13th centuries. Roundels and squares of inlaid tesserae were rhythmically spaced with white marble borders; colored marble mosaic with its rich surface served to fill out the spaces where one would ordinarily expect to see an icon. These aniconic planar modules provided a rich surface ornamentation that was employed on chancel barriers, ambos, episcopal thrones, altar frontals, ciboria, cornices of doorways, etc.

The façade of S. Miniato al Monte, Florence (Fig. 5), erected in three successive periods (*c.* 1100, 1150, and 1200) achieves its clarity through an antique geometry whose schematization excludes an image. Rectangular and circular surfaces have an abstract life of their own that provides the appropriate experience of church façade. Areas that receive sculptured and painted figuration in contemporary French Romanesque receive abstraction here. The other privative "iconic" niches of the cosmatesque marblework and the abstract tympana of S. Miniato provided the experience of "void" familiar to much modern abstraction such as that of M. Rothko; the suggested infinitude and richness of texture of the numerous tesserae placed in the mosaic fields have the "all-over" articulation also frequently found in contemporary abstraction.

A comparison between the vaulting of Kings College Chapel (1446–1515) and the ceiling of the Sistine Chapel (1508–12; Fig. 6) provides a clear juxtaposition of the aniconic and the iconic in religious art.

The Gothic vaulting has a rich Gothic tracery intentionally presented to be seen and experienced in itself without figurative reference to Biblical event or dogma. It is aniconic. The visual drama created there is understood to be suitable articulation of a worship space, and capable of inspiring the faithful to devotional ends. On the other hand the drama of creation, represented by Michelangelo on the Sistine ceiling, presents a highly sophisticated iconography based on the Biblical account of creation with the attendance of Prophets alternated with Sybils. The fresco engages the viewer in an architectural space extended into a believable figurative illusion that provides an anthropomorphic conception of creation. These two examples, both symmetrical structures, indicate the force achieved by both iconic and aniconic art in religious art and architecture.

Fig. 1. Page with foliate decoration, "Lindisfarne Gospels," c. 698–721 (Cotton MS Nero D. iv, fol. 26v).

Fig. 2. Sanctuary of the 12th-century Cistercian abbey church at Le Thoronet, France, with 20th-century altar.

ABSTRACT ART IN THE CHURCH

Fig. 3. Twelfth-century white glass window in the Cistercian abbey church at Obazine.

Fig. 4. Pontifical throne of Cosmati work, 13th century, in the basilica of San Lorenzo fuori le Mure, Rome.

Fig. 5. The façade of the basilica of San Miniato al Monte, Florence, 12th to 13th centuries.

Fig. 6. Comparison details of the ceilings of (a) Kings College Chapel, Cambridge, and (b) the Sistine Chapel.

The Aniconic in the 20th Century

Despite the few scattered renewal efforts of the late 19th century, art remained for the most part separated from the Church at the turn of the century. Following cubism and the initial interests of the constructivists and surrealists, the artist who wished to work in "religious art" was in an ambiguous position. On the one hand, his creative interests were generally oriented to the analysis of structure or a presentation of reality that became less and less "referential"; on the other hand, ecclesiastics wished to have a referential religious art (figurative and established symbol). As a result, by the 1930s and 1940s there had emerged a proliferation of "modern" liturgical art that was unresolved. Modern images of saints and symbols were presented with trappings of cubist division or expressionistic intensity; the referential aspect of image was either partly or totally lost while the ends of the styles employed were sacrificed for the sake of the referential. Artists who made the greatest progress with pure abstraction (Kandinsky, Malevich, Mondrian) remained distant from institutional patronage (the Church and State), which they saw as a harmful interference in the purity of form that they sought. After World War II a number of factors came together to create a new atmosphere; a merging of contemporary artistic thought with the needs of the Church began to occur. Important factors were the postwar rebuilding, which demanded that a great number of churches be built; the return of a number of artists to religious interest; the inherited influence of the Bauhaus (the dispersion under Hitler of Bauhaus teachers spread its influence); the directives of the German bishops for church architecture published in 1947, which provided intelligent guidelines for use of contemporary art in the Church; and in America the postwar suburban growth along with the growth of art consciousness.

Conceptual Basis. Although the modern renewal of religious art within the Church has experienced many directions of interest, the core of success, where it has been felt, has accompanied a deep understanding of key concepts of 20th-century art and architecture. The key concepts may be assembled under two categories that bear importantly on the aniconic: (1) the conception of the total work as an inseparable integrity of function, signification, material, and sensitive organization; (2) the potential of visual and spatial elements to be experienced immediately (without intermediate reference) as suitably significative or expressive of an assigned function (e.g., the fenestration by A. Manessier for the convent chapel at Hem, France). The first concept derives from an examination of function from technical and aesthetic aspects; it tends to eliminate the concept of decoration as additive and lends great importance to total visual control. The second concept reduces the role of referential symbols and figurative representation to achieve significative ends; the architect tends to design elements earlier assigned to artists (or engage artists of like sensibility) to achieve the visual signification in the structure itself (articulation of surface, spatial modulation, light control, etc.).

The insights offered by the pioneer work of L. H. *Sullivan and F. L. *Wright and the important work of de *Stijl and the *Bauhaus with subsequent institutes of design have all contributed to an understanding of artistic integrity as a total conception.

Liturgical art, industrial design, and architecture today are understood to achieve integrity when the artist manages this maximum interpenetration of function, signification, and plastic sensibility. In this sense the baptistery of the St. John's Abbey church (Collegeville, Minn.) attempts to integrate the architectural program of baptistery with the meaning and function of the rite of Baptism and the total program of the Church (for

Fig. 7. A. Manessier, mosaic marquee of the chapel of Ste-Thérèse, Hem, France, 1958.

Fig. 9. J. M. Subirachs, "Cross," 1963.

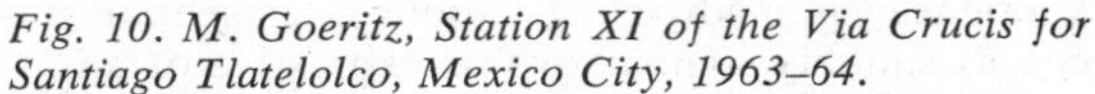

Fig. 10. M. Goeritz, Station XI of the Via Crucis for Santiago Tlatelolco, Mexico City, 1963–64.

Fig. 8. Harry Bertoia, reredos of the chapel at M.I.T., Cambridge, Mass., 1955.

ABSTRACT ART IN THE CHURCH

Fig. 11. R. Lippold, "Trinity," church of the Priory of St. Gregory the Great, Portsmouth, R.I., 1961.

Fig. 12. G. Meistermann, sanctuary mural, Maria Regina Martyrium, Berlin, Germany, 1962.

Fig. 13. R. Sowers, two of sixteen windows in Holy Trinity Chapel, New York City, 1965.

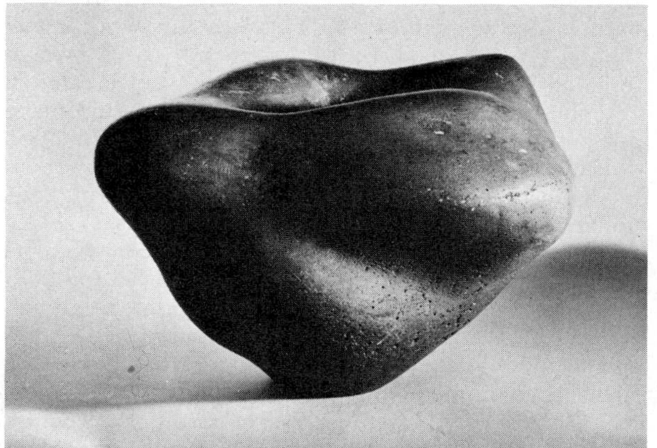

Fig. 14. F. Stahly, font, Vatican Chapel, Brussels World's Fair, 1958.

Fig. 15. F. Stahly, window relief for the church at Baccarat, France, 1957.

illustration *see* BAPTISMAL FONT). Thus the font rises with its living water from the ground (floor); one steps down to the "pool" to be reborn (baptized; one dies, descends into the grave with Christ in order to rise with Him; death to life); the font itself is crafted as basin containing water; signs of life, living plants, are placed in the font area; the baptistery is located as an experience of entrance to the Church (one enters the life of the Church through Baptism). These considerations alone do not create a work of art. However, the intelligent and sensitive incorporation of all these elements in the total plastic conception may create a work of art where there is nothing to be added or subtracted; one does not distinguish minor arts or decorative arts from the fine arts here since the conception of all elements is intimately merged with the whole (distribution of light, modulation of spaces and surfaces). The conception is aniconic since it does not attempt to use figuration or referential symbol to achieve its end. The interest of the architect is to create the program of elements necessary for a meaningful experience of the ritual of Baptism; the experience of the visual and spatial elements in itself in the context of "entering church," "being baptized," or "witnessing Baptism" provides a directly sensed awareness of the inward effects of the Sacrament. What is obvious in the example of the baptistery is less obvious elsewhere. Therefore it is important to give attention to the nonreferential expressive abilities of the aniconic. (*See* CHURCH ARCHITECTURE, 1, for a discussion of nonreferential symbolism.)

Nonreferential Expression in the Aniconic. Even in totally nonfigurative art there are degrees of reference beyond the work itself. The reference might be in some degree to nature, or to other human experience, or to concepts that are either literary or structurally symbolic. Thus a literary reference by way of title, or color and delineation in a mode analogous to some visual structure in nature, or even the conception of the work in a specific context (stained glass in a baptistery) might serve to lend the work some referential subject. However, in nonfigurative art, such reference remains minimal.

Reference to other material, visual or conceptual, does not necessarily constitute an important element in experiencing the work; it may, however, in its discovery, serve for a more complete experience of the work. The content (expression) in aniconic religious art remains as elusive as it does in representational art if one makes the careful distinction between subject matter and content. Thus one perceives that the subject represented on the 12th-century tympanum of Autun is the Last Judgment, but one cannot easily isolate its content. What a work employs iconographically does not identify content though it may serve as an important means for its comprehension. The iconographic subject is, as it were, the clothing and face of a person that help identify him (subject), but this does not necessarily tell much about him as a person (content). In this sense the content of nonimage art must be studied by the same methods employed for representational art; these are iconological methods that are synthetic rather than analytic [Panofsky, *Studies in Iconology* (Oxford 1939)].

In aniconic religious art there is no subject as one finds in representational art (e.g., Majestas Domini, Madonna). It is precisely this leap to content without subject representation that provides difficulty for many in regard to abstract religious art. It does not initiate its structure and content on the basis of a representation (reference to another visual reality, imaginary or real); it initiates its visual structure on the basis of the plastic elements employed and the significative architectural and liturgical context of the work itself. The creative resourcefulness of the artist based on his experience and knowledge of the visual world serve in its realization.

The example of the mosaic marquee (Fig. 7) designed by A. Manessier for the entrance to the chapel of Hem (dedicated March 30, 1958) provides an example of the expressive abilities of the aniconic. Here the subject is a marquee entrance to a chapel dedicated to St. Thérèse. This work is not totally nonreferential; the artist had, in fact, created the marquee on the theme of alleluia. It is a joyful entrance announcement that employs colorful mosaic patterns in an organic structure with forms closely related to nature. S. Stehman refers to it as a kind of "hymne végétal" marked with rather solem accents [*Art d'Eglise* 104.3 (1958) 89]. Inside the church the south wall (Epistle side) is made entirely of cement and slab-glass composed by the same artist. This abstract composition of brilliant light provides a mounting of experience from the entrance marquee to the sanctuary (for illustration *see* FRANCE). Both the stained glass and the marquee have structural elements (color, form, rhythmic occurrences) that are familiar to forms in nature (flower, plant, tree). However, the work is substantially nonreferential; its reference is to its own internal organization of elements. These are created to complement and fulfill the structural needs of the chapel as house of God, the place of worship and meditation.

Harry Bertoia's reredos (screen) for the interdenominational chapel at the Massachusetts Institute of Technology (architect Eero *Saarinen, 1955) is even less referential (Fig. 8). Executed with pieces of metal spaced rhythmically to form a screen behind the altar, the work complements and fulfills the architectural conception of a place suitable for meditation. The gentle spatial modulation of the metal is a visual "sound" in silence; a continual interplay of convergence and expansion is achieved through the reflection of the central shaft of light on the pieces of metal. Bertoia's intentions are clearly aniconic. He does not strive to create a religious image but rather, in the process of assembling an art work from the wealth of plastic possibilities, he strives to "sing a song of celebration to the glory of creation"; and, in the M.I.T. work, "to make a work conducive to meditation" ("Abstract Art and the Church," Archives, St. Vincent Archabbey).

Still there are other works, substantially abstract, that employ a symbol or other implied reference and, at the same time, remain strongly aniconic because their reference is to expressive plastic qualities in the work as much as to signification through sign; figural representation is excluded entirely. The cross (Fig. 9) by J. M. Subirachs (b. 1927) executed in 1963 is such a work. The sign of the cross is made by the crossed tension of ropes; the INRI (Jesus of Nazareth King of the Jews) is stencil marked in the upper right corner, a package "signing" method commonly used today in industrial packaging departments. What occurs here is a metaphysical "tripping" of the mind to see a new series of associations: first, awareness of tension effected by the stretched rope and the reddened wood compressed as in a vise by the two vertical end bars drawn together with steel bolts; secondly the signification of this plastic

Fig. 16. Sanctuary of the Grailville Oratory, Loveland, Ohio. The building was formerly a barn and was renovated by R. Tweddell, architect, and W. J. Schickel, liturgical designer. The structural members of the building and the laminated wood altar are the only permanent decoration.

ABSTRACT ART IN THE CHURCH

Fig. 17. R. Ubac, Station I of the Via Crucis, chapel of Fondation Maeght, Saint Paul de Vence, France, 1961.

drama through the stenciled INRI (black) and the cross sign. The visual experience signifies crucifixion (plastically and referentially) that may be seen and identified thereafter thousands of times in an industrial culture. Subirachs believes that such abstraction is most suitable for religious art today because: (1) it is a more faithful translation of metaphysical themes and (2) it seeks to signify (not portray) with a language of signs in accord with the times; the language of traffic signs, emblems, and visual advertising devices tends to replace other communication methods such as allegorical images and situation representation ("Abstract Art and the Church" *loc. cit.*).

Breadth of Realization. Although a number of non-image works in religious art might be singled out before World War II, it was not until after the war that strict abstraction in the contemporary sense began to appear in churches. The controversial church at *Assy was dedicated as late as 1950 yet all the contemporary art represented there is figurative or strongly referential symbolism. A. *Gleizes painted pure abstract paintings for contemplation in the 1930s, but his quite abstract "Eucharist" fresco (Chantilly) was realized only as early as 1952.

An occasional abstract work with religious interest occurred in studio painting before the war, but the acceptance of modern abstraction in churches (aside from what was considered "ornament") followed the war. Strong aniconic tendencies were already manifest in churches such as D. *Böhm's St. Engelbert, Cologne (1932; aniconic façade and interior), and Dom *Bellot's convent of Ste-Bathilde, Vanves, France (1930–35; aniconic sanctuary vaulting, fenestration, and passageways). However, the absence of image art here was more a purifying negation than a positive search for a genuine integration of abstraction and church architecture.

Important postwar monuments that led in the use and integration of abstraction in churches were: Sacred Heart at Audincourt, France (1950–52; abstract façade mosaic and baptistery windows by J. Bazaine; the windows and tapestry by F. *Léger employ referential symbolism); Notre-Dame du Haut, *Ronchamp, by Le Corbusier (1952–55; abstraction through relationship of space, light, color, and surface; some symbols are used on the windows and enameled doors); Maria Königin, Cologne-Marienburg, Germany, by D. Böhm (1954; wall of abstract stained glass includes symbols of Mary Litany); Interfaith chapel, Massachusetts Institute of Technology (1955; with altar screen by H. Bertoia); Madonna of the Poor, by L. Figini and G. Pollini (1952; fenestration, suspended cross, and spatial program of sanctuary). Each of these examples (among many) attempted in some way to integrate the abilities of abstraction in sculpture, stained glass, and mosaic with church architecture. The significance of a specific structure and its relationship to others in the first 15 years following the war remains obscured by the number of churches built in such a short time. Building activity that incorporated abstraction to some extent flourished in Italy, France, Spain, the northern countries, and England.

Postwar growth in the U.S. and renewed activity in Latin America all produced an important deposit of church architecture with tendencies toward the aniconic. (*See* CHURCH ARCHITECTURE, 10, 11, 12.)

Individual artists who concerned themselves with the problems of pure abstraction in religious art have collaborated with architects in church architecture with greater frequency and success since 1955. Some artists who have been more active in this sense are:

J. Albers (1888–), window for the abbot's chapel, "The White Cross," St. John's Abbey, Collegeville, Minn. (1955); dossal screen wall, St. Patrick's Church, Oklahoma City, Okla., Haydite concrete blocks, gold leaf surface. Jean (Hans) Arp (1887–), baptismal font, La Toussaint, Basel, Switzerland (1950). J. Barillet (1912–), numerous windows often in collaboration with others; with Manessier, church of Hem, France (1958); with A. Rattner, New Loop Synagogue, Chicago (1960); an excellent example with architect P. Damaz, windows in Our Lady of Florida, Palm Beach, Fla. (1962). J. Bertholle (1909–), numerous stained-glass windows such as in the church of Notre Dame de la Route Blanche, Segny (Ain), France (1949) and the Carmelite chapel, Ville de la Réunion, Paris (1962); also illuminations, mosaic, and tapestry. E. Gilioli (1911–), meditation sculptures such as "Prayer" (1958); "Friendship" (cross; 1964); "Angel" (1947). M. Goeritz (1915–), between 1958 and 1964, executed stained-glass windows for the cathedrals of Cuernavaca and Mexico City (more than 100 for the latter); decorations and windows for San Lorenzo, Mexico City; the Via Crucis (abstract) for Santiago Tlatelolco, Mexico City (1963–64); windows for church of Atzapotzalco, Mexico City (1962–63). W. Kaufmann (1920–), stained glass and mosaic in various churches; designed monumental stained-glass walls for projected New Norcia Cathedral of the Holy Trinity, Australia, with architect P. Nervi; windows incorporate a symbolic Trinitarian theme. G. Lardeur, window for *Civitas Dei* pavilion, Brussels World's Fair (1958). J. Le Moal, (1909–) stained-glass, baptistery windows in the church of St. Martin of Brest (1957) and crypt window, Sacred Heart, Audincourt, France (1958). R. Lippold (1915–), "Trinity" above main altar, monastery church of St. Gregory, Portsmouth, R.I. (1961), gold and stainless steel wire, 60 by 40 by 50 feet. A. Manessier (1911–), numerous paintings, tapestry, stained glass, lithography; important leader in the problem of image and content in religious art; of his many windows are those at St. Pierre Triquetaille, Arles, France (1953); church of Pouldu (with Le Moal; 1958); and the crypt of St. Gereon, Cologne, Germany (1964). M. Martens, stained glass, "Heavenly Jerusalem," chapel of the College of Notre Dame, Antwerp, Belgium (1963). H. *Matisse, windows and vestments at *Vence, France. G. Meistermann (1911–), stained-glass window, Holy Cross, Bottrop, Germany (1957); apocalyptic sanctuary mural for Maria Regina Martyrium, Berlin (1962). J. Perrot, slab-glass and concrete, church of St. Joan of Arc, near Belfort, France. J. Reynal (1903–), now Mrs. Thomas Sills, mosaic, 30 feet by 20 feet, Our Lady of Florida, Palm Beach, Fla. (1962); also meditation mosaics. L. Schaffrath, stained glass. Ursulinenkloster St. Angela, Wipperfürth, Germany (1962); baptistery window, St. Walburga, Overath, Germany (1954). R. Sowers (1923–), stained glass, Stephens College Chapel, Columbia, Mo. F. Stahly (1911–), water font, sanctuary wall, and ceiling for Vatican Chapel, Brussels World's Fair (1958), architect, P. Pinsard; window relief for church of Baccarat (1957); important for his establishment of a collective studio school at Meudon, France, which works to integrate sculpture with architecture through collaboration of artist and architect. R. Ubac (1910–), windows, church of Ezy-sur-Eure, France (1958; symbolizing crucifixion) and, among others, the windows and stations in the chapel of the Fondation Maeght à Saint Paul de Vence. J. Weinbaum (1926–), ceramic mosaic and stained glass; among others are stained glass and mosaic, St-Pierre du Regard, Calvados, France (1957), and windows for church in Escherange, Moselle, France (1962). L. Zack (1892–), numerous sculptures and stained glass for churches among which are windows for the chapel of Notre Dame des Pauvres at Issy-les-Moulineaux, France (1955), and the church of St. Vincent de Paul at Strasbourg, France (1964); tabernacles in collaboration with T. Zack, basilica of Ste-Jeanne d'Arc, Paris (1964) and St-Pierre de Charonne, Paris (1964). P. Szekely (1923–), numerous sculptures in churches for tabernacle, altar, etc.; "Signe Métaphysique" (1956), ab-

Fig. 18. Sanctuary of the church of St. John Capistrano, Munich, Germany, designed by the German architect Sep Ruf. Nonfigurative patterning of the brickwork provides the only decoration.

ABSTRACT ART IN THE CHURCH

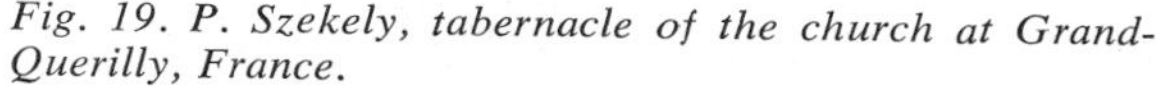

Fig. 19. P. Szekely, tabernacle of the church at Grand-Querilly, France.

Fig. 20. P. Szekely, model for the church of the Carmel de Valenciennes, France; architect, C. Guislain.

stract sculpture, cemetery at Albenc in Isère (about 3 feet high); nonfigurative spiritual portrait of St. Ferreol (1958), church of Pinet d'Uriage, France, dedicated by D. Ropps; sculpture for the Carmel of Valenciennes, France (1963–64); 16 signs, concrete rubbings for Lourdes exhibition (1964).

Summary of the Problem. Although much exists by way of nonimage art in the decoration of churches, as mentioned above, it must be noted that this work often exists in conjunction with the use of image (e.g., crucifix, patron saint, or other). What has been observed concerning art in contemporary church architecture is first that the tendency has been to reduce the role of image and sometimes to eliminate it entirely; and secondly the positive use of nonfigurative abstraction has gradually assumed an important place in architectural conception. The reasons for the ascendance of the aniconic tendency are related to the radical changes that occurred in architectural and artistic theory in general since the mid-19th century. Added to this was the interest of the Church in employing suitable contemporary artistic expression in the construction and decoration of churches. This attitude was particularly well expressed in the 1947 directives issued by the German bishops; the encouragement of the 1952 instruction on sacred art issued by the Holy See and the further intentions of Vatican II (ch. 7, *Constitution on the Sacred Liturgy*) have all contributed to the growth of a healthy use of abstraction (*see* LITURGICAL ART, 2).

For P. Szekely the artist works at a junction of matter and spirit; his task is to tie the very low with the Most High by creating a work that of itself is a sign of this union, and thus a religious sign. Szekely and others have attempted to achieve these ends with a nonfigurative art. The church edifice with all its elements (space, light, color, etc.) is a sign of the New Jerusalem and incorporates the aspirations of the Christian community in the viable context of its growth toward fulfillment; contemporary artistic abilities may create a sign of Christian hope and a suitable environment for the function of liturgy without employing representational reference to history or diagrammatic explications of dogma.

The didactic role of art in church decoration (e.g., depiction of Biblical events) has lost part of its function in modern societies that are almost entirely literate. Since the great achievements of the medieval and Renaissance periods man's view of the world and of himself has expanded and the artistic expression of it tends to disenchantment with pictorial description. Descriptive landscape has been replaced by artistic structure influenced by the scientific exploration of the microcosmic, the macrocosmic, and the internal processes of growth; moreover, anthropology, psychoanalysis, sociology, and vast communication systems have created a self-awareness that contributed to the displacement of the descriptive representation by various kinds of expressionism and constructivism. Such structural and expressive exploration, when employed to create worship environment, has helped extend the Christian belief of transformation in Christ to those aspects of reality (within man, society, and structure of the universe) that challenge contemporary man.

Representational art, and consequently the useful employment of existing Christian iconography, does not lend itself easily to the creative interests of mid-20th-century artists. Even in the light of a significant deposit of promising abstraction in postwar church construction the realization of a healthy and widely accepted religious art has not been achieved in the 20th century. The resolution of this problem lies, for the most part, in the ability to create within Christianity itself a meaningful artistic expression that can absorb and transform the contemporary artistic vision.

Bibliography: For bibliog. on the teaching of the Church on images and art, *see* IMAGES, VENERATION OF; LITURGICAL ART, 2; for bibliog. on modern movements, *see* AMERICAN ART; ART, MODERN EUROPEAN, 3; CHURCH ARCHITECTURE, 1, 10, 11, 12. Annotated annual listings of liturgical literature appear in YrBkLit Stud. "Abstract Art and the Church," Archives, St. Vincent Archabbey, Latrobe, Pa. (unpub. papers; 1964), papers of 16 contemporary artists on abstraction in religious art. Mercier Art Abstr includes app. of directives and church teaching on image, also select bibliog. M. AUBERT et al., *Le Vitrail français* (Paris 1958). A. CHRIST-JANER and M. M. FOLEY, *Modern Church Architecture* (New York 1962). M. A. COUTURIER, *Art et liberté spirituelle* (Paris 1958). Gilson Arts, ch. 8, 185–205. A. HENZE and T. FILTHAUT, *Contemporary Church Art,* ed. M. LAVANOUX, tr. C. HASTINGS (New York 1956). T. MATHEWS, "Toward an Adequate Notion of Tradition in Sacred Art," LiturgA 32 (1964) 43–49. J. PICHARD, *L'Art sacré moderne* (Paris 1953); *Modern Church Architecture,* tr. E. CALLMANN (New York 1960). J. R. RAMSEYER, *La Parole et l'image* (Neuchâtel 1963), esp. ch. 7, 181–184. P. R. RÉGAMEY, *Religious Art in the Twentieth Century* (New York 1963); "Debat sur l'art non figuratif," *La Vie intellectuelle* 19 (July, 1951) 40–62. R. SCHWARZ, *The Church Incarnate,* tr. C. HARRIS (Chicago 1958). G. E. KIDDER-SMITH, *The New Churches of Europe* (New York 1964). R. SOWERS, *Stained Glass: An Architectural Art* (New York 1965). R. J. VEROSTKO, "Abstract Art and the Liturgy," LiturgA 30 (1962) 129–132. W. WEYRES and O. BARTNING, eds., *Kirchen: Handbuch für den Kirchenbau* (Munich 1959). Periodicals. *Art d'église* (Bruges 1932–). *Arte cristiana* (Milan 1913–). *Art Sacré* (Paris 1935–). *Art Chrétien* (Paris 1934–). *Fede e arte* (Vatican City 1953–). *Liturgical Arts* (New York 1931–). *Das Münster* (Munich 1947–). **Illustration credits:** Fig. 1, Courtesy of the Trustees of the British Museum. Fig. 2, Franceschi-Zodiaque. Fig. 3, Photo Zodiaque. Figs. 4 and 5, Alinari-Art Reference Bureau. Fig. 7, Courtesy of L'Art d'Église. Fig. 8, M.I.T. photo. Fig. 10, Kati Horna. Fig. 11, Joseph W. Molitor. Fig. 12, G. E. Kidder Smith. Fig. 14, Paul Facchetti. Fig. 15, P. Willi. Fig. 17, Galerie Maeght. Fig. 18, Photo Archives, Das Münster. Fig. 19, Courtesy of Art Chrétien. Fig. 20, Pierre Joly-Véra Cardot.

[R. J. VEROSTKO]

ABSTRACT EXPRESSIONISM

The first major American school of art to effect an international style, developed in the U.S. in the 1940s and 1950s. It was a revolution in art in which aesthetic values and concepts were revised. Its aesthetic premise emphasized individuality and viewed art as a private language with personal symbols based on the artist's innermost feelings of the world.

The New York school developed after World War II as a reaction against the prevalent ideas of art as being regional in scope or as serving propaganda in intent; it resisted the manacle of cubist ideology, the dominance of the school of Paris, and surrealism. Members of the group were concerned with the subconscious and techniques of chance as a tool for probing the inner life. They utilized the two-dimensional picture plane of cubism, Miro's free forms, *Klee's primitivism, *Matisse's color, and *Mondrian's search for the ultimate. Their ideological concerns stressed the emotional significance of pure color and free form. The idea was posited that the artistic experience is immediate and inward as well as outward. This broke down the barrier between inspiration and execution and prohibited intellectual editing and conformity to preconceived ideas. Thus a new concept of the artist's self as a natural, self-conscious innocence developed.

ABSTRACT EXPRESSIONISM

Fig. 1. Willem de Kooning, "Woman I," oil on canvas, 75⅞ by 58 inches, 1950–52.

Fig. 2. Philip Guston, "Native's Return," oil on canvas, 65 by 76 inches, 1957.

Fig. 3. Franz Kline, "Chief," oil on canvas, 58⅜ by 73½ inches, 1950.

The early leaders were Gorky, Tomlin, *Pollock, Kline, *Baziotes, Rothko, Still, Newman, Motherwell, DeKooning, Gottlieb, Brooks, Guston, McNeil, and Hoffman. Others who participated in the movement were Tworchov, Reinhardt, Nevelson, Ferber, Hare, Lipton, Smith, Lassau, Rivers, Marca-Relli, and Burlin.

In 1940 the MacMillan Gallery showed Pollock and DeKooning. In 1943 Pollock had his first show at "Art of this Century" Gallery. In 1946 his "drip" paintings were shown, and they evoked the idea of a continuum in which the viewer was enveloped by a canvas where the painting flowed off and on the canvas. He became the iconoclast for American painters, and this free style became known as "action painting." Art in this style became a vehicle for liberating the artist from political or moral values and utilized a vital action in which the artist could act with his total personality. Art was the result of this encounter, and the action on the canvas became an event in place of the traditional notion that the canvas was space to analyze, or in which to design or reproduce objects. The method eliminated sketches and the separation between art and life. Current phrases were: "It's not a picture of a thing, it is the thing itself." "It doesn't reproduce nature, it is nature." "The painter doesn't think, he knows." The "Artists Club" on Eighth Street, N.Y., was formed to discuss the new ideology.

In 1958 the movement became international with the "New American Painting" exhibition at the Museum of Modern Art. Within this free conceptual framework many diverse directions were pursued so that artists as different as Reinhardt and Rothko, Smith and Roszack could work within it. The liberating influence of these concepts paved the way for younger artists such as Rauschenberg, Stankiewicz, Warhol, Indiana, Rosenquist, Kelly, Noland, Albert, Mallary, Parker, Chamberlin, Bontecu, and Stella. Out of their work have come assemblage, *pop art, optical art, happenings, environments, and a new style of hard-edge painting.

See also AMERICAN ART.

Bibliography: H. HOFMANN, *Search for the Real, and Other Essays* (Andover, Mass. 1948). H. E. READ, *A Concise History of Modern Painting* (New York 1959; repr. pa. 1962). F. O'HARA, *Jackson Pollock* (New York 1959); "Franz Kline Talking," *Evergreen Review* 2.6 (1958–59) 58–68. H. ROSENBERG, *Tradition of the New* (2d ed. New York 1960); "The American Action Painters," *Art News* 51.8 (1952) 22–23, 48–50; "Critic within the Act," *ibid.* 59.6 (1960) 26–28. A. H. BARR, in New York Museum of Modern Art, International Program, *New American Painting* (New York 1959) 15–19, catalogue. W. DEKOONING, in "What Abstract Art Means to Me," *Bulletin of the New York Museum of Modern Art* 18.3 (1951) 4–8, symposium. J. FERREN, "Epitaph for an Avant-Garde," *Arts Magazine* 33.2 (1958) 24–26, 68. P. G. PAVIA, "The Unwanted Title," *It Is* 5 (1960) 8–11. B. HELLER, "The Roots of Abstract Expressionism," *Art in America* 49.4 (1961) 40–49. **Illustration credits:** Fig. 1, Collection, The Museum of Modern Art, New York; Purchase. Fig. 2, The Phillips Collection, Washington, D.C. Fig. 3, Collection, The Museum of Modern Art, New York. Gift of Mr. and Mrs. David M. Solinger.

[R. L. WICKISER]

ABSTRACTION

Generally, a mental separation of things not, or at least not necessarily, separated in the real. Looked at from this point of view, abstraction is understood as the psychological act of discarding all but one facet of a thing (or things) to cognize that facet without the others. To be legitimate this psychological act presupposes an appropriate object: the facet cognized through abstraction must be in itself knowable apart from that from which it is mentally separated. Just as the term abstraction is used to name the psychological act of mentally separating one thing from another, it can also be used to name the abstractability of that which is mentally separated. Thus one may speak of a man abstracting a given object from certain nonessential data, and one may speak of that object itself abstracting from these data. This article considers first the abstraction of the intelligible from the sensible, as well as alternative theories in the history of thought that propose to account for the discovery of the intelligible. It then explains how the intelligible as abstracted is universal, and concludes with a consideration of the various kinds of abstraction.

Abstraction of the Intelligible. Of the different, though not necessarily unrelated, instances of abstraction the most radical is the abstraction of the intelligible object from the data of sense experience. This abstraction is meaningful, of course, only within a philosophical frame that sees such a thorough difference between the sensible and the intelligible that they are recognized as objects pertaining to irreconcilably different orders. And even among those who admit this difference there is an abstraction only so long as the sensible and intelligible are somehow given together, with the intelligible somehow cognized by way of an insight in and through the sensible. The sensible is the fluctuating, kaleidoscopic data of man's original cognitive contact with the things of the physical world: their colors and shapes; their sounds, odors, flavors; their temperatures, weights; their motions and rest; and the like. The intelligible, on the other hand, is the stable, definable, potentially scientific object of a cognitive vision radically different from an experience of the sensible. If the sensible is the phenomenal in things, the intelligible is the meaningful in them. The sensible as a datum of experience is exclusively singular, tied to an individual thing in this place at this time. The intelligible is, at least as object of the direct act of intellection, universal; i.e., it can be said of many, indifferent to individual differences, indifferent to shifts in place and time.

Empiricist View. For those who fail to admit the distinction between the sensible and the intelligible there is no question of an abstraction of an intelligible object from sense data. This is the case, for example, with those empiricists (such as J. *Locke and D. *Hume) who limit knowledge effectively to the realm of sense experience. They may speak of an abstraction, but at best they mean some more or less subtle reworking of sense impressions that yields an image involving an outline simple enough to stand for many things. This notion also underlies the use of the term abstraction by those working in *cybernetics. The refined impressions here spoken of remain on the same plane as the impressions from which they came, the plane of the sensible. There is no question of penetrating to the radically different plane of the meaningful. There can be in this, therefore, no abstraction from the sensible to the intelligible.

Nonabstractive Theories. There are some in the history of thought, however, who do admit the radical difference between the sensible and intelligible, but who, nevertheless, explain man's knowledge of each without recourse to a theory of abstraction. Plato is one of these, St. Augustine another.

For *Plato, envisioning the intelligible is not the result of seeing into and through the data of sense experience to an underlying intelligibility, but rather of turning from what is sensible to intelligibles that are defined apart from, and exist independently of, the sensible. Plato distinguishes between a preexistence in a realm of pure intelligibles, wherein a vision of these intelligibles has been once achieved, and this life, in which there takes place, by way of reminiscence, a conversion from the data of sense experience to these intelligibles. If Plato can be taken literally, for him learning is but a process of remembering ideas from another existence, temporarily forgotten in this existence, but innately present nonetheless.

For St. *Augustine, intelligibles are not innate; they are not apprehended by way of reminiscence, but neither are they seen by way of abstraction from sensible data. In his view, there is a realm of intelligibles to which the human intellect is naturally subject and which a man can know so long as his intellectual vision functions in virtue of an incorporeal light supplied by God. The intellect is thought to be related through this divine *illumination to the intelligible as the sense of sight is related through corporeal light to the visible. For St. Augustine, as well as for Plato, there is an infinite metaphysical distance between the sensible and the intelligible, but there is no abstraction because the intelligible is not known in and through the sensible. For *Aristotle and for St. *Thomas Aquinas, there is this infinite metaphysical distance between the sensible and the intelligible, and yet the latter can be cognized only through the former; for them a theory of abstraction is a noetic necessity.

Thomistic Account. According to the Thomistic *epistemology, some things are sensibly endowed as well as intelligibly endowed, e.g., men, trees, and rocks; others, only intelligibly endowed, e.g., angels. Men can know both, but the human condition is such that the latter are known only in function of the former, and the intelligible in the former only in function of the sensible. In other words, the sensible characteristics of the sensibly endowed things are immediately knowable, but the intelligible are knowable only mediately by way of the sensible.

In Thomistic terms, the thing is said to be actually sensible and only potentially intelligible. As actually sensible the thing can be actually sensed as it stands; but the potentially intelligible must be rendered actually intelligible before it can be actually understood. The *senses are capacities for actually sensing the actually sensible; the *intellect (i.e., the possible intellect) is the capacity for actually understanding the actually intelligible. The senses need no help since the thing as it stands is actually sensible. The possible intellect stands in need of another capacity on the intellectual level that is able to make the potentially intelligible actually intelligible. This capacity is called the agent intellect. The thing—which is potentially intelligible—is originally present in knowledge through its sensory re-presentation, which is called the *phantasm. Through this phantasm in sensory experience only the sensible characteristics of the thing are actually present to the knower; but just as the thing, while being actually sensible, is potentially intelligible, so through the phantasm the intelligible aspect of the thing is potentially present to the knower. The agent intellect is a spiritual light that, by illuminating the phantasm, actualizes the intelligible so that it can be actually cognized by the possible intellect.

The possible intellect, like the senses, is a passive power, able to operate only after being reduced from potency to act. The thing as it stands, as physical, is able to reduce the senses, themselves in a way physical, from potency to act: no agent sense is needed. But the thing itself, as physical, cannot reduce the wholly spiritual possible intellect to act: only something spiritual can do this, and this is the agent intellect. But the agent intellect is an unspecified light; and since there is no knowing except of something determinate, that which actualizes the possible intellect must simultaneously specify it for the act of knowing something determinate. Thus the agent intellect, as principal cause, uses the phantasm of the thing as instrumental cause (*see* INSTRUMENTAL CAUSALITY). Together they actualize the possible intellect, which—once reduced from potency to act in reference to a given intelligible aspect of some thing—can posit the act of knowing that intelligible object. The intelligible remains an object irreducibly other than the sensible. Intellection is never reduced to sensation. But the intelligible is known only in and through sense experience by way of an intuitive penetration that is most strictly an abstractive act.

The Intelligible as Universal. The object cognized in the abstractive intuition just described can be distinguished from the data of sense experience in several ways, as has already been noted. Perhaps the most obvious difference is that the characteristics present in sense knowledge are incorrigibly singular, while the object intellectually cognized is characteristically universal. This difference demands further comment. For one thing, though this is an obvious difference between the sensible and the intelligible in man's experience, it is not the essential difference. If it were, the intellect would be defined as an appetite for the universal; it is, rather, an appetite for the meaningful. In fact, there is an inverse ratio between the meaningful content of an object and its universality (man being an object much richer in content than substance, but considerably less general). If one were to define the intellect as transcendentally related to universality rather than to intelligible content or meaning, this would strongly suggest that the crowning achievement of the intellectual life would come in the possession of an object involving next to nothing in the way of intelligible content.

It remains true, however, that the object cognized intellectually is, as cognized, universal. The reason is that that which in the thing shrouds its intelligibility (so that it is only potentially intelligible) is *matter, and this coincidentally is the principle of the *individuation of the physical thing. To get to the intelligible, man must (and does, through the light that is the agent intellect) slough off matter as a principle of nonintelligibility. In doing so, of course, he also sloughs off the principle of individuation and cognizes an object that is universal. The intellect is essentially ordered to the intelligible, but the price of knowing the intelligible is knowing it as a universal.

Further comment is required in reference to the universal character of the object of intellection. It might seem, perhaps, that since in the realm of real subjects only singulars exist, the abstraction that renders an object universal somehow precludes the possibility of knowing things as they are. The question is: Is there something inherently falsifying in the process of abstraction? Not at all. A *quiddity that is universal in the mind as object need not be in itself intelligibly different from this same quiddity individualized in things. Natures or quiddities in themselves are neither singular nor universal, but as such are open to either state. In things in a first existence outside the mind natures are in the state of singularity; in the mind in a second existence as objects they are invested with the relation of reason that is the form of universality. Universality is not real; it is a being of reason. But the nature as known, to which universality accrues in the process of being known, need in no sense be itself intelligibly de-realized simply because it takes on a nonreal relation in the mind. The nature remains identically the nature of the thing. However, even though abstraction does not falsify things, man does pay a price because he knows by way of abstraction. Things as they exist as subjects, independently of a mind's knowing them, are highly sophisticated complexes of many intelligible aspects as well as all that is sensible in them and the existential act that makes them be more than a mere possibility. In any given act of abstractive intuition some one (more or less meaningful) intelligible aspect, abstracted from all else, is cognized. Thus knowledge by way of abstraction, in any given instance of abstractive intuition, may be seriously incomplete. However, there is an infinite difference between knowledge that is incorrigibly false and knowledge that is less than complete. (*See* UNIVERSALS.)

Kinds of Abstraction. Discussion thus far has been limited to the abstraction of the intelligible from the sensible. There are other abstractions to consider and certain distinctions to be made, viz, between abstraction by way of simple consideration and abstraction by way of negative judgment, between precisive and nonprecisive abstraction, between total abstraction and formal abstraction, and between the abstraction of a whole, the abstraction of a form, and separation.

Simple Consideration vs. Negative Judgment. One important distinction between types of abstraction is that between abstraction by way of simple consideration and abstraction by way of negative judgment. To abstract one thing from another by way of simple consideration is to cognize it without simultaneously cognizing the other. This is legitimate only if the first is definable or able to be understood without the other entering into its definition or meaning. There is no need here for the first to be existentially independent of the other. Some things (e.g., a nature such as man) are definable apart from something else (e.g., individuating characteristics) without being able to exist apart from them. They can, of course, be abstracted from these by way of abstraction through simple consideration.

To abstract one thing from another by way of negative judgment is not simply to cognize it independently of the other but to think that it exists without the other. An abstraction of this sort is legitimate only if what is abstracted from another is not only independent in meaning from the other but even existentially independent. The nature of man cannot be abstracted by way of negative judgment from individuating characteristics because, though man is definable apart from them, man cannot exist apart from them. However, man can be abstracted from tree by way of negative judgment because man is independent of tree both in meaning and in existence; for tree does not enter into the definition of man, and men can be without there being trees. This distinction is important, as the examples should make clear, for any solution to the problem of the universal. As Aquinas frequently points out, it was a failure to distinguish between abstraction by way of simple consideration and abstraction by way of negative judgment that forced Plato to posit *existing* Forms and Mathematicals.

Precisive vs. Nonprecisive Abstraction. Another distinction between types of intellectual abstraction is that between the precisive abstraction that renders an object abstractly expressed and the nonprecisive abstraction that renders an object concretely expressed. The difference between "man" and "humanity" (for an example from the category of *substance) and between "pious" and "piety" (for an example of an *accident) is at stake. "Pious" and "piety" do not differ in intelligible content; their difference is one of mode of conception. The formality that is precisely "piety" is conceived as belonging to a bearer (in general) in the conception of "pious." "Pious" is equivalently "subject-having-piety." Identically this same formality, but abstracted from any reference to a bearer—i.e., positively cut off from any subject—is conceived in the notion of "piety." "Pious" names a whole, i.e., the whole subject that is the bearer of piety, but only from the point of view of its piety. "Piety" names the formality as a part, which, with other parts, makes up the whole. "Pious" can be said of a concrete subject, such as Tom, so long as Tom has piety. "Piety" cannot be said of Tom; though it is no less real than "pious," it is conceived in such fashion as to be, as conceived, cut off from concrete subjects.

Formal vs. Total Abstraction. Important among the traditional distinctions between types of intellectual abstraction is that between formal abstraction and total abstraction. In this matter it is necessary to clarify the usage of terms, for "total abstraction" and "formal abstraction" are used by different philosophers to stand for a variety of different abstractions. Reference here is exclusively to the use to which T. de Vio *Cajetan and *John of St. Thomas put them when they discuss abstraction in reference to the specification of the sciences (*see* SCIENCES, CLASSIFICATION OF). Although these commentators on St. Thomas claim to be repeating a distinction already made by St. Thomas, a careful investigation of the relevant texts in St. Thomas suggests this is not the case. Be that as it may, the point they make is consonant with the Thomistic theory of science and helpful in understanding it.

Formal abstraction (*abstractio formalis*) is an abstraction of an intelligible content of thought from the matter that shrouds its intelligibility. Total abstraction (*abstractio totalis*) is the abstraction of a logical whole from its subjective parts. Formal abstraction yields an object qua intelligible; total abstraction, qua universal. Given the inverse ratio between meaningful content and universality the two abstractions work in opposite directions. And yet they are both necessary for human *science (*scientia*). Human science, as science, needs an object able to be intellectually analyzed. For science the real must be present to the mind in abstraction from whatever matter stands in the way of its being understood. Formal abstraction abstracts from matter as a principle of nonintelligibility to yield an object rich enough in intelligible content to satisfy the scientific mind. Human science, as human, is achieved in discourse. The objects of scientific analysis must be present to the mind as able to fit into a discursive pattern: they must be present in the state of universality or of communicability. Total abstraction abstracts from matter as the principle of incommunicability to yield an object that is universal and as such able to fit into a discursive pattern.

To the extent that objects are differently freed from the restrictions of matter as a principle of nonintelligibility they are differently scientific. Freedom from individual sensible matter yields an object that is scientifically relevant on the level of natural science. Freedom from all sensible matter yields an object that is scientifically relevant on the level of mathematics. And freedom from all matter yields the object of metaphysical inquiry. Thus one may speak of the first order of formal abstraction, i.e., physical abstraction; the second order of formal abstraction, i.e., mathematical abstraction; and the third order of formal abstraction, i.e., metaphysical abstraction. These three orders or degrees of formal abstraction respectively constitute the different levels of theoretical science.

Total abstraction admits of different degrees also: some objects are more general, some less general, than others. These differences do not constitute differences *among* sciences; they function exclusively *within* a given science. Two objects on the same level of formal abstraction are studied in the same science, but the more general is studied before the more specific. Total abstraction does not help to specify the sciences, then; but it is a common condition for all the sciences; and, within a given science, it determines the order of proceeding in its particular subject matter.

Abstraction vs. Separation. In distinguishing between the types of speculative science, St. Thomas speaks of an abstraction of a whole (*abstractio totius*) that yields the object of natural science, of an abstraction of a form (*abstractio formae*) that yields the object of mathematics, and a separation (*separatio*) that yields the object of metaphysics. The first two of these are called abstractions in a strict sense because they are abstractions by way of simple consideration. The third is more sharply referred to as a separation because it is an instance of the more radical abstraction by way of negative judgment.

The first of these three abstractions is the abstraction of the whole essence of the natural thing from the matter that individuates it. It yields an object sufficiently free from matter to be intelligible, but an object defined nevertheless in terms of common sensible matter. The second yields the form of *quantity that is abstracted from all matter save common intelligible matter. The third yields an object abstracted from all matter and an object seen to be independent of matter both in meaning and existence. The significantly different stances in reference to matter for these objects—resulting in significantly different modes of defining—put each on a different level of theoretical science. St. Thomas, with his distinctions between the abstraction of a whole, the abstraction of a form, and separation, covers the same ground as do Cajetan and John of St. Thomas with their distinctions between physical abstraction (the first degree of formal abstraction), mathematical abstraction (the second degree of formal abstraction), and metaphysical abstraction (the third degree of formal abstraction).

See also KNOWLEDGE, PROCESS OF; KNOWLEDGE, THEORIES OF; KNOWLEDGE; EPISTEMOLOGY; UNIVERSALS.

Bibliography: THOMAS AQUINAS, *The Division and Methods of the Sciences: Questions 5 and 6 of Commentary on the De Trinitate of Boethius,* tr. with introd. and notes A. MAURER (Toronto 1953), bibliog. 86–93. J. F. PEIFER, *The Concept in Thomism* (New York 1952). E. D. SIMMONS, "In Defense of Total and Formal Abstraction," NewSchol 29 (1955) 427–440; "The Thomistic Doctrine of the Three Degrees of Formal Abstraction," *Thomist* 22 (1959) 37–67. C. DE KONINCK, "Abstraction from Matter," *Laval Théologique et Philosophique* 13 (1957) 133–196; 16 (1960) 53–69, 169–188. F. A. CUNNINGHAM, "A Theory on Abstraction in St. Thomas," ModSchoolm 35 (1958) 249–270. L. FERRARI, *"Abstractio totius* and *abstractio totalis," Thomist* 24 (1961) 72–89. M. D. PHILLIPE, "'Ἀφαίρεσις, πρόσθεσις, χωρίζειν dans la philosophie d'Aristote," RevThom 48 (1948) 461–479. G. VAN RIET, "La Théorie thomiste de l'abstraction," RevPhilLov 50 (1952) 353–393. L. B. GEIGER, "Abstraction et séparation d'après S. Thomas: *In De Trinitate,* q.5, a.3," RevScPhilTh 31 (1947) 3–40.

[E. D. SIMMONS]

ABSURDITY

Absurdity is a basic notion for a number of modern thinkers such as A. Malraux (1901–), J. P. Sartre (1905–), A. *Camus (1913–60), F. *Kafka (1883–1924), E. Albee (1928–), F. Arrabal (1932–), S. Beckett (1906–), J. Genet (1910–), E. Ionesco (1912–), and H. Pinter (1930–). Whereas dictionaries define the absurd as that which is contrary to reason, as used by these writers it designates that which is without a reason. The absurd is a situation, a thing, or an event that really is, but for which no explanation is possible. Because the affair is inexplicable, it offends reason; it is senseless; it is absurd.

Søren *Kierkegaard (1813–55) is the source for this type of thought. Kierkegaard's writings are a constant protest against the excessive *rationalism of G. W. *Hegel, who taught that all the mysteries of the Christian faith could be comprehended by reason. To indicate that the Incarnation was beyond the understanding of human reason, Kierkegaard called it the absurd, meaning by that something unintelligible and incomprehensible to reason. He insisted that Christian absurdity was neither nonsense, nor irrationality, nor something meaningless; for notions such as these follow on the judgment of reason examining its legitimate data, whereas the Christian accepts the Incarnation by faith. In the light of faith he sees that the Incarnation is in no way absurd.

The notion was then taken up by modern thinkers, especially by existentialists, but in an atheistic context. Thus, absurdity for Sartre arises from the absolute contingency and complete gratuity of the world. Because there is no God, Sartre argues, there are no reasons for things. Things just are; and because they are without any reason for being, they are absurd. Ultimately all things come from nowhere and are going nowhere. Camus gives a different meaning. Admitting that there are scientific explanations for the various parts of the universe, Camus denies that there is any ultimate reason for the whole. Absurdity is a feeling that arises from the confrontation between man, who is looking for a unified explanation of all things, and a world that has no basic meaning.

Because of their preoccupation with the absurd, playwrights like Genet, Ionesco, Beckett and the like have been called collectively the Theater of the Absurd. To indicate the role of absurdity in the human situation these dramatists create sections of dialogue that are incoherent; they depict scenes in which the actions of the actors directly contradict the words they are speaking; they construct plays around the weird fantasies of deranged minds. In this they resemble Kafka, whose exuberant and enigmatic symbolism describes man as caught in a nightmare of existence; truth and illusion are so intertwined in his works that life is there seen as wearisome, uncertain, and senseless.

The Christian can well appreciate the loneliness, frustration, and the emptiness engendered by *atheism in these men. He can also be grateful for his faith, which enables him to see atheism as the most absurd of all absurdities; for the visible things of this world do declare the hidden attributes of God (Rom 1.20).

See also EXISTENTIALISM; EXISTENTIALISM IN LITERATURE; FRENCH LITERATURE 6; ENGLISH LITERATURE 9.

Bibliography: P. PRINI, EncFil 1:416–417.

[V. M. MARTIN]

ABŪ 'L-BARAKĀT,

ABŪ 'L-BARAKĀT, Coptic author; d. May 10, 1324. His full name was Shams al-Ri'āsa abū 'l-Barakāt ibn Kabar. He seems to have taken the added name of Barsauma on the occasion of his priestly ordination. He was a Coptic priest attached to the church called al-Mu'allaqa in Old Cairo. He held, besides, the post of secretary to the prince and Mameluke officer Ruqn al-Dīn Baibars al-Manṣūri and collaborated with him on his history of Islam, which comes up to 1325, the year of Ruqn's death. Other works that he left are: a Coptic-Arabic dictionary; a large number of elegant sermons for feasts and occasions; and his principal work, a theological encyclopedia entitled *The Lamp of Darkness and the Exposition of the Service.*

The latter presents all that clergy and laity need to know about the doctrines of the faith, the Scriptures, Canon Law, liturgy. The work has a practical teaching purpose and seeks to hand on the genuine religious tradition. Of 24 chapters the first 7 deal with doctrine (1–3), items of church history (4), a list of collections of Church law (5), introduction to the Scripture and an account of the liturgical books (6), and an account of Christian literature in Arabic (7). The remaining chapters treat of cult and Church customs and practices.

Bibliography: Graf GeschChArabLit 2:438–445. E. TISSERANT, DTC 8.2:2293–96; *Revue de l'Orient chrétien* 22 (1920–21) 373–394. M. JUGIE, EncCatt 1:149. J. ASSFALG, LexThK[2] 1:101.

[J. A. DEVENNY]

ABŪ 'L-FAḌL (FAẒL) 'ĀLLAMĪ,

ABŪ 'L-FAḌL (FAẒL) 'ĀLLAMĪ, court official, historian, and one of the most learned and liberal-minded men of his age in Moslem India; b. Agra, India, Jan. 14, 1551; d. Orchha, Aug. 22, 1602. He attended the school of his father, Shaykh Mubārak Nāgawrī, at Agra, from which he was graduated at the age of 15. While teaching in this school, he educated himself by reading, contemplating, and discussing religious problems. For years he wavered, like al-Ghazzālī (*Algazel), between skepticism, orthodoxy, asceticism, and *Sufism. At the age of 23 he was presented to the great Mogul Emperor Akbar (1556–1605) and soon found favor with him. Akbar was then under the political and religious influence of conservative ulema, from which abū 'l-Faḍl gradually freed him. He meantime incurred the jealousy of Akbar's son Salīm (the future Jahāngīr, 1605–27), who succeeded in having him sent to Deccan on a mission. On his way back he was assassinated at Salīm's instigation.

Abū 'l-Faḍl's principal title to fame rests on his authorship of *Akbar Nāma* (book of Akbar). The book, in Persian, consists of two parts, the first dealing with the life and reign of Akbar and the second giving a complete account of the political institutions and the administration of the empire. In addition, it has encyclopedic information about Hindu philosophy, science, literature, and customs, some of which can be found in few other places.

Bibliography: N. HASAN, EncIslam[2] 1:117–118. C. A. STOREY, *Persian Literature* (London 1939) 2.3:541–551.

[P. K. HITTI]

ABŪ 'L-FARAJ 'ABDALLĀH IBN AṬ-ṬAYYIB,

ABŪ 'L-FARAJ 'ABDALLĀH IBN AṬ-ṬAYYIB, an outstanding figure of the first half of the 11th century, philosopher, physician, monk, and priest; d. Baghdad, 1043. Few facts of his life are known. He studied and practiced medicine at al-'Aḍudīya Hospital in Baghdad (1015–16). He was patriarchal secretary to the Catholicos Yuḥanna ibn Nuzuk (1012–22). He enjoyed the favor of the Buwayhid ruler Jalāl al-Dawla. He was in charge of the synod in which Elias I (1028–49) was elected Catholicos. As Elias's secretary he prepared in 1028 the ecclesiastical approval for Elias of Nisibis to record his religious discussion with the Moslem *wazir* Abū 'l-Qāsim al-Maghribī.

He wrote in Arabic: in the field of philosophy—commentaries on Aristotle's logic and metaphysics (devoting 20 years to the latter) and on Porphyry's *Isagoge;* in the field of medicine—texts, explanations, and excerpts of the scientific and medical works of Hippocrates and Galen; in the field of ecclesiastical studies—commentaries on the Scriptures, works on apologetics, dogma, moral theology, and Canon Law. Withal he managed to lead the life of a dedicated and edifying priest and ecclesiastical administrator. His passionate concern to put at the disposition of his contemporaries the scientific riches of the past had a motivation familiar to American Catholics; he was driven to compensate for the lack of education and culture among laity and clergy.

Bibliography: Graf GeschChArabLit 2:160–177, with full bibliog. and an acount of his writings in print and MSS. P. MOUTERDE, LexThK² 5:591. P. SFAIR, EncCatt 1:149–150. E. TISSERANT, DTC 11.1:276–277.

[J. A. DEVENNY]

ABUNDIUS OF COMO, ST., bishop and patron of Como, Italy; d. April 2, between 462 and 489, probably 468 (feast, April 2). Abundius (also called Abundantius), assistant and successor of Bishop Amantius, was consecrated Nov. 17, 449, and sent by Pope Leo I in 450, along with Bishop Eutherius of Capua and the priests Basilius and Senator, to Constantinople to discuss the orthodoxy of its patriarch *Anatolius. Theodosius II died before their arrival, but Marcian and Pulcheria received them kindly. On Oct. 21, 450, a synod was held in the baptistery of Hagia Sophia in which all the bishops of the patriarchate, beginning with Anatolius, signed the Tome of Leo to Flavian anathematizing the doctrines of *Nestorius and *Eutyches. Abundius performed a similar papal mission to Bishop Eusebius of Milan and his suffragans, and then devoted himself to the conversion of pagans in his own diocese.

Bibliography: R. MAIOCCHI, *Storia dei vescovi di Como* (Milan 1929). A. P. FRUTAZ, EncCatt 1:35–37; LexThK² 1:101–102, P. GINI, BiblSanct 1:23–30.

[M. J. COSTELLOE]

ABYSS (IN THE BIBLE), an important region in ancient Near Eastern cosmography. According to the Babylonian creation narrative **Enuma elish* (Pritchard ANET² 60–72), in the beginning there were two huge bodies of water, Apsu (male) and Tiamat (female), from whose mingling streams the first gods were begotten. Soon hostilities broke out between the newly formed gods and their parents. Apsu decided to annihilate his offspring; but Ea, the god of magic, cast a spell on him and killed him. Tiamat, bent on avenging her consort, organized her forces, formed 11 terrible monsters, and advanced toward her rebellious children. This time Ea's powerful spell proved ineffective, and the gods were thrown into panic, aware that they were no match for Tiamat in open combat. Only Marduk, the youngest and most powerful among them, stood a chance against her, and the divine assembly rallied around him, agreeing to give him supreme authority if he consented to do battle. Marduk armed himself and rode out on his storm chariot. The battle was fierce, but Marduk prevailed and Tiamat perished. He cut her body in two like a shellfish, and with one half he formed the firmament, sealing her waters above it; with the other half he shaped the earth. From this narrative, it is clear that Apsu and Tiamat represent the threatening forces of chaos and destruction over which the gods had to triumph before establishing order in the cosmos. Out of the chaotic waters a heavenly ocean (Tiamat) and a subterranean one (Apsu) were formed.

In Gn 1.2 the primeval watery abyss that God divided in two in order to form the heavenly and terrestrial oceans is called *tᵉhôm,* rendered ἄβυσσος (abyss) in the Septuagint. Philological and conceptual similarity with Babylonian *ti'âmat* have led most scholars since Gunkel to recognize a link of dependence between the two. The Biblical tradition apparently borrowed this element from Mesopotamian mythology and transformed it to meet the demands of Israelite faith. The transformation, however, was radical; *tᵉhôm* was reduced to the status of a purely natural element, offering no resistance whatever to God's creative activity. Elsewhere in the Bible the word *tᵉhôm* is applied only to the waters below the firmament, i.e., the visible ocean and the subterranean reservoir that feeds springs and streams (Gn 7.11; 49.25; Ez 31.4, 15). Even the word *tᵉhôm* itself is not a perfect philological equivalent of *ti'âmat*. These important differences recommend caution in the assessing of the degree of dependence of Genesis ch. 1 on the Babylonian creation epic. The latter, however, has closer parallels in other sections of the Bible.

See also DRAGON; LEVIATHAN; RAHAB (PRIMEVAL MONSTER).

Bibliography: H. GUNKEL, *Schöpfung und Chaos in Urzeit und Endzeit* (2d ed. Göttingen 1921). A. HEIDEL, *The Babylonian Genesis* (2d ed. Chicago 1951). O. KAISER, *Die mythische Bedeutung des Meeres in Ägypten, Ugarit und Israel* (Berlin 1959). H. JUNKER, "Die theologische Behandlung der Chaosvorstellung in der biblischen Schöpfungsgeschichte," in *Mélanges André Robert* (Paris 1956) 27–37.

[L. F. HARTMAN]

ACACIAN SCHISM

The Acacian Schism (484–519) was caused by a change of policy on the part of the Patriarch of Constantinople, Acacius (472–489), who despite his intimacy with the Monophysites had opposed the anti-Chalcedonian encyclical of the Emperor *Basiliscus in 475. Upon the restoration of the Emperor Zeno (August 476), he collaborated in the deposition of the Monophysite bishops, including Peter the Fuller of Antioch and John Codonatus of Apamea. In 479 he consecrated the Chalcedonian Calandion as bishop of Antioch at the Emperor's behest and drew a protest from Pope *Simplicius (468–483) for interfering in another patriarchal jurisdiction (*Epist.* June 22, 479).

In 482, in concert with Peter Mongus, he composed a doctrinal statement called the **Henoticon,* or Decree of Union, which Zeno promulgated for the province of Egypt. It was intended to conclude the Christological disputes by citing the authority of the first three ecumenical councils, condemning Nestorius and Eutyches, but it did not mention the natures in Christ. Contrary teaching, "be it of the Council of Chalcedon or any other council," was condemned. Though the symbol of Chalcedon and Leo's *Tome* were not rejected, anti-Chalcedonians were admitted to communion, and Peter Mongus was reinstated as patriarch in Alexandria.

Pope *Felix III wrote a letter of protest to Acacius, then excommunicated him in a Roman synod (July 28, 484) when Acacius recognized Peter Mongus at Alexandria. When the excommunication was reiterated in 485, Acacius erased the name of Felix from the diptychs. The two successors of Acacius, Fravita (490) and Euphemius (490–495), were not hostile to the decrees of Chalcedon. They announced their election to the Pope for recognition; but Felix demanded that Acacius's name be struck from the diptychs, and relations were again suspended between Rome and Constantinople. The Patriarch Euphemius, having forced the new Emperor *Anastasius I (491–518) to accept the decisions of Chalcedon before his accession to the throne, attempted to heal the rupture with Pope *Gelasius (492–496), but without success since the new Pope renewed the demand made by Felix. Meanwhile acceptance of the *Henoticon,* though not universal among the Monophysites, was considered an anti-Chalcedonian gesture. Gelasius, however, entered relations with Constantinople through an embassy sent by the Roman senate (492 and 494); but his successor, *Anastasius II (496–498), proved adamant in the request for the removal of Acacius's name from the diptychs.

Emperor Anastasius was encouraged in his anti-Chalcedonian policy during the 3-year sojourn in Constantinople (508–511) of the Monophysite propagandist *Severus, the future patriarch of Antioch (512–518) and a fervent supporter of the *Henoticon*. The Emperor published his *Type,* or formula for union, which he attempted to impose upon the Chalcedonian Patriarch, Flavian of Antioch (510). In 512 Pope *Symmachus responded to an imperial letter that attempted, among other accusations, to charge him with favoring Manichaeism.

When the rebel general Vitalian forced the Emperor to agree to call a council at Heraclea with the Pope presiding, Anastasius was compelled to enter into relations with Rome. But after the defeat of Vitalian, legations sent to Constantinople in 515 and 517 by Pope *Hormisdas were unsuccessful. However the advent of *Justin I occasioned immediate negotiations between Hormisdas and the pro-Chalcedonian Emperor. The schism was brought to an end on March 28, 519, when Patriarch John in a letter to the Pope indicated his acceptance of the formula of Hormisdas and the removal of the names of Zeno and Acacius as well as the latter's five successors from the diptychs. Opposition throughout the East endured only briefly.

Bibliography: E. Schwartz, *Publizistische Sammlungen zum Acacianischen Schisma* (AbhMünchAk NS 10; 1934). F. Hofmann, Grill-Bacht Konz 2:43–94. R. Haacke, *ibid.* 117–146. H. Bacht, *ibid.* 266–291. P. Charanis, *Church and State in the Later Roman Empire* (Madison, Wis. 1939). S. Salaville, "L'Affaire de l'Hénotique," ÉchosOr 18 (1916–19) 255–266, 389–397; 19 (1920) 49–68, 415–433. L. Salaville, DTC 6.2: 2153–78. Stein-Palanque HistBEmp 2:24–39, 224–228.

[H. CHIRAT]

ACACIUS OF BEROEA, bishop in the province of *Antioch who took part in all major ecclesiastical controversies between 360 and 433; b. Syria?, *c.* 322; d. Beroea, after 433. He had been a monk under *Asterius of Amasea at Gindarus near Antioch, and was renowned as a bishop for his austere life and discipline. He fought Arianism and Apollinarianism at Antioch in the persecution of Valens from 369 to 377. He was consecrated bishop of Beroea in 378, and attended most later councils, including *Constantinople I in 381. He took part in two legations from the East to Rome to settle the Antiochian schism, and he was prominent in the intrigues (401–404) that led to the exile of St. *John Chrysostom. He did not attend the Council of Ephesus in 431, but played an important part in the *Nestorian controversy and helped restore peace between Alexandria and Antioch through the Union formula of 433. When he died shortly after, he was more than 110 years old. Of his writings only six letters remain.

Bibliography: Quasten Patr 3:482–483. G. Bardy, "Acace de Bérée et son rôle dans la controverse nestorienne," RevScRel 18 (1938) 20–44.

[V. C. DE CLERCQ]

ACACIUS OF CAESAREA, disciple and successor of *Eusebius and leader of the Homoean faction in the Arian controversy; d. after 365. Nothing is known of him before he succeeded Eusebius *c.* 340. He was present at the Council of Antioch in 341 and became one of the foremost bishops of the anti-Nicene party. As such he was condemned by name by the orthodox assembly of *Sardica in 343. Later he was involved in a bitter feud with St. *Cyril of Jerusalem on jurisdictional and doctrinal grounds. His career reached a climax when the Homoean confession (the Son is "like to" the Father) became the official creed of the empire at the Synod of Constantinople in 360. When orthodoxy prevailed under the Emperor Jovian, Acacius had no scruples in signing the Nicene creed; but he returned to Homoean doctrine when *Valens became Emperor of the East in 364. However, he was condemned by the Homoiousian synod of Lampsacus in the summer of 365 but retained his see until his death (*c.* 366). He was noted for his eloquence and Biblical scholarship. He renovated the famous library of Caesarea, and he composed several works that are lost, except for a few exegetical fragments on Romans and the Octateuch.

Bibliography: Quasten Patr 3:345–346. J. Lebon, "La Position de saint Cyrille de Jérusalem dans les luttes provoquées par l'arianisme," RHE 20 (1924) 181–210, 357–386.

[V. C. DE CLERCQ]

ACADEMIC DEGREES

An academic degree is a title or rank conferred by an educational authority in recognition of scholarship or for some outstanding achievement. The degrees now commonly used in the U.S. are associate, bachelor, master, and doctor; Catholics add the licentiate. Such titles are either earned, i.e., awarded upon completion of a program of study, or honorary, i.e., awarded in recognition of service or attainment.

History. Just as the origin and development of universities are somewhat obscure, so a certain vagueness surrounds the earliest use of academic degrees. The ancient world did not award degrees in any sense analogous to that of modern usage. The custom of granting degrees originated with the rise of medieval universities. The first recorded instance is the conferral of a doctorate at the University of Bologna *c.* 1150 A.D. The medieval titles were bachelor, licentiate, master, doctor, and professor. The last three were at first used interchangeably, and, with the licentiate, indicated the right to teach. There is a parallel between the use of these titles and advancement in a guild from the status of apprentice to that of master, which was awarded for technical skill. Gradually, "doctor" was reserved for the faculties of theology, law, and medicine, while "master" or licentiate came to be associated with the faculty of arts. Both signified completion of a course of study and indicated that the holder was qualified to teach or practice.

From the Continent the use of degrees spread to Oxford and Cambridge and from these universities to America. Harvard and the other colonial colleges followed the English pattern, which did not include a licentiate. From the very beginning, both civil and ecclesiastical authorities chartered colleges and universities, and gave them broad powers to grant "the usual degrees." The Holy See still exercises this power particularly in the fields of theology, philosophy, Scripture, and Canon Law. In the U.S. many Catholic institutions secure degree-granting charters both from the civil authority and the Holy See.

Types. Five principal types of academic degrees, i.e., associate, bachelor, licentiate, master, and doctor, are recognized throughout the academic world. The first two, designated as undergraduate degrees, imply completion of work on the college level; the others, called graduate degrees, imply work done beyond the 4 years of college.

Associate Degree. This degree may be traced to the University of Durham, England, *c.* 1865. It was first used in the U.S. in 1900, when the University of Chicago granted 83 such degrees. It marks successful completion of 2 years of work beyond high school. Most common titles are the associate in arts (A.A.), and the associate in science (A.S.), though about 130 varieties exist. The associate is often referred to as a "junior college degree," but many 4-year institutions grant it.

Bachelor's Degree. This degree, conferred on nine graduates of Harvard in 1642, is the oldest academic degree used by American institutions. Practically no other earned degree was conferred in America until 1800. It generally denotes completion of a 4-year program after high school. While the most common forms are still the bachelor of arts (B.A.) and bachelor of science (B.S.), a striking feature is the proliferation of hundreds of varieties. Because institutions currently grant some 450 types of B.S. degrees alone, their real significance can be obtained with certainty only by an investigation of a particular program. The actual title no longer offers a clue to the course work involved.

Master's Degree. This generally represents 1 or 2 years' work after the baccalaureate. In colonial times it was often an honorary degree, or conferred automatically after the English fashion. Requirements vary considerably, but usually include a program of courses, examinations, and less frequently a thesis. There are approximately 400 types of master's degrees, which require individual investigation for evaluation.

Licentiate. This was a fairly common degree in medieval universities where it represented a level of achievement approximating the master's degree. It survives in the U.S. chiefly among Catholics in the fields of philosophy, theology, Scripture, and Canon Law, although it is still well known in modern Europe and in Latin America. It represents 1 or 2 years of work beyond the baccalaureate.

Doctorate. This is the highest earned degree, requiring 3 to 4 years or more of mature study and research after the baccalaureate. Professional doctorates, classified as first degrees, e.g., doctor of medicine (M.D.), doctor of dental medicine (D.M.D.), doctor of laws (LL.D.), have long-established traditions, but usually do not imply research. Research doctorates, e.g., doctor of philosophy (Ph.D.), doctor of science (D.Sc.), doctor of literature (Litt.D.), require an original or significant dissertation, as well as advanced study. Most important is the Ph.D. degree, no longer limited to philosophy but referring to any field. There are several other earned doctorates, e.g., doctor of education (Ed.D.), doctor of business administration (D.B.A.), doctor of sacred theology (S.T.D.), and doctor of divinity (D.D.).

Honorary Degrees. These are granted for service or achievement, rather than completion of formal requirements. They became very common in the 19th century, but today an honorary B.A., M.A., or Ph.D. is rare. The most common awards are D.Litt., LL.D., and D.Sc. By custom bishops are awarded an honorary D.D. degree.

Certain degrees carry ecclesiastical rights and privileges. Canon 1387 of the Code of Canon Law gives preference to doctors in appointment to benefices. A degree may entitle one to voting rights, offices, or distinct garb, e.g., a special biretta or ring.

Bibliography: H. RASHDALL, *The Universities of Europe in the Middle Ages,* ed. F. M. POWICKE and A. B. EMDEN, 3 v. (Oxford 1936). U.S. Department of Health, Education and Welfare, *Academic Degrees Earned and Honorary Degrees Conferred by Institutions of Higher Education in the United States* (Washington 1961). L. J. DALY, *The Medieval University, 1200–1400* (New York 1961).

[A. J. CLARK]

ACADEMIC DRESS

A costume generally consisting of cap, gown, and occasionally hood, sometimes worn at institutions of higher learning. Like judicial dress, it originated with

Fig. 1. The "cappa clausa."

medieval clergy, whose ecclesiastical dress probably derived in turn from civilian attire at an earlier age. Medieval scholars were almost completely clergy, whose sober form of dress was loosely termed *vestimentum clausum* (clothing closed). The earliest illustrations

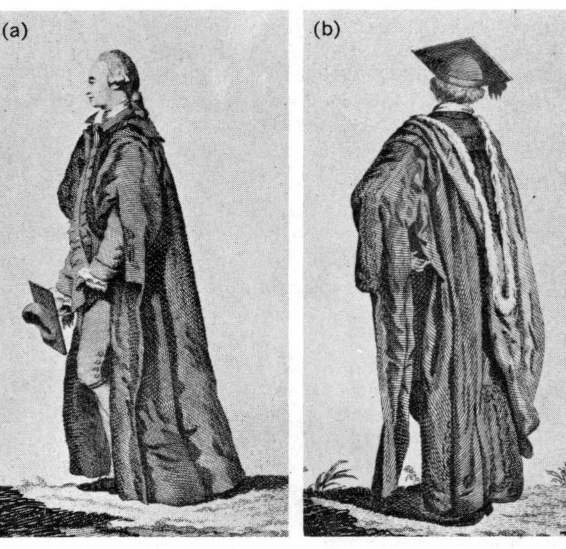
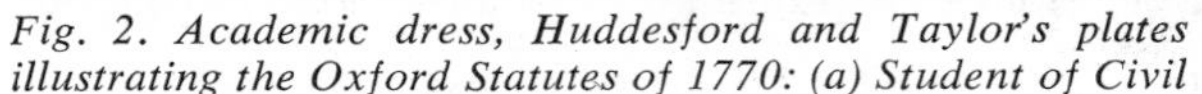

Fig. 2. Academic dress, Huddesford and Taylor's plates illustrating the Oxford Statutes of 1770: (a) Student of Civil Law. (b) Bachelor of Music. (c) "Determining" Bachelor of Arts. (d) Bachelor of Arts with ordinary hood.

Fig. 3. Twentieth-century academic dress of the U.S.: (a) The traditional Master's costume. (b) Bachelor's cap, gown, and hood. (c) Doctor's cap, gown, and hood. The hood lining is folded back to show the colored lining.

available show gowns that somewhat resemble cassocks. It is improbable that a distinction was made at first between dress and various academic levels. In fact, academic levels of scholar, bachelor, and master (sometimes called doctor or professor) do not seem to have originated until the 13th century.

European Origins. The gown probably originated in the everyday cape of the clergy, which was made obligatory for all church dignitaries in England by Stephen Langton, Abp. of Canterbury, at the Council of Oxford in 1222. Later, at the Universities of Bologna, Italy, Paris, France, Oxford, England, and subsequent universities, this *cappa clausa* came to be regarded as academic dress—especially when the clergy consistently disregarded Langton's rule. For the convenience of the hands, there were one or two open slits, which later extended to the ground. The gown was originally black, but as universities passed further from ecclesiastical control, it often assumed brighter colors. By 1500 all doctors wore scarlet hoods and copes, while masters and bachelors of divinity retained the black.

The hood, which was originally worn by everybody, with no academic significance, was certainly lay in origin. Originally it apparently served a threefold purpose: head covering, shoulder cape, and bag for alms. In front was a liripipe, a piece of material for pulling it on and off. From about 1432, masters and doctors evidently wore two kinds: silk-lined for summer, and miniver-lined at other times. The undergraduate hood is mentioned in literature as early as the 1480s. From about 1675, principally masters and doctors retained the silk-lined hood; the miniver-lined hood served as pro-doctoral insignia only. Later, at Cambridge, a distinction was made between hoods of regent masters (those actively engaged in teaching at a university), which were lined with miniver, and those of nonregents, lined with silk.

The cap originated in the skull cap worn by ecclesiastics to protect their tonsured heads against the weather. This in turn was a shallow form of the cap of liberty that the Roman freedman used to cover his new-shaven head: the Synod of Bergamo (1311) ordered the clergy to wear it "after the manner of laymen." In academic usage, originally at Oxford and Cambridge, only doctors in the superior Faculties wore a cap (*pileus*), a tight round skull cap with a little point at the crown. All others then wore hoods. Tudor times seem to have added other varieties: the round velvet cap (*pileus rotundus*) for graduates in secular Faculties, surviving today as part of the full dress of doctors (except in theology), and the square cap (*pileus quadratus*) after 1520 from the University of Paris. The Paris cap was probably formed by sewing together four pieces of cloth, the seams producing raised, squaring ridges. From it, two types evolved: the biretta or priest's cap, and the velvet cap of doctors of theology. Bachelors and others were not authorized to wear caps until 1575–80.

In those places in which it prevailed, the Protestant revolt brought about less and less concern for academic dress. After the Laudian code of 1636, there were few far-reaching changes. By the 18th century, when France was beginning to fall victim to anticlericalism, recognized academic dress was worn at universities only in England (due to an insular conservatism as well as a determination to keep intact the "Establishment" in Oxford and Cambridge) and in Spain and Portugal (where strong Church discipline preserved it). There is today not much uniformity in academic dress in Europe.

U.S. Adaptations. King's College, the present Columbia University in New York City, established in 1754, imported many British regulations for academic dress. Use of academic dress in the U.S. widened especially toward the end of the 19th century. Essentially this was a student movement to provide a senior badge, to dress up commencement week and other exercises, and to overcome differences of dress. In 1893, a regulatory Intercollegiate Commission was formed. In 1895 this commission presented the Intercollegiate Code, since adopted by about 95 per cent of U.S. colleges and universities. It granted a charter to Cotrell and Leonard Inc., Albany, N.Y., to act as sole depositary for the authoritative Intercollegiate Bureau of Academic Costume; this company still maintains a library and register of propriety. In 1932 the American Council on Education appointed a Committee on Academic Costumes and Ceremonies to study the 1895 Code; in 1935, and again in 1959, it recommended minor revisions.

The Code oversees academic dress. Concerning the black gown, the bachelor's, which is worn closed, is distinguished by its long, pointed sleeves; the master's, designed to be worn open, has a long oblong sleeve; the doctor's, also to be worn open, carries in addition velvet panels around the neck and down the front edges, with three bars of the same across the sleeves (all of which facings may also be of the color distinctive of the field to which the degree pertains). In the U.S., however, the most distinctive feature is the hood. Its shape and size mark the college degree of the wearer. The shape of the bachelor's and master's hoods is similar, but the former is 3 feet long, the latter 3½. The doctor's has a rounder base, and an overall length of 4 feet. The color of the hood lining officially represents the institution conferring the degree. Some have one solid color and others have two. The two colors are supplied by a chevron or by the parti-per (one color in the upper part of the lining, another in the lower). In assigning colors to respective Faculties, the Intercollegiate Commission retained, as far as possible, their historical association.

Bibliography: W. N. HARGREAVES-MAWDSLEY, *A History of Academical Dress in Europe until the End of the Eighteenth Century* (New York 1963). O. J. HOPPNER, *Academic Costume in America* (Albany, N.Y. 1948), pamphlet. **Illustration credits:** Figs. 1*a*, 1*b*, 1*c* and 1*d*, By permission of the Bodleian Library, Oxford.

[H. A. BUETOW]

ACADEMIC FREEDOM

A term more widely used to advocate than to define cautiously the removal of constraint from higher education. Contemporary discussion places it in these contexts: (1) freedom of inquiry by scholars and research workers; (2) absence of nonacademic controls over teaching and library resources; (3) tenure for professors and in part for administrators; and (4) student liberties, particularly in the form of freedom of speech and assembly. *Lehrfreiheit* (freedom to teach) and *Lernfreiheit* (freedom of study), as sponsored by German universities during the 19th century, are usually considered the basic modern formulations, though neither has great relevance for the current situation in the U.S. The first was designed to protect duly appointed professors from harassment by political authorities; the second sought to free university students from the rigid discipline of the secondary schools. For historical background, *see* EDUCATION, I (HISTORY OF), 3–5.

The Issue of Academic Control. In the U.S., overall control of academic institutions, insofar as these are not conducted by religious denominations or orders, has normally been entrusted to boards of regents, overseers, or trustees. The issue therefore early became one of defining the limits of their authority. Sometimes, notably at Harvard, discussion of faculty autonomy began during the early decades of the 19th century. But it was a spate of well-publicized dismissals or resignations of academicians between 1890 and 1914, for holding unpopular or "controversial" views on economic problems, pacifism, and biological evolution, that aroused public concern and that seemed to indicate that in the pluralistic society then prevailing the right to judge scholarship and teaching should be reserved to the faculties themselves. Impetus was therewith given to the formation in 1915 of the American Association of University Professors (AAUP). A committee of this organization was entrusted with the definition and defense of academic freedom and soon became widely known for the moderation and practicality of its views. It stressed tenure as the major concern, and so became no mere policy-making body. Any professor who contended that his tenure rights had been violated could appeal to the committee, which then conducted an investigation; and an institution found seriously at fault could be publicly listed by the association. Such listing made recruiting more difficult for the offending institution.

Protection of Tenure of Professors. Tenure in office results from appointment until a stipulated retirement age and is not revocable except for due cause. It is normally granted after service over a period of 3, 5, or 7 years and is not transferable from one institution to another. In some states it is held binding for institutions under public control as of the date of award, regardless of subsequent loss of efficiency. Interpretations of "due cause" vary, but the favored practice is to grant a hearing by a faculty committee, which makes a recommendation to the president of the institution, who, however, may retain the right to review and decide cases involving moral turpitude or (sometimes) subversive activity. When dismissal is deemed by the individual affected to have been based on prejudice or insufficient information, an appeal may be made through professional or civil liberties organizations or through the courts. Inability to further finance a given academic activity is often a reason for abrogating tenure. Sudden drops in enrollment, for example, may affect the status of departments of instruction. Some institutions make provision for the retraining of faculty members so affected; others do not. Hence the right to tenure is not absolute, but it remains the most important gain in the history of academic freedom.

More recently legislative bodies and the courts have, to an increasing extent, been concerned with academic freedom. Sometimes the action has been restrictive. A famous case of 1940 involved the revocation by a court of the appointment of Bertrand Russell to a New York municipal college on the ground that his views flouted American mores. But it was a real or alleged subversive activity that most engaged the attention of Federal and state legislative bodies. As a result of reports by investigative agencies, notably the Un-American Activities Committee of the House of Representatives, actions to dismiss professors were taken, sometimes based on perjury. Requirements of *loyalty oaths aroused no serious protests in some states but in others, notably California, created widespread faculty revolt. The courts upheld the constitutionality of the Federal Smith Act (1940) and the New York Feinberg Law (1949), both of which sanctioned procedures to abrogate tenure in cases in which active subversive activity was established. More far-reaching though often beneficent are the curbs on the liberties of academic institutions imposed by *civil rights legislation. In many states questions concerning race, creed, or even national origin cannot appear on appointment forms; and the courts have reviewed a number of cases in which there was question of discrimination, even in one case involving alleged failure to promote because of religious bias. Supreme Court decisions drawing a sharp distinction between religious education and the public interest have likewise been restrictive. On the other hand, the courts have also vigorously supported academic freedom. They have reviewed dismissal actions when requested to do so and have ordered reinstatement when the evidence appeared inconclusive or when the educational authorities were deemed at fault. In California the highest court invalidated the dismissal of professors who had refused to take the loyalty oath. Thus the intervention of legislative bodies and the courts has not been an unmixed blessing or an unalleviated curse.

Claims have also been made that there exists a presumptive right to tenure. Persons not retained beyond the period of probation may air their grievances through the press or seek to obtain the support of professional organizations. But they cannot seek redress in the courts, which have consistently held that college administrators must have the right to determine the appropriateness of permanent appointment. Some rights are, however, now normally conceded. Those who are not reappointed are held entitled to notice of the termination of their service in time to permit finding employment elsewhere. Trustees may also investigate seriously charges that dismissals of nontenure employees are due to discrimination. Conversely, tenure does not in any way imply that the one granted it cannot accept employment elsewhere, often on very short notice. The problem thus created has been one of the most serious faced by academic institutions, particularly during the decades after 1945.

Scope of Faculty Control. Nonacademic controls of teaching and library resources have generally ceased to be important in American higher education. A dissident professor may encounter public disapprobation of his views, and undoubtedly bias of various kinds exists on campuses, particularly in departments of instruction. Occasionally the adoption of certain textbooks or the use of educational films is opposed by one pressure group or advocated by another. So far as it is possible to determine, political influence is now seldom used to secure appointments to academic staffs, although the selection of senior administrators is still affected by taboos. The situation was once far less favorable, and the improvement is an important result of the widespread recognition of professional standards in higher education.

The right to tenure is believed to have numerous important implications, though there is no consensus concerning all of them. Professors are to be granted the right to freedom of inquiry and to publication of the results; the right to air their views in public, if these are within the scope of their professional competence; freedom to join professional organizations and to establish chapters of them on their campuses; a share in the administration of the institution, particularly insofar as the course of study or the appointment of new faculty are concerned; and in many instances a measure of responsibility for the promotion of colleagues. Increasingly, boards of trustees confer with the faculty when a new president is being selected.

Student Liberties. Since the foundation of the National Student Association (1947) and similar bodies, the more traditional forms of student self-government have frequently been modified to permit grants of freedom and autonomy to campus organizations. The most controversial of these involve publications and the selection of extern speakers. Student editors demand the right of free comment on campus affairs, and indeed on the world as a whole, sometimes even the abrogation of censorship in any form. Student organizations point to their citizenship in the community as a whole when inviting speakers, however obnoxious a given orator may be to the president or the board. Sometimes, as at the University of California in 1964, rioting has taken place when quite abnormal student demands have been opposed. Less widely commented on but no less important are student demands for *Lernfreiheit* in the German sense, namely, for the privilege of choosing professors under whom they wish to study and the right to stay away from classes without incurring penalties.

Policies of Catholic Institutions. Catholic institutions generally have been slow to accept academic freedom as outlined, although marked changes have taken place since a report by W. M. Mallon, SJ, to the National Catholic Educational Association (1942) indicated that 65 per cent of the Catholic colleges responding to the questionnaire reported making no provision for tenure. The great majority of such institutions have been conducted by religious orders whose members are under obedience and therefore without permanent tenure in any position. In earlier times laymen were usually appointed only when no religious were available, but a tradition of according a measure of security gradually developed. Institutional survival has since come to depend on quality of instruction, now unobtainable without professionally competent lay faculties; indeed, in some well-known Catholic universities four-fifths of those in instructional ranks are laymen. As a result, tenure is granted and respected. Branches of the AAUP have been established and function as they do on secular campuses. The ever-growing number of religious educated in universities of distinction bring back to their campuses an awareness of the dominant American outlook in the area of scholarship. The number of laymen appointed to administrative positions is likewise increasing. On the basis of the information available in 1965, Catholic colleges seem to confer a large measure of autonomy on department chairmen, sometimes larger even than normal, but to concede to the faculty as a whole less opportunity to influence or modify the policies of the administration.

Restrictions on Students. Catholic institutions, like Protestant denominational colleges, have been relatively slow to concede the legitimacy of student requests for a larger measure of autonomy. Invitations to extern speakers are more rigidly controlled, and censorship of publications is generally the rule. This reluctance to remove restrictions has in general not been disadvantageous in the more permissive Catholic institutions, which have seldom witnessed the excesses reported elsewhere. But in more conservative colleges there may well have been fostered undue narrowness of outlook and excessive respect for authority. At all events, Catholic student organizations have not attained the results expected of them, and the reason may well be a lack of confidence on the part of their elders. On the other hand, many colleges have striven to introduce an equivalent of the "honors system," with good results; there is more intellectual ferment, and a noticeable improvement of publications has taken place.

Freedom of Inquiry. More important is the question of freedom of inquiry. This has been the most important single target of attack by both friends and enemies of Catholic education. The criticism has taken many forms: the allegation that the teaching of theology and philosophy has been too didactic, that library resources have been controlled, that effective self-study of the institution has been avoided, and that religious bias manifests itself in the presentation of both the humanities and the social sciences. That these strictures were once justified may be conceded, and that there is still room for improvement is true. Obviously the faculty of an educational institution under Catholic auspices will profess respect for, though on the part of its Jewish and Protestant members not acceptance of, Catholic teaching. This will include recognition of the right of the Church to use spiritual sanctions to oppose ideas considered to be injurious to faith and morals. But at least until very recently limitations on freedom of inquiry have been insisted upon that are widely held not to be in consonance with the purposes of a contemporary university. One of these limitations is the *Index of Forbidden Books. It has been observed that if the deviant literature of today were placed outside the pale, as Victor Hugo's *Les Miserables* once was (it was thought too humanitarian in outlook), the Index would be lengthy, indeed. For some time counselors believed it prudent to refer to the Index as infrequently as possible, lest students be tempted to flout authority; but Catholic colleges in the U.S. have generally kept the indicted works under lock and key, thus providing occasion for ironic comment by students and faculty alike. Recommendations that the Index be discontinued began to be made by north European scholars after World War I, when there was a notable revival of Catholic academic activity, but became more numerous and vocal with the convening of Vatican Council II.

This Council accorded unprecedented freedom for some forms of inquiry. These may be grouped under the headings of Biblical studies and ecumenicism (*see* BIBLICAL THEOLOGY; ECUMENICAL MOVEMENT). The new emphasis on the value of archeological research and textual criticism for well-informed reading of the Scriptures has rejuvenated Catholic scholarship in this basic field of inquiry. The corollary, however, is greater latitude in related areas. The acceptance of *aggiornamento* in the study of the history of salvation has given new life to Catholic thinking about moral theology, the sociology of religion, speculative philosophy, and the relationships between religion, philosophy, and science. Ecumenicism, on the other hand, has prepared the way for more candid and thorough studies of ecclesiastical history and of divergent religious views. The study of comparative religion is now a matter of genuine concern. Thus new goals have been set for the Catholic college and university of the future. Recognition of the fact that modern society is uniquely the product of scholarly research, not in the natural sciences merely, has led to invigorating insight into the mission of the Church as the divinely appointed teacher of perennial wisdom and truth, freely given by God and freely acquired. Finally, recognition of the importance of participation in the liturgy cannot help but bring about a new sense of sharing, with mind and heart, in the total mission of the Church, which is also a mission to the intelligence.

These are changes of the greatest significance, and it is therefore not surprising that they should be leaving their mark on Catholic higher education. Understanding and acceptance of them are of necessity uneven. But changes in orientation are taking place rapidly. Since the value of monasticism, in whatever form, is a major source of the strength of the Catholic life, religious communities are restudying their educational practices and processes of formation. Princes of the Church have advocated changes of outlook and practice for which there were few spokesmen some decades ago. That there should be a stirring of faculty and students to share in the new sense of freedom is natural, and unrest has unsettled some Catholic campuses as it has others. Older patterns of institutional behavior must be modified and new ones created. The time has come when the best fruits of the struggle for academic freedom will ripen in Catholic universities and colleges as they have elsewhere.

Bibliography: R. HOFSTADTER and W. P. METZGER, *Development of Academic Freedom in the United States* (New York 1955). R. M. MACIVER, *Academic Freedom in Our Time* (New York 1955). R. KIRK, *Academic Freedom* (Chicago 1955). Amer. Assoc. of University Professors, "General Report of the Committee on Academic Freedom and Academic Tenure," *Bulletin* 1 (1915) 15–43; "Academic Freedom and Tenure," *ibid.* 45 (1959) 107–112. S. HOOK, *Heresy, Yes—Conspiracy, No!* (New York 1953). Natl. Assoc. of Student Personnel Administrators, Commission viii, draft report of 1964 (unpub. Urbana, Ill.). W. M. MALLON, "Faculty Ranks, Tenure and Academic Freedom," *National Catholic Educational Association Bulletin* 39 (1942–43) 177–194. G. N. SHUSTER, *Education and Moral Wisdom* (New York 1960). J. B. MCGANNON et al., eds., *Christian Wisdom and Christian Formation* (New York 1964). R. F. DRINAN, *Religion, the Courts and Public Policy* (New York 1963). J. D. DONOVAN, *The Academic Man in the Catholic College* (New York 1964).

[G. N. SHUSTER]

ACADEMIES, LITERARY

Unlike most academies of music or art, literary academies are institutions of research, not of education. Their origins can be traced to groups of humanists working together during the *Renaissance. With the growth of modern literatures, discussion groups known as academies multiplied, particularly in Italy. These were very different from the national academies of today, which began to emerge in the 17th century and are now generally bodies of some authority, regulated by statute and limited in membership.

Renaissance Academies. Though it is doubtful whether the humanists themselves used the name "academy," there is evidence that it was applied to them by their contemporaries. Meetings between Greek and Western scholars at the Council of Florence (1438–39) did much to promote the study of Greek literature and philosophy; the group of Hellenists that frequented the household of Cardinal *Bessarion in Rome after the council is often referred to as Bessarion's Academy. Pope Nicholas V drew his team of translators of the Greek classics from this circle. Another group, formed under the patronage of Alfonso I in Naples in 1442 and at first led by Antonio Beccadelli, "il Panormita," became known as the Academia Pontaniana after the name of its second president, Giovanni Gioviano Pontano, and met until 1543. Another, founded in Rome *c.* 1460, was called the Academia Romana or Pomponiana after its leader, who had assumed the name *Pomponius Laetus. The members, who included Bartolomeo Sacchi, known as "il Platina," and Filippo Buonaccorsi, took Latin names and devoted themselves in particular to the study of ancient Rome. Their activities continued until 1468, when Pomponius Laetus and Platina were charged with conspiring to revive pagan practices and were imprisoned by Paul II. Many of their adherents were protected by Bessarion until the two leaders were released after the death of the Pope (1471).

The first group to choose the name "academy" for itself was probably the Academia Platonica of Florence. Under the enthusiastic patronage of Cosimo, and later of Lorenzo, de' Medici, the members took Plato's Academy for their model and their meetings followed the form established in the *Symposium.* The first formal meeting took place on Nov. 7, 1474, in the Villa Careggi, but Marsilio *Ficino, the effective leader of the group, had held similar assemblies there since about 1459. The academy survived until 1522 and counted among its most distinguished members Angelo Poliziano, Leon Battista *Alberti, and Giovanni *Pico della Mirandola.

The passage from classical to Italian studies was marked by the Accademia Aldina, founded in Venice between 1494 and 1500 by Aldus Manutius. Its well-defined rules were drawn up in Greek, the language used at meetings, and its purpose was to edit and print not only the ancient classics but also Italian literary works. It did not long survive the founder's death in 1515. In Rome the Academia Romana was revived by Sixtus IV (1471–84) and reached its greatest luster during the pontificates of Julius II (1503–13) and Leo X (1513–21), when it was frequented by such writers as Paolo Giovio, Pietro *Bembo, Baldassare *Castiglione, and Jacopo *Sadoleto. The sack of Rome in 1527 put an end to these activities. In Florence, Ficino's academy was revived in 1540 by Cosimo I. The Welsh scholar William Thomas, who lived in Italy from 1544 to 1549, describes one of the meetings and concludes, "I never heard reader in school nor preacher in pulpit handle themselves better than I have heard some of these in the harangue" [*History of Italy* (1549) 139].

Later Italian Academies. The high standard of the early academies was not long maintained. From the 16th to the 18th centuries, academies for the discussion of literature and science proliferated in Italy. Oratory gave place to declamation and poetic contests attracted displays by ingenious poetasters. These literary clubs, each identified by its own badge or symbol, often adopted extravagant titles (e.g. Accademia degli Immobili, Florence, 1550; degli Oziosi, Naples, 1611; dei Fantastici, Rome, 1625), and members used fictitious names, often anagrams of their own. The reason for this may have simply been conceit, but it is not unreasonable to suppose that these harmless titles were intended to constitute some form of defense against possible charges of political or religious intrigue. Few of these academies survived the Napoleonic era. Their pretensions brought Italian literature into some disrepute both at home and abroad, and Giuseppe Baretti, a staunch defender of his country's institutions, had to admit that "arts and sciences are not generally forwarded much by our academies, as far as I can observe: yet they are upon the whole rather useful than pernicious, and answer the ends of society if not of science" [*An Account of the Manners and Customs of Italy* (1769) ch. 15].

In reaction against the mannerism and frivolities of these societies, the Arcadia was founded in Rome in 1690. A literary group that had met at the house in Rome of Queen Christina of Sweden decided at her death in 1689 to form a regular association, whose object was to rid Italian poetry of the excesses of *secentismo.* A set of statutes was adopted in 1696, and the first president, or *custode generale,* was Giovanni Mario Crescimbeni, who later published the history of the academy (1712). Under his leadership the members, each of whom assumed a pastoral name, held regular meetings on the Gianicolo, at which poetry contests were staged. Membership increased rapidly, and the academy enjoyed considerable patronage from the Church, notably from Clement XI (1700–21), who was styled "Pastore Massimo." Well over 100 branches were established throughout Italy and even abroad, and the *Rime,* or collections of verse, of the Arcadi were published in 13 volumes from 1716 to 1780. As the century progressed, the influence of the movement became steadily less, but the Arcadi were still active after the Napoleonic period. In 1925 Arcadia was renamed Accademia Letteraria Italiana, and occasional summer meetings are still held on the Gianicolo (*see* ARCADIANISM).

Origins of National Academies. The academies so far described were for the most part short-lived, but the same period saw also the beginnings of the more permanent institutions we know today. The Accademia della Crusca, founded by Antonfrancesco Grazzini in Florence in 1582, was intended specifically for the study of Italian literature and language, and it survives for this purpose today. As its name implies, it undertook to sift the true grain of the language from the husks. The result was the *Vocabolario degli Accademici della Crusca,* the world's first major dictionary (Venice 1612), now in its fifth edition (1863–1923. A–O only). The Accademia dei Lincei (Rome 1603), dedicated mainly to the study of science, was the ancestor of two present-day academies. After many vicissitudes, it was remodeled in 1826 by Leo XII and again in 1847 by Pius IX, only to be taken over by the Italian state in 1870, when it became the Accademia Nazionale dei Lincei. From the vestiges arose the present Pontificia Academia Scientiarum, known by this name since 1936.

In Spain and Portugal, a number of academies, modeled on the Italian, were established for short periods in the 17th century and later, though the movement did not develop to the same extent. Those in Spain most frequently mentioned are the Academia de los Nocturnos (Valencia 1591–94); the academy headed by Francisco de Medrano, which met in Madrid from 1617 to 1622 and numbered among its members Lope de *Vega, *Tirso de Molina, and *Calderón; and the Academia de los Anhelantes (Zaragoza *c.* 1628–53). Of the Portuguese academies, perhaps only the Academia dos Generosos (Lisbon 1649), the Academia dos Singulares (Lisbon 1663), and the Academia dos Anónimos (Lisbon, early 18th century) deserve note. The present national academies of these countries were founded also at this time. The Real Academia Española (Madrid 1714) has produced a dictionary, a grammar, and various editions of the Spanish classics, and is in correspondence with academies in Latin America. The Portuguese national academy, the Academia das Ciências de Lisboa (1779), has collaborated with the Academia Brasileira de Letras (Rio de Janeiro 1897) to produce an orthographic dictionary.

In France the place of the minor Italian academies was taken by the salons, which were not, however, the earliest assemblies of this nature. The oldest surviving academy is the Académie des Jeux Floraux (Toulouse), which has held contests for verse in both French and langue d'oc since 1323. It was granted the title of academy by Louis XIV in 1694, together with a set of statutes that fixed the number of members, or *mainteneurs,* at 40. (Outside France, a similar institution was the Jocs Florals de Barcelona, first held in 1393 and revived from 1859 to 1936. Political conditions at present do not favor a restoration. In Wales, *eisteddfodau,* or bardic contests, can be traced to the 10th century, and the National Eisteddfod has been held yearly since 1860, with contests in poetry, prose, drama, and music.) At Paris Jean Antoine de Baïf drew up statutes for an Académie de Poésie et de Musique, for which Charles IX granted him letters patent in 1570, but this academy ended with the death of the King in 1574. Its place was taken by the Académie du Palais, under Henry III, from 1576 to 1584. St. Francis de Sales founded the Académie Florimontane at Annecy in 1606 for the study of sciences and languages; but no records were kept and it is unlikely that it remained long in existence.

The most important academy in France, and the most generally renowned elsewhere, is the Académie Française. It grew from a small private literary circle that came under the protection of Richelieu and received letters patent from Louis XIII in 1635. Its task was to "donner des règles certaines à notre langue et la rendre pure, éloquent et capable de traiter les arts et les sciences." For this purpose it issued a dictionary in 1694 (now in its 8th edition, 1931–35), and a grammar, though this was not published until 1932. Its first publication was *Les sentiments de l'Académie Française sur la tragi-comédie du Cid* (1638), an adjudication in the literary controversy between *Corneille and Scudéry. It is now one of the five academies that together form the Institut de France. Membership is limited to 40 and is confined to those authors whose services to French literature are thought to be outstanding and to other persons of eminence in the life of the nation.

There are also numerous provincial academies in France, as well as a smaller number of private literary academies of which the Académie Goncourt is the most important. It was endowed by Edmond de Goncourt, who died in 1896, leaving a sum sufficient to provide an annuity for each of the 10 members and a prize of 5,000 francs to be awarded annually for a work of fiction. It was intended that the members should be young writers of promise, unlike the more mellow "immortals" of the Académie Française, which the irreverent tend to regard as a literary Valhalla. The Prix Goncourt is now one of the highest literary honors in France.

In Germany the triviality of the lesser Italian academies was not well viewed, though the merits of the various native *Sprachgesellschaften* have also been disputed. The first and most important of these was the Fruchtbringende Gesellschaft (Weimar 1617–80). Like the Accademia della Crusca its purpose was language reform. Germany now has several general academies (Akademien der Wissenschaften), including those founded at Berlin (1700), Munich (1759), and Leipzig (1846).

Other important academies of continental Europe are the Österreichische Akademie der Wissenschaften (Vienna 1847); Académie Royale des Sciences, des Lettres, et des Beaux Arts (Brussels 1772); Académie Royale de Langue et de Littérature Françaises (Brussels 1920); Koninklijke Nederlandse Akademie van Wetenschappen (Amsterdam 1851); Svenska Akademien (Stockholm 1786), which awards the Nobel prize; and Akademiya Nauk SSSR (Moscow 1725).

In Great Britain there is no strictly literary academy. During the 18th century fashionable hostesses attempted to introduce literary levées and salons, but their influence was small. After a tour of the Continent, Lady Anne Miller held a series of contests in *bouts-rimés* at her villa at Batheaston from 1775 to 1781. These were modeled upon the *giuochi olimpici* of the Roman Arcadia, but the Batheaston assembly could scarcely be called an academy. In his essay on "The Literary Influence of Academies" (*Essays in Criticism,* first series, 1865), Matthew Arnold put forward a case for the establishment in Britain of a body similar to the Académie Française, though he thought that the British genius would be better served by a rather less authoritarian tribunal. His plea was not heeded, but in 1901 the British Academy (240 fellows) was founded for research in the humanities. The Royal Society (London 1662), whose membership originally included men of letters, now deals exclusively with the sciences.

In the U.S. the most important early foundation was the American Academy of Arts and Sciences (Boston), established by act of Congress in 1779. Its purpose, according to its statutes, is "to cultivate every art and science which may tend to advance the interest, honor, dignity, and happiness of a free, independent, and virtuous people." A more recent institution is the American Academy of Arts and Letters, founded in New York in 1904.

Characteristics of Modern Academies. It will be seen from the foregoing that national academies are now very different from the early foundations. They have clearly defined constitutions and are generally divided into at least two classes, dealing respectively with the humanities and the various branches of science. Membership is limited and, being subject to election or appointment, is somewhat of an honor. Papers containing the results of research are published regularly in transactions or proceedings, and many academies also award literary prizes. Financial needs are met from trusts or public funds. With this means at its disposal an authoritarian government may well use the academy as an instrument of policy and even limit the freedom of expression of its members.

International collaboration between academies is a comparatively recent development. The Conseil International de la Philosophie et des Sciences Humaines, founded at Brussels (1949) under the auspices of UNESCO, is a coordinating body to which several international learned institutes are affiliated. Among them are the Union Académique Internationale, founded in 1919 to promote collaboration between academies concerned with humanistic learning, and the Fédération Internationale des Langues et Littératures Modernes (1928), which coordinates the study of modern literary history.

Bibliography: Details of modern academies are to be found in: *The World of Learning* (London 1947–). *Minerva: Jahrbuch der gelehrten Welt* (Berlin 1891–).

M. MAYLENDER, *Storia delle accademie d'Italia,* 5 v. (Bologna 1926–30). A. DELLA TORRE, *Storia dell' Accademia Platonica di Firenze* (Florence 1902). G. TOFFANIN, *L'Arcadia* (3d ed. Bologna 1958). Académie Française, *Trois siècles de l'Académie française* (Paris 1935). F. A. YATES, *The French Academies of the Sixteenth Century* (London 1947). W. F. KING, "The Academies and Seventeenth-Century Spanish Literature," PMLA 75 (1960) 367–376. J. SÁNCHEZ, *Academias literarias del Siglo de Oro español* (Madrid 1961).

[R. S. PINE-COFFIN]

ACADEMY, DEVELOPMENT OF

The term academy has been applied to a variety of educational institutions. In popular usage several types of secondary schools bear the title. In the new context of American educational history, the academy was a private or semipublic institution designed to meet the need for a practical preparation for life that the changing American economy demanded. It was a transitional institution, bridging the gap between the colonial Latin grammar school and the modern American high school and sharing some of the characteristics of each. Between 1750 and 1880, and spreading into every section of the country, the academy became the dominant secondary school in the interval between the Revolution and the Civil War. In curriculum and fees it catered primarily to the needs of a growing middle class.

History. The first type of secondary school in America was the Latin grammar school designed for boys of the so-called upper classes who planned to attend college or enter the ministry. A Renaissance product, the Latin school's curriculum was rigidly classical, and as such failed to meet the needs of the new nation with its rapidly expanding commerce and industry. Demands for a curriculum more adequately adapted to the affairs of practical living received a forceful response in Benjamin Franklin's *Proposals Relating to the Education of Youth in Pensilvania,* published in 1749.

These proposals set forth an elaborate plan for a new type of school, practical in aim and content, to be known as an academy. The plans took concrete form with the establishment of his model academy in Philadelphia, 1751. The philosophy of the late 17th-century sense realism found a channel of expression in Franklin's academy, which provided vocational training and a practical preparation for life in society, government, and the professions. He gave the study of the English language primary consideration. Mathematics; social studies, which included various aspects of history; geography; and natural science, also had a place in the curriculum. Greek and Latin, as well as modern languages, were not required but were taught to those who asked for them. Franklin introduced practical experiences in agriculture and work with machines and showed concern for the cultivation of manners and morals. He based his ethical standard, however, on the needs of human nature and society rather than on any appeal to religious sanctions. The Philadelphia academy was intended to provide a terminal program suitable for the commercial and productive classes. Tradition was strong, however, and Franklin's associates insisted upon a classical curriculum parallel to the realist program.

Franklin's educational views had a lasting impact upon the developing pattern of American education. They stimulated the movement toward universal education, they initiated the nonsectarian concept of secondary education; they weakened the hold of the classics; and obtained a foothold for practical subjects in the secondary school curriculum.

The academy movement spread rapidly. The two Phillips academies, at Andover, Mass., 1780, and at Exeter, N.H., 1781, respectively, were the first chartered academies in New England. Both put particular emphasis on the "great and real business of living." Within a comparatively short time, institutions similar to the Phillips academies were founded throughout the colonies from New England to North Carolina and, following the Westward movement, eventually appeared in every section of the country. The peak of growth was reached about 1850 when there were more than 6,000 schools of the academy type. They were not always designated as academies but were sometimes called seminaries, institutes, or halls.

Characteristics. Although the academies charged fees, they frequently received state, county, and local grants. Private donors also contributed to their support and many were richly endowed. States often gave grants of land. The state-chartered academies were generally nonsectarian in spirit and content and governed by self-perpetuating boards. Many academies were owned and managed by religious denominations; others by private stock companies. Most of the early academies were coeducational. Beginning with John Poor's academy for young ladies in Philadelphia, which was chartered in 1792, girls' academies flourished, and a number of them later developed into colleges for women. The curriculum of the academies proliferated with time. The classics, English, and, in girls' schools, domestic science courses were stable offerings. Methods of teaching and school management provided limited professional training for boys and girls before normal schools began.

Catholic Academies. Restrictions upon Catholics during the colonial period had greatly limited their educational efforts. Under the freedom guaranteed by the Constitution and the guidance of the hierarchy, Catholic higher education in the U.S. was initiated with the establishment of Georgetown College, which opened in 1791 (*see* GEORGETOWN UNIVERSITY). The same year saw the foundation of Georgetown Visitation Academy, a school for girls (*see* GEORGETOWN VISITATION CONVENT). This was the first of many similar institutions, whose growth kept pace with the increasing Catholic population. Academies for Catholic boys likewise multiplied. By 1852 Catholic schools offering education above the elementary level numbered 100 for girls and 47 for boys.

The curriculum of the Catholic establishments was similar in content to that of other contemporary academies with one exception. In aim, the Catholic schools adhered staunchly to the objectives of Catholic education. Religious and moral instruction was, therefore, the basic and integrating element of the entire program. The majority of academies were under the direction of religious communities of men or women. The contribution to American life of these early Catholic secondary schools is best seen in the lives of their students who took their places among the rank and file of American citizens.

The growth of academies fostered secondary education and broadened its popular appeal. Their demand for well qualified teachers also hastened the advent of normal schools. However, they continued to be restrained by tradition and failed to meet the needs of an expanding America. Although many still exist, toward the last decade of the 19th century they gave way to the modern American high school.

Bibliography: E. E. Brown, *The Making of Our Middle Schools* (New York 1903). B. FRANKLIN, *Proposals Relating to the Education of Youth in Pensilvania.* (facsimile reprint Philadelphia 1931). E. J. GOEBEL, *A Study of Catholic Secondary Education During the Colonial Period, up to the First Plenary Council of Baltimore, 1852* (New York 1937). R. F. SEYBOLT, *The Private Schools of Colonial Boston* (Cambridge, Mass. 1935); *The Public Schools of Colonial Boston 1635–1775* (Cambridge, Mass. 1935).

[R. MC LAUGHLIN]

ACADEMY OF AMERICAN FRANCISCAN HISTORY, research organization composed of Franciscan scholars interested in the contributions of Spain and Portugal to the development of the New World; established in 1944; located in the suburban area of Washington, D.C. It seeks to further understanding of the colonial background of regions of the U.S. once subject to Spain. The Academy has accumulated an extensive microfilm and microprint collection of the letters and other writings of Franciscan missionaries in North America. From this collection it translates and publishes important items such as the writings of Junípero *Serra and Fermín Lasuén. An important part of its work is the editing and publishing of historical classics such as the chronicles of Diego de Córdova and of Isidro Félix de Espinosa. The Academy publishes the *Americas,* a quarterly review devoted to the history and culture of Latin America. Each year it confers the Serra Award on a distinguished writer in the field of Latin American studies.

[F. KENNEALLY]

ACCA, ST., bishop of Hexham; d. Hexham, England, Oct. 20, 740 (feast, Oct. 20). A Northumbrian, he was fostered by Bosa (d. 705), who was afterward appointed bishop of *York (678), and he became the devoted disciple and companion of *Wilfrid. When the latter was reinstated at Hexham in 705, he made Acca abbot of St. Andrew's monastery there (*see* HEXHAM, MONASTERY OF). Acca succeeded Wilfrid as bishop of Hexham in 709. In addition to ruling the diocese with zeal, he concerned himself with the promotion of the liturgy in all its splendor by procuring the service of the cantor Maban (fl. 720), who had inherited the Roman tradition of psalmody of *Gregory the Great, brought to England by the monks of *Augustine of Canterbury. He completed, decorated, and richly furnished the churches begun by Wilfrid. He promoted learning, built and equipped a famous library, and, above all, encouraged *Bede, who wrote about him and dedicated several books to him. He was expelled from Hexham in 732 for some unknown reason; he sought refuge in Galloway but returned to die and be buried in his diocese.

Bibliography: BEDE, *Eccl. hist.* 5:19–20; ed. C. PLUMMER 1:330–332. M. CREIGHTON, DNB 1:56–57. J. GODFREY, *The Church in Anglo-Saxon England* (Cambridge, Eng. 1962), *passim.* A. S. COOK, "The Old-English Andreas and Bishop Acca of Hexham," *Transactions of the Connecticut Academy of Arts and Sciences* 26 (1924) 245–332. A. M. ZIMMERMANN, LexThK² 1:103. Zimmermann KalBen 3:200–203.

[C. MC GRATH]

ACCARON (EKRON), the most northern city of the pentapolis of the *Philistines. Though near the conflux of the borders of Juda, Dan, and Ephraim (Jos 13.3; 15.11; 19.43), it was not controlled by the Israelites (Jgs 1.18) until given to Jonathan by Alexander Balas in Machabean times (1 Mc 10.89). Accaron does not figure greatly in the OT. The captured Ark of the Covenant was brought there (1 Sm 5.10). After Goliath's death, the Israelites chased the Philistines into Accaron (1 Sm 17.52). Some of the Prophets denounced it and its sister cities (Jer 25.20; Am 1.8; So 2.4; Za 9.5, 7), perhaps because of its *Beelzebub worship (see 4 Kgs 1.2–6). It was one of the cities captured by *Sesac *c.* 917 B.C.; *Sennacherib's inscriptions (Pritchard ANET[2], 287–288) mention the capture of the city after its officials and patricians had rebelled against their King, Padi, who was loyal to Sennacherib. Padi later received some Judean towns from Sennacherib after the Assyrian invasion of Juda in 701 B.C. The exact site of the city is disputed. Recent identifications are modern *Qatra, 'Aqir,* and *Khirbet al-Muqanna',* all within several miles of one another on a line west of Jerusalem near the Mediterranean.

Bibliography: EncDictBibl 19–20. W. F. STINESPRING, Inter DictBibl 2:69.

[E. MAY]

ACCELERATION

Acceleration is an administrative provision that quickens the usual progression of instruction. Its purpose is to meet the need of the academically talented or gifted student to advance at his own speed. It is basically, therefore, a method of coping with individual differences.

Acceleration always has been an emotionally charged issue in American education. Until the 1920s educators generally held that pupils who had attained similar levels of educational achievement should be placed together and acceleration was common. With the growing concern for social adjustment, however, in the mid-1930s, acceleration fell into almost complete disfavor on the grounds that it caused social and emotional maladjustment, and pupils were grouped according to age rather than achievement.

In the 1950s there was a resurgence of interest in the very able pupil that received additional impetus from the advent of the space age. Previous research was reexamined and new investigations launched. Research in the 1960s can be succinctly summed up as consistently favorable to acceleration, since the claim that it is harmful intellectually, socially, or emotionally has not been proved valid.

Acceleration is feasible on all academic levels if properly planned. By its very nature, it is an individualized process and should take place only after all aspects of the student's development have been carefully appraised. Where such an approach has been used, research shows that the pupils involved maintained excellent records of achievement and sound adjustment following acceleration.

Procedures such as early admittance to kindergarten or first grade and the more common double promotion have proved sound educational practices during the elementary grades. This supports the recommendation that acceleration of no less than 1 year and probably no more than 2 is a satisfactory procedure for most bright students.

On the secondary level, accelerated students, especially when grouped, have been found to make faster progress without sacrifice of achievement or social relationships. In addition, acceleration can include courses that build up advanced college credit. This practice is especially effective when a strong guidance program fosters articulation between college and high school.

Advanced placement, early admission, and other acceleration procedures are more accepted on the college level than in the elementary and secondary schools. Although difficulties have been encountered, acceleration has generally found favorable reception in higher education.

Research since the 1950s has led experimentally oriented educators to conclude that pupils of similar social, physical, emotional, and intellectual maturity and achievement should be placed together and that acceleration can aid in accomplishing this end. That view, however, is not shared by the majority of teachers and administrators. Its adherents, moreover, hold that acceleration should be considered as one of several techniques recommended for the top 2 per cent of the student population, and then only when used in conjunction with other methods.

Bibliography: L. M. TERMAN et al., *Genetic Studies of Genius,* 5 v. (Stanford 1925–59). NEA, *Project on the Academically Talented Student* (Washington 1958–61) 12 monographs.

[H. C. SCHWEITZER]

ACCEPTANTS, members of the clergy, especially in France and in the Netherlands, who accepted the bull **Unigenitus,* dated Sept. 8, 1713, and known in France as early as September 25. At this time, in France, a pontifical declaration had no effect until after it had been accepted by parliament and the Assembly of the Clergy. Parliament discussed the bull *Unigenitus* on September 27 and 28. The opposition was led by Attorney General H. F. Daguesseau, who maintained that he saw in it proof of the fallibility of the popes, and parliament refused to endorse the bull, at least for the time being. The King then brought together the bishops present in Paris in an Assembly of the Clergy. The debates began on October 16. The Acceptants were immediately in the majority; supported by those in power and influenced especially by Cardinals A. G. de Rohan and H. de Bissy, they were nevertheless unable to attain unanimity and subdue their opponents, grouped around Cardinal L. A. de Noailles, Archbishop of Paris. Louis XIV, annoyed, sent the opponents to their dioceses and on Feb. 15, 1714, by a *lettre de cachet,* imposed on parliament the acceptance of the bull. In August 1714, 112 bishops had accepted it, while only 16 refused it. Some Acceptants retracted their submission in 1716, during the brief period in which the Regent was favorably disposed toward Jansenism; but shortly afterward the Acceptants again had the support of those in power, and the Archbishop of Sens, Languet de Gergy, assumed a leading position in the group. The victory was practically assured them after the royal declaration of March 24, 1730, which made the bull *Unigenitus* a law of the land.

See also APPELLANTS; JANSENISM.

[L. J. COGNET]

ACCESSUS. In order to expedite the papal election, each cardinal, immediately after an inconclusive ballot, was allowed an additional vote in favor of a candidate other than the one for whom he had voted in the ballot; such additional votes were added to those cast in the ballot in the hope of effecting a two-thirds majority. This procedure was known as *accessus,* i.e., acceding to the latter candidate. A cardinal could use this right of accessus only once after each ballot; after 1621 he could not use it in his own favor. The complications involved in ensuring that a cardinal did not use it in his own favor or in favor of the candidate for whom he had already voted in the ballot prompted St. Pius X in 1904 to abolish it, replacing it with a second ballot that should take place immediately after each morning and evening ballot.

See also CONCLAVE; POPES, ELECTION OF.

Bibliography: PIUS X, "Vacante Sede Apostolica" (apostolic constitution, Dec. 25, 1904), CIC, Document 1, par. 76. Pastor 27:117.

[B. FORSHAW]

ACCHO (ACRE), ancient Canaanite bay and city state north of Mount Carmel. The coastal plain of Accho (Heb. *'aqqô*) is about 4 miles wide and so protected by the mountains as to form one of the best natural harbors along the Palestinian coast. Modern Accho, or Acre (called by the Crusaders St. Jeanne d'Acre), has lost its importance to Haifa, located on the same plain a little farther south. Accho is mentioned several times in the Amarna, Egyptian, and Assyrian texts. The Israelites never succeeded in capturing it from the Canaanites, but descendants of the tribe of *Aser (Asher) dwelt in the surrounding region (Jgs 1.31–32). In the early 15th century B.C. it was conquered by *Thutmose III, and toward the end of the 14th century, by Seti I. *Ramses II desolated the town in the 13th century. In 701 B.C. Accho paid tribute to *Sennacherib, but it rebelled against *Assurbanipal (Ashurbanipal), who killed and deported many of its inhabitants (*c.* 640 B.C.). During the Hellenistic period the city, which was then known also as Ake, was renamed Ptolemais, probably in honor of Ptolemy II Philadelphus (285–246 B.C.), who enlarged and beautified it. Antiochus III, the Great (223–187), seized it from the Ptolemies. The town then became the leader of several Phoenician cities that harassed the Jews of Galilee (2 Mc 6.8; 13.24–25). About 165 B.C. Simon Machabee defeated the men of Ptolemais, but he could not capture their city (1 Mc 5.14–21, 55). Alexander Balas seized it from Demetrius I about 150 B.C. (1 Mc 10.1). At that time it was offered to Jonathan, but he refused it (1 Mc 10.56–60). According to Flavius Josephus (*Ant.* 13.12), Alexander Jannaeus attempted in vain to seize Accho. In 65 B.C. Ptolemais was incorporated into the Roman Province of Syria. St. Paul visited the Christian community in Ptolemais at the end of his third missionary journey (Acts 21.7). During the Crusades the city was the main port of entry to the Holy Land and the last stronghold to be surrendered to the Moslems.

Bibliography: A. LEGENDRE, DBSuppl 1:38–42. D. BALDI, Enc Catt 12:198–199. R. NORTH, LexThK[2] 1:238–239. Abel GéogrPal 2:235–237. EncDictBibl 20–21. O. CRUSIUS, Pauly-Wiss RE 1.1 (1893) 1171–73. N. MAKHOULY and C. N. JOHNS, *Guide to Acre* (2d ed. Jerusalem 1946).

[C. H. PICKAR]

ACCIAIOLI

A celebrated Florentine family whose name (spelled also Acciaiuli or Acciajuoli) derives from *acciaio* (steel), in which the family dealt in the Brescia-Bergamo area until Frederick Barbarossa's depredations against the Guelfs of Lombardy forced them to move into Tuscany. From the year 1161, when Guigliarallo Acciaioli settled in Florence, until his last male descendant died in 1834, the family was renowned for its merchants, bankers, scholars, statesmen, and patrons of the arts. Wealth amassed in their mercantile enterprises,

Cardinal Angelo Acciaioli, detail of his tomb by Donatello, in the Certosa in Florence.

which extended into North Africa and the eastern Mediterranean, became the capital for a lucrative banking business that counted kings and popes among its clients. The most important churchmen in the family were Angelo, Niccolò, and Filippo.

Angelo, cardinal, supporter of the Roman popes during the Great *Western Schism (1378–1417); b. Florence, April 15, 1340; d. Pisa, May 31, 1408. In 1375 he was named to the bishopric of Rapolla in the Kingdom of Naples by Gregory XI (1371–78), and in 1383 he was appointed archbishop of Florence by Urban VI (1378–89). During this period his eloquent defense of the Roman Pontiff against the pretensions of the Avignon claimant, Clement VII (1378–94), was rewarded by his elevation to the cardinalate with the titular see of S. Lorenzo in Damaso. In the papal election of 1389 Angelo was the choice of half of the cardinals, but he directed this support to Cardinal Pietro Tomacelli, who assumed the tiara as Boniface IX (1389–1404). The Pope entrusted Angelo with several difficult missions, especially that of assuring the accession of Prince Ladislaus to the throne of Naples and of Hungary, as well as conducting the young King's coronations at Gaeta and at Zara. Angelo restored peace between the Pope and the powerful Orsini family and settled ecclesiastical difficulties in Germany and in the Balkans. In common with other cardinals, hitherto unquestioningly loyal to the Roman pontiff, he concluded that a council was the only solution to the Western Schism and was attending a preliminary session of the Council of Pisa at the time of his death. His body was transferred to the Certosa in Florence in the 16th century.

Niccolò, cardinal, papal diplomat; b. Florence, 1630; d. Rome, 1719. Niccolò attended the Roman Seminary and completed his clerical studies at the Roman College, where he received a doctorate in law. Under Alexander VII (1655–67), Niccolò had charge of paying and equipping the militia of the Papal States. In 1667 he administered the papal treasury and 2 years later was made cardinal deacon of SS. Cosmas and Damian by Clement IX (1667–69). During the reign of Alexander VIII (1689–91), Niccolò, with the clumsy assistance of Cosimo III, Grand Duke of Tuscany, attempted to prevent the marriage of his nephew Roberto Acciaioli to Elizabeth Mormorai, a widow. When Elizabeth was forcibly placed in a convent, her fiancé delivered an uncomplimentary account of his uncle's part in the episode to each of the cardinals who had assembled to elect a successor to Alexander VIII. The embarrassing narrative did much to defeat Niccolò's otherwise excellent chances of election. In the conclave of 1700 Niccolò, who was identified with the "Zelanti," was again among the favored candidates but was ruled out of contention by the powerful "Imperialist" faction. For 12 years Niccolò served as papal legate to Ferrara, and in 1715, 4 years before his death, he was made bishop of Ostia and dean of the Sacred College.

Filippo, cardinal, papal nuncio to Portugal at the time of the expulsion of the Jesuits; b. Rome, March 12, 1700; d. Ancona, July 4, 1776. Filippo's first ecclesiastical appointment was as vice legate to Ravenna (1724), where he remained for 4 years. This was followed by other minor assignments until 1743, when he was made titular archbishop of Petra in Transjordan and sent to Lucerne as papal nuncio to Switzerland. In 1753 he was appointed nuncio to Portugal, where Sebastião *Pombal was beginning his campaign of vilification against the Jesuits. Filippo endeavored to refute or mitigate each charge against the society and kept Pope Benedict XIV (1740–58) informed of developments. Filippo was advised by Benedict to remain near the Spanish border so that he could escape if necessary and send or receive messages with less danger of their interception. Despite Filippo's efforts, all Portuguese Jesuits were either jailed or expelled in January 1759, 8 months before Filippo was elevated to the cardinalate by Clement XIII (1758–69), with the titular see of S. Maria degli Angeli. The following year he was ordered to leave Portugal. After his return to Rome, Filippo was made bishop of Ancona.

Bibliography: C. Ugurgieri della Berardenga, *Gli Acciaioli di Firenze,* 2 v. (Florence 1962). E. Santovito and A. Cattani, EncCatt 1:190–191. E. Sapori et al., EncIt 1:259–261. Espasa 1:967–971. F. Bock, LexThK[2] 1:103–104. Pastor, v.36, 37. G. Mollat and P. Richard, DHGE 1:263–265. A. D'Addario and G. Pampaloni, DizBiogItal 1:76, 82–83. P. Litta et al., *Famiglie celebri italiane,* 14 v. (Milan 1819–1923). **Illustration credit:** Alinari-Art Reference Bureau.

[R. F. COPELAND]

ACCIDENT

A word with various meanings in ordinary usage and with precise technical significations in law, philosophy, and theology. The term may mean generally a chance occurrence, or it may be used to describe a fall or collision, as in vehicular traffic, with or without personal injury. The adjectival form, moreover, is frequently used to refer to the less important or more superficial aspect of a thing or event. Different though these meanings may be, there is a common element among them. If used as *chance, accident contrasts with the stability of *order; if used as less important, accident contrasts with the essential or the necessary. The note of contrast, then, is implicit in most usages of the term. Its varied meanings are set over against a more basic, more important, usually more enduring reality that is implied in the very usage itself.

Ancient and medieval philosophers thus employed the term in enumerating accident among the *predicables and in contrasting accident with *substance. In their analysis, man is essentially what his substance is. While this substance remains unchanged, man remains. But man does change accidentally. He may gain weight, increase in size, become tanned in the summer, develop his knowledge, exercise his muscles, and move about from place to place in time. All of these changes are real. The essential sameness of man throughout change of this type indicates a difference of levels, that of independent and dependent, basic and proximate, fundamental and phenomenal, substantial and accidental.

When modern philosophers rejected substance and substituted phenomenon for accident, they eliminated any contrasting note from phenomenon. The phenomenon began to play the dual role of substance or *subject as well as the manifestation or appearance of that subject. Hence, the terms accident and phenomenon cannot always be read simply as translations of each other or as necessarily contrasted with their correlatives, substance and noumenon respectively (*see* NOUMENA; PHENOMENA). The context must be consulted before deciding how the term accident is being used by a particular author.

This article first discusses the historical development of the concept and then presents a systematic analysis that justifies its understanding in the Aristotelian-Thomistic tradition and explains its uses in Catholic theology.

Historical Development

The main stages in the evolution of the concept of accident include its origins in Greek philosophy; its development in the medieval period, particularly by St. Thomas Aquinas; and later formulations that led to the gradual rejection of the concept in modern and contemporary philosophy.

Greek Notions. The key to the historical development of the meaning of accident is the kind of relation an accident bears to a more fundamental subject. The relative and dependent character of accident was clearly taught by *Aristotle in his classic resolution of the Greek philosophical controversy over the fact and nature of *change. Accident was to substance as the superficial to the fundamental. But *Plato had prepared for the Aristotelian answer by asking in what sense being (εἶναι, οὐσία) could be predicated of things that were different, such as rest and motion. For Plato, the problem also centered on a plurality of predicates for one subject. In the *Sophist* (255C) he states that "of those which are, some are per se, and some are related to others."

Aristotle developed these insights. He says in his *Metaphysics* (1030a 20–23), "For as 'is' belongs to all things, not however in the same sense, but to one sort of thing primarily and to others in a secondary way, so too 'what a thing is' belongs in the simple sense to substance, but in a limited sense to the other categories." In contrast with οὐσία for substance as primary being, Aristotle used συμβεβήκος for accident. This Greek term connoted "going along with" or "occurring with" something else. For Aristotle, there were nine different ways, classes, or categories in which there was an "occurring with" the primary being, substance. These nine classes of accident together with substance constitute the ten *categories of being. When the Greek συμβεβήκος came to be translated into the Latin *accidens,* the latter's etymology of "happening" or "falling upon" accented the notion of relative and dependent; it also provided the form for the later English term.

Thomistic Concept. St. *Thomas Aquinas further emphasized the relative and dependent aspect of accidents. "In the definition of an accident something is placed which is outside the essence of the thing defined; for it is necessary to place the subject in the definition of an accident" (*In 2 de anim.* 1.1). The reason for this necessity is that accidents "do not have a perfect essence; whence it follows that they must admit into their definition the subject, which is outside of their genus" (*De ente* 2).

Essence of Accidents. Accident is said not to have a perfect *essence; yet it does have some kind of essence. Its very state of imperfection or of being a lesser essence emphasizes a dual character: its reality as distinct from substance and its dependence on substance. In the Aristotelian and Thomistic view, an accident has always a dependent mode of existence. An accident expresses more than itself in its very aspect of lacking independence: its referent is not size alone, but the size of something; not shape alone, but the shape of something.

Though having an imperfect essence, accident nonetheless has an essence and thus may be compared to substance. As essences, both substance and accident are alike in that they have a capacity for *existence. "In its own nature being is substance or accident" (*De nat. gen.* 2). Substance and accident are distinguished from each other by the precise, opposite modes of existence proper to each. The mode of existence proper to substance is *per se,* or independent, whereas that proper to accident is *in alio,* or dependent. "Similarly, 'to exist in a subject' is not the definition of accident, but on the contrary 'a thing which is due to exist in another' " (*In 4 sent.* 12.1.1.1 ad 2). What is properly characteristic of accident is its need or aptitude for existence in another. Even in the Eucharist, after the change of the substance of the bread and wine into the Body and Blood of Christ, the accidents of bread and wine do not cease to have aptitude for inherence in a subject; thus, although sustained by divine power, they never cease to be accidents (ST 3a, 77.1 ad 2).

In both the natural and supernatural orders, accident is within the order of *being, and it most properly is called a being of a being (*ens entis*) to emphasize its ever-present dependent mode. It is characterized also as a being *secundum quid* (i.e., relatively) in contrast with substance, which is a being *simpliciter* (i.e., absolutely). This latter contrast also emphasizes a development in the terminology of St. Thomas for substance and accident. In his commentary on the *Sentences,* he uses *res* (*thing) when speaking of substance or accident; in his later writings, however, his terminology indicates that substance and accident are principles within the order of being. Each is an essence, but only substance is perfect; accident is imperfect. By reason of the different status of their essence, they have differing capacities for existence. Substance is essence in its capacity for an independent, or *per se,* mode of existence. Accident is essence in its capacity for a dependent, or *in alio,* mode of existence. They are distinguished by their differing capacities for distinct modes of existence, while remaining interrelated as the dependent on the independent.

Distinct Existence of Accidents. This principle of distinction between substance and accident serves also to answer the controverted question of the distinct existence of the accident. The majority of St. Thomas's commentators, including *John of St. Thomas and T. de Vio *Cajetan, hold that in a thing there is one substantial existence with many distinct accidental existences. Some distinguished contemporary commentators, however, point to various passages in St. Thomas and advance their reasons for holding that the one substantial existence is also that whereby accidents exist [see R. G. Fontaine, *Subsistent Accident in the Philosophy of St. Thomas and in His Predecessors* (Washington 1950) 74–76]. The author of this article takes the position that substance and accident have distinct existences within the one concrete thing. The argument for this view may be put as follows: "An accident really exists as a modification of a really existent substance. Only in real dependence upon substantial existence can the accidental existence be had. An identical existence could not be really dependent and really independent in the same respect. The one has to be really distinct from the other" [J. Owens, *An Elementary Christian Metaphysics* (Milwaukee 1963) 159–160].

Thomistic Classification. In treating of the real distinction between substance and accident, one may easily create the false impression that there is but a single kind of substance and a single kind of accident. Actually, there are many specifically different substances, and it is the substance itself that specifies the difference. "For when we say that some substance is corporeal or spiritual, we do not compare spirituality or corporeity to substance as forms to matter, or accidents to a subject; but as differences to a genus. Thus it is that a spiritual substance is not spiritual through something added to its own substance, but is such through its own substance. In the same way, corporeal substance is not corporeal through something added to substance, but according to its own substance" (*De subs. sep.* 6).

In a somewhat similar fashion, accident in general is distinguished into ultimate classes or genera. Aristotle, Augustine, and Aquinas treat of the nine genera of accidents as classifications of real being. Of these nine genera, Aquinas observes that two points must be noted. "One is the nature belonging to each of them considered as an accident, which commonly applies to each of them as inherent in a subject, for the existence (*esse*) of an accident is existence in another (*inesse*). The other point to note is the proper nature of each one of these genera" (ST 1a, 28.2).

St. *Augustine has given examples of the nine genera. "When the question is asked, how large is he? and I say he is . . . four feet in measure, I affirm according to quantity . . .. I say he is white, I affirm according to quality . . .. I say he is near, I affirm something according to relation . . .. I affirm something according to position when I say he lies down . . .. I speak according to condition (*habitus*) when I say he is armed . . .. I affirm according to time when I say he is of yesterday . . .. And when I say he is at Rome, I affirm according to place . . .. I affirm according to the predicament of action when I say he strikes . . . and when I say he is struck, I affirm according to the predicament of passion" (*Trin.* 5.7).

A list of the predicamental accidents in more precise terminology would include *quantity, *quality, *relation, *action and passion, position in time (*quando*), *location (*ubi*), *situation (*situs*), and condition, or habit (*habitus*). It is well, however, to remember that "the original terms that Aristotle used to name the accidental categories were not substantive in form. . . . The proper designation of the category of quantity, for instance, was *to poson,* the quantitative. That of quality was *to poion,* the qualitative. Corresponding to these adjectival forms, adverbial and verbal forms were used to name the other categories. . . . 'the quantitative' helps keep in mind that it designates not something self-contained and as it were standing in its own right, but rather a way in which a substance happens to be" (Owens, 166).

Absolute and Intrinsic Accidents. Of these predicaments, quantity and quality are absolute accidents and the rest are relative. While each of the predicamental accidents is, as an accident, related to the subject or substance on which it depends, only the accidents other than quantity and quality put the substance in which they inhere into relation with other things. Quantity and quality alone modify the substance in itself, i.e., without further reference to other substances. Quantity confers *extension on corporeal substance. Quality modifies a substance, whether spiritual or corporeal, either in itself or in its operation. Both quantity and quality thus serve in an absolute or intrinsic way for the immediate grounding of relative or extrinsic accidents; these enable substance further to relate to other things and to manifest itself in a variety of ways.

Relative and Extrinsic Accidents. The accidents other than quantity and quality are sometimes designated as extrinsic, a term that serves to contrast them with the two intrinsic accidents. Just as all accidents are in a sense relative, because their very essence is to have aptitude for inherence in a subject, so too are all accidents in a sense intrinsic. A real accident of its very nature belongs to a substance, and in this way is intrinsic. Those accidents, however, that put their substance into relation with other substances are properly called extrinsic. Their role and function are directed outward toward other substances, even though the accident itself is rooted in the relating substance.

The most obvious of the extrinsic or relative accidents is relation. As real, predicamental relation is distinguished from the logical relation or the relation of reason, which exists only within the mind. As predicamental, it is distinguished from the transcendental relation, which is the very nature of some essence or principle as this relates to a complementary principle. Predicamental relation is a distinct reality by means of which the substance to which it belongs is related to another subject; its very essence is reference or order to another. Such a relation must be distinguished from the foundation that serves as the cause of relation. For example, the quality of tallness is the foundation for the real relation of *similarity between tall people.

The correlative accidents action and passion are related to the operation of an *agent, although each stands in different relation to that agent. Action is the second actuality of the creature at the operational level. Since it involves the exercise of *causality, it cannot be understood without an appreciation of the notion and reality of cause. Action is a further perfection of the agent, but it is extrinsically denominated by reference to the patient upon which the agent operates. Passion, on the other hand, is the accidental modification that the patient undergoes by receiving in itself the efficiency of the agent. Action and passion are really distinct categories, although both are intimately related to the *efficient causality of the agent.

Finally, there are four extrinsic accidents based on quantity. The accident "when" (*quando*) is sometimes, although incorrectly, identified with *time. Time is based on the reality of *motion, whose inner relationships provide the basis for the measuring or numbering in which time consists. Corporeal objects, existing in the changing world of time, have a type of accidental existence by reason of their temporal situation. "When" is thus a category of real being; it has extrinsic denomination from time as a measure.

Location in *place provides the basis for another category, the accident "where" (*ubi*). This inheres in a subject through its quantity, because of the circumscriptive containment of the subject arising from the surrounding quantities of other bodies.

The ninth category, situation or posture, is an accident presupposing the category "where," which it further determines by specifying the order of parts of the body in place. Being a passenger on the subway or bus would answer to the category "where," whereas the various stances one chooses or is forced to take on the vehicle as it becomes crowded are examples of the further determination that is situation or posture.

The tenth category, condition or habit (*habitus*), is the accident proper to a body by reason of something extrinsic and adjacent to it that does not measure it, as does place. An example would be "clothed," in which case the body that is the subject of the accident is denominated by something extrinsic to it, namely, clothing.

Later Conceptions. St. Thomas reconciled the unity of a thing with its many divergent characteristics, activities, and changes by acknowledging complexity within the structure of a finite thing. The unity is preserved through the uniqueness of a specific substantial nature with its proportioned substantial existence, which in turn allows for a variety of lesser perfections or accidents that have a basic exigency for inherence in the substance. Though having real status in the order of being, the accident is nonetheless a lesser being; as has been said, it is but a being of a being.

This delicate balancing of unity and plurality within the one concrete thing was not preserved by much of 14th-century scholasticism. The most prominent spokesman was *William of Ockham, who rejected any real distinction other than between thing and thing. "In creatures there cannot be any distinction whatsoever outside the soul, except where there are distinct things" (*Summulae in lib. phys.* 1.14). Renaissance scholasticism, in the person of F. Suárez, lost still more the Thomistic appreciation for unity within complexity. Suárez's distinctive teaching was that "being can be predicated absolutely and without qualification of the accident" (*Disp. meta.* 32.2.18).

The extreme view of the distinction of accident from substance that thus developed evoked opposing reactions in modern philosophy. Authors tended to suppress either the reality of accident or the reality of substance. Although it would be simplistic to ascribe these two tendencies solely to the teaching of Suárez, it may be noted that R. *Descartes and G. W. *Leibniz read him and that I. *Kant knew his teaching through the *Ontologia* of C. *Wolff. The more basic reason for these opposing tendencies in modern philosophy, however, lies in the differing epistemologies of *rationalism and *empiricism. Rationalism, by exalting the intellectual power of man, freed man's reason from dependence on the data of sense and ascribed to reason the power of attaining easily the essences of things. Empiricism, reacting against this abandonment of the sense origins of knowledge, so deeply immersed itself in the conditions of the empirical that it precluded any intellectual discovery of the substantial essence.

Thus Descartes opted for two kinds of substance, the bodily and the spiritual, each of which he really identified with its primary property, extension and thought respectively. All other properties he regarded as but varieties of the primary property. B. *Spinoza sought to resolve the basic problem of unity and plurality in things by considering the Cartesian extension and thought as two modes of a unique, infinite substance. Yet Spinoza carefully refrained from calling the modes accidents. All multiplicity and apparent finiteness, for him, are mere modifications of the two attributes of extension and thought that are characteristic of the one, infinite, divine substance.

J. *Locke opposed the innate ideas of Descartes but accepted the Cartesian criterion of truth as the clear and distinct idea. He applied the criterion of distinctness to the point of isolating empirical qualities from any known bond with the thing of which they were supposed to be qualities. Instead of stressing the interdependence and interrelation between quality and substance, he gave to each a separate and independent status. One may speculate what influence Locke's training in Ockhamist philosophy at Oxford had on this extreme separation of substance and accident.

Whereas Locke would allow that substance is at least an unknown support of qualities, D. *Hume, going further than G. *Berkeley in the rejection of material substance, could find no philosophical need for substance in any sense whatever. Restricting his knowledge to distinct perceptions, each of which he considered as existing independently, Hume in effect identified the accidental with the substantial. Since "every perception may exist separately, and have no need of anything else to support their existence, they are therefore substances, as far as this definition explains a substance" (*Treatise* 1.1.5).

Modern and contemporary philosophers have tended to repeat the position of Hume. A common view is that there is no need of substance to explain reality because everything that substance is supposed to contribute can be ascribed to phenomena. Hence, although Kant provided for the unknowable thing-in-itself, the noumenon, in contradistinction to the empirically known phenomenon, the more dominant theme in contemporary thought has been a rejection of substance.

Systematic Analysis

While many contemporary philosophers thus tend to disregard the distinction between substance and accident, and therefore to reject the concept of accident itself, this concept continues to be important in scholastic philosophy and theology. The following more systematic explanation may serve to justify the retention of the concept in philosophy and to outline its many important uses in Catholic theology.

Justification in Philosophy. The various philosophical positions with respect to accident in modern thought may be grouped under four headings, viz, (1) rationalist, (2) empiricist, (3) Kantian, and (4) contemporary scientific. Though differing superficially, these positions have much in common; moreover, they must all confront the perennial problem of reconciling unity and plurality as these are found in the concrete existing thing.

Rationalism, as exemplified in the thought of Descartes and Spinoza, really identifies substance and accident or substance and mode while accenting the reality of substance. Empiricism, as exemplified in Hume's formulation, rejects substance while ascribing to perceptions or phenomena the substantial mode of independent existence. Kantian criticism explicitly retains the unknown noumenon, or thing-in-itself, and the known phenomena that, together with the space-time forms within the knower, are materially constitutive of sensible intuition; with the noumenon unknown and unknowable, however, for all practical purposes only the phenomena are retained. Hence rationalism, empiricism, and Kantian criticism effectively retain only one ultimate level of reality. The same may be said of the contemporary scientific view; so far as it accords any objectivity to accident, it regards phenomena such as light, color, heat, and sound as various types of motion. Physical scientists and contemporary naturalistic philosophers speak of systems rather than of substance, although they continue to designate the entities and particles within their systems in terms once used to describe substance. Since this manner of thinking equivalently rejects a substance-accident dualism, it amounts to maintaining that matter and motion (or matter in motion) exist either independently or dependently—in other words, are either substances or accidents. Hence, the contemporary scientific position, like its three predecessors, reductively retains but one ultimate level of reality.

The basic issue is whether reality is sufficiently explained when only one level of reality is retained or whether the facts expostulate a radical dualism that accentuates the relatedness and dependence of realities at different levels. In effect, the philosophical problem may be stated either as the problem of substance or as the problem of accident. If substance is rejected, either theoretically or practically, its intelligible characteristics, both generic and specific, are transferred to the phenomena. But then what is to be said of the phenomena? A duality of levels of reality is denied while a term is retained, viz, phenomenon, whose etymological meaning is "that which appears or is manifest," and which itself connotes the presence of something else that does not appear or is not manifest. The same is true of the term accident, which means "occurring with" or "happening to" something else.

The resulting inference is more than a carry-over of Aristotelian prejudices that have been inherited along with a Greek-derived language. What it indicates is, rather, that the mind dealing with the data of experience recognizes two complementary, mutually related roles within a thing, one of which is dependent, the other independent. Plato sought answers to the problem that arises when one subject is considered to be the recipient of many different predicates. The full answer is more than the substance-accident dualism as elaborated by Aristotle, but this dualism is integral to the solution of the problem. As Aquinas has demonstrated, beneath such diversity there must be something basic, primary, and independent, for this alone can account for the unity that is known. The alternative is a meaningless regression to infinity. The basic and independent source of a thing's unity and the ultimate subject of all predication is substance (ST 1a, 11.1 ad 1).

Substance-accident dualism cannot be appreciated in any epistemology that severs the bond of relatedness between substance and accident and presumes to treat of either as though it were independent of the other. Original knowledge of substance and accident in any explicit way is a simultaneous recognition of the independent-dependent duality found in the things of experience. By a gradual process of increasingly perfected knowledge, the mind comes to know the precise characteristics of substance and of accident in general. Proper knowledge of the specific kind of substance, while varying in its degree of difficulty, corresponds to the perfection of knowledge of its accidents, for these both manifest the substance and are dependent on it.

Uses in Catholic Theology. A proper understanding of the nature of accident is of special importance for Catholic theology and doctrine. For example, a sound theological statement of the mystery of human and angelic supernatural participation in the divine life requires the utmost precision regarding the substantial and accidental orders, for only if this distinction is maintained can both the reality of the divine indwelling be preserved and the error of *pantheism be avoided. The meaning of created grace as a prerequisite for man's living union with God involves a new mode of accidental existence within man, while preserving intact man's essential humanity and God's transcendent deity.

Eucharistic Doctrine. The doctrine most commonly associated with philosophical teaching on substance and accident is that of the *Eucharist. Of this mystery, the Council of Trent declares: "This Council teaches the true and genuine doctrine about this venerable and divine sacrament of the Eucharist—the doctrine which the Catholic Church has always held and which she will hold until the end of the world, as she has learned it from Christ our Lord himself, from his Apostles, and from the Holy Spirit, who continually brings all truth to her mind. . .. The Council forbids all the faithful of Christ henceforth to believe, teach, or preach anything about the Most Holy Eucharist that is different from what is explained and defined in this present decree" (Denz 1635). "If anyone says that the substance of bread and wine remain in the holy sacrament of the Eucharist together with the body and blood of our Lord Jesus Christ and denies that wonderful and singular change of the whole substance of the bread into the body and the whole substance of the wine into the blood, while only the species of bread and wine remain, a change which the Catholic Church has most fittingly called transubstantiation: let him be anathema" (Denz 1652).

Four hundred years after Trent, Pope Pius XII stated in *Humani generis* (1950): "Some even say that the doctrine of transubstantiation, based on an antiquated philosophical notion of substance, should be so modified that the real presence of Christ in the Holy Eucharist be reduced to a kind of symbolism, whereby the consecrated species would be merely efficacious signs of the spiritual presence of Christ . . ." (Denz 3891). In 1965 some Catholic theologians continue to question the relevance of the substance-accident dualism for Eucharistic theology. They deny that the Council of Trent used substance as a technical philosophical term and maintain, on the basis of contemporary science, that fundamental changes within a thing, such as bread, are not substantial changes. Further, their argument calls attention to the fact that Trent did not use the term accident but the term species.

In reply, one must distinguish the scientific, the philosophical, and the theological levels involved in this questioning. The critique given for the rejection of substance-accident dualism by contemporary science and by modern philosophy may be taken on face value for purposes of argument. But one may add a further question: What evidence is there that contemporary scientists use the expression *substantial change in the same way as philosophers use it, especially scholastic philosophers whose terminology is a requisite for understanding the statements of the Council of Trent. As Pope Pius XII insisted in *Humani generis,* "the things that have been composed through common effort by Catholic teachers over the course of the centuries to bring about some understanding of dogma are certainly not based on any such weak foundation. These things are based on principles and notions deduced from a true knowledge of created things. . . . Hence, it is not astonishing that some of these have not only been used by the Ecumenical Councils, but even sanctioned by them, so that it is wrong to depart from them" (Denz 3883).

Historical Development. The fact is that the Eucharistic teaching of the Council of Trent represents a definitive formulation culminating the gradual growth of the Church's understanding of its traditional belief in the real presence of Christ in the Eucharist. The Fathers of the Church all taught that after the consecration Christ is truly present and that bread and wine are no longer present. Further statements seeking greater understanding of the mystery were a later development beginning with *Paschasius Radbertus, who in 844 published the first monograph on the Eucharist, *De corpore et sanguine Domini.* Paschasius raised the problem of the objectivity of the appearances of bread and wine while affirming the real presence of the Body and Blood of Christ. Two centuries later *Berengarius of Tours, maintaining that his position had the support of the New Testament and the Fathers, taught that the doctrine of the real presence and of substantial conversion is against reason. *Lanfranc, in his *De corpore et sanguine Domini,* replied: "We believe that the earthly substances . . . are converted . . . into the essence of the Lord's body, the species of the things themselves being preserved and certain other qualities." The teaching of Berengarius was condemned by several synods, including those at Paris, Tours, and Rome, and also by the

Sixth Council of Rome (1079) at which Pope Gregory VII required that Berengarius profess his belief that "the bread and wine . . . are substantially changed into the true, proper, and life-giving flesh and blood of our Lord Jesus Christ" (Denz 700; cf. 690).

From the middle of the 11th century onward, theologians used accident interchangeably for appearances, species, and qualities when dealing with the Eucharistic transformation of bread and wine into the Body and Blood of Christ. The term *transubstantiation was used by *Alan of Lille in his *Theologicae regulae* (*c.* 1200) to indicate the type of *change that is there taking place.

It remained for St. Thomas Aquinas to treat extensively of substance and accident as these relate to the intelligibility of statements concerning the Eucharist. By developing Aristotelian insights on the interdependent, but really distinct, character of substance and accident, and their simultaneous knowability through the natural functioning of the intellect in its dependence on the senses, Aquinas was able to formulate an acceptable accounting of the mystery of transubstantiation. The divine power in and after the consecration, in a manner transcending man's comprehension, sustains the real accidents of bread and wine without their connatural substances. Since the species of bread and wine are the natural objects of the senses and declare to reason the presence of bread and wine, the species serve as a sacramental sign; these require an act of faith in the presence of the Real Food, who is the living Christ physically present beneath the appearances. St. Thomas in his explanation uses the terms accidents and species interchangeably (ST 3a, 75.5).

The formulations of the dogma of the Eucharist as proposed by Trent should thus be understood against the background of their development within the living theology of the Church, which includes not only the work of the great scholastic theologians, but especially other conciliar teachings, such as those of the Councils of Rome, Constance, and Florence.

See also EUCHARIST (AS SACRAMENT); SUBSTANCE; ACT; FORM; QUALITY.

Bibliography: C. FERRO, EncFil 1:29–38. R. J. DEFERRARI et al., *A Lexicon of St. Thomas Aquinas* (Washington 1948–53) 1:9–10. R. E. MCCALL, *The Reality of Substance* (Washington 1956). L. DE RAEYMAEKER, *The Philosophy of Being,* tr. E. H. ZIEGELMEYER (St. Louis 1954) 195–204. C. A. HART, *Thomistic Metaphysics* (Englewood Cliffs, N.J. 1959) 215–239. M. M. SCHEU, *The Categories of Being in Aristotle and St. Thomas* (Washington 1944). A. J. OSGNIACH, *The Analysis of Objects* (New York 1938). C. DAVIS, "The Theology of Transubstantiation," *Sophia* (Melbourne, Austral. April 1964). H. B. GREEN, "The Eucharistic Presence: Change and/or Signification," Down Rev 83 (1965) 32–48. PAUL VI, "Mysterium fidei" (encyclical, Sept. 3, 1965), *The Pope Speaks* 10 (1965) 309–328.

[R. E. MC CALL]

ACCLAMATION, vocal approval, praise, felicitation, or, occasionally, denunciation of a person or action by a crowd, a legally constituted group, or a congregation. Although Eastern in origin, acclamation became common in the Roman Republic: the senate sometimes passed decrees by acclamation, and some emperors were elected by acclamation, e.g., M. Claudius Tacitus in 275; by this method *Fabian was chosen pope in 236, and *Ambrose of Milan became bishop in 374. In 451 the Council fathers at Chalcedon deposed by acclamation *Dioscorus of Alexandria for his part in the Robber Council of Ephesus. Acclamations were frequent at synods and councils, the coronations of kings, and the consecrations of bishops.

Liturgical acclamation in the early Church was probably borrowed from Jewish liturgy, but secular acclamations also influenced ritual usage. Liturgical acclamations usually refer to the collection of brief formulas that express desires, affirmations of faith, invocations, or petitions used in the divine service, such as the litanies, the reproaches of Good Friday, and doxologies. Acclamation is a valid form of papal election and occurs when the cardinal electors, without previous consultation or the formality of balloting, unanimously proclaim a candidate supreme pontiff.

Bibliography: F. CABROL, DACL 1.1:240–265. A. MOLIEN, *Catholicisme* 1:72–73. B. OPFERMANN, LexThK[2] 1:238. PIUS XII, "Constitutio apostolica de sede apostolica vacante," ActApS 38 (1946) 85–86.

[P. W. HARKINS]

ACCLAMATIONS

The term principally designates the musical salutations addressed on a variety of ceremonial occasions to the Byzantine emperor, his family, the patriarch of Constantinople, and other dignitaries of Church or state. The antecedents of these acclaims may be found in the imperial ceremonies of pagan Rome. Under Nero and his successors the spontaneous cheering of the crowd at the appearance of the emperor in the circus was supplanted, or at least supplemented, by organized applause, in which certain phrases became standard formulae; it also became the practice of the Roman Senate to hail the emperor, upon his entrance, with various ritual expressions. In similar fashion the Byzantine emperors attending the Hippodrome at Constantinople were greeted with hymns and panegyrics by the alternating choirs of the Blue and Green factions; and the emperor-salutations preserved in the records of the Church councils seem the lineal descendants of the old Senatorial acclaims—with the difference that, here, the Christian God is invoked as the One who is to preserve the ruler in his holy kingdom. A particularly common formula of acclamation is that which wishes the emperor a long life; such a formula would begin with the word *Polychronion* (long-lasting)—which thus became the term designating the entire genre—and conclude with the phrase "for many years," used also independently as a short form of acclamation.

The earliest full account of the Byzantine acclamations and their manner of performance is provided by Emperor Constantine VII Porphyrogennetus (913–959) in a book describing the court ceremonies of his time—though it is probably in large part a compilation from older sources. Acclamations, it appears, were performed by different bodies of singers according to the nature of the occasion: at secular ceremonies (receptions and the like) they were sung by a group of laymen of the court, known as *kraktai*; on religious occasions, as in acclaiming a high ecclesiastic, the singers were clerics, called *psaltai.* In either case the usual mode of performance was antiphonal: the choir was divided into two alternating groups, each with its leader. Instruments were regularly used in the court performances, but were forbidden in the church save for rare exceptions, e.g., Christmas Eve, with the emperor attending church, when the *kraktai* and *psaltai* together with various instruments (trumpets, horns, etc.) united in performing the imperial acclamations.

Music for these acclamations is preserved only in late sources, none earlier than the 14th century; the melodic tradition there recorded may, of course, be much older than the documents themselves. The musical style tends to be fairly florid, particularly in the setting of the words "many years"; however, the portion of text that simply names the emperor and enumerates his various dignities is recitationlike in character.

Acclamations were used on a great variety of occasions—not only coronations, but royal visitations, seasonal feasts such as the blessing of the grapes, promotions of court functionaries, etc.—so long as the empire survived. After its fall, their function was restricted to the celebration of ecclesiastical dignitaries. The common position in the liturgy for episcopal acclamation was at the procession with the Gospel Book, a part of the opening ceremonies of the Mass.

There exists a Western counterpart to the Byzantine imperial acclamations: the *laudes regiae* (royal praises), a formulary that makes its first appearance in the Gallican ritual in the second half of the 8th century, in conjunction with the Litany of the Saints, to which it is in many formal respects analogous. Its use thereafter in the Middle Ages, in a diversity of connections and forms, was widespread; vestiges of it have remained in the acclamations for popes and certain secular rulers of modern times. Musical settings of the *laudes* are preserved in medieval MSS dating from the 10th century onward. While they differ in many points of individual detail, it may be said in general that the style is simple rather than ornate, with extensive use of a reciting tone.

Bibliography: Wellesz ByzMus. H. J. W. TILLYARD, "The Acclamation of Emperors in Byzantine Ritual," *Annual of the British School at Athens* 18 (1911–12) 239–260. *Constantin VII Porphyogénète: Le Livre des cérémonies,* ed. and tr. A. VOGT, v.1 (Paris 1935), v.2 (Paris 1939–40). J. HANDSCHIN, *Das Zeremonienwerk Kaiser Konstantins und die sangbare Dichtung* (Basel 1942). E. H. KANTOROWICZ, *Laudes Regiae: A Study in Liturgical Acclamations and Mediaeval Ruler Worship* (Berkeley 1946). F. CABROL, "Acclamations," DACL 1:240–265. E. PETERSON, Εἷς Θεός: *Epigraphische, formgeschichtliche und religionsgeschichtliche Untersuchungen* (Göttingen 1926). H. HUCKE, "Eine unbekannte Melodie zu den *Laudes regiae*," *Kirchenmusikalisches Jahrbuch* 42 (1958).

[I. THOMAS]

ACCOLTI, MICHAEL, Jesuit missionary; b. Conversano, Italy, Jan. 29, 1807; d. San Francisco, Calif., Nov. 7, 1878. Both of his parents were of ancient and noble families. In 1830 he was appointed to the Pontifical Academy of Noble Ecclesiastics in Rome and enrolled for 2 years. He then entered the Jesuit novitiate of Sant' Andrea in Rome, and was ordained on Sept. 24, 1842, in the Basilica of St. John Lateran. A year later he was assigned to accompany a group of Jesuits led by Pierre *De Smet to work among the Flathead Indians in the Northwest of North America.

Accolti spent several years working in Jesuit missionary stations in Oregon. With the discovery of gold in California by James Marshall on Jan. 24, 1848, the rapid increase in population there made the need for priests imperative. Accordingly, Accolti and a companion, John *Nobili, arrived in San Francisco on Dec. 8, 1849, marking the first return of the Society of Jesus to California since its expulsion in 1768 from the lower, or Mexican, part of the area.

Within a few months Accolti was recalled to Oregon as superior of the Jesuits of the Northwest. Because he was convinced of the need to establish the Jesuits permanently in California, he went to Rome in 1853 and secured from the father general, Peter Beckx, a decree (1854) assigning the Jesuit effort in the Oregon country and California to the care of the Italian Jesuit province of Turin. This arrangement ensured a flow of manpower to the missions confided to Accolti. In 1855 he was relieved of his office of superior in Oregon and returned to San Francisco, where he assisted Anthony Maraschi, SJ, to found St. Ignatius College (later University of *San Francisco). From 1860 until his death he served alternately in San Francisco and at Santa Clara College (later University).

Bibliography: G. J. GARRAGHAN, *Jesuits in the Middle United States,* 3 v. (New York 1938). J. W. RIORDAN, *The First Half Century of St. Ignatius Church and College* (San Francisco 1905).

[J. B. MC GLOIN]

ACCOLTI, PIETRO AND BENEDETTO, members of a Tuscan family notable for its ecclesiastics and poets.

Pietro, cardinal of Ancona; b. Florence, March 15, 1455; d. Rome, Dec. 12, 1532. In 1505 he was consecrated bishop and received the See of Ancona. Pope Julius II made him a member of the college of cardinals on March 17, 1511. Leo X placed Cardinal Accolti in charge of the papal letters during his pontificate, and in this capacity he drew up *Exsurge Domine,* which condemned Martin Luther on 41 accounts of heresy. In keeping with the pluralism of the times, Cardinal Accolti held the bishoprics of suburban Albano and Sabina, and the Sees of Maillezais, Arras, Cadiz, and Cremona. In 1524 Clement VII bestowed upon him the archbishopric of Ravenna. The cardinal resided in Rome during the last years of his life. He was survived by his brother Bernardo (1465–1536), who gained considerable fame as a poet. Because of confusion with respect to the Accolti family in the 15th and early 16th centuries, Pietro has been mistaken for his nephew Benedetto.

Benedetto, cardinal-archbishop of Ravenna, papal secretary; b. Florence, 1497; d. there, Sept. 21, 1549. Benedetto, the son of Michele Accolti, was named cardinal in 1527 by Clement VII. Much of the confusion resulted from the granting of several of the bishoprics held by Pietro to Benedetto upon his uncle's death. Furthermore, Benedetto has been identified also with the 15th-century jurist and historian who bears the same name (Benedetto Accolti, 1415–66). Cardinal Benedetto Accolti made a reputation as a poet and defender of papal rights in the early years of the Protestant revolt.

Bibliography: A. POSCH, LexThK^2 1:104–105. P. RICHARD, DHGE 1:270–271. P. CIPROTTI and G. SANITÀ, EncCatt 1:199–201. Pastor v.7, 9–12, *passim.* G. B. PICOTTI, *La Giovinezza di Leone X* (Milan 1928). G. K. BROWN, *Italy and the Reformation to 1550* (Oxford, Eng. 1933). E. P. RODOCANACHI, *Histoire de Rome: Le Pontificat de Léon X* (Paris 1931).

[J. G. GALLAHER]

ACCOMMODATION

Adaptation of the divine to the possibilities of man and the conditions of his existence. There is doctrinal accommodation and practical (liturgy and rule of life), pedagogical (the active subject of accommodation, knowing perfectly its object, presents it gradually to the passive subject, individual or group, according to its mental and moral development) and evolutive (in accommodating doctrine or practice to new ideas, mentalities, and situations, the knowledge of doctrine or the meaning and form of practice are thereby further developed).

Pedagogical accommodation is a gradual initiation into the mysteries of faith and the sacramental cult. In matters of doctrine it means to teach provisionally only a part of the *truth or to give it a simplified or imaginative expression in order to secure an easier apprehension and a readier acceptance. Its catechetical necessity at home and in the missions is self-evident. Hence it was practiced from the beginning by Christ and the Apostles (Jn 16.12; Rom 6.19; 1 Cor 3.1, 2; 9.19–22).

In the theology of revelation accommodation means that revelation is adapted to the general human condition. Salvation through Christ and the sacramental Church is adapted to the condition of a being that by nature ascends to the invisible by means of the visible. Revelation is also adapted to the changing historical situations. It is an old Christian idea that the method of revelation is an economy, a presentation adapted to the mental and moral capacities of the recipient. From beginning to end it proceeds on the principle of clarifying development (*see* ECONOMY, DIVINE). Some Protestant theologians of the 18th century expounded the view that Christ and the Apostles did not share the contemporary beliefs of Judaism but used them as a means of accommodating revelation to the Hebrew mind. They often proceeded to a far-reaching demythologization: messianism and eschatology, angels and devils, sacrifice and atonement were explained as Jewish thought-forms.

Nowadays one is rather inclined to think that the Apostles and even Christ in His acquired human knowledge did share those contemporary ideas that they assumed in their preaching. To be a man is not only to have a soul and a body, but also to be present through the body to a human and historical world. True humanity involves a conscious life marked by historicity. Therefore, if the doctrine of faith is revealed truth, the historical thought-forms in which it was given must express it truly, however much they may be inadequate and consequently subject to a process of explicatory development.

Besides the idea of historicity another modern idea contributed to a dialectical conception of divine accommodation: a revelation can be apprehended and assimilated by a human mind only if it meets there with a previous existential questioning, however dim and unuttered, and if its expression is sufficiently prepared in human language that is the reflection of self-questioning existence. Historical revelation, then, is a dialogue in which the word of God falls in with the existential self-questioning of His chosen people, bringing that questioning itself to fuller consciousness and provoking answers leading to new experiences and questions, which in return prepare the moment for a fuller revelation. In this manner historical existence and revelation form a dialectical unity: from the nature of the human recipient revelation could not but be progressive, and revelation in return progressively educated the receptivity of Israel.

The same basic principles explain the nature of ecclesiastical accommodation. If human thought is of such a nature that even absolute truth can be apprehended by it only in historical thought-forms, it follows that, once historical revelation is closed, man's understanding and expression of it must nevertheless continue to develop. Ecclesiastical accommodation has a twofold dimension: time and space. Every form of ecclesiastical life, doctrinal as well as liturgical and pastoral, must be continually retranslated into the actual forms of human thought and language, of common sensibility and social life. The reason is obvious: in all its aspects human reality, so far as it is human, is the outcome of a self-creating activity. It is culture, not nature. History is not the account of what happened to an unchangeable man but an account of the changes by which man makes, perfects, or deteriorates the excellences that constitute his self-realization. Nothing can stop that process because it is mankind itself in the exercise of its being. To refuse accommodation is to become out of tune with living humanity and to lose gradually all real influence on human life.

For the same reason contemporary ecclesiology and missiology begin to proclaim the necessity of a far more radical accommodation of the Church to the differences offered by the great cultural areas of man's globe. If realized humanity is culture, not nature, then the great cultures that divide humanity are not extrinsic differentiations of a human being that is everywhere the same, but intrinsic modes of human self-realization that permeate and characterize the whole of human existence. Therefore it is now theoretically clear, as it has been proved long since by practice, that the Church cannot become firmly rooted in the great non-Western cultures without a far-reaching accommodation of its doctrinal, liturgical, and social self-expression.

From the special viewpoint of ecclesiology it should be added that the *unity of the Church, perfectly incarnated in the multiplicity of existing cultures, is the true and full manifestation of its *catholicity.

See also APOLOGETICS; APOLOGETICS, PRACTICAL; DOCTRINE, DEVELOPMENT OF; MISSIOLOGY; PREEVANGELIZATION; REVELATION, THEOLOGY OF; SYMBOL IN REVELATION.

Bibliography: Surveys. J. NEUNER and K. MÜLLER, LexThK[2] 1:240–244. T. OHM, Fries HbThGrdbgr 1:25–30. Y. M. J. CONGAR, *Catholicisme* 5:775–782. A. MULDERS, *Missiologisch bestek* (Hilversum 1962) 301–316. FR. OPTATUS, *Katholiek archief* (1953) 265–312. H. OTT, ThRu 21 (1953) 63–96. Studies. J. DANIÉLOU, *Essai sur le mystère de l'histoire* (Paris 1953). P. RICOEUR, *Histoire et vérité* (Paris 1955). G. VOSS, *Missionary Accommodation* (pa. New York 1947). *Missions et cultures non-chrétiennes* (Semaine de missiologie de Louvain 29; Louvain 1959).

[J. H. WALGRAVE]

ACCREDITATION, EDUCATIONAL

The recognition granted to an educational institution by a competent professional, state, or regional agency to indicate that the institution has met the accrediting agency's requirements and standards of quality.

Historical Background. A unique feature of education in the U.S. is the absence of Federal control. The Constitution does not specifically include education among the responsibilities of the Federal government. In accordance with the 10th Amendment to the Constitution, this power rests with the individual states, or the people at large. Each state has, consequently, established its own system of public education and has made provision for the recognition and chartering of private institutions.

To remedy the lack of authorized, universal educational standards, in 1910 Congress created the post of specialist in higher education within the Bureau of Education. The specialist's first move was to establish as a criterion of excellence the ability of an institution to prepare students for graduate study (as indicated by the records of its students in graduate schools) and on this basis, to prepare a tentative list of approved colleges to be submitted to the universities for their evaluation. This list was suppressed Feb. 19, 1927, by an executive order of the President. This incident is of interest to educators for two reasons: (1) it represents the initial use of a purely qualitative factor in the evaluation of educational institutions; (2) it marks the closest approach to centralized Federal control of education in the history of the U.S.

Although in 1953 the Federal government created an Office of Education in the Department of Health, Education, and Welfare, its administrative functions are limited to the expenditure of funds appropriated by Congress for the maintenance of colleges of agriculture and mechanical arts (land-grant colleges) in the several states and in Puerto Rico. The office also conducts investigations of special educational problems, disseminates information, and acts as a clearinghouse for educational groups or individuals. It has not controlled education, nor has it made any move in this direction. On the other hand, evaluation of academic institutions on the basis of qualitative standards has steadily progressed into the 1960s.

State Systems of Education. In 1820 the humanitarian movement took up the cry "free schools for all children." With the advent of free schools came compulsory school attendance laws and the necessity to decide what schools to attend to fulfill the law. Thus several states became approving agencies, thereby precipitating the movement to develop state systems of education. New York, by establishing the first state office of education in 1813, became the first so-called accrediting agency. Others followed, with Maryland in 1825, Vermont in 1827, Pennsylvania in 1833, Michigan in 1836, and Massachusetts in 1837. By 1850 free schools, chiefly elementary and secondary, under state control were general in the northern and middle eastern states.

Each state has its state superintendent of public instruction, with the trend moving away from local township responsibility toward a county system of organization and stronger state supervision. States and towns had long since established normal schools and teachers colleges, the former giving way to the latter. Nearly all states and some cities had universities that include college, graduate, and professional schools; while after the 1950s there was a sweeping movement in towns and counties to establish junior or community colleges.

State Accreditation. As the states became more interested in developing complete educational systems through graduate and professional levels, they became more concerned with setting up standards for institutions of all types and in establishing agencies of control for all education within their borders. They recognized that accreditation would serve to promote high standards of education in the arts and science, in professional preparation, and on all levels of instruction; to inform the public regarding the quality of educational programs; to facilitate the transfer of students from one institution to another; to encourage experimentation and self-evaluation in institutions of higher learning; to secure competent scholars and teachers and adequate facilities; and to protect educational institutions from political interference.

The State of New York is unique in the strength of its centralized control of all educational enterprises within its borders and its influence on education outside its boundaries. By maintaining lists of approved institutions many states control all intrastate education at a level of excellence regularly lower than that of private accrediting associations. The majority of states, in order to facilitate the transfer of students and to enforce compulsory school attendance laws, have set up approved lists of elementary and secondary schools and thus exercise some measure of control over education up to the college level. In states such as California and Michigan, the actual approval of institutions is effected by the state university, which thereby becomes the powerful center of control. In other states, such as Wyoming and Mississippi, the state department of education cooperates with the state university in maintaining supervision over education. In others, college associations within the state conduct the necessary accrediting procedures.

In general, it may be said that the departments of education of the several states are the approving agencies for elementary and secondary schools, and the state universities for institutions of higher learning. The trend, however, is toward state department of education, rather than state university approval.

Regional Accreditation. In the absence of a central national control and in view of state organization of systematic supervision on a comparatively low academic level, colleges and universities began to form associations of their own. Their main purpose was to discuss common problems and to form lists of approved secondary schools and institutions of higher learning in order to facilitate both the admission of college freshmen and the acceptance of transfer students from other institutions of equal standards. By 1900 associations of colleges and secondary schools in various regions were well established and for the most part functioning effectively.

The New England Association of Colleges and Secondary Schools, established in 1886, did not at first regard itself as an accrediting agency, nor in general operate as one until 1954. The Middle States Association of Colleges and Secondary Schools, which extends its services to Puerto Rico and some foreign countries, was organized in 1887 and since 1950 has done the most to improve the process of accreditation. The North Central Association of Colleges and Secondary Schools, established in 1895, has been of great influence within its own region and has been a leader for other approving agencies in developing improved techniques for evaluating schools and colleges. This association more than any other has influenced approving agencies generally to break away from purely quantitative measurements and to turn to measuring the worth of an institution largely through a study of its product and the success with which it attained its aims. The Southern Association of Colleges and Secondary

Schools, established in 1895, became an important factor in improving educational opportunities throughout the South, and especially in establishing teachers colleges and teacher-training centers. The Northwestern Association of Secondary and Higher Schools (1917) and the Western Association of Schools and Colleges (1924), which became an accrediting body in 1948, are of comparatively recent date, but since 1950 have taken their places with the older and more experienced groups.

On a nationwide scale is the Association of American Universities, a North American group of universities mainly interested in graduate studies. Membership is determined by the quality and extent of work accomplished by the graduate department and limited to institutions elected by the association.

The youngest of the accrediting agencies, the National Commission on Accrediting, was formed in 1949 in protest against apparent abuses and the accrediting procedures, practices, and policies of professional accrediting agencies. The commission succeeded in reestablishing order and in pointing the way to the solution of many problems inherent in accreditation.

Despite certain limitations and the thorny problems inherent in the establishing of criteria and procedures, educational accreditation has greatly contributed to raising academic standards on both secondary and higher educational levels. By promoting a shift from purely quantitative or measurable standards to qualitative criteria, accreditation procedures jolted educational institutions out of the rut of complacency and lit a new spark of endeavor in the direction of academic excellence. By emphasizing objectives, rather than policies and procedures, accrediting agencies encouraged self-studies and analyses that enabled the institutions to view critically and objectively their own strengths and weaknesses and led to greater diversity and flexibility in curricula and methods.

A more recent trend in the 1950s, an outgrowth of the self-evaluative process, is to substitute a purely supervisory role for one of service: to offer consultative assistance when needed; to act as a clearinghouse for institutions engaged in self-study; to provide the joint cooperative inspection of several accrediting agencies in order to render the best possible service according to need.

Bibliography: Catholic University of America, Workshop on Administration in Higher Education in Relation to Self-Evaluation and Accreditation, 1958, *Self-Evaluation and Accreditation in Higher Education*, ed. R. J. DEFERRARI (Washington 1959). J. F. NEVINS, *A Study of the Organization and Operation of Voluntary Accrediting Agencies* (Washington 1959). W. K. SELDEN, *Accreditation: A Struggle over Standards in Higher Education* (New York 1960).

[R. J. DEFERRARI]

ACCUSATION, commonly, the act of charging one with a fault or offense (from the Latin *accusare,* to call to account).

In moral theology accusation can be either evangelical (*see* CORRECTION, FRATERNAL) or judicial; the latter is the type of accusation considered here. Public officials, who have been appointed for the preservation of the common good, are obliged, more or less gravely, depending on the possibility of injury to the community resulting from silence, to make accusations against those who violate the law. Such officials, if bound by oath to the fulfillment of their office, are the more gravely obliged. However, such oaths of office are generally understood to impose no graver obligation than is proportionate to the importance of a case and to its bearing on the common good.

Private individuals also may be bound to accuse violators of the law. Every member of society is obliged to come to the aid of the society when peace and order are endangered. There are times when this duty makes it seriously obligatory to accuse criminals. For example, to keep silent when one has information about persons who are a threat to the community's peace can be a grave sin. Duty to oneself or one's family may also indicate an obligation to lodge an accusation against a wrongdoer. Apart from obligations in justice, anyone may be gravely obliged in charity to save another from a grave evil, especially if this can be done without serious inconvenience to self.

Bibliography: Prümmer ManThMor 2:159.

[J. D. FEARON]

ACEDIA

Acedia, more commonly called sloth through confusion with its most notable effect, is a disgust with the spiritual because of the physical effort involved. If the spiritual good from which acedia recoils has a necessary connection with the divine good, which should be the subject of Christian joy, it can be a sin, and even serious. Moreover, acedia is one of the capital sins, a common distraction from virtue, producing other, even quite distinct, sins.

The word describing this constant human phenomenon is found not only in the Septuagint Bible (e.g., Sir 6.26) but in Greek and Latin pagan authors; etymologists show that the word should not be derived from Latin *acidus* but from the Greek α-κήδος (not caring). Whatever its possibly Stoic origins may be, the psychology of the temptation received most careful attention from the desert fathers of the 4th century, who discussed it in the context of other evil thoughts as the *daemon meridianus* (Ps 90.6). Evagrius Ponticus in 383 seems to be the first to have written a description of acedia in his *De octo vitiosis .cogitationibus* (PG 40:1274), obviously drawing more from actual experience than literary antecedents. The loneliness of the hermitage in the barren desert, a body worn out by fasting, and a mind fatigued by long prayers were conditions calculated to bring on the ennui and restlessness that was called acedia. John Cassian faithfully reported this fairly common trouble to the West in his *On the Spirit of Acedia* (Conferences 10; PL 49:359–369). The description of Cassian luxuriates in psychological detail, showing that acedia can express itself not simply in laziness but even in nervous activity. Evagrius, Cassian, and in fact the entire Oriental tradition had spoken of melancholy (λυπή) as a distinct sin though closely connected with acedia. St. Gregory the Great in his commentary of Job (*Moralia* 31.45; PL 76:620) omitted acedia from his list of principal sins and included only sadness (*tristitia*). Nevertheless, as later commentators have pointed out, in one respect the more ancient tradition—the use of the word acedia, or its corruption *accidia*—prevailed. Moreover six "daughter-sins" are for the first time explicitly named in connection with this melancholy: malice, rancor, pusillanimity, despair, torpor concerning commandments, and a wandering of the mind around forbidden things. Finally, St. Gregory, or at least the Gregorian pastoral tradition, is responsible for the removal of acedia from its original context in which it was a special temptation for monks, and for viewing it as an interior malaise that expressed itself most frequently in a tardy and slothful performance of religious and other duties (cf., e.g., Rabanus Maurus, *De ecclesiastica disciplina,* PL 112:1251–53; Jonas of Orleans, *De institutione laicali* PL 102:245–246; Alcuin, *Liber de virtutibus* c.32, PL 101:635; St. Antoninus, *Summa theologiae moralis* 2.10:933–938).

St. Thomas Aquinas opposed acedia to the joy of charity, and in a precise study demonstrated its sinfulness by showing the evil of sadness over a genuinely good object and likewise the excessiveness of even legitimate sorrow when it impedes the performance of duty. The specificity of acedia St. Thomas sees in its opposition to the divine good as man may participate in it, but the intimate connection of the other virtues with charity permits a wide scope for acedia. Nevertheless, acedia's direct attack on charity's act of rejoicing in the divine good makes it serious matter, although imperfect acts of acedia are found even in the holy. Finally, St. Thomas justified acedia's right to be called capital from its ability to produce other sins. The "daughter" sins associated with acedia in the Gregorian tradition, as well as their proliferation in the encyclopedic effort of St. Isidore (*In Deut.,* PL 83: 366), are ingeniously explained (ST 2a2ae, 35; *De malo* 11). While the commentators have remained faithful to the Thomistic synthesis, a popular tendency to confuse acedia with its principal external effect, sloth (*pigritia*), developed. Those aware of more profound interior implications attempted the spiritualization of acedia by "baptizing" it spiritual sloth. This terminology, adapted from St. John of the Cross (*Dark Night . . .* 1.7), has the disadvantage of making acedia appear to be an exotic sin reserved for the spiritual elite, whereas the tradition and experience show it to be a very common difficulty.

Bibliography: E. VANSTEENBERGHE, DTC 11.2:2026–30. G. BARDY, DictSpirAscMyst 1:166–169. For an interesting survey of the development of the idea, A. L. HUXLEY, "Accidie," in *On the Margin* (London 1923), and for contemporary attitudes, E. WAUGH, "Sloth," in A. WILSON et al., *The Seven Deadly Sins,* ed. I. FLEMING (New York 1962). A series of five articles by I. COLOSIO in *Rivista di ascetica e mystica* 2 (1958) 266–287, 495–511; 3 (1959) 185–201, 528–546; 4 (1960) 22–33, 159–169.

[U. VOLL]

ACERENZA, ARCHDIOCESE OF (ACHERUNTINUS), in Lucania, south Italy. A bishopric since the 4th century, archbishopric since 1059, metropolitan since 1106, it was united *aeque principaliter* with *Matera (1440–1954). In 1963 the see, 377 square miles in area, had 69,508 Catholics in 22 parishes with 45 secular and 4 religious priests. Its three suffragans had 187,480 Catholics, 159 priests, and 284 sisters: Muro Lucano (founded *c.* 1050); Potenza (*c.* 495) and Marsico Nuovo (5th century), united in 1818; and Venosa (5th century). The first known bishop, St. Justus, attended the synod of Rome in 499. Strategically located, Acerenza was taken from the Ostrogoths by the Byzantines in the 6th century and in the 10th century attached to the Greek archdiocese of *Otranto. Normans conquered it in 1041. A famous cathedral built by Bp. St. Leo II in the 8th century was rebuilt after a fire in 1082. In 799 the relics of St. Canio, the patron of the diocese, were translated to Acerenza. The city was almost abandoned in 1203 and its bishops then moved to the cathedral of St. Peter in Matera, which itself became a diocese in 1440, the bishop residing in each see for 6 months. In the 16th century the population of the area declined considerably.

Bibliography: J. FRAIKIN, DHGE 1:290–293 with list of bishops. N. C. SCIPIONI, EncCatt 1:211–213. Eubel HierCath. *Rivista di storia della Chiesa in Italia* (Rome 1947–). AnnPont (1964) 15, 1414.

[G. A. PAPA]

ACH, NARZISS, German experimental psychologist; b. Ermershausen, Oct. 29, 1871; d. July 25, 1946. Ach pursued his studies at Göttingen, at Berlin, and finally at Würzburg, where he earned his doctorate under O. *Külpe, with a dissertation entitled *Über die Willenstätigkeit und das Denken* (Leipzig 1905). Experimenting on the *will, Ach succeeded in isolating the constituents of the will act: the sensory element, the intellectual element, the essential element or the awareness of ego activity in willing, and the dynamic element or awareness of effort. In interpreting his work, he postulated "determining tendencies," predispositions that operate to control thought and action, and yet do not appear as such in consciousness. He refuted the charge of G. E. Müller (1850–1934) that these tendencies were nothing but the phenomenon of "perseveration," claiming that the intentionality present in determining tendencies was entirely missing in perseverations. Ach's work constituted a significant experimental study of the will.

See also IMAGELESS THOUGHT, THEORY OF; INTROSPECTION.

Bibliography: H. MISIAK and V. M. STAUDT, *Catholics in Psychology* (New York 1954). R. MÜLLER-FREINFELS, *The Evolution of Modern Psychology,* tr. W. B. WOLFE (New Haven 1935).

[M. G. KECKEISSEN]

ACHAB, KING OF ISRAEL, *c.* 869 to *c.* 850 B.C., son and successor of *Amri (Omri; *c.* 876–*c.* 869). The reign of Achab (or Ahab; Heb. *'aḥ'āb*) is recounted in considerable detail in 3 Kgs 16.29–22.40, although much of this is concerned primarily with the activities of the contemporary Prophet *Elia (Elijah). In some ways Achab seems to have been an even more vigorous ruler than his father, Amri. At the Battle of Qarqar on the Orontes River in Syria his army was one of the largest in the South Syrian confederacy that checked the advance of *Salmanasar (Shalmaneser) III in 853 B.C. (see Pritchard ANET[2] 279). Later Achab broke with Damascus and forced its King, *Ben-Adad (Ben-Hadad) II, to make a number of important concessions, including the establishment of an Israelite market in Damascus to replace the market that the Syrians had set up at Samaria in Amri's time. He likewise obtained important territorial concessions. Although the details are not given, there is evidence that he also held Moab in subjection [4 Kgs 1.1; Moabite Stone, line 8 (Pritchard ANET[2] 320–321); *see* MESHA INSCRIPTION].

Part of his success was due to his friendly relations with King Josaphat (Jehoshaphat) of Juda (*c.* 873–*c.* 849), to whose son Joram (Jehoram; King *c.* 849–*c.* 842) he gave his daughter Athalia in marriage (4

Kgs 8.18, 26). But even more useful to him were his close ties with Tyre; his wife, *Jezabel, was the daughter of Ethbaal (Ittobaal), King of Tyre. In the eyes of the Deuteronomistic editor of Kings, however, this marriage was a disaster for Israel because Jezabel, a zealous promoter of the worship of the Phoenician gods, exercised much influence over her husband, as evidenced, for instance, in their theft of Naboth's vineyard (3 Kgs 21.1–21).

Actually, although the prophet Elia accused Achab of being a worshiper of Baal (3 Kgs 18.18), he seems to have been a fairly sincere if not altogether consistent Yahwist. At more than one critical juncture in his career he had recourse to the prophets of Yahweh (e.g., 3 Kgs 22.6–8), including Michea ben Jemla (22.7–23), an avowed enemy of Jezabel. Later, however, he threw Michea into prison for his unwelcome prophecy. Apparently Elia's great contest with the prophets of Baal (18.16–45) met with no interference from the King, who even permitted a prophet to reprimand him for his lenient treatment of Ben-Adad after the latter's defeat at Aphec (20.35–43).

The Bible says little about Achab's extensive building operations, but the excavations at *Samaria have shown these to have been considerable and on quite a lavish scale. In short, he succeeded in making Israel a first-class power for its time, an achievement in which he was not surpassed by any of the other kings of Israel, except, perhaps, *Jeroboam II (*c.* 786–*c.* 746). Achab was killed in battle at *Ramoth in Galaad, which, against the advice of Michea ben Jemla, he was trying to wrest from the Syrians with the help of Josaphat of Juda. He was buried in Samaria, and in fulfillment of the prophecy of Elia (3 Kgs 21.19) the dogs licked up the blood washed from the chariot in which he had been slain (22.38).

Bibliography: S. Garofalo, EncCatt 1:215. A. Alt, RGG³ 1: 189–190. EncDictBibl 21–23.

[B. MC GRATH]

ACHAIA, ROMAN PROVINCE OF, in NT times the portion of Greece south of Macedonia. Before the Roman conquest in 146 B.C. Achaia was the name of the Greek territory bordering on the southern side of the Gulf of Corinth. After their conquest, the Romans united this region to the adjacent northern Greek territories; this larger region then formed the Roman province of Achaia. After it became a senatorial province in 27 B.C. it was governed by a proconsul who had previously been a praetor. In A.D. 15 Tiberius made it an imperial province, but in 44 Claudius gave it back to the senate. This agrees with Luke's narrative (Acts 18.12), which gives the title of proconsul to *Gallio, the official before whom Paul was brought by the Jews. Corinth, the capital of Achaia, was the residence of the proconsul (Acts 18.12). From the fragmentary inscription of Delphi it is known that Gallio was the proconsul of Achaia *c.* A.D. 51–53. It was during his proconsulship there that Paul was arrested for sedition (Acts 18.12–21). The date of Gallio's proconsulship is thus important for Pauline chronology. From Paul's Epistles it is known that there was a flourishing Christian community in Achaia. In his Second Epistle to the Corinthians (1.1) Paul sends greetings to the Christians of all Achaia. When he writes to the Thessalonians, he praises them for giving a good example to all the Christians in Macedonia and Achaia (1 Thes 1.8). The principal cities of Achaia were Athens, Corinth, and Cenchrea, the eastern seaport of Corinth, whence Paul sailed to Syria (Acts 18.18).

Bibliography: E. Jacquier, DB 1:126–128. Hastings DB (1963) 7. Pauly-Wiss RE 1.1 (1893) 190–198.

[P. P. SAYDON]

ACHARD (AICHARDUS), BL., commemorated by the Cistercians on Sept. 15; d. *c.* 1170. From *Clairvaux, St. Bernard sent him as architect to several new monasteries. The Romanesque church of *Himmerod was one of Achard's buildings. Two of his writings as novice master, "On the Seven Deserts" and "On All the Saints," are extant in manuscript (Montfaucon 1299).

Bibliography: Zimmermann KalBen 4:88. P. Fournier, DHGE 1:306. A. Schneider, *Die Cistercienserabtei Himmerod im Spätmittelalter* (Himmerod 1954) 131–132. Konrad von Eberbach, *Exordium magnum Cisterciense,* ed. B. Griesser (Rome 1961).

[A. SCHNEIDER]

ACHARD OF SAINT-VICTOR, theologian, bishop; b. England, early 12th century; d. Avranches, France, 1171 or 1172. A Canon Regular of Saint-Victor, Paris, he was its abbot in 1155 and was consecrated bishop of Avranches in 1162. His major treatise, *De Trinitate,* was known for a long time only through two citations in the *Eulogium ad Alexandrum III* [ed. N. Häring, MedSt 13 (1951) 267] by John of Cornwall (*c.* 1125–*c.* 1199). It is preserved in a Padua MS [cf. M. T. d'Alverny, RechThAm, 21 (1954) 299–306]. Achard is undoubtedly the author of the treatise on spiritual psychology entitled *De discretione animae, spiritus et mentis,* even though Häring, who edited the work, has tried without sufficient evidence to attribute it to *Gilbert de la Porrée [MedSt 22 (1960) 148–191]. Also extant are 15 of his sermons, some of which are really treatises, remarkable for their rich philosophical and theological content. Two of his letters are published in PL 196:1381–82.

Bibliography: J. Châtillon, "Achard de Saint-Victor et les controverses Christologiques du 12ᵉ siècle," *Mélanges F. Cavallera* (Toulouse 1948) 317–337; "Les Régions de la dissemblance selon A. de S-V.," *Recherches Augustiniennes* 2 (1962) 237–250; "A. de S-V. et le *De discretione animae, spiritus et mentis,*" ArchHistDoctLitMA 31 (1965). F. Bonnard, *Histoire de l'Abbaye royale et de l'ordre des chanoines réguliers de Saint-Victor,* 2 v. (Paris 1904–08) 1:120, 144, 203–209. P. Delhaye, LexThK² 1:107.

[J. CHÂTILLON]

ACHARIUS OF NOYON, ST., bishop; d. Nov. 27, 640? (feast, Nov. 27). Though no medieval hagiographer has left a life of St. Acharius (Aigahardus), he is mentioned in several Merovingian sources. He was a monk at *Luxeuil under St. *Eustace of Luxeuil, the successor of St. *Columban. In 626–627 he signed the acts of the synod of Clichy as Aigahardus, Bishop of Tournai-Noyon. Most probably he was responsible for the appointment of St. *Omer to the See of Thérouanne by King Dagobert I. He encouraged the missionary activities of St. *Amandus, who in turn asked Acharius to have Dagobert force the rebellious pagans to receive Baptism. St. Acharius's successor at Noyon was St. *Eligius of Noyon.

Bibliography: MGSrerMer 4:123 (Colomban); 4:695 (Eligius); 5:437 (Amand); 5:755 (Omer). Baudot-Chaussin 11:923–924.

[B. L. MARTHALER]

ACHAZ, KING OF JUDA. Achaz (Hebrew *'āḥāz*, abbreviated form of *yᵉhô'āḥāz*, "Yahweh takes hold"), ruled Juda from 736 to 716 B.C. During the last days of his father, Joatham, the Aramaeans of Damascus and the Northern Kingdom of Israel organized an anti-Assyrian coalition. When Joatham refused to join, the league threatened to use force. Joatham died before actual hostilities began, and Achaz was left to face the league's ultimatum. When he refused to act counter to the desires of the pro-Assyrian party in Juda, the coalitionists were determined to depose him.

Ignoring Isaia's warning and famous prophecy (Is 7.1–17; *see* MESSIANISM), he refused to trust in God and bought aid from the Assyrian King *Tiglath-Pileser III with gold from the temple and palace. The immediate purpose of his appeal to Assyria was achieved when the league was defeated; however, Juda became one of the many small states of the west over which Assyria was master.

As a vassal of Assyria, Achaz acknowledged the religion of the Assyrian Empire. The adoption of the foreign cult, however, did not mean that it replaced the traditional worship of Yahweh, but the two cults existed together. Because he had encouraged illegal Yahweh-worship on the high places and had instituted Assyrian idolatry into Juda, Achaz was most severely reproached by the inspired writers.

Bibliography: B. W. ANDERSON, *Understanding the Old Testament* (Englewood Cliffs, N.J. 1957) 265–273. J. BRIGHT, *A History of Israel* (Philadelphia 1959) 256–290. W. F. ALBRIGHT, "The Son of Tabeel (Isaiah 7:6)," BullAmSchOrRes 140 (1955) 34–35. C. C. TORREY, "A Hebrew Seal from the Reign of Ahaz," BullAmSchOrRes 79 (1940) 27–28.

[J. E. BRUNS]

ACHÉRY, JEAN LUC D', Benedictine monk noted for his collections of medieval manuscripts; b. Saint-Quentin, France, 1609; d. Paris, April 29, 1685. He first entered the Abbey of St. Quentin but later transferred to the congregation of St. Maur and was professed in the Monastery of the Trinity in Vendôme on Oct. 4, 1632. Because of poor health he was transferred to the Abbey of St. Germain des Prés in Paris, where he became head librarian. He was diligent in his work, made a complete inventory of the library and added many unedited texts gathered from other Benedictine monasteries. These he used in his editions of *Lanfranc and Guibert Nogent, and in his *Spicilegium.* In 1664 he became teacher and guide of Jean Mabillon. He is noted for his promotion of learning in the congregation of St. Maur. His principle works are *Spicilegium sive collectio veterum aliquot scriptorum* (13 v. Paris 1655–77; ed. 3 v. 1723); *Grimlaici regula solitariorum,* (Paris 1653); *Acta sanctorum ordinis S. Benedicti* (3 v. Paris 1688–1701).

Bibliography: R. NAZ, DDC 4:1013–14. U. BERLIÈRE, DHGE 1:309–310; DTC 1.1:310–311.

[H. A. LARROQUE]

ACHTERFELDT, JOHANN HEINRICH, theologian; b. Wesel, June 1, 1788; d. Bonn, May 11, 1877. He taught moral and pastoral theology at Bonn in 1826. He was a disciple of Georg *Hermes (d. 1831), whose teachings he publicly championed in the *Zeitschrift für Philosophie und katholische Theologie,* which he founded in 1832. Together with J. W. J. Braun, he published Hermes's theological lectures in three parts as *Christkatholische Dogmatik* (Münster 1834–36; incomplete). Since Achterfeldt did not submit to the condemnation of Hermesianism, Clemens August Droste Vischering (d. 1845), Archbishop of Cologne, in 1837 was obliged to forbid him the exercise of the ministry and the continuation of his lectures. Moreover, Johannes von Geissel (d. 1845), the coadjutor, suspended him in 1843. He finally submitted in 1873, and was reinstated by the Church.

Bibliography: Hurter Nomencl 3:1262. H. SCHRÖRS, *Geschichte der katholisch-theologischen Fakultät zu Bonn, 1818–1831* (Cologne 1922); *Die Kölner Wirren* (Berlin 1927). A. SCHRÖER, LexThK[2] 1:110–111.

[A. SCHRÖER]

ACOLYTE

The word acolyte (one who follows, a companion) refers to a cleric who has received the fourth and highest of the minor orders. His functions bring him into close relation with liturgical services. The ministry of the acolyte, as well as that of the subdeacon, has resulted from a division of the ministry of the deacon. The chief duties of the acolyte are to carry candles in procession, to light the candles on the altar, and to minister wine and water for the Holy Sacrifice of the Mass.

Order of Acolyte. Since this is an order instituted by the Church, it is not considered a Sacrament, but a sacramental participating in the order of deacon. The rite of ordination for the acolyte consists of two parts, both essential. For the first part of the ceremony the remote matter is a candlestick with an unlighted candle. For the second part the remote matter is an empty cruet. The handing of these objects to the candidate constitutes the proximate matter; the form consists of the two formulas indicated by the Pontifical for the double rite. As the ordaining prelate completes the words of each form, the candidate answers "Amen." Instead of one prayer, as in the case of the other minor orders, two rather lengthy prayers follow the ordination of the acolyte. These facts suggest the importance of the order of acolyte as the immediate preparation for receiving major orders. The instruction of the ordaining prelate

Investiture of altar boys into the Knights of the Altar.

stresses the obligation of the acolyte to serve faithfully at the altar and to manifest in his service of the Church the virtues symbolized by the light that has been placed in his hands.

See also ORDINATIONS IN THE ROMAN RITE.

Bibliography: V. MAURICE, DTC 1.1:312–316.

[T. J. RILEY]

Altar Boys. The functions of the acolyte today are normally performed by altar boys who have not received the order of acolyte. The substitution of altar boys for minor clerics dates back more than 1,000 years. In the 9th century at the Synod of Mainz it was decreed that "Every priest should have a cleric or boy (*scholarem*) to read the epistle or lesson, to answer him at Mass, and with whom he can chant the psalms" (*Admonitio Synodalis,* PL 132:456). The origin of altar boys, therefore, seems to have been due more to necessity than to choice, since originally it was the mind of the Church to reserve her ceremonies for those in major and minor orders. From the day this privilege was granted, altar boys have had an active part in divine worship, and yet little has been recorded about them, and scarcely any legislation issued concerning them. Indeed, one can go so far as to say that they have no written history. Perhaps this is because since they have taken over the duties of minor clerics, whatever was written in the past for or about these clerics is, with few exceptions, applicable to altar boys.

Today, boys are selected for the altar at 10 or 11 years of age. They are chosen for their goodness, intelligence, faithfulness, and a willingness to assist in the sacred ceremonies. The method of training is left to the discretion of the teacher. For the induction of new altar boys some parishes have a special ceremony. This ceremony consists of having the boys dressed in cassocks and kneeling on the predella while the pastor or another priest places the surplices over their shoulders. This investiture is then followed by an appropriate instruction. The duties of altar boys range from lighting candles to filling the minor offices at pontifical Mass. The length of time that boys serve on the altar varies. In some places they serve until the completion of eighth grade, while in others they remain until the upper years of high school or even later in life.

The dress of altar boys has not been determined by the Congregation of Rites. The *Ritus Servandus* of the Missal directs the server to wear a surplice (title 1, par. 2). A surplice presupposes a cassock and, in view of this, many authors agree that the cassocks should be black and that the surplices should be of white linen. Custom, no doubt, has sanctioned the wearing of red, white, and purple cassocks. It is forbidden, however, to attire boys as miniature prelates, with rochets and mozzettas, or zucchettos and pontifical sashes; nor may they wear gloves.

Various societies, having parish units with their own officers, have been established to help in the formation of faithful and competent servers. They outline methods of selecting and training boys, and of advancing and rewarding those who are dutiful and proficient. Among those still extant is the St. John Berchmans' Sanctuary Society, founded by Vincent Basile, SJ, apostolic missionary of South Slavonia, and approved by Pius IX in 1865. A similar society is the *Knights of the Altar, founded by Francis E. Benz in 1938 with the approval of Abp. John G. Murray of St. Paul, Minn. The official publication of this society is the *Catholic Boy* (Notre Dame, Ind.).

Bibliography: Miller FundLit. P. PARSCH, *The Liturgy of the Mass,* tr. and adap. H. E. WINSTONE (St. Louis 1957). Manuals for use of altar boys are: W. A. O'BRIEN, *How to Serve Low Mass and Benediction* (New York 1962). J. W. KAVANAGH, *Altar Boy's Ceremonial* (New York 1955). *Manual of St. John Berchmans' Society* (New York 1945). *Knights of the Altar* (Notre Dame, Ind. 1939).

[J. W. KAVANAGH]

ACOSTA, GABRIEL (URIEL)

Jewish rationalist and religious dissenter; b. Oporto, Portugal, *c.* 1590; d. Amsterdam, Holland, April 1640. He was called originally Gabriel da Costa, and he himself always used the family name of Da Costa, but he is more generally known by its Latinized form of Acosta. He was born into a family of *Marranos, his father having escaped the stake by accepting Catholicism. However, according to Uriel's autobiography, his family observed the tenets of the Catholic faith punctiliously. Young Uriel was reared as a noble; he studied law and prepared himself for an ecclesiastical career. Despite this background he began to doubt the truth of Christian dogma, became increasingly disenchanted, and found no solace in the resolute doctrines of the Catholic Church. Circumstances, however, had compelled Acosta to conceal his theological views, for in 1615, after the death of his father, in order to support his family, he accepted a semiecclesiastical office as chief treasurer of an abbey, the collegiate church of Oporto. But his spirit became more restless and his conscience more disquieted. Secretly he began to delve into the faith of his ancestors, and the doctrines of Judaism brought repose to his mind. Uriel then determined to forsake Catholicism and return to Judaism. Cautiously, he conveyed his intention to his mother and brothers, and they too resolved to expose themselves to the great danger of secret emigration and to the perils of an uncertain future. About 1617 the Acosta family arrived in Amsterdam, where they were admitted into the covenant of Abraham and where the baptismal name Gabriel was exchanged for the name Uriel.

Soon, however, it became apparent that in Judaism as well, Uriel's wayward disposition could find no satisfaction. From his readings of the OT he had constructed an ideal of Judaism that clashed sharply with the realities of Jewish life. Liberal Mosaic and prophetic doctrines, he believed, were being discarded for rigid and prosaic ritual and observance, and the religious life of Judaism seemed to be as clogged with petty detail as the Catholic faith that he had abandoned. He had expected that Judaism would resolve for him the puzzles that the Church could not solve and that the rabbis could offer what he could not obtain from his Catholic confessors. Acosta had sacrificed much for his convictions, and he believed he had earned thereby his right to protest and to propagate his views. In a lengthy pamphlet (*Proposals against Tradition*), which he had written from Hamburg and directed to the Sephardic community of Venice, he challenged and denounced the "offensive" traditional laws and customs, and with arrogant expressions he decried their rabbinic guardians and cavilled at their authority. His revolutionary ideas had aroused a vigorous opposition, and upon his refusal to recant he was promptly placed under the ban at Hamburg and publicly excommunicated at Venice (Aug. 14, 1618).

In the interim he had returned to Amsterdam, where he was held in great contempt and isolated from all human intercourse. This forced severance only served to increase his passion for speculation, and he resolved to publish a work in which he would deny the doctrine of immortality and indicate the "glaring contrasts" between the Bible and rabbinical Judaism. But Acosta's intention was anticipated by his former friend, the physician Samuel da Silva, who in 1623 had published a book in Portuguese entitled *A Treatise on the Immortality of the Soul in order to Confute the Ignorance of a Certain Opponent, Who in Delusion Affirms Many Errors*. Believing that the opposition had commissioned Da Silva, he hastened to publish his retort (1624), also in Portuguese, *An Examination of the Pharisaic Traditions Compared with the Written Laws, and a Reply to the Slanderer Samuel da Silva*. He now denied not only the belief in immortality but also the doctrines of the resurrection and of reward and punishment. By denying such concepts he had challenged Christian dogma as well. He was again denounced, arrested, imprisoned for several days, and fined 300 florins, and his work was condemned to the flames. For 15 years (1618–33) Acosta lived as an outcast; unable to bear it any longer, he agreed to recant and to be, as he phrased it, "an ape among apes."

He had submitted not from conviction but from despair, and consequently he became embittered to the point of disbelief in the divine origin of the Bible itself. Word had now gotten out that he dissuaded three Christians from their intention of embracing Judaism, and he was once more placed under the ban. After 7 years of total ostracism he succumbed. His tortured spirit now longed for tranquility, and the price required of him this time was severe and cruel. Before huge audiences he was ordered to recite his public penance, was given 39 lashes, and then trampled upon as he lay prostrate upon the threshold of the synagogue. His proud and indomitable spirit had now been broken; with shame and humiliation he arrived home, poured out his feelings in a short autobiographical sketch entitled *Exemplar Humanae Vitae* (*A Specimen of Human Life*), and then shot himself. A refutation of the *Exemplar* was made by Philip Limborch, a Dutch theologian, as an appendix to his *Amica collatio cum erudito Judaeo* (Gouda 1687; repr. 1847).

Bibliography: S. Bernstein, UnivJewishEnc 1:72–74. F. de Sola Mondes, JewishEnc 1:167–168. C. Gebhardt, EncJudaica 5:678–680. J. Cantera, LexThK[2] 1:113. A. Romeo, EncCatt 1:230. I. Sonne, "Da Costa Studies," JewishQuartRev 22 (1932) 247–293. H. H. Graetz, *History of the Jews*, ed. and tr. B. Löwy, 6 v. (Philadelphia 1945) 5:56–65. J. Whiston, *The Remarkable Life of Uriel Acosta* (London 1740).

[N. J. COHEN]

ACOSTA, JOSÉ DE

Philosopher and theologian; b. Medina del Campo, Spain, September or October 1540; d. Salamanca, Feb. 15, 1600. He took vows in the Society of Jesus Sept. 24, 1570. In 1572 he went to Peru, where he was provincial and rector of the Colegio of Lima. He served as theologian of the Third Provincial Council of Lima (1582–83), and participated in the composition and publishing of the books ordered by the Council. In 1586 he went to Mexico, where he remained until his return to Spain in May 1587. He was visitor of the provinces of Aragon and Andalusia, and, in 1592, provost of the Casa Profesa of Valladolid. In connection with the convocation of the Fifth Congregation of the Society of Jesus he was in Rome until 1594, engaged in negotiations that caused him difficulties with Father General Claudio Aquaviva. He spent the rest of his life in Spain. In 1597 he was named rector of the Colegio of Salamanca.

Acosta's writings are many and varied, but the following works brought him fame: *De natura novi orbis, De procuranda indorum salute,* (both published Salamanca 1588), and the *Historia natural y moral de las Indias* (1590; new ed. Mexico City 1962). He translated *De natura* into Spanish and included it with the *Historia* as books 1 and 2, so that those two works came to form a single whole.

In the *De procuranda* Acosta examined the fundamental problems of evangelization in America in his day. He discussed the doubts as to the capacity of the Indian (book 1), the legality of the employment of force (book 2), the rights and obligations of the civil authority and of the colonists (book 3), the special requisites for being a missionary in America (book 4), the parochial functions of the missions (book 5), and the casuistic difficulty in the administration of the Sacraments to the Indians (book 6). This work was the first systematic and complete presentation of the missionary problems provoked by the appearance of a new and unforseeable pagan world in the midst of the inhabited world. It is noteworthy, also, for the practical and balanced solutions proposed by its author, in contrast to the unfair exaggerations of impassioned men such as Fray Bartolomé de *Las Casas and Ginés de Sepulveda. The *Historia* (including the *De natura*) reflects Acosta's scientific concerns, which were never divorced from his missionary interests. A new entity, America, had appeared within the heart of Christendom, and it was necessary to show that, despite its novelty, it did not mean any derogation of the order God had assigned to nature and the course of history. This was the great task Acosta performed in his *Historia.* The highly varied subjects are grouped in accordance with the scientific view of reality then current, and thus the author placed the American world within the system of the universe (book 1), the sphere of the world (book 2), the concept of matter (book 3), the hierarchy of living beings (book 4), the idea of man as a spiritual being (book 5) and man as a rational being (book 6), and, finally, within the providential system of history (book 7).

Acosta's two great works represent the ideological culmination of the initial period (16th century) of the religious conquest and the philosophical and scientific conquest of the New World, of the great historical and ontological process of its incorporation into Western culture. For this reason, both works occupy unique positions in early American bibliography and have a historical value that is both irreplaceable and permanent.

[E. O'GORMAN]

ACQUAVIVA

Prominent Neapolitan family, which gave several leading members to the Church.

Giulio, cardinal, of the family of the Duke of Atri; b. Naples, 1546; d. Rome, July 21, 1574. In 1568 he was sent to Spain to settle a controversy between (St.) Charles Borromeo and the governor of Milan, and to offer the Pope's condolences to Philip II, recently bereft of his third wife and his son Don Carlos. On May 9, 1570, he was created cardinal deacon of St. Callistus, and later of St. Theodorus, by Pius V, who held him in great esteem and asked for his spiritual assistance at his deathbed.

Ottavio (the elder), cardinal; b. Naples, 1560; d. there, 1612. He was summoned to Rome by Sixtus V, and held various offices under him and his successors. On March 16, 1591, Gregory XIII created him a cardinal and sent him as vice-legate to Campania. Two years later, Clement VIII sent him to Avignon as his representative, a difficult mission because at that time relations were tense between the Church and the neighboring Protestant subjects of Henry IV. The conversion and coronation of this monarch took place while Ottavio was in Avignon. As a tactful and efficient administrator, he reorganized the administration of justice, implementing reforms that lasted until the end of the papal administration. On his return to Rome in March 1597, he was given impressive popular acclaim. Leo XI appointed Ottavio archbishop of Naples in 1605, in which office he distinguished himself by his ability and charity. He sought to alleviate the consequences of the famine of 1607, built two monasteries for the Minorites, and left a few manuscripts, one a commentary on the *Summa.*

Ottavio Acquaviva (the elder).

Ottavio (the younger), cardinal; b. Naples, 1608; d. Rome,1674. As governor of Jesi (1638), Orvieto (1642), and Ancona (1643), he organized the defense of these cities against Parma and the French. Innocent VI summoned him to Rome, where he held various posts. In March 1664 he became cardinal with the title of St. Bartholomew-of-the-Island, and later of St. Cecilia (1668). As a papal legate in Bologna, he led a campaign against outlaws; in 1655 he was host to Christine of Sweden.

Trojano, cardinal; b. Naples, Jan. 24, 1695; d. Rome, March 24, 1747. A vice-legate to Bologna under Clement XI, Trojano was appointed governor of Ancona by Innocent XIII, and master of the Sacred Palace by Benedict XIII. Titular archbishop of Larissa, he was created cardinal of St. Cecilia by Clement XII in 1732. At the request of Philip V he became archbishop of Toledo; in 1739, of Monreale. He was on friendly terms with Charles III, and represented Spain and Naples in the Roman Curia. He favored the reforms of B. Tanucci and negotiated the concordat of 1741, which abolished certain privileges of the clergy, among them, exemption from taxation. He played a major role in the conclave of 1740, which elected Benedict XV. The 1744 edition of Giambattista Vico's *Scienze Nuova* was dedicated to him.

Bibliography: P. RICHARD, DHGE 1:359–363. L. CARDELLA, *Memorie storiche dei cardinali,* 9 v. (Rome 1792–97). Pastor v.17, 18. M. DE CAMILLIS and G. MESEGUER, EncCatt 1:244–246.

[E. J. THOMSON]

ACQUAVIVA, CLAUDIUS

Fifth general of the Jesuits; b. Atri, Sept. 14, 1543; d. Rome, Jan. 31, 1615. He was the youngest son of the Duke of Atri, Giovanni Antonio Donato A. d'Aragona. He studied jurisprudence in Perugia, entered papal service and was appointed a chamberlain by Pius IV. On July 22, 1567, he entered the Society of Jesus after learning about it from Francis Borgia and Juan de Polanco. In 1574 he was ordained, and became a professor of philosophy at the Roman College. The next year he was named rector of the Collegium Maximum in Naples. In 1576 he was provincial of the Neapolitan province and 3 years later, of the Roman province. On Feb. 19, 1581, with 32 of the 57 votes, Acquaviva was elected general of the society; he had the longest term of office to 1964. His administration was marked by a very sharp increase of the society in Europe and in the missions. The number of members grew from approximately 5,000 to more than 13,000, and colleges, from 144 to 372. To the tasks posed by this expansion, Acquaviva brought a disciplined handling of his office, judged by many to have been too authoritative. He molded the society as no other general had since its founder, Ignatius of Loyola. His chief concern was the maintenance and promotion of religious spirit during this period of rapid growth. In the resultant regimentation that seemed necessary, the individual initiative envisioned by Ignatius was perforce retarded. During his long term the standardization that had actually begun earlier was conclusively established, e.g., a binding regulation for the daily hour of mental prayer, annual repetition of the Exercises, a 1-year tertianship. Significant is his letter *Quis sit orationis et paenitentiae usus* of 1590, in which Acquaviva, as did his predecessor Everard Mercurian, takes an open-minded attitude on the question of extent and type of mental prayer and external penitential exercises. Differences of opinion on this point led to a clash with the German assistant and admonitor, Peter Hoffaeus, who subsequently was relieved of his office.

In 1599 appeared the final *Directorium* for making and conducting the Spiritual Exercises, which, although in use for centuries, is today not considered to correspond completely with the intentions of St. Ignatius.

Acquaviva also provided the definitive text of the Ratio Studiorum, which regulated Jesuit learning and higher studies until the society's suppression on Aug. 16, 1773. He issued as well, the *Industriae . . . ad curandos animae morbos*, directed to superiors and reflecting wide experience and genuine piety. Among the many difficulties that tested his brilliant talent for diplomacy and administration were: the movement among Spanish Jesuits toward a national independence, which was supported by Phillip II and had an influential advocate in Francesco Toletus, elevated to the cardinalate in 1593; the intention of Sixtus V to amend the constitution of the society on very significant points; the plan of Clement VIII to name Acquaviva archbishop of Naples in order to remove him from control of the society. There were also the controversies on theological questions, such as the doctrine stated by St. Robert *Bellarmine on the *potestas indirecta* of the pope; the debates on grace caused by Luis *Molina's *Concordia liberi arbitrii cum gratiae donis* that led to the **Congregatio de Auxiliis;* the doctrine of Juan de Mariana on the murder of tyrannical leaders. Through these difficulties Acquaviva was able to consolidate the society into its ultimate stability with circumspection and tenacity.

Bibliography: Sommervogel 1:480–491; 8:1669–70; 12:46–48, 318–319, 910–911. B. SCHNEIDER, ArchHistSocJesu 26 (1957) 3–56; 27 (1958) 279–306. J. DE GUIBERT, *La Spiritualité de la Compagnie de Jésus,* ed. E. LAMALLE (Rome 1953). M. ROSA, DizBiogItal 1:168–178.

[B. SCHNEIDER]

ACROSTIC, an anglicized Greek word signifying a composition, usually in verse, in which initial (or occasionally middle and final) letters are arranged in such an order as to form words. When middle and final letters are so employed, there is question rather of mesostichs and telestichs respectively. The word type, as well as the alphabetical form of acrostic, is Oriental in origin. The earliest Greek example dates from the beginning of the 2d century B.C. The word form of acrostic was a characteristic feature of the pagan Sibylline Oracles (see Cicero, *Div.* 2.54.171–) and other oracular or magicoreligious texts. Hence, it was only natural that the Christian Sibylline books should make use of the same device. In bk. 8, 217–250 (written near the end of the 2d century A.D.), one finds the well-known acrostic: Ἰησοῦς Χρειστὸς Θεοῦ Ὑιὸς Σωτὴρ σταυρός (Jesus Christ, Son of God, Savior, Cross), which—with the omission of σταυρός—furnishes also the widespread acrostic IXΘYC (in Greek, fish, a basic early Christian symbol). The passage from the Sibyllines is presented in Latin translation by St. Augustine (*Civ.* 18.23) in such a way that the initial letters of each Latin verse reproduce the Greek verse cited—but without the word σταυρός—in Latin transliteration. In the Pectorius inscription found near Autun, the initial Greek letters of the first five verses furnish the acrostic IXΘYC also. In keeping with the Oriental background, frequent use of acrostics is noted likewise in Christian Syriac poetry, especially in the hymns of St. Ephrem. Optatianus Porphyrius (first half of 4th century A.D.), Ausonius, and Commodian employed elaborate acrostics, and acrostics became common as a device for indicating the name of the deceased in Christian funeral epigrams, especially the name of a martyr.

The alphabetic acrostic, familiar from the Lamentations of Jeremia and from a number of Psalms, is the obvious source for Christian Greek and Latin acrostics of this kind. St. Hilary of Poitiers has two abecedarian hymns, and St. Augustine made use of this form as a memory aid in his famous *Psalmus abecedarius contra partem Donati.* The abecedarian hymn (*A solis ortus cardine*) of Sedulius has become a part of the Christmas liturgy. In the tradition of Optatianus Porphyrius, acrostics were developed to a fantastic degree in the *carmina figurata* of Rabanus Maurus in the Carolingian age. Acrostics of the earlier and simple form continued to flourish throughout the Middle Ages and have had a sporadic life down to the present time (*see* PECTORIUS, EPITAPH OF).

Bibliography: A. KURFESS and T. KLAUSER, ReallexAntChr 1:235–238, an excellent treatment with bibliog. A. FERRUA, Enc Catt 1:251–253, with bibliog. H. LECLERCQ, DACL 1.1:356–372, with full texts and plates. F. DORNSEIFF, *Das Alphabet in Mystik und Magie* (2d ed. Leipzig 1925) 146–151. Manitius, Indexes s.v. "Akrosticha."

[M. R. P. MC GUIRE]

ACT

Considered analogically and in its own right, act denotes perfection just as *potency denotes imperfection. Hence, potency plays a determining, limiting role in relation to act. Thus we say that God is *Pure Act, because He is not limited by any potency, while created being is a mixture of potency and act. Since act in itself is said to denote perfection, it is not limited except by a principle distinct from itself, namely, potency; wherefore the axiom: *actus non limitatur a seipso.* Both potency and act should be considered as principles of being, not as beings themselves. It is also important not to confuse potency and act as principles in the structure of being with two successive stages in the development of a being, as when one speaks of being first in potency (*in potentia*) and then in act (*in actu*).

Kinds of Act. To make use of the following classification one must be aware of the ontological scope of its application. The notions of potency and act are basically analogical. Hence, what might perfectly fulfill the notion of act from one point of view might also at the same time, but from another point of view, be considered as potency. Thus the form of a being is act in relation to the matter that it actuates, while the essence of that which is composed of matter and form, in its turn, is potency in regard to the *esse* that actuates it.

Act That Is neither Received nor Receptive. This is pure act, subsistence act, which is neither received into a limiting potency nor susceptible of receiving an act superior to it.

Act That Is Received but Is Not Receptive. This is substantial existence or *esse,* limited by essence that, in turn, plays the role of limiting potency in its regard. *Esse,* as such, is not in its own turn susceptible of receiving an act in the substantial order that would be superior to it. What is composed of essence and *esse,* however, is said to be ordered to activity as to an accidental act that perfects an individual substance. Operation is also an act in this category, for it perfects the faculty and through it the individual in which it is received and from which it emanates. But it too, in itself and in its own right, is not ordered to a superior act.

Act That Is Receptive but Not Received. The separated form belongs to this classification. It is not received into quantitatively signed matter (*signata quantitate*), which would otherwise make it some type of individual being, but it does receive an act to which it is ordained and which is its proper substantial *esse*. An act that is not received, inasmuch as it is pure form, is called "infinite" because it is not limited by matter. Yet it is "finite" in the order of existence since it is not *esse subsistens,* but has a finite mode of existing. This category of act has the role of being a limited potency to *esse*.

Act That Is Received and Receptive. This is the category of all forms received into a limiting principle that, in their turn, are ordained to a further act that perfects them. Such, for example, is the form of a composite being received in the limiting matter that it actuates, but that, together with this matter, is ordained to the act of the composite, viz, the substantial *esse*. The same applies to any accidental form that is act in relation to its subject but is also potency in relation to a superior act that perfects it. An example would be a faculty that perfects an individual but is ordained to operation as to a superior act that in turn perfects the individual.

Pure and Mixed Act. What has been said thus far leads to the distinction between pure act and mixed act (*purus* and *non purus*). In itself the first is not received and limited, whereas the second is. Again one must specify the given context in stating whether an act is pure or not. In relation to *esse,* God alone is Pure Act. In the order of essence, separated forms, i.e., beings that are not composed, can be called pure and infinite inasmuch as they are not limited by potency.

First and Second Act. First act is often opposed to second act (*actus primus* and *actus secundus*). This usage designates either form or essence in relation to the *esse* that perfects them, or the individual in relation to the operation that perfects it. That which perfects as an ultimate actualization is called second act.

One can sum up the different kinds of act as follows: (1) *motion, act of the changeable, (2) substantial or accidental *form (faculty, *habit); (3) *esse* (*existence), and (4) operation. Each in its own way is act and as such conveys the notion of perfection. Substantial *esse* and operation are alone, strictly speaking, terminal acts and are not further receptive in their own proper order.

Historical Development. The notion of potency as opposed to act and as uniquely definable by it was introduced into philosophy by *Aristotle. He first used these notions in the *Physics* to explain change, which he defined as "the act of that which is in potency, precisely as such" (201a 10). In the *Metaphysics* he introduced act and potency as general divisions of being (1045b 34). Here also he arrived at the notion of pure act (1071b 20).

Scholastic Thought. St. *Thomas Aquinas applied the notions of potency and act in a context to which Aristotle could not have given thought, that of the real distinction between essence and existence. Here the notions attain a level of ontological profundity never before known (*see* ESSENCE AND EXISTENCE). Potency and act are also basic to the Thomistic thesis on *participation and to the notion of *being proper to St. Thomas (see below).

With John *Duns Scotus one finds an early attempt to introduce an entity, unknown to Aristotle and St. Thomas, intermediate between potency and act, i.e., virtual act (*actus virtualis*). This is act that, without the agency of any extrinsic causality, reduces a being from potency to act. Thus it is the complete power to pass into act by itself; all being that possesses it is self-moved. Wherefore, Scotus reasons, the inefficacy of Aristotle's attempt to prove that whatever is moved is moved by another; for Scotus, the fact that motion involves passage from potency to act is no proof of that. For arguments against the virtual act of Scotus, see Sylvester of Ferrara: *Comm. in 1 C. gent.,* Leon. ed., c. 13, p. 35, nn. 6–7. Francisco *Suárez rejects the distinction between essence and existence as part of his refusal to use the principle of the limitation of act by potency to prove the real distinction. Suárez admits neither this distinction nor the Thomistic concept of being upon which it is based. Instead he attempts to base the fundamental distinction between God as infinite and creature as finite on the notions of *ens a se* and *ens ab alio*. But he does not perceive the ties that unite the thesis of the distinction between *ens a se* and *ens ab alio* with the distinction in the Thomistic tradition between pure act and created being that is necessarily composed of potency (essence) and act (existence). Finally, Suárez subscribes to the notion of *virtual act,* with the consequences inherent in it (cf. *Disp. Meta.,* disp. 29, sect. 1, n. 7, ed. Vives, 26:23).

Leibniz and Descartes. Gottfried *Leibniz is situated, consciously or not, in the line of Scotus and Suárez inasmuch as he employs the notion of "active force" and replaces the notion of potency with that of "impeded act." For Leibniz, forces are always active. If they appear to be at rest, it is because their activity is impeded.

René *Descartes' elimination of the notions of potency and act is part of his deliberate rejection of all ontology. He combines both scientific reasons (e.g., the principle of inertia) and philosophical arguments to condemn the principle that whatever is moved is moved by another. His reasoning rests generally on his opposition to the notions of potency and act. In all this there is a conscious rejection, a reflective break with the world of the ancients and the Middle Ages, in which the notions of being, act, and potency occupy a central place. The consequences of this break were destined to become immeasurable.

Modern and Contemporary Period. Little by little, the notion of act came to be employed in one of its many senses. The moderns designate activity by it and, more particularly, the free intellectual activity of self proper to man. The metaphysics of act now becomes subjectivistic, and this phenomenon is realized most characteristically in such philosophies as those of *Hegel or *Gentile. The latter attacks Aristotle, gratuitously at that, for regarding act as static, as an object, whereas it is grasped interiorly by consciousness. Louis *Lavelle shows a different emphasis; while maintaining the interiorization of act, he views act in relation to being, potency, and voluntarity, and thus avoids the strictly idealistic viewpoint of Gentile.

Recent Thomism. Since the appearance of *Aeterni Patris* there has been a revival of the classic doctrine of potency and act. At the same time, discussions relative to its interpretation, its role in the Thomistic synthesis, its value in itself, and its applications have been encouraged. The same can be said for the principle *actus non limitatur a seipso* and the conclusions that can be drawn from it.

Outside of *scholasticism, the analogical notions of potency and act have, on the whole, lost their significance. One cannot, without great equivocation, connect scholastic usage with what contemporary thinkers make of these notions. Regrettable though this may be, it is a fact that must be faced.

Act and Being. The first of all notions is that of being, not of act. Potency and act divide being as such. Also, being is defined as that which is either in potency or in act, and not as that which exists; whence, the definition: *ens est id quod habet relationem ad esse sive actualitatis sive possibilitatis.* With St. Thomas the notion of being is profoundly "existentialized" by the fact that for him *esse* is the act of acts, the most profound, intimate, and formal element in being. Unless one reverts to "essentialism," being is inconceivable without this reference to *esse.* Thus the whole metaphysics of St. Thomas is founded upon the notion of being understood with explicit relation to *esse* as act. This notion is what enables him to argue to the real distinction of essence and existence in *finite being.

Act and Participation. The problem of the one and the many is at the heart of metaphysics. As St. Thomas saw it, *participation is in turn basic to the solution of the problem of the one and the many. Numerically multiplied and limited beings are possible because they are beings by participation. They are not instances of *esse per se subsistens,* which is necessarily unique (God), but of *esse* received into limiting potencies, i.e., into essences. The notions of potency and act, Aristotelian in origin, enabled St. Thomas to systematize the doctrine of participation, of Platonic origin, into a conceptualization that is precise and free from equivocation. St. Thomas's stroke of genius consists in having united these two perspectives into a new and irreducible synthesis that profoundly transformed the elements it assimilated, thanks in no small part to his distinctive notion of *esse* as act.

This notion also gives to his metaphysics of *causality an essential profundity. For St. Thomas, the efficient cause touches the *esse rerum,* allowing him to conceive God as cause of this *esse,* and even its proper cause. Creatures merely confer *esse* as secondary causes under God's premotion (*see* PREMOTION, PHYSICAL). Thus God is not merely a final cause, moving by desire (as was taught by Aristotle), nor merely the first formal and exemplary cause (as for the Platonists). It is in these perspectives that one must locate the *secunda via* of St. Thomas.

Act and Change. Historically in Aristotle and psychologically in human consciousness, act and potency are linked with the perception of movement and with one's own activity. This includes continuous movement, substantial change, and the personal operation that precedes any discovery. To be grasped intelligibly and without contradiction, change presupposes: (1) a point of departure—potency; (2) a point of arrival—act; and (3) the imperfect act (*actus imperfectus*) between these—essentially act in relation to the prior potency, that of the point of departure, and at the same time potency in relation to the perfect act (*actus perfectus*) at the terminal point of the movement. Wherefore, the classical definition of *motion as "the act of a being in potency precisely as such."

See also POTENCY AND ACT; POTENCY; ACTION AND PASSION; ACTUALISM (IN PHILOSOPHY); ENERGY; ENTELECHY; EXISTENCE; FORM; PURE ACT; HUMAN ACT; MOTION; PARTICIPATION.

Bibliography: C. A. HART, *Thomistic Metaphysics: An Inquiry into the Act of Existing* (Englewood Cliffs, N.J. 1959). H. REITH, *The Metaphysics of St. Thomas Aquinas* (Milwaukee 1958). F. VAN STEENBERGHEN, *Ontology,* tr. M. FLYNN (New York 1952). A. FOSSATI, EncFil 1:464–475. A. SMEETS, *Actus en potentie in de Metaphysica van Aristoteles* (Conférences d'Histoire et de Philologie ser. 3.49; Louvain 1952). G. MANSER, *Das Wesen des Thomismus* (Thomistische Studien 5; 3d ed. Fribourg 1949). C. GIACON, *Atto e potenza* (Brescia 1947). W. N. CLARKE, "The Limitation of Act by Potency," NewSchol 26 (1952) 167–194. J. D. ROBERT, "Le Principe: Actus non limitatur nisi per potentiam subjectivam realiter distinctam," RevPhilLov 47 (1949) 44–70. G. GENTILE, *Genesis and Structure of Society,* tr. H. S. HARRIS (Urbana 1960). L. LAVELLE, *La Dialectique de l'éternel présent: de l'acte* (Paris 1946).

[J. D. ROBERT]

ACT, FIRST, as used in theology indicates the universal principle of all actuality, namely, God. Whatever is finite actuality is so because it participates in the infinite actuality of the first act (St. Thomas, ST 1a, 75.5 ad 1). Creatures can no more act without a positive divine influence than they can begin or continue in existence independently of it. God as the first act is the cause of created action, not only by giving the created agent its form, which is the principle of action, but by conserving that form and its powers, and by concurring in the operations that flow from those powers. Since every reduction of power to operation, whether in the material or spiritual order, is a transition from *potency to *act, effected by something in act, God must be the first act (ST 1a, 2.3).

While God is first act, the acts of creatures as secondary agents, nevertheless, are real, efficacious, and according to their proper forms and powers (ST 1a, 105.5). However since the cause of an action is more the one whose power effects it than the one who acts, God as first act is more the cause of created action than its secondary agents. How God moves the created free will freely, yet efficaciously, so that it acts freely under divine influence, is a problem about which theologians have speculated through the centuries.

See also CAUSALITY; CAUSE, FIRST; FREE WILL AND GRACE; PURE ACT.

Bibliography: A. GARDEIL, DTC 1.1:337–339. DTC, Tables générales 1:557–560. J. MÖLLER, LexThK[2] 1:118–119. T. T. PAINE, Davis CDT 1:23–25.

[M. R. E. MASTERMAN]

ACT OF SETTLEMENT, IRISH

The decisive legislative measure of 1662; it began the reduction of land owned by Irish Catholics from 61 per cent in 1641 to 22 per cent in 1688 and 15 per cent in 1703. Consequently, the Protestant ascendancy dominated Ireland until, after Catholic Emancipation (1829), Daniel *O'Connell compelled the English government to give equality to Catholics. Socially and economically, the landed system of Ireland remained stereotyped except for the brief Catholic ascendancy under James II, for 200 years, from Oliver *Cromwell until after the famine of the 1840s.

Provisions of the Act. The act, which was passed on July 31, 1662, virtually confirmed the Cromwellian settlement in favor of the adventurers who invested money in the parliamentarian war in Ireland and the soldiers who fought against the Catholics and Royalists. Charles II was restored on terms that maintained political power in the hands of the English conquerors in the Irish Civil War (1641–53), except for the regicides. Some initial endeavor was made to be favorable to those Catholics who had supported the King in arms, notably in the King's declaration of Nov. 30, 1660, but in Ireland pressure from the ex-Cromwellians was so great as to diminish the chances of Catholic Restoration in succeeding months. Finally, even those who were made secure by the Act of Settlement were denied justice. The government became alarmed at the Puritan Castle Plot of May 1663, which nearly succeeded in capturing James, Duke of Ormond, the Lord Lieutenant; and as a result, before the end of 1665 the Act of Explanation was passed, restricting to some 50 the restoration of Catholics under the preceding act, but also compelling the new Protestant interest to surrender one-third. The Declaration of November 1660 had promised to restore royalist Irish, "innocent" of rebellion against Charles I, but it also had confirmed to the adventurers all lands possessed by them on May 7, 1659, with provision for deficiencies claimed before the following May. As regards the soldiers, the lands already assigned to them to compound for wages due even if only in valuation at 13/ in every pound sterling (20/) were confirmed, except where it could be established, before the following December twelvemonth, that there had been bribery or false admeasurements in allotting their land.

Exceptions involved those regicides and others exempted from pardon by the English Act of Oblivion (1660), the Protestant Church of *Ireland lands, the estates of those opposing the Restoration, and the estates restored to "innocent" owners by decree of the King's courts although previously set out to adventurers and soldiers. Satisfaction would be given to adventurers and soldiers holding lands, when it could be proved that these properly belonged to legal encumbrancers from before Oct. 22, 1641 (the day before the outbreak of the Irish Catholic Rebellion). Provision was to be made where this had not already been done for those officers who had served Charles II or his father before June 5, 1649, at a rate comparable to the provision for parliamentarian soldiers, but they were to be satisfied with sixpence in the pound less. Protestants were to be restored to their estates where these had been taken from them under the Cromwellian Settlement, and a reprisal of equal value was to be assigned to the adventurers and soldiers who would have to be removed for this purpose. There was to be no benefit for those persons who entered the rebellion before Sept. 15, 1643 (the date of the cessation of hostilities between the Catholic Confederates of Kilkenny and King Charles I, leading to their payment of subsidies and lending of troops to him). Nor was there to be any benefit for those who had taken out decrees in land in Connaught or Clare (under the Cromwellian provision transporting innocent Catholics from their lands east of the Shannon so as to leave the three other provinces for the adventurers and soldiers).

Special provisions in favor of the Earl of Ormond and his wife and the Earl of Inchiquin safeguarded such actions as they had taken in mortgaging their lands. "Innocent papists" who had never acted against the King since Oct. 22, 1641, were to be restored by May 2, 1661 (subsequently extended by a further Act for 1 year), provided they restored to the King those transplantees' lands to which they had been removed compulsorily in Connaught and Clare. This provision marked them off from those who had voluntarily taken out decrees for Connaught and Clare land as these were held bound by their own decision. Again "innocent popish inhabitants" of towns, especially of Cork, Youghal, and Kinsale, were not to be restored specifically to their own property but instead were to be allotted undisposed lands near these towns. Lands set out to persons for money lent for the army in the beginning of the rebellion were still to remain disposable for the most deserving.

Lands allotted by the Cromwellians to certain persons, notably George Monck, Duke of Albemarle; Roger Boyle, Earl of Orrery; and the orphans of Owen O'Connolly, who had revealed the 1641 rising plans, were confirmed. The Declaration provided for a sequence of priorities in accommodating these various interests. Those who had adhered to the articles of peace deserved consideration, but not those who rejected or abandoned them or those who took Connaught certificates, unlike those who served the King's ensigns abroad, some of whom were specifically named for restoration. Many others were also named ("nominees") but not for immediate restoration.

Enactment. The Declaration of 1660 had provided for action in this order. First, the English who were to be dispossessed were to be settled; then precedence was to be observed in restitution as follows: (1) innocent Protestants and papists without decrees in Connaught and Clare; (2) those with such decrees being innocents; (3) transplanted persons dispossessed hereby of lands decreed in Connaught and Clare; (4) Irish papists who served the King's ensigns abroad. After these reprisals, the debts for the army before 1649 were to be satisfied. Rents were reserved on lands of every adventurer, soldier, and person settled, restored, or reprised. The Declaration was followed by a commission for its execution on April 30, 1661. Meanwhile, the Catholic position had been worsened by the production at court of the Catholic Confederates' negotiations with Urban VIII in the 1640s, making him their final court of appeal in their disputes with the King. In consequence, the instruction for the execution of the commission discriminated specifically against those who had supported the papal nuncio Giovanni Battista *Rinuccini or who, having opposed him, subsequently sought absolution from excommunication. The act itself, incorporating the Declaration and the commission, was passed only under threat that the government would not pardon activities during the interregnum. Subsequently, the court of claims to determine those who were innocent operated for 9 months before the termination of such restorations by the Act of Explanation. An abortive attempt to reopen the question in 1672 by individual royal grants led to parliamentary pressure in England to banish the Catholic clergy. In 1864 a Commission of Grace restored a few others, and the abortive Irish Parliament of James II attempted to repeal the Restoration acts. The Act of Settlement remained a standing grievance with the Catholic aristocracy.

Bibliography: *Statutes at Large, Passed in the Parliaments Held in Ireland,* 20 v. (2d. ed., Dublin 1786–1801). W. S. MASON, *Collation of the Irish Statutes* (Trinity College, Dublin, MSS Add. w.8). *Calendar of the State Papers Relating to Ireland . . . 1625–1670,* 8 v. (London 1900–10). Irish Manuscripts Commission, *The Civil Survey . . . 1654–1656,* 10 v. (Dublin 1931–61). J. G. SIMMS, *Williamite Confiscation in Ireland, 1690–1703* (London 1956). W. F. T. BUTLER, *Confiscation in Irish History* (Dublin-London 1917).

[R. D. EDWARDS]

ACTA APOSTOLICAE SEDIS, the official publication of the Holy See. Its first issue appeared Jan. 1, 1909. It was established in accord with the constitution *Promulgandi* of Pius X, Sept. 29, 1908, and is the exclusive and prescribed means for promulgating the laws of the Holy See, unless the Holy See itself provides otherwise (ActApS 1:6). At first, no provision was made regarding any length of time during which subjects were not bound by the newly promulgated laws. Since the Code of Canon Law, however, these laws begin to bind only 3 months after the date of the issue of ActApS in which they are published, unless from the nature of the case their binding force arises at once, or a shorter or longer interval is expressly prescribed in the law itself (CIC c.9). The publication appears at least once a month and forms an annual volume of about 1,000 pages. It is printed in Latin but usually contains documents in other languages. Its contents consist of encyclical and decretal letters, any motu proprio issued, and other writings as well as addresses of the Holy Father; the decrees and decisions of the various Congregations, tribunals, and commissions; a diary of the Roman Curia; a list of all the officials throughout the world appointed or honored by the Holy See; and a necrology of the bishops and cardinals.

Bibliography: Abbo 1:9. Woywod-Smith 1:9. Vermeersch-Creusen EpitCanIur 1:85.

[F. LOMBARD]

ACTION AND PASSION

Two of the ten Aristotelian *categories of being—ποιεῖν and πάσχειν in Greek, *actio* and *passio* in scholastic Latin. The history of these concepts reveals a shift of emphasis between *Aristotle himself and modern Aristotelians. In Aristotle action and passion are uniformly taken for granted. The *Categories*—presumably because action and passion are assumed to be obvious—merely gives examples, "to lance," "to cauterize," "to be lanced," "to be cauterized" (2a 3). The *Physics* is concerned directly with questions about motion, and detailed consideration of action is given only because of a difficulty based on the reality of action (202a 16, 202b 22). The same is true in the *Metaphysics,* where the difficulty is based on the actuality of action (1050a 30). Among the Greek and Latin commentators there is no dissent with respect to Aristotle's answer to these difficulties, that action is in the "patient" or recipient of the action, nor is there in St. *Thomas Aquinas. However, St. Thomas does give an occasion for later controversies (1) by devoting a separate, formal consideration to action as being in the patient (*In 3 phys.* 5), and (2) by making incidental statements that seem to contradict Aristotle's opinion (e.g., *C. gent.* 2.9; *De pot.* 7.9 ad 7, 7.10 ad 1, 8.2). These apparent contradictions escaped early Thomistic commentators, and it was left to T. de Vio *Cajetan to uncover the latent difficulty—though, curiously enough, even this discovery was not based on the difficult texts (*In ST* 1a, 25.1). After Cajetan, the shift in emphasis of the discussion was complete, and the focus was then on various theories with respect to the subject of inherence of action considered as an *accident.

This brief history omits the opinion of John *Duns Scotus (*Oxon.* 4.13.1) and the Scotists, which, considering action as an extrinsic relation to the patient, maintains against Aristotle that action is in the agent.

Definitions. Action and passion, in this context, are limited to the sphere of physical or predicamental action. Predicamental action is regularly distinguished from another type, called "immanent action": the former constitutes the category of action and is often called "transient" (or "transitive") action because, of its nature, it affects something outside the *agent, whereas immanent action perfects the agent itself and belongs to one of the species of *quality. In general, predicamental or transient action has the meaning of physical activity—any activity that of its nature brings about some *change or *motion in another body. Thus, pushing, striking, painting, and even feeding are transient actions; knowing, willing, and feeling, on the other hand, are not (St. Thomas, *C. gent.* 1.100; *In 9 meta.* 8.1862–65; etc.).

In the older Aristotelian tradition (with the exception of the Scotists), it was generally accepted that Aristotle meant this predicamental action when he said action is in the patient. His argument is straightforward: "A thing is capable of causing motion because it *can* do this, it is a mover because it actually *does* it. But it is on the movable that it is capable of acting. Hence there is a single actuality of both" (*Phys.* 202a 16–19). The conclusion is stated clearly in the *Metaphysics* in terms of a concrete example: "The act of building is in the thing being built" (1050a 30).

Passion, in this understanding, is simply the reception of the single actuality, motion-action. The sole reality in all three—motion, action, and passion—is the motion itself, though each is distinct from the others in definition (*In 3 phys.* 5.7, 5.10). Accordingly, in this straightforward view, action is defined simply as "motion from an agent"; passion, as "motion [received from an agent] in a patient."

It is clear that this doctrine has a direct bearing on the Aristotelian notion of *efficient causality—an agent, according to St. Thomas, is denominated such precisely because of its effect on the patient (*In 3 phys.* 5.15). It would seem clear also that such a notion, of agents' being determined from the effects they produce, could be of service in responding to difficulties raised by D. *Hume against the perception of *causality in the physical order.

Subject of Predicamental Action. In controversies about the subject of inherence of predicamental action, after the time of Cajetan, the straightforwardness of Aristotle's view is lost. Cajetan did not deny Aristotle's single actuality of action and motion, nor did he deny that this actuality is in the patient; but he added to it a second actuality—the perfecting of the agent whereby it actually comes to affect something else—and it is this that he claims is essential to action as a category and is subjected in the agent (*In ST* 1a, 25.1). This subtlety, distinguishing two actualities with respect to action, one in the patient and one in the agent, led to a new definition of action as "the second act by which an agent is rendered actually causing" [as opposed to first act, in which it is only a potential agent; see F. Suárez, *Disp. meta.* 48.1.15–20 (Vivès, 26:872–

873); John of St. Thomas, *Nat. phil* 1.14.3–4 (*Curs. phil.* 2:304–305, 310)].

In the aftermath of Cajetan's formulation, three well-defined schools of thought have grown up relative to the subject of inherence of transient action: (1) Many Thomists (e.g., *Ferrariensis, F. *Suárez, and P. *Fonseca) continued to maintain the older view, that action is in the patient, and the view still has proponents (T. S. McDermott). (2) At the opposite pole, some Thomists [e.g., J. P. Nazarius (1555–1646) and S. *Maurus], followed the lead of Cajetan, holding that action in the true sense is not in the patient but in the agent, and again the view has contemporary proponents (J. Gredt, *Elementa philosophiae* 1.281). (3) Finally, *John of St. Thomas developed an intermediate position, maintaining that action is in both the agent and the patient, though in different senses, a view that also has present-day proponents (W. D. Kane).

Arguments can be proposed both for and against each of these positions, as follows.

Action Is in the Patient. Two arguments are presented in favor of this position. The first is based on the authority of Aristotle, and maintains that the doctrine that action is in the patient was universally held (with the exception of the Scotists) up to the time of Cajetan. Aside from the slighting of the Scotist position, this argument has little force apart from its further doctrinal justification; it can easily be countered, as is implicitly done by Cajetan: the traditional doctrine is not denied, but only complemented by a further consideration not touched on explicitly by the older tradition (*In ST* 1a, 25.1.6).

The formal argument in favor of action as in the patient is more cogent. In one form or another, it usually recapitulates the argument of Aristotle: Since the whole reality of action is motion as from an agent (it is defined as *motus ab agente*), it follows that action will be found where motion is found. Therefore, since it is solid Aristotelian doctrine that motion is in its subject and not in the agent, action also must be in the subject (now denominated "patient," as receiving motion from the agent). The counterargument proposed against this is that this action is not denied, but it is not the essential constituent of predicamental action. Such a counterargument is not in every way convincing, if only because it is precisely this notion of action in the patient that St. Thomas uses to establish action in his derivation of the categories (*In 3 phys.* 5.15).

Action Is in the Agent. The first argument in favor of this view, proposed by Cajetan, is based on a difficulty in theology. All the divine perfections are in reality identified with the divine essence. If, therefore, the perfection of an agent is in the patient, it is difficult to see how the action of God producing effects in creatures without the intermediate cause can be identified with the divine essence. If, on the contrary, action is taken to be the perfection of the agent as actually causing, the difficulty vanishes. It is hard to see this as a serious difficulty; the question here is clearly one of an action properly immanent and only virtually transient.

What then of the argument occasioned by this difficulty? It states that, because action is the perfection of the agent as actually (and no longer only potentially) causing, it must be in the agent. Confirmation is sought from St. Thomas's statement that action is the actualization of a power (*actualitas virtutis*—*ST* 1a, 54.1).

Against this it can be argued that: (1) The distinction between immanent and transient action cannot be adequately sustained in such a formulation. (2) St. Thomas finds no difficulty in placing the perfection of a power in its affecting something outside itself—he does just this, in fact, precisely in order to distinguish transient from immanent action (*In 9 meta.* 8.1864). (3) In Aristotelian doctrine the primary type of motion is local motion; in such motion it is difficult to see what added perfection a moving body would acquire by moving another body in a collision—obviously a most important case of the action of a physical agent.

Action Is in Both Agent and Patient. To this formulation is usually added: in the agent "inchoatively," in the patient "formally and terminatively [*consummative*]." Before arguments can be proposed in favor of this position, the very terms in which it is stated must be clarified.

John of St. Thomas, the chief proponent of this view, explains the term "inchoatively" in two ways. First he says that it means "after the manner of an emanation" (though obviously he does not mean this to exclude a secondary aspect of inherence in a subject). Then he shows how it is possible for something to be in two subjects at once, provided that it is formally or *simpliciter* in only one, by appeal to the way in which a virtue can be in the will as imperating and yet at the same time be formally in the sense appetites (ST 1a 2ae, 50.3; 56.2).

The terms "formally and terminatively" are then clear from the preceding account: action receives its ultimate formality in producing its effect in the patient, and this formality lies in the completing of the emanation from the agent in the patient.

In defending this position, John of St. Thomas feels that the principal burden falls on the defenders of action as only in the patient, to explain away the apparently contrary texts in St. Thomas and to show that an aspect in the agent is unnecessary. (He feels that the position of those holding for action in the agent need not lead them to deny that it is also in the patient, but only to affirm that it is in some way in the agent.) His refutations of arguments in favor of action as only in the patient can be reduced to a distinction between "action-as-effected" and "action-as-effecting," and he is forced to say that both Aristotle and St. Thomas, in the majority of texts, wished to lay such stress on the terminative and formal aspect that they passed over the inchoative or emanational aspect [*Nat. phil.* 1.14.3–4 (*Curs. phil.* 2:304–314)]. Such an argument seems odd for a professed Aristotelian and Thomist, and this aspect of the whole position can be countered by the same arguments proposed earlier against action as in the agent.

A Simpler Position. Finally, against all three positions adopted after the time of Cajetan, it can be objected that they are needlessly subtle and are based on a false notion of what is required to constitute a category (P. Hoenen, 237–247). This view has much to recommend it, both in its simplicity and its return to the traditional view. However, it must explain away the difficulties in St. Thomas's texts if it is to be completely successful as a Thomistic interpretation. In summary, this explanation runs as follows. For St. Thomas and the earlier scholastics in general, a purely extrinsic denomination—without any instrinsic form as foundation—was sufficient to establish the last six categories. And St. Thomas is explicit in affirming that action and passion are based on extrinsic denomination and not on any intrinsic form. Nevertheless, it is still the agent that is denominated by this extrinsic reality, and it is this aspect—the agent as denominated from its effect and as subject of predication—that is referred to whenever St. Thomas refers to action as in the agent (Hoenen, 245–246).

Importance. Whether in its simple or in its subtle form, this question has an important bearing on several areas of scholastic philosophy. One aspect, in the defense of a realistic view of causality against Hume, has already been touched upon. In addition, the theory has an important bearing on the proofs for the existence of God as an unmoved mover and on the way in which free agents move and are moved by God (*see* MOTION, FIRST CAUSE OF). Further, the doctrine is of supreme importance both in explaining the difference between physical action and the acts of knowledge and affectivity and in explaining the interaction of soul and body, knower and known, in psychology.

See also ACTION AT A DISTANCE.

Bibliography: P. H. J. HOENEN, *Cosmologia* (5th ed. Rome 1956). T. S. MCDERMOTT, "The Subject of Predicamental Action," *Thomist* 23 (1960) 189–210. W. D. KANE, "The Subject of Predicamental Action according to John of St. Thomas," *ibid.* 22 (1959) 366–388. J. A. MCWILLIAMS, "Action Does Not Change the Agent," *Philosophical Studies in Honor of the Very Rev. Ignatius Smith,* ed. J. K. RYAN (Westminster, Md. 1952) 208–221.

[P. R. DURBIN]

ACTION AT A DISTANCE

The action of one material body on another across empty space, i.e., without mutual contact or without the presence of a third body or medium that is in contact with both. Whether such action is possible or not is discussed by both philosophers and scientists. The more common answer is that such action is impossible on both philosophical and empirical grounds; agreement is not unanimous largely because of differences over what is meant by "action," "matter" or "material," and "empty space" (*see* ACTION AND PASSION; MATTER; SPACE). The possibility of a spirit's exercising influence upon a material body is not in question because the notions of action, distance, and contact—derived as they are from material and extended being—do not apply to a spirit except in an analogical sense. Two reasons are usually adduced for the necessity of mutual contact or for the presence of an intermediate body: first, to make it possible to speak of localization and distance; and second, to make possible the action of the *agent upon the receiving subject. The present article discusses only the second reason, the first being treated elsewhere. *See* PLACE; LOCATION (UBI).

Various Positions. Among the philosophical proponents of the possibility of action at a distance are usually enumerated dynamists such as I. *Kant (1724–1804), with his concept of attractive forces (*Anziehungskräfte*), R. *Boscovich (1711–87), and I. J. J. Carbonnelle (1829–89); and various philosophers of science or of nature, including B. *Bolzano (1781–1848), R. H. *Lotze (1817–81), K. Gutberlet (1837–1928), and J. Schwertschlager (1853–1924). Chief among those who oppose the possibility are the early Greek philosophers—particularly the atomists, the pre-Socratic cosmologists, and the Hippocratic medical writers—and 17th-century Cartesians and mechanists. Similar opposition stems from *Aristotle, St. *Thomas Aquinas, and most medieval and scholastic thinkers, all of whom reject the possibility on metaphysical grounds.

The founders of modern science were against action at a distance, generally because of the atomist and mechanist suppositions that underlay their thought. Supporters for the concept of such action first arose from the Newtonian theory of *gravitation, although *Newton himself opposed it. The express formulation of the concept came in the 19th century with various interpretations of the experimental work of A. M. *Ampère (1775–1836) and Michael *Faraday (1791–1867), and the mathematical theories of J. C. *Maxwell (1831–79) and H. R. Hertz (1857–94). At the end of the century, the failure of the Michelson-Morley experiment to detect an *ether gave further support to the concept. More recent thinkers variously accept the possibility because of the purely mathematical way in which they interpret field concepts, or reject it because of a realist commitment to fields as existent entities, or regard it as a pseudo-problem because of a positivist view of modern science in its entirety.

Metaphysical Impossibility. The various arguments for the metaphysical impossibility of action at a distance may be summarized as follows: (1) action requires the presence of an agent; (2) contact is necessary for the exercise of influence; (3) action, as an *accident of both agent and recipient, requires that both be present in the same place; (4) cause and effect must be together; and (5) the actual dependence of the recipient upon the agent requires local contact. Since a number of these arguments are considered elsewhere (*see* ACTION AND PASSION; CAUSALITY; MOTION, FIRST CAUSE OF), only the last is explained here. The argument may be formulated in the following terms.

The action of one subject upon another requires that the recipient be dependent upon the agent in such a way that it be able to receive the agent's action. Where material bodies are involved, however, such dependence is possible only when there is local contact between agent and recipient. Therefore, action at a distance is impossible.

The major premise is universally true of action in general, even that of a spirit upon matter. The mere existence of two subjects is not sufficient for one to act upon the other, but a certain conditioning of the one for the other is required and this conditioning is prior in nature to the action itself.

In order for such mutual conditioning to occur, as stated in the minor premise, the agent and recipient must form one system in a material sense, i.e., one corporeal system with internal local relations. But such a system can be obtained only through local contact, and this either immediately or mediately, i.e., through a material medium that is again in immediate contact with both agent and recipient. If such contact does not exist, the bodies cannot influence one another. Moreover, while an inactive medium can register place and relative direction, it cannot determine an event that originates from one body and influences another at a particular time and with a particular intensity. Thus, when a medium is involved, it must play both an active and a passive role in the bodily interaction.

This argument is metaphysical in the sense that it presupposes the validity of such concepts as action, being, and causality, all of which are verifiable in ordinary experience without recourse to the experimental and conceptual developments of modern science. Those who reject metaphysics, of course, do not subscribe to an argumentation of this type (*see* METAPHYSICS, VALIDITY OF).

Physical Arguments. Physical proofs of the impossibility of action at a distance attempt to show that, as a matter of fact, such action does not take place in the physical universe. For this purpose, one may classify actions as either chemical, or mechanical, or those involving some type of field interaction. Regarding chemical activity, it seems generally agreed that chemical interaction occurs only if reagents are brought into contact, and thus there is no action at a distance. Again, if physical action is transmitted mechanically, either by streams of particles or by collision of macroscopic bodies, there is no action at a distance. This leaves only actions associated with field concepts—among which may be enumerated electricity, magnetism, electromagnetism, gravity, and nuclear and other forces—for detailed discussion.

One characteristic of such actions is their dependence upon the distance between agent and recipient, as, for example, the magnitude of the gravitational force between bodies being inversely proportional to the square of their distance. Again, in the case of the electric and magnetic phenomena, intermediary bodies can exercise influence, as in shielding effects. Moreover, such actions are propagated with a finite velocity, and the implied dependence on space and time is incompatible with action at a distance. Yet again, the existence of standing waves and of radiation quanta cannot be explained solely in terms of empty space. Finally, a field theory itself is opposed to the concept of action at a distance. Fields have properties that differ from point to point and that are describable in terms of potentials; they also contain a definite amount of *energy. Thus they function as operational media and have a degree of reality corresponding to the action they transmit. Whatever phenomena urge scientists to admit the action of a field also urge the acceptance of a medium that supports such activity.

Such arguments, while not absolutely conclusive, argue strongly against the hypothesis of action at a distance.

See also VACUUM; VOID.

Bibliography: P. H. VAN LAER, *Actio in distans en aether* (Utrecht 1947); *Philosophico-scientific Problems,* tr. H. J. KOREN (Pittsburgh 1953). M. B. HESSE, "Action at a Distance," *The Concept of Matter,* ed. E. MCMULLIN (Notre Dame, Ind. 1963) 372–390; *Forces and Fields: The Concepts of Action at a Distance in the History of Physics* (New York 1962).

[W. A. WALLACE]

ACTION FRANÇAISE

Action Française (A.F.) is the name of a political league and also its journal, which attempted during the first 4 decades of the 20th century to reestablish the monarchy in France.

Program and Influence. A first committee of A.F. was born in 1898 during the *Dreyfus affair. It was transformed in 1905 into a league of A.F., which proposed to combat every republican regime and to reestablish the monarchy. It edited a biweekly periodical, called *L'Action française.* (1899–), and in 1908 launched a daily newspaper, with the same name. An institute of A.F. took charge of doctrinal propaganda. Charles *Maurras was the unquestioned head and the theorist of the movement, which counted several other very talented leaders, such as Léon *Daudet, Henri Vaugeois, and Jacques Bainville.

A.F. was never a mass movement, and played only a minor legislative role although Daudet was for a time elected a deputy. But its intellectual influence was considerable, especially among Catholics. Although its principal directors were atheists, they believed that if French society was to prosper as it had in the past, it must return to both the political form and the religious practice of earlier times. The Church quickly became disturbed by the organization's influence over a section of the French clergy and faithful. Its journal taught that political laws proceed from experience, and that the national interest has an absolute primacy in moral matters. Its young partisans grouped under the name *"camelots,"* and swore to promote royalist restoration by any means whatsoever. In brief it was a political school whose concepts derived from a naturalist view of man, society, and religion; and this intellectual outlook obliterated the moral sense of its members in their concepts of foreign and domestic politics.

Attitude of the Church. Because of the complaints of French bishops, the Holy Office prepared a prohibition of seven books by Maurras, and the periodical, but not the newspaper, of the movement (Jan. 26, 1914). However, A.F.'s combat against anticlerical republicans and its struggle for a conservative type of Catholicism then in favor at the Vatican produced interventions in its favor at Rome. As a result, Pius X (1903–14) suspended publication of the decree. Benedict XV (1914–22) adopted the same attitude because of World War I. Pius XI (1922–39) received new complaints as a result of an investigation that revealed the extraordinary ascendancy of the movement over Belgian youth, and asked Cardinal Andrieu, Archbishop of Bordeaux, to publish a letter of disapproval, which appeared on Aug. 25, 1926, and received papal approbation. The *Osservatore Romano* printed articles on this subject to which A.F. replied violently, branding the editors a "small band of demoniacal agents," and pretending in an article entitled *"Non possumus"* that treason and parricide were being asked of it. A decree of the Holy Office (Dec. 29, 1926) published the text of the 1914 condemnation, and added to it, with the ratification of Pius XI, the newspaper *L'Action française* "as it is published today" because of articles written "these recent days especially . . . namely by Charles Maurras and Léon Daudet, articles which every sensible man is obliged to recognize as written against the Holy Apostolic See and the Roman Pontiff himself."

Reacting with fury, A.F. vilified the *Osservatore Romano* as *"Diffamatore Romano,"* and "an infamous rag"; resurrected all the familiar specters of anticlericalism, such as Galileo, St. Bartholomew's Massacre, Alexander VI, and the Borgias; and accused the Pope of being the victim of a plot to restore the Holy Roman Germanic Empire. This led Bishop Ruch of Strasbourg to classify *L'Action française* the most anticlerical newspaper in France.

Subsequent to the condemnation of Dec. 29, 1926, the Holy See published other documents that fixed the manner of treating the unsubmissive. Priests were forbidden to administer the Sacraments to them and were threatened with canonical sanctions if disobedient. Marriages of the rebellious were merely to be blessed in the sacristy, like mixed marriages. Dying rebels must make honorable amends or be deprived of the last rites, and go to their graves without the Church's prayers.

Several French bishops remained sympathetic to A.F., and at first refrained from commenting on the Roman condemnation or made very fine distinctions in their observations. Undoubtedly at the Holy See's demand, a long declaration appeared with 116 episcopal signatures (March 8, 1927), but without the names of three bishops. One of these was later regarded by the Holy See as having resigned. Sanctions were taken against important ecclesiastics, such as Cardinal *Billot, who was removed from the Sacred College and went to finish his days at the Jesuit novitiate in Gallora. Priests suspected of favoring the movement were gradually removed from influential posts, especially those dealing with young people. Jacques Maritain, in collaboration with P. Doncoeur and four other ecclesiastics, published a book defending the Holy See, *Pourquoi Rome a parlé* (1927). Maurice Pujo replied to it in a series of articles later gathered in book form as *Comment Rome est trompé* (1929), which drew from V. Bernadot and five authors the reply *Clairvoyance de Rome* (1929). Some bishops closed their eyes; but others applied the sanctions rigorously. Many cases gained notoriety and with the passage of time contributed to build hopes for a gradual appeasement of the affair. Some interventions occurred in Rome. Maurras wrote to Pius XI (January 1937), and received a reply. He then wrote two more letters to the Pope. Their correspondence made it clear, however, that their viewpoints remained irreconcilable.

The pontificate of *Pius XII (1939–58) opened new perspectives. After long negotiations, the directive committee of A.F. sent a letter to the Pope expressing their sincerest sorrow for anything in their polemics and controversies that had been injurious and even unjust. The Catholics on the committee rejected all their erroneous writings and every precept and theory contrary to Catholic teachings. Pius XII had not demanded the type of retraction required by his predecessor, but the text signed by the committee constituted an implicit retraction since it admitted that the prohibition's motives were just.

The Holy See triumphed in the end, for Catholic youths ceased joining the movement. Its defeat became more evident when the Duke of Guise, pretender to the throne, disassociated himself from A.F. (November 1937). The liberation government forbade in 1944 the publication of *L'Action française* because of its attitude during World War II.

Bibliography: N. FONTAINE, *Saint-Siège: Action française et catholiques intégraux* (Paris 1928). D. GWYNN, *The "Action Française" Condemnation* (London 1928). L. WARD, *The Condemnation of the Action Française* (London 1928). J. BRUGERETTE, *Le Prêtre français et la société contemporaine,* 3 v. (Paris 1933–38) v.3. Dansette 2. S. M. OSGOOD, *French Royalism under the Third and Fourth Republics* (The Hague 1960). E. J. WEBER, *Action Française* (Stanford 1962). E. R. TANNENBAUM, *The Action Française* (New York 1962). H. DANIEL-ROPS, *L'Église des révolutions: Un Combat pour Dieu, 1870–1939* (Histoire de l'Église du Christ 6.2; Paris 1963). J. GRISAR, LexThK[1] 1:71–74. H. DU PASSAGE, LexThK[2] 1:116–117. A. DA LANGASCO, EncCatt 1:255–258.

[A. DANSETTE]

ACTION POPULAIRE, or Institut Social Action Populaire, an institute of French Jesuits at Vanves (Seine) founded in 1903 to diffuse among French Catholics the social teachings of the Church. After World War I an Institut d'Études Sociales was established at the Institut Catholique de Paris, under the direction of Gustave Desbuquois, SJ, to train priests, religious, and lay persons in the social sciences; in 1965, nearly half of the students were from African, Asian, and Latin American countries. In 1926 Action Populaire was asked to send one of its members permanently to the International Labor Organization established at Geneva in 1919. Through contacts with trade union leaders and industrial managers, participation in national or diocesan social weeks, publication of two periodicals, and the editing of a large number of books and commentaries on the social encyclicals, Action Populaire assumed leadership in the training of French clergy and laity in organized and responsible Catholic *social action. After World War II, it developed into a center for research and action in economics, politics, and sociology. In 1961 a branch of the institute was founded at Abidjan, Ivory Coast, West Africa, as the Institut Africain pour le Développement Économique et Social (INADES); now autonomous with its own staff and activities, it conducts correspondence courses for social workers from the entire African continent and receives encouragement from most of the new African governments for its programs of courses, summer schools, and services relating to the rural economy and economic development. In 1965 the Action Populaire staff of 20 Jesuits was engaged in research and in teaching at the Institut Catholique, at the Gregorian University in Rome, or as visiting professors or consultants in various foreign universities and centers. The main fields of research include social philosophy and ideology, the sociology of religion, demography, the sociology of the family, the regional economy, the rural economy, economic and social development, social legislation, international relations, and Soviet studies. The monthly *Revue de l'Action Populaire* is devoted to specialized study of social doctrine, social structures, and social change; the fortnightly *Cahiers d'Action Religieuse et Sociale,* to information and the training of Catholic leaders.

See also SOCIAL MOVEMENTS, CATHOLIC, 2.

[R. BOSC]

ACTIVE LIFE, SPIRITUAL

A life of external activity as opposed to contemplation. In the 3d century, Origen identified the active life with Martha and the contemplative life with her sister Mary. Before the Christian Era the Greeks had differentiated the theoretical from the practical. The practical life was that which busied itself with affairs of family or city. To express the practical matter of working out one's salvation, of striving for perfection, or making a spiritual effort to purify one's conscience in the sight of God, St. Paul used the Greek word "askein." Gradually this word had acquired the meaning of an exercise of the spiritual faculties in the acquisition of the virtues of learning, or exercise in a physical sense. St. Paul often made reference to the efforts of athletes in the games when urging his Christians to the practice of perfection.

Origen again was first to apply the word "ascetic" to Christians who practiced virginity and devoted themselves to works of mortification. With St. Augustine the term active life became almost synonymous with ascetical striving by making it consist of the practice of virtues, as apart from contemplation of truth. St. Gregory the Great seconded this doctrine by identifying the active life with the practice of the corporal works of mercy and to some extent the spiritual works, and this tradition persisted through St. Thomas and Suárez.

The active life reaches a new plane when it concerns itself with the care of souls. From the time of Augustine authors point out that bishops, to whom the care of souls properly belongs, lead the active life in its fullest sense, as well as the contemplative life, since all their activity must be richly impregnated with contemplation. It follows that those who are not bishops more fully lead the active life the more they participate in the care of souls, a work that is proper to bishops. That is why St. Thomas can rank in the first place those religious orders whose concern is to give to others the fruit of their contemplation. Historically, religious orders, at the beginning, were concerned only with the perfection of their own members. Gradually, the needs of souls forced them into the apostolate proper to bishops. Religious orders, such as the Franciscans and Dominicans in the 13th century, were even founded with a view of doing work bishops no longer could handle alone. The revolutionary Society of Jesus (1540), which set the pattern for many of the more modern religious institutes, moved into whatever area was necessary for the good of souls, whether it was the corporal and spiritual works of mercy, or preaching and the administration of the Sacraments. In modern times, the next logical step was taken by the participation of the laity in the apostolate of the hierarchy or what is known as Catholic Action, a way of living the active life of the spirit while remaining in the world.

The secret of the successful practice of the active life is charity in action. As St. Thomas teaches, charity is the root of merit. Affective charity, consisting in internal acts of the love of God is common to both the active and the contemplative lives, and must be made effective in the external worship of God in the contemplative life. St. Augustine says that it is "only the compulsion of charity that shoulders necessary activity" (*Civ.* 19.19). Affective charity is the real measure of perfection, but is itself gauged best by this effective charity of good works. Effective charity means carrying out God's commands. The whole purpose of the active life is to attain union with God by service to neighbor, whom God has commanded us to love. One leading the active life does not so much leave God for God, as the popular phrase puts it, but finds God always and everywhere in activity done for the love of God.

Obviously the term "active life" is an analogous term. In a nonspiritual sense it would be the opposite of quiet. In the spiritual sense it is ambiguous, for it can mean either the opposite of the contemplative life or the life that flows from contemplation. When used in the context of the spiritual as a univocal term, it usually refers to the life of virtue, the pursuit of virtue, the life of the corporal and spiritual works of mercy, and all those things that are indirectly connected with charity.

Bibliography: E. C. BUTLER, *Western Mysticism* (2d ed. London 1927). P. T. CAMELOT and I. MENNESSIER, "The Active Life and the Contemplative Life," *The Virtues and States of Life,* ed. A. M. HENRY, tr. R. J. OLSON and G. T. LENNON (Theology Library 4; Chicago 1957) 645–683. J. DE GUIBERT, *The Theology of the Spiritual Life,* tr. P. BARRETT (New York 1953). E. CORETH, "Contemplative in Action," TheolDig 3 (1955) 37–45.

[J. F. CONWELL]

ACTIVISM

A teaching or orientation that emphasizes action in contradistinction to passivity. Thus, in a learning situation, the functionalism advocated by John *Dewey or the method of teaching children promoted by Maria *Montessori is sometimes called activism. As a philosophic notion, it is opposed to intellectualism and gives precedence to practice and activity over theory. In this sense contemporary *existentialism can be called activism in that it repudiates speculation in favor of action.

However, in Catholic circles, particularly in the U.S., it has come to denote an excessive activity of the apostolate that is detrimental to the spiritual life, especially in religious orders and congregations: exterior work of the apostolate absorbs the interest of the one engaged in it to the extent that his interior life suffers as a consequence. It is also referred to as naturalism. Although such activism is not a formal doctrine, but rather a tendency of human nature, it is sometimes called the "heresy of action" and may be said in a general way to have a spirit opposed to the *Quietism promoted by Miguel de *Molinos and condemned by Innocent XI in 1687 (Denz 2201–69).

Activism should not be confused with the salutary work of the apostolate performed with the proper spiritual motives. Far from being an obstacle to spiritual growth, the giving of oneself in the service of others out of charity fosters the interior life of the soul. Activism, therefore, should not be equated with activity or a multiplicity of works. In its modern connotation, it has reference only to spiritual activity prompted by an indiscreet zeal and lacking a spiritual foundation. In the encyclical *Menti nostrae* Pius XII refers to it as "that kind of activity which is not based on divine grace and does not make constant use of the aids provided by Jesus Christ for the attainment of holiness" [ActApS 42 (1950) 677].

Safeguards against activism include proper spiritual formation, the constant exercise of humility and prayer, and a wholesome spiritual outlook concerning the work of the apostolate. Those engaged in the apostolate should keep the words of St. Paul foremost in mind: "So then neither he who plants is anything, nor he who waters, but God who gives the growth" (1 Cor 3.7). The avoidance of activism should not, on the other hand, give way to a negativism characterized by a turning away from the performance of good works. In fact, there is great necessity for an increase in apostolic work to counteract growing materialistic tendencies.

Activism is also called *Americanism. Such a spiritual pragmatism was condemned by Leo XIII in the apostolic letter **Testem benevolentiae,* addressed to Cardinal James Gibbons in 1899. While the Pope praised the Church and the people of the U.S. for their spirit of progress and accomplishment, he nevertheless cautioned them, among other things, not to place too great an emphasis on externals and outward activity to the detriment of the spiritual life. Thus the term Americanism is often used, especially by European writers, to denote an excessive apostolic activity lacking the proper spiritual motivation.

See also APOSTOLATE AND SPIRITUAL LIFE; FUNCTIONALIST SCHOOL; GRACE.

Bibliography: N. SAMMARTANO, EncCatt 2:340–355. M. BLONDEL, "Theory and Practice of Action," tr. J. M. SOMERVILLE, *Cross Currents* 4 (1954) 251–261. J. B. CHAUTARD, *The Soul of the Apostolate,* tr. J. A. MORAN (Trappist, Ky. 1941). J. AUMANN, "The Heresy of Action," CrossCrown 3 (1951) 25–45. L. J. PUTZ, "Toward a Spirituality of Action," *Proceedings of the 1958 Sisters' Institute of Spirituality* 6 (1959) 96–105. R. BRADLEY, "Activity or Activism," *Sister Formation Bulletin* 4.2 (1957) 1–6. F. KLEIN, *Americanism: A Phantom Heresy* (Cranford, N.J. 1951) reproduced from W. ELLIOTT's *Life of Father Hecker* (4th ed. New York 1898).

[L. F. BACIGALUPO]

ACTIVITY PROGRAM (EDUCATION)

Although the activity program varies from situation to situation, its salient features may be described as "a type of curriculum based on experiential learning in line with the interests and needs of the child; organized around units of work or pupil enterprises that reproduce or approximate life situations; often involve a large measure of overt activity, such as gardening, shopwork, singing, and dramatizing" (DictEdu 311). To this general definition must be added as a necessary element of the program the social aspect of working together.

Origin and Development. Known variously as the activity program, the activity movement, and in Europe as the activity school, the program represents the contributions of many philosophers and educational practitioners over many years and in several countries. The movement developed largely as a protest against the verbalistic learning prevalent in schools and their dependence on books as a primary or sole source of the curriculum. The originators of activity pedagogy, J. A. *Comenius, J. J. *Rosseau, J. H. *Pestalozzi, and F. W. *Fröbel, each added to the growing body of theory emphasizing pupil activity, manual training, social interdependence, and reliance on nature as basic to sound education. Because of their influence and the work of able administrators, the activity school became the form of public education in both Austria and Germany in 1920.

In America, John *Dewey, pragmatic philosopher and educational experimenter, gave the activity movement its American expression in the child-centered school. In 1896, in his laboratory school at the University of Chicago, he organized the curriculum around children's interests and needs and attracted wide attention from educators and laymen alike. From 1904 on, as professor of philosophy at Columbia University, he strongly influenced his students, particularly Boyd Bode and William Kilpatrick, who popularized his ideas and inaugurated the *progressive education movement in 1919, which in some respects went far beyond Dewey's own conception of the activity program.

Beginning in a few private schools and laboratory schools of teachers' colleges, the movement spread across the country until nearly every school, public and nonpublic, adopted many or at least some of its principles. Recently, however, there has been a gradual diminution of enthusiasm for activity programs and a growing emphasis on tool subjects. A golden mean between the traditional book-centered learning and the progressive child-centered school is apparently gaining acceptance.

Content and Method. The activity-school curriculum veered away from classical materials and assigned subjects toward a program based on child interests, child-centered instead of subject-centered. Since everything is changing in the world, said the activist, schools should emphasize process rather than content as such, and the most procedural subjects, the social studies, should receive the greatest stress. Science became important, not because of its content, but because of its problem-solving techniques; and the graphic arts became an integral part of the curriculum. With the extremists, instead of required pupil texts, a variety of references for consultation were to be used according as "felt needs" or developmental periods of growth dictated.

The method of the activity program stressed creativity, learning by doing, as opposed to listening and reciting. The activity began with a real-life problem, which the child solved by following the five steps in the scientific method. During this inquiry, he sought information in reference books; and developed skill in reading, composing, and reporting. The child-centered school opposed all ability grouping as undemocratic, preferring projects, units of work, and socialized recitation, and opportunities to work together in social situations. Some schools adopted modified activity programs, introducing the best features of content and method of the child-centered schools.

Evaluation—Catholic Viewpoint. Concerning content, Catholic educational philosophy approves many aspects of the activity program: its variety, flexibility, relevance to daily living, and concern for individual needs and interests, as long as religion is accorded first place in the curriculum. The Church recognizes personal experience and activity, as opposed to acquiescent passivity, as a sound basis for learning and favors various educational methods that involve pupil participation. It rejects, however, the extreme permissiveness of some child-centered schools that, overestimating the innate goodness of man, forget that the child's fallen nature, wounded but not essentially vitiated, requires adequate guidance in curbing unruly impulses, and correction as well as motivation.

On the other hand, three elements of the activity program are contrary to Catholic philosophy: the faulty concepts of the nature of man; the nature of truth; and the respective roles of child, parent, and Church. The Church teaches that man, created by God, is composed of body and soul substantially united and destined to live with God hereafter. The basic false naturalism pervading much of the activity program, however, denies the whole concept of the supernatural and ignores redemption, grace, and original sin. The Church, moreover, teaches that truth exists and can be known, and that supernatural truth, revelation, should be taught; that religion must be an integral part of the educational system that has as its primary aim right living here and supernatural life hereafter. The activity program, however, eschewing all knowledge of ultimate principles of truth and morality, accepts only the principles of *pragmatism or instrumentalism; and rejecting those divine truths that must be taken on faith, holds only those facts that are scientifically demonstrated. Finally, in making the child the measure of all things, the activity program tends to diminish adult authority represented by the teacher and parent, and to overlook the dynamic role of the Church as the guardian of truth and the dispenser of God's graces.

Thus the naturalism undergirding the child-centered school and expressed in the activity program is untenable for Catholics, although various features of it can be adopted to improve the traditional schools of the past.

Bibliography: W. McGucken, "The Philosophy of Catholic Education," *Philosophies of Education,* ed. N. B. Henry (National Society for the Study of Education, 41st Yearbook, pt. 1; Chicago 1942) 251–288. V. C. Morris, *Philosophy and the American School* (Boston 1961). G. G. Schoenchen, *The Activity School* (New York 1940). H. O. Rugg and A. Shumaker, *The Child-Centered School* (Yonkers-on-Hudson, N.Y. 1928). Pius XI, *Divini illius magistri* (Encyclical, Dec. 31, 1929) ActApS 21 (1929) 723–762; Eng. *The Christian Education of Youth* (New York 1936).

[M. J. CORCORAN]

ACTON, CHARLES JANUARIUS, cardinal; b. Naples, Italy, March 6, 1803; d. there, June 23, 1847. He was the son of Sir John Acton, sometime prime minister of the Kingdom of Naples. After his father's death (1811), Charles went to England, where he studied at Westminster School and then at Magdalene College, Cambridge (1819–23). He then returned to Rome to attend the Academy of Noble Ecclesiastics previous to ordination. In 1828 he was made a papal chamberlain and was appointed secretary to the nuncio in Paris. His next appointment was that of vice legate at Bologna. Before the uprising in Bologna (1831), Gregory XVI named him secretary to the Congregation of Regulars. Later he became auditor of the Apostolic Chamber. He was proclaimed cardinal (June 24, 1842) after being created *in petto* nearly 3 years previously. At the meeting between Gregory XVI and Czar Nicholas I (1845), Acton was the interpreter and sole witness. Later he wrote an account of the conversation at the Pope's request. As adviser to the Holy See on matters concerning England, he recommended in 1840 an increase in the number of English vicars apostolic from four to eight but opposed the restoration of the hierarchy (1850). Although urged by the King of Naples to do so, he refused to accept the archiepiscopal See of Naples.

Bibliography: C. S. Isaacson, *The Story of the English Cardinals* (London 1907). B. N. Ward, *The Sequel to Catholic Emancipation,* 2 v. (New York 1915) 1:154–166. DictEngCath 1:3–6.

[B. FOTHERGILL]

ACTON, JOHN EMERICH EDWARD DALBERG

Historian; b. Naples, Italy, Jan. 10, 1834; d. Tegernsee, Bavaria, June 19, 1902. The later eighth Baronet and first Baron, Acton was the only child of Sir Richard Acton and Marie Louise Pellini de Dalberg. At the age of 3, upon the death of his father, he succeeded to a baronetcy in England. With his mother as his guardian, he was brought to his estate at Aldenham. After spending a year at St. Nicholas, a preparatory school near Paris (1842), he enrolled for 4 years at St. Mary's College, Oscott, whose president was Nicholas (later Cardinal) *Wiseman. Acton continued his studies at Edinburgh under a private tutor, Dr. Logan, a former vice president of Oscott. Unable to gain admission to Cambridge University, Acton went to Munich in 1850 to become the pupil and traveling companion of Johannes Ignaz von *Döllinger. He traveled widely throughout Europe and visited the U.S. in 1855. His German training developed in him a profound love for historical learning and critical scholarship. His cosmopolitan background and knowledge of languages assisted him greatly in his historical pursuits.

John Emerich E. D. Acton, portrait by F. S. von Lenbach.

Acton returned to England in 1859 with the intention of introducing the isolated English Catholic community to progressive Catholic thought. He believed that England, better than any other Western country, had preserved a true Catholic spirit in its political institutions and that Catholics had a special duty to maintain the Christian character of the English constitution. He sat as a Whig member of Parliament for Carlow, an Irish constituency (1859–65). During this period he formed a close friendship with William *Gladstone and became his lifelong political supporter and confidant. With his interests and talents, Acton found the world of practical politics thoroughly uncongenial, and he took little part in parliamentary affairs. In 1858 he purchased part ownership of a liberal Catholic journal, the *Rambler* (called in 1862 *The Home and Foreign Review*). Until 1864 he devoted most of his energies to writing articles and reviews for this enterprise. This was his most prolific period as a writer and saw the production of some of his best works.

Encouraged by *Newman and ably assisted by Richard *Simpson, Acton followed a progressive line that gave offense to the ultraconservatives who represented the dominant group in the Church. Because of his insistence, often in provocative, arrogant fashion, that the Catholic scholar should be free to discuss without restriction all religious questions that were not defined doctrines, and his coolness toward the papal *temporal power, the English hierarchy and Rome viewed him with suspicion. By 1864, when Pius IX issued the *Syllabus of Errors, Acton was convinced that the Holy See favored a restrictive policy that ran counter to his own deepest convictions. In a spirit of frustration he withdrew from Catholic journalism. He continued to contribute to the *Chronicle* (1867–68) and the *North British Review* (1867–71), but his most productive period was at an end. On Gladstone's recommendation he was raised to the peerage in 1869.

During *Vatican Council I, Acton was one of the most vociferous opponents of a solemn definition of papal primacy and infallibility. Despite his close association with Döllinger, he refused to identify himself with the German scholars who repudiated the conciliar definitions of the papal prerogatives and who were, as a result, excommunicated (*see* OLD CATHOLICS). Although fanatically opposed to the growing *ultramontanism, he taught his son in 1890: "A Church without a pope is not the Church of Christ." He remained a devout Catholic in his private life, but after 1875 he grew more isolated from his coreligionists.

Contemporary ideas of progress and human perfectibility exercised a powerful influence on his thoughts. Acton came to view the course of history as one of progress toward freedom. With a fervor that at times approached hysteria he denounced all forces, past or present, that restricted liberty. He subjected the popes to special condemnation, and he was no less severe on saints who had countenanced the *Inquisition. He collected voluminous notes for a major work on the history of liberty that was never completed. He was one of the founders of the *English Historical Review* (1886). On the nomination of Lord Rosebery, Acton was appointed (1895) regius professor of modern history at Cambridge. As his final project Acton drew up the plans and acted as editor for the *Cambridge Modern History,* but this 14-volume monument of cooperative scholarship appeared (1902–12) only after his death.

Apart from periodical articles, Acton published little during his lifetime. Since his death, however, most of his major essays and lectures have appeared in book form. His writings reflect immense learning and moral earnestness, but they are marred occasionally by a Whig bias that led him to be unfair in his historical judgments. His influence on Catholic thought during his lifetime was minimal, but he has since been recognized as the most farsighted Catholic historical thinker of his generation.

Bibliography: Works. *Lectures on Modern History,* ed. J. N. FIGGIS and R. V. LAURENCE (London 1906; repr. 1930); *Historical Essays and Studies,* ed. J. N. FIGGIS and R. V. LAURENCE (London 1907); *Essays on Freedom and Power,* ed. G. HIMMELFARB (Boston 1948); *Essays on Church and State,* ed. D. WOODRUFF (New York 1953); *Letters to Mary Gladstone,* ed. H. PAUL (New York 1904); *Selections from the Correspondence of the First Lord Acton,* ed. J. N. FIGGIS and R. V. LAURENCE (London 1917); *Lord Acton and His Circle,* ed. F. A. GASQUET (New York 1906). A. WATKIN and H. BUTTERFIELD, "Gasquet and the Acton-Simpson Correspondence," CambHistJ 10 (1950–) 77–105, points out defects in Gasquet's editing. V. CONZEMIUS, ed., *Ignaz von Döllinger: Briefwechsel 1820–90* (Munich 1963–), to be completed in 5 v., contains D's correspondence with Acton.

Literature. U. NOACK, *Katholizität und Geistesfreiheit nach den Schriften von J. Dalberg-Acton, 1834–1902* (Frankfurt 1936). F. ENGEL-JANOSI, "Reflections of Lord Acton on Historical Principles," CathHistRev 27 (1941) 166–185. F. E. LALLY, *As Lord Acton Says* (Newport, R.I. 1942). D. MATHEW, *Acton: The Formative Years* (London 1946), to 1864. H. BUTTERFIELD, *Lord Acton* (London 1948), pamphlet; "Acton: His Training, Methods, and Intellectual System," in *Studies in Diplomatic History and Historiography in Honour of G. P. Gooch,* ed. A. O. SARKISSIAN (London 1961) 169–198. G. HIMMELFARB, *Lord Acton* (Chicago 1952). H. A. MACDOUGALL, *The Acton-Newman Relations* (New York 1962). G. E. FASNACHT, *Acton's Political Philosophy* (London 1952). L. KOCHAN, *Acton on History* (London 1954). J. L. ALTHOLZ, *The Liberal Catholic Movement in England* (London 1962). **Illustration credit:** National Portrait Gallery, London.

[H. A. MAC DOUGALL]

ACTS, NOTIONAL

In Trinitarian theology notions are characteristics proper to each Divine *Person, by which man is able to know the Persons as distinct. These are innascibility, paternity, filiation, active and passive spiration (ST 1a, 32; Scotus adds the inspirability of the Second Person: *In 1 sent.* 28.1–3). The adjective notional is applied to whatever is proper to one Person and not common to all. In God "all is one, save where there is relative opposition" (Council of Florence; Denz 1330); therefore all that is notional is really identical with the divine *relations of origin, but man's abstractive mode of thought makes it necessary to introduce further mental distinctions if he is to think or speak of this mystery.

By the term notional acts theologians designate those divine acts that enable one to come to the knowledge of the distinct Persons; these are the *generation of the Word and the *spiration of the Spirit. The magisterium unhesitatingly applies the corresponding verbs (*generare, gigni, procedere*) to each Person (Fourth Lateran Council; Denz 800, 804). Considered as the way by which the Persons and their opposed relations originate, these enable one to discern each Person. Some theologians speak simply of two acts (generation, spiration); the majority speak of four, considering each act both as emanating from a principle (active generation, spiration) and as received in a term (passive generation, spiration).

Certain conceptual problems arise (ST 1a, 40.4; 41.1–6). (1) One cannot think of origin save in terms of action, but, applied to God, man's concept of action must be purified of all created imperfection. God's immanent activity of knowing and loving is identical with His essence, pure act; one must exclude all idea of motion, passive potency, and determinability and speak simply of God's active power, exercise of activity, the active and actual influence of principle on term. Thus, by a mental distinction, one expresses the dynamic aspect of the relation of producing principle to term produced. (2) Notional acts are necessary, for God's activity is identical with His essence. This is not to suggest coercion; indeed notional acts are voluntary, not that the Father could have refrained from begetting the Son, but because God wills and loves all the perfection that He necessarily is. (3) Does the notional act presuppose (logically) the corresponding property, or vice versa? When one considers generation and spiration as received in the Son and the Spirit, the act is clearly prior to the property (filiation, passive spiration). Active spiration, common to two Persons, obviously presupposes those Persons. But what of active generation? This presupposes the First Person, constituted by the property of paternity. How can that property be logically prior to the act of generation? St. Thomas answers (ST 1a, 40.4 ad 1) by distinguishing between paternity as a property of the First Person (prior to generation) and as a relation to the Second Person (subsequent to generation).

See also PROPERTIES, DIVINE PERSONAL; RELATIONS, TRINITARIAN; PROCESSIONS, TRINITARIAN; TRINITY, HOLY, ARTICLES ON.

Bibliography: A. MICHEL, DTC 11.1:802–805. Commentaries on ST 1a, 41. *Somme théologique: La Trinité,* ed. and tr. H. F. DONDAINE, 2 v. (Paris 1942–46) 2:354–366. P. VANIER, *Théologie trinitaire chez saint Thomas d'Aquin: Évolution du concept d'action notionelle* (Montreal 1953).

[R. L. STEWART]

ACTS OF THE APOSTLES

A book of the Bible containing a theological history of the first 30 years of Christianity. This article will first consider the origin and authorship of Acts, and then give a thematic summary of the work.

Origin and Authorship. That Luke wrote Acts is not seriously questioned. Tradition dating back to the 2d century (*Muratorian Canon, Irenaeus, ancient Latin prologue to the pre-Jerome Latin translation) and to the 3d century (Clement of Alexandria, Origen, Tertullian) attests to his authorship. Acts was composed as a companion volume to Luke's Gospel (*see* LUKE, GOSPEL ACCORDING TO ST.). The prologues of both are addressed to the same Theophilus. Luke's desire to bring the two works into close unity is evident in the care he has taken to tie the first chapter of Acts to the last chapter of the Gospel: Acts 1.4 corresponds to Lk 24.49; Acts 1.8 corresponds to Lk 24.47; Acts 1.9 corresponds to Lk 24.51. The two works were separated early in their history, when the NT works were collected, so that the four Gospels might be placed together. The title, Acts of Apostles (so, without the article, in the Greek), was probably invented at that time.

Date. The precise date of composition is unknown. St. Jerome believed that Acts was written shortly after Paul's first Roman imprisonment (A.D. 61–63), the last event described in it. This opinion is still popular and explains the lack of any mention of Paul's later imprisonment and martyrdom. A still older opinion is that Acts was written only after Paul's death *c.* A.D. 67. The solution to the question depends on the dating of Luke's Gospel. It preceded Acts and depended on the Gospel of Mark. Mark seemingly wrote after the death of Peter, *c.* A.D. 64. A suggested sequence is: death of Peter *c.* A.D. 64; Gospel of Mark shortly afterward; Gospel of Luke; Acts of the Apostles. This would date Acts *c.* A.D. 70 at the earliest. This question of the date of composition is of secondary importance once the Lucan authorship is granted. He was an eyewitness of part of what he relates. For the rest he shows himself a careful investigator. (The studies of Sir William Ramsay have proved how precise a historian Luke was.)

Sources. It is evident that sources were needed, since Luke was not a witness of the greater part of the material he narrates. That some of this source material was in written form is very probable. Experts differ on whether there were two parallel sources, or various complementary sources, or one principal source. Modern research has not yet identified positively any written sources, since Luke has reworked them into his own style and vocabulary. It is possible, however, to point to his own personal sources of information. The "we sections" in which Luke speaks in the first person plural (16.10–17; 20.5–2.18; 27.1–28.16) arose from his own experiences as Paul's companion. His acquaintance with Mark (Col 4.10, 14) and with Philip the Deacon (21.8) must have provided much information. Mark could have been a source for the Petrine material in the first half of Acts. From Philip he could have learned the details of the choosing of the deacons, the martyrdom of Stephen, and the ministry of Philip himself (ch. 6–8). From Philip, too, or some other Caesarean (23.33), he could have heard the story of Cornelius (ch. 10) and of the death of Agrippa (12.19–23). From Paul he could have gathered the information on Paul's conversion and his first missionary journey. Mnason, a Cypriot (21.16), could have been a source of information on the important work of the Cypriots in the early apostolate (11.19–20). All these personal sources would have enabled Luke to control any written sources that came into his possession.

Texts. The ancient manuscripts of Acts fall into two general classes, Eastern and Western. The Eastern, or Alexandrian, text usually has a shorter reading. It is represented by the famous codices S (Sinaiticus), B (Vaticanus), and A (Alexandrinus), and also by citations in the writings of Clement of Alexandria, Origen, and the majority of writers from the 4th century on.

The Western text, about 8 per cent longer, is found in the Vetus Latina, the Syriac, Codex D (Beza), and in many of the ancient Church writers of the West, such as Irenaeus, Tertullian, and Cyprian. It is not as reliable as the Eastern, though some of the readings in which it differs from the Eastern may be authentic. Study must be made in each such instance to determine, if possible, what the original reading was.

Form. Acts is a travel story, if any one name suffices to describe it. It is an account of how and why Christianity moved from Jerusalem to Rome, from the center of the Jewish world to the center of the Roman. This form was determined to some extent by the materials used. Paul, hero of the second half as Peter was of the first, was surely a traveler. Yet the point of the story is not so much how Paul got to Rome as how his gospel arrived there. This form may account for the abrupt ending of the book. The book, as well as the journey, is finished once Rome is reached.

Thematic Summary. The major problem of the infant Church was integration. Were the Gentiles to be integrated into the Church, and if so, in what fashion? For the first Christians these questions were serious and difficult. All the first Christians had been Jews with noticeable religious and national bias. The Jews were a people set apart by God. Their social and dietary laws made impossible any vital contact with Gentiles. As a result, their prejudice against the Gentile world was deep rooted and militant.

The Prophets had, indeed, spoken of the salvation of the Gentiles and of their acceptance into the unity of God's faithful worshipers. But the assumption was always that this would happen through the pagans' acceptance of Judaism. And Jesus had not cast sufficient light upon this question for His disciples to solve it easily by reference to His words. He had spoken of foreigners coming into the Kingdom from the East and the West, displacing the children of the kingdom of God (Mt 8.10–12). He had also spoken in parables of the laborers called into the vineyard late in the history of salvation (Mt 20.1–16), and of the invitation given to those in

St. Paul's conversion on the road to Damascus (Acts 9.1–9). An illumination in the "Ada" group of manuscripts from the Benedictine Abbey of St. Emmeram in Regensburg, now in the Bavarian State Library, Munich.

the highways and byways to attend the marriage feast (Mt 22.1–10). His baptismal command, too, was universal: Baptism should be extended to all nations (Mt 28.19). But these teachings might signify that the pagans would become followers of Christ by first becoming Jews, members of the chosen people to whom the Christ had been promised, for Jesus had said that He was sent only to the lost sheep of the house of Israel (Mt 15.24). Such was the situation at the time of Jesus' Ascension. It was clear that salvation was offered to the Gentiles. But the problem was, must they become Jews to receive it? Acts tells us how the Holy Spirit solved it.

Theme. From beginning to end Acts speaks of the growth of the Church in numbers and in the understanding of its own catholic character. Starting as a small Jewish group in Jerusalem, the Church developed rapidly over the period of 30 years described. The development was horizontal, taking the Church from Jerusalem, through Palestine and Syria, into Cyprus and Asia Minor, over into Macedonia and Greece, and then to Rome, the center of the world. It was a vertical development, too, in the sense of a Spirit-guided realization of the newness of the Church, of its separateness from Judaism, of its catholicity, its hierarchy, its theology, and its sacramental life. In all this the Holy Spirit had a special role. He is the main personage in the story.

Development of the Theme. Acts 1.6 quotes as the Apostles' final words to Jesus, "Lord, wilt thou at this time restore the kingdom of Israel?" This clearly indicates a still imperfect grasp of the spiritual nature of the kingdom of God. The Apostles were awaiting the restoration of Israel's kingdom, a political kingdom resembling, but surpassing, that of David and Solomon. And thus the story of Acts begins. A small group of Jews in Jerusalem believed in Jesus, but its outlook was limited, political. This group considered itself a special unit, for care was taken to elect a successor to Judas so that the Twelve, the chosen witnesses to Jesus, might remain at full strength. They would be the leaders, the new patriarchs, of the group that accepts Jesus as the Messiah. As they awaited the promised Spirit (1.8), they wondered what He would bring to pass.

The question was soon answered. On Pentecost (ch. 2) the Spirit was given to them, and Peter, who assumed leadership from the beginning, addressed the multitude of Jews gathered from all parts of the known world. His message was that Jesus is risen from the dead, that He is the Holy One of God, the fulfillment of the prophecies, that He has taken His place at God's right hand as Lord and has sent down the Spirit, the sign and gift of the messianic age. The results were spectacular. About 3,000 were baptized. The Church became a flourishing community. Though it was still tied to Judaism and still worshiped at the Temple (2.46; 3.1; 5.42), it was something special, too, with a community life based on the leadership of Peter, the teaching of the Apostles, communal prayer, the *breaking of bread, and common property (2.42–47).

Opposition soon formed, an opposition that served the purpose of making the followers of Christ analyze more carefully their relationship to Judaism. Chapters 3 to 5 note the resistance of official Judaism to the preaching of Peter and the others. The reaction of Peter was firm: "We must obey God rather than men" (5.29).

Stephen. The incident of Stephen (ch. 6–7) constituted the next important step in the history of Christianity's coming into being. A Jewish *Hellenist, Stephen is one of the heroes of Acts. With the aid of the Spirit—for he was "a man full of faith and of the Holy Spirit" (6.5)—he realized that the externals of the Old Testament, the Temple, the Mosaic Law, Palestine itself, were not essential elements of religious worship. His sermon shows how God approached men and was accepted by them apart from the Temple, apart from the Law, apart from Palestine. The conclusion he aimed at is that salvation, although through the Jewish religion, is not to be confined to it. This is the first expression of Christian catholicity, of Christian universalism. It is the full development of the universalism of the Prophets. To Stephen it brought the reward of the Prophets, persecution and death. His stoning was witnessed by and perhaps engineered by Saul of Tarsus, a former student of the famous Rabbi Gamaliel, and a zealous Pharisee.

Stephen's theology and death had a profound influence on the horizontal-vertical development of the Church. His closest associates, the other Christians among the Hellenists, were driven from Jerusalem (8.1). They carried with them the message of universal Christianity, which they preached with fiery zeal.

From this point in Acts, the movement of the vertical development of the Church is rapid. In ch. 8 the deacon Philip, also a Hellenist, evangelizes the Samaritans, themselves only half-Jewish. He also baptizes the Ethiopian official, seemingly a Jewish proselyte. *See* PROSELYTES (BIBLICAL). In ch. 9 Saul the persecutor becomes Saul the Christian. This man, says the Lord, will be "a chosen vessel to me, to carry my name among nations and kings and the children of Israel" (9.15).

First Gentiles in the Church. In ch. 10–11 the question of Christianity's relationship to Judaism and to the Gentiles becomes critical. The pagan Cornelius, directed by the Spirit, sent to Peter for spiritual assistance. Peter, also directed by the Spirit, went to him at Caesarea. The question, how this Gentile should be received into the church, is answered soon enough; for, as Peter speaks to Cornelius and his family, the Spirit descends upon them. Peter concludes: "Can anyone refuse the water to baptize these, seeing that they have received the Holy Spirit just as we did? And he ordered them to to be baptized" (10.47–48). Here was the revelation needed by the primitive Church. Just as the Spirit had come upon non-Jews, so were the Jewish Christians to baptize them and bring them into the Church. "To the Gentiles also," concluded the Jerusalem Christians, "God has given repentance unto life" (11.18).

In ch. 11.19–12.17, two other events of importance are described. The activities of the Church at Antioch are told in 11.19–30. There the Hellenists were preaching Christianity even to the Gentiles. Barnabas, another Hellenist, but one highly respected by the Jerusalem Christians, was sent to Antioch to inspect the proceedings. He is another hero of the Acts, again a man "full of the Holy Spirit and of faith" (11.24). He endorsed the orthodoxy of the Antiochean apostolate and, further, sought out Saul, whom he had known at Jerusalem. The second event of importance in this section is the persecution of Peter and his exile from Jerusalem (12.1–17). With his departure Jerusalem began to decline in importance as the Christian center.

Paul's Journeys. Chapters 13 and 14 narrate the first missionary journey of Paul and Barnabas. It included Cyprus (of which Barnabas was a native) and the southern and central section of Asia Minor. Even more important than this geographical extension of Christianity was the preaching experience of the two missionaries. In general the Jews resisted their gospel, while the Gentiles accepted it with enthusiasm. This experience made a profound impression on Paul in particular. His realization of the Church's catholicity deepened. And, as the second coming of Christ receded into the distant future with the Jewish refusal to accept Christianity, Paul was forced to give closer consideration to the here-and-now life of the Church.

Paul and Barnabas returned from their trip ardent universalists. God "had opened to the Gentiles a door of faith" (14.26). But serious trouble faced them when the ultratraditionalist Jewish Christians, newly arrived from Judea, insisted on the necessity of the Mosaic Law (15.1). To be a Christian, one must first become a Jew. The Church was not catholic, it was Jewish.

This is the point of discussion at the Council of Jerusalem (*c.* A.D. 50), which is decribed in Acts 15 (*see* JERUSALEM, COUNCIL OF). When Peter and James agreed with Paul and Barnabas that the Gentile Christians should remain free of the Law, the question was decided. Paul and the other missionaries were now free to carry the life and liberty of the gospel to the furthest outposts of the pagan world.

The final 13 chapters (16–28) of Acts are the story of the further geographical spread of the Church. They recount Paul's second and third voyages, which carried the gospel deeper into Asia Minor and across the Hellespont into Macedonia and Greece. At the end of Paul's third journey he was taken prisoner in Jerusalem (ch. 21) and then transferred to Caesarea, where he was held for 2 years. From there he is sent to Rome for another 2 years of imprisonment. And with that Acts come to a sudden end. Perhaps Luke used his leisure time as Paul's companion in Rome to write the history of the Church up to this point and set aside his pen just as Paul came up for trial. Or perhaps Luke wrote Acts some years later and was simply satisfied to bring it to an end once he had traced the gospel to Rome through Paul's arrival there. It is impossible to decide which alternative is correct.

See also PETER, APOSTLE, ST.; PAUL, APOSTLE, ST.; CHURCH, I; STEPHEN (PROTOMARTYR), ST.

Bibliography: Commentaries. A. WIKENHAUSER, ed., *Regensburger Neues Testament* 5 (3d ed. rev. Regensburg 1955). A. STEINMANN, ed., *Die Heilige Schrift des Neuen Testaments* 4 (4th ed. rev. Bonn 1934). A. BOUDOU (Paris 1933). J. DUPONT and L. CERFAUX, BJ (1953) 35. E. JACQUIER (2d ed. Paris 1926). G. RICCOTTI (Rome 1951) tr. L. E. BYRNE (Milwaukee 1958). N. M. FLANAGAN (Collegeville 1960). Studies. L. PIROT, DBSuppl 1:42–86. Jackson-Lake 5. W. L. KNOX, *The Acts of the Apostles* (Cambridge, England 1948). J. DUPONT, *Les Sources du Livre des Actes* (Bruges 1960). H. J. CADBURY, *The Book of Acts in History* (New York 1955). W. M. RAMSAY, *St. Paul the Traveller and the Roman Citizen* (3d ed. Grand Rapids 1949). **Illustration credit:** Bavarian State Library, Munich.

[N. M. FLANAGAN]

ACTS OF THE MARTYRS

The official court records of the trials of early Christians for their faith. Taken in a broader sense, the Acts of the Martyrs, or *Acta Martyrum,* include all the varied accounts (*acta, gesta, passiones, martyria,* and *legenda*) of the arrest, interrogation, condemnation, execution, and burial of the martyrs of the first centuries. These narratives make up an extensive and important body of Christian literature, but are of unequal value, ranging from authentic accounts of trustworthy eyewitnesses to complete fictions and even forgeries. The Bollandist H. *Delehaye has divided the Acts into six categories accepted by other hagiographers, even though differences of opinion exist as to the value to be assigned to particular Acts.

Acta, or Court Proceedings. In a Roman criminal court the questions asked by the judge and the responses of the defendants, along with the official verdict, were taken down in shorthand by professional notaries (*notarii, exceptores,* or *censuales*). These notes were then transcribed in regular characters and deposited in the archives (*instrumentum provinciae*), where they could be consulted years and even decades later, as is attested by Eusebius (*Hist. Eccl.* 5.18.9; 7.11.6), St. Augustine (*Contra Cresconium* 3.70), St. Jerome (*Adv. Rufinum* 2.3), and Lydus (*De magistratibus populi Romani* 3.29). Copies of the proceedings could be obtained for private circulation and were used for public reading in the liturgy. Within less than a year after Cyprian's first interrogation at Carthage the *acta proconsulis* were in the hands of confessors in the mines of Numidia (Cyprian, *Epist.* 77.2). The earliest of the authentic Acts are those of *Justin Martyr and his six companions executed at Rome *c.* 164 by order of Junius Rusticus, prefect of the city. The *Acta Martyrum Scillitanorum* report the trial and condemnation of 12 Christians from Scilli on July 17, 180, by the proconsul Saturninus at Carthage.

The *Proconsular Acts of Cyprian,* one of the most important and moving documents of the early Church, contains a transcript of his first trial in 257; another of his second the following year; and a description by an eyewitness of his execution on Sept. 14, 258. The *Acts of Fructuosus* preserve the protocol of the trial of the bishop and his two deacons, Augurius and Eulogius, along with a description of their deaths by fire (Jan. 21, 259). Other authentic Acts from the time of Diocletian are those of Maximilianus, who was executed at Theveste in Numidia in 295 for refusing to enter military service, and of the centurion Marcellus, beheaded at Tangier in Mauretania in 298 for throwing away his military belt. A number of other Acts are occasionally placed in this first category, but in general they seem to be interpolated or to be of somewhat doubtful authenticity.

Passiones and Martyria. Accounts of eyewitnesses or well-informed contemporaries are frequently called *passiones* in Latin and in Greek *martyria.* They were written by Christians and are of a more personal and literary character than the *acta.* The earliest of these writings is the *Martyrdom of *Polycarp* of Smyrna, composed by a certain Marcion and sent in the name of the Church of Smyrna to the Christian community at Philomelium in Greater Phrygia. These Acts describe the arrest, trial, and heroic death of the aged bishop in the arena at Smyrna, most likely on Feb. 22, 156. Another report of this same type is the encyclical letter preserved by Eusebius (*Hist. Eccl.* 5.1.1–2.7), which was sent by the Churches of Lyons and Vienne to the Churches in Asia and Phrygia, describing the persecution of the Christians at Lyons in 177. Among the numerous victims was Bishop Pothinus "over ninety years of age"; Blandina, a slave girl; Sanctus, a deacon of Vienne; and Ponticus, a boy of 15. This famous letter, the first important document of Gallic Christianity, may have been composed by St. *Irenaeus of Lyons, disciple of Polycarp and successor of Pothinus. The *Passio SS. Perpetuae et Felicitatis* gives an engaging account of the imprisonment and death in the amphitheater at Carthage on March 7, 202, of Saturus Saturninus, Revocatus, and two young women, a slave Felicitas and her mistress, Vibia Perpetua, 22 years of age, "well born, liberally educated, honorably married, having father and mother and two brothers, one like herself a catechumen, and an infant son at her breast." The longest portion of the *passio* (ch. 3–10) was written by Perpetua herself; and another section, by Saturus (ch. 11–13) while they were waiting execution. The two documents were given an introduction and conclusion describing the deaths of the saints by a contemporary of considerable literary talent, possibly *Tertullian.

The *Acts of SS. Carpus, Papylus, and Agathonice* is a description of the trial and deaths of three saints at Pergamum under Marcus Aurelius and Lucius Verus (A.D. 161–169) or, more likely, during the persecution of Decius (250–251). A similar chronological problem is connected with the death of Pionius at Smyrna. His *passio* was taken by an unskilled editor from three sources: a memorial left by Pionius himself or one of his companions, and two official interrogations. The structural and ideological resemblances between the *passio* of Marion and James, that of Montanus and Lucius, who suffered in Africa (*c.* 259), and that of Perpetua and Felicitas have raised questions regarding their authenticity; but they are probably genuine. The *Acts of Phileas,* Bishop of Thmuis, condemned by

Culcianus, Prefect of Egypt, at Alexandria early in the 4th century also belong to this category.

Interpolated Accounts. The third class of martyrs' Acts is much more extensive. It consists of accounts drawn from written documents that have been more or less extensively edited at a later date to suit the purpose of the author. An example of this type of development may be seen in seven different redactions of the *Acts of the Scillitan Martyrs.* Among the pieces in this class are the *passiones* of Maximus, *Crispina, Irenaeus, Pollio, Euplus, Philip, Quirinus, Julius; of *Agape and Chionia; of Saturninus, Dativus and their companions, Claudius, Asterius and their companions; and of the Persian martyrs Simeon, Pherbuta, Sadoth, and Bademus. Many of the narratives in the Menology of *Symeon Metaphrastes also belong here. Since mid-19th century numerous attempts have been made, using both internal and external criteria, to sift the facts from the fiction in these Acts, but the conclusions reached are often uncertain.

Historical and Imaginative Romances. These are late works based on neither written documents nor definite oral traditions. A few facts are set down in an elaborate, imaginary framework. Usually what is historical in these compositions is the saint's name, the date of his feast, and the existence of his shrine. Acts of this type are very numerous. They include those of Vincent, Peter Balsam, George, Cyricus and Julitta, Lucianus and Marcianus, Firmus and Rusticus, and the series of cycles of the Roman *legendarium* that include the martyrdoms of SS. *Agnes, *Cecilia, *Hippolytus, *Lawrence, Sixtus, *Sebastian, *John and Paul, and *Cosmas and Damian. Here also belong the Acts of St. Felicitas and her seven sons. The execution of seven martyrs at Rome on July 10 (their feast) is guaranteed by the Philocalian calendar (354); the account of their kinship is probably due to the influence of the Biblical story of the heroic Jewish mother and her seven sons tortured to death by Antiochus the Great (2 Mc 7.1–42).

Imaginative romances were likewise written using the martyr story as a theme. In legends of this type not only are the narrated events fictitious, but the saint's existence has no foundation in fact. The Acts of Didymus and Theodora, of *Genesius the comedian, who was converted while ridiculing Baptism, and of SS. *Barbara and *Catherine of Alexandria are apparently of this category. The Acts of Theodotus of Ancyra were woven about an ancient tale already known to Herodotus (*Hist.* 2.121); and the story of *Barlaam and Joasaph, which contains the greater portion of the *Apology* of the 2d-century *Aristides, is essentially a Christian retelling of the ancient Buddha legend from the East. Stories of this type, which followed the tradition of the Hellenistic novel, were extremely popular in the 6th and 7th centuries. Unfortunately, Christians of later times took these tales for history.

Hagiographical Forgeries. These accounts about the death of martyrs were written for neither the edification nor the amusement of readers but to deceive them. The *Acts of Paul and Thecla* are the earliest examples of this type. They were composed out of excessive devotion to St. Paul by a priest of Asia who was later deposed for his pains (Tertullian, *De baptismo* 17). Such stories were also fabricated to substantiate the Apostolic founding of Gallic sees; and in most instances it is impossible to determine the real authors of the frauds since the writer may simply be elaborating an already current tale.

Growth of Martyr Literature. Several factors contributed to the growth of martyr literature. There was, first of all, the natural desire to preserve the memory of those who had died for a cause. Jewish counterparts of the Christian Acts are found not only in the Book of Machabees but also in the martyrdoms of Akiba and Jehuda ben Baba. Pagan parallels existed in the political martyrs of the *Acta Alexandrinorum* and in the trial of Secundus, the Silent Philosopher, at Athens by the Emperor Hadrian. There was an appreciation of the apologetic value of martyrdom as a proof of the divine origin of Christianity (Tertullian, *Apologeticum* 50; Justin, 2 *Apology* 13) and of the theological notion that the martyr was the perfect imitator of Christ in his passion; and there was the edification that could be derived from a reading of the sufferings of the saints.

In Africa, Gaul, and Spain the custom quickly rose of reading in the liturgy the Acts of the martyrs on their feasts. The practice was not introduced at Rome until a much later date. This seems to explain why, with the exception of the account given by Justin Martyr of the condemnation of three Christians by Lollius Urbicus (*c.* 160; *2 Apology* 2) and the Acts of Justin and his companions, there are no authentic records of the trials and executions of the numerous Roman martyrs. During the centuries following the persecutions anonymous writers tried to make up for this deficiency. According to a late 5th-century document, the so-called *Decretum Gelasianum* 1 (PL 59:171–172), the *gesta sanctorum martyrum* were not read in church at Rome since their authors were unknown and they could be a source of ridicule. Later centuries were less critical; and by the end of the 8th, a martyr's Acts were liturgically read at Rome on his feast (Hadrian I, *Epist. ad Carolum Regem;* PL 98:1284).

The legendary Acts of the martyrs are historically useful for the knowledge that they supply regarding popular beliefs and social, political, and legal institutions of the centuries in which they were composed. The authentic Acts are important for the direct and indirect evidence they afford of practices and beliefs traditional in the early Church: a reverence for Scripture (*Passio SS. Scillitanorum* 12); the preservation of relics (*Acta Procons. Cypriani* 5); infant Baptism (*Martyrdom of Polycarp* 9); martyrdom as a second Baptism (*Passio SS. Perpetuae et Felicitatis* 21; *Passio SS. Jacobi et Mariani* 11); prayers for the souls of the departed (*Passio SS. Perpetuae et Felicitatis* 7–8); devotion to "Mother" Church (*Letter of the Churches of Lyons and Vienne;* in Eusebius, *Hist. Eccl.,* 5.2.6–7); the observance of fasts (*Acta SS. Fructuosi, Eulogii et Augurii martyrum* 3), particularly before the reception of the Eucharist (*Passio SS. Jacobi et Mariani* 8); and the essential difference in the veneration shown to Christ and to the saints: "For Him, who is the Son of God, we adore; but the martyrs, we love as disciples and imitators of the Lord" (*Martyrdom of Polycarp* 17). Even more intimately than the arguments of the apologists and the speculations of the Alexandrian theologians, the authentic Acts make contact with our spiritual ancestors, the common Christians called to make a heroic confession. They present the moving spectacle of men and women of every age and every walk of life dying for their faith in the firm hope of attaining everlasting life.

Bibliography: E. C. E. OWEN, ed. and tr., *Some Authentic Acts of the Early Martyrs* (Oxford 1927). H. DELEHAYE, *The Legends of the Saints* tr. D. ATTWATER (New York 1962). H. LECLERCQ, DACL 1.1:373–446. P. PASCHINI and I. ORTIZ DE URBINA, Enc Catt 2:327–338. A. HAMMAN, LexThK[2] 7:133–134. W. H. C. FREND, *Martyrdom and Persecution in the Early Church* (Oxford 1965).

[M. J. COSTELLOE]

ACTUALISM (IN PHILOSOPHY). Actualism is a term employed in both generic and specific senses to designate various systems of philosophy. Generically it refers to philosophical positions having as their center the notion of pure act. These positions in turn may be divided into two groups: (1) those that conceive pure act as fully realized or actualized being, free of potency (save of the active kind), and immune to intrinsic change; and (2) those that conceive pure act under the aspect of the infinite self-positing and self-transcendence of being through the dialectic of nonbeing. Examples of the first, according to various interpretations, are *Parmenides, *Plato, and *Aristotle, from the classical world, and St. *Thomas Aquinas and *Spinoza from the medieval and modern respectively. Representative of the second are *Heraclitus among the ancients; the proponents of philosophical romanticism, e.g., *Fichte, *Schelling, and *Hegel; and among recent thinkers, Giovanni *Gentile.

In its specific historical sense, actualism is used to designate the philosophical position of Gentile, which he himself called actual idealism. Gentile drew upon the spiritualism of *Berkeley and the idealism of the romantics—as interpreted by the Italian Hegelians of the mid-19th century, Donato Jaja and Bertrando Spaventa—to develop his distinctive view. He defined this as "the theory that mind, the spiritual reality, is the act which posits its object in a multiplicity of objects reconciling their multiplicity and objectivity in its own unity as subject" [*The Theory of Mind as Pure Act,* tr. H. W. Carr (London 1922) 241].

See also ACT; PURE ACT; IDEALISM; SPIRITUALISM; HEGELIANISM AND NEO-HEGELIANISM.

[A. R. CAPONIGRI]

ACTUALISM (IN THEOLOGY) stresses the gracious activity of God toward man. It neglects consideration of any created effect produced by this activity that could be classified as a thing of some perdurance.

Most contemporary Protestant theologians, especially in Germany, are influenced by actualism. Creation, revelation, ecclesiology, predestination, faith, justification, and grace are interpreted solely as "events" or "decisions" having meaning only for the present moment. There is no emphasis on any permanent dependent being that results from the divine activity in these matters. The word of God is event, never a doctrine that one might take for speculative development. Faith is never knowledge, acquired once for all, but an act of decision that one may have to modify at any given moment.

Actualism distrusts Catholic doctrine, especially its notion of nature as a permanent endowment of the individual or person from which specific activity flows, and its conception of sanctifying grace as a physically permanent quality possessed by the justified person. It sees here the putting of an abstract image in the place of God. It holds the religious relationship between God and man to be always an event, an "encounter of man with God," not a thing put at the disposal of man. Catholic theology, it thinks, by tending to give permanent reality to what is only event, misunderstands divine activity.

There is an element of truth in the actualist conception of the relationship between God and man, namely, the absolute transcendence of God and dependence of man on God's continuous activity for every moment of created existence. The relationship thus is a continuous event or encounter; for the creature, even *grace, must be conserved in being by the Creator, and conservation is a continuous creation—a truth that Catholic thinkers have always recognized. But at the same time every divine activity terminating outside God results in a created being, transient or permanent.

If one speaks of grace as the gracious activity of God toward men, one does not thereby exhaust the riches of the Biblical word. It has such a meaning (Lk 1.30), but grace means also a lasting gift (Rom 5.15, etc.) resulting from, but distinct from, the gracious action of God, a gift possessed by man and of a higher perfection than is due to any creature.

The Catholic concept of sanctifying grace as a physically permanent quality inherent in the justified person (Denz 1529) is therefore a concept both Biblically sound and based on a realistic and coherent philosophy. Not all the relations between man and God can be adequately explained in terms of God's gracious activity alone. Actualism flees reality other than that of change. The actualist notion of faith would seem easily to lead to the vagaries of *situational ethics.

See also ACTUALISM (IN PHILOSOPHY); HABIT (IN THEOLOGY); JUSTIFICATION; NATURE.

Bibliography: A. HALDER and H. VOLK, LexThK[2] 1:260–262. H. BOUILLARD, *Karl Barth,* 2 v. in 3 (Paris 1957) v.2. R. MARLÉ, *Bultmann et l'interprétation du N.T.* (Paris 1956). H. U. VON BALTHASAR, *Karl Barth: Darstellung und Deutung seiner Theologie* (2d ed. Cologne 1962).

[F. L. SHEERIN]

ACUÑA, CRISTÓBAL DE, Spanish Jesuit missionary, explorer of the Amazon; b. Burgos, 1597; d. Lima, Peru, Jan. 14, 1670. He entered the Jesuit Society in 1612 and made his profession in 1634. In 1630 he was the first rector of the College of Cuenca (Ecuador), the base for the Jesuit mission of Maynas in the upper Amazon. Acuña was appointed by the royal court to take part in a scientific expedition to the Amazon River because he had "journeyed through almost all Provinces of Peru, Quito, Chile, Tucumán, and Paraguay, including the coast of Brazil, La Plata, and Pará," according to reports from his superior, Francisco Fuentes. Acuña and a companion, Father Andrés de Artieda, left Quito on Feb. 16, 1639, investigating the characteristics of the Amazon River, native population, products, and various other items of interest. They arrived in Pará Dec. 12, 1639, and in March 1640 both returned to Spain. In Madrid Acuña gave an account of his observations to Philip IV and the Council of the Indies, and requested permission and assistance to carry out further evangelization along the great river. A result of his exploration was the *Nuevo descubrimiento del Gran Río de las Amazonas* (Madrid 1641), immediately translated into several languages. With the political separation of Portugal from Spain in 1640, projects of colonization and missionary work came to a standstill, and Acuña returned to South America in 1644. He stayed in the New Kingdom of Granada and Quito, until he was persuaded to return to Lima in 1659.

Bibliography: J. JOUANEN, *Historia de la Compañía de Jesús en la antigua provincia de Quito, 1570–1774,* 2 v. (Quito 1941–43). E. TORRES SALDAMANDO, *Los antiguos Jesuítas del Perú* (Lima 1882).

[F. MATEOS]

AD BESTIAS. Beast hunts and fights were a favorite entertainment at Rome from the middle of the 2d century B.C. and subsequently throughout the cities of the Roman world. Gladiators—who were slaves—and criminals were required to fight various kinds of ferocious wild animals in the amphitheater. The gladiators often survived, but criminals, who were under the formal sentence, *datio* or *damnatio ad bestias,* were doomed to die in the arena. This criminal sentence was imposed on men guilty of tampering with coinage, of parricide, murder, or treason, and to some extent also on prisoners of war. In the age of the persecutions, Christians, who were accused of treason for not worshiping the emperor, were often condemned *ad bestias,* as is evident from numerous references to this form of punishment in the passions of the martyrs and in the works of early Christian writers. As the Christians were unpopular, the cry, *Christiani ad leones,* was often raised by spectators. See Ignatius of Antioch (*Epist. ad Rom.* 4), *Martyrium Polycarpi* (12), Tertullian (Apol. 40, and *De fuga in pers.* 5), St. Cyprian (*Epist.* 55), and Eusebius (*Hist. Eccl.* 4.15). Contrary, however, to the modern widespread view, the majority of the early Christian martyrs did not perish in the arena, but were executed by the sword.

Bibliography: E. JOSI, EncCatt 1:288–289. H. LECLERCQ, DACL 1.1:449–462, with full presentation of the literary, epigraphical, and archeological evidence. A. PILLET, *Étude sur la "damnatio ad bestias"* (Lille 1902).

[M. R. P. MC GUIRE]

AD LIMINA VISIT, more properly called *visitatio ad limina apostolorum,* refers to the periodic visit to Rome required of each residential bishop (CIC c.341) and military vicar approved by apostolic authority (Consistorial Congregation, Feb. 28, 1959, ActApS 51:273). Canon Law requires that residential bishops, not, however, titular bishops, make such a visit every 5 years if the diocese is in Europe, every 10 years if the diocese is outside Europe (CIC c.341). This visit should be made by the bishop in person or through his coadjutor if he has one. For a just reason, approved by the Holy See, the bishop may delegate a worthy priest of his diocese (CIC c.342). The ad limina visit consists of three acts, which are distinct but closely related in purpose and in time of fulfillment: (1) the visit to the basilicas of St. Peter and St. Paul to pray at the tombs of the Apostles, signing the register kept in the sacristies of these basilicas, and receiving a document of proof of the visit for presentation to the Consistorial Congregation; (2) a personal visit to the Holy Father, offering to him acts of homage and obedience and a verbal report of the visitor's diocese; (3) the presentation of a written report (or *relatio de statu dioecesis*) concerning the status of the diocese. This report is submitted to the Consistorial Congregation, unless it is for a diocese of a missionary country, in which case it is presented to the Congregation for the Propagation of the Faith. This report must be submitted every 5 years, even by those bishops who are required to make the actual visit only every 10 years. The ad limina visit is not traceable to a single specific act of legislation, but was a natural development from the infant Church.

Bibliography: J. J. CARROLL, *The Bishop's Quinquennial Report* (CUA CLS 359; Washington 1956). A. LUCIDI, *De visitatione sacrorum liminum . . .,* 3 v. (3d ed. Rome 1883).

[J. GOEKE]

AD MAJOREM DEI GLORIAM (A.M.D.G.), often taken to be the sign manual of the Society of Jesus (*see* JESUITS), from its frequent use in the writings of St. *Ignatius of Loyola, the founder. Father Brou says: "The haunting idea which summons a formula to the tip of a writer's pen reveals the dominant thought of his soul: in the *Constitutions* alone, St. Ignatius makes mention of the greater glory of God 259 times, almost once for every page." Another writer, Father Lawlor, says: "I have made the count twice over, and the truth is that Ignatius uses the formula about 135 times . . . locutions such as 'ad majus servitium Dei,' 'ad majus Dei obsequium,' etc., are repeated about 157 times in the *Constitutions.*" Probably the most dramatic presentation of the formula is seen in the silver statue, modeled in Rome by Francisco de Vergara and erected in 1741 as an *ex voto* over the high altar in the Basilica of St. Ignatius at Loyola. The saint is represented bearing a large open book on his left forearm, and pointing with his right hand to the formula inscribed across both pages. It can be safely assumed that in St. Ignatius's vocabulary, the words *obsequium, servitium,* and *gloria Dei* are practically synonymous, and that consequently the idea occurs 1,000 times or more, if to the *Constitutions* we add the occurrences in the 12 volumes of his letters. Most interpreters agree that the dynamic word is the qualifier *Majorem.*

Bibliography: A. BROU, *The Ignatian Way to God,* tr. W. J. YOUNG (Milwaukee 1952). F. X. LAWLOR, "The Doctrine of Grace in the *Spiritual Exercises,*" ThSt 3 (1942) 513–532. H. RAHNER, LexThK^2 1:149.

[W. J. YOUNG]

AD PERENNIS VITAE FONTEM, the first line of the *De gaudio paradisi,* the first part of a rhythmical eschatological tetralogy traditionally ascribed to *Peter Damian. Its meter is accentual trochaic tetrameter, maintained flawlessly throughout the 20 three-lined strophes of this rhythm on the joys of paradise, and continued in the 35 additional strophes on death, judgment, and hell. The *Ad perennis* has received several excellent translations into English. Abounding in Biblical imagery, the poem captures the longing of the soul to be released from the bonds of earth to abide in the heavenly Jerusalem, especially in the unending possession of the Source of life itself. Damian's authorship is questioned, not only because of a doubt in the MS ascription in Vat. lat. 3797, fol. 362–363, and of the admittedly dubious claim of *Peter the Deacon of Monte Cassino that it was written by *Alberic of Monte Cassino, but for the further reason that its meter seems to be foreign to that appearing in the poetic works of Damian that have been definitely authenticated.

Bibliography: AnalHymn 48:66–67. O. J. BLUM, "Alberic of Monte Cassino . . .," *Traditio* 12 (1956) 87–148, esp. 128–130. S. A. HURLBUT, *The Song of St. Peter Damiani . . .* (Washington 1928). Raby ChrLP 250–256. Raby SecLP 1:369–374. Julian DictHym 1:13. J. LECLERCQ, RevBén 67 (1957) 151–174. P. MEYVAERT, *ibid.*, 175–181. K. REINDEL, *ibid.*, 182–189. Szövérffy AnnLatHymn 1:391–397.

[O. J. BLUM]

AD REGIAS AGNI DAPES, an Ambrosian hymn by an unknown author; it is used for Vespers on the Saturday after Easter and subsequent Sundays and ferials until the feast of the Ascension. The Roman *Breviary has an earlier version, *Ad coenam agni providi,* which seems to reflect the Ambrosian Milanese thought of the 6th century or earlier. It may very well be the work of *Nicetas of Remesiana, a near contemporary of St. Ambrose (*see* HYMNOLOGY). When this hymn was included in the reform of the Breviary entrusted by Pope *Urban VIII to the Jesuit commission, it lost in its revision much of the rhythm of the primitive text, only three original lines being retained unchanged. The hymn is the song of a people newly redeemed, glorying in the triumph of their Leader, who invites them to a banquet celebration. As the Israelites were spared by the avenging angel (Ex 12.23) and as they passed miraculously through the Red Sea (Ex 14.22–23), so Christ has become Pasch and Victim (1 Cor 5.7–8) to break the bonds of Satan and offer the faithful the trophies of the spirit, especially joy.

See also DIVINE OFFICE.

Bibliography: H. A. DANIEL, *Thesaurus hymnologicus,* 5 v. (Halle-Leipzig 1841–56) 1:88, text. AnalHymn 51:87. C. TESTORE, EncCatt 1:332–333. Raby ChrLP 41. Connelly Hymns 140–143, Eng. tr. Szövérffy AnnLatHymn 1:95.

[M. M. BEYENKA]

AD SANCTAM BEATI PETRI SEDEM, a bull of Alexander VII dated Oct. 16, 1656, that states precisely that the five propositions condemned in 1653 by the bull **Cum occasione* of Innocent X came from C. *Jansen and that they had been condemned in the sense in which Jansen understood them. The Pope recalled that he had, while cardinal, taken part in the commissions held in 1653 and that he had thus formed a personal opinion on the subject. Nevertheless, in Jansenist circles there was a persistent rumor that, in order to obtain this bull, their adversaries had showed the Pope a falsified copy of **Augustinus* into which had been introduced the last four propositions, which were not there expressed in proper terms. For somewhat obscure reasons, the bull *Ad sanctam* was held in reserve for quite a long time, and it was not until March 2, 1657, that the nuncio Piccolomini sent it to Louis XIV. Cardinal Mazarin had it immediately accepted by the Assembly of the Clergy, and in the following November, not without some difficulty, by parliament.

See also JANSENISM.

Bibliography: Denz 2010–12.

[L. J. COGNET]

ADALAR, ST., priest and martyr; d. Dokkum, Netherlands, June 5, 754 (feast, April 20, translation). He was a companion of St. *Boniface and shared the martyrdom of that great missionary in Frisia. Little more is known of him, but there is an unsubstantiated tradition that he was the first bishop of Erfurt, consecrated by Boniface himself in 741. The *Acta sanctorum,* however, lists him as only a priest in its account of Boniface's last days. Adalar's relics were taken to Erfurt *c.* 756, and he was honored by special veneration in that city during the Middle Ages. His relics, along with those of St. *Eoban, rediscovered during the construction of a new church in 1154, were translated, and are now in the Erfurt cathedral.

Bibliography: ActSS June 1:450. M. OPPERMANN, *Der hl. Adelarius, Erfurts erster und einziger Bischof* (Paderborn 1897). Zimmermann KalBen 2:78–80. A. BIGELMAIR, "Die Gründung der mitteldeutschen Bistümer," in *Sankt Bonifatius: Gedenkgabe z. 1200. Todestag* (Fulda 1954) 247–287, esp. 279. U. TURCK, LexThK[2] 1:119.

[B. J. COMASKEY]

ADALARD, ST., Carolingian abbot of Corbie, author (known also as Adalhard of Corbie); b. *c.* 750; d. Jan. 2, 826 (feast, Jan. 2). The grandson of *Charles Martel and the nephew of King *Pepin III, Adalard was educated at the Frankish court. At the age of 20, in protest over *Charlemagne's repudiation of his wife, the daughter of the Lombard king *Desiderius, Adalard left the court and entered the *Benedictine monastery of *Corbie. But for ascetic-monastic, and perhaps, dynastic reasons he soon transferred to *Monte Cassino. Later, probably *c.* 780, the monks of Corbie in conjunction with Charlemagne himself brought Adalard back to the Frankish kingdom and made him abbot at Corbie. Thenceforth Adalard, himself an important representative of the *Carolingian Renaissance, was in active intellectual contact with *Paul the Deacon, *Alcuin, *Angilbert of Saint-Riquier and others, and was reputed to be one of the more influential advisers of Charlemagne. In 809 and 810 Adalard was in Rome on the Emperor's business and met with Pope *Leo III to consider the differences between Rome and the Franks on the *filioque question. Possibly chief minister of the young King Pepin of Italy even at this time, Adalard was the tutor of Pepin's son Bernard, and was Charlemagne's *missus* to the Lombard Kingdom from 811 to 814, the year he was banished by Emperor *Louis the Pious for unknown reasons (perhaps at the instigation of *Benedict of Aniane). He was not recalled from the island monastery of Noirmoutier until 821. Thenceforth he was active in the reorganization of his Abbey of Corbie, in founding (with *Wala) the new Abbey of *Corvey in Saxony, and as adviser to Louis the Pious on questions of ecclesiastical policy (e.g., his penance at *Attigny, 822). As monk and abbot, Adalard enjoyed great prestige (whence his sobriquet "Antonius"), but he preserved some practices of the monastic *regula mixta* and came out, sometimes rather sharply, against Benedict of Aniane. His remains were elevated Oct. 10, 1040; since then he has been locally venerated as a saint. Adalard's writings include a *De ordine palatii,* now lost [but see M. Prou in *Bibl. de l'École des Hautes Etudes* 85 (Paris 1885) and MGCap 2:517–530]. His *De ratione lunae paschalis* is also lost (cf. MGEp 4:566.9 and *Flodoard of Reims in MGS 13:531). Extant are Adalard's *Statuta seu brevis Corbeiensis monasterii* [ed. J. Semmler, Corpus Consuetudinum Monasticarum 1 (Siegburg 1963) 355–408] and his

Capitula . . . de admonitionibus in congregatione (ed. J. Semmler, *ibid.* 408–418).

Bibliography: Sources. *Vita* by PASCHASIUS RADBERTUS, PL 120:1507–56. *Vita II* and Miracles, Mabillon AS 5:289–355. MGEp v.4, 5, see index. Literature. S. ABEL and B. VON SIMSON, *Jahrbücher des fränkischen Reiches unter Karl dem Grossen,* 2 v. (v.1 2d ed. Leipzig 1883–88), *passim.* B. VON SIMSON, *Jahrbücher des fränkischen Reiches unter Ludwig dem Frommen,* 2 v. (Leipzig 1874–76), *passim.* U. BERLIÈRE, DHGE 1:457–458. Baudot-Chaussin 1:35–38. P. LEHMANN, NDB 1:48–49. Wattenbach-Levison 3:316–318, 340–342, sources and literature. D. A. BULLOUGH, "*Baiuli* in the Carolingian Regnum Langobardorum and the Career of Abbot Waldo," EngHistRev 77 (1962) 625–637. J. SCHMIDT, *Hinkmars De ordine palatii und seine Quellen* (Diss. Frankfurt 1962). A. E. VERHULST and J. SEMMLER, "Les Status d'Adalhard de Corbie de l'an 822," *Moyen-âge* 68 (1962) 91–123, 233–269. L. WEINRICH, *Wala: Graf, Mönch und Rebell* (Lübeck 1963). H. PELTIER and H. WIESEMEYER, in *Corbie, abbaye royale* (Lille 1963) 61–94, 105–133. J. SEMMLER, "Die Beschlüsse des Aachener Konzils im Jahre 816," ZKirchgesch 74 (1963) 15–82, esp. 76–82. C. BRÜHL, "Hinkmariana," Deutsch v.1 (Düsseldorf 1965) 81.

[J. SEMMLER]

ADALBALD, ST., nobleman; d. near Perigueux in Aquitaine, *c.* 650 (feast, Feb. 4). Information about Adalbald of Ostrevand is mainly derived from the 9th-century *Life of St. Rictrude* by *Hucbald of Saint-Amand (ActSS May 3:81–89). It relates that Adalbald was the grandson of St. Gertrude of Hamage, and the husband of St. Rictrude, by whom he had four children. He was the brother-in-law of St. Bertha, and friend of St. *Amandus, the Apostle of Belgium, with whom he founded the abbey of Marchiennes in Flanders. He had been very active in the court of Dagobert I. Vindictive in-laws assassinated him.

Bibliography: MGSrerMer 6:91–94. L. VAN DER ESSEN, *Étude . . . saints merovingiens* (Louvain 1907). Baudot-Chaussin 2:44–46. Butler Th Attw 1:236. E. EWIG, LexThK² 1:119. P. F. X. DE RAM, *Biographie nationale,* 29 v. (Brussels 1866–1957) 1:18–21.

[B. L. MARTHALER]

ADALBERO OF AUGSBURG, BL., bishop; d. April 28, 909 (feast, Oct. 9). He was highly regarded for his great erudition and his proficiency in liturgical chant, and through his zeal for regular observance the Abbey of *Lorsch became a model of monastic discipline under his guidance. He was instrumental in obtaining royal favors for the monastery of *Sankt Gallen, with which he maintained close spiritual ties. Little is known of his activity while bishop of Augsburg from 887 to 909. *Regino of Prüm sent his *Chronicon* (MGS 1:543–612) to Adalbero for approval and correction where such might seem necessary to the bishop. This prominent churchman supervised the education of Louis the Child (d. 911), the last of the *Carolingian dynasty to rule in Germany, and was his trusted adviser and loyal supporter. The tomb of Adalbero is in the church of St. Afra in Augsburg.

Bibliography: L. BOITEUX, DHGE 2:429–430. Baudot-Chaussin 10:252–253. F. ZOEPFL, NDB 1:39–40; LexThK² 1:119. Szövérffy AnnLatHymn 1:268. Zimmermann KalBen 3:155, 158. F. ZOEPFL, *Das Bistum Augsburg und seine Bischöfe im Mittelalter* (Augsburg 1955) 55–59.

[H. DRESSLER]

ADALBERO OF METZ, two bishops of the See of Metz.

Adalbero I, bishop, statesman, monastic reformer; d. Saint-Trond, Belgium, April 26, 962. Son of Count Wigerich and brother of Duke Frederick of Upper Lorraine, Adalbero succeeded *Benno as bishop of *Metz, the chief see of Lorraine, in 929. Always politically active, he joined the rebellion against *Otto I (938–940), with the intention of transferring Lorraine to French suzerainty. Failing in this enterprise, he thereafter remained on close, friendly terms with the German court. In 950 Adalbero intervened in France as mediator between Hugh the Great and Louis IV. He gave vital support to the monastic reform movement by reforming *Gorze Abbey in 933 and appointing Abbot Ainald. Subsequently he introduced Gorze monks into his own cathedral chapter at St. Arnulf's, and reformed other houses including *Moyenmoutier and *Saint-Trond, of which Adalbero himself was abbot.

Adalbero II, bishop, monastic reformer; b. between 955 and 962; d. Dec. 14, 1005. Nephew of Adalbero I, and son of Duke Frederick, he was reared at Gorze and elected bishop of Verdun in 984. He was then transferred immediately to Metz through his mother's influence. More ascetic and less interested in politics than his uncle, he devoted his attention chiefly to his spiritual tasks. He introduced the *Cluniac reform into Lorraine, rebuilt the dilapidated Abbey of St. Symphorian, founded three abbeys for women, and seconded, but not always wisely, Emperor *Henry II's ecclesiastical policy. He promoted education and made Metz the intellectual center of Upper Lorraine. He enjoyed a local, unofficial cult.

Bibliography: MGS 4:348, 658–672. J. DALSTEIN, DHGE 1:431–433, 436–437. R. PARISOT, DictBiogFranc 1:384–390. E. EWIG, NDB 1:40–41. Wattenbach-Holtzmann 1.2.

[R. H. SCHMANDT]

ADALBERO OF REIMS, archbishop, reformer; d. Reims, Jan. 23, 989. Adalbero came from an important noble family in Lorraine and was educated in the monastery of *Gorze. He became a canon at Metz and was made archbishop of Reims in 969. Adalbero worked vigorously to protect his church from the depredations of the feudal nobility and to reform the secular and monastic clergy of his diocese. He placed the cathedral school under the direction of the celebrated scholar, Gerbert of Aurillac (*see* SYLVESTER II, POPE). Because Adalbero opposed the designs of the French kings in Lorraine and supported the Ottonian emperors, he was accused of treason and brought to trial, but the proceedings were frustrated by Hugh Capet (*see* CAPETIAN DYNASTY). When the Carolingian Louis V died (987), Adalbero presided over the assembly that elected Hugh, and subsequently he conferred the royal anointing on both Hugh and his son *Robert II.

Bibliography: M. SEPET, DHGE 1:433–436. A. BIGELMAIR, LexThK² 1:120.

[F. BEHRENDS]

ADALBERO OF WÜRZBURG, ST., bishop; b. *c.* 1010; d. Lambach Abbey, Oct. 6, 1090 (feast, Oct. 6). Last of the Carinthian counts of Lambach-Wels, he studied at Paris, became a canon of the cathedral of Würzburg, and, named by Emperor *Henry III, was consecrated bishop of Würzburg (June 30, 1045). He was a zealous if litigious bishop, maintaining his episcopal rights against both the monastery of *Fulda (1049) and the Diocese of *Bamberg (1052). During the struggle between King (later Emperor) *Henry IV and Pope *Gregory VII, he remained loyal to the imperial cause until Henry "excommunicated" the Pope (1076). He then broke with Henry and participated actively in his deposition (1077). In 1085, forced from his see by an antibishop, Meginhard, he found final refuge at *Lambach, his ancestral monastery, which he himself had reestablished as a Benedictine abbey.

Bibliography: D. W. WATTENBACH, MGS 12:127–147. L. BOITEUX, DHGE 1:439–440. Hauck 3:580 and *passim*. P. J. JORG, LexThK² 1:120. W. ENGEL NDB 1:41–42.

[S. WILLIAMS]

ADALBERT OF BREMEN, archbishop of Bremen-Hamburg, royal adviser; b. Thuringia, *c.* 1000; d. Goslar, March 16, 1072. Born of noble parents, he was educated at Halberstadt, where he became canon and, by 1032, provost. Then through royal favor he was made archbishop of *Bremen-Hamburg (1045–72). Under him the see's efforts to convert the northern Slavs and Scandinavians were intensified. Denmark was deeply influenced by Bremen, Sweden only temporarily, and Norway hardly at all; missionaries sailed to Iceland, Greenland, the Orkneys, and Finland; in 1060 Slavic sees were erected at Mecklenburg and Ratzeburg. After the Council of *Sutri (1046) Adalbert refused Emperor *Henry III's offer of the papacy. He hoped instead to establish his see as a patriarchate (probably over a Danish archbishop), but was only appointed papal agent for the evangelization of northern Europe, i.e., he was made legate, and then vicar in 1053. In German politics he played a leading role as adviser to Henry III and guardian to young *Henry IV, and virtually ruled (1064–66) until rival nobles exiled him from court (1066–69). This reversal prevented the realization of his greatest ambition, to make his see into a compact duchy in which the archbishop would be the leading economic, religious, and political power; nonetheless, he enlarged its power and prestige substantially. He is typical of the great German prelates who served the Salians on the eve of the *investiture struggle. *Adam of Bremen's history is the best source for Adalbert's life.

Bibliography: E. N. JOHNSON, "A. of Hamburg-Bremen: A Politician of the Eleventh Century," *Speculum* 9 (1934) 147–179. O. H. MAY, *Regesten der Erzbischöfe von Bremen,* v.1 (Hanover 1928–37) 53–79, with full bibliog.; NDB 1:42–43. H. FUHRMANN, "Studien zur Geschichte mittelalterlicher Patriarchate," ZSavRGKan 41 (1955) 120–170.

[R. KAY]

ADALBERT THE DEACON, ST., missionary; b. England, late 7th century; d. Egmond, Holland, June 25, 705 (feast, June 25). Possibly a member of the English royalty, he devoted himself to missionary work. Under the leadership of St. *Willibrord, Adalbert left his monastery in 690 to evangelize Friesland. Though he never advanced beyond the rank of deacon, Adalbert's patience and kindness made him an effective witness to the faith. He became archdeacon of *Utrecht, a position entailing considerable responsibility. In about 702 he went to preach in northern Holland and built a church in Egmond, where he is buried. After his death his tomb became a place of pilgrimage, and his cult had the support of the counts of Holland, who in 923 founded the Abbey of *Egmond in his honor. Adalbert's first biographer, Rupert, wrote almost 200 years later, and hence the details of his vita are largely conjectural. He should not be confused with the Abbot Adalbert of Echternach.

Bibliography: Mabillon AS 3:586–600. ActSS June 7:82–95. Butler Th Attw 2:641–642. Zimmermann KalBen 2:357–360. C. DEEDES, DCB 1:32. R. BIRON, DHGE 1:441.

[J. F. FAHEY]

ADALBERT OF PRAGUE, ST., bishop, martyr; b. probably at Libice, the ancestral stronghold of his family, 956; d. near Danzig, April 23, 997 (feast, April 23). He was baptized Vojtech and was a member of the East Bohemian princely dynasty of Slavnik. At confirmation he took the name Adalbert, the name of the first archbishop of Magdeburg, who had supervised his education. Because of his great piety and demonstrated ability, the young Adalbert was chosen bishop of Prague in 982, after the death of Thietmar, the first bishop of Prague, a German by birth. Thus Adalbert was the first Czech to occupy the See of *Prague. His position was particularly important owing to the great influence of the Slavnik family to which he belonged. A man of austerity, energy, and zeal, Adalbert strove to improve and reform his clergy, to suppress abuses and pagan survivals, and to spread Christianity throughout Bohemia (*see* CZECHOSLOVAKIA) and neighboring Hungary. His activity, however, aroused the enmity of the extreme nationalists, who sympathized with the old pagan traditions, and led to a conflict with the Duke of Bohemia, Boleslas II. Adalbert, when forced to leave Prague, went to Rome, where he became a monk at the *Benedictine Abbey of SS. Alexius and Boniface. In 992 he was persuaded to return to Prague, but found it nec-

St. Adalbert of Prague receiving the crosier from Otto II, detail of bronze doors, cathedral at Gniezno, c. 1175.

essary to leave again in 995. In that same year Boleslas II treacherously attacked Libice and massacred all the members of the Slavnik family and their principal supporters. Refused permission to return to his see, Adalbert obtained a release from his episcopal obligations from *John XV and dedicated himself entirely to missionary activity. A close friend of Emperor *Otto III, Adalbert was his trusted adviser on problems concerned with the progressive Christianization of the *Slavs. Adalbert was also a close friend and collaborator of SS. *Romuald and *Bruno of Querfurt. In 995 he accepted the invitation of King Boleslas I the Great of Poland to organize missionary work among the heathen Prussians on the Baltic coast, where he met a martyr's death. His body was ransomed by King Boleslas and buried at Gniezno, Poland, and in 1039 was translated to Prague.

Bibliography: JOHANNES CANAPARIUS, *Vita s. Adalberti* in v.1 of *Fontes rerum Bohemicarum,* 7 v. (Prague 1873–1932). BRUNO OF QUERFURT, *Vita s. Adalberti, ibid.* H. G. VOIGT, *Adalbert v. Prag* (Berlin 1898). Butler Th Attw 2:152–153. F. DVORNIK, *The Making of Central and Eastern Europe* (London 1949); *The Slavs: Their Early History and Civilization* (Boston 1956). **Illustration credit:** Marburg-Art Reference Bureau.

[O. P. SHERBOWITZ-WETZOR]

ADALDAG, ST., seventh archbishop of Bremen-Hamburg; b. *c.* 900; d. Bremen, Germany, April 28 or 29, 988 (commemorated, April 28). A Saxon and canon of Hildesheim, Adaldag was the chancellor of Emperor *Otto I when he succeeded *Unni as archbishop of the great northern See of *Bremen-Hamburg in 937. Adaldag remained one of Otto's principal advisers, and when Otto deposed and abducted Pope *Benedict V (964), it was Adaldag who served as the Pope's custodian. As archbishop, Adaldag proved energetic and effective and carried on extensive missionary activities. Under him the Danish suffragan Sees of Schleswig, Ribe, Aarhus, and Odense were founded. The Diocese of Oldenburg in Holstein was set up as a base for a reinvigorated mission to the Wends. He successfully warded off the claim of the archbishop of *Cologne to metropolitan jurisdiction over Bremen.

Bibliography: ADAM OF BREMEN, *History of the Archbishops of Hamburg-Bremen,* tr. F. J. TSCHAN (New York 1959). O. H. MAY, *Regesten der Erzbishöfe von Bremen,* v.1 (Hanover 1928); NDB 1:47–48, bibliog. G. DEHIO, *Geschichte des Erzbistums Hamburg-Bremen* (Berlin 1877). G. GLAESKE, *Die Erzbischöfe von Hamburg-Bremen als Reichsfürsten (937–1258)* (Hildesheim 1962).

[J. F. FAHEY]

ADALGAR OF BREMEN, ST., third archbishop of *Bremen-Hamburg; d. Bremen, May 9, 909 (feast, May 15). Having proved a pious, wise, and zealous monk and deacon at *Corvey, he was assigned (865) by his abbot—also named Adalgar—to assist Abp. *Rembert of Bremen-Hamburg. Adalgar became Rembert's coadjutor and then his successor (889) after confirmation by King Louis II and his sons Louis III and Carloman, by Emperor *Arnulf, by the abbot and monastery of Corvey, and by a local synod. He received the *pallium from Pope *Stephen V, was consecrated by Abp. Sundrold of Mainz, and received his crozier from Arnulf. Adalgar traveled throughout his see and attended the royal court; his missionary activity was somewhat limited by the Norman wars. He was involved in a dispute with Abp. Herman of Cologne, who forced Bremen into the status of suffragan bishopric by means of the Synod of Tribur (895) presided over by Abp. Hatto of Mainz. However, Pope *Sergius III abrogated this decision at the end of Adalgar's life. Adalgar appointed a coadjutor, *Hoger of Bremen-Hamburg, and five bishops. He is buried in the basilica of St. Michael in Bremen. *Trithemius was the first to call him a saint (*De Viris illustribus* 3.214); northern writers say nothing of canonization. There is a baroque statue of him in the choir at Corvey.

Bibliography: ADAM OF BREMEN, *History of the Archbishops of Hamburg-Bremen,* ed. and tr. F. J. TSCHAN (New York 1959). *Leben der Erzbischöfe Anskar und Rimbert,* ed. W. WATTENBACH (Die Geschichtschreiber der deutschen Vorzeit 22; 3d ed. Leipzig 1939). Zimmermann KalBen 2:174. O. H. MAY, NDB 1:48.

[G. SPAHR]

ADALGIS OF NOVARA, ST., bishop; d. *c.* 850 (feast, Oct. 7). According to a constant tradition, Adalgis (or Adelgis) was of Lombard origin and possibly belonged to the same family as *Desiderius, the last Lombard king. Though nothing is known of his early life, it is likely that Adalgis was a canon of the church of St. Gaudence in Novara. It is not clear whether his nomination to the episcopacy (*c.* 830) was because of his merits or his family connections. He seems to have been a man of considerable importance, for his name is found on many documents during the years 835 to 848. He was buried in the church of St. Gaudence, which he had endowed a short while before; his remains were transferred to the cathedral *c.* 1590.

Bibliography: ActSS Oct. 3:945–947. M. BESSON, DHGE 1:456. Baudot-Chaussin 10:188. V. G. GREMIGNI and A. CARDINALI, BiblSanct 1:194–196.

[J. E. LYNCH]

ADALGOTT, SS., two abbots of *Disentis with this name.

Adalgott I, abbot; d. Nov. 1, 1031 (feast, Oct. 26). A *Benedictine monk from the abbey of *Einsiedeln, he became abbot of Disentis in 1016. He was interested in monastic reform and the elaboration of the liturgy. According to the Einsiedeln chronicler, who preserves a verse epitaph of him, he was popularly honored as a saint immediately after his death. In 1672 his relics were enshrined in a new church at the abbey.

Adalgott II, abbot, and bishop of Chur; d. abbey of Disentis, Switzerland, Oct. 3, 1160 (feast, Oct. 3). A disciple of *Bernard of Clairvaux, he became abbot of Disentis and bishop of Chur, Switzerland, in 1150 and served in both offices with outstanding devotion until his death. He appears to have been a great benefactor of other religious houses, such as Münster and Schännis, where commemoration of him was later made. He was a figure of some importance in the affairs of the time, being connected with Emperor *Frederick I Barbarossa and the prince bishop of Constance and also with Pope *Stephen III, whose fellow student he had been. His feast is still kept in the Diocese of Chur, and his relics were enshrined along with those of Adalgott I in the abbey church in 1672.

Bibliography: Adalgott I. R. BIRON, DHGE 1:456. ActSS Nov. 1:385. I. MÜLLER, *Disentiser Klostergeschichte* (Einsiedeln 1942) 75, 81, 236, 268; LexThK² 1:124. Zimmermann KalBen 3:222, 224.

Adalgott II. M. BESSON, DHGE 1:457. I. MÜLLER, LexThK²

1:124. J. G. MAYER, *Geschichte des Bist ums Chur* (Stans 1907) 206–212. L. BURGENER, *Helvetia sancta,* 2 v. (New York 1860) 1:7–9. Zimmermann KalBen 3:133, 135.

[J. L. GRASSI]

ADAM (IN THE BIBLE)

The name given in the genealogical lists of Gn 4.25–5.5 to the first human being, identical in form with the Hebrew word for man, *'ādām.* He is named simply Man, not merely because he was the first man, but rather because he was regarded as the type of all mankind (Gn 5.2). However, in the story of *Paradise and the *Fall of man in Gn 2.4b–3.24 the term is always preceded by the definite article in Hebrew, *hā-'ādām,* "the man," and therefore in this section it should not be translated as if it were a proper noun. [The Confraternity Version is wrong in following the faulty vocalization of the Massoretic Text in Gn 3.17, 21, where *'ādām* (Adam) is read, instead of *hā-'ādām,* "the man."] The Hebrew word *'ādām* means man in the sense of "mankind"; to designate an individual man, Hebrew must use the term *ben 'ādām,* son, i.e., member, of the human race. This fact is of some importance in the interpretation of the story of the fall of man, in which the inspired author is speaking, not so much about an individual man, as about the whole human race typified by this individual.

The derivation of the Hebrew word *'ādām* is uncertain. Probably there is nothing more than a folk etymology in Gn 2.7 where it is implied that man is called *'ādām* because God formed him out of the dirt of the *'ădāmâ* (ground). But in any case, the author of Gn 2.4b–3.24 makes skillful use of this derivation: because man (*'ādām*) was formed from the ground (*'ădāmâ*), he is destined to till the ground (Gn 2.5) in hard labor (3.17, 23) and ultimately go back to it in death (3.17).

According to the genealogies of the *Patriarchs, Adam lived for 930 years (Gn 5.5). The children that *Eve bore him were *Cain, Abel and *Seth (4.1–2, 25).

Adam on a 12th-century Byzantine ivory panel, seated before a stylized palm tree, apparently before the creation of Eve. His dejected appearance illustrates God's words: "It is not good that man should be alone" (Gn 2.18).

After these first few chapters of Genesis, Adam is not mentioned again in the OT until the books written in the last few centuries before Christ (1 Chr 1.1; Tb 8.6; Sir 17.1–4; 49.16; Wis 2.23–24; 9.2–3; 10.1–2), when people began to speculate about the first man. Several curious tales are told about Adam in the apocryphal and rabbinical writings.

In the NT, besides the passing references in Lk 3.38; Acts 17.26; Jude 14, Adam is mentioned in connection with the Christian doctrine on marriage (Mt 19.4–6; Eph 5.31), the subordinate position of women in the Church (1 Cor 11.7–12; 1 Tm 2.13–14), and especially the teachings of St. Paul on the universality of grace (Rom 5.12–21), the resurrection of the dead (1 Cor 15.21–22), and the state of the glorified body (1 Cor 15.45–49). Paul draws an important contrast between "the first, the old, the earthly Adam" of Genesis and "the second, the new, the heavenly Adam" who is Christ; the former is the "figure" (τύπος) of the latter (Rom 5.14). The Christian must "strip off the old Adam and his deeds and put on the new Adam, so that he may be renewed unto perfect knowledge according to the image of his Creator" (Col 3.9–10).

Bibliography: L. PIROT and J. B. FREY, DBSuppl 1:86–134. J. JEREMIAS, Kittel ThW 1:141–143. J. DANIÉLOU, *From Shadows to Reality,* tr. W. HIBBERD (Westminster, Md. 1960). A. VITTI, "Christus-Adam," *Biblica* 7 (1926) 121–145, 270–285, 384–401.
Illustration credit: Walters Art Gallery, Baltimore, Maryland.

[E. H. PETERS]

ADAM (IN THEOLOGY)

Both Greek and Latin Fathers affirmed a privileged state for Adam, head of the human race, before his sin, but the enumeration and analysis of his gifts were arrived at slowly. Some, such as Gregory of Nyssa, tended to elaborate; others, such as Irenaeus, to attenuate the Genesis paradisal passages. Augustine formulated the traditional gifts: immortality, *impassibility, *integrity, a marvelous knowledge. He made the gift of original justice seem the same as sanctifying *grace. Anselm followed Augustine but saw *original justice as pertaining to the nature of man. Aquinas taught that Adam was created in grace but left room for a distinction between sanctifying grace and original justice, the former regarded not as a formal constituent of original justice but as efficient cause. He followed Augustine's enumeration of the gifts, as did most scholastics up until the present century. A triple subordination existed in Adam. His reason was subject to God, the lower powers to reason, the body to the soul; and the first subjection was the cause of both the second and third (ST la, 95.1). The Church is more cautious than its theologians. Nowhere are the gifts singly defined. Trent uses the phrase "holiness and justice" to indicate them (Denz 1511).

The theory of evolution and the findings of paleontology have proposed many questions about the first man (*see* EVOLUTION, HUMAN). Were there many Adams or just one? Was Adam the paragon of creation or a cave man? Did he know the natures of all created things or was his knowledge very primitive? Contemporary sciences dealing with the origin of man seem to contradict the traditional concept of Adam. "If the details of the evolutionary theory regarding man are still hypothetical, its general direction is uncontestably

Adam as lord of creation, leaf of an ivory diptych of the 4th century, in the Museo Nazionale Bargello, Florence.

shown [and] the conception of a primitive paradisal state would seem to be absolutely outside the facts" (Gardeil).

Contemporary theology on Adam has accepted, in general, this trend in scientific thought and is now engaged in a reexamination of the fonts of revelation to work out seeming incompatibilities. Pius XII in 1950 reminded Catholics that "the Catholic faith obliges us to believe that souls are immediately created by God" and that Adam cannot be regarded as representing a certain number of first parents since "it is in no way apparent how such an opinion can be reconciled with what the fonts of revelation and the pronouncements of the magisterium of the Church set forth concerning original sin" (Denz 3896–97). Speculation on the last point is open.

Toward a harmony of science and revealed truth, theologians make many points. Three may be mentioned here. There is a parallel between the production of the first man and that of any man. As in the latter case biology cannot ascertain the fact of the infusion of the soul by God, so in the former paleontology cannot ascertain the fact of the divine intervention. Again, sanctifying grace is not to be judged or measured by technology. The first man may indeed have been a primitive; this does not rule out his *friendship with God. Finally, the special endowments of Adam may be interpreted now as "germs or possibilities rather than perfections actually realized" (Gardeil).

See also: ADAM (IN THE BIBLE); EVE; CREATION, ARTICLES ON; MONOGENISM; ORIGINAL SIN; POLYGENISM; PREADAMITES.

Bibliography: DTC, Tables générales 1:30–33. J. SCHILDENBERGER, LexThK[2] 1:127–130. Robert-Tricot[2] 1:174, excellent bibliog. on European and American lit. to 1960. THOMAS AQUINAS, ST 1a, 90–102, and commentary by H. D. GARDEIL in *Somme théologique I.90–102: Les Origines de l'homme,* tr. A. PATFOORT (Paris 1963) 423–451. J. COPPENS, *La Connaissance du bien et du mal et le péché du Paradis* (Louvain 1948), also in RevBibl 56 (1949) 300–308. J. DE FRAINE, *The Bible and the Origins of Man* (New York 1962). A. M. DUBARLE, *Le Péché originel dans l'Écriture* (Paris 1958). C. HAURET, *Beginnings: Genesis and Modern Science,* tr. and ed. E. P. EMMANS (2d ed. Dubuque 1964). M. M. LABOURDETTE, *Le Péché originel et les origines de l'homme* (Paris 1953). J. L. MCKENZIE, *Myths and Realities* (Milwaukee 1963) 146–181. R. J. NOGAR, *The Wisdom of Evolution* (Garden City, N.Y. 1963). H. RENCKENS, *Israel's Concept of the Beginning,* tr. C. NAPIER (New York 1964). L. F. HARTMAN, "Sin in Paradise," CathBiblQuart 20 (1958) 26–40, with fine bibliog. C. REILLY, "Adam and Primitive Man," IrTheolQ 26 (1959) 331–345. C. VOLLERT, "Evolution and the Bible," *Symposium on Evolution* (Pittsburgh 1959) 81–119. **Illustration credit:** Alinari-Art Reference Bureau.

[T. R. HEATH]

ADAM OF BREMEN, historian and geographer; d. Bremen, *c.* 1081. He is noted for his Latin chronicle of the archbishops of *Bremen-Hamburg (text completed *c.* 1076). His obscure career began in East Franconia (Würzburg or Bamberg?), but *c.* 1066 he went to Bremen, where he lived as canon and head of the cathedral school until his death. Soon after his arrival, he began to collect materials for the history; 10 years later the first version was completed, but he continued to add material and revise the text until his death. The work is divided into four books. The first two cover the 250 years previous to the archiepiscopate of *Adalbert of Bremen (1045–72), whose biography (bk. 3) is Adam's masterpiece. A valuable geographical appendix (bk. 4) describes the world of the northern seas.

Bibliography: Earlier eds. of *Gesta Hammaburgensis ecclesiae pontificum* superseded by Adam von Bremen, *Hamburgische Kirchengeschichte,* ed. B. SCHMEIDLER (3d ed. Leipzig 1917), Eng. tr. F. J. TSCHAN, *History of the Archbishops of Hamburg-Bremen* (New York 1959), with useful introd. and extensive bibliog. G. MISCH, *Geschichte der Autobiographie* (3d ed. Frankfurt a.M 1949–) v.3.

[R. KAY]

ADAM OF BUCKFIELD

Aristotelian philosopher of Oxford; b. Bockenfield, Northumberland, *c.* 1220; d. between 1279 and 1294. He was a student at Oxford in 1238, and by 1243 he became a master in arts. In 1249, then a subdeacon, he was recommended by *Adam Marsh to *Robert Grosseteste for the rectory of Iver, Buckinghamshire, and was praised highly for his piety and learning. In 1264 he held a canonry and prebend at Lincoln, probably having abandoned the schools of Oxford. There is no contemporary evidence that he was a master in theology.

All his extant writings relate to his teaching career in the faculty of arts at Oxford. The precise determination of his writings is a delicate matter. Some are ascribed to Adam Buckfield, some to Adam Bouchermefort, others vaguely to *Magister Adam Anglicus;* and six works survive in two versions. M. *Grabmann, the first to consider the problem seriously, assumed that Buckfield and Bouchermefort were distinct individuals and assigned one set of writings to each on the basis of the manuscript tradition. Later, Grabmann himself acknowledged that Buckfield and Bouchermefort are the same person. A diversity of names for a single individual is not unusual, since medieval scribes were frequently unfamiliar with the place name being copied; Emden has noted 22 different forms for Adam of Buckfield.

His works, commonly called *notulae, glosae,* or *sententiae,* cover all the *libri naturales* of Aristotle and the *Metaphysica nova,* the version from the Arabic. His method of exposition was one early used in the schools and later popularized by *Averroës. It consists in a literal exposition and analysis of each section of the text that had been divided and subdivided. Buckfield's exposition is remarkable for its clarity, conciseness, and accuracy. He used the Latin version of Aristotle known as the *corpus vetustius,* although he sometimes referred to other versions. Occasionally he inserted short questions to clarify difficult points. A notable one, the only fully developed *quaestio,* occurs at the end of *De anima,* bk. 1. Although he utilized *Avicenna, *Algazel, and others, his principal source was Averroës, often to the point of simply paraphrasing him. However, unlike Averroës, Buckfield maintained a plurality of forms in material substance (*see* FORMS, UNICITY AND PLURALITY OF).

Besides commenting on Aristotle he also wrote glosses on the pseudo-Aristotelian *De plantis* and *De differentia spiritus et animae,* and a *Quaestio de augmento.* The authenticity of *In metaph. vetus* and *De causis,* sometimes ascribed to him, is doubtful. The *De anima* in the Berlin manuscript is a compilation drawn from Buckfield and *Albert the Great.

The 45 surviving manuscripts, widely scattered, indicate that his works were considerably popular in the Middle Ages. The importance of Buckfield lies in the range of his commentaries, the perfection of his technique, and the indication of the curriculum of arts at Oxford in the middle of the 13th century.

Bibliography: ADAM OF BUCKFIELD, "Super secundum Metaphysicae," ed. A. A. MAURER in *Nine Medieval Thinkers,* ed. J. R. O'DONNELL (Toronto 1955) 99–144. D. A. CALLUS, RevNéosc Phil 42 (1939) 413–424, 433–438; "Introduction of Aristotelian Learning to Oxford," *Proceedings of the British Academy* 29 (1943) 255–256. M. GRABMANN, *Mittelalterliches Geistesleben,* 3 v. (Munich 1925–56) 138–182, 614–616. F. PELSTER, *Scholastik* 11 (1936) 196–224. S. H. THOMSON, MedHum 2 (1944) 55–87; 3 (1945) 132–133; 12 (1948) 23–32. L. BATAILLON, *ibid.* 13 (1960) 35–39. Emden 1:297.

[D. A. CALLUS]

ADAM EASTON,

English cardinal, theologian responsible for the papal condemnation of John Wyclif in 1377, author of several important spiritual and liturgical works; b. Easton, England, *c.* 1330; d. Rome, Sept. 20, 1397. Easton, a monk of Norwich cathedral priory, studied at Oxford and graduated there as master of theology in 1366. Two years later he accompanied the Benedictine cardinal, *Simon Langham, Archbishop of Canterbury, to the papal Curia at *Avignon and completed there by 1377 his *Defensorium ecclesiastice potestatis,* a systematic refutation of the antipapal writings of *Marsilius of Padua and John *Wyclif. He was an eyewitness of the disputed election of Pope *Urban VI, the validity of which he consistently maintained. In 1381 he was promoted to cardinal and wrote the *Office of the Visitation of the BVM,* promulgated in 1389 in the cause of Church unity. Another major work, *Defensorium s. Birgittae* led to the canonization of *Bridget of Sweden in 1391. Easton's extant writings reveal him to have been one of the greatest Biblical scholars and Hebraists of the 14th century.

Bibliography: L. MACFARLANE, DictSpirAscMyst 4.1:5–8; *The Life and Writings of Adam Easton,* 2 v. (U. of London thesis, 1955). Emden 1:620–621.

[L. MACFARLANE]

ADAM OF EBRACH, BL.,

abbot; b. near Cologne, *c.* 1100; d. Nov. 20, 1161 (feast, Feb. 25). He is probably to be identified with Adam, monk of *Morimond, to whom *Bernard of Clairvaux wrote two surviving letters (PL 182:91–105). Adam was originally a monk of *Marmoutier who by 1121 had become a *Cistercian at Foligny, whence he went to Morimond and became abbot. In 1125 he and many of the monks abandoned Morimond, and only considerable pressure from Bernard induced them to return. Adam founded the Abbey of *Ebrach, near Mannheim, in 1127 and became its first abbot. His high and saintly reputation so assured the house of success that he was able to make new foundations: at Reun (1129), *Heilsbronn and Langheim (1133), Nepomuk (1145), Alderspach (1146), and Bildhausen (1158). In his final years he was a correspondent of the mystic St. *Hildegarde of Bingen and an ardent supporter of the *Crusades. His cult has never been officially recognized, but his feast is kept by the Cistercians.

Bibliography: F. X. VON WEGELE, "Relacio . . . et . . . Narratio fundationis monasterii Eberacensis," *Monumenta Eberacensia* (Nördlingen 1863) 3–7. R. TRILHE, DHGE 1:461–463. F. J. SCHMALE, LexThK^2 1:131–132. SELNER, *Brevis notitia monasterii B.M.V. Ebracensis* (Rome 1749) 99–102.

[J. L. GRASSI]

ADAM OF FULDA,

church composer, author of a famous tract, *De Musica;* b. Fulda, Germany, *c.* 1445; d. Wittenberg, 1505. In 1490 he was in a Benedictine monastery at Vormbach, but in the same year was *ducalis musicus* at the court of the Elector of Saxony. From 1492 to 1498 he was court poet, historian, composer, and teacher in Torgau, and from 1502 to his death (of the plague) he was professor at the University of Wittenberg. His one work as a theorist discusses the elements of music, plainchant, and notation; it is filled with references to authority, and obviously falls within the quadrivium and the university approach. As composer he produced a Mass, a Magnificat, motets, and several antiphons and hymns, and is also credited with three secular songs. These reveal a reliance on techniques developed by Burgundian composers of earlier dates, particularly *Dufay and *Busnois, thus providing evidence of cultural contact between musicians of southern Germany and those of Burgundy.

Bibliography: ADAM OF FULDA, *Musica,* Gerbert ScriptEccl MusS v.3. W. EHMANN, MusGG 1:79–81. W. S. ROCKSTRO, Grove DMM 1:50. Eitner QuellLex 1:37–38.

[A. SEAY]

ADAM OF HOUGHTON, bishop, and English royal servant; b. probably near Whitchurch, Pembrokeshire; d. Saint David's, Feb. 13, 1389. He became a doctor of civil law at Oxford *c.* 1340. He was canon of Saint David's and of Hereford (1347), archdeacon of Chichester (1350), and held many other benefices before being papally provided to the bishopric of *Saint David's, Sept. 20, 1361. He served King *Edward III as a diplomat in France, 1360–62 and 1377. A trier of petitions in Parliament, 1363–72 and 1384–85, he was one of 12 magnates appointed by the Commons to draft reforms in May 1376. From January 1377 to October 1378 he was chancellor of England. Five sets of his episcopal statutes survive. He founded the College of St. Mary at Saint David's in 1365 and also the cathedral choir school.

Bibliography: C. L. KINGSFORD, DNB 9:1313. Emden 2:972–973. G. WILLIAMS, *The Welsh Church from Conquest to Reformation* (Cardiff 1962).

[G. WILLIAMS]

ADAM MARSH, English theologian (also known as de Marisco); b. in Diocese of Bath and Wells, late 12th century; d. Nov. 18, 1258. He studied arts under *Robert Grosseteste at Oxford, where he had become master by 1226. He became a Franciscan at Worcester in 1232 or 1233. He returned to Oxford to study theology under Grosseteste until the latter became bishop of Lincoln in 1235. As intimate friend and adviser of Grosseteste, he accompanied the bishop to the Council of Lyons (1244–46). Around 1247, he became the first Franciscan master in theology at Oxford, where he taught until 1250. He was constantly summoned by King *Henry III for official business; by *Boniface of Savoy, Archbishop of Canterbury, for counsel; and by the Pope for settling local disputes. In 1256, the King and the archbishop tried unsuccessfully to secure his appointment to the See of Ely. He explored the possibilities of making peace with France in 1257. In his lifetime he had the title of "Doctor illustris." *Roger Bacon spoke of Adam and Grosseteste as "the greatest clerics in the world," (*Opus Tertium,* 22, 23, 25). His 247 letters, published by J. S. Brewer [*Monumenta Franciscana* (RollsS 1858) 1:77–489], are of unusual historical interest, but the theological and exegetical works ascribed to him have not yet been studied or edited.

Bibliography: A. G. LITTLE, *The Gray Friars in Oxford* (Oxford 1892) 134–139; "The Franciscan School at Oxford in the 13th Century," ArchFrancHist 19 (1926) 831–838. D. DOUIE, "A. de Marisco," *Durham University Journal* 32 (1940) 81–97. G. CANTINI, "Adam de Marisco," *Antonianum* 23 (1948) 441–474. M. CREIGHTON, DNB 1:79. A. DE SERÉNT, DHGE 1:482–484. Emden 2:1225–26.

[J. A. WEISHEIPL]

ADAM OF ORLETON, master of arts, doctor of Canon Law, Oxford (1310), bishop of Hereford (1317), Worcester (1327), Winchester (1333); d. Farnham Castle, Hampshire, July 18, 1345. He sided with the Mortimers against *Edward II and engineered the escape of Roger Mortimer of Wigmore from the Tower (1323). When charged with treason, Orleton refused to plead before a civil court and was condemned in absence (1324). Protected meanwhile by the other bishops, he joined Queen Isabella's forces (1326) and played a leading part in securing Edward's abdication (1327). He served on *Edward III's regency council and as treasurer, and he represented Edward in dealings with *John XXII and with France, retaining the King's favor even after Mortimer's fall (1330). His conviction was annulled (1329). He quarreled with Abp. *John Stratford (1341) and may have written the King's answer to Stratford's criticisms of the government. Modern writers tend to accept the view of the chronicles of Geoffrey le Baker (ed. E. M. Thompson, Oxford 1889) that Orleton was able, but opportunist and unscrupulous.

Bibliography: *Registrum Ade de Orleton, Episcopi Herefordensis, A.D. MCCCXVII–MCCCXXVII,* ed. A. T. BANNISTER (Canterbury and York Society; London 1908). H. R. LUARD, DNB 1:79–81. J. C. DAVIES, *Baronial Opposition to Edward II* (Cambridge, Eng. 1918). E. L. G. STONES, "The Date of Roger Mortimer's Escape from the Tower of London," EngHistRev 66 (1951) 97–98. Emden 2:1402–04. M. MCKISACK, *The Fourteenth Century, 1307–1399* (Oxford 1959).

[R. W. HAYS]

ADAM OF PERSEIGNE, Cistercian abbot, spiritual writer; b. Champagne; d. Perseigne, 1221. After entering the clerical state, Adam received an excellent education in philosophy and theology. He was first attached to the court of the Count of Champagne as chaplain and confessor of Countess Marie. The chronology of Adam's life is uncertain but it is generally assumed that he successively joined the Canons Regular, the Benedictines of *Marmoutier, and finally the Cistercians at *Pontigny, where he served as master of novices. In 1188 he was elected abbot of Perseigne near Alençon. Adam's public career reached its climax in the service of Innocent III. In 1199 he mediated the feud over royal succession following the death of King *Richard I, the Lionhearted. In 1200 he participated in the organization of the Fourth Crusade (*see* CRUSADES); in 1203 he arbitrated the disputed episcopal election at Reims; and in 1208 he acted as peacemaker between *Philip II Augustus of France and King *John of England. He was venerated in his abbey as blessed. Much of Adam's literary work has been lost. The surviving portion consists of letters of spiritual guidance and of sermons on the Blessed Virgin or on various scriptural passages. He was a master of medieval Latin style, was well acquainted with the Bible and with patristic and Cistercian sources such as the works of St. Bernard and St. Aelred. He was warm, sympathetic, and sincere, a man of piety and practical wisdom.

Bibliography: Sources. *Lettres* (SourcesChr 66; Paris 1960–) v.1, *Texte latin, introduction, traduction et notes,* ed. J. BOUVET;

PL 211:579–779. J. BOUVET, "Correspondance d'Adam, Abbé de Perseigne, 1188–1221," *Archives Historiques du Maine* 13 (1953) 101–160. Literature. L. T. MERTON, "La Formation monastique selon Adam de Perseigne," CollOCistR 19 (1957) 1–17. J. BOUVET, "Biographie d'Adam de Perseigne," CollOCistR 20 (1958) 16–26. B. LOHR, "The Philosophical Life According to Adam of Perseigne," CollOCistR 24 (1962) 225–242; 25 (1963) 31–43. A. MIGNON, DTC 1:387–388. L. CALENDINI, DHGE 1: 488–490. A. LE BAIL, DictSpirAscMyst 1:198–201.

[L. J. LEKAI]

ADAM PULCHRAE MULIERIS, secular master of theology at Paris; fl. 1210 to 1250. The personage designated by this perennially enigmatic name is gradually becoming better identified. He was Master Adam who read the *Sentences* at Paris (1243 to 1245) under Peter of Lamballe (d. 1256), the text of which is preserved in Paris MS, Bibl. Nat. Lat. 15652. He was a contemporary of Eudes Rigauld (fl. 1236–75), Peter the Archbishop (fl. 1245–48), Stephen of Poligny (fl. 1242–48), and John Pagus (fl. 1231–46), but older than Bertrand of Bayonne (fl. 1240–59), *Albert the Great, *Eudes of Rosny, and John Pointlasne (*Pungens asinum;* fl. 1245–48). Having been a master of arts, he was probably fairly well known in his day, for he composed *De intelligentiis* (or *Memoriale rerum difficilium*) between 1210 and 1240. In it he manifests knowledge of various writings of *Aristotle, notably the *Metaphysics,* and at least one treatise by *Avicenna. He seems to have been inspired by the hierarchical illumination theme of *Pseudo-Dionysius and to have had a profoundly voluntaristic conception of man and life. His activities and influence cannot be fully appreciated until publication of numerous treatises attributed to "Master Adam," including those of *Adam of Buckfield or Bouchermefort.

Bibliography: Glorieux R 1:288. P. GLORIEUX, "Les Années 1242–1247 à la Faculté de Théologie de Paris," RechThAMéd 29 (1962) 234–249. C. BAEUMKER, *Witelo, ein Philosoph und Naturforscher des XIII. Jahrhunderts* (BeitrGeschPhilMA 3.2; 1908); *Miscellanea Francesco Ehrle,* v.1 (StTest 37; 1924) 87–102.

[P. GLORIEUX]

ADAM OF SAINT-VICTOR, Victorine canon, liturgical poet; b. probably in Britain or Brittany, *c.* 1110; d. apparently *c.* 1180. Little exact biographical information is known about Adam since no account of his life was written before that by William of Saint-Lô (d. 1349). Educated in Paris, he entered the monastery of *Saint-Victor *c.* 1130; there he followed the lectures of *Hugh of Saint-Victor. His theological ideas are Augustinian, as is evidenced in his poem on mankind, *Haeres peccati* (PL 196:1422), which served as his epitaph. At one time he was thought to be the author of scholastic and Biblical works, but this is now challenged (Stegmüller RB 1:14). However, he is known and praised for the composition of approximately 45 *Sequences, rhythmic pieces to be used in the liturgy of the Mass preceding the Gospel. At the Fourth *Lateran Council (1215) *Innocent III gave Adam's Sequences a general approbation. He is credited with having brought to perfection the Sequence poetry that had been initiated by *Notker Balbulus and nurtured at Saint-Victor even before Adam's time. His poetry is based on accent, rhyme, and a fixed number of syllables, 4, 6, 8, 10, or 12 (Ghellinck Essor 2:295–298). After the invocation of the first strophe, his Sequences describe the virtues and the miracles of the saint whose feast is being celebrated (e.g., St. Geneviève, the patron of Paris, Sequence 10). In his Sequences on Christ and the Blessed Virgin, Adam made use of the allegory typical of his day (Raby ChrLP 345–375).

See also HYMNOLOGY.

Bibliography: *Oeuvres poétiques,* ed. L. GAUTIER, 2 v. (Paris 1858–59); *Les Proses: Texte et musique,* ed. E. MISSET and P. AUBRY (Paris 1900); *Sämtliche Sequenzen, lateinisch und deutsch,* ed. and tr. F. WELLNER (2d ed. Munich 1955). Anal Hymn 8:53–55. HistLittFranc 15:40–45; 29:589–598. Manitius 3:1002–08. Raby ChrLP 345–375. H. SPANKE, "Die Kompositionskunst der Sequenzen Adams von St. Victor," StMed 14 (1941) 1–29.

[P. DELHAYE]

ADAM SCOTUS (ADAM OF DRYBURGH), spiritual writer, preacher; b. Berwickshire, Scotland; d. Witham Charterhouse, Somerset, England, probably 1212. As a young man he joined the *Premonstratensians at *Dryburgh Abbey, Berwick, Scotland, where he rose to the office of abbot, or at least coadjutor, *c.* 1184. There he wrote his *De ordine,* 14 "sermons" that describe early Premonstratensian life and include a commentary on the Rule of St. *Augustine. Several years after this (in 1179 or 1180) he produced his most extensive work, the *De tripartito tabernaculo,* which illustrates Adam's adherence to a scriptural exegesis based on the four senses of the Bible. His *De triplici genere contemplationis* is a less extensive work but reveals the essence of Adam's mysticism. The *De instructione animae,* a dialogue between the heart and the mind, examines monastic life. Just before leaving Dryburgh, Adam, who had gained a reputation as a preacher among the Premonstratensians both at home and at the motherhouse in France, made a collection of 100 of his sermons, most of which are for feasts of the temporal and sanctoral liturgical cycles, but 14 of which specially pertain to religious. Attracted to the *Carthusian way of life while in France, Adam returned to England *c.* 1188 and entered *Witham, the only charterhouse in the British Isles. There he was a friend of Bp. *Hugh of Lincoln and on at least one occasion preached before Abp. *Hubert Walter of Canterbury. Of the numerous works from this Carthusian period listed in his biography [AnalPraem 9 (1933) 215–232], only his *De quadripertito exercitio cellae,* a commentary on early Carthusian spiritual life, is extant. Though neither a theologian nor a spiritual writer of the front rank, Adam is, nevertheless, one of the finer monastic representatives of the Anglo-Norman culture of 12th-century Britain.

Bibliography: Works. PL 198:97–872; 184:869–880; 153:799–884; *Sermones Fratris Adae . . .,* ed. W. DE GRAY-BIRCH (Edinburgh 1901); *Ad viros religiosos,* ed. F. PETIT (Tongerloo 1934). Literature. ADAM OF EYNSHAM, *The Life of St. Hugh of Lincoln,* eds. D. L. DOUIE and H. FARMER, 2 v. (New York 1961–62). T. A. ARCHER, DNB 1:81–83. A. WILMART, "Magister Adam Cartusiensis," *Mélanges Mandonnet,* 2 v. (BiblThom 13, 14; 1930) 2:145–161. E. M. THOMPSON, *The Carthusian Order in England* (New York 1930). F. PETIT, *La Spiritualité des Prémontrés aux XIIe et XIIIe siècles* (Paris 1947). J. BULLOCH, *Adam of Dryburgh* (New York 1958). M. J. HAMILTON, tr., *Adam of Dryburgh: Six Christmas Sermons* (Doctoral diss. microfilm; CUA 1964).

[M. J. HAMILTON]

ADAM WODHAM, English Franciscan theologian; b. *c.* 1295; d. Babwell, England, 1358. There are many variations of the name of his town of origin (see Emden 3:2082). He seems to have studied at Oxford (*c.* 1317–19), for he attended disputations given by

*William of Ockham and *Walter of Chatton. He lectured on the *Sentences* in the Franciscan friary in London (1328–30) before presenting a revised version at Oxford (1330–32). A marginal note in MS Vat. lat. 955, fol. 1v, refers to a collection of the lectures made at Oxford in 1331. Later Adam prepared a definitive text (*Ordinatio*) and a shorter version (*Editio media*). He also lectured on the *Sentences* at Norwich (1332–34). The *Editio media* was abbreviated by *Henry (Totting) of Oyta *c.* 1373 (ed. Paris 1512). Adam is also credited with a revised text of disputed questions (*Determinationes*); however, there is no MS evidence for the writings on Scripture attributed to him by L. Wadding and others. Adam is frequently called an Ockhamist. Not only did he accept the dedication of Ockham's *Summa logicae,* but he seems to have written the prologue to the work, stating that he is not ashamed to have been under the rod of such a master. Because of this intimacy, he is often called the "imitator of Ockham." However, Adam belonged to no one school, for he criticized Ockham as well as *Duns Scotus. He was an independent thinker, quoted by *Peter of Candia as on a par with *Thomas Aquinas, Duns Scotus, Ockham, and *John of Ripa.

Bibliography: Sbaralea 1:1–3. C. MICHALSKI, "Die vielfachen Redaktionen einiger Kommentare zu Petrus Lombardus," *Miscellanea Franz Ehrle* 1 (Rome 1924) 219–264. L. BAUDRY, *Guillaume d'Occam,* v.1 *L'Homme et les oeuvres* (Paris 1949). A. G. LITTLE, *The Grey Friars in Oxford* (Oxford 1892) 172–173. L. MACALI, EncFil 4:1782.

[I. C. BRADY]

ADAMNAN OF IONA, ST., abbot; b. Drumhome, County Donegal, Ireland, *c.* 625; d. Iona, 704 (feast, Sept. 23). He embraced the monastic life and later went to Scotland to the abbey of *Iona, becoming its 9th abbot in 679. When required to go to England in 685 on behalf of some Irish held captive there, he was converted to the Roman system in the *Easter controversy and to the Roman tonsure. He went back to Iona and later to Ireland pleading for this latter change, and it was adopted in many places, though not in Iona. At the Synod of Tara (697) he insisted that women should not take part in warfare, and the Old Irish *Cáin Adamnáin* (Canon of Adamnan) is attributed to him. He wrote also the life of his predecessor, *Columba of Iona, as well as the treatise *De locis sanctis,* an account of Arculfus's trip to the Holy Land. The ascription of a Vergil commentary to him is uncertain, and the Old Irish *Fís Adamnáin* is certainly not his. An Old Irish life, the *Betha Adamnáin,* is still extant.

Bibliography: ADAMNAN, *The Life of Columba,* ed. W. REEVES (Dublin 1857), ed. and tr. A. O. and M. O. ANDERSON (New York 1961); *De locis sanctis,* ed. D. MEEHAN (Scriptores latini hiberniae 3; Dublin 1958); *Cáin Adamnáin,* ed. and tr. K. MEYER (Oxford 1905); "Betha Adamnáin," ed. R. I. BEST, in *Anecdota from Irish Manuscripts,* ed. O. J. BERGIN et al., 5 v. (Halle 1907–13) 2:10–20, tr. M. JOYNT *Celtic Review* 5 (1908–9) 97–107. ActSS Sept. 6:642–649. Manitius 1:236–239. J. T. GILBERT, DNB 1:92–93. Kenney 283–287.

[R. T. MEYER]

ADAMS, HENRY BROOKS

Writer, novelist, and historian; b. Boston, Mass., Feb. 16, 1838; d. Washington, D.C., March 27, 1918. He was descended on both sides from wealthy and distinguished New England ancestors, two of whom were presidents of the United States. He was raised as a Unitarian, but rejected his Protestant orientation because he felt it was complacent ("Boston had solved the universe . . .") and unrealistic ("all the problems which had convulsed human thought from earliest recorded time . . . were not worth discussing"). His most significant effort in a lifetime of inquiry was to understand and recover the religious instinct.

Henry Brooks Adams.

At Harvard College (1854–58) he was influenced by Louis *Agassiz to devote himself to the intellectual life. He sailed for Germany to study law, but decided to become a writer instead. He returned to America in 1860, and served as private secretary to his father, Charles F. Adams, who had been reelected to Congress. When the elder Adams was appointed minister to Great Britain, Henry accompanied him to London (1861–68). To strike the strongest blows for reform, he became a freelance journalist and covered the Washington political scene (1868–70). He was appointed assistant professor of medieval history at Harvard (1870) and was named editor of the *North American Review* (1870–76). In 1872 he married Marian Hooper.

In 1877, Adams moved back to Washington, where he devoted full time to writing and to his self-appointed function as "stable-companion to statesmen." The next 8 years were highly productive. He started the monumental *History of the United States During the Administrations of Jefferson and Madison* (9 v. 1889–91), which has been hailed by some as the greatest work of its kind since *Gibbon's. He was also an able biographer, author of *Albert Gallatin* (1879), a study of Jefferson's secretary of the treasury, and *John Randolph,* a partisan view of the brilliant Southern spokesman. In later life Adams returned to biography, publishing *The Life of George Cabot Lodge* (1911). Both of his novels were published anonymously. *Democracy, An American Novel* (1880), a best-selling *succès de scandale,* was a satire on the Washington of his time, centering on the career of Mrs. Lightfoot Lee. *Esther* (1884) also features a cultivated and charming heroine, probably modeled on his wife, who makes an earnest but futile effort to accept a religious view of life.

His wife's suicide in 1885 was a severe blow to his psychic equilibrium. Although Adams was by nature an inveterate traveler, his journey to Japan (1886) with his close friend, artist John *LaFarge, was meant, in part, to be recuperative. With LaFarge he visited Hawaii, the Pacific Islands, Australia, and Europe (1890–92). This journey occasioned one of his most interesting and curious volumes, *Memoirs of Marau Taaroa* (1893), a history of Tahiti from a non-Western perspective, revised and reprinted (1901) as *Memoirs of Arii Taimai E.* During the 1890s he spent much of his time abroad, traveling from the Near East to Russia and Scandinavia. In his mid 60s he undertook the completion of his two most important books—*Mont-Saint-Michel and Chartres* (1902), a study of medievalism rather than medieval history, and *The Education of Henry Adams* (1906), at once an intellectual autobiography in the third person and a study of 20th-century multiplicity. Both books were privately printed. "The Rule of Phase Applied to History" (1908) and "A Letter to American Teachers of History" (1910) were collected along with an earlier essay, "The Tendency of History" (1894), in *The Degradation of the Democratic Dogma* (1919). In 1912 he suffered a heart attack, but recovered sufficiently to go to France, where he remained until the outbreak of World War I. In 1918 he returned to Washington and died there.

Adams was not generally regarded as a literary figure until *Mont-Saint-Michel and Chartres* and *The Education* won an audience after his death. He prophesied the "darkening chaos of the modern world" in *The Education,* predicting the moral bankruptcy of a materialistic society. Using the 12th century, presented poetically and passionately in *Chartres,* as a touchstone by which to judge the 20th century, he looked with nostalgia at the unity of that far time, the Middle Ages, and with fear at the "multiplicity" of the time to come. The Virgin was the chief symbol in his studies of 13th-century unity, "the point of history when man held the highest idea of himself as a unit in the unified universe"; the Dynamo symbolized 20th-century multiplicity, marked by a "great influx of new forces . . . violently coercive" and "rapid in acceleration."

Bibliography: J. BLANCK, *Bibliography of American Literature,* 4 v. (New Haven 1955–63) v.1 contains a descriptive listing of separate editions. *Literary History of the United States,* ed. R. E. SPILLER et al., 3 v. (New York 1948) v.3 and its *Bibliography Supplement,* ed. R. M. LUDWIG (New York 1959), the best general bibliography. H. ADAMS, *Letters of Henry Adams, 1858–1918,* ed. W. C. FORD, 2 v. (Boston 1930–38); *Henry Adams and His Friends,* ed. H. D. CATER (Boston 1947). W. C. FORD, ed., *A Cycle of Adams Letters, 1861–65,* 2 v. (Boston 1920). E. SAMUELS, *The Young Henry Adams* (Cambridge, Mass. 1948); *Henry Adams: The Middle Years* (Cambridge, Mass. 1958); *Henry Adams: The Major Phase* (Cambridge, Mass. 1964). E. STEVENSON, *Henry Adams, a Biography* (New York 1955). W. H. JORDY, *Henry Adams: Scientific Historian* (New Haven 1952). J. C. LEVENSON, *The Mind and Heart of Henry Adams* (Boston 1957). Y. WINTERS, *In Defense of Reason* (New York 1947). **Illustration credit:** Harvard University Archives.

[J. SCHWARTZ]

ADAPTATION, MISSIONARY

The adjustment of the mission subject (the older churches) to the cultural requirements of the mission object (the newer churches). Missionary adaptation is known also as "accommodation," "nativization of local churches," and "the principle of cultural relevancy."

History. From the earliest times, despite opposition in some particular situations, missionary adaptation has been the accepted policy of the Church, as was affirmed by Pius XII in his encyclical *Evangelii praecones.* St. Paul summed up the policy in his motto "all things to all men" (1 Cor 9.22). Nativization was encouraged by St. Paul especially through local leadership and through a sympathetic appreciation of local ways. Thus, he ordered Titus to ordain local Christians for the new Cretan church (Ti 1.5); and while insisting that Timothy (a Jew) be circumcised, he nevertheless attacked those who imposed the law of circumcision on Gentile converts. The view of the infant Church in the matter was made unquestionably clear when the Apostolic Council of Jerusalem, confronted with problems stirred up by overzealous Judaizers, officially proclaimed the supranational character of Christianity (Acts 15.10–30).

During the following centuries, the Fathers of the Church, in expounding Christian doctrine and in defending the Faith, had frequent recourse to the non-Christian literature and to the so-called "pagan" philosophy of the time. To many, if not to most, Church Fathers, a "pagan" heart was not corrupt but basically good, suitable material for Christianization (*anima naturaliter Christiana*). Many present-day usages, such as incense, candles, priestly vestments, certain liturgical symbols, holy water, some aspects of Christian art and music, processions, holydays, and liturgical seasons are traceable to the sympathetic attitude of the early Church toward local traditions.

In the following period of Church history, as Christianity spread to the barbaric tribes of northern Europe, the practice of employing traditional rites and customs to express Christian beliefs and sentiments was strongly encouraged by the missionaries and Church authorities, including such outstanding figures in mission history as SS. Boniface, Cyril and Methodius, and Augustine. The advice of Gregory the Great given to Abbot Mellitus, a fellow missionary of St. Augustine of Canterbury, is regarded even by modern applied anthropologists as sound and commendable:

> Tell Augustine not to destroy the temples of the gods but only the idols housed therein. Tell him to purify the temples with holy water and then to set up altars and place relics of Saints [into those same temples] . . .. Why should not the building be converted from the service of demons to the service of the true God? The people will see that their places of worship have not been destroyed and will, therefore, be more inclined to renounce their error and recognize and adore the true God, for the places to which they will come will be familiar to them and highly valued. Moreover, since they have the custom of sacrificing oxen to demons . . . let them on the occasion of the dedication of their churches and on the feast of the martyrs whose relics are preserved in them . . . celebrate the occasion with religious feasting. Let them slaughter and eat the animals not as offerings to the devil but unto the glory of God to Whom they will give thanks as the Giver of all things. Thus, if they are not deprived of such external joys, they will understand more easily the inner joys of faith. [Bede, *Historia Ecclesiastica,* 1.30.]

In the following period of Church history, especially in the earlier part of the age of discoveries, the policy of missionary adaptation was almost invariably disregarded, a fact easily understood in the light of the ethnocentrism of the times. Rapidly expanding Europe was regarded as the home of everything that was good, civilized, and Christian, while missionary work was looked upon as an all-out war on "savagery" and "superstition," an essentially negative attitude incompatible with the spirit of accommodation.

The outstanding champions of missionary adaptation appeared in the 16th and 17th centuries. St. Francis Xavier's sermons to the Japanese, Matteo Ricci's attitude toward the Chinese ancestor cult and Confucianism,

Roberto de Nobili's involvement in Hindu thought, and many of the devices employed in the Jesuit Reductions reflect the appreciation of the missionaries of this period (especially of the Jesuits) for the good in traditional ways and for the potential role cultural relevancy can play in effective evangelization and in making Christianity truly "at home" with the people.

The Congregation for the Propagation of the Faith has from its inception insisted upon nativization, strongly admonishing missionaries not to interfere with traditional ways, unless the customs in question were clearly contrary to Christian faith and morals. As early as 1659 this was emphasized by the Congregation: "Can anyone think of anything more absurd than to transport France, Italy or Spain or some other European country to China? Bring them your faith, not your country" [*Collectanea* 1 (1907) 130–141].

In recent times, the Church has laid an even greater stress upon missionary adaptation. Benedict XV in his *Maximum illud,* Pius XI in his *Rerum ecclesiae,* Pius XII in his *Evangelii praecones* and *Fidei donum,* and John XXIII in his *Princeps pastorum* leave no doubt about the supranational character of the Church and of the role indigenous clergy and laity are to play not only in governing their churches but also in making Christianity truly "at home." "Unity in diversity!" is one of the basic goals of Vatican Council II, a goal that cannot be realized except through accommodation.

Justification of the Policy. The reformers considered man's whole nature as corrupt through sin. Consequently, paganism was to be regarded as essentially superstitious and immoral. Error permeates all that a pagan thinks, says, feels, and does. Accommodation to pagan ways thus becomes compromise between truth and error. Modern Protestantism, however, takes a milder position with respect to pagan customs, admitting that through God's grace, man has been saved from complete corruption. Man's rebellion against God, Protestant missionaries admit, has not resulted in total deterioration, and, consequently, degrees of remoteness from truth among the various beliefs and practices of pagans must be recognized.

This later view approaches Catholic teaching regarding grace and nature, and, therefore, also in regard to the correct attitude toward pagan cultures. Pius XII in his *Evangelii praecones* (§88) points out that "although human nature by Adam's unhappy sin has been tainted with an hereditary blemish, it still retains a naturally Christian propensity. If this is illumined by divine light and nurtured by divine grace, it can in time be raised to genuine virtue and supernatural activity." According to Catholic teaching, then, there is much in pagan mentality and ways that is neutral or good in the natural sphere. Moreover, the pagan can, through his own reason, attain at least a limited knowledge of God, which, although not sufficient in itself, is nonetheless not wrong in all respects. The missionary can, therefore, adapt such naturally good and true beliefs, values, and practices to Christian living without thereby compromising divine truth. Man's natural goodness can be thus supernaturalized and Christianized.

Aims of Missionary Adaptation. Some missiologists have regarded accommodation as mere human wisdom, purely practical and pedagogical in nature. More recently, however, theological and moral reasons are being emphasized by mission experts. The aims of missionary adaptation can be summed up under three heads: (1) justice, (2) consistency with the supranational character of the Church, and (3) missionary effectiveness.

(1) One of man's most basic rights is his right to his own national distinctiveness and culture. In the words of Pius XII: "The right to existence, the right to the respect from others, the right to one's own good name, the right to one's own culture and national character . . . are exigencies of the law of nations dictated by nature itself" [Allocution, Dec. 6, 1953, ActApS (1953) 794–803]. The first aim of accommodation, therefore, is not merely to be "obliging" or "accommodating," as the term might imply, but to be just.

(2) The supranational nature of the Church calls for missionary adaptation. Wherever the Church happens to be, there it must be "at home." As Pius XII expressed it in his Christmas Message of 1945: "The Catholic Church is supranational by her very nature . . .. She cannot belong exclusively to any particular people, nor can she belong more to one than to another . . .. She cannot be a stranger anywhere."

(3) Modern applied anthropology shows that the most effective communication across cultures (such as is involved in the direct or indirect apostolate) is the one geared most closely to the sociocultural structure and to the underlying psychology of those with whom one wishes to communicate. History, too, shows that the most effective missionaries were the ones most deeply immersed in local cultures. Modern culturological, sociological, and psychological theory emphasizes the importance of directing culture change as much as possible in accord with existing socially shared patterns of thought, evaluation, and action, so as to avoid unnecessary and serious disorganization. Moreover, effective communication of the Christian message aims not only to inform the non-Christian about the true religion but to show him how to live a life of religion. This essential task requires of the missionary that he preach the Gospel in a way that is relevant to the time and place.

Object of Missionary Adaptation. The object of accommodation is the particular people's socially shared system of coping with its physical, social, and ideational environment. In a word, the object of missionary adaptation is culture as understood by anthropologists today. Culture includes the total inventory of a way of life, and therefore missionary adaptation must not be restricted to the so-called "lofty" aspects of human life—art, music, philosophy, and ritual—although missionaries do place emphasis on adaptations in regard to liturgy, catechetics, art, and philosophy. But the adjustment called for by the policy of accommodation refers to the total way of life in all its aspects—food, housing, clothing, ornamentation, etiquette, gardening techniques, family life, ownership, trade, government, law, etc. By the same token, local cultures must adjust themselves to Christian norms not only in regard to the "lofty" aspects of human life but in regard to all aspects, for religion affects the whole of life.

Culture, the object of accommodation, includes not only isolated elements of a way of life but also its total structure, the manner in which the various elements are interlocked into a system. In other words, whether it be a question of the older churches adjusting to the newer or vice versa, accommodation becomes a difficult policy to carry out because the adjustment must be made in regard to a complex, integrated whole. To "retain what-

Missionary adaptation in the art form of the dance.

ever is neutral or good in the native culture" is an oversimplified rule of thumb. Because of the systematic arrangement of cultural components and because of the close interlocking patterns of behavior, even practices that are in themselves neutral or good may have to be, at times, removed, substituted, or in some way modified.

Underlying a culture and giving it a special direction is the so-called configuration of culture, the philosophy or psychology of a people. The socially shared basic assumptions, values, and goals that form this philosophy are likewise the object of accommodation.

Subject and Limits of Missionary Adaptation. Although the definition of missionary adaptation proposed above speaks of older churches adjusting themselves to the cultural requirements of the newer, the definition should not be understood to imply that accommodation is one-sided. On the contrary, the definition presupposes certain limits beyond which the Church may not go. The Church goes as far as it can go, and while doing this expects the new Christian community to come the rest of the way.

The policy of accommodation, therefore, presupposes on the part of the new church a spirit of sacrifice and generosity, and on the part of the older churches genuine empathy. Empathy is the sympathetic understanding of the local way of life. It does not necessarily mean approval or actual adoption of all native ways; rather, it consists in viewing all local behavior in full native context, fully understanding and appreciating why the local people behave as they do.

However, when speaking of approval and actual adoption of local ways and values, definite limits must be observed. These limits are dictated by faith, reason, and the goals of the apostolate. In regard to faith, one must carefully distinguish between what is essential for the unity of faith, and what might be termed as the accidentals of the Church. The Church has the obligation of preserving the deposit of faith in its entirety and purity. Under no circumstances can it compromise where revealed truth or natural law are concerned. A double standard (one for the "mature" churches and one for the churches of so-called "mission areas") is contrary to the true meaning of accommodation. Thus, to accommodate in regard to fetishism, polygamy, or infanticide is impossible. On the other hand, those purely human aspects of the constitution of the Church and Canon Law that are deemed essential by the Church to maintain her external unity, important as they may be, are nonetheless accidental to the Church and are therefore not to be blindly insisted upon, as if they were dogmas of faith. Accidentals contributing only to the external unity of the Church, e.g., the ritual, the seminary curriculum, do not enjoy precedence over the principle of missionary adaptation; rather, they must be constantly reexamined and kept up to date—always, however, with a view not only to the local needs and advantages but also to the needs and advantages of the universal Church. Accidentals considered nonessential even for external unity (the so-called "garb" of the Church) constitute the least limited area for missionary adaptation, e.g., catechetical methods, nonliturgical devotions, ecclesiastical art.

With the policy of accommodation the goals of the missions are never overlooked. Thus, any approval or adoption of local ways that, although perhaps good or neutral in itself, might lead to untheological amalgamations or that might be a serious drag on the missionary effort is to be regarded as a risk to be carefully weighed against the possible advantages that the particular accommodation promises.

Manner of Adapting. Three distinct steps are involved in missionary adaptation: (1) a recognition of an inconsistency between local ways and those of older churches; (2) an unbiased decision as to who must make the adjustment, the older churches or the newer; (3) the discovery of the best concrete approach toward integrating the local ways with Christianity or, as the case may be, the discovery of the best concrete approach in directing the desired change in the pagan culture. Such a change is in the realm of ideas, rather than things, and is effected through communication and free choice. Involved are such cultural processes as loss, increment, substitution, and fusion.

See also CATECHESIS, MISSIONARY.

Bibliography: L. J. LUZBETAK, *The Church and Cultures: An Applied Anthropology for the Religious Worker* (Techny, Ill. 1963). T. J. M. BURKE, ed. *Catholic Missions: Four Great Missionary Encyclicals* (Incidental Papers of the Institute of Mission Studies, New York 1957). J. J. CONSIDINE, *Fundamental Catholic Teaching on the Human Race* (World Horizon Reports 27; Maryknoll, N.Y. 1961). **Illustration credit:** Maryknoll Sisters.

[L. J. LUZBETAK]

ADAPTATION, RELIGIOUS. The modification of religious life necessary to accommodate it to the contemporary environment. In recent times this has been considered a more acute need for societies of religious women than for those of men. The evident demands of the apostolate had already forced a greater amount of spontaneous adaptation in the case of religious men, whereas the women tended, on the whole, to be more conservative. For this reason attention is here confined to adaptation in communities of women.

Religious life in the 20th century faced many problems: the dynamic socioeconomic changes following two world wars; the effects of these upon the physical and mental health of the new generations; the call from ever widening mission fields for more and better trained workers; a growing scarcity of religious vocations; an increasing number of requests for dispensation from final vows; the establishment and spread of secular institutes, which led many to question the relevance of traditional religious congregations to modern society.

In view of these problems the Holy See urged a modernization of attitudes and customs among religious. While proclaiming the great value to the world of religious life as a sign of man's true subjection to God, the popes distinguished carefully between unchanging essentials of religious life and unessential, outmoded customs. Pius XII urged the importance of better trained, more apostolic minded religious. He established yearly national conferences of religious superiors to pool experiences and solve common problems; in 1952 he assembled the first international congress of superiors in Rome and a national congress in the U.S. John XXIII and Paul VI continued this program of yearly national conferences in a growing number of countries.

Local institutes, seminars, books, and periodicals studied the conflict between modern and traditional views on religious obedience, chastity, poverty, communal life, and the apostolate; and attempted to clarify to superiors the physical and psychological needs of modern youth.

The chief obstacles to adaptation in the U.S. seem to be lack of a clear conception of the role of religious women in the Church today, commitments that cannot simply be dropped in favor of new fields of apostolate, legitimate fears that hasty changes and headlong activity will destroy the contemplative spirit so necessary for development of love of God and men.

Adaptation has been slow, but changes are apparent and undoubtedly will multiply following Vatican Council II. National congresses are building a strong spirit of unity and mutual cooperation among religious, a greater sense of responsibility for the missions, and a fuller realization that God's will for religious is expressed in the needs of the Church today. Some congregations have simplified their horarium, adopted less confining habits, and are using lay workers and labor-saving devices to provide additional time and personnel for truly apostolic work. The training of sisters is improving. (*See* SISTER FORMATION MOVEMENT.) A trend toward some form of the Divine Office in place of nonliturgical prayers indicates a growing appreciation of Holy Scripture and liturgy.

Such changes should lead to a more complete dedication of religious to the spread of Christ's kingdom and so to a new flowering of holiness and a deeper penetration of the spirit of Christ into contemporary society.

Bibliography: *Religious Life* (London 1950–). *Religious Life in the Modern World* (Notre Dame, Ind. 1960–). L. J. SUENENS, *The Nun in the World,* tr. G. STEVENS (Westminster, Md. 1963).

[M. J. BARRY]

ADDAI AND MARI, SS. According to Syrian Christian legend, Addai (Thaddeus) and Mari were two of the Lord's 72 Disciples, and were sent by Christ to establish the Church in Syria and Persia. Addai is named in the *Acta Edessena,* partly preserved by Eusebius (*Hist. eccl.* 1.13), which recounts the legends of *Abgar and part of the "Doctrine of Addai." The Doctrine is a 4th-century apochryphal account of the founding of Christianity in Edessa; it gives the story of the finding of the holy *cross by Protonica, describes the Emperor Tiberius as punishing Jews for the crucifixion of Christ, and mentions Palut as one of the earliest bishops of Edessa. The Edessan portrait of Christ attributed in the account to Ananias, the messenger of King Abgar V, must be later than 394 for it is not mentioned by Aetheria in her *Peregrinatio ad loca sancta.*

Mari is considered the disciple of Addai and one of the 72. He is said to have founded the Persian Church in Kōkē near *Seleucia-Ctesiphon, and the monastery at Dair Qunnā. The *Acta S. Maris* was written probably in the 7th century. The Nestorians trace the foundation of their liturgy to SS. Addai and Mari.

Bibliography: LABUBNĀ BAR SENNĀK, *The Doctrine of Addai,* ed. and tr. G. PHILLIPS (London 1876). H. RAHNER, LexThK[2] 1:136. J. ASSFALG, *ibid.* 7:24. E. PETERSON, EncCatt 1:290–291. É. AMANN, DBSuppl 1:510–512. A. BAUMSTARK, *Geschichte der syrischen Literatur* (Bonn 1922). B. BOTTE, "L'Anaphore Chaldéene des Apôtres," OrChrPer 15 (1949) 259–276. Beck KTLBR 238.

[F. X. MURPHY]

ADDICTION

The use of a chemical agent to a degree which although it is harmful to the individual and to society, becomes more frequent through psychological compulsion, physiological dependence, and physical tolerance.

The compulsive quality of addiction appears in an overpowering psychological need to acquire and to use the addictive agent. If the drug cannot be obtained, psychic tension increases to a pitch which is seemingly unbearable; it is a severe psychological dependence. Physiological dependence is the second factor present; the addict acquires a new biological need through the use of the drug. As a result of this altered physiological state, the body reacts to the cessation of drug usage. This withdrawal, or abstinence syndrome, may vary from a mild to a severe state and may prove fatal. Tolerance, the third characteristic of addiction, is the gradual physical resistance to the effectiveness of the drug. Increasing amounts must be taken to produce an effect of equal intensity.

Addiction must be distinguished from habituation, which refers to the acquisition of an emotional dependence on the use of a chemical agent. Habituation may have a compulsive character, but tolerance is not established and withdrawal symptoms do not occur.

Addiction is a multifaceted problem. Although there is need for further research on etiological factors, there is general agreement regarding some influences. Both internal and external factors are involved in addiction.

Internal Factors in Addiction. Among the internal factors are constitutional predisposition, differential susceptibility, and emotional immaturity.

Constitutional Predisposition. Constitutional predisposition, of genetic origin, cannot be discounted in evaluating the addictive process. Some individuals remember clearly their first encounter with the addictive agent, and that from that time they have been addicted. The drug seems to supply a previously unsatisfied need.

Even though the addict may be cured, in the sense that he is free of his addictive agent and his psychic equilibrium has reached a normal range, his tendency to relapse is lifelong. The addiction-prone individual cannot use a narcotic in the same way that the normal individual can.

Although the addict may change from one narcotic to another, or from alcohol to a narcotic, the common denominator of all these agents is their powerful influence on the central nervous system. This common site of action suggests a physiological predilection.

Differential Susceptibility. The differential susceptibility of the addict includes, in addition to constitutional predisposition, the factor of psychological prejudice. Investigation into the personality structure of the addict reveals a deep, primitive craving for narcissistic gratification of needs. The addict desires satisfaction of needs without having to give anything of himself to others, without having to invest anything of himself in external reality. Typically, he wants to be the passive recipient of pleasure. The pharmacogenic attainment of pleasure is reminiscent of the physiological comfort that came from the warmth and nourishment of nursing. The addict desires the psychological state which his addiction provides, but he also has a primitive need for the physical sensations which he frequently describes in vivid detail.

Of all those who are given narcotics for the relief of pain, only a small percentage come under the mastery of the drug. Unfortunately, nothing is known to enable a physician to predict which person may be susceptible to an addicting agent.

Emotional Immaturity. The emotional immaturity of the addict refers to his poor impulse control, his pursuit of immediate relief from inner tension, his experience of intolerable threat when deprived, and his inability to deal with his aggressive and sexual impulses in a mature manner. His immaturity is manifested by inability to cope with external reality unless it is diluted by his addictive agent. The motivational aspect of his emotional immaturity is extremely important, because it is this specific defect in his personality which makes the addict such a therapeutic problem, perpetuates his poor prognosis, and contributes to the high rate of recidivism. His infantile inability to postpone gratification, to tolerate discomfort, both physical and psychological, makes him repeatedly susceptible to his addictive relief.

External Factors in Addiction. Among the external factors are availability of the agent, cultural tolerance, and environmental stress.

Availability. The availability of the drug is an important factor in the development of addiction and in the specificity of the addiction. It is estimated that there were 175,000 narcotic addicts in the U.S. prior to the enactment of the Harrison Act in 1914. Presently, the estimate is 60,000. With this decrease in incidence, there was a reversal of sex ratio. Prior to the Harrison Act, female narcotic addicts outnumbered males 3 to 1; presently, the ratio is 4 males to 1 female. Among alcoholic addicts, the ratio also favors males, 6 to 1.

The factor of availability is not of such significance that exposure to a drug is tantamount to addiction. Only a minority become addicted, even in areas where drugs are readily available. In addition, some who try the use of drugs break the habit spontaneously.

Availability of the drug plays an important role in the treatment of addiction, however. Treatment must begin in an environment where the agent cannot be obtained. Availability is a significant factor also in the relapse rate. The proportion of narcotic addicts who become so through the medicinal use of drugs is estimated to be about 15 per cent. The therapeutic availability of drugs is undoubtedly a factor in their addiction, but for every one who becomes addicted in this way, there are numerous other patients who do not. Obviously other factors are involved.

Cultural Tolerance. The low incidence of alcoholism among Jews and the high incidence among Irish are examples of cultural influence. On a smaller scale, the influence of peer groups may foster addiction or may oppose or even interdict such behavior. There are juvenile gangs which forbid members to use narcotics or alcohol, and other gangs that promote their use among members. Various minority groups, unable to deal effectively with the hostility engendered by their second-class position, adopt the use of alcohol or narcotics as a means of anesthetizing their hurt, of increasing the distance between themselves and society, and of expressing, indirectly, their antagonism toward their oppressors.

Environmental Stress. Environmental stress includes many elements, some referable to the early life of the individual and others related to his present milieu. Examination of the background of the addict frequently reveals an unstable or broken home, in which one or both parents displayed delinquent behavior, and from which the father was often absent, either constantly, due to desertion or divorce; periodically, due to episodes of pathological behavior; or psychologically, due to inconsistency and inadequacy. The mother was often overindulgent toward the child, and through her attitude failed to confront the child with reality in such a way that he could acquire the ability to control his impulses and to postpone the gratification of his needs.

In regard to contemporary environmental factors, poverty, illiteracy, and social disorganization show a positive correlation to addiction. Addiction rates are higher in areas of poor housing, overcrowding, and shifting family life. There are higher rates of juvenile delinquency and greater numbers on relief roles among addicts.

Interrelationship of Factors. Addiction is not an emotional disease *sui generis.* There is no true addictive personality. The psychological characteristics that are consistently found among addicts are found also in nonaddicted populations. There is no distinctive emotional trait, no specific personality pattern that satisfactorily delineates the addict and distinguishes him from the nonaddict.

Addiction has no one cause. There are many factors involved and the relative weight of each factor varies from one individual to the next. In addition, there is accumulating evidence that the various factors have different weights for different people in determining the depth of the addiction and the danger of recidivism following treatment. When the external factors are more influential in establishing the addiction, the possibility of successful treatment is favorable, especially when society helps in correcting the external influences. It is probably from among those addicts who have been influenced largely by external factors that the spontaneous remissions occur. When the internal factors of predisposition, susceptibility, and immaturity predominate, the prognosis for remission, even with treatment, is less sure and the relapse rate is high.

A better understanding of these factors and their relative and specific influence on addiction must be developed through extensive research and careful analysis before the problem of addiction will be solved.

Bibliography: M. Nyswander, "Drug Addictions," *American Handbook of Psychiatry,* ed. S. Arieti, 2 v. (New York 1959) 1:614–622. I. Zwerling and M. Rosenbaum, "Alcoholic Addiction and Personality," *ibid.* 1:623–644. W. C. BIER, ed., *Problems in Addiction: Alcohol and Drug Addiction* (Pastoral Psychology Series 2; New York 1962). D. P. AUSUBEL, *Drug Addiction: Physiological, Psychological, and Social Aspects* (Random House Studies in Psychology; New York 1958). "Special Issue on Drug Addiction," *Comprehensive Psychiatry* 4.3 (1963).

[R. J. MC ALLISTER]

ADDIS ABABA, ARCHDIOCESE OF (NEANTHOPOLITANUS)

Metropolitan see of the *Ethiopian rite since 1961, in central *Ethiopia, east central Africa. In 1963 it had 18 secular and 33 religious priests, 49 men in 5 religious houses, 47 women in 9 convents, and 23,900 Catholics in a population of 7,259,000; it is 121,000 square miles in area. Its suffragans Adigrat and Asmara, both of the Ethiopian rite and both created in 1961, had 185 priests and 44,400 Catholics in a population of 4,300,000. The country also included the Latin Vicariates of Asmara (created in 1959), Gimma (1937), and Harar (1937), and the Latin Prefectures of Hosanna (1940) and Neghelli (1937); they had 137 priests, 376 sisters, and 57,200 Catholics in a population of more than 10 million. Addis Ababa, built in 1887, expanded under Italian rule (1936–41) and today has 450,000 people.

Monophysitism, introduced in the 6th century, now claims some 8 million Ethiopians. Many Jews entered the land (1st to 7th centuries) and converted the Agau tribes in the north; these became Christian in the 16th century bringing with them many Jewish practices, but the Falacha group is still Jewish. Islam encircled the Christian kingdom of Aksum from 640, the pressure being especially strong from the 12th century, and in 1268 the Christian capital was moved south into Shoa (the area of Addis Ababa). When the Hamitic Gallas invaded the country from the south *c.* 1540, royal authority declined until reestablished by Theodoros II (1855).

Ethiopian monks affirmed the union of the Ethiopian Church with Rome at the Council of *Florence (1441) but could not reenter their country. Portugal renewed Ethiopia's contact with the Christian world (1520–26), and Jesuit missionaries from 1555 prepared the official acceptance of Catholicism (1626). The intransigence of the Jesuit patriarch Alfonso Mendez, however, led to persecution of Catholics and the closing of the country to missionaries (1632). Repeated attempts by missionaries, especially Franciscans, to restore contact with Rome in the 17th and 18th centuries ended in their deaths. Bl. Giustino de *Jacobis secretly entered Ethiopia (1839) to convert Coptic priests, and missions were restored.

After the establishment of the Latin Vicariate of the Gallas under Vincentians (1846) and the Ethiopian Vicariate of Abyssinia under Capuchins (1849), the Prefectures of Eritrea (1903) and Kaffa (1913) were created and that of French Somaliland detached (1914). In 1930 a Catholic bishop of the Ethiopian rite was appointed for Asmara; on his death in 1951 his successor resided in Addis Ababa. In 1937 under the Italians, eight ecclesiastical territories were established: the Vicariates of Addis Ababa, Harar, and Gimma; the Prefectures of Tigre, Gondar, Dessié, and Neghelli; and the Exarch of Asmara. In 1940 the Prefectures of Endeber and Hosanna were created. Non-Italian missionaries had been expelled from Ethiopia in 1935, and Italians were expelled in 1941. A papal envoy arrived in Addis Ababa in 1947, Capuchins returned to the Gallas in 1955, diplomatic relations were established with the Holy See in 1957, Vincentians received the Vicariate of Gimma in 1958, and the Ethiopian hierarchy was established in 1961. The seminary in Addis Ababa is under Vincentians.

There is a Greek Orthodox metropolitan in Addis Ababa. Scandinavian and German Lutherans have been active in the country since 1866. The Lutheran radio station in Addis Ababa (1963) for Africa and the Near East is the most powerful in Africa. Protestants (except Germans) were expelled by the Italians (1935–41), but returned after World War II. The University of Hailé Selassié I (1961) is in Addis Ababa.

Bibliography: MissCattol 83–87. G. CARACI et al., EncCatt 5:683–708. R. AUBERT, DHGE 15:1176–81. I. GUIDI and H. FROIDEVAUX, *ibid.* 1:210–235. *Bilan du Monde* 2:358–364. Ann Pont (1964) 16.

[E. P. COLBERT]

ADELA, ST., Benedictine abbess; b. *c.* 675; d. near Trier, *c.* 734 (feast, Dec. 24). Probably the daughter of Dagobert II, she is quite surely identical with the abbess Adola, to whom a letter of Abbess Alffled (MGEpSel 1.3: letter 8) is addressed. She is said to have founded the Abbey of Pfalzel at Trier. In 722 *Boniface visited her and took her grandson (later Gregory of Utrecht) away as a student. She died about 734, but her remains were not discovered until 1072. Other information about Adela is based on a will, regarded as unauthentic by Pertz, but accepted by some scholars today. Her cult has not been confirmed, and she is not generally venerated in the liturgy of the Church.

Bibliography: Hauck 1:431. R. AIGRAIN, *Catholicisme* 1:136–137. A. HEINTZ, LexThK[2] 1:140. G. ALLMANG, DHGE 1:525.

[L. MEAGHER]

ADELAIDE OF TURIN, marquise of Turin; b. *c.* 1020; d. Canischio, Italy, June 29, 1091. Adelaide and her two younger sisters, Immilla and Bertha, were the daughters of Count Olderic Manfredi of Turin (d. 1035) and Bertha of Obertenga. After the death of her father she assumed the regency of his lands and married Hermann (d. 1038), the step-son of Emperor *Conrad II. Her sister Immilla was married to a German Prince, Otto of Schweinfurt. After the death of her first husband Adelaide married Henry of Aleràmico di Monferrato (d. 1045), by whom she came into possession of the march of Turin. When her second husband died, Emperor *Henry III assigned the march of Turin to Otto (d. 1057–58), the son of Count Humbert of Savoy; and in order to secure the peaceful possession of the march, Otto married Adelaide. Her being twice widowed and married three times caused much contemporary criticism, and some later historians have questioned whether there were not two Adelaides of Turin. That there was only one, is substantiated by a letter of *Peter Damian, who refers to her as *multivira* and as one who still can hope to reach the kingdom of heaven (PL 145:421–422). There were five children from her last marriage: Peter, Amadeo, Otto, Bertha, and Adelaide. When Otto of Savoy died, his wife resumed the regency of the march of Turin together with her eldest son Peter (d. 1078). Adelaide played an important political role, mostly in support of the imperial court, but nevertheless trying to reduce the opposition against Pope *Alexander II. Her relations with the papacy fluctuated, for she was once praised by Peter Damian and on another occasion forced to go to Rome to be reconciled and obtain absolution. Adelaide arranged the marriage of her children for political reasons, and in 1066 her daughter Bertha (d. 1089) was married to Emperor *Henry IV. When in 1069 the Emperor informed a diet of princes that he intended to seek a divorce from Bertha, Adelaide's opposition was strong enough to defeat his plans, and for a time the relations between the Marquise and the imperial party were somewhat strained. Later, in 1077, when Henry IV had gone to Canossa, it was Adelaide, together with Countess *Matilda of Tuscany and the Abbot *Hugh of Cluny, who conducted the negotiations with Pope *Gregory VII and finally was able to reconcile her son-in-law with the Pope. Her political interest continued until her death; for even after her son Peter died and the march nominally came under the rule of her son-in-law Federico di Montbéliard, she continued to control it and play an important role in Italian politics.

Bibliography: C. A. Gerbaix di Sonnaz, *Studi storici sul contado di Savoia e marchesato in Italia,* 3 v. (Turin 1883–1902). C. W. Previté Orton, *The Early History of the House of Savoy* (Cambridge, Eng. 1912). F. Cognasso, *Umberto Biancamano* (Turin 1929); EncCatt 1:295–296.

[W. M. PLÖCHL]

ADELAIDE OF VILICH, ST., abbess; b. Cologne, last half of the 10th century; d. Cologne, Feb. 5, probably 1015 (feast, Feb. 5). She was the daughter of Count Megingoz of Gelder. At an early age, Adelaide (Adelheid) entered the convent of St. Ursula in Cologne, where the Rule of St. Jerome was observed. As first abbess of the convent founded by her parents in Vilich (today Beuel, near Bonn), on the Rhine River, she introduced the *Benedictine Rule, which she considered stricter than that of St. Jerome. It was said that she had her nuns learn Latin so that they might better understand the Divine Office. While remaining abbess of Vilich, Adelaide succeeded her sister Bertrada, after the latter's death, as abbess of St. Maria im Kapitol in Cologne. She was buried in Vilich, where her relics are preserved. Adelaide was the friend and adviser of *Heribert, Archbishop of Cologne; and according to legend, she showed great prudence in providing for the poor during a severe famine.

Bibliography: ActSS Feb. 1:719–727. Zimmermann KalBen 1:170–173. A. Schütte, *Handbuch der deutschen Heiligen* (Cologne 1941) 27–28. A. Groeteken, *Die hl. Aebtissin Adelheid von Vilich* (2d ed. Kevelaer, Ger. 1956). J. Torsy, LexThK² 1:142.

[M. F. MC CARTHY]

ADELAIDE, ARCHDIOCESE OF (ADELAIDENSIS), metropolitan see of the State of South *Australia; diocese (1844), archdiocese (1887), whose suffragans are Darwin and Port Pirie. Founded by a British chartered company (1836) as a free (nonconvict) colony, Adelaide was planned as an exclusively Protestant settlement, but there were a few Catholics among the first immigrants. The first Mass in Adelaide was offered (June 1840) for a congregation of 50 by William *Ullathorne in a store lent by a Protestant. The first resident priest was William Benson (1841–44). Its first bishop, Francis Murphy, was also the first prelate consecrated in Australia. Years of great hardship followed, culminating in the almost complete exodus of the adult male population to the gold fields of the neighboring colony of Victoria. This temporarily impoverished the diocese, already burdened with debt. But years of great progress soon followed, including the foundation (1866) of the Australian Sisters of St. Joseph by Mother Mary *McKillop. When Adelaide was created an archdiocese in 1887, part of its vast territory became the suffragan Diocese of Port Augusta (since 1951, Port Pirie). The Diocese of Darwin, covering the Northern Territory of Australia, became a suffragan in 1938. (*See* AUSTRALIA for statistics and map.)

Bibliography: *The Official Year Book of the Catholic Church of Australasia* (Sydney). AnnPont (1964) 16.

[J. G. MURTAGH]

ADELARD OF BATH, English translator, writer of scientific treatises, philosopher; b. *c.* 1070; d. after 1142–46. A Benedictine, he was educated at Tours, taught at Laon, and then spent 7 years traveling in Italy, Sicily, possibly Spain, and Jerusalem, learning as opportunity offered. He is thought to have taught again in France, and an entry in the Pipe Roll for 1130 indicates that he had already returned to England.

A letter to his nephew, *De eodem et diverso* (On the Identical and the Diverse), written between 1105 and 1110, and dedicated to William, Bishop of Syracuse, records a conversation of the author with Philosophia and Philocosmia—the former representing the realm of reason, possibly the liberal arts and unchanging values, the latter the shifting world encountered through the senses. Its main interest lies in its remarks on *universals.

His *Quaestiones naturales* or *76 Questions on Nature* composed 1111–16, deal with a variety of the natural sciences based on Arabic learning. [An English translation by H. Gollancz is included in Berechiah Ben Natronai, *Dodi ve-nichdi—Uncle and Nephew* (Oxford 1920)]. He acquired an Arabic copy of Euclid's *Elements c.* 1120, and being competent in both Greek and Arabic, he was the first to translate this work into Latin. He also rendered into Latin an Arabic *Introduction to Astronomy,* the astronomical tables, and an *Introduction* by Mohammed ben Moses al Khwarizmi (fl. *c.* 830) either to astronomy or to the quadrivium as a whole, as well as other works of Greco-Arabic science. He is the author of *Rules for the Abacus, Function of the Astrolabe* (*c.* 1141–46), and a treatise *On Falconry.*

Adelard was the first of the 12th-century scholars to give learning in England its bias toward the investigation of nature and mathematics, a bias later conspicuous in the works of *Robert Grosseteste and *Roger Bacon.

Bibliography: H. E. Willner, ed. "Des Adelard von Bath Traktat De eodem et diverso," BeitrGeschPhilMA 4.1 (1903). Thorndike 2:19–49. C. H. Haskins, *Studies in the History of Medieval Science* (2d ed. Cambridge, Mass. 1927). M. Müller, "Die Quaestiones naturales des Adelardus . . .," BeitrGeschPhil MA 31.2 (1934). F. P. Bliemetzrieder, *Adelhard von Bath* (Munich 1935). D. A. Callus, "Introduction of Aristotelian Learning to Oxford," *Proceedings of the British Academy* 29 (1943) 229–281. A. C. Crombie, *Augustine to Galileo* (London 1952). E. J. Dijksterhuis, *The Mechanization of the World Picture,* tr. C. Dikshoorn, (Oxford 1961).

[E. A. SYNAN]

ADELELM OF BURGOS, ST., known also as Lesmes, patron of *Burgos and one of four famous Benedictine abbots in Castile in the 11th century; b. Loudon, near Poitiers, date unknown; d. Burgos, Jan. 30, 1097 (feast, Jan. 30). His vita was written soon after his death by Rudolph, a monk of *Chaise-Dieu in Auvergne. Adelelm gave up wealth and a military life and at Chaise-Dieu became famous for asceticism and miracles. He sent the Queen of England (Matilda of Flanders) blessed bread that reportedly cured her lethargy. At the request of Alfonso VI and his wife Constance, he came to Burgos about 1081 and ministered to pilgrims and the sick. He crossed the swollen Tagus River Moses-like (reputedly without getting wet) in front of Alfonso's army when it took Toledo in 1085. The miracles attributed to him in France and in Spain were chiefly cures of sickness effected by means of blessed bread or water.

Bibliography: A. DE VENERO, *Vida del confessor San Lesmes* (Burgos 1563). Flórez EspSagr 27:87–98. M. LEGENDRE, DHGE 2:77. L. SERRANO, *El obispado de Burgos,* 3 v. (Madrid 1935) v.2. K. LECHNER, LexThK² 1:141.

[E. P. COLBERT]

ADELHELM I, BL., abbot; d. Feb. 25, 1131 (feast, Feb. 25). A *Benedictine monk at the Abbey of *Sankt Blasien, he was chosen *c.* 1122 to be the first abbot of Engelberg, near Stans in Switzerland, soon after its foundation by Conrad of Seldenbüren (d. 1125). He worked to secure the exemption of his abbey from outside controls and won royal and papal confirmation of its status in 1124. Although his life was reputed to have been a saintly one and miracles and wonders were reported at his tomb, almost no details beyond his activity as abbot are known. Having been venerated from the middle of the 12th century, his relics were enshrined in a chapel at the abbey at Engelberg in 1744.

Bibliography: M. BESSON, DHGE 1:528. A. M. ZIMMERMANN, LexThK² 1:142. ActSS Feb. 3 (1863) 490. L. BURGENER, *Helvetia Sancta,* 2 v. (New York 1860). H. MAYER, *Geschichte des Klosters Engelburg* (Ei 1891). Zimmermann KalBen 1:252–254.

[J. L. GRASSI]

ADELMANNUS (ALMANNUS), theologian, bishop of Brescia (*c.* 1050 to the time of his death, probably in 1061), known chiefly for his literary activity during his earlier career as schoolmaster at Liège (*c.* 1028–48) and at Spire (*c.* 1048–50). A cleric of the church of Liège, and apparently a Walloon by birth, he studied under *Fulbert of Chartres, with *Berengarius of Tours as a fellow student. Two certainly authentic works of his are extant (PL 143:1289–98): *Rhytmi alphabetici de viris illustribus,* an acrostic poem celebrating literary figures of the entourage of Fulbert; and a letter to Berengarius in which he rehearsed the traditional doctrine concerning the Eucharist. An anonymous letter of an inhabitant of Spire to Abp. Hermann of Cologne (1036–56) protesting the abuse of the practice of general absolution has also been ascribed to him (PL 151:693–698).

Bibliography: K. HAMPE, "Reise nach England," NeuesArch 22 (1897) 378–380. U. BERLIÈRE, DHGE 1:530. Manitius 2: 103–105, *passim.* L. C. RAMÍREZ, *La controversia eucarística del siglo XI* (Bogotá 1940) 19–40.

[A. H. TEGELS]

ADELPHUS OF METZ, ST., bishop; d. Aug. 29, sometime in the 5th century (feast, Aug. 29; in Neuweiler, Sept. 1). Apart from the undoubted existence of his cult in Metz from an early date, everything about Adelphus is conjectural. He is believed to have succeeded St. Rufus as bishop of Metz in the 5th century, and to have ruled the diocese for 17 years, converting many pagans. The solemn translation of his relics to Neuweiler in 836 was an occasion of great popular rejoicing. Neuweiler became a center of pilgrimage. A great church was built in the 11th century to enshrine the relics, but during the Reformation they were restored to their former repository in the abbey church.

Bibliography: ActSS Aug. 6:504–512. BHL 1:76. *Pauli Warnefridi Liber de episcopis Mettensibus,* MGS 2:260–270. *Gesta episcoporum Mettensium,* ed. G. WAITZ, MGS 10:531–551, esp. 536. *Translatio et miracula S. Adelphi episcopi Mettensis,* ed. L. DE HEINEMANN, MGS 15.1:293–296. Duchesne FÉ 3:45–54. L. PFLEGER, "Zur Gesch. des Adelphikultus in Elsass," *Archiv für elsässische Kirchengeschichte* 2 (1927) 443–444. J. M. B. CLAUSS, *Die Heiligen des Elsass* (Düsseldorf 1935). A. M. BURG, LexThK² 1:144.

[M. B. RYAN]

ADEN, called in Arabic *'Adan,* a coastal city in southwestern Arabia and capital of the Aden (British) crown colony and of the Aden (British) Protectorates. Aden city, of about 99,000 inhabitants (mostly Moslem Arabs), is located on the east side of a small extinct peninsular volcano (Jebel Shamsân). Aden harbor, the most important in southern Arabia, is formed by Jebel Shamsân and Jebel 'Iḥsân (Little Aden). Known by ancient Greek authors as "Arabia emporium," Aden may well be *mrb* (Marab) in the kingdom of *Ḥiṣâṣatân* (the reservoirs) mentioned by the Sabaean text Jamme 576 (*c.* 40 B.C.). The famous tanks of Aden (in the eastern part of Jebel Shamsân) were undoubtedly built by ancient South Arabians. In more recent times, Aden was under the domination of the Turks from 1558 until 1630, then of the Sultan of Laḥej (22 miles north-northwest of Aden) from 1735 until 1839, and since then of Great Britain.

Aden Colony, a crown colony since April 1, 1937, is about 75 square miles in size and has about 200,000 inhabitants. It is composed of Aden, Little Aden, Shekh Othman (Arabic *Šayḫ 'Uṯmân;* of about 30,000 inhabitants), and surrounding territories. Its two dependencies are Perim Island (Arabic *Barîm;* of about 5 square miles, in the Straits of Bâb-el-Mandeb) and the Kuria Muria Islands (Arabic *Jizâ'ir Hûryân Mûryân;* of 30 square miles, east of Dhofâr).

Aden Protectorates, about 112,000 square miles in size, are divided into the Eastern and Western Protectorates with about 450,000 and 550,000 inhabitants, respectively (mostly Moslem Arabs). The two main cities are Al-Mukallâ (of about 200,000 inhabitants; seaport in the east) and Laḥej (of about 11,000 inhabitants). The British Protectorates date from the 19th century. In 1959 the Federation of the Arabs and the Ḥimyarites of the South was created; it became the Federation of South Arabia (composed of 11 states) in 1962.

Bibliography: *Bilan du Monde* 2:21–23. W. PHILLIPS, *Qataban and Sheba* (New York 1955). D. VAN DER MEULEN, *Aden to the Hadramauth* (London 1947).

[A. JAMME]

ADENULF OF ANAGNI, secular Parisian scholastic; b. Anagni, *c.* 1225; d. Paris, Aug. 26, 1289. A nephew of *Gregory IX, he studied arts and theology at Paris, being regent master in theology *c.* 1272 to 1288. Of his works there are extant 2 commentaries on Aristotle, a quodlibet, about 10 sermons, and a canonical treatise. He may have written the commentaries on the Psalms and Apocalypse published under the name of *Albert the Great. A canon of Paris, provost of Saint-Omer, a rich and liberal man, he fostered studies, students, and the transcription of MSS, among them the commentary of St. *Thomas Aquinas on St. John. He was twice proposed for a bishopric (Narbonne and Paris), but found refuge among the canons of Saint-Victor. He bequeathed almost 40 magnificent MSS to Saint-Victor and the Sorbonne.

Bibliography: Glorieux R 1:376–377. Glorieux L 1:99–100. M. GRABMANN in *Traditio* 5 (1947) 269–283. G. MOLLAT, DHGE 1:541.

[P. GLORIEUX]

ADEODATUS (DEUSDEDIT) II, POPE, April 11, 672, to June 17, 676; b. Rome, the son of Jovinian. He succeeded *Vitalian and, like him, defended orthodoxy against *Monothelitism. He was remarkable for his generosity and for inaugurating the practice of dating events in terms of his reign. He enlarged and enriched the Benedictine monastery of St. Erasmus on the Coelian Hill, where he had been a monk. Two letters defending monastic exemptions are attributed to him (PL 87: 1141–46). Some martyrologies celebrate his feast on June 26, but the *Bollandists say he had no cult.

Bibliography: Duchesne LP 1:346–347. Jaffé E 166. Kehr ItalPont 1:43,176. Mann 1.2:17–19. Caspar 2:587. I. DANIELE, EncCatt 1:304. G. SCHWAIGER, LexThK² 1:144.

[C. M. AHERNE]

ADESTE FIDELES, hymn used during the Christmas season, found neither in the Breviary nor in the Missal. It has been called "a second sequence for Christmas." Its origin is variously accounted for, although it is generally thought that both hymn and music were composed together in the early 18th century. Many scholars today think that it was written by John Francis Wade (1711–86), who was a teacher of Latin and church song at Douai, France, between 1740 and 1743. J. Stéphan in 1947 bolstered a plausible theory of Wade's authorship of an earlier version of the hymn and chorus, *Venite, adorate,* and the later more liturgical *Venite, adoremus.* He maintained that the hymn antedated 1744, when in a disguised form it was used as an "Air anglais" in a Paris vaudeville *Acajou.* It exists today in three versions, the first, with four strophes beginning with the words (stanza 1) *Adeste,* (2) *Deum de Deo,* (7) *Cantet,* and (8) *Ergo qui natus;* the second, with additional strophes inserted beginning (3) *En grege relicto,* (4) *Stella duce,* (5) *Magi aeterni patris,* and (6) *Pro nobis egenum;* a third version used in France has strophes 1, 3, 5 and 6. The hymn urges the faithful to approach the crib of the Word made Flesh, in the company of shepherds, magi, and angels. There are more than 40 English translations of the hymn.

Bibliography: J. STÉPHAN, *The Adeste Fideles* (Buckfastleigh, Eng. 1947). A. MOLIEN, *Catholicisme* 1:140–141. P. DEARMER, *Songs of Praise Discussed* (New York 1952). M. BRITT, ed., *The Hymns of the Breviary and Missal* (new ed. New York 1948). Julian DictHym 1:20–22.

[M. M. BEYENKA]

ADHÉMAR OF CHABANNES, Benedictine chronicler of French history; b. Limousin, France, 988; d. while on a pilgrimage to Palestine, 1034. Placed as a child in the monastery of Saint-Cybard, near Angoulême, he spent most of his life there. He became widely known for his deep faith and love of study and writing. Some of his sermons, his writings on the liturgy, and two historical works have survived. Some of his manuscripts that he left at Saint-Martial of Limoges still exist. His most important works are the three books of the *Historia* [ed. J. Chavanon (Paris 1897)] and the *Commemoratio,* or chronicle of Saint-Martial of Limoges [ed. H. Duplès-Agier (Paris 1874)]. Even though only the third book of the *Historia* is original, the work is important for the history of Aquitaine. The *Commemoratio,* written after 1025, gives a biography of each abbot of Saint-Martial from 848 onward.

Bibliography: L. DELISLE, "Notice sur les manuscrits originaux d'Adhémar de C.," *Notices et extraits des manuscrits da la Bibliothèque Nationale* . . . 35.1 (1896) 241–358. HistLittFranc 7:300–308. Molinier SHF 2:3–6. Manitius 2:284–294.

[J. A. CORBETT]

ADHÉMAR OF PUY, *Adhémar de Monteil;* b. a nobleman, probably related to the Counts of Valentinois; d. Antioch, Aug. 1, 1098. Adhémar became bishop of Le Puy shortly after 1080. During his early years as bishop, he fought vigorously and successfully to regain the lands which, under the laxer rule of his predecessors, had been taken from his see by neighboring feudal lords. Adhémar appears to have made a pilgrimage to the Holy Land in 1086–87. When *Urban II proclaimed the first Crusade at the Council of Clermont (Nov. 27, 1095), Adhémar was the first person to take a vow to go on crusade. On the following day, he was named by Urban to be his legate and deputy with the crusading armies. In October 1096, Adhémar commenced his journey, traveling with the army of Raymond IV of Saint-Gilles, Count of Toulouse. (*See* RAYMOND OF TOULOUSE.) Adhémar's functions as the papal legate on the Crusade were varied. As a military adviser, he played an important but secondary role, although in the Battle of Dorylaeum (July 1, 1097) his intervention at a crucial moment was decisive. More important was his activity as a mediator between the rival Western princes in the crusading army. Most important of all was his effort to establish harmonious relations between the Crusaders and the Eastern Christians in the territories conquered by the Crusaders. He strove consistently to integrate Eastern and Western clergy into a single ecclesiastical establishment in the Holy Land. While he lived, relations between native Christians and Western churchmen in the *Crusaders' states were close and friendly.

Bibliography: S. RUNCIMAN, *A History of the Crusades,* 3 v. (Cambridge, Eng. 1951–54) v.1. K. M. SETTON, ed., *A History of the Crusades* (Philadelphia 1955–) v.1. J. H. and L. L. HILL, "Contemporary Accounts and the Later Reputation of Adhemar, Bishop of Puy," MedHum 9 (1955) 30–38. J. A. BRUNDAGE, "Adhemar of Puy: The Bishop and his Critics," *Speculum* 34 (1959) 201–212.

[J. A. BRUNDAGE]

ADJUTOR, ST., crusader and Benedictine monk; b. late 11th century; d. Tiron, France, April 30, 1131 (feast, April 20). His parents were Jean, Seigneur de Vernon, and Rosemonde de Blaru. A devoutly religious youth, he attempted to live as austerely as possible, and *Hugh of Amiens, Archbishop of Rouen, his friend and biographer, recounts his compassion and charity in great detail. He was one of a group of Norman knights who in 1095 set out on the First *Crusade. The expedition was reputedly attended by many miraculous ocurrences including Adjutor's escape from a Moslem prison. On his return to France, he became a monk at the Abbey of *Tiron, where he earned a reputation for sanctity. He spent his last years as a hermit in a small cell he had built near the monastery. His cult is celebrated in the Dioceses of Rouen, Évreux, Chartres, and Paris.

Bibliography: ActSS April 3:832–836. A. CLERVAL, DHGE 1: 571–573. Zimmermann KalBen 2:78–81. H. LAHRKAMP, LexThK² 1:147. J. THÉROUDE, *La Vie et l'office de s. Adjuteur* (Rouen 1864), hist. and bibliog. introd. by R. BORDEAUX; repr. of *Vie de s. Adjuteur,* pub. .by D. LANGLOIS in 1638 and of *Officium s. Adjutoris* (Paris 1639).

[V. L. BULLOUGH]

ADLER, ALFRED

Depth psychologist and founder of *individual psychology; b. Vienna, Feb. 17, 1870; d. Aberdeen, Scotland, May 28, 1937. Adler was one of the earliest associates of Sigmund *Freud. Gradually, however, the two came to differ radically in their theories, and in 1911 Adler broke definitively with Freud. In 1919 he set up the Vienna school system's first child guidance clinics. Having been a frequent visitor to the U.S., he settled there in 1935. His death came while on a lecture tour. Although not perpetuated in a homogeneous school, Adler's individual psychology has influenced the development of depth psychology, and his ideas have been incorporated into other systems. He differs fundamentally from Freud on the source of neuroses, regarding the will to power, rather than the libido, as the basic driving force in human nature. Neurosis occurs, according to Adler, when an individual's drive to dominate is excessive or is frustrated. This is particularly likely to happen with persons who suffer from some physical inferiority; but since the will to power is a universal characteristic of human nature, it may lead to neurosis in any case where it is too intense or is frustrated. The basic trait of the neurotic character is the desire to become all-powerful, in short, to be like God.

Adler's system lays great stress on the finalistic element in neurosis. What purpose does the neurosis serve? His general answer is that the neurosis is a security measure adopted by the individual to avoid frustration and defeat. Through neurosis, the person seeks to provide himself with an alibi by which to justify his actions and omissions on the grounds that his illness makes him incapable of responding to life's challenges in a normal manner.

Adler assigns major importance to the role of environmental factors in the development of the individual's psychological life. It is the external world, the community, that frustrates the will to power. Thus, where Freud's approach is biological, and in particular, sexual, Adler's is strongly sociological. His therapeutic method also emphasizes this aspect. Giving relatively little attention to the unconscious, his psychotherapy instead aims to awaken healthy community feelings in the individual. In this reeducative approach, the analyst tries to restore the patient's confidence and security by encouraging his sense of fellowship with others at the expense of his egotistic power drive.

With its emphasis on environmental and sociological factors, Adler's system provides a useful balance to Freud's one-sided insistence on biological, sexual elements. At the same time, however, in part because of his Marxist ideological convictions, Adler exaggerates the importance of milieu factors. In its stress on the determining role of environment, his system is quite as deterministic as Freud's.

Alfred Adler.

Adler and Freud differ little in their ideas about religion. For Adler, religion is of no advantage to mental health. Rather, it is regarded as a flight from reality, one of the neurotic's subterfuges in his quest for false security.

Bibliography: J. H. VAN DER VELDT and R. P. ODENWALD, *Psychiatry and Catholicism* (2d ed. New York 1957). P. BOTTOME, *Alfred Adler* (2d ed. London 1946). **Illustration credit:** Library of Congress, Washington, D.C.

[R. P. ODENWALD]

ADLER, FELIX, educator, social reformer; b. Alzey, Germany, Aug. 13, 1851; d. New York City, April 24, 1933. He received his higher education at Columbia University, New York City, and Heidelberg University, Germany.

After rejecting Jewish worship and also belief in a personal God, he founded the New York Society for Ethical Culture in 1876. He stressed the need for cooperative action among all men, regardless of creeds, in the correcting of social injustices. He was one of the founders of the National Child Labor Committee and the Good Government Club, and worked also for better housing, district nursing, labor arbitration, and vocational education. From 1902 to 1933 he was professor of political and social ethics at Columbia University.

Bibliography: F. ADLER, *An Ethical Philosophy of Life* (New York 1918). H. NEUMANN, *Spokesmen for Ethical Religion* (Boston 1951). H. L. FREISS, DAB 21:13–14.

[H. BISCHOFF]

ADMINISTRATIVE LAW (U.S.)

The administrative process is the most significant legal development of the 20th century. A brief sampling of what it does supports its significance. The price and quality of vital consumer goods and services are regulated by the administrative process. The price paid for electricity, gas, telephone service; the rates and schedules of railroads, airlines, buses; the protection of the public interest in radio and television programming; the establishment of minimum standards to protect against impure food, deceptive advertising, unsafe appliances; compensation for workmen injured on the job—these and innumerable other areas of the daily lives of Americans are affected by the administrative process.

Definition. In the U.S., it is traditional and convenient to divide the governmental process into its three classical parts: legislative, executive, and judicial. The legislature makes law; the executive initiates the action of law in a particular case; the judiciary interprets and applies the law in a specific case. But each of the three branches performs functions in certain situations that belong to another branch. The judicial branch makes law in certain situations; the executive operates in a legislative capactiy when it issues tax regulations; and the legislative performs both judicial and executive functions on occasion. Notwithstanding the actual encroachment by one branch of government on the powers exercised by another, the concept of separation of powers is deeply engrained in the American polity. Any conscious attempt to combine the three powers in one agency of government was doomed to meet with the disapproval of those who remembered the concept of separation as an important ingredient in the democratic society of the U.S. To this formalistic disapproval, the one-word answer that can and has been given is expediency.

Late in the 19th century, it became apparent that existing legislative pronouncements regulating railroads, enforceable in the traditional fashion, were inadequate to cope with abuses in this indispensable form of transportation. Governmental supervision of a specialized nature was required to investigate, prosecute, and issue regulations, thus combining several governmental functions. Several state legislatures established regulatory commissions with such powers. When the U.S. Supreme Court held that the states did not have the power to regulate interstate railroad rates, however, a Federal regulatory agency became imperative. In response, the Interstate Commerce Commission (ICC) was established in 1887. The initial function of the ICC was merely negative, to correct abuses. It soon became apparent that the Commission could best perform its function if its powers were expanded, enabling it to operate in an affirmative manner, to supervise closely the railroad situation, thereby assuring a system of transportation which the country required. As to other needed goods and services, convenience and necessity indicated that similar regulatory agencies, with appropriate *expertise* in given areas, would assure the efficient fulfillment of the needs of society.

Attributes. The most convincing argument in favor of the administrative process in certain areas is awareness of the alternatives. The Congress of the United States performs most efficiently when it is deciding major policy questions. It becomes hopelessly bogged down in the necessary mass of detail found in the supervision of various regulated industries. Thus, Congress gradually developed the system of legislating only the basic policy skeleton and delegating to adminstrative agencies the job of constant supervision with its necessary corollaries: the rule-making (legislative), investigative and prosecutive (executive), and adjudicatory (judicial) functions. The other alternative would be supervision by the courts, but courts are manned by judges who would necessarily have to spend a great deal of time and effort making themselves aware of the technical matters that would be presented for adjudication in the absence of certain governmental agencies. If, for example, the area of adjudication were railroads, judges would lack the expertness of members of the ICC. If the matter involved radio or television broadcasting, judges would lack the engineering skills to understand the complicated nature of some of the controversies that arise in this area. On the other hand, an experienced body such as the Federal Communications Commission can bring to such a controversy all the tools of specialization that it possesses, since it works exclusively in this area. It should be able to resolve the dispute more efficiently than a court, and more justly, since it would not be overwhelmed by the mass of necessary detail that such controversies often present.

One of the leading scholars in the field of administrative law, Prof. Kenneth Davis, suggests: "Another major reason for the legislative preference for the administrative process has been the belief that the judicial process is unduly awkward, slow and expensive. The public has demanded a speedy, cheap and simple procedure, a procedure which keeps the role of the lawyers to a minimum." Some indication of the success or failure of the administrative process is indicated by statistical comparisons of the quantity of work done by administrative agencies as compared with legislatures and courts. The amount of legislation emanating from the Federal administrative agencies greatly exceeds the output of Congress. It has been estimated moreover that such agencies adjudicate three to four times as many matters as do Federal courts. As for state courts, they would unquestionably be overwhelmed if they had to add to their already overcrowded dockets the immense quantity of adjudication now handled by state administrative agencies. There is little question that the administrative process is more efficient at least in quantitative terms than alternative methods. It is argued, however, that there is too great a sacrifice of theoretical ideals that may ultimately affect the quality of results reached through the administrative process.

Constant Scrutiny. Regarding a blending of powers, there is no question that the administrative process does violence to our theoretical, constitutional concept of separation. As late as 1937, a committee, appointed by President Franklin D. Roosevelt, affirmed this position. Yet the U.S. Supreme Court has held that blending is not unconstitutional, and the best reply to the charge against it is that of Professor Davis: "The principle whose soundness has been confirmed by both early and recent experience is the principle of check. . . . We have learned that danger of tyranny or injustice lurks in unchecked power, not in blended power." The principle of check is applied in the Federal agencies.

The personnel are appointed by the executive; the purse strings are within the control of the legislature to whom the agencies must report; and agency actions are subject to *judicial review.

The administrative process in America has been subjected to powerful attacks, and has withstood them because it is a necessary device to perform functions in our society that could not be performed as well, if at all, by existing branches of our government. There should be less concern about the so-called evils of the administrative process because of the constant scrutiny to which it is subjected. In 1933, the American Bar Association appointed a special committee to investigate the administrative process. A series of critical reports followed, and in 1939 the President asked the attorney general to appoint a committee to investigate the need for procedural reforms in the field of administrative law. After the interruption of World War II, the quest for reforms culminated in the Adminstrative Procedure Act of 1946 (APA), which strengthened rather than weakened the administrative process. The constant concern about administrative law continued, however, with further studies, reports, and recommendations in the 1950s, capped by the 1956 recommendation of the American Bar Association for a new Code of Administrative Procedure.

More recently, when a Florida lawyer and businessman, Louis J. Hector, resigned as a member of the Civil Aeronautics Board in 1959 after 2 years of service, his long memorandum of resignation to the president, in which he severely criticized the independent regulatory commission, caused great controversy. Responses to the "Hector Memorandum" were prolific and widespread. Even more recently, in one of his first acts after being elected president, John F. Kennedy requested James M. Landis, a recognized scholar in the field of administrative law, to investigate and report on the Federal regulatory agencies. The Landis Report has added to the ever-present dialogue about the administrative process.

Bibliography: K. C. DAVIS, *Administrative Law Text* (St. Paul 1959). C. A. AUERBACH et al., *The Legal Process* (San Francisco 1961) 883–1049. L. L. JAFFE and N. L. NATHANSON, *Administrative Law: Cases and Materials* (2d ed. Boston 1961).

[J. E. MURRAY]

ADMINISTRATOR, APOSTOLIC

An apostolic administrator is a cleric, usually a bishop, who, by an extraordinary measure, is assigned by the pope to govern a diocese in serious spiritual or temporal difficulty. The nature of his mission, the history of the office, and its present discipline in the Code of Canon Law (CIC cc.312–318), mark him as a papal "trouble shooter" sent to a distressed diocese.

Mission. An administrator could be sent to a diocese filled by a resident bishop who might be, for example, under a canonical penalty suspending his jurisdiction, or who is guilty of gross mismanagement in financial affairs, incapacitated by bodily or mental illness, physically prevented from exercising jurisdiction because of banishment or detention, etc. An administrator's appointment to a vacant diocese might be prompted, for example, by the need for special investigation into past administration, for close supervision over the cathedral chapter in the election of a vicar capitular, or for delicate diplomacy during a period of political discord.

Unlike a residential bishop, the administrator has only vicarious power (CIC c.197.2), governing not in his own name, but as deputy of the pope whose jurisdiction he exercises (CIC c.218.2). When the situation in the diocese has been normalized, administration is resumed by a resident bishop who rules by proper power in his own name, not as a delegate of the pope (CIC cc. 197.2, 329.1). The office of apostolic administrator, therefore, is not a permanent governing structure for a given diocese. A person called a "permanent" apostolic administrator is one whose term of office has not been fixed in his mandate, but left indefinite; hence, "permanence" regarding his office must be understood negatively.

Historical Evolution. Although the title "apostolic administrator" was stabilized only in 1908 by Pius X's constitution *Sapienti Consilio*, the existence of the office that it represents is discernible as far back as the 5th century. The Fifth Council of Carthage (401) and the Council of Macriana (419) in Africa speak of the interventor or intercessor, appointed by the metropolitan or a provincial council to oversee the smooth succession of government in a vacant diocese. He was usually the bishop of a neighboring diocese whose task as interventor was to conduct the funeral of the deceased bishop, to administer provisionally the affairs of the diocese, and to supervise the election of the new bishop.

In Italy and France a similar office was called that of visitator, the earliest record of which appears in the Council of Riez (439). From this time it became the common practice in France for the metropolitan to send a visitator to a diocese immediately upon its vacancy in order to prevent, among other things, the plundering of the bishop's property by clergy and laity alike. The prerogative of appointing visitators soon devolved to the papacy. From the time of Pope St. Gregory the Great (590–604) well into the 9th century there were numerous examples of papal visitators sent throughout Italy and France, as well as Spain where the similar office of commendator had been common since the Council of Valencia (524).

From the 8th century the office began to suffer limitations as the institute of the cathedral chapter developed. When the Second General Lateran Council in 1139 granted the cathedral chapter the right to hold episcopal elections, the office of visitator became one of extraordinary and less frequent application, and in 1298 Boniface VIII reserved the appointment of administrators to the Holy See (CorpIurCan VI° 1.8.4). Sixtus V in 1588 assigned competence over such appointments to the Congregation of Bishops and Regulars, and in 1908 Pius X, in reorganizing the Roman *Curia, reassigned competence to the Congregation of the Consistory and consecrated the title apostolic administrator, which, since the time of decretal law, had been used interchangeably with the title *vicar apostolic. The two are now distinct offices, the former denoting a papal deputy sent to a canonically erected diocese (CIC c.312); the latter, a deputy sent to a missionary territory (CIC c.293.1).

Law Governing the Office. In default of special contrary provisions of the Holy See in a particular case, the *Code of Canon Law determines various details in the office of apostolic administrator. If he is appointed to a diocese held by an incumbent bishop, he takes possession of the government of the diocese by presenting his letter of appointment to the bishop (unless he be absent or mentally incapacitated) and to the cathedral chapter (CIC c.313.1). At that moment the jurisdiction of the bishop and his *vicar-general is suspended (CIC c.316.1). The administrator becomes local ordinary (CIC c.198.1) and is in no way subject to the resident bishop, but he may not concern himself with court action in which the bishop may be involved, nor may he pass judgment against the vicar-general for past administration (CIC c.316.2). The administrator's jurisdiction does not cease on account of the death of the bishop or the pope; normally it expires according to the wishes of the Holy See and generally, when a new bishop takes possession of the see (CIC c.318). If the administrator, in turn, should be prevented from exercising jurisdiction, or if his jurisdiction is extinguished, the Holy See should be notified immediately; meanwhile, the bishop resumes administration if he is able. If the diocese has since become vacant, the cathedral chapter assumes government of the diocese and elects a vicar capitular within 8 days (CIC c.317).

If, however, the administrator is sent to a vacant diocese, he takes possession in the manner of a residential bishop (CIC cc.313.2, 334.3). Unless the Holy See should provide otherwise, the actual government of the diocese, should the administrator be impeded, or the succession of powers when his jurisdiction ceases, proceeds according to the usual norms (CIC cc.429–444).

Unless there are contrary conditions in his mandate, the permanent apostolic administrator enjoys the same rights, honors, and duties as a residential bishop (CIC c.315.1), while the office of temporary administrator is generally identical with that of the vicar capitular (CIC c.315.2n1). If the temporary administrator is a bishop, he enjoys the honorific privileges of a *titular bishop; otherwise, he has those of a prothonotary apostolic (CIC c.315.2n2).

Bibliography: T. J. McDonough, *Apostolic Administrators* (CUA CLS 139; Washington 1941). P. Hofmeister, "Von den Apostolischen Administratoren der Diözesen und Abteien," ArchKathKRecht 110 (1930) 337–392.

[J. R. KEATING]

ADMINISTRATOR, DIOCESAN (VICAR CAPITULAR)

The diocesan administrator is a priest elected by the board of diocesan consultors to provide temporarily for the needs of a see made vacant by the death, resignation, transfer, or removal of the bishop. Although the bishop's position is unique and his place is not filled until his successor assumes office, the diocese is never left without a source of authority. Jurisdiction passes immediately to the cathedral chapter or, if there is none, to the board of diocesan consultors, who are empowered to administer the diocese for a short time. Within 8 days, however, they must elect a vicar capitular or a diocesan administrator. While he acts in their place, he is responsible not to the chapter or the board of consultors, but to the new bishop. The Code of Canon Law does not distinguish between the diocesan administrator and the vicar capitular, either in name or in the power exercised.

Rights and Duties. The duties of the diocesan administrator are defined in general law (CIC cc.432–444), and the apostolic administrator, named by the pope for some extraordinary reason, enjoys only those powers specified in his letter of appointment. The authority exercised by the diocesan administrator arises from the office he holds. It is vicarious ordinary jurisdiction. For the duration of his office, he is the local ordinary. He can make laws, administer justice through the diocesan tribunal, punish crimes, and establish penalties. He can execute apostolic rescripts and exercise habitual faculties entrusted to the former bishop, not, however, those given to the bishop in view of his personal qualifications (*industria personae*). He can allow extern bishops to pontificate in the diocese, and he may do so himself, if he has the episcopal order, but without the use of the throne and baldachin. If he is a titular bishop, the diocesan administrator continues to use the insignia and precedence of his order; otherwise, during his term of office, he holds the rank of a titular prothonotary apostolic and takes precedence over all the clergy of the diocese except bishops. The law explicitly forbids him from altering or removing documents from the episcopal curia or doing anything to prejudice the rights of the diocese and its bishop. Although the vicar capitular's powers are extensive enough to provide for normal administration, they are limited by law in specific areas as well as by the general rule so that no innovations are to be introduced until the new bishop assumes his office.

History. The vicar capitular, as the diocesan administrator is more generally known, has a long history as the representative of the chapter of canons assigned to the cathedral church. In Europe and elsewhere the cathedral chapter is considered a regular diocesan institute. The canons celebrate the divine liturgy and form a bishop's council. When the see becomes vacant, the chapter assumes responsibility for its administration, just as a *presbyterium* did in the early church.

Prior to the Council of Trent the cathedral chapter was free to exercise its interim authority collectively, through the agency of one or more canons acting in turn, or through a vicar removable at the chapter's discretion. Since diversity gave rise to abuse, the Council of Trent determined that within 8 days the chapter had to elect a vicar capitular, to whom its jurisdiction completely and irrevocably passed (ConcTrid, sess. 24, cap. 16, de ref).

Where there were no cathedral chapters, other measures had to be taken to provide for temporary administration. In the U.S. bishops satisfied the most urgent need by delegating their apostolic faculties to one or more priests, with instructions that these powers should be used in administering the affairs of the diocese during the interim. This became the rule of the Second Plenary Council of Baltimore in 1866 (Conc. Plen. Balt. II, 96) and was confirmed by the Third Plenary Council of Baltimore in 1884 (Conc. Plen. Balt. III, *Tit. Praev.*).

Furthermore, it became the custom for bishops in the U.S. to designate several priests to act as their advisers in administrative matters. By 1866 most, if not all, bishops had their diocesan councils instituted for this purpose. The Congregation for the Propagation of the Faith urged the American hierarchy at the Third Plenary Council of Baltimore to establish a cathedral chapter in each diocese. Judging this inopportune, the bishops decided instead to enact detailed laws governing the appointment and duties of diocesan consultors (Conc. Plen. Balt. III, 17–22).

In 1918 the Code of Canon Law made it mandatory for the universal Church that a diocese having no cathedral chapter should create in its place a board of diocesan consultors to advise the bishop and assume administration of the vacant see. This abrogated the right of American bishops to designate the diocesan administrator in advance and supplied a uniform and effective norm for interim administration of dioceses.

Bibliography: L. A. JAEGER, *The Administration of Vacant and Quasi-vacant Dioceses in the United States* (CUA CLS 81; 1932). P. TORQUEBIAU, DDC 3:530–595. J. DESHUSSES, DDC 4:469–473. Wernz-Vidal 2:708–713.

[J. H. HACKETT]

ADMONT, ABBEY OF, Benedictine abbey on the Enns River, Diocese of Graz-Seckau, central Austria; dedicated to the Blessed Virgin and St. *Blaise. The place (*in valle Ademundi*) is first mentioned in a document of Louis the German (859). In 1074 Abp. *Gebhard of Salzburg built the abbey on an earlier cloister of St. Emma of Gurk (d. 1045), who also endowed the monastery of Gurk (1043). A reform cloister in the spirit of *Cluny, Admont reached its first peak under Abbots Gottfried (1138–65) and Irimbert (1172–77) with a scriptorium famous for illuminations and script. The abbey cleared land, founded parishes, opened mines, fostered viticulture, and kept a hospital for the poor, the sick, and lepers; 13 monks became abbots elsewhere. From the 12th century the abbot was archdeacon of the Enns, Palten, and Liesing valleys. A brief decline was followed by economic and spiritual revival under Henry II (1275–97) and *Engelbert (1297–1327). Protestantism and the Turks caused great harm; and the cloister of Benedictine nuns, founded in 1120, came to an end. Johann IV Hoffmann (1581–1614), Mathias von Preininger (1615–28), and Urban Weber (1628–59) restored and rebuilt Admont. The Latin school was succeeded by a Gymnasium (1644) and a school of theology (1711); monks from Admont taught in the state Gymnasiums of Graz, Leoben, and Judenburg (1750–1900). During the Napoleonic Wars the abbey was plundered four times (1798–1809). Benno Kreil (1823–63) restored its finances, but a fire destroyed part of the cloister, the abbey church, and the nearby market (1865). Admont was rebuilt, only to be expropriated by Nazis (1938).

The Abbey of Admont with the Alps in the distance.

Since 1945 Admont has been slowly rebuilding and regaining its lost possessions and art treasures. It now has extensive farms and forests with modern equipment, workshops, and two power plants. The ornate library (236 by 46 feet and 36 feet high) has seven ceiling frescoes by B. Altomonte (1776) and baroque carvings by J. T. Stammel (d. 1765); it holds 130,000 volumes, 1,100 MSS, and 900 early printed works. The archives, a natural history museum with a collection of insects, and an art museum with a 1,000-year-old collection are noteworthy. The neo-Gothic abbey church (1869) has sacred art objects, a Christmas crib by Stammel (1745), and precious vestments from the abbey's embroidery school (17th–18th centuries). With 51 monks in 1964, Admont cared for 29 parishes, a Gymnasium and boarding school, and a seminary.

Bibliography: P. J. WICHNER, *Geschichte des Stiftes Admont,* 4 v. (Graz 1874–80). P. A. KRAUSE, *Die Stiftsbibliothek in Admont* (Linz 1962). U. BERLIÈRE, DHGE 1:574–576. A. KRAUSE, LexThK[2] 1:150. Cottineau 1:19–20. Kapsner BenBibl 2:184. P. A. KRAUSE, *Das Blasiusmünster in Admont* (Linz 1965).

[A. KRAUSE]

ADO OF VIENNE, ST., historian, archbishop of Vienne; b. Archdiocese of Sens, France, *c.* 800; d. Vienne, France, Dec. 16, 875 (feast, Dec. 16). He was born of a Gâtinais family, who offered him as a child to the Benedictine Abbey of *Ferrières-en-Gâtinais, where he was trained under Abbot *Lupus of Ferrières. He later spent some time studying at *Prüm under Abbot Markward, and went also to Rome or Ravenna for some years—perhaps 5—to gather hagiographical materials. Given charge of the parish of Saint-Romain in Lyons, Ado was later promoted to the See of *Vienne some time between July 6, 859 (when Aglimar, his predecessor, died), and Oct. 22, 860 (when Ado signed the acts of the Council of Thusey). As archbishop of Vienne he won the esteem of Popes *Nicholas I and *Adrian II, and Kings *Charles II the Bald and *Louis the German alike, especially for his firm stand against the divorce of King *Lothair II (MGEp 6:175–177). He was active in his archdiocese as well, holding councils to reform clerical morality and to regulate the celebration of the Divine Office. The acts of these reforming councils have disappeared except for a fragment from one held in 870. Ado is also important as an author. In his *Chronicum sive Breviarium de sex mundi aetatibus ab Adamo usque ad annum 869* (PL 123:23–138; MGS 2:315–323), a chronicle of world history that depends on similar works by Bede, Orosius, and Isidore and on contemporary Frankish sources, he treated in interesting detail the Diocese of Vienne, listing 47 bishops accurately (Duchesne FE 150–162), but he identified the first bishop, Crescens, with the person of that name mentioned by St. Paul (2 Tm 4.10). However, Bishop Crescens actually lived in the 3d century. Ado himself may have wrenched the chronology or may simply have repeated an earlier legend. He reedited a life of St. *Desiderius of Vienne, one of his predecessors in the See of Vienne, who died as a result of courageously rebuking the redoubtable *Brunhilde, and composed a life of St. Theuderius, a 6th-century abbot in Vienne. Ado published a martyrology called

Passionum codices undecumque collecti (PL 123:143–436), nine-tenths of which was taken from a similar work by *Florus of Lyons. The remaining text Ado claimed to have derived from an ancient collection copied by him when he was in Italy at Ravenna. This portion of the text has been condemned as sheer forgery on Ado's part; it only added to the already complicated problems concerning *martyrologies. *Usuard was much influenced by Ado's work.

Bibliography: Mabillon AS 6:278–290. W. L. KREMERS, *Ado von Vienne* (Steyl 1911). M. BESSON, DHGE 1:585–586. Butler Th Attw 4:571–572. Baudot-Chaussin 12:482–494. A. M. ZIMMERMANN, LexThK² 1:150–151.

[C. M. AHERNE]

ADOLESCENT PSYCHOLOGY

The exact boundaries of adolescent psychology are as difficult to define as the limits of adolescence itself. Its field is distinguishable from other areas of psychological investigation by its concentration on the behavior and personality characteristics of young persons commonly referred to as teen-agers. The study of the child prior to adolescence is then identified as *child psychology or child development, although this area is sometimes joined to the study of adolescence in order to make up the field of investigation called *developmental psychology.

The subject matter of adolescent psychology includes the behavior, psychic life, and emerging personality and interpersonal relationships of boys and girls who have passed through puberty but have not yet reached the threshold of adulthood. Methodologically, the psychology of the adolescent derives its information from a direct study of adolescents themselves, but maintains close liaison with other fields of investigation that can shed light on adolescent problems. The fields of child, developmental, genetic, adjustment, abnormal, and *social psychology are important adjuncts to the study of adolescents, as are less directly related fields such as physiology, sociology, and social and *mental health. Because the approach is developmental, and extends over a period of time, the techniques used in this study are objective rather than subjective, and longitudinal rather than cross-sectional in nature. *See* METHODOLOGY (PSYCHOLOGY). Since the emerging personality of the adolescent must be studied in transition, the developmental method is preferred. Yet the contributions that literature, biography, diaries, and other sources of information might make to the understanding of the adolescent cannot be overlooked.

Nature of Adolescence. Adolescence has a fairly well-defined boundary that distinguishes it from the preceding stage of childhood. This boundary is determined by the phenomenon referred to as puberty, which is marked by the emergence of definite physical characteristics and the ripening of the capacity for reproduction. When puberty is completed, childhood has receded into the past.

The boundary at the other end of adolescence is not so clearly defined, because of considerable vagueness in the criteria used to discern adulthood or maturity. From the physical point of view it is possible to identify the signs of adulthood, because the person actually becomes physically mature. This normally occurs between 20 and 23 years of age. For political, economic, and social reasons, therefore, adulthood may be regarded as starting at age 21, although in some instances the dividing year is lowered to 18. Since puberty varies with age as well as with other factors (e.g., personality, race, sex, nationality, and cultural differences), the chronological boundaries of adolescence extend roughly from 12 to 20 years, thus corresponding closely with the teen-age period. While some adolescents mature earlier than 12, and others extend their youth well into the period of adulthood, these boundaries certainly include the great majority of adolescents.

Statistics indicate that adolescents comprised about one-tenth of the American population in 1964. Population figures provided by the Bureau of the Census show that for the census year of 1960 there were about 16,800,000 youths in the 14-to-19-year age bracket. In 1958, there were 8,868,586 boys and girls enrolled in grades 9 to 12. By 1961 this figure had increased to 11,161,000, which comprised 91.4 per cent of all children 14 to 17 years of age. To appreciate how sharply school enrollment decreases with increasing age, one should compare this figure with the 1,952,000 teen-agers enrolled in school during their 18th and 19th years; the 91.4 per cent there drops to 38.0 per cent. Finally, in 1961 there were 196,000 males and 939,000 females in the 14-to-19-year age bracket who were already married. Obviously, school "dropouts" and early marriages of 1,135,000 adolescents have important implications for the study of the problems of adolescents.

Adolescent Personality. The study of adolescence revolves around the adolescent personality. This gradually emerging personality forms the matrix for the conflicts and frustrations, the difficulties and problems of the adolescent period. What is such a personality like? This question is not easily answered, because the adolescent personality is in constant transition, shifting from day to day, from week to week, even from one moment to the next. Traditionally, the adolescent has been characterized as idealistic, unstable, rebellious, uncertain, loving, dependent, conforming; and, above all, as sexually confused. All of these descriptive adjectives are applicable to one or another adolescent at some point in his development. While it is not improbable that some adolescents, and perhaps the majority of them, manage to survive this period of storm and stress without noticeable damage, it is known from the complaints of parents and teachers, from the large number of school dropouts, from early marriages, unhallowed pregnancies, rising statistics on juvenile crime, increases in teen-age drinking, and similar evidence, that many adolescents do not survive the transitional period without considerable trouble.

To draw a clear picture of the adolescent personality, one must understand something about the dynamics of personality formation (*see* PERSONALITY). For example, the average adolescent is driven by powerful needs (or drives) to act in certain ways toward himself and others. The adolescent needs acceptance and love, independence, security, sex identity, self identity, and experience; but he also needs participation, approval, achievement, and conformity. These needs indicate why the peer group is so important to the adolescent: he is rescued from his rebellious independence by the acceptance and the conformity afforded by his peers. The adolescent is also strongly influenced by basic feelings, particularly those of sex, anxiety, guilt, and self-rejection, that serve to reinforce the dynamics of his personality needs. Again, he is motivated by certain tasks that he feels must be fulfilled, particularly the achievement of maturity, responsibility, self-direction, and vocational identity. To the extent that these tasks remain unfulfilled, the adolescent finds it impossible to cross the border into adulthood, feeling threatened by a reality for which he is poorly equipped. The fulfillment of these needs and tasks, on the other hand, leads to personal integration and wholeness, which complete the process of personality growth.

Problems of Adolescents. Out of such needs and expectations, imposed on adolescent boys and girls by an unyielding nature and a sternly demanding environment, grow many of the problems encountered by adolescents. For convenience these problems can be grouped into five categories: personal, social, moral-religious, educational, and vocational. All such problems are closely intertwined, so that one is likely to lead to others. Typically, the "sex problem" readily extends into the moral, religious, and social areas of the adolescent's life; and so for others.

Among personal problems, the most prominent are associated with sex, aggression, rebellion, sex identity, and uncontrolled feelings like guilt, anger, and inferiority. Within the category of social problems are those involved in relating to the opposite sex, conformity to family standards and expectations, and attempting to fit into the social milieu with its somewhat rigid system of values. The moral and religious difficulties encountered by teen-agers are occasioned by such personal and social experiences and developments. In his confrontation with accepted moral codes, in his conflicts with his parents, and in his inability to cope with strong feelings, the adolescent is powerfully urged toward reorienting all of his basic values. The simple schema of childhood is no longer adequate for the more complex demands and expectations, and the adolescent begins to take a close look at the values previously set for him by parents, teachers, and society. This reorientation causes anxiety, anguish, and sometimes rebellion.

The adolescent is confronted also with educational and vocational expectations and demands. Society frowns on the boy or girl who drops out of high school before graduation, and there is tremendous pressure on youths to continue their education into college, and even graduate school. Yet many youths are intellectually and temperamentally unsuited to education, find it extremely difficult to apply themselves to academic requirements, and often consciously or unconsciously "fail themselves" out of school. In later adolescence they are faced also with vocational expectations relating to military service, to a career, and to marriage. For all such decisions and demands the average youth may be very poorly equipped by disposition, talent, or experience, and thus may find himself on the threshold of adulthood beset by confusion and anxiety. By comparison, one may note the steady, forward progress toward mature, adult living of young people who have settled their minds about marriage, have decided how to handle military service, have entered the religious life or determined other career goals for themselves.

Catholics and the Adolescent. The Catholic Church has been keenly aware of the needs and problems of its youth, and the popes have directed their attention on numerous occasions to them. The Church has sponsored and encouraged many organizations and activities such as the Catholic Youth Organization, the Catholic Family Movement, the Sodality Movement, Newman Clubs, Pre-Cana Programs, and released-time classes for religious instruction. Through the numerous high schools and colleges associated with the Church, Catholic youth is offered extensive opportunity for religious instruction, moral development, and education in values. In addition, the Church sponsors numerous moral and religious facilities and practices for the spiritual growth of youth; no one can complain that it has been negligent in this regard.

On the side of research publication in the area of adolescent psychology, however, Catholic scholarship is not particularly distinguished. Here and there some research has been done on adolescent behavior, and a few publications have appeared in more recent years; but on the whole Catholic institutions of higher learning, and special agencies of the Church, can look only to the future for accomplishments in this field.

In the area of *guidance and *counseling also, Catholic schools are mediocre when compared to the best in secular education. Many Catholic high schools are poorly equipped to handle typical guidance and counseling problems, and Catholic institutions of higher learning seem to give little support to formal programs in this direction. The reasons for this are many and varied; at least part of the explanation, however, seems traceable to lack of interest in modern psychology and its techniques. For the guidance of youth presupposes a well-developed psychology of adolescence, and in this field much still remains to be done.

Bibliography: W. C. Bier, ed., *The Adolescent: His Search for Understanding* (Pastoral Psychology Ser. 3; New York 1963). W. A. Connell and J. D. McGannon, *The Adolescent Boy* (Notre Dame, Ind. 1958). C. A. Curran, *Counseling in Catholic Life and Education* (New York 1952). J. P. Finn, *A Study of the Problems of Certain Catholic High School Boys as Told by Themselves and Their Teachers* (Washington 1950). U. H. Fleege, *Self-Revelation of the Adolescent Boy* (Milwaukee 1945). R. B. Fullam, ed., *The Popes on Youth* (New York 1955). J. R. Gallagher and H. I. Harris, *Emotional Problems of Adolescents* (New York 1958). J. M. Gillespie and G. W. Allport, *Youth's Outlook on the Future* (Garden City, N.Y. 1955). A. M. Greeley, *Strangers in the House: Catholic Youth in America* (New York 1961). G. A. Kelly, *The Catholic Youth's Guide to Life and Love* (New York 1960). M. Knoebber, *The Self-Revelation of the Adolescent Girl* (Milwaukee 1936). B. Morrison, *Character Formation in College* (Milwaukee 1938). J. A. O'Brien, *Sex-Character Education* (New York 1953). G. H. J. Pearson, *Adolescence and the Conflict of Generations* (New York 1958). J. S. Plant, *The Envelope: A Study of the Impact of the World Upon the Child* (New York 1950). H. H. Remmers and D. H. Radler, *American Teenager* (New York 1957). H. V. Sattler, *Parents, Children, and the Facts of Life* (Paterson, N.J. 1952). A. A. Schneiders, *Personality Development and Adjustment in Adolescence* (Milwaukee 1960); *Adolescence and the Challenge of Maturity* (Milwaukee 1964). R. J. Steimel, ed., *Psychological Counseling of Adolescents* (The Proceedings of the Workshop on Psychological . . .; Washington 1962). R. M. Strang, *The Adolescent Views Himself: A Psychology of Adolescence* (New York 1957). A. Wheelis, *The Quest for Identity* (New York 1958). E. G. Williamson, *Counseling Adolescents* (New York 1950). R. M. Wittenberg, *Adolescence and Discipline* (New York 1959).

[A. A. SCHNEIDERS]

ADONAI, comes from the Canaanite and Hebrew word *'ādôn,* which means lord. The word is a plural form to which the personal suffix "my" has been added. In order to distinguish this form, which means "my lords," from the same word used in speaking of the one Lord, a special plural form featuring a long "a" before the "i" was evolved. (For an example of these different forms cf. Gn 18.3 with 19.2, Hebrew text.) The suffix "my" gradually lost its significance, as happened also in the case of the word Rabbi (my Master). For Adonai as a substitute for Yahweh, *see* YAHWEH; JEHOVAH; ELOHIM.

Bibliography: B. W. ANDERSON, InterDictBibl 2:414. H. JUNKER, LexThK[2] 1:152. P. VAN IMSCHOOT, *Théologie de l'Ancien Testament,* 2 v. (Tournai 1954–56).

[R. T. A. MURPHY]

ADONIA, fourth son of *David, born to him of Haggith at Hebron (2 Sm 3.4; 1 Chr 3.2). The first two chapters of 3 Kings relate in considerable detail the attempt of Adonia [Heb. *'adōnîyāh(û)*, my lord is Yahweh] to succeed his father. Since he was the oldest living son of the aged King and had the support of David's general, *Joab, and the priest *Abiathar, he had himself crowned at En-Rogel. Whether this action had the approval of David is uncertain, but it is clear that the Prophet *Nathan and David's favorite wife *Bethsabee (Bathsheba) promptly induced the dying King to nominate *Solomon as his successor. This was quickly arranged, and thereupon Adonia lost most of his supporters. At first he was leniently treated by Solomon, but later, when he tried to take David's young *concubine Abisag as his wife and thus press his claim to the throne, Solomon ordered that he be put to death.

Bibliography: A. PETER, LexThK[2] 1:153. A. PENNA, EncCatt 1:319. F. E. GIGOT, CE 1:146–147. EncDictBibl 35–36.

[B. MC GRATH]

ADOPTION (IN THE BIBLE), the legal action by which a minor is made the equivalent of a child born in a family and given corresponding inheritance rights. Adoption was practiced in the ancient Near Eastern civilizations of the 2d millennium, and traces of the custom can be found in the Bible, especially in the stories of the *Patriarchs. For example, Abraham's expectation that Eliezer would be his heir (Gn 15.2–3) seems to reflect the practice of the *Hurrians preserved in the *Nuzu (Nuzi) documents. From these texts it appears that even a slave could be made an heir when there was no son. Such a person would be considered an adopted child. The action of Sara in giving her servant girl *Agar (Hagar) to Abraham as a concubine in order that Sara might accept the child born of this union as her own (Gn 16.2–5) is a case of adoption paralleled in the Nuzu texts. The same is true of the story of the birth of Jacob's sons Dan and Nephthali, whom Bala, Rachel's maid, bore on her mistress's "knees" (Gn 30.3–8), and of the account of Israel's action in regard to Joseph's sons (Gn 48.5–20); the sons of Machir (the son of Manasse) also "were born on Joseph's knees" (Gn 50.23). These parallels to the Hurrian practice reflect the ancient Near Eastern background of the patriarchal narratives and are not surprising since *Haran, a patriarchal center, was part of the Hurrian territory. However, it would seem that these practices of adoption were not made part of the Israelite legal traditions, since there is no trace of them in the Biblical law codes. Other examples of adoption in the OT are the cases of Moses (Ex 2.10), Genubath (3 Kgs 11.20), and Esther (Est 2.7, 15); these, however, took place in foreign lands and do not necessarily reflect Israelite practice.

Another instance of adoption customs that appears in the Bible is the relationship of the king to Yahweh, expressed by the formula of Ps 2.7, "You are my son; this day I have begotten you," which, in turn, is based on Nathan's oracle to David (2 Sm 7.8–16). Since the king represented the people, the people as a whole share in the adoption. This is not a new idea in Israel, for in the Exodus from Egypt God had already entered into a father-son relationship with the people (Ex 4.22; Dt 32.6). The use of the metaphor of Yahweh as father to Israel is expressed in many other texts (Is 63.16; Jer 3.19; 31.9; Os 11.1; etc.).

This concept reached its full flowering only in the NT. There Our Lord taught His disciples to address God as their Father (Mt 6.9; Lk 11.2). Similar references are found in the Gospel of St. John (Jn 20.17), and St. Paul refers to the Christian adoption as sons of God as the result of the indwelling of the Holy Spirit (Rom 8.15, 23; Gal 4.5; Eph 1.5).

See also ADOPTION, SUPERNATURAL.

Bibliography: EncDictBibl 36–37. De Vaux AncIsr 51–52. E. A. SPEISER, *Genesis* (Anchor Bible 1; Garden City, N.Y. 1964) 112, 120–121, 230. R. T. O'CALLAGHAN, *Aram Naharaim* (Anal Or 26; 1948) 73–74. R. J. TOURNAY, "Nouzi," DBSuppl 6:646–674. S. O. MOWINCKEL, *The Psalms in Israel's Worship,* tr. D. R. AP-THOMAS (Nashville 1962) 54–58.

[S. M. POLAN]

ADOPTION (IMPEDIMENT TO MARRIAGE). Adoption in Roman law constituted a diriment impediment to marriage (CorpIurCivInst 1.10.1,3; Dig 23.2.55). According to the response of Pope Nicholas I (858–867) to the Bulgars, the Church "canonized" this impediment of Roman law (CorpIur Can C.30 q.3 c.1). The reason for the impediment is expressed in the Roman-law principle *adoptio naturam imitatur* (adoption imitates nature).

In Church law, the impediment to marriage caused by legal relationship coincides with the impediment as it obtains in the civil law of the region. Accordingly, legal relationship may be no impediment, an impedient impediment (CIC c.1059; CrebAllat c.47), or a diriment impediment (CIC c.1080; CrebAllat c.71). In the Oriental code, legal relationship constitutes a minor grade impediment (CrebAllat c.31n5). Of the United States and its territories, Puerto Rico alone maintains a diriment impediment of legal relationship (Civ. Cod. of Puerto Rico 1911–13, n 3205,3.4).

See MARRIAGE, CANON LAW OF, 3.

Bibliography: Wernz-Vidal 5:188. BENEDICT XIV, *De synodo diocesana,* 4 v. (Rome 1842) 2.9.10. C. B. ALFORD, *Ius civile matrimoniale comparatum,* 2 v. (Rome 1937) 1:162–163.

[J. F. GALLAGHER]

ADOPTION (U.S. LAW OF)

The practice of taking a child into one's home and rearing it as one's own existed in ancient times. Sargon, the founder of the city of Babylon, was an adopted child. Oedipus, Paris, Tristan, and other notables of early literature were reared as adopted children. Moses was brought up by someone other than his natural parents. The Apostle Paul in his several epistles makes frequent reference to adoption and places special significance on the practice (e.g., Rom 8.14–17; Gal 4.5–7).

The Romans had a procedure for adoption, and their law is the source of early American legislation of adoption. There was no common law regarding it. In fact

England enacted its first adoption act in 1926 (16, 17 Geo. 5, c. 29; 17 Halsbury, *Laws of England 1406–23*, 2d ed. 1935), long after many American states had legislated in the matter. Under the Roman system the primary concern of adoption was the continuity of the adopter's family. Emphasis was placed on inheritance and succession. The earliest adoption laws in the U.S. appeared in Louisiana and Texas, states that inherited much of their legal systems from the Roman law. In the early adoption laws of these states the motivating interest was the inheritance of property.

Early adoption statutes were predominantly legislative acts authenticating and making public records of private agreements of adoption. There was little concern, as there was later, for the general welfare of the child. Massachusetts, in 1850, was the first state to require judicial machinery to effect an adoption. In contrast to the laws of Louisiana and Texas, the Massachusetts act provided judicial supervision over adoptions to insure that the adoptive parents would rear the adoptive child properly. The other states that soon followed Massachusetts in enacting legislation with emphasis on judicial supervision over adoption were Pennsylvania (1855), Indiana (1855), Georgia (1855–56), Wisconsin (1858), Ohio (1859), Michigan (1861), New Hampshire (1862), Oregon (1864), Connecticut (1864), Kansas (1868), California (1870), Maine (1871), Rhode Island (1872), North Carolina (1872–73), and New York (1873). Currently all jurisdictions in the U.S. require that adoptions be effected by a judicial proceeding.

Adoption has become a more common method of increasing one's family than it was in the past. The number of children adopted annually in the U.S. rose from an estimated 80,000 in 1951 to about 107,000 in 1960.

Adoption procedures and practices have become steadily more complex. Today adoption cannot be defined as merely the juridical act creating certain civil relations between people. It is really a social process by which a child becomes a member of another family. It involves a number of community institutions, such as the legislature, the court, social welfare agencies, and religious institutions.

Social Service Aspects. Many jurisdictions require that before an adoption is decreed by a court, the court must have a study made of the child and of his natural and adoptive parents. The purpose of the study, called the social investigation, is to help the court to decide the best disposition of the case. It has brought into the adoption process social welfare agencies and social workers, who are trained in understanding human behavior, evaluating family relationships, and interviewing. Generally it is a social worker who prepares the report of the investigation for the court. This report is general in nature and concerns the character, personality, and health of the adoptive parents; the condition of their home and neighborhood in which they live; and an opinion on whether the child's best interests will be furthered by the adoption. The judge uses the social investigation as a guide in reaching his decision.

Social workers and child welfare agencies may enter the adoption process at any stage. If a couple contacts a child welfare agency in order to obtain a child, a social worker becomes involved early in the adoption process by doing an adoption study. The study is made after an applicant has been interviewed and has formally applied for a child at a child welfare agency. Normally it includes the following material: information about the applicants' health, the physical condition of their home, the neighborhood where they live, their reputation in the community, their developmental history, the history and current functioning of their marriage, their conceptions and expectations about parenthood, their age, sex, nationality, and class preference in relation to the child they hope to adopt, and their expectations about that child.

The contacting of a child welfare agency first and having the agency place a child with an applicant and counseling the applicant about adoption is called an agency placement. Not using this route to obtain a child, but acquiring a child through private sources, such as through the family physician, clergyman, lawyer, or friend is called a private or independent placement. Of the 107,000 children who were adopted in 1960 by unrelated persons, 59 per cent were placed through social agencies and 41 per cent were placed independently.

Agency Services. The use of agencies to obtain children for adoption is increasing. In some states the courts are prohibited from entering a decree of adoption for any child not related to the petitioners in some way, unless the placement is made by a licensed child welfare agency. Other states discourage private placement of children through their child-placement laws, making it a crime for certain persons unrelated to the natural parents to place a child with a family for adoption.

Adoption services in a social welfare agency have as their function the promotion of the well-being of the child to be adopted and a recognition of the needs and interests of the natural and adoptive parents. One aspect of these services consists in casework services to the natural parents. If the natural parent is an unwed mother, she is counseled by a social worker who takes the necessary steps to ensure that the expectant mother is properly cared for either at home or in an institution. The social worker helps the expectant mother plan for the child's future and assists her in deciding whether she wants to keep the child or give up the child for adoption. If she decides to relinquish her child, a formal procedure is followed to obtain her consent properly according to the state adoption statute. If she decides to keep the child, the social worker makes her aware of the legal problems that may arise pertaining to the child's status and financial support and informs her of the necessity for seeking legal counsel.

The services to the child usually take the form of a social study of him, including his developmental history, his family history, and a medical and psychological examination. The child is placed in the home of a suitable adoptive family, where there is supervision by the agency.

Matching Parent and Child. Services to the adoptive parents usually include help in determining whether they will be fit parents, the selection of a child suitable for them if their home can be used, assistance in the legal steps necessary to effect the adoption, and postadoption counseling. The major question facing agencies in selecting adoptive parents is whether the proposed adoptive parents will be satisfactory for parenthood not only immediately but for the total span of childhood years and thereafter. Factors taken into account are the applicants' physical and emotional health, their family history, their work history, the condition of their home and neighborhood, and their reputation in the community. When a child becomes available for adoption, the agency makes a further determination regarding the applicants' suitability for the particular child, and it endeavors to match the particular adoptive parents with a particular child. Physical and emotional characteristics of both parents and child are considered. A child with special needs (through physical handicap, membership in a minority group, or advancement past infancy) requires parents with special qualifications and characteristics.

In matching the parent with the child, ethnic characteristics are considered. Social welfare agencies are aware that difficulties might arise if adoptive parents and children are of different racial origins. It has been the practice in many agencies in most parts of the U.S. to place children in adoptive homes with similar racial characteristics because it is felt that these children can thus become more easily integrated into the family group and community. Some agencies do not follow this policy, however. In fact some agencies foster the placement of minority-group children (e.g., Negroes, Indians, and Asiatics) with white parents. The reason for this policy is the large number of minority-group children available for adoption and the relative fewness of acceptable applicants with the same racial characteristics. It is thought that children should be placed as soon as possible where they can benefit from a permanent family relationship rather than in a temporary setting such as a foster home or an institution.

Child welfare agencies use religion as a factor in the placement of children. Nonsectarian agencies judge that a child should ordinarily be placed in a home where the religion of the adoptive parents is the same as that of the child unless the natural parents have specified that the child may be placed with a family of another religion. Catholic adoption agencies are committed to the basic principle that a Catholic child being placed for adoption can have his total needs met only in a Catholic adoptive home. This view is based on the Catholic conviction that religion is something more than an external value to the child. It is an obligation basic to his very nature. However, the practice of Catholic adoption agencies varies somewhat where applicants representing a marriage between a Catholic and a non-Catholic are concerned. Some Catholic agencies will consider such applications, particularly in instances where the mother is Catholic, or in families in which the non-Catholic party is willing to take instructions in the fundamental teachings of the Catholic Church. On the whole, however, these agencies seek adoptive couples both of whom are Catholic.

Legal Aspects. Individual state statutes specify the nature, content, and formalities of adoption procedures within their own jurisdictions. What follows is a general overview of basic similarities in the diverse state statutes. Traditionally adoption proceedings have been conducted in a juvenile, family, or probate court or in the court of the highest general trial jurisdiction within the state. Generally the adoption proceedings are brought in the court of the county or district where: (1) the petitioners—the adoptive parents—reside or are domiciled; (2) where the child resides, is domiciled, or is physically located; or (3) where the natural parents are domiciled. Jurisdiction for adoption might consist in any one or combination of these factors, depending on the statutes of the particular state involved.

Adoption proceedings are begun by the filing of a petition by the adoptive parents. This petition usually consists of information (viz, names, ages, place of residence) about the petitioners and the child to be adopted. The natural parents must consent to the adoption, and their consent must be filed with the court. Under some circumstances (e.g., parental abandonment, neglect, unfitness, mental disability), which must be proved, parental consent is unnecessary. A social study is usually made by court-appointed personnel and assists the judge in determining whether the proposed adoption is in the best interests of the child. There is a hearing following the general civil procedure of the state. Some states, however, provide for an informal hearing. Under certain conditions adoption statutes provide for notice to the natural parents. Usually there is an opportunity for appellate review of an adoption decree.

The goal of adoption is to integrate the adopted child fully into the family. Essentially, modern adoption legislation and other laws affecting the family incorporate this goal. The relationship that is established between the adopted child and his adoptive parents is a permanent one. In most states the adopted child is afforded the same treatment, so far as the law is concerned, as if he were the adoptive parents' natural child.

Each state in the U.S. has enacted an adoption statute, and each statute must be studied in order to learn the rights and responsibilities of an adopted child in a particular state. In most states the adopted child is considered, for legal purposes, to be the actual child of the adopting family. Thus the same reciprocal legal rights and duties of the natural parent-child relationship exist for the adoptive parent when the child has been adopted.

The rights of an adopted child to inherit from his adoptive and natural parents vary. In some states he inherits from both his natural and adoptive parents. In others, he does not inherit from his natural parents, their issue, collateral relatives, etc., but only from his adoptive parents, their issue, collateral relatives, etc. This latter position reflects the modern view of the adopted child's total integration into his new family and his complete legal break with his natural parents and family.

Bibliography: I. E. Smith, ed., *Readings in Adoption* (New York 1963). H. L. Witmer et al., *Independent Adoptions* (New York 1963). F. V. Harper and J. H. Skolnick, *Problems of the Family* (rev. ed. Indianapolis 1962). Child Welfare League of America, *A Study of Adoption Practice,* 3 v. (New York 1956) v.2. S. N. Katz, "Judicial and Statutory Trends in the Law of Adoption," *Georgetown Law Journal* 51 (1962) 64–95. L. A. Huard, "The Law of Adoption," *Vanderbilt Law Review* 9 (1956) 743–763. S. N. Katz, "Community Decision-Makers and the Promotion of Values in the Adoption of Children," *The Social Service Review* 38 (1964) 26–41.

[S. N. KATZ]

ADOPTION, SUPERNATURAL

The elevation and restoration of man to a particular relationship with God beginning on earth in *grace and ordered to eternal union in glory. *Supernatural adoption is a gratuitous conferring of the status and title of son and heir on one not such by natural generation. Unlike human adoption, which supposes a nature common to father and son, divine adoption, through *faith and Baptism, causes the son to partake of the divine nature as a fruit of Christ's redemptive *Incarnation. (*See* DIVINE NATURE, PARTAKER OF.)

Sacred Scripture. The word adoption (υἱοθεσία), found four times in St. Paul (Gal 4.5; Rom 8.15; 9.4;

Eph 1.5), appears nowhere else in the Bible. In Rom 9.4, "adoption" refers to the Israelites under the Law; elsewhere it occurs in Resurrection contexts referring to Redemption or justification, which, like adoption, are forensic concepts in Roman law. In itself adoption might seem to be simply a metaphor, but evidence indicates that a reality is involved. In its chronological use there is a progressive determination of teaching: Gal 4.5 reads, "that we might receive the adoption of sons"; Rom 8.15, "you have received a spirit of adoption as sons"; Eph 1.5, "He predestined us to be adopted through Jesus Christ as his sons."

In a wider context, Gal 3.15–4.9, Rom 8.9–17, and Eph 1.3–14 employ a basic vocabulary with ever-increasing comprehension, Eph 1.3–14 being a hymn of praise and thanksgiving for our adoption. As a hymn, this pericope is a finished product, an epitome of Pauline teaching possibly enshrined in the liturgy. In this it is like St. John's prologue, which also climaxes in a traditional proof-text, Jn 1.12–13, "the power of becoming sons of God." Actually John's prologue subsumes the three Pauline citations, and all four reflect the parabolic movement found in the early liturgy: from the Father, through the Son, in the Spirit, to the Father—a movement identifying Christ as the mediator through whom all things descend to earth and rise to heaven. In the Pauline passages the concrete terms declare the truth of our adoption, and these same concepts all appear later in the Johannine tradition, which, following 1 Pt 1.23 and Jas 1.18, describes sonship in terms of generation. We have been changed from slaves to sons and heirs, and constitute the family of God.

In each final summary it is glory that is invoked, and in the NT glory may be equated with divinity (cf. Jn 17.21–23). In Romans ch. 8 the leading thought is the gift of the Spirit as the vital principle of Christian life; this is also the meaning of the Passover mystery of Christ in John (12.16, 23, 28; 7.39): the Crucifixion, by which the humanity of Christ is glorified, is the sign of the beginning of the mission of the Spirit (Jn 15.26) and the birth of the Mystical Body (Jn 19.27–30), in which we too, Paul concludes, will be glorified, "provided, however, we suffer with him" (Rom 8.17). It is through Christ that a consubstantiality of the flesh, a sonship and brotherhood is attained: as God, Christ communicates His Spirit in Baptism, which is our identification with His Passover; as man, He communicates Himself to us corporally in the Eucharist (1 Cor 11.23–26). Thus Christ's presence in us is not just the presence of His Spirit; we are bound to the Godhead in the bodily Christ, too. Incorporated into the glorified humanity of the Son, we glorify the Father by extending the mystery of His paternity (Eph 3.15), the personal property of the First Person. For Jesus declared to the Father, "I have manifested thy name" (Jn 17.6), conveying to the Semite the revelation of the Person. If the name is Father, paternity is the mystery revealed: for some scholars, "Father" replaces the Tetragrammaton (Ex 3.14) in the Christian dispensation.

John totally authenticates the Pauline teaching in which the individualistic use of adoption seems suggested to Paul in association with other legal terms. However, its use accomplishes a double purpose: it emphasizes the unique divine quality of the sonship of the God-Man in contrast to ours; it poses the paradox that theologically is resolved by our supernatural elevation to all that is intrinsically necessary in legal adoption—a sharing of the same nature so that "sons," or "heirs," has meaning as knowledge, love, divinity of Persons that can be truly participated.

Theological Development. The Greek Fathers especially (EnchPatr, *Index theol.* 359) wrote enthusiastically of this revelation of love that is the Triune God and of our divinization by filiation, adoption, and union through the wedding of the divine and human in the Incarnation, which had its term in the Resurrection, signifying the glorification of Christ's humanity—which glorification is the cause of ours. We are certain that Paul presented no fiction in declaring our adoption, but it is debated whether the Fathers' affirmations concerning the Persons are mere *appropriations. Development of dogma in the West, however, did not follow the Greek Fathers' lead. Instead, Tertullian's juridical orientation of the Church, the historical exigencies of Arianism, and Anselm's theory of the infinite *satisfaction of Christ with subsequent concentration on the suffering Christ accentuated the negative aspects of Redemption and culminated in the definitions of the Council of Trent.

This Council decreed (Denz 1520–83) that *justification is a passing from the state in which a man is born a son of the first Adam to a state of grace and adoption of sons of God and heirs of eternal life. The formal cause of justification it declared to be that by which God makes us just, and this in the scholastic tradition is called sanctifying grace. An infused ontological accident, sanctifying grace inheres in the soul, elevating it to the *supernatural order and effecting our partaking of the divine nature, supernatural adoption, and the divine *indwelling. God as efficient cause educes this grace from the *obediential potency of the soul and not from its natural power; it is declared created insofar as it causes its subject to begin to be in a new way. Our supernatural adoption is thus seen to follow from our participation in the divine nature, whereby we are ordained to glory and the *beatific vision of God; for this sanctifying grace physically and formally but analogically disposes us.

In this analysis the divine indwelling is an accidental union with the Holy Spirit, or more properly with the divine nature, since all *ad extra* activities are by definition common to the three Persons. Yet insofar as the divine indwelling is not considered as act (having a beginning in time) but as gift (conferred in the act) it is, like the hypostatic union and the beatific vision, uncreated. Whenever either created grace or uncreated grace is present to the soul, so is the other. The theological explanation of this and its consequences in the post-Tridentine period caused much speculation. These years marked a gradual return to the sources with subsequent Biblical, patristic, and liturgical movements and renewals, such as neo-Thomism, that have all affected contemporary understanding of supernatural adoption. Thomists, for instance, turned again to the Angelic Doctor's scriptural commentaries (e.g., *In Rom,* ch. 8, lect. 6), which in conjunction with his ST 3a 3.5 ad 2 presents adopted sonship as an extension of the natural sonship of the *Word, a conclusion supplying a basis for true morality: the children of God must have the family traits that John describes (Jn 1.4–5, 7–9; 8.12; 12.36; 1 Jn 3.3, 5, 9–10, 16; 4.8, 16, 20) and spiritual theology elaborates. J. Arintero, C. Marmion, Sister Elizabeth of the Trinity, B. Häring, C. Spicq, and even

P. Teilhard de Chardin have all in the 20th century underlined the centrality of this mystery, a fact not unrelated to modern study of psychology. Another factor that has increasingly if unconsciously modified thinking on this subject has been the impact on the common teaching of the Church by the schema "On the Principal Mysteries of the Faith" (CollLac 7.1:555–567) prepared for Vatican Council I but never voted on.

Speculative Questions. At the speculative level there are two complex and widely discussed questions regarding supernatural adoption. One of these is the relation of *grace and nature, the very possibility of the natural being adopted into the supernatural. Is there a basis for this in human nature or the divine plan? Some say that *original sin's being a hindrance to supernatural adoption posits its being internal and therefore, metaphysically speaking, in opposition to something intrinsic to man, such as an orientation to the beatific vision. The "extrinsicists," however, say the latter is a free grace not due to nature. St. Thomas drew a strict line between the natural and the supernatural. Currently a group of theologians inclining to the Scotist position sees the Incarnation as the original act of God that presupposes grace already existent. The desire of God is thus innate or quasi-intuitive in man. Grace as founded in Christ explains His mediatorial role and makes personal God's love and man's response. Those who see this openness to God as preceding sanctifying grace and as distinct from human nature, though affecting man intrinsically, include K. Rahner, R. Guardini, H. U. von Balthasar, L. Malevez, H. de Lubac, E. Gutwenger. If we are made for the beatific vision, the means to it, they argue, cannot be wholly extrinsic and accidental; yet as gift it depends on God's free will. (*See* SUPERNATURAL EXISTENTIAL.)

The other question follows from what is regarded as the inadequacy of the metaphysics of causality in the Aristotelian-Thomistic system, which by explaining our supernatural life in terms of efficient causality provides an unsatisfactory basis for the interpersonal relations affirmed in Scripture and the Fathers. A solution in the guise of a quasi-formal cause dates from D. Petau, but most theologians opting for this today have been influenced by M. de la Taille's theory of *created actuation by uncreated act, though in varying ways (F. Bourassa, Rahner, M. Donnelly, P. De Letter). Relative to the possible personal principle of our adoption two views exist. From the late 16th to the 20th century, union with the Spirit as the basis of sonship has been proposed (L. Lessius through Petau, M. J. Scheeben, T. de Régnon, G. Waffelaert). In a more recent view, perhaps stemming from K. Schrader at Vatican Council I, the glorification of Christ's humanity and its consubstantiality with ours is seen by some as the basis of filiation (É. Mersch, H. Lyons, S. Dockx).

See also ELEVATION OF MAN; GRACE, ARTICLES ON; INCORPORATION IN CHRIST; REBIRTH (IN THEOLOGY).

Bibliography: Scripture. P. BONNETAIN, DBSuppl 3:946–953, 971–991, 1006–33, 1050, 1107–24. M. W. SCHOENBERG, "St. Paul's Notion on the Adoptive Sonship of Christians," *Thomist* 28 (1964) 51–75. J. GIBLET, "La Sainte Trinité selon l'évangile de saint Jean," LumetVie 29 (1956) 95–126. F. AMIOT, *The Key Concepts of St. Paul,* tr. J. DINGLE (New York 1962). G. SCHRENK and G. QUELL, Kittel ThW 5:946–1004.

Theological development. E. DES PLACES et al., DictSpirAsc Myst 3:1370–1432. A. MICHEL, DTC, Tables générales 1:37–40. W. J. BURGHARDT, *The Image of God in Man according to Cyril of Alexandria* (Washington 1957) *passim.* R. GLEASON, *Grace* (New York 1962) 75–171. R. GARRIGOU-LAGRANGE, *Grace,* tr. Dominican Nuns, Menlo Park, Calif. (St. Louis 1952) *passim.*

Speculative questions. G. ROTUREAU, *Catholicisme* 1:154–157. W. M. SHEA and M. J. WREN, "The Relationship of the Christian to the Trinity," *Dunwoodie Review* 1 (1961) 38–68, 111–136. H. P. C. LYONS, Davis CDT 1:36–38. K. RAHNER, *Nature and Grace,* tr. D. WHARTON (New York 1964).

[M. M. LOUGHRAN]

ADOPTIONISM

A heresy that proclaimed a double sonship of Christ, and maintained that as divine He was the natural Son of God, but as man He was only the adopted Son. In origin, the heresy goes back to *Paul of Samosata, though it has been ascribed to *Theodore of Mopsuestia, and *Nestorius. Adoptionism was first officially taught by *Elipandus, Archbishop of Toledo, Spain, *c.* 785, in his attempt to correct the errors of Migetius concerning the Incarnation. Elipandus believed that he could best safeguard the distinction between the divine and human natures in Christ by designating the eternally begotten Logos as God's natural son; and the Son of Mary, which the Logos assumed, as God's adopted son. Two monks, Beatus and Etherius, challenged the orthodoxy of this explanation and referred the matter to Pope *Adrian I. In a letter to the Spanish hierarchy the Pontiff condemned the term "adopted son" as applied to Christ because it was contrary to Sacred Scripture and to the teaching of the most reliable Greek and Latin theologians, and because it constituted a revival of Nestorianism.

Elipandus refused to submit and found a staunch supporter in Felix, bishop of Urgel. Since the latter's diocese was in Charlemagne's kingdom, Felix was obliged to appear before a council at Ratisbon in 792, and to swear never to employ the words "adopted son" in speaking of Christ. At this point the Spanish hierarchy intervened and wrote a defense of Elipandus to Charlemagne and the bishops of Gaul. The King, with the approval of the Sovereign Pontiff, summoned a council at Frankfort in 794 to settle the controversy.

The council was one of the largest assemblies in the history of the Church, with two papal legates present and representatives of every country of western Europe except Mozarabic Spain. It opened with the reading of a letter from Pope Adrian in which he unconditionally condemned Adoptionism as heretical. In accordance with the papal teaching a definition was drawn up, which may be summarized as follows: "The Son of God became the Son of man, but He still kept the title of a real son; there is only one Son and He is not an adopted son." It indicated the basic fallacy of Adoptionism, which applied the word son to a nature and not to a person. Finally, texts from Scripture and quotations from the Fathers of the Church were cited to prove the correctness of this definition. This patristic section seems to have been the work of the scholarly monk *Alcuin. The condemnation of Adoptionism at Frankfort was repeated at councils in Friuli, Italy (796), Rome (799), and Aix-la-Chapelle (800). As far as is known, Elipandus and the Spanish bishops adhered to their opinion, but did not break formally with the Holy See.

In the 12th century Abelard, Folmar of Trier, and Gilbert de la Porée maintained that the union between the Logos and His human nature could be only external and accidental; for, if it were substantial, it would constitute a finite quality in the Blessed Trinity. Hence they concluded that Jesus Christ as man was not the natural but only the adopted son of God. On Feb. 18, 1177, Pope Alexander III condemned the teaching that Jesus Christ as man is not a substantial reality, and added, "as He is truly God, so He is also truly man, composed of a rational soul and a human body." Two centuries later Durandus and some Scotists taught that Jesus Christ is, at the same time, the natural and the adopted Son of God, because He has received the fullness of sanctifying grace. But this opinion is also to be rejected, for adoption implies that the one adopted was previously a stranger to the person who adopted him, and Christ, as at once God and man, could never be a stranger to His heavenly Father. Besides, one and the same person cannot be both the natural and the adopted son of the same father.

Bibliography: H. QUILLIET and E. PORTALIÉ, DTC 1.1:403–421. J. POHLE, *Christology,* v.4 of *Dogmatic Theology,* tr. and ed. A. PREUSS, 12 v. (St. Louis 1950–53). É. AMANN, Fliche-Martin 6:129–152. Denz 595, 610–611.

[S. J. MC KENNA]

ADORATION

The reverential attitude of man toward God, by which he acknowledges, with his whole being, soul and body, God's absolute immensity, holiness, and glory and subjects himself to Him with such intensity that this disposition manifests itself in proper words and perceptible physical acts. Adoration, basically, is the directing of one's whole being toward God, so that in all its diversity it is to the praise and glory of God—*gloria Dei externa materialis* (Eph 1.6, 12, 14). The expression and fulfillment of this attitude is the reverential, loving praise of God, in extolling words, in hymns, in thanksgiving (*eucharistia*), as well as in reverential external gestures (*gloria Dei externa formalis*). Thus man, in the awareness of the works of God, transforms this praise of God the Creator (who manifests Himself in His works, but exceeds them immensely) into reverence and love, which is strictly speaking the aim of the creative act of God. God in no way needs this praise, but on the contrary possesses in Himself all glory and is externally happy and sufficient in Himself. For the person whose conduct is directed to the divine rule, the bestowal of such praise is a moral duty. St. Thomas considered this attitude realized in the total frame of the inner and external acts of the virtue of religion. Adoration in the narrower sense of the word was, for him, that attitude "by which someone disposes his body to worship God" (ST 2a2ae, prol. 84), whereby the exterior act is ordered to the interior, in order to incite the spirit to a perfect devotion to God (ST 2a2ae, 84.2). Contemporary theology accepts this definition, but seeks to connect more emphatically adoration with acts by which God is worshipped (St. Augustine, *Enchir.* 3) and to look to adoration to produce a deeper effect upon the entire body and soul of man.

Man is here mainly for the praise and the glory of God. The high point of man's existence is the real act of the cult of adoration. It is above all an interior disposition of devotion (ST 2a2ae, 82) and the act of prayer (ST 2a2ae, 83) proceeding from faith, hope, and charity. This inner act is concretized in the form of adoration, awesome reverential praise, humility, and devotion. Obviously the continuation and completion of oral adoration is the physical gesture, especially devout posture—standing, prostration, genuflection, bowing, kissing, and other manifold reverential acts accompanied by prayerful attention. The physical gesture, to be sure, obtains its significance as adoration primarily through the interior state of mind as it is formed by the individual or the custom of the community. Because of the precedence of the inner disposition, adoration is essentially a personal act. However, since a person is by nature inclined toward association with others, the act of adoration of the individual extends itself, especially in its perceptible utterances, to an act of adoration in company with all the faithful, within the framework established in the New Testament. The faithful can and should be built "on the foundation of the apostles and prophets with Christ Jesus Himself as the cornerstone into a dwelling place for God in the Spirit" (Eph 2.20–22) in the unity of the one sacrificial banquet of the Eucharist, mindful of the Lord and His act of redemption. They should offer to the Father, in and through Christ, true adoration "in spirit and in truth" (Jn 4.23). In virtue of the presence of the one sacrifice of Christ, which is taken over in the divine service of the Church, the whole life of those attending, body and soul, their self-denial and penance, are included in this sacrifice—and become a sacrificial offering to the Father—*per eam (hujus oblationis hostiam) nosmetipsos tibi perfice munus aeternum.*

This cult of adoration may and can be paid only to the one true God, the Most Holy Trinity, each of the three divine Persons together being one God. The same adoration is due the Incarnate Word, since Christ's humanity is taken up in the subsistence of His divine Person. It is due also to parts of His human nature, insofar as in them, the God-Man manifests Himself to us; to the Sacred Heart of Jesus as to the embodiment and symbol of the divine love of Jesus; to His precious blood as the seat of His life; to His holy wounds as the signs of His suffering. The same adoration is offered to the Sacrament of the Eucharist, in which, under the exterior appearances of bread and wine, the whole God-Man is really present. This cult of adoration is called *latria* (adoration in its strict sense), which, if given to a creature, would be sacrilegious idolatry. It is to be sharply distinguished from the cult of *dulia,* which is veneration by which the saints are honored, i.e., those among the perfect Christians who are designated by the Church for veneration, admiration, praise, intercession, and imitation. It is likewise to be distinguished from *hyperdulia,* by which Mary, the Mother of God, is venerated in a special measure. In these forms of veneration and adoration absolute and relative forms of cult are distinguished. A relative form of cult, for example, is given to pictures of Christ and the pictures and relics of the Saints. In such circumstances veneration does not terminate in the picture but is directed beyond it, to the reality represented.

External acts and gestures do not always signify the same things in different times and cultures. At one time an action such as genuflection or prostration might be understood as a sign of the kind of adoration that is due only to God. If such is the case, then that gesture of reverence must be denied to any creature. At other times and in other cultures the same sign could be understood as an expression of reverence such as could reasonably be shown to a picture, to a saint, or even to a civil or ecclesiastical dignitary.

Bibliography: THOMAS AQUINAS, ST 2a 2ae, 84–100; 3a, 25. É. BEURLIER, DTC 1.1:437–442. A. CHOLLET, DTC 3.2:2404–27. O. KARRER, LexThK² 1:500–501. B. NEUNHEUSER, LexThK² 6:665–667. F. HEILER et al., RGG³ 1:356–360. B. HÄRING, *The Law of Christ,* tr. E. G. KAISER (Westminster, Md. 1961–) v.2.

[B. NEUNHEUSER]

ADORATION, NOCTURNAL, the homage paid during the night hours to the Blessed Sacrament exposed on the altar or reserved in the tabernacle. The practice developed especially in connection with the exposition of the Blessed Sacrament during the Forty Hours devotion.

At its inception, the devotion of the Forty Hours consisted in an exposition of the Blessed Sacrament for 40 consecutive hours, thus necessitating and fostering adoration during the night. (*The Clementine Instruction* does not permit exposition of the Blessed Sacrament without adoration.)

There were isolated cases of nocturnal adoration as early as the Middle Ages. In 1226 the Holy See approved adoration of the Eucharist, veiled on the altar at Avignon, by request of Louis VII to give thanks for his victory over the Albigenses.

In the 13th or 14th century the practice of adoring the Blessed Sacrament in the Easter Sepulcher, a direct forerunner of the Forty Hours devotion, entailed the practice of nocturnal adoration.

Nocturnal adoration, being held at Sacred Heart Church, Washington, D.C.

In 1810 Giacomo Sinibaldi, Canon of Santa Maria in Via Lata, organized what was to become the Nocturnal Adoration Society, to pay homage to Our Lord during the night in the various churches in which Forty Hours were being held successively. Herman Cohen, a Jewish-convert Carmelite, founded a similar society in Paris in 1848. Canonically approved as a pious union in 1851 and raised to the title of archconfraternity in 1858, the Nocturnal Adoration Society promotes the practice of nocturnal adoration throughout the year and independently of the Forty Hours devotion. In September 1963 the Nocturnal Adoration Society in the U.S. numbered 638 affiliated units, with a membership of more than 100,000.

Bibliography: F. BÉRINGER, *Les Indulgences: Leur nature et leur usage,* tr. P. MAZAYER, 2 v. (4th ed. Paris 1925). J. CORBLET, *Histoire dogmatique, liturgique et archéologique du sacrement de l'Euchariste,* 2 v. (Paris 1885–86). **Illustration credit:** Trinity Missions.

[E. R. FALARDEAU]

ADORATION, PERPETUAL

The practice of maintaining uninterrupted worship of the Blessed Sacrament, preferably with the Sacrament solemnly exposed on the altar. Its historical connection with *Forty Hours devotion is evident from the *Graves et diuturnae* of Pope Clement VIII (Nov. 25, 1592) asking for public and uninterrupted prayer to "ascend without intermission before the face of the Lord" through "the salutary devotion of the Forty Hours." The first adoration society instituted for men was the Congregation of the Blessed Sacrament, established by St. Pierre Julien *Eymard in Paris (1856). The pioneers appear to have been groups of pious laymen, such as the Beguines of Liège (12th century) and the members of the Confraternities of the Blessed Sacrament (13th century). They were zealous for the honor of the Holy Eucharist, keeping vigil in the churches, decorating the altar, and burning candles before the tabernacle night and day. The practice of exposition of the Sacrament began gradually, strongly influenced by the movement to institute the feast of Corpus Christi. For this at first only the tabernacle door was opened; then the ciborium was exposed on the altar; and finally the monstrance, needed in the processions that originated at this time, came into use. Two German bishops of the 14th century mention ostensoria in their last wills. In 1395 at Munich a sum of money was bequeathed for the construction, behind the main altar, of a tabernacle "where the most Blessed Sacrament will be prepetually exposed in a monstrance with a candle always burning before it." Such upheavals as the French Revolution interrupted the spread of this devotion, but by the end of the 19th century many Eucharistic associations flourished. At Rome, in 1809, Nocturnal Adoration was reorganized in various churches so as to be perpetual.

The Archconfraternity of Nocturnal Adoration was established there in 1824. In Brussels a movement started in 1848 under the inspiration of Anna de Meeûs, which in 5 years became the Archconfraternity of Perpetual Adoration of the Blessed Sacrament and the Work for Needy Churches. From this society in 1872 came the Congregation of Perpetual Adorers. At Marseilles in 1859 Eymard established the People's Eucharistic League so that the laymen might share the Eucharistic spirit and work of the religious congregation he had founded. In 1897 this league acquired the status of Archassociation and in 1962 had more than a million members. Each member makes at least 1 hour of adoration per month; those belonging to the Guard of Honor make a Holy Hour at a specified time. The Priests' League for Adoration of the Blessed Sacrament, founded in 1879, was canonically erected and approved at Rome in 1887. There were 8,000 members enrolled at that time. In 1962 there were almost 300,000 priests enrolled. Each member promises to make a weekly hour of adoration before the Blessed Sacrament. Headquarters for the U.S. are in New York City. In 1950 a society for Perpetual Adoration of the Blessed Sacrament for diocesan priests, which had been founded 8 years earlier in the diocese of Aosta (Italy), was canonically erected, with headquarters at Rome.

Bibliography: G. Vassali et al., DictSpirAscMyst 4.2:1637–48.

[F. COSTA]

ADORATION OF THE BLESSED SACRAMENT, SISTERS OF THE, popularly known as the Adoration Sisters (SABS), a religious congregation of the Syro *Malabar rite, founded at Chambakkulam, Kerala, India, in 1908, by Bp. Thomas Kurialasserry of Changanacheri, assisted by Mary Shantal. Members take simple perpetual vows. The special objects of the institute are to make reparation to the Sacred Heart of Jesus in the Blessed Sacrament, and also to teach and to engage in various works of charity. The sisters wear a white habit, white coif, black veil, and a medal of the Blessed Sacrament. Upon the founder's death in 1925, Father J. Kandathiparampil directed the congregation. In 1930, when the congregation numbered 138 members in 9 houses, it was introduced into the Archdiocese of Ernakulam. The diocesan groups united in 1963 under a single superior general, who resides at Changanacheri. Papal approval of the institute has been sought. The congregation is divided into 4 commissariats, each under a provincial. In 1964 there were 1,618 sisters in 85 convents who staffed 30 educational and 4 charitable institutions of their own. They worked also in 76 educational and 9 charitable institutions under the direction of others.

Bibliography: *The Silver Jubilee of the Sisters of Adoration and the Inauguration of Perpetual Adoration* (Mannanam, India 1936).

[A. M. MUNDADAN]

ADORERS OF THE PRECIOUS BLOOD, SISTERS (RPB), a cloistered, contemplative community with papal approbation, founded in Canada in 1861 for the twofold purpose of adoration of the Precious Blood and the salvation of souls. The foundress, Catherine Aurélie Caouette, and three companions began the congregation at St. Hyacinthe, Quebec Province, with the approval of Bp. Joseph LaRocque (1860–65) and under the direction of Msgr. J. S. Raymond. Mother Catherine Aurelia of the Precious Blood, as she was known in religious life, died July 6, 1905. The constitutions of the community were approved by Leo XIII in 1896, after several foundations had been made in Canada and one in the U.S., in Brooklyn, N.Y. (1890).

The sisters chant the Office in choir, have perpetual adoration of the Blessed Sacrament, and rise at midnight for an hour of reparation. The Blessed Sacrament is exposed all day on the first Sunday of each month and during the Forty Hours' Devotion, which, by special privilege, is held three times a year. The sisters also engage in making altar breads, vestments, and altar linens and in doing art work. Their apostolate of prayer and sacrifice has been extended to 28 foundations in Canada, 5 in the U.S., and 1 each in Cuba, Italy, and Japan. A convent that had been established in China in 1924 was suppressed by the Communists in 1948. Originally each convent was independent, but in 1945 the French-speaking Canadian convents formed a federation under the motherhouse in St. Hyacinthe. A similar federation of the English-speaking convents in Canada was formed in 1949 with its motherhouse in London, Ontario. By 1964 there was a total of 841 sisters in the congregation, 159 of them were in the U.S.

Bibliography: *The Life of Mother Catherine Aurelia of the Precious Blood* (St. Louis 1929).

[M. M. RYAN]

ADORO TE DEVOTE, a rhymed prayer marked by deep personal faith and theological insight, and addressed to Christ in the Blessed Sacrament. Although never a part of the Breviary, it appeared in various collections of popular devotions until Pope *Pius V inserted it in the Roman Missal among the prayers of thanksgiving after Mass. All extant MSS attribute the poem to St. *Thomas Aquinas; however, his authorship has been contested. No MS is known from the first 50 years after Aquinas's death, nor does anyone during that time refer to Thomas as its author. Two of the 14th-century codices state that Thomas composed or recited the prayer on receiving Viaticum. On this point the silence of the saint's biographer, William de Tocca, is significant. Dom André *Wilmart, who made the most thorough study of the manuscript and literary tradition of the *Adoro Te,* concluded that documentary evidence is insufficient to affirm Aquinas's authorship. Furthermore, some theologians doubt Thomistic origin because of divergences of thought and expression between the *Summa* and this poem. However, M. *Grabmann has maintained the genuineness of authorship because all MSS indicate it, and in his judgment the poem breathes the Eucharistic theology of Aquinas. F. Raby pointed out that a certain poem of *Jacopone da Todi (written *c.* 1280–94) would be unexplainable had the *Adoro Te* not existed. Although this fact does not prove Thomistic origin, it makes possible the assigning of a date that falls within the lifetime of Thomas (d. 1274). In Raby's opinion the earliest MSS may be correct in stating that Aquinas wrote the *Adoro Te,* even if they report incorrectly the circumstances of its composition. There are many English translations. One of the most effective is that of Gerard Manley *Hopkins beginning "Godhead here in hiding, Whom I do adore."

Bibliography: AnalHymn 50 (1907) 589–591. Julian DictHym 1:22–23; 2:1549, 1600. A. Wilmart, "La Tradition littéraire et textuelle de l'*Adoro te devote,*" RechThAMéd 1 (1929) 21–40, 149–176; repr. with appendices in *Auteurs spirituels et textes dévots du Moyen Âge latin* (Paris 1932) 361–414. F. J. E. Raby, "The Date and Authorship of the Poem *Adoro Te Devote,*" *Speculum* 20 (1945) 236–238. M. Grabmann, *Die Werke des heiligen Thomas von Aquin* (3d ed. Münster 1949) 367–370, with refs. cited in nn. 184–186. J. P. Cavarnos, "Greek Translations of the *Adoro Te Devote* and the *Ave Verum,*" *Traditio* 8 (1952) 418–423.

[M. I. J. ROUSSEAU]

ADRAGNA, ANTONIO MARIA, theologian; b. Trapani, Sicily, Oct. 1, 1818; d. Rome, Oct. 14, 1890. He entered the Conventual Franciscans in 1834 and was ordained in 1841. He taught in Würzburg and Assisi, was named consultor of the Holy Office in 1861, and member of the dogmatic commission for Vatican Council I in 1866. Adragna was given the task of preparing a schema on the temporalities of the Church for the council. From 1872 to 1879 he was minister general of his order. As a result of the religious suppressions in Rome he was forced to live in Holland (1876–78). None of his works have been published, and many have been lost. He was generally considered a conservative in his theology.

Bibliography: L. DI FONZO, EncCatt 1:331. DizBiogItal 1:306. D. SPARACIO, *Frammenti bio-bibliografici di scrittori ed autori minori Conventuali dagli ultimi anni del '600 al 1930* (Assisi 1931).

[P. FEHLNER]

ADRIAN, ST., 9th-century bishop and martyr; b., according to legend, in Hungary, of royal stock. Adrian (Hadrian, Odhran) is supposed to have been consecrated bishop there. No reliable information on him is extant. Apparently he went to the British Isles and as a missionary bishop had no settled see, but preached especially to the Picts of Fifeshire. Legend has it that he was archbishop of *St. Andrews in Scotland. However, it may well be that this is the Irish St. Odhran who reputedly arrived in Scotland with 6,606 companions of various nationalities, possibly driven out of Ireland by the invading Danes. Adrian established a monastery on the Isle of May (Firth of Forth). In 875 the Danes and the Scots fought at the Firth of Forth, and most of the Scots were killed. The Aberdeen Breviary (1509) commemorated the martyrs who had died in the monastery on the Isle of May on Holy Thursday.

Bibliography: ActSS March 1:324–326. L. MACFARLANE, Lex ThK² 4:1310–11. W. F. SKENE, *Celtic Scotland,* 3 v. (2d ed. Edinburgh 1886–90) 2:311–316.

[R. T. MEYER]

ADRIAN I, POPE

Pontificate, Feb. 1, 772, to Dec. 25, 795; b. Rome. Of a socially prominent family, Adrian became pope by unanimous acclaim when he was still only a deacon. On the day of his election he proclaimed an amnesty for all who had been either imprisoned or exiled by Paul Afiarta, secret agent at Rome of the Lombard King *Desiderius. Through Afiarta, the new Pope signified to Desiderius his willingness to continue relations of friendliness, provided the King would restore papal properties as he had promised. Desiderius kept up an exchange of envoys on the matter, even after the trial of Afiarta for the murder of Roman officials disclosed that the *Lombards had meddled in the internal affairs of Rome. Meanwhile the King went ahead secretly with further usurpations of papal territory. Adrian made an equally secret appeal for help to *Charlemagne; but when Desiderius suddenly moved on Rome with an army, the Pope met the emergency himself with the levying of troops, repair of the city wall, and a threat of excommunication. The Lombard King turned back, and Charlemagne's proposal of a compromise settlement failed to satisfy him. He fortified himself in Pavia where he endured siege by Charles's troops from October 773 to June 774. Desiderius capitulated finally,

Pope Adrian I, stylized portrait on a silver denarius of his pontificate, in the Vatican Library.

and thereafter Charles styled himself "King of the Franks and Lombards."

With Pavia still under blockade, Charles had gone to Rome for the celebration of Easter. The following Wednesday (April 6), he met with Adrian and gave him hearty assurance that the promises (754) of his father, *Pepin, in regard to the papal patrimony would be respected. Charles's subsequent temporizing in the matter, however, gave the Pope much cause for grievance. A second Easter visit (781) added to the papal territory Sabina and Narni to the east and Terracina to the south; and finally, a third encounter (787) granted considerable territory to the north. From that date, the *States of the Church had much the same borders that they would retain until their disintegration in 1860.

Adrian undertook extensive construction and repair of buildings in Rome, beautifying the city and providing employment through public works. Outside the city he founded a great agricultural colony, from the excess yield of which he was able to feed 100 poor persons each day. Collaborating with Charlemagne in the reform of the Church, he sent him (774) the *Dionysio-Hadriana* (**Dionysiana*) collection as an official expression of Roman disciplinary practice. He effectively countered the *Adoptionist heresy in Spain. But, more important (for art as well as for doctrine), he urged the Empress *Irene's convocation of the Second Council of *Nicaea (787), which condemned *iconoclasm. A faulty translation of Nicaea's acts into Latin drew from the regional Council of Frankfurt a counter condemnation (*see* LIBRI CAROLINI); but Adrian was able to set matters right by explaining the true meaning of Nicaea II, whose acts he sanctioned.

Bibliography: Duchesne LP 1:486–523; 3:105–107. PL 96: 1167–1204; 128:1163–98. MGEp 3:567–657; 5.1:1–57. F. LOT et al., *Les Destinées de l'empire en Occident de 395 à 888,* 2 v. (Histoire générale. Histoire du Moyen-Âge 1; new ed. Paris 1940). Fliche-Martin 6:49–70, 107–153. M. JUGIE, EncCatt 1: 338–341; DHGE 1:614–619. O. BERTOLINI, DizBiogItal 1:312–323. W. OHNSORGE, "Der Patricius-Titel Karls des Grossen,"

ByzZ 53 (1960) 300–321. P. VIARD, *Catholicisme* 5:471–473. **Illustration credit:** Leonard Von Matt.

[J. E. BRESNAHAN]

ADRIAN II, POPE

Pontificate, Dec. 14, 867, to November or December 872; b. Rome, 792. He was of a distinguished Roman family, from which two previous popes had come—*Stephen IV (816–817) and *Sergius II (844–847). In 842 Adrian was named cardinal priest of San Marco. He was elected pope as a compromise candidate in the struggle between those who favored and those who opposed the strong policies of his immediate predecessor, *Nicholas I (858–867). After approval by the German Emperor *Louis II, Adrian was consecrated on Dec. 14, 867. Though he attempted to maintain the policies of Nicholas, the papal power declined during his reign, for conciliatory by nature and already advanced in age, he was confronted with serious conflicts. Great influence was exercised in papal affairs by the pontifical secretary and archivist, *Anastasius the Librarian, member of a powerful family with which Adrian had personal differences. The reason for this difficulty was his daughter, born to him in a marriage contracted before he was ordained a priest. Believing Anastasius to be in part responsible for the subsequent murder of both the daughter and her mother in 868, Adrian dismissed him under the severest ecclesiastical penalties. Not long afterward, however, the secretary was reinstated, and he continued to dominate.

Pope Adrian II in the procession of the translation of the relics of St. Clement, detail of an 11th-century fresco in the lower basilica of S. Clemente.

Among Adrian's conflicts with the German princes was that over the attempted divorce of *Lothair II, King of Lorraine, who sought to put away his wife Theutberga in order to marry his concubine Waldrada. Adrian's efforts at reconciliation were unsuccessful, and the problem was resolved only upon the death of Lothair in 869. In the subsequent contention over the kingdom of Lorraine, Adrian supported the claims of Louis II against those of *Charles II the Bald, who was supported by the redoubtable Bishop *Hincmar of Reims. Louis II was excluded when the German princes, Charles the Bald and *Louis the German, came to an agreement among themselves at the Treaty of Mersen in 870. Later efforts by Adrian to intervene in the civil and ecclesiastical disputes in the Carolingian domains met with strong rebuffs from Hincmar. Anastasius, then in control of the papal chancellery, was found to be the true author of these attempts at intervention although papal prestige was somewhat restored when Adrian reaffirmed Louis II's imperial title in 872, following a revolt in Benevento.

In his relations with the *Byzantine Empire, Adrian was only partially successful. A synod held at Rome in June of 869 severely condemned *Photius and his partisans. Three papal legates were dispatched to the Council of Constantinople (*see* CONSTANTINOPLE IV) in 869 and 870, where the position taken by Adrian and his predecessor, in regard to Photius, was upheld. Rome's claims to jurisdiction in the Balkan area were defeated, however, when *Ignatius, Patriarch of Constantinople, accepted the invitation of *Boris I of Bulgaria to evangelize his people. This defeat was to a degree offset by Adrian's sponsoring of the mission of *Cyril (Constantine) and Methodius among the Slovak people of Central Europe and his allowing the use of old Slavonic in the liturgy.

Bibliography: PL 122:1245–1320. Jaffé E 368–375. O. BERTOLINI, DizBiogItal 1:323–329. A. NOYON, DHGE 1:619–624. Fliche-Martin 6:395–412. I. DANIELE, EncCatt 1:341–344. F. DVORNIK, *The Photian Schism* (Cambridge 1948); *The Patriarch Photius in the Light of Recent Research* (Munich 1958). G. SCHWAIGER, LexThK[2] 4:1306–07. Seppelt 2:289–306, 433–434. *Archivium historiae pontificiae* 1 (1963) 524. **Illustration credit:** Alinari-Art Reference Bureau.

[A. J. ENNIS]

ADRIAN III, POPE, ST., May 17, 884, to *c.* September 885; b. Rome; d. near Modena, Italy (feast, commonly given as July 8). Little is known of him; he was the son of Benedict, member of a Roman family. His brief reign was disturbed by the continuing conflict of contending factions in Rome. It appears that he represented the policies of Pope *John VIII (who was assassinated in 882) rather than those of Pope *Marinus I, Adrian's immediate predecessor. In the spirit of the age, Adrian dealt severely with the opposition: by his order a certain George, an official of the Lateran palace, was blinded and a woman named Mary, a member of the aristocracy, was subjected to disgraceful punishment. Adrian's policy regarding the problems with the Byzantine Emperor, and especially with *Photius, was probably a conciliatory one, but he did not live long enough to accomplish anything of note. Emperor *Charles III the Fat, who at that time was in control of nearly all of the former empire of Charlemagne, invited Adrian to come to an imperial diet, chiefly for the purpose of settling the question of the imperial succession, since Charles had no legitimate male heir. Leaving an imperial *missus* in charge of the government of Rome, Adrian set out for Germany. En route, he fell ill and died. He was buried in the nearby Abbey of Nonantola. His cultus, which developed in the locality, was approved by the Holy See in 1891.

Bibliography: Jaffé L 1:426–427; 2:705. Duchesne LP 2:225; 3:127. Mann v.3. O. BERTOLINI, DizBiogItal 1:329–330. G. SCHWAIGER, LexThK² 4:1307. P. VIARD, *Catholicisme* 5:474.

[A. J. ENNIS]

ADRIAN IV, POPE

Pontificate, Dec. 4, 1154, to Sept. 1, 1159, the only Englishman who occupied the papal throne; b. Nicholas Breakspear between 1110 and 1120. His beginnings are obscure, but it seems fairly certain that he came from a low social class. At an early age he left England to join the *Canons Regular of St. Rufus near Valence. There his ability and intelligence were recognized, and he rapidly attained positions of authority. As abbot, he came into conflict with his community, and the fact was brought before Pope *Eugene III, who clearly recognized Nicholas's stature. Resolute and farsighted as Nicholas was, Eugene removed him from his community, but created him cardinal bishop of Ostia (1149). Afterward Nicholas was sent to Scandinavia to regularize the relations of the Northern Church with the papacy. The mission was effectual, lasting several years and culminating in the erection of important sees and the ordering of diocesan matters.

Upon the death of *Anastasius IV, Nicholas was unanimously elected pope. Although his pontificate lasted less than 5 years, it was important in the history of the papacy. The times were particularly insecure, owing to repeated attempts by the Byzantines to reconquer Italy; the menacing designs of the Staufen Emperor Frederick I; the restless if not rebellious climate in Rome itself resulting from the demagogic oratory of *Arnold of Brescia; the emergence of the new dialectical methods of inquiry and the concomitant spiritual disquietude resulting from the conflicts between *Abelard and St. *Bernard of Clairvaux; the equally unsettling effects of the Crusades; and the repeated attacks of the Sicilian King upon the Papal State. These were only some of the challenges that confronted the new Pope. Adrian was quite equal to the task, resting as he did upon the traditional principles of the papacy, especially on those enunciated by *Gregory VII. The first measure of his pontificate showed the courage and resolution of the man: he laid the city of Rome under an interdict for the first time in its history, and insisted upon fulfillment of his conditions before the measure was withdrawn (Easter 1155).

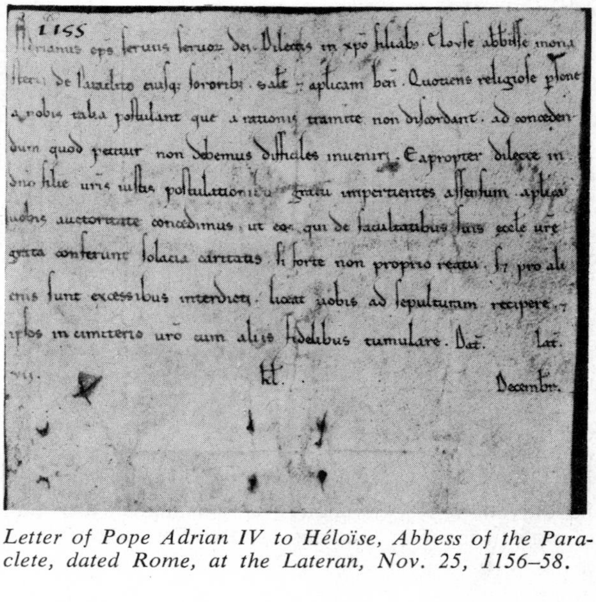

Letter of Pope Adrian IV to Héloïse, Abbess of the Paraclete, dated Rome, at the Lateran, Nov. 25, 1156–58.

His relations with Frederick Barbarossa, though at first correct, soon deteriorated. As he had little confidence in Frederick's protestations of obedience to the Roman Church, Adrian considered it prudent to come to terms with the Sicilian King, William I, now acknowledged as papal vassal. Pope and Emperor were guided by entirely different aims and principles. Barely 2 years after Frederick's coronation the noted incident at Besançon occurred (1157), in which in a letter to the Emperor the Pope allegedly referred to the Empire as a "fief" of the papacy. This allegation, if not malicious, at least revealed the ignorance of those who made it, especially the Imperial Chancellor *Rainald of Dassel. The term *beneficium,* used by the Pope in his communication and translated as "fief," never had feudal meaning as it was employed in papal language. The allegation was simply a diplomatic subterfuge of the Staufen government used against the papacy. The activity of Frederick I in Northern Italy in the following year and the Diet of Roncaglia (1158) were again clear indications of the eventual Staufen designs, and matters reached a serious impasse when Adrian forbade Frederick to meddle in a dispute between Bergamo and Brescia about territorial possessions of these churches. Everything seemed set for an open conflict between Empire and Papacy when the Pope died suddenly at Anagni. He left behind a College of Cardinals far from united, which led to the troubles at the beginning of *Alexander III's pontificate.

In English affairs Adrian is remembered chiefly for his benevolent attitude toward King *Henry II. Although much disputed, his bull **Laudabiliter,* in which *Ireland was granted to the English king, seems, on balance, a genuine document. In Adrian's pontificate the term *Vicar of Christ for the pope became current. Sound, dedicated to essentials, clear-sighted, firmly grounded in papal principles of government, Adrian IV steered the papacy safely through a very difficult period: his pontificate begins the steep ascent of the papacy to the heights of *Innocent III.

Bibliography: CARDINAL BOSO, Duchesne LP 2:388–397. H. K. MANN, *Nicholas Breakspear* (London 1914). M. E. VON ALMEDINGEN, *The English Pope* (London 1925). P. FEDELE, ed., *Fonti per la storia di Arnaldo da Brescia* (Rome 1938). W. ULLMANN, "Cardinal Roland and Besançon," *Miscellanea Historiae Pontificiae* 18 (1954) 107–125; "The Pontificate of Adrian IV," CambHistJ 11 (1953–55) 233–252. M. MACCARRONE, *Papato e Impero, dalla elezione di Federico I alla morte di Adriano IV, 1152–1159* (Rome 1959). **Illustration credit:** H. P. Krauss, New York.

[W. ULLMANN]

ADRIAN V, POPE, pontificate, July 11, 1276, to Aug. 18, 1276; b. Ottobono Fieschi, in Genoa, Italy, early 13th century; d. Viterbo, Italy. He came from an influential Italian family and was created cardinal deacon of S. Hadrian by his uncle, Pope *Innocent

Monument of Pope Adrian V, by the 13th-century sculptor Arnolfo di Cambio, in the basilica of S. Francesco, Viterbo, Italy.

IV, in September 1244. In May 1265 he was sent to England as the envoy of Pope *Clement IV to defend the rights of the Holy See there and to resolve the conflict between King *Henry III and his barons. He successfully completed this task and returned in June 1268 to the Roman *Curia, where he worked in support of the Angevin policy in Italy. Elected to the papacy on the death of *Innocent V, he died before he could receive either ordination to the priesthood or episcopal consecration. His attempt to repeal the second canon of the Second Council of *Lyons concerning papal elections was ignored by his successors. Adrian was buried in the basilica of S. Francesco at Viterbo, where his epitaph may still be seen.

Bibliography: R. GRAHAM, "Letters of Cardinal Ottoboni," EngHistRev 15 (1900) 87–120. Duchesne LP 2:457. N. SCHÖPP, *Papst Hadrian V* (Heidelberg 1916). A. VACANT, DTC 1.1:458–459. É. GRIFFE, *Catholicisme* 5:476–477. Potthast Reg 2:1709–10. G. SCHWAIGER, LexThK² 4:1308–09. Seppelt 3:536–540. **Illustration credit:** Alinari-Art Reference Bureau.

[B. J. COMASKEY]

ADRIAN VI, POPE

Pontificate, Jan. 9, 1522, to Sept. 14, 1523; b. Adrian Florensz Dedal, Utrecht, March 2, 1459. He is the last non-Italian and first reforming pope of the 16th century. His widowed mother secured a good education for him with the Brothers of the Common Life at Zwelle and Deventer, and this enabled him to enter the University of Louvain when he was 17. There he studied and taught theology; in 1497 he became dean of St. Peter's Church, Louvain, and chancellor of the university, of which he was twice rector magnificus. One of his students published his notes on the *Sententiarum Petri Lombardi* (1512), and some of his disputations (*Quaestiones quodlibeticae,* 1515.)

In 1515 Margaret of Burgundy chose him as a member of her household, and Emperor Maximilian appointed him tutor to his grandson, the future Emperor Charles V, who remained grateful throughout his life for Adrian's religious instruction. In the same year Adrian was sent on a difficult diplomatic mission to Spain, where he became the friend of Cardinal *Ximénez of Cisneros. At the death of *Ferdinand V of Castile in 1516, he was appointed sole administrator of the kingdom until the arrival of Charles I. He was named bishop of Tortosa (1516), viceroy of Spain (1517), and inquisitor of Aragon and Navarre (1517) and Castile and Leon (1518). Through the urgent request of Emperor Charles he was created cardinal of Utrecht on June 1, 1517.

In Rome, at the death of Leo X and after turbulent deliberations, he was unanimously elected pope, though absent from the conclave. He was shocked by the news, conveyed to him in Spain, but accepted the will of God and took his own name as Pope Adrian VI. As he had labored in Spain in complete ignorance of the language and customs of the country, so in Italy he was a stranger to his environment. He had little sympathy with Renaissance art and culture, though he valued the learning of the humanists, Johann *Eck and Juan Luis *Vives, and tried to secure the support and advice of Erasmus. The difficulties he encountered in Rome were overwhelming. The principal Catholic princes, Francis I of France and Emperor Charles V, whose help he needed, were at war with one another. In the Turkish advance, Belgrade had fallen, and the Island of Rhodes was threatened. He was the first pope to

Adrian VI, 16th-century portrait by an unknown artist, in the collections of the Galleria Uffizi, Florence.

face the full impact of the Lutheran revolt, which was making rapid advances, and to deal with the pressing necessity of reform of the Church.

With confusion in the Papal States, lack of financial resources, and reluctant allies, he failed to save Christianity from disunity and from the Turks. The Island of Rhodes fell in December 1522, and the way to Hungary was open. His honest demand for reform alienated the cardinals as well as the members of the Diet of Nuremberg (1522–23), where his "Instructio" to the German nation was ill-received and unheeded. Practically alone and exhausted by the opposition on all sides, he died, only 20 months after his accession to the papacy.

Bibliography: Pastor v.9. L. P. GACHARD, ed., *Correspondance de Charles-Quint et d'Adrien VI* (Brussels 1859). C. BURMAN, *Hadrianus VI* (Utrecht 1727). E. H. J. REUSENS, *Syntagma Doctrinae Theologicae Adriani sexti* (Louvain 1862). L. E. HALKIN, *La Réforme en Belgique sous Charles-Quint* (Brussels 1957). A. MERCATI, ed., *Dall'Archivio vaticano: . . . Diarii di concistori del pontificato di Adriano VI* (Rome 1951). EphemThLov 35 (1959) 520–629 (commemorative issue on the 500th anniversary of his birth). C. A. C. VON HÖFLER, *Papst Adrian VI* (Vienna 1880). P. MAARSCHALKERWEERD, EncCatt 1:348–349. P. RICHARD, DHGE 1:628–630. **Illustration credit:** Alinari-Art Reference Bureau.

[K. M. SAUM]

ADRIAN OF CASTELLO (DE CORNETO), cardinal and humanist; b. Corneto, 1458 or 1459; d. 1521. In 1488 Innocent VIII sent him to Scotland as papal nuncio to reconcile James III and his dissident nobles. James was killed before Adrian's arrival, but Adrian reached England, where he gained favor with King Henry VII and became his agent in Rome. He returned to England in 1489 for the collection of Peter's pence. He was made bishop of Hereford in England, Feb. 14, 1502, and was raised to the cardinalate, May 31, 1503, by Alexander VI. He also acted as secretary of the Papal Treasury and ambassador of Henry VII. After the death of Alexander VI, his involvement in politics incurred the displeasure of Julius II. In 1509 he left for Venice and later for Trent, where he remained until the death of the Pope. In 1511 he returned to Rome for the election of Leo X; became implicated with Cardinal Alfonso Petrucci in a plot to poison Leo X; confessed to being privy to it, and although forgiven by Leo, found it safer to reside in Venice. At the insistence of Henry VIII, he had been deprived of his office as collector of Peter's pence, and on July 5, 1518, he was degraded from the cardinalate and the bishopric of Bath, England, which honors were given to Wolsey. A probable rumor mentions that he was murdered in 1521 on his way to Rome after the death of Leo X. Among his writings are *De vera philosophia ex quatuor doctoribus ecclesiae* (Bologna 1507) and *De sermone latino et modo latine loquendi* (Basel 1513).

Bibliography: B. GEBHARDT, *Adrian von Corneto* (Breslau 1886). J. WODKA, LexThK[2] 1:158. R. ORAZI AUSENDA, EncCatt 3:1019–20.

[M. I. C. DUFFEY]

ADRIANUS, exegete of the Antiochene School; fl. 1st half of the 5th century A.D. He was a Greek-speaking Syrian and author of a little work remarkable both in method and content, Εἰσαγωγὴ εἰς τὰς θείας γραφάς, (Introduction to Holy Scripture), the first extant work to bear this title. No details whatever are available about his life. He was monk and priest, if he is to be identified with the Adrianus (or Hadrianus) to whom St. Nilus (d. *c.* A.D. 430) addressed three letters. He was certainly mentioned by Cassiodorus in his list of exegetes as coming after St. Augustine, but before Eucherius and Junilius (*Inst.* 1.10.1). Photius (A.D. *c.* 820–891) also speaks of Adrianus in his *Bibliotheca* and characterizes his work as a "book useful to beginners" (PG 103:45 C). The Εἰσαγωγή deals with figures of thought (chiefly anthropomorphisms), word figures, and figures of composition (τῆς συνθέσεως) and their subdivisions. By way of illustration he quotes the Septuagint about 360 times, and the New Testament about 60 times. He was influenced clearly in his work by Theodore of Mopsuestia and Theodoret of Cyr, and possibly by St. John Chrysostom.

Bibliography: PG 98:1273–1312. ADRIANUS, Εἰσαγωγὴ εἰς τὰς θείας γραφάς, ed. F. GOESSLING (Berlin 1887), this is the modern critical edition that should be used. Bardenhewer 4:254–255. G. MERCATI, "Pro Adriano," RevBibl NS 11 (1914) 246–255.

[M. R. P. MC GUIRE]

ADSO OF MONTIER-EN-DER, Benedictine author and teacher (called also Azo, Asso, Hermericus); b. Jura, France, first half of the 10th century; d. at sea, 992. He was a monk at Luxeuil, then schoolmaster at Saint-Evre (Aper) at Toul, and later abbot at Montier-en-Der (Haute-Marne) *c.* 960, before finally becoming abbot of Saint-Bénigne at Dijon. While on pilgrimage to the Holy Land, he died at sea and was buried in the Cyclades. The friend of such important figures as *Abbo of Fleury, Gerbert (later Pope *Sylvester II), and *Adalbero of Reims, Adso is remembered especially for his writings. The most important is *De Antichristo* (PL 101:1291–98), among the writings attributed to *Alcuin; it is addressed to Gerberga, wife of Louis IV of France. He wrote many lives of saints, viz, St. Frodobert (ActSS Jan. 1:505–513), St. Mansuetus (ActSS Sept. 1:637–651), St. Basolus (PL 137:647–668), St. Bercharius (ActSS Oct. 7.2:1010–31), and St. Waldebert (ActSS, May 1:282–287).

Bibliography: PL 137:599–700. MGS 4:487–490, 509–520. Potthast Bibl 1:16. E. MARTIN, DHGE 1:636. G. HOCQUARD, *Catholicisme* 1:164–165. S. HILPISCH, LexThK[2] 1:159.

[C. DAVIS]

ADUARTE, DIEGO FRANCISCO, Dominican chronicler and bishop in the Philippines; b. Zaragoza, Spain, 1569; d. Nueva Segovia, 1636. He took the Dominican habit in 1586 and made his profession in the order the next year in Alcalá de Henares. He was already a priest when he went to the Philippines in 1594. In Manila he taught Christianity to the Chinese residents. From there his missionary zeal took him to Cambodia, Canton, Malacca, and Cochin China, where he underwent many hardships and met only failures for his efforts. He was convinced of the need for more missionaries in the Far East and made trips to Spain in 1603 and in 1607 to get them. On the second trip he went to France and got two missionary expeditions sent out. He himself prepared a third group and accompanied it as far as Mexico; he then returned to Spain for a fourth expedition, which he led to Manila. He was named bishop of Nueva Segovia in 1632 and governed wisely and charitably. He died a holy death. His body was found incorrupt, even though it had been buried in such damp soil that the casket was full of water. His chief work was *Historia de la Provincia del Santo Rosario de la Orden de Predicadores en Filipinas, Japón y China,* 2 v. (Manila 1640; Zaragoza, Spain 1693). It was reprinted with many additions in 1742, 1783, and 1870–72. In 1962 an edition containing a biography and bibliography of the author was published in Madrid.

[E. GÓMEZ TAGLE]

ADULT EDUCATION

Despite various definitions, authorities agree that adult education is a life-learning process that deals with the needs and aspirations of adult people as individuals and as members of the community. It implies continuous experiences organized for the purpose of adult learning. Generally speaking, it has no established norms such as entrance requirements, credits, or mandatory participation. It had only a marginal status in our educational system until the early years of the present century, when it became a separate movement and grew in numbers and stature. The Adult Education Association of the United States, established in 1951, through its two major journals, *Adult Leadership* and *Adult Education,* began to disseminate information and suggest effective ways of improving adult education at national, regional, and local levels. By 1955, Malcolm Knowles, first executive director of the Association, reported that there were more than 49 million people in the United States engaged in some form of adult education.

Other countries made significant advances at an earlier date. In 1949 the United Nations Educational, Scientific, and Cultural Organization (UNESCO) created an adult education section and called an international conference at Elsinore, Denmark. In 1952, UNESCO published the *International Dictionary of Adult Education,* which describes programs in 50 countries. In August 1960 a second world conference was held in Canada at which representatives from 49 countries and 46 international nongovernmental organizations were present.

Aims. The aims of adult education, as stated by its proponents, are, in general, to enable adults to assume the responsibilities that the circumstances of mature life have brought them and to cope with the exigencies of the age in which they live. Under Catholic auspices the goals are much the same, but with apostolic intent. Catholic adult education aims to increase knowledge of the teachings of the Church and their application to present-day problems. In 1954, in an address entitled "Teaching Authority of the Church," Pius XII said that these problems may relate to every phase of life, that the jurisdiction of the Church is not limited to matters strictly religious, that it also includes both social and political questions, and national and international issues, since these touch on ethics and morals. [*Catholic Mind,* 53 (1955) 316.]

The primary concern of adult education is to satisfy man's needs, the greatest of which are moral and spiritual. Since Catholic resources are limited, however, educators feel that concentration should be placed on courses that will enable Catholics to enlarge their intellectual horizon and acquire a rich Christian culture, leaving other fields (vocational, technical, and recreational) to secular auspices. To achieve this end, theology and philosophy are usually included in all Catholic adult education programs. Through them the fundamentals of the Catholic faith are brought to adults in their contemporary setting, and the laity are given an opportunity to direct their intellectual efforts to the study of the problems of human life and man's final destiny.

Through the social sciences, adult education programs train people to understand more clearly the nature and claims of society, economic and political issues, and the social doctrine of the Church. To this end courses are offered in the encyclicals, current social and political problems, the family, man and society, and foreign relations. Institutes of industrial relations and labor schools under Catholic sponsorship aim to clarify the position of the Church with regard to labor and management. Cultural courses designed to encourage a study of the best in literature, drama, art, and music form a significant part of an adult education program. World literature, literary types, great books, music appreciation, art appreciation, glee-club singing, and contemporary drama are frequently offered as courses.

Vocational studies, especially those relating to business, are sometimes a part of Catholic adult education programs, when they are needed or requested either for self-improvement, or to obtain advancement in the student's field of work. Accounting, salesmanship, typewriting, shorthand, business law, marketing, etc., are popular and practical. Other vocational subjects (engineering, drafting, shop work, home economics) are adapted to local needs in certain communities. Recreational courses and hobbies are at times added to the programs.

Through study and research in gerontology, the problems of the aging have become a matter of major concern with many adult educators. Frequently, when men and women retire, they lose interest in life, become lonely, and feel unneeded and unwanted. Many educational projects, rather uneven and irregular in pattern, have been introduced to assist these older people to adjust, and to make their lives more interesting and useful. In the Catholic field some excellent work has begun in several localities. Golden-age clubs, elders clubs, and senior citizen clubs have been organized and diversified programs have been worked out. These projects have brought older people security and peace and have made them realize the possibilities of filling their declining years with mental, moral, and spiritual riches.

Catholic adult education programs are sponsored by various agencies: colleges and universities, dioceses, high schools, parishes, special centers, and libraries. The programs vary in size from a few offerings in theology and philosophy to a broad schedule covering many fields and a wide selection of courses.

Administration. This depends on the type, sponsorship, and scope of the program. In a college or a university, a director is usually appointed who has assistance according to his need. In a diocese, high school, or special center, the person in charge is frequently a director who is responsible to the bishop or superintendent of schools. In a parish, either the pastor administers the program himself or assigns it to an assistant or to a capable layman. The director organizes the faculty, which is generally composed of volunteer members of the college staff supplemented by religious and laymen, professional men, and businessmen of the area. They must not only be competent in their fields and dedicated to their profession, but must also have a sympathetic understanding of adults and an acquaintance with methods adapted to mature minds. The success of adult education rests largely with the teacher, since the students vary greatly in age and background, earn no credits, have no attendance requirements, and may tend to drop out unless the teaching is good.

There are many other activities conducted by the Catholic Church that are not called adult education, but that make an important contribution to the education of adults. Among these are the Cana Conferences, the Rural Life Movement, study clubs in the Confraternity of Christian Doctrine, the Christian Family Movement, the Grail program, Te Deum forums, and the extensive work of the National Councils of Catholic Men and Women. Hundreds of Catholics participate in these apostolic works, which are definitely educational in their scope. Some would include under adult education night classes for credit. These evening programs are usually a modified schedule of the regular day programs with textbooks, examinations, and credits. They are undoubtedly an effective way of educating adults, but do not come under the present use of the term adult education, which denotes short, noncredit courses not leading to a baccalaureate degree.

Catholic Commission. In 1954, the National Catholic Educational Association established a Commission on Adult Education to study its present position and future possibilities in the Catholic environment. Msgr. Joseph Cox was chairman of the commission until his death in 1959. That same year, a workshop on adult education was held at The Catholic University of America and the workshop papers were published under the title *Principles and Problems of Catholic Adult Education.* Immediately after the workshop, the commission was reorganized under the name National Catholic Adult Education Commission; a constitution and bylaws were drawn up, officers were elected, and the first number of a bulletin was published. The general purpose of the commission is to encourage and coordinate adult education activities among Catholics, to disseminate information, to act as a clearinghouse for the exchange of ideas, and to promote interest in the field. A *Handbook of Catholic Adult Education* was published in 1959.

Bibliography: C. H. GRATTAN, *In Quest of Knowledge: A Historical Perspective on Adult Education* (New York 1955). J. KEELER, ed., *Handbook of Catholic Adult Education* (Milwaukee 1959). M. S. KNOWLES, ed., *Handbook of Adult Education in the United States* (Chicago 1960). M. MACLELLAN, *The Catholic Church and Adult Education* (Washington 1935). CATHOLIC UNIVERSITY OF AMERICA, *Principles and Problems of Catholic Adult Education,* Proceedings of the Workshop on Principles and Problems of Catholic Adult Education—1958, ed. S. MIKLAS (Washington 1959). UNITED NATIONS EDUCATIONAL, SCIENTIFIC AND CULTURAL ORGANIZATION, *International Directory of Adult Education* (Paris 1952). J. J. WRIGHT, "Goals for Catholic Adult Education," *Catholic World* 193 (1961) 13–19. G. WEIGEL, "Challenge of Adult Education," *National Catholic Education Association Bulletin* 56 (1959) 406–414. P. J. HALLINAN, "Adult Education for Catholics: The Necessity and the Challenge," *National Catholic Education Association Bulletin* 59 (1962) 513–517.

[J. KEELER]

ADULT RELIGIOUS EDUCATION

The continuation for adults of the religious formation received in the schools or elsewhere in earlier life. Catholic adult education aims primarily to develop the individual in terms of his total nature—intellectual and spiritual—through increase of knowledge of Christian principles and growth in grace and virtue.

Years before Vatican Council II gave serious consideration to the increasing and unique importance of the laity, Pius X declared, "the chief cause for the present indifference and the serious evils that result from it is to be found above all else in ignorance of divine things, not only among the young, but also among adults and those advanced in years." In a similar vein Pius XII, writing to the American hierarchy, said that "the needs of our times require that the laity procure for themselves a treasure of religious knowledge, one that will have solidity and richness through the medium of libraries, discussion groups and study clubs."

Although the value of adult education in Christian teachings has long been recognized in this country, the period of the past 25 years has witnessed an extraordinary growth in the various media for conducting programs in this field. Noncredit courses for adults, predominantly religious in character, are offered in more than 60 colleges and universities. These courses include theology for the laity, study of the Scriptures and Bible-reading, liturgy, ecumenism, social teachings of the Church, marriage and family life, and spiritual formation. A number of dioceses offer complete religious education courses for adults. Some have a priest-director for the various centers where the program is carried out. In many cities throughout the country Catholic libraries provide adult lectures and forums on current themes and problems relating to religion. These courses are attended by the laity to the number of tens of thousands. Other courses are sponsored by individual parishes. There is a growing conviction among Catholic leaders that the parish, the vital organizational and spiritual unit of the people of God, should form a center of adult education with emphasis on the new role of the laity in the Church. It is felt that from this source of adult learning, adequately established and financed, will come the solution to many problems that face Catholic laymen, the Catholic home, and the Church at large; such a center will take the strain from the Catholic school system, which remains the chief concern of the present-day parish.

An adult religious education program through parish discussion clubs has been developed by the Confraternity of Christian Doctrine (CCD), which, according to a recent survey, counted nearly a quarter million participants. Texts for these groups vary from a 2-year course on the life of Christ based on the Gospels to a 4-year program on Christian doctrine. Experienced discussants and college-trained members take up the Catholic "classics" of modern literature. The typical Confraternity discussion club consists in a small group of 10 or 12 members who meet weekly for 10 sessions in the fall and for the same time in the spring. Each group has a trained leader who directs the discussion on a text that has been selected usually by a local parish or diocesan director of the CCD. Cooperative study and discussion often follow the procedure *think, judge, act,* familiar in Catholic Action groups. Information is not the only goal of discussion clubs; motivation of the members to active participation in some form of the lay apostolate is emphasized.

A wide variety of correspondence courses to instruct others in the Catholic faith are available. These courses, many of which are carried out by seminarians and, in at least one noteworthy case, by the Knights of Columbus, reach many thousands annually. Moreover, the new media of communication, radio and television, are used increasingly by such organizations as the National Council of Catholic Men in the teaching apostolate of the Church.

Bibliography: Catholic University of America, School of Nursing Education, *Dynamics in Group Discussion* (Washington 1952). H. KEMPFER, *Adult Education* (New York 1955). M. MACLELLAN, *The Catholic Church and Adult Education* (Washington 1935). Confraternity of Christian Doctrine, *Manual of the Parish Confraternity of Christian Doctrine* (10th ed. rev. Washington 1962). Catholic University of America, Workshop on Principles and Problems of Catholic Adult Education, 1958, *Principles and Problems of Catholic Adult Education,* ed. S. MIKLAS (Washington 1959).

[J. B. COLLINS]

ADULTERY

Defined by moral theologians as the act of sexual intercourse between a married man and a woman not his wife, or between a married woman and a man not her husband. The special note here is that at least one of the two parties concerned is married. If both are married, the guilt, of course, is compounded. As to the specific guilt of adultery, it adds a sin against justice to the intrinsically grave malice of fornication, which in itself is a deordination of sex from its true and appointed end. The victim of the injustice is, of course, the innocent spouse, whose marital rights are violated by the sinning parties.

Authors are agreed that the special malice of adultery remains even if the injured spouse should consent to the evil action. The reason is that marriage is an indissoluble contract, and hence no one can waive his rights in this matter, and they are in fact inalienable.

As to the consequences of adultery, Canon Law makes it clear that if one party is guilty of adultery, the other has the right to effect a permanent separation, and this indeed without any intervention of ecclesiastical authority. The marriage bond itself remains, however, and precludes remarriage. Canon 1129 of the Code notes also that this right is forfeited if the other party consented to the crime, was the cause of it, expressly or tacitly condoned it, or was guilty of the same crime. The innocent party is considered to have condoned the crime if, having learned of it, he or she continued to live with the guilty one in marital relations. The law presumes this to be the case unless the innocent party within 6 months has turned the adulterer out of doors, or has left, or brought legal action against, him or her.

When separation has taken place because of adultery, the innocent party is never again under obligation to readmit the adulterer to a community of married life. If the innocent party freely desires this readmission, however, it is his privilege to grant it, unless the adulterer in the meantime, with the consent of the innocent party, has assumed new obligations, such as the vows of the religious state. In general, it may be said that the Church favors the condoning of the adultery by the innocent party for the sake of keeping the family together, unless circumstances clearly make this inadvisable.

The question may be asked: must the adultery be public, or does it suffice that the injured party knows for certain of the crime? That there must be certainty seems clear; to act on mere suspicion would be a serious mistake. However, according to commentators, it does not seem to be the meaning of Canon Law in permitting separation that the offense must be a matter of public knowledge.

Nevertheless, if the party accused of adultery denies the crime, objects to the departure of the spouse, and takes his case to an ecclesiastical court, the other party must furnish proof of the adultery.

The right to separate belongs to the innocent party, not to the guilty one, and the adulterer must stay with his spouse if the latter desires this. Once the innocent party has decided on this course of action, the adultery ceases to be a cause of separation, and the innocent party may not at some future disagreement or quarrel threaten to separate because of the adultery.

Bbiliography: J. AERTNYS and C. A. DAMEN, *Theologia moralis,* 2 v. (16th ed. Turin 1950). Woywod-Smith.

[L. G. MILLER]

ADULTERY (IN THE BIBLE). Adultery was forbidden by the Mosaic Law and penalties were prescribed, yet it seems to have been common. It was prohibited by the Sixth and Ninth Commandments (according to the enumeration of Ten *Commandments common among Catholics: Ex 20.14, 17; Dt 5.18, 21). Even pagans acknowledged its gravity (Gn 12.11–19; 20.2–7; 26.7–11). Death to both parties was commanded in Lv 20.10, but the manner of death was not specified. Stoning is mentioned in Dt 22.24 (cf. Jn 8.5–9), a variety of penalties in Ez 16.38–40, burning in Gn 38.24; but there is no Biblical record of any of these punishments having been inflicted. Intercourse with a female slave was not a capital offense.

When polygamy was permitted, the woman owed perfect fidelity to her husband, for she belonged to him alone, and if she had culpable intercourse with another man she was guilty of adultery. The husband's fidelity was not so strict, for he did not belong entirely to her, and could take other wives. A husband was guilty of adultery only when he had intercourse with a married (Ex 20.17; Dt 5.21; 22.22; Lv 20.10) or betrothed (Dt 22.23–27) woman, but not if he had relations with an unbetrothed maiden (Dt 22.28–29), a slave, or a prostitute. Thus, by adultery a woman violated her husband's rights; a man violated the rights only of another man. Only women were described as subject to a trial by ordeal for suspected adultery (Nm 5.11–31). The repeated prohibitions against adultery both in the OT (e.g., Prv 2.18; 5.1–23; 6.26) and in the NT (Mt 19.3–12; 1 Cor 6.9; 2 Pt 2.14) are an indication of its frequency.

By reason of the spiritual union existing between Yahweh as bridegroom and Israel as bride, the Prophets used the term adultery figuratively to designate apostasy from God or the worship of idols and Israel's infidelity to its covenant with God (Is 57.3–7; Jer 3.8–9; 5.7; 23.10; Ez 23.37, 43; Os 2.2–13).

The NT not only reestablished the original view of marriage (Mt 19.3–9), but proclaimed equal rights of both partners (1 Cor 7.4; Eph 5.25–33). Jesus and the Apostles renewed the prohibitions of the Old Law (Mt 5.27; Mk 10.11, 19; Lk 18.20; Rom 7.2; 13.9) and classed adulterers with murderers and other sinners who would be excluded from heaven (Mt 15.19; Mk 7.21; 1 Cor 6.9, 18; 1 Thes 4.3–8; Heb 13.4; Jas 4.4). Though the Decalogue already forbade adulterous desires (Ex 20.17; Dt 5.21), Jesus placed such desires on the same level with adultery itself (Mt 5.28). In Jn 8.11 Jesus pardoned the sinner but did not condone the sin.

In keeping with the figurative usage of the Prophets, the disbelieving contemporaries of Our Lord (Mt 12.39; 16.4; Mk 8.38), the lovers of this world (Jas 4.4), and evildoers generally (Ap 2.22) were called adulterers.

See also MATRIMONY, I.

Bibliography: EncDictBibl 37–39. W. KORNFELD, "L'Adultère dans l'Orient antique," RevBibl 57 (1950) 92–109.

[J. J. DAVIS]

ADVENT

From Latin *adventus* meaning coming, the season immediately before Christmas, beginning on the Sunday nearest the feast of St. Andrew and lasting for 4 weeks. In about the 9th century the First Sunday of Advent became the beginning of the Church year. (*See* LITURGICAL YEAR IN ROMAN RITE.)

Meaning. Because Advent is so closely related to Christmas it can scarcely be understood apart from that feast. For one thing, it was not until the birthday of Christ was celebrated throughout the Church that Advent came into existence at all. For another, its very name is derived from the ancient name for the feast, for *Adventus, Epiphania* and *Natale* are all synonymous first for the Incarnation itself, then for the feast that commemorates and celebrates the Incarnation. Christmas (Epiphany as well) is not only the commemoration of the birth of Christ as a historical event, it is also and much more the celebration of the coming of God in the flesh as a saving event. The very celebration itself is a saving event that brings about the coming of Christ in men's souls.

The term Advent, originally applied to the feast itself, gradually came to designate the time before Christmas. The oration for the Second Sunday of Advent is a survival of this usage: "Stir us up, O Lord, to make ready for your only-begotten Son. May we be able to serve you with purity of soul through the coming of him who lives and reigns . . .." Here the word coming refers to the Feast of Christmas. Furthermore the ancient Introit for the Epiphany begins with the words "Ecce *advenit* Dominator Dominus" (Behold the Lord the Ruler is come). Advent, then, is first of all a comprehensive name for the Incarnation and all that the Incarnation accomplishes.

History. The remote beginning, or at least the prototype, of Advent is to be found in the Gallican custom of having a time of preparation for the Feast of the Epiphany, which was a baptismal feast in that part of the West and consequently had its season of preparation for Baptism similar to Lent. This took the form of a period of fasting and prayer that at first lasted 3 weeks but in time was lengthened to 40 days in obvious imitation of Lent. In fact, it came to be known as "St. Martin's Lent" because it began on that saint's feast (Nov. 11). The main point to note is that this primitive Advent was an ascetical rather than a liturgical season.

In 380 the Council of Saragossa ordered that there be a 3-week fast before the Epiphany. About 100 years later the Diocese of Tours kept a fast three times a week beginning with St. Martin's Day, a custom that the Council of Mâcon (581) extended to all the dioceses in France. During the next 2 centuries the practice found its way to England also.

At Rome the situation was different. Since the Epiphany was never a baptismal feast there, the same reason for having a "Lent" before it did not exist. When Advent first appeared at Rome it was a preparation for Christmas and not the Epiphany, and it was a liturgical season rather than an ascetical period. In any case there was no trace of anything resembling Advent at Rome until the 6th century. The Gelasian Sacramentary (6th century) was the first to provide an Advent liturgy as it exists today, although the idea of an Advent liturgy may have originated not at Rome but in Ravenna in the 5th century.

The real author of the developed Roman Advent liturgy was Gregory I. He shortened the season from 6 weeks to 4, composed prayers, antiphons, and responses for the season, and also arranged the Lectionary for the Mass and the Office. When the Roman rite was introduced into Gaul in the 9th century, Gregory's Advent went along with it, to be enriched there with Gallican prayers and rites. It was the Gallicans who did most to bring about the emphasis upon the Second Coming, which is so striking an element of the present Advent liturgy.

This fusion of the Roman and the Gallican Advents found its way back to Rome in the 10th century, giving the Church the rich Advent liturgy it has today. Whatever the object of the original Roman Advent may have been, its scope has been widened to include not only a preparation for the anniversary of the first coming of Christ, but also the expectation of His Second Coming in power and majesty. Neither aspect can be excluded if one is to be faithful to the texts actually in use.

Too exclusive an insistence upon either point of view fails to take into account the important fact that Advent is a liturgical season, that it is therefore a mystery in the ancient sense of the word, a sense that has been so strikingly recovered in the 20th century. That is to say, it is a present reality that contains and mediates salvation. It deepens and strengthens the awareness of Christ's presence in His Church and in its members.

Advent is not so much a preparation for Christmas or an expectation of the Second Coming (although it is both) as a kind of anticipation of the Feast of Christmas, a celebration viewing the mystery of the Incarnation in the light of its full and final achievement.

Because Christ has come once, He will come again; indeed He has never left, but is continuously present in His Church. For this reason Advent is at once a celebration of His first coming and His presence in the midst of His Church and a looking forward to the full and final coming when He will complete the work of the Redemption. The word Advent must therefore be taken in the fullest sense: past, present, and future.

This is the basis for speaking of the three comings of Christ. Since the time of St. Bernard, Christian spirituality has maintained this way of approaching Advent, an approach that finds its best justification in the liturgy itself; for between the first and the Second Coming of Christ, the present coming in grace is constantly taking place, His coming by grace in men's hearts. The Church not only prepares to welcome Him at Christmas time or to greet Him in the hour of His final triumph; it rejoices even now in the possession and the presence of its Lord in its midst. All through the year men are summoned to prepare the way of the Lord, to hear the voice of Him who is even now in their midst, to prepare for his Second Coming by living the mystery of Christ in the present.

Bibliography: Miller FundLit. A. G. MARTIMORT, *L'Église en prière* (Paris 1961) 734–738.

[W. J. O'SHEA]

ADVENTISTS, various groups of Christians who since apostolic times have believed that the Second Coming of the Lord was imminent (*see* PAROUSIA). Adherents of *Montanism in the 2d century looked for an early end of the world, as did the *Anabaptists during the Reformation. Modern adventism began in the early 19th century in America with the Biblical prophecies of William *Miller (1782–1849). Seeing signs of widespread moral deterioration, Adventists believe that the world is evil and must soon be destroyed. They foresee a final battle between the forces of good and evil, usually identified as the battle of *Armageddon, and the victory of Jesus Christ, who will then establish a kingdom of righteousness that will last for 1,000 years. Miller set definite dates for the Second Coming in 1843 and 1844 but when these dates passed, his followers became disillusioned. Only a remnant continued to proclaim the imminent Second Coming and these adventists usually refused to specify a date.

Largest of the adventist bodies that stem from Miller's preaching is the *Seventh-day Adventist Church. Along with adventism it teaches the observance of the Jewish Sabbath, conditional immortality, and the prophethood of Mrs. Ellen G. White (1827–1915). The general conference of the church was organized in 1863 and since then Seventh-day Adventism has spread throughout the world. Most of its adherents live outside the U.S. A much smaller adventist body, the Advent Christian Church, reported 30,000 members in 1964. This church was organized in 1855 by Jonathan Cummings, who taught doctrines similar to those of the Seventh-day Adventists, but his followers observed Sunday instead of Saturday. *Jehovah's Witnesses is an adventist body that denies the Trinity and the deity of Jesus Christ. The founder of this sect, Charles Taze *Russell, was influenced by adventist preachers early in his career. Most of the 1 million Witnesses live outside the U.S. The Church of Jesus Christ of *Latter-day Saints originally stressed adventism, but this emphasis in Mormonism gradually diminished. Many of the *Pentecostal churches include a strong adventist position among their beliefs, as do the *Catholic Apostolic Church and the *New Apostolic Church. Other small adventist bodies include the Life and Advent Union, the Church of God (Abrahamic Faith), the Primitive Advent Christian Church, and the United Seventh Day Brethren; altogether these number fewer than 10,000 members.

[W. J. WHALEN]

ADVERTENCE, the act of the mind heeding, attending to, or taking note of something. The term is used by moralists to signify actual attention given by an agent to what he is doing or to some morally significant circumstance. Thus a man who is habitually aware of his obligation to abstain from meat on Friday may eat meat without adverting to the fact that it is Friday. Advertence admits of varying degrees of clarity and of distinctness. Inadvertence is a kind of actual ignorance, and the general principles governing its effect upon the morality of human action are the same as those that determine the influence of ignorance.

See also IGNORANCE; ATTENTION; DISTRACTIONS.

Bibliography: THOMAS AQUINAS, ST 1a2ae, 6.8. H. DAVIS, *Moral and Pastoral Theology,* 4 v. (rev. ed. New York 1958) v.1. B. H. MERKELBACH, *Summa theologiae moralis,* 3 v. (8th ed. Paris 1949) 1:351–352, 355–356, 435–438.

[F. D. NEALY]

ADVERTISEMENTS, BOOK OF, was a set of instructions regulating the conduct of religious services, issued in 1566 by Matthew *Parker, Archbishop of Canterbury, as a means of securing uniformity in public worship. The legislation of 1559 had brought about a church compounded of Protestant doctrine and Catholic ceremonial. This compromise was abhorrent to the extreme Protestant reformers who wished to see a form of worship that was purified from all taint of popery (the so-called *Puritans). The Puritan dispute with the established church developed slowly. In its early stages it was concerned with the vestments prescribed for use by the Royal Injunctions of 1559, which the Puritans regarded as the "livery of Antichrist." Neither side was prepared to yield; the Puritan objections were grounded in conscience, and Elizabeth I refused to waive the exercise of her prerogative to regulate worship. Other items were, in time, added to the list of Puritan objections, such as the use of organs, the ring in the marriage service, the sign of the cross in Baptism, and other "dregs of popery." Sympathy with the Puritans was considerable; in 1563 articles embodying their objections were introduced into the lower house of convocation, where they were rejected by only one (proxy) vote.

The disorder prevailing in the church alarmed the Queen, and on Jan. 25, 1565, she instructed Parker to secure "one manner of uniformity through our whole realm" and to eradicate variety "by order, injunction, or censure according to the order and appointment of such laws as are provided by act of parliament." Accordingly, in March 1566, he issued a set of instructions, known as the *Book of Advertisements,* which laid down fixed rules for the conduct of public services. The delay in issuing the *Advertisements* was due to the fact that Parker had been anxious, in order to lessen his own difficulties, to obtain royal authority for them; this was, however, withheld by the Queen. From the outset they met with opposition. At a meeting held at Lambeth on March 26, 1566, to which more than 100 of the London clergy were summoned, 37 refused to comply with the *Advertisements;* these men were suspended from office and then deprived. Nevertheless, they continued to preach and conduct services, and they may be regarded as the first English Nonconformists.

Bibliography: R. W. DIXON, *History of the Church of England,* 6 v. (Oxford 1878–1902) v.5, 6. J. STRYPE, *The Life and Acts of Matthew Parker,* 3 v. (Oxford 1821) v.1. V. J. K. BROOK, *A Life of Archbishop Parker* (Oxford 1962). H. GEE and W. J. HARDY, comps., *Documents Illustrative of English Church History* (London 1896) 467–475 (text).

[G. DE C. PARMITER]

ADVERTISING

Use of paid announcements directed to the public, generally designed to influence the purchase of goods and services. Informative advertising helps to bring buyers and sellers together by showing consumers when, where, and how they can satisfy existing needs. Persuasive advertising attempts to stimulate latent needs and to strengthen desires for goods and services. In practice both forms often go together and even informative advertising is persuasive in some way. Institutional advertising does not aim directly at sales but tries to render the public, the government, or potential investors favorable to the company itself.

In the U.S., advertising, a $13 billion business in 1964, uses television, radio, magazines, newspapers, handbills, posters, billboards, direct mail, and point-of-purchase displays. Since advertising pays for nearly all radio and television programs and for a major part of all magazines and newspapers, it has cultural and political as well as moral and economic significance.

Economic Significance. The economic effect of advertising in general is difficult to measure. Some informative advertising is absolutely necessary in any extended market. In most cases it is also the cheapest and fastest way for producers to build a mass market and realize economies of sale. There is, however, considerable doubt about the economic utility of advertising that softens competition by creating merely subjective values and consumer preferences or by substituting publicity for price reductions and quality improvement. While such advertising can stabilize the operation of the firm and even the quality of some products, the kind of competition it fosters does not further the welfare of consumers.

Despite the undesirable economic effects of some advertising, most of it is a necessary and useful service that enables a company to produce and market more efficiently and the public to buy more cheaply and more quickly than they otherwise would. Indeed, good informative advertising saves the public so much time and energy that its economic productivity is probably far greater than statistics would indicate.

The actual effects of particular advertising campaigns depend not only on the intention and skill of the advertiser, but on the state of the economy, the nature of the product, and the tactics of competitors. Thus, if the demand for a product is increasing, effective advertising can help all firms in an industry to raise sales and to lower unit costs up to a certain point. However, in a falling or stable market or when advertising saturation has been reached, it may only shift customers from one producer to another without effecting any decrease in costs.

Persuasive advertising is often defended on the grounds that it is necessary for economic growth. There is little evidence for this position and most economists believe that it diverts resources from areas where needs are more vital. In practice, such waste, real or potential, is probably due more to the carelessness of consumers and to the free enterprise system than to the power of advertising itself. Indeed, because advertising is a marginal, though essential, force that reinforces rather than creates needs and desires, it seldom bears the chief responsibility for the effects attributed to it.

In industries where competition is largely a question of advertising, the necessity of having large sums for promotion can make entry into the market difficult and so reduce competition. In the same industries advertising may be wasteful since it serves to protect the market position of a firm rather than to inform the public. Unfortunately, there is no practical way of estimating the extent of such effects.

Consumer Freedom. The range of consumer choices is increased by truthful informative advertising. Untruthful or persuasive advertising does not appear to diminish freedom notably except where the consumer cannot judge for himself or where he is so emotionally involved that he refuses to use his reason. These conditions are often present with regard to such heavily advertised but relatively useless products as tobacco goods, alcoholic drinks, and cosmetics, so that such advertising is often a cause of both waste and the decrease in freedom.

The support of mass media by advertising has helped to free the press of control by political parties and government. At the same time, although advertisers exercise little or no direct control over the media, the economic relationship has produced two results. First, most media must appeal to a mass audience in order to attract heavy advertising. Secondly, the media have become as much a business as an educational force with the result that editorial positions tend to correspond with those of the advertisers on many economic questions.

Regulation. Advertising is regulated by both private and governmental groups. The Better Business Bureaus and such trade associations as the National Association of Broadcasters and the Direct Mail Advertising Association have drawn up codes for advertising. In addition to the laws of individual states, agencies such as the Federal Trade Commission and the Food and Drug Administration supervise advertising that involves certain products in interstate commerce. The most important laws governing advertising are the Federal Trade Commission Act (1914) as amended, the Clayton Act (1914), and the Robinson-Patman Act (1936).

Bibliography: N. H. Bordan, *The Economic Effects of Advertising* (Chicago 1942). T. M. Garrett, *An Introduction to Some Ethical Problems of Modern American Advertising* (Rome 1961). M. J. Simon, *The Law for Advertising and Marketing* (New York 1956).

[T. M. GARRETT]

ADVERTISING (MORAL ASPECT)

From the standpoint of morality, two extreme positions with regard to advertising must be rejected: (1) The position that holds that advertising, as a part of the economic enterprise, enjoys absolute autonomy from the norms of morality. No sphere of human activity can be legitimately divorced from the moral order. It is always the human person who acts, and his decisions are subject to the norms of morality. They must be carried out and answered for as human acts. (2) The position that considers all advertising intrinsically immoral. Sweeping statements to this effect are not uncommonly made, but they are without validity. Advertising, which is a form of human communication aimed at influencing other people, is *in se,* neither morally evil nor morally good. Its morality must be judged from the intention of the advertiser and from other significant circumstances, especially the manner in which advertising is carried on.

Truthfulness. In regard to the truthfulness of advertising, certain clarifications are desirable. First, an advertisement does not pretend to give complete information about a product or service, nor can complete information be reasonably expected. Second, advertisements are sometimes directed to a particular group in the society; misunderstandings that may arise on the part of those outside the group cannot necessarily be blamed on the advertisement. Third, common sense dictates that the truthfulness of advertising be judged on the basis of the total context of the advertisement, not on each word or picture in literal isolation. These things being understood, the following moral principle applies: Those responsible for advertising have a moral obligation to tell the truth about the product or service advertised. On his part, the consumer has an objectively founded right to the truth. One may distinguish, of course, between a serious violation of the truth and a slight violation. Catholic moral theologians agree that a substantial misrepresentation of the truth, designed to deceive the consumer in an important and significant way about the value or effectiveness of a product or service, constitutes a serious violation of the norm of truthfulness. A misrepresentation of the truth in regard to accidental features or matters of little import, is a slight violation of the truth. Small exaggerations about the excellence of one's product or service (sometimes called "puffery") seems morally permissible, since the average person expects this and takes it into account.

Modesty. Concerning modesty, certain clarifications are necessary. Reference is not made here to advertisements that in the opinion of many are tasteless, vulgar, or artistically crude. Nor is there any categorical rejection of the natural beauty of the human female as a legitimate means of attracting attention to a product or service. Rather, reference is made to those advertisements that are pornographic or obscene, that is, those that contain an intrinsic tendency to arouse the sexual passions. Such advertisements may not always and in all circumstances have an erotic effect upon all individuals, but if an advertisement, taken as a whole and in its intrinsic nature, tends commonly to produce such an effect, it is obscene. Advertisements of this kind are morally wrong because they are scandalous, that is, likely to provide an occasion of sin to others. As such, they are gravely forbidden by the moral law. Advertisements that are suggestive or have a double meaning, but are not properly pornographic or obscene, would not be likely to provide an occasion of sin to an average adult; hence, a less severe moral judgment applies to them. The matter is complicated, however, when such advertisements are presented indiscriminately to all age groups. Those responsible for advertising have an obligation to exercise prudence in this area. Since community standards and legal criteria are in a constant state of flux, it must be emphasized that those responsible for advertising are bound to adhere to the principles of natural law and divine revelation governing chastity and modesty.

Charity. Advertisers have a moral obligation to address themselves to others with genuine respect. Some advertising fails against this dictate of charity. Thus, vulgar and tasteless advertisements often offend the common sensibilities of men and women. So, too, many people are annoyed by that type of advertising that relies on raucous shrieks and yells, off-key music, and the frequent repetition of banal slogans. It is admittedly difficult to determine with precision the obligations of charity in this matter. The fact that such advertising is sometimes effective does not necessarily justify it.

Cooperation. Since much modern advertising is due to "team" effort, the question of cooperation in immoral advertising often comes up. The many complications of this question cannot be dealt with here. The individual must make his judgments of conscience in the light of the accepted moral principles governing formal and material cooperation. It must be pointed out, however, that even those who may be justified in cooperating materially with immoral advertising have a social responsibility to do what they can to improve the moral condition of their profession. The practical ways in which this responsibility can be exercised will depend on concrete situations and circumstances.

Materialism. It has often been stated that the most immoral aspect of advertising is its fostering of a materialistic philosophy of life. The critics maintain that much advertising influences people to consider a high material standard of living as the end of human life, as if human happiness depends on the possession or prestige value of material things.

The fostering of materialism, it is said, manifests itself especially in the advancement of planned obsolescence. This term is used to describe the yearly or other regular superficial changes in products and styling, or prestige-selling appeals that are made to persuade the consumer to purchase new items before the old are worn out. The problem of economic waste, stemming from planned obsolescence, is very complicated and beyond the scope of this article. Advertising evidently plays an important role in planned economic waste, since advertising advances the plan and to some extent determines its success. From the moral point of view, there are divergent opinions on the morality of economic waste and planned obsolescence. It is difficult to justify economic waste as a normal feature of the economy, although there are some who think it possible. For present purposes, the following conclusion will have to suffice: If economic waste in the form of planned obsolescence as a normal feature of the economy is morally wrong, then the advertising that promotes this practice is also morally wrong.

Some moralists argue that advertising is simply an effect of a set of values already professed by the majority in a society. Thus, if the majority considers a high material standard of living as the end of life rather than as the means to more spiritual ends, advertising in that society will reflect this set of values. Advertising is not the cause of a materialistic philosophy of life, but an effect of it. While there is some truth to such an argument, it seems more than probable that advertising, though not totally responsible for a widespread materialistic philosophy of life, does *de facto,* contribute to the spread of this philosophy.

Subliminal Techniques. Certain psychological techniques are sometimes used to influence the consumer in "subliminal" or "hidden" ways. Although these techniques have been widely publicized, there is little evidence that they are successful. Moreover, there are good reasons to believe that many responsible members of the advertising profession are not seriously interested in them. Many moralists would view with misgiving a procedure aimed at moving people to act on impulses activated by sensory impressions that have not crossed the threshold of consciousness, because this would seem to involve an attempt to dehumanize in some degree the response of the public. But no clear case can be made against it. All advertising that seeks to build up an impulse to act by associating a product with urges and feeling responses essentially irrelevant to its merits, tends to make the response of the buying public less human and rational. And all would agree that subliminal, as well any other form of advertising, is wrong when it is aimed at arousing morally objectionable impulses.

Bibliography: T. M. GARRETT, *An Introduction to Some Ethical Problems of Modern American Advertising* (Rome 1961). F. J. CONNELL, "Ethics of the Advertising Business," *National Catholic Almanac* (1960) 229–233.

[D. LOWERY]

ADY, ENDRE, Hungarian poet; b. Érmindszent, Nov. 22, 1877; d. Budapest, Jan. 27, 1919. He was of a noble Protestant family; his father, Lawrence, traced his genealogy back to Árpád, who, in the 10th century, led the Hungarians into their present-day homeland. Ady first attended the Gymnasium of the Piarist fathers in Nagykároly, then the Protestant College of Zilah. He studied law at Debrecen and Budapest and began his literary career as a small-town journalist. His first book, *Versek* (Poems), was published in 1903. The following year he went to Paris and thereafter had alternating homes in Paris and Hungary. His *Új Versek* (1906, New Poems) is filled with admiration for the progress he saw in Paris. He accused his native land of backwardness and advocated cooperation with neighboring countries. Many critics disapproved his radicalism and dynamic symbolism. In 1908 he became the cofounder of *Nyugat* (Occident), the magazine that profoundly revitalized Hungary's intellectual life. In 1915 he married Berta Boncza, the "Csinszka" of his poems. Ady was near death when Béla Kun's Communist regime seized power at the end of World War I. "This is not my revolution," he said shortly before his demise. His influence on Hungarian literature was great, for he dared to write about problems that transgressed the prevailing aesthetic rules. He confessed himself a sinner who craved wealth and sensual pleasures (in his *Léda* poems), but he also showed the utmost humility, praying for forgiveness, purity, and union with God. His best poems appeared in *Vér és Arany* (1907, Blood and Gold), *Az Illés Szekerén* (1908, On the Chariot of Elias), *Szeretném Ha Szeretnének* (1909, I Would Love to Be Loved), *Minden Titkok Versei* (1910, The Poems of All Secrets), and *A Magunk Szerelme* (1913, Love of Ourselves).

Bibliography: S. SIK, *Gárdonyi, Ady, Prohászka* (Budapest 1928). A. SCHÖPFLIN, *Ady Endre* (2d ed. Budapest 1945). G. FÖLDESSY, *Ady minden titkai* (Budapest 1949). J. RÉVAI, *Ady* (Budapest 1949). M. KOVALOVSZKY, ed., *Emlékezések Ady Endréröl* (Budapest 1961–).

[O. J. EGRES]

AELFRIC OF CANTERBURY, ST., archbishop; d. Nov. 16, 1005. A monk of *Abingdon and possibly of Glastonbury, he was abbot of St. Alban's and bishop of Ramsbury and Wilton (*c.* 990) before his election to *Canterbury on Easter Day 995. Installed in 996, he received *Gregory V's own pallium in Rome (997). The expulsion of secular clergy and the substitution of monks at Canterbury Cathedral are now generally attributed to either Aelfric or his predecessor, Sigeric. Buried at Abingdon, his body was translated to St. John's, Canterbury, and (after 1067) to his Cathedral. His will is extant. Reference to Aelfric is found in the *Anglo-Saxon Chronicle,* the *Vita Dunstani auctore B* (dedicated to Aelfric), in Florence of Worcester, the *Chronicon monasterii de Abingdon,* and the *Chronicon monasterii sancti Albani.* Matthew of Paris, however, is unreliable.

Bibliography: J. M. KEMBLE, ed., *Codex diplomaticus aevi saxonici,* 6 v. (London 1839–48). W. HUNT, DNB 1:162–163. C. COTTON, *The Saxon Cathedral at Canterbury and the Saxon Saints Buried Therein* (Manchester 1929). A. TAYLOR, DHGE 2:416. Knowles MOE 50, 696–697.

[W. A. CHANEY]

AELFRIC GRAMMATICUS, Benedictine abbot of Eynsham, greatest Anglo-Saxon author of the 10th and 11th centuries; b. *c.* 950 to 955; d. Eynsham, *c.* 1020. He was trained in the ideals of the 10th-century English Benedictine revival by *Ethelwold at *Winchester and as a monk and priest was sent (*c.* 987) by *Alphege of Canterbury, Ethelwold's successor, to Cerne (Dorset), founded by ealdorman Aethelmaer. There Aelfric conducted the monastic school. In 1005 he became first abbot of Eynsham, another foundation of Aethelmaer. His Anglo-Saxon writings, composed in lucid, precise, often alliterative style, included, among other works: the *Catholic Homilies* (991–992), two series of 40 sermons each, dedicated to Abp. Sigeric of Canterbury, derived mainly from Church Fathers and intended for use throughout the liturgical year; *Lives of the Saints* (before 998), a third homiletic collection, concerning saints "whom monks honor"; paraphrases of parts of the Heptateuch; and a treatise on the Old and New Testaments. His Latin *Grammar,* the source of his appellation "the Grammarian," was the first in a medieval vernacular. This work, his Latin *Glossary* and the famous *Colloquy,* with its informative and amusing conversations, were all educational works for monastic schools. Aelfric also condensed the *Regularis concordia* for Eynsham; he authored a vita of Ethelwold and pastoral letters for Bp. Wulfsige of Sherborne and Abp. Wulfstan of York. Sixteenth-century English reformers believed his Easter homily on the Real Presence supported their views against transubstantiation; but his position, influenced by *Ratramnus of Corbie and affirming the "spiritual" (*gastlice*) presence in the Eucharist, antedated the precise distinctions of medieval scholasticism.

Bibliography: W. HUNT, DNB 1:164–166. C. L. WHITE, *A.: A New Study of His Life and Writings* (Boston 1898). S. H. GEM, *An Anglo-Saxon Abbot: A. of Eynsham* (Edinburgh 1912). M. M. DUBOIS, *A.: Sermonnaire, docteur et grammairien* (Paris 1943). P. CLEMOES, "The Chronology of A.'s Works," *The Anglo-Saxons,* ed. P. CLEMOES (London 1959) 212–247.

[W. A. CHANEY]

AELFRYTH, ST., Anglo-Saxon virgin, recluse; d. after 833 (feast, Aug. 2). She was the daughter of King *Offa of Mercia, but unfortunately neither he nor his family found a biographer. Aelfryth (Elfriede, Etheldreda, Etheldritha, etc.) is said to have been betrothed to St. *Ethelbert, King of East Anglia, who was executed on her father's orders *c.* 790. Surviving her father (d. 796) by many years, she seems to have lived a solitary life at *Crowland, one of the great Midland monasteries. She is often confused with her sister Aelfleda, whose husband was murdered through treachery.

Bibliography: ActSS August 1:173–175. Dugdale MonAngl 2:109–111. H. DAUPHIN, DHGE 15:158–159. R. STANTON, *A Menology of England and Wales* (London 1887) 22. Zimmermann KalBen 2:527.

[E. JOHN]

AELRED (AILRED), ST.

Abbot and writer; b. Hexham, Northumberland, 1110; d. Rievaulx, Jan. 12, 1167 (feast, Jan. 12; in the Dioceses of Liverpool, Hexham, and Middlesbrough and in Cistercian houses, March 3).

Life. He was of a noble family, the son of Eilaf, the last of the hereditary priests of Hexham in Northumberland on the English-Scottish border. He attended schools at Hexham and Durham, and possibly at the old Scottish capital, Roxburgh. Much of his youth he spent at the court of the half-English King David I of Scotland. Aelred entered the Cistercian Abbey of Rievaulx in Yorkshire probably in 1134. His monastic life falls into three periods: for 9 years he was at Rievaulx as novice, monk, and confidential adviser to Abbot William; for about 4 years he was abbot of Revesby, a newly established daughterhouse of Rievaulx; and from the end of 1147 until his death he was abbot of Rievaulx.

Aelred was known to his contemporaries as the "Bernard of the North" because of the warmth of his sentiment, the attractive power of his mind, and his wondrous gift of writing and preaching for monks and clergy. He was one of the most influential persons of his time. His life was marked by tireless activity, even during the chronic illness that plagued his later life. The duties of administering a large and prosperous community and the many visitations to the daughter-houses of Rievaulx were a constant responsibility. Moreover, he kept up an extensive correspondence and was much in demand as friend and counselor to abbots, bishops, and kings. His writings reveal Aelred as a person of warmth and simplicity, deeply imbued with the Christian humanism of his day.

His life, the *Vita Aelredi*, was written by a contemporary monk, Walter Daniel, who lived for 17 years under Aelred's rule and who sought to illustrate Aelred's sanctity. The supposed canonization of Aelred by Celestine III in 1191 is false. In 1476 the general chapter at Cîteaux allowed a more solemn celebration of Aelred's feast in England and gave a formal authorization of the local cultus.

Writings. Only part of the literary heritage of Aelred is extant. His extensive correspondence with popes and kings, his rhythmic prose in honor of St. Cuthbert, his homily for the feast of St. Edward the Confessor have been lost. The *Vita Aelredi* is the starting point for the authentic list of Aelred's works. This list does not include the *Oratio pastoralis* and four historical works, although these are well attested by 12th-century Rievaulx manuscripts. The manuscript tradition of the *corpus aelredianum* tells an interesting story. Some 180 manuscripts have been listed. The great number of 13th-century manuscripts (71) is due partly to the fact that several works of Aelred were ascribed to St. Bernard and St. Augustine. The greatest number of manuscripts were copied at the Benedictine Abbey of Reading, and most are preserved today in England.

The first attempt to edit a series of Aelredian works was made by Richard Gibbons in the 17th century, but until the present time the works of Aelred have not been gathered together. A complete and critical edition of the *Opera Omnia* was in preparation for the *Corpus Christianorum Continuatio Medievalis* for 1967, the 800th anniversary of Aelred's death.

The writings of Aelred are usually divided into ascetical or devotional works and historical works.

Ascetical Works. Aelred's first work, *Speculum caritatis,* was written at the instigation of St. *Bernard of Clairvaux while Aelred was novice master. In a fluent and fine style, he treated of the excellence and practice of charity. The *De Iesu puero duodenni* was written at the request of a friend, Ivo of Wardon. Quoting the text of Luke (2.41–52), Aelred gave a literal, an allegorical, and a spiritual or moral exposition. His most famous work, *De spiritali amicitia,* was based on Cicero's *De amicitia* but was influenced also by Augustine and Bernard. Written in dialogue form, it has as its theme that truly spiritual friendship never concerns two persons only. It always involves Christ, who is the source from which the friendship springs, the framework in which it grows, and the final end at which it aims.

The *De institutione inclusarum* is a rule for recluses, written at the request of Aelred's sister. According to

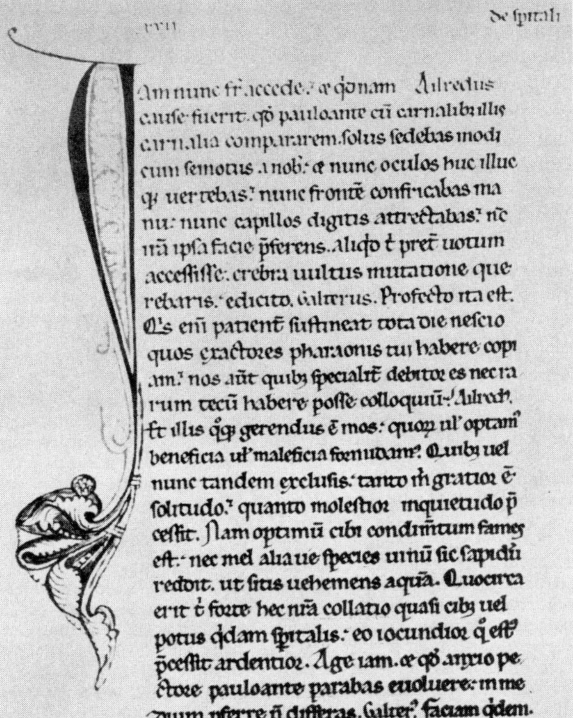

xvii De spitali

Iam nunc fr. accede. et qo nam Ailredus
cause fuerit. qd pauloante cu carnalibus illis
carnalia compararem. solus sedebas modi
cum semotus a nob. et nunc oculos huc illuc
q uertebas. nunc fronte confricabas ma
nu. nunc capillos digitis attrectabas. nc
ira ipsa facie pferens. aliqd t pret uotum
accessisse. crebra uultus mutatione que
rebaris. edicito. Galterus. Profecto ita est.
Q's enī patient sustineat tota die nescio
quos exactores pharaonis tui habere copi
am. nos aut quib specialit debitor es nec ra
rum tecū habere posse colloquiu. Ailred.
Et illis qq gerendus ē mos. quo ul optam
beneficia ul maleficia formidam. Quib uel
nunc tandem exclusis. tanto m gratior ē
solitudo. quanto molestior inquietudo p
cessit. Nam optimū cibi condimentum fames
est. nec mel alia ue species uinū sic sapidu
reddit. ut sitis uehemens aquā. Quocirca
erit t forte hec nra collatio quasi cib uel
potus qdam spitalis. eo iocundior q est
pcessit ardentior. Age iam. et qd anxio pe
ctore pauloante parabas euoluere. in me
dium pferre n differas. Galter. Faciam qdem.

Page from a 13th-century manuscript of St. Aelred's "De spiritali amicitia" in the Bibliothèque Municipale at Saint-Omer, France (MS 86, fol. 17r).

the author's own words, it contains "a way of life to govern the body, a way of purifying the inward man of vices, and an example of three-fold meditation." The *De anima* consists solely in a synthesis of Augustinian doctrine and deals with fundamental questions concerning the nature of the soul—a common preoccupation for contemporary Cistercian psychologists. Aelred's ascetical works include also *Sermones de tempore et de sanctis,* 31 *Sermones de oneribus,* and a fine pastoral prayer of the abbot for his monks.

Historical Works. The historical writings of Aelred have long been neglected on the assumption that they are not of spiritual interest. However, they reveal much of Aelred's personality and of the spiritual environment of the country in which he lived. In chronological order, they are: *Genealogia regum anglorum, Vita s. Niniani, De bello standardii, De sanctimoniali de Watton, Vita s. Eduardi Confessoris, De sanctis Ecclesiae Hagulstadensis.*

Doctrine. Aelred's love for Ciceronian literature could no longer predominate after he entered the cloister. The *lectio divina* led him to a love of the Scriptures. As a monk he was orientated toward the writings of the fathers of the desert, the Rule of St. Benedict, and the whole patristic learning, especially the *Confessions* of St. Augustine. Faithful to the Cistercian formation, he showed great devotion to the humanity of Christ, wrote with Bernardine accents about charity and spiritual friendship, composed a treatise on the nature of the soul, and wove beautiful prayers into his sermons for the monks. His meditation on the incidents of Our Lord's life and Passion had a remarkable influence on the later development of Christian spirituality. Aelred's insistence on monastic experience as a way that leads to God, his affective spirituality, his Christocentric devotion, especially to the Child Jesus, make him one of the greatest monastic writers of medieval England.

Bibliography: Life. W. DANIEL, *The Life of Ailred of Rievaulx,* ed. and tr. F. M. POWICKE (New York 1950). Cross ODCC 27–28. M. A. CALABRESE, BiblSanct 1:276–279.

Works. PL 195:209–796. C. M. SAGE, "The MSS of St. Aelred," CathHistRev 34 (1949) 437–445. A. HOSTE, *Bibliotheca Aelrediana* (The Hague 1962), a survey of the MSS, old catalog., eds., and studies of Aelred. R. GIBBONS, ed., *Opera divi Aelredi Rievallensis* (Douai 1618; repr. 1655), includes most of the ascetical works. Critical eds. of individual works. *De Iesu puero duodenni,* ed. A. HOSTE, tr. J. DUBOIS, as *Quand Jésus eut douze ans* (SourcesChr 60; 1959); Eng. tr. G. WEBB and A. WALKER, *On Jesus at Twelve Years Old* (London 1956). *De institutione inclusarum,* ed. C. H. TALBOT, in AnalOCist 7 (1951) 167–217; Eng. tr. G. WEBB and A. WALKER, *A Letter to His Sister by Saint Aelred of Rievaulx* (London 1957). *De anima,* ed. C. H. TALBOT, in MedRenSt Suppl 1 (1952). *De spiritali amicitia,* see A. HOSTE, "The First Draft of Aelred of Rievaulx' *De spiritali amicitia,*" SacrErud 10 (1958) 186–211. For 13th- and 14th-century summaries of *De spiritali amicitia,* see A. HOSTE, "*Le Speculum spiritalis amicitiae,* compilation du XIIIe siècle de deux traités d'Aelred de Rievaulx par Thomas de Frakaham," *Studia monastica* 3 (1961) 291–323, Eng. tr. H. TALBOT, *Christian Friendship by S. Aelred of Rievaulx* (London 1942). C. DUMONT, ed. and tr., *Saint Aelred de Rievaulx* (Les Écrits des saints; Namur 1961), extracts of the ascetical writings. R. TWYSDEN, ed., *Historiae anglicanae scriptores X* (London 1652), includes most of the historical writings. See also A. SQUIRE, "Historical Factors in the Formation of A. of R.," CollOCistR 22 (1960) 262–282. R. L. G. RITCHIE, *The Normans in Scotland* (Edinburgh 1954) 246–257.

Doctrine. A. LE BAIL, DictSpirAscMyst 1:225–234. A. HALLIER, *Un Éducateur monastique: Aelred de Rievaulx* (Paris 1959). C. DUMONT, "L'Équilibre humain de la vie cistercienne d'après le Bs. A. de R.," CollOCistR 18 (1956) 177–189; "A. de R.," *Théologie de la vie monastique* (Paris 1961) 527–538. A. HOSTE and S. ROSE DE LIMA, *For Crist Luve: Prayers of Saint Aelred, Abbot of Rievaulx* (The Hague 1965).

[A. HOSTE]

AEMILIAN, SS. The Roman martyrology lists eight saints by this name; other martyrologies list more. The most noteworthy are the following: Aemilian (feast, July 18), martyred at Dristra (Romania) under the Emperor Julian the Apostate. Aemilian of Cogolla, hermit, parish priest; d. Tarazon, Aragon, 574 (feast, Nov. 12); the abbey of S. Millán de la Cogolla was built at his hermitage and has his relics. His life was written by *Braulio; he is regarded as a patron of Spain. Aemilian, Bishop of Cyzicus, 9th century (feast, Aug. 8); he opposed Emperor Leo V the Armenian in the controversy over *iconoclasm and died in exile as a result. Aemilian, Bishop of Nantes, perhaps in the 8th century (feast, Sept. 3); though he is not named in the early lists of bishops of Nantes, legend claims he fought against the Saracens near Autun. Aemilian of Lagny, abbot, d. *c.* 648 (feast, March 10); an Irish disciple of St. *Fursey (Furseus), he succeeded him as abbot of *Lagny-Sur-Marne.

Bibliography: ActSS July 4:370–376. J. DUBOIS, *Catholicisme* 4:52. I. M. GOMEZ, DHGE 15:406–412. Butler Th Attw 4:321–322. A. M. ZIMMERMANN, LexThK[2] 1:438. ActSS Aug. 2:353; Oct. 11:196. V. GRUMEL, *Catholicisme* 4:51–52. BHL 1:105. Baudot-Chaussin 9:75–76. G. BARDY, *Catholicisme* 4:52–53. ActSS March 2:45.

[B. L. MARTHALER]

AENNON, a place near Salim, Palestine, having an abundant supply of water etymologically connected with Heb. for "spring," *'ayin.* It was one of the sites where John habitually baptized (Jn 3.23). The exact locations of Aennon and Salim are uncertain. Some have situated it near *Sichem or even as far south as the environs of *Hebron. Most moderns follow Eusebius in placing it 8 miles south of *Beth-San and west of the Jordan River (modern *Umm el-Amdān*).

Bibliography: InterDictBibl 1:152. EncDictBibl 39.

[E. MAY]

AEON

An indefinitely long period of time. The Biblical use of the term can be seen best by examining how it is employed in the OT, in intertestamental Judaism, and in the NT.

In the Old Testament. The Greek word *αἰών,* from which the English word is derived, first occurs in the Greek versions of the Bible as a translation of the Hebrew word *'ôlām,* meaning an indefinitely long period of time of greater or lesser extent. The terms express especially the notion of the duration of time in which one generation succeeds another (Eccl 1.4) or indefinite periods of time long since past (Jos 24.2) and thus come to mean age (Ez 26.20). Moreover, *'ôlām* and *αἰών* come to take on the more precise meaning of eternity or unlimited, endless time in some passages in which Yahweh is said to live "from of old" (*mê-'ôlām*), as one generation succeeds another. He is "the everlasting God" (*'ēl 'ôlām:* Gn 21.33). He swears "As I live forever . . ." (*l[e]'ôlām:* Dt 32.40). The eternal King (*melek 'ôlām:* Jer 10.10) is, in the later, deuterocanonical books, He who lives forever (*hê-'ôlām:* Dn 12.7; Sir 18.1).

In Intertestamental Judaism. In addition to the two meanings of *αἰών,* "long duration of time" and "eternity," that later Judaism received from the OT, two new and often related meanings emerged: (1) The apocalyptic literature in particular distinguishes between the present "age," which is "the aeon of injustice" (Ethiopic Enoch 48.7) and the future "age" of holiness (Syriac Baruch 15.7–8). In the eschatology of this period [*see* ESCHATOLOGY (IN THE BIBLE)] there is postulated a moral difference between the present evil aeon and the future aeon with its promise of happiness for the just (cf. even the deuterocanonical Tb 14.5). (2) The present "age" was easily identified with the world that has existed from creation up to the present [*see* WORLD (IN THE BIBLE)] or to the future golden "age," and thus the temporal meaning of *αἰών* tends sometimes to merge with a purely spatial sense of this material world (4 Esdras 7.50).

In the New Testament. The NT authors use *αἰών* to mean (1) age in the sense of a certain period of time of greater or lesser duration, (2) age meaning an indefinite period of years or of generations, (3) eternity properly speaking, and (4) world either as the present material world, especially the world of sin and darkness that is opposed to the kingdom of God, or the "world to come" that has already begun.

(1) The word *αἰών* sometimes means simply age or era as a more or less defined number of years or generations. Thus in 1 Cor 10.11 St. Paul refers to the limited "ages" of the past when he says that "the end of the ages" has come.

(2) As an indefinite duration of time, *αἰών* may have been used several times (e.g., in 1 Cor 2.7, where "before the ages" may refer to the limited but indefinite period of time between creation and the end of the world), but such usage readily passes over into the following meaning.

(3) The term *αἰών* can signify eternity in the sense of an unlimited, endless period of time, either backward and forward or simply the future duration of time without end. Thus in Col 1.26 *ἀπὸ τῶν αἰώνων* apparently means "from all eternity," but perhaps equivalently, "before the foundation of the world," as in Eph 1.4; Jn 17.24; 1 Pt 1.20; see also *εἰς τὸν αἰῶνα* (forever) in Jn 6.51; *εἰς τὸν αἰῶνα τοῦ αἰῶνος* and *εἰς τοὺς αἰῶνας τῶν αἰώνων* in Heb 1.8; Gal 1.5; 1 Tm 1.17 meaning "forever and ever," and *αἰώνιος* (everlasting) in Rom 16.26; Heb 9.14.

(4) Finally, *αἰών* very frequently has the sense of world (Heb 1.2; 11.3), especially in those passages where "this present aeon" is contrasted with "the aeon to come" (Mt 12.32; Mk 10.30; Rom 12.2). As in Jewish usage there is often a moral difference between "this aeon" and "the aeon to come"; so in Lk 16.8, "the children of this aeon" are distinguished from "the children of light." St. Paul expressly speaks of "the present evil aeon" (Gal 1.4), and Jesus refers to its end (Mt 13.39). The future aeon has, indeed, already begun in the present aeon by means of Christ's Redemption (Gal 1.4; Heb 6.5), but there remains the tension between the present world and the growing realization of the kingdom of God.

Bibliography: H. SASSE, Kittel ThW 1:197–209. O. CULLMANN, *Christ and Time,* tr. F. V. FILSON (rev. ed. Philadelphia 1964). J. BARR, *Biblical Words for Time* (Naperville, Ill. 1962). A. LUNEAU, *L'Histoire du salut chez les pères de l'église* (Paris 1964). EncDictBibl 662–664. F. J. SCHIERSE, LexThK² 1:680–683.

[J. L. RONAN]

AEONIUS OF ARLES, ST., bishop; fl. 494–500 (feast, Aug. 18). Little is known of his life before he became bishop and metropolitan of *Arles on Aug. 23, 494. On Sept. 29, 500, he was succeeded at his own request by his friend *Caesarius of Arles, with whom he had founded Chalon-sur-Saône. Two important items were settled during his episcopacy, the diocesan boundary with *Vienne and the primacy of the See of Arles (Jaffé K 753, 754). Popes *Anastasius III and *Symmachus corresponded with him on *traducianism and the date of Easter in certain doubtful cases (Jaffé K 751, 754). There are also letters to him from Ruricius I of Limoges (d. 507; PL 58:87, 97). Aeonius contributed much to the development of monasticism in France and was instrumental in bringing Caesarius to Arles. His name does not appear in the Roman Martyrology.

Bibliography: MGSrerMer 3:460–462, 469. PL 67:1005–06. *Sancti Caesarii opera omnia,* ed. G. MORIN, 2 v. in 3 (Maredsous 1937–42) 2:300. E. EWIG, LexThK² 1:683. G. BARDY, *Catholicisme* 4:279–280. Jaffé K.

[T. P. HALTON]

AERTNYS, JOZEF, Redemptorist moral theologian (known also as Josef Aertnijs); b. Eindhoven, in the Diocese of 's Hertogenbosch, Holland, Jan. 15, 1828: d. Wittem, Holland, June 30, 1915. After being educated by the Redemptorists, Aertnys made his profession Oct. 15, 1846, and was ordained Sept. 14, 1854. He served as professor of moral theology at Wittem from 1860 to 1898 and was a consultant in theological and canonical problems for the bishops and priests of his native land. Among his writings, the more important were: *Caeremoniale solemnium functionum juxta liturgiam Romanam* ('s Hertogenbosch 1880; 3d ed. 1921); *Compendium liturgiae sacrae* (Tournai 1895; 11th ed. 1943); *Theologia moralis juxta doctrinam S. Alphonsi* (Tournai 1886–87), a work that went through 17 editions, of which the 9th to 16th were made by A. Damen and the 17th was provided by J. Visser (1956–58), professor at the Urbaniana University in Rome. The 18th edition is being prepared. He also wrote *Theologia pastoralis* (Tournai 1892; 6th ed. 1916). He published many articles in scholarly publications and served as one of the original founders of the *Nederlandse Katholieke Stemmen,* for which he wrote frequently on moral questions of the day.

Bibliography: "In Memoriam," *Nederlandse Katholieke Stemmen* 15 (1915) 210–211. M. DE MEULEMEESTER et al., *Bibliographie générale des écrivains Rédemptoristes,* 3 v. (Louvain 1933–39) 2:9–11; 3:246.

[A. SAMPERS]

AESCULAPIUS, CULT OF. Greek hero and god of healing, known also by the Greek form of his name, Asklepios. He is mentioned in the *Iliad* and by Pindar (*Pyth.* 3) and is treated extensively by Pausanias (*Description of Greece,* bk 2). The town of Epidaurus claimed to be his birthplace and here was built the greatest of the temples and healing establishments dedicated to him. Other outstanding centers were on the island of Cos and at Pergamum and Smyrna in Asia Minor. The cult was brought to Rome in 293 B.C.

The practice of healing at temples of Aesculapius usually required that the patient stay within the sacred enclosure of the temple, where the god would send dreams prescribing treatments to effect cures. The treatments prescribed were frequently of an unexpected character and involved physical exertion, regardless of the patient's condition. In addition to balms, poultices, warm baths, purges, bloodletting, diet and fasting, the god frequently prescribed horseback riding, cold baths, going barefoot, smearing the body with mud from the

Tombstone of Xanthippos. The foot in his hand is probably a votive offering to Aesculapius.

sacred spring, and outdoor exercises, even in the coldest weather.

Many votive inscriptions from the temple at Epidaurus are known (published in *Inscriptiones Graecae* v.4 and in other collections). These, along with the data supplied by Aristophanes (*Plut.* 653–747) and the great 2d-century Sophist Aelius Aristides (*Sacred Discourses*) and others, furnish a fairly full literature on the kind of ailments treated and miraculous cures attested. These include cures of barrenness, paralysis of the fingers, blindness, dumbness, removal of branding marks, kidney stones, tumors, skin diseases, fevers, and bronchial ailments—in fact almost all the diseases known to man.

Some modern scholars have maintained that priests at the temples of Aesculapius often administered medicines and sometimes even performed operations, inducing the patient to believe that such events had occurred while they were asleep and were due to the intervention of the god himself. It is indeed probable that much of the medical lore contained in the so-called Hippocratic Corpus was collected, and perhaps used, at temples of this deity. The cult of Aesculapius was very popular and flourished until it was suppressed by Christian emperors.

Bibliography: F. R. WALTON, OxClDict 16, 106–107. Prümm RelHdbh 447–453. E. J. and L. EDELSTEIN, *Asclepius*, 2 v. (Baltimore 1945). A. M. J. FESTUGIÈRE, *Personal Religion Among the Greeks* (Berkeley 1954) 85–104. **Illustration Credit:** Trustees of the British Museum.

[T. A. BRADY]

AESTHETIC DISTANCE

A term used to indicate the psychological distance that the artist must preserve between his audience and his work in order to enable the audience to contemplate the work as an aesthetic object and not become engaged in an existential participation in it.

This is a general rule for proper aesthetic appreciation, but when the subject presented for contemplation involves sex, the task of preserving this distance is especially difficult. Ordinarily the artist must employ every available device to help his audience fully recognize the human situation presented for contemplation. In the presentation of situations involving sex, however, the problem is to control rather than stimulate the imagination to such an extent that it lingers on details at the expense of the main context. Human curiosity in this area is quite natural, and emphasis on physical detail can easily pass from imaginative stimulation to actual sexual involvement, psychological or physical. The true artist respects human nature in this matter—if he does not, he destroys the aesthetic distance that is absolutely necessary for aesthetic contemplation.

There are various ways to maintain this necessary distance. A certain reticent suggestion rather than blatant and sustained statement is one technique. The general context, the way in which the whole work frames an episode and gives it perspective, can also pervade and control even when the episode in question is frankly and realistically developed. Finally, aesthetic distance can often be successfully maintained by handling sex humorously or satirically. Laughter does not invite to identification and participation, but to aloofness and criticism.

To make the sexual situation real, detailed enough to be convincing, and at the same time to preserve the proper aesthetic distance is admittedly one of the most difficult tasks confronting a creative artist—and a touchstone of his claim to the title.

See also LITERATURE, NATURE AND FUNCTION; EROTIC LITERATURE; AESTHETICS; MODESTY.

Bibliography: G. MEHLIS, "The Aesthetic Problem of Distance," in *Reflections on Art,* ed. S. K. LANGER (New York 1958). M. B. MCNAMEE, "Esthetic Distance and Sex," *America* 102 (Dec. 19, 1959) 372–373. W. C. BOOTH, *The Rhetoric of Fiction* (Chicago 1961).

[M. B. MC NAMEE]

AESTHETICS

The term has been used in several significantly different ways since it was first introduced by A. G. Baumgarten (*Meditationes philosophicae de nonnullis ad poema pertinentibus*, 1735), who defined it as "the science of sensory cognition." In one more recent but well-established use (as in the *Journal of Aesthetics and Art Criticism*, Cleveland), it embraces all comparatively broad and searching questions about art, its nature, conditions, and consequences, and is roughly equivalent to the philosophy and psychology of art. Many modern thinkers maintain a sharp distinction between psychological aesthetics, considered as a branch of empirical psychology, and philosophical aesthetics. Of these thinkers, some regard the latter as a special application of philosophical analysis to those problems that arise from reflection on the presuppositions and methodological principles of criticism, i.e., the description, interpretation, and evaluation of works of art. Others would define philosophical aesthetics as the investigation of the nature of art, of beauty, and of aesthetic value.

Each of the arts (and, it might be added, certain aspects of nature and of man) presents its own special problems to the aesthetician, for example, the alleged "meaning" of music, the relation between representation and design in visual art, and the relevance of truth and credibility to the greatness of literature. But there are also general problems that cut across these special ones. The aesthetic study of literature may begin with an examination of the foundations of literary criticism and with such questions as: Are explications of poems objective and interpersonally valid? What reasons can be given for judging a poem to be good, or better than another poem? Such questions, persistently pursued, lead to fundamental problems about the essential nature of poetry and of literature, about the relation of literature to the other arts, and about the values that may be ascribed to art in general. This article reviews three of these broad problems.

Theories of Art. The concept of the fine arts as a special class (comprising such major arts as painting, sculpture, architecture, music and literature as well as hundreds of minor arts, such as flower arranging and the fashioning of jewelry) is a modern achievement. It first clearly appears in *Les beaux arts réduits à un même principe* (1746), by the Abbé C. Batteux, and in D'*Alembert's *Discours préliminaire* to the *Encyclopédie* (1751). The formation of this concept made it possible to state one of the fundamental aesthetic problems in the modern way: What is the common and central character of works of fine art (or art, for the purposes of the present discussion)? Much of the thinking about aesthetics in the past 200 years has been a search for a general theory of art. But the earliest sustained reflections on aesthetic problems, by Plato and Aristotle, as well as later medieval and Renaissance discussions of the similarities and differences among the arts, had led to important ideas (such as the idea of "imitation," Batteux's "single principle") that could be put to use by later aestheticians.

The various answers to the question, What is art?, may be placed in three main categories, though it will be evident that within each category there are many divergent views; and it must be borne in mind that individual philosophers may straddle two theories.

Referentialism. It was plain to those who first philosophized about art that at least some works of art are partly derivative from what is to be found in the world: the sculptor gives his figure a recognizable human visage; the dramatic poet presents the words and deeds of actual or possible people. The theory that art is essentially *mimesis* (still, for want of a better term, translated as imitation) was a reasonable generalization from these observations, since ancient visual art was representational and ancient music was wedded to dance and song. Under Plato's dialectical manipulations, *mimesis* took on several senses—most prominently and pejoratively, the sense that the artist makes an image (*phantasma*) or deceptive semblance (see *Soph.* 236B; *Tim.* 19D; *Gorg.* 463–65; *Rep.* 600C). In Aristotle's use of the term (*Poet.* 1447a, 1460b), as applied to poetry and painting, no such denigration is implied.

Whatever else it has come to mean—and it has meant many things in the course of its long history—imitation involves some kind of reference of the work of art to the outside world by means of an important similarity between them, though with something left out or added (abstraction or distortion). Thus *Hegel's view that art embodies the Ideal in sensuous form (see *Philosophy of Fine Art*, tr. F. P. B. Osmaston, London, 1920, 1:53, 77, 154) and *Schopenhauer's that art embodies the Platonic Ideas (see *The World as Will and Idea,* bk. 3, tr. R. B. Haldane and J. Kemp, 4th ed. London, 1896, esp. 1:231, 252, 272) may be regarded as variants of the same theory (*see* PLATO; PLATONISM). Sophisticated 20th-century versions of the theory of "imitation" hold that a work of art is an "iconic sign" [see C. W. Morris, "Esthetics and the Theory of Signs," *Journal of Unified Science* (*Erkenntnis*), Leipzig, 8:131–50] or "presentational symbol" (see S. Langer, *Philosophy in a New Key*, Cambridge 1942). A musical composition, for example, is said to designate a type of mental state or process in virtue of its kinetic similarity to its referent; in this view, every work of art is or contains a reference to the world outside it.

Expressionism. The source of the artist's creative impulse was the subject of speculation in the earliest times, as for example by Homer and Hesiod, who ascribed it to divine inspiration. Plato's observations on the "madness" or "frenzy" of the poet (see *Phaedrus* 245A; *Ion* 533E, 536B; *Meno* 99C) emphasized the artist's irrationality and lack of genuine wisdom. In this light a work of art has been understood by many as a manifestation, or objectification, of its creator's feelings.

The view of art as essentially expression of emotion was widely accepted during the Romantic period (cf. Wordsworth's description of poetry as "the spontaneous overflow of powerful feelings," 1800 Preface to the *Lyrical Ballads*). In a more complicated form, as developed by Benedetto *Croce (*Estetica,* Milan 1902) and clarified by others (e.g., R. G. Collingwood, *The Principles of Art,* Oxford 1938), the expression theory has become a pervasive influence in 20th-century aesthetics. Croce's identification of expression and intuition is variously interpreted; but his primary thesis, that through the act of expression the artist becomes able to articulate his own feelings and impressions, has been widely accepted.

Formalism. The self-containedness and self-sufficiency (that is, the high degree of unity and order) of works of art were somewhat emphasized by St. Augustine (see *Vera Relig.* 23.59; 41.77; *Musica* 1.13.28; *Ordine* 2.15.42; *Lib. Arb.* 2.16.42). Drawing on suggestions from Plato (*Philebus* 64E, 66AB) and Plotinus (*Enneads* 1.6.2), he developed the connection between beauty, order, and numerical proportion and related art to the divine order. The same interest in the internal nature of the aesthetic object is seen in St. Thomas's three conditions of beauty, *integritas sive perfectio*, *debita proportio sive consonantia*, and *claritas* (ST 1a, 39.8; cf. 2a2ae, 145.2, 180.2).

These formal concepts—but detached from metaphysical and theological contexts—commended themselves to some 19th-century aestheticians who were eager to defend the autonomy of art against various encroachments: the neo-Hegelian reduction (or elevation) of art to a sensuous form of religion and philosophy; the realist theory that art is a mirror of social and cultural conditions; the socialist theory that art exists mainly to promote justice and human understanding. Éduard Hanslick, in his highly significant work, *Vom Musikalisch-Schöne* (Leipzig 1854), argued that the beauty of music is peculiar and internal to it, not depending on its relation to anything else.

This so-called formalist theory was generalized to the fine arts by Clive Bell (*Art*, London 1914) and Roger Fry (*Vision and Design*, London 1920) and has been defended in various qualified versions. Its insistence that literary works, for example, should be respected as objects in their own right has inspired such movements as Russian formalism of the prerevolutionary and early postrevolutionary period, and the New Criticism of England and the U.S., and it is reflected in such works of the phenomenological school as Roman Ingarden's *Das Literarische Kunstwerk* (Halle 1930).

Highly generalized theories like the foregoing are not always incompatible with each other. Indeed, they may be construed as attempts to answer different questions: the first group, questions about the semantics of art; the second group, questions about the pragmatics of art; and the third group, questions about the syntax of art (to borrow the terminology of C. Morris, "Foundations of the Theory of Signs," *Encyclopedia of Unified Science*, Chicago 1938). Nevertheless, these positions reflect significant differences of opinion about the factors that are basic and decisive in art; and the critic's assumptions about the precise nature and degree of autonomy that can be ascribed to art will have consequences for his practical criticism.

Aesthetic Value. The existence of criticism as a distinctive intellectual activity appears to presuppose that there is a certain "point of view" from which aesthetic objects are most appropriately regarded (the aesthetic point of view) and a special kind of "value" (aesthetic value) to be found, or at least looked for, in them. Criticism has almost always been taken to include the evaluation, or appraisal, of aesthetic objects, issuing in such judgments as "*The Windhover* is a good poem," or "This is a poor painting," which are normally supported by reasons ("The poem is subtle and profound," "The painting is disorganized"). Many of the fundamental issues in the philosophy of criticism concern the logic of critical reasoning—whether, for example, originality or success in fulfilling the author's intention ought to count as a relevant and convincing ground for judging a work to be good.

To justify the critic's appeal to certain reasons—or, in other words, his use of certain criteria of judgment—seems to require the discrimination, or isolation, of aesthetic value. Once we are clear concerning what sort of goodness is to be sought in art, we can ask what features of the work are likely to enhance or to diminish that goodness. This is essentially the procedure followed by Aristotle when he asked what is the proper pleasure (*oikeia hedone*) of tragedy, and proceeded to analyze those elements of tragedy that bear upon its tendency to provide this pleasure (see *Poet.* 1453b, 1459a, 1462b).

The attempt to work out a satisfactory account of aesthetic value encounters a number of very difficult problems, some of them pervasive in general value theory, some of them peculiar to aesthetics. They can be only very briefly indicated here. (*See* VALUE, PHILOSOPHY OF.)

Value and Beauty. Is aesthetic value the same as beauty? Until the concept of the sublime came to be considered seriously and carefully in the 18th century, judgments of aesthetic value were characteristically stated as judgments of beauty. In this usage, "This is a beautiful poem" means the same as "This is a good poem." Beauty is today more often considered as a ground of aesthetic value (the painting is good *because* it is beautiful), but not necessarily the sole ground, since expressive distortion may approach *ugliness (or, some would say, achieve it); yet its power and vitality may make the painting great. (On this issue, contrast J. Maritain, *Art and Scholasticism*, tr. J. F. Scanlan, New York 1930, with S. C. Pepper, *Aesthetic Quality* New York 1937.)

Value and Naturalness. Is aesthetic value natural or nonnatural? For some, to give a naturalistic definition of aesthetic value is to equate it with a psychological fact, such as giving pleasure or being desired. Whether it is inherently fallacious to propose such a definition has been much discussed. Many philosophers contend that a normative term (such as value or good) can never be reduced to nonnormative terms (such as pleasure or satisfaction), for any of several reasons: (1) that normative terms refer to a special nonempirical property, (2) that normative terms have a commending function that is absent from nonnormative terms, (3) that normative terms express attitudes and nonnormative terms do not. Others hold that a naturalistic definition framed with sufficient care—that is, by qualifying the conditions of the pleasure, or the nature of the satisfaction, involved—can correctly indicate what a normative term actually means in ordinary usage.

Value—Objective or Subjective? The objectivist regards the aesthetic value of an object as an internal property of it, which it possesses independently of any relation to a human perceiver who enjoys, approves, or admires it. The subjectivist takes aesthetic value to consist in some relation between the object and the perceiver (including the reader). The principal defense of subjectivism is that it is difficult to conceive of an object as having any value apart from some interest that is taken in it or apart from some desire that is satisfied by it. Objectivism, on the other hand, is often supported by the claim that it provides the only escape from relativism.

Value—Relative or Nonrelative? To say that aesthetic value is relative is to say that there can be two persons, one of whom says that a work of art is good and the other that it is not good, yet without really contradicting each other. If aesthetic value is objective, then it is not relative; but the subjectivist can choose between relativistic and nonrelativistic definitions. For example, if the subjectivist can first formulate the concept of the "perfect critic," as one who has all the desirable qualifications we could ask for in a critic—sensitivity, learning, sympathy, impartiality, etc.—then he might define the term "has aesthetic value" as "would be approved and admired by a majority of all perfect critics." This definition is subjective, but it is not relative, since whenever A says that a poem is good in this sense and

B denies it, A and B are contradicting each other, no matter who A and B may be. On the other hand, the subjectivist might define aesthetic value in relation to a particular culture or historical epoch; by this definition, when a critic praises a poem, he is saying that it is, or will be, or under certain conditions would be, enjoyed and approved by sensitive people in his own culture. According to such a definition, if A and B belong to different cultures, they cannot contradict each other by respectively affirming and denying that the poem is good.

The relativist usually argues that tastes vary and that what can be enjoyed by some people cannot be enjoyed by others; he urges that our definition of aesthetic value reflect this fact. In rebuttal it may be pointed out that there are all sorts of factors that affect this variability and no particular definition can accommodate them all. The only safe recourse for the relativist, then, is complete personal relativism, which transforms the critical judgment "This is a good poem" into something like "I now like this poem." This personal definition does bring out the alleged "noncognitive" features of critical evaluations: that their utterance reveals the speaker's attitude, his desire to commend something, or his hope of influencing others. But it seems to leave out the logical features of critical evaluations that allow disputes to arise over them; and it is implausible to claim that the personal definition correctly describes what most people mean when they praise poems.

Value a Capacity? It is also argued that we must distinguish between aesthetic value as something available to those properly prepared for it and the actual realizations of this value in experience. This distinction can be preserved by defining aesthetic value as the capacity to provide a certain kind of (presumably desirable) experience or a certain kind of (desirable) pleasure. This instrumentalist definition of aesthetic value would be subjective, but nonrelative; it would not be a naturalistic definition, since a normative term (desirable) would be retained in the definiendum. Then critical disputes over, say, the merits of a poem, would concern the question how great an aesthetic experience (or how intense an aesthetic pleasure) can be obtained from it under optimum conditions. If someone actually does derive a genuine aesthetic experience of some magnitude from the work, that will be sufficient evidence of its aesthetic value. If no such experience occurs, the critic may be able to show, by an analysis of the work, either that it is unlikely to occur or that it may occur in more adequately prepared perceivers. In any case, it will be possible to support the critical evaluation by reasons. But the appeal to such reasons will presuppose, what the aesthetician must also at some point justify, that the aesthetic experience is itself desirable.

Aesthetic Experience. The experience of listening to music or contemplating a painting is more different from the experience of reading a poem or novel than these are from each other. This is evident to the careful observer, even though there is much that we do not yet understand (but hope in time to learn by psychological investigation) about the exact nature of these experiences. The aesthetician asks whether there is such a thing as an aesthetic experience common to all the arts. It is important to know this if we wish to group all the arts together in one genus, and especially if aesthetic value is to be defined in terms of aesthetic experience.

There is general agreement that aesthetic experience is characterized at least by unusually intense absorption in a phenomenal object—in visual or auditory patterns or, in the case of prose fiction, the ostensible world of the work. Beyond this, the chief point at issue is the remoteness of aesthetic experience from the experiences of everyday life. A number of questions and positions are on hand, difficult to sort out satisfactorily. They range from Clive Bell's claim (in *Art*, 3–7) that there is a unique "aesthetic emotion"—the response to "significant form"—utterly different from any other emotion and owing nothing to life experiences, to I. A. Richards's contrary insistence (*Principles of Literary Criticism*, London and New York 1924, ch. 2, 32) that art differs only in degree from other things in its effects upon us.

"Moving" Quality of Art. Ancient and medieval philosophers were aware of something puzzling about the state of mind induced by works of art. That this response involves the emotions in a central way was suggested (and deplored) by Plato, who noted the excited state of the rhapsode (in the dialogue *Ion*) and of the theater audience (*Rep.* 603–10). When psychological aesthetics came into its full development during the 18th century, a major aim of British aesthetic investigation was to explain the characteristic effects of art—its capacity to move us and the special sort of enjoyment it provides. Various contributions to a solution of this problem were made by J. Addison, in his account of the "pleasures of the imagination" (*Spectator*, Nos. 409, 411–21; 1712), by F. Hutcheson (*An Inquiry into the Original of Our Ideas of Beauty and Virtue*, London 1725) and by E. *Burke (*A Philosophical Inquiry into the Sublime and the Beautiful*, London 1756), and by A. Alison (*Essays on the Nature and Principles of Taste,* Edinburgh 1790), among many others. These writers aimed to discover (some of them with the aid of associationist psychology) the nature of our feelings about the beautiful and the sublime and the basis of our pleasure in these qualities.

Detachment of Aesthetic Experience. It was Kant (*Critique of Judgment*, Berlin 1790) who attempted a radical separation of aesthetic enjoyment from ordinary enjoyments and identified the experience of beauty as one in which we take "pleasure without interest" in an object exhibiting "purposefulness without purpose," an object capable, by its form, of arousing the "free play" of the reproductive imagination in harmony with the general cognitive conditions of the understanding. By emphasizing this disinterestedness of aesthetic experience, Schopenhauer made of art an escape from the horror of life under the dominion of the Will to Live, with its ceaseless alternation between boredom and unsatisfied desire. He described aesthetic experience as a state of "will-less contemplation" of timeless Ideas, when the drives are laid temporarily to rest, as the self loses consciousness of itself and is no longer constrained to view the world under the "principle of sufficient reason."

This opposition between the aesthetic point of view and the practical point of view—between, for example, the painter's and the real-estate developer's way of looking at a landscape—has been widely emphasized in modern aesthetics. Several writers have stressed the "isolation" and "detachment" of aesthetic experience, its wholeness and self-sufficiency—notably E. Bullough in his famous paper " 'Psychical Distance' as a Factor in Art and an Aesthetic Principle" (*British Journal of Psychology*, 5, Cambridge 1912–13, 87–118). An object, according to Bullough, is psychically "distanced" when disconnected from ordinary practical needs and ends and regarded for its surface qualities and internal form. Nearly any object can be so regarded, but aesthetic objects are designed to facilitate this response —though they differ considerably in their degree of distance, ranging from geometrical abstraction to pictorial realism.

Intensity of the Aesthetic Experience. Schopenhauer's emphasis on denial of the Will was violently rejected by Nietzsche (see the posthumously collected notes, *The Will to Power,* tr. A. M. Ludovici, 2d ed., New York 1910–11). Art, he insisted, does not induce resignation but "affirmation" of life in all its aspects; it is an expression of the Will to Power. Later writers have tried to make room for something of this view in stressing the intensity of aesthetic experience, its "heightened consciousness" and the sense of increased vitality—not the absence of emotion, or its release, but its ordering into a harmonious tension. This has been called "synaesthesis," the balance or poise of impulses, opposed without frustration (see I. A. Richards et al., *The Foundations of Aesthetics,* London 1922, 72–91).

Attempted Synthesis. A significant attempt to do justice to these divergent (though not necessarily incompatible) points, as well as others, is that by John Dewey in *Art as Experience,* New York 1934, esp. ch. 3. Dewey's aim was to show how the special traits of aesthetic experience, those we cherish most, grow out of a natural setting, as intensifications of traits found valuable in all experience. The organism interacts with its environment, doing and undergoing. Sometimes stretches of continuing experience take on an unusual degree of completeness: the impulses that are aroused at the start run their course; there is consummation and fulfillment. Then we have, not just experience, but "an experience." And when an experience is controlled by attention to sensuous quality, and takes on a pervasive and distinct character, it is aesthetic experience, continuous but articulated, coherent but rhythmic, dynamic, cumulative, and inherently satisfying.

The Thomistic Tradition. This tradition also, as carried on by a number of contemporary thinkers (see e.g., J. Maritain, *Art and Scholasticism;* É. Gilson, *Painting and Reality,* New York 1957), has aimed to do justice to the dominant traits, as well as the wide range, of aesthetic experiences and to correct other accounts by keeping more firmly in view the intellectual aspect of aesthetic enjoyment. St. Thomas's pregnant definition of beauty as *id quod visum placet* (ST 1.5.4 ad 1; cf. 1a2ae, 27.1) implies that in the perception of beauty, the exquisite intelligibility of the object, its possession of a form proportionate to the intellect itself (*proportio sive consonantia*), affords that delight mixed with exaltation that characterizes aesthetic experience. This relation to the cognitive faculty, which is essential to beauty, explains its restriction to sight and sound—we derive sensuous pleasure from perfumes, for example, but odors are not (strictly speaking) beautiful.

General Conclusion. These theorists and others have guided us to an understanding of many important features of aesthetic experience, though some questions remain unsettled. Roughly speaking, we can locate the peculiar character of that experience in the combination of two distinguishable objects of delight. First, we respond to pattern or gestalt as such; we desire the perception of order: symmetry, geometrical regularity, rational arrangement. Second, we respond to human qualities that emerge in the phenomenal field: to embodied energy, calmness, joy, force, tenderness, etc. With the first is connected the unity and repose of aesthetic experience; with the latter, our capacity to be moved and shaken. Works of art differ enormously according to which aspects are dominant. But speaking generally, in art we confront and cognize a complex of elements and relations making up, through formal cooperation, a satisfactory whole. Out of this whole emerge certain qualities, of various degrees of intensity, that engage our attention and our feelings. In a way subtly different from the feeling of ordinary life, we are lifted to a fresher and more vital plane of awareness, the joy of the spirit answering to the radiance of the object.

See also ART (PHILOSOPHY); BEAUTY; LITERATURE, NATURE AND FUNCTION OF; LITERARY CRITICISM, HISTORY OF.

Bibliography: Among the useful anthologies in English are E. VIVAS and M. KRIEGER, eds., *The Problems of Aesthetics* (New York 1953). M. M. RADER, ed., *A Modern Book of Esthetics* (3d ed. New York 1960). M. WEITZ, ed., *Problems in Aesthetics* (New York 1959). W. ELTON, ed., *Aesthetics and Language* (New York 1954). W. E. KENNICK, ed., *Art and Philosophy* (New York 1964). A. HOFSTADTER and R. KUHNS, eds., *Philosophies of Art and Beauty* (New York 1964). K. ASCHENBRENNER and A. ISENBERG, eds., *Aesthetic Theories* (New York 1965). A. SESONSKE, ed., *What is Art?* (London 1965).

On the history of aesthetics, see K. E. GILBERT and H. KUHN, *A History of Esthetics* (rev. ed. Bloomington 1953). M. C. BEARDSLEY, *A Short History of Western Aesthetics* (New York 1965). E. DE BRUYNE, *Études d'esthétique médiévale,* 3 v. (Bruges 1946). A. FONTAINE, *Les Doctrines d'art en France* (Paris 1909). S. H. MONK, *The Sublime: A Study of Critical Theories in 18th Century England* (New York 1935; Ann Arbor pa. 1960). E. CASSIRER, *The Philosophy of the Enlightenment,* tr. C. A. KOELLN and J. P. PETTEGROVE (Princeton 1951). W. J. HIPPLE, *The Beautiful, the Sublime, and the Picturesque in Eighteenth-Century British Aesthetic Theory* (Carbondale, Ill. 1957). G. MORPURGO-TAGLIABUE, *L'Esthétique contemporaine* (Milan 1960).

On classical and contemporary problems of aesthetics, see M. C. BEARDSLEY, *Aesthetics* (New York 1958). F. E. SPARSHOTT, *The Structure of Aesthetics* (Toronto 1963). J. STOLNITZ, *Aesthetics and Philosophy of Art Criticism* (Boston 1960).

[M. C. BEARDSLEY]

AETERNA CAELI GLORIA, the hymn for Lauds in the ferial office on Fridays throughout the year in the present Roman *Breviary (1965). Originally the initial letter of each line was in alphabetic sequence through the letter "T," except that the fourth line repeated initial "C." To maintain the correct alphabetic sequence the orthography of the manuscript tradition must be retained in lines 9 and 11 (see Anal Hymn 51:33). The text printed in the Roman Breviary does not preserve the alphabetic structure in its entirety. The meter of the hymn is the iambic dimeter. The author, once thought to be Pope Gregory I (the Great), is unknown. In content this hymn is a prayer to Christ for light to see one's duties and for the increase of the three theological virtues of faith, hope, and charity.

Bibliography: Julian DictHym 24–25. AnalHymn 51:32–34. A. S. WALPOLE, ed., *Early Latin Hymns* (Cambridge, Eng. 1922) 276–279. M. BRITT, ed., *The Hymns of the Breviary and Missal* (new ed. New York 1948) 68–69. Szövérffy AnnLatHymn 1:142, 214.

[H. DRESSLER]

AETERNA CHRISTI MUNERA, an Ambrosian hymn written in iambic dimeter. Nearly all modern scholars unhesitatingly assign the authorship of this hymn to St. *Ambrose. The author intended this composition of eight strophes to be used on the feast days of martyrs. In the course of time, however, the hymn was selected for use on the feast days of Apostles also, and this entailed certain changes in the sequence of lines and adaptations especially notable in the first strophe. In the present Roman *Breviary (1965) the first (with adaptations), second, sixth, and seventh strophes, with an added doxology, form the hymn for Matins in the Common of Apostles outside of Eastertide. In the Common of Many Martyrs both in and out of Easter time the first (with adaptations), third, fourth, fifth, and eighth strophes are used for the hymn at Matins. In each case the hymn praises the victory of the Apostles or martyrs and expresses admiration for their constancy in specifically described trials and sufferings.

See also HYMNOLOGY.

Bibliography: Julian DictHym 24–25. A. S. WALPOLE, ed., *Early Latin Hymns* (Cambridge, Eng. 1922) 104–108. M. BRITT, ed., *The Hymns of the Breviary and Missal* (new ed. New York 1948) 325–326. W. BULST, ed., *Hymni Latini antiquissimi LXXV* (Heidelberg 1956) 52, 185. Szövérffy AnnLatHymn 50–52, 62, 66, 116, 174.

[H. DRESSLER]

AETERNE RERUM CONDITOR, the words of the opening line of the first strophe of the hymn for Lauds in the present Roman Breviary, for the Sundays from January 14 to the first Sunday in Lent and from October 1 to the first Sunday in Advent. The use of this hymn at the early canonical hours goes back to *Caesarius of Arles (d. 542), who prescribed its use in his Rule (*Sanctarum virginum regulae* 69; *S. Caesarii opera omnia* 2:121). The text in the Breviary follows the revisions introduced under Pope Urban VIII (d. 1644), changing the older reading in the second, third, and seventh strophes. This hymn is acknowledged by all as an authentic work of St. *Ambrose. *Augustine (*Retract.* 20.2; CSEL 36:97–98) quotes two lines of the fourth strophe and names Ambrose as the author. The thought and at times the very wording of several lines bear a striking similarity with passages in Ambrose's *Hexaemeron* (CSEL 32.1:201). The meter of the hymn is the iambic dimeter. In five successive strophes, Ambrose gives a mystical interpretation of the significance of the crowing of the cock (*gallicinium*). Barring the purely scriptural animal metaphors, such as the lamb, the wolf, and the lion of Juda, the usage of this hymn is one of the few animal motifs in early Latin hymnology.

Bibliography: Chevalier RepHymn 1:647. Julian DictHym 1:26. A. S. WALPOLE, ed., *Early Latin Hymns* (Cambridge, Eng. 192) 27–34. A. M. BRITT, ed., *The Hymns of the Breviary and Missal* (new ed. New York 1948). Raby ChrLP 33–41. W. BULST, ed., *Hymni Latini antiquissimi LXXV* (Heidelberg 1956) 39, 162. Szövérffy AnnLatHymn 1:56–58.

[H. DRESSLER]

AETERNE REX ALTISSIME, opening words of three hymns written in iambic dimeters. The best known is that employed in the Roman liturgy for the Feast of the Ascension. There are two forms of this hymn; the one of eight strophes is the basis for the text currently used in the Breviary. The author of this hymn is unknown. F. J. Mone conjectured that originally it consisted of the present first four strophes written by St. *Ambrose and that an inferior 5th-century poet added four more strophes. The longer text of 14 strophes (including those in the Roman usage) is the form of the hymn as it is found in the *Mozarabic rite. The current Roman Breviary assigns the hymn of eight strophes for use at Matins in the ferial and Sunday Offices during Ascension time. The Breviary text is a much-altered version; only the third and sixth strophes follow the manuscript reading. In content the hymn celebrates Christ's victory over death, recalls the homage due to Him from those in heaven, on earth, and beneath the earth, and begs Him as man's future judge for forgiveness and the crown of eternal glory.

The second hymn dates from the 13th century and was written for use at Vespers on the feast of Christ's *crown of thorns, which was reputedly brought to France by King *Louis IX and venerated in the Ste. Chapelle in Paris. The author is unknown. The hymn has five strophes, of which the first four have alternating rhyme. The composition expresses the great joy of Paris at being the repository of Christ's crown, which mystically signifies Christ Himself, the crown of men and women living in chastity and the reward of those living in the married state.

The third hymn also honors the crown of thorns. Similar in structure and content to the previous composition, it incorporates two complete strophes from yet another hymn in honor of the crown of thorns, *Corona Christi capitis*.

Bibliography: F. J. MONE, ed., *Lateinische Hymnen des Mittelalters*, 3 v. (Freiburg 1853–55) 1:228–229. AnalHymn 12: 20–21; 27:96–97; 51:94–95; 52:15. G. M. DREVES and C. BLUME, eds., *Ein Jahrtausend lateinischer Hymnendichtung*, 2 v. (Leipzig 1909) 2:136. Julian DictHym 1:26–27. A. S. WALPOLE, ed., *Early Latin Hymns* (Cambridge, Eng. 1922) 361–364. M. BRITT, ed., *The Hymns of the Breviary and Missal* (new ed. New York 1948). Connelly Hymns 102–103. Szövérffy AnnLatHymn 2: 202–203; 254–255; 258; 449.

[H. DRESSLER]

AETERNI PATRIS, the name of two papal documents of Pius IX and Leo XIII. The first is the apostolic letter of June 29, 1868, convoking the Vatican Council I; it indicates the office of the pope as guardian of faith and morals, the role of ecumenical councils, and summarizes the then prevailing dangers to faith and morals. The second document is the encyclical of Leo XIII dated Aug. 4, 1879, and written to restore scholastic philosophy in general and that of St. Thomas Aquinas in particular. Beginning with a consideration of the Church's concern for teaching true philosophy because of its relation to theology, the Pope declares that many modern evils stem from false philosophy. The encyclical mentions the esteem in which St. Thomas has been held and urges the revival of St. Thomas's philosophy and of his spirit of investigation.

See also SCHOLASTIC METHOD; SCHOLASTIC PHILOSOPHY; SCHOLASTICISM.

Bibliography: PIUS IX, *Acta Pii IX* 4:412–423. R. AUBERT, *Le Pontificat de Pie IX, 1846–1878* (Paris 1952). LEO XIII, *Acta Leonis XIII* 1 (1878–79) 255–285. Denz 3135–40. L. FOUCHER, *La Philosophie catholique en France au XIXe siècle avant la renaissance thomiste et dans son rapport avec elle, 1800–1880* (Paris 1955) 237–268. B. M. BONANSEA, "Pioneers of the Nineteenth Century Scholastic Revival in Italy," NewSchol 28 (1954) 1–37. J. COLLINS, "Leo XIII and the Philosophic Approach to

Modernity," *Leo XIII and the Modern World,* ed. E. GARGAN (New York 1961) 181–209. C. A. HART, "America's Response to the Encyclical *Aeterni Patris,*" *American Catholic Philosophical Association Bulletin* (1929) 98–117. G. F. RITZEL, "Some Historical Background of the Encyclical *Aeterni Patris,*" *Nuntius Aulae* 38 (1956) 135–155. A. ALEXANDER, "Thomas Aquinas and the Encyclical Letter," *Princeton Review* N.S. 5 (Jan. 1880) 245–326.

[W. F. HOGAN]

AFFILIATION, EDUCATIONAL

A term applied in education denoting the relationship of an educational institution associated with another but independently operated. The affiliating institution is usually larger and has set certain academic standards which must be met by the affiliate. Such a program was established for Catholic secondary schools and colleges by The Catholic University of America in 1912 and continues to function as a voluntary consultative service for Catholic institutions of the U.S. and those conducted by American religious communities in foreign countries. Its primary purpose is to render to Catholic institutions above the elementary level such assistance as is possible through the intelligent, informed, and alert leadership found within the affiliates themselves. Thus, the affiliate in no way becomes dependent upon the University, but rather operates independently and entirely on its own merits, working with the University to improve and develop in accord with the affiliate's own objectives. Cooperative and voluntary in nature, affiliation is aimed at the individual and collective improvement of Catholic education through a series of specific and practical services adapted to the needs of Catholic institutions.

Historical Background. In the later part of the 19th century and the early 1900s, systems of affiliation were used as an accrediting technique whereby an institution of higher education, especially state universities, recognized and approved such secondary schools as were able to meet its curricular and instructional standards. Since these standards were usually set in terms of the institution's own admission requirements and were maintained within the affiliate by the application of one or more sanctions (e.g., inspections, reports, testing, and scholarship ratings), two benefits commonly accrued: (1) improved articulation between school and college with graduates of the affiliate being admitted to the college by certification rather than by examination, and (2) the standardization and unification of the public school systems of the country. With the later development and wide acceptance of the accrediting system, however, educational institutions in general no longer considered affiliation necessary; although in individual cases, some colleges continued to be affiliated with state, municipal, or private universities (*see* ACCREDITATION, EDUCATIONAL).

During these same years Catholic educators recognized similar needs for the growing number of Catholic schools but feared the influence of the secular system because of the materialistic philosophies then so prevalent. It was this situation that prompted the bishops of the Third Plenary Council of Baltimore in 1884 to set up machinery for enlarging and improving Catholic educational opportunities and to found a national Catholic university not only as the crown of the system but also as a potential unifying and guiding agent for it. Thus the original constitutions of The Catholic University of America (1889), approved by the Congregation of Seminaries and Universities, authorized the affiliation of other Catholic educational institutions to the University, and Pope Leo XIII, in his apostolic letter of the same year, *Magni nobis gaudii,* emphasized affiliation as a function of the new University: "We exhort you all that you shall take care to affiliate with your university, your seminaries, colleges, and other Catholic institutions according to the plan suggested in the Constitutions, in such a manner as not to destroy their autonomy."

Although it was not practical for the new University to implement these directives immediately by a comprehensive program of affiliation, the first three University rectors actively promoted the general cause of Catholic education and took positive steps toward such a goal. Early efforts included encouraging the locating of religious houses of studies near the University and the affiliating of St. Paul Seminary (Minn.) in 1894, the beginning of a plan of affiliation for the theological curricula of major seminaries, one which has remained entirely distinct from the 1912 school-college plan.

By the 1910s a phenomenal growth in the number of Catholic schools had taken place so that the need for unification had become more acute and minimal standardization of the system by a Catholic agency was viewed by many as highly desirable. By this time also the University had expanded and strengthened its academic program to include a full course of professional education so that Rev. Thomas Edward *Shields, then dean of the university's Catholic Sisters College, and Right Rev. Edward A. *Pace, university director of studies, saw in the original directives from Rome regarding affiliation an answer to the problem. Thus on April 17, 1912, the fourth rector of the University, Most Rev. Thomas J. *Shahan, submitted to the board of trustees a detailed practical plan devised by Shields, and the first comprehensive plan of affiliation under Catholic auspices was established.

Scope and Growth. While the 1912 plan, following the affiliation pattern of its day, adopted reports and testing as sanctions to maintain quantitative and qualitative standards among affiliates, Shields sought goals broader than merely recognition for Catholic institutions. He viewed affiliation as part of a master plan for up-grading curricula and improving instructional outcome, and as supplementary to university efforts in the field of teacher training and in the production of a body of Catholic educational literature. By placing emphasis on the high school as the middle school of the system and developing its curriculum and psychologically sound teaching principles, he was able to make a substantial contribution to the overall quality and articulation of the total system.

By the 1920s the pioneering stage in the unification and coordination of the Catholic system of the U.S. was fast coming to an end. The accreditation movement had also progressed to a point at which it was no longer felt that a form of accreditation apart from the secular agencies was advantageous to Catholic education. Since after Shields' death in 1921, however, little was done in recognition of these new trends, by the 1930s reorganization of the program was acutely overdue. In 1938 the rector, Most Rev. Joseph M. Corrigan, appointed a new committee, with Roy J. Deferrari, then secretary general, serving as chairman. By 1939 the affiliation program was completely revised and considerably expanded in scope.

The accreditation function was replaced by an emphasis on systematic, cooperative development of an affiliate leading to proper accreditation by the secular agencies. The visitation-evaluation, patterned after current accrediting procedures, was adopted as the primary supervisory technique for the individualized servicing of an affiliate. The other services of affiliation were viewed as means to reinforce this fundamental objective. At this time also the program was expanded to include junior colleges, teacher training institutions, and hospital and collegiate schools of nursing, and the minor seminary (secondary school and junior college) and the philosophy division of the major seminary (general college) were officially included within the regular academic categories of affiliation.

Reorganization. During the 1950s and 1960s, working out of the secretary general's office, the 1939 plan was developed and strengthened. The old high school testing program, which had fallen into disrepute, was rebuilt on new scientific testing principles and its use was made optional to affiliates. Institutional evaluation techniques with special concern for the Catholic character of the affiliate and its special purposes were perfected. The common and special problems of Catholic education were systematically treated by regular quarterly bulletins and comprehensive documents, and University workshops were initiated for the discussion of academic problems by representatives of the affiliates themselves. By 1960, with Deferrari's appointment as full-time director of the program, the direct cooperative participation of affiliates in carrying on the program was further emphasized by inviting qualified affiliates to serve as members of evaluating teams and on curriculum and textbook committees. In 1963 the affiliation of schools of nursing was dropped in order to redouble efforts to keep affiliates abreast of new trends and developments in the field of general education.

Quantitative growth since 1939 has also been steady: the number of high schools increased from 151 to 440 in 1963; 4-year general colleges from 54 to 184; and the new categories of junior college and teacher training institutions reached totals of 88 and 30 respectively. Of the grand total of 767 affiliates in 1963, 130 were seminaries or included seminary departments and 105 were for the education of sisters only. All episcopal provinces in the U.S. were represented with affiliated institutions located in 127 archdioceses and dioceses, as well as 2 dioceses in Puerto Rico and 22 foreign dioceses. In assisting these affiliates, the University reached a student population of more than 250,000 and a total faculty population of approximately 20,000. Geographically, the affiliates are distributed throughout 45 states, the District of Columbia, and 8 foreign countries.

Administrative Structure. The comprehensive and individualized approach of affiliation to Catholic educational problems requires an equally comprehensive administrative structure. This is obtained by drawing on the general resources and personnel of the University while a desired unity and continuity of operation is achieved through a trained affiliation office staff working directly under the director of the program, who serves also as chairman of a standing committee of affiliation. This committee of University faculty and administrators functions as a policy-making group under the academic senate and the rector of the University and serves in a consultative capacity on academic and professional matters. Qualified evaluators, subject-matter experts, and other needed specialists are obtained from among the affiliates themselves and from other educational and scholarly associations.

Bibliography: R. J. DEFERRARI, "The Affiliation of Catholic Educational Institutions with the Catholic University of America," *Catholic University of America Bulletin* 28.2 (Oct. 1960). *The Programs of Affiliation of The Catholic University of America* (Washington 1960). Catholic University of America, *Courses of Study for Affiliated High Schools* (Washington 1912); *Affiliation of High Schools and Colleges* (Washington 1913–38); *Program of Affiliation* (Washington 1939–). R. WATRIN, *The Founding and Development of the Program of Affiliation of The Catholic University of America: 1912–1939* (Washington 1965).

[R. J. DEFERRARI]

AFFINITY

Affinity is a relationship of persons deriving from marriage. It arises from a valid marriage, whether consummated or not, between two baptized persons, and constitutes a diriment impediment to subsequent marriages between a man and blood relations of his wife, and vice versa. According to the Code of Canon Law (CIC cc.97, 1077), affinity does not beget affinity; therefore, the blood relations of a man are not impeded by affinity from contracting marriage with the blood relations of his wife, nor are those of the woman with the blood relations of her husband.

In the direct line, the impediment of affinity extends indefinitely either ascending or descending, while in the collateral line it extends only to the second degree inclusive. No generations exist in affinity as they do in consanguinity. Hence the husband and wife are not affines to each other, but are the source or stipes of affinity. The terms of computation or relationship are "line" and "degree" as in consanguinity, and refer to the blood relations of the respective consorts. The determination of the line and degree of affinity follows that of consanguinity, except that a person related to one consort by a certain line and degree of consanguinity becomes related to the other consort in the same line and degree. (*See* CONSANGUINITY.)

In the first degree of the ascending direct line, affinity would exist as a diriment impediment to marriage with one's father-in-law, mother-in-law, stepfather, and stepmother; in the second degree with one's wife's or husband's grandmother, wife's or husband's grandfather, the grandmother's husband, and the grandfather's wife; in the third degree with the wife's or husband's great-grandfather, wife's or husband's great-grandmother. In the first degree of the descending direct line, the affines whom one could not marry would be the son-in-law, daughter-in-law; stepson, stepdaughter; in the second degree, the granddaughter's husband, the grandson's wife, the husband's grandson, the wife's granddaughter. In the first degree of the collateral line the affines are the brother-in-law, sister-in-law, husband's uncle, wife's aunt; in the second degree they are the husband's first cousin, wife's first cousin, husband's nephew, wife's niece.

History. Affinity was an impediment to marriage already in the Mosaic Law. A man was prohibited in the direct line from marrying his stepmother (Lv 18.8, 20.11; Dt 22.30, 27.20); his daughter-in-law (Lv 18.15, 20.12), his stepdaughter, stepson's daughter and stepdaughter's daughter (Lv 18.17), his mother-in-law (Lv 18.17, 20.14, Dt 27.23), and his stepsister (Lv 18.11); in the collateral line, his paternal uncle's wife (Lv 18.14, 20.20), his brother's wife (Lv 18.16, 20.21) except where the levirate law would apply, and the sister of his wife, the latter still living (Lv 18.18). Contrary to the last example, a man could marry two sisters simultaneously before the time of Moses; e.g., Jacob married Lia and Rachel simultaneously (Gn 29).

Although the above texts are addressed to the male, they are applicable reciprocally to the female also. Affinity in each case did not cease through death or divorce of the spouses who created it. The penalty for disregarding the impediment in the direct line was most frequently death (Lv 20.11, 12, 14). In the collateral line the penalty probably did not exceed the legal illegitimizing of offspring.

Carnal relations, licit or illicit, did not produce affinity. Nor was it marriage alone that created affinity but rather the contract of solemn engagement or Sponsalia, which would be the equivalent of a ratified marriage. Reasons for declaring affinity an impediment might be cited as: (1) the respect and reserve that a person should naturally possess toward near relatives through blood or marriage, for marriage identified husband and wife in their unity of flesh (Gn 2.24); (2) the scandals that could arise from marriages between persons of close familial ties, in view of Oriental residence customs.

The Tree of Affinity in a French manuscript of the "Decretum" of Gratian, c. 1180. Noe supports the lower branches of the tree, while at the top Adam and Eve steady the uppermost of the series of small roundels which carry the names of the family relationships.

In the New Testament two instances reflect application of affinity bars to marriage. The first was Herod Antipas's marriage with his brother's wife, Herodias (Mt 14.3, 4). The union was both adulterous, since Herod's brother was probably still living, and incestuous, as violating the Mosaic Law of affinity, which also obligated strangers living among the Jews (Lv 18.26). The second was the case of incest at Corinth mentioned in 1 Cor 5.1, in which a man was rebuked for marrying his stepmother, a crime punished by excommunication. Outside of these two cases, nothing more anent affinity appears in the New Testament.

Roman Law. The Roman law concerning affinity (*adfinitas*) was founded upon valid marriage (*justae nuptiae*) and related one consort to the kin of the other (CorpIurCivDig 38.10.4.3, 8; Inst 1.10.6–10). Apparently affinity was considered an impediment only in the direct line reaching to infinity, but not in the collateral line (Dig 23.2.14.4). Prohibition of marriage was limited to affinity involving one's stepfather or stepmother and stepdaughter or stepson; and between father-in-law or mother-in-law and daughter-in-law or son-in-law (Dig 38.10.4.3–5), not descending one from another or from a common stock.

Conciliar Decrees. The Mosaic Law and Roman law were the sources used by the Church to formulate its own rules of affinity. For the first 3 centuries, the Mosaic Law was probably the only source. With decrees of Church councils such as those of Elvira (300–306) and Neo-Caesarea (314–325), and the Council of Rome (402), there were departures made from the Mosaic law, extending the impediment beyond the limits set by the Old Tesatment. Elvira forbade marriage with a stepdaughter and stepsister (c. 61, 66; Mansi 2.15, 16; Hefele-Leclercq 1.256–257); Neo-Caesarea forbade marriage of a woman with her brother-in-law (c. 2; Mansi 2.540; Hefele-Leclercq 1.328). The Council of Rome forbade marriage with the deceased wife's sister and a deceased uncle's wife (c. 9, 11; Mansi 3.1137; Hefele-Leclercq 2.136–137). These decrees easily passed into the civil codes in the middle of the 4th century (CorpIurCivCod 1.5.5.9). Later councils extended the impediment still further to the widow of the paternal or maternal uncle, reaching as far as the seventh degree, and civil codes followed suit (e.g., Law of Visigoths 1.3.5.1 in MGL 1).

The ambit of affinity gradually evolved, particularly in the collateral line. From the 8th century the basis of affinity was changed from the marital contract (*justae nuptiae*) to carnal intercourse (*unitas carnis*). With corroboration from Scripture (Gn 2.24; 1 Cor 6.16), St. Basil (379) had condemned marriage between a brother-in-law and sister-in-law (Letter 160, PG 32: 623). St. Augustine mentioned the case later (*Contra Faustum* 1.22.61; PL 42:438; CSEL 25.1.656–657; *Civ* CSEL 40.2), and so did the author of a letter attributed by St. Bede to St. Gregory (Mansi 10.407; Bede, *Hist. Eccl.* 1.27 in PL 95.60). The practical rule that resulted from this was that *unitas carnis*—carnal intercourse—made two persons one and established identity of relationship between oneself and relatives of a spouse, hence putting affinity on a plane with consanguinity. The Synod of Rome (721) then made this a juridic rule (Mansi 12.263), and Gratian made it an adage of law (CorpIurCan C.35 q.2, 3 c.15; C.35 q.5 c.3). The classical definition of affinity through Gratian became relationship of persons emanating from carnal intercourse.

By the 10th century the similarity between the impediments of affinity and those of consanguinity became complete. Roland Bandinellus (Pope Alexander III, 1159–81), a disciple of Gratian, concerning their mutual computation of degree stated: "The first type of affinity walks abreast [*aequis passibus ambulat*] with consanguinity" (CorpIurCan C.35 q.1). In the many vicissitudes during this period the two impediments reached as far as the seventh degree, although the actual force of the last two degrees fluctuated from one area to the next between diriment and impedient.

Since carnal relations (*unitas carnis*) alone formed the basis of affinity, it was calculated identically with consanguinity. Most commentators became adherents of this principle with, however, some notable exceptions such as St. Thomas, who maintained against the majority that it was marriage and not copula that formed the true basis of affinity (ST Suppl. 55.4.2). From the basis of *unitas carnis,* logic pushed the experts to develop their speculations about affinity unhindered. They distinguished four kinds of affinity. The first was that arising from marital (licit) or extramarital (illicit) sexual relations. Just when or where the concept of illicit affinity arose is unknown; however, some authors find the first trace in the Pseudo-Isidorian decretals of the 9th century. Once affinity was based upon sexual intercourse, the lack of ecclesiastical precepts respecting a public form of marriage created the difficulty of distinguishing between licit and illicit affinity.

The second kind of affinity arose between the man and the affines of the woman by the first type of affinity and vice versa. In this type a man could become related to the affines of a widow whom he married, and vice-versa. Extending this still further, the third kind of affinity would appear in a marriage between a man and the affines related to the woman by the second kind of affinity. These three main classes of affinity are illustrated by this example: Roger and Sylvia are married. The latter's first cousin, Catherine, is married to Julius. Catherine is associated with Roger by the first kind of affinity, Julius with Roger by the second kind of affinity, and following the death of Julius's wife and his remarriage, his new wife will be associated to Roger by the third type of affinity. The fourth type arose not from the sexual act but from generation and touched the offspring born of a second marriage, making them affines to the relatives of the first parent within the fourth degree (*soboles ex secundis nuptiis*).

The principle of exogamy was not without benefit in the fusing of diverse peoples, but it caused inconveniences also in its subtle and complicated computations. The fourth Council of the Lateran (Mansi 22.1028) in its 50th canon abolished all but the first kind of affinity and restricted its prohibitive power to the fourth degree in the collateral line arising from conjugal or extramarital carnal intercourse. The ancient rule had stated: affinity begets affinity. The new position stated the contrary: affinity does not beget affinity. The simple ancient definition of affinity, "relationship of persons proceeding from sexual intercourse" had to be augmented to read, "between a man and the blood relations of the woman, and vice versa." However valuable were these changes, illicit affinity remained to vex legalists. Also, legitimate affinity upheld to the fourth degree in the collateral line and to infinity in the direct line was still somewhat awkward to deal with.

The Council of Trent (1563) was unsatisfied with the work of the Lateran Council. In the collateral line it limited illicit affinity to the second degree. It upheld licit affinity to the fourth degree, as had the Lateran Council. It did not completely solve the difficulties of which it so vehemently complained in reforming the former law, and subsequent appeals from many bishops appeared in the Curia for relaxation of the impediment. The Council of the Vatican (1869–70) made no further changes.

It was left to the *Code of Canon Law to make radical and far-reaching changes. Its most extreme modification was the change of the very basis of affinity from sexual intercourse to valid marriage entered into according to proper form. This represented a regression to the Roman civil law. As an impediment, it bound each spouse to the blood relations of the other. In the direct line the impediment extended to infinity but was limited in the collateral line to the second degree of affinity (CIC c.1077).

Multiple Affinity. Affinity can become multiple in only two cases: (1) where the consanguinity from which affinity arises is itself multiple; e.g., John marries Apollonia; if Apollonia is twice related to Miriam in two different degrees of consanguinity, John is also twice related to Miriam in the same degree of affinity; (2) by successive marriage with the blood relations of a deceased consort; e.g., if Peter marries Josephine, and after her death marries Rita, her sister, he would have double affinity with a third sister, Margaret, in the first collateral degree and with a daughter of Margaret in the second collateral degree. Since affinity does not exist between the blood relations of the husband and those of the wife, two brothers might marry two sisters, or a father and son might marry a mother and daughter, or a son might marry a mother and his father the daughter of that mother.

Extent of Impediment. Since the wording of CIC canon 97.1 is not clear, it was formerly a disputed question whether affinity arises from every valid marriage or only from a sacramental marriage. Now, after a reply from the Holy Office (ActApS 49:77), it is settled that the word "valid" is not limited to sacramental marriages, i.e., between two baptized persons. If affinity would be contracted between unbaptized persons, however, it would automatically become an impediment to marriage when even one of the parties became baptized. With the unbaptized, civil codes determine the binding force of the impediment of affinity where the divine law does not certainly hold. If two infidels marry, although bound by affinity that is pronounced a diriment impediment by the state, they marry invalidly. In the United States, each state has its own law concerning affinity, and it must be studied to determine its force. In the District of Columbia, for example, a man may not marry his stepmother, a stepdaughter, grandfather's wife, grandson's wife, mother-in-law, wife's grandmother, wife's granddaughter, son's wife [D.C. Code (1940) 30.101].

Dispensation. Affinity is perpetual as an impediment and is not extinguished by passage of time or death of one of the parties. It is certain that it is an impediment of merely ecclesiastical law, therefore, the Church can and has dispensed from it in every degree. However, she does not as a rule dispense from affinity in the first degree of the direct line in a consummated marriage; the persons can neither enter into nor revalidate a contract, although some rare cases of such dispensation have appeared. When the marriage is not consummated, dispensation may be obtained from the apostolic delegate.

Collateral affinity in the second degree is a minor impediment; consequently, a dispensation once granted from it is valid despite error and regardless of obreption or subreption. It is common opinion among canonists that this impediment serves little purpose and could be expunged without harm to the Church or society. If collateral affinity is partially in the third degree, it does not constitute an impediment; however, first degree mixed with the second is a major impediment.

For a just reason the local ordinaries may dispense from the impediment of affinity in the second degree of the equal collateral line, which is a minor impediment. For a grave and urgent cause where there is danger in delay, and no possibility of postponing a marriage to receive dispensation from the Holy See, ordinaries may dispense also from the first degree of the equal collateral line and from the first degree mixed with the second.

Oriental Law. Among the Orientals, there are three types of affinity. The first type is the only one identical with the Latin rite, existing between each spouse and the blood relations of the other. It arises from a valid marriage, consummated or not, and is called affinity from digeneia (CrebAllat 68.1nn1–3). This kind binds all Orientals and is an impediment in the direct line in all degrees, and in the collateral line to the fourth degree inclusive. The Orientals follow their own method of calculation of degrees. In the direct line it is identical with the Latins; in the collateral line it is computed by counting the number of persons on both sides, instead of one side as in the Latin rite. Multiple affinity is computed as in the Latin rite.

The second species of affinity exists between the blood relations of one consort and blood relations of the other (CrebAllat 68.2). It is an impediment only to the fourth degree inclusive and binds the following Orientals: Chaldeans, Melchites, Rumanians, Bulgarians, Russians, Greeks from Greece and Turkey, and Ethiopians. It is not multiplied. The local hierarch can dispense from this impediment in any degree. It is computed by determining the degrees each affine is distant from each of the spouses from whose marriage affinity arose and adding them together.

The third species of affinity arises from trigeneia, i.e., from three marriages: two completed, a third contemplated but impeded (CrebAllat 68.3), and is the relationship existing between relations by affinity of one spouse and the blood relations of the other spouse. This might result in two cases: (1) when two persons successively contract marriage with a same third person with the previous bond dissolved; (2) when two persons successively marry two others who are blood relatives. Subject to this rule are Catholic Russians, Bulgarians, and Greeks from Greece and Turkey, as well as many dissident Oriental groups. Each consort acquires affinity by trigeneia with those who are affines to the other spouse through the second marriage from digeneia. The degree of affinity in trigeneia is computed by determining the degree of affinity of each spouse with affines from the second marriage through digeneia, which relates them in the same degree to the other spouse in trigeneia. The impediment does not exceed the first degree and is never multiple. The local hierarch has ordinary power to grant dispensations.

Bibliography: P. DIB, DDC 1:264–285. *See* CONSANGUINITY.
Illustration credit: H. P. Kraus, New York.

[C. HENRY]

AFFLIGEM, ABBEY OF, Benedictine abbey in Hekelgem, Brabant, Archdiocese of *Mechelen-Brussels, Belgium; dedicated to SS. Peter and Paul. It owes its origin to the conversion (*c.* 1083) of six thieving knights who were moved by the preaching of Wéry, a monk of Saint-Pierre (Ghent). They were soon joined by two monks from Saint-Airly (Verdun), one of whom, Fulgentius, became the first abbot (1088). In 1519 monks from *Egmond introduced at Affligem the reform of *Bursfeld. Affligem was incorporated into the episcopal *mensa* (mensal income) of Mechelen (1560) and governed thereafter by provosts, among whom was Benedict of Haeften. In 1628 Affligem adopted the reform of Lorraine and affiliated with the Congregation of the Presentation of Notre Dame, which was dissolved in 1654. The abbey was suppressed by French Revolutionaries (1796), but the community regrouped at Termonde (1838) and affiliated with the Congregation of Subiaco (1857). A colony from Termonde regained possession of the ruins of Affligem (1870). Many priories depended on this abbey; three of them became abbeys—Vlierbeek (near Louvain), *Maria Laach, and *Saint-André-lez-Bruges. Currently the monks of Affligem participate actively in the *liturgical movement in the Dutch-speaking provinces of Belgium. Affligem missionaries have gone to South Africa.

Bibliography: U. BERLIÈRE, DHGE 1:672–674. A. M. ZIMMERMANN, LexThK² 1:168–169. Cottineau 1:23–24.

[N. N. HUYGHEBAERT]

AFFRE, DENIS AUGUSTE, archbishop of Paris; b. Saint-Rome-de-Tarn (Aveyron), Sept. 28, 1793; d. Paris, June 27, 1848. He completed his studies at the seminary of Saint-Sulpice in Paris and was ordained May 16, 1818. After joining the *Sulpicians, he was appointed professor of theology at the Paris seminary (1819). His *Gallicanism obliged him to seek a post among the diocesan clergy (1820). He became chaplain of a foundling home, meanwhile editing the periodical *La France chrétienne.* He became vicar-general of the Diocese of Luçon (1822); then of the Diocese of Amiens (1823–34), helping to reorganize the latter diocese. In 1834 he was named honorary vicar-general of Paris and member of the council of Archbishop de *Quelen. In this capacity his chief concern was with intellectual questions. He supported Father *Lacordaire when the latter was given charge of the conferences in Notre Dame Cathedral. He became coadjutor bishop of Strasbourg (Dec. 9, 1839). After the death of De Quelen (Dec. 31, 1839), he was named Capitulary Vicar of Paris, and soon after, archbishop (May 27, 1840). If his episcopate was marked by conflicts with the chapter and with several religious congregations, it was noted also for a serious adminis-

tration, the founding of a school for advanced ecclesiastical studies, and the publication of remarkable pastoral letters. He defended academic freedom, despite opposition from the government of *Louis-Philippe. He recognized the Republican regime (February 1848). During the June insurrection, his effort to restore peace led him to the barricades of Faubourg Saint-Antoine, where he was fatally wounded (June 25) by a bullet. He published many canonical and philosophical works, including *Traité de l'administration temporelle des paroisses* (1826), *Essai historique sur la suprématie temporelle des papes* (1829), *Traité de la propriété des biens ecclésiastiques* (1837), *Introduction philosophique à l'étude du christianisme* (1844), and *De l'appel comme d'abus* (1845).

Bibliography: J. Leflon, *Études* 258 (1948) 212–216. R. Limouzin-Lamothe, "Documents nouveaux sur la mort de Mgr. Affre," RevHistÉglFrance 35 (1949) 66–68. P. Pisani, DHGE 1:684–698. A. Isnard, DictBiogFranc 1:667–669. G. Jacquemet, *Catholicisme* 1:184–185. A. Amanieu, DDC 1:285–288.

[R. LIMOUZIN-LAMOTHE]

AFGHANISTAN, landlocked, mountainous country in Asia, bounded by Iran, West Pakistan, and the Union of Soviet Socialist Republics, 250,000 square miles in area. The country, known in ancient times as Aryana or Khorasan, formed part of the Kingdom of Bactria *c.* 150 B.C. Persia and India later influenced Afghanistan, which was overrun by *Islam in the 7th century A.D. and has remained Moslem since then. Political unity was achieved in 1747. Great Britain gained control over Afghan foreign affairs in 1880, but in 1919 the country gained complete independence. It is governed by a constitutional monarchy. Its population, estimated at 14 million in 1964, was almost entirely Moslem.

There is a tradition that the Apostles Thomas and Bartholomew first brought Christianity to this region. Mention is made of the Diocese of Herat, which existed in the 5th century and which was a metropolitan see in the 6th, 10th, and 11th centuries. Christian communities, largely Nestorian, flourished in Afghan cities located on the caravan routes, but they eventually disappeared. Balkh, in the northern section, served as an important mission center, whence Christians of the Syrian rite spread the faith to China. Jesuit missionaries came to Kabul in the 17th century, but the number of conversions seems to have been small. At the present time Christian missionaries are forbidden to enter the country to proselytize. Since 1932 there has been a Barnabite priest attached to the Italian embassy and resident in Kabul, the capital. Catholic chaplains from Quetta and Peshawar in Pakistan regularly visit Afghanistan to minister to the few Catholics there, mostly foreign personnel engaged in technical work. The Little Sisters of Jesus work in a hospital in Kabul.

Bibliography: Latourette v.1, 6. *Bilan du monde* 2:23–24.

[L. MASCARENHAS]

AFRA, ST., martyr at Augsburg during the persecution of *Diocletian, patron of the Diocese of Augsburg (feast, Aug. 7). The *Martyrology of St. Jerome witnesses to her life and martyrdom, and this information is confirmed by Venantius *Fortunatus, who visited her grave in 565. A *passio* represented by a long and short recension and a *conversio* depict her as a repentant prostitute. This legend began apparently in the 8th century and spread rapidly (there is even an Armenian version) but has no historical foundation. It arose through confusion with the martyr of Antioch, Venerea, whose name was interpreted in relation to Venus, and was inscribed in the Martyrology of St. Jerome on the same day as Afra's. Several ancient calendars of Augsburg assert that Afra was a virgin. The body of a woman discovered in a sarcophagus in the Roman Church of St. Afra in the 11th century is honored today under the altar dedicated to the saint. In a later *passio* the martyrdom of an Afra at Brescia is fused with that of SS. Faustinus and Jovita. It is

St. Afra, 16th-century reliquary bust from Würzburg.

obviously a version developed from the original legend of the 8th century.

Bibliography: A. BIGELMAIR and A. P. FRUTAZ, LexThK[2] 1:169–170. A. BIGELMAIR, "Die heilige Afra," *Lebensbilder aus dem bayerischen Schwaben,* ed. G. VON PÖLNITZ, 4 v. (Munich 1952–55) 1:1–29. H. GOUSSEN, *ThGlaube* 1 (1909) 791–794. H. ROSENFELD, Archiv für Kulturgeschichte 37 (1955) 306–335. F. SAVIO, AnalBoll 15 (1896) 5–72, 113–159, Afra of Brescia.
Illustration credit: Bayerisches Nationalmuseum, Munich.

[P. ROCHE]

AFRICA

This article surveys the modern development of the Catholic Church in Africa. For the earlier Christian centuries, *see* NORTH AFRICA, EARLY CHURCH IN. Separate articles treat the history and current status of the Church in this area. *See* ALGERIA; ANGOLA; ASCENSION ISLAND; BASUTOLAND; BECHUANALAND; BURUNDI; CAMEROUN; CANARY ISLANDS; CAPE VERDE ISLANDS; CENTRAL AFRICAN REPUBLIC; CHAD; COMORO ISLANDS; CONGO-BRAZZAVILLE; CONGO-LÉOPOLDVILLE; DAHOMEY; EGYPT; ETHIOPIA; FERNANDO PO; GABON; GAMBIA; GHANA; GUINEA; GUINEA, PORTUGUESE; IFNI; IVORY COAST; KENYA; LIBERIA; LIBYA; MADEIRA ISLANDS; MALAGASY REPUBLIC (MADAGASCAR); MALAWI; MALI; MAURITANIA; MAURITIUS; MOROCCO; MOZAMBIQUE; NIGER; NIGERIA; RÉUNION; RHODESIA; RIO MUNI; RWANDA; SAHARA, SPANISH; SAINT HELENA; SÃO TOMÉ AND PRINCIPE; SENEGAL; SEYCHELLES ISLANDS; SIERRA LEONE; SOMALIA; SOMALILAND; SOUTH AFRICA; SOUTH-WEST AFRICA; SUDAN; SWAZILAND; TANGANYIKA; TOGO; TUNISIA; UGANDA; UPPER VOLTA; ZAMBIA; AND ZANZIBAR.

FROM 1400 TO 1850

After the tide of *Islam had swept over North Africa, Christianity, which had been so flourishing, disappeared progressively, save in Egypt and Ethiopia, where it survived in heretical and schismatic forms.

Along the Mediterranean coast, *Franciscans in Morocco, *Trinitarians and *Mercedarians in the ports of Barbary carried on a precarious, often heroic ministry among the Christians found there as traders, merchants, and above all, as slaves. During the entire medieval period relations between Europe and the Africa of the Negroes were practically severed.

Portuguese Crusade. Relations reopened in the 15th century as a result of the efforts of the Portuguese. They took possession of Ceuta in Morocco (1415), erected a diocese there, then another at Tangier (1468), and a third at Safi (1487). Under the impulse of *Henry the Navigator there had already begun those audacious expeditions that carried the Portuguese flag to the Far East and led to the discovery and exploration of the entire African coast. Propagation of the faith was one of the chief motives of these expeditions. The kings of Portugal took seriously the mission confided to them by the popes. Priests accompanied the navigators. A cross was planted on newfound shores. Conversion of the Africans began without delay.

Successively the gospel was spread to the Azores and Cape Verde Islands, then southward along the west coast to Guinea, Sierra Leone, territories bordering the Gulf of Guinea, São Tomé and the neighboring islands, the Congo, and Angola. On the east coast the Portuguese missionaries reached Mozambique, and the islands in the Indian Ocean. The first apostles were often Franciscans, but the other orders established in Portugal soon joined them. The *Jesuits played a very active role from their foundation. The secular clergy also furnished a considerable number of men. Missionaries did not hesitate to recruit priests among the natives, even when they could only give them a formation that was too rapid and summary.

Cape Verde Islands and Guinea. The evangelization of these regions was confided by Henry the Navigator to the *Order of Christ. There is mention of a parish on the island of Santiago in 1462. Two Franciscans arrived (1466) and began preaching in the Casamance region and Portuguese Guinea (1469). A bishopric of Cape Verde was erected (1533), dependent on the See of Funchal in the Madeira Islands, which had been established in 1514; and an ecclesiastical organization was formed, which reproduced faithfully that in Portugal. The jurisdiction of this see extended on the continent from Senegal to the Ivory Coast. In 1539 the Diocese of Cape Verde became a suffragan of *Lisbon. It had the good fortune to have several remarkable bishops. A school was opened in 1510, destined to become much later a seminary. Unfortunately the rigors of the climate, severity of life, and frequent incursions of English and French corsairs led to progressive depopulation of the archipelago and decadence of Christianity. Vain attempts at revivification were essayed by Jesuits from 1604 to 1642, and by Capuchins after 1656; but decline continued. By mid-19th century there was no bishop; the entire clergy consisted of 28 priests, 7 being Portuguese.

The Guinea mission was confided by Pope Pius II (1462) to the Franciscan Alfonso de Bolano. It depended on that of Cape Verde, whose priests went to the continent occasionally to assure religious services for the Portuguese colonists and to seek the conversion of the natives. In this way Christian communities extended along the coast from Gambia to the Gold Coast, where the Portuguese had an important settlement. In 1489 a Wolof chieftain was invited to Lisbon, where he received Baptism with all his retinue. Upon his return he was accompanied by a band of missionaries. He was later killed by a Portuguese commander during a dispute. This ended the mission.

With the absorption of Portugal by Spain (1580–1640), and the attacks by the Dutch, French, and English, Portuguese influence and evangelization declined in these regions. Spanish Capuchins appeared in 1647, but the local authorities would not accept them. Portuguese Capuchins replaced them and enjoyed some success. In 1663 many local kings received Baptism or showed favor to the mission. In 1694 occurred the first episcopal visit, made by Vitoriano de Porto, the very zealous bishop of Cape Verde. He found many flourishing communities of Christians. When a bishop, accompanied by two Franciscans and 18 secular priests, set out on a second visit (1741), they were shipwrecked off Casamance. Those who were not drowned were imprisoned by the natives. Afterward these Christian communities received no more visits, especially along the Slave Coast, except from transient priests who were half apostles, half adventurers. One of these sent to Paris the son of the king of Assinie, who was solemnly baptized by Bishop Bossuet with King Louis XIV as sponsor (Aug. 1, 1691). In Sierra Leone, following the first missionaries, came the Jesuits from the end of the

16th century. Franciscans from Andalusia tried a century later without much success to reanimate the missions.

Benin and São Tomé. Upon his first contacts with the Portuguese in 1485, the King of Benin asked for priests. His motives were mixed, however, and the mission had no great result. Spanish religious arrived *c.* 1655, but the Portuguese forced them to leave. Christianity vegetated, served only intermittently by clergy from São Tomé. This latter island was the center of Portuguese colonization in this vast area. Many churches were built there, staffed by both regulars and seculars. In 1534 Pope Paul III established there a see whose jurisdiction extended to the Congo and Angola. When these two countries were detached, the Diocese of São Tomé lost its importance, more so when in 1753 the seat of government was shifted to Principe Island. The last bishop died in 1800.

Congo and Angola. It was in the Congo and Angola that Portuguese missions flourished most. Diogo Cão discovered (1484) the mouth of the Congo River, and brought the region's nobles to Lisbon, where they were instructed in the Catholic faith. Upon their return they converted their king. Systematic evangelization began in 1490, conducted by Franciscans, Canons Regular of St. Augustine, and secular priests. From the start its success was remarkable. King Nzinga was baptized under the name Dom João (1491). A church was built in his capital, which was named São Salvador. A truly Christian kingdom, closely modeled on that of Portugal, arose on the left bank of the river. During the reign of King Afonso (1506–43) Christianity spread widely. Missionaries arrived regularly from Portugal; and young Congolese were sent to Portugal for instruction. Dom Henrique, son of the King, was consecrated bishop of Utica (1518). He soon returned to the Congo, but died *c.* 1535. Dominicans, Discalced Carmelites, and Jesuits sent missioners. São Salvador became an episcopal see in 1597.

Angola was first evangelized in the second half of the 16th century. Christian beginnings were not as brilliant there as in the Congo; but by the end of the century, the city of Luanda (São Paulo de Loanda) was founded. The region counted in 1590 about 20,000 Christians. It came to supplant São Salvador as the political capital. Since 1675 it has been the religious metropolis.

Missions in the Congo and Angola experienced alternating successes and reverses. Responsibility for failures can be ascribed to extreme dependence on Portugal, shortcomings in mission methods, hostility of the Dutch Calvinists who occupied these coasts (1641–48), the slave trade, which proved very demoralizing, incessant tribal wars, and pagan resistance. The Christian kings of the Congo frequently petitioned the Holy See for missionaries, but they had to contend with the opposition of the Portuguese government, which relied on its right of *Patronato Real and sought to admit into its territories none but Portuguese as missionaries, even though it became less and less capable of furnishing them. Finally (1640) the Congregation of the *Propagation of the Faith (Propaganda) erected a Prefecture Apostolic of the Congo, which it confided to the Capuchins. After many difficulties these friars, mostly Italians, disembarked (1645) and received an enthusiastic welcome. Their arrival substantially reinforced existing missionary forces and marked clearly a renewal of evangelization in this area.

A seminary, erected in 1682, supplied an appreciable number of native priests. From 1693 the *Junta das Missoes* strove to look after the interests of the mission. However, the suppression of the Jesuits in Portugal (1759), and the anticlerical policy of *Pombal proved most injurious. Portuguese Carmelites and Italian Capuchins continued to supply some missioners into the first third of the 19th century, but they could not halt the mission's rapid decline.

East Africa. Missions prospered less in East Africa than on the west coast because of the influence of Islam and the concentration of Portuguese interest on the Indies. Churches were built in the coastal cities and staffed with chaplains to serve resident and transient Catholics. Missions sought to penetrate the interior. Thus Jesuits from India advanced to the kingdom of Monomotapa. One of them, Gonçalo de Silveira (1526–61), baptized the King, the Queen, and 300 persons of the court; but he was put to death during a reversal of opinion.

From 1577 Dominicans were in Mozambique, and from there spread to other Portuguese settlements along the coast. Pope Pius IV authorized (1563) the Portuguese kings to name apostolic administrators for Ormuz, Mozambique, and Sofala. Dominicans were in Sofala in 1586. By 1591 this mission counted 20,000 Christians. The territory of Mozambique, stretching from Cape Gardafui to the Cape of Good Hope, was removed from the jurisdiction of *Goa in 1613 and confided to administrators who were bishops *in partibus,* and carried the title "Prelate of Mozambique."

During the 17th century the Dominicans again evangelized Monomotapa, whose king was baptized in 1652. The Jesuits returned and opened a college and seminary. Augustinians labored in Mombasa and Malinda. Franciscan Regular Tertiaries, Brothers of St. John of God, and secular priests also aided this work. In the 18th century decadence set in among the Christian communities and missionaries. The number of missionaries kept declining until by 1855 none remained.

The general suppression of religious orders promulgated in Portugal in 1834 increased to such an extent the damage caused by the suppression of the Jesuits in 1773 that it destroyed the *patronato* and the Portuguese mission. This nation, which had done so much to evangelize Africa, furnished scarcely any more missionaries. Those she did supply, like so many of the native clergy, proved unworthy. Not until the opening of the mission seminary at Cernache de Bonjardim in 1855 was there a renewal of Portuguese missionary action.

French Missions. The French also played a part, although much less important than that of Portugal, in evangelizing Black Africa. In the 17th century Capuchins from Normandy worked along the coast of Senegal, and their fellow religious from Britanny, along the coast of the Gulf of Guinea. Neither group seemingly had much success. During the 18th century Saint-Louis and Gorée had chaplains who assured a ministry among the whites and the half-breeds, and sometimes visited Christian communities along the coast. In 1776 there arrived in Saint-Louis two *Messieurs du St. Esprit* who were sailing to Guiana when they were shipwrecked and captured by the Moors. After being ransomed by the Christians they returned to France. Two years later

CICM Immaculate Heart of Mary Mission Society
CM Vincentians
CMF Claretians
CSSp Holy Ghost Fathers
OCarm Carmelites
OFM Franciscans
OFMCap Capuchins
OMI Oblates of Mary Immaculate
OP Dominicans
OPrem Premonstratensians
OSA Augustinians
OSB Benedictines
OSFS Oblates of St. Francis de Sales
SAC Pallottines
SJ Jesuits
SPF Society for the Propagation of the Faith
SVD Society of the Divine Word
WF White Fathers

The Church in Africa South of the Sahara, 1964
7,096 Parishes: 25,847,582 Catholics
ARCHBISHOPRICS and Suffragan Sees
Sees underlined have been established since 1959.

A-1 **DAKAR,** Senegal 26: 104,548
A-1 Ziguinchor 14: 31,804
A-1 Kaolack, Pref. Apost. 1: 5,107
A-1 Saint-Louis, Pref. Apost. 8: 9,055
A-1 Bathurst, Gambia (immed. subj.) 6: 5,585
B-2 Bissau, Portuguese Guinea, Pref. Apost. 15: 26,499

C-1 **BAMAKO,** Mali 6: 8,353
B-1 Kayes 7: 3,664
C-1 Ségou 4: 4,400
C-2 Sikasso
D-1 Gao, Pref. Apost. 7: 1,708

B-2 **CONAKRY,** Guinea 16: 14,286
C-2 N'Zérékoré 8: 4,353
C-2 Kankan, Pref. Apost. 8: 7,516
B-2 Freetown and Bo, Sierra Leone, (immed. subj.) 16: 23,493
B-2 Makeni, Sierra Leone (immed. subj.) 9: 3,109
C-3 Cape Palmas, Liberia, Vic. Apost.
B-3 Monrovia, Liberia, Vic. Apost. 5: 5,335

C-3 **ABIDJAN,** Ivory Coast 28: 157,710
D-3 Abengourou
C-2 Bouaké 16: 46,982
C-3 Daloa 15: 7,000
C-3 Gagnoa 14: 46,097
C-2 Katiola 16: 26,607

D-2 **OUAGADOUGOU,** Upper Volta 12: 38,892
C-2 Bobo-Dioulasso 15: 48,170
D-2 Koudougou 8: 20,697
D-2 Koupelá 10: 20,563
D-1 Nouna 11: 25,285
D-2 Ouahigouya 4: 5,444
D-2 Fada-N'Gourma, Pref. Apost. 10: 4,916

D-3 **CAPE COAST,** Ghana 23: 230,600
D-3 Accra 122: 81,818
D-3 Keta 21: 160,000
D-3 Kumasi 24: 142,581
D-2 Navrongo 6: 11,735
D-2 Tamale 5: 4,381
D-2 Wa 7: 46,488

D-3 **LOMÉ,** Togo 26: 231,598
D-2 Sokodé 16: 21,765
D-2 Dapango, Pref. Apost. 4: 2,664

E-3 **COTONOU,** Dahomey 19: 130,500
E-3 Abomey 10: 69,685
E-3 Porto-Novo 12 (93 churches, 21 priests): 61,545
E-2 Parakou, Pref. Apost. 17: 13,123
E-1 Niamey (immed. subj.) 7: 12,800

E-2 **KADUNA,** Nigeria 12 (80 churches): 33,000
F-2 Jos 12: 56,000
F-2 Makurdi 15: 48,204
F-2 Yola 14: 11,279

E-3 **LAGOS,** Nigeria 15: 93,189
E-3 Ibadan 10: 43,000
E-3 Ondo 11: 83,504
E-2 Oyo 9: 32,013
E-3 Benin 10: 176,415

E-3 **ONITSHA,** Nigeria 28: 236,078
F-3 Calabar 22: 100,798
E-3 Enugu 19: 183,525
F-3 Ikot Ekpene 240 (31 priests): 38,061
F-3 Ogoja 20: 90,939
E-3 Owerri 39: 446,537
E-3 Port Harcourt 8: 63,632
E-3 Umuahia 26: 210,339
E-2 Ilorin, Pref. Apost. 4: 5,950
E-2 Kabba, Pref. Apost. 11: 24,670
F-2 Maiduguri, Pref. Apost. 4: 5,678
E-1 Sokoto, Pref. Apost. 9: 9,245

G-2 **FORT-LAMY,** Chad 11: 132,298
G-2 Fort Archambault 9: 7,500
G-2 Moundou 10: 60,450
G-2 Pala, Pref. Apost. 19: 5,076

F-3 **YAOUNDÉ,** Cameroon 49: 290,159
F-3 Buea 30: 104,671
F-3 Douala 32: 118,950
G-3 Doumé 18: 48,133
G-2 Garoua 30: 12,000
F-3 M'Balmayo 18: 61,000
F-3 Nkongsamba 29: 137,135
F-3 Sangmélima 23: 78,838
F-3 Fernando Poo, Spanish Guinea, Vic. Apost.

F-4 **LIBREVILLE,** Gabon 17: 145,229
F-4 Mouila 15: 69,246

G-5 **BRAZZAVILLE,** Congo 18: 134,537
G-4 Fort-Rousset (138 churches): 47,123
F-5 Pointe-Noire 21: 118,379

G-3 **BANGUI,** Cent. Afr. Rep. 24: 98,528
G-3 Berberati 11: 28,680
H-3 Bangassou, Pref. Apost. 7: 19,653
G-3 Bossangoa, Pref. Apost. 7: 18,400

G-4 **COQUILHATVILLE,** Congo 4: 98,401
H-4 Basankusu 19: 64,380
G-4 Bikoro 11: 23,734
H-4 Ikela 7: 23,000
H-3 Lisala 28: 319,869
H-3 Lolo 8: 36,742
H-3 Molegbe 21: 198,714

I-4 **STANLEYVILLE,** Congo 20: 217,794
H-3 Bondo 3: 61,575
I-4 Bunia 1,226 (106 priests): 389,787
I-3 Buta 15: 71,232
H-4 Isangi 10: 42,841
J-3 Mahagi 3: 1,867
I-3 Niangara 15: 167,095
I-3 Wamba 18: 49,935
I-3 Doruma, Pref. Apost. 9: 12,814

G-5 **LÉOPOLDVILLE,** Congo 23: 250,000
F-5 Boma 24: 317,765
G-4 Idiofa 27: 175,260
G-4 Inongo 3: 91,946
G-5 Kenge 15: 101,432
G-5 Kikwit 32: 424,698
G-5 Kisantu 14: 158,800
G-5 Matadi 30 (767 churches): 195,757
G-5 Popokabaka 14: 128,636

H-5 **LULUABOURG,** Congo 6: 250,818
H-5 Kabinda 11: 96,740
H-5 Luebo 11: 89,987
H-5 Tshumbé : 44,220
H-4 Kole, Pref. Apost. 4: 12,120
H-5 Mweka, Pref. Apost. 6: 27,483

I-4 **BUKAVU,** Congo 13: 222,836
I-4 Beni 21: 351,345
I-4 Goma 11: 105,164
I-5 Kasongo 13: 76,621
I-4 Kindu 181: 39,245
I-4 Uvira 9: 40,452

I-6 **ELISABETHVILLE,** Congo 32: 199,025
I-5 Baudouinville 15: 98,961
I-5 Kamina : 60,000
I-5 Kilwa 11: 24,640
I-5 Kongolo 12: 52,755
I-6 Sakania 11: 50,912

K-2 **ADDIS ABABA,** Ethiopia 13: 23,900
K-1 Adigrat 16: 7,000
K-1 Asmara 84: 37,400
K-1 Asmara Latinorum, Vic. Apost. 10: 27,000
K-2 Gimma, Vic. Apost. 4: 5,200
L-2 Harar, Vic. Apost. 12: 8,300
K-3 Hosseina, Pref. Apost. 13: 16,455
K-3 Negelli, Pref. Apost. 1: 250
L-2 Djibouti, French Somaliland (immed. subj.) 4: 5,500
L-3 Mogadishu, Somali Rep., Vic. Apost. 13: 2,450

J-4 **RUBAGA,** Uganda 31: 299,239
J-3 Arua 19: 252,304
I-4 Fort Portal 11: 132,298
J-3 Gulu 20: 230,105
J-4 Kampala 32: 238,252
J-4 Masaka 23: 230,304
J-4 Mbarara 18: 315,384
J-4 Tororo 40: 390,514

K-4 **NAIROBI,** Kenya 77: 137,788
J-4 Eldoret 18: 52,988
J-4 Kisii 18: 136,152
J-4 Kisumu 41: 396,425
K-4 Kitui 7: 4,578
K-4 Meru 19: 77,067
K-5 Mombasa-Zanzibar 15: 47,880
K-4 Nyeri 28: 157,508
K-4 Ngong, Pref. Apost. 3: 2,070

I-4 **KABGAYI,** Rwanda 31: 489,096
I-4 Butare 19: 264,729
I-4 Nyundo 18: 155,537
I-4 Ruhengeri 13 99,640

I-4 **KITEGA,** Burundi 19 (247 churches): 545,000
I-5 Bururi 8: 106,383
I-4 Ngozi 20: 536,361
I-4 Usumbura 166: 380,000

J-5 **TABORA,** Tanganyika 21: 41,385
J-4 Bukoba 17: 180,928
J-5 Karema 21: 177,300
I-5 Kigoma 14: 46,033
J-5 Mbeya 14: 43,620
J-4 Musoma 17: 47,862
J-4 Mwanza 71: 80,661
J-4 Rulenge 11: 74,927
J-4 Shinyanga 20: 24,902

K-5 **DAR ES SALAAM,** Tanganyika 30: 103,295
K-4 Arusha 8: 6,300
J-5 Dodoma 82: 67,426
J-5 Iringa 30: 144,046
J-5 Mbulu 13: 34,308
K-5 Morogoro 37: 150,312
K-4 Moshi 36: 190,281
K-6 Nachingwea
K-5 Tanga 10: 30,526
K-6 Ndanda, Abbey nullius 32: 66,476
J-6 Peramiho, Abbey nullius 45: 216,325

J-7 **BLANTYRE,** Nyasaland 19: 226,542
J-6 Dedza 11: 85,510
J-6 Lilongwe 13: 93,660
J-6 Mzuzu 10: 20,663
J-7 Zomba 24: 91,558

I-7 **LUSAKA,** Rhodesia 16: 45,800
J-5 Abercorn 13: 52,544
J-6 Fort Jameson 14: 65,683
I-6 Fort Rosebery 12: 82,537
J-6 Kasama 13: 118,866
I-7 Livingstone 14: 27,676
I-7 Monze 8: 32,700
I-6 Ndola 25: 97,735

J-7 **SALISBURY,** Rhodesia 35: 107,205
I17 Bulawayo 21: 43,608
I-7 Gwelo 22: 92,661
J-7 Umtali 14: 39,190
I-7 Wankie 11: 8,013
I-6 Solwezi, Pref. Apost. 4: 1,702

F-5 **LUANDA,** Angola 49: 485,000
G-6 Luso 7: 20,200
G-6 Malanje 15: 144,462
G-6 Nova Lisboa 57: 669,034
G-6 Sa da Bandeira 32: 247,702
E-4 São Tomé e Principe 10: 50,000
G-6 Silva Porto 28: 200,000

J-8 **LOURENCO MARQUES,** Mozambique 65: 382,243
J-7 Beira 28: 73,888
J-8 Inhambane 17: 123,000
K-7 Nampula 45: 69,769
K-6 Porto Amelia 19: 65,452
K-7 Quelimane 28: 62,932
J-7 Tete 14: 43,626
J-6 Vila Cabral 11: 30,000

M-6 **DIÉGO-SUAREZ,** Madagascar 19: 61,412
M-6 Ambanja 13: 16,262
L-7 Majunga 19: 41,265

L-7 **TANANARIVE,** Madagascar 49: 238,060
M-7 Ambatondrazaka 10: 33,696
L-7 Antsirabe 20: 212,799
L-7 Miarinarivo 8: 47,204
M-7 Tamatave 17: 70,231
L-7 Tsiroanomandidy 188: 28,087

L-8 **FIANARANTSOA,** Madagascar (128 priests): 323,124
L-8 Farafangana 11: 64,000
L-8 Fort-Dauphin 10: 23,815
L-8 Morombe : 8,209
L-7 Morondava (17 priests): 17,444
L-8 Tuléar 8: 22,000

I-8 **PRETORIA,** South Africa 32: 40,367
I-9 Johannesburg 78: 217,779
I-8 Lydenburg 19: 15,847
J-9 Manzini 13: 25,142

I-9 **BLOEMFONTEIN,** South Africa 17: 35,049
I-9 Bethlehem 12: 21,090
H-9 Keimoes 18: 26,102
H-9 Kimberley 46: 31,500
I-9 Kroonstad 12: 36,200

I-9 **MASERU,** South Africa 36: 187,000
I-9 Leribe 35: 171,772
I-9 Qacha's Nek 9: 53,103

I-9 **DURBAN,** South Africa 63: 116,663
J-9 Eshowe 22: 28,518
I-9: Kokstad 9: 28,454
I-9 Mariannhill 37: 153,113
I-9 Umtata 19: 25,154
I-9 Umzimkulu 11 (51 churches): 29,658

G-10 **CAPE TOWN,** South Africa 40: 64,243
I-9 Aliwal 15: 14,918
H-10 Oudtshoorn 22: 9,024
I-10 Port Elizabeth 33: 37,281
I-10 Queenstown 20: 10,499
H-9 De Aar, Pref. Apost. 6: 4,988
J-9 Ingwavuma, Pref. Apost. 5: 4,087
I-8 Louis Trichardt, Pref. Apost. 8: 4,873
I-9 Volksrust, Pref. Apost. 18: 24,000
I-8 Pietersburg, Abbey nullius 8: 32,127

J-1 El Obeid, Sudan, Vic. Apost. 8: 2,351
J-2 Juba, Sudan, Vic. Apost. 15: 228,115
J-1 Khartoum, Sudan, Vic. Apost. 7: 6,824
I-3 Rumbek, Sudan, Vic. Apost. 5: 25,846
I-2 Wau, Sudan, Vic. Apost. 17: 56,356
J-2 Malakal, Sudan, Pref. Apost. 7: 7,661
I-3 Mopoi, Sudan, Pref. Apost. 10: 88,224
I-8 Francistown, Bechuanaland, Pref. Apost. 9: 7,842
G-9 Keetmanshoop, South West Africa, Vic. Apost. 21: 14,507
G-8 Windhoek, South West Africa, Vic. Apost. 26: 56,966

INSERT OF AREA
WEST OF LAKE VICTORIA I J 4

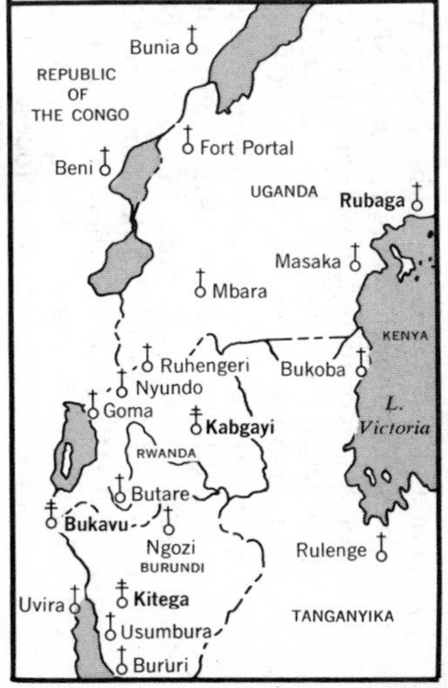

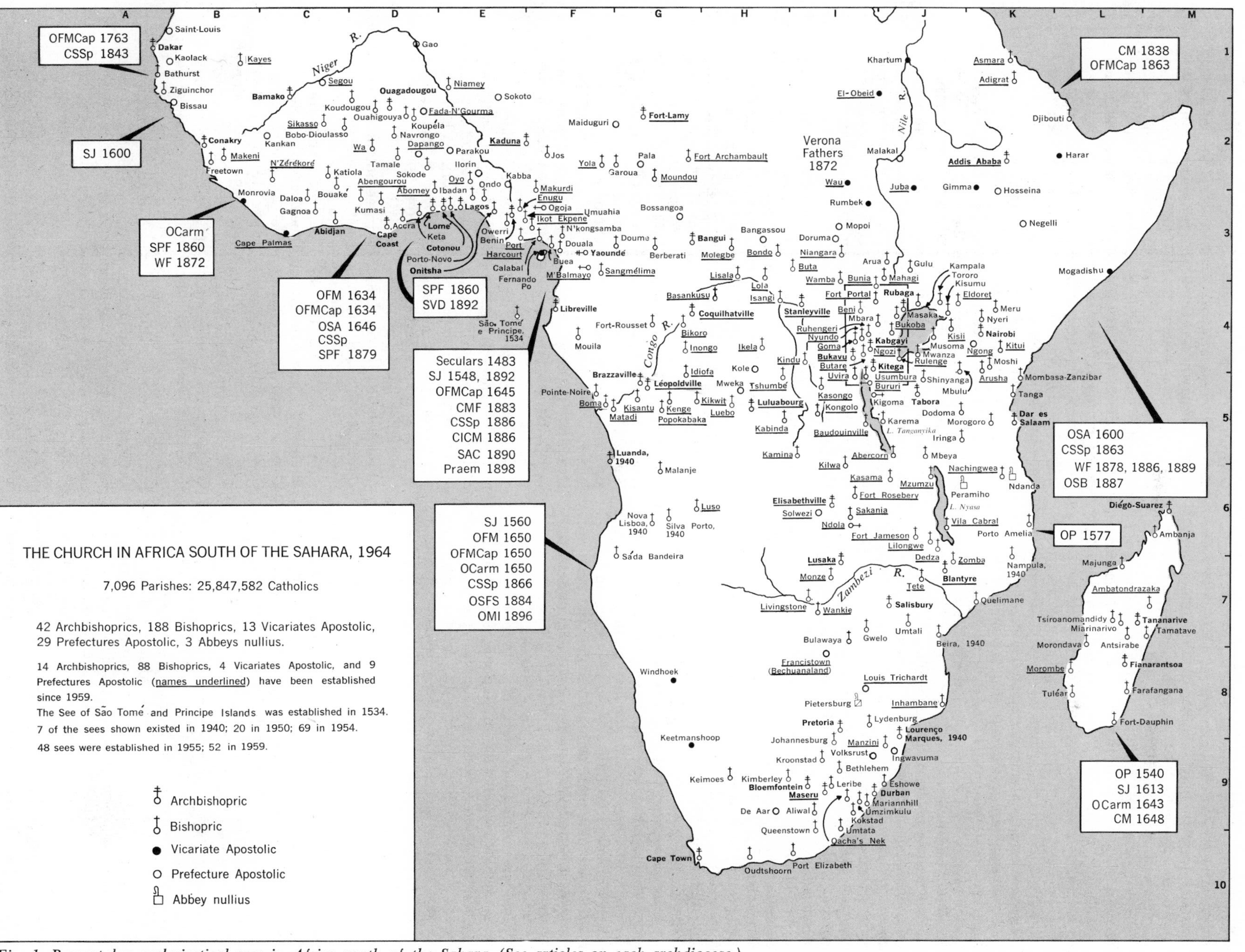

Fig. 1. Present-day ecclesiastical sees in Africa south of the Sahara. (See articles on each archdiocese.)

one of them, M. de Glicourt, returned to Senegal as prefect apostolic and remained until 1783. After the enactment of the *Civil Constitution of the Clergy during the French Revolution, Saint-Louis received as pastor one of the "constitutional" clergy who cast aside his clerical garb. At Gorée the church was profaned and the parish registers were burned in the public square.

At the end of the 18th century some French priests crossed to the right bank of the Congo River and entered the kingdoms of Loango and Kakongo to renew the attempt by the Capuchins a century earlier. The Holy See created a prefecture apostolic, whose prefect, M. de Bellegarde, arrived in 1766. The mission led a precarious existence until 1776. It had only about 10 missionaries. Most of them died there; the others returned to France.

Madagascar and the Mascarene Islands were visited, soon after their discovery, by Portuguese priests en route to or from the Indies. The first missionaries seem to have been Franciscans, who were followed by Dominicans. Neither group enjoyed much success. Jesuits began to work there in 1613. Propaganda confided the mission to Discalced Carmelites in 1647, but these religious were unable to manage it. St. Vincent de Paul sent Vincentians, who inaugurated a mission in 1648 that lasted until 1651 without much result. Two later attempts by them were more successful. In 1671 the Vincentians departed. Some small-scale endeavors followed until the French Revolution ended missionary work.

Vincentians worked in Réunion (then called Bourbon) subsequent to the French occupation (1665). The island of Mauritius, then called the Île de France, had no resident priest until a Vincentian came in 1721. In 1752 it became a prefecture apostolic. The Vincentians remained until 1810, when the British occupation began.

Ethiopia. One of the principal points in Portuguese strategy concerning Islam was to circumvent it by working in conjunction with the mysterious *Prester John, who was supposed to be ruling in Ethiopia. For this reason the kings of Portugal tried their best to enter into relations with the Abyssinian rulers. Ambassadors were exchanged from 1487. Portugal also sent military aid when Ethiopia was attacked by Moslems or by pagan tribes, as happened in 1541. Jesuits sought to convert the Monophysites. They organized the first mission in 1554. Pope Julius III erected a Latin bishopric in Ethiopia in 1555. A second mission began in 1603. Father Afonso Mendes converted the negus Sessenos, but the influence of the schismatic clergy produced a violent persecution of Catholics. Jesuit missionaries were expelled, and Bishop Appolinario de Almeida was put to death. This ended the mission.

Renewal of the Missions since 1850

After the exuberant flowering of the early Christian centuries in Egypt and in Roman Africa, and the later attempts during the 17th and 18th centuries following the Portuguese discoveries, Christianity had almost completely disappeared from the African continent by the beginning of the 19th century. Everything had to begin anew.

Africa remained a closed continent. Along the Mediterranean coast Turkish corsairs prevented penetration. If some succeeded in breaking this barrier, they were confronted by an immense desert. Along the other coasts from Cape Verde south to the Cape of Good Hope and northward from there to Zanzibar, the slave trade with the blacks brought many Europeans into contact with the river tribes who served them as dealers, but it rendered difficult relations with those in the interior. Moreover the African rivers, barred by rapids near their mouths, were scarcely adapted to navigation. The trails to the interior were sprinkled with so many ambushes that men dared not adventure upon them. Then too, both nature and climate were so hostile that white men were unable to adapt themselves or to make any durable establishment.

With the 19th century other factors intervened. After Europe recovered from the convulsions of the French Revolution and the Napoleonic era, romanticism became the vogue. It was perceived that there was at hand an almost unknown continent. Travelers, adventurers, traders, soldiers, politicians, and literary men began for various and sometimes contradictory reasons to interest themselves in Africa and its inhabitants. It was the golden age of explorations.

European governments were not slow to grasp the practical value of these expeditions. Each of the great powers supported its nationals. The continent was carved into zones of influence, determined at the Berlin Congress (1885–86), which gave rise to colonies that lasted to mid-20th century. Most of these colonies acquired autonomy after World War II without altering notably their artificial frontiers (*see* COLONIALISM).

At the foundation in Brussels of the International Association for the Exploration of Africa (1876), as at the Berlin Congress, the missions were not forgotten. This association promised that all governments with sovereign rights in these territories would protect and favor all religious, scientific, and charitable institutions and enterprises, and give special protection to Christian missionaries.

Missionaries did not delay in following explorers and colonizers. This was one result of the European religious revival, notably in France, after 1815, and of the missionary renewal initiated by Pope Gregory XVI.

The contemporary evangelization of Africa can be divided into three periods: (1) 1850 to 1918; (2) 1918 to 1939; and (3) since 1945.

1850 to 1918. This first period was one of attempts and experiences. Its point of departure was the abolition of *slavery and the suppression of slave trading. After the Civil War, the U.S. repatriated 3,000 former slaves near Cape Palmas where they set up the Republic of Liberia. The hierarchy in the U.S. was concerned about Catholics in this group and sent to them in 1841 two priests, Edward *Barron and John Kelly, along with a layman Denis Pindar, who acted as a teacher. When they found in Monrovia only 18 Catholics among the former slaves, they turned to the native population and met a good reception. Barron went to Rome to inform the Holy See about the possibilities. As a result he received episcopal consecration (Sept. 28, 1842) and accepted charge of the immense territory of the newly created Vicariate of the Two Guineas, extending from Senegal to the Orange Free State without limits in the interior.

While recruiting personnel in France, Bishop Barron met François *Libermann, who had recently founded a congregation to convert the Africans, and from him obtained seven priests and three lay brothers. Soon after the group arrived at Cape Palmas (Nov. 29, 1842) disaster overcame it. Within a few months most of the missionaries were dead. All the survivors had to be repatriated except Father Bessieux and Brother Grégoire, who found refuge in Libreville, Gabon. There they founded the first modern African mission.

In Central and East Africa slave trading still persisted. Military expeditions were needed to curb Arab slave traders. From 1868 when the mission of Bagamoyo, near Zanzibar, was founded, redemption of slaves was a main preoccupation of the missioners. Cardinal *Lavigerie was the apostle of the struggle against slavery. Under his inspiration was established the society that supplied funds to redeem slaves, and to set up "liberty villages" to shelter liberated slaves. These villages were then regarded as the first elements of the Christian future, but matters did not always turn out thus. This method risked discrediting Christianity among free men, but it was often the only one possible.

The care of slaves did not absorb all the energies of the missionaries. They also traveled through the bush country penetrating villages and parleying with native chieftains to win them to Christianity. This direct approach rarely succeeded. Africans scarcely felt a need to change their religion, especially when this involved changes in morals such as the renouncing of polygamy. Confronted with the reticence of adults, missionaries had to address themselves to youth, and organize schools, especially boarding schools. It was realized that Christianity could only be grafted on a certain level of civilization; and that, as a result of traditional pagan influence on the whole of society, it was necessary to modify some fundamental structures. This required the education of new generations (*see* ANIMISM AND ANIMATISM; RELIGION IN PRIMITIVE CULTURE).

The educational work of the missions affected only the boys. African custom did not accept the education of girls, which would lead to feminine emancipation. There was also a lack of competent teachers, and few congregations of religious women then undertook this type of apostolate.

The boarding-school system was good but costly; it immobilized a large part of the personnel and did not always produce the desired results. It was supplemented, therefore, by direct evangelization of the bush districts by means of catechists, native auxiliaries who took up residence in pagan villages, taught the catechism to children, and tried to inspire adults with the desire to become Christians. When a Christian community began to arise, the catechist instructed the catechumens, presided over pious gatherings, regulated discussions at religious gatherings, assisted the dying, and guided and counseled Christians, thereby ensuring the permanence of the Church in his village. He worked in conjunction with a missionary priest who supervised and encouraged him during periodic visits (*see* CATECHIST, MISSIONARY).

To perfect their methods the pioneers had to study native languages, customs, and material needs in order to establish or create resources, or merely to survive in a period when vast regions had scarcely been opened to outside contacts, when communications with Europe were rare and slow, when dispositions of the inhabitants were not always favorable, and when tropical hygiene was in a primitive state. The apostolate was carried on mostly by the *Holy Ghost Fathers, the Society of the *African Missions, and the *White Fathers.

1918 to 1939. After World War I, conditions improved. Colonization became more effective; it brought peace, order, and economic development beneficial to the missions. The prestige enjoyed by the whites helped Christianity, without involving necessary connivance between colonization and evangelization. The missions received an impetus from the encyclicals *Maximum illud* in 1919 and *Rerum ecclesiae* in 1926 (*see* MISSIONS, PAPAL LETTERS ON). Pius XI's activity supplied further stimulus. The result was an increase in missionary personnel and resources. Papal missionary works were reorganized. New institutes of religious men and women appeared. Between 1918 and 1933 the baptized in Africa increased from 1,873,000 to 4,945,000; catechumens from 548,630 to 2,614,000; missionaries from 1,868 to 3,539; native priests from 90 to 281; sisters from 4,077 to 10,019 (1,982 Africans); catechists and instructors from 12,666 to 67,102; minor seminaries from 10 with 384 students to 80 with 3,080 students; major seminaries from 12 with 134 seminarians to 29 with 748 seminarians.

In this period a hunger for education manifested itself among youth in many African territories. The missionaries reacted by multiplying schools of all kinds, from humble ones in the bush conducted in native languages to highly organized ones conformed to official programs, with instruction in the language of the colonial power. Not only did the apostolate gain in breadth and depth, but many students from the mission schools were able to elevate their standard of life, rise to better positions, and join the elite class that slowly developed. Teaching of girls progressed also, although more slowly than that of boys. In general the colonial administration in the British, Belgian, and Portuguese territories practiced a policy of assistance and collaboration in regard to missionary education, which was not the case in the French colonies.

Alongside their educational work, the missions accomplished a remarkable work of assistance and beneficence. There was scarcely a station without a dispensary. There were also hospitals, leprosaria, nurseries, and orphanages. Religious women were the ones most devoted to this apostolate. It was not only a means of gaining souls by caring for the body, but also an exercise of pure charity, which many African peoples urgently needed (*see* MEDICAL MISSIONS; MISSIONS, SOCIAL ACTION OF).

From the material viewpoint also, the situation improved during this period. The missions owed this mainly to the work of lay brothers, and also to donations from European and American benefactors, and often from local populations. In this way the missionaries were able to situate their missions in material surroundings favorable to success and also to give an example of industriousness in regions where this virtue was often held in disdain.

Formation of an indigenous *clergy was a basic task, but great obstacles impeded it. In 1923 there were 88 native African priests; in 1939, one bishop, one prefect apostolic, and 300 priests from Africa, plus one bishop from Madagascar. Many native congregations of brothers and sisters had appeared in different regions.

Since 1945. World War II directly affected Africa only in Ethiopia and North Africa; yet its impact was considerable elsewhere, and it had important repercussions on the missionary apostolate. The war was followed by a rapid transformation that affected the most basic structures of the continent. It led also to the intellectual, social, and political emancipation of the Africans, and put an end to colonialism. Missionaries had to adjust their methods to this new situation.

Evangelization of the bush country by groups of catechists was not abandoned, but catechetical procedures had to be revised. The rapid growth of towns and cities necessitated an urban apostolate resembling that in the great cities of Europe and America, with parishes, *Catholic Action, *youth organizations, and societies of various kinds. The *Legion of Mary enjoyed great success. There was also a need to link charitable works with the social apostolate. This required social secretariats, social study groups, institutes for research and study (such as INADES at *Abidjan), Christian *Syndicalism (Pan-African Union of Believing Workers), the formation of teachers and technicians, and war against hunger, illiteracy, and tyrannical customs. There was also a need to develop a Christian laity that would not only live the faith, but make it radiate in all sectors of life, especially in those where spiritual and temporal were intertwined.

Catholic education needed to be completed by the erection of colleges and professional schools, and crowned by the establishment of universities, such as *Lovanium University near Léopoldville, and the University College of Pius XII at Roma, in Basutoland. Numerous African students completed their higher education in Africa, Europe, or the U.S. Educational development made clear the need for a Catholic press. Previously missionaries had published numerous religious works in African languages. It became necessary to add newspapers and other periodicals, published most often in the language of the former colonial power, which had become the official language and the vehicle of instruction. Catholic bookshops and libraries appeared in the most important centers. Similar attempts were made in the realms of the cinema and radio (*see* CATHOLIC PRESS, WORLD SURVEY, 1).

This rapid development of the apostolate demanded a more intense effort by the Catholic world. Pius XII appealed to it in his encyclicals *Evangelii praecones* (1951) and *Fidei donum* (1957). In response numerous religious institutes of men and women, including contemplative ones, went to Africa. Christian countries prepared priests for this mission. Catholic organizations in Europe and America sent specialists and technicians.

John XXIII, in *Princeps pastorum* (1959), addressed especially the laity, and urged them to participate actively in the missionary apostolate, and to collaborate in the formation of a model African Catholic laity.

The coming of independence to numerous former colonies posed delicate ecclesiastical problems. The Church was prompt in disassociating itself from colonialism and adapting itself loyally to the new structures. This was not always easy, because of the authoritarian susceptibilities and tendencies of the young governments and the convulsive movements that here and there accompanied the birth of the new states. In places missionaries were persecuted, expelled, or even put to death. In some countries schools were nationalized, Catholic Action movements stifled, and the Catholic press suppressed. On the whole, however, the missions emerged from this crisis without too much damage.

Other Developments Since 1850

A conspectus of mission developments throughout the continent reveals great developments, much more so in some regions than others.

North Africa. For centuries North Africa has been overwhelmingly Moslem. Modern Catholic missions have caused relatively few changes in the religious affiliations of the native populations. Catholic gains have resulted from the increased presence of Europeans.

In 1830 King Charles X of France sought to conquer Algeria. With the troops arrived chaplains, who were slowly replaced by missionaries from various religious institutes who occupied themselves with the military personnel and the colonists. *Anticlericalism, which was rampant in France after the revolution of 1830, prevented all proselytism among the local populace. "The Gospel for the colonists, the Koran for the natives" was the policy. In 1838 the Diocese of *Algiers was created, followed in 1866 by those of Oran and Constantine. Archbishop Lavigerie obtained (1867) from Emperor Napoleon III permission to open orphanages, in which Arab children would have an opportunity to become Christians. To promote the apostolate among the Moslems he founded two missionary religious institutes. The color of their garb, inspired by that of the Arabs, caused them to be called *White Fathers and *White Sisters. Lavigerie also traced the method to be pursued by these religious: exercise of charity, care of the sick, and instruction of children.

The White Fathers came to Tunisia in 1876. Leo XIII restored the ancient See of *Carthage and bestowed it on Lavigerie, already archbishop of Algiers and cardinal, who received the title Primate of Africa. Charitable and educational works developed, as a result of a regime more liberal than in Algeria. The great majority of Catholics in these two predominantly Moslem countries were French, Spanish, Italian, or Maltese in origin. In 1961 Algeria had about 900,000 Catholics among its 10 million inhabitants. Algerian independence (1962) caused about 600,000 of them to leave the country by 1964. Tunisia, which became independent in 1956, had about 40,000 Catholics in 1964 among a population of 4.5 million.

Since the days of St. Francis of Assisi Moslem fanaticism has several times annihilated missionary enterprises in Morocco. In 1802 there remained only one Franciscan in *Tangier. The Morocco mission, made a prefecture apostolic in 1630, disappeared in the 18th century, to be reestablished in 1859. Not until 1862, however, as a result of a treaty with Spain, were missionaries able to enjoy relative peace. After 1907 France began to extend its authority among the Berbers and permitted French Franciscans to evangelize them. In 1908 the Prefecture of Morocco became a vicariate, which in 1923 was divided in two, Tangier and *Rabat. Christians were recruited almost exclusively among persons of European descent. Yet the influence of the monastery of Toumliline and of the publications and schools directed by religious congregations permitted contacts with a Moslem elite. The 12 million inhabitants in 1961 included about 375,000 Catholics.

The first apostles of the Sahara were Jesuits, established at Laghouat (1868). White Fathers replaced them in 1872 and advanced southward. Touaregs offered to conduct three missionaries to Tombouctou but massacred them during the journey (1876). A second attempt (1881) also failed. Missionaries were content to occupy the oases along the northern border of the desert. In 1901 there was set up the Prefecture Apostolic of the Sahara, which became the Vicariate Apostolic of Ghardaïa (1948) and the Diocese of Laghouat (1955). In this area the sole apostolate possible is that of disinterested assistance and patient waiting, as defined in theory and practice by Charles Eugène de *Foucauld, the hermit of the Sahara. His disciples continued his work. The industrialization of some desert areas offered new mission opportunities. Missionaries strove to relieve the extreme poverty of the populace and also to prepare the people to live by their labor and to benefit from the region's economic changes. The Diocese of Laghouat had 29,000 Catholics in 1963 among a population of 1.1 million Moslems.

Christianity was reintroduced in Libya only in 1911 as a result of the Italian occupation. The preponderant influence of the Moslem Sanusi sect prevented any conversions. Foreigners have been the sole Catholics. Franciscans and Salesians ministered to the 37,000 Catholics in this country of 1.1 million Moslems.

West Africa. During the Restoration period in France (1815–30) the Congregation of the Holy Spirit sent some priests from Paris to Senegal, where a mission had been established in 1763, but with stations only at Saint-Louis and Gorée. The intrepid Anne Marie *Javouhey, foundress of the Sisters of St. Joseph of Cluny sent her daughters there and also came herself. She was instrumental in having the first three Sengalese priests ordained (1840). In 1849 Father Bessieux, the sole survivor of Edward Barron's enterprise in Liberia, was named vicar apostolic of the Two Guineas; but since he dwelt at Libreville, he received for the northern part of the vicariate a coadjutor who resided in Senegal in a small village, which became the modern *Dakar. In 1848 the fusion between the Congregation of the Holy Spirit and that of the Sacred Heart of Mary founded by François Libermann created the *Holy Ghost Fathers and assured unified action. Later the Lamennais Brothers and the Sisters of Castres arrived. By 1872 the mission counted six Senegalese priests and a congregation of native religious women.

After establishing some coastal stations and carrying the gospel to Casamance, the Holy Ghost Fathers approached the populace of the interior, touched as yet only by Islam. In Upper Senegal they were relieved (1895) by White Fathers who advanced toward Segou, Bamako, and Tombouctou. The Sudan was thus encompassed in the vast Vicariate of Sahara-Sudan, which was divided and subdivided into numerous jurisdictions after 1901. The progress of the missions in Senegal and Sudan was unfortunately fettered by the policy of the French administration, often anticlerical and always pro-Moslem. Yet splendid Catholic communities were founded among the Mossis in Upper Volta, and elsewhere. In these regions Moslem propaganda was especially active.

The evangelization of Sierra Leone was confided (1858) to Melchior de *Marion-Brésillac, founder of the Society of the African Missions. Six weeks after his arrival he and his companions contracted yellow fever. The Vicariate of Sierra Leone was then entrusted to the Holy Ghost Fathers, who settled in Freetown (1864). In 1897 the Prefecture of French Guinea was detached and in 1903 that of Liberia. In these countries Catholicism was implanted rather quickly in the coastal or

Fig. 2. Bronze crucifix from West Africa, thought to have been made there in the 16th or 17th century.

forest regions, but in the interior it was balked by a tenacious paganism or submerged almost entirely by Islam. In Guinea, after the winning of independence (1958) political difficulties for a time hindered the apostolate.

In 1860 Father Planque, second founder of the Society of the African Missions, sent missionaries along the coast from Cape Palmas to the delta of the Niger River, inhabited by vigorous and intelligent peoples who were thoroughly pagan and attached to barbarous customs. A mission was opened at Ouidah (1861), and another at Porto Novo (1864). Former slaves, repatriated from Brazil, often formed the first elements of the Church. Thirty years of open or covert struggles with the despots and sorcerers of Dahomey was the lot of the pioneers, such as the heroic Father Dorgère, until French occupation (1892). The mission of Lagos was founded in 1868. In 1870 the Vicariate of the Coast of Benin was erected; it extended from the mouths of the Volta to those of the Niger. Despite the climate and other sources of difficulty these missions were increasingly successful, leading to the erection of 23 dioceses in Dahomey, Togo, and Nigeria by 1964.

A similar development occurred in the mission to the Gold Coast (Ghana) and the Ivory Coast. After painful beginnings, they too realized prosperity. In Ghana the mission has suffered considerably from authoritarian tendencies of the government.

Nigeria is the country in West Africa with the densest population (about 39 million in 1965) and the most rapid development. In its southwest and even more in its southeast, African Mission Fathers and Holy Ghost Fathers, aided by several other congregations, have established flourishing centers, but Protestants have also been active. The northern part has been won in great part to Islam, but it contains islands of paganism that can be converted to Christianity with great difficulty. Nigeria had 1.8 million Catholics and 596,000 catechumens in 1961.

West Africa, comprising the coastal states of Senegal, Gambia, Portuguese Guinea, Guinea, Sierra Leone, Liberia, Ivory Coast, Ghana, Togo, Dahomey, and Nigeria, along with the inland countries of Niger, Upper Volta, and Mali, had a population of 71.8 million in 1961, the vast majority of which was Moslem or pagan. Catholics totaled 3.6 million and catechumens 965,000, accounting for 17 per cent of the inhabitants in Togo but only 0.5 per cent in Niger.

Equatorial Africa. From *Libreville in present-day Gabon, the Holy Ghost Fathers extended their field of action gradually along the coast, and then toward the interior of the country. In 1865 they were placed in charge of the Prefecture of the Congo and established themselves at Landana. From there they ascended the coast to the former kingdom of Loango, where resided Father Carrie, later the first vicar apostolic of the French Congo. In 1875 Savorgnan de Brazza began the explorations that led him across Gabon to the Congo. At his request Prosper Augouard left Landana and arrived at Stanley Pool (1881). In 1883 he founded the mission of Linzolo and in 1887, that of Mfoa, the later *Brazzaville. In 1890 he became bishop of a territory extending from Stanley Pool to the Nile basin. In his own boats "the bishop of the cannibals" ascended the Congo, Alima, and Ubangi Rivers redeeming slaves and opening mission stations. In 1894 he came to *Bangui, the center of a prefecture in 1909, and of a vicariate in 1938, which extended to Chad and Sudan. Capuchins and Jesuits later came to aid the Holy Ghost Fathers. This entire region on the frontiers of Islam was eventually opened wide to the gospel.

Meanwhile the mission of Gabon tried to enter Cameroun (1884), but German occupation of this territory blocked it. Evangelization could begin only in 1890, as a result of the efforts of the German *Pallottines. Priests of the Sacred Heart of St. Quentin made a foundation in Adamaoua (April, 1914). As a result of World War I the country fell under the control of France and England. The Pallottine Fathers had to give way to the Holy Ghost Fathers in the French sector, and to the *Mill Hill Missionaries in the English. The Sacred Heart Fathers remained in the Bamiléké region. After World War II the *Oblates of Mary Immaculate began mission work in northern Cameroun among Moslems and numerous, very primitive pagans. By 1964 more than one-third of the 4 million inhabitants were Christians (900,000 Catholics, 550,000 Protestants). The rapid progress of Christianity in southern Cameroun caused it to be said that "the Holy Spirit had breathed there in a tornado."

In Fernando Po and Spanish Guinea diverse missionaries labored, notably Jesuits (1857–76). After 1883 the mission was confided to the *Claretians. Christianity has continued to flourish there. In 1961 90 per cent of the 246,000 inhabitants were Catholics. The vast Portuguese territory of Angola, south of the Congo, was the most flourishing Christian area in Africa in the 17th and 18th centuries. Everything, or almost everything, had to begin anew in the 19th. This was the work of the Holy Ghost Fathers. From Landana Father Duparquet set out to explore the southern part of the country. As a result of his activity the Holy See erected the Prefecture of Cimbebasia (1879), which included not only Angola but the entire southeast of Africa. In 1892 Cimbebasia's area was restricted to Portuguese territories, which it shared with the See of *Luanda. Since the missionary agreement (May 7, 1940) between Portugal and the Holy See, Angola has comprised one archdiocese and six dioceses. Secular priests from Portugal and Goa, Benedictines, Capuchins, LaSalette, and Holy Ghost Fathers have been very successful in their labors. Catholics comprised 37 per cent of the 4.6 million inhabitants in 1961.

The islands of São Tomé and Principe are also Portuguese territories. In 1961 88 per cent of the 64,000 inhabitants were Catholics.

The evangelization of that portion of the Congo basin, which was first an independent state, then the Belgian Congo, and since 1960 the Republic of the Congo-Léopoldville, was undertaken by the Holy Ghost Fathers, who opened stations on the left bank of the Congo River between 1873 and 1880, and also by the White Fathers to whom the Holy See confided (1886) two mission centers in the upper Congo, the southernmost of which embraced the entire Congo basin from its source to Stanley Pool. The Berlin Conference (1884), which partitioned the Congo basin between the European powers, created the Congo Free State and confided it to the king of the Belgians Leopold II, who obtained from Pope Leo XIII the creation of a vicariate corresponding to his new domain. Since the King wanted only Belgian missionaries, the vicariate was confided to the Congregation of the *Immaculate Heart of Mary (Scheut Fathers), a Belgian institute. In 1893 Jesuits entered the Kwango region. Many other institutes of men and women followed. Despite early difficulties, the missions of the Belgian Congo, to which were joined after 1918 those of Rwanda and Burundi, progressed rapidly. Favored by the intelligent attitude of the Belgian government, they attained great prosperity. Unfortunately the troubles that started soon after the coming of independence in 1960 have proved a setback to the missions.

The region of Equatorial Africa, comprising Cameroun, Fernando Po, Spanish Guinea, Gabon, Congo-Brazzaville, Congo-Léopoldville, Rwanda, Burundi, Central African Republic, Angola, São Tomé, and Principe, includes the most Catholic section of the continent. Nearly 40 per cent of its 31 million inhabitants in 1961 were Catholics or catechumens. Although the Central African Republic, with 1.2 million inhabitants was only 16 per cent Catholic, Rwanda and Burundi were about 50 per cent Catholic and other sections almost entirely Catholic.

South Africa. Catholicism came to South Africa rather late. European colonization there was from the start mostly Protestant. The first colonists were Dutch

Fig. 3. Doors of the Catholic chapel of the University, Ibadan, Nigeria, carved by Lamidi Fakeye in 1954.

Calvinists, who were joined by French Huguenots and German Lutherans in the service of the Dutch East India Company. The Anglo-Saxons who came later were in the majority Protestants. Three priests who arrived at Cape Town in 1805 were expelled the following year. In 1818 the Holy See designated a Benedictine, Bede Slater, as the first bishop of Cape Town, with residence on the island of Mauritius. The lack of discipline in the small Catholic community prevented any durable ministry. To regulate matters, Rome detached South Africa from the Vicariate of Mauritius and confided it to a Dominican, Patrick *Griffith, who succeeded in redressing the situation. During this period the small number of priests could occupy themselves only with white Catholics.

In 1847 the Vicariate of Western Cape of Good Hope was established and confided to Bishop Devereux. Oblates of Mary Immaculate heeded his appeal, and took charge of the Vicariate of Natal (1850). The first bishop, Marie Jean Allard, began work among the Zulus without success. He met a better reception among the Basutos to whom he turned next. He was also interested in the Orange Free State and Transvaal, where the discovery of diamonds (1867) had started intense immigration.

In 1874 Rome created the Prefecture of Central Cape of Good Hope, which was first confided to the society of the African Missions, later to the Oblates of St. Francis de Sales. Until 1922, however, it was administered by the Vicariate of Western Cape of Good Hope, with Pallottines in charge.

The Vicariates of Western and Eastern Cape of Good Hope made rapid progress. Schools multiplied. Many congregations of religious women entered. Trappists under Franz *Pfanner established themselves at Mariannhill, which became the cradle of a new mission institute. In 1886 the Prefecture of Transvaal was erected and also the Vicariate of Kimberley for the Orange Free State and Basutoland. Mass was first celebrated in Johannesburg Feb. 21, 1887.

To the west, Father Duparquet landed at Walvis Bay and founded (1878) the mission of Omaruru and then the one at Mafeking to the north, on the border of Bechuanaland (1888).

The German colony of Southwest Africa was confided to the *Oblates of St. Francis de Sales in its southern part, and to the Oblates of Mary Immaculate in its northern part. These two congregations moved into Bechuanaland in 1892. The Prefecture of Bechuanaland was erected in 1894 and progressed flourishingly.

The Boer War hindered progress only temporarily. The same was true during and after World War I, which had repercussions in German Southwest Africa. During this period ecclesiastical jurisdictions multiplied after the arrival of new missionaries belonging to various congregations. Secular priests, mostly Irish, continued to assure pastoral care in regions of the Cape of Good Hope and Port Elizabeth.

In this vast region the pastoral aspects of the Church varied greatly; there were parishes of the European or American type in the great cities, humble missions in the veld. The successes of a century have been spectacular, but grave problems have been posed to Christians by *racism and by the *segregation (apartheid) imposed by the government. South African Catholicism has opposed, especially in schools, apartheid as a policy contrary to justice and charity.

Mozambique and Zambezi (Rhodesias) on the east coast were evangelized earlier by the Portuguese. Only in 1879, however, did the Jesuits enter the immense region to the north of the Limpopo and Zambezi Rivers, which constituted the Prefecture of Rhodesia. Liberty in this apostolate was accorded them only in 1887. Their work did not begin to bear fruit until 1889, after the conquest of the warlike Matabeles. The Jesuits centered at Vleeschfontein, where their mission recalled the famous *reductions of Paraguay.

The Holy See asked Bishop Allard, already occupied with the Vicariate of Natal, to take charge of the Catholics of *Lourenço Marques, who were being cared for intermittently by four of five priests from Goa. However, the governor of Mozambique opposed the coming of Allard, claiming that this territory belonged to the See of Goa and that instructions from Propaganda did not concern it, in virtue of the rights conferred by the Portuguese *padroado*. However, this step was not useless, for the government of Lisbon hastened to construct a chapel and send a priest of its own choice. A little later the Jesuits came to Mozambique and began to restore the former missions from their ruins; but they were expelled after the Portuguese revolution of 1910. German priests of the Society of the Divine Word, who succeeded them, had to leave the country after World War I. The mission was abandoned until the nationalist restoration in Portugal, which gave the signal for a vigorous recovery. Since the Portuguese missionary agreement of 1940, the rate of progress has accentuated. The Archdiocese of Lourenço Marques was the first in black Africa to be headed by a cardinal. Secular priests, aided by various mission orders, now minister to the area.

South Africa, including the Republic of South Africa, Southwest Africa, Basutoland, Swaziland, Bechuanaland, Rhodesia, Zambia, Malawi, and Mozambique, is much less Catholic than Equatorial Africa. The 2.7 million Catholics and 460,000 catechumens in 1961 constituted about 10 per cent of the 31 million inhabitants. In Basutoland, however, they comprised more than 40 per cent of the 700,00 inhabitants and in Zambia about 20 per cent of the 2.5 million inhabitants; but in Mozambique, long in Portuguese hands, only about 12 per cent of the 6.7 million inhabitants—this represents, however, a sharp rise from the 4,000 Catholics there in 1900.

Insular Africa. In the Indian Ocean east of Mozambique are located the islands of Madagascar, Réunion, and Mauritius.

Mauritius, the former Île de France was evangelized during the *ancien régime* by the Vincentians. English Benedictines replaced them after England seized the island (1810). Bishop Collier (1840–63) was the most remarkable of the English missionaries. He brought to the island the first disciples of Father Libermann, notably Jacques Désiré Laval, called the Peter Claver of Mauritius. Since then, Holy Ghost Fathers have shared the work with secular priests among the Creole population, while other missionaries have been occupied with the sizable Chinese and Indian groups. Clergy from Mauritius serve the small neighboring islands. The Seychelles Islands depended on Mauritius until 1852. In 1863 the mission was confided to the Capuchins.

Vincentians came in 1714 to Réunion, called the Island of Bourbon before 1848. After the French Revolution Christian life was reanimated as a result of the efforts of a colonial clergy recruited and formed in the Seminary of the Holy Spirit in Paris and placed under the authority of a prefect apostolic. The sons of Father Libermann and the daughters of Mother Javouhey also had a beneficent influence, notably at the time of the liberation of the slaves. In 1850 the island became a diocese suffragan to Bordeaux. Since 1916 it has been under the jurisdiction of Propaganda and entrusted to the Holy Ghost Fathers.

From Réunion the gospel passed to Madagascar (now the Malagasy Republic), which in 1789 was part of the Prefecture of Bourbon. In 1818 it was attached to the Vicariate of the Cape of Good Hope, which was incapable of providing missions at that time when Protestants were solidly implanted among the Hovas. In 1820 Catholicism was found only in the small islands of Mayotte, Nossi-Bé, and Sainte-Marie near Madagascar. The Seminary of the Holy Spirit occasionally sent priests to them. In 1829 Madagascar became part of the Prefecture of the South Sea Islands, whose center was at Bourbon and whose domain reached to Oceania. The titular was the vicar-general of Pamiers Monsignor de Solages. He tried to go to Tananarive but was impeded by the order of the Queen, who had become a Protestant. He died (1832) of fever and hunger at Andevoranto on the east coast.

From 1841 the island had its own prefect apostolic dependent on the island of Bourbon. In 1848, along with the neighboring small islands, it became a vicariate confided to the Holy Ghost Fathers, who were replaced in 1850 by the Jesuits. Access to Madagascar remained forbidden to Catholics. In 1855 Father Finaz entered the capital in disguise and remained there nearly 2 years. Not until 1861 were Jesuits able to reside in Tananarive. Their ministry was almost constantly in difficulty, caused first by Protestants, then by the Franco-Madagascar wars (1885–86), and finally by the often flagrant sectarianism of the colonial administration. In 1896 the Vicariate of South Madagascar was erected and confided to the Vincentians; in 1898, that of North Madasgascar, confided to the Holy Ghost Fathers. Other religious orders came later and helped produce the flowering of Catholicism, which was not withered by the rebellion of 1947. The number of Catholics, the development of Catholic Action, social works, education, witness the deep implanting of Catholicism.

In 1961 the 400,000 inhabitants of Réunion and the Seychelles Islands were well over 90 per cent Catholic; the 675,000 on Mauritius, about 31 per cent; and the 5.4 million in the Malagasy Republic, about 22 per cent.

East Africa. It was from Réunion also that Catholicism passed to the continent because of the zeal of Bishop Maupoint of Saint-Denis. In 1859 he sent his vicar-general, Abbé Fava, with two priests, a physician, and six religious to lay the bases of a mission. A house was purchased in Zanzibar, where the Catholics, 60 in all, attended a Mass (Dec. 25, 1860).

In 1862 the Prefecture Apostolic of Zanguebar (Zanzibar) was erected, covering all this section of the coast, with Bishop Maupoint as apostolic delegate. Holy Ghost Fathers came to help him, notably Father Horner who proposed first to seek the abolition of the slave trade and then to establish along the coast, which had been won to Islam, bases whence missionaries could penetrate to the pagans of the interior.

Zanzibar was then the most important slave market in all Africa. More than 60,000 slaves passed through there annually and many more died en route. Those who arrived in too poor health to be sold with profit were cast on the shore to be eaten by jackals or carried off to sea. Father Horner sought to gather these unfortunates, especially children, and to redeem those whom he could. After the official suppression of the traffic, the British confided to Father Horner those who were seized aboard the ships of the slave traders. Thus was born the orphanage at Bagamoyo, which became an important establishment. From there departed numerous groups of explorers and missionaries. Bagomoyo has been the mother of all missions on the east coast, just as Libreville has performed the same function for those of the west coast.

The prefecture was erected into a vicariate in 1883, extending to the region of Kilimanjaro. In 1887 the southern part was detached to constitute the Vicariate of Southern Zanguebar, which was confided to the Benedictines of Bavaria, replaced after World War I by Swiss Capuchins. When England and Germany divided the country (1906) there were erected the Vicariate of Central Zanguebar, corresponding to the German part and that of Northern Zanguebar, corresponding to the British section. In 1905 the Consolata Missioners from Turin received the Prefecture of Kenya, near Mt. Kenya.

Bishop Lavigerie was entrusted by Leo XIII in 1878 with the entire region of the large lakes. The first group of missionaries left Marseilles (1879) for Nyanza, Uganda, and Tanganyika.

In Tanganyika beginnings were difficult because of the opposition from Protestants and Arab slave traders. Despite the rebellion of 1905 and World War I, the mission flourished remarkably. Numerous religious institutes collaborated with the White Fathers, and created one of the strongest sectors of the Church in Africa. In 1961 about 18 per cent of its 9.4 million inhabitants were Catholics.

In Uganda beginnings were still more difficult. Father Lourdel reached its capital in 1879. The first adult baptisms occurred in 1880. Moslem intrigues obliged the missionaries to depart (1882–85). In their absence, however, Catholicism continued to grow. The hatred of the prime minister unleashed a persecution that resulted in the martyrdom of 38 Catholics, 22 of whom have been canonized (*see* UGANDA, MARTYRS OF). Despite two later persecutions, in 1888 and 1892, Catholicism has enjoyed such spectacular progress that Uganda has been termed the pearl of the African missions. Of its 6.8 million inhabitants in 1961, 30 per cent were Catholics. Mission progress in the neighboring kingdoms of Burundi and Rwanda, entered by missionaries *c.* 1900, has been even more successful, since about half of their 5 million inhabitants in 1961 were Catholics.

Since internal troubles interrupted communications between Zanzibar and the missions of Nyanza and Tanganyika, Cardinal Lavigerie tried to join the two latter ones. In 1889 the Portuguese ambassador proposed to him in Rome the foundation of a mission on the border area between Mozambique and Nyasaland, and an agreement was signed for the establishment of a station at Mponda. In 1891 Anglo-Portuguese rivalries forced the missionaries to settle further north. The Vicariate of Nyasa was erected in 1897. From it was detached in 1904 Shire, which was confided to the care of the Montfort Fathers.

In 1894 the Holy Ghost Fathers founded a station in Kenya at Mombasa, and in 1899, one at *Nairobi. Consolata Fathers and Mill Hill Missionaries joined them later. World War I turned German East Africa into a battlefield, which tested many missions. World War II provoked other difficulties because of the very active Moslem propaganda in certain regions and also because of the revolutionary aspirations of budding nationalism. Conflicts ensued that were embittered by racism and communism. The gravest conflict was the insurrection in the 1950s of the Mau Mau in Kenya, who were violently anti-Christian, and caused veritable martyrdoms among the faithful. Yet Christianity prospered in eastern and central Africa. Numerous ecclesiastical jurisdictions were erected, many of which were confided to native bishops and priests. By 1961 the missionaries had won to Catholicism about 14 per cent of the 7.6 million Kenyans.

Northeast Africa. Catholicism is very meagerly represented in this predominantly Moslem area comprising French Somaliland, Somalia, Ethiopia, Sudan and Egypt. Only about 1 per cent of the 58 million dwellers in these countries were Catholics in 1961.

It was long impossible for missionaries to penetrate British Somaliland, which pertained nominally to the Vicariate of Arabia. The two missionaries who were installed at Berbera in 1890 were expelled in 1910. Not until 4 decades later were they authorized to settle in Hargeisa (now in Somalia). In French Somaliland, Capuchins from the Vicariate of Arabia opened the first mission at Obock (1885), which became a prefecture (1914) embracing a vast part of Ethiopia. In Italian Somaliland the Prefecture of Benadir was erected in 1904 and confided to the Trinitarians, later to the Consolata Fathers. In 1927 the prefecture took the name of Mogadiscio and was transferred to the Franciscans. Since 1960 British and Italian Somalia have formed an independent state. Islam continues to enjoy a religious monopoly. Communist influences also have existed.

Abyssinian *Monophysitism rather than Islam has impeded Catholicism in Ethiopia. Pope Gregory XVI charged the Franciscans in 1834 to restore this former mission field, but it was not until 1839 that this could be accomplished, and then by Italian Vincentians. Promising beginnings (1840–45) were succeeded by persecution, which resulted in martyrdoms, such as that of Bl. *Ghebre Michael. The prefect apostolic Bl. Giustino de *Jacobis was also put to death (July 30, 1860). French Vincentians restored the mission and have remained there with alternating successes and failures. The arrival of Italians at Massaua (1885) led to the creation of the Prefecture of Eritrea (1895), which became a vicariate in 1911. A hierarchy of the Oriental rite was created in 1930.

In southern Ethiopia a mission in the Galla region began in 1846, directed by Guglielmo *Massaja. Despite serious difficulties, it spread to Choa, Godham, and Kaffa. In 1880 Massaja returned to Europe and became a cardinal. After him Bishop Taurin inaugurated the mission of Harar, which progressed under Bishop Jarosseau, his successor (1900–37). In 1937 the Italian conquest permitted the erection of three vicariates and six prefectures. All this advance was endangered by Ethiopia's recovery of autonomy (1941). The eviction of Italy failed to result in that of Catholicism. Missions have since renewed their activities. Eritrea, which has federated with Ethiopia, has retained its missionary personnel. Relations with the Vatican were established in 1957. Among the Catholic jurisdictions, those of the *Ethiopian rite are exarchates under the Congregation for the Oriental Church; those of the Latin rite are vicariates or prefectures dependent on Propaganda.

Upper Egypt and Sundan lacked relations with the Western world *c.* 1900 and constituted a source of slaves for Moslem slave traders. In 1842 one of the companions of Bishop De Jacobis, obliged to flee Ethiopia, went to Khartoum. In 1846 Gregory XVI created the immense Vicariate of Central Africa, which he confided to Bishop Casolani, a Maltese, and later to a Polish Jesuit, Bishop Ryllo. The first missionaries arrived in 1848, but none remained by 1854. Attempts were later made without much success to renew the work by Dom Mazza, a priest from Verona, and then by Austrian Franciscans. During 20 years, 75 missioners died, most of them under 30 years of age. In 1866 the Holy See suppressed the Vicariate of Central Africa.

Daniele *Comboni, one of Dom Mazza's companions, founded his own missionary congregation, the *Verona Fathers, and in 1872 obtained the reestablishment of the vicariate. He became the first vicar apostolic (1877) but died in 1881. The Madhi revolt prevented activity by the mission for 17 years. Not until 1898 were the Verona Fathers able to work amid its ruins. In the northern part, predominantly Moslem, results were meager, but in the southern section the pagan populations of the Upper Nile and of Bahr-el-Ghazal willingly accepted Catholicism. Since 1956 the Sudan has been an independent state with Moslem influence predominant. Under the pretext of promoting national unity, they have tried to turn the peoples of the south into Moslems. In 1964 the missions were undergoing persecutions and all missionaries who were foreigners were expelled. Less than 3 per cent of the 12 million Sudanese in 1961 were Catholics.

Egypt was the sole African country in which Christ dwelt and the first to receive the gospel. In 1900 Catholicism was represented there only by foreigners and by a handful of native faithful, more or less contaminated by the decadence of the Coptic Church. When Egypt was opened to European influences in 1835, the apostolic delegate appealed for French missionaries. In 1839 the vast Vicariate of Egypt and Arabia was created. To it came Vincentians and Daughters of Charity (1844), Christian Brothers (1857), the society of the African Missions (1876), and Jesuits (1879). These religious set up numerous charitable and educational establishments. The anti-European reaction of 1882 and the English seizure of the country compromised Catholic influence but only temporarily. In 1895 Leo XIII established the Catholic hierarchy of the Coptic rite. In 1923 the constitution promulgated by King Fouad I assured Christians equality of rights. But after 1937 the militant nationalism and Islamism of the Egyptian government created a difficult situation. The new constitution (1956) made Mohammedanism the state religion. Schools and the great majority of establishments held by religious were nationalized. While engaging in educational and charitable works, especially in the Delta region, the missionaries did not neglect the Coptic Christian com-

Fig. 4. "The Descent from the Cross," panel of the doors of the cathedral at Ibadan, Nigeria, carved by L. Fakeye.

munities along the Nile to Upper Egypt. Work among the Copts has been conducted especially by the Jesuits. In 1879 a minor seminary was opened, whose students completed their studies at Beirut. The Coptic clergy has its major and minor seminary at Maadi. About 0.6 per cent of the 25 million Egyptians in 1961 were Catholics.

Conclusion. Thus it is clear that the Catholic Church has become present everywhere in Africa, and that this presence is the result of only 1 century of apostolate. The 50,000 Catholics in 1800 increased to 26 million by 1961. In 1800 ecclesiastical divisions were rare; in 1964 there were 312 dioceses, vicariates, or prefectures, of which 276 were dependent on Propaganda, 16 (in Portuguese territories) on the Congregation of *Extraordinary Ecclesiastical Affairs, 15 on that of the Oriental Church, and 5 on the Consistorial Congregation. The 50 missionaries of 1800 increased to 13,500 priests (2,500 Africans), 5,000 teaching brothers (1,200 Africans), 23,000 religious women (7,000 Africans), and more than 100,000 African catechists or teachers.

The African territories where Catholic missions have been most prosperous are the following: Dahomey, Togo, southern Nigeria, southern Cameroun, Gabon, Congo, Rwanda, Brundi, Angola, Basutoland, Mozambique, Tanganyika, Uganda, and Madagascar. In several regions the era of clearing and seeding continues; in many others the Church has developed mature communities. The Holy See has recognized this by establishing the ecclesiastical hierarchy in British West Africa (1950), South Africa (1951), British East Africa (1953), Rhodesia (1955), French Africa (1955), Morocco and southern Algeria (1956), Belgian Congo and Rwanda and Burundi (1959), and Zambia and Malawi (1959).

More significant has been the nomination of more and more Africans as ordinaries. There were 78 in December 1963, including the first African cardinal, Laurean Rugambwa, Bishop of Bukoba, Tanganyika, created cardinal in 1960. To coordinate the apostolate six apostolic delegations have been instituted. Much remains to be done. In a total population of 230 million in 1964, Christians numbered 50 million (26 million Catholics, 19 million Protestants; 5 million Orthodox); Moslems, 95 million; pagans, 85 million. Catholics represented about 12 per cent of the population.

The task before the Church is immense and the difficulties many. Paganism sometimes enjoys a resurgence as it assimilates Christian elements. Islam remains indomitable and carries on an active, successful proselytism. Laicism and materialism, imported with colonialism, penetrated the most highly educated classes and the youthful group in the population. *Nationalism, often implicated with racism, continues to provoke political storms injurious to the missions. Communism extends its propaganda, and utilizes discontents, resentments, and disorders. In short, the Church faces a continent in ferment, which is awakening from centuries of slumber and moving gradually but fitfully into the turmoil of the modern world.

The success of the missions accentuates the penury of personnel and resources. The care of more and more Christian communities restricts the apostolate among non-Christians. The native clergy and laity are far from adequate for the needs in countries where, despite an abundance of baptisms, the outlook and social structures are not yet Christianized. In seeking to adapt the Christian message to African realities, African Catholics are open to the ideas and methods of older sections of the Church from which they await effective aid. Vatican Council II has shown that the new Church of Africa, succeeding to that of the early centuries, can make its voice heard in the concert of Christianity.

Bibliography: Streit-Dindinger, v.17–20. J. ROMMERSKIRCHEN and J. DINDINGER, *Bibliografia missionaria* (Rome 1936–), annual. Delacroix HistMissCath. Mulders. Latourette. Latourette Christ19th-20thCent, v.3, 5. C. P. GROVES, *The Planting of Christianity in Africa,* 4 v. (London 1949–58). J. BECKMANN, *Die katholische Kirche im neuen Afrika* (Einsiedeln 1947). P. W. BÜHLMANN, *Afrika* (*Die Kirche unter den Völkern,* v.1; Mainz 1963). J. MULLEN, *The Catholic Church in Modern Africa* (London 1965). R. A. OLIVER, *The Missionary Factor in East Africa* (New York 1952). J. CONSIDINE, *Africa: World of New Men* (New York 1955). E. DAMMANN, *Die Religionen Afrikas* (Stuttgart 1963). H. EMMERICH, *Atlas Missionum* (Vatican City 1958), to be used with L. SCHORER'S *Data statistica* (Vatican City 1959). A. FREITAG et al., *The Universe Atlas of the Christian World* (London 1964). B. ARENS, *Manuel des missions catholiques* (Louvain 1925). MissCattol. *Bilan du Monde.* AnnPont has annual data on all dioceses, vicariates, and prefectures. Complete list in AnnPont (1965) 1423–27. **Illustration credit:** Fig. 2, Courtesy of the May Company.

[J. BOUCHAUD]

AFRICAN MISSIONS, SOCIETY OF THE

The Society of African Missions (SMA), of pontifical right, was founded in Lyons, France, on Dec. 8, 1856, by Bp. Melchior de *Marion-Brésillac for the conversion of Africa and Negroes of African origin. Its members—priests, students, and coadjutor brothers—live a common life but have no vows, although they take a solemn perpetual oath of obedience.

In 1858, as its first mission, the society was given the vicariate apostolic of *Sierra Leone, where, the following year, Brésillac and most of his missionaries perished during a fever epidemic. Leadership then passed to Father Augustin Planque, whom Pius IX confirmed as the first superior general of the society. In 1861 a group of missionaries left for the newly erected vicariate of Dahomey, where successful foundations were made at Ouidah, Porto-Novo, and Lagos. The missionaries established stations along the West Coast of Africa, from Liberia to the Niger River. In 1875 Planque founded the Congregation of Our Lady of the Apostles to provide sisters to assist in establishing schools, orphanages, dispensaries, model farms, and workshops, in order to improve the conditions of the native people and to attract them to the Catholic religion.

The society spread throughout Europe and the U.S.; in 1912 the Irish province was established; in 1923 the Dutch province; in 1927 Eastern France (Alsace); in 1941 the American province. The motherhouse was transferred to Rome in 1937. By 1961, there were houses in England, Italy, Canada, Belgium, and Spain, while a total of 1,778 members of the society engaged in missionary activities in 18 ecclesiastical divisions in Liberia, the Ivory Coast, Ghana, Togo, Dahomey, Nigeria, and Egypt. In addition, the society served in four other African territories entrusted to the native African hierarchy. In the U.S., Bp. Benjamin J. Keiley of Savannah, Ga., appealed to the society for priests to work among the Negroes of his diocese. From the Savannah mission, begun in 1904 and directed by Rev. Ignatius Lissner, priests spread to various parishes throughout the U.S. In 1917, Lissner founded the *Franciscan Handmaids of the Most Pure Heart of Mary, a congregation for colored sisters. In 1941, when the American province was canonically erected in Tenafly, N.J., he was named its first provincial.

The Society of African Missions has a minor seminary in Dedham, Mass.; a novitiate in Doylestown, Pa.; and a house of studies in Washington, D.C. The 80 priests of the American province work in the Archdioceses of Atlanta, Ga.; Boston, Mass.; Los Angeles, Calif.; Newark, N.J.; Philadelphia, Pa.; and Washington, D.C.; and the Dioceses of Belleville, Ill.; Charleston, S.C.; Savannah, Ga.; and Tucson, Ariz. In Africa, they staff the vicariate apostolic of Cape Palmas, Liberia.

Bibliography: R. F. GUILCHER, *La Société des missions africaines: Ses origines, sa nature, sa vie, ses oeuvres* (Lyon 1956). J. BONFILS, *L'Oeuvre de Msgr. De Marion Brésillac en faveur du clergé local dans les missions de l'Inde au XIX*[e] *siècle* (Lyon 1959). M. J. BANE, *Catholic Pioneers in West Africa* (Dublin 1956); *Heroes of the Hinterland* (New York 1959). J. M. TODD, *African Mission* (London 1962).

[E. J. BIGGANE]

AFTERLIFE

Although belief in a continuing or new life after death is widespread among the peoples of the world, there are profound differences among cultural traditions in conceptions of this afterlife; and even in those civilized societies in which a sharp division between the here and the hereafter is theologically postulated and conventionally accepted, there are personal variations in specific images of the afterlife. Despite the latter, two elements—belief in a final moral judgment of personal conduct in the world and belief in the specific existence of an afterworld distinct from this world—define Christian, Christian-influenced, and to a lesser degree Jewish and Islamic conceptions of the afterlife. For the developed doctrinal and theological concepts, *see* HEAVEN (THEOLOGY OF); HELL (THEOLOGY OF); JUDGMENT, DIVINE (IN THEOLOGY); PURGATORY. This article treats within the perspective of the comparative study of *religion the differing conceptions found (1) in primitive societies, (2) in the Bible, and (3) in Greco-Roman religion.

1. IN PRIMITIVE SOCIETIES

Generally speaking, primitive peoples do not share the twin assumptions of a final moral judgment of behavior in the world and the specific existence of an afterworld. Accordingly, most anthropologists would not agree with Wilhelm *Schmidt's assumption of moral judgment and an associated belief in an afterworld as coextensive with primitive *monotheism (274–). It seems more acceptable historically to reason that as society becomes increasingly secularized, and in the literal sense civilized, the sphere of moral action contracts and grows more complex; correlatively, the idea that the ultimate *loci* of the consequences of morality and immorality are in the afterworld emerges with great clarity.

Continuity of the Self. Primitive societies are, as Robert Redfield and Paul Radin have indicated, moral at their core; persons relate to each other in a moral nexus, not as contracting partners in a legal, technical, commercial, that is, civilized order (*see* ETHICS IN PRIMITIVE SOCIETIES). This *sacred* quality of primitive life is evident in the ritually celebrated cycles of birth, death, and rebirth of the person, of society, and of nature at large. In these primitive rites of passage and ritual dramas, persons may be, for example, conceived as dying to a given status in the world and being reborn into another status, but without destroying the continuity of self. The self is never merely reduced to the status; rather, it is enriched by experiencing the pain of internal growth and diversification. In a sense, the passage of the person through primitive societies can be understood as a progressive spiritualization. In the Winnebago medicine rite described by Radin, the goal is what Mircea Eliade has called the "perpetual regeneration of the initiate," the "eternal return" to mythical origins, implying an abolition of time and a "reinstatement of the miraculous moment of creation" (*Shamanism* 319–320). Historical, progressive, lineal time, central to the modern scientific world view and expressed in the Hebraic and Christian cosmogonies (in the Christian context based on the historicity of Jesus), is not a primitive conception.

The cyclic and sacred character of primitive life is similarly evident in the common belief, as among the Anaguta of Northern Nigeria, that an infant is the reincarnation of an ancestral spirit in the grandparental generation; hence the person, who has literally died to the world, begins a new spiritual existence, is reborn. The critical point is that primitive society itself emerges as the arena of the original drama of creation and transcendence, of Eliade's "irruption of the sacred into the world" occurring in "primordial" time (*The Sacred and the Profane* 72). The passage through life takes on the aspect of a moral drama, culminating, as among the Winnebago Indians of Wisconsin, in the initiate's ultimate effort to grasp the meaning of creation and so win eternal life or rebirth. In these primitive rites, the forerunners of the more explicit and historically specific Christian Sacraments, that which Eliade terms a "nostalgia for Paradise" (*Shamanism* 508), for the instant of pure being, is evident.

Identity of World and Afterworld. It is clear that the antinomies life-death, natural-supernatural, sacred-profane, and spirit-flesh that weigh so heavily in civilized Christian thought are, in primitive societies, largely irrelevant. Life moves on all levels simultaneously. Ordinary events are suffused with sacred meaning, everything has personality; God, spirits, ancestors—dreamt of, seen, or felt—*exist*. The mode of primitive thinking is existentialist in the most comprehensive sense. Therefore, the split between this world and the afterworld is of little moment. Where conceptions of the afterlife are present, they typically assimilate, as Franz Boas put it, the "social life of the dead [to] . . . the living" (606–607). The deceased may maintain an active position in the kinship structure. The afterworld is, with minor exceptions, quite the same as this world; throughout North Asia, as elsewhere, the former is simply a mirror image of the latter. Frequently, the souls of the dead, on their passage to this inverted world, must pass over some obstacle or across a narrow bridge. But this seems to be related to the psychology of mourning and the consequent need for ritualizing the trauma of separation, rather than to a permanent journey to a distinctly conceived afterworld.

Despite the contradictions inherent in certain technical aspects of the primitive view of the afterlife (e.g., the social immediacy of souls versus their indeterminate existence in a "double" of this world), neither the idea of hell nor of other-worldly reward for moral behavior are important themes in primitive religions. This is true even where, as among the Anaguta, there is a clear cut belief in an accessible supreme creator.

See also RELIGION (IN PRIMITIVE CULTURE).

Bibliography: F. BOAS, *Race, Language and Culture* (New York 1940). S. DIAMOND, "Plato and the Definition of the Primitive" in *Culture in History: Essays in Honor of Paul Radin,* ed. S. DIAMOND (New York 1960) 118–141; "The Search for the Primitive" in *Man's Image in Medicine and Anthropology,* ed. I. GALDSTON (New York 1963) 62–115. M. ELIADE, *The Sacred and the Profane,* tr. W. R. TRASK (New York 1959; Torchbk 1961); *Shamanism: Archaic Techniques of Ecstasy,* tr. W. R. TRASK (Bollingen Series 76; rev. ed. New York 1964). R. FIRTH, "Fate of the Soul" in *Anthropology of Folk Religion,* ed. C. M. CHARLES (pa. New York 1960). P. RADIN, *The World of Primitive Man* (New York 1953; repr. 1960). R. REDFIELD, *The Primitive World and Its Transformations* (Ithaca, N.Y. 1953). W. SCHMIDT, *The Origin and Growth of Religion,* tr. H. J. ROSE (2d ed. London 1935).

[S. DIAMOND]

2. IN THE BIBLE

The Israelites believed in some kind of ghostlike afterlife. According to their ideas, all the dead go to *Sheol, the nether world. Kings and slaves, old and young, "all go to one place" [Eccl 6.6; Ps 88(89).49; Jb 3.13–19; 30.23].

Location and Nature of the Abode of the Dead. The Babylonians refer in their myths, e.g., the *Gilgamesh Epic, to the abode of the dead as a place under the earth or on the other side of the world sea. The dead reach it by descending into the earth or by traveling to the farthest point west. Before entering, they must cross the underground river or the "waters of death." The Scriptures, too, refer to its locality by the direction in which the dead go, "down to Sheol" (Is 38.18; Ez 31.14; 3 Kgs 2.9). Even the NT localizes the abode of the dead in the depths of the earth (Mt 16.18; Lk 16.26; Acts 2.24, 27, 31; Rom 10.7; Ap 1.18; 20.13). According to mythicodynamic thinking, this realm of death is constantly overflowing its banks. It is present wherever death exercises its sovereignty. Consequently, not only the grave [Ps 39(40).3; 54(55).24; 142(143).7; etc.] and the depth of the earth are linked with it [Ps 62(63).10; 138(139).8; Is 7.11], but also the sea [Ps 68(69).2, 16; Jon 2.4] and the desert (Jer 2.6, 31; Os 2.5). These "three non-worlds" (J. Pedersen) are considered manifestations of death and belong to the realm of death. In each diminishing of life, the realm of death disrupts the world of the living. Thus illness [Psalms 12(13); 21(22); 29(30); 87(88); etc.], captivity [Psalms 141(142); 142(143)], persecution and hostility [Psalms 17(18); 143(144)], misfortune, poverty, and hunger are all a foretaste of the descent into Sheol and abandonment by Yahweh. The sinner is already living in Sheol (Ps 9A.16–18).

The texts of the preexilic as well as most of the postexilic books draw a most uninviting picture of Sheol. This realm of death is described as an eternal house (Eccl 12.5) with chambers and rooms (Prv 7.27) and gates [Ps 9A.14; 106(107).18; Jb 38.17; Sir 51.9; Wis 16.13; Is 38.10; Mt 16.18; Ap 1.18], a prison (Eccl 9.10) with bars (Jon 2.7) and bolts and bonds [Ps 115(116).3], the land of oblivion [Ps 87(88).13; 114(115).17], a land whence no one can return (Jb 7.9–10; 10.21; Prv 2.19; Sir 38.21). Sheol is called the "no more" (Is 38.11), destruction [Ps 87(88).12], dust [Ps 21(22).30; 29(30).10; 145(146).4; Is 26.19; Jb 17.16; Dn 12.2]. It is a place of horror [Ps 115(116).3], complete darkness [Jb 10.21–22; 17.13; 18.18; 38.17; Ps 87(88).7; 142(143).3], and remoteness from Yahweh. Even so, Satan does not have any influence in the abode of the dead, but Yahweh controls Sheol through His power [Ps 138(139).8; Jb 26.6; Prv 15.11; Is 7.11; Am 9.2].

State of the Dead in the Afterlife. In the OT, death is conceived as the end of the entire living man. Yet this basic conception does not exclude a further existence of the deceased in the realm of the dead, as can be shown by the frequent mention of the dead, of graves, and of funeral customs. For the Israelite, life is life only as it is filled with joy, fortune, wealth, and Yahweh's presence. [*See* LIFE, CONCEPT OF (IN THE BIBLE).] These marks of life are not present in the deceased, who are referred to as *r^epā'îm*, the "weak" [Jb 26.5; Ps 87(88).11; Is 14.9] or as those who have descended into the pit [Ps 27(28).1; 29(30).4; Is 38.18; Ez 26.20; 31.14, 16]. In Sheol, the dead were thought to remain in a state of suspended animation, phantoms of the entire former living man, devoid of all power and vitality (Is 14.10). There is no activity (Eccl 9.10), no pleasure (Sir 14.11–17), no participation in or knowledge of what is happening on earth (Eccl 9.5; Jb 14.12–17; 21.21). In the older books of the OT there is no doubt that the deceased are taken away from the vital union with Yahweh. In the nether world, no one praises God any more [Ps 6.6; 29(30).10; 113B(115).17; Sir 17.22–23; Is 38.18b].

However, the older, pessimistic concept of Sheol as the one place for all the dead, irrespective of the moral value of their lives, begins to change in the later books of the OT. The doctrine of *retribution gradually leads to a distinction between the lot of the good and that of the wicked [Ez 32.17–32; Is 26.8, 14–21; 66.24; Ps 33(34).22–23; Wis 3.2–10, 19; Prv 14.32]. The just man has hope because there will be a reward for his work (2 Chr 15.7; Wis 4. 7–17, 20). In the writings of the postexilic period, a real change in the attitude toward afterlife is observable in the expectancy of resurrection (*see* RESURRECTION OF THE DEAD, 1). Israel's faith in its election by Yahweh and in His mercy and omnipotence, a faith that was justified by His constant intervention in the nation's history and by its experience of the loving union between God and the pious man, had to develop into a trust in Yahweh that amounted to an undocumented guarantee of resurrection and immortality (*see* SOUL, HUMAN, IMMORTALITY OF, 3). This doctrine developed gradually [Jb 14.14–17; Os 13.14; Is 25.9; 57.1–2; Wis 1.13–16; Ps 36(37).3–7; 64(65).5a], and some of its theological reasonings were worked out by Isaia. One finds it in plain words in Dn 12.1–3; Jb 19.25–27; Is 26.19–21; 2 Mc 7.9–11, 14, 22–23, 34–36. However, even at the time of Christ, the doctrine of individual resurrection, which was explicitly rejected by the *Sadducees, was not commonly accepted in Israel (Mt 22.23–34 and parallels; Acts 23.6–10). The NT hardly speaks about the state of the dead. The afterlife was of little concern for the primitive Christian community because the parousia of the Lord (*see* PAROUSIA, 1) and the fulfillment of the eschatological promises were really the heart of the Christian expectation for the future: union with Christ, experienced in faith and in the sacramental life, is but an anticipation of eschatological salvation; this union will be continued, intensified, and fulfilled in the life to come (Phil 1.21–26; etc.).

See also HEAVEN (IN THE BIBLE); HELL (IN THE BIBLE); PURGATORY; ABRAHAM'S BOSOM; HADES; TARTARUS; GEHENNA; PARADISE; JUDGMENT, DIVINE (IN THE BIBLE).

Bibliography: EncDictBibl 508–510. P. ANTOINE, DBSuppl 2:1063–76. J. SCHMID, LexThK² 5:890–892. H. EISING, *ibid.* 9: 391–393. A. ROMEO, EncCatt 11:349–353. H. J. KRAUS and B. REICKE, RGG³ 3:403–406. A. JEREMIAS, *Die babylonisch-assyrischen Vorstellungen vom Leben nach dem Tode* (Leipzig 1887). P. DHORME, "Le Séjour des morts chez les Babyloniens et les Hébreux," RevBibl 16 (1907) 59–78; "L'Idée de l'au-delà dans la religion hébraïque," RevHistRel 123 (1941) 113–142. J. P. E. PEDERSEN, *Israel: Its Life and Culture,* 4 v. in 2 (New York 1926–40; repr. 1959). E. F. SUTCLIFFE, *The Old Testament and the Future Life* (2d ed. Westminster, Md. 1947). O. KUSS, *Der Römerbrief* (Regensburg 1957) 1:241–275, with bibliog. A. FEUILLET, "Mort du Christ et mort du chrétien d'après les épîtres pauliniennes," RevBibl 66 (1959) 481–513. R. H. CHARLES, *Eschatology* (New York 1963).

[H. KÖSTER]

3. IN GRECO-ROMAN RELIGION

At the outset, from an extrinsic point of view, it should be observed that Greco-Roman beliefs on the life after death did not come from a revealed religion; they were not fixed once and for all in sacred books; nor were they dictated, maintained, and controlled as dogmas by a religious authority. They were the product of a slow and steady evolution that corresponded closely, although often with marked lags and uncertainties, to the trends or stages in the development of classical culture in general. Belonging as they did to the domain of tenacious traditions no less than to that of innate anxieties and forebodings, they were in no wise monolithic. New beliefs were superimposed on old conceptions without adjustment or elimination. Rites that belonged to an outmoded faith continued to be performed, even when no one any longer understood their precise bearing or original signification. Conceptions that were basically divergent were found not only side by side in a given cultural period but also together, apparently without conflict, in the soul of one and the same individual.

In General. The mingling of markedly diversified ethnic elements, especially in the great Hellenistic and Roman centers, created a mixture of opinions and beliefs that would be difficult to reduce to its primary components. In view of the shortcomings of official religion in the sphere of death and the hereafter, religious conceptions were so exposed to the strong influences of old wives' tales, superstitions, and black magic, that, in the Hellenistic Age and under the early

Hermes bringing a dead woman to Charon, who will ferry her across the River Styx; watercolor rendering after the decoration on a Greek lekythos that dates from the 5th century B.C.

empire, the educated classes abandoned themselves to unbelief, skepticism, or indifference. The masses, who were long isolated from the progress of philosophy and literature, were too deeply engulfed in the precarious conditions of material subsistence to attempt—at least on their own initiative—a separation of religious rites from superstitious practices or of sound religious sentiments from chimerical fictions.

Intrinsically, Greco-Roman views on the life beyond the grave were conditioned by the evolving ideas of ancient man respecting anthropology, the image of the universe, ethics, and human destiny. From the viewpoint of the earliest beliefs on death, the earliest notions on man were neither spiritual nor materialistic in the modern sense of the terms, but simply "human," in the sense that man did not originally think of himself as a being composed of two "principles." The human being was one, possessing a unity that death did not split into a "lifeless body" and a "surviving soul." The shade in the lower world or the soul in heaven was most commonly only man in his entirety, viewed from the angle of his corporeal dematerialization. The development of the concept of man gradually arrived at an increasingly sharp dichotomy between body and soul. The explanation for the distinction is not to be sought in the different opinions that were held on the nature of the vital principle (breath, blood, heat, eidolon, spark), but rather, on the one hand, in the practice of incineration, which by the very fact that it destroyed the body emphasized the soul, and, on the other, in the influence exercised by dualistic currents in philosophy.

The ancient image of the world passed from the stage in which the earth was looked upon as a flat disk floating on the waters of Ocean to the lofty concept of a universe consisting of concentric spheres in harmonious movement, circumscribed by the sphere of the fixed stars. Yet it did not detach itself from the proud and touching idea that the earth, where man reigned as master, formed the center of the universe in question. Since what survived of man did not attain a degree of dematerialization that would have permitted it to escape the category of "place," the soul found a localization beyond the grave in the precise region to which the scientific image of the world and the ideas on the survival and nature of the soul suggested that it be assigned.

Ethical concepts acquired real influence only from the time when death ceased to be considered a mere passage to another world, where the lot of the dead man was simply a repetition of his social condition on earth. Notions of moral responsibility, of personal conscience, of virtuous conduct, and of sinful life could not make their appearance, however, before the individual as such became conscious of himself. From that time he had to abandon the idea that life was lived on earth only, and he had to submit to moral demands with their inevitable sanctions whereby he could hope, in an existence beyond the grave, for the stern justice and the strict recompense that he had vainly expected on earth.

Human destiny was at first confined within the narrow limits of a terrestrial life, from which man escaped only to the extent to which he, on his part, assured the continuity of his family, tribe, and community. When this restricted cadre was broken to the benefit of the emerging individual human person, the way was open for a concept of survival that, in combining the idea of a reward beyond the grave with the notion of an immortal soul, eventually far surpassed in both duration and intensity the possibilities of life on earth. Thus, the true life could begin or rebegin only after death, which, far from diminishing the significance of the human soul, sent it back to its heavenly and divine home.

Early and Classical Greek Beliefs. According to a notion that was held for many centuries, the dead man survived in his tomb. This notion was the source of the meticulous care devoted to funerals, funeral furniture and offerings, and the cult connected, on certain days of the year (e.g., at the *Anthesteria* at Athens), with the tomb of the dead individual or with the tombs of the dead in general. This was the source too, from Mycenaean times, of the family cult, and then of the community cult of dead men who were especially significant, namely, the "heroes." Subsequently, society, cut off from its ancestral tombs by emigration, apparently was not acquainted with either the cult of the dead or that of heroes. Hence arose the general Greek belief—reinforced by the authority of Homer—that the dead were all found together in the subterranean realm of Hades. In the absence of any moral perspective, Hades was not yet a place of retribution. Given the absolute value of life on earth, it was the exact negative replica of that life. It was marked by the absence of the positive features of earthly existence both on the physical plane—countryside, light, warmth, color, and sound—and on the psychological plane—security, freedom, and joy of existence. It was a life in which, by the law of repetition, shades continued the shadow of their earthly sojourn. However, Minoan religion had postulated the existence of Isles of the Blest, located at the end of the world beyond Ocean, to which the gods transported men of divine lineage while they were still alive. This transatlantic eden of living heroes was subsequently changed into the underworld Elysium of the blessed dead—most probably under the influence of the Mysteries of Eleusis. The initiates, in keeping with the law of repetition, continued to celebrate their joyous feasts in their new abode, while the noninitiates had to be satisfied with a shadowy existence in mire (ἐν βορβόρῳ). This, however, was not yet a form of punishment in the strict sense but a deprivation of true life.

Orphic Conceptions. From the 7th to the 6th century B.C., the Orphics, taking over certain popular beliefs regarding the hereafter, went beyond the ritual demands of the Eleusinian Mysteries and substituted for them prescriptions of moral purity. They spread the idea that the noninitiates would be punished in hell for their unworthy lives. Developing also a vague popular notion respecting the transmigration of the soul, the Orphics, from the 6th century, adopted the doctrine of metempsychosis. They maintained that the soul, divinely immortal and essentially independent of the body in which it was entombed (σῶμα, σῆμα), was able, by virtue of upright conduct in the course of successive incarnations, to free itself finally from all dependence on a carnal body. It could then live its own proper and true life in an Elysium, which Orphic "teaching" (except in Pindar) has not described in detail.

Pythagorean Conceptions. From the end of the 6th century, Pythagoreanism borrowed from the Orphic Mysteries its views on metempsychosis and the popular notion of a recompense after death. It thus contributed in its turn to the establishment of the belief according to which, in the lower world, Elysium was reserved for the pious, while Tartarus in Hades was a place of punishment for sinners.

Judgment, and Reward or Punishment in the Hereafter. In the classical period (5th and 4th centuries B.C.) the Orphico-Pythagorean belief in the punishment of Hades spread widely, as is evidenced by literature (Aristophanes, Plato) and art (vase paintings). The majority of people were hardly reached by the philosophical arguments of Plato, who sought to prove scientifically the immortality of the soul, but they were deeply influenced by the mythicoreligious representations of a rewarding hereafter, of which they learned from mythology and the mysteries. Thus most probably *c.* 400 B.C., the idea of a *iudicium post mortem* took definite shape, as is known through the writings of Plato and the south Italian funerary vases of the 4th century. After death every soul appeared before a tribunal in Hades, where a college of three heroes (Minos, Rhadamanthus, and Aeacus) judged it according to its merits. Pious souls were rewarded with the Elysian dwellings as their abode; those of less perfect conduct had to undergo a kind of purgatory; and hardened sinners were condemned for all eternity to the punitive and exemplary tortures of Tartarus.

Hellenistic Beliefs. Plato's affirmation of the divine affinity and immortal nature of the soul ended in the skepticism of the New Academy, while *Epicurus, following the atomic theory of Democritus, taught that after death the soul, like the body, dissolved into atoms. The early Stoics recognized in their vital principle, which was related to the fiery ether, a vague form of survival, but it was quite impersonal and limited in time. However, with Posidonius and his Platonic leanings, the soul regained a true immortality. The mystery religions and the strong Orphico-Pythagorean beliefs in Magna Graecia promised a hereafter to their adherents. The aspects of this paradise were not so much an indication of a relatively low level of morality as they were a reflection of and transfer of deep longings for a felicity that was no longer threatened by trials or death. According to popular belief, the firmness of which was not influenced by skepticism or by the denials of the educated class, the hereafter was usually located under the earth. This fact is indicated by metrical epitaphs, curse tablets consigning their victims to the infernal deities, Orphic gold plates found in south Italy, and paintings on funerary vases from the same region, etc. Similarly, the allegorical interpretation of the punishments of Tartarus as worked out by the Pythagoreans had no effect whatever on the popular notions respecting reward or punishment in the next world.

Nevertheless, the progress of Hellenistic civilization brought about marked changes regarding the location of the hereafter. On the one hand, in accordance with the new scientific theories on the structure of the earth and the universe, Hades had to be moved either to the dark antipodes of the inhabited earth or to the nonilluminated hemisphere of the world. On the other hand, philosophicoreligious teaching on the divine, and therefore heavenly, origin of the soul; astrological cosmology, which turned man's eyes heavenward; the increasing importance of the symbolism of fire and light; and the astral myths telling of great mortals being changed into stars, all combined to exert an influence on beliefs. Men gradually adopted the revolutionary idea that after death souls were changed into stars, or rather flew off to the

Gravestone of Aurelius Hermia and Aurelia (Philematium), c. 60 B.C., *from the Via Nomentana, Rome (CIL I*[2] *1221).*

starry sky. Under the Roman Empire, this lunisolar or astral immortality received support from solar pantheism. It would be wrong, however, to exaggerate the expansion of the new belief. Only limited circles were affected. In the leisured class as a whole, skepticism was the rule, whereas the lower strata of the population continued to stick to their old idea of an underworld Hades.

In Early Rome. Primitive Roman beliefs regarding the hereafter were very restricted in scope and character. The dead man was placed in a tomb that was built in the form of a house. He led there a kind of weak existence, and the living had to sustain him by funeral offerings. At the same time he was to be feared, as is evidenced by references to apparitions in dreams, to ghosts, to the role of the *ahori* or premature dead, and to necromancy. On certain days of the year, too, the dead had official access to the world of the living by the removal of the *lapis manalis* covering the entrance to the lower world (*mundus*). In so far as the dead man was a link in the long chain of his *gens* or clan, he belonged to the divine ancestral spirits, the *Di Parentes*. Mixed in the mass of the dead, he formed a part of the *Lemures,* spirits of the dead who were divided into *Lares* and *Larvae* according as they were benevolent or malevolent, respectively. Furthermore, these various connections were all brought under the head of *Di Manes,* to whom specific rites were assigned: the *Parentalia, Lemuria, Larentalia,* and later the *Rosalia* and *Dies Violares.*

Before the 4th century B.C., the Romans do not seem to have been familiar with an infernal lower world common to all the dead nor with any form of punishment beyond the grave. From this time the Etruscans acquainted them with the Greek representation of Hades, but in the form that the terrifying Etruscan demonology had given it. In the course of the 3d century B.C., Magna Graecia invested this Etrusco-Roman world of the dead, *Orcus,* with all its rich infernal mythology and with all the Orphico-Pythagorean acquisitions to which the Greek genius had given birth. Through the direct contact between the Greco-Oriental and Roman civilizations, all these ideas and beliefs became more and more thoroughly acclimated at Rome. They received a quasi-sacred and definitive expression in the 6th book of Vergil's *Aeneid.*

Greco-Roman Beliefs. From the end of the republic, the Greco-Oriental and Roman worlds were fused into a great cultural commonwealth in which the active, general circulation of religious ideas occasioned the flourishing of various forms of syncretistic religion. Still, old conceptions persisted, whether they took on a new life under their old patrons (the various philosophies), whether they adjusted themselves to the form and organization of religious practices coming from the East (the mystery cults), or whether they simply maintained themselves against the winds and waves of innovation, firmly anchored as they were in the hearts of the masses (popular beliefs).

With regard to the concern of philosophy with the problem of the hereafter, Neo-Pythagoreanism (1st century B.C.–2d century A.D.) and Neoplatonism (*c.* A.D. 250–*c.* 500)—despite some Oriental elements—represented basically currents and ideas of Greek origin. According to the Neo-Pythagoreans, souls, on being freed from the body, escaped into the atmosphere, where they were purified by the winds before they re-entered their original home, the starry spheres. The Neoplatonists taught that the soul, buffeted in some way between the material many and the spiritual One, had the duty to apply itself to the noble task of regaining suprasensible divine life. The syncretistic teachings of the Hermetic literature and of Gnosticism (2d and 3d centuries A.D.) held in common that the soul, having once been cast into matter, could return to its heavenly source only through "true knowledge." Besides the old mysteries, whose promise of immortality was reinforced through contact with Orphico-Pythagorean and Neoplatonic elements, various cults, under a flexible form of mystery religion probably borrowed from the Greek mysteries, honored divinities imported from the East (Cybele-Attis, Isis-Osiris, Sabazios, Mithras), and they attracted the intensely emotional devotion of the masses, among whom the earlier native stock was being submerged by cosmopolitan elements.

It is desirable, however, to give a just evaluation of the expansion of the philosophicoreligious doctrines, which appealed strictly to the intellectual aristocracy insofar as it had not limited its hopes to the immortality of fame, and also to appraise the content of the message of salvation afforded by the mystery religions. Several lofty ideas that belonged to philosophy and the mysteries—freedom from death of the body by resurrection, deliverance from the death of the soul by spiritual rebirth and divine illumination, deification, divine filiation—had little or no influence on the rank and file of people before Christianity spread among them. Such ideas acquired their real efficacy, expansion, depth, and, in a certain measure, their existence only through the victorious progress of Christianity.

The popular conceptions, which are so vividly revealed by the metrical funeral inscriptions, indicate that common people were practically impervious to the Pythagorean idea that placed Hades in the sublunary region or in the moon itself, and that they had no interest in the system of solar pantheism or in the Gnostic teachings on the fall and ascent of souls through the planetary spheres. The old believers clung obstinately to the cult of the dead at the tomb and to the idea of a lower world in which the shades lived the barest kind of existence in darkness, although they granted that in rare cases the dead, as a reward for a pious life, enjoyed in the Elysian Fields a happy existence of eternal feasting. However, as the gods—and light—had their abode in the heavens, the blessed Hereafter tended to be moved to the celestial heights. There the elect received as their portion the immortal happiness that the philosophicoreligious teachings, the mysteries of Gnostic coloring, and imperial apotheosis had offered to a select few. Hell, in the modern sense, remained fixed in the traditional lower world; its punishments, to which Christianity made its contribution (e.g., in the *Apocalypse of Peter*), attained a diversity and refinement that emanated less from a conscience motivated by the unfulfilled desire for perfect justice than from the lower level of human thinking, over which neither the noblest pagan ideas nor the Christian gospel of salvation had effective control.

See also CRETAN-MYCENAEAN RELIGION; ETRUSCAN RELIGION; GREEK PHILOSOPHY (RELIGIOUS ASPECTS); GREEK RELIGION; MYSTERY RELIGIONS, GRECO-ORIENTAL; NEOPLATONISM; NEO-PYTHAGOREANISM; ORPHISM; ROMAN RELIGION; STOICISM.

Bibliography: J. T. ADDISON, *Life beyond Death in the Beliefs of Mankind* (Boston and N.Y. 1932). F. CUMONT, *Lux perpetua* (Paris 1949). A. DIETERICH, *Nekyia* (2d ed. Leipzig 1913). L. R. FARNELL, *Greek Hero Cults and Ideas of Immortality* (Oxford 1921). F. HEILER, *Unsterblichkeitsglaube und Jenseitshoffnung in der Geschichte der Religionen* (Munich 1950). O. KERN, *Die Religion der Griechen*, 3 v. (2d ed. Berlin 1963). K. LATTE, *Römische Religionsgeschichte* (Munich 1960). R. A. LATTIMORE, *Themes in Greek and Latin Epitaphs* (2d ed. pa. Urbana, Ill. 1962). Nilsson GeschGrRel. W. F. OTTO, *Die Manen oder von den Urformen des Totenglaubens* (3d ed. Darmstadt 1962). C. PASCAL, *Le credenze d'oltretomba nelle opere letterarie dell' antichità classica*, 2 v. (Catania 1912). G. PFANNMUELLER, *Tod, Jenseits und Unsterblichkeit* (Basel 1953). E. ROHDE, *Psyche: The Cult of Souls and Belief in Immortality among the Greeks*, tr. W. B. HILLIS from 8th Ger. ed. (New York 1925). **Illustration credits:** Fig. 1, Reproduced from "Weissgrundige Attische Lekythen," Fürtwangler and Riezler, Munich, 1915. Courtesy of F. Bruckmann KG, Munich. Fig. 2, Courtesy of the Trustees of The British Museum.

[G. SANDERS]

AGABUS, an early Judaeo-Christian endowed with the charism of prophecy. Agabus (Ἄγαβος, of uncertain derivation) is first mentioned in Acts 11.27–28, where he is spoken of as accompanying a group of prophets who journeyed from Jerusalem to Antioch. There he predicted that a famine would soon overtake the world. Luke notes the fulfillment of his prophecy in the reign of the Emperor Claudius (A.D. 41–54). This is most probably the famine of Judea that Josephus describes in *Ant.* 3.15.3; 20.2.5; 5.2. As a result of Agabus's prediction, the Antiochian community collected alms for the Jerusalem Church, which had become impoverished through its charity to the poor. Agabus is almost certainly the same prophet who met Paul at Caesarea *c.* A.D. 58 and, through a symbolic action, predicted that Paul would be imprisoned in Jerusalem and given over to the Gentiles (Acts 21.10–11). In the Eastern Church Agabus is venerated as a martyr whose feast day is celebrated on March 8.

Bibliography: A. WIKENHAUSER, LexThK[2] 4:1314; *Die Apostelgeschichte und ihr Geschichtswert* (Münster 1921) 407–409. A. ROMEO, EncCatt 1:418–419. EncDictBibl 39. B. H. THROCKMORTON, InterDictBibl 1:52. K. S. GAPP, "The Universal Famine under Claudius," HarvThRev 28 (1935) 258–265.

[J. A. GRASSI]

AGAPE, SS. The name of several saints honored as martyrs in the early Church. The name Agape (Charity) is sometimes confused with Agatha.

Agape, daughter of St. Sophia (Wisdom), is associated with SS. Faith and Hope and, according to a 7th- or 8th-century *passio* written by John the Priest, she was allegedly put to death at Rome during the persecution of Hadrian. The *Itineraria located her grave on the Via Aurelia, while the *Notula* of Olea of Monza placed it on the Via Appia. Ansa, wife of King Desiderius of the Lombards (756–774), gave her relics to the monastery of St. Giulia in Brescia. Her feast is celebrated August 1 in the Roman Church, and September 17 in the Greek Church. (See A. Frutaz, LexThK[2] 1:182; G. de Tervarent, AnalBoll 68:419–423; *Passio* in BHL 2966–73.)

Agape of Thessalonika, honored with her sisters SS. Chionia and Irene in the Syrian Breviary on April 2, in the Roman Martyrology on April 3, and among the Greeks on April 16. The sisters, after a legal process under the Roman prefect Dulcitius on April 1, 304, were allegedly burned to death for refusing to eat food sacrificed to the Roman gods and for hiding Christian books. The Basilica of Thessalonica was erected in their honor. The acts of the three judicial processes have been preserved. (See A. Palmieri, DHGE 1.876; H. Delehaye, SynaxConst 605–606.)

Agape, associated with St. Marina, is mentioned in the Syrian martyrology as having been martyred at Antioch on March 11, 411. According to later Spanish

The breaking of bread at a funeral banquet, or agape, 2d-century fresco in the Catacomb of Priscilla, Rome.

legends she is said to have been put to death with the Bithynian martyrs in Spain during the Decian persecution, but this story resulted from a misreading of the Roman martyrology by the Spanish hagiographer Galesinius. (See S. Salaville, DHGE 1:875–876.)

Agape of Terni, mentioned in the Roman martyrology as a virgin and martyr for February 15. A protégé of Bishop Valentine of Terni, she was reputedly beheaded in the Aurelian persecution on Feb. 15, 273, and her body buried on a spot known as *Inter Turres.* In 550 Bishop Anastasius erected a church there in her honor, confiding the body to a Benedictine monastery. In 1174 the church was in ruins; St. Agape's head was then sent to Rome and kept in the Basilica of the Apostles.

St. Jerome's martyrology mentions another St. Agape for August 8, supposedly honored at Trier, but there is no mention of her in the liturgical books of the diocese.

Bibliography: A. PALMIERI, DHGE 1:876–877. H. DELEHAYE, "Les Martyrs d'Interamna," *Bulletin d'ancienne littérature et d'archéologie chrétiennes* 1 (1911) 161–168. F. DE' CAVALIERI, ed., "Nuove note agiografiche: Martyrium SS. Agapes, Irenes et Chiones," StTest 9 (1902) 1–20.

[E. G. RYAN]

AGAPE

Technical name for a love feast in the early Christian Church.

Origin of the Term. The verb ἀγαπάω (to love) was common in classical Greek, but the derivative noun ἀγάπη was unknown. Borrowed from the popular Egyptian dialect, the noun occurred in the Septuagint (LXX) version of the Scriptures (e.g., Jer 2.2; Ct 3.5, 10). In the NT it was used to designate a beneficent love, a predilection of God for men, or a love of men for God or of men among themselves, i.e., a fraternal charity. In all three meanings it was suitable for appropriation by the early Christians as a technical term or proper name for various forms of fraternal meals of a semiliturgical nature. Although not without certain analogies in the Jewish and pagan world of antiquity (e.g., *The Letter of* **Aristeas* 187–300; the sacred meals of the *Qumran Community, *Manual of Discipline* 1QS 6.2–5; Plato's *Symposium;* and the meals of Greek religious fraternities), the Christian love feasts had as their specific and basic purpose a practical imitation of Christ's love for men (Lk 14.12–14; 22.26–27) by expressing and fostering fraternal love. The poor and widows were invited to share in both the charitable agapae and those celebrated to honor the dead and the martyrs. Since they were inspired by Christ's love for men, the agapae were related also to the Eucharist, even when they did not include a Eucharistic banquet. *See* EUCHARIST (BIBLICAL DATA). Jesus had instituted the Eucharist at the *Last Supper in the form of a banquet at which His love attained its full perfection (Jn 13.1), and it was at Eucharistic feasts that the union of Christians in Christ's love was most concretely manifested (1 Cor 10.16–17).

Agape in the New Testament. If agape is understood in a wide sense, many of the communal meals in the NT may be classified as love feasts. The only certain instance of the use of agape as a technical term for love feast in the NT is found in the Epistle of St. Jude, v. 12, "These men are stains [or hidden reefs] at your love feasts, carousing impudently and feeding themselves alone." (The plural form ἀγάπαις occurs here for the first time in extant Greek literature and for the only time in the NT.) However, in a passage suggesting literary dependence, 2 Pt 2.13 reads, "These men are stains and blemishes, reveling in their deceits [or lusts, ἀπάταις, instead of ἀγάπαις, which occurs in some MSS as a variant reading], while they carouse with you" (author's translations).

According to Acts 2.42–47 the primitive Jerusalem community habitually practiced the *breaking of bread, an early name for the Eucharist. This Eucharistic rite was probably the essential part of a fraternal meal that recalled and continued the meals of Jesus' public ministry (Mk 6.34–44; Jn 12.1–2), the Last Supper (at which Jesus had gathered with His disciples according to Jewish custom in a *ḥăbûrâ,* a religious fellowship, for the *Passover Meal), and the joyful, post-Resurrection feasts with the risen Lord (Lk 24.30–35, 41–43; Jn 21.9–13; Acts 1.4). It was quite fitting and convenient that such feasts, since they reenacted Christ's loving and victorious presence among His disciples, should have included the Eucharist, as a general rule. In Acts 6.1–6, however, the "daily ministration" to widows was simply a work of mercy rather than a liturgical service that included prayer, preaching (the service of the word), and, very likely, the Eucharist. (*See* MEAL, SACRED.)

That abuses occurred when such fraternal feasts were being adapted for recently converted Greeks is clear from 1 Cor 11.17–34. Drunkenness, factions, and dishonoring of the poor at these meals led St. Paul to complain that the sacred meaning of the Lord's Supper was being ignored and corrupted; he insisted on the reform of such gatherings (on their complete elimination according to W. Goossens and L. Thomas) and reemphasized the traditional doctrine about the Eucharist: it was a proclamation of the value of the Lord's death in view of His final *Parousia (v. 26). Their meals were to be sober and sacred feasts, convoked not to satisfy hunger (v. 34), but to express fraternal love: "Wherefore, my brethren, when you come together to eat [the meal that signifies your unity], wait for one another" (v. 33). In this way they would not ". . . despise the church of God and put to shame the needy" and would merit Paul's commendation (v. 22). A communal breaking of bread at Troas is also described in Acts 20.7–11.

Agape in the Post-Apostolic Church. The letter of Pliny the Younger to Trajan (10.96, *c.* A.D. 112) describes a Christian fraternal meal, at which food of a "common and innocent" kind was eaten. The quoted words do not necessarily exclude an accompanying Eucharist. In the **Didache* (ch. 9–10) certain prayers have been interpreted as referring either to the Eucharist, or an agape, or both together, a fact that indicates the rites were similar and not mutually exclusive. The phrase, "to celebrate an agape," of St. *Ignatius of Antioch's Epistle to the Smyrnaeans (8.2) refers apparently to a love feast that was related to, but distinct from, the Eucharist. Other Ignatian references to agape as a meal (e.g., *Smyrn.* 6.2; 7.1) are uncertain. *Tertullian (*Apology* ch. 39, late 2d century), after speaking of monetary contributions for the relief of the poor, gives the name agape to a meal of which the main purpose, probably on private initiative, was such relief. In this most celebrated description of an agape, prayers were said, food was eaten in moderation, the Scriptures were read, and hymns were sung, although there is no mention of an officiating cleric. In the *First Apology* of St. *Justin Martyr (ch. 65–67) it is the Eucharist itself, not an agape, that served as the occasion for social relief of the needy. An agape for widows is mentioned in the *Apostolic Tradition* of *Hippolytus of Rome (early 3d century), as well as in the dependent *Canons of Hippolytus* (183). Other forms of agapae in which the poor could share were adapted from pagan funeral feasts, such as those on the Roman feast of the *Parentalia* held in honor of the dead, or on the feasts of martyrs (*Canons of Hippolytus* 169). The so-called *fractio panis* (breaking of bread) scene of the Cappella Greca of the catacomb of Priscilla illustrates a Christian funeral banquet. Such a banquet symbolized the heavenly meal desired for the dead in the place of peace and refreshment (**refrigerium*) and recalled Jesus' words, ". . . that you may eat and drink at my table in my kingdom" (Lk 22.29–30). The Church defended the legitimacy of such practices (St. Augustine, *Contra Faustum Manichaeum* 20.21; *De civitate Dei* 8.27), but abuses often caused their regulation or suppression (St. Augustine, *Conf.* 6.2; Council of Laodicea cc.27–28). After the 4th century, social changes and the growth of ecclesiastical organization brought about the gradual disappearance of the agape. (*See* BURIAL, I.)

The fragmentary nature of the early texts and their difficulty of interpretation make it impossible to trace a really systematic view of the history of the agape. As seen from the foregoing considerations, the practice seems to have followed few general rules and differed widely according to the various local churches. Never a universal custom, it was replaced by more efficient, if less personal, manifestations of Christian charity.

Bibliography: B. REICKE, *Diakonie, Festfreude und Zelos in Verbindung mit der altchristlichen Agapenfeier,* UppsUArs No. 5 (1951), a fundamental work with many penetrating insights. C. SPICQ, *Agapè: Prolégomènes à une étude de théologie néotestamentaire* (Studia hellenistica 10; Louvain 1955), presenting the pre-Christian background of the term. W. GOOSSENS, *Les Origines de l'Eucharistie: Sacrement et sacrifice* (Paris 1931) 127–146. A. ROMEO, EncCatt 1:420–425. DENIS-BOULET, *Catholicisme* 1:192–193. J. A. JUNGMANN, LexThK[2] 1:180–181. J. LEIPOLDT, RGG[3] 1:169–170. L. THOMAS, DBSuppl 1:134–153. H. LECLERCQ, DACL 1.1:775–848. **Illustration credit:** Pontificia Commissione di Archeologia Sacra.

[C. BERNAS]

AGAPETUS I, POPE, ST.

Reigned May 13, 535, to April 22, 536 (feast, April 22 and Sept. 20). The successor of Pope *John II was the archdeacon Agapetus, member of an old Roman family and the son of Gordianus, priest of the titular church of SS. Giovanni e Paolo. He appears to have been the candidate of the party that had supported *Dioscorus some years before. Immediately after the election, a council was held, and the document that Pope *Boniface II had made the supporters of Dioscorus sign was solemnly burned. This was intended as a repudiation of the uncanonical attempts of recent popes to appoint their own successors.

Justinian I decided to use the assassination of Queen Amalasuntha by King Theodatus (535) as an excuse for liquidating Ostrogothic rule in Italy, since Amalasuntha had placed herself under imperial protection. He ordered his commanders to occupy Sicily and Dalmatia. When King Theodatus threatened to put to death all the Roman senators, with their wives and children, unless the Emperor desisted from his purpose, Pope Agapetus was dispatched to Constantinople to persuade the Emperor to give up his plans. The Pope was received triumphantly, but failed in his endeavor. Nothing could deflect the Emperor from his designs, and *Belisarius began the reconquest of Italy in July 536. During his brief stay in Constantinople, however, Agapetus was able to accomplish a few successes. Either shortly before or soon after his arrival, he was informed by some of the clergy that Patriarch *Anthimus, installed on the throne of Constantinople through the influence of Empress *Theodora (1), was tainted by the Monophysite heresy. When the fact came to light, Agapetus ordered the patriarch's deposition on the grounds that he had been uncanonically translated from the See of Trebizond to Constantinople. Agapetus then secured the election of an orthodox patriarch, *Mennas, whom he personally consecrated (March 13, 536).

Agapetus praised the profession of faith that the Emperor submitted to him, but refused to acknowledge the right of laymen to teach in the Church. Shortly afterward he became ill and died. Before expiring, he begged the Emperor to summon a general council to condemn Anthimus and submitted to him a petition from the monasteries of Constantinople, Syria, and Palestine, urging that the Monophysites, protected by Empress Theodora, should be expelled from Constantinople. His body was sealed in a leaden coffin and taken back to Rome, where he was buried in the portico of St. Peter's. Agapetus converted his own family house on the Clivus Scauri into a library, which was intended to form part of a Roman university he hoped to found with the help of *Cassiodorus. The library was later incorporated by Pope *Gregory I in his own monastery nearby on the Caelian. Six genuine letters of Agapetus are extant.

Bibliography: Dekkers CPL 1693. PL 66:35–76. Duchesne LP 1:287–289; 3:91. Caspar 2:200–226. L. Bréhier, Fliche-Martin 4:453– . H. Leclercq, DACL 13.1:1217–18. O. Bertolini, *Roma di fronte a Bisanzio e ai Longobardi* (Bologna 1941); DizBiogItal 1:362–367. T. G. Jalland, *The Church and the Papacy* (SPCK: 1944). I. Daniele, EncCatt 1:428–429. T. Cecchetti, *ibid.* 10:1248, Bibliotheca Agapiti. F. Dvornik, *Byzance et la primauté romaine* (Paris 1964).

[J. CHAPIN]

AGAPETUS II, POPE, May 10, 946, to Dec. 955; b. Rome. He was lauded in contemporary sources as "sanctissimus" and as a man "of wondrous sanctity." Interested in monastic reform, Agapetus, with the help of the despot of Rome, *Alberic II of Spoleto, established a Cluniac foundation at *St. Paul-Outside-the-Walls with monks from the Abbey at *Gorze. Despite the political preponderance of Alberic in Rome, Agapetus—at least at the beginning of his pontificate—made some notable decisions demonstrating independent papal action and real authority. A struggle over the archbishop of *Reims had developed when Count Herbert of Vermandois appointed his 5-year-old son Hugh as archbishop. Raoul, one of the later Carolingians, conquered Reims and appointed the monk Artaud archbishop. At first the Pope supported Artaud; then deceived by forged documents, he turned to Hugh. But when several synods (Verdun, 947; Mousson, 948) and especially the council of Ingelheim (948) called by *Otto I and presided over by Marinus, papal legate, decided in favor of Artaud, Agapetus confirmed their decisions at a council in Rome (949). The Pope in effect ratified Otto's wide powers of administration over Danish bishops in a bull of 948 extending the jurisdiction of the metropolitan of Hamburg (*see* BREMEN-HAMBURG) over Denmark. Within Germany he likewise gave Otto broad jurisdiction over monasteries and sent Otto's brother, Abp. *Bruno of Cologne, the *pallium, which he permitted Bruno to wear at will. But in spite of the Pope's desires to crown Otto I emperor during Otto's Italian expedition (951–952) to rescue Adelaide, dispossessed widow of Lothair II of Italy, Alberic would have none of it. Alberic effectively controlled Rome until his death in 954, and Agapetus played a continually diminishing role in Roman affairs. In the Pope's presence Alberic had the nobles and clergy swear they would elect his son Octavian (later *John XII) as Agapetus's successor. Octavian succeeded to the temporal government of Rome in 954 and awaited only the Pope's death to gain the papacy itself. Agapetus was buried in the Lateran basilica.

Bibliography: Duchesne LP 2:245. Jaffé L 1:459–463. Hefele-Leclercq 4.2:757–788. Mann 4:224–240. J. P. Kirsch, DHGE 1:890–892. Seppelt 2:357–362, 366. P. Brezzi, *Roma e l'Impero medioevale* (Bologna 1947).

[C. M. AHERNE]

AGAPIOS OF HIERAPOLIS, bishop of Hierapolis in Syria (Manbij, northeast of Aleppo), whose Arabic name was Maḥbūb ibn Qusṭanṭin, a contemporary of *Eutychios of Alexandria (877–940), whom he outlived by some years. His general history, *Kitāb al- 'Unwān* (Book of the Title), for which he is known, is quite independent of the *Annals* of Eutychios. It covered the period from the beginning of the world to A.D. 941 or 942. The original text is no longer extant, however, beyond the year 776 or 777, the second year of the caliphate of al-Mahdī. For the ancient history of Christianity Agapios uses, without criticism, a great deal of the apocryphal and popular legendary literature. For later ecclesiastical and profane history, he uses the Syrian sources, including the Maronite chronographer Theophilos of Edessa (785), whose *World Chronicle* was amply exploited by Agapios in explaining the downfall of the dynasty of the *Umayyads and the rise of the *'Abbāsids. He knew also the *Church History* of Eusebius of Caesarea, which he uses indirectly by short citations. His special merit lies, however, in his sometimes unidentifiable source materials, offering at times historical details no longer preserved in other extant sources. Most important are: his list of the Eastern Metropolitans, and his references to the famous text of Papias of Hierapolis in Phrygia (whom he does not cite by name) concerning the four Gospels. Agapios is *Michael I the Syrian's source on Bardesanes.

Bibliography: Agapios of Hierapolis, *Kitāb al- 'Unwān,* ed. and French tr. A. Vasiliev, PatrOr 5:565–691; 7:459–591; 8: 399–547. C. Karalevsky, DHGE 1:899–900. Graf GeschCh ArabLit 2:39–41.

[L. MALOUF]

AGAR (HAGAR), Egyptian slave girl of Abraham's wife Sara. When Sara gave up hope of providing Abraham with an heir, she offered Agar to her husband, a procedure which, according to marriage contracts found at Nuzi, was expected of a barren wife (see Gordon, 3). In both of the Genesis accounts (Yahwist source in 16.1–16; Elohist source in 21.9–21), Agar, after incurring Sara's jealousy, is driven out of the household with her young son, *Ismael. In the desert she is visited by an *angel of the Lord, who, besides saving her from perishing, promises that Ismael will grow into a powerful nation. Thus, as mother of the 12 tribes of Ismael (Gn 25.12–26; cf. Bar 3.23), Agar is the first in a series of non-Israelite women (Tamar, Rahab, Ruth) singled out for a special role in salvation history.

In Gal 4.21–31 St. Paul utilizes the Agar story "by way of allegory" to illustrate the contrast between the Old Law and the New. Just as the offspring of Agar are slaves, since they are born of a slave, so, too, they who are offspring of the Old Law are slaves. The New Law, however, like Sara, gives birth to free offspring. In contrast, Agar's offspring was "born according to the flesh," i.e., as a purely natural phenomenon, whereas the birth of Sara's son Isaac was in fulfillment of a divine promise; so, the Jews are but the natural descendants of Abraham, whereas Christians are "the children of the promise." Finally, St. Paul contrasts the Old Covenant given on Sinai, which is "a mountain in Arabia," the land of Ismael, with the New Covenant, which is bestowed from the New Jerusalem above. These contrasts are climaxed by the Pauline conclusion: "cast out the slave girl and her son."

Bibliography: M. NEWMAN, InterDictBibl 2:508–509. EncDict Bibl 40–41. J. GABRIEL, LexThK[2] 4:1314. G. KITTEL, Kittel ThW 1:55–56. C. H. GORDON, "Biblical Customs and the Nuzu Tablets," BiblArchaeol 3 (1940) 1–12. R. T. O'CALLAHAN, "Historical Parallels to Patriarchal Social Custom," CathBiblQuart 6 (1944) 391–405. J. BRIGHT, *A History of Israel* (Philadelphia 1959).

[E. MARTIN]

AGASSIZ, LOUIS, geologist and ichthyologist; b. Motier, Switzerland, May 28, 1807; d. Cambridge, Mass., Dec. 12, 1873. He was reared in the poverty and simplicity of a Protestant parsonage, the son of cultured parents. He pursued science at Zürich, Heidelberg, and Munich Universities, earning both a Ph.D. and an M.D. As a student, he took over research on fish begun by C. F. P. von Martius and J. B. Spix, publishing (1829) the results as *Selecta Genera et Species Piscium.* While studying in Paris, he was given a professorship at Neuchâtel (1832–46), during which he published his important *Recherches sur les Poissons Fossiles,* which raised to nearly 1,000 the number of named fossil fishes. He also studied the glacial movement in Switzerland, publishing his *Études sur les glaciers* in 1840. He came to the U.S. in 1846, lecturing at Boston and Charleston, S.C., and studying geology and natural history; in 1848 he was named to a professorship of zoology at Harvard. He continued his writings, organized the museum of zoology at Harvard, and undertook several expeditions to study natural history. After the death of his first wife, Cecile Braun, he married Elizabeth Cabot Cary, noted Boston writer and promoter of education for women (1850).

Agassiz was especially renowned as a teacher because of his great interest in his students and his advocation of learning from nature itself rather than from books. His contributions embraced significant work in geology, ichthyology, embryology, natural history, science education and revision of zoological nomenclature. For 50 years after his death practically all leading zoologists in America had been directly or indirectly trained by him. Abhorring the hypothesis that seemed to exclude a Creator, he opposed Darwinism throughout his lifetime. His important works are: *Recherches sur les Poissons Fossiles* (Neuchâtel 1833–44); *An Essay on Classification* (London 1859); *Études sur les glaciers* (1840); *Contributions to the Natural History of the United States* (1857–63).

See also DARWIN, CHARLES; EVOLUTION, ORGANIC.

Bibliography: E. C. AGASSIZ, ed., *Louis Agassiz: His Life and Correspondence,* 2 v. (Boston 1885). J. D. TELLER, *Louis Agassiz* (Columbus, Ohio 1947).

[L. P. COONEN]

AGATHA, ST., martyr and patroness of Catania, Sicily; d. possibly in the Decian persecution, 249 to 251 (feast, Feb. 5). The martyrology of Carthage and that of St. Jerome mention her death on February 5. Legend alleges that she was sent to a brothel to induce her to repudiate her faith. After the removal of her breasts, the Apostle Peter is supposed to have appeared and cured her; but the next day she died in prison of new cruelties. From the 6th century, claims were made for Palermo as the place of her birth; but the older versions of the legend testify for Catania. Her *passio* is recorded in many Greek and Latin versions, but the Greek seems to be the oldest.

St. Agatha, 12th-century mosaic, Capella Palatina, Palazzo Reale at Palermo, Sicily.

The cult of St. Agatha quickly spread beyond Sicily,

and her name was inscribed in the Canon of the Roman Mass. It is probable that her remains were translated to Constantinople. Pope Symmachus had a church erected in her honor on the Via Aurelia; and Gregory I (d. 604) reconsecrated an Arian church as S. Agata dei Goti in her name. Her intervention was credited with stilling an eruption of Mt. Etna the year after her burial; and in the Middle Ages, particularly in south Germany, bread, candles, fruits, and letters were blessed in her name to ward off destruction by fire. The popular merrymaking that accompanied her cult in Sicily was probably related to ancient pagan festivals, but the claim that her cult prolonged that of Isis is untenable. She is considered the patron of foundrymen, miners, Alpine guides, and nurses. Since the 14th century she has been depicted with her severed breasts on a plate, with a candle, or with a house in flames.

Bibliography: M. SCADUTO et al., EncCatt 1:432–436. B. KÖTTING, LexThK[2] 1:183–184. H. DÖRRIE, ReallexAntChr 1: 179–184. **Illustration credit:** Anderson-Art Reference Bureau.

[P. ROCHE]

AGATHO, POPE, ST., June 27, 678, to Jan. 10, 681 (feast, Jan. 10). He helped conclude the struggle against *Monothelitism, supporting the council convened by *Constantine IV Pogonatus, 680–681 (*see* CONSTANTINOPLE III, COUNCIL OF). Agatho achieved fullest Western participation through local synods in Milan, England, Gaul, and in Rome (Easter, 680), where 125 bishops, mostly from Italy, met and appointed three legates to Constantinople. Presiding over the council, which also condemned *Honorius I, they signed its acts and delivered a letter from the Roman synod describing the lack of clerical education resulting from poverty in the western Church and the consequent obligations upon clerics to support themselves. A second letter from Agatho to Constantine IV, inspired by the *Tome* of *Leo I, combined clear teaching with a firm proclamation of Roman infallibility. He likewise praised Constantine's toleration of Monothelites. Agatho upheld Bishop *Wilfrid of York's appeal to Rome against his metropolitan's unexpected division of Wilfrid's diocese, sent the archcantor John to introduce the Roman liturgy into England, secured the remission of an imperial tax on newly elected popes, and regularized the See of *Ravenna.

Bibliography: Duchesne LP 1:350–358. Jaffé E 1:238–240; 2: 699, 741. Hefele-Leclercq 3.1:475–484. J. P. KIRSCH, DHGE 1:916–918. Mann 1.2:23–48. Haller 1:332–339; 545. G. SCHWAIGER, LexThK[2] 1:185.

[C. M. AHERNE]

AGAZZARI, AGOSTINO, baroque church composer and theorist; b. Siena, Italy, Dec. 2, 1578; d. there, April 10. 1640. Nothing certain is known of his early career, but from March 1602 until at least October 1603 he was *maestro di cappella* at the German College in Rome, and in 1606 he held the same post at the Roman Seminary. It is thought that he was maestro at the Siena cathedral from *c.* 1630 until his death. In his important treatise on thorough bass (*basso continuo*), *Del sonare sopra il basso* (1607), he championed the cause of *stile moderno* in church music. In his own sacred compositions, which included numerous Masses, motets, Psalms, and other settings, he employed monody and the *concertato* style (both baroque techniques). As a transition figure, however, he was clearly indebted to the Roman conservative tradition and its *stile antico* techniques. In addition to religious music he composed one of the earliest operas, *Eumelio,* first produced at the Roman Seminary (1606).

Bibliography: Samples of his music appear in *Musica Divina,* ed. K. PROSKE and J. SCHREMS, 8 v. (Regensburg 1853–69); *Canticum Vetus,* ed. K. G. FELLERER (Mainz 1936), and other modern eds. Strunk SourceR 424–431. A. ADRIO, MusGG 1:132–137. E. H. PAYNE, Grove DMM 1:68. O. KINKELDEY, *Orgel und Klavier in der Musik des 16. Jahrhunderts* (Leipzig 1910). Buk MusB.

[T. CULLEY]

AGE (CANON LAW)

In the Church's legal system, as in all others, juridical personality and capacity for performing legal acts are modified by one's age.

In the Latin rite a person who has completed his 21st year is an adult; otherwise he is a minor (CIC c.88.1). In the Oriental rites, unless some regulation in a particular law demands a more advanced age, a person who has completed his 18th year is an adult; one below that age is a minor (ClerSanc c.17.1). All rites agree in presuming by law that a minor of the male sex reaches puberty at the end of the 14th year, and one of the female sex at the end of the 12th year (CIC c.88.2; ClerSanc c.17.2).

Before attaining the age of puberty one cannot vote in ecclesiastical elections (CIC c.167.1n2; ClerSanc c.109.1n2), choose his own church or place of burial (CIC c.1223.2), testify in ecclesiastical court (CIC c.1757.1; SollNostr c.279.1), or incur *latae sententiae* penalties (CIC c.2230). In criminal matters, and especially in those in which a *latae sententiae* penalty is involved, a woman is considered lacking the age of puberty until the competion of her 14th year.

A person before puberty who has not yet completed the 7th year is called an infant or a child, and he is regarded as not being capable of performing human acts; after the completion of the 7th year, however, he is presumed to have the use of reason (CIC c.88.3; ClerSanc c.17.3n1). Both of these presumptions regarding the use of reason are rebuttable by evidence, which may show that it was attained earlier or not until a later age. All persons without the use of reason are juridically in the same class as infants (CIC c.88.3; ClerSanc c.17.3n2). Infants are not subject to purely ecclesiastical laws (CIC c.12) and are incapable of crime if they actually lack the use of reason (CIC c.2201.1).

An adult enjoys the full exercise of his rights; the minor remains subject to the authority of his parents or guardians in the exercise of his rights, with the exception of matters in which the law considers minors exempt from parental authority (CIC c.89; ClerSanc c.18).

Minors are expressly exempt from parental authority in these matters: after the age of 7, they may acquire a quasi-domicile (CIC c.93.2; ClerSanc c.21.2); after the age of puberty, they may choose a church for their funeral services and a place of burial (CIC c.1223.2); and after the age of reason, they may act as parties in spiritual causes (CIC c.1648.3; SollNostr c.163.3). A minor may also without parental consent, by an implicit exemption of the law, embrace the religious or the clerical state (CIC cc.976.1, 555; PostApost c.88).

Those who certainly have the use of reason and have not reached the age of 7 are not subject to purely ecclesiastical laws, including all the Church's penal laws, unless the law expressly states otherwise (CIC c.12). The Code does expressly provide otherwise regarding the reception of the Sacraments in danger of death (CIC cc.854.2, 940.1), the precept of Easter Communion (CIC c.859.1), and the precept of annual confession (CIC c.906). Hence, in these matters one is bound by the Church law if he has the use of reason, regardless of the actual completion of the 7th year.

In relation to Baptism, those who have the use of reason are to be considered as adults and are to be baptized only after they seek Baptism of their own volition (CIC c.745.2n2).

The law of fasting begins to bind only after the completion of the 21st year (CIC c.1254.2).

For eligibility to certain ecclesiastical offices the law requires a specified minimum age. Thus, for example, bishops must be 30 years of age (CIC c.331.1n2; ClerSanc c.394.1n3); masters of novices, 35 (CIC c.559.1; PostApost c.92.1); and the confessors of women religious, 40 (CIC c.524.1; PostApost c.56.1).

In the case of adults, maturity is succeeded by old age, which also modifies the juridical condition of the persons concerned (CIC cc.1254.2, 2218.1).

Bibliography: J. A. McCloskey, *The Subject of Ecclesiastical Law According to Canon 12* (CUA CLS 165; Washington 1942). Pospishil PersOr. Bousc-Ellis.

[J. D. MC GUIRE]

AGE (IMPEDIMENT TO MARRIAGE). In legislating for the minimum age at which her subjects are capable of a valid marriage contract, the Church declares that 2 years must elapse after canonical puberty is attained. Hence, in order to marry validly, males must have completed (according to CIC c.34.3n3; Post Apost c.324.3n3) their 16th year and females (CIC c.1067.1; CrebAllat c.57.1) their 14th year of age. Nonage is, therefore, one of the diriment impediments to marriage in the Latin Church as well as in all of the Oriental Churches; it has its origin in Roman law that required puberty for *iustae nuptiae*. Natural law imposes no such impediment of nonage; it requires only that the parties to a marriage have sufficient mental capacity to give matrimonial consent. Impuberty together with its physical incapacity to use marriage does not prevent the contracting of marriage as far as the natural law is concerned. Since the impediment of nonage established in the CIC is purely one of ecclesiastical law, it does not bind the unbaptized. The unbaptized are, however, bound by a reasonable and just impediment of nonage established by the competent civil authority, when they contract marriage with the baptized, as well as among themselves. Further, as a matter of ecclesiastical law, this impediment can be dispensed by the Holy See if the occasion and sufficiently grave causes warrant it. It ceases entirely, of course, upon the completion of the required years, but a marriage contracted before attaining the canonical age and without a dispensation is not thereby validated. Such a marriage is validated by a renewal of consent, or in an extraordinary case by a radical sanation. The Church, while regulating the minimum age for a valid marriage, establishes no age beyond which a marriage would be invalid.

Bibliography: J. C. O'Dea, *The Matrimonial Impediment of Nonage* (CUA CLS 205; Washington 1944). Abbo 2:1067.

[J. D. MC GUIRE]

AGED, CARE OF THE

The term "aged" is now conventionally used to designate persons who have completed their 65th year. Most such persons live out their allotted time in reasonably sound health and without need of specialized help; others decline with advancing years and need special care. It is with this latter group in the U.S. that this article is especially concerned.

The provision of adequate care for the aged has become a pressing social problem. The medical, economic, and social advances of this century have added years to the normal life span, with the result that the number of elderly people has increased rapidly. Between 1900 and 1960 the number of people 65 years of age and older in the U.S. increased from 3.1 to 16.6 million. Moreover, urbanization and industrialization, by changing the family structure and employment pattern, has aggravated the problem. The household of the past, especially the agricultural household, often consisted of three generations and included unmarried adult relatives; with the women, and often the men, working at home it was usually able to care for infirm members. The contemporary urban family, by contrast, usually consists of two generations while the children are at home and of one generation after they have married. The increased mobility of modern life tends to separate married children from their parents by great distances. Women, both unmarried and married, often work outside of the home, and unmarried women frequently establish independent households. This development, while increasing the independence of all generations, leaves the contemporary family limited ability to care for its aged.

Background. Prior to the 20th century, as has already been indicated, care of the aged was primarily a family responsibility. In the predominantly agricultural society of the Middle Ages, elderly people themselves were not viewed as, and in fact were not, a class needing special help. The Christian conscience usually operating through the Church and its institutions—monasteries, convents, and parishes—and through guilds, took seriously its obligation to the poor, including the infirm. As the Middle Ages drew to a close, however, the developing commercial revolution, and in England, especially, the beginning of an agricultural revolution, disrupted social structures and brought vast numbers of indigent people crowding into the growing towns. From Spain to England, the contemporary literature bore witness to this new problem and to the inability of existing charitable organizations to cope with it. The suppression of many monasteries, convents, and at a later period, guilds, occasioned by the Reformation disrupted the traditional channels for collecting and distributing alms, and destroyed the more important charitable institutions and refuges of the poor, thus intensifying the problem of relief. Governments were gradually forced to assume increasing responsibility for the alleviation of distress.

The English poor laws from the 16th to the 19th century illustrate how difficult it is for an age to understand its own problems. Underlying this legislation, more marked as we move closer to the 19th century, there seems to be a conviction that poverty and unemployment are always voluntary. And the lack of sympathy of the legislators for the able-bodied idle carried over into the programs for succor of both the young and the old. In the 18th and early 19th centuries in the U.S., where the tradition of the English poor laws prevailed—similar situations existed in most European countries—the indigent aged were generally institutionalized in almshouses or poorhouses or, occasionally, in understaffed public hospitals. Care in these institutions was generally inadequate—administration was frequently harsh and even punitive, the environment was unstimulating and custodial in nature, and medical care was minimal or nonexistent. The elderly were housed with other public wards, such as orphans, the feeble-minded, and the sick. When these latter groups began to be cared for in specialized institutions (about 1870 in the U.S), care of the aged also began to improve. But such was the lingering reputation of the poorhouse that the needy accepted institutionalization only as a last resort.

Catholic Homes for the Aged. The first Catholic home for the aged, the Lafon Asylum of the Holy Family, in New Orleans, was established in 1842. It is still conducted by the Sisters of the Holy Family, a Negro congregation, and admits aged people of the Negro race. About the same time, the Sisters of the Third Order of St. Francis, in Buffalo, N.Y., began caring for the elderly sick in their own homes, and in 1855 they established the St. Francis Asylum in Buffalo. Other homes were opened in several cities by various religious communities and national immigrant groups, but care of the aged became an important part of Catholic welfare work in the U.S. only with the establishment here of homes for the aged by the Little Sisters of the Poor.

The Little Sisters of the Poor. This congregation, founded by Jeanne Jugan in France in 1845 for the care of indigent men and women, began its work in the U.S. with the establishment of a home for the indigent aged in Brooklyn in 1868. In that same year other groups of these French sisters established homes in Cincinnati and New Orleans. By 1874 this congregation was operating 13 homes in the U.S., and 39 by 1917.

Other Foundations. The Little Sisters of the Poor were permitted by rule to admit only the indigent. But many elderly people who had means of their own required special care, and other religious communities opened homes to fill this need. Many such homes, however, encountered serious financial difficulties. They accepted lump-sum payments with the understanding that they would give the patients life-term care. This policy proved to be a shortsighted one. The contributions were often inadequate; the patients lived much longer than had been anticipated. As a result the institutions not only suffered severe financial hardship, but were criticized by the public who knew that the contributions had been made in advance but who underestimated the costs of operating the homes. To solve this problem some religious communities associated their home for the aged with another charitable work, such as a hospital. Others continued to accept prepayments, but attempted to estimate the costs on an actuarial basis; the outcome, however, was rarely wholly satisfactory. As a result, few of these homes made genuine progress and some were forced to dissolve.

Aid from Diocesan Charities. After World War I the officials of many dioceses came to realize that religious communities could not continue to carry unaided the increasing burden of caring for the aged and began to contribute financial help. When in the late 1920s a home for the aged in Erie, Pa., conducted by the Sisters of St. Joseph, was destroyed by fire, the bishop replaced it at the expense of the diocese. In Syracuse, N.Y., a similar home was built with funds collected in a Catholic Charities campaign in 1924. At about the same time the Diocese of Green Bay, Wis., assumed the financial responsibility for a home for the aged, and soon many other dioceses assumed financial responsibility for homes for the aged.

Carmelite Sisters for the Aged and Infirm. In New York City during the 1920s, a superior of one of the homes operated by the Little Sisters of the Poor, Rev. Mother Angeline Teresa, became persuaded from the many appeals made to her that better provision should be made for the care of aged persons with some financial means; these, too, needed the security that care by the sisters afforded. As the Little Sisters could admit only the indigent, the challenge of providing homes for those aged who could pay for their care led to the formation of a new religious community. In 1929 Mother Teresa and six companions founded the Carmelite Sisters for the Aged and Infirm, and in 1930 with a grant from the Catholic Charities purchased a building in the Bronx that became St. Patrick's Home for the Aged and Infirm. The effort of these sisters to keep abreast of the ever changing and improving methods in institutional care of the aged is exemplified in the structure of each new home and in the continued efforts of the community to train its sisters in the special skills needed for proper care of the aged.

Increase in Number. While the Carmelite Sisters and the Little Sisters of the Poor are today the leaders among religious congregations in operating homes for the aged, many homes are conducted by other communities also. There were 98 Catholic homes for the aged in 1910; 142, in 1930; 171, in 1940; 314, in 1958; and 355, in 1962. In 1956 about 200,000 persons were cared for in various types of homes for the aged in the U.S.; probably less than one-sixth of these were in Catholic homes. The 355 Catholic homes operating in 1962 cared for about 34,000.

In recent decades, intensified research on the problems of aging has led to greater appreciation of the needs of the elderly. Many homes for the aged have thus enlarged their services to meet the particular social and medical needs of each resident. This, of course, has added to the overall cost of care.

Governmental and Industrial Programs for the Aged. After 1935 the Federal-State Old Age Assistance program and the Federal Old Age and Survivors Insurance (OASI) program made important changes in programs for the aged and in their financing. The progressive liberalization of benefits under OASI and the gradual expansion of its coverage, together with the rapid growth since World War II of industrial pension programs, have given a large measure of security to a substantial proportion of the elderly in the U.S. Incomes from these sources have enabled more and more of the aged to maintain independent living arrangements while in good health and to defray in whole or in part the costs of institutional care should they need it. The Hospital Survey and Construction Act of 1946 (Hill-Burton Act), through which Federal grants are made for the expansion of hospitals and associated services, benefited homes for the aged by helping them meet the increased demand for nursing-care facilities.

Social Programs in the U.S. Since 1950, social centers for the aged have spread throughout the U.S., being sponsored by municipal welfare departments, voluntary agencies, fraternal and civic organizations, labor unions, and other groups. For many older people such centers provide the social and recreational stimulus necessary for a well-rounded life and for fruitful utilization of leisure time. The first Catholic elders' center in the U.S. was established in St. Paul the Apostle parish in New York City in 1951 through the efforts of the Paulist Fathers who conduct the parish and of the Catholic Charities of the archdiocese. Similar centers have since been organized in several dioceses throughout the country. Parish centers appear to outnumber elders' centers sponsored by other Catholic groups. They afford the advantages of proximity to the person's home—particularly important for the partially disabled—and of close contact of the older parishioner with his parish priest. Often the elderly person in a large city is known only to the priests of the parish and the other members of the center.

Social Programs Abroad. European countries have organized similar programs for older people. Outstanding examples are the parish clubs in the Netherlands. These clubs, begun in 1950, were later organized into the "Union of Diocesan Associations of Old People" and, by 1960, had a membership of 40,000. Besides meetings and other affairs to provide companionship and leisure-time activity, these associations organize retreats, give advice on pension and financial programs, and encourage exchange of visits by older people for mutual spiritual support. Such clubs are financed by the parish and diocese, by municipal governments, and by trade and industrial associations; members also pay a small fee.

Other Services for the Aged. The National Council of Catholic Charities for years has promoted studies, conferences, and workshops on the aged and their needs and has cooperated with other groups in planning better services for them. The Catholic Charities in many dioceses maintains family service divisions that, in addition to providing material help, endeavor to allay the feelings of frustration and insecurity experienced by many of the aging.

Religious communities and volunteer groups devoted to caring for the sick in their own homes render a widespread and invaluable service to the elderly sick, often making it possible for them to postpone admission to a home. Around the turn of the century this work was undertaken by several religious communities including the Sisters of Bon Secours in Baltimore, Md.; the Little Sisters of the Assumption and the Dominican Sisters of the Sick Poor in New York City; and the Sisters of the Infant Jesus, generally known as the Nursing Sisters of the Sick Poor, in Brooklyn.

An increasing number of parishes are giving attention to the particular needs of their aged parishioners. Among other innovations, there are provisions for hearing aids in confessionals and in some pews; front pew reservations for the aged who cannot climb the steps to the altar rail; ascending plane walks and banisters; space for wheel chairs; and reserved entrance and exit doors.

Dimensions of the Problem of Adequate Care. During the 20th century the aged have increased at an unprecedented rate, both in numbers and as a percentage

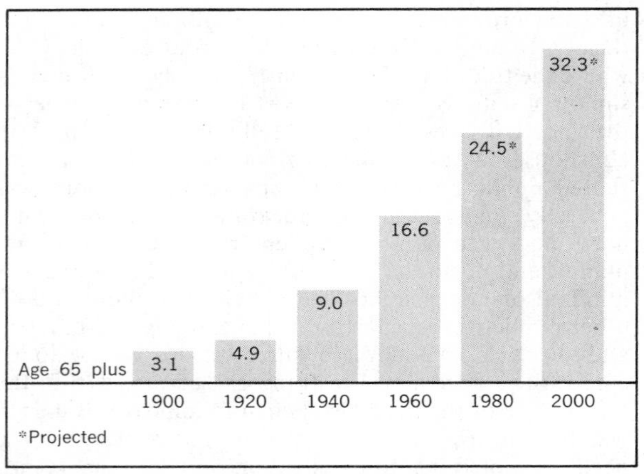

Twentieth-century increase in population of older Americans (in millions).

of the population, in all industrialized nations of the West. As shown in the chart, the number of people aged 65 and over increased more than fourfold between 1900 and 1960; while the rate of increase is declining, it is estimated that the number of people in this age group will have reached 32.3 million by 2000. West European nations show similar patterns. Between 1850 and 1950 the proportion of the aged in their populations doubled, being between 8 and 12 per cent in most of these countries in 1950. In predominantly agricultural countries, by contrast, the age group 65 and over has shown little relative increase, generally comprising about 4 per cent of the populations.

Two statistics, already cited, may help in forming some broad estimate of the dimensions of the problem that proper care for the aged will present in coming years. In 1960 there were 16.6 million people in the U.S. aged 65 and over. In 1956 there were about 200,000 persons in homes for the aged in the U.S. It has been estimated that in the future the number of aged requiring institutional care will range from 4 to 12 per cent. It is obvious that providing proper care for the aged is an urgent social problem that will demand the sustained and determined efforts of public and private agencies and of the society as well.

Bibliography: T. RUDD, *Caring for the Elderly* (London 1956). E. W. BRUGESS, ed., *Aging in Western Societies* (Chicago 1960). President's Council on Aging, *The Older American* (Washington 1962–63). J. T. DRAKE, *The Aged in American Society* (New York 1958). J. O'GRADY, *Catholic Charities in the United States: History and Problems* (Washington 1931). M. B. DE LOURDES, *Where Somebody Cares* (New York 1959). L. L. LAUERMAN, "Concerning the Aging," AmEcclRev 138 (1958) 173–185. A. J. APP, *Making the Later Years Count* (St. Paul, Minn. 1960). **Illustration credit:** 1900 through 1960, census of population; 1980, U.S. Bureau of the Census, "Current Population Reports; Estimates," Series P-25, No. 251; 2000, Division of the Actuary, Social Security Administration.

[M. A. MC BRIDE]

AGEN, DIOCESE OF (AGENNENSIS), suffragan to Bordeaux (suffragan to Toulouse, 1802–22); patron, St. Stephen. Agen's Romanesque and Gothic cathedral is named for St. Caprasius (martyred *c.* 300 with St. Foy). St. Phoebadius, the first known bishop of Agen, condemned the Arians in 357, and presided at two local councils (374, 380). *Gregory of Tours mentioned Agen's Christians; they were persecuted by the Romans and Arian Visigoths until 507, and were raided by Saracens (732) and Normans (848). Nothing is known of the period from *c.* 670 until 1021, when both the monasteries and the heretics began to flourish. The *Templars appeared in Agen in about 1154, and after 1249 mendicant orders repaired some of the inroads of the Albigensians, who had a church there (*see* ALBIGENSES). Agen was a prosperous entrepôt between Bordeaux and Narbonne, and a battleground for the counts of Toulouse and the French and English kings until the end of the Hundred Years' War. The plague, the absence of its bishops, religious and civil wars (1550–1650), Jansenism, and Gallicanism hindered ecclesiastical reform. In 1652 Agen came under royal administration; in 1790 it was temporarily called Lot-et-Garonne. Of Agen's 1963 population of 265,648, 246,000 were Catholics, served by 439 parishes, 306 clergy, and 398 religious in 65 convents.

Bibliography: *Revue de l'Agenais* (1874–). A. DURENGUES, DHGE 1:933–941. E. JARRY, *Catholicisme* 1:203–205. AnnPont (1963) 17.

[E. P. COLBERT]

AGENNĒTOS. In the early formative period of Christian doctrine prior to *Nicaea I (325), ἀγέννητος was a Greek adjective employed to signify the self-existence or uncreatureliness of the Godhead. And ἀγέννητος (spelled with two ν's) was indeed a term used in the philosophy of the day to designate God's self-existence. Etymologically, however, the adjective with the two ν's would not have meant self-existence or uncreatureliness—as ἀγένητος (spelled with one ν)—but ungenerateness.

Now if, regardless of etymology, the sense is to be uncreated, ἀγέννητος must be said of both Father and Son. But if, on the other hand, etymology is restored and the sense is ungenerated, then ἀγέννητος can be said only of the Father. For obviously, the Son, precisely as Son, is generated from the Father. *Arianism, however, almost systematically blurred this difference: first, by using the term in the etymological sense of ungenerated; but then, by taking ungenerated to mean the same thing as uncreated. But the Son was generated, not ungenerated; hence, the Son was a creature.

In its rejection of Arianism, *Nicene Creed clarified the problem (Denz 125–126). The Son is generated (γεννηθέντα); by implication, ἀγέννητος in this context can be said only of the Father. Yet, if the Son is "begotten," the Son is nevertheless "not made" (οὐ ποιηθέντα); again by implication, ἀγέννητος in this further context, that of creation, characterizes not only the Father but the entire Godhead as such.

See also ASEITY; GOD THE FATHER; PATERNITY, DIVINE; PROPERTIES, DIVINE PERSONAL; GENERATION; GENERATION OF THE WORD; LOGOS; SON, GOD THE; TRINITY, HOLY; TRINITY, HOLY, ARTICLES ON; WORD, THE.

Bibliography: M. SCHMAUS, LexThK^2 1:187–188. J. N. D. KELLY, *Early Christian Doctrines* (2d ed. New York 1960) 226–237. G. W. H. LAMPE, ed., *A Patristic Greek Lexicon* (New York 1961–).

[R. L. RICHARD]

AGENT, a transliteration of the scholastic Latin *agens,* in general having the same meaning as mover (*movens*), efficient cause, or simply cause. St. *Thomas Aquinas regularly uses agent and efficient cause indiscriminately, often combining them as *causa agens* or *causa movens.* In dependence on Aristotle, he defines an agent as "that whereby a change or state of rest is first produced" (*a quo est principium motus vel quietis—In 2 phys.* 5.5). In this St. Thomas differs in no significant respect from the general scholastic tradition. At least the older scholastic tradition is also in agreement that agents in the physical order are denominated such from the effect produced by their action in the "patient," or recipient (*see* ACTION AND PASSION).

Other aspects of the scholastic notion of agent can be seen in the various assertions commonly accepted with respect to agents: "Every agent acts for an end." "Every agent acts insofar as it is in act, and according to its form." "An agent, precisely as such, is more noble than its patient or effect." "Every agent produces an effect similar to itself." "Agent and patient must exist together," and "every physical agent acts by contact" (*see* SCHOLASTIC TERMS AND AXIOMS).

The principal kinds of agent recognized by the scholastics include: (1) The perfecting (*perficiens*), counseling (*consilians*), and disposing agents—the last being subdivided into primary (*praeparans*) and secondary (*adjuvans*). (2) Equivocal (or analogical) and univocal agents, depending on whether or not the agent is on the same metaphysical level as the patient; this distinction is closely related to that between universal and particular agents and that between incorporeal and corporeal agents. (3) Principal or instrumental and primary or secondary (sometimes "first" and "second") agents. (4) Natural and nonnatural agents, the latter including many other types, such as violent, chance, artificial, and voluntary; a related distinction contains necessary, chance, and free agents. (5) Finally, agents that are causes of *being or causes merely of *becoming, according as the effect continues to depend on the cause after it is produced or not.

Intellectual agents are included in this list, especially under artificial and voluntary nonnatural agents, but the "agent intellect" (*intellectus agens*) is not. The latter is the intellectual faculty rendering abstract knowledge possible, and it is treated under *intellect.

See also CAUSALITY; EFFICIENT CAUSALITY.

Bibliography: R. J. DEFERRARI et al., *A Lexicon of St. Thomas Aquinas* (Washington 1948–53). L. SCHÜTZ, *Thomas-Lexikon* (New York 1957).

[P. R. DURBIN]

AGGAI (HAGGAI), BOOK OF

The 10th of the 12 *Minor Prophets according to the Biblical arrangement of books, but the first of the postexilic Prophets. His name (spelled Aggaeus in the Vulgate and Aggeus in the Douay OT, Haggai in Jewish and Protestant editions) is a derivative from the Hebrew *ḥag,* meaning feast. Though probably not a priest himself (Ag 2.11), he may have exercised some official duties at the national sanctuary of Jerusalem, perhaps as a cult prophet or preacher.

A wholly new style of prophetic preaching is discernible in the short compilation of Aggai's sermons. While the earlier Prophets upbraided the nation for excessive concern over Temple ritual and called for a return to strong and sincere morality (Os 6.4–6; Is 1.11–17; Jer 7.1–8.3), Aggai, instead, was entirely preoccupied with the reconstruction of the Temple and the correct compliance with ceremonial laws (Ezr 5.1; 6.14). Here, as in almost all postexilic writing, the preponderant influence of the priest-prophet Ezechiel is manifest. Not only do Aggai's ideas manifest little or no originality, but his style is prosaic and unimpressive, especially when compared with the poetic rhythm and rich imagery of the earlier Prophets. Attempts to versify his lines remain hypothetical.

An ancient editor of the book indicates that the Prophet spoke four or possibly five times in the 2d year of *Darius I, King of Persia, between Aug. 29 and Dec. 18, 520 B.C. [Ag 1.1; 2.1, 10, 15, 20; conversion of the dates are based on R. A. Parker and W. H. Dubberstein, *Babylonian Chronology 625 B.C.–A.D. 75* (Providence 1956) 30]. The land of the Jews in Palestine had shrunk to about 20 by 25 miles, with a population no greater than 20,000. It belonged to the province of Samaria, which was part of the fifth Persian satrapy of 'Abar Nahara ["across the River" (Euphrates)]. The country was harrassed with drought and depression (Ag 1.6, 9–11; 2.15–17); grasping, quarreling Jews were guilty of much injustice, even selling their fellow citizens into slavery (Nehemia ch. 5; Mal 3.5). The neighboring districts, Samaria to the north and Edom to the south, were despised and hated (Ezra ch. 4; Mal 1.3; Abdia); and they, in their turn, threatened to invade Juda.

The first discourse (Ag 1.1–15a) presents Aggai's blunt condemnation of the people for living in "paneled houses, while this house [the Temple] lies in ruin" (1.4). The prophet attributed the crop failures to the nation's religious laziness and therefore demanded immediate action on the Temple's reconstruction. He obtained a favorable reaction from the people. Some exegetes transfer the speech of 2.15–19 immediately after 1.15a, which is regarded as the date introducing it, on the basis that a date is prefixed to every one of Aggai's discourses. In that case, this short book would contain five instead of four sermons.

Initial letter to the Book of Aggai in the Great Bible of Demeter Nekcsei-Lipocz executed in Hungary, c. 1350, in an atelier headed by a Bolognese artist (MS Pre. Acc. 1, vol. II, fol. 194v).

The second discourse (1.15b–2.9), the most important of all from a theological point of view, was spoken on the second-last day of the octave of the Feast of *Booths (cf. Lv 23.34; Dt 16.13). Aggai's words ring with high messianic hopes, possibly because the feast included a thanksgiving service at the Temple for the year's harvest (Lv 23.39–41; 3 Kgs 8.2). He would have thought of the final harvesting of messianic blessings at the same Temple. The messianic hopes can also be accounted for by international events: Darius's quick seizure of the throne and his repulsive measures against all rebels. God too could act as decisively and quickly as Darius. Although the Vulgate recognizes a personal Messiah in 2.7, e.g., "the Desired One of all the nations," the Hebrew text and the Greek Septuagint refer to "the treasures," i.e., the contributions and talents of all nations flowing into the Temple and having a part in the liturgy.

The third discourse (2.10–14 or 2.10–19) centers on the power of evil to spread and propagate more surely than goodness. Aggai may here be rejecting the Samaritan offer to help on the reconstruction of the Temple (Ezr 4.1–5) for fear that they might contaminate the chosen people.

In the last discourse (2.20–23) Aggai reiterated the hope in a marvelous intervention when Yahweh would save His people through a Davidic king.

Bibliography: P. R. ACKROYD in *Peake's Commentary on the Bible*, ed. M. BLACK and H. H. ROWLEY (New York 1962) 562a–563i. S. BULLOUGH, CathComHS 543a–544k. T. CHARY, *Les Prophètes et la culte à partir de l'Exil* (Tournai 1955) 118–138. A. GELIN, "Introduction aux prophètes," BJ^2. T. H. ROBINSON and F. HORST, *Die zwölf kleinen Propheten* (HAT 14; 2d ed. 1954). J. SCHILDENBERGER, LexThK^2 1:188. G. RINALDI, EncCatt 1:448–449. R. BACH, RGG^3 3:25–26. EncDictBibl 42–43. **Illustration credit:** Library of Congress.

[C. STUHLMUELLER]

AGGRESSION, an act of hostility in which the individual clashes with some facet of reality (persons, things, himself) to reduce tension arising from frustration. This distinguishes aggression from aggressiveness, which aims at the completion of a task with energy, initiative, and determination. Aggressive behavior ordinarily fits the pattern of normal adjustment, while aggression veers toward maladjustment and abnormality. Aggression is direct if the attack is against the frustrating object; displaced, if against a neutral object. Sometimes it is directed inward, and the aggressor punishes himself. When fear inhibits a frontal attack, displaced aggression occurs. The object of the displaced aggression must resemble the original and yet be dissimilar enough that the inhibitions against the act of aggression are overcome.

Some signs of aggression are fighting, bullying, teasing, swearing, carrying of grudges, and ridiculing. They range from self-assertiveness and dominance to revenge and brutality. Some internal determinants of aggression are feelings of guilt, inadequacy, and inferiority; some external are lack of discipline and self-control, rejection, overprotection, and frustrating home or school situations. To the extent that aggression is disruptive of social, psychological, or moral life, it is maladjustive and abnormal.

Bibliography: A. A. SCHNEIDERS, *The Anarchy of Feeling* (New York 1963) 65–79; *Personal Adjustment and Mental Health* (New York 1955) 329–363. N. R. F. MAIER, *Frustration: A Study of Behavior without a Goal* (New York 1949). J. DOLLARD, et al., *Frustration and Aggression* (New Haven 1939). L. J. SAUL, *The Hostile Mind: The Sources and Consequences of Rage and Hate* (New York 1956).

[E. J. RYAN]

AGIL, ST., missionary and abbot; b. Franche-Comté, *c.* 580; d. Abbey of Rebais near Meaux, France, *c.* 650 (feast, Aug. 30). At the age of about 7 he was received at the abbey of *Luxeuil by *Columban and trained there in the religious life by *Eustace of Luxeuil. He probably followed Columban into exile in 610, returning to Luxeuil with Eustace, and after his ordination as a priest accompanying Eustace on a missionary journey to Bavaria *c.* 617. When elected bishop of Langres in 628, Agil refused the dignity. *Ouen of Rouen chose him to be the first abbot of his new foundation at Rebais, and Agil was consecrated in the presence of Dagobert I at Clichy in 636, when the King also granted the abbey a charter of immunity (MGD 1:16). Agil died at the age of 66 and was buried in St. Peter's church at Rebais. There are two biographies of the saint, one from the late 7th century and the other a composite of the 11th and 12th centuries.

Bibliography: Mabillon AS 2:301–320. ActSS Aug. 6:574–597. BHL 148–149. E. VACANDARD, *Vie de saint Ouen, évêque de Rouen* (Paris 1902) 61–69, 169. P. FOURNIER, DHGE 1:957–958. Zimmermann KalBen 2:634. R. AIGRAIN, *Catholicisme* 1:245–246.

[B. J. COMASKEY]

AGILITY, that quality or endowment in virtue of which the risen body of the just "will be freed from the heaviness that now presses it down and will take on a capability of moving with the utmost ease and swiftness wherever the soul pleases" (*Catechism of the Council of Trent* 1.12.13). According to St. Paul, in the resurrection of the just "what is sown in weakness rises in power" (1 Cor 15.43). In these words Catholic theologians have seen a reference to the agility of the risen *glorified body.

St. Thomas explains why this quality is postulated and what its nature is: "The soul which will enjoy the divine vision, united to its ultimate end, will in all matters experience the fulfillment of desire. And since it is out of the soul's desire that the body is moved, the consequence will be the body's utter obedience to the soul's slightest wish. Hence, the bodies of the blessed when they rise are going to have agility . . .. For weakness is what we experience in a body found wanting in the strength to satisfy the desire of the soul in the movements and actions which the soul commands, and this weakness will be entirely taken away then, when power overflows into the body from a soul united to God" (*C. gent.* 4.86). Traditional scholastic authorities are in substantial agreement with St. Thomas concerning the nature of this mysterious quality; its future existence, they maintain, is implicitly contained in the revealed fact of the glorious resurrection at the world's end. Agility therefore will be present in the complete and definitive transformation of the body of man's lowliness, which "our Lord Jesus Christ . . . will refashion . . . conforming it to the body of his glory by exercising the power by which he is able to subject all things to himself" (Phil 3.21).

See also RESURRECTION OF THE DEAD.

Bibliography: A. CHOLLET, DTC 3.2:1879–1906. J. F. SAGÜES, SacTheolSumma BAC 4.6:295–309. M. A. GENEVOIS, *Entre dans la joie* (Paris 1960).

[C. J. CORCORAN]

AGILULF OF COLOGNE, ST., bishop; d. 750 or 751 (feast, July 9). He became bishop of Cologne after 745–746, supported the reforms of St. *Boniface, and attended the Frankish Synod in 747. The cult of St. Agilulf did not flourish until after July 9, 1062, when Abp. *Anno II of Cologne translated the relics of St. Agilulf from the Abbey of *Malmédy to St. Maria ad Gradus in Cologne, where they remained until their removal to the cathedral in 1846. According to the *Passio sancti Agilolfi,* composed probably before 1062, this Agilulf was a simple monk, martyred by the Neustrians at Amblève (Amel) on March 31, 716. Later sources wrongly identified him with Bishop Agilulf. Thus, *c.* 1160, Dietrich of Deutz added the title "martyr" to the entry *Agilolfus episcopus* in the list of bishops of Cologne. According to another account, the *Miracula sancti Quirini,* written at Malmédy late in the 11th century, Agilulf was a Benedictine monk at the Abbey of *Stavelot under Abbot Anglinus, whom he succeeded, apparently in 745, remaining abbot even after he became bishop of Cologne. This, too, is plainly inaccurate, since Anglinus was certainly abbot as late as 751.

Bibliography: W. NEUSS, ed., *Geschichte des Erzbistums Köln,* v.1. *Das Bistum Köln von den Anfängen bis zum Ende des 12. Jahrhunderts* (Cologne 1964) 134–135. W. LEVISON, "Bischof Agilolf von Köln und seine *Passio,*" *Annalen des hist. Vereins für den Niederrhein* 115 (1929) 76–97; repr. in W. LEVISON, *Aus rheinischer und fränkischer Frühzeit. Ausgewählte Aufsätze* (Düsseldorf 1948) 76–95. A. STEFFENS, *Der heilige Agilolfus* (Cologne 1893). MGS 11:438–439, 482; 13:293. ActSS July 2:714–726.

[M. F. MC CARTHY]

AGNELLI, GIUSEPPE. Jesuit writer of catechetical and devotional works; b. Naples, April 1, 1621; d. Rome, Sept. 8, 1706. Agnelli entered the Society of Jesus in 1637. For a time he was professor of moral theology, and was later rector of the colleges of Montepulciano, Macerata, and Ancona, where he was also consultor of the Inquisition of the March of Ancona. He spent the last 33 years of his life in the professed house in Rome. His chief writing was *Il Catechismo annuale* (Macerata 1657), or *Il Parrocchiano istruttore* (Rome 1677, Venice 1731), which was an adaptation for parish priests and contained an explanation of the Gospel for every Sunday in the year. In addition he wrote a week's devotion to St. Joseph for the Bona Mors Sodality, four commentaries on the *Exercises* of St. Ignatius, a collection of meditations for a triduum, a 10-day retreat for Jesuits about to make profession, and a series of sermons for Advent and Lent.

Bibliography: T. J. CAMPBELL, CE 1:212. A. M. FIOCCHI, EncCatt 1:458–459. Sommervogel 1:65–68.

[B. CAVANAUGH]

AGNELLUS OF PISA, BL., first Franciscan superior in England; b. Pisa, *c.* 1194; d. Oxford, March 3, 1232. He was sent (*c.* 1217) by St. *Francis to France, where he became *custos* of Paris. As a deacon in

1224 he was appointed to introduce the *Franciscans into England, where he became the first minister provincial. At the urging of his superior, he became a priest (before 1229). He successfully defended the rights of his order against the claims of the bishops (1231). He propagated the order throughout much of England and is chiefly responsible for the reputation for science of the English Franciscans, since he obtained *Robert Grosseteste as a teacher for the Franciscan house of studies in Oxford. Agnellus was declared blessed in 1892.

Bibliography. THOMAS OF ECCLESTON, *De adventu Fratrum Minorum in Angliam,* ed. A. G. LITTLE (2d ed. Manchester, Eng. 1951). C. MARIOTTI, *Il b. Agnello da Pisa ed i Frati Minori in Inghilterra* (Rome 1895). L. HARDICK, ed., *Nach Deutschland und England* (Werl 1957) 115–214.

[L. HARDICK]

AGNES, ST., virgin and martyr of Rome (feast, Jan. 21). Little is known about this popular Roman saint who was martyred in the middle of the 3d or in the early 4th century. Her feast is recorded in the *Depositio martyrum* contained in the Chronograph of 354 (*see* CHRONOGRAPHER OF 354). She is mentioned

St. Agnes, detail of a 6th-century mosaic in the church of S. Apollinare Nuovo, Ravenna.

by Ambrose (*De virginibus* 1.2; *De officiis* 1.41), in the Ambrosian hymn *Agnes beatae virginis,* by Pope *Damasus in a still extant epitaph, and by Prudentius (*Peristephanon* 14). According to Ambrose and Prudentius she was beheaded, according to Damasus, burned to death, and according to the *Agnes beatae virginis,* she was strangled. Despite this contradictory evidence, the sources agree in that she was young, only 12 or 13, when martyred. A fully developed legend of the 6th century describes her as a beautiful young girl with many rivals for her hand. When she rejected them, she was delated to the governor as a Christian and sent to a house of prostitution. Those who came to see her were struck with awe. One who looked lustfully at her lost his sight but regained it through her prayers. Brought before the judge, she was condemned and executed and buried on the Via Salaria, in a catacomb eventually named after her. Before 349 a basilica was built over her tomb by Constantina, daughter of Constantine. This was restored by Pope *Symmachus (498–514) and completely rebuilt by *Honorius I (625–638). In the 4th century, Agnes was represented as an orant with arms outstretched in prayer. From the 6th century on she was portrayed as a young girl with a lamb in her arms or at her feet. Before the 9th century her head was removed from her tomb to the *Sancta Sanctorum* of the Lateran palace. When this was examined on April 19, 1903, it was seen to be that of a girl about 12 years old. Pius X gave the relic to the church of St. Agnes *in Agone* on the Piazza Navona in Rome.

Bibliography: A. P. FRUTAZ, EncCatt 1:467–474. E. JOSI, BiblSanct 1:382–407. Butler Th Attw 1:133–137. **Illustration credit:** R. V. Schoder, SJ.

[M. J. COSTELLOE]

AGNES OF ASSISI, ST., Poor Clare abbess; b. Assisi, 1197; d. there, Aug. 27, 1253 (feast, Nov. 16). Sixteen days after her older sister, *Clare of Assisi, fled from home to follow (St.) *Francis of Assisi, Agnes joined her, first at San Angelo di Panzo, where she heroically withstood family opposition, and then at San Damiano. When the Benedictines of Monticelli asked to become *Poor Clares, Francis sent Agnes to them as abbess (1219 or 1221). After returning to San Damiano in 1253, she witnessed the death of Clare and died soon after. She is said to have had a vision of the Christ Child, which her iconography sometimes depicts. Benedict XIV approved her cult in 1753. She is buried in S. Chiara, Assisi.

Bibliography: "Vita . . .," AnalFranc 3 (1897) 173–182. THOMAS OF CELANO, *Legenda Sanctae Clarae virginis,* ed. F. PENNACCHI (Assisi 1910). Wadding Ann 1:141–142; 2:18–19; 3:350–351. *Vita di. s. Agnese di Assisi, compilata da una suora Clarissa* (Lecce 1913). Butler Th Attw 4:358–359. *Leben und Schriften der heiligen Klara von Assisi,* ed. E. GRAU (2d ed. Werl 1953), legend ascribed to Thomas of Celano; Eng. tr. I. BRADY and M. F. LAUGHLIN (St. Bonaventure, N.Y. 1953) 35–37.

[M. F. LAUGHLIN]

AGNES OF BOHEMIA, BL., Poor Clare abbess; b. Prague, 1205?; d. Prague, March 2, 1281 or 1282 (feast, June 8). Agnes, daughter of Ottokar I, King of Bohemia, and Constance of Hungary, built a hospital for the poor, founded an order of hospitallers to staff it, and in 1232 built a Franciscan friary and a *Poor Clare convent in Prague. Wishing to become a Poor Clare herself, she appealed to Gregory IX against negotiations for her marriage, rejecting, according to some authorities, both Henry III of England and Emperor Frederick II. She took the veil in her own convent in 1234 or 1236. As abbess she was closely associated with *Clare of Assisi, and four letters to her from Clare are extant. She is portrayed in art as a Poor Clare abbess. Pius IX beatified her on Dec. 3, 1874.

Bibliography: ActSS March 1:501–531. W. W. SETON, *Some New Sources for the Life of Bl. Agnes of Bohemia . . .* (Aberdeen, Scotland 1915); "The Letters from Saint Clare to Bl. A. of B.," ArchFrancHist 17 (1924) 505–519. E. GILLIAT-SMITH, *Saint Clare of Assisi: Her Life and Legislation* (New York 1914). A. DE SÉRENT, DHGE 1:977–979. C. TESTORE, EncCatt 1:475. *The Legend and Writings of Saint Clare of Assisi,* ed. I. BRADY and M. F. LAUGHLIN (St. Bonaventure, N.Y. 1953) 9–10, 88–98, 157–159. M. FASSBINDER, *Die selige Agnes von Prag, eine königliche Klarissin* (Werl 1957).

[M. F. LAUGHLIN]

AGNES OF MONTEPULCIANO, ST., Dominican nun, patroness of Montepulciano; b. Agnes Segni, Gracciano-Vecchio, Tuscany, *c.* 1268; d. Montepulciano, Italy, April 4, 1317 (feast, April 20). At the age of 9 she induced her parents to let her join a community at Montepulciano called "Sisters of the Sack" because of their coarse garments. Her holiness and intelligence impressed the nuns, and she was made bursar when only 14. A year later she accompanied an older nun to Proceno to found a new convent. She was soon elected abbess. In her new position she increased her austerities, fasting on bread and water, and sleeping on the ground. The citizens of Montepulciano, desiring her return, offered to build a convent in a place formerly occupied by a house of ill fame. Agnes became prioress there (1306) and placed the convent under Dominican patronage. She was a competent administrator, often providing miraculously for the needs of her sisters. Simplicity and ardor were the keynotes of her spirituality. Her vita reports that she was favored by apparitions of the Blessed Virgin, the Christ Child, and the angels, and that showers of white, cross-shaped particles "like manna" fell upon her and the places where she prayed. She died after a painful illness. As patroness of Montepulciano, she is represented with a model of the city in her hands; in Italian art she is associated with *Catherine of Siena and *Rose of Lima.

Bibliography: RAYMOND OF CAPUA, *Vita,* ActSS April 2:790–810. *Année Dominicaine,* 23 v. (Lyons 1883–1909) April 2: 519–546. A. WALZ, *Die hl. Agnes v. Montepulciano* (Dülmen 1922). Butler Th Attw 2:135–137. G. DI AGRESTI and D. VALORI, BiblSanct 1:375–381.

[M. J. FINNEGAN]

AGNES OF POITIERS, ST., abbess; d. *c.* 589 (feast, May 13, in the Diocese of Poitiers). She was the adopted daughter of St. *Radegunda, the wife of Chlotar I, King of the Franks (d. 561). In 550 Radegunda fled from her husband after he had killed her brother. She found temporary refuge in several communities and finally founded the convent of the Holy Cross in Poitiers, which was consecrated by St. *Germain in 561. About 570 Radegunda and Agnes visited Arles to study the rule of St. *Caesarius. Subsequently the rule was adopted at Poitiers, and Agnes became the first abbess, but she was replaced in 589 after a revolt by dissatisfied elements in the convent. Agnes is remembered for her connection with the poet *Fortunatus, who was also a correspondent of her mother. Her relics are preserved in the church of St. Radegunda, and her tomb is a popular place of pilgrimage in the area.

Bibliography: GREGORY OF TOURS, *Historia Francorum* 9.39–42 in MGSrerMer 1:393–404. F. G. HOLWECK, *A Biographical Dictionary of the Saints* (St. Louis 1924) 33. R. AIGRAIN, *Catholicisme* 1:216. Mercati-Pelzer DE 1:56. P. DE MONSABERT, DHGE 1:973–974. G. ALLEMANG, LexThK[2] 1:199.

[J. F. FAHEY]

AGNESI, MARIA GAETANA, mathematician; b. Milan, May 16, 1718; d. Milan, Jan. 9, 1799. Maria Agnesi, one of 23 children of a rich and cultured family, had mastered eight languages before her 13th year. At 20 she began the work that resulted in the publication of *Le Instituzioni Analitiche* (1748), a precise summary of the mathematical knowledge of the time. In volume 1 appeared the cubic curve, given earlier by *Fermat in the form $(a^2 - x^2)\ y = a^3$ and discussed by Guido Grandi in his *Quadratura circuli et hyperbolae,* 1703 and 1710. Although the formula did not originate with Maria Agnesi, it attracted the attention of mathematicians through her publication and was known subsequently as the "Witch of Agnesi" or the "Curve of Agnesi." She also translated, but did not publish, the *Traité analytique des sectiones coniques* of *L'Hospital. Maria Agnesi served 2 years as professor of mathematics at the University of Bologna. She desired to enter the Augustinians, but during her lifetime this community was suppressed. On the request of Pope Benedict XIV, she directed the women's section of the Pio Istitutio Trivulzio, a home for aged and sick poor.

Bibliography: F. CAJORI, *History of Mathematics* (2d ed. rev. New York 1919). F. F. MULCRONE, "The Names of the Curve of Agnesi," *American Mathematical Monthly* 64 (1957) 359–361. A. REBIÈRE, *Les Femmes dans la science* (Paris 1897). T. KLOYDA, "The Walking Polyglot," *Scripta Mathematica* 6 (1939): 211–217.

[T. À K. KLOYDA]

AGNOSTICISM

An attitude of mind toward man's knowledge of God; namely, that God is humanly unknowable. Etymologically, agnosticism (Gr. *agnostos*) means an unknowing, a profession of ignorance. Historically, the word "agnostic" was first used by T. H. *Huxley in 1869. Having joined the Metaphysical Society, a society whose members professed knowledge on all kinds of mysteries, and wishing to show his opposition to such extravagant claims, Huxley adopted the name "agnostic." Since his time the term has been used to designate anyone who denies man a knowledge of immaterial reality, and especially of the existence and nature of God.

Kinds of Agnosticism. An agnostic is not an atheist. An atheist denies the existence of God; an agnostic professes ignorance about His existence. For the latter, God may exist, but reason can neither prove nor disprove it. Agnostics have been divided into two groups: those who deny that reason can know God and make no judgment concerning that existence; those who deny that reason can prove it but nonetheless profess a belief in God's existence. A well-known contemporary instance of the first group is Bertrand *Russell; a famous example of the second is Immanuel *Kant. With few exceptions, modern and contemporary agnostics belong to the second group.

Another division of agnosticism may be made in terms of the philosophical commitments that cause their adherents to deny the possibility of knowing God. These commitments are many and varied, but the principal ones in the history of thought may be enumerated as nominalism, empiricism, Kantianism, the theory of the unconditioned, logical positivism, and existentialism. The remainder of this article explains the philosophical grounds for agnostic attitudes within these schools and gives a critical evaluation of each.

Nominalism. *William of Ockham, the father of philosophical *nominalism, denied that the human intellect could with certitude demonstrate the existence of One, Infinite God. For Ockham, universality or community is only a condition of thought and in no sense a truth about being. There is nothing in things that allows the mind to transcend from them to God.

Argument. The line of reasoning for Ockham and his followers is clear. Unless there resides in the beings of man's experience a *relation that orders them to God, the mind cannot demonstrate the existence of God from the existence of these beings. For the nominalist no such relation exists. Relation bespeaks an order between two things. And since order must include the things ordered, it implies a pattern of inclusiveness, or universality. Universality, however, cannot be part of the structure of being, but only of the signification of words. Nominalism thus erases universality from being. Each individual is simply itself—a singular instance of existence. To put universality in things, argue the nominalists, is to confuse the order of being with the order of signification. Things may be really dependent on God, but the mind could know this only if it could intuit some relation between things and God. But because of the atomistic (nonuniversal) nature of the singular, this is impossible. The singular can reveal to the intellect no illative force, no moment of trancendence. Analysis of the singular never uncovers objective universality. Thus does nominalism block off any philosophical ascent to God by way of intellectual inference. The fruit of nominalism in natural theology is agnosticism. (*See* OCKHAMISM; UNIVERSALS.)

Evaluation. What the nominalists fail to recognize is that, while each being is indivisibly singular, the *intellect has the power to consider one aspect of the singular while leaving others out of consideration. Thus the intellect can attain universal notions, such as man, animal, substance, and so forth. Universality is in the thing, in the sense that the perfection that is considered is in the thing; but *as* in the thing, the perfection is inseparable from the very singularity of the thing. Moreover, the order that results from received existence is an intelligible datum that can be grasped by the intellect, though not by the *senses. Change, imperfection, limitation, composition—these are all intelligible facts about the things of man's experience that spell out for his intellect the contingent condition of their being. Contingency, and hence order and dependence, may be impervious to his senses, for they are not sensible facts; but they are open to his intellect, because they are facts of existence. Thus the intellect is not only justified but necessitated to make an inference from caused to Uncaused Being.

Empiricism. The central teaching of *empiricism is that all knowledge comes through experience. While such a truism need not lead to agnosticism, historically it did so, and this because of the empiricists' quarrel with rationalism.

Argument. *Rationalism maintained that such terms as "contingent" and "necessary" were both true in what they defined and actually descriptive of the real world. For the empiricist this is impossible. Man experiences what happens in the world, not that it must so happen, that is, happen contingently or necessarily. "Necessity," writes D. *Hume, "is something that exists in the mind, not in objects." And since man does not experience necessity, he cannot say that the causal proposition, "every event has a cause," has been gained from experience. The necessity and universality found in the causal proposition is not grounded in objects, but in some condition of man's thinking about objects. Empiricism explains the origins of the causal proposition in terms of human habits of thought. Repeatedly experiencing B following A, one comes to anticipate B whenever he experiences A. But since he does not experience a connection between them, he cannot say that B *must* follow A.

This obviously means that the human mind can never reason with certitude to the existence of God. For this would be asserting a necessary connection between mundane events and a supramundane Being, a connection that falls outside human experience. To assert this connection is to commit the fallacy of rationalism; one inserts a necessity derived from his concepts into the world of events. As with nominalism, empiricism precludes a transcendence from effect to cause by rejecting for knowledge the objective value of the causal principle or of *causality.

Evaluation. The empiricists are guilty of a one-dimensional interpretation of human experience. As has been seen, imperfection, limitation, composition, relations, differences, and so forth, are just as clearly facts about a thing as are its color, size, shape, motion, etc. While the former are not sense data, it would be arbitrary to argue that they are not facts of human experience. To limit experience to what is directly perceptible by the five senses is to eliminate a large part of experience and to go against experience itself. It is true that man does not sense causality, that he does not sense relations; but he does experience them, not with his senses but with his intellect. Sense experience is only one kind of experience. The activities one experiences among beings is attended by the intellectual *insight that these beings are really related and hence are true causes and effects. The demonstration for the existence of God is grounded, above all, in an intellectual, rather than sensible, experience of reality. (*See* EXPERIENCE.)

Kantianism. Kant subscribed to the Humean critique of causality. Yet he viewed the construction of his critical philosophy as the proper synthesis of rationalism and empiricism. The importance of Kant in the history of agnosticism cannot be overstressed. In the minds of most non-Catholic thinkers, Kant's *Critique of Pure Reason* has given the *coup de grâce* to any possible proof for the existence of God.

Kant's Criticism. In removing necessity from things themselves, Hume seemed to be destroying the objective value of the necessary truths of the physical sciences, mathematics, and metaphysics. To justify the necessity and universality of such truths (at least for science and mathematics), Kant proposed his theory of the synthetic a priori judgment. A judgment is synthetic, rather than analytic, when its content refers to empirical reality; and it is a priori when it involves elements not drawn from that reality. "Every event has a cause," is an example of a synthetic a priori judgment. It is a judgment that deals with events and hence refers to empirical reality; but it has elements not drawn from empirical reality, namely, universality (*every* event) and necessity (has a *cause*), and so is a priori. For as Hume had correctly pointed out, universality and necessity are not concepts drawn from the object. (*See* CRITICISM, PHILOSOPHICAL; KANTIANISM.)

The important fact about such a judgment is that, though not drawn completely from empirical reality, it is always applicable to it. This is so because the judgment "every event has a cause" expresses a condition for the very experiencing of events, at least in a unified way. In a word, a synthetic a priori judgment contains two elements: one formal, the work of the understanding; the other material, the product of experience. Since such judgments express the very conditions that make knowledge of the world possible, they have objective validity whenever applied to this world. The way man knows empirical reality, and must know it, is as objective as the thing known. It now remains to see how this view of knowledge leads of necessity to agnosticism.

Argument. In order, to be perceived, a thing must be experienced here and now. The here and now, or space and time, are not intrinsic properties of the thing, but necessary conditions for perceiving the thing. In like manner, cause, substance, and relation are not intrinsic properties of the thing, but necessary conditions for understanding it. And only those things that can be perceived in space and time can be understood. But God is a reality that is entirely outside space and time, and so there are no conditions that could make any knowledge of Him possible. There is no way for the intellect of man to have an objective knowledge of God.

But obviously, says Kant, man can form an idea of God. The mind forms such an idea whenever it seeks for the cause of causes, for the ultimate unifying principle of all beings and of all thought. But God as a unifying principle is merely an idea, that is to say, a concept formed by the transcendental activity of human reason with no guarantee of an objective correlate outside the reason. To form an idea of God, then, is in no way to prove that there is a God. For as not subject to the conditions of space and time, God is not perceivable; and as unperceivable through sensibility, He must remain forever unknowable to understanding.

If all Kant were saying is that God in His own Being in no way is subject to the senses or intellect of man, so that one can never have any direct natural knowledge of Him, he would be no more agnostic than the most orthodox Catholic philosopher. His agnosticism consists in his absolute refusal to give to the understanding of man even an indirect knowledge of God. God cannot be known either in Himself (which all admit) or through creatures. The objective reality of God can never in any sense become a term for human understanding. Since God is outside all the conditions for human understanding, no category of the mind can be applied to Him. Thus the category of cause cannot be applied to Him. The application of causality is valid among the beings of empirical reality (*phenomena), but not among those of transempirical reality (*noumena). God's existence cannot be inferred or concluded to; for the reason in passing from phenomenal reality to noumenal steps outside the conditions of human understanding. Hence this transition results in no objective knowledge of reality, but only in empty concepts.

It is true that Kant, on moral grounds, saw the necessity for postulating a belief in God (or in the idea of God), but since such a postulate has no cognitive content and does not guarantee the actual existence of God, this aspect of Kant's critical philosophy in no way mitigates his agnosticism.

Evaluation. An analysis of Kant's epistemology makes it clear that he equated *being with "being-sensible." If an absolute condition for knowing anything is that it be *first* perceived in human sensibility, then, of course, only sensibles are knowable. This would mean that all other facts in man's knowledge of being, for example, its distinction from other beings, its limitations, its composition, and so forth, belong not to the thing but only to the way man knows the thing. He could not predicate them about the thing itself, but only about the thing as in his knowledge. He could not say "man *is* limited," but only "man must be *known* as limited." In the view of Kant, one cannot say that limitation, imperfection, and composition (all the facts of being that lead one to God) are facts about being independent of the knowing process. And this is to equate being with "being-sensible." Admittedly, to grasp these facts (including the fact of existence itself) an intellect is needed; the senses are not enough. But to say that therefore they are the product of the intellect, they are due *merely* to the way the intellect knows, is a false conclusion. The way the eye sees color or the ear hears sound is certainly not the way color or sound is present in objects; but no one denies that there is in the object the proper and sensible correlate of color and sound. So, too, with the intelligible elements of being. They will yield their presence only to an intellect, and in an intellectual way. But they are as much facts about a being as are its sensible facts. To deny this is to deny the very existence of things, for existence is not a sensible fact.

Theory of the Unconditioned. Under the influence of Kant, agnosticism began to assume the form of a philosophical theory, the theory of the unconditioned. The two names most commonly associated with this theory are Sir William *Hamilton and Herbert *Spencer. The former develops it in his main work, *Philosophy of the Unconditioned* (Edinburgh 1829), and Spencer devotes the first 100 pages of his *First Principles* (London 1862) to "The Unknowable." While neither man is read much in the mid-20th century, their influence during their lifetime was considerable, and their views on man's knowledge of God have become accepted teaching.

Argument. The theory of the unconditioned is, in its essentials, Kantian, and briefly it comes to this. To think of an object is to condition it, either by putting it into some class, as when one says "God is a substance," or by relating it to some other object, as when one says "God is a cause." Since all knowledge goes from the known to the unknown, every object must be known in terms of something else. An object that cannot be conditioned by either classification or relation is unknowable. For to know is to condition. But God, as Infinite and Absolute Being, transcends every condition. Thus God is unknowable and is the very negation of thought. To classify the infinite is to make it finite; and to relate the absolute is to make it relative. To say, therefore, that God is a substance, or a cause, or a being, are so many meaningless statements. There is only one meaningful statement that can be made about the unknowable—it cannot be known.

If this teaching simply meant that man can have no direct knowledge of God, in the sense that God in Himself can never be grasped as a term within man's knowledge, it would be acceptable. But it means more than this. For in an indirect knowledge of God through creatures, either God becomes a term of knowledge or not. If He does not, man does not know God, but only creatures; if He does, then He has been conditioned by a relation (cause), and so once more it is not God man is thinking about but only some subjective notion he calls God.

Evaluation. How does one break through the dilemma presented by this theory? By a close look at the act of existing of a finite being and a closer look at what it means to know. The very *contingency of an imperfect act of existing demands that it has grounds for existing that are outside itself. Its *existence is received existence. Contingent existence is a contradiction in terms unless it has its source in Necessary Existence. But can man know this Necessary Being? He cannot know it in itself, but he can know that there must be such a Being. In affirming the necessity of such a Being, what terminates his knowledge is not the being of God but the truth of the proposition "There must be a God." Thus the being of God is left unconditioned, but man's knowledge has been conditioned and determined to a *truth* about God, namely, that He exists. Moreover, this is a truth about an actually existing being (and not an empty concept), for man's knowledge has been determined by actually existing beings precisely as caused by God. And in this sense one can say that God is the indirect object, and the object that logically terminates one's thinking, for it is through His being that the things that determine one to know Him exist. The error of the theory of the unconditioned is that it equates conditioning in knowledge with conditioning in being. Man can know God through creatures without affecting God's being. In fact, though this is not the present concern, even a direct vision of God such as the angels and saints have in heaven, leaves the divine being completely unconditioned, unaffected; for the whole act of knowledge as such is in, and hence affects, the knower. Conditions concern the way one knows, not what one knows. The agnostics fail to make this important distinction.

Logical Positivism. A fashionable form of contemporary agnosticism, especially in the U.S. and Britain, is *logical positivism. This school, whose methodology is *linguistic analysis and whose theory of knowledge is empiricism, teaches that a proposition is true if its language elements are reducible to, or verifiable in terms of, some direct or indirect sense experience. Propositions that make no claim to describe reality, such as those of logic and mathematics, are true if consistent with themselves. Factual propositions belong to the empirical sciences, and formal propositions to the logical and mathematical sciences. Both sets of propositions can be either true or false, and both have their proper meaning; for they can be seen as either reducible to sense experience, as in the case of factual propositions, or as self-consistent, as with formal propositions.

Argument. Statements about God are neither factual nor formal. Since the subject of such propositions falls outside both direct and indirect sense experience, the elements of such propositions are not verifiable in terms of any knowable experience. They can be shown to be neither true nor false. Thus they are empty of all meaning; they are meaningless, "nonsensical" bits of language. Nor are they formally true, since they claim to bear upon a real object. If no such claim were made, the logical positivists would grant that statements about God would have formal (not factual) truth. For they could be viewed as instances of a consistent use of language or a possible way that ideas could be related.

Evaluation. As is clear, the agnosticism espoused by the logical positivists is simply a restatement, in terms of the analysis of *language, of the basic positions of Hume on the origin of knowledge and of Kant on the noncognitive value of "transcendental ideas." (*See* ANALYTICAL PHILOSOPHY; VERIFICATION.)

Existentialism. The most important philosophical movement of the mid-20th century is undoubtedly *existentialism. Briefly, this doctrine teaches that the only essence the individual man has is that which he freely creates for himself through the decisive realization of his human possibilities. Man in his existence is free tendency. He makes himself what he is. To say that he possesses a stable and determined essence is to rob him of his freedom and to make his being a fixed and formalized unfolding of a predetermined pattern. Moreover, as a continual flux of existential tendencies, man cannot grasp himself through any conceptual knowledge; for a concept immobilizes, and so falsifies, reality. Man's being, rather, is grasped by an encounter of experience with himself and others, and not by an insight into intelligible patterns, for there are none.

Argument. Existentialism is agnostic for several reasons. First, it refuses to man any rational or conceptual understanding of God. Second, even when some awareness of a ground of Being is suggested, one can never identify this ground with God. For these objects of "transcendence" (the All-Embracing in K. Jaspers, Being Itself in M. Heidegger, Nothingness in J. P. Sartre) are described in terms philosophically incompatible with a personal and genuinely transcendent God. Furthermore, one can never be sure, because of the type of awareness involved in *phenomenology, that these objects are not the product of one's own *consciousness. Third, existentialism is agnostic because in the horizontal movement of phenomenological awareness one never attains a moment of seen inference to a source of being. The roots of intelligibility having been removed from being, nothing remains in the flux of existential moments by which man can grasp a relationship to a Being that transcends the flux. In spite of their great concern for the freedom and openness of the human spirit, existentialists are still the victims of Humean empiricism; but now it is an inverted empiricism, the empiricism of consciousness.

Evaluation. The error of the existentialists is twofold. First, they fail to recognize that a *finite being without an *essence is a contradiction. For finite existence is always the existence of something, and this from its very beginning. Man without an intrinsic limit or essence would be an act of infinite existence. The second error is their failure to recognize that unless human *freedom is grounded in intelligence and dependent upon it, man cannot know the possibilities among which he *can* choose. Finally, these possibilities of man are really surreptitiously reintroduced essences; for an essence is a *potency that can be realized (made actual) through existence. There are many excellent and profound things in existentialism. But the suppression of the human essence and the apotheosis of freedom are not among them.

Conclusion. An interesting phenomenon attends the writings of an agnostic. He describes the Unknown God in the same terms as the theist: infinite, absolute, necessary, transcendent, and so forth. The impression is given that the agnostic knows no less about God than the theist and the theist no more than the agnostic. If God is unknowable, why does the agnostic know so much about Him? The touchstone of an agnostic is not what he says about God, but what he intends these statements to mean. The all-important difference is this: the theist claims his statements about God legitimately bear upon an existing object and give him true and valid knowledge of this object. The agnostic denies that his statements about God have any of these characteristics. They are not statements about an existing object at all, but only about an idea wholly constructed by his mind.

See also GOD 4, 5, 7, 9; GOD, PROOFS FOR THE EXISTENCE OF; ATHEISM; DEISM; HUMANISM, SECULAR; NATURALISM; THEISM; THEOLOGY, NATURAL.

Bibliography: Hastings ERE 1:214–220. R. FLINT, *Agnosticism* (London 1903). J. WARD, *Naturalism and Agnosticism,* 2 v. (New York 1899). J. D. COLLINS, *God in Modern Philosophy* (Chicago 1959). H. DE LUBAC, *The Drama of Atheist Humanism,* tr. E. M. RILEY (New York 1949). R. JOLIVET, *The God of Reason,* tr. M. PONTIFEX (New York 1958). A. G. N. FLEW and A. MACINTYRE, eds., *New Essays in Philosophical Theology* (New York 1955). A. E. TAYLOR, *Does God Exist?* (New York 1947). E. S. BRIGHTMAN, *The Problem of God* (New York 1930). A. C. COCHRANE, *The Existentialists and God* (Philadelphia 1956). F. E. ENGLAND, *Kant's Conception of God* (New York 1930). T. H. L. PARKER, *The Doctrine of the Knowledge of God* (London 1952). F. R. TENNANT, *Philosophical Theology,* 2 v. (New York 1928–30). C. C. J. WEBB, *Studies in the History of Natural Theology* (Oxford 1915).

[M. R. HOLLOWAY]

AGNOSTOS THEOS, Greek term meaning "unknown god." It was used by St. Paul in his speech on the *Areopagus of Athens (Acts 17.23) when he said that he had seen in Athens an altar with the inscription ΑΓΝΩΣΤΩ ΘΕΩ [to (the) unknown god]. His statement has caused much discussion since no exact parallel has been found in actual inscriptions. Several examples in the plural are known, such as the inscriptions mentioned by Pausanias ("Attica," *Description of Greece,* LoebClLib 1:6–7): *βωμοὶ θεῶν τε ὀνομαζομένων ἀγνώστων καὶ ἡρώων* (and altars of gods called "unknown" and of heroes) and by Philostratus (*The Life of Apollonius of Tyana,* LoebClLib 2:12): *ἀγνώστων δαιμόνων βωμοί* (altars of unknown divinities). There are also inscriptions with the noun in the singular, but with other adjectives, such as "to the appropriate god," and "to the nameless god." It is therefore certain that honor was often paid to gods whose names were not known to the worshiper but who may have done him favors and must not be overlooked. Tertullian (*Ad nationes,* CorpChrist 1:55) notes: "nam et Athenis ara est inscripta 'ignotis deis' " (for at Athens there is an altar inscribed "to the unknown gods"), and St. Jerome (*In Titum* 1.12; PL 26:572–573) refers to a phrase *Diis ignotis et peregrinis* (to unknown and strange gods) as probably the inscription that Paul actually saw. Apparently Paul adapted for his purpose of teaching monotheism some such inscription he had seen in Athens and used it as an opportunity to make known to his audience the one true God whom, unknowingly, they had in fact, in the midst of all their fictitious divinities, been seeking and worshiping. The phrase cannot mean "to the unknowable God," nor could it mean to the pagans, "to the [one true but] unknown God," even if the inscription were in the singular. Its reference would be to any god overlooked because not known.

Bibliography: E. NORDEN, *AGNOSTOS THEOS* (Leipzig 1923), esp. 115–124. O. JESSEN, " *Ἄγνωστος θεός,*" Pauly-Wiss RE Suppl. 1 (1903) 28–30. T. BIRT, " *Ἄγνωστοι θεοί* und die Areopagrede des Apostels Paulus," *Rheinisches Museum für Philologie* 69 (1914) 342–392. Jackson-Lake 5:240–246. W. ELTESTER, RGG[3] 1:176.

[R. V. SCHODER]

AGNUS DEI

A chant to accompany the breaking of the Host at Masses in Latin (*Fractio panis; see* MASS, ROMAN). The chant is intoned immediately after the people's response to the *Pax Domini* of the celebrant and sung three times as the celebrant recites the three Communion prayers before receiving Communion. The final petition substitutes the words "dona nobis pacem" for the "miserere nobis" of the two preceding petitions. According to the Liber pontificalis (ed. Duchesne 1:376) it was Pope Sergius I (687–701) who first ordered that during the time of the Fraction of the Lord's body the clergy and people should sing "Lamb of God [Agnus Dei], who take away the sins of the world, have mercy on us." (In the *Milanese rite a variable *confractorium* is chanted at this point in the liturgy). According to J. Froger, it is possible that Pope Sergius did nothing more than replace a variable chant in the earlier Roman liturgy with this fixed formula. Righetti (3:444 and n.81), on the other hand, insist that the variable texts for the Fraction contained in many early Roman documents are of a later Gallican origin (*see* GALLICAN RITES). Thus, up to the time of Pope Sergius the Roman rite Fraction would have been carried out in silence. The *Capitulare* (ed. Silva-Tarouca, 200), which dates from a few years after the prescriptions of Pope Sergius, states that the Agnus Dei was to be sung by the entire assembly. Soon afterward, however, the *Ordo Romanus* I (ed. Andrieu, *Les Ordines Romani* 2:101) and the *Ordo of St. Armand* (ed. Andrieu, 2:165) direct that the clergy or the **schola cantorum* (also composed of clerics) are to sing the Agnus Dei. It seems, therefore, that by the second half of the 8th century it was a chant reserved to the clerics.

The phrase "dona nobis pacem" does not occur in any of the ancient texts. The petition "miserere nobis" was always the same, and the entire invocation was repeated as often as needed until the fraction was finished. When multiple fractions disappeared in the 9th century, the petitions were gradually reduced to the hallowed number three. The phrase "qui tollis peccata mundi, miserere nobis" is found also in the Gloria; both texts, however, are based on the testimonial of John the Baptist (Jn 1.29) with two grammatical changes. The vocative form "agnus" is treated as indeclinable because of a sense of reverence for religious terms. The plural "peccata" is substituted for the Biblical "peccatum."

According to classic Roman usage, only one all-inclusive petition, "miserere nobis," is added to the invocation. This is still the practice in the Latin liturgy of the Lateran basilica and on Holy Thursday for the Roman rite in general. Since the 10th and 11th centuries the petition "dona nobis pacem" is substituted as the third and final response. The first occasion for this substitution was most probably the transfer of the Agnus Dei to accompany the Kiss of Peace (see Rabanus Maurus, *De inst. cler.* 1:33; PL 107:324). As early as the 11th century the words "dona eis requiem" are found in *requiem Masses, while the third petition closes with "requiem sempiternam."

The oldest melody for the Agnus Dei (Mass 18 in the *Graduale romanum*) is identical to that given for the same text in the Litany of the Saints (*see* LITANY,

A page from the 14th-century Graduale of the monastery of Saint-Corneille at Compiègne, France (MS lat. 16823, fol. 222v). Two tropes for the "Agnus Dei" can be seen in the right-hand column.

LITURGICAL USE OF). The only change is the addition of a note on the accent of "nobis" in the Mass melody. The "Agnus Dei" at the end of the litany is a self-sufficient song, giving a festive climax to the litany. The close connection of this chant with the litany is further clarified by the fact that it is omitted in the Easter Vigil Mass because it was sung in the litany.

The dating (12th century) given in the *Graduale romanum* for the Agnus Dei of Mass 18 is very misleading, since it refers to the earliest MS in which this melody is found; whereas the melody is actually of a much earlier origin. According to A. Gastoué (*Le Graduel et l'antiphonaire* 278), it is related to ancient Byzantine psalmody. The Agnus Dei in the Mass of the Dead is an adaptation of that of Mass 18. This melody is known as the *minor* in a 12th-century Rheinau MS, to distinguish it from a more complex one (the *major*) in the same MS, destined to be sung by the *schola* on great feast days [M. Gerbert, *De cantu et musica sacra* (St. Blasien 1774) 1.1:457].

The simple Agnus melodies (Mass 18, Mass of the Dead, Mass 16) show a structural relation to the simple Sanctus melodies (Masses 15, 16, 18) by their use of recitative patterns. Just as these simple Sanctus melodies are an extension of the dialogue recitation of the Preface, so also the Agnus melodies are an extension of the dialogue recitation of the Pax Domini. Among the chant settings (*c.* 300) of the Ordinary, as B. Stäblein notes, the Agnus melodies are most often related to the Sanctus but very seldom to the Kyrie melodies (MusGG 1:150).

*Tropes for the Agnus Dei began to appear as early as the 10th century. Eighty-six of these have been found, consisting mostly of three verses and, in great part, hexameters. One verse was inserted each time between the invocation and the petition. The following is an example (from MS BN lat. 16823, fol. 1.222v):

Agnus Dei . . . Fons indeficiens pietatis—Miserere nobis.

Agnus Dei . . . Actor summe bonus bonitatis—Miserere nobis.

Agnus Dei . . . Pax eterna dator claritatis—Dona nobis pacem.

Bibliography: J. FROGER, *Les Chants de la Messe aux VIIIe et IXe siècles* (Tournai 1950). J. A. JUNGMANN, *The Mass of the Roman Rite,* tr. F. A. BRUNNER, 2 v. (New York 1951–55) 2: 332–340. Righetti 3:444–446. B. STÄBLEIN, MusGG 1:148–156. Apel GregCh. **Illustration credit:** Bibliothèque Nationale, Paris.

[C. KELLY]

AGOBARD OF LYONS, archbishop; b. Spain, 769; d. Lyons, France, 840. In 782 he moved to Narbonnaise, Gaul, and in 792 he went to Lyons as a companion to *Leidradus, Charlemagne's *missus* (delegate), on one of his tours of duty in the region of Narbonne and Seo de Urgel. Ordained a priest in 804 and named *chorbishop for Leidradus in 813, Agobard ruled the See of Lyons at the retirement of Leidradus to Soissons (814), and in 816 was named his successor. Agobard was one of the greatest prelates of his day. Because of his opposition to Emperor *Louis the Pious in the Council of Compiègne (833), he was compelled to leave Lyons after the Emperor's coronation in 835, taking refuge with *Lothair I in Italy. In the meantime his position in Lyons was given to his opponent, *Amalarius of Metz. In 838, after his reconciliation with the Emperor, Agobard returned to Lyons. He composed many theological writings, e.g., against Felix de Urgel (*see* ADOPTIONISM), *De insolentia Judaeorum* against the Jews (*see* ANTI-SEMITISM), and numerous political, juridical, and liturgical works. He wrote also against superstition. The *Liber de imaginibus,* often attributed to him, was composed by *Claudius of Turin. His other authentic works—official documents from his see—are the product of collaboration with his deacon *Florus of Lyons. The *De divina psalmodia, Contra libros IV Amalarii,* and the hymn *Rector magnificus* are exclusively the work of Florus. His presence at the Council of Paris in 825 is uncertain, but it is clear that he did not participate in drawing up the synodal *Libellus* against images addressed to Pope *Eugene II.

Bibliography: *Annales Lugdunenses,* in MGS 1:110, autobiographical notes from the margin of Codex Vallicellianus E 26. PL 104:29–352. MGS 15.1:274–279. MGEp 5:150–239. A. BRESSOLLES, *Saint Agobard, évèque de Lyon, 769–840,* v.1 of *Doctrine et action politique d'Agobard* (Paris 1949). J. A. CABANISS, *Agobard of Lyons* (Syracuse 1953). P. BELLET, "El *Liber de imaginibus sanctorum* bajo el nombre de Agobardo de Lyon obra de Claudio de Turín," AnalSacTarracon 26 (1953) 151–194. L. SCHEFFCZYK, LexThK[2] 1:204.

[P. BELLET]

AGONY IN THE GARDEN

The account of Jesus' agony in the garden is found in Mk 14.32–42; Mt 26.36–46; Lk 22.40–46. Mark's account is identical in substance with Matthew's and very similar to it in words. Each account has 11 verses. Luke's account, of seven verses, is considerably different and partially from an independent source. The stark presentation of Jesus' humanity, as well as the shameful portrait of the sleeping "pillars" of the Church (Gal 2.9), Peter, James, and John, argue for the historicity of the event and for the very primitive tradition that preserved it. Mark and Matthew single out the three eyewitnesses to Jesus' terror. The slight differences, even between Mark and Matthew, testify to the freedom with which each account was developed.

Commentary. In Mark the locale is called *Gethsemani (oil press), a place just to the east of Jerusalem at the base of the *Mount of Olives. It had been frequently visited by Jesus and His Disciples (Lk 22.39; Jn 18.1). Upon His arrival Jesus left the main group of the Apostles in one spot while he went apart with Peter and the two sons of Zebedee, James and John. In their presence, says Mark, Jesus fell into a state of terror. This picture is softened a bit by Matthew, but it is reinforced by Luke's description of the bloodlike sweat that was wrung from Jesus by the thought of the chalice of woe He was soon to drink. All three Evangelists speak of this figurative chalice.

Eventually Jesus separated Himself a short distance from the three Apostles, "about a stone's throw," says Luke, and there He prayed to His father. This prayer could hardly have been heard by the Apostles. They were removed from Jesus at the time. Even more significantly, they were asleep. The substance of Jesus' prayer, therefore, is intended simply to reflect His conformity to the Father's will, even in the most desperate of circumstances. It is a concretizing of the "Our Father . . . Thy will be done" of the Lord's Prayer. (The words "Thy will be done" in Mt 26.42 are identical with those in Mt 6.10.) Mark and Matthew visualize Jesus as face to the ground to indicate the abject horror and sorrow

"Christ in Gethsemani," pen and brush drawing by the German artist Wolf Huber, c. 1518.

into which His humanity was plunged. Luke's picture of Jesus on His knees dramatizes the heroic acceptance of a cross chalice as almost too overpowering for any man to drink. Luke alone (22.43–44) speaks of the messenger from heaven sent to strengthen Jesus and of His bloodlike sweat. These two verses present textual difficulty; they are missing in many MSS, including the two best ones, *Codex Vaticanus* and *Codex Alexandrinus.* They are retained, however, in most modern English versions.

Mark and Matthew tell of Jesus' returning three times to His sleeping Disciples. (Luke mentions only one return.) It is significant that in Mark Jesus, at His initial return, addresses Peter as Simon, the first time Peter has been so called since Mk 3.16, when his name was changed to Cephas-Rock-Peter. In Gethsemani Peter was no rock of support to his Master. His proud assurance in Mk 14.29–31 proved an empty boast.

All three Evangelists recount Jesus' counsel to the Apostles to pray lest they enter temptation (another echo of the Our Father). This temptation would be a sharing in Christ's climactic struggle against Satan as the "hour" (Mk 14.41; Mt 26.45) of battle that was His Passion and glorification began (*see* HOUR OF JESUS).

In both Mark and Matthew it is possible to understand the customary "Sleep on now and take your rest" as an interrogation, "Do you continue to sleep and rest?" This would be a more logical phrasing.

Theology. The agony account is the most realistic portrait of Our Lord's humanity in the NT. Mark does not hesitate to present to his readers a terrified Christ who stands clothed in weak humanity before the excruciating vision of His Passion. Jesus, "one tried as we are in all things except sin" (Heb 4.15), one who "has suffered and has been tempted" (Heb 2.18), is the astounding model of the martyr who, with trembling hands, accepts a horrifying destiny for love of God and man. The reference to the expiatory death of Isaia's suffering servant (Is 52.13–53.12; *see* SERVANT OF THE LORD ORACLES) is strong throughout the whole scene and is underlined in Mk 14.41 and Mt 26.45.

Echoes in John's Gospel. In Jn 18.1 mention is made of the garden beyond the valley of the *Cedron (Kidron) into which Jesus and His Disciples entered after the Last Supper. But not a word is said in John of any profound agitation that Jesus underwent there. Strangely enough, however, striking echoes of the agony scene can be found in different parts of the Fourth Gospel. For example, Jn 12.27 reads like Mk 14.34, 36; Jn 12.28 reads like Lk 22.43; Jn 14.31 is the same as Mk 14.42 and Mt 26.46; and Jn 18.11 is the equivalent of Mt 26.42 plus the chalice motif of Mk 14.36. This is an amazing phenomenon. One of three explanations is possible. Perhaps John and the Synoptics are all historically accurate, and the likenesses are simply coincidental. This is unlikely. Or the Synoptics have used facts of Our Lord's public life to fill out the Gethsemani event. Or John, who insists on the kingship of Christ during the whole of His Passion account, has removed the theological message of Gethsemani to other places in Jesus' life, especially to the incident in John ch. 12.

Bibliography: G. FILOGRASSI, EncCatt 1:497–499. K. T. SCHÄFER, LexThK[2] 2:546–547. A. DURAND, DTC 1.1:615–619. V. TAYLOR, ed., *The Gospel according to St. Mark* (London 1952) 551–557. G. S. SLOYAN, *The Gospel of St. Mark* (pa.

Collegeville, Minn. 1960), on Mk 14.32–42. D. M. STANLEY, *The Gospel of St. Matthew* (pa. Collegeville, Minn. 1963), on Mt 26.36–46. C. STUHLMUELLER, *The Gospel of St. Luke* (pa. Collegeville, Minn. 1960), on Lk 22.39–46. R. BROWN, *The Gospel of St. John and the Johannine Epistles* (pa. Collegeville, Minn. 1960), 13.8a and on Jn 18.1; "Incidents That Are Units in the Synoptic Gospels But Dispersed in St. John," CathBiblQuart 23 (1961) 143–148. **Illustration credit:** Kupferstichkabinett, Berlin.

[N. M. FLANAGAN]

AGOSTINI, PAOLO, Italian composer of the colossal baroque; b. Vallerano, Italy, 1593; d. Rome, Oct. 3, 1629. A student and son-in-law of G. B. Nanino, he in turn taught Francesco *Foggia, who became his son-in-law. After providing music for several important Roman churches, Agostini was *maestro di cappella* at St. Peter's (following *Ugolini) from February 1626 until his death, as well as a composer of Masses, psalms, Magnificats, and motets. His sacred music exhibits his once-famous ability to combine the polychoral writing of the Roman colossal baroque school with authentic *stile antico* counterpoint. He was regarded by some as among the most ingenious musicians of the century, by reason of his skill in harmonic, contrapuntal, and canonic writing. Very little of his total output has been published, and very little of that is available in modern editions. Most of his works are preserved in the Vatican and Corsini libraries.

Bibliography: E. H. PEMBER, Grove DMM 1:70–71. Eitner QuellLex 1:53–54. F. J. FÉTIS, *Biographie universelle des musiciens et bibliographie générale de la musique,* 8 v. (2d ed. Paris 1860–65; suppl. 2 v. 1878–80) 1:28–29. R. CASIMIRI, "'Disciplina musicae' e 'Mastri di capella' dopo il Concilio di Trento nei maggiori istituti ecclesiastici di Roma," *Note d'archivio per la storia musicale* 15 (Jan.–April 1938). Fellerer CathChMus. Buk MusB.

[T. CULLEY]

AGRA, ARCHDIOCESE OF (AGRAENSIS), metropolitan see since 1886, in Uttar Pradesh (United Provinces) and Rajasthan (Rajputana), north India. The city of Agra, on the right bank of the Jumna River, was the Mogul capital of India (1526–1658) and, taken by the British (1803), was the capital of the North-West provinces until the end of the Sepoy Mutiny (1859); it is famous for Indian Moslem architecture, especially the Taj Mahal (*c.* 1631–45). In 1963 the archdiocese, 40,000 square miles in area, had 9 parishes, 5 secular and 14 religious priests, 3 men in one religious house, 69 women in 9 convents, and 4,600 Catholics in a population of 11,500,000. Its five suffragans, which had 184 priests, 843 sisters, and 37,720 Catholics in a population of 71 million, were: Ajmer and Jaipur (created in 1955), Allahabad (1886), Jhansi (1954), Lucknow (1940), and Meerut (1956). *See* INDIA.

Portuguese and other Jesuits from 1597 until 1773 undertook missions to Agra, from which they sought to evangelize *Tibet. Present results date from the Capuchin mission of 1773, detached from the Vicariate of *Bombay in 1784 to form with Tibet and Tibet-Hindustan mission. In 1808 this mission was made a vicariate which included most of Tibet, Kashmir, Punjab, Gwalior, and the east half of the North-West provinces. Patna (1845), Tibet (1816), and Punjab (1880) were detached from the Vicariate, and prefectures were carved from the Archdiocese of Agra in 1887 and 1892. A provincial synod was held in 1894. Ignatius *Persico was vicar (1856–60). The Capuchin Dominic R. B. Athaide was the first Indian prelate (1956–).

Bibliography: H. FROIDEVEAUX, DHGE 1:1010–13. T. POTHACAMURY, *The Church in Independent India* (Bombay 1961). C. DA TERZORIO, *Le missioni dei Minori Cappuccini,* v.9 (Rome 1935). *The Catholic Directory of India, 1962* (Allahabad, India 1962). AnnPont (1965) 17.

[E. R. HAMBYE]

AGRAPHA, a Greek word (ἄγραφα) meaning "unwritten" words or sayings of Jesus not recorded in the canonical Gospels, but in other NT writings, patristic sources, papyri fragments, and rabbinic writings. This technical meaning was first given to them by A. Resch in 1889. The last Gospel verse, Jn 21.25, opens the way for authentic agrapha; hundreds are considered, but few if any can be proved objectively authentic. Paul's obvious agraphon in Acts 20.35 is questioned (see Jeremias, 37); variant readings of Gospel MSS that offer new sayings of Jesus (e.g., in Lk 6.5) are not well attested; most of the sayings from the Fathers, the apocryphal Gospels [*see* BIBLE, III (CANON), 5], early sectarian writings (some of these with a tendentious or heretical turn), the Talmud, and Mohammedan sources merely paraphrase some canonical text.

Resch's *Agrapha* (1889) was the first scholarly probe for authenticity; he considered 74 sayings authentic; his second edition reduced the number to 35. By 1929 A. Vaganay hesitatingly accepted only 4 or 5. The papyri discoveries have given new impetus to agrapha study, but little or no authentic material. J. Jeremias selected 18 likely authentic texts for examination and careful study. Probably the sober view of G. MacRae on the latest agrapha from the Gospel of Thomas of the Coptic papyri, that one will probably never be able to say that any given logion is a genuine and hitherto lost saying of Jesus, should be extended to the earlier agrapha.

Bibliography: A. RESCH, *Agrapha: Aussercanonische Evangelienfragmente* (Leipzig 1889). A. VAGANAY, DBSuppl 1:159–198. G. W. MACRAE, "The Gospel of Thomas: *Logia Iesou?*" CathBiblQuart 22 (1960) 56–71. J. JEREMIAS and O. HOFIUS, *Unbekannte Jesusworte* (3d ed. Gütersloh 1963). J. JEREMIAS, RGG³ 1:177–178. A. ROMEO, EncCatt 1:568–570. J. SCHMID, LexThK² 1:206. EncDictBibl 43. M. S. ENSLIN, InterDictBibl 1:56.

[C. LOUIS]

ÁGREDA, MARY OF, also known as Mary of Jesus, Poor Clare mystical writer; b. Ágreda, province of Burgos (Spain), April 2, 1602; d. Ágreda, May 24, 1665. Mary was one of the 11 children of Francisco Coronel and Catalina de Arana. She is said to have made a vow of chastity at the age of 8 and to have had a desire for religious life from early youth. In 1619 she became a Poor Clare at Ágreda. Her mother and one of her sisters entered with her; her father, although 63 years of age, took the Franciscan habit and thus made her mother's admission possible. Mary was made abbess at the age of 25 by papal dispensation. Except for a period of 3 years she remained in office for life. In 1633 she founded a new monastery outside Ágreda, to which she transferred her nuns. In 1672, 7 years after her death, Mary's cause was introduced at the request of the Spanish court and she was declared venerable.

Mary of Ágreda's principal work was *The Mystical City of God and the Divine History of the Virgin Mother of God* (3 v. Madrid 1670). A concise narrative, written in a polished style (though critics differ on this), it is a life of Our Lady as seen by Mary in vision. It aroused considerable opposition in the Sorbonne, particularly the chapter on the Immaculate Conception, which, though perhaps crude, was not, as was alleged, immoral. Mary supported the doctrine. The book was condemned by the Inquisition and put on the Index, June 26, 1681. Almost immediately there were earnest appeals from Spain, and at the request of the King, Innocent XI suspended the decree of condemnation and had it removed Aug. 4, 1681. Some held that this suspensory decree was intended only for Spain, but a decree of the Holy Office (Sept. 19, 1713) in reply to a query put by the bishop of Ceneda appears to have declared the decree to have the force of law throughout the whole Church.

Prominent among the opponents of the book were Bossuet and particularly Eusebius Amort. It was alleged that more importance was given to private revelations than to the Incarnation, that the term "adoration" was used for devotion to Our Lady, that the government of the Church was attributed to her, etc. On the other hand, it is said that the Sorbonne condemnation was based on a faulty translation and that evidence exists that Amort misunderstood the Spanish in 80 places.

Though the *Mystical City of God* was attacked, even Mary of Ágreda's enemies respected her holy life, and no accusation was ever made against her sincerity. In 1729, after a new examination, the work was approved by the universities of Salamanca, Alcalá de Henares, Toulouse, and Louvain.

Mary's letters to Philip IV cover a period of 22 years and deal with morals, asceticism, and politics. She is said to have been instrumental in the dismissal of the Conde-Duque de Olivares.

Bibliography: T. J. CAMPBELL, CE 1:229–230. J. VAN DEN GHEYN, DTC 1.1:627–631. EncUnIlEurAm 3:430–431. F. TINIVELLA, EncCatt 1:570–571. H. THURSTON, *Surprising Mystics,* ed. J. H. CREHAN (Chicago 1955) 122–132.

[K. E. POND]

AGRICIUS OF TRIER, ST., 4th-century bishop of Trier; d. *c.* 335 (feast, Jan. 19; originally Jan. 13). Agricius took part in the Council of Arles (314) and was possibly the master and predecessor of Bishop Maximinus, who welcomed the exiled (St.) *Athanasius to Trier. The name of Agricius is connected with the legend of the "Holy Tunic of Trier," which he allegedly received from the Empress (St.) *Helena and brought to Trier along with the bones of St. *Matthias and other relics. An 11th-century legend speaks of him as originally bishop of Antioch and says he changed Helena's palace into a cathedral.

Bibliography: ActSS Jan. 2:55–63. H. V. SAUERLAND, *Trierer Geschichtsquellen des XI. Jahrhunderts* (Trier 1889) 55–212. E. EWIG, *Trierer Zeitschrift* 21 (1952) 30–33. A. HEINTZ, LexThK² 1:207.

[P. ROCHE]

AGRICOLA, ALEXANDER, Renaissance composer, Flemish school; b. Flanders, *c.* 1446; d. Valladolid, Spain, 1506. Agricola spent a few years (1471–74) providing chapel music for the Duke of Milan (Lorenzo de'Medici). Apart from a short stay as *petit vicair* at Cambrai cathedral (1476), and another with the Duke of Mantua (*c.* 1491), we know only of his final activities (1500–06) at the court of Archduke Philip of Austria, ruler of the Netherlands. According to Agricola's epitaph, he succumbed to cholera while traveling through Philip's newly acquired Castilian territory. His works consist of Masses, motets, and secular songs (French, Flemish, and Italian), the Masses receiving particularly artistic treatment. In this emphasis he relates most closely to his famous predecessor Jan van *Okeghem. Agricola generally manifested little interest in songlike melodies, preferring long, rhythmically intricate lines made up of short fragments linked by frequent cadences. Only in his late compositions does he give the text the important role it plays in the mature works of his greatest contemporary, *Desprez.

Bibliography: *Opera omnia,* ed. E. R. LERNER (CorpMensMus 22; 1961–). E. R. LERNER, *The Sacred Music of Alexander Agricola* (Doctoral diss. unpub. Yale U. 1958). N. BRIDGMAN, "The Age of Ockeghem and Josquin," NewOxHMus 3:277–279. Reese MusR 207–211.

[E. R. LERNER]

AGRICOLA, GEORGIUS (GEORG BAUER), forerunner of geological, mineralogical, and metallurgical investigators; b. Glauchau, Saxony, March 24, 1494; d. Chemnitz, Saxony, Nov. 21, 1555. Little is known of his early life. He obtained a bachelor of arts degree in the classics (Leipzig University, 1517 or 1518); taught Latin and Greek at Zwickau until 1520; and studied medicine at Leipzig, Bologna, Padua, and Ferrara, where he took his medical degree (1526). In Italy he met *Erasmus who became a lifelong friend. Erasmus, as director of the Forben Press in Basel, published most of Agricola's works after 1530. Agricola practiced medicine in Zwickau, and became public physician of Joachimsthal and Chemnitz.

The dukes of Saxony gave him several public posts and supported publication of his works on everything from geology to religion and political science. He founded a new school in education, based on observation of natural processes in the field. Many modern concepts of geology and ore deposition were first stated by him. Long after his death, his works were generally unknown. Interest in his geologic work was aroused by the publication of Hofmann's biography (1905) and translations of his works. For Americans, he holds the unique distinction of having been translated by a president (H. C. Hoover) and his wife.

His first work on mining, *Bermannus* (1530), was written in Joachimsthal. In 1544 followed *De ortu et causis subterraneorum* and, in 1546, *De natura fossilium* (the first modern textbook of mineralogy according to the Bandy's), *De veteribus et novis metallis,* and *Interpretatio,* all included in the second edition of *Bermannus* (1546). His most important work, *De re metallica,* appeared posthumously in 1556.

Bibliography: G. AGRICOLA, *De natura fossilium,* tr. M. C. and J. A. BANDY (New York 1955), Eng. tr. of 1546 ed.; *De re metallica,* tr. H. C. and L. H. HOOVER (London 1912; reprint New York 1950), Eng. tr. of 1556 ed.

[A. LA ROCQUE]

AGRICOLA, RODOLPHUS FRISIUS (HUYSMAN), father of German *humanism; b. Baflo, near Groningen (Holland), Feb. 17, 1444; d. Heidelberg, Oct. 27, 1485. Agricola studied at St. Martin's School in Groningen under the influence of the *Brethren of the Common Life and at the Universities of Erfurt, Louvain, and Cologne. From 1469 to 1479 he experienced Italian *Renaissance culture in Pavia and Ferrara. After returning to Groningen, he spent the last 3 years of his life in Heidelberg, lecturing informally on rhetoric and the classics. Agricola's major work, *De inventione dialectica,* sought to demonstrate the true function of logic as an element basic to rhetoric. His greatest contribution, however, lay in the personal inspiration that he gave to German humanists of the next generation.

Bibliography: F. VON BEZOLD, *Rudolf Agricola, ein deutscher Vertreter der italienischen Renaissance* (Munich 1884). H. E. J. M. VAN DER VELDEN, *Rodolphus Agricola* (Leiden 1911). J. PIETSCH, DHGE 1:1025–26. W. KOCH, LexThK[2] 1:208.

[L. W. SPITZ]

AGRICULTURAL ECONOMICS

A branch of economics in which the laws and principles of the broader science are applied to the phenomena typical of the narrower field of agriculture. This branch itself may be subdivided into specialized areas such as price analysis, production economics, land economics, and marketing.

Beginnings of the Science. Although since the time of Cato men of affairs have written at length about effective ways of tilling the soil and managing farm estates, their works must generally be classed as manuals of practical husbandry rather than as treatises on agricultural economics. Likewise, while some of the thinkers who helped to fashion modern economic theory, as it took shape between Adam Smith's *Wealth of Nations* (1776) and Alfred Marshall's *Principles of Economics* (1890), often developed their propositions against an agricultural background, agricultural economics is for the most part a product of the late 19th and early 20th centuries.

Europe. During the second half of the 19th century universities and governmental and private institutes in Europe began offering courses and undertaking studies that contributed to the improvement of agricultural methods and to the development and execution of a national farm policy. Much of this work was of a practical nature designed to meet specific needs. Toward the end of the century, however, many German universities began offering courses of a more general nature in the economics of agriculture. These courses were of two types: those taught by professors with a background in political economy, with emphasis upon the political and national-welfare aspects of farming (*Agrarpolitik*) and those that dealt primarily with the efficient organization and operation of the individual farm (*Landwirtschaftliche Betriebslehre*).

The United States. Agricultural economics developed along similar lines in the U.S. The professors who began offering courses in farm management after the turn of the century were usually trained agronomists who felt the need of basing managerial choices in farming upon relative costs and receipts, rather than upon yields and volume of output alone. These men attacked the problem not of making two blades grow where one grew before, but of finding the most profitable of the various alternatives in a given set of cost and price conditions.

One of the earliest among them was W. J. Spillman, who after receiving a master's degree at the University of Missouri in 1889, taught agriculture at various universities in succeeding years. He studied and brought to the attention of his students, as a teaching device, the methods used by the most successful farmers. Invited in 1902 to organize the Office of Farm Management in the U.S. Department of Agriculture, he promoted studies of this kind in all parts of the country. His emphasis upon managing a farm with the aim of maximizing the farmer's income is evident from the Department of Agriculture bulletins issued under his direction. An example is Bulletin 370, *Replanning a Farm for Profit,* by C. B. Smith and J. W. Froley, issued in 1909.

Meanwhile other social scientists began to devote attention to problems of agriculture. In 1905 H. C. Taylor published *Introduction to the Study of Agricultural Economics,* the first American textbook on the subject. About the same time Thomas Nixon Carver was offering a course in agricultural economics at Harvard University, and in 1907 he published his *Principles of Rural Economics.* Other pioneers were Thomas L. Hunt, who offered a course in rural economics at the University of Ohio as early as 1892; George F. Warren at Cornell University, L. C. Gray and B. H. Hibbard at the University of Wisconsin, and W. M. Hayes and Andrew Boss at the University of Minnesota.

Formation of Professional Associations. The widening interests in economics of the individual farm led to the formation in 1910 of the American Farm Management Association, and in 1916 economists interested in the wider aspects of theory and policy organized the National Association of Agricultural Economists. Both associations met annually in conjunction with the American Economic Association, and in 1919 merged to form the American Farm Economic Association.

This Association brought together men doing research and teaching in the economics of agriculture at various levels—that of the individual farm, that of the industry as a whole, and that of the industry in relation both to the national and to the world economy. This collaboration resulted in a regular interchange of ideas and techniques and in the development of fruitful hypotheses, all of which were fostered by the association through its annual meetings and its quarterly journal, the *Journal of Farm Economics,* founded in 1919.

Research and discussion of all phases of agricultural economics, which had been expanding for over a decade, were powerfully stimulated by the establishment in 1922 of the Bureau of Agricultural Economics in the U.S. Department of Agriculture. Members of this agency continued and expanded their cooperation with agricultural economists elsewhere, with the result that a fraternity of teachers and research workers developed who collaborated in exploring phases of the economic life and activity of the American farm people and in publishing their findings in a stream of books, reports, bulletins, and periodicals. No industry or occupation of comparable size has been more intensively studied. This scholarly interchange became worldwide with the establishment of the International Association of Agricultural Economists in 1929.

Unification of the Science. The relations between the two areas of specialization—farm management and agricultural economics—were outlined by Prof. E. G. Nourse as early as 1916. Writing in the *Journal of Political Economy,* Nourse defined agricultural economics as "the application of general economics to the particular business of agriculture, rather than an independent set of doctrines built up out of a specialized body of data." Just as agricultural chemistry is the application of supposedly universal principles to the special field of agriculture, as labor economics is the application of general economic laws to the relations between employer and employed, and as international economics is the application of these laws to international relations, he argued, so agricultural economics is the application of general economic principles to the phenomena associated with the production of food and fiber.

The general laws and principles of economics are in turn derived from the observation of patterns of uniformity in human behavior associated with the administering of scarce resources in order to achieve a maximum of desired ends. Since the phenomena studied by the economist are not ordinarily adaptable to controlled experiment, his typical method is to construct a model by making simplifying assumptions that permit him to abstract from the complexity of real life the few variables whose interrelations he wishes to observe, eliminating mentally the effects of those he wishes to ignore. Once these fundamental relations have been explored, the investigator can bring his analysis more closely into accord with reality by introducing into his model one after another the variables that he had hitherto neglected.

Such an analytical procedure is known as economic analysis, or economic theory. It is generalized and abstract and does not purport to present any specific situations in the real world. If the investigator applies the general laws and principles developed by such analysis to the special field of agriculture, where the units of output can be pictured as bushels of grain or heads of cattle, he moves into agricultural economics. Nevertheless, it is still a pure science in that it is investigation without reference to the use to which the findings are to be put.

But people are interested in science and knowledge not only for its own sake, but also for its practical uses. When knowledge developed in theoretical agricultural economics is used to guide the combination of resources on a farm in such a way as to derive a maximum value return, it is called farm management. It is an applied science in that it uses scientific knowledge for practical ends.

Economic Characteristics of Agriculture. The justification for making agriculture a special field in which to observe the working out of general economic laws lies in the peculiar conditions that characterize it. Agriculture is one of the few industries in economically developed countries operating under conditions approaching pure *competition. It is generally characterized by an inelastic demand; that is, the increase in the sales of a product brought about by a fall in its price is relatively smaller than the fall in price. Practically, this means that a nation's farmers tend to realize smaller incomes as they increase output. These two characteristics, the competitive market and the inelastic demand for the product, create special problems for agriculture. In the competitive market the only way the individual producer can improve his economic position (apart from abandoning agriculture altogether) is to adopt cost-reducing methods of production. The fall in unit costs resulting from such methods usually leads to an increase in production. The enterprising operator may make a temporary gain by anticipating his neighbors in the adoption of innovations, but when they follow suit, as they must to stay in business, the output of the product in question will increase. But as a result of the inelastic demand for the product the larger output brings not a rise but a fall in farm income. As farmers improve their methods of production, they tend to be rewarded in the long run by a steady fall in individual and aggregate incomes.

Agricultural Economics and Public Policy. An understanding of the way in which the general laws of economics work out under the conditions peculiar to agriculture is indispensable to the development of sound public policy. Without it, it is impossible to shape properly the framework within which individual farmers operate or to legislate programs for their welfare and that of society as a whole. Economic analysis furnishes the conceptual apparatus needed to assess the costs and benefits of alternative courses of action. Thus on the basis of his analysis of the supply and demand for farm products, the economist may point out that allowing competition to have free play in agricultural markets following a period of price support by the government—as has been widely advocated in the U.S. and other industrial countries—will not automatically or quickly bring about a reduction in output so that prices may rise to remunerative levels. Instead, farmers in the U.S. and other industrially developed countries, accustomed to innovation, may accelerate their adoption of cost-reducing techniques and thus increase the output of farm products. As a result prices may fall to very low levels and remain there for an extended period before enough farmers abandon agriculture to bring about the desired adjustment in production. Confronted with such analysis, the statesman must decide on the basis of ethical values whether to allow the adjustment to be brought about by unaided market forces, with the accompanying hardship to farm families and the sacrifice of their investments built up over a period of years, or to interfere with the operation of those forces and spread the resulting social cost, in order to bring about some other kind and rate of adjustment.

Agriculture and Economic Growth. In mid-20th century increased emphasis was placed upon the role of agriculture in economic growth. It is now recognized that economic development in nonindustrial countries requires a concomitant development in agriculture. Industrial and agrarian revolutions go together, each influencing and stimulating the other.

A rapid advance in agricultural productivity has far-reaching repercussions. First, it assures relatively low prices for food. This means that the industrial population will have relatively more purchasing power to devote to other goods and services. The increase in effective demand for such items provides an incentive for capital investment in their production, while low prices for food, by dampening demands for higher wages, results in relatively lower prices for industrial products and indirectly in further increase in investment. Second, as productivity in agriculture progresses farm workers are released to provide the manpower for developing industries. So vital to economic growth is the transfer of farm workers to industrial employment that ratios such as the percentage of the labor force in agriculture or the farm share of the national income can be taken as indexes of the degree of economic development of a nation.

Increased productivity in farming aids economic development in other ways. It generates surplus income that can be used to provide savings needed for capital formation; and by making possible an increase in exports or reduction in imports of food and fiber, it helps to conserve foreign exchange to pay for imported raw materials, equipment, and other goods essential to economic development.

Agriculture contributed in this way to the economic development of the U.S. and most western European countries, and is now repeating the process in countries ready for what W. W. Rostow calls the take-off stage. In the U.S., agricultural output increased steadily but at varying rates from 1870 to the 1920s, part of the increase being due to improvements in labor efficiency and part to the increase in the amount of land and capital used for farming. The drought and Depression of the 1930s checked the upward trend, but by the late 1930s, under the impetus of demands generated by World War II, total output and output per man-hour began to increase rapidly. Labor productivity on farms more than tripled between 1940 and 1960, increasing twice as fast as in industry.

Manpower Trends in U.S. Agriculture. As expenditures for food do not increase greatly, either in response to a fall in price or an increase in income, expansion in demand for farm products must depend for the most part on such slowly changing factors as population growth, increase in exports, and new uses for farm products. Consequently, our needs for food and fiber can be supplied by a steadily declining farm labor force. It is estimated that the increase in inputs of capital for machinery and other nonhuman resources, e.g., fertilizer, since the 1920s has just about been offset by the decreases in the use of labor, making possible a net migration from farms averaging over 1 million persons per year in the 2 decades following the outbreak of World War II. This is an annual rate of 5 per cent. By the early 1960s the farm population had fallen to less than 15 million, i.e., to less than 8 per cent of the total population.

Migration from farms involves the sons and daughters of large farm families who are not needed on the mechanized farms of today and of low-income farmers and their families who are seeking to better their economic condition. That the latter category is largely responsible for the decline in the number of farms in the U.S.—from 5.4 million in 1950 to 3.9 million in 1959—is evident from the fact that farms with annual sales of less than $2,500 decreased more than 40 per cent in that period, while farms with annual sales of $5,000 to $9,999 declined by less than 10 per cent, and those with annual sales of $10,000 or more increased by nearly two-thirds. It should be noted, however, that despite the increase in the number of larger farms, most farms are still family enterprises, the farm family supplying most of the labor and capital and making all of the managerial decisions.

Views of John XXIII. The movement of workers from farm to industry was recognized by John XXIII as a necessary consequence of economic development. When discussing the problems of agriculture in *Mater et Magistra* (1961), he observed that "as economic life progresses and expands, the percentage of rural dwellers diminishes, while the great number of industrial and service workers increases" (124). Because of his appreciation of the values associated with rural living, the Pope expressed regret over this uprooting of rural populations and suggested programs and policies that will make rural living more attractive as well as economically possible.

Pope John recognized also the role of food and agriculture in economic progress; in his encyclicals *Mater et Magistra* and *Pacem in terris* (1963), he commends people of developed countries for giving concrete witness to the fact of human solidarity through programs of foreign aid, including in particular donations of farm products. He urges that such programs be expanded and accompanied by technical assistance: "It is hoped that in the future the richer countries will make greater and greater efforts to provide developing countries with aid designed to promote sciences, technology, and economic life" (*Mater et Magistra* 165).

See also COMMON MARKETS; ECONOMIC GROWTH; ECONOMICS, DEVELOPMENT OF; ECONOMIC AID, INTERNATIONAL; MIGRATION, INTERNAL; RURAL SOCIETY; URBANIZATION.

Bibliography: H. C. and A. D. TAYLOR, *The Story of Agricultural Economics in the United States, 1840–1932: Men, Service, Ideas* (Ames, Iowa 1952). E. G. NOURSE, ed., *Agricultural Economics: A Selection of Materials in Which Economic Principles Are Applied to the Practice of Agriculture* (Chicago 1916). T. N. CARVER, *Principles of Rural Economics* (Boston 1911). J. D. BLACK, *Economics for Agriculture: Selected Writings,* ed. J. P. CAVIN (Cambridge, Mass. 1959). L. C. ROBBINS, *An Essay on the Nature and Significance of Economic Science* (2d ed. London 1935). L. A. BRADFORD and G. L. JOHNSON, *Farm Management Analysis* (New York 1953). G. F. WARREN, "The Origin and Development of Farm Economics in the United States," *Journal of Farm Economics* 14 (1932) 2–9. R. L. COHEN, *The Economics of Agriculture* (London 1959). E. O. HEADY, *Economics of Agricultural Production and Resource Use* (Englewood Cliffs, N.J. 1960).

[M. E. SCHIRBER]

AGRICULTURE

An intentional human effort to produce food and fiber by growing plants and breeding animals. It involves two kinds of activities: (1) organic, in which men try to control biological events, and (2) mechanical, in which men use tools and machines.

Prehistoric Agriculture. Neolithic men first appeared about 10,000 B.C., although they did not begin agriculture until sometime later. They probably began farming in response to the desiccation of their food collecting territories, which began around 9000 B.C. Most likely these neolithic farmers were comparatively settled fishing people rather than nomads. The first farmers probably developed seed grain culture and later animal husbandry. Animal taming gave way to domestication as men selectively bred animals to secure desired characteristics, and domestication most likely developed after men had an assured food surplus. Herding cultures almost certainly arose on the fringe of stable agricultural societies, for herdsmen have never been found independently of settled farmers.

The oldest agricultural site in the Old World dates from about 8000 B.C. in Iran. New World sites date from about 6000 B.C. in Central America. Old World man developed barley, rye, wheat, millet, and sorghum and also domesticated pigs, sheep, cattle, and horses in about that order. Horticulture, particularly viticulture, flourished from the very beginning of agriculture. Olive groves appeared in the Mediterranean by at least 3500 B.C. Plows for breaking the soil first appeared

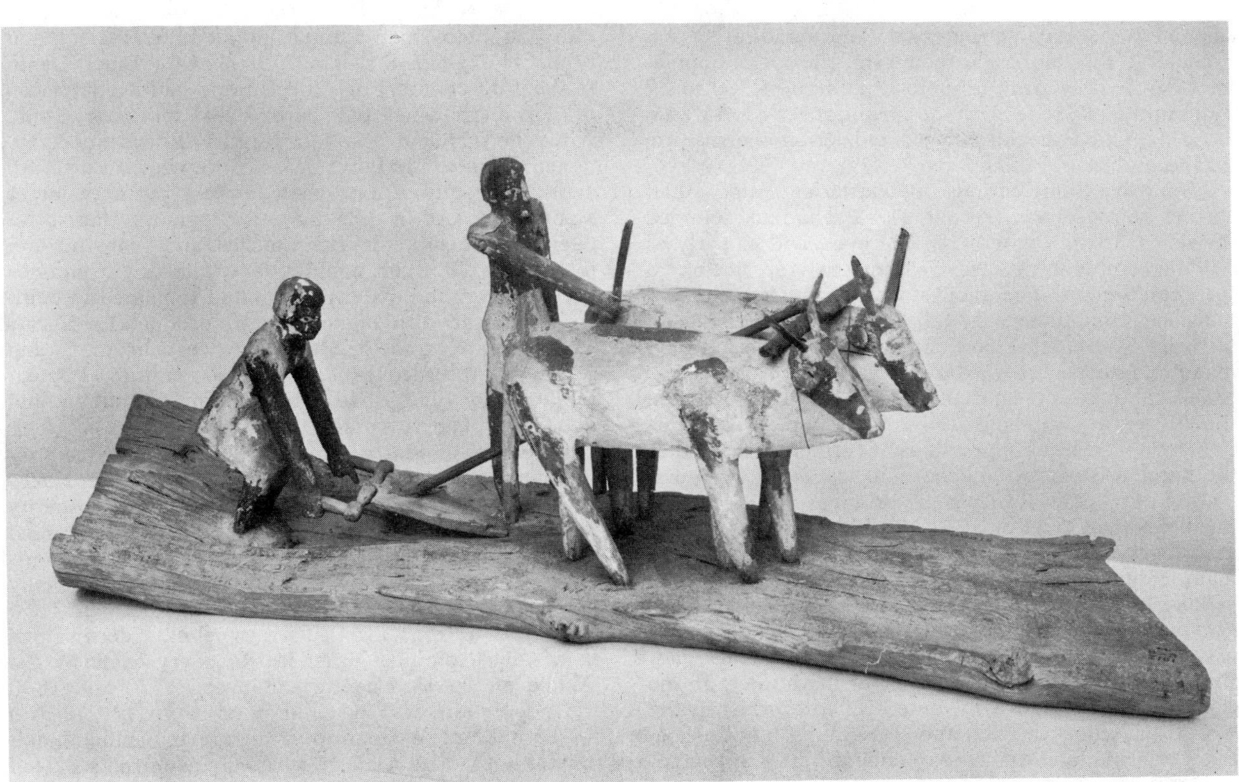

Men plowing with oxen, painted wooden tomb model, from an Egyptian tomb of the Middle Kingdom, c. 2000 B.C.

in Sumer, from whence they spread to Egypt by about 3000 B.C. and to China by about 1500 B.C. The American Indians independently developed the high-yielding crops of maize, potatoes, and manioc, among others.

The Bronze Age began in Mesopotamia before 3500 B.C., spread to Egypt, and appeared later in the Indus and Yellow River valleys. The Sumerians of Mesopotamia developed towns and the idea of town life, both of which were copied in Egypt and India. Around 3500 B.C. metal-using migrants entered the Upper Nile, pushed into lower Egypt, began irrigation, and started living in villages. Towns created markets and led to the development of partial commercial farming. Towns also created urban wealth, which men invested in farm land and irrigation works. Great landlords appeared, first in Mesopotamia, then elsewhere. Chinese farming probably derived from the Middle East. Farming peoples first became active in the Yellow River Valley around 2500 B.C. When they arrived they already knew something about irrigation and had some small domesticated animals, barley, and millet. In Central America maize agriculture was well advanced in the tropical rain forest by 4000 B.C. In the Old World river valleys silt deposits restored soil, but depletion continually plagued Americans who lived away from streams and had no animal manures. American Indians adjusted by alternately clearing and abandoning fields. Andean farmers may have introduced the potato; in any case the extravagantly yielding potato soon flourished in the Andean society. Andean farmers also depended heavily on beans. These legumes helped maintain soil fertility throughout the Americas.

On fertile land, in a favorable climate, people crowded into a limited area. Under primitive technology vast tracts of land went unused, while other areas became unfit for farming because of overuse and had to be abandoned. Farmers sometimes allowed stock to graze in the fallow fields and so discovered that manure helped restore fertility. Fallow fields could not feed enough animals, however, so farmers put some land in forage crops. Some of these were legumes that incidently helped restore or even increased fertility. A forage legume rotation appeared early in the Mediterranean, while in China and America farmers grew legumes such as peas and beans.

Slavery and Serfdom. In both the Old and New Worlds slavery probably developed as peasants secured loans with the promised labor of the borrower or some member of his family. Soon urbanites took up trade in captives, and by the dawn of Hellenic history enslavement of farm workers was already well established. Abundant slave labor inhibited technical advances nearly everywhere, although reapers did appear in Rome in the Christian Era.

The early Christian Church was urban and had little immediate impact on agricultural society. Christians tolerated slavery but did not encourage it, and as Christianity spread into rural areas, slavery gradually became more humanized and consequently more expensive. In the 200 years after Christ, estates with free but exploited tenants gradually supplanted the older plantations worked by slaves. As economic activity in the empire slowed down between 200 and 400, both the tenants and slaves became serfs on the large farms in most of the empire. As the empire declined after 400, city markets shrank or disappeared, barter replaced a money economy, and self-sufficiency supplanted commercial farming. Agricultural science and technology stagnated and even retrogressed. The manorial system gradually arose alongside feudalism. European population fell steadily from around 67 million in 200 to 27 million in 700. Huge amounts of land reverted to waste, some of which the farmers grazed, using the manure on the arable.

Monastic Contributions. Monasteries helped halt further retrogression. About 318 Pachomius founded the first Christian monastery in Egypt, and as early as 370 the emperor ordered peasants to stop fleeing to the monasteries. The monks were frontiersmen, and indeed in the 6th century SS. Columban and Benedict virtually insisted that new monasteries be started only in remote areas. Where the monks went, peasants followed, and a slow agricultural revival began. From the 9th century on, secular lords forcibly made peasants into serfs, and legal oppressions of farmers increased as the rural aristocracy advanced its civil-military jurisdiction. The chief agricultural problem of the Middle Ages was maintenance of soil fertility. Oxen and small animals, such as sheep and pigs, were kept for their manure and because they foraged well in the wilds. Wool, almost a side product at first, became more important in trade. As trade grew, full self-sufficiency gave way to partial self-sufficiency. Technology also advanced. The horse collar, which put the burden on the chest of the horse, was invented by Europeans in the 9th century. Between 500 and 1000 the iron horseshoe, the water mill, and the fixed moldboard plow appeared. The moldboard plow cut deeply, turned a furrow, and greatly reduced soil erosion. By making more types of soil usable it greatly expanded this limited resource. The advances let farmers handle more land and more crops. European population rose to about 42 million in 1000 and to 48 million in 1100.

In the 10th and 11th centuries the Cluniac monasteries came to dominate the monastic life of Europe. These monasteries had international interests and could mobilize great resources for great purposes. The monks worked with secular lords to develop land and utilize resources. These activities expanded in the 11th and 12th centuries under the Cistercians and Carthusians, who turned deserts into gardens on a vast scale. The Knights Hospitallers alone created 40 villages on the Garonne between 1100 and 1110. The monks also opened rivers to commerce and helped speed the economic life of Europe. English Cistercians sold wool abroad, and monasteries in Lombardy sold surplus in Pavia and Venice. The commercial rebirth of the Middle Ages began with the monasteries, which could mobilize capital on a scale no other institution could match. Towns grew, and markets for farm produce reappeared as a money economy and commercial farming revived. Furthermore, after the Crusades began in the 12th century, agriculture achieved new levels of prosperity. The Crusades also weakened the nobility, and the serfs demanded and got concessions. In the 12th and 13th centuries the old manorial system decayed. The nobility slowly replaced it with the seignorial system in which the serfs paid in cash and kind rather than in labor.

Depopulation and Recovery. A 13th-century metropolitan explosion brought ever greater returns to the peasants and encouraged rapid population increases. Eventually population grew so large that it could not be properly fed with the then known technology. Malnutrition more than famine afflicted the society and probably explains the dreadful toll of the Black Death in the 14th century. In 1300 Europe had a population of 73 million, which fell sharply to 45 million by 1400. After the middle of the 14th century, Europeans abandoned villages, and farms reverted to wilds. In the 14th and 15th centuries European farmers put ever larger amounts of land in peas and other legumes, thus introducing more proteins into the diet and more nitrates into the soil. Farmers could reduce fallowing from once every 2 years to once every 5. Land remained in cultivation longer with higher overall production. Everywhere greater trade led to greater urbanization, and prosperity returned to European agriculture. Population rose; by 1450 it had reached about 60 million, and by 1500 it had risen to 69 million.

Influence of Early America. In the 16th century the expansion of commerce and voyages of discovery spurred the European economy. Most of the prosperity resulted from the population rise, which accompanied growing international trade. A truly commercial agriculture evolved in Europe as prices rose. Then suddenly an agricultural depression struck Europe between 1650 and 1750. Europe avoided overwhelming decline primarily by exploiting America. Recovery came by the middle of the 18th century. Between 1750 and 1800 the population of Europe shot up from 140 million to 188 million. Across Europe men reclaimed land, and animal husbandry declined relatively as farmers shifted to the more lucrative grain and industrial crops. The potato supported a larger peasant population than would otherwise have been possible. Maize and potatoes also affected European animal husbandry. Animals feeding on these and other fodder crops produced manure, which farmers applied to the land, and fallowing nearly ceased in more advanced areas. From the 16th to the 18th centuries Europeans merged the great American crops with the superior European technology. As a result, Europe rapidly moved beyond the rest of the world in agricultural production.

The 19th-century Technology. Judged by innovations alone, no other century approached the 19th in originality and diversity of undertaking. Organic discoveries and applications multiplied. Justus von Liebig began the science of soil chemistry in the 1830s, although Edmund Ruffin had already shown the need for lime fertilizer in 1821. In 1859 Charles Darwin presented evolution with its implications for human selection of plants and animals, and in 1865–66 the Austrian monk Gregor Mendel developed the science of genetics. In the 1860s Louis Pasteur showed the bacterial origin and possible prevention of several diseases. Auguste Goffart presented the earliest scientific work on silos in 1877. Theobald Smith proved cattle fever to be tick borne in 1889 and paved the way for later successes with malaria and yellow fever. S. M. Babcock invented a chemical butterfat test in 1890 with immense influence on dairying.

Mechanical advances also altered agriculture. The steamboat, perfected in 1807, and the railroad, beginning with the first line in 1822, permitted speedy and cheap transport of farm products. Jethro Wood devised an iron plow with interchangeable parts for easy repair in 1817, and Obed Hussey made the first successful horse-drawn reaper in 1833. Both inventions reduced the man-hours needed in grain production. In

1837 John Deere began making plows with steel shares, which swiftly broke prairie soils. A threshing machine patented by the Pitts brothers in 1837 cut time and labor in harvesting wheat, and facilities for handling the huge seasonal influxes of grain appeared with the grain elevator built by Joseph Dart at Buffalo, N.Y., in 1842. Mechanical refrigeration was perfected in the 1860s. J. F. Glidden patented barbed wire in 1874, greatly reducing the cost of fencing for farmers everywhere. The German Gottlieb Daimler devised a light internal combustion engine in 1883, which was used in 1892 in the first successful tractor.

The 19th-century Socioeconomic Changes. In short, 19th-century scientific and technical advances replaced men with machines and made two blades of grass grow where one grew before. Human exploitation, long opposed by the Church, became neither necessary nor useful. The final Catholic statement came with Leo XIII's *Rerum novarum* in 1898, which proclaimed principles of justice for the new technical era and pointedly reasserted the right of farmers to own their own land. Ideas about human dignity changed in many parts of the world, and in Christendom, at least, slavery ended. The British outlawed the slave trade in 1808, and most of Latin America ended slavery between 1806 and 1821. The United States ended slavery in 1865. Agricultural productivity rose throughout 19th-century Christendom. The greatest increase occurred in the U.S., which also experienced the greatest expansion of farm land. Even in Europe, however, more land came under the plow. Relatively, the number of farmers in the population began to fall, and at the same time millions ate better than ever before. In Christendom total grain consumption rose from an average of 804 pounds per capita for the decade 1831–40 to 1,193 pounds in 1888. Western meat consumption rose from an annual average of 69.3 pounds in the decade 1831–40 to 71.4 pounds in 1888. The figures, although largely estimates, do suggest the trends of the century. Still, malnutrition and famine afflicted most of mankind in the 19th century. In Asia and Africa the ancient village system persisted with few changes into the 20th century. Population levels reflected degrees of change in farming, and by far the largest increases of the 19th century came in Europe and America.

Government and Agriculture in the 20th Century. Agriculture in the 20th century has been most changed by the spread of democratic government, a revolution in human expectations, and serious breakdowns in the free market. Many times in history the market economy failed to produce acceptable living standards for most people, but in the 20th century men refused to accept the failure. Famine, widespread malnutrition, ruinous farm prices, and industrial depressions seemed not only unnecessary but intolerable. Typically, 20th-century governments responded to popular demands by trying to overcome economic obstacles to earthly happiness. Everywhere governments established bounties, price supports, and tariff protection for farmers. The Depression of the 1920s and 1930s accelerated the process, even though economic aid brought regulations. In one of the few encyclicals to deal at length with modern agriculture, Pope John XXIII welcomed governmental involvement in agrarian life. Indeed, in his *Mater et Magistra* of 1961 Pope John urged governments to assist farmers more directly and more often, and he encouraged farmers to get help in reducing the harshness of the free market.

Science and Agriculture in the 20th Century. Scientific and technological changes continued in the 20th century. Gasoline tractors replaced draft animals everywhere, but especially in the U.S. The shift to tractors dramatically released land for food that had formerly been used to grow fodder. Spectacular organic discoveries changed every aspect of farming. Both humans and animals benefitted from the discovery of vitamins in 1915. Between 1916 and 1918 D. F. Jones made genetics an applicable science with his hybridization of corn. Applied genetics also led to Kanred wheat in 1917 and the commercial production of hybrid seed corn in 1926. In 1939 Swiss scientists discovered DDT and opened the way to the discovery of other insecticides. In 1945 herbicides first appeared with the introdiction of 2,4-D The drudgery and losses caused by weeds and insects seemed at an end. A host of animal diseases succumbed to penicillin, first used in 1944, and the discovery of more antibiotics continued virtually without end. Gamma-ray sterilization of male screwworms on Curaçao resulted in the eradication of that pest in 1955. Potentially the method could be applied to insects elsewhere. These startling changes could not but have profound influence on food production as they came to be applied around the world. Meanwhile, scientific discoveries proliferated endlessly. The changes of the 20th century could be seen everywhere in rising levels of food production. Nutritional standards rose around the world in the 20th century, even though they were very low in some places. The diet of the people

WORLD AVERAGE YIELDS
(100 kilograms per hectare)

Selected commodities	1948–49 to 1952–53	1961–62
Wheat	10.1	11.7
Maize	15.8	20.8
Rice	16.0	20.3
Potatoes	107.0	112.2

SOURCE: *Production Yearbook, 1962* (Food and Agriculture Organization of the United Nations; Rome 1963).

ESTIMATED CALORIE AND PROTEIN CONTENT OF REGIONAL AVERAGE FOOD SUPPLIES PER CAPITA*

Region	Calories per day		Proteins daily in grams	
	1948–49 to 1950–51	1961–62	1948–49 to 1950–51	1961–62
Europe	2,860	3,007	85	87
North America	3,150	3,100	91	93
Far East	1,916	2,142	46	54
Africa; Near East	2,550	2,667	78	81
Oceania	3,290	3,330	98	99

* Excluding Russia, China, Latin America, and most of Africa, for which there were no applicable data.

SOURCE: *Production Yearbook, 1962* (Food and Agriculture Organization of the United Nations; Rome 1963).

of the world steadily improved through the third quarter of the 20th century. The specter of famine through overpopulation remained real, but somewhat distant.

See also AGRICULTURAL ECONOMICS; NATIONAL CATHOLIC RURAL LIFE CONFERENCE.

Bibliography: N. S. B. GRAS, *A History of Agriculture in Europe and America* (2d ed. New York 1940). B. H. SLICHER VAN BATH, *The Agrarian History of Western Europe, 500–1850,* tr. O. ORDISH (New York 1963). W. D. RASMUSSEN, *Readings in the History of American Agriculture* (Urbana, Ill. 1960). J. H. HAWKES and L. WOOLLEY, *Prehistory and the Beginnings of Civilization,* v.1 of *History of Mankind,* 2 v. (New York 1962). R. COULBORN, *Origin of Civilized Societies* (Princeton, N.J. 1959). C. O. SAUER, *Agricultural Origins and Dispersals* (New York 1952). **Illustration credit:** Courtesy of the Trustees of the British Museum.

[J. T. SCHLEBECKER]

AGRIPPA I AND II

The last two Jewish Kings of Palestine. Agrippa I, b. *c.* 10 B.C.; d. A.D. 44. His father was Aristobulus, son of *Herod the Great and Mariamme I, and his mother was Berenice, daughter of Herod's sister Salome and her second husband, Costobar. Agrippa came to the throne of his grandfather Herod by a series of fortunate chances and useful friendships. His mother Berenice was intimate with Antonia, Tiberius's sister-in-law, and Agrippa during his education in Rome cultivated his contemporaries in the Emperor's family, Germanicus, Drusus, and Claudius. When the premature deaths of Germanicus and Drusus disappointed his prospects, Agrippa, with Cyprus, his wife, went to *Idumea and later accepted a post in *Tiberias under his uncle *Herod Antipas, who had married Agrippa's sister *Herodias. A quarrel with Antipas caused Agrippa to go to Flaccus, the Roman legate in Syria; expelled for bribery, he made his way with difficulty back to Italy in A.D. 36, at every turn borrowing money on his expectations and his connections with Antonia. During Tiberius's last year, Agrippa cultivated a friendship with the Emperor's grandnephew Gaius Caligula. An indiscreet remark, expressing the hope that Gaius would soon succeed Tiberius, put Agrippa in prison for 6 months, but he was saved by Tiberius's death (A.D. 37) and Gaius's accession. Agrippa was awarded a kingship over the tetrarchy of his late uncle *Philip and the tetrarchy of *Abilene, with the titular rank of praetor; to this was added, in A.D. 39, the tetrarchy of Antipas, whom he had accused of treason. As king, Agrippa resisted Gaius's insistence that his imperial image be set up in Jewish places of worship, especially in the Jerusalem temple, and strove to protect the traditional privileges granted Jews throughout the Empire. To win approval of the Pharisaic party, Agrippa persecuted the Christians in Palestine (Acts 12.1–6). Gaius's assassination (A.D. 41) found Agrippa in Rome, and by his immediate support of the reluctant Claudius he ensured his favor as emperor. Claudius added Judea, Samaria, and Idumea to Agrippa's kingdom and raised him to the titular rank of consul. Agrippa thus ruled over a territory equal to that of Herod the Great. His reign was, however, inefficient and extravagant. Moreover, by taking initiatives forbidden to a vassal king, Agrippa foolishly strained relations with Rome. He died prematurely, after being seized by a sudden illness at a public event in Caesarea (Acts 12.20–23).

Agrippa II, b. A.D. 27; d. probably *c.* 93. Since he was only 17 at the death of his father Agrippa I, he was too young to succeed to the throne. Claudius placed the whole of the kingdom again under a Roman procurator; supervision of Jewish religious affairs was given over to Herod, King of Chalcis, Agrippa I's brother. In A.D. 50, 2 years after the latter's death, Claudius appointed Agrippa to take his uncle's place, and 3 years later he enlarged his holdings by substituting for Chalcis the former tetrarchy of Philip and the tetrarchies of Abilene and Noarus; Nero in the following year added four toparchies in Galilee and the *Perea. Agrippa, though using the Roman name M. Julius Agrippa, conformed externally to the Jewish Law. He required that his sisters' non-Jewish husbands be circumcised; yet his sister Berenice lived with him, giving scandal to his Jewish subjects. In A.D. 60 the newly appointed Roman procurator Porcius Festus asked Agrippa to help him assess the case of Paul (Acts ch. 25–26). The high-handed behavior of Festus' successor Gessius Florus stirred the people to rebellion, and Agrippa was unable to persuade them to submit to Roman authority. In the revolt Agrippa consistently took the side of Rome; he accompanied both Cestius Gallus and Vespasian in their campaigns. Agrippa's close ties to both Vespasian and Titus served him well after the end of the revolt. Visiting Rome in A.D. 75 with Berenice, he was given the titular rank of praetor. He remained king until his death; his territory was afterward put under direct Roman administration.

Bibliography: J. BLINZLER, LexThK² 5:265–266. B. MARIANI, EncCatt 1:580–582. EncDictBibl 43–45. A. ROSENBERG, Pauly-Wiss RE 10.1 (1917) 143–150. A. H. M. JONES, *The Herods of Judaea* (Oxford 1938) 184–261. S. H. PEROWNE, *The Later Herods* (New York 1959).

[J. P. M. WALSH]

AGRIPPA VON NETTESHEIM, HEINRICH CORNELIUS, occultist and critic of Church, society, and learning; b. Cologne, Germany, Sept. 14, 1486; d. Grenoble, France, Feb. 2, 1535. He was educated at Cologne, Paris, and Pavia, and claimed doctorates in law and medicine; he became famous for omnifarious learning. He lectured on Cabala at Dôle (1509) and in 1510 dedicated *De occulta philosophia* to Trithemius of Sponheim (expanded and published, 1533). He spent 7 years in Italy (1511–18), fighting for the Emperor

Heinrich Cornelius Agrippa von Nettesheim.

Maximilian I and studying and lecturing at Pavia. In 1518 he returned north, subsequently serving as *advocatus* of Metz (1518–20), director of the Geneva hospital (1521–23), and town physician at Fribourg

(1523–24). He next became physician to the French King's mother, Louise of Savoy, residing at Lyons; then, having lost favor and being unpaid, he moved to the Low Countries. There he lived (1528–32) at Antwerp and Malines, practicing medicine and working as imperial historiographer under Margaret of Austria. Again neglected by a royal patron, he served the Archbishop of Cologne, Hermann von Wied (1532–35), until he returned to France and died probably at Grenoble. His study of esoteric literature, Cabalistic, Hermetic, Neoplatonic, and magical, produced *De occulta philosophia.* His second major work, *De incertitudine et vanitate scientiarum et artium* (1526; printed 1530) expressed his rejection of all human learning and his blind faith in the Bible. Though recklessly anticlerical and at first inclining toward Luther, he refused to abandon the old faith.

Bibliography: *Opera,* 2 v. (Lyon n.d.), including an extensive correspondence. C. G. NAUERT, *Agrippa and the Crisis of Renaissance Thought* (Urbana 1965). A. PROST, *Les Sciences et les arts occultes au XVIe siècle: Corneille Agrippa, sa vie et ses oeuvres,* 2 v. (Paris 1881–82). W. LEIBBRAND, LexThK² 1:209–210. **Illustration credit:** Library of Congress.

[C. G. NAUERT JR.]

AGUADO, PEDRO DE, chronicler of the conquest of Venezuela and Colombia; b. Valdemoro (Madrid), 1538; d. probably Bogotá, 1609?. He became a Franciscan and in 1560 was included in an expedition of 50 missionaries who were being sent to Peru. He left Spain in 1561 and disembarked in Cartagena. After doing missionary work among the Indians, he became guardian of the Franciscan convent in Bogotá and enlarged the establishment. As provincial, he went to Spain in 1573 on important business. He must have just written the *Recopilación historial,* based on Medrano's account, for he referred to it as having been completed in the petition he presented at court in 1575. After reworking the chronicle, he presented it in 1579 to obtain permission for publication. Although permission was granted, the work was not published then. In 1583 he was back in Bogotá and in 1589 he was commissary in Cartagena.

Aguado wrote with the ideas of the Counter Reformation, presenting events as being the work of men in the exercise of their free will and asserting that therefore men were subject to disciplinary punishment if they acted against the right conscience. The work was divided into two parts, and it was not until 1906 that a partial version of the first part was published in Bogotá. In 1913 and 1915 the second part was published in Caracas. The entire work was published by the Academy of Madrid as *Historia de Santa Marta* (1916–17) and *Historia de Venezuela* (1918–19). It was published under the title *Recopilación historial* in Bogotá in 1956. The manuscripts have been preserved in the Academy of Madrid, and copies are in the library of the Royal Palace.

Bibliography: P. DE AGUADO, *Recopilación historial,* 4 v. (Bogotá 1956–57), see J. FRIEDE, "Estudio preliminar," 1:14–23. A. LÓPEZ, "Historiadores franciscanos de Venezuela y Colombia: Fray Pedro de Aguado y Fray Pedro Simón," *Archivo Ibero-Americano* 14 (1920) 207–235. G. MORÓN, *Los cronistas y la historia* (Caracas 1957). O. FALS BORDA, "Odyssey of a Sixteenth-Century Document: Fray Pedro Aguado's *Recopilación historial,*" *Hispanic American Historical Review* 35 (1955) 203–220. D. RAMOS, "El cronista Pedro Simon," in *Noticias historiales* (Caracas 1963).

[D. RAMOS]

AGUESSEAU, HENRI FRANÇOIS D', Chancellor of France; b. Limoges, Nov. 27, 1668; d. Paris, Feb. 5, 1751. His father was the intendant of Languedoc, and introduced Henri early to the affairs of government. Five years after he began studying law in Paris in 1685, he was named advocate general of the Parlement of Paris. In 1700 Aguesseau was elevated to the office of procurator general, and managed during the closing years of Louis XIV's reign to retain the royal favor while fostering the cause of the Parlement and opposing the papal bull **Unigenitus.* In the troubled Regency period, he served two short terms as chancellor, 1717 to 1718, and 1720 to 1722. On each occasion, after removal from office, he was exiled to Fresnes where he turned to religious and philosophical writing. With the appointment of Cardinal Fleury as Prime Minister in 1726, Aguesseau was recalled to the chancellorship. With Fleury he brought stable government to France, and restored public respect for law. Until his resignation in 1750 he was one of the most influential members of the government, highly regarded for his ability and integrity. In general, he refrained from politics and made his most lasting contribution in the area of law reform. As chancellor he was in charge of the publishing trade and granted the permission for the publication of the *Encyclopédie.*

Bibliography: *Oeuvres complètes,* ed. J. M. PARDESSUS, 16 v. (Paris 1819). A. A. BOULLÉE, *Histoire de la vie et des ouvrages du chancelier d'Aguesseau,* 2 v. (Paris 1848). F. MONNIER, *Le Chancelier d'Aguesseau* (2d ed. Paris 1863). H. REGNAULT, *Les Ordonnances civiles du chancelier Daguesseau* (Paris 1929).

[C. B. O'KEEFE]

AGUIAR Y SEIYAS, FRANCISCO, archbishop of Mexico; b. Betanzos, Spain, in the Province of Galicia (date unknown); d. Mexico City, Oct. 14, 1698. He went to Mexico in 1679 as bishop-elect of Michoacán and 3 years later was appointed archbishop of Mexico City, where he became widely known for his spirit of charity and fiery zeal. He waged an unceasing fight against gambling, cockfighting, bullfighting, and the theater. As a diligent pastor of souls, he built a hospital for mentally deranged women and made visitations of his entire diocese in 1684 and in 1696. Disturbed that the Crown, despite the decrees of the Council of Trent, had made no provision for an archdiocesan seminary, he directed all his efforts to obtaining royal approval to erect one; it was completed in 1691. During his term of office, many churches and convents were built in Mexico City, the most famous being the Colegiata of Guadalupe whose first stone was laid in 1695. Of note also is the warm abiding friendship that existed between the archbishop and the celebrated Mexican savant, Carlos *Sigüenza y Góngora, who received many favors from Aguiar y Seiyas.

Bibliography: F. SOSA, *El episcopado mexicano* (Mexico City 1877). I. A. LEONARD, *Baroque Times in Old Mexico: Seventeenth Century Persons, Places, and Practices* (Ann Arbor 1959).

[C. E. RONAN]

AGUILAR, NICOLÁS, priest and revolutionist; b. Tonacatepeque, El Salvador, Dec. 15, 1741; d. San Salvador, Sept. 12, 1818. In 1755 he was sent to Guatemala, where he studied under the Jesuits. On April 18, 1767, he was ordained in Olocuilta, El Salvador. Shortly afterward, in a competition, he won the post of pastor of San Salvador, and performed his duties faithfully there until his death. In 1811 when San Salvador was governed by the unpopular intendant Don Antonio Gutiérrez Ulloa, Aguilar and José Matías *Delgado led a group that rose, on November 5, in armed rebellion in favor of independence. Their plan was to depose the intendant and take possession of 1,000 new muskets in the court of arms and some 200,000 pesos in the royal treasury. The insurrection failed because it was not well planned. Later, from the pulpit, Aguilar urged the populace to be tranquil and urged obedience to the captive King, Ferdinand VII. Although he continued to be active, he vacillated: sometimes he harangued the crowds to rise up in arms; other times he tried to subdue them, preaching love of neighbor and pardon of one's enemy. In 1814 he directed a new uprising, which failed also. In his last years, although he was respected because of his advanced age, he suffered bitterly because of what happened to his two brothers, Manuel and Vicente, exemplary priests and patriots. Manuel was deported to Guatemala, and Vicente, who was blind, was imprisoned.

[S. MALAINA]

AGUSTÍN, ANTONIO, humanist, scholar, reform bishop; b. Saragossa, Feb. 26, 1517; d. Tarragona, May 31, 1586. He studied at Alcalá, Salamanca, Bologna (1536) and Padua (1537). In 1541 he became a doctor of laws at Bologna and 3 years later, at the request of Emperor Charles V, was appointed auditor of the Roman Rota. In 1555 Paul IV dispatched him to England as nuncio to Queen *Mary Tudor and councilor to Cardinal Reginald *Pole. The following year he was appointed bishop of Alife, Kingdom of Naples, and in 1561 was made bishop of Lérida in his native Spain. His participation in and support of the Council of *Trent and its ecclesiastical reforms prompted Gregory XIII to create him archbishop of Tarragona (1576). Throughout his life Agustín was concerned with the history and study of Roman and Canon Law; his best-known work in Roman law is *Emendationum et opinionum libri IV ad Modestinum.* His critical work, *De emendatione Gratiani,* is noteworthy in Canon Law. Agustín was also a scholar of liturgical and catechetical theology, classical philology, and heraldry. His collected works were published in eight volumes at Lucca (1768–74).

Bibliography: Schulte 3.1:723–728. L. SERRANO, DHGE 1: 1077–80. E. MAGNIN, DDC 1:628–630.

[C. L. HOHL, JR.]

AHIKAR (ACHIOR)

Hero of a story found in several forms and in many places of the ancient Near East. The story itself is accompanied by a long series of maxims typical of the wisdom literature of that part of the world [*see* WISDOM (IN THE BIBLE)]. This article will first treat of the story and then consider the relationship between the Ahikar of the story and the Achior of the Books of Tobit and Judith.

Ahikar of the Aramaic Story. The narrative portion of the text relates the experiences of Ahikar who was purportedly chancellor and adviser of the Assyrian Kings Sennacherib (705–682 B.C.) and Esarhaddon (681–670). Being childless, he adopted a nephew, Nadan (Nadab), to whose education he devoted much time and effort. Thanks to this careful grooming, Nadan was chosen his uncle's successor. Once established in power, Nadan forgot his benefactor and eventually became so antagonistic toward him that he had him condemned to death. By a clever ruse, however, Ahikar escaped execution and found safe refuge in a cave.

Sometime later, the Pharao of Egypt sought the aid of Esarhaddon in his quest of a man wise enough to solve several profound riddles (such as, how to construct a castle in the air). Esarhaddon turned to Nadan, but he declined the challenge; whereupon the King sorely regretted having consented to Ahikar's execution. At this propitious moment, the executioner presented himself and told how the doomed man had been spared. Ahikar was found, he readily solved all the riddles and was promptly restored to power. Nadan was flogged and cast into prison, where he died miserably.

As might be expected, the 142 maxims that accompany the story are sage observations on such matters as education, obedience, filial respect, gratitude, and retribution. Both the story and the maxims enjoyed extraordinary popularity, as is evidenced by the traces of those that have been found in such varied sources as the Arabic **Thousand and One Nights*, the Greek edition of *Aesop's Fables*, the *Koran, and the Bible.

The oldest known text of the story is a fragmentary Aramaic version found among the *Elephantine Papyri and dated in the late 5th century B.C. (tr. by H. L. Ginsberg, Pritchard ANET 427–430). Other texts are available in Syriac, Arabic, and other languages (see F. C. Conybeare, J. R. Harris, and Agnes S. Lewis, *The Story of Ahikar from the Syriac, Arabic, Armenian, Ethiopic, Greek and Slavonic Versions*, 2d ed., Cambridge 1913).

Scholars generally agree that the original story was written in Aramaic, in an Akkadian (Mesopotamian) milieu, perhaps as early as the 7th century B.C. and certainly no later than the 6th century B.C. They vary considerably, however, on their estimate of its historical reliability. All admit a degree of literary embellishment; some maintain that the essential elements of the narrative should be accepted as factual. This position has been strengthened by a text recently discovered at Uruk in which there is reference to a certain "Ahuqar" who was royal adviser under Esarhaddon. [Text first published by J. J. van Dijk. See report by J. C. Greenfield in JAmOrSoc 82 (1962) 293].

Ahikar and the Achior of Tobit and Judith. A certain Achior is mentioned in four passages of the Book of *Tobit. He is presented as chief administrator and royal adviser ("keeper of the seal") under Esarhaddon and is claimed as Tobit's nephew (1.21–22) and friend (2.10). Both Achior and his nephew, Nadab, were among the guests at Tobias's wedding (11.18), and explicit mention is made of Nadab's ingratitude and disgrace (14.10). In view of these striking similarities there can be little doubt that this Achior is to be identified with Ahikar of the Aramaic Story. Moreover, the spelling of the name in the Greek text ['Αχι(α)χαρος] eliminates any difficulty on that score.

Some scholars have suggested that the story of Tobit was in fact a mere adaptation of the Ahikar story. However, a careful reading of Tobit reveals almost no similarity between the themes of these two works. In Tobit, there are no riddles to be solved and, more important, there is no ungrateful nephew; rather, there is a most obedient son. There is some slight evidence of literary influence (e.g., 4.17); beyond that, one can say only that the author of Tobit wished to associate his hero with a famous sage who had also known adversity and was rewarded at the end.

In the Book of *Judith, one of the main characters is an Ammonite leader called Achior (᾿Αχιωρ). He expounds at length on the theological implications of Israel's history for the benefit of a skeptical Holofernes (5.5–21), is scorned and reproached for his efforts (6.2–13) and is forced to share Israel's lot (6.14–21). Thus he shares eventually in her victory also (14.6–10). There does not appear to be any demonstrable connection between this Achior and the Ahikar of the Aramaic Story.

Bibliography: DBSuppl 1:198–207. A. E. Goodman, in *Documents from Old Testament Times,* ed. D. W. Thomas (London 1958) 270–275. T. Nöldeke, *Untersuchungen zum Achiqar-Roman* (Berlin 1913).

[D. R. DUMM]

AHMADIYYAH, a sect claiming to represent true Islām although repudiated by both the *Sunnites and the *Shiïtes (*see* ISLAM). The Aḥmadiyyah movement was founded by Mīrzā Ghulām Aḥmad (1839–1908) at Qādiyān in the Punjab (India). In 1891 he formally claimed the titles "al-*Mahdī" (the leader who is to return to mankind according to Moslem and, more emphatically, Shiïte doctrine) and "al-Masīḥ" (the Messiah; a Moslem reincarnation or second coming of Jesus Christ). The main lines of his doctrine, embodied in the *Bay'ah,* followed Islam more or less closely. However, his personal claims and certain details (for instance the "revelation" that Christ's tomb is located on Khan Yar Street in Srinagar, Kashmir) were so offensive and so far exceeded the bounds of Islamic orthodoxy that the Aḥmadiyyah came to be regarded generally as simply another syncretistic sect of a type frequently bred in western India (*see* SIKHISM). After the death of Mīrzā Ghulām Aḥmad's first caliph (Arabic *khalīfah,* "successor") in 1914, the Aḥmadiyyah was split by a schism that separated from the so-called Qādiyāni Aḥmadiyyah certain dissident elements repudiating some of the founder's claims and the political activity of the movement. Since then, further schisms have occurred, notably in its African missions. At the time of the partition of India in 1947 the principal center of the parent sect was moved to Rabweh in Pakistan.

The Ahmadiyyah sect in all its variations has exhibited an energetic proselytism, which is uncommon in modern Islam and which has spread it throughout the world, achieving notable success in East and West Africa. Its adoption of certain Christian evangelical methods has proved successful in Nigeria, Dahomey, Ghana, and Sierra Leone in the west, and Kenya and Tanganyika in the east. At the same time it represents an alien and unwelcome element that conflicts with orthodox Islam and menaces wider Islamic penetration of Africa. It is impossible to estimate the numerical strength of the Ahmadiyyah sect, but it is clear that it has established itself with considerable security.

Bibliography: H. A. Walter, *The Ahmadiya Movement* (London 1918). M. Bashir-al-Din, *The Ahmadiyya Movement in Islam* (Chicago n.d.). J. S. Trimingham, *Islam in West Africa* (Oxford 1959) 230–232.

[J. KRITZECK]

AHURA MAZDA (OHRMAZD) AND AHRIMAN, the good God and the Evil Spirit in Zoroastrianism. In *Zoroaster's *Gāthās,* Ahura Mazda, "The Wise Lord" (the ancient name of Ohrmazd, and used by Darius and his successors), was the father of the twin-spirits—the Holy One (Spenta Mainyu) and

Ahura Mazda symbol on north jamb of eastern doorway of Council Hall, Persepolis, Iran.

the Destructive One (Anra Mainyu, hence Ahriman), who at the origin of the world made a choice, respectively, in favor of good and evil. Later, in more recent parts of the *Avesta,* Ahura Mazda became identified with the Holy One, thus becoming the direct opposite of Anra Mainyu, and on a level with him. The origin of evil is no longer explained as the consequence of a choice, but is either left unaccounted for, Ohrmazd and Ahriman being coeval, or reinterpreted in the light of *Zervanism, a Persian speculative doctrine on time. Zervan, "Time," is said to have offered sacrifice for 1,000 years before the world existed, in order to have an offspring. At the end of this period, Ohrmazd was born to him, but also Ahriman—the latter as the result of a doubt that came to Zervan about the efficacy of his sacrifice.

Bibliography: R. C. Zaehner, *The Dawn and Twilight of Zoroastrianism* (New York 1961). J. Duchesne-Guillemin, *La Religion de l'Iran ancien* (Paris 1962). **Illustration credit:** Erich F. Schmidt, Oriental Institute, University of Chicago.

[J. DUCHESNE-GUILLEMIN]

AIALON (AJALON), a strategically located town of ancient Palestine, about 12 miles west and slightly north of Jerusalem, near the Philistine border (1 Sm 14.31). Originally an Amorrite town, it is mentioned in the *Amarna letters and in *Sesac's list of conquered cities. Though assigned to the tribe of Dan in Jos 19.42, to Ephraim in 1 Chr 6.69, and to Benjamin in 1 Chr 8.13, it continued in Amorrite hands until David conquered it. It was a levitical city (Jos 21.24) and a city of refuge (1 Chr 6.54) situated in Solomon's second district (3 Kgs 4.9). Roboam fortified it (2 Chr 11.10), but the city fell to the Philistines in Achaz's reign (2 Chr 28.18). It is identified with modern Yālō near 'Amwās (*Emmaus). The Valley of Aialon, an important means of access to the mountains of Juda, figured in Josue's battle with the five Canaanite kings (Jos 10.12).

Bibliography: EncDictBibl 46.

[E. MAY]

AIBLINGER, JOHANN KASPAR, church composer, scholar, and conductor; b. Wasserburg (Bavaria), Germany, Feb. 2, 1779; d. Munich, May 6, 1867. After 4 years' training in piano and organ at the monastery at Tegernsee (where he was also a choirboy), he went on to the Gymnasium in Munich and the university at Landshut. When his entrance into the monastery was frustrated by the secularization of Bavarian cloisters in 1803, he traveled and studied for 16 years in Italy, and was then recalled to direct the Italian Opera in Munich. In 1826 he was named director of the court chapel. He returned to Italy in 1833 to gather a collection of ancient music now housed in the Bavarian Staatsbibliothek in Munich. Except for an opera, *Rodrigo and Ximene* (1821), and three ballets, he composed only religious music of astute craftsmanship in almost every medium and for every religious function. His music was regarded highly by church musicians in the latter half of the 19th century as a welding of Renaissance and contemporary techniques.

See also CAECILIAN MOVEMENT.

Bibliography: O. URSPRUNG, MusGG 1:174–175; *Münchens musikalische Vergangenheit von der Frühzeit bis zu Richard Wagner* (Munich 1927). F. X. WITT, "Ein vergessener Komponist" in his *Ausgewählte Aufsätze zur Kirchenmusik*, ed. K. G. FELLERER (Cologne 1934). C. F. POHL, Grove DMM 1:76–77. Fellerer CathChMus.

[F. J. MOLECK]

AICHINGER, GREGOR, baroque church composer of the *concertato* style; b. Regensburg, Germany, 1564; d. Augsburg, Feb. 21, 1628. At 13 he was singing in Munich under *Lasso, and a year later, was studying at the University of Ingolstadt, center of the Counter Reformation in South Germany. The influence of the student sodality of the Blessed Virgin there later permeated his music, as he asserted in the foreword to his *Vespertinum* of 1603. He took Holy Orders after a visit to Rome during the Holy Year 1600. From 1584 he made Augsburg the center of his activities. There he was closely associated with the *Fugger family, having been a classmate of Jacob II at the University. In 1590 he studied polyphony under Giovanni *Gabrieli, in Venice, and his subsequent compositions reveal his mastery of vocal scoring, structure, and tonal texture. These compositions include three books of *Sacrae cantiones, Tricinia Mariana,* and other collections of the standard Renaissance sacred forms. His *Cantiones ecclesiasticae cum basso generali et continuo* (Dillingen 1607) are some of the earliest German works to contain a *basso continuo,* a baroque innovation.

Bibliography: *Ausgewählte Werke,* ed. T. KROYER (Leipzig 1909); T. KROYER, "Gregor Aichingers Leben und Werke," *ibid.,* pref. Reese MusR. E. F. SCHMID, MusGG 1:177–183.

[F. J. GUENTNER]

AIDAN OF LINDISFARNE, ST., monastic bishop; d. Bamborough, Aug. 31, 651 (feast, Aug. 31). Aidan was of Irish descent and while a monk at *Iona, was invited by King *Oswald to reconvert the lapsed Northumbrian race. Consecrated bishop in 635, he established his see in *Lindisfarne. *Bede, almost the sole source of knowledge of the saint, praised his ascetic life and evangelical fervor, and told of his many miracles, but regretted his adherence to the schismatic practices of the Celtic Church, especially over the dating of Easter. *See* EASTER CONTROVERSY. Aidan had several famous pupils including St. *Chad, Eata, and Hild. Cuthbert, while keeping sheep, saw his soul being carried to heaven by angels. Some of his relics were taken to Ireland in 664. Others were removed from Lindisfarne in 875; in 995 they were translated to *Durham with the body of St. *Cuthbert of Lindisfarne.

Bibliography: BEDE, *Eccl. Hist.* 3.5, 14–17. ActSS Aug. 6: 688–694. L. GOUGAUD, *Christianity in Celtic Lands,* tr. M. JOYNT (London 1932). M. CREIGHTON, DNB 1:182–183. Zimmermann KalBen 2:644. Butler Th Attw 3:451–452.

[B. COLGRAVE]

AIGUANI, MICHELE (ANGUANI, ANGRIANI), theologian; b. Bologna, *c.* 1320; d. Bologna, Nov. 16, 1400. He is commonly known as Michael of Bologna. After joining the Carmelite Order, he studied Scripture (1360) and theology (1362–63) at Paris, where in 1364–65 he obtained his master's degree. For years he taught theology at Bologna. He was elected definitor (1372) and provincial (1375 and 1379) of his own province of Bologna. In 1380, when the *Western Schism had divided also the Carmelite Order, Aiguani was nominated vicar-general of the whole order by Urban VI (d. 1389). In 1381 he was elected prior general, an office he retained until 1386 when Urban deposed him, probably because he was unjustly accused of opposition to the Pope. However, he was vindicated by Boniface IX (d. 1404), who in 1395 nominated him again as vicar-general for the province of Bologna. Aiguani held a philosophical position between voluntarism and seminominalism. He long remained one of the main theologians of his order; this explains why so many manuscripts of his works are extant and why his principal works have been reprinted so often. His chief works were: *Lectura Sententiarum* (Milan 1510), *Lectura super Psalterio* (Compluti 1524).

Bibliography: B. M. XIBERTA Y ROQUETA, *De Scriptoribus scholasticis saec. XIV ex Ordine Carmelitarum* (Louvain 1931) 324–393. A. DI SANTA TERESA, EncCatt 1:597.

[H. SPIKKER]

AIGULF OF LÉRINS, ST., abbot; b. Blois *c.* 630; d. *c.* 674 (feast, Sept. 3). At 20, Aigulf entered the monastery of Fleury (*see* SAINT-BENOÎT-SUR-LOIRE). Abbot Mummolus commissioned Aigulf to go to *Monte Cassino, which had been ravaged by the Lombards, and to bring back the remains of SS. Benedict and Scholastica. The success of his mission is questionable (Leccisotti, *Il Sepolcro di s. Benedetto,* Monte Cassino, 1951). In 671 Aigulf was made abbot of Lérins. His severe rule led to his abduction and martyrdom on Capri.

Bibliography: *Vita,* Mabillon AS 2:627–643, see also 338–344 for account of the *translatio. Passio,* ActSS Sept. 1:728–763. H. LECLERCQ, DACL 5.2:1709–60. Baudot-Chaussin 9:77–79. R. AIGRAIN, *Catholicisme* 1:244–245. E. EWIG, LexThK[2] 1:226. C. LEFEBVRE, BiblSanct 1:633–634.

[B. F. SCHERER]

AIKENHEAD, MARY, foundress of the Irish Sisters of Charity; b. Cork, Ireland, Jan. 19, 1787; d. Dublin, July 22, 1858. Because of her early attraction toward the service of the poor, Daniel *Murray, then coadjutor bishop of Dublin and later archbishop there, persuaded her to form a religious congregation and received authorization from the Holy See to establish it. Mary and one associate then spent a 3-year noviceship at the Bar Convent of the Institute of the Blessed Virgin Mary, York, England. The Irish Sisters of Charity (*see* CHARITY, SISTERS OF) began their institutional existence when the two women returned to the North William Street Orphanage, their new home in Dublin, and took the usual three vows of religion, plus a fourth vow of dedication to the poor. The sisters cared for the orphans, set up a day school, and visited neighboring poor families. Steady growth in numbers of recruits and of houses enabled the congregation to teach religion in parochial schools and to staff additional free schools and a Magdalen refuge. In 1834 the sisters opened St. Vincent's Hospital in Dublin, the first Catholic hospital in Ireland. In 1838 they became the first religious women to labor in Australia. For the last 27 years of her life, Mother Aikenhead directed her institute while prostrate on her bed with chronic spinal

Mary Aikenhead, a commemorative stamp.

trouble. The decree introducing her cause of beatification in Rome was issued in 1921. Since her death the congregation has spread to England, Scotland, the U.S., and Africa.

Bibliography: M. B. BUTLER, *A Candle Was Lit: The Life of Mother Mary Aikenhead* (Dublin 1953). ActApS 13 (1921) 234–238.

[E. MC DERMOTT]

AIMERIC OF ANGOULÊME, Latin poet and metrist; b. Gastinaux, France; fl. late 11th century. He was educated in Senlis and was a friend of Bishop Adhemar of Angoulême (d. 1101), to whom he dedicated at least one of his works. He probably became a monk at *Saint-Maur-des-Fossés. Aimeric is best known for his treatise on quantity and accent in Latin words. His *Ars lectoria,* written in 1086, drew on the most important ancient writings on the subject and was intended to insure the correct use of quantity and accent in the Latin of the liturgy and other forms of public speaking. It is valuable for its evidence concerning earlier and contemporary pronunciation, and as a revelation of Aimeric's extensive knowledge of ancient literature, including such little-known poets as Luxorius (6th century A.D.).

Bibliography: *Ars lectoria,* brief selections in C. THUROT, *Notices extraits de divers manuscrits latins pour servir à l'histore des doctrines grammaticales au moyen âge* (Paris 1868) 2, 13–14, 508. Manitius 3:180–182.

[M. M. MC LAUGHLIN]

AIMERIC OF PIACENZA, Dominican master general; b. Lombardy; d. Bologna, Aug. 19, 1327. He entered the *Dominicans at Bologna (1267), studied at Milan, and taught for 24 years at Bologna. As provincial of the province of Greece, he attended the general chapter at Toulouse May 1, 1304. He was active in organizing studies in the order, but is best known for his role in the trial of the *Templars. Ordered by *Clement V (1309) to proceed against the Templars in Castile and Leon, Aimeric exonerated them after an investigation conducted without torture. He believed that his order's exemption allowed him to dispense with torture, evidently unaware that Clement had explicitly ordered it in a bull dated March 17, 1310. He was summoned to the Council of *Vienne but did not attend. It is probable that he resigned as master general (May 30, 1311) rather than take part in the process against the Templars.

Bibliography: Quétif-Échard 1.2:494–496. D. A. MORTIER, *Histoire des maîtres généraux de l'ordre des Frères Prêcheurs,* 8 v. (Paris 1903–20) 2:421–473. R. COULON, DHGE 1:1179–80. A. WALZ, EncCatt 1:601–602.

[P. M. STARRS]

AIMERIC OF SANTA MARIA NUOVA, cardinal deacon of S. Maria Nuova; d. May 28, 1141. Of Burgundian origin, he was elevated to the cardinalate by Pope *Callistus II in 1120 and served as chancellor of the Roman Church from 1123 until his death. A friend and correspondent of such eminent monastic reformers as *Bernard of Clairvaux, *Guigo I, and *Peter the Venerable, he played an important, though in certain respects a controversial, role in the ecclesiastical politics of his time, notably in the events surrounding the death of Pope *Honorius II and the election of Pope *Innocent II, which precipitated the schism of 1130 to 1138.

Bibliography: BERNARD OF CLAIRVAUX, *Epistolae* 15, 20, 48, 51–54, 157, 160, 181, 338 in PL 182:118–119, 123, 154–157, 158–160, 315, 320, 344, 542–544. H. WOLTER, LexThK^2 4:1324–25. Fliche-Martin 9:50–53. H. W. KLEWITZ, "Das Ende des Reformpapsttums," DeutschArch 3 (1939) 371–412; *Reformpapsttum und Kardinalkolleg* (Darmstadt 1957).

[M. M. MCLAUGHLIN]

AIMERICH, MATEO, Jesuit philologist and historian of Latin literature; b. Bordil, Spain, Feb. 25, 1715; d. Ferrara, Italy, 1799. He entered the Society of Jesus on Sept. 27, 1733, and at the completion of his clerical studies, taught philosophy and theology in several Jesuit colleges. He was appointed rector at Barcelona and Cervera, and chancellor of the University of Gandia. When Charles III of Spain expelled the Jesuits (1767), Aimerich found refuge in Ferrara, where he spent his remaining years in writing and research. Besides writing treatises in philosophy and ascetics, biographies, and funeral orations, he compiled the *Nomina et acta episcoporum Barcinonensium* (Barcelona 1760). His fame rests principally upon his writings on philology and the history of Latin literature. Of these the most noted is *Novum lexicon historicum et criticum antiquae romanae literaturae* (Bassano 1787).

Bibliography: Sommervogel 1:712–714. É. VAN CAUWENBERGH, DHGE 5:1298.

[W. C. HAUSMANN]

AIN-TRAZ, SYNODS OF. Ain-Traz is the summer residence of the Melchite patriarch of Antioch when he is in Lebanon. This residence was purchased in 1811 by Patriarch Agapios Matar to be used as a seminary for married priests. It is here that the Melchite patriarch convenes with his bishops to study, discuss, and decide on the major issues concerning their community. In the course of modern Melchite history, two of the synods held at Ain-Traz deserve particular attention.

Ain-Traz Synod I was convoked and presided over by the then newly elected Patriarch Maximos Mazloum on Dec. 13, 1835. The canons outlined by this synod relate to the Melchite discipline. They regulate Baptism, Confirmation, the Liturgy of the Presanctified, confession, Extreme Unction, Holy Orders, Matrimony, communication in sacris, the holy days of obligation, the clergy (garb, commerce, residence, catechism, exercise of medicine, inheritance), the religious (garb, exclaustration), pastoral visits of the bishops, alms to the seminary of Ain-Traz, charitable foundations, fast and abstinence, pilgrimages to different churches, usury, etc. The Congregation for the Propagation of the Faith confirmed *in forma generali* the 25 canons listed above with few modifications of the text submitted. In this manner the Melchite discipline, outlined at the Synod of Saint-Sauveur in 1790 and reaffirmed at the Synod of Qarqafee in 1806, received the official stamp of the Church on Jan. 13, 1838.

While the Congregation for the Propagation of the Faith was studying the acts of this synod, Patriarch Maximos Mazloum received a diploma from the Sultan in Constantinople recognizing him as the sole civil leader of all the Melchites in the Turkish Empire, and from the Holy See in Rome, the right to add to his title the words "Alexandria and Jerusalem." As a result, his jurisdiction was extended to encompass the territories of the old patriarchates of the East.

Ain-Traz Synod II was called by Patriarch Cyril Jeha and was held from May 30 to July 8, 1909. The acts are not printed. They were submitted to Rome in due time, but, as of 1964, they had not been confirmed. However, it is certain that they have served as *fontes* to the modern codification of the Oriental Church as it concerns the Melchite congregation.

Besides these two official synods, each successive patriarch meets regularly with his bishops at Ain-Traz to discuss current events. Their directives are printed in the major publications of the community, mainly: *Al Masarrat,* published by the Paulist Fathers at Harissa; *Ar Risalat Al Muhalisiat,* published by the Salvatorian Fathers at Saida; and *Le Lien,* published by the Patriarchal clergy in Cairo.

Bibliography: Hefele-Leclercq 11:339–379. J. CHAMMAS, *Hulasat Tarîh al-Kanîsat al-Malakîyat,* 3 v. (Sidon, Leb. 1952) 3:185.

[L. MALOUF]

AĬNALOV, DMITRIĬ VLAS'EVICH, Russian art historian; b. Mariupol, 1862; d. 1939. He was appointed *Privatdozent* at the University of Kazan in 1891 and professor at the University of St. Petersburg in 1903. While continuing and consolidating the cause of the scientific study of Byzantine art, founded by his master Kondakov, he gave it a new orientation. Attacking the view that Rome was the birthplace of Byzantine art, his book *The Hellenistic Origins of Byzantine Art* compellingly emphasized the generating role of the great Hellenistic cultural centers of the Near East. This contribution, with modifications, has been confirmed by subsequent findings and has formed the basis for all standard texts on early Christian and Byzantine art. But his theory that 14th-century Byzantine art was a byproduct of the Italian Dugento has not found support in modern research. His interests included also early Russian and Italian Renaissance art.

Bibliography: Sources. *The Hellenistic Origins of Byzantine Art,* tr. E. and S. SOBOLEVITCH (New Brunswick, N.J. 1961). *Mozaiki IV i V vekov* (St. Petersburg 1895). *Vizantiiskaia zhivopis XIV stoletiia* (Petrograd 1917). *Geschichte der russischen Monumentalkunst der vormoskovitischen Zeit* (Berlin-Leipzig 1932). *Geschichte der russischen Monumentalkunst zur Zeit des Grossfürstentums Moskau* (Berlin-Leipzig 1933). Literature. K. MIJATEV, "D. V. Ainalov," *Bulletin de l'institut archéologique Bulgare* 13 (1939–41) 302–303.

[G. GALAVARIS]

AINAY, ABBEY OF, former *Benedictine monastery of Saint-Martin and former collegiate church, located in the marshy peninsula between the Rhone and the Saône, slightly upstream from the junction of the two rivers, in present-day Lyons, France, Diocese of Lyons (Latin, *Athanacum monasterium* or *Interamnense mon.*). Founded in the 6th century, it suffered a serious crisis in the mid-9th century, and was resettled by Benedictine monks who came apparently from the Paris area. The abbey church, wholly preserved today, was consecrated by Pope Paschal II on Jan. 27, 1107. The abbey prospered in subsequent centuries, and at the end of the 13th century it controlled 200 parishes in the southeastern part of present-day France. Yet this powerful abbey produced no great ecclesiastical writer and gave the Church no saint. Its temporal power, as well as its spiritual influence, was severely curtailed by the *Wars of Religion. It was secularized by a papal bull of Dec. 4, 1685, becoming a collegiate church; the former religious became a chapter of *canons. During the French Revolution three of its canons were guillotined. The church is still used as a parish church and is the seat of an archpriest of the city of Lyons. It has been elevated to the rank of a minor basilica.

The 12th-century church of Saint-Martin d'Ainay.

Bibliography: GallChrist 4:233–241. H. A. CHARPIN-FEUGEROLLES and M. C. GUIGUE, eds., *Grand cartulaire de l'abbaye d'Ainay,* 2 v. (Lyons 1885). J. B. VANEL, DHGE 1:1195–1201. R. GAZEAU, *Catholicisme* 1:248–249. **Illustration credit:** Archives Photographiques, Paris.

[L. GAILLARD]

AIRVAULT, MONASTERY OF, former monastery of Canons Regular of St. Augustine in the Diocese of *Poitiers, west central France. It was founded as a collegiate chapter *c.* 991 by Audéarde (d. *c.* 1013) and reformed with Augustinian canons from Lesterp by Bp. Peter II of Poitiers (1087–1115). It declined and was impoverished by the Hundred Years War; the conventual buildings were destroyed in the Wars of Religion (1568). In 1477 the first commendatory abbot appeared, and by 1546 Airvault was definitely in *commendation. The community of 12 canons, appointed by the abbot, joined none of the reform congregations of canons in the 17th century. The suppression ordered in 1768 by the *Commission of Regulars was not enforced, and the canons continued their services in the church of St-Pierre until 1791. The 11th-century church, redone in the 13th century, now serves a parish.

Bibliography: Cottineau 1:39. P. DE MONSABERT, DHGE 1: 1219–23. H. BEAUCHET-FILLEAU, "Recherches sur Airvault: Son château et son abbaye," *Memoires de la Société des antiquaires de l'Ouest* 24 (1857) 177–369. J. BERTHELÉ, "Les Voûtes Plantagenet des églises d'Airvault et de St. Jouin," *Revue poitevine et Saintongeaise* 4 (Melle 1887) 1–15.

[N. BACKMUND]

AISTULF, KING OF THE LOMBARDS, 749 to 756. Elected on the deposition of his brother *Rachis, Aistulf reigned until his accidental death. His policies aimed at consolidating Italy under Lombard control. The Exarchate of *Ravenna was taken in 751 and a number of towns formerly a part of the Byzantine Exarchate but currently claimed by the papacy were either taken or threatened by the *Lombards. An appeal by Pope *Stephen II to the *Franks, under the new *Carolingian dynasty, brought invasions by *Pepin III in 755 and 756. The Lombards were defeated but not overthrown, although most of the land in dispute between the Lombards and the papacy was formally conferred by Pepin on the Pope (*see* DONATION OF CONSTANTINE; STATES OF THE CHURCH). Aistulf was succeeded by *Desiderius.

Bibliography: J. B. BURY, *A History of the Later Roman Empire*, 2 v. (New York 1889). L. DUCHESNE, *The Beginnings of the Temporal Sovereignty of the Popes, A.D. 754–1073*, tr. A. H. MATHEW (London 1908). O. BERTOLINI, *Roma di fronte a Bisanzio e ai Longobardi* (Bologna 1941).

[K. F. DREW]

AIX, ARCHDIOCESE OF (AQUENSIS IN GALLIA)

Metropolitan see since 445, in southeast France, 20 miles north of *Marseilles; it corresponds to the arrondissements of Aix and Arles in Bouches-du-Rhône department and is 1,768 square miles in area. Since 1822 the archbishop has held also the titles of *Arles (once a metropolitan and for a while a primatial see) and Embrun (once a metropolitan). In 1963 the See of Aix had 128 parishes, 217 secular and 30 religious priests, 522 women in 69 convents, and some 300,000 Catholics. Its five suffragans, which had 1,391 parishes, 874 secular and 278 religious priests, 2,487 sisters, and 1,350,000 Catholics, were: Ajaccio in *Corsica (created in the 3d century), Digne (*c.* 400), *Fréjus-Toulon (*c.* 374), Gap (5th century), and *Nice (3d century). The area of the diocese has varied greatly. Until 1789 it corresponded to the old Roman *civitas* (96 parishes). In 1802 it included the departments of Var and Bouches-du-Rhône. In 1822 it lost Marseilles arrondissement and Var department. Its suffragans *c.* 800 (Apt, Fréjus, Gap, Riez, and Sisteron) comprised the old Roman province *Narbonensis II,* less Antibes. *Algiers (1838–67) and Nice (1860) were added later.

The 11th-century legend that the sees of the lower Rhône were founded by disciples of Christ (Lazarus, Mary Magdalen, and Martha) is without value. The first known bishop dates from *c.* 379. Until *c.* 1000 the history of Aix is very obscure. Many lacunae in its list of bishops correspond with the domination of the Arian Goths and to the years Saracens raided from their base at Garde-Freinet (until 972). After the Moslems were expelled, Aix revived and became the capital of the County of Provence, with which its history then merged. Despite Abp. Jean de Saint-Chamond, who in 1566 announced from the episcopal throne his apostasy to Protestantism and married, the diocese remained strongly Catholic. The Catholic reform followed the rulings of the Council of Aix (1585); but Jansenism, supported by members of the Parlement of Provence (1501–1789), troubled the diocese, especially in the 17th century.

Of 34 synodal statutes known (1362–1760), 22 date from the 18th century. Provincial councils were held in 1103, 1112, 1409, 1585, 1838, and 1850. The most important was that of 1585, under Abp. Alexandre Canigiani (1576–91), an Italian who attended the Councils of Milan held by St. Charles *Borromeo, whose disciple he was. The decisions at Aix in 1585 contained the essence of Borromeo's rules and spirit: definition of an ideal bishop, rules of the episcopal life, and relations with clergy and faithful; pastoral duties, which were also insisted upon, included preaching, administration of the Sacraments, pastoral visitations, validation of Baptism, strict rules on the Sacrament of Penance, the spirit of Rome in the liturgy, rules for seminaries (Canigiani founded one in 1580), and division of the diocese into itinerant vicariates with regular inspection. Borromeo's spirit and methods thus were introduced before the spirit of French reform developed. Other archbishops of Aix were *Peter Aureoli (1321–22), Guillaume *Fillastre (1420–22), Gilbert *Génébrard (1593–97), Alphonse du Plessis de Riche-

Aix, the 17th-century Church of the Madeleine.

lieu (1626–29, Carthusian brother of Cardinal Richelieu and later archbishop of Lyons), Jérôme de Grimaldi (1648–85, who left his goods to the seminary he started), Charles de Vintimille (1708–29, transferred to Paris), Jérôme Champion de Cicé (1771–1801, ecclesiastical minister of Louis XVI who played a role in the Estates General of 1789), and François Xavier Gouthe-Soulard (1886–1900).

Famous people in Aix's history include St.*Eucherius of Lyons (d. *c.* 450); St. *Elzéar of Sabran (1285–1323), canonized with his wife Delphine in 1369; Abp. Honoré de Laurens of Embrun (1600–12); Ignace Cottolendi, vicar apostolic of *Nanking (1630–62); and Cardinal Abp. J. H. Guibert of Paris (1871–86). The former Cistercian Abbey of Silvacane (1147–1440) and the 12th-century Benedictine *Montmajour in Arles were distinguished. The archbishop was chancellor of the university founded in Aix (1403) by the Pisan Pope Alexander V, with faculties of theology, law, and medicine. Aix, once known for baths (*Aquae Sextiae,* after the consul Sextius who founded it in 123 B.C.), has beautiful monuments: the 12th-century Cloister of Saint-Sauveur; the composite (5th–16th century) Cathedral of Saint-Sauveur with a 5th-century tomb of St. Mitrias (d. *c.* 300) and a 5th-century baptistery; Sainte-Madeleine and the Jesuit chapel (17th century); and Saint-Jean-de-Malté (13th–15th century). Arles has the church and cloister of Saint-Trophime (11th–15th century), Notre-Dame de la Major (12th century), and the Romanesque Saint-Honorat. Sainte-Marthe is a shrine in Tarascon. Among other shrines in the diocese, many to the Blessed Virgin, is that of Saintes-Maries of the Sea (for gypsies) in honor of St. Sarah, the gypsy (servant) of Mary Magdalen and Martha.

Bibliography: GallChrist 1:297–348. GallChrist novissima (Montbéliard 1899) 1:1–171. A. RASTOUL, DHGE 1:1235–41, incomplete and mediocre but has list of bishops. *Bouches-du-Rhône conseil général: Encyclopedie départementale,* v.14 (Marseilles 1935). É. GRIFFE, *La Gaule chrétienne à l'époque romaine,* 2 v. (Paris 1947–58; rev. ed. 1965–). AnnPont (1965) 19. **Illustration credit:** Arthur O'Leary.

[E. JARRY]

AKATHISTOS

From the Greek ἀ-κάθιστος, meaning not seated, standing. It is perhaps the most celebrated hymn of the Byzantine Church, and belongs to the poetical genre known as kontakion (*see* BYZANTINE RITE, CHANTS OF). It is performed at the vigil service of the fifth Saturday in Lent, a calendar position that it occupied from an early date; its original association, however, was more probably with the Feast of the Annunciation, March 25.

The body of the poem comprises 24 stanzas (*oikoi*) linked by an alphabet acrostic—the first 12 treating of the Incarnation and the infancy of Christ, the last 12 alternating the praises of God and His Mother in the even- and odd-numbered stanzas respectively; the concluding stanza, by exception, is addressed to the Virgin. Each of the stanzas presents the same seven-line metric pattern, but the odd ones add to this a series of salutations to the Virgin: 12 lines in metrically matching pairs, each line beginning with Χαῖρε (Hail), and the entire stanza concluding with the unvarying refrain Χαῖρε, νύμφη ἀνύμφευτε (Hail, unwedded Bride). The even stanzas have simply "Alleluia" as refrain. As an introduction (*prooimion*) to the 24 stanzas, early MSS give another stanza, of independent metrical design and standing outside the alphabet acrostic: τῇ ὑπερμάχῳ στρατηγῷ . . . (To the invincible Leader . . .), a hymn of thanksgiving to the Virgin for the delivery of Constantinople from siege; in fact, the chronicles mention several such occasions at which the *Akathistos* was presumably sung. It has been conjectured that the original *prooimion* was not this but another stanza, now found as an independent hymn for the same office: Τὸ προσταχθὲν μυστικῶς λαβὼν . . . (Receiving secretly the command . . .), which corresponds more closely to the 24 stanzas in wording and theme. But quite possibly neither stanza was part of the original composition of the hymn.

The authorship and date of the *Akathistos* have been the subject of much discussion; the medieval sources offer different attributions, and modern scholars in turn have advanced the claims of various candidates for the honor: Romanos in the 6th century, Patriarch Sergios and George Pisides in the 7th, Patriarchs Germanos and Photios in the 8th and 9th centuries respectively. The latest of these claimants has been eliminated by the discovery of a Latin translation of the *Akathistos* that can hardly be later than the early 9th century. As for the others, the prevailing tendency in more recent scholarship has been to assign the hymn to the 6th century, or even somewhat earlier; and the case for the authorship of Romanos himself has been forcefully argued, notably by Wellesz, despite its weakness in the MS tradition. For other scholars the hymn remains anonymous, perhaps the work of some imitator of Romanos; thus the question of attribution seems unlikely to receive any definitive solution.

The earliest extant musical sources for the *Akathistos,* completely notated, date from the 13th century; there is little reason to suppose that the music they contain was that originally accompanying the text. The melody conforms to the highly ornate and formulaic style characteristic of the kontakion in that period; the service book in which it occurs was, in all likelihood, of a type designed for the use of soloists. The music is written out in full over the individual stanzas, suggesting that, at a time when virtually all kontakia had been reduced to *prooimion* and a single *oikos,* the *Akathistos,* at least on occasion, was performed in its musical entirety. In the present-day service the medieval melody has been replaced by one of more recent origin, and the stanzas succeeding the first are generally read, not sung.

As mentioned previously, the *Akathistos* existed in a Latin version by the late 8th or early 9th century; thereafter, its rhetoric and imagery appear as the inspiration of a considerable repertory of Latin hymns. The subject is given detailed exposition in the study of G. G. Meersseman cited below.

Bibliography: Wellesz ByzMus. *The Akathistos Hymn,* introd. and transcribed by E. WELLESZ (*Monumenta musicae byzantinae, Transcripta* 9; Copenhagen 1957). E. WELLESZ, "The 'Akathistos': A Study in Byzantine Hymnography," DumbOaksP, 9 and 10 (1956) 141–174. C. DE GRANDE, *L'Inno acatisto* (Florence 1948). G. G. MEERSSEMAN, "Der Hymnos Akathistos im Abendland," in *Spicilegium Friburgense,* v. 2–3 (Fribourg 1956–60). P. MAAS, "Das Kontakion," ByzZ 19 (1910) 285–306. P. F. KRYPIAKIEWICZ, "De Hymni Acathisti auctore," ByzZ 18 (1901) 357–382. M. HUGLO, "L'Ancienne version latine de l'hymne acathiste," *Muséon* 64 (1951) 27–61.

[I. THOMAS]

AKHNATON (AMENHOTEP IV)

Akhnaton is the name that Amenhotep IV gave to himself, although Egyptologists, following the practice of Manetho, usually call him Amenophis IV. He was the son and successor of Amenhotep III and ruled for some 17 years, about the middle of the 14th century B.C. (1372–1354, according to E. Drioton-J. Vandier, *L'Égypte,* 3d ed., 631; 1353–1336, according to W. Helck-E. Otto, *Kleines Wörterbuch der Ägyptologie* 37). His mother was Tiye. His wife, Nefertiti, cannot be identified, as some have claimed, with Princess Tadukhepa, the daughter of the Mitannian King Tushratta; her nurse was Teye, the wife of Ay, and she had a sister in Egypt named Benremut. The history of the reign of Amenhotep IV is dominated by the religious revolution that he unleashed against Amon and the other Egyptian gods. This revolt so engaged his energies that it caused the collapse of the empire that Thutmosis III had built up in Syria and Phoenicia.

The Aton Reform. From the beginning of his reign, Amenhotep IV showed his devotion to a particular form of the sun-god, the solar disk, which was called Aton. Aton appears more and more frequently on the monuments and in the texts that date from the beginning of the New Empire, especially under Amenhotep III; but from this it does not follow that the solar disk had already been the object of a special cult. East of the temple of Amon at Karnak, Amenhotep IV built for Aton a solar temple like the one in Heliopolis. Its god was represented under the form of a solar disk, the rays of which ended in human hands. It is important to note that the colossal statues of the king that adorned this temple were made in a new style that was to become characteristic of the Amarna Art, as it is called. In the tombs of his officials, e.g., that of the vizier, Ramose, the traditional art is also suddenly replaced by this realistic style. This shows that the sovereign was able to impose his novel ideas on his contemporaries, and we can suppose that these art forms served merely as means to express his equally revolutionary notions in religious matters. Thereupon the conflict that this involved with the traditionalists reached a critical point, and things began to happen quickly. In the 6th year of his reign Amenhotep IV left Thebes and founded a city, halfway between Luxor and Cairo, on a site that is currently known as el-Amarna, but that he called Akhetaton (the Horizon of Aton). Here he surrounded himself with officials who were *homines novi* and were totally devoted to him. Soon he proscribed the cult of most of the other gods, particularly that of Amon. Their temples were closed, their statues smashed, and their names chiseled out of every monument, whether big or little. His own name, Amenhotep, "Amon is merciful," he changed to Akhnaton, "Useful to Aton."

Akhnaton's new doctrine finds its best expression in the famous hymn to Aton that appears in certain tombs of his officials at el-Amarna, most notably the tomb of Ay, who later succeeded Tut-ankh-Amon on the throne of Egypt (see Pritchard ANET 369–371). Akhnaton himself is credited with its composition. The tenor of this hymn is thoroughly monotheistic; yet a careful study of it shows that it does not really contain much that had not been said before in the hymns to Amon and various other gods. Actually, the traditional cults also showed a strong monotheistic tendency (*see* EGYPT, ANCIENT, 1), but the syncretism that is the basis of the old religion is entirely absent here, and it is precisely this that constitutes, above all else, the novelty of the hymn. The new faith ignored all the old gods that were venerated under animal or human forms and worshiped only the sun-god, under the form of the solar disk. An exception, however, must be made for the cult of the bull, Mnevis, which was also introduced at Akhetaton. This detail shows how much the religion of Akhnaton was indebted to the Heliopolitan cult. The conclusion can be drawn that what the King really did was to carry to its extreme the ideology of the ancient solar religion by abolishing, as E. Drioton expresses it, "the contradiction, that had always been felt by the more enlightened thinkers, between the monotheism professed by the educated classes and their official polytheism" ["Le monothéisme de L'Ancienne Égypte" *Cahiers d'histoire égyptienne* (Cairo 1949) 167]. There is no need, therefore, to look outside of Egypt, as some have done, for the motives that inspired this reform.

The relations with Heliopolis are evident also in the plan of the sanctuary at Akhetaton, which, though more complicated, belongs to the general type of solar temples. The first part consisted of the *per-hat,* "house of jubilation," a courtyard with two altars, and of the *gem-Aton,* "Aton was found," a series of courtyards with altars. The second part, the house of *benben,* likewise comprised two courtyards, one of which was enclosed with a peristyle within which was probably an obelisk.

End of the Reign. Such simple and rational doctrine, however, proved insufficient, even though it was propagated by a fanatical prophet, who was at the same time both a poet and an originator of a new aesthetic ideal. Immemorial tradition showed itself still stronger. The Aton doctrine won few adepts apart from Akhnaton himself, and scarcely was he dead when even his former friends returned to the old religion. The last years of his life were not happy. His second daughter, Meketa-

Limestone sketch of Akhnaton (Eighteenth Dynasty) from el-Amarna; sculptor's trial or model for other sculptures.

ton, died. His wife, Nefertiti, fell into disgrace, and in her palace to the south of Akhetaton her name and image were everywhere replaced by those of her oldest daughter, Meritaton, the wife of Akhnaton's younger brother, Smenkhkarē, who began to make conciliatory gestures to the Amon priesthood. Tut-ankh-Aton, the husband of Akhnaton's third daughter and later his successor, changed his name to Tut-ankh-Amon for his short reign at Thebes, during which he officially restored the Amon cult. Horemheb, when ascending the throne, wiped out the last traces of the Aton heresy. It was probably at this time that Akhnaton suffered his *damnatio memoriae* and that his body was doomed to destruction, though perhaps secretly saved by some of the small group of his loyal followers. Succeeding generations regarded him merely as "the enemy at Akhetaton."

Bibliography: J. A. Wilson, *The Burden of Egypt: An Interpretation of Ancient Egyptian Culture* (Chicago 1951) ch. 9; also available as *The Culture of Ancient Egypt* (Chicago 1956). A. H. Gardiner, *Egypt of the Pharaohs* (Oxford 1961) ch. 9. L. G. Leeuwenberg, *Echnaton* (The Hague 1946). **Illustration credit:** The University Museum, the University of Pennsylvania.

[J. VERGOTE]

AKIBA BEN JOSEPH, the leading rabbi of his time and one of the founders of Talmudic *Judaism; b. Palestine *c.* A.D. 50; d. there, *c.* 135. He took no interest in learning until he was well on in years, when he studied under Rabbi *Johanan ben Zakkai at Jabneh (Jamnia). Later he founded his own academy, first at *Lydda (Lod) and then at Bene Barak. He was the main spiritual force behind *Bar Kokhba in the latter's revolt against the Romans (132–135). After being arrested and tortured by the Romans, he died reciting the Shema Yisrael ("Hear, O Israel . . ."—Judaism's profession of faith, citing Dt 6.4).

Rabbi Akiba (Akiva, Aqiba) was the first to make a systematic collection of the halakic traditions (*see* HALAKAH) of the Tannaim ("repeaters," the rabbis of the first two Christian centuries) who handed down the Oral Law (as distinct from the Written Law of Moses); this work of his, as continued by his disciple Rabbi Meïr and still in oral form, was further systematized and recorded in writing in Rabbi *Judah ha-Nasi's *Mishnah. Another original contribution made by Akiba was his doctrine that the Oral Law was not immutable, but could be adjusted to changing conditions; since this is the basic principle guiding all Talmudic development, he is regarded as father of the *Talmud.

Bibliography: L. Ginzberg, JewishEnc 1:304–310. D. J. Bornstein, EncJudaica 2:7–22. S. Cohen, UnivJewishEnc 1: 144–150. J. Schmid, LexThK[2] 1:778–779. A. Romeo, EncCatt 1:1719–20. L. Finkelstein, *Akiba: Scholar, Saint and Martyr* (New York 1936). A. Guttmann, "Akiba, 'Rescuer of the Torah'," HebUCAnn 17 (1942–43) 395–421. S. A. Birnbaum, "Bar Kokhba and Akiba," PalExFQS 86 (1954) 23–32. P. Benoit, "Rabbi Aqiba ben Joseph, sage et héros du Judaïsme," RevBibl 54 (1947) 54–89.

[J. J. DOUGHERTY]

AKKADIAN LANGUAGE AND LITERATURE

Akkadian is the earliest recorded *Semitic language, spoken in ancient Mesopotamia from the early 3d millennium down to the middle of the 1st millennium B.C. and surviving as a written language as late as A.D. 75. Its two principal dialects were Babylonian and Assyrian. The name Akkadian (Assyro-Babylonian *akkadû*) is derived from the name of the city of Akkad (Agade), capital of the first Semitic Empire in Mesopotamia, founded by Sargon in the 24th century B.C.

Akkadian Language

Akkadian is generally regarded as the eastern branch of the Semitic family of languages as opposed to the western branch, which includes such tongues as *Hebrew, *Arabic, *Aramaic, Ugaritic (*see* UGARIT), and *Ethiopic. With these it shares the typical Semitic phonology (preponderance of laryngeals and emphatics), consonantal root structure (chiefly triconsonantal), stem structure, interlocking morpheme patterns, pronominal suffixes, lack of real word compounds, and preference for coordinate rather than subordinate clauses.

Phonology. The Akkadian consonants were ', *b, d, g, ḫ, k, l, m, n, p, q, r, s, ṣ, š, t, ṭ, z* (also ʿ and *ś* in the earliest periods). The primary vowels were *a, i, u;* a secondary vowel, *e,* was derived from either *a* or *i,* usually in combination with certain consonants; these vowels could all be either long or short. There is no clear evidence for the existence of diphthongs or of the vowel *o.*

Writing. The Akkadian cuneiform script consisted of more than 500 simple and compound signs, almost all originally borrowed from the Sumerian writing system (*see* WRITING, ANCIENT SYSTEMS OF). As in *Sumerian, a single cuneiform sign could stand for either (1) an entire word, (2) a syllable, (3) a phonetic indicator (i.e., an unpronounced sign used to indicate how an ambiguous preceding or succeeding sign should be pronounced), or (4) a determinative (indicating the class to which a preceding or succeeding word belonged, e.g., prefixed *ālu* identified the name of a town or city). Also as in Sumerian, many of the signs were polyvalent or homophonous or both; the complicated writing system discouraged literacy except among the highly trained professional scribal class. In certain periods,

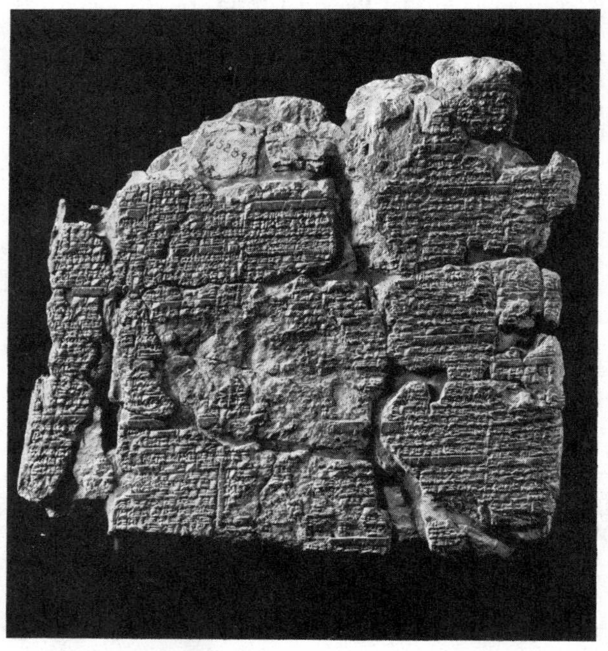

Cuneiform tablet inscribed in Akkadian with parts of the Law Code of Hammurabi, original text c. 1700 B.C.

such as the Old Assyrian (19th century B.C.), a simplified and more phonetic system of writing was developed, in which slightly more than 100 signs were used and polyvalency and homophony were practically unknown.

Morphology and Syntax. Both nouns and verbs were formed chiefly around a triconsonantal root with interlocking morpheme patterns; e.g., the root *prs* meant "decide" and *pārisu* meant "one who decides"; *lpt* meant "touch" and *lāpitu,* "one who touches," etc. Noun and verb forms were both built on patterns of this type. Nouns distinguished gender (masculine, feminine), number (singular, plural, also dual in early periods and in later isolated forms), case (nominative, genitive, accusative; also dative and locative in the earlier periods), and state (regular, construct, absolute). There was also a series of forms termed the permansive that turned a noun into a quasi verb, e.g., noun *bēlu* "lord," permansive *bēlēku* "I am lord." Adjectives were much like nouns in form, but they had no dual, no dative or locative, and no construct or absolute state. Personal pronouns were either independent (nominative, dative, accusative) or suffixed (genitive, dative, accusative).

Verb forms were likewise built around a usually triconsonantal root (sometimes artificially augmented from a biconsonantal original), though quadriconsonantal verbs also occurred. There were four basic stems of the verb, usually labeled the *G, D, Š,* and *N*. The *G* (*Grundstamm*) expressed the basic meaning of the root. The second (*D,* because it doubled the second consonant of the root) usually had a factitive or intensive meaning for verbs whose *G* stems were respectively intransitive or transitive. The third stem, which inserted *-š-* before the three root consonants, was causative in meaning. The fourth stem, which added *-n-* before the three root consonants, expressed the passive. Further stems were derived from these four by introduction of a *-ta-* infix (reciprocal, reflexive, or passive meaning) or a *-tan-* infix (iterative). Within each of these original or derived stems there were three tenses (present, preterite, and perfect, all of which might have either aspectual or temporal connotations), an imperative, and three nominal forms: participle, infinitive, and permansive. There were two moods: the subjunctive (for verbs in subordinate clauses) and the ventive (usually denoting action with relation toward the speaker or point of reference).

Syntax remains a largely uncharted area in Akkadian studies, perhaps because of its seeming simplicity. Subordinate clauses were relatively few, but there was an astonishing range of nuance in paratactic clauses. Because of the existence of permansive forms and the restricted use of the verb "to be" (*bašû*), nominal sentences were common, as were ellipses in letters.

Dialects and Distribution. The classical division of the Akkadian language into various dialects has usually been made along the following lines. Old Akkadian, the most primitive form of the language known, was used in 3d-millennial Mesopotamia when the non-Semitic Sumerian was the predominant language of the land; the dialect is known largely from personal names or from loanwords in Sumerian, except for the brief period of the empire of Sargon of Akkad and his successors, when longer inscriptions were composed entirely in Akkadian. In the 2d and 1st millenniums, two major branches of Akkadian are usually distinguished —Assyrian in the north and Babylonian in the south. These are further subdivided into Old Assyrian (1950–1750), Middle Assyrian (1500–1000), and Neo-Assyrian (1000–600) in the one branch; Old Babylonian (2000–1595 or 1950–1530), Middle Babylonian (1595-1000 or 1530–1000), and Neo-Babylonian (1000–625) in the other. (The double series of numbers is due to a disputed point of chronology.) There was a purely literary dialect, Standard Babylonian (1000–500), and also Late Babylonian (625 B.C.–A.D. 75), which was heavily influenced by Aramaic and was soon replaced by it except as a written legal and scholarly language. Within these groups, various subdialects may sometimes be distinguished; for example, different forms of Old Babylonian were used in northern and in southern Babylonia, in the Diyala region, at *Susa, *Mari, and Alalakh, besides the formal language of the Old-Babylonian chancellery, the consciously archaizing language of the official royal inscriptions, and the so-called hymno-epic dialect of literary compositions. Except for the learned and poetic Standard Babylonian dialect, a linear development is usually assumed from Old Akkadian, separately, to Old Babylonian and to Old Assyrian, which both then altered in the course of time into the later dialects of Babylonian and Assyrian.

This neat but inadequate view of Akkadian is now gradually being replaced by one more in accord with the findings of modern linguistics. Though it is still too early to attempt definitive classifications before the pertinent studies are finished—or, in some cases, even begun—the gaps between Old Akkadian and Old Babylonian or between Old Assyrian and Middle Assyrian (to mention two of the more obvious examples) seem to preclude linear descent. Furthermore, it is becoming increasingly clear that the so-called Standard Babylonian was really literary Old Babylonian with the inevitable minor adjustments of a later generation; and such cherished discoveries as the hymno-epic dialect are now seen not to have been dialects at all, but rather a congeries of scribal conventions. The coming decades of study will undoubtedly produce further revisions in the classical picture of the Akkadian dialects.

Besides its use in Babylonia and Assyria, Akkadian also spread as a second language to many other countries of western Asia, especially during the days of widespread political and cultural contact, in the 2d millennium. It was used at many places in Syria, including Mari, Qatna, Alalakh, Ugarit, *Byblos, and Aleppo, and as a scholarly and diplomatic language for the *Hittites in Hattusha. Fragments of Akkadian epics have been found in Palestine and Egypt as well. For a time Akkadian was the diplomatic language of the ancient Near East; and the celebrated *Amarna Letters of the correspondence of 18th-dynasty Egypt with the kingdoms of Babylonia, *Mitanni, Hatti, and Assyria and with numerous cities and towns in Syria, Palestine, and perhaps even Cyprus and Anatolia were written almost entirely in Akkadian. International treaties of the period were drafted in Akkadian, and it was used also as the language for legal documents in Alalakh, Ugarit, and Susa. Akkadian cuneiform writing was also adopted and adapted for expressing the native languages of foreign peoples: *Hittite, Ugaritic, *Hurrian, Elamite (*see* ELAM), Old Persian, and Urartian; and the use of clay tablets for writing found favor in the Minoan and

Mycenaean civilizations and with later Aramaic scribes as well. (*See* CRETE.)

Akkadian Literature

Because of the durable and inexpensive material on which most Akkadian was written, a unique epigraphic record of many various phases of Mesopotamian civilization has been preserved. The clay on which records were inscribed was easily obtainable, and its smooth and plastic surface when wet could be readily impressed with a stylus (usually made of reed, but sometimes of wood or other material). These impressions became permanent when the clay dried in the sun or was baked in a kiln. The sizes and shapes of tablets ranged from thin squares the size of a postage stamp to large rectangles almost 3 feet long, on which several hundred lines could be written. Occasionally tablets were imitated in stone or metal, especially for recording royal inscriptions. Because of the number and variety of tablets that have survived, scholars are better able to reconstruct a complete picture of society in Mesopotamia than that in Egypt or Palestine, from which a much smaller range of documentation is extant.

Administrative Texts. The most common types of tablets are utilitarian economic documents, household or business memoranda, and administrative texts dealing with the disposition of men, real estate, or goods of a private house, estate, temple, or palace. Common, too, are official legal contracts, sealed and witnessed, necessary to attest the validity of any private transaction, such as a sale or loan, a marriage, or an adoption. There are likewise many letters touching on business affairs, directives of merchants to their agents in distant parts, and reports of goods being imported or exported. Nonbusiness letters between private persons are comparatively rare, undoubtedly because of the low literacy level among the general population.

Royal Archives and Inscriptions. Light is thrown on national and international affairs also from the palace archives. There are pronouncements of the king governing the realm: the law "codes" (not really codifications but rather recurrent royal attempts to reform portions of the existing customary law); charters, land grants, and declarations of tax exemption issued to cities, temples, or private individuals; and edicts of a more personal nature issuing from the king in his role as chief judge (and final court of appeals) in the land or regulating such activities as the operation of the royal harem. There are reports coming into the capital from local subordinate officials throughout the provinces and orders sent out to them; this correspondence contains both the prosaic handling of ordinary government affairs and more than occasional displays of personal intrigue and rivalry for the royal favor. In time of unrest or war, there are reports of events in the troubled areas, requests for more troops or supplies, and even diplomatically worded royal letters attempting to dissuade defecting cities from rebellion. On the international plane, there are the well-known vassal treaties as well as parity treaties, arrangements made for political marriages between the royal houses of lands like Egypt and Babylonia, and the usual royal correspondence between courts. Here too, one often finds surprising personal touches, such as the complaint of the King of Babylonia that the gifts he had received from the King of Egypt were not as good as those he himself had sent, or his inquiry after his sister who had been married many years before into the Egyptian court.

The achievements of the Assyrian monarchs were chronicled in detail in their royal annals, year-by-year accounts of their military campaigns and conquests of foreign lands; these accounts were preserved sometimes in great display rooms of the palace and sometimes on steles deposited in temples in thanksgiving to the national gods. The king of Assyria was also ex officio the chief priest of the god Assur, and splendid liturgies and hymns surrounded the royal figure in his ritual duties. Some of the rulers, especially *Assurbanipal (Ashurbanipal; 668–627 B.C.) of Assyria, amassed huge heterogeneous collections of tablets. It is largely from the libraries of such bibliophile monarchs that the present-day knowledge of the intellectual, scientific, and literary history of ancient Mesopotamia has been gained.

Scribal Lore. The complicated character of the cuneiform writing system favored the development of a specialized class of scribes, who underwent a long and arduous training and then held key positions in the economic and political life of the land as secretaries and interpreters for their often illiterate masters. The contents of the curriculum in the scribal schools can be gauged from the surviving elementary manuals (syllabaries containing cuneiform signs with their phonetically written names and pronunciation) and encyclopedic dictionaries (Sumerian words and their Akkadian equivalents arranged in classes according to meaning). At first, the fledgling scribes were set to copying these texts, and then, as they progressed, they were allowed to copy more advanced texts such as sample letters, the repetitious omen series, and literary texts. The scribes kept alive the bilingual tradition of Sumerian and Akkadian, and original inscriptions were still being composed for antiquarian-minded kings in Sumerian more than 1,000 years after the death of Sumerian as a living language. In general, Sumerian influence is evident in many aspects of later Akkadian: the borrowed writing system, loanwords from Sumerian, and especially words found in the legal, scientific, literary, and religious tradition.

Magical and Omen Literature. Akkadian magical literature has survived in abundance: conjurations, incantations, charms, magic amulets, and so forth. Sometimes epic texts of cultic significance, such as the Irra Epic, were inscribed on tablets and hung on the wall of a home as a sort of household blessing. Texts dealing directly with the performance of the cult, such as descriptions of the care and feeding of the gods or rituals for consecrating a newly made statue so as to insure in it the presence of the pertinent deity, provide further interesting testimony to Assyro-Babylonian religious practices.

The most active branch of Akkadian "science"—to judge from the volume and variety of texts that have survived—was the interpretation of omens. For the ancient Mesopotamian who was eager to divine what the future held in store, there was a vast written tradition for the interpretation of various natural phenomena: birds flying, ants on a wall, animals encountered on the street, the shape of the *exta* (abdominal organs, especially the liver) of a slaughtered sheep, the birth of animal or human monstrosities, the weather, eclipses—each had some significance for the future of the country or the individual. A properly trained diviner would consult the large clay handbooks of his trade and tell king or commoner what any of these happenings portended. To a certain extent, even the practice of medicine was handled in this way; the diviner would take note of the patient's physical symptoms and then ascertain from his tablets whether the patient was likely to recover or die.

Scientific Texts. Fortunately not all Mesopotamian science was of this type. There were also medical practitioners who could do more than give an oral diagnosis or prognosis and who actually prescribed pharmaceutical remedies for the sufferer, and there were specialists such as eye doctors. For glassmakers, there were tablets recording the complicated chemical processes and firing required for producing different types of glass. For mathematicians, there were handbooks of tables for multiplication, division, reciprocals, coefficients, square and cube roots, and collections of "problem" texts, which described by means of a concrete example the procedure for measuring the area of an irregular field, etc. In geography, there were maps with names in cuneiform and descriptions of the various regions of the known world. From the astronomers, we have records of their observations as well as computation texts, which contain the methods for computing certain celestial phenomena, such as the positions of the moon or planets or the time of an eclipse, and the results of such computations, i.e., ephemerides. Since until the time of the Seleucid era (312 B.C.) there were no fixed methods of computing years, there were long chronological texts listing the lengths of the reigns of various kings or, from earlier periods, recording the names given each individual year (usually from a significant contemporary event).

Belles Lettres. There were also genres in Akkadian letters that come closer to what we would term literature. These included epics such as the *Gilgamesh Epic (saga) and the cultic creation epic known from its first words as the **Enuma elish;* epics surrounding divine or semidivine mythological figures (Anzu, Adapa, Atrahasis, Irra, Etana, Ishtar); and epic cycles concerning kings, such as Naram-Sin, Tukulti-Ninurta I, or Nebuchadnezzar I. There was also fictional didactic and narrative verse such as the Dialogue of Pessimism, the Theodicy, and the *Ludlul bēl nēmeqi* ("I will praise the lord of wisdom," sometimes misnomered the Babylonian Job). There was a rich literature of religious songs and hymns, among which one may often encounter a rare beauty, such as the hymn of Assurbanipal to the sun god and the prayer to the gods of the night. From Mesopotamian folk literature have been preserved fables, proverbs, and a more sophisticated "disputation" genre, in which various animals, plants, or metals debated their relative usefulness. From extensive catalogues listing just the titles of literary pieces such as hymns, one can see how much Akkadian literature has not yet been recovered. In the later periods, when the spark of creativity waned among the scribal class, elaborate commentaries and explanations of obscure words in earlier literature were compiled; these are of help today in ascertaining the meaning of the frequent obscure passages in Akkadian poetry.

The richness and wealth of Akkadian literature has just begun to be exploited for the appreciation of the intellectual and material culture of the Babylonians and Assyrians. But as the knowledge of the Akkadian language grows (*see* ASSYRIOLOGY), and an ever-increasing number of Akkadian texts can be interpreted with greater facility, ancient Mesopotamia emerges into an ever clearer picture. One sees more and more its striking influence on countries such as Palestine, Syria, Anatolia, and even, via intermediaries, on Greece. Thus it affected the base of the cultural heritage of the modern Western world.

Bibliography: W. VON SODEN, *Grundriss der akkadischen Grammatik* (AnalOr 33; Rome 1952), the standard grammar of Akkadian. For dictionaries of Akkadian, *see bibliography of* ASSYRIOLOGY. A. L. OPPENHEIM, *Ancient Mesopotamia: Portrait of a Dead Civilization* (Chicago 1964). S. A. PALLIS, *The Antiquity of Iraq* (Copenhagen 1956). E. I. GORDON, "A New Look at the Wisdom of Sumer and Akkad," BiblOr 17 (1960) 122–132. W. G. LAMBERT, *Babylonian Wisdom Literature* (Oxford 1960). O. NEUGEBAUER, *The Exact Sciences in Antiquity* (2d ed. Providence 1957). For Eng. trs. of selections from Akkadian literature, see Pritchard ANET[2] 60–119, 161–188, 217–222, 265–317, 331–345, 383–392, 425–427, 434–440, 482–490. **Illustration credit:** The University Museum of The University of Pennsylvania.

[J. A. BRINKMAN]

AKUTAGAWA, RYŪNOSUKE, Japanese writer; b. Tokyo, March 1, 1892; d. Tokyo, July 24, 1927. He graduated from Tokyo Imperial University in 1916, and for several years taught at the Japanese Navy Engineering School. With the publication of some works written in his student days, he early acquired a reputation as an intellectual. His writings reveal the influence of the English and French literatures of the end of the century, his themes being death and the anguish of egoism, first treated in his earliest work, *Rōnen* (1914, Old Age). Aestheticism reigned in Japanese literary circles at the time; poets like Hakushū Kitahara, Mokutarō Kinoshita, and Kōnosuke Hinatsu expressed the quest for beauty in poems about the early Catholics in Japan. Furthermore in some 10 short stories delineating those early Catholics, Akutagawa dealt mainly with martyrs' selfless deaths. They include "Hōkyōnin no Shi" (1918, The Death of a Catholic), "Jashūmon" (1918, Heathendom), and "Juriano Yoshisuke" (1919, Yoshisuke Julian).

After the introduction of Protestantism to Japan in 1853, many writers became Christian, only to apostatize.

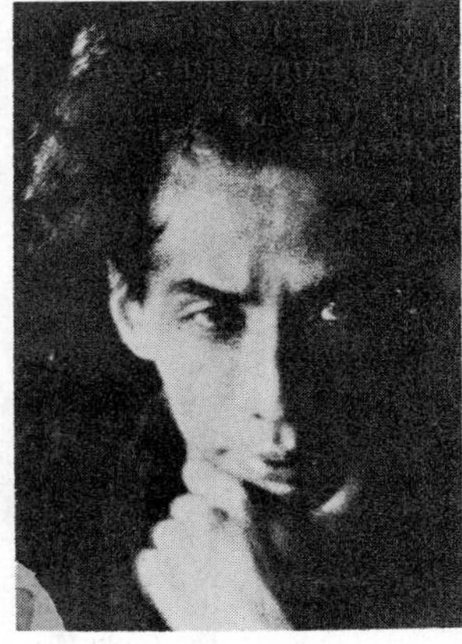

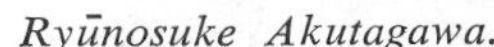

Ryūnosuke Akutagawa.

None of these wrote of Christ; Akutagawa did, although he was not baptized. He spent the month before his suicide in setting down his concept of Christ in the two essays, "Seihō no Hito" (1927, The Man from the West), and "Zoku Seihō no Hito" (1927, The Man from the West, II). Here he explains that his first interest was Christianity, especially Catholicism, an interest which then turned to Christians, and finally to Christ. He viewed Christ as a gifted journalist, poet, communist, Bohemian, and cultured man; he thought of Christianity as a didactic art created by Christ. And in the crucified Christ he saw himself, though with a deep doubt that resulted in his suicide on July 24, the night after he had completed the second essay on Christ. A Bible was found by his bed, yet his essays were not confessions of faith; despite his fascination with Christ he was not conscious of sin. To him faith seemed irrelevant. Akutagawa may be viewed as an agnostic who at once denied and recognized God. His concepts were closer to the spirit of Catholicism than those of any of his fellow writers.

Bibliography: Major works in Engl. tr. *Tales Grotesque and Curious,* tr. G. W. SHAW (Tokyo 1953); *Kappa,* tr. S. SHIOJIRI (Tokyo 1961). Collected works. *Akutagawa Ryūnosuke zenshū,* 20 v. (Tokyo 1954–56). Criticism. S. YOSHIDA, *Akutagawa Ryūnosuke* (Tokyo 1954).

[K. KODAMA]

ALABAMA

A state in the southeastern U.S., admitted to the Union (1819) as the 22d state. It has an area of 51,609 square miles and is bounded on the north by Tennessee, on the east by Georgia, on the southeast by Florida, on the south by the Gulf of Mexico, and on the west by Mississippi. The capital is Montgomery, and the largest city is Birmingham, with other centers of population at Mobile, Huntsville, Tuscaloosa, and Gadsden.

History. Cree, Cherokee, Choctaw, and Chickasaw Indians inhabited the area, which was explored by the Spanish in the 16th century. The first permanent settlement was made by the French at Mobile (1702). The Confederate States were organized at Montgomery (Feb. 4, 1861). The post-Civil War period marked the rise of Alabama industry, with the expansion of coal and iron mining. Industrialization was greatly increased during and after World War II, and Huntsville became a center for rocket research.

Religious affiliation in Alabama is largely Protestant; in the total state population of 3,061,743 in 1952 Catholics constituted only 1.6 per cent, while Protestants accounted for 32.2 per cent; Jews, 0.3 per cent; and all others, 65.9 per cent (*see* CHURCH MEMBERSHIP, U.S.). In 1964 Catholics numbered 124,731 in the state's total of 3,696,234 (*see* MOBILE-BIRMINGHAM, DIOCESE OF).

The state's institutions of higher learning include Tuskegee Institute, founded by Brooker T. Washington, and three under Catholic auspices, which in 1964 enrolled more than 2,000 students. There were 15 Catholic secondary schools (5,194 students) and 86 elementary schools (20,440 students), with an additional 6,321 students receiving religious instruction under Confraternity of Christian Doctrine programs.

Church-State Relations. References to and provisions affecting religion are incorporated in the state constitution and in acts of the legislature and the judiciary.

Constitution. Alabama is governed by the Constitution of 1901, as amended. The preamble invokes "the favor and guidance of Almighty God." Article 1, sec. 1, states that all men "are endowed by their Creator with certain inalienable rights." The oath of office required of all members of the legislature and all officers, executive and judicial, ends with "so help me God" (art. 16, sec. 279). Article 1, sec. 3, on religious freedom states "that no religion shall be established by law; that no preference shall be given by law to any religious sect, society, denomination, or mode of worship; that no one shall be compelled by law to attend any place of worship; nor to pay any tithes, taxes, or other rate for building or repairing any place of worship, or for maintaining any minister or ministry; that no religious test shall be required as a qualification to

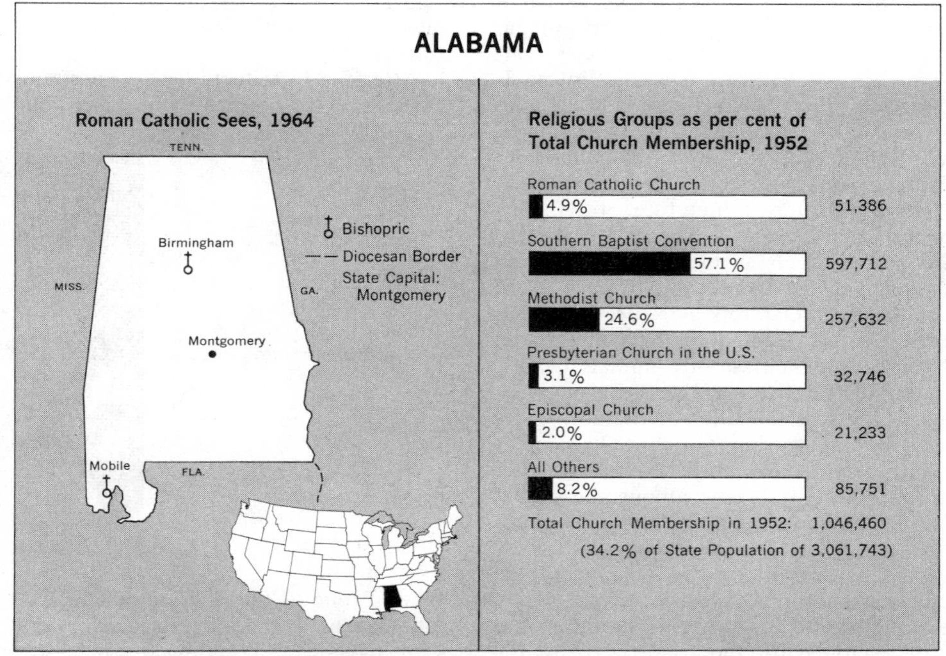

Church-membership statistics were compiled by the Bureau of Research and Survey of the National Council of the Churches of Christ in the U.S.A.

Spring Hill College, built in 1830 by Bishop Portier, first bishop of Mobile, mid-19th-century lithograph.

any office or public trust under this state; and that the civil rights, privileges, and capacities of any citizen shall not be in any manner affected by his religious principles."

There is a prohibition against the use of public school funds for the support of sectarian schools (art. 14, sec. 263). Appropriations made to charitable or educational institutions, not under the absolute control of the state, must be passed by a two-thirds vote of the senate and house of representatives (art. 4, sec. 73). Provision is made for the exemption from taxation of religious, educational, or charitable institutions (art. 11, sec. 217).

The legislature is prohibited from authorizing the marriage of a white person to a Negro (art. 4, sec. 102).

Lots 1 mile or more from town, with buildings used exclusively for religious worship and not exceeding 5 acres, are exempt from taxation (art. 4, sec. 91).

Registrants and electors must take an oath (art. 8, sec. 186, 188). All officers, executive and judicial, and members of the legislature must take an oath or affirmation ending in the words "So help me God" (art. 16, sec. 279).

Marriage and Divorce. Marriages of men under 17 and women under 14 are forbidden. The parents' consent is required if the male is under 21 and the female is under 18, unless the minor was previously married. A license and a blood test are needed. Marriages may be celebrated by clergymen and certain public officials. Common-law marriages are recognized.

Marriages are void if either party is bound by a prior subsisting marriage, unless the mate has remained absent for 5 years preceding the second marriage and it was not known if he was living; if the parties are related by blood in any degree of the direct line, and up to but not including first cousins; between a white person and a Negro (any person having Negro ancestors). Marriages may be annulled on the grounds of insanity, fraudulent intent not to perform the marriage vows, bigamy, incest, miscegenation, and nonage.

The grounds for absolute divorce are: incapacity; adultery; physical violence; abandonment for 1 year; imprisonment in the penitentiary for 2 years under a 7-year sentence; a crime against nature before or after marriage; 5 successive years in the insane asylum after marriage with the spouse confined and hopelessly and incurably insane when the bill is filed; final decree of divorce from bed and board or final decree of separate maintenance in effect over 4 years; the wife's pregnancy at time of the marriage without the husband's knowledge or agency; nonsupport for 2 years. If a wife abandons her husband, he is entitled to custody of the children after they reach 7 years of age if he is a suitable person. The court may, in its discretion, enjoin the divorced wife from use of the given name or initials of her divorced husband. Neither party may remarry (except each other) within 60 days after the decree or pending appeal. In certain cases the guilty party may not remarry for a longer time. *See* MARRIAGE, U.S. LAW OF; DIVORCE (U.S. LAW OF).

Abortion, Birth Control, Sterilization. The law forbids *abortion unless it is necessary to preserve the mother's life or health. Any person who willfully administers to any pregnant woman any drug or substance or uses or employs any means to produce an abortion, miscarriage, or premature delivery, or aids, abets, or prescribes for the same shall be confined for a period of up to 1 year.

Property and Taxation. Religious societies may incorporate under the nonprofit corporation statute or the religious corporation statute or other general or special laws. Charities may incorporate under the nonprofit corporation statute. The bishop of a diocese may become a corporate sole and hold the property and use it to conduct the business of the diocese. The incorporation of a church is not necessary to the existence of the church.

Real and personal property of religious societies and charities not run for profit is exempt from taxation.

There are no mortmain or fund-raising statutes.

Prisons and Reformatories. Chaplains are appointed by the governor. They devote their entire time to the moral improvement and religious instruction of the convicts. The prison director, with the governor's approval, must procure a sufficient number of Bibles and other reading matter for the convicts, not to exceed in cost $500 in any 1 year; it is the duty of the chaplain to distribute the same among the convicts.

Holidays and Sunday Observance. Sunday, Christmas, and New Year's Day, Thanksgiving Day, Mardi Gras Day, January 19, February 22, April 13, April 26, June 3, July 4, Labor Day, October 12, and November 11 are holidays. When holidays fall on Sunday, the next day is a holiday. Contracts are void if made on Sunday, except in cases of necessity or when they are contracts of a religious or charitable character. Shooting, hunting, gaming, card playing, and the holding of public markets and trading therein are forbidden. There is nothing that forbids the retailing of beer and whisky on Sundays by cafes and hotels that have a license to sell such beverages. Certain other activities depend on the size of a municipality and on local option.

Morality, Public Health, and Safety. No state condones polygamy. An Alabama statute forbids the disturbance of religious worship. It is unlawful for any person to display, exhibit, handle, or use any poisonous or dangerous snake or reptile in such a manner as to endanger the life or health of any person. This reptile statute does not violate either the Federal or state constitutional guarantees of freedom of religion [*Hill v. State* 88 So. (2) 880 - (1956); the Alabama supreme court refused to review the case].

Various Constitutional Freedoms. An ordinance requiring a reasonable license fee of transient distributors of books or pamphlets for sale on the streets, taking no account of the particular calling of the distributor, whether minister or layman, was found to be not unconstitutional as denying freedom of speech, press, or worship (*Jones v. City of Opelika* 242 Ala 549; See also 316 U.S. 584).

In a first-degree murder prosecution the solicitor for the state was permitted to ask each juror, during *voir dire* examination, whether such juror had any moral or religious scruples against capital punishment and whether the juror believed that the Bible taught that capital punishment was immoral. The court held that this was not reversible error and did not deny freedom of worship or due process of law [*Redies v. State* 9 So. (2) 914].

Bibliography: T. M. OWEN, "A Bibliography of Alabama," *Amer. Hist. Assoc. Annual Report 1897* (Washington 1898) 777–1248. J. H. PARKS and R. E. MOORE, *Story of Alabama* (Atlanta 1952). C. G. SUMMERSELL, *Alabama History for Schools* (Birmingham 1957). M. T. A. CARROLL, *A Catholic History of Alabama and the Floridas* (New York 1908). M. KENNY, *Catholic Culture in Alabama: Centenary Story of Spring Hill College* (New York 1931). *The Code of Alabama, 1940* (recompiled, Charlottesville, Va. 1958–).

[O. H. LIPSCOMB]

ALABASTER AND MARBLE

Alabaster (Greek, ἀλάβαστρος; Latin, *alabaster*), or limestone, a fine-grained variety of gypsum (calcium sulfate) often used for vases and other ornamental pieces. The best kind of alabaster is pure white, but translucent. Through a process of heating in nearly boiling water, it can be made nearly opaque, resembling marble (see below). Oriental alabaster, or the *alabastrides* of the classical writers, is obtained from stalagmitic or stalactitic calcium carbonate. It resembles certain kinds of onyx or onyx marble and is found in areas where limestone abounds. It is usually yellow in color, and its banded structure gives it a likeness to marble. Vases made of Oriental alabaster were highly prized by the Romans and the Greeks as containers for perfumes and precious ointments. Egyptians used it in their sarcophagi and as a lining for tombs, and on the walls of their temples for decorative purposes. This is the type of alabaster that is mentioned in the OT in 1 Chr 29.2: "I will have prepared . . . onyx and stones like alabaster." David left it with the other precious stones to Solomon for the building of the Temple. In the NT it is mentioned in Mt 26.7, Lk 7.37, and Mk 14.3 in connection with the anointing of Christ by the sinful woman. "There came to him a woman having an alabaster box of precious ointment and poured it on his head as he was at table" (Mt 26.7). This vase, though probably alabaster, was not necessarily so; for, because of the wide use of alabaster vases as containers for precious ointments, any container used for this purpose came to be known as an "alabaster," even though it might be made of some other material. Such alabaster usually had a narrow lip or spout for pouring the precious ointment and an elongated body rounded at the bottom.

The term marble (Greek, μάρμαρος) is technically confined to granular limestones and dolomites that have been recrystallized by nature under heat, pressure, and aqueous solutions. The most famous marble quarry in late antiquity was located at Carrara; it still produces exceptionally white marble. The so-called onyx marbles consist of concentric zones of calcite or argonite and constitute the *giallo antico* (ancient yellow) of Italian quarries, the reddish mottled Siena marble, and the Algerian onyx used in ancient Carthage and Rome.

Marble was used in ancient times particularly for sculpture and architectural ornamentation. Colored

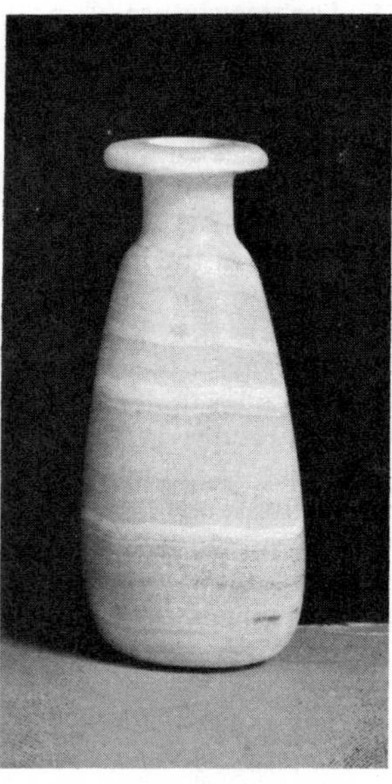

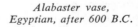

Alabaster vase, Egyptian, after 600 B.C.

marble was used by the Egyptians, while the earlier Greek and Roman sculptors preferred white marble for its sheer beauty. Christian sarcophagi (*see* SARCOPHAGUS) of marble have been discovered dating from the

The Holy Trinity, alabaster, English School, 14*th century, height* 33⅝ *inches, greatest width* 14 *inches.*

4th century, for example, the tombs of St. *Helena and of Constantia now in the Vatican Museum. Christian craftsmen continued the techniques of the classic marble trade, although most of the marble found in the earlier churches was appropriated from the ancient temples for pavement, wall ornamentation, and columns. During the Middle Ages, Christian architects sought a sober polychromic effect, usually associating one color with white marble. Churches in Tuscany and Liguria had both the façade and interior done in alternating bands of green and white (churches of Pistoia) or black and white (the cathedrals in Genoa, Milan, and Florence; St. Peter's, Portovenere). Roman churches abandoned the use of colored marble decor on the exterior in the late Renaissance, but Raphael's use of polychrome marble in the church of S. Maria del Popolo started a new fashion. During the baroque period there was an excessive use of marble decorations particularly in columns and wall decorations. The diaspore marble of Sicily was used at Rome in the churches of St. Mark and S. Maria in Via Lata; the yellow of Verona was employed in the Cybo Chapel of S. Maria del Popolo; while precious marbles were utilized for altars such as that of the Gesù and the Pauline Chapel in St. Mary Major, as well as for baldachinos and pulpits, reredos and various types of tables. Italian church styles were imitated in various parts of the world, and marble became a sign of elegance until the contemporary revolution in church architecture.

See also SCULPTURE.

Bibliography: O. BOWLES, *The Stone Industries* (2d ed. New York 1939). A. HERBECK, *Der Marmor* (Munich 1930). M. ZOCCA, EncCatt 8:169–171. **Illustration credits:** Fig. 1. Courtesy of the Walters Art Gallery, Baltimore, Md. Fig. 2. National Gallery of Art, Washington, D.C., Samuel H. Kress Collection.

[E. E. MALONE]

ALACOQUE, MARGARET MARY, ST., contemplative nun of the Visitation order (*see* VISITATION NUNS); b. Lauthecourt, France, July 22, 1647; d. Paray-le-Monial, Oct. 17, 1690 (feast, Oct. 17). Margaret was the fifth of seven children of Claude Alacoque, a royal notary, and Philiberte Lamyn. The family was esteemed by members of the nobility, whose names appear frequently as sponsors on the Baptism register. Margaret's education was limited to the training received in the home of her godmother and, after the death of her father, to the 2 years spent at the boarding school of the Urbanists, where she made her first Communion. Illness required her withdrawal, and the next 15 years were spent with her mother in painful dependence on near relatives. During this period, her attraction to suffering and her grace of contemplative prayer were intensified. On July 20, 1671, Margaret Mary entered Paray-le-Monial, and was professed November 6 of the next year. Between 1673 and 1675 she received the revelations. The first commissioned her to spread devotion to the *Sacred Heart; the second requested Communion and the *Holy Hour of reparation; the last expressed a wish for a special feast day in honor of the Sacred Heart. Margaret Mary lived the devotion, and amid contradiction and opposition worked for its recognition within her order. The exterior apostolate was confided to the Jesuits, among whom Bl. Claude de *La Colombière had been chosen to sanction the revelations. She was beatified by Pius IX, Sept. 18, 1864, and canonized by Benedict XV, May 13, 1920.

Bibliography: M. M. ALACOQUE, *Letters,* tr. C. A. HERBST (Chicago 1954); *The Autobiography,* tr. V. KERNS (Westminster, Md. 1961). L. GAUTHEY, ed. *Vie et oeuvres de la b. Marguerite-Marie Alacoque,* 2 v. (Paris 1915). P. BLANCHARD, *Sainte Marguerite-Marie: Expérience et doctrine* (Paris 1961). A. HAMON, *Vie de Ste. Marguerite Marie* (Paris 1924), with full bibliography. Butler Th Attw 4:134–138. J. BAINVEL, DTC 3.1: 320–351.

[M. L. LYNN]

ALAIN (ÉMILE AUGUSTE CHARTIER)

French philosopher, essayist, and schoolmaster, one of the great intellectual forces in France during the first half of the 20th century; b. Mortagne, France, March 3, 1868; d. Le Vésinet, June 3, 1951. Of Norman ancestry, he inherited the rugged common sense and obstinancy of the Norman peasant. Of Catholic parentage, he gave up his religious beliefs in youth and never became fully reconciled with Catholic dogma. After graduation from École Normale Supérieure, he taught in various lycées, finally becoming a professor of philosophy at Lycée Henry IV in Paris. His renown as philosopher and teacher extended to all parts of France, and many of his pupils attained eminence, among them the later biographer and historian André Maurois. Although after his retirement his home became a rendezvous for distinguished Frenchmen, he is not well-known outside his own country.

He wrote daily *propos* for the *Dépêche de Rouen.* These short essays, embodying his views on a variety of subjects, were collected from time to time and reissued. They form about half of his complete works and include *Les propos d'Alain* (1920), *Propos de littérature* (1933), and *Propos de politique* (1934). Among Chartier's other published works are *Le Citoyen contre les pouvoirs* (1925) and *Histoire de mes pensées* (1936).

Although his life was devoted to teaching and many of his works contain references to education, he wrote only one book on the subject, his *Propos sur l'éducation.* The style, though informal, is forceful, displaying an original mind. His educational philosophy shows the influence of G. F. Hegel rather than of J. J. Rousseau. His educational views followed few of the accepted patterns of his day. The task of the school was twofold: (1) making of citizens; and (2) integration, by which he meant the maintenance of the moral and intellectual man, who in turn makes the nation. To achieve this end, he favored the Napoleonic system of centralized control in education and austere educational surroundings. He advocated the early intense and detailed study of the best literature, and stressed mathematics, history, and geography with particular emphasis on geometry and Latin. He aimed to induce pupils to think long and deeply on worthwhile things and insisted that progress be slow and thorough with excellence as the main goal.

Chartier was mainly a conservative and looked askance at the "new education." He objected to observation lessons, so much insisted upon in the Decroly system (*see* DECROLY, OVIDE). He considered wasteful many of the motivational devices used in the modern school, holding that the child responds best to something challenging, and lightly dismissed the findings of psychology on individual differences. His own ideas on pupils' capacities were formed from his experiences with the select group that attends the French lycée. The concept of equality of opportunity did not interest him. The aim, he insisted, should be to discover and concentrate on excellence. He disregarded parental rights in education, holding that centralized state authority was best fitted to use the school as an instrument for achieving the "glory of France."

In France, between World Wars I and II, his teaching and extensive publications exercised a wide influence. This lay largely in strengthening and conserving the prevailing classical and French tradition of an elite excelling in scholarship and indirectly, therefore, obstructed the liberalizing and democratizing efforts of other educational leaders. He contributed nothing to furthering distinctly Christian ideals in French education.

Bibliography: J. CHATEAU, ed., *Les Grands pédagogues* (Paris 1956). A. MAUROIS, *Alain* (Paris 1949). G. PASCAL, *La Pensée d'Alain* (Paris 1946). "Hommage à Alain," *Mercure de France* 313 (1951) 581–661, made up of seven articles on various phases of Chartier's life and thought. C. L. HALL, "Alain, 1868–1951," SchSoc 76 (1952) 289–292.

[M. R. MC LAUGHLIN]

ALAIN, JEHAN, French organist and composer; b. Saint-Germain-en-Laye, Feb. 3, 1911; killed in action at Petit-Puy, near Samur, June 20, 1940. A member of a family of organists (including his father, Albert, and his sister, the prominent concert organist Marie-Claire), Jehan began his organ studies with his father, then at 16 entered the Paris Conservatory, where he took first prize in fugue and harmony. In 1934 he became a member of Marcel Dupré's organ class, taking first prize in organ in 1939; his composition teachers were Paul Dukas and J. J. Roger-Ducasse. He was organist of the church of Saint-Nicholas de Maisons Lafitte (1935–39) and received the *Prix des amis de l'orgue* in 1936 for his "Introduction, variations, scherzo et chorale." His works show a fresh vitality and originality without a conscious break with the tradition of the French organ school. Several of his organ works, such as the "Litanies," "Le Jardin suspendu," and "Postlude for the Office of Compline," have become staples of the recital repertoire. He also wrote extensively for piano, chorus, and various chamber combinations.

Bibliography: Organ works, 3 v. (Paris 1929–39); piano works, 3 v. (Paris 1929–38). B. GAVOTY, *Jehan Alain, musicien français* (Paris 1945). N. DUFOURCQ, *La Musique d'orgue française de Jehan Titelouze à Jehan Alain* (2d ed. Paris 1949). C. ROSTAND, *French Music Today,* tr. H. MARX (New York 1958). J. COMBARIEU and R. DUMESNEL, *Histoire de la musique,* 5 v. (Paris 1953–60) 5:283. F. GOLDBECK, Grove DMM 1:86. Baker 14.

[A. DOHERTY]

ALAMÁN, LUCAS

Mexican statesman and historian; b. Guanajuato, Oct. 17, 1792; d. Mexico City, June 2, 1853. He was in his native town when the war of independence broke out in 1810. The entrance of the insurgents in Guanajuato and their excesses impressed him and determined the critical attitude he held during the rest of his life toward that war and its leaders. That same year he began to study mineralogy, chemistry, and natural sciences in Mexico City. His passion for scientific knowledge never weakened his religious faith and his loyalty to the Church as frequently happened with other men of his time. In 1814 he went to Europe and visited Spain. While in Paris he studied in the Collège de France where he met Benjamin Constant, Mme. Récamier, Chateaubriand, and Mme. de Staël. In 1815 he traveled in England, Italy, and Germany. In 1820 he sailed for Mexico when Riego's revolution in Spain was restoring the liberal regime of the 1812 Constitution. The Spanish revolution opened an important chapter of his life. As soon as he reached Mexico, he was elected deputy in congress, and in that capacity he went to Spain in 1821.

While Alamán was traveling, *Iturbide brought about the independence of Mexico. Alamán came back in 1823 when the ephemeral Empire was falling, and the new provisional government appointed him secretary of foreign and internal affairs. Two legal projects date to that time: the first, to restrict the entry of colonists into Texas; the second, to establish the independence of Guatemala, then part of the Mexican Empire. He gave up the ministry in 1824, but the following year, at the inauguration of the republic, its first president, Guadalupe Victoria, recalled him for the ministry of foreign and internal affairs. There he contended with Joel R. *Poinsett, the U.S. ambassador, who was interested in concluding agreements adverse to the territorial and commercial interest of Mexico. Alamán left the ministry in September 1825 to devote himself to planning and executing industrial business projects, to studying, and to writing. In 1830 during the presidency of Bustamante, Alamán was again in charge of the ministry of foreign and internal affairs. He held this position until May 1832.

While away from the government for 20 years, he founded the spinning and weaving plant of Celaya, and gathered material for the historical works that were to make him famous. As a traditional Catholic with monarchial inclinations, he organized the Conservative Party, which brought *Santa Anna to the presidency in 1853. Alamán, destined to be the mastermind in the new regime, was minister for the last time. He died almost immediately, and Santa Anna, unrestrained, started a rule of personal dictatorship until the Ayutla revolution accomplished his ultimate expulsion from the country.

Alamán's *Disertaciones* (3 v., 1844–49) and above all, his *Historia de México* (5 v., 1849–52), are among the most important works of Mexican historiography.

Bibliography: J. C. Valadés, *Alamán: Estadista e historiador* (Mexico City 1938). J. Gurría Lacroix, *Las ideas monárquicas de don Lucas Alamán* (Mexico City 1951).

[J. FUENTES MARES]

ALAMANNI, a federation of West German tribal units that occupied the lands between the Upper Rhine and Danube during the Germanic migrations. The confederation originated among the Elbe-Saale *Suevi; the name first occurs in A.D. 213 when the Emperor Caracalla repulsed them from his frontier. By 258, however, they were flowing steadily into southwestern Germany, and the efforts of *Julian in 359 and the victories of *Valentinian I in 369–370 and Gratian in 378 failed to dislodge them, as they seized Raetia, modern Switzerland. After 443 the Burgundians blocked their expansion beyond Lake Geneva. They were neutral during Attila's campaign of 451. They invaded Alsace and took Trier in 480. Until *Clovis defeated them decisively in 496 (506?) at Tolbiac, they seemed to threaten Frankish expansion. The Ostrogoths protected them from a complete Frankish conquest, but after 526 Alamannia and Raetia became Frankish provinces.

The chief weakness of the Alamanni was their federal organization, which prevented a centralized government. During the Merovingian period, however, political power was gradually concentrated in a duke. The earliest version of their law, the *Pactus Alamannorum,* dates from *c.* 630; the final *Lex Alamannorum,* from the time of Duke Lantfrid (710–730). The Alamannic duchy lost its semiautonomy in 746 but reemerged in 911 as Swabia. The Alamanni remained pagan until at least 600, but they tolerated the Catholicism of their relatively few Roman subjects. The history of the bishoprics of Chur, Constance, and Basel during this period is obscure. St. *Columban, St. *Gall, and other Irish monks visited Lake Constance *c.* 610. The Alamannic conversion to Catholicism occurred inconspicuously during the 7th century.

Bibliography: O. Feger, *Geschichte des Bodenseeraumes* (Lindau 1956–) v.1. L. Schmidt, *Geschichte der deutschen Stämme* (2d ed. Munich 1940). H. Tüchle, LexThK[2] 1:264.

[R. H. SCHMANDT]

ALAMANNI, COSMO, Italian philosopher, theologian, and commentator on the works of St. *Thomas Aquinas; b. Milan, Aug. 30, 1559; d. there, May 24, 1634 (according to Sotwell) or July 24, 1634 (according to Ehrle). Alamanni entered the Jesuit novitiate at Novellara on Sept. 11, 1575, one of five brothers to do so; he studied theology at the Roman College under F. *Suárez and G. *Vázquez, and taught at Brera College in Milan. In 1590 he prepared for publication a theological opusculum entitled *Correctiones in Fonescam,* but it remained in MS only. Delicate health forced him to interrupt his teaching career in Milan after 17 years. In 1606 he was called to be the bishop's theologian at the Pavia curia, where he remained for 17 years also. During his sojourn in Pavia, Alamanni completed his *Summa totius philosophiae e divi Thomae Aquinatis doctrina* (Pavia 1618–23). This was edited a second time with augmentations by J. Frontenau (Paris 1640) and again by F. Ehrle (Paris 1885–94). The *Summa* presented a clear and accurate exposition of the teaching of St. Thomas, and was considerably influential in the revival of *Thomism in the 20th century.

Bibliography: *Summa philosophiae,* ed. F. Ehrle, 3 v. (Paris 1885–1894), pref. vi–viii. N. Sotwel, *Bibliotheca scriptorum Societatis Jesu* (Rome 1676) 161–162, 519. Sommervogel 1:113–114. L. Morati, EncFil 1:118. E. M. Rivière, DHGE 2:89. U. Viglino, EncCatt 1:621. B. Schneider, LexThK[2] 1:264–265.

[F. J. ROENSCH]

ALAN OF LILLE, Doctor Universalis; b. Lille, *c.* 1114–20; d. Cîteaux, 1202. Alan, one of the most original personalities of the 12th century, was well read and possessed of almost encyclopedic learning. He was a philosopher, theologian, preacher, polemist, poet, spiritual writer, and canonist; he was never submerged in any school. Nothing is known of Alan's first 40 years. It is possible that he was an auditor of *Gilbert de la Porrée. Allusions in his works indicate that he first lived and taught in *Paris *c.* 1157–70. This period was followed by residence and teaching in the Midi (Montpellier and perhaps Le Puy *c.* 1171–85). Then, perhaps, he returned to Paris. He finally retired to *Cîteaux where he died, seemingly as a simple Cistercian lay brother. He has been venerated within the order as blessed. His remains were exhumed June 22, 1960, and the well-preserved skeleton was that of a man 88 to 92 years of age. Most of Alan's theological writing dates from his first residence in Paris. The *Summa, Quoniam homines,* unfortunately incomplete (ed. P. Glorieux, 1954), is remarkable for its Dionysian and Platonic inspiration. Though somewhat later than the *Sentences* of Peter Lombard, it is completely original. Numerous *Questiones disputatae,* as yet unedited, also date from this period at Paris. Alan's *Theologicae regulae* inaugurated a new form of axiomatic theology. To this epoch belongs also the first of Alan's great poetical works, the *De planctu naturae,* half verse, half prose. Alan's next work, a near classic, the *Liber parabolarum,* consisted of proverbs on moral conduct, in verse. More than 70 of Alan's sermons are extant; his *Summa de arte praedictoria* is one of the earliest works on preaching theory. To Alan's years in the Midi belong the *Contra haereticos,* which refutes the theses of the *Waldenses, *Albigenses, Jews, and Saracens; the *Liber distinctionum theologicarum,* a kind of Biblical dictionary; and the popular *Penitential,* the present edition of which is very defective. One of Alan's greatest works, the *Anticlaudianus* (ed. R. Bossuat, 1954), was written *c.* 1184, probably in the Midi but perhaps at Paris. This vast epic, which inspired *Dante and *Chaucer, depicts Nature as she strives to create the perfect man.

The hero of the Epic is not Christ but the chevalier of the *chansons de geste*. Two spiritual treatises, *De sex alis Cherubim,* and *Elucidatio super Canticum Canticorum,* are extant. The authenticity of the *Commentarium . . . Merlini* and the *Liber de naturis animalium* is questionable. The *De articulis catholicae fidei* has been restored to Nicholas d'Amiens.

Bibliography: Works. PL 210. O. Lottin, "Le Traité d'Alain de Lille sur les vertus, les vices et les dons du Saint Esprit," MedSt 12 (1950) 29–45. Literature. Manitius 3:794–804. Cross ODCC 28. A. M. Landgraf, LexThK[2] 1:266. P. Glorieux, RRG[3] 1:212. S. Vanni-Rovighi, EncFil 1:118–119.

[P. GLORIEUX]

ALAN DE LA ROCHE, or Alanus de Rupe, founder of the modern rosary devotion and of the Confraternities of the Rosary; b. somewhere in Brittany, date unknown; d. Zwolle (Holland), Sept. 8, 1475. Although called blessed, he was never officially beatified. Little information about his life is historically certain. He entered the Dominicans probably at an early age at Dinan in Brittany. After his profession he was sent to the convent of St. Jacques in Paris for his philosophical and theological studies, and subsequently he lectured there. The date of his ordination is not known. He filled professorships in different convents of his order: from 1462 he was at Lille, where, from 1464, the Dominican convent belonged to the *Congregatio Hollandica;* in 1464 he was at Douai, and in 1468, at Ghent. It is questionable whether he went to the University of Rostock (Germany) in 1470. In 1474 he went to Zwolle. Along with his teaching he may have preached often, though there is no solid historical information on this point. His works on the rosary were not printed until after his death; e.g., by J. A. Coppenstein, OP (*B. Alanus de Rupe Redivivus,* Freiburg 1619), but this edition exhibits a worked-over text and is uncritical and incomplete. Alan gave the Hail Mary, which existed in various forms, the precise form in which it became popular. He divided 150 Ave's into 3 series of 50, introduced the Our Father before each 10, and treated in accompanying articles or statements the mysteries of the birth, Passion, and glory of Christ. In 1470 he founded at Douai the first Confraternity of the Rosary. His fantastic visions, in which, for example, it was said that the Blessed Virgin commissioned St. Dominic to institute the rosary, should be regarded as a quite normal means of religious propaganda in Alan's period.

Bibliography: *Beatus Alanus de Rupe Redivivus,* ed J. A. Coppenstein (Naples 1630), the most accessible ed. and later reprints. R. Coulon, DHGE 1:1306–12. Quétif-Échard 1.2: 849–852. B. de Boer, "De Souter van Alanus de Rupe," *Ons Geestelijk Erf* 29 (1955) 358–388; 30 (1956) 156–190; 31 (1957) 187–204; 33 (1959) 145–193, best study to date, with detailed bibliog.

[C. BRAKKEE]

ALAN OF TEWKESBURY, Benedictine abbot, writer; d. 1202. Alan entered the monastery at Canterbury in 1174 on his return from Benevento where he had been a canon. When Herlewin resigned in 1179, Alan became prior. He incurred the enmity of *Henry II because he supported Thomas *Becket, obtained the privilege of collecting *Peter's Pence, and objected to the choice of *Baldwin as archbishop of Canterbury. Though Alan later recognized Baldwin, the latter transferred him to the abbey of *Tewkesbury, where he was abbot in 1186. Alan wrote a life of Becket and an account of the Clarendon Council (*see* CLARENDON, CONSTITUTIONS OF). Also extant are his letters to Henry concerning the translation of Becket's remains, and to Baldwin claiming for Canterbury certain rights over the see of *Rochester.

Bibliography: *Materials for History of Abp. Thomas Becket,* ed. J. C. Robertson, RollsS 67.2:299–352. Gervaise of Canterbury, *Historical Works,* ed. W. Stubbs, RollsS 73.1:293. J. B. Mullinger, DNB 1:214–215. R. Biron, DHGE 1:1318. Ghellinck Essor 1:132; 2:174–175.

[M. L. MISTRETTA]

ALAN OF WALSINGHAM, monk, reputedly an architect of *Ely, England; d. Ely *c.* 1364. He became subprior, sacristan (1321–41), and prior (1341) at Ely. In these offices he was concerned with cathedral building projects and has been spoken of as architect of the Lady chapel (now Trinity Church, Ely), the chapel of Prior Cranden, and the famous "Lantern," the cathedral's octagonal central dome erected after the Norman tower fell (1322). Recent emphasis on the role of the medieval master mason as designer casts some doubt upon the architectural role of the monk, even if the idea to build was his. Master masons William Ramsey and William Hurley are now considered the probable designers of the 14th-century additions. Alan was twice elected bishop of Ely by the monastic chapter and twice put aside by Rome, in favor of Thomas Lisle in 1344 and *Simon Langham in 1361.

Bibliography: E. I. Bell, DNB 1:215–216. J. H. Harvey, *The Gothic World, 1110–1600* (London 1950). H. Dauphin, DHGE 15:363, 366. E. Miller, *The Abbey and Bishopric of Ely* (Cambridge, Eng. 1951).

[F. M. BEACH]

ALANS, a nomadic Iranian people occupying the steppe region between the Caucasus Mts. and the Don and Ural Rivers early in the Christian era. They figured occasionally in Roman affairs before falling under the domination of the Huns *c.* A.D. 350, with whom they moved westward into Ostrogothic territory. One group advanced into central Germany, joined the Vandals in Gaul 406–409, and crossed into Spain under their chieftain Respendial. Decimated there by Visigothic *foederati* in 418, the survivors merged with the Vandals and accompanied Gaiseric into Africa. Another Alan contingent near Orleans fought with the Roman general Aetius against Attila in 451. Liberated from the Huns after 455, the main body of Alans drifted back to the steppes. Moslems and Mongols dominated them during the Middle Ages. They finally withdrew into the central Caucasus where their descendants survive as the Osset nation. The only ancient report of the Alans' religion says that they worshipped a sword fixed in the ground. Those who associated with the East Germans probably absorbed some Arianism, but their conversion as a tribe came only after Patriarch *Nicholas I of Constantinople (901–925) sent the monk Euthymius to evangelize them. Nicholas then established the metropolitan see of Alania whose Orthodox history can be traced to 1590.

Bibliography: S. Vailhé, DHGE 1:1334–38. E. A. Thompson, *A History of Attila and the Huns* (Oxford 1948). F. Dvornik, *The Making of Central and Eastern Europe* (London 1949). G. Deeters, LexThK[2] 1:265.

[R. H. SCHMANDT]

ALANUS ANGLICUS

A medieval canonist of Welsh origin, date and place of birth and death unknown. He was one of the leading professors at Bologna in the decade preceding the Fourth Lateran Council (1215); possibly he and his fellow countryman *Gilbertus Anglicus ended their days as Dominicans. Both *decretist and *decretalist, his collection of decretals suggests English affiliations: he may have studied or taught law in England before the Bologna period or at least may have had some connection with John of Tynmouth and his associates in the English schools (*see* CANON LAW, HISTORY OF, 4). *Tancred, in the preface of his *Apparatus* to the *Compilatio tertia antiqua,* speaks of him simply as an English professor in the schools of Bologna. The extant works of Alanus are: *Collectio decretalium* (*c.* 1206), a critical register of which has been published by R. von Heckel (see bibliography); *Apparatus* to *Compilatio prima antiqua* (after 1207); glosses on *Compilatio secunda antiqua* (shortly after 1210 or 1212); *Apparatus Decretorum* (*Ius naturale*). Some have held that he was the author of *Compilatio quarta antiqua,* but this was definitely *Joannes Teutonicus.

The apparatus *Ius naturale* is one of four great apparatuses on Gratian's *Decretum* that appeared at Bologna between 1190 and 1210. A first recension dates from about 1192, a second from some 10 years later. As Stickler has shown (1959), the two recensions differ doctrinally: whereas, for example, Alanus originally was in the Gelasian-Gratian tradition of the juridical independence of the spiritual and secular powers, he had shifted by 1202 to a theocratic position. However, although some consider Alanus to be the architect of those curialist doctrines of papal sovereignty that eventually crystallized in the **Unam sanctam* of Boniface VIII, he was simply responding to a wind that was blowing from the *Summa* of *Huguccio. (*See* CHURCH AND STATE.) The *Collectio Decretalium* of Alanus is one of the many systematic collections of decretals that appeared about this time (*see* DECRETALS, COLLECTIONS OF). A first version had an appendix of 111 chapters; in a second version, which was that "received" at Bologna, Alanus inserted these chapters into the body of his collection, distributing 412 decretals in 484 chapters. Except for a division into six books instead of the classic five and some additional decretals, it follows the layout of the collection (1202–03) of Gilbertus Anglicus and appears to owe something to Anglo-Norman collections. With that of Gilbertus, the *Collectio Alani* is the principal source from which *John of Wales formed his *Compilatio secunda antiqua* (1210–12) after the publication of Innocent III's official *Compilatio tertia antiqua* in 1210 (*see* QUINQUE COMPILATIONES ANTIQUAE).

Bibliography: Schulte 1:84, 188–189. Kuttner 67–75, 316, 325, 346. R. VON HECKEL, "Die Dekretalensammlungen des Gilbertus und Alanus nach den Weingartener Handschriften," ZSavRGKan 29 (1940) 116–357. Stickler 231. S. KUTTNER, "The Collection of Alanus: A Concordance of Its Two Recensions," *Rivista di storia del diritto italiano* 26–27 (1953–54) 39–55. A. M. STICKLER, "Alanus Anglicus als Verteidiger des monarchischen Papsttums," *Salesianum* 21 (1959) 346–406; LexThK[2] 1:265–266. See also "Bulletin of the Institute for Research and Study in Medieval Canon Law," *Traditio* 16 (1960) 557–558; 17 (1961) 534–536.

[L. E. BOYLE]

ALARCÓN Y MENDOZA, JUAN RUIZ DE,

Spanish dramatist; b. Mexico City, 1581?; d. Madrid Aug. 4, 1639. By 1600 he had qualified at the Royal and Pontifical University of Mexico for the bachelor's degrees in both civil and Canon Law, but he did not take either. Instead, he journeyed to the University of Salamanca, then the foremost university in Spain, where he was granted the degrees of Bachelor of Canon Law on Oct. 25, 1600, and of civil law on Dec. 3, 1602.

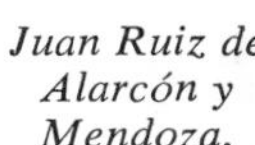

Juan Ruiz de Alarcón y Mendoza.

In 1606 he moved to Seville, where he practiced law until his return to Mexico (1608). A year later he received his licentiate in law from the University of Mexico and attempted unsuccessfully to obtain a professorial chair at that university. By 1614 he had taken up permanent residence in Madrid.

Between 1614 and 1626 Alarcón wrote the plays that have won for him an enduring place among the great Spanish dramatists. When in 1626 he was appointed to a post with the Council of the Indies, he withdrew from the literary scene, although he subsequently published two collections of his works, one containing 8 plays (Madrid 1628), the other containing 12 (Barcelona 1634). From his last will and testament, drawn up 3 days before his death, we learn that he had a daughter, Lorenza de Alarcón.

Living as he did in an age when physical defects were seldom greeted with sympathetic understanding, Alarcón continually received from his fellow writers jeers and taunts directed at his short stature, bowed legs, and humped back and chest. Perhaps because he was thus repeatedly exposed to a lack of charity, he concentrated in his plays upon the problems of human conduct and gave to his drama an ethical significance that has led some critics to call him the greatest moralist of the Spanish classic theater. His dramatic corpus—20 authentic plays, 9 others attributed to him—seems slight compared to the prolific work of the three other major dramatists with whom he is ranked, Lope de *Vega, *Tirso de Molina, *Calderón de la Barca; yet the heritage he left to Spanish drama is scarcely less significant than theirs. His plays, often didactic in intent, show striking originality of plot, lively dialogue, sensitive character delineation, and a highly polished versification.

Two of Alarcón's most famous plays are *La verdad sospechosa,* which attacks the vice of lying, and *Las* *paredes oyen,* which demonstrates the reprehensibleness of slander. The first of these directly influenced French comedy; *Corneille translated and adapted it as *Le Menteur* (1643) and often said that he would give two of his best works to have written it. Other well-known plays by Alarcón are *Los favores del mundo, Mudarse por mejorarse, El Tejedor de Segovia* (*segunda parte*), *La prueba de las promesas,* and *El examen de maridos.*

Bibliography: *Obras completas,* ed. A. MILLARES CARLO (Mexico City 1957–). A. CASTRO LEAL, *Juan Ruiz de Alarcón: Su vida y su obra* (Mexico City 1943). W. POESSE, "Ensayo de una bibliografía de Juan Ruiz de Alarcón y Mendoza," *Hispanofila* 14 (Jan. 1962) 1–21; 15 (May 1962) 29–56; 17 (Jan. 1963) 36–78. **Illustration credit:** Embassy of Spain, Washington, D.C.

[R. R. LA DU]

ALASKA

A vast peninsula with its network of islands in northwest North America, admitted to the Union (1959) as the 49th state. It is the largest (571,065 square miles) state in the U.S.; its southern part borders on the Pacific Ocean, while its main territory comprises all of North America west of the 141st meridian. The area, including the Aleutians, is known for its fishing, pulp mills, and mining, and it contains the capital *Juneau, which is also the see city of Alaska's first diocese. The northern part, a wide expanse of tundra sloping gently westward toward the Bering Sea and on the north toward the Arctic Ocean, constituted a vicariate apostolic from 1916 to 1962, when it became the Diocese of *Fairbanks. On Feb. 9, 1966, the Archdiocese of *Anchorage was established.

History. The first known Christian missionaries in Alaska were the Franciscans Juan Riobo and Matias de Santa Catarina y Noriega who sailed with the Spanish Arteaga expedition in 1779. They landed on the southern coast of Prince of Wales Island, Bay of Bucareli, and Riobo celebrated a high Mass of thanksgiving (May 13, 1779), the first recorded act of public worship in present Alaska. Priests of the Russian schismatic church first established missions in Alaska. In 1787 Shelikoff of the Russian American Company petitioned the Holy Synod for missionaries to the Aleuts. The Archimandrite Ivassof with nine companions arrived in Kadiak in 1794 and from this base they penetrated the Alaskan archipelago, the Bering Coast, and finally the interior, reaching Yukon and Kuskokwim villages. Protestant missionaries followed the Russians, and as early as 1853 a Lutheran parish had been established in Sitka. Six years later Archdeacon Robert McDonald of the Church of England left La Pierre House on the Porcupine in Canada to visit Alaskan villages. Other Episcopalian clergymen who followed him founded missions at Nukluroyit, Anvik, and other places. After the U.S. acquired Alaska (1867), Moravians, Presbyterians, Methodists, Swedish Evangelicals, and Congregationalists established missions there. The Presbyterians, who arrived in 1878, have been the most active and also the most successful.

The first Catholic missionaries to penetrate into Alaska were the Oblates of Mary Immaculate. In 1862 Rev. Jean Sequin proceeded from northwestern Canada into Russian Alaska to Fort Yukon, arriving there on

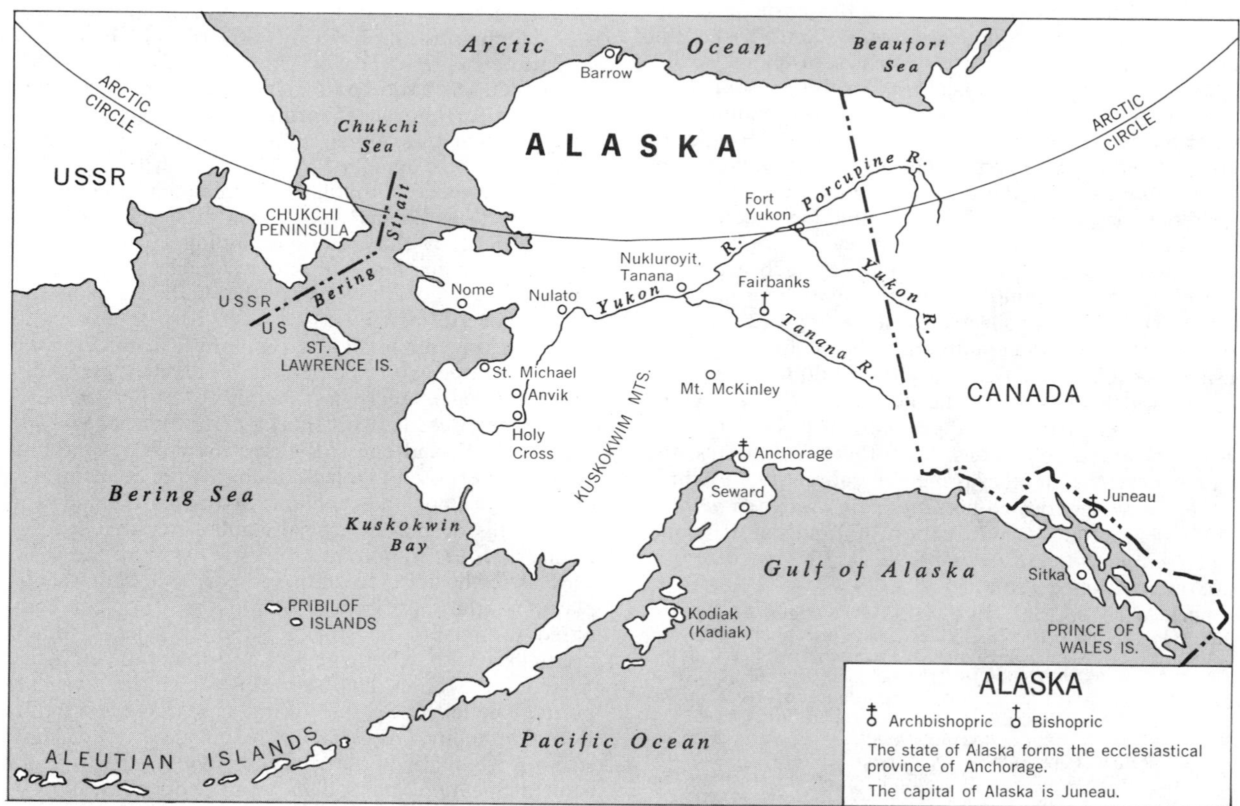

Fig. 1. Map of Alaska showing sites important in the development of the Church in the area.

Fig. 2. Joseph Raphael Crimont, first bishop of Alaska.

Fig. 3. Mission of Our Lady of the Snows, Nulato, on the Yukon, founded 1887

ALASKA

Fig. 4. Ursuline nuns and school children at St. Mary's Mission, Akulurak, 1912.

September 23. He spent a depressing winter and left the following June, having accomplished nothing. In 1870 Rev. Emile Petitot traveled from the same base at Good Hope to a new Fort Yukon built by the Americans. He was cordially received but achieved little. Two years later Bp. Isidore Clut with August Lecorre, then a secular priest, arrived at Fort Yukon to establish a mission. Disappointed with results, they left the following spring for St. Michael, where success awaited them. When Bishop Clut left for Canada on July 7, 1873, Lecorre remained at St. Michael. He too returned to Canada during the following year when he was informed that Alaska was attached to the Diocese of Vancouver Island.

Archbishop Charles Seghers of Vancouver Island made five journeys to Alaska: to the southern panhandle in 1873, 1879, and 1885; to the interior with Rev. Joseph Mandart in 1877; and finally to the interior in 1886 when he was murdered. On this last trip he was accompanied by two Jesuits, Aloysius Robaut and Paschal Tosi, who returned the following year with two other Jesuits and missions were established at Holy Cross, Nulato, and other places. From this time (1887) the Catholic development of Alaska was slow and painful. Its rigors of climate, vastness of area, sparseness of population, and high cost of material means have made it one of the most difficult mission areas in the world. By the 1960s advanced means of travel and communication had made the work of pastor and missionary more effective, but the more intimate relations with secular developments in the states had created new problems of adjustment. In 1951 Catholics represented 15 per cent of the total population. Ten years later when the total population was about 227,000, Catholics numbered approximately 35,500.

Church-State Relations. References to and provisions affecting religion are incorporated in the state constitution and in acts of the legislature and the judiciary.

Constitution. Alaska is governed by the Constitution of 1956. The preamble states that the people are "grateful to God" and that they want to "secure and transmit" their religious liberty. "No law shall be made respecting an establishment of religion, or prohibiting the free exercise thereof" (art. 1, sec. 4). There is a prohibition against the use of public funds for the direct benefit of any religious or private educational institution (art. 7, sec. 1). All property used exclusively for nonprofit religious, charitable, cemetery, or educational purposes is exempt from taxation (art. 9, sec. 5).

Impeachments of civil officers and judges are tried in the house of representatives (art. 2, sec. 20 and art. 4, sec. 12). All public officers must take a designated oath or affirmation before taking office (art. 12, sec. 5.

Marriage and Divorce. Marriages of men under 18 and women under 16 are forbidden. The consent of parents is needed for men under 19 and women under 18. A license and blood test are necessary. The ceremony may be performed by clergymen and certain public officials; no particular form is needed.

Marriages are void if either party is bound by a prior subsisting marriage, or if the parties are related by blood in any degree of the direct line, and up to, but not including, first cousins.

Marriages may be annulled upon suit of the injured party on the ground of nonage, insufficient understanding, force, or fraud. Common-law marriages are not recognized if attempted since 1917.

The grounds for absolute divorce are: impotency from the time of marriage up to the action for divorce; adultery; conviction of a felony; willful desertion for 1 year; cruelty impairing health or endangering life or person; unbearable indignities; incompatibility of temperament; habitual and gross drunkenness, continuing for 1 year before the commencement of the action; willful neglect by the husband in not providing the common necessities; incurable mental illness when the spouse has been confined to an institution for at least 18 months preceding the commencement of the action; addiction after marriage to the habitual use of drugs. There are no restrictions on remarriage. *See* MARRIAGE, U.S. LAW OF; DIVORCE (U.S. LAW OF).

Abortion, Birth Control, Sterilization. The law forbids *abortion unless it is necessary to preserve the mother's life. A person administering to a pregnant woman any medicine, drug, or substance whatever, or who uses an instrument or other means, with the intent to destroy the child, before or after quickening is, if the death of the child or mother is thereby produced, guilty of manslaughter.

There are no references to birth control, contraception, anovulants, or sterilization in the state code.

Property and Taxation. Religious societies may incorporate either under the nonprofit corporation statute or the religious corporation statute. Charities may incorporate under the nonprofit corporation statute. The property of such congregation, parish, or mission is held by the bishop as a corporation sole. A bishop also holds the property for an unincorporated religious society.

Real and personal property of religious societies and charities, not run for profit, is exempt from taxation. There are no fund raising statutes.

Prisons and Reformatories. There are no statutes concerning chaplains or religious matters.

Holidays and Sunday Observance. Sunday, Christmas and New Year's Day, Labor Day, Thanksgiving Day, and Memorial or Decoration Day, February 12, February 22, March 30, July 4, October 18, and November 11 are holidays. If a holiday falls on a Sunday, the next day is also a holiday. Places serving alcoholic beverages keep the same hours on Sunday as they do the rest of the week. They close from 5 A.M. to 8 A.M. each day.

Morality, Public Health, and Safety. No state condones polygamy. Alaska's disorderly conduct and disturbance of the peace statute does not specify disturbance of religious meetings. The chapter on basic science excludes from its restrictions the practice of the religious tenets of a church by mental or spiritual means exclusively. Generally a physical examination of children in elementary and secondary schools is required, but no child is obliged to submit to a physical examination if his parent or guardian objects on the grounds of religious principles.

Various Constitutional Freedoms. The right to picket peacefully and truthfully is one of organized labor's lawful means of advertising its grievances to the public, and as such is guaranteed by the constitution under freedom of speech (*Glover v. Retail Clerk's Union Local 1382,* 10 Alaska 274).

Bibliography: C. L. ANDREWS, *The Story of Alaska* (Seattle 1931; repr. Caldwell, Idaho 1938). E. H. GRUENING, *The State of Alaska* (New York 1954). C. C. HULLEY, *Alaska: Past and Present* (rev. ed. Portland, Ore. 1958). J. E. CHAMPAGNE, "First Attempts at the Evangelization of Alaska," *Études Oblates* 2 (Jan.–March 1943) 13–22. G. MOUSSEAU, "L'Affaire d'Alaska," *ibid.* 5 (July-Sept. 1946) 161–188. *The Constitution of the State of Alaska, 1956* (Fairbanks 1956), Index (Juneau 1960). *Alaska Statutes Annotated, 1962* (Charlottesville, Va. 1962–).

[W. P. SCHOENBERG]

ALB, a long white linen tunic worn as an undergarment for most liturgical functions. It is gathered in about the waist by means of a cincture. It has its origin in the Greco-Roman *tunica talaris,* a garment of daily use reaching to the ankles and decorated at the bottom and extremities of the sleeves with colored bands. Even though the influence of the short garments of the Germanic peoples brought about a change in fashion, the clergy did not follow it, continuing instead to dress in the traditional Roman style. By the 6th century, the wearing of albs was an established custom for the celebration of the liturgy. Although the interest in color during the Gothic period brought about the appearance of colored albs, white has always been traditional. The 16th century saw the rise of the lace industry; only then did lace appear on albs—an innovation that was a regression from the masculine and dignified robe of the past. Eventually lace, at first a mere ornament, covered most of the garment. The liturgical renewal of the 20th century has brought about the return of the all-linen alb.

Alb tied with cincture.

Bibliography: H. NORRIS, *Church Vestments* (New York 1950). E. A. ROULIN, *Vestments and Vesture,* tr. J. MCCANN (Westminster, Md. 1950). J. BRAUN, *Die liturgische Gewandung im Occident und Orient* (Freiburg 1907).

[M. MC CANCE]

ALBAN, ST., protomartyr of the English Church (feast, June 22). He was a pagan soldier serving in the Roman army at Verulamium (now the city of Saint Albans, Hertfordshire, England). *Gildas and *Bede, both of whom wrote their histories long after the episode, relate Alban's martyrdom to the persecution of Diocletian (302–305). Some historians doubt that this movement reached England and have attempted to connect the death with the earlier persecution of Decius (249–251). Still others have suggested that the execution was carried out under martial law in 283 or 286 and not as a result of a general edict against Christians. According to tradition Alban protected a Christian priest from his persecutors and was converted by him. Alban was then summoned before a military tribunal, where he admitted to being a Christian and was scourged and later beheaded. A church and, later, the Abbey of *Saint Albans were erected on the site of his martyrdom.

Bibliography: J. A. DUKE, *The Columban Church* (London 1932; repr. 1957). R. G. COLLINGWOOD and J. N. L. MYRES, *Roman Britain and the English Settlements* (2d ed. Oxford 1937). C. E. STEVENS, "Gildas Sapiens," EngHistRev 56 (1941) 353–373, esp. app. W. LEVISON, "St. Alban and Saint Albans," *Antiquity* 15 (1941) 337–359. Butler Th Attw 2:612–614.

[B. F. BYERLY]

ALBANI, distinguished Umbrian family of Urbino who were prominent in the Church in the 18th and 19th centuries. The most influential member of the family was Pope *Clement XI (1700–21); three of his nephews and a grandnephew were cardinals, all of them closely associated with the papal curia.

Annibale, papal diplomat; b. Urbino, Aug. 15, 1682; d. Rome, Sept. 21, 1751. He was created cardinal in 1711 by his uncle and was appointed bishop of Sabina in 1730. During most of Clement's reign, Annibale was one of the most active diplomats in the Vatican service, occupying in succession the post of nuncio in Vienna, Dresden, and Frankfurt. He exerted considerable influence in the elections of both Innocent XIII and Benedict XIV. He left a valuable library, gallery of paintings, and a collection of coins and antiques to the Vatican collection. Among his literary works was the edition of the writings of Clement XI.

Alessandro, brother of Annibale; b. Urbino, Oct. 19, 1692; d. Rome, Dec. 11, 1779. He was created cardinal by Innocent XII (1721), after he had distinguished himself in the papal diplomatic service. While he was always involved in the political life of the curia, he was primarily a scholar, and after 1761 he was director of the Vatican Library. He was a patron of the arts and a friend of the foremost collectors of antiques; he gained renown for his building of the Villa Albani in Rome, in which he housed a valuable collection of Greek and Roman sculpture.

Giovanni Francesco, a third nephew of Clement; b. Rome, Feb. 26, 1727; d. Rome, Sept. 1803. He was cardinal bishop of Ostia. He was spokesman for the Austrians in the papal curia, and toward the end of his career, was dean of the Sacred College of Cardinals and particularly influential in the election of *Pius VII.

Giuseppe, Giovanni Francesco's nephew; b. Rome, Feb. 26, 1750; d. 1834. He, too, was created cardinal (1801) after some years of service in Vienna. He was secretary of state to *Pius VIII.

Bibliography: E. RE, EncIt 2:95. Pastor v. 33, 34, 35. M. DECAMILLIS, EncCatt 1:638–641. P. RICHARD, DHGE 1:1369–73.

[C. B. O'KEEFE]

ALBANIA

European country in the Balkans, 11,100 square miles in area, bordered by Yugoslavia, Greece, and the Adriatic Sea. A census in 1961 registered 1,660,000 inhabitants, of whom 140,000 dwelt in Tirana, the capital. The Albanians are descendants of the ancient Illyrians and refer to themselves as *Shquipëtars* and to their country as *Shqipëria.* Besides those dwelling in Albania there are 900,000 Albanians in Yugoslavia, 100,000 in Greece, 100,000 in Italy, 10,000 in the U.S., and 5,000 elsewhere. The Albanian language belongs to the Indo-European family, and is written in Latin characters with many diacritical signs. Albanians retain a tribal system and a special manner of life; they are noted for courage, a warlike but religious spirit, and moral integrity. After the Roman occupation in the 2d century B.C., Albania was subjected to Latinizing influences that came from the North. At the same time Hellenizing influences penetrated from the South. Both of these cultural factors are still perceptible in the Albanian language. The two influences meet at the Skhumbi River. When Gratian made an administrative division of the Roman Empire (379), Albania was placed in the eastern section, then later pertained to the Byzantine Empire. As part of the Prefecture of Illyricum Orientale, it formed the provinces of Epirus Vetus (with its capital in Nicopolis, modern Preveza), Epirus Nova (with its capital in Dyrrhacium, modern Dürres), and Praevalitana (with its capital in Scodra, modern Shkodër). During the Middle Ages this area

Map of Albania showing Latin and Orthodox sees.

changed masters several times, being subject to Goths, Slavs, Avars, Serbs, Bulgaro-Macedonians, Normans, and Venetians. From the 15th century to 1912 it was under Turkish rule. Albania became a principality in 1912, a republic in 1925, and a kingdom in 1928. Since 1946, with the Communists in control, it has been known as the People's Republic. Albania supported the U.S.S.R. in 1949 when the latter broke with Yugoslavia. This alliance weakened after Stalin's death, and was replaced by a close understanding between Albania and Communist China.

Christianity in Albania. Christianity came to Albania from Rome in the form of the *Latin rite and from Greece in the form of the *Byzantine rite. There is, however, no evidence about the time and manner of its arrival. It antedated the Council of Sardica (343–344), since five bishops attended this synod from Epirus Nova and Dardania. The Slav invasion (*c.* 600) destroyed the ecclesiastical organization and caused the inhabitants to retire to the mountainous districts, where they lived as shepherds, gradually reverting to primitivism. There is a void of historical records concerning the Albanians from the 7th to the 11th centuries. After the 11th century groups moved southward and settled extensively in Greece as far south as Attica, where they adopted the Byzantine rite and adhered to the *Eastern Schism. Northern Albania remained Catholic and retained the Latin rite. After the formation of the Slav principality of Dioclia (modern Montenegro), the metropolitan See of *Bar was created (1089). Dioceses in northern Albania became its suffragans. From 1019 Albanian dioceses of the Byzantine rite were suffragans of the autocephalous Archdiocese of Ohrid (or Okhrida) until Dyrrhacium and Nicopolis were reestablished as metropolitan sees. Thereafter only the dioceses in inner Albania remained attached to Ohrid. In the 13th century during the Venetian occupation, the Latin Archdiocese of Dyrrhacium was founded.

Turkish invaders in the 15th century met heroic resistance in northern Albania from the Catholic tribes under the leadership of George Castriota (1403–68), known as *Scanderbeg. After Scanderbeg's death the Turks occupied Albania, except for some sections held by Venice, until 1912. During the centuries of Turkish rule the majority of the Albanians became Moslems, especially in central Albania during the 17th and 18th centuries. Frequently this change of religion was merely external. Many families remained crypto-Catholics and preserved Christian traditions and usages, such as Baptism, veneration of saints, pilgrimages, and dietary regulations. As a result there evolved a kind of Islamo-Christian syncretism. The expansion of Islam diminished during the 19th century under Austrian protection, but it did not cease until 1912.

Latin-rite Catholics. For several centuries the care of Catholics in northern Albania was confided almost exclusively to the Franciscans. Pope Clement XI (1700–21) was particularly eager to help these Catholics, because his family, the Albani, had migrated from Albania to Italy in the 15th century. At his insistence the first Albanian national synod convened in Shkodër in 1703. Attempts to establish a seminary were made in the 18th century, but they did not succeed until 1856, when Italian Jesuits opened in Shkodër a pontifical college, to which a seminary was later attached. The Jesuits set up a printing press. In their popular missions they

The 14th-century church of St. Nicolas, Lezh, Albania.

strove to abolish the custom of blood vendetta. The Archdiocese of Bar became part of the newly established principality of Montenegro in 1878, and by the terms of the concordat with Montenegro (1886) it ceased to be the metropolitan see for Albania. Shkodër replaced it the same year as metropolitan see, with all Albanian dioceses except Durrës as its suffragans.

Byzantine-rite Christians. The Byzantine rite prevails in southern Albania and among the Albanians in Greece and Italy. The Eastern Schism entered Albania gradually. Union with Rome persisted in some mountainous districts until the 17th century; it was supported by national opposition to the Greek and Slav hierarchy, by some archbishops of Ohrid, and especially by the populace in the Chimarra district that sent several petitions during the 16th and 17th centuries to have clergy sent there from Rome. In 1628 the Congregation for the Propagation of the Faith dispatched to Chimarra graduates of the Greek College in Rome and Basilian monks from southern Italy. Athanasius II, Archbishop of Ohrid and a refugee in Chimarra, united with Rome in 1660 and consecrated one of the missionaries as bishop of the Byzantine rite. This mission was abandoned in 1765 when entry was barred to Catholic missionaries; it was not restored until Basilian monks came from Italy (1938–45).

After the Turkish occupation of the 15th century, a large number of Albanians migrated to southern Italy to preserve their faith and to escape Turkish oppression. Many eventually adopted the Latin rite. Their descendants still dwell as Catholics in Calabria and Sicily. In 1963 there were 33,000 belonging to the Latin rite and 70,000 pertaining to the Byzantine rite (*see* ITALO-ALBANIAN RITE).

Most present-day Albanians in the Byzantine rite are Orthodox. For centuries the hierarchy and the liturgical language of this rite in Albania was Greek. When Albania proclaimed its independence in 1912, the Albanian Orthodox, under the leadership of Fan Noli, a priest, claimed the status of an autocephalous church and introduced the vernacular into the liturgy. Not until 1937, however, did the Patriarchate of *Constantinople officially recognize this situation. The Orthodox in Albania have four dioceses under the metropolitan of Tirana. Orthodox Albanians in Greece are members of the Greek Orthodox Church. In the U.S. an autonomous Albanian Orthodox diocese exists whose archbishop resides in Boston. Fan Noli occupied this post from 1930 to 1965. Following the Communist victory in Albania, this U.S. see proclaimed its independence.

Since 1945. In 1945 the Communists began a severe persecution of the Catholic Church on the pretext that Catholics sided with Italy, which occupied Albania in 1939. All Italian missionaries were imprisoned. Several of them were eventually put to death, and others were banished, including the apostolic delegate. The persecution extended equally to the native hierarchy and clergy and to Catholic schools and the seminary. Two Albanian bishops were sentenced to death; others were imprisoned. The Albanian Catholic Church was cut off from all contact with Rome or with other countries. In 1951 the clergy was given a special status in accordance with Communist laws. Three Catholic bishops were residing in the country in 1964.

The Orthodox Church imitated the Russian Church and adapted itself to the changed situation by recognizing the Communist government and its proceedings. As a result it received better treatment than the Catholic Church; yet religious conditions in Albania are among the worst in Communist countries.

Reliable religious statistics have been unavailable since 1945. In 1944 about 830,000, constituting 70 per cent of the inhabitants, were Moslems, at whose head was a mufti in Tirana. At that time the 120,000 Catholics made up 10 per cent of the populace. All but 400 of them belonged to the Latin rite. There were 131 parishes, 93 secular and 94 regular priests, and 230 religious women. Since 1938 northern Albania has been under the jurisdiction of Propaganda; southern Albania, under the Oriental Congregation. Catholic Albanians in the U.S. had no priests or parishes in 1964. An Apostolic Administration of South Albania was established in 1939 for Catholics of the Byzantine rite. Until his expulsion in 1945 the apostolic delegate filled the post of administrator. The Catholic Church of this rite was destroyed by the Communist persecution. For the Latin rite there exists the metropolitan See of *Shkodër, whose suffragans are Lesh (Lezhë), Pult, and Sapë; the Archdiocese of *Durrës, immediately subject to the Holy See; and the Abbey *nullius* of Orosh.

The Orthodox Church, with about 250,000 adherents, constituted 20 per cent of the population in 1944. It retains a metropolitan see in Tirana, whose suffragan sees are Berat, Korrçë (Korçë), and Gjinokastër. The Albanian Orthodox diocese in the U.S. had about 5,000 members in 1964.

Bibliography: D. FARLATI and G. COLETI, *Illyricum sacrum,* 8 v. (Venice 1751–1819), v.7. L. VON THALLÓCZY et al., *Acta et diplomata res Albaniae mediae aetatis illustrantia,* 2 v. (Vienna 1913–18), contains documents for period 344–1406. M. ŠUFFLAY, "Die Kirchenzustände in vortürkischen Albanien," *Illyrisch-albanische Forschungen,* ed. K. JIREČEK, 2 v. (Munich 1916) 1:188–281. M. E. DURHAM, *Some Tribal Origins, Laws, and Customs of the Balkans* (London 1928). G. PETROTTA, "Il cattolicesimo nei Balkani. L'Albania," *La Tradizione* 1 (1928) 165–203; *Popolo, lingua, e letteratura albanese* (2d ed. Palermo 1932). F. W. HASLUCK, *Islam and Christianity under the Sultans,* ed. M. HASLUCK (Oxford 1929). H. LECLERCQ, DACL 7.1:89–180. M. SPINKA, *A History of Christianity in the Balkans* (Chicago 1933). N. BORGIA, *I monaci basiliani d'Italia in Albania,* 2 v. (Rome 1935–42). G. CARACI et al., EncCatt 1:644–650. G. STADTMÜLLER, "Altheidnischer Volksglaube und Christianisierung in Albanien," OrChr Per 20 (1954) 211–246; "Die Islamisierung bei den Albanern," *Jahrbücher für Geschichte Osteuropas,* NS 3 (1955) 404–429; "Das albanische Nationalkonzil vom Jahre 1703," OrChrPer 22 (1956) 68–91; LexThK[2] 1:271–272. **Illustration credit:** Eastfoto.

[M. LACKO]

ALBANIAN LITERATURE

The Sons of the Eagle (Shqyptár), as Albanians call themselves, are among the oldest peoples of Europe. Of Illyrian and partly Thracian descent, they inhabit the region between Greece and Yugoslavia, on the west coast of the Balkan Peninsula. There are about 3 million Albanians, of whom more than a third live in the bordering countries. The Albanian language is an independent member of the Indo-European language group. There are two main dialects, Geg and Tosk, with little difference between them; a common phonetic Latin alphabet was adopted (1908, Congress of Monastir).

Albanians have a rich oral literature of heroic and lyric songs, tales, and proverbs. The heroic songs are called *Kangë Trimnijet* (Songs of Valor); among the best are those of the cycle around the legendary heroes, Mujo and Halil. The highest ideals of the hero are honor, loyalty, magnanimity, hospitality, and the protection of the innocent. The finest collection of heroic songs is in the 15-volume *Visaret e Kombit* (Nation's Treasure).

Beginnings to 19th Century. The oldest known written document in Albanian, preserved in the Bibloteca Laurentiana in Florence, is a baptismal formulary contained in a pastoral letter written Nov. 8, 1462, in Latin, by Paul Engjelli, Archbishop of Durci. As a result of the Turkish conquest in 1479, many Albanian intellectuals emigrated to Italy and elsewhere. They wrote mainly in Latin and Italian, but supply valuable information about the cultural conditions of Albania at that time. Martin Barleti, a priest (*c.* 1450–1512), wrote the *Siege of Shkoder,* a history of the Turkish conquest, and *The Life of Scanderbeg,* the national hero in the struggle against the Turks. After a century of Turkish domination, few Albanians could understand Latin or Greek; the clergy were obliged to translate liturgical books and catechisms into the vernacular. The translation in 1555 of the Missal, by Gjon Busuku, a priest, is fundamental for a knowledge of the development of the Albanian language. The first poem in Albanian was written by Lekë Matranga (1562–1619), a priest born at Hora e Arbereshëve, Sicily; he published this together with a translated short catechism by Pedro *Ledesma, SJ.

Pjeter Budi (1566–1623), Bishop of Sapa and Sarda, a champion of liberation, is considered the first original writer in prose, though even some of his poems show unmistakable talent. His main work is *Doktrina e Krishtênë* (1618, *Christian Doctrine*). Frano Bardhi (1606–43), Bishop of Sapa, compiled and edited the first Latin-Albanian dictionary, which contained more than 5,000 words and a life of Scanderbeg in Latin. Pjeter Bogdani (1625–89), Bishop of Shkoder and later Archbishop of Shkup, wrote *Çeta e Profetve* (1685, Phalanx of the Prophets), a landmark in the development of Albanian prose. During the 18th century, there was hardly any new work in Albanian literature worth mentioning if we except Gjon Kazazi's *Catechism* (1743), De Lece's *Grammar,* and especially *Gjella e Shën Mrís Verjin* (1762, Life of the Virgin Mary), by Jul Variboba.

About 200,000 Albanians fled to different parts of Europe before the Turks. Those settling in southern Italy and Sicily developed a literature of their own, which reached its peak with Jeronim De Rada (1814–1903), whose chief work was the romantic *Kangjellet e Milosaos,* a love story of two simple people. Other Italo-Albanians followed in the steps of De Rada: Anton Sartory (1819–94), a priest, wrote the first original drama in Albanian, *Emira* (1886), and a book of poems, *Valle Hares Madhe* (1848, Hymms to the Great Joy); Zef Serembe (1843–1901) was a talented, romantic poet; Leonardo da Martino, OFM (1830–1923), a missionary in Albania and teacher of *Fishta, published his poems in *Arpa e nji Italo-Arebreshit* (1881, The Harp of an Italo-Albanian); and Zef Schirò published at the turn of this century his idyl, *Mily e Haidhija* and *Te Dheu i Huej.* In Albania itself, literary production up to 1880 was small. There are some works of religious and didactic character, especially those of Prênk Doçi (1846–1917), Abbot of Mirdita, best known for his patriotic poems, *Zâni i Kasnecave* (1867, The Voice of the Heralds), and for founding the literary society *Bashkimi* (1899). Filip Shiroka (1859–1935) wrote poetry in a romantic-elegiac vein, and Luigj Gurakuqi (1879–1925), writer and statesman, was famous for oratory and romantic poetry.

19th Century and After. For most of the 19th century, Albanian literature was dominated by Catholics, especially priests and religious. Toward the end of the century, other elements of Albanian society entered the literary scene, but the Catholic voice was still strong, especially in the work of Mjeda and Fishta.

Naim Frashëri (1846–1900) was one of the outstanding poets of the Tosk dialect. His masterpiece is *Bagëti e Bujqësi* (1886, Cattle and Land) and his lyrics are gathered in *Lulet e Verës* (1890, Spring Flowers). His writings show Persian and Arab influence and his philosophy is pantheistic, with a mixture of religious ideas from the Moslem sect Bektashism. The fame of Konstantin Kristoforidhi (1827–95), an Albanian of the Orthodox church, is connected with the translation of the Bible (1867), which is considered a classic in Albanian prose. Faik Konitza (1875–1942), a Moslem, was one of the best prose writers of Albania. From 1897 to 1909, he published his review, *Albania,* where many of his works can be found. He became prewar minister of Albania to Washington. Çajupi (pseudonym for Andon Çako, 1866–1930) wrote lyric poetry and is renowned for his *Baba Tomory* (1902, Father Tomori). Ndre Mjeda (1866–1937), priest, teacher, and pastor, published his first poem, *Vaji i Bylbylit* (Lamentation of the Nightingale), in 1887; his *Juvenilia* (1917) includes his finest poems. Though predominantly a romantic, he imitated the classics in his later years. Vincenc Prennushi (1885–1954), Franciscan, Bishop of Sapa and later Archbishop of Durc, published an important collection of folksongs, *Kangë Popullore Gegnishte* (1911, Popular Songs in the Geg Dialect). His best lyrics were collected in *Gjeth e Lule* (1931, Leaves and Flowers). The towering figure in the 20th century is Gjergj Fishta. Among others of the period Ernest Koliqi (1903–) excels. His fame rests chiefly on his short stories, *Hija e Maleve* (1929, The Shade of Mountains) and *Tregtar Flamuish* (1935, Merchant of Flags), and his lyric poems, *Symphonija e Shqypeve* (Symphony of Eagles).

Bibliography: G. Schirò, *Storia della letteratura albanese* (Milan 1959). S. E. Mann, *Albanian Literature* (London 1955). G. Petrotta, *Svolgimento storico della cultura e della letteratura albanese* (Palermo 1950).

[A. NARGAJ]

ALBANY, DIOCESE OF (ALBANENSIS)

Suffragan of the metropolitan See of *New York embracing 10,419 square miles of east-central New York. As originally established on April 23, 1847, the diocese was 30,000 square miles in area; it was subsequently reduced by the creation of separate sees at Ogdensburg (1872) and Syracuse (1886).

Early History. Among the pioneer missionaries of the area were Isaac Jogues, SJ, and his companions, whose work with the Iroquois Confederacy began in 1642 (*see* NORTH AMERICAN MARTYRS). French missionaries under the jurisdiction of the bishops of Quebec, Canada, continued to labor north of Fort Orange (Albany); one of them, Jacques de Lamberville, baptized Kateri *Tekakwitha, the "Lily of the Mohawks," whose cause for beatification was introduced in 1943. When the English gained control of the Hudson River Valley (1664), Fort Orange became Albany in honor of James, the Duke of York and Albany. A Catholic, Thomas *Dongan, became first governor in 1682. From 1688 to the Revolutionary War, Catholics in the English colonies were under the ecclesiastical jurisdiction of the vicar apostolic of London. In 1790 John Carroll was consecrated the first bishop of the U.S. and his Diocese of Baltimore, Md., included all territory east of the Mississippi River except Florida. In 1808 New York State and half of New Jersey were made a diocese.

Diocese. Population in the Albany area increased during the first half of the 19th century because of expanded steamboat travel, the building of the Erie Canal, and the construction of railroads. Political, economic, religious, and social upheavals in Europe forced refugees to America, many of whom settled along the Hudson-Mohawk Valley. Thus in 1847 the Holy See established the Diocese of Albany and named John J. McCloskey, then coadjutor bishop of New York, as Albany's first ordinary, May 21, 1847. The new diocese had a Catholic population of approximately 60,000 served by 38 priests in 47 parishes. The cornerstone for Immaculate Conception Cathedral was laid July 2, 1848; meanwhile St. Mary's Church served as temporary cathedral. By 1864, when McCloskey was transferred to New York, the Albany diocese had a Catholic population of 290,000, with 95 priests, 120 churches, and 27 schools. Under his immediate successors, John J. Conroy, who was consecrated Oct. 15, 1865, and retired Oct. 16, 1877, and Francis McNierney (d. 1894), the diocese was reduced in size by the erection of separate sees at Ogdensburg and Syracuse. Albany's fourth bishop, Thomas M. A. Burke, was consecrated July 1, 1894, and governed until his death on Jan. 20, 1915. The Cathedral of the Immaculate Conception, completed by McNierney, was consecrated by Burke on Nov. 16, 1902. Thomas F. Cusack, former auxiliary to the archbishop of New York, ruled as fifth bishop of Albany from 1915 to 1918 and was succeeded by Edmund F. Gibbons (d. 1964), who was consecrated March 25, 1919, and governed until his retirement on Nov. 10, 1954. During his administration the number of parishes increased to 195, high schools to 21, and elementary schools to 83. Gibbons established the *Evangelist* (1926), a diocesan weekly newspaper; was cofounder with Bp. John Cantwell of Los Angeles, Calif., of the National Legion of Decency; and established the first Albany diocesan seminary (1954). He was succeeded by William A. Scully, who had been appointed coadjutor Aug. 21, 1945. On June 27, 1957, Edward J. Maginn was appointed auxiliary bishop.

In 1964 the diocese had a Catholic population of 397,894 served by 437 diocesan and 283 religious priests, 144 brothers, and 1,875 sisters. There were 11 parochial, 4 diocesan, and 9 private high schools; 104 elementary schools; and 4 colleges—College of St. Rose, Albany; St. Bernardine of Siena College, Loudonville; College of Holy Names, Albany; and Maria College, Albany. Diocesan priests staff Mater Christi Seminary; separate seminaries are maintained by the Missionaries of La Salette; Vincentians; Franciscans, Minor Conventuals; Mill Hill Missionaries; and Franciscans, Friars Minor. Two Newman Centers serve Catholic students attending New York State Teachers College at Oneonta, and Hartwick College and State University College at Albany. Sixteen other secular colleges have Newman chaplains. Five retreat houses serve men, women, and high school boys and girls. The diocese supervises five summer camps and four day camps.

Lay organizations include the Legion of Mary, Nocturnal Adoration Society, St. Vincent de Paul Society, First Friday Luncheon Clubs, Knights of Columbus, Catholic Daughters of America, Knights of St. John, Catholic War Veterans, National Council of Catholic Nurses, Ladies Catholic Benevolent Association, Catholic Central Union of America, National Catholic Women's Union, Catholic Young Adult League, Catholic Interracial Council, Catholic Society for the Deaf, Christian Family Movement, Communication Arts Guild, St. Luke's Guild, and Young Christian Workers.

Six shrines located in the diocese are dedicated to Our Lady of La Salette (Altamont), North American Martyrs (Auriesville), Kateri Tekakwitha (Fonda), Immaculate Conception (Haines Falls), Our Lady of Lourdes (New Lebanon), and St. Jude (Schodack Landing). The National Office of the Family Rosary Crusade, under the direction of Patrick Peyton, CSC, is located in Albany.

Bibliography: *Centenary Dedication of the Cathedral, Albany, New York* (1952). J. J. DILLON, *The Historic Story of St. Mary's, Albany, N.Y.* (New York 1933). J. H. KENNEDY, *Thomas Dongan: Governor of New York, 1682–1688* (CUA StAmChHist 9; Washington 1930). M. A. LEARY, *The History of Catholic Education in the Diocese of Albany* (Washington 1957). M. C. SEVIER, *History of the Albany Cathedral of the Immaculate Conception, 1852–1927* (Albany 1928). F. J. ZWIERLEIN, *Religion in New Netherlands* (Rochester, N.Y. 1910).

[J. P. BERTOLUCCI]

ALBAR OF CÓRDOBA, the foremost example of Latin culture in Moslem Spain; b. Córdoba?, *c.* 800; d. date and place unknown. In five of his letters he calls himself *Paulus,* the Little One, rather than Paul. He was a landowner, probably of the highest nobility, a layman trained in law, it seems, active in religious and secular affairs. In his correspondence (20 letters) he debated about the Messiah with the apostate to Judaism, Bodo-Eleazar (840); disputed over theology and the use of rhetoric with John of Seville (*c.* 850); and engaged the Abbot Esperaindeo in a discussion of heterodox ideas (*c.* 851). The remaining letters reveal Albar's legal difficulties over land given to a monastery and difficulties with his ordinary, Bishop Saul, about spiritual discipline. Albar wrote 540 of the 613 metrical lines of rather bad descriptive verse of this period in Córdoba (ed. L. Traube, MGPoetae 3.1:122–142). The *Indiculus luminosus* (854) attacked critics of the martyrs of Córdoba and contains one of the earliest known polemics against Islam. Albar's spiritual works, the vita of his friend, the martyr *Eulogius of Córdoba (*c.* 860), and the *Confessio,* a devotional manual for contrition apart from the Sacrament of Penance, contain traces of mystical thought.

Bibliography: Flórez EspSagr 10. PL 121:397–566. C. M. SAGE, *Paul Albar of Córdoba* (Washington 1943). E. P. COLBERT, *The Martyrs of Córdoba (850–859)* (Washington 1962).

[E. P. COLBERT]

ALBELDA, ABBEY OF, former Benedictine monastery of St. Martín in the Diocese of Calahorra, Spain, 6 miles south of Logroño. The fortress *Albailda* (Arabic: "white") built by Muza II of Saragossa in 850 was destroyed by Ordoño I of Oviedo in 851. However, hermits, there as monks probably before 850, formed a monastery soon afterward and in 924 grouped themselves under the Benedictine Rule with a large number of monks sent there from León by Ordoño II. In 951 the abbey had 200 monks and was a famous center of learning. In 976 the monks (Vigila) completed the beautifully illuminated codex *Albeldensis* (Escorial d-I-2) that contains a collection of 61 councils, the valuable *Chronicle of Albelda* of 883, and other items in Visigothic script. A copy of the *Albeldensis* (Escorial d-I-1) completed in 994, a *Liber ordinum* of 1052 (now in *Silos) sent to Rome in 1064 for the approval of the *Mozarabic liturgy, several other extant codices of the 10th century, and several lost codices (including works by Salvus, d. 962) gave the scriptorium of Albelda a fame that *Alfonso X recognized in 1270. From 1033 to 1092 the bishops of Calahorra-Nájera resided in Albelda, and the monks became secularized canons. In 1435 the canons, the treasure, and many documents of Albelda were moved to Santa María la Redonda in *Logroño. The cartulary of the abbey (891–1092) went to Simancas. Archeological remains of the monastery, recently discovered, seem to be Visigothic in style.

Bibliography: C. J. BISHKO, "Salvus of Albelda . . .," *Speculum* 23 (1948) 559–590. M. ALAMO, DHGE 11:327–333.

[J. PÉREZ DE URBEL]

ALBERDI, JUAN BAUTISTA

Argentine lawyer and political theorist; b. Tucumán, Aug. 29, 1810; d. Neuilly, France, June 19, 1884. His Spanish father, Salvador Alberdi, a liberal and a fervent admirer of Rousseau, was granted Argentine citizenship by the Congress of 1816 for his support of the revolutionary cause. After completing his elementary studies, Alberdi was sent to Buenos Aires in 1824 to enter the Colegio de Ciencias Morales on a scholarship provided by *Rivadavia. He dropped out before the end of the year to go into commerce, but on the advice of Florencio Varela, he returned to school. There he became acquainted with Miguel Cané, who, seeing that he was alone and without relatives, invited him into his house. When the Colegio was closed in 1830, Alberdi and his companions transferred to the University of Buenos Aires, where he participated in the cultural activity of the university and the city in that period.

Literary Apprentice. He began writing about music, which he never ceased to practice despite his predilection for politics. In 1832 he published *El espíritu de la música* and *Ensayo sobre un método nuevo para apren-*

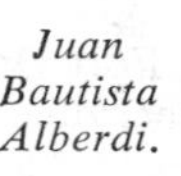

Juan Bautista Alberdi.

der a tocar el piano con toda facilidad, which opened the doors of the salons to him. His prose style was more fully developed in his *Memoria descriptiva sobre Tucumán* (1834). His *Contestación al Voto de América* (1835) answered José Rivera Indarte's work and showed his legal talent. He demonstrated that talent also in *Fragmento preliminar al estudio del derecho* (1837), in which he developed the theories of the historical school, applying them to his country. He participated in the literary salon and contributed to *La Moda.* He was a member of the Young Argentina group and drafted the 15th symbolic article of the *Dogma socialista* of Esteban Echeverría, which reflected the ideas of the earlier Unitarists and Federalists.

Literary Protagonist. In August 1838 Alberdi emigrated to Montevideo and collaborated on *El Iniciador,* directed by Andrés Lamas and Miguel Cané. In association with these two friends and José Rivera Indarte, he edited *El Nacional* and then went on to start the periodicals *El Talismán, Muera Rosas, El Corsario,* and *El Porvenir,* in collaboration with Cané. In 1839 they published *La Revista del Plata,* a journal to support the plans of Lavalle and to oppose Rosas. Alberdi obtained his law degree in 1840 and at once attracted attention in the courts. About this time he wrote his theatrical work *La Revolución de Mayo* and, in 1841, *El Gigante Amapolas.* He defended the French intervention in La Plata and supported the campaign of Fructuoso Rivera and Lavalle against Rosas, as secretary of Lavalle's expedition. Before Oribe laid siege to Montevideo, Alberdi went to Europe. In France he visited General José de *San Martín, of whom he wrote a moving literary portrait. In 1844 he went through Rio de Janeiro and settled in Chile. He revalidated his law degree in Santiago with his *Memoria sobre la conveniencia y objeto de un Congreso General Americano,* which was destined to lay the foundations of American international law. In Valparaíso he was active in his profession and continued to produce forceful writings. Some of his defenses were famous. His ideas attracted the leading men of Chile. In 1845 he published *Veinte días en Génova*, and in 1846, the *Biografía del General don Manuel Bulnes* and other works.

Political Theorist and Practitioner. On May 1, 1852, he published his celebrated *Bases y puntos de partida para la organización política de la República Argentina*, placing at the end of this work the draft of the constitution that he thought should be adopted by the country. His work was most useful in the period of national organization. In 1854 the government of Uruguay named him chargé d'affaires in England and France, later extending his territory to include Spain and Rome. In the aftermath of the battle of Pavón, he lost his post, and he remained in Europe. After an absence of more than 4 decades, he returned to Argentina in 1879 as a national deputy for Tucumán. The next year he wrote a work of singular interest: *La República Argentina consolidada* . . . . Not being able to overcome the old antagonisms, he returned to France. There he received word of his appointment as Argentine minister in Chile, but his health did not permit him to travel, and he became commissioner of immigration, a position he held until his death in a sanatorium in Neuilly. He was one of the greatest political thinkers of his age.

Bibliography: J. Mayer, *Alberdi y su tiempo* (Buenos Aires 1963). E. Quesada, *La figura histórica de Alberdi* (2d ed. Buenos Aires 1919). A. Salvadores, *Juan Bautista Alberdi* (Buenos Aires 1948). B. Canal Feijoo, *Constitución y revolución: Juan Bautista Alberdi* (Buenos Aires 1955). **Illustration credit:** Library of Congress.

[V. O. CUTOLO]

ALBERDINGK THIJM, JOSEPHUS ALBERTUS, Dutch poet and pioneer of Catholic emancipation; b. Amsterdam, Aug. 13, 1820; d. Amsterdam, March 17, 1889. He grew up in a middle-class family and embarked on a business career, but he soon started to write romantic poems with a mystical tinge. He later developed a theory that the connection of art and beauty with religion should be an intrinsic part of human life and of society. A militant Catholic, he combatted the mediocrity and narrow-mindedness of many fellow Catholics. Against them he defended the necessity of good theater and a friendship with non-Catholic authors, in whose periodicals he wrote essays and poetry. He equally contested growing agnostic materialism, for example, in *Het Voorgeborchte* (1851) and *Magdalena van Vaernewijck* (1851). In this respect he followed his admired master, Willem Bilderdijk (1756–1831), Holland's first romantic poet and the protagonist of a Protestantism based on sentiment. The poet E. J. Potgieter (1808–75) gave his friend Thijm the title of Catholic romantic and encouraged him to elevate Catholic culture.

Under this impulse, Thijm began to understand the greatness of Holland's 17th-century "golden age," a period he had considered pagan and heretical. He became the enthusiastic admirer of *Vondel, Holland's greatest poet. Thijm's *Portretten van Joost van den Vondel* (1876) inaugurated a long series of studies of Vondel by Catholic scholars. Prior to his interest in the 17th century, Thijm had seen in the Middle Ages, then generally thought of as "dark," support for his ideals of Catholic unity and harmony. Several of his short stories recapture medieval life and thought, e.g., *De klok van Delft* (1846), *Legenden en Fantasien* (1847), *De organist van de Dom* (1849), *Karolingische verhalen* (1851, Carolingian Tales), and *Geertrude van Oosten* (1853). He was also active in the field of art, especially in architecture. One of his best essays, *De heilige Linie* (1875, The Holy Line), discusses the symbolism of church architecture. In 1876 he was appointed professor in art history at the Academy of Arts in Amsterdam. He was unable to understand younger authors, however, including his own son, Karel (pseudonym, Lodewijk van Deyssel), and lost contact with the young painters, who, like the authors, tended toward naturalism. They in their turn respected him, but considered him the representative of an era that had lost its reason for existence.

Bibliography: *Werken*, ed. J. F. M. Sterck, 7 v. (The Hague 1908–20). A. J. (pseud.), *J. A. Alberdingk Thijm* (Amsterdam 1893), biog. by his son. W. Bennink, *Alberdingk Thijm: Kunst en Karakter* (Nijmegen 1952). G. Brom, *Alberdingk Thym* (Utrecht 1956).

[J. I. MENDELS]

ALBERGATI, NICCOLÒ, BL., Carthusian bishop and cardinal; b. Bologna, 1375; d. Siena, May 9, 1443 (feast, March 3). Nobly born, Albergati abandoned the law for the Carthusian house of San Girolamo di Casara, where he became prior (1407) and visitor (1412). Appointed bishop of Bologna (1417), cardinal (1426), and eventually grand penitentiary and camerlengo, he served both *Martin V and *Eugene IV as legate to England, France, Germany, and Italy and at the councils of *Basel, *Ferrara, and *Florence. For example, in 1422 Martin V sent him—albeit unsuccessfully—to reconcile the rulers of England, France, and Burgundy. Later (1435), Albergati won Philip the Good of Burgundy over to *Charles VII, thus contributing materially to the Peace of Arras. He was buried in the Charter House at Florence. *Benedict

Bl. Niccolò Albergati, silverpoint (Jan van Eyck, 1431).

XIV authorized his cultus when he beatified him on Oct. 6, 1744.

Bibliography: H. M. ZANOTTI, *Vita del b. Niccolò Albergati* (Bologna 1757). S. AUTORE, DHGE 1:1396–97. P. DE TÖTH, *Il beato cardinale Niccolò Albergati e i suoi tempi, 1375–1444,* 2 v. (Acquapendente 1934). J. G. DICKINSON, *The Congress of Arras, 1435* (Oxford 1955) *passim.* **Illustration credit:** Staatliche Kunstsammlungen, Dresden.

[J. G. ROWE]

ALBERIC OF MONTE CASSINO, rhetorician, author, monk of Beneventan origin; d. *c.* 1105. He entered Monte Cassino as an adult (*c.* 1060) during the time of Abbot Desiderius (*see* VICTOR III). One of the earliest medieval proponents of the **Ars dictaminis,* he is credited in the *Chronicon Casinense* (with interlinear interpolations in the handwriting of *Peter the Deacon) with numerous *vitae* (St. *Scholastica, MS Vat. lat. 1202), political and theological pieces. The hymns ascribed to him by Peter the Deacon— for whatever reason—are identical in title with works found in the MSS of *Peter Damian. The influence of his Latin style, acquired by *imitatio* or perhaps personally from Damian, spread through the work of his students, especially that of Pope *Gelasius II. Most of his writings, among them his letters to Peter Damian, on the controversy of *Berengarius of Tours, and on the *investiture struggle are lost. Alberic belonged to the learned Cassinese milieu of *Alphanus, *Leo Marsicanus, and *Constantine the African.

Bibliography: PL 173:1032–33. MGS 7:728. L. VON ROCKINGER. ed., *Briefsteller und Formelbücher des 11. bis 14. Jahrhunderts* (Munich 1863). A. LENTINI, "A. di Monte Cassino nel quadro della riforma gregoriana," StGreg 4 (1952) 55–109. O. J. BLUM, *ibid.* 5 (1956) 291–298; "Alberic of Monte Cassino and the Hymns and Rhythms . . . ," *Traditio* 12 (1956) 87–148. J. LECLERCQ, "Inédits de S. Pierre Damien," RevBén 67 (1957) 151–174. P. MEYVAERT, "Alberic of Monte Cassino or Saint Peter Damian?" *ibid.* 175–181. K. REINDEL, "Zur handschriftlichen Überlieferung der Gedichte des Petrus Damiani," *ibid.* 182–189. Szövérffy AnnLatHymn 1:391–393.

[O. J. BLUM]

ALBERIC OF OSTIA, cardinal bishop, papal legate; b. Beauvais, France, *c.* 1080; d. Verdun, 1148. Alberic became a monk in *Cluny, where he rose to the rank of subprior; he held the same office at the Abbey of Saint-Martin-des-Champs. At the instance of *Peter the Venerable, he was appointed abbot of *Vézelay (1131) despite the opposition of the monks of that abbey. In the schism of Anacletus II (*see* PIERLEONI) he supported Pope *Innocent II, who created him cardinal bishop of Ostia and papal legate (1138) to England. A strong representative of the *Gregorian Reform, Alberic was the first papal legate in more than 70 years to enter England with unrestricted powers. In Scotland he won the clergy to recognition of Innocent (Synod of Carlisle, Sept. 26, 1138); but his primary business was to visit the chief monastic and episcopal centers of England and Scotland, to hold a council in which recent reform decrees might be applied, and to supervise the election of the Archbishop of Canterbury. Assisted by two assessors, the Austin Canon Robert of Hereford and Abbot Richard of *Fountains, he brought the mission to a successful conclusion with the synod of Westminster (Dec. 11, 1138) and the election of *Theobald of Canterbury, the former abbot of *Bec. After affording his good offices to the establishment of peace between England and Scotland, he returned to Rome (January 1139), where he participated in the Second *Lateran Council. Appointed legate to Antioch, he deposed Radulph, the second Latin patriarch (Nov. 30, 1139), and in 1140 presided at a synod in Jerusalem. His last years were spent as legate in southern France, where he opposed the *Albigenses, *Éon of Stella, and the followers of *Henry of Lausanne.

Bibliography: JOHN OF HEXHAM, *Chronicle* in *The Priory of Hexham,* ed. J. RAINE, 2 v. (Surtees Society 44, 46; London 1864–65) 1:107–172. RICHARD OF HEXHAM, *ibid.* 1:63–106. Hefele-Leclercq 5:721, 745–746, 817. U. ROUZIÈS, DHGE 1: 1408–09. H. TILLMANN, *Die päpstlichen Legaten in England* (Bonn 1926). P. MIKAT, LexThK[2] 1:275–276. Knowles MOE 237, 253.

[O. J. BLUM]

ALBERIC OF ROSATE, Italian jurist; b. Rosciate, near Bergamo, Italy, 1290; d. Bergamo, Sept. 14, 1360. He was descended from a family of judges and notaries, and he studied law in Padua under Oldradus de Ponte and Richard Malombra. After returning to Bergamo in the 2d decade of 1300, he practiced law and continued to cultivate juridical and literary studies, though it appears he never taught. He was one of the principal exponents of the Italian juridical school of commentators at the time of its most glorious flourishing and was the promoter of the first real lexicographic attempt in the juridical field.

Between the downfall of the Commune and the rise of the Viscounty in Bergamo, he was one of the protagonists of the city's public life. In 1331 and 1333 he reformed the statutes of the city of Bergamo; and in the years 1335, 1337–38, and 1340, he served as ambassador for Bergamo and the Visconti family to the Pope in Avignon. In the holy year 1350 he and his family made a pilgrimage to Rome. Alberic protected the Celestine monastery in Bergamo and the adjoining Holy Spirit hospital, and gave generous assistance also to the poor through the Consortium of Mercy.

In his *Quaestiones statutorum,* which had several reprints, he left a fundamental work in statutory legislation, and perhaps the first doctrinal treatise on private international law. His contemporaries and posterity described him as *summus practicus;* he wrote commentaries on various parts of Justinian's Digest and Code. The influence of the *De regulis iuris,* included in the *Liber Sextus* of Boniface VIII, is clearly evident in Alberic's commentary on title *De regulis iuris* of the *Digesta* (CorpIurCivDig 50.17). His *Dictionarium iuris,* which was reprinted several times, is the first ample lexicon of civil and Canon Law. Finally, he revised in Latin the commentary of Jacopus della Lana to Dante's *Comedy* (the work is not edited).

Bibliography: G. CREMASCHI, "Contributo alla biografia di Alberico da Rosciate," *Bergomum* 30 (1956) 3–102. L. PROSDOCIMI, DizBiogItal 1:656–657. G. BILLANOVICH, "Epitafio, libri e amici di Alberico da Rosciate," *Italia Medioevale e Umanistica* 3 (1960) 251–261.

[R. ABBONDANZA]

ALBERIC OF SPOLETO, two dukes, father and son, in the 10th century.

Alberic I, Duke of Spoleto and Count of Camerino and Tuscany; d. *c.* 925. He was a Lombard adventurer who married *Marozia, daughter of *Theophylactus and *Theodora and thus became associated with the family that exercised effective power in Rome during the early 10th century. He was part of the alliance that under the leadership of Pope *John X drove the Saracens from their strongholds in Italy by the victory on the Garigliano River in 915.

Alberic II, called also Alberic of Rome, Roman senator; b. *c.* 905; d. 954. He was probably the natural son of Alberic I and Marozia. In 932 on the occasion of Marozia's third marriage, to Hugh of Provence (d. 947), Alberic led an uprising, expelled Hugh and imprisoned both Marozia and Pope *John XI, his half-brother. Alberic's power was based on Roman opposition to Hugh, who tried unsuccessfully to gain Rome up until his death. *Liutprand of Cremona termed Alberic's government *monarchia,* but, as leader of the Roman nobility, Alberic adopted the unusual title of *princeps,* and used it especially on his coinage, usurping the imperial prerogative by placing his name with the Pope's. The details of his government over Rome and its territory are not adequately known, but the unusually peaceful era of Roman politics from 932 to Alberic's death in 954 attests to an effective rule. During this period he replaced the popes as temporal rulers, but his influence over individual popes varied. *Leo VII, Alberic, and *Odo of Cluny, on Alberic's invitation, cooperated in a restoration of Roman monasteries, a revival spurred by restored security after the expulsion of the Saracens and by Alberic's attempt to gain further support for his rule at Rome. The visit of Hugh of Provence to Rome in 941 indicates a weakening of Alberic's influence under *Stephen VIII. It was said that *Marinus II dared not act without Alberic, who called himself, in 945, *Domini gratia humilis princeps.* *Agapetus II allowed Alberic only his hereditary title of senator, and probably during this pontificate Alberic had to put down a conspiracy. It is not known whether Agapetus was influenced by Alberic in refusing *Otto I's request for a visit to Rome in 951. Before his death in 954, Alberic had arranged for the papal election of his illegitimate son, Octavian, who became pontiff as *John XII.

Bibliography: O. Gerstenberg, *Die politische Entwicklung des römischen Adels im X und XI Jahrhunderts* (Berlin 1933). L. Bréhier, DHGE 1:1404–06. J. Gay, *L'Italie méridionale et l'empire byzantine* (Paris 1904) 218–223. L. Duchesne, *The Beginnings of the Temporal Sovereignty of the Popes, A.D. 754–1073,* tr. A. H. Mathew (London 1908). Duchesne LP 2:243–249. G. Fasoli, *I re d'Italia, 888–962* (Florence 1949). W. Kölmel, *Rom und Kirchenstaat im X und XI Jahrhunderts* (Berlin 1935). Haller 2:194–204, 546–550. Seppelt² 2:354–362.

[C. B. FISHER]

ALBERIC OF TROIS-FONTAINES, Cistercian historian of Trois-Fontaines (Diocese of Châlons-sur-Marne); d. after 1251. The author of a universal *Chronicle* of events during his lifetime, he began work on his history *c.* 1232, utilizing in part an earlier work by the Cistercian Giles of Orval. He also depended on many other sources that are no longer extant. Although Alberic is often uncritical, his *Chronicle* is valuable because of the information it gives about events that are not found in any other surviving work. The *Chronicle* is printed in the MGS 23:631–950.

Bibliography: HistLittFranc 18:279–292. G. Müller, EncCatt 1:666. U. Berlière, DHGE 1:1413–14. B. Griesser, LexThK² 1:276–277.

[V. L. BULLOUGH]

ALBERIC OF UTRECHT, ST., Benedictine monk, bishop of Utrecht; d. Aug. 21 or Nov. 14, 784 (feast, Nov. 14, March 4, Aug. 21). He was a nephew of an earlier bishop of Utrecht, St. *Gregory, the successor of *Boniface. Alberic participated in the mission to the Frisians, directing *Ludger of Münster's activity there. He was a friend of such intellectual leaders of the Carolingian Renaissance as *Alcuin and Ludger. He received episcopal consecration in 780 at Cologne. As bishop of Utrecht he reorganized the cathedral school, dividing the teaching among four masters. Alberic's relics are preserved at Susteren.

Bibliography: Sources. MGS 16:497. Literature. J. Torsy, LexThK² 1:277.

[R. BALCH]

ALBERONI, GIULIO

Cardinal and statesman; b. Firenzuola d'Arda, Piacenza, Italy, May 31?, 1664; d. Piacenza, June 27, 1752. Although of humble origins, Alberoni was educated by Barnabites and Jesuits and enjoyed the protection of Bishop Barni, who sponsored his ecclesiastical career. Alberoni, ordained and appointed a canon (1698), began his diplomatic apprenticeship as a secretary to the Duke of Vendôme, supreme commander of the French army in Italy, whom he followed to France (1706), Holland, and Spain (1711). After the general's death (1712), Alberoni remained in Madrid as an agent of the duchy of Parma. In 1714 he successfully negotiated the marriage of Philip V, a widower, to Elizabeth Farnese of Parma. As prime minister (1716) and cardinal (July 12, 1717), Alberoni implemented domestic reforms in agriculture, trade, manufacturing, and welfare that were decidedly in advance of his times. In foreign policy, fully cognizant of the ambitions of Philip V, he boldly sought to restore Spanish prestige in Italy and to vindicate his sovereign's rights to the French throne. To this end,

Giulio Alberoni, portrait by Mulinaretto in the Galleria Alberoni, Piacenza.

he reorganized the army and navy and engaged in intrigues against the Empire and its allies. Compelled to declare war prematurely by the irresponsible actions of Parma and the urging of Philip, Alberoni ordered the invasion of Sardinia (1717) and Sicily (1718), in spite of formal assurances to the contrary given to Clement XI. Diplomatic and military disasters followed. Alberoni failed to secure the support of Russia and Sweden in restoring James Stuart, "the Old Pretender," and in overthrowing Philip, Duke of Orléans. The Quadruple Alliance (Empire, France, England, and Holland) reconquered the islands of Sardinia and Sicily and invaded Navarre. Alberoni, held responsible by the King, the Pope, and the Quadruple Alliance for this ill-starred venture, was expelled from Spain (Dec. 5, 1719). Hiding in Italy, he evaded arrest and assassination, while a commission of 15 cardinals investigated charges of treason brought against him. Alberoni attended the conclave that elected Innocent XIII (1721); he was given a relatively mild sentence of 4 years' imprisonment but was completely exonerated by the Pope (Sept. 18, 1723). When created bishop of Malaga and reconciled with Philip V (1725), the aging cardinal hoped to spend his remaining years in peaceful retirement in his estate of Castelromano. Instead, he was appointed by Clement XII to the legation of Ravenna (1735), where he promoted public works. In 1739 he occupied San Marino, a controversial move that was later disavowed by the Pope for political reasons. His last post was the legation of Bologna (1740–43). He spent the last years of his life in Piacenza in charitable and scholarly pursuits. Alberoni is buried in the church of the college San Lazzaro-Alberoni, which he founded in 1732 for the education of clerics.

Bibliography: S. BERSANI, *Storia del Cardinale G. Alberoni* (Piacenza 1861). A. ARATA, *Il processo del Cardinale Alberoni* (Piacenza 1923). P. CASTAGNOLI, *Il Cardinale G. Alberoni,* 3 v. (Piacenza 1929–32). S. HARCOURT-SMITH, *Cardinal of Spain: The Life and Strange Career of Alberoni* (New York 1944). P. DALLA TORRE, EncCatt 1:670–672, bibliog. E. BOURGEOIS, *Le Secret des Farnèse: Philippe V et la politique d'Alberoni* (Paris 1909). P. RICHARD, DHGE 1:1425–28. **Illustration credit:** Photo Manzotti, Piacenza.

[E. J. THOMSON]

ALBERS, WILLIAM, philanthropist, pioneer in supermarket merchandising; b. Cincinnati, Ohio, May 23, 1880; d. Cincinnati, June 6, 1954. After his education in St. Joseph Parochial School and Hughes High School, Cincinnati, and a brief employment in his father's grocery store, he became associated with the Schneider Brothers Company, which was consolidated with the Kroger Grocery and Baking Company. As assistant secretary (1910), vice president and general manager (1915), and president (1928), he was chiefly responsible for the growth of Kroger's from 185 to 5,600 stores before he resigned in 1929. In 1933 he opened the first of Albers Super Markets, Inc., and founded 67 supermarkets in Ohio and Kentucky. In Chicago he established and headed the Super Markets Institute, which developed advanced techniques of supermarket operations. During World War II, he served on the National Food Advisory Council and War Food Council. Albers was active in cultural and educational associations, and was director of the Catholic Youth Organization and National Council of Catholic Men; trustee of The Catholic University of America, Washington, D.C.; member of the lay advisory board of Xavier University, Cincinnati; treasurer of the Board of Trustees of Cincinnati College of Music; and finance chairman of the Greater Cincinnati Television Education Foundation. His services merited him investiture as Knight Commander, Order of St. Gregory (1934), several honorary degrees, and the annual citation of the National Conference of Christians and Jews in 1954.

[A. G. STRITCH]

ALBERT BEHAIM, papal legate, anti-imperialist; b. Bavaria, *c.* 1180; d. probably in Passau, *c.* 1260. In 1212 Albert received a canonry at Passau, the first of many benefices he accumulated, shortly after entering the papal Curia, where he served under *Innocent III and *Honorius III. Later, after returning to Germany, he became a violent agitator against the Hohenstaufen dynasty even before the final papal controversy with *Frederick II. When *Gregory IX excommunicated the Emperor in 1239, he commissioned Albert to promulgate the sentence in Bavaria and compel obedience, which brought Albert into conflict with almost all the Bavarian clergy. Albert employed so many excommunications and interdicts that Duke Otto expelled him in 1241. He finally found refuge at Lyons in 1244 with *Innocent IV, whom he advised on German affairs, playing a part in the election of the antikings. Not until 1250, after the Emperor's death and the forceful deposition of Albert's chief foe, Bp. Rudiger of Passau, could he return home and recover his prebends. Always aggressive and anxious to promote his own interests, Albert continued to make enemies. His own bishop imprisoned him for some obscure reason, but in 1258 Pope *Alexander IV intervened to secure his release. Details of his death are not known.

Bibliography: *Alberts von Beham Conceptbuch,* ed. C. HÖFLER (Stuttgart 1847). R. BAUERREISS, *Kirchengeschichte Bayerns,* 5 v. (St. Ottilien, Ger. 1949–55; 2d ed. 1958) v.4. Hauck v.4. J. OSWALD, NDB 2:1.

[R. H. SCHMANDT]

ALBERT THE GREAT (ALBERTUS MAGNUS), ST.

Dominican bishop, Doctor of the Church, patron of scientists, philosopher; b. Lauingen on the Danube, near Ulm, *c.* 1200; d. Cologne, Nov. 15, 1280; variously referred to as Albertus Magnus, Albert of Lauingen, Albert of Cologne, and Albert the German; honored under the scholastic titles of *Doctor universalis* and *Doctor expertus.* His feast is celebrated on November 15 in the Latin Church. Although in his own right Albert was an outstanding figure of the Middle Ages, he is best known as the teacher of St. *Thomas Aquinas and as a proponent of *Aristotelianism at the University of Paris. He combined interest and skill in natural science with proficiency in all branches of philosophy and theology.

Early Life. Albert was the eldest son of a powerful and wealthy German lord of military rank. After his elementary training, he studied the liberal arts at Padua, while his father fought in the service of Frederick II in Lombardy. Early in the summer of 1223, *Jordan of Saxony, the successor to *Dominic as master general of the Order of Preachers, came to Padua in the hope of bringing young men into the order by his preaching. At first he found "the students of Padua extremely cold," but 10 of them soon sought admission, "among

Fresco of St. Albert the Great, by Fra Angelico, in the Priory of San Marco, Florence.

them two sons of two great German lords; one was a provost-marshall, loaded with many honors and possessed of great riches; the other has resigned rich benefices and is truly noble in mind and body" (Jordan, *Epist.* 20). The latter has always been identified as Albert of Lauingen.

After overcoming fierce opposition from his family, he entered the novitiate and later was sent to Germany to study theology. Shortly after 1233 he was appointed lecturer of theology in the new priory at Hildesheim, then, successively, at Freiburg im Breisgau, at Regensburg for 2 years, and at Strassburg. During these years he wrote his treatise *De natura boni,* influenced largely by *Hugh of Saint-Victor and *William of Auxerre.

Teaching at Paris. Around 1241 he was sent to the University of Paris to prepare for the mastership in theology. The intellectual climate of Paris, "the city of philosophers," was vastly different from his native Germany, for here he encountered the "new Aristotle," recently translated from Greek and Arabic, and the wealth of Arabic learning introduced from Spain. Albert arrived in Paris just as the commentaries of *Averroës on *Aristotle were becoming available. At the Dominican convent of St. Jacques, he fulfilled the university requirements for bachelors in theology, lecturing cursorily on the Bible for 2 years, responding in disputations, and then expounding the *Sentences* of *Peter Lombard for 2 years (*c.* 1243–45). But Albert was more interested in acquiring the new learning than in lecturing on the *Sentences.* In 1245 he incepted as a master in theology under Guéric of St. Quentin, and continued to lecture as master in the Dominican chair "for foreigners" until the end of the academic year 1248. Albert was, in fact, the first German Dominican to become a master.

Most probably it was at Paris that he began his monumental presentation of the whole of human knowledge to the Latin West, paraphrasing and explaining all the known works of Aristotle and pseudo-Aristotle, adding contributions from the Arabs, and even entirely "new sciences" (*Phys.* 1.1.1). Apparently asked by his younger confreres to explain Aristotle's *Physics* in writing, he undertook to explain systematically all the branches of natural science, logic, rhetoric, mathematics, astronomy, ethics, economics, politics, and metaphysics. "Our intention," he said, "is to make all the aforesaid parts of knowledge intelligible to the Latins" (*ibid.*). This vast project took about 20 years to complete and is one of the marvels of medieval scholarship. While working on it, he probably had among his disciples the young Aquinas, who arrived in Paris in the autumn of 1245.

Years in Germany and Italy. In the summer of 1248 Albert was sent to Cologne to organize and preside over the first *studium generale* in Germany, which had been authorized by the Dominican general chapter in June. At Cologne he devoted his full energies to teaching, preaching, studying, and writing until 1254. Among his disciples at this time were Thomas Aquinas, who studied under Albert from 1245 until 1252, and *Ulric of Strassburg. In 1253 Albert was elected provincial of the German Dominicans, a position he faithfully filled for 3 years. Despite the administrative burdens, the yearly visitation of each priory and nunnery, and lengthy journeys on foot, he continued his prolific writing and scientific research in libraries, fields, ore mines, and industrial localities.

In 1256 he was in the papal curia at Anagni with Aquinas and *Bonaventure to defend the cause of mendicant orders against the attacks of *William of Saint-Amour and other secular masters. Here also he held a disputation against Averroist doctrine on the intellect (*see* INTELLECT, UNITY OF). He lectured to the curia on the whole of St. John's Gospel and on some of the Epistles; for this reason he is listed among the "Masters of the Sacred Palace." Resigning the office of provincial, he resumed teaching in Cologne (1257–60). In 1259 the general chapter requested him and four other masters in theology to draw up a plan of study to be followed throughout the order.

Late that same year irregularities in the Diocese of Regensburg led to the appointment of Albert to succeed the removed bishop. His own reluctance and the pleadings of Humbert of Romans, general of the order, were of no avail. On Jan. 5, 1260, Alexander IV ordered his installation as bishop of Regensburg. With the settling of conditions in this diocese and the election of a new pope, he was able to resign in 1262; he then chose the house of studies at Cologne for his residence. Albert voluntarily resumed teaching, but in the following year he was ordered by Urban IV to preach the crusade throughout Germany and Bohemia (1263–64). From 1264 to 1266 he lived in the Dominican house in Würzburg. In 1268 he was in Strassburg, and from 1269 until his death he resided in Cologne, writing new works and revising earlier ones.

Only two more times, as far as is known, did he undertake long journeys from Cologne. He took part in the Council of Lyons in 1274, and in 1277 he traveled to Paris at the height of the Averroist controversy to forestall the hasty condemnation of certain Aristotelian doctrines that both he and Thomas (d. 1274) held to be true (*see* AVERROISM, LATIN; FORMS, UNICITY AND PLURALITY OF). This last journey, apparently, was a failure. Some time after he drew up his last will and testament in January 1279, his health and memory began to fail him. Weakened by manifold labors, austerities, and vigils, he

St. Albert the Great by Sister Gertrude, OP, of Rosary College. Statue is in the priory cloister of St. Rose Priory, Dubuque, Iowa.

died at the age of "eighty years or more," to quote *Bartholomew of Lucca and *Bernard Gui. His body was laid to rest in the Dominican church at Cologne where it remains today.

Cult and Canonization. Not only was Albert the only man of the High Middle Ages to be called "the Great," but this title was used even before his death (*Annal. Basil.,* MGS 17:202). Long before the canonization of Thomas in 1323, Albert's prestige was well established. *Siger of Brabant, a contemporary, considered Albert and Thomas "the principal men in philosophy" (*De anim. intel.* 3). In the words of Ulric of Strassburg, Albert was "a man so superior in every science, that he can fittingly be called the wonder and the miracle of our time" (*Sum. de bono* 4.3.9).

In Germany there has always existed a deep devotion to the venerable bishop. He was beatified by Gregory XV in 1622. By the decree *In Thesauris Sapientiae* (Dec. 16, 1931) Pius XI declared him a saint of the universal Church with the additional title of doctor. In the solemn decree *Ad Deum* (Dec. 16, 1941) Pius XII constituted him the heavenly patron of all who cultivate the natural sciences.

Aristotelianism. The Christian centuries preceding Albert were fundamentally Augustinian in philosophy and theology, transmitting the Christian Platonism of the Fathers through the monasteries and the schools (*see* AUGUSTINIANISM; PLATONISM). The 12th-century Latin translations of *Avicenna, *Avicebron, *Costa ben Luca, *Isaac Israeli, and the **Liber de Causis,* together with the paraphrases of *Dominic Gundisalvi, could easily be accommodated to Christian philosophy, since Platonic thought was a common element. When the new Aristotle reached the schools, the obscure Latin versions of the Stagirite from Arabic and Greek were studied and taught with every aid at hand, including *John Scotus Erigena, Avicenna, Avicebron and *Augustine. The earliest teachers of the Aristotelian books at Paris, *Amalric of Bène and *David of Dinant, made a pantheist of Aristotle, and incurred a deserved censure until the new Aristotle could be examined more carefully. Later masters in the faculty of arts, such as *Robert Grosseteste, *John Blund, *Adam of Buckfield, Geoffrey of Aspall, *Robert Kilwardby and *Roger Bacon, were more orthodox, though they interpreted Aristotle through the teaching of Avicenna and in Platonist fashion.

However there is a fundamental divergence between Platonic and Aristotelian views, particularly concerning scientific thought and the nature of man. For *Plato the study of nature is not strictly scientific, but only problematic, a "likely story"; for certainty one must go to mathematics, and thence to the contemplation of pure forms in metaphysics. Further, Plato conceived man as a soul imprisoned in a body, rather than a unique composite of body and soul. Aristotle, on the other hand, considered the study of nature to be autonomous in its own domain, independent of mathematics and metaphysics, worthy of pursuit in its own right, and truly "scientific" in the technical sense employed by the Greeks. Moreover, Aristotle was the first to elaborate fully the doctrine of potency and act, using this to explain how the body and soul of man constitute an absolute unity in nature. The arrival of Averroës's commentaries in the schools after 1230 helped to bring out the difference between the two Greeks, for Averroës was the most Aristotelian of the Arabic commentators.

Among the Latin schoolmen, Albert was the first to make the Aristotelian approach to the physical world his own and to defend its autonomy against "the error of Plato" (*Meta.* 1.1.1, *et passim*) maintained by his contemporaries. Strictly speaking, Albert's expositions of Aristotle are neither commentaries nor paraphrases; they are really original works in which "the true view of Peripatetic philosophers" is rewritten, erroneous views refuted, new solutions proposed, and personal observations (*experimenta*) incorporated. This, at least, was the opinion of Roger Bacon's contemporaries at Paris, who thought that "now a complete philosophy has been given to the Latins, and composed in the Latin tongue" (*Opus tertium* 9). For this reason, as Bacon tells us, Albert's views had as much authority in the schools as those of Aristotle, Avicenna, or Averroës, "and he is still alive and he has had in his own lifetime authority, which man has never had in doctrine" (*ibid.*).

Scientific Method. Yet Albert did not blindly follow the authority of Aristotle. In his philosophical as well as theological works, he does not hesitate to reject certain views, such as the eternity of the world and the animation of the spheres, and observational errors. "Whoever believes that Aristotle was a god, must also believe that he never erred; but if one believes that Aristotle was a man, then doubtless he was liable to error just as we are" (*Phys.* 8.1.14). In matters of experimental science, he frequently rejects a supposed observation of the Stagirite, saying that it is contrary to his own observations (*Meteor.* 3.4.11, *Animal.* 23.1.1. 104, etc.). In his treatise on plants he insists, "Experiment is the only safe guide in such investigations" (*Veg.* 6.2.1). In practice as well as in theory he realized that "the aim of natural science is not simply to accept the statements of others, but to investigate the causes that are at work in nature" (*Mineral.* 2.2.1).

Albert was an indefatigable student of nature, and applied himself so sedulously that he was accused of neglecting the sacred sciences (*Henry of Ghent, *De script. eccles.* 2.10). Even in his own lifetime incredible legends were circulated, attributing to him the power of a magician or sorcerer. In later generations such legends were multiplied and spurious treatises were circulated under his name. The real influence of Albert, felt throughout the Renaissance, comes from his establishing the study of nature as a legitimate science in the Christian tradition. *See* SCIENCE (IN THE MIDDLE AGES).

Sacred Theology. In theology he was not so successful as his illustrious disciple in presenting a new synthesis. Aquinas's famous *Summa* is a perfect application of Aristotle's *Posterior Analytics* to the deposit of faith, employing from the very beginning the profound implications of Aristotelian metaphysical principles. This cannot be said of Albert's theological works. Nonetheless these are outstanding in medieval literature for their sound scholarship, breadth of inquiry, and clarity of presentation. Considering the milieu in which he wrote, it is most significant that he defended strongly the distinction between the realm of revelation and that of human reason (*see* FAITH AND REASON).

Unlike many of his contemporaries, he defended the autonomy of philosophical investigation, insisting that no truth of reason could contradict revelation. At the same time, he maintained the superiority of revelation and the right of theologians to use all of human knowledge to search the divine mysteries. This view was continued by Aquinas and others so that today it is an integral part of Catholic theology.

Albertists. Among the immediate students of Albert, apart from Aquinas and Ulrich of Strassburg, should also be enumerated Hugh of Strassburg, *John of Freiburg, *John of Lichtenberg, and *Giles of Lessines. Other German Dominicans favorably disposed toward Neoplatonic thought developed mystical elements in Albert's teaching. These were transmitted through *Theodoric of Freiberg and Berthold of Mosburg to Meister *Eckhart and other 14th-century mystics, namely, Johannes *Tauler, *Henry Suso, and Jan van *Ruysbroeck. In the 15th century small groups of thinkers at Paris and Cologne, identifying themselves as "Albertists," set up a philosophical school in opposition to Thomism. Founded by Heymericus de Campo (Van de Velde), they opposed the traditional Thomistic teaching on the real distinction between essence and existence, as well as that on universals. In so doing they actually returned to the teaching of Avicenna, and made extensive use of Albert's commentaries on the *Liber de Causis* and the works of *Pseudo-Dionysius.

That Albert's teaching is not to be completely identified with that of his famous student is clear from his response to the 43 questions of *John of Vercelli (*43 Problemata determinata*), one of his last writings. Some have even held that an occasional *quidam* in the works of Albert is a disparaging reference to Thomas. But on the whole there is broad doctrinal agreement between master and student. This has led to a gradual assimilation of the Albertist tradition within the Dominican Order into the mainstream of Thomism, with the result that Albertism and Thomism have become practically indistinguishable.

Writings. The reputation of Albert was so widespread that not only were his authentic works frequently copied in manuscript and abundantly reproduced in print, but an incredible number of spurious works, some even fantastic, have been attributed to him. On the other hand many works known to have been written by him have not yet been discovered. Two editions of "complete works" have been published: one at Lyons in 1651, in 21 folio volumes edited by Peter Jammy, OP; the other at Paris (Vivès), 1890–99, in 38 quarto volumes edited by the Abbé Auguste Borgnet, of the Diocese of Reims. The first volume of a new and critical edition that will comprise 40 volumes, under the direction of Bernhard Geyer, President of the Albertus Magnus Institute of Cologne, appeared in 1951. The following list gives the volume of the Borgnet edition (B), and the projected volume of the Cologne edition (C). The dates in brackets are the certain or probable dates of composition.

Logic. *Super Porphyrium de 5 universalibus,* B.1, C.1; *De praedicamentis,* B.1, C.1; *De sex principiis,* B.1, C.1; *De divisione,* C.1; *Peri hermeneias,* B.1, C.1; *Analytica priora,* B.1, C.2; *Analytica posteriora,* B.2, C.2; *Topica,* B.2, C.3; *De sophisticis elenchis,* B.2, C.3 [all between 1248–1264].

Natural Science. *Physica,* B.3, C.4 [between 1245–48]; *De caelo et mundo,* B.4, C.5 [between 1248–60]; *De natura locorum,* B.9, C.5 [before 1259]; *De causis proprietatum elementorum,* B.9, C.5 [between 1248–59]; *De generatione et corruptione,* B.4, C.5 [before 1260]; *Meteora,* B.4, C.6 [before 1259]; *Mineralia,* B.5, C.6 [before 1263]; *De anima,* B.5, C.7 [*c.* 1256]; *De nutrimento,* B.9, C.7 [before 1263]; *De intellectu et intelligibili,* B.9, C.7 [before 1259]; *De sensu et sensato,* B.9, C.7 [before 1260]; *De memoria,* B.9, C.7 [before 1263]; *De somno et vigilia,* B.9, C.7 [before 1259]; *De spiritu et respiratione,* B.9, C.7 [before 1259]; *De motibus animalium,* B.9, C.7 [before 1259]; *De aetate,* B.9, C.7 [before 1259]; *De morte et vita,* B.9, C.7 [before 1259]; *De vegetabilibus et plantis,* B.10, C.8 [before 1259]; *De animalibus,* B.11–12, C.9–11 [1258–62]; *De natura et origine animae,* B.9, C.12 [*c.* 1263]; *De principiis motus processivi,* B.10, C.12 [*c.* 1261]; *QQ. super de animalibus,* C.12 [*c.* 1258].

Moral Sciences. *Ethica,* B.7, C.13 [before 1261]; *Super Ethica commentum et quaestiones,* C.14 [between 1248–52]; *Politica,* B.8, C.15 [between 1265–75].

Metaphysics. *Metaphysica,* B.6, C.16 [between 1261–66]; *De causis,* B.10, C.17 [between 1266–71]; *De unitate intellectus,* B.9, C.17 [*c.* 1270]; *De 15 problematibus,* C.17 [*c.* 1270]; *43 Problemata determinata,* C.17 [April 1271].

Sacred Scripture. *Super Iob,* C.18 [1272 or 1274]; *Super Isaiam,* C.19; *Super Ieremiam* (frag.), C.20; *Super Threnos,* B.18, C.20; *Super Baruch,* B.18, C.20; *Super Ezechielem* (frag.), C.20; *Super Danielem,* B.18, C.20; *Super Prophetas minores,* B.19, C.20; *Super Mattheum,* B.20–21, C.21 [definitive version after 1270]; *Super Marcum,* B.21, C.22 [definitive version between 1272–5]; *Super Lucam,* B.22–23, C.23 [1261–62; rev. 1270–75]; *Super Ioannem,* B.24, C.24 [1256; rev. 1272–75]. Albert's commentaries on St. Paul and on Apocalypse have not yet been found; the printed Apocalypse is spurious.

Systematic Theology. *De natura boni,* C.25 [before 1240]; *Super 4 sententiarum,* B.25–30, C.29–32 [rev. version completed in 1249]; *QQ. theologicae,* C.25 [1245–48]; *De sacramentis, De incarnatione, De resurrectione,* C.26 [1245–50]; *De 4 coaequaevis,* B.34, C.26 [1245–50]; *De homine,* B.35, C.27 [1244–48]; *De bono,* C.28 [1244–48]; *In corpus Dionysium,* B.14, C.36–37 [1248–60]; *Summa theologiae,* B.31–33, C.34–35 [after 1270]; *De mysterio missae,* B.38, C.38 [after 1270]; *De corpore domini,* B.38, C.38 [after 1270].

Sermons and Letters. C.39 (see J. P. Schneyer).

Spurious and Dubious Works. C.40. It is certain that Albert wrote on mathematics, astronomy, and rhetoric, but these writings have not yet been found. Among the definitely spurious works, the best known are the *Compendium theologiae veritatis,* B.34, which is by Hugh of Strassburg; *De laudibus B. Mariae Virginis,* B.36; *Mariale,* B.37; *Biblia Mariana,* B.37; the *De secretis naturae, De secretis mulierum,* and other occult works. The authenticity of many other works is still disputed among scholars, principally that of the *Speculum astronomiae.*

See also THOMISM; SCHOLASTICISM; NEOPLATONISM.

Bibliography: M. ALBERT, *Albert the Great* (Oxford 1948). T. M. SCHWERTNER, *Saint Albert the Great* (Milwaukee 1932). Copleston 2:293–301. Cross ODCC 30. Ueberweg 2:400–416. EncFil 1:121–127. A. PAZZINI, EncCatt 1:698–706. W. KÜBEL, LexThK² 1:285–287; see also 284 under "Albertismus." P. MANDONNET, DTC 1.1:666–675. P. G. MEERSSEMAN, *Introductio in opera omnia Beati Alberti Magni* (Bruges 1931). "De vita et scriptis B. Alberti Magni," ed. P. DE LOË, AnalBoll 19 (1900) 257–284; 20 (1901) 273–316; 21 (1902) 361–371. Quétif-Échard 1:162–183. H. C. SCHEEBEN, "Albertus der Grosse: Zur Chronologie seines Lebens," *Quellen und Forschungen zur Geschichte des Dominikanerordens in Deutschland* 27 (Vechta 1931). "Le Bienheureux Albert le Grand," RevThom 36 (1931), esp. M. H. LAURENT and Y. CONGAR, "Essai de bibliographie albertinienne," 422–468. M. SCHOOYANS, "Bibliographie philosophique de saint Albert le Grand (1931–60)," *Revista da Universidade Católica de São Paulo* 21 (1961) 36–88. J. P. SCHNEYER, "Predigten Alberts des Grossen in der Hs. Leipzig, Univ. Bibl. 683," Arch FrPraed 34 (1964) 45–106. **Illustration credit:** Fig. 1. Alinari photo.

[J. A. WEISHEIPL]

ALBERT OF JERUSALEM, ST., patriarch of Jerusalem; b. Parma, Italy, *c.* 1149; d. Acre, Holy Land, Sept. 14, 1214 (feast, Sept. 25). He studied theology, civil law and Canon Law before becoming a canon regular in the monastery of the Holy Cross in Mortara. In 1184 he was made bishop of Bobbio whence he was soon transferred to *Vercelli in Lombardy. A skilled diplomat, he served as mediator between Pope *Clement III and Emperor *Frederick I Barbarossa, and later as a legate of Pope *Innocent III in the north of Italy, where he brought about peace between Parma and Piacenza. His reputation for diplomacy and piety led to his selection as patriarch of Jerusalem in 1205. Since the Moslems held Jerusalem after 1187, he established his residence in St. Jean d'Acre where he worked hard to keep peace between all factions. In his capacity as patriarch he was requested by Burchard (d. 1221), prior of the hermits living on Mt. Carmel, to give them a rule, which he did in 16 short chapters (*see* CARMELITES). He was assassinated on the Feast of the Exaltation of the Cross by a disgruntled former master of the Hospital of the Holy Spirit at Acre whom he had deposed (*see* HOSPITALLERS). His feast was first introduced by the Carmelites in 1411 and was formally approved in 1666.

Bibliography: ActSS April 1:764–799. P. MARIE-JOSEPH, DHGE 1:1564–67. J. BAUR, LexThK² 1:279.

[V. L. BULLOUGH]

ALBERT OF PISA, Franciscan minister general 1239–40; d. Jan. 23, 1240. According to tradition he was received into the Order by St. *Francis in 1211. He rapidly advanced to positions of responsibility, and so acquired wide administrative experience. Albert's appointments as provincial minister ranged from Tuscany and other regions of Italy, to Germany, Spain, Hungary, and England. He valued and enforced the precepts of St. Francis and became a leading opponent of *Elias of Cortona. When Elias was deposed in 1239, Albert was elected minister general. The constitutions passed under his presidency at the chapter, though later revised, permanently affected the Order's government and development.

Bibliography: THOMAS OF ECCLESTON, *De adventu Fratrum Minorum in Angliam,* ed. A. G. LITTLE (2d. ed. Manchester 1951). *Chronica Fratris Jordani,* ed. H. BOEHMER (Paris 1908). A. DE SERENT, DHGE 1:1544–45. R. B. BROOKE, *Early Franciscan Government* (Cambridge, Eng. 1959).

[R. B. BROOKE]

ALBERT OF PONTIDA, ST., monastic reformer; d. Pontida, Italy, Sept. 12, 1095 (feast, Sept. 12; in Pontida, Sept. 2). After recovering from a near mortal wound, he gave up the life of a soldier, made a pilgrimage to *Santiago de Compostela, and entered the *Benedictine Order during the height of the reform movement led by *Hugh of Cluny. He founded the monastery of Saint James at Pontida, located between the towns of Bergamo and Lecco, *c.* 1080 and became its first prior. He continued to direct the fortunes of this foundation as part of the Cluniac organization until his death, and he was buried there. When the monastery was destroyed by fire in 1373, his remains were transferred to the church of St. Mary Major in Bergamo, where they were honored until 1911, when they were returned to Pontida to the restored abbey church.

Bibliography: J. MABILLON, *Annales Ordinis S. Benedicti,* 6 v. (Lucca 1739–45) 5:322. L. SECOMANDI, *S. Alberto di Pontida ed il suo monasterio* (Bergamo 1895). Kehr ItalPont 6.1:392–394. R. BIRON, DHGE 1:1545–46. G. MORIN, in RevBén 38 (1926) 53–59. J. BAUR, LexThK² 1:280.

[K. NOLAN]

ALBERT I OF RIGA, bishop; b. near Bremen, *c.* 1165; d. Riga, Jan. 17, 1229 (feast, prior to the Reformation, June 1). He came from a Buxhövden ministerial family, was a canon at Bremen after 1189, and was consecrated bishop of Livonia by Archbishop Hartwig II on March 28, 1199. After negotations with the Pope, the King, and Denmark, he landed at the mouth of the Düna in 1200 with a large force of crusaders. He founded the city of Riga in 1201 and made it a bishopric. By 1207 the area between the Düna and the Aa (Lielupe) Rivers was under his control. Soon Albert became involved in the great controversies of that period and territory. The Roman Curia wished to establish a protective state (Marienland) itself and distrusted Albert because of his connection with the Hohenstaufen, who had recognized him as an imperial prince in 1207 and 1225; therefore the Holy See strengthened the Order of the *Knights of the Sword, which was supported by the empire (1210) as well. Although Riga remained a bishopric, it was no longer a suffragan of Bremen after 1214, and received metropolitan privileges over mission dioceses. It became an archbishopric only in 1253. Rome supported the Danes in Estonia. Meanwhile Albert, forced against his will by the Knights of the Sword to submit temporarily (1219–22) to Waldemar II, came into conflict with the Russians, who supported an aimless pagan revolt (1217–24). This ultimately led to a compromise among the Germans, so that the conquered territory was divided between Albert and the Knights. This division became a source of future weakness for the region, a part of which the city of Riga later claimed as its territory.

Bibliography: HEINRICUS LETTUS, *Chronicon Livoniae*, ed. A. BAUER (2d ed. Würzburg 1959). *Baltische Lande* 1 (Riga 1939). F. KOCH, *Livland und das Reich bis zum Jahre 1225* (Posen 1943). H. LAAKMANN, NDB 1:130. M. HELLMANN, *Das Lettenland im Mittelalter* (Münster 1954); LexThK² 1:280–281. G. ALLMANG, DHGE 1:1440–41.

[H. WOLFRAM]

ALBERT II OF RIGA, archbishop of *Riga; b. Cologne, late 12th century; d. 1273. Albert Suerbeer is frequently said to have been a Dominican, though this is probably an error. The assertion that he studied at Paris and took a master's degree there is also doubtful. He taught at the cathedral school in Bremen and in 1229 was nominated bishop of Livonia, but the chapter at Riga refused to accept him, choosing instead a Premonstratensian, Nicholas. In 1240 Albert was appointed archbishop of *Armagh, where he supported the English King, *Henry III, against the rebellious barons in the struggle over church property and promoted the canonization of *Edmund of Abingdon. Albert took part in the First Council of *Lyons, 1245, and in 1246 was appointed archbishop of Prussia, Livonia, and Esthonia and papal legate for these countries and adjacent lands. Local opposition prevented him from exercising his authority in these posts, and from 1247 to 1253 he acted as apostolic administrator of the See of Lübeck. In 1253, on the death of the incumbent Nicholas, he was elected by the chapter to the See of Riga; 2 years later he was confirmed by *Alexander IV as archbishop and metropolitan. His efforts to extend the influence of his see met with strong opposition from the powerful local military order, the *Knights of the Sword, which in 1238 had been assimilated to the *Teutonic Knights. This opposition caused the archbishop to be imprisoned briefly in 1268, though his cause was supported by the citizens of Riga.

Bibliography: P. VON GOETZE, *Albert Suerbeer, Erzbischof von Preussen, Livland, und Ehstland* (St. Petersburg 1854). M. H. MACINERNY, *A History of the Irish Dominicans* (Dublin 1916). G. ALLMANG, DHGE 1:1563. M. HELLMANN, LexThK² 1:281.

[P. M. STARRS]

ALBERT OF SARTEANO, BL., Franciscan missionary; b. Sarteano, near Siena, Italy, 1385; d. Milan, Italy, Aug. 15, 1450 (feast, Aug. 15). He received his early education from *Guarino of Verona and in 1415 joined the *Franciscan Order. From 1435 to 1437 he worked as a preacher under the direction of *Bernardine of Siena in the Holy Land. As a delegate of Pope *Eugene IV, Albert made a second journey to the Near East (1439–41), during which he helped win the good will of the Coptic Patriarch John of Alexandria, and so prepared the way for the reunion realized at the Council of *Florence in 1442. He was vicar general of the Franciscan Order from 1442 to 1443. His cult has not been publicly approved, but he is honored in the Franciscan Order as blessed.

Bibliography: B. NERI, *La vita e i tempi beato Albertio da Sarteano* (Florence 1902). A. DE SÉRENT, DHGE 1:1554–56. Wadding Ann v.9, 10, 11. G. HOFMANN, "Kopten und Aethiopier auf dem Konzil von Florenz" in OrChrPer 8 (1942) 5–39. E. MARTIRE, EncCatt 1:694–695. G. FUSSENEGGER, LexThK² 1:282.

[K. NOLAN]

ALBERT OF SAXONY, nominalist philosopher of Paris and bishop; b. Rickmersdorf, lower Saxony, 1316; d. 1390. He was an outstanding master in arts at the University of Paris from 1351 to 1362 and rector of the University in 1357 and 1362. In his *Quaestiones super libros Physicorum* (Venice 1504), *Quaestiones in libros de caelo et mundo* (Venice 1520), and *Quaestiones in libros de generatione* (Venice 1504) he was much influenced by the teaching of *John Buridan and *Nicholas Oresme, notable on the theory of *impetus and on the configuration of forms that can be increased and decreased. In his *Logica* (Venice 1522), *Quaestiones super libros Posteriorum* (Venice 1497), and *Sophismata* (Paris 1489) he was greatly influenced by the *nominalism of *William of Ockham. His *Tractatus obligationum* and *Insolubilia* (Paris 1490) clearly show the influence of Oxford logicians. He promulgated and developed the new physics initiated by *Thomas Bradwardine and John Buridan. He wrote a number of short treatises on proportionality and the square of the circle that became popular textbooks in universities. In his unedited commentary on the *Nicomachean Ethics* of Aristotle he followed closely the commentary of *Walter Burley. In 1365 he was named the first rector of the new University of Vienna. In 1366 he was nominated and consecrated bishop of Halberstadt; he served in this office until his death. His writings in natural philosophy were widely read until the 17th century.

Bibliography: B. NARDI, EncFil 1:128. A. MAIER, *Die Vorläufer Galileis im 14. Jahrhundert* (Rome 1949); *An der Grenze von Scholastik und Naturwissenschaft* (2d ed. Rome 1952). M. CLAGETT, *The Science of Mechanics in the Middle Ages* (Madison, Wis. 1959). Gilson HistChrPhil 516–520. P. HOSSFELD, Lex ThK² 1:281. U. VIGLINO, EncCatt 1:695–696.

[J. A. WEISHEIPL]

ALBERT OF TRAPANI, ST., Carmelite; b. Trapani, Sicily, *c.* 1240; d. Messina, Sicily, Aug. 7, 1307 (feast, Aug. 7). By 1280 he had entered the *Carmelite monastery in his native town, and despite his own humble opinion of himself he prepared for the priesthood and was ordained by 1289. He effected numerous conversions throughout Sicily and was made religious superior of the Sicilian province in 1296. By the time of his death, he had gained an extraordinary reputation for sanctity. He was buried at Messina, where he is honored as the patron because of his miraculous assistance to the city during a siege in 1301. His head is preserved at Trapani. His cult was approved by *Callistus III in 1457 and by *Sixtus IV in 1476. His relics are widely disseminated because of the currently used blessing of the water of St. Albert in the Carmelite ritual; his aid is invoked against fever. The oldest biography dates from 1385, and few details of his life are certain. He is often shown holding a lily, or receiving the Christ Child from Our Lady. There are paintings of him by Francesco Francia and Bernardo Monaldi.

Bibliography: L. M. SAGGI, DizBiogItal 1:740–741. B. M. XIBERTA Y ROQUETA, "Catalogus sanctorum ordinis carmelitarum," *De visione sancti Simonis Stock* (Rome 1950) 281–307. P. MARIE-JOSEPH, DHGE 1:1558–59. G. MESTERS, LexThK² 1:282–283. Réau IAC 3.1:47. AMBROGIO DI SANTA TERESA, EncCatt 1:696. "Vita s. Alberti confessoris ordinis carmelitarum," Anal Boll 17 (1898) 317–336. ActSS Aug. 2:215–239.

[E. R. CARROLL]

ALBERTARIO, DAVIDE, journalist; b. Filighera (Pavia), Italy, Feb. 16, 1846; d. Carenno (Bergamo), Italy, Sept. 21, 1902. He became a journalist in the year of his ordination (1868), after earning the doctorate in theology at Rome's Pontifical Gregorian University. In 1872, he became part owner and associate editor, then editor, of the daily *Osservatore Cattolico,* of Milan and of the weekly *Il Popolo Cattolico*. He defended zealously, if not always temperately, the principles of the *Syllabus of Errors and of *Vatican Council I, and opposed not only liberal intolerance and "irreligious tyranny" but also the "liberal Catholicism" of some priests and bishops. This position set him against men of such outstanding reputation as Bishop *Bonomelli of Cremona and Bishop *Scalabrini of Piacenza, and such well-known priests as the noted geologist, Antonio Stoppani. In 1894, at a time when relations between Church and State had become less stormy, Albertario invited to the *Osservatore Cattolico* Filippo Meda, who was to succeed him as editor and give a new impetus to public action by Catholics. During this period the paper continually advised its readers to prepare for the time when the Holy See might permit Italian Catholics to reenter political life (*see* MARGOTTI, GIACOMO). In 1898, during a disproportionate reaction of the government to certain social movements, which led to the temporary dissolution of Catholic organizations, Albertario, who had bravely defended the poorer classes, was arrested. Together with certain Syndicalist Socialists, he was tried and condemned to 3 years in prison, a sentence generally regarded as unjust. After a year he was released following the lively agitation that the sentence had aroused among Italian Catholics. He told the story of his imprisonment in two volumes entitled *Un anno di carcere* (1900).

See also CATHOLIC PRESS, WORLD SURVEY, 16.

[E. LUCATELLO]

ALBERTI, LEANDRO, Italian Dominican, historian and Inquisitor; b. Bologna, 1479; d. Bologna, 1552?. As a young religious at Forlì and then at Bologna, he studied under the humanist G. Garzoni and the theologian S. Mazzolini of Priero. In 1514–15 and in 1525 as socius to two masters general, the celebrated *Cajetan and the noted theologian Francesco Silvestri of Ferrara, called "*Ferrariensis," he traveled through Italy, France and Germany. After 1532, apart from a brief period as vicar of Santa Sabina in Rome, he was involved almost exclusively with duties of the office of the Inquisition at Bologna. During the transfer of the Council of Trent to Bologna (1547), Alberti was frequently consulted. Among Alberti's literary productions, several works have merited distinction: *De viris illustribus Ordinis Praedicatorum* (Bologna, 1517), still profitably consulted; *Descrittione di tutta Italia* (Bologna, 1550), his principal work, published in 12 editions; and the *Historie di Bologna* (Bologna and Vicenza, 1541–91).

Bibliography: Quétif-Échard 2.1:137–139. G. M. MAZZUCHELLI, *Gli scrittori d'Italia,* v.1 (Brescia 1753) 306–310. A. L. REDIGONDA, DizBiogItal 1:699–702.

[A. L. REDIGONDA]

ALBERTI, LEONE BATTISTA, Renaissance architect and theoretician; b. Genoa, 1404; d. Rome, 1472. Educated in Padua and a graduate in Canon Law from the University of Bologna, he became a leading Italian humanist. During his lifetime his fame rested on the book *Della famiglia* (1437–41). Subsequently he became known best for his writings on the arts: *On Painting* (1435) is the first and basic theoretical exposition of 15th-century Italian art, and his treatise *On Architecture* (1450) played an important role in the development of Renaissance buildings. He derived the guiding principle of his aesthetics from the ancient Aristotelian postulate, revived by St. Thomas Aquinas, that art imitates nature. Accordingly, in *Della famiglia* he wrote that children ought to be brought up with attention to their individual natures. Similarly, in *On Architecture* he maintained that architecture imitates nature in its employment of materials and adherence to structural laws. Painting, on the other hand, meant for Alberti an illustration and characterization of the *istoria;* that is, the painter had to remain faithful to the nature of the narrative subject matter.

As an architect Alberti was more a designer-aesthete trained in the liberal arts than a builder. Inspired by antiquity, he created the Palazzo Rucellai (1446), the façade of S. Maria Novella (1456) in Florence, and the Tempio Malatestiano (1447) at Rimini. In Mantua he designed the centrally planned church of St. Sebastian (1460) and the church of St. Andrea (1470). In the latter he used the monumental Roman triumphal arch for the façade, and in lieu of traditional columns he repeated the same motif in the interior to create the rows of side chapels. This single-nave interior remained the model for Catholic churches in succeeding centuries.

Bibliography: *Opere volgari . . .,* ed. A. BONUCCI, 5 v. (Florence 1843–49). P. H. MICHEL, *Un Idéal humaine au XVe siècle: La Pensée de L. B. Alberti* (Paris 1930), bibliog. M. L. GENGARO, *Leon Battista Alberti: Teorico e architetto del rinascimento* (Milan 1939). I. GALANTIC, *Sources and Analysis of Alberti's Theory of Art* (Doctoral diss. unpub. Harvard U. 1965).

[I. GALANTIC]

ALBERTINUS OF FONTE AVELLANA, ST., abbot; d. April 13, 1294 (feast, April 13). He became a *Benedictine monk *c.* 1250 and was an outstanding prior general of the congregation of *Fonte

Avellana in the Marches from 1275 until his death. He was buried in the monastery church at Fonte Avellana and was soon honored as a saint. His cult was approved by Pope *Pius VI on Aug. 21, 1782. He is regarded as a holy protector against hernia.

Bibliography: G. B. MITTARELLI and A. COSTADONI, *Annales Camaldulenses,* v.5 (Venice 1760) 207–210. A. GIBELLI, *Monografia dell'antico monastero di S. Croce di Fonte Avellana: I suoi priori ed abbati* (Faenza 1895). R. BIRON, DHGE 1:1585–86. Zimmermann KalBen 2:50–51. Mercati-Pelzer DE 1:80. A. M. ZIMMERMANN, LexThK[2] 1:283.

[K. NOLAN]

ALBERTO CASTELLANI, historian and editor; b. *c.* 1459; d. 1552. He entered the Dominican priory of SS. John and Paul in Venice, and although the details of his life are obscure, his name appears often in connection with writings that cover a wide field of interest, most of them concerned with the history of his order. These include the *Catalogus sanctorum a Petro de Natalibus Veneto e regione Castellana episcopo Equilino concinnatus* (Venice 1501), *Catalogus illustrium Ordinis virorum* (Venice 1501), and *Chronica brevis ab initio Ordinis usque ad praesens tempus* (Venice 1504). Besides these historical accounts of the prominent Dominicans from the foundation of the order to his own time, he edited the constitutions of the Order of Preachers; the formularies for the election of priors, visitation of convents, and conduct of chapters; and the valuable *Tabula super privilegia papalia Ordini Praedicatorum concessa* (1507). In 1519 he edited a Biblical concordance of the Old and New Testament, and he is famous for his revision of the *Pontificale Romanum.* (*See* PONTIFICAL, ROMAN.) Among the many ascetical, patristic, and apologetical works he published were some of the sermons of Caesarius of Arles and Zeno, Bishop of Verona (Venice 1508), and an interesting example of devotional iconography, the *Rosario de la gloriosa Vergine Maria* (Venice 1521), in which the mysteries of the Rosary were incised in wood for popular use.

Bibliography: Quétif-Échard 2:48–49. U. MANNUCCI, EncIt 2:192–193. A. WALZ, EncCatt 3:1018–19, bibliog.

[E. D. MCSHANE]

ALBERTUS MAGNUS COLLEGE

Founded in 1925 in New Haven, Conn., by the Dominican Sisters of St. Mary of the Springs, Albertus Magnus College is the oldest residential, 4-year liberal arts Catholic college for women in New England. The College received its charter from the state of Connecticut in 1925 and was subsequently accredited by the New England Association of Colleges and Secondary Schools, Connecticut State Department of Education, University of the State of New York, and American Medical Association. It is affiliated with The Catholic University of America, and holds institutional membership in the Association of American Colleges, American Council on Education, Association of College Admissions Counselors, College Entrance Examination Board, National Catholic Educational Association, National Commission on Accrediting, American Alumni Council, and American Association for University Women.

The Dominican Sisters administer the College through a board of trustees and a staff of administrative officers, all of whom are appointed from within the congregation by the major superior in Columbus, Ohio. In legal, financial, and public relations matters, the administration receives counsel and guidance from an advisory board, which consists of men and women of varied professional, business, and civic backgrounds. In 1954 the formation of a lay development council was begun to aid the College in the specific task of planning and coordinating activities toward a long-range program of expansion.

In 1964 administrative and teaching faculty comprised 7 priests, 22 sisters, and 27 laymen, holding 20 doctoral, 2 professional, and 28 master's degrees. Enrollment numbered 495 students from 25 states and 3 foreign countries, an increase of 75 per cent over the 5 previous years. Faculty-student ratio was approximately 1 to 10, while resident-day student ratio averaged 55 to 45. Financial aid in some form was distributed to 31 per cent of students during 1963–64.

The College derives its income from tuition, fees, and gifts, except for a modest return from a small endowment fund. Administered as an independent entity, it receives no regular financial support either from the motherhouse or from ecclesiastical sources. A full-time lay director of development is in charge of a fund-raising program for expansion.

The curriculum covers a broad range of academic disciplines in languages, literature, fine arts, and the natural and social sciences with emphasis on the traditional Dominican ideal of liberal education. A demonstrated competence in a selected field of concentration is a prerequisite for all degree candidates. Begun in the junior year, the field of concentration is a combination of a major and related subjects and is designed to develop depth and proficiency in a specific area of knowledge. The curriculum, which contains 195 courses, offers 18 subjects for the required intensive study leading to the B.A. degree. Preprofessional programs are offered in medicine, law, and teacher-training for secondary education. Additional academic opportunities and advanced programs of study open to superior students include the early decision plan, an honors at entrance program, advanced placement, foreign study and independent study, and national scholastic honor society membership.

In 1964 the College library contained 44,000 volumes supplemented by more than 375 subscriptions to American and foreign periodicals and magazines. Special collections include *Dominicana; Connecticutiana;* books of special presses; first editions of the works and letters of New England writer Louise Imogen Guiney; the works of American author Donald G. Mitchell; and facsimiles of the *Book of Kells, Lindisfarne Gospels,* and *Gutenberg Bible.*

In 1961 the College completed the first phase of a master plan of expansion to reach total completion by 1975, the golden jubilee of Albertus Magnus College.

[A. F. KOHUT]

ALBI, ARCHDIOCESE OF (ALBIENSIS)

Metropolitan see since 1678, in southwest France, 2,232 square miles in area, corresponding to Tarn department. In 1961 it had 506 parishes, 416 secular and 132 religious priests, 234 men in 15 religious houses, 1,363 women in 127 convents, and 297,000 Catholics (with some 10,000 Protestants). Its four suffragans, which had 1,588 parishes, 1,662 priests, 2,350 sisters, and 723,000 Catholics, were: Cahors (3d century) with a university (1332) that united with that of *Toulouse

Albi, the cathedral of Sainte-Cécile, 1282–1514.

in 1751; Mende (4th century); Perpignan (Elne in Aragon, 571; moved to Perpignan in 1602) with a university (1350) that was suppressed in the French Revolution; and Rodez (475). The city of Albi, on the left bank of the Tarn River, has a population of 34,700 and is the capital of the Tarn department.

Albi was detached from the *civitas Ruthenorum* (Rodez) in the 4th century as the *civitas Albigensium* and included in *Aquitania I.* The see was created after the *civitas,* at the end of the 4th century; the first known bishop, Diogenianus, appears in the 5th century. Albi was held by the Visigoths (who detained St. Eugene, bishop of Carthage, there in 475) until *Clovis took it (507). Feudal lords seized the bishopric in the 10th century, but in the 11th-century Gregorian reform the churches were freed. Rather unjustly, Albi's name has been given to the Manichaean heretics (*Albigenses) of the 12th and 13th centuries, rampant throughout south France. Bishops and mendicant orders (Dominicans and Franciscans) fought the heresy, and Simon de Montfort and *Louis VIII led crusades against its protectors. In 1264 the bishops became temporal lords of the city under the suzerainty of the Holy See. The 16th-century Wars of Religion brought grave troubles, but a religious renaissance took place at the end of the 16th and in the 17th century (convents and episcopal activity). Albi's bishops include St. Salvius (574–584), the reformer Louis d'Amboise (1474–1503), the reformer Hyacinthe Serroni (1678–87) who founded the seminary, Cardinal François de *Bernis (1764–94), and Eudoxe *Mignot (1900–18) who renewed ecclesiastical studies.

The red-brick, fortified Cathedral of Sainte-Cécile (1282–1514) symbolized the temporal power of the bishops. The late 13th-century episcopal palace (*La Berbie*) adjoins it. The 6th-century monastery of Saint-Salvy, with a 10th–13th century church, has a crypt and a cloister of note.

Albi, suffragan to *Bourges, was divided in 1317 to form Castres, and in 1678 was made an archbishopric by Innocent XI. Suppressed by the *Concordat of 1801 and united to Montpellier, it was restored as a see and a metropolitan with its present suffragans (1817–22). The diocese now comprises the old See of Albi and the former Sees of Castres and Lavaur (1317). Former monasteries outside the city include Vieux (a double monastery founded by St. Eugene), Troclar (the late 7th-century double monastery of St. Sigolène), Castres (7th-9th century, which became a see), Gaillac (10th century), Sainte-Marie of Vielmur (10th), Sainte-Marie of Ardorel (12th, Cistercian in 1138), and Sainte-Marie of Candeil (12th century). The council of 1254, attended by bishops of the provinces of *Narbonne, Bourges, and *Bordeaux, dealt with heresy, ecclesiastical discipline, usury, and the rights and obligations of Jews. Albi has 10 diocesan statutes (1230–1762).

Outside the city are the cathedrals of Castres (17th–18th century) and Lavaur (14th–16th, fortified), the former abbey church of Saint-Michel in Gaillac (16th-century Romanesque, fortified), and the fortified church of Rabastens (13th–14th). There are shrines to Our Lady near Albi and in Grazac, as well as Saint-Crucifix at Cordres. Among the schools of the diocese is the College of Sorèze, where *Lacordaire was superior.

Bibliography: C. DE VIC and J. VAISSETE, *Histoire générale de Languedoc,* ed. E. DULAURIER et al., 16 v. in 17 (new ed. Toulouse 1872–1904). L. DE LACGER, DHGE 1:1600–17; *États administratifs des anciens diocèses d'Albi, de Castres, et de Lavaur* (Paris 1921). E. JARRY, *Catholicisme* 1:273–275. AnnPont (1965) 22. **Illustration credit:** French Embassy, Press and Information Division, New York City.

[E. JARRY]

ALBIGENSES

Followers of the Catharist heresy, which was already existing in Bulgaria (*see* BOGOMILS) in the mid-10th century; they professed a form of *Manichaeism, which had gradually spread westward along the trade routes. The areas in which the heresy enjoyed its greatest strength were the Balkan peninsula, northern Italy, and southern France. Brought from northern France to Albi (County of Toulouse) between 1145 and 1155, it spread from there through all of Languedoc, acquiring in the process the name of Albigensianism, by which it is better known.

Albigensian doctrine is neo-Manichaean in character, but its relationship to the earlier heresy cannot be traced. In its stricter and more characteristic form, Albigensianism teaches that the devil is not only the creator of matter but even a rival god. The Christian God is the creator of spirit-being only. The human soul, created good, had rebelled and was expelled from heaven. The devil at once imprisoned it in matter. Salvation for the soul consists in liberation from matter (a result attainable only by ceaseless struggle against material allurements) and return to its original heavenly state. It was to teach men this truth that Christ came to earth.

Christ is not God but an angelic spirit whose "body" had only a corporal appearance. He therefore did not really die or rise again. There will, likewise, be no final resurrection of the body for the rest of the human race; nor is there any hell or purgatory. Purgation is to be achieved on earth. For those already purified, death is the longed-for release from matter; to hasten the time of its coming by suicide (*endura*) would be permissible and even laudatory. Those who by the time of death have not achieved purgation will have to do so through *metempsychosis.

The Catholic Mass, Sacraments, and other religious practices involving the use of material things were condemned as vain and sacrilegious. And yet, in addition to public reading and explanation of the Scriptures (New Testament, mainly), the Albigenses themselves indulged in a rite of public confession (*apparelhamen-*

tum) and a ritual meal (agape). Of chief importance was the *consolamentum,* a rite of initiation by which one passed from the rank of ordinary believer to that of the Perfect (*Katharoi;* *Cathari: the "pure"); the rite was believed to efface all sin and impart the Holy Spirit (identified as a helping angel).

Ordinary believers (Believers, Hearers) had only to "venerate" the Perfect (*melioramentum*) and pledge to seek the *consolamentum* when death seemed imminent. The Perfect, however, were bound to fulfill all the ascetical requirements of the sect: never to lie; to refuse to take an oath (particularly subversive to medieval society, bound together as it was by oaths); never to take human life even in war or self-defense; to abstain from meat or animal products; and never to marry (or if already married, to desert the wedded state). The sexual act was considered the greatest of evils because it added to the number of souls that were incarnate. The Perfect were the preachers of the sect. From their number were drawn bishops and suffragans of dioceses and the local deacons, whose role was somewhat that of pastors.

Contacts with the Orient resulting from the *Crusades had added to the luxurious living of Languedoc and had intensified the tradition of courtly love that already existed there. This atmosphere had a baneful effect also on clerical and monastic life. The simple and disciplined lives of the Catharist preachers stood in marked contrast to the clergy of southern France, and their words, accordingly, had greater weight. That they won many converts, however, was attributable equally to the easy morality permitted the ordinary Catharist believer.

The history of the Church's reaction to the heresy is chiefly that of the rise of the papal *Inquisition and, *pari passu,* of the origin and early development of the *mendicant orders. The details of the military undertaking known as the Albigensian Crusade belong, similarly, more to the account of the final unification of France (*see* LOUIS VIII, KING OF FRANCE). The political strength of Catharism was definitively broken by the taking of Montségur in 1245. By that time, moreover, the Inquisition had been all but finally perfected as a counteragent; and though the Albigenses continued to press their cause with great zeal and subtlety, they lost ground steadily, and nothing was heard of them after the close of the 14th century.

Albigensian heretics disputing with Dominicans, detail of a 14th-century fresco by Simone Martini in the church of Santa Maria Novella at Florence.

Bibliography: Sources. J. J. I. VON DÖLLINGER, *Beiträge zur Sektengeschichte des Mittelalters,* 2 v. in 1 (Munich 1890; repr. New York 1960). C. DOUAIS, ed., *Documents pour servir à l'histoire de l'Inquisition dans le Languedoc,* 2 v. (Paris 1900). *Cahiers d'études cathares* (Arques, France 1949–). Literature. J. GUIRAUD, *Histoire de l'Inquisition au Moyen Âge,* 2 v. (Paris 1935–38). A. C. SHANNON, *The Popes and Heresy in the 13th Century* (Villanova, Pa. 1949). H. SÖDERBERG, *La Religion des Cathares: Études sur le gnosticisme de la basse antiquité et du moyen âge* (Uppsala 1949). Fliche-Martin 9.2:330–351; 10:112–147, 291–340. S. RUNCIMAN, *The Medieval Manichee* (Cambridge, Eng. 1947; repr. 1955). A. BORST, *Die Katharer* (Stuttgart 1953). P. DE BERNE-LAGARDE, *Bibliographie du catharisme languedocien* (Textes et documents 1; Toulouse 1957). S. SAVINI, *Il catarismo italiano ed i suoi vescovi nei secoli XIII e XIV* (Florence 1958). F. NIEL, *Albigeois et Cathares* (Paris 1956). **Illustration credit:** Alinari-Art Reference Bureau.

[J. E. BRESNAHAN]

ALBINUS (AUBIN) OF ANGERS, ST., abbot and bishop; b. Vannes, France, 469; d. March 1, 550 (feast, March 1). He entered the monastery of Tincillac at an early age and was elected abbot in 504; he was then 35 years of age. Under his rule the community prospered, and in 529 he was made bishop of *Angers. In that office he proved himself zealous and capable as well as devout. As bishop, Albinus gave particular attention to the poor, spending large sums for the ransoming of captives. He was energetic in putting into effect the decrees of the Synods of Orleans (538 and 541), in which he had participated. His remains are enshrined in the church dedicated to his memory in 556, and his intercession is credited with many miracles, as a result of which he has become the object of popular veneration, not only in France, but throughout Europe. His vita was composed by *Fortunatus (MG AuctAnt 4:27–33).

Bibliography: ActSS March 1:54–63. F. UZUREAU, DHGE 5: 254–255. Zimmermann KalBen 1:273. R. AIGRAIN, *Catholicisme* 1:1012–13. Mercati-Pelzer DE 1:83. Butler Th Attw 1:452. G. ALLEMANG, LexThK[2] 1:289.

[J. F. FAHEY]

ALBO, JOSEPH, Spanish-Jewish philosopher, theologian, and polemicist; b. *c.* 1380; d. *c.* 1440. Not much is known of his life. He lived for a while at Daroca (province of Saragossa) and later at Soria (province of Castile). One of his teachers was Ḥasdai *Crescas. At the celebrated theological Disputation of Tortosa (1413–14), which had been convoked by the antipope *Benedict XIII during his self-imposed exile in Spain, Albo was one of the leading spokesmen in defense of Judaism against the attacks on it by the convert from Judaism, Gerónimo de Santa Fe (called before his conversion Joshua ben Joseph ibn Vives de Lorca and commonly known as Lorki).

As a result of the debate, Albo, recognizing the need for a good theological work for the defense of Judaism, composed his best-known book, the *Sefer ha-Ikkarim* (Book of Principles), completed in 1425. It soon became one of the most popular works on Jewish theology. It was first printed at Soncino in 1485, and later editions with commentaries were published at Fribourg (1584) and at Venice (1618). In this work Albo attempted to determine precisely the essential beliefs of Judaism. Four tractates make up the work. The first, which serves as a general introduction, treats of the bases of all true religion, which are Albo's three "principles": the existence of God, divine revelation, and reward and punishment. In the three following tractates the author studies in detail each of these three basic principles and their consequences. In this way he sets forth a complete system of Jewish theology, sometimes following *Maimonides and sometimes Crescas and borrowing much from his contemporary Simeon ben Tzemaḥ Duran. Like Crescas, he detached himself from the pure intellectualism of the earlier Jewish philosophers and placed the goal of human life not only in intellectual but also in religious and moral perfection. Jewish writers, e.g., Isaac *Abrabanel, have noted Albo's seeming indifference toward the Jewish belief in a coming Messiah.

See also JEWISH PHILOSOPHY.

Bibliography: J. ALBO, *Sefer ha-Ikkarim,* tr. I. HUSIK, 5 v. in 4 (Philadelphia 1929–30), a critical ed. of the Hebrew text with Eng. tr. I. HUSIK, *A History of Medieval Jewish Philosophy* (2d ed. New York 1930; pa. 1958); "Joseph Albo: The Last of the Jewish Mediaeval Philosophers," *Proceedings of the American Academy for Jewish Research* 1 (1928–30). G. VAJDA, *Introduction à la pensée juive du moyen âge* (Paris 1947) 186–189, 286. A. TÄNZER, *Die Regionsphilosophie des Joseph Albo* (Frankfurt 1896). E. ZOLLI, EncCatt 1:714.

[A. BRUNOT]

ALBORNOZ, GIL ÁLVAREZ CARRILLO DE, Archbishop of Toledo, cardinal legate, restorer of the Papal States; b. Cuenca, Spain, *c.* 1295; d. near Viterbo, Italy, Aug. 23, 1367. He studied Canon Law in Toulouse and rose in the service of Alfonso XI to succeed his uncle as archbishop of Toledo in 1338. As royal chancellor and ecclesiastical primate, he pursued reforms in his diocese, crusaded against the Moslems, and played an important part in the unification of Castile. When Peter I (1350–69) reversed the policies of Alfonso, Albornoz in June 1350 left a vicar in his see and went to Avignon, where *Clement VI made him a cardinal in December 1350. In June 1353 *Innocent VI gave him extensive powers as legate in Italy to prepare the Papal States for the return of the popes. By mid-1357 Albornoz had defeated the petty tyrants and modernized the government of the *States of the Church, centralizing authority territorially and favoring parliaments and communal rights against individual privileges. Innocent then yielded to the Visconti of Milan, to whom Albornoz would not cede Bologna, and replaced him. Albornoz, however, returned to Italy in October 1358 to regain the papal position. His second mission was made difficult as foreign powers became involved in the dispute over Bologna and the return of the popes to Rome. In November 1363 *Urban V replaced Albornoz a second time. The cardinal remained in the Papal States as legate to Naples; he died escorting Urban to Rome. The *Constitutiones Aegidianae,* which Albornoz promulgated for the Marches of Ancona in 1357, were later extended to all the Papal States and lasted until 1816. He bequeathed his enormous wealth in four countries to a multitude of pious causes. In 1365 he founded a college for Spanish students in Bologna where many of his papers remain to be studied.

Gil Álvarez Carrillo de Albornoz.

Bibliography: P. SELLA, *Costituzioni Egidiane dell' anno 1357* (Rome 1912). G. MOLLAT, DHGE 1:1717–25; 2:1770–73. F. FILIPPINI, *Il cardinale Egidio Albornoz* (Bologna 1933). J. BENEYTO PEREZ, *El cardenal Albornoz* (Madrid 1950). G. MOLLAT, *Popes at Avignon, 1305–1378* (Camden, N.J. 1963). **Illustration credit:** Embassy of Spain, Washington, D.C.

[E. P. COLBERT]

ALBRECHT OF BRANDENBURG, cardinal archbishop of Mainz, elector of the Holy Roman Empire; b. Berlin, June 28, 1490; d. Mainz, Sept. 24, 1545. He was the younger son of Johann Cicero, Elector of Brandenburg, and Margareta, daughter of Duke Wilhelm III of Saxony; his brother, Joachim I, succeeded to the electorate upon the father's death. Through the influence of his father and brother, Albrecht became archbishop of Magdeburg (1513) and bishop of Halberstadt. When the archbishopric of Mainz, which carried with it the title of Elector, became vacant in 1514, Albrecht put forth his candidacy. In order to raise the necessary 24,000 ducats (14,000 to pay the installation tax for Mainz and 10,000 to receive the needed dispensation for the plural holding of sees), he made an arrangement with the *Fugger banking house. Genial Jacob Fugger advanced the money to Pope *Leo X in return for one-half of the sum that would be collected from the preaching of an indulgence in Albrecht's dioceses. As the indulgence (for the building of St. Peter's in Rome) had not been allowed to be preached in these dioceses as yet, it was believed that large sums would be raised. In January 1517 Albrecht authorized Johann *Tetzel to preach the indulgence. Martin *Luther posted his 95 theses in protest against the indulgence, Tetzel, and the archbishop.

Albrecht had been strongly influenced by the humanistic atmosphere of the University of Frankfurt-on-der-Oder, which his brother, Joachim I, founded with Albrecht's assistance in 1506. As an admirer of Erasmus he did not hesitate to criticize the Church and advocate reform. Thus he was not unsympathetic to the attacks upon the Church by Luther and his followers in their early stages. However, there was more of Erasmus than Luther in the young humanist and, rather than break with Rome, as did the latter, he supported reform within the Church. As the Protestant Revolt gained momentum, Albrecht aligned his religious and political policies closer to those of his brother in support of the papacy. He founded the University of Halle (papal permission granted in 1531) and introduced reforms in the University of Mainz. In 1541 he invited (Bl.) Peter Faber, SJ, to Mainz, where the Jesuit quickly became the heart of the Counter Reformation in western Germany. A lover of the arts and music, with good taste in architecture,

Albrecht of Brandenburg, miniature portrait in the so-called "Glockendonsches Gebetbuch," commissioned by Albrecht in 1530 for presentation to the Neue Stift at Hälle (Hofbibliothek, Aschaffenburg, Germany MS 9).

Albrecht is one of the finest examples of a 16th-century German Renaissance prince.

Bibliography: J. JANSSEN, *History of the German People at the Close of the Middle Ages,* tr. M. A. MITCHELL and A. M. CHRISTIE, 17 v. (London 1896–1925). J. HEIDEMANN, *Die Reformation in der Mark Brandenburg* (Berlin 1889). Pastor. J. LORTZ, *Die Reformation in Deutschland,* 2 v. (Freiburg 1940). H. HOLBORN, *A History of Modern Germany: The Reformation* (New York 1959). E. W. ZEEDEN, LexThK[2] 1:291–292. J. PIETSCH, DHGE 1:1494–96. W. DELIUS, RGG[3] 1:218. **Illustration credit:** Foto-Samhaber Inh. Hesse, Aschaffenburg, Germany.

[J. G. GALLAHER]

ALBRECHT OF BRANDENBURG-ANSBACH, first duke of Prussia, margrave of Ansbach, and last grand master of the Teutonic Knights; b. Ansbach, May 17, 1490; d. Tapiau, East Prussia (present-day Gvardiesk, Russia), March 20, 1568. A distinguished member of the Hohenzollern family, he was, through his mother, the nephew of King Sigismund of Poland. He was already Margrave of Ansbach when in 1511 he was elected grand master of the *Teutonic Knights of East Prussia, a position he held until April 9, 1525, when he announced his conversion to Lutheranism, suppressed the order, and secularized its property along with the adjacent lands of Samland and Ermland as his personal fief under the suzerainty of the king of Poland. His initial contact with Lutheranism came at the Diet of Nuremberg in 1522, when he met Andreas *Osiander. Later, at *Luther's suggestion, he married (1526). His first wife was Dorothy of Denmark, and by this union he linked *Lutheranism with the Scandinavian countries. His second wife, whom he married in 1550, 3 years after the death of his Danish wife, was Marie of Braunschweig-Calenberg. Under Albrecht's active leadership Lutheranism spread into Kurland, Livonia, and Estonia. His brother William became archbishop of Riga and in 1539 emulated the actions of Albrecht. The University of Königsberg (*Collegium Albertinum*) was founded by Albrecht in 1544 as an academic institution to study and propagate the Lutheran faith. In 1549 he appointed Osiander as professor of theology, and immediately the university was plunged into theological controversy over Osiander's preaching. In the controversy Albrecht supported Osiander and thus helped to widen the split within the ranks of Lutheranism. He died in 1568 lamenting, "We have, alas, very few pastors of souls, but quite a swarm of hirelings and storks." His biographers agree that he saved Prussia from possible absorption by Poland and paved the way for the eventual union of Brandenburg and Prussia in 1618, thus contributing to the rise of Prussia.

Bibliography: ALBRECHT OF BRANDENBURG-ANSBACH, *Vertrau Gott allein,* ed. E. ROTH (Würzburg 1956). P. G. THIELEN, *Die Kultur am Hofe Herzog Albrechts von Preussen* (Göttingen 1953). W. HUBATSCH, RGG[3] 1:218–219. E. M. WERMTER, ed., *Kardinal Stanislaus Hosius, Bischof von Ermland, und Herzog Albrecht von Preussen* (Reformationsgeschichtliche Studien und Texte 83; Münster 1957); LexThK[2] 1:292.

[C. L. HOHL, JR.]

ALBRECHTSBERGER, JOHANN GEORG, influential composer, theorist, and virtuoso of the classical school; b. Klosterneuburg (near Vienna), Austria, Feb. 3, 1736; d. Vienna, March 7, 1809. After receiving music training as a chorister in St. Martin's Church in Klosterneuburg and at the Abbey of *Melk, he was a fellow student with M. *Haydn at the Jesuit college in Vienna and later a student of F. J. *Haydn. He was organist successively in Raab (Hungary), Maria-Taferl (Lower Austria), and Melk (to 1766). His musicianship had been noted by Joseph II as crown prince, and he was named court organist in Vienna in 1772 and also choirmaster at St. Stephen's Cathedral from 1793 until his death. Among his students were *Eybler, *Hummel, and notably *Beethoven, who profited immensely from his contrapuntal exercises. Although he turned out a considerable body of sacred vocal and organ music as well as concert compositions, he was more important for his theoretical writings, such as *Gründliche Anweisung zur Composition* and *Clavierschule für Anfänger.* As with J. J. *Fux, in theory he preferred *stile antico,* yet often applied *stile moderno* in his instrumentally accompanied sacred music. Many of his settings of the Mass Proper and the Office make use of Gregorian **cantus firmi;* all of them exhibit his great contrapuntal skill. Yet in neither his creative nor his theoretic work was he successful in synthesizing the vocal polyphonic style of Palestrina with that of subsequent instrumental polyphony, and in his oratorios he dropped counterpoint in favor of the *galant* style that was then emerging into fashion.

Bibliography: *Organ and instrumental compositions,* ed. O. KAPP, DenkmTonkÖst 33. Individual works also pub. in modern eds. *Complete Works,* ed. I. RITTER VON SEYFRIED (Vienna 1826–37), with biog. E. TITTEL, *Österreichische Kirchenmusik* (Vienna 1961). H. GOOS, MusGG 1:303–307. F. GEHRING, Grove DMM 1:97.

[K. G. FELLERER]

ALBRIGHT, JACOB, founder of the Evangelical Association; b. Pottstown, Pa., May 1, 1759; d. Pottstown, May 18, 1808. The son of German immigrants, he received little formal education, was apprenticed to a brickmaker, and followed this trade throughout his life. Albright was originally a Lutheran, but was converted to Methodism in 1790 and began to preach in German among his neighbors. In 1796 he was licensed as an exhorter and preached among the German settlers of Pennsylvania, Maryland, and Virginia. He began forming classes on the Methodist pattern in 1800, and 3 years later he was ordained a minister by his congregation. When the language barrier separated his German congregations from the mainstream of American Methodism, Albright organized his followers as "The Newly Formed Methodist Conference" (1807) and was chosen by them as their first bishop. The Methodists made no effort to unite with them; and in 1813 the independent conference, subsequently known as the Evangelical Association and still later as the *Evangelical Church, severed its nominal ties with Methodism.

Bibliography: R. YEAKEL, *Albright and His CoLaborers* (Cleveland 1883); *History of the Evangelical Association* (Cleveland 1909). R. W. ALBRIGHT, *History of the Evangelical Church* (Harrisburg 1942).

[R. K. MAC MASTER]

ALBUIN OF SÄBEN-BRIXEN, ST., bishop; d. Feb. 3 or 5, 1005 or 1006 (feast, Feb. 5). Albuin (or Albwin), one of the aristocratic Aribonen family of Carinthia, received his education in the cathedral school at Brixen. He became bishop of Säben in the Tirol about 977, and transferred the episcopal residence to nearby, more accessible Brixen. In 978 Emperor *Otto II confirmed and enlarged the bishopric's immunity. Albuin was on excellent terms with Otto II and the Emperor *Henry II, and received extensive grants of land from them and other nobles. He played a considerable part in political life, since his see lay on the main route from Germany to Italy. Shortly after his death Albuin was venerated as a saint. In 1141 he was proclaimed one of the diocesan patron saints. His relics are in the cathedral.

Bibliography: A. W. A. LEEPER, *A History of Medieval Austria* (New York 1941). A. SPARBER, *Kirchengeschichte Tirols* (Innsbruck 1957).

[R. H. SCHMANDT]

ALBUQUERQUE, UNIVERSITY OF, a coeducational 4-year college in Albuquerque, N.Mex., founded in 1920 by the Poor Sisters of St. Francis Seraph to provide educational facilities for teaching sisters during the summer months. It was chartered as a full-time training school in 1940 and named the Catholic Teachers College of New Mexico. In 1949 it became a liberal arts college and until March 1966 was known as the College of St. Joseph on the Rio Grande.

The University is accredited by the North Central Association of Colleges and Secondary Schools, and affiliated with The Catholic University of America. It is approved by the New Mexico State Department of Education for the certification of elementary and secondary teachers, and by the U.S. Department of Justice to receive foreign students. It is approved for the training of veterans under the several public laws governing educational benefits.

The institution is under the administration of the Poor Sisters of St. Francis, whose motherhouse is in Colorado Springs, Colo. Administrative officers and faculty include Franciscan sisters, priests, and laymen. In 1964 the staff comprised 3 priests, 19 sisters, and 41 laymen, holding 15 doctoral and 41 master's degrees. Enrollment numbered 915 students from nearly every state and from several foreign countries. The University is financed through tuition and fees, and the contributed services of the religious.

A liberal arts and science curriculum includes all subjects ordinarily offered for the bachelor degree. The business administration curriculum affords concentration areas in accounting, economics, general business, and the secretarial sciences. Complete courses of study for the training of elementary and secondary teachers and medical technologists are offered, as well as preprofessional programs in architecture, dentistry, engineering, law, and medicine. The University confers the B.A., B.S., B.S. in business administration, B.S. in education, B.S. in medical technology, associate of arts degree in nursing, and the M.A. and M.S. in education.

The science department maintains modern laboratories for the several fields of chemistry, physics, and the natural sciences, including laboratories for general basic courses and an additional facility for advanced work in these fields. A language laboratory is equipped with complete monitoring and intercommunication systems. In 1965, of particular value in the 38,500-volume library were collections of the history, fiction, art, and culture of the U.S. Southwest; Shakespearean recordings; a collection of classical music recordings; and spoken-word recordings in education, language, and poetry. The library subscribed to 290 current periodicals.

[M. V. SCHULLER]

ALCALÁ, UNIVERSITY OF

An institution of higher learning founded in 1509 in the ancient Spanish city called Complutum by the Romans and renamed Alcalá de Henares (Alkalá Nahar, fortress or castle) by the Moors. In 1836 the University was transferred from Alcalá to the Spanish capital, where it was replaced by the Central University of Madrid, a state institution under the jurisdiction of the Ministry of Education.

The original idea of a university dates back to 1293, when the Archbishop of Toledo, Gonzalo Gudiel, obtained from the King of Castile, Sancho IV, surnamed the Brave, permission to found a *studium generale* in Alcalá. In 1459, during the reign of John II, Abp. Alonso Carrilo y Acuña, with the approval of Pius II, established and endowed three chairs of grammar and the arts. The true founder of the University, however, was the renowned Franciscan Archbishop of Toledo, Francisco *Ximénez de Cisneros, Prime Minister of Spain, to whom the Spanish Pope, Alexander VI, granted a bull on April 13, 1499, for the erection of the College of San Ildefonso.

At the outset, only clerical studies were planned: liberal arts and philosophy, theology, the elements of Canon Law, classical and Biblical languages required for the direct study of Sacred Scripture and the Fathers of the Church. Civil law, considered less useful for clerics, was expressly forbidden by the founder, who for the same reason also omitted medicine, which was later added (1514) with the approval of Leo X. Civil law, however, was not included by royal commission until 1672.

The University of Alcalá was a Renaissance institution, a characteristic that differentiated it from all other then existing Spanish universities, and particularly from the famous University of *Salamanca, which adhered to scholastic ideals (*see* SCHOLASTICISM). Alcalá's involvement in the renaissance movement is seen in its two most important accomplishments: the establishment of chairs of Biblical languages that constituted the Trilingual College and the publication of the *Polyglot Bible prepared by masters incorporated with the University.

In keeping with Cisneros' plans, a major college and 18 minor colleges made up the university city. The major college, San Ildefonso, occupied the same building as the University. The minor colleges were built on nearby streets. Since the plan was carried out in haste (the University was to open in 1508), inferior materials were used. However, in 1543 the original building was replaced by an imposing stone structure, the work of Rodrigo Gil de Ontañon. Besides classrooms and dining hall for the major college, the University complex included a richly ornamented college hall, the Chapel of San Ildefonso, a library so large that "not even the majority of European [libraries] could vie with it," and a prison, neither dark nor often used, a kind of detention room for fatherly correction. In addition, among the minor colleges was St. Luke's, a student infirmary that later became a student hospital. One college was founded in 1590 by a Portuguese nobleman, Jorge Sylveira, a descendant, through his mother, of the MacDonnels of Ulster in Ireland. He bestowed on the college an endowment of £2000 and at the cost of £1000 built a chapel dedicated to his patron, St. George.

There is some question regarding the authentic statutes, and several dates of issue are cited. The statutes, however, generally accepted as those regulating the first 10 years of the University, are those dated Oct. 17, 1517. The date of inauguration was certainly July 26, 1508, and the first scholastic year 1508–09. The course of studies, organized the following year, included the Faculties of Philosophy, Theology, Letters, and Medicine, modeled very closely after the University of Paris.

University of Alcalá, main building, constructed in 1543 by the architect Rodrigo Gil de Ontañon.

Administration was vested in the rector of the College of San Ildefonso and the vice rectors of the minor colleges, the councilors, and eventually the visitors sent by the king. The curriculum was controlled by the chairmen of the various departments, also called regents or masters. The rector of the major college (San Ildefonso) was elected each year by the students and received his authority from the pope rather than from the king, according to the constitutions. The students were exempt from all other authority. The rector acted as "ordinary and proper judge," a custom that gave rise to the "university forum" or "tribunal."

A rigid system of examinations, which was completely separate from teaching, was entrusted to a board of doctors not connected with instruction. This necessitated choosing the best-prepared students for the severe ordeal of examination. Those who passed were awarded successively the degree of bachelor, licentiate, and doctor, or in philosophy, master.

Among outstanding masters at the University of Alcalá were Antonio de Nebrija in humanities; *Thomas of Villanova and Gaspar Cardello in philosophy; and Francisco Valles in medicine—all of whom were deans of their Faculties and had the satisfaction of teaching students who were also outstanding in sanctity, such as *Ignatius of Loyola and *John of Avila; in diplomacy, Próspero Espínola Doria; in the pacification of Peru, Pedro Lagasca; in Sacred Sciences, Diego *Laínez, theologian at Trent, and Luis de *Molina, founder of Molinism; and in letters, Francisco de *Quevedo, and perhaps Felix de Vega Carpio.

The reform, introduced by the centralized state in the 18th century, sapped the autonomous vitality of the University and finally, in the early 19th century, brought to an end this famous center of culture.

Bibliography: H. RASHDALL, *The Universities of Europe in the Middle Ages,* ed. F. M. POWICKE and A. B. EMDEN, 3 v. (new ed. Oxford 1936). J. URRIZA, *La preclara Facultad de Arte y Filosofía de la Universidad de Alcalá de Henares en el siglo de oro, 1509–1621* (Madrid 1941). F. C. SÁINZ DE ROBLES, *Esquema de una historia de las universidades españolas* (Colección Crisol 74; Madrid 1944). C. M. AJO G. Y SÁINZ DE ZÚÑIGA, *Historia de las universidades hispánicas* (Madrid 1957–). S. D'IRSAY, *Histoire des universités françaises et étrangères des origines à nos jours,* 2 v. (Paris 1933–35). I. CECCHETTI, EncCat 1:718–721. L. A. MUNOYERRO, *La Facultad de Medicina de Alcalá de Henares* (Madrid 1945). **Illustration credit:** Photo MAS, Barcelona.

[J. URRIZA]

ALCALÁ DE HENARES, city 19 miles northeast of *Madrid, *Spain. The Roman *Compluto* was Christianized early, for in the persecution of Diocletian *c.* 300 Justus and Pastor (6 and 9 years old) were martyred there. St. *Paulinus of Nola *c.* 396 wished to bury his infant son beside their tomb, and Bishop Asturius of Toledo came to the city because of devotion to the martyrs (thus, it seems, beginning a new diocese). Seven bishops are known before the Arab invasion (579–711), and *c.* 850 Venerius *episcopus Complutensis* received *Eulogius of Córdoba. After the Reconquest, Alcalá (the Arabic name) again became part of the See of *Toledo. In its episcopal palace councils were held: 1379 on the Western Schism, 1422, 1434, and 1479 under Abp. Alfonso Carrillo to condemn the errors of Peter of Osma.

In 1459 Carrillo, by grant of Pius II, established a *studium generale* with three chairs. Cardinal *Ximénez de Cisneros incorporated this *studium* into the university he founded by grant of Alexander VI (three bulls in 1499, three more 1500–01), with faculties of the arts, philosophy, theology, elements of canon law, and classical and Oriental languages; medicine was added in 1514. In the same building with the university was founded the College of San Ildefonso; 7 of 18 lesser colleges planned for 216 students on scholarships were realized. The first courses were offered in 1509–10. The university, distinguished for humanism and its Renaissance character, had important professors and students: Melchor *Cano, Francisco *Suárez, Benito Arias Montano (1527–98; Orientalist, exegete, and collector of MSS for the *Escorial), the humanist Elio Antonio de Nebrija (1441–1522), St. *Thomas of Villanova, St. *Ignatius of Loyola, and others.

Alcalá, which depended on the university, at its peak had 60,000 inhabitants, 38 churches, 21 convents, and 27 colleges (one, under Franciscan sisters, for women; another, the trilingual college that prepared the *Complutense* *polyglot Bible). The Discalced Carmelites composed the **Complutensis artium cursus* in their philosophical college (17th–18th century). The rich library went to Madrid with the university and diocese in 1851. St. *Didacus died in Alcalá (1463). The university building (1523) and the episcopal palace, with a magnificent ceiling in the *Mudejar* salon, are preserved. Since 1955 the Jesuit philosophical faculty for Castile (10 professors) has been in Alcalá. The city had a population of some 20,000, two parishes, and eight religious houses (1965).

Bibliography: Flórez EspSagr v.7. S. D'IRSAY, *Histoire des universités françaises et étrangères des origines à nos jours,* 2 v. (Paris 1933–35), v.1. J. URRIZA, *La preclara facultad de artes y filosofía de la Universidad de Alcalá de Henares en el siglo de oro 1509–1621* (Madrid 1941). L. ALONSO MUÑOYERRO, *La facultad de medicina en la universidad de Alcalá de Henares* (Madrid 1945). C. M. AJO G. Y SAINZ DE ZÚÑIGA, *Historia de las universidades hispánicas* (Madrid 1957–60) v.1–2.

[J. VIVES]

ALCEDO, ANTONIO DE, enlightened American scholar who compiled geographic and historical information on 18th-century Spanish America; b. Quito, Ecuador, 1734 or 1735; d. Coruña, Spain, 1812. He was the son of a Spanish colonial official, Dionisio de Alcedo y Herrera, who served in America from 1728 to 1736 and again from 1742 to 1750. Antonio received his early education from his father. He studied mathematics at the Imperial Institute of Madrid, attended the faculty of medicine in Paris, and later devoted himself to the study of languages, history, numismatics, and physics. Simultaneously he had a military career, entering the Royal Infantry Regiment before he was 18 and retiring in 1800 with the rank of field marshal. In 1787 he was made a member of the Academy of History. In 1792 he was appointed political and military governor of Alciza and in 1802 governor of Coruña, where he spent the last years of his life. Until 1921 the only known work of Alcedo was *El diccionario geográfico histórico de las Indias Occidentales o América* (5 v. in 4, Madrid 1786–89). In these volumes he made extensive use of the statistics and information gathered by his father during his residence in America and his frequent trips. It is not distinguished in style, but it includes many interesting, if sometimes too numerous, details on the description of the provinces of the New World. This geographer was not content to give an exact detailed statistical report of these areas but, according to his subtitle, included information on the most important events in the various places: "fires, earthquakes, sieges, invasions which they have undergone and the famous men they have produced." A monograph by Alcedo, also based on data accumulated by his father, is *Historia del Reino de Tierra Firme.*

In 1921 the critic Gonzalo Zaldumbide called attention to a title, *Biblioteca Americana o catálogo histórico de todos los autores que han escrito sobre materiales de América en varios idiomas con una noticia de sus vidas,* in the Bibliothèque Nationale, Paris. Another copy is in the Lenox American Collection of the New York Public Library. This copy includes additions made by the author that fill in some of the omissions found in the earlier copies. Two other holograph copies, dated 1791 and 1807, belong to the John Carter Brown Collection at Brown University, Providence, R.I.

Alcedo also collaborated with Casimiro de Ortega on a report for the Academy of History discussing the merits of the *Historia del reino de Quito* by Juan de *Velasco y Petroche. The report made it possible to correct a number of errors in the work before it was published.

Bibliography: I. J. BARRERA, *Historia de la literatura ecuatoriana* (Quito 1960). *Biblioteca Mínima Ecuatoriana.* J. R. PÁEZ, "Don Antonio de Alcedo y su Biblioteca Americana," *Boletín de la Academia Nacional de la Historia* 37 (Quito 1957) 90–91.

[J. TOBAR DONOSO]

ALCHEMY

Alchemy is a pseudo-science based on the premise that base matter can be transmuted into gold by chemical means. Although scattered individuals may still be found who take the idea seriously, alchemy as an important cultural movement died out in the 18th century. The "Work" (as it came to be called) has always had both a practical and a mystical side. Realistic (or greedy) experimenters conceived their "gold" as identical with mined gold, while their more mystical brethren, adapting their design to the fact that genuine gold was never produced in the laboratory, vaguely envisioned the end product as a marvelous substance, either solid (hence, "philosopher's stone") or liquid (the "elixir" or the "tincture"), which could variously heal, ennoble, sanctify, or multiply wealth. Alchemy enjoyed no historical "development" as a science; one can, for instance, find that a typical treatise written in the 17th century is no more than a vague congeries of notions drawn from ancient and medieval authors, uncorrected by observation and experiment. The ensuing outline, therefore, consists of only a brief chronological sketch, emphasizing important names and places, followed by a summary of the basic principles of alchemy, a discussion of its theological and mystical pretensions, and, finally, a brief register of the attitudes taken toward alchemy by responsible thinkers from the 13th to the 17th centuries, when the science flourished most widely.

Historical Outline. The term "alchemy" comes from medieval Latin *alchimia,* a version of Arabic *al-kimia,* which is in turn connected with *Khem* (black earth), the old Egyptian term for their own land, through Greek χημία, although this was probably confused with Greek χυμεία, which refers to the pouring or casting of metals. This etymology epitomizes the history of the science, which may be said to have been born in Hellenistic Alexandria from the imposition of Greek philosophy (mainly the Aristotelian doctrines of *entelechy and of the four elements with their "quintessence,"—and later, Gnostic theology) on the arts of metalworking and glassmaking as they had developed in Egypt. (*See* GNOSTICISM.) The original alchemists were probably members of a secret cult whose practices derived largely from the mystical lore of the Hebrews, Egyptians, and Chaldeans. To this period (*c.* A.D. 200–400) belong the writings of a pseudo-Democritus and of Zosimos the Panopolitan; these contain recipes for the superficial coloring of metals to resemble gold, but they also express a belief in the possibility of genuine transmutation. After the fall of the Alexandrian schools alchemists continued to work in Syria and Byzantium (e.g., Theophrastos and Stephanos of Alexandria), but their treatises simply transmit Alexandrian teaching. The rise of Islam saw the translation of Greek alchemical works into Arabic, and the further elaboration of the mystical element by Jâbir ibn Hayyân (9th century) and by his Sufite sect (*See* SUFISM). More practical aspects, especially the classification of mineral and animal substances and the development of pharmaceuticals, were extended by the physician *Rhazes (865?–925). Arabic treatises, brought into Sicily and Moorish Spain in the 12th century, were turned into Latin by Robert of Chester and other translators of the Toledo school, while a number of original pseudonymous works were composed also, notably the *Summa perfectionis* of Geber, probably the most widely known alchemical treatise of the Middle Ages. Geber's work has a specious sort of scholastic logic to it, and on practical matters such as the preparation of reagents or the design of a sublimatory furnace he shows a commendable accuracy. But the *Summa* is filled with mystical cant and is finally vitiated by the misguided hope of producing the elixir. Except for *Paracelsus, who turned alchemy to the service of medicine (iatrochemistry), practically nothing was added to the ideas found in Geber, and in the Enlightenment of the 18th century, interest in the science almost entirely died out. There was a parallel growth in China, although it was there related to *Taoism and the notion that Tao-infused substances were productive of long life. Chinese and Western alchemy have a number of secondary features in common, namely, the theory that metals grow in the earth, the doctrine that physical discipline is essential to the successful alchemist, the idea of planetary influence, and frequent allegorical and mystical designations for ingredients and processes.

Relationship to Orthodox Science. In a justly famous phrase, "the story of alchemy is the history of a mistake." From the standpoint of the modern chemist its solid achievements are few. Some pieces of equipment—special furnaces, stills, water-baths, the mortar and pestle—owe their invention to alchemists; a few elementary processes, like sublimation, go back to the earliest days of experimentation; and there are scattered instances of unusually precise technique, as in the distillation of alcohol (*aqua ardens*) in 12th-century Salerno. But these were merely by-products of a quest that was destined to fail because it was founded on a faulty idea and bedeviled by the habit of analogical thinking. In theory, a substance had its individualizing properties removed by heating, so that it became a *prima materia,* a black, formless mass, which could then have qualities added to it in successive stages (represented by changing colors) until it took on the characteristics of gold. Experiment by inductive methods was precluded on principle, the pattern of the "Work" being altered only as chance or fashion caused one allegorical statement to succeed another. Even the most widely acknowledged principles of the science were clouded by the same sort of allegorical obscurantism. Such was the doctrine of "contraries," which directed that the "Work" must be initiated with a union of contrary substances (e.g., mercury, principle of liquidity, and sulfur, principle of fire). This may go back ultimately to primitive superstitions concerning the origin of the universe from an original splitting of a primal chaos. The persistent belief that metals grow in the ground, slowly approaching the perfection of gold, led alchemists to think that they could accelerate nature's processes in the laboratory. The great stress on a color sequence (normally: *nigredo, albedo, rudedo*) probably stems from a primitive animistic belief patterned on the yearly cycle of nature. So, too, the idea of a sympathetic relationship between the macrocosm and the microcosm, perhaps best known for its influence on medieval medicine, was an ancient doctrine implicit in alchemical theory from the earliest times, as in the *Emerald Table of Hermes* (probably composed as early as the 2d century), a cryptic "revelation" expounding a vague declaration that "that which is above

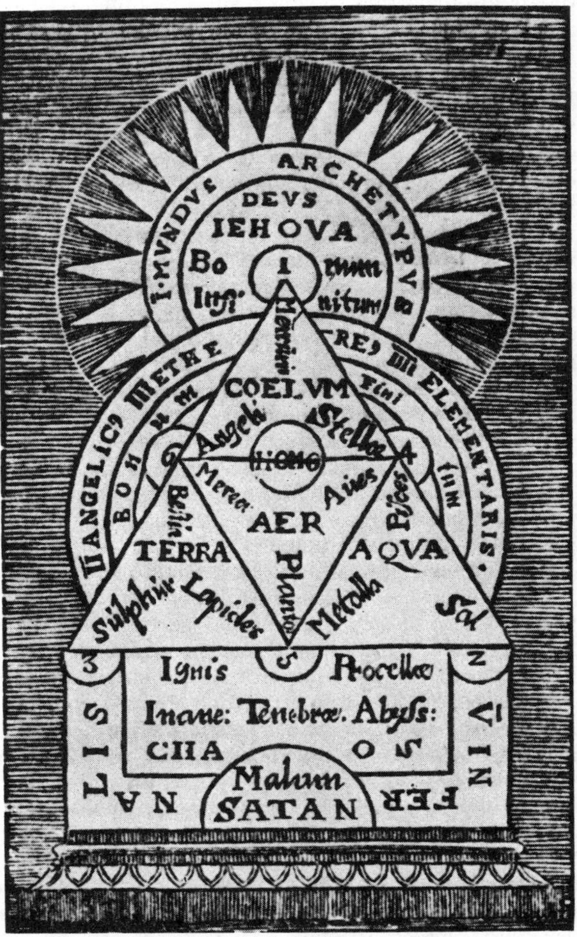

Woodcut illustrating the alchemical concept of the world.

is like to that which is below . . . to accomplish the miracles of one thing." The correspondence between the seven metals and the seven planets with their related deities (e.g., Sun = gold, Venus = copper) also tended to inhibit free experimentation. The few refinements in equipment and processes were small recompense for this expenditure of misdirected energy, and it was not until the appearance of Boyle's *The Sceptical Chymist* (A.D. 1661) that chemistry had a chance to flourish.

Mystical and Theological Aspects. Such analogies as the above, supported by a natural leaning toward mythopoeic expression and by an alleged desire to conceal the secrets of alchemy from the "unworthy," produced an esoteric jargon and a flood of allegorical explanations of the "Work." And there was an astonishing multiplication of alchemical books in the 13th and 14th centuries, as interest in alchemy kept pace with the burgeoning scientific spirit. There was, however, this important difference—the composition of an alchemical treatise was very much a rhetorical exercise in which the author "amplified" his matter by stock figures like the following: rules of conduct (e.g., the "philosopher" had to carry on the "Work" in isolation, or with absolutely trustworthy assistants); extended citations of ancient authorities such as Hermes, Moses, and Mary the Jewess; inordinately lengthy inventories of ingredients; formulas recommending ceaseless study or perseverance, and others stressing the unity of the "Work" (in one treatise it is said to consist of "*one* thing, *one* substance, *one* vessel, *one* essence, and *one* agent, which begins and ends the "Work"), the commonness of the stone, or the need of assiduous care of the fire. The tone of address varies from intemperate abuse of foolish "sophists" who do not understand what they read to opaque flights of mystical fancy. The quasi-theological element fell into a bizarre combination with the allegorical, at least as early as the 13th century, in works such as the *Pretiosa margarita novella* of Petrus Bonus and the *Aurora consurgens* attributed (certainly wrongly) to St. *Thomas Aquinas, in both of which it is difficult to tell whether the author is speaking of Christian or alchemical mysteries. Two most curious manifestations of this strain can be seen in the alchemical "mass" of Nicholas Melchior (fl. A.D. 1500) and in the triptych, "The Millennium," of Hieronymus *Bosch, whose interest in alchemy was inspired by the teachings of the heretical Adamites of the 15th century.

Attitudes toward Alchemy. In every age most serious thinkers tended to be critical of both the theory and the practice of alchemy, although occasional strong voices defended the basic idea. Both St. *Albert the Great and St. Thomas Aquinas admitted the possibility of the transmutation of elements, yet they believed that it had not yet been accomplished. Dante placed the alchemists in the lowest circle of the Inferno because they "ape creative Nature by their Art"; and Petrarch, Jean de Meun, Langland, Chaucer, Sebastian Brant, Erasmus, and Ben Jonson are in the mainstream of a tradition of vitriolic satire against alchemy, based mainly on its antisocial effects but frequently stressing its theoretical absurdity. The decretal of Pope *John XXII, beginning "Spondent quas non exhibent," is directed against the illegal practice of alchemy, yet the conclusion of Oldrado da Ponte, consistorial advocate in the papal Curia under John, namely, that alchemy is a true art and that alchemists do not sin as long as they attribute their power to God, was quoted with approval by a number of later canon lawyers. The 14th century saw a spate of trials against ecclesiastics for practicing alchemy and other "occult arts"; in 1323 a sentence of excommunication was passed against all Dominicans who did not renounce alchemy and burn their books within 8 days; and the Inquisitor Nicholas Eymeric carried on a vigorous prosecution of alchemists for their heretical beliefs. The religious heretic later gave way to the charlatan, who flowered in the 16th and 17th centuries in such famous quacks as Edward Kelly and John Dee, succeeded in our own day by relatively obscure and harmless mystery-mongers who busy themselves in the attempt to prove that great medieval works of literature and art were in reality designed as alchemical hieroglyphs. Stimulating modern approaches to the problems of alchemy are those of Carl Gustav *Jung, who sees in the "Work" a version of the psychological process of individuation, and Mircea Eliade, who has examined alchemy as a "spiritual technique." These investigators, while they make it clear that alchemy is no mere "prelude to chemistry," both raise problems for the theologian.

A proper history of alchemy awaits the cataloguing and identification of alchemical treatises—a massive undertaking, which is far from complete. It now seems unlikely, however, that the greater part of the treatises attributed to St. Albert the Great, St. Thomas Aquinas, Raymond *Lull, and *Arnold of Villanova have been correctly ascribed, although *Michael Scot and *Roger Bacon did have unusual interests and may have composed works on alchemy. The difficulty of achieving scholarly objectivity in texts and studies is compounded by the fact that the freakish history of alchemy has a strong attraction for occultists as well as a legitimate interest for students of chemistry, theology, psychology, and literature. Finally, mention should be made of the frequent claim that modern transmutation of matter through nuclear transformation is a justification of the alchemists' dream. This is certainly not transmutation in any sense comparable to that sanguine hope of elevating base substances to golden perfection comprised in the "philosophers'" command to "cook, cook, cook, and weary not of it." Such comparisons merely obscure the essentially antiscientific character of alchemy.

Bibliography: E. O. VON LIPPMANN, *Entstehung und Ausbreitung der Alchemie,* 3 v. (v.1, 2, Berlin 1919, 1931; v.3, Weinheim 1954) a basic scholarly study. Thorndike. H. M. LEICESTER, *The Historical Background of Chemistry* (New York 1956) a lucid account of chemical operations known to early alchemists. E. J. HOLMYARD, *Alchemy* (Baltimore, Md. 1954) a readable short history from a chemist's standpoint. C. G. JUNG, *Psychology and Alchemy,* tr. R. F. HULL (New York 1953), v.12 of *Collected Works* (Bollingen Series 20; New York 1953) contains a useful bibliography of collections and individual works in Latin of the medieval period. M. ELIADE, *The Forge and the Crucible,* tr. S. CORRIN (New York 1962). O. S. JOHNSON, *A Study of Chinese Alchemy* (Shanghai 1928). J. READ, *Prelude to Chemistry* (New York 1937) an interesting survey of the vagaries of the alchemical mind, though it relies to some extent on the writings of occultists such as A. E. Waite.

[J. E. GRENNEN]

ALCHER OF CLAIRVAUX, Cistercian monk at the Abbey of Clairvaux *c.* 1150 to 1175. Certain works that have been attributed to him fall within the framework of the monastic literature of the day; one that seems the most authentic is a treatise on the love of God (*De diligendo Deo;* PL 40:847). He is known chiefly for the opusculum *De spiritu et anima,* written in the tradition of speculative mysticism as a treatise on the nature and functions of the soul and ordered to the practice of the virtues of a Christian and religious life (PL 40:779–832). During the high scholastic era this work was attributed to St. *Augustine; hence its importance in the history of psychology. In their commentaries on the *Sentences, c.* 1250, *Albert the Great (*In 1 sent.* 8.25) and *Thomas Aquinas (*In 4 Sent.* 44.4.3) recognized that it could not be the work of Augustine, but it had already exerted strong influence.

The *De spiritu et anima* is "a compilation of the doctrines of Augustine" (Aquinas) with additions from Boethius, Macrobius, Hugh of Saint-Victor, Cassiodorus, and St. Isidore of Seville. Alcher limited himself to juxtaposing the borrowed elements; as a result the coherence of his work suffered. Yet from this confused mass some great ideas emerged. The soul is a unique substance, and its so-called powers are only the functions by which its activity is manifested without impinging upon its absolute simplicity. The soul governs everything that constitutes human life, even its most humble functions. The higher functions are affectivity and knowledge: the first operates through the concupiscible and irascible appetites, which act as the seat of the four passions of love, hate, hope, and fear and which give birth to vice or to virtue, according to the use that men make of them. Knowledge includes five hierarchical degrees, from sense, whose object is material things, to intelligence (*intelligentia*), which is direct contact with God. Alcher insisted also that the images of the Trinity are realized in the soul.

Bibliography: Gilson HistChrPhil 168–169, 632, 658. P. Michaud-Quantin, "Une Division 'augustinienne' des puissances de l'âme au moyen-âge," RevÉtAug 3 (1957) 235–248. G. Théry, "L'Authenticité du *De spiritu et anima* dans S. Thomas et Albert le Grand," RevScPhilTh 11 (1921) 373–377. L. Lewicki, Coll OCistR 18 (1956) 161–164, summary of Polish theses.

[P. MICHAUD-QUANTIN]

ALCIMUS, a renegade Jew and leader of the pro-Hellenistic party in Judea from *c.* 164 to *c.* 159 B.C. Alcimus (Ἄλκιμος, Hellenized form of Heb. *'elyāqîm,* "God will raise up . . .") belonged to the Oniad priestly family (1 Mc 7.14; 2 Mc 14.7), although this is disputed by Josephus (*Ant.* 12.9.5; 20.10.3). He was probably appointed high priest by *Lysias in 164 B.C. (2 Mc 14.3, 7). When he was prevented by *Judas Machabee from taking office, he appealed to the Syrian King Demetrius I (1 Mc 7.5), who confirmed his claim to the high priesthood and sent him into Judea in 161 B.C. with an army commanded by Bacchides (1 Mc 7.8–9). In Judea Alcimus won over the *Hasidaeans to his side, but soon afterward he executed 60 of them and lost their support completely (1 Mc 7.12–18). Driven from Judea by Judas Machabee, Alcimus returned to Demetrius, who made two attempts to restore him. The first attempt failed when Judas defeated the Syrian army under Nicanor (1 Mc 7.26–50). The second succeeded when Baachides defeated Judas in 160 B.C., and power passed to Alcimus and the Hellenizers (1 Mc 9.1–53). Alcimus, however, died of a stroke in the following year while engaged in tearing down the wall in the Temple area that served to separate the Gentiles from the Jews (1 Mc 9.54–56).

Bibliography: A. Tcherikover, *Hellenistic Civilization and the Jews,* tr. S. Applebaum (Philadelphia 1959). F. M. Abel, *Histoire de la Palestine depuis la Conquête d'Alexandre jusqu'à l'invasion Arabe,* 2 v. (ÉtBibl 1952) 1:156–159. EncDictBibl 48. J. Swaim, InterDictBibl 1:76. E. L. Ehrlich, LexThK² 1:338.

[P. F. ELLIS]

ALCOBAÇA, ABBEY OF, former Cistercian abbey, once the greatest in *Portugal, 2 miles from the Atlantic, near Leiria. It was founded in 1153 by King Alfonso Henriques after the reconquest of Estremadura and settled from *Clairvaux, but it had to be rebuilt after a Moorish raid in 1195. The church, consecrated in 1252, was modeled after that of Clairvaux. The abbey, which reached its peak in the 14th century with 300 monks, founded many daughter houses in Portugal; its possessions included 13 towns and 3 seaports. The abbot belonged to the Cortes, was Grand Chaplain of the court, and had spiritual jurisdiction over the *Orders of Christ and of *Aviz. Alcobaça was of major importance in the cultural and economic history of Portugal. Besides promoting the foundation of the University of *Lisbon, it established the first public college (1269), the first pharmacy, and one of the first printing presses in Portugal; it maintained an agricultural school and model farms, opened mines, and pioneered in metallurgy, ceramics, glasswork, weapons manufacture, and other industries. From 1475 the abbatial title, with some of the revenue, was granted in *commendation to Portuguese nobles, while monastic life was directed by triennial abbots. In 1567 Alcobaça became the head of the Portuguese Congregation of St. Bernard with its own abbot general and triennial chapters. It lost its moral leadership in the 17th and 18th centuries but prospered until the Napoleonic invasion. After a Liberal revolution the abbey was suppressed and sacked (1834). The buildings were unharmed, but the rich library and archives suffered irreparable damage. Most surviving MSS are in Lisbon's National Library. Alcobaça is now a

The façade of the church of the Abbey of Alcobaça.

national monument; the medieval cloister is a tourist attraction, the vast baroque complex is a home for the aged, and the church serves a parish.

Bibliography: VIEIRA NATIVIDADE, *O monasterio de Alcobaça* (Porto 1937). A. GUSMÃO, *A Real Abbadia de Alcobaça* (Lisbon 1948). M. COCHERIL, "L'Ordre de Cîteaux au Portugal. Le problème historique," *Studia Monastica* 1 (1959) 51–95. Chevalier TB 44. Cottineau 1:50–51. R. TRILHE, DHGE 2:25–29. M. HARTIG, LexThK² 1:297–298. **Illustration credit:** Photo SNI-YAN, courtesy of Casa de Portugal, New York City.

[L. J. LEKAI]

ALCOCK, JOHN, Cambridge scholar, bishop; b. Beverley, Yorkshire, England, 1430; d. Wisbech Castle, Isle of Ely, Oct. 1, 1500. The son of William Alcock of Beverley, he studied at *Cambridge, where he was a doctor of civil law by 1459. In 1461 he became rector of St. Margaret's, Fish street, London, after which he rapidly accumulated benefices. In 1472 he became bishop of *Rochester by papal provision, keeper of the great seal (until June 1473), tutor of Edward, Prince of Wales, and president of his council. He was translated to the bishopric of *Worcester in 1476 and to *Ely (1486), where he proved an able administrator. At Ely cathedral he began his own chantry chapel in 1488 and built the great hall in the episcopal palace; at Downham he rebuilt the episcopal residence. His greatest fame rests in his founding of Jesus College, *Cambridge (1496), upon the site of the dissolved convent of St. Radegund. His original endowment was small, and the College was limited to six priest-fellows in residence; a boys' grammar school was attached to the college. Still in evidence, decorated with his device of a cock on a globe, are the College buildings, principally remodeled conventual structures. His educational interests are further revealed by his residing at Peterhouse, Cambridge, in the early 1490s and by his foundation of a chantry and grammar school at Hull, Yorkshire. His literary remains include: (1) *Mons perfeccionis, the hyll of perfeccion,* (2) *In die innocencium sermo pro episcopo puerorum,* (3) an English sermon on the text of Lk 8.8, (4) *Desponsacio virginis Christo: Spousage of a virgin to Cryste* (all printed by Wynkyn de Worde, 1496–97), (5) *Gallicantus ad confratres suos curatos in sinodo apud Barnwell,* Sept. 25, 1499, (6) *The Abbay of the Holy Gost,* an English commentary on the seven penitential Psalms, and (7) *Castle of Labour* by P. Gringoire, translated from the French.

Bibliography: J. ALCOCK, Register as Bishop of Worcester in the Worcester Diocesan Record Office, St. Helen's Church, Worcester; Register as Bishop of Ely in the University Library, Cambridge, with a printed calendar by J. H. CROSBY in *Ely Diocesan Remembrancer* (1908–1910). J. B. MULLINGER, DNB 1:236–237. *The Victoria History of the County of Cambridgeshire and the Isle of Ely,* ed. L. F. SALZMAN et al. (London 1938–59) v.2, 3, 4. A. GRAY and F. BRITTAIN, *A History of Jesus College, Cambridge* (London 1960). Emden Cambr 5–6, 669.

[H. S. REINMUTH, JR.]

ALCOHOLICS ANONYMOUS

A society, commonly referred to as AA, established to help victims of alcoholism. AA assumes that alcoholism is a disease, which, though basically incurable, can nevertheless be arrested, but only by total abstinence from alcohol. The only requirement for membership in AA is a sincere desire to stop drinking. There are no dues or fees. AA, though it makes a strong point of religious motivation, is not allied with any particular faith, sect, or denomination.

AA was established in 1935 in consequence of a fortuitous conversation between two alcoholics at Akron, Ohio. One was a New York broker; the other, an Akron physician. The first AA group consisted of these two men, and they were shortly joined by a third, who gave up drinking as a result of meeting with them. A second small group quickly took shape in New York, and a third was begun in 1936 in Cleveland, Ohio. By late 1937, the number of members having a substantial record of sobriety was sufficient to convince the membership that their program offered new hope to the alcoholic.

To bring the message of the group to those who needed it, a book entitled *Alcoholics Anonymous* was published in 1939. At that time recoveries from alcoholism within the group numbered about 100. The basic program of AA is found in this book. In it, alcoholism is described from the point of view of the alcoholic. The spiritual ideas were codified in the Twelve Steps, and their application to the alcoholic dilemma is made clear. The message of the society came to the attention of many through this book, which was given wide and continuous publicity by magazines and newspapers throughout the world. Clergymen and physicians alike rallied to the movement, giving it strong support and endorsement. AA in 1964 had a worldwide membership of more than 100,000.

The basic principles of AA were borrowed mainly from the fields of religion and medicine, though some ideas that have contributed to its success came from experience within the fellowship. The Twelve Steps are principles spiritual in nature, which, if practiced as a way of life, can expel the obsession to drink and enable the sufferer to become happily and usefully integrated. The Twelve Suggested Steps of Recovery are the following:

1. We admitted we were powerless over alcohol—that our lives had become unmanageable.
2. We came to believe that a Power greater than ourselves could restore us to sanity.
3. We made a decision to turn our will and our lives over to the care of God, as we understood Him.
4. We made a searching and fearless inventory of ourselves.
5. We admitted to God, to ourselves, and to another human being, the exact nature of our wrongs.
6. We were entirely ready to have God remove all these defects of character.
7. We humbly asked Him to remove our shortcomings.
8. We made a list of all persons we had harmed, and became willing to make amends to them all.
9. We made direct amends to such people whenever possible, except when to do so would injure them or others.
10. We continued to take personal inventory and when we were wrong promptly admitted it.
11. We sought through prayer and meditation to improve our conscious contact with God as we understood Him, praying only for knowledge of His Will for us and the power to carry that out.

12. Having had a spiritual awakening as the result of these steps, we tried to carry this message to alcoholics, and to practice these principles in all our affairs.

The AA also has its Twelve Traditions. These succinctly explain the organizational operation of the society and its means of achieving unity and of relating itself to the world about it.

Alcoholics Anonymous has been established in more than 80 countries. In 1962 it was estimated that more than 300,000 alcoholics had been rehabilitated through its program.

Bibliography: *Alcoholics Anonymous Comes of Age: A Brief History of A.A.* (New York 1957). *Partners in A.A.: An Informal Handbook for Members and Groups* (New York 1958). *The Al-Anon Family Groups: A Guide for the Families of Problem Drinkers* (New York 1955).

[E. M. ROGERS]

ALCOHOLISM

The general disordered condition of those who have been addicted to grave excess in the use of alcoholic beverages over a long period of time. Also called alcoholism at times is the excessive drinking itself, to the extent that it is marked by a lack of control. In either case alcoholism is a behavior as well as a medical or psychiatric problem. It should be distinguished from mere drunkenness, in which the element of compulsion or addiction is absent. These terms are not used technically in their psychiatric or pharmacological meanings, but with the moral connotation of interference with human freedom and responsibility. They connote habits or urges that have assumed pathological proportions.

Traits of Alcoholics. Alcoholics are characterized quite generally by three traits: (1) excessive drinking over a period of years; (2) serious life problems caused by or connected with the excessive drinking; and (3) an element of compulsion or addiction, or lack of control in the drinking situation, or an inability to put a permanent stop to one's drinking without special help. This broad description is applicable to the great majority of drinkers in the U.S. who would be classified by scientific writers as alcoholics, chronic alcoholics, alcohol addicts, inebriates, etc., although still broader meanings are given to the term, especially in Europe. The description would also be recognized as applicable to the vast majority of those persons who, because of problems connected with their drinking, seek help from physicians, psychiatrists, clergymen, clinics, and Alcoholics Anonymous, and to the many others who need such help but do not seek it.

Excessive drinking means frequent drunkenness, at least partial, over a period of years. It does not mean frequent complete drunkenness as theologians understand that term. Large numbers of true alcoholics never, or only on rare occasions, become completely drunk in the theological sense. Usually a heavy drinker cannot be diagnosed as clearly alcoholic (or at least cannot be convinced of such a diagnosis) until after several years of excess.

The serious problems range all the way from disruption of family harmony to complete deterioration of the individual. Typical problems are: intolerable home conditions caused by drinking, loss of job, loss of family, loss of health, loss of moral ideals, loss of faith, loss of self-respect, commitment to jails or mental institutions.

The element of compulsion or addiction operates with more or less frequency and more or less force, not with rigid, mechanical necessity, even after the person has become an alcoholic. It is a factor that affects, but does not automatically negate, freedom and responsibility. When all three of these traits are present together, experts in the field would not hesitate to conclude that the person is an alcoholic, that he will never learn to drink normally and moderately, and that the goal of treatment is total abstinence for life.

Incidence in the U.S. The U.S. has almost the highest, if not the highest, rate of alcoholism among those nations for which reliable information is available. It is estimated that about 80 million people in the U.S. use beverage alcohol at least occasionally. Of these about 5 million are alcoholics in the broad sense described. Many of the other 75 million drink to excess at times, or even frequently, and there is no sharp dividing line separating these excessive drinkers from the alcoholics who are recruited largely from their ranks. It is estimated variously that out of every 15 or 20 persons in the U.S. who use alcoholic beverages at least occasionally, one becomes an alcoholic. The magnitude of the problem of alcoholism is revealed not only by these statistics but by the staggering economic and industrial losses and by the incalculable human suffering in broken lives and broken homes caused by alcoholic excess.

Alcoholics are numerous in all classes of society in the U.S., and it is a mistake to consider the "skid row" alcoholic as typical. Clinical statistics based on sufficiently large samples indicate that large numbers of male alcoholics display a relatively high degree of social and occupational integration. They are married, living at home, and are gainfully occupied, many of them in jobs requiring special skills or responsibility. The great majority of alcoholics are between 30 and 55 years of age. The average age of those coming to the clinics for help is 42. It has been estimated that one out of six alcoholics in the U.S. is a woman, but others believe this proportion is too low; and there are indications that alcoholism among women is on the increase, especially in cities. The incidence of alcoholism in various races differs widely. Although systematic studies on a large scale have yet to be made, available statistics show, for example, that alcoholism is relatively infrequent among Chinese, Italians, and Jews, while Irish-Americans are among the racial groups that show a disproportionately high incidence.

Alcoholism as a Disease. To be distinguished from the disease of alcoholism are certain other diseases, both bodily and mental, that occur with some frequency among alcoholics. The condition of many alcoholics is complicated by diseases such as cirrhosis of the liver, alcoholic polyneuropathy, alcoholic beri-beri, pellagra, delirium tremens, and Korsakoff's psychosis. These diseases are due in large part to nutritional deficiencies in the alcoholic and, though not exclusively characteristic of alcoholism, are found in alcoholics with much greater frequency than in the general population. In addition, the average alcoholic, especially in the later stages, is often in poor physical condition, and

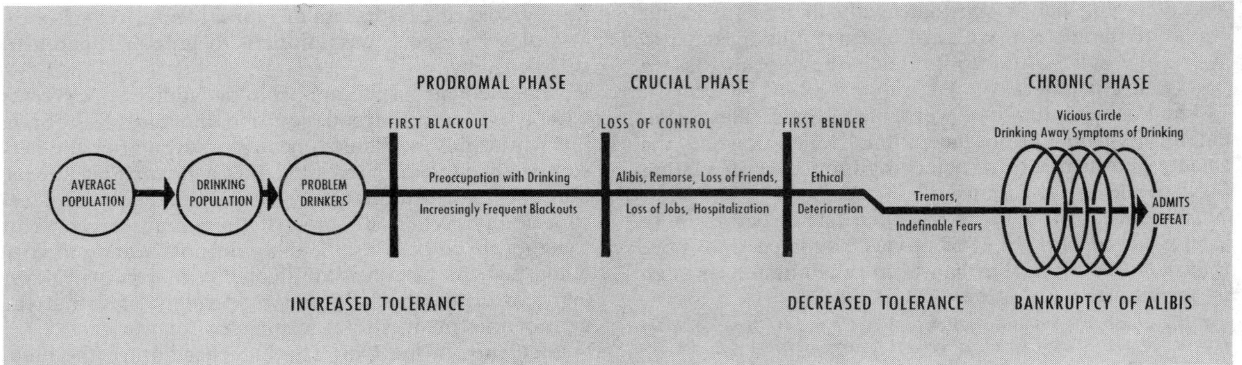

Schematic diagram of three phases of alcohol addiction as evidenced in males.

almost always in a painfully confused state of mind—a confusion that does not generally clear up until after several months of sobriety.

But when alcoholism is called a disease, it is meant that the abnormal drinking itself is a disease, or that the general disordered condition of the alcoholic should be called a disease or illness. This disease concept has not met with universal acceptance. First, it is impossible at present to identify a definite disease entity that all alcoholics have in common. Alcoholism is not like tuberculosis or diabetes or the various heart diseases in this respect. Second, the disease concept is resisted by those who feel that this gives the alcoholic a good excuse to go on drinking and say: "I can't help it; I'm sick"; and by those who feel that the condition of alcoholism is not adequately described as a disease since it involves behavior and misbehavior that it is within the power of the alcoholic to control.

On the other hand, justification is offered for referring to the abnormal drinking or the general disordered condition of the alcoholic as a disease. (1) The professions of medicine and psychiatry see in the alcoholic a condition that by their norms deserves to be called a disease. Those qualified in these professions are the judges of what the label "disease" means, and of whether the condition called alcoholism deserves that label. (2) Alcoholics who have recovered cannot learn to drink normally. After years of sobriety they still react abnormally if they start drinking again. Why is this so, unless there is something inside them, physiological or psychological, or both, that makes them react that way? That something is rightly called pathological. (3) Many scientists believe they have discovered a physiological basis for the alcoholic's abnormal drinking. Although researchers in physiology have not been able to agree as yet upon a clear, definite, organic, or functional pathology in alcoholics generally, there is nevertheless some reason for believing that in many alcoholics the abnormal drinking results from a bodily pathology; and that in most alcoholics, once they have become addicts, physiological changes have occurred that prevent them from ever becoming normal drinkers. (4) The psychological—with or without physiological—mechanisms involved in addiction, considered generally, can properly be called pathological. The alcohol addict, once he has become an addict, has acquired a dependence on alcohol that is usually beyond his power to control without help. This addiction is often just as strong as drug addiction, and as an addiction can be considered an illness or disease. (5) The work of E. M. Jellinek and others provides formidable evidence that the alcoholism here described must be called a disease or sickness by medical standards (see E. M. Jellinek, *The Disease Concept of Alcoholism,* New Haven 1960).

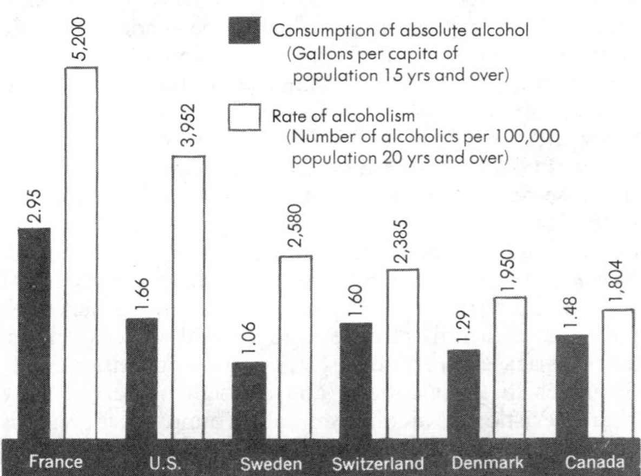

Consumption of alcohol compared to rate of alcoholism in six countries.

Psychiatrists more frequently speak of alcoholism as a symptom of mental illness rather than as itself a mental illness. But it can be both. For many alcoholics are persons who before they started drinking excessively suffered from mental illness more or less severe, many being neurotics and some being psychotics. Their drinking is an attempt to escape from their mental pain or an attempt to solve their problems of adjustment to life. Often such persons become addicts much more quickly than others. When they learn to solve their drinking problem by not drinking at all, they still have their mental troubles to contend with. Then there are those who begin their excessive drinking without any marked abnormality or personality disorder. They seem to become alcoholics as a result of long-continued overindulgence and self-pampering; but once they become addicts they display many characteristics in common with the first type. Their prognosis is more favorable because once they solve their drinking problem they have solved their principal problem. Some students of the problem think that most alcoholics are of the first type; others think that most belong to the second group. But both types are addicts, that is, victims of a habit so severe and so strong that it has assumed pathological proportions. The addiction itself is considered a form of mental illness by those who speak of alcoholism as a disease.

Moral Deterioration of Many Alcoholics. In addition to the disorders of body and mind that are characteristic of the alcoholic's condition, many alcoholics go through a process of gradual moral and spiritual deterioration. Consequently the Massachusetts Commission on Alcoholism in its 1951 report considers alcoholism to be "not only a medical and psychiatric problem, but also a behavior problem." The fibers of the alcoholic's character gradually become weakened. He regresses in his emotional attitudes and his moral outlook. A great many alcoholics, especially of the second group, begin their drinking by way of harmless self-indulgence. But this indulgence soon becomes so attractive that it leads to sinful excess. Sins of deliberate drunkenness become habitual. Little by little one moral ideal after another is allowed to grow dim. Honesty goes. Humility goes. Purity goes. There ensue increasing selfishness and egocentricity, increasing self-deception, increasing neglect of family, business, and friends, increasing resentments and cynicism, neglect of the Sacraments, neglect of Mass, and finally, in many cases, a rejection of God. The lessons learned in childhood are disdained. What began as harmless self-indulgence has degenerated into addiction. The alcoholic finds himself morally and spiritually bankrupt, at odds with God, at odds with his own conscience, and finally deprived of his own self-respect.

This is not true of all alcoholics by any means. But the gradual process of deterioration, for which they are in varying degrees responsible, is true of so many that it must be considered characteristic of the condition. This position has been confirmed by the experience of Alcoholics Anonymous (AA), which has been more successful than any other agency in the U.S. in the large-scale rehabilitation of alcoholics. Their central program, the "Twelve Suggested Steps of Recovery," is a program of moral and spiritual regeneration. If this medicine of the soul is so successful in arresting alcoholism, it is fair to conclude that the alcoholic's sickness is, in part at least, a sickness of the soul. And so there is a growing tendency to describe alcoholism as a triple sickness, of the body, of the mind, and of the soul.

Moral Responsibility of the Alcoholic. Supposing alcoholism to be a pathological condition, is it a condition for which the alcoholic himself is responsible? Objectively, many alcoholics are little responsible for their condition, either because their addiction has a physiological basis over which they never had control, or because they were compulsive drinkers almost from the beginning. Their condition is not the result of long overindulgence, and they are not more responsible for it than a neurotic is responsible for his neurosis. Many other alcoholics are responsible objectively for their condition, because it is the result of long-continued excessive drinking for which they were responsible. To the extent that they foresaw addiction as the end-result or probable end-result of their excess, they are responsible for not having prevented it. But very few actually foresee addiction. There is nothing more insidious and blinding than alcoholic excess. Apparently, therefore, it is a comparatively rare case where the future alcoholic sees and recognizes the danger he is in with sufficient clarity to be mortally guilty *in causa* of the addiction when it finally sets in.

But when the stage of addiction has been reached, the addict's freedom not to drink is frequently diminished to a notable extent. Habit is recognized by theologians as an obstacle to free human acts (*see* SINNER, HABITUAL). A habit that has degenerated to the pathological proportions of addiction interferes notably with freedom: hence the compulsion to drink mentioned above. The word compulsion is not used in a technical, psychiatric sense, but in the ordinary sense: a person acts by compulsion when he is compelled to act as he does, or cannot help acting as he does. The alcoholic experiences at times an attraction for alcohol that is well-nigh irresistible when he is left to himself. But in saying that the alcoholic drinks compulsively, it is not meant that he always does so, or that when he does the compulsion is always complete. Accordingly, the alcoholic's compulsion to drink was described above as operating with more or less frequency and more or less force. Very often, after having had a few drinks, the alcoholic finds himself in the grip of this compelling addiction, and at times even after weeks or months of sobriety he appears to start drinking without being responsible or with only partial responsibility for what he is doing.

The alcoholic's responsibility for his excessive drinking, therefore, is generally diminished to a considerable extent and sometimes eliminated; but each alcoholic, each drinking episode, and even each act of drinking must be judged separately. The honest and enlightened testimony of the drinker's own conscience is the best criterion of his subjective responsibility; and in the final analysis, after making allowance for the pathological character of his addiction, judgment must be left to a merciful God (Ford, *Depth Psychology,* 76).

As for other sins committed by the alcoholic, the norm laid down by the Code of Canon Law for the imputability of ecclesiastical crimes committed under the influence of liquor provides an excellent general rule for estimating moral responsibility for sins committed under the influence of liquor (*see* RESPONSIBILITY). If a person, alcoholic or not, foresees that sins of impurity, or the danger of traffic accidents, or fighting, etc., are likely to happen, and deliberately goes on drinking regardless of consequences, he is guilty. But a person is not guilty of the acts done while completely drunk—unless he foresaw the probability that they would happen and was deliberately willing to go ahead and take a chance that they would happen; in which case he is guilty of them in the sight of God, whether or not they actually happen. The alcoholic or other drinker often does not fully contract this guilt subjectively, because in spite of past experience he is convinced firmly, if unreasonably, that this time will be different.

But if a person is not completely drunk and does not foresee the evil consequences, then his guilt depends on how much control he has left when he causes them. Merely because a man is drinking, and even on an extended bout, one should not conclude that he is without the use of reason and entirely without responsibility for what he does. This is true of both alcoholics and nonalcoholics. Some alcoholics go on drinking for days or weeks or months without ever being completely drunk in the theological sense, except perhaps at the end of the day. The rest of the time they are under the influence of liquor but they know what they are doing. Their misconduct and sins are imputable to them frequently not only *in causa* but *in se,* with a variation in the responsibility according as the alcohol has sharpened or dulled their faculties. The average alcoholic feels himself more or less responsible for the things that happen while he is in this state, although his general confusion of mind is an extenuating circumstance. He may feel that if he had not been drinking he never would have done these things; but he feels that even though drinking he did not have to do them. It is remarkable that he often feels just the opposite as to the drinking itself: that was something he could not help doing; at least the continuation of the drinking was inevitable once he got started. At other times, however, he feels that the reason he was drinking was in order to have the courage to do these very things. At still other times he feels that he was so under the influence of alcohol that he was not responsible, even though he was not entirely drunk. For instance, a man in an alcoholic blackout (temporary amnesia) behaves rationally, and those with whom he deals have no idea he is drinking heavily, but afterward he remembers nothing of what has happened. Theologians have yet to treat of the morality of the blackout itself (supposing it is brought on deliberately) and of the acts performed while in this abnormal state (Ford and Kelly 1:295–300).

Although the alcoholic may be more or less powerless over alcohol and unable at times directly to resist the craving for drink, yet it is within his power, generally speaking, to do something about his drinking. He is therefore responsible for taking the necessary means to get over his addiction. Some need psychiatric help; many need medical help; almost all need spiritual help. However, the same elements of confusion, ignorance, hopelessness, and despair may modify considerably the subjective responsibility in this matter, too. But today there is new hope for the alcoholic because the kind of help he needs is more and more available to him.

Rehabilitation of Alcoholics. Many alcoholics are in very poor condition or even have some of the diseases of alcoholism; they need medical treatment for their condition or for their diseases just as other patients do, and they may even need hospitalization for this treatment. As for the alcoholism itself, the treatment of the acute toxic condition of drunkenness and hangover is only the first step to the long-range treatment of the alcoholic's drinking problem. Sometimes the alcoholic himself "tapers off" or "sweats it out cold turkey"; sometimes with a little medical help he manages to conclude the drinking episode at home. Many cases, however, need 5 to 10 days of hospitalization to break the alcoholic episode and get a new start toward sobriety.

In treating acute alcoholism and hangover, the withdrawal of alcohol is accompanied by sedation of various types that is diminished and eliminated as soon as possible. Drugs have been used effectively; nutritional deficiencies are remedied by vitamins and diet. The treatment of acute alcoholism often can be handled best in a hospital; and the highest hopes for eventual recovery can be entertained for those who voluntarily undergo hospitalization with the type of treatment pioneered at St. Thomas's Hospital in Akron, Ohio. During the 5-day treatment the patient is introduced to the methods and members of AA, and his hospitalization is merely the first step in a complete program of rehabilitation in AA. He is referred for further medical, psychiatric, and religious help where indicated.

Since alcoholism is frequently marked by three types of breakdown in the individual—physical, mental, and moral—the long-range treatment is most successful when it proceeds on all three levels. Some treatments emphasize one aspect more than another, and undoubtedly in individual alcoholics one aspect may be much more in need of treatment than another.

Physical Treatment. Various types of aversion treatment attempt to induce a conditioned reflex of disgust for alcohol. When the treatment is successful, the alcoholic is nauseated by the sight or smell or taste of alcoholic beverages for some time. Antabuse, known internationally as disulfiram, is a drug that will make anyone violently sick if alcohol is taken while it is in the system. The alcoholic who takes antabuse is afraid to drink as long as he keeps taking it. It is a somewhat dangerous drug and should be used only as prescribed by qualified medical men and only in cases where continued supervision is possible by physicians experienced in the problems of alcohol. Aversion treatments and antabuse are always used in conjunction with psychotherapy for best results. Further research may show that new drugs, nutritional supplements, etc., have an important role to play in the long-range treatment of alcoholism, but so far there is no such thing as a cure, or a magic pill. In particular, scientific research does not justify any promises that by use of drugs or medicines the alcoholic can be so cured that he can learn to drink again in moderation.

Psychiatric Treatment. The psychiatrist can help the alcoholic to understand himself and his problems and to learn to live with himself, to accept himself as he is, and to accept the fact that the only solution for him is complete abstinence. Group therapy has been used to expose, clarify, and relieve the emotional conflicts and personality disorders that usually underlie alcoholic drinking. Further enlightenment as to the deeper causes of alcoholic drinking may perhaps be provided in the future by psychoanalyisis. But at present there is not enough clinical material; and the guesses of one analyst seem to be as good or as bad as those of another. Deep analysis has been tried in only a limited number of reported cases and apparently without notable success. Many psychiatrists support their own psychotherapeutic measures with medicine and drugs, and a great many encourage their patients to join AA.

Moral and Spiritual Help. Pastoral counseling has been effective in many cases. Since alcoholism is a problem of human behavior, which involves choices on the part of the individual, and often very difficult choices, it is clear that divine grace must play a leading role in restoring the alcoholic to spiritual health. Men cannot observe the law of God very long without the help of grace. The alcoholic may be a neurotic and may suffer from a compulsive or addictive urge to drink. But it is possible for the same person to be both an addict and a sinner, and his misconduct may be at times the product of his compulsion and at other times the product of his willfulness. The many alcoholics who do not want to be helped (or at least think they do not) and who with great stubbornness refuse to do anything about their drinking may be in need of conversion just as much as they are in need of a cure. Moral disorders and conflicts of conscience sometimes underlie the abnormal drinking. Consequently, the means of divine grace, prayer, and the Sacraments, especially Penance and Holy Communion, are all-important in helping the alcoholic. The administration of the pledge, for short periods and to those whose alcoholism is not too far advanced, also has been recommended and found useful. But the more advanced the alcoholism, the less likely it is that the pledge by itself will be effective; for an advanced alcoholic makes a resolution that he is literally unable to keep, unaided. The pledge, therefore, seems to be more effective as a preventive of alcoholism than as a remedy.

Alcoholics Anonymous and Clinics. Alcoholics Anonymous has been very successful in restoring alcoholics to permanent, contented sobriety. For an account of this remarkable organization and its program, *see* ALCOHOLICS ANONYMOUS.

The recognition of alcoholism as a public health problem has been brought about largely through the influence of AA, of the Yale Center of Alcohol Studies, and the National Council on Alcoholism. The latter organization is the national clearinghouse for information on developments and activities in the field of alcoholism. It disseminates the latest scientific and medical findings in this field and also guides and stimulates the establishment of community programs on alcoholism. Many local affiliates operate such programs throughout the U.S. Most of the states now maintain public outpatient clinics or special inpatient facilities. In some states a percentage of the taxes on alcoholic beverages goes toward the support of the state program or state facilities. Besides offering medical and psychiatric help to the alcoholic, the clinics are valuable in educating the family of the alcoholic to the nature of his problem and in ways of dealing with it. Like other agencies, the clinics generally work in close cooperation with AA. Large industries also have begun to establish clinics for the help of their alcoholic employees.

Outlook. The problems of rehabilitating the alcoholic are far from solved. There is no such thing as a cure for alcoholism. But the illness can be successfully arrested, and the present outlook is more hopeful. Successful treatment often depends on recognizing the manifold character of the average alcoholic's problems, and on the cooperation of those who can offer medical, psychiatric, social, and religious help. The availability of this varied cooperative assistance spells new hope for the alcoholic today.

Prevention of Alcoholism. The absolute legal prohibition of alcoholic beverages is favored by very few Catholics in the U.S. Catholics generally consider that even if this would reduce the amount of alcoholism and other evils connected with the use of alcohol, the price paid in restricting the liberty of large numbers of temperate users of alcohol, and in the inevitable lawlessness that would accompany attempted enforcement, would be too high. It is recognized by everyone, however, that some legal controls are necessary, and all the states have legal machinery to regulate the hours and conditions under which alcoholic beverages can be procured or dispensed. To the extent that legal regulation makes it more difficult and more expensive to drink, the number of drinkers and the amount drunk are diminished. Fewer drinkers and less drinking, especially of hard liquor, presumably result, in the course of time, in decreasing the number of alcoholics.

Advertising. A growing dissatisfaction with the amount of advertising of alcoholic beverages, especially the wine and beer advertising on radio and television, is likely to lead to further legal restrictions in this regard. Such curtailment of advertising would hardly be reflected in an immediate or measureable decrease in alcoholism. But it is the opinion of many that much of this advertising engenders, especially in young people, false and exaggerated ideas as to the place and prestige of social drinking in contemporary society, and thus reinforces dangerous drinking customs prevalent in the U.S. Like others who appeal to sense appetites, the beverage alcohol advertisers have the advantage, in their pursuit of profits, of being able to cater to the lower, pleasure-seeking instincts of human beings. Human nature being what it is, these instincts are easily and frequently abused. The advertisers of such products, therefore, have a special social responsibility. When they fail to fulfill it, and when the abuses become intolerable, the industry becomes an easy and inevitable mark for further legal restrictions.

Education. An important role in the prevention of alcoholism, as in any other public health problem, must be played by education. The dramatic success of AA in rehabilitating alcoholics has roused public interest and focused attention on alcohol problems. This in itself has had immense educational impact. The National Council on Alcoholism conducts a nationwide campaign of popular education. The Yale Center of Alcohol Studies and the Yale Summer School of Alcohol Studies have done pioneer work in research and publications, both scientific and popular. The entire Yale Center, including the Summer School and the publications department, was relocated at Rutgers, The State University, New Brunswick, N.J., in 1961 and became known as the Rutgers Center of Alcoholic Studies. Other scientific centers are doing similar research in the U.S. and in Canada; and the U.S. government, through the National Institutes of Mental Health, is beginning to subsidize fundamental alcohol research.

The Association for the Advancement of Instruction about Alcohol and Narcotics has as its object to assist private and public school educators to discharge effectively their responsibility to inform students concerning alcohol and narcotics. As a rule the states require alcohol education by law, but the teaching has often been haphazard and ineffective. The high school grades are in particular need of this instruction and orientation, but it is appropriate also at the college level. There are available now text materials for schoolroom use that present the facts and the problems in a scientific, unemotional, and unprejudiced way. The Diocese of Syracuse, N.Y., has pioneered in introducing such materials into its school system. In seminaries, students for the priesthood should receive more thorough and realistic information and training about alcohol and alcoholism and about practical methods of dealing pastorally with alcohol problems. The National Clergy Conference on Alcoholism conducts annual pastoral institutes in various dioceses of the U.S. for priests to help them to deal with problem drinkers. Medical schools are beginning to recognize the urgent need of more adequate preparation of physicians to deal with the medical aspects of alcoholism.

Education can help to prevent alcoholism, not merely by giving the scientific facts, by pointing out the dangers of excess and the warning signs of oncoming addiction, but especially by influencing social attitudes toward drinking. There are social pressures that almost force people, especially young people, to drink. There are drinking customs that tend to condone and even to promote excessive drinking, especially of hard liquors. Scientific education can help to modify these pressures and customs. Further studies of the causes of alcoholism from the sociological and psychiatric points of view should be welcomed, since such information can give intelligent direction to a movement aimed at eliminating excess and abuse. Since one of the causes of alcoholism is often found in the maladjusted personality of the victim, it is hoped that practical principles of mental hygiene can be developed and applied that will enable such personalities to come to terms with life without resorting to the delusive solution that alcohol appears to offer for their problems. Nor should there be any conflict between the principles of true Christian asceticism and sane mental hygiene. Both recognize self-discipline as fundamental. Consequently education in the virtue of temperance, which inculcates self-denial and self-discipline in drinking as in other sense pleasures, should be part of any educational program that deals with a problem of human behavior.

Total Abstinence. The practice of total abstinence from supernatural motives (self-denial, penance, good example, reparation to Our Lord for sins of intemperance, etc.) has the highest approval of the Church and its theologians. The idea is current, however, that there is something Jansenistic or puritanical about it, or that it is a Protestant, or at least an un-Catholic, ideal. This is far from the truth. This mistaken idea has been engendered by the fact that some Protestant denominations take the false position that total abstinence is obligatory on all Christians, and many of them have been active crusaders for absolute prohibition. Besides, such organizations as the Women's Christian Temperance Union, the Anti-Saloon League (now known as the Temperance League of America), Allied Youth, etc., are of Protestant origin or inspiration. However, Catholic total abstinence societies both in Europe and America have received papal approval and strong encouragement, and their members have been granted special indulgences by the Holy See (*see* TEMPERANCE MOVEMENTS).

Given the size of the alcohol problem in the U.S. (not merely of alcoholism but of excess and abuse that falls short of alcoholism), the voluntary pledge for years or for life, based on solid motives such as the supernatural ones mentioned above, or even based on a reasonable fear of excess and addiction, and supported by a program of social activities, could become again as it was in the past a potent preventive of alcoholism. And for those segments of the population in which excess is more prevalent, or where the incidence of alcoholism is disproportionately high, total abstinence is a peculiarly appropriate and effective means of prevention. The total abstainer who remains such will never become an alcoholic.

Virtuous Moderation. Total abstinence does not exclude virtuous moderation as a preventive measure; for it is equally true that the moderate drinker who remains a moderate drinker will never become an alcoholic. Since the call to a voluntary work of supererogation based on supernatural motives is not likely to reach the mass of the population, and since the fear of excess and addiction in the remote future is not a very effective deterrent for the average young person, reliance on the total abstinence movement alone as a preventive of alcoholism does not seem to be sufficient. In addition there is required a strong temperance movement in the literal sense of the word temperance: virtuous moderation. An effective movement for such moderation would include the educational program referred to above and would attempt to change the dangerous drinking customs and attitudes of society, thus diminishing the social pressures that lead people to drink immoderately. There is no intrinsic reason why two social movements, one for total abstinence and one for virtuous moderation, should not work side by side as friendly allies in a common cause. There are no contradictory principles involved that would make the two natural enemies.

It will only be by the constant, wholehearted cooperation of many diverse elements in society that alcoholism and excess can be prevented to a significant degree. Sane legal controls, scientific education, mental hygiene, total abstinence, true moderation, and the other factors mentioned, all must be brought to work together and to contribute their share to the prevention of alcoholism. In practice it is of the first importance to keep in mind that the prevention of alcoholism is a problem altogether distinct from that of the recovery of alcoholics. Programs of prevention will not work well when linked to or confused with therapeutic programs.

In the last analysis it must not be forgotten that the excessive drinking of alcohol is a problem of human behavior. Like every such problem it has theological implications, illustrating vividly the mysterious interplay of free will and divine grace within the human soul. The grace of God is all-important to the recovery of the alcoholic. It is not less important in the more general problem of the prevention of alcoholic excess and alcoholism. That is why a religious program of prevention should be aimed principally and directly at inculcating the Christian virtue of sobriety, which can be practiced with the help of God's grace either by total abstinence from or true moderation in the use of beverage alcohol.

Bibliography: *Classified Abstract Archive of the Alcohol Literature,* at Rutgers Univ., containing more than 50,000 titles and about 10,000 abstracts of pertinent writings in use throughout the U.S., Canada, and Europe. *Quarterly Journal of Studies on Alcohol* (1940–), contains full bibliog. of current literature. E. M. JELLINEK, *The Disease Concept of Alcoholism* (New Haven 1959). J. C. FORD and G. KELLY, *Contemporary Moral Theology* (Westminster, Md. 1958–) v.1. J. C. FORD, *Depth Psychology, Morality and Alcoholism* (Weston, Mass. 1951). S. P. LUCIA, ed., *Alcohol and Civilization* (New York 1963). R. G. MCCARTHY, ed., *Alcohol Education for Classroom and Community* (New York 1964). **Illustration credits:** Fig. 1, Adapted from World Health Organization charts based upon E. M. Jellinek's lectures at the European Seminar on Alcoholism, Copenhagen, 1955. Fig. 2, Courtesy of Blackwell Scientific Publications, Oxford.

[J. C. FORD]

ALCUIN

Educator and theologian, adviser and friend of *Charlemagne; b. Northumbria, England, *c.* 735; d. Tours, France, May 19, 804. Alcuin (in Saxon Ealh-wine, Latinized as Alcuinus and Albinus) was educated in the tradition of Anglo-Saxon humanism at the *cathedral school of *York (the old Roman legionary fortress of Eboracum), of which he became librarian and magister in 778 as the successor of his teacher Aelbert. Charlemagne met Alcuin at Parma and secured his services for the Frankish state, where he lived and worked, with the exception of two journeys to his native England, from 782 until his death at his abbey of St. Martin at Tours, to which he had retired in 796. Though he extolled the monastic ideal, he never became a monk, and his career as a secular cleric never went beyond the diaconate.

Alcuin as Educator. Alcuin's activities profoundly influenced the cultural development of a rude, if not barbarous age. His active contribution as a scholar in speeding up the intellectual, religious, and political regeneration and growth of a period commonly called the *Carolingian Renaissance was not paralleled by any of his learned contemporaries and friends in the Frankish *palace schools attended by members of the royal family and their entourage. His writings—except perhaps his voluminous correspondence of more than 250 letters and his occasional poetry—lay no claim to special artistic merit; they are for the most part the practical result of his educational and political endeavors in the service of Charlemagne. His originality as an educator found expression in his mastery of the traditional learning according to *Cassiodorus's formula of the seven *liberal arts; emphasizing the trivium he compiled textbooks on grammar, *rhetoric, *dialectic (*see* DIALECTICS IN THE MIDDLE AGES), and orthography. *See* EDUCATION, I (HISTORY OF), 2. Alcuin's edition of the pseudo-Augustinian *Categoriae decem* is the first contribution to the study of the Latin Aristotle since *Boethius. Commentaries on Genesis, on certain Psalms, the Canticles, and Ecclesiastes, on John, the Apostolic letters, and the Apocalypse, may have been intended as reading texts designed to acquaint clerics with traditional patristic exegesis. Lives of SS. *Martin of Tours, Richarius, *Vedast, and *Willibrord are older vitae rewritten by Alcuin in a better Latin.

The real stature of Alcuin as Charlemagne's counselor in political matters is apparent in the activities undertaken by him either at the King's express request or with his obvious approval.

Theological and Liturgical Writings. The *Adoptionism of Felix of Urgel and *Elipandus of Toledo was refuted by Alcuin in three apologetic treatises. He publicly rebuked heretical doctrines at synodal meetings, and is now recognized as the author of the Frankish episcopate's *Synodica* and of Charlemagne's letter sent from the Council of Frankfurt to Spain in 794. Alcuin, not *Theodulf of Orléans, was the author of the **Libri Carolini* in which Charlemagne rejected Byzantine veneration of *images restored by the seventh ecumenical council (*Nicaea II) in 787 (*see* ICONOCLASM).

Alcuin's various reforms introduced into liturgical service books used in the Frankish empire culminated in his edition of a lectionary, and especially in his revision of the Gregorian *Sacramentary with his appended supplement and the famous preface *Hucusque*. This revision preserved elements of the *Gallican rites and inserted them into the Roman Missal. Irish-Northumbrian customs such as the chanting of the Creed at Mass and the celebration of the Feast of *All Saints were introduced by him into the Frankish liturgy. Some of the liturgical texts and formulas used in his revision and supplements are drawn from the *Mozarabic rite, whose textual traces he encountered in his fight against the writings and doctrines of the adoptionists. Recent research has shown for the first time Alcuin's share in the writing of some of Charlemagne's *capitularies and letters. This constitutes important evidence for the leading role played by the foreigner from Northumbria in the political life of the Frankish empire. Alcuin's recension of Jerome's Vulgate undertaken upon Charlemagne's wish was presented by Alcuin's pupil Fredugise to the Frankish King at Rome on Christmas Day, 800—the same day on which he became emperor. The contributions of Alcuin to the editing of better Latin texts undoubtedly led to increased activities in Frankish scriptoria, and his name is therefore connected with the creation of the Carolingian minuscule, the new calligraphic book hand that became the prototype of the modern Roman script (*see* PALEOGRAPHY, LATIN). But such a dependence is far from certain, and cannot be maintained conclusively. The leading position occupied by Alcuin in the events preceding the coronation of Charlemagne as emperor rests upon firmer grounds. There is much information concerning Alcuin's per-

Alcuin, medallion border miniature in the so-called "Alcuin Bible" written probably during the time of the abbot Adalhard at St. Martin's, Tours (Bamberg, MS Bibl. 1, fol. 5v, detail).

sonal influence on the Frankish King, who had visited him at Tours toward the end of May 800 on his way to Italy. On the other hand, recent research has now made it possible to recognize rather clearly the influence exerted on the events of Dec. 25, 800, by a group of Alcuin's friends who were then in attendance at Rome. The contention, first made by A. Kleinclausz in 1902, that Charlemagne's coronation was the work of imperialistic clerics led by Alcuin and his circle has been accepted in the meantime by both French and German historians. To be sure, Alcuin was neither a meek stay-at-home nor "a dedicated bookworm" (*ein Stubengelehrter*), but (as E. E. Stengel observes) a scholar who was thoroughly grounded in the management of political affairs.

Bibliography: Sources. Alcuin's works in PL v.100 and 101; modern critical editions of letters, saints' lives, poems, and treatises by E. Dümmler, B. Krusch, K. Halm, W. Levison, A. Marsili, A. Poncelet are listed by L. WALLACH, *Alcuin and Charlemagne: Studies in Carolingian History and Literature* (Cornell Studies in Classical Philology 32; Ithaca 1959) 286–287; newly found letters and documents written by Alcuin: *ibid.* 273–274. *Libri Carolini,* ed. H. BASTGEN, MGConc 2, suppl. Pseudo-Augustine, *Categoriae decem,* ed. L. MINIO-PALUELLO, *Aristoteles latinus I 1–5: Categoriae vel praedicamenta* (Bruges–Paris 1961) 129–192.

Literature. H. LÖWE, *Die karolingische Reichsgründung und der Südosten* (Stuttgart 1938), ch. on Alcuin rejected by F. L. GANSHOF, *Revue belge de philologie et d'histoire* 17 (1938) 977 and by P. GRIERSON, EngHistRev 54 (1939) 525–526. A. KLEINCLAUSZ, *Alcuin* (Paris 1948). E. S. DUCKETT, *Alcuin, Friend of Charlemagne: His World and His Work* (New York 1951). Wattenbach-Levison 2:225–236, and the *additio* in the review by L. WALLACH, *Speculum* 29 (1954) 820–825. G. ELLARD, *Master Alcuin: Liturgist* (Chicago 1956). F. C. SCHEIBE, "Alcuin und die *Admonitio generalis,*" DeutschArch 14 (1958) 221–229; "Alcuin und die Briefe Karls des Grossen," *ibid.* 15 (1959) 181–193. B. FISCHER, *Die Alkuin Bibel* (Freiburg 1957). E. BOURQUE, *Études sur les sacramentaires romains,* pt. 2, *Les Textes remaniés,* v.2, *Le Sacramentaire d'Hadrien: Le Supplément d'Alcuin et les Grégoriens mixtes* (Rome 1958). L. WALLACH, *op. cit.;* "Libri Carolini and Patristics, Latin and Greek: Prolegomena to a Critical Edition," in his *The Classical Tradition: Literary and Historical Studies in Honor of Harry Caplan* (Ithaca 1966). P. MUNZ, *The Origin of the Carolingian Empire* (Leicester 1960). E. E. STENGEL, "Imperator und Imperium bei den Angelsachsen," DeutschArch 16 (1960) 45. F. L. GANSHOF, "Le Programme de gouvernement impérial de Charlemagne," *Renovatio Imperii: Atti della Giornata internazionale di studio per il millenario: Ravenna, 4–5 novembre 1961* (Faenza 1963) 63–96. R. FOLZ, *Le Couronnement impérial de Charlemagne: 25 Décembre 800* (Paris 1964). **Illustration credit:** Staatliche Bibliothek, Bamberg.

[L. WALLACH]

ALDEBERT AND CLEMENT, pseudosaints; fl. first half of the 8th century, in Neustria. Aldebert (or Adalbert) had himself and his Irish disciple Clement ordained by ignorant Gallic bishops in defiance of regular canonical forms. He claimed to have visions, to have special knowledge of the angels, to be able to read consciences, and to perform miracles. As proof he exhibited a letter from Christ, which he said had fallen from heaven at Jerusalem. Ignorant country people, especially women, proclaimed his virtues those of a saint and a prophet. At the urging of *Boniface he was condemned (March 744) at the Synod of Soissons. The condemnation was repeated at general Frankish councils in 745 and 747 and at a Roman council in October 745. After 747 Aldebert and Clement disappear from history.

Bibliography: *Die Briefe des heiligen Bonifatius und Lullus,* ed. M. TANGL, MGEpSel 1:109–118, 160. MGConc 2.1:33–50. Hefele-Leclercq 3:846, 874. C. DE CLERCQ, *La Législation religieuse franque . . .,* 2 v. (Paris-Antwerp 1936–58) 1:123–124. T. SCHIEFFER, *Winfrid-Bonifatius und die christliche Grundlegung Europas* (Freiburg 1954). A. M. LANDGRAF, LexThK[2] 1:298.

[C. P. LOUGHRAN]

ALDEGUNDIS, ST., abbess; b. *c.* 630; d. Jan. 30, 695 or 700 (feast, Jan. 30). She was the daughter of SS. Walbert, Count of Hainaut (d. *c.* 660), and Bertilda, and the sister of *Waldetrud. Aldegundis became the foundress and first abbess of the convent of Maubeuge, where her niece, *Aldetrude, received spiritual formation and later succeeded her in office. The many biographies of Aldegundis, all rather legendary, report numerous visions with which she is said to have been favored. There is, however, no doubt about the continuous and widespread cult of this saint, whose intercession is sought for the cure of diseases of the eye and the illnesses common to childhood. She is invoked also as the patroness of cancer victims, probably because she is reported to have suffered greatly from this malady in the last years of her life. Her cult was already well established by the 10th century.

Bibliography: PL 132:858–876. ActSS Jan 3:655–662. Mabillon AS 2:773–782. MGSrerMer 6:85–90. E. LEROY, *Histoire de sainte Aldegonde* (Valenciennes 1883). L. VAN DER ESSEN, *Étude critique et littéraire sur les Vitae des Saints Mérovingiens* (Louvain 1907) 219–231. H. DUBRULLE, DHGE 2:46–47. Zimmermann KalBen 1:144–146. A. M. ZIMMERMANN, LexThK[2] 1:141. Baudot-Chaussin 1:619–621. P. BAYERSCHMIDT, NDB 1:37. J. DUBOIS, AnalBoll 79 (1961) 270, 287. M. COENS, *ibid.* 80 (1962) 149. R. AIGRAIN, *Catholicisme* 1:285.

[H. DRESSLER]

ALDEIAMENTO SYSTEM IN BRAZIL. *Aldeiamento* was the name given to a plan to domesticate and Christianize nomadic Indians by gathering them into village mission-settlements (*aldeias*). In the early years of Portuguese settlement there was no concerted effort to congregate Indians. Christianization of a few Indians was attempted through visitation by missionaries in the wilderness. Soon after the arrival of the Jesuits in 1549 a more determined effort was made. Members of the Society, not knowing the Indian language, at first trained young boys, both Indian and Portuguese, to act as interpreters. The youths were taught to read and write, to sing plainchant and other music, to read aloud in Portuguese, and to serve Mass and play musical instruments. With these boys, the Jesuits visited the existing Indian villages and attempted to introduce Christianity. This method was also unsatisfactory.

Finally the system of *aldeias,* or reductions, was tried. Through persuasion and, at times, a show of force by soldiers, Indians were gathered into new strategically placed villages. There was catechetical instruction morning and evening for all. After 1583 afternoon instruction was kept for those already Christian or those who were preparing for Holy Communion. The morning instruction consisted mainly of the learning of essential prayers. The afternoon instruction treated of the articles of faith and preparation for confession and Communion. It was felt that only in this way could the Europeans Christianize and civilize these Stone Age Indians. The Indians were treated as minors and not as adults. It was particularly important to keep the neophytes from contact with the pagans. As Manuel *Nóbrega expressed it: "We want to congregate all those baptized and keep them separated from the rest." Through force of circumstances the missionaries were compelled to allow their Indians to perform manual labor for the Portuguese, but they always strove to limit this concession and to shield their neophytes from whites and mestizos as far as possible. In the 17th and 18th centuries, the Jesuits and other religious established the *aldeias* far in the interior, at greater distances from white settlements, in order to protect their charges still more from demoralization.

Aldeiamento was used particularly in Maranhão, Pará, and Amazonas, and, farther south, in the São Paulo area. The system, which was relatively successful after 1680, including as many as 60,000 Indians in the Amazon area, came to an abrupt end between 1755 and 1759 with the secularization of all missions by Pombal.

See also MISSIONS IN COLONIAL AMERICA, I (SPANISH MISSIONS), 1.

Bibliography: S. LEITE, *História da Companhia de Jesús no Brasil,* 10 v. (Lisbon 1938–50). C. R. BOXER, *Race Relations in the Portuguese Colonial Empire, 1415–1825* (London 1963).

[M. C. KIEMEN]

ALDEMAR, ST., Benedictine abbot; b. Capua, Italy, *c.* 950; d. in village of San Martino near Bucchianico, Italy (feast, March 24). As a youth he became a monk at *Monte Cassino and was ordained deacon. Aloara of Capua (d. 992), widow of Pandolf of Benevento (d. 981), put him in charge of the Capuan monastery of San Lorenzo, which she had founded in 982. Later he moved to Boiano, where he was ordained a priest. Persecutions drove him first to San Liberatore and then to Farafiliorumpetri, where he built the monastery of Santa Eufemia; and he founded other monasteries in the region of Chieti and in Piceno. After his death his body was translated to Bucchianico, where it rests today, and he is venerated locally as a patron saint.

Bibliography: BHL 251–252. ActSS March 3:487–490. E. GATTOLA, *Historia abbatiae Cassinensis,* 2 v. (Venice 1733). L. TOSTI, *Storia della badia di Montecassino,* 3 v. (Rome 1888–90) 1:98. Zimmermann KalBen 1:367–369. U. BERLIÈRE, DHGE 2:47. J. BAUR, LexThK[2] 1:298.

[A. LENTINI]

ALDERICH, VEN., Premonstratensian lay brother; d. Diocese of Cologne, Feb. 6, *c.* 1200 (commemoration, Feb. 6). According to his legend Alderich (or Aldric) was of French royal birth. After various pilgrimages he became a lay brother and swineherd at the *Premonstratensian nunnery of Füssenich near Zülpich, Diocese of Cologne, where he died when he was about 20 years of age. His claim to sanctity seems to have been based on confusion with the Cistercian saint Alexander of Foigny (ActSS May 1:434) whose life was in many respects similar. *Fusniacum,* the Latin name for Foigny, stands also for Füssenich, which was in close relation with the Cistercian convent of Hoven. Alderich's cult, observed in the Diocese of Cologne, does not antedate the 16th century.

Bibliography: ActSS Feb. 1:930–933. U. ROUZIÈS, DHGE 2:51. Backmund MonPraem 1:165–166; 3:556–557. N. BACKMUND, LexThK[2] 1:298–299.

[J. J. JOHN]

ALDETRUDE, ST., abbess; b. between 628 and 639; d. Feb. 25, *c.* 696 (feast, Feb. 25). She was the daughter of *Vincent Madelgarius and *Waldetrud. At an early age she was placed in the convent of Maubeuge, where *Aldegundis, her aunt, was abbess. The *Vita Aldetrudis* (ActSS Feb. 3:514–516), written by a 10th-century monk, contains so many legendary elements that it is practically impossible to gain an accurate account of the spiritual formation of the saint. It is generally agreed, however, that she succeeded her aunt in the office of abbess at Maubeuge and creditably fulfilled the duties of this position for more than a decade. If the early hagiographers are worthy of belief, Aldetrude came from an exceptional family in which father, mother, and four children are venerated as saints.

Bibliography: L. VAN DER ESSEN, *Études critique et littéraire sur les Vitae des saints mérovingiens* (Louvain 1907) 237–240. H. DUBRULLE, DHGE 2:52. Baudot-Chaussin 2:526–527. R. AIGRAIN, *Catholicisme* (Paris 1948) 1:286. G. ALLEMANG, Lex ThK[2] 1:299. A. D'HAENENS, BiblSanct 1:750–751.

[H. DRESSLER]

ALDHELM, ST., abbot, bishop, first notable Anglo-Saxon writer; b. *c.* 640; d. Doulting (Somerset), 709 (feast, May 25). Kinsman of *Ine, King of Wessex, he was educated by Maildubh, Irish founder of *Malmesbury, and in Kent by the African Abbot *Hadrian, companion of St. *Theodore of Canterbury. As abbot of Malmesbury (from *c.* 675) he rebuilt the church and monastery and made foundations at Frome and Bradford-on-Avon. When the Wessex Diocese was divided in 705, he ruled the western half (roughly Wiltshire, Dorset, and Somerset) while remaining abbot of Malmesbury. He built churches in his cathedral town of Sherborne and on his Dorset estates at Corfe and Wareham, near which a headland still bears his name. He was buried at Malmesbury, whose principal saint he remained for the Middle Ages, in spite of the short suspension of his cult by *Lanfranc.

His principal works include: *De virginitate,* a study of saints of the Bible and the early Church in both prose and verse; *De metris et enigmatibus ac pedum regulis,* a treatise on grammar; *Letters,* including one to the Britons on the date of Easter and one to the clerics of St. *Wilfrid on loyalty in persecution; *Carmina ecclesiastica,* a collection of religious poems. All of these were widely read in England and on the Continent until the 11th century. Their turgid Latin influenced St. *Boniface and charter writers. King *Alfred highly praised his Anglo-Saxon poems, sung to harp accompaniment

St. Aldhelm and the nuns of Barking, marginal drawing in a 9th-century manuscript of "De laudibus virginitatis" in the Lambeth Palace Library, London (MS 200, fol. 68 v.).

to attract hearers to church, but these have not survived. Highly esteemed by St. *Bede, Aldhelm's learning and piety inspired many followers, including *William of Malmesbury.

Bibliography: *Aldhelmi opera,* ed. R. Ehwald, MGAuctAnt 15. Bede, *Historia ecclesiastica,* ed. C. Plummer (Oxford 1896, reprint 1956) 5:18. William of Malmesbury, *Gesta Pontificum Anglorum,* ed. N. E. Hamilton, RollsS 52 (1870) 330–443. G. F. Browne, *St. Aldhelm* (London 1903). A. S. Cook, *Sources of the Biography of Aldhelm* (Transactions of the Connecticut Academy of Arts and Sciences 28; New Haven 1927). E. S. Duckett, *Anglo-Saxon Saints and Scholars* (New York 1947). **Illustration credit:** Reproduced by permission of the Archbishop of Canterbury and the Trustees of Lambeth Palace Library.

[H. FARMER]

ALDOBRANDINI

Distinguished Italian family prominent in Vatican affairs in the 16th and 17th centuries.

Silvestro, jurist; b. Florence, 1499; d. 1558. Of old Florentine nobility, he studied law at Pisa under Filippo Decio and received his doctorate in 1521. Active politically against the Medici, he was forced into exile in 1531. His distinguished career as a jurist led him to Venice, to Faenza, and to Rome (1534), where Paul III appointed him to various legal and administrative offices. He then served the dukes of Ferrara and Urbino before being appointed consistorial advocate in 1548. Under Paul IV he rose with the influence of the Pope's nephew Cardinal Carafa and enthusiastically supported anti-Spanish policy. However, in 1557 he was disgraced and lost his position. His writings include *Addizioni ai commentarii di Filippo Decio sulle Decretali* (Lyons 1551) and *Trattato dell'usura* (Venice 1604).

Funeral monument of Silvestro Aldobrandini by Giacomo della Porta in S. Maria sopra Minerva, Rome.

By Silvestro's marriage with Lisa Deto he had one daughter, Julia, and six sons, four of whom held high positions in the Vatican. *Tommaso* (d. 1572) was secretary of briefs under Paul IV. *Giovanni* (d. 1573) became bishop of Imola under Pius V and was made cardinal in 1570. *Pietro* (d. 1587) was a distinguished jurist and succeeded his father as fiscal advocate in 1556. *Ippolito* became *Clement VIII. During Clement's pontificate, three of his nephews were raised to prominence.

Two of the nephews, *Cinzio Passeri* (b. Sinigaglia, 1551; d. Rome, Jan. 1, 1610), Julia's son, and *Pietro* (b. Rome, 1571; d. there, Feb. 21, 1621), son of Clement's brother Pietro, were made cardinals on Sept. 17, 1593, and were appointed to administer jointly the office of secretary of state. Although Cinzio was the elder and the earlier favored by Clement, Pietro soon established himself as the real authority in the office and the most powerful man in the Vatican next to the Pope. He had the natural skills of a diplomat combined with prudence, zeal, and strength of mind. He was a man of affable disposition, deftly handling intricate political affairs and always retaining the close confidence of Clement. As legate *a latere* he received the annexation of the Duchy of Ferrara to the Papal States in 1598. He cultivated harmony with Henry IV of France, personally blessing Henry's marriage to Marie de' Médicis; in 1600 Pietro also secured peace between France and Savoy. Clement rewarded him by making him camerlengo and in 1604, archbishop of Ravenna. After the death of Clement, Pietro fell from papal favor and retired to Ravenna, where he effected important Church reforms.

A third nephew, *Gian Francesco* (1545–1601), also favored by Clement, was made general of the papal armies. He died while commanding troops against the Turks in Hungary. Of his many children, the eldest son, *Silvestro* (1587–1612), at the age of 16 years was made cardinal by Clement. *Ippolito,* the younger (1592–1638), became cardinal under Gregory XV. The male line died out in 1638, but the granddaughter of Gian Francesco, Olympia, married Paolo Borghese in 1638, and the Aldobrandini fortunes thereby passed to the Borghese family.

Other distant relatives include Giacomo Aldobrandini (d. 1606), bishop of Troia and nuncio to Naples; Cardinal Baccio Aldobrandini (1613–1665), protégé of Ippolito the younger; and Alessandro Aldobrandini (1667–1734), nephew of Baccio.

Bibliography: P. Litta et al., *Famiglie celebri italiane,* 14 v. (Milan 1819–1923). P. E. Visconti, *Città e famiglie nobili e celebri dello stato pontificio,* 3 v. in 4 (Rome 1847). P. Richard, *La Légation Aldobrandini et le traité de Lyon* (Lyons 1903); et al., DHGE 2:55–60. L. Passarini, *Memorie intorno alla vita di Silvestro Aldobrandini* (Rome 1878). Pastor v.23 and 24, *passim.* E. Santovito, EncCatt 1:739–740. F. Bock, LexThK² 1:300–301. **Illustration credit:** Alinari-Art Reference Bureau.

[J. C. WILLKE]

ALDRIC OF LE MANS, BL., bishop; b. *c.* 800; d. March 24, 856 (feast, Jan. 7). The son of half-Saxon, half-Bavarian parents, Aldric spent his youth at the court of *Charlemagne at Aachen, where he became a friend of *Louis the Pious. Bishop *Drogo of Metz ordained him priest, named him precentor, and placed him in charge of the cathedral school. But when Louis the Pious became emperor, he recalled Aldric to

Aachen, making him his chaplain and confessor. Named bishop of Le Mans and consecrated Dec. 22, 832, by the metropolitan of Tours, Aldric received the Emperor, who came to celebrate Christmas with him. As bishop Aldric distinguished himself by his charity, disciplined his clergy, and built the monastery of Saint-Martin in his city, as well as the Saint-Julian fountain. He fought with the monks of *Saint-Calais, compelling them to recognize his authority over their abbey. On the death of Louis the Pious (840) they allied themselves with the enemies of Emperor *Charles II the Bald and had Aldric exiled from Le Mans. In 846, however, a royal charter restored him to his see. However, when Rainald became abbot of Saint-Calais he succeeded, a few years before Aldric's death, in winning from Charles the Bald and the synod of Bonneuil recognition of his abbey's episcopal *exemption (855). Aldric is buried in the abbey church of Saint-Vincent in Le Mans. In addition to three testaments (the first two confirm legacies to various churches and counsel on how to maintain peace between clerics and monks; the third is an ascetic piece) the bishop composed the *Gesta Aldrici,* in which he reports on his management of the diocese in the first 44 chapters, the rest of the work being a later addition.

Bibliography: Molinier SHF No. 8121–22. *Gesta domni Aldrici,* ed. R. CHARLES and L. FROGER (Mamers 1889). J. P. E. HAVET, *Oeuvres,* 2 v. (Paris 1896) 1:271–317, the *Actus pontificum* usually attributed now to the Chorbishop David. Duchesne FÉ v.2. Butler Th Attw 1:48. M. BESSON, DHGE 2:68–69.

[J. DAOUST]

ALDRIC OF SENS, ST., monk, abbot, then archbishop of Sens; b. Gâtinais, 775; d. Ferrières, Oct. 10, either 836, according to *Duchesne and Levillain, or 841, according to Stein and others (feast, June 7). He was of noble birth, and was educated at Saint-Martin of Tours, became monk at *Ferrières (Gâtinais), was appointed to the clergy of Sens by its Archbishop Jeremiah, was called to the court of Aachen by King *Louis the Pious, and was named director of the *Palace School and member of the Council. In 821 he succeeded Abbot Adalbert at Ferrières; in 828 he was chosen archbishop of Sens, and was consecrated at the Council of Paris in 829. Concerned about clerical discipline, he effected a reform at the abbey of *Saint-Amand in Flanders, and with *Ebbo of Sens he reformed *Saint-Denis. He sent his disciple Servatus *Lupus of Ferrières to complete his studies with *Rabanus Maurus at *Fulda. Preoccupied with the prosperity of his own abbey, he obtained during a visit of Louis the Pious to Ferrières the monastery of Saint-Josse in Ponthieu. He participated in the Council of *Thionville rehabilitating Louis the Pious. He was buried at the abbey of Ferrières. His magnificent reliquary disappeared, and his remains were scattered when the Calvinists pillaged the abbey in 1569.

Bibliography: Mabillon AS v.2. GallChrist 12:19–21. PL 105: 809–811. E. JAROSSAY, *Histoire d'une abbaye à travers les siècles: Ferrières en Gatinais* (Orléans 1901). L. LEVILLAIN, "Étude sur les lettres de Loup de Ferrières," BiblÉcChartes 63 (1902) 85–86. H. STEIN, DictBiogFranc 1:1361. G. HOCQUARD, *Catholicisme* 1:288.

[P. COUSIN]

ALDROVANDI, ULISSE, one of the great zoological encyclopedists of the 16th century; b. Bologna, Italy, 1522; d. there, May 4, 1605. Although born to nobility, and destined for business, he entered the University of Bologna in 1539 after traveling in France and Spain; later (1548) he studied at Padua. About 1549 he was suspected of doctrinal deviation, but, after a hearing in Rome, was exonerated by Pope Julius III. His contacts with the zoologist Rondelet in Rome and the botanist Ghini at Bologna attracted him to biology. In 1553, at Bologna, he received his M.D. A few years later he began a 40-year professorship of natural history at Bologna. Botany was his prime interest: he lectured in pharmacology, established the botanic garden (1567–68), collected plants for a comprehensive herbarium that failed to materialize, and published (1574) his *Antidotarii . . .* on medical botany.

Henceforth, his time and fortune were invested in vast programs of data collecting and illustrating, mostly zoological, for his proposed *Natural History.* Volume 1, on birds, a well-illustrated 900-page work, appeared in 1599. Two more volumes on birds (1600, 1603) and one on insects (1602) were published shortly before his death. His prestige and the momentum of his massive project are suggested by the publication of nine more large tomes during the 63 years (1606–68) following his death. The total bulk (14 folio volumes) of Aldrovandi's *Natural History* was greater than Gesner's, its illustrations better, its taxonomy somewhat superior; but animal fables included in it made it less authoritative. All volumes were reprinted, and its influence persisted throughout the 17th and 18th centuries. The vast collections of his museum items and dried plants were bequeathed to the University of Bologna, where many of them remain today. His unpublished MSS are so numerous that no full bibliography exists in any language.

Bibliography: G. SARTON, *The Appreciation of Ancient and Medieval Science During the Renaissance* (Philadelphia 1953).

[L. P. COONEN]

ALEANDRO, GIROLAMO, cardinal-bishop and humanist; b. Motta, Italy, Feb. 13, 1480; d. Rome, Feb. 1, 1542. He studied in Padua and taught in Venice, where he belonged to the circle of A. *Manutius and knew Erasmus. From 1508 he taught classical and oriental languages at Orleans and at Paris, where he became rector in 1513. Aleandro went to Rome in 1516 as secretary of Eberhard de la Mark, Bishop of Liège. Leo X sent him in 1520 as apostolic nuncio to Charles V to combat Luther, whose condemnation as a heretic he secured in the Diet of Worms in 1521. Clement VII made him archbishop of Brindisi and nuncio to Francis I. After becoming a cardinal in 1538, he spent his remaining years in vain endeavors to fulfill Paul III's plans for a general council. He published numerous scholastic works in Greek and Latin. His own treatises and letters are valuable sources of the history of his time.

Bibliography: E. SANTOVITO, EncCatt 1:741–742. Mercati-Pelzer DE 1:87. H. JEDIN, LexThK[2] 1:301–302. H. LIEBING, RGG[3] 1:224. *Nuntiaturberichte aus Deutschland,* Abt. 1, suppl. 1: *Legation Lorenzo Campeggios 1530–1531 und Nuntiatur Girolamo Aleandros* 1531, ed. G. MÜLLER (Tübingen 1963).

[E. A. CARRILLO]

ALEGAMBE, PHILIPPE, historiographer and bibliographer; b. Brussels, Jan. 22, 1592; d. Rome, Sept. 6, 1652. At the completion of his literary studies, he traveled to Spain where he entered the service of the Duke of Osuna. In 1611 Alegambe accompanied the duke to Sicily. On Sept. 7, 1613, Alegambe was admitted into the Jesuit novitiate at Palermo. He studied theology at the Roman College and was sent to the University of Graz, Austria, to lecture in philosophy and theology. Then, as tutor of the young Prince of Eggenberg, he traveled for 5 years throughout Europe until he was called to Rome by the Jesuit General Mutius *Vitelleschi to become secretary to the German assistant. After 4 years he was relieved of this post and worked on the continuation of the *Bibliotheca scriptorum S.J.* (Antwerp 1643), begun by P. Ribadeneira, SJ. He also published the *Mortes illustres et gesta eorum de S.J. qui in odium fidei . . . confecti sunt* (Rome 1657), *Heroes et victimae charitatis S.J.* (Rome 1658), and the *Compendium vitarum SS. Justini, Felicis, Florentii et Justae . . . ex MSS. ecclesiae colleg. S. Justae Aquilae.*

Bibliography: Sommervogel 1:151–153. E. M. RIVIÈRE, DHGE 2:80–81. B. SCHNEIDER, LexThK[2] 1:302.

[E. D. MCSHANE]

ALEGRE, FRANCISCO JAVIER, historian and Latinist of Mexico; b. Veracruz, Nov. 12, 1729; d. near Bologna, Aug. 16, 1788. He entered the Society of Jesus, March 19, 1747, and was ordained on Sept. 29, 1754. He taught classics and mathematics in Havana (1755–62) and Canon Law in Mérida, Yucatán (1762–64). Then he was summoned to Mexico City by his provincial superior to write a history of the Jesuit Mexican province. By 1766 he had finished the first draft into which he incorporated hundreds of original documents. Because of his great talent for writing, Alegre rarely had to correct any part of the text, some 1,500 folio pages. Titled *Historia de la provincia de la Compañía de Jesús de Nueva España,* it spans 2 centuries, for it prefixes to the history of the Mexican province proper (1572–1766) the tragic Florida mission (1566–72). This thoroughly documented history in which he preserved a vast number of documents now lost or unavailable is Alegre's greatest contribution. Even in the unsatisfactory edition of Bustamante (Mexico City 1841–42) it furnished the principal source of information on northern colonial Mexico to historians from H. H. Bancroft to P. M. Dunne. After the expulsion of the Jesuits in 1767, Alegre went into exile in Bologna,

Francisco Javier Alegre.

Italy. Here he devoted his last 2 decades to literary and scientific studies and publications.

Bibliography: F. J. ALEGRE, *Historia de la provincia de la Compañía de Jesús de Nueva España,* ed. E. J. BURRUS and F. ZUBILLAGA, 4 v. (Rome 1956–60). E. J. BURRUS, "Francisco Javier Alegre: Historian of the Jesuits in New Spain," ArchHist SocJesu 22 (1953) 439–509. **Illustration credit:** Library of the Hispanic Society of America, New York City.

[F. ZUBILLAGA]

ALEMANY, JOSEPH SADOC

Dominican missionary, first archbishop of San Francisco, Calif.; b. Vich, Spain, July 13, 1814; d. Valencia,

Joseph Sadoc Alemany.

Spain, April 14, 1888. He joined the Order of Preachers in 1829. Six years later secularization laws closed the Spanish religious houses, and he completed his studies in Italy. Ordained at Viterbo, Italy, in March 1837, he engaged in further study and pastoral work in Rome.

In 1840 Alemany was sent to the U.S. to serve the Dominican foundations in Ohio, Kentucky, and Tennessee. He soon perfected his English and became an American citizen (1845) while gaining experience as curate and pastor in several frontier parishes and as rector of Nashville's diocesan seminary. In 1849 he was named American provincial and left for Rome the following spring to attend a general chapter of his order. While there he learned of his appointment by Pius IX as bishop of Monterey in Upper California. After remonstrating unsuccessfully with the Pope, Alemany was consecrated in the Church of San Carlo al Corso, Rome, on June 30, 1850 (9 weeks before California became a state). En route to California, he stopped in France and Ireland to seek recruits and help for his distant see. He arrived in San Francisco in December 1850, and by the end of January 1851 was established at Monterey, where the chapel of the presidio served as cathedral. As bishop of Monterey, the 36-year-old Dominican had jurisdiction over both Upper and Lower California as well as much of the land now comprising Nevada and Utah. The Mexican government protested his control over Lower California (Mexican territory) and withheld the proceeds of the *Pious Fund, an important source of income. Although he had few priests and fewer usable churches in the area, he was still able to report some progress at the First Plenary Council of Baltimore (1852).

On July 29, 1853, Alemany was named archbishop of the new provincial See of San Francisco, and Lower California was removed from his jurisdiction. As archbishop, he attended Vatican Council I (1869–70), where he was a member of the 24-man commission to explore the teaching on papal infallibility. At the Third Plenary Council of Baltimore (1884), he was chairman of the commission of bishops reporting on the expediency of a uniform catechism. After directing his rapidly growing archdiocese for 3 decades Alemany requested a coadjutor, and on Sept. 16, 1883, Patrick William Riordan, of Chicago, was consecrated for this post. In November, Alemany traveled 1,000 miles to Ogden, Utah, to meet Riordan and welcome him to San Francisco, and from that meeting a close friendship developed. On Dec. 28, 1884, Alemany resigned his charge into the hands of his coadjutor and retired to Spain. He was appointed titular archbishop of Pelusium and devoted his efforts to restoring the Dominican Order in his native country. He served in the parish of Nuestra Señora de la Pilar, Valencia, until his death. At his request, his remains were entombed in the ancient church of Santo Domingo in Vich, where he had been received into the Dominican Order 60 years before. In 1965 Alemany's remains were returned to San Francisco for interment in nearby Holy Cross Cemetery.

Bibliography: A complete biographical study is J. B. McGloin, *California's Pioneer Archbishop: The Life of Joseph Alemany, O.P., 1814–1888* (New York 1965). An earlier monograph is F. J. Weber, *A Biographical Sketch of Right Reverend Joseph Sadoc Alemany, Bishop of Monterey 1850–1853* (Van Nuys, Calif. 1961). **Illustration credit:** Historical Archives, University of San Francisco.

[J. B. MC GLOIN]

ALEMBERT, JEAN D', mathematician who had a profound influence on the development of mechanics, man of letters; b. Paris, November 1717; d. Paris, Oct. 29, 1783. He was a foundling abandoned on the steps of a church near Notre Dame Cathedral, and was cared for by Mme. Suhard, who bestowed upon him the name of Jean le Rond, in memory of the church where she found him. He was the son of Marie de Tincin and the Chevalier Destouches; his father provided for his education.

At 12 he matriculated at the College of Four Nations, which was under Jansenist administration. He developed a taste for mathematics, and his writings in mathematical physics followed in quick succession after his publication of *A Memoir on Integral Calculus.* By means of these treatises, he gained admittance to the French Academy of Science (1742). His *Dynamics* (1743), in which he reduced questions of motion to those of equilibrium, includes the principle that bears his name.

His address on celestial mechanics won for him the prize of the Berlin Academy of Science (1746). His collected works comprise eight volumes, and include every area of the mathematics of his day, as well as some diverse literary works, among which are his famous eulogies of members of the French Academy. Not only was D'Alembert a great mathematician, but he was also noteworthy as an encyclopedist. He was an associate of Diderot in the preparation of the *Dictionnaire Encyclopédique* and from 1743 to 1754 was occupied with the great *Encyclopédie*, for which he wrote the celebrated *Discours préliminaire*. In his philosophy he followed John Locke, but he can be considered a forerunner of positivism rather than a materialist.

See also ENCYCLOPEDISTS; DEISM.

Bibliography: Works. *Oeuvres et correspondances,* ed. M. C. Henry (Paris 1887); *Éléments de Musique* (new ed. Lyon 1762); *Éloges lus dans les séances publiques de l'Académie française* (Paris 1779); *Mélanges de littérature, d'histoire et de philosophie,* 2 v. (Berlin 1753); *Oeuvres philosophiques, historiques et littéraires,* ed. J. F. Bastien, 5 v. (new ed. Paris 1821–22); *Traité de dynamique* (Paris 1743); *Traité de l'équilibre et du mouvement des fluides* (Paris 1744). General studies. M. M. Marie, *Histoire des sciences mathématiques et physiques,* 12 v. (Paris 1883–88). Copleston 6:39–58.

[M. S. REGIS]

ALEN, JOHN, archbishop of Dublin, chancellor of Ireland; b. Cottenshall, Norfolk, 1476; d. Hollywood's of Artane, Ireland, July 28, 1534. Alen (Alan, Allen) was the son of Edward Alen and Catherine St. Leger. He took his M.A. degree at Cambridge and was ordained Aug. 25, 1499. His doctorate of civil and canon law was acquired at Rome, where for 11 years he acted as proctor of the archbishop of Canterbury. He held a variety of benefices, among them the treasurership of St. Paul's and the living of Galby in Leicestershire into which he was intruded by Wolsey. He played his part as minister of the royal supremacy in reducing the clergy to subjection and in the dissolution of the monasteries. After he was consecrated archbishop of Dublin on March 13, 1529, his indefatigable interest in the rights of his see resulted in the *Reportorium Viride,* a full description of the diocese in 1532–33, and his register (*Liber Niger Alani*). His end came violently, as a result of a false rumor that Gerald Fitzgerald, ninth Earl of Kildare, had been put to death. He sought refuge at Hollywood's of Artane but two retainers of the Fitzgeralds murdered him there.

Bibliography: F. E. Ball, *The Judges in Ireland 1221–1921,* 2 v. (London 1926) 1:125–127, 155–156, 198–199, *passim.* C. MacNeill, ed., *Calendar of Archbishop Alen's Register* (Dublin 1950). *Analecta Hibernica* 10 (1941) 173–222. J. Gairdner, DNB 1:305–307.

[J. J. MEAGHER]

ALENI, GIULIO, Italian missionary; b. Brescia, 1582; d. Fuchow, China, Aug. 3, 1649. He entered the Jesuits in 1600. In 1610, having been assigned to the Chinese mission, he arrived at Macao, where he spent 3 years before gaining entrance into the southeastern provinces of China. Meanwhile he taught mathematics and published his observation of a lunar eclipse, *Resultat de l'observation sur l'éclipse de lune du 8 Novembre, 1612, faite à Macao.* He was the first Christian missionary in Kiang-si and Fukien and labored in those provinces for 30 years. To promote good will toward Christianity, he adopted the dress and manners of the Chinese and became, after Matteo Ricci, the most famous Italian missionary to China; he was honored with the title of "Confucius of the West." He wrote a number of books, mainly theological in content, which were published in Chinese. His chief work, *The Life of God, the Savior, from the Four Gospels* (8 v. Peking 1635–37) was often reprinted and used even by Protestant missionaries. Also notable is a cosmography *Tchi fang wai ki* (The True Origin of 10,000 Things, 6 v. Hangchow 1623).

Bibliography: Sommervogel 1:157–160; 8:1603; 12:915. E. LAMALLE, EncCatt 1:747–748. E. M. RIVIÈRE, DHGE 2:99–100. G. H. DUNNE, *Generation of Giants* (Notre Dame, Ind. 1962).

[J. V. MENTAG]

ALEP, Syrian city (in Arabic, Halab), the ancient Beroea. The first known bishop of Beroea was Eustathius, who had become bishop of Antioch before the Council of *Nicaea I (325). The city became a Monophysite center and after the Arab invasion had Melchite, Jacobite, and Maronite Christians, who (*c.* 727) each had a bishopric there. The Byzantine schism in the 11th century separated the Greek Catholics from Rome; and the Armenians set up their own bishopric there (*c.* 1200). The Capuchins, Jesuits, and Carmelites, who arrived in Alep during the first quarter of the 17th century, labored for reunion with Rome; but, as this effort proved unsuccessful, a Catholic community was eventually established, and in 1762 an apostolic vicariate was inaugurated for the Chaldean Catholics. In 1901 it became a patriarchal vicariate.

At present (1964), five Catholic and three non-Catholic bishops have sees at Alep. The Melchite archbishopric of Alep, or Beroea (*Aleppensis Melkitarum*), has seven parishes with 15 secular and 3 religious priests and 17,500 Catholics. The Syrian Catholic diocese (*Aleppensis Syrorum*) has 6 parishes with 6 secular priests and some 7,150 Catholics. The Maronite Catholics (*Aleppensis Maronitarum*) have 3 parishes with 7 secular priests and some 2,500 Catholics. The Armenians (*Aleppensis Armenorum*) have 7 parishes with 11 secular and 1 religious priest and 15,500 Catholics. The Chaldean Catholics (*Aleppensis Chaldaeorum*) have 6 parishes with 3 secular and 5 religious priests and some 6,000 Catholics. There are also Orthodox, Armenian, and Jacobite bishoprics there.

Bibliography: W. DE VRIES, LexThK[2] 1:303–304. F. TOURNEBIZE, DHGE 2:101–128; *Études* 134 (1913) 351–370. J. SAUVEGET, *Alep* (Paris 1941). AnnPont (1964) 22–23.

[F. X. MURPHY]

ALEP, ARCHDIOCESE OF (ALEPPENSIS OR BEROENSIS)

There are four Catholic archbishoprics, a bishopric of the *Chaldean rite created in 1957, a Latin vicariate apostolic created in 1762, and three schismatic sees (*Orthodox, *Armenian, and *Jacobite) located in Alep, which in the 17th century under French influence became the Catholic stronghold of Syria.

The four Catholic archbishoprics, of the *Melchite, *Syrian, *Maronite, and *Armenian rites, in 1963 had 23 parishes, 39 secular and 3 religious priests, 15 men in 3 religious houses, 42 women in 7 convents, 8,270 pupils in 21 schools, and 42,650 Catholics; their areas in square miles are respectively 8; 2,420; 28,958; and 47,104. The Chaldean bishopric, 732 square miles in area, had 6 parishes, 3 secular and 5 religious priests, 6,000 Catholics in a population of 4 million; and the Latin vicariate, 509,652 square miles in area, had 12 parishes, 2 secular and 56 religious priests, 78 men in 22 religious houses, 350 women in 25 convents, 22,000 pupils in 34 schools, and 10,200 Catholics in a population of 4,500,000.

The city of Alep, which lies 70 miles from the Mediterranean between the Orontes and Euphrates valleys at an important crossroads, was the capital of a kingdom taken by the *Hittites (1758 B.C.) and long contested by Egypt. Assyrian influence was asserted there (854 B.C.). From *c.* 300 B.C. until the Arab conquest (A.D. 638) the city was called Beroea after the Macedonian town near Thessalonica. In the late 10th century it was taken by Byzantium but soon recognized the Fatimites of Egypt; it was captured by *Seljuk Turks (1084). Crusaders besieged it in 1118 and 1124 but could not take it. It was a stronghold of *Saladin (1183). *Mamelukes held it from 1291 until it fell to the *Ottomans (1516). Following the opening of the Suez Canal (1869) Alep declined in importance. British and Arab troops captured it in 1918, and it became part of the French mandate of Syria (1920), which became independent (1941–45). Of 483,000 people in Alep (1962), 30 per cent are Christian.

Bishop Eustathius of Alep, which was Christian probably in the 3d century, was transferred by the Council of Nicaea I (325) to *Antioch, to which Alep was suffragan. By the 6th century Alep and six other sees were archbishoprics, i.e., subject to the patriarch rather than to a metropolitan. In the Middle Ages, when suffragan sees practically disappeared, Alep assumed the title of metropolitan. This ambiguous title, confirmed in a synod for the Melchite see in 1790, lacks canonical support but has been accepted in practice. There are no suffragan sees for any of Alep's archbishoprics.

Melchite Patriarchs, some of whom recognized the primacy of Rome, left Antioch for Damascus (1366). A few of them resided in Alep, whose episcopal list has lacunae from the 10th to the 17th century, when the archives of the Congregation for the *Propagation of the Faith were begun (1622). Archbishop Meletius Karmë (*c.* 1612–35), who became patriarch and died in 1635, was in communion with Rome before the arrival of Capuchins, Jesuits, and Carmelites in Alep (1625–26). In 1686 a disputed Melchite election resulted in a patriarch, Cyril, in Damascus and another, Athanasius, in Alep (1694), which also had an archbishop, Gregory. All three prelates were eventually recognized by Rome. On Cyril's death (1720) Athanasius, sole patriarch, continued to reside in Alep. When Athanasius died (1724), most of Alep's Melchites were Catholic. But *Istanbul introduced a Greek Orthodox as patriarch and as archbishop of Alep, causing a schism that by 1750 resulted in Catholic and Orthodox Sees of Alep. From 1760 Rome appointed most of the Catholic Melchite prelates. A vacancy of the Catholic see (1810–16) was followed by a persecution that brought exiles, confiscations, and deaths (1817–31), and the Orthodox see appropriated the possessions of the Catholic Melchites. Other persecutions of Catholics occurred in 1850 and 1908 but the Orthodox see has now lost much of its importance. In 1829 the Chouerite *Basilian monks in Alep separated from the Lebanese order and called themselves Basilians of St. John; the Basilian Chouerite sisters separated in the following year.

Besides its Melchite prelate, Alep, which had had Monophysite bishops previously, had a Jacobite archbishop from 543. From the first known Jacobite prelate, Matthew (644–669), to *c.* 1300 the episcopal list is regular; it includes *Bar-Hebraeus (1258–64). The Catholic community in Alep probably had its origins in the successful discussions there between the papal legate Leonard Abel and schismatic groups (1583–87). Jacobite Abp. Denis Constantine (1599–1649) became Catholic before his death, and Andrew Akijian (1656–77), the first Catholic Syrian Patriarch of Antioch in 1662, was consecrated by the Maronite patriarch. After his election Syrian Catholics underwent severe persecution. Jacobite Abp. Michael Giarweh of Alep became Catholic (1774) and was elected Patriarch of Antioch (1781–82); but he had to flee from Mardin, seat of the Jacobite patriarchate until World War II, to Lebanon where he began an uninterrupted series of Catholic Syrian patriarchs. The patriarchate moved to Alep (*c.* 1831–52) and then back to Mardin. Patriarch Mar Ephraim II Rahmani (1898–1929) and his successors have resided in Beirut. Alep hosted a synod of Syrian Catholics in 1866.

Maronites split from Monothelite Melchites in Alep in 727, but were persecuted and declined until Lebanese immigrants swelled their numbers in the early 17th century. The Maronite episcopacy of Alep, which began probably in 1638, was filled by Lebanese until 1725. Hendyye Ajjeymi, a visionary who founded a Congregation of the Sacred Heart, disturbed Maronite religious life in Alep from *c.* 1750 until a synod dissolved the congregation (1780). It was revived, however, and caused some difficulties for the Melchite Church until 1847.

Armenians were in Alep from the 12th century. Their bishop recognized the primacy of Rome at the Council of *Florence (1439), and in 1585 a profession of faith was sent to Rome. Western missionaries won many Armenians back to Catholicism, and by 1661 most Armenians were Catholic. Armenian Catholic bishops date from 1710. The schismatic Armenian *catholicos of Sis frequently resided in Alep. The election of the Armenian Catholic Bp. Abraham Ardzivean of Alep as catholicos in 1740 led to the reunion of Armenians with Rome (*see* CILICIA OF THE ARMENIANS, PATRIARCHATE OF). The schismatic catholicos of Sis, a refugee from persecution in Turkey (1921), resided in Alep before moving to Beirut. In 1899 the Armenian Catholic Diocese of Alep was made an archbishopric.

A Latin Bishopric of Alep (1644–50) had little success, and Latin Catholics in Syria reverted to the jurisdiction of the custodian of the Holy Land. In 1762 a Latin vicariate was established in Alep with the authority of apostolic delegate for the territories of the former Patriarchates of Antioch and Jerusalem, plus Cyprus and the Armenian Patriarchate of Cilicia. The first vicar, formerly vicar in *Algiers, left in 1774 and the vicariate was vacant until 1816. Since 1836 the vicars, mostly Franciscans, have resided in Lebanon more than in Alep; they now reside in Damascus.

Nestorians are not mentioned in Alep until *c.* 1500. A group of them became Catholic in 1627 but had disappeared 100 years later. The Chaldean patriarchal vicariate created for some 250 members (1901) became a diocese in 1957.

Bibliography: J. SAUVAGET, Alep (Paris 1941). I. ORTIZ DE URBINA, EncCatt 1:749–751. W. DE VRIES, LexThK² 1:303–304. C. KARALEVSKY and F. TOURNEBIZE, DHGE 2:101–128. Orient Catt. AnnPont (1965) 22–23.

[J. A. DEVENNY]

ALER, PAUL, theologian and dramatist; b. Saint Vith, Belgium, Nov. 9, 1656; d. Düren, Germany, May 2, 1727. He entered the *Jesuits in 1676, obtained his *magister artium* degree from the University of *Cologne, and taught philosophy and moral theology at Tricoronatum College there. He devoted his life to the teaching and training of the young and was called to direct various colleges. The Tricoronatum was equipped with a modern theater where locally produced Latin tragedies of a sacred character and other works involving choral music were presented. Aler's own creative work in this field made enemies for him, but the Roman *Rota approved what he was doing (*see* JESUIT DRAMA). He spent the last years of his life in works of piety. His literary output consists of dramas, tragedies (only one in German), orations in Latin, also a course of lectures in philosophy, one in poetry, and a valuable German-Latin dictionary.

Bibliography: A full list of Aler's works is given in J. N. PAQUOT, *Mémoires pour servir à l'histoire littéraire des dix-sept provinces des Pays-Bas de Principauté de Liége . . .*, 18 v. (Louvain 1763–70) 12:132–140. Sommervogel 1:160–167; 8:1603–04; suppl. 321, n.990. J. KUCKHOFF, *Die Geschichte des Gymnasium Tricoronatum* (Cologne 1931) 458–519. A. FRITZ, in *Das Marzellen-Gymnasium in Köln 1450 bis 1911* (Cologne 1911) 123–140. J. HARTZHEIM, *Bibliotheca coloniensis* (Cologne 1747) 263–265. A. DE NOUE in *Biographie national de Belgique* 1:213–214. W. KRATZ, NDB 1:191. H. KERN, ADB 1:335–336. E. M. RIVIÈRE, DHGE 2:129–130. F. BRUNHÖLZL, LexThK² 1:304.

[M. MONACO]

ALERDING, HERMAN JOSEPH, bishop, historian; b. Ibbenbueren, Westphalia, Germany, April 13, 1845; d. Fort Wayne, Ind., Dec. 6, 1924. He was the son of Bernard Herman and Theresa (Schrameier) Alerding, who settled in Newport, Ky., during his infancy. He entered St. Gabriel Seminary, Vincennes, Ind., in 1858, and continued his studies at St. Thomas Seminary near Bardstown, Ky., and St. Meinrad Seminary, St. Meinrad, Ind. After he was ordained for the Diocese of Vincennes on Sept. 22, 1868, he did pastoral work in Terre Haute, Ind., and Cambridge City, Ind., until 1874. That year he was transferred to Indianapolis, Ind., where he served as procurator of St. Joseph Seminary during the 1 year of its existence, and as pastor of St. Joseph Church. On Nov. 30, 1900, Alerding was consecrated as bishop of Fort Wayne by Abp. William H. Elder of Cincinnati, Ohio. The new bishop promoted secondary schools and furthered consolidation of the parochial system. During his episcopacy the Catholic population in the diocese almost doubled, largely because of the influx of foreign-born Catholics to work in the steel mills of northern Indiana.

Alerding gained recognition among Church historians with the publication of *The History of the Catholic Church in the Diocese of Vincennes* (1883). It was the first general history of the Church in Indiana, and, although not scientifically written or well organized, it contained a wealth of material. He published a second work, *The Diocese of Fort Wayne,* in 1907.

Bibliography: C. BLANCHARD, ed. *History of the Catholic Church in Indiana,* 2 v. (Logansport, Ind. 1898). J. F. NOLL, *The Diocese of Fort Wayne: Fragments of History* (Fort Wayne 1941).

[M. C. SCHROEDER]

ALÈS, ADHÉMAR D', Jesuit theologian and patrologist; b. Orléans, France, Dec. 2, 1861; d. Paris, Feb. 24, 1938. He entered the Society of Jesus in 1880 and was ordained in 1896. As a scholastic and young priest he taught philosophy and both Greek and Latin literature. In collaboration with P. Bainvel he inaugurated the *Bibliothèque de théologie historique* and published detailed theological studies on *Tertullian (1905), *Hippolytus (1906), the Edict of Callistus (1914), *Cyprian (1922), and *Novatian (1925). He became professor of theology at the Institute Catholique in Paris in 1907 and dean of the faculty in 1925. He served as principal director of the *Dictionnaire Apologétique de la Foi Catholique* (4 v. Paris 1911–28), to which he contributed many articles dealing with the development of theology in the early and medieval Church. He was an exact and careful scholar whose analyses of theological problems in their historical development have proved invaluable. As a result of a controversy over divine providence and free will he published *Providence et libre arbitre* (Paris 1927). He also contributed to the *Bibliothèque des sciences religieuses* with: *Baptême et Confirmation* (Paris 1928), *Eucharistie* (Paris 1930), *Le Dogme de Nicée* (1925), *Le Dogme de Éphèse* (1931), *De Verbo Incarnato* (1930), and *De Deo Trino* (1935) and wrote articles and reviews for scholarly periodicals.

Bibliography: R. METZ, LexThK² 1:304–305. DTC Tables générales 1:70–71. J. LEBRETON, *Catholicisme* 1:294–295; *"In Memoriam:* Le R. P. D'Alès," RechScRel 28 (1938) 129–133.

[F. X. MURPHY]

ALEXANDER I, POPE, ST., 107? to 116? (feast, May 3). He was the fifth successor to Peter. Ancient lists make him successor to Evaristus. Eusebius says that he became bishop in the 8th year of Trajan's reign (*Chron.*) and died in the 3d year of Hadrian (*Hist. Eccl.* 4.1, 5.6). Jerome says that he became bishop in the 12th year of Trajan. These dates do not agree with Eusebius's statement (*Hist. Eccl.* 4.4) that Alexander reigned 10 years: the Liberian catalogue says 7; the Liber pontificalis, 10. It also says he was a Roman, the son of an Alexander, and ascribes to him the introduction of the *Qui Pridie* into the Canon of the Mass, an arbitrary attempt to assign an early origin to a liturgical practice. The custom of blessing houses with holy water and salt was inherited from pagan practices rather than introduced by Alexander. The Roman tradition that he was decapitated and buried near Rome apparently confuses him with the Roman martyr Alexander whose tomb was discovered in 1855. *Irenaeus knows of no martyrdoms among Roman bishops before Telesphorus.

Bibliography: Duchesne LP 1:lxxxix–xcii, 54–55, 127. ActSS May 1:371–380. Caspar 1:8–16. Haller 1:18–20. A. DUFOURCQ, DHGE 2:204–206. P. GOGGI, EncCatt 1:787. G. SCHWAIGER, LexThK² 1:315.

[E. G. WELTIN]

ALEXANDER II, POPE

Pontificate, Sept. 30, 1061, to April 21, 1073; b. Anselm, son of Arderico of Baggio, in Baggio, near Milan, date unknown. Educated and ordained priest in Milan (1055), and onetime disciple of *Lanfranc at *Bec (1045), he cooperated with the reform aims of the *Patarines. He was made bishop of Lucca in 1057, retaining the see as pope, and served *Nicholas II as legate to Milan, with Cardinals Hildebrand (*Gregory VII) in 1057 and *Peter Damian in 1060, in support of the reform and papal authority there. Disorders after the death of Nicholas II (July 27, 1061) delayed election of a successor. Upheld by Hildebrand and protected by Norman arms, Anselm was elected in Rome and enthroned without participation of the German King, whose role had been canonically recognized, if not clearly defined, in the *Papal election decree of 1059. Certain Roman civilians and dissident bishops, seconded by the German court, elected Cadalus of Parma (antipope Honorius II), who was proclaimed by the future emperor *Henry IV at a Basel synod, October 28, and was abandoned only after condemnation by the Council of Mantua in 1064. Despite this harassment, the reform objectives and vigorous exercise of papal authority were pressed throughout Latin Christendom, under the steadily increasing influence of Hildebrand, through a growing volume of papal correspondence and the unprecedented activity of legates: in Lombardy, France, Spain (*Hugh of Remiremont), England (where *William I's conquest was approved), Germany, Bohemia, Croatia-Dalmatia, and Scandinavia. Relations with the Church of *Constantinople, in 1061 and 1062 were the first since Patriarch *Michael Cerularius was excommunicated in 1054 (cf. Grumel). *Peter of Anagni was sent to Emperor *Michael VII Ducas after his accession in 1071, but unhappily, ecclesiastical concord was not achieved. The Latinization of Greek sees proceeded with the Norman conquest of Byzantine territories in south Italy, in some instances in the name of reform (cf. Holtzmann). The reconquest of Moslem dominions, begun at this time with full papal sanction, was an important prelude to the *Crusades (*see* SPAIN, 2). In 1063 the Pope intervened in defense of the Jews in southern France and Spain, who suffered grievously in these campaigns, and renewed the prohibition of Pope *Gregory I against their maltreatment (Jaffé L 4528, 4532, 4533). The claim that the territories conquered by French knights in Spain and by *Normans in Sicily respectively were to be held of the Pope in feudal tenure (*ex parte s. Petri*) rested in part on the spurious *Donation of Constantine, in wider use from that time on. After a confident appeal to Henry IV for military aid in a conflict with the Pope's Norman supporters (settled at the synod of Melfi, 1067), relations with the German court deteriorated. A dispute over the See of Milan (*see* ATTO OF MILAN) was among the causes of growing tension inherited by his successor, Gregory VII, that culminated in the *investiture struggle.

Bibliography: Jaffé L 1:566–592. PL 146:1271–1430, letters. Mann 6:261–369. Fliche-Martin v.8. C. VIOLANTE, *La pataria milanese e la riforma ecclesiastica* (Rome 1955); DizBiogItal 2:176–183, both essential. V. GRUMEL, "Le Premier contact de Rome avec l'Orient après le schisme de Michel Cérulaire," *Bulletin de littérature ecclésiastique* 43 (1942) 21–29. W. HOLTZMANN, "Il Papato, i Normanni e la Chiesa greca," *Almanacco calabrese* 13 (Rome 1963) 53–66. F. BAIX, DHGE 11:53–99.

[J. J. RYAN]

ALEXANDER III, POPE

Pontificate, Sept. 7, 1159, to Aug. 30, 1181; b. Rolando Bandinelli, at Siena, Italy, *c.* 1105; d. Rome. A student of theology and Canon Law, Rolando was professor at Bologna *c.* 1140 and had written the *Summa (Stoma) magistri Rolandi,* a commentary on the *Decretum* of *Gratian and a theological treatise, the *Sententiae Rolandi Bononienses magistri,* before Pope Eugene III named him cardinal deacon (1150), car-

The seal of Alexander III, Archives of the Vatican.

dinal priest (1151), and appointed him chancellor (1153). He was one of the legates sent to negotiate the Treaty of Constance (1153) with *Frederick I Barbarossa. One of Pope *Adrian IV's most trusted advisers, he favored a pro-Norman diplomatic orientation and was a member of the legation sent to King William of Sicily, which drew up the Treaty of Benevento (1156). In the celebrated incident at Besançon (1157), the word *beneficia,* used by Rolando to mean "benefits" bestowed by the pope on the emperor, but translated as "fiefs" by the German chancellor, *Rainald of Dassel, aroused serious opposition.

Frederick Barbarossa. In the election of 1159 following Adrian IV's death, a majority decided for Rolando, who took the name of Alexander III; but a determined minority chose Cardinal Octavian, who, as Victor IV, was shortly afterward endorsed at a council dominated by the Emperor at Pavia (Feb. 10, 1160). Moreover, with the Emperor's power increasing in Italy and especially with his reduction of Milan (1162), Alexander was forced to seek refuge in France, where he arrived April 12, 1162. But even though Frederick had so far succeeded in keeping all but one or two German bishops at least outwardly in line, and was influential in certain peripheral areas, Alexander, assisted by some exceptionally able legates, had won wide support for himself. With a few exceptions the regular clergy remained behind him. Especially significant was the Council of Beauvais (July 1160), where, despite certain hesitations, *Louis VII of France and *Henry II of England had declared for Alexander, setting an example followed by other rulers. As a consequence, though in exile, Alexander could preside over the important Council of Tours (1163); and at Sens, where the Curia settled from 1163 to 1165, he conducted the normal business of ecclesiastical administration. The Pope returned to Rome Nov. 22, 1165. Meanwhile, resistance to the imperially supported schism was gaining ground in Italy, imperial Burgundy, and somewhat tentatively in Germany. And so Frederick, at the Diet of Würzburg (May 1165) ordered all princes and ecclesiastics to take an oath to antipope Paschal III, who had succeeded Victor IV in April 1164, and prepared once again to enter Italy in force. In the summer of 1167 Frederick occupied Rome, despite heroic resistance organized by Alexander. On July 22 he and his wife, Beatrice, were crowned by Paschal III. Plague, however, soon decimated the Emperor's forces, taking, among other notables, Rainald of Dassel. Moreover, moves already under way among certain north Italian cities resulted in the formation of the anti-imperial *Lombard League. Alexander, who had escaped to Benevento, gave the League his diplomatic support, and a new city, Alessandria, was named in his honor. About this same time, the Byzantine Emperor *Manuel I Comnenus proposed that he be accepted as ruler of a revived empire of east and west in return for assistance to the Pope. Though Alexander politely declined this proposal, legates were sent to continue discussion of the religious problems involved.

Alexander, therefore, never closed the door to eventual reconciliation with Frederick's empire, and his inexhaustible patience gradually bore fruit. An increasing number of German ecclesiastics was becoming uneasy, and Frederick's own conscience seems not to have been entirely tranquil. Despite the choice of a third imperial antipope, Callistus III (Sept. 20, 1168), mediation efforts especially by the Cistercians, and then military reverses, notably the victory of the Lombard League at Legnano (1176), made possible the Peace of Venice (1177), where in solemn ceremony the Emperor publicly reconciled himself with Alexander. Though adamant on essentials, such as his position as rightful pope, his jurisdiction over the church in the Empire, Alexander was willing to negotiate on other matters, e.g., the Matildine lands, and individual cases of schismatic ordinations or appointment to German sees. When Alexander returned to Rome in August 1177, he treated the schismatic clergy of the city and the final antipope Innocent III leniently.

Becket. During part of this same period, notably 1164 to 1170, Alexander was also concerned with the affair of Thomas *Becket. The Pope had received the archbishop of Canterbury in France, had supported him,

Alexander III returns to Rome, 1177, detail of a fresco by the 15th-century artist Aretino Spinello, Palazzo della Signoria, Siena. At the head of the Pope's horse are Frederick Barbarossa and the Doge Sebastiano Ziani.

and had condemned several of the Constitutions of *Clarendon. Alexander's preoccupation with the schism and his fear that King Henry II might go over to the antipope help to explain what some of Becket's adherents regarded as the Pope's failure to back the archbishop more vigorously. It must, however, be added that, as with the schism, Alexander remained insistent that the way to reconciliation be kept open. By means of several legations he attempted to bring about a settlement. In the years following Becket's murder (1170) a *modus vivendi* between the papacy and the English government was reached.

Evaluation. Despite the crises in England and the Empire, Alexander was able to make many significant contributions to the development of ecclesiastical government. His directive that the *licentia docendi* be given to deserving candidates without fee and the decree of the Third *Lateran Council that each cathedral maintain a teacher indicate a concern for education. He was abreast of developments in Spain and promoted missions and ecclesiastical organization in Scandinavia. Hoping to enlist aid for the Holy Land, he reissued the crusade bull, albeit without result (*see* BULLA CRUCIATA). Although little inclined to arbitrary measures personally, Alexander was aware of the dangerous growth of the *Cathari in southern France, and those procedures authorized toward the end of his pontificate or at the Third Lateran Council foreshadowed both the legatine inquest process and the cooperation of Church-State power (*see* INQUISITION) that would be utilized in the Church's antiheresy campaign.

Perhaps because of his moderation and patience, it has sometimes been suggested that Alexander did not stand fully in the line of development of the medieval *papacy that led from *Gregory VII to *Innocent III. It is true that he avoided broad statements on papal authority over secular rulers. But he was emphatic on papal supremacy within the Church. Moreover, his dealings with England and the Empire reveal a canon lawyer's concern with the legitimate rights of the ecclesiastical power within kingdoms and an awareness of the impact of contemporary developments in civil government on the ecclesiastical establishment. In the years following his death, the judgments he made on a surprisingly wide variety of cases found their way into the collections of decretals. The Third Lateran Council (1179), which bears the imprint of his mind, was a fitting climax to the pontificate of the first great lawyer-pope.

Bibliography: PL 200. J. M. WATTERICH, ed., *Pontificum Romanorum . . . vitae* (Leipzig 1862) 2:377–649. Jaffé L 2:145–418. CARDINAL BOSO, in Duchesne LP 2:397–446. F. THANER, ed., *Die Summa magistri Rolandi* (Innsbruck 1874). A. GEITL, ed., *Die Sentenzen Rolands, nachmals Papstes Alexander III* (Freiburg 1891). H. REUTER, *Geschichte Alexanders des Dritten und der Kirche seiner Zeit,* 3 v. (Leipzig 1860–64). Mann 10:1–238. P. BREZZI, *Roma e l'Impero medioevale 774–1252* (Bologna 1947). Haller 3:145–252. Fliche-Martin 9.2:50–188. Seppelt 3: 222–290, 607–609. M. PACAUT, *Alexandre III* (Paris 1956). M. W. BALDWIN, *Alexander III and the Twelfth Century* (Westminster, Md. 1966). **Illustration credit:** Fig. 2, Alinari-Art Reference Bureau.

[M. W. BALDWIN]

ALEXANDER IV, POPE, Dec. 12, 1254, to May 25, 1261; b. Rainaldo dei Conti di Segni. His illustrious family had produced two earlier popes, *Innocent III and *Gregory IX. He was named cardinal deacon (1227) by his uncle, Gregory IX, and became cardinal bishop of Ostia in 1231. Although by nature devout and peaceful, Alexander IV nevertheless prosecuted the war begun by his predecessor, *Innocent IV, against the heirs of Emperor *Frederick II in Germany, Italy, and Sicily. He allocated Sicily to Alfonso of Castile, and Conradin's heritage he assigned to Edmund, son of *Henry III of England. Alexander spent much of his pontificate outside Rome, because of the *Guelf-Ghibelline struggles in central Italy and *Manfred's war against the *States of the Church. During the interregnum in Germany, Alexander at first supported the claims of William of Holland to the imperial throne; after 1257 he switched his support to Richard of Cornwall. In negotiations with the Byzantine Emperor Theodore II Lascaris, Alexander attempted to reunite the Greek and Latin Churches. In Cyprus he successfully settled the rival claims of the two churches. In Syria he made the head of the recently reconciled Maronites patriarch of Antioch. A patron of the *Franciscans, Alexander restored to them many privileges that his predecessor had suppressed. He died at Viterbo and is buried in the cathedral.

Bibliography: ALEXANDER IV, *Les Registres,* ed. C. BOUREL DE LA RONCIÈRE et al., 3 v. (Paris 1902–53). Potthast Reg 2:1286–1473, 2124–29. F. TENCKHOFF, *Papst Alexander IV* (Paderborn 1907). Haller 4:272–296. G. SCHWAIGER, LexThK[2] 1:316–317.

[J. A. BRUNDAGE]

ALEXANDER VI, POPE

Pontificate, night of Aug. 10–11, 1492, to Aug. 18, 1503; b. Rodrigo Borja (Borgia) in Játiva (Xátiva), Valencia, Spain, *c.* 1431; d. Rome. His uncle, Pope *Callistus III, showered him with ecclesiastical benefices, sent him to study law in Bologna (1455), and, along with his cousin Lluís-Joan del Milà, made him a cardinal (Feb. 22, 1456). He was bishop of Valencia (June 30, 1458) and vice chancellor of the Church under Popes Callistus III, *Pius II, *Paul II, *Sixtus IV, and *Innocent VIII, even though his private life brought stern rebukes from Pius II. *See* BORGIA (BORJA). A man of great political talent, he was elected pope in the conclave of Aug. 6–11, 1492, not without employing a form of simony. Ruling in an era of turbulence for both Italy and the papacy, he pursued before 1498 a papal, Italian, and family policy that was quite different from his course of action during the last 5 years of his pontificate.

Italian Policy before 1498. Until 1498 he strove to restore and consolidate the Italian league, a project dear to Callistus. This league with Venice and Milan, joined eventually by Siena, Ferrara, and Mantua, was made public April 25, 1493. Then, threatened with an invasion of Italy by King *Charles VIII of France, Alexander sealed a treaty of friendship with Alfonso II of Naples through marriage of Alfonso's daughter, Sancha of Aragon, with Jofré Borja; the couple received the principality of Squillace from Alfonso. Alexander gained the support of King *Ferdinand V (II of Aragon) and Queen *Isabella I of Castile by the marriage of Joan (Juan) Borja, Duke of Gandia, to María Enríquez, first cousin of Ferdinand, and by granting the famous bulls that regulated Castilian and Portuguese conquests in America and granted the **patronato real* over all new churches in the Americas.

But when Charles VIII invaded Italy with the support of Ludovico el Moro of Milan and the approval

Pope Alexander VI, detail of a fresco of the Resurrection by Pinturicchio, in the Borgia rooms of the Vatican.

of Florence, Alexander was forced to give him free passage for the expedition, in which Charles conquered the Kingdom of Naples (February 1495). Charles entered Rome on Dec. 31, 1494. But eventually papal troops and the *condottiere* Virginio *Orsini drove the French and their allies out of Italy. After the battle of Fornovo (July 6, 1495) and the retreat of Charles to France, Alexander continued his policy of alliance with Spain (he granted the sovereigns the title "Catholic" in 1496), and with Naples. He sent his son, Cesare Borja, as cardinal-legate for the coronation of Frederick III of Naples in 1497 and arranged the marriage of his daughter, Lucrezia (whose first marriage with Giovanni *Sforza, Lord of Pesaro, he had annulled as unconsummated) with Alfonso of Aragon, Duke of Bisceglie and brother of the above-mentioned Sancha. It was during these years (1495–98) that Alexander was engaged in his struggle with Girolamo *Savonarola, who, after his excommunication, was tried and condemned by the government of Florence, then in the hands of his enemies, the *arrabbiati*.

French-Papal Alliance. In 1497 Alexander made serious plans for the reform of the Church, but his own irregular life and the ambitions of Cesare, who resigned the cardinalate in 1498 and took up politics in a practical way, frustrated his good intentions. In preferring Cesare's marriage to Charlotte d'Albret rather than Naples' Carlotta of Aragon, Alexander initiated his new policy in which he relied more on *Louis XII of France. It was further characterized by the abandonment of the Kingdom of Naples to its fate, and by the plan to unify the Romagna, Emilia, Umbria, and the Marches, the four feudatories (at least nominally) of the Holy See. Cesare, then Duke of Valentinois, accompanied Louis XII in the occupation of Milan (1499), and later undertook the conquest of central Italy, a campaign comparable to that waged by Alexander in Rome against the feudal nobility (Orsini and *Colonna). The Renaissance plan for greater cohesion in the *States of the Church shows Alexander's political ability, but the execution of the plan is open to serious criticism, e.g., the excesses of Cesare and his troops, the danger of a greater separation of central Italy from Rome under Cesare, and the open support of a French king who, after conquering Milan, aspired to Naples as well. Although Cesare's rule of the Romagna vanished like a dream on the Pope's death, and feudal anarchy returned, the later conquests of Pope *Julius II and his reorganization of the States of the Church were made possible by the internal collapse of those provinces in the wake of Cesare's conquests. Amid such fighting, however, the *Holy Year of 1500 could still be celebrated with some splendor.

After fruitless talks in Rome with ambassadors of various European states, Alexander—as had his uncle Callistus III—published a bull proclaiming a crusade against the *Ottoman Turks (June 10, 1500). But only Venice and Spain took part, conquering the islands of Cephalonia and Leukas. On the excuse that Frederick III of Naples was intriguing with the Turks, Louis XII and Ferdinand of Aragon and Castile divided his Neapolitan kingdom by the Treaty of Granada (Nov. 11, 1500). When the two kings disputed over the border that should separate their lands, Alexander sided with Louis, for whom Cesare campaigned in Naples. During Cesare's domination of central Italy, Lucrezia married (1501) Alfonso d'*Este, firstborn of Ercole I, Duke of Ferrara, as a guarantee of the independence of the duchies.

Evaluation. In August 1503 Alexander and Cesare both fell ill during an epidemic in Rome. The Pope died after confessing and receiving Viaticum and Extreme Unction. Despite his dissipated life, both as cardinal and pope, Alexander can be credited with several achievements during his pontificate. Better educated and more refined than Callistus III, he entrusted the decoration of the main floor of the *Vatican palace to Pinturiccio, restored the Castel Sant' Angelo, and provided a new building for the University of Rome. Michelangelo created his Pietà for Alexander. The monumental chancery palace was built during his pontificate.

In the evangelization of the New World, his actions conformed to the best papal traditions: he promoted the re-Christianization of *Greenland, supported Portuguese missionary work, and with his *Alexandrine bulls, ensured peace between Portugal and Castile in both the Far East and the Americas, as well as the spread of the Gospel. (*See* PAPAL LINE OF DEMARCATION.) Criticism of the bulls has, perhaps, not always taken into account the political rights claimed by popes from the Middle Ages or the interplay of ecclesiastical, papal, and family policies involved in their concession. Alexander's piety seems to have been more sincere than his life would indicate. Still, any overall judgment of him and his pontificate from an ecclesiastical and religious point of view will always be negative, even though his enemies have often calumniated him through exaggeration. Recent uncritical excesses of those seeking naively to vindicate him have provoked a reaction, frequently as unrestrained as that of the revisionists.

Bibliography: Sources. O. RAYNALDUS, *Annales ecclesiastici,* ed. J. D. MANSI, 15 v. (Lucca 1747–56) 11:208–416. BullRom v.5. A. DE LA TORRE, ed., *Documentos sobre relaciones internacionales de los Reyes Católicos,* 4 v. (Barcelona 1949–62). J. FERNÁNDEZ ALONSO, *Legaciones y nunciaturas en España de 1466 a 1521,* 2 v. (Rome 1963–66). For further source material, *see* BORGIA.

Literature. Pastor v.5, 6. M. GIMÉNEZ FERNÁNDEZ, "Las bulas alejandrinas de 1493 referentes a las Indias," *Anuario de estudios americanos* 1 (1944) 171–387. G. SORANZO, *Studi intorno a papa Alessandro VI (Borgia)* (Milan 1950); *Il tempo di Alessandro VI papa e di Fra Girolamo Savonarola* (Milan 1960). G. B. PICOTTI, in RivStorChIt 5 (1951) 169–262; 8 (1954) 313–355. A. M. ALBAREDA, "Il vescovo di Barcellona Pietro Garsias bibliotecario della Vaticana sotto Alessandro VI," *La bibliofilia* 60 (1958) 1–18. A. GARCÍA GALLO, "Las bulas de Alejandro VI y el ordenamiento jurídico de la expansión portuguesa y castellana en Africa e Indias," *Anuario de historia del derecho español* 27–28 (1957–58) 461–829. C. M. DE WITTE, "Les Bulles pontificales et l'expansion portugaise au XVe siècle," RHE 53 (1958) 443–471. P. DE LETURIA, *Relaciones entre la Santa Sede e Hispanoamérica,* 3 v. (AnalGreg 101–103; 1959–60), v.1. M. BATLLORI, *Alejandro VI y la casa real de Aragón, 1492–1498* (Madrid 1958); *Estudis d'història i de cultura catalanes,* v.2 *L'humanisme i els Borja* (Rome). *At the Court of the Borgia, Being an Account of the Reign of Pope Alexander VI Written by . . . Johann Burchard,* ed. and tr. G. PARKER (Folio Society; London 1963). **Illustration credit:** Alinari-Art Reference Bureau.

[M. BATLLORI]

ALEXANDER VII, POPE

Pontificate, April 7, 1655, to May 22, 1667; b. Fabio Chigi, Siena, Feb. 13, 1599. The Sienese Chigi family had been prominent since the Middle Ages. Fabio was a brilliant boy, given to writing verses; for 9 years he studied philosophy, law, and theology at the University of Siena. He received his doctorate in theology in 1626. After 2 years more of private study at Rome, where he became acquainted with a number of intellectual leaders, Chigi entered the papal service. He rose steadily

Pope Alexander VII, tomb by Bernini in the Basilica of St. Peter at Rome.

from a referendary in 1629 to vice-legate of Ferrara, bishop of Nardo, and apostolic visitor to Malta. When appointed a bishop he became a priest. His diplomatic ability was to receive a sterner test when Urban VIII sent him to troubled Germany. He spent 13 years as nuncio to Cologne, and also served as the Pope's representative at the Peace Conference of Münster. This was a most difficult task and if Chigi did not bring about the success of the papal policy, he did win the esteem of Pope and Curia. Innocent X made him secretary of state in 1651 and a year later he received the red hat. The Conclave of 1655 that followed the death of Innocent X was a long one—January 17 to April 7. Upon election Chigi took the name Alexander VII in memory of the great 12th-century pope, *Alexander III. Alexander suffered a great deal from poor health, but he was a hard worker. He was charitable to the poor and was a great help to his people in the plague of 1656. He encouraged scholarship and aided the work of historians by setting up sensible regulations for the use of archival materials. A truly splendid patron of the arts, Alexander is remembered for commissioning the construction of the great colonnade of Bernini.

Alexander and Louis XIV maintained poor relations, and the King went to some pains to humiliate the Pope over a clash between Alexander's Corsican guards and the French embassy. But this was not all the trouble Louis caused Alexander. The Pope tried hard to help beleaguered Christians beat back the Turks, but Louis XIV, more interested in weakening the Hapsburgs, did not cooperate; thus, papal plans foundered on Bourbon ambitions.

Like his predecessors, Alexander was forced to take action against the Jansenists. Innocent X had condemned the Five Propositions, but then Antoine *Arnauld, the great Jansenist leader, decided that while the Five Propositions were indeed wrong, and one could accept the Pope's condemnation of them, they were not to be found in Cornelius *Jansen's **Augustinus*. Alexander countered by a bull in which he said that the Five Propositions were contained in Jansen's *Augustinus* and condemned Jansen's presentation of them.

Alexander welcomed the illustrious convert, *Christina, Queen of Sweden, and gently corrected some of her odd ideas. He encouraged foreign missions and gave increased power to the Congregation for the Propagation of the Faith.

Bibliography: Pastor 31:1–313. A. L. ARTAUD DE MONTOR, *The Lives and Times of the Popes,* 10 v. (New York 1910–11) 6:71–106. N. J. ABERCROMBIE, *The Origins of Jansenism* (Oxford 1936). BullRom, v.16–17. J. ORCIBAL, *Les Origines du jansénisme,* 5 v. (Louvain 1947–62). G. I. DELLA ROCCHETTA, EncCatt 1:801–803. K. REPGEN, LexThK[2] 1:318. H. HEMMER, DTC 1.1:727–747. **Illustration credit:** Alinari-Art Reference Bureau.

[J. S. BRUSHER]

ALEXANDER VIII, POPE, Oct. 6, 1689, to Feb. 1, 1691; b. Pietro Vito Ottoboni, Venice, April 22, 1610. He was descended from a noble Venetian family; his father Marco was chancellor of Venice. Pietro showed brilliance in his studies and at 17 won a doctorate in civil and Canon Law at the University of Padua. In 1630 he went to Rome and was made governor of Terni, Rieti, and Spoleto and auditor of the Rota. Innocent X named him cardinal in 1652 and bishop of Brescia 2 years later. Under Innocent XI, he became grand inquisitor of Rome and secretary of the Holy Office. When elected pope in 1689, Alexander was an octogenarian. He used the 18 months of his pontificate to diminish the tensions with France, and in a mood of conciliation brought *Louis XIV to restore Avignon, seized during the reign of *Innocent XI, and to renounce the privilege of diplomatic residence. He did not give way, however, on the four articles of the *Assembly of the French Clergy of 1682. In the bull *Inter multiplices,* signed Aug. 4, 1690, but promulgated just 2 days before his death, he declared them null and invalid. His improved relations with France decreased his friendship with Emperor Leopold I, who recalled his ambassador from the Vatican court and refused to receive the papal chargé d'affaires in Vienna. He was interested also in a possible Stuart restoration in England and established a group to study English affairs. His reign was conspicuous for generous aid to Venice in the Turkish wars, for excessive nepotism, and for his patronage of the Vatican Library. He is also remembered for his condemnation of 31 Jansenist propositions (Denz 2301–32), certain errors about the so-called philosophical sin (Denz 2290–93), and errors about the love of God (Denz 2311–13, 15).

Monument of Pope Alexander VIII, designed by Arrigo di San Martino, in St. Peter's Basilica, Rome.

Bibliography: Pastor 32:530–560. P. RICHARD, DHGE 2:243–251. X. M. LE BACHELET, DTC 1:747–763. G. A. HANOTAUX, *Recueil des instructions données aux ambassadeurs et ministres de France,* 3 v. (Paris 1888–1913). BullRom 20:1–167. **Illustration credit:** Alinari-Art Reference Bureau.

[S. V. RAMGE]

ALEXANDER I, EMPEROR OF RUSSIA; b. St. Petersburg, Dec. 12, 1777; d. Taganrog, Nov. 19, 1825. Alexander, the son of Czar Paul I (1754–1801) and Sophia Dorothea of Württemberg, was much influenced by his Swiss tutor Frédéric Laharpe, a rationalist. Until 1812 Alexander inclined toward deism and was affected also by traditional Russian autocracy. After succeeding to the imperial throne upon his father's assassination (1801), he relaxed some of the rigid state controls and initiated important government reforms. During the first half of his reign, Russia was involved in the Napoleonic wars. At the subsequent Congress of *Vienna, Alexander I was the most powerful monarch. Influenced by *Metternich, he became extremely conservative both in domestic and foreign policy after 1815.

Alexander I was deeply impressed by *Rousseau's adulation of humanity and envisioned a syncretistic Christianity united under his political rule. He sought unsuccessfully to have Pope *Pius VII bless the *Holy Alliance. Within his own realm, he maintained a policy of tolerance toward Latin Catholics but seriously interfered with the correspondence between Rome and the bishops. He supported the scheme, originated under *Catherine II, to make the metropolitan of *Mogilev a veritable Latin patriarch for Russia, with power to nominate and to dispose bishops, to inspect and even to suppress religious houses, and to be the ultimate court of appeal in ecclesiastical cases. By the decree of Nov. 9, 1801, the Czar established the Roman Catholic Ecclesiastical College, which lacked the approval of the Holy See but regulated the affairs of the Latin Church, as the *Holy Synod did for the Orthodox Church. Alexander I pursued the policy of subjecting the Ruthenians to Latin jurisdiction. He expelled the *Jesuits from St. Petersburg (1815) and from the empire (1820). During his reign, however, he never objected to the conversion of his courtiers to Catholicism, and he even maintained a correspondence with Madame *Swetchine. At the time of Alexander's death, General Michaud, his aide-de-camp, was in Rome requesting that Pope *Leo XII send a trustworthy priest to St. Petersburg. It was thought that Alexander was contemplating reunion. But he died before a papal mission could be organized. The story that Alexander became a Catholic upon his deathbed lacks foundation.

See also UNION OF SOVIET SOCIALIST REPUBLICS.

Bibliography: L. I. STRAKHOVSKY, *Alexander I of Russia* (New York 1947). P. PIERLING, *La Russie et le Saint-Siège,* 5 v. (Paris 1896–1912) v.5. A. BOUDOU, *Le Saint-Siège et la Russie,* 2 v. (Paris 1922–25). M. J. ROUËT DE JOURNEL, *Nonciature d'Arezzo, 1802–1806,* 5 v. (Rome 1922–57) v.3, 4. Koch JesLex 37–38, 1574–78. S. FURLANI, EncCatt 1:805. I. SMOLITSCH, LexThK[2] 1:311–312.

[R. F. BYRNES]

ALEXANDER, PATRIARCH OF ALEXANDRIA, ST.

Patriarchate, 312 to April 328, during which the controversy over *Arianism erupted; b. *c.* 250; d. Alexandria, April 18, 328 (feast, Feb. 26). He served prominently under Bishops Peter and Achillas and was probably rector of the famous school of Alexandria. In 312 he was elected to succeed Achillas: *Philostorgius affirmed that *Arius supported the candidacy of Alexander; *Epiphanius of Constantia blamed Arius's frustrated ambition for the subsequent enmity. Alexander gave Arius charge of the important parish of Baucalis. He first encountered opposition from Meletius of Lycopolis, whose rigoristic attitude toward the lapsed (*see* LAPSI) had led him into schism against the former bishop, Peter; Alexander had difficulty also with the priest Kolluthus, who had usurped the power to ordain priests and deacons. In about 318 he received complaints concerning the teachings of Arius, who denied the true divinity of Christ.

Alexander first called a conference of the local clergy, and Arius was asked to explain his views. When discussion and persuasion failed to convince him of his errors, Alexander convened a synod of all Egyptian bishops, which condemned and excommunicated Arius. There followed a period of feverish activity on both sides. Arius went to Palestine and Bithynia, where he received support from both Bp. *Eusebius of Caesarea and Bp. *Eusebius of Nicomedia, who wrote to many fellow bishops in Arius's favor. To counteract this propaganda, Alexander circulated numerous letters to expose the erroneous doctrine of Arius and to defend his own course of action. In these he showed himself an adherent of moderate Origenism and insisted especially on the natural, eternal generation of the Son and on His perfect likeness to the Father.

After conquering the East in 324, *Constantine I intervened in the conflict and sent *Hosius of Córdoba, his ecclesiastical adviser, to Egypt with a letter for Alexander and Arius, exhorting them to make peace. On Hosius's arrival, Alexander informed him of the true issue at stake and gained a powerful ally. Another Egyptian synod was called; when it failed to bring Arius to submission both prelates suggested holding a general council. At *Nicaea I (325), Alexander was among the leaders of the orthodox party and may have had a hand in the inclusion of the term homoousios in the *Nicene Creed.

After the Council, Alexander met with continued opposition from the Meletians, although they had been treated leniently by the decisions of Nicaea. He designated *Athanasius as his successor. Alexander is venerated as a saint in the Coptic Church. Epiphanius mentions a collection of 70 letters of Alexander, but only 2, dealing with the Arian crisis, have survived. A sermon on the soul and body, and one on the Passion of Christ, and fragments of others are also preserved in Coptic and Syriac translations.

Bibliography: H. G. OPITZ, ed., *Athanasius' Werke,* v.3.1 (Berlin 1934) 6–11; 19–29, works. X. LE BACHELET, DTC 1.1:764–766. R. JANIN, DHGE 2:182–183. J. N. D. KELLY, *Early Christian Doctrines* (2d ed. New York 1960) 224–225. Quasten Patr 3:13–19. V. C. DE CLERCQ, *Ossius of Cordova* (Washington 1954) 189–206. J. R. PALANQUE, Fliche-Martin 3:69–80, Eng. in J. R. PALANQUE et al., *The Church in the Christian Roman Empire,* tr. E. C. MESSENGER, 2 v. in 1 (New York 1953) 1:73–109.

[V. C. DE CLERCQ]

ALEXANDER OF ABONOTEICHOS

Founder and prophet of a pagan oracle and mystery cult in Paphlagonia, Asia Minor, *c.* A.D. 105–175. Except for a few coins of Lucius Verus and Marcus Aurelius, and inscriptions attesting the fact of his existence, our knowledge of him comes from a bitterly antagonistic biography by Lucian of Samosata called *Alexander the False Prophet.* The Alexander ambiguously mentioned by Athenagoras in his *Embassy for the Christians* (ed. J. H. Crehan, AncChrWr 23:65–66, 157) may be the same man, although the identity is disputed. As a youth he consorted with a healer who was a disciple of the philosopher Apollonius of Tyana. Later he conspired with a charlatan named Cocconas to found an oracle and begin a cult.

At Chalcedon Alexander invented several prophecies to the effect that the god Asclepius or Aesculapius, the son of Apollo, would become incarnate at Abonoteichos and that Alexander would be his prophet. He then arranged a spectacular "birth" of the god, whom he called Glycon, in the form of a snake emerging from a goose egg. Using a tame serpent, a network of spies and helpers, and an ingenious method of opening sealed scrolls with heated needles, he began to issue oracles in return for payment (a drachma and two obols).

The renown of Glycon and Alexander spread through Asia Minor and reached Rome, where the influential Rutilianus became an ardent follower and was inveigled into marriage with Alexander's daughter "by the goddess Selene." With the oracle firmly established, Alexander introduced an annual 3-day celebration of some of the classical mystery themes and some invented by the prophet himself. His chief opponents apparently were the Epicureans, whom he fought through oracles and through the influence of his followers. By his own orders, Epicureans, Christians, and atheists were rigidly banned from attending the mysteries or consulting Glycon. The cult of Glycon was not confined to healing, but was more properly a form of worship and an imitation of the great oracles of the ancient world.

After amassing wealth, Alexander died of an infection when he was nearly 70. The cult outlasted him by at least a century, as 3d-century coins of the region show.

Bibliography: LUCIAN, *Alexander the False Prophet,* ed. and tr. A. M. HARMON (LoebClLib 4) 173–253. S. DILL, Hastings ERE 1:306. K. PRÜMM, *Religionsgeschichtliches Handbuch für den Raum der altchristlichen Umwelt* (2d ed. Rome 1954) 460–462. J. LEIPOLDT, ReallexAntChr 1:260–261.

[G. W. MAC RAE]

ALEXANDER OF COMANA, ST., "the charcoal burner," first bishop of Comana in Pontus; martyred *c.* 275 (feast, Aug. 11). According to *Gregory of Nyssa (PG 46:933–940), St. *Gregory Thaumaturgus, when invited to organize a Christian community and preside over the election of a bishop in Comana, rejected all the proposed candidates, pointing out that the Apostles had been poor and ordinary men. Someone proposed Alexander, and Gregory questioned him to discover that beneath the grime of his trade he was an educated man of good birth, who had given up his possessions to follow Christ. Alexander was consecrated. Later, he was burned to death, probably under Aurelian (270–275). As the patron of charcoal burners, he was first inserted into the Roman martyrology by *Baronius.

Bibliography: G. ELDAROV, BiblSanct 1:776–777.

[M. J. COSTELLOE]

ALEXANDER OF FIESOLE, ST., bishop and martyr; b. Fiesole?; d. near Bologna, *c.* 833–841 (feast, June 6). Having been consecrated in Rome, he succeeded to the episcopacy of his native city. In that office he was remarkable for all the pastoral virtues. He persuaded the Emperor *Lothair I to restore certain properties of which the Church had been despoiled. As Alexander was returning from this successful mission, he was attacked by those who had been forced to surrender their ill-gotten possessions. In the encounter he was drowned in the River Reno. His relics were brought to Fiesole where he quickly became one of the principal patrons.

Bibliography: ActSS June 1:738–740. BHL 1:278. Baudot-Chaussin 6:105. G. RASPINI, BiblSanct 1:781–782.

[J. E. LYNCH]

ALEXANDER THE GREAT

King of Macedon (336–323); b. Pella (northeastern Greece), 356 B.C.; d. Babylon, June 13, 323. The son of Philip II of Macedonia and Olympias of Epirus, Alexander (III) succeeded to the throne at the age of 20 after the assassination of Philip. After he had demonstrated his ability as general in consolidating the kingdom bequeathed to him by his father, he was named ἡγεμών (general) by the council of the Greek League for the war it had declared against Persia to avenge the sacrilege of Xerxes against the temples of the Greek gods. In 334 B.C. he led an army of Macedonians and Greeks across the Hellespont, met and defeated at the River Granicus an army led by Persian satraps, and proceeded on his way through Asia Minor, liberating the Greek city-states as he went. The following year he was met at Issus by an army led by the Persian King Darius III (335–330 B.C.), which he routed and put to flight. The favorable terms of peace offered by Darius he refused, thus giving the first indication that he intended to go beyond his commission and become king of Persia. Instead of pursuing Darius immediately, Alexander turned south in order to seize control of the Mediterranean coast and so neutralize the powerful Persian fleet. Tyre, the island naval power that had withstood Nabuchodonosor for 13 years, fell to Alexander in 7 months, and Egypt was occupied by him without opposition. Turning then toward Persia, Alexander met Darius at Gaugamela and again defeated him (331 B.C.); Darius fled and was later killed by his own subjects. Alexander thereupon occupied the great cities of the Persian Empire, set fire to Xerxes' palace at Persepolis, and was crowned king of Persia. His campaign into India (327–325 B.C.) extended the borders of his empire to the lower Indus. He was barred from further conquests only by the refusal of his own army, which, having followed him for 11,000 miles and through several major battles, demanded to be allowed to return home. Alexander returned to Babylon, where he died after a 10-day fever, being not yet 33 years old. He left no heir and his empire was divided among his generals (*see* PTOLEMIES; SELEUCID DYNASTY); a posthumous son born to Roxane, one of Alexander's wives, never ruled, but was murdered at the age of 12 years.

Alexander the Great with Amon horns, four-drachma silver coin issued by Lysimachus, c. 300 B.C.

Alexander's lasting importance lies not so much in his military victories as in the steps he took to realize the dream (present at least in his last years) of a great world state. He was convinced of the superiority of Greek language and culture and wished it to be the basis of unity among the lands and races he ruled; this was accomplished at least in part through the many cities (traditionally numbered at 70) that he founded. Yet he rejected the notion of Aristotle (who had been his teacher from the age of 13) that all barbarians were slaves by nature; he recognized the qualities of the Persians and wanted to make them partners with the Macedonians and Greeks in his empire. He married Roxane, a daughter of a Bactrian baron, and Barsine, a daughter of Darius, and encouraged marriages of his officers and men with Persian women; he took Persians (and others) into his army and often left Persians in charge of the satrapies that he took over. Although his early death prevented the realization of many of his plans, the Hellenization of the East was the most important result of his labors and one that even the division of his empire and the strife that followed did not destroy. When the OT was translated for the sake of the Jewish *diaspora, it was into Greek that it was translated, even though the work was done in Egypt [*see* BIBLE, IV (TEXTS AND VERSIONS), 5]. Hellenism continued to take root and spread, so that during the 1st Christian century the common culture and language throughout what was by then the Roman Empire facilitated the spread of the gospel. Some of Alexander's followers had more zeal and less moderation than he in imposing Greek culture. The attempt of *Antiochus IV Epiphanes to do this in Palestine through threats and persecution led to the Machabean revolt [*see* MACHABEES (MACCABEES), HISTORY OF THE] and forms the background of the Books of the *Machabees and the Book of *Daniel.

Bibliography: G. T. GRIFFITH and W. W. TARN, OxClDict 32–34. H. E. STIER, ReallexAntChr 1:261–270; LexThK[2] 1:310; RGG[3] 1:229–230. C. A. ROBINSON, *Ancient History: From Prehistoric Times to the Death of Justinian* (New York 1951) 315–351. J. B. BURY, *A History of Greece to the Death of Alexander the Great,* rev. R. MEIGGS (3d ed. New York 1951; repr. 1959) 724–821. N. G. L. HAMMOND, *A History of Greece to 332 B.C.* (Oxford 1959) 596–642. W. W. TARN, *Alexander the Great,* 2 v. (Cambridge 1948); CAH 6:352–437, with bibliog. of modern works. H. BERVE, *Das Alexanderreich auf prosopographischer Grundlage,* 2 v. (Munich 1926). G. A. RADET, *Alexandre le Grand* (Paris 1931). **Illustration credit:** Hirmer Verlag München.

[J. F. DEVINE]

ALEXANDER OF HALES

English Franciscan theologian known by the scholastic titles of *Doctor irrefragabilis* and *Doctor doctorum;* b. Hales Owen, Shropshire, *c.* 1185; d. Paris, Aug. 21, 1245.

Life. Born of a wealthy agrarian family, he studied arts at the University of Paris, where he became a master before 1210. About 1210 he began to study theology and became regent master *c.* 1220–22. He retained his professorship until 1241, when he relinquished it to *John of La Rochelle. As a theologian he acquired a considerable reputation. Early in his teaching career as regent master in theology he replaced the custom of lecturing on the Bible with lectures on the *Sentences* of *Peter Lombard. Because of this unprecedented procedure, *Roger Bacon, who originally had the highest admiration for him, mentioned Alexander's innovation as one of the causes for the decline of theology. In fact, however, Alexander's emphasis on speculative theology, use of philosophy, and study of the Fathers initiated the golden age of medieval scholasticism (*see* SCHOLASTICISM, 1). Later this custom was reserved for bachelors in theology. Between 1226 and 1229 he became a canon of St. Paul's in London with the prebend of Holborn, even though he remained in Paris. He played an important part in the struggle between university and crown; the reorganization of the university effected by the bull *Parens scientiarum* of *Gregory IX, April 13, 1231, was partly the work of Alexander. Toward the end of 1231 and the beginning of 1232 he was in England, where contemporary documents record him as canon of Lichfield and archdeacon of Coventry. From August 1235 until February 1236 he helped to negotiate peace between France and England. At the beginning of the academic year 1236–37, Alexander, already more than 50 years of age, disposed of his wealth and entered the Franciscan Order, thereby securing a chair in the university for the order. Among his outstanding Franciscan disciples were John of La Rochelle, *Odo Rigaldus, and St. *Bonaventure. As a Franciscan master he participated in the general chapter at Rome, collaborated on the first exposition of the Rule (1241–42), and was probably dean of regent masters. He took an active part in censuring doctrines of the Dominican Étienne de Venizy (1241) and of the secular John Pagus (1244). Attending the Council of Lyons in 1244, he and *Robert Grosseteste were part of a commission charged with examining documents preparatory to canonizing St. *Edmund of Abingdon. His sudden death was mourned throughout Paris. The solemn funeral rites, held on Aug. 25, 1245, were presided over by *Odo of Châteauroux, papal legate to France. The poet *John of Garland sang his praises (HistLitFrance 21:372).

Works. Five major writings can be ascribed to him with certainty. (1) *Exoticon,* a youthful work about difficult words, is attributed to him in Cambridge, Glanville, and Caius College MS 136. (2) *Glossa in 4 libros sententiarum* (BiblFranSchMA 12–15, Quaracchi 1951–57), apparently a *reportatio* that was discovered in 1946, is a *lectio cursoria,* midway between a literal commentary and a fully developed series of questions on the text of Peter Lombard. (3) *Quaestiones disputatae 'antequam esset frater'* (BiblFranSchMA 19–21, Quaracchi 1960), including 68 questions of various length, were written between 1220 and 1236. They touch almost the whole domain of theology and demonstrate convincingly the author's propensity for speculative theology. (4) *Quaestiones quodlibetales,* of which four are known to be extant (Glorieux L 2:57–59, 289, 319), are being prepared for publication at Quaracchi. (5) The *Summa theologica,* sometimes known as the *Summa pseudo-Alexandri* (4 v. Quaracchi 1924–48), must be discussed in terms of the *Summa* left incomplete by Alexander in 1245 and the expanded version issued in 1260 and published at Quaracchi. Of the present version only the following seem to have been in the original *Summa fratris Alexandri:* bk. 1, all except perhaps q. 74, *De missione visibili;* bk. 2, all except the tracts *De corpore humano* and *De coniuncto;* bk. 3, fragments. The work is called *Summa fratris Alexandri* in the MS tradition and in the bull *De fontibus paradisi* of Alexander IV, Oct. 7, 1255. The bull ordered that the *Summa* be completed by the Franciscans. *William of Melitona (Middleton) and his collaborators worked until 1260 without completing it. They utilized Alexander's *Glossa* and *Quaestiones disputatae* and incorporated many parts of their own writings, as well as those of Prevostino, or

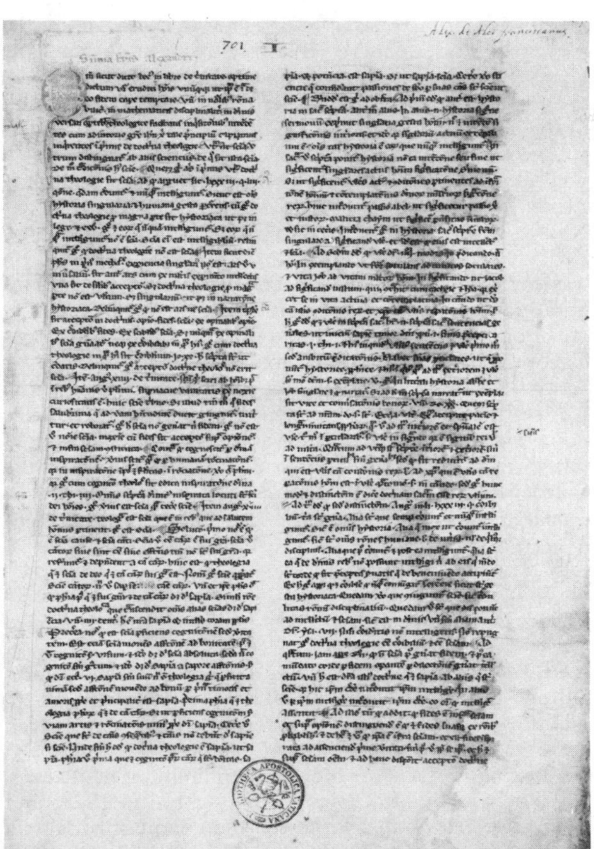

The beginning of the first part of the "Summa" of Alexander of Hales in a manuscript in the Vatican Library (Vat. lat. 701, fol. 3 r).

Praepostinus (*c.* 1145–1210); *William of Auxerre; and *Philip the Chancellor. The final version of the *Summa* was imposed on the Franciscan school by two ministers general, Guiral Ot in 1331 and Leonard of Gaffoni in 1373. Alexander collaborated with John of La Rochelle, Robert of La Bassée and Odo Rigaldus in the *Expositio super regulam* of 1241–42 (ed. L. Oliger, Rome 1950). Although numerous Biblical commentaries have been attributed to him (Stegmüller RB nn. 1117–57), only a *Postillae super quatuor Evangelia* and a *Commentarius super Psalmos* are generally accepted as his; but this question needs to be further investigated. Three *Sermones* can also be attributed to him with some certainty.

Thought. Although Alexander quoted freely from almost all the works of *Aristotle, including the pseudo-Aristotelian *De causis,* and had access to the full text of these works, he had no clear idea of the true meaning of Aristotelian philosophy. In his writings he adapted fragmentary texts of Aristotle to the teaching of St. *Augustine. His work belongs to a period when no collective theological effort had been made to assimilate the newly discovered Aristotelian world. His main theological authorities were Augustine, *Pseudo-Dionysius, *Boethius, and many 11th- and 12th-century theologians, notably St. *Anselm of Canterbury, St. *Bernard of Clairvaux, *Gilbert de la Porrée, and the pseudo-hermetic *Liber 24 philosophorum.*

His psychological notions, introduced when he was discussing the image of God in man, are strictly Augustinian or are inspired by the pseudo-Augustinian *De spiritu et anima.* Against William of Auxerre, Alexander maintains that the powers of the soul are not distinct from the substance, but only from the essence. Since essence is that by which the soul is what it is, its powers are not what makes the soul to be what it is; on the other hand, since substance is what makes a thing subsist in its indivisible unity, the soul cannot be complete without its powers or faculties (*see* FACULTIES OF THE SOUL). This position was characteristic of the Franciscan school until the time of *Duns Scotus. Alexander followed Augustine in his discussion of the problem of evil and in his notion of wisdom. The *Summa theologica* of 1260 remarkably illustrates what may be called the spirit of the 13th-century Franciscan school of theology at the University of Paris.

Bibliography: Glorieux R 2:15–24. Stegmüller RS 1:31–34. I. HERSCHER, "A Bibliography of Alexander of Hales," Franc Studies 5 (1945) 434–454. Gilson HistChrPhil, *passim.* L. MASCALI, EncFil 1:140–142. V. DOUCET, EncCatt 1:784–787; "A New Source of the *Summa fratris Alexandri:* The Commentary on the Sentences of Alexander of Hales," FrancStudies 6 (1946) 403–417; "Prolegomena" to Alexander of Hales, *Summa theologica,* in v.4 (Quaracchi-Florence 1948); "Prolegomena" in each v. of *Glossa in quattuor libros Sententiarum Petri Lombardi,* BiblFranSchMA 12–15 (1951–57); "Prolegomena" to Alexander of Hales, *Quaestiones disputatae "Antequam esset frater", ibid.* 19 (1960) 1:5*–41*.

[A. EMMEN]

ALEXANDER OF JERUSALEM, ST., bishop and martyr; d. Caesarea, Palestine, 250–251 (feast, March 18 and Jan. 30). One of the great bishops of the early Church, he was trained in *Alexandria, where he was a pupil of Pantaenus (d. *c.* 200) and *Clement of Alexandria and where he became the friend of *Origen. After becoming bishop of an unknown see in Cappadocia *c.* 200, he was imprisoned *c.* 204 during the persecution of Septimius Severus (d. 211) and not released until 211. In the following year he was made coadjutor and later successor of the aged Narcissus (d. 222), Bishop of *Jerusalem, both unusual proceedings at that early date. At Jerusalem he founded the library later used by *Eusebius of Caesarea in preparing his great history of the early Church. When Origen was condemned by the bishop of Alexandria, Alexander invited him to Jerusalem, ordained him, and put him in charge of the teaching of Scripture and theology in the diocese. Alexander died in prison at Caesarea during the persecution of Decius (d. 251).

Bibliography: EUSEBIUS, *Hist. eccl.* 6.8, 11, 14, 19, 39, 46. G. BAREILLE, DTC 1.1:763–764. C. VAN HULST, EncCatt 1:783–784.

[J. L. GRASSI]

ALEXANDER NECKHAM, Augustinian theologian, scientist, and poet (also spelled Neckam; nicknamed *Nequam,* meaning worthless); b. Sept. 13, 1157, St. Alban's, Hartfordshire; d. March 31, 1217, Kempsey, Worcestershire. He studied arts at Paris, probably between 1175 and 1182, and taught at Dunstable (*c.* 1182) and St. Alban's (*c.* 1183–90). Having studied theology at Oxford between 1190 and 1197, he entered the Order of the Augustinian Canons about 1200. He acted as papal judge delegate (1203 and 1205), and became abbot of Cirencester in 1213. His works include *De nominibus utensilium; Novus Aesopus* and *Novus Avianus; Super Marcianum de nuptilis Mercurii et Philosophiae; Repertorium vocabulorum Bibliae; De naturis rerum libri duo* (RollsS 34:1–354); *Commen-*

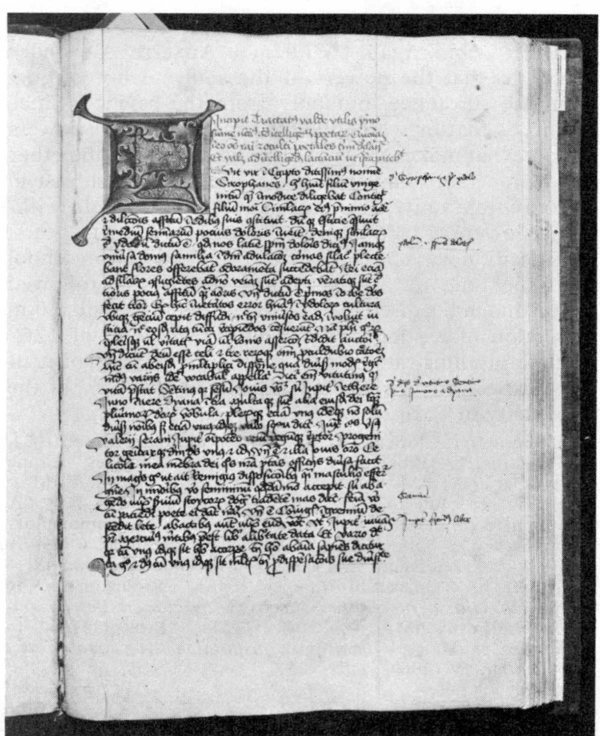

Folio from a manuscript of Alexander Neckham's "Mithologie, sive Sintillarium" written in Germany in 1486 (fMS Lat. 193, p. 1, Houghton Library, Harvard University).

tarius in Ecclesiastem (cf. Stegmüller RB 2:1172); *Commentarius in Canticum; Corrogationes novi Promethei,* or *Summa super Bibliam; De laudibus divinae sapientiae* (RollsS 34:357–503); *Glossae in Psalterium; Commentarius in Parabolas Salomonis; Speculum speculationum; Quaestiones de rebus theologicis; Sacerdos ad altare;* as well as some sermons. Alexander, as a typical exponent of encyclopedic learning in medieval England, influenced later English thought, particularly that of the poet, Edmund *Spenser [cf. St Philol 22 (1925) 222–225]. His works display considerable erudition, including knowledge of the natural sciences. His prestige may be judged from the fact that his change of opinion in favor of the celebration of the Virgin Mary's conception [EngHistRev 47 (1932) 260–268] was influential in spreading that feast in England [cf. FranzStud 39 (1957) 115, 179].

Bibliography: F. M. Powicke, "Alexander of S. Albans," *Essays in History Presented to Reginald Lane Poole* (London 1927) 246–260. H. Kantorowicz, "A Medieval Grammarian on the Sources of Law," TijdschrRG 15 (1937) 25–47. P. W. Damon, "A Note on the Neckham Canon," *Speculum* 32 (1957) 99–102. Stegmüller RB 2:1158–72. LexThK² 1:308. Emden 2:1342–43.

[A. EMMEN]

ALEXANDER NEVILLE, archbishop of York, bishop of Saint Andrews; b. *c.* 1332; d. May 16, 1392. Having studied at Oxford by 1348–49, he was a master of arts by 1357 and a scholar of civil law by 1361. He became master of the hospital of St. Thomas the Martyr at Bolter-in-Allendale, Northumbria, that year, and he was made archbishop of *York in 1374. A clerk of King *Edward III by 1361, he was a royal curialist from 1386 when he became a member of Parliament's continual council under King *Richard II. As such he was involved in the crisis of 1387–88 that issued in the Merciless Parliament of 1388. Neville supported the King; hence the chronicler Knighton described him as one of the *nephandi seductores regis.* A bitter opponent of the chief Lord Appellant, Thomas, Duke of Gloucester, he was four times appealed of high treason: at a preliminary meeting of the Appellants at Waltham Cross, Nov. 14, 1387; before Richard at Westminster, Nov. 17, 1387; before Richard in the Tower of London, Dec. 28 or 29, 1387; in Parliament, Feb. 3, 1388. He was found guilty of treason and his property and temporalities were declared forfeit. Neville's life was spared, but Pope Urban VI translated him from the archbishopric of York to the Diocese of *Saint Andrews, Scotland, at the Appellants' request (bull of translation, April 30, 1388). But since Scotland did not recognize Pope Urban (*see* WESTERN SCHISM), Neville sought refuge in Louvain. He is buried in the church of the Carmelites, Louvain, Belgium.

Bibliography: W. Hunt, DNB 14:243–244. T. F. Tout, *Chapters in the Administrative History of Mediaeval England,* 6 v. (New York 1920–33). A. B. Steel, *Richard II* (Cambridge, Eng. 1941; repr. 1963). M. McKisack, *The Fourteenth Century* (Oxford 1959). Emden 2:1346–47.

[V. MUDROCH]

ALEXANDER NEVSKI, Grand Duke of Vladimir and Kiev, 1252 to Nov. 19, 1263; b. May 30, 1220. The son of Grand Duke Yaroslav II, Alexander proved to be the most outstanding of the Russian princes at the beginning of the Mongol domination of Russia. His father made him Prince of Novgorod in 1228, and from there Alexander witnessed the conquest of Russia by the Mongol armies of Batu Khan (1237–42). The mongol invasion destroyed completely the southern part of Russia (Kiev and Chernigov) and a great part of east Russia (Riazan); but northern Russia, centered around Novgorod, was protected by swamps and woodland and fared better, becoming the pivot of consolidation for whatever survived the Mongol disaster. On the western borders of Novgorod Alexander was eminently successful in repulsing the attacks of Swedes, Lithuanians, and the Livonian Knights—it was his victory over the Swedes on the Neva River that gained him the surname Nevski (of the Neva). Recognizing, however, the hopelessness of any open resistance to the overwhelming power of the *Mongols, Alexander remained a loyal vassal of the Mongol Empire, and discouraged all insubordination and rebellion; he was thus able to reduce further Mongol ravages and to protect his people. He journeyed to the court of the Great Khan in Mongolia and to the Golden Horde, settling disputes and pleading the cause of his country. In 1252 the Great Khan appointed him Grand Duke of Vladimir and Kiev and thus the senior Russian Prince. He is venerated as a saint in the Russian Church (feasts, Nov. 23 and Aug. 30).

Bibliography: V. O. Klîuchevskiĭ, *A History of Russia,* tr. C. J. Hogarth, 5 v. (New York 1911–31) v.1. A. Palmieri, DHGE 2:261–262. N. de Baumgarten, "Généalogies des branches régnantes des Rurikides du XIIIe au XVIe siècle," *Orientalia Christiana* 35 (1934) 5–150.

[O. P. SHERBOWITZ-WETZOR]

ALEXANDER OF VILLA DEI, grammarian; b. Villedieu, Normandy, *c.* 1170; d. Avranches, *c.* 1250. He studied and later taught orthography and prosody at Paris. He was tutor for some time to the two nephews of the bishop of Dol in Brittany, and in order to engrave Latin grammar upon their memories, he composed the *Doctrinale puerorum,* or the *Grammatica versibus descripta.* The poem consists of 2,645 hexameter verses dealing with declension, gender of nouns, verbal forms, defective and anomalous verbs, government, syntax, quantity, accent, and figures of speech. It was based on ancient grammarians such as *Priscian and *Donatus, as well as on contemporaries such as *Peter Riga. More than 200 manuscripts and almost 300 early printed editions of the 15th and 16th centuries attest its popularity. It reigned supreme as a grammar for more than 3 centuries, until branded barbaric by the humanists. Alexander's career both as a student and as a teacher at Paris lay in the period when there was considerable rivalry between the University of *Paris, which was largely conservative, theological, and philosophical in attitude, and the schools of *Orléans with their humanistic and classical tendencies. The *Doctrinale* was intended to keep students from the harmful fables of such pagan poets as Maximianus, a poet of the 6th century, who might be read at Orléans. Another work of Alexander's, a sort of ecclesiastical calendar called the *Ecclesiale,* important for the history of liturgy had similar motivation. Alexander wrote it to counterattack the humanists of Orléans; just as Ovid had written the *Fasti* to commemorate the feasts of the pagan gods, he wrote the *Ecclesiale* to recognize Christian feasts: "Falsum de fastis fatuus legat; ecclesialis/Vera calendaris sit cura scientia nobis" (*Prol.*). Alexander had planned to write also a great encyclopedia, but there are only fragments of a metrical glossary to the *Alphabetum maius.* There exist copies of a *Computus* and the *Algorismus,* which have been ascribed to him.

Bibliography: *Das Doctrinale des Alexander de Villa-Dei,* ed. D. REICHLING (Berlin 1893). E. DUPONT, DHGE 2:278–279. HENRI D'ANDELI, *The Battle of the Seven Arts,* ed. and tr. L. J. PAETOW (Berkeley 1914). Manitius 3:756–761. R. R. BOLGAR, *The Classical Heritage and Its Beneficiaries* (Cambridge, Eng. 1954) 208–210. Raby SecLP 2:86–88. L. R. LIND, ed. and tr., *Ecclesiale* (Lawrence, Kans. 1958), with notes.

[R. T. MEYER]

ALEXANDER, ARCHIBALD, Presbyterian theologian; b. Lexington, Va., April 17, 1772; d. Princeton, N.J., Oct. 22, 1851. He was the son of William and Ann (Reid) Alexander. After studying at Liberty Hall College (later Washington College), Chestertown, Md., under Rev. William Graham, he was ordained in 1794. He served as president of Hampden-Sydney College, Virginia, from 1796 to 1807, when he accepted a call to Pine Street Presbyterian Church, Philadelphia, Pa. As moderator of the general assembly (1807), he advocated the establishment of Princeton Theological Seminary. Installed as its first professor in 1812, he taught didactic and polemic theology there until his death. With the works of Turretini and other Calvinist scholastics as the basis of his courses, Alexander was the chief theologian of the Old School party, opposing the New School in his *Thoughts on Religious Experience* (1841) and in the columns of the *Biblical Repertory,* which he founded in 1825. His *Brief Outline of the Evidences of the Christian Religion* (1825) was widely adopted as a college text. In *The Canon of the Old and New Testaments* (1826) he taught verbal inspiration and inerrancy. He was also influential in advocating foreign missions and in the American Colonization Society.

Archibald Alexander.

Bibliography: J. W. ALEXANDER, *The Life of Archibald Alexander* (New York 1854). H. T. KERR, ed., *Sons of the Prophets* (Princeton 1963).

[R. K. MAC MASTER]

ALEXANDER, SAMUEL

English educator and neorealist philosopher; b. Sydney, Australia, Jan. 6, 1859; d. Manchester, England, Sept. 11, 1938. Alexander was educated at the University of Melbourne and at Balliol College, Oxford, and served as a teaching fellow of Lincoln College from 1882 to 1893. He was then professor of philosophy at Victoria University of Manchester until 1924, during which time he was president of the Aristotelian Society (1908–11), fellow of the British Academy (1913), and Gifford lecturer at the University of Glasgow (1916–18). In 1927, he was appointed the Herbert Spencer lecturer at Oxford. He published many philosophical and literary works, among which *Space, Time, and Deity* (2 v., London 1920) is the most important.

In revolt against traditional materialism, Alexander formulated his epistemology and metaphysics in the context of naturalism and realism. His principal synthesis may be summarized as follows: (1) space and time are infinite, continuous, and inseparable—the universal matrix of all reality; (2) all being originates by "emergent evolution," an intrinsic urge (*nisus*) to develop into a more complex form of reality; (3) reality is creative; each emergent level is known by the "perspective" enjoyed by the mind; (4) just as mind emerges from life, and life from a lower physicochemical level of existence, so the values of truth, beauty, freedom, and goodness emerge from mind; (5) deity is not a transcendent Creator, but the last emergent quality of mind.

While Alexander's pantheistic evolutionism directly opposed the materialistic, agnostic evolutionism of Spencer and T. H. Huxley, it can be identified with other currents of contemporary thought. Alexander associated his space-time matrix with the four-dimensional continuum arrived at mathematically by Einstein. He allied his "emergent evolution," a concept used independently by the British zoologist, C. Lloyd Morgan, with H. Bergson's "creative evolution." His empirical "perspectivism" was closely akin to the direct realism of G. E. *Moore, B. *Russell, and the pragmatists, while leaving place for the a priori and nonempirical as found in Plato and Kant. His concept of value, human freedom, and deity has much in common with the pantheistic naturalism of B. *Spinoza, the French philosophy of the spirit, and the absolute idealism of F. H. *Bradley and B. Bosanquet. Again, his psychic evolutionism is not unlike that proposed by A. N. *Whitehead.

The defects of Alexander's evolutionism were two: his system remained basically eclectic and he never unified in principle, logically or ontologically, the world of spirit and of matter. In spite of his instinct against materialism and agnosticism, his thought never truly attained to spiritual substance and the transcendence of God.

See also EVOLUTIONISM; PANTHEISM.

Bibliography: Works. *Moral Order and Progress* (3d ed. London 1899); *Locke* (London 1908); *The Basis of Realism* (London 1914); *Space, Time, and Deity,* 2 v. (London 1920); *Artistic Creation and Cosmic Creation* (London 1928); *Spinoza and Time* (London 1921); *Spinoza* (Manchester 1933); *Philosophical and Literary Pieces,* ed. J. LAIRD (London 1939), bibliog. Literature. P. DEVAUX, *Le Système d'Alexander* (Paris 1929). M. R. KONVITZ, *On the Nature of Value: The Philosophy of Samuel Alexander* (New York 1946). A. F. LIDDELL, *Alexander's Space, Time, and Deity* (Chapel Hill, N.C. 1925). J. W. MCCARTHY, *The Naturalism of Samuel Alexander* (New York 1948), bibliog.

[R. J. NOGAR]

ALEXANDRIA

Greek, Ἀλεξάνδρεια; Latin, Alexandria. "The Paris of the ancient Mediterranean world," it was founded by Alexander the Great in 331 B.C. and became an important commercial, industrial, and cultural center and the chief city of Egypt.

Greek Learning. The museum and library founded by Ptolemy I *c.* 280 B.C., providing for 100 research scholars in the humanities and sciences, made the city one of the most influential centers of Greek learning. A flourishing Jewish colony produced the important scholar *Philo Judaeus and made Jewish doctrine available to Gentiles and to Jews ignorant of Hebrew through the translation of the Old Testament into Greek, known as the Septuagint, which was completed in the 2d century B.C. Thus Alexandria was to some extent prepared for the arrival of Christian teaching, which, according to tradition, was brought there by St. Mark,

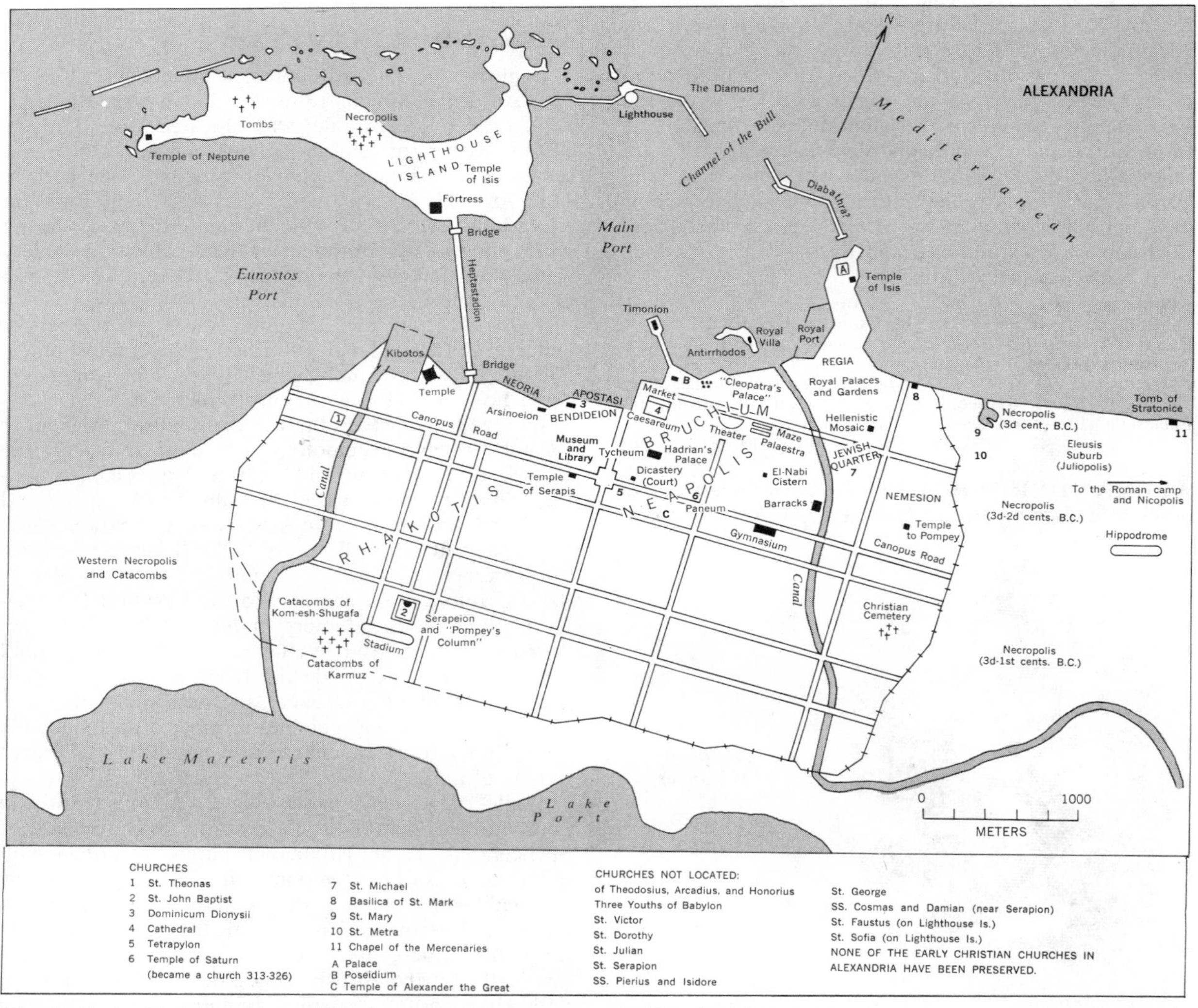

Fig. 1. Early Christian Alexandria. A cosmopolitan commercial center since its foundation, the city was taken by Caesar (48 B.C.), by the Arabs (A.D. 640), by the Turks (1517). Lighthouse Island is now connected to the city by an isthmus. The map is based upon structural remains above ground and archeological excavations.

who was buried in the city. Apollos, one of St. Paul's collaborators, was a Jew of Alexandria (Acts 18.24), and Paul on the voyage to Rome could talk with the sailors on two Alexandrian ships (Acts 27.6; 28.11). The Gnostic teachers *Basilides, Isidorus, and *Carpocrates found followers at Alexandria.

A landmark in the local Christian history was the founding of a Christian school of philosophy by *Pantaenus (late 2d century). Under its famous directors *Clement of Alexandria (d. *c.* 215) and *Origen (185–254), the school became an influential center of Christian scholarship. Alexandria was still a center of Greek learning, and Ammonius Saccas (*c.* 175–242), the founder of Neoplatonism, lectured there. In this setting one of Clement's important achievements was to show that Greek learning could be put to the service of Christianity. Origen after a distinguished career was obliged to leave for Palestine over the question of his qualifications to be a teacher and a priest, and an Alexandrian council of 231 supported his bishop's disapproval of his activities.

Alexandrian Christians suffered persecution under Septimius Severus (202 and after), attacks from the pagans of the city under Philip (249), and persecution again under Decius (250), Valerian (257–262), Diocletian (304–305), and Maximinus Daia (310–312). The *Meletian schism arose when Meletius, Bishop of Lycopolis, performed ordinations in Alexandria although it was not his diocese. He was condemned at a council at Alexandria in 306.

Heresies. Much of the ecclesiastical history of Alexandria was concerned with the conflicts caused by the heresies of *Arianism, *Nestorianism, *Eutychianism, and *Monophysitism. Arius, a parish priest of the city, began his heretical teaching about 319, and after disputes with *Alexander, Patriarch of Alexandria, he was excommunicated by a local synod (321) and left the city. The opposition to Arianism was vigorously led by (St.) *Athanasius of Alexandria, who, succeeding Alexander, served as bishop from 328 to 373, with several intervals when he was driven into exile or had to flee for safety. A council was called in 362 to deliberate on the divinity of the Holy Spirit, and two councils in 363 and 364 formulated definitions of the faith addressed to the Emperor Jovian. An anti-Arian council met in 370. Bishop *Theophilus of Alexandria (385–412) led a campaign against paganism that included the destruction (389) of the temple of Serapis, one of the most venerated pagan shrines. In 415 Hypatia, a noted pagan teacher of classical philosophy, was killed by a Christian mob. *Synesius of Cyrene, later bishop of Ptolemais (*c.* 410–*c.* 414), was one of her pupils before his conversion to Christianity.

The next important chapter in Alexandrian Church history was the patriarchate of St. Cyril (412–444), who led the fight against Nestorianism. Nestorius's teaching was rejected by a council at Alexandria in 430, and Cyril presided at the Council of Ephesus (431), where Nestorianism was condemned. This condemnation caused a breach between Antioch and Alexandria, which was healed on the basis of a council at Antioch (432).

Out of the controversy over Nestorianism grew the heretical doctrine of Eutyches concerning the nature of Christ (448), which was the real beginning of the Monophysite heresy. At the Council of Chalcedon

Fig. 2. The mummy of Archbishop Timothy of Alexandria (d. 385) and his successor Theophilus (385–412), drawings on a papyrus fragment of the so-called "Alexandrian World Chronicle," a 5th-century manuscript now in the Pushkin State Museum for Pictorial Art, Moscow.

(451) *Dioscorus, Patriarch of Alexandria, was deposed for his support of Eutyches, and his condemnation was followed by rioting and bloodshed in Alexandria. The Monophysite teaching found strong support in Alexandria and the rest of Egypt, as it did in Syria. To the ancient ecclesiastical rivalry between the sees of Alexandria and Constantinople was added the theological antagonism of the Egyptians to the orthodox leaders who represented the imperial government and were dispatched from Constantinople to impose official orthodoxy on the Alexandrian Church. Further friction arose out of the racial aversion of Upper Egypt to the Greek culture of Alexandria and out of the ancient nationalistic sentiment of the Egyptian people, who had long been subjected to foreign domination. There were protracted disorders in Alexandria, and the Monophysites kept control of the local Church by violent means, especially under the Monophysite patriarchs Timothy "the Cat" (457–477) (*see* TIMOTHY AELURUS, MONOPHYSITE PATRIARCH) and Peter "the Stammerer" (477–490). The orthodox Emperor Justinian (527–565), intent on restoring peace in the empire, supported the orthodox regime in Alexandria by force, and the orthodox patriarchs were protected by troops. The result of this prolonged experience was that Egypt, like Monophysite Syria, developed well-recognized separatist tendencies; and when the Arabs invaded Egypt (648),

Fig. 3. Fragment of an ivory carving found at Alexandria showing a carpenter at work, 3⅝ by 3⅛ inches, 3d or 4th century A.D.

they were welcomed as prospectively less oppressive than the hated Byzantine government.

A celebrated figure in the Church at Alexandria at this time was the Patriarch (St.) *John the Almsgiver, noted for the simplicity of his personal life and for his extensive charities, which he supported from the profits of the patriarchate's properties and commercial activities, notably, the cargo fleet owned by the Church.

The final years of the local Church before the Arab conquest were troubled by an outgrowth of Monophysitism, the heresy of *Monothelitism, which recognized the existence of only one will in Christ. A Monothelite council was held in the city in 633. In 828 some Venetian merchants, visiting Alexandria, secretly carried off the body of St. Mark to Venice.

Liturgy. The Liturgy of St. Mark, which seems to be not older than the 5th century, represents the usage of the orthodox Church at Alexandria, with additions from other sources. There are three Coptic liturgies (in the native Egyptian tongue, called Coptic during the Christian period) that preserve the Monophysite usage of Alexandria. These are called respectively the Liturgies of St. Cyril of Alexandria, of St. Gregory of Nazianzus, and of St. Basil, though they have no real connection with the personages named. (*See* COPTIC RITE, LITURGY OF; COPTIC RITE.)

Theological School. The museum and library had attracted leading classical scholars, and the Christian theologians of Alexandria were naturally influenced by the local pagan scholarly tradition. Philo Judaeus (d. *c.* A.D. 50) conceived an effort to harmonize Greek philosophy and the Old Testament with a philosophical mysticism that strongly influenced Alexandrian theology. His method of allegorical exegesis of the Bible spread to Christian theological schools elsewhere. Christian thought in Alexandria was strongly influenced also by the Platonic tradition. Clement, Origen, and their colleagues adapted the Platonic tradition and the allegorical method to Christian thought. The contribution of Alexandria to the development of systematic theology was also important; Origen's *De principiis* was the first systematic exposition of Christian doctrine. Alexandrian thought differed from Antiochene theology, which was Aristotelian, pragmatic, and critical. Similarly, Biblical exegesis at Alexandria was allegorical and mystical, while that at Antioch was historical and literal. Platonic dualism was reflected in the emphasis upon the transcendence of God and the divinity of Christ in Alexandrian teaching. This was the basis of Alexandrian controversies with *Antioch, where the humanity of Christ was stressed. Thus Athanasius was the Alexandrian champion of orthodoxy against the Arian teaching, favored at Antioch, that the Son of God was a creature. The same perspective was the basis of the opposition of Cyril to the doctrine of Nestorius of Antioch that there were separate divine and human persons in Christ. The extreme form of the Alexandrian tendency resulted in Monophysitism, which maintained that there was only one, divine, nature in Christ. One of the distinguished Alexandrian scholars of the early 5th century was *John Philoponus, typical of his time in working simultaneously as theologian, commentator on Aristotle, and grammarian.

Art and Archeology. Hellenistic Alexandria, with its wealthy and cultivated atmosphere, developed a distinctive artistic style of its own that reflected the sophisticated and cosmopolitan character of the city. The artistic tradition of classical Greece served as the basis for the new Alexandrian manner, but the Alexandrian artists, with a realism unknown in classical Greece, sought to emphasize the individuality of their subjects.

When Christian art appeared in Alexandria, the Christian artists naturally worked in the local style. The earliest preserved Christian monuments in the city are the frescoes in the catacomb of Karmuz, painted in a characteristic style that was carried to Rome and used in the catacombs there. In Egypt and Italy in the early centuries Christ was portrayed as a youthful Hermes, with short curly hair; the bearded oriental type emerged later in Syria and Palestine. The illustrated *Christian Topography* of *Cosmas Indicopleustes is a typical example of Alexandrian theology and art of the 6th century. The Christian artists of Alexandria, like their pagan predecessors, produced elegant textiles, glass, gold and silver work, and ivory carving, which they exported throughout the ancient world. There was always opposition between the Hellenic artistic tradition of Alexandria itself and the indigenous *Coptic art of the rest of Egypt, which represented a totally different artistic tradition.

Bibliography: J. FAIVRE, DHGE 2:289–369. J. PARGOIRE et al., DTC 1:786–824. H. LECLERCQ and F. CABROL, DACL 1:1098–1210. W. SCHUBART, ReallexAntChr 1:271–283. H. A. MUSURILLO, ed., *The Acts of the Pagan Martyrs: Acta Alexandrinorum* (London 1954). C. BIGG, *The Christian Platonists of Alexandria* (2d ed. London 1913). R. B. TOLLINTON, *Alexandrine Teaching on the Universe* (New York 1932). E. MOLLAND, *The Conception of the Gospel in the Alexandrian Theology* (Oslo 1938). R. V. SELLERS, *Two Ancient Christologies* (London 1940). E. R. HARDY, *Christian Egypt: Church and People* (London 1952). J. MASPERO, *Histoire des patriarches d'Alexandrie* (Paris 1923). C. R. MOREY, *Early Christian Art* (2d ed. Princeton 1953). E. A. PARSONS, *The Alexandrian Library* (New York 1952). G. DOWNEY, "Coptic Culture in the Byzantine World," *Greek and Byzantine Studies* 1.2 (1958) 119–135. H. I. BELL, *Cults and Creeds in Graeco-Roman Egypt* (Liverpool 1953). **Illustration credits:** Fig. 2, Gertrud Pappert, courtesy of Villa Hügel, Essen, Germany. Fig. 3, The Art Museum, Princeton University.

[G. DOWNEY]

ALEXANDRIA, DIOCESE OF (ALEXANDRINENSIS), suffragan of the metropolitan See of New Orleans, comprising the northern part of Louisiana, an area of 22,212 square miles. It was originally established as the Diocese of Natchitoches by Pius IX on July 29, 1853, but was changed to Alexandria, Aug. 6, 1910. In 1963 Catholics numbered more than 87,000 in a total population of about 1,005,000. Catholic missionary work in the territory dates from 1682, when the Franciscan Zenobius Membre, chaplain to R. *La Salle's expedition down the Mississippi River, stopped at the village of the Tensas Indians, near present-day Newellton, La. The next missionaries in Northern Louisiana were priests from the Seminary of Quebec, Canada, who arrived in the Lower Mississippi Valley in 1699. Francis de Montigny, their superior, took up residence among the Tensas Indians, and in the vicinity of Newellton built what was probably the first chapel within the future Diocese of Alexandria. The oldest town in the diocese and in the entire state originated in 1716 when J. B. le Moyne de *Bienville sent a military force to establish Fort St. John the Baptist on an island in the Red River. The settlement became known as "Le Poste de Natchitoches."

In 1853 when Louisiana's second diocese was created from the Archdiocese of *New Orleans with Natchitoches as its see city, Auguste Marie Martin was named first bishop. At that time the diocese, covering three-fifths of the state, had 5 priests, 6 parish churches, about 3 mission chapels, 1 school, and 22,000 Catholics. Martin died Sept. 29, 1875, and was succeded by Francis Xavier Leray, who was consecrated April 22, 1877. Two years later he was named coadjutor of New Orleans, but he remained administrator of Natchitoches until 1883 when he became ordinary of New Orleans. Successive ordinaries included Antoine Durier (1885–1904), Cornelius Van de Ven (1904–32), Daniel F. Desmond (1933–45), and Charles P. Greco, who was appointed Jan. 15, 1946, and consecrated February 25. In the spring of 1910, Bishop Van de Ven petitioned

Auguste Marie Martin.

the Holy See to transfer the see city of the diocese to Alexandria, citing the latter's advantages of better road and railroad communications to all parts of Northern Louisiana, and its closer proximity to the large percent-

St. Joseph's Seminary, Natchitoches. Bought in 1837 for a rectory, used as diocesan seminary from 1854 to 1878, still in use in the 1960s by priests of nearby Immaculate Conception Church.

age of French Catholics living in the southern part of the diocese.

Under Greco the diocese entered a period of significant growth and development. Between 1946 and 1963 the Catholic population increased about 80 per cent, as compared with a 13 per cent increase in the total population. The number of parishes totaled 84 and missions 63, served by 180 priests, including 53 religious (Franciscans, Dominicans, Benedictines, Jesuits, Holy Ghost fathers, and Immaculate Heart of Mary Missioners). Also serving the diocese were 21 brothers (Sacred Heart and Holy Eucharist) and 348 sisters representing 17 communities. There were 11 high and 42 elementary schools, 6 general hospitals, 3 orphanages, and a home for the aged.

Bibliography: R. BAUDIER, *The Catholic Church in Louisiana* (New Orleans 1939).

[C. M. CLAYTON]

ALEXANDRIA, PATRIARCHATE OF

First patriarchate to be formed in the early Church. In the Council of *Constantinople I (381) the patriarch of Alexandria was granted second place of honor after the pope of Rome, and his jurisdiction spread over Egypt, Libya, and Pentapolis, which at that time possessed more than 100 bishoprics. *Alexandria was a city of capital importance as a civil center and for its rich libraries and renowned schools of philosophy and theology. It possessed a tightly organized hierarchy that radiated its jurisdiction over thousands of monks in the Egyptian desert who were renowned all over the then Christian world.

From the Council of Chalcedon to the Eastern Schism. Its unity split asunder after the Council of Chalcedon (451) condemned *Monophysitism as a heresy. The majority of the Christians living in Alexandria followed their patriarch, Dioscorus, thus forming what today is called the indigenous Coptic Dissident Church (*see* COPTIC RITE). Those in the minority who remained faithful to the teachings of Chalcedon formed the Melchite Church (*see* MELCHITE RITE). From 457 there existed two parallel hierarchies: the Hellenic element, faithful to Orthodoxy and Constantinople, and the Egyptian element, which gradually became a nationalism and expressed itself in the heterodox teaching of Monophysitism. The Melchites who remained faithful, both politically and theologically, to the Byzantine emperors were settled in the large cities and were always a minority.

The patriarchal see was disputed between the Melchites and the Coptic Monophysites, and from 482 to 538 the latter prevailed. After 538 there was a double patriarchal hierarchy, Melchite Catholic and Coptic Monophysite. The Coptic patriarchs were frequently forced into exile under *Justinian I (527–565), who supported the Melchites. *Heraclius (610–641) strove to establish *Monothelitism as a compromise between Monophysitism and Catholicism to create at least the outer appearance of religious unity.

During the Arab conquest of Egypt the Coptic patriarch was allowed to exercise his jurisdiction, and through financial and social pressure the number of Melchites was greatly reduced, principally because the Arabs distrusted Melchite loyalty to the Byzantine rulers. The Melchite patriarchal see, still Monothelite in sentiment, remained vacant from 652 to 737; and candidates for the episcopacy had to be sent to Tyre for consecration.

The two churches preserved the same liturgical rite, that of the primitive liturgy of Alexandria (*see* ALEXANDRIAN RITE, LITURGY OF), but gradually the rite of the Byzantine emperor was accepted by the Melchites. From 639 to 1811 the Copts were oppressed as much as the Melchites under the domination of the Mussulman caliphs. The year 1811 marks the beginning of contemporary history of Egypt under the Sultan Mohammed Ali and his successors, who granted religious liberty to all Christians.

From the Eastern Schism to 1964. The close relationship between the Melchite Patriarchate of Alexandria and the Patriarchate of Constantinople, which still existed at the time of Michael Cerularius (1054), caused the Melchites to go into schism, though the exact time of the break with Rome cannot be determined. In 1219 the Latin Crusaders established a Latin patriarch for Alexandria in expectation of their capturing the city, but he was never able to reside there. During the Latin occupation the Melchite patriarch took up residence in Constantinople, thus increasing his dependence on the Byzantine Church. The Alexandrian patriarch, together with those of Antioch and Jerusalem, sent a representative to the Council of *Florence (1439) and through him accepted union with Rome. It is difficult to know whether the Melchite patriarch of Alexandria repudiated this union with Rome along with the Antiochene patriarch in the Synod of Constantinople in 1484. But the Alexandrian Melchites finally severed relations with Rome after the Turkish conquest of Alexandria in 1517. It is probable that a faction favoring union with Rome always existed and that from time to time one of them held the patriarchal see. But by decision of the Turkish caliph, the patriarch of Constantinople became head of all Orthodox subjects in the Ottoman Empire. From this point, the Alexandrian Orthodox patriarchate was completely Hellenic.

With the reunion of 1724 (*see* ANTIOCH, PATRIARCHATE OF; MELCHITE RITE) a Catholic Melchite patriarchate was established in Antioch. In 1833 Patriarch *Maximos III Mazlūm obtained from Gregory XVI the personal privilege (which has been handed down uninterruptedly) of adding the title of patriarch of Alexandria and Jerusalem along with jurisdiction over the Melchite Catholics in these areas. From 1895, when a Coptic Catholic patriarchate was established for the Alexandrian patriarchate, until the present there have been four separate patriarchal sees of Alexandria: the Monophysite Coptic, the Catholic Coptic, the Orthodox, and the Melchite Catholic. The Dissident Copts representing the indigenous Christian group of Egyptians number 2,500,000 faithful, and the Catholic Copts are a minority of 82,894. The Orthodox Hellenes, supported mainly by Greek immigration, have been greatly reduced in number since the rise of Gamal Abdel Nasser. They number only 35,000. The Melchite Catholics, mostly emigrants from Lebanon and Syria, number 26,000. Since the Melchite Catholic patriarch is the same for all three Melchite patriarchates of Antioch, Alexandria, and Jerusalem, the Melchite patriarchate of Alexandria is governed by a vicar patriarch, who resides in Cairo; the patriarch resides in Damascus, Syria.

Bibliography: D. ATTWATER, *The Christian Churches of the East,* 2 v. (rev. ed. Milwaukee 1961–62). C. DE CLERCQ, *Les Églises unies d'Orient* (Paris 1934). J. FAIVRE, DHGE 2:289–369. R. JANIN, *Les Églises Orientales et les Rites Orientaux* (Paris 1955). C. KARALEVSKIJ, *Histoire des Patriarcats Melkites,* 3 v. in 2 (Rome 1909–10). A. A. KING, *The Rites of Eastern Christendom,* 2 v. (London 1950). J. PARGOIRE, DTC 1.1:786–801. E. R. HARDY, *Christian Egypt* (New York 1952). W. DE VRIES et al., eds., *Rom und die Patriarchate des Ostens* (Freiburg 1963).

[G. A. MALONEY]

ALEXANDRIA, SCHOOL OF

The name for both the catechetical institution and the theological tradition characteristic of Alexandria during the patristic age. Alexandria was one of the most important cultural centers of the ancient world and the focal point for the mutual influence exercised in the conjunction of *Christianity and Hellenism. Before the introduction of Christianity, Alexandria possessed great libraries in its museum, the Serapeum, and the Sebasteon. It was likewise the center of Hellenistic Judaism. The Books of Ecclesiasticus and Wisdom were probably produced there before the Christian Era. *Philo Judaeus, the great doctor of Hellenistic Judaism, worked there. Hence it is not astonishing that Alexandria early became a Christian intellectual center.

Catechetical School. The origin of the Christian School of Alexandria is obscure. It is obvious that, from the start, the bishops of Alexandria used collaborators in preparing the catechumens for Baptism, although none of these is known. In the late 2d century *Pantaenus, a convert philosopher, is cited as the head of a Christian school in Alexandria (*c.* 150); and *Clement of Alexandria has been considered his successor. These scholars conducted philosophical schools in which they taught the Christian faith as a philosophy (*gnosis*) or way of life. They do not appear to have had anything to do with the catechetical school as such. This was conducted by the bishop; and the first certain information is supplied in relation to *Origen, whom Bishop Demetrius charged with the instruction of catechumens (*c.* 203). Origen enlisted the aid of Heraclas, who evidently gave the basic instruction in the *Christian way of life while his master concentrated his attention on the formation of a superior school of sacred science (*didascaleion*) that is generally designated as the School of Alexandria. *Gregory Thaumaturgus, Origen's student in Caesarea, described the courses taught in the *didascaleion,*—logic, dialectic, and physics (including mathematics and astronomy)—as a propaedeutic to Christian theology. This included the analysis of current philosophies but principally the exegesis of the Scriptures.

*Philip Sidetes, a 5th-century historian, records the names of the so-called heads of the school. He does not mention Pantaenus or Clement, but cites Athenagoras; Origen; Heraclas, who was bishop of Alexandria in 232; Dionysius, bishop in 248; Theognostus (247–282); Pierius; and Peter, bishop from 300. Although it is known that many 4th-century Fathers of the Church, such as *Jerome, *Gregory of Nazianzus, and *Basil of Caesarea, studied for a time at Alexandria, the only 4th-century teacher of whom there is positive knowledge is *Didymus the Blind.

Theological School. The current of Christian thought represented by a group of scholars and propagandists with similar intellectual interests, and a more or less uniform procedure in exegesis of the Scriptures, formed what is generally referred to as the theological School of Alexandria. Its members did not necessarily belong to the catechetical school. The relationship between Athanasius and Cyril of Alexandria and this school, for example, is not known; both Apollinaris and Eutyches represent Alexandrian Christological thought, though Apollinaris originated in Laodicea, near Antioch, and Eutyches was from Constantinople. The School of Alexandria is represented by two distinct phases: Clement and Origen were intent on presenting the Christian religion to the cultivated people of their epoch, Christians and non-Christians alike, and wanted to show them that Christ was the summit of all human knowledge; the authors of the 4th and 5th centuries, such as Athanasius and Cyril, on the other hand, had to defend the Christian truths concerning the Trinity and the divinity of Christ against heretical Christian theologians.

From the start, Alexandrian exegesis distinguished itself from that of Antioch. The latter was in general attached to the literal sense of the Bible. The Alexandrians recognized this sense, but their primary interest was concentrated on the mystery of divine revelation revealed in the historical and literary details of the Old Testament. It was therefore a question of discovering Christ in the older revelation. With joyful sagacity, the Alexandrian authors sought out in the Old Testament *symbols of the New. Their preference lay in the more profound, mystical, spiritual sense that is still termed typological or allegorical. Philo placed them on the path of this exegesis, which was, however, immediately inspired by a distinctly Christian principle, that of the unity of the two Testaments, such as Christ Himself had expressed it when He said that it was of Him that Moses and the Prophets had spoken.

In their Trinitarian doctrine, Clement and Origen were influenced by the Platonism of their epoch. They insisted on the divine transcendence. This at times forced them into expressing themselves as if the Son and the Holy Spirit were inferior to the Father. Origen emphasized the distinction of the divine Persons and spoke of three *hypostases.* Denis the Great did the same, and in so doing was accused of destroying the unity of the divine nature. But the Alexandrian tradition as presented by Athanasius went directly the other way: against Arius, who likewise lived in the Egyptian capital, Athanasius defended the consubstantiality of the Father and the Son; and although he recognized the possible orthodoxy of the formula of the three hypostases, he personally held to the Nicene terminology of the single *ousia,* or substance, and of the single hypostasis.

In Christology the Alexandrians were guided by the Fourth Gospel. For them, as for St. John, Christ was above all the Word. Their soteriology controlled this conception. For them, Redemption consists essentially in the divinization that Christians are to obtain in Christ. This insistence on the divinity of Christ left the aspect of His humanity somewhat obscure. The Alexandrians generally did not see, for example, the importance of attributing a human soul to Christ. However, this aspect was appreciated by *Didymus the Blind, who stressed the perfect human consubstantiality of Christ. Cyril defined Christ as one nature of the Word Incarnate. This formula was repeated literally by Eutyches and the *Monophysites, and tended to be interpreted by their adversaries as the negation of the human nature in Christ.

Bibliography: R. Nelz, *Die theologischen Schulen der morgenländischen Kirchen* (Bonn 1916). G. Bardy, RechScRel 27 (1937) 65–90; *Catholicisme* 1:310–314; *Vivre et penser* 2 (1942) 80–109. A. Knauber, TrierThZ 60 (1951) 243–266. F. Pericoli Ridolfini, *Revista degli studi orientali* 37 (1962) 211–230. Bardenhewer 2:5–10. Quasten Patr 2:2–4. H. Rahner, LexThK² 1:323–325. Cross ODCC 35. J. Daniélou, *Origène* (Paris 1948). H. de Lubac, *Origène: Homélies sur l'Exode* (SourcesChr 16; 1947); "'Typologie' et 'allégorisme,'" RechScRel 34 (1947) 180–226; 47 (1959) 5–43. J. Guillet, *ibid.* 34 (1947) 257–302. W. J. Burghardt, ThSt 11 (1950) 78–116. W. Gruber, *Die pneumatische Exegese bei den Alexandrinern* (Graz 1957). E. Molland, *The Conception of the Gospel in the Alexandrian Theology* (Oslo 1938). R. V. Sellers, *Two Ancient Christologies* (London 1940).

[A. VAN ROEY]

ALEXANDRIAN RITE, LITURGY OF. This rite, parent of all other Egyptian liturgies, is said to have come from St. Mark the Evangelist (d. 74?), who probably brought the Antiochene rite into Egypt. Before the Council of Chalcedon (541) the rite of Alexandria, Greek-speaking capital of the Diocese of Egypt and cultural center of the Eastern Roman Empire, was the liturgy of St. Mark in Greek. After Chalcedon and the rapid spread of the Monophysite heresy throughout the Patriarchate of Alexandria, the Greek liturgy of St. Mark was used only by the Melchites, while the Copts and the Ethiopians set up modified forms of the Alexandrian rite in their own languages, Coptic and Ge'ez. Constantinople's subsequent importance among the

Orthodox Christians of the East caused the Byzantine liturgy to intrude upon and finally displace the Alexandrian liturgy among the Melchites. Since the 12th century, the liturgy of St. Mark in Greek, commonly identified with the original Alexandrian rite, has been used by no one. By distilling from the present Coptic rite additions coming from Monophysitism, as well as the Byzantine additions that followed upon the Arab conquest, one can reconstruct an approximation of the original Alexandrian rite. Earliest known documents containing the original rite are a papyrus, *Fragment of the Anaphora of St. Mark* (4th century), the *Dêr-Balyzeh Papyrus* (6th–7th century), and an 11th-century manuscript of the *Euchologion* of Serapion of Thmuis (d. 362).

Bibliography: D. ATTWATER, *The Christian Churches of the East,* 2 v. (Milwaukee 1961). Miller FundLit 50. I. H. DALMAIS, *Eastern Liturgies* (New York 1960). Quasten MonE 37–67.

[E. E. FINN]

ALEXANDRINE BULLS, name usually given to two bulls of Alexander VI (1492–1503), both called *Inter caetera* and dated respectively May 3 and 4, 1493. They were addressed to the Catholic Kings in order to establish the legal basis for the Spanish dominion over the islands found on Columbus's first voyage. In the second bull, the Alexandrine Line was set at 100 maritime leagues "west and south" of the Azores and Cape Verde Islands, in order to separate the new jurisdictional area from that created in papal bulls dating from 1454 to 1481 in favor of Portugal, whose sailors had already begun the search for a direct route to the Indies. The line was moved 370 leagues to the west of the Azores in the Treaty of Tordesillas between Spain and Portugal (1494), on which basis the Portuguese crown later claimed possession of eastern Brazil. The papal concessions were made on condition that the Iberian rulers assume the obligation of converting to Christianity the natives of areas discovered. The *Dudum siquidem* bull (October 1493) of Alexander VI reaffirmed and broadened the concessions made to the Spanish crown. At the time the Alexandrine Bulls were issued, it was thought that the islands discovered by Columbus were located along the eastern coast of Asia. Therefore, those documents must be regarded as "pseudo-Asiatic," more than American, and could not really have provided any basis for an exclusive right of sovereignty over the Western Hemisphere on the part of Spain and Portugal. The remote antecedent of the bulls is found in the *Donation of Constantine, a famous 8th-century forgery, in which that Roman Emperor is said to have given the popes, among other privileges, dominion over "the various islands." On this basis, the papal chancery elaborated what is now called by medievalists an "omni-insular doctrine," applied for the first time in 1091 when Urban II gave the Archipelago of Lipari to a local abbot and the island of Corsica to the bishop of Pisa. Afterward, Adrian IV and other popes granted dominion over various islands in European seas to several princes, demanding in exchange the payment of feudal tribute. In some of the final stages of its evolution during the Middle Ages, the collection of Peter's pence was linked to papal sovereignty over islands. Among the areas feudatory to the Holy See were England, Sicily, Sardinia, Cyprus, Castelrosso, the archipelagos of the Tyrrhenian and North African seas, Scandinavia (considered an island by the imperfect geography of the time), and finally, in the 14th century, the Canary Islands. The "omni-insular doctrine" was still a part of the public law of Europe when America was discovered. (For illustration, see following page.)

See also PAPAL LINE OF DEMARCATION.

Bibliography: L. WECKMANN, *Las bulas alejandrinas de 1493 y la teoría política del Papado medieval* (Mexico City 1949).
Illustration credit: Library of Congress.

[L. WECKMANN]

ALEXIAN BROTHERS

The Congregation of Cellites, or Alexian Brothers (CFA), evolved from the needs of the victims of the Black Death of 14th-century Europe. The work of caring for the sick and burying the dead fell to the lot of men and women whose heroic charity overcame the natural fear of infection and death. One such group, founded in Brabant, Belgium, became known as the Poor Brothers, Bread Brothers, or Cellite Brothers. Those living in St. Alexius House at Aix-la-Chapelle (Aachen, Germany) bound themselves by the vows of religion, according to the Rule of St. Augustine. In 1469 the Holy See raised the society to a religious order. They chose St. Alexius, who worked among the poor, as their chief patron and have since been known as the Alexian Brothers. There are no priest members.

Despite European wars and political upheavals, the congregation at its peak had several thousand brothers working in Germany, Holland, Belgium, Luxemburg, and northern France, in establishments that were closely affiliated but locally independent. At a low point, following the French Revolution, the Alexians were revitalized chiefly through the efforts of the superior of the Aachen house, Brother Dominic Brock, known as the "Pater." In 1854 he and four others renewed their vows, which had become almost meaningless because of government interference. Vocations increased and new institutions for the physically and mentally ill were established. In 1870 Clement Wallrath (Pater Dominic's successor) obtained full papal approval from Pius IX, becoming the first superior general responsible directly to the Holy See. Leo XIII urged the independent Alexian houses to unite under Pater Clement, but few actually did so.

Meanwhile, Brother Bonaventure Thelen, who in 1865 was sent to establish the congregation in the U.S., opened Alexian Brothers Hospital in Chicago, Ill., the following year. During the next few years, the brothers pioneered many medical advances and erected hospitals in St. Louis, Mo.; Oshkosh, Wis.; and Elizabeth, N.J. Under Brother Aloysius Schyns, they incorporated their school of nursing in Chicago in 1898, the only Catholic school of nursing for men students in the nation. In 1938 a home for retired men and women was opened in Signal Mountain, near Chattanooga, Tenn.; in 1955 the brothers took over the operation of the clinic for Father Edward *Flanagan's Boys Home at Boys Town, Nebr. In 1951 the novitiate for the American province was permanently established at Gresham, Wis., where a modern building was constructed in 1955. The same year a new school and residence for the school of nursing was completed in Chicago. Hospitals have been erected also in San Jose, Calif., and Cook County, Ill.

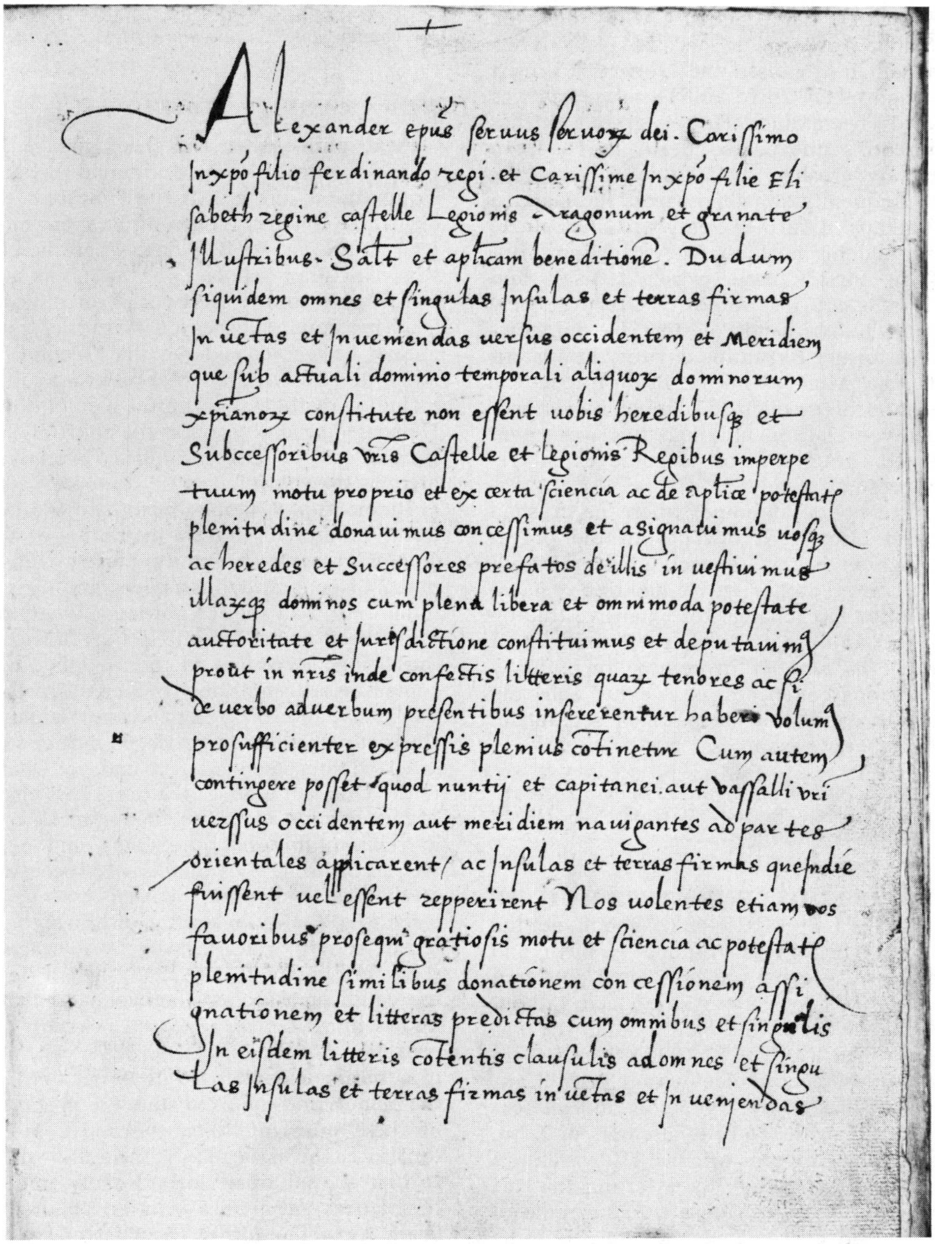
Alexander epus seruus seruorum dei. Carissimo
in xpo filio ferdinando regi et Carissime in xpo filie Eli
sabeth regine castelle Legionis Aragonum et granate
Illustribus. Salt et apticam benedictione. Dudum
siquidem omnes et singulas Insulas et terras firmas
Inuentas et inueniendas uersus occidentem et Meridiem
que sub actuali dominio temporali aliquorum dominorum
xpianorum constitute non essent uobis heredibusque et
Successoribus vris Castelle et legionis Regibus imperpe
tuum motu proprio et ex certa sciencia ac de aptice potestatis
plenitudine donauimus concessimus et asignauimus uosque
ac heredes et Successores prefatos de illis inuestiuimus
illarumque dominos cum plena libera et omnimoda potestate
auctoritate et iurisdictione constituimus et deputauimus
prout in nris inde confectis litteris quarum tenores ac si
de uerbo ad uerbum presentibus insererentur haberi volum
pro sufficienter expressis plenius cotinetur Cum autem
contingere posset quod nuntij et capitanei aut vassalli vri
uersus occidentem aut meridiem nauigantes ad partes
orientales applicarent/ ac insulas et terras firmas que inibi
fuissent uel essent repperirent Nos uolentes etiam uos
fauoribus prosequi gratiosis motu et sciencia ac potestatis
plenitudine similibus donationem concessionem assi
gnationem et litteras predictas cum omnibus et singulis
in eisdem litteris cotentis clausulis ad omnes et singu
las insulas et terras firmas inuentas et inueniendas

First page of the bull "Dudum siquidem" of Pope Alexander VI, in an early 16th-century manuscript. This manuscript, which contains transcriptions of 34 hereditary grants, charters, and privileges awarded to Columbus by Ferdinand and Isabella, and two papal bulls, is thought to be one of four copies made for Columbus before his fourth voyage to America in 1502. One copy is lost, the three others are in the Municipal Palace, Genoa; the Archives of Foreign Affairs, Paris; and the Library of Congress, Washington, D.C.

In Europe the brothers concern themselves chiefly with the care of the mentally ill and with home patients, while their work in the U.S. is primarily the operation of modern general hospitals. For this reason the brothers are educated in all phases of hospital work: nursing, administration, X-ray technology, laboratory technology, pharmacy, engineering, physical therapy, accounting, and dietary procedures.

Bibliography: Heimbucher, 1:591. G. Pou y Marti, EncCatt 5:1706.

[A. SANFORD]

ALEXIUS I COMNENUS, BYZANTINE EMPEROR, 1081 to 1118, theologian; b. 1048. The third son of John Comnenus, the brother of Isaac I Comnenus, Alexius belonged to a military family and fought with distinction against both Seljuk Turks and various Byzantine rebel uprisings. In April 1081 he proved himself victor in the struggle for the throne. He was supported by his mother, Anna Dalassena, by his elder brother Isaac, and by his wife, Irene, who came from the influential Ducas family. His diplomatic and military ability enabled him to avert the disasters facing the Empire. He made a treaty with Suleiman, ruler of the Seljuk Turks of Iconium (1081). Then with Venetian help he repulsed the Norman *Robert Guiscard, who had taken Corfu and Durazzo and was advancing toward Thessalonica. He was given a further respite by Guiscard's unexpected death in 1085. In 1091 he effectively crushed the Turkic nomads, the Patzinaks, who frequently swarmed across the Danube to ravage the Balkans. A further treaty with the Seljuks (1095) strengthened his position in Asia Minor. But the arrival of the First Crusade was a setback, and Alexius failed to assert his authority over the new Latin principalities in Syria and Palestine. He did, however, regain some former Byzantine territory in western and southeast Asia Minor, and in 1108 forced the Norman Bohemund of Antioch to admit his overlordship by the treaty of Devol, although this was never fully implemented. Thus Alexius to some extent restored imperial prestige.

Despite his firm policy at home, where he crushed all his rivals and also tried to root out the prevalent dualist *Bogomil heresy, he could not re-create a really effective central authority. He had to buy naval support from Venice in exchange for extensive trading privileges, and he appears to have used the system of making grants *in pronoia* in return for military service. Thus the apparent success of Alexius' able rule was only a façade concealing deep-seated separatism and inadequate imperial resources.

Bibliography: CMedH² v.4.1. Ostrogorsky 315–333. J. M. Hussey, *Church and Learning in the Byzantine Empire, 867–1185* (Oxford 1937). A. Comnena, *The Alexiad,* tr. G. A. S. Dawes (London 1928). Beck KTLBR 610–612.

[J. M. HUSSEY]

ALEXIUS THE STUDITE, PATRIARCH OF CONSTANTINOPLE (1025–43), abbot at the monastery Studion (hence "the Studite"); birth and death dates unknown. Alexius was appointed patriarch by Emperor Basil II on the latter's death bed without the sanction or knowledge of the metropolitan; he was immediately enthroned (Dec. 15, 1025). As his appointment was not in accordance with Canon Law, his entire reign was marred by arguments and altercations. In 1037 Alexius withstood the attempts of John, brother of the reigning Emperor Michael IV, to remove him from the patriarchal throne by asserting that his removal would automatically bring about the removal of the bishops he had consecrated and the priests he had ordained. When John, eager to secure the patriarchy for himself, persisted in efforts to unseat him, Alexius threatened to declare his coronation of Michael IV null and void, and thus he successfully maintained his throne.

The importance of his patriarchate lies in his administrative policies, which were marked in numerous edicts, synods, and disciplinary laws. He concerned himself extensively with the doctrines of the Monophysites and the Messalians and with Byzantine marriage laws; but he showed weakness by not opposing the second and third marriages of Empress Zoë, daughter of Constantine VIII; these marriages were against Canon Law and the tradition of his monastery. In 1034, Alexius founded a monastery patterned after those of the Studite Order and devoted to the Blessed Virgin; it was later named after him.

Bibliography: PG 119:744–748, 827–850. T. Balsamon, *ibid.* 137:1245. S. Pétridès, DHGE 2:398. K. Baus, LexThK² 1:328. É. Amann, Fliche-Martin 7:136–138. G. Ficker, *Erlasse des Patriarchen von Konstantinopel Alexios Studites* (Kiel 1911).

[G. LUZNYCKY]

ALFARABI (FĀRĀBĪ, AL-)

Arab philosopher and theologian, fuller name Abū Naṣr Muḥammad ibn Muḥmmad al-Fārābī; b. Wasig, Transoxania, in the district of Fārāb, *c.* 870; d. Damascus, 950. Of Turkish descent, he spent most of his life in Iraq and Syria. At Baghdad, where he came in contact with Christian scholars, he acquired a knowledge of Greek philosophy. His works on philosophy, particularly his commentaries on Aristotle, gained him wide notice; he was considered the "second Teacher" after Aristotle himself. He wrote on other subjects, however, including mathematics, music, medicine, and astronomy. He passed several years at the court of Saif ad-Dawlah, ruler of Aleppo, engaged mostly in study. Otherwise his life was uneventful.

Emanation. *Neoplatonism and the Islamic religious tradition offered Alfarabi the notion of a first being, the One, who is absolute unity, perfect transcendence, and pure existence, and thus a necessary being who is present to himself in an act of knowledge where intellect, object of intellect, and act of intellect are absolutely one. From this being, according to the Neoplatonic principle accepted by Alfarabi, only one creature could derive immediately, and this by a process of "emanation" (Faiḍ). Emanation, however, proceeds by degrees. Thus a first intellect, supremely perfect and yet essentially inferior to the One, is the first creature. He is also the first form of multiplicity, for his essence is necessary when viewed in relation to God (the One) and contingent when viewed in itself. This duality of aspect, distant ancestor of the real distinction between essence and existence, leads to a duality in the act of knowledge. The first intellect knows God and itself by two acts, which themselves are creative: the act by which he knows God is the cause of a second intellect, and that by which he knows himself gives rise to a heavenly sphere with its own soul and body. The process continues, according to common Neoplatonic doctrine, until the spheres of the planets and the fixed stars are produced. The lowest of these pure intellects, the active intellect, tenth in rank after the first cause, is the author of the matter and form in the sublunar world. Finally, under the influence of the heavenly bodies, common matter is prepared to bring forth the forms given it by the active intellect (*dator formarum*). A gradual growth in perfection takes place, culminating in the emergence of the human soul, the highest form associated with matter.

Man and Society. At this point, Alfarabi describes the growth of human consciousness. The activity of the senses furnishes the materials for universal ideas, and illumination by the active intellect puts the human intellect in act. Man's grasp of universals grows as he frees himself from matter and comes more under the influence of the active intellect. The final step in the process is reached when man has an "acquired intellect," which for Alfarabi is almost on a level with the active intellect.

In all this Alfarabi depends heavily on his Greek predecessors, above all on Alexander of Aphrodisias. But there is present in most of his writing a mystical element that reminds one of *Plotinus. The difference, of course, lies in the fact that Alfarabi considers union with the active intellect as the highest form of existence for man, and not union with the One, as Plotinus held. Alfarabi defines man's happiness as a permanent state of being wherein he is freed from matter and enjoys the society of pure spirits. He insists on the collaboration of intellect and will in the tendency toward this goal.

Moreover, for Alfarabi man is a social being who needs the society of other men to grow toward happiness. In his notion of society Alfarabi is greatly indebted to Plato, particularly to the *Republic.* The "virtuous state" he sees as analogous to the human body, with the ruler as the heart. The ideal ruler is both philosopher and prophet—philosopher to have attained the perfection of the theoretical intellect, prophet to be able to receive inspiration that will lead men to happiness. Since this ideal is almost impossible to realize, Alfarabi was satisfied if the ruler were to possess only the essential qualities. Again, like Plato, he contrasted the ideal state with its imperfect imitations, e.g., democracy, timocracy, and tyranny.

Appreciation. In general, Alfarabi relied heavily on the Greek tradition as he knew it. Although he made frequent references to Plato and Aristotle, the extent of his knowledge of their works is not easy to assess. He did write a commentary on Aristotle's *De interpretatione,* gave a summary of the *Metaphysics,* and claimed to have read nine books of Plato's *Laws.* But in most cases his knowledge came from the commentators Alexander and Themistius and from the many manuals of philosophy then available.

Alfarabi's influence in Islam was considerable, for he determined the principal lines of its philosophical speculation. He was generally appreciated by his successors, despite the attacks of *Algazel. His works were frequently translated into Latin and Hebrew in the Middle Ages. He seems to have influenced the political theories of *Maimonides, but for the most part ranks far behind Avicenna and Averroës in importance for medieval philosophy.

See also ARABIAN PHILOSOPHY; JEWISH PHILOSOPHY; SCHOLASTICISM, 1.

Bibliography: Works. *Philosophische Abhandlungen,* ed. and tr. F. H. DIETERICI (Leiden, Arab. text 1890; Ger. tr. 1892); *Abhandlung: Der Musterstaat,* ed. and tr. F. H. DIETERICI (Leiden, Arab. text 1895; Ger. tr. 1900); *De intellectu et intellecto,* critical ed. of Arab. text M. BOUYGES (Beirut 1938); *Commentary on Aristotle's "De interpretatione,"* ed. W. KUTSCH and S. MARROW (Beirut 1960); *Católogo de las ciencias,* ed. and tr. A. GONZÁLEZ PALENCIA (2d ed. Madrid 1953), Span., Arab. and 2 Lat. versions; *De Platonis philosophia,* ed. F. ROSENTHAL and K. WALZER (Plato arabus 2; London 1943), Lat. and Arab.; *Compendium legum Platonis,* ed. and tr. F. GABRIELI, (*ibid.* 3; 1952), Lat. and Arab. *Alfarabi's Philosophy of Plato and Aristotle,* tr. with introd. M. MAHDI (New York 1962). Eng. selections in R. LERNER and M. MAHDI, *Medieval Political Philosophy: A Sourcebook* (Glencoe, Ill. 1963).

Literature. M. STEINSCHNEIDER, *Al-Farabi des arabischen Philosophen Leben und Schriften* (Memoires de l'Academie Imperial des Sciences de St. Petersburg 13.4; 1859). I. MADKOUR, *La Place d'al- Fârâbi dans l'école philosophique musulmane* (Paris 1935). E. I. J. ROSENTHAL, *Political Thought in Medieval Islam* (Cambridge, Eng. 1958). N. RESCHER, *Al-Fārābī: An Annotated Bibliography* (Pittsburgh 1962). R. WALZER, EncFil 2: 269–270.

[J. FINNEGAN]

ALFERIUS, ST., Cluniac abbot; b. Salerno; d. La Cava, April 12, 1050 (feast, April 12). He was a member of the Pappacarbone family and received an excellent education. Introduced to the court of Prince Waimar III of Salerno, he was sent on diplomatic missions to France and Germany, *c.* 1002–03. While traveling, he fell ill and stopped at the monastery of S. Michele della Chiusa (Piedmont), where he met *Odilo of Cluny. To fulfill a vow, Alferius became a monk at *Cluny in 1003. He was recalled to Salerno by Waimar III and charged with the reform of the monasteries in this area. His hermitage became the Abbey of *La Cava (SS. Trinità) when he was joined by a number of disciples. His cult was approved by Leo XIII in 1893.

Bibliography: HUGH OF VENOSA, *Vitae quatuor priorum abbatum Cavensium,* ed. L. MATTEI CERASOLI in Muratori RIS[2] 6.5:3–12. ActSS April 2:96–101. Kehr ItalPont 8:311. F. M. MEZZA, *L'ambasciatore che fondò un monastero* (Cava, Italy 1952), popularization. Butler Th Attw 2:80.

[R. GRÉGOIRE]

ALFIERI, PIETRO, proto-Caecilian composer and scholar of Renaissance church music; b. Rome, June 29, 1801; d. Rome, June 12, 1863. Choral director at the English College and a Camaldolese monk, Alfieri was led to his studies in vocal polyphony through the influence of G. *Baini, whose biography of Palestrina (1828) fomented the church-music reform that climaxed in the *Caecilian movement, and of F. Santini, who had amassed the greatest collection of 16th- to 18th-century church music (now held by the University of Münster, Westphalia). His own contribution to the reform movement consisted in his editions of Palestrinia (*Raccolta di musica sacra,* 7 v. 1841–46), Vittoria, Allegri, and other Renaissance masters and his important theoretical and practical writings, among them *Ristabilimento del canto e della musica ecclesiastica* (1843), *Accompagnamento coll'organo, Trattato di armonia di Catel,* two works of special relevance to the art of chant—*Saggio storico teoretico-pratico del canto gregoriano* (1855) and *Prodromo sulla restaurazione de'libri di canto gregoriano* (1857)—and numerous periodical articles. He published also a brief history of the Accademia di Santa Cecilia, Rome, and a life of Niccolo *Jommelli (both 1845). Although (or, more properly, because) his compositional ideal, to which every new work, he believed, must aspire, was Palestrina, his own compositions, comprising Masses, motets, Marian hymns, settings of litanies and Sequences, and much more, are undistinguished.

Bibliography: K. G. FELLERER, MusGG 1:316. Riemann. Kornmüller.

[F. HABERL]

ALFIERI, VITTORIO

Italian poet and dramatist; b. Asti, in the Piedmont, Jan. 16, 1749; d. Florence, Oct. 8, 1803. Every biography of Alfieri challenges comparison with his autobiography, *Vita di A. V. da Asti scritta da esso,* written in Paris (1790) and redone in Florence (1803) with the addition of 11 chapters. His account is not the colorful kind of chronicle that other Italian writers of the 18th century (*Goldoni, Casanova, Mazzei, Gorani, Gozzi, and Da Ponte) elaborated as flattering self-portraits. Alfieri was motivated by a grave concept of himself and his literary calling; he related no comic anecdotes, but rather mapped the austere road he trod to become a tragic author. In fact, he deliberately set himself to renew the moral conscience of his people by means of the theater.

Alfieri came of patrician family, and until he was 25 lived like the youth of his class: he spent 8 years of what he calls *ineducazione* at the Academy of Turin, was an officer in the service of the King of Sardinia, and for many years traveled through Italy and the whole of Europe. In Tuscany, where he had withdrawn to study the Italian language in its origins and to purify himself of every trace of French influence, he met the Countess of Albany, the wife of Prince Charles Edward Stuart, pretender to the English throne, and attached himself to her for the rest of his life, residing with her in Alsace, Paris, and Florence.

Vittorio Alfieri

Dedication to Tragedy. After the production of his first play, *Cleopatra* (1775), he determined to devote himself to tragedy. He denounced all his previous education and disciplined himself by study of the classics, which he wrongly conceived as models of a new culture, a new style. Further, his love of poetry, his proud and even naïvely overbearing awareness of his own worth, and a thirst for action so at variance with the melancholy of the times, all impelled him toward tragedy and made him a poet-prophet who foreshadowed the Italy of the *Risorgimento. He was not as much a solitary as he portrayed himself, and his impassioned voluntarism ("I wanted, always I wanted, most strenuously I wanted") linked his "pre-Romanticism" to the *Sturm und Drang* of the contemporary Germans. But his vague yearning for profound truths, his almost religious cultivation of poetic revelation, and the sense of mystery sunder him as much from *arcadianism as from that rationalistic, scientistic, and propagandistic encyclopedism that had pervaded Europe through French culture.

The new times seemed to encourage Alfieri's revolutionary drive, but he was soon disillusioned. He had welcomed the American revolution in *L'America libera,* a sequence of five odes (1781–83) in honor of Washington and Lafayette, and hymned the French revolution in *Parigi sbastigliata* (1789); but in the same year he gave evidence of an evolution in his political thinking: the revolution seems betrayed and liberty slowly takes shape in his thought as a more profound matter of moral and religious life. He fought against political absolutism in the treatise *Della Tirannide* (1777) and in the politicoliterary essay *Del principe e delle lettere* (1785–86), wherein he rejects patronage and celebrates poets as the supreme heroes, founders of religions and the founders also of nations.

Setting himself in opposition to the dogmas and the illusions of the *Enlightenment, he vented his anger in the *Satire* (1788–89) at Voltaire, "irreligiosity," and the hypocrisy of the "liberty, equality, and fraternity" that had led to a blood bath, progressivism, commercialism, and the rise of the middle class. The *Misogallo* (1796), a collection of anti-French writings, is one of the first evidences of nascent Italian nationalism. The six *Commedie* (1800–02) also have more political than poetic interest. The *Rime* (1775), however, modeled on the Petrarchan manner as recovered in his own times, are splendid lyrics. Among so many bitter conflicts in a spirit that sought truth and life in the secret of the imagination, even his adjustment to Catholicism swung from enthusiasm to indifference. In his maturity, however, he returned to observance of his faith, profoundly influenced by the liturgy.

Import of the Tragedies. The 19 tragedies, structured according to the strictest neoclassical principles, deal predominantly with political themes, thus bridging the separation between politics and literature that had long been the fashion in Italy. Of the tragedies, *Filippo* (1775) is the cry of young love smothered by family and government tyranny; *Virginia* (1777) celebrates the sacrifice of an innocent girl deceived by the tyrant but avenged by the forces of liberty inspired by her death; the hero of *Oreste* (1776) rebels against the tyrant, but his mad violence plunges him into matricide. In *Merope* (1782), Alfieri softened the portrait of the tyrant and dramatized the conflicts of a mother intent on revenge but restrained by pity; *Saul* (1782), his masterpiece, analyzes the magnanimous power of the Biblical King caught between the "terrible ire" of the Almighty and the serene grace of the young David; the heroine in *Mirra* (1784) strives to hide a fatal passion, but, under duress from pitying relatives, she confesses and dies. *Bruto primo* (1786), dedicated to George Washington, and *Bruto secondo* (1789), dedicated to the "Italian people of the future," round out his most important tragedies.

Alfieri's Significance. Modern Italian literature begins with Alfieri, and the Italian theater became his heir, whether through his influence on the opera (especially on Giuseppe *Verdi) or on the traditions of the great actors (Gustavo Modena, Adelaide Ristori). Before Alfieri, European culture had been most alert to even mediocre values of Italian literature; after him it remained unaware of too many genuine values. Italian culture, however, won from his pioneering example an awareness that poetry is a way of knowing and revealing the truths of the human heart and soul that underlie any ideology or propaganda.

Bibliography: *Opere,* 22 v. (Pisa 1805–15); ed. L. FASSÒ et al., 20 v. (Centro Nazionale di Studi Alfieriani; Asti 1951–); *Lettere edite ed inedite,* ed. G. MAZZATINTI (Turin 1890); *Scritti giovanili inediti o rari,* ed. A. PELLIZZARI (Naples 1916); *Appunti di lingua e traduzionaccie prime,* ed. C. JANNACO (Turin 1946); *Tragedie,* 2 v.; *Commedie; La vita; Le rime,* ed. F. MAGGINI (Florence 1926–33). G. BUSTICO, *Bibliografia di V. Alfieri* (3d ed. Florence 1927). C. CAPPUCCIO, "V. Alfieri," *I classici italiani nella storia della critica,* ed. W. BINNI, 2 v. (Florence 1954–55) v.2. C. DEJOB, *De la tendresse dans le théâtre d'Alfieri* (Paris 1895). B. CROCE, "Alfieri," *Poesia e non poesia* (Bari 1923). M. FUBINI, *V. Alfieri: Il pensiero, la tragedia* (Florence 1937); DizBiogItal 2:273–319. W. BINNI, "La rivoluzione alfieriana," *Preromanticismo italiano* (Naples 1948). **Illustration credit:** Italian Information Center, New York City.

[M. APOLLONIO]

ALFONSO X, KING OF CASTILE, b. Toledo, 1221; d. Seville, 1284. He was the son of St. *Ferdinand III and Beatrice of Suabia, and was king of Castile and Leon (1252–84). His political career was unfortunate, but during his reign Spanish culture and literature reached one of its high-water marks and he became known as El Sabio. He established schools in Seville, Murcia, and Toledo, in which learned Christians, Moslems, and Jews cultivated the arts and sciences. He continued the famous school of translators founded at Toledo in the 12th century by Archbishop Raimundo (1130–50). He was no mere patron, but selected the works for translation and took part in their final editing. Castilian prose reached flexibility and full development during his reign, especially in historical and legal works. To Alfonso himself are attributed the *General estoria* (unfinished; reaching only to the birth of Christ); *Estoria de España* (*Primera crónica general*), an account up to the reign of his father; and a legal work, *Las siete partidas*. The *Cantigas de Santa María* is also ascribed to Alfonso. It is a collection of 420 lyrics in Galician, with a stanza system of Hispano-Arabic origin (the *zejel*), composed to be sung; its basic theme is the miracles of the Blessed Virgin.

Bibliography: ALFONSO X, *Cantigas de Santa María,* ed. W. METTMAN, 3 v. (Coimbra 1959–64). J. RIBERA Y TARRAGÓ, *Music in Ancient Arabia and Spain* (Stanford 1929). E. S. PROCTER, *Alfonso X of Castile: Patron of Literature and Learning* (Oxford 1951). G. MENÉNDEZ-PIDAL, "Cómo trabajaron las escuelas alfonsíes," *Nueva Revista de Filología Hispánica* 5 (1951) 363–380.

[J. M. SOLA-SOLE]

ALFONSO DE CASTRO, theologian; b. Zamora, Spain, 1495; d. Brussels, Feb. 3, 1558. De Castro entered the Franciscan Order at Salamanca in 1511; he studied theology there and later at the University of Alcalá. He occupied a chair of theology at Salamanca for 30 years, meanwhile doing occasional preaching in Germany, England, and at the court of Charles V. In 1530 he took part in a debate on the validity of the marriage of Henry VIII and wrote a treatise on the subject that was posthumously published at Lyons in 1568. As theologian to Cardinal Pacheco at the first session of the Council of Trent, he was active in the discussions of original sin and the canon of Sacred Scripture. He became so skilled in the knowledge of penal law that he came to be known as "princeps poenalistarum." In 1557 he was named archbishop of Compostela, but died before being consecrated. Among his works are: *Adversus omnes haereses lib. XIV* (Paris 1534), which catalogues and refutes the heresies from the time of the Apostles to the 16th century; *Homiliae 25 in Ps. 50* (Salamanca 1537); *Homiliae 24 in Ps. 31* (Salamanca 1540); *De justa haereticorum punitione* (Salamanca 1547); and *De potestate legis poenalis* (Salamanca 1550).

Bibliography: Wadding Ann 18:132–134. E. CAGGIANO, Enc Catt 1:856–857.

[B. CAVANAUGH]

ALFONSO OF MADRID, Franciscan spiritual writer; b. Madrid, between 1475 and 1500; d. after 1521. Little is known about the details of his life. Evidently gifted with sound psychological insight, he was a practiced and popular spiritual director in the aristocratic circles in which he moved. At the request of a noble lady, probably one of his penitents, he wrote *Espejo de ilustres personas* (Burgos, 1542), a treatise on spiritual perfection written especially for the wealthy and noble; the *Memorial de la Vida de J.C.,* meditations on the life of Jesus, written for wealthy women; and *Siete meditaciones de la Semana Santa* (Paris 1587), meditations on the events of Holy Week. His masterpiece, however, was the *Arte para servir a Dios* (Seville 1521), which is ranked among the great spiritual treatises by both SS. Teresa of Avila and Francis de Sales. It has special significance, for it was one of the first ascetical works to be written in the vernacular. The book has three parts, dealing, respectively, with: the principles of the Christian life, the intellect, and the will; the establishment and ordering of prayer and virtue, and the control of natural dispositions; charity, God's mercy, love of neighbor based on the love of God, and the three degrees of the spiritual life. The work is traditional in doctrine but is expressed in a highly personal style, with great clarity and beauty. It was reprinted many times in the original and translated into other tongues. In 1560 it was translated into Latin by the Louvain Dominicans and it is considered to have had much influence in the Catholic reform.

Bbiliography: P. GUILLAUME, "Un Précurseur de la Reforme catholique, Alonso de Madrid," RHE 25 (1929) 260–274. E. CAGGIANO, EncCatt 1:860. J. GOYENS, DictSpirAscMyst 1:389–391.

[B. CAVANAUGH]

ALFONSUS BONIHOMINIS, or de Buenhombre, Spanish Dominican Hebraist and Arabist; b. Cuenca or Toledo; d. before Aug. 12, 1353. He is known chiefly for his Latin translation of two Arabic works of a Jewish Rabbi converted to Christianity: *Tractatus Rabbi Samuelis ad Rabbi Isaac per quem probatur adventus Christi,* translated while he was in Paris in 1339 (many eds.; *Bibl. vet. Patrum* 18:518); and *Disputatio Abutalib Saraceni et Samuelis Judaei quae fides praecellat* (uned. MS Madrid Nac. 4402 f. 103–110), translated while he was bishop of Marrakech in Morocco (1344 to death). Both are Christian apologies in dialogue form. His other translations from Arabic into Latin (*see* TRANSLATION LITERATURE, GREEK AND ARABIC) are *Historia Joseph* (uned.), done probably in Egypt (1336) and the *Legenda s. Antonii abbatis Thebaidis* (ed. *Bibl. vet. Patrum* 18).

Bibliography: Quétif-Échard 1:594–595. S. RUIZ, DHGE 9: 1135–36. M. H. LAURENT, *ibid.* 10:1061. F. STEGMÜLLER, Lex ThK² 1:334.

[M. J. FINNEGAN]

ALFORD, MICHAEL, Jesuit historian; b. London, 1587; d. Saint-Omer, Flanders, Aug. 11, 1652. After a novitiate begun at Louvain (1607), and after the usual course of philosophy in the English College, Seville, and theology at Louvain, during which he was ordained, Alford (originally Griffith), spent 2 years among the English at Naples. For 5 years (1615–20) he was English penitentiary at St. Peter's, Rome. He was socius to the master of novices at Liège (1620) and later rector of the tertians at Ghent before going to England in the winter of 1628–29. Upon landing, he was mistaken for Richard Smith, Bishop of Chalcedon, and arrested, but he was released at the intervention of Queen Henrietta Maria. Alford worked in Leicestershire and Herefordshire, becoming superior of the residence of St. Anne in 1636. He spent his leisure mainly in historical studies and writing, and retired to Saint-Omer in 1652 to finish his three-volume *Fides Regia Britannica sive Annales Ecclesiae Britannicae* (Liège 1663). He wrote also a life of St. Winefride (1635) and *Britannia Illustrata* (1641).

Bibliography: H. More, *Historia Provinciae anglicanae Societatis Jesu* (Saint-Omer 1660) 394–395. G. Oliver, *Collections toward Illustrating the Biography of the Scotch, English, and Irish Members of the Society of Jesus* (London 1845). A. de Backer, *Bibliothèque des écrivains de la compagnie de Jésus*, 3 v. (Paris 1869–76) 1:71. T. Cooper, DNB 1:284. Sommervogel 1:175–176.

[F. EDWARDS]

ALFRED THE GREAT, KING OF ENGLAND

Reigned 871 to 899; educator, pioneer of vernacular prose; b. Wantage, 849; d. Winchester, Oct. 26, 899. He was the son of King Aethelwulf and Osburh and succeeded to the throne as King of the West Saxons. By his Mercian wife, Ealhswith, Alfred had two sons and three daughters. He had been second in command of the army under Aethelred, his brother, and became king when Wessex had first to repel the invading Danes. After the Danish protectorate of Mercia was established in 874, Alfred faced constant danger. Driven into hiding in the Somerset fens in the winter of 878, he returned in the spring and defeated the Danes at Edington. Their leader, Guthrum, was baptized, and the Danes left for East Anglia in 880. Further invasions were intercepted at sea.

In 885 Alfred repulsed a Danish invasion at Rochester and attacked East Anglia with Kentish ships. He occupied London in 886, and all the English people not subjected to the Danes submitted to him. This marked the beginning of a united English monarchy. Another Danish invasion in 892 renewed the wars. In spite of their oaths, the Danes of Northumbria and East Anglia joined the invaders in campaigns (893–895), but Alfred's determined opposition forced them to retire. They continued to ravage the southern coast, and in 896 Alfred built special long ships to oppose them. He defended his people successfully, raiding as far as Bridgnorth and Chester, but not attacking the permanent Danish settlements.

Alfred, King of England, on the gold, enamel, and crystal "Alfred Jewel," c. 871–901 (reproduced actual size).

Alfred's exceptional achievement was to add to his military concerns a personal desire to stimulate an intellectual renaissance for his people. Like other kings of Wessex, he maintained close links with Rome, which he had twice visited as a boy, and he invited Continental clergy to help him in England to plan a pattern of education on Christian foundations to include the elite laity as well as the clergy. Alfred's court became a cultural center in which he, by providing essential texts in OE translations of Latin authorities, brought about the beginnings of OE prose.

By 885, when the Welsh priest Asser, whose biography of the King is the first-known work of the kind about a layman, joined Alfred as friend and mentor for Latin studies, the King had begun working through the Vulgate; and in what Asser calls an *Encheiridion,* or handbook, he carried about everywhere a copy of the Office Psalms and especially valued religious citations. Indeed his austere and almost saintly personal life must have contributed greatly to his success as leader. Daily Mass and the canonical Hours were his regular practice.

In his final decade Alfred translated or directed a version of the *Liber pastoralis curae* by Pope St. *Gregory I to serve as a textbook for bishops and their priests; then *Bede's *Historia ecclesiastica gentis Anglorum,* so that the history of their own Church might be properly known; next, to provide a soundly Christian view of world history, the Spanish priest *Orosius's *Historiae adversum paganos* (to which Alfred added his famous description of the geography of northern Europe); and finally, for training in Christian philosophy, Boethius's *De consolatione philosophiae.* In these works, especially in Orosius and Boethius, there is a beginning of literary prose; the King's impressive personality shines through his prefaces to these works and in those passages he interpolated for added clarity or for bridging lacunae—this evidence shows Alfred as an original composer. In his last days he was concerned with his personal philosophical problems; thus he freely adapted from St. Augustine's *Soliloquies,* which he mixed with meditations of his own in what he called his *Blostman,* or blooms.

Bibliography: Asser, *Life of King Alfred,* ed. W. H. Stevenson (Oxford 1904), Latin text with introd. and commentary; Eng. tr. L. C. Jane (Oxford 1924). E. S. Duckett, *Alfred the Great* (Chicago 1956). The OE versions of the *Pastoral Care,* with tr., Orosius' *Histories* and Bede's *Historia ecclesiastica* are in eds. pub. by the EEngTSoc (1871–72, 1883, 1890–98). Version of Augustine's *Soliloquies* is ed. H. L. Hargrove in *Yale Studies in English* (New York 1902) with tr. (1904). Alfred's version of Boethius's *Consolations,* is ed. and tr. W. J. Sedgefield (Oxford 1900). Trs. of important passages in EngHistDoc v.1. **Illustration credit:** Courtesy of the Ashmolean Museum.

[D. J. A. MATTHEW; C. L. WRENN]

ALFRED OF SARESHEL (Alfredus Anglicus), English scientist; fl. *c.* 1210. He was one of the English scholars who reinforced 13th-century science with new texts from antiquity, especially those of Aristotle. Alfred is known only through his writings. He was the author of glosses on Aristotle's *Parva naturalia* and *De anima,* and also on the pseudo-Aristotelian work of Nicholas of Damascus on plants, *De plantis* (or *De vegetalibus*), which he first translated from Arabic. His *Liber de congelatis* is a translation of the appendix of Avicenna's *On Meteors.* No evidence supports the thesis that his glosses *On Plants* and *On Meteors* represent his teaching at Oxford. His commentary *On Meteors* was used by both *Adam of Buckfield and *Roger Bacon. His original work *De motu cordis* (*On the Motion of the Heart*) [C. Baeumker, "A. von S . . ." BeitrGeschPhilMA (1923) 23.1–2], dedicated to *Alexander Neckham (d. 1217), cites principally Aristotle, but also such physiological authorities as *Galen, *Costa ben Luca, *Avicenna, and *Hippocrates. *De motu Cordis* was the study, unattempted theretofore, of the heart as chief organ of the soul, or, more precisely, as the domicile of life. Alfred combined Aristotelian science with that of Galen and helped to shift the scientific center of gravity to physiology and medicine.

Bibliography: A. PELZER, "Une Source inconnue de Roger Bacon, A. de S.," ArchFrancHist 12 (1919) 44–67. Thorndike 2:195. Sarton 2.2:561–562. D. A. CALLUS, "Introduction of Aristotelian Learning to Oxford," *Proceedings of the British Academy* 29 (1943) 229–281. Gilson HistChrPhil 235, 260, 658, 661.

[E. A. SYNAN]

ALGAZEL (GHAZZĀLĪ, AL-)

Arab philosopher and theologian; b. Ṭūs, province of Khorāsān, Persia, 1058; d. Ṭūs, 1111.

Life. Algazel received his early education in his native city and at Jurjan, where the teaching of the mystics, or Sufis, was emphasized (*see* SUFISM). The decisive period of his formation began, however, when he attended the lectures of a famous theologian, al-Juwaynī, at Nisāpour. There he acquired a deep knowledge of Islamic theology and law and was initiated into the philosophical speculations of *Alfarabi and *Avicenna. From the beginning, Algazel shared with his teacher a distrust for authority in matters of religion. This distrust accompanied him all his life, explaining in great part the distinctive features of his intellectual and spiritual evolution.

When al-Juwaynī died in 1085, Algazel joined the scholars whom the vizier, Niẓām al-Mulk, had gathered around him. After 6 years in this group, he was named professor of Moslem law at the famous Niẓāmiya College in Baghdad. In 1095 he resigned his post, left Baghdad, and on the pretext of making the pilgrimage to Mecca retired to Damascus. In his *Al-Munqidh min aḍ-ḍalāl* (Deliverance from Error), he explains this decision on religious grounds as a need to deepen his spiritual life and to free himself from worldly preoccupations; scholars suggest, however, that political considerations had something to do with his retirement. Following this, he spent 2 years in Syria, made the pilgrimage to Mecca, visited Jerusalem, and lived the life of an ascetic, studying and practicing mysticism. He then returned to Ṭūs, probably before 1098 or 1099. He abandoned his life of private teaching and ascetical practices in 1106 when, on demand of the vizier, Fakhr al-Mulk, he returned to Nisāpour as professor at the Niẓāmiya College there. This second period of teaching lasted until 1109, when he retired to Ṭūs, to remain until his death.

Thought. Algazel is among the profound religious teachers of Islam. A polemist of first rank, he is mainly responsible for the intellectual orientation taken by orthodox Islam since his day. He assured the triumph of the theology of al-*Ash'arī; at the same time, he contributed to the decadence of philosophical speculation by his attacks on certain classical Neoplatonic doctrines held by Alfarabi and Avicenna. He also endorsed mysticism, thitherto the object of suspicion and condemnation by the orthodox followers of Islam.

Algazel's writings, especially *Al-Munqidh min aḍ-ḍalāl,* show that his conversion expressed itself in the form of universal doubt, somewhat similar to that of R. *Descartes but arising in a different context. Algazel was convinced that there is in man an innate ground of religious experience that is generally oriented by parental authority. Thus children born of Christians become Christians; those born of Jews become Jews. Such influence cannot be justified, particularly since it would put all religions, Islam included, on the same footing. To found his own religious life and to work for the revival of the true religion, for him Islam, it was necessary for Algazel to uncover the fundamental experience that would justify all the rest. In describing his search for this, he follows a logical rather than a chronological pattern. He begins by doubting sense knowledge, which, as the intellect shows, contains contradictory elements. But he holds that even clear intellectual concepts cannot be accepted at face value, for they too might be found wanting if they could be examined by a higher faculty.

Algazel finally escapes from these harassing doubts not by argument and demonstration, but by the light that God has given him. Once received, this light from God allows him to evaluate the four principal positions that have been defended by the theologians, the philosophers, the Batinites, and the mystics. In weighing each position, Algazel is not purely negative, but seems conscious that the shortcomings of any one explanation do not render it valueless. It is this attitude that caused Algazel to be accused of insincerity, for his adversaries were not slow to point out that, after attacking them, he incorporated much of their doctrine in his own synthesis.

Algazel criticizes the theologians for adopting principles admitted by their adversaries and for using arguments based merely on universal consent. His criticism of the philosophers is that they have some excellent logical principles but fail to live up to them in proving their own positions, being content merely to echo a long tradition taken over from the Greeks. The third group whose doctrine Algazel rejects is the Batinite Sect, which claimed that all religious truth must be received for no other reason except the infallible authority of a teacher (their infallible Imām, at that time the Fatimite Caliph of Cairo); their position is a radical denial of his own, which claims that authority can never replace experience. The fourth group, the mystics, receives Algazel's full adherence. In his view, purity of heart obtained by recollection is the first condition of progress in the mystic way, which leads to complete absorption in God (*fanā*). At this point there is a period of visions and revelations, later reaching its perfection in a nearness to God. The prophets are those who reach the highest degree of experience and are thus constituted physicians of the heart. It is through their influence and the following of their precepts that a man can eventually hope to attain light.

Works. A great number of works have been attributed to Algazel (see Bouyges). During his first teaching period, up to 1095, he wrote some treatises on logic and composed the *Maqāṣid al-Falācifa,* a summary of philosophical doctrines, which he then refuted in the *Tahāfut al-Falācifa* (Incoherence of the Philosophers). He wrote also some works on Moslem canon law and a treatise on theology, the *Iqtisād.* During his retreat (1095–1105) he composed his principal work, *Iḥyā 'Ulūm ad-Dīn* (Revival of the Religious Sciences), together with numerous minor works dealing with the spiritual life. In 1105–06, while teaching at Nisāpour, he wrote his intellectual autobiography and later *Mishkāt al-Anwār* (Niche of Lights), a highly esoteric account of his religious thought. In the years preceding his retirement from teaching in 1095 and immediately following it, he wrote several works against the Batinite Sect, among others, *Al-Qisṭās al-Mostiqīm* (The Just Balance).

See also ARABIAN PHILOSOPHY; ISLAM.

Bibliography: Works in translation. *The Faith and Practice of al-Gazālī,* tr. W. MONTGOMERY WATT (London 1953); *Streitschrift des Gazali gegen die Bātinijja-Sekte,* ed. I. GOLDHIZER (Leiden 1916; repr. 1956); *The Alchemy of Happiness,* tr. C. FIELD (London 1910); *Mishkat al-Anwār (The Niche for Lights),* tr. W. H. T. GAIRDNER (London 1924; Lahore 1952); *O Disciple* (Beirut 1951); *Al Qistās al Mostiqīm* (Damascus 1955–57); *Worship in Islam,* tr. and commentary E. E. CALVERLY of *Book of the Iḥyā on the Worship* (Madras 1925; 2d ed. London 1957); *Iḥyā ouloûm ed-din ou Vivification des sciences de la foi,* analyzed H. BOUSQUET (Paris 1955). AVERROËS, *Tahāfut al-Tahāfut,* tr. S. VAN DEN BERGH, 2 v. (London 1954), contains text of Algazel's *Tahāfut* quoted by Averroës.

Studies. A. BOUYGES, *Essai de chronologie des oeuvres de al-Ghazali* (Algazel) (Beirut 1960). A. J. WENSINCK, *La Pensée de Ghazzâlî* (Paris 1940). D. B. MACDONALD, "The Life of al-Ghazzālī with Especial Reference to His Religious Experiences and Opinions," JAmOrSoc 20 (1899) 71–132. S. M. ZWEMER, *A Moslem Seeker after God* (New York 1920). M. ASIN-PALACIOS, *"Algazel" dogmatica, moral, ascetica* (Zaragoza 1901); *La Mystique d'al-Gazzali* (Beirut 1914); *La espiritualidad de Algazel y su sentido Cristiano,* 4 v. (Madrid 1934–41). J. OBERMANN, *Der philosophische und religiöse Subjektivismus Ghazalis* (Vienna 1921). M. SMITH, *Al-Ghazālī: The Mystic* (London 1944). F. JABRE, La Notion de la ma'rifa chez Ghazali (Beirut 1958).

[J. FINNEGAN]

ALGEBRA

The division of mathematics that deals with the study of finite structures; its branches include theory of equations, number theory, matrix theory, and algebraic systems (group, ring, field . . .).

Mathematics is the study of basic structure. This includes structures of *number systems and of *geometries and of *topologies and of *calculi. Mathematicians study the abstract structure of problems in engineering, physics, chemistry, and logic. The basic structure of an economy, of a political system, or of a language are also part of modern mathematical investigation. The arithmetic and symbol manipulation performed by a modern *computing machine is *not* mathematics, but the analysis of computer problems before they are placed on the computer is mathematics. Many different disciplines, including mathematics itself, apply theory developed by mathematicians. However, the study of abstract structures is the mathematician's primary field of research.

In the finite structure theory known as algebra, it may at first seem that little of practical importance has been lost since this book and the table on which it rests, and indeed the entire universe, are each composed of only a finite number of subatomic particles. That conclusion, however, would be incorrect. Although analysis assumes a continuous (infinite) structure, its elegant theory has many applications to finite, real-life situations—indeed, it is only the existence of the modern computer, born in the last half of the 20th century, that has made the extensive use of finite methods feasible on a large-scale basis.

Historical Survey. Originally algebra arose in problems relating to numbers. Babylonian tablets (*c.* 3100 B.C.) contain algebraic problems. The Rhind (Ahmes) Papyrus (a *c.* 1700 B.C. copy of an earlier manuscript) contains abstract problems such as "a number and a quarter of that number together give 15, what is the number?" as well as practical problems involving the equitable distribution of wages to laborers, the calculation of the amount of grain needed to produce bread and beer for a given number of people, and area and volume problems such as the number of bricks needed to construct a building ramp of given dimensions.

About 2,500 years later (*c.* A.D. 800) a more favorable notation permitted the serious study of algebraic equations; and eventually, in the 16th century, the solution of the cubic equation by a school of Italian mathematicians including G. *Cardano led gradually to semimodern notation, and the basic structural theory of polynomial equations developed. The fundamental theorem of elementary algebra (that a polynomial equation of degree n has at least one root) was not proved until almost 1800 by K. F. Gauss.

By 1900 every university had a course devoted to the structural theory of equations, but modern abstract algebra was in the main still untaught. By 1920 invariant theory, matrices, group and field theory were studied in most graduate programs, but undergraduate programs in abstract algebra did not begin to appear regularly until about 1940. By 1960 almost every college and university provided undergraduate courses in modern abstract algebra and thousands of high school students studied Boolean algebra, matrices, groups, fields, and rings as well as systems of linear equations. More good structural algebra is currently being taught in some high schools than was available in the finest graduate schools 100 years ago.

Although algebra is one of the oldest branches of mathematics, more algebraic theory was developed in the 50 years from 1900 to 1950 than in the 5,000 years between 3100 B.C. and A.D. 1900. Furthermore, more algebraic (finite) mathematical theory was published in the 15 years from 1950 to 1965 than in the previous highly productive 50-year period. Abstract algebra is an interesting, growing branch of mathematics.

Recent Developments. Some of the most important recent contributions to modern abstract algebra will be found in libraries under the name Nicholas Bourbaki, a pseudonym (pilfered from an obscure Napoleonic general) used by a coalition of some of the best French mathematicians. The actual members of the coalition change, but the production of high quality mathematics continues. Not only are new areas of mathematics being explored, but very ancient areas are flowering in fashions that would have been unbelievable even in the mid-1940s.

Ancient Babylonian tablets discuss problems that in modern notation, require the solution of

$$3x + y = 19$$
$$2x - y = 1$$

Modern schoolboys still solve similar systems of two linear equations in two unknowns and even systems of three or four equations in three or four unknowns, but until recently only the hardy ventured beyond this. Today's computers make it possible to solve, as routine problems, systems of 700 equations in 700 unknowns that arise in modern economic theory. Systems of 1,728 equations in 1,728 unknowns arise daily in vibration theory and flutter analysis in modern rocket and jet design. Much larger systems arise in the heat transfer problems of atomic physics. With the new vistas come new problems. Although a great deal is known about continuous variables (analysis) and much has been learned about certain finite algebraic systems such as groups, fields, rings, and integral domains, no one has yet completely studied the basic structure of the arithmetic used in any major computer now in operation. Modern computers are amazing arithmetical engines, but they violate many basic postulates of high school algebra. High school algebra assumes for all a, b, c that

$$(a + b) + c = a + (b + c)$$
$$(ab)c = a(bc)$$
$$s(a + b) = sa + sb$$

It assumes also that if $a \neq 0$ and $ax = ay$, then $x = y$; and if $a + x = a + y$, then $x = y$; and if $ab = 0$, then either $a = 0$ or $b = 0$. However, none of the above rules can be assumed in computer arithmetic. In spite of this, computers provide the majority of the arithmetic answers needed in today's engineering and science. Mathematicians must study the basic structure of computer algebras if science is to make reasonable use of this vital new tool.

Abstract algebra has many other problems of even more interest to mathematicians than the ever-changing structure of computer arithmetic. Modern economics, psychology, business administration, physics, chemistry, and engineering—all lean heavily on mathematics. Each brings new problems for the mathematician's study.

See also MATHEMATICS, NATURE OF.

Bibliography: Introductions to modern abstract algebra. R. V. ANDREE, *Selections from Modern Abstract Algebra* (New York 1958). R. A. BEAUMONT and R. W. BALL, *Introduction to Modern Algebra and Matrix Theory* (New York 1954). R. E. JOHNSON, *First Course in Abstract Algebra* (Englewood Cliffs, N.J. 1960). Advanced presentations. G. BIRKHOFF and S. MACLANE, *A Survey of Modern Algebra* (rev. ed. New York 1953). N. JACOBSON, *Lectures in Abstract Algebra,* 3 v. (Princeton 1951–64) v.1 *Basic Concepts,* v.2 *Linear Algebra,* v.3 *Theory of Fields and Galois Theory.*

[R. V. ANDREE]

ALGER OF LIÈGE (ALGER OF CLUNY, ALGERUS MAGISTER)

Theologian, whose writings influenced the development of Canon Law; b. Liège, Belgium, in the mid-11th century; d. Cluny, France, about 1131 or 1132. According to his biographer, Nicholas of Liège, Alger received his education in his native city and was first appointed deacon and teacher at St. Bartholomew's, Liège. About 1101 he was transferred to St. Lambert's Cathedral, became a canon, and served as secretary to Bishop Otbert (1092–1117) and his successor, Frederick (1119–21). After Frederick's death on May 27, 1121, Alger entered Cluny and, though already advanced in years, was ordained.

Writings. Presumably while he was at St. Lambert's (1101–21), Alger wrote the *Tractate Concerning the Legal Rights of the Cathedral.* Before 1094 he had written a more important work, *On Mercy and Justice* (*Liber de misericordia et justitia*), in which he criticized certain sacramental doctrines of St. *Peter Damian (d. 1072) as too lax, and advocated a more thorough study of St. Augustine's sacramental teaching. Some 124 quotations from the works of St. Augustine serve to underline his own effort in this regard.

In later life, Alger wrote *On The Sacraments of the Lord's Body and Blood* (*De Sacramentis corporis et sanguinis dominici*), generally dated 1110 to 1121. Much of its source material is derived from Ivo's *Decretum.* In addition to these works, his short treatise, *On Free Will* (*Libellus de libero arbitrio*), of unknown date, and a number of Alger's letters are still extant. But it is more than doubtful that the little tract *On the Sacrifice of the Mass,* attributed to him, and the so-called *Sentences of Master A.,* also often assigned to him, are actually his works.

Although Alger's work on the Eucharist was considered by *Peter the Venerable to be far superior to the writings of *Lanfranc (d. 1089) and *Guitmand of Aversa (d. 1095) on the same subject, its influence on later authors was not strong. His work *On Mercy and Justice,* however, lived on through Gratian's *Decretum* (*see* GRATIAN, DECRETUM OF). It has been estimated that Gratian borrowed about 100 texts from it. More important, the *Dicta Gratiani* contain numerous explanations often copied verbatim from Alger. When Peter Lombard used Gratian's *Decretum* in the compilation of his *Sentences,* Alger's influence on theology was further intensified.

Doctrinal Teachings. In his search for a solution to the doctrinal problems conjured up by the contradictory claims of the *Gregorian Reform, Alger points to the "invocation of the divine name" in Baptism as a constructive sacramental principle. Accordingly, he formulates the general rule: "All sacraments, no matter who administers them in the name of the Trinity, are in themselves true and holy" (*De Sacramentis* 2.10). He considers it "a crime to believe that the invocation of the divine name in His sacraments may be frustrated" (*De Sacramentis* 3.2). If administered by heretics, sacraments are valid but without divine grace. An exception to this rule is Baptism administered even by a pagan in case of necessity, for "necessity knows no law" (*De Misericordia* 1.55). In Alger's time the word "sacrament" was neither clearly defined nor restricted to only seven liturgical rites; it must also be noted that in formulating his rule Alger had Baptism, Holy Orders, and the celebration of the Mass in mind.

Alger heavily underlines the importance of faith and intention. By faith, he holds, all sacraments of the Church are brought to completion. The perfection and sum total of the Christian faith are found in the use of the Trinitarian name. Although Alger insists that God examines our intention and faith rather than our external actions, he stresses that to be valid the liturgical rite of the Church must be observed. Any ritual changes made outside the Church must be rejected as heretical. However, regional differences in the liturgical customs of the Church do not affect sacramental validity, for the unifying element is the unity of faith and changes should be judged according to the intention of those responsible for them. Similar clarifications account for an unusual amount of casuistry in Alger's work on the Eucharist. Unfortunately Hugh of Saint-Victor, Gratian, and Peter Lombard did not make use of this work, but a number of manuscripts still extant in the libraries of Europe attest to its widespread popularity in the 12th century. The *Sentences of Master A.,* which provided source material for the compilation of Gratian's *Decretum,* dates back to the School of *Anselm of Laon rather than to Alger of Liège.

Bibliography: Alger's works are collected in PL 180:739–972; his letters in P. JAFFÉ, *Bibliotheca rerum germanicarum,* 6 v. (Berlin 1864–73) 5:262–267, 373–379. The *Eulogy* by Nicholas of Liège is found in PL 180:737–738. G. LE BRAS, "Le liber de misericordia et justitia d'Alger de Liège," NouvRevHistDrFranÉtr 45 (1921) 80–118; "Alger de Liège et Gratien," RevScPhilTh 20 (1931) 5–26. S. KUTTNER, "Zur Frage der theologischen Vorlagen Gratians," ZSavRGKan 23 (1934) 243–268. L. BRIGUE, *Alger de Liège* (Paris 1936). N. M. HARING, "The *Sententiae Magistri A.* and the School of Laon," MedSt 17 (1955) 1–45; "A Study in the Sacramentology of Alger of Liège," MedSt 20 (1958) 41–78.

[N. M. HARING]

ALGERIA

Republic in northwest *Africa, bordered by *Tunisia, *Libya, *Niger, *Mali, *Mauritania, Spanish *Sahara, *Morocco, and the Mediterranean Sea; 952,444 square miles in area, of which 838,315 square miles are Sahara. The capital of Algeria is *Algiers. Algeria became independent of France on July 5, 1962, and this event was followed by a mass exodus of the European population; in 18 months more than 800,000 Catholics left Algeria. In 1963 Algeria had 402 secular and 279 religious priests, 348 men in 70 religious houses, 1,606 women in 168 convents, and about 100,000 Catholics (more than half of them in Algiers itself) in a population of 10 million. Algiers (Roman *Icosium*), one of many small early Christian dioceses in North Africa, was restored in 1838 and became a metropolitan archdiocese in 1866. Another early Christian see, Constantine (Roman *Julia Cirta*), which unites to its title that of *Hippo, became, together with Oran, the suffragan sees in 1866. Laghouat, embracing the southern nine-tenths of Algeria, was created in 1955 immediately subject to the Holy See; previously it was the Prefecture of Ghardaïa (1901), detached from the Prefecture of the Sahara and the Sudan, called Ghardaïa in the Sahara (1921) and made a vicariate (1948–55).

Algeria, a land of Berber tribes, had early Phoenician settlements on the coast and came under the sway of *Carthage before it flourished under Roman rule as *Numidia* and *Mauretania Caesarea.* It suffered from *Donatists and was ruined by Vandals, who were besieging Hippo when St. Augustine died there (430). Byzantine rule was restored (533), but the tribes would not accept Christianity. The Arab conquest (709) was military, but Islam was accepted. Christian communities under bishops, having ties with Rome, lasted until *c.* 1150; Gregory VII appointed a bishop of Bône in 1076. Missionaries, especially from Spain, cared for Christian captives, soldiers, and merchants along the coast; but by 1512 there were so few Christians in Algeria that a bishop of Constantine appointed by Julius II did not venture to occupy his see. Spain attempted to hold the Algerian coast (1505–29), *Ximénez de Cisneros restoring the See of Bougie and planning to restore that of Oran; but the Mediterranean was abandoned as a field of expansion in favor of the New World. Oran, a refuge of Moors forced out of Spain, was held by Spain (1509–1708, 1732–91); but the rest of the Algerian coast was in the hands of Barbary pirates under the Ottoman Empire until French troops in 1830 took Algiers, the main port from which the pirates had menaced European coasts and shipping.

French and Spanish Trinitarians from 1580 and French Vincentians from 1646 had cared for Christian slaves in Algeria and functioned as French consuls. The Vincentian Vicariate Apostolic of Algeria (1650–1827) made little effort to convert Moslems or Christian renegades. The bishopric of Algiers created under the French in 1838, which included all Algiers, cared

mostly for immigrant French settlers and was deterred by the government from extending its activity to the Moslem population until Cardinal *Lavigerie, founder of the White Fathers and White Sisters (1868), became archbishop (1867–92). The first bishop of Algiers and the first bishop of Constantine resigned because of financial difficulties. Jesuits, called into Algeria in 1939, began missionary work in Kabylia (1839), which had been conquered in 1857. Vincentians returned in 1842 to direct seminaries in Algiers, Constantine, and Oran. Charles de *Foucauld was slain at Tamanrasset in Algeria (1916).

Bibliography: H. Froidevaux, DHGE 2:424–433. A. Pons, *La Nouvelle Église d'Afrique* (Tunis 1930). *Annuaire du diocese d'Alger* (1930–). L. E. Duval, *Messages de Paix 1955–1962* (Algiers 1961). E. Jarry, *Catholicisme* 1:317–319; 3:100–102. *Bilan du Monde* 2:41–49.

[J. CUOQ]

ALGIERS, ARCHDIOCESE OF (ALGERIENSIS), metropolitan see since 1866, in north central *Algeria on the Mediterranean. In 1963 it had 177 secular and 109 religious priests, 140 men in 34 religious houses, 815 women in 77 convents, and 75,000 Catholics in a population of 3,500,000; it is 21,120 square miles in area. Its suffragan sees, Contantine and and Oran, were created in 1866. The city of Algiers, with a population of 884,000, is the capital of Algeria and, after Alexandria in Egypt, the most important port in Africa. The present city, founded by Berbers *c.* 950, succeeded the Roman *Icosium,* originally founded by Phoenicians and destroyed by Vandals *c.* 430; from 1529 it was a stronghold of Barbary pirates in the Ottoman Empire, until taken by France in 1830.

Three early Christian bishops of *Icosium* are known, and Christianity in the region probably lasted for many centuries under Moslem rulers. Missionaries from Spain cared for Christian captives, soldiers, and merchants in medieval Algiers and Bougie, a seaport 115 miles east where Raymond *Lull died (1325). Vincentian vicars apostolic resided in Algiers caring for Christian slaves and serving as French consuls (1650–1827); Jean *Le Vacher (1668–83) is particularly noteworthy. The See of Algiers, created in 1838, suffragan to *Aix, was occupied by Antoine Dupuch (1838–45, d. 1856) and Antoine Pavy (1846–66). The first archbishop, Charles *Lavigerie (1867–92), exercised a primacy over all Africa from Algiers. On his death the Vicariate of the Sahara and the Sudan (1868) and the Archbishopric of *Carthage (1884) were detached from the jurisdiction of Algiers. The Basilica of Our Lady of Africa (1857) is a pilgrimage shrine. The seminary (1842) is under Vincentians. The University of Algiers, founded in 1909, has 6,500 students. Political events leading to Algerian independence in 1962 hurt religious life in the archdiocese. The main religious congregations represented are Vincentian, Trappists, Jesuits, and Cardinal Lavigerie's White Fathers.

Bibliography: A. Rastoul, DHGE 2:420–423. E. Jarry, *Catholicisme* 1:317–319. AnnPont (1964) 24. *Annuaire du Diocèse d'Alger* (1930–).

[J. CUOQ]

ALI ('ALĪ IBN ABĪ ṬĀLIB), son-in-law of Mohammed; b. Mecca, *c.* A.D. 600; d. Kufa, Jan. 24, 661. 'Alī was taken into his cousin Mohammed's household at 10, and became one of the first converts to Islam from paganism. He joined the *Hegira to Medina A.D. 622, was married to the Prophet's daughter Fāṭima, and fathered the Prophet's only surviving grandsons, al-Ḥasan and al-Ḥusayn. Mohammed's unexpected death in 632 was the first great crisis of Islam. Political, judicial, and religious head of the new Islamic state, Mohammed left no sons and apparently had appointed no successor. While 'Alī and his kin prepared the body for burial, a group of the Prophet's companions elected Abū Bakr, father of Mohammed's favorite wife, 'Ā'isha, as successor to the Prophet. 'Alī kept aloof, but the choice was ratified by the people of Medina. Abū Bakr (d. 634) appointed 'Umar, once an enemy, later father-in-law to Mohammed, as his own successor; and under their leadership Egypt, the Fertile Crescent, and Persia were taken by Arab armies. 'Umar was assassinated in 644 and the electoral conclave of the six most prominent companions of the Prophet passed over 'Alī in favor of 'Uthman ibn 'Affān, an early convert of the aristocratic Banū Umayya family, who had led the Meccan opposition to the Prophet. In 656 'Uthmān, in the face of general discontent with his caliphate, was blockaded in Medina and murdered when he refused to abdicate.

'Alī, then acclaimed caliph, defeated his opponents who accused him of illegal election and collusion with the murderers, and made his capital in Kūfa. Mu'āwiya, Governor of Syria, claiming vengeance for his cousin 'Uthmān, maneuvered 'Alī into a position in which he felt constrained to negotiate. At this, some of 'Alī's party withdrew allegiance, accusing him of forsaking Islam by negotiating on what should be religious principle. 'Alī was forced to take up arms against these "Seceders," (Khārijites) and in revenge was assassinated by one of them in 661. A mosque called Meshed 'Alī was afterward erected to his memory near the spot.

From 'Alī's reign came a major sectarian rift in Islamic theology. The "Partisans" (*Shī'a*) of 'Alī formed the chief division of Islam opposed to the "Traditionalist" (*Sunnī*) majority (*see* SHIITES; SUNNITES). After his death, his followers did not accept Mu'āwiya's claim to the caliphate. They insisted that 'Alī and his heirs were divinely appointed *imāms, leaders of the Moslem community.

While first an Arab political faction, the Shī'a came to differ markedly from the Sunnīs in metaphysics and doctrine; they have seen the imāms as infallible and impeccable, and at times even as emanations of the Godhead. The Shī'a have subdivided repeatedly over the claims of descendants of 'Alī, and have formed new sects and versions of the doctrine, ranging from the Zaydīs of Yemen, who simply hold that some descendant of 'Alī should rule, to the Nuṣayrīs of North Syria, for whom 'Alī is a member of a Gnostic divine trinity. The Sunnīs hold that he was one of the pious first caliphs, who came legally to power in a troubled time and died a tragic death. The polemic has led to much forged documentation.

Bibliography: L. Veccia Vaglieri, EncIslam² 1:381–386. L. Caetani, comp., *Annali dell'Islam,* 10 v. (Milan 1905–26) v.9 and 10.

[J. A. WILLIAMS]

ALIPIUS, ST., b. Tagaste, North Africa, *c.* 360; d. after 429 (feast, Aug. 15 or 18). Alipius was a student and close friend of *Augustine of Hippo and a fellow Manichean, who pursued a law career at his parents' wish. He joined Augustine at Rome in 383 and journeyed with him in 384 to Milan, where they were baptized by *Ambrose in 387. Returning to Africa (388) Alipius spent 3 years at Tagaste in prayer and penance before going to Hippo to be ordained a priest. On a pilgrimage to Palestine he met *Jerome and was instrumental in fostering a relationship between Jerome and Augustine. Upon his return to Africa, Alipius became bishop of Tagaste (*c.* 394) and struggled against the Pelagians and the Donatists. He visited Italy again in 419 and 428, on business for the Church and the government. During much of his life, he served as Augustine's assistant in his public activities. Augustine, writing in 429, called him old; and Alipius seems not to have survived long after that.

Bibliography: ActSS Aug. 3:201–208. AUGUSTINE, *Conf.* 6, 8, 9. Tillemont 12:565–580. A. P. FRUTAZ, LexThK[2] 1:410. F. MOURRET, *A History of the Catholic Church,* tr. N. THOMPSON, v.2 (St. Louis 1935) 416.

[R. K. POETZEL]

ALKMAAR, MARTYRS OF, eight Franciscans put to death in Alkmaar, near Amsterdam, Holland, June 20, 1572, and Nov. 12, 1573, because of their belief in the Eucharist. Religious animosity characterized the Dutch struggle for independence from Spain. When Alkmaar fell into the hands of the "Sea Beggars," as the partisans of the Prince of Orange called themselves, a renegade Catholic, Gerard of Brokenrode, betrayed five Franciscans into their hands: Daniel of Arendonck, guardian of the monastery in Alkmaar, Cornelius of Diest, John of Naarden, Louis of Arquennes, and the lay brother Adrian of Gouda. They were imprisoned and tortured because they would not abandon their belief in the Real Presence, and then hanged before the town hall. Their bodies were cast on the seacoast, where miraculous lights appeared afterwards. The lay brother Engelbert of Terborg was then captured and killed, and the next year Eylard Dirksz of Waterland and David Leendertsz were hanged after torture. The process of their beatification is pending.

Bibliography: F. V. D. BORNE, *De Katholike Encyclopaedie* 2:13. W. LAMPEN, LexThK[2] 1:338–339.

[F. D. S. BORAN]

ALL SAINTS, FEAST OF

A feast in honor of all the saints, celebrated in the West on November 1. The origins of this feast are uncertain. From a hymn composed by St. Ephraem in 359, it appears there was a commemoration of all the martyrs at Edessa on May 13 (*Carmen* 6; CSCO 219:27). By 411, however, the East Syrians kept this commemoration on the Friday after Easter [*Breviarium Syriacum,* ed. Mariani (Rome 1956) 34]. A sermon of St. John Chrysostom reveals that Antioch commemorated all the martyrs on the first Sunday after Pentecost (PG 50: 705). In the West, St. Maximus of Turin (5th century) preached in honor of all the martyrs on the same Sunday (*Hom.* 81; PL 57:427). The commemoration soon included nonmartyrs as well, for the *Comes of Würzburg* (7th century) lists this Sunday as *domi. in nat. scorum* or Sunday of the Nativity of the Saints (DACL 8.2:2292).

In 609 or 610, Boniface IV received the Roman Pantheon from the Emperor Phocas (d. 610) and dedicated it under the title *S. Maria ad Martyres* [*Liber Pontificalis,* ed. L. Duchesne (Paris 1955) 1:317]. The dedication occurred on May 13, and the anniversary was later observed with great festivity. Many see in this the origin of All Saints' Day. It may be, however, that the feast of May 13 was simply the anniversary of the dedication, or that Boniface chose this date because it was already associated with all the martyrs in the East. P. Radó accepts, while M. Righetti rejects, the theory that the date was chosen to offset the pagan *Lemuria* (placating of the gods), observed on May 9, 11, and 13.

How a feast of all the saints came to be celebrated on November 1 has not yet been demonstrated. Gregory III (731–741) dedicated an oratory in St. Peter's Basilica to all the saints (*Liber Pontificalis* 1:417). The date of the dedication is not known, but from this time on, a feast of all the saints is found in England on November 1 (see the martyrology of St. Bede, PL 94: 1087). Egbert of York had been ordained deacon in Rome in 732 and had received the pallium from Gregory himself. If Egbert is the founder of the English feast, he may have accepted November 1 as the dedication of Gregory's oratory.

In 799, Alcuin, who was educated at Egbert's cathedral of York, commended Arno, Archbishop of Salzburg, for observing the feast of November 1 (*Epist.* 91; PL 100:296). The feast, however, does not appear in Alcuin's supplement to the Gregorian Sacramentary.

According to John Beleth (d. *c.* 1165), Gregory IV (827–844) transferred the feast of May 13 to November 1 because provisions were inadequate for the numerous pilgrims coming to Rome for the feast in May (*Rationale divinorum officiorum,* 127; PL 202:133–134). G. Dix [*Shape of the Liturgy* (2d ed. Westminster 1954) 379] and J. H. Miller seem to accept this, while H. Schmidt, denying any connection between the two dates, believes the November feast originated in Gaul and was immediately adopted in Rome.

According to Ado of Vienne (800–875), this same pontiff asked Louis the Pious (778–840) to extend the feast of November 1 throughout the empire (*Martyrologium,* PL 123:387). Sigebert (d. 1112) in his chronicle, for some unknown reason, assigns the year 835 to this event (PL 160:159). In fact, in the 9th and 10th centuries, November 1 is listed as *Natale omnium sanctorum,* e.g., in the Sacramentary of Corbie (PL 78: 146). According to Sicard of Cremona (d. 1215), it was Gregory VII (1073–85) who definitively suppressed the feast of May 13 in favor of November 1 (*Mitrale,* PL 213:414). Indeed, in the 12th century, May 13 disappears from the liturgical books.

Other scholars, however, with good reason oppose such attempts to connect May 13 and November 1. J. Hennig believes May 13 was simply the anniversary of a dedication and not a feast of all the martyrs. He thinks that the oratory in St. Peter's has little to do with All Saints' Day, for there is no record of a celebration of the anniversary of this oratory, which was merely a side chapel and dedicated principally to Our Lady. Hennig places the origin of November 1 in Ireland, whence the feast passed to Northumberland and then to the Continent. There is an allusion to a feast of all the saints on November 1 in the oldest Irish martyrology, the *Félire of Oengus.* This book also gives a feast of all the saints of Europe on April 20 and of all the saints of Africa on December 23. Ireland and Britain were considered

Miniature in an "Horae B.V.M.," c. 1495, from a French atelier showing the beginning of the Litany of the Saints.

apart from Europe and so would want a feast of their own saints. The Irish often assigned the first of the month to important feasts, and since November 1 was also the beginning of the Celtic winter, it would have been a likely date for a feast of all the saints.

The texts of the Mass are borrowed from other feasts and commons of the martyrs. The second nocturn lessons, wrongly attributed to St. Bede, were written by Helisacher (9th century). The feast had a vigil from early times, and an octave was introduced by Sixtus IV (1471–84). Both vigil and octave were suppressed in 1955.

Bibliography: Miller FundLit 418–419. P. Radó, *Enchiridion liturgicum,* 2 v. (Rome 1961) 2:1391–95. Righetti 2:207–209. H. A. P. Schmidt, *Introductio in liturgiam occidentalem* (Rome 1959). J. Hennig, "The Meaning of All The Saints," MedSt 10 (1948) 147–161. P. Jounel, "Le Sanctoral romain du 8e au 12e siècles," *Maison-Dieu* 52 (1957) 59–88. Oengus the Culdee, *Martyrology* (*Félire*), ed. W. Stokes (HBradsh Soc 29; London 1905). **Illustration credit:** Philadelphia Museum of Art, Philip S. Collins Collection.

[C. SMITH]

ALL SOULS' DAY

A liturgical day of the Roman rite, commemorating all the faithful departed. It is observed on November 2 unless this be a Sunday, in which case it is transferred to November 3. On it the *Office for the Dead and *Requiem Masses are celebrated in suffrage for the deceased to help them attain the final purification necessary for being admitted to the *beatific vision. The Byzantine Churches observe a similar feast on the Saturdays before Septuagesima and Pentecost, the Armenian Church on Easter Monday.

Although the Church has always encouraged prayers for the deceased, she was slow in introducing a special liturgical day for this purpose. This may have been due to the tenacity with which superstitious pre-Christian rites for the dead continued to keep their hold on the faithful. Attempts of local churches to observe such a day can be traced back to the early Middle Ages, possibly arising in imitation of the commemorations of deceased members customary in monastic communities. In Spain, for example, Pentecost Monday was dedicated to the commemoration of the deceased in the time of St. Isidore of Seville (d. 636).

The choice of November 2 is traditionally attributed to St. *Odilo, the fifth abbot of Cluny (d. 1048), because of his decree that all Cluniac monasteries should follow the example of Cluny in offering special prayers and singing the Office for the Dead on the day following the feast of *All Saints. Due to the influence of Cluny the custom spread and was finally adopted universally in the Latin Church.

The custom of having each priest celebrate three Masses seems to have originated among the Spanish Dominicans during the 15th century. After this privilege was approved by *Benedict XIV in 1748, it was rapidly adopted throughout Spain, Portugal, and Latin America. During World War I, *Benedict XV, impressed by the number of war casualties and mindful of the numerous founded Masses that could no longer be fulfilled, granted to all priests the privilege of celebrating three Masses: of these one can be said for a particular intention, another must be celebrated for all the faithful departed, and the third for the intentions of the pope.

Throughout the Middle Ages it was popular belief that the souls in purgatory could appear on this day as will-o'-the-wisps, witches, toads, etc., to persons who had wronged them during their life. True Christian concern for the deceased along with superstition were the reasons for the great number of pious foundations for Masses and prayers on their behalf. Many different folkloric and popular customs and practices, especially various forms of food offerings, were associated with All Souls' Day. Among religious traditions, the parish procession to the cemetery, visiting the graves of relatives and friends, and leaving flowers and lights on the graves have remained almost universal.

Bibliography: K. A. H. Kellner, *Heortology* (St. Louis 1908) 326–328. T. Maertens and L. Heuschen, *Doctrine et pastorale de la liturgie de la mort* (Bruges 1957). C. A. Kneller, "Geschichtliches über die drei Messen am Allerseelentag," ZKathTh 42 (1918) 74–113. A. Dörrer, LexThK^{2} 1:349–350.

[A. CORNIDES]

ALLAMANO, GIUSEPPE, founder of the *Consolata Missionary Fathers and Consolata Missionary Sisters; b. Castelnuovo d'Asti, Italy, Jan. 21, 1851; d. Turin, Italy, Feb. 16, 1926. He was a nephew of St. Joseph *Cafasso. While a secondary school student he was under the spiritual guidance of St. John *Bosco. He studied at the seminary in Turin and was ordained (1873). In 1880 Allamano became rector of the Sanctuario della Consolata, a Marian shrine in Turin, to which a residence for priests was attached. Under his direction the Consolata became an important center of Marian piety. In 1883 he became a canon of Turin. He promoted many charitable works and won wide popularity as a preacher and confessor. He founded the Institute of the Consolata for Foreign Missions (1901) and a companion Missionary Sisters of the Consolata (1910), and directed both congregations until his death. He sent missionaries to Kenya (1902), Mozambique (1905), Ethiopia (1913), and Tanganyika (1922). The *decretum super scripta* in his cause for beatification was issued in 1960.

Bibliography: L. SALES, *Il servo di Dio Giuseppe Allamano* (3d ed. Turin 1944); *La dottrina spirituale del servo di Dio Can. G. Allamano* (Turin 1949). U. VIGLINO, EncCatt 1:892–893, with photo.

[T. P. JOYCE]

ALLARD, PAUL, French archeologist and historian; b. Rouen, Sept. 15, 1841; d. Senneville-sur-Fécamp, December 1916. Having been educated in literature at Rouen and in law at Paris, Allard served as a lawyer in Rouen, journeyed through Europe (1861–68) studying art and social conditions, particularly in Scotland and Holland, and was introduced to the catacombs and the study of Christian antiquity in Rome by G. B. de *Rossi. His career combined historical studies with an interest in the Christian social apostolate. As an admirer of Lacordaire, A. de Broglie, and Alexis de Tocqueville, he wrote articles and monographs on social problems, founded L'union catholique de la Seine-inférieure, and took an active part in four Catholic international scientific congresses held in France between 1888 and 1897. In 1872 Allard published a French adaptation of W. R. Brownlow and J. S. Northcote's edition of G. B. de Rossi's *Roma Sotterranea* (2d ed. Paris 1873); he then devoted his attention to a study of the acts and passions of the martyrs with the intention of preserving the substance of these legend-infested documents by means of archeological discoveries. Under the influence of E. Le Blant (d. 1897), the recorder of the Christian epigraphy of Gaul, he produced *Histoire des persécutions* (Paris 1885–90), *Ten Lectures on the Martyrs* (Eng. tr. London 1906), and the article "Martyre" in the *Dictionnaire Apologétique* 3 (Paris 1916) 334–492, which gave new impetus to the scientific study of the evidence whose import was generally exaggerated by pious writers and denied by rationalist historians. His earlier monographs dealt with *L'art païen sous les empereurs chrétiens* (Paris 1879) and *Esclaves, serfs et mainmortables* (Paris 1884) and had a bearing on contemporary anti-Christian polemics, as did *Julien l'Apostat* (3 v. Paris 1900–02) and his critiques of L. Havet, A. von Harnack, and F. Cumont. His *Saint Basile* appeared in 1903 and *Saint Sidoine Apollinaire* in 1909. Named director of the *Revue des questions historiques* in 1904, he contributed a large number of monographs and reviews to that journal, continuing its reputation for scholarly excellence.

Bibliography: *Répertoire de Bibliographie française,* v.1 (Paris 1937) 803–805. G. BARDY, *Catholicisme* 1:326. E. VACANDARD, *Dictionnaire pratique des connaissances religieuses,* ed. J. BRICOUT, 6 v. (Paris 1925–28) 1:138–139. P. J. HEALY, CE 1:317. H. LECLERCQ, DACL 6.2:2670–80. B. PESCI, EncCatt 1:893–894. J. GUIRAUD, RevQuestHist 3d ser. (1924) 381–423.

[J. BEAUDRY]

ALLEGORY. The word may be used of a type of literary work using allegory (e.g., *Pilgrim's Progress* or *Gulliver's Travels*), or it may apply more specifically to one kind of meaning. Based on literal meaning, allegory presents something not directly expressed; e.g., a Christian's trip through life built upon a traveler's trip through a country. It is an extension of *symbol (not of *metaphor, as is commonly supposed) and has been constantly used by literary artists from the earliest recorded times.

The treatment of allegory by medieval thinkers has been widely influential. St. Thomas Aquinas, dealing with the levels of meaning in Scripture (ST, I, a 1.10), sets forth four levels of meaning: the historical or literal, which expresses the thing the words directly speak of, and which furnishes the base for all other meanings; the allegorical, in which the thing referred to directly expresses also something else, for instance the blood of the Lamb saving the firstborn of the Jews expresses the salvific blood of Christ; the moral, in which what is literally expressed touches us directly and urges us to activity; and the anagogic, which expresses realities beyond time and space.

Thus in *Pilgrim's Progress,* the literal sense is the trip of the pilgrim through the countryside and its varied perils; the allegorical sense is the progress of a Christian from his baptism through all trials to heaven; the moral sense is the incentive to courage, to trust, and to effort; and the anagogic sense is the providence of God and the worth of the goal. (*See* BUNYAN, JOHN.)

*Dante applied these four levels to his own work, and since then critics, especially in our own time, have used them for discussion of allegory, particularly in complicated modern allegories such as those of T. S. Eliot and of *Joyce. Joyce's *Ulysses,* for example, has been dealt with according to the literal sense, the wanderings of Stephen and Bloom in Dublin on June 16, 1904; the allegorical sense, referring both to the *Odyssey* and to man's trip through life; the moral sense, referring to such things as avoiding Stephen's painful scruples and imitating Bloom's kindness; and the anagogic sense, referring to the mysterious goals toward which man's nature urges him, expressed negatively here in these lost Irish souls.

See also BIBLE, VI (EXEGESIS).

Bibliography: H. DE LUBAC, *Exégèse médiévale,* 2 v. (Paris 1959–64). N. ARVIN, *Herman Melville* (New York 1950) ch. "The Whale." J. C. JOOSEN and J. H. WASZINK, ReallexAntChr 1:283–293, with bibliog. J. PÉPIN, *Mythe et allégorie* (Paris 1957).

[R. BOYLE]

ALLEGORY, PAGAN USE OF. In the earliest Greco-Roman tradition allegory probably had a twofold origin: the popular use of riddles and puzzles and that of ambiguity in oracular replies. The anonymous *Rhetorica ad Herennium,* from the age of Cicero, distinguishes three types of allegory (*Rhet.* 4.34.46): a series of linked metaphors, the use of fictional names for historical persons, and irony. Quintilian (*Institutes of Oratory* 8.6.52) also includes riddles and puzzles. The allegorical interpretation of Homer arose as early as the 5th century B.C. when philosophers and later grammarians used allegory to prove that Homer was the first moral philosopher (see, e.g., Horace, *Epistles* 1.2.1–31). The early Stoics in particular emphasized allegory in the explanation of Homer and in etymology. The later Stoics were more circumspect in employing allegorical interpretation. In late paganism, the Neoplatonists—with the exception, however, of Plotinus—revived the allegorical method of interpretation and used it widely in their works. Through the use of allegorical interpretation they gave late paganism a comprehensive, systematic form.

The main influence on Christian allegory was undoubtedly the eclectic method of *Philo Judaeus of Alexandria (d. A.D. 45). Well read in Plato and the Stoics, he developed the rabbinical system of exegesis to the point of appealing to a higher, spiritual sense called the "enigma" in dealing with difficult passages in the Pentateuch. It was largely from Philo that the Alexandrian school (*see* ALEXANDRIA, SCHOOL OF) developed its exegetical method, employing allegorical interpretation in a universal and highly elaborate manner.

Bibliography: J. TATE, OxClDict 38–39. H. A. WOLFSON, *The Philosophy of the Church Fathers,* v.1 (Cambridge, Mass. 1956) 24–72. J. C. JOOSEN and J. H. WASZINK, ReallexAntChr 1:283–293, with bibliog.

[H. MUSURILLO]

ALLEGORY IN THE BIBLE. In the terminology of Greek rhetoric allegory is distinguished from parable (*see* PARABLES OF JESUS). An allegory is a developed metaphor; a parable is a developed simile. Allegory tends to portray abstract truth in symbolic guise, and in an allegory the details and characters of the narrative have an assigned meaning. In the OT there is no such distinction, for the Hebrew *māšāl* covers the gamut of figurative language, including parable and allegory. We do not find prolonged allegories, although some have attempted (rather unsuccessfully) to see consistent allegorical narrative in the *Canticle of Canticles. There is an allegory of old age in Eccl 12.1–7. Ezechiel is adept at simple allegories, e.g., 17.2–24, where the birds represent kings. The visions of apocalyptic literature, e.g., Daniel ch. 7, are akin to allegory. In the NT there is a Pauline allegory on the armor of salvation in Eph 6.13–17. Although the Synoptic Gospels use the Greek term παραβολή (parable), this term is much wider than parable and covers simple allegory as well. Some of the parables have allegorical features, and the explanations offered in the Gospels for some of the parables are allegorical in their identification of details and characters. The imagery found in John is a blend of allegory and parable.

[R. E. BROWN]

ALLEGRANZA, JOSEPH, theologian, archeologist; b. Milan, 1713; d. there, 1785. He belonged to the Milanese Dominican monastery of San Eustorgio and took the habit at Brescia in 1731. After teaching theology at Novara and Vercelli, he took his doctorate in theology at Rome in 1746. He then directed his efforts particularly to archeological researches. His extensive travels in Italy, southern France, and on the Island of Malta provided him with many archeological finds as well as useful friendships. After 1755 he lived almost entirely at Milan, where in 1765 he had the responsibility for cataloging the Pertusati library. For this he was awarded a gold medal from the Empress Maria Theresa. Among his numerous writings of a historical-archeological and antiquarian nature are: *Spiegazione, e riflessioni sopra alcuni sacri monumenti antichi di Milano* (Milan 1757); *De sepulcris christianis in aedibus sacris* (Milan 1773); and *Opusculi eruditi latini ed italiani* (Cremona 1781).

Bibliography: R. COULON, DHGE 2:489–493. G. FERRETTO, *Note storico-bibliografiche di archeologia cristiana* (Vatican City 1942) 280–282, 339.

[A. L. REDIGONDA]

ALLEGRI, GREGORIO, priest, composer of the Roman baroque; b. Rome, 1582; d. Rome, Feb. 17, 1652. As a boy he sang under G. B. Nanino at S. Luigi dei Francesi church in Rome from 1591 until his voice changed; he also sang and studied under G. M. *Nanino. In 1629, after he had established his reputation as a composer, he was appointed to the papal choir by Urban VIII. As a composer of the late Roman school, Allegri favored the *stile antico,* with a view to preserving the *Palestrina tradition, already regarded as the model for liturgical purposes. His most notable work is the nine-voice, two-choir *Miserere,* which was written down from memory by both *Mozart and *Mendelssohn and is still performed in the Sistine Chapel during Holy Week. Many other sacred works exist in MS, and concertini for various voice groupings, motets for two to six voices, and a forerunner of the string quartet were published during his lifetime.

See also MUSIC, SACRED, HISTORY OF, 5.

Bibliography: G. ALLEGRI, *Miserere,* ed. F. HABERL (Augsburg 1936). A. CAMETTI, *Rivista musicale Italiana* 22 (1915) 596–608. K. G. FELLERER, MusGG 1:329–330.

[F. J. GUENTNER]

ALLELUIA

A Hebrew word derived from *hallelû* (imperative of *hillel,* to praise) and *Jah* (abbreviated form of *Jahvè:* God) that is used in Christian liturgies. This article treats (1) the present use of the Alleluia in the Roman rite, (2) the history before musical notation, and (3) the various musical and liturgical uses.

The Present Use in the Roman Rite. Because of its joyful character, present usage excludes it from the liturgy of the dead and from Septuagesima Sunday to the Easter Vigil Mass. It is found in the following forms: as a responsory, as an acclamation added to or inserted in a liturgical text, and as an antiphon. As a responsory it is an ornate chant found in the Roman rite only in the Mass and is preceded by the Gradual and followed by the Gospel. In the Easter season the Gradual is omitted and a second Alleluia is sung. On the principal feasts of the year and in the Easter season one, two, or three Alleluias can be added to the standard Mass and Office texts. During the Easter season the standard texts of antiphons may even be dropped and the world alleluia substituted instead.

History before Musical Notation. From the beginning of the Christian liturgy there seemed no need to translate this Hebrew word of joy. The present spelling is taken from the Septuagint form Ἀλλελούια. Many patristic texts show that the primitive Church preserved the melismatic character of the Alleluia as found among the Hebrews. "Nam sicut in melodia hoc compositum nomen [Alleluia] diversos tonos recipit, ita et multiplices causas ad vim suae praedicationis assumit" (Cassiodorus, PalLat 70.811). *Jubilatio, melodiae tropi,* and even *toni* are terms used to express the musical vocalizations characteristic of the execution of the Alleluia. Other texts indicate the early use of the word as an acclamation. (See Ap 19.1–7.) "Diligentiones in orando subjungere in orationibus Alleluia solent" (Tertullian, Pal Lat 1.1304). Later, Cassian and St. Benedict indicate the frequent addition of the word to Psalm verses in the recitation of the Office. Amalarius, writing about 840, is the first to describe the substitution of the word Alleluia for the texts of standard antiphons. "Antiphonae aliquae sunt post responsorios collectae, quarum sonus redactus est in sola Alleluia sibi invicem conjuncta" (*Studi e testi* 140:108).

Two problems have been much discussed by scholars: the role of St. Gregory in specifying the times when the Alleluia could be used and the origin of the verse of the Mass Alleluia. The theory generally accepted is that the Alleluia became a part of the Mass by order of Pope Damasus (368–384) at the request of St. Jerome and in imitation of the Church of Jerusalem. Later it was restricted to Easter, but in the 5th century extended to the whole Easter season. St. Gregory, in turn, extended its use to the entire year with the exception of the penitential season. (For the controversy see Froger and Wellesz in the bibliography.) The oldest references to the Alleluia do not mention the verses, but they are always present in the MS tradition. From the evidence available it is impossible to establish the exact date when the Alleluia as a responsory assumed the form it now has.

The Various Musical and Liturgical Uses of the Alleluia. A study of the Alleluia in each of the Western rites shows both interesting parallels and significant differences.

Gregorian Chant. In the earliest chant MSS only the Alleluias for Masses on principal feasts were written in the body of the MS; the others were placed in a special fascicle at the end. The selection of the Alleluia for the Sundays and most of the feasts was left to the cantor. For this reason, the first attempts to assign a specific Alleluia for each Mass were not uniform and resulted in various medieval traditions, important for determining the scriptorium from which a MS comes.

The responsorial Alleluia of the Roman Mass is sung as follows: Alleluia (intoned by soloist), alleluia with jubilus (sung by choir), verse (sung by soloist with the choir joining in at the end), alleluia with jubilus (sung by the choir). In the Middle Ages the Alleluia was not repeated after the verse on ferial days, and on special feasts two veses were sometimes sung as in the Byzantine tradition. The musical structure of the Alleluia and its verses shows great variety. The Alleluia melody may be simple or contain several melodic repetitions, especially in the melisma or jubilus, while the melody of the verse may be new or derived from the Alleluia melody. Frequently the end of the verse repeats the jubilus only, sometimes it repeats the entire melody of the Alleluia plus jubilus, while other verses show no melodic relationship to the Alleluia and jubilus but have a different melody (such as *Venite exultemus, Te decet,* and *Paratum cor*). The frequent statement that the form of the Alleluia is a simple A-B-A is textually correct but musically erroneous. The protus and tetrardus modes are most frequent; the tritus—as in Byzantine chant—is rare. The responsory Alleluia is used only at Mass in the Roman rite, although Amalarius mentions (*op. cit.* 105) three Alleluia responses he had found but had not copied into his own antiphonary.

The addition of two or three Alleluias to the texts of the Mass and Office is common in Gregorian chant. Musically they are distinct from the responsory Alleluia in that they are more simple; if they have a melisma it is generally found on the syllable "le" and not the last syllable. Some of these are thought to be of Gallican origin. The substitution of the word Alleluia for the texts of antiphons is most common in the Roman rite as the example shows.

Di - - xit Do - mi - nus Do - mi - no me - - o:
Se - de - a dax - tris me - is. Al - le - lu - ia,
Al - - le - - lu - - ia, Al - - le - - lu - ia.

In the Old Roman repertory (*see* GREGORIAN CHANT) the number of Alleluias in the Mass is indeed much smaller, only 13 melodies being found for the Alleluia that precedes the verse. When the Alleluia is repeated after the verse, a new and longer jubilus is found on larger feasts, but one that is generally related musically to the first jubilus in that it is enlarged by melodic repetitions and ornaments. The jubilus melisma is not found at the end of the verse except for the Alleluia *Beatus vir.* The interesting Alleluias for Vespers of Paschal week have two or three verses and highly developed melismas.

Mozarabic Chant. The Alleluia of the Mass was sung after the Gospel, not before. More than one verse is not found, and frequently the jubilus is also found at the end of the verse. The Alleluia jubilus when repeated after the verse may be new (as in *Vincenti dabo* and *In die resurrectionis*) or a development of the first. The Mozarabic repertory of Mass Alleluias is richer than the Old Roman and Ambrosian. The addition of Alleluias to the *Sono* (verse sung at beginning of Vespers) and *Sacrificium* (Offertory) show long and varied melismas on the syllable "le." The substitution of the text Alleluia for standard antiphons, however, is not found.

Ambrosian Chant. The Ambrosian Mass Alleluias ignore the tritus modes and, like the Old Roman, are few in number. Each one, however, has three different melismas or jubiluses. The first has no name, but the second is called *melodiae primae* and the third *melodiae secundae,* the latter being quite developed. A special melisma called the *francigena* is sometimes added to make a fourth. The ritual for singing all of this was complicated and cannot be totally unraveled. The same type of responsorial Alleluia is found also in the Ambrosian Office, especially at Vespers. The other phenomena, i.e., additional Alleluias and substitution for standard texts, are also found in the Ambrosian chant.

The "Longissimae Melodiae." As early as the 9th century there developed in the Gregorian chant a body of elaborate Alleluia melodies, not confused with the liturgical Alleluias but written as a separate collection; they were given strange and suggestive names—*Frigdola, Graeca, Hypodiaconissa, Organa, Nostra tuba, Romana,* etc. They were called "longissimae melodiae" by

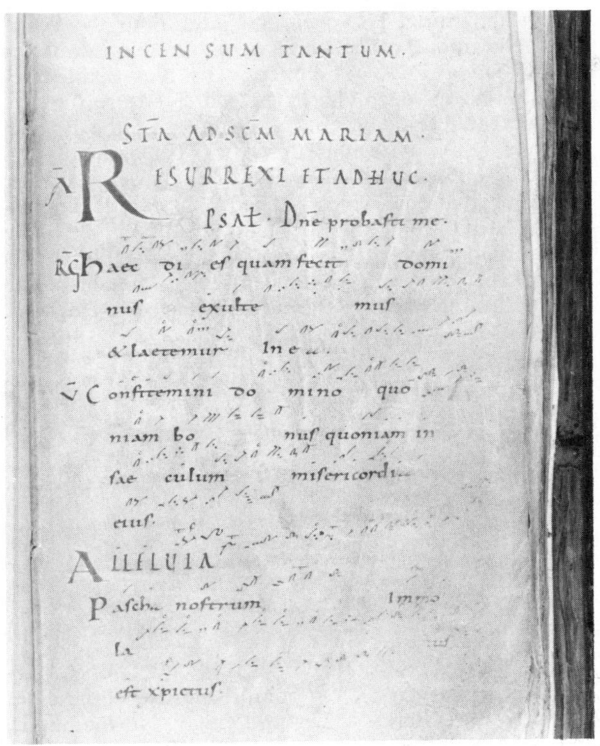

"Allelulia Pascha nostrum" in a cantorium written c. 900 (Codex San. 359, page 107, detail).

Notker and certainly are related to the phenomenon of the longer melismas of the Old Roman, Mozarabic, and Ambrosian liturgical Alleluias. These "longissimae melodiae" are important for the history of the *Sequence into which they developed.

Bibliography: J. Glibotic, "De cantu Alleluia in patribus saeculo VII antiquioribus," EphemLiturg 50 (1936) 101–123. J. Froger, "L'Alleluia dans l'usage romain et la réforme de St. Grégoire," *ibid.* 62 (1948) 6–48. E. Wellesz, "Gregory the Great's Letter on the Alleluia," *Annales musicologiques* 2 (1954) 1–26. B. Stäblein, MusGG 1:331–350. L. Brou, "L'Alleluia dans la liturgie mozarabe," *Annuario musical* 6 (1951) 3–90. P. Wagner, DACL 1:1226–29. F. Gennrich, *Grundiss einer Formenlehre des mittelalterlichen Liedes* (Halle 1932) 107–118. Apel GregCh 375–392. **Illustration credit:** Fig. 2, Stiftsbibliothek St. Gallen.

[R. G. WEAKLAND]

ALLEN, EDWARD PATRICK, bishop; b. Lowell, Mass., March 17, 1853; d. Mobile, Ala., Oct. 21, 1926. The son of John and Mary (Egan) Allen, he attended the public schools of Lowell and Lowell Commercial College before entering Mt. St. Mary's College, Emmitsburg, Md., where he received the M.A. (1878). After completing his studies for the priesthood, he was ordained at Emmitsburg on Dec. 17, 1881, by Bp. Thomas A. Becker. Allen first taught at Mt. St. Mary's, then worked for 2 years in the Archdiocese of Boston, Mass., returning to Emmitsburg in 1884. After serving briefly as vice president and treasurer of the college, he was elected president in June 1885. On Jan. 26, 1897, he was appointed fifth bishop of Mobile (redesignated *Mobile-Birmingham in 1954); he was consecrated by Cardinal James Gibbons in Baltimore, Md., on May 16 and installed in his diocese on May 30. During the next 30 years the Catholic population in the diocese increased from 17,000 to 48,000; Allen's administrative ability and sound fiscal policy enabled the diocese to keep pace with this growth by an adequate expansion of clergy, churches, and social services. Particular effort was made in the Negro apostolate through the introduction of the *Josephite fathers, and significant progress was achieved in the hitherto undeveloped rural areas of the diocese.

Bibliography: Archives, Diocese of Mobile-Birmingham.

[O. H. LIPSCOMB]

ALLEN, FRANCES MARGARET, SISTER, nurse; b. Sunderland, Vt., Nov. 13, 1784; d. Montreal, Canada, Dec. 10, 1819. She was the first daughter of Revolutionary War hero Ethan Allen and his second wife, Frances Montresor Buchanan. Three years after her birth, the family moved to Burlington, Vt., and 2 years later her father died. She grew up in a period of religious revival prompted in part by reaction against her father's deistic work, *Reason: The Only Oracle of Man* (1784). Although the revival affected her mother and her stepfather, Jabez Penniman, she remained skeptical. In 1807 she entered the school of the Sisters of Notre Dame in Montreal, where she experienced a spiritual crisis that led her to embrace Catholicism. When she announced her desire to become a nun, Dr. and Mrs. Penniman brought her home. Nevertheless, she returned to Montreal, accompanied by her mother, and on Sept. 20, 1809, entered the nursing order of the Sisters of the Hôtel-Dieu of St. Joseph. She pronounced her vows on March 18, 1811, and devoted herself to pharmacy. During the War of 1812, when the Hôtel-Dieu became a military hospital, she was instrumental in bringing converts into the Catholic Church. Long after her death, a hospital was erected (1894) on a plot that once formed a part of her father's farm, and the Sister Hospitallers of the Hôtel-Dieu were requested to operate it.

Bibliography: Archives, Hôtel-Dieu, Montreal. L. Gibson, *Some Anglo-American Converts to Catholicism Prior to 1829* (Washington 1943) 171–190. H. Morrissey, *Ethan Allen's Daughter* (Quebec 1941).

[L. GIBSON]

ALLEN, GEORGE, educator, author; b. Milton, Vt., Dec. 17, 1808; d. Worcester, Mass., May 28, 1876. Although his parents, Herman and Sarah (Prentiss) Allen, were Protestant, they sent him to Canada to study French in the household of a Catholic priest. In 1823 Allen entered the University of Vermont, Burlington, from which he graduated in 1827. He was professor of languages at Georgia, Vt., from 1828 to 1830. Following a brief career as a lawyer and his marriage to Mary Hancock Withington in 1831, he turned his attention to religion. He began to study theology and was ordained an Episcopal minister in 1834. He served as rector of a church in St. Albans, Vt., until 1837, when he returned to teaching as professor of languages at Delaware College, Newark. In 1845 he was named to the chair of Latin and Greek at the University of Pennsylvania, Philadelphia. There he was influenced by the *Oxford Movement and became a convert to Catholicism (1847). Allen was the author of several books, including *The Remains of W. S. Graham* (1849) and *The Life of Philidor* (1863).

Bibliography: T. Woody, DAB 1:190. [J. L. MORRISON]

ALLEN, WILLIAM

Cardinal, founder of the college at Douai; b. Rossall, Lancashire, 1532; d. Rome, Oct. 16, 1594. He was admitted to Oriel College, Oxford (1547) and took his M.A. in 1554. He became principal of St. Mary's Hall, Oxford, in 1556 but resigned soon after the accession of Elizabeth I. He remained in Oxford until 1561 and then went to Louvain to join the distinguished group of English scholars in exile. He returned to England for health reasons in 1562 and spent 3 years in Lancashire, Oxfordshire, and Norfolk attempting to stiffen Catholic resistance to the religious changes, taking what was then an unusual line among English Catholics, that it was not permissible to be present at Anglican services. He went into exile for the second time and was ordained in 1565. In 1568, with the help of John Vendeville, one of the professors in the new University of *Douai (Douay), he established, by his own initiative and in the face of considerable criticism and opposition, a college at Douai for the training of priests for England. Douai became the major educational center for English Catholics, and its long-term significance is summed up by Philip Hughes's comment: "Here, under God, was the principal means of preserving the Catholic Church in England for the next two hundred years."

Leader of the Exiles. William Allen was regarded as the leader of English Catholics and was called to Rome as adviser on English affairs in 1575, 1579, and 1585, after which he remained in Rome until his death. In 1587, at the request of Philip II, King of Spain, and because of the role he was intended to play as archbishop of Canterbury and Lord Chancellor if the Armada succeeded, Sixtus V made him a cardinal.

Probably from about the mid-1570s Allen was deeply involved in various enterprises to overthrow the Elizabethan government and to support a rival claimant to the throne when Elizabeth I was removed from the scene. With Robert *Persons and others he was a leader of the "Spanish party" among English Catholics abroad. Allen maintained that the seminary priests sent to England came purely for religious reasons and had no political intentions. In his *Defence of the English Catholics* (1584), he argued that the priests were not traitors and were not working for the overthrow of the regime. With few exceptions this is undoubtedly true, but Allen and his associates were certainly using political means to try to secure their end—the preservation of the Catholic religion in England. They believed that unless action were taken by Catholic rulers in Europe, English Catholicism would be destroyed. Allen's own actions from the mid-1570s and his own statements in his *Defence of Sir William Stanley's Surrender of Deventer* (1587) and in his *Admonition to the Nobility and People of England and Ireland* (1588), which was intended for distribution if the Armada secured a bridgehead, show clearly that he considered that Elizabeth had forfeited any claim to the loyalty of Catholics. This attitude is logical and understandable, but it placed the seminary priests and the Jesuits in an awkward position in relation to the government and lent weight to the charge that the priests were softening up English Catholics so that they would become traitors as soon as the invaders landed.

Allen's Achievements. Allen's varied activities included important contributions to contemporary controversial writing. His profound interest in the Scriptures led, among other work, to the production of the Rheims-Douay New Testament. His remarkable personality and his deep charity helped to ensure the success of Douai and the holding together of the English Catholic body. After his death the College ran into many difficulties, partly because of the absence of any formal regulations, which he had considered unnecessary. The divisions among English Catholics at home and abroad, which were already considerable in his lifetime, became even more deep-seated after his death and did lasting harm to the Catholic cause in England.

Bibliography: Works. *Letters and Memorials,* ed. T. F. KNOX (London 1882); *The First and Second Diaries of the English College, Douay,* ed. T. F. KNOX (London 1878); "Some Correspondence of Cardinal Allen, 1579–85," ed. P. RYAN in Cath RecSoc (Aberdeen 1911) 7:12–105, additional letters. Literature. P. K. GUILDAY, *The English Catholic Refugees on the Continent 1558–1795* (New York 1914). A. C. SOUTHERN, *Elizabethan Recusant Prose, 1559–1582* (London 1950). B. CAMM, *Cardinal William Allen* (New York 1909). M. HAILE, *An Elizabethan Cardinal* (New York 1914). G. MATTINGLY, *The Armada* (Boston 1959); "William Allen and Catholic Propaganda in England" *Travaux d'Humanisme et Renaissance* 28 (1957) 325–339. Hughes RE. T. COOPER, DNB 1:314–322. C. TESTORE, EncCatt 1:901–903. F. STEGMÜLLER, LexThK² 1:346–347.

[P. MCGRATH]

ALLENTOWN, DIOCESE OF (ALANOPOLITANA), a jurisdiction comprising five counties in Pennsylvania (Berks, Carbon, Lehigh, Northampton, and Schuylkill) established Jan. 28, 1961, by separation from the Archdiocese of *Philadelphia. Bishop Joseph McShea, who had served 9 years as auxiliary of Philadelphia, was installed as Allentown's first bishop April 11, 1961. In 1964 the diocese numbered 242,828 Catholics in a total population of 935,617; there were 151 parishes and the Cathedral of St. Catharine of Siena, 289 diocesan priests, 66 religious priests, 1,116 sisters, 31 brothers, and 141 seminarians. In 1962 a total of $10.5 million was raised to construct a college, three new high schools, and additions to three existing high schools. The Allentown College (1965), located in Center Valley, and Alvernia College (1958), Reading, head an educational system numbering, in 1964, 15 secondary schools (8,378 students) and 101 elementary schools (30,824 students). An additional 16,539 public school students received religious instruction. One protective institution for girls, four hospitals with a total of 1,159 beds, three orphanages and infant asylums, and four homes for the aged served the charitable and

Cathedral of St. Catharine of Siena, Allentown, Pa.

hospital needs of the diocese. A central social agency office in Allentown maintains branch offices in Reading and Shenandoah.

[D. B. THOMPSON]

ALLERS, RUDOLF, philosopher and psychiatrist; b. Vienna, Jan. 13, 1883; d. Hyattsville, Md., Dec. 18, 1963. He studied at the Vienna Gymnasium and at the Medical School of the University of Vienna, where he was taught by S. *Freud. He received his M.D. in 1908, then did his hospital internship while working in a chemical laboratory. This training was of value in his later experimental work in neurophysiology and perception. From 1908 on Allers specialized in psychiatry and in 1913 became an instructor in psychiatry at the Medical School of the University of Munich. During World War I he served in the surgeons' corps of the Austrian Army. From 1918 to 1938 he combined teaching and laboratory research at the Medical School of the University of Vienna with private practice. Encouraged by A. *Gemelli, he studied philosophy at Milan and in 1934 received a doctorate in philosophy. In 1938 he became professor of psychology at The Catholic University of America; in 1948, professor of philosophy at Georgetown University. He was awarded the Cardinal Spellman–Aquinas Medal by the American Catholic Philosophical Association in 1960.

Allers worked always in the context of his theory that the continuity between the medieval and modern worlds is greater than has been suspected. He believed that one cannot deal with man theoretically for any length of time without developing at least an implicit philosophical framework of interpretation, and stressed the need for a distinctive psychological method of treating the problems of man. *The Psychology of Character* is his major treatise in the study of man as a moral personality. His writings reflect a lifelong concern with phenomenology and existentialism.

Bibliography: Works. *Über Schädelschüsse* (Berlin 1916); *Das Werden der sittlichen Person* (Freiburg 1929), tr. E. B. STRAUSS, *The Psychology of Character* (New York 1931); *Self Improvement* (New York 1939); *Character Education in Adolescence* (New York 1940); *Sex Psychology in Education*, tr. S. A. RAEMERS (St Louis 1937); *The New Psychologies* (New York 1933); *The Successful Error* (New York 1941); *Existentialism and Psychiatry* (Springfield, Ill. 1961). Literature. J. COLLINS, "The Work of Rudolf Allers," NewSchol 38 (1964) 281–309.

[J. C. CUNNINGHAM]

ALLGEIER, FRANZ ARTHUR, Biblical scholar; b. Wehr (Baden), Germany, Oct. 23, 1882; d. Freiburg im Breisgau, Germany, July 4, 1952. After his seminary studies (1902–06) and ordination (1906), he did graduate work in classical languages at the University of Freiburg (1907–10) and in Semitic languages at the University of Berlin (1912–14), receiving the doctorates in theology in 1910 and in philosophy in 1915. In this year he was appointed instructor in Biblical languages in the theological faculty at Freiburg, and in 1919 he succeeded his former teacher G. *Hoberg as professor of OT literature at the same institution. Because of his special training and the obstacles then placed by ecclesiastical authorities on the way toward the publication of exegetical works, he chose as his chief field of work the study of the transmission of the Greek and Latin versions of the Bible, while showing a strong interest in general historical research. From 1929 to 1941 he was general secretary of the *Görres-Gesellschaft; in 1937 he was made a papal domestic prelate, in 1941, consultor of the *Pontifical Biblical Commission, and in 1945, rector of the University of Freiburg. He retired in 1951.

Allgeier's publications include (among others): *Über Doppelberichte in der Genesis* (1911); *Die westsyrische Überlieferung des Siebenschläferlegende* (1915); *Das Buch des Predigers* in the "Bonner Bibel" (1925); *Die altlateinischen Psalterien* (1928); *Bruchstücke eines altlat. Psalters aus St. Gallen* (1929); *Biblische Zeitgeschichte* (1937); *Die Chester Beatty-Papyri zum Pentateuch* (1938); *Die Psalmen der Vulgata* (1940); *Die neue Psalmenübersetzung* (1940).

Bibliography: A. DEISSLER, *Oberrheinisches Pastoralblatt* 53 (1952) 281–287; LexThK[2] 1:352.

[A. DEISSLER]

ALLIES, THOMAS WILLIAM, writer; b. Midsomer Norton, Somersetshire, Feb. 12, 1813; d. London, June 17, 1903. He was the son of the Rev. Thomas Allies and his first wife Frances Elizabeth Fripp. Introspective and bookish, he distinguished himself at both Bristol Grammar School and Eton College. After obtaining his M.A. degree (1832) at Wadham College, Oxford, he became a fellow there. He took Anglican orders (1838), and became examining chaplain to Bishop Bloomfield of London. This work he found congenial, but the bishop considered his views influenced by the *Oxford Movement, and soon presented him with the small rural parish of Launton. Here, Allies began an intensive study of the *Fathers of the Church, which ultimately led him into the Roman Catholic Church (1850). He married (1840) Eliza Hall Newman, who preceded him into the Church. After his conversion he taught private pupils until Cardinal *Wiseman appointed him (1853) secretary to the Catholic Poor School Committee. In this post he rendered distinguished service until 1890. *Newman offered him the chair of modern history in the Catholic University of Ireland, but the offer did not reach fruition. Of his many publications, the most important are his *Journal in France* (1849) and the *Formation of Christendom* (8 v. 1861–95).

Bibliography: T. W. ALLIES, *A Life's Decision* (London 1880). M. H. ALLIES, *Thomas William Allies* (London 1907). G. DONALD, *Men Who Left the Movement* (London 1933).

[V. A. MC CLELLAND]

ALLIOLI, JOSEPH VON, Scripture scholar; b. Sulzbach, Germany, Aug. 10, 1793; d. Augsburg, Germany, May 22, 1873. After studying theology at Landshut, he was ordained at Regensburg in 1816. He studied Oriental languages at Vienna, Rome, and Paris from 1818 to 1820 and became professor in the university at Landshut in 1824. Two years later Allioli was transferred to the University of Munich. In 1835, because of a weak throat, he had to resign, and he accepted a canonry at Regensburg. In 1838 he became dean of the chapter at Augsburg. Allioli's most important work was his German translation of the Bible, *Übersetzung der heiligen Schriften Alten und Neuen Testaments, aus der Vulgata, mit Bezug auf den Grundtext, neu übersetzt und mit kurzen Anmerkungen erläutert* (6 v. Nuremberg 1830–32; 10th ed., A. Arndt, ed., Regensburg 1899–1901). On May 11, 1830, this work received a papal commendation, and for a century it was the most widely used Catholic version of the Bible in German. Among his other works are: *Aphorismen über den Zusammenhang der heiligen Schrift Alten und Neuen Testaments, aus der Idee des Reichs Gottes* (Regensburg 1819); *Häusliche Alterthümer der Hebräer nebst biblischer Geographie* (Landshut 1821); *Biblische Alterthümer* (Landshut 1825); and *Handbuch der biblischen Alterthumskunde* (in cooperation with P. *Gratz and D. B. *Haneberg, Landshut 1843–44).

Bibliography: K. STAAB, LexThK² 1:352. P. DE AMBROGGI, EncCatt 1:905. F. VIGOUROUX, DB 1.1:388–389.

[M. C. MC GARRAGHY]

ALLO, ERNEST BERNARD, Scripture scholar, who won renown in the fields of Biblical exegesis and comparative religion; b. Quintin, France, Feb. 3, 1873; d. Saulchoir, Paris, Jan. 19, 1945. He interrupted medical studies to enter the Dominican order. In 1900 he went to Mossul, Iraq, to teach theology in the Chaldean seminary and in 1903 to the École Biblique in Jerusalem. In 1905 Allo was assigned to the University of Fribourg, Switzerland, where he spent his entire teaching career. In 1930 the university named him to the newly created chair of the history of religions. In 1938 he retired to the Saulchoir where he died. Allo was considered one of the foremost Catholic exegetes of his time. His commentaries on the Apocalypse and 1 and 2 Corinthians are regarded as representative of modern scientific exegetical approach. In his *Foi et Systèmes* (1908), he defended orthodox positions against *Modernism with a moderate reasonableness. He became expert in the history of religions to show the transcendence of Christian revelation above other religions and published *Plaies d'Europe et baumes de Gange* (1931), a study of Hinduism. His final work was *Évangile et Évangelistes* (1944).

Bibliography: C. SPICQ, LexThK² 1:355.

[A. SMITH]

ALLOUEZ, CLAUDE JEAN, Jesuit missionary; b. Saint Didier-en-Forez, France, June 6, 1622; d. near Niles, Mich., Aug. 27–28, 1689. He joined the Jesuits at Toulouse (1639), studied there and at Billom and Rodez, and was ordained in 1655. He was 36 when he arrived in Canada, where he spent the next 7 years ministering to the settlers in the Saint Lawrence area. In 1665 he was named vicar-general to Bp. F. de M. Laval of Quebec. Allouez's assignment to the Great Lakes region marked the first step toward the organization of the hierarchy in the central part of what later became the U.S. From 1665 to 1689 he traveled the Great Lakes region in all directions—Huron, Superior, Erie, Michigan—covering 3,000 miles, preaching to more than 20 Indian tribes, and, it is said, baptizing about 10,000 persons. In 1667 he went to Lake Nipigon and celebrated the first Mass to be offered within the boundaries of the present Diocese of Fort-William, Ontario. He worked among the Illinois, prepared a prayer book in Illinois and French, laid the foundations for St. Francis Xavier Mission (1673), and wrote *Récit d'un 3ᵉ voyage fait aux Illinois* (*c.* 1679). The *Relations* of 1667 to 1676 have preserved numerous extracts from his journals; the edition of 1671 contains a portion of the address he delivered the preceding year at Sault Sainte Marie, Mich., when M. S. F. de Saint-Lusson took possession of the territories of the West in the name of the King of France. Allouez is honored in the U.S., especially in Wisconsin, where in 1899 the Wisconsin Historical Society raised a monument to him at De Pere, the center of his missionary activities.

Bibliography: "Narrative of a 3rd Voyage to the Illinois made by Father Claude Allouez," *Jesuit Relations and Allied Documents,* ed. R. G. THWAITES, 73 v. (Cleveland 1896–1901; New York 1959–) 60:148–167, and general intro. Garraghan JMUS 1:3–4. T. J. CAMPBELL, *Pioneer Priests of North America,* 3 v. (New York 1908–19) 3:147–164. F. J. NELLIGAN, "The Visit of Father Allouez to Lake Nipigon in 1667," *Canadian Catholic Historical Association Report* (1956) 41–52.

[L. POULIOT]

ALMA

The Hebrew word *'almâ* used to describe the mother of *Emmanuel in the divine oracle delivered to King Achaz of Juda (735–715 B.C.) by the prophet *Isaia (Is 7.14). The Hebrew substantive is the feminine counterpart of the rare *'elem,* "young lad," and ordinarily designates a young girl of marriageable age until the birth of her first child, prescinding entirely from her actual marital or virginal status. (The Hebrew word for expressing "virgin" as such is *bᵉtûlâ.*) A Ugaritic cognate, *ǵlmt,* is attested in approximately the same meaning as *alma;* but the Ugaritic literary parallel adduced for the prophecy in the poem of Nikkal is based on a highly questionable textual restoration. In the OT itself, this prophecy exhibits the literary characteristics of the genre known as "birth *oracle" (*Geburtsorakel*), foretelling a child's birth, name, food, and future circumstances of life (cf. Jgs 13.3–5; Lk 1.13–17).

The Septuagint translation in choosing to render *alma* in this passage by παρθένος (rather than νεᾶνις) furnishes a pre-Christian interpretation and greater specification of the somewhat neutral Hebrew expression by making explicit the notion of "virginity" connected with the mother of Emmanuel. In Mt 1.23 the angel appearing to Joseph in a dream is portrayed as citing the Septuagint version of the prophecy of Emmanuel and his virgin mother and applying it to Mary and her expected child. Subsequent Christian translations and interpretations of the passage in antiquity generally followed the lead of the Septuagint.

Because of its use in Matthew, this prophecy has usually been held to refer to Mary and her Son in at least a typical sense (implicitly demanded by Pius VI in his brief *Divina,* Sept. 20, 1779, EnchBibl 74). But the literal sense of the passage has often been disputed, and no single theory has been able to win general acceptance. The following points describe briefly the four opinions most commonly held at present. (1) The prophecy may be taken as literally messianic (*see* MESSIANISM). Isaia was promising as a sign for the King a future savior of Israel, even though the prophet may not have fully understood the import of his words. (2) The literal sense of the prophecy may involve no specific woman and child, but may simply be a figurative way of expressing passage of time in a broader context. Isaia 7.14–16 should be interpreted as a whole: "Before the unborn child of any woman now pregnant has had time to reach the age of discretion, the two kings whom [Achaz] fears will be destroyed." (3) The prophecy may be viewed as referring to Isaia's own wife (cf. Is 8.3) and his own unborn child. The child's birth and naming are wholly within the prophet's power because Emmanuel is in fact to be his own son. This opinion sees ch. 6–8 of Isaia as the proper context for interpreting the oracle and tends to regard 7.18–25 (and perhaps also 7.15, 17) as later literary additions. (4) The oracle may refer literally to Achaz's queen Abi(a) and the unborn prince who will reign as Ezechia (715–686 B.C.). The birth of the heir to David's throne would be a mighty portent for the King and provide a fitting type for the Messiah to be born of the same Davidic royal line. The prophecies of the "Prince of Peace" and the "Root of Jesse" in ch. 9 and 11 of Isaia would thus be fulfilled in varying degrees in both the literal, present heir and in his messianic antitype.

See also VIRGIN BIRTH.

Bibliography: J. LINDBLOM, *A Study of the Immanuel Section in Isaiah* (Lund 1957). N. K. GOTTWALD, "Immanuel as the Prophet's Son," VetTest 8 (1958) 36–47. J. J. STAMM, "Neuere Arbeiten zum Immanuel-Problem," ZATWiss 68 (1956) 46–53. M. MCNAMARA, "The Emmanuel Prophecy and Its Context," *Scripture* 14 (1962) 118–125; 15 (1963) 19–23, 80–88.

[J. A. BRINKMAN]

ALMA REDEMPTORIS MATER. One of the four Marian antiphons, this chant is sung at the end of Compline from the Vespers of Saturday before the first Sunday of Advent to the second Vespers of the Purification. *Hermannus Contractus, a monk of Reichenau (1013–54), is believed to have composed both the words and the music. Although now sung as an independent piece, this chant was originally performed in the manner characteristic of antiphons, i.e., it preceded and followed the chanting of a psalm or canticle on a simple formula. The 13th-century MS Worcester Cathedral F. 160 (PalMus 12:303), assigns it to Terce of the Feast of the Assumption and provides it with a *differentia,* an ending formula for the psalm tone to be used with it. The more elaborate of the two melodies found in the *Liber usualis* for this antiphon is apparently the original one; it served as the basis for numerous medieval and Renaissance compositions. It is found as the tenor of 13th-century motets in the Montpellier, Bamberg, and Las Huelgas MSS; in these works the upper voices have different texts. One of the earliest settings of the polyphonic Mass Ordinary (first half of the 15th century) in which the various movements are unified by the presence of the same tenor melody in each of them is a *Missa super Alma Redemptoris Mater* by Lionel *Power. *Dufay composed a three-part setting in which the plainsong is present in slightly ornamented form in the highest voice; in *Okeghem's four-part setting the chant—again ornamented—forms the alto voice; in *Obrecht's setting it is in the bass. Joaquin *Desprez used the melody in two works: in one the chant is paraphrased and presented in canon between the alto and tenor voices; in the other it is combined with the melody of *Ave Regina caelorum.* *Palestrina based a six-part Mass on the theme and two eight-part motets. The chant is composed in the major scale rather than in one of the medieval modes, and has often been said to be of particular beauty.

Bibliography: Reese MusMA. Reese MusR. Apel GregCh. Wagner GregMel. B. STÄBLEIN, "Antiphon," MusGG 1:523–545.

[R. STEINER]

ALMAIN, JACQUES, theologian whose works influenced Gallican theories; b. Sens, *c.* 1480; d. Paris, 1515. At first he taught dialectics and natural philosophy at the University of Paris, but then entered the College of Navarre in 1508 to pursue theology, and 3 years later received his doctorate. In 1512 he was commissioned to teach theology at the college, a task he continued until his death, expounding, as was the custom of the day, the *Books of Sentences.* Almain's rise to prominence was occasioned by Cajetan's treatise *De comparatione auctoritatis papae et concilii,* in which the eminent Thomist personally defended the authority of the pope at the pseudo-Council of Pisa against the advocates of the conciliar theory. *See* CONCILIARISM. Almain was assigned the task of censuring Cajetan's position. His work, *De auctoritate ecclesiae et conciliorum generalium adversus Thomam de Vio,* appeared in 1512. Among other doctrinal points, he maintained that the authority of a general council is superior to that of the pope. Invoking Mt 18.17, he argued that the bishops gathered in a general council have divine power to judge all the faithful including the pope, because the latter is a member of the Church; that they have the right to impose their will upon him and even to depose him if need be; that the pope is superior to bishops taken individually, but inferior to them gathered in a council. Besides several purely philosophical works, seven of Almain's theological treatises, of unequal value and interest, are extant.

Bibliography: C. TESTORE, EncCatt 1:910. V. OBLET, DTC 1:895–897.

[G. M. GRABKA]

ALMEIDA, MIGUEL CALMON DU PIN E, Brazilian statesman; b. Santo Amaro, Bahia, Dec. 22, 1796; d. Rio de Janeiro, Oct. 5, 1865. After studying humanities in his province, Du Pin e Almeida went to Coimbra University, where he graduated in law in 1821. He started his career as a judge in Pôrto de Moz, Portugal. However, at the beginning of 1822 he was in Bahia, fighting for the independence of Brazil against Portuguese troops; he was also a member of the provisional government of the province. He was elected to the Constitutional Assembly of 1823, the first parliament of independent Brazil. In 1825 he was elected to the provincial assembly and in 1826, to the general assembly and was reelected several times thereafter. He was minister of finance in 1827, 1837, and 1841; minister of foreign affairs in 1829 and 1862. Du Pin was sent on official missions to Vienna in 1836, and in 1844 to London, Paris, and Berlin. He sought an agreement with England and France to protect Paraguay and Uruguay against the ambition of Rosas of Buenos Aires. In Berlin he negotiated a treaty of commerce between Prussia and Brazil. He studied the administration, public instruction, and military organization of Prussia and other European states to see what could be applied in Brazil. *The Viscount of Abrantes' special mission from October 1844 to October 1846* (Rio 1853) is his account of this trip. To further the economic progress of the country, Du Pin e Almeida fostered immigration and founded societies of agriculture and colonization. He was cofounder of the Academy of Music and the National Opera. He wrote several essays on the making of sugar, the cultivation of tobacco, and ways of promoting colonization. From 1840 he was senator from the Province of Ceará, and in 1843 he became a member of the Council of State. Though a man of liberal and modern ideas, he was one of the leaders of the Conservative party, whose ideology was often difficult to distinguish from that of the Liberal party. A good Catholic and a moderate among so many regalistic-minded politicians of his time, Du Pin e Almeida was one of the most gifted leaders in public life under the Brazilian Empire. He was made marquis of Abrantes in 1854.

Bibliography: P. CALMON, *O marquez de Abrantes* (Rio de Janiero 1933).

[T. BEAL]

ALMICI, CAMILLO, Oratorian scholar; b. Brescia, Italy, June 2, 1714; d. there, 1779. Camillo, inclined from boyhood to learning and piety, joined the Brescia Oratory at the age of 19. After his ordination he spent his life in this community, becoming a distinguished theologian, apologist, and critical scholar, expert particularly in Hebrew, Greek, and Scripture. He was also well acquainted with church history and patristic writings, in fact with the whole field of secular history and archeology. As a scholar, he made himself accessible to other scholars and students, and was much consulted. As an Oratorian priest, he was a popular preacher and confessor. His writings include *Riflessioni su di un libro di Giustino Febronio* (Lucca 1766); *Critica contro le opere del pericoloso Voltaire* (Brescia 1771); *Dissertazione sopra i martiri della Chiesa cattolica* (Brescia 1765); *Meditazione sopra la vita e gli scritti di Paolo Sarpi* (Brescia 1765), in which he points out the tendentiousness and unreliability of Sarpi's history of the Council of Trent; and a dissertation on the art of writing biography and autobiography. Almici published some small works under the anagrammatic pseudonyms Callimaco Limi, and Callimaco Mili.

Bibliography: C. TOUSSAINT, DTC 1.1:898. P. GUERRINI, *Le Congregazione dei Padri della Pace* (Brescia 1933). *Hurter Nomencl* 5.1:224–225. A. PALMIERI, DHGE 2:658.

[J. CHALLENOR]

ALMOND, JOHN, BL., English martyr; b. Allerton, near Liverpool, *c.* 1577; d. Tyburn, Dec. 5, 1612 (feast, Dec. 5). At the age of 8, having already attended Much Wootton Grammar School, he went to Ireland, where he remained until 1597. He then entered the English College at Rome and in April 1601 he was ordained. To gain his D.D. degree he gave a public disputation that won great applause, since he was exceptionally clever and quick at debate. Almond left Rome for England in September 1602 and became a successful missionary—discreet, forceful, and holy. In 1607 he was tracked down by pursuivants in Holborn, taken to Newgate, and then transferred to the Gatehouse Prison. He either escaped or was released, for he was heard of in Staffordshire in 1609. In 1612 he was again arrested and brought before Dr. John King, Bishop of London. Part of the extant record of the examination reads:

BISHOP: In what place were you born?
JOHN ALMOND: About Allerton.
BISHOP: About Allerton! Mark the equivocation; then not in Allerton?
JOHN ALMOND: No equivocation. I was not born in Allerton but on the edge or side of Allerton.
BISHOP: You were born under a hedge then were you?
JOHN ALMOND: Many a better man, than I or you either, has been born under a hedge.
BISHOP: You cannot remember that you were born in a house?
JOHN ALMOND: Can you?
BISHOP: My mother told me so.
JOHN ALMOND: Then you remember not that you were born in a house but only that your mother told you so. So much I remember too.

He was committed to Newgate, where the prisoners were in danger of suffocation from the stench of the dungeon. Because of his reputation for cleverness and sanctity, Protestant ministers, including the archbishop of Canterbury, carried on disputes with Almond in the hope of winning a recantation; but they always retired, beaten in argument. On Dec. 3, 1612, he was brought for trial under his own name and two aliases, Mollinax and Ladome. Although no proof was brought, he was found guilty of being a priest and on December 5 he was drawn to Tyburn. His last words on the scaffold were, "In manus tuas Domine . . ."; he was beatified on Dec. 15, 1929. (*See* MARTYRS OF ENGLAND AND WALES.)

Bibliography: Butler Th Attw 4:502–503. J. H. POLLEN, *Acts of English Martyrs* (London 1891) 170–193. R. CHALLONER, *Memoirs of Missionary Priests,* ed. J. H. POLLEN (rev. ed. London 1924). DictEngCath 1:26–27. W. J. STEELE, *Blessed John Almond* (Postulation pamphlet; London 1961).

[G. FITZHERBERT]

ALMS AND ALMSGIVING (IN THE BIBLE)

A religious act, inspired by compassion and a desire for justice, whereby an individual who possesses the economic means helps in a material way his less fortunate neighbor. In the earlier history of Israel when society was predominantly seminomadic and all members were more or less economically equal, there was no need of almsgiving. But with the possession of landed property, the growth of aristocracy, and the centralization of government, a large mass of debt-ridden farmers arose in contrast to a small urban nobility. Such a society offended the ideal of social justice that the covenant of Yahweh demanded. Hence, the Prophets, beginning with Amos, denounced oppression of the poor (Am 5.11–12, 24; 8.4; Is 10.2; Mi 2.2) and vigorously demanded social justice (Am 5.24).

Throughout the OT the notion of alms (concrete aid given the poor) is understood primarily in the context of justice; just as Yahweh acts with justice, so, too, must his worshipers. The Hebrew word for alms, *ṣ*[e]*dāqâ*, means justice or righteousness; giving to the poor helps reestablish the right order; it produces justice. To return to the poor man his pledged cloak at nightfall that he may sleep in comfort is justice (*ṣ*[e]*dāqâ*) before Yahweh (Dt 24.13). Mindful of the poor, the Law prescribed that the land should lie fallow every 7th year (Ex 23.11) and that the gleanings from the harvest should be left for the poor in the field and vineyard (Lv 19.9–10; 23.22; see also Ru 2.2–8). After the Exile there was a growing emphasis on the religious nature of personal almsgiving. Job, in his plea of a clean conscience, asserts that his reverence for God prompted him to give food, clothing, and shelter to the needy (Jb 31.16–23). Alms purge away sin, deliver from death (Tb 12.9; see also Dn 4.24), and bring God's favor on the giver (Tb 4.7); on the other hand, refusing alms to the poor brings a just retribution (Prv 21.13) because God, who created the poor man, too, will hear the latter's cry (Sir 4.1–6).

In the NT almsgiving is considered primarily as an act of religion springing from love and compassion; its note of social justice also is alluded to, especially in the writings of St. Luke and in the Epistle of James. Jesus enjoins unostentatious almsgiving, together with prayer and fasting, as one of the pillars of the religious life (Mt 6.1–2, 5, 16, 19). It merits a heavenly reward (Mt 6.4, 20; 19.27–29; 25.40; Lk 12.33; 16.1–9) and

Jesus points out to His disciples the poor widow putting her last two mites in the almsbox at the Temple, illumination, 9th- or 10th-century Armenian Gospel Book.

makes the donor a true son of the Most High (Lk 6.35). Luke's writings, in particular, commend almsgiving; he alone relates the stories of Zachaeus, a chief tax collector, who gave half his possessions to the poor (Lk 19.1–10), of the Baptist's advice to share food and clothing with the needy (Lk 3.11), and of Christ's advice to lend money without thought of return (Lk 6.35). Luke also takes the opportunity of relating that Paul worked with his hands to provide for the needs of others as well as his own (Acts 18.3; 20.34–35). St. Paul organized collections for the poor (Rom 15.25–28; 1 Cor 16.1; 2 Cor 8–9), in order not only to alleviate want, but to break down prejudices between Jew and Gentile and to knit the members of Christ into a community of good will. According to St. James, true religion demands that those in the Christian community who possess the means should help their needy brethren (Jas 1.27; 2.14–17; see also 1 Jn 3.17; 1 Pt 4.8–10).

Bibliography: EncDictBibl 55–56. InterDictBibl 1:87–88. O. CONE, *Rich and Poor in the N.T.* (New York 1902). R. BULTMANN, "*ἐλεημοσύνη*," Kittel ThW 2:482–483. H. J. CADBURY, *The Making of Luke—Acts* (2d ed. London 1958) 260–263. **Illustration credit:** Courtesy of the Smithsonian Institution, Freer Gallery of Art, Washington, D.C.

[M. RODRÍGUEZ]

ALMS AND ALMSGIVING (IN THE CHURCH)

The word alms can be traced back to the Greek word ἐλεημοσύνη (pity). This word is found in the Septuagint, a fact of importance since it is especially in Holy Scripture that the divine perspective on alms can be seen. From this point of view, the Christian is led to reflect on his duties in regard to those less favored than himself, and especially on the responsibilities of his Christian stewardship over material goods. St. Thomas Aquinas considered almsgiving the general and principal work of mercy (ST 2a2ae, 32).

The Value of Alms. Alms assume so large a place in the design of eternal love that Holy Scripture considers a heart attentive to the poor a genuine blessing. "Happy is he who has regard for the lowly and the poor; in the day of misfortune the Lord will deliver him. The Lord will keep and preserve him, He will make him happy upon the earth, and not give him over to the will of his enemies. The Lord will help him on his sick bed, He will take away all his ailment when he is ill" [Ps 40(41). 1–4]. Such blessings are hardly surprising since an alms given to a fellow man is received by God Himself. As the OT puts it, "He who has compassion on the poor lends to the Lord, and He will repay him for his good deed" (Prv 19.17). But the NT incomparably enhances this value of alms since there it is Jesus Christ Himself who is the recipient of alms. This truth is repeatedly illustrated in the legends of the saints. For example, Christ, disguised as a poor man who was clothed by St. Martin of Tours, was to make Martin a great missionary to the pagans and the founder of the Church of Gaul. The first miracle after Pentecost, which had an enormous effect in Jerusalem, was performed by Peter, who, when asked for an alms, gave not silver and gold, but what he had (see Acts 3.6).

Since God sees as His own the needs of the poor, alms have an eternal value, meriting a treasure in heaven. "Sell what you have and give alms. Make for yourselves . . . a treasure in heaven" (Lk 12.33). Alms also have the redemptive value of blotting out sins. "Water quenches a flaming fire and alms atone for sin" (Sir 3.29). In this spirit Daniel gives advice to a king who is in agony over his own weakness: "Atone for your sins by good deeds and for your misdeeds by kindness to the poor, then your posterity will be long" (Dn 4.24). The Archangel Raphael affirms this value of alms to the family of Tobit; in fact, this is one of the most important lessons given by this Biblical work. "Prayer is good with fasting and alms more than to lay up treasures of gold, for alms delivereth from death, and the same is that which purgeth away sin, and maketh to find mercy and life everlasting" (Tb 12.8–9). Another aspect of the value of alms is that of sacrifice, as taught by Sirach. "In works of charity one offers fine flour, and when he gives alms he presents his sacrifice of prayer" (Sir 35.2).

Alms Purify the Heart. The portions of personal possessions so shared are detached from what is kept, and this tends to create an interior detachment. This may be the meaning of the somewhat obscure text of St. Luke: "Nevertheless, give that which remains as an alms; and behold, all things are clean to you" (Lk 11. 41).

Alms have still other values, for they enrich not only the giver, but the Church, since its charity is in this way enlarged. Alms increase brotherly love in the recipient, who in his turn prays for his benefactor. More particularly, in the exchange of mutual aid between the churches, the entire Mystical Body is blessed. This idea was the foundation of St. Paul's totally apostolic concern for Jerusalem's poor. He considered alms to be a means of eliminating the causes of disunity among Christians. "Now, however, I will set out for Jerusalem to minister to the saints. For Macedonia and Achaia have thought it well to make a contribution for the poor among the saints at Jerusalem" (Rom 15.25–26). Such an idea might have splendid applications to the bonds between parishes and dioceses with the help of papal direction. It would be a witnessing before the world to the mutual aid existing among Christ's disciples so that at least among them there would be no distinction based either on race or on country.

The final words of Paul lead to an even higher sphere: human alms become a divine revelation since God both inspires the good action and is glorified by it. "He . . . will increase the growth of the fruits of your justice that, being enriched in all things, you may contribute with simplicity of heart, and thus through us evoke thanksgiving to God; for the administration of this service not only supplies the wants of the saints, but overflows also in much gratitude to the Lord. The evidence furnished by this service makes them glorify God for your obedient profession of Christ's gospel and for the sincere generosity of your contributions to them and to all; while they themselves, in their prayers for you, yearn for you, because of the excellent grace God has given you" (2 Cor 9.11–14).

Qualities of Alms. In order to have such value and to merit these promises, alms should correspond to the divine pattern. First, the primacy of intention must be emphasized, for intention is the soul of human action and gives it its real value. Christ Himself emphatically taught that alms should be given "in secret and thy Father, who sees in secret, will reward thee" (Mt 6.2–4). Christian alms then, should be a communion in merciful love. From this point of view, almsgiving has a delicacy that excludes ostentation and avoids the display of any superiority. St. Jerome once said that alms should be given as if the giver were the real recipient (*Letter to Hedibian*). More emphatically yet, the Lord taught, "When thou givest alms, do not let thy left hand know what thy right hand is doing" (Mt 6.3).

Almsgiving must also be totally disinterested, "not hoping for anything in return" (Lk 6.35; cf. Lk 14.4). The OT had already mentioned the importance of promptness in the reception of a needy friend: "Refuse no one the good on which he has a claim when it is in your power to do it for him. Say not to your neighbor, 'Go and come again tomorrow, tomorrow I will give,' when you can give at once" (Prv 3.27–28).

Almsgiving was commanded by the Lord, but not simply in the sense of material assistance; it includes rather, the realization of the compassionate intention of love. St. Paul expressly adds joy to the eagerness of generosity: "He who shows mercy [should do so] with cheerfulness" (Rom 12.8). In a word, alms should reflect the realism of a love that is attentive in its search for the opportunity of fraternal service, since the brother with whom we share what we have is a child of the same Father from whom we have all received. The example of Christ Himself speaks volumes. Living on alms, He nonetheless gave alms to those poorer than Himself (Jn 13.29). Even more, Christ is God's gift for the enrichment of the world: "For you know the graciousness of our Lord Jesus Christ—how being rich he became poor for your sakes, that by his poverty you might become rich" (2 Cor 8.9).

Obligation to Give Alms. St. John has formulated the principle: "He who has the goods of this world and sees his brother in need and closes his heart to him, how does the love of God abide in him?" (1 Jn 3.17). True love demands a sharing when there is an abundance on one hand and a need on the other. To refuse to meet this demand is incompatible with charity. In the parable, the priest and the levite saw the unfortunate Samaritan; they could have helped him, but they passed by. It is seldom that a man's life depends so entirely on help from his neighbor, but when it does, the obligation is quite clear. This obligation would be so great that to refuse or deny it would be to destroy charity.

Conditions for the Obligation. "Abundance" exists when one has more than is necessary and strictly useful for his own life, for that of his family, or for the maintenance of his social position. Provision for one's social position is not necessarily a matter of snobbery or ostentation. Social life can impose real obligations. What these may be in any particular case may be determined by reasonable custom and special circumstances as these are evaluated by the Christian conscience of the individual. The logic of his faith and the operation of the gifts of the Holy Spirit will enable him to reach decisions about what is necessary to himself and what should be shared with his neighbor.

Extreme necessity means the absence or insufficiency of goods required for human life. The *standard of living varies in different situations. Three stages and forms of theological thought upon this subject can be distinguished. The Fathers were preoccupied with preaching the necessity of almsgiving; the scholastics, with the analysis of its theological foundations; the casuists, with the practical application of the theological conclusions.

The Fathers, as in fact Christian preachers of every age have done, sought to inspire love of the poor and horror of greed and selfishness. They insisted upon the responsibility of the rich, who, as stewards of God, owed their superabundance to the poor. St. Thomas and the scholastics in general worked out the connection between mercy and alms and analyzed the essential reasons why almsgiving is obligatory. From the 14th to the end of the 18th century the major concern of moralists was the problem of conscience in the determination to the extent of the obligation in concrete situations. An effort was made to achieve precision. When exactly is there real abundance? When are alms a matter of strict precept, and when are they more a matter of counsel? St. Alphonsus Liguori studied, edited, and criticized the thought of his predecessors; and his conclusions on the subjects of extreme need and abundance have become classic. With a view to the circumstances of his own time and society, St. Alphonsus taught that the rich should give in charity a 50th part, that is, 2 per cent, of what they could save. In defense of this and other similar theological conclusions in this matter—some propositions were in fact condemned by the Church as too lax—it should be noted that although the sum demanded for charity appears small, these authors did not lose sight of the wider horizons of the Gospel; and they were striving to determine what charity required as a matter of course and independently of extreme need. Confronted by a neighbor in extreme need, no Christian is really faithful to the Gospel when he is not prepared to sacrifice his abundance.

Alms are a matter of counsel when fraternal charity can be genuine without them, for instance, when the necessity of one's neighbor is not at the moment so pressing that a refusal to help him would be equivalent to a denial of love. On the other hand, there would be a serious obligation when the withholding of help would keep another from a good absolutely necessary to him. In this case, the lack of love would constitute a mortal sin against fraternal charity.

Generally speaking, then, the obligation of almsgiving is measured both by the extent of one's abundance, and by the kind of necessity the abundance would alleviate. If this necessity is extreme and one's assistance is the only possible way to relieve it, the duty is strict. But if the condition of need is known to others or if it is not really extreme, determination of the extent and force of the obligation calls for the exercise of prudence. The obligation itself is clear because of its connection with fraternal charity; the assessment of the obligation in concrete situations is often not easy to make.

Difficulty in Assessing. This may be due not only to variable circumstances but also, perhaps, to the very nature of things. An adequate Christian judgment in this matter can proceed only from a genuinely spiritual estimate of one's own resources. Certainly God's plan involves the provision of room in human life for creativeness and the generous use of freedom. However, this should not be used as a pretext to evade imperative duty where it clearly exists. Any uncertainty about the extent of a man's obligation should move him to develop the habit of seeing Christ in those poorer than himself. One's final welcome into the kingdom—or his rejection—will depend upon the criterion of his effective love for his brethren (Mt 25.34–46). The complexity of life's circumstances shows only that Christ wants His disciples to be free and to use their real liberty in a life of charity, with their conscience enlightened by the divine mercy.

Application to Contemporary Life. The two roots of the obligation of almsgiving indicated by St. John are having the goods of this world and seeing the need of a brother (1 Jn 3.17). In the contemporary world the "having" and "wanting" are viewed in relation to an expanding economy that is not only national but international in scope. In the scale of needs there is almost infinite variation, and while the duties of love have not lost their ancient urgency, their application must undergo modification.

The State's Assumption of the Burden of Providing for Many Needs. Modern civilization has become conscious of at least some of the human rights consonant with human dignity, and in genuine democracies these rights are clearly seen. The state either directly or indirectly takes over more and more of the responsibility for meeting such needs as arise from unemployment, illness, old age, and so on. In consequence of this, many people do not require the help of private charity. To pay taxes or to take out insurance is to participate in the assistance the state and other institutions offer. When these factors are taken into consideration, it can be seen that there has been reduction in the frequency of instances of clearly assessable obligation to give alms.

Nevertheless, there will always be cases in which a Christian cannot rely on the community to assume his personal duty to give alms any more than he can expect the community to assume his personal obligation to love his brother. Laws cannot cover every situation (unforeseen accidents, immediate urgencies, and the like). In addition to obligations arising in such circumstances, a sense of charitable responsibility for his brethren should penetrate and illumine the Christian's performance of his civic duties and particularly the exercise of his right to vote.

Personal Knowledge of the Universality of Human Misery. The newspapers, radio, and television present the public with a spectacle of worldwide need, and this the Christian will see as a call upon his charity. No national or political limits exist for Christian charity. In most situations, only well-organized community effort can make an adequate response to the enormous needs. In the multitude of appeals and of possibilities offered, a 20th-century Christian may need to make a choice; bearing in mind the order of charity, he may have to consider which neighbors are closest to him spiritually. One such spiritual consideration might be "his brethren in the faith." "Therefore, while we have time, let us do good to all men, but especially to those who are of the household of the faith" (Gal 6.10). Those of the household will recognize the help more clearly as an expression of faith. But in general, discernment and an interior spirit become increasingly necessary for the Christian as he finds himself assailed with more multiple and varied appeals.

Need for Collective Organizations. In the mid-20th century it was said that almost any aid project involves so many costly measures that only an organization could undertake it. This was true, especially in cases in which aid had to be sent to distant places. This kind of situation should broaden the scope of a Christian's compassionate intentions. He should be conscious of the complexities of the problem and take these into account in his thinking about economics, politics, and international relations. He may feel himself (and be) obligated to personal participation in collective effort and in interesting others by information and appeal. Yet in all this the Christian must take constant care that his participation remains an expression of fraternal love, without which no alms are pleasing to God. The qualities, stated above, that should mark Christian almsgiving, should also characterize participation in the different forms of collective effort to bring aid to others. Otherwise these efforts will degenerate into mere philanthropic enterprises.

While he busies himself by having a share in large and collective undertakings, the Christian will try to keep alert in order not to miss the occasional opportunity that may occur to exercise charity in a direct, immediate, and personal way. He will remember that alms can be in forms other than money. His time, influence, friendliness, sympathy, and encouragement can also be a kind of alms and will give him much opportunity to prove his love for Christ and His Gospel.

See also MERCY; MERCY, WORKS OF; CHARITY.

Bibliography: THOMAS AQUINAS, ST 2a2ae, 30–33. ALPHONSUS LIGUORI, *Theologia moralis,* ed. L. GAUDÉ, 4 v. (new ed. Rome 1905–12) 1.2:3.2. A. BEUGNET, DTC 1.2:2561–71. R. BROUILLARD, *Catholicisme* 1:1050–56; "La Doctrine Catholique de l'aumône," NouvRevTh 54 (1927) 5–36. L. BOUVIER, *Le Précepte de l'aumône chez saint Thomas d'Aquin* (Montreal 1935). G. J. BUDDE, "Christian Charity, Now and Always: The Fathers of the Church and Almsgiving," AmEcclRev 85 (1931) 561–579. J. D. O'NEILL, CE 1.1:328–331.

[J. M. PERRIN]

ALMSGATHERING (CANON LAW)

Almsgathering in its common historical and juridical connotation is a privilege of collecting alms granted to religious for the needs of their respective institutes and for the promotion of charitable causes specifically entrusted to their care. In a wider significance, as understood and contained in canon 1503 of the Code of Canon Law, almsgathering includes also the ecclesiastical authorization given to seculars, clerical or lay, of orally soliciting aid for any pious purpose or ecclesiastical institution that is in need of such aid.

Law for Religious. Almsgathering by religious is of a definite type and does not embrace all modes of enlisting aid. It entails: (1) a privilege granted by common law to mendicant orders that are such in name and in fact, by special apostolic concession to other orders and congregations, and by written permission of the local ordinary to diocesan institutes; (2) a going from place to place, from house to house, or any similar manner of publicly and generally collecting alms not from a few but from many persons; (3) an oral petitioning, excluding other methods, such as the sending of written or printed circulars through the mails or the making of appeals on radio or television.

The privilege implies: (1) that it be exercised personally by members of the religious institute, except in institutes of religious women where the local ordinary is regularly to select trustworthy persons to solicit the alms; (2) that the method followed and the rules observed be in conformity with instructions issued by the Holy See on this subject; (3) that the alms obtained be used exclusively for the needs of the religious community. Any soliciting of funds that are beyond the privilege is governed either by CIC c.1503 or by particular legislation. The latter may include other methods of soliciting alms.

Regulars who by the nature of their institute are mendicants in name and in fact can, with the sole permission of their superiors, collect alms in the diocese in which their religious house is situated; outside of the diocese they need also the permission of the ordinary of the place in which they propose to collect alms (CIC c.621.1). The privilege of such mendicants is a juridical one, based upon the very nature of the institute professing absolute poverty. The local ordinary has no direct control over its exercise. Indirectly he does, insofar as he determines whether or not such a house is to be canonically erected in his diocese.

All other religious institutes of pontifical right are forbidden to seek alms without first obtaining the privilege from the Holy See. Those who have obtained the privilege require also the written permission of the local ordinary, unless it is otherwise stated in the privilege itself. Some institutes with the right of proprietorship have the privilege solely in virtue of approved constitutions, with no further obligation of obtaining the permission of the local ordinary. Religious of congregations of diocesan approval are strictly forbidden to seek alms without the written permission of the ordinary of the place in which they propose to collect (CIC c.622.1, 2). Permission is granted readily to mendicants collecting outside the diocese in which their house is situated; to others only when the need is real and cannot be met in some other suitable manner.

Oriental Rites. Ordinaries of the Latin rite must not permit any member of an Oriental rite of whatever order or dignity to collect money in their territory without an authentic and recent rescript of the Oriental Congregation, nor may they send any of their subjects to Oriental dioceses for the same purpose without a similar document (CIC c.622.4). The Code of Oriental Law, motu proprio *Postquam Apostolicis,* canons 171–173, presents a more restrictive attitude toward every exercise of the privilege of almsgathering. The permission for habitual collecting of alms is to be granted only exceptionally and with the permission of the highest extern superior. The permission of the Holy See is always required to solicit alms outside Oriental regions. Oriental regions include any countries where the Oriental rite is established since ancient times, although no ecclesiastical hierarchy may be in existence today.

General Norms. The Holy See has issued instructions on the method to be followed in collecting alms and the rules to be observed. The principal decrees are *Singulari quidem* (for religious women) of March 27, 1896, and *De eleemosynis colligendis* (for religious men) of Nov. 21, 1908. A special instruction of the Congregation for the Propagation of the Faith governing the collecting of money for the missions was issued on June 29, 1952.

Almsgathering in its wider significance is the collecting of alms by private persons, clerical or lay, and may not be undertaken without the permission of the Holy See or of their own ordinary, as well as that of the local ordinary where alms are to be solicited. Private persons includes religious men and women when they solicit funds beyond the privilege itself. Persons holding an office with territorial jurisdiction, e.g., a parish priest, may gather funds without permission, subject only to existing particular legislation.

Appeals made through the mails and other modern means of communication do not come under the common law of almsgathering. Such methods may be regulated by particular law and, in the absence of such law, are tempered by acceptable custom. The decree of the Third Plenary Council of Baltimore (ActDecrConcPlen BaltIII n.295) requires that the local ordinary withhold permission from a collector of alms until the proper ordinary or religious superior has first obtained it for the collector and (ActDecrConcPlenBaltIII n.296) forbids the soliciting of Mass stipends through advertisements in newspapers or circulars.

Bibliography: U. Manucci, "De iure et ratione quaestuandi," *Analecta Ecclesiastica* 17 (1909) 72–80, 288–293. L. G. Meyer, *Alms-gathering by Religious* (Washington 1946).

[L. MEYER]

ALOGOI, the name given to heretics who denied the divinity of Christ as the Logos, as in St. John's Gospel, Epistles, and the Apocalypse. They were first named by *Epiphanius of Constantia (*Panarion* 51; *Ancor.* 13.5). They were mentioned by *Irenaeus (*Adv. haer.* 3.11. 9–17) as Montanists misusing the Johannine teaching on the Paraclete. Eusebius (*Hist. eccl.* 3.28.1) and Hippolytus (GCS 1.2:241–247) described the Roman priest Gaius in the reign of Pope *Zephyrinus (199–217) as attributing the Johannine writings to the Gnostic Cerinthus. A type of enthusiastic spirituality, the Alogoi doctrine was current in the West in the 2d and 3d centuries; the necessity of defending the Johannine writings then is evident in Hippolytus and the *Muratorian Canon (lines 16–26). The name Alogoi has a double meaning: men denying the Logos, and lacking reason.

Bibliography: A. Grillmeier, LexThK[2] 1:363–364. C. Schmidt and J. Waynberg, eds. and trs., *Gespräche Jesu* (TU 3d ser. 13; 1919) 420–452. A. Bludau, *Die ersten Gegner der Johannesschriften* (Biblische Studien 22; Fribourg 1925). G. Bareille, DTC 1.1:898–901. A. Wikenhauser, *Einleitung in das Neue Testament* (3d ed. Freiburg 1959).

[F. X. MURPHY]

ALOYSIUS GONZAGA, ST.

Patron of youth; b. Castiglione, near Mantua, March 9, 1568; d. Rome, June 21, 1591 (feast, June 21). The firstborn of Ferrante Gonzaga, Marquis of Castiglione and Prince of the Empire, and Marta Tana Santena, Aloysius grew up amid the brutality and license of

St. Aloysius Gonzaga, a portrait from life.

Renaissance society, which witnessed the murder of two of his brothers. Between Aloysius and his devout mother a tender affection developed, while his father began early to prepare him for the military life envisioned for him. In Pierfrancesco del Turco he had a wise and competent tutor. In 1577 Aloysius was sent to attend the court of Francesco de' Medici, Grand Duke of Tuscany. In 1581, he accompanied his parents, who joined Empress Maria of Austria on a visit to Spain. At the court of Philip II he acted as page to the heir apparent, Don Diego, and pursued the study of philosophy. At Alcalá he was invited to participate in a public debate. Aloysius while in Spain decided to enter the Society of Jesus. His father firmly resisted his decision and began a struggle of wills that lasted for several years and still continued after their return to Castiglione in 1584. Aloysius prevailed, renounced the rights to his inheritance, and entered the novitiate in Rome on Nov. 25, 1585. As a novice he studied philosophy at the Roman College and gave a public defense in that subject. He pronounced his first vows on Nov. 25, 1587. For 4 years he studied theology, having as one of his masters the brilliant Gabriel Vázquez. In 1589 he returned to Castiglione for a brief stay in order to settle some intricate family affairs. While attending the sick during an epidemic in Rome in March 1591, he contracted the plague, and died three months later.

The steps in the spiritual growth of Aloysius are clear. At 7 he manifested a strong sense of responsibility and love for vocal prayer. A book by Gaspar Loarte, SJ, and his later reading of Louis of Granada, opened up for him the area of mental prayer to which he gave several hours a day. With intensity, calmness of judgment, and power to face facts he firmly decided on a life of holiness. His calm purpose to conquer himself was expressed in severe penance. At Florence, before the Madonna in the Church of Annunziata, he made a vow of virginity. A distaste for court life at Mantua led him to read the lives of the saints. In 1580 he received First Holy Communion from St. Charles Borromeo, and this inspired him to a lasting devotion to the Holy Eucharist. He showed his basic humility and obedience in the novitiate by surrendering his own ideas about prayer and penance. His charity, which was practical, was revealed in the catechetical lessons he gave and in his care for the sick. While he was at the Roman College his spiritual director was St. Robert Bellarmine. His letters, uneffusive and unpretentious, reveal a direct and calm soul.

He never signed himself Aloisio or Aloysius, but Aluigi or Luigi. Francesco Sacchini, competent historian of the early Society of Jesus, objected to the form Aloysius in 1612, arguing for Ludovicus or Louis. However, Francesco Gonzaga, head of the family at the time, insisted on Aloysius. Benedict XIII canonized Aloysius in 1726, and 3 years later declared him patron of youth, an honor confirmed by Pius XI in 1926.

Bibliography: ALOYSIUS GONZAGA, *Lettere ed altri scritti,* ed. E. ROSA (Florence 1926). C. C. MARTINDALE, *The Vocation of Aloysius Gonzaga* (New York 1927). V. CEPARI, *Life of Saint Aloysius Gonzaga,* tr. F. SCHROEDER (Einsiedeln 1891). E. DELPIERRE and A. NOCHÉ, *St. Louis de Gonzague et la Renaissance italienne* (Le Puy 1945). A. LAMBRETTE, *St. Louis de Gonzague* (Museum Lessianum, Section Ascétique et Mystique 22; Louvain 1926). M. MESCHLER, *Leben des hl. Aloysius von Gonzaga* (Freiburg 1891). **Illustration credit:** Kunsthistorisches Museum, Vienna.

[W. V. BANGERT]

ALOYSIUS RABATÁ, BL., Carmelite prior; b. Monte San Giuliano, Sicily, *c.* 1430; d. Randazzo, Sicily, 1490 (feast, May 11). He entered the *Carmelite Order at Trapani and became prior of the Randazzo monastery. Even as superior he continued to engage in manual labor and begging. He was noted especially for his love of neighbor and for the forgiveness of his enemies, as was exemplified in his refusal to reveal the identity of the assailant from whose wounds he died. The process of beatification was begun in 1533, the cult approved in 1841, and an Office and Mass assigned in 1842. His relics were translated to the collegiate church of St. Mary, Randazzo, in 1912.

Bibliography: ActSS May 2:707–721. L. M. SAGGI, $LexThK^2$ 1:365. Butler Th Attw 2:275–276.

[E. R. CARROLL]

ALPHA AND OMEGA, the first and the last letters of the Greek alphabet, used as a self-designation of God (the Father) in Ap 1.8; 21.6 (where it is explained by the parallel "the beginning and the end") and of Christ in Ap 22.13 (with the parallel of 21.6 and also "the first and last"). The use of the term in 22.13 is an example of the common NT device of applying to Christ what is said elsewhere (e.g., in the OT) of God (the Father) in order to affirm the Son's divinity. The parallels allude to Is 41.4; 44.6; 48.12, where God's eternity is emphasized. "Alpha and Omega" is more comprehensive than "the first and the last" (of Christ also in Ap 1.17; 2.8), suggesting that God (and Christ) includes all, not only in time and space but in other dimensions and aspects, just as the two termini of the alphabet include all its letters. The thought is similar to that of Rom 11.36: God the creator takes in all duration in His eternity; He is the origin, the sustainer, and the end of all things. John's use of Alpha-Omega

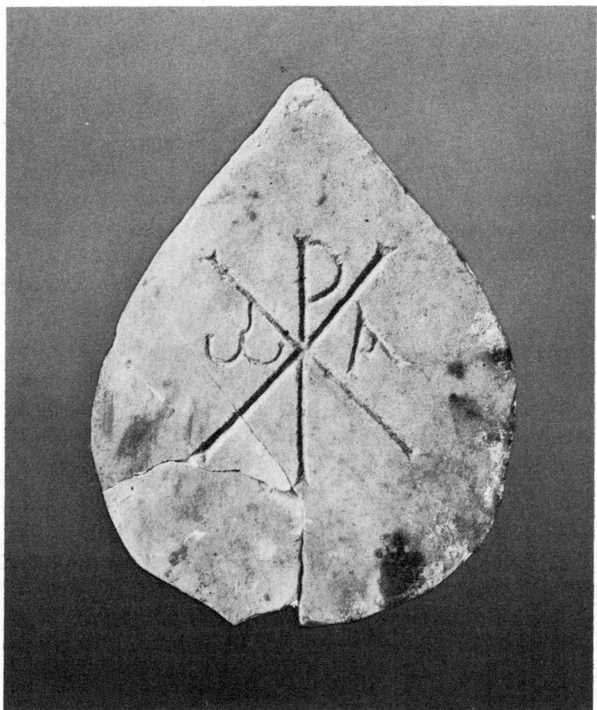

Alpha and Omega suspended from a Chi-Rho, inscription on a tear-shaped stone slab, c. 409, in the cemetery of Commodilla at Rome.

has a Jewish background; some rabbinic writings use aleph-tau (later also aleph-mem-tau = *'ĕmet,* truth or fidelity) as a symbol for the *Shekinah, the visible manifestation of God's presence.

Bibliography: Kittel ThW (Eng) 1:1–3. EncDictBibl 56. E. B. ALLO, *L'Apocalypse* (Paris 1921) 28. **Illustration credit:** Pontificia Commissione di Archaeologia Sacra.

[E. F. SIEGMAN]

ALPHABET

Alphabet writing developed from simplified representations of common objects or pictograms. These eventually came to represent syllables, from which an alphabet script was later devised. The history of alphabetic writing, therefore, must be distinguished from the broader and more complex history of writing (*see* WRITING, ANCIENT SYSTEMS OF). This article will treat of the origin of alphabetic writing, and the development of the Ugaritic cuneiform alphabet and the Phoenician linear alphabet.

Origin. In the 4th millennium B.C., the Sumerians, a non-Semitic people in lower Mesopotamia, had already devised a system of writing with a stylus on soft clay tablets, from which, like the later Babylonians, they finally developed their cuneiform (from Latin *cuneus,* a wedge) writing into a fully conventionalized syllabic script. Cuneiform, moreover, during its long history and its unusually wide diffusion, was used to write totally different languages, both Semitic and non-Semitic. It was even employed for the primary element in forming the characters of the Ugaritic alphabet script, whose existence was completely unknown before 1929. The Semitic alphabet, however, progenitor of all the Western world alphabets, can now be studied inductively through inscriptional material. Thanks to the genius of some unknown Semite(s) from the Syria-Palestine area, a far simpler alphabetic system has replaced the cumbrous machinery of pictographic and syllabic writing through the revolutionary innovation of representing a consonant with a single sign. The earliest known examples of this alphabet, called "Proto-Canaanite," are found in three short Palestinian inscriptions from *Gazer (Gezer), Lachis (Lachish), and *Sichem (Shechem), all dating between 1700 and 1500 B.C. Originating in a pictographic script, it developed into a true alphabet on the basis of acrophony; i.e., the first consonant of the name of the pictured object was taken as the phonetic value of the sign. Thus the value of *beth* was *b,* of *gimel, g,* of *daleth, d,* etc. This acrophonically devised script, on which Egyptian hieroglyphic writing exercised a direct or indirect influence, radiated from the Syria-Palestine area, probably from Phoenicia proper. It is, moreover, from this Proto-Canaanite alphabet, a purely consonantal form of writing, that Phoenician, Aramaic, Hebrew, and the different South Semitic scripts developed.

Ugaritic and Phoenician Alphabets. There are two alphabetic scripts known to have been used in Palestine and Syria in the Late Bronze Age (*c.* 1500–1200 B.C.), both of which owe their origin to the inventiveness of the Canaanites. These are the cuneiform alphabet of Ugarit (modern Ras Shamra) and the so-called Phoenician linear alphabet, ancestor of our Greek alphabet. In 1929 C. F. A. Schaeffer, the French archeologist, discovered the Ugaritic literature written on clay tablets in a hitherto unknown alphabetic script. Besides the literature, the excavators found several abecedaries (ABC tablets) from *c.* 1400 B.C. that confirm other evidence that both the names of the Proto-Canaanite signs and their order stem at least from the 14th century B.C. Our knowledge of the origin and development of the linear Phoenician alphabet, also indigenous to Syria-Palestine, has likewise gained immensely by an accumulation of inscriptional evidence. We have already mentioned three of these inscriptions from Middle Bronze Palestine. To these may be added a number of short inscriptions from Late Bronze, between 1400 and 1200 B.C. The Proto-Sinaitic inscriptions, discovered near the turquoise mines of the Sinai Peninsula, and written in the same alphabet, can now be dated between 1500 and 1450 B.C. A more developed conventionalized form of the same alphabetic script is attested in the 10th-century B.C. Phoenician inscriptions from Babylon. The Greeks, in turn, *c.* 800 B.C., borrowed the alphabet in form, names, and order from the Phoenicians, whose trading ventures were famous throughout the Mediterranean. L. H. Jeffery (see bibliography) has shown that the earliest Greek alphabetic script came from the Greek colony living in the Phoenician city at the site now known as Al-Minah, near the later city of Seleucia, the port of Antioch, on the northern coast of Syria; around 800 B.C. this Phoenician trading center was Aramaic-speaking, which explains the Aramaic names of the letters of the Greek alphabet. Since all subsequent Western alphabets are derived ultimately from the Greek alphabet, the Western world is indebted for its alphabet to the Mediterranean cradle of its civilization.

Bibliography: D. DIRINGER, *The Alphabet* (2d ed. New York 1953). G. R. DRIVER, *Semitic Writing* (rev. ed. London 1954). F. M. CROSS and T. O. LAMBDIN, "A Ugaritic Abecedary and the

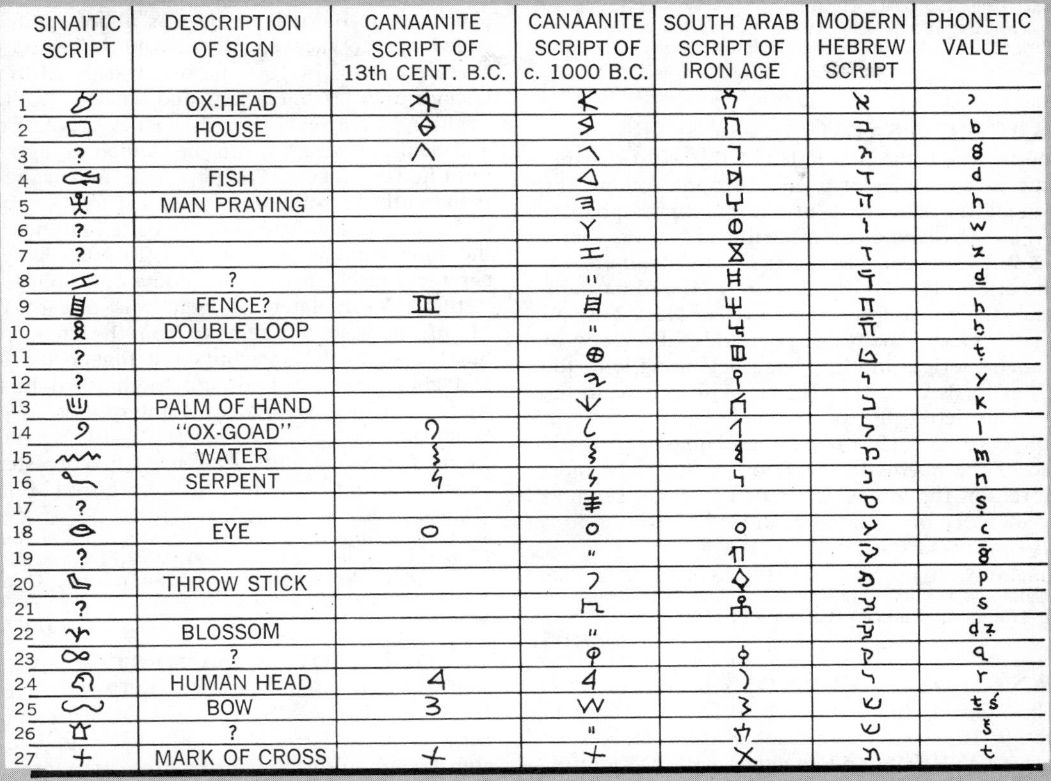

	SINAITIC SCRIPT	DESCRIPTION OF SIGN	CANAANITE SCRIPT OF 13th CENT. B.C.	CANAANITE SCRIPT OF c. 1000 B.C.	SOUTH ARAB SCRIPT OF IRON AGE	MODERN HEBREW SCRIPT	PHONETIC VALUE
1		OX-HEAD				א	ʾ
2		HOUSE				ב	b
3	?					ג	g
4		FISH				ד	d
5		MAN PRAYING				ה	h
6	?					ו	w
7	?					ז	z
8		?		"		ד̱	ḏ
9		FENCE?				ח	ḥ
10		DOUBLE LOOP		"		ח̄	ḫ
11	?					ט	ṭ
12	?					י	y
13		PALM OF HAND				כ	k
14		"OX-GOAD"				ל	l
15		WATER				מ	m
16		SERPENT				נ	n
17	?					ס	s
18		EYE				ע	ʿ
19	?			"		ע̇	ǵ
20		THROW STICK				פ	p
21	?					צ	ṣ
22		BLOSSOM		"		צ̇	ḍẓ
23		?				ק	q
24		HUMAN HEAD				ר	r
25		BOW				ש	ṯś
26		?		"		ש	š
27		MARK OF CROSS				ת	t

The chart above shows the earlier alphabet containing 27 characters; the chart below shows the later development that had only 22 characters. The numbers on the left show the correspondence of the individual characters.

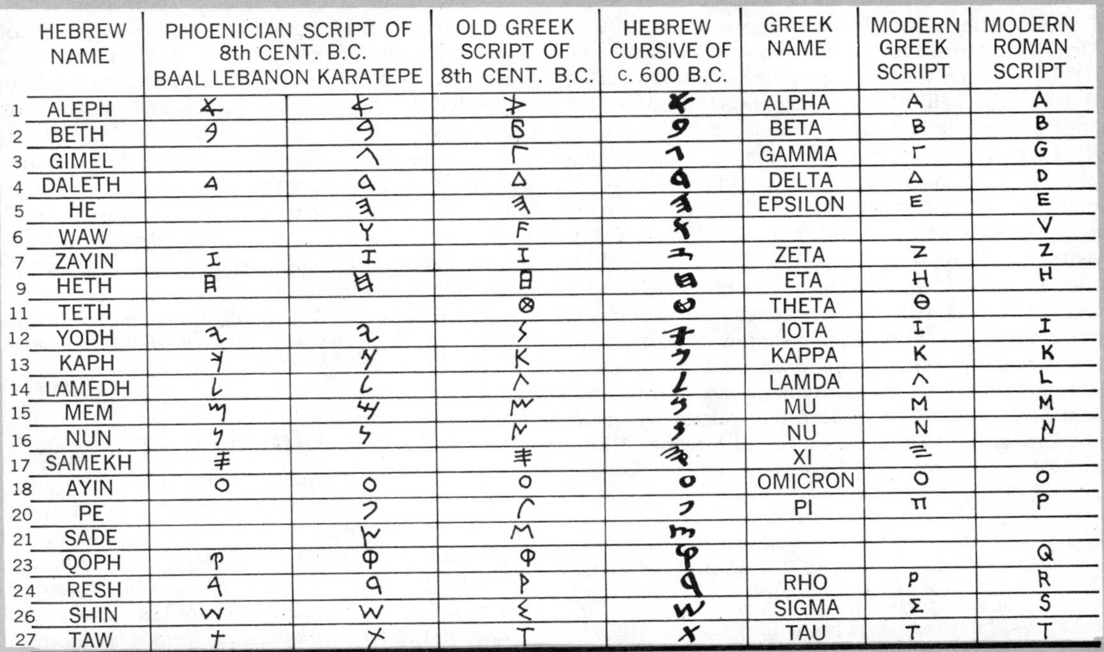

	HEBREW NAME	PHOENICIAN SCRIPT OF 8th CENT. B.C. BAAL LEBANON	KARATEPE	OLD GREEK SCRIPT OF 8th CENT. B.C.	HEBREW CURSIVE OF c. 600 B.C.	GREEK NAME	MODERN GREEK SCRIPT	MODERN ROMAN SCRIPT
1	ALEPH					ALPHA	A	A
2	BETH					BETA	B	B
3	GIMEL					GAMMA	Γ	G
4	DALETH					DELTA	Δ	D
5	HE					EPSILON	E	E
6	WAW							V
7	ZAYIN					ZETA	Z	Z
9	HETH					ETA	H	H
11	TETH					THETA	Θ	
12	YODH					IOTA	I	I
13	KAPH					KAPPA	K	K
14	LAMEDH					LAMDA	Λ	L
15	MEM					MU	M	M
16	NUN					NU	N	N
17	SAMEKH					XI	Ξ	
18	AYIN	O	O	O		OMICRON	O	O
20	PE					PI	Π	P
21	SADE							
23	QOPH							Q
24	RESH					RHO	P	R
26	SHIN					SIGMA	Σ	S
27	TAW					TAU	T	T

Development of the alphabet from the Proto-Canaanite script, as illustrated by the Sinaitic inscriptions of the first half of the 15th century B.C.*, through the older Phoenician scripts, to the Phoenician script of the 8th century* B.C.*, when it was borrowed by the Greeks. About 600* B.C. *a Western form of the script used by the Greeks was borrowed in turn to write Latin, and from this Latin script most modern alphabets are derived. Hebrew uses an alphabet derived from the same Phoenician script, but differently developed through the Aramaic.*

Origins of the Proto-Canaanite Alphabet," BullAmSchOrRes 160 (1960) 21–26. A. G. WOODHEAD, *The Study of Greek Inscriptions* (Cambridge, Eng. 1959). L. H. JEFFERY, *The Local Scripts of Archaic Greek* (Cambridge, Eng. 1961). **Illustration credit:** From W. F. Albright, *The Archaeology of Palestine* (Penguin Books, Baltimore 1949).

[F. L. MORIARTY]

ALPHABETIC PSALMS, poems of an acrostic formation in which the first letter of the word that begins a line or a couplet or even a strophe follows the succession of the 22 letters of the Hebrew alphabet: *'ālep, bêt, gīmel, dālet,* etc. This artificial form is found in Psalms 9; 24; 33; 36; 110; 111; 118 (Vulg enumeration), and also in Prv 31.10–31; Lam 1–4, and partially (because of the poorly preserved text) in Na 1.2–8 and Sir 51.13–30. Occasionally the poet adds, at the end of the alphabetic series, another verse beginning with the letter *pē',* as in Ps 24(25); 33(34). With regard to the choice of this letter, P. W. Skehan has pointed out [CathBiblQuart 23 (1961) 127] the quasi-alphabetic form also of the poems in the Book of Job. The most plausible reason for the device is that it might serve as an aid to memory or some other didactic purpose.

See also PSALMS, BOOK OF.

Bibliography: S. HOLM-NIELSEN, "The Importance of Late Jewish Psalmody for the Understanding of Old Testament Psalmodic Tradition," *Studia Theologica* 14 (1960) 1–51.

[R. E. MURPHY]

ALPHANUS OF SALERNO, scholar and archbishop; b. Salerno, Italy, between 1015 and 1020; d. there, Oct. 9, 1085. He was a teacher at the University of *Salerno (*c.* 1050), and together with Desiderius, later Pope *Victor III, he entered the *Benedictine Order at the monastery of *Monte Cassino in 1056. This foundation was, under the abbacy of Desiderius (1058–1087), the most advanced center of culture in Italy. In 1057 Alphanus was an abbot in Salerno, and in 1058 he became archbishop. Salerno's fame rested essentially in the field of medicine, the study of which Alphanus strongly encouraged; he also established for himself a considerable reputation as a theologian, hagiographer, and hymnist. He showed unusual skill in the meter of his Latin verse, which covers a wide variety of subjects and indicates considerable acquaintance with the Roman poets (AnalHymn 22.24, 50). An ode addressed to Hildebrand, while the future *Gregory VII was still an archdeacon, calls on the papacy to crush with spiritual weapons the forces of barbarism that opposed the Church, and it compares Hildebrand himself to the Roman heroes of the past. It was in Salerno that the Pope found refuge when the army of Emperor *Henry IV forced him to flee Rome (1085). Alphanus was an important figure both in politics and in the development of Christian humanism in the 11th century.

Bibliography: F. UGHELLI, *Italia sacra,* ed. N. COLETI, 10 v. in 9 (2d ed. Venice 1717–22). Raby ChrLP. Raby SecLP. C. DAWSON, *Religion and the Rise of Western Culture* (New York 1950). I. CECCHETTI, EncCatt 1:838–840. J. M. VIDAL, DHGE 2:401–403. A. LENTINI, "Rassegna delle poesie di Alfano da Salerno," *Bulletino dell' Istituto storico italiano* 69 (1957) 213–241. Szövérffy AnnLatHymn 1:398–402.

[B. D. HILL]

ALPHEGE OF CANTERBURY, ST., Benedictine, archbishop, honored as a martyr; b. 954; d. Greenwich, England, April 19, 1012 (feast, April 19). Alphege, who is known also as Aelfheah, Elphege, or Godwine, entered the monastery of Deerhurst in Gloucestershire against his parents' wishes. He left to become an anchorite near Bath; later he was abbot until *Dunstan called him to succeed *Ethelwold as bishop of *Winchester in 984. In 1006 he was translated to the archbishopric of *Canterbury and visited Rome for his *pallium. Five years later the Danes sacked Canterbury and held Alphege for ransom, which he agreed to pay until he remembered the poor who must raise the sum. Apparently he sometimes preached to his captors, who in 1012 during a drunken orgy pelted him to death with the bone remains of their feast. In 1023 King *Canute ceremoniously carried the body of Alphege to Canterbury. Years later Alphege was one of the saints *Lanfranc wished to remove from the English calendar, but *Anselm of Canterbury felt that to die for justice and charity was tantamount to martyrdom. The best sources include Osbern of Canterbury's *Life* (ed. H. Wharton, *Anglia Sacra,* 2:122–147), the *Anglo-Saxon Chronicle* and *Florence of Worcester, for the year 1012, and *Thietmar of Merseburg (MGS 3:849).

Bibliography: W. HUNT, DNB 1:150–152. C. COTTON, *The Saxon Cathedral at Canterbury and the Saxon Saints Buried Therein* (Manchester, Eng. 1929). W. A. PANTIN in *For Hilaire Belloc,* ed. D. WOODRUFF (London 1942). Butler Th Attw 2:129–131. Knowles MOE, *passim.*

[E. J. KEALEY]

ALPHEGE OF WINCHESTER, ST., called Aelfheah, "the Bald"; d. March 12, 951 (feast, Sept. 1; March 12 in *Winchester). A priest and monk, perhaps at *Glastonbury although the date and circumstances of his monastic profession are unknown, he was chaplain and secretary to his kinsman King Athelstan. Alphege, who succeeded Byrnstan as bishop of Winchester (934), is important primarily for his influence on the English monastic revival, encouraging and eventually investing his relative *Dunstan as monk. He ordained Dunstan and *Ethelwold, the latter commended to Alphege by Athelstan, on the same day, prophesying their future episcopates (*c.* 939). Dunstan may have been offered Alphege's see on the latter's death, but Aelfsige succeeded to it. The chief sources are: The *Anglo-Saxon Chronicle;* the *Vita Dunstani auctore B;* Aelfric, *Vita sancti Aethelwoldi;* Adelard, *Vita sancti Dunstani;* *William of Malmesbury; and *Simeon of Durham.

Bibliography: W. BIRCH, ed., *Cartularium Saxonicum,* 4 v. (1885–99). E. S. DUCKETT, *Saint Dunstan of Canterbury* (New York 1955). Butler Th Attw 1:577.

[W. A. CHANEY]

ALPHONSUS LIGUORI, ST.

Theologian, founder of the Congregation of the Most Holy Redeemer, bishop, Doctor of the Church; b. Marianella, near Naples, Sept. 27, 1696; d. Pagani, near Salerno, Aug. 1, 1787 (feast, Aug. 2).

Life. He was the eldest son of Giuseppe de Liguori, of a noble and ancient Neapolitan family and an officer of the royal navy, and Anna Cavalieri. After receiving his early education at home under the care of tutors, Alphonsus was enrolled in 1708 at the University of Naples, where he studied until Jan. 21, 1713, when at the age of 16 he received his doctorate *in utroque jure.* He practiced at the bar for some years, leading the while an exemplary Christian life under the direction of the Oratorians. When charged in 1723 with the defense of the interests of the Duke of Gravina against the Grand Duke of Tuscany, he lost confidence in the justice of his client's cause, perhaps in consequence of intrigues. Shocked by this experience he renounced the world and put on clerical dress, Oct. 23, 1723. He began his theological studies at home under the direction of Don Julio Torni and joined a group of secular priests (Congregation of the Apostolic Missions), in whose missionary activities he took part from 1724. Ordained Dec. 21, 1726, he devoted himself in a special way to the work of hearing confessions and preaching. In 1727 he organized the Evening Chapels (*Cappelle Serotine*), an association of workers and artisans formed for the purpose of mutual assistance, religious instruction, and works of apostolic zeal. In 1729 he left his home and took up residence in the College of the Holy Family, known also as the Chinese College, founded in Naples by Matteo *Ripa. There he devoted himself to the pastoral ministry by giving missions and working in the church connected with the college. After a sojourn at Scala and providential meetings with Thomas Falcoia of the society of *Pii Operarii,* who was made bishop of Castellamare di Stabia in 1730, and Sister Maria Celeste Crostarosa (1696–1755), he took an effective part in the foundation at Scala of the Institute of the Most Holy Savior, an order of contemplative nuns dedicated to the imitation of Jesus Christ, which was approved by Benedict XIV in 1750. On Nov. 9, 1732, he founded at Scala, under the direction of Bishop Falcoia, a congregation of priests under the title of the Most Holy Savior (known, after 1749, as the Congregation of the Most Holy Redeemer). It was intended as an association of priests and brothers living a common life and sharing in the desire to imitate Jesus Christ, particularly in the work of preaching the divine word. This congregation was formed with a special view to the needs of country people, who so often lacked the opportunities of missions, catechetical instruction, and spiritual exercises. Alphonsus gave himself to the work of the missions, to the organization of his congregation, and to the composition of his rule. His first companions deserted him, but he stood firm and before long vocations increased in number and new foundations multiplied; among the earliest were Villa Liberi (1734), Ciorani (1735), Pagani (1742), Deliceto (1745), and Mater Domini (1746).

On Feb. 25, 1749, Benedict XIV by his brief *Ad pastoralis dignitatis fastigium* approved the Congregation of the Most Holy Redeemer. Alphonsus was elected superior general for life at the general chapter held that same year. In consequence of the hostility of Marquis Tanucci and of the government, which was opposed to religious orders, Alphonsus could not obtain the royal exequatur in Naples to the brief of Benedict XIV. A royal decree of Dec. 9, 1752, gave limited assurance to the future of the institute, which at the time was extending its activity in the Papal States and in Sicily. Alphonsus governed his congregation, preached missions, and busied himself in writing and other apostolic work. He was appointed bishop of Sant' Agata dei Goti and was consecrated in Rome, June 20, 1762. As a bishop he soon distinguished himself for his work of reform. He put a stop to abuses, restored churches, fought for the liturgy, reformed his seminary, visited his diocese, promoted missions and often took a personal part in them, and exercised charity toward all, especially during the great famine of 1763–64. He kept an eye on the government of his congregation, which at the general chapter of 1764 adopted the completed constitutions, and continued with his writing. He was stricken in 1768 with a painful illness that made the pastoral ministry difficult; he offered his resignation from his see, and it was accepted by Pius VI in 1775. He then retired to Pagani, where he devoted himself to the governing of his congregation. Troubles concerning the rule caused by authorities of the Kingdom of Naples saddened his last years. The future of the congregation seemed precarious after the suppression of the Jesuits. He negotiated through an intermediary with the government to obtain its approbation, but the rule approved by the King and imposed on the congregation—the *regolamento*—differed notably from the rule approved by Benedict XIV. The Holy See, in its struggle with the Kingdom of Naples, took their canonical status away from the houses in the kingdom and gave to the houses in the Papal States their own superior. Alphonsus died before the reunion of the two branches of his congregation, which subsequently expanded to the whole world. Beatified Sept. 15, 1816, by Pius VII, canonized May 26, 1839, by Gregory XVI, declared Doctor of the Church by Pius IX in 1871, Alphonsus was finally made patron of confessors and moralists by Pius XII, April 26, 1950.

The Man. Ardent and richly endowed by nature, of delicate sensibility, tenacious of will, and profoundly intelligent, Alphonsus was given more to practical thinking than to pure speculation. He had to a rare degree an awareness of the concrete, a sense of the practical. In his relationship with others he combined nobility

St. Alphonsus Liguori, portrait by an unknown Italian artist, painted in 1768 and preserved in the College of the Redemptorist Fathers at Pagani, Italy.

of manner with affability and benevolence toward all, especially the poor, and smiling good humor: "a model of moderation and of gentleness" [B. Croce, *Uomini e cose della vecchia Italia,* v.21 (Bari 1927) 123].

The will of God, obeyed even in its most crucifying demands, was the only rule of his life. His prayer attained the summit of union with God, but it also expressed itself in apostolic action. He could in fact be described as a mystic of action. All his activity is explained by his determination to consecrate himself to the work of the Redemption and to the salvation of men. In this cause he employed all his artistic gifts. He was a talented musician and composed, in the style of the great Neapolitan school of the 18th century, a duetto of merit called *Duetto tra l'anima e Gesù Cristo.* He composed *Tu scende dalle stelle,* the lovely Christmas hymn that is still the most popular of Italian carols. In his *Canzoncine spirituali* he expressed in authentic poetry the sentiments of his mystical soul. An excellent picture of his psychology and intimate life can be gathered from the three volumes of his letters (Rome 1887–90).

Missions. Popular missions were for Alphonsus the means par excellence of procuring the salvation of souls. As a member of the Congregation of Apostolic Missions he took part in missionary work before he was a priest. His apostolate intensified with his ordination, and still more with the foundation of his congregation, which was dedicated in a special way to that work. It is estimated that he gave no fewer than 150 missions, and he himself once acknowledged that he had had 34 years of missionary experience. As a bishop he promoted missions in his diocese, and until his death he remained interested in the work. Alphonsus borrowed many of the elements of existing systems of conducting missions, but two features marked his own: (1) its concern that in the general structure of the mission and in the plan of the sermons there should be a continual adaptation to the concrete situation of the faithful; and (2) its effort to assure the perseverance of the participants by putting a major stress upon the love of God as the principal motive for conversion, and by calling for "renewals of the mission" to be preached some months after a mission, this last point being an original contribution to mission planning that won much acclaim.

Writing. No complete listing of the literary productions of St. Alphonsus is possible. Between 1728 and 1778 there appeared 111 works, and in addition to these there were posthumous publications. As to editions and translations, P. De Meulemeester in 1933 counted 4,110 editions of the original text (402 appeared before the death of Alphonsus) and 12,925 editions of translations into 61 languages. Since that time the number has continued to grow.

Works on Preaching. His principal work in this field was his *Selva di materie predicabili . . .* (1760), a complete treatise on sacerdotal perfection, the pastoral work of the missions, and the substance and form of preaching. In addition to this he published *Lettera ad un religioso amico ove si tratta del modo di predicare* (1761) in which he insisted on the necessity of preaching the gospel in a simple manner, without superfluous ornamentation, so that all, even the simplest of men, could understand the preacher. Mention should also be made of his sermons, and especially the *Sermoni compendiati per tutte le domeniche del anno* (1771), which were much admired by Newman.

Spiritual Works. These were markedly ascetical in character, but were solidly founded upon theology. They were the fruit of his interior life and of his preaching. The point of departure for his spirituality was the revelation of the love of God for man. Contrary to the teaching of the Jansenists, God offers to every man the possibility of salvation and of sanctification. This consists essentially in the loving response that man makes to the gift of God's love. To man turning toward God and detaching himself from creatures and the disordered impulses of concupiscence, Alphonsus presented the themes proposed by St. Ignatius in the First Week of the **Spiritual Exercises:* death, judgment, heaven, and hell. Such was the subject of his *Apparecchio alla morte* (1758) and of the *Via della salute* (1766). But the supreme motive of the Christian's love for God is Christ, the perfect revelation of God's love for man. The spirituality of St. Alphonsus was resolutely Christocentric. In his works devoted to the mysteries of Christ—*Santo Natale* (1758), *Riflessioni ed affetti sopra la passione di Gesù Cristo* (1761), *Riflessioni sulla passione di Gesù Cristo* (1773), and *Novena del Cuore di Gesù* (1758)—it is always the love of Christ that is emphasized, a love that man must requite by loving Christ in return. The most perfect synthesis of this spirituality is to be found in the *Pratica di amar Gesù Cristo* (1768), written in the manner of a commentary on the hymn of charity of St. Paul (1 Corinthians ch. 13). The love of God is not authentic if it does not express itself—here one can recognize the characteristically Alphonsian propensity for concreteness—in doing the will of God in the state and condition to which one is called. Hence the importance of the choice of state. Alphonsus developed this doctrine for all the states of life in his little work *Uniformità alla volontà di Dio* (1755). A fortiori, this principle is applicable to particular vocations: sacerdotal, as in the above mentioned *Selva;* religious, as in *Avvisi spettanti alla vocazione* (1749), and *La vera sposa di Gesù Cristo* (1760–61), a complete treatise on religious perfection.

What means did God give to Christians to attain holiness? The Sacraments, first of all. Alphonsus insisted particularly upon Penance and the Eucharist. In his volume *Del sagrificio di Gesù Cristo* (1775) he studied the essence of the Mass and the means of participating in it fully. Against the Jansenists he recommended frequent Communion (*see* COMMUNION, FREQUENCY OF). Devotion to the Blessed Sacrament occupied a place of prime importance in his spirituality. His book *Visita al SS. Sacramento* (1745) became a best seller and went through 40 editions during his lifetime. It gave to the practice of the visit a form that thenceforth became classic and definitive, and by means of it generations of Christians have come to find the nourishment of their daily prayer in the Eucharistic presence.

Prayer has a place of central importance in the economy of salvation and sanctification. Alphonsus gave magisterial treatment to the topic in what was, from the theological point of view, his most important work, *Del gran mezzo della preghiera* (1759). The first, and ascetical, part shows the absolute necessity of prayer for salvation. The second, and theological, part is directed against the Jansenist teaching on salvation and predestination. God wills the salvation of all men; Christ died for all; God gives to all the grace necessary for salvation, and one will certainly be saved if he corresponds with it. Faced with Jansenism and the teaching of the different theological schools on the subject of grace, Alphonsus expounded his own understanding of it. On the one hand there is an efficacious grace necessary for salvation; normally this acts by a kind of moral movement, determining infallibly by its own intrinsic power the consent of man's will, but leaving his liberty intact. But there is also a sufficient grace, which is truly active and gives man the power to perform psychologically easy acts in the order of salvation, such as that of imperfect prayer. One who corresponds with this sufficient grace will necessarily obtain efficacious grace. But sufficient grace is fallibly active. Man can fail to correspond with it and so in effect deprive himself of it. How is this grace fallibly active? St. Alphonsus never pretended to resolve this question explicitly; it is a point upon which one is simply referred to the conclusions of the commentators. F. *Marin-Sola, OP, and J. Maritain have proposed possible metaphysical extensions of the Alphonsian doctrine. As in other matters, St. Alphonsus was inspired by a number of authors and incorporated their teaching into his own view of the problem. But if, in fact, he often cited H. *Noris and Claude-Louis de Montaigne, the continuator of H. *Tournely, he went back beyond these and other immediate sources to the scholasticism of the 12th and 13th centuries and to St. Augustine. "Never did anyone bring together so compactly and so accurately the thought of St. Augustine on prayer and its necessity. The bishop of Sant' Agata was only an echo of the bishop of Hippo on this subject. . . . He had the genius to read with suprising clarity what the intellectual Jansenists had neglected in the writings of St. Augustine" [F. Cayré, *Patrologie et histoire de la théologie* v.3 (Paris 1944) 294].

The object of Christian prayer was first the love of God—i.e., the fulfillment of His will—then perseverance in that love, and finally the grace to pray always. Among the forms of prayer recommended by the saint was liturgical prayer (for which in 1774 he edited an Italian translation of the Psalter, *Traduzione de' Salmi e Cantici*) and mental prayer. For him mental prayer was morally necessary to assure the effective practice of prayer and consequently for perseverance in the grace of God, progress in charity, and union with God. The extremely flexible and easy method of mental prayer described in a number of his works led to the little masterpiece *Modo di conversare continuamente ed alla familiare con Dio* (1753). He would not hesitate to lead a disciple who corresponded with the grace of God to the height of mystical union with God by means of infused prayer [see *Pratica del confessore* (1755)].

The Virgin Mary appears in all the spiritual works of Alphonsus. To her he devoted the most elaborate of his books, *Le glorie di Maria* (1750), which is one of the great works of Catholic Mariology. Replying to L. A. *Muratori's criticism of the deviation of Marian devotion, Alphonsus firmly established the role of Mary in the history of salvation and solidly based devotion to her on theology. By the grace of the Redeemer

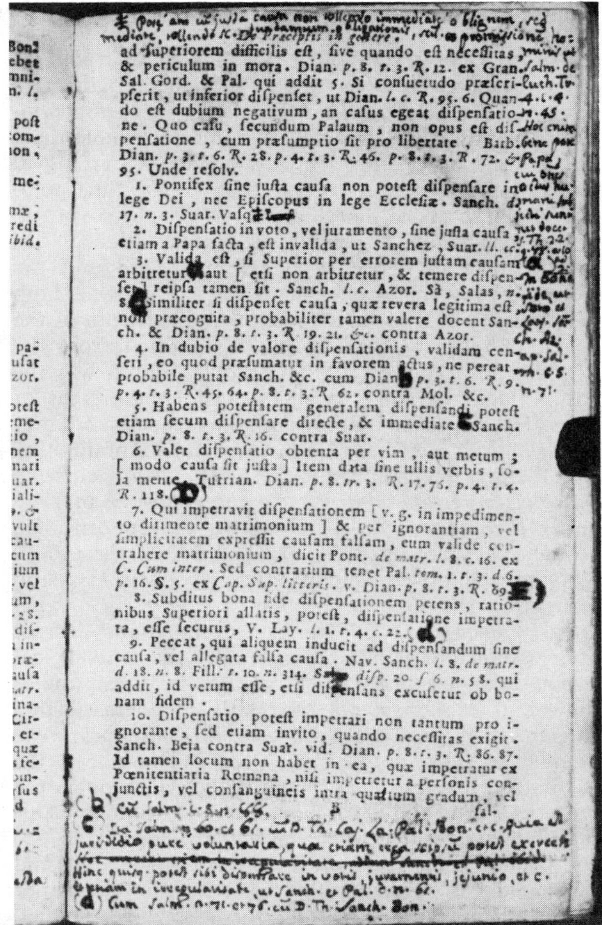

ad superiorem difficilis est, sive quando est necessitas & periculum in mora. Dian. *p.* 8. *t.* 3. R. 12. ex Gran. Sal. Gord. & Pal. qui addit 5. Si consuetudo præscripserit, ut inferior dispenset, ut Dian. *l. c.* R. 95. 6. Quando est dubium negativum, an casus egeat dispensatione. Quo casu, secundum Palaum, non opus est dispensatione, cum præsumptio sit pro libertate, Barb. Dian. *p.* 3. *t.* 6. R. 28. *p.* 4. *t.* 3. R. 46. *p.* 8. *t.* 3. R. 72. & 95. Unde resolv.

1. Pontifex sine justa causa non potest dispensare in lege Dei, nec Episcopus in lege Ecclesiæ. Sanch. 17. *n.* 3. Suar. Vasq.

2. Dispensatio in voto, vel juramento, sine justa causa etiam a Papa facta, est invalida, ut Sanchez, Suar. *ll. cc.*

3. Valida est, si Superior per errorem justam causam arbitretur, aut [etsi non arbitretur, & temere dispenset] reipsa tamen sit. Sanch. *l. c.* Azor. Sà, Salas, *n.* 8. Similiter si dispenset causa, quæ revera legitima est, non præcognita, probabiliter tamen valere docent Sanch. & Dian. *p.* 8. *t.* 3. R. 19. 21. &c. contra Azor.

4. In dubio de valore dispensationis, validam censeri, eo quod præsumatur in favorem actus, ne pereat probabile putat Sanch. &c. cum Dian. *p.* 3. *t.* 6. R. 9. *p.* 4. *t.* 3. R. 45. 64. *p.* 8. *t.* 3. R. 62. contra Mol. &c.

5. Habens potestatem generalem dispensandi potest etiam secum dispensare directe, & immediate. Sanch. Dian. *p.* 8. *t.* 3. R. 16. contra Suar.

6. Valet dispensatio obtenta per vim, aut metum; [modo causa sit justa] Item data sine ullis verbis, sola mente. Tutrian. Dian. *p.* 8. *tr.* 3. R. 17. 76. *p.* 4. *t.* 4. R. 118.

7. Qui impetravit dispensationem [v. g. in impedimento dirimente matrimonium] & per ignorantiam, vel simplicitatem expressit causam falsam, cum valide contrahere matrimonium, dicit Pont. *de matr. l.* 8. *c.* 16. ex *C. Cum inter*. Sed contrarium tenet Pal. *tom.* 1. *t.* 3. *d.* 6. *p.* 16. §. 5. ex *Cap. Sup. litteris*. v. Dian. *p.* 8. *t.* 3. R. 89.

8. Subditus bona fide dispensationem petens, rationibus Superiori allatis, potest, dispensatione impetrata, esse securus, V. Lay. *l.* 1. *t.* 4. *c.* 22.

9. Peccat, qui aliquem inducit ad dispensandum sine causa, vel allegata falsa causa. Nav. Sanch. *l.* 8. *de matr. d.* 18. *n.* 8. Fill. *t.* 10. *n.* 314. Sa *disp.* 20. *f* 6. *n.* 58. qui addit, id verum esse, etsi dispensans excusetur ob bonam fidem.

10. Dispensatio potest impetrari non tantum pro ignorante, sed etiam invito, quando necessitas exigit. Sanch. Beja contra Suar. vid. Dian. *p.* 8. *t.* 3. R. 86. 87. Id tamen locum non habet in ea, quæ impetratur ex Pœnitentiaria Romana, nisi impetretur a personis conjunctis, vel consanguineis intra quartum gradum, vel fal-

Page of St. Alphonsus Liguori's personal copy of the "Medulla" of Hermann Busenbaum with marginal notes in the saint's own hand.

immaculate in her conception (by his argumentation Alphonsus helped prepare the way for the definition of this dogma by Pius IX), Mary directly cooperated in the redemption of the world effected by Jesus on Calvary; she is the Co-Redemptress and consequently the universal, but not exclusive, mediatrix of grace. Through her one obtains especially the grace of prayer, and thus prayer to Mary leads to Jesus. St. Alphonsus considered authentic devotion to Mary an assurance and sign of salvation. *Le glorie di Maria* had an enormous influence on the 19th century and contributed to the great development of Marian devotion at that time.

In the development of his spiritual teaching Alphonsus was inspired by the spiritual writers of the 16th to the 18th centuries and freely incorporated things gathered from them into his own writings. In the *Biblioteche predicabili* and the *Prontuarii* he drew abundantly from these writers, the authors most frequently cited being the Jesuits Alfonso *Rodriguez, G. B. *Scaramelli, and J. B. *Saint-Juré, who transmitted to him the spirituality of the *Exercises* of St. Ignatius, and the spiritual doctrine of SS. Teresa of Avila, Francis de Sales, and, in lesser measure, that of John of the Cross.

Dogmatic Works. These, for the most part, were composed during his episcopate, and they are principally works of controversy. With a pastoral end in view, Alphonsus refuted the principal errors of his time and addressed himself to unbelievers for the purpose of showing them the truth of the Catholic religion. He resorted to psychological and moral as well as to intellectual arguments, wishing to reach the whole man. His *Verità della fede* (1767) is divided according to a threefold purpose, a structure not common in apologetical works of the time. For materialists he sought to prove, against the arguments of Hobbes, Locke, and Spinoza, the existence of a personal God and the spirituality of the soul; for theists, he showed both the necessity of a revealed religion and the truth of the Christian religion; for Christians separated from the Church, he argued that the Catholic Church was the only Church of Christ authenticated by the signs of truth. He stressed the necessity of a supreme authority in the Church provided with the privilege of infallibility. This theme was developed in the *Vindiciae pro suprema pontificis potestate contra Febronium,* printed in 1768 under the pseudonym of Honorius de Honoriis. He brought decisive support to the doctrine of the infallibility of the pope, which Vatican Council I was to recognize. His *Opera dommatica contro gli eretici pretesi riformati* (1769) took the canons and decrees of the Council of Trent and expounded their theological import as opposed to Protestant doctrine. These studies show that Alphonsus was an excellent dogmatic theologian. In his *Trionfo della Chiesa ossia istoria delle eresie colle loro confutazioni* (1772) he traced the history of heresies and their refutation through the centuries from antiquity to Jansenius and Molinos. In his *Condotta ammirabile della divina Providenza* (1775) he expounded his views on the history of salvation and on the unity and perpetuity of the Church in the manner of the *Discours sur l'histoire universelle* of Bossuet, but in a manner that made his thought much more accessible to the generality of Christians.

Moral Works. A third of the writing of Alphonsus was devoted to moral theology, and this fitted smoothly into place in the ensemble of his pastoral and spiritual thought. Writing with an eye upon the daily pastoral necessities of the ministry, he elaborated his moral theology for the use of his religious and of priests engaged in pastoral work, especially that of the confessional. It complemented his spiritual doctrine inasmuch as it searched out the will of God in all the circumstances of life. His great work in the moral field was his *Theologia moralis,* which began as simple annotations on the *Medulla theologiae moralis* of H. *Busembaum (1st ed., 1748); in the second edition (1753–55) it became more properly the work of Alphonsus himself, although it adhered to the plan of the *Medulla* and the *Institutiones morales.* With the appearance of the third edition (1757) the *Theologia moralis* in three volumes took on its definitive aspect. Alphonsus, however, labored unceasingly to perfect the successive editions (4th ed., 1760; 5th, 1763; 6th, 1767; 7th, 1772; 8th—which Alphonsus considered definitive—1779; 9th, 1785). From 1791 to 1905, the date of the critical edition by P. Gaude, there were 60 complete editions. In 1755 there appeared his *Pratica del confessore per ben esercitare il suo ministero,* which constituted the soul, so to speak, of his great work on moral theology. The *Istruzione e pratica per un confessore* (1757), translated into Latin under the title *Homo apostolicus,* was an original work, the most perfect, perhaps, of all the writings of the saint for its unity of tone and the firmness of its thought; it was intended as an example of what a manual of moral theology ought to be. *Il confessore diretto per le confessioni della gente di compagna* (1764) was written by the bishop of Sant' Agata for the priests of his diocese. A series of notes and "dissertations," 18 in all, devoted to probabilism and the exposition of his own system of *morality, was published between 1749 and 1777. The most important of these was entitled *Dell' uso moderato dell' opinione probabile* (1765). Certain of these papers were written against the theories of Giovanni Vincenzo *Patuzzi, OP, with whom Alphonsus engaged in vigorous controversy. The work of St. Alphonsus contained numerous citations, as did all the works of moral theology of the time. In the *Theologia moralis* more than 800 authors were cited, and the number of citations amounted to 70,000. All could not have been made at firsthand. No moralist after 1550 escaped Alphonsus' attention. His work, therefore, provides a complete panorama of the literature of moral theology of that time. His most immediate sources were St. Thomas Aquinas, Lessius, Sanchez, Castropalao, Lugo, Laymann, Bonacina, Croix, Roncaglia, Suarez, Soto, Collet, Concina, and most especially the *Cursus moralis* of the Salmanticenses.

Equiprobabilism. Alphonsus gave much time to the elaboration of his system, known as *equiprobabilism, which sought to steer a middle course between *probabilism and *probabiliorism. Having used F. Genet (1640–1703), a probabiliorist, as his guide at the beginning of his missionary experience, Alphonsus was won over to ordinary probabilism in practice. But he was not satisfied with it. Beginning in 1749 he wrote a series of dissertations on the subject. His thought became definitively fixed between 1759 and 1765, during his controversy with Patuzzi, which proved to be a fruitful experience for Alphonsus and provided him with an occasion for the consolidation of his thought. From 1767 to 1778, when his literary activity came to an end, he was constrained to veil his thought somewhat because of the anti-Jesuit persecutions, but he did not modify it substantially. Equiprobabilism, opposed to either a lax or a rigorous moral position, was not a compromise between the two, but a higher equilibrium. In recognizing the obligation of the more probable opinion in favor of the law, Alphonsus recognized also the law as a moral value. Rejecting probabilism as a universally valid and mechanically applicable solution of cases of conscience, Alphonsus proclaimed the necessity of a personal decision of conscience. In the case in which two equiprobable opinions, one favoring the law and the other liberty, are presented, Alphonsus, in leaving a man free to make his own decision, affirmed at the same time the moral value of human liberty. Man, who is created to the image of God, imitates his Creator in doing good freely. In support of his system, St. Alphonsus appealed to E. *Amort and St. Thomas. A. G. Sertillanges has said of it: "Equiprobabilism, properly understood, can rightly pass for a Thomist solution" [*La Morale de saint Thomas d'Aquin* (Paris 1942) 401].

In Alphonsian moral theory the study of the concrete circumstances of action rules out the mechanical application of a system, however sound it may be. Always disposed to prefer reason to the authority of moralists, he resolved most of his cases in terms of intrinsic evidence and in the light of Christian charity and prudence. As a result of his labor the Christian world was presented with a compilation of truly sound moral opinion, equally removed from the extremities either of laxism or rigorism, scrupulously weighed by the conscience of a saint. This has been a brilliant service to the Church [M. Labourdette, RevThom 50 (1950) 230].

Influence. The influence of St. Alphonsus on moral theology has proved durable, and the practical direction traced by him has been substantially adopted by the Church (Lanza-Palazzini). Among the major events in the history of the Church in the 19th century was the progressive rallying of moralists and of the clergy to the moral thinking of St. Alphonsus. In eliminating rigorism, in facilitating access to the Sacraments, he infused a new youth into Christianity. In France the penetration of Alphonsian thought was perhaps more rapid than elsewhere. Among its propagators in that country were Jean Marie de Lamennais; Bruno Lanteri, the apostle of Turin; and Cardinal Gousset, Archbishop of Reims, who evoked in 1831 the response of the Sacred Penitentiary favorable to Alphonsian moral theology. The Curé d'Ars mitigated his rigor after coming to know Liguorian principles. At the same time the Swiss, Belgians, Germans, and Spaniards welcomed this moral doctrine, the proclamation of St. Alphonsus as a Doctor of the Church lending encouragement to the movement. To the criticism of the system by A. Ballerini, SJ, the Redemptorists responded with a voluminous dossier, *Vindiciae alfonsianae* (1873). Among the manuals of moral theology written by Redemptorists were those of J. *Aertnys, C. *Marc, and, in the U.S., A. *Konings. Many of the manuals used in the seminaries of Europe and America either adopt the Alphonsian system or are marked by its influence in their solutions of cases.

It can be said that the influence of St. Alphonsus on Catholicism in the 19th century was very generally and very deeply felt. What he had written contributed to the definition of the dogmas of the Immaculate Conception and of the infallibility of the pope. He did much to shape the form that popular devotion took, especially the devotion toward the Eucharist and the Virgin Mary. His teaching on prayer reached even beyond the Church to thinkers such as Kierkegaard. He defended the Church against rationalism and enlightened despotism. Above all, he gave Jansenism in its practical form a blow from which it could not recover. His spirituality recalled the great message of the love of God for all men; his moral doctrine, inspired by the gospel, made it possible for Christians everywhere to deal with perplexities that had to be faced if they were to adjust successfully to the world in which they found themselves. "St. Alphonsus was more than a great personage of history. He is a symbol, and a very significant one" [H. X. Arquillière, *Histoire illustrée de l'Eglise,* v.2 (Geneva-Paris 1948) 196].

Bibliography: *Complete Works,* ed. E. GRIMM, 22 v. (New York 1886–97; 2d ed. of v.1–5, 12, Brooklyn 1926–28); *Opere ascetiche,* ed. F. DELERUE et al. (Rome 1933–); *Opera dogmatica,* Lat. tr. A. WALTER, 2 v. (Rome 1903); *Theologia moralis,* ed. L. GAUDÉ, 4 v. (Rome 1905–12; repr. 1953); *Lettere,* 3 v. (Rome 1887–90); *Canzoniere Alfonsiano,* ed. O. GREGORIO (Angri 1933); *The Way of Saint Alphonsus Liguori,* ed. B. ULANOV (London 1961), selected writings.

Bibliographies. M. DE MEULEMEESTER et al., *Bibliographie générale des écrivains Rédemptoristes,* 3 v. (Louvain 1933–39) v.1, 3. A. SAMPERS, "Bibliographia Alphonsiana 1938–53," *Spicilegium historicum C.SS.R.* 1 (1953) 248–271; "Bibliographia scriptorum de systemate morali S. Alphonsi et de probabilismo in genere, ann. 1787–1922 vulgatorum," *ibid.* 8 (1960) 138–172.

Biographies. A. TANNOIA, *Della vita ed istituto del ven. servo di Dio, Alfonso M. de Liguori,* 3 v. (Naples 1798–1802; new ed. Turin 1857). R. TELLERÍA, *S. Alfonso Maria de Ligorio,* 2 v. (Madrid 1950–51). O. GREGORIO et al., *S. Alfonso de Liguori: Contributi biobiliografici* (Brescia 1940). A. BERTHE, *St. Alphonsus de Liguori,* tr. H. CASTLE, 2 v. (Dublin 1905). D. F. MILLER and L. X. AUBIN, *Saint Alphonsus* (Brooklyn 1940). M. DE MEULEMEESTER, *Origines de la Congrégation du Très Saint Rédempteur,* 2 v. (Louvain 1953–57). H. CASTLE, CE 1:334–341. G. CACCIATORE, EncCatt 1:864–873. B. HÄRING and E. ZETTL, LexThK² 1:330–332. G. LIÉVIN, DictSpirAscMyst 1:357–389. S. O'RIORDAN, David CDT 1:60–62.

Literature. K. C. M. VAN WELY, *Gestalte en structuur van de Missie bij S. Alfonsus* (Amsterdam 1964). G. CACCIATORE, *S. Alfonso de' Liguori e il giansenismo* (Florence 1944). J. F. HIDALGO, *Doctrina alfonsiana acerca de la acción de la gracia actual eficaz y suficiente* (Rome 1951). K. KEUSCH, *Die Aszetik des hl. Alfons von Liguori* (2d ed. Paderborn 1926). H. MANDERS, *De liefde in de spiritualiteit van Sint Alfonsus* (Brussels 1947). D. CAPONE, "Dissertazioni e note di S. Alfonso sulla probabilità e la coscienza," *Studia moralia* 1 (Rome 1963) 265–343; 2 (Rome 1964) 89–155; 3 (Rome 1965) 82–149. C. DILLENSCHNEIDER, *La Mariologie de Saint Alphonse de Liguori,* 2 v. (Fribourg 1931–34). R. S. CULHANE, "Alphonsus and the Immaculate Conception," IrEcclRec 82 (1954) 391–401. J. A. CLEARY, "The Return to St. Alphonsus," IrTheolQ 18 (1951) 161–176.

[L. VEREECKE]

ALPINI, PROSPERO, Italian physician and botanist whose study of the sexual differences in plants aided Linnaeus in the foundation of his system of classification; b. Marostica, Republic of Venice, Nov. 23, 1553; d. Padua, Feb. 6, 1617. Alpini studied medicine at Padua where he received his doctor's degree in 1578; he then practiced medicine in Campo San Pietro for about 2 years. He spent 3 years in Egypt as physician to the Venetian Consul, George Emo. This appointment left him with ample time to continue his study of botany. Alpini became interested in the management of date trees and seems to have deduced the principle of sexual difference of plants. He noted that the female date palms do not produce fruit unless dust found in the male flowers was sprinkled over the female flowers. As a practicing physician in Cairo he made various studies in epidemiology. He was a strong believer in the doctrine of contagious diseases of which little was known at the time. Sarton in his *Introduction to the History of Science* lists Alpini as the first European to mention trachoma (*c.* 1580).

On his return to Italy in 1586 Alpini resided at Genoa as physician to Andrea *Doria, Prince of Melfi, but in 1593 he returned to Padua, where he held the chair of botany for many years. Alpini's best known work is *De Plantis Aegyptii liber* (Venice 1592), which contains numerous descriptions of plants and many illustrations. His *De Medicina Aegyptorum* (Venice 1591) contains the first account of the coffee plant published by a European writer. The genus *Alpinia* of the order Zingiberaceae was named in his honor by the Swedish botanist Linnaeus.

Bibliography: J. VON SACHS, *History of Botany,* tr. H. E. F. GARNSEY (Oxford 1890). A. CASTIGLIONI, *History of Medicine,* ed. and tr. E. B. KRUMBHAAR (2d ed. New York 1947). G. LUSINA, DizBiogItal 2:529–531.

[M. A. STRATMAN]

ALPIRSBACH, ABBEY OF, former *Benedictine abbey in Württemberg, Germany, former Diocese of Constance, present-day Diocese of Rottenburg. Its name came either from the demesne of Count Adalbert I of Uffgau (1041–45) or, according to another interpretation, from the phrase "old deer-hunting." Its founders were Ruotmann of Hausen, Adalbert of Zollern, and Alwig of Sulz. The first monks and the first abbot, Kuno, were of the *Fruttuaria-Sankt Blasien tradition; the third abbot came from *Hirsau. Lands were granted the abbey by Bp. *Gebhard III of Constance when the temporary wooden church was dedicated in 1095; the dedication of the extant Romanesque church followed on Aug. 28, 1099. In 1101 Adalbert of Zollern entered the abbey and donated more land. The foundation was confirmed in 1101 by Pope Paschal II as an abbey with free election of abbot and bailiff (*Vogt*); it received confirmation and protection from Emperor Henry V in Strasbourg on Jan. 23, 1123. The abbey bailiffs included the counts of Zollern, the dukes of Teck, and the counts of Württemberg. It was noted for its liturgy and pastoral work; it assarted the forests of the Kinzigtal area. Alpirsbach reached the high point of its development in the 12th century. It had a worthy and able abbot in Bruno (1338–80). In 1482 it was incorporated into the *Bursfeld congregation; the dormitory, abbot's quarters, and cloister were remodeled; the south aisle of the church was widened; the bell tower was completed; and the high altar was commissioned. The abbey was much damaged by fires in 1508 and 1513 and by the *Peasants' War. In 1534 the *Reformation came to Alpirsbach in the person of Ambrose *Blarer, a former Alpirsbach monk become Württemberg reformer. From 1556 to 1595 the abbey was a Protestant convent-school. From 1629 to 1648 it was inhabited by Catholic monks from Ochsenhausen, then it again became Protestant. In 1807 all church property was secularized, including Alpirsbach's holdings in 297 localities. The abbey church is now Lutheran; the refectory, a Catholic chapel.

Bibliography: G. ALLMANG, DHGE 2:765–768. W. HOFFMANN, *Die ehemalige Benediktinerabtei Alpirsbach* (Munich 1955). *Weingarten, 1056–1956,* ed. G. SPAHR (Weingarten 1956). K. HOFMANN, LexThK[2] 1:367.

[G. SPAHR]

ALT, ALBRECHT, OT scholar and Biblical historian; b. Stübach, Bavaria, Sept. 20, 1883; d. Leipzig, April 24, 1956. From 1922 until his death he was a member of the OT faculty at the University of Leipzig. But he often sojourned in Palestine. For some time he edited the *Palästinajahrbuch.* He knew Palestine well, and this familiarity pervaded his geographical and topographical studies; in such historical studies as *Die Landnahme der Israeliten in Palästina* (1925) Alt made much of regional or territorial history and its continuity. In his celebrated collection of historical essays, *Kleine Schriften zur Geschichte des Volkes Israel* (1953–59), Alt's competence extended to the histories of the neighboring peoples also, especially to the histories of Egypt and Syria. A master epigraphist and philologist, he interpreted not only Semitic and cuneiform material but also late Greek, Roman, and Byzantine sources. He was a coeditor of the fourth edition of R. Kittel's *Biblia Hebraica.* In 1929 he published *Der Gott der Väter* on the early religion of the Hebrews.

Alt made major contributions to the understanding of Israelite legal and political institutions. In *Die Ursprünge des israelitischen Rechts* (1934) he distinguished clearly between the types of apodictic law and casuistic law in the Pentateuchal legislation. *Die Staatenbildung der Israeliten in Palästina* (1930) and related studies advanced understanding of Israel's political institutions.

Bibliography: K. H. MANN, "Bibliographie Albrecht Alt," *Beiträge zur historischen Theologie* 16 (1953) 211–223. "Festschrift A. Alt zum 70. Geburtstag," *Wissenschaftliche Zeitschrift* 3 (1953–54) 173–178. M. NOTH, RGG[3] 1:247–248.

[T. W. BUCKLEY]

ALTAMIRANO, DIEGO FRANCISCO DE, Jesuit missionary; b. Madrid, Oct. 26, 1625 (or possibly Oct. 18 or 26, 1626); d. Lima, Dec. 22, 1715. He entered the Society of Jesus in 1642. For some 10 years he lived as a member of the province of the Philippines, and he made his solemn profession on Sept. 11, 1661. He was professor of theology at the University of Córdoba del Tucumán, Argentina, and rector of the major seminary. As a missionary to the Chaco, he founded the reduction of St. Francis Xavier, and he was provincial of Paraguay from 1677 to 1681. He served as procurator for Madrid and Rome in 1683, visitor of the Nuevo Reino (Colombia and Ecuador), visitor and provincial of Peru, and rector of the College of Lima. An outstanding religious superior, he was a staunch advocate of Jesuit rights in their internal government and in their relationship with the crown and the bishops. He was a historian of the society in the regions with which he was personally acquainted. His contribution to missionary activity ranged from writing a catechism in the Mocobí tongue to supervising the strategic location of missions as far south as the Strait of Magellan. He supported military protection for missions and protected the missions against the incursions of the Paulistas and of other Indian tribes. He tried to stop the king from compelling the Indians to grow maté and to export it from their own territory.

Bibliography: E. TORRES SALDAMANDO, *Los antiguos Jesuítas del Perú* (Lima 1882). Sommervogel 1:208–209.

[A. DE EGAÑA]

ALTANER, BERTHOLD, Catholic historian and patristic scholar, educator, author; b. St. Annaberg (Silesia), Sept. 10, 1885; d. Bad Kissingen (Bavaria), Jan. 30, 1964. After being ordained in 1910, he took his doctorate in theology at the University of Breslau, where he began to teach church history in 1919; in 1929 he was appointed ordinary professor of patrology, ancient church history, and Christian archeology. He was the first theologian to be deprived of his university position by the Nazi government for political reasons (1933). Cardinal Bertram thereupon provided him with a position at the cathedral of Breslau in order to enable him to continue his research. But he lost his very valuable library when the Gestapo expelled him from Breslau in 1945. He found refuge in Bavaria and after the war was appointed to the chair of patrology and the history of the liturgy at the University of Würzburg, which he occupied until his retirement in 1950. His early works deal with the history of the Dominican Order: *Venturino von Bergamo O.P.* (Breslau 1911), *Der hl. Dominikus* (Breslau 1922), *Die Dominikanermission des 15. Jahrhunderts* (Habelschwerdt 1924), and *Die*

Briefe Jordans von Sachsen (Leipzig 1925). He became best known by his one-volume textbook *Patrologie,* which he published in 17 editions and 6 languages (Eng. ed. by H. Graef, New York 1960). The volume *Kleine patristische Schriften* (TU 83; Berlin 1965) collects 48 articles dealing with the influence of Eastern theology on Western writers, especially St. Augustine, published previously in various periodicals.

Bibliography: B. ALTANER, *Verzeichnis meiner Veröffentlichungen 1907–53* (Würzburg 1953); "Bibliographie B. Altaner," HistJb 77 (1958) 576–600. J. QUASTEN, ThRev 51 (1955) 213–214; CathHistRev 50 (1964) 92–93.

[J. QUASTEN]

ALTAR

This article covers the employment of the altar in pagan religions with emphasis on antiquity, in the Bible, and in the Church. The treatment is confined to the liturgical use, as the altar in art is treated in the articles devoted to the history of art. The article is divided as follows: (1) historical background, (2) in the Bible, (3) in the liturgy, and (4) consecration.

1. HISTORICAL BACKGROUND

A place designated by custom or tradition for the presentation of sacrifices or other offerings to superhuman beings (God, ancestors, etc.), which reveals and guarantees communication with the other world, whether above or below the earth. An altar is usually a fixed place belonging to the sanctuary of a deity. In contrast to primitive hunter cultures, in which, generally, offerings are not burned for the deity or shared by the participants, but simply exposed *in toto* for the god in the open, the more differentiated cultures—agricultural or pastoral—are typified by religious systems in which altars function. Hence, a treatment of altars should be limited to such religions.

The altar is variously employed. It can be used as the slaughter place of a sacrificial victim (*mizbēaḥ,* the Hebrew word for altar, connotes "a place of slaughter"); as an altar on which the sacrificial part meant for the deity is burnt; as an offering place where the sacrifice is tendered to the deity for some time before the participants consume it; as the place where the participants (sacrificers and priests) partake of their part of the sacrifice (sacrificial meal).

It should be noted that the bringing of sacrifices is much wider and older than the use of altars, and also, that even in complex cultures, not all sacrifices require formal altars. Some ancient Teutonic tribes practiced human sacrifice by drowning and hanging. Furthermore, there are altars for unbloody offerings, e.g., agricultural products, although it is in conjunction with bloody sacrifices that we find the most characteristic examples. The use of a special altar for incense is found at an early date, but its origin is obscure. Finally, altars do not serve exclusively to maintain contact with gods. Thus, every Hindu temple, for example, has a special elevated place on which offerings are placed for the *bhūtas,* "beings," "spirits," but not gods. The most important forms of altar may be grouped under four heads.

The Place of Divine Presence and Communication. The place where a man has had a meeting with God is often marked by a stone or heap of stones to show that it is an appropriate place for communication with God (see Gn 28.10–22; 35.1–3). The most primitive of altars is accordingly a stone or heap of stones. The altar can mark the throne of the deity, as in West African and ancient Nordic religion, or the place to which the gods are invited or summoned, as in Hinduism. In each case, communication is possible because of the divine presence. Significantly, the Old English word for altar, *wīgbed,* literally means "table of the idols." The importance of communication with the divine is further stressed by the gigantic size of some altars in classical antiquity, as those of Syracuse, Parium, and Pergamum. This size is explained not only by the quantity of offerings for the deity, but also by the great number of celebrants sharing in the meat roasted. The widespread conviction that a man taking refuge at the altar, as in ancient Greece and Israel, must not be harmed has its natural explanation in the divine presence in its own domain.

Central Place as Representation of the Earth. This idea is at the heart of all altar symbolism. Hence the most archaic altars are made of earth or of natural stone, which stands for the earth. In ancient Indian religions the altar (*vedi*) consists of a piece of ground strewn with a special grass. The earth symbolism is never totally abandoned, even when altars become larger and even elaborate structures. The Roman temples had elevated altars for celestial deities and low altars or excavations in the earth for chthonic deities. Greek religion made a similar distinction between the altar for the cult of the celestial gods (βωμός) and, for that of the chthonic divinities, (ἐσχάρα), the low altar or fireplace; or βόθρος, a pit or trench in which sacrifices were burned or libations poured. Whether high or low, the earth was represented.

Among the Indo-Europeans generally the hearth (deified as Vesta in Rome) appears to be the prototype of the altar. This is not in contradiction with the earth symbolism, because the earth is the basis of human dwellings. In Hinduism the *Gārhapatya* fire (domestic fire) is used to ignite the other two fires required by the ritual.

The Place of Re-Creation and Consecration. The symbolic identification of altar and earth is variously expressed. Religions that have a cosmogonic myth concerning the killing of a monster (such as Tiamat in Mesopotamia and Vṛtra in Vedic religion) cultically reenact this deed and thus reestablish the world. The altar is the center of the re-creation and consecration of life.

In cults of the *manes* and in chthonic cults generally the burial mound is used as an altar, particularly in ancient Greece, for libations. In Germanic religion also traces have been found of sacrificial cults on graves. The meaning is to be sought in the same area as that of all chthonic cults: death leads to life.

Similarly, the great significance of fire altars is based on the capacity of fire to die and rise again. *Ara,* the common Latin word for altar derives from a root *ās* "to burn." Its use and purpose is *sacrificium,* "to make sacred," "to consecrate." An integral part of the Hindu ritual is the drilling of the fire for the altar.

The Center of Action. None of the images by which the altar can be presented—*tumulus,* table, seat, throne, trench, etc.—is complete if the dynamic is disregarded. All dynamics of human life find their center here. In ancient Greece children were accepted by carrying them

Fig. 1. Great altar of Zeus from Pergamum, c. 180 B.C., as reconstructed in the State Museum of (East) Berlin.

around the hearth, ἑστία. They thus shared in the sacredness of the altar. Especially among the Teutons, but also elsewhere, the altar was the proper place for the swearing of oaths. Everywhere altars are surrounded and covered with instruments of action: receptacles for the sacrificial fire, priestly tools and attire, the sacrificial kettle, or whatever custom prescribes. The altar is *the* earth where *the* action takes place.

Bibliography: L. Ziehen, "Altar I (griechisch-römisch)," and K. Galling, "Altar II (orientalisch)," ReallexAntChr 1:310–334, with bibliog. G. van der Leeuw, *Religion in Essence and Manifestation,* tr. J. E. Turner (London 1938; 2 v. Torchbks New York 1963). L. H. Gray et al., Hastings ERE 1:333–354. C. G. Yavis, *Greek Altars, Origins and Typology* (St. Louis 1949). E. D. Van Buren, "Akkadian Stepped Altars," *NUMEN* (1954) 228–234. V. Grønbech, *The Culture of the Teutons* (London 1932). J. Bayet, *Histoire politique et psychologique de la religion romaine* (Paris 1957). Nilsson GeschGrRel 1:78, 269–271. J. de Vries, *Altgermanische Religionsgeschichte,* 2 v. (2d ed. Berlin 1956–57) v.1. J. Gonda, *Die Religionen Indiens I, Veda und älterer Hinduismus,* v.11 of *Die Religioner der Menschheit,* ed. C. M. Schröder (Stuttgart 1960–). **Illustration credit:** Fig. 1, German Information Center, New York.

[K. W. BOLLE]

2. In the Bible

The article will be developed in four parts: terminology, pagan altars in the Bible, altars of Israel, and altars in the NT.

Terminology. The most common Hebrew word for altar in the OT is *mizbēaḥ* from the root *zbḥ,* meaning "to slaughter." Though *mizbēaḥ* probably meant at first that upon which the victim was slaughtered (Gn 22.9), later the victim was slaughtered at a distance from the altar and then placed upon it (Lv 9.13). The altar came to be even more dissociated from slaughter when grain offerings were made upon it, and when the term *mizbēaḥ* was applied to the altar of incense and even to the altar of the Transjordanian tribes, a mere memorial not used for sacrifice (Jos 22.26–27). Less common is *šulḥān,* the "table" of the Lord (Mal 1.12). The Greek equivalent of *mizbēaḥ* is θυσιαστήριον, likewise linked with the root "to sacrifice," θύω. In the Books of Machabees θυσιαστήριον is the characteristic word for the altar of the true God, carefully distinguished from βωμός, a pagan altar (1 Mc 1.54, 59, in Septuagint). In the NT altars of sacrifice are called both θυσιαστήριον (Mt 5.23) and τράπεζα, "table" (1 Cor 10.21), the first term being applied also to the altar of incense (Lk 1.11).

Pagan Altars in the Bible. Solomon offered sacrifice at the "great high place" in *Gabaon (3 Kgs 3.4), most likely an ancient Canaanite sanctuary. Danger of harmful pagan influence, however, led to laws calling for the destruction of pagan altars (Ex 24.13; Dt 7.5), an attack renewed in the postexilic hostility to the small pagan incense altars known as *ḥammānîm* (2 Chr 34.4). In time, the contamination of pagan worship became so abhorrent that the altar of holocausts defiled by Antiochus Epiphanes (1 Mc 1.57) was entirely dismantled and a new altar constructed in its place (1 Mc 4.44–47).

The Altars of Israel. A large stone in its natural condition could serve as an altar (1 Sm 6.14); most often, however, altars were constructed either of mud brick or unhewn stones. The ancient legislation of Ex 20.24–26 permitted either material, but there is no clear indication as to which was more generally used. Just as a heifer not yet yoked to the plow was suitable for sacrifice (Nm 19.2), so unhewn stones not yet removed from the divine sphere by human industry were proper altars. This desire to separate the divine from the human is probably the origin of the law against steps leading up to the altar (Ex 20.26): such steps would have been hewn out by human labor and would also have been trodden by the priest. The danger of indecent exposure as the priest mounted the steps clad in just a loincloth seems to be a secondary explanation. In time the ancient prescriptions lost their force, and the most sacred parts of the altar became the carved horns at its four corners (Ex 29.12), while the priest, now fully clad, used steps to ascend to the altar (Ex 28.42–43).

Despite changing custom, the symbolism of the altar remained constant. Above all, it was a symbol of God's presence. Thus Abraham and Jacob built altars to commemorate a theophany (Gn 13.18; 35.7), as did Gedeon, even giving a theophoric name to his altar: "Yahweh-Peace" (Jgs 6.24). At the altar, communion was achieved with God, as the offerings were removed from the human sphere to the divine, and blessings were received from God in return (Ex 20.24). The sprinkling of blood (*see* BLOOD, RELIGIOUS SIGNIFICANCE OF) on the worshipers and the altar brought the people into communion with God Himself (Ex 24.6).

The horns of the altar were a special sign of God's protective presence, and thus afforded sanctuary to the fugitive who grasped them (3 Kgs 2.28). Their origin is not clear. Perhaps they are vestiges of the ancient memorial pillars (Gn 28.18). They may have been used originally for holding the animal in place, or may merely be considered the altar's extremities prolonged to express a religious respect parallel to that shown for the extremities of the priest's body (Ex 29.20). In any case, they were characteristic of the two altars in the Temple of Jerusalem, the altar of holocausts and the altar of incense. *See* TEMPLES (IN THE BIBLE).

Fig. 2. Horned altar in the ruins of Mageddo, limestone, 10th century B.C.

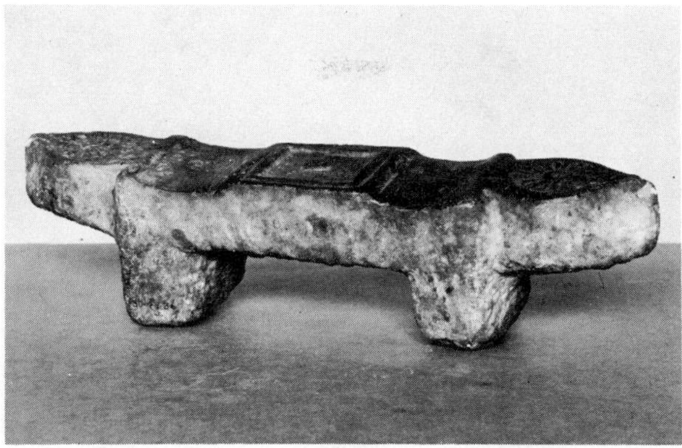

Fig. 3. Portable alabaster incense altar from South Arabia, Sabaean era, 3d to 1st centuries B.C.

The Altar of Holocausts. Although traditions about sacrifice date from the desert period (Ex 10.25; 18.12; 32.6, 8), there is no proof that such sacrifices were performed on a fixed altar. The desert altar of holocausts described in Ex 27.1–8 and 38.1–7 is more accurately understood as a movable likeness of the Temple's altar, which the author assumes to have been in use in the desert period. Since it was wooden and hollow, high but without steps, it is not clear how such an altar could have been used for holocausts. It also contained a bronze grating that gave it the name "the bronze altar." It is not clear what the position or function of this grating was.

The Books of 3 and 4 Kings contain several allusions to the altar of holocausts in Solomon's Temple, though it is noticeably absent from the lengthy description of the temple furnishings in 3 Kgs 6–7. It was made of bronze (3 Kgs 8.64) and was movable (4 Kgs 16.14); similar altars are familiar from Phoenician inscriptions. The sacred writer may have omitted his description of the altar because of its Phoenician origin. Data on the altar measurements are supplied by 2 Chr 4.1; however, these may be taken from the altar built later by Achaz (4 Kgs 16.10–11) or from the postexilic altar of the author's own time. The precise relationship between this altar in 2 Chronicles, ch. 4, Achaz's altar, the altar in Ezechiel's vision (Ez 43.13–17), and the postexilic altar of holocausts remains obscure. Achaz moved Solomon's altar somewhat to the north and installed a much larger one, built on different levels and modeled on one he had seen in Damascus, and therefore probably Syrian in origin. Whether it should be related to Ezechiel's altar, also constructed on various levels but Babylonian in its inspiration, is doubtful. The names Ezechiel gives his altar's different levels ("bosom of the earth," "the divine mountain") came from the various levels of Babylonian temples and were employed by Ezechiel to make the altar a temple in miniature. The altar in 2 Chr 4.1 has almost the same dimensions as Ezechiel's but its description may have been taken from the postexilic altar, about which further information is lacking.

The Altar of Incense. The incense altar of the *Tent of Meeting is described in Ex 30.1–5 and 37.25–28, but is probably a projection of the Temple altar into

the desert period. The arrangement of the Tent's furnishings is found in Ex 25–27, but, here, there is no mention of the incense altar, described later and out of context in Ex 30.1–5. Nor is it mentioned in texts describing the offering of *incense in the desert (Nm 16.6–7, 17–18; 17.11–12), where individual *censers are used. Like the desert altar of holocausts, it is a portable altar, built of wood and carried with poles. It is, however, also plated with gold, and so is known as "the golden altar."

The existence of this altar just outside the Holy of Holies in Solomon's Temple is well documented in 3 Kgs 7.48 and Is 6.6. Excavations in Mageddo and Sichem have also yielded small stone incense altars that can be said to date back as early as the 10th century B.C.

No mention is made of the incense altar among the precious appurtenances restored by Cyrus to the returning exiles (Ezr 1.6–11), but Antiochus Epiphanes later removed the golden altar when he plundered the second Temple (1 Mc 1.23). Under the Machabees, an incense altar was reinstalled (1 Mc 4.49), undoubtedly the same one at which Zachary offered incense (Lk 1.8–10).

In the New Testament. The ancient symbolism of the altar as the sign of God's presence is reflected in the words of Jesus: the altar sanctifies the gift (Mt 23.18). The symbolism now lessened the altar's importance, for the NT sacrifice was already sanctified without the altar. The new sacrifice is Jesus who sanctifies Himself (Jn 17.19). Thus, in 1 Cor 10.16–17, St. Paul affirms that Christians partake of the Lord's Body and Blood without reference to the altar. In Hebrews also the author shows no concern for an altar for the Eucharistic sacrifice. When he asserts, "We have an altar, from which they have no right to eat who serve the tabernacle" (Heb 13.10), he means the cross, or more likely he means the person of Jesus Himself.

The imagery of the Apocalypse recalls the Temple's altars, although it is not always clear which is meant, the one for holocausts or for incense. In Ap 11.1, the author is told to measure the Temple and the altar. In its context the image refers to the small group of men who remain faithful to Christ. Other references to altars found in the Apocalypse (Ap 6.9; 8.3, 5; 9.13; 14.18; 16.7) seem to envisage the altar of holocausts from which the prayers of the martyred saints arise. In any case, even in the Apocalypse, the altar's value is ultimately eclipsed, for in the vision of the new Jerusalem there is no temple or altar, "for the Lord God almighty and the Lamb are the temple thereof" (Ap 21.22).

Bibliography: De Vaux AncIsr 406–414. K. GALLING, Inter DictBibl 1:96–100; 2:699–700. "Le Mystère de l'Autel," *Maison-Dieu* 29 (1952) 9–31. **Illustration credits:** Fig. 2, Palestine Archaeological Museum. Fig. 3, The University Museum of the University of Pennsylvania.

[P. J. KEARNEY]

Fig. 4. (a) Wooden three-legged table altar or "Tribadion," 3d-century fresco, Cemetery of St. Callistus, Rome. (b) Early Romanesque table altar of stone in the church of San Pedro de Rocas, Spain. (c) Box-shaped altar above the martyr's grave in the church of San Alessandro in Rome, 5th century. The opening in the front gives access to the relics within.

3. In the Liturgy

The early Church continued to speak of the Lord's table (τράπεζα κυρίου; 1 Cor 10.21), which stressed the meal aspect of the Eucharist. A less common term, θυσιαστήριον (Heb 13.10), emphasized the sacrificial aspect of the Eucharist. With the gradual separation of the agape and Eucharistic rites in the 2d century, the idea of sacrifice received more emphasis. Latin Christians then spoke of an *altare* (sing.), distinct from the pagan form, *altaria* (pl.). *Ara* remained a predominantly pagan term for altar.

Historical Development. The altars in the first 3 centuries were wooden, and only rarely stone, tables. A 3d-century representation of a wooden altar exists in the cemetery of St. Callistus (Fig. 4*a*). Deacons moved the table to and from the place of the liturgy; however, fixed altars did exist.

Transition to Fixed Stone and Metal Altars. Fixed altars became customary in the 4th century when stone and metal altars began to replace the wooden altars. In 517, the Council of Epaon in Bourgogne forbade wooden altars (can. 26), yet some were still used in the 12th century. Various reasons exist for the transition from wood. The danger of persecution no longer necessitated movable altars, basilicas called for more fitting altars, and the rock or stone theme in Scripture, as well as increased reverence for altars, possibly exerted some influence. Down to the Carolingian era the altar remained small with space enough for the chalice, bread, and book (Fig. 4*b*). The mensa (top part) was usually square, but sometimes rounded. Frequently, till the 13th century, it was slightly concave.

Association with Relics. The cult of martyrs provoked the next important development in the history of the altar. It was an ancient custom to honor deceased heroes; with all the more reason did Christians honor their martyrs (*Martyrium Polycarpi* 17.1; 18.2). Cyprian tells of the Eucharist being celebrated at grave sites (*Epist.* 39.3; 12.3). The tombs themselves, however, were not used as altars; instead, portable altars were used. Later, churches and altars were built over the tombs (e.g., St. Peter's and St. Paul's at Rome). Among the reasons for associating relics with the altar were: reverence, a desire to retain communion with the martyrs, obtain their intercessory protection, and highlight the relation of their sacrifice to the altar's (see Ap 6.9–11).

This association took place when many new churches were being built. Since not all the new churches could be built over martyr tombs, relics were brought to altars. In Rome and parts of Gaul, however, recourse was often had to second-class relics, pieces of cloth touched to reliquaries (*brandea, palliola*), for Roman law strictly forbade the disturbance of the dead. Though it is said that the threat of barbarian invasions (5th to 6th centuries) led to the translation of some relics to safety within cities, we know that Popes Hormisdas (514–523) and Gregory I (590–604) forbade any such translation. Yet Boniface IV (608–615) brought a large number of relics to Rome for the dedication of St. Mary of the Martyrs. In any event, the spread of relics from Rome was slow. In the East and in northern Italy relics were divided and translated with little hesitation. Though Theodosius I (375–395) outlawed it (*Cod. Theod.* 9.7.7), his law was ineffective; the practice continued and eventually prevailed in the West. From the 9th century on, even the Eucharist and corporals were sometimes misused as altar relics till this practice was forbidden in the 14th century.

Fig. 5. The confession before the high altar of the Basilica of St. Peter at Rome. The altar itself stands directly over the site of St. Peter's tomb.

Types of Altars Resulting from the Association with Relics. This association caused some changes in the structure of altars. Three forms of altars became common. (1) The table altar continued in use with the relics placed either in the base of its main support or in a hollowed out part of the mensa. This type of altar became less common in the Carolingian era because it was impractical for the entombment of relics. (2) There appeared a hollowed box-shaped altar with a window opening on its front or back, permitting access to the reliquary within it (Fig. 4*c*). (3) A solid box-shaped altar was built over tombs. Access to the tomb below could be had through a confession in front of the altar (Fig. 5). If there were no tomb below the altar, a sepulcher for the relics might be carved out of the mensa, or a niche in the front of it used to house them. Only in the late Middle Ages did the present practice of placing the sepulcher in the mensa prevail. In 1596 Church law required a sepulcher for every altar.

Altars made out of, or in the form of, sarcophagi did not exist before the 16th century, and were in vogue only during the baroque and rococo period. Wooden portable altars used by missionaries are mentioned as early as the 6th century. The earliest example of one comes from the tomb of St. Cuthbert in Durham (d. 687). Only in the 14th century did the portable altar-stone become common (Fig. 6).

From One Altar to Many Altars. One altar to a church was the rule in the early Church (Ignatius, *Ad*

Fig. 6. Portable altar of ivory and enamel with a stone top, from Melk, Austria, second half of the 11th century; height 10.7 cm, length 23.8 cm, width 15.5 cm.

Phil. 4.1; Eusebius, *Hist. Eccl.* 10.4.68); and this remains the practice in the East. The one altar gave symbolic expression to the oneness of the Church and of her worship. Only in the 5th and 6th centuries did altars begin to multiply in the West. Though the orations *super oblata* (Secret prayers) in the Leonine Sacramentary speak of *altaria* (pl.), this plural reference was to the altars used to receive the offerings. Altars were first multiplied to provide a place for the numerous relics. This change occurred in the time of Pope Symmachus (498–514), and possibly even before. In the 7th century an increase in the number of low Masses for votive intentions and the practice of ordaining monks were factors in the multiplication of altars, especially since it was often the custom to celebrate only one Mass a day at an altar. Gregory I had no objection to a church with 13 altars (*Epist.* 6.49). A Carolingian prescription did try to control this multiplication, but at the end of the Middle Ages the Cathedral of Magdeburg and the Marian Church of Danzig each had 48 altars. Nevertheless, the principle of one altar has been preserved to the extent that there still is only one main altar to a church.

Position of Altar and Celebrant (Orientation, Retables, and Chancels). In the pre-Carolingian period the altar was situated away from the apse wall: at the edge of the apse, between the apse and the nave, or in the middle of the nave. Moreover, it might be built on the floor of the elevated apse or on the floor of the nave, in either case with or without a few steps elevating it. At all events it was most visible. Two developments played a large part in shifting the altar to the rear or apse wall: orientation and the development of retables. Perhaps an exaggerated reverence for the Eucharistic mystery also played a part in moving the altar away from the people.

As regards orientation, the basilicas in Rome were usually portal-oriented, i.e., the church entrance faced the east (vs. apse-oriented churches). When the bishop went to the altar from his throne in the apse, he would be facing the people. However, the Eastern custom of apse-oriented churches spread to the West, especially from the early 5th century on. The apse-oriented churches in Gaul and the emphasis on orientation in prayer there caused changes in the ceremony books, which originally came from Rome. The celebrant then stood facing the apse, leading the people behind him. The use of this position was brought to Rome with the Roman-Germanic ceremony books of the 10th century. It was eventually accepted by Roman churches, unless other conditions prevented celebrating Mass on the people's side of the altar (e.g., the confession at St. Peter's). This change brought the bishop's throne from behind the altar to the front gospel side of the altar. The clergy moved to the front or people's side of the altar. Thus orientation contributed to moving the altar to the rear. *See* CHURCH ARCHITECTURE, 1.

However, a second factor contributed to this movement of the altar, namely, the placing of martyr's relics on it in reliquaries that were often quite large (Fig. 7). Churches without first-class relics began to substitute for them retables, vertical structures of varying height, built onto the rear of the altar (or later, from the floor up). At first they were of modest dimensions and painted with religious scenes, especially scenes from the life of a saint. They appeared gradually in the 10th and 11th centuries and flourished in the Gothic period (12th–15th centuries). The oldest retables extant come from the 12th century. They grew in size as paneled retables became common (triptychs and polyptychs). Carved figures were added to them. Some retables allowed for changes in keeping with the liturgical season. By the end of the Middle Ages hardly an altar was without a retable. Some cathedral churches built in the 12th and 13th centuries continued to place the bishop's throne behind the altar. In these churches the retable was a subsequent development that blocked out the bishop's throne and made its location useless for the liturgy. The retable in these instances was an additional factor in moving the throne from behind

Fig. 7. Reconstruction of the altar formerly in the Abbey church of St. Denis at Paris. The altar is enclosed with curtains and a reliquary rests under a canopy behind and above the gradine.

the altar and thus permitting the location of the altar against the apse wall, farther from the congregation.

The distance between the laity and altar was further accented by the chancel or rood screen. Even in the early churches a division of some sort separated laity and clergy (Eusebius, *Hist. Eccl.* 10.4). In both East and West this dividing piece grew. In the East it developed into the iconostasis (*see* ICON) that blocked out the view of the altar except when its center door was opened. In the West the altar could still be seen, but the chancel grew large enough to provide an elevated platform for Scripture readings, preaching, cantors, even the organ (Fig. 8*a*). Since in the late Middle Ages the bishop's throne and choir of canons or monks separated the laity from the altar, an altar for the laity (rood altar) was placed in front of the chancel in many churches. The baroque period was largely responsible for clearing the churches of chancels; all that remains of them today is the altar railing (*see* COMMUNION TABLE).

Tabernacles and Gradines. Down to the 16th century the Eucharist was reserved in various parts of the church. Only in the 16th century did the *tabernacle become a permanent fixture of the altar. Its presence on the main altar is now required by Church law, though provision is made for reserving the Sacred Species elsewhere if there is another place more convenient and fitting for veneration and worship (Fig. 10). The presence of the tabernacle has distracted attention from the altar and to some extent made of it a support for the tabernacle and a place for exposition of the Blessed Sacrament.

Also, in the 16th century one or more gradines (steps) were added to the rear of the mensa. These gradines have served as pedestals for candles, flowers, relics, statues, etc. Again, they tend to obscure the nature of the altar.

In the Renaissance and baroque periods, large paintings flanked with pillars and statuary served as retables. Another favorite motif, especially in the baroque period, was the exposition throne for the Blessed Sacrament. The retables often became monumental in their proportions so that the altar seemed a mere appendage. This development, with various modifications, persisted until recent times when the altar has again begun to receive the emphasis it deserves, especially with the 20th century trend to celebrating Mass facing the people.

Altar Accessories. Retables, chancels, and tabernacles have been discussed in treating the historical development of the Altar. But there are many other altar accessories that deserve special mention.

Civory and Baldachino. The civory is a canopy structure over the altar supported by four columns. Various reasons have been given for its use, but most likely it was adopted from profane use to express the sovereign dignity and liturgical importance of the altar. This

Fig. 8. (a) The nave of the church of St. Étienne du Mont, Paris. The choir screen separating the sanctuary from the nave was built between 1540 and 1545. (b) Square altar completely covered with a linen cloth, detail of a 6th-century mosaic in the Basilica of San Vitale at Ravenna, Italy. The mosaic is an early representation of the sacrifices that were offered by Abel and Melchisedec.

seems especially true for the small altar in the large 4th-century basilicas. The popularity of the civory, however, lessened in proportion to the growth of retables. In the late 15th century the *baldachino developed from the civory as a canopy supported from above or from behind the altar. Even though Church law prescribed some kind of canopy for cathedral main altars and altars at which the Eucharist is reserved, the law has not been well observed.

Curtains are sometimes related to the civory. St. John Chrysostom (344?–407) speaks of curtains in conjunction with the liturgy (*Homil. in 1 Cor.* 36.5). In the East, they were frequently attached to the chancel rather than to the civory (Fig. 7). They served to hide the altar from catechumens and, later, to hide the mysteries themselves from the laity, as the iconostasis does today. In the West, curtains attached to the civory are mentioned in the time of Sergius I (687–701), but they served a decorative, not liturgical, purpose.

Altar Cloths. A cloth completely covering the altar dates back to at least the 4th century (Fig. 8*b*). Sometimes a separate white linen cloth, the ancestor of the corporal, was placed on this covering cloth. The back part of the upper cloth was raised and folded back over the chalice to serve as a pall (Fig. 9). But soon the pall became a separate piece. By the 8th century two or four linen cloths were being used to cover the altar in case of spillage. At this time also the uppermost cloth came to be called "corporal" since it held the Body (*Corpus*) of Christ. Meanwhile, when the altar received a retable and was moved against the back wall, the original cloth that covered the altar completely became the frontal (or *antependium), for only the front could then be covered. Besides cloth, there were also metal and wooden frontals. It is prescribed by law that the altar front be covered unless it is of precious material and highly decorative.

Fig. 9. Celebration of Mass; the corporal is folded over the chalice as a pall, illumination in the 13th-century Missal of Jumièges in the Municipal Library at Rouen, France (MS 299, fol. 152r).

Candles and Cross. *Candles (*see* LIGHT, LITURGICAL USE OF) provided light for the altar from earliest times, but did not appear on the altar until the 11th century. The *cross appeared on the altar at the same time; the *crucifix became increasingly common from the 14th century on.

Secondary Elements. Altar cards were added in the 16th and 17th centuries as a memory aid. Decorative flowers were long traditional, but only in the 16th century were they tolerated on the altar. A Missal stand is known as far back as the 6th century. In the 13th century cushions became common, at least in Europe, as stands.

Church Law. A number of references have been made above to Church law regarding the altar. J. B. O'Connell sumarizes (218) the law for the perfect altar:

> It is a consecrated altar, standing clear of its surroundings, with no reredos—or with one that does not interfere with the correct structure of the altar, the full veiling of the tabernacle, the proper position of the cross—and no fixed exposition throne. It is fully clothed with its frontal and altar cloths, and surmounted by a canopy (civory, baldaquin, or tester). If the altar has a tabernacle, this will be entirely detached and fully veiled by its conopaeum. The altar cross will be such as to be clearly visible in all parts of the church.

The Altar's Symbolism. The Church in various ways reminds her children that the altar is a sign of Christ. She marks it with five wounds, and, in general, treats it with utmost respect (anoints, incenses, kisses it). Its stone aspect is symbolic of Christ the mystic cornerstone (Acts 4.11; Mt 21.42; 1 Pt 2.4–7), the rock source of living water (1 Cor 10.4). But the altar is not a passive sign of Christ. Here God comes to man and man to God as the covenant is daily renewed in meal and sacrifice. The table aspect of the altar recalls the Last Supper, the family meal with Christ our Brother, in a spirit of peace, joy, and love. The stone aspect of the altar recalls Christ's sacrifice, which continues to be applied today. It also reminds men, as do the relics entombed therein, of the sacrifices they should offer in union with His. The ciborium calls attention to the sovereignty of our King, and reminds us of our allegiance to Him and His Kingdom.

Unfortunately, in the history of the altar, secondary elements (relics, retables, chancels, etc.) have received too much emphasis. They have distracted attention from the true nature of the altar. Even the reservation of the Blessed Sacrament on the altar, important as it is, has its proper relation to the altar, as coming from the altar to communicate the life of the altar's meal and sacrifice. For the altar remains a sign of Christ's meal and sacrifice, the center of the Church's life and worship.

Bibliography: J. BRAUN, *Der christliche Altar in seiner geschichtlichen Entwicklung,* 2 v. (Munich 1924). E. BISHOP, *Liturgica historica* (Oxford 1918; repr. 1962) 20–38. Eisenhofer Lit 120–127. A. M. ROGUET, "L'Autel," *Maison-Dieu,* no.63 (1960) 96–113. *Maison-Dieu,* no.70 (1962). A. G. MARTIMORT, ed. *L'Église en prière* (Tournai 1961) 170–176. Miller FundLit 99–110. J. B. O'CONNELL, *Church Building and Furnishing* (Notre Dame, Ind. 1955) 133–218. P. RADÒ, *Enchiridion liturgicum,* 2 v. (Rome 1961) 1:337–341. Righetti 1:295–333. M. M. HASSETT, CE 1:346–367. H. LECLERCQ, DACL 1.2:3155–89. A. ROMEO et al., EncCatt 1:919–928. T. KLAUSER, LexThK[2] 1:369–375. J. P. KIRSCH and T. KLAUSER, ReallexAntChr 1:334–354. H. CLAUSSEN, RGG[3] 1:255–267. **Illustration credits:** Fig. 4*a*, Pontificia Commissione di Archeologia Sacra. Fig. 4*b*, Photo

Fig. 10. The altar of sacrifice and the altar of reservation, chapel of Mt. Savior Monastery, Elmira, N.Y.

Zodiaque. Fig. 4*c*, Leonard Von Matt. Figs. 5 and 8*b*, Alinari-Art Reference Bureau. Fig. 6, Courtesy of the Dumbarton Oaks Collections, Washington, D.C. Fig. 8*a*, Archives Photographiques, Paris. Fig. 9, Bibliothèque Nationale. Fig. 10, Charles L. Hickey.

[R. X. REDMOND]

4. CONSECRATION OF

The consecration of an altar is the purification and hallowing of a fixed or portable altar by a solemn rite that sets it aside permanently for its sacred purpose—the offering on it of the sacrifice of the Mass (CIC cc.822, 1199, 1202).

A fixed altar may be consecrated either during the consecration of a church or separately (CIC c.1165.5). The rite of consecration is found in the Roman Pontifical. It is normally carried out by the bishop of the diocese (CIC c.1155.1). Any bishop can validly consecrate an altar, but for the lawful consecration of a fixed altar the permission of the local bishop is needed (CIC cc.1155.2, 1199.2). An abbot can consecrate an altar only by apostolic indult.

A consecrated altar—at least a fixed one—is to have a title of dedication. This may be the Blessed Trinity, Our Lord under the title of a mystery of His life or of a name already used in the liturgy, the Holy Spirit, Our Blessed Lady, an angel, or any canonized saint.

An altar may be consecrated on any day, but it is more becoming that the ceremony should be on a Sunday or a solemn feast of a saint. The rite may not, however, be performed on certain greater feasts.

The consecration of a fixed altar is lost by the separation, even momentarily, of the table from its support, to which it is inseparably joined by a special anointing at its consecration. Either a fixed or a portable altar loses its consecration if it suffers a serious break, or if the relics are removed from it, or the lid of the "sepulchre" (the cavity in which the relics are buried) is broken or removed, except in one case, i.e., when the bishop or his delegate removes the lid to repair or fasten it, or for the purpose of inspecting the relics (CIC c.1200).

The present rite of consecration is derived from the combination of two separate rites that were fused in about the 10th century: (1) the Roman ceremony for the translation and "deposition" of the relics of saints (a ceremony that follows the order of the liturgy of the dead) and the first celebration of Mass on the altar (which alone was necessary for its consecration in the Roman rite up to the 6th century); and (2) the Jewish-Gallican ceremonies of lustration (purification by prayer with the sprinkling of blessed water), incensation, and ritual anointing, chiefly derived from 7th- and 8th-century Gallican texts, which took their inspiration from the rite of the dedication of a Jewish altar (Ex 29; Lv 8). This composite rite was added to by innovations in the Roman Pontifical of the 13th century and that of William Durandus of Mende (d. 1296).

After an introduction in which the Litanies of the Saints are sung, the rite of the consecration of a fixed altar is made up of three parts: (1) lustration of the altar with blessed Gregorian water (a mixture of water, salt, ashes, and wine) sprinkled around it and marked on five spots on the table, accompanied by the chanting of antiphons and psalms; (2) deposition of relics of the saints (among them that of at least one martyr) brought in solemn procession and enclosed by the bishop in the sepulchre, whose lid is sealed by cement mixed with the Gregorian water and blessed while antiphons are sung; (3) consecration by anointing with chrism of five places on the table-top of the altar, its front, and the junction of the table with its supports at the four corners; the incensation of the altar; the burning of blessed incense grains on its table; the invocation of the Holy Spirit; and three prayers—the last one being a consecratory Preface.

Fig. 11. Consecration of an altar. (a) *Burial of saints' relics in the altar table.* (b) *Burning grains of incense on corner of altar previously anointed with chrism.* (c) *Anointing of the altar stone for a wooden altar.*

The altar is then clothed in blessed altar cloths and the requisites for Mass prepared on it. The consecration concludes with Mass celebrated in honor of the altar's title, and the imparting of a plenary indulgence by the consecrating prelate.

Bibliography: A. TESIO, EncCatt 1:924. P. OPPENHEIM, Enc Catt 4:1292–93. C. BRAGA, "In novum codicem rubricarum," EphemLiturg 74 (1960) 217–257. P. JOUNEL and A. M. ROGUET, *Consécration d'un autel* (Paris 1963). Righetti 4:325–327.

[J. B. O'CONNELL]

ALTDORF, ABBEY OF, former Benedictine abbey in Alsace, Diocese of *Strasbourg, France; it was important for pastoral care and as a pilgrimage center. Founded by Count Hugo III as a cloister and burial place for his family, it was built under Count Eberhard V and rebuilt several times—*c.* 1192; after it had been pillaged by Strasbourgers, 1262; after the Peasants War; *c.* 1600; and in 1700. The wooden cloister church, consecrated by Bp. Erchenbald of Strasbourg in the presence of Abbot Maiolus of Cluny, was dedicated to St. Bartholomew (974); a member of the family had taken part in Rome at the translation of relics of St. Bartholomew, who became the family patron saint. Before 1049, it seems, Bishop Werner reconsecrated the church in honor of St. Cyriacus (d. 303), a favorite with Benedictines, and the *Fourteen Holy Helpers. Pope Leo IX, a member of the family, consecrated the altar. In the 12th century Altdorf was a double monastery (*see* MONASTERIES, DOUBLE). The Romanesque church was built *c.* 1200; choir and transept were rebuilt by the Vorarlberg Peter Thumb (1720–33). The Cluniac cloister joined the congregations of Mainz-Bamberg (1417), *Bursfeld (1607), and Strasbourg (1608). In the 15th century Altdorf was individually united with *Sankt Gallen. Frescoes of the 12th century, whitewashed when the abbey was suppressed (1790), have been uncovered recently.

A second Abbey of Altdorf in south Württemberg, west Germany, originally housed Benedictine nuns or canonesses (*sanctimoniales*); it seems to have been founded after 934. The cloister was the burial place of the founder's family. The present cemetery of the Abbey of *Weingarten occupies the site. Altdorf seems to have died out *c.* 1000; but clerics, perhaps canons, continued divine services. It was revived as a convent of women (1036), which moved to Weingarten after a fire (1053) and then to Altomünster (1056).

Bibliography: A. SIEFFERT, *Altdorf: Geschichte von Abtei und Dorf* (Strasbourg 1946). G. SPAHR, "Die Reform im Kloster St. Gallen," in *Schriften des Vereins für Geschichte des Bodensees* 76 (1958) 1–62. C. BUHL, "Weingarten-Altdorf," in *Weingarten, 1056–1956,* ed. G. SPAHR (Weingarten 1956) 22.

[G. SPAHR]

ALTENBURG, ABBEY OF, Benedictine abbey in the Diocese of St. Pölten, Austria; its patron is St. Lambert. It was founded (1144) by Countess Hildburg of Rebgau-Poigen and settled with 12 monks from *Sankt Lambrecht in Styria, and has always been the pastoral and cultural center of the former "Horn County." Six incorporated parishes include the pilgrimage parish Maria Dreieichen and the city parish of Horn. In 1964 the abbey had a boys' choir school and a boarding school, and 20 monks devoted themselves to pastoral care and scholarship. The cloister, one of the most splendid baroque monuments in Austria, was built (1650–1742) after its total destruction (1645) in the

The nave of the abbey church at Altenburg, Austria.

Thirty Years' War. Its present form is the work of the architect Joseph Mungenast (1729–41). There are many frescoes by Paul Trogers (church, library, prelates' hall, and emperors' stairway) and valuable stucco work of the *Wessobrunn school (Franz Josef Holzinger and Michael Flor). Excavations in 1932 revealed part of the early Romanesque cloister.

Bibliography: *Urkunden der Benedictiner-Abtei zum heiligen Lambert in Altenburg,* ed. H. BURGER (Fontes rerum Austriacarum 21; Vienna 1865). H. BURGER, *Geschichtliche Darstellung der Gründung und Schicksale des Benedictinerstiftes St. Lambert zu Altenburg in Nieder-Österreich* (Vienna 1862). F. ENDL, *Stift Altenburg* (Augsburg 1929). G. SCHWEIGHOFER, *Stift Altenburg* (Vienna 1963). Kapsner BenBibl 2:184–185. Cottineau 1:68–69.
Illustration credit: Foto-Westmüller, Linz.

[G. SCHWEIGHOFER]

ALTENSTAIG, JOHANNES, humanist and theologian; b. Mindelheim, Bavaria, Germany, *c.* 1480; d. *c.* 1525. He attended Heinrich *Bebel's courses in poetry and rhetoric at the Universtiy of *Tübingen. He divided his time between teaching and scholarly research, first at Tübingen and from 1509, at Polling. In 1518 the bishop of *Augsburg commissioned him to compile a study on the churches of Bavaria. He became friends with various humanists and theologians, among them Johann *Eck, with whom he conducted an intensive cultural exchange. Following Bebel's teaching and example, Altenstaig aimed at restoring classical purity to the debased Latin language of his day. Though opposing the *Reformation, like his master he was critical of the prevailing ecclesiastical customs and practices, expressing his dissatisfaction in such works as, e.g., his *Kommentar zum Bebels Triumphus Veneris* (Strasbourg 1515). He was the author of several theological and philological treatises, and tried his hand also at poetry.

Bibliography: Works. *Vocabularius vocum* (Hagenau 1508); *Dialectica* (Hagenau 1514); *Vocabularius theologiae* (Hagenau 1517); *Opusculum de amicitia* (Hagenau 1519); *De felicitate triplici* (Hagenau 1519); *Isokrates von dem Reich* (Augsburg 1517); *Ain nutzlich vnnd in hailiger geschrifft gegründte vnderricht* (Augsburg 1523); *Von der Füllerey* (Strasbourg 1525).

Literature. V. STEGEMANN, NDB 1:215–216. F. ZOEPFL, *Johannes Altenstaig: Ein Gelehrtenleben aus der Zeit des Humanismus und der Reformation* (Münster 1918); LexThK² 1:380–381; *Geschichte der Stadt Mindelheim in Schwaben* (Munich 1948); "Der Humanismus am Hof der Fürstbischöfe von Augsburg," HistJb 62–69 (1942–49) 671–708. N. ELLENBOG, *Briefwechsel,* ed. A. BIGELMAIR and F. ZOEPFL (Münster 1938). J. PIETSCH, DHGE 2:797–798. A. STEICHELE, ADB 1:363.

[M. MONACO]

ALTERNATIVA, an institution found in Spain, later transplanted to Spanish America. In Spain, it demanded that an office or offices be alternated between members of different regions or nations. In Spanish America, it usually meant the alternation in office between a native of Spain, called *chapetón* (tenderfoot), and a native of America, called Creole. In Spanish America, the *alternativa* is found both in civil and in Church life; however, it was employed most widely in Spanish America in the religious orders. There it meant that the most important offices in a province had to be filled alternately by Spanish and Spanish-American religious respectively: the head of the province, at least half the members of his council, the heads of the more important houses as well as the occupants of the key posts in the province, such as regent of studies and master of novices. In other words, 10 to 12 posts alternated in each chapter by force of law. In the state of present research, it is not known when the *alternativa* was first established in Spanish America. The earliest known date is 1601, when it was imposed on the Dominicans of Quito. Soon thereafter, it was found officially in Mexico, Central America, Colombia, Venezuela, Peru, Bolivia, and in the Philippines. In 1627 the Franciscans in Mexico even received the *alternativa,* the alternation of office between three parties: the friars who had received the habit in Spain, Spanish boys who entered the order in Mexico, and the Mexicans. The *alternativa* was not found among either the Mercedarians or the Jesuits; the first were governed usually by Spanish superiors, and the second by direct appointees of their general. Most frequently, the *alternativa* was requested by the Spanish friars because they were the minority party. In Guatemala, however, both the native Dominicans and Franciscans asked for it because they were the minority. Theoretically, the *alternativa* could have been advantageous since it could have ensured broadening intellectual contacts. Actually, it was a source of endless friction and dissension and is one of the factors which helped to weaken and corrupt the religious orders in Spanish America wherever it was found. Essentially, it predicated that election to office was less dependent on merit than on race.

Bibliography: A. S. TIBESAR, "The *Alternativa:* A Study in Spanish-Creole Relations in Seventeenth Century Peru," *Americas* 11 (1954–55) 229–283. J. GONZÁLES ECHENIQUE, "Notas sobre la *Alternativa* en las provincias religiosas de Chile indiano," *Historia* 2 (1962–63) 178–196.

[A. S. TIBESAR]

ALTMANN OF PASSAU, ST., bishop; b. Westphalia, Germany, *c.* 1015; d. Zeiselmauer, near Vienna, Austria, Aug. 8, 1091 (feast, Aug. 8). He became canon and teacher at *Paderborn, provost of the canons of *Aachen *c.* 1051, and then chaplain to Empress Agnes (d. 1114). After a pilgrimage to Jerusalem, he was named bishop of Passau in 1065. His concern for the purity and pastoral zeal of his clergy made him a champion of the *vita communis* according to the Rule of St. *Augustine, and he introduced this rule when founding Sankt Nikola outside Passau (*c.* 1070) and *Göttweig (1083) and when reforming *Sankt Florian (1071) and Sankt Pölten (1081). He was also instrumental in the foundation of the Augustinian houses of Rottenbuch (1073) and *Reichersberg (1084). Altmann courageously published the papal decrees against married priests in 1074 and was the first to announce Emperor *Henry IV's excommunication in Germany in 1076. As papal legate, he attended the princes' meeting at Tribur in October 1076. Driven from his diocese in 1077 or 1078 by the imperial party, Altmann fled to Rome, but in 1080 he returned to the eastern part of his diocese, where he continued his political and pastoral efforts under the protection of Margrave Leopold II (d. 1095) until his death. He was buried in the Abbey of Göttweig, and a monk of this monastery wrote his vita (MGS 12:226–243). Since the late 19th century, his cult has been permitted in the Dioceses of Passau, Linz, and Sankt Pölten.

Bibliography: ActSS Aug. 2:356–389. ALTMANN OF PASSAU, *Streitschriften,* ed. M. SDRALEK (Paderborn 1890). A. LINSENMAYER, *Zur Erinnerung an den seligen Bischof Altmann v. Passau, 1065–1091* (Munich 1891). E. TOMEK, *Kirchengeschichte Österreichs* (Innsbruck 1935–59) 1:138–143. J. HALLER, "Der Weg nach Canossa," HistZ 160 (1939) 229–285, esp. 280–283. Wattenbach-Holtzmann 1:385–389, 541–545. R. BAUERREISS, *Kirchengeschichte Bayerns,* v.2 (St. Ottilien 1951) 98–103, 233–236. J. OSWALD, NDB 1:225–226; LexThK² 1:402–403, bibliog. G. ALLMANG, DHGE 2:826–827.

[A. A. SCHACHER]

ALTO, ST., hermit and monastic founder; d. *c.* 770 (feast, Feb. 9). He was not, it would appear, one of the early missionaries who labored with *Virgilius of Salzburg in southern Bavaria. According to tradition he came to the region near modern Dachau shortly after the middle of the 8th century and lived for a time as a hermit on some forest land given him by *Pepin III. After a few years he built the monastery of Altomünster, which was destroyed in the 10th century during the Hungarian invasion. St. *Boniface is said to have consecrated the monastic church erected during the lifetime of Alto. The authenticity of the saint's relics preserved today at Altomünster is not fully established. Sometime in the 11th century *Othloh of Sankt-Emmeram wrote his *Vita s. Altonis* (MGS 15:843–846), which preserved the local traditions concerning the life of the saint.

Bibliography: A. BAYOL, DHGE 2:830–831. Manitius 2:101. Zimmermann KalBen 1:190, 192. Baudot-Chaussin 2:216. R. BAUERREISS, LexThK² 1:403.

[H. DRESSLER]

ALTOONA-JOHNSTOWN, DIOCESE OF (ALTUNENSIS-JOHNSTONIENSIS). Suffragan of the metropolitan See of Philadelphia, established May 27, 1901, as the Diocese of Altoona, and redesignated Altoona-Johnstown Oct. 9, 1957. The 6,674-square-mile area includes the counties of Cambria, Blair, Bedford, Huntingdon, and Somerset, which were separated from the Diocese of *Pittsburgh, and Center, Clinton, and Fulton counties, taken from the Diocese of *Harrisburg. In the latter part of the 18th century Jesuits from Conewago, Pa., ministered in the area that was then part of the St. Francis Regis mission circuit. In 1799 the famous Russian convert missionary Demetrius Augustine *Gallitzin founded and named the mission of Loretto in Cambria County from Conewago. Taking up permanent residence there in July of that year he expended his labors and fortune for his people until his death May 6, 1840, at Loretto, where his remains are entombed.

Old St. John's, Altoona, Pa., procathedral until 1924.

Interior of the Cathedral of the Blessed Sacrament, Altoona.

With the establishment of the see in 1901, St. John the Evangelist Church, Altoona, was used as the procathedral until 1924, when the Cathedral of the Blessed Sacrament was begun. This early Renaissance style cathedral was finally completed in November 1960. Three years earlier St. John Gaulbert's Church, Johnstown, dedicated in 1896, had been raised to the rank of cocathedral.

When Eugene A. Garvey was chosen first bishop of the new see and consecrated Sept. 8, 1901, there were 44,000 Catholics cared for by 59 priests. Garvey died Oct. 22, 1920, and was succeeded in turn by John J. McCort (1920–36); Richard T. Guilfoyle (1936–57); Howard J. Carroll (1957–60); and J. Carroll McCormick, former auxiliary of Philadelphia, who was appointed to Altoona-Johnstown June 25, 1960. By 1964 the diocese numbered 154,153 Catholics in a total population of about 626,700. There were 119 parishes and 319 priests, 38 brothers, and 495 sisters serving in the diocese, which had 61 elementary and 5 high schools, 1 general hospital and a school for nurses, 1 orphanage, and 1 home for the aged. There were two colleges: *St. Francis College, Loretto (1847), a coeducational institution under the direction of the Franciscan fathers, Third Order Regular; and Mt. Aloysius Junior College for women, Cresson, conducted by the Religious Sisters of Mercy.

Bibliography: Archives, Diocese of Altoona-Johnstown. A. A. LAMBING, *A History of the Catholic Church in the Diocese of Pittsburgh and Allegheny* (New York 1880). J. T. REILY, *Conewago: A Collection of Catholic Local History . . .* (Martinsburg, W.Va. 1885). M. WIRTNER, *The Benedictine Fathers in Cambria County, Pennsylvania* (Carrolltown, Pa. 1926).

[R. F. HEMLER]

ALTÖTTING, MONASTERY OF, famous place of pilgrimage in honor of Our Lady, located in Upper Bavaria near the Austrian frontier, in the present Diocese of Passau, former Diocese of Salzburg. The name "Oetting" is said to derive etymologically from *Otto,* name of a Bavarian leader baptized by St. *Rupert of Salzburg (*c.* 700); the prefix *Alt-* (Old) was added in 1231 to distinguish the original structure from the new church built at that time. It is estimated that more than 600,000 pilgrims a year now visit the Holy Chapel (*Gnadenkapelle*) at Altötting, which contains the 13th-century statue of Our Lady of Grace (about 26 inches high, of linden wood, vested in jewel-studded robes).

The chapel, octagonal in shape and possibly modeled on the cathedral at *Aachen, was enlarged (1499–1511) by a small nave and arcade. Among its art treasures, special mention should be made of the "Golden Horse," a work of French Gothic workmanship dating from *c.* 1400. Attached to the Bavarian ducal palace in the Carolingian period, the Holy Chapel was endowed in 876 by King Carloman of Bavaria (d. 880), who erected a Benedictine monastery and church adjacent to it. In 907 the chapel survived the attack of the Hungarians that destroyed the Benedictine foundation. Nothing further is known of it until 1231, when Duke Louis the "Kelheimer" founded a new collegiate church there; the provost and the chapter of *canons were in charge of pilgrimages until 1803, when they were suppressed.

Present-day religious houses in Altötting include St. Mary Magdalene, which has been served successively by Jesuits (1591–1773), secular priests (1773–1841), Redemptorists (1841–1873), and now the Capuchins. St. Anne was a Franciscan friary from 1653 to 1803, when it became a provincial house of Capuchins, who were put in charge of the pilgrimages. St. *Conrad of Parzham (d. 1894) was lay-brother and porter at this Capuchin friary. St. Anne's new church, built in 1911, was made a minor basilica in 1913. The Mary Ward Sisters (*Englische Fräulein*) and the Missionary Sisters of the Holy Cross both have their motherhouses there; the Sisters of St. Vincent de Paul have been in Altötting since 1862.

Bibliography: L. Boiteux, DHGE 2:834–841. H. Geiselberger, *Der Gnadenort Altötting* (6th ed. Altötting 1950). H. M. Gillett, *Famous Shrines of Our Lady,* 2 v. (Westminster, Md. 1952) v.2. M. A. König, LexThK[2] 1:404–405.

[M. F. MC CARTHY]

ALTRUISM

In its extended sense, altruism refers to any attitude or position that favors benevolence. As ordinarily used in *ethics, it applies to any system that reduces all morality to love of neighbor, makes the quest of the happiness of one's fellow man the basic moral value, and defines the good simply as whatever furthers the well-being of others. Altruism is thus opposed to *egoism, and to other systems that grant to the love of self or of God a priority over love of neighbor.

Historical Development. Historically, altruism is a result of the progressive secularization of Christian morality in modern times. The Church has always emphasized Christ's teaching that the first and greatest Commandment is to love God, and that the second is to love one's neighbor as oneself. After the renaissance of *materialism in the 16th century, some philosophers (e.g., T. *Hobbes) denied the validity of both these precepts. Among those who reacted to this were the precursors of altruism. Anthony Ashley Cooper, third Earl of Shaftesbury (1671–1713), being a Deist, spurned theological argument. Yet he pointed out that unselfish tendencies are as natural as the selfish, and that virtue consists of the harmony of both—with the predominance of the former. His disciple, Francis Hutcheson (1694–1746), made benevolence the essence of moral good. He was also the author of the celebrated formula, "the greatest happiness of the greatest number." David *Hume (1711–76), who greatly influenced Comte, and Adam *Smith (1723–90) both emphasized the role of benevolence and sympathy in moral action.

Auguste *Comte (1798–1857), the founder of *positivism, coined the word altruism as the most proper name for his new morality and religion. Dismissing Catholic dogma as outdated, he saw in its law of love for neighbor the necessary principle and bond of the developing social order. While rejecting God, he nevertheless understood that men need something greater than themselves to honor and serve. He therefore substituted the glorification and love of Humanity for that of God, making benevolence the source and criterion of all morality. In addition he instituted a positivistic hierarchy, ritual, and code, hoping thereby to channel all of men's emotions and ideals into the service of the newly recognized Supreme Being.

The earlier English utilitarians had accepted benevolence as a source of pleasure. It was John Stuart *Mill (1806–73), however, who developed altruistic or social *utilitarianism. This is an incongruous amalgam of the views that pleasure, or happiness, is what all should seek, and that "In the golden rule of Jesus of Nazareth we read the complete spirit of the ethics of utility. To do as you would be done by, and to love your neighbor as yourself, constitute the ideal perfection of utilitarian morality" [*Utilitarianism, Liberty, and Representative Government* (New York 1910, 1947) ch. 2].

Herbert *Spencer (1820–1903) concluded from his positivistic, utilitarian, and evolutionary ideas that the ultimate development of man and of morality consists in finding one's egoistic pleasure in altruistic acts. Many materialists of the time, like Ludwig Büchner (1824–99) and E. H. *Haeckel, adopted similar views.

The idealists of the 19th century in general emphasized the dignity of the individual; the counterpart of this in ethics was a greater or lesser insistence on benevolence. Thus, for Arthur *Schopenhauer (1788–1860), compassion is the only motive that gives man's acts moral value.

The 20th century has seen yet other types of altruism flourish. Léon Bourgeois (1851–1925) proposed his ethics of solidarity, which identified moral good with the exigencies of the interdependence binding all men. *Socialism probably owes most of its success to its appeals to altruism. The totalitarians are selectively altruistic: the Nazis and Fascists limit it racially; the Communists, to the proletariat.

Evaluation. The deficiencies of altruism stem from its rejection of God as the ultimate end and from its substitution of some surrogate, often regarded as divine. Thus arises the tragedy of atheistic humanism: "modern" men adoring either themselves or an abstraction of their own making. As a result altruists have no way of adequately substantiating real obligations. They are always open to the unanswerable objection, "Why should I be altruistic if I don't want to ?" Many altruists are also utilitarians, and so are subject to all the difficulties that this view entails. Again, altruistic systems have a rather arbitrary and narrow basis. Some one aspect of life is taken, for instance, one's natural feelings of sympathy, compassion, or solidarity, and on this the whole of morality is erected.

Another telling consideration against altruism is its logically ultimate result, the complete subordination of the individual to the group as in totalitarian societies. For if moral good consists essentially in service to one's fellow men, then a good state is one that takes whatever means are necessary to assure that everyone complies. This means the loss of all natural rights and of human dignity.

The love and service of neighbor is indeed a major duty and a main purpose for man's existence; nevertheless it has a subordinate role in conduct that can be rightly understood only in a theistic context. Man's primary end and duty is to know, love, and serve God. He serves God by seeking his own personal development and happiness. But he must also love his neighbor, because it is God's will that all help each other to fulfill the divine plan. As a social being, he realizes himself most fully by submerging himself in the service of God and neighbor.

See also ETHICS, HISTORY OF; SOCIETY.

Bibliography: J. D. COLLINS, *A History of Modern European Philosophy* (Milwaukee 1954). R. A. TSANOFF, *Ethics* (rev. ed. New York 1955). J. LECLERCQ, *Les Grandes lignes de la philosophie morale* (new ed. Paris 1954). H. DE LUBAC, *The Drama of Atheist Humanism,* tr. E. M. RILEY (New York 1950). Eisler 1:40–41.

[G. J. DALCOURT]

ALUMBRADOS (ILLUMINATI)

Name given to the adherents of a Spanish pseudomysticism of the 16th century and deriving from their claim to act always under the immediate illumination of the Holy Spirit. The name was first so used in a letter from a Franciscan friar to Cardinal *Ximénez de Cisneros in 1494. The movement itself was but a recurrence of the bizarre parody of true mysticism that is never long absent from the Church in the world. Proximately, its sources would most probably be found in the voluntarism of medieval Teutonic theology and in the Averroistic strains of Arabian mysticism, as well as in a Reformation anticlericalism. The movement was confined mostly to the Dioceses of Cadiz and Seville. Its doctrines, which are known in later times chiefly in the form of opinions condemned by the Inquisition in 1623, seem to have infected all classes of people.

The basic flaw in the teaching of the Alumbrados lay in the exaggerated importance they attached to mental prayer. They held that mental prayer is commanded by divine law and that in it all other precepts are fulfilled. Thus not even attendance at Mass, obligations arising from charity, or obedience to lawful authority must be allowed to impede the existence of mental prayer. This devotion was described simply as the recollection of God's presence, in which there is no discursive movement of the mind, no meditation properly so called, and no reflection on mental images such as the Sacred Passion or humanity. It is by the practice of this quietistic prayer of nothingness that the soul arrives at a state of perfection in which its faculties are so submerged that the soul can no longer act. To one constituted in this highest degree of spirituality, there comes the ravishment of the Spirit, so that in ecstasy the soul sees the divine essence, beholds the Blessed Trinity even as the elect in heaven. When this beatifying vision has been achieved, all the properties of beatitude logically follow. The soul is freed from the weakness of wounded nature; it is rendered impeccable; it is, in short, consciously confirmed in grace. Thus elevated, a man does not act as of himself; willingly or unwillingly he is moved by the illumination of the Spirit.

In the moral order, such principles could lead only to catastrophe. The investigations of the Inquisition provide a sordid account of the grossest carnal sins indulged in by the "perfect" under the guise of "communications of the Holy Spirit and divine love between souls." As a result of these shocking disclosures, it is not surprising that the Inquisition's judgment of the type of mysticism practiced by the Alumbrados was extremely unfavorable. Certainly the hypercritical attitude of some of the theologians of the next century toward even true spirituality was a result in no small degree of the aberrations of the Alumbrados.

Bibliography: P. POURRAT, DTC 13.2:1552–54. F. CAYRÉ, *Manual of Patrology and History of Theology,* tr. H. HOWITT, 2 v. (Paris 1936–40) 2:790. R. A. KNOX, *Enthusiasm* (New York 1950; repr. 1961) 241–242. V. BELTRÁN DE HEREDIA, "La Beata de Piedrahita no fué alumbrada," *Ciencia tomista* 63 (1942) 294–311.

[T. K. CONNOLLY]

ALVA, DUKE OF (FERNANDO ÁLVAREZ DE TOLEDO)

Spanish soldier and statesman; b. Piedrahita, Ávila, Oct. 29, 1508; d. Tomar, near Lisbon, Portugal, Dec. 12, 1582. After 1510 Fernando was raised by his grandfather Federico Álvarez, from whom he was said to have derived his zeal for religion, politics, and stern discipline. As a youth he entered the military service of Emperor *Charles V and saw action against the French and against the Turks in Hungary before his 20th year. In 1535 Alva (Alba) led the Spanish troops at the siege and conquest of Tunis. Later (1541) he had charge of an unsuccessful expedition against Algiers, yet Charles showed his confidence by conferring on him the chief command of the Spanish army and by naming Fernando personal instructor to his son and successor, Philip.

Early Military Campaigns. In 1546 Alva led the imperial forces that sought to put down the rebellious Lutheran princes in southern Germany. This campaign culminated in Alva's victory at Mühlberg (April 24, 1547), in which John Frederick the Magnanimous, Elector of Saxony, was captured and forced to sign the Capitulation of Wittenberg. Less successful was Alva's attempt at regaining Metz, which the Lutheran princes had illegally ceded to the French, together with Toul and Verdun. Accompanied by the Emperor, Alva besieged Metz from November 1552 to January 1553, when the imperial forces withdrew. Charles became disillusioned with imperial affairs after this setback and devoted the remaining years of his reign to Spain and the Netherlands.

After Charles V's abdication in 1556, the Duke of Alva continued to serve Philip II in key posts in Italy and the Netherlands, and later in the war against Portugal. Previously (1554) he had accompanied Philip to

Fernando Álvarez de Toledo, the Duke of Alva, portrait by Antonio Moro in the Royal Museum at Brussels.

England on the occasion of Philip's marriage to Queen *Mary Tudor. In 1555 Alva received the chief military command in Italy, having as main objective the halting of French expansion into the peninsula. The following year Alva moved against the forces of Francis, Duke of Guise, and Pope Paul IV, then the ally of the French. Already at the gates of Rome with victory assured, Alva was embarrassed by orders from Philip to halt and make terms with the Pontiff. The Spanish King was content with the diplomatic victory of securing a break in the Franco-papal alliance, which resulted in Paul IV's withdrawal from political entanglements and Spanish supremacy in the peninsula. Three years later (1559), Alva played a major role in concluding the Franco-Spanish peace of Cateau-Cambrésis, and Philip sent him at the head of a large embassy to Paris, where he acted as proxy for the Spanish King in his marriage to Princess Elizabeth, daughter of Henry II of France.

Regent of the Netherlands. In 1567 Philip decided that a stronger hand was needed to cope with the religious and political situation in the Spanish Netherlands. The Duke of Alva received orders to proceed north from Genoa with an army of 10,000 men. Arriving in Brussels on August 22, he assumed the post of captain general under the regent, *Margaret of Parma. Margaret, whose rule had been mild and conciliatory, now served as regent in name only, with Alva formally succeeding as regent and governor general by the end of the year. Alva's 6-year regime was to be an unforgettable reign of terror in which the Spanish government attempted forcibly to uproot the now firmly entrenched Protestantism of the northern provinces. Instead of seeking the support of the Catholic Netherlanders, Alva's harshness and severity, coupled with arbitrary tax impositions, alienated them. In order to crush the rebellious Dutch nobles, Alva immediately formed a 10-man Council of Troubles (dubbed the Council of Blood by the Netherlanders) to try all accused heretics or malcontents. In June 1568, on orders from the Council, more than 20 nobles were beheaded; they included two of the principal instigators of rebellion, Count Lamoral of *Egmont and Philip de Montmorency, Count of Hoorn. The most dangerous adversary of Spanish policy, William the Silent, Prince of Orange, refused to appear before the Council and fled to Germany to recruit mercenaries to fight Alva. In July Alva had no trouble in crushing a mercenary force led into the country by Louis of Nassau at Jemmingen. A second army under William of Orange was likewise defeated and quickly withdrew across the frontier into Germany. Alva was determined that the Netherlanders themselves would have to finance the cost of the civil war, and in 1569 he imposed both a property and a sales tax. This proved to be a psychological blunder that united Catholic subjects with the Protestants against him.

William of Orange meanwhile organized a fleet of privateers manned by exiles, the Sea Beggars, who harassed Spanish-held coastal towns and seized Spanish ships at sea. In April 1572 the Sea Beggars succeeded in taking Utrecht, Brielle, and Flushing, thus setting off a widespread popular uprising against the Spanish government. William of Orange moved his land forces into Brabant, while his brother Louis of Nassau seized Mons and Valenciennes. Suspending the tax levy, Alva organized a massive counterattack that ruthlessly attacked, subdued, and pillaged without any mercy Mons, Malines, Zutphen, Naarden, and Haarlem (1572–73). The sack of Haarlem was followed by an attack on Alkmaar, in which the tide once more turned in favor of the rebels; 2,000 citizens repelled 16,000 Spaniards with severe Spanish loss. "From Alkmaar, victory begins" became a popular cry as new uprisings took place on every side.

Return to Spain. Alva, now in poor health and largely dependent on his son Don Federigo for leadership in the field, sought a recall from Philip II. The Spanish King, dissatisfied with the course of affairs in the Netherlands, willingly acceded, and Alva returned to Spain in December 1573, to be succeeded by Don Luis de Requesens, whose subsequent policy of moderation was to be no more successful. Alva, at first received with favor by Philip, subsequently incurred the King's hostility and was banished to the castle of Uzeda. Factors probably responsible were royal disapproval of Don Federigo's marriage, personality clashes between Philip and Alva, and the influence of the rival court faction, the Eboli-Perez group, which had long regarded Alva as dangerous. When the need again arose in 1580, Philip recalled his now aging general to lead the Spanish army in a dynastic war against Portugal. On Aug. 25, 1580, at the bridge of Alcantara, Alva won a crushing victory over the Portuguese, led by Diego de Meneses. Alva entered Portugal and effected the Spanish overlordship of the country that lasted until 1640. He died a little more than a year after his Portuguese victory.

Bibliography: G. G. Dept in *Biographie nationale de Belgique* 4 (Brussels 1930) 380–404. P. Geyl, *The Revolt of the Netherlands, 1555–1609* (2d ed. N.Y. 1958). R. B. Merriman, *The Rise of the Spanish Empire in the Old World and in the New,* 4 v. (New York 1934) v.4. L. Berra, EncCatt 1:631–633. L. E. Halkin, LexThK[2] 1:268–269, bibliog. H. Pirenne, *Histoire de Bel-*

gique, 7 v. (Brussels 1911–32) 4:3–46. **Illustration credit:** Institut Royal du Patrimoine Artistique, Bruxelles.

[W. KELLER]

ALVA Y ASTORGA, PEDRO DE, lecturer on theology, procurator general of the Franciscans in Rome, one of the most outstanding figures of the 17th century in the debates on Immaculate Conception; b. 1602; d. 1667. He was of Spanish origin, and belonged to the Franciscan Province of the Twelve Apostles of Peru. With the aid of his own press in the Low Countries he was able to publish his copious theological writings. All these centered about the tradition of the Immaculate Conception; he was critic, debater, and editor of collected writings on this subject. Some of these compilations are still of basic interest (compare X. Le Bachelet, "Immaculée Conception," DTC, 7:1094). With his contribution the controversy entered upon a decisive period. Another phase of his work, less studied, is his contribution to the history of his order, with his great *Bullarium* in 10 volumes and 16,000 documents. The *Indiculus* and a draft of it are well known, but the major work remained unedited, and its present whereabouts are unknown.

Bibliography: A. EGUILUZ, "Fr. Pedro de Alva y Astorga, O.F.M., en las controversias inmaculistas," *Verdad y Vida* 12 (1954) 247–272; "El P. Alva y Astorga y sus escritos inmaculistas," *Archivo Ibero Americano* 15 (1955) 497–594. L. CEYSSENS, "Pedro de Alva y Astorga, O.F.M., y su imprenta de la Inmaculada Concepción de Lovaina (1663–66)," *ibid.* 11 (1951) 5–35.

[A. EGUILUZ]

ALVARADO, FRANCISCO, DE, Dominican missionary; b. Mexico, 1560?; d. Teposculula, March 1603. Practically nothing is known of the life of this Dominican friar. He took the habit in the convent of Santo Domingo in Mexico City and made his profession on July 24, 1574. He was a missionary among the Mixtec Indians in Mexico and learned their language well. He wrote *Vocabulario Misteco,* a Mixtec lexicon printed in Mexico before 1595. According to Dominican historians, Alvarado compiled the information from works of other Dominican missionaries, corrected it, and enlarged upon it from his own experience. These early vocabularies and grammars were of great importance in the training of Indian missionaries.

Bibliography: A. FRANCO, *Segunda Parte de la Historia de la Provincia de Santiago de Mexico Orden de Predicadores en la Nueva España* (Mexico 1900). Quétif-Échard 2.1:298.

[A. B. NIESER]

ÁLVARES, FRANCISCO

Priest and missionary; d. *c.* 1540. As chaplain of the first official Portuguese royal embassy to Ethiopia (1520–26), he wrote a monumental description of the Eastern Christian nation, *Verdadera* [sic] *informaçam das terras do Preste Joam,* published in reduced form in Portuguese in 1540. Translated into several European languages, it provided 16th-century Europe with frank, honest, accurate information that supplemented what Damião de *Góis had made available at second hand. It is highly esteemed in Ethiopia today.

Ethiopia's ambassador to Portugal reached Lisbon early in 1514. The following year King Manuel I sent his mission in reply, and the Ethiopian ambassador was in the company as the group proceeded to Goa. In 1517 they tried to land in the Massaua area on the west side

Title page, first Portuguese edition (1540) of Francisco Álvares's "Verdadera informaçam das terras do Preste Joam" (True Information about the lands of the Prester John).

of the Red Sea, but bad weather and worse leadership nearly wrecked the whole expedition, and the Portuguese ambassador, Duarte Galvão, died. The survivors returned to India, and only in April 1520 did the embassy, now headed by Dom Rodrigo de Lima, finally land at Massaua.

Álvares's narrative, published in Lisbon long after his return, begins at this point. Its lengthy first book, the major part of the entire volume, concerns the 6 years the embassy spent in Ethiopia. It ends in April 1526, when the Portuguese, returning home, were picked up by a Portuguese fleet from India. The second book describes the subsequent journey to Goa and the passage to Lisbon, where the travelers arrived in July 1527.

The Ethiopian Emperor, Lebna Dengel (David II), had sent Zagazabo on this same journey as his ambassador to King João III, who had succeeded Manuel in 1521. Perhaps more important, he named Álvares his ambassador to the Pope and instructed him to render Ethiopian obedience to the Holy See. For reasons of his own João III forced Álvares to wait in Portugal for 5 years before permitting him to proceed to Rome in the company of João's ambassador to the Pope, Dom Martinho de Portugal.

Finally on Jan. 29, 1533, at a consistory in Bologna, in the presence of Emperor Charles V, Álvares rendered David II's obedience to Pope Clement VII. News of this event electrified Europe, where it circulated in a little Latin book published in Bologna within a month and reprinted many times in several languages. The Latin volume, at least partly written by Paolo Giovio, contains information on Ethiopia unquestionably taken from Álvares's larger treatise.

Nothing came of the Ethiopian submission, for the Pope (Giulio de' Medici) had other matters on his mind, as did the Portuguese. Álvares remained in Italy, apparently in Rome, where he is said to have died. His great treatise remained unpublished and is lost. The version printed in 1540, probably without his authorization, is only a portion of the larger study. Published at the King's order, it reveals the workings of a great mind, tolerant and critical, Portuguese and ecumenical.

Bibliography: F. ÁLVARES, *The Prester John of the Indies,* tr. H. E. J. STANLEY, ed. C. F. BECKINGHAM and G. W. B. HUNTINGFORD, 2 v. (Cambridge, Eng. 1961). F. M. ROGERS, *The Quest For Eastern Christians: Travels and Rumor in the Age of Discovery* (Minneapolis 1962). **Illustration credit:** Library of Congress.

[F. M. ROGERS]

ÁLVAREZ OF CÓRDOBA, BL., Dominican preacher and reformer; b. Córdoba (Lisbon) 1360; d. Córdoba, Feb. 19, 1430 (feast, Feb. 19). He preached extensively in Andalusia and in Italy. Once the Spanish kingdoms broke with the antipope *Benedict XIII, Álvarez preached tirelessly against him. Having been counselor for a brief period to King Henry III of Castile, he was instrumental at Henry's death, 1406, in securing the election of King John II in preference to Ferdinand, the King's brother. Álvarez acted as confessor and counselor to Queen Catherine and King John until his retirement to Córdoba in 1423, when he founded the observant priory of Scala Coeli. His devotion to the Passion of Christ, which had been engendered during a pilgrimage to Palestine in 1405, moved him to erect in the priory gardens tableaux of the Passion that were forerunners of the *Way of the Cross. In 1427, Martin V appointed him vicar of the Spanish Dominican Observants. He was beatified in 1741.

Bibliography: D. A. MORTIER, *Histoire des maîtres généraux de l'ordre des Frères Prêcheurs,* 8 v. (Paris 1903–20) 4:210–214. P. ÁLVAREZ, *Santos, bienaventurados, venerables de la orden de los Predicadores,* 4 v. (Vergara, Spain 1920–23) 1:495–508. G. GIERATHS, LexThK² 1:408.

[A. H. CAMACHO]

ÁLVAREZ, BALTASAR, Jesuit spiritual writer; b. Cervera del Rio Alhama (Logroño), 1533; d. Belmonte, July 25, 1580. Álvarez entered the Society of Jesus at Alcalá, May 3, 1555. After a period in the apostolic ministry in Avila (1558–66), he was made rector in Salamanca (1573–76) and from 1576 to 1580 held the posts of both rector and novice master at Medina del Campo and Villagarcía. He was also visitor for the province of Aragón, designated provincial of Peru, and finally, for a few months, provincial of Toledo. St. Teresa of Avila called upon him for counsel in certain critical moments of her life, and for 6 years he was her confessor.

Álvarez's prayer of silence was considered incompatible with the spirit of the society and was condemned by the Superior General E. Mercurian at the instigation of the provincial Juan Suarez and the visitor Diego Avellaneda. The opposition stemmed in part from caution begotten by the then recent condemnation of the illuministic ideas of the Alumbrados, and in part from the disfavor with which superiors in the society at the time viewed the tendency of some Jesuits to encourage involvement in contemplation at the expense of the apostolic ministry, which was the principal end of the society.

The influence of the spiritual doctrine of Álvarez was due not only to his own accomplishment but also to the popularity of his biography, which was written by Luis de *La Puente, SJ. His frequent assignments to administrative office in the society prevented him from dedicated and extensive writing. His works include commentaries on the rule for novices; retreat sermons; two "reports" about his prayer, short but valuable treatises on the prayer of silence. He excelled in the expression of true fervor and the intensity of his personal spiritual experience.

Bibliography: B. ÁLVAREZ, *Escritos espirituales: Introducción biográfica,* ed. C. M. ABAD and F. BOADO (Barcelona 1961), complete ed. of his works. L. DE LA PUENTE, *Vida del v. p. B. Álvarez* (new ed. Madrid 1882). I. IPARRAGUIRRE, *Répertoire de spiritualité ignatienne* (Rome 1961) 177–178. E. HERNÁNDEZ, DictSpirAscMyst 1:405–406. Brémond 8:228–269. J. TARRAGO, "La oración de silencio . . . del Padre Baltasar Álvarez y los ejercicios . . . ," *Manresa* 4 (1928) 165–174, 258–270.

[I. IPARRAGUIRRE]

ÁLVAREZ, DIEGO, theologian; b. Medina del Rio Secco (Diocese of Palencia), unknown date; d. Trani, 1631 (and not in 1635). He entered the Dominican Order at Medina, and taught theology at Burgos, Palencia, Toto, and Valladolid. On Nov. 7, 1596, he arrived at Rome where his superiors had sent him to defend the Thomist school in the controversies on grace and free will. While serving as regent of theological studies at the Minerva, he participated in the work of the **Congregatio de Auxiliis* with Tomás de *Lemos. He was named bishop of Trani (Southern Italy) in 1606; there he remained until his death. His main works deal with the controversies on grace: *Commentarii in Isaiam* (Rome 1599), *De auxiliis divinae gratiae et humani arbitrii viribus et libertate* (Rome 1610), *Responsiones ad obiectiones adversus concordiam liberi arbitrii cum divina praescientia* (Trani 1622), *De origine pelagianae haeresis et eius progressu* (Trani 1629). All these works were edited several times in the 17th century. Álvarez also published his courses on theology, on the third part of the *Summa theologica* of St. Thomas, *De incarnatione divini verbi* (Lyons 1614), and on the second part, *Disputationes theologicae in primam secundae S. Thomae* (Trani 1617). His *Manuale concionatorum* (Rome 1622) deals more directly with his episcopal activity. There are many texts and documents at the archives of the order in Rome that remain unedited.

Bibliography: Quétif-Échard 2.1:481–482. P. MANDONNET, DTC 1.1:926–927. D. RESTANGE, EncCatt 1:951. R. COULON, DHGE 2:872–873.

[A. DUVAL]

ÁLVAREZ DE PAZ, DIEGO, Jesuit spiritual writer; b. Toledo, 1560; d. Potosí, Jan. 17, 1620. Álvarez de Paz entered the Society of Jesus in Alcalá, Feb. 24, 1578, and in 1589 went to Peru as a student of theology and remained there for the rest of his life. He began his active career as professor of philosophy, theology, and Sacred Scripture, and then served as rector in different colleges, vice provincial in Tucumán (1605–07), and provincial in Peru from 1616 until his death.

His work as a spiritual writer is contained in three extensive volumes that treat, respectively: perfection; the overcoming of sin, vices, passions, and the practice of virtues, especially humility; the search for peace through prayer. This trilogy is like a vast spiritual encyclopedia, noteworthy for the depth of insight, theological precision, clearness, and richness in dogmatic content, although from a literary viewpoint it is somewhat too profuse. His doctrine on affective prayer was based on the influence of A. Cordeses, SJ. De Paz was the first Jesuit to make a detailed study of infused contemplation.

Bibliography: Sommervogel 1:252–258. J. E. DE URIARTE and M. LECINA, *Biblioteca de escritores de la Compañía de Jesús a la antigua asistencia de España desde sus orígenes hasta el año de 1773,* v.1 (Madrid 1925) 155–162. I. IPARRAGUIRRE, *Répertoire de spiritualité ignatienne de la mort de S. Ignace à celle du P. Aquaviva, 1556–1615* (Rome 1961). J. DE GUIBERT, *The Jesuits: Their Spiritual Doctrine and Practice,* tr. W. T. YOUNG (Chicago 1964). A. ASTRÁIN in Greg 1 (1920) 394–424. E. UGARTE DE ERCILLA in *Razón y Fe* 58 (1920) 465–473; 59 (1921) 186–187. E. HERNÁNDEZ, DictSpirAscMyst 1:407–409.

[I. IPARRAGUIRRE]

ALVARO PELAYO, Franciscan (1304), doctor of Canon and civil law in Bologna; b. Galicia, *c.* 1275; d. Seville, *c.* 1349. As papal penitentiary in *Avignon (1330–32) and as bishop of Silves in Portugal (1332), he knew firsthand the evils plaguing Christendom that are described in his writings. He sought to open the eyes of his readers with exhaustive examinations of conscience (potentially political constitutions) so that reason under canonical guidance might achieve a state of universal order in society. His thought, for the most part theocratic, accords certain basic rights to the state. The first part of *De statu et planctu ecclesiae* (Avignon 1330–32; revised, 1335–40) is a defense of *John XXII and the papacy against *Louis IV of Bavaria and *Marsilius of Padua. The second part deals with the condition of the Church as it was and as it should be. The *Speculum regum* (*c.* 1341), citing classical authors more frequently than Christian, was meant for the Spain of Alfonso XI, and perhaps his chancellor, Archbishop *Albornoz. Alvaro urges Alfonso to continue the Reconquista into Morocco, *de iure* Christian. The *Collirium fidei adversus hereses* (1344) is an annotated catalogue of heresies, ancient and medieval. Although widespread in MSS and in print, Alvaro's writings lack definitive editions and studies. A *Quinquagesilogium* dealing with the Franciscan rule and a commentary on St. Matthew exist in MSS. A sermon on the beatific vision and a commentary on the *Four Books of Sentences* are lost.

Bibliography: *Bibliographia Franciscana* 9–11 (1954–63). G. DELORME, DHGE 2:857–861. A. MICHEL, *Dictionnaire de sociologie* 1:488–491. A. VACANT, DTC 1.1:926. L. OLIGER, EncCatt 1:954–955. J. LAHACHE, DDC 6:1312. L. AMORÓS, LexThK[2] 1:409. M. A. SCHMIDT, RGG[3] 1:301.

[E. P. COLBERT]

ALVASTRA, ABBEY OF, a former *Cistercian monastery dedicated to Our Lady, situated near Lake Vättern in the Province of Östergötland, Sweden, in the old Diocese of Linköping. The oldest and most important Cistercian monastery of medieval Sweden, it was founded in 1143 on the advice of Archbishop *Eskil of Lund by King Sverker the Elder (d. 1156), who granted property for its erection on the estate of his late wife Ulfhild. At her request St. *Bernard had already sent monks from *Clairvaux. Alvastra was the 40th ab-

Excavations of the medieval Alvastra Abbey.

bey to be affiliated with Clairvaux. From Alvastra the monasteries of Varnhem, Julita (Saba), and Husby (Gudsberga) were founded. A monk from Alvastra, Stephen (d. 1185), was appointed the first archbishop of *Uppsala in 1164. Both the Sverker family and the succeeding Folkung dynasty were favorably disposed toward the monastery, and the royal tomb of the Sverker family was later built in front of the high altar of the abbey church. St. *Bridget received visions during her stay at Alvastra, and her husband and one of her sons are buried in its chapel. One of her most devoted friends and her confessor was the prior, Peter Olavi (d. 1390), who recorded most of her revelations from her own dictation. The abbey was abandoned in 1527 when Gustavus I Vasa (d. 1560), who was moving toward imposing the Protestant *Reformation in Sweden, took control of its estates. Only a few volumes remain from the old monastic library, but parts of the buildings and of the church are still preserved. Layers from fires in 1312 and 1415 have been of importance for the dating of the many articles found during excavation projects carried on at the site since the end of the 19th century.

Bibliography: Cottineau 1:75–76. U. BERLIÈRE, DHGE 2:892. E. ORTVED, *Cistercieordenen og dens klostre i Norden,* 2 v. in 1 (Copenhagen 1927–33) 2:53–141. K. SPAHR, LexThK[2] 1:409. I. SWARTLING, *Alvastra kloster* (Stockholm 1962). H. JOHANSSON, *Ritus cisterciensis* (Lund 1964). **Illustration credit:** Swedish Information Service, New York City.

[O. ODENIUS]

ALVERNIA (LA VERNA), a mountain in the valley of the Casentino in the Tuscan Apennines, halfway between Arezzo and Florence, which became a place of pilgrimage after the time of St. *Francis of Assisi. In 1213 Count Orlando of Chiusi had given the friars a piece of land on Alvernia on which he built a chapel, St. Mary of the Angels (1216). While making a retreat there, Francis received the stigmata, Sept. 14, 1224 (*see* STIGMATIZATION). It was probably here also that Francis wrote his famous blessing to Brother *Leo of Assisi. In 1263 a Church of the Stigmata was built, and a third church, the Chiesa Maggiore, was begun in 1348 and completed in 1459. The church, which now belongs to the municipality of Florence, had originally been in the care of the Conventual *Franciscans. In 1430 Martin V entrusted it to the Observants. After Martin's death the Conventual Franciscans were temporarily in charge, but in 1433 Eugene IV again entrusted it to the Observants, and the *Franciscans serve the church today. The Chiesa Maggiore was made a minor basilica in 1921 by Benedict XV.

Bibliography: V. FACCHINETTI, *La Verna nel Casentino . . .*, v.1 of *I Santuari francescani*, 3 v. (Milan 1925–27). R. M. HUBER, *A Documented History of the Franciscan Order* (Washington 1944–). S. MENCHERINI, *Guida illustrata della Verna* (3d ed. Quaracchi-Florence 1921); *Bibliografia Alvernina* (Città di Castello 1914). *La Verna* 11 (1913), excellent bibliog.

[J. J. SMITH]

ALVERNIA COLLEGE. A liberal arts college for women located in Reading, Pa., Alvernia was founded in 1958 by the Bernardine Sisters of the Third Order of St. Francis. Since their establishment in the U.S. in 1894, the sisters have had the education of youth as one of their important objectives. The training of teachers for the elementary schools began as early as 1908 when Mother M. Veronica, the acting superior general, engaged qualified lay instructors to prepare prospective teachers. By 1926 the community's own graduate teachers assumed part of the teaching program. In affiliation with *Villanova University, an extension center known as the Teachers Seminarium was established at the motherhouse in Reading. Here the sister-students earned part of their credits toward degrees that they received either at Villanova or at other institutions of higher learning. In view of these antecedents, in 1958 superiors decided to establish a college that would afford the young sisters professional preparation with a strong liberal arts background and planned course sequences. A further incentive was the need for a college for women in the Reading area. Alvernia College was chartered by the Commonwealth of Pennsylvania and approved by the state Department of Public Instruction. It is affiliated with The Catholic University of America and holds membership in the National Catholic Educational Association.

The corporate powers of Alvernia are vested in and exercised by a board of trustees composed entirely of Bernardine sisters. All the officers of the administration are members of the religious community. In 1964 the faculty consisted of 22 sisters, 1 priest, and 2 laymen. Staff-held degrees included 16 master's degrees and 3 doctorates.

The curriculum includes a standard program in the liberal arts and sciences, with philosophy and theology as integrating subjects. Majors leading to the B.A. and B.S. degrees are offered in the fields of natural sciences and mathematics, the humanities, the social sciences, and education. The College has approved programs for the preparation of elementary and secondary teachers based on a common core of general education. College enrollment in 1964 numbered approximately 133 students and the 1963 summer session registered 111.

While Alvernia subscribes to the traditional methods of teaching, it utilizes modern educational techniques and explores approaches to independent study. It has a planned developmental program.

[M. A. PEZYNSKA]

ALVERNO COLLEGE

A day and resident college for lay and religious women in Milwaukee, Wis. Established in 1887 as St. Joseph Normal School by the School Sisters of St. Francis, it was reorganized in 1936 as a 4-year college under the name of Alverno Teachers College. Ten years later, it was reorganized again as Alverno College, a 4-year liberal arts college. By 1951 three separate schools (teacher education, music, and nursing) had been merged within the framework of the College.

Alverno provides curricula in the liberal arts, education, business education, home economics, medical technology, music, and nursing. Degrees conferred are the B.A., Mus.B., and B.S. Majors are offered in art and art education; business education; elementary and secondary education; the liberal and fine arts, including liturgical music; modern languages; mathematics; the natural and social sciences; home economics; speech; medical technology; and nursing.

The department of nursing was established in 1946. It offers a 4-year basic degree program, with state approval and National League for Nursing accreditation. There is a nursing collection of 1,255 volumes in the library. Total library holdings at Alverno in 1964 numbered 50,799 volumes. There were 452 current periodicals received.

Through the Institute of European Studies, Alverno students may spend a single semester or the entire sophomore and junior years either at the University of Paris or the University of Vienna. The Alverno honors seminar, fine arts series, and contemporary affairs lecture series bring to the campus scholars, artists, and eminent lecturers.

Administration of the College is carried out through a board of directors composed of nine members of the religious community. The archbishop of Milwaukee is chancellor of the College. The administrative personnel, all members of the religious community, is made up of the president; dean; business officer; registrar and assistant; and directors of nursing, music, admissions, and student personnel services. In 1964 the part- and full-time administrative and teaching staffs totaled 99, and included 5 priests, 86 sisters, and 8 laymen. The staff held 73 master's degrees and 17 doctorates. The setting of Alverno College is a 50-acre campus with facilities housed in nine units. In 1964 its enrollment numbered 1,180 students, of whom 927 were full time. The 1963 summer session registered 1,063.

The College is accredited by the North Central Association of Colleges and Secondary Schools, the National Council for Accreditation of Teacher Education for the preparation of elementary and secondary school teachers, the Wisconsin State Board of Nursing, the National League for Nursing, and the University of Wisconsin. It is recognized by the Wisconsin State Department of Public Instruction. It holds membership in the American Association of University Women, the National Catholic Educational Association, the American Council on Education, the National Commission on Accrediting, the American Association of Colleges for Teacher Education, the Association of American Colleges, the National Association of Schools of Music, the National Music Council, and the National Conference of Catholic Schools of Nursing.

[M. P. PUETZ]

ALZATE, JOSÉ ANTONIO, Mexican philosopher, journalist, and scientist; b. Mexico City, November 1737; d. there, Feb. 2, 1799. While the exact date of birth is not known, Alzate, son of Joseph Phelipe de Alzate and Josepha Ramírez, was baptized Nov. 21, 1737. His family provided for his early education. Later he received a *capellanía* in Mexico City, which enabled him to study further. He went to the University of

Mexico, where he received the bachelor of arts degree in 1753 and the bachelor in theology in 1756. Any money he had went into books and scientific instruments. Alzate was a man of the Enlightenment, strongly influenced by Diderot and Condorcet. He had an encyclopedic mind and a tremendous curiosity about physical and natural science. He was very critical of Spanish policy, which interefered with the investigation and development of natural science. He helped in the reform of teaching in Mexico, which began with the establishment of the Royal School of Mines in 1792. Humboldt compared him to Antonio León and Joaquín *Velazquez y Cárdenas. Much of his work is unknown; some of the manuscripts have been lost; many remain unpublished. The results of his studies were usually published in popular form, as the *Gacetas de literatura de Mexico*. Essentially Alzate was a scientific editor, a kind of Mexican Benjamin Franklin. These publications are collections of scientific and technological information. The *Gacetas* described machines and instruments and announced discoveries and inventions useful in agriculture, mining, and industry. Alzate was a naturalist and devoted much time to the observation of birds and insects, especially of the cochineal. He made experiments with electricity and recorded his meteorological observations, particularly of the aurora borealis of 1789. He investigated the Indian ruins and wrote archeological accounts of them. Alzate's reports were frequently verified by scientific commissions, and he was honored by a number of scientific academies. A portrait of him is owned by the National Academy of Sciences in Mexico City.

José Antonio Alzate.

Bibliography: J. A. ALZATE, *Gacetas de literatura de Mexico,* 4 v. (Puebla 1831). A. ARAGÓN LEIVA, *Elogio a Alzate* (Mexico City 1942). **Illustration credit:** Courtesy of the Library of Congress.

[J. HERRICK]

ALZEDO, JOSÉ BERNARDO, pioneer Peruvian theorist and composer; b. Lima, *c.* 1788; d. Lima, Dec. 28, 1878. After music study with the Augustinian Cipriano Aguilar and the Dominican Pascual Nieves, both of Lima, he composed his first Mass (1806). In the next year he was professed as a Dominican tertiary. His patriotic hymn was chosen by General José de *San Martín in a contest for a *marcha nacional*. The fever of the times led him to join the Chilean battalion Aug. 15, 1822, and he served the army as a musician. From 1823 to 1864 he resided in Santiago de Chile, and from 1847 as chapelmaster of the cathedral. His rich output of Masses, Salve Reginas and motets (now preserved in Peru's National Library) testifies to the quality of cathedral music endorsed by Abp. Rafael Valentín Valdivieso. By virtue of a papal brief, Alzedo married Juana Rojas of Santiago on March 6, 1857. Upon his final return to Lima, he published with government subvention a valuable theory text, *Filosofía Elemental de la Música* (1869). The Peruvian national conservatory bears his name.

See also LATIN AMERICA, MUSIC IN.

Bibliography: C. RAYGADA, *Historia crítica del himno nacional,* 2 v. (Lima 1954), biog., 2:15–105, list of compositions, 60–64. E. PEREIRA SALAS, *Historia de la música en Chile, 1850–1900* (Santiago de Chile 1957). N. FRASER, Grove DMM 1:129–130. Chase LatAmMus.

[R. STEVENSON]

ALZOG, JOHANN BAPTIST, theologian, historian, and patrologist; b. Ohlau, Silesia, June 29, 1808; d. Freiburg, Germany, March 1, 1878. Alzog studied at Breslau and at Bonn. He was ordained in Cologne, July 4, 1834, and received the doctor's degree at Münster in 1835. He then taught at Posen (1836–44) and Hildesheim until called to the University of Freiburg im Breisgau (1853), where he remained until his death.

Alzog was a voluminous writer of sure theological sense and scientific method in research. In 1841 he published his *Lehrbuch der Kirchengeschichte,* which went through nine editions and was translated into seven languages. In 1866 he published his *Handbuch der Patrologie,* a model of exactness in biographical detail, conciseness of doctrinal exposition, and bibliographical citation. He edited the *Oratio apologetica de fuga sua* of St. Gregory of Nazianzus, and also contributed to various periodicals and lexica. He vigorously supported the archbishop, Martin de Dunin, in the controversy over mixed marriages. In 1869 he was called to Rome by Pius IX to take part in the preparation for Vatican Council I. Alzog's work was noted for impartiality and equanimity. After Johann A. *Möhler, he was a principal influence in the revival of studies concerned with positive theology in Germany. He also helped to found the *Görres-Gesellschaft.

Bibliography: H. HEMMER, DTC 1:931–932. P. SÄGER, LexThK[2] 1:410–411.

[F. MURPHY]

ALZON, EMMANUEL D', founder of two religious congregations; b. Vigan (Gard), France, Aug. 30, 1810; d. Nîmes (Gard), France, Nov. 21, 1880. Emmanuel Marie Joseph Maurice d'Alzon was born of an aristocratic family. Influenced by Hugues Félicité de *Lamennais, he studied for the priesthood at Montpellier and Rome, and was ordained (Dec. 26, 1834). He became vicar-general of the Diocese of Nîmes (1835), preached extensively, and became responsible (Jan. 1844) for the administration of the College of the Assumption, a secondary school that he sought to raise to university status to break the state monopoly on higher education. Until his death he continued to serve as college president and vicar-general. After taking the vows of religion privately (June 1844), he received episcopal permission to do so publicly, along with five teachers from his college, thereby inaugurating the *Assumptionists (Dec. 27, 1850), whose superior general he remained during his lifetime. In 1865 he was cofounder of the *Oblate Sisters of the Assumption.

Emmanuel d'Alzon.

Upon the suggestion of Pius IX he oriented his activities after 1862 toward Catholics of the Byzantine rite. D'Alzon was a friend of *Montalembert, *Ozanam, and *Veuillot. His interest in Catholic journalism was evidenced by his collaboration in several publications. He attended *Vatican Council I as theologian to Bp. Claude *Plantier and labored vigorously for the definition of papal infallibility. As a spiritual director D'Alzon was very influential. His letters to Mother Marie Eugénie de Jésus, foundress of the Congregation of the *Assumption, are esteemed for their literary and spiritual excellence. An immense amount of D'Alzon's personal correspondence and many manuscripts of sermons and meditations survived him; some of them have since been published.

Bibliography: S. Vailhé, *Vie du P. Emmanuel d'Alzon,* 2 v. (Paris 1927–34). S. Peitavi, DHGE 2:908–913. S. Salaville, DictSpirAscMyst 1:411–421. M. H. Laurent, DictBiogFranc 2:370–371.

[G. H. TAVARD]

AMABILIS, ST., priest of Auvergne; b. probably Riom (Auvergne), France *c.* 397; d. Nov. 1, *c.* 475 (feast, June 11; Clermont, Oct. 19). In the 6th century, *Gregory of Tours (*In gloria confess.* 33) described the popular belief in this saint's power over serpents as well as the veneration at his tomb. Gregory reports that he himself witnessed two miracles there. Amabilis served as precentor at Clermont and later as parish priest at Riom where, in 1120, a church was dedicated to him. In the 7th century his relics were transferred to Riom; in the 18th century a dispute occurred over these relics between neighboring Clermont and Riom, where Amabilis is patron. Public processions in his honor have been traditional in Riom.

Bibliography: ActSS June 2:460–467. L. Bernet-Rollande, *Saint Amable: Sa vie, son église, son culte* (Clermont-Ferrand 1891). M. Prevost, DHGE 2:913. R. Aigrain, *Catholicisme* 1:387–388.

[L. M. COFFEY]

AMADEUS VIII OF SAVOY (FELIX V, ANTIPOPE); b. Chambéry, Sept. 4, 1383; d. Ripaille, Jan. 7, 1451. Although piety and personal tragedy had led the Count (Duke of Savoy, 1416) to retire from his inherited domains to enter the Order of St. Maurice, which he had founded at Ripaille on Lake Geneva, Amadeus nevertheless accepted his election as Pope (crowned July 24, 1440) by the Council of *Basel. He obtained only scattered support from Christendom. His relations with the Council deteriorated, and he left Basel (Nov. 17, 1442) for Lausanne and then Geneva. The last antipope, he abdicated April 7, 1449, receiving from the magnanimous *Nicholas V the rank of cardinal bishop, a pension, and the titles of papal vicar and legate in Savoy and adjacent dioceses.

Bibliography: G. Mollat, DHGE 2:1116–74, sources and literature; "La Légation d'Amedée VIII de Savoie, 1449–1451," Rev ScRél 22 (1948) 74–80; *Catholicisme* 4:1151–52. J. Grisar, LexThK² 1:413.

[J. G. ROWE]

AMADEUS IX OF SAVOY, BL., Duke of Savoy; b. Thonon, France, Feb. 1, 1435; d. Vercelli, Italy, March 30, 1472 (feast, March 30). He was the first of 18 children born to Louis I of Savoy and Anne of Cyprus. In 1451 he married the daughter of Charles VII of France, Yolanda, to whom he had been betrothed as an infant. He succeeded to the throne in 1456, but later (1469) relinquished control to his wife because he was subject to epilepsy. He was a wise and able ruler, a friend of the poor, and a peacemaker. He meditated and attended Mass daily and received the Sacraments more frequently than was the common practice in his time. He showed great forbearance and forgiveness toward his adversaries, the *Sforzas, and some of his own brothers. He was beatified in 1677.

Bibliography: E. Fedelini, *Les Bienheureux de la Maison de Savoie* (Chambéry 1925). Butler Th Attw 1:706–707. J. Grisar, LexThK² 1:413.

[N. G. WOLF]

AMADEUS OF LAUSANNE, ST., Cistercian abbot of Hautecombe (1139–44), bishop of Lausanne (1144 or 1145–59); b. chateau of Chatte in the Dauphiné, Jan. 21, 1110; d. Lausanne, Aug. 27, 1159 (feast, Jan. 28). Schooled at the imperial court, Amadeus followed the example of his father, Amadeus the Elder of Clermont-Hauterive, in quitting noble rank for cloistered anonymity (1125), but he did not find the obscurity he sought, for his abbot, St. *Bernard of Clairvaux, urged him into posts of leadership. He was often imperial counselor, papal legate, and local arbiter. As bishop he put into practice the monastic ideals of personal piety, devotion to communal peace, and attention to practical detail. He was the author of eight homilies in honor of the Blessed Virgin, the seventh of which was cited twice in the 1950 papal definition of the Assumption. After his death he was acclaimed blessed by his people and his order, and his cult was confirmed by St. Pius X. In 1911 his tomb was discovered in the old Lausanne cathedral, and his relics were taken to Fribourg.

Bibliography: *Huit homélies mariales,* ed. G. Bavaud et al. (SourcesChr 72; Paris 1960). A. Dimier, *Amédée de Lausanne, disciple de saint Bernard* (S. Wandrille 1949). CollOCist 21:1–65, commemorative issue, 8th centenary of St. Amadeus's death.

[P. EDWARDS]

AMALARIUS, liturgist; b. in the area of Metz, *c.* 775; d. Metz, *c.* 850. He was trained by Alcuin's school. From 809 to 813 he was archbishop of Trier, then teacher at the palace school at Aix-la-Chapelle. He administered the Archdiocese of Lyon from 835 to 838. In 838 the

Synod of Quierzy, following the leadership of *Florus of Lyons, removed him from this administration because of his theology, which was contrary to tradition. Amalarius's most significant work is the *Liber officialis* (823), which became the most influential liturgical book of the early Middle Ages in the West. Though not the father of the allegorical method of interpreting the liturgy, he decisively contributed to its breakthrough in the West and thereby in the long run brought about a shift of emphasis in piety—certainly not to its advantage. In place of the one mystery of cult with which ancient Christian piety was impregnated, Amalarius and his innumerable followers artfully excogitated many "mysteries."

See also LITURGY, ALLEGORICAL INTERPRETATION OF.

Bibliography: J. M. HANSSENS, *Amalarii episcopi opera liturgica omnia,* 3 v. in StTest 138–140 (1948–50). A. KOLPING, "Amalar von Metz und Florus von Lyon," ZKathTh 73 (1951) 424–464. J. A. CABANISS, *Amalarius of Metz* (Amsterdam 1954). I. CECCHETTI, EncCatt 1:959–962. E. DEBROISE, DACL 1.1: 1323–30.

[B. FISCHER]

AMALBERGA, SS. Two saints with this name are venerated on the same day (feast, July 10), and since the events of both their lives have been embellished with legendary details, it is quite difficult to distinguish between them, much less to separate fact from fiction in their biographies. It seems quite clear, however, that one St. Amalberga (7th century) was the wife of Count Witger and mother of *Gudula, Reinelde, and Bishop Emebert of Cambrai (d. *c.* 715). When her husband became a *Benedictine monk at the Abbey of *Lobbes, she entered the convent at Maubeuge. She died at Maubeuge, and her body was later transferred to Lobbes.

The second Amalberga (8th century) was a nun of the community of Münsterbilzen in Belgium. Because of her beauty she was approached by King *Pepin III who wished her to marry his son Charles (*Charlemagne). Reportedly she once suffered a broken arm in resisting Charles's attentions, and perhaps for that reason her name has been invoked for the cure of bruises. She died at the convent of Tamise in Flanders, but her relics were solemnly translated to the church of St. Pierre in Ghent in 1073.

Bibliography: Butler Th Attw 3:64–65. A. PONCELET, "Les Biographes de Ste. Amelberge," AnalBoll 31 (1912) 401–409. ActSS July 3:61–68, 70–107. MercatiPelzer DE 1:108, 109. U. BERLIÈRE, DHGE 2:924–925. L. VAN DER ESSEN, *Études critique et littéraire sur les vitae des saints mérovingiens de l'ancienne Belgique* (Louvain 1907) 177–182, 301–302. Zimmermann Kal Ben 2:427–431.

[J. F. FAHEY]

AMALECITES, ancient tribe of southern Palestine, deriving its name from an eponymous ancestor Amalec. They first appeared in the patriarchal narratives; as early as the era of Abraham, the eastern kings raided "the country of the Amalecites" (Gn 14.7). Yet Gn 36.12 would suggest that Amalec was a descendant of Esau. The long, bitter feud between the Hebrews and Amalecites dated back to the latter's provocative attack on the Israelites at Raphidim near Mt. Sinai (Ex 17.8–16). The scouts who reconnoitered the Promised Land likewise encountered Amalecites living in southern Juda and the *Negeb, who barred Jewish entrance from the south (Nm 13.29). Even after the Hebrews had entered Canaan from the east, they still had fierce encounters with these seminomadic raiders who threatened the settled land and its inhabitants (Jgs 3.13; 6.3; 7.12). As the Hebrew state gained strength, Saul and David were able to carry out the complete *ban enjoined by Yahweh against this people (Dt 25.17–19) by exerting pressure from the north. A series of victories (1 Sm 15.7–8; 30.1–18) finally forced the Amalecites to become denizens of the wild steppe of the Negeb. This resulted in the practical extinction of Amalec, though there survived a remnant that was annihilated during the reign of Ezechia (1 Chr 4.42–43).

Bibliography: De Vaux AncIsr. N. GLUECK, *Rivers in the Desert* (New York 1959).

[T. KARDONG]

AMALFI, ARCHDIOCESE OF (AMALPHITANUS), in south Italy; diocese in the 6th century; archdiocese in 987 with suffragan Sees of Capri, Lettere, Scala, Ravello, and Minori; the last three were suppressed in 1818 and united with Amalfi, which today is immediately subject to the Holy See without suffragans. The first known bishop was Pimenius in 596. Amalfi was a thriving maritime republic ruled by doges from 839 to 1073 but in 1131 came under Norman rule. In 1020 Amalfi merchants founded the Knights of St. John in Jerusalem. In 1208 Bp. Peter of Capua translated relics of St. Andrew the Apostle, patron of Amalfi, from Constantinople. The cathedral built in the 9th century was redone in Arab-Norman style in 1202 and in baroque in 1700. A bell tower begun in 1180 was completed in 1276. Very many Benedictine monasteries flourished in the 9th, 10th, and 11th centuries, but thereafter (until 1700) declined, suffering impoverishment as did the city itself. The famous Cistercian monastery of St. Peter of Tozcolo (1212) became Carthusian in 1583 and is today an inn. In 1048 or 1059, and in 1597, provincial councils were held. In 1964 the diocese had 62 secular and 23 regular priests and 55 parishes for an all-Catholic population of 40,000.

Bibliography: J. FRAIKIN, DHGE 2:926–930. P. F. PALUMBO, EncCatt 1:964–967. Gams. Eubel HierCath. RivStorChIt. Ann Pont (1964) 26, 1414.

[G. A. PAPA]

AMALRIC AUGERIUS, 14th-century historian and theologian; b. Béziers, France, date unknown; d. after 1362. He was a doctor of theology from the University of *Montpellier, prior of Santa Maria de Aspirano in the Diocese of Perpignan, and chaplain to *Urban V. Although he is commonly identified as an *Augustinian, A. Zumkeller claims that this is uncertain. His only known work, *Actus romanorum pontificum a primo usque ad Johannem papam XXII sive annum 1321,* is an alphabetical chronicle of the popes, written at Avignon in 1362 (*see* AVIGNON PAPACY) and dedicated to Urban V. It has been edited by J. G. Eccard, *Corpus historicum medii aevi* (Leipzig 1723) 2:1641–1824, and by L. A. Muratori, *Rerum italicarum scriptores* (Milan 1734) 3.2.

Bibliography: Zumkeller 90. L. BOEHM, LexThK[2] 1:415. Hurter Nomencl[3] 2:644. A. PALMIERI, DHGE 5:387.

[A. J. ENNIS]

AMALRIC OF BÈNE, theologian, with pantheistic and materialistic inclinations; b. Bène, near Chartres, mid-12th century; d. Paris, *c.* 1206. He was known also as Amaury, and was a student and later teacher of theology at Paris. He showed the influence of the school of *Chartres and derived his ideas partially from misinterpreted writings of *John Scotus Erigena, but especially from *Aristotle. Amalric was called to Rome by *Innocent III who censured his theories. Amalric retracted them upon his return to Paris. Although he left no writings, he attracted a number of disciples called *Amalricians, whose writings indicate that basically Amalric identified God with the universe. In 1210 his body was exhumed and, by order of a council of Paris, was reburied in unconsecrated ground.

Bibliography: F. G. HAHN, *Über Amalrich von Bena und David von Dinant* (Villach, Austria 1882). G. C. CAPELLE, *Amaury de Bène* (Paris 1932). F. VERNET, DictSpirAscMyst 1:422–425.

[B. CHUDOBA]

AMALRICIANS, an early 13th-century sect centered in Paris, disciples of *Amalric of Bène. The disciples were more extreme than their master. Their pantheistic concept of a God who is identical with the universe made them reject *transubstantiation, as they held that God was already present in the bread and wine. Their abstract pantheism ultimately led them to a denial of the essential difference between good and evil, and to the substitution of knowledge of the natural processes for faith. According to their Trinitarian concept of history, the Father ruled over ancient times and the Son over the first 12 centuries of Christianity, while the reign of the Holy Ghost began with Amalric. Having been condemned by a council in Paris (1210) as heretical, and 5 years later by the Fourth *Lateran Council, the sect quickly disappeared (*See* JOACHIM OF FIORE).

Bibliography: See references under AMALRIC OF BÈNE. Hefele-Leclercq 5.2:1303–05. M. T. D'ALVERNY, "Un Fragment du procès des Amauriciens," ArchHistDoctLitMA 25 (1950–51) 325–336. E. HAMMERSCHMIDT, LexThK² 1:415–416.

[B. CHUDOBA]

AMAN, prime minister of the Persian King Assuerus (Xerxes I, 485–465) and an enemy of the Jews in the Book of *Esther. He was the son of Amadathi of the race of Agag (Est 3.1). This Agag may designate the king of the *Amalecites (1 Sm 15.1–33). Thus, Aman (Heb. *hāmān*) would represent another in a long line of Israel's bitter enemies dating from her desert wanderings (Ex 17.14, 16; Dt 25.17–19). Because Esther's uncle *Mardochai, a Jew, refused to bow before him, Aman persuaded the King to destroy all the Jews of Persia. But Esther, the Jewish wife of Assuerus, saved her people, and Aman was hanged on the gallows he had prepared for Mardochai. In the subsequent massacre by the Jews of their former oppressors, Aman's 10 sons were also killed (Est 9.6–10).

Bibliography: P. RENARD, DB 1.1:433–437. J. SCHILDENBERGER, LexThK² 4:1337. A. PENNA, EncCatt 1:969. EncDictBibl 63–64.

[E. A. BALLMANN]

AMANA SOCIETY, known also as the Community of True Inspiration, one of the oldest and largest of the successful communal sects in America (*see* COMMUNAL MOVEMENTS). Deeply influenced by German *Pietism of the early 18th century, Johann Rock and Eberhard Grüber protested against what they considered the rigid dogmatism and ritualism of the Lutheran Church. Claiming that divine inspiration had been given to them, they organized a community of True Inspirationists in 1714. Its principal tenets maintained that God deals directly with man through inspiration and revelation and that true Christian living is characterized by simplicity. At first Rock and Grüber gained many adherents, but after their deaths the community steadily declined because no one claimed the charism of inspiration. In 1817, however, the sect experienced a revival, when Christian Metz and Barbara Heineman, both claiming inspiration, became its leaders. Metz, an excellent organizer, set about establishing communities, but the Inspirationists soon ran into difficulties with the German government because of their pacifist beliefs. In 1842 they immigrated to America, establishing themselves in Erie County, N.Y., as a cooperative type community, called Ebenezer. In 1850 they adopted a pure communistic form of living that was closer to their ideal of Christian simplicity.

When more land was needed to support its 1,200 members and to maintain its "isolation from worldliness," the sect migrated west (1854), purchasing 25,000 acres near Iowa City, Iowa. Five years later the settlement, Amana, or "Believe Faithfully," was incorporated under Iowa State laws. For the next 70 years the communal economy proved successful, but in 1932 the community voted in favor of conversion to a joint stock corporation. Legally known as the Amana Society, it holds all real property; ecclesiastical matters are handled by the Amana Church Society, which is governed by elected elders. Members of the Amana community are Christians in the Evangelical tradition, but distinguished by the following: "We believe . . . in the Holy Ghost . . . who has spoken and operated through the prophets of old and who even now operates audibly through the instruments of true inspiration. . . ." Their worship is simple; the Lord's Supper, with the washing of feet, is celebrated only rarely. They do not baptize with water, since they hold that baptism is a spiritual practice. Celibacy is highly recommended, but marriage is permitted and divorce is prohibited. Older rules against participation in warfare have been modified. In 1964, although no one in recent years had claimed inspiration, the Amana community continued to prosper.

Bibliography: B. M. SHAMBAUGH, "The Amana that was and the A. that is," *Palimpsest* 31 (1950) 215–248. B. S. YAMBURA and E. W. BODINE, *A Change and a Parting* (Ames, Iowa 1960).

[T. HORGAN]

AMANDUS, ST., apostle of Belgium; b. Aquitaine, France, late 6th century; d. Feb. 6, after 676 (feast, Feb. 6 and Oct. 26). His life is known principally from the *Vita prima* (MGSrerMer 5:428–449), which Krusch assigns to the latter half of the 8th century, but which Stracke attributes to Amandus's contemporary Baudemund (d. *c.* 700), and de Moreau [AnalBoll 67 (1949) 449] places in the late 7th or early 8th century. Here the saint is depicted as a native of Aquitaine, son of Serenus and Amantia, who became a monk at Yeu, was tonsured at Tours, and lived as an ascetic at Bourges under Bishop Austregisil (d. *c.* 624). A visit to Rome *c.* 620 launched him on a missionary career in the northern Frankish domains where, probably before 630, he was consecrated a bishop without fixed see. There followed a second journey to Rome and an apostolate along the River Schelde and at Ghent, wherein he was sustained by King Dagobert I (d. 638). It is not certain that his censure of this monarch's

St. Amandus, figure on a copper gilt and champlevé enamel reliquary of 13th-century Flemish workmanship.

morals brought about his exile or that he preached in the Danube region, in the Pyrenees, and in the country about Narbonne. During the years from 639 to 642, operating out of his monastery at Elnone (later to be known as *Saint-Amand-les-Eaux), he had the aid of *Jonas of Bobbio in evangelizing along the Scarpe and Schelde Rivers as far as the North Sea (MGSrerMer 4:62). That Amandus was constrained to accept the bishopric of Tongeres-Maastricht seems to find support in a 649 letter of Pope *Martin I dissuading him from resigning his see (Jaffé E 2059). De Moreau sees evidence that Amandus founded monasteries at Elnone, Ghent, Nivelles, and Barisis-au-Bois (MGD 1:25), and probably also at Marchiennes, Leuze, Renaix, and Moustier-sur-Sambre. At Elnone, on April 17, 674 or 675, he drew up his *Testament* (MGSrerMer 5:483–485), but the year of his death is unknown. Medieval calendars [see AnalBoll 79 (1961) 80] keep his feast on Feb. 6, the traditional date of his death, or on Oct. 26, the date of his episcopal consecration.

Bibliography: MGPoetae 3:561–610. É. DE MOREAU, *S. Amand, le principal évangélisateur de la Belgique* (Brussels 1942); *Histoire de l'église en Belgique* (2d ed. Brussels 1945–) 1:78–92; "La Vita Amandi prima," AnalBoll 67 (1949) 447–464. D. A. STRACKE, "Over de *Vita sancti Amandi,*" *Handelingen van den Kon. geschieden oudheidkundigen Kring van Kortrijk* NS 26 (1953) 99–179. E. LESNE, DHGE 2:942–945. W. LAMPEN, LexThK[2] 1:416–417. R. AIGRAIN, *Catholicisme* 1:398–400. **Illustration credit:** Courtesy of the Walters Art Gallery, Baltimore.

[H. G. J. BECK]

AMANDUS OF WORMS, ST., bishop; fl. 7th century (feast, Oct. 2). A royal charter of doubtful authenticity by Dagobert I (d. 639) in 627 supposedly granted certain lands and revenues to the church of Worms, of which Amandus, an apostolic man, was said to be bishop (MGD 1:139). According to later reports, *Rupert of Salzburg brought the relics of the saint to the monastic church of *Sankt Peter in Salzburg during the 8th century. Subsequently doubts arose whether these relics were those of the holy bishop of Worms or of another *Amandus, the apostle of Belgium, and only in a 17th-century notice in the *Catalogus abbatum S. Petri* are the relics clearly identified as those of St. Amandus, the Bishop of Worms. The first reference to a church at Worms in honor of the saint dates from the early 11th century, and the original cult of the bishop kept his feast day October 26.

Bibliography: ActSS Oct. 11:910–922. G. ALLMANG, DHGE 2:937–938. H. SCHMITT, LexThK[2] 1:417. I. POLC, BiblSanct 1: 924–925. E. ZÖLLNER, *Geschichte Österreichs* (Munich 1961) 49–50.

[H. DRESSLER]

AMANN, ÉMILE, theologian and historian; b. Pont-à-Mousson, France, June 4, 1880; d. Strasbourg, Jan. 10, 1948. He studied for the priesthood at Nancy. In the Institut Catholique of Paris he pursued courses leading to the doctorate in theology. In 1910 with other scholars at the Institut he started a collection of apocryphal New Testament writings. In this series he himself edited a text of the *Protévangile de Jacques* (Paris 1910). With L. Vouaux he published the *Actes de Paul* (Paris 1913). His contribution to this collection was completed with his edition of the *Actes de Pierre* (Paris 1920). After 1913 he was on the editorial staff of the *Dictionnaire de théologie catholique,* and in 1922 he assumed the direction of this publication. He was responsible for the appearance of about 90 fascicles representing almost 20 volumes. Amann himself contributed over 100 articles to the project. In 1919 he joined the faculty of theology at the University of Strasbourg as professor of ancient Church history. Other works of importance are *Le Dogme catholique dans les Pères de l'Église* (Paris 1922), *L'Église des premiers siècles* (Paris 1928), and v.6 and half of v.7 in the Fliche-Martin series *Histoire de l'Église: L'Époque carolingienne* (Paris 1934) and *L'Église au pouvoir des laïques* (Paris 1940).

Bibliography: RevScRel 22 (1948) 5–8. G. JACQUEMET, *Catholicisme* 1:399. M. A. MICHEL, LexThK[2] 1:418. S. GAROFALO, EncCatt 1:971.

[C. R. MEYER]

AMANTIUS OF RODEZ, ST., bishop of Rodez, France; fl. 5th century (feast, Nov. 1 and 13 in Martyrology of St. Jerome, Nov. 4 in the Roman Martyrology). Nothing is known of his life and episcopate beyond the fame of his miracles. His name seems to be the first known for the See of Rodez where he was bishop before 471, when Euric (d. 484), King of the *Visigoths, took the city. His biography, attributed falsely to *Fortunatus, is from at least the 7th, probably the 9th century, and is not trustworthy. A near successor in Rodez, *Quinctian of Clermont, who attended the synod of Agde in 506, paid great honor to his relics, building a church over his tomb.

Bibliography: ActSS Nov. 2.1:270–287. GREGORY OF TOURS, *Vitae patrum* 4.1 in MGSrerMer 1:674. BHL 1:351–352. R. AIGRAIN, *Catholicisme* 1:400–401. A. P. FRUTAZ, LexThK[2] 1:418. U. ROUZIÈS, DHGE 2:949–950.

[M. C. MC CARTHY]

AMARCIUS, medieval Latin poet; fl. last half of the 11th century. A shadowy figure who has been variously supposed to have been a Frenchman, a Rhinelander, or a Swiss, he may have studied in the schools at Spiers and may have been active as early as 1043 and as late as 1092. In one of his poems he styles himself Sextus Amarcius Gallus Piosistratus. From the same poem it may be deduced that he was in Orders, had some knowledge of medicine, and was versed in classical literature. It seems probable also that he was at one time in the entourage of Emperor *Henry III. His main poem, which survives in a single manuscript, is the *Sermones,* a work of remarkable freshness and vitality, which, cast in the form of a dialogue, deals with the sufferings of contemporary man and is based on a similar work by *Odo of Cluny.

Bibliography: *Sexti Amarcii Galli Piosistrati sermonum libri IV,* ed. M. MANITIUS (Leipzig 1888). Manitius 2:569–574. Wattenbach 2:2–3.

[J. L. GRASSI]

AMARILLO, DIOCESE OF (AMARILLENSIS)

Suffragan of the metropolitan See of *San Antonio, comprising 44,500 square miles in northwestern Texas. The original territory of the diocese, erected Aug. 25, 1926, covered 73,000 square miles; it was reduced in 1961 when 24 southern counties were incorporated into the new Diocese of San Angelo. Amarillo's first bishop was Rudolph A. Gerken (1927–33), who was named archbishop of Santa Fe, N.Mex., June 2, 1933, and was succeeded in Amarillo by Robert E. Lucey (1934–41). Having been consecrated May 1, 1934, Lucey was installed in his see city May 16. He instituted a strong program of Catholic Action and organized a Diocesan Council of Catholic Women, the Confraternity of Christian Doctrine, Holy Name Society, and Catholic Youth Organization. He established the Catholic Welfare Bureau and founded a diocesan newspaper, the *West Texas Register*. The Diocesan Council of Catholic Men was organized in 1960. When Lucey was named archbishop of San Antonio in 1941, his successor in Amarillo was Laurence J. FitzSimon (1941–58), who was consecrated Oct. 22, 1941, and installed November 5. Material expansion of the diocese, delayed by economic depression and wartime restrictions, proceeded rapidly after 1947. In 10 years 20 churches were built in new parishes and missions. A diocesan children's home was opened in Panhandle in 1953.

Sacred Heart Cathedral, Amarillo, Tex.

St. Mary's Church, Clarendon, Tex., built 1890, the first Catholic church in the Texas Panhandle.

John L. Morkovsky, who had been appointed auxiliary bishop in 1955, succeeded to the see Aug. 18, 1958, six weeks after the death of FitzSimon. During Morkovsky's episcopacy the number of Catholics increased to 60,520 in 1963, in a total population of 750,000. There were 48 parishes, 30 missions, and 7 stations, served by 88 priests, of whom 22 were religious, including Vincentians, Capuchins, Franciscans, Dominicans, and Pallottines. Brothers of the Christian Schools and sisters of the Benedictine, Dominican, Franciscan, Mercy, St. Joseph, Incarnate Word, and Our Lady of Victory communities also worked in the diocese. The *Catholic Church Extension Society provided considerable help in building up the Church in the area. On April 16, 1963, Morkovsky was transferred to Galveston-Houston, Tex., and Lawrence M. de Falco was consecrated Amarillo's fifth bishop, May 30, 1963.

St. Mary's Academy, the first Catholic school in the diocese, was established in Clarendon in 1899 by Sisters of Charity of the Incarnate Word; it was moved to Amarillo in 1913. Price College, a diocesan boys' high school, was established in Amarillo in 1928. A diocesan development campaign in 1961 provided funds to establish a minor seminary, St. Lucian's, in Amarillo, and initiated plans for interparish high schools in Amarillo and Lubbock, and a home for the aged in Panhandle. The Incarnate Word Sisters directed St. Anthony's Hospital, Amarillo, and maintained a nurses' training school. Smaller hospitals at Lubbock, Slaton, and Wellington were operated by the St. Joseph, Mercy, and Dominican sisters, respectively. The School Sisters of the Third

Order of St. Francis, whose motherhouse is in Vienna, Austria, have their American aspirancy and novitiate at Panhandle; the Franciscan Sisters of Mary Immaculate of Pasto, Colombia, have their American aspirancy and novitiate with junior college (Our Savior) at Amarillo. Other institutions in the diocese included 18 elementary schools, which in 1963 enrolled a total of nearly 4,000 students. More than half of the diocese's Catholic population were Latin Americans. In addition, large numbers of migrant seasonal laborers, mostly Catholics of Mexican descent, were employed annually in cotton and vegetable production; mechanization reduced their numbers in the late 1950s. Special services provided for Latin Americans included the *cursillo (retreat) movement and the establishment of a lay missionary training center and clinic at San Jose Mission, Hereford.

Bibliography: C. E. CASTAÑEDA, *Our Catholic Heritage in Texas, 1519–1936,* 7 v. (Austin 1936–58).

[M. N. ROONEY]

AMARNA LETTERS

Diplomatic correspondence of the 14th century B.C. discovered in 1887 at El-Amarna, a plain on the east bank of the Nile about 190 miles south of Cairo. The place now called El-Amarna was the site of the capital of Egypt, Akhet-Aton, during most of the reign of *Akhnaton (Amenhotep IV); and the letters came from the diplomatic correspondence with Mesopotamia, Syria, and Asia Minor in the last years of *Amenhotep III (1413–1377 B.C.) and in the reign of Amenhotep IV (1377–1358 B.C.). Perhaps a few letters may be dated to the reign of Smenkhere (1358 B.C.). In 1907, J. A. Knudtzon collated virtually all the letters, which had been divided among various museums and private collections, and together with some scribal exercises and a few Akkadian literary texts from El-Amarna, published them in transliteration and translation (abbreviated EA). Later about 20 more texts were found either in museums or through excavation, so that the number of the Amarna Letters now stands at 377.

Linguistic Features. The language of the letters is Akkadian and written in syllabic cuneiform script on clay tablets; exceptions are two letters written in a Hittite dialect (EA 31–32) and one very long letter in Hurrian (EA 24). At this period Akkadian was the lingua franca of the Near East, as it had been for several centuries. From a linguistic viewpoint the letters written from Palestine and the Phoenician coast are especially important. Written by scribes with little knowledge of Akkadian, they contain many Canaanitisms reflecting the scribes' native speech: glosses (e.g., Akkadian *nīru,* "yoke," is glossed *ḫullu* representing Hebrew *'ol*—the *ḫ* because Akkadian had no sign for West Semitic *'ayin*), hybrid forms partly Akkadian, partly Canaanite (e.g., *yuwaššira,* "let him send," is Akkadian *uwaššir* with Canaanite *y-* verbal preformative and *-a* suffix indicating a wish), and Canaanite syntax in sentence structure. For this reason, though written in Akkadian, the Amarna Letters are a valuable source for the Canaanite language, of which Biblical Hebrew was a dialect, in the 14th century B.C.

Historical Background. From *c.* 1450 B.C. all of Palestine and Syria were under Egyptian hegemony, while to the east, across the Euphrates, lay the kingdom of *Mitanni. This balance of power was destroyed in the Amarna period. A new power appeared on the international scene, the *Hittites, who under Suppiluliuma (*c.* 1380–46) moved east against Mitanni and south into Syria, eventually forming a string of small vassal states. Another power also began to make itself felt; led by Assur-uballit I (*c.* 1363–28), Assyria shook off the Mitanni yoke and finally held what the Hittites failed to subject.

The Amarna Letters bear witness to these events and to Egyptian inaction. Neither Amenhotep III nor his successor, who was absorbed in a religious revolution, seems to have understood the gravity of the situation. Other interests, complacency born of almost a century of unquestioned power, perhaps doubts arising from the conflicting reports of vassals and corrupt Egyptian officials—these resulted in Egypt's loss of power in Syria and along the Phoenician coast and in political chaos in Palestine.

Correspondence with Major Powers. Only a small part of the letters is from or to major powers. In EA 17–29 Tuishrata of Mitanni writes to Amenhotep III, his widow Teye, and Amenhotep IV; relations are cordial, and the principal topic is Tuishrata's daughter as Amen-

Amarna letter, now in the British Museum, from King Tuishrata of Mitanni to King Amenhotep III of Egypt, partly concerned with plans for a marriage of the latter with Tuishrata's daughter. The reverse is also inscribed.

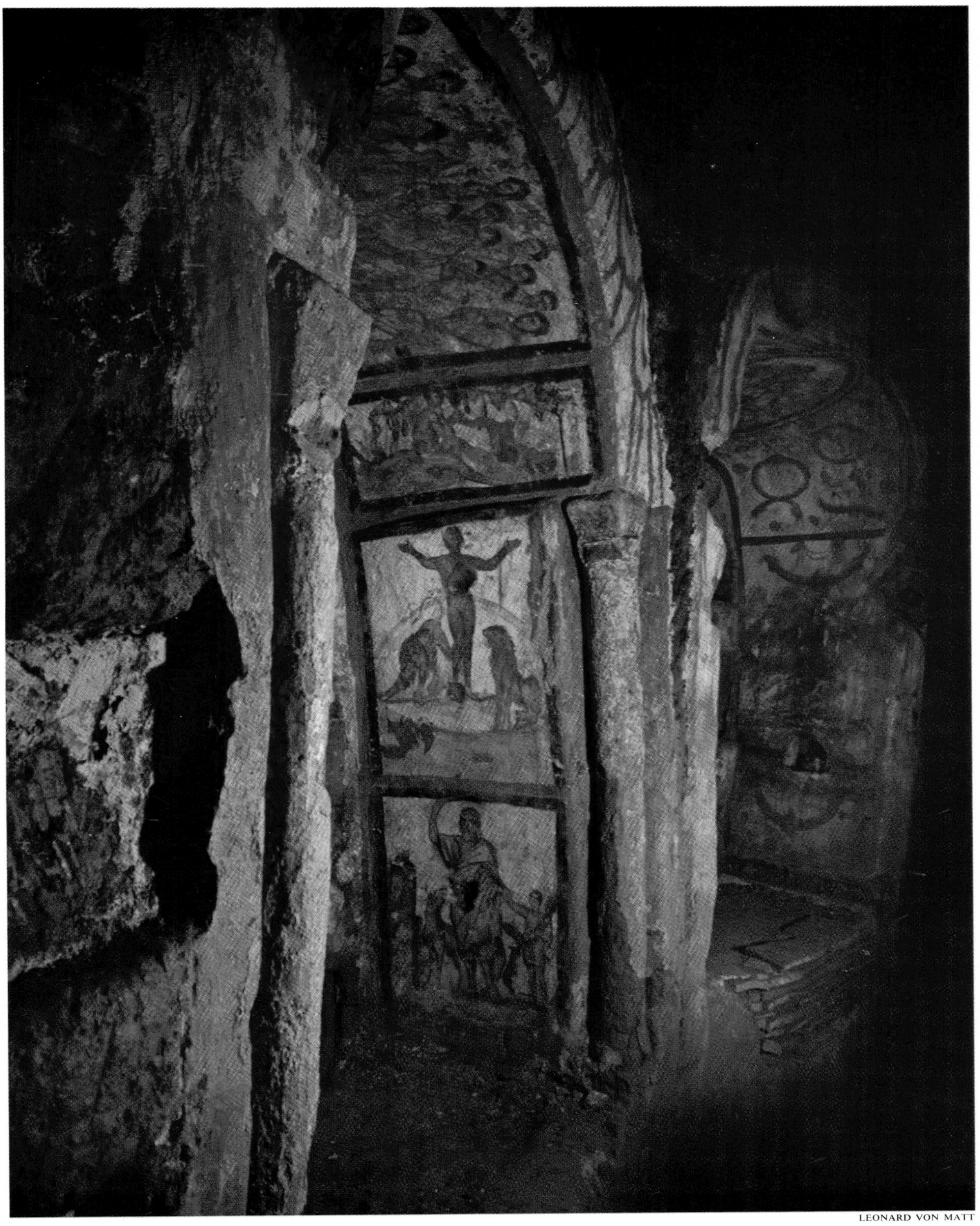

LEONARD VON MATT

A partial view of the Catacomb of the Giordani at Rome. The arcosolium is decorated with 4th-century frescoes of Christ with the Apostles, Jona under the gourd vine, Daniel in the lions' den, and the sacrifice of Isaac.

hotep III's prospective wife. Behind the cordiality loom the Hittites, though they are mentioned only once to record an early Mitanni victory, of which a part of the booty is sent to Egypt (EA 17). Alliance through marriage is also the subject of the correspondence of Amenhotep III with Kadashman-Enlil of Babylon (EA 1–5), whose successor, Burnaburiash, is eager to continue the good relations (EA 6–11). Significantly, the latter complains of the presence of Assyrians at the Egyptian court and wants them sent away empty-handed. However, only two of the Amarna Letters come from Assyria (EA 15–16); they are written by Assur-uballit I and are to be dated to the end of the reign of Amenhotep IV. In EA 15 announcement is made of the sending of a treaty along with gifts. This desire to be leagued with Egypt undoubtedly reflects the Hittite menace in nearby Mitanni.

Correspondence with Vassal States. The remaining Amarna Letters, more than 300, are mostly from, or to, vassals. The letters from Syria and the Phoenician coast concern chiefly the efforts of Amurru, a small state in central Syria south of Kadesh, to expand through exploitation of Egyptian weakness and Hittite support. Its rulers, 'Abd-Ashirta (EA 60–64) and 'Aziru (EA 156–161, 164–168), protest their loyalty, but the letters from their neighbors, especially those from Rib-Adda of Byblos [EA 68–95, 102–138; RevAssyrArch 19 (1922) 102–103], reveal their attacks and eventual control of the coast as far as Beirut. Pleas for help and decisive intervention go unheeded; even the murder of a high Egyptian official leaves the court unmoved. As a result of this lethargy Amurru became a vassal of the Hittites along with other states to the north. By *c.* 1350 Hittite power extended south of Byblos and inland to the Syrian desert.

Even in nearby Palestine confusion reigned: the kinglets of *Jerusalem, *Sichem (Shechem), *Mageddo (Megiddo), Lachish, and *Gazer (Gezer) were at war with each other—plundering caravans, filling their letters with recriminations—or joined in uneasy alliance by the threat of a common enemy. The Egyptian yoke weighed heavily and unrest was deep. Exactions were severe; the fertile lands of Mageddo and Sharon, worked by Canaanites under *corvée,* were crown property and their produce was stored in royal granaries. Egyptian garrisons were to be fed and clothed, and troops passing northward were also to be supplied.

The population of Palestine, confined largely to the plains and low hills—the coastal plain, the Plain of Esdraelon, and the Jordan Valley—was small. W. F. Albright estimates it at around 200,000. The central mountain range, apart from a few centers like Hebron, Jerusalem, and Sichem, was largely unoccupied. Except in the extreme north, Transjordan was the home of seminomads. Ethnically, the population was very mixed. Biridiya of Mageddo and Intaruda of Achshaph (cf. also Arzaya, Yashdata, Rusmanya, etc.) bore Indo-Aryan names, while Abdi-Kheba of Jerusalem, in name at least, was "The Servant of Kheba," a Hurrian goddess. This was the Palestine that the Israelites entered a century later, and with this background much of the Biblical narrative, especially their initial confinement to the hill country, becomes clear.

Bibliography: Pritchard ANET[2] 483–490, selected letters in translation and bibliography. E. F. CAMPBELL, "The Amarna Letters and the Amarna Period," BiblArchaeol 23 (1960) 2–22. W. L. MORAN, "The Hebrew Language in Its North-West Semitic Background," *The Bible and the Ancient Near East,* ed. G. E. WRIGHT (Garden City, N.Y. 1961) 54–72. P. DHORME, DBSuppl 1:207–225. **Illustration credit:** Trustees of the British Museum.

[W. L. MORAN]

AMASIA, KING OF JUDA, *c.* 800 to *c.* 783 B.C., son of King Joas (or Jehoash; *c.* 837–*c.* 800). The story of his reign is told in 4 Kgs 14.1–22 and 2 Chr 25.1–28. On the score of his fidelity to the worship of Yahweh, Amasia [Heb. *'ămaṣyah(u),* Yahweh is strong] is treated more kindly in the former passage than in the latter. After winning a victory over Edom to the south (*see* EDOMITES), he engaged in war with King Joas (Joash) of Israel (*c.* 801–*c.* 786), probably over a border dispute. In this he was crushingly defeated, and he was forced to abdicate in favor of his son *Azaria (Ozia or Uzziah). Later he was assassinated at Lachis, where he had been exiled; but he was buried in Jerusalem.

Bibliography: S. LANDERSDORFER, LexThK[2] 1:419. A. PENNA, EncCatt 1:974–975. EncDictBibl 67.

[B. MC GRATH]

AMAT, THADDEUS, missioner, educator, second bishop of Monterey (Calif.) diocese, now the Archdiocese of *Los Angeles; b. Barcelona, Dec. 31, 1811; d. Los Angeles, May 12, 1878. Son of Pedro and Maria (Brusi) Amat, he entered the Congregation of the Mission (Vincentians) in Barcelona on Dec. 30, 1831, pronounced his vows there on Jan. 16, 1834, and after further training in Barcelona and at Saint Lazare in Paris, was ordained on Dec. 23, 1837. Upon arriving in the U.S. in 1838, he did missionary work in Louisiana for 3 years. From 1841 to 1847 he was superior at St. Mary's Seminary in Perryville, Mo., and St. Vincent's College, Cape Girardeau, Mo., also serving briefly (1842–43) as pastor of Holy Trinity Church and administrator of the diocesan seminary in St. Louis. In 1848 he became superior of St. Charles Seminary, Philadelphia.

When on July 29, 1853, Bp. Joseph Alemany was transferred to the new See of San Francisco, Amat was named bishop of Monterey, where his familiarity with Spanish and American cultures was useful. He was consecrated in Rome on March 12, 1854. After stopping in Spain to enlist clergy and religious and in San Francisco (November 1855) to deliver the pallium to Archbishop Alemany, he hastened to his own diocese with the personnel he had recruited. Amat had headquarters at Santa Barbara, but soon perceived that the rapidly growing Los Angeles would become the population nucleus of his area. In 1856 he sent Blasius Raho, CM, there as his vicar-general. While in Rome in 1859, he obtained authorization to entitle his diocese Monterey-Los Angeles and to reside in Los Angeles. He secured legal recognition of diocesan claims to mission properties in 1856, and later, to the *Pious Fund of the Californias. In 1862, 1869, and 1876 he held synods to cope with the problems of the growing diocese. He attended the Second Plenary Council of Baltimore (1866) and Vatican Council I (1869–70). There he participated actively in discussions on the constitutions "On Catholic Faith" and "On Primacy." When a spinal injury restricted his activity, he asked for a coadjutor, and his vicar-general, Francis Mora, was appointed and consecrated Aug. 3, 1873. Amat was buried in St.

Vibiana Cathedral, whose cornerstone he had laid and whose dedication on April 30, 1876, he had witnessed.

Bibliography: R. BAUDIER, *The Catholic Church in Louisiana* (New Orleans 1939). G. E. O'DONNELL, *Saint Charles Seminary, Overbrook,* 2 v. (Philadelphia 1943–53). R. BAYARD, *Lone-Star Vanguard: The Catholic Reoccupation of Texas, 1838–1848* (St. Louis 1945).

[N. C. EBERHARDT]

AMATOR, SS., *Amator of Auxerre,* bishop; d. May 1, 418 (feast, May 1). The details of the 6th-century biography written by an African priest, Stephen, are quite fabulous. There is, however, ample evidence of Amator's historical existence as an early bishop at Auxerre. *Amator,* priest and martyr; d. April 30, 855 (feast, April 30). He had gone to study at Córdoba, and with SS. Peter and Louis he was killed there by the Mohammedans, according to the *Memoriale Sanctorum* (PL 115:814) of *Eulogius of Córdoba. *Amator of Lucca,* hermit (feast, Aug. 20). He is considered a saint in San Michele in Borgo San Lorenzo. Another (the same?) St. Amator is honored on Aug. 20 in Quercy and in the Limousin. Probably the two may be identified, but the historical existence of either is most improbable.

Bibliography: Amator of Auxerre. ActSS May 1:51–61. Duchesne FÉ 2:430. M. BESSON, DHGE 2:981–982. R. LOUIS, Dict BiogFranc 2:439–442. Amator, Martyr. ActSS April 3:815. P. SICART, DHGE 2:982. E. P. COLBERT, *The Martyrs of Córdoba, 850–859* (Washington 1962). Amator of Lucca. ActSS Aug. 4:16–25. E. ALBE, "La Vie et les miracles de s. Amator," Anal Boll 28 (1909) 57–90; DHGE 2:920–922, 990.

[W. A. JURGENS]

AMATUS OF MONTE CASSINO, historian, poet; b. Salerno, Italy, *c.* 1010; d. *Monte Cassino, Italy, March 1, before 1105. He had been bishop, probably of Pesto-Capaccio; if this conjecture be true, he presumably became a monk at Monte Cassino after his episcopacy, *c.* 1060. He was one of the group of eminent writers at the abbey during the tenure of Abbot Desiderius (*see* VICTOR III, POPE). His works include the following: *Historia Normannorum,* much abridged in a popular French version of the 14th century (antedating all other histories of the *Normans, it treats of events critically and with specific detail, making it a work of great importance); the *Liber in honore s. Petri,* in four books of Leonine hexameter, which gives various accounts of the Apostle from Scripture and Apocryphal writings; *De laude Gregorii VII,* a lost work that was probably in verse; *De duodecim lapidibus et civitate caelesti Hierusalem,* probably to be identified with the diffuse rhythm *Cives caelestis patriae.*

Bibliography: *Storia dei Normanni di Amato di Montecassino,* ed. V. DE BARTHOLOMAEIS (Rome 1935); *Il poema di Amato su S. Pietro Apostolo,* ed. A. LENTINI, 2 v. (Montecassino 1958–59). *Chronica monasterii Casinensis* 3.35, MGS 7:728. PETER THE DEACON, *De viris illustribus Casinensis coenobii* ch 20, PL 173: 1032. Manitius 3:449. F. NOVATI, *Le origini,* ed. A. MONTEVERDI (Milan 1900–26) 402, issued in parts. W. SMIDT, "Die *Historia Normannorum* von A.," StGreg 3 (1948) 173–231. A. LENTINI, "Ricerche biografiche su A. di M.," *Benedictina* 9 (1955) 183–196; "Il ritmo *Cives caelestis patriae . . .,*" *ibid.* 12 (1958) 15–26; DizBiogItal 2:682–684.

[A. LENTINI]

AMATUS OF NUSCO, ST., bishop and abbot; b. Nusco, Italy, *c.* 1104; d. 1193 (feast, Sept. 30 in Nusco, Aug. 31 in Benedictine martyrology). The chronology of his life and many of its details are uncertain because there are two quite different versions, the earliest of which was written after 1460. The later version appears the more reliable and was favored by the *Bollandists. According to this account (ActSS Aug. 6:901–928) Amatus was born at Nusco in southern Italy of noble parents. He entered the religious life and after a short period as archpriest of Nusco became a *Benedictine. In 1142 he founded the Abbey of Fontignano near Orvieto, and in 1154 he was made bishop of Nusco. He was a zealous and popular bishop and a generous benefactor of religious houses. He is said to have worked many miracles both before and after his death. The other version of the saint's life (ActSS Aug. 6:844–847) states that he was born in the early 11th century, was consecrated bishop in 1048 or 1071, when the Diocese of Nusco was created, and died in 1093.

Bibliography: A. PALMIERI, DHGE 2:993–994. A. M. ZIMMERMANN, LexThK[2] 1:420. Zimmermann KalBen 2:642, 644. G. TAGLIALATELA, *Orazione panegirica di s. Amato, primo vescovo e patrono di Nusco* (Naples 1890). *Enciclopedia ecclesiastica,* ed. A. BERNAREGGI (Milan 1942–) 1:130.

[J. L. GRASSI]

AMATUS OF REMIREMONT, ST., abbot; b. Diocese of Grenoble, France, between 565 and 570; d. Abbey of Remiremont, France, *c.* 628(feast, Sept. 13). About 581, while still very young, he entered the monastery at Agaunum, now known as the Abbey of *Saint-Maurice, and he eventually became a hermit there. In 614 he went to the monastery of *Luxeuil with its abbot, *Eustace of Luxeuil, but he left *c.* 620 with his friend and convert Romaric (d. 653) to found a monastery at Castrum Habendi that soon became known as the Abbey of *Romarici Mons,* or *Remiremont. This foundation became one of the most fruitful of the foundations from Luxeuil, and Romaric succeeded Amatus as abbot. In the dispute between the monk Agrestius and the followers of St. *Columban and Abbot Eustace of Luxeuil, the two founders sided with Agrestius, but after a series of misfortunes and the downfall of Agrestius, they made peace with their former superior. Amatus died shortly afterward in semiretirement at Remiremont. He is sometimes mistakenly identified with another Amatus, Bishop of Sion, who died near the close of the century.

Bibliography: *Vita Sancti Amati,* Mabillon AS 2:120–127. E. EWIG, LexThK[2] 1:420–421. A. M. BURG, *ibid.* 9:25–26. Mercati-Pelzer DE 1:111. J. MABILLON, *Lettre . . . touchant le premier institut de l'abbaye de Remiremont* (Paris 1687). M. A. GUINOT, *Étude historique sur l'abbaye de Remiremont* (Paris 1859) 377–388. M. BESSON, *Monasterium Acaunense* (Fribourg 1913) 173–184. Zimmermann KalBen 3:49–50. BHL 1:358. Butler Th Attw 3:549–550.

[G. E. CONWAY]

AMBARACH, PETER (MUBARACH, BENEDICTUS), 17th-century Maronite Jesuit, Oriental scholar; b. Gusta, Lebanon, June 1663; d. Rome, August 25, 1742. Ambarach, known in Italy as Pietro Benedetti, studied at the Maronite College in Rome (1672–85), and was ordained in Lebanon by the Maronite Patriarch Stephen al-Duwaihi (Aldoensis) who sent him back to Rome in 1691 to defend the validity of Syriac ordinations against the charges of Jean *Morin. Cosimo III, Grand Duke of Tuscany, named him director of the Oriental Press at Florence, and he accepted the chair of Sacred Scripture at Pisa. He entered the Jesuit novitiate in Rome on Oct. 30, 1707, and became a member of Pope Clement XI's commission for the critical edition of the Greek Bible. At the request of Cardinal Querini he started a Latin translation of the work of St. *Ephrem, which he left unfinished. Among his publications are a Latin translation of Stephen al-Duwaihi's *Defense of Syriac Ordinations and the Maronite Liturgy;* a *Vita Arabica S. Alexii* [ActSS July 4 (1725) 266–270]; a partial edition of the Menologium of the Emperor *Basil II in Greek and Latin (completed by Clement XI and published, Urbino 1727); a history of the persecutions under the Persian King Sapor and his successors, written with the aid of C. Maiella; a revision of the *Works of St. Ephraem* in Greek and Syriac (3 v. 1737–43; *see* ASSEMANI, JOSEPH SIMON); and some verse and letters, including an exchange with Apollonio Bassetti.

Bibliography: Sommervogel 1:1295–98. E. M. Rivière, DHGE 2:1014–15. P. Sfair, EncCatt 2:1225. A. Fabroni, *Vitae Italorum doctrina excellentium,* 18 v. (Pisa 1778–99) 11:174–185.

[P. JOANNOU]

AMBIGUITY, an obscurity of meaning that leaves a statement open to contrary interpretations, often as a result of faulty grammar or insufficient context (*see* FALLACY). The phrase "systematic ambiguity" has been used by Bertrand *Russell to characterize the function of certain key words in formal logic. According to Russell the word "true," for example, applies to statements belonging to a number of logically distinct types. If we apply it to a sentence that combines statements of different types, contradiction may result. By avoiding such combinations the logician can guard against this (*see* ANTINOMY). Some scholastic philosophers speak of the systematic ambiguity of terms used in metaphysics. Such everyday words as "being" and "good" can be applied to the divine order, but at the risk of hidden equivocation. To eliminate this risk, the metaphysician takes note of whatever in the term's original signification carries over into its other uses (*see* ANALOGY).

[H. A. NIELSEN]

AMBITION

Ambition has two extreme senses, one good, the other bad, with interesting mixtures of legitimate thrustfulness and self-regarding pride falling between the two. The term comes from Latin *ambitio* (*ambire, ambitus*), a going about seeking votes for an office; and as representing a desire for success according to the order of right reason, it is laudable and indeed obligatory, for such a desire is inseparable from a brave tackling of difficulties. Thus a man should resolutely prosecute the causes that will give him a full and rounded life, promote the standing of his family, enlarge and dignify the work on which he has set his heart, redound to the credit and glory of his country, and show forth the beauty of the Church. Above all, in a Christian sense, he will not be half-hearted in his response to the call to holiness and the apostolate: "Let your light shine before men" (Mt 5.16).

So considered, ambition is characteristic of the great-hearted man of the Nichomachean Ethics, of the *magnanimity that is the first potential part of the cardinal virtue of *fortitude as described in the *Summa theologiae* of St. Thomas Aquinas (ST 2a2ae, 129), or the large-mindedness and grandeur praised by Massillon and the court preachers in the high century of Louis Quatorze. Found in people of spirit who seek nothing but the best, its character, according to Aristotle, the Stoics, and the medieval theologians, appears both from its positive notes and the contrary vices it disdains. It is the love of honor as this implies the resplendence of virtue rather than its fame. Indeed on occasion magnanimity will fight with the enterprise and doggedness of fortitude, and the authors note its special connection with *fiducia* in the sense of the keeping of one's word whatever befalls, and with *securitas,* the steady confidence that is never down-hearted. Yet always it keeps a sense of proportion and acts between the vices of excess and defect. On the one hand it avoids the pushfulness (*praesumptio*) of acting for what is out of the question or not deserved, and the vaingloriousness (*inanis gloria*) that sets too great a store on human approbation. On the other hand it masters the faint-heartedness (*pusillanimitas*) that causes one to fail to attempt to do what he can. "The kingdom of heaven suffers violence" (Mt 11.12). Yet as bound up with men's contending emotions, the passions of the irascible appetite, magnanimity is turned into sin. So the poet sees ambition as the last infirmity of a noble mind, and St. Thomas treats *ambitio* as a disorder and vice.

Charity is not ambitious; it does not seek its own (1 Cor 13.5). This indeed is the keynote of the sin, a self-seeking that takes honor out of its context and isolates it as a good for oneself, wanting praise for an excellence that is not possessed, or hugging the praise to oneself as if one's efforts deserved it without the help of God, or as if it could be hoarded and not turned to the benefit of others. It is this inordinateness that makes it a moral failure or sin, and it is this extravagance in honor-seeking that makes it a sin against magnanimity.

Bibliography: Thomas Aquinas, ST 2a2ae, 131. R. A. Gauthier, *Magnanimité: L'Idéal de la grandeur dans la philosophie païenne et la théologie chrétienne* (Paris 1951); "Fortitude," *The Virtues and States of Life,* ed. A. M. Henry, tr. R. J. Olsen and G. T. Lennon (Theology Library 4; Chicago 1957) 487–531. A. Beugnet, DTC 1:940–942. R. Brouillard, *Catholicisme* 1:407–409.

[T. GILBY]

AMBIVALENCE, FEELINGS OF

Ambivalence is a psychological reaction in which opposing emotions and feelings, such as love and hate, joy and sorrow, or desire and fear, exist at the same time within the same individual. The person is moved by both emotions; the relative strength of each may be equal or nearly equal, resulting in conflict. At times both emotions are present on the level of awareness, producing inner turmoil; at other times, one emotion remains on the level of awareness while the other is repressed. For example, a daughter who must care for an invalid mother experiences love and a true desire to be helpful but at the same time feels annoyance, resentment, and even *hostility. For moral reasons, however, she does not allow herself to acknowledge the existence of the destructive feelings and emotions. In her struggle to keep these repressed, she may intensify her overt manifestation of love.

Ambivalent feelings are not limited just to the affective sphere but exert an influence on judgment and action. They produce contrary impulses, whereby an individual may desire two things that are incompatible. Since both impulses seem equally acceptable, he is faced with a dilemma. The healthy person, after a brief period of hesitation, is able to arrive at a decision, which consists of either a clear-cut choice or a compromise. The mentally ill person is unable to weigh the value of his opposing feelings and then come to a decision. He shifts back and forth between two opposing modes of action. At one time he settles on one mode of action, only at a later date to shift his choice to the opposing mode. He is unable to commit himself fully to any plan of action.

The early development of human relationships sets the stage for future feelings of ambivalence and the manner of handling these feelings. The very young child has loving feelings toward the "giving" mother while he experiences hostility toward the frustrating and punishing mother. Since both types of treatment are the usual fare of the growing child, he must learn how to handle these opposing emotional responses. He quickly discovers that any open manifestation of hostility meets with immediate opposition. Consequently, he learns to repress these undesirable feelings, lest he provoke the anger of his mother even more and perhaps lose her love. The child repeats the same experience when a new brother or sister enters the home. He is expected to love the newcomer; hostile, jealous feelings are unacceptable. For fear of the consequences, he refuses to acknowledge his true emotional reactions. However, these emotions still exert an influence on his overt behavior.

Since ambivalent feelings and emotions influence judgment and action, they have a direct bearing on morality. In the case of the average normal individual, ambivalence lessens the flexibility of choice but does not take away freedom of choice; in the case of the mentally ill, it can produce such indecision as to make a judgment impossible.

Bibliography: R. DALBIEZ, *Psychoanalytical Method and the Doctrine of Freud,* tr. T. F. LINDSAY, 2 v. (London 1941). J. C. FORD and G. A. KELLY, *Contemporary Moral Theology* (Westminster, Md. 1958).

[R. P. VAUGHAN]

AMBROS, AUGUST WILHELM, musician and scholar whose history of music implemented the church music reform of the 19th century (*see* CAECILIAN MOVEMENT); b. Mauth (near Prague), Czechoslovakia, Nov. 17, 1816; d. Vienna, June 28, 1876. His father, a civil official, had a background of culture; his mother, an accomplished pianist, was a sister of R. G. Kiesewetter (1773–1850), a distinguished music antiquarian. Ambros pursued musical studies while preparing for his doctorate in law. In 1850 he became councilor of state, and later a member of the governing board of the Prague conservatory and author of serious studies in music and art. From 1872 he was a professor in the Vienna conservatory and a justice department official. His essay *Die Grenzen der Musik und Poesie* [Leipzig 1856; tr. by J. H. Cornell as *The Boundaries of Music and Poetry* (New York 1893)] offered an alternative to Eduard Hanslick's view that the beauty of a musical composition depends exclusively on tonal relations and can express no extramusical reality. His five-volume *Geschichte der Musik* (1862–82), appearing concurrently with *Proske's anthology, *Musica Divina,* revealed the artistic past of the Church (with emphasis on Renaissance polyphony) and provided aesthetic principles for the reform movement. The fourth volume, unfinished at his death, was completed from his notes by C. F. Becker and G. Nottebohm. A fifth volume consists of musical examples, some from Ambros's collection of 800 transcriptions, and others supplied by the editor, Otto Kade. Ambros's own compositions did not survive him.

Bibliography: A. ADLER, MusQ 17 (1931) 360–363. F. BLUME, MusGG 1:408–413. E. DANNREUTHER, Grove DMM 1:133–134. Kornmüller. E. TITTEL, *Österreichische Kirchenmusik* (Vienna 1961). F. L. HARRISON et al., *Musicology* (Englewood Cliffs, N.J. 1963).

[E. LEAHY]

AMBROSE, ST.

Bishop of Milan, Father, and Doctor of the Church; b. Treves, *c.* A.D. 339; d. Milan, April 4, 397 (feast, Dec. 7). His family, perhaps in part ultimately of Greek origin, belonged to the high Roman aristocracy. At the time of his birth his father was praetorian prefect of the Gauls, one of the chief civil offices in the Roman Empire. Following his father's death, his brother *Satyrus, his sister Marcellina, and he were brought to Rome, where the brothers received an excellent education in the liberal arts and in law. Their education both in the family household and at school included a thorough training in Greek, which was to stand Ambrose in good stead later. He must have received a solid training in Christian doctrine also in a household in which Christian conduct and piety were emphasized. His sister Marcellina took the veil from Pope Liberius in 353. About 365 Ambrose and Satyrus entered the civil service as advocates, and *c.* 370 both were promoted to provincial governorships, Ambrose being made *consularis,* or governor, of Liguria and Aemilia with his residence at Milan, the imperial capital of the Roman Empire. He soon acquired a reputation for uprightedness in administration and for blameless character. On the death of the Arian Bishop Auxentius, he had to quell the violence that arose regarding the choice of a successor among Catholics and Arians, and then, much against his will, he was unanimously chosen as bishop by both sides. Although brought up in a Christian family, he was still a catechumen. Within a few days after his Baptism he was ordained to the priesthood and consecrated as bishop of Milan (Dec. 7, 374).

Episcopate. He immediately distributed his share of the family wealth to the poor and set an example of strict asceticism in the episcopal household, which was organized on a kind of semimonastic basis. In the administration of his charities he received the enthusiastic and self-sacrificing support of his brother Satyrus (d. 378). Under the tutelage of the learned priest Simplicianus, who later succeeded him in the See of Milan, he applied himself to the systematic study of theology. In exegesis he was profoundly influenced by the allegorical method of interpretation as developed by Philo and Origen. His chief guides in theology were St. Athanasius, Didymus the Blind, St. Cyril of Jerusalem, St. Basil, and Hippolytus. The investigations of P. Courcelle have shown, too, that he was well acquainted with Plotinus and made fruitful use of Neoplatonic ideas in his development of Christian thought.

However, Ambrose remained typically Roman in thought and language, and as a man of action. In his exegesis and in his theological expositions, as well as in the homilies that underlie most of his works, and even in his letters, he exhibits a marked predilection for moral teaching and exhortation. All his writings were composed at short notice, as the occasion demanded, in the course of an extraordinarily busy and difficult episcopate. From the days of his election, he was repeatedly involved in problems of the gravest import for the Church and for the State, and he soon came to be recognized throughout the Western Empire as the great champion of orthodoxy and of the rights of the Church.

Altar of Victory. On his accession the young Emperor *Gratian (375–383) refused to accept the pagan title *pontifex maximus;* and some years later (381), in his second edict against paganism, he ordered the removal of the altar and statue of Victory from the Senate house in Rome. The powerful pagan party sent a delegation headed by *Symmachus to Milan to protest; but, under the influence of Ambrose, it was refused an audience at court. In the summer of 384, after the murder of Gratian (383), a new delegation under the leadership of Symmachus, then Praetorian Prefect, presented an eloquently written *Relatio,* or *Memorial,* to the imperial consistory and the boy-emperor *Valentinian (383–392), again pleading for the restoration of the altar and statue. Ambrose hastily prepared a strong refutation of the petition, and the request for restoration was denied. Both the *Memorial* of Symmachus and the reply of Ambrose (*Epist.* 18) are extant—at least in the revised form that was eventually given them.

Conflict with the Arian Empress Justina. Despite the aid rendered to the position of Valentinian by Ambrose's mission to the usurper Maximus at Treves in 383, Valentinian's mother, the Empress Justina, fearing the growing ascendancy of the bishop over her son, and as a staunch Arian, organized a coalition against Ambrose. She raised an issue by demanding that one basilica in Milan, namely, the Basilica Portiana outside the walls, be given to the Arians. Ambrose was summoned to the imperial palace near the beginning of Lent in 385, but refused to give up the basilica. The incident created a riot in the city, and Ambrose himself had to be asked to calm his people. A few weeks later, just before Easter, Justina boldly demanded that the new basilica within the walls, Ambrose's own cathedral church, be turned over to the Arians, but he refused with the curt statement that "a bishop cannot give up the temple of God" (*Epist.* 20.1). Beginning on Palm Sunday there was a series of clashes between the imperial troops and Ambrose's congregations at the new and old basilicas, and at the Portiana, accompanied by destruction of property. The bishop, however, stood his ground, and on Holy Thursday news was brought to him at the Portiana that the court had abandoned its attempt to seize any of his churches at that time.

The struggle was not over. With the help of the Arian Bishop Mercurinus Auxentius, Justina had an imperial edict passed against the Catholics in January 386, and Ambrose was summoned to appear before the Emperor and his council to dispute the points at issue with Auxentius. He refused, explaining his position at length, and finally, to avoid arrest, remained within the pre-

St. Ambrose, mosaic of the 5th century in the chapel of S. Vittore in Ciel d'Oro, Milan.

cincts of the new basilica. For several days and nights the church was surrounded by imperial troops, but they did not force an entrance. To relieve tension and to encourage his flock, Ambrose introduced the antiphonal singing of Psalms and of hymns of his own composition. It was on this occasion also that he delivered his *Sermon against Auxentius,* in which, in terse juridical style, he enunciated the epoch-making principle in the relations of Church and State: *imperator enim intra ecclesiam, non supra ecclesiam est* (par. 3). The court was forced to capitulate; the anti-Catholic edict was rescinded, and no further action was taken against Ambrose. After the deaths of Maximus (388) and Justina, the young Emperor Valentinian again turned to Ambrose for counsel, and Ambrose treated him with fatherly affection until his murder in 392.

Ambrose and the Emperor Theodosius (379–395). Only two incidents marred temporarily the cordial relations of Ambrose and *Theodosius, the greatest personalities of their age in Church and State, namely, the Callinicum affair and the massacre of Thessalonica. At Callinicum on the Euphrates the Christian congregation with the connivance of their bishop had burned a Jewish synagogue (late in 388), and Theodosius ordered that the bishop restore the synagogue at his own expense. Ambrose opposed this order in vehement terms on the ground that Christians, in rebuilding a synagogue, would be committing an act of apostasy, and the Emperor reluctantly withdrew his order. In this case, however, excessive zeal led Ambrose to neglect the demands of strict justice, for he suggested no possible alternatives for redressing the wrong done.

In 390 several imperial officers were killed in a riot at Thessalonica, and Theodosius, influenced primarily by his Master of the Offices, Rufinus, ordered a savage reprisal that led to the massacre of 7,000 defenseless persons in the circus of the Macedonian city. Ambrose left Milan at the news, but in a letter to the Emperor he reproached him for his crime and told him that, under threat of excommunication, he must do public penance. Theodosius complied some months later, even if some of the dramatic details furnished by the historian *Theodoret are to be discounted. A few years later (in 392 and 395) Ambrose delivered his great funeral orations on Valentinian II and Theodosius, which contain so much precious information on his part in the political affairs of his time.

Ambrose as Pastor. Despite his heavy involvement in political affairs of concern to the Church, Ambrose was a zealous defender of orthodoxy and, above all, a zealous pastor of souls. In his homilies he attacked severely all the social abuses of his age. With the courage and eloquence of a Hebrew Prophet, he denounced especially evil conduct in the upper classes and its deplorable results. But he also expounded theological doctrine very effectively in his homilies. Augustine came to listen to his eloquence, but was led to a new understanding of the Scriptures and of Christian faith by the bishop's explanations (*Confessions* 6.1.1–6.4.6). Augustine was baptized by Ambrose at Easter 386. Ambrose had distributed his own wealth to help the poor and urged others to do the same. Following the battle of Hadrianople in 378, and the subsequent Gothic invasion, he did not scruple to sell the sacred Church vessels to redeem captives. In his advocacy of Christian ideals, he was one of the most zealous and influential promoters of virginity in his age. He gave a new impetus to the cult of the martyrs with the discovery of two skeletons, which were thought to be those of *Gervase and Protase, in the course of the excavations for his own great basilica in 386.

St. Ambrose barring Theodosius from the cathedral at Milan, painting by Ambrogio Borgognone (c. 1450 or 1460 to 1523) in the Accademia Carrara at Bergamo, Italy.

Writings. The volume of his extant works is noteworthy when one considers that they were all written in the midst of an extraordinarily demanding episcopate. They often reveal, on the dogmatic and scriptural side, especially, a heavy dependence on Greek works, but the borrowing is freely acknowledged. Ambrose was primarily concerned not with originality but with meeting the practical needs of dogmatic and moral instruction and exhortation. For the most part his treatises were assembled from homilies, and the revision was hastily done. However, he was splendidly trained in Latin literature, and many passages in his works exhibit Christian Latin literary style at its best. Like Leo the Great, he had a happy facility for coining clear and pithy phrases and definitions.

Exegetical Works. All his Old Testament exegesis is based essentially on Philo and Origen. Even the most literal of scriptural texts is given an allegorical or typological meaning. In view of the homiletic origin of his exegetical works, moral application is invariably a primary concern. His major contributions are: *Exameron* (6 bks.), based on the corresponding work of St. Basil; *Expositio evangelii secundum Lucam* (10 bks., of which 1 and 2 are taken over directly from Origen);

and *Expositio in Psalmum 118*. His shorter works include *De Cain et Abel, De Noe, De Abraham* (2 bks.), *De Isaac et anima, De bono mortis, De Iacob et vita beata* (2 bks.), *De Ioseph, De patriarchis, De fuga saeculi, De Helia et ieiunio, De Nabuthae, De Tobia, De interpellatione Iob et David, Apologia prophetae David,* and *Explanatio super Psalmos 12*.

Moral-Ascetical Works. The *De officiis* (3 bks.), written for the clergy of Milan, is the most important. As its title indicates, it is modeled on the corresponding predominantly Stoic treatise of Cicero. However, resemblance is more external than real. The work is thoroughly Christian and, as is usual in Ambrose, relies heavily on Scripture for examples and authority. The other writings in this category are: *De virginibus ad Marcellinam sororem* (3 bks.), *De viduis, De virginitate, De institutione virginis,* and *Exhortatio virginitatis*. In these treatises Ambrose reveals greater independence in developing his arguments in favor of the life of virginity. Through his emphasis on the Blessed Virgin as the ideal and patron of virginity, he is one of the chief founders of devotion to Mary in this respect. The *De lapsu virginis consecratae* is definitely recognized as pseudo-Ambrosian.

Dogmatic Works. Three of these are against Arianism: *De fide ad Gratianum* (5 bks.), on the divinity of the Son; *De Spiritu Sancto* (3 bks.), based essentially on Didymus the Blind, St. Athanasius, and St. Basil; and *De incarnationis dominicae sacramento*. Three others deal primarily with the exposition of the Sacraments and of the faith to catechumens and are of great importance for the history of the liturgy: *De sacramentis* (6 bks.), *De mysteriis,* and *Explanatio symboli*. The last two are now definitely assigned to Ambrose. Finally, he composed the *De paenitentia* to refute Novatianism.

Orations and Letters. The two orations *De excessu fratris* (*Satyri*), the *De obitu Valentiniani,* and *De obitu Theodosii* are masterpieces of their genre. The invective *Sermo contra Auxentium de basilicis tradendis* is to be regarded also as a formal oration. Only 91 of Ambrose's *Epistulae* are extant. Apart from a few private letters, they are official or semiofficial in character, or are little exegetical or moral treatises in epistolary form.

Hymns and Other Works. Of the numerous hymns ascribed to Ambrose, the *Deus Creator omnium, Aeterne rerum conditor, Iam surgit hora tertia,* and *Intende, qui regis Israel* are certainly genuine. By these compositions he has justly earned the title "father of liturgical hymnody" in the West. He seems also to have given definitive form to the *Exsultet. Several inscriptions and 21 Tituli in verse also have good claims to Ambrosian authorship (see Faller, 999). The *Hegesippus sive de bello Iudaico* (5 bks.), a free translation and adaptation of the *De bello Iudaico* of Flavius Josephus, may be regarded with some probability as being a work from the early life of Ambrose.

Appreciation. Ambrose exhibited little originality in the field of dogma or exegesis, but he was a courageous and effective defender of orthodoxy, a great moral teacher, and an exemplary pastor of souls. Above all, he was the first of the Fathers and Doctors of the Church to deal formally with the relations of Church and State. He enunciated the principle that the Church is supreme in its own domain and is the guardian of morality. Even the emperors, despite their lofty dignity and absolutism, are subject to the moral laws as defined and put into practice by the Church. The penance of Theodosius and the principle underlying and demanding it were phenomena found in the sacred history of Israel. However, they were entirely new in the Greco-Roman world, and they were to be of the greatest significance for the future.

See also MILANESE RITE; HYMNOLOGY.

Bibliography: Dekkers CPL Nos. 122–183. J. HUHN, LexThK[2] 1:427–430, with bibliog. O. FALLER, EncCatt 1:984–1000, excellent. A. LARGENT, DTC 1.1:943–951, and A. MICHEL, Tables générales 1:111–115, with bibliog. H. VON CAMPENHAUSEN, RGG[3] 1:307–308. A. GASTOUÉ and P. DE LABRIOLLE, DHGE 1:1091–1108. G. BARDY, DictSpirAscMyst 1:425–426. W. WILBRAND, ReallexAntChr 1:365–373. Altaner 443–457, with an excellent summary of Ambrose's teachings and copious bibliog. F. CAYRÉ, *Manual of Patrology and History of Theology,* tr. H. HOWITT, v.1 (Paris 1936) 520–547. Bardenhewer 3:498–547. J. R. PALANQUE, *Saint Ambroise et l'Empire romain* (Paris 1933), with bibliog. F. H. DUDDEN, *The Life and Times of St. Ambrose,* 2 v. (Oxford 1935). A. PAREDI, *St. Ambrose,* tr. J. COSTELLO (Notre Dame, Ind. 1963). C. MARINO, *Chiesa e stato nella dottrina di S. Ambrogio* (Rome 1963). J. HUHN, *Das Geheimnis der Jungfrau-Mutter Maria nach Ambrosius* (Würzburg 1954). P. COURCELLE, *Recherches sur les "Confessions" de Saint Augustin* (Paris 1950), esp. 91–174 and 211–221. On the language and style of St. Ambrose, see esp. CUA PatrSt v.10, 12, 15, 19, 20, 27, 29, 30, 35, 40, 43, 49, 56, and 58, and C. MOHRMANN, "Langue et style de la poésie chrétienne," *Études sur le latin des chrétiens* v.1 (Rome 1961) 151–168, esp. 165–168. For new Eng. tr. see FathCh v.22, 26, 42, and 44. On the *Vita S. Ambrosii,* written at the suggestion of St. Augustine by Ambrose's former secretary, Paulinus of Milan, in 422, see A. STUIBER, LexThK[2] 8:208, with bibliog. **Illustration credits:** Fig. 1, Soprintendenza, Monumenti Lombardia. Fig. 2, Anderson-Art Reference Bureau.

[M. R. P. MC GUIRE]

AMBROSE OF CAHORS, ST., bishop?; d. near Bourges, France, *c.* 770 (feast, Oct. 16). In the account of his life that has come down to us it is impossible to sort out any certain historical information. According to a doubtful tradition he held his episcopal office at Cahors under *Pepin III the Short. Slandered and persecuted despite his works of charity, he gave up his see and lived for 3 years in a cave near the Lot River. While returning from a pilgrimage to Rome, he died in the neighborhood of Bourges. His cultus, dating from the 10th century, is perhaps the best evidence for his saintly career.

Bibliography: ActSS Oct. 7.2:1031–50. BHL 1:369–374. Duchesne FE 2:13. E. ALBE, DHGE 2:1110–11. C. LEFEBVRE, BiblSanct 1:943. Baudot-Chaussin 10:484–485.

[J. E. LYNCH]

AMBROSE OF MASSA, VEN., Franciscan; b. near Massa Marittima, Tuscany, Italy; d. Orvieto, April 17, 1240. He was a secular priest in the Tuscan Maremma when in 1222 he was led to reform his life by the preaching of Moricus (d. 1236), one of the first companions of *Francis of Assisi. After 3 years as parish priest at Cotone near Scansano in the Province of Grosseto, Ambrose joined the *Franciscans (1225) in the friary of Massa Marittima. For the next 15 years he devoted himself to penance and charitable works, living mostly at Orvieto. Many miracles were performed at his tomb in the church of St. Francis there, so that the citizens petitioned the Holy See for his *canonization. The cause was opened and is still in existence, never having been brought to a conclusion. In the Franciscan Order Ambrose is venerated with the title of blessed, though this has not officially been confirmed by the Church.

Bibliography: Wadding Ann 2:470–472; 3:266–268. ActSS Nov. 4:568–608. L. FUMI, "Processo della canonizzazione del b. Ambrogio da Massa," *Miscellanea Francescana* 1 (1886) 77–81, 129–136. M. BIHL, DHGE 2:1121. W. FORSTER, LexThK² 1:430.

[S. OLIVIERI]

AMBROSE TRAVERSARI, BL., Camaldolese monk and early Christian humanist; b. Portico, southwest of Ravenna, Sept. 16, 1386; d. Fontebuono, Nov. 17, 1439. He entered the Camaldolese cenobitic monastery, St. Mary of the Angels, at Florence, Oct. 8, 1400, and was professed Nov. 6, 1401. Soon Florentine humanists such as Niccoli, Strozzi, and Cosimo de Medici visited his cell to discuss classical and patristic literature, philosophy, and theology. Ambrose gathered and emended ancient texts and translated many works of the Greek Fathers. He became subprior in January 1431, and prior general of his order on Oct. 26, 1431, because of his interest in reform. The *Hodoeporicon* is a diary of the resulting visitations from December 1431 to 1433. He represented Pope *Eugene IV at the Council of *Basel, and before Emperor *Sigismund. At Ferrara and *Florence in 1438 he effectively employed his knowledge of Greek in negotiating with Byzantine representatives leading to reunion of the Roman and Orthodox Churches.

Bibliography: A. DINI-TRAVERSARI, *Ambrogio Traversari e i suoi tempi* (Florence 1912). G. MERCATI, *Ultimi contributi alla storia degli umanisti,* 2 v. (StTest 90, 91; 1939) v.1. C. SOMIGLI, EncCatt 12:453–454. J. WODKA, LexThK² 1:431.

[N. G. WOLF]

AMBROSIANS

A term applied to various religious congregations under the protection of St. *Ambrose, Bishop of Milan (374–397), especially to two groups of women and three groups of men, although neither Augustine nor Ambrose's biographer, Paulinus, says that Ambrose himself founded a religious order. His *Treatises on Virginity* are exhortations to purity of life and personal sanctity, but not a rule for a religious community.

1. The first known "Ambrosians," the *Oblationaries of St. Ambrose,* appeared in the 9th century in Milan. It exists today as a group of 10 poor men and 10 poor women at the Scuola dei Vecchioni in Milan who have the task, on feast days, of bringing the people's oblation of bread and wine to the altar at the offertory of an Ambrosian-rite Mass.

2. In the 14th century, three Milanese noblemen, Alexander Crivelli, Anthony Pietrasancta, and Alber Besozzi, sought retreat and solitude in a wooded glen outside the city walls. Clothed in a chestnut-colored habit of tunic, scapular, and cowl, they practiced works of charity and preached to the people. They were joined by others, and in 1375 Gregory XI, before his return from Avignon, gave the growing community of priests and solitaries the Rule of St. *Augustine, the Ambrosian rite, and a special constitution under the title of *Fratres Sancti Ambrosii ad Nemas*. Similar groups began to dot the countryside but the only bond of unity was community custom. In 1441, Eugene IV merged all members into the *Congregatio Sancti Ambrosii ad nemus Mediolanensis,* designating the original monastery as the motherhouse. Laxity of discipline led to a reform by St. Charles *Borromeo in 1579. Sixtus V in 1589 added to the congregation the monasteries of the Brothers of St. Barnabas, which had been founded by John Scarpa, and included the name of St. Barnabas in the title. The congregation was dissolved by Innocent X in 1646.

3. In 1408, the *Annunciatae of Lombardy,* or Nuns of St. Ambrose, were founded by Dorothea Morosini, Eleanore Contarini, and Veronica Duodi at Pavia. Daughterhouses spread throughout Lombardy and Venetia. Guided by the Rule of St. Augustine, the nuns lived a cloistered life of prayer and poverty under the jurisdiction of the local bishop. Nicholas V and Pius V approved their constitutions. They were suppressed by Napoleon; only one house remains today.

4. Another congregation of Ambrosian sisters was founded by Catherine Morigia in 1474 at Mt. Varese in Lombardy, as a branch of the Ambrosian *Fratres.* These sisters, dedicated to a life of prayer and penance, wore a chestnut-colored habit, followed the strict rule of St. Augustine, lived in cloister, and used the Ambrosian liturgy. In 1474 they were given canonical status by Sixtus IV under the title *Nuns of St. Ambrose.* A rapid decline in the 17th century led Innocent X to abolish them, also in 1646.

5. In implementing the decrees of the Council of Trent in his Diocese of Milan, Charles Borromeo, the "second Ambrose," organized a society of priests under the patronage of Our Lady and St. Ambrose, called *Oblates of St. Ambrose,* in 1578. He consulted Philip *Neri and *Felix of Cantalice on the rule for his community, which was approved by Gregory XIII. Living in community and owing obedience to the bishop, they became the bishop's associates in the work of the ministry. In 1810, Napoleon dispersed the congregation but Archbishop Romilli restored it in 1854. The oblate ideal spread to Poitiers in France, to Paderborn in Germany, and, in 1857, to England, under Cardinal Nicholas *Wiseman, where the community became known as the *Oblates of St. Charles.*

Bibliography: Heimbucher 1:598–599, 625–626; 2:560. P. FOURNIER, DHGE 3:412. F. BERTOGLIO, EncCatt 5:1705. E. CATTANEO, *ibid.* 9:26–27. C. GREINZ, LexThK² 1:424–425.

[M. A. MULHOLLAND]

AMBROSIASTER, the name coined by *Erasmus to designate the author of a commentary on the Epistles of St. Paul that had traditionally been ascribed to St. Ambrose, but that Erasmus was convinced could not be by him. Most scholars agreed that the commentaries were quite unlike the work of Ambrose, and in 1905 A. Souter proved to general satisfaction that a collection of 127 *Quaestiones Veteris et Novi Testamenti,* commonly attributed to Augustine, was in fact by the same author as the Pauline commentaries. In 1908 Souter produced a critical text of this work (CSEL v.50). It was planned that a similar edition of the Pauline commentaries should be produced by H. Brewer, but Brewer died before the work was far advanced. The Maurists' edition (reproduced in PL v.17) was made from 13 MSS, all of French provenance. In recent years a survey of H. J. Vogels has shown that some 72 MSS exist and that they show that there were three versions of the commentary on Romans produced by the author himself: two versions of what he had to say on 1 and 2 Corinthians and a single version of the commentary on the other Epistles, except Hebrews, for which the commentary has been supplied by Alcuin. In the *Quaestiones* Souter indicated that the same procedure was followed. There was a first edition of 150 *quaestiones* by the author himself; then a definitive 127 *quaestiones;* and finally, though much later, a version in which only 115 are found. Souter considered that the author worked on Romans and on 1 and 2 Corinthians and finally made the first edition of his *Quaestiones*. He then turned to the rest of Paul and brought out the second edition of the *Quaestiones,* and all this between 370 and 384. The silence of St. *Jerome about such an important work on the Epistles is hard to explain and has been put down to jealousy. Augustine did cite the work (*contra duas epp. Pelagii* 4.4.7; CSEL 60:528) but ascribed it to *Hilary of Poitiers. The Irish knew it as Hilary's, for the *Codex Ardmachanus* has *Incipit prologus Hilari in Apostolum* as a heading, and the library at Bobbio had a copy of *Hilarii in ep. ad Romanos*. Guesses have been made as to the identity of the author, but without achieving any firm result. He was versed in Roman law, betrayed an interest in things Jewish (but was not of Jewish origin), had lived in Rome, disliked allegorical interpretations of Scripture, wrote astringently in Latin, and had read Irenaeus, Tertullian, Cyprian, Victorinus of Pettau, and Eusebius of Vercelli.

Bibliography: A. SOUTER, *A Study of Ambrosiaster* (Texts and Studies 7.4; Cambridge, Eng. 1905); *The Earliest Latin Commentaries on the Epistles of St. Paul* (Oxford 1927). G. BARDY, DBSuppl 1:225–241. H. J. VOGELS, "Die Überlieferung des Ambrosiasterkommentars zu den Paulinischen Briefen," *Nachrichten der Akademie der Wissenschaften in Göttingen. Philologisch-historische Klassé* 1.7 (1959) 107–142; "Ambrosiaster und Hieronymus," RevBén 66 (1956) 13–19; ed., *Das Corpus Paulinum des Ambrosiaster* (Bonn 1957).

[J. H. CREHAN]

AMBROSIUS CATHARINUS (LANCELOT POLITI), Dominican theologian and bishop; b. Siena, *c.* 1484; d. Naples, Nov. 8, 1553. A doctor of civil and Canon Law and consistorial lawyer under Leo X, he became a Dominican in 1517 because of Savanarola's preaching. Recognizing the dangers of nascent *Lutheranism, he was one of the first (1520, 1521) to write against it. While prior of Siena, he waged a controversy with his superiors in favor of the feast of the Immaculate Conception. This resulted in his removal from office. In 1532 he went to France where, prior to the Council of Trent, he published several works on problems raised by Protestantism—predestination, justification, purgatory, veneration of the saints, and episcopal residency. Pallavincino declared that Catharinus "was second to none among his contemporaries in contest with heretics." He attended the Council, 1545 to 1547, as papal theologian, manifesting his intellectual independence, especially in controversies with his confreres Carranza, D. *Soto and B. Spina. At the petition of the Conciliar Fathers, Catharinus was appointed bishop of Minori in 1546; he was made archbishop of Conza in 1552. During the Tridentine period he produced many works concerning the problems that arose during the sessions. His original and extensive writings (50 edited and unedited works), often concerned with uncharted areas of theology, contained flaws. Concerning the intention of the minister in conferring the sacraments, he defended the thesis of external intention; on the value of the words *Hoc est corpus meum,* he held that the consecration is effected by the preceding epiclesis, "Quam oblationem . . ." of the Roman Mass. His juridico-moral theory concerning the transmission of original sin found adherents among such theologians as *Banez, *Billuart, *Suarez and the *Salmanticenses. His works are characterized by an emphasis upon the teaching authority of the Church and a thematic return to the Scriptures and the Fathers.

Bibliography: J. SCHWEIZER, *Ambrosius Catharinus Politus* (Münster 1909). M. M. GORCE, DTC 12.2:2418–34.

[J. R. COONEY]

AMBRY (ARMARIUM), a niche, usually in the wall, with or without a door, for storing or showing books, clothes, food, jewelry, money, precious objects, small statues, vessels, etc. This function was known from antiquity. In Christian usage, the ambry served for the reservation of altar bread and wine, sacred vessels, liturgical books, *holy oils, *relics, and the *Eucharist. From the 4th century, sacred objects were kept in church (preferably in the sanctuary or high up in a nearby pillar) or *sacristy. At least from the early 6th century, ambries were made in the stems of *altars. After the decree *Sane* of *Innocent III, the doors of eucharistic ambries had locks and keys. As devotion to the Holy Eucharist grew, ambries were placed in more prominent places in church and often had barred windows. The *tabernacle for reservation upon the altar (9th century) superseded the ambry from the 16th century onward. Documentary and archeological evidence of many varieties of ambry abounds all over the West from the 12th century.

Bibliography: DU CANGE 1:701–702; 3:372. L. KÖSTER, *De custodia sanctissimae Eucharistiae* (Rome 1940). E. MAFFEI, *La Réservation eucharistique jusqu' à la Renaissance* (Brussels 1942). G. DIX, *A Detection of Aumbries* (4th ed. London 1955). S. J. P. VAN DIJK and J. H. WALKER, *The Myth of the Aumbry: Notes on Medieval Reservation Practice and Eucharistic Devotion* (London 1957) 15–66.

[S. J. P. VAN DIJK]

Modern use of the ambry (St. Marien, Olter, Switzerland).

AMELRY, FRANCIS, Carmelite spiritual writer and mystic; b. *c.* 1498; d. *c.* 1552. Not much is known of his life except that he held a bachelor's degree in theology and was prior at the Carmel at Ieper. The Index of 1558 mentions a mystery play of his, and he is known to have written about 10 spiritual works in which love and its mystical experience is the dominant theme. Two of his tracts, *Wat de Liefde Gods can bedrgven* (What the Love of God Can Do) and *Een Dialogus of Tsame sprekinghe der ziele* or *De minnende ziel* (The Loving Soul), have been transposed from Old Dutch into modern Dutch and are published in the series "Bloemen von One Geestelijk Erf." The first tract is a handbook of the spiritual life. The second work, his masterpiece, has been translated into Latin by Antonius von Hemert (1552) and into other languages. It is a systematic and logical presentation of the stages of love, in seven steps, which describe love's progressively enveloping nature. Although based on sound theology, his mystical doctrine was much influenced by personal experience and is expressed in a mystical, ardent, forceful, analogous style.

Bibliography: A. AMPE, *Franciscus Amelry, de edele zanger der liefdle* (Antwerp 1951). C. JANSSEN, *Carmelklius en Carmelwereld* (Bussum 1955) 111–112. *De katholieke encyclopaedie,* ed. P. VAN DER MEER et al., 25 v. (Amsterdam 1949–55) 2:187.

[B. CAVANAUGH]

AMEN, a Hebrew word from a root (*'mn*) meaning "to be trustworthy," used to signify "surely," "so it is," "so may it be," "I ratify." (*See* FAITH, 1.) In the OT, the term has several significations. In Nm 5.22 it is used to signify assent to an administered oath, the one using the term thereby agreeing to accept the consequences of a curse or punishment in the event the crime be committed. In Dt 27.15–26 the word is used to indicate ratification of each of 12 curses for 12 specified possible crimes. It is similarly used in Neh 5.13 and Jer 11.5. In 3 Kgs 1.36, Tb 9.12, and Jer 28.6, it is used to signify agreement with a blessing. In synagogue practice, Amen was used by the people to ratify a prayer or doxology pronounced by the rabbi or leader [Neh 8.6; Ps 105(106).48]; often in such usage it was doubled [Ps 40(41).14; 71(72).19; 88(89).53].

In the NT, Christ's statements are often introduced with Amen, thereby guaranteeing their absolute certitude and divine authority. Such meaning was unknown in previous usage of the word. In the Gospel of St. John, such statements are introduced by a double Amen (Jn 1.51; 13.16, etc.), the other Evangelists retaining single use of the term. The word was pronounced in apostolic liturgical assemblies to ratify the priestly Eucharistic prayer (1 Cor 14.16), even by Greek-speaking Christians. Frequent passages in the Epistles indicate the use of the word to conclude private petitions and doxologies, as well as liturgical ones (Rom 1.25; 9.5; 1 Tm 1.17; Heb 13.21; 1 Pt 4.11; 5.11; 5.14; Jdt 1.25; Phil 1.25; 2 Pt 3.18; 1 Thes 5.28; 2 Thes 3.18; etc.). According to St. Paul, through Christ "also rises the 'Amen' to God unto our glory" (2 Cor 1.20), since all the divine promises find their fulfillment and ratification in the Word Incarnate. The Apocalypse states that those in glory, when hearing the heavenly doxologies before the throne of God, will respond with Amen (Ap 5.14).

Bibliography: F. CABROL, DACL 1.1:1554–73. I. CECCHETTI, EncCatt 1:1030–32. J. BAUR, LexThK[2] 1:432–433. EncDictBibl 67–68. L. GILLET, EphemThLov 56 (1944–45) 134–136.

[M. R. E. MASTERMAN]

AMEN-EM-OPE, WISDOM OF

An ancient Egyptian literary work best known for its close connection with the Book of *Proverbs in the Bible. Within Egyptian literature it ranks as a late example of the "wisdom" teacher's manual of conduct for aspiring scribes. *See* WISDOM (IN THE BIBLE); EGYPT, ANCIENT, 3. Its date of composition is uncertain; some would put it about 1300 B.C. The author describes himself as Amen-em-Ope, son of Kanakht, a local functionary in Abydos. His work is currently known to us from a hieratic papyrus in the British Museum (first published in 1923) and from fragmentary scribal exercises on a writing board and on an *ostracon. The most satisfactory dating for any of these copies would seem to be that for the pottery fragment (ostracon), which is ascribed to the latter half of the Twenty-first Egyptian Dynasty, thus about 1000 to 946 B.C. Divided into an introduction and 30 "houses," or chapters, the Wisdom of Amen-em-Ope resembles, even in this external form, the "Sayings of the Wise" in Prv 22.17–24.34, with which it has close contacts also in themes treated and imagery employed. The links between Amen-em-Ope and Proverbs are not confined to this part of Proverbs, however, but are clearly present also between Prv 1–9, the work of the final editor of Proverbs, and the Egyptian book. Literary dependence in some degree is certain, though it has been disputed on which side the dependence lies. Since wisdom literature is notoriously derivative and compilatory, this question admits of no facile solution, though the dates now favored for Amen-em-Ope's work would seem to give it priority. The most recent attempt (by É. Drioton, an excellent Egyptologist) to establish the priority of the Semitic—not necessarily Hebrew—side, is open to criticism from the standpoints of both literatures, and must be adjudged unsuccessful. The editor of Proverbs is well known for his use of sources; Deuteronomy, Isaia, and Jeremia can be seen at almost every line underlying his first nine chapters. The materials scattered in no particular order in the rather diffuse work of Amen-em-Ope are reflected in small compass in the one section (22.17–24.34) of the composite book of Proverbs. Moreover, it would seem most likely that the final editor of Proverbs consciously adapted selected data of the Egyptian work to his own religious and cultural milieu. This was the easier to do, in that the references to "the god" in this Egyptian book are most of the time without mythological and polytheistic overtones.

Bibliography: J. A. WILSON, in Pritchard ANET 421–424, with basic references. Excerpts and references. J. M. PLUMLEY in D. W. THOMAS, ed., *Documents from Old Testament Times* (Torchbooks; New York 1961) 172–186. Studies. J. M. MCGLINCHEY, *The Teaching of Amen-em-ope and the Book of Proverbs* (Washington 1939). P. W. SKEHAN, "Proverbs 22:17–24:34," CathBiblQ 10 (1948) 120–125. É. DRIOTON, "Sur la Sagesse d'Aménémopé," *Mélanges bibliques . . . A. Robert,* ed. H. CAZELLES (Paris 1957) 254–280; "Le Livre des Proverbes et la Sagesse d'Aménémopé," *Sacra pagina,* ed. J. COPPENS et al., 2 v. (Paris-Gembloux 1959) 1:229–241. R. J. WILLIAMS, "The Alleged Semitic Original of the *Wisdom of Amenemope,*" JEgypt Arch 47 (1961) 100–106. B. COUROYER, "Aménémopé I, 9:III, 13: Égypte ou Israel?" RevBibl 68 (1961) 394–400.

[P. W. SKEHAN]

AMENHOTEP III, king of *Egypt, 1402 to 1364 B.C. The reign of Amenhotep (Amenophis) III, son of Thutmose IV (1409–1402), was the most splendid of those of the great Egyptian emperors of the Eighteenth Dynasty (1570–1304), whose policy was to undo the

Head of Amenhotep III, wearing a war crown. Granite, New Kingdom, Eighteenth Dynasty.

work of the Hyksos kings and restore Egypt to its place among its neighbors. To do this it had been necessary to conquer and hold Cyprus and Crete and a considerable part of Asia, including Syria and the Phoenician coast (Palestine), as tributary kingdoms. Although Amenhotep launched no new military campaigns, he had the power and wealth to retain the conquests that had been made especially by *Thutmose III (1490–1436). In Asia his supremacy was unchallenged. Babylon, Assyria, and *Mitanni sought his favor. This period offers the first documentation of world diplomacy through the *Amarna Letters, which include correspondence with the above-mentioned kingdoms, some of it relating to Amenhotep's marriage alliances with foreign princesses. As a young man he had married a commoner, Tiye, and he associated her name with his own in the titles of royal documents, a practice not known among his predecessors. During his reign a certain democratization of the Pharao's person may be noticed. He was a great hunter, and more than 30 *scarabs commemorating one of his lion hunts have been discovered. Others celebrate his marriage to a Mitanni princess.

Amenhotep's reign was one of prosperity and luxury. Trade flourished with Syria, the East, and the Mediterranean world. He built extensively in Egypt, Nubia, and the Sudan, and his constructions were memorable and colossal. He patronized the fine arts, particularly in the decoration of the palace he built at the south of the western plain of *Thebes (Biblical No-Amon). The capital itself was transformed into the first example in antiquity of a monumental city. In religion he seems to have anticipated somewhat the policy of his son and successor, the so-called heretic Pharao *Akhnaton (Amenhotep IV; 1364–1347); for when he removed his palace to the left bank of the Nile, he erected a chapel there to the sun-god, Aton, without reference to the national god, Amon. Serious threats to his empire arose toward the end of his reign. The Hittites encroached on the north, but the Pharao's troops were able to repel them for the time being. Invasions of desert Semites, the *Habiru, related to the Hebrews of the Bible, began to inundate Syria and Phoenicia. His tomb in the Valley of the Kings west of Thebes was plundered in antiquity.

Bibliography: CAH v.2, ch. 5. J. H. Breasted, *A History of Egypt,* 2 v. (2d ed. New York 1909; repr. 1956). J. A. Wilson, *The Burden of Egypt: An Interpretation of Ancient Egyptian Culture* (Chicago 1951; pa. repr. *The Culture of Ancient Egypt* 1956). É. Drioton and J. Vandier, *L'Égypt* (4th ed. Paris 1962). A. H. Gardiner, *Egypt of the Pharoahs* (New York 1961).
Illustration credit: Courtesy, The Cleveland Museum of Art.

[V. P. MALLON]

AMERBACH, JOHANNES AND BONIFATIUS. Johannes, renowned German printer; b. Amerbach (Franconia, West Germany), probably 1440; d. Basel, Dec. 25, 1513. He took his M.A. degree in 1461 in Paris, and became a resident of Basel in 1475 and a citizen there in 1482. His printing shop, made famous through numerous editions of the Church Fathers (especially of SS. Ambrose and Augustine), of the Bible with commentary, and of the *Corpus juris canonici,* attracted the interest and labors of renowned scholars. Amerbach's edition of St. Jerome was so far advanced at the time of his death that Johannes Froben, assisted by Erasmus, was able to publish it by 1516. His printing business was continued by his sons, Bruno and Basil, together with Froben.

Bonifatius, son of Johannes, close friend and heir of Erasmus, humanist and professor of Roman law; b. Basel, Oct. 11, 1495; d. there, April 24, 1562. He took his M.A. degree in Basel in 1513 and was a jurist there till 1519. After studies in Freiburg, he was in residence in Avignon (after 1520). Made a professor in Basel in 1524, Amerbach took a very critical attitude toward the Reformation, especially in regard to its preaching and compulsory Communion. He remained in Basel to the end of his life and had a decisive part in the renewal of the university, of which he was rector many times.

Bibliography: Johannes. J. Heimberger, *Amerbacher Persönlichkeiten* (Basel 1929). R. Wackernagel, *Geschichte der Stadt Basel,* 3 v. (Basel 1924). A. Hartmann, NDB 1:247; ed., *Die Amerbachkorrespondenz,* 4 v. (Basel 1942–53). O. Vasella, LexThK[2] 1:433. Bonifatius. *Die Matrikel der Universität Basel,* ed. H. G. Wakenagel, 2 v. (Basel 1951–56). E. Dürr and P. Roth, eds., *Aktensammlung zur Geschichte der Basler Reformation in den Jahren 1519 bis Anfang 1534,* 6 v. (Basel 1921–50).

[G. J. DONNELLY]

AMERBACH, VEIT, humanist and Lutheran convert to Catholicism; b. Wembding, 1503; d. Ingolstadt, Sept. 13, 1557. Amerbach (known also as Trolman) studied at Ingolstadt, Freiburg, and Wittenberg, taught in the Latin school at Eisleben, and in 1530 was made professor on the arts faculty in Wittenberg. He became disaffected with his colleagues, concluded that the patristic writings did not support Luther's doctrine of justification by faith, and was moved by Johann Eck's arguments for the primacy of the pope. In November 1543 he left Wittenberg and embraced Catholicism. He taught briefly in the Latin school in Eichstätt, and then became a professor of philosophy and rhetoric at Ingolstadt. He published commentaries on Cicero, Ovid, Chrysostom, and other writers of classical and Christian antiquity.

Bibliography: L. FISCHER, *Veit Trolmann von Wemding, genannt Vitus Amerpachius, als Professor in Wittenberg* (Freiburg 1926). T. FREUDENBERGER, LexThK[2] 1:433–434. M. SIMON, RGG[3] 1:310.

[L. W. SPITZ]

AMERICAN ART

Art in America has been a mirror of its life, a reflection of the times in which it was created. Those artists who arrived with the early settlers in the 16th century were intent on recording the discoveries of the New World. By the 17th century, art served the vanity of wealthy families who were able to commission likenesses for posterity. Eighteenth-century painting can be called the age of portraiture, for it opened with paintings of colonial family groups and closed with portraits of Revolutionary War heroes and the first president.

American art of the 19th century is characterized by the landscape. Beginning among Hudson River Valley artists, the attraction of the natural beauties of America led artists westward along pioneer routes to the Mississippi, the Rockies, and beyond. In the early years of the 20th century, cityscapes gained prominence as American life was once again concentrated in urban centers; artists then focused on the landscape of the Middle West during the years of the Dust Bowl and the Depression.

Waves of modernism flowing from Europe affected American art at the time of World War I. As lines of communication drew the continents closer together, an International Style resulted, and following World War II U.S. artists competed for artistic leadership of the world community.

Fig. 1. Unknown artist, "Alice Mason," canvas, 38½ by 24⅞ inches, 1670.

BEGINNINGS AND THE REVOLUTION

The first artists in America were those who accompanied the explorers; artists whose primary purpose was to record the native inhabitants, the flora and fauna, and to send back the results of their find to an eager public in Europe.

Some of these early recorder-artists concentrated also on mapmaking, while others depicted the events they observed firsthand. Jacques Le Moyne came to Florida with the Huguenots in the 1560s and was witness to a night raid by one group of savage Indians upon the village of another. His subsequent creation of an illustrative painting, however, was executed from the safety of Europe when he returned.

In 1585 John White produced the first pictorial impressions made by a white man in America. Accompanying an English expedition to Sir Walter Raleigh's colony in Roanoke, White made on-the-spot drawings of American Indians, their villages and rituals. Though his noble savages often look more Renaissance than real, the fish, fowl, and food are accurate to the most minute detail.

White's black-and-white drawings were sent back to Europe, where they were tinted by colorists of fantastic imagination. Thus an ear of corn would appear with alternating stripes in barber pole fashion.

The Limners. Oil painting in the New World began in the 17th century, when portraits represented one of the only forms of worldly vanity for the early settlers. The first portraitists were itinerant limners, untrained "professional" painters who roamed the Eastern Seaboard, moving from one community to another as the available portrait commissions ran out. Limner, the old English word for painter, is applied to these men, who were often sign painters by profession and created likenesses as a sideline.

The limners, whose identities are now unknown, are traditionally given the names of the people they painted. The "Gibbs Limner" painted three portraits in 1670 of the stern-faced Gibbs children; the "Mason Limner" is known through his painting of little Alice Mason (Fig. 1). The limner who painted "Elizabeth Freake and Baby Mary" (1674) created one of the earliest family portraits in America.

The limners painted by formula, employing a darkened background and a checkerboard floor as dictated by the European painting tradition with which they were familiar. The body and background in a painting might be done beforehand, while the limner was on the road between towns; thus the sitter posed only for the head. The resultant effect is often disconcerting, with a three-dimensional head attached to a flat and lifeless body.

First Professionals. John Smibert (1688–1751) was the first well-trained painter to come to America (1728), and in 1729, in Boston, he held the earliest art exhibition. The artist immigrated to the New World in the company of Bp. George Berkeley, whom he intended to assist in establishing a college for the Indians in Bermuda. Though the grandiose scheme never materialized, Smibert created an ambitious 6- by 8-foot

Fig. 2. John Singleton Copley, "Paul Revere," canvas, 35 by 28½ inches, c. 1769.

canvas of "Dean George Berkeley and His Entourage" (1729, Yale University Art Gallery), which attempts a natural grouping of eight life-size figures, one of them a self-portrait.

The next generation of New England artists felt the influence of Smibert, but one of his disciples, Robert Feke (b. *c.* 1706–10; d. after 1750), soon eclipsed the older painter. Feke produced backgrounds of naturalistic landscapes for his sitters, with trees, hills, and sky rendered in a most convincing manner. His handling of textural variations, such as in the silken waistcoat, rippled and shining, worn by "James Bowdoin II" (1748, Bowdoin College Museum of Fine Arts), had no equal until Copley.

Early Painters in the South. Though the Southern colonies boasted fewer painters than New England, they, too, attracted trained artists from abroad. In 1708 Justus Engelhardt Kühn (d. 1717) left his native Germany to settle in Annapolis; in 1711 the Swede Gustavus *Hesselius arrived in Delaware; and in 1740 the Swiss artist Jeremiah Theüs (*c.* 1719–74) settled in Charleston. Of the three, Hesselius's reputation became the most widespread, for he traveled the Philadelphia and Chesapeake Bay regions painting portraits of Indian chieftains and an occasional religious subject, such as a "Last Supper" for the church of St. Barnabas near Annapolis.

By the middle of the 18th century, Gustavus Hesselius and his son John had become the principal portrait painters in the Philadelphia area, with their strongest competition coming in the late 1740s from London-trained John Wollaston (active 1751–69) and his fellow countryman William Williams (active 1746–65).

America's Old Masters. By then Philadelphia and Boston were established as major colonial towns. In 1738 two great artists were born to these communities: John Singleton Copley (d. 1815) in Boston, and Benjamin West (d. 1820) in a Quaker village near Philadelphia.

Copley was initially exposed to art through the mezzotints of his stepfather, Peter Pelham (*c.* 1695–1751), the first well-trained engraver in America. This early exposure to light and shade is apparent in his marked facility to manipulate the contrasts of light and shadow

Fig. 3. John Hesselius, "Charles Calvert," canvas, 50¼ by 40¼ inches, 1761.

Fig. 4. Gilbert Stuart, "Mrs. Richard Yates," canvas, 30¼ by 25 inches, 1793.

AMERICAN ART

Fig. 5. Benjamin West, "Penn's Treaty with the Indians," canvas, 75½ by 108¾ inches, c. 1771.

on the faces and clothing of his subjects. He achieved a three-dimensional illusion superior to the efforts of his predecessors.

Individual portraits, such as his "Paul Revere" (Fig. 2), display his concern for chiaroscuro. This particular canvas presents the unpretentious sitter in a natural, informal pose, surrounded by the tools and product of his trade. The painter's outstanding group portrait, "The Copley Family" (*c.* 1775, Museum of Fine Arts, Boston), a masterpiece of composition, far surpasses similar subjects by Smibert and Feke. In it the four Copley children affectionately surround their mother, while their artist father looks on approvingly. It includes Copley's father-in-law, W. Clark, an importer whose tea was dumped in the Boston harbor in 1773. In one corner of the canvas a discarded doll and Mrs. Copley's plumed hat are rendered with skillful understatement. Though Copley predicted victory for the colonies, he left America before the Revolution and went to England, where he spent the rest of his years. There he was influenced by Thomas Gainsborough and Sir Joshua Reynolds and gained international fame.

Like Copley, Benjamin West went to England before the Revolution. He was destined to become the most influential American artist abroad; his London studio was the training ground for a generation of American painters, including Gilbert Stuart, Charles Willson Peale, and John Trumbull.

West was originally inspired to follow a career in art after successfully copying the figure of Saint Ignatius from a painting he had seen in his native Pennsylvania. By the time he was 30, in his meteoric rise to fame he had been summoned to exhibit his canvases before King George III of England. His final triumph came in 1792 when he became the second president of the Royal Academy.

He was nicknamed the "American Raphael" because he painted with a classical sensibility. His painting of "The Death of Wolfe" (1770, National Gallery of Canada, Ottawa) presents the fallen English hero of the Battle of Quebec as though intended to be a contemporary version of the "Dying Gaul." Surrounding groups of junior officers look posed and unlifelike, while in the foreground a pensive Indian completes the entourage, despite the fact that no Indians accompanied the British forces during that phase of the French and Indian War. Paintings such as this and his "Penn's Treaty with the Indians" (Fig. 5) of the following year helped establish interest in realistic and contemporary historical painting. West's pupil John Trumbull (1756–1843) created action-packed battle scenes that glorify the American Revolution and mark him as one of America's first Romantic painters. During the war Trumbull had served briefly as one of Washington's aides, and his firsthand observations furnished the inspiration for the stirring re-creation of such events as the "Battle of Bunker Hill" and the "Death of General Montgomery at the Siege of Quebec" (1786, Yale University Art Gallery).

Another important West student, Gilbert Stuart (1755–1828), developed brilliant portraiture. Born in Rhode Island, Stuart went to England in 1775 and became a successful portrait painter, returning after 18 years to America for the avowed purpose of painting President Washington. The chief executive sat for him three times, the results being the so-called "Vaughan," "Landsdowne," and "Athenaeum" portraits. Stuart's fame derives from the more than 100 copies he made of three initial presidential portraits. His genre paintings of English rural life are noteworthy also.

Although the sitter was customarily decked in elaborate finery, and the painting background permeated with lush foliage or classical columns, Stuart inaugurated a new portrait style by minimizing these elements in order to focus attention on the subject's physiognomy. Thus his popular Athenaeum portrait of George Washington achieves an unencumbered probity. The subject of another, "Mrs. Richard Yates" (Fig. 4), stares out from her seemingly Puritan environment, a needle and thread the sole concessions to an otherwise barren background.

From the Revolution to Late 19th Century

By 1776, West, Copley, and Stuart ("America's Old Masters") had all taken up residence in Europe. During the Revolution and immediately thereafter the production of art in the U.S. appeared to be dominated mostly by one family, the Peales. Charles Willson Peale (1741–1827) and his lesser-known brother James sired a total of 16 children, 9 of whom became artists. There was never any doubt about the profession that four of Charles Willson Peale's sons would follow, for he named them Rembrandt, Rubens, Raphaelle, and Titian.

He had a Renaissance-like diversity of interests. Originally apprenticed to a saddle maker, he soon showed artistic talent and was sponsored for European studies under Benjamin West by a group of eminent residents of his native Maryland, including Charles *Carroll of Carrollton, a signer of the Declaration of Independence.

When he returned to America, the city fathers of Philadelphia wooed him there by promises of portrait commissions. Realizing the need for art schooling in America, Peale was instrumental in establishing the Pennsylvania Academy of Fine Arts in Philadelphia (1805), the oldest art school in the U.S. Among his fellow founders was the first native sculptor, William Rush (1756–1833), a carver of ships' figureheads, whose full-length statue of George Washington (1814) earned the approval of the president's nephew Bushrod.

The studio of Charles Willson Peale became the headquarters for his varied activities. First it was expanded to include a picture gallery. Having painted the earliest known portrait of then Colonel Washington in 1772, he decided a decade later to create an entire gallery of Revolutionary War heroes.

Then, in 1786, the artist added a museum of natural history. Years later, when the Peale Museum was incorporated, the 81-year-old Peale painted "The Artist in his Museum" (Fig. 6) in the Grand Manner. The impressive canvas shows Peale proudly drawing back the curtain on history to reveal neatly arranged rows of stuffed birds. There was also a huge mastodon skeleton, the pride of his collection. The unearthing of the mammoth animal in New York State had been financed and supervised 2 decades earlier by Peale himself, who created an ambitious painting of the drama entitled "Exhuming the First American Mastodon" (1806–08, Peale Museum, Baltimore).

The Columbianum exhibition (1795), organized by Charles Peale, contained one of the earliest examples of still life in America, by James Peale (1749–1831). In

Fig. 6. Charles Willson Peale, "The Artist in His Museum," canvas, 103½ by 80 inches, 1822.

Fig. 7. Thomas Cole, "The Oxbow of the Connecticut," canvas, 51½ by 76 inches, 1846.

Fig. 8. Albert Bierstadt, "Rocky Mountains," canvas, 73¼ by 120¾ inches, 1863.

AMERICAN ART

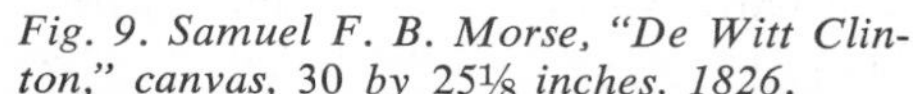

Fig. 9. Samuel F. B. Morse, "De Witt Clinton," canvas, 30 by 25⅛ inches, 1826.

Fig. 10. George Caleb Bingham, "Fishing on the Mississippi," canvas, 29 by 36 inches, 1851.

the years that followed Raphaelle (1774–1825) and Rubens Peale (1784–1865) carried on the tradition inaugurated by James. Raphaelle painted simple arrangements of fruit, bread, and kitchenware on a table that reveal a sure grasp of and an honest delight in the form and texture of everyday objects.

Rembrandt (1778–1860), the most prominent of Charles' sons, studied in England under West (1802) and while in France (1808–10) was influenced by the classicism of *David. His large canvas, "The Court of Death" (1820, Detroit Institute of Arts), suited the taste of the period and displayed the artist's range of technical abilities. His many portraits include the "Self Portrait" (1828), which epitomizes his work in the vein of romantic realism.

Early 19th-century Portrait Painters. The next generation of artists was the first to show no recollection of colonial times. The art of South Carolina–born Washington Allston (1779–1843) represented an additional break with the past, for he was the first American visionary who injected his work with subjective reverie and dramatic mood. This Harvard-trained painter also helped establish the tradition of the Grand Tour for American artists, the route that took them to Paris and Rome, as well as to Benjamin West's London, in search of inspiration, subject matter, and schooling.

Allston often painted subjects from the Old Testament, and his rich use of color earned him the nickname "American Titian." In dramatic paintings such as "The Moonlight Landscape" (1819, Museum of Fine Arts, Boston), with its large, dreamy areas in shadowy darkness and sailboats silhouetted against the brilliant light of a full moon, the artist anticipated the work of a later 19th-century visionary, Albert Pinkham Ryder.

The best-known pupil of Washington Allston was Samuel F. B. Morse (1791–1872), a Massachusetts-born painter who, like his master, studied with Benjamin West. In 1825 Morse helped to found the National Academy of Design (New York), then served as its president for 15 years. Also in 1825, 7 years before he first experimented with the telegraph, Morse created his masterpiece, the "Marquis de Lafayette" (1825, Art Commission of the City of New York). Lafayette stands full-length and triumphant, enveloped in a flowing cape that separates him from a brilliant sunset. Sculptured busts of Washington and Franklin are shown on pedestals beside him, while he leans upon a third base that remains vacant, waiting to display his own likeness.

Although Morse was on the way to becoming a successful artist, he refused to produce hack portraits lacking in depth of expression. In 1837, expressing disappointment in the level of artistic acceptance in America, he gave up painting and concentrated on invention.

In the generation following the Peales, the leading Philadelphia portrait painter was Thomas Sully (1783–1872). Born in England, he spent his youth in Charleston, S.C., and New York City before finally locating in Philadelphia in 1810. For the next half-century he romanticized the art of portraiture by combining the style of Gilbert Stuart with his love for the theatrical. Whether depicting the young actress Fanny Kemble (1833) or Andrew Jackson in the year the president died (1845, National Gallery of Art, Washington), Sully demonstrated his preoccupation with surface effects that achieved an elegant grace but failed to penetrate to the inner character of his sitters.

Sully's son-in-law, John Neagle (1796–1865), also a successful Philadelphia painter, is remembered for his painting "Pat Lyon at His Forge" (1829, Pennsylvania Academy of the Fine Arts, Philadelphia). Probably the earliest example of American genre painting, it shows the sturdy blacksmith poised in front of his anvil, his life-size figure dramatically highlighted by the glow from red-hot coals.

By the early 19th century, America's professional portrait painters were firmly established in each community of the new nation, having abandoned the nomadic life of the earlier itinerant limner. Yet the limner tradition had never really died. From the 1720s until Civil War days it was continued in the work of the so-called "Primitive" or folk artists, those uncounted scores of painters who plied their trade among rural patrons whose standards were not so exacting as their counterparts in the cities. Largely self-taught, the folk artists combined a straightforward approach with bold color and naïve charm. There was no pretense that their works possessed the competence of drawing and the subtlety of modeling of their professional competitors; but then the remuneration they sought was also modest—one "Primitive" who, typically, toured the countryside in a wagon-turned-studio offered a likeness in oil, mounted complete with frame and glass, for as little as $2.92.

In the years following the Revolution, national pride was displayed in countless portraits of Revolutionary heroes and the battles in which they were victorious. Following the War of 1812, romantic nationalism seemed to be best expressed in the painting of the American landscape, with its vast, untamed, natural beauty and sprawling, breathtaking vistas.

The Hudson River School. In 1825, when the Erie Canal was opened to connect the Great Lakes and New York City, the Hudson River took on new commercial importance. Within a year, a 25-year-old English-born artist, Thomas Cole (1801–48), settled in the Hudson River region, declaring it more beautiful than either his native land or the West Indies, to which he had already traveled.

Cole seemingly never tired of painting the inspiring Hudson River Valley and the Catskills, incorporating their lush forests and rolling hills into both naturalistic and allegorical landscapes. Ironically, however, his five best-known paintings, illustrating the rise and fall of ancient Rome ("The Course of Empire," 1832–36, New York Historical Society), were executed following a trip to Italy, and his most famous single canvas, "The Oxbow of the Connecticut" (Fig. 7), dramatizes the unusual, almost circular bend in the Connecticut River, not the Hudson.

Yet the "Oxbow" is typically Cole, a symphony of contrasts. The drama is heightened by gathering storm clouds in an otherwise cloudless sky, and the rich forest in the foreground is contrasted with a large, gnarled, and dying tree, a Cole trademark. The observer cannot avoid experiencing a sense of discovery in Cole's work, for as the canvas is scrutinized, small figures—an Indian with upraised spear here, an artist at his outdoor easel there—emerge as if from hiding among the thickets.

By the 1830s enough painters specialized in the Hudson River Valley that years later, they might be called America's first native landscape group, the "Hudson River School." Thomas Doughty (1793–1856) was drawn to such subject matter because of his love for hunting and fishing; and in his small canvases of views along the Hudson he usually included a solitary figure with fishing pole or rifle in hand.

Asher B. Durand (1796–1886), originally an engraver, turned to painting along the Hudson River in the 1830s. He applied the meticulous technique of printmaking to the minute details of foliage in his landscapes. Durand was one of the first American artists to paint outdoors, advising others to forsake the studio for the experience of working in direct sunlight. His painting "Kindred Spirits" (1849, New York Public Library) portrayed and gave tribute to both Thomas Cole, the artist who passed away the previous year, and William Cullen Bryant, the poet whose verses glorifying the beauty of nature inspired contemporary landscape painters.

Another Hudson River artist, John Kensett (1818–72), specialized in panoramic vistas. In such works as his "View from West Point," sailboats and an occasional steamer executed in careful detail ply the Hudson like toys.

The first landscape painter to develop outside the "Hudson River School" tradition was George Inness (1825–94). Born in upstate New York, his early works were influenced by the Hudson River canvases of Cole and Durand. However, several trips to Europe exposed him to the Barbizon painters, and his best creative efforts, displayed in such works as the "Delaware Water Gap" (1861) and "Peace and Plenty" (1865, The Metropolitan Museum of Art), are closer to the spirit of Rousseau and Corot than to that of the Americans.

Despite the grandeur and seemingly unending variety of the Hudson River Valley, it could not hold the undivided attention of artists for long. Frederick E. Church (1826–1900), Connecticut-born and a student of Cole's, did paint an occasional scene in the Catskills, but his best-known works resulted from roaming the world in search of the picturesque: "View of Cotopaxi" (1862) features a volcano in Ecuador, while other canvases depict the Alps, the Acropolis, or the Aegean Sea.

The Western Landscape. With all his wanderings Church did not record the majestic drama of the Rocky Mountains, a subject that has since become identified with the paintings of Albert Bierstadt (1830–1902). A naturalized American of German birth, Bierstadt studied art in his native Düsseldorf before immigrating to America, where in 1858 he accompanied an expedition to the untamed and uncharted West. Bierstadt made numerous sketches that preserved the awe-inspiring vistas he had seen. After returning East he executed paintings that suitably re-created the Rockies in panoramic fashion. Such monumental canvases as the "Last of the Buffalo" and the "Rocky Mountains" (Fig. 8) awe the viewer with their 10 feet of horizontal expanse.

Following Bierstadt 10 years later, Thomas Moran (1837–1926), an English-American, visited the Grand Canyon and the Yellowstone Valley. Exceeding Bierstadt's works at least in size, Moran presented the spectacle of the West in paintings more than 15 feet in length, to which he applied the atmospheric effects explored by his countryman Turner.

Bierstadt and Moran were typical of a generation of artists who moved West with surveyors and explorers, painter-pioneers whose record of romantic and realistic scenes must have enticed many Easterners to migrate with the wagon trains. Pennsylvania-born George Catlin (1796–1872) had been one of the first artists to head West (1830). He journeyed along the Missouri River, stayed for a time among the Indians, and produced more than 500 pictures featuring nearly 50 Indian tribes, their ceremonies and customs. Seven years later Alfred Jacob Miller (1810–74), a Baltimore-born student of Thomas Sully, set out to sketch the uncharted lands of the Louisiana Territory. Miller returned with more than 300 drawings, some in watercolor, from which hundreds more were painted in subsequent years.

For several decades artists traveled in the West. One of the last to travel the Plains while the journey could still be referred to as adventuresome was Frederic Remington (1861–1909), the best known painter of cowboys. Remington was the most prolific pictorial historian of the old West; although he lived to be only 48, he is credited with 2,800 drawings and paintings and 24 pieces of sculpture. Unlike Bierstadt and Moran, who specialized in wondrous landscapes, or Catlin and Miller, who did numerous portraits of Indian villagers and chieftains, Remington depicted the action-packed drama of supply wagons under attack and cavalry charges on the southern plains. His canvases are virtually alive with the crack of gunfire, whooping tribal yells, and the hoofbeats of the thundering herd.

American Genre. Still another facet of the "Golden West" was recorded by George Caleb Bingham (1811–79), a Virginia-born artist, largely self-taught, who grew up along the banks of the Missouri. Bingham immortalized the river's fur traders and raftsmen, fellow pioneers whom he first meticulously sketched individually in pencil, then incorporated into carefully planned compositions in oil. In such paintings as his "Fishing on the Mississippi" (Fig. 10), the artist showed himself a veritable Mark Twain of the paint brush.

Bingham's view of "The County Election" (1851–52, City Art Museum, St. Louis) contains the excitement of frontier politics in which he participated. His paintings of everyday life find parallels in the genre of David G. Blythe (1815–65), who recorded the Pittsburgh scene, and Richard Caton Woodville (1825–56), whose subjects were culled from the life of his native Baltimore.

The true Eastern counterpart of Bingham, however, was William Sidney Mount (1807–68). Mount, born on a Long Island farm, also lacked formal art training. He attended the National Academy of Design just briefly when it first opened its doors. During the 1830s and 1840s, while the "Hudson River School" held sway in New York State, he recorded another variety of rural scene, epitomized by men whittling while bargaining for a horse, or in "Eel Spearing at Setauket" (1845, New York State Historical Society, Cooperstown), the latter a compositional parallel to Bingham's "Fur Traders Descending the Missouri" (1845, The Metropolitan Museum of Art). Mount's genre includes also some of the earliest paintings of the American Negro ("The Power of Music," 1847, The Century Association, New York).

Another genre painter who portrayed the Negro sympathetically in the years immediately preceding the

Fig. 11. Frank Duveneck, "Whistling Boy," canvas, 28 by 21½ inches, 1872.

AMERICAN ART

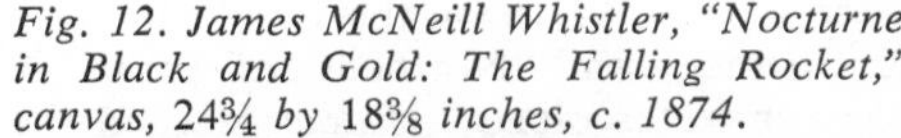

Fig. 12. James McNeill Whistler, "Nocturne in Black and Gold: The Falling Rocket," canvas, 24¾ by 18⅜ inches, c. 1874.

Fig. 13. John Singer Sargent, "El Jaleo," canvas, 91½ by 140 inches, 1882.

Fig. 14. Albert Pinkham Ryder, "Toilers of the Sea," canvas, 10 by 12 inches, c. 1900.

Fig. 15. Winslow Homer, "Breezing Up," canvas, 24⅛ by 38⅛ inches.

Civil War was Eastman Johnson (1824–1906), a Maine-born artist who established himself in New York City. His "Old Kentucky Home" (1859, New York Historical Society) is compositionally confusing, yet its 13 singing, dancing, banjo-playing figures reveal a slice of life that many artists preferred to ignore.

The Munich Men; American Expatriates. Johnson's meticulous technique can be attributed in part to his early apprenticeship to a Boston lithographer, but perhaps more properly to the training he received in Düsseldorf. In the 1840s and 1850s Düsseldorf became a mecca for American art students abroad. Bierstadt had been a product of its school, as had Richard Caton Woodville, and Emanuel Leutze (1816–68), whose popular historical subjects included "Washington Crossing the Delaware" (1851, The Metropolitan Museum of Art).

In the Düsseldorf school, as in the ateliers of Paris, a premium was placed on competence in drawing. Color was subordinated to draftsmanship, a characteristic that had a significant influence on Americans trained there. However, after the Civil War, Munich replaced Düsseldorf, and by the early 1870s there were more than 80 "Munich men," as they were called, including Frank *Duveneck, William Merritt Chase (1849–1916), Walter Shirlaw (1838–1909), and J. Frank Currier (1843–1909). Duveneck's "Whistling Boy" (Fig. 11) typifies the new technique, in which drawing was done directly with the brush and the paint applied impasto. This style of execution, with its spontaneity and slashing brushwork, was enthusiastically received when displayed in America.

John Singer Sargent (1856–1925), though Paris-trained, became the leading American exponent of such direct painting. A brilliant draftsman, he had established his reputation as a painter of portraits of prominent people. Sargent had a knack for capturing the humanity of his subjects through informal poses; his portrayal of a striding "Robert Louis Stevenson" (1885, Mr. and Mrs. John Hay Whitney, New York) appropriately characterizes the literary figure.

Sargent was born in Italy of American parents and spent his formative years wandering with his family throughout Europe. He never lost his love for travel, and following a visit to Spain in 1880 he painted "El Jaleo," an Andalusian dance (Fig. 13), a bold composition with dramatic lighting effects in chiaroscuro.

After 1884 Sargent lived in London, the adopted home of another American expatriate, James McNeill *Whistler. Like Sargent, Whistler had nomadic early years; born in Massachusetts, he had lived in St. Petersburg (Russia), Paris, and London by the time he was 25. Japanese prints appeared in Paris shortly before Whistler arrived there, and he was inspired by the flat, two-dimensional pattern of Oriental art. This influenced his creation of such works as "Arrangement in Gray and Black" (portrait of his mother, *c.* 1871, Louvre, Paris) and "Nocturne in Black and Gold: The Falling Rocket" (Fig. 12).

Whistler's landscapes were often vague and colorless, virtually nonobjective for their day. When the English art critic John Ruskin pronounced judgment on one of them by saying that he never expected a coxcomb to ask 200 guineas for flinging a pot of paint in the public's face, the artist sued for libel. Whistler's caustic wit aided his case, and although the court awarded him damages of only a farthing, the decision proved a moral victory for the artistic cause of personal expression.

The third of the famous trio of American expatriates is Mary *Cassatt, the U.S.'s first internationally significant woman artist. Pittsburgh-born and Philadelphia-bred, she went to Paris to study at 23, but then adopted France as her home. Enlisting in the Impressionist camp before that movement became respectable and popular, Cassatt, like Manet, Degas, and Whistler, displayed the influence of Japanese prints in her work. "The Bath" (*c.* 1892, Art Institute of Chicago) is a tender portrayal of the mother-and-child theme.

LATE 19TH CENTURY TO THE PRESENT

While Sargent, Whistler, and Cassatt were acquiring artistic reputations abroad, Ryder, Homer, and Eakins were making the greatest strides in the U.S.

Albert Pinkham *Ryder was a mystic, a visionary, and a recluse. He was born in the Massachusetts whaling port of New Bedford. His paintings (numbering only about 150) have a rich luminous quality and a sense of lonely experience of landscape and sea. In such typical seascapes as "Moonlit Cove," "Moonlight Marine," and "Toilers of the Sea" (Fig. 14), details merge and dissolve among the darkened shadows over a paint surface that has today become a network of cracks due to years of reworking by the artist.

Winslow Homer (1836–1910) was one of America's leading realist genre painters. The Boston-born Homer served his apprenticeship as a Civil War illustrator for *Harper's Weekly,* sketching in competition with the photographs of Matthew Brady. As a painter he began working in oils in the 1860s, creating such homely rural scenes as children playing "Snap the Whip" or youngsters struggling with an unruly calf. One of his earliest seascapes, "Breezing Up" (Fig. 15), shows a group of boys relaxing topside on a catboat, but his subsequent marine subjects are preoccupied with drama, as suggested by such titles as "Lost on the Grand Banks," "The Signal of Distress," and "Northeaster." From his mother, an amateur watercolorist, Homer learned the technique that has since become associated with his name.

Thomas Eakins (1844–1916) also found great interest in water scenes, but his are limited to subjects such as "Turning Stake-Boat" (Fig. 16), which features sculling on the Schuylkill River in his native Philadelphia. Eakins was a scientific realist whose methodical mind required that one of the racing boats be brought into his studio, in order that he might resolve the problems of perspective and reflections. His very first commission, a portrait of Pres. Rutherford B. Hayes, upset Philadelphia Republicans who expected an idealized pillar of strength and received instead a shirt-sleeved likeness of the chief executive, his face flushed by the summer heat. Eakins painted a well-known surgeon performing an operation before a gallery of medical students ("The Gross Clinic," 1875, The Jefferson Medical College, Philadelphia), only to find his masterpiece condemned by an art critic who objected to the prominent display of blood on the surgeon's hands. After he had taught at the Pennsylvania Academy for a decade, Eakins was forced to resign in 1886 because of constant friction with the school's directors over his

Fig. 16. Thomas Eakins, "Turning Stake-Boat," canvas, 40¼ by 60¼ inches, 1873.

Fig. 17. John Henry Twachtman, "Snowbound," canvas, 25¼ by 30⅛ inches, 1885.

AMERICAN

ART

Fig. 18. George Bellows, "Stag at Sharkey's," canvas, 36¼ by 48¼ inches, 1909.

Fig. 19. Robert Henri, "Old Johnnie," canvas, 24⅛ by 20⅜ inches, c. 1913.

Fig. 20. John Sloan, "Backyards, Greenwich Village," canvas, 26 by 32 inches, 1914.

Fig. 21. John Marin, "Movement, Fifth Avenue," watercolor, 16⅝ by 13½ inches, 1912.

Fig. 22. Grant Wood, "American Gothic," beaver board, 29⅞ by 24⅞ inches, 1930.

Fig. 24. Edward Hopper, "Early Sunday Morning," canvas, 35 by 60 inches, 1930.

AMERICAN

ART

Fig. 23. Georgia O'Keeffe, "Ranchos Church," canvas, 24 by 36 inches, 1930.

Fig. 25. Marsden Hartley, "Rising Wave, Indian Point, Georgetown, Maine," board, 22 by 28 inches, 1937–38.

use of nude models in the anatomy classes. Untiring in his search for truth, Eakins received scarce public acceptance either of his art or of his teaching during his lifetime.

Influence of Impressionism; "The Ten." In the year 1884 the work of the French Impressionists, scorned in their native land, was shown in New York City for the purpose of raising funds to purchase a pedestal for the Statue of Liberty, and American collectors rallied to the cause. When their patronage of such European art continued a decade later, 10 American Impressionists banded together and raised their voices in protest. "The American Ten," as they were patriotically named, included Childe Hassam (1859–1935), J. Alden Weir (1852–1919), and Thomas Dewing (1851–1938). Beginning in 1898 they inaugurated a series of annual exhibitions in order to promote their own brand of Impressionism.

Several of "The Ten," had gained recognition as the "Munich men" of the 1870s, but by the 1890s their earlier gravy-brown colors were replaced with the dazzling brightness of Impressionism. John Twachtman (1853–1902) was one of them, and his painting entitled "Snowbound" (Fig. 17) is an Impressionist canvas in which a blanket of snow covers the landscape, its melting and dissolving surface becoming blurred in the face of the warming sun.

"The Eight" (Ashcan School). A decade after "The Ten" was formed, another group called "The Eight" was organized to gain artistic freedom for all. Theirs was a crusade to break the monopolistic tendency of New York's staid National Academy of Design, which sought to mold public taste along academic lines. Robert Henri (1865–1929), leader of "The Eight," though himself academy-trained in Philadelphia and Paris, employed bravura brushwork. In such canvases as "Old Johnnie" (Fig. 19) the ruddy-faced portrait comes to life through spontaneously painted though deftly placed brushstrokes.

During the 1890s Henri attracted to him a group of painters that included John *Sloan, William Glackens (1870–1938), George Luks (1867–1933), and Everett Shinn (1876–1953), who later became four of "The Eight." These men were newspaper artist-reporters whose quick sketches of riots, coal mine disasters, and fires accompanied news stories much as the newspaper photograph does today. It was Henri who urged them to paint, and when they adopted his dark Munich-type palette, academicians derisively referred to the group as the "Revolutionary Black Gang."

The "revolutionary" aspect of their work involved depicting the life of the city, which Henri contended was as suitable for subject matter as the rural landscapes chosen by the academicians. A significant teacher and painter, Henri insisted that everything was ready subject matter for the artist. He prodded his students to invade saloons, dance halls, and tenements in order to paint the life about them; and each chose his own approach: George Bellows (1882–1925) was captivated by the city's vigorous side; Edward Hopper (1882–), by its loneliness. Guy Pène du Bois (1884–1958) reflected on its satirical nature; Glenn Coleman (1887–1932) viewed it with affection.

Bellows found ready subject matter half a block from his art classes, at Tom Sharkey's Athletic Club, where the boxers in combat became the feature of several dynamic paintings, such as "Stag at Sharkey's" (Fig. 18). Among other Henri students who became prominent Realist painters of the next generation were Rockwell Kent (1882–), Eugene Speicher (1883–1962) and Gifford Beal (1879–1956).

Henri and his colleagues in "The Eight" likewise chose their subjects from the life of the city, ranging from Luks's dancing street urchins ("The Spielers," 1905, Addison Gallery of American Art, Phillips Academy, Andover, Mass.) and Glackens' children sledding ("Central Park—Winter," 1905, The Metropolitan Museum of Art) to compositions of the East River embankments and plying tugboats by Henri and Shinn.

John Sloan remained the most devoted practitioner of the cityscape, whether recording a bustling crowd under the Sixth Avenue elevated tracks or the intimate confines of McSorley's Bar. In Sloan's painting of "Backyards, Greenwich Village" (Fig. 20) he demonstrated, through honest realism, the beauty of the commonplace; ironically, such subject matter was responsible for the group becoming known, years later, as the "Ashcan School."

Also included among "The Eight" were Maurice Prendergast (1859–1924), the first American to be influenced by Cézanne; the Impressionist Ernest Lawson (1873–1939); and a painter of sylvan nudes, Arthur B. Davies (1862–1928).

The Armory Show. The sole exhibition of "The Eight" was held in 1908. Two years later they arranged a show open to all artists. This independent movement led to the still more liberal policy of including the work of European painters as well, an idea that Davies masterminded into the famous Armory Show of 1913, the first comprehensive exhibit of modern European art ever displayed in America. The Armory Show, so-called because it was held in New York's 69th Regiment Armory, aroused curiosity over the contemporary innovations of Cubism, Fauvism, and nonobjectivism as embodied in the works of such artists as Picasso, Duchamp, *Matisse, and *Kandinsky. These avant-garde Europeans, whose controversial canvases attracted all the attention, eclipsed the efforts of American painters, whose creations seemed conservative by comparison.

While "The Eight" had been waging and winning the battle against the Academy at home, America's pioneers of modernism were absorbing the latest art styles in Europe. Max Weber (1881–1961) studied with Matisse in Paris in 1907 and became one of the U.S.'s earliest Cubists. Alfred Maurer (1868–1932) joined a group centered around the experimental writer Gertrude Stein, and his use of Expressionistic color qualified him as the only American Fauve. Arthur G. Dove (1880–1946) was the first American to paint nonobjectively when, in 1910, he created his initial canvases completely devoid of subject matter. In 1912 Morgan Russell (1886–1953) and Stanton MacDonald-Wright (1890–) produced Cubist-inspired color abstractions and became the cofounders of "Synchromism," which, though short-lived and lacking wide significance, was hailed as the first international art movement originated by Americans.

Another of the small group of American moderns was John Marin (1870–1953), who had gone to Europe in 1905, drawn by the work of Whistler, only to return 5 years later prepared to interpret New York City in

Cubist terms. The most important 20th-century American watercolorist, Marin was one of the earliest painters to apply the theory of analytic Cubism to the American scene to create the excitement and pulsation of the big city (Fig. 21).

Few American artists had been prepared for what they saw at the Armory Show. When World War I erupted, temporarily halting the importation of European art to this country, American artists had time to close the cultural gap and assimilate the modern art movements prevalent abroad. Yet in the 1920s the realist tradition continued to dominate American art.

Some of the older artists, such as Jerome Myers (1867–1940) and Eugene Higgins (1874–), held to the style of "The Eight," while others, such as Charles Sheeler (1883–1965) and Charles Demuth (1883–1935), became fascinated with a more precise brand of realism, which traced its roots to the machine age. With cameralike accuracy Sheeler, a former photographer, created oils of the wheels and drive shaft of a railroad locomotive or geometrically inspired building forms piled one against another. Demuth preferred to superimpose a thin criss-crossing of Cubist forms over his industrial scenes or across a monumental grain elevator ("My Egypt," 1927, The Whitney Museum of American Art). Because the elimination of the human element allowed them to concentrate on sharp-edged shapes, precisely painted, Sheeler and Demuth are referred to as "Precisionists."

Regionalism. In the 1930s Grant Wood (1892–1942) of Iowa, John Steuart Curry (1897–1946) of Kansas, and Thomas Hart Benton (1889–) of Missouri were the triumvirate of artists who epitomized "Regionalism," an art movement born of the Depression, the Dust Bowl, and American isolationism. Wood, the satirist, painted the "Daughters of the American Revolution" as three pompous New England matrons, while his sense of local pride created in "American Gothic" (Fig. 22) the simple dignity and elegance of a pair of typical Middle Westerners.

Curry's Kansas provided him with subjects ranging from a baptism to a tornado, always painted with prominence given to the farm folk. Benton, the muralist of the group, in individual works depicted farmers haying, an oil-derrick-filled boom town, or composite montages representing the arts of the West.

In the years before World War II, American artists could follow several established courses. On the one hand, the American scene painting was continued in the Coney Island beach scenes of Reginald Marsh (1898–1954) and the gaunt-faced city dwellers of Moses and Raphael Soyer (1899–). "Regionalism" was extended to Chicago by Aaron Bohrod (1907–), who depicted junk-filled lots and isolated houses on the outskirts; and to Salem, Ohio, by Charles Burchfield (1893–), who recorded such subjects as a family having dinner behind the walls of an unpretentious frame row house ("Six O'Clock," 1936, The Syracuse Museum of Fine Arts).

Many of Edward Hopper's subjects, from a sparsely filled movie theater to an all-night restaurant on a deserted street, illustrate the loneliness of the big city. His "Early Sunday Morning" (Fig. 24) is the ultimate in urban desolation, but the artist instills interest into the otherwise monotonous subject through a varied arrangement of window shades and awnings and the creative use of color.

Hopper's art stands apart from most because, though painted in realistic terms, it incorporates a skeleton of abstract design beneath the surface. This Hopper brand of realism is present also in the dynamically designed compositions of Andrew Wyeth, Ben Shahn, and Walter Stuempfig.

Another group of painters applied the styles of various European art movements to the American scene. Stuart Davis (1894–1964), a fellow student with Hopper under Robert Henri, was first exposed to the art of *Gauguin and Matisse at the Armory Show. From this experience evolved a personal style of brightly colored, flat-patterned shapes inspired by the city: its jazz music, neon signs, and five- and ten-cent store gadgets, a style typified by his painting "Something on the Eight Ball" (Fig. 26).

Marsden Hartley (1877–1943) had experimented with German Expressionism before World War I, then spent much of the next 3 decades applying its heavy-lined masses and powerful visual impact to subjects found in his native New England (Fig. 25). Georgia O'Keeffe (1887–), America's best-known woman artist of the first half of the 20th century, fused Cubism with the hard-edged realism of the "Precisionists," then applied her style to a wide range of subjects: the starkly silhouetted skull of a cow, the subtle curvilinear involvement of floral forms, the panoramic view of skyscrapers, and the magnified side of a barn.

That her subjects often possess cameralike preciseness is evidence of the influence of her husband, photographer Alfred *Stieglitz. Stieglitz provided a major source of encouragement for America's other pioneer modernists. In a small gallery that he opened on New York's lower Fifth Avenue he had arranged the initial displays of work by Marin, Maurer, Hartley, Weber, and Dove.

During the 1930s, social and political commentary found its artistic outlet in the satires of lawyers and senatorial debates by William Gropper (1897–) and Joseph Hirsch (1910–), the putty-faced gangster types of Jack Levine (1915–), and the plight of the Southern Negro as depicted by Robert Gwathmey (1903–).

European Artists Come to America. During and between the two World Wars, a steady stream of European artists migrated to America, bringing with them the fruits of European experiments. Joseph Stella (1880–1946) brought the excitement of Italian *Futurism; Hans Hofmann (1880–1966) brought from Germany the spirit of Expressionism, which took dynamic form in his teaching, as well as his painting. Jules Pascin (1885–1930), Josef Albers (1888–), George *Grosz, and Lyonel *Feininger were among the arrivals, as were Piet *Mondrian, Max Beckmann (1884–1950), and Raoul Dufy (1877–1953). America had become the artistic melting pot of the world, fusing and assimilating all the art movements that had been associated with the various European countries.

Abstract Expressionism. Following World War II a new type of art called Abstract Expressionism was born. This was the first significant international art movement to originate in America (*see* ABSTRACT EXPRESSIONISM). Sometimes referred to as "Action Painting" because of the spontaneous action of its execution, Abstract Expressionism is chiefly non-objective. It is related to qualities of Oriental calligraphy and is often associated with

Fig. 26. Stuart Davis, "Something on the Eight Ball," canvas, 56 by 45 inches, 1953–54.

the amorphous shapes of ink blots. Theoretically it rejects preconceptions of structure and lodges its validity in the direct, immediate act of painting itself as a means of probing the inner life. It does not, therefore, represent but becomes in itself the event to experience. Works of this type are characterized by largeness (related to human scale), accidental effects of the media employed, personal calligraphic strokes, and immediacy and intensity of relationship in the pictorial elements employed. The term came to be applied to the work of artists influenced by the ideology of a free conceptual framework; consequently no single descriptive element can be applied to all its manifestations. The term Abstract Expressionism itself, though objected to by some, seemed apt to others since works were characterized by both abstraction and highly expressionistic elements.

Jackson *Pollock is the artist most closely associated with Abstract Expressionism. In 1948 he created the first "drip-and-dribble" painting by pouring enamel house paint directly from cans onto a large canvas spread horizontally on the studio floor, then allowing smaller amounts of the flowing pigment to trail from sticks that were directed like wands, weaving a new visual world, a labyrinth of calligraphic markings.

Pollock's initial effort in this direction was titled "Number 1, 1948" (1948, Museum of Modern Art, New York). Among the many paintings that followed, "Convergence" (Fig. 29) is typical of his original, vigorous, free-flowing style; it measures 13 feet in length and is not a picture for a wall but becomes the wall itself.

Pollock's highly individualistic style was anticipated by that of another innovator, Mark Tobey (1890–). A devoutly religious man who is a follower of the Baha'í World Faith, Tobey, in the early 1930s, made several visits to the Orient, where he was influenced by Zen and sumi painting. Upon his return, he began creating, in "white writing," such compositions as "Broadway" (Fig. 27), which conveys the movement and vitality of Manhattan through strictly calligraphic means.

When Tobey settled in Seattle, he, together with the Oregon-born painter Morris Graves (1910–), assumed the leadership of the so-called "Northwest

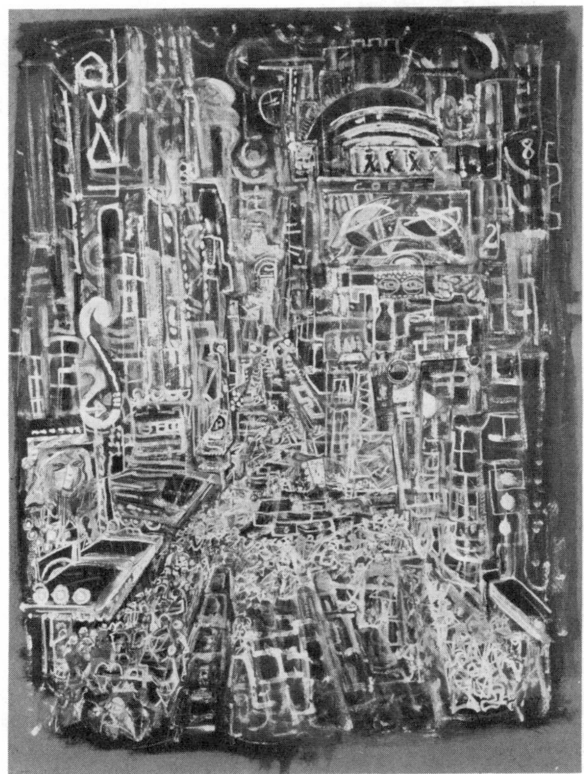

Fig. 27. Mark Tobey, "Broadway," tempera on masonite, 26 by 19$\frac{3}{16}$ inches, 1936.

Fig. 28. Willem de Kooning, "Asheville," canvas, 28$\frac{5}{8}$ by 31$\frac{7}{8}$ inches, 1949.

AMERICAN ART

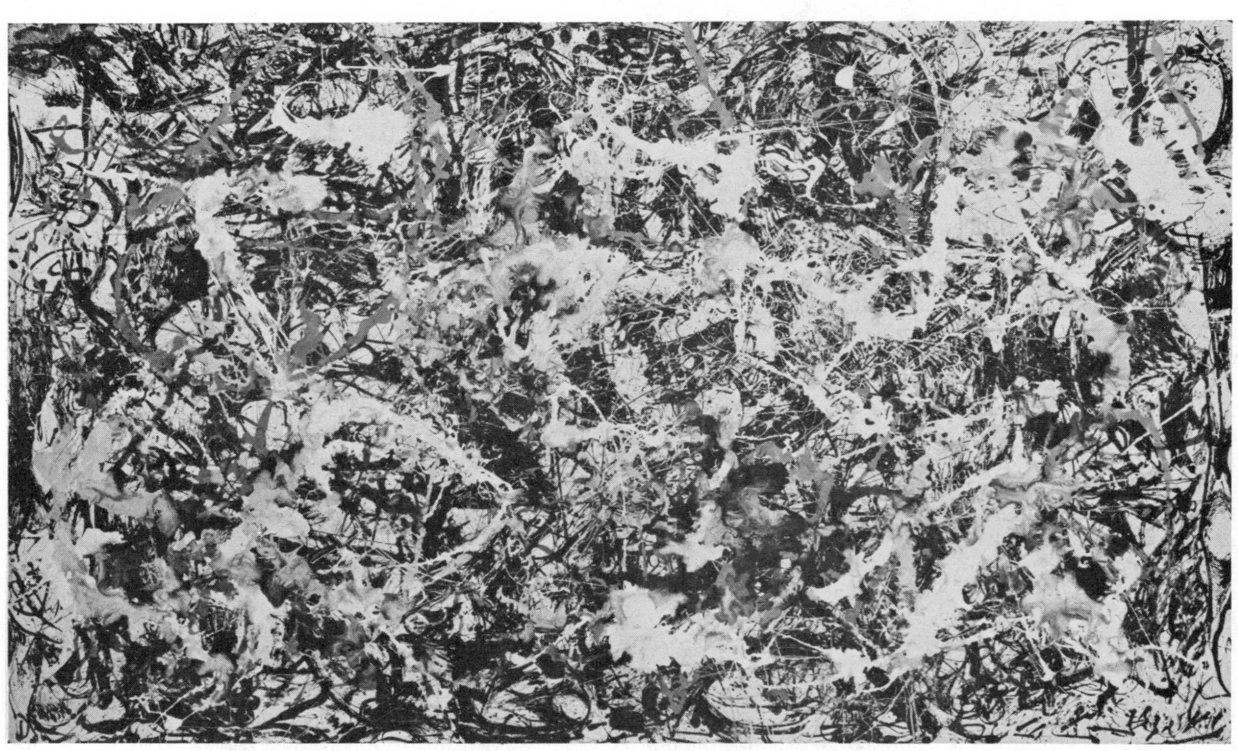

Fig. 29. Jackson Pollock, "Convergence," canvas, 93$\frac{1}{2}$ by 155 inches, 1952.

Fig. 30. Richard Diebenkorn, "Figure on a Porch," canvas, 57 by 62 inches, 1959.

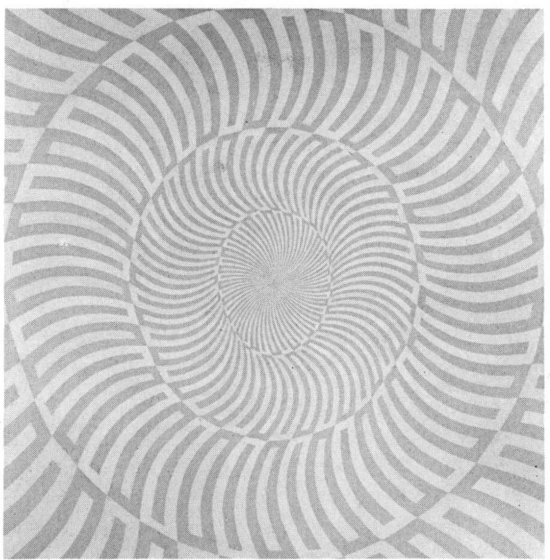

Fig. 31. Richard Anuszkiewicz, "Water from the Rock," canvas, 56 by 52 inches, 1961–63.

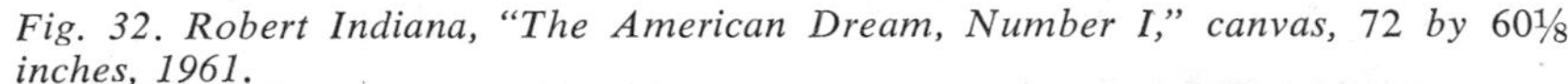

Fig. 32. Robert Indiana, "The American Dream, Number I," canvas, 72 by 60⅛ inches, 1961.

School," artists who convey in their work a sense of Oriental mysticism.

Following the death of Pollock in 1956, Dutch-born Willem de Kooning (1904–) emerged as an important figure in Abstract Expressionism. In contrast to Pollock, De Kooning applies paint to the canvas with brushes, and in many of his best-known works, such as the dozen versions in the "Woman" series, subject matter once again becomes discernible. In his nonfigurative expressions, such as "Asheville" (Fig. 28), one is caught up in the violence of a brutal brushstroke that discharges a disturbing energy.

The practitioners of Abstract Expressionism are so varied in their approaches that they are often grouped under the broader term, "The New School." Franz Kline (1910–59) engaged giant calligraphic markings in black on the pure white canvas. Sam Francis (1923–), painting in Paris, superimposes swirling black forms on a bright red-and-yellow background, allowing the brilliant underpainting to shine through like dazzling sunlight. The brushwork of Joan Mitchell (1926–) is an intense personal jotting of curving lines; Bradley Walker Tomlin (1899–1953) dry brushed bold, dark vertical and horizontal strokes over multicolored patches of unmodeled pigment; and James Brooks (1906–) fuses the brushed, the dripped, and the palette-knifed application of paint into a varied, visually intriguing surface structure.

Another facet of "The New York School" can be classified as either soft- or hard-edged abstraction. The former is found in the canvases of Mark Rothko (1903–) that show floating, muted-colored rectangles (like voids) or the paintings of William *Baziotes and Theodoros Stamos (1922–); the latter is found in the powerful, collagelike forms of Robert Motherwell (1915–). Other artists, such as Hans Hofmann and Adolph Gottlieb (1903–), combine the vigorous paint handling of Abstract Expressionism with more restrictive hard-edged forms. Arshile Gorky (1904–48), one of the most influential painters of the group, evolved stylized, linear, articulated shapes in which flat paint surfaces are partially hidden by an energetically scrubbed overpainting.

Mid-Century Directions. By mid-century, art trends in America were no longer controlled by the painter. Art had become big business. With corporations and individual collectors investing millions of dollars annually in the purchase of contemporary art, the country's museums, galleries, and critics refused to follow the artists' lead and determined instead to be the tastemakers. In 1954 New York's Museum of Modern Art announced an open exhibition dealing with "The Figure," and then was credited with hastening the return of figurative painting.

The leaders of this trend back to the figure were Richard Diebenkorn (1922–), Elmer Bischoff (1916–), and David Park (1911–), all California residents who were soon labeled "The San Francisco School." These artists, and others who followed their lead, sought to reintroduce the figure to painting without having to abandon the surface quality and exploration of paint application that had been vigorously expanded by the Abstract Expressionists.

The result, as exemplified by Diebenkorn's "Figure on a Porch" (Fig. 30), attempts a successful marriage of these two elements in a new approach that seems to have begun where the Munich school of the preceding century had left off.

During the 1950s Piet Mondrian's theory of the simplification of nature reached an extreme limit when Robert Rauschenberg (1925–) painted white-on-white, and Ad Reinhardt (1913–), black-on-black. Just about the time that Abstract Expressionism had spent itself, a new art form, *pop art, appeared.

Pop Art; Junk Sculpture. Pop art appeared as a reaction against the intellectualism of Abstract Expressionism, substituting an emphasis on the commonplace, which the man in the street was capable of understanding. As may be expected, some of the pop artists emerged from the commercial art field: Andy Warhol (1930–), for instance, specialized in drawing women's apparel before he began creating larger-than-life size Coca-Cola bottles, Campbell Soup cans, and Brillo boxes. James Rosenquist (1933–) had been an itinerant billboard painter, then turned to magnifying, on canvas, fragments of the larger-than-life commercial sign images he had formerly reproduced and observed at close range.

Roy Lichtenstein (1923–) enlarged comic strips, Jim Dine (1935–) emphasized the textural patterns of oversized neckties and coats, Jasper Johns (1930–) made paintings of the American flag, and pop sculptor Claes Oldenburg (1929–) produced mammoth plaster-of-paris hamburgers.

Robert Indiana (1928–) was initially inspired by a set of commercial brass stencils discovered in a deserted lower Manhattan loft he rented as a studio. His stencil style resulted in such works as "The American Dream, Number I" (Fig. 32). Short, commonplace words, such as "Tilt," "Eat," and "Gas," done in flat, bright colors form bold commercial patterns stenciled in oils on canvas or on wood constructions resembling packing crates.

The creations of Marisol (1930–) are interpenetrations of sculpture and painting. When she produces a 66-inch-high painting of the "Mona Lisa" on a wood panel with plaster-of-paris hands, or a life-size, part-plaster, part-wood, part-painted group portrait, such as "The Family" (1962, Museum of Modern Art, New York), the observer must look twice to determine where the chisel has left off and the paint brush taken over.

Pop art attempts a comment on the aesthetic of the commonplace, making *objets d'art* out of simple, everyday visual experience; it also mirrors the American image of a commercial-oriented Coke and hamburger society.

Similarly, a parallel art form of the 1950s, "junk sculpture," elevates the discarded, while simultaneously commenting on America's destruction of its natural grandeur through planned ugliness (e.g., automobile graveyards). Richard Stankiewicz (1922–), a leader of the movement, welds rearranged odds and ends of iron and steel into compositions that often suggest natural shapes; while Jason Seley (1919–) suggests similar forms derived from nature by welding together steel automobile bumpers.

Op Art. Following pop art, op art represents another type of reaction to or extension of Abstract Expressionism. "Op" stands for optical; it is an art that is usually mechanical in appearance and based on geometric patterns of contrasting colors that cause visual agitation. Like the *moiré* patterns of "watered silk" or taffeta, op art plays visual tricks on the beholder; sometimes shimmering, sometimes pulsating, sometimes causing forms to appear, to advance, and to recede.

Josef Albers, considered the father of op art in America, has been experimenting with optical illusions since the 1930s. He has created more than 100 color variations of "Homage to the Square," a basically unchanged composition of three diminishing squares placed one within another, which owe their variety and visual impact to a fixed geometric progression of proportion and the subtle interplay of color.

Richard Anuszkiewicz (1930–), a former Albers student at Yale, is one of the leaders of the op art movement. His paintings feature complementary colors of full intensity; in such works as "Water from the Rock" (Fig. 31) the interlocking shapes seem to gyrate with never-ending motion.

See also CANADIAN ART; SANTO.

Bibliography: History. V. BARKER, *American Painting: History and Interpretation* (New York 1950); *From Realism to Reality in Recent American Painting* (Lincoln, Nebr. 1959). A. H. BARR, ed., *Masters of Modern Art* (New York 1954). J. I. H. BAUR, *American Painting in the 19th Century* (New York 1953); *Revolution and Tradition in Modern American Art* (Cambridge, Mass. 1951); ed., *Nature in Abstraction* (New York 1958). Y. BIZARDEL, *American Painters in Paris* (New York 1960). W. BORN, *American Landscape Painting* (New Haven 1948); *Still Life Painting in America* (New York 1947). P. BOSWELL, *Modern American Painting* (New York 1939). M. W. BROWN, *American Painting, From the Armory Show to the Depression* (Princeton, N.J. 1955). A. BURROUGHS, ed., *A History of American Watercolor Painting* (New York 1942); *Limners and Likenesses: Three Centuries of American Painting* (Cambridge, Mass. 1936). H. CAHILL, ed., *American Folk Art: The Art of the Common Man in America, 1750–1900* (New York 1932). H. CAHILL and A. H. BARR, eds., *Art in America: A Complete Survey* (New York 1935). P. A. CHEW, ed., *Two Hundred and Fifty Years of Art in Pennsylvania* (Greensburg, Pa. 1959). H. DORRA, *The American Muse* (New York 1961). E. H. DWIGHT, *American Painting, 1760–1960* (Milwaukee 1959). A. ELIOT, *Three Hundred Years of American Painting* (New York 1957). J. T. FLEXNER, *America's Old Masters* (New York 1939); *First Flowers of Our Wilderness* (Boston 1947); *The Light of Distant Skies, 1760–1835* (New York 1954); *A Short History of American Painting* (Boston 1950); *That Wilder Image* (Boston 1962). M. L. FRIEDMAN, *The Precisionist View in American Art* (Minneapolis 1960). L. GOODRICH, ed., *A Century of American Landscape Painting, 1800–1900* (New York 1938); *Pioneers of Modern Art in America* (New York 1963). *Young America: Thirty American Painters and Sculptors under Thirty-five* (Whitney Museum of Art; New York 1957–). L. GOODRICH and J. I. H. BAUR, *American Art of Our Century* (New York 1961). J. GORDON, *Geometric Abstraction in America* (New York 1962). O. F. L. HAGEN, *The Birth of the American Tradition of Art* (New York 1940). T. B. HESS, *Abstract Painting: Background and American Phase* (New York 1951). *American Art since 1950* (Brandeis University, Poses Institute of Fine Arts; Waltham, Mass. 1962). S. HUNTER, *Modern American Painting and Sculpture* (New York 1959). Isham. M. KAROLIK, *M. and M. Karolik Collection of American Paintings, 1815 to 1865* (Cambridge, Mass. 1949). O. W. LARKIN, *Art and Life in America* (rev. ed. New York 1960). J. MELLQUIST, *The Emergence of an American Art* (New York 1942). D. C. MILLER and A. H. BARR, eds., *American Realists and Magic Realists* (New York 1943). B. B. PERLMAN, *The Immortal Eight: American Painting from Eakins to the Armory Show, 1870–1913* (New York 1962). W. H. PIERSON and M. DAVIDSON, eds., *Arts of the United States: A Pictorial Survey* (New York 1960). N. POUSETTE-DART, *American Painting Today* (New York 1956). Richardson. E. P. RICHARDSON, *American Romantic Painting* (New York 1944). A. C. RITCHIE, *Abstract Painting and Sculpture in America* (New York 1951). W. C. SEITZ, *The Responsive Eye* (New York 1965), on op art. J. T. SOBY, *Contemporary Painters* (New York 1948). F. A. SWEET, *The Hudson River School and the Early American Landscape Tradition* (Chicago 1945). R. TAFT, *Artists and Illustrators of the Old West: 1850–1900* (New York 1953). J. WALKER, *Paintings from America* (Baltimore 1951). J. WALKER and M. JAMES, *Great American Paintings from Smibert to Bellows, 1729–1924* (New York 1943). *Metropolitan Museum of Art Bulletin* 23 (April 1965), issue on American art. A. T. GARDNER and S. P. FELD, *American Paintings: A Catalogue of the Collection of the Metropolitan Museum of Art: Painters Born by 1815* (Greenwich, Conn. 1965). A. T. GARDNER, *American Sculpture: A Catalogue . . .* (Greenwich, Conn. 1964). H. GELDZAHLER, *American Painting in the Twentieth Century* (Greenwich, Conn. 1965). J. W. MCCOUBREY, *American Art 1700–1960* (Englewood Cliffs, N. J. 1965).

Literature, arranged by artists. F. BUCHER, *Josef Albers: Despite Straight Lines* (New Haven 1961). E. P. RICHARDSON, *Washington Allston: A Study of the Romantic Artist in America* (Chicago 1948). P. BOSWELL, *George Bellows* (New York 1942). T. H. BENTON, *An Artist in America* (New York 1937), autobiog. J. F. MCDERMOTT, *George Caleb Bingham: River Portraitist* (Norman, Okla. 1959). J. I. H. BAUR, *Charles Burchfield* (New York 1956). F. A. SWEET, *Sargent, Whistler and Mary Cassatt* (Chicago 1954). G. I. QUIMBY, *Indians of the Western Frontier: Paintings of George Catlin* (Chicago 1954). E. I. SEAVER, *Thomas Cole* (Hartford, Conn. 1949). J. T. FLEXNER, *John Singleton Copley* (Boston 1948). J. GORDON et al., *Arthur B. Davies, 1862–1928: A Centennial Exhibition* (Utica, N.Y. 1962). E. C. GOOSSEN, *Stuart Davis* (New York 1959). T. B. HESS, *Willem de Kooning* (New York 1959). A. C. RITCHIE, *Charles Demuth* (New York 1950). W. S. SIPLE, *Frank Duveneck* (Cincinnati 1936). L. GOODRICH, *Thomas Eakins, His Life and Work* (New York 1933). D. C. MILLER, ed., *Lyonel Feininger . . . Marsden Hartley* (New York 1944). L. GOODRICH, ed., *Robert Feke* (New York 1946). I. GLACKENS, *William Glackens and the Ashcan Group* (New York 1957). F. S. WIGHT et al., *Morris Graves* (Berkeley, Calif. 1956). E. MCCAUSLAND, *Marsden Hartley* (Minneapolis 1952). C. BRINTON, *Gustavus Hesselius* (Philadelphia 1938). A. T. E. GARDNER, *Winslow Homer, American Artist* (New York 1961). L. GOODRICH, ed., *Edward Hopper Retrospective Exhibition* (New York 1950). E. MCCAUSLAND, *George Inness, An American Landscape Painter, 1825–1894* (New York 1946). J. I. H. BAUR, *An American Genre Painter: Eastman Johnson, 1824–1906* (New York 1940). F. S. WIGHT, *John Marin . . ., Frontiersman* (Berkeley, Calif. 1956). O. W. LARKIN, *Samuel F. B. Morse and American Democratic Art* (Boston 1954). M. B. COWDREY and H. W. WILLIAMS, *William Sidney Mount, 1807–1868* (New York 1944). C. C. SELLERS, *Charles Willson Peale,* 2 v. (Philadelphia 1947). S. HUNTER, "Jackson Pollock," *New World Writing* 9 (New York 1956). H. H. RHYS, *Maurice Prendergast* (Cambridge, Mass. 1960). P. SELZ, *Mark Rothko* (Garden City, N.Y. 1961). L. GOODRICH, *Albert P. Ryder* (New York 1959). C. M. MOUNT, *John Singer Sargent* (New York 1955). C. SHEELER, *Charles Sheeler: Paintings, Drawings, Photographs* (New York 1939). V. W. BROOKS, *John Sloan: A Painter's Life* (New York 1955). H. W. FOOTE, *John Smibert, Painter* (Cambridge, Mass. 1950). J. T. FLEXNER, *Gilbert Stuart* (New York 1955). E. BIDDLE and M. FIELDING, *The Life and Works of Thomas Sully, 1783–1872* (Philadelphia 1921). C. L. ROBERTS, *Mark Tobey* (New York 1959). T. SIZER, *The Works of Colonel John Trumbull: Artist of the American Revolution* (New Haven 1950). L. GOODRICH, *Max Weber* (New York 1949). R. HIRSCH, *The World of Benjamin West* (Allentown, Pa. 1962). G. M. SMITH, *Andrew Wyeth* (Buffalo, N.Y. 1962). **Illustration credits:** Fig. 1, Adams National Historic Site. Photo–Worcester Art Museum. Fig. 2, Courtesy, Museum of Fine Arts, Boston. Figs. 3 and 19, The Baltimore Museum of Art. Figs. 4 and 15, The National Gallery of Art, Washington, D.C., Mellon Collection. Figs. 5 and 6, Courtesy of the Pennsylvania Academy of the Fine Arts. Figs. 7 and 9, The Metropolitan Museum of Art, Rogers Fund, 1909, 1907. Fig. 8, The Metropolitan Museum of Art, Gift of Mrs. Russell Sage, 1908. Fig. 10, Nelson Gallery–Atkins Museum (Nelson Fund), Kansas City, Mo. Fig. 11, Collection of the Cincinnati Art Museum. Fig. 12, Collection of the Detroit Institute of Arts. Fig. 13, Isabella Stewart Gardner Museum, Boston. Fig. 14, Addison Gallery of American Art, Phillips Academy, Andover, Mass. Figs. 16 and 18, The Cleveland Museum of Art, Hinman B. Hurlbut Collection. Figs. 17 and 22, Courtesy of the Art Institute of Chicago, Friends of American Art Collection. Figs. 20 and 24, Collection of the Whitney Museum of American Art, New York. Fig. 21, Courtesy of the Art Institute of Chicago, Alfred Stieglitz Collection. Fig. 23, The Metropolitan Museum of Art, Alfred Stieglitz Collection, 1949. Fig. 25, The Baltimore Museum of Art, Edward J. Gallagher, III, Memorial Collection. Fig. 26, Philadelphia Museum of Art. Fig. 27, The Metropolitan Museum of Art, Arthur H. Hearn Fund, 1942. Fig. 28, The Phillips Collection, Washington, D.C. Figs. 29 and 31, Albright-Knox Art Gallery, Buffalo, New York.

Fig. 30, Oakland Art Museum. Gift of the Anonymous Donor Plan of the American Federation of Arts. Fig. 32, Collection, The Museum of Modern Art, New York, Larry Aldrich Foundation Fund.

[B. B. PERLMAN]

AMERICAN BOARD OF CATHOLIC MISSIONS

The ABCM traces its origins back to 1919, when 17 directors of Catholic home and foreign missionary societies met at the University of Notre Dame, Ind., to discuss feasible ways of cooperating in the solicitation of contributions. They recommended a plan of organization to the bishops of the U.S., who at their annual meeting the same year appointed a committee to coordinate and stimulate the missionary endeavors of the whole country. This committee, under the chairmanship of Henry Moeller, Archbishop of Cincinnati, Ohio, assumed the title of American Board of Catholic Missions.

Although the board, with the assistance of an advisory council of priests representing various missionary bodies, intended to aid and promote Catholic missions in every part of the world, it had to alter its program and to confine its support to the home missions after the Holy See (1922) reorganized the Pontifical Society for the *Propagation of the Faith, which was thenceforth in the U.S. and elsewhere to operate independently under its own director for the benefit of the foreign missions. After negotiations with the Holy See a new plan of organization, drawn up under the leadership of Francis C. Kelley, Bishop of Oklahoma, was adopted by the American hierarchy at their annual meeting of 1924 and was approved by Pius XI on November 7 of the same year. At their next annual meeting the bishops elected a new board of six members; the first meeting was held in Washington, D.C., Sept. 15, 1925, and Cardinal George Mundelein, Archbishop of Chicago, Ill., was chosen as president, Bishop Kelley as secretary, and John Francis Noll, Bishop of Fort Wayne, Ind., as treasurer; headquarters were located permanently in Chicago. In 1946 it was resolved that the archbishop of Chicago should be *ipso facto* the president of the ABCM; at the same time William D. O'Brien, Auxiliary Bishop of Chicago and president of the *Catholic Church Extension Society, was appointed permanent secretary, and Bishop Noll was appointed permanent treasurer; they both held these offices until their deaths in 1962 and 1956 respectively. In 1965 there were nine nonpermanent members, elected for 5-year terms by the bishops of the U.S. at their annual meetings. The board meets regularly once a year, usually in November; it issues a printed financial report to the bishops of the U.S.

The ABCM serves principally as a center for the collection and distribution of funds for the "missions in the territory and for the inhabitants of the United States and of its possessions which do not receive aid from the Society for the Propagation of the Faith." As its main source of income it receives 40 per cent of the dues paid for membership in the Society for the Propagation of the Faith and of the collection taken up in all the parishes once a year on Mission Sunday. In distributing the money the board correlates its allotments with those of the Extension Society and other Catholic national institutes and agencies. The board gives two sorts of grants, namely, ordinary grants to bishops who have requested subventions for the missions in their dioceses and extraordinary grants for work among the Spanish-speaking Catholics in the Southwest and among Negroes in the South. Moreover, even after the Philippines became independent, the board continued to send subsidies to the Church in that country until 1964. In that same year it was also decided that bishops who have priests or laymen working in Latin America may be given some financial aid upon application. In 1964 the various grants reached a total of nearly $3 million.

[R. TRISCO]

AMERICAN CATHOLIC PHILOSOPHICAL ASSOCIATION (ACPA), a national society for the study of philosophy, founded at The Catholic University of America, Washington, D.C., where it has since retained its national offices, and incorporated in the District of Columbia. On Jan. 5, 1926, the association elected its founders Msgr. Edward A. *Pace as first president and Rev. James H. Ryan as first secretary-treasurer. For 28 of the ensuing years the national secretary was Msgr. Charles A. Hart. The objectives of the association as stated in the current constitution are to promote philosophical scholarship, to improve the teaching of philosophy, and to communicate with other individuals and groups of like interest. The original constitution included the phrase "with special emphasis on scholastic philosophy."

The second largest philosophical association in the U.S., the ACPA in 1965 numbered over 1,500 institutional and individual members, grouped in twelve sectional conferences, which hold periodic meetings through the academic year. A 3-day annual congress is held in a different city each year. The publications of the ACPA include *New Scholasticism,* a quarterly journal containing current research articles, book reviews, and a 25-page Chronicle of philosophy; the *Proceedings of the American Catholic Philosophical Association,* an annual volume of more than 250 pages containing addresses and research papers from the annual convention; and periodic volumes of "Philosophical Studies." In 1963 and 1965, respectively, a Personnel Placement Service and a Speaker's Bureau were initiated. The ACPA is affiliated with the International Federation of Philosophical Societies and the World Union of Catholic Philosophical Societies.

[G. F. MC LEAN]

AMERICAN CATHOLIC PSYCHOLOGICAL ASSOCIATION (ACPA), a professional society devoted to furthering interest and competence in psychology among Catholics. Following preliminary discussions concerning the formation of a Catholic Psychological Association, a formal attempt was made to bring together prospective members during the 1947 convention of the American Psychological Association, when an organizational meeting was held at Mercy College, Detroit, on Sept. 11, 1947. Those present at this meeting voted to form the projected organization, leaving the details in the hands of a committee on organization under the chairmanship of W. C. Bier, SJ, who subsequently became the executive secretary of the Association, a post he still held in 1965. A constitution for the new organization was submitted for consideration during a meeting at Boston College, Sept. 18, 1948, and adopted by a mail ballot later in the year. The charter members of the Association (231 in number) were those who voted on the adoption of the Constitution and who met the membership requirements. In establishing the Association care was taken to mitigate the tendency that might be created thereby to draw Catholics away from the main body of psychologists. Two principal antidotes were employed: (1) the policy (written into the constitution) of holding the annual meeting at the time and place of the convention of the American Psychological Association, taking only a portion of a day out of the main convention for a separate ACPA meeting; and (2) the membership requirements adopted, which were those of the American Psychological Association. The ACPA has two classes of members: constituent, who are members of the APA; and associate, who either are associates of the APA or have the qualifications to become so. The basic requirement for constituent membership is the doctorate in psychology, and for associate membership, the master's degree. The aims of the ACPA are twofold: (1) to interpret to Catholics the meaning of psychology and to advance its acceptance in Catholic circles; and (2) to provide a forum for the discussion of psychological questions of special interest to Catholics. The Association seeks to attain these aims mainly by its annual meeting and by its publications. It has two regular publications: the quarterly ACPA *Newsletter,* begun in 1950, and the semiannual *Catholic Psychological Record,* begun in 1963. Between 1956 and the start of the *Record* in 1963, the Association issued a series of volumes containing papers given at the annual meetings. The Association was incorporated under the laws of the state of New York on Aug. 11, 1964. As of Jan. 1, 1965, it had 567 constituent and 189 associate members; its headquarters were located at Fordham University, N.Y.

[W. C. BIER]

AMERICAN CATHOLIC SOCIOLOGICAL SOCIETY, a professional association that aims "to stimulate concerted study and research among Catholics working in the field of sociology, to create a sense of solidarity among Catholic sociologists, to present the sociological implications of Catholic thought and to encourage its members to recognize their professional responsibilities as sociologists" (Constitution). It was founded in 1938 by Ralph A. Gallagher, SJ (1896–1965), and a group of Middle Western Catholics. Father Gallagher was elected the first president and served as executive secretary from 1939 to 1962, when he was named honorary vice president for life; he served also as editor of the *American Catholic Sociological Review* from its first issue in 1940 until 1956, and as managing editor from 1956 until the end of 1960. Immediately after its foundation, the society was affiliated with the *National Catholic Welfare Conference; Bp. Edwin V. *O'Hara was its honorary president until his death in 1956, and he was succeeded the following year by Bp. John J. Wright. Membership in the society grew from 93 at the end of 1938 to 369 at the end of the first decade; there were nearly 500 members in 1965. This growth reflected increasing interest in *sociology in Catholic circles, especially in Catholic higher education, an interest attributable in part to the activities of the society itself. Annual conventions have been held from the beginning, except during the war years of 1944 and 1945, when regional meetings were substituted. Committees on the *Industry Council Plan and on sociology in college and seminary curricula have been especially active. The quarterly *American Catholic Sociological Review* provided articles and reviews on varied subjects, not only in the field of sociology but also in social philosophy, social welfare, social work, and Catholic social action. Special issues were devoted to such topics as juvenile delinquency, minority groups, the sociology of religion, and the thought of Pierre Teilhard de Chardin. In 1964 its name was changed to *Sociological Analysis,* and the scope was narrowed to "focus primarily on the sociological analysis of religion."

Bibliography: W. E. BROWN, "American Catholic Sociologists," AmCathSocRev 8 (1947) 44–46. R. ROSENFELDER, "March 26, 1948: Ten Years Old," *ibid.* 9 (1948) 46. P. MUNDY, "Sociology and American Catholics," in *Contemporary Sociology,* ed. J. S. ROUCEK (New York 1958) 304–320, esp. 308–315. H. W. ODUM, *American Sociology* (New York 1951) 369–370, 418–419.

[E. J. ROSS]

AMERICAN COUNCIL OF CHRISTIAN CHURCHES, the agency of a group of American fundamentalist Protestant denominations, churches, associations, and individuals, organized on the basis of a commonly accepted statement of Biblical truths and on the need to unite against what they consider the errors of other churches and groups of churches. Its constitution and bylaws provide that "the Council shall have no authority over its members, but shall be their servant and voice in matters requiring joint testimony and united action" (art. 6, sec. 1).

The Council began in New York City Sept. 17, 1941, with two founding denominations, the Bible Presbyterian Church (after 1961 the Evangelical Presbyterian Church) and the Bible Protestant Church. Since then it has grown to include 15 denominations with a general constituent membership of approximately 260,000. In addition, the Council lists other membership classifications to raise the total to about 1,510,000. The latter figure includes all those who belong as adherents, i.e., those who are included within the *National Council of the Churches of Christ in the U.S.A. but who wish representation in the American Council.

Council organization includes officers, an executive committee, an annual convention, a radio committee, a commission on chaplains, an associated mission committee coordinating activities of member mission boards, and various other committees formed for the needs and interests of the Council. Headquarters are in New York City; regional and state councils assist in carrying out the work. The American Council is itself a member of the International Council of Christian Churches.

A major preoccupation of the Council is opposition to the National and World Councils of Churches. Specifically, the American Council declares that these bodies attempt to build a "one-world church" and a "one-world government"; advocate peaceful coexistence with godless communism; promote the philosophy of pacifism; and claim to represent the whole of Protestant Christianity. The American Council strongly opposes all of these positions, especially through the "Twentieth Century Reformation Hour," a radio program, and the *Christian Beacon,* a weekly religious newspaper.

The Bible Protestant Church is a typical member of the Council. This denomination, the Eastern Conference of the Methodist Protestant Church, changed its name to the present one in 1940. In 1964 it had 42 churches, a membership of 2,634, and 37 clergy having charges. Its general organization meets annually, and it supports a monthly periodical called the *Bible Protestant Messenger*. Since the inception of the Council, Dr. Carl McIntire has played an important part in its work. Through his activities the most prominent aspect of the Council has been an uncompromising campaign against what are considered the errors of others in a manner characteristic of a radical right organization.

[R. MATZERATH]

AMERICAN FEDERATION OF CATHOLIC SOCIETIES

Catholic societies existed in the U.S. as early as the 1830s, but the notion of a federation of these societies developed only after Pius IX commended the work of the Belgian Catholic Union in 1871. Influenced by the Pope's recommendation that unions be formed throughout the world, Richard Clarke, a New York lawyer, drafted a constitution for local unions, hoping to federate them into a national union. Although this hope was not realized, attempts to unite Catholics continued. In 1889 and 1893 Catholics met at *Lay Congresses where the delegates were urged to join Catholic societies. Before the first congress, Martin *Griffin, editor of the Irish Catholic Benevolent Union *Journal,* suggested a federation of Catholic societies, and a diocesan federation began in Pittsburgh, Pa., in 1890. For the next 11 years agitation continued for a national federation to muster forces against the "violation of Catholic rights" in education, Indian missions, employment, and other areas. Finally in 1900 and 1901 organizational meetings were held for this purpose in Philadelphia, Pa.; New York, N.Y.; and at Trenton and Long Branch, N.J.

The result of these efforts was the American Federation of Catholic Societies, a loose union of organizations that retained their autonomy and identity. It existed until 1920, although the last public meeting took place in 1917. Except for 1905, annual conventions were held; between conventions Anthony *Matre, national secretary, handled routine matters, aided by the executive and advisory boards composed of officers and members of the hierarchy. In 1911 the federation formed a social service commission with Bp. Peter *Muldoon, of Rockford, Ill., and Rev. Peter *Dietz, of Milwaukee, Wis., as chairman and secretary, respectively. During its 18 active years, the federation tried to mold Catholic public opinion; it informed its members on pertinent topics, both Catholic and secular, and worked to block harmful and aid helpful legislation both locally and nationally. Outstanding Catholic laymen such as James Edward *Hagerty, sociologist at Ohio State University; Frederick Kenkel of the *Catholic Central Union; and David *Goldstein, converted socialist, were featured by the federation in its *Bulletin,* in its *Weekly Newsletter,* and on its lecture platforms. The federation also conducted a campaign of decency in entertainment and inaugurated an early system of evaluating the morality of motion pictures. To some extent it contributed to the Americanization of immigrant Catholics and provided some early precedents for cooperation between the clergy and laity.

When Catholic action was needed at the beginning of World War I, the federation failed to take the initiative because it was busy reorganizing. However, it did pledge its wholehearted support to the Knights of Columbus and the newly formed National Catholic War Council. When the latter was continued after the war as the *National Catholic Welfare Conference (NCWC), the federation was absorbed into it and eventually disappeared with the formation of the National Councils of Catholic Men and Women, NCWC.

Bibliography: A. F. GORMAN, *Federation of Catholic Societies, 1870–1920* (Doctoral diss. unpub. U. of Notre Dame 1962).

[A. F. GORMAN]

AMERICAN INDIAN, EDUCATION OF

From the earliest days of American colonization Catholic missions and schools have made a signal contribution to the education of Indian youth. *See* AMERICAN INDIAN MISSIONS (CANADA); AMERICAN INDIAN MISSIONS (U.S.). Since the ratification of the Bill of Rights in 1791 more than 100 Catholic schools have been established to provide academic instruction and vocational training for Indian children.

The first Indian schools founded in the new republic were Spring Hill Academy near Detroit, Mich., established in 1808 by Gabriel *Richard, SS, and a small Jesuit establishment near Florissant, Mo., begun in 1824. Both were short-lived but were followed during the next 50 years by more than 20 other schools in Michigan, Wisconsin, Kansas, and North Dakota.

Until 1870 Protestant and Catholic schools bore the entire burden of Indian education. All received small but irregular subsidies from federal or tribal funds. After 1870, following the enactment of the Indian Peace Policy, the U.S. government made contracts with almost all mission agencies guaranteeing them a stipulated per-capita payment for a specified number of Indian pupils. Mission schools subsequently multiplied rapidly in the Northwest, the Great Plains and Great Lakes areas, and in the Southwest, many of them with funds munificently provided by Katherine *Drexel. Jesuits, Franciscans, Benedictines, and various sisterhoods supplied the personnel.

In the 1880s the U.S. government also began to provide schools of its own at a still greater rate, making itself less dependent upon mission schools as collaborators. In 1896 Congress enacted legislation outlawing the use of public funds after 1900 for the education of Indians in sectarian schools, and as a consequence, deprived 48 of the 56 Catholic schools of their main, and

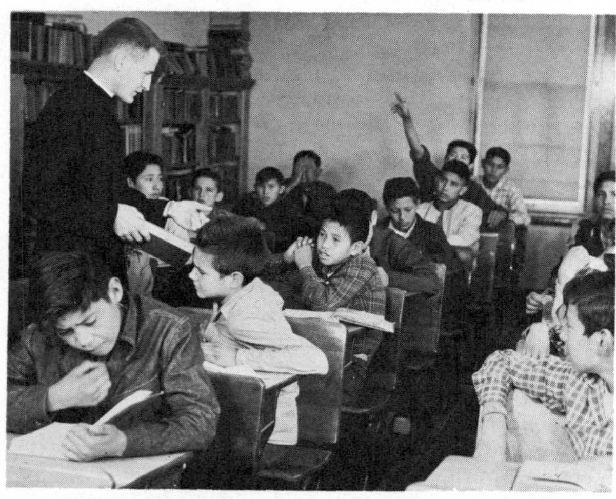

The seventh-grade class at St. Francis Mission School, Rosebud Sioux Reservation, S.Dak.

almost only, means of financial support (*see* BUREAU OF CATHOLIC INDIAN MISSIONS).

There followed a quarter of a century of both stress and progress, during which time aid from tribal funds was at first denied the mission schools but later allowed; and Catholic aid gradually increased. Small and less promising schools were perforce allowed to succumb, while the larger and better schools suffered but were maintained and, on the whole, were gradually strengthened. Meanwhile new schools were established, and before long Catholic mission schools were serving more Indian children than they had at the previous peak of their success. Pupil enrollment in 1896 was 3,600; in 1910, nearly 5,000.

Although the boarding school, a government favorite, was also the mission favorite, it was meeting growing criticism. Gradually, as the real or apparent need of its services lessened and the day school proved to be more feasible and more beneficial, the pendulum swung heavily in favor of the latter. Since the 1930s the majority of mission boarding schools have been converted into day schools; and by 1964 new day schools had been established that serve two-thirds of the Indian pupils enrolled in Catholic schools.

Meanwhile schools of both types have been gradually brought to a higher degree of efficiency and usefulness. Boarding schools have changed aims, methods, and clientele; day schools enjoy improved facilities, wider coverage, and provide more extensive services to pupils.

Administrative Problems. Religious orders of men and women, subject to the direction and supervision of local bishops, are in immediate charge of these. Laymen have only advisory roles in their operation. Unlike Federal Indian schools and public schools that accommodate Indian pupils, which are also assisted by the government, only 10 mission schools receive limited aid from public or tribal funds. Indians themselves contribute little or nothing.

The problems common to all Indian schools, varying only in degree, arise from the background of their Indian and part-Indian pupils. Most of these are not so ready as white children to enter school. Many have little or no knowledge of the English language and have formed habits that make their adjustment to any school regime difficult. Deficiency in comprehending and using the language handicaps many pupils for years.

Although Indians are generally docile in school, most of them lack real interest in studies and ambition to learn, thereby reflecting the attitude of their parents, who do not cooperate with the school or become involved in the education of their children. Drop-outs from all schools are consequently numerous with only half as many Indian children enrolled in grade 12 as in grade 8. This problem, however, which stems from the Indian background, like all the others has become much less acute than it was in the past.

Curriculum. No uniform curriculum is prescribed for Catholic mission schools or followed by them, nor would this be desirable. Their programs of study conform to the requirements of the local educational authorities of the State and Church, with minor adaptations designed to meet the special needs of Indian children. Their high school courses are largely academic, with some vocational and home economic courses. As to methods, teachers use those in general use in Catholic schools.

Since the *raison d'être* of the Catholic Indian school is the religious instruction and training of its pupils, its best efforts are directed to this end. Most of the time and effort, however, are seriously given to instruction in secular subjects, in which the Catholic school aims to offer the pupils an education comparable in value to the opportunities offered by other schools. Differences naturally exist, nevertheless, between mission schools and public schools; between one mission school and another. The variables at play are the native talent of administrators and teachers, their training, experience, vision, aims, and dedication.

The senior high school class at St. John's Indian School, Pima Reservation, Laveen, Ariz.

In 1964 Catholic Indian schools were 54 in number. Of these 39 were day schools; 11, boarding schools; 4, mixed boarding and day; 15 had high school units. Their staffs were composed of 522 religious and 106 lay teachers. Reported enrollment (1963–64), the highest on record, was 9,105 Indian children; a small number of white pupils attended several schools. Twenty-five per cent of the Catholic Indian children between the ages of 6 to 18 were enrolled in these schools at that time.

As has been noted, the backgrounds of Indian and part-Indian children and the influence that experiences outside the school exert upon them also notably affect their educational development. The three following extensive surveys made in recent years assess from this point of view the achievements of large numbers of pupils in mission, Federal, and public schools: S. Peterson, *How Well Are Indian Children Educated?* (Washington 1948); K. Anderson, G. E. Collister, and C. E. Ladd, *The Educational Achievement of Indian Children* (Lawrence, Kans. 1953); M. Combs, R. Kron, G. E. Collister, and K. Anderson, *The Indian Child Goes to School* (Lawrence, Kans. 1958).

Bibliography: Bureau of Catholic Indian Missions, *Reports of the Director* (Washington 1883–1910). *The Indian Sentinel* (Washington 1902–). E. C. ADAMS, *American Indian Education* (New York 1946). **Illustration credits:** Catholic Indian Missions, Washington, D.C.

[J. B. TENNELLY]

AMERICAN INDIAN MISSIONS (CANADA)

In 1961 there were 220,121 Indians and Eskimos in Canada, more than half of whom lived in the provinces of Ontario and British Columbia; their annual increase totals about 5,000. They live on 2,200 reservations, i.e., certain areas that are assigned to them as living space. With the exception of a small number who have been integrated into the Canadian community, they depend on the Ministry of Citizenship and Immigration, whose department of Indian affairs devotes itself exclusively to their concerns. Since the end of World War II, the department has sought to raise the level of education and standard of life of the Indians. In the pursuit of its ultimate goal—the integration of the Indians as equal partners in the Canadian community—it has constructed hospitals, provided social workers, designed a building program to replace the wretched traditional huts with modern housing, organized placement bureaus, and encouraged the different tribes to assume the administration of their own affairs. Some progress has been made; thus, the tribe of the Six Nations (Iroquois) near Brantford, Ontario, elects its own municipal council and governs itself. Furthermore, experience has proved that an Indian properly educated is quite capable not only of holding a permanent position in the manual arts but also of being successful in administration, business, and the liberal professions. Unfortunately, however, the various tribes do not experience to the same degree the desire or the need to adopt the culture and the way of life of the whites. Meanwhile, each year numbers of Indians ask for and obtain their integration; during 1960–61 they totaled 954, of whom the majority were women who had married non-Indians.

Religious Care. In 1964 about 55 per cent of the Indians and Eskimos of Canada were Catholic; they were cared for by 500 missionary priests, assisted by 250 lay brothers and numerous sisters. In the district of the MacKenzie alone, more than 100 Gray Sisters of the Cross (Ottawa) devote themselves to hospitals and schools. Their apostolate is a difficult one, especially in the Arctic, where a missionary must on occasion travel a distance of 200 miles to celebrate Mass and administer the Sacraments to a small number of Eskimos. Aircraft and snowmobiles are frequently lacking; often sleds drawn by dogs are the sole means of transport. The bishops of these regions are responsible for the spiritual well-being of the Indians and Eskimos who live within the limits of their jurisdictions; they have delegated this task principally to the religious orders. Thus, the Oblates of Mary Immaculate serve as missionaries to the various nations of the western provinces, and the Jesuits are responsible for the Iroquois of Caughnawaga and Saint Regis, Quebec, as well as for the Ojibwa of northern Ontario.

Education. The Church operates 41 boarding schools, most of which belong to the government, in which 6,500 children receive a Catholic education. In addition, there are five hostels in the northwestern territories, where the children attend state schools with non-Indians. Originally the Indian Act provided that no Catholic child could be forced to enroll in a Protestant school and vice versa. However, later circumstances rendered difficult the application of this article of the law and, in fact, several provinces do not recognize the denominational schools and refuse them any financial assistance whatever. In such cases, the children have a choice between nonsectarian and pagan schools. Although the Church has tried to maintain its rights in matters of education, it has not been completely successful. The government sponsors no organized instruction beyond high school, but it does assume the expenses of students who wish to continue their studies at a university.

Integration. The Church hopes for the complete integration of the Indians into the population of Canada. It maintains, however, that any integration worthy of the name must be peaceful, freely accepted, and not imposed by the will of those in power. Moreover, it does not subscribe to any methods that would constitute a grave danger to the faith of Catholics.

Bibliography: Indian Affairs Branch, *The Indian in Transition: The Indian Today* (Ottawa 1962). *The Work of the Roman Catholic Church among the Indian and the Eskimo People of Canada* (Oblate Fathers Indian and Eskimo Welfare Commission; Ottawa n.d.).

[L. POULIOT]

AMERICAN INDIAN MISSIONS (U.S.)

The Catholic Indian heritage in the early days of the new Republic was slight. There existed only a few small groups of Catholic Indians, such as the Penobscots and Passamaquoddies in Maine, the Kaskaskias in Illinois, the St. Regis Iroquois in northern New York, the Ottawas at Arbre Croche near Mackinac, Mich., and the Potawatomies in northern Indiana. Descendants of the Indians who had been served by other discontinued colonial missions had then but vague remembrances of the faith, except for a few mixed-bloods here and there. *See* MISSIONS IN COLONIAL AMERICA, I (SPANISH MISSIONS), 4; MISSIONS IN COLONIAL AMERICA, III (FRENCH MISSIONS); MISSIONS IN COLONIAL AMERICA, IV (ENGLISH MISSIONS).

18th- and 19th-Century Development. Persistent appeals from Maine's 400 Catholic Indians moved Bp. John Carroll to send them the Sulpician Francis Cinquard in 1791. He was followed, first by one, then by two, and finally by three devoted pastors. Three churches and day schools have long been maintained for these Indians, numbering 900 in 1965.

The Catholic Indians in New York presented no problem. These survivors of the flourishing Sulpician Mission of the Presentation, the last of the colonial Iroquois missions, occupied the small St. Regis–Mohawk Reservation, bisected by the U.S.–Canadian boundary. The half of the tribe living in New York was then and has since been served by the Canadian pastors of the entire tribe.

Missions of the Middle West. At the request of Pres. George Washington, Bishop Carroll assigned Rev. John F. Rivet to Vincennes, Ind., in 1795 to pacify the roving, warlike tribes in the area and to foster the faith among them. The spiritual results of his zealous but discouraging ministry of 9 years were slight. With him went Rev. Peter Janin to Kaskaskia, Ill., another trouble spot. During his brief stay, he was unable to bring back to the practice of their religion the demoralized Illinois Indians, nor were the pastors of nearby parishes any more successful in the following 20 years, when the last Indians drifted westward.

The first Catholic Indian school, Spring Hill Academy (1809–12), was the work of the Sulpician Gabriel Richard, pastor of nearby Detroit, Mich. This venture was too short-lived to prove its value. Meanwhile, Richard and his assistants paid frequent visits to the Ottawas at Arbre Croche, Mich. Their devout chief, Blackbird, educated at the Sulpician mission at Oka, exerted great influence over them, as was manifest in their upright, temperate, and religious lives. The resident priest they had constantly pleaded for was assigned to them in 1827. Rev. Peter Dejean opened a small school, staffed by trained lay teachers. He was followed in 1829 by Rev. (later bishop) Frederic *Baraga, who was remarkable for his zeal and influence over the Indians. He made converts on Beaver and Washington Islands, and on the Manistique River in Michigan. In 1833 he established missions at Grand Rapids and Muskegon, places then also in Indian country. He was sent in 1835 to the Chippewas on Lake Superior, where he established missions at LaPointe, Grand Portage, Fond du Lac, and Bad River. Baraga later resided at L'Anse, where he set up a model Indian village.

Notable among his successors at Arbre Croche were Francis *Pierz, likewise an indefatigable missionary, and Rev. (later bishop) Ignatius *Mrak. Chapels were multiplied, and in 1840 nine small schools were in operation. By successive treaties, the Ottawa and Chippewa Indians in Michigan and Wisconsin surrendered more and more of their hunting grounds and were gradually surrounded by whites. Both the Indians and the missions remained, however, and continue to exist.

Work among the Potawatomies, survivors of the old Jesuit mission of St. Joseph's near Niles, Mich., was begun by Rev. Stephen *Badin in 1831. The Indians immediately proved the sincerity of their frequent appeals for a resident priest. Badin's successors, Revs. Louis Deseilles and Benjamin Petit, established other missions in villages south of St. Joseph's but their work was destroyed by the harassment of white settlers and by the deportation of 700 earnest and well-instructed Indians to the West (1836–38). There they formed the foundation of the Jesuit Potawatomi mission in eastern Kansas.

The Menominee mission in Wisconsin was initiated by the Dominican Samuel *Mazzuchelli at Green Bay in 1831. His work was continued successfully by Revs. Theodore *van den Broek, OP, and Florimond Bonduel. After 1854, when these Indians moved to their present (1965) reservation, they were served by resident priests or neighboring pastors until 1880, when the Franciscans took charge of the mission. They conduct two large parishes and parish schools for this Catholic tribe.

Among the mixed-blood Winnebagos, then on Turkey River in Iowa, visiting missionaries had some apparent success during the 1840s. When that part of the tribe moved to Minnesota in 1850, a mission with resident pastor and school met with small response. Work among these frequently transported Indians was resumed only in 1908 on their reservation in Nebraska. Catholic Winnebagos are few.

Missionary work among the Sioux in Minnesota was begun in 1842 and zealously continued for several years by Rev. Augustin *Ravoux near St. Paul, but he had no successor. His Sioux prayerbook and catechism, however, were later of great service to the pioneer Sioux missionaries in the Dakotas. Meanwhile, Father Pierz, who went to Minnesota in 1852, established a small mission at Crow Wing on the fringe of Chippewa territory. He extended his work by visits to other Chippewa settlements, but none of these small clusters of converts had a resident priest until 1874. They were afterward placed under the care of Benedictines, who established schools at White Earth and at Red Lake, and later resident missionaries elsewhere in northern Minnesota. They continue to serve 19 Indian congregations with a reported membership (1965) of 5,000.

The fruitful mission among the Chippewas at Pembina, N.Dak., begun in 1818 by a Canadian, Rev. Severe Dumoulin, was interrupted when this post was dis-

Fig. 1. St. Mary's Mission to the Potawatomies, Kansas, drawing by an unknown 19th-century Jesuit missionary.

covered to be in U.S. territory. Work was resumed there in 1848 by Rev. George A. *Belcourt, who established two promising missions and schools and a native religious community, the Sisters of the Propagation of the Faith. All this was discontinued soon after he returned to Canada in 1859. The Turtle Mountain missions, inaugurated in 1882 by Rev. John F. Malo and continued by the Benedictines, are the successors to these missionary efforts.

The Jesuit undertaking in St. Louis, Mo., St. Regis Indian Seminary at Florissant, disappointed the hope of its founders. During its short career (1824–30), it was beset by difficulties in recruiting and keeping pupils. Expected results did not materialize. Jesuits, as well as diocesan priests, made brief excursions before and after this to various tribes in the then Indian territory to the west. Nothing was effected thereby, except slight spiritual help to a few Catholic traders and mixed-bloods.

Beguiled by specious appeals made by traders or a few half-breeds, the Missouri Jesuits ventured upon several more pretentious undertakings that proved to be equally disappointing. The Kickapoo Mission (1836–39), near Fort Leavenworth, Kans., headed by zealous, overoptimistic Rev. Charles *Van Quickenborne, was a hopeless failure. The next venture, St. Joseph's Mission (1838–41) at Council Bluffs, Iowa, might have been effective had it not been frustrated by frequent outbreaks of Indian drunkenness. Only a few half-breeds among these Potawatomies, recent emigrees from northern Illinois, were responsive. A third venture, a mission and school among the Miamis (1839–41), was rendered futile also by the apathy and excessive intemperance of the Indians.

Fig. 3. Insula, a Flathead chief, drawing by G. Sohom, dated 1854. The artist's note quotes Father De Smet as calling him a "great man and warrior." It also states that he was noted for his piety and officiated at the burial of the dead.

Fig. 2. A Kickapoo Indian using a Christian prayer stick, early 19th-century watercolor by George Catlin.

A bright chapter in the Jesuits' record in nearby Indian country was the outstanding success of their missionaries among the Potawatomies, lately uprooted from Indiana (1837–67). With its large group of already well-instructed Catholics and its well-conducted schools for boys and girls, St. Mary's Mission in Kansas, under capable Rev. J. B. Duerinck, made steady progress. After the Indians had sold most of their reservation, the great majority drifted into Oklahoma.

St. Francis Hieronymo Mission, among the wild, roving Osages, began with manual training schools for boys and girls in 1847, directed by the Jesuit John Schoenmaeker. The schools, which were the chief activity of the mission, attracted large numbers of mixed-blood children, but few regular full-blood pupils. Many of the mixed-bloods became practicing Catholics and took up farming. Success with the full-bloods was slight. They, too, sold their Kansas reservation in 1867 and moved to northeast Oklahoma. Their former missionaries visited them from time to time until the local Benedictines assumed charge of them and the Potawatomies in 1875.

Missions of the Northwest. In response to repeated invitations from the Flatheads in the heart of the Rocky Mountains, Pierre *De Smet, SJ, was sent to investigate the situation in 1840. Deeply impressed by the attitude of these Indians and with great expectations, he set out the following year with two other Jesuit priests and three lay brothers. The beginnings of St. Mary's Mission (near Stevensville, Mont.) fulfilled his hopes. Five years later, however, troubles sprang up, discouragement set in, and the mission was abandoned in 1850. Years later the Flatheads were visited occasionally by Jesuits, and eventually, in 1891, the Flatheads joined the Kalispel Indians.

Nicholas Point, SJ, companion of De Smet, was assigned in 1841 to open a mission for the small Coeur d'Alene tribe in northern Idaho. This developed under the care of Rev. Joseph Joset into an excellent mission and long remained so. De Smet discovered another promising opportunity among a small Kalispel group in the northeast corner of Washington; they, too, received a resident missionary, Adrien Hoecken, SJ, in 1845. He and his neophytes moved to a fertile valley in Montana (later called the Flathead Reservation) in 1854, where St. Ignatius Mission was established, long the pride of the Jesuits. A school, begun there in 1864, continues to function. In 1845 Point made the first of several ineffective attempts to win over the Blackfeet or Piegans, who lived north of the Flatheads and were their perennial enemies, but these wild marauders were not ready for the gospel.

St. Paul's and St. Francis's Missions, provided with resident priests, met with success among several Selish groups living along and near the Columbia River in the Northwest. John *Nobili, SJ, extended this work into Canadian territory. Transfers of mission personnel to California after 1850, however, soon reduced active Jesuit missions in the Northwest to two, although a revival was to take place later. Francis N. *Blanchet (later archbishop), and Modeste Demers (later bishop), sent from Canada in 1837 principally to evangelize the Indians in the Oregon Country, had preceded the Jesuits. But burdened by the care of white settlers, they made only occasional excursions up the Columbia River and along Puget Sound, ministering to Catholic traders, mixed-bloods, and their families, but arousing merely momentary interest among the Indians. Other Canadian priests who joined them later accomplished scarcely more.

A heroic chapter began with the coming of Rev. John *Brouillet and four Oblates of Mary Immaculate to Fort Walla Walla, late in 1848, to establish missions among the sturdy, independent, seminomadic Yakimas, Cayuses, Umatillas, and Walla Wallas. Brouillet had scarcely begun St. Ann's Mission among a few interested Cayuses when the nearby Presbyterian missionary, Dr. Marcus Whitman, his wife, and others were murdered. This precipitated a punitive war against the Cayuses and their allies. St. Ann's Mission was continued under great difficulties and danger for 4 years by Casimir Chirouse, OMI. It was later resumed and developed by Rev. Adolph Vermersch and his successors. Placed under the Jesuits in 1888, it was renamed St. Andrew's, as it is currently called.

The Oblates of Mary Immaculate had built three log chapels in Yakima territory and developed small devout congregations. When the Yakimas were set upon by poorly disciplined militia in 1856, bloody conflicts ensued and the chapels were plundered and burned. Revs. Charles Pandosy and Peter Durieu—though mistrusted by both whites and pagan Indians, mistreated and often in danger of death—remained fearlessly among the Indians until expelled in 1858. The chapel at Ahtanum was rebuilt 10 years later by Rev. Louis St. Onge and missionary work was resumed. After 1871 the work was continued, until recent times, by the Jesuits. A diocesan priest then took charge of the small Yakima congregation at White Swan, Wash.

The energies of the Oblates of Mary Immaculate found a new outlet along Puget Sound. Little, however, was accomplished in the 10-year-old St. Joseph's Mission at Olympia until the arrival of Chirouse in 1858. Together with various Oblate assistants he established and maintained St. Francis Xavier Mission and a school among the Snohomish at Tulalip, chapels for the Lummi and the Suquamish Indians (1861), St. Mary's among the Swinomish (1868), and St. Clare's on the Muckelshoot Reserve (1869). When recalled to Canada, the Oblate missionaries left behind them 2,000 Indian converts. Among their successors, Revs. John Boulet and Paul Gard deserve special mention. The only other significant activity in the Northwest at that time was the 40 years of devoted ministry by Rev. Adrian Croquet to the small mixed tribal groups on the Grande Ronde Reservation, in western Oregon, beginning in 1859.

Missions of the Southwest. The annexation of New Mexico, Arizona, and California in 1848 brought critical Indian problems to the new vicars apostolic. Wholesale murders by incoming gold seekers and greedy land grabbers, widespread epidemics, starvation, and alcoholism had reduced to a small fraction the California Indians formerly under the care of the suppressed Franciscan missionary establishments. The attention of Rev. Antonio Ubach and of other devoted priests was soon directed to the small groups in the mountains of San Diego and Riverside Counties. Gradually more and more priests were able to give the Indians more adequate care. St. Anthony's Boarding School near San Diego (1887–1907) and St. Boniface's at Banning (1890–1940) provided care and education for a limited number of children. Mission chapels were built from year to year and more frequent services held in them. By 1965 about 5,000 Catholic Indians in southern California, with 28 chapels of their own, were under the care of 10 priests. Missionary work on a small scale, beginning in 1870, was carried on in Lake and Mendocino Counties. About 1,000 Catholic Indians in six villages were cared for by two Capuchin priests (1965).

In New Mexico, Bp. John B. *Lamy found about 5,000 industrious, baptized Pueblo Indians, but few of them were willing to practice their religion. The Spanish Franciscan friars had been able to do but little, during their long tenure, to break the tenacious hold

Fig. 4. "Mission of San Carlos, near Monterey, California, 1792," watercolor by William Alexander.

Fig. 5. Music book for instruction of Indians at Mission Santa Barbara, Calif., 18th century. Each part was written in a different color as an aid to learning.

of the native religion on these Indians. The Pueblos had allowed their children to be baptized and to attend religious instructions, but this had been of little avail. At first only a few priests could be assigned to attempt their reformation. Their number gradually increased until, by 1965, there were 13 priests engaged in serving the Indians at their 24 villages. Two boarding and three day schools are provided for their children. Gradual progress has been made in reforming some of the 10,000 Indians, but many others remain only nominal Catholics.

Late 19th-century Expansion. A surge in interest and activity in older mission fields and the extension of missionary work into large new fields during the last quarter of the 19th century put the Catholic Indian missions far ahead of others. Up to that time they had lagged behind the similar efforts made by Protestant groups. The cooperation of the Federal government in Indian educational work; the establishment and effectiveness of the *Bureau of Catholic Indian Missions; the generous contribution of personnel by Jesuits, Franciscans, Benedictines, and many sisterhoods; and the financial assistance of Mother Katharine *Drexel were important factors in this development. In 1900, 140 priests were engaged on the missions, 175 chapels had been provided, 60 schools were operated, and approximately 50,000 Indians were counted as Catholics; whereas in 1875, only 20 priests, 55 chapels, and 7 small schools were to be accounted for and baptized Catholic Indians numbered scarcely more than 25,000.

The late 19th century was for the Jesuits the golden era of missions in the Northwest. The Jesuits improved and enlarged the boarding schools and opened a day school on the Flathead Reservation; established missions and schools on the Blackfeet, Fort Belknap, Northern Cheyenne, and Crow Reservations; and initiated work on the Fort Peck Reservation, all in Montana. They established a school on the Coeur d'Alene Reservation and a mission on the Nez Perce Reservation, both in Idaho. They reactivated and extended their work among the Colville Indians, established a school near their reservation, conducted a mission for the Spokane Indians, and took charge of the Yakima Reservation, all projects in Washington. Jesuits assumed the care of the Umatilla Reservation in Oregon and established a school there. A boarding school for the Puget Sound Indians was opened near Takoma, under diocesan auspices, and other missionary work among these Indians was continued and expanded.

Systematic work among the Sioux Indians in the Dakotas, heretofore scarcely possible, began with the establishment of a mission and school on the small Devil's Lake Reservation in North Dakota in 1874, followed shortly afterward by missions and schools on the Grand River (later Standing Rock) Reservation in the same state, and on the small Crow Creek Reservation in South Dakota, under Benedictine auspices. Meanwhile, Jesuits had opened schools and missions on the large Rosebud and Pine Ridge Reservations in western South Dakota, and a school and mission for the Arapahos of Wyoming. Francis M. Craft, an experienced missionary and founder of the second Indian Sisterhood, the Congregation of American Sisters, established the first permanent mission among the Mandans, Arickarees, and Gros Ventres in North Dakota. All of these foundations were to experience notable expansion and success in later years. Missionary work was attempted, but with little success, among the Sisseton and Yankton Sioux in South Dakota.

In Minnesota the Benedictines expanded their Chippewa missions. In Wisconsin the Franciscans took charge of the small Red Cliff and Bad River Chippewa and the Menominee missions, began the Court Oreille mission, and established schools at all of these. They assumed the care also of the Ottawa missions and schools in lower Michigan, while Canadian Jesuits accepted the small Chippewa missions in upper Michigan. A small mission was opened on the Oneida Reservation, near Green Bay, Wis.

In former Indian Territory (later included in Oklahoma), Benedictines, entrusted with the Catholic Potawatomies and Osages, established four schools among them, and a mission and school on the Kiowa Reservation. They and diocesan priests also undertook itinerant missionary work among other tribes in the area. The diocesan priests established also a mission and school on the Quapaw Reservation.

Modest beginnings were made in the Southwest among the Papago, Pima, and Navaho Indians in Arizona and the Mescalero Apaches in New Mexico. Work in southern California was increased and extended into the Yuma Reservation.

20th Century. The progress of the Indian apostolate as a whole during the 20th century may be judged by the following indications. From 1900 to 1965 there was a 150 per cent increase in the number of Catholic Indians living on or near reservations. They numbered 125,000 persons, served by 230 priests in 360 churches and chapels maintained for their special benefit. Nearly twice the number of Indian children as in 1900 attended greatly improved mission schools, despite the termination of Federal grants for the education of Indian children in private schools at the beginning of the 20th century. Missions were initiated and maintained on 16 small reservations not previously cared for. Progress was not uniform, however, throughout the country in time or in space. Effort was intensified in several areas, well sustained in others, but faltering in some places.

In the Middle West solid and notable progress was made among the Sioux Indians, of whom 18,000 were reported to be Cathoics. They were served by 59 priests at 77 churches and outlying stations with chapels. All parts of all the Sioux reservations had resident priests. Nine schools were maintained for their children. The older missions developed well, as did new missions and schools established more recently on the Yankton and Sisseton Reservations. The Benedictines in charge of the Turtle Mountain Chippewa reported notable success. A mission and school were established on the Winnebago Reservation in 1908. An Indian sisterhood, Oblate Sisters of the Blessed Sacrament, established at St. Paul's, S.Dak., had 15 professed members. The Mandan and the Arapaho missions also steadily advanced.

Long delayed misionary work in the Southwest assumed large proportions. Missions among the Navahos in Arizona and New Mexico, modestly begun in 1898 by the Franciscans, numbered 12 resident priests, who also attended 13 outmissions with chapels and numerous missionary stations. Two schools were conducted for Navaho children. Navahos, however, have been slow to come into the Church, although a significant number of conversions were made in recent times. Much more successful in this respect were the Pima missions, begun in 1901, and the Papago missions, begun in 1907. These 58 missions and 6 schools were served by 12 Franciscans. The greater part of these fairly large tribes was Catholic by 1965. The Apache missions on the San Carlos and Fort Apache Reservations, begun in 1918 and 1922 respectively, had relatively few converts. Progress in various degrees was noted in the Pueblo missions. Three day-schools for their children had increasing numbers of pupils. The California Mission Indians, 4,000 Catholics, were well ministered to by the six priests resident among them and by several nearby pastors.

Fig. 6. Indians performing a ceremonial dance in honor of the Virgin at Isleta Pueblo, N.Mex., July 1948.

Both the Indians and the missions in the Northwest were affected unfavorably by the large-scale sale of Indian lands to incoming white settlers. Such contacts were usually not beneficial to the Indians. Both religious and economic progress was slow. The older missions, however, continued, but under heavy handicaps. The Jesuits relinquished their missions on five reservations to diocesan priests, but increased their activity on the Colville Reservation in Washington. Nearly all the older schools remained in operation and the total number of Catholic Indians slowly increased.

A similar situation developed in Michigan, Wisconsin, and Minnesota. In addition, the Chippewa missions on the diminished reservations suffered the loss of many Catholic Indians to more prosperous towns and cities. But Franciscans, Benedictines, and Jesuits maintained a record of devoted service to the 8,000 Catholic Indians under their care in 31 missions, as did the sisters in six mission schools. The Ottawa missions in lower Michigan were even more seriously depleted in membership. Six small missions and one school suffice for the remaining Indians. By contrast, the two Menominee missions and schools in Wisconsin prospered.

The surge of interest in Indians in Oklahoma, manifested in the 10 Indian mission boarding schools operated during the first quarter of the 20th century, later receded. The dissolution of the reservations and the dispersal of their occupants made the former schools and missions appear largely unnecessary. Most of the 5,000 Catholic Indians in the state were absorbed into white parishes. Only three small schools and missions remain.

Besides new missions already mentioned, others have been undertaken (since 1900) and sustained on the following small reservations: Mille Lacs and Nett Lake in Minnesota; Santee in Nebraska; Rocky Boy in Montana; Klamath, Siletz, Warm Springs, and the Ute colony in Oregon; Southern Ute and Ute Mountain in Colorado; Maricopa and Fort Mohave in Arizona; Uintah and Ouray in Utah; and Jicarilla Apache in New Mexico.

The apostolate to the Indians reaches into Indian reservations in 40 Northern, Middle Western, and Western dioceses. It reaches into all the large and medium-size reservations and into many of the smaller ones. No other home mission project is relatively better provided with religious workers.

Bibliography: J. G. SHEA, *History of the Catholic Missions among the Indian Tribes in the United States, 1529–1854* (New York 1855). Garraghan JMUS. W. N. BISCHOFF, *The Jesuits in Old Oregon* (Caldwell, Idaho 1945). C. DURATSCHECK, *Crusading Along Sioux Trails: A History of the Catholic Indian Missions of South Dakota* (St. Meinrad, Ind. 1947). R. L. WILKEN, *Anselm Weber: Missionary to the Navaho, 1898–1921* (Milwaukee 1955). M. J. GEIGER, *The Kingdom of St. Francis in Arizona, 1539–1939* (Santa Barbara, Calif. 1939). Bureau of Catholic Indian Missions, *The Indian Sentinel* (Washington 1916 to date), organ of the Catholic Indian missions. **Illustration credits:** Fig. 4, Newberry Library, E. E. Ayer Collection, Chicago. Fig. 5, Academy of American Franciscan History. Fig. 2, The Thomas

Gilcrease Institute of American History and Art, Tulsa, Okla. Fig. 3, The Smithsonian Institution. Fig. 1, The Kansas State Historical Society, Topeka.

[J. B. TENNELLY]

AMERICAN LITERATURE

The literature of the U.S. is the subject of the following survey. Though it should more properly be called U.S. literature, custom sanctions the use of the adjective American; other literatures of American (i.e., Western hemisphere, exclusive of Canada) provenance will be found surveyed under Argentinian, Brazilian, Chilean, Mexican, and Latin American literatures. In comparison with other great national literatures, American (U.S.) literature is a relative latecomer; hence it seems more practical to survey it not by periods (as is done for English, French, German, Italian, and Spanish), but by genres. Accordingly, the survey following is divided into: (1) Nonfiction, (2) Drama, (3) Poetry, (4) Fiction to 1900, and (5) Fiction from 1900.

1. NONFICTION

In a nation carving for itself a place in a physical wilderness and establishing its political, religious, and cultural identity, nonfiction writing always plays a large part; for it is a method of describing the nature of the emerging nation in pragmatic terms and of defining its goals in terms of idealistic activism. A great amount of nonfiction has been written in what is now the U.S. Much of it has been done with skill, but relatively little of it for other than utilitarian reasons. Under the historical stresses peculiar to a new land, writing is frequently instructive or hortatory, often sparse, and usually without much belletristic quality. Certainly the Declaration of Independence (1776), the Constitution of the U.S. (1787), *The Federalist papers* (1787–88) by Alexander Hamilton (assisted by James Madison and John Jay), and many other utilitarian works are primary documents in any definition of American experience without being true parts of the literature of the U.S.

In the 3½ centuries during which the English colonies on the Atlantic Seaboard grew from clusters of imperiled pilgrims and planters into a mighty continental nation, unique in its concept of the role of the citizen in the governing of the state, many different kinds of nonfiction have been written, and each stage in this growth has called forth different kinds of writing. There have been travel writing, first about the U.S. and later about other lands; history; biography and autobiography; polemical essays that are political, religious, social, and economic; humorous and satiric comment; lectures on religious and cultural subjects; literary criticism; and philosophy. A mere catalog of the writers of significant nonfiction in the U.S. would exhaust the limits of a survey such as this. The attempt is made, therefore, to mention the major types and principal writers of nonfiction in each of the large periods or trends in U.S. history: colonial, Revolutionary and Federalist, romantic, realistic, and modern.

Colonial Period. During the colonial period, which extends from the founding of the first permanent English colony at Jamestown in 1607 to the Stamp Act in 1765—an event that forced the colonies to a widespread awareness of themselves as somehow separate from their motherland—the bulk of the writing was concerned, for obvious reasons, with practical affairs. The earliest writings were by Englishmen reporting their experiences in the New World. The most notable of these records, almost all of which are in the form of travel reports, were those of Capt. John Smith (1580–1631), whose *A True Relation of . . . Virginia* (1608), *A Description of New England* (1616), and *The Generall Historie of Virginia, New-England, and the Summer Isles* (1624) recorded, with some questionable heroics by Smith himself, the events of this early colonization. A second large body of early material dealt with the historical records, both private and public, of the new colonies. The most notable among these were the *Journal* by John Winthrop (1588–1649), which covered the years 1630 to 1649 and described the attempt to create in the Massachusetts Bay Colony a theocratic government with God as ruler and the Bible as constitution, and William Bradford's (1590–1657) *The History of Plimmoth Plantation,* which told the story of the Pilgrim colony from 1620 to 1646, and which remained in manuscript for 2 centuries until its publication in 1856.

Pilgrim and Puritan alike were enforcing a kind of government that some subjects felt to be too restrictive, and this resentment occasioned the series of controversial pamphlets arguing freedom of conscience and tolerance of religious belief written by Roger Williams (1603–83) between 1643 and 1652. Williams's revolt resulted in the Providence Plantation settlement in Rhode Island. These early writers wrote very much as their English contemporaries did and usually in terms of the practical considerations of the world they lived in. The missionary activities of the Jesuits in Spanish, French, and Portuguese settlements in the New World were recorded in *The Jesuit Relations and Allied Documents, 1601–1791* (tr. R. G. Thwaites, 73 v. 1896–1901).

The 18th century produced three major American writers of nonfiction: Cotton Mather (1663–1728), Jonathan Edwards (1703–58), and Benjamin Franklin (1706–90). Mather's *Magnalia Christi Americana* (1702) was a learned book describing the acts of the "Puritan saints" in the New World. His *Manductio ad Ministerium* (1726), a set of directions for ministers, was a vigorous defense of a way of life already yielding its previously strong position; it also contained a significant digression on literary style. Mather's extensive writing had great intellectual integrity and some distinction of style. His *Bonifacius; or, Essays to Do Good* (1710) influenced Franklin. Jonathan Edwards, who in a long series of writings reiterated the Calvinistic concepts of depravity, of unmerited grace, and of election and reprobation, was one of the first and greatest of American philosophers. Among his many works the most notable was *The Freedom of the Will* (1754), which attempted to reconcile the old belief and the new knowledge. He is too often remembered exclusively for his famous "hell-fire" sermon, "Sinners in the Hands of an Angry God," and too little for the literary effectiveness and charm of his *Personal Narrative*.

Benjamin Franklin was a man endowed with an almost incredible variety of interests and abilities. He edited *Poor Richard's Almanac,* noted for its pithy practical advice, annually from 1733 to 1758, and between 1771 and 1789 he wrote his clear and remarkably effective *Autobiography*. He also produced a number of ef-

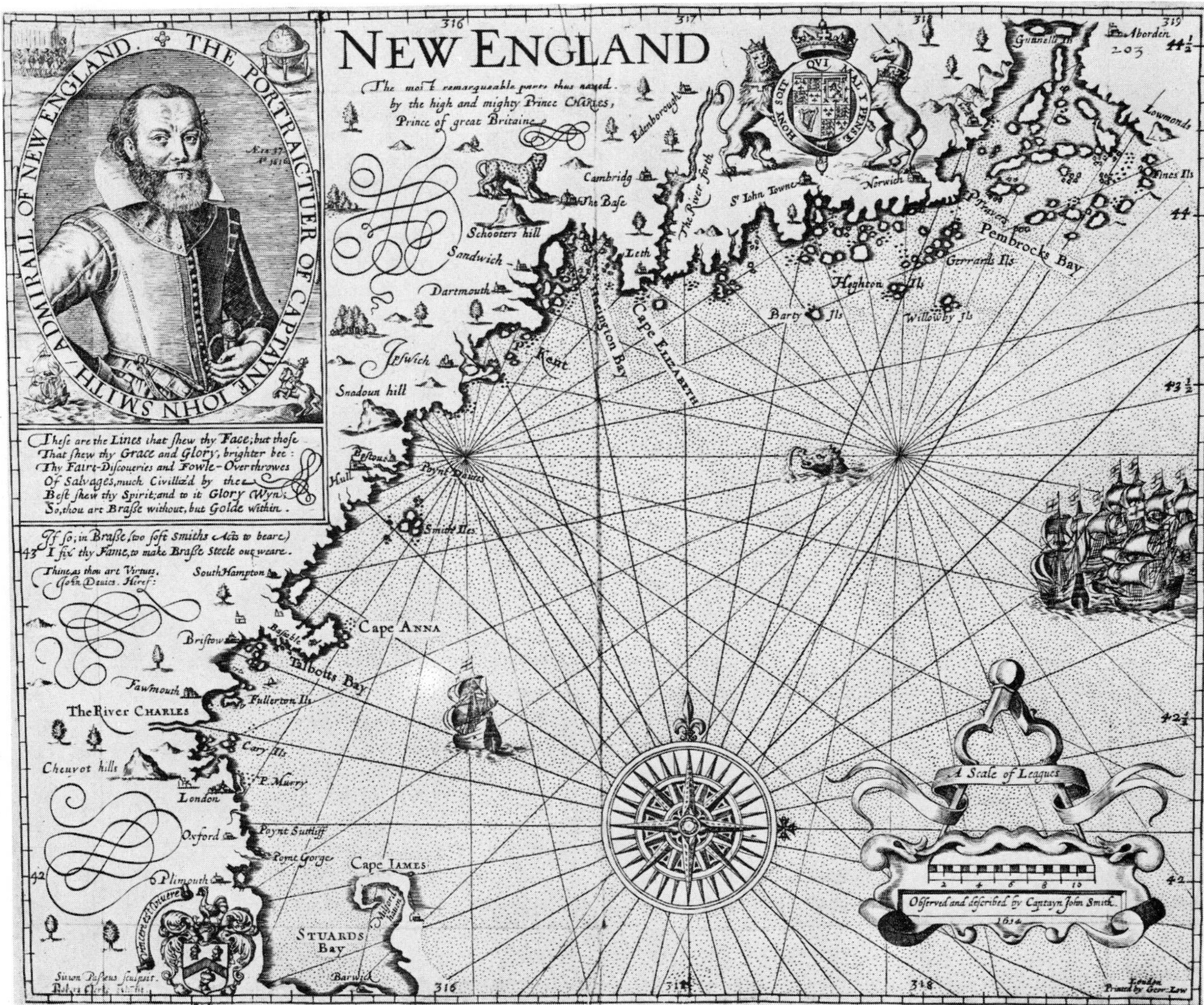

Fig. 1. John Smith and a map of New England from book 6 of his "General History" published in London, 1624.

fective and graceful brief essays. After Edwards, Franklin was the finest prose writer in America before the formation of the nation.

Other writings of some literary merit were already beginning to oppose these older ways. Most illuminating for the period as social history are the *Diary* of Samuel Sewell (1652–1730), a daily record of life in commerical New England, and the almost equally valuable journal of another Bostonian, Sarah Knight, which describes a journey from Boston to New York in 1704. John Woolman (1720–72) argued the Quaker position effectively in many documents on social issues and in his *Journal* (1774) produced an autobiography of great beauty of style and of value as a picture of the "inner life."

The people of the South were of essentially Episcopalian leanings, except in the colony of Maryland, where there were strong Catholic influences. William Byrd II, the master of Westover Plantation in Virginia, produced an amusing *History of the Dividing Line* (1728), describing a survey establishing the line between Virginia and North Carolina, and *A Journey into the Land of Eden* (1733), a record of his travels to his frontier lands. Byrd's *Secret Diaries,* written in his private shorthand, were not deciphered and made public until the 20th century; they reveal a remarkably robust, learned, and typically 18th-century man.

Revolutionary and Federalist Era. The period between the Stamp Act in 1765 and the "second American revolution" in Andrew Jackson's dramatic victory for the frontier egalitarianism in 1828 was marked by vigorous polemical writings. Thomas Paine (1737–1809) in *Common Sense* (1776) and in his series *The Crisis* (1776–83) helped to create and to strengthen the spirit of revolt out of which the triumphant nation came. Michel-Guillaume Jean de Crèvecoeur in *Letters from an American Farmer* (1782) made an early, graceful, and largely successful attempt to define the essence of Americanism. With the formation of the new nation came a continuing dialogue in the form of polemical writings. The 85 essays of *The Federalist* are eloquent arguments for the Federal view of the government. Thomas Jefferson (1743–1826), whose Declaration of Independence crystallized the physiocratic egalitarianism upon which the nation rested, continued in many papers, in letters, and in his inaugural addresses to argue

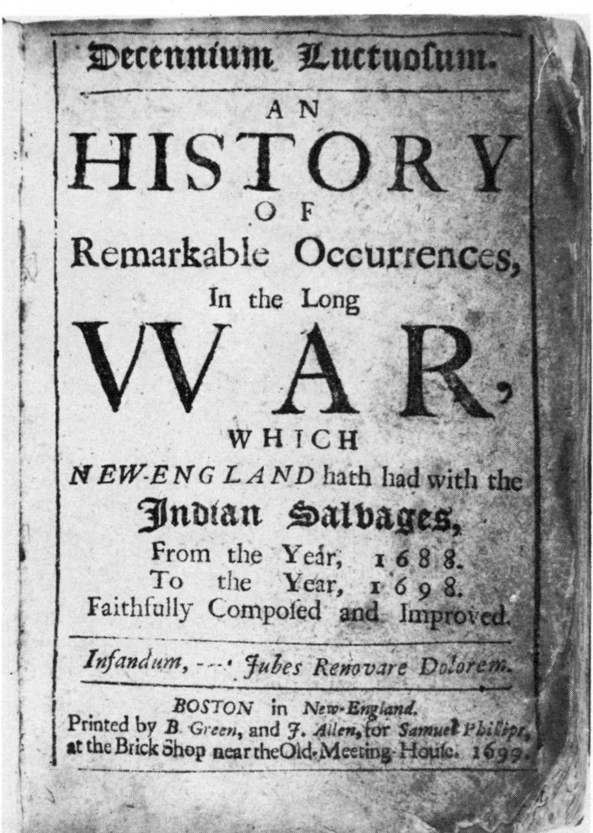

Decennium Luctuoſum.

AN

HISTORY

OF

Remarkable Occurrences,

In the Long

WAR,

WHICH

NEW-ENGLAND hath had with the

Indian Salvages,

From the Year, 1688.

To the Year, 1698.

Faithfully Compoſed and Improved.

Infandum, ---- Jubes Renovare Dolorem.

BOSTON in *New-England.*

Printed by *B. Green*, and *J. Allen*, for *Samuel Phillips*, at the Brick Shop near the Old-Meeting-Houſe. 1699.

Fig. 2. Title page of Cotton Mather's "Decennium Luctuosum" (1699).

against the Federalists and for individual freedom and local autonomy.

The first truly successful American writer of belletristic materials was Washington Irving (1783–1859). In his *Salmagundi Papers* (1807–08) he transferred the Addisonian essay to the New World. In his burlesque *History of New York* by "Diedrich Knickerbocker" (1809) he followed the English neoclassic writers in the production of a fine and most amusing example of literary parody. In his *Sketch Book* (1819–20), in addition to some early short stories, he included numerous essays that reflected his feelings as a traveler in England and at home; and in *Bracebridge Hall* (1822) he described with great charm a typical English squirearchy. In *The Alahambra* (1832) he wrote with deep feeling of Spanish life and legend. Though the vein Irving worked was small and thin, he mined it with skill and grace and, when he had exhausted it, turned to biography and history and produced studies of Christopher Columbus (1828), Oliver Goldsmith (1849), and George Washington (5 v., 1855–59); a history, *The Conquest of Granada* (1829); and a record of frontier life in *Tour of the Prairie* (1835).

Dominance of Romanticism. In the period between the election of Andrew Jackson (1829) and the end of the Civil War (1865), European romanticism dominated American literature. Poetry and fiction, both long and short, had begun to play an important part in American writing, but this first great period in national literature was also marked by extensive and distinguished work in the essay.

Transcendentalists. The major group of writers were the Transcendentalists, who were associated with Concord, Mass. (*see* TRANSCENDENTALISM, LITERARY). The greatest figure of the period was Ralph Waldo *Emerson, whose address "The American Scholar" at Harvard (1837) was a declaration of independence from English influences, whose essay *Nature* (1836) is still the clearest definition of the postulates of the transcendental unitarians, and whose "Divinity School Address" (1838) is a clear statement of his philosophy of the intrinsic divinity of all men. He was a frequent lecturer as well, and his essays were primarily lectures adjusted to book form. They appeared as *Essays* in two series (1841, 1844), as *Representative Men* (1850), and as a travel record in *English Traits* (1856).

Emerson's closest associate was Henry David *Thoreau, who in many essays expressed his interest in the nature of both his inner and the outer world. His most distinguished works were *A Week on the Concord and Merrimack Rivers* (1849) and *Walden* (1854). The latter is the story of his ascetical sojourn at Walden Pond in an effort to push life into a corner and make it reveal its true nature. His famous lecture on "The

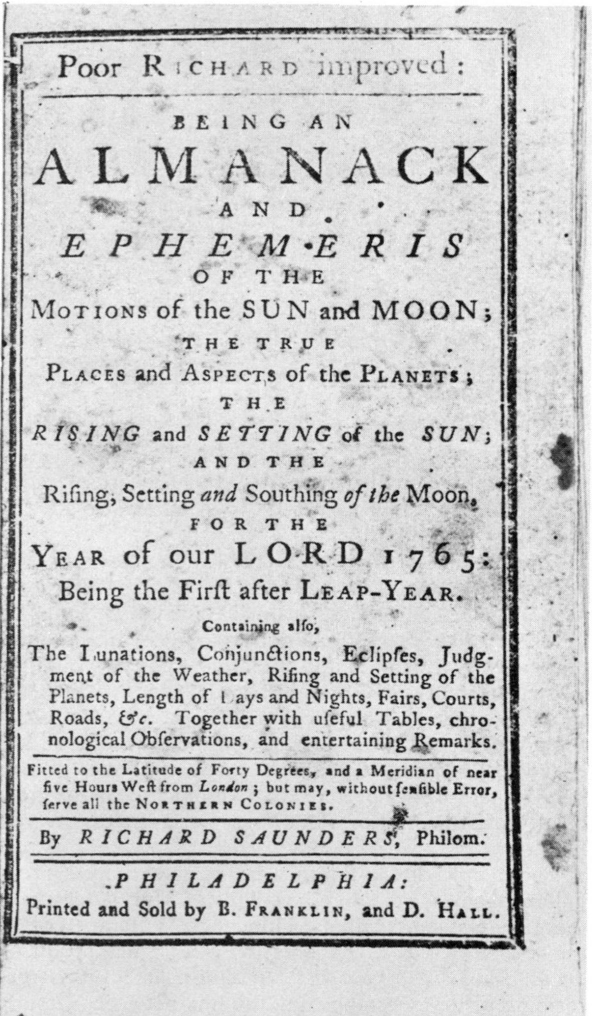

Poor RICHARD improved:

BEING AN

ALMANACK

AND

EPHEMERIS

OF THE

MOTIONS of the SUN and MOON;

THE TRUE

PLACES and ASPECTS of the PLANETS;

THE

RISING and *SETTING* of the *SUN*;

AND THE

Riſing, Setting *and* Southing *of the* Moon,

FOR THE

YEAR of our LORD 1765:

Being the Firſt after LEAP-YEAR.

Containing alſo,

The Lunations, Conjunctions, Eclipſes, Judgment of the Weather, Riſing and Setting of the Planets, Length of Days and Nights, Fairs, Courts, Roads, &c. Together with uſeful Tables, chronological Obſervations, and entertaining Remarks.

Fitted to the Latitude of Forty Degrees, and a Meridian of near five Hours Weſt from *London*; but may, without ſenſible Error, ſerve all the NORTHERN COLONIES.

By *RICHARD SAUNDERS*, Philom.

PHILADELPHIA:

Printed and Sold by B. FRANKLIN, and D. HALL.

Fig. 3. Title page of a "Poor Richard's Almanac" (1765).

Duty of Civil Disobedience" has been, through its annunciation of the doctrine of passive resistance, one of the great germinal statements for various protest movements in the modern world, influencing such different leaders as *Gandhi and Martin Luther King. Margaret Fuller (1810–50) in *Women in the Nineteenth Century* (1845) made an early and significant statement in the feminist movement. Other Transcendentalists included Amos Bronson Alcott (1799–1888), best known for his gnomic *Orphic Sayings,* published in the *Dial* magazine (1840–44), the major organ of the movement, edited by Emerson; Margaret Fuller; and Orestes *Brownson. Brownson, who became a Catholic in 1844, was a critic, editor, and philosopher; among his many works were the lively essays published in his own and other magazines; *The Convert, or, Leaves from My Experience* (1857); and *Conversation on Liberalism and the Church* (1870). At this time, too, an extensive argument against the institution of slavery was carried on in the work of many men, notably William Lloyd Garrison (1805–79), whose weekly newspaper the *Liberator* (1831–65) was a rallying point for the movement. A form of writing popular in the 1840s and 1850s was the "slave narrative," autobiographical accounts of the horrors of slavery told by former slaves. The best-known of these works was the *Narrative of the Life of Frederick Douglass* (1845), notable both for its subject matter and the moving simplicity of its style.

The New England Brahmins and the group associated with *Knickerbocker Magazine* (New York 1832–65) joined against the "Young America" critics who clustered about Evert A. Duyckinck (1816–78) and debated the issue of an internationally oriented as opposed to a native and regional literature. Among those involved were Edgar Allan *Poe, the author of trenchant critical essays in many journals; James Russell Lowell (1819–91), whose critical essays were collected in a number of volumes, the best-known being *Among My Books* (1870) and *My Study Window* (1871); and William Gilmore Simms (1806–70), who vigorously defended nationalism in *Views and Reviews* (2d series 1845).

History and Biography. History, too, came to be increasingly important during this period. George Bancroft (1800–91) produced his monumental *History of the United States* (1834–76). John Lothrop Motley (1814–77) wrote *The Rise of the Dutch Republic* (3 v. 1856) and the *History of the United Netherlands* (4 v. 1860–67). In terms of literary value the major historians of the age were William H. *Prescott and Francis Parkman. Prescott's major accomplishments were *The Conquest of Mexico* (3 v. 1843) and *The Conquest of Peru* (2 v. 1847), both beautifully written accounts of Spain in the New World. Parkman devoted his major energies to a fascinatingly detailed record of the struggle between the French and the English in the colonial U.S. Among his many works are *The History of the Conspiracy of Pontiac* (1851), *Pioneers of France in the New World* (1865), about the conflict of French Huguenots and Spanish Catholics over Florida, and *The Jesuits in North America in the Seventeenth Century* (1867), recounting the struggle to Christianize the Indians.

Biography, too, became important. Jared Sparks (1789–1866) wrote a good study of George Washington (1834); Simms, mentioned above, treated Francis Marion (1844), John Smith (1846), and the Chevalier Bayard (1847). Narratives of personal experience were also popular. Notable among them were Herman *Melville's accounts of his life among the Polynesians, *Typee* (1846) and *Omoo* (1847), and Richard H. Dana, Jr.'s (1815–82), record of his experiences on a merchant marine ship in *Two Years Before the Mast* (1840).

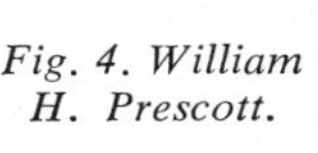

Fig. 4. William H. Prescott.

The light essay attracted the attention of Oliver Wendell Holmes (1809–94), whose *Autocrat of the Breakfast Table* series (1858–72) was a highlight in the 19th-century familiar essay. The use of the materials of American experience for humorous treatment, by such men as Joseph Glover Baldwin (1815–64), whose *Flush Times of Alabama and Mississippi* (1853) wryly comments on American frontier life, and Henry W. Shaw (1818–85), whose "Josh Billings" was a fine example of the cracker-barrel philosopher, also began to be important during the age when Americans embraced romantic idealism, examined it with a critical eye, and found much in it to admire, and no small amount to laugh at.

Journalism. Much of the finest American nonfiction in the first half of the 19th century appeared in literary magazines, frequently modeled on the great British reviews. The *North American Review,* founded in 1815 and numbering among its editors Jared Sparks, Edward Everett, James Russell Lowell, and Henry *Adams, published contributions from most of America's finest writers until its demise, after a long period of slow decay, in 1940. A surprisingly brilliant magazine of similar form, the *Southern Review,* edited by Hugh Swinton Legaré, had a short life (1828–32), but a long influence, especially on the *Southern Quarterly Review* (1842–57), the best-known of whose several editors was William Gilmore Simms, and on the spritelier *Southern Literary Messenger* (1834–64), whose best-known contributor and editor was Edgar Allan Poe. The *Knickerbocker,* edited by the vitriolic Lewis Gaylord Clark, spoke for conservative New York from 1832 to 1865, while the shorter-lived *Democratic Review* (1837–51) was the voice of liberal nationalism and numbered among its contributors almost every major American writer of its age, including Poe, *Hawthorne, Brownson, Whittier, Bryant, and Simms. Brownson himself published two important magazines, the *Boston Quar-*

terly Review (1838–42) and *Brownson's Quarterly Review* (1844–65; 1872–76).

Any account of the literature of this epoch must include mention of the superb addresses and letters of Abraham Lincoln; the most famous single piece from his pen is undoubtedly *The Gettysburg Address* (Nov. 19, 1863), though his Second Inaugural Address (March 4, 1865) is perhaps an even greater masterpiece.

Age of Realism. The realistic period in American nonfiction extends from the close of the Civil War (1865) to the beginnings of World War I (1914). During this period there was a substantial growth in U.S. interest in travel writing.

Travel and Autobiography. Travel literature had been initially designed for European audiences interested in America. During the romantic period a number of major writers had described their experiences abroad, notably Emerson in *English Traits* and Hawthorne in *Our Old Home* (1863), or described personal adventures in remote places, as Melville and Dana had done. In the period after the Civil War, a newly confident nation, deeply interested in itself and in the larger world, produced a number of descriptions of America, Europe, and England. Bayard Taylor (1825–78) wrote interestingly about many different journeys he made to California, Egypt, Turkey, India, China, and other exotic spots. Mark *Twain in *The Innocents Abroad* (1869), *Roughing It* (1872), *Following the Equator* (1897), *A Tramp Abroad* (1880), and *Life on the Mississippi* (1883) employed the travelbook structure for his humorous and perceptive comments on American views of the world at large. Henry *James used the travel form in such works as *Italian Hours* (1909), *Portraits of Places* (1883), and *A Little Tour of France* (1885). When James's travel writings, his criticism—notably in the volumes *The Art of Fiction* (1884), *French Poets and Novelists* (1878), and in the prefaces to the New York Edition of his *Novels and Tales*—and his autobiography (1913–17) are viewed as a whole, James is seen as one of the major and most effective writers of nonfiction whom America produced after the Civil War.

William Dean Howells (1839–1920) wrote in the early portion of his career on *Venetian Life* (1866) and *Italian Journeys* (1867); and in later years, many charming accounts of voyages to England and to the Continent. He is like James in the variety of his interests; he wrote good critical studies attempting to define realism, which are scattered through numerous journals with which he was associated. He gathered some of them in *Criticism and Fiction* (1891), *Heroines of Fiction* (1901), and *Literature and Life* (1902). He also produced seven volumes of autobiography, among them *A Boy's Town* (1890) and *My Year in a Log Cabin* (1893).

Autobiography found its most effective American spokesman perhaps in Henry *Adams, whose *History of the United States During the Administrations of Jefferson and Madison* (1889–91) was an outstanding accomplishment, whose *Mont-Saint-Michel and Chartes* (1904) is a philosophical attempt to reconstruct the essence of medieval life, and whose *Education of Henry Adams,* privately published in 1906, is, along with Franklin's autobiography, one of the two most distinguished examples of the form written by Americans.

"Literary Comedians." This was also the era of the literary comedians, who, in dialect, in the essay, and in exaggeration, found sources for significant humorous expression that is peculiarly American. Charles Farrar *Browne, who wrote as "Artemus Ward"; David Ross Locke (1833–88), who used the pen name "Petroleum V. Nasby"; Charles H. Smith (1826–1903), who commented as "Bill Arp"; and Edgar W. Nye (1850–96) all found large national audiences and told them much that was not only amusing but also pertinent both as comment and criticism. One of the most significant practitioners in the genre in this and the following century was Finley Peter *Dunne.

Social Criticism. New to the interest of post–Civil War America was the growing dissatisfaction U.S. writers felt with the burgeoning capitalistic industrialism that was given an unchecked role as the dominant force in the nation's life by the Civil War and by the removal from serious debate of an agrarian as opposed to an urban culture. One of the early clear expressions of this concern was Walt *Whitman's *Democratic Vistas* (1871), a prophetic indictment of the emptiness of modern America. Much of the writing in this period is concerned with economic and social reform. About the beginning of the 20th century a group of writers critical of the direction and nature of American life wrote extensively in *Collier's, Cosmopolitan, McClure's,* and other magazines and in books attacking the political and business organization of early 20th-century America. Called muckrakers, they expressed serious social and political dissatisfaction. The most distinguished of their books were Ida M. Tarbell's (1857–1944) *History of the Standard Oil Company* (1903) and Lincoln Steffens' (1866–1936) *The Shame of the Cities* (1904). Steffens later, in his *Autobiography* (1931), continued to do distinctive work, with a marked emphasis on social criticism.

Essay and Literary Criticism. The familiar essay continued to find practitioners, notably Agnes *Repplier, whose many volumes of witty and graceful essays included *In Our Convent Days* (1905), *Books and Men* (1888), and *Points of View* (1891). Louise Imogen *Guiney, in her several volumes of essays, notably *A Little English Gallery* (1894) and *Patrins* (1897), was devoted to restoring to fame forgotten literary worthies. Other prolific essayists were Donald Grant Mitchell (1822–1908), John Muir (1838–1914), and John Burroughs (1837–1921), all of whom wrote well on nature.

The literary criticism of the age was centered in the long controversy between the supporters of a sentimentalized romantic world, such as that defended by the novelist F. Marion *Crawford in *The Novel—What It Is* (1893), and those who demanded that all writing, imaginative or factual, bear a definable and undistorted relationship to the actualities of the real world. This conflict, known as "the realism war," resulted in many essays that debated the issue, the most distinctive of these being the work of Hamlin Garland (1860–1940) in *Crumbling Idols* (1894), William Dean Howells, and to a limited degree Henry James. Certainly the group of prefaces that James prepared for the New York edition of his *Novels and Tales* remains one of the most impressive single bodies of critical material by an American writer in all of U.S. literary history.

Conflict between Idealism and Science. The period after the Civil War saw the philosophical questions that

Transcendentalism had tended to treat as basically epistemological undergo the shift that was, as many have pointed out, inevitable as an outgrowth of the conflict of idealism and science. The most seminal mind of the age was that of William *James, who defined *pragmatism with clarity and grace and probed the essence of truth and value. In such works as *The Will to Believe* (1897), *Pragmatism* (1907), *A Pluralistic Universe* (1909), and *The Varieties of Religious Experience* (1902), where the truth of religion is measured by the degree of emotional satisfaction it offers, he gave expression to an essentially optimistic view of man in society. One of his disciples, John *Dewey, made extensive applications of James's basic principles to the nature of man, art, and society, with unusual emphasis on the role of education in shaping the future. The controversy over evolution led John Fiske (1842–1901), in works such as *The Outline of Cosmic Philosophy* (1874) and *Darwinism and Other Essays* (1879), to try to transplant the ideas of Herbert *Spencer to American soil. George *Santayana, a Catholic (as he said) in everything except faith, presented counterviews to those of James and Dewey, concentrating on aesthetic experience in works such as *The Sense of Beauty* (1896) and formulating an essentially idealistic philosophy in many other works. Toward the end of his life he published his charming and thoughtful memoirs (3 v. 1944–53).

The period between the Civil War and World War I has justly been called "the age of the magazine." In 1850 *Harper's* began a fruitful life that still continues. In 1857 it was joined by the *Atlantic Monthly,* still an active force in American writing. The *Catholic World* began in 1865, as did the *Nation,* edited until 1881 by E. L. Godkin (1831–1902). *Scribner's Monthly,* in its brief career (1870–81), was probably the first truly national magazine in America, and it revolutionized an always fluid medium. In 1914 the *New Republic* began. In these journals and in hundreds like them, the magazine became not only a major vehicle for fiction and poetry, but the principal publishing forum for the familiar essay, the critical review, and the informative article.

After World War I. In the period following World War I, U.S. literature of a belletristic nature came into its own. Eugene *O'Neill established drama as a major form, and the "new poetry" vigorously expressed its discontent about America and Americanism. The American novel had become a major art form of international proportions. The familiar essay continued in the work of many writers and proved to be a device for humorous and often profound comment by authors such as E. B. White (1899–), James Thurber (1894–1961), Christopher Morley (1890–1957), and a number of others.

Literary and Social Criticism. The most important single type of writing in this age, however, was literary and social criticism. Important among the literary critics were Paul Elmer More (1864–1937), whose *Shelburne Essays* (14 v. 1904–36) defined an essentially Platonic and Thomistic view of life and art, and Irving Babbitt (1865–1933), whose *Rousseau and Romanticism* (1919) and *Democracy and Leadership* (1924) became basic documents in a critical movement, the new humanism, which aimed at restoring the humane tradition, although without firm religious foundation. H. L. Mencken (1880–1956), in his work on the magazines *Smart Set* and *American Mercury,* wrote trenchantly about life and art in America, later publishing many of these essays in *A Book of Prefaces* (1917) and in a series of volumes entitled *Prejudices* (1919–27). Mencken's three-volume autobiography, *Happy Days* (1940), *Newspaper Days*

Fig. 5. H. L. Mencken.

(1941), and *Heather Days* (1943), is distinguished for its pungent style. Van Wyck Brooks (1886–1963) was also a critic of American life as a subject for art and America as a home for the artist. In *America's Coming of Age* (1915) and *The Pilgrimage of Henry James* (1922) he argued for Americans' need to discover their useful past. Brooks grew mellow as he aged, and out of this mellowness and his concern for the past he fashioned his five-volume history of writing in 19th-century America, *Finders and Makers,* each published under a separate title (1936–52).

Vernon L. Parrington (1871–1929), a literary historian with an effective style, described the course of American literary and cultural history in *The Main Currents of American Thought* (1928–30). V. F. Calverton (1900–40) in *The Liberation of American Literature* (1932) and Granville Hicks (1901–) in *The Great Tradition* (1933) applied liberal political stances to the examination of the literary past.

The "new critics" during the 1930s and 1940s developed a highly intensive, analytical, and formal approach, particularly to poetry, based upon the examination of the work as autonomous in itself. Among these critics were R. P. Blackmur (1904–), Allen Tate (1899–), Robert Penn Warren (1905–), John Crowe Ransom (1888–), and Cleanth Brooks (1906–). Warren, Tate, and Ransom, together with Donald Davidson (1893–), were leaders in the group that as "Twelve Southerners" published *I'll Take My Stand* (1930), a volume that argued the virtues of the agrarian way of life and insisted on a strong religious orientation essentially Catholic in nature. Ransom also wrote feelingly about the spiritual emptiness of modern America in *God without Thunder* (1930). Other approaches to the problem of religion in the modern world included Reinhold Niebuhr's (1892–) *The Nature and Destiny of Man* (2 v. 1941, 1943) and Paul Tillich's (1886–) *Systematic Theology* (2 v. 1951, 1959). Each attempted to relate man significantly to a God-centered order through applications of Protestant assumptions.

Travel, Biography, History. Ernest Hemingway (1899–1961) continued the travel tradition with *The Green Hills of Africa* (1932) and *Death in the Afternoon* (1935); his posthumously published *A Moveable Feast* (1964) was a distinctive memoir. Other important records of personal experience included John Reed's (1887–1920) *Ten Days That Shook the World* (1919), an excellent eyewitness account of the Bolshevik revolution; Floyd Dell's (1887–) *Homecoming* (1933); and Gertrude Stein's (1874–1946) personal record under the persona of her secretary-companion, *The Autobiography of Alice B. Toklas* (1933).

A great deal of biographical writing has been done in America since World War I. Gamaliel Bradford (1863–1932), a prolific writer of biographical studies who aimed at uncovering inner motive—he called his works "psychographs"—was typical of a widespread interest in the psychological springs of action and in the debunking of major historical figures. His best-known book was *Damaged Souls* (1923). Of a different order was the vast study of Abraham Lincoln undertaken by Carl Sandburg (1878–), the first two volumes of which appeared in 1926 and the remaining four in 1939. Douglas Southall Freeman (1886–1953) in *Robert E. Lee* (4 v. 1934), *Lee's Lieutenant's* (3 v. 1942–44), and *George Washington* (6 v. 1948–54) joined Sandburg as an outstanding American biographer of the century.

Among the many historians, four make unusually strong claims on the basis of literary merit. Charles A. Beard (1874–1948) and Mary R. Beard (1876–1958) joined their talents in the production of the beautifully written *The Rise of American Civilization* (2 v. 1927). Bernard De Voto (1897–1955) wrote with great effectiveness of the cultural history of the early Middle West in works such as *Mark Twain's America* (1932), *The Year of Decision* (1943), and *Across the Wide Missouri* (1947). The considerable work of Peter *Guilday and William Thomas *Walsh spanned several decades in this era. Guilday's studies (*The Life of John Gilmary Shea,* 1926; *The Life and Times of John England,* 1928; and *The Life and Times of John Carroll, Archbishop of Baltimore,* 1954) were pioneer ventures

Fig. 6. Carl Sandburg.

in the history of U.S. Catholicism; Walsh's biographies of Spanish figures (e.g., *Isabella of Spain: The Last Crusader,* 1930; *Philip II,* 1937), if somewhat partisan, were stylistically distinguished. A similar distinction marks the work of Garrett Mattingly (e.g., *Catherine of Aragon,* 1930). Arthur M. Schlesinger, Jr. (1917–) wrote with great skill in *The Age of Jackson* (1945) and had completed in 1965 three volumes (1957, 1959, 1960) in his study of *The Age of* [Franklin D.] *Roosevelt.* Great gifts for catching the essential spirit of a period are evident in the work of Paul Horgan (1903– ; e.g., the Pulitzer prize winning *Great River: The Rio Grande in North American History,* 1954; *The Centuries of Santa Fe,* 1956), in Thomas Merton's (1915–) *The Seven Storey Mountain* (1948), and in Charles Lindbergh's (1902–) *The Spirit of St. Louis* (1953). Lindbergh's wife, Anne Morrow (1906–), was lyrically philosophical in *Gift from the Sea* (1955). Samuel Eliot Morison (1887–), whose specialty is naval history, wrote a superb life of Columbus, *Admiral of the Ocean Sea* (1942), and a beautifully effective record of his nation in *The Oxford History of the American People* (1965). One of the most charming and significant autobiographies was *The Manner is Ordinary* (1957) by John *LaFarge, SJ, a pioneer in race relations and other social movements.

Nonfiction continues to be the most popular vehicle for the communication of ideas, the study of movements, and the comprehension of the self and the nation. Although today it takes itself with great seriousness and indeed on occasion with an oppressive earnestness, in the hands of some of the best writers it still can and does lift itself on the appealing wings of grace and humor and thus enriches and delights while it instructs.

Bibliography: The best study of and guide to nonfiction in the literature of the U.S. is Spiller LitH; v.1. contains essays by more than 50 experts, and v.2 is the best bibliog. guide. J. BLANCK, comp., *Bibliography of American Literature* (New Haven 1955–). C. L. F. GOHDES, *Bibliographical Guide to the Study of the Literature of the U.S.A.* (2d ed. Durham, N.C. 1963), indispensable. A. H. QUINN, ed., *The Literature of the American People* (New York 1951), excellent, judicious, and thorough. F. L. MOTT, *A History of American Magazines,* 4 v. (New York 1930–38; repr. Cambridge, Mass. 1957). H. W. SCHNEIDER, *A History of American Philosophy* (New York 1946) and M. E. CURTI, *The Growth of American Thought* (2d ed. New York 1951) for philos. and religion. S. PERSONS, *American Minds* (New York 1958), for the history of ideas. F. STOVALL, ed., *The Development of American Literary Criticism* (Chapel Hill, N.C. 1955). W. BLAIR, ed., *Native American Humor (1800–1900)* (San Francisco 1960), with a long excellent introd. **Illustration credits:** Figs. 1 and 3, Rare Book Department, Free Library of Philadelphia. Fig. 2, Tracy W. McGregor Library, University of Virginia. Fig. 4, Library of Congress, Brady-Handy Collection. Fig. 5, Courtesy of Alfred A. Knopf. Fig. 6, William A. Smith, Pinesville, Pa.

[C. H. HOLMAN]

2. DRAMA

The history of dramatic art in the U.S. roughly parallels that of the struggle for political independence: like the Republic, the drama had to throw off a foreign yoke; it had to choose between expediency and idealism; if it faltered on occasion, yet it was sustained by individual, strong men; if its representatives gave way at times to sentimentality and empty oratory, it finally found its own voice and spirit. The following survey traces the stages of this development.

Early History—17th and 18th Centuries. The first recorded drama on the North American continent—apart from Indian ceremonials—was a Spanish religious play performed on Corpus Christi Day in 1538, in what is now Mexico. The first play inside U.S. limits was a *comedia* "on a subject connected with the conquest of New Mexico," performed on the banks of the Rio

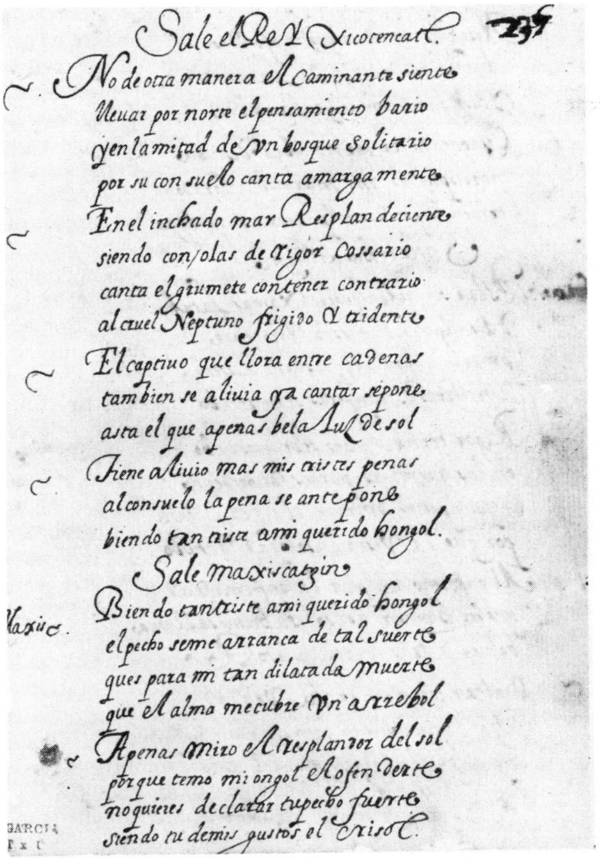
Sale el Rey Xicotencatl
No de otra manera el caminante siente
llevar por norte el pensamiento vario
y en la mitad de un bosque solitario
por su consuelo canta amargamente
En el inchado mar resplandeciente
siendo consolas de rigor cossario
canta el grumete contener contrario
al cruel Neptuno fingido el tridente
El captiuo que llora entre cadenas
tambien se aliuia ya cantar se pone
asta el que apenas bela luz de sol
tiene aliuio mas mis tristes penas
al consuelo la pena se antepone
biendo tan triste a mi querido bongol.
Sale Maxixcatzin
Biendo tan triste a mi querido bongol
el pecho se me arranca de tal suerte
ques para mi tan dilatada muerte
que el alma me cubre un arrebol
Apenas miro el resplandor del sol
porque temo mi ongol el ofendente
no quieres declarar tu pecho fuerte
siendo tu demis gustos el crisol.

Fig. 7. Page from the unique manuscript of the play "Coloquio de la nueva conbersion y bautismo de los quator ultimos reyes de Tlaxcala en la Nueva España," first performed in what is now Texas in 1598.

Grande (1598). In Canada, a French masque was recorded in 1606. The first play in English was *The Bear and The Cub,* acted in Accomac County, Va. (1665). William Darby, its author, and two fellow actors were called before a magistrate to explain their dalliance with the dubious art of drama but were found not guilty; it is supposed that the Cavalier South was more hospitable to the art than the Puritan North. In 1702 students at William and Mary College recited a "pastoral colloquy" before their Governor Berkeley, who is said to have written plays himself. Since the first play printed in America (*Androboros,* 1714) is attributed to Robert Hunter (d. 1734), Governor of the Province of New York, it is apparent that tolerance of drama gradually crept north. The first professional playwright was a vagabond actor named Anthony Aston, who wrote in his journal (1703): "We arrived in Charles-town, full of Lice, Shame, Nakedness, Hunger, and Poverty. I turned Player and Poet and wrote one play on the subject of the Country." There were to be many efforts to write such a play, efforts that formed the early period of colonial drama.

Williamsburg had a theater in 1716, and Charleston one in 1736, but playhouses were improvised in New York until Lewis Hallam's (1714–56) American Company opened a theater there on Nassau Street in 1753. In every colony players suffered from "legal statutes, clerical frowns, exigencies of war, yellow fever, and the copyright bogey," though all these plagues did not descend at once. Hallam countered "clerical frowns" with the advertised contention that plays such as Shakespeare's were "moral lectures."

The First Native Play. If history were neater, the first play by an American to be acted would have been *Ponteach* (1766), written by Major Robert Rogers (1731–95), an Indian fighter who in his plays treated his old enemy with sympathy and admiration; but Rogers could not find a producer. Instead, the first was *The Prince of Parthia,* by Thomas Godfrey (1736–63), an imitative, neoclassic pseudotragedy written in 1759 and performed by Hallam's company in 1767. It was written as a substitute for *The Disappointment,* a comic opera that the younger Lewis Hallam (1740–1808) cancelled because he feared that its satire of American types would give offense. Godfrey's play is the sort of exotic romance that held the stage for a century.

In 1774 the Congress drew up a resolution that forbade such extravagances as stage plays, gaming, and cockfighting. The British boasted that playhouses remained open in Tory territory, and Fanueil Hall in Boston was converted into a theater, where a farce by Burgoyne is supposed to have been interrupted by news of the Battle of Breed's Hill. Eventually, the political conflict affected all dramatic activity. Satires were written on both sides: those of Mrs. Mercy Warren (1728–1814), *The Adulateur* (1773) and *The Group* (1775), were among the most distinguished of the colonial contributions; but because they were circulated only in print and not staged, they were hardly drama in any serious sense. Addison's *Cato* was performed, however crudely, for the soldiers at Valley Forge; *The Recruiting Officer* was in rehearsal there when more pressing matters intervened. And John Leacock wrote an unproduced chronicle-pageant, *The Fall of British Tyranny* (1776). In these various ways the drama did its bit in the fight for freedom, usually in the colonial taverns that often served as impromptu theaters during these years.

The Real Beginning. The Contrast (1787) by Royall Tyler (1757–1826) marks the true beginning of American drama. Like many subsequent plays, it copied a foreign model (Sheridan's *The School for Scandal*), and its "contrast" of the honest, upright Yankee, Colonel Manly, with the pompous, deceitful Dimple was repeated many times in later plays; another of its characters, Jonathan, the shrewd, down-to-earth, cracker-barrel American, became a stock figure in much subsequent drama. When the play was printed (1790), George Washington's name headed the subscription list, indicating a measure of respectability, though when it was acted in Boston it was still announced as a "moral lecture." Even though born in Boston, Tyler overcame Puritan abhorrence of the drama and wrote other plays, two of which were produced; none were as influential as his first.

If Tyler was the pioneer, William Dunlap (1766–1839) was the first settler. He was a producer, a playwright, and the first historian of the native drama (*A History of American Drama,* 1832). His practices set a pattern for the next century: He wrote romantic dramas on American history (*Major Andre,* 1789); he provided vehicles for actors (*Darby's Return,* 1789); he dramatized gothic novels (*Fontainville Abbey,* 1795); and adapted foreign plays (Kotzebue's *The Stranger,* 1798). Even his dreams and his economic destiny were

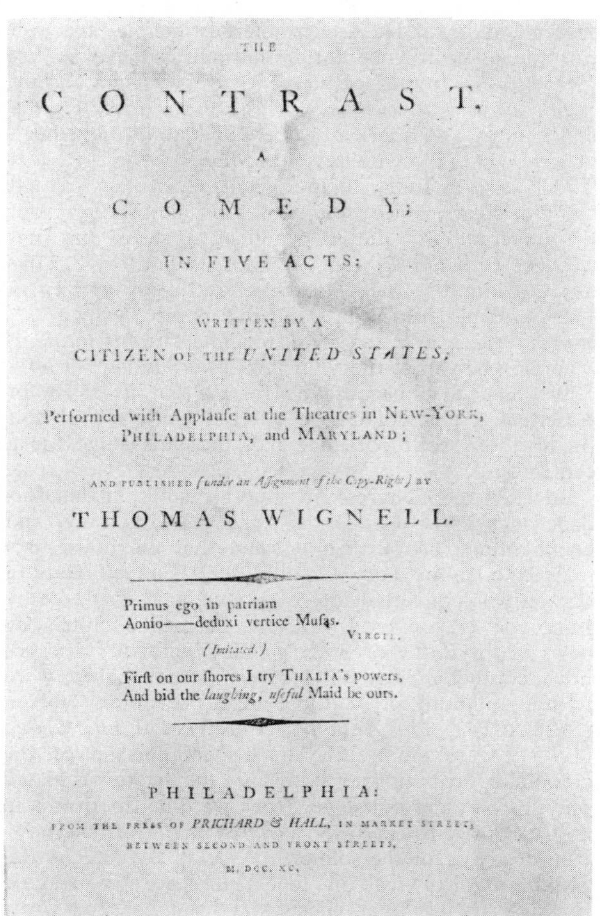
THE

CONTRAST,

A

COMEDY;

IN FIVE ACTS:

WRITTEN BY A

CITIZEN OF THE UNITED STATES;

Performed with Applaufe at the Theatres in NEW-YORK, PHILADELPHIA, and MARYLAND;

AND PUBLISHED (under an Affignment of the Copy-Right) BY

THOMAS WIGNELL.

Primus ego in patriam
Aonio——deduxi vertice Mufas.
VIRGIL.

(Imitated.)

Firft on our fhores I try THALIA's powers,
And bid the laughing, ufeful Maid be ours.

PHILADELPHIA:

FROM THE PRESS OF PRICHARD & HALL, IN MARKET STREET, BETWEEN SECOND AND FRONT STREETS.

M. DCC. XC.

Fig. 8. Title page of an edition of "The Contrast" printed in Philadelphia in 1790, shortly after its successful first performance in 1787.

prophetic, for he had visions of a government-supported theater. After many tribulations as a manager Dunlap went bankrupt in 1805, but he had earned his title of Father of the American Theater.

The 19th Century. Translations from the French or German, English adaptations, and truncated versions of Shakespeare's work dominated the stage at the beginning of the 19th century, but those American plays that were written and performed were in many cases no worse than the foreign imports. Susanna Rowson (1762–1824) was the first woman playwright whose work was acted; her farce, *The Female Patriot* (1795), is based on Philip Massinger's *Bondman.* John Murdoch's *The Triumph of Love* (1795) satirized the Quakers and introduced an early version of a standardized Negro character, Sambo.

More expert was the work of James Nelson Barker (1784–1858), later the mayor of Philadelphia. His *Tears and Smiles* (1807) was an echo of *The Contrast;* it even contained a character named Nathan Yank, blood brother of Jonathan. Barker's version of the Pocahontas story, *The Indian Princess* (1808), was the first play by an American to be presented in London. Foreign authors were still preferred in America, however, and Barker's dramatization of Scott's *Marmion* (1812) was announced as the work of an Englishman.

John Howard Payne (1791–1852), who improved his popularity by frequent productions in London, wrote *Brutus* (1818) in imitation of British neoclassic plays; his *Clari, or The Maid of Milan* (1823) introduced "Home, Sweet Home," a song America sang for a century. Payne collaborated with Washington Irving on *Charles II* (1824), but Irving's part was kept secret, indicating the reluctance of a respectable man of letters to be associated in public with the muse of drama.

Indians, Burlesque, Rhetoric. In 1828 the popular actor Edwin Forrest (1806–72), who was regarded by many theatergoers as "their champion against English superiority," offered a prize for a play about an "aboriginal." He received 200 manuscripts and chose *Metamora, or The Last of the Wampanoags,* by John Augustus Stone (1800–34). Forrest acted the role of the noble, eloquent savage off and on for the rest of his career. Indian plays became so plentiful that one commentator complained (1845) that "Indian plays have of late become perfect *nuisances.*" Burlesques impeded their growth, but did not stop them; the most famous of these was by John Brougham (1810–80), an Irish-born comedian whose *Po-ca-hon-tas* (1855) was subtitled "an Original, Aboriginal, Erratic, Operatic, Semi-civilized and Demi-savage Extravaganza," evidence in itself of an Irish contribution to the national sense of humor. Forrest had a voice of "prodigious volume and melody" and looked for plays in which to exercise it. Similar rhetorical opportunity was provided by Robert M. Bird's *The Gladiator* (1831), which clothed abolitionist sentiments in Roman trappings, and in *De Soto* (1857) by George Henry Miles (1824–71), a teacher at Mt. St. Mary's College, Emmitsburg, Md., and the first Catholic playwright of significance. It was a time of orators, on and off the stage, which partly explains the popularity of Shakespeare, whose plays were trimmed to accentuate the "big speeches."

Domestic Melodrama. The domestic scene often replaced the exotic as a setting for melodramatic thrills. The novel by Harriet Beecher Stowe (1811–96), *Uncle Tom's Cabin* (1852), was dramatized within 6 months of publication. The New York *Herald* commented, "The thing is in bad taste . . . a firebrand of the most dangerous character," and the play closed. A year later it began a spectacular career in a version by George Aiken (1830–76) commissioned by actor-manager George Howard, who starred his wife and daughter as Topsy and Eva. It was acted in every U.S. theater and also in London and Paris; in New York, at one point, three performances a day were given. The play was reputed to have won many new patrons for the theater; certainly its popularity continued long after the Civil War. Its final significance may be seen more in the effect it had on popular melodrama than in its abolitionism. In like manner, the success of W. H. Smith's *The Drunkard* (1844) may have been a result more of the evil of excessive sentimentality than the evil of excessive drink. A dramatization of Mrs. Henry Wood's novel *East Lynne* (1863), *The Old Homestead* (1886) by Denman Thompson, *Way Down East* (1898) by Lottie Parker, and like pieces carried the domestic melodrama to the end of the century, just as William Young's dramatization of Lew Wallace's *Ben Hur* (1889) perpetuated the exotic thriller.

Comedy Types and Improving Tastes. Comedy created its recognizable types, the opposite numbers of the public and domestic heroes. The plays in which they appear are trivial, but that matters little since, portrayed as they were by popular actors who specialized in certain "lines," they seldom have much to do with the plot. Tyler's Jonathan appeared in various guises under such names as Zachariah Dickerwell, Solomon Swap, Industrious Doolittle, and Jedediah Homebred, and outwitted the city (or foreign) slicker every time. As the focus of American life shifted to the city, urban types sprang up, notably Mose the fire boy, who, with his red hat and black boots, moved through a series of sequels. The melting pot was reflected in the depiction of immigrant types, as in the Mulligan Guard plays of Edward Harrigan (1845–1911); this interest culminated, in the next century, in Anne Nichol's *Abie's Irish Rose* (1922), the despair of critics and the delight of audiences; it set the long-run record of its day.

There were exceptions: plays that followed the pattern but were distinguished by careful observation or skillful playmaking. Anna Cora Mowatt's (1819–70) *Fashion* (1845) is a genuine comedy of manners. If Mrs. Tiffany is a cousin of Mrs. Malaprop, she at least is freshly drawn. Edgar Allan Poe, whose parents were actors and whose drama criticism for the Broadway *Journal* was the voice of taste in a wilderness of mediocrity, called *Fashion* "in many respects superior to any American play." It was performed for three consecutive weeks at a time when protracted engagements were rare.

Francesca da Rimini (1855) was a conscious attempt by George Henry Boker (1823–90) to elevate the drama by casting a story taken from Dante into blank verse. Poe had said: "The Elizabethan theatre should be abandoned. We need thought of our own. . . ." But since Shakespeare's work was both popular and highly regarded, it is easy to understand Boker's desire to imitate the best. He has been highly praised, even by modern scholars of American drama. The play was revived in 1882; but its light has dimmed, and it is now almost indistinguishable from *The Prince of Parthia.*

Impact of the Civil War. The Civil War had very little immediate effect on drama. Edwin Booth (1833–93) shone as Macbeth and Richard III, and Joseph Jefferson III (1829–1905) developed a definitive version of *Rip Van Winkle.* When Booth's brother, John Wilkes, assassinated President Lincoln during a performance of *Our American Cousin* (an English comedy reminiscent of *The Contrast*), feeling ran high for a time against actors; but when the crisis passed, Edwin returned to act Hamlet more gloriously than ever. Plays written in the period ignored the terrible tensions of the conflict, and 20 years elapsed before its dramatic possibilities were explored.

Managers made attempts to lure literary men into the theater. Mark Twain and Bret Harte collaborated on a comedy called *Ah Sin* (1877), but the play is distinguished chiefly for Twain's witty curtain speech. When an otherwise successful literary man failed in the theater—as William Dean Howells and Thomas Bailey Aldrich did—it was assumed that the fault was an inherent shallowness in drama itself. "The history of American playwriting," said Joseph Wood Krutch, "was never a very important part of the history of American literature until after the twentieth century had well begun." It is true that there is nothing in 19th century American drama to compare with *Moby Dick* or *The Scarlet Letter* or *Huckleberry Finn;* but clearly the drafting of novelists to write plays was no cure.

Dionysius (Dion) Boucicault (1820?–90) was typical of the sort of journeyman writer who lured audiences with thrills and kept the pot boiling until there was meat to put into it. Both his method and value are indicated by his adaptation of a French play, *Les Pauvres de Paris,* into *The Poor of New York;* subsequently, in England, he reworked it into *The Poor of Liverpool* and *The Streets of London;* local color was something he could spray on at will. His Negro and Irish characters, regarded as authentic in his own day, now hardly seem more than stereotypes. In adapting Mayne Reid's (1818–83) novel *The Quadroon* (1856), he further fractioned the heroine's percentage of Negro blood, called the play *The Octoroon* (1859), and accomplished the dubious trick of writing a play about race that offended neither North nor South.

John Augustin *Daly was a force both in raising the level of production and in encouraging native writers. Responsible for some 90 plays, Daly was an adapter and arranger rather than an original writer, though in *Horizon* and *Divorce* (both 1871) he tried to deal with indigenous subjects. He was a superb if tyrannical stage director; his passion for detail and his insistence on

Fig. 9. Cordelia Howard as "Little Eva" in the Aiken production of "Uncle Tom's Cabin," cover to the sheet music for a song in that production.

intensive rehearsal were revolutionary in America. Like other playwrights of the day, he was fond of the "sensation scene" and he and Boucicault waged a legal battle over prior right to tying the hero to railroad tracks (Daly was incontestably the first to feed a heroine into a buzzsaw). William Gillette (1855–1937), a brilliant actor, wrote the first substantial play about the Civil War, *Held by the Enemy* (1886). His eye for stage effect and his feeling for character, however, were more clearly demonstrated in *Secret Service* (1889). Gillette, Boucicault, and Daly were all "practical men of the theatre," artists of real if limited talent who built a tradition and an audience for later writers.

Social Problems. As manager, Daly introduced the work of Bronson Howard (1842–1908) to the stage. "The American dramatist of today," Howard wrote at the end of the century, "has come to make a closer study of American society than his predecessors did." He himself studies big business in *The Henrietta* (1887), and the Civil War in *Shenandoah* (1889). Clyde Fitch (1865–1909) began by writing plays to managerial order (*Nathan Hale,* 1898; *Barbara Frietchie,* 1899); but, encouraged by Howard's lead and affected by the new naturalism emanating from Europe, he turned to the native scene and topical problems in *The Truth* (1907) and *The City* (1910). Sentimentality still ruled in these plays, and the sensation scene remained, though it was transferred from scenic tricks to startling twists of character; still, the advance was noticeable. The old tears and the new purpose coexisted for some time, so that Edward Sheldon (1866–1940) could picture slum life in *Salvation Nell* (1908), big-city politics in *The Boss* (1911), and racial prejudice in *The Nigger* (1909) and yet enjoy his greatest success with *Romance* (1913), a sentimental love story.

Augustus Thomas (1857–1934) began with routine regional plays (*Alabama,* 1891; *In Mizzoura,* 1893), but moved to a topical theme in *The Witching Hour* (1907), which makes melodrama out of occult phenomena. *As a Man Thinks* (1911) challenged the double standard of sexual morality. William Vaughn Moody (1869–1910), a poet of whom much was expected, perceived and presented in *The Great Divide* (1906) the significance of the contrast between the rugged Westerner and the genteel Eastern tradition and created a remarkable study of these materials; his characters have complexity unique in the period. Although it is possible to argue that the melodramatists (Boucicault, Daly, Gillette) possessed a skill and effectiveness lacking in their more serious-minded colleagues, it was in the direction of the social problem play that American serious drama moved.

As melodrama shifted from thrill to problem, so comedy passed from slapstick to satire. The horseplay of Edward Harrigan (1845–1911) and Charles Hoyt (1860–1900) gave way to the engaging sophistication of Langdon Mitchell's *The New York Idea* (1906), which commented sardonically on casual attitudes toward marriage, and of Jesse Lynch Williams's (1871–1929) Pulitzer prize play, *Why Marry?* (1917), which reminded some critics of Bernard *Shaw. Revolution was not total, however, and Booth Tarkington (1869–1946) and George Ade (1866–1944) continued to produce their soft-edge comedies, perpetuating American types. George M. Cohan (1878–1942) was perhaps the most interesting of light comedy writers in the first half of the century. In the old tradition of actor-playwrights, he reconstituted the stage Yankee under the guise of his own cocky, urban, show-business personality in genial rogue farces that ended in reform. He combined folk wisdom with the wise-crack and used the American flag as a prop (he was born on the 4th of July); his plays *Little Johnny Jones* (1904) and *The Yankee Prince* (1908) are a stage in immigrant comedy. He picked up the burlesque tradition in *The Tavern* (1920), which makes fun of the extravagant use of coincidence and the overt passion of the domestic thrillers. Cohan provided a link with the new spirit by appearing in O'Neill's *Ah! Wilderness* (1933) and as President Franklin D. Roosevelt in George Kaufman (1889–1961) and Moss Hart's (1904–61) *I'd Rather be Right* (1937).

The 20th Century. At the turn of the century, when control of industry generally was passing into the hands of small but powerful groups of men, the "syndicate" moved into the theater as well. A band of five men pooled their resources and exercised almost complete sway over American theatrical production. They owned a chain of theaters, prepared their own plays, discouraged innovation, and smashed competition. David Belasco (1853–1931), a lone-wolf producer-director, was the last of a disappearing breed. Known for his clerical collar and his cunning stage effects, Belasco wrote (or had written) plays to fit actors or to exploit ingenious lighting displays. *The Heart of Maryland* (1895) and *The Girl of the Golden West* (1905) contain impressive but superficial detail and are only variants of the old "sensation" play.

"Little Theater" and Other Movements. All promises were fulfilled in Eugene *O'Neill, whose work is the result of what was admirable in the old tradition cross-fertilized by the fresh conceptions of character and social significance imported from Europe; these conceptions had their greatest influence through the "little theater movement." This is a label given to various groups of enthusiastic amateurs who aspired to set up art theaters free of commercial entanglements. *Theatre Arts* magazine was founded (1916) to give voice to the new aspirations, and many amateurs became professionals. The same impetus led to the study of drama in universities, an academic innovation peculiar to the U.S. O'Neill enrolled in the 47 Workshop in Drama under George Pierce Baker (1866–1935) at Harvard, and pioneer departments were set up at Carnegie Tech (1913) and Yale University (1925). In the 1930s, the National Theatre Conference was established to unite college and community theaters. Both these movements have Catholic counterparts: the Loyola Community Theatre in Chicago and the Blackfriars' Guild in New York (which had branches in a dozen cities by 1940) stimulated the organization of the Catholic Theatre Conference in 1937, the same year that a department of speech and drama began at The Catholic University of America in Washington, D.C. (*see* CATHOLIC THEATER MOVEMENT).

O'Neill's plays were first produced by the Provincetown (Mass.) Players, and later by the Theatre Guild of New York, which was founded (1918) "to produce plays of artistic merit not ordinarily produced by commercial managers." O'Neill treated tragic themes without compromise and tailored his work neither to popular actors nor to audience complacency. *The Great God Brown* (1926), which was highly experimental, and *Long Day's Journey into Night* (1956), which was relentlessly naturalistic, show the range of his interest. He was the first American dramatist to win world fame; in 1936 he was awarded the Nobel prize for literature. In Europe the "free theaters" often had a political tinge; this was not true of influential American parallels until the Group Theatre, an offshoot of the Theatre Guild, came into being in 1931. The Group produced the plays of Clifford Odets (1906–63), whose *Waiting for Lefty* (1935) was blatant propaganda, but whose *Golden Boy* (1939) emphasized character rather than message. Dunlap's old dream of a subsidized theater was in a way realized in the Federal Theatre Project (1935) set up to occupy theater artists idled by the Depression. This project at one time employed 10,000 persons in the presentation of all sorts of plays to all sorts of audiences—some seeing live drama for the first time—and developed the "living newspaper" documentary technique for dramatizing social conditions; Arthur Arent's *One Third of a Nation* (1938), the best-known of these, took its title from a phrase in a speech by Pres. Franklin D. Roosevelt. The Federal Theatre ran afoul of congressional suspicion of its radicalism and was abolished in 1939. The American National Theatre and Academy, chartered by Congress in 1935, was actually more like what Dunlap had in mind, but it was entirely dependent on private funds and has never fulfilled the promise of its title.

The formation of the Playwrights' Company (1938) was an attempt to get the reins of production away from businessmen (the Theatre Guild had by then mellowed into cautious middle age), and the dramatists who composed it are convenient representatives of trends between the World Wars. Maxwell Anderson's (1888–1959) *Winterset* (1935) was a bold attempt to write contemporary tragedy in blank verse; it was a fictional account of the aftermath of the celebrated Sacco-Vanzetti trial and hence had a journalistic as well as a poetic interest. Anderson, like Boker before him, was acclaimed in his time but his reputation has since declined. Robert Sherwood (1896–1955) revealed the temper of the time with an allegory that pitted an intellectual against a gunman (who acts suspiciously like a fascist) in *The Petrified Forest* (1935); when the intellectual won, a new cast was given the American hero figure. Sherwood also paid tribute to a traditional hero in *Abe Lincoln in Illinois* (1938). Sidney Howard (1891–1939), who had made an early mark with domestic character studies (e.g., *The Silver Cord,* 1926), caught the excitement of medical research in *Yellow Jack* (1934). Elmer Rice (1892–) is more likely to be remembered for *Street Scene* (1929), a naturalistic drama of tenement life, and for *The Adding Machine* (1931), an expressionistic play about the mechanization of modern man, than for his later work.

Comedy of Manners. Samuel N. Behrman (1893–), the fifth member of the Playwrights Company, shared with George Kelly (1887–) and Philip *Barry the distinction of keeping alive the comedy of manners in a time when most playwrights were recollecting emotion in indignation. The new realism after World War I led to comedies such as Laurence Stalling's (in collaboration with Anderson) *What Price Glory?* (1924), and Ben Hecht and Charles MacArthur's *The Front Page* (1928), which struck a robust, iconoclastic note typically American. George S. Kaufman (1889–1961) took up this hard-bitten tradition and in a series of collaborations produced sharp-tongued comedies satirizing middle-class complacency. He reached a peak of accomplishment with Morris Ryskind in *Of Thee I Sing* (1931), for which George Gershwin wrote the music. This play provided a merrily cynical view of a presidential campaign in which the candidate was elected on a platform of romantic love, and its blows were aimed at the broad sentimental streak that runs through American life—and American drama. Kaufman wrote impolite comedy but stopped short of Aristophanic insult. Howard Lindsay (1899–) and Russel Crouse (1893–) offered a classic comic view of the 19th-century no-nonsense, areligious, businessman in *Life with Father* (1939).

Fig. 10. A scene from the 1956 New York production of Eugene O'Neill's "Long Day's Journey into Night."

Kelly, Barry, and Behrman were literate makers of polite comedy. Kelly was the most enigmatic of the three: his short play *The Torchbearers* (1922) makes fun of the antic fringes of the Little Theater Movement; *The Showoff* (1924) caricatured the self-made braggart. There was in his work no obvious trace of his Catholic background. Barry, also a Catholic, whose play *The Joyous Season* (1934) was remarkable because it departed from stereotyped religious characters in its presentation of an intelligent and witty nun, revealed a compassion for the rich in *Holiday* (1928) and in *The Philadelphia Story* (1929). Behrman combined a sense of social responsibility with a sense of high comedy in *End of Summer* (1938) and objectified the dilemma of the comic writer in a time of crisis with *No Time for Comedy* (1939). William Saroyan (1908–) created a brief flurry with such whimsical plays as *The*

Time of Your Life (1939) and belied his Armenian ancestry with the thoroughly American advice to other writers: "Forget anybody who ever wrote anything."

Musical Comedy. In the 1930s musical comedy, thought by many historians to be the most original and artistic American contribution to drama, became immensely popular. It had begun accidentally in a girl-show called *The Black Crook* (1867) and had survived with fluctuating value as a combination of vaudeville, burlesque, and Viennese light opera. Edna Ferber's (1887–) *Show Boat* (1928), with Jerome Kern's music and Oscar Hammerstein II's (1895–1960) book and lyrics, showed what soaring music and a vigorous story could accomplish. George Gershwin's (1898–1937) *Porgy and Bess* (1936) is folk opera with a jazz beat and vivid characters. Richard Rodgers (1902–) carried the form into two distinct areas: sardonic and clever in his work with Lorenz Hart (*Pal Joey,* 1940), and sunny and sentimental in his collaborations with Oscar Hammerstein II, of which *Oklahoma* (1943) is the most influential because it welds story, score, and dancing into an artistic whole. *My Fair Lady* (1956), by Alan Lerner (1918–) and Frederick Loewe (1904–) illustrates the range of the form by capturing the quality of Shaw's *Pygmalion.*

Mid-Century Development. After World War II, two general lines of dramatic development can be traced. Thornton Wilder (1897–) reaffirmed the possibility of the American dream; Arthur Miller (1915–) and Tennessee Williams (1914–) questioned it. Miller achieved middle-class tragedy in *Death of a Salesman* (1949), a terrifying account of the nightmare into which the dream can turn. Williams added verbal splendor to the greatest talent since O'Neill in *The Glass Menagerie* (1945) and *A Streetcar Named Desire* (1947). After these men the drama passed, in the 1960s, into another period of European imitation, evident in the "off-Broadway" devotion to foreign plays and in native versions of the *theater of the absurd. Wilder was one of the few American playwrights of whom it can be said that the Christian tradition informs his work (*Our Town,* 1939, and *The Skin of Our Teeth,* 1942). He was a unique figure also because, as both successful dramatist and leading novelist, he apparently realized the desire of 19th-century managers and critics to reconcile American literature in general with American drama.

Fig. 11. Scene from the original New York production of Thornton Wilder's "Skin of Our Teeth," 1942.

Bibliography: O. S. Coad and E. Mims, *The American Stage* (New Haven 1929). B. Hewitt, *Theatre U.S.A., 1668–1957* (New York 1959). J. W. Krutch, *The American Drama since 1918* (rev. ed. New York 1957). G. C. D. Odell, *Annals of the New York Stage,* 15 v. (New York 1927–49). A. H. Quinn, *A History of the American Drama,* 2 v. (2d ed. New York 1943) v.1 *From the Beginning to the Civil War,* v.2 *From the Civil War to the Present Day.* C. M. Smith, *Musical Comedy in America* (New York 1950). A. S. Downer, *Fifty Years of American Drama: 1900–1950* (Chicago 1951). I. Goldberg, *The Drama of Transition* (Cincinnati 1922). G. Hughes, *A History of the American Theater: 1700–1950* (New York 1951). G. J. Nathan, *The Theatre in the Fifties* (New York 1953). A. S. Downer, ed., *American Drama* (New York 1960). J. Gassner, ed., *Best American Plays [1916–1962]* (New York 1939–63); suppl. v. *1918–1958* (New York 1961). A. H. Quinn, ed., *Representative American Plays* (New York 1917). C. J. Stratman, *Bibliography of the American Theatre, excluding New York City* (Chicago 1965). W. Rigdon, ed., *The Biographical Encyclopaedia and Who's Who of the American Theatre* (New York 1966). **Illustration credits:** Fig. 7, The Garcia Collection, The Library of the University of Texas. Fig. 8, The New York Public Library, Theatre Collection. Fig. 9, Museum of City of New York. Fig. 10, New York Public Library, Theatre Collection; photo by Gjon Mili. Fig. 11, New York Public Library Theatre Collection; photo by George Karger of Pix, Inc., N.Y.C.

[L. BRADY]

3. POETRY

"Beware of a boundless and sickly appetite for the reading of poems which now the rickety nation swarms withal . . .," was the advice of Cotton Mather in 1726 to young men preparing for the ministry.

Puritan Culture. Such counsel suggests that although poetry was not completely ignored in the Puritan culture, it assuredly had a limited place. *The Bay Psalm Book* (1640), the first book issued in the English colonies of North America, was intended to be a literal translation of the Psalms, in which accuracy was more important than poetic excellence: "God's Altar needs not our polishings." The most widely read poetic work was Michael Wigglesworth's (1631–1705) *The Day of Doom* (1662), written to renew the orthodox Puritan view of God's way with the damned and the elect. Although much of her verse is dull and didactic, some of the poetry of Anne Bradstreet (1612?–72) is still worthy of attention. Her *Contemplations* skillfully evoke the physical beauty of New England; the personal poems (pub. 1678), reveal the things close to her heart. The most significant Puritan poet, however, was Edward Taylor (1645?–1729), a minister, whose poems were not published until the 20th century. His poetry, more sensuous and highly colored than that of his U.S. contemporaries, resembles that of George Herbert and Richard *Crashaw, yet he is equally able to use well homely images and simple experience. His religious

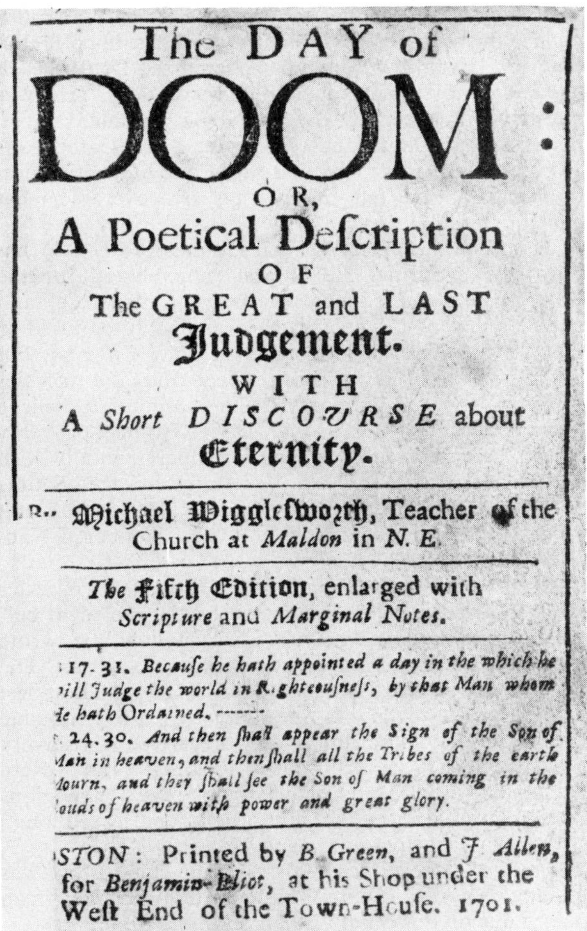

The DAY of

DOOM:

OR,

A Poetical Description

OF

The GREAT and LAST

Judgement.

WITH

A Short DISCOURSE about

Eternity.

...Michael Wigglesworth, Teacher of the Church at *Maldon* in *N. E.*

The Fifth Edition, enlarged with *Scripture* and *Marginal Notes.*

17.31. *Because he hath appointed a day in the which he ...ill Judge the world in Righteousness, by that Man whom ...e hath Ordained.* -------

24.30. *And then shall appear the Sign of the Son of ...an in heaven, and then shall all the Tribes of the earth ...ourn, and they shall see the Son of Man coming in the ...ouds of heaven with power and great glory.*

...STON: Printed by *B. Green*, and *J. Allen*, for *Benjamin Eliot*, at his Shop under the West End of the Town-House. 1701.

Fig. 12. Title page of "The Day of Doom" by Michael Wigglesworth, published in Boston, 1701, 5th edition. This copy is the earliest known of the American editions.

fervor is the major impulse for most of his poems, especially the famous *Meditations*. With his strong sense of emotion and his powerful imagination, he was the most gifted poet in America before Bryant. (*See* PURITANISM AND LITERATURE.)

Reason and Revolution. There was no dearth of poetic activity during the era of the Enlightenment and the revolutionary period, although little of the verse produced had enduring qualities. The Connecticut (or Hartford) Wits devoted themselves dutifully to the creation of a national literature. John Trumbull (1750–1831) is best remembered for his satires; Timothy Dwight (1752–1817), for *Greenfield Hill* (1794); and Joe Barlow (1754–1812), for his attempt at an American epic, *The Columbiad* (1807).

From about 1807 until 1837 American literary activity was centered in New York City in the hands of a group known as the Knickerbockers. They, too, were concerned with the creation of a national literature, although their efforts are of interest primarily to scholars. James Kirke Paulding (1778–1860), second only to Washington Irving in the group, produced two volumes of verse. Samuel Woodworth (1784–1842), principally a journalist, caught the public fancy with some of his lyrics. Fitz-Greene Halleck (1790–1867) showed a genuine gift for adroit satire in the "Croaker" poems, and his close friend and collaborator, Joseph Rodman Drake (1795–1820), is still remembered for "The Culprit Fay" (1835) and "The American Flag" (1835). Nathaniel Parker Willis (1806–67) wrote some competent *vers de société*. Philip Freneau (1752–1832) is, however, the eminent poet of this period. At his best (as in "The Wild Honey Suckle," 1786) he is a gifted lyric poet. Because he spent a great deal of his strength on political and polemic occasional poetry, the early promise of his genuine romantic gifts was never quite realized. Nevertheless, his ardent Americanism was not equaled until the appearance of Walt Whitman. The first Catholic poet of any consequence, John Milton Harney (1789–1825), was a contemporary. A convert who became a Dominican, he published a number of poems in periodicals.

The American Renaissance. Subject to the contemporary influences of European *romanticism, American poets from Bryant to Whitman are roughly classified as romantics. The term, often vaguely used, means many things: a tendency toward idealism, the portrayal of the marvelous and mysterious, the recovery of the past, a dependence upon the imagination, the celebration of emotion, the revolt against authority, the sanctity of individual rights, new interest in humble life, the rise of humanitarian sympathy, and a renewed appreciation of nature. No one poet incorporated all these themes equally in his work, but they may serve in part as touchstones for the American romantic movement.

Bryant and Emerson. William Cullen Bryant (1794–1878) is the major transitional figure in the movement away from the Enlightenment to the new thought. His stoic poem "Thanatopsis" (pub. 1817) shows his debt to the 18th-century English "Graveyard School." After reading Wordsworth, however, he turned more and more to nature as "the abode of gladness." "Inscription for the Entrance to a Wood" (1815) and "To a Waterfowl" (1818) are representative of his best nature poems; "A Pennsylvania Legend," of his use of romantic themes. He combined a genuine love for America with a belief in personal immortality, in the changeless life of the spirit, and in the permanence of that which is "noble and truly great." His essentially conservative Christian view is expressed in "The Flood of Years" (1876).

Although Ralph Waldo *Emerson wrote some of the most important nonfictional prose of the 19th century, he is equally famous as one of America's finest poets. His best poetry has an inventive brilliance not obscured by the fogginess so often found in his prose. Like the young Wordsworth, he was a poet of the divinity of nature. The fundamental articles of his belief can be briefly stated: first, the Unity of Being in God and man; second, the physical world as a symbol of the spiritual world; and the third, the existence of a universal moral law in the spiritual and physical universe. These doctrines are given poetic expression in "Woodnotes," "Threnody," his famous elegy, "Days," one of his finest poems (1857), "The Sphinx," "Hamatreya," "Uriel," and "Brahma." One of the first (and best) of the American symbolists, he was especially sensitive to images; the piling of one image upon another is, in fact, one of his major techniques (*see* SYMBOLISM, LITERARY). He is highly conscious of the suggestive qualities of individual words, even though his versification and structure are occasionally weak. His technical experimentation and his bold, unsystemized thought were powerful influences on the greatest practitioners of the "new poetry"—Walt Whitman and Emily Dickinson.

The New England Group. Though no other New England poet of the period was of Emerson's stature, the region was fertile in poetic activity during the first half of the 19th century, and each practitioner made a significant contribution to the development of American poetry. Henry Wadsworth *Longfellow was an industrious scholar, a sound craftsman, and a fluent versifier who did much to transmit the culture of the Old World to the New—his translation (1865–67) of Dante's *Divina Commedia* was a prodigious achievement. He stands out among many 19th-century writers for his sympathetic understanding and appreciation of at least the cultural aspects of Catholicism. He transmuted historical material of America's young culture into verse in *Hiawatha* (1855), *The Courtship of Miles Standish* (1858), *Evangeline* (1847), and *Tales of a Wayside Inn* (1863). His *Christus* (1872) is more ambitious than successful. The vogue of the long poem of epic pretensions also affected the Catholic poet, John Delevau Bryant (1811–77), who contributed *The Redemption.* Longfellow expressed lyrically, if too often didactically, the simple and homely thoughts of an unsophisticated people. Few American poets have written the sonnet with greater authority; one of the high points of his art can be seen in the *Divina Commedia* sonnets. Finally, he taught many readers still living in the remains of a Puritan culture to enjoy verse; his poems sank deep into the national memory, where they continue to endure.

Like Longfellow, James Russell Lowell (1819–91) was an erudite man, competent in many languages. He became an established literary critic in his time and one of America's foremost men of letters. He, too, was enamored of the past, as in "The Vision of Sir Launfal" (1848), but even this work reflects his concern for contemporary America. His best work remains *The Biglow Papers* (1848 and 1862), a truly indigenous American poem in Yankee dialect. Lowell's poems, however lacking in concentration and force many of them may be, give abundant evidence of his humanitarianism, his balanced nationalism and his hopeful humanism. His faith was in a depersonalized Deity: "each age must worship its own thought of God." He was strongly influenced by the values of Catholicism (cf. his essay on Dante and his poem, "The Cathedral," 1869), but in this "age that blots out life with question marks," he felt finally "t'is irrecoverable, that ancient faith."

Fig. 13. James Russell Lowell.

The fame of Oliver Wendell Holmes (1809–94) has been less enduring. He is best remembered for the urbanity and wit so characteristic of his prose, and occasionally, of his poetry. He was deeply opposed to the Calvinistic strain still alive in New England, but his passion for science did not lead into the excesses of some of his contemporaries; he continued to believe in a beneficent, if impersonal, Deity. Holmes probably would have been more at home temperamentally with the English classicists of the Augustan age. Satires such as "The Deacon's Masterpiece" (1858) are still vital, as is the fragile charm of "The Chambered Nautilus" (1858).

A rural New Englander, John Greenleaf Whittier (1807–92) was largely unaffected by the prevalent cultural urban atmosphere. Like Longfellow, he wrote some historical and legendary narratives, such as "The Barefoot Boy" and "Maud Muller" (1856). The finest of his Yankee idylls was *Snow-Bound* (1866), notable for its homely description and sincerity. Antislavery poems such as "Massachusetts to Virginia" (1842) were passionately felt. Many of his poems reveal a religious sentiment guided by an inner light and based on a strong sense of divine immanence.

Poe and the Southern Writers. The South, too, was making its contribution to the mainstream of American poetry during this time. William Gilmore Simms (1806–70), a symbol and chief spokesman of the Southern literary type, was a prolific poet, novelist, biographer, and editor. But Edgar Allan *Poe is the dominant figure among Southern writers. Although he composed less than 50 poems, he remains one of the most original figures in the history of American poetry. Abroad, and in France particularly, because of his influence on *Baudelaire and the French symbolists, he is considered one of America's most important poets. He appears an isolated figure on the American scene, more perhaps because of his life and his personality than because of his poetry. The poems themselves are often highly romantic, richly suggestive, and sometimes a trifle vague. While "To Helen" (1831) and "The Raven" (1845) are probably his most anthologized pieces, other representative poems are "The Sleeper" (1831), "The City in the Sea" (1831), "Ulalume" (1847), and "Israel" (1831). His longest work, *Eureka* (1848), seems to be in prose, but the reader is advised to take Poe's advice: "It is as a Poem only that I wish this work to be judged. . . ." Although his religious views have little coherence, one senses in this work a gigantic egotistic personalism, which is secular romanticism carried to its ultimate point. Poe's best work, however, together with that of Emerson, remains the high point of 19th-century symbolism in the U.S.

The most gifted poet of the 19th-century South after Poe was Sidney Lanier (1842–81). He was an excellent musician, and the pronounced melodic line of his poetry and his famous theory of prosody (*The Science *of English Verse,* 1880) have attracted wide attention. His work is lavishly evocative, sensuous, rich in harmony and descriptive power. "The Symphony" (1875) is an excellent illustration of his attempt to wed music and verse. "Corn" (1874) shows his concern with the practical aspects of postwar Southern life. His best work as a lyric poet of nature can be seen in the lush "The Marshes of Glynn" (1878) and in "Sunrise" (1880). Lanier's deep sense of moral idealism is apparent in his work, even though his expression of religious feelings is often sentimental.

Henry Timrod (1828–67) and Paul Hamilton Hayne (1830–86) deserve mention, though Timrod felt that his mission as a poet was to deal with the South as a separate civilization, and Hayne was too often merely a sentimental regionalist. A group of Southern Catholic poets was deeply moved, too, by the Civil War and its consequences; they wrote some of their best poetry in patriotic response to this national calamity. Father John Bannister *Tabb composed many short poems that have an exquisite, cameolike finish. Father Abram *Ryan became known as the poet-priest of the South and was one of its most widely read spokesmen. Of Theodore O'Hara's (1820–67) work, "The Bivouac of the Dead" is still read. The most famous poem of James Ryder Randall (1839–1908) is "Maryland, My Maryland" (1861).

Approach to Modern Poetry. Because the individual states of the U.S. were still only loosely joined in a federal relationship, most poets before the Civil War were identified with a particular region, place, or class. Because he was less attached to any specific region, place, or class, it can be said that Walt *Whitman was the first poet to speak for all America.

Walt Whitman. Whitman's *Leaves of Grass* (1855–82), altered and modified through nine editions, was his single work of poetry. Of it Whitman said, "It has mainly been . . . an attempt . . . to put *a Person,* a human being (myself, in the latter half of the Nineteenth Century, in America), freely, fully and truly on record. I could not find any similar personal record in current literature that satisfied me." The poem was of a time but for all time, of a place as a summary of all places, and of a person as a composite of all persons. Perhaps this last, Whitman's personalism, was the most important. He made himself the voice of democracy and found within himself that "divine average" which he so conspicuously celebrated. The strands of 19th-century liberalism, quasi-mystical Quakerism, and a powerful Emersonian transcendentalism are mingled in the poem.

Later editions show, however, a significant deepening of Whitman's unsystematized religious feeling. Although marred by an overdramatization of the self and by crude sexuality, *Leaves of Grass* was, as Emerson said, the poem for which America had been waiting. Whitman felt obliged to abandon the ordinary idiom and technique of poetry for his deeply felt personal statement. The long, flowing lines create the illusion of a sense of freedom from form. Despite his dislike for revising and polishing, however, the form is meaningful and appropriate to his subject and method. There may be few better poems in American literature than "Out of the Cradle Endlessly Rocking" (1859) and "When Lilacs Last in the Dooryard Bloom'd" (1865–66), which are clearly Whitman at his best.

Emily Dickinson. No two people were more different in temperament and personality than Whitman and Emily *Dickinson. Yet the two will always be linked as pioneer figures in the creation of "the new poetry." Dickinson's work was not finally published until the 20th century; her poetry reveals a woman enamored of solitude but unafraid to deal with the profoundest elements of the thought of her day. Her major concern was the difference between what merely seems to be and what actually is, a philosophic dualism that escaped the monistic mind of Whitman. Her nature poetry invariably moves from the natural object to the concerns of man. She was no stranger to human suffering or happinness. Perhaps God, or the ways of God, was her ultimate subject, the base of her art. That she was witty and piquant about theological matters should not blind the reader to her comfortable intimacy with the Creator. Although her certitude lacked a formal base, it was deeply felt and not nearly so vague as Emerson's Over-Soul. The cryptic, even splintered, character of her style has made her of special interest to contemporary critics and poets. She was, like Whitman, although in a totally different direction, a harbinger of the future.

The Minor Poets. Of the many minor poets after the Civil War, some reflected a kind of new regionalism, but most were at best imitative of the verse of 50 years before. John Hay (1838–1905) is remembered for his *Pike County Ballads* (1871), Eugene Field (1850–95) for his children's poetry, Richard Hovey (1864–1900) because of his association with E. A. Robinson and for his "Songs of Vagabondia" (1894–1901) written with Bliss Carman (1861–1929). Edwin Markham's (1852–1940) "Man with a Hoe" (1899) still can be found anthologized together with some of the poems of Joaquin Miller (1837–1913) and James Whitcomb Riley (1849–1916). William Vaughn Moody's (1869–1910) reputation was much greater in his own day than it is now; the work of George Cabot Lodge (1873–1909) showed promise before his early death. Two Catholic poets of the time are still remembered, perhaps more as historical figures than as poets. John B. *O'Reilly wrote four volumes of verse. George Parsons Lathrop (1851–98), Hawthorne's son-in-law who also acted as his editor, wrote *Rose and Roof-tree* (1875).

The 20th Century. At the turn of the century the future of American poetry appeared bleak. The worst of the general characteristics of the late 19th century were still influential: poetry was genteel, conventional, imitative, and strongly moralistic.

Crane and Frost. The first change can be seen in two volumes by Stephen Crane (1871–1900), *Black Riders* (1895) and *War Is Kind* (1899). His style was impressionistic, tense, bare, and spontaneous. That the breakthrough was an accomplished fact, however, became evident in the poetry of Edwin Arlington Robinson (1869–1935). Although seemingly isolated from the mainstream of American culture, he captured the best of the New England tradition in a modern idiom. His sensitive, often eccentric poetry was filled with psychological insights in which a new realism is evident; his rhythms are those of the speech of the New England townsman of his day. His reputation continues to grow; his ability may be noted especially in those brief poems such as "Miniver Cheevy" (1907) and

"Luke Havergal" (1897), in which he captures the essence of man's entire character.

If Robinson revitalized and bodied forth the tradition of the townsman, Robert *Frost can be said to be spokesman for the tradition of the New England countryman. Like Robinson he is one of the major links between the conventions of poetry inherited from the past and the experimentation to come. An unforced lyric charm is evident in the best of his early poems, but there is also a vein of striking realism that led to the tragic power of his best narrative poems. *North of Boston* (1914) was a high point of his work, and only at times in succeeding collections did he reach its acute insight. Lyrics such as "Stopping by Woods" (1923) and "Mending Wall" (1914) have become ingrained in the American consciousness; some of his best work is demonstrated in the dramatic scenes of some of his poems such as "Death of the Hired Man" (1914).

Lesser Poets. A group of minor poets helped to make the transition from the 19th century to the 20th, and produced a durable body of work. Lizette Woodworth Reese (1856–1935) brought to her lyric poetry an emotional honesty not always inhibited by convention. Louise I. *Guiney, a Catholic New Englander, has a like exquisite lyric power, although her range is wider and more dramatic. Joyce and Aline *Kilmer made their Catholicism an integral part of their subject matter. Although more famous as a philosopher, George *Santayana wrote some verse that compares well with that of Robinson.

Major Experimenters. In 1912 Harriet Monroe (1860–1936) began the publication of *Poetry: A Magazine of Verse,* and from this date the renaissance of the 20th-century poetry can be said to have begun. Two poems by Ezra Pound (1885–), one of the seminal figures of the 20th-century poetry, appeared in the first issue. As poet and critic, Pound is a symbol of the dedicated artist; he is one of the finest American lyricists, a brilliant and original translator, and one of the few modern poets capable of the long, sustained poem. "Hugh Selwyn Mauberly" (1920) dramatizes as does no other poem the problem of the artist in this century. The monumental *Cantos,* although overly immersed in sources, too concerned with polemics, and crippled by a philosophical materialism, may well be

Fig. 14. William Carlos Williams.

the most original poem of the time. One of the many movements in which Pound was involved was *imagism, dedicated to the sharpening of the texture of poetry and the use of free verse. Among the more important partisans attracted to this movement were Richard Aldington (1892–), Hilda Doolittle (1886–1961), and John Gould Fletcher (1886–1950). Eventually Amy Lowell (1874–1925) took over the movement, and Pound passed on to other things.

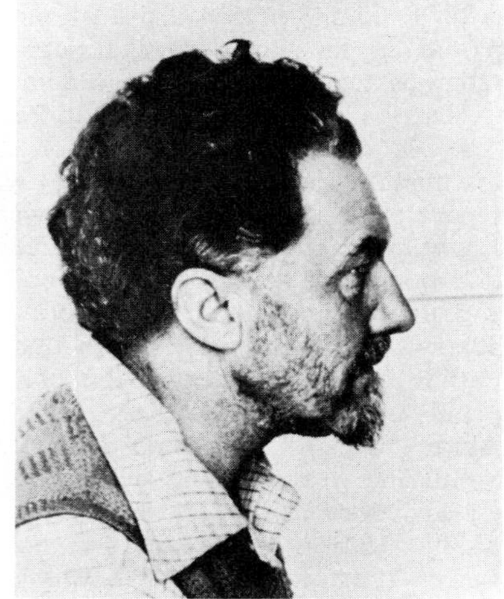

Fig. 15. Ezra Pound.

Both William Carlos Williams (1883–1963) and Marianne Moore (1887–) were as interested in experimentation as was Pound. Originally influenced by imagism, Williams became more concerned with a continuing effort to find the essential meaning of his immediate American surroundings. From this effort came his long poem, *Paterson* (1946–51), a celebration of his home town in the speech rhythms of the American people. Marianne Moore was an experimenter in her syllabic verse, producing a very prose-like poetry, as can be seen in "Observations" (1924). "Odd" and "striking" are words regularly used to describe her poems. Her later poetry seems more concerned with fundamental human problems, e.g., "Like a Bulwark" (1956).

The Contribution of T. S. Eliot. In 1914 Pound discovered the work of T. S. *Eliot, the man destined to become the greatest poet of the century. Eliot's early work revealed a self-conscious irony that gradually modulated into the universal perspective so richly evident in *The Waste Land* (1922). This poem, completely free of the mannerisms of the 19th century, has been called "the greatest poem of the era." In it Eliot revealed, as had no one before him, the moral, spiritual, and social disintegration of the West, a fragmentation that he understood by basing the poem upon a coherently organized mythical framework. His work is vitally concerned with the values of the past, especially the great significance of its formal religious base. "Ash Wednesday" (1930) is a devotional poem that celebrates the Anglo-Catholicism to which Eliot had been converted. *Four Quartets* (1932–34), the culmination of his nondramatic poetry, is one of the most deeply felt and brilliantly executed spiritual testimonies in the English language. Like Dante, his admired master, Eliot had found the fullness of his expression, progressing from a cultural inferno through a personally felt purgatory to the completeness of an encompassing spiritual certainty: Time and the Timeless reconciled.

With a strong sense of Christian certitude now defined, Eliot turned to the poetic drama. His plays are an attempt to dramatize the good news of the Christian message. His high point in this genre was *The Cocktail Party* (1949), for which he had prepared himself by the writing of the successful *Murder in the Cathedral* (1935) and the boldly experimental *The Family Reunion* (1939). He was less successful later (and less bold) in *The Confidential Clerk* (1954) and *The Elder Statesman* (1959).

Other Voices of Faith. Although the quest for spiritual certitude in its broadest sense may well be the dominant note in poetry of the first half of the 20th century, specific religious themes, except in Eliot's work, were not common until the '50s and '60s. A group of minor Catholic poets, however, kept insisting—and not always in a provincial manner—that such subject matter was truly amenable to poetry. James J. Daly, SJ (1872–1953), earned a large enough reputation to be regularly anthologized. Charles L. O'Donnell, CSC (1884–1934), and William T. Walsh (1891–1949) had an almost exclusively Catholic reading public. The prolific Theodore *Maynard, well known also for his biographies and criticism, had the widest audience for his verse.

Impressed by the experimentalism of their time, another group of poets moved in a direction not so obviously dominated by Pound. Although stylistically divergent, Carl Sandburg (1878–), Vachel Lindsay (1879–1931), Edgar Lee Masters (1868–1950), and Stephen Vincent Benét (1898–1943) tried to discover the peculiar native quality among American folk heroes, folk patterns, and folklore. Lindsay was rhythmic and enthusiastic, a reformer; Masters discovered free verse and some neglected facts of small town life; Sandburg was coarse, vernacular, sentimental, and romantic; Benét tried to turn folk materials into an epic in *John Brown's Body* (1928).

Fig. 16. Marianne Moore.

The Lyric Vein. That there were many doors opened by the new century can be seen in the vein of lyricism represented by a distinguished group of feminine poets. Sara Teasdale (1884–1933), who achieved a remarkable spoken effect in her poetry, is notable for her unsentimental, passionate, and direct idiom. Elinor Wylie (1885–1929), a brilliant technician, was richly emotional and complex. Edna St. Vincent Millay (1892–1950) was a revolutionist in ideas and a traditionalist in form. Despite her excessive sentimentality, she became a symbol of the emancipated woman. Leonie Adams (1899–), a Catholic, was as formal as Millay, but wrote with a mature intensity that makes her verse seem richer and deeper. She may be regarded by history as the best of this group. Phyllis McGinley (1905–), also a Catholic, was as much appreciated as any poet of her time because of her technical skill, lucidity, and fresh wit.

Singularly impressive is the appearance in the 20th century of a group of nuns who exhibited genuine power as lyricists. Sister M. *Madeleva, scholar and poet, established her reputation in the '20s as a lyric poet of genuine eloquence. Sister M. Maura, Jessica Powers (Sister Miriam of the Holy Spirit), Sister Maris Stella, and Sister M. Thérèse, among others, have been recognized as gifted minor poets since that time. Neither fragmentary nor sentimental, their lines are melodious, brave, and certain.

It appears, however, that the two finest lyric poets were men. Conrad Aiken (1889–) is an artist of the first order, a master of exotic and purposeful diction. E. E. *Cummings, the outstanding lyric poet of his time, combined a freshness of feeling with a decidedly experimental form. His eccentric use of typography is more often genuine than not. He is also one of America's gifted satirical poets, even though his satire is often more earthy than witty.

Regionalism Revived. The 20th century, with its large sense of hospitality, found room for a revived regionalism, the most notable group being the "Fugitives" at Vanderbilt University—John Crowe Ransom (1888–), Robert Penn Warren (1905–), and Allen Tate (1899–). While Ransom's highly intellectual verse has a great measure of calm dignity about it, Warren, although often idea-centered, is more deliberately coarse and common. Tate was the "genius" of the group. He was keenly sensitive to the tormented nature of his time and place, and he accurately caught in his "Seasons of the Soul" (1944) the mood of desolation generated by lack of belief. After his conversion to Catholicism in 1950 he wrote a series of poems tracing the religious quest of the modern intellectual, "The Swimmers" and "The Buried Lake." Robert Fitzgerald (1910–), a Catholic of the "Tate Generation" and one of the finest translators of the century, is a classic poet of the Horatian mood. Fray Angelico Chavez, OFM, a contemporary of Fitzgerald, has been a very prolific poet who deftly employs the materials of the Southwest with a heightened emphasis upon its setting.

Crane and Jeffers. Tate was a close friend of Hart Crane (1899–1932), the apotheosis of the romantic spirit in America and the successor of Whitman in idea if not in form. Misunderstanding Eliot's *The Waste Land* as a pessimistic poem, Crane determined to answer it by celebrating an optimism based upon the progress in technology that characterized American culture. The result was his masterpiece, *The Bridge* (1930). Although Crane did not have the intellectual power to meet adequately the problems raised by Eliot, *The Bridge,* despite the failure of some of its parts, was sustained by an impressive lyric power and by a natural poetic sense that finally redeems its most extravagant faults.

Whitman was also a strong influence on a few able, Marxist-oriented poets of the '30s: Kenneth Fearing (1902–61), Muriel Rukeyser (1913–), and Archibald MacLeish (1892–). Standing alone outside the mainstream of American poetry was the West Coast eccentric, Robinson Jeffers (1887–1962). He constructed his bitter, misanthropic view of reality in a number of dramatic poems set against the untamed Pacific shoreline. Considered a dilettante by critics after the publication of his first volume, *Harmonium* (1923), Wallace Stevens (1879–1955) took almost 20 years to establish a reputation as a serious poet. In *The Man with the Blue Guitar* (1937) Stevens found a theme—the overwhelming importance of the imagination as the organizing principle in an otherwise chaotic world. To him it was the poet's special task to keep in proper poise the distinct worlds of reality and imagination. By the time of his death, Stevens was considered one of the five or six most important American poets of the first half of the 20th century.

After World War II. Numerous young poets emerged after World War II and continued to write distinguished poetry through the '50s and '60s. Also an acute critic of poetry, Randall Jarrell (1914–) was clever and ironic. Karl Shapiro (1913–) tended to use ordinary situations in his attempt to plumb the commonplace. Peter Viereck (1916–) is an excellent satirist of the tired pretensions of much "modernism." Richard Wilbur (1921–), enamored of traditional form like all these poets, has demonstrated a fresh lyric power.

One of the most interesting of these emerging figures is Robert Lowell (1917–). After his conversion to Catholicism, his subject matter became increasingly the story of this conversion and its meaning to himself as a representative figure in a confused world; his conversion, unfortunately, seems not to have been too stable. Both lyric and dramatic, his mannered style approaches a kind of modern rococo. An excellent craftsman, he was able to create a genuine sense of tragic feeling in *Land of Unlikeness* (1944) and *Lord Weary's Castle* (1946).

Young Catholic Poets. More prolific than Lowell was Thomas Merton (1915–), the young intellectual who announced his conversion to Catholicism and his entry into the Cistercian Order in a moving autobiography, *The Seven Storey Mountain* (1948). Merton's reputation has grown steadily. He has moved away from imitation and toward a style uniquely personal. He has demonstrated more successfully than others had done that religious feelings can be presented without sentimentality or false piety; his lyric power is often used to give new lustre to common attitudes. Perhaps his work set an example for a very different kind of poet, Brother Antoninus, OP (William Everson), also a convert. In his formless style, reminiscent of Whitman, there is a primitive music; his major theme appears to be his genuine recollection of the ecstasy of the discovery of God. John Frederick Nims (1913–) expresses his Catholicism in the idiom of his time in closely controlled verse marked by a significant attention to form. He writes especially well of the romantic ambivalences of men and women. Formerly an editor of *Poetry,* Nims is very much aware of the currents in contemporary poetic activity. Dunstan Thompson (1918–), a Catholic like Nims, was much concerned with the handling of complex forms and with the kind of surface brilliance in vogue during the '40s. Although he has published no verse since 1947, his two early volumes established his reputation as a romantic poet of more than passing interest.

Modern Movement. T. S. Eliot remarked that both the capacity for writing poetry and the capacity for intense religious emotion are rare, and that the existence of both in the same individual is rarer still. Thus, one is amazed to discover the number of excellent Catholic poets who have emerged in the '50s and '60s: Father John Lynch (1904–), Father Raymond Roseliep (1917–), Ned O'Gorman (1929–), Kathleen Rains (1908–), John Fandel (1925–), Samuel Hazo (1925–), John Logan (1923–), Daniel Berrigan, SJ (1921–), and Galwey Kinnell. Each has produced at least one significant volume of poems; it remains to be seen how much these poets will grow. If the middle decades do mark the beginning of a renaissance, considerable credit for the maturing of the Catholic poet in America goes to the Catholic Poetry Society of America and its periodical, *Spirit,* edited by J. G. Brunini (1899–). This movement has raised the quality of much religious verse through the standards it has set for the appreciation and understanding of poetry.

Bibliography: For bio-bibliog. materials the indispensable starting point is Spiller LitH, esp. its bibliog. J. BLANCK, comp., *Bibliography of American Literature* (New Haven 1955–). C. L. F. GOHDES, *Bibliographical Guide to the Study of the Literature of the U.S.A.* (2d ed. Durham, N.C. 1963). Works that deal explicitly with U.S. poetry are not numerous. G. W. ARMS and J. KUNTZ, *Poetry Explication: A Checklist of Interpretation since 1925 of British and American Poems, Past and Present* (New York 1950), bibliog. *Explicator* (Fredericksburg, Va. 1942–), the June issue contains an annual checklist. H. H. CLARK, ed., *Major American Poets* (New York 1936), contains a useful bibliog. and notes for major 19th-century poets. A. TATE and K. KILMER, eds., *Sixty American Poets, 1896–1944* (Washington 1954), lists selected books by and about the poets.

Partial histories of poetry in the U.S.: L. BOGAN, *Achievement in American Poetry, 1900–1950* (Chicago 1951). B. DEUTSCH, *Poetry in Our Time* (New York 1952). R. H. PEARCE, *The Continuity of American Poetry* (Princeton 1961). H. W. WELLS, *The American Way of Poetry* (New York 1943). Two studies of significant value: W. V. O'CONNOR, *Sense and Sensibility in Modern Poetry* (Chicago 1948; pa. New York 1963). H. H. WAGGONER, *The Hell of Elohim: Science and Values in Modern American Poetry* (Norman, Okla. 1950). **Illustration credits:** Fig. 12, Houghton Library, Harvard. Fig. 13, Harvard University Archives. Fig. 16, George Platt-Lynes.

[J. SCHWARTZ]

4. FICTION TO 1900

Physical and social conditions in the nascent U.S. understandably delayed for some time the beginnings of creative fictional writing.

Early Fiction. Joseph Morgan's *The History of the Kingdom of Basaruah* (Boston 1715) was the first fictional work published in the U.S. This Calvinist allegory was the cautious beginning of a genre that Puritanism was to view later with mistrust. The first novel by an American, *Adventures of Alonzo,* did not appear until 1775. The author, Thomas Atwood Digges, a Catholic Marylander, published his work only in England, however, and did not use an American theme. It is usual to date novel writing in the U.S. from William Hill Brown's *The Power of Sympathy* (1789); this book emulated the fiction of the English novelist Richardson, whose rectitude had edified even New England's Jonathan *Edwards. The domestication of the Richardson heroine in America was completed by Susannah Rowson's *Charlotte Temple* (1794) and Hannah Foster's *The Coquette* (1797). Lest the watchful should denounce them as pernicious, these books and others like them were carefully presented as moral instruction intended for the young; and they exalted the sentiments of honor, virtue, and religion on nearly every page. To placate moralists further, the villains of these sagas of seduction invariably were blackhearted and the heroines, virtuous.

Later Development. The avowals of pious intentions by these novelists who dramatized the problems of chambermaids had little to do with popularity, but their forbidden themes did, and a market for livelier fiction was created. Royall Tyler's *Algerine Captive* (1797), itself a successful picaresque novel, relates that readers "with one accord forsook the sober sermons and practical pieties of their fathers for the gay stories and splendid impieties of the traveller and the novelists." H. H. Brackenridge's *Modern Chivalry* (1792–1815), our first back-country novel, and Gilbert Imlay's engagingly candid *The Emigrants* (1793) were very popular. Of still less ethical pretext were the Gothic novels of Charles Brockden Brown (1771–1810). Brown called himself "a story-telling moralist" and "the ardent friend and willing champion of the Christian religion," but believed literature should be plausible and exciting as well as moral. *Wieland* (1798), his best work, heavily assails *Calvinism's cheerless tenets. As the first native novel to merit critical notice, it won its author the title of father of the U.S. novel.

Romanticism

Washington Irving's *The Sketch Book* (1819) was the first American book to win acclaim abroad. Not only did it establish Irving (1783–1859) as archspokesman of Romanticism (*see* ROMANTICISM, LITERARY) in the U.S., but it selected the themes American authors would write about for the next 40 years. Irving was not an intellectual; he was a keen student of the romantic temperament and frankly catered to it, though his later works did not have the success of *The Sketch Book*. Other writers were to tap the emotional lode he had uncovered. Although *Poe, *Hawthorne, and even *Dickens were his debtors, Irving's influence was strongest on scores of popular writers, whose works, once much admired, are now forgotten.

Among these are Donald Grant Mitchell's *Reveries of a Bachelor* (1850), George W. Curtis's *Prue and I* (1857), Timothy Shay Arthur's *Ten Nights in a Barroom and What I Saw There* (1854), Josiah Holland's novels, Mrs. E. D. E. N. Southworth's novels, and those of many prolific if unexceptional Catholic novelists including Anna Dorsey (1815–96), Isaac Henderson (1850–1909), John Boyce (1810–64), Jedediah Huntington (1815–62), Henry Harland (1861–1905), C. C. Pise (1801–66), and A. H. Brisbane. Brisbane's *Ralphton* (1848) solicited favor by advocating an Americanized Catholicism stripped of "pomp and pageantry." The Catholic novelists traded heavily on such themes of sentiment as domestic felicity, self-sacrifice, the humanitarian impulse, motherhood, and the "clinging-vine" ideal of conduct. Though of these writers only Jedediah Huntington and the militant Father Pise showed the appetite for apologetics that characterized Orestes *Brownson's *Charles Elwood* (1840), many of them joined Brownson in putting Calvinism under sharp rebuke.

Fig. 17. Washington Irving.

Shift to Sentimentalism. Romantic novels held favor late into the 19th century in the U.S. Horatio Alger's alone sold more than 20 million copies. Popular favorites included Lew Wallace's *Ben Hur* (1880), F. Marion *Crawford's epical Saracinesca tetralogy (1887–96), and the novels of Mary Tincker (1833–1907), whom Crawford alone, among Catholic novelists of that era, outsold. None of these works, however, was to approach *Uncle Tom's Cabin* (1852) as an expression of evangelical sentimentalism. Indeed, no other novel in history ever made so compelling an appeal to the common conscience and humanity of its readers, or had a greater practical influence. Harriet Beecher Stowe's aim had been to create a moral revulsion against slavery; her hope, to overwhelm it by a general upsurge of Christian sentiment. She wrote with a skill and passion further illustrated in the competence of her later fictional studies of the New England mind. Among the best of these was *The Minister's Wooing* (1859), a severe castigation of Calvinism.

Frontier Historical Fiction. This genre flourished beside sentimental romance and sometimes cohabited with it. Indians, a prominent element as fictional characters in American frontier literature, first appeared in C. B. Brown's *Edgar Huntly* (1799); there they are little more than animals. John Davis's *The First Settlers of Virginia* (1802) was the first clear delineator of American settings, and the first book to treat Indians idealistically. It anticipated James Fenimore Cooper, whose Indians, most notably portrayed in *The Last of the Mohicans* (1826) and *The Deerslayer* (1841), were to illustrate *Rousseau's ideal of the noble savage. Those

Fig. 18. Harriet Beecher Stowe.

who did not were offered as examples of civilization's deleterious influence on man.

Prominent among Cooper's emulators were James Kirke Paulding and Catharine Maria Sedgwick. Both shared his dislike of Calvinism, as may be seen in Mrs. Sedgwick's *Hope Leslie* (1827) and Paulding's *The Puritan and His Daughter* (1849). William Gilmore Simms (1806–70), who, although he had a Southerner's righteousness nevertheless deplored Puritanism's rigid exactions, was Cooper's chief competitor. As a realist, Simms let himself be limited by Romantic tradition, except in his characterization of Captain Porgy in his best novel *Woodcraft* (1852), where he triumphed over it. His *The Yemasse* (1835), is one of the first American novels to make apt, if unamiable, use of Spanish-English encounters in the southern U.S. in the colonial era. Timothy Flint's *Francis Berrain* (1826), J. P. Kennedy's *Rob of the Bowl* (1838), and Mrs. Stowe's *Agnes of Sorrento* (1862) gave evidence of efforts to treat Catholicism impartially.

Counter-Romanticism

Since Romanticism did not find a foothold in the U.S. until realism had already begun to supplant it abroad, little American fiction of the Romantic period was entirely devoid of realistic elements. Some, such as *Uncle Tom's Cabin* and J. P. Kennedy's *Swallow Barn* (1832), blended both elements.

Local Color. Formal beginnings of realism in U.S. literature, however, must properly be ascribed to the local colorists. W. A. Caruther's *The Kentuckian in New York* (1834) was, in fact, the first local-color work, but it is customary to assign this distinction to A. B. Longstreet's *Georgia Scenes* (1835), which was really neoclassical. Local-color writing began properly with Bret Harte whose "The Luck of Roaring Camp" (1868) was the first of his many popular Western tales, all of them contrived and pulsating with sentiment. The genre was moved forward by Edward Eggleston, whose didactic and candid *Hoosier Schoolmaster* (1871) strenuously opposed Calvinism. Two Catholic contributors to the tradition were R. M. Johnston, whose *Dukesborough Tales* (1871) stressed character and setting, and Frances Tiernan ("Christian Reid" 1846–1920), whose *The Land of the Sky* (1876) attracted attention to North Carolina. Three New England women, Helen Hunt Jackson (*Ramona,* 1884), Mary E. Wilkins Freeman (*A New England Nun,* 1891), and Sarah Orne Jewett (*The Country of the Pointed Firs,* 1896) took up the tradition of local-color fiction from its first New England development—Mrs. Stowe's *The Pearl of Orr's Island* (1862). Miss Jewett alone of these local colorists shunned didacticism. Her dignity and gentle charity are unsurpassed by any other local-color writer, but they are matched by Joel Chandler Harris, a convert to Catholicism. Harris's *Uncle Remus: His Songs and His Sayings* (1880) was the first of eight volumes of Negro folk tales that have earned him a place beside the Grimm brothers as a preserver of a folk heritage; his storyteller stands among the great characters of world literature. Kate Chopin was another Catholic local colorist; her *Bayou Folk* (1894) and *A Night in Acadie* (1897) interpret Cajun life with remarkable sensitivity.

Allegory. The local colorists had registered their disapproval of Romanticism's artificiality and shallowness by working with characters, settings, and situations drawn from the world around them. The great allegorists of the same era concerned themselves primarily with ideas, and struck at Romanticism's benevolent appraisal of human nature and the inevitable corollary, the denial of original sin. First in the field was Edgar Allan *Poe, father of the short story, whose *Tales* (1840, 1845) instantly brought the Gothic mode to maturity. Using the device of the symbol in such tales as "Ligeia," "The Fall of the House of Usher," and "The Masque of the Red Death," Poe passes beyond the mere act of storytelling to develop an idea. Through such themes as double identity and premature burial he sought to probe man's relationship to conscience and the question of the soul's survival after death. Poe pursued horror not for its own sake but as a means of bringing his readers to a confronting of evil, an affirmation, thought *Baudelaire, that redeemed human dignity from the shallow optimism of the Romantic movement. Poe was not only American literature's first symbolist, but its first critic of stature and the first of its writers to think of literature in terms of beauty.

Nathaniel *Hawthorne was another who did not support the Romantic view of man. A constant sense of the loss of Eden echoes in his short stories and novels. Hawthorne saw original sin as a factor of psychological necessity but, unlike his Puritan forebears, thought sinners could hope for grace through repentance. Though his masterpiece, *The Scarlet Letter* (1850), explores a situation that originated in an act of adultery, it has as its main theme not illicit love, but consequent sins of hypocrisy and revenge, and their effect on the soul. In the resolution he allies himself not with the romantic individualism of his heroine, but with the claims of law and conscience acknowledged by her lover. Hawthorne, in his last completed novel, *The Marble Faun* (1860), deliberates the question of sin's regenerative power and conjectures that sin may be an element of human education antecedent to high moral results. Hawthorne's passion for ethics was at once the glory and the bane of his art. While preoccupied with shaping truth in the moral sphere, he often let his characters become abstractions of moral qualities, or sacrificed narrative interest to moral content. This very quality lets Melville speak of "the ever-moving dawn that forever advances through Hawthorne's darkness, and circumnavigates his world."

The early novels of Herman *Melville, *Typee* (1845) and *Omoo* (1846), with mild hedonism berated Christian missionary efforts in the Pacific islands and contrasted invidiously the white man and the savage. But Melville soon came to ponder deeply the problem of evil, its origins and meaning, and concluded that "In certain moods, no man can weigh this world without throwing in something, somehow like Original Sin, to strike the uneven balance." His preoccupation with evil received such frank expression in *Mardi* (1849) that it alienated his generally devoted readers. In *White Jacket* (1850) he went back to his popular themes, though in its climax he portrayed the fall of Adam. Urged to return to allegory by Hawthorne (who found Melville could "neither believe, nor be comfortable in his unbelief") Melville responded with *Moby Dick* (1851) in which he reached the summit of achievement in American fiction. *Moby Dick* recounts the voyage of a U.S. whaling ship the "Pequod," in pursuit of a white whale that has maimed the "Pequod's" captain, Ahab, and has become to him "all evil . . . visibly personified . . . and practically unassailable." In order to revenge himself on Moby Dick, Ahab, a Yankee *Faust, allies himself with Satan. At the end of this black grail quest, insolently begun on Christmas day, it is apparent that it is not the whale, which has acted merely in accord with nature, that is evil, but Ahab himself. *Moby Dick* is an extraordinary work in which vast patterns of allegory and symbol blend with Biblical allusions, and all interpenetrate each other in surging yet ordered complexity; it is a masterful repudiation of Romanticism's deification of the self. Of Melville, Lewis Mumford aptly said: "In depth of experience and religious insight there is scarcely any one in the 19th century, with the exception of *Dostoevsky, who can be placed beside him."

Fig. 19. Charles Brockden Brown.

Romantic Realism. Not every writer who rejected the Romantic compact had the wit or ability to strike at it obliquely through the symbol. Fitz-James O'Brien's Gothic tale, "The Diamond Lens," subtly caricatured the romanticism of Nature, but the usual practice of those opposing Romantic themes was to pit against them a truthful presentation of life. Thus the sketches of Charles Farrar Browne ("Artemus Ward," 1834–67) excoriated, with devastating accuracy, the foibles of *sentimentalism; Robert Montgomery Bird's *Nick of the Woods* (1837) depicted America's Indians as savage degenerates; and Theodore Winthrop, who shared Hawthorne's fascination with the theme of moral ambiguity, depicted the West with unusual forthrightness in *John Brent* (1862). Elizabeth Barstow Stoddard's attempts, in *The Morgesons* (1862) and *Two Men* (1865), to use familiar Romantic themes with restraint and plausibility were a novelty; but Bayard Taylor, in *John Godfrey's Fortunes* (1864) and *The Story of Kennett* (1866), reshaped such themes with a probity of purpose that exhibited the essential shallowness of the Romantic view. Though melodramatic and sententious, Oliver Wendell Holmes's *Elsie Venner* (1861) and *The Guardian Angel* (1867) broke with Romanticism by suggesting that heredity and environment substantially limit man's moral responsibility. But Holmes was no naturalist; he presented his case as an attack against the doctrine of total depravity on which so many ethical and educational procedures in 19th-century America were based.

Another early adherent to the realistic movement was George Washington Cable, despite his brilliance of description and fierce moral earnestness. Dedication to truth and constant bearing on ethics gave his work an honesty that few contemporary novelists approached. His best work was *The Grandissimes* (1880).

Outposts of Modern Fiction

In 1898, depressed by the grief and self-reproach that personal problems engendered in him, Mark *Twain wrote three works, *What Is Man?, The Mysterious Stranger,* and "The Man That Corrupted Hadleyburg," thus bequeathing American literature that curious legacy—a national humorist who was a self-confessed nihilist and scientific determinist. It was not the Twain of these later years that his readers remember, however, but the creator of Huck Finn and Tom Sawyer, and the prince and pauper. Usually Twain was a deist. Certainly his greatest character, Huckleberry Finn, whom T. S. Eliot ranked with "Ulysses, Faust, Don Quixote, Don Juan, Hamlet, and other great discoveries man has made about himself," was a responsible figure. Huck's decision to accept damnation rather than surrender the slave Jim to society was, as an example of moral choice, "one of the most powerful

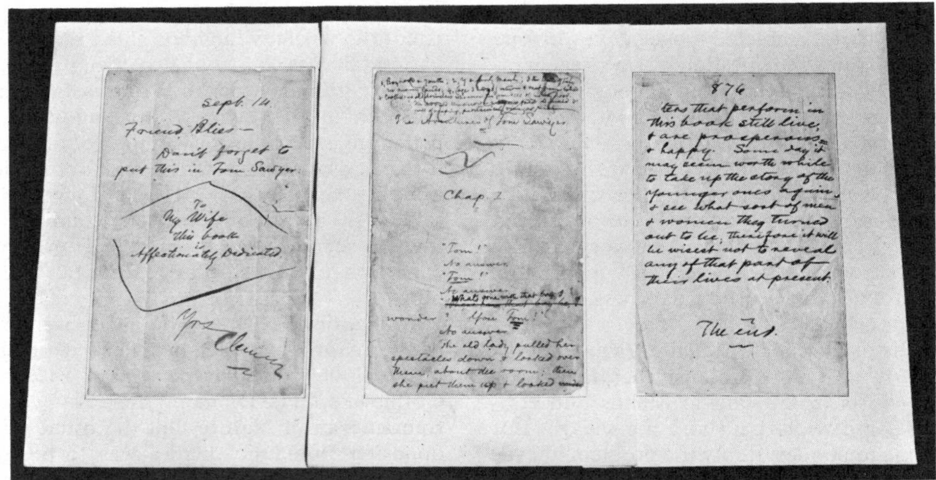

Fig. 20. Original manuscripts of "Tom Sawyer," in archives of Georgetown University.

antinaturalistic declarations in all literature," said Randall Stewart. Twain's rejection of the benevolent theory of human nature and his free-wheeling assaults on sentimentalism and preaching might seem to put him outside the pale of Romanticism. Yet there persisted a reverence for Nature that showed his work to be, if intrinsically apart from the Romantic identity, at least circumscribed by it.

In Graham Greene's opinion, Twain's contemporary Henry *James bore the same relationship to the novel that Shakespeare bore to drama. James's acute perceptions equipped him to analyze human sensibilities penetratingly, and he did so with consummate artistry. He wrote of people living in an exquisite world where evil was the more horrid for never flaunting itself. James's approach freed the novel from its amorphous sentimentality without divorcing it from morality. His basic grasp of the meaning of Christianity was implicit in the major actions of all his principal characters—in Isabel Archer's confrontation of life in *Portrait of a Lady* (1881), in Millie Theale's confrontation of death in *The Wings of the Dove* (1902). James's tribute to the power of truth and goodness, in the latter book, had no parallel in the realm of the sophisticated novel. Because of his restraint, the extent to which moral life preoccupied James is not always credited. Like Hawthorne, whom he reverenced, James admitted the psychological necessity of original sin. Apparently, however, he thought that belief in free will was indispensable even if it could not be proved, since only upon that postulate could moral life exist. As a symbolist James invites comparison with Hawthorne and Melville, but he is identified with another age.

Realism. Not until William Dean Howells (1837–1920) published his first novel in 1872 could the age of realism be said to have begun in the U.S. Yet at least one man, John W. De Forest (1826–1906), had anticipated Howells. De Forest might seem to have been merely a precursor of realism if his latent censoriousness had been the only evidence; but his emphatic break with the Romantic traditions of war in *Miss Ravenel's Conversion* (1867), anticipating Stephen Crane by nearly 30 years, was hailed by Howells himself as "of an advanced realism before realism was known by that name." Thus he was somewhat more than a precursor.

Harold Frederic, whose *The Damnation of Theron Ware* (1896) told relentlessly the story of a Methodist minister led to spiritual shipwreck by his shallow idealism, stood with De Forest and Howells entirely in the realm of realism in this period. Although Howells's status as a major writer is sometimes disputed, his role as father of American realism never is, for his success in introducing James, Twain, Norris, Crane, Garland, Jewett, and others to the methods of European realism was complete. Howells, convinced that it was fiction's primary role to express life, spurned open didacticism, sentimentalism, plot manipulation, and pseudo-Romantic attitudes. He considered a novel to be no better than the moral values that went into it. Although he was a firm advocate of traditional standards of morality, he wrote with a caution that led him to call his method "reticent realism." Habitually Howells's focus was not on sin but on its ethical implications, a concern that betrayed him into occasional moralizing. Howells was orthodox in the compassion that motivated his moral decisions, but the influence of naturalism appeared in his theory of "complicity," a belief that responsibility for sin is dispersible. Although his social conscience was already active when he wrote *A Modern Instance* (1882) and *The Rise of Silas Lapham* (1885), Christian idealism received its strongest expression in *A Hazard of New Fortunes* (1890). Subsequently, critics judged Howell's continence, wholesomeness, and nobility to be anchoritic. Yet he was, in his way, very advanced.

Transition to Naturalism. The closing years of the 19th century showed the first, timorous stirrings of naturalism in U.S. fiction. To the literary naturalist, man is a mere pawn, his every move dictated by circumstances he cannot control. Reason and morality are but pitiable illusions man throws between himself and reality. For guidance in this mode American writers looked to *Zola.

The earliest naturalistic novels in the U.S. were E. W. Howe's *The Story of a Country Town* (1883) and Joseph Kirkland's *Zury* (1887). Howe's book, though hobbled by Gothicism, routed the Romantic idealization of Western life; *Zury* focused with unsettling conviction on the joyless reality of Western farm life. *Zury's* impact on Hamlin Garland produced *Main Traveled Roads*

(1891), which continued the presentation of farm life in the western U.S. with graphic earnestness. But Garland was a realist. His people, no matter how downtrodden, were never degraded morally. Nor did he consistently deny them free choice. *Crumbling Idols* (1894) proffered his "veritism," a plan to describe reality exactly while simultaneously depicting in man moral and spiritual values beyond environment's reach.

Stephen Crane (1871–1900) was once thought to be a writer without literary antecedents. Now the influence of Zola is conceded. Crane's *Maggie* (1893) presented a strong case for environmental determinism; his masterpiece, *The Red Badge of Courage* (1894) portrayed compassionately an unheroic protagonist and stripped the glory from war. "The Open Boat" (1897), his finest short story, carried the revolt against Romanticism to new lengths in its insistence that Nature is indifferent to man's welfare. But Crane did not believe man altogether incapable of moral decisions; accordingly, his naturalism is not total.

McTeague (1899), by Frank Norris (1870–1902), was the most naturalistic novel written in the U.S. in the 19th century. But a stubborn strain of idealism and lyricism controlled Norris's later novels, *The Octopus* (1901), the most ambitious novel of its generation, and *The Pit* (1903). Norris often showed man sunk to the level of the beast, but he did not make them equals. He had faith in man's aspiring nature and expected truth, justice, and happiness to win eventually.

Fiction in the U.S. throughout its history to 1900 was either rigidly orthodox or uneasy in its apostasy. During the 19th century those writers who sought most earnestly to understand man's spiritual identity—Hawthorne, Melville, Twain, and James—wrote the best books, a fact that supports the wisdom of Lionel Trilling's contention that the greatness and practical usefulness of the novel is found in its "unremitting work of involving the reader in the moral life." The essentially moral character of U.S. fiction receives 20th-century affirmation, despite the vogue of naturalism, in the stature attained by Southern writers, products of a milieu in which strong spiritual convictions have held their ground against the assault of materialism.

See also AMERICAN LITERATURE, 5; ROMANTICISM, LITERARY; NATURALISM, LITERARY.

Bibliography: H. R. BROWN, *The Sentimental Novel in America: 1789–1860* (New York 1959). A. COWIE, *The Rise of the American Novel* (New York 1951). G. A. DUNLAP, *The City in the American Novel, 1780–1900* (Philadelphia 1934). E. W. GASTON, *The Early Novel of the Southwest* (Albuquerque 1961). R. STEWART, *American Literature and Christian Doctrine* (Baton Rouge 1958). A. H. QUINN, *American Fiction: An Historical and Critical Survey* (New York 1936). C. C. VAN DOREN, *The American Novel, 1789–1939* (New York 1940). E. C. WAGENKNECHT, *Cavalcade of the American Novel* (New York 1952). L. AHNEBRINK, *The Beginnings of Naturalism in American Fiction* (Cambridge, Mass. 1950). **Illustration credits:** Figs. 17–19, Library of Congress. Fig. 20, Georgetown University News Service.

[J. J. MC ALEER]

5. FICTION FROM 1900

Though the first 2 decades in no way foreshadowed the coming glory, the 20th century has been an extraordinarily rich one for American fiction, both novel and short story. If it has no Hawthorne or Melville, it can offer a larger number of truly fine novelists than the preceding century. During the interval between the two world wars, American novelists not only dominated world fiction but exported themes and techniques on a scale comparable to that of the great French and Russian masters in the time of Balzac and Dostoevskiĭ.

The Foundations. Nevertheless, for all this energy and innovation, the foundations of American fiction remained substantially what they had been. As each new group came into prominence—Middle Westerners, Southerners, Irish, Jews, Negroes—it assimilated itself to the themes that had come before and were, as *Moby Dick* has it, of the "straight warp" of American necessity. Now, however, these old themes were given fresh form by new artists plying their several shuttles on a "Loom of Time" that never once ceased to be American time. Henry James's great dictum held true: "It's a complex fate, being an American." As self-conscious as their predecessors, these novelists did their best to define that fate anew, whether they happened to be expatriate or, Antaeuslike, rooted in native ground. The basic instrument they used for this never-ending quest after American identity remained that curious hybrid, the metaphysical romance, to be distinguished from that lesser thing, the historical romance. The alienated hero —Cooper, not Camus, invented him—continued to prevail, and naturally served to connote a certain tension between inner concept and outer fact. T. S. Eliot's "dissociation of sensibility," after all, had come about in the Puritan 17th century, the seminal American century; to this moment the American novel has stayed Puritan, if only *à rebours*. The alienation theme made possible a bravura prose as remote from the prosaically real as Hawthorne's gothicized paragraphs and as incongruously rococo as the gingerbread ornamentation on a Nantucket home's "widow's walk." The resultant odd mixture appears as often in John Updike as in Herman Melville.

As the century opened, its fiction rapidly became dominated by the facile escapism of what Willa *Cather contemptuously termed "dreary dialect stories" and "machine-made historical novels." It was the hour of George Barr McCutcheon's (1866–1928) Graustark in Indiana, of Mary Johnston (1870–1936), Harold Bell Wright (1872–1944), John Fox, Jr. (1863–1919), and, several cuts above these, the American Winston Churchhill (1871–1947). Yet two gods from the great past, Mark *Twain and Henry *James, and one half-god, William Dean Howells (1837–1920), had survived into these opening decades. Indeed, the densely textured masterpieces of James's final period, *The Wings of the Dove, The Ambassadors, The Golden Bowl,* belong to 1902–04. The influences of these three remained great all during the century, cutting across the newer traditions of naturalism, realism, and the local color movement that would soon mutate into the more valuable impulse of regionalism.

Influx of Naturalism. For the moment, harsher flavors attracted the common reader's palate. European naturalism became "naturalized" in the most massive of American naturalists, Theodore *Dreiser; in Jack London (1876–1916), now more popular in Russia than the U.S., who crossed Marxism with the adventure story and whose splendid animal tales, *The Call of the Wild* (1903) and *White Fang* (1906), remain his enduring literary legacy; in Upton Sinclair (1878–) whose *The Jungle* (1906) still stands as the archetypal "muckraking" documentary and whose later Lanny Budd stories formed a Tom Swift's–eye view of the world between 1925 and 1945. Brooding, powerful, maladroit, philosophically puerile but possessed of deep compassion for the human predicament, Dreiser made naturalism temporarily a major force in American letters. His best books are the first two volumes of the Cowperwood trilogy, *The Financier* (1912) and *The Titan* (1914); and *An American Tragedy* (1925). *See* NATURALISM, LITERARY.

Aspect of Social Involvement. Though it produced a number of notable books, naturalism has never really been native to the American genius, which characteristically resists any ideological straitjacket. It performed one historical service, however, in helping make the American imagination, with its ingrained bent toward anarchy, more involved in society. Before the naturalistic wave had spent its force, it partially determined certain important American talents. Sherwood Anderson (1876–1941) poeticized it in the grotesques of that seminal volume, *Winesburg, Ohio* (1919). Sinclair Lewis (1885–1951) was its humorist and satirist. Never merely a naturalist, Lewis, like Cervantes, came to love the butts of his satiric scorn. Sentimentalism vitiated his novels after *Dodsworth* (1929). The once revolutionary *Main Street* (1920) has not stood the test of time. *Babbitt* (1922), which gave a new name to literature's emblematic gallery, survives, as does *Arrowsmith* (1925).

Fig. 21. Sinclair Lewis.

The books of James Farrell (1904–) are doggedly honest, devoid of charm, numbing in their grey earnestness. The *Studs Lonigan* trilogy (1932–35) was, among other things, a devastating indictment of urban American Catholicism's shortcomings, and marks Farrell's major achievement. The most relaxed and mellow of America's naturalists is John Steinbeck (1902–), who grafts Darwin onto Emerson to produce a kind of pastoral wherein the Life Force is protagonist, animals are drawn more arrestingly than men, the Skid Row bums philosophize with golden-hearted prostitutes in a California forest of Arden. *The Grapes of Wrath* (1939), this century's *Uncle Tom's Cabin,* made Steinbeck's contemporary reputation. It may well be that he will be remembered as the author of the less ambitious *Tortilla Flat* (1935) and of *The Red Pony* (1945).

Decay of Naturalism. The naturalistic wheel came full circle in the work of John Dos Passos (1896–), a congenital Iberian anarchist perpetually trying to fit himself into a Jeffersonian mold. Moving in an ideological half-circle from left to right, midway in his career Dos Passos assembled the dazzling gadgetry of his sociopolitical trilogy, *U.S.A.* (1938). The characters, however, are thin; and the component novels, however brilliant as blueprints, in the end remain blueprints. During the 1930s naturalism was employed, with no great degree of success, as an instrument of the class struggle in the listless proletarian fiction of Michael Gold (1896–) and Jack Conroy (1899–). It also leavened the two most successful novels dealing with World War II, *The Naked and the Dead* (1948) by Norman Mailer (1923–) and *From Here to Eternity* (1951) by James Jones (1921–).

Early Women Fiction Writers. Hawthorne stigmatized lady writers of his day as a "damned mob of scribbling women," an outburst that could not conceivably be applied to three patrician talents that may be said to have dominated fictional sensibility for the greater part of the 1920s, overshadowing such not inconsiderable male writers as Booth Tarkington (1869–1946) and Joseph Hergesheimer (1880–1954). The *doyenne* of the trio, Edith Wharton (1862–1937), an aristocrat to the manner born, employed her very Jamesian art to register the subtlest nuances of caste in *The House of Mirth* (1905) and *The Age of Innocence* (1920). She was also the chronicler of frustrated passion, an excellent writer of short stories (including a quite un-American specialty, ghost stories), and true mistress of that extremely taxing form, the *novella.* Mrs. Wharton's *Ethan Frome* (1911) and *The Old Maid* (1924) belong on the small shelf that houses the few masterpieces of this most exquisitely modulated of all fictional genres: Fitzgerald's *The Great Gatsby* (1925) and *Rich Boy* (1926); O'Hara's *Appointment in Samarra* (1934); Faulkner's *The Bear* (1942); Hemingway's *The Old Man and the Sea* (1952); and Katherine Anne Porter's (1894–) *Pale Horse, Pale Rider* (1939) and *The Leaning Tower* (1944)—both of which are so much better than her disappointing foray into longer fiction, *Ship of Fools* (1962).

Virginia-born Ellen Glasgow (1874–1945), whose astringent realism turned the Southern novel away from escapist nostalgia, wrote high comedy in the tradition of Meredith and Jane Austen. *Barren Ground* (1925), *The Romantic Comedians* (1926), and *Vein of Iron* (1935) rank high among her books. Her fellow Virginian by birth, Willa Cather, early became Nebraskan by adoption and, through such novels as *O Pioneers!* (1913) and *My Ántonia* (1918), established herself as the historian of Swedish and Bohemian immigrants. Miss Cather, who began her literary career as a follower of Ibsen, ended it as an American Vergil celebrating, through her natural piety and poetry of place, the timeless land. The grave moral music of her prose is scored with Flaubertian precision. Like the heroine of her *A Lost Lady* (1923), she too was a lady lost in time—a time recovered through the divining rod of art—but this turned sociological critics against her delicate classicism. History remains an important human dimension, nevertheless, and Cather's distillate of bygone greatness will continue to be of significance. Her *Death Comes for the Archbishop* (1927) is a uniquely American book.

Other Novelists. One of the most widely praised novelists in the early 1920s now virtually forgotten, was that American-Anatole France, James Branch Cabell (1879–1958), whose *Jurgen* (1919) became a censorship *cause célèbre* and whose *The Cream of the Jest* (1917) deserves revival. Better known as a playwright, Thornton Wilder (1897–) may well be the century's most underrated novelist. His fastidiously ironic inventions, *The Cabala* (1926) and *The Ides of March* (1948), tease the imagination; and *Heaven's My Destination* (1934) joins Allen Tate's (1899–) *The Fathers* (1938) and Glenway Wescott's (1901–) *The Grandmothers* (1927) among the unaccountably neglected American classics.

Impact of World War I. The world did not break in two in 1922, as Cather thought, but in 1914–18. World War I is the watershed of the modern consciousness, though the split did not really become apparent until the new young sensibilities, fused in the European crucible yet showing marked affinities with the mannered writing of the 1890s, began to make their impact felt. Meanwhile shifts of emphasis went on back home. Middle Western writers continued to take over from New England, the first American region to have become self-conscious. In a certain sense, nevertheless, New England's "iron dark," as Faulkner phrased it, remained the archetypal home of the moral imagination, if only as a foil to Southern lushness, which, as early as the beginning of the 1930s began a long reign over the American sensibility. Its power lasted a full 30 years until the pendulum swung again, back in the direction of the great Eastern cities.

Insofar as its chroniclers were part of it, the "lost generation" was not lost at all except, as Arthur Mizener pointed out, in "the sense that all maps were useless, and that they had to explore a new-found land for themselves." Lost or not, Ernest *Hemingway was the new generation's amphibious Neptune; William *Faulkner, its Mars in anachronistic Confederate gray; F. Scott *Fitzgerald, its silver-footed Hermes; and Thomas Wolfe (1900–38), its untidy Titan.

Hemingway, Faulkner, Fitzgerald, Wolfe. It is in Europe that American writers, like Columbuses reversing the westward passage, tend to discover themselves most memorably. The more vitally American for his periodic bouts of expatriation, Hemingway dowered the novel with a new idiom, stylized yet vernacular, and a prose technique that owed at least as much to painting as to literature. His themes were honor, courage, and war; his typical hero was an existentialist saga-warrior at bay before a world he never made. His aesthetic—"to make instead of describe"—was as severe as James's. He has to his credit the best World War I novel in English, *A Farewell to Arms* (1929), a bittersweet tragicomedy of love in the postwar wasteland, *The Sun Also Rises* (1926), and a good dozen great short stories. Of his three volumes of more or less autobiographical revelation, *A Moveable Feast* (1964) is the best.

Though Faulkner wrote of other things as well, his lasting accomplishment is the linked series of novels, *novelle,* and short stories known as the Yoknapatawpha material. Like the Mississippi in flood, it rolls across 3 decades of novelistic development. Faulkner's love-hate relationship with his native region is sociologically valuable and historically illuminating; but what gives his best work its cosmic significance is the way in which he managed to make the South surrogate for the human condition. *Light in August* (1932), *Absalom, Absalom!* (1936), *The Hamlet* (1940), and *The Bear* (from 1942's *Go Down, Moses*) represent his torrential art at its most intense.

While Faulkner must be acclaimed the prophet of what may loosely be called the Southern school, he is by no means its only writer of merit. In *Tobacco Road* (1932) and *God's Little Acre* (1933), Erskine Caldwell (1903–) served as its somewhat squalid sociologist. Robert Penn Warren (1905–), major critic and poet, provided the movement with a metaphysic that was at times too overtly symbolized. This did not prevent his *All the King's Men* (1946) from being the best political novel of its decade. Perhaps the two most vivid talents after Faulkner are the fantasists, Eudora Welty (1909–) and Carson McCullers (1917–), both of whom bring a haunting ballad note into their strange tales of humans figured as freaks and grotesques. The most recent significant Southern writer was Flannery *O'Connor (1925–64), a Catholic whose chosen field is an exploration of the Protestant fundamentalist temperament. Other names that ought not be overlooked in a long roster of Southern literary attainments are: Elizabeth Madox Roberts (1886–1941), William March (Campbell; 1893–1954), Conrad Aiken (1889–), Marjorie Kinnan Rawlings (1896–1953), Hamilton Basso (1904–64), Harper Lee (1926–), the sometimes too lurid Calder Willingham (1922–), and William Styron (1925–), author of *Lie Down in Darkness* (1951).

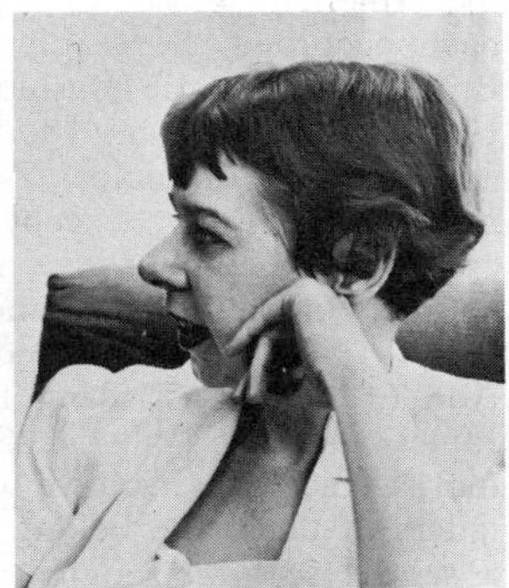

Fig. 22. Carson McCullers.

Given the grace of his prose, the charm of his literary personality, and the dark fascination of his Furies-haunted life, it is hard to be objective about F. Scott Fitzgerald. All but ruined by early adulation, unfairly neglected while still at the height of his powers, restored to critical favor shortly after his premature death, Fitzgerald has now very likely been overpraised. But he will never lose the wreath that designates him laureate of the First Jazz Age. *The Great Gatsby* (1925), as perfect in form as it is organically symbolic in content, remains a moral history of the American dream, as does a handful of consummately lyric short stories headed by "Crazy Sunday" and "Babylon Revisited."

The onetime enormous reputation of Thomas Wolfe has not weathered as well as those of his greater contemporaries. A sprawling giant of a man, he wrote his gigantesque novels after the fashion of ecstatic Whitmanesque catalogues. In essence, they were paeans of praise addressed to the American earth. The best of them—*Look Homeward, Angel* (1929), *Of Time and the River* (1935), *You Can't Go Home Again* (1940)—make up in reality one long novel; and they have but one hero, Wolfe himself.

The Short Story. Faulkner, Hemingway, and Fitzgerald are not the only good short story writers the 20th century has produced. In fact, those prophets who have been predicting the imminent demise of the novel seem to accept the American short story as vigorously alive; and so it has been, on several levels. Since the Puritan leaven has gone on working strongly within the American ethos, popular entertainers have rarely been accorded the credit they are freely granted in Britain. So it is still "fashionable" to look down on O. Henry [W. S. Porter (1862–1910)], even though such a tale as "A Municipal Report" sets him among the masters. Similarly, except in the world of musical comedy, the comic verve and poetry of slang one encounters in the fairy-tale underworld of Damon Runyon (1884–1946) goes unacknowledged by critics. George Ade (1866–1944), Ring Lardner (1885–1933), and James Thurber (1894–1961), America's greatest humorist since Twain, have all been luckier, as have the tellers of tales who belong to the *New Yorker* school, a school so wide-ranging that it must be declared a university of the contemporary conte: Irwin Shaw (1913–), J. D. Salinger (1919–), J. F. Powers (1917–), John O'Hara (1905–). Nor are practitioners of the short story within the Southern school without honor; nor those attached to what, for convenience only, may be described as the newest school, a Jewish one, whose leading members will be discussed below in another context.

The Novel of Social Concern and of Manners. In common with the rest of the world, the 1930s in America were marked by economic distress and the beginnings of ideological rigidity. As in England (though not in Europe), the American protest was intermingled with an emotional pacifism, and seemed more tentative than ordered. The avowedly Marxist novels of this period are mere curiosities today. Just as in Britain, left-wing emotion, much of it quite generous, came through more effectively in poetry. Except for Steinbeck's *Grapes of Wrath,* only one of these protests survives: the acridly symbolic, almost dadaistic personal satire of the four short novels by Nathanael West (1904–40), of which *Miss Lonelyhearts* (1933) may be taken as representative.

The period was similarly devoid of political novels capable of exploring the political demonisms then stalking over the Continent of Europe. There was no American writer comparable to André Malraux, Ignazio Silone, Arthur Koestler, or George *Orwell in this respect, though Hemingway's *For Whom the Bell Tolls* (1940) displayed a surprising objectivity toward the complex issues of the Spanish Civil War. Lionel Trilling's (1905–) *Middle of the Journey* (1947) represented an intellectual's *amende* for the political naïveté of what he had elsewhere finely termed the "liberal imagination." Intelligent, honest, overschematized, it pales beside the dark insights of Koestler's *Darkness at Noon* (1940).

The 1930s witnessed an important shift in the concept of the hero in the novel. The proletarianized Byronic adventurer came in with Hemingway's Harry Morgan in *To Have and Have Not* (1937). More importantly, after the economic debacle of 1929, Howells' and Dreiser's business-man-as-protagonist, sociological subject, and moral problem gave way to the sensitive young *homme moyen sensuel,* who finds the business round complicating his spiritual and emotional life. It was a Jamesian reversion, in a way, on the part of certain new novelists-as-social-historians who maintained the novel's central preoccupation. Beyond holding up to their age a mirror reflecting the way men really live at a particular point in space and time, they had no sociological pretensions.

The best of these historians of manners was John Marquand (1893–1960), historian of the latter-day Brahmins, chronicler of the fated consequence of choice, and satirist of two cities, New York and Boston. The titular hero of his *The Late George Apley* (1937) gave American letters the second of three emblematic types of the century, the other two being George Babbitt and Holden Caulfield. Marquand's *Wickford Point* (1935) is a Chekhovian comedy. *H. M. Pulham, Esq.* (1941) and *Point of No Return* (1949) are both major novels. Marquand's son, who writes under the name of John Phillips, acquitted himself of a brilliant "sport" in *The Second Happiest Day* (1953), a wry comedy of marriage that is closer to Evelyn Waugh and Fitzgerald than to the work of his father.

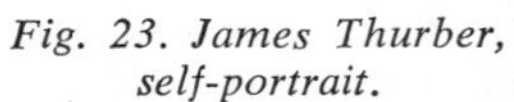

Fig. 23. James Thurber, self-portrait.

John O'Hara's coarser talents are characterized by an even more extensive social mobility but a more limited emotional range; there are times when his perception seems essentially that of a perfectly tooled tape recorder set to transcribe the confidences of bedroom, servants' entry, and men's locker room. More adept in the short story, O'Hara has written both essential and overstuffed novels. His dominant themes are the attrition of love in modern marriage and the newcomers tilting with the Establishment. The short stories in *The Cape Cod Lighter* (1962) are as high in quality as those in 1935's *Butterfield 8*. Two other social historians of more than a little merit are James Gould Cozzens (1903–) whose best-selling *By Love Possessed* (1957) was not nearly so good as his earlier novel on the law, *The Just and the Unjust* (1942), or the army novel, *Guard of Honor* (1948); and Louis Auchincloss (1917–), whose somewhat slender analytic gift shows to advantage in *The Great World of Timothy Colt* (1956), and in *The Rector of Justin* (1964).

World War II and Changing Moral Standards. The 1940s and early 1950s were overshadowed by war. For a complex of reasons, 20 years after World War II ended no war masterpiece had yet emerged from any national literature comparable to Hemingway's *A Farewell to Arms,* Remarque's *All Quiet on the Western Front* (1929), or *Werfel's *The Forty Days of Musa Dagh* (1934). In addition to the previously mentioned *The Naked and the Dead* and *From Here to Eternity,* these slighter American examples are worthy of note: Harry Brown's (1917–) *A Walk in the Sun* (1944); Thomas Heggen's (1919–49) *Mister Roberts* (1946); and Irwin Shaw's (1913–) *The Young Lions* (1948). The single epic reflex of World War II arose from the travail of world Jewry. The U.S. made one considerable contribution to this "matter of Israel" in John Hersey's (1914–) heroic *The Wall* (1950).

As had happened also after World War I, the 1950s witnessed a further relaxation of sexual reticence. After James Joyce and Virginia Woolf, the novel of individual sensibility had been "old hat" in Britain. Now, in the guise of the "self" that determines its own "identity," it tardily emerged in the U.S. One unpleasant—even, at times, sinister—minor reflex, which showed signs of having run its course by the mid-1960s, was the novel of sexual deviation, more particularly male homosexuality. As had happened much earlier in Continental fiction, so now in American the Marquis de Sade began to serve as an antimuse, presiding over a coldly schematic sort of novel ranging from Proustian ambivalence, through transvestite nightmare, to proselytizing for the aberrations in question. The image of woman became defaced. Fantasy turned onanistic. The sensibility of Russian-born Vladimir Nabokov (1899–) introduced the word "nymphet" to the American vocabulary in his novel *Lolita* (1955); and in *Naked Lunch* (1959) William Burroughs (1914–) proved that it was quite possible to out-Genet Jean Genet.

With one exception, the emotional recidivism implicit in the deviate's monocular view of reality was foredoomed to flatness and mediocrity for the reason Hemingway once gave: "In general they lack drama as do all tales of abnormality since no one can predict what will happen in the normal while all tales of the abnormal end much the same." The single exception is the kind of command Truman Capote (1924–) exerts over his imaginative miniature universe of childhood—a Hans Christian Andersen world minus its tenderness and sense of "otherness"—in *Other Voices, Other Rooms* (1948), *The Grass Harp* (1951), and *A Tree of Night* (1956).

Exponents of another minority phenomenon, Jack Kerouac (1922–) and his fellow "beats," wrote a species of autobiography in fiction (*see* "BEAT" WRITING). More effective in "hipster" poetry and off-beat music, the beat aesthetic, to call it that, can be seen in Kerouac's *On the Road* (1957) and *The Dharma Bums* (1960). They are loose-gaited, spastic books that looked to Henry Miller (1891–) for their father image and to his cloacal trilogy, *Sexus, Plexus, Nexus* (1949–60), as the holy books of the part of their mystique that might be described as scatalogy-into-eschatology. A cognate preoccupation with Zen Buddhism somewhat tenuously linked J. D. Salinger (1919–) with these self-styled "holy barbarians." But Salinger, who became an international culture-hero in the 1950s and 1960s, is a much more considerable and likable phenomenon than just this. Perhaps there is less than meets the eye in his pint-sized saga of those seven mystical buds sprung from *Abie's Irish Rose,* the Glass children. Perhaps there is something a little facile in the escape into contemplation that, on closer view, looks more like mere religiosity, offered by *Franny and Zooey* (1961). But even if Salinger turns out to have been a man of one book, there can be no reservations about the excellence of *The Catcher in the Rye* (1951) with Holden Caulfield, the incarnation of every boy's adolescence, setting down his own wincing view of life in a marvelously convincing vernacular.

The Groves of Academe, Thrillers, and Westerns. Among minor fiction that ought not be overlooked was the emergence of the "academic" novel in two senses of the word: the novel *about* academe, such as Mary McCarthy's (1912–) *The Groves of Academe* (1952) and Randall Jarrell's (1914–65) *Pictures from an Institution* (1954); and the novel *by* academics, usually overloaded with symbols. Wright Morris's (1910–) *Ceremony in Lone Tree* (1960) might be taken as representative of this too elaborately conscious kind of "construct." The historical novel, always a popular but never a major genre in America, enjoyed two spectacular successes in Hervey Allen's (1889–1949) *Anthony Adverse* (1933) and Margaret Mitchell's (1900–49) *Gone With the Wind* (1936). Mention should also be made of Kenneth Robert's (1885–1957) successful cycle dealing with the Revolutionary period through the War of 1812; Walter Edmonds's (1903–) *Drums Along the Mohawk* (1936) and *Chad Hanna* (1940); the *Bounty* trilogy (1932–34) of Charles Nordhoff (1887–1947) and James Norman Hall (1887–1951); and the Dumaslike cloak-and-sword contrivances of Samuel Shellabarger (1888–1954), such as *Captain from Castile* (1945).

As a part of their Puritan inheritance, Americans tend to take their literary pleasures rather sadly. The country that sired the detective story through Poe's Dupin has never really accepted the thriller as a legitimate branch of literature. Unlike the English variety, American detective stories move in the direction neither of poetry nor of fantasy; nor do they offer themselves, *à la* Graham Greene, as symbols for the human plight. Nevertheless, the "hard-boiled" *roman policier,* which was to reach its *reductio ad absurdum* in the sadistic wish-fulfillments of Mickey Spillane and Ian Fleming, had its genesis in an American pulp magazine in 1929. Marking the transition from gentleman sleuth to professional private eye, *Black Mask* published the early stories of the only two masters to raise their work above the general ruck of this unstable subgenre. Dashiell Hammett (1894–1961) created the sardonic private operative, Sam Spade. Raymond Chandler (1888–1959) was somewhat Hemingwayesque in his feeling for Los Angeles as it was in the 1930s; but his half-Hamlet, half-Horatio Philip Marlowe owed much to Joseph Conrad's narrator-detective of human motive, the Marlow of *Youth* and *Lord Jim.* Through his Perry Mason series Erle Stanley Gardner (1889–) popularized the Hammett-Chandler formula with great success. The Rex Stout (1886–) Nero Wolfe stories followed the beaten path of the omnicompetent sleuth.

Given the provenance of the western story, which happens to be the U.S.'s original contribution to the romance cycles of the Western world, it is more than a little disappointing that this century's western hardly measures up to the derivative German Wild West tales of Karl May or to what James Thurber used to call the French *Aventures du Wild Bill dans le Far-Ouest.* Now and then, to offset the tepidities of a Zane Grey (1875–1939), an occasional fine book did put in an appearance: Owen Wister's (1860–1938) *The Virginian* (1902), for example, or Walter Van Tilburg Clark's (1909–) *The Ox-Bow Incident* (1940). On the whole, however, the kind of imaginative energy that begot the first true western in Cooper's *The Prairie* went into the Remington-and-Meissonier detail that movie director John Ford lavished on such pictures as *Fort Apache* and *The Horse Soldiers.*

Every era has its popular fictioneers; their books enjoy enormous vogues for a few decades, then become footnotes in literary histories. They are usually women; and their great exemplar, the single work of genius created in this vein, remains Charlotte Brontë's *Jane Eyre.* The 20th century's successors to last century's Augusta Jane Evans, author of *St. Elmo,* and England's Mrs. Henry Wood of *East Lynne* fame are Frances Parkinson Keyes (1885–), Edna Ferber (1887–), and Taylor Caldwell (1900–). Three of Ferber's entertainments, *So Big* (1924), *Show Boat* (1926), and *Cimarron* (1930), managed to transcend the stereotype this sort of commodity usually demands.

In a subterranean way, subliterary developments can be of enormous cultural importance. On this plane, Edgar Rice Burroughs (1875–1950) was the century's demiurge. After his own crudely sensational fashion, he was a master of archetypes; and primary narrative vigor made his Tarzan, blood-brother of Gilgamesh and Beowulf, an even more widely known folk hero than Arthur Conan Doyle's Sherlock Holmes.

Again because of its Puritan antecedents, American literature almost invariably tends to be a literature of power rather than of delight. As was true of the 19th century, the 20th has produced little fantasy as such. Nor has there been memorable writing for children, except for the first few *Oz* books of L. Frank Baum (1856–1919), and the exquisite original fairy tales that James Thurber (1894–1961) produced between *Many Moons* (1943) and *The Thirteen Clocks* (1950). One cannot help but note, too, that a deposit of first-rate science fiction is wanting; and, on another plane, that there has not existed a viable conception of society upon which novelists might repose, as Trollope and C. P. Snow have done, without the necessity of protest or dissent. Except for Peter De Vries (1910–), and the somewhat Rabelaisian view he takes of life in suburbia in *Tunnel of Love* (1954) and *Comfort Me With Apples* (1956), the American comic novel was virtually nonexistent.

Fiction from Catholic Authors. Since novelists who happen to be Catholic have a way of resenting being categorized as Catholic novelists, perhaps it is better to speak of fiction by Catholics rather than by the more constricting label "Catholic fiction." Indeed, unlike the Augustinian example of Britain's Graham Greene and France's François Mauriac, there is no American metaphysical tradition of Catholic writing. On the plane of fiction, it has had a tendency to move in the direction of ethnic and national local color. By whatever name, fiction by American Catholics in the 20th century has described, on the whole, a gratifying parabola between the Biedermeyer decorations on *The Cardinal's Snuff Box* (1900), by the *Yellow Book's* Henry Harland (1861–1905), and Flannery O'Connor's contemporary empathetic reconstructions of Southern Calvinism.

Between the termini of this trajectory, there were certain developments, some of them quite encouraging in the light of what seemed to be an American Catholic culture lag. Myles Connolly (1897–1964) produced his Chestertonian whimsy, *Mr. Blue,* in 1928. As accomplished in history as in fiction, Paul Horgan (1903–) has shown great psychological delicacy both in *novella* and essential novel. His Harper prize novel, *The Fault of Angels* (1933), represented one facet of a discriminating sensibility. *A Distant Trumpet* (1960) was a Vergilian evocation of the U.S. Cavalry in the last Indian war. For his chosen terrain Edwin O'Connor (1918–) selected an area Trollope had not disdained: that of Irish priests and politicians. Up to 1964 his two important books were *The Last Hurrah* (1956) and the Pulitzer prize winner, *The Edge of Sadness* (1961). J. F. Powers (1917–) tilled an even narrower plot: that of the priest's life viewed departmentally as across a rectory breakfast table. Of the three books Powers produced over a period of nearly 20 years, two of them, *Prince of Darkness* (1947) and *The Presence of Grace* (1956), were made up of distinguished short stories. His single novel, *Morte d'Urban* (1962), a National Book award winner, displayed at one and the same time robust humor, delicate probing of motive, and a Balzacian density of selective detail that made it the best clerical comedy Catholicism had seen since Balzac's *Le Curé de Tours.*

Influence of the Indian, the Negro, and the Jew. Although the Indian stayed almost as aloof from the white man's culture as he had in Tocqueville's day, there was a growing body of excellent fiction about him: e.g., James Boyd's (1888–1944) *Shadows of the Long Knives* (1928), Oliver *LaFarge's *Laughing Boy* (1929), Mary Austin's (1868–1934) *One-Smoke Stories* (1934), August Derleth's (1909–) *Wind Over Wisconsin* (1938), A. B. Guthrie's (1901–) *The Big Sky* (1947), and Conrad Richter's (1890–) *The Light in the Forest* (1953). More importantly, if more and more the Negro was becoming the nation's conscience, the Indian had always stood for its imagination—what Thoreau once called the "red face of man." One had only to open the pages of Cather's *The Professor's House* (1925) or Faulkner's *Go Down, Moses* (1940) to recognize that Indian empathy with the wilderness and Indian freedom from the clogs of civilization blew like a calumet's smoke through 20th-century literature every bit as much as through the century of Cooper and Chateaubriand.

Negro Protest. The Negro, on the other hand, far from staying aloof, had from the beginning patiently tried to assimilate himself to the dominant culture he had encountered, as a slave, in the New World. From Cooper's *Littlepage* trilogy (1845–46) on, Negro characters had been depicted by white writers with varying degrees of sympathy and sensitivity, a one-way traffic that culminated in the power and depth Twain and Faulkner brought to their heroically conceived portraits of black men. But, inspired as Jim and Lucas Beauchamp were, they were still black men seen through the eyes of white men. As James Baldwin sardonically remarked about Faulkner's dichotomy in the representation of Negroes: "He could control them in his imagination, but not in life." The time had come for the Negro to write his own novels. He did so according to the manifesto James Baldwin directed to his fellow novelists: "You have to force the world to deal with you, not the white man's image of you." The Negro novelist's attempt to establish his own identity as a human person marks one of the novel's two major developments since 1950. The other is the even more successful effort on the part of an emergent school of Jewish novelists.

Both developments were the result of the classic American quest. The "secret sharer" who serves as every American novelist's psychic double continues to be America itself; this is a characteristic that American culture shares with Russian culture and with no other. Every new ethnic group, every new minority culture must engage in this Laocoön struggle to prove its identity as native son; and the Negro's necessity is simultaneously the most urgent and the most difficult of all. For he has to affirm what other groups can assume: his essential humanity as a man, not just his particular status as a black man. This is why, up to 1965, the Negro novel, for all its power and integrity, remained in a propaganda phase, however incandescent the special pleading that illuminates it. It is still thesis fiction keeping pace with the nascent black self-consciousness that marked the 1950s and 1960s, expressing itself within Africa, for instance, in the *négritude* of poetry written in the one-time French colonies and in the English vernacular fiction of such a transitional figure as Amos Tutuola (*see* NEO-AFRICAN LITERATURE).

Putting aside such interesting cognate phenomena as fiction by Negroes about the genre subjects of jazz and dope, important Negro fiction began with *Native Son* (1940), a novel tracing the black American's socioeconomic curve from sharecropper to urban proletarian, by Richard Wright (1908–), a writer who afterward belied his early promise. Ralph Ellison (1914–) took the next step with the pregnant symbol of his *Invisible Man* (1952). James Baldwin (1924–), who read Wright and Ellison in his Harlem boyhood, inherited

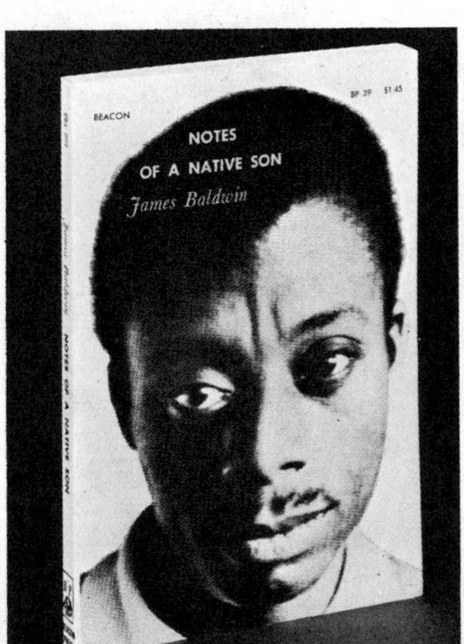

Fig. 24. James Baldwin.

their tradition of polemic and dissent. As much pamphleteer and essayist as novelist, Baldwin deployed his eloquently troubling fiction—*Go Tell It on the Mountain* (1953), *Another Country* (1961)—as a way of realizing "a bigger world than the world in which I lived," as an escape hatch, for both his race and himself, from the Harlem ghetto, where "I hung in limbo," not knowing "precisely where I belonged or what I was." This kind of impulse once powered Dickens's generous indignation; and there is every evidence that, once the necessity for revolutionary protest has passed, the Negro novel will come of age as a rounded, three-dimensional consideration of human problems.

The more things change, the more they stay the same. Behind the classic tradition of the American novel lies an Adamic vision of man; and every bit as much as the 19th-century masters, the new Jewish novelists strive to induct this primal perception into their fresh alignments of experience. The biggest novelistic displacement since the end of World War II has been the growing ascendancy of a group of these new Jewish writers.

Jewish Moral Concern. Possessed of energy, biological *élan,* and a sense of life's inner significance, Jewish writers have been reshaping the novel into a thing that is new and yet old, into an aesthetic entity that has Chagall and Sholom Aleichem in its vigorous pedigree as well as Tolstoy, the Transcendentalists, and the great Victorians. Budd Schulberg (1913–), Jerome Weidman (1913–), Gerald Green (1922–), Irwin Shaw (1913–), Leo Rosten (1908–), Daniel Fuchs (1909–), Herman Wouk (1915–), Leon Uris (1924–), all in their very different ways demonstrate range and power. But the three leaders in 1965 appeared to be Bernard Malamud (1914–), Saul Bellow (1915–), and, though his output had so far been slight, Philip Roth (1933–). Bellow's notable achievement, in the picaresque *The Adventures of Augie March* (1953) and *Henderson the Rain King* (1959) which mixes surrealist fancy and symbol to provide a full-blooded, yet cerebral comedy. His *Herzog* (1965) won the National Book Award. Malamud, too, utilizes an idiosyncratic use of fantasy in his baseball novel, *The Natural* (1952), and in one of the century's great short story collections, *The Magic Barrel* (1959). His "straight" fiction, *The Assistant* (1957) and *A New Life* (1961), is not quite so effective. Till now Roth has confined his attention to shorter fiction; the title *novella* in *Goodbye Columbus* (1959) is most notable.

Two New Talents. As Hawthorne had done before them, two rather considerable new talents naturalize the gods in contemporary contexts. Like a silver snail out of Walter De la Mare, John Updike (1932–) has traced a glistening track across the 1960s in novel, short story, and light verse. A Keatsian romantic and virtuoso of language, he tilts an almost overbrimming cornucopia of essay richness onto the pages of *The Poorhouse Fair* (1959), *Rabbit Run* (1960), and *Pigeon Feathers* (1962). His more ambitious *The Centaur* (1963) does not succeed quite so well.

If Updike is Fair Harvard incarnate, John Cheever (1912–) is New England redivivus. Like Updike, Cheever is a laureate of domestic love and a celebrator of monogamy; his Westchester suburbanites pursue lost innocence and the good life. Cheever's earlier work was in the short story; *The Enormous Radio and Other Stories* (1953) is representative here. He broke impressive new ground in his two *Wapshot* chronicles (1957 and 1963).

Portents for the Future. From Edith Wharton to John Updike stretch five writing generations. Halfway through the 1960s there appeared to be no major portents of change; consolidation, not experimentation, seemed to be the current mode. Though the novel has never mediated tragedy with the authority of drama, there were signs that a further flight away from tragedy

Fig. 25. John Updike.

into the grotesque, after the fashion of Eudora Welty's and Carson McCuller's Dickensian monsters, might be in the immediate offing. There were indications, too, that the symbolism syndrome had not yet run its course. For the rest, the protean form that Emerson mistrusted and paid the ultimate compliment of labeling "sorceries" will go on being written for the predictable future. As Thoreau put it, "creation is here and now." The American novel is very far from having reached its 7th day.

Bibliography: J. ALDRIDGE, *After the Lost Generation* (New York 1951). W. E. ALLEN, *The Modern Novel in Britain and the United States* (New York 1964). J. W. BEACH, *American Fiction: 1920–1940* (New York 1941). M. BEWLEY, *The Eccentric Design* (New York 1959). V. W. BROOKS, *The Confident Years: 1885–1915* (New York 1952). R. CHASE, *The American Novel and Its Tradition* (Garden City, N.Y. 1957). A. COWIE, *The Rise of the American Novel* (New York 1951). M. COWLEY, ed., *After the Genteel Tradition* (Gloucester, Mass. 1959). L. A. FIEDLER, *Love and Death in the American Novel* (New York 1960). W. M. FROHOCK, *The Novel of Violence in America: 1920–1950* (Dallas 1950). H. C. GARDINER, ed., *Fifty Years of the American Novel: 1900–1950* (New York 1951). M. D. GEISMAR, *Writers in Crisis* (Boston 1942); *Last of the Provincials* (Boston 1947); *Rebels and Ancestors* (Boston 1953). F. J. HOFFMAN, *The Modern Novel in America* (Chicago 1956); *The Twenties* (New York 1955). A. KAZIN, *On Native Grounds* (abr. ed. Garden City, N.Y. 1956). A. MIZENER, *The Sense of Life in the Modern Novel* (Boston 1964). **Illustration credits:** Fig. 21, Courtesy, Underwood and Underwood; Photo, Library of Congress. Fig. 22, Photograph by Werner J. Kuhn. Fig. 23, Harper & Row. Fig. 24, Beacon Press. Fig. 25, W. Earl Snyder.

[C. A. BRADY]

AMERICAN PHILOSOPHY

In a strict sense, there is no American philosophy just as there is no French or German philosophy; all the major philosophical schools have been and continue to be represented in philosophical thought in America. In a broad sense, however, American philosophy may be taken to mean the history of philosophical ideas in the U.S., and particularly their relation to the complex totality of American intellectual history, i.e., to its social, economic, political, literary, and religious aspects and to the Western tradition as a whole. Just as American civilization is not specifically new but is a distinctive part of the great Western culture whose components are Greek and Roman thought and the Hebraic and Christian religious traditions, so philosophical thought in America is part of the complex unity of the Western intellectual tradition. The proximate origins of philosophical speculation in the English-speaking colonies of North America are traceable to the colleges of the 17th century. The coming of age of American philosophy in the period following the Civil War was preceded by a long period of development whose principal stages were the theological thought of colonial times, the encyclopedic and political thought of the Enlightenment, and the religious and literary humanism of the Romantic era.

Colonial Times. A year before Descartes's *Discourse on Method* appeared (1637), the Puritans of New England were founding Harvard College. Varied influences from abroad, particularly British, French, and German, helped to shape the early American intellectual tradition. Important though the French influence in the 18th century and the German influence in the 19th were, the British influence was pervasive and immeasurable from colonial times. The colonials were nurtured upon the writings of British theologians and philosophers, particularly John *Locke. Yet from the earliest period, native forces also were powerful in the formation of a nation of continental proportions. "The Puritan came to the New World and became a Yankee."

First Philosophers. The early colonial colleges provided the rudiments of philosophical instruction through the medium of Latin manuals. There were many learned divines in early New England whose ideas are still of interest, but the first philosophers of note appeared in the 18th century. Thus Samuel Johnson (1696–1772), a native of Connecticut, who was the first president of King's College (later Columbia University), has been called America's first college philosophy professor. An Anglican minister, he championed free will against the

Fig. 1. Samuel Johnson, before 1757, by John Smibert.

Calvinists and taught a theory of idealism similar to that of G. *Berkeley. His philosophical works, chiefly *Elementa philosophica* (Philadelphia 1752), though not markedly original, contributed greatly to the spread of a deeper knowledge of philosophy in the colonial institutions. Similarly, Jonathan *Edwards is known as America's first great philosophical thinker. He was one of the last of the great Puritan divines, and his mentality, if not his theology, reminds one of the scholastics. He utilized his knowledge of philosophy to defend *Calvinism against *Arminianism and *Deism. His idealistic doctrine was original with him, but it has much in common with the teachings of the *Cambridge Platonists and of Berkeley. Among his most important works is the *Inquiry into the Freedom of the Will* (Princeton 1754), which defends the thesis that, while it is free in the sense of possessing a spontaneity of inclination, the will is determined by the motives presented to it by the understanding and ultimately by God. For some critics, such as V. Parrington, he was a great thinker but a failure because he sought to enslave souls to an outworn creed. To others, such as P. E. More, he is a giant of the intellect comparable to Calvin and a master of religious emotion.

Influence of the Enlightenment. The "Age of Reason" in the colonies was part of a large-scale movement emanating from Europe and extending to North and South America. Among the outstanding representatives of the *Enlightenment are men famous as founders of the new republic: Benjamin Franklin, John Adams, Thomas Jefferson, Thomas *Paine, and Ethan Allen. Indebted to European political philosophy, these men were inspired by the age-old tradition of English liberties and by the experience of living in a pioneer land. Despite certain weaknesses in their political thought, the Founding Fathers created a reasonable and workable political instrument in the Constitution of the U.S., which ranks among the notable achievements of mankind.

The religious philosophy of the Enlightenment thinkers was predominantly Deistic. While most of them adhered personally to a religious creed, their interpretation of religion reduced it to a religion of nature, a kind of "Christianity not mysterious." Their views on God and providence differ widely, but the principle guiding their philosophical speculation is indicated by the title of Allen's *Reason the Only Oracle of Man.* One of the most extreme attacks on supernatural revelation and authority is delivered in Paine's *The Age of Reason.* (*See* ENLIGHTENMENT, PHILOSOPHY OF.)

Between 1800 and 1870. The early 19th century was an age of optimism and idealism. Despite the gathering clouds of war, it was a kind of springtime. An unbounded confidence in the power of men to cooperate with their fellows in building an ideal society, particularly in the new lands opening up for settlement, was characteristic of the most generous minds. This attitude was in part a development of the Enlightenment faith in reason, but in even greater part it was an outgrowth of the influence of European Romanticism (*see* ROMANTICISM, PHILOSOPHICAL). The idealism of the time is illustrated in somewhat exaggerated form by the numerous utopian societies and communitarian experiments that were tried under the auspices of both religious and irreligious "free-thinking" groups. Of greater significance for the development of philosophy was the influence of the *Scottish School of Common Sense on many academic centers. This type of realism was regarded as providing support for orthodox Protestant theology. Among the leading members of the movement were John *Witherspoon, James McCosh (1811–94), and Noah Porter (1811–92). At this time, the professor of mental and moral philosophy was usually both college president and professor of divinity.

Like the American Enlightenment, *transcendentalism was part of a worldwide movement of Romanticism. It is in many respects the most significant movement in the general cultural life of the 19th-century America. Partly a reaction against Calvinism, partly a reaction against the *rationalism of the Enlightenment, it was deeply influenced by Romanticism, German *idealism, Plato, and the Orient. Nevertheless, it had deep native roots and corresponded to the aspirations of its generation; the ideas it took from Europe were those for which it felt an affinity. Among its leading lights were R. W. *Emerson, H. D. *Thoreau, A. B. Alcott (1799–1888), Margaret Fuller (1810–50), T. *Parker, G. Ripley (1802–80), and O. *Brownson. The most eminent, Emerson, was for Europe as for America the representative American philosopher of the age. Indebted to the great minds and poets of many lands, he made his own what he absorbed. Emersonian philosophy is a kind of intuitive and mystical wisdom, expressed aphoristically rather than systematically. While Emerson preached the characteristic American virtue of self-reliance, it has not always been recognized that for him self-reliance is achieved in the measure in which one becomes united to the Over-Soul. Self-reliance is God-reliance. In communing with Nature, one comes close to Universal Being, to God. Emerson cannot and should not be compared with Kant and Plato, but he continues to have a message for American culture; he personifies "man thinking."

From 1870 to World War I. After the Civil War, America entered a period of rapid expansion, in which higher education participated. Many colleges developed into universities and established graduate schools. Scholars in greater numbers than ever went to Germany for higher studies. The philosophers among them returned and set up separate departments of philosophy. Historians of American philosophy view this period as philosophy's coming of age. It seems premature to refer to it as a classic period, but it was undoubtedly a golden age. An outstanding generation of distinguished teachers and scholars, the mere listing of whose names would be unduly long, elevated philosophical pursuits in the U.S. to a level of greater professional proficiency. They brought to the task vision as well as technique. Several of them are ranked by common consent among the greatest of American philosophers: C. S. *Peirce, J. *Royce, W. *James, and J. *Dewey. To complete the list of "six classic philosophers," the names of G. *Santayana and A. N. *Whitehead should be added. Santayana was born in Spain and lived abroad for many years; he was educated and taught at Harvard, however, and published *Realms of Being* and other important works, particularly on aesthetics, in the U.S. Whitehead, an eminent British mathematician and philosopher, came to the U.S. late in life, after World War I, but for almost a quarter of a century he was exceptionally influential on the younger generation of philosophers. He felt that the American experience prompted him to state his philosophy in its definitive form.

Evolutionism. Among the most significant developments contributing to a decided change in philosophical outlook was the debate over *evolutionism. As Dewey brought out in his *Influence of Darwin upon Philosophy* New York (1910), philosophy was never the same after the appearance of Darwin's *Origin of Species* (1859). There was a shift, to use the graphic expression of Peirce, from "seminary philosophy" to "laboratory philosophy." However, not all theologians rejected evolutionary theories, nor did all scientists accept them.

Fig. 2. Borden Parker Bowne.

The Harvard scientist Louis *Agassiz adhered steadfastly to the doctrine of fixed types. Asa Gray, a botanist, was among the leading defenders of Darwinism and maintained that it was reconcilable with religious belief. The leading philosopher engaged in the controversy was John Fiske (1842–1901), who was influenced by Herbert *Spencer but elaborated his own version of evolutionary philosophy in *Outlines of Cosmic Philosophy* (London 1874) and *The Idea of God as Affected by Modern Knowledge* (Boston 1885).

Idealism. For the greater part of this period the predominant philosophy in America was idealism. Of its numerous varieties the principal schools were (1) personal idealism (G. H. Howison, B. P. Bowne); (2) speculative or objective idealism (J. E. Creighton); (3) dynamic idealism (G. S. Morris); and (4) absolute idealism (J. Royce). The most distinguished of American idealists is undoubtedly Royce, who characterized his own system as absolute idealism, absolute voluntarism, and absolute pragmatism. He stressed the role of the will in the activity of thought and argued that the need for the eternal is among the deepest of all man's practical needs. Among the more recent idealists may be mentioned W. E. Hocking and B. Blanshard.

Pragmatism. Peirce and James are the recognized founders of *pragmatism, though there is a considerable difference in their interpretations of pragmatic method. Peirce, who eventually called his own version pragmaticism, aspired to erect a philosophical edifice that would outlast the vicissitudes of time, but he was unable to complete his system. The seminal ideas contained in his *Collected Papers* (8 v.) have won him recognition in the 20th century as one of America's greatest philosophers. James made such significant contributions to the young science of psychology that he is often referred to as the "Father of American Psychology." He was noted for his lively style, warm personality, and zest for living; and his writings evoked new interest in philosophical questions among the educated public. He interpreted the pragmatic principle in moral and in psychological rather than in strictly logical terms, and employed it as a method for resolving puzzling philosophical issues. He tried to sketch a metaphysics of pure experience in his radical *empiricism, but he had room in his philosophy for a divinity of limited power, a future life, and the reality of human freedom.

In his journey "from absolute idealism to experimentalism," Dewey was influenced by Darwin, Peirce, and James. He emphasized the need for a complete "reconstruction *in* philosophy" and the development of experimental naturalism based on experience and the empirical method. With sober earnestness, a somewhat plodding style, and dogged determinism, he undertook this task in a score or more of books and numerous other studies. In his thought education and democracy, philosophy and civilization are closely related; he sought to make philosophy count for something in a practical world. Dewey vies with James for the title of America's most representative philosopher.

From World War I to World War II. At the beginning of the 20th century, idealism continued to dominate the philosophical scene as it had for much of the 19th century. However, pragmatism soon forced it to assume a defensive posture. The controversy over the epistemological issues involved in idealistic metaphysics contributed to a resurgence of realism. Even before World War I, the "new realists" (E. B. Holt, W. T. Marvin, W. P. Montague, R. B. Perry, W. B. Pitkin, and E. G. Spaulding) issued their manifesto, *The New Realism* (New York 1912). Dissatisfied with the difficulties in the presentationalistic theory of the new realists, the "critical realists" (D. Drake, A. O. Lovejoy, J. B. Pratt, A. K. Rogers, Santayana, and R. W. Sellars) stated their position in *Essays in Critical Realism* (London 1920). During the 1920s and 1930s a lively debate ensued, then subsided somewhat inconclusively as the participants went on to develop their own highly divergent metaphysical doctrines. Montague formulated an "animistic materialism"; and Sellars, an "evolutionary naturalism and new materialism." (*See* REALISM, AMERICAN.)

Fig. 3. Ralph Barton Perry.

World War II and After. American philosophers have on the whole recognized their responsibility to be concerned with the social and political problems of their times. They have frequently been, as this account shows, in the ranks of reformers. Up to the time of World War I a note of optimism about social progress continued to prevail. The disillusionment following the war and the shock of the great economic Depression of the 1930s, however, affected the outlook of the philosophers in the academic community; they took stock of the role

Fig. 4. Sidney Hook.

of philosophy and education in a period of crisis, and sought to set down solid foundations for a social and economic democracy. Tough-minded naturalists and Christian philosophers alike were more often than not found in the ranks of the liberals, though they differed profoundly on basic principles. After World War II, the space age, and the period of the cold war, many philosophers seemed for a time to be overawed by the colossus of science and accepted the role of working on highly specialized problems calling for proficiency of technique rather than range of vision. Eventually, more and more of them came to recognize the need for the restoration of a philosophy more humanistic, even more metaphysical. Meanwhile, as an institution in American higher education, philosophy flourished more than ever. It had to its credit a number of distinguished philosophers respected internationally; it made notable contributions to every branch of philosophy and its history. Of increasing importance was the philosophy of science (*see* SCIENCE, PHILOSOPHY OF). Yet something of the buoyant confidence and broad vision of the giants of the golden age seemed wanting.

Among the prominent developments of this period are *naturalism, *logical positivism, *existentialism and *phenomenology, *Thomism, and the renewal of metaphysics. Naturalism continues to be one of the strongest movements in American philosophy. Vigorous new spokesmen (S. Hook, E. Nagel) have succeeded the older generation (M. R. Cohen, F. J. E. Woodbridge, Sellars). C. I. Lewis's conceptualistic pragmatism synthesized ideas from diverse sources. Just before World War II, logical positivism was introduced into the U.S. by R. Carnap and others from Continental circles. It appealed to many empirically minded philosophers who were no longer satisfied with the older type of pragmatism. After the war, the increasing interest extended to the other principal form of *analytical philosophy, *linguistic analysis, and was aroused chiefly through the writings of British scholars, some of whom came to teach in the U.S. Positivism and analysis appeared for a time on the way to dominating the scene completely. The preponderant role of the sciences in education, culture, and the national life generally does much to explain the philosophical attraction exerted by the proponents of an "encyclopedia of unified science."

Although the International Society of Phenomenology and the *Journal of Philosophy and Phenomenological Research* were founded in 1939 and 1940 respectively, only recently have phenomenology and existentialism had any wide influence. It was unlikely that existentialist philosophy, which has generally risen in a society afflicted with defeat and anxiety, would appeal to an affluent society. However, the growing sense of a vacuum in the sphere of human values as the rift between the "two cultures" widened may explain the attraction existential phenomenology has had, particularly in Protestant theological circles and for some Catholic scholars. The American Catholic philosophical enterprise, which enjoys a long tradition of teaching scholastic and Thomistic philosophy in a large number of colleges and universities and which established the *American Catholic Philosophical Association in 1926, came of age after World War II as its members took an increasingly active part in common philosophical pursuits (*see* SCHOLASTICISM, 3). These factors contributed to a genuine renewal of metaphysics, typified by the thriving Metaphysical Society of America, founded in 1950. Among leading metaphysicians are P. Weiss, J. Wild, and J. Feibleman.

Critique and Evaluation. This brief sketch cannot even mention by name all the philosophers and movements worthy of note; at best it conveys a sense of the variety and vitality of the American philosophical tradition. Is there a unifying theme in its history? To discover one is not an easy matter, as H. Schneider points out. Scholars have held up Scottish realism, transcendentalism, and especially pragmatism as *the* American philosophy. Meanwhile the philosophical enterprise in America continues to be vigorously pluralistic. All the schools of thought are represented in its ranks. While there is thus no one American philosophy, there are nevertheless certain common traits that characterize the American philosophical tradition. There is above all a practical emphasis, with a zeal for reform and renewal; there is a unity that is moral rather than doctrinal. American philosophy has traditionally conserved a religious and humanistic orientation, even in pragmatism. Yet the danger confronting it lies in an increasingly naturalistic ethos, indifferent if not hostile to religious values. As American philosophy faces the challenge of existence in a technological culture, what it most needs is not less technique but more vision.

Bibliography: Histories. M. R. COHEN, *American Thought,* ed. F. S. COHEN (Riverside, N.J. 1954). M. F. CURTI, *The Growth of American Thought* (2d ed. New York 1951). G. DELEDALLE, *Histoire de la philosophie américaine . . .* (Paris 1954). D. A. GALLAGHER, "American Philosophic Thought and the Western Tradition" in J. HIRSCHBERGER, *The History of Philosophy,* tr. A. N. FUERST, 2 v. (Milwaukee 1958–59) v.2. S. PERSONS, *American Minds* (New York 1958). V. L. PARRINGTON, *Main Currents in American Thought,* 3 v. (New York 1927–30). N. PORTER, "Philosophy in Great Britain and America" in F. UEBERWEG, *History of Philosophy,* tr. G. S. MORRIS from 4th

Ger. ed., 2 v. (New York 1872–74) 2:349–460, app. A. J. RECK, *Recent American Philosophy* (New York 1964). W. RILEY, *American Thought from Puritanism to Pragmatism and Beyond* (New York 1915; repr. 1941). H. W. SCHNEIDER, *A History of American Philosophy* (2d ed. New York 1963). J. SMITH, *The Spirit of American Philosophy* (New York 1965). H. TOWNSEND, *Philosophical Ideas in the U.S.* (Cincinnati 1934). W. H. WERKMEISTER, *A History of Philosophical Ideas in America* (New York 1949). R. C. WHITTEMORE, *Makers of the American Mind* (New York 1964).

Readings and sources. G. P. ADAMS and W. P. MONTAGUE, eds., *Contemporary American Philosophy: Personal Statements,* 2 v. (New York 1930). P. R. ANDERSON and M. H. FISCH, eds., *Philosophy in America from the Puritans to James* (New York 1939). J. L. BLAU, ed., *American Philosophic Addresses, 1700–1900* (New York 1946). M. FARBER, ed., *Philosophic Thought in France and the U.S.* (Buffalo, N.Y. 1950), original essays by noted scholars. M. H. FISCH, ed., *Classic American Philosophers* (New York 1951). S. HOOK, ed., *American Philosophers at Work* (New York 1956), essays. W. G. MUELDER, et al., eds., *The Development of American Philosophy* (2d ed. Boston 1960).

Illustration credits: Fig. 1, Columbia University. Fig. 2, Boston University. Fig. 3, Fabian Bachrach, Boston. Fig. 4, New York University.

[D. A. GALLAGHER]

AMERICAN PROTECTIVE ASSOCIATION

A secret anti-Catholic organization, active especially in the Middle West during the period 1893 to 1896. Like the earlier Know-Nothing Movement, the A.P.A. relied primarily on political activities to combat the alleged menace of Catholicism in America (*see* KNOW-NOTHINGISM).

The A.P.A. was founded in 1887 in Clinton, Iowa, by Henry F. Bowers. About 70,000 members had been recruited in the upper Mississippi Valley by 1892. The following year a number of factors inspired a great surge in A.P.A. activity and strength. These included the appointment of Abp. Francis Satolli as first permanent papal delegate to the U.S.; the replacement of Bowers by William J. Traynor, a more practical and politically astute leader; and most important, the Panic of 1893, which A.P.A. propagandists ascribed to papal plots.

These developments occurred at a time when Irish political power was increasing in such cities as Boston and New York and when the prolonged school controversy was aggravating anti-Catholic sentiment. The rapid expansion of parochial schools after the Third Plenary Council in 1884 had induced several states to attempt public regulation of private schools. Compromise solutions, such as the *Poughkeepsie Plan and the *Faribault Plan, only provoked further controversy.

Encouraged by these circumstances the A.P.A. launched a membership drive and by 1896 claimed a total of 2,500,000 members. To aid its campaign the society established the *A.P.A. Magazine* and about 70 weekly newspapers, including Traynor's *Patriotic American,* which published a bogus encyclical in which the date was set for American Catholics to slay their fellow citizens in a holy massacre. Propaganda efforts were reinforced by economic pressure against Catholic businessmen and workers.

Political action, however, was the principal A.P.A. concern. Usually endorsing Republican candidates, the A.P.A. influenced elections in 1894 in Ohio, Wisconsin, Indiana, Missouri, and Colorado. In Michigan the society elected a congressman, William S. Linton. Yet, in a year of Republican victories, the strength of the A.P.A. was deceptive. Many of the candidates endorsed by its state and municipal advisory boards ignored the organization after the election. Most of its triumphs were confined to purely municipal offices. Nationally the A.P.A. was denounced by numerous responsible leaders, notably Washington Gladden, a Congregational clergyman. Its appeal was further limited by a legislative program that included little more than opposition to federal grants secured by the Bureau of Catholic Indian Missions and by its objection to Congressional acceptance of the Marquette statue presented by Wisconsin.

The A.P.A. was weakened also by internal strife. A growing nativist faction clashed with the Scotch-Irish and Scandinavian membership. The A.P.A. was then hopelessly wrecked by disagreement over the election of 1896. Traynor refused to endorse William McKinley and attempted, unsuccessfully, to create a third party. McKinley's victory virtually ended the career of the A.P.A., although, again under Bowers's leadership, it remained in existence until 1911.

Bibliography: J. HIGHAM, *Strangers in the Land* (New Brunswick 1955) 62–63, 80–87. C. WITTKE, *We Who Built America* (New York 1940) 498–505. H. J. DESMOND, *The A.P.A. Movement* (Washington 1912). D. L. KINZER, *The American Protective Association: A Study of Anti-Catholicism* (University Microfilms 8097; Ann Arbor 1954; Seattle 1964).

[J. L. MORRISON]

AMERICAN SCHOOLS OF ORIENTAL RESEARCH

The organization known as the American School of Oriental Research in Jerusalem was founded in 1900. When, in 1921, the organization formed a second school, located in Baghdad, the two were incorporated under the title, American Schools of Oriental Research (ASOR).

The ASOR was formed to promote the study and to extend the knowledge of Biblical literature, and of the history, geography, archeology, and ancient and modern languages and literatures of Palestine, Mesopotamia, and other Near Eastern regions. The society fulfills its purpose by undertaking original research, explorations, and excavations. These projects may be carried out by the ASOR alone, in cooperation with other institutions, or jointly. The organization also provides opportunities for qualified students to pursue studies at one of its two schools.

The institutional corporate members of the ASOR, numbering about 130, are selected from the higher educational institutions in the U.S. and Canada, including Catholic, Protestant, and Jewish theological seminaries. Membership includes individuals also. The society is financed by membership fees as well as by revenue from publications, gifts, and endowments.

The Jerusalem and Baghdad Schools are under the same trustees and president. Each school has its own supervisory committee, a director, an annually appointed professor, one or more annually appointed fellows when funds are available, and research students.

The Jerusalem School is located near the Old City, in the Hashemite Kingdom of Jordan. Its facilities provide living quarters, a library, and a base for field expeditions.

The long-term directors of the school, William F. Albright (1920–29 and 1933–36) and Nelson Glueck (1932–33, 1936–40, and 1942–47), were particularly active in undertaking excavations and surface explorations, which established the sites and periods of occupation of many ancient settlements (*see* PALESTINE, 7.).

Research by the Jerusalem School has yielded much new knowledge concerning the early history of the alphabet and of Islamic and early Christian archeology. Representatives of the Jerusalem School have been outstanding in the research and exploration connected with the *Dead Sea Scrolls.

The Baghdad School does not have permanent quarters. The Iraqi Department of Antiquities houses the school's library and often provides work space in the Iraqi Museum.

The Baghdad School usually focuses its activities upon Iraq, but work has been undertaken also in Iran and Turkey. Besides conducting many excavations, representatives of the Baghdad School have prepared important bodies of Sumerian and Assyro-Babylonian texts for publication.

The ASOR publishes a *Bulletin;* an *Annual;* the *Biblical Archaeologist;* the *Journal of Cuneiform Studies;* and a variety of texts, monographs, and archeological reports.

Bibliography: *American Schools of Oriental Research: Jerusalem-Baghdad* (New Haven 1963), a catalogue published by the society.

[R. G. VINCENT]

AMERICANISM

The name given to certain doctrines reprobated by Leo XIII in his apostolic letter *Testem benevolentiae* of Jan. 22, 1899. The pope carefully excluded from condemnation the legitimate use of the word to signify "the characteristic qualities which reflect honor on the people of America." As indicated in the papal letter, the censured doctrines had been discussed in France as a result of the French translation and adaptation of *The Life of Isaac Thomas Hecker* by Walter *Elliott, CSP. The basic principle of the censurable Americanism was that the Church should modify her doctrines to suit modern civilization, to attract those not of the faith to the Church, passing over some less attractive doctrines and adapting the Church's teachings to popular theories and methods. Leo summarized five specific errors: the rejection of external spiritual direction as no longer necessary; the extolling of natural over supernatural virtues; the preference of active over passive virtues; the rejection of religious vows as not compatible with Christian liberty; and the adoption of a new method of apologetics and approach to non-Catholics.

U.S. Elements. While the immediate controversy that brought about the papal letter existed chiefly in France it also had roots in the U.S. Bishops and priests there were divided between those who advocated greater Catholic participation in American public life, particularly the public movements for social and economic reform, and the more conservative group who thought American life was Protestant and tainted with the liberalism condemned in the *Syllabus of Errors of Pius IX. In November 1886 certain German priests led by Father P. M. *Abbelen, of Milwaukee, Wis., presented a petition to the Congregation of the Propagation of the Faith in Rome, protesting the treatment of foreign language groups and members of national parishes in the U.S. Bishops (later Archbishops) John *Ireland, of St. Paul, Minn., and John J. *Keane, then of Richmond, Va., in Rome at the time to prepare for the foundation of The Catholic University of America, Washington, D.C., published a refutation of the Abbelen petition and sent a warning to Cardinal James *Gibbons, of Baltimore, Md. Gibbons called a meeting of the eastern archbishops in Philadelphia, Pa., December 19, to protest the petition, which was rejected by the Congregation of Propaganda June 8, 1887.

In 1890 and 1891 certain European societies interested in immigrants to the U.S. met in Lucerne, Switzerland, under the chairmanship of Peter Paul *Cahensly, and petitioned Rome for better representation of foreign nationalities in the American hierarchy. Archbishop Ireland protested publicly. At a meeting of the National Educational Association in St. Paul in 1890, he praised the public schools and expressed regret that there had to be separate Catholic schools. When he inaugurated the *Faribault and Stillwater school plans to get state aid, he was accused of being opposed to Catholic parochial schools. After defending himself at the meeting of the archbishops in 1891 at St. Louis, Mo., he went to Rome to clarify his position on the school question.

In these controversies Ireland's chief associates were John J. Keane, since 1889 rector of Catholic University, and Denis O'Connell, rector of the North American College in Rome. The leaders of the conservatives were Abp. Michael A. *Corrigan, of New York, and Bps. Bernard *McQuaid, of Rochester, Winand *Wigger of Newark, and the German bishops of Wisconsin, especially Abp. Frederick *Katzer and Bp. Sebastian *Messmer. Moreover, among the faculty of Catholic University, the chief conservatives were Msgr. Joseph *Schroeder, Joseph *Pohle, and Abbé Georges Périès. Professors supporting Keane were chiefly Thomas *Bouquillon, Charles P. Grannan, and Edward *Pace. Others who supported the conservatives were Thomas *Preston, vicar-general of New York, and René *Holaind, SJ. Gibbons, despite his friendship for Ireland, endeavored to keep peace between the two groups. The N.Y. *Freeman's Journal,* the *Northwestern Chronicle* of St. Paul, and the *Western Watchman* of St. Louis supported Ireland. The *Review* of Chicago and later of St. Louis, edited by Arthur *Preuss; *Church Progress,* edited by Condé *Pallen of St. Louis; and most of the German Catholic papers opposed Ireland's policies.

European Influence. In France, Ireland and Gibbons were admired by the more progressive Catholics, especially those who had accepted the urging of Leo XIII for a reconciliation between the Church and the French Republic, called the **ralliement*. When they invited him to speak in Paris in the spring of 1892, Ireland praised the democracy and civic activities of the American priests and gave them credit for the remarkable progress of the Church in the U.S. After he left France a young lecturer in the Institut Catholique, Abbé Félix *Klein, gathered a selection of Ireland's speeches and translated them into a small volume published in 1894.

Back in the U.S., Ireland welcomed Abp. Francesco Satolli as the papal legate to the World's Fair in Chicago, and heard Satolli support his program for Catholic schools at the archbishops' meeting in New York in November 1892. Suddenly on Jan. 14, 1893, Satolli announced the erection of the Apostolic Delegation to the U.S. in Washington, with himself as the delegate. In September 1893 the delegate appeared in Ireland's company at the Catholic Columbian Congress in Chicago, but refused to take part in the World's Congress of Religions in which Ireland, Keane, Gibbons, and other Catholics participated against the wishes of the conservatives. Two years later, the delegate announced that Rome had forbidden Catholic participation in further congresses of religions. The occasion of this prohibition was the effort of certain French clergymen to promote such a congress at the Paris World's Fair in 1900. In 1895 O'Connell was forced to resign as rector of the North American College, followed in September 1896 by Keane's enforced resignation from the rectorship of Catholic University. Keane's supporters in the University in turn brought about the resignation of Schroeder, whom they accused of being the chief factor in the rector's removal.

The Catholic Press. During the next 2 years, the Catholic press carried frequent exchanges between the two groups, with the conservatives making vague charges that their opponents were guilty of the condemned liberalism of the Syllabus, and the progressives insisting that the conservatives were *refractaires,* opposing the policies of Leo XIII. In 1890–91, Father Elliott published in the *Catholic World,* and later in book form, a biography of the founder of the Paulists, Father Isaac *Hecker, with an introduction by Archbishop Ireland. Elliott also arranged for a French translation. In 1897 the more progressive Catholics in Paris decided to publish the French translation and asked Klein to shorten it and make it more attractive. He complied, adding an enthusiastic preface in which he praised Hecker as the priest of the future and lauded the American Catholic way of life. The book went quickly into six printings and received wide notice in the religious press.

In addressing the International Scientific Congress in Fribourg, Switzerland, in August 1897 O'Connell, now rector of Cardinal Gibbon's titular church, Santa Maria in Trastevere, Rome, took as his theme the Americanism in the life of Father Hecker, stressing Hecker's acceptance of American democracy and relations between Church and State. Bp. Charles Turinaz of Nancy, France, demanded permission to answer him. The next fall, beginning November 6, a series of sermons were given in Paris churches by Jesuits who attacked certain dangers to the Church from within, especially "Father Hecker's Americanism." In *La Vérité,* the conservative Catholic newspaper of Paris, under the pen name "Martel," an article appeared March 3, 1897, entitled "L'Americanism Mystique" and was followed by other articles on "Americanism." "Martel" was Abbé Charles Maignen, a priest of the Society of the Brothers of St. Vincent De Paul, a writer who opposed the *ralliement.* Abbé Georges Périès, the former professor of Canon Law at The Catholic University of America, under the name "Saint Clement" occasionally contributed an article to the series but for the most part the articles were composed by Maignen.

The articles ridiculed the claim of Ireland and Klein that Hecker exemplified the priest of the future, and quoted in derision passages from the biography on Hecker's illnesses and his dismissal from the Redemptorists. Maignen also attacked O'Connell's speech at Fribourg, an article by Keane in the *Catholic World,* some of the articles written to sell the Hecker biography, and the writings of clergymen who had left the Church, such as Abbé Victor Charbonnel. In April other articles in *La Vérité* described "Les Champaignes de L'Américanisme," and how the Americanists were undermining the defense of the Church. The campaigns included the Congress of Religions; the efforts of Charbonnel to hold a second Congress of Religions at the Paris Fair; the activities of Keane in Rome; an article of M. Brunetière praising American Catholicism in *Revue des Deux Mondes;* a newspaper story predicting that Cardinal Gibbons would be the next pope; and an article in the *Contemporary Review* by "Romanus," who Maignen implied was an Americanist.

Maignen found other evidence of the Americanists' doctrines in Keane's addresses at the Congress of Religions and his defense of that congress at the Brussels International Catholic Congress of 1894. Maignen collected these articles, to which he added a few other essays, for a book entitled *Études sur l'Américanisme, Le Père Hecker, est-il un Saint?* When Cardinal Richard of Paris refused his imprimatur to the book, Maignen took it to Rome, where he obtained the imprimatur of the Master of the Sacred Palace, Père Albert Lepidi, OP, which some interpreted as a papal approval of the book. The controversy over the biography and the movement vaguely described as Americanism raged through the French Catholic press and was mentioned in the secular press. The discussion reached into Belgium. Some discussions appeared also in Germany, and then the controversy moved into Italy, where it became confused with the local quarrel over the temporal power of the papacy.

Testem Benevolentiae. Leo XIII opposed the move to put the Hecker biography on the Index and appointed a committee of cardinals to study the question. The committee reported adversely on the doctrines called "Americanism." The Pope changed the report in its opening and closing passages so that no one was accused of holding the condemned doctrines, and the ordinary political and social Americanism were exempted from the disapproval. Although Gibbons sent a cable to stop the condemnation and Ireland rushed to Rome, both arrived too late to head off the papal letter, *Testem benevolentiae,* which was dated Jan. 22, 1899. Ireland, Keane, and Klein immediately submitted but denied that they held the condemned doctrines. The Hecker biography was withdrawn from sale. The conservative bishops in the U.S. thanked the Pope for saving the American Church from the dangerous doctrines. Gibbons, to whom the Pope's letter was addressed, denied in his reply that any educated American Catholic held the condemned doctrines.

Bibliography: T. T. McAvoy, *The Great Crisis in American Catholic History 1895–1900* (Chicago 1957) with annotated bibliography in "Essay on Sources."

[T. T. MC AVOY]

AMESHA SPENTA, "the Beneficent Immortals," as they are called in the Avesta. According to the teaching of Zoroaster they are the "archangels" of Ahura Mazda. From the Indo-Iranian period, the classes and functions of society were threefold, and each had divine patrons. The most important function, sovereignty, had as patrons two principal gods, Varuna, guardian of the True Order, and Mitra (the Contract, the Friend). In Zoroaster's system, Ahura Mazda combines the two aspects of sovereignty. However, this function, like the other functions, continues to be under a hierarchy of archangels in which the True Order, Arta, holds the highest place, above Vohu Manah (Good Mind), which holds the position previously held byMitra. The second function, physical force and fighting, had Indra as patron. In Zoroaster's system, Khshathra (Dominion) corresponds to it, while Indra himself persists as a *daēva.*

The third function, fecundity, had as patron a variable and multivalent goddess, to whom the archangel Ārmaiti (Devotion) corresponds. The counterparts of the twin patrons, Nāsatya (Healers), are the archangels Haurvatāt and Ameretāt (Health and non-Death). One of the twins survived as a *daēva* named Nāonhaithya. Also there is the god Vāyu (Cosmic Wind), a kind of Janus, ruling over ambiguous beginnings, which in Zoroaster became the initial Choice between Good and Evil, represented by the two Mainyus or Spirits, *Spenta Mainyu* (the Beneficent or Holy Spirit) and Anra Mainyu (the Destructive Spirit).

See also DAEVAS; PERSIAN RELIGION, ANCIENT; ZOROASTER (ZARATHUSTRA).

Bibliography: G. DUMÉZIL, *Les Dieux des Indo-Européens* (Brussels 1952); *L'Idéologie tripartie des Indo-Européens* (Brussels 1958). J. DUCHESNE-GUILLEMIN, *La Religion de l'Iran ancien* (Paris 1962).

[J. DUCHESNE-GUILLEMIN]

AMETTE, LÉON ADOLPHE, cardinal, archbishop of *Paris; b. Douville (Eure), Sept. 6, 1850; d. Antony (Seine), Aug. 29, 1920. Born in very modest circumstances, he studied at the seminary of Saint-Sulpice in Paris, was ordained (1873), and became a private secretary to Bishop Grolleau of Evreux (1873) and then vicar-general under a succession of bishops (1889–98). He became bishop of Bayeux (1898); coadjutor to Cardinal *Richard de la Vergne of Paris (Feb. 21, 1906), whom he succeeded (Jan. 28, 1908); and cardinal (Nov. 27, 1911). In both sees he had to confront the results of the law separating Church and State (1905) but he adopted a peaceful attitude toward the civil power in order to prepare a reconciliation. During World War I he was a promoter of the *Union sacrée* and frequently served as intermediary between the French government and the Holy See. In his archdiocese he erected 16 new parish churches and 29 chapels and gave a great impetus to diocesan works. Amette was very pious, a Dominican tertiary, and a talented orator. He published a number of his pastoral letters and sermons as well as several short tracts on varied religious topics and current problems.

Bibliography: C. CORDONNIER, *Le Cardinal Amette, archevêque de Paris,* 2 v. (Paris 1949). J. RUPP, *Histoire de l'Église de Paris* (Paris 1948) 303–311. H. CHOMON, DictBiogFranc 2:637–640.

[R. LIMOUZIN-LAMOTHE]

AMICE, a rectangular piece of linen used to wrap around the neck and shoulders of the wearer to protect the outer liturgical garments from being soiled by the face and neck. In medieval days, the alb was the first vestment to be put on. The amice was added as a scarf, part of which covered the head, keeping the hair in place until the stole and chasuble were put on and arranged properly. There was no common usage as to when the amice thus worn should be brought back off the head. Some removed it after putting on the chasuble; others kept it on the head until the beginning of the Canon of the Mass. When resting on the shoulders the amice was thought to look untidy. This problem was taken care of by the ornamentation of the upper edge with a band of stiff, rich material, or a narrow strip of embroidery that formed a collar called *Aurifrisium* or apparel. Today the amice is put on before the alb. This gives the desired neat appearance. It is not worn on the head at any time, except by members of religious orders who wear a cowl as part of their habit. There is, however, a rubric in the Roman Missal that directs the wearer to lay the amice on his head for a moment, before tucking it around his neck.

Bibliography: Miller FundLit 115–116. E. A. ROULIN, *Vestments and Vesture,* tr. J. MCCANN (Westminster, Md. 1950). J. BRAUN, *Die liturgischen Paramente in Gegenwart und Vergangenheit* (2d ed. Freiburg 1924); *Die liturgische Gewandung im Occident und Orient* (Freiburg 1907). V. ERMONI, DACL 1.2:1597–99.

[M. MC CANCE]

Amice: (a) Amice as it is put on over the cassock before vesting with the alb. (b) Amice as worn around the cowl by some religious orders. (c) Aurifrisium, or apparel used to decorate the upper edge of an amice.

AMICO, FRANCESCO, Jesuit theologian; b. Naples, April 5, 1578; d. Graz, Austria, Jan. 31, 1651. He entered the Society of Jesus on Oct. 27, 1596, and after teaching the humanities, philosophy, and theology, he became chancellor of the University of Graz. Adapting his theological treatises to a 4 years' course of seminary teaching, he wrote his famous *Cursus theologici juxta scholasticam hujus temporis methodum.* The fifth volume of this work (*De iure et iustitia*) contained three propositions censured by the Congregation of the Index, June 18, 1651, and later condemned by Alexander VII and Innocent XI (Denz 2037, 2132–33). A decree of July 6, 1655, permitted the reading of a corrected edition of the work, such as the Antwerp edition of 1650.

Bibliography: Sommervogel 1:280–282. E. M. RIVIÈRE, DHGE 2:1234. I. TAROCCHI, EncCatt 1:1066–68. Hurter Nomencl 3:933–934.

[F. C. LEHNER]

AMICUS CURIAE

Under the common law system, the *amicus curiae* (Latin "friend of the court"), either an attorney or layman, assisted the court in the proper determination of cases before it by calling the court's attention to pertinent facts or applicable law that might otherwise escape that tribunal's consideration. The impartial *amicus* served the court in those instances where the litigants failed to present all aspects of a case with sufficient clarity either because of their own inadequacies, collusion, or indifference, or because the court itself was possessed of limited knowledge or skill in the matter at hand. The term has been applied also to persons who conduct investigations or act in the capacity of master or referee at the request of the court.

Permission to appear as *amicus curiae* is not a matter of right, but rests solely with the discretion of the court. If a matter of public concern is involved, the courts usually exercise great liberality in granting the *amicus* permission to appear. In some jurisdictions, the consent of the litigants is a prerequisite to the participation of the *amicus,* while in others, the court is the sole determining factor. The *amicus curiae* is not considered a party to the litigation and therefore is not bound by the judgment; he is regarded as a neutral individual, even though one of the parties may incidentally benefit from his appearance.

The genesis of the *amicus curiae* appears to be lost in antiquity. One trace is found in early Roman law where the judge, when in doubt as to a point of law, was accustomed to seek the advice of a *consilium* or jurisconsult. In the middle of the 14th century, a similar institution is discernible in the English law, the term *amicus curiae* being mentioned in the Year Books of Edward III. The English practice was somewhat contrary to the Roman in that the right to volunteer unsolicited advice was recognized. Under the modern practice, the Roman and English procedures have been combined so that the court has the right both to appoint an *amicus curiae* as well as to grant an *amicus* permission to appear upon his own application.

Until approximately the middle of the 18th century, the function of the *amicus curiae* was relatively well defined and limited to the neutral, disinterested role of guardian of the integrity of the courts, viz, ensuring the complete presentation of matters inadequately covered or omitted by the parties, or those not within the realm of the court's competence. At that time, however, the *amicus curiae* was permitted to assume a function that presaged the modern trend from strict neutrality to straightforward advocacy and partisanship.

In present-day practice, the *amicus curiae* is no longer the impartial tutelary of the courts. In most instances, the *amicus* is rather the partisan of one of the litigants or the representative of interests and parties not otherwise represented.

Bibliography: H. F. JOLOWICZ, *Historical Introduction to the Study of Roman Law* (2d ed. Cambridge, Eng. 1952). L. WENGER, *Institutes of the Roman Law of Civil Procedure,* tr. O. H. FISK (rev. ed. New York 1940). E. R. BECKWITH and R. SOBERNHEIM, "Amicus Curiae: Minister of Justice," *Fordham Law Review* 17 (1948) 38–62. S. KRISLOV, "The Amicus Curiae Brief: From Friendship to Advocacy," *Yale Law Journal* 72 (1963) 694–721.

[J. S. CASTELLANO]

AMIDISM, a form of Mahāyāna Buddhism popular among the laity and especially important in Japan. It was founded by the Pure Land (Ch'ing T'u) or Lotus School in China in the 4th century A.D., if not earlier. Its three basic tenets are contained in three Skt *sūtras* that were translated into Chinese, whence they passed into Japanese. Amita is the Japanese adaptation of the Skt epithets of Buddha: *Amitābha,* "immeasurable light," and *Amitāyus,* "immeasurable life." The idea of the Pure Land is central in the Chinese Lotus School and in the *Jôdo* (Pure Land) doctrine developed in Japan in the 12th and 13th centuries. Salvation is offered to all men who have faith in Amita and invoke his name as "the Lord of immeasurable light and immeasurable life." Through this faith and repeated invocation the humblest layman is assured a rebirth in the Pure Land, the Western paradise. Amidism is the largest Buddhist sect in Japan.

See also BUDDHISM; JAPANESE RELIGION.

Bibliography: R. MASUNAGA, "Amida," König RelwissWbh 47–48. J. A. HARDON, *Religions of the World* (Westminster, Md. 1963) 124–126. A. LLOYD, *The Creed of Half Japan* (New York 1912). H. DE LUBAC, *Amida* (Paris 1955). F. KIICHI, "Die Jōdo-Lehre," König Christus 3:428–432. A. HAUCHECORNE, "Les Religions du Japon" in *Histoire des religions,* ed. M. BRILLANT and R. AIGRAIN, v.2 (Paris 1954) 212–215.

[M. R. P. MC GUIRE]

AMIENS

City on both banks of the Somme River in north France; capital of Somme department, which comprises the present diocese, and of Picardy, which comprised the medieval diocese. The see, suffragan to *Reims, in 1963 had 248 parishes with 367 secular and 78 religious priests and was 2,380 square miles in area. Of the city's 120,000 inhabitants, in 18 parishes with 58 priests, one-fourth attended Mass and received the Sacraments regularly.

The Celtic *Samarobriva* was the capital of the Gallic *Ambiani,* in the Roman province of *Belgica II c.* 400. Its commercial, military, and industrial importance meant an early Christian evangelization, but neither dates nor data can be assigned to the two SS. *Firmin, traditionally the first apostles of Amiens. The first St. Firmin seems to have been a traveling missionary from Navarre who left traces in *Pamplona, *Agen, Clermont, *Angers, *Beauvais, and Amiens, where he is supposed to have been martyred *c.* 303; his relics may have been translated to Pamplona (1186) after Philip II Augustus added Amiens to the French realm in 1185. Amiens considers him the founder and first bishop of

Amiens and its Gothic cathedral.

its church. There is also a tradition of the evangelization of Amiens from Rome, marked by the martyrdoms of SS. Fuscian, Victoricus, and Quentin.

St. *Martin of *Tours cut his cape to give half of it to a poor man; the site was marked by a chapel that became the Abbey of Saint-Martin-aux-Jumeaux (1073). No bishops are known between Eulogius (346) and Edibius (511). Until the 11th century Amiens, a prize for Normans (859, 881, 883, 891) and a strongpoint in the war between Flanders and Normandy, kept within its Roman walls. Bishop Jesse (799–830, 833–834) was one of Charlemagne's *missi.* The bishop *c.* 1000 shared seigneurial rights with the count, who in the 12th century was his vassal. Episcopal holdings, shared with the chapter, were few outside the city, where the Abbeys of *Corbie (622) and *Saint-Ricquier (625) held most of the land; in 1301 the bishop disposed of far fewer benefices than did the abbeys. St. Simon, count of Amiens (1072–77), became a monk at St. Claude in the Jura mountains and died in Rome (1082). *Peter the Hermit, preacher of the First Crusade, was from Amiens. Bishop St. Godefroy (1104–15) supported church reform. When the cathedral was built (1220–69), Amiens was a town rich from the cloth trade.

Picardy was a center of Calvinism, combatted by Bp. Geoffroy de la Marthonie (1577–1601). A seminary was founded in 1655. After the revocation of the Edict of Nantes (1685) many of the Huguenots fled to London and Edinburgh. Jansenism was opposed by Bps. François Faure (1653–87), Pierre Sabatier (1706–34), and François Gabriel d'Orléans de la Motte (1734–74). Only two clerics were executed in the French Revolution, when Amiens was a Constitutional see under *Rouen. The *Concordat of 1801 made Amiens, united with Beauvais and *Noyon, suffragan to *Paris. In 1822 it became suffragan to Reims again. The major seminary was reorganized in 1805, the minor in 1828. Most of the 12 bishops of the 19th century were in transit to other sees. Pastoral problems differ in the many agricultural villages and in industrial centers.

The beautiful Gothic cathedral ranks with Reims and Chartres; built by the architect Robert de Luzarches, it has five monumental portals (three on the west façade and two at ends of the transept) and two towers 215 feet high. Its treasure includes a replica of a relic of the head of St. John the Baptist brought from Constantinople (1206). Former abbeys include the Benedictine Saint-Valery (613), Saint-Sauve in Montreuil (7th century), Saint-Josse-sur-Mer (793), Forestmontier (10th century), Saint-Fuscien (1105), and Saint-Vast in Moreuil (1109) for men; and Sainte-Austreberte in Montreuil (7th century), Bertaucourt (1095), and Saint-Michel in Doullens (12th century) for women; the Cistercian Le Gard, Cercamp, Valloire (all 1137), and Lieu-Dieu (1191) for men; and Villancourt (12th century), Épagne (1178), and the Paraclet (1219) for women; the Augustinian Saint-Acheul (1085) and Clerfay (1136) for men; and the Premonstratensian Saint-Jean (1115), Dommartin (1120), Séry (1127), Selincourt (1131), and Saint-André-au-Bois (12th century).

Bibliography: H. Macqueron, *Bibliographie du département de la Somme,* 2 v. (Amiens 1904–07). A. de Calonne, *Histoire de la ville d'Amiens,* 3 v. (Amiens 1899–1906). H. Pelletier, *Histoire religieuse de la Picardie* (Abbeville 1961). F. I. Darsy, *Bénéfices de l'église d'Amiens,* 2 v. (Amiens 1869–71). G. Durand, *Monographie de l'église Notre-Dame, cathédral d'Amiens,* 3 v. (Amiens 1901–03). *Cartulaire du chapitre de la cathédral d'Amiens,* 2 v. (Amiens 1905–12). F. Vercauteren, *Étude sur les civitates de la Belgique seconde* (Brussels 1934). H. P. Eydoux, *Réalités et énigmes de l'archéologie* (2d ed. Paris 1964). M. Godet, DHGE 2:1254–72. E. Jarry, *Catholicisme* 1:466–469. G. Bardy, *ibid.* 4:1318–19. AnnPont (1965) 29.
Illustration credit: French Embassy, Press and Information Division, New York City.

[J. ESTIENNE]

AMIOT, JEAN JOSEPH MARIE, missionary to China; b. Toulon, Feb. 8, 1718; d. Peking, Oct. 8, 1793. He entered the Jesuits in 1737 and spent 42 years as a priest in China. He was a prolific writer on Chinese and Tartar art and history. As an astronomer and mathematician he served at the court of the Emperor Ch'ien Lung. His Paris correspondent, Bertin, published many of his writings in *Memoires concernant l'histoire des Chinois, par les missionaires de Pekin* (16 v. 1776–1814), of which volume 12 is his study of Confucius, based on the best Chinese accounts of the philosopher. Amiot translated a history of Chinese music and compiled a Manchu-French dictionary. The Manchu grammar attributed to him is a translation and abridgement of a Latin work, probably by F. Verbiest.

Bibliography: H. Cordier, *La Grande encyclopédie* 2:758–759. E. M. Rivière, DHGE 2:1275–77. H. Chomon, DictBiogFranc 2:674–677. *Enciclopedia de la Religion Católica,* 7 v. (Barcelona 1951–56) 1:567. J. A. Otto, LexThK² 1:439.

[B. LAHIFF]

AMISH CHURCHES, a reform group founded under the leadership of a Swiss Mennonite bishop, Jacob Amman, who withdrew from the Mennonite fellowship in 1693, accusing his fellow *Mennonites of laxity in doctrine and practice. In particular he advocated the strict enforcement of "shunning" excommunicated persons. Following this practice, the Amish avoid all social intercourse with such persons, even if they are members of their own family.

Amish immigrants began arriving in America in 1720. They settled in Pennsylvania and later in Indiana, Ohio, Illinois, Nebraska, and Canada. They were popularly known as the "hooks and eyes" Mennonites because they oppose the use of buttons. The Old Order Amish refuse to use such inventions as electricity, telephones,

Old Order Amish of Lancaster County, Pa., gathering at a farmhouse for one of their biweekly services.

radio and television, and automobiles. They wear plain black clothing, drive buggies, insist on marriage within the sect, oppose participation in war, and try to educate their children in their own schools up to the eighth grade. The men cut their hair in a bob and let their beards grow; the women wear capes and bonnets. Amish farmers attempt to preserve their Swiss-German culture and continue to speak their own "Pennsylvania Dutch" dialect.

The Old Order Amish Mennonite Church was organized in 1865 and reported 19,864 members in 1964. Church government is of the congregational type, and there are three grades of clergy: *Voll Diener* (bishop), *Diener zum Buch* (preacher), and *Armen Diener* (deacon), all of whom are chosen by lot. Biweekly morning services of worship are held, including hymns, sermons, scriptural reading, testimonies, liturgical prayers, and benediction. During the benediction, everyone genuflects when the name of Jesus Christ is mentioned. Afternoon meetings are scheduled only on the days when the Lord's Supper is celebrated; then the service is in two parts—before and after dinner. The Old Order Amish worship in private homes, subscribe to the Confession of Dortrecht (1632), prescribe strict shunning of backsliders, and try to remain free from the secular community.

Over a period of years some Amish separated from the Old Order Amish and formed the Conservative Mennonite Conference. They held their first conference at Pigeon, Mich., in 1910. These Amish introduced meetinghouses, Sunday schools, and the use of English in worship. They use modern conveniences and cooperate with the larger Mennonite Church.

A smaller group of Amish who also left the parent body formed the Beachy Amish Mennonite Churches. This schism originated in Somerset County, Pa., in 1927 and was led by Bp. Moses M. Beachy. The Beachy Amish have abandoned restrictions against modern inventions and offer a mitigated discipline. They numbered 3,116 in 1964.

Bibliography: J. A. Hostetler, *Amish Society* (Baltimore, Md. 1963). C. G. Bachman, *The Old Order Amish of Lancaster County* (Lancaster, Pa. 1961). *The Mennonite Encyclopedia,* ed. H. S. Bender and C. H. Smith, 4 v. (Scottdale, Pa. 1955–60). **Illustration credit:** Photo by Mel Horst, *Among the Amish* (Witmer, Pa. 1964).

[W. J. WHALEN]

AMMANATI, BARTOLOMMEO, Italian mannerist sculptor and architect; b. Settignano, 1511; d. Florence, 1592. He trained under Baccio Bandinelli in Florence and with Jacopo Sansovino in Venice. By the mid-1540s further travels had taken him to Padua, where his works include the Benavides tomb in the Eremitani with its classical, Sansovinesque seated allegories. Throughout the reign of Julius III (1550–55), he collaborated with *Vasari and *Vignola on the papal projects in Rome. The flaring, shimmering draperies of his niche figures in the Del Monte Chapel of S. Pietro in Montorio reflect Vasari's *mannerism; the Nymphaeum, his semicircular structure in the garden of the

Villa Giulia, echoes the plan of Vignola's villa. Returning to Florence in 1555, he became chief court architect to Cosimo I Medici. For the duke Ammanati executed, among other architectural and sculptural works, the wings and garden façade decorated with rusticated orders, which he added to the Palazzo Pitti (1558–70), and the colossal, planarly conceived marble Neptune atop the fountain in the Piazza della Signoria (1563–75). Late in life he worked for the Florentine Jesuits (S. Giovannino, 1579), until sickness and failing eyesight restricted the activities of his final years.

Bibliography: F. KRIEGBAUM, "Ein verschollenes Brunnenwerk des Bartolomeo Ammanati," *Mitteilungen des Kunsthistorischen Institutes in Florenz* 3 (1932) 71–103, bibliog. E. VODOZ, "Studien zum architektonischen Werk des Bartolomeo Ammanati," *ibid.* 6 (1940) 1–141, bibliog.

[H. V. NIEBLING]

AMMANATI DE' PICCOLOMINI, JACOPO, cardinal, patron of the arts, papal official; b. Villa Basilica near Lucca, Italy, March 8, 1422; d. San Lorenzo, Sept. 10, 1479. Jacopo Ammanati, who came from a poor family, owed his advancement to his classical studies in Florence. Cardinal Domenico Capranica made him his private secretary in 1450. Subsequently, he became secretary of briefs under *Callistus III and *Pius II. Pius valued him highly, adopting him into the Piccolomini family, and investing him with the rights of a citizen of Siena. In turn he had great admiration for Pius and wrote a continuation of his *Commentarii,* which gives much information about the intrigues in the papal court. He was named bishop of Pavia in 1460 and cardinal in 1461. He soon disagreed with *Paul II and was even imprisoned on a charge of conspiracy. In 1470 he was transferred to Lucca and named papal delegate to Umbria. Pope *Sixtus IV sent him as legate to Perugia in 1471. He was a conscientious ecclesiastic and a Christian humanist.

Bibliography: S. PAULI, *Disquisizione istorica della patria, e compendio della vita di Giacomo Ammanati Piccolomini* (Lucca 1712). G. CALAMARI, *Il confidente di Pio II,* 2 v. (Rome 1932). I. DANIELE, EncCatt 1:1079. J. WODKA, LexThK^2 1:439–440.

[N. G. WOLF]

AMMEN, DANIEL, naval officer; b. Brown County, Ohio, May 15, 1820; d. near Washington, D.C., July 11, 1898. He was the fourth child of David and Sally (Houtz) Ammen. While a boy, Ammen formed a lasting friendship with a neighbor, Ulysses S. Grant, and once saved him from drowning. In 1836 Ammen received an appointment as a midshipman in the Navy—the first awarded in his county. He prepared for his career by 3 months of study at the U.S. Military Academy, West Point, N.Y., since there was no naval academy in existence then. A brief tour of duty on the storeship "Relief" followed before he went to sea in the "Macedonian" in 1837, beginning a naval career that lasted more than 49 years (including more than 21 years at sea), during which he rose from midshipman to rear admiral. During the Civil War he served with the Union blockading squadrons and participated in attacks on Confederate coastal forts. After the war his friendship with President Grant won him assignments in the Navy department as chief of the Bureau of Yards and Docks (1869–71) and of the Bureau of Navigation (1871–78). Ammen retired at his own request in 1878 and spent the rest of his life at his estate near Washington, D.C. He was married first to Mary Jackson; after her death he married Zoe Atocha, who bore him five children and who survived him.

Bibliography: D. AMMEN, *The Old Navy and the New* (Philadelphia 1891). L. R. HAMERSLY, *The Records of Living Officers of the U.S. Navy and Marine Corps* (Philadelphia 1870); *Hamersly's Naval Encyclopaedia* (Philadelphia 1881). E. W. CALLAHAN, ed., *List of Officers of the Navy of the U.S. and of the Marine Corps, 1775–1900* (New York 1901).

[H. D. LANGLEY]

AMMIANUS MARCELLINUS, Roman historian; b. Antioch, between A.D. 325 and 335; d. probably in Rome, *c.* 400. A Greek of a prominent upper-middle-class family, he served as a military officer under Ursicinus in Italy, on the Rhine, and in the East (353–360); took part in the Persian campaign of *Julian the Apostate (363); spent time in Antioch; and settled in Rome after 378. Intense Roman patriotism led him to write in Latin and fill the void after Tacitus. His *Res gestae* in 31 books runs from Nerva to the death of Valens (96–378); extant are bks. 14 (353) to 31, published between 392 and 397.

Ammianus's sources were his memory, notes, interrogations of eyewitnesses (often mentioned by name), and a complex variety of written material. His general accuracy is great as checked against the independent history of Faustus of Byzantium. His knowledge of ancient history and literature is impressive. The *History* reveals a general "faithfulness to facts, based on clear proofs." He is usually objective and fair-minded. Closeness to Ursicinus sometimes clouded his judgment, and he did not do complete justice to Gallus, but his eulogistic tone toward Julian did not blind him to that Emperor's faults. The oppression of the pagans by *Theodosius I (392) made Ammianus cautious in treating him and his family. His many, though frequently uncritical, excursuses reflect in part his wide travel. His tone is critical of the luxury of the times, but he was blind to the real decline of Rome and the seriousness of the barbarian threat. In style he shows best in his excellent characterizations and the vitality of his dramatic narratives, but he is often excessively rhetorical. His language is diffuse and poetical, anticipating the style of the literature of the century to follow.

A pagan, Ammianus is respectful of martyrs and generally fair to Christianity insofar as it is a "plain and simple religion." Although critical of Julian for an edict against Christian teachers of rhetoric, he is just as critical of ecclesiastical politics, the "deadly hatred" of Christians for one another, the bloody rivalry of specific bishops, and the widespread luxury of the urban hierarchy. De Labriolle classes him with those cultured pagans, so numerous at the time, who from contempt or indifference looked at the contemporary Christian revolution without understanding it or being impressed by it. For all his limitations, Ammianus is one of the greatest of the Roman historians.

Bibliography: *Rerum gestarum libri,* ed. C. U. CLARK, 2 v. (Berlin 1910–15); Lat.-Eng. edition, ed. and tr. J. C. ROLFE, 3 v. (LoebClLib; rev. ed. 1950–1956). E. A. THOMPSON, *The Historical Work of Ammianus Marcellinus* (Cambridge, Eng. 1947). M. L. W. LAISTNER, *The Greater Roman Historians* (Berkeley 1947) 141–161, 180–183. P. C. DE LABRIOLLE, *La Réaction païenne* (6th ed. Paris 1942) 433–436. G. B. PIGHI, ReallexAnt Chr 1:386–394.

[W. R. F. TONGUE]

AMMONITES, a people centered in OT times around the fortress city of Rabbath-Ammon in Transjordan. In Gn 19.38, Ammon, as the eponymous ancestor of this people, is begotten by Lot's incestuous union with his own daughter, thus indicating, by punning on the name Ammonites (*beṇê 'ammôn,* "sons of Ammon," as if it were *beṇê 'ammî,* "sons of my people"), the tribal relationship between the Ammonites and the Israelites.

Early History. Surface explorations by N. Glueck have shown an almost complete absence of permanent settlement in the Ammonite section of Transjordan from 1900 to 1400 B.C. Thus the Ammonites probably spent their earlier years as a seminomadic people. Some notion of the Ammonite settlement is evident in Dt 2.19–21, where Yahweh recounts His favors to Ammon because of its origins.

That the Ammonites had achieved some measure of sedentary life by the 13th century B.C. is clear from the fact that the Israelites were unable to penetrate their frontiers (Nm 21.24). At the time of the Exodus the Ammonites were confined to the area around Rabbath-Ammon in upper *Jaboc (Jabbok) Valley. Earlier, their domain had extended to the Jordan (Jgs 11.13–27). The Israelites, however, found the Amorrites lodged between Ammon and the Jordan. Since Gad and Manasse replaced the Amorrites, the Ammonites could not regain their original possessions save for brief periods (1 Sm 11.1–11). Rabbath-Ammon, however, was always secure, because of the strong line of fortresses placed strategically in a semicircle to the west of the city.

Relations with Israel. Although the Israelites and Ammonites were often at odds, only at the height of its power, under David, could Israel subdue the principal city (2 Sm 12.29–30). Early relations were sometimes amicable (2 Sm 10.2), but Ammon generally served as a foil, both material and spiritual, against the Israelites. Jephte (Jgs 11.32), Saul (1 Sm 11.1–11), David, Josaphat (2 Chr 20.1–25), and others engaged the Ammonites in battle. Whenever possible, the Ammonites allied themselves with conquering invaders against the Israelites, probably in order to regain what they considered rightfully theirs (4 Kgs 24.2).

The Ammonites proved to be an even more dangerous spiritual foe. An Ammonite woman and her god Milkom found a place in Solomon's harem (3 Kgs 11.5-7). The prophets denounced Ammon in the most violent terms (Am 1.13; Jer 49.1–6) for her moral corruption. The Ammonites were also among those who hindered Nehemia in his efforts to rebuild Jerusalem after the Exile (Neh 4.3–7). The Ammonites as such ceased to figure as an organized kingdom after the Babylonian occupation in the 6th century B.C. Their capital, however, served as the seat of many subsequent governments and lives on today as Amman, the capital of the Hashemite Kingdom of *Jordan.

Bibliography: N. GLUECK, *The Other Side of the Jordan* (New Haven 1940). G. E. WRIGHT, *Biblical Archaeology* (rev. ed. Philadelphia 1963). G. M. LANDES, "The Material Civilization of the Ammonites," BiblArchaeol 24 (1961) 66–86.

[T. KARDONG]

AMMONIUS, ANDREAS, humanist; b. Lucca, Italy, 1478; d. London, England, Aug. 16, 1517. He spent several years in Rome, where he acquired a fine literary reputation, and in 1504 he moved to England, where his first years were spent in privation and difficulties. A friend of Thomas *More and Desiderius *Erasmus, who both had a high opinion of his writing, Ammonius contributed greatly to the spread of *humanism in England. After being named secretary of Latin letters to *Henry VIII in 1511, he celebrated in verse the King's victorious campaigns against *Louis XII of France and James IV of Scotland (d. 1513). He was named papal collector in England by *Leo X in 1515. The chief source on his life is his correspondence with Erasmus between 1511 and 1517. Ammonius wrote various literary pieces, but almost all were thought to have been lost. It was believed that of his writings nothing had survived except 12 letters included in the 1713 edition of Erasmus's correspondence and an eclogue contained in the collection *Bucolicorum auctores* (Basel 1546). In 1784, however, a printed volume of his poetry was discovered in the Bibliothèque Nationale in Paris; another copy is to be found in the Bodleian library, Oxford.

Bibliography: Sources. *Opus epistolarum Des. Erasmi Roterdami,* ed. P. S. ALLEN et al. (Oxford 1906–) v.1–3. J. BALE, *Scriptorum illustrium . . . catalogus,* 2 v. in 1 (2d ed. Basel 1557–59), 13th century, No. 45. Literature. Cosenza DictItHum 1:168–169. H. VAN LAUN, DNB 1:363. E. G. LÉDOS, "Les Poésies latines d'Andrea Ammonio della Rena," *Revue des bibliothèques* 5 (1897) 161–176. C. LUCCHESINI, *Della storia letteraria del ducato lucchese libri sette,* 2 v. in 1 (Lucca 1825–31) 1:180–182. G. M. MAZZUCHELLI, *Gli scrittori d'Italia,* 2 v. (Brescia 1753–63) 1.2: 646. C. PIZZI, *Un amico di Erasmo, l'umanista Andrea Ammonio* (Florence 1956); ed., *Andreae Ammonii Carmina omnia, accedunt tres epistolae nondum editae* (Florence 1958).

[M. MONACO]

AMNESIA. The most familiar of the various types of dissociative reactions, amnesia might be defined as a gap of memory that embraces a part of the individual's previous life and at times also the awareness of his own identity. Amnesia is distinguished from ordinary types of passive forgetting in that the attack of amnesia possesses all the characteristics of active forgetting or *repression. Like repression, amnesia is an active psychological process appearing suddenly and proceeding indeliberately, forcefully, and almost blindly to blot out of consciousness psychological data that are emotionally unpleasant or painful. Thus it forces them outside the pale of ordinary recall. The entire amnestic process takes place automatically and unintentionally, resembling a reflex and self-protective reaction.

Just as fainting occurs in the presence of unbearable physical *pain, so analogously amnesia occurs in the presence of unbearable psychological pain. Both serve as temporary protective devices. Amnesias provide insulation to the unstable and immature personality and at the same time offer a way of escape from the precipitating cause, often an acute, emotionally charged conflict situation. In this way the frustrating conflict is temporarily, however unsatisfactorily, resolved by the process of dissociative forgetting. Ordinarily the amnesia is restricted to a definite span of time so that events prior to the memory gap and subsequent to it are subject to normal recall. The great majority of dissociative amnesias are of relatively short duration, from about 3 hours to several months, although some cases of extended duration are on record.

Usually, when memory returns, the return is complete and sudden. In many cases the return of memory occurs spontaneously, sometimes on the experiencing of a highly charged emotional incident. In other cases the clearing of the amnesia requires psychotherapy. Hypnotism has proved the quickest technique for clearing the memory gap.

Amnesia has been treated above as a dissociative reaction pertaining to a *psychoneurotic disorder that is produced by psychogenic factors or without clearly defined tangible cause or structural change. The term amnesia is also used to cover losses of memory caused by organic factors. The inability to recall past events or the inability to store up new impressions can be caused by a blow on the head followed by a period of unconsciousness. The events immediately preceding the blow will remain a permanent blank. Other organic factors responsible for temporary or permanent memory gaps or defects are a wide variety of acute toxic conditions. If and when the toxic condition clears, the amnesia usually vanishes also. One common type of amnesia due to organic causes can be found in the seizures of true *epilepsy.

Bibliography: A. H. MASLOW and B. MITTELMANN, *Principles of Abnormal Psychology* (New York 1941; rev. ed. 1951) 397–409. F. J. BRACELAND and M. STOCK, *Modern Psychiatry* (New York 1963) 155–160. T. V. MOORE, *Cognitive Psychology* (New York 1939) 412–428. P. JANET, *The Major Symptoms of Hysteria* (2d ed. New York 1920). M. PRINCE, *The Dissociation of a Personality* (New York 1906).

[E. J. RYAN]

AMON, national god of Egypt. His name is spelled also as Amun. Amon was originally one of the local gods of *Thebes (Noh), but when that city became prominent in the Twelfth Dynasty (1991–1786 B.C.),

Amon, gold statuette, 900 B.C., *from Thebes.*

he became the chief god of Thebes, which then became known as No-Amon (City of Amon), as it is called in Na 3.8; see also Jer 46.25. St. Jerome translated *nō' 'āmôn* in Na 3.8 erroneously as *Alexandria populorum* (Alexandria of the nations); therefore Amon's name does not appear in the Vulgate. In the Eighteenth Dynasty (1570–*c.* 1304) Amon emerged as the supreme god of the whole nation, having been identified with *Ra (Re) the sun-god and called Amon-Ra, "the King of the gods." The main sanctuary of Amon was the enormous temple in the section of Thebes now known as Karnak, but he was worshiped throughout Egypt and even in Libya and Nubia (Biblical Ethiopia). His wife Mu (the mother) and his son Chonsu (the wanderer, i.e., the moon) formed a triad of gods. Amon's name (Egyptian *i'mn,* "hidden") stresses his mysterious and inscrutable nature; he was difficult to find and was often associated with the invisible wind that could only be heard and that, as breath, was the mysterious source of life in man and beast. Amon was also worshiped under several names with different attributes. As Khen or Kin he was the god of reproduction, and as Khnum he was "the maker of gods and men." He was sometimes represented by a human body with the head of a ram, the animal sacred to him, or simply by a pair of ram's horns. More often, however, he was featured in wholly human form with two long feathers on his head. The Greeks and Romans identified Amon with Zeus or Jupiter and called the Egyptian city of Thebes Διόσπολις (city of Zeus).

See also EGYPT, ANCIENT, 1.

Bibliography: EncDictBibl 70–71. H. JACOBSOHN, RGG[3] 1:327. H. STOCK, LexThK[2] 1:464. K. SETHE, *Amun und die acht Urgötter von Hermopolis* (AbhBerlAk 4; 1929). J. A. WILSON, *The Burden of Egypt: An Interpretation of Ancient Egyptian Culture* (Chicago 1951) 130–131, 169–172. H. FRANKFORT, *Ancient Egyptian Religion* (New York 1961). **Illustration credit:** The Metropolitan Museum of Art, Carnarvon Collection, Gift of Edward S. Harkness, 1926.

[H. MUELLER]

AMORRITES

This name suggests that the Amorrites (Amorites) of the OT were the same as the Amorrites who invaded Mesopotamia and Syria *c.* 2000 B.C. At the time of the invasion they were a nomadic people; Egyptian paintings represent them with short beards and dressed in sandals and varicolored tunics. They became urbanized in ancient *Mesopotamia, and the OT does not represent them as nomadic. The name is connected with Sumerian MAR.TU and Akkadian Amurru, "west"; Amurru appears in Assyrian records only as a geographical designation. Hence the name must have entered the Israelite vocabulary from Mesopotamia, since the Amorrites did not enter Palestine from the west. The term in Syria and Palestine has its own meaning, which is not derived from Mesopotamian usage. In the *Amarna Letters, Amurru signifies both a geographical district in Syria (north of modern Beirut) and a state ruled by Abdi-Ashirta that does not clearly lie in the same geographical district. The Hittite King Mursilis made a treaty with Duppi-Tešub, King of Amurru; the name of this ruler is not Amorrite. The district of Amurru was the objective of a campaign of Seti I of Egypt (1318–1301 B.C.).

Data on Amorrites in Syria and Palestine do not indicate such a wide diffusion as is suggested by Biblical occurrences of the name. The Amorrites are classified with certain Canaanite tribes as sons of Canaan and descendants of Ham (Gn 10.16). The classification is geographical, however, not ethnic; the Amorrites lived in the territory of Canaan but were not of the same ethnic origin as the Canaanites. They are mentioned as living near the Dead Sea at Hasason-Thamar (Gn 14.7), and Mamre is called an Amorrite (Gn 14.13). Mamre, however, is not a personal name but a place name. There are signs that Genesis ch. 14 does not preserve historical memories in their purity. *Sichem (Shechem) is called an Amorrite city, but only once (Gn 48.22). Other data are not entirely consistent. The Amorrites dwelt in the mountains (the central highlands of Palestine) while the Canaanites dwelt in the Jordan Valley and on the coastal plain (Nm 13.29). The Amorrite kings of western Palestine mentioned in the narratives of the conquests of Joshua resided in the highlands (Jos 5.1; 10.5–7). According to Jgs 1.34–35, on the other hand, the Amorrites of the coastal plain prevented the tribe of Dan from expanding westward and retained cities which they held in the foothills of the central highlands. In Nm 21.21–23 there is an Amorrite kingdom of eastern Palestine east of the Dead Sea and north of the Arnon. It is to be noted, however, that the tradition placed the fall of this kingdom before the Israelite settlement in Palestine. A later writer connects Jerusalem with the Amorrites (Ez 16.3, 45). Hence the Amorrites appear to be distributed over much of the territory of Palestine.

Glazed tile from Medinet Habu, representing an Amorrite captive of Ramses III.

The identity of these Amorrites with the Amorrites of Mesopotamia would be more assured if a representative number of their personal names were mentioned in the Bible. The type of small kingdoms that they established in Palestine corresponds to the type of state that the Amorrites established in northwest Mesopotamia and north Syria. Archeology so far has not disclosed any specifically Amorrite traces; however, the nomadic incursions into Transjordan and the Jordan Valley, particularly at Jericho, that are evidenced for the 21st to 19th centuries B.C. conform very well to what is known of Amorrites from elsewhere. But the allusions to the diffusion of the Amorrites in other sources suit their presence and diffusion in Palestine, where they seem to have survived longer as a distinct group than elsewhere. It is probable that the OT use of the name is somewhat loose, particularly in documents considerably removed in time from the living traditions of the settlements, and that the Amorrites were mistakenly said to have been in some places where they never actually were.

Bibliography: W. F. ALBRIGHT, *From the Stone Age to Christianity* (2d ed. New York 1957). J. BRIGHT, *A History of Israel* (Philadelphia 1959). J. FINEGAN, *Light from the Ancient Past* (2d ed. Princeton 1959). K. KENYON, *Archaeology in the Holy Land* (New York 1960) 135–161. **Illustration credit:** Courtesy, Museum of Fine Arts, Boston.

[J. L. MC KENZIE]

AMORT, EUSEBIUS, philosopher, theologian; b. Bibermühle, Bavaria, Nov. 15, 1692; d. Polling, Feb. 5, 1775. He received his early education from the Jesuits at Munich and entered the canons regular at Polling, where in 1717 he was assigned to teach philosophy and, later, theology and Canon Law. In 1722 he founded an influential scientific and literary review, *Parnassus boicus,* which he continued for some years. Amort spent the years from 1733 to 1735 as theologian to Cardinal Lercari in Rome, where he became acquainted with many distinguished scholars and theologians. Among his correspondents were numbered such men as Benedict XIII and Benedict XIV, Cardinals Lercari, Orsi, and Galli, St. Alphonsus Liguori, and Daniel Concina. After his return from Rome, Amort devoted the last 40 years of his life to writing. Seventy volumes came from his pen, embracing an almost encyclopedic range of subjects: philosophy, apologetics, dogmatic, moral, and mystical theology, history, Canon Law, prayer books, catechisms, and hagiography. Engaging in the controversy on *probabilism, he sought to maintain a middle course between rigorism and laxism, and he is credited with being a cofounder of *equiprobabilism, inasmuch as St. Alphonsus appealed to his authority in support of that system. He took a very critical view of the *Mystical City of God* of Mary of *Agreda, against which he devoted the best known of his works, *De revelationibus, visionibus et apparitionibus regulae tutae . . .* (Augsburg 1744), a book that brought him into conflict with the supporters of Mary. Amort also entered into the controversy that was being waged at the time with regard to the authorship of the **Imitation of Christ.* He vigorously defended the claims of Thomas à Kempis against the Benedictine champions of Jean Gerson, and filled seven books with his views upon the matter. His more important moral treatises were: *Theologia eclectica, moralis et scholastica* (4 v. Augsburg 1752), an edition of which, revised by Benedict XIV, was published in Bologna in 1753; *Theologia moralis inter rigorem et laxitatem media* (Augsburg 1739); and *Ethica christiana* (Augsburg 1758). His *Vetus disciplina canonicorum regularium et saecularium* (Venice 1748) is still considered a valuable contribution to the history of religious orders.

Bibliography: No thorough biographical study of Amort has been written. Hurter Nomencl 5.1:228–232. C. TOUSSAINT, DTC 1.1:1115–17. L. HERTLING, DictSpirAscMyst 1:530–531. T. J. SHAHAN, CE 1:434–435.

[P. K. MEAGHER]

AMOS, BOOK OF

The third in the series of the 12 *Minor Prophets, though actually the earliest one. Although the institution of prophecy was already ancient in the days of Amos, the book bearing his name represents the first written collection of a prophet's oracles, thus ushering in a new epoch in the literature of Israel. *See* PROPHECY (IN THE BIBLE). The book is composed almost wholly of oracles pronounced by Amos in the middle of the 8th century B.C. primarily predicting doom for the Northern Kingdom because of social injustice and perversion of cult, emphasizing as it does Yahweh's ethical demands. It also holds some promise of hope, although this is not elaborated on by the prophet. This article will treat of the book in Israel's history, its division, composition, content, and doctrine.

Historical Setting. About midway in the reign of *Jeroboam II (783–743), when Israel had reached the zenith of its recovered prosperity, the spirit of the Lord summoned the shepherd Amos from Thecua, an obscure village on the margin of the desert of Juda, to pronounce impending doom upon the Northern Kingdom (Am 1.1; 7.14). Like the roaring of a lion, as described in 3.8, the message of the prophet resounded through the sanctuary at Bethel and in the gates of the capital. The response was an angry rejection of Amos by officialdom in the person of Amasia, priest of the sanctuary (7.13), as had happened on previous occasions (2.12). Yet the call of Amos to the office of prophet was the providential work of Yahweh; it was neither by reason of personal choice nor inheritance that Amos prophesied at the sanctuary of Bethel. He emphatically denied that he was a prophet by profession, i.e., a member of the prophetic guilds that ministered at the sanctuaries (7.14; see H. H. Rowley, 114–115). Rather, his call was immediately from Yahweh, who had taken him from following the flock and from dressing sycamore trees to prophesy to Israel (7.15). The oracles of Amos were soon written down, probably by a disciple, and, for the first time in Israel, the force of the written word was effectively carrying the prophetic message. The prophetic faith had found a new instrument to convey its message and succeeding prophets built upon the solid foundation set by Amos.

Division. In an introduction (1.1–2), the editor identifies the prophet and the general period of his ministry, and with a single verse characterizes the tenor of the entire prophecy.

In the first part (1.3–2.16) is presented a series of oracles, all of the same literary construction and directed against the hostile neighbors of Israel. This reaches a dramatic climax in the judgment of the Lord against the Northern Kingdom itself (2.6–16).

The second part (3.1–6.14) contains a collection of oracles that elaborate upon the sinfulness of Israel and the determination of Yahweh to chastise these transgressions. A third group of minatory oracles (8.4–14) logically pertain to this section, but apparently have been misplaced, since they interrupt the continuity of the passage in which they now stand.

The last part (ch. 7–9) is taken up with a succession of visions, each of which depicts a dire punishment about to overtake the people. Inserted after the third vision is a brief biographical account of Amos (7.10–17). A messianic epilogue concludes the book (9.8c–15).

Composition. Modern scholarship attributes the bulk of the prophecy to Amos (see W. S. McCullough, 247–248). There is evidence of certain later additions, e.g., the references to Juda (1.2; 2.4–5) and several lyrical passages that may be fragments of a hymn glorifying Yahweh as Lord of the physical universe (4.13; 5.8; 8.9; 9.5–6). The messianic promise of restoration of the "fallen hut of David" at the end of the prophecy (9.8c–15) breathes an optimism difficult to harmonize with what precedes it, which seems to presuppose the destruction of both kingdoms. This messianic part was perhaps added during the Exile. Thus the work as we now possess it comes from the hands of a redactor, probably a disciple of the prophet, who collected the oracles and arranged them in an order that is not necessarily chronological. This work was very likely done in the Southern Kingdom after the fall of Samaria. The text of Amos has been preserved in good condition with a few minor exceptions.

Content and Doctrine. Amos exposes with rustic candor the sins of the wealthy of Samaria, particularly their avarice and greed (2.6; 8.5–6), the perversion of judgment (5.7, 12), oppression of the weak (2.7; 3.10; 5.11), and sensuality (2.7; 6.4–6). These excesses outrage Amos's sense of justice because they are enjoyed at the expense of the defenseless poor of the land.

The sanctuaries of *Bethel, *Galgal, and the city of *Dan are objects of God's displeasure (4.4–5; 5.5, 21–23; 7.9; 8.10, 14). Here cult is offered to foreign deities (5.26; 8.14) in a kind of syncretism with the religion of Moses. The priests are guilty of fostering formalism in worship rather than a true religion of the heart (5.21–24). Indeed, they have become so self-complacent in their privilege as the chosen people that they have forgotten the obligations that election carries with it (3.2).

Jeroboam II shares this guilt (6.13) and his dynasty will fall (7.9); so too, will the lives of his officials be forfeited (6.1, 7). The whole nation must suffer for the sins of its leaders at the hands of an unnamed oppressor (6.14), which is clearly Assyria (7.17).

A sincere repentance and return to Yahweh could save them (4.6–11). "Seek me, that you may live" is the plaintive refrain of God's last desperate plea (5.4, 6, 14–15). But amidst a people enamoured of luxury, these overtures fall upon deaf ears. Amos, abandoning hope of any true conversion, proclaims a punishment approaching with inexorable certainty (4.12; 5.26–27; 8.3; 9.1–4). In this context, the "*day of the Lord," longed for by the Israelites as a glorious event, is given a new and terrifying meaning by Amos (5.18, 20). It is henceforth to be a day of wrath when Yahweh will visit just retribution upon all sinners (8.9–14). Intimately allied with this is the inchoate theme of the *remnant of Israel to be spared (3.12; 5.15; 9.8).

The leitmotif of Amos's prophecy is "righteousness," the necessary condition for worship that is acceptable to God (5.24). Amos in insisting upon justice con-

Amos prophesying the fall of Samaria, illuminated initial in a 14th-century Latin Bible from Alsace-Lorraine.

trasts with his contemporary, Hosea, who extols God's steadfast love (Heb. *ḥesed*), a term that never occurs in Amos. See N. Snaith, *The Distinctive Ideas of the OT* (Philadelphia 1946) 65–69.

Amos professes strict monotheism. Yahweh is the sole ruler of the universe (4.13; 5.8; 8.9, 11). He requites evil among the pagans (ch. 1–2), directs the course of the history of Israel as well as the nations (9.7), and uses the Assyrians as His instrument (6.14). His wonderful deeds in behalf of His people, especially in the Exodus (2.10; 3.1; 4.10; 5.25; 9.7), increase the responsibility of the Israelites to observe the moral precepts of the covenant.

Bibliography: InterDictBibl 1:116–121. W. R. Harper, *Amos and Hosea* (ICC; New York 1905). R. S. Cripps, *The Book of Amos* (ICC; 2d ed. London 1955). T. H. Sutcliffe, *The Book of Amos* (2d ed. London 1955). J. Morgenstern, *Amos Studies*, 3 v. (Cincinnati 1941–). H. H. Rowley, "The Nature of Old Testament Prophecy in the Light of Recent Study," *The Servant of the Lord and Other Essays on the O. T.* (London 1952). A. Neher, *Amos: Contribution à l'étude du prophétisme* (Paris 1950). W. S. McCullough, "Some Suggestions about Amos," JBiblLit 72 (1953) 247–254. J. D. W. Watts, "The Origin of the Book of Amos," ExposTimes 66 (1954–55) 109–112. A. S. Kapelrud, *Central Ideas in Amos* (Oslo 1961). B. Vawter, *The Conscience of Israel* (New York 1961) 61–97. **Illustration Credit:** Rare Book Department, Free Library of Philadelphia.

[J. K. SOLARI]

AMPÈRE, ANDRÉ MARIE, French physicist; b. Polémieux-les-Mont-d'Or, near Lyon, Jan. 22, 1775; d. Marseille, June 10, 1836. His father was executed in the Revolution as an aristocrat. Ampère was a precocious child, and he began teaching while yet a student. At 24 he married Julie Carron, and he never recovered from the loss when she died 4 years later. At 26 he obtained the physics and chemistry professorship at Bourg; and at 29, at the Lyon Lyceum. Two years later, in 1807, he became professor at l'École Polytechnique in Paris, as well as general inspector of the University. As a mathematician he developed probability and variation analysis and integration of partial differential equations. Better known as a physicist, he discovered independently Avogadro-Ampère's law: "gases at equal pressures and volumes contain an equal number of molecules." He studied and codified Oersted's discoveries of interaction between electrical conductors, using rotating loops pivoting in mercury pools. He found that a coil of parallel loops, which he called a "solenoid," behaved like a magnet, advancing the theory that the earth could be considered like one. The theory that magnets are formed by molecular currents susceptible of orientation is his also.

Bibliography: *Journal et correspondence* (Paris 1869); *Correspondence et souvenirs,* ed. H. CHEUVREUX, 2 v. (Paris 1875). C. A. VALSON, *André-Marie Ampère* (4th ed. Paris 1936). L. DE LAUNAY, *Le grand Ampère* (Paris 1925). D. F. J. ARAGO, *Oeuvres complètes,* ed. J. H. BARRAL, 12 v. (Paris 1854–59), v.2, eulogy on Ampère.

[E. T. SPAIN]

AMPHILOCHIUS OF ICONIUM, 4th-century bishop of Iconium, in Pisidia; b. Caesarea, *c.* 340; d. after 394 (feast, Nov. 23). Amphilochius studied rhetoric under Libanius at Antioch, practiced as a lawyer in Constantinople for 6 years, and decided to become a hermit. His decision was frustrated by *Basil of Caesarea, who forced on him the Diocese of Iconium. As bishop, Amphilochius campaigned against *Arianism and the crypto-Manichean ascetical sects of the Apotactites, Encratites, and Messalians.

Basil dedicated his *De Spiritu Sancto* to Amphilochius, who used it to combat the propaganda of the Macedonians, against whose teachings he summoned a council at Iconium in 376. Amphilochius himself wrote a similar treatise on the Holy Spirit, but it has not been preserved. Basil's letters 190, 218, 188, 199, and 217 were addressed to Amphilochius; but virtually all of Amphilochius's letters and almost his entire literary output have been lost. A notable exception is his synodal letter to the bishops of another province, following the Council of Iconium (376), in which he explicitly defended the divinity of the Holy Spirit (PG 39:93–98). In 381 Amphilochius attended the Council of *Constantinople I; he revisited the capital in 383 and 395, the last time probably shortly before his death and just after presiding at the anti-Messalian Council of Side in 394.

His 333 iambic verses to Seleucus are a treatise on the combination of the devout life with contemplative study that was preserved among the works of *Gregory of Nazianzus. It has special importance for the history of the canon of the Bible. Eight of his sermons also have been preserved, dealing primarily with liturgical feasts. His authority as a theologian grew during the early 5th century, and all the major councils after Ephesus (431) appeal to him as a source of patristic doctrine.

Bibliography: PG 39:9–130. K. HOLL, *Amphilochius von Ikonium in seinem Verhältnis zu den grossen Kappadoziern* (Tübingen 1904). G. FICKER, ed., *Amphilochiana* (Leipzig 1906). Altaner 357–358. J. QUASTEN, LexThK² 1:448–449. H. M. WERHAHN, ByzZ 47 (1954) 414–418. G. BARDY, DictSpirAscMyst 1:544.

[A. G. GIBSON]

AMPHITHEATER (COLOSSEUM), originally called the Amphitheatrum Flavianum, in Rome, Italy. Since its construction (A.D. 72–80) this gigantic amphitheater has been regarded both as a symbol of Rome's power and as one of the world's greatest wonders. The structure, built of travertine blocks upon the site of Nero's Golden House by the Emperors Vespasian and Titus, is an ellipse 1,719 feet in circumference and 159 feet in height, with an arena 282 by 177 feet. In its best preserved section it is four stories high. The first three stories are formed by arcades with pillars of Doric, Ionic, and Corinthian orders respectively; the fourth is a tier of blind arcading, broken by alternate panels and windows. The interior had three tiers of marble seats for about 50,000 spectators. Beneath the sanded arena was an elaborate structure of rooms, vaults, passageways, and drains.

The intricate system of substructures beneath the arena seems to indicate that it could be flooded for mock naval battles. There were efficient devices for the drainage of the entire interior, which have been in part restored. Surrounding the arena was a low wall surmounted by a railing high enough to protect the audience from wild animals and combatants. The primary purpose of the huge arena was entertainment, such as gladiatorial fights, naval clashes, and wild-beast fights. While it has been venerated as the scene of numerous Christian martyrdoms since the 17th century, this late tradition has been seriously questioned by recent scholars, especially the Bollandist H. *Delehaye, as the ancient Christian sources make no mention of such martyrdoms.

Because of earthquakes and its use as a stone quarry, the Colosseum continued to deteriorate until Pope *Benedict XIV (1740–58) forbade further demolition. Because of periodic stories of buried treasure in the Colosseum, Pope *Pius IX, in 1864, gave permission for excavations. Nothing of intrinsic value was found. However, the excavations did give R. Lanciani an opportunity to examine the foundations of the vast structure. He found that the substructures were arched like those of the structure above the ground, and that

The Colosseum, built in the 1st century A.D., Rome.

underneath them was a very thick bed of concrete. Further excavations were begun in 1938. The outbreak of World War II in the following year suspended the work. Since then, after years of preliminary study, the excavations have been resumed, and are intended to prepare for a restoration of the building.

Bibliography: G. Rodenwaldt, CAH 11 (1936) 775–805. H. Leclercq, DACL 1.2:1648–82. G. Lugli, EncIt 10:887–888. E. Kirschbaum and L. Hertling, *The Roman Catacombs and Their Martyrs,* tr. M. J. Costelloe (Milwaukee 1956). Cross ODCC 313, s.v. Colosseum. **Illustration credit:** Foto-Enit-Roma.

[T. J. ALLEN]

AMPLEFORTH, ABBEY OF, St. Laurence's Abbey, Ampleforth, near York, Diocese of Middlesbrough, of the English *Benedictines. It has an unbroken tradition from *Westminster Abbey (suppressed in 1559) through Sigebert Buckley, the last survivor of that abbey, who aggregated monks to Westminster (1607), some of whom helped found the monastery of Dieulouard in Lorraine (1608). When Dieulouard was dispersed (1793), some of its monks returned to England, settling at Ampleforth in a priory (1802) which became an abbey (1900). A boys' school established soon after 1802 achieved high standards and large enrollment (807 students in 1964) under the headmasters Edmund Matthews (1903–24) and Paul Nevill (1924–54). Today Ampleforth is a liturgical, educational, and monastic center with 160 monks. The library contains many incunabula and the works of D. A. *Baker in MSS. Abbot Oswald Smith (1900–24) emphasized monastic observance and Abbots Matthews (1924–39) and Herbert Byrne (1939–63) undertook a major building program. Notable figures include Abbot J. McCann, Bp. Slater of Mauritius, Bp. J. C. *Hedley, and Bp. P. A. *Baines. Its foundations are St. Benet Hall, Oxford (1897), and St. Louis Priory, St. Louis, Mo. (1955). Monks from Ampleforth still work on the English mission, as Bl. Alban *Roe once did from Dieulouard.

Bibliography: J. McCann and C. Cary-Elwes, eds., *Ampleforth and Its Origins* (London 1952).

[C. CARY-ELWES]

AMPULLAE, the diminutive of amphora [properly, amp(h)orula, from *amphi,* or both, and *phero* or *porto,* bear], a small globular flask with two handles for carrying, another name for cruets. The term is used of those clay or glass vessels found at tombs in the catacombs. It is probable that these vessels were used to preserve portions of the oil or perfume used to anoint the bodies of the dead. Another class of this type of vessel was used to preserve oil for the lamps burning at the shrines of martyrs, a custom generally observed in the Middle Ages. Some image or symbol usually identified the saint from whose tomb the ampullae were taken. Several of those containing oil from the tombs of famous Roman martyrs are still preserved at the Cathedral of Monza. These were the gift of Pope Gregory the Great to Queen Theodolinda. A greater number of ampullae of this type were brought to Europe by pilgrims from the tomb of St. Mennas in Egypt. A third class of ampullae made of clay, metal, or glass was used to preserve the oils consecrated by the bishop (Optatus of Milevis, *Contra Parmenianum Donatistam* 2.19, "Ampulla Chrismatis").

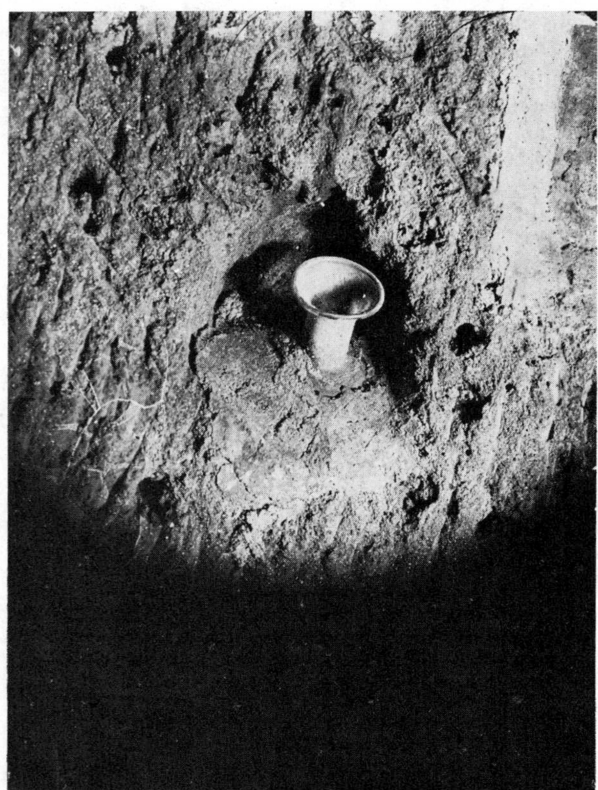

A small glass ampulla of the 3d century, in situ, embedded in a tomb wall in the Cemetery of Panfilo, Rome.

Of the ampullae found in the catacombs, many contained a dark-red sediment that was thought to be blood, thus marking the tomb of a martyr. Negative results obtained by chemical analysis have rendered this theory untenable. The sediment found in a test group of so-called blood vases revealed the presence of elements vastly disproportionate to those that might be found in blood. While it is not improbable that a few of the "ampullae sanguinis" did contain blood, they cannot be considered one of the marks of a martyr's tomb, since a number of such ampullae were found at the tombs of children under 7, and many date from the latter half of the 4th century, long after the era of persecution. Moreover, ampullae have been found in Jewish catacombs, e.g., on the Via Labicana, fastened to the tombs in the same way as in the Christian cemeteries.

Bibliography: H. Leclercq, DACL 1.2:1722–78. E. Dante and E. Josi, EncCatt 1:1113–15. Cross ODCC 45. F. Oppenheimer, *The Legend of the Ste. Ampoule* (London 1953). **Illustration credit:** Pontificia Commissione di Archeologia Sacra.

[M. A. BECKMANN]

AMRAPHEL, king of Sennaar (Shinar), ancient name of Babylonia, who joined three other kings—Arioch of Ellasar (Larsa), Thadal (Tidal) of Goyyim, and Chodorlahomor of *Elam, in a war against Elam's rebellious subjects, five kings of southern Canaan (Gn 14.1–11). *Lot, *Abraham's nephew, was taken prisoner by the invaders, but later rescued by his uncle (14.12–16). Formerly Amraphel was commonly identified with the well-known king of Babylon, *Hammurabi (Hammurapi), but this opinion is now abandoned by almost all scholars. None of the kings in the account can be certainly identified with any known historical figures. Similar names, however, have been found in historical records of the ancient Near East from the first half of the 2d millennium B.C. The passage in Genesis preserves other traces of its ancient origin. The view once held by some that the account was a late fabrication of the author to glorify the ancestor of the Hebrews is now rightly rejected. Yet the differences of vocabulary and tone do indicate that Gn 14.1–16 was not part of one of the principal sources of the *Pentateuch, but was inserted by the inspired author, who added from another source the account of Abraham's meeting with *Melchisedec. The faithfulness with which he preserved his ancient sources makes it possible to date Abraham with some probability between the 19th and 17th centuries B.C.

Bibliography: G. CASTELLINO, EncCatt 1:1118. H. JUNKER, LexThK[2] 1:451. EncDictBibl 75–76. F. M. T. DE LIAGRE BÖHL, RGG[3] 1:332–333. C. F. JEAN, DBSuppl 3:1380–82. R. DE VAUX, "Les Patriarches hébreux et les découvertes modernes," RevBibl 55 (1948) 326–337.

[J. F. MATTINGLY]

AMRI (OMRI), KING OF ISRAEL, *c.* 876–*c.* 869, and founder of a dynasty that numbered three more kings [*Achab (*c.* 869–*c.* 850), Ochozia (Ahazia; *c.* 850–*c.* 849), and Joram (*c.* 849–*c.* 842)]. Although Amri (Heb. *'omrî;* Assyrian *ḫumri*) was allotted only a dozen verses in the Bible (3 Kgs 16.16–28), he was certainly one of the most effective rulers Israel ever had. Long after his dynasty was a thing of the past the Assyrians continued to call Israel *māt ḫumrī* (the land of Amri) or *bīt ḫumrī* (the house of Amri) and an Israelite was called *mār ḫumrī* (son of Amri). Amri came to the throne during the time of great trouble and confusion following the murder of King Ela (*c.* 877–*c.* 876) by the usurper Zamri (Zimri). Amri had to contend for power with him, as well as with another contender, Thebni ben Gineth. Yet within a year of Ela's death, Amri was in sole command. To strengthen his position he built a new capital at Samaria on a strategically situated hill at the fork of the highway where one road went north over the Carmel range and the other went west to the Mediterranean Sea (*see* SAMARIA, CITY OF). This was in keeping with the policy of military and commercial alliance with the Phoenician cities of *Sidon and *Tyre, rather than with *Damascus. To cement his bonds with the Phoenicians, he married his son Achab to *Jezabel, the daughter of King Ethbaal (Ittobaal) of Tyre—a marriage that had disastrous results for the worship of Yahweh in Israel. For his impiety Amri is roundly condemned by the Deuteronomistic editor of Kings—a sentiment that was expressed at an earlier age by the Prophet Michea (Mi 6.16).

Bibliography: F. SPADAFORA, EncCatt 1:1119. EncDictBibl 76–77. R. BACH, RGG[3] 4:1630.

[B. MC GRATH]

AMSDORF, NIKOLAUS VON, Lutheran theologian and bishop, important for the early organization of Protestantism; b. probably Torgau, Dec. 3, 1483; d. Eisenach, May 14, 1565. Amsdorf received his M.A. at the University of Wittenberg and lectured there on philosophy and theology. When Luther arrived at Wittenberg the two became close friends and coworkers, Amsdorf assisting in the translation of the Bible. Amsdorf became an evangelical preacher in Magdeburg, Goslar, Einbeck, Meissen, and elsewhere. In 1542 Elector John Frederick appointed him first bishop of the Lutheran diocese of Naumburg-Zeitz (1542–47), a post that he lost at the outset of the *Schmalkaldic War. After a period in Weimar, he lived in Eisenach from 1552 until his death, the unofficial leader of the Lutherans there. He was unwavering in holding to a conservative Lutheran position in theology and was instrumental in founding the University of Jena, a Lutheran stronghold.

See also GNESIOLUTHERANISM; INTERIMS; CONFESSIONS OF FAITH, PROTESTANT.

Bibliography: *Ausgewählte Schriften,* ed. O. LERCHE (Gütersloh 1938). O. LERCHE, *Amsdorf und Melanchthon: Eine kirchengeschichtliche Studie* (Berlin 1937). P. BRUNNER, *Nikolaus von Amsdorf als Bischof von Naumburg* (Gütersloh 1961). F. LAU, RGG[3] 1:333–334.

[L. W. SPITZ]

AMULETS, charms and other objects worn for magical use, to protect against witchcraft, the evil eye, sickness, accidents, and all other conceivable dangers or maladies. The use of amulets can be traced to remote prehistoric times and has a world distribution. The ultimate source of belief in their efficacy is undoubtedly the primordial concept of *mana. Not only persons but objects can be protected by amulets or charms. Any kind of material, stone, wood, metal, may be used, and even parts of animals. Signs, figures, or symbols, as well

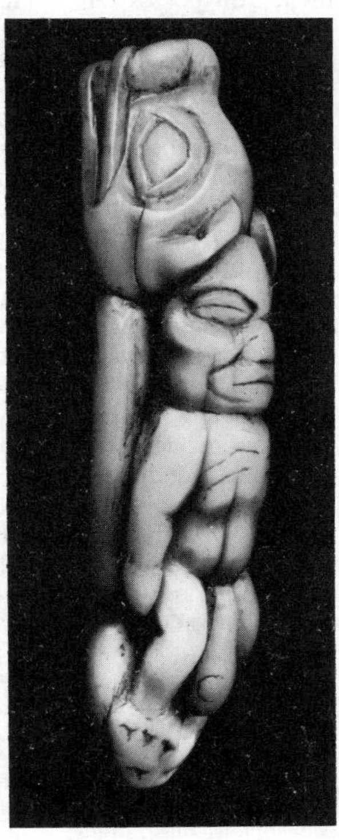

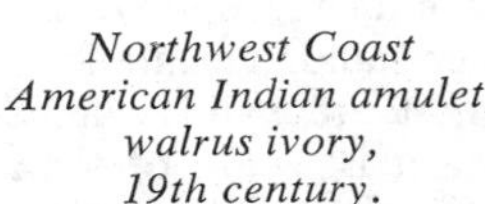

Northwest Coast American Indian amulet, walrus ivory, 19th century.

as magical formulas, magic words, inscriptions, anagrams, and cryptic phrases, may be engraved or even written upon the surface of the object employed. Magical potency can be secured or increased by consecration of the object according to a special ritual or by the

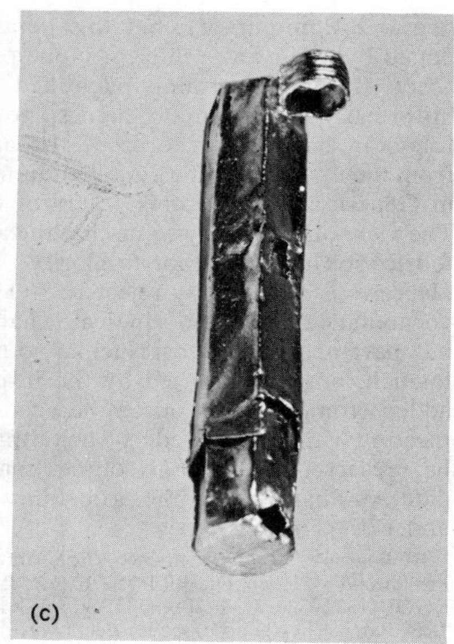

Amulets: (a) Figure of the cat-headed goddess, gold, Egyptian, Twenty-sixth Dynasty. (b) Early Christian mezuzah type, gold, 3rd century, and (c) gold case of the type used with it when worn around the neck.

peculiarity of the place or circumstances of its origin or fabrication.

In all cases involving the use of amulets, it is the object itself that, in some way or another, has acquired magical powers. It may be that its form or shape or the circumstances of its discovery has fulfilled the requirement for possession of magical properties. In other cases the words, signs, or symbols are prescribed in some religious ritual as carrying with them a peculiar control over pertinent deities and spirits.

The wide use of amulets in pagan cultures has led many specialists in comparative religion to put the Christian use of sacramentals in the same category. However, Christian belief is radically different because no magical properties or powers are assigned to the object or action concerned. The sacramental is primarily efficacious through promoting in the user a religious habit of mind and personal piety, which in themselves may have a decided influence upon Christian manner of life. On the other hand, an amulet in pagan belief possesses powers that are valid whether or not the one using or handling it is aware of them. It is believed that contact, even unknowingly, with an amulet calls forth the operation of its magical powers, which are both inherent and intrinsic. For the Jewish and Christian use of amulets see references given in the bibliography of this article.

See also MAGIC; SUPERSTITION.

Bibliography: A. CLOSS and M. HAIN, LexThK² 1:462–464. C. H. RATSCHOW, RGG³ 1:345–347. F. ECKSTEIN and J. WASZINK, ReallexAntChr 1:397–411. B. FREIRE-MARECO et al., Hastings ERE 3:392–472, a comprehensive world survey; 413–430, section on Christian usage by E. VON DOBSCHÜTZ needs qualification or correction in a number of places, esp. 425–430. H. LECLERCQ, DACL 1.2:1784–1860, with bibliog. and copious illustrations. E. R. GOODENOUGH, *Jewish Symbols in the Graeco-Roman Period* (Bollingen Ser. 37; New York 1953–), Indexes *s.v.* "Amulets" and the pls. at end of each v.
Illustration credits: Fig. 2*a*, University Museum, Philadelphia. Figs. 2*b*, 2*c*, Courtesy of the Dumbarton Oaks Collections. Fig. 1, Robert H. Lowie Museum of Anthropology, University of California, Berkeley.

[T. A. BRADY]

AMYOT, JACQUES, bishop of Auxerre, one of the four great French prose stylists of the 16th century; b. Melun, France, Oct. 30, 1513; d. Auxerre, Feb. 6, 1593. His parents, it seems, were of some means, and he studied at the Collège de France, graduating at 19 more as the result of hard work than brilliance. He was at Bourges from 1534 to 1547 teaching Greek and Latin. Francis I, to whom he dedicated his first works, conferred on him the abbey of Bellozane-en-Bray, March 18, 1547 (N.S.; 1546 O.S.). It is not known when or where he was ordained. He was in Rome (1550–51) and performed a diplomatic mission of a few days to the Council of Trent before he became tutor to the sons of Henry II. Charles IX made him grand chaplain of France, Dec. 6, 1560, an office he held until Henry IV deposed him in 1590. He received other royal favors from Charles, including the See of Auxerre in 1570. In 1578 Henry III made him grand chaplain of the Order of the Holy Spirit. Charges that he held Protestant beliefs have not been established. His literary work consists mostly of translations: *Histoire aethiopique d'Heliodorus* (1547), *Sept livres des histoires de Diodore Sicilien* (1554), *Amours pastorales de Daphnis et Chloé* (1559), and Plutarch's *Lives* and *Morals* (1559, 1565, 1579), the translation of which by Sir Thomas North in 1579 was used by Shakespeare. Amyot's translations are quite free and contain errors, but it seems that he used the Greek rather than Latin or Italian translations available. The works became very popular and exerted an influence on French moral thought and literary style for some time. Amyot wrote several original works, including prayers before and after Holy Communion, published after his death.

Bibliography: R. STUREL, *Jacques Amyot: Traducteur des Vies parallèles de Plutarque* (Paris 1908). C. URBAIN and M. CITOLEUX, DictBiogFranc 2:751–761.

[D. R. PENN]

AMYRAUT, MOÏSE, Calvinist theologian; b. Bourgeuil, Touraine, September 1596; d. Saumur, Jan. 8, 1664. He was intended for a legal career and became at 21 a licentiate of law at Poitiers; but, having been introduced to Calvin's *Institutes,* he studied theology at Saumur under John *Cameron, whose doctrine of divine election he was to develop and defend. After pastorates at Saint-Agnan and Saumur, he was from 1633 a professor in the Saumur academy. For the Synod of Charenton, 1631, he presented King Louis XIII with a memorandum on infractions of the Edict of *Nantes. A man of courtly manners, he moved with ease among eminent persons and was on occasion consulted by Richelieu and Mazarin. He was twice acquitted of heresy before national synods of his church. He was a prolific and in his time an influential writer, firm in his principles and courteous to his opponents. His "hypothetic universalism" on divine election is set forth in his *Echantillon de la doctrine de Calvin sur la prédestination* (*c.* 1634), and other treatises. His ecumenical proposals appear best in his Εἰρηνικόν (1662), but his whole work is irenic in tone.

Bibliography: E. and É. HAAG, *La France protestante,* 10 v. (Paris 1846–59) 1:72–80, lists and describes his works. R. STAUFFER, *Möise Amyraut: Un Précurseur français de l'oecuménisme* (Paris 1962). O. E. STRASSER, RGG[3] 1:347–348. J. DEDIEU, DHGE 2:1380–81.

[J. T. MC NEILL]

ANABAPTISTS

The term Anabaptist, meaning literally "rebaptizer," occurs from the 4th century onward and was first used to designate those who insisted on the rebaptism of persons baptized by heretics or by clergy who had fallen away from the faith under persecution.

In the 16th century it was applied to those elements in the Reformation movement who denied the validity of infant baptism. It became a pejorative term, used by their Catholic and Protestant opponents to associate them with a heresy condemned for centuries by both ecclesiastical and civil law and incurring the death penalty according to the Justinian Code, and was applied indiscriminately to a heterogeneous group of the "left wing" of the Reformation. The association with *Donatism was inaccurate, since the 16th-century Anabaptists were not concerned with the validity of the administration of the Sacrament of Baptism but rather denied its sacramental character. Their attitude toward baptism with water ranged from seeing it as an important act of public confession (e.g., Swiss Brethren) to the denial of the necessity of any physical baptism (e.g., Schwenckfeld). Thus the Schleitheim Confession of the Swiss Brethren (1527) states: "Baptism shall be given to all those who have learned repentance and amendment of life, and who believe truly that their sins are taken away by Christ and to all those who walk in the resurrection of Jesus Christ." By contrast, Caspar Schwenckfeld asserts summarily: "God does not tie his grace to water." Since the differences among those who rejected infant baptism are vast, it is advisable to divide the so-called Anabaptists into four separate but related groups: (1) New Testament–oriented pacifists, (2) Old Testament–oriented revolutionaries, (3) spiritualists, and (4) rationalists. It should be noted, however, that in the 16th century the lines between these groups were somewhat fluid and that they exerted considerable influence upon each other.

New Testament–oriented Pacificists. This segment had its origin in lay Bible study groups in Zürich, Switzerland (1523–25). The movement was led by men close to *Zwingli (Conrad *Grebel, Felix Manz, Georg Blaurock, and later Balthasar *Hubmaier), impatient with Zwingli's hesitation and vacillation in his interpretation and administration of the sacraments, his attitude toward political authority, and the nature of the church. On Jan. 21, 1525, Grebel baptized Blaurock, and "believer's baptism" became the outward mark of the movement. When those rebaptized were soon expelled from Zürich, they spread their new teaching all over central Europe. Later some, following the example of the early Christian community in Jerusalem (Acts 4.32–35), organized Christian communist communities that have survived to the present (*see* HUTTERITES). In northern Europe the New Testament–oriented pacifist Anabaptists eventually found an eloquent leader in Menno Simons (1496–1561). *See* MENNONITES.

The theology of the group was expressed in the Schleitheim Confession. Besides condemning infant baptism and favoring adult baptism as confession of faith, it advocated the "ban" (the strict discipline of the community of the baptized), a memorial view of Holy Communion, complete separation from all who did not share their views, and the refusal to bear arms and participate in political life.

Old Testament–oriented Revolutionaries. This group originated in Zwickau in Saxony (*c.* 1520) among the impoverished weavers of that town. Led by Nicholas Storch, they were soon joined by Thomas *Münzer, who became one of their most voluble spokesmen, and participated actively in the Peasant War. While they also opposed infant baptism, they distinguished themselves from the pacifist Anabaptists by their emphasis upon the Old Testament call to war against the "Canaanites," their stress upon direct revelations from God independent of the Bible, and their elaborate millennial speculations based on an allegorical interpretation of the Book of Daniel and the Apocalypse. Although Münzer perished (1525) in the fiasco of the Peasant War, views similar to his own were later expressed by the Münster Anabaptists, who, influenced by the millennial hopes of Melchior *Hoffmann and under the leadership of Anabaptist refugees from the Netherlands, the "prophet" John Mathijs and his successor "king" John Beukels (John of Leiden), attempted to establish a communist and polygamous "kingdom of God" in this Westphalian city by force of arms (1533–35). After the utter collapse of this "kingdom" the surviving Anabaptist elements were absorbed in the New Testament–oriented pacifist Anabaptists under the leadership of Menno Simons.

Spiritualist Anabaptists. This group, whose rejection of infant baptism was not accompanied by an equally clear endorsement of baptism for adults, saw in the organizational structures of the church, as well as the sacraments and even the Bible, regulations applicable only to the infancy of God's people. Thus Sebastian *Franck (1499–1542) suggested that in its childhood the church could not dispense with such crutches, but when it discarded them in its maturity, the Father would be pleased rather than angered. Similarly Caspar Schwenckfeld (1489–1561) advocated the suspension of infant baptism, since he considered it so utterly immersed in superstition and abuses as to be worthless (*see* SCHWENCKFELDERS).

Central in the thought of Spiritualist Anabaptists such as Franck and Schwenkfeld was the denial of the absolute claims of all the contending religious movements of the time, from the Roman Catholics and Lutherans to the pacifist and revolutionary Anabaptists. They believed in an invisible church, which might well include not only sincere Christians but also good Moslems and pagans obedient to the "inner Word" wherever they might be. Such emphasis upon the inner Word of the Spirit distinguished the Spiritualist Anabaptists from the other groups and their Biblical literalism.

Rationalist Anabaptists. This last body had its roots primarily in the Romance lands. The Spaniard Michael *Servetus (1511–53) as well as the Italians Laelius (1525–62) and his nephew Faustus Socinius (1539–1604) were not only opposed to infant baptism but rejected the Trinitarian theology of the ancient Church as well (*see* SOCINIANISM). In this they were influenced by the Arianizing tendencies of Renaissance humanism (e.g., Florentine Academy under Marsilio *Ficino), by the Biblical literalism and the rejection of non-Biblical language typical of Anabaptists, which brought the complex Christological formulations of Nicaea and Chalcedon into disrepute, and by the confidence in the God-given ability of human reason to comprehend and follow the council of God. The rationalist Anabaptists tended to identify "spirit" with "reason" and saw Biblical truth as that which contributed to the moral improvement of humanity. Thus they tended to depreciate the confession of Christ as God and Savior, considering Him the great ethical teacher and example.

Anabaptists have survived in some contemporary denominations. Mennonites, Amish, and Hutterites carry on the tradition of the New Testament–oriented pacifists. The Schwenckfelder Church originated in the spiritualist tradition, and the Society of Friends (Quaker) has incorporated many of its teachings. Unitarians are loosely related to the rationalists. Only the Old Testament–oriented revolutionaries have found no permanent institutional expression although some of their millennial claims can be found in groups at the fringe of Protestantism. In the scholarly investigation of the Anabaptist movement, the following questions have been debated: (1) the influence of medieval sects on Anabaptists (e.g., L. Keller); (2) the place of origin in Switzerland (e.g., E. Troeltsch) or Saxony (e.g., K. Holl); (3) the definition of Anabaptism restricting it to the New Testament–oriented pacifists (e.g., H. Bender); (4) Anabaptist contributions to the doctrine of the church (e.g., F. Littell); (5) Anabaptist contributions to concept of separation of Church and State (e.g., G. H. Williams).

While the influence of medieval sectarianism is vague, the origin of the 16th-century movement can be considered settled if the distinction between the various groups of Anabaptists is maintained. Switzerland applies to the New Testament–oriented pacifists, and Saxony, to the Old Testament–oriented revolutionaries. The attempt to restrict the term Anabaptist to the pacifists must be considered special pleading. The Anabaptist contribution to a voluntaristic view of the church and separation of Church and State has been demonstrated. In these matters, Anabaptists have exerted an influence upon Christian thinking in general and Protestant thinking in particular quite out of proportion to their numbers.

Bibliography: H. E. FOSDICK, ed., *Great Voices of the Reformation* (New York 1952). H. J. HILLERBRAND, *A Bibliography of Anabaptism, 1520–1630* (Elkhart, Ind. 1962). MENNO SIMONS, *Complete Writings,* tr. L. VERDUIN, ed. J. C. WENGER (Scottdale, Pa. 1956). G. H. WILLIAMS, *The Radical Reformation* (Philadelphia 1962); ed., *Spiritual and Anabaptist Writers* (Philadelphia 1957). *The Mennonite Encyclopedia,* 4 v. (Scottdale, Pa. 1955–60). K. HOLL, "Luther und die Schwärmer," *Gesammelte Aufsätze zur Kirchengeschichte,* 3 v. (Tübingen 1927–28) 1:420–467. F. H. LITTELL, *The Origins of Sectarian Protestantism* (New York 1964). J. LORTZ, *Die Reformation in Deutschland,* 2 v. (Freiburg 1949). E. TROELTSCH, *The Social Teaching of the Christian Churches,* tr. O. WYON, 2 v. (New York 1931; repr. 1956). A. L. E. VERHEYDEN, *Anabaptism in Flanders, 1530–1650,* tr. M. KUITSE et al. (Scottdale, Pa. 1961). H. FAST, RGG[3] 6:601–604, bibliog. A. BAUDRILLART, DTC 1.1:1128–34. Y. CONGAR, *Catholicisme* 1:500–501. P. BERNARD, DHGE 2:1383–1405, bibliog. P. J. KLASSEN, *The Economics of Anabaptism, 1525–1560* (The Hague 1964).

[G. W. FORELL]

ANACLETUS (CLETUS), POPE, ST., pontificate, *c.* 79 to 92. He appears in the Liber pontificalis and the Roman martyrology as two popes, both martyrs, with feasts on April 26 and July 13. St. Irenaeus (*Adv. haer.* 3.3) and the liturgy of the Mass make him the second successor of Peter (*see* POPES, LIST OF). Eusebius (*Hist.* 3.13, 15, 21; 5.6) says that he died in the 12th year of Domitian's reign after a 12-year episcopate. The Liber pontificalis probably mistakes Anacletus for *Anicetus as the builder of a burial monument for Peter. Modern excavations show that Anacletus was not buried near Peter in the Vatican.

Bibliography: Duchesne LP 1:xix–xx, 52–53. J. P. KIRSCH, DHGE 2:1407–08. Caspar 1:8–16. L. KOEP, ReallexAntChr 2: 410–415. E. KIRSCHBAUM, *Tombs of St. Peter and St. Paul,* tr. J. MURRAY (New York 1959). G. SCHWAIGER, LexThK[2] 1:524.

[E. G. WELTIN]

ANALGESIA, the absence of sensibility to pain. Other sensations may remain intact. Localized analgesia is a concomitant of certain nervous diseases or may result from injury of specific nervous elements.

Analgesia is achieved therapeutically through certain surgical procedures, by hypnosis, and with drugs capable of obtunding pain. Analgetics or analgesics are drugs that relieve pain by means other than reduction or removal of the causative factor. The central nervous system is considered the primary site of their systemic action.

The use of drugs for alleviation of pain antedates recorded history. Opium from the poppy plant indigenous to Asia Minor was known to physicians of Greece and the Near East, centuries before Christ. Morphine, the prototype of potent analgetics, was isolated in 1803 by F. W. A. Sertürner, a German pharmacist, from the mixture of alkaloids in opium. Numerous other opiate analgetics have been prepared, such as methylmorphine (codeine), dihydromorphinone (Dilaudid), methyldihydromorphinone (Metopon), dihydrocodeinone (Hycodan), Pantopon, and diacetylmorphine (heroin). The term, narcotic, as applied to these drugs connotes (1) their ability to produce lethargy and (2) control of their prescription in the U.S. by the Department of Internal Revenue under the Harrison Narcotic Act.

Synthetic, opiatelike narcotics, termed opioids, include meperidine (Demerol), methadone (Dolophine), levorphan (Levo-Dromoran), and alphaprodine (Nisentil).

A popular group of less potent, nonnarcotic drugs including acetanilid, acetophenetidin (phenacetin), aminopyrine (pyramidon), and the salicylates, especially acetylsalicylic acid (aspirin), are constituents of numerous proprietary preparations. Although commonly employed for relief of pain, their classification as analgetics is questionable since they may be effective through their alteration of the cause of pain.

See also ANESTHESIA; HYPNOSIS; DOUBLE EFFECT, PRINCIPLE OF.

Bibliography: L. S. GOODMAN and A. GILMAN, *The Pharmacological Basis of Therapeutics,* 3d ed. (New York 1965) 247–344. E. G. GROSS and M. J. SCHIFFRIN, *Clinical Analgetics* (Springfield 1955). J. BONICA, *Management of Pain* (Philadelphia 1953). G. A. KELLY, *Medico-moral Problems* (St. Louis 1958) 12–16, 115–127, 270–281, 288–293; *Medico-moral Problems,* pt. 4 (St. Louis 1952) 22. POPE PIUS XII, "Anesthesia: Three Moral Questions," (Address, Feb. 24, 1957) *The Pope Speaks* 4 (1957) 33–49; French text ActApS 49 (1957) 129–147.

[C. PITTINGER]

ANALOGY

Analogy, a technical, philosophical, and theological term, commonly designates a kind of predication midway between univocation and equivocation. Thus it denotes a perfection (the "analogon") that, though found similar in two or more subjects called "analogates," is neither simply the same nor simply different. As a technical notion, analogy must be distinguished from "argument by analogy." The latter has the following structure: if a given perfection *a* is possessed by two individuals, *B* and *C,* and if *a* is accompanied by another perfection *d* in *B,* then *d* will also be found in *C.* This argument is heuristic, or suggestive; of itself it is not and cannot be certain.

HISTORY OF THE CONCEPT OF ANALOGY

The term analogy was first used by Greek mathematicians in the sense of proportion. *Plato is generally conceded to have been the first to use it philosophically to designate proportions between the elements of the world and between kinds of knowledge and types of reality. Plato also applies it to similarities of function in different things, and occasionally to a likeness between two things that is not an identity.

These uses were expanded and developed by *Aristotle. In biology, the "analogy" between different organs that perform similar functions became an important concept. In his ethical writings, Aristotle uses the term analogy in a similar way. Thus, there is no single "idea of the good"; "the good" designates something found in unequal degrees in different subjects. In the *Metaphysics* the principles, elements, and causes of things are said to be common "analogously," that is, proportionately common. In his logical writings, analogy is sometimes used in the sense of similar proportions. However, when Aristotle says that the most common classes of terms are analogous, he refers rather to a general similarity which cannot be further analyzed into common genera and specific differences. In his psychological works he notes that actual knowledge is analogous to the object known. This is a type of proportion in the sense of suitability, "adaptation to" rather than similarity. Although these uses of analogy are clearly not identical, Aristotle does not explain how they are related, probably because he has no explicit theory of analogy.

One other discussion is important in Aristotle for the doctrine of analogy (though here he himself does not use the term): *being* is a word with many meanings, but all the meanings are somehow reduced to a primary one. Aristotle explains this by saying that all the things that are called being are so called by reference to one subject that is being in the primary sense; this is the so-called πρὸς ἕν equivocity.

The Greek and Arabian commentators on Aristotle gathered these comments together, but did not develop a full theory of analogy. In the same way the later Platonists, especially Pseudo-Dionysius, extended Plato's use of analogy and adopted some of the Aristotelian terminology.

Medieval Development. In the Augustinian tradition, no formal, explicit doctrine of analogy is to be found; since intellectual knowledge does not arise from the sensible world, such a doctrine is not necessary. But prominent among St. Augustine's themes are the inability of our language to express the perfection of God, and the similarity-in-dissimilarity of creatures in relation to God.

The doctrine of St. *Thomas Aquinas will be considered in great detail below. He used analogy more than any of his predecessors and made a number of formal analyses of it. There is, however, no single, adequate summary. Some of his uses reflect the original meaning of proportion; one usage (analogy of Scripture) is derived from the grammatical meaning of agreement. Such usage is irrelevant to analogy as a philosophical doctrine.

St. Thomas's immediate predecessors, like his teacher St. Albert the Great and his contemporaries, used analogy only incidentally. In St. Bonaventure we find instead a highly developed doctrine of creatures as vestiges and images of God. Even such authors as Henry of Ghent do not elaborate a doctrine of analogy; he, for example, is content to say that there are two types of being.

John *Duns Scotus is aware of Aquinas's doctrine of analogy as well as of equivalents like that of Henry of Ghent's double notion of being. His arguments for the univocity of being rest on his view of metaphysics (univocal being is its object), the possibility of a proof for the existence of God (only from being as being can the existence of a transcendent God be proved), and the principle of contradiction and the laws of logic (if being is not univocal, formal contradictions are impossible; arguments employing "being" would have four terms). However, along with the univocity of being, Scotus holds an analogy of beings in themselves insofar as they are related and ordered.

In the hands of *William of Ockham, the univocity of being becomes the logical univocity of a name or a sign. A word is "common" to many things; if it is not univocal, it must be equivocal. In addition to words; there are also signs, and signs are very like the words which conventionally express them. But there can be no question of any analogy of beings in themselves, since things are radically singular and unrelated to each other.

Thomistic Commentators. Against this background, the great commentators on St. Thomas Aquinas, John Capreolus excepted, systematized and developed the doctrine of their master. In the 15th century, Cardinal Tommaso de Vio *Cajetan wrote his famous *On the Analogy of Names.* Cajetan holds that there are three basic types of analogy, according to the division of analogy given by St. Thomas in *In 1 sent.* 19.5.2 ad 1. These are analogy (1) according to being alone and not according to intention, (2) according to intention alone and not according to being, (3) according to both being and intention. Analogy according to being alone and not according to intention is also called analogy of inequality and analogy of genus. In St. Thomas, the example is the term "body," predicated of terrestrial and celestial bodies. A logician always defines this term in the same way, but the philosopher of nature and the metaphysician define the two kinds of bodies differently. Cajetan considers that a similar difference can be found in all generic predicates; he therefore concludes that such predication is not really analogy at all. The second analogy, according to intention and not according to being, is called analogy of attribution. In it, the perfection exists only in one analogate, the *primary* analogate, but is attributed to other things, the *secondary* analogates, which have some relation to the primary one (cause, effect, sign, exemplar, and so on).

The third kind of analogy, according to both being and intention, is the most important for metaphysics. According to Cajetan, this analogy is the analogy of proportionality, discussed by St. Thomas in *De ver.* 2.11. In this analogy there is no direct relation between the two analogates; instead, there is a relation within each of the analogates, and it is these relations that are similar and are the bases for analogical predication. In the two analogates which are unlike, there are four *relata* which are also unlike, but the two relations, or proportions, are similar (schematically: $A{:}B{::}C{:}D$). The analogon thus seems at first sight to be a similar function, or relation, but it is sometimes also called a common perfection. This analogy can be of two types: proper (intrinsic) and improper (extrinsic, metaphorical). Cajetan also asks whether there is one concept (*una ratio*) corresponding to the single analogous term. He answers with a distinction: first, there is a clear concept that perfectly represents the relation in one of the analogates and imperfectly represents the others; this concept is simply many concepts and only proportionately one concept. Secondly, there is a "confused" concept which only imperfectly represents the relation in the analogates and so is simply one concept, though it is proportionately many. The clear multiple concepts become the common concept by a special abstraction in which the particular modes are run together (con-fused); the single, common but confused concept becomes one of the clear concepts by way of fuller expression.

Cajetan considers two objections against analogy from the viewpoint of his own systematization. One is that analogy leads to agnosticism. He answers that only in the analogy of proper proportionality is the perfection intrinsic to both analogates, and yet not in such a way as to destroy the inequality of the analogates. His other objection is that the use of an analogous term in reasoning makes that reasoning formally invalid. He answers that the term, when confusedly conceived, does have a true unity and so is not used equivocally.

*John of St. Thomas, the third of the great commentators, is principally concerned with defending the doctrine of Cajetan. He does, however, differ on one point: it seems to him that individuals in the same species are univocal, for example, that many men are univocally beings.

Sylvester of Ferrara (*Ferrariensis), the fourth great commentator, takes exception to one of Cajetan's statements about the analogy of proper proportionality. Because many texts of St. Thomas assert that there is a primary analogate in every analogy, he holds that even in the analogy of proper proportionality there is a first analogate, though Cajetan had denied this.

Later Scholastics. The next major writer on analogy is Francisco *Suárez. He is not usually considered among the commentators of St. Thomas, though he does regard his theory of analogy as that of the Angelic Doctor. Suárez disagrees on many counts with Cajetan. He holds, first, that attribution is not necessarily extrinsic; in an intrinsic analogy the perfection exists perfectly and independently in one analogate, and imperfectly and dependently on the first in the secondary analogates. Secondly, he holds that proportionality is always extrinsic. He therefore holds that the relation between God and creatures cannot properly be expressed by the analogy of proportionality except in metaphorical language. Suárez considers the same objections which Cajetan had considered; these objections seem to him to require a strict unity of the objective concept which abstracts from the differences of the modes.

Later scholastic writers on analogy fall into three categories. There are followers of both Cajetan and Suárez; in addition, many Thomists and some Suarezians have adopted elements of both theories. In particular, these Thomists make use of an idea already mentioned by Cajetan: that a single pair of real beings may be related by several analogies; thus, God and a creature are analogously beings by both analogy of attribution and of proportionality. God is prior to the creature inasmuch as the analogy of attribution is made use of; both are intrinsically beings because of the analogy of proper proportionality.

Apart from Suárez and the Suarezians, most scholastics could be considered followers of Cajetan. Not until the 1920s were there signs that any Thomist began to question Cajetan's interpretation. Since then, a number of writers have tried to work out anew the actual texts of St. Thomas. Here several views have been stressed. Some authors have emphasized the so-called Platonic strains in St. Thomas, and in the light of this new point of view the doctrine of *participation has been stressed. Participation is a real, intrinsic analogy which is not proportionality because it does not involve four terms. Similarly, the analogy of proportion has reappeared in many authors, and this, too, is a direct, intrinsic analogy. Finally, several authors depart from Cajetan in another direction; they assert that analogy is an affair of language, not of conceptions nor of being, and therefore pertains to logic, not to metaphysics.

Recent Thought. The historical movement has been considered as staying within the scope of scholastic thought. Analogy for many years was of no interest to nonscholastic thinkers; rationalists, idealists, and their followers restricted scientific language to univocal terms. Kierkegaard here represents a break; he considered univocal language to belong to science whose proper field is that of objects. But persons, and especially God, cannot be known objectively; the only valid knowledge here is "subjective." In the Danish thinker himself there is no theory of predication or of knowledge which systematically considers this difference. Karl Barth, and after him, Paul Tillich, considers the possibilities of analogy in solving this problem. It seems to both that any real analogy reduces God to the category of finite things. We can speak about God only through symbols.

The notions of symbol and of myth have been exploited by many writers who feel, on the one hand, that abstractive organized knowledge is not the only kind of knowledge man has, and on the other, that any direct, purely intellectual knowledge is necessarily abstractive. Knowledge through symbol and myth is direct, profound, and vitally moving, but it is not a grasp of the intrinsic reality of the thing known. Thomistic criticism of this theory generally centers on the issue of intrinsic vs. extrinsic knowledge. A being that is known only through symbol, myth, or metaphor is not known in itself; hence we can never make any statement about that being in itself, but only statements about ourselves and objects of direct experience. While this is not sufficient for religious language, it must be recognized as playing some partial role.

Something similar to analogy has been reached by an altogether different road. The movement called *positivism considered that only scientific language was worthy of analysis, and so all non-univocal terms that deserved consideration had to be reducible to univocal ones. Moreover, univocal terms were restricted to things of immediate experience or to logical and mathematical terms. In the last decade or so, *linguistic analysis began to consider common language rather than scientific language. In common language, there are of course many univocal terms; but a great number of terms are found to have many meanings, and in some of their usages no single meaning can be pinned down. This usage has been called systematic ambiguity. Several Thomistic writers have seen in the theory of systematic ambiguity a contemporary approach to the same problem that St. Thomas and his followers handled through the notion of analogy. A few think that the modern approach is better than the traditional one. For, they point out, traditional discussions of analogy, at least since Cajetan, have been metaphysical. They think, however, that this is a mistake; analogy is and remains a matter of terms. Properly, therefore, analogy is to be treated by logic. There has been as yet no general and sharply focused Thomistic critique of this theory, but it would seem to raise serious difficulties with the traditional notion of logic as a science of second intentions, as well as to question the possibility of sciences other than logic, such as theology, to attain valid knowledge of the real. In the last analysis, ambiguous terms may serve to confuse or to persuade, perhaps even to suggest; but they would seem to have no place in anything like a science whose object is to know. Only if analogy reaches into our knowledge and even into the objects of our knowledge can analogical predication be admitted as scientific.

Doctrine of St. Thomas on Analogy

For St. Thomas analogy is a kind of predication midway between univocation and equivocation. Since analogy is the use of a term to designate a perfection found in a similar way in two or more subjects in which it is found partly the same and partly different, the first step is to clarify what is meant by the words "partly the same, partly different." (ST 1a, 13.5; *In 4 meta.* 1.534–539; *In 1 eth.* 7.95–96.) In univocal predication, predicates have an absolute meaning and can be accurately and distinctly defined in themselves. But strictly analogous predicates cannot be so defined; their meaning is proportional to the subjects of which they are predicated. The reason for this difference is that univocal terms arise by abstraction from the particular subjects in which the perfection is present, so that the difference in the subjects does not enter into their meaning. Analogous terms do not arise by abstraction but rather by "separation," or negation (*In Boeth. de Trin.* 5.3–4), and so retain a relation to a concrete subject. A consequence of this is that there is no single clear meaning for an analogous predicate (ST 1a, 13.5 ad 1). Nevertheless, analogous terms can be validly used in argumentation on condition that they are not mistaken for univocal concepts of essences. Even if we cannot judge the conclusion of a univocal argumentation without considering the premises from which it was derived, we can use that conclusion without keeping the original premises in mind as a premise for further argumentation. But in an argument using an analogous term, the conclusion cannot be abstracted from its premises, because the secondary analogate arrived at by the argument must include the primary in its definition (ST 1a, 13.6). That is why our statements concerning the existence and nature of God are limited in scope (ST 1a, 2.2 ad 3; 3.4 ad 2) and why St. Thomas made no concessions to rationalism, whether heterodox or Christian in intent, Averroistic or Anselmian.

The kind of abstraction called separation arrives at terms which in all their major uses are analogous and which can therefore be considered primarily analogous terms. In addition, some terms are first univocal but become analogous in other applications; these are secondarily analogous terms. Thus, some qualities of sensible things can be simply abstracted and are therefore univocal; but they can also be used to signify something that is primarily analogous. "Life," for instance, is a primarily univocal term. But in a second use, it can signify the kind of being that lives, and thus we use the term analogously when we speak of intellectual life.

Kinds of Analogy. Analogical predication therefore involves a relation to, and between, the analogates themselves. The most fundamental division of analogy is into intrinsic, or proper, and extrinsic, or improper (*De prin. nat.* 6; *In 1 sent.* 19.5.2 ad 1; *De ver.* 21.4 ad 2). An analogy is intrinsic when the perfection which is predicated is really found in both of the analogates; it is extrinsic when it is really found in only one but imposed by the mind on others. Thus the term "living" is analogously applied to angels and animals by an intrinsic analogy, for both live but in an irreducibly different way. But when it is applied to the language of Shakespeare, it is applied by an extrinsic analogy; for life is only attributed, it is not found there in reality (cf. ST 1a, 18.1).

Various Relationships. The second way of dividing analogy is based on the relation between the analogates themselves (*De pot.* 7.7; ST 1a, 13.5; *De ver.* 2.11; *In 5 eth.* 5.939–945). This relation can be directly between the two analogates, a "one-to-one," two-term analogy, as substance and accident are related to each other. Again, it can be a relation, not between the analogates themselves but between the analogates and some third object, as two accidents of a thing may be unrelated to each other but both be related to the same substance; this is a "many-to-one," three-term analogy. Finally, there may be no direct relationships of the analogates at all, but each of them may contain a relation that is similar to the relation in the other, a "many-to-many," four-term analogy, also called "proportionality." For example, when one understands something immediately, he says that he *sees* it. What he means is that as vision is to the power of sight, so direct understanding is to the intellect, not that the intellect is similar to the eye or vision to understanding.

Two-, Three-, and Four-Term Analogies. In two- and three-term analogies there is necessarily an inequality between the terms, so that the terms can always be compared to each other as greater and lesser (*De prin. nat.* 6; *De subs. sep.* 8). Consequently one of the analogates will be "prior" to the other or others in time, in understanding, in perfection, in causality (*In 3 meta.* 8.437–438; *In 4 meta.* 1.534–539; *In 5 meta.* 1.749). Moreover, when there is a direct order between the terms, one of them will be defined by the other; that is, all the posterior analogates will be defined through the first. But since definition is relative to knowledge (*In 5 meta.* 5.824), the first analogate will be the one which is first in our knowledge, not necessarily the first in reality. Thus we define accidents through their dependence on substance, for we know substance as prior; but we "define" God through the creatures' dependence on Him, for creatures are first in our knowledge and we know God only through them (ST 1a, 13.6).

In four-term analogies, on the other hand, there is no direct relationship between the analogates; hence, priority of one over the other is not necessary, and one is not defined through the other (*De ver.* 2.11).

Mutual Determination and Eminence. Two- and three-term analogies can be further divided according to the kind of relation that is in question. Two-term analogies are sometimes definite proportions which are mutually determining (*In 1 sent.* prol., 1.2 ad 2; *In Boeth. de Trin.* 1.2 ad 3; *De ver.* 2.11). For example, knowledge can be possessed habitually or actually exercised. In the former case, "knowing" is predicated as in potency (and potency is always proportioned to the act of which it is the potency); in the latter, as in act (in creatures, an act is always the act of some potency). So, too, analogous causes are often strictly proportioned to their effects (*In 4 meta.* 1.534–538).

A direct relationship, however, need not be understood as a definite, interdetermining proportion. Indeed, the term "proportion" itself is often used by St. Thomas to indicate an indefinitely greater perfection in the prior analogate (*In 3 sent.* 1.1.1 ad 3; ST 1a, 12.1 ad 4). In such cases, the prior analogate possesses a perfection eminently, in a higher degree, more perfectly; whereas the others possess it deficiently, in a lesser degree, less perfectly (*C. gent.* 2.98; *De pot.* 7.5; *De ver.* 4.6; *In 1 sent.* 8.1.2; ST 1a, 13.2, 104.1; *Comp. theol.* 2.8). This language must not be allowed to mislead us. The expression "degree of difference" may refer to a difference that is directly quantitative or at least based on a directly quantitative one; and then there is no analogy, but univocation, for the perfection in question is reducible to a single one (ST 1a, 42.1 ad 1). But at other times we speak of degrees of difference when the differences are greater than merely specific ones and cannot be reduced to univocal genera and differences (*De pot.* 7.7 ad 3). Similarly, we sometimes use the terms "perfect" and "imperfect" to refer to stages of one and the same perfection, as when we say that a baby has only an imperfect control of his limbs, whereas the grown man has perfect control; this also is univocation. On the other hand, we might say that animals have an imperfect spontaneity because they are not merely passive to outside influences; whereas the spontaneity of a man is perfect, in the sense that his spontaneity is truly a freedom, not only from external violence, but also from other predeterminations (cf. ST 1a, 4.1, 2; *Comp. theol.* 1.101; *De ver.* 8.1).

Participation. One kind of analogy of eminence has additional characteristics. For the prior analogate can be more eminent because it is the analogous perfection by its essence, whereas the imperfect analogates are such because they possess that perfection as distinct from themselves, as received, and so as limited by their own proper nature. The primary analogate, then, is identically its perfection and so is unlimited in its order; if we are talking about being and the properties of being, the being by essence is simply infinite. The secondary analogates, which have the perfections as received and limited, are being, good, and so on, by participation (*De pot.* 3.5, 7.7 ad 2; *C. gent.* 2.15, 53; 3.66, 97; ST 1a, 3.8, 44.1, 47.1, 75.5 ad 1 and 4; 79.4; *In Ioann.* prol.; *Quodl.* 2.2.1). In other perfections, too, a similar relation can be found. Thus, the acts of reason itself are reasonable by their essence, whereas the desires of a virtuous man are reasonable—truly enough and intrinsically—only by participation, inasmuch as through obedience to reason they possess some order, structure, and so forth, that is derived from reason (*De virt. in comm.* 12 ad 16).

Three-term analogies are sometimes a set of two-term analogies with a common primary analogate which is numerically one and the same, as medicine, health, food, and complexion are each called "healthy" by their various relations to the health of the animal (*C. gent.* 1.34). Such a form of analogy is not really distinctive, since it can be simply reduced to the two-term analogies which make it up. At other times, however, the common term is not itself one of the analogates that are immediately understood but is entirely outside the predication or is a whole made up of all the analogates (*In 1 sent.* prol. 1.2 ad 2, 35.1.4; *De nat. gen.* 1). In the latter case, evidently, the parts cannot be equal or quantitative parts; otherwise there would simply be univocation.

Chief Applications of Analogy. For St. Thomas, analogy is not simply a formal structure of predication to be treated in logic. When analogy is "applied" to a particular case, the content, or matter, of what is said must be taken into account. For this reason, analogy is properly treated in metaphysics.

Being. The analogon most often and most fully discussed by St. Thomas is *being. But there is no single analogy of being; rather, the various beings have different relations to each other. Following the lead of Aristotle, St. Thomas finds in each being a set of internal components. Of these, the most thoroughly discussed principles are substance and accident. Substance is being in the primary sense, and the act of being (*esse,* existence) properly pertains to it. Accident is proportioned to substance, and its being consists in its actual inherence in substance (*In 4 meta.* 1.534–539; *In 7 meta.* 4.1334–38; *De ver.* 2.11; *In 1 eth.* 7.95–96). Thus, substance and accident stand in a one-to-one, two-term analogy, the analogy of proportion. However, we can also consider that accidents are not beings by themselves but rather by their relation or reference to substance, and that the being attributed to them is the being of substance; we would then call this an analogy of reference or attribution (*De prin. nat.* 6; *In 4 meta.* 1.543; *In 11 meta.* 3.2197). The various internal principles of being and substance are similar pairs of proportioned analogates and so can all be understood as act and potency; the act-potency correlation is itself the proportional relationship (*In 5 meta.* 9.897; *In 9 meta.* 7-10.1844–94). The act-potency correlation itself is first discovered in motion; it is again found in substance (potency) and accident (act), in matter (potency) and form (act), faculty (potency) and operation (act), and essence (potency) and the act of being, *esse* (act).

Causality. Beings are also related to each other as cause and effect. Though many causes are univocal, having the same perfection as their effects, these are only the proximate causes of beings. More ultimate causes are not specifically the same as their effects; nevertheless, they can be denominated extrinsically from these effects by causal reference (ST 1a, 6.4, 16.6). In addition, these equivocal causes must be in some sense "more perfect" than their effects (ST 1a, 4.2). This is the analogy of eminence—but merely by knowing this we are unable to determine whether the perfection of the effect is intrinsically in the equivocal cause, or whether the equivocal cause is more perfect inasmuch as its perfection is simply different. After the existence of God is known and His nature as pure act is apprehended, then His causal eminence in regard to His creatures is seen to consist in this, that He is being, goodness, and other similar perfections by His essence and therefore infinitely; whereas creatures both are and are *what* they are by participation (ST 1a, 14.6, 25.2 ad 2, 45.5, 57.2, 79.4, 93.2 ad 1 and 4; *In Dion. de div. nom.* 1.3, 2.4). Inasmuch as the being-by-essence is simple and self-identical, the analogy of participation in being is necessarily an intrinsic analogy. Hence, whatever is predicated of God according to this analogy is truly a knowledge of God, even though it remains a knowledge of Him through His creatures. Because God is the cause of the world through intellect and will (ST 1a, 44.3), He is the exemplar of all things; and created things are related to Him as images (ST 1a, 3.3 ad 2, 35.1 ad 1, 93.1; *In 1 Cor.* 11.1), as representations (ST 1a, 45.7), and as similar to Him (*De pot.* 7.7 ad 4 *in contrarium;* ST 1a, 4.3 ad 4). At the same time, created beings as individuals are seen to be related to each other as diverse participants in the One Being that is being by essence.

Good. The good that is convertible with being is predicated according to the analogy of participation, as is being (ST 1a, 6.1, 2); this transcendental good is, however, only a qualified good and as such, a secondary analogate (in an analogy of proportion) to the unqualified good, which is the "proper" good (ST 1a, 5.1 ad 1). The proper good is itself divided into the moral good, the pleasurable, and the useful (ST 1a, 5.6 ad 3). Whereas the good is in things, truth is primarily in the intellect and only secondarily in things (ST 1a, 16.1). As it is in things, it is analogous according to their intrinsic perfection (ST 1a, 16.3); as it is in the mind, it is dependently and imperfectly in created minds, absolutely and perfectly in the divine mind (ST 1a, 16.5). Perfections such as life and wisdom (ST 1a, 18.3, 14.1, 9.1 ad 2, 13.9 ad 3, 41.3 ad 4) are also predicated by essence and by participation.

God. The transcendentals, and those perfections which are called pure perfections (which do not necessarily include a mode of participation, ST 1a, 13.3 ad 1), are the concern of both natural theology and revealed theology. Negative statements about God are no problem. But affirmative statements can also be made about God (ST 1a, 13.12), both on the basis of the perfections of creatures and on the basis of revelation. A theory of analogy is the only way in which we can be sure of the *meaning* (not the truth) of these statements. St. Thomas's fullest explanation is given in regard to the predicate "living" (ST 1a, 18.3). Living can mean (1) a kind of substance capable of certain activities, (2) the activities themselves, (3) the way of existing proportioned to such a nature and such activities. The first two senses are univocal; only the third is analogous. In the richest sense the phrase "God is living" means: being the cause of life as we know it and having the perfection of life intrinsically, not as a limiting essence, but as identical with an unlimited existence and as expressing what we conceive as a mode of being. Surely we can form no simple concept of this or any other perfection that is drawn into the analogy of being (ST 1a, 13.1), yet we can understand what we mean by saying "God is living," and "God is life"; we can also show why we make such a statement.

On the other hand, *what* we can say significantly about God is often metaphorical. St. Thomas shows us how we can determine the abstract philosophically analyzed meaning of metaphorical statements (ST 1a, 4.2), and his commentaries on Sacred Scripture provide many instances of such analysis. But he does not engage in an investigation of the psychological, or subjective, meaning of these metaphors. For such analysis, fruitful recourse can be had to phenomenological and existentialist, as well as to psychological and literary, studies of metaphor and symbol. Many modern writers on Sacred Scripture are successfully doing this.

See also ANALOGY, THEOLOGICAL USE OF; BEING; ACT; SUBSTANCE; ACCIDENT; GOOD; PARTICIPATION; CAUSALITY; TRANSCENDENTALS; GOD.

Bibliography: History. J. F. ANDERSON, *The Bond of Being* (St. Louis 1949). H. LYTTKENS, *The Analogy between God and the World* (Uppsala 1952). J. OWENS, *The Doctrine of Being in the Aristotelian Metaphysics* (Toronto 1951) 58–60. Doctrine. CAJETAN, *The Analogy of Names and the Concept of Being,* tr. E. BUSHINSKI and H. KOREN (Pittsburgh 1953). T. M. FLANAGAN, "The Use of Analogy in the Summa Contra Gentiles," ModSchoolm 35 (1957) 21–37. JOHN OF ST. THOMAS, *The Material Logic,* tr. Y. R. SIMON et al. (Chicago 1955) 152–208. G. P. KLUBERTANZ, *St. Thomas Aquinas on Analogy* (Chicago 1960). E. L. MASCALL, *Existence and Analogy* (New York 1949). R. MASIELLO, "The Analogy of Proportion in the Metaphysics of St. Thomas," ModSchoolm 35 (1958) 91–105. A. MAURER, "St. Thomas and the Analogy of Genus," NewSchol 29 (1955) 127–144. R. MCINERNY, *The Logic of Analogy* (The Hague 1961). M. T.-L. PENIDO, *Le Rôle de l'analogie en théologie dogmatique* (Bibliothèque Thomiste 15; Paris 1931). G. PHELAN, *St. Thomas and Analogy* (Milwaukee 1941). J. M. RAMIREZ, "De analogia secundum doctrinam aristotelico-thomisticam," *La Ciencia Tomista* 24 (1921) 20–40, 195–214, 337–357; 25 (1922) 17–38.

[G. P. KLUBERTANZ]

ANALOGY, THEOLOGICAL USE OF

Analogy is a word that stands for many different meanings. The most important are: (1) a form of reasoning, i.e., reasoning by analogy, also called argument from *convenience; (2) a mode of explanation (the parable); and (3) a mode of predication, i.e., analogous predication. The present article is concerned with analogy as a form of predication and with the use of analogy in *theology.

Aristotle. Called by some scholars the father of analogy [see A. Goergen, *Kardinal Cajetans Lehre von der Analogie* (Speyer 1938) 86], Aristotle was the first to deal systematically with analogy as a form of predication. In the *Organon* (106a–108b) he divides the predicates, according to their modes of signification, into three classes. To the first class belong the terms that are predicated of many subjects according to the same meaning, to the second the terms that are predicated of many subjects according to meanings that are entirely different, and to the third the terms that are predicated of many subjects according to a meaning that is partly the same and partly different. Aristotle calls the terms of the first class univocal and the terms of the second class equivocal. Then one would expect him to call analogous the terms of the third class. But this use of the term analogy does not go back to Aristotle, who defines this class of words as terms that do not differ by way of equivocalness. It is only later, in the Middle Ages, that the word analogy is used for this form of predication.

Aristotle did not content himself with elaborating a perfect logical theory of analogy: in his metaphysical and ethical works he applies this theory to metaphysical and ethical language, and says that terms such as being, substance, cause, good, etc., are predicated neither univocally, nor equivocally, but according to a certain analogy (κατ' ἀναλογίαν). However, he did not go so far as to elaborate a systematic theory of theological language. But from what he said about metaphysical language (of which theological language is the most conspicuous part) and about God's transcendence it is necessary to draw the conclusion that the words used when one talks about God have, according to Aristotle, an analogous meaning.

Aquinas. The Angelic Doctor distinguishes three kinds of predicative analogy. There is (1) attributive analogy, e.g., when "healthy" is predicated of Peter, medicine, food, climate, color, etc. In attributive analogy a quality is predicated properly and intrinsically of the first analogate, and it is predicated of the other analogates because of the relation that they have to the first analogate. There is also (2) metaphorical analogy, e.g., when "to smile" is predicated of Peter and of the meadow. In metaphorical analogy a quality is predicated properly only of the first analogate; of the others it is predicated only because of some similarity between their situations and the situation of the first analogate. There is, finally (3), proportional analogy, e.g., when "substance," "nature," "being," "cause" are predicated of man, animals, trees, stones, etc. In proportional analogy a perfection is predicated properly and intrinsically of each analogate.

According to Aquinas all three kinds of analogy may be used in theology. Attributive and metaphorical analogies help one to talk about God's dynamic perfections. Proportional (and also attributive) analogy enables one to talk about God's entitative perfections, i.e., about God's nature as it is in itself (see *C. gent.* 1.30–34; ST 1a, 13).

Bonaventure and Scotus. The other great scholastics, also, especially Bonaventure and Scotus, have made careful studies of analogy, the former more from an ontological, the latter more from a logical standpoint.

According to Bonaventure every creature bears some analogy to God because every creature is an imitation of God inasmuch as it is caused by God and is conformed to Him through the divine idea. Bonaventure distinguishes between two main levels of likeness: the vestige and the image. The vestige is the likeness that irrational creatures bear to God. The image is the likeness of rational creatures to God.

Duns Scotus, in his study of theological language, recognized that it is essentially analogical, but he insisted that analogy presupposes univocity since one could not compare creatures with God unless he had a common concept of both. God is knowable by man in this life only by means of concepts drawn from creatures, and unless these concepts were common to God and creatures one would never be able to compare the imperfect creatures to the perfect God: there would be no bridge between creatures and God.

After the Middle Ages analogy tends to disappear from philosophy but continues to be used by both Catholics and Protestants in theology. The main effort of Catholic theologians is to interpret and systematize Aquinas's teaching, whereas the aim of Protestant theologians is to elaborate a theory of theological language consistent with their views of the relationship between God and man, nature and grace.

Cajetan, Suárez, and the Modern Thomists. The official interpretation of Aquinas's teaching has been for centuries that of Thomas de Vio, better known as Cardinal Cajetan (d. 1534), who in his famous little book *De nominum analogia* "solved the more metaphysical difficulties concerning analogy so thoroughly and subtly that no room is left to find out anything further" [John of St. Thomas, *Cursus philosophicus thomisticus* (Marietti ed. 1:481)]. Cajetan's interpretation (an interpretation based on an isolated text of St. Thomas—*In 1 sent.* 19.5.2 ad 1) starts out with a threefold division of analogy: attributive, metaphorical, and proportional. He then goes on to show that attributive and metaphorical analogies can be of little use in metaphysics (and in theology): the first because it is always extrinsic, the second because it is always improper. Therefore the only analogy capable of saving metaphysics (and theology) is analogy of proportionality, since it is the only analogy apt to express the true being of something.

Although this interpretation of Aquinas's doctrine of analogy became for centuries the official interpretation, there was from the very beginning a powerful dissenting voice, the voice of Suárez, who was not willing to grant to Cajetan either that attribution is only extrinsic or that proportionality is the safeguard of metaphysics and theology. In his *Disputationes metaphysicae* (Vivès ed. 26:13–21) Suárez attempts to prove that Cajetan misinterprets Aquinas's doctrine of analogy on two main points. The first misinterpretation, according to Suárez, is of his doctrine on analogy of proportionality, since this analogy includes an element of metaphor and of impropriety, just as "smiling" is said of a meadow through metaphorical reference. Therefore Cajetan would be wrong in giving such prominence to the analogy of proportionality. And he is wrong, claims Suárez, also on another point: his identification of Aquinas's analogy of attribution with analogy of extrinsic attribution. Now, shows Suárez, analogy of attribution can be intrinsic and extrinsic, and Aquinas teaches both of them. Besides analogy of extrinsic attribution (i.e., the analogy where the denominating form exists only in the primary analogate), Aquinas teaches also analogy of intrinsic attribution, i.e., the analogy where the denominating form exists in all the terms, in one absolutely and in the others relatively, through a relation of efficient and exemplary causality of the latter to the former. The analogy between God and creatures is of this type. Therefore, to leave it out, as Cajetan did, is a fatal blow for theology.

For centuries Suárez's view was an isolated one. But in recent years many students of St. Thomas have joined him in his criticism of Cajetan's version of analogy. The reaction was led by É. Gilson's important essay, "Cajétan et l'existence" [*Tijdschrift voor Phil.* 15 (1953) 267–286], in which he attacked Cajetan's Aristotelian and essentialist interpretation of Aquinas, as well as the "minor" problem of Cajetan's version of analogy. This interpretation of the philosophy of St. Thomas, says Gilson, has been "the main obstacle to the diffusion of Thomism." By explaining Aquinas in the light of, and according to, Aristotle, Cajetan misses the great novelty of his philosophy, the discovery of being (*esse*). To Cajetan the supreme perfection continues to be essence, not existence. He is an essentialist, not an existentialist.

Encouraged by Gilson's authority, more and more Thomists have denounced Cajetan's version of analogy and have propounded some new interpretation of Aquinas's teaching. The interpretation that is now receiving almost universal consent (it is supported by É. Gilson, C. Fabro, J. Nicolas, B. Montagnes, A. Hayen, and many other scholars, as well as the present writer) can be summarized as follows. Aquinas teaches both analogy of intrinsic attribution and proper proportionality. At the beginning of his theological career he seems to emphasize proportionality more than attribution, but toward the end of his life his preference is for attribution, although he never rejects proportionality. He prefers attribution, because proportionality is inadequate to express at the same time God's transcendence and immanence. Proportionality is certainly able to express God's transcendence, but fails to express His immanence adequately, since it cannot express the dependence of the finite on divine causality. In analogy of proper proportionality there are no primary and secondary analogates. All analogates are primary. For this reason Aquinas came to the conclusion that analogy of proper proportionality cannot give an adequate interpretation of the God–creature relationship, and dropped it in theology but kept it in metaphysics.

Aquinas believes that an adequate interpretation of the God–creature relationship can be provided by analogy of intrinsic attribution. Analogy of intrinsic attribution is able to signify both that there is a likeness between primary and secondary analogates, and that the secondary analogates are imperfect imitations of the primary. Intrinsic attribution is able to stress the likeness between analogates as much as their difference. It says that the analogous perfection is predicated of the primary analogate essentially and of the secondary analogate by participation.

Analogy in Protestant Theology. Up to 1965 no systematic historical study of the doctrine of analogy in Protestant theology has been made [although there is an outline drawn up by the author of the present article in *The Principle of Analogy in Protestant and Catholic Theology* (The Hague 1963)]. However, it is probable that a good history of analogy in Protestant theology could be written by distinguishing three periods: (1) the period of the reformers and orthodoxy, during which Protestant theologians were still attached to Catholic tradition and considered analogy as the only proper way of talking about God; (2) the period of Hegelian and Kierkegaardian theology, during which analogy was replaced by dialectic; and (3) the period of the great modern theologians, K. Barth, P. Tillich, and R. Bultmann, during which a remarkable revival of analogy has taken place. These theologians recognize that analogy is the only proper way of talking about God, but do not agree about its nature: Tillich conceives it as symbolic, Barth as an analogy of faith (*analogia fidei*), and Bultmann as an existential analogy.

Both classical and modern Protestant theologians have tried to elaborate a theory of analogy coherent with their doctrine of the relationship between nature and grace, which are conceived as opposites that can never be reconciled. Sin has caused in human nature a corruption that cannot be healed; it has raised between God and man an infinite qualitative difference that will last forever. This principle of the infinite qualitative difference is reflected in the Protestant theories of theological language: in the theory of analogy of extrinsic attribution of classical theology, in the Hegelian theory of dialectic, in Tillich's theory of symbolic analogy, in Barth's theory of analogy of faith, and in Bultmann's theory of existential analogy. While in the Catholic theory of analogy it is legitimate to use human concepts and human language when one talks about God because of a permanent analogy existing between God's being and man's being, according to the Protestant theories of analogy any such use is condemned, because after the Fall there is no longer an analogy of being between God and man. Therefore men's words are such that they can never, of themselves, be properly predicated of God. They can express divine reality either by a purely extrinsic attribution, or dialectically, or symbolically, or mythically, or by a divine choice.

What should one say of these Protestant theories of theological language? Are they satisfactory? Are they such as to give one some knowledge of God? Catholic and Protestant theologians generally agree that the very possibility of any knowledge of God, both natural and revealed, rests on analogy: in the natural knowledge it is man who takes some concepts from nature and applies them to God; whereas in the supernatural knowledge it is God Himself who chooses some of the concepts used by man in order to tell him something about Himself. The first kind of analogy is called *analogia entis,* the second, *analogia fidei.* According to the Catholic doctrine on the relationship between *grace and nature, there is no conflict, but harmony, between the two analogies: grace does not destroy analogy, but, by raising it into analogy of faith, fulfills it. On the contrary, according to the Protestant doctrine on the relationships between nature and grace, there can be no harmony between the two analogies but only conflict: analogy of being cannot be redeemed and therefore it cannot be raised into analogy of faith. Between analogy of being and analogy of faith there is a permanent "ontological" conflict.

From the Catholic point of view such a conflict is inadmissible: "to separate the supernatural from the natural knowledge of God in this radical way is to render the former unintelligible and impossible, since revelation, and this is clear, does not change our natural mode of knowing, but utilizes the natural instruments of our knowledge, our acquired concepts, and our mental constructions" [J. H. Nicolas, "Affirmation de Dieu et connaissance," RevThom 64 (1964) 201].

See also ANALOGY; ANALOGY OF FAITH; ANTHROPOMORPHISM (IN THEOLOGY); DIALECTIC IN THEOLOGY; DOGMATIC THEOLOGY; METHODOLOGY (THEOLOGY); REASONING, THEOLOGICAL; THEOLOGICAL CONCLUSION; THEOLOGICAL TERMINOLOGY; THEOLOGY, HISTORY OF; THEOLOGY, INFLUENCE OF GREEK PHILOSOPHY ON; THEOLOGY, ARTICLES ON.

Bibliography: The use of analogy in theology. G. P. KLUBERTANZ, *St. Thomas Aquinas on Analogy* (Chicago 1960), full bibliog. A. CHOLLET, DTC 1.1:1142–54. Y. M. J. CONGAR, *ibid.* 15.1:382–386, 389–390, 452–453. E. CORETH and E. PRZYWARA, LexThK² 1:468–473. E. PRZYWARA, *ibid.* 473–476. K. BARTH, *Anselm: Fides quaerens intellectum,* tr. I. W. ROBERTSON (London 1960); *Nein! Antwort an Emil Brunner* (Munich 1934); *Church Dogmatics* (New York 1955–). J. BITTREMIEUX, *De analogica nostra Dei cognitione* (Louvain 1913). Y. M. J. CONGAR, *La Foi et la théologie* (Tournai 1962). M. T. L. PENIDO, *Le Rôle de l'analogie en théologie dogmatique* (Bibl Thom 15; Paris 1931). I. T. RAMSEY, *Religious Language* (New York 1963). G. SÖHNGEN, *Analogie und Metapher: Kleine Philosophie und Theologie der Sprache* (Freiburg 1962). V. BRUSOTTI, "L'analogia di attribuzione e la conoscenza della natura di Dio," RivFilNeosc 27 (1935) 31–66. K. FECKES, "Die Analogie in unserem Gotteskennen," in *Probleme der Gotteserkenntnis,* ed. A. DYROFF et al. (Münster 1928). L. LE ROHELLEC, "Cognitio nostra analogica de Deo," DivThomP 30 (1927) 298–319. G. M. MANSER, "Die analoge Erkenntnis Gottes," DivThomF 6 (1928) 385–403. J. F. ROSS, "Analogy as a Rule of Meaning for Religious Language," *International Philosophical Quarterly* 1 (1961) 468–502. A. D. SERTILLANGES, "Agnosticisme ou anthropomorphisme," *Revue de philosophie* 8 (1906) 129–165.

Aquinas's theory of analogy. J. F. ANDERSON, *The Bond of Being* (St. Louis 1949). B. M. BELLERATE, *L'analogia Tomista nei grandi commentatori di S. Tommaso* (Rome 1960). C. FABRO, *Partecipazione e causalità secondo S. Tommaso d'Aquino* (Turin 1960). J. FEHR, *Das Offenbarungsproblem in dialektischer und thomistischer Theologie* (Fribourg 1939). J. HABBEL, *Die Analogie zwischen Gott und Welt nach Thomas von Aquin* (Berlin 1928). H. LYTTKENS, *The Analogy between God and the World* (Uppsala 1952). R. M. MCINERNY, *The Logic of Analogy* (The Hague 1961). B. MONTAGNES, *La Doctrine de l'analogie de l'être d'après saint Thomas d'Aquin* (Louvain 1963). G. PHELAN, *St. Thomas and Analogy* (Milwaukee 1941). O. A. VARANGOT, *Analogia de atribución intrínseca y analogia del ente segun Santo Tomas* (Buenos Aires 1957). F. A. BLANCHE, "La Notion d'analogie dans la philosophie de S. Thomas d'Aquin," RevSc PhilTh 10 (1921) 170–193. B. LANDRY, "L'Analogie de proportion chez S. Thomas d'Aquin," RevNéoscPhil 24 (1922) 257–280. A. MARC, "L'Idée thomiste de l'être et les analogies d'attribution et de proportionnalité," *ibid.* 35 (1933) 157–189. E. WINANCE, "L'Essence divine et la connaissance humaine dans le Commentaire sur les Sentences de S. Thomas," RevPhilLouv 55 (1957) 171–215. H. A. WOLFSON, "St. Thomas on Divine Attributes," in *Mélanges offerts à Étienne Gilson de l'Academie française* (Toronto 1959) 673–700.

[B. MONDIN]

ANALOGY OF FAITH

Originally a mathematical term, the Greek word for *analogy means "proportion" and was borrowed by philosophers to refer to the relationship between concepts of things that are partly the same and partly different. It took on special importance in the concept of analogy of being (*analogia entis*). The analogy of faith (*analogia fidei*) must not be confused with this more philosophic concept. The phrase analogy of faith is Biblical: Rom 12.6 speaks of the *charism of prophecy, along with such similar gifts as ministering, teaching, exhorting. Prophets exercised one of several "offices" within the primitive church (Acts 11.27; 13.1); guided by the Spirit, they gained insight into the faith or recognized tasks to be undertaken. The Pauline injunction is given that this gift of prophecy must be exercised "according to the proportion [ἀναλογίαν] of faith." No prophet is to be accepted who proclaims anything opposed to the "one faith" proper to the "one body in Christ." Such preaching would be out of proportion to, or beyond, the objective truth entrusted to the Christian community.

The analogy of faith, therefore, has always been associated with the one unchanging faith of the Church; it is closely related to the notion of *tradition and soon became a norm for the early Christian writers. They saw a "proportion" in the manner in which the New Testament complements the Old Testament, and in which each particular truth contributes to the inner unity of the entire Christian revelation. Thus the phrase came to indicate a rule or guide for the exegesis of Scripture. *See* BIBLE, VI (EXEGESIS). In difficult texts, the teachings of tradition and the analogy of faith must lead the way. The Catholic exegete, conscious of his faith, recognizes the intimate relationship between Scripture and tradition; he strives to explain Scriptural passages in such a way that the sacred writers will not be set in opposition to one another or to the faith and teaching of the Church (cf. Leo XIII, Denz 3283; Pius X, Denz 3546; Pius XII, Denz 3887).

Karl Barth's violent rejection of the *analogia entis* "as the invention of Antichrist" and his insistence that in questions of revelation only the *analogia fidei* is acceptable occasioned further study of this problem. In its reaction against the extremes of liberal Protestantism, *dialectical theology (or crisis theology) built upon *Kierkegaard's notion of God as "completely other" than man, and as totally transcendent. *Analogia fidei* means for Barth that we possess a "theological language" in which God and not man gives meaning to the words. His great fear is that philosophy (represented by *analogia entis*) will sit in judgment on the Word of God.

Söhngen points out that Barth misunderstands the Catholic notion of *analogia entis,* and that it does not make philosophy master over faith [*Catholica,* 3 (1934) 113–136, 176–208; 4 (1935) 38–42]. Though not convinced, Barth admits the pertinence of Söhngen's remarks. Barth's fear of rationalistic "proofs" for the mysteries of faith may indicate here an identification of the Catholic doctrine with the admittedly too rationalistic theories of *faith of the post-Cartesian era; a clearer grasp of the Thomist-Suarezian approaches might remove this fear. Barth seems to be more concerned here with certitude, so that he looks upon the *analogia entis* as something on the level of knowledge rather than being —noetic rather than ontic. The Catholic will not hesitate to admit that it is God who gives His meaning to the human words used to express the divine; an *analogia fidei* in this sense is essential. The Christian vocabulary has only gradually been formed throughout the life of the divinely guided Church. To reject the *analogia entis* entirely, however, cuts man off so radically from God that, as Emil Brunner points out, the end result can be nothing but the most advanced form of Nominalism, in which human words take on divine meanings that are purely arbitrary and are in no way reflected in a reality already existing in the midst of creatures.

See also BARTHIANISM.

Bibliography: K. BARTH, *Church Dogmatics,* tr. G. T. THOMSON (New York 1955–). H. U. VON BALTHASAR, *Karl Barth: Darstellung und Deutung seiner Theologie* (2d ed. Cologne 1962). H. BOUILLARD, *Karl Barth,* 3 v. (Paris 1957) 2:190–217. J. L. MURPHY, *With the Eyes of Faith* (Milwaukee 1965). B. NEUNHEUSER, "La teologia protestante in Germania," in *Problemi e orientamenti di teologia dommatica,* 2 v. (Milan 1957) v.1. E. PRZYWARA, LexThK[2] 1:473–476.

[J. L. MURPHY]

ANALYSIS AND SYNTHESIS

Transcriptions of the Greek ἀνάλυσις, from ἀνὰ and λύω, meaning resolution, and σύνθεσις, from σύν and τίθημι, meaning composition. Analysis and synthesis are methods of inquiry and processes of things. Logical statements of analysis and synthesis, therefore, reflect basic metaphysical and epistemological theories.

Greek Thought. *Epicurus, building on the atomic philosophy of *Democritus, rejected dialectic for a canonic of sensations, preconceptions, and passions. All man's notions are derived from sensations by contact, analogy, likeness, and synthesis (Diogenes Laertius, 10.31–32). *Plato distinguished two methods in dialectic: division (διαίρεσις) and bringing together (συναγωγέ); and later commentators, such as Ammonius, *Proclus, and Diogenes Laertius, enumerate three or four dialectical methods that include "analysis" but not "synthesis."

*Aristotle, who frequently contrasted the methods of Democritus and Plato, made use of both analysis (but not in the sense of dichotomous division) and of synthesis (but not in the sense of combination of atomic parts). Aristotle distinguishes between a mixture, or composition (σύνθεσις), and a compound, or combination (μίξις; *Gen. et cor.* 328a 5–17); but he also uses "synthesis" more broadly to include three kinds: compositions of elements in simple substances, compositions of simple substances in homoeomerous substances (bones, flesh, etc.), and compositions of these in more complex organic and inorganic bodies (*Part. animal.* 646a 12–24; *Topica* 151a 20–31). Thinking is true or false by a synthesis (or division) of objects of thought (*Anim.* 430a 26–b 4); synthesis and division are essential to truth and falsity, and nouns and verbs are related by synthesis and division in propositions (*Interp.* 16a 9–18). In general, a synthesis is a combination of parts in a whole, and its opposite is division rather than analysis. Analysis is resolution in two senses for Aristotle. In the *Prior Analytics* it is the resolution of all syllogisms to the perfect, or universal, syllogisms of the first figure (47a 2–5). In the *Posterior Analytics* it is the resolution of demonstrative syllogisms to true premises (78a 6–8). In the latter sense practical deliberation, like mathematical inquiry, is an analysis: what is sought is assumed and the means of achieving it are sought. What is last in the order of analysis is first in the order of genesis (*Eth. Nic.* 1112b 11–24).

Commentators. Mathematical analysis is presented by Euclid, Pappus, and Proclus as Aristotle formulated it. Analysis is the method of assuming what is sought and tracing its consequences to something admitted to be true. These thinkers added, however, that synthesis is the contrary method of assuming that which is admitted to be true and tracing its consequences. Alexander of Aphrodisias attributes this geometrical conception of analysis and synthesis to Aristotle in his commentary on the *Prior Analytics.* Synthesis is the way from principles to that which is derived from the principles, and analysis is the return from the ends to the principles. Greek commentators tended to accept this interpretation, and it was reinforced by Galen's inclusion of analysis and synthesis among the methods of medicine. Cicero, on the other hand, distinguished two methods, "invention" and "judgment"; and since the method of invention is developed in the *Topics,* the method of judgment was sought in the *Analytics.* After the translation of the *Analytics* and the *Topics* in the 12th century, the terms *resolutio* (analysis) and *compositio* (synthesis) took their places beside *inventio* and *judicium* in the interpretation of Aristotle's logic. *Thomas Aquinas distinguishes three applications of these terms: (1) nouns and verbs are related in propositions by composition and division; (2) inferences involving certainty depend on judgment and are treated in the *Analytics,* those short of certainty depend on invention, and inventions concerned with probabilities are treated in the *Topics;* and (3) inference from experienced composites to simple principles is resolution, and inference from principles or simples to conclusions or composites is composition.

Renaissance and Modern Thought. During the Renaissance, problems of method assumed a central place in the arts and sciences and in logic. *See* METHODOLOGY (PHILOSOPHY). All the varieties of classifications of methods in logic and rhetoric, mathematics and medicine, science, practice, and the arts were brought into complex opposition. Two pairs of distinctions—analysis and synthesis, and judgment and invention (or discovery)—emerged as dominant, sometimes in opposition, sometimes merging. Peter *Ramus held that there is a single method and that invention and judgment are phases of its employment. His opponents, e.g., J. Schegk (1511–87) and J. *Zabarella, differentiated analysis and synthesis, resolution and composition. Basic issues of philosophy and scientific method were involved in the oppositions. Analysis and synthesis may be conceived in terms of parts and wholes or in terms of principles and conclusions. By the first approach analysis proceeds from wholes to parts, and synthesis arranges parts in wholes; by the second approach analysis proceeds from effects to causes, and synthesis from principles to conclusions. The first constitutes a single method in which discovery is a synthesis of elements analyzed, and knowledge is conceived as empirical and a posteriori; the second distinguishes two processes, the analytic discovery of causes and principles and the synthetic derivation of conclusions; knowledge is conceived as universal and a priori. These differences emerged in formulations of scientific method when F. *Bacon sought a method of discovery in topics or tables of observations and a synthesis in the increase and organization of the sciences, while R. *Descartes sought a method of discovery in the methods of mathematical analysis and a synthesis in mathematical deduction.

Differences of method underlie the treatment of simple, clear, and distinct ideas by the philosophers of the 17th and 18th centuries. I. Kant abandoned dogmatic philosophy for the methods of critical philosophy and emphasized the need to distinguish (as many philosophers beginning with Aristotle had) between analytic and synthetic as applied to propositions or judgments and analytic and synthetic methods. He argued against D. *Hume that significant, and therefore true, judgments must be synthetic and that mathematical truths are synthetic, not analytic; he also sought to establish synthetic judgments a priori in mathematics, physics, and ethics by deriving them from principles synthetically.

Contemporary Usage. The oppositions of analytic and synthetic in contemporary philosophy apply the same distinctions to experience, nature, phenomena, and language; and the prominence of "analysis" in many 20th-century philosophies is conditioned by the same contradictory oppositions of definition. The truths of mathematics are analytic in an "analysis" related to the language of the *Principia Mathematica,* and they are derived, as the truths of any formalized science can be, from logical primitives. The analysis of language may be of formal languages or of actual languages, and it may proceed by constructing operational rules of use and of interpretation or by uncovering meanings of basic terms and of their coherences and incoherences. Phenomenological and existential analysis, on the other hand, seeks to avoid deduction and returns at each point to direct experience of phenomena without abstract separation of language, thought, and thing. Mathematics, psychology, and all the special sciences are subject to the same phenomenological analysis, but for that reason analysis does not depend on the conclusions of any of the sciences. The analysis of the phenomenologically given may adumbrate a transcendent ontological reality, or it may proceed creatively and operationally to the discovery of ontological essences emergent from existences. In both forms of analysis there is a tendency to refute or destroy the errors of past philosophers. Error is a mistaken synthesis, but there are many forms of analysis and, therefore, many errors of analysis owing to the fact that by one analysis other analyses are frequently seen to be undetected syntheses.

See also DEDUCTION; INDUCTION; ANALYTICAL PHILOSOPHY; LINGUISTIC ANALYSIS.

Bibliography: S. CARAMELLA, EncFil 1:185–190. Eisler 1:45–46, 3:201–204. S. E. DOLAN, "Resolution and Composition in Speculative and Practical Discourse," *Laval Théologique et Philosophique* 6 (1950) 9–62. L. M. RÉGIS, "Analyse et synthèse dans l'oeuvre de saint Thomas," *Studia Mediaevalia in honorem A. R. P. Martin* (Bruges 1948) 303–330.

[R. MC KEON]

ANALYTICAL PHILOSOPHY

The philosophical movement known as analytical philosophy, which conceives the main task of philosophy to be the logical analysis of meaning, is not so much a unified and coherent school of philosophy as it is a general trend discernible in contemporary English philosophy and *American philosophy. According to analytical philosophers, the function of the philosopher is not to invent speculative systems or world views in the fashion of traditional metaphysics, but rather to clarify what is already known by piecemeal logical analysis of what propositions "mean" (*see* SEMANTICS). A great many (if not all) of the traditional philosophical problems arise, so it is claimed, from logico-linguistic confusions about meaning, and when one analyzes the conditions that propositions must satisfy in order to have meaning, then these problems simply "dissolve." From this point of view, the function of philosophy is predominantly critical or therapeutic in character. Analysis enables one, it is said, to delimit the sphere of meaningful propositions without becoming involved in the metaphysical or epistemological presuppositions of traditional philosophers. This hope (more or less optimistically entertained and more or less explicitly professed) of discovering a purely "neutral" philosophical method has been a constant ideal of most analytical philosophers.

For the analyst, then, *philosophy does not attain a superior kind of knowledge of transcendental entities, such as God, the Absolute, mind, soul, or substance, that is inaccessible to natural science; rather it is a "second-order" activity. This applies also to ethics; the philosopher can by "meta-ethical" analysis clarify the conditions of meaningful ethical discourse, but he cannot help man (at least by rational means) make a specific moral option of a way of life. It is important to emphasize, however, that the various thinkers who share this view of the nature and function of philosophy do so for very different reasons and motives and with all kinds of reservations about the proper scope of analysis.

Historical Origins. Within the general movement of analytical philosophy two main streams of thought can be discerned. The first was initiated by G. E. *Moore and Bertrand *Russell in the early years of the 20th century and continued through L. *Wittgenstein to contemporary Oxford philosophers. The second stream takes its origin from the Vienna Circle of *logical positivism, and continues in the work of the logical empiricists and their allies, mainly in the U.S.

Common Sense Philosophy. Moore was led to an analytic view of philosophy mainly by way of exasperated reaction against the neo-idealism of F. H. *Bradley and others, which had been the dominant influence in English philosophy since the 1870s. Moore reacted against the inflated metaphysical speculations of these philosophers in favor of *common sense and a more modest view of the function of philosophy as the clarification of the kinds of questions man asks and of the reasons relevant to answering them. This involves continual reference to what is known by common sense and also to the usages of ordinary *language. Since the latter is most often the vehicle of common sense truths, any philosophical propositions that violate ordinary language, violate, *prima facie,* common sense itself. However, Moore did not make this reference to ordinary language into a formal criterion of meaning, as some later analysts have tended to do. Moore, in fact, does not provide a systematic theory of analysis such as Wittgenstein was to develop later; his view of analysis is largely a common sense and pragmatic one that takes seriously certain truisms of method, such as defining terms and being clear about their meaning. The living example Moore gave as a scrupulous practitioner of analysis in this sense made him quite influential in the growth of analytical philosophy.

Symbolic Logic and Analysis. Moore's views were shared in the early 1900s by Bertrand Russell, who had also reacted against neo-Hegelianism in favor of common sense and the view of philosophy that made its main task the clarification of uncritically accepted notions. But Russell was also profoundly influenced by the new symbolic logic of which, with G. *Peano, G. *Frege and A. N. *Whitehead, he was one of the principal founders (*see* LOGIC, SYMBOLIC). Symbolic or mathematical logic has in fact had far-reaching influence upon the development of philosophical analysis. First, the example of the logicians' formal calculi suggested the possibility of constructing an "ideal language" where the grammatical and syntactic structure would faithfully mirror the logical structure, with the result that confusions could no longer arise within it. Second, the formal systems of the logician suggested a clear and sharp distinction between the formal and material elements of language, and further that the philosopher should properly concern himself with the formal structure of conceptual systems. Third, symbolic logic has tended to suggest that logical rules and axioms, like the rules of formal calculi, have purely conventional status, that is to say, they are true because defined to be so. And this in turn has suggested that all necessary truths, including fundamental philosophical axioms such as the principle of causality, are conventional in character.

Analytical philosophy is not directly and necessarily tied up with symbolic logic, however, and the use made of it by the analysts varies greatly. Rudolf Carnap and Willard V. O. Quine, for example, pay considerable attention to symbolic logic, while Oxford philosophers, such as Gilbert Ryle, J. L. Austin and P. F. Strawson, view it almost as a bad influence on philosophy. That symbolic logic does not entail any one philosophical position, whether that of analysis or otherwise, is shown by the example of Whitehead, Russell's collaborator in the pioneer work, *Principia Mathematica* (1910). Whitehead's philosophy is in the tradition of the great metaphysical syntheses and quite at variance with the analytical conception of philosophy.

Ideal Language. Mainly from the suggestions of symbolic logic, Russell derived his fundamental distinction between grammatical form and logical form, and the conception of analysis this distinction implied. He claimed that confusions arise in philosophical discourse because the grammatical and syntactic form of common language misleads one concerning its logical form or structure. The task of analysis is to expose these confusions by revealing the real logical form of propositions, and to construct an "ideal language," i.e., a language in which the grammatical structure would mirror the logical structure and in which, by definition, no confusions, and therefore no philosophical problems, could arise. However, Russell, like Moore, did not claim that "all" the traditional metaphysical problems were thus answerable nor that the "sole" function of philosophy consisted in analysis. Since the 1920s Russell has in fact been concerned to elaborate a more or less "traditional" empiricist position—a combination of Humean ideas with modern logic—and he has become increasingly critical of the English analysts' emphasis upon ordinary language.

Wittgenstein's Development. The tentative ideas of Moore and Russell on the function of analysis were developed by Wittgenstein into a formal philosophical position. Wittgenstein's early work, the *Tractatus Logico-Philosophicus* (1921), came to much the same conclusion as did the logical positivists of the Vienna Circle, namely, that only the propositions of the natural sciences are meaningful, all other propositions being meaningless or "nonsense." Nevertheless the whole basis of Wittgenstein's method was different from that of logical positivism for, whereas the latter's method rested upon an arbitrary (and metaphysical) assumption that only empirically verifiable propositions are factually meaningful, Wittgenstein claimed that his criterion of meaning rested upon a purely logical examination of the structure of language. For him, "nonsense" results from attempting to think beyond the "limits of language" and to say what cannot be said in language. From this point of view, philosophy in the traditional sense, the investigation of the ultimate principles of thought and reality, is "nonsense." The sole task of philosophy is a negative or critical one; it is "the logical clarification of thoughts."

In his later work, *Philosophical Investigations* (1953), instead of speaking about the structure of language as a unitary whole, as he had done in the *Tractatus,* Wittgenstein now spoke of particular "language-games," that is, the sets of concepts we use in talking about, for example, perceptions of color or mental states. The meaning of a word was now defined in terms of its "use" in a particular "language-game," and the task of analysis was to remind us of the context in ordinary language in which the word is used, for there, by definition, it is used meaningfully. The philosopher "cures" us of philosophical puzzlement by showing us how it originates in a misunderstanding of "the workings of our language." Philosophy is, then, not explanatory but rather descriptive in function.

In the *Tractatus* Wittgenstein had questioned himself about the philosophical status of his own propositions and had there adopted the heroic solution (if hara-kiri is a form of heroism!) of admitting that they were also "nonsense." In the *Philosophical Investigations,* however, Wittgenstein adopts a kind of pragmatic justification of his method of analysis. That is to say, the method is justified so far as it works in clearing up philosophical puzzles. The possibility of meaningful metaphysical propositions is not ruled out a priori, but it is strongly implied that since a great number of the traditional metaphysical problems have been shown to be dissolvable by analysis, all such problems are as a matter of fact dissolvable.

Linguistic Analysts. John Wisdom at Cambridge has extended Wittgenstein's idea of philosophy as a therapeutic activity like that of psychoanalysis, and has also tried to show how metaphysical statements, though meaningless if taken literally, may nevertheless have a function in accenting aspects of the familiar world in an unfamiliar way. Again, Wittgenstein's ideas on ordinary language have been exploited by the so-called linguistic analysts at Oxford, particularly by J. L. Austin (*see* LINGUISTIC ANALYSIS). Gilbert Ryle has developed Wittgensteinian ideas in his celebrated work, *The Concept of Mind* (1949), on the relation between mind and body, and another important Oxford philosopher, P. F. Strawson, has strongly criticized the "ideal languages" of "constructionists," such as Carnap and Quine, in favor of ordinary language. In his book, *Individuals* (1959), Strawson has also argued for the possibility of a "descriptive metaphysics."

Other significant philosophers in the Wittgensteinian tradition are G. E. M. Anscombe; H. L. A. Hart, who has brought analysis to bear upon jurisprudential questions; R. M. Hare; and S. Hampshire. In the U.S., philosophers such as N. Malcolm, M. Black and M. Lazerowitz may be said to belong to the same tradition.

Ethics and Religion. Wittgenstein said almost nothing about *ethics, but his Oxford followers have attempted to apply his theory of meaning to ethical propositions. Such propositions, it is claimed, can be meaningful without being factually or descriptively true or false, for they are not used to describe some peculiar kind of entity, e.g., goodness, as thinkers like Moore had assumed, but are used rather to express an "emotive" attitude (A. J. Ayer, *Language, Truth and Logic,* 1936) or a "pro-attitude" (P. Nowell-Smith, *Ethics,* 1957). So also ethical reasoning has its own function and is not reducible either to scientific or mathematical reasoning (S. Toulmin, *An Examination of the Place of Reason in Ethics,* 1950). For the analysts, ethics becomes "meta-ethics" or the philosophical examination of the logic of ethical propositions and reasoning, and it is not concerned with giving reasons favoring one particular moral "way of life" over another.

A similar view of religious language has been suggested by R. B. Braithwaite (*An Empiricist's View of the Nature of Religious Belief,* 1955), R. M. Hare, and others. Religious propositions, so it is claimed, are factually neither true nor false, but they may nevertheless be meaningful in that they declare a certain attitude toward life and the world. However, on the whole question of the possibility of a natural *theology the English analysts adopt widely differing views. Some hold with the logical positivists that propositions about God are meaningless (A. J. Ayer, A. N. Flew); others assert that such propositions are neither true nor false but are nevertheless meaningful in other ways (R. B. Braithwaite, R. M. Hare); others argue that analysis cannot say anything one way or the other about the options we make for or against belief in God (e.g., Wittgenstein); others again seem to admit the possibility of a rational proof of the existence of God (e.g., N. Malcolm). For these views, see *New Essays in Philosophical Theology,* ed. A. Flew and A. MacIntyre, 1955; and *Faith and Logic,* ed. B. Mitchell, 1957.

Logical Positivism. The second stream of analytical philosophy derives from the study of scientific methodology by philosophers of science such as J. H. *Poincaré, P. *Duhem, and above all Ernst *Mach. Studies on the nature of scientific concepts and on the foundations of mathematics by Frege, G. *Cantor, and Russell had focused attention on problems of meaning and verification. These, together with the influence of symbolic logic and the radical scientific positivism of Mach ("we experience only sensations"), prepared the way for the emergence of the Vienna Circle in the 1920s (M. Schlick, R. Carnap, F. Waismann, H. Feigl, V. Kraft). The ideas of the Vienna Circle were put into English dress by A. J. Ayer in his influential book, *Language, Truth and Logic.*

The heart and soul of logical positivism is the so-called "verification principle," which states that a proposition is meaningful only if it is scientifically verifiable (*see* VERIFICATION). The propositions of *logic and mathematics are conventional rules that do not say anything about the real world (*see* MATHEMATICS, PHILOSOPHY OF); and all other metaphysical propositions (about God, soul, etc.) are nonsense. For the logical positivists, then, analysis consists in using the verification principle to discriminate between empirical and nonempirical propositions and, from these latter, to eliminate the metaphysical ones as nonsensical. Second, apart from the elimination of metaphysics, the positive task of philosophy lies in the analysis and clarification of scientific concepts. Difficulties concerning the verification principle (since it is not itself scientifically verifiable must it not be meaningless or at best true merely by definition?) have caused divergences among logical positivists. K. R. Popper, for example, has evolved a criterion of meaning based on "falsifiability," but he restricts its use to scientific propositions and is cautious about making it a general criterion of meaning (*The Logic of Scientific Discovery,* 1959). And A. J. Ayer, under pressure from the Wittgensteinians, has mitigated his earlier logical positivism (see *The Problem of Knowledge,* 1956; *The Concept of a Person,* 1963).

Logical Empiricism. The more orthodox strain of logical positivism has continued in the school of logical empiricism set up by a number of Continental philosophers (R. Carnap, H. Feigl, H. Reichenbach, R. von Mises) who emigrated to the U.S. after the breakup of the Vienna Circle in the 1930s. The logical empiricists continue to exploit the positivist criterion of meaning in more or less sophisticated forms, with the consequent elimination of metaphysics as nonsense; and again they also conceive the main task of philosophy to be the critique of science. Closely allied with this school is the Unified Science Movement, whose aim is to establish a uniform basic scientific language and eventually some kind of unification of the laws of the natural sciences.

Another ally of logical empiricism is the movement of *semiotics, or the philosophical analysis of signs. Logical syntax, that part of semiotics concerned with the formal structure of theoretical language, has been developed especially by Carnap (*The Logical Syntax of Language,* 1937). A more independent sympathizer is C. I. Lewis, who has been much influenced by symbolic logic. In such logic a number of self-consistent logical calculi can be constructed, and one is preferred to another solely on pragmatic grounds. Lewis claims that the same is true of the conceptual schemes that we use for interpreting experience. The laws of logic, mathematical axioms, the fundamental laws of science, even the distinction between what is real and unreal, are all man-made conceptual constructions, by means of which the mind puts order into experience and makes it intelligible. Philosophy is the critical analysis of these schemes or constructions in order to make them more consistent and useful (*Mind and the World-Order,* 1929).

Influence and Critique. Analytical philosophy has been the dominant influence in English philosophy since the 1930s, and since the 1940s it has had increasing influence in the U.S. In these two countries the movement is of great importance and cannot be disregarded. However, apart from Austria and Scandinavia, it has had very little effect in Continental philosophical circles. Both the movement of analysis and the Continental movement of *phenomenology are philosophies about philosophy, and each claims to have discovered a revolutionary philosophical method. Consequently there are very few possible points of contact between the two movements.

Two main claims are made by analytical philosophers: (1) that so-called philosophical problems are due to logico-linguistic confusions; (2) that from a logical analysis of the conditions of meaning one can derive a "neutral" philosophical method capable of analyzing or dissolving these problems. These claims may be put forward in either a "weak" or "strong" form. Thus, for example, it may be claimed that "some" philosophical problems arise from logico-linguistic confusion and that these problems are dissolvable by analysis, while allowing the possibility that "some other" philosophical problems may be genuine ones solvable only by properly philosophical means of a traditional kind. This "weak" form of analysis is quite unexceptionable. In fact, no one would now dispute that the analysts have performed a service in making philosophers sensitive to differences of logical structure in the various "realms of discourse" (differences already remarked in part by *Aristotle and *Thomas Aquinas), and again, to the subtle but important part that logico-linguistic confusion plays in the genesis and complication of philosophical problems.

On the other hand it may be claimed, either explicitly or implicitly, that "all" philosophical problems have their origin in logico-linguistic misunderstandings that are dissolvable without remainder by analysis, so that the "sole and exclusive" task of philosophy consists in therapeutic analysis, with the further consequence that philosophy cannot have any positive "transcendental" role of its own as, for example, in the formulation of a proof of the existence of God (*see* GOD, 7). This "strong" form of analysis is obviously exposed to grave objections. Unless some form of verification principle is arbitrarily and surreptitiously assumed, no "logical" inspection of the conditions of meaning can ever enable one to infer what there is in the world and what there is not —whether, for instance, the limits of reality are coterminous with the empirical world or not. Such an inference from the logical order to the real order is in fact a form of *ontologism. As for those varieties of analysis (e.g., logical empiricism) that directly or indirectly assume the verification principle, they are obviously open to the same fatal objection as can be made to that principle, namely, that it is self-refuting in the sense that not being itself empirically verifiable it must be meaningless as to fact or at best a conventional or arbitrary definition of "meaning."

See also PHILOSOPHY, HISTORY OF; LINGUISTIC ANALYSIS; LOGICAL POSITIVISM; SCIENCE, MODERN PHILOSOPHERS OF; METAPHYSICS, VALIDITY OF.

Bibliography: M. BLACK, ed., *Philosophical Analysis* (Ithaca, N.Y. 1950). M. J. CHARLESWORTH, *Philosophy and Linguistic Analysis* (Pittsburgh, Pa. 1959). H. FEIGL and W. SELLARS, eds., *Readings in Philosophical Analysis* (New York 1949). J. A. PASSMORE, *A Hundred Years of Philosophy* (London 1957). D. F. PEARS, ed., *The Nature of Metaphysics* (New York 1957). A. J. AYER et al., *The Revolution in Philosophy* (New York 1956). J. O. URMSON, *Philosophical Analysis: Its Development Between the Two World Wars* (Oxford, Eng. 1956). G. J. WARNOCK, *English Philosophy Since 1900* (New York 1958). ProcAm CathPhilAssoc 34 *Analytic Philosophy* (1960).

[M. J. CHARLESWORTH]

ANALYTICAL PSYCHOLOGY

The theory and practice of the psychological doctrine of C. G. *Jung. This article outlines the essential elements of the theory, which is concerned with the structure of the psyche, then discusses the practice associated with it in terms of psychotherapy and its goal in individuation, and concludes with a critique and evaluation.

Structure of the Psyche. Like the *psychoanalysis of Sigmund *Freud and the *individual psychology of Alfred *Adler, analytical psychology is based on the psychotherapeutic triad: (1) corporeal symptom (e.g., paralysis in writing); (2) unconscious cause (e.g., repression); and (3) mental problem (e.g., attitude with regard to authority). Jung's investigation begins with the second element, the role of the *unconscious. However, whereas Freud and Adler presented a merely negative evaluation of the unconscious ("a wastepaper basket for the soul's refuse"), Jung succeeded by his theory of archetypes in broadening the concept of the unconscious and in disclosing its positive contents.

Layers of the Unconscious. The upper layer of the unconscious is formed during the lifetime of each individual. It contains things that have been forgotten, things that have been stored in one's memory ("the palaces of memory," St. Augustine), things that have been repressed (these were studied by Freud and Adler), and things that have been assimilated unconsciously. Because this layer is different in each man, Jung calls it the "personal unconscious." The contents of the "personal unconscious" that have their origin in repression are the complexes.

The phenomena that came to light in the treatment of *neuroses, however, called for a broader concept of the unconscious. Below the "personal unconscious" are layers that can be found in each individual psyche and thus are common to all men; as a consequence, Jung calls these the "collective unconscious." Moreover, analysis of the *dream disclosed constantly recurring themes that could not be explained on the basis of the personal unconscious; these were often found in an archaic context, "dressed in symbols." They included such figures as father, mother, brother, sister, and bride; friend, traitor, king, and hero; and God, savior, devil, saint, and priest. Again, there were situations such as a dragon in the form of a whale, an alliance, and a liberation from captivity, and objects such as a bridge, a rainbow, and a mountain pass. All of these themes are found not only in the dreams of modern man but also in the myths and religions of different nations, and, in code, even in alchemy. Jung calls them archetypes; together they form the contents of the collective unconscious.

Role of the Archetypes. Being an empirical researcher, Jung works with the archetypes as operative factors in the life of the soul without committing himself as to their origin. Whether they are "the sediment of innumerable experiences or a given presupposition of human experience" (H. Portmann) remains an open question. They are variously described as "the psychic aspect of the brain structure," "ways in which the instincts manifest themselves," "dominant elements of the psyche," "prototypes," "primary patterns of behavior," "complexes of experience," and "organs of the prerational psyche." When they become virulent by reason of an appealing situation—either occurring in the external circumstances of life or arising in analysis —they pass into *consciousness in a fascinating way as archetypical images and put consciousness to the task of interpreting their symbolic meaning.

The archetypes are related to the most important steps in the development of human nature, viz, the successive discoveries of the "I," of the "Thou," of the "We," and of God. At the same time they constitute typical tasks of human life by confronting man with different spheres of life, viz, individuality, sex, community, and religious reality.

Particular Archetypes. The discovery of the "I" is, for example, related to the myth of the whale (cf. Jonas). The best known archetypes, "anima" and "animus," correspond to the discovery of the "Thou." "Anima" (in man, "animus" in woman) is the soul's organ for establishing a loving relationship toward persons, situations, and things; it grants the capacity for everything related to the Muses, sensitivity, tenderness, intuition—in short, for the feminine aspect in the cosmos (in woman, for the masculine aspect). After "anima" (or "animus") has taken form and shape and has entered the realm of consciousness, it contains the features of the ideal partner of the opposite sex. An orderly and cultivated formation of love and sexual life (both within and outside marriage) is needed in order to connect the "anima" to the conscious direction of the self. But if a man evades the life of love and sex, he hardens, dries up, and acquires a "soulless" attitude. This explains why Jung chose the concept of "anima" for this part of the soul. It is a purely psychological concept that indicates only a particular realm of the soul's activity and is to be clearly distinguished from the metaphysical concept of *anima* as this is used in scholastic philosophy (*see* SOUL; SOUL, HUMAN). In like manner Paul *Claudel uses these concepts in a different sense when he makes his famous comparison of *animus* and *anima.* For him, *animus* represents consciousness, the conscious mind, whereas *anima* represents the unconscious, the depth dimension of the soul.

The discovery of the "We" is connected with the archetypes of community life, such as father, mother, neighbor, enemy, physician, and king.

The religious archetypes, which are related to the discovery of God, constitute a new disclosure by Jung; the divine Child, the Virgin Mother, the Savior, the overwhelming and bright God and His dark adversaries, etc., are the psychic organs for the perception of the *numinosum,* the *tremendum,* and the *fascinosum.* Whereas Freud dissolves everything religious in the *sublimation of the desire for pleasure, Jung teaches that there is an autonomous religious disposition in the soul.

The Self. The structure of the psyche reaches completion only in the light of still another discovery by Jung. To the two parts of the soul, consciousness and the unconscious, he adds a third part in which both are united: this is the *self, the authentic center of the psyche (the *ego is merely the center of consciousness). The self is closely related to the concept of "summit of the soul" in Christian mysticism. According to the measure in which the four tasks of human life are being accomplished, the self becomes more and more the center, man starts living more from within himself, he finds himself and reaches his own personal development. The triad of consciousness, unconscious, and self constitutes the specific element of Jung's concept of the soul.

Theory of Types. A side product of Jung's work is his theory of types (*see* TYPOLOGY). In order to explain the apparent mutual exclusiveness of Freud's and Adler's theories, Jung saw himself forced to introduce an opposition between extraversion and introversion. A man is extraverted if an object determines him; in that case, all his energy is directed outward. In the case of the introverted person, on the other hand, the subject is determining; his energy is concentrated upon the ego and directed inward. Freud and Adler each described and absolutized his own type, which explains their opposition. Jung points to other pairs of types: Plato and Aristotle, St. Augustine and St. Thomas Aquinas, F. von Schiller and J. W. von Goethe, F. W. Nietzsche and Richard Wagner. Introversion and extraversion are universal and basic attitudes with regard to the four fundamental functions: (1) thinking, which makes learning possible; (2) feeling, in which the evaluative judgment is formed; (3) experiencing, which is the conscious perception of the senses; and (4) intuition, which is the unconscious perception of possible events. Because these four functions may be found in either an extraverted or an introverted form, many variants may result. Thus one arrives at a possible and systematic way of measuring and of orienting oneself in the psychic realm, similar to the geographical system of the four compass points.

Psychotherapy. Against the background of this structure of the soul Jung defines neurosis as a disunion between consciousness and the unconscious. Accordingly, his *psychotherapy endeavors to make the disjoining element conscious, to dissolve it by a change of attitude, and to reconstruct the unity of the psyche. This work of analysis receives the help of various additional concepts, viz, projection, transfer, dream analysis, "persona" and shadow, and training analysis.

Projection. At first the repressed or split-off contents of the unconscious bypass consciousness and are projected toward the outside world. For example, in a person who has fallen in love, the "anima" (or "animus") is projected toward the beloved, overlaying the real person and overestimating his size. The beloved is identified with the projected archetype. The lover remains blind with regard to the other until this identification is dissolved, the projection is recognized as such, and the reality of the other distinguished from the archetype "anima," which then is connected with consciousness. In like fashion, the father image is projected toward people in authority. One must similarly acquire an understanding of the projection and consciously come to grips with the father image, starting from his first experiences of childhood and proceeding until he arrives at an insight into the essence of fatherhood. Such are typical of the phases one must go through in the case of projected archetypes.

Transfer. During the analytical process the archetypes are projected toward the psychotherapist, thereby creating a bond that is charged with both positive and negative emotional elements. The communication between doctor and patient that results from such a transfer constitutes a helpful therapeutic atmosphere in which the neurosis can be treated. Knowledge and maturity are required by the therapist if he is to give direction to such a transfer. What here takes place in the realm of the intrapsychic frequently takes place on a smaller scale in the relationship between the priest and his spiritual child.

Dream Analysis. Dreams are the language of the unconscious and are always related to the individual state of consciousness. A distinction must be made between dreams originating in the personal unconscious and those originating in the collective unconscious. The contents of dreams may be interpreted either on the level of objects in the outside world, or on the level of the subject, i.e., as the dreaming person represents himself, or on both levels. In any event, the interpretation requires knowledge of mythology (*see* MYTH AND MYTHOLOGY).

"Persona" and Shadow. One's customary mechanical and unconscious mode of behavior in relation to the outside world surrounds his consciousness with a kind of protective shield that may become an isolating armor. Jung calls this shield the "persona" (Lat. *persona,* the mask through which the classical actor spoke). This purely psychological concept must be clearly distinguished from the metaphysical concept of *person, which stands not for one part of the soul but for both the totality and the centrality of the individual. According to Jung, penetrating and loosening this "persona" brings into consciousness the repressed and mostly negative and dark aspects of the soul; these are the shadow of the bright ego. The integration of this shadow into consciousness constitutes a challenging task for the patient, but it is a necessary presupposition for the work of the therapist and, indeed, for anyone who engages in guidance and *counseling.

Training Analysis. To be able to practice analytical psychology as therapy and as psychagogy one must undergo special study for 2 years in course work and training analysis. Centers of training are various Jungian institutes in Switzerland, England, Italy, Israel, and Germany, and, in the U.S., the Society of Jungian Analysts in Los Angeles and San Francisco and the Association for Analytical Psychology in New York.

Individuation. A cure consists in more than becoming free from symptoms of illness; it involves coming round to oneself, i.e., developing and discovering oneself. This process of individuation leads to the integration of all layers of the soul, including the religious. The only person who can live a sound and healthy life is one who allows the religious layers of his soul to develop and becomes himself religious, in the sense of making the religious archetypes conscious. The completeness and unity of the psyche in the self is expressed in religious symbols (mandalas). Jung leads the person along the path of individuation not only toward health but also toward salvation. He characterizes the experience of the self in an individuated soul as "the kingdom of God within us."

Critique and Evaluation. In the line of development of *depth psychology, analytical psychology should be located somewhere between Freudian psychoanalysis and *existential psychology. Jung's greatness as a psychologist lies principally in his discoveries, which surpass his interpretation of them. The latter breathes the positivism of the 19th century and is based upon the Kantian assumption of the impossibility of knowing metaphysical realities. Concepts from revelation, such as "the kingdom of God," are thus reduced to the level of the comparative study of *religion.

Jung's investigation of the collective unconscious has added to the knowledge of man's creative potentialities. It would seem, however, that the psychological notion of the self, despite Jung's interpretation, should be equated with the person. What is signified in philosophy by person and the actualization of the person, comes closer to concrete experience when the notions of self and individuation are incorporated into their content. The structure of the psyche in the triad of consciousness, the unconscious, and the self (cf. the triads in St. Augustine's psychological doctrine on the Trinity) thus has points of contact with the Christian idea of the human person. *Conscience, too, is to be located in the self, for this is the sphere where free decisions are made. Discovering the self is therefore a matter of forming one's conscience, in the sense of orienting it according to the norms of moral doctrine.

In summary, one may say that analytical psychology offers important material for a Christian anthropology. A special subject for theological study would be the investigation of the suitability of employing the Jungian archetypes in Christian preaching; for these would seem to touch on important elements in the process of any conversion.

Bibliography: Sources. C. G. JUNG, *Collected Works,* ed. H. READ et al., tr. R. F. C. HULL, 18 v. (Bollingen Ser. 20; New York 1953–), Ger. ed. (Zurich 1958–); *Memories, Dreams, Reflections,* recorded and ed. A. JAFFÉ, tr. R. and C. WINSTON (New York 1963), autobiography.

Studies. J. GOLDBRUNNER, *Individuation* (New York 1956). J. JACOBI, *The Psychology of C. G. Jung: An Introduction with Illustrations,* tr. R. MANHEIM (rev. ed. New Haven 1951); *Complex, Archetype, Symbol in the Psychology of Jung,* tr. R. MANHEIM (Bollingen Ser. 57; New York 1959). V. WHITE, *Soul and Psyche: An Enquiry into the Relation between Psychiatry and Religion* (New York 1960). J. RUDIN, *Psychotherapie und Religion: Seele, Person, Gott* (Freiburg 1960). J. GOLDBRUNNER, *Realization* (Notre Damė, Ind. 1966).

[J. GOLDBRUNNER]

ANAMNESIS

From the Greek ἀνάμνησις, meaning remembrance, commemoration, memorial; anamnesis refers especially to the *Unde et memores* in the Latin Mass and its analogs in other liturgies. It takes up Christ's injunction, "Do this in remembrance of me" (1 Cor 11.24), and recalls the purpose of the Eucharistic rites as a commemoration of Christ and His salvific work.

Liturgical Use. The anamnesis follows the Consecration and is usually linked with it by a conjunction, such as *unde, igitur,* or *ergo.* It is found in almost all liturgies (Serapion's is a marked exception). The oldest extant text is in the 3d-century *Apostolic Tradition* of Hippolytus: "Memores igitur mortis et resurrectionis eius offerimus tibi panem et calicem" (4; Botte LQF 16). In other Latin liturgies this prayer is called *post pridie, post mysteria,* or *post secreta.* The Gallican liturgies generally limit themselves to an anamnesis of Christ's death; the Resurrection is already mentioned in Hippolytus; and the Ascension is cited in the 4th-century *De Sacramentis.* Oriental rites often add other mysteries.

History of the Term. The word anamnesis is variously translated "memory," "remembrance," or "commemoration," but it is not easy to render the word accurately in English, since it implies both a subjective and an objective element. Greek versions of the Bible use the word to translate various forms of the Hebrew root *zkr.* Such passages as Prv 10.7, Jb 18.17, and Ps 134 (135).13 show that memory and memorial are closely connected with the Hebrew conception of the "name," which connotes the personality and power of God. From Nm 15.40 and Ps 102(103).18 it is clear that remembering is inseparably linked with action of some kind. A memorial sacrifice is suggested by *'azkārâ* in Lv 24.7 and *zikkārôn* in Nm 10.10. Anamnesis and its cognate verb have the sense not merely of remembering something absent but of recalling or representing before God an event of the past so that it becomes present and operative. Thus the sacrifice of a wife accused of adultery (Nm 5.15) is an ordeal that recalls her fault to God's remembrance, and the widow in 3 Kgs 17.18 complains that Elia had come only to recall to God's remembrance the record of her sin. Finally, remembering is further related to the covenant (1 Chr 16.17–18; Ex 6.5–6) and to the theme of the Passover feast (Ex 12.14; Dt 16.1–3); but we cannot deduce much from this association.

St. Paul may have been influenced by the use of *zikkārôn* in Ex 13.9, when in 1 Cor 5.7–8 he declares: "Christ our passover has been sacrificed. Let us celebrate . . . with the unleavened bread of sincerity and truth." The use of the word anamnesis by later Christian writers was probably affected by Hellenism; both the word and the idea played a part in the mystery cults of Hellenist-Roman religious life.

Function in the Eucharist. The anamnesis interprets the mystery of the Mass, tying it to the events of salvation history; it serves to bring out a basic aspect of the Mass, that it is a memorial of Christ and His salvific acts. Because it is a relative sacrifice, the Eucharist not only recalls by reflection the personal relationship God established by Christ's death and Resurrection, but also represents these acts sacramentally, so that the worshiping community enters effectively into the everlasting sacrifice of the risen Lord, which is thus made present on earth. St. John Chrysostom is typical of early writers and subsequent tradition alike in his emphasis on the relation of Christ's sacrificial death and Resurrection: "We offer even now what was done then, for we perform the anamnesis of His death" (*In Hebr. Hom.* 17.3; PG 63:131). The anamnesis in the Roman Mass makes clear, too, the role of the Church: "We thy servants and thy holy people" join in offering Christ's sacrifice.

In the light of OT and early Christian usage, it is evident that the celebration of the Eucharist is certainly more than a mere recollection or subjective memory (μνεία or μνήμη; cf. Rom 1.9–10); the Lord's Supper was not continued as a sort of funeral banquet, implying a mere mental commemoration. Nor is it some pale and powerless imitation of the *dromena* of the pagan mysteries, for it is the memorial that proclaims the Lord's sacrificial death (1 Cor 11.26). It is rather an anamnesis, an objective memorial directed Godward, releasing Christ's personality and power afresh; it is the experience of a fellowship with Christ in His eternal sacrifice. Since Christianity is a historical religion, based on the Incarnation of the Son of God and His redemptive death and Resurrection, it is these paschal mysteries that are sacramentally perpetuated in the Mass, the sign of Christ's new covenant with men.

Bibliography: J. A. JUNGMANN, *The Eucharistic Prayer: A Study of the Canon Missae,* tr. R. L. BATLEY (Notre Dame, Ind. 1956) 1–14. W. J. LALLOU, "Unde et memores," AmEcclRev 113 (1945) 81–93. Miller FundLit 210–214. A. SCHLITZER, "A Protestant Ecumenical on the Eucharist," YrbkLitStud 3 (1962) 119–135.

[F. A. BRUNNER]

ANANIAS, high priest, appointed to his office *c.* A.D. 47 by Herod, King of Chalcis, and removed from his office in 59 by King Agrippa II. When St. Paul was arrested in Jerusalem and arraigned before the Sanhedrin, *c.* 58, Ananias had him slapped on the mouth. After being struck, Paul called Ananias a "whitewashed wall," accused him of breaking the Law in the very act of condemning him for a transgression of the Law, and foretold his violent death (Acts 23. 1–5). A few days later Ananias was Paul's chief accuser before the Roman governor, Felix, at Caesarea (Acts 24. 1). Hated by the people both because of his avarice and cruelty and because of his pro-Roman politics, he was assassinated by *sicarii* ("daggermen") of the *Zealots at the beginning of the Jewish Revolt in A.D. 66.

Bibliography: EncDictBibl 1:542–544. A. BÜCHLER, JewishEnc 1:557–558.

[E. J. HODOUS]

ANARCHISM

A doctrine that teaches the necessity to eliminate political authority in order to realize social justice and individual freedom. It is usually accompanied by opposition to private property and organized religion. Anarchism is rooted in these assumptions: (1) that man is good and essentially altruistic by nature; (2) that he is free only when he follows his powers and prescribes a rule to himself; (3) that he has been corrupted by the *state and by *law, which are always instruments of class or personal exploitation and oppression; and (4) that a natural, interpersonal harmony of interests exists in the economic and the moral order in the absence of the state. These assumptions lead to the following conclusions: (1) that social injustice and moral evil can neither be cured nor diminished by state action; (2) that the division of labor should always be on a voluntary basis; (3) that the state should be replaced by voluntary cooperation arising from below, that is, proceeding from individuals to groups, and, on the federal principle, to higher forms of human association; and (4) that voluntary association implies the right of secession.

History. Anarchist ideas extend back at least as far as Zeno (*c.* 320–*c.* 250 B.C.), the founder of *Stoicism. Building on the principle of self-sufficiency, Zeno prescribed an ideal society wherein men would live without family, property, or courts of law. In medieval Europe the pantheistic *Brothers and Sisters of the Free Spirit rejected all authority and advocated communism of goods and women. During the Hussite wars, Petr Chelčický (*c.* 1390–*c.* 1460) taught that since all compulsion is from the devil, the state is evil and must disappear along with class distinctions. *Anabaptists of the 16th century believed themselves freed from all law by Christ's grace, refused to pay taxes or tithes, and held wives and property in common. The French writers Rabelais (*c.* 1495–1553) and *Fénelon (1651–1715) expressed anarchist ideas that were later shared by some 18th-century *philosophes*. A couplet of *Diderot is typical: "La nature n'a fait ni serviteurs ni maitres/Je ne veux ni donner ni recevoir des lois."

Systematic Anarchism. Modern anarchist thought draws on the classical liberal belief in a natural economic order (*see* LIBERALISM, ECONOMIC) and on the philosophy of Ludwig *Feuerbach (1804–72), which emphasizes the need to eliminate man's alienation from his true self by a reduction of all barriers and a reclamation of the material world. William Godwin (1756–1836), in his *Enquiry Concerning the Principles of Political Justice* (1793), considered government and property acquired by exploitation as basic evils, and he advocated a stateless society of self-governing communities with goods in common. He conceded that if the most natural and just associations were established, the conduct of some men would need to be restrained for a lengthy period until their corrupted instincts were corrected. The left-wing Hegelian Max Stirner (1806–56), in his *Der Einziger und sein Eigentum* (1844), argued that only the individual is real and that restraints such as the state, property, religion, and philosophical abstractions are detrimental to his self-realization. He advocated replacing the state with a voluntary association of egoists. The term anarchism was used for the first time by a systematic anarchist thinker, Pierre Joseph Proudhon (1809–65), in his *Qu'est-ce que la propriété?* (1840). He defined property, in the sense of goods obtained by usurpation and monopoly, as theft. He urged its elimination not by expropriation but by the establishment of banks of exchange that would operate on a basis of mutuality of individual services calculated in units of labor. He thought that such banks would lead to further free associations of persons having the same interests, which would ultimately eliminate the exploitative economic order and the state. Proudhon recognized that a complete removal of the state could not be readily realized, and he argued that the practical aim should be a minimization of coercion and decentralization, and the encouragement of voluntary groups.

Collectivist Form. With Michael Bakunin (1814–76), anarchism assumed a decidedly collectivist form. He argued that political authority, private property, and religion are natural institutions in the lower stages of human evolution, and proclaimed: "L'Eglise et l'Etat sont mes deux bête noires." The state is harmful because it supports an exploitative economic order and acts by coercion. Bakunin held that society should be built on voluntary association and cooperation, with common ownership in land and the means of production—"there will be a free union of individuals into communes, of communes into provinces, of provinces into nations, and finally of nations into the United States of Europe, and later of the whole world." Bakunin introduced into the anarchist movement an emphasis on terroristic violence that was brought to Russia and merged with *nihilism by his pupil Sergei Netschayev. Prince Peter Kropotkin (1842–1921) wedded anarchism to a communism based on the commune, an autonomous unit owning all means of production and consumption. He believed coercive authority unnecessary because the new society would accord with the natural cooperative impulse in man and because free agreements need not be enforced. That modern anarchist thought is not uniformly antithetical to religion is evidenced in the thought of Count Leo *Tolstoi (1828–1910). Although he rejected the divinity of Christ and personal immortality, Tolstoi taught that the Gospels indicate that religion means altruistic love of neighbor and that this is negated by political authority, which proceeds from egoism and violence.

Contemporary Significance. Proponents of anarchism have differed over means of implementation. Godwin rejected violence and advocated education; Proudhon did not preach violence but believed outbreaks to be inevitable; the collectivists Bakunin and Kropotkin preached its necessity while Tolstoi repudiated it, emphasizing noncooperation with the state. With the spread of the ideas of Bakunin and Kropotkin, propaganda by the deed of terroristic violence was accepted by many and rationalized as a proper means to capture the imagination of the masses. Unquestionably the invidious connotation given the term anarchist in the popular mind is due principally to acts of terror, such as the assassination of Pres. William McKinley. Generally speaking, violence (and atheism) has been most associated with anarchism in the Latin countries. Allied with *syndicalism as a mass movement, it reached a high point for a short period in the Spanish Civil War in Catalonia when anarchosyndicalists assumed authority. In the contemporary world, however, anarchism has little significance as a political movement. It survives principally in intellectual circles as an ideal to be approximated, if not realized, and as a means of protest against the mass society and centralized economic and political order (*see* MASSES).

Critique. Anarchism's fundamental assumption of man's natural goodness is contradicted not only by the theological doctrine of original sin but also by historical experience. Although the antagonistic tendencies in men may be less strong than the cooperative, it is unwarranted to attribute the former solely to the institutional environment while deeming the latter completely natural. Further, legal power subserving the common good is not an avoidable hindrance to, but a necessary precondition of, the full development of human freedom and the attainment of social justice. Finally, it is inconceivable that the state can be destroyed without violence; if violence is used, a new coercive state will necessarily succeed.

Bibliography: M. NETTLAU, *Bibliographie de l'anarchie* (Brussels 1897); *Der Anarchism von Proudhon zu Kropotkin* (Berlin 1927). E. V. ZENKER, *Anarchism* (New York 1897). E. H. CARR, *Michael Bakunin* (London 1937). R. ROCKER, *Anarcho-Syndicalism* (London 1938). H. READ, *The Philosophy of Anarchism* (London 1940). G. D. H. COLE, *Socialist Thought: Marxism and Anarchism* (London 1954). J. JOLL, *The Anarchists* (London 1964). I. L. HOROWITZ, ed., *The Anarchists* (New York 1964). D. NOVAK, "Place of Anarchism in the History of Political Thought," RevPol 20 (1958) 307–329.

[A. J. BEITZINGER]

ANASTASIA, SS. Anastasia is the name of a martyr saint commemorated in the Canon of the Roman Mass and in the second Mass of Christmas. The only known fact regarding Anastasia is that during the persecution by *Diocletian a woman of that name suffered martyrdom at *Sirmium, where the faithful constructed

Martyrdom of St. Anastasia, miniature in the 11th-century Menologion of Basil II (Vat. Cod. gr. 1613, fol. 110).

a church in her honor. Gennadius, Patriarch of Constantinople (458–471), had her body translated to a sanctuary in the Byzantine capital. Various theories have arisen to explain her connection with Rome. In the 4th century Pope Damasus decorated a Roman basilica known under the title of "Anastasia," which apparently served the Palatine and imperial palace. Thus, the Church of Anastasia is an important Roman edifice having some connection with the emperor and the pope. Since the word "Anastasia" means Resurrection, H. *Grisar suggested that the church may have been built to commemorate that Christian mystery. But P. Whitehead believes it took its name from the founder, probably the Emperor Constantine's sister, Anastasia. The name Anastasia was added to the Canon of the Mass late in the 5th century, and in the 6th century the basilica is referred to as a title church. The basilica, constructed between the Circus Maximus and the Palatine palace, seems to have originally been cruciform in style. It underwent various reconstructions and is an imposing structure with three aisles.

The Roman Martyrology cites another Anastasia, on April 15, who, with Basilissa, supposedly buried the bodies of SS. Peter and Paul and was beheaded by *Nero. No evidence supports the existence of Anastasia and Basilissa.

Bibliography: C. CECCHELLI, EncCatt 1:1150. H. GRISAR, *Analecta Romana* 1 (Rome 1899) 595–610. L. DUCHESNE, *Mélanges d'archéologie et d'histoire* 7 (1887) 387–413. P. B. WHITEHEAD, "The Church of S. Anastasia in Rome," AmJArch 2d ser. 31 (1927) 405–420. R. KRAUTHEIMER, *Corpus basilicarum christianarum Romae* (Vatican City 1937–) 1:42–61. Butler Th Attw 2:98; 4:613–614. **Illustration credit:** Biblioteca Apostolica Vaticana.

[E. G. RYAN]

ANASTASIUS, ST., Hungarian archbishop; d. Nov. 12, between 1036 and 1039 (feast, Nov. 12). A German disciple of Bp. *Adalbert of Prague, Anastasius (or Ascherich; Radla-Astericus) became abbot of Adalbert's newly founded monasteries at Brevnov, near Prague (993), and then at Miedzyrzecz, Poland. He later undertook a mission to *Hungary at the request of King *Stephen I of Hungary, according to Stephen's vita (MGS 11:232–33). There Anastasius became abbot of St. Stephen's foundation at *Pannonhalma, and later archbishop of *Esztergom, possibly the only Hungarian metropolitan see (K. Schünemann). In 1007 Anastasius attended the Synod of Frankfurt, and in 1012 he was at the consecration of the church of St. Peter in Bamberg. His possible German origin and his certain presence at German synods is witness to the continued close links between Germany and the Christianization of Hungary under Duke Geza and Stephen I.

Bibliography: K. SCHÜNEMANN, *Die Deutschen in Ungarn bis zum 12. Jahrhundert* (Berlin-Leipzig 1923) 35–37, 46–48. A. BRACKMANN, *Kaiser Otto III. und die staatliche Umgestaltung Polens und Ungarns* (AbhBerlAk; 1939) 23–26; *Zur Entstehung des ungarischen Staates* (*ibid.* 1940) 17–19. R. BÄUMER, LexThK² 1:494. Butler Th Attw 4:325–326. F. DVORNIK, *The Making of Central and Eastern Europe* (London 1949).

[V. I. J. FLINT]

ANASTASIUS I, POPE, ST., Nov. 27, 399, to Dec. 19, 401. He was apparently a Roman. St. Paulinus of Nola, whom he received in Rome and invited to attend his anniversary in 400, praised his charity and zeal.

Pope St. Anastasius I, effigy from the 9th-century series of frescoes formerly in the basilica of St. Paul at Rome.

Jerome likewise held him in high esteem, particularly as he favored the anti-Origenist group of Jerome's friends in Rome.

After Rufinus of Aquileia translated Origen's *Peri Archon* in 398, omitting or correcting heterodox doctrines ascribed to Origen, Jerome was encouraged to make a literal translation, thus renewing the controversy over the orthodoxy of Origen. Rufinus had enjoyed the confidence of Pope Siricius, but evidently Jerome's friends in Rome, particularly Marcella, and Eusebius of Cremona alerted Anastasius to the dangers of Origen's teachings. When he received from *Theophilus of Alexandria a cautionary letter, probably instigated by Jerome, he wrote to Simplicianus, Bishop of Milan, and to his successor, Venerius, proscribing Origenistic heresies. Rufinus, feeling himself implicated, wrote an *Apologia* addressed to Anastasius in which he gives an orthodox explanation of his faith and justifies his translations of Origen. Anastasius further wrote to *John of Jerusalem, and in mentioning Rufinus declared himself disinterested in the latter's fate, as long as he did not propagate Origenism (*see* ORIGEN AND ORIGENISM).

Anastasius had also written to the Council of Carthage, which convened on Sept. 13, 401, to urge the African bishops to continue the battle against the Donatists (Mansi 3:1023; 4:491). *See* DONATISM. He died on Dec. 19, 401 (Duchesne LP 1:219) and was buried "ad ursum pileatum."

Bibliography: Jaffé K 273–284. J. P. KIRSCH, DHGE 2:1471–73. Duchesne LP 1:218–219. F. CAVALLERA, *Saint Jérôme,* 2 v. (SpicSavLov 1, 2; 1922). Caspar 1:285–287, 291. **Illustration credit:** Pontificia Commissione di Archeologia Sacra.

[P. T. CAMELOT]

ANASTASIUS II, POPE, Nov. 24, 496, to Nov. 19, 498. When *Gelasius I was succeeded by the conciliatory Anastasius II, hopes were raised that the *Acacian Schism could be brought to an end. Papal legates were dispatched to Constantinople to announce the Pope's election and to sound out the Emperor

*Anastasius I. The Pope was prepared to make a notable concession by recognizing the baptisms and ordinations performed by Acacius but required that Acacius' name be removed from the diptychs. The success of the mission was compromised by the senator Faustus, the emissary of King *Theodoric, who led the Emperor to believe that Rome could be won over to acceptance of the *Henoticon.

The Pope's conciliatory efforts in his friendly reception of the deacon Photinus, sent to Rome by the archbishop of Thessalonica, who had been one of the most determined supporters of Acacius, displeased some of the Roman clergy and they renounced communion with Anastasius II. The Pope died at this juncture, "struck dead by the divine will" according to the Liber pontificalis. This statement perpetuated the legend of the Pope's "apostasy" during the Middle Ages. Dante placed him among the heretics in the sixth circle of hell. Pope Anastasius II wrote a letter to the bishops of Gaul condemning traducianism. A letter to King *Clovis I congratulating him on his conversion is apocryphal, as Clovis was not baptized until after the Pope's death. Anastasius II was buried in the portico of St. Peter's.

Bibliography: A. THIEL, ed., *Epistolae Romanorum pontificum* (Braunsberg 1868) 1.615–639. Duchesne LP 1:258–259; 3:87. L. DUCHESNE, *L'Église au VIe siècle* (Paris 1925). H. LECLERCQ, DACL 13.1:1212–13. Caspar 2:82–87; 758. G. BARDY, Fliche-Martin 4:340–341. P. GOGGI and A. P. FRUTAZ, EncCatt 1:1155. W. ULLMANN, *The Growth of Papal Government in the Middle Ages* (2d ed. New York 1962). R. U. MONTINI, *Le tombe dei papi* (Rome 1957) 105.

[J. CHAPIN]

ANASTASIUS III, POPE, *c.* June 911 to *c.* August 913; b. Rome; d. there. He was the son of Lucian, but little is known of him, except that he was a man of good repute. He succeeded *Sergius III and ruled in a time of turmoil when the government of Rome was dominated by *Theophylactus, *consul et senator,* and his energetic wife, *Theodora. The papal throne was at that time entirely in the control of this powerful family (*see* TUSCULANI). There is extant only one authentic document of Anastasius' reign, a bull granting the *pallium to Ragembert, Bishop of Vercelli. Another bull, purporting to grant extensive jurisdiction to the bishop of Hamburg, is spurious. Anastasius was buried in *St. Peter's Basilica.

Bibliography: P. BERTOLINI, DizBiogItal 3:24. G. SCHWAIGER, LexThK[2] 1:493. Jaffé L 448. A. CLERVAL, DHGE 2:1475. Seppelt 2:350. G. HOCQUARD, *Catholicisme* 1:510–511.

[A. J. ENNIS]

ANASTASIUS IV, POPE, July 8, 1153, to Dec. 3, 1154; b. Conrad de Suburra, Rome. As cardinal bishop of Sabina (named probably 1126), he actively supported the election of Innocent II in 1130 and served as his vicar in Rome when that Pope was absent in France. Already old and experienced, he was elected pope without opposition on the day of Eugene III's death and consecrated on July 12, 1153. Anastasius was charitable to the Romans during famine, and he built a papal residence near the Pantheon. During his pontificate *William Fitzherbert was reinstated and Sweden began to pay *Peter's Pence. When his legate to Germany failed to settle the matter of Frederick I Barbarossa's translation of *Wichmann from Naumburg to the See of Magdeburg, a move already denounced by Eugene, Anastasius accepted Wichmann and bestowed the *pallium* on him in Rome. He was criticized for his overly compliant attitude.

Bibliography: PL 188:989–1088. Jaffé L 2:89–102. Duchesne LP 2:388. Mann 9:221–231. Haller 3:116–120. Seppelt 3:212, 606ff.

[M. W. BALDWIN]

ANASTASIUS I, BYZANTINE EMPEROR, 491 to 518; b. Epidamnus, modern Durrës, Albania, 431; d. Constantinople, July 9, 518. He married the widowed Empress Ariadne and was named emperor after a successful administrative career. At heart he was a Monophysite, who as a layman had engaged in preaching and had exhibited traits of religious scrupulosity. Before being crowned emperor, he was forced to sign a profession of faith in the Council of Chalcedon by the patriarch of Constantinople, Euphemius. His reign was troubled by the strife wrought by the *Henoticon. An able administrator, he did much to reorganize the interior administration and settle the external problems of the Empire. He attempted to impose *Monophysitism on the Eastern bishops, aided mainly by *Severus of Antioch and *Philoxenus of Mabbugh. In 496 he succeeded in deposing Euphemius, the patriarch of Constantinople, on surreptitious charges that stemmed from his intransigent support of the Council of Chalcedon; he deposed also Patriarch Macedonius (511), as well as Flavian of Antioch (512) and Elias of Jerusalem (516). The imposition in the liturgy of the Monophysite Trisagion brought strong reactions in Constantinople, and one of the imperial officers on the Danube, Vitalian, revolted (513–515). His attempts at reconciliation with Rome did not put an end to the *Acacian Schism; and only in Syria and Egypt were the religious policies of Anastasius temporarily successful. However, he proved to be one of the most efficient and remarkable Byzantine emperors, despite the failure of his religious policy.

Bibliography: L. BRÉHIER, DHGE 2:1447–57. P. CHARANIS, *Church and State in the Later Roman Empire: The Religious Policy of Anastasius* (Madison, Wis. 1939). Stein-Palanque Hist BEmp 2:77–217.

[P. ROCHE]

ANASTASIUS, PATRIARCH OF CONSTANTINOPLE, 730 to 753. At the dismissal of Germanus as Patriarch of Constantinople because of his opposition to *iconoclasm, the Emperor *Leo III appointed the syncellus Anastasius as Patriarch (Jan. 22, 730). Anastasius was excommunicated by Pope *Gregory III as a heretic and intruder, and the Emperor in turn detached the Hellenized provinces of Sicily, Calabria, and the Balkan Peninsula from Roman allegiance, attaching them to the Patriarchate of Constantinople. Thus a further step was taken in the rupture between Rome and Byzantium. In 741 Anastasius supported the revolt of usurper Artabasdus, crowned him emperor, and agreed to the restoration of the holy icons in the city's churches. On suppression of the rebellion by the Emperor *Constantine V (742–775) Anastasius was severely punished and humiliated publicly, but retained the patriarchal throne. His subsequent reign was marked by an intensification of iconoclastic propaganda directed by the

Emperor himself. The patriarch died while preparations were being made for the Iconoclast council of 754.

Bibliography: B. KOTTER, LexThK² 1:491. Ostrogorsky, 145–147, 152–153. Grumel Reg 1.2:8–9.

[F. DE SA]

ANASTASIUS, PATRIARCHS OF ANTIOCH, SS.

Anastasius I, St., Patriarch of Antioch; d. *c.* 599 (feast, April 21). He was *apocrisiarius* of the See of Alexandria at Antioch and was elected patriarch in 559. He showed himself an intrepid defender of orthodoxy, opposing strenuously Emperor *Justinian I's edict on Aphthartodocetism (565), and was exiled to Jerusalem in 570 by Emperor *Justin II. Pope *Gregory I, then *apocrisiarius* of Pope *Pelagius II at Constantinople, sent several consoling letters to the exile, and on becoming pope interceded with Emperor Maurice for Anastasius' reinstatement (593). In exile Anastasius wrote much against heresy; five of his philosophical works are available in Latin translations. Because of the diversity of his argumentation, he is considered a precursor of scholasticism. He exercised great influence on later Greek theologians.

Anastasius II, St., Patriarch of Antioch; d. *c.* 609 (feast, Dec. 21). His letter to Pope Gregory I announcing his election and profession of faith is lost, but Gregory's reply exists (MGEp 7:48). His Greek translation of Gregory's *Liber regulae pastoralis* also has disappeared. He was killed during an insurrection of the Jews when Emperor Phocas attempted to convert them by force. Baronius inserted his name into the Roman Martyrology for December 21.

Bibliography: Anastasius I. PG 89:1293–1308. A. RAES, Bibl Sanct 1:1064–65. E. STOMMEL, LexThK² 1:490–491. S. VAILHÉ, DTC 1.1:1166. R. JANIN, DHGE 2:1460. M. SCADUTO, EncCatt 1:1158–59. Altaner 619. L. DUCHESNE, *L'Église au VIe siècle* (Paris 1925). R. DEVREESSE, *Le Patriarcat d'Antioche* (Paris 1945) 81, 83, 99, 118, 119. Anastasius II. A. RAES, BiblSanct 1:1052–53. H. RAHNER, LexThK² 1:491. R. JANIN, DHGE 2:1460. M. SCADUTO, EncCatt 1:1152. Altaner 559, 619. Mart Rom 596. R. DEVREESSE, *op. cit.* 100, 118, 119.

[F. DE SA]

ANASTASIUS THE LIBRARIAN

Enigmatic personality very influential behind the scenes in Rome from the 840s to 870s; b. probably Rome, *c.* 810–817; d. *c.* 878. By his own account he was the nephew of Arsenius, the influential bishop of Orte, rather than his son, as *Hincmar of Reims held (*Annales Bertiniani,* ann. 868). His knowledge of Greek, which he learned at an early age, brought him into prominence. The beginning of his career was stormy and even scandalous. Created cardinal priest of St. Marcellus by *Leo IV in 847 or 848, Anastasius soon abandoned his church for motives still obscure but in which ambition must have played a part; he was excommunicated (Dec. 16, 850), anathematized (May 29, and June 19, 853) and deposed (Dec. 8, 853). Between the election and the consecration (Sept. 29, 855) of *Benedict III, successor to Leo IV (d. July 17, 855), Anastasius attempted to secure the pontifical throne by force and for a few days stood as antipope. Benedict III later admitted him again to lay communion. Anastasius henceforth altered his whole attitude, becoming a zealous defender of the succeeding popes. It is this change that explains why, up to the time of *Hergenröther, Lapôtre, and Perels, the existence of two men named Anastasius (Anastasius the cardinal and Anastasius the librarian) was admitted. Anastasius became abbot of S. Maria in Trastevere under *Nicholas I (858–867), was freed from his suspension on the day of the consecration of *Adrian II (Dec. 14, 867), and immediately afterward was named librarian of the Holy Roman Church, a post he retained under *John VIII (872–882) until his death (the last official mention of him is May 29, 877, the first allusion to his successor, Zacharias of Anagni, March 29, 879).

It is hard to exaggerate the part Anastasius played from 861 onward in drawing up papal letters, especially those dealing with the Byzantine Church and the Patriarch *Photius, whose determined opponent he was. At the beginning of 868 Anastasius was acting patron to SS. *Cyril (Constantine) and Methodius on their arrival in Rome with the Slavonic liturgy. When Eleutherius, the son of Arsenius, shortly afterward (March 10, 868) ravished the daughter of Adrian II and a few months later killed her and her mother, Stephania, Anastasius was accused of complicity in the murder, whereupon the previous condemnations were at once reimposed. After being rehabilitated, probably before the middle of 869, he was sent by Emperor *Louis II to Constantinople, on the occasion of the 8th ecumenical council, *Constantinople IV (869–870), to arrange a marriage between Louis's daughter Ermengard and the eldest son of the Byzantine Emperor *Basil I. The project did not succeed, but Anastasius made good use of his stay, now in questioning *Metrophanes of Smyrna, the bishop whom Photius had once exiled to Cherson, about the discovery there of the relics of Pope St. *Clement I by Cyril (Constantine), now by helping the official delegates of the Holy See to the Council, at whose last session (Feb. 28, 870) he also assisted. As the *acta* of the official delegates perished, it was his personal copy that was accepted in Rome; in 871 Anastasius offered Adrian his Latin translation of these *acta,* preceded by a long dedicatory epistle. He was to do precisely the same thing, at the beginning of the pontificate of the new Pope *John VIII, with the *acta* of the 7th ecumenical Council (*Nicaea II, 787). During John's pontificate Anastasius' literary activity was particularly intense, consisting mainly of translations (of unequal value) from Greek into Latin. Thus, he composed for *John the Deacon of Rome (Hymmonides) a *Chronographia tripertita* out of extracts from the Byzantine chronicles of Patriarch *Nicephorus I, *George Syncellus, and *Theophanes and a *Collectanea* relating to the history of *Monothelitism. For Emperor *Charles II the Bald, both before and after his coronation (Christmas 875), he translated the *Scholia* of St. *Maximus Confessor and of Patriarch *John III Scholasticus to the works of *Pseudo-Dionysius and the life of the latter by Patriarch *Methodius of Constantinople (BHG 554d), as well as summaries of liturgical treatises attributed to Maximus and to Patriarch *Germanus I of Constantinople and a *passio* of St. *Demetrius. His hagiographical work over 20 years included versions of lives, miracles, or translations relative to SS. *John the Almsgiver, Patriarch of Alexandria, Basil of Caesarea, John Calybites, Bartholomew the Apostle, Pope Martin I, Stephen the protomartyr, Peter of Alexandria, Cyrus and John, and the 10,000 martyrs of Mt. Ararat. His translations of two short works of Cyril (Constantine) and his letter to Photius when he was restored to favor by John VIII are lost. Of the *Liber Pontificalis, the composition of which was once gratuitously attributed to Anastasius, probably only the notice on Pope Adrian II is from his hand.

Bibliography: ANASTASIUS THE LIBRARIAN, *Epistolae sive praefationes*, ed. E. PERELS and G. LAEHR, MGEp 7:395–442. U. WESTERBERGH, *Anastasius Bibliothecarius. Sermo Theodori Studitae de sancto Bartholomaeo apostolo* (Stockholm 1963). J. HERGENRÖTHER, *Photius Patriarch von Konstantinopel*, 3 v. (Regensburg 1867–69). A. LAPÔTRE, *De Anastasio bibliothecario sedis apostolicae* (Paris 1885). E. PERELS, *Papst Nikolaus I und Anastasius Bibliothecarius* (Berlin 1920). G. LAEHR, "Die Briefe und Prologe des Bibliothekars Anastasius," Neues Arch 47 (1928) 416–468. F. DVORNIK, *The Photian Schism: History and Legend* (Cambridge, Eng. 1948). P. DEVOS, "Anastase le bibliothécaire: Sa Contribution à la correspondance pontificale. La date de sa mort," *Byzantion* 32 (1962) 97–115; "Une Passion grecque inédite de S. Pierre d'Alexandrie et sa traduction par Anastase le bibliothécaire," AnalBoll 83 (1965) 157–187.

[P. DEVOS]

ANASTASIUS SINAITA, ST., 7th-century Palestinian monk, theological controversialist, and exegete revered as a saint by the Byzantine Church; d. Mt. Sinai, *c.* 700 (feast in Orthodox Church, April 21). He is of unknown origin and is confused with other authors. Anastasius was a monk on Mt. Sinai who left the monastery to dispute with heretics in Egypt and Syria and became known as the New Moses. His writings are edited uncritically and do not permit a fair judgment. The *Hodegos,* or *Viae Dux,* in 24 chapters, was composed in the desert against the *Monophysites (*c.* 685). The arguments on which it is based are buttressed by Aristotelian definitions and citations from the Fathers and the councils that are frequently faulty, indicating that he quoted from memory. In the *Hodegos* he mentions four other works: a Dogmatic Tome, the Apologetic Tome, the Treatise against Nestorius, and a Treatise against the Jews, which are now lost. A *Quaestiones et Responsiones* (*Eratopokriseis*) is in substance the work of Anastasius, but in its present form it shows signs of later additions. It deals with the whole gamut of monastic life and secular culture, and answers objections to the faith with Biblical and patristic texts. Eleven books of an exegetical work, Commentary on the Hexameron, are preserved in Latin, and only the 12th is in the original Greek. The author depends on *Pseudo-Dionysius and engages in exaggerated allegorism. A Dialogue on the Jews (PG 89:1203–72) is not authentic.

Bibliography: PG 89:35–1288. M. JUGIE, EncCatt 1:1157–58. Altaner 633, 644. G. BARDY, RevBibl 42 (1933) 339–343; Dict SpirAscMyst 1:546–547. J. B. PITRA, *Iuris ecclesiastici Graecorum historia et monumenta,* 2 v. (Rome 1868) 2:238–294. R. JANIN, DHGE 2:1482–83. U. RIEDINGER, LexThK² 1:492. Beck KTLBR 442–446. M. SALSANO, BiblSanct 1:1059–61.

[F. DE SA]

ANATHEMA, a Greek term (ἀνάθεμα) found in the sense of accursed or separated from the fold in Rom 9.3 or 1 Cor 16.22, is in Church law (CIC c.2257.2) synonymous with *excommunication, or exclusion from the Church's fold. Theologically, the anathema in the canons of councils generally means that the doctrine so condemned is heretical and its contradictory defined as revealed truth (*see* DEFINITION, DOGMATIC). Such is the case for the canons of Vatican I. However, P. Fransen's study of the anathema as used in Trent has shown that not only revealed doctrine but also *dogmatic facts or disciplinary laws can be covered by a condemnation under anathema of their denial. In such a case, the anathema expresses repudiation of an inadmissible doctrine or practice.

Bibliography: A. VACANT, 1.1:1168–71. A. BRIDE, *Catholicisme* 1:516–517. H. VORGRIMLER, LexThK² 1:494–495. P. FRANSEN, "Réflexions sur l'anathème au concile de Trente," EphemThLov 29 (1953) 657–672.

[P. DE LETTER]

ANATHEMAS OF CYRIL

A summary under 12 heads (hence the alternative names, κεφάλαια, *capitula*) of St. *Cyril of Alexandria's teaching against *Nestorius. They were worded in such a way that refusal to accept any of them is to be regarded as a denial of the Catholic faith. "If anyone does not confess . . . let him be anathema."

Nestorius was condemned in Rome in 430, and Pope Celestine commissioned St. Cyril of Alexandria to obtain from him a retraction of his errors. On receiving the papal instructions, Cyril took it upon himself to draw up 12 propositions and send them with a covering letter to Nestorius. This action was unfortunate. He went beyond his brief in drawing up what amounted to a new profession of faith, and the way he formulated his doctrine was misunderstood in Antioch and Constantinople. At this time the use of certain terms in *Christology was not yet stabilized. Moreover, there were current two different approaches to the theology of the Word Incarnate. Both were legitimate, both were based on Scripture; but whereas Alexandria stressed the unity of Christ and thence proceeded to consider the divine and human elements, Antioch began with the humanity and then turned attention to the mystery that this man was also God. Cyril seems to have been unaware of the difference in terminology and emphasis of the two schools. What is more, the sources of some of his phrases were suspect. Both the μία φύσις (one *physis*) and the analogy between the human and divine nature in Christ and the union of body and soul in man were taken from Apollinarist works on the mistaken assumption that they were Athanasius'. It was not surprising then, that the Anathemas met with opposition. Theodoret of Cyr and Andrew of Samosata wrote refutations, and Cyril was obliged to defend his views in three apologies: *Against the Eastern Bishops* (PG 76:315–386); *Letter to Eutropius* (PG 76:385–452); *Explanation of Twelve Chapters Pronounced at Ephesus* (PG 76:293–312). The text of the Anathemas can be found in Denz 252–263.

Contents. The first Anathema deals with the chief objection to Nestorius, since it defends Mary's title of *Theotokos, Mother of God. The second and third show the inadequacy of Cyril's vocabulary. In describing the unity of Christ he speaks indiscriminately of a physical or hypostatic union. For him the terms *physis* and *hypostasis are interchangeable, and they are used to stress the fact that Christ is truly one, that there is a real union, not a mere association or harmony of two distinct realities. At Antioch these terms *physis* and hypostasis were also interchangeable, but there they were applied to the humanity and to the divinity to convey the idea that Christ is not only truly man but truly God as well. And so whereas Cyril maintained there was but one *physis* or hypostasis, Antioch maintained that there were two. Yet both views were within the realm of orthodoxy.

Some of the Anathemas have to do with predication. Both divine and human attributes are to be referred to the same Christ (4). The divine Word really suffered and died (12). St. Cyril later allowed that it was lawful to distinguish between statements concerning the human nature and those concerning the divine. The Nestorian heresy meant the need for caution in the use of certain titles and expressions in reference to Christ. He would not allow Christ to be called Theophoros, God-bearer. Some of the Fathers did use this name, but it does not sufficiently indicate the intimate union of the divine and human in Christ (5). Although Scripture speaks of Christ as a servant, one cannot allow the Word of God to be called the master of Christ as Nestorius had done (6). Similarly Nestorius had misconstrued Heb 3.1. The High Priest of men is not a man, but the Incarnate Word Himself (10). Neither is Christ an instrument of the Word; He is the Word (7). And so there is to be a single adoration of Christ, the Word Incarnate, not a coadoration of the man and the Word (8). Cyril brings out the fact that the Holy Spirit is not an alien power but the very Spirit of Christ (9). In the eleventh Cyril states that the flesh of the Lord has power to vivify, since it is the flesh of the divine Word. Antioch suspected such sentiments of *Apollinarianism, not recognizing that by flesh was meant the living, animated flesh.

Subsequent History. At the Council of *Ephesus in 431 approval was given to Cyril's letter to Nestorius (no. 4 in collected letters; PG 77:44–49), and this was accepted as the authentic interpretation of Nicaea I. But the other letter of Cyril (no. 17; PG 77:105–121) to which the 12 Anathemas were appended did not receive such formal recognition. Later, at the time of Pope Vigilius, there was to be confusion as to which of the letters was solemnly approved. As Galtier has shown, the Anathemas are not to be taken as the solemn dogmatic teaching of the Council of Ephesus, although they are to be found in the acts of the Council. This is not to say that one can disregard the Anathemas. The first one with its defense of Theotokos was certainly accepted, and even the others reflect the mind of the Council. But the true meaning of these propositions was clouded by the lack of terminological precision; and when *Monophysitism arose, the Church defended its position without recourse to the Anathemas. Cyril himself recognized their inadequacy in the discussions after Ephesus; and when union was achieved in 433 with John of Antioch, there was no mention of them. The contention that Monophysitism was a natural outcome of Cyril's teaching cannot be maintained; and if certain less happy terms of his were dropped at Chalcedon, it is incorrect to say that there was an abandonment of his theology.

In the changed conditions of the 6th century there was an attempt to incorporate into the Church's teaching certain formulas of Cyril that had been omitted at Chalcedon, including the Anathemas. But much of this stemmed from a desire to find agreement among the various contending parties. When the good name and traditions of *Alexandria and *Antioch were at stake, much depended on the official recognition of the orthodoxy of the great figures in these Churches. Consequently, the mention of the Anathemas in subsequent documents is often motivated by reasons other than theology. Now that the terminology has been stabilized, it is only the Monophysite churches that keep to the Cyrilline way of speaking.

See also JESUS CHRIST, II (IN DOGMATIC THEOLOGY); CHRISTOLOGICAL CONTROVERSY, EARLY; JESUS CHRIST, ARTICLES ON.

Bibliography: DTC, Tables générales 2:2642–43. G. JOUSSARD, LexThK[2] 1:495–496. Quasten Patr 3:116–142. J. N. D. KELLY, *Early Christian Doctrines* (2d ed. New York 1960). H. DU MANOIR DE JUAYE, *Dogme et spiritualité chez saint Cyrille d'Alexandrie* (Paris 1944) 491–523. E. L. MASCALL, *Via Media: An Essay in Theological Synthesis* (Greenwich, Conn. 1957) 79–120. J. H. NEWMAN, *Historical Sketches,* 3 v. (New York 1903–06) 2:307–362 (Theodoret). P. T. CAMELOT, *Éphèse et Chalcédoine* (Histoire des conciles oecuméniques 2; Paris 1962). H. M. DIEPEN, "Les Douze anathématismes au concile d'Éphèse et jusqu'en 519," RevThom 55 (1955) 300–338. P. GALTIER, "Les Anathématismes de saint Cyrille et le concile de Chalcédoine," RechScRel 23 (1933) 45–57; "L'unio secundum hypostasim chez saint Cyrille," Greg 33 (1952) 351–398. J. LEBON, "Autour de le définition de la foi au concile d'Éphése," EphemThLov 8 (1931) 393–412.

[M. E. WILLIAMS]

ANATHOTH, a Levitical city (Heb. *'ănātôt*) of Benjamin (Jos 21.18), the modern Khirbet Rās el-Kharrūbeh near 'Anātā, about 3 miles northeast of Jerusalem. The deposed chief priest Abiathar was banished to this city (3 Kgs 2.26). It was the birthplace of Jehu (1 Chr 12.3) and Abiezer (2 Sm 23.27), two of David's valiant warriors. It is perhaps most famous as the birthplace of the Prophet Jeremia (Jer 1.1), who later bought his cousin's land there when it was already in the hands of the Babylonians who were besieging Jerusalem. This "parable in action" predicted the new covenant and the return from exile when real estate transactions could again take place (Jer 32.1–44).

Bibliography: InterDictBibl 1:125. EncDictBibl 79.

[E. MAY]

ANATOLIUS OF CONSTANTINOPLE, patriarch; b. Alexandria *c.* 400; d. Constantinople July 3, 458. He was a disciple of St. Cyril, who ordained him deacon and sent him to Constantinople as his apocrisiary. Anatolius was chosen by Dioscorus of Alexandria and the eunuch Chrysaphius to succeed Flavian as bishop of Constantinople after the Robber Synod of Ephesus in August 449. His good faith was challenged by Pope Leo I, who sent legates to Constantinople demanding that he condemn Eutyches and Nestorius explicitly and subscribe to Leo's *Tome to Flavian* (Leo, *Ep.* 80, 85).

On the accession of Marcian and Pulcheria as Emperors in late August 450, Anatolius accepted Leo's conditions, agreed to the rehabilitation of the bishops deposed at Ephesus in 449, and exhumed the body of Flavian for burial in the Church of the Holy Apostles in Constantinople. He encouraged the Emperor Marcian to call the Council of Chalcedon in 451 and played a critical part in its decisions, taking his position immediately after the papal legate. In agreeing to the condemnation of Dioscorus for his unjust activity at the Robber Synod, not for doctrine, he was instrumental both in convincing the Illyrian and Egyptian bishops of the orthodoxy of Leo's *Tome* and in formulating the statement of faith that became the Council's decision. Anatolius, accused by Pope Leo of ambition in promoting canon 28 of the Council, which declared the See of Constantinople second after Rome, protested his innocence but eventually wrote a letter of submission and entered into full communion with Rome. He was rebuked by Leo for exceeding his authority in consecrating Maximus successor to Domnus of Antioch, but in general he cooperated with the Pope in pursuing an anti-Monophysite policy, particularly after the accession of the Emperor Leo I in 457. His part in the coronation of Marcian as Emperor is not clear, but the ceremony for the Emperor Leo set the precedent for all subsequent Byzantine coronations.

Bibliography: M. JUGIE, DHGE 2:1497–1500. LEO I, *Epistularum Collectiones,* ActConcOec 2.4. Jaffé K 452–540. Tillemont 15:588–832.

[P. T. CAMELOT]

ANATOLIUS OF LAODICEA, ST., 3d-century bishop; d. Alexandria, *c.* 282 (feast, July 3). Founder of a school for Aristotelian philosophy, Anatolius achieved public honors in his native city. Consecrated coadjutor bishop by Theotecnus of Caesarea in Palestine, he became bishop of Laodicea in 268. He was the author of a work on the dating of Easter, a manual of arithmetic in 10 books, and one of theology (Eusebius, *Hist. eccl.* 7.32).

Bibliography: ANATOLIUS OF LAODICEA, *Fragmenta ex libris arithmetic,* PG 10:231–236. ActSS July 1:571–585. Bardenhewer 2:227–230. J. QUASTEN, LexThK² 1:497. M. ANDRIEU, DHGE 2:1493–94.

[F. X. MURPHY]

ANAXAGORAS

Greek philosopher; b. Clazomenae in Asia Minor, *c.* 500 B.C.; d. Lampsacus in Ionia, *c.* 428 B.C. As a young man, he was probably acquainted with the work of Anaximenes. During the Persian invasion of Ionia, he settled at Athens, where he engaged in scientific inquiry, wrote, and taught such personages as Pericles and Euripedes. He appears to have been the first thinker to bring the scientifico-philosophical spirit from Ionia to Athens. He was celebrated for his astronomical investigations, especially his discovery of the true cause of eclipses, and respected for his high moral character. In middle life, after 30 years at Athens, he was indicted by Pericles's political foes on a charge of impiety, namely, claiming the sun was but an incandescent stone. Through the persuasive influence of Pericles, he was released. However, having been compelled to leave Athens, he retired to Lampsacus, a Milesian colony, where he may have founded a school.

Teaching. Anaxagoras most likely wrote only one book, probably under the customary title *On Nature.* It was composed in an attractive and lofty style and was sold at Athens for one drachma during the time of Socrates's trial. From a critical examination and interpretation of the extant fragments, a rather self-consistent cosmological system can be constructed.

In his study of the physical universe, Anaxagoras was confronted with two interrelated problems: stability and change, unity and plurality. Among his predecessors and contemporaries, the Milesians, Pythagoreans, and *Heraclitus emphasized becoming and multiplicity, whereas *Parmenides, *Zeno of Elea, and Melissus stressed permanency and oneness. Anaxagoras attempted to bridge the gulf between these extremes with a compromise solution.

Stability and Change. In his explanation of the special qualities of individual things, Anaxagoras assumed the existence of as many original qualitative principles as there are qualitative determinations in perceptible things. On the empirical ground of innumerable phenomena, he pluralized the Parmenidean being into an unlimited number of seeds (Frg 4, Diels FrgVorsokr 59A). Each seed is infinitesimal, infinitely divisible, eternal, qualitatively unchangeable, stable, and homogeneous, for this simple principle, however much it is divided, always separates into parts qualitatively the same as its whole; accordingly, Aristotle called them ὁμοιομερῆ or "like things" (Phys. 187a 25). Agreeing with Parmenides that coming-to-be and ceasing-to-be are only apparent, Anaxagoras explained the generation and corruption of complex things as simply the mixing and unmixing of seeds (Frg 17).

Unity and Plurality. Anaxagoras's account of unity and plurality logically develops from his theory of stability and change in accordance with Parmenides's two canons: the exclusion of real change and the impossibility of deriving plurality from unity. Anaxagoras reasoned that the manifold different sense objects can be adequately explained only by a plurality of originally different seeds, each a qualitative unit. Although all the primordial seeds—e.g., flesh, bone, and hair—are mixed in individual things, there being "a portion of everything in everything" (Frg 6), yet each complex thing is (and is called) whatever preponderates. Anaxagoras theorized that in the far distant past all the seeds coexisted in the unity of a primeval agglomerate, and that, through the powerful forces of vortex motion, they were separated and then organized to form the present visible cosmos (Frgs 2, 9, 15).

Mind. Although the seeds are movable in space, they are not in motion of themselves. Rather they require an ultimate, universal principle of their orderly movement—Nous or Mind (Frgs 12, 13). Alone in motion of itself, Mind communicates orderly movement to the seeds, separating them from the pristine conglomerate. Mind is no less illimitable than the chaotic congeries. Like the seeds, it is eternal (Frg 14); simple, "mixed with no thing" (Frg 12), homogeneous; quantitatively divisible, yet qualitatively unchangeable; participated by some things, yet remaining essentially identical with itself. Unlike other things, however, Mind is the finest and purest being; it is independent, since it is self-ruling and self-moving, the first principle of motion and order in the cosmos, with "complete understanding of everything" and it "has the greatest power" (Frg 12).

Influence and Critique. Anaxagoras's conception of Mind represents a major contribution in the history of philosophy. For his supreme psychophysical principle, transcendent being of beings and unifying cause of all becoming, he was justly commended by *Aristotle as "a sober man in contrast with the random talk of his predecessors" (*Meta.* 984b 15–18). Both *Plato (*Phadeo* 98) and Aristotle (*ibid.* 985a 18), however, criticized Anaxagoras for failing to go beyond the function of Mind as the initiator of cosmic motion to its subsequent causal influence in the production of natural phenomena. Once Mind originates movement, its causality—somewhat suggestive of teleology—becomes less direct and rather obscure, and then purely mechanical factors seem to assume hegemony.

Nevertheless, in Anaxagoras's thought there is the emergence of a dualism between Mind and nonmental reality. Although Mind is still conceived as something material, it is a distinct, independent, universal, primary cause of orderly motion in the cosmos. This notion is given a central role and greatly enriched in the natural theology of subsequent Greek and Christian philosophers.

See also GREEK PHILOSOPHY.

Bibliography: K. FREEMAN, *The Pre-Socratic Philosophers: A Companion to Diels, Fragmente der Vorsokratiker* (2d ed. Cambridge, Mass. 1959); *Ancilla to the Pre-Socratic Philosophers* (Cambridge, Mass. 1957). G. S. KIRK and J. E. RAVEN, *The Presocratic Philosophers: A Critical History with a Selection of Texts in Greek and English* (Cambridge, Eng. 1957). J. BURNET, *Early Greek Philosophy* (4th ed. London 1930; reprint 1957). W. W. JAEGER, *The Theology of the Early Greek Philosophers,* tr. E. S. ROBINSON (Oxford 1960). J. OWENS, *A History of Ancient Western Philosophy* (New York 1959). Copleston 1:66–71.

[P. J. ASPELL]

ANCESTOR WORSHIP

An important special form of worship of the dead found in certain cultures. It is concerned with dead relatives, particularly blood relatives. Although ancestors of the larger kinship groups are also included, the cult involves especially the immediate members of the family to the third generation. Families and clansmen, through their veneration of ancestors, maintain solidarity and a sacred dignity. Although the cult of ancestors is, for the most part, characteristic of the primitive religions of the matriarchal agricultural peoples, and is connected especially with planting and harvesting, in general it is the patriarchal feature that is dominant in it.

Of the early higher cultures, the Chinese was the one in which ancestor worship attained its greatest development. It exercised influence on Japanese Shintoism; although in Japan, as in Peru, ancestor worship had its own root in the existing clan system. Among the Finns, a corner in the house was regarded sacred to ancestors. The pagan Scandinavians set out barley and beer on fixed days for their farmer ancestors. The "cult of the fathers," i.e., the worship of male forbears, was widely practised not only among the ancient Germans but also in Aryan India; in fact it is so well attested for other Indo-European peoples that it must go back to the age of primitive Indo-European unity. In Greece, the dead were believed to become incarnate in snakes, and if these creatures appeared in a house, they inspired a feeling of special awe.

H. *Spencer (1820–1903) held that manism was the primitive form of religion, but his theory has received no corroboration from investigations of even the lowest and simplest cultures. Mythical ancestors or more or less mythical forbears were given the status of heroes. However, historical members of families were not raised immediately to divine status by their people. On the other hand, it is known that even higher cosmic beings, like Amaterasu, the Japanese sun-goddess in the imperial palace, became ancestor divinities.

Images of ancestors were especially significant in ancestor worship. The ancestor tablets of the Chinese probably go back to such representations. In rites at the grave, these were marked with sacrificial blood by the son of the dead man. They had their place at the domestic altar, before which all significant family happenings were reported. The chief place of cult was the grave, but the temple dedicated to ancestors was important also. The priestly function in the ancestor cult was performed originally by the head of the house.

The "Feast of All Souls," celebrated among the ancient Germans in the Yule Festival, the Feast of Lights held in July in the Far East, and the Urabon Feast of the Japanese are all connected with the reception and entertainment of the spirits of ancestors.

Bibliography: F. HAMPL et al., König RelwissWbh 25–30. W. CROOKE et al., Hastings ERE 1:425–467. C. M. EDSMAN, RGG[3] 6:959–961. J. HAEKEL, LexThK[2] 1:222–223. W. SCHMIDT, *The Origin and Growth of Religion,* tr. H. J. ROSE (2d ed. London 1935) 61–72. W. OTTO, *Die Manen* (Berlin 1923). F. KRAUSE, *Maske und Ahnenfigur: Ethnologische Studien* (Leipzig 1931). H. FINDEISEN, *Das Tier als Gott: Dämon und Ahne* (Stuttgart 1956). A. E. JENSEN, *Myth and Cult among Primitive Peoples,* tr. M. T. CHOLDIN and W. WEISSLEDER (Chicago 1963). F. HERRMANN, *Symbolik in den Religionen der Naturvölker* (Stuttgart 1961) 109–111.

[A. CLOSS]

ANCHARANO, PETRUS DE, lay canonist and teacher; b. Ancharano, Tuscany, *c.* 1330; d. Bologna, May 13, 1416. Little is known of his teaching career except that he taught in Bologna in 1384, Siena from 1387 to 1390, and again in Bologna and other universities. He held positions in the civil governments of Bologna and Venice and took part in the proceedings of the Council of Pisa and the opening sessions of the Council of Constance; but he returned to Bologna where he died. His most important work is the *Commentaria in Decretales* (Lyons 1535–43), which reproduces earlier literature on the Decretals and finds its place with the great commentaries of Baldus and Zabarella. Other works include: *Lectura super Sexto* (Lyons 1517), *Lectura super Clementinas* (Venice 1483, Lyons 1534), and *Consilia* or *Responsa* (Turin 1496, Lyons 1539, Venice 1585). He is also the author of many *Repetitiones,* studies on particular points of law.

Bibliography: C. LEFEBVRE and R. CHABANNE, DDC 6:1464–71. Van Hove 1:496. Schulte 2:278–282.

[H. A. LARROQUE]

ANCHIETA, JOSÉ DE

Missionary and linguist, called the "Apostle of Brazil"; b. San Cristobal de la Laguna, Tenerife, March 19, 1534; d. Reritiba (today Anchieta), Brazil, June 9, 1597. He was related to the family of Ignatius Loyola. He studied at Coimbra and entered the Society of Jesus on May 1, 1551. When his novitiate ended, he was appointed to the missions in Brazil. He left for Brazil in 1553 and worked in the missions until his death.

At first he was in the captaincy of São Vicente and was one of the founders of the village of São Paulo de Piratininga and the Jesuit school there, in which he was a teacher of humanities. He learned Tupi, the language in general use on the coast, and prepared a grammar for it, printed years later. He also wrote catechetical texts and many canticles, dialogues, and religious plays in Tupi and in Portuguese for teaching the faith to the Indians.

In 1567 Anchieta was appointed superior of the Jesuits in the captaincy of São Vicente. He had been ordained the year before. In 1577 he was made fifth provincial of Brazil, a post he held until 1587. The last years of his life he spent in the captaincy of Espíritu Santo. The bishop of Bahia preached at his funeral and gave him the name "Apostle of Brazil."

Although Anchieta was an excellent writer, he was above all a man of action. In his 44 years as Brazilian apostle he held first rank among the missionaries. During his life he was the object of popular veneration because of his apostolic work, his lofty ideals, and a certain untenable and unsubstantiated reputation for heroic deeds. He was said to have had the courage to suppress cannibalism practiced on enemy captives, who were eaten at ritual banquets, and to have protected the chastity of Christian Indian women against the lust of pagan barbarians. He was famed for other apparently extraordinary deeds bordering upon the supernatural and miraculous. No one has been so openly termed a saint, apostle, and father of Christianity in colonial Brazil as has Anchieta. Biographers of the 17th century, Sebastián Beretario who wrote in Latin and Simão de Vasconcellos who wrote in Portuguese, reflect the feeling of veneration then current in Brazil; they present Anchieta as a saint, apostle, and great miracle worker. This devotion continues to be strong among Brazilian Catholics as shown in pilgrimages made to the house of his birth in Tenerife and in the bronze statue erected in La Laguna in 1960. It is said that he baptized 2 million Indians, a number not substantiated but which assuredly testifies to his reputation for numerous baptisms.

The cause for the beatification of Anchieta was introduced in 1615 in a petition of the Brazilian Jesuits. The decree stating the heroic virtues of the venerable servant of God was issued in Rome on Aug. 10, 1736. However, in the second half of the 18th century, after the suppression of the Society of Jesus, the cause was abandoned, and the documents were deposited in the archives in Rome.

Bibliography: S. DE VASCONCELLOS, *Vida do veneravel padre José de Anchieta,* 2 v. (Rio de Janeiro 1943). C. VIEIRA, *El padre Anchieta* (Buenos Aires 1945). H. G. DOMINIAN, *Apostle of Brazil: The Biography of Padre José de Anchieta, S.J., 1534–1597* (New York 1958). S. BERETARIO, *Iosephi Anchietae Societatis Iesu sacerdotis . . . vita* (Lyons 1617).

[F. MATEOS]

ANCHIN, ABBEY OF, near Douai, Flanders, north France; a Benedictine foundation (1079) by two (later nine) local noblemen on land donated by several persons, including the bishop of *Cambrai, the suzerain lord, who confirmed the donation, and the cantor of Cambrai. To teach the monastic rule, Bishop Gerard II sent two monks from Hasnon, one of whom he made abbot. After a fire (1083), Hugh, dean of Cambrai and a skilled architect, used his wealth to rebuild the abbey. The church, consecrated in 1086, was soon too small and was rebuilt (1182–1230) with four towers and a magnificent interior (350 by 85 by 85 feet); 14 columns enclosed a choir 43 feet wide. Conventual buildings and an abbot's house also were built. Abbots Pierre Toulet (1449–64) and Hugh of Lobbes (1464–90) enriched the church with marble statues, alabaster, paintings, organs, sacred vessels, and a miter and cross of great value. Divine services were of unusual splendor in the 15th century. Abbot Charles Coguin (1511–46) began a new cloister which was decorated with sculpture, stained glass, and Biblical frescoes—one of the most beautiful in Europe.

Abbot Alvisus (1120–30, d. 1148), once prior of *Saint-Vaast in Arras, devoted himself to the Cluniac reform and to temporal affairs. Callistus II confirmed new donations (1123), and the abbey came under papal protection. The virtuous and learned *Goswin (1130–65) fostered an active scriptorium and continued Alvisus's work after the latter became bishop of Cambrai. Jean de Batheries (1414–48) and Charles Coguin acquired many MSS. Jean Letailleur (1555–74) established a school of theology where Greek and Hebrew were taught, furnishing professors for the new University of *Douai (1562). Gaspard de Bovincourt (d.

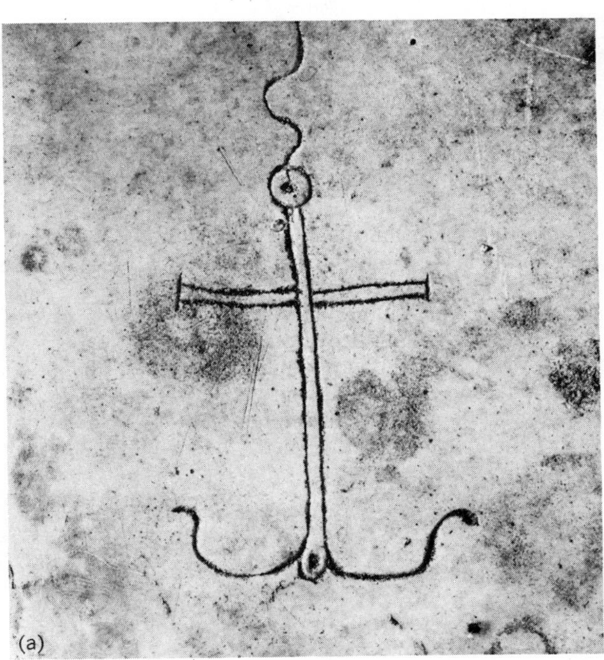

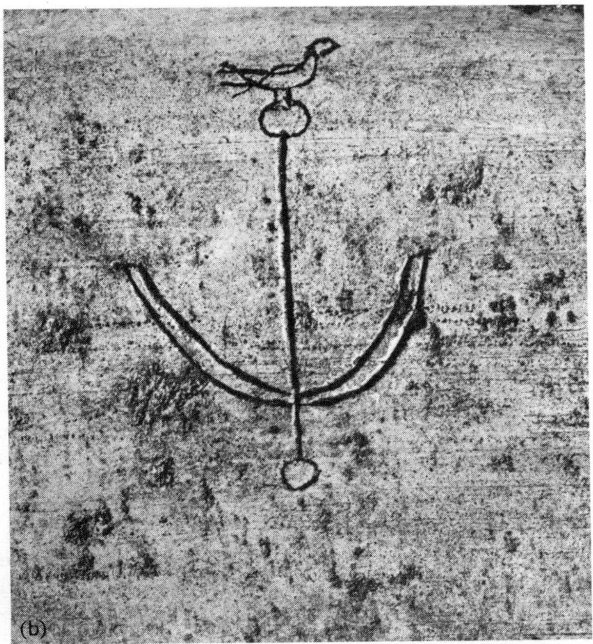

Anchors (a) with a shank in the shape of a cross, 4th century, in the cemetery of Domitilla, and (b) surmounted by a dove, 3d century, in the cemetery of Praetextatus, both at Rome.

1577), François de Bar (d. 1606), and Jean Despierres (d. 1664) were prominent authors.

Powerful and rich, Anchin had pontifical privileges from 1219; it was under the bishop of Arras but also was a member of the estates of Flanders and the Netherlands. It held many properties and houses, received tithes, and named pastors to 53 churches. It contested abbatial rights and privileges with lords and the bishop of Arras (1252–54). Philip II of Spain appointed Warnier de Daure abbot (1574–1610), and the kings of France appointed commendatory abbots from 1681 (*see* COMMENDATION). The zeal of the abbots offset the effects of disasters and wars. At the time of the *French Revolution monastic observance was good. Despite the desire of the 30 monks to remain at Anchin, the abbey was razed, gold and silver work and bells were melted down, and the community was dispersed.

Bibliography: A. ESCALLIER, *L'Abbaye d'Anchin, 1079–1790* (Lille 1852). M. G. BLAYO, DHGE 2:1516–24. P. HELIOT, "Quelques monuments disparus de la Flandre wallonne: L'Abbaye d'Anchin," in *Revue belge d'archéologie et d'histoire de l'art* 28 (Brussels 1959) 129–173.

[P. COUSIN]

ANCHOR, a symbol of safety, so regarded because of its importance in navigation. The Christians in using the anchor on funeral monuments, jewels, and rings as a symbol of hope in a future existence, gave a loftier signification to an already familiar sign. In early Christian thought, hope in the salvation assured by Christ was of paramount importance, and it is exemplified by the association of the anchor with the *monogram of Christ. The author of the Epistle to the Hebrews is the first to connect the idea of hope with the symbol of the anchor: "We have hope set before us as an anchor of the soul, sure and firm" (Heb 6.19–20). *Clement of Alexandria mentions its use on jewels and rings (PG 8:633). The anchor, appearing in the epitaphs of the catacombs and the cemeteries of SS. Priscilla, Domitilla, and Callistus during the 2d and 3d centuries, was an expression of confidence that those departed had arrived at the port of eternal peace. Seldom used as a symbol in medieval ornamentation, the anchor reappeared in the baroque period associated with the patrons of seamen, with ports, and particularly with representations of Pope St. *Clement I. In the sepulchral ornamentation of the late baroque and the classical periods, it reassumed its original Christian character as the symbol of hope in life eternal. (Illus., preceding page.)

Bibliography: A. LEGNER, LexThK[2] 1:567–568. P. STUMPF, ReallexAntChr 1:440–443. J. P. KIRSCH, DACL 1.2:1999–2031. **Illustration credits:** Pontificia Commissione di Archeologia Sacra.

[M. A. BECKMANN]

ANCHORAGE, ARCHDIOCESE OF (ANCORAGIENSIS), metropolitan see comprising 138,985 square miles in the state of Alaska. The archdiocese was established Feb. 9, 1966, from territory taken from the Dioceses of *Fairbanks and *Juneau; these sees, previously included in the ecclesiastical Province of Seattle, Wash., were made suffragans of Anchorage. Right Rev. Joseph T. Ryan, National Secretary of the Catholic Near East Welfare Association, was named ordinary of the newly created archdiocese and was consecrated in his native city of Albany, N.Y., on March 25, 1966. His see had a population of 130,000, of whom

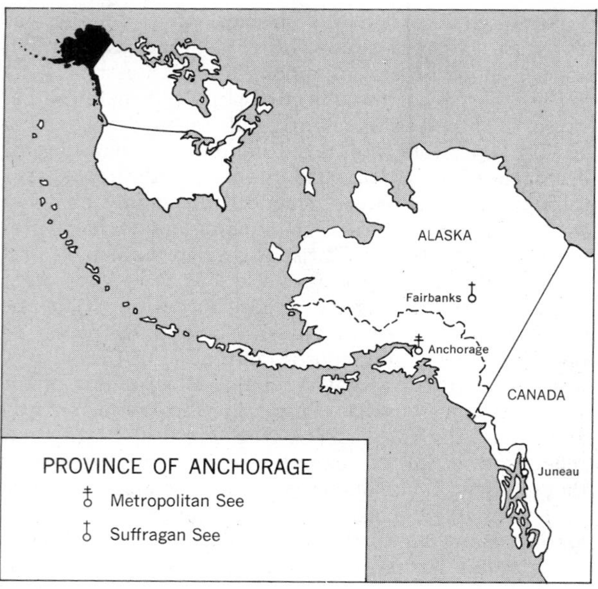

Province of Anchorage, comprising the Archdiocese of Anchorage, called the metropolitan see, and two dioceses known as suffragan sees. The archbishop has metropolitan jurisdiction over the province.

17,000 were Catholics; there were 21 priests and 30 sisters for 8 parishes, 6 missions, and 7 stations. A high school at Anchorage was staffed by the Sisters of Providence, and one at Glenallen by the Sisters of St. Ann. There were two general hospitals under Catholic auspices.

[M. P. CARTHY]

ANCHORITES, persons who have retired into solitude to live the religious life. The term is derived through the Latin and French from the Greek ἀναχωρητής, from ἀναχωρεῖν (to withdraw, to retire). In practice the Latin words *anachorita* and *eremita* have been used synonymously, and the same holds for the modern language derivatives of these two words. If a slight nuance of distinction is discernible, however, it is that *hermit refers to one who has retired into a place far from human habitation, whereas anchorite refers to one living in a cell adjacent to a community. In both East and West, this latter kind of solitary has been more numerous than the former kind. With the Justinian reforms of the 6th century, the Eastern solitaries were gathered in to dwell near a community, although other and more dramatic forms of eremitical life continued to exist by way of exception. In the Eastern Orthodox Church today, all anchorites live adjacent to a community and in some way are dependent upon it, although a few noncanonical hermits continue to exist. In the West, the medieval anchors and anchoresses, solitaries who lived usually in cells built against the walls of churches, have ceased to exist; but the anchoritic life has been preserved by congregations such as the Carthusians and the Camaldolese.

Bibliography: C. LIALINE, DictSpirAscMyst 4.1:936–953. P. DOYÈRE, *ibid.* 953–982. R. M. CLAY, *The Hermits and Anchorites of England* (London 1914).

[A. DONAHUE]

ANCONA AND NUMANA, ARCHDIOCESE OF (ANCONITANUS ET NUMANENSIS),

archbishopric without suffragans, immediately subject to the Holy See, since 1904; in the Marches, on the Adriatic, central Italy. In 1965 it had 80 secular and 106 religious priests, 152 men in 12 religious houses, 270 women in 30 convents, and 135,000 Catholics; it is 79 square miles in area. The city of Ancona, one of the best ports in Italy, was founded by Greeks from *Syracuse (*c.* 390 B.C.) and became a Roman naval base and port for Dalmatia. It was the chief city of the Pentapolis, taken from Byzantium by the Lombards and given to the *States of the Church by Charlemagne (774). Saracens destroyed it (848), but it was rebuilt under the popes (876) and, although in competition with Venice, flourished until the 16th century. It was part of the States of the Church from 1532 to 1860, except from 1797 to 1815.

The first cathedral was dedicated to St. Stephen, probably in the 4th century. The present cathedral is dedicated to St. Cyriacus, the first reputed bishop, who is obscurely known. Gregory the Great recounts a miracle of Bishop Marcellinus (*c.* 550). Bishop Leopardus (861–878) was an envoy of Adrian II to the Bulgars, and Bishop Paul performed missions for John VIII to Germany (873) and to Constantinople (878), where he sided with *Photius. Under the popes Ancona flourished as a semiautonomous maritime republic, and it was long a center of Italian Jews. The diocese formerly had its own rite. In 1422 Ancona was united with the 5th-century See of Numana.

Ancona natives were St. Benvenuto Scotivoli (d. 1282), Franciscan bishop of Osimo; Bl. Gabriel Antonio Ferretti (d. 1456), a Franciscan preacher; Bl. Antonio Fatati (d. 1484), bishop; and the hermit Girolamo Ginelli (d. 1506). The Byzantine-Romanesque basilica of S. Ciriaco (11th–12th century) became a minor basilica in 1926. Early mosaics and frescoes were found beneath the Romanesque S. Maria della Piazza.

Bibliography: M. NATALUCCI, *Ancona attraverso i secoli,* 3 v. (Città di Castello 1960). E. RICCI et al., EncIt 1:151–159. S. PRETE, EncCatt 1:1172–73. AnnPont (1965) 30. **Illustration credit:** Alinari-Art Reference Bureau.

[R. BROWN]

The Byzantine-Romanesque basilica of St. Cyriacus, Ancona, The Marches, Italy.

ANCRENE RIWLE

A medieval code of rules for the life of anchoresses or recluses. The *Ancrene Riwle,* or *Ancrene Wisse,* was written specifically for three sisters (not nuns) who had retired to a life of prayer and penance. Seven copies of the text are extant in English. The best known is the British Museum Cotton MS Nero A.xiv, which furnished the basis of James Morton's original edition for the Camden Society in 1853. Two French versions, several Latin versions, and some adaptations of material taken from the Rule show the popularity of this much-read classic of Middle English prose. The Early English Text Society is well on its way toward offering reliable texts of all MSS of the Rule, along with critical apparatus. Once these editions are available a full investigation of the relationships between the MSS can be begun, and a solution of problems connected with the Rule may be possible. Date, authorship, place of composition, and names of the women for whom the Rule was written are unknown. The general approach to these questions, particularly that of date, is being made through a study of the theological background of the work. Scholars agree generally that the original text (probably not extant) existed in English not long after 1200.

The *Ancrene Riwle* contains interesting details of domestic arrangements and the daily horarium of medieval recluses. Commonly an anchoress lived alone, but the three sisters addressed here lived within a single enclosure in separate cells. Each had a window looking into the sanctuary of the adjoining church so that she could see the Blessed Sacrament exposed over the altar. The parlor window, through which she spoke to visitors, was to be heavily draped. The author warns his spiritual charges against possible abuses from outside their cloister. Daily life consisted of prayer (chiefly oral), spiritual reading, and plain sewing. The two meals permitted were to be eaten in silence. Each anchoress had a "maiden" to look after her material needs. She was responsible for instructing her servant in religion and general behavior.

The *Ancrene Riwle* is divided into eight parts: Divine Service, Keeping the Heart, Moral Lessons and Examples, Temptation, Confession, Penance, Love, and Domestic Matters. The first and last parts form the "outer rule"; and the other parts, the "inner rule."

The style and tone show that the author had rather wide scholarly interests. He refers to the Bible, Lives of the Fathers, Cassian, Gregory the Great, works of Anselm and Bernard; he quotes Ovid and Seneca; he appears to know Geoffrey of Monmouth's *History.* He seems, moreover, from the practical, moral aim of the work, to have been kindly and devout. His prose is easy, lively, and concrete, with imagery suggestive of the world of feudalism. He stresses the inner life that the outer rule is to foster. The *Ancrene Riwle* throws light on the religious aspirations of late 12th-century England, and reflects indirectly much secular life of the time.

The *Ancrene Riwle* is one of six prose treatises in the Katherine Group, so-called from a work in the group, *Lifode of Seint Katheryn.* The Katherine Group is evidence that after the Conquest a "school" of Middle English prose writing continued the Old English

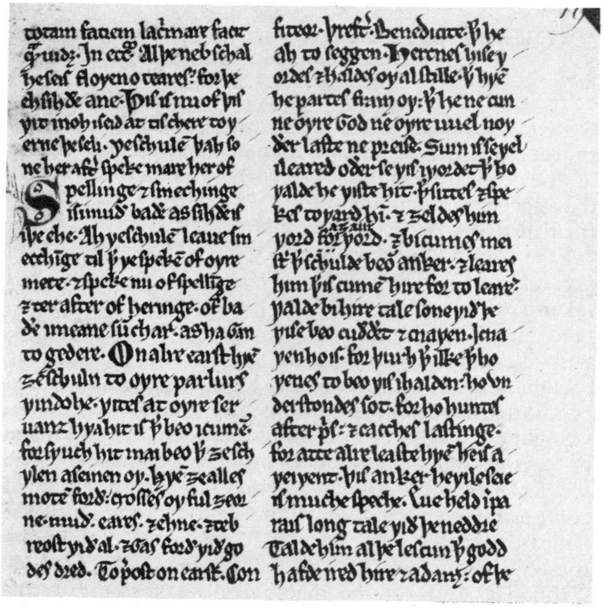

Folio from a medieval copy of the "Ancrene Riwle," originally written in England in the first half of the 13th century (Cotton MS Titus D. xviii).

homiletic prose tradition. The works in the Katherine Group are in the same dialect and are somewhat uniform in style. The *Ancrene Riwle* is the outstanding member of the group.

Bibliography: *Ancrene Wisse: Parts 6 and 7,* ed. G. Shepherd (London 1959–60). J. E. Wells, ed., *Manual of the Writings in Middle English,* and supplements 1–8 (New Haven 1916–41). F. W. Bateson, ed., *Cambridge Bibliography of English Literature,* 5 v. (Cambridge, Eng. 1940–57). Modern Humanities Research Association, *Annual Bibliography of English Language and Literature* (Cambridge, Eng. 1921–), see v. for 1938. **Illustration credit:** Courtesy of the Trustees of the British Museum.

[M. M. BARRY]

ANCYRA, two ancient cities of Asia Minor, important for early Church history.

Ancyra in Galatia is the modern city of Ankara, Turkey. St. Paul visited Galatia twice, in 51 or 52 (Acts 15.30–18.1) and 54 or 55 (Acts 18.23) and addressed an Epistle to the *Galatians from Corinth in 57. Crescens, its first known bishop, founded the church of *Vienne in Gaul. Ancyra had a number of early martyrs, including Theodotus, the brothers Plato and Antiochus, and Clement, to whom a 6th-century church with cupola was dedicated. Its temple of Augustus was converted into a Christian church, and the city served as a monastic center (Palladius, *Hist. Laus.* 66–68). It was early troubled by heretical movements, as St. Paul testifies (Epistle to the Galatians), and *Montanism and other sects spread from there (Council of Constantinople I, c.7; In Trullo, c.95). Synods were conducted in 273 and 277. The acts of the synod in 314 deal mainly with apostates, or *lapsi,* and moral discipline (Mansi 2:513–540); that of 358, called by George of Iconium and presided over by *Basil of Ancyra, adopted the homoiousian formula against the Anomeans, avoiding the *homoousios for fear that it favored *Sabellianism, while the semi-Arians opposed the formula "similar in all things" (Mansi 3:265–290). The synod of 375 deposed the Catholic Bp. Hypsis of Parnassus and attempted to arrest *Gregory of Nyssa. As a metropolitan see of Constantinople, Ancyra in the 7th century had seven or eight suffragans and was considered fourth in rank. It lost importance after the Arab invasions, and its Greek population became Turkish-speaking. It was colonized by the Armenians in the 13th century. In the 19th century Pius IX created a bishopric for the Armenians, who had been united to Rome since 1735. The massacre of the Armenians in 1917 and the treaty of Lausanne following the Greco-Turkish war in 1923 put an end to Christianity in the region.

Ancyra in Phrygia (known also as *Ancyra ferrea* or Ancyra of Synaos), originally in the province of Lydia, formed part of Laodicea in the 6th century and *c.* 900 was suffragan of Hierapolis. Florentius, its first known bishop, participated in the Council of Nicaea I (325). Philip of Ancyra was at Chalcedon (451); Cyricus, at Constantinople III (680–681) and in Trullo (692); Constans, at Nicaea III (787); and Michael, at the Photian Council of Constantinople (879). Ancyra had two Latin bishops in the 15th century: Francis (d. 1434) and Gonsalvus of Curiola. Its ruins were discovered by Hamilton near the modern village of Klisse-Keuï not far from Synaos (modern Simaoul); they include a theater and temple.

Bibliography: K. Gross, LexThK² 1:568. C. Karalevsky, DHGE 2:1538–43. M. Jugie, EncCatt 1:1169–71. Hefele-Leclercq 1.1:298–326; 1.2:903–908. P. Joannou, *Discipline générale antique (IIe–IXe s.)* (Fonti CICO; 1962–) 1.2:54–73. H. Grotz, *Die Hauptkirchen des Ostens* (OrChrAnal 169; 1964) 126–133, 158–159. G. de Vries, *Cattolicismo e problemi religiosi nel prossimo oriente* (Rome 1944) 131–138. L. Robert, *Hellenica* 9 (1950) 67–77. S. Vailhé, DHGE 2:1546–48. Le Quien 1:799–802. T. Wiegand, "Reisen in Mysien" *Mitteilungen des kaiserlichen deutschen archaeologischen Instituts: Athenische Abteilung* 24 (1904) 311–339. For Ancyra, Armenian Catholic bishopric, see F. Tournebize, DHGE 2:1543–46, and *see* ARMENIA.

[P. JOANNOU]

ANDECHS, ABBEY OF, former Benedictine abbey in the Diocese of *Augsburg, Bavaria, south Germany. It was founded by Duke Albrecht III of Bavaria (1455–56) during the reform of his friend *Nicholas of Cusa and dedicated to St. Nicholas; monks from *Tegernsee settled it. Originally Andechs was a castle of the powerful Counts of Diessen-Wolfratshausen (of Andechs after 1130), who had extensive holdings in Bavaria, Main-Franconia, the Tyrol, Istria, and Burgundy, and who produced many saints and bishops before becoming extinct in 1248. The relics the counts had collected in the Holy Land and Italy were kept in a chapel, cared for by Benedictines, which in 1248 came under the bishop of Augsburg. Chapel and relics survived the destruction of the castle (1248), and the relics, after discovery, were exhibited (1388). Many illustrious monks lived in Andechs before it was suppressed (1803); as a rule, there were 25 to 30 monks (1750–1802). In 1846 Louis I of Bavaria gave Andechs to the newly founded St. Boniface Abbey in Munich, to which it still belongs. The 15th-century Gothic hall church has furnishings of 1755. Among the famous relics, a host consecrated by Pope Gregory I (d. 604) attracts many pilgrims.

Bibliography: Cottineau 1:94–95. A. Bayol, DHGE 2:1552–56. R. Bauerreiss, LexThK² 1:505–506. Kapsner BenBibl 2:185–186.

[W. FINK]

ANDERSEN, HANS CHRISTIAN

Novelist, poet, playwright, author of fairy tales; b. Odense on Funen, Denmark, April 2, 1805; d. Copenhagen, Aug. 4, 1875. His father was a poor shoemaker who could provide for his son only the education usual for children in that milieu. This included elementary instruction in the Lutheran faith of the Danish State Church, to which Andersen belonged all his life. His writings show that throughout his life he remained faithful to these religious views, at a time when the rationalism of the Enlightenment was all-pervasive. In 1819 he left for Copenhagen, in the hope of becoming an actor, and received some education in the schools of singing and dancing of the Royal Theatre. His apprentice years in the theatrical world ended without success in 1822. These apparently fruitless years, however, helped shape his career, and he always considered them steppingstones toward the fame he craved. Benefactors in Copenhagen put him through secondary school (1822–28), and in 1829 he published the first of his books to win attention, a tale called *A Journey on Foot from Holmen's Canal to the East Point of Amager.*

Andersen's fame rests almost exclusively on his fairy tales, but early in his career he regarded himself as a playwright and novelist. Most of his plays were unimportant, though a few—*Mulatten* (1840, The Mulatto), and *Ole Lukøje* (1850, The Sandman)—were quite successful. His first novel *Improvisatoren* (1835, The Improvisators), like many of his works, contains autobiographical elements. Andersen traveled widely and wrote a number of charming travel books, such as *En Digters Bazar* (1842, A Poet's Bazaar). His obsession to win fame sometimes led him to identify himself with his own "ugly duckling," much to the embarrassment of his benefactors and wellwishers. Posterity, however, has recognized Andersen, if not as the greatest of all Danish writers, at least as the one most widely known. His tales (*Eventyr*), the first of which appeared in 1835, have been widely translated and are classics in their genre. Better, perhaps, they are a genre of their own with inspirations borrowed from folk tales, *kindermärchen,* exempla, fables, allegories, and myths, all fused by his genius as a story teller. The best known of them are probably *Fyrtøjet* (The Tinder-Box), *Den grimme Ælling* (The Ugly Duckling), *Den standhaftige Tinsoldat* (The Steadfast Tin Soldier), *Prinsessen paa Ærten* (The Princess on the Pea). Though his stories are often considered to be only for children, Andersen deliberately put into most of them a double meaning which only the adult reader can perceive, and a few of his tales like *Klokken* (The Bell), and *Skyggen* (The Shadow) were not for children.

See also CHILDREN'S LITERATURE.

Hans Christian Andersen, memorial statue in Central Park, New York City.

Bibliography: H. C. ANDERSEN, *Eventyr og Historier,* ed. S. LARSEN, 16 v. in 8 (Copenhagen 1943–45); *Romaner og Rejseskildringer,* ed. H. G. TOPSØE-JENSEN, 7 v. (Copenhagen 1943–44). S. DAHL and H. G. TOPSØE-JENSEN, eds., *A Book on the Danish Writer, H. C. Andersen,* tr. W. G. JONES (Copenhagen 1955). B. F. NIELSEN, *H. C. Andersen Bibliografi: Digterens danske Værker 1822–1875* (Copenhagen 1942). C. S. PETERSEN and V. ANDERSEN, *Illustreret dansk litteraturhistorie,* 4 v. (Copenhagen 1924–34) v.3, 4. H. G. TOPSØE-JENSEN, "H. C. Andersens Religion," *Anderseniana* 5.2 (1963) 155–174. **Illustration credit:** By Courtesy of New York City Park Department.

[H. BEKKER-NIELSEN]

ANDERSON, HENRY JAMES, mathematician and astronomer; b. New York, N.Y., Feb. 6, 1799; d. Lahore, India, Oct. 19, 1875. Little is known of his family except that it was of comfortable means. After education privately, he attended Columbia College (University), New York City (1814–18), and then the College of Physcians and Surgeons, graduating with a medical degree in 1823. His talent for mathematics attracted the attention of Dr. Robert Adrian, professor of mathematics and astronomy at Columbia, who recommended Anderson as his replacement when he retired in 1825. Anderson retained the post until 1843 when he resigned to take his ailing wife abroad. After her death, he remained abroad and joined a U.S. government expedition to the Holy Land. His report on its findings, *Geological Reconnaissance of Part of the Holy Land,* was published by the government (1848). While abroad, he became a Roman Catholic. After his return to the U.S., he actively promoted Catholicism, serving in many lay posts, including that of president of the Society of St. Vincent de Paul. In 1851 he was elected trustee of Columbia. Throughout his life he retained his interest in astronomy and in 1874 journeyed to Australia with a scientific expedition to conduct observations of Venus in transit. A year later he went to explore the Himalayas and died while in India.

Bibliography: Columbia University, The Columbiana Collection.

[J. P. SHENTON]

ANDERSON, LARS (LAURENTIUS ANDREAE), founder of a national Protestant ecclesiastical polity in Sweden; b. Strängnäs, *c.* 1480; d. there, April 29, 1552. He studied at Rostock, Leipzig, and Greifswald and made several trips to Rome. A canon of Strängnäs, he became the secretary of Bishop Mathias, received the title of apostolic notary, and finally became head of the cathedral chapter in Strängnäs. He was converted to Lutheran views under the influence of the deacon Olaus *Petri. Anderson, a talented administrator, became King Gustavus Vasa's chancellor in 1523 and aided Olaus and Laurentius Petri in their reforming endeavors, working for a break with Rome and for a Swedish national church, and fully establishing the Reformation at the Council of Oerebro in 1529. In 1540 he opposed Vasa's effort to transform the Swedish church in the direction of Presbyterianism; he was sentenced to death, was pardoned, and lived out his days in retirement. He wrote one theological treatise on *Faith and Good Works*.

Bibliography: H. Holmquist, *Die Schwedische Reformation 1523–1531* (Leipzig 1925) 24–27, 32 and *passim*. H. Sandberg, *Kring Konflikten mellan Gustav Vasa och reformatorerna,* (Uppsala 1941) 127–146. P. B. Watson, *The Swedish Revolution under Gustavus Vasa* (Boston 1889). J. Wordsworth, *The National Church of Sweden* (Milwaukee 1911).

[L. W. SPITZ]

ANDERSON, MARY ANTOINETTE, American actress; b. Sacramento, Calif., July 28, 1859; d. London, England, May 29, 1940. She attended the Academy of the Presentation in Louisville, Ky., until she saw a performance by Edwin Booth in *Richelieu,* whereupon she determined to educate herself for a stage career. She was encouraged in this by the great American actress Charlotte Cushman. On Nov. 27, 1875, she appeared professionally for the first time at the Macauley Theater in Louisville as Juliet, and made her New York debut 2 years later as Pauline in *The Lady of Lyons* at the Fifth Avenue Theater. During the next 12 years she became one of the leading actresses of the American and English stage. She was noted for her portrayals of Parthenia in *Ingomar,* Galatea in W. S. Gilbert's *Pygmalion and Galatea,* Julia in *The Hunchback,* Meg Merrilies in *Guy Mannering*—all typical heroines of the drama of the day. She played the parts of many Shakespearean heroines, notably Juliet, and undertook a double role in *The Winter's Tale* as Hermione and Perdita. In 1889, at the height of her fame, she retired from the theater, married Antonio de Navarro, and went to England to live. She returned to the stage during World War I for a few benefit performances. Her writings include *A Few Memories* (1896) and *A Few More Memories* (1936).

[J. MC G. CALLAN]

ANDERTON, ROGER AND LAWRENCE, 17th-century English Catholic writers and controversialists.

Roger, son of Christopher Anderton of Lostock and cousin of Lawrence; b. place and date unknown; d. 1640?. Roger came into possession of Birchley Hall near Preston, *c.* 1615, and was probably the patron of the Catholic secret press in Lancashire, later called the Birchley Hall press. It operated from 1615 to 1621, when it was discovered and seized by the government. Several of the books printed at this press were issued under the pseudonym "John Brereley, Priest," who has sometimes been identified with Lawrence Anderton, though the evidence is far from conclusive.

Lawrence, Jesuit controversialist; b. County of Lancashire, England, *c.* 1575–76; d. there, April 17, 1643. He was the son of Thomas Anderton of Chorely, Lancashire, and was educated at Blackburn Grammar School and Christ's College, Cambridge, where he earned a reputation for intellectual brilliance and received his B.A. in 1596 or 1597. Anderton went abroad, probably on becoming a Catholic, and apparently returned to England in 1602 as a priest. He joined the Society of Jesus in 1604. Anderton spent much of his missionary life in his native Lancashire and was superior of the Lancashire district for several years after 1621. He labored principally in London and the South *c.* 1627 to 1642. He wrote several notable works of controversy against the English Protestants.

Bibliography: T. Cooper, DNB 1:396–397. DictEngCath 1:34–38, 39–41. A. F. Allison and D. M. Rogers, *A Catalogue of Catholic Books in English . . . 1558–1640,* 2 v. (London 1956).

[A. F. ALLISON]

ANDÍA Y VARELA, IGNACIO, Chilean priest and artist; b. Santiago, Feb. 2, 1757; d. there, Aug. 13, 1822. In 1784 he entered the colonial administration; he held the posts of Secretario de la Capitanía General and Administrador de Correos y Tabacos. His skill in penmanship and his wide technical knowledge were constantly in demand. He accompanied Governor O'Higgins (1788) on his inspection tours of the country. His experiences resulted in a valuable map of Chile and drawings of the meeting with the Indians at Lonquilmo. Overwhelmed by responsibility for 18 children and by official lack of understanding, he sought other employment. In 1803 he was commissioned to do the monumental Escudo de España, which was to have adorned the Palacio de la Moneda built by his brother-in-law, the Italian architect Joaquin Toesca, and which decorates the entrance of the Cerro Santa Lucía. The plans for the Casa de Fundición and the Túmulo Funebre of Carlos III, considered a masterwork, were his. Unfortunately most of his works, including the Primer Escudo Nacional (1813), with its curious symbolism, have been lost. The artistic copy of the MS *La Venida del Mesías en Gloria y Majestad* by the Jesuit theologian Manuel Lacunza, prefaced by an excellent pen portrait, remains as proof of his talent. At the age of 62 he achieved his desire of entering the Church. Later he was a priest in San Felipe, where the so-called Gallery of the Monk, from which he made botanical and geological excursions, is still preserved. His last work was the construction of the Casa de Ejercicios de San José.

Bibliography: E. Pereira Salas, *Historia del arte en el Reyno de Chile* (Buenos Aires 1964). Toledo Museum of Art, *Chilean Contemporary Art* (Toledo, Spain 1942).

[E. PEREIRA SALAS]

ANDORRA

A principality of 179 square miles in the east Pyrenees, bordered by the Spanish provinces of Lérida and Gerona and by the French departments of Ariège and Pyrénées Orientales. The population of 11,500 (1964) is entirely Catholic. The 55 scattered churches and chapels testify to the regular religious practice of the majority of the inhabitants. Catholicism is the official religion; no other recognized or organized confession exists. Governmental power lies in a General Council of 24 members elected by males of 25 years and over. From time immemorial Andorra has been divided into six communes or parishes named in the acts of consecration of the cathedral of Seo de Urgel (839): Andorra la Valla (the capital), Canillo, Encamp, La Massana, Ordino, and Sant Julià.

Part of the Roman Empire and of the Visigothic kingdom, Andorra, like the rest of the Pyrenees, was little affected by the Arab invasion. With the creation

Andorra (a) Churches of Santa Coloma (10th century, restored in the 12th) and (b) St. Cerni de Nagol (11th–12th century).

of the Spanish March it came under Carolingians as part of the county of Urgel. Bishops of Urgel from the 9th century gained feudal lands and rights in Andorra, where they established, with the consent of the counts of Urgel, an ecclesiastical domain. From the 11th century it was a fief of the Caboet family, which transmitted it by marriages to the Castellbó and then to the Foix family (1208). Henry of Navarre, Count of Foix and Viscount of Bearn, brought his rights to the crown of France when he became king in 1589. The present indivisible condominion over Andorra exercised by the French president and the Spanish Bishop of Urgel is based on the agreement (*Pareatges*) of Bp. Pedro de Urg of Urgel and Count Roger Bernard III of Foix (1278, 1288) after long and bitter dispute.

The isolated location high in the Pyrenees has allowed Andorra to keep its political constitution and traditional institutions from the Middle Ages, notwithstanding recent economic progress resulting from immigration and tourism. Its laws and customs are codified in the *Manual Digest* (1748) of A. Fiter Rosell and the *Politar* (1763) of A. Puig, both written in Catalan, the official language. Andorra has long been part of the Diocese of Urgel, whose bishops hold spiritual and administrative authority. An archpriest in the capital is one of 10 priests in the country. There are two schools under Holy Family sisters. Spaniards and French, paid by their governments, care for preuniversity education; students then go to Spain or France for higher studies. Andorra has no higher school of religious studies nor charitable and social work apart from parochial institutions.

There are pre-Romanesque (9th–11th century) and Romanesque (11th–12th century) churches of archeological interest; most of the murals have disappeared or are in museums and private collections. Our Lady of Meritxell, proclaimed principal patroness of Andorra in 1873, has a shrine with a 12th-century Romanesque image, probably the oldest from the Pyrenees.

Bibliography: C. Baudon de Mony, *Relations politiques des comtes de Foix avec la Catalogne jusq'au commencement du XIVe siècle,* 2 v. (Paris 1896). J. A. Brutails, *La Coutume d'Andorre* (Paris 1904). F. Pallerola y Gabriel, *El Principado de Andorra y su constitución política* (Lérida 1912). P. Pujol, "L'acta de consagració i dotació de la catedral d'Urgell," *Estudis romànics* 2 (1917) 1–28. F. Valls Taberner, *Privilegis i ordinacions de les valls pirinenques,* v. 3, *Vall d'Andorra* (Barcelona 1920). J. M. Vidal, *Instituciones políticas y sociales de Andorra* (Madrid 1949). J. M. Font i Rius, "Els origens del co-senyoriu andorrà," *Pirineos* 11 (1955) 77–108. J. M. Guilera, *Una història d'Andorra* (Barcelona 1960). J. Capeille, DHGE 2:1585–87. *Bilan du Monde* 2:70.

[C. BARAUT]

ANDRADA E SILVA, JOSÉ BONIFÁCIO DE

Brazilian savant and patriarch of the independence of Brazil; b. Santos, São Paulo, June 13, 1763; d. Niterói, Rio de Janeiro, April 6, 1838. Like his older brother, he planned to follow an ecclesiastical career. He changed from his original intention, matriculated at Coimbra in 1783, and received his bachelor of law and philosophy in 1787. In Lisbon, 2 years later, he was admitted to the Academia Real de Ciencias, and there he published his first scientific work, *Memória sôbre a pesca das baleias,* in 1790. After extensive travel in Europe, he returned to Portugal in 1800. There he was appointed (1801) to hold the chair of metallurgy created especially for him at the University of Coimbra. He held also a number of government positions. The numerous scientific articles he wrote were well accepted by various European learned societies, to many of which he belonged as a regular or honorary member.

In 1819 he returned to Brazil. In 1821, having been chosen parochial elector of Santos, he was made vice president of the junta of the Province of São Paulo, thus initiating a brief but extraordinary political career. He went to Rio de Janerio at the beginning of 1822 to support the stay in Brazil of Pedro, the prince-regent, whose return to Portugal was sought by the Côrtes. Pedro appointed him minister of the kingdom and of foreign affairs, the first Brazilian to hold those offices. As the principal figure in the government, with profound influence on the prince, he contributed decisively to the separation of Brazil from Portugal, becoming the patriarch of independence, which was proclaimed on Sept. 7, 1822.

After the acclamation of the prince-regent as Emperor Pedro I on October 12, José Bonifácio became minister of the empire and of foreign affairs. As actual leader of the government, he gave abundant proof of his qualities as administrator and statesman. Among the Brazilian problems that preoccupied him were those of the enslavement and civilization of the Indians, about which he wrote a *Representação* for the Constituent Assembly and *Apontamentos,* both later published. Because of his many political adversaries, he left the government in July 1823. With his brothers Antônio Carlos and Martim Francisco he went over to the opposition through the newspaper *O Tamoio,* which they directed. The Andradas were arrested and deported to Europe in November 1823. José Bonifácio remained in France until 1829, when he returned to Brazil, where, without taking up political activities, he went to live on the island of Paquetá in Guanabara Bay.

In April 1831, when Pedro I abdicated the throne of Brazil, he appointed José Bonifácio tutor of his son Pedro II and of the latter's three sisters, whom he left in Rio de Janeiro on his return to Europe. Although the appointment was approved by the General Assembly, the Minister of Justice, Diogo Antônio *Feijó, tried to

José Bonifácio de Andrada e Silva.

dismiss Andrada in 1832 on the pretext that he had been part of an uprising promoted by those in favor of the return of Pedro to Brazil. Feijó did not succeed at that time, but the dismissal was accomplished by force in December 1833.

Bibliography: O. T. DE SOUSA, *José Bonifácio, 1763–1838* (Rio de Janeiro 1945); *José Bonifácio,* v.1 of *História dos fundadores do Império do Brasil,* 10 v. (Rio de Janeiro 1957–58); ed., *O pensamento vivo de José Bonifácio* (São Paulo 1961); *Obras científicas, políticas e sociais de José Bonifácio de Andrada e Silva,* 3 v. (Santos 1965).

[H. VIANNA]

ANDRADE, ANTONIO DE, Portuguese missionary; b. Oleiros, Portugal, 1580; d. Goa, India, March 19, 1634. He entered the Society of Jesus in 1596, went to India in 1600, and became rector of the colleges at Goa, and in 1621 superior of the Mogul mission at Agra. Lured by reports of Christian communities to the north, he became the first European to cross the Himalayas into Tibet in 1624, and in 1625, with six other Jesuits, five Portuguese and one French, he established a mission at Tsaparang, on the Sutlej River. The accounts of his two trips were quickly translated into several European languages. In 1629 he returned to Goa as provincial superior. The Tsaparang mission was destroyed in 1631 during a revolt inspired by hostile lamas; the Christian community had numbered about 400. Andrade was preparing to return to Tibet when he died, probably from poison.

Bibliography: C. WESSELS, *Early Jesuit Travelers in Central Asia* (The Hague 1924) 43–91. ArchHistSocJesu, Index generalis (1953) 299. E. LAMALLE, EncCatt 1:1182.

[M. B. MARTIN]

ANDRADE Y PASTOR, MANUEL, surgeon who introduced the Sisters of Charity of St. Vincent de Paul into hospital work in Mexico; b. Mexico City, 1809; d. there, 1848. After graduating from the College of Surgery in 1831, he spent some years in the Hôtel-Dieu in Paris working in Dupuytren's clinic. On his return he published two extensive reports on medical organization in France and later, a biography of Dupuytren. From 1838 on he was professor of surgery in the Establecimiento de Ciencias Médicas, and later he also taught anatomy. He was named director of the College of Surgery the same year. In Paris he had been impressed with the efficiency and abnegation of the Sisters of Charity, and he worked to have them brought to Mexico. He published a long report on their work in hospitals and the rules of the order. With the aid of the Countess de la Cortina, permission was obtained on Oct. 9, 1843, to bring a group to Mexico. Andrade and the Countess paid for the journey of 11 sisters who arrived in Mexico City Nov. 15, 1844. When Mexico was invaded in 1847, the Surgeon General of the U.S. warmly praised Andrade for his work as director of the Hospital de Jesús. While working in the hospital during the campaign, Andrade was struck in the face by a bullet and shortly thereafter he died of a "malignant fever." He kept up an active scholarly life and founded the Mexican Academy of Medicine in 1836, serving as its secretary in 1837 and vice president in 1840. At its meetings he presented a number of papers, some quite outstanding. All his writings have appeared in the *Periódico* of the Academy. Andrade's most famous pupil was Miguel Jiménez, the celebrated and skilled Mexican physician of the 19th century.

[G. SOMOLINOS]

ANDRÉ, BERNARD (ANDREAS), 15th-century *Augustinian poet and historiographer; b. Toulouse, France, *c.* 1450; d. London, England, after 1521. Although he was a doctor of civil and canon law, his fame was that of a poet and humanist. He went to England, perhaps *c.* 1485, and came under the patronage of Richard *Foxe, later bishop of Winchester. It was probably Foxe who introduced André to the court, where *Henry VII appointed him poet laureate and royal historiographer. André directed the education of Arthur, Prince of Wales, and possibly also that of the future *Henry VIII. He wrote a life of Henry VII, begun in 1500 but never fully completed (ed. J. Gairdner, London 1858). Most of his writings are in Latin, although he has left a few French poems. His work, most of which is unedited, has value chiefly as a source of contemporary information, for its literary value is disputed. In official records André is frequently referred to as "the blind poet."

Bibliography: J. GAIRDNER, DNB 1:398–399. F. ROTH, *History of English Austin Friars 1249–1538,* 2 v. (New York 1961), v.2 *Sources.* A. PALMIERI, DHGE 2:1722–23.

[A. J. ENNIS]

ANDREAS CAPELLANUS, author of the treatise *De amore;* lived in France in the 12th century. Andreas is known only from his own work, written about 1186, in which he refers to himself indirectly as chaplain of the royal court. Manuscript rubrics call him chaplain of the King of France. Some critics identify him with André, chaplain of Countess Marie of Champagne from 1182 to 1186, but nothing of his life is firmly established. The *De amore,* also called *De arte honesti amandi,* is a long Latin prose treatise in three books on love as passion. The first two books are in appearance a manual of seduction; the first contains eight sample dialogues between men and women of different ranks, and the second includes 31 Rules of Love and the amatory judgments of various noble ladies. The third book apparently reverses the first two; it contains traditional antifeminist arguments on why love should be avoided. Modern critics are divided on the interpretation of the work. Some see it as a serious exposition of *courtly love, others as a humorous description of actual practices, and still others as a condemnation of concupiscence, humorous and ironic at the beginning, straightforward at the end.

Bibliography: *Andreae Capellani regii Francorum de amore libri tres,* ed. E. TROJEL (Copenhagen 1892); tr. by J. J. PARRY as *The Art of Courtly Love by Andreas Capellanus* (New York 1941). F. SCHLÖSSER, *Andreas Capellanus* (2d ed. Bonn 1962). J. F. BENTON, "The Court of Champagne as a Literary Center," *Speculum* 36 (1961) 551–591. D. W. ROBERTSON, *A Preface to Chaucer* (Princeton 1962) 391–448.

[J. F. BENTON]

ANDRELINI, PUBLIO FAUSTO, Renaissance humanist and poet; b. Forlì, Italy, 1461; d. Paris, Feb. 25, 1518. Andrelini was crowned poet laureate at Rome, April 20, 1483, and in 1488 he established himself in Paris. Rivalry marked by acrimonious literary exchanges arose between him and a fellow Italian, Girolamo *Balbi, who ultimately was forced to leave Paris. In 1489 Andrelini was authorized to teach literature at the University of Paris and later he obtained a canonry in Bayeux. As court poet from 1492, he composed many occasional poems; e.g., on the death of Charles VIII, on the captivity of Ludovico *Sforza, on Louis XII's victory over the Venetians, and a panegyric on Queen Anne of Brittany. Andrelini has been described as the characteristic humanist—presumptuous and mediocre. Though admired highly by his contemporaries, his poetry lacks originality and is often obscene. A man of vulgar spirit, he gave to humanism a gross and unchristian direction.

Bibliography: G. C. KNOD, *Aus der Bibliothek des Beatus Rhenanus* (Leipzig 1889). P. S. ALLEN, "Hieronymus Balbus in Paris," EngHistRev 17 (1902) 417–428. L. DELARUELLE, *Études sur l'humanisme français: Guillaume Budé . . .* (Paris 1907). A. CLERVAL, DHGE 2:1747–48. E. PICOT, "Les Italiens en France au XVIe siècle," *Bulletin italien* 17 (1917) 61–75. H. STEIN, Dict BiogFranc 2:972–973. W. KOCH, LexThK^{2} 1:521.

[M. G. MC NEIL]

ANDREW, APOSTLE, ST.

Brother of Simon *Peter and, like him, once a fisherman on the Sea of *Galilee. His name in Greek (Ἀνδρέας) means "manly, courageous." Andrew is first mentioned in the Gospel of Mark. Both Mark (1.16–18) and Matthew (4.18–20) relate how Jesus, "passing along by the Sea of Galilee, saw Simon and his brother Andrew casting their nets into the Sea" and called them to follow Him. In the lists of the 12 Apostles, Andrew is always mentioned with the group of the 4 closest to Jesus, although he is separated from his brother in Mark (3.16–18) and Acts (1.13) by *James and *John,

The Apostle St. Andrew, wood carving by Tilman Riemenschneider (c. 1460–1531).

who appear more prominent among the Apostles. Mark mentions Andrew by name in two other episodes: first, when having left the synagogue of Capharnaum, the first four disciples "came to the house of Simon and Andrew" (Mk 1.29), where Peter's mother-in-law was cured by Jesus; second, on the fatal trip to Jerusalem when the same four disciples asked Jesus "sitting on the mount of Olives when the destruction of Jerusalem and the end of the world would take place" (Mk 13.3–4). The fact that Matthew and Luke, in their retelling of both stories (see Mt 8.14 = Lk 4.38; Mt

24.3 = Lk 21.7), independently omit Andrew is significant of the lesser importance of this disciple among the first Christian communities. However, the Fourth Gospel provides more details on Andrew, an old companion of the author. Before their call by Jesus, both Andrew and the Evangelist were disciples of John the Baptist, and they were the first to follow Jesus (Jn 1.35–40). It is Andrew who led his brother Simon to Jesus (Jn 1.40–42). The two brothers were born in Bethsaida, located a few miles north of Carpharnaum (Jn 1.44). In the account of the feeding of the five thousand as given in Jn 6.5–14, the first of the two Marcan accounts of the miracle (Mk 6.32–44) is expanded by a question of Andrew (Jn 6.8–9) that has no precise parallel in the Synoptics. Finally, in the story of the Greeks' coming to Jesus (Jn 12.20–34), Andrew appears as a prominent person. The Greeks "approached Philip," who in turn "came and told Andrew"; and both "spoke to Jesus." No further mention is made of Andrew in the NT. The apocryphal writings, especially *The Acts of the Apostle Andrew,* have preserved some historical details that are difficult to demythologize. According to later traditions, Andrew preached in northern Greece, Epirus, and Scythia, and was crucified at Patras in Greece *c.* 70. His cult, very popular in the Greek Church, spread to Rome in the 5th century, and from there to France and England. He is the patron saint of Russia and Scotland. His feast is celebrated November 30. In iconography, beginning in the 15th century, St. Andrew was commonly represented with an X-shaped cross as the instrument of his martyrdom, although a few examples of this are found as early as the 10th century. This notion of his crucifixion probably arose from a misunderstanding of the legend of his martyrdom.

Bibliography: P. M. PETERSON, *Andrew, Brother of Simon Peter* (NovTest Suppl. 1; 1958). F. DVORNIK, *The Idea of Apostolicity in Byzantium and the Legend of the Apostle Andrew* (Cambridge, Mass. 1958) 138–328. L. VAGANAY, *Catholicisme* 1:522–523. B. MARIANI, EncCatt 1:1183–84. B. KRAFT and H. SCHAUERTE, LexThK² 1:511–513. EncDictBibl 80. B. ZIMMERMAN, DACL 1.2:2031–34. Iconography. Réau IAC 3.1:76–84. Künstle Ikonog 2:58–62. K. RATHE, EncCatt 1:1184. **Illustration credit:** Samuel H. Kress Collection, Atlanta Art Association Galleries, Atlanta, Georgia.

[A. LEGAULT]

ANDREW ABELLON, BL., teacher, reformer, and artist; b. Saint-Maximin-la-Saint-Baume, France, *c.* 1375; d. Aix, France, May 15, 1450 (feast, May 17). He joined the *Dominican Order in his native village and taught philosophy and theology in various Dominican priories until 1408, when he became master of theology. From 1408 to 1419 he devoted himself exclusively to preaching in southern France, but found time to minister to the victims of the plague that broke out at Aix in 1415. While prior of *Saint-Maximin (1419–22 and 1425–29), he restored observance in that house and completed and embellished its buildings. As vicar of observance appointed by Master General Bartholomew Texier (d. 1449), Abellon introduced reform in the priories of Aix, where he was prior from 1438 to 1442, and Marseilles, where he was prior from 1444 to 1448. An artist, he used his talents to teach the eternal truths by paintings. He was beatified in 1902.

Bibliography: H. M. CORMIER, *Le Bienheureux André Abellon* (2d ed. Rome 1902). D. A. MORTIER, *Histoire des maîtres généraux de l'ordre des Frères Prêcheurs,* 8 v. (Paris 1903–20) 4:145, 193–210. G. GIERATHS, LexThK² 1:513.

[A. H. CAMACHO]

ANDREW CACCIOLI, BL., Franciscan, early companion of St. Francis; b. Spello, near Assisi, Italy, 1194; d. Spello, June 3, 1254 (feast, June 3). These dates (ActSS, 1869, June 1:356–362) are to be preferred to those (1181–1264) suggested by *Wadding (Wadding Ann 1256, n. 50 and 1264, n. 11). The name Caccioli is puzzling as it can scarcely have been a family name, for at that time it was not usual to use surnames, especially in the case of *mendicants. In 1223, after the death of his parents and sister, Andrew received the habit at the hands of *Francis of Assisi. He was thus one of his early companions, and we are informed that he was the first priest to join the group (*inter quos fuit primus sacerdos*). He received permission in writing from Francis to win souls for Christ by preaching, and in 1226 he was present at the founder's death. His interpretation of the rule, which he shared with many of the saint's early companions, twice earned for him imprisonment under *Elias of Cortona. On the first occasion he was set free by *Gregory IX on the intercession of *Anthony of Padua and the second time by *John of Parma; thus, there seem to be no grounds for asserting that he died in prison. He was present at the general chapter held at Soria in Spain in 1233. His remains lie under the altar of the chapel dedicated to his honor in the church of Saint Andrew the Apostle in Spello and his cult was confirmed by Pope *Clement XII in 1738.

Bibliography: ActSS June 1:356–362. *Martyrologium Franciscanum,* ed. ARTURUS A MONASTERIO, rev. I. BESCHIN and J. PALAZZOLO (Rome 1939). O. BONMANN, LexThK² 1:514. *Acta Ordinis Fratrum Minorum* 69 (1950) 129. Butler Th Attw 2: 466–467.

[T. C. CROWLEY]

ANDREW DE COMITIBUS, BL., Franciscan brother; b. Anagni, Italy, *c.* 1240; d. convent of San Lorenzo al Piglio, Rome, Feb. 1, 1302 (feast, Feb. 17; in order, Feb. 1). He was a member of the noble family of the Conti (de Comitibus) and a close relative of Popes *Innocent III, *Gregory IX, *Alexander IV, and *Boniface VIII. Pope Boniface wished to create him cardinal, but Andrew's humility and holiness of life led him to refuse the proffered dignity; some chronicles suggest that he was actually created cardinal and renounced the office.

Andrew is said to have been the author of the treatise *De partu Beatae Mariae Virginis,* which has since been lost. Andrew was famous during his lifetime for his many miracles, and Boniface VIII is quoted as saying that, had Andrew died during his reign, he would have canonized him. He was eventually beatified by Innocent XIII in 1724, and his cause is still under consideration. He is buried in the church of San Lorenzo al Piglio.

Bibliography: *Compendium chronicarum Fratrum Minorum scriptum a patre Mariano de Florentia,* ArchFrancHist 2 (1901) 457–472. B. MARINANGELI, "Memorie del convento di S. Lorenzo al Piglio (Roma)," *Miscellanea Francescana* 20 (1919) 148–154. S. PELLEGRINI, *Il beato Andrea Conti, 1250–1302* (Piglio 1959). M. BIHL, DHGE 2:1654–55. W. FORSTER, LexThK² 1:514–515. Mercati-Pelzer DE 1:139.

[T. C. CROWLEY]

ANDREW CORSINI, ST., bishop of Fiesole; b. Florence, Italy, Nov. 30, 1302; d. Fiesole, Italy, Jan. 6, 1373 (feast, Feb. 4). After a misspent childhood he donned the *Carmelite habit *c.* 1317. He was sent to study at the University of Paris in 1329 and was named provincial of his order for Tuscany in 1348. He was most active in this office both during the plague that struck *Florence and later in undertaking an extensive campaign to rebuild the hard-hit religious communities and restore their spiritual fervor and monastic discipline. He was nominated as bishop by the cathedral chapter at Fiesole, and the election was confirmed by *Clement V in a bull of Oct. 13, 1349. Andrew Corsini was an able and wise administrator; he visited the parishes of his diocese, founded confraternities of priests in honor of the Trinity, and provided for restoration and construction of churches. He also mediated quarrels between the families of the Florentine nobility. His cult became popular shortly after his death; and papal approval, several times requested, was finally granted by *Urban VIII on April 22, 1629, and the bull of canonization was promulgated June 4, 1724, by *Benedict XIII. *Alexander VII extended his veneration to the whole Church, although he is especially honored in Florence, where he is buried and where his intercession is credited with the repulse of Filippo Maria *Visconti's attack on Pope *Eugene IV and the fathers of the Council of *Florence in 1440.

Bibliography: ActSS Jan. 2:1061–77. S. MATTEI, *Vita di Santo Andrea Corsini* (Florence 1872). P. CAIOLI, *S. Andrea Corsini carmelitano* (Florence 1929). F. CARAFFA and S. ORIENTI, Bibl Sanct 1:1158–69. Butler Th Attw 1:246–247. P. MARIE-JOSEPH, DHGE 2:1655–59. AnalBoll 48 (1930) 432–434. ANASTASIO DI S. PAOLO, AnalOCarmD 4 (1930) 232–250.

[M. MONACO]

ANDREW OF CRETE, ST., archbishop; b. Damasus, *c.* 660; d. Erissos, July 4, 740 (feast, July 4). A monk in Jerusalem (678), he became a deacon in Constantinople (*c.* 685) and head of a refuge for orphans and the aged. He later became archbishop of Gortyna in Crete (692). At the Monothelite Synod of Constantinople (712), he subscribed to the repudiation of two wills in Christ defined by the Council of *Constantinople III. In 713 he retracted, explaining his doctrine in a metrical confession, and participated in the quarrels over *Iconoclasm. He was remarkable as an orator; 22 of his homilies and panegyrics have been published, while some are still unedited. He furthered the development of the Byzantine Liturgy, inaugurating a type of penitential hymn or Great Canon still in use, and he is respected as one of the principal hymnographers of the Oriental Church.

Bibliography: ANDREW OF CRETE, *Opera Omnia,* PG 97:805–1443. S. VAILHÉ, ÉchosOr 5 (1901–02) 378–387. E. MERCENIER, *A propos d'Andrée de Créte* (Alexandria 1953). Bardenhewer 5:152–157. Altaner 645. H. RAHNER, LexThK² 1:516–517. Beck KTLBR 500–502.

[L. VEREECKE]

ANDREW DOTTI, BL., Servite preacher; b. Sansepolcro, Tuscany, Italy, 1256; d. Vallucola, Italy, Aug. 31, 1315 (feast, Aug. 31). He belonged to the noble Italian family of Dotti, and he received an excellent education. Touched by a sermon of *Philip Benizi, he entered the *Servite Order in 1278 at Florence, where Alexis *Falconieri, one of the seven founders, was superior. His progress in religious virtue was rapid, and after his ordination he was sent to a convent near Sansepolcro, where his zeal manifested itself in preaching, prayer, and penance. He received permission to join a group of hermits at Vallucola, whom he united with the Servites in 1294. Between 1297 and 1310 Andrew preached with extraordinary results throughout Italy. After the death of Alexis Falconieri he returned to the hermitage of Vallucola, where he led a life of charity, mortification, and contemplation. He was buried in a church in his native town. Pope *Pius VII approved his cult on Nov. 29, 1806.

Bibliography: M. POCCIANTI, *Chronicon rerum totius sacri ordinis servorum beatae Mariae virginis* (Florence 1567). C. BATTINI, *Vita del beato Andrea Dotti dei Servi di Maria* (Bologna 1866). P. SOULIER, *Vie de saint Philippe Benizi* (Paris 1886); P. SOULIER et al., eds., *Monumenta servorum sanctae Mariae,* 20 v. (Brussels 1897–1930) v.2. S. M. LEDOUX, *Histoire des sept saints fondateurs* (Paris 1888). T. ORTOLAN, DHGE 2:1663–64. G. M. ROSCHINI, EncCatt 4:1899.

[M. B. MORRIS]

ANDREW OF FIESOLE, ST., archdeacon of Fiesole, Italy; of Scottish or possibly Irish birth; d. *c.* 877 (feast, Aug. 22). He accompanied (St.) Donatus (feast, Oct. 22) to Rome on a pilgrimage. On their return they passed through the town of Fiesole near Florence, where the episcopal see was vacant. The clergy and people were assembled in the cathedral praying for a pious and worthy bishop when they entered. At once, reportedly, the bells began to ring and candles and lights were illumined by superhuman power. Donatus was elected bishop, and he ordained Andrew as his archdeacon. Andrew restored the church of San Martino di Mensola at Fiesole and built a monastery there. In 1284 his relics were found in the church where they are still preserved. His *acta* of the 14th or 15th century are too late to be of any value.

Bibliography: A. M. TOMMASINI, *Irish Saints in Italy,* tr. J. F. SCANLAN (London 1937). ActSS Feb. 1:245–248; Aug. 4:539–548. A. M. ZIMMERMAN, LexThK² 1:515–516. Butler Th Attw 3:382.

[R. T. MEYER]

ANDREW FRANCHI, BL., preacher and bishop; b. 1335, Pistoia, Italy; d. there May 26, 1401 (feast: May 26 in Pistoia, May 30 in Dominican Order). He was born of the noble family of Franchi-Boccagni, took the Dominican habit *c.* 1351 and graduated as doctor in theology at Rome. He was successively prior (1370–75) at Pistoia, Orvieto, and twice at Lucca, and was noted as a teacher, preacher, and spiritual director. Exceptionally austere, Franchi was devoted to Christ Crucified, the Madonna and Infant, and the Magi. As bishop of Pistoia from about 1380 to his resignation in 1400, he lived as a religious, preached, spent his income on the poor and on pious causes, converted many sinners, and healed factional strife. His body, buried in San Domenico, Pistoia was found incorrupt in 1911. Benedict XV (1921) and Pius XI (1922) approved his cult.

Bibliography: Quétif-Échard 1.2:717–718. ActApS 13 (1921) 549; 14 (1922) 16–19. I. TAURISANO, *Beato Andrea Franchi* (Rome 1922).

[W. A. HINNEBUSCH]

ANDREW OF LONGJUMEAU, Dominican missionary, papal ambassador; b. Longjumeau, France, early 13th century; d. France, *c.* 1270. In 1238 King

*Louis IX commissioned him to bring the Crown of Thorns back to France from Constantinople. Innocent IV made use of his proficiency in Oriental languages and sent him to negotiate the return of the Jacobite and *Nestorian Churches to unity with Rome. While on the Crusades with King Louis (1248–54) he went on a mission to the Great Khan at Karakorum to investigate his reported conversion to the Faith. In 1256 he was in Tunis working for the conversion of the Sultan, but sometime before 1270 he returned to France, where he died.

Bibliography: P. PELLIOT, "Les Mongols et la papauté," *Revue de l'Orient Chrétien* 23 (1922–23) 1–30; 24 (1924) 225–335; 28 (1931–32) 3–84. J. S. DE JOINVILLE, *The History of St. Louis*, ed. N. DE WAILLY, tr. J. EVANS (New York 1938) 39–41, 142–148. Quétif-Échard 1.1:140–141. A. DUVAL, *Catholicisme* 1: 530–531.

[J. D. CAMPBELL]

ANDREW OF PESCHIERA, BL., Dominican; b. Peschiera on Lake Garda, Italy, *c.* 1400; d. Morbegno, Switzerland, Jan. 17–18, 1485 (feast, Jan. 19). At an early age Andrew Grego entered the *Dominicans at Brescia and was sent to San Marco, Florence, for his studies. He had a special attraction for the virtue of obedience. His life work was the evangelization of Vatellina, a district in southern Switzerland, where he labored so zealously for 45 years that he became known as its apostle. He assisted in the foundation of two Dominican houses, in Morbegno (1457) and in Coire. At times he acted as inquisitor at Como. He was especially solicitous for the poor. Solemn veneration was accorded him at the translation of his remains to the chapel of St. Roch in 1497. His cult was approved Sept. 23, 1820, by Pius VII.

Bibliography: R. COULON, DHGE 2:1690–91. A. WALZ, Enc Catt 1:1198. Baudot-Chaussin 1:392. Butler Th Attw 1:123–124.

[M. G. MC NEIL]

ANDREW OF RINN, BL., peasant child, alleged martyr; b. Nov. 16, 1459; d. Rinn, near Innsbruck, Austria, July 12, 1462 (feast, July 12). At his father's death, his mother entrusted Andrew, then 2 years old, to his uncle's care. Andrew disappeared July 12, 1462, and his mother found his body hanging from a tree in a nearby wood. The uncle claimed he had sold the child to Jews returning from a fair. The child's body was buried in a cemetery of Ampass without any extant evidence of a juridical investigation. Veneration was first given to the remains when the inhabitants of Rinn, imitating the citizens of Trent who honored a boy Simon murdered by Jews in 1475, solemnly transferred Andrew's body to Rinn. His cult spread through northern Tyrol. Benedict XIV approved his equivalent beatification Dec. 25, 1752, but refused canonization Feb. 22, 1755.

Bibliography: E. VACANDARD, DHGE 2:1700–02. Butler Th Attw 3:86–87. M. MAYER, LexThK[2] 1:519. Baudot-Chaussin 7:282.

[M. G. MC NEIL]

ANDREW OF SAINT-VICTOR, canon regular, abbot, and exegete whose critical and scholarly exposition of the literal sense of the OT was responsible for sending later exegetes to the original Hebrew; b. England, *c.* 1110; d. Wigmore Abbey, Herefordshire, England, Oct. 19, 1175. He entered the monastery of *Saint-Victor in Paris *c.* 1130 and studied under *Hugh of Saint-Victor (d. 1141), whom he later succeeded as Scripture teacher. After serving for a while as the first abbot in the new abbey at Wigmore (beginning *c.* 1147), he returned to the academic life of Saint-Victor's; but he later (*c.* 1162) returned to Wigmore as abbot (*c.* 1161–63) and remained there until his death. Following Hugh, Andrew put all his energies into expounding the "letter." He was the first medieval commentator who systematically used Jewish sources in his exposition of the OT. He commented on the first seven books of the Bible, on the Prophets, Proverbs, and Ecclesiastes. Andrew's works were used by *Peter Comestor, *Peter Cantor, *Stephen Langton, *Hugh of Saint-Cher, and *Nicholas of Lyra, and influenced their exposition of the literal sense.

See also EXEGESIS, MEDIEVAL.

Bibliography: B. SMALLEY, *The Study of the Bible in the Middle Ages* (2d ed. New York 1952) 112–195; "Andrew of St. Victor, Abbot of Wigmore: A Twelfth Century Hebraist," RechThAMéd 10 (1938) 358–373; "The School of St. Victor," *ibid.* 11 (1939) 145–167. C. SPICQ, *Esquisse d'une histoire de l'exégèse latine au moyen âge* (Paris 1944) 130–131. L. OTT, LexThK[2] 1:519. C. EGGER, EncCatt 1:1205.

[J. J. MAHONEY]

ANDREW OF STRUMI, BL., abbot and church reformer; b. Parma, Italy, first half of the 11th century; d. Parma, March 10, 1097 (feast, March 10). A disciple of the deacon *Arialdo, he took part in the church reform movement at *Milan, and at great personal risk he recovered the body of his master who had been slain at the instigation of the simoniacal archbishop Guido of Velate (d. 1071). About 1069, while still in his 40s, Andrew joined the *Vallombrosans and was in close contact with their founder, *John Gualbert, for some years. He became abbot of *Strumi *c.* 1085, when the Vallombrosans replaced the *Benedictine community there. He was called upon to mediate between *Florence, which was supporting *Urban II, and *Arezzo, partisan of Emperor *Henry IV. Andrew wrote a life of Arialdo (PL 143:1437–86) and also one of John Gualbert (PL 146:765–960). There is in the latter work a reference to one of the saint's miracles that could have been performed only after 1106, and this has cast some doubt on the date usually given for Andrew's death. In the late 13th century Andrew's relics were enshrined in the church of S. Fedele at Strumi.

Bibliography: Sources. ActSS March 2:47–49. Literature. B. ALBERS, "Die aeltesten Consuetudines von Vallumbrosa," Rev Bén 28 (1911) 432–436. G. DOMENICI, "La badia di S. Fedele di Strumi presso Poppi," *Rivista storica benedettina* 10 (1915) 72–92, esp. 87–89. U. ROUZIÈS, DHGE 2:1716. Zimmermann KalBen 1:309–310. Butler Th Attw 1:549–550. A. M. ZIMMERMANN, LexThK[2] 1:520.

[B. J. COMASKEY]

ANDREWE, RICHARD, dean of York, English royal servant; b. Adderbury, Oxfordshire; d. 1477. He was educated at Winchester and New College, Oxford, where he was a fellow (1421–33). A doctor of civil law in 1432, he practiced as a canon lawyer, becoming an official of the court of Canterbury (1439 and 1441), and chancellor of Abp. Henry *Chichele. He was a king's clerk as early as 1433. His reputation with King *Henry VI and the archbishop led to his nomination on May 20, 1438, as first warden of Chichele's new College of All Souls, Oxford, an office he held until 1442. He then became a king's secretary (1443–55). He served on many diplomatic missions, including the negotiations, in 1444, for Henry's marriage. His services were rewarded with appropriate preferment: he held several canonries at York, Salisbury, and Saint David's, and became archdeacon of Salisbury (1441–44) and of Buckingham (1447–49). Imposed on a reluctant chapter by King and Pope, he became dean of *York, serving from 1452 until June 2, 1477. His political career ended with the fall of Henry VI, but in his later years he acted as vicar-general of the archbishop of York. He founded chantries at Deddington, Oxfordshire, and Chipping Sodbury, Gloucestershire, and gave a number of Canon Law books to All Souls and New College, Oxford.

Bibliography: *Testamenta Eboracensia,* 6 v. (Surtees Society 4, 30, 45, 53; Newcastle 1836–1902) v.3 (1865). A. J. Otway-Ruthven, *The King's Secretary . . . in the XV Century* (Cambridge, Eng. 1939). Emden 1:34–35.

[C. D. ROSS]

ANDREWES, LANCELOT

Anglican bishop of Winchester, prominent prelate, preacher, and apologist for the Church of England as reformed yet still Catholic, equally opposed to the extremes of Romanism and Puritanism; b. London, 1555; d. Winchester, 1626. He was the son of a master mariner. Andrewes's early promise showed rapid development at Cambridge, where he acquired a critical knowledge of 15 languages that he later used to good purpose as a principal translator of the Authorized Version (King James) of the Bible (1611). He was ordained in 1580, and withstood the influence at Cambridge University of the strong Puritan party eager to win his support. His attraction to Calvinism was only to the devotional side and he showed himself a conservative in Church affairs, appealing in his *Catechetical Lectures* for "apostolic handsomeness and order." Although he retained altar, candles, and incense, then despised as "popish furniture," he yet toured the north (1586) with the Puritan Earl of Huntingdon to win over Catholic recusants. Having been appointed canon penitentiary at St. Paul's, London, in 1589, he began the series of sermons that won him the title "an angel of the pulpit." Andrewes refused two offers of bishoprics from Elizabeth in protest against the policy of alienating episcopal revenues to the crown but was persuaded by King James to accept the See of Chichester (1605), whence he moved to Ely (1609) and to Winchester (1613). He took no umbrage at being passed over for Canterbury, probably realizing, as did others, that he had no bent for the ecclesiastical politics necessary in the primatial see. When James I was involved in controversy with Cardinal (St.) Robert Bellarmine over the divine right of kings and the oath of allegiance imposed on English papists after the Gunpowder Plot (1605), Andrewes rallied to his king's support in *Tortura Torti* (1609) and *Responsio ad Apologiam Cardinalis Bellarmini* (1610), upholding the orthodoxy of the reformed Church of England and ridiculing the term Roman Catholic as a contradiction in terms, serving only "to distinguish your Catholic Church from another Catholic Church which is not Roman." His equal dislike of Calvinism explains his absence from the Anglican delegation to the Synod of the Dutch Reformed Church at Dort (1618), though the previous year he had gone with James I to Scotland to try to persuade the Presbyterians to accept episcopacy. Andrewes himself was a dedicated bishop, intervening in public affairs only when he thought it necessary. He remained a bachelor, and was a lifelong student, acquiring a profound knowledge of patristic theology. His charming delivery and classical style made him a popular and famous preacher. He was a saintly man with a gift for composing prayers, and his *Preces Privatae* have retained their appeal. His importance in the theological development of the Anglican Church is as a forerunner, with his friends Richard Hooker and George Herbert, of the *Caroline Divines.

Lancelot Andrewes, from a portrait by an unknown artist, Jesus College, Oxford.

Bibliography: *Works,* ed. J. P. Wilson and J. Bliss, 11 v. (*Library of Anglo-Catholic Theology;* Oxford 1841–54.) A. T. Russell, *Memoirs of the Life and Works of Lancelot Andrewes* (London 1863). T. S. Eliot, *For Lancelot Andrewes* (London 1928). J. H. Overton, DNB 1:401–405. M. Schmidt, RGG^3 1:369. **Illustration credit:** By kind permission of the Principal and the Fellows of Jesus College, Oxford.

[G. ALBION]

ANDRIEU, MICHEL, liturgist; b. Millau, May 28, 1886; d. Strasbourg, Oct. 2, 1956. He took his theology as an Oratorian in Fribourg from 1907 till ordination, July 18, 1910. Studies in Christian archeology in Rome and literature in Paris fitted him for his more than 30-year career of liturgical scholarship. L. Duchesne, his first master, opened to him the virginal field of the Ordinals. Invited to the faculty of Catholic theology at Strasbourg in 1918, he remained there until his forced retirement in 1956, his 70th year. At the University while patiently pursuing research in the manuscript traditions of the Ordinals, he poured into the faculty review (*Revue des sciences religieuses*) the stream of his monumental essays on Roman liturgy, by-products of his main investigation. He brought to his work an exacting scientific method and an awareness that the liturgy of the past, once restored critically, would be a vital source of theology. He also feared that the fast-growing liturgical movement would bypass the heritage of the past centuries. His method, spirit, and fears were contagiously transmitted, personally to his associates, and by his writings to his careful readers. His two great works, *Ordines Romani,* 5 v. (Louvain 1931–61) and *Pontifical Romain,* 5 v. (Vatican City 1938–63), map out the course taken by the Roman liturgy in its growth from the 6th to the 15th century.

Bibliography: C. VOGEL, LexThK² 1:522; "L'Oeuvre liturgique de Mgr. M. Andrieu," RevScRel 31 (1957) 7–19. B. CAPELLE, "L'Oeuvre liturgique de Mgr. Andrieu et la théologie," Nouv RevTh 79 (1957) 169–177. *Mélanges en l'honneur de Monseigneur Michel Andrieu* (Strasbourg 1956).

[R. T. CALLAHAN]

ANDRONICUS II PALAEOLOGUS, BYZANTINE EMPEROR, 1282 to 1328; b. Constantinople, 1256; d. May 24, 1332. He was the son of Michael VIII Palaeologus and Theodora Ducas. At 15 he was married to the daughter of Stephen V of Hungary and associated in the Emperorship (1271). Breaking with his father's conciliatory policy toward Rome after the *Sicilian Vespers had destroyed the anti-Constantinopolitan designs of Charles of Anjou, he deposed *John XI Beccus and restored the deposed anti-union Patriarch, Joseph. On Joseph's death (March 1283), he imposed Gregory of Cyprus (d. 1289) in the patriarchate, forcing his mother Theodora to renounce communion with Rome.

Because of his devotion to theology and ecclesiastical politics, he tried to pacify the followers of the deceased Patriarch Arsenius, deposed by *Michael VIII, and to institute a reform of clergy and monasteries under the hermit Athanasius, who became patriarch in 1289 but abdicated in 1293. Under the patriarch John (Comus) in 1295 the Emperor convoked a reform synod; when he attempted an alliance with the Serbs and espoused his daughter to the already married Kral Stephen Urosh II he was reproached in a synod (1300)

Obverse of gold seal of Andronicus II on profession of faith dated April 9, 1277.

and ceded. He restored Athanasius as patriarch (1304–12) and deposed Niphon of Cyzicus as patriarch in 1315 for simony, replacing him with a layman, John XIII Glycas (1315–19), then with Gerasimus (1320–21), and then with the monk Isaac (1323).

The reign of Andronicus was accompanied by a series of disasters including interior religious quarrels, the continual threat of western crusading attacks, Italian colonizing enterprises, and Turkish invasions. The attempt to exclude his grandson, *Andronicus III, from the throne resulted in civil war and on May 24, 1328, he was deposed and finished his life in a monastery.

Bibliography: L. BRÉHIER, DHGE 2:1782–92; CMedH 4 (1923) 613–614. F. DÖLGER, LexThK² 1:523. I. SYKUTRES, *Hellenika* 2 (1929) 267–333; 3 (1930) 15–44, on the Schism of Arsenius (in Greek). Ostrogorsky 426–444. **Illustration credit:** Archivio Segreto Vaticano.

[J. GEIGER]

ANDRONICUS III PALAEOLOGUS, BYZANTINE EMPEROR, May 5, 1328, to June 15, 1341; b. Constantinople, 1296?; d. Constantinople. He was the eldest son of Michael IX Palaeologus, and was coemperor with his grandfather *Andronicus II, who on Michael's death in 1320 attempted to exclude Andronicus III from the succession. He joined John Cantacuzenus against the government at Constantinople, and in a civil war forced the abdication of Andronicus II. He married Irene of Brunswick (d. 1324), then Jeanne (later Anne) of Savoy (1326). Andronicus was an outstanding military leader who sought the assistance of Pope *Benedict XII against the Turks, promising to join a crusade. In 1339 he dispatched Stephen Dandolo and *Barlaam the Calabrian to Avignon for aid. There, in regard to the question of Church reunion, the Latin hatred for the Greeks, rather than dogmatic differences, was cited as the obstacle, and the question of an ecumenical council was raised. Andronicus increased the influence of the Church in the juridical system of the empire by the establishment of an ecclesiastical law court under the patriarch, and in the disputes over *Hesychasm he attempted to act as pacifier but accepted the judgment of Cantacuzenus in favor of *Palamas.

Bibliography: F. COGNASSO, EncCatt 1:1215. F. DÖLGER, LexThK² 1:523–524. L. BRÉHIER, DHGE 2:1792–97. BARLAAM CALABRO, *Epistole greche,* ed. G. SCHIRÒ (Palermo 1954). Ostrogorsky 444–454.

[J. H. GEIGER]

ANEIROS, LEÓN FEDERICO, 18th bishop, and 2d archbishop of Buenos Aires; b. Buenos Aires, Aug. 28, 1828; d. there, Sept. 4, 1894. He was appointed bishop of Aulon *in partibus* in 1870, and chosen archbishop on July 24, 1873; he remained in that capacity until his death. He was educated at the San Ignacio College when it was directed by the Jesuits. In 1848 he received his doctorate in theology and civil and Canon Law. After having taught at the University of Buenos Aires, he was simultaneously a delegate for the province of Buenos Aires and the secretary of Bishop Escalada. One of his major concerns was to foster the Catholic press. In 1853 he founded the newspaper *La Religión* and in 1855, *El Orden,* both directed by Félix Frías. Aneiros contributed to them until 1858 and 1861, when they ceased publication. From the time he occupied the See of Buenos Aires, he was obliged to combat secularism, which was gaining ground. His need of clergy led him to be lenient in receiving unworthy priests from France, Italy, and especially Spain, who in the end did more harm than good. He fostered Catholic education and facilitated the establishment of the colleges of San José and of El Salvador. In 1878, because he wished to return the church of San Ignacio to the Jesuits, a mob led by a renegade Spanish priest tried to set fire to the archiepiscopal curia, and did in fact burn El Salvador College. When a persecution against the Church and its institutions was initiated in 1883–84, Archbishop Aneiros endorsed the brave and determined action of the Catholic delegates, who personally upheld Christian interests in the Parliament, but he did little himself. It was said that he did not wish to offend the men who governed the country at that time. He was a holy man but rather short-sighted and not very energetic.

Bibliography: R. D. CARBIA, *Mons. León Federico Aneiros* (Buenos Aires 1905). E. LAMAREA, "Mons. León F. Aneiros," *Archivum: Revista de la Junta de Historia Eclesiástica Argentina* 2 (1944) 165–173.

[G. FURLONG]

ANERIO, FELICE AND GIOVANNI FRANCESCO, baroque composers of the Roman school. Felice; b. Rome, *c.* 1560; d. Rome, Sept. 27, 1614. As a youth Felice sang at St. Mary Major under G. M. Nanino from 1568 to 1574, and in the Julian choir under Palestrina from 1575. In 1585 he was appointed director of music at the English College in Rome, and in 1594 was called by Clement VIII to the post of composer to the Papal choir, previously held by Palestrina. He was also associated with the Sodalitas musicorum, whose purpose was to provide training for church musicians and further the cause of good music. Felice composed four books of madrigals, as well as numerous works in the standard forms of the period. His style follows the principles of balance and clarity that are the hallmarks of Palestrina's music. After 1600, however, the baroque ideal of contrasting sounds becomes noticeable, especially in the larger works. Toward the end of his career he worked with *Suriano in the revision of plainchant, which resulted in the now discredited Medicean edition (1614; *see* CHANT BOOKS, PRINTED EDITIONS OF).

Giovanni Francesco; b. Rome, *c.* 1567; d. Poland, June, 1630. Giovanni sang under Palestrina at St. Peter's from 1575 to 1579 and subsequently was music director at the Lateran and at the court of Sigismund XI of Poland before holding the post of maestro of the Jesuit church of S. Maria dei Monti, from 1613 to 1620. In 1616, at 49, he received Holy Orders. He died on the way from Poland to Italy and was buried at Graz, Austria. Like his brother, Giovanni adhered to the Palestrinian technique, but in later compositions employed some of the newly developed methods of baroque expression. A collection of spiritual madrigals for from five to eight voices was written for the Congregation of the Oratory in 1616; his numerous works include also Masses, motets, hymns, and similar forms of church music.

Bibliography: Modern eds. of music by F. X. HABERL, K. PROSKE, J. SCHREMS, et al. F. X. HABERL, "Felice Anerio," *Kirchenmusikalisches Jahrbuch* 18 (1903) 28–52; "Giovanni Francesco Anerio," *ibid.* 1 (1886) 51–66; 6 (1891) 97; 10 (1895) 93. K. G. FELLERER, MusGG 1:470–474. Reese MusR. BukMusB.

[F. J. GUENTNER]

ANESTHESIA, the loss of feeling. Although the condition may result from disease, the term commonly refers to the clinical state produced for elimination of pain during surgery and childbirth. Anesthetics are drugs capable of producing anesthesia.

General anesthesia denotes loss of consciousness due to the action of anesthetics upon the brain. General anesthetics include gases and volatile liquids that are administered by inhalation and solutions of drugs that are injected intravenously or infused rectally. Diethyl ether (ether), nitrous oxide, cyclopropane, halothane (Fluothane), trichlorethylene, trifluoroethylvinyl ether (Fluoromar), methoxyflurane (Penthrane), divinyl ether (Vinethene), ethylvinyl ether (Vinamar), ethylene, and chloroform are inhalation anesthetics. The barbiturates, thiopental sodium (Pentothal) and thiamylal sodium (Surital), are intravenous anesthetics. Tribromethanol with amylene hydrate (Avertin), ether, and barbiturates are used rectally.

Local anesthesia refers to loss of feeling in part of the body. Local anesthetics are drugs used to produce this effect through application to peripheral aspects of the nervous system. They are applied topically to mucous membranes, infiltrated around nerve endings, or injected around nerves to provide regional anesthesia. Among the many local anesthetics are the hydrochlorides of cocaine, procaine (Novocain), chloroprocaine (Nesacaine), piperocaine (Metycaine), hexylcaine (Cyclaine), tetracaine (Pontocaine), dibucaine (Nupercaine), lidocaine (Xylocaine), butethamine (Monocaine), and mepivacaine (Carbocaine).

Anesthesia may also be achieved by *hypnosis or through application of physical means such as refrigeration (crymoanesthesia). Modern surgical anesthesia implies obtundation of reflex movements and provision of adequate muscle relaxation in addition to comfort for the patient.

Anesthesia is an important American contribution to medicine. Since the first use of ether by Crawford Long in 1842 and its classic demonstration by William Morton in 1846, the use of anesthesia has progressed markedly. Recent developments in the specialty have made feasible hitherto impossible surgery. Research on xenon anesthesia has stimulated the current interest in molecular action of anesthetics.

See also ANALGESIA; HYPNOSIS; MEDICINE; DOUBLE EFFECT, PRINCIPLE OF.

Bibliography: J. ADRIANI, *The Pharmacology of Anesthetic Drugs* (4th ed. Springfield 1960). R. D. DRIPPS et al., *Introduction to Anesthesia* (2d ed. Philadelphia 1961). T. E. KEYS, *The History of Surgical Anesthesia* (rev. ed. Dover; New York 1963). G. A. KELLY, *Medico-Moral Problems* (St. Louis 1958) 12–16, 288–293.

[C. PITTINGER]

ANESTHESIA (MORAL ASPECT)

The generic medical notions of anesthesia and analgesia are not so sharply defined as to offer a clear-cut and always mutually exclusive distinction between the two terms. Anesthesia is described as the loss of feeling or sensation. The term is understood primarily of tactile sensation but is likewise used in relation to the other senses. Analgesia is described simply as the loss of sensibility to pain.

As more commonly used today, anesthesia signifies both the systemically induced narcosis and muscle relaxation known as "general anesthesia" as well as the more restricted and localized desensitizing procedures that do not suppress consciousness and are known as regional or local anesthesia. Analgesia, however, is used to represent the other pharmacological approaches to pain or discomfort, whether physical, psychic, or both, through systemic sedation short of general anesthesia.

Throughout the known history of man the ingestion of alcoholic concoctions has been used for the relief of pain. The same can be said of a number of roots, seeds, and fumes that achieved their effect by being eaten, chewed, or inhaled. But all these crude substances had dangerous and inappropriate side effects, and their action was, for the most part, unpredictable and difficult to control.

Nearer to modern times, "ether binges" and "nitrous oxide jags" had become the sport of medical students and the stock-in-trade for sideshow performers. But anesthesia became a clinical entity in its own right in the first half of the 19th century, and it was on Oct. 16, 1846, that a group of serious physicians first stood in the surgical theater of the Massachusetts General Hospital with an etherized patient before them, prepared for surgery. But it was not until World War II, with its large-scale battle casualties demanding surgery on patients already in deep shock, that research opened the way to modern technique and control.

The voluntary acceptance of suffering, supernaturally motivated, has a definite place in authentic Christian asceticism, and there can be times and circumstances in which physical suffering is not only implied in the pursuit of Christian perfection but may even be demanded in adherence to basic Christian morality. These considerations, however, do not posit any basic moral problem regarding the use of anesthesia or analgesia; as Pope Pius XII pointed out in his address to The Italian Society of Anesthesiology (Feb. 24, 1957):

> The fundamental principles of anesthesiology, as a science and an art, and the end it pursues, give rise to no difficulties. It combats forces which, in a great many respects, produce harmful effects and hinder greater good. . . . The patient desiring to avoid or relieve pain can in good conscience use those means discovered by science which, in themselves, are not immoral. . . . Within the limits laid down, and provided one observes the required conditions, narcosis involving a lessening or suppression of consciousness is permitted by natural morality and is in keeping with the spirit of the Gospel. [Pope Speaks, 4 (1957) 33–39.]

Although general anesthesia is never without some risk, the danger presents no moral problem. There are established procedures and adequate controls to prevent or counteract most of the difficulties that may arise, and whatever risk there might be is justified by the benefit to the patient in any circumstance that constitutes a proper medical indication for anesthesia.

With regard to analgesia, there is some moral danger in the use of the amphetamines, barbiturates, barbiturate derivatives, and various tranquilizers because of the sometimes injudicious prescription of them by physicians, or their inadequately controlled availability, or their abuse by patients who take them too often or in too large doses independently of medical direction. Aside from injury or death due to overdosage, the danger is addiction. In the late 1950s 20 per cent of the addicts admitted to the Public Health Service Hospital in Lexington, Ky., were addicted as a result of the clinical application of narcotics (Faucett, "Drug addiction"). Here emerges the moral responsibility of the physician to spend extra time and care in many cases in order to reduce the need for analgesics by encouragement, sympathy, and understanding, as well as to adapt medication to the best interests of the individual patient.

Finally, in terminal illness complicated by severe pain and anxiety, there is sometimes a need to distinguish between a veiled euthanasia and a legitimate application of drugs. If the analgesic regimen required to control pain is likewise debilitating and life-shortening, there need be no moral difficulty as long as the control of the pain is the purpose of the medication and the debilitating side effects, although foreseen, are not sought (*see* EUTHANASIA).

Bibliography: R. D. DRIPPS et al., *Introduction to Anesthesia* (2d ed. Philadelphia 1961). S. C. CULLEN, *Anesthesia* (6th ed. Chicago 1961). PIUS XII, "Address to the International College of Neuro-Psychopharmacology," OssRom Sept. 13, 1958. T. J. O'DONNELL, "Moral Principles of Anesthesia: A Re-evaluation," ThSt 21.4 (1960) 626–633. J. F. FAZEKAS and T. KOPPANYI, "Are Barbiturates Used Promiscuously in Therapy?," *Postgraduate Medicine* 16.6 (1954) A52–A62. E. R. BLOOMQUIST, "Addiction, Addicting Drugs and the Anesthesiologist," *Journal of the American Medical Association* 171.5 (Oct. 3, 1959) 518–523. J. C. FORD, "Chemical Comfort and Christian Virtue," AmEcclRev 141.6 (1959) 361–379. R. I. FAUCETT, "Drug Addiction and Other Considerations in the Management of Pain with Narcotic Drugs," *American Practitioner and Digest of Treatment* 8.8 (1957) 1230–31.

[T. J. O'DONNELL]

ANFREDUS GONTERI, Franciscan theologian, *Doctor Providus,* also known as Alfredus, Aufredus, or Gaufredus Gontier; b. *c.* 1270 in Brittany. He studied at Paris between 1302 and 1307, and was there a disciple of *Duns Scotus, whom he repeatedly calls "my master." A contemporary document records him, in 1303, as a signatory of an appeal to the council against Pope *Boniface VIII in the latter's conflict with Philip the Fair. He twice commented on the *Sentences,* in 1322 at Barcelona and in 1325 at Paris, where he became a master in theology. Further information about his life is wanting.

Only Book 2 of his first commentary on the *Sentences* has been identified, while of his Paris commentary we possess Books 1–3. In addition, we have a *Quaestio de paupertate Christi,* written at Barcelona *c.* 1322 [*Studi Francescani* 33 (1936) 240–291]. His *Quaestiones quodlibetales* is cited by *William of Vaurouillon. Anfredus himself mentions his *Quaestiones ordinariae* and his *Quaestiones disputatae de beatitudine, super IVm,* but these have not been discovered.

Vaurouillon (*In 4 sent.* 45.1) calls Anfredus "an outstanding disciple of Scotus." He himself confesses in his commentary on the *Sentences:* "I am not quite willing to contradict the *Doctor Subtilis,*" but in fact depends substantially on the anti-Scotist, *Henry of Harclay, in the same work. In Anfredus's first book, the more than 200 questions utilize almost exclusively the first book of Harclay. His borrowings, here as in the second book, are for the most part as good as literal; even when he contests Harclay's opinions, he depends upon him in literary and technical matters. In addition there are indications that Anfredus utilized the first book of *John of Reading. He often cites *Peter Aureoli, as well as the work of a friend, a certain "Frater Franciscus"—probably *Francis of Marchia or *Francis of Meyronnes. (*See* SCOTISM.)

Bibliography: JOHN DUNS SCOTUS, *Opera Omnia,* ed. C. BALIĆ (Vatican City 1956) 4:15*–28*. J. ALFARO, "La Inmaculada Concepción en los escritos inéditos de un discipulo de Duns Escoto, Aufredo Gontier," Greg 36 (1955) 590–617.

[A. EMMEN]

ANGEL OF THE LORD

A theophanic messenger of God, mentioned mainly in ancient texts of the Pentateuch and the Historical Books of the OT, distinct from, and posing a different problem than, the angels in general.

Summary of Usage. The Hebrew word *mal'āk* (messenger) may be used of human messengers (Gn 32.4), prophets as spokesmen for God (2 Chr 36.15–16; Ag 1.13), or God's superhuman envoys (Gn 19.1, 15), but its use in the phrase *mal'ak yahweh* or *'elohim* (the messenger of Yahweh or God) has a more specific meaning that has not yet been satisfactorily explained.

In a series of passages taken from the Yahwistic and Elohistic traditions that formed the nucleus of the Pentateuch and in other early texts, the messenger of the Lord is presented not as a created heavenly envoy, distinct from God, but as Yahweh or God Himself appearing to men in sensible form (Gn 16.7–13; 21.17–20; 22.11–18; 31.11–13; Ex 3.2–6; 14.19, 24–25; Nm 22.22–35; Jgs 2.1–5; see also Jos 5.13–15; Jgs 6.11–24; 13.3–23). In a few other passages (Ex 23.20–23; Gn 24.7; 48.16; Nm 20.16) a messenger sent by God and apparently distinct from Him performs salvation acts that are attributed directly to God in other places. Other passages ascribe vengeance to messengers from God, who are distinct from Him, e.g., the Exterminator of Ex 12.23 (see also 1 Cor 10.10; Heb 11.28; Gn 19.1; 2 Sm 24.16; 4 Kgs 19.35). Finally, David is compared to an angel of the Lord because of his goodness and wisdom (1 Sm 29.9; 2 Sm 14.17–20; 19.27). The burden of the rest of this article is to determine what the angel of the Lord in the first series of texts means.

Original Meaning of Yahweh's Messenger. There are three theories that attempt to explain the origin and meaning of these texts: (1) the messenger is one who represents the Lord, transmits His will and promises, and therefore speaks God's message in the first person singular as the Prophets also did (Jerome and Augustine); (2) the messenger is the ubiquitous God Himself who directly but in human form manifests His message to His chosen leaders (see the Greek and early Latin Fathers of the Church who affirmed that the angel was a manifestation of the Logos); and (3) the messenger is the result of later theological speculation and was interpolated into ancient, naïve traditions relating direct, nonmediated appearances of God to man that clashed with the evolved concept of God's transcendence and the angels' mediation.

Each theory has valid elements that aid in the understanding of the individual passages, but none of them solves all the problems concerned with the messenger of the Lord wherever it appears. The third theory mentioned above (interpolation) cannot by itself explain why vestiges of the direct intervention of God were left uninterpolated. But it does explain how postexilic Jews must have understood the passages into which they did not interpolate the angel of the Lord. The first theory mentioned above (representation) is certainly Biblical and is to be applied to the second and third series of texts cited above, and perhaps even to the fourth where David is praised as God's representative; but in the first series the messenger is certainly not distinct from God Himself.

The second theory mentioned above (identity) appears to offer more solutions than the other two, especially when one considers that the original meaning of *mal'āk* may not have been messenger but a sending or a message. Certainly in other ancient passages no mediation whatsoever is found when God communicates with His elect (Gn 12.1–3, *passim*). "The angel of the Lord is therefore a form in which Yahweh appears . . .. He is God himself in human form" [G. Von Rad, *Genesis,* tr. J. H. Marks (Philadelphia 1961) 188]. God appearing in human form then is a type of the Logos, Christ, who fulfills the directness and mediation of this mysterious "message" of Yahweh. In Mal 3.1 the messenger of the Lord and messenger of the covenant appear to be both Yahweh Himself and the messenger sent before Him.

In the NT (Lk 1.11; 2.9; Jn 5.4; Acts 5.19; etc.) the angel of the Lord is distinct from God, "sent from God" (Lk 1.26).

Bibliography: J. TOUZARD, DBSuppl 1:242–255. EncDictBibl 87–90. W. G. HEIDT, *Angelology of the Old Testament* (Washington 1949).

[T. L. FALLON]

ANGELA OF FOLIGNO, BL.

Mystic; b. *c.* 1248, Foligno, Italy; d. Jan. 4, 1309. She married and lived a worldly and even sinful life until she was nearly 40 years of age. At this time she underwent a sudden conversion, the reason for which has remained unknown, and immediately afterward became a Franciscan tertiary. Her desire for an austere life of chastity, cloistered from the world, could not be fulfilled while her husband and children were alive, so, according to her own account, she prayed for their deaths, an extraordinary fact that can be explained only by the possibility that she had had some special revelation. Her prayer was heard, and soon a circle of disciples grouped around her. She is recorded to have had mystical graces, an account of which her Franciscan confessor caused her to dictate to him, and he translated her words into Latin. The book was later circulated as the *Book of Visions and Instructions.*

In a penetrating analysis Angela traces the "twenty steps of penitence" by which she was led to the threshold of the mystical life. She lays particular stress on the importance of self-knowledge, which is the first step leading to perfect penitence. Through this she was enlightened on the magnitude of her sins and she learned to pray with great ardor and love. She then received an entirely new understanding of the Our Father, the words of the prayer being explained to her in her heart, and she penetrated more deeply into the teaching of the Gospel. "And I began to have constantly," she wrote, "whether waking or sleeping, a divine sweetness in my soul."

After this she entered into the mystical life proper, which is described as a sequence of seven steps. Now Angela received revelations on the inner life of the divine Trinity, on the extension of the Incarnation in the Eucharist, and on the greatness and power of God, doctrines that she had first accepted through the teaching of the Church, but that she now assimilated mystically "through the taste of the mind." This flood of intellectual illumination was followed by 8 days of ecstasy, during which time she lay motionless and was unable to speak.

After this experience Angela received a further increase of graces, and her fear of being deceived was allayed by the divine promise that she would now be able to accept suffering and contradiction with joy. In the third step she was constantly aware of the presence of God; then, after a brief period of desolation, she entered in spirit into the side of Christ; as she puts it, she "saw" the ineffable power and will of God and was filled with sublime joy. In the fifth step she was granted the revelation of the divine union and love, a revelation that was accompanied by profound ecstasies that renewed her soul. At this stage she recognized the divine presence by a certain unction that renewed her soul and even "softened the limbs of her body," a mystical experience frequently described as "liquefaction."

The sixth step was characterized by almost complete spiritual darkness and distress, during which her soul was assailed by most painful temptations and God seemed entirely absent, leaving her to fight—apparently unassisted—against the evil spirits. This night of the spirit prepared her for the final step of transforming union. It began with a vision of God in darkness, "because He is a greater good than can be thought or understood . . . and she saw nothing, and she saw all"—language recalling pseudo-Dionysius and "negative theology," according to which God is more adequately defined in terms of ignorance than of knowledge. This final step culminated in her vision of herself in God, when she heard the words: "In you rests all the Trinity, all Truth, so that you hold Me and I hold you," a perfect description of the mystical marriage.

Angela's doctrine, which has been praised by such authorities as St. Francis de Sales, St. Alphonsus Liguori, and Benedict XIV, is in the authentic Franciscan tradition with its stress on poverty and its passionate love of the crucified Christ, which Angela both lived and taught to perfection. She was beatified in 1693. Her feast day is January 4; in the Franciscan Order, March 30.

Bibliography: *The Book of Divine Consolation of the Blessed Angela of Foligno,* tr. M. G. STEEGMAN (New York 1909); *Le Livre de la bienheureuse Angèle de Foligno,* ed. P. DONCOEUR, (Paris 1926). M. FALOCI PULIGNANI, *La Beata Angela da Foligno* (Gubbio 1926). L. LECLÈVE, *Sainte Angèle de Foligno* (Paris 1936). J. M. FERRÉ, "Les principales dates de la vie d'Angèle de Foligno," *Revue d'histoire franciscaine* 2 (1925) 21–34.

[H. GRAEF]

ANGELA MARIA OF THE IMMACULATE CONCEPTION, VEN., reformer of the Rule of the Order of the Holy Trinity; b. Cantalapiedra (Salamanca), March 1, 1649; d. El Toboso (Toledo), April 13, 1690. Her family, though prosperous and devout, opposed her entry into religious life. Nevertheless, she entered the Carmelites in Valladolid and, later, the Order of the Holy Trinity in Medina del Campo (Valladolid). She then went to El Toboso, founded the Trinitarian convent there and reformed the rule. She was gifted with the discernment of souls and extraordinary administrative ability. Her theological knowledge astounded the theologians of her time. Her autobiography, *Vida de la Venerable Madre Sor Angela Maria de la Concepcion,* was written at her confessor's direction, published in Madrid in 1691, and subsequently reissued in 1773, 1854, and 1901. Her *Riego Espiritual para Nuevas Plantas* went through three editions. Still unedited are other manuscripts in the archives of El Toboso Convent. In iconography, she is represented kneeling before an angel who offers her the scapular of the Order of the Holy Trinity, while the Holy Spirit, in the form of a dove, hovers over her head.

Bibliography: *Enciclopedia de la Religión Católica,* 7 v. (Barcelona 1950–56) 1:660.

[S. A. JANTO]

ANGELICO, FRA (GIOVANNI DA FIESOLE)

Famous Florentine painter of the early Renaissance, known also as Guido da Vicchio; b. Province of Mugello, Tuscany, 1378; d. Rome, 1455. At 20 he entered the Dominican monastery at Fiesole. Shortly thereafter, because of the strained relations with Florence resulting from the schism in the Church, the Fiesole Dominicans fled first to Foligno, then later, because of a pestilence, to Cortona. In 1418, after the schism was healed, they returned to Fiesole.

When and where Fra Angelico began his training in painting is uncertain. His earliest-known work, dating in the period from 1418 to the mid-1430s, betrays a close relationship to the *International Gothic style with its use of gold backgrounds, its elegant, delicate figures, and its rhythmically swinging drapery.

Examples from this early period ("Coronation of the Virgin," Uffizi, Florence; "Last Judgment," S. Marco

Fig. 1. Tombstone of Fra Angelico in the church of S. Maria sopra Minerva, Rome.

(a)

(b)

Fig. 2. (a) "The Meeting of SS. Francis and Dominic," panel, 10¼ by 10½ inches. (b) "Deposition from the Cross," panel, 1433, in the Museum of S. Marco, Florence.

Fig. 3. "Christ Appears to Mary Magdalene," fresco in the Museum of S. Marco, Florence.

museum, Florence) are evidences of Angelico's interest in a Neoplatonic negative mysticism. According to this, the soul by contemplation and intense concentration sloughs off all material experiences in its attempt to return to paradise, the great source of Light from which it had originally emanated (see Dante, *Paradiso,* canto xxiii); hence the striated gold backgrounds like sunbursts and the childlike, naïve figures that fill Angelico's paintings at this time ("Except ye . . . become as little children ye shall not enter the Kingdom of Heaven"—Mt 28.3).

Another type of mysticism, a positive type, is present in the "Deposition from the Cross" (1433, S. Marco Museum, Florence). The scene takes place in a flowery Tuscan meadow, not against an abstract gold background. This type of mysticism is present also in the frescoes in the cloister and cells of the remodeled monastery of S. Marco (1437), Florence; the Crucifixion and other episodes from Christ's life are set in natural surroundings. Past and contemporary religious personalities are often present contemplating the event. For the positive mystic, salvation and paradise are attained by contemplating and imitating the life of Christ on this earth according to the words of the Savior: "I am the Way . . . ."

During the last 10 years of his life Angelico was much in demand. In 1445 Eugene IV summoned him to the Vatican to work on the frescoes in the chapel of the Sacrament. These frescoes were later destroyed. In 1447 he began the "Last Judgment" frescoes in the S. Brixio Chapel, Orvieto cathedral (finished years later by *Signorelli), but was almost immediately resummoned to the Vatican by *Nicholas V to paint scenes from the lives of SS. Stephen and Lawrence in the Nicholas Chapel. He demonstrated there his command of the contemporary interest in light and shade, perspective and foreshortening. In 1449 he returned to Fiesole to become prior of San Domenico for 3 years. He rejected an offer to decorate the choir of Prato cathedral, later to be undertaken by Fra Filippo *Lippi. Instead he returned to Rome to finish work there. He lies buried in S. Maria sopra Minerva.

Bibliography: R. L. DOUGLAS, *Fra Angelico* (2d ed. London 1902). F. SCHOTTMÜLLER, *The Work of Fra Angelico da Fiesole* (New York 1913). J. POPE-HENNESSY, *Fra Angelico* (New York 1952). M. SALMI, *Il beato Angelico* (Spoleto 1958). DeWald ItPaint. **Illustration credits:** Figs. 1, 2*b,* and 3, Alinari-Art Reference Bureau. Fig. 2*a,* Samuel H. Kress Collection, M. H. De Young Museum, San Francisco, Calif.

[E. T. DE WALD]

ANGELINA, ST., Serbian princess; b. 15th century; d. Fruška Gora (Yugoslavia), *c.* 1510 (feast, June 30). She was the daughter of Ivan Tsrnoievič, Prince of the independent state of Zeta. From her marriage to the despot Stephen Branovič she had two sons, Jörg and Hanns. After the death of the despot Vonk, she ruled the Zetans (1497–99) and fought against the Turks to preserve Zetan independence. She became a heroine to the Serbians, who called her the mother and queen of Montenegro. Her piety and devotion attracted much admiration, and her cult is still popular in Yugoslavia, where folk poems and songs commemorate her holiness and her patriotism. She was buried in the monastery of Krusedol in the Fruška Gora Mts., where her son Jörg had become a monk. He was later metropolitan of Belgrade (d. 1516).

Bibliography: Z. KOSTELSKI, *The Yugoslavs* (New York 1952). J. MATL, LexThK[2] 1:532–533.

[F. J. LADOWICZ]

ANGELINA OF MARSCIANO, BL., founder of a congregation of Third Order Regular *Franciscans; b. Angelina Angioballi in Montegiove near Orvieto, 1377; d. Foligno, July 14, 1435 (feast, July 21); known also as Angelina of Corbara or of Foligno. She was married to John of Terni, Count of Civitella, at 15 and was a widow at 17. She became a Franciscan tertiary and converted her castle in the Abruzzi into a home for a community of tertiaries. She was so successful in persuading young girls of the area to choose a state of virginity and to enter the convent that she was denounced as a sorcerer and a Manichaean to Ladislaus of Durazzo, King of Naples (*see* ANJOU). He dismissed the charges against her, but in 1395 he exiled her. She and her companions went to Assisi and then to Foligno, where they formed a community of which she became the abbess; in 1398 they made solemn profession and set up strict enclosure. Pope Martin V united her 16 foundations into one congregation, making her superior general in 1428. Evidences of her sanctity were noted at her death, and her body was found incorrupt in 1492. Pope Leo XII approved her cult in 1825.

Bibliography: Butler Th Attw 3:160–161. O. BONMANN, Lex ThK[2] 1:532.

[N. G. WOLF]

ANGELO OF ACRI, BL., famous Capuchin preacher; b. Luke Anthony Falcone, Acri, Italy, Oct. 19, 1669; d. Acri, Oct. 30, 1739 (feast, Oct. 31). He was born of poor parents in southern Italy. After two attempts and two failures, he was invested a third time in the Capuchin Order in 1690; this time he persevered and was ordained in 1702. While Leonard of Port Maurice won fame by his preaching in northern Italy, Angelo did the same in southern Italy. Until his death, he preached home missions and at Forty Hours Devotions. His confreres elected him provincial of the Capuchin province of Cosenze in 1717. In Acritania he founded a convent of Capuchinesses (1725), for whom he wrote his only work, a book of prayers on Christ's sufferings. On Oct. 24, 1739, he became ill of a fever; he died a few days later. He was beatified by Pope Leo XII on Dec. 18, 1825. His cause of canonization was reintroduced in 1853 and is still active.

Bibliography: Lexikon Capuccinum (Rome 1951) 71–72. A. RANGE, "Angelus of Acri," *Round Table of Franciscan Research* 24 (1959) 42–48; "Makings of a Saint," *ibid.* 13–19. ActSS Oct. 13:658–682. AnalCap 1–70, see index.

[C. KRONZER]

ANGELO CARLETTI DI CHIVASSO, Franciscan moral theologian and canonist; b. Chivasso, Piedmont, probably in 1411; d. Cuneo, April 12, 1495. He came of a wealthy and distinguished family and studied at the University of Bologna. After receiving his doctorate in civil and canon law, the youth was soon entrusted with responsibilities that gave promise of a distinguished career in civil government. But at the age of 30 he gave up his worldly expectations and entered the Franciscans of the Cismontane Observance, taking the name Angelo in place of that of Antonio, which he had been called at Baptism. His learning and holiness quickly won the confidence of his brethren. He was four times chosen vicar general of his order and was held in great esteem outside the order. In 1450 Sixtus IV commissioned him to preach the crusade against the Turkish invaders of Otranto, and in 1491 he was appointed by Innocent VIII to work against the spread of the Waldensian heresy in Savoy and Piedmont. He was a zealous champion of the poor and the oppressed, doing much by his preaching and writing to promote the **Montes Pietatis.*

Chivasso's reputation as a moralist rests chiefly on his *Summa casuum conscientiae,* which was first published by Chivasso himself at Venice in 1486. A second edition followed in 1488, and thereafter for the rest of the century republications appeared almost annually. Many new editions throughout the following century are evidence of its continuing popularity. The work came to be known as the *Summa angelica* because of the author's name. Its doctrine, sound and exact, was expressed with rare perspicuity. The arrangement and presentation of topics in alphabetical sequence made it, in effect, a kind of dictionary or encyclopedia of practical moral theology and Canon Law, which proved most helpful to confessors. Luther detested the work and consigned it to the flames at Wittenburg, along with the bull of his excommunication, a collection of the decretals, and the *Summa theologiae* of St. Thomas Aquinas (Dec. 10, 1520).

Chivasso enjoys the title Blessed, his cult, which began shortly after his death, having been confirmed by Benedict XIV in 1753.

Bibliography: Hurter Nomencl 2:1072–73. Wadding S 19. Wadding Ann 13, 14, 15 *passim.* A. BEUGNET, DTC 1.1:1271–72. G. POU Y MARTI, EncCatt 1:1256–57.

[P. K. MEAGHER]

ANGELOLOGY

The theology of angels is a science that studies in the light of divine revelation the invisible world of spiritual intelligences (good angels) created by God who assist man in the attainment of his salvation and share with him the divine call to supernatural grace and glory.

It is a true science: it (1) is based on the certainty that angels exist (Denz 800, 3891); (2) attains through an intellectual study of the causal influence exercised by angels upon corporeal beings a knowledge of angelic nature; and (3) is established under the precise modality whereby angels realize substance, i.e., immateriality (St. Thomas, *In meta.,* prooem.; *In 7 meta.* 11.1536). It is a systematic science which, by means of theological and philosophical reflection, has developed and coordinated into a coherent system the divinely revealed data. The theology of angels is not merely a metaphysics of angels; it also shows the relationship of angels to the government of the universe (ST 1a, 110.1) and the Christian economy. Although angelology is a kind of microtheology which pays special attention to Christ's employment of angels in His Redemption of mankind, it properly sees a continuity in the role of the angels in both the Old and New Testaments, a role that is continuously salvific. Indeed, in the Bible the world of angels appears as tangential to the world of the Jewish people, of Christ, and of His Church. It may be added that angelology implicitly refutes opinions that reject existing reality beyond the empirically scientific.

Patristic Tradition. The Fathers Christianized angelology by subordinating angelic ministry to Christ's unique mediation. In their concepts they went beyond the Judaic notion of the angelic mediator of God and messenger of God. They decidedly opposed syncretistic efforts to identify angels with the pagan messengers of gods or impersonal protective deities. In addition, they developed important points of doctrine related to the angels: their existence and nature, call to grace and glory, society, missions, and functions in the government of the world.

The *Celestial Hierarchy* of *Pseudo-Dionysius proffered the first complete systematic theory of an angelic society (*c.* A.D. 600). Before that time the Fathers did not approach an angelology. They were slow to arrive at an exact concept of the true spirituality of angels, particularly because they lacked a clear philosophical distinction between body and spirit. In this question the Latins lagged behind the Greeks. In general it may be said that there was no apparent progress in systematized angelology from the 7th to the 13th centuries.

Scholastics. The interest of early scholastics, largely of theological import, centered on the place of angels in the divine plan of creation and Redemption. In the West, theological *summae* of the 12th century affirmed the personal character of angels, their knowledge and liberty, but failed to develop these notions. The 13th century witnessed a more philosophical treatment of the being and operations of angels. St. Thomas Aquinas, with his genius and the advantage of the Greek, Arabian, Jewish, and Christian philosophical studies upon the existence of separated substances, offered an extensive synthesis of thought in his angelology; in his system, angels are pure spirits, subsistent separated substances, forms not joined with body (ST 1a, 50.2, 4, 5; *C. gent.* 2.45–56). Scotus, holding an opposite view, considered angels as incorporeal but composed of matter and form (see DTC 1.2:1230–48 for a comparative study of three systems of angelology, i.e., of St. Thomas, Suárez, and Scotus).

Contemporary Angelology. Since the 17th century angelology has not been limited to the studies of the scholastics; it has come into its own positive theology. Treatises on the angels are normally found in dogmatic treatments of God the Creator. Of particular note are the contributions of Cardinal A. *Lépicier, R. *Garrigou-Lagrange, Jean Daniélou, and Karl Rahner. Synthesis has advanced but there is need for additional study to understand better the relationship of angelic mediation and intervention with Christ's unique mediation. Further studies have already determined a specific distinction between the patronages of angels and saints (human), based on a "movement" peculiarly angelic. This "movement," involving operations of the angelic will and intellect whereby inferior creatures are moved toward their respective ends, is ordinary to angels but extraordinary to the nonangelic beings.

Magisterium of the Church. The basic truths about angels are accepted on faith; their existence, creation, and spirituality (Denz 800, 3002, 3021, 3025); their personal nature (Denz 3891); their not emanating from the divine substance (Denz 3024). For an extensive account of conciliar teaching on angels see DTC 1.2:1264–71. The Church's teaching is shown best on the practical level in the liturgy. Here especially it is made clear that the role of angels in man's salvation is not of prime importance, that Christ is the one Mediator.

See also ANGELS; ANGELS, GUARDIAN (IN THE BIBLE); ANGELS OF THE CHURCHES; DEMON (IN THE BIBLE); DEMON (THEOLOGY OF); DEMONOLOGY.

Bibliography: A. VACANT et al., DTC 1.1:1189–1271. DTC, Tables générales 1:153–165. K. RAHNER, LexThK² 1:533–538. R. HAUBST, *ibid.* 3:867–872. J. DUHR, DictSpirAscMyst 1:580–625. H. LECLERCQ, DACL 1.2:2080–2161. A. A. BIALAS, *The Patronage of Saint Michael the Archangel* (Chicago 1954). J. D. COLLINS, *The Thomistic Philosophy of the Angels* (Washington 1947). J. DANIÉLOU, *The Angels and Their Mission . . .* , tr. D. HEIMANN (Westminster, Md. 1957). P. P. PARENTE, *The Angels* (St. Meinrad, Ind. 1958) also pub. as *Beyond Space* (New York 1961). P. DE LETTER, "Trends in Angelology," *Clergy Monthly* 24 (1960) 209–220. P. MILWARD, "Angels in Theology," Ir TheolQ 21 (1954) 213–225.

[A. A. BIALAS]

ANGELRAM, abbot and scholar; b. Saint-Riquier, Somme, France, *c.* 975; d. Dec. 9, 1045. A member of a knightly family of Ponthieu, Angelram (also Ingelram, Angalram) joined the *Benedictine Order at the Abbey of Saint-Riquier *c.* 884. He studied there under Abbot Ingelard and later at the school of Chartres under *Fulbert. He was ordained to the priesthood and maintained a wide variety of interests. He later paid homage to his master in Chartres in the salutation: "Fulberto praeptori et domino Ingelramnus monachus ipsius scholasticorum vilissimus." Angelram accompanied King *Robert II of France on a trip to Italy in 1016 or 1020. On Ingelard's death in 1022, he became abbot at Saint-Riquier, and continued in that office until his death. A man of administrative and organizational skill, he was also a scholar who so distinguished himself in music, grammar, and dialectic as to win the surname "the wise." His poetic *Vita Richarii* (PL 141:1423–34) survives, but lives of SS. Vincent and *Austreberta have been lost. The *Vita Richarii* shows reminiscences of Vergil and Sedulius. An extensive biography of Angelram survives, the work of the chronicler Hariulf, Abbot of Oldenburg (PL 141:1402–22), and it includes an epitaph by Angelram's pupil Guido, later bishop of Amiens (d. 1076). He has at times been given the title saint, although there is no cult.

Bibliography: L. BOUTHORS, *Histoire de St-Riquier* (Abbeville 1902). HistLittFranc 7:352. P. FOURNIER, DHGE 3:70–71. Manitius 2:533–535. Zimmermann KalBen 3:409–410, 412–413. S. HILPISCH, LexThK² 1:538.

[W. C. KORFMACHER]

ANGELS

Celestial spirits who serve God in various capacities. This article treats of (1) the angels in the Bible, (2) theology of the angels, (3) devotion to the angels, and (4) iconography of the angels.

1. IN THE BIBLE

The word angel ultimately is derived from the Greek ἄγγελος, which is the translation of Hebrew *mălʼāk,* messenger. The primary significance of angel, therefore, is messenger from God, a significance describing function rather than being or nature. A few other Hebrew words sometimes signify angels, and some of these are more indicative of being, e.g.: *ʼabbîrîm,* the mighty [Ps 77(78).25]; *ʼĕlohîm* (gods) of Ps 8.6, which is still translated angels, but as such is questionable; *bᵉnē ʼĕlohîm* of Jb 1.6; 2.1 and *bᵉne ʼēlîm* (*sons of God) of Ps 88(89).7; 28(29).1, which surely mean angels in Job and probably in the Psalms, but the designation "sons" is one of association and identity of wills rather than similarity of natures; *mᵉšārᵉtîm* [Ps 102(103).21], ministers, which refers to the heavenly spirits or angels; *ʽăbādîm* (Jb 4.18), servants, which is used in parallel with angels; the Aramaic *ʽîr,* watchers, of Dn 4.10, 14, 20, which is interpreted by the Septuagint (LXX) as angels; *ṣābāʼ* (3 Kgs 22.19; 2 Chr 18.18; Neh 9.6; Ps 148.2), host(s), which indicates the ordered service of the angels; *qᵉdōšîm* [Ps 88(89).6, 8; Jb 5.1; 15.15; Dn 8.13], holy ones, the angels as "set apart" for the service of God.

Angels in the Old Testament. The angel is an object of divine faith. Knowledge of their existence must come from God. Therefore, the intelligence concerning angels that one may garner from Hebrew Scripture is not a human fabrication or an evolution of religious thought resulting in the projection upon human consciousness of images not truly extramental. The angels are real, possessors of real objective natures, whose appearances and functions are real.

It is true that in the Scriptures, to some degree in the OT, more noticeably in the NT, a development can be discerned in the way man comprehends the angelic world. It is true also that God undoubtedly used the cultural and religious content of man's knowledge as a screen on which to project knowledge of His messengers and their work. Thus, the disturbed course of Israel through eras and empires was influenced by foreign ideas that God willed to use, as catalysts and elements, to communicate His truth of beings superior to man, instruments of His government of His people. To classify Israel's angels merely as the residue of former polytheism, the extravagances of religious élan, or the

Jewish expropriations of Persian ideas is to deny Judaeo-Christian belief in them. Polytheism, devout speculation, and Persia were all present, but as catalysts speeding the development of the essential relationship of God's people to Himself and His heavenly court.

Nature of Angels. Hebrew mentality paid little heed to the abstract and did not advert to the spiritual defined as nonmaterial. The Israelite never thought of God as being philosophically supernatural. Hence one does not find in the OT a sophisticated theological definition of the nature of angel or a formally developed angelology. Angels are mentioned frequently, however, and on the whole are understood to be superhuman, heavenly beings whose normal habitat is Yahweh's court (Jb 1.6; 2.1), where they enter into divine counsels (3 Kgs 22.19–22) yet always in subordination to God [Tb 12.18; Ps 102(103).20–21]. Like Yahweh they are normally invisible, unapproachable, and unaffected by human needs (Tb 12.19). Thus, without philosophical advertence to them, angels are assigned to God's extramundane place and manner of being (Gn 28.12). Though there is no explicit mention of their creation, they belong to God (Ex 23.23; 32.34). In the OT there is no mention of fallen angels or of battles in heaven, although Satan, the Adversary of Job, is gradually thought of as an evil force (Jb 1.6–12; 2.1–7; Za 3.1–2; 1 Chr 21.1).

Appearance of Angels. For the most part the angels sent by God to intervene in men's lives appeared to them in human form (Gn 18.2; 19.1; Dn 8.15). Because of the editorial layers of Genesis ch. 18 and 19 it is difficult to determine whether there was something in the appearance of the "three men" that revealed them to be angels (19.1). In Gn 18.2 Abraham saw three men, yet Yahweh alone appeared to him in 18.1, and again Yahweh spoke alone in 18.13, 17, 20, etc. Samson's mother, however, asserted that a man of God, who appeared to her, had the "appearance" of an angel of God (Jgs 13.6), as though there was a standard way to recognize an angel in human guise, but Manoe does not know him to be the Angel of the Lord who is later identified as Yahweh Himself (Jgs 13.3–23). Only one angel is said to be able to fly (Dn 9.21).

Function of Angels. The primary function of angels is to do God's will (Tb 12.18). They serve and praise God and are closer to Him than men [Ps 102(103).20–21; Dn 7.10]. Yet God's will has them also intervene in human affairs, by the exercise of power over nature without any apparent material energy (Genesis ch. 19), by communicating God's messages (Gn 31.11; Zacharia ch. 4), by destroying and punishing (4 Kgs 19.35; 2 Sm 24.16), and by helping and saving [3 Kgs 19.5–8; Ps 33(34).8; 90(91).11–12; Dn 6.23].

Angels in the New Testament. With the advent of the Son of God into the world, the prime office of the angel, mediation between God and men, was overshadowed by Our Lord's perfect mediation. Whereas the Old Law came through the ministry of God's angels (Gal 3.19; Heb 2.2), the new dispensation came through His Son, superior to the angels and adored by them (Heb 1.1–8). The Christian dispensation is not subject to angels but to the Lord Jesus (Heb 2.5–18). Also, a greater knowledge of angels and their functions in God's government has been revealed to Christians, which has led to the development of the more elaborate doctrine of Christian angelology.

Fig. 1. Basalt relief, c. 1000 B.C., of a six-winged creature, excavated at Tell Halaf, Palestine. Such non-Hebrew images were probably the basis for the descriptions of seraphim and angels found in the Old Testament.

Nature of Angels. Angels are spirits (Heb 1.14). Their spirituality is not simply immateriality but is totally above human experience so that a worthy man's spiritualization at the resurrection will make him the angel's equal, i.e., unmarried, immortal, and the son of God and of the resurrection (Lk 20.36; Mt 22.30; Mk 12.25). Angels see, praise, and worship God in His presence (Mt 18.10; Ap 5.11–13; 7.11–12; 8.2). They experience joy (Lk 15.10); they desire to bend over and get a better look at the mysteries of salvation (1 Pt 1.12)—obvious anthropomorphic expressions applied to angelic activity. They are stronger and more powerful than men (2 Pt 2.11) and instill fear by reflecting God's glory (Acts 10.4). Yet, at some time they were capable of rebelling against God, for some sinned (2 Pt 2.4; Jude 6). The consequence of the evil angels' defection is described in a mysterious battle won by Michael and his angels over *Satan and his angels (Ap 12.7–9; cf. Mt 25.41). The NT texts suppose that the evil angels are unalterably opposed to God and incapable of redemption.

The notion of angelic rank and gradation, adopted from Jewish literature, also began to crystallize (Jude 8–9; Lk 1.19; Eph 1.21; Col 1.16; see section 2, below). As to the number, Christ speaks of 12 legions (Mt 26.53); the author of Hebrews, of many thousands (Heb 12.22); and John, of thousands of thousands of angels (Ap 5.11). The actual multitude of the angels is

Fig. 2. The angel casting the millstone into the sea (Ap 18.21), miniature in the "Bamberg Apocalypse" illuminated at Reichenau, c. 1020, and preserved in the Staatliche Bibliothek, Bamberg (Codex bibl. 140, fol. 46).

vast, therefore, but beyond that nothing else is known.

Appearance of Angels. Of themselves, spiritual beings are invisible and intangible to men. Hence when angels communicate with men, they ordinarily assume a human form that is either indicated or presumed in the text, e.g., the angelic appearances to Zachary (Lk 1.11), to Mary (Lk 1.26, 28), to the shepherds (Lk 2.9, 13), to the witnesses at the tomb (Mt 28.2–7; Mk 16.5; Jn 20.12; Lk 24.4), and to Peter (Acts 12.7). In some of these appearances there is an aura of glory, i.e., light, radiance, and whiteness. The angels mentioned so frequently in the Apocalypse are described with the imagery of the OT apocalypses, adapted to the author's purposes (Ap 10.1). These descriptions of angelic appearances to men are anthropomorphic accounts of supernatural experiences, and as a result, it is impossible to determine their material objectivity in detail.

Functions of Angels. "Are they not all ministering spirits, sent for service, for the sake of those who shall inherit salvation?" (Heb 1.14). The angels are subject to Christ (Eph 1.20–22; 1 Pt 3.22), and their prime role is to minister to Jesus and His kingdom. They announce its preparation and its actual commencement (Lk 1.11, 19, 26–37). They obviate obstacles to the King's advent (Mt 1.20; 2.13, 19–20); they are the first heralds of the gospel of peace (Lk 2.9–13); and they minister to and strengthen the King (Mt 4.11; 26.53; Lk 22.43). As harbingers of glory, they roll back the stone from the tomb's mouth (Mt 28.2–4), wait for those who would seek the living among the dead, and give them the first news of the victory of the light over darkness (Mt 28.5–7; Mk 16.5–7; Lk 24.4–7; Jn 20.12–13). For the children of light, the little ones, they are advocates before God (Mt 18.10; Acts 12.11) and bearers of prayers to God (Ap 8.3). Through the good offices of angels, the Prophets of the new and eternal Covenant are delivered from bondage (Acts 5.19; 12.7–11). The vital force of God's Kingdom, the grace of its King, is spread through angels' instrumentality to new peoples and in new directions (Acts 8.26; 10.3, 22; 27.23–24).

They avenge God's honor (Acts 12.23), and on the day of judgment the angels of His power (2 Thes 1.7) will accompany the King in His *Parousia (Mk 8.38), when they will be part of Christ's and His Father's glory and gather together the elect (Lk 9.26; Mt 25.31). They will gather also the workers of evil and cast them into the fire (Mt 13.41), thus separating the wicked from the just (Mt 13.49). Jesus will acknowledge before the angels those who in their lives have acknowledged Him before men (Lk 12.8–9), and Christians will enter the heavenly Jerusalem in the company of myriads of angels (Heb 12.22). They are not, however, to be worshiped by the citizens of God's Kingdom (Col 2.18); rather, the saints, who belong to Jesus, will judge the angels (1 Cor 6.3).

The angelic panoply of the *Apocalypse deserves special mention, but it is much too intricate for detailed treatment here. Since almost everything in *apocalyptic literature is symbolic, undoubtedly the angels of many of this book's visions also are symbolic, e.g., the seven *angels of the churches (Ap 2.1–3.14, *passim*). At least this much may be said of the angels of the Apocalypse: they are servitors of God's power, glory, and judgment and are constantly active in God's government of apocalyptical and eschatological battle.

See also ANGEL OF THE LORD; CHERUBIM; SERAPHIM; ANGELS, GUARDIAN; MICHAEL, ARCHANGEL; GABRIEL, ARCHANGEL; RAPHAEL, ARCHANGEL.

Bibliography: CathCommHS. A. LEMONNYER, DBSuppl 1: 255–262. J. BONSIRVEN, *ibid.* 4:1161–66. EncDictBibl 81–87. K. RAHNER, LexThK[2] 1:533–538. J. MICHL, *ibid.* 3:863–867. W. G. HEIDT, *Angelology of the Old Testament* (Washington 1949). J. L. MCKENZIE, "The Divine Sonship of the Angels," CathBibl Quart 5 (1943) 293–300. **Illustration credits:** Fig. 1, Courtesy of the Walters Art Gallery, Baltimore. Fig. 2, Hirmer Verlag München.

[T. L. FALLON]

2. THEOLOGY OF

Christian theology drew on Holy Scripture, both the Old and the New Testament, for its angelology, but in the beginning it was also guided by extra-Biblical, Judaic ideas as well as by prevailing views on nature-spirits. In this way opinions about the angels that were contemporary and popular gained, at times, a wide circulation. Gradually, however, in the course of a long development and refinement, theology time and again pared away these accretions, until finally, through speculative elaboration of the concepts contained in Holy Scripture, there evolved an angelology that, with varying degrees of certitude, has become the doctrine of the Church.

Nature of the Angels. In pre-Christian Judaism there already existed the conviction that angels were spiritual beings without bodies (1 Enoch 15.6; Philo, *De sacrif. Abelis et Caini* 5), and that, consequently, they were visible to men only as apparitions and did not appear in material bodies (Tb 12.19). For this reason, angels were always known in Christendom as spiritual beings (Irenaeus, *Adv. haer.* 2.30.6–7; Pseudo-Dionysius, *Cael. hier.* 1.3; *Eccl. hier* 1.2; Gregory the Great, *Moralia* 2.8; 4.8), and were called simply "spirits" (Tertullian, *Apol.* 22.8; Clement of Alexandria, *Str.* 5.36.3; 7.82.5; Origen, *C. Cels.* 4.24–25; 6.18; cf. Heb 1.14). They were said not to have a body of flesh (Irenaeus, *Adv. haer.* 3.20.4; Eusebius *Praep. ev.* 4.3.18), which did not mean, however, that they had no body of any kind, i.e., absolute spirituality as opposed to some sort of corporeality. It was said rather that angels had an immaterial body corresponding to their nature (Tertullian, *De carne Christi* 6.9: "constat angelos . . . substantiae spiritalis, etsi corporis alicuius, sui tamen generis"; see also Gregory of Nazianzus, *Orat.* 28.31; Ambrose, *De Abrahamo* 2.58; Augustine, *Lib. arb.* 3.11.33; *Gen. ad litt.* 3.10). These bodies were considered to be in some way vaporous or firelike (Basil, *Spir.* 38: *ἡ μὲν οὐσία αὐτῶν ἀέριον πνεῦμα, εἰ τύχοι, ἢ πῦρ ἄυλον*; Fulgentius, *Trin.* 9: the good angels have a *corpus aethereum, id est igneum,* the bad a *corpus aerium*). This was not to say, however, that they were material in any sense known to man's experience (Gregory of Nazianzus, *Orat.* 38.9). At that time the view prevailed that everything created was corporeal; the angels, then, could be no exception (cf. Gennadius, *Liber ecclesiasticorum dogmatum* 12: "creatura omnis corporea est: angeli et omnes caelestes virtutes corporeae, licet non carne subsistant; ex eo autem corporeas esse credimus intellectuales naturas, quod localitate circumscribuntur"). Augustine, to be sure, already knew of the opinion concerning the pure spirituality of angels, but he did not think that it could be accepted inasmuch as occasionally they became visible in visions (*Epist.* 95.8). Pseudo-Dionysius was the first to teach the complete spirituality of angels (*Cael. hier.* 2.2–3; 4.2–3; *Eccl. hier.* 1.2; *Div. nom.* 7.2) and following him was Gregory the Great (*Moralia* 2.8; 4.8; 7.50; cf. *Dial.* 4.3.29). But this doctrine still encountered long opposition because of the contrary views of many Fathers in the East as well as in the West, where it was opposed by the authority of Augustine. Then, Rupert of Deutz espoused the notion that the bodies of angels were vaporous (*De victoria Verbi Dei* 1.28, PL 169:1241–42; *In Gen.* 1.11; PL 167, 208–209), while Bernard of Clairvaux took no stand on the question (*De consideratione* 5.4.7; cf. *In Cant. sermo* 5.7). It was first in the period of high scholasticism (e.g., Thomas Aquinas, ST la, 50.1) and then, subsequently, that a spirituality of angels, no longer burdened by any corporeality, was generally taught.

Holy Scripture and the history of the Church tell of the appearances of angels. This led to the question of how spiritual beings could be seen. It was thought that an angel was perceived in an ethereal body that was proper to it (Augustine, *Trin.* 3.5; *Enchir.* 59; Fulgentius, *Trin.* 9), or that he assumed a material body for the apparition (Augustine, *Trin.* 3.5; Augustine took this possibility into consideration but avoided making a decision on the question), perhaps a body from air (Gregory the Great, *Moralia* 28.3: "ad tempus ex aere corpora sumerent"; so also Thomas Aquinas, ST 1a, 51.2), all of which were inadequate hypotheses. In any case, so it was said, an angel never showed himself in a body of flesh (John Chrysostom, *C. Anom.* 7.6), nor in his true form, but in a special form suited to the apparition (ἐν μετασχηματισμῷ: John Damascene, *Fide orth.* 2.3; PG: 94, 869).

Angels as Moral Beings. The doctrine that God had created the angels was, in general, firmly held from the beginning [Justin, *Dial.* 88.5; 141.1; Athenagoras, *Leg.* 24.3; Irenaeus, *Adv. haer.* 2.2.3; Clement of Alexandria, *Prot.* 63.2; Augustine, *Civ.* 9.23; 12.26(25)], and, in fact, through the power of the preexisting Christ (Tatian, *Orat.* 7.1–2; Irenaeus, *Adv. haer.* 2.2.4; 3.8.3; Origen, *Princ.* 1.7.1; Athanasius, *C. Ar.* 1.62; cf. Col 1.16). The angels, moreover, came into being before any other creature [Basil, *Hex.* 1.5; Augustine, *Conf.* 12.13 (according to these explanations the concept heaven in Gn 1.1 would include the creation of the angels); *Civ.* 11.9, 32; Gregory the Great, *Moralia* 28.34] as beings gifted with reason and given freedom for forming personal, moral decisions (Justin, *Dial.* 102.4; Tatian, *Orat.* 7.3; Athenagoras, *Leg.* 24.4; Irenaeus, *Adv. haer.* 4.37.1, 6; Augustine, *Civ.* 22.1; Gregory the Great, *Moralia* 6.20).

The angels, therefore, could also sin (Augustine, *Enchir.* 15). Origen was of the opinion that all the heavenly spirits had sinned, and, according to the gravity of the offense, they had then become demons, souls of men, or angels (*Princ.* 1.8.1). Other sources supposed that only a part of the angels had sinned. For the most part, in the beginning, their sin was considered in conjunction with a Judaic opinion (*Book of Jubilees* 4.22; 5.1, 6, 10; 1 *Enoch* 6–7 and frequently; *Syriac Apocalypse of Baruch* 56.12–13; Philo, *De gigantibus* 6; Flavius Josephus, *Ant.* 1.3.1.73) to be one of sexual union with human women [Justin, 2 *Apol.* 4(5).3; Athenagoras, *Leg.* 24.5; Irenaeus, *Adv. haer.* 4.36.4; Clement of Alexandria, *Str.* 3.59.2; 5.10.2; Tertullian, *De cultu fem.* 1.2.1–4; 1.4.1; Cyprian, *De hab. virg.* 14; Ambrose, *De virginibus* 1.52–53; *De Noe et Arca* 4; cf. Jude 6; 2 Pt 2.4]. This opinion was based on a specific interpretation of the "Sons of God" in Gn 6.2, 4, but there were also other interpretations assigned to the passage (Origen, *C.Cels.* 5.55; Augustine, *Civ.* 15.22–23; John Chrysostom, *Hom. 22 in Gen.* 2). The sin of the angels was then connected with abuse of the service that God had intrusted to them (Origen, *Hom. 4 in Ezech.* 1; *In Jo.* 13.59.412), and especially with pride (Athenagoras, *Leg.* 24.4; John Chrysostom, *Hom. 22 in Gen.* 2; Augustine, *Gen. ad litt.* 11.15; *Enchir.* 28; Gregory the Great, *Moralia* 4.8; 27.65). According to those who held for a sexual transgression, the sin of the angels occurred in the course of human history, namely, before the flood; according to those who presumed a sin of a different kind, it had already occurred at the beginning of the world (Augustine, *Civ.* 15.23). This view then prevailed generally. The sin of Satan and the sin of the bad angels had to be considered different things as long as the sin of the angels was presumed to be sexual, because the devil existed, as the seducer, in Paradise (Gn 3.1–5, 13–14) long before the fall of the angels. Already from the 2d century, however, the two offenses were linked in such a way that the other angels were thought to have been taken up in the sin of the one angel who through pride became Satan (Tatian, *Orat.* 7.5; Augustine, *Enchir.* 28; Gregory the Great, *Moralia* 4.15). It also continued to be the view of later times (e.g., Thomas Aquinas, ST 1a, 63.8; Suárez, *De angelis* 5.12.13).

According to an early opinion, the rest of the angels, who had not sinned the previous time, did not yet experience the full beatitude of heaven, but they had first to undergo a period of trial like humans on earth (cf. Ignatius, *Smyrn.* 6.1; Clement of Alexandria, *Str.* 7.5.2). They were not without guilt (Ambrose, *Expos.* Ps 118.8.29; *De Spir. Sancto* 3.134; Jerome, *In Micheam* 2 at 6.1–2, concerning the angels of the Churches in Apocalypse ch. 2 and 3, who are praised and reprimanded) and required the forgiveness of God (Cyril of Jerusalem, *Catech.* 2.10). Gradually, however, another opinion prevailed according to which the angels were absolutely spotless and happy beings (Methodius, *Symp.* 3.6; Gregory of Nazianzus, *Orat.* 38.9; Augustine, *Civ.* 10.26; *Enchir.* 57; Pseudo-Dionysius, *Cael. hier.* 7.2; *Eccl. hier.* 6.3, 6; Gregory the Great, *Moralia* 18.71; 27.65); they were sanctified by the Holy Spirit from their creation (Basil, *Hom. in Ps.* 32.4; John Damascene, *Fide Orth.* 2.3, PG 94:869); they had never been involved in sin (Gregory the Great, *Moralia* 18.71), and they live in blessed communion with God [Gregory of Nazianzus, *Orat.* 28.31; Augustine, *Civ.* 7.30; 11.13; *Doct. christ.* 1.31(30); Pseudo-Dionysius, *Cael. hier* 4.2].

Service of the Angels. According to the general view, the angels serve God (Clement of Rome, 1 *Clem.* 34.5–6; Clement of Alexandria, *Str.* 7.3.4; Origen, *C.Cels.* 8.13, 25; Athanasius, *C.Ar.* 1.55, 62; Augustine, *Civ.* 10.26), who works in creation through them (Tertullian, *De anima* 37.1; Origen, *C.Cels.* 8.47; Augustine, *Civ.* 7.30; 10.12). The angels, however, also serve men, especially Christians [Hermas, *Vis.* 4.2.4; *Sim.* 5.4.4; Clement of Alexandria, *Str.* 5.91.3; Origen, *C.Cels.* 1.60; Athanasius, *C.Ar.* 1.61; Augustine, *Civ.* 7.30; *Doctr. christ.* 1.33(30); cf. Heb 1.14]. It was believed that God even appointed a guardian angel for every man (Clement of Alexandria, *Str.* 6.157.5; Origen, *Orat.* 11.5; *C.Cels.* 5.57; *Princ.* 1.8.1; Ambrose. *Explan. Ps.* 38.32; Jerome, *In Matth.* 3 at 18.10; John Chrysostom, *Hom. 59 in Mt.* 4; cf. Mt 18.10; Acts 12.15) or, according to another explanation, at least for the baptized (Origen, *C.Cels.* 6.41; *Princ.* 2.10.7; Basil, *Adv. Eun.* 3.1; John Chrysostom, *Hom. 59 in Mt.* 4). While Pseudo-Dionysius and Gregory the Great, theologians very influential in angelology, never mention a personal guardian angel, in the Middle Ages the view prevailed that every man had such a spirit at his side (e.g., Thomas Aquinas, ST 1a, 113.2–5). An echo of a prior Judaic view (Qumran, *Manual of Discipline* 3.18–19) was the opinion that every man had at his side an angel of justice and an angel of wickedness (Hermas, *Mand.* 6.2.1–10; Origen, *Princ.* 3.2.4; Cassian, *Conl.* 7.13; 8.17 13.12).

According to an early Christian view nations also have their angels (Irenaeus, *Adv. haer.* 3.12.9; Clement of Alexandria, *Str.* 6.157.5; Origen, *C.Cels.* 5.29–32; *Princ.* 1.5.2; 3.3.3; John Chrysostom, *Hom. 59 in Mt* 4; Jerome, *In Dan.* at 10.13; Augustine, *In ps. 88 sermo* 1.3; Pseudo-Dionysius, *Cael. hier.* 9.2–4; Gregory the Great, *Moralia* 17.17; cf. Dan. 10.13, 20–21; 12.1), cities likewise (Clement of Alexandria, *Str.* 6.157.5; Origen, *Hom. 12 in Luc.*, Rauer 87; Jerome, *In Ierem.* 6.7 at Jer 30.12) and the Christian communities (Hermas, *Sim.* 5.3; Tertullian, *De pudicitia* 14.28; Origen, *Orat.* 11.3; 31.6–7; *Princ.* 1.8.1; Ambrose, *In Luc.* 2.50; cf. Ap 1.20; ch. 2–3).

Various duties in creation were attributed to the angels (Justin, 2 *Apol.* 4(5).2; Athenagoras, *Leg.* 10.3–4; 24.3; Origen, *C.Cels.* 8.31–32, 36; Gregory of Nazianzus, *Orat.* 28.31; Augustine, *Civ.* 7.30; *Gen. ad litt.* 8.24: "sublimibus angelis . . . subdita est omnis natura corporea, omnis inrationalis vita, omnis voluntas vel infirma vel prava, ut hoc de subditis vel cum subditis agant, quod naturae ordo poscit in omnibus iubente illo, cui subiecta sunt omnia"; *ibid.* 8.45, 47). They were said to move the stars (Clement of Alexandria, *Str.* 5.37.2), and to be placed over the four elements: earth, water, air, and fire (Origen, *Hom. 10 in Jer.* 6; cf. Ap 7.1–2; 14.18; 16.5), over plants (Origen, *Hom. 10 in Jer.* 6) and animals (Hermas, *Vis.* 4.2.4; Origen, *Hom. 10 in Jer.* 6; *Hom. 14 in Num.* 2). But this concept of nature-angels also met with rejection, because it was thought unworthy in the Christian view of their contemplation of God (Jerome, *In Hab.* at 1.14). In refined form, however, it still perdured in the Middle Ages and even in Thomas Aquinas, according to whose doctrine all things corporeal were governed by angels (ST 1a, 110.1–3).

What is more, it was thought that the procreation of living creatures could not be explained except by the participation of angels (Origen, *C.Cels.* 8.57; *Hom. 14 in Num.* 2); even human beings were said to originate with their help [Tertullian, *De anima* 37.1; Clement of Alexandria, *Excerpta ex Theo.* 53.3; Origen, *In Jo.* 13.50 (49).326–327, 329, 335]. They were, indeed, not considered for this reason to be creators of life (Augustine, *Civ.* 12.25–26(24–25); *Trin.* 3.8.13], but to be helpers in a manner that men were not capable of discerning (Augustine, *Gen. ad litt.* 9.16).

Angels punish men (Hermas, *Sim.* 6.2.5–7; Clement of Alexandria, *Str.* 7.12.5; Cyprian, *Ad Demetrianum* 22; Ambrose, *De Abraham* 2; Gregory the Great, *Hom. in evang.* 38.5; *Moralia* 19.46); these angels were thought by some to be evil spirits (Jerome, *In Is.* 6 at 13.3), by others good spirits (Eusebius, *H.e.* 5.28.12; Ambrose, *Epist.* 34.10; Augustine, *Civ.* 9.5).

Angels take part in the Divine Service with Christians (Origen, *Orat.* 31.5–6; Ambrose, *In Luc.* 1.12; *Const. App.* 8.4.5; Gregory the Great, *Dial.* 4.58) and celebrate with the Church on earth the feasts of Christendom (Gregory of Nazianzus, *Orat.* 38.17; John Chrysostom, *Sermo de resurrectione* 3). The angels also bring the prayers of men before God (Clement of Alexandria, *Str.* 7.39.3; Origen, *Orat.* 11.1, 5; *C.Cels.* 5.4; 8.36; Ambrose, *In Luc.* 8.61; Augustine, *In psalm.* 78.1) and watch over men from heaven (Clement of Alexandria, *Str.* 7.20.4; Tertullian, *De spectaculis* 27.3; Basil, *Hom. de ieiunio* 2.2).

Finally, it was expected that at men's death angels would come and lead the souls of the deceased into the next world (Tertullian, *De anima* 53.6; Origen, *Hom. 5 in Num.* 3; John Chrysostom, *Laz.* 2.2; Gregory the Great, *Hom. in evang.* 35.8; *Moralia* 8.30; *Dial.* 2.35; 4.7, 19; in the Roman rite, the "Ordo commendationis animae" and the Offertory of the Mass for the dead; cf. Lk 16.22).

Groupings of Angels. From Judaic tradition (Tb 12.15; 1 *Enoch* 20.2–7; 61.10; *Testament of Levi* 3.2–8) and from the New Testament (Rom 8.38; 1 Cor 15.24; Eph 1.21; Col 1.16) the view was taken that there were various orders of angels. The princes of the angels, who are usually called ἀρχάγγελοι, archangels, command a leading role [*Epistula Apostolorum* 13(24); Irenaeus *Adv. haer.* 5.25.5; Clement of Alexandria, *Str.* 6.41.2; Pseudo-Dionysius, *Cael. hier.* 9.2]. As was already true in Judaism, so also at this time their numbers fluctuated. Four such angels are mentioned (*Orac. Sib.* 2.215), six (Hermas, *Vis.* 3.1.6–7), or seven (Clement of Alexandria, *Str.* 6.143.1). Under the influence of the Book of Tobias (12.15) and the Apocalypse (ch. 8 and 9; cf. 1.4), the number was finally fixed at seven, and they have been revered, especially in the religion of the common people, throughout the entire Middle Ages in the East and West and even down into modern times. It was, however, only the three archangels mentioned in Holy Scripture, *Michael, *Gabriel, and *Raphael, who received attention in theology and who were also gradually honored in the liturgy (Gregory the Great, *Hom. in evang.* 34.9; Lateran Synod of 745, Mansi 12:380A).

Since the 4th century the choirs of angels have been reckoned at nine both in the East (Cyril of Jerusalem, *Catech. mystag.* 5.6; Chrysostom, *Hom. 4 in Gen.* 5) and in the West (Ambrose, *De apologia prophetae David* 5.20). This number prevailed because the five groups named in the Pauline Epistles (δυνάμεις, *virtutes,* virtues; ἐξουσίαι, *potestates,* powers; ἀρχαί, *principatus,* principalities; κυριότητες, *dominationes,* dominations; θρόνοι, *throni,* thrones) were looked upon as good heavenly spirits, and they were placed together with the angels and archangels [their numbers were estimated at a gradually increasing figure (*Const. Ap.* 8.12.27: a million archangels)] along with the cherubim and seraphim. This series, somewhat schematic and not fully in accord with the Bible, was speculatively developed under Neoplatonic influence by Pseudo-Dionysius into a hierarchical structure of three triads (*Cael. hier.* 6.2; 7–9; *Eccl. hier.* 1.2). Thus elaborated, this doctrine of nine choirs of angels was commonly held in the West

Fig. 3. Christ enthroned among the nine choirs of angels, miniature in a manuscript of the "Canticle of Canticles" illuminated at Reichenau, c. 1000, and now in the Staatliche Bibliothek, Bamberg (Cod. bibl. 20, fol. 5r).

from the time of Gregory the Great (*Hom. in evang.* 34.7; *Moralia* 32.48; *Epist.* 5.54). It received widespread attention chiefly from John Scotus Erigena's Latin translation of the writings of Pseudo-Dionysius in the 9th century (see, e.g., Thomas Aquinas, ST 1a, 108.5–6; a vision and description of the nine choirs by Hildegard of Bingen, *Scivias* 1.6; and a poetical description by Dante, *Paradiso* 28.88–129).

Names of Angels. Most frequently mentioned are the names that occur in Holy Scripture: Michael, Gabriel, and Raphael (Origen, *C.Cels.* 1.25; Gregory the Great, *Hom. in evang.* 34.9). People were especially fond of linking the names of Michael and Gabriel (Tertullian, *De carne Christi* 14.3; Origen, *C.Cels.* 8.15). In Syria the sign XMΓ—usually rendered Christ, Michael, Gabriel (see ReallexAntChr 5:182)—was frequently found on tombs, doorframes, and rings. Another name for one of the princes of the angels that is encountered with relative frequency is Uriel. It comes from the Judaic angelology [*Orac. Sib.* 2.215; *Epist.Apost.* 13(24); Ambrose, *De fide* 3.20]. Over and above the names found in the Bible, popular belief, and particularly superstition, attributed still further names to the princes of angels and other angels. These were names borrowed from the Jews, or even invented arbitrarily or out of ridicule. The Church, however, condemned these tendencies in the Lateran Synod of 745 (Mansi 12:379–380) and in further decrees of the 8th and 9th centuries. When similar attempts were made in the 15th century and again later, the Church once more took steps against them (see ReallexAntChr 5:188).

Teaching of the Church. The Church has defined as dogma that besides the visible world God also created a kingdom of invisible spirits, called angels, and that He created them before the creation of the world (Lateran Council IV, 1215, ch. 1, Denz 800; repeated at Vatican Council I, 1870, Denz 3002; cf., earlier, the Nicene Creed of 325, Denz 125: Πιστεύομεν εἰς ἕνα θεόν . . . πάντων ὁρατῶν τε καὶ ἀοράτων ποιητήν). In conformity with Holy Scripture and with the whole Christian tradition, these angels must be regarded as personal beings and not as mere powers or the like. Pius XII rejected a contrary opinion as being opposed to Catholic doctrine (encyclical *Humani generis,* Aug. 12, 1950; Denz 3891). Only those three names for angels that occur in the Bible may be used.

The Church has further declared as dogma that God created the devil and the demons good by nature, and that they became bad through a fault of their own (Lateran Council IV, ch. 1; Denz 800). The Church, however, has never declared authoritatively the way in which the angels sinned to become the devil and demons.

Moreover, in evaluating the accounts taken from the Bible and from Christian tradition, two extremes are to be avoided: on the one hand not everything that is therein contained can be taken as fact, because much of it belongs simply to the philosophy of life in antiquity and must be discarded; so, too, the existence and efficacy of angels cannot be denied out of hand simply because it is possible today, because of more accurate knowledge, to explain by natural causes what was once attributed to the angels. In the interpretation of Biblical passages, the literary type must be taken into consideration, that is, whether it intends simply the communication of a fact, e.g., that angels are helpers of the Christians (Heb 1.14); or a narrative that popular

Fig. 4. "The Fall of the Angels," panel from the retable of the high altar of the cathedral of Laon, France, by the 15th-century artist Nicolas Frances.

imagination has embellished (e.g., the Book of Tobia); or symbolic visions whose true message must first be discovered through the veil of symbolic experiences that are presented in images proper to the period (e.g., in the Apocalypse). In expressions drawn from tradition, however, one must take into consideration that in the course of time theology has purified the obscurity and error contained in traditional views about angels. In this way theology has now come to a point of distinguishing exactly among angels, stars, and the powers of nature, and specifies that the nature of angels is completely spiritual and no longer merely a very fine material, firelike and vaporous. Up to now it has not yet been defined as dogma that every man has a guardian angel. This opinion does, however, have a basis in Holy Scripture and has been maintained in the Church since ancient times, despite the uncertainty of the question in the first 1,000 years. The Church has never declared itself on whether the angels are divided into orders, nor has it said what kinds of orders there might be. Still, it can be drawn from the New Testament that angels exist and are effective in various ways, as can be detected there within certain limits. Many questions, however, that are raised in Scripture and tradition relating to the angels, cannot be answered or, at least, cannot be answered convincingly, because the necessarily certain knowledge is not possible.

Modern Attitudes toward the Belief in Angels. In the modern mind angels are considered to be tenuous creatures who, with the passage of time, are more and more being relegated to the sphere of legend, fairy tale, and child's fancy. Then, of course, there was rationalism, which thought that all belief in the existence of angels should be repudiated. Inasmuch as they are considered to be products of the imagination, their existence is widely denied. The believing Christian, however, will even today maintain that there are angels because the Bible and the Church teach it. What is more, he is convinced that the assertions of the Bible must be understood and evaluated in terms of the basic principles laid down in the previous section. Some reservations are also required in regard to many of the expressed views of the Fathers or other theologians. The old opinion that events in the world were caused by spiritual beings has been replaced in favor of a mechanical explanation arising from insight into the play of cause and effect. Therefore, the Christian can no longer postulate angelic activity where he knows that impersonal forces are at work. Furthermore, he will reject each and every embellishment of the concept of angels. He also believes that the angels, inasmuch as they are pure spirits, can never appear in a real body; that as spiritual beings they act on earth as causes in a manner that is unknown to men but verified in Scripture and in the experience of the Christian life of grace. Such spiritual beings can evoke in the phantasms of men a vision structured in accordance with the concepts of the times (a similar explanation was already attempted in the Middle Ages and was rejected by Thomas Aquinas, ST 1a 51.2 by an appeal to Scripture, but clearly from an outdated exegesis). Finally, one must be aware that the profane sciences can never prove either the existence or the activity of angels. One knows that angels exist, as St. Augustine once said, through faith ["esse angelos novimus ex fide" (*In psalm. 103 serm.* 1.15)].

See also ANGELOLOGY; ANGELS, GUARDIAN; ANGELS OF THE CHURCHES; APOCALYPSE, BOOK OF; CHERUBIM; DEMON (IN THE BIBLE); DEMON (THEOLOGY OF); ORIGINAL SIN; SERAPHIM.

Bibliography: See tracts on the angels in the manuals of dogma. J. TURMEL, "Histoire de l'angélologie des temps apostoliques à la fin du Ve siècle," *Revue d'histoire et de littérature religieuses* 3 (1898) 289–308, 407–434, 533–552, "L'Angélologie depuis le faux Denys l'Aréopagite," *ibid.* 4 (1899) 217–238; 289–309, 414–434, 537–562; *Histoire des dogmes*, 6 v. (Paris 1931–36) 4:45–119. W. LUEKEN, *Michael: Eine Darstellung und Vergleichung der jüdischen und der morgenländisch-christlichen Tradition vom Erzengel Michael* (Göttingen 1898). G. BAREILLE et al., DTC 1:1192–1271. P. PERDRIZET, "L'Archange Ouriel," *Seminarium Kondakovianum* 2 (Prague 1928) 241–276. J. DUHR, DictSpirAscMyst 1:580–598, 622–625. C. VAGAGGINI, EncCatt 1:1248–51. E. PETERSON, *Das Buch von den Engeln: Stellung und Bedeutung der hl. Engel im Kultus* (2d ed. Munich 1955). O. HOPHAN, *Die Engel* (Luzern 1956). J. DANIÉLOU, *The Angels and Their Mission . . .*, tr. D. HEIMANN (Westminster, Md. 1957). A. WINKLHOFER, *Die Welt der Engel* (Ettal 1958). R. HAUBST, LexThK^{2} 3:867–872. C. D. G. MUELLER, *Die Engellehre der koptischen Kirche* (Wiesbaden 1959). P. GLORIEUX, ed., *Autour de la spiritualité des anges: Dossier scripturaire et patristique* (Tournai 1959). B. NEUNHEUSER, "Die Engel im Zeugnis der Liturgie," ArchLiturgwiss 6 (1959) 4–27. J. MICHL, ReallexAnt Chr 5:115–258. **Illustration credits:** Fig. 3, Hirmer Verlag, München. Fig. 4, From the collection of the Cincinnati Art Museum.

[J. MICHL]

3. DEVOTION TO

In the strict sense, cult of (devotion to) angels denotes a religious practice flowing from the virtue of *religion (St. Thomas Aquinas, ST 2a2ae, 82.2) and constituting an external manifestation of honor and reverence to angels in recognition of their excellence and of one's own reasonable dependence on them. It is an act of secondary veneration (dulia). In general, any religious act of venerating angels can be termed angelic devotion; however, where such an act possesses the required internal (intellect and will) and external (reverence and subjection) elements, it will coincide with angelic cult as defined above. When associated with divine faith, cult of the angels belongs to the supernatural order and has its place in the spiritual life.

Sacred Scripture. The Christian concept of angelic cult is verified only in practices of genuine, divinely revealed, religion and has no equivalent in pagan cults associated with "angels." Assyrians, Persians, and Egyptians paid honor to protective deities, in Accadian *kāribu,* but there is no identity between these pagan deities and the Hebrew *k^{e}rûbîm.*

The OT offers some manifestations of angelic cult, e.g., by Balaam (Nm 22.21–35), Tobit (Tb 12.16), and Daniel (Dn 10.9), but such practices did not constitute the principal object of prophetic teaching; nor did people, though conscious of angels, consider their existence relevant. In the NT, the Gospels mention angels but do not specifically recommend or reject devotion to them; St. Paul implicitly teaches veneration of angels (1 Cor 11.10; Gal 4.14), but such cult is to be given in a manner that does not derogate from Christ, the one and unique mediator; he shows displeasure at false or exaggerated cult to angels. In Ap 22.8–9 St. John is rebuked and corrected for offering excessive veneration to an angel but not for venerating him.

Patristic Era. Fathers of the East and West showed their approval of angelic cult and testified to its early existence. They warned against idolatrous cult of angels (see Aristides, *Apol.* 14; PG 96:1121), condemned latreutic acts of worship toward angels (see Origen, *Cels.* 8.13, 57; PG 11:1533, 1601), defended angelic cult as distinct from adoration reserved to God alone, latria (see Eusebius, *Praep. evang.* 7.15; PG 21:553). There was a period when reserve and restriction had to be urged especially because of false cults and charges of "atheism" against Christians for not worshiping pagan deities [Justin Martyr, 1 *Apol.* 6, PG 6:336; Athenagoras, *Leg.* 10, *Ante-Nicene Fathers* (New York 1903) 2:133]. St. Augustine deserves credit for the excellent formula of honor and love as proper cultic dispositions for venerating angels, distinct from the worship given to God: ". . . we honor them out of charity not out of servitude" (*Vera relig.* 55.110; PL 34:170). The acceptance of the *angelology of Pseudo-Dionysius (5th–6th century), taught especially in his *Celestial Hierarchy* (PG 3:119–370), is largely responsible for angelic cult becoming firmly and universally established in the Church.

The earliest known devotion to angels was principally centered on the Archangel *Michael, the only individual angel honored in liturgical feasts in the Church before the 9th century. In the East, Michaeline devotion was evidenced by the 4th century in the churches and sanctuaries in and near Constantinople. It then spread to Italy and to the rest of Europe.

In the West, the feast of St. Michael and the angels was celebrated as early as the 5th century in the church of the same name outside Rome (see the Leonine Sacramentary, 7th century; Masses and prayers in honor of St. Michael are also mentioned). Devotion at two presently active Michaeline sanctuaries began with separate apparitions of St. Michael in the early centuries: one at Monte Gargano (*c.* 490), near Foggia, Italy, and the other at Mont-Saint-Michel (708), Manche, France.

Fig. 5. Fourteenth-century Byzantine icon of the Archangel Michael, in the Museo Civico at Pisa, Italy. Such paintings were used in the Eastern Liturgies and were also objects of great personal devotion.

Beginning with St. Benedict (543), in the West, there was a steadily growing tradition of angelic cult of faith, love, and devotion from the time of Pope Gregory the Great to St. Bernard of Clairvaux (d. 1153). The latter was the principal and most eloquent exponent of cult of the guardian angels; with him angelic cult assumed that form which has continued unchanged in the Church.

Scholasticism. Theologians of the school were less occupied with devotion to angels and more with a study of their nature, intelligence, and will. Even so, angelic cult was not dormant. The scholastic period was noted for prayers to the guardian angels (13th century), growth of associations and confraternities formed to honor the angels (15–16th centuries), development and popularization of angelic devotion—in which religious orders (Dominican, Franciscan, Jesuit) and individuals [Pierre Caton (d. 1626), Johannes Tauler, Ludolph of Saxony] played prominent roles. Of particular note, also, were a popular treatise on angels by Fra Francesco Eiximenis (d. 1409) and a collection of the practical counsels of mystics on angels by Denis the Carthusian (d. 1471). By 1630 the cult of angels was widespread.

19th and 20th Centuries. Devotion to the angels has been perpetuated in various ways in the last 2 centuries but in particular through: (1) associations and societies, such as the Archconfraternity of St. Michael Archangel (formally erected by Leo XIII, 1878), and the episcopally approved association of Philangeli ("Friends of Angels," founded in England, 1950, by Mary Angela Jeeves—hqs., 1212 E. Euclid, Arlington Heights, Illinois); (2) patronages under the titles of holy and guardian angels in general, and of SS. Michael, *Gabriel, and *Raphael in particular; (3) publications, such as the two currently (1965) published—*L'Ange gardien* (Clerics of St. Viator, 28 rue du Bon-Pasteur, Lyons, France) and *Les Annales du Mont Saint-Michel* (Mont-Saint-Michel, Manche, France); and (4) a variety of liturgical and nonliturgical rites or practices—Masses and Divine Offices in honor of guardian angels and the Archangels Michael, Gabriel, and Raphael; prayers in the Mass, e.g., Preface, *Supplices te rogamus, Per intercessionem, Domine Jesu Christe;* the prayer in the Communion of the Sick, *Exaudi nos;* in the burial service of adults, *In paradisum;* in the blessing of homes, *Exaudi nos;* the Litany of All Saints and novenas [see *The Raccolta* (New York 1957) 440–455 and *The Roman Martyrology*].

Magisterium of the Church. Whatever had contributed to the original establishment and development of angelic cult, however it was associated with the beliefs of the faithful and even subjected to Jewish-Gnostic influence, it is evident that the Church, through its official magisterium, unified and clarified belief in the angels and guided this cult (see J. Michl, ReallexAntChr 5:199–200). The positive teaching of the Church treats of veneration due to angels, the benefits of angelic intervention, and the man-angel relationships in the communion of the saints (blessed). It encourages the faithful to love, respect, and invoke the angels (see Nicaea II, Denz 600; Benedict XIV, Denz 2532; *The Raccolta*); on the other hand, the Church guards its subjects against false and dangerous practices, e.g., by rejecting all names of individual angels except Michael, Gabriel, and Raphael [see the Council of Rome under Pope St. Zachary (745); c.35 of the Council of Laodicea (4th century); the Synod of Aachen (789); the Council of Trent, Denz 1821–25].

Orthodox Churches. The devotion to angels among the Orthodox is found particularly in their Liturgy (Mass and Divine Office) and their observance of special feasts; it is directed especially to Michael, Gabriel, and Raphael.

See also ANGELS, 1, 2, 4; ANGELS, GUARDIAN (IN THE BIBLE); DEMON (THEOLOGY OF).

Bibliography: J. MICHL and T. KLAUSER, ReallexAntChr 5:53–322. A. VACANT et al., DTC 1.2:1189–1271. K. RAHNER, LexThK² 1:533–538. R. HAUBST, *ibid.* 3:867–872. J. DUHR, DictSpirAsc Myst 1:580–625. H. LECLERCQ, DACL 1.2:2144–59, bibliog. 2159–61. EncDictBibl 81–87. Hefele-Leclercq v.1, 4, 5. A. A. BIALAS, *The Patronage of Saint Michael the Archangel* (Chicago 1954). J. DANIÉLOU, *The Angels and Their Mission . . .*, tr. D. HEIMANN (Westminster, Md. 1957). J. DANIÉLOU, *Theology of Jewish Christianity*, ed. and tr. J. A. BAKER (Chicago 1964). 147–187. L. M. O. DUCHESNE, *Christian Worship: Its Origin and Evolution*, tr. M. L. MCCLURE (5th ed. repr. New York 1949). W. G. HEIDT, *Angelology of the O.T.* (Washington 1949). P. P. PARENTE, *The Angels* (St. Meinrad, Ind. 1958), also pub. as *Beyond Space* (New York 1961). J. W. MORAN, "St. Paul's Doctrine on Angels," AmEcclRev 132 (1955) 374–384. M. A. JEEVES, "The Friends of Angels," *Life of the Spirit* 8 (1953–54) 159–163. **Illustration credit:** Fig. 5, Hirmer Verlag München.

[A. A. BIALAS]

4. ICONOGRAPHY

The concept of angels originated in the Orient, but the figural type of the Christian angel was derived from the winged Greek goddess of Victory, or Nike (Fig. 6). During and after the Italian Renaissance, pagan putti, Cupids, or Amors served as models for new types of Christian angels. (Illustrations on following pages.)

Gender, Garments, and Wings. According to Scripture, angels are masculine, youthfulness and virility being their general attributes (Fig. 7). It was only in the late Gothic period that artists began to depict angels of an ideal beauty; this development led to the invention of the purely feminine angel in the Renaissance. The infant angel, also created in the late Gothic period (Fig. 8), was used widely during the Italian Renaissance. In early Christian times angels were represented in long white tunics and palliums, which symbolized both the divine light emanating from angels and the purity of angels (Figs. 9 and 10). At times they were represented in togas with the chlamys of the Roman senator to give them an air of dignity. During the Byzantine period the influence of imperial ceremony increased; often they were represented in the guise of imperial court guards, i.e., in loro and military chlamys and holding standards (Fig. 11). In the West, the early Christian type was used continuously during the Middle Ages, often with additions such as a diadem, a scepter, a codex or roll, or taenia, all symbolic of divine power. From the 13th century the influence of the liturgy and mystery plays became stronger, and their garments imitated various liturgical costumes according to their liturgical functions. At the beginning of the early Christian period angels were represented as wingless youths; it was only in the 4th century that they were depicted with wings. The earliest Christian example of a winged human figure is found in S. Pudenziana in Rome as the symbol of St. Matthew. In St. Mary Major in Rome winged angels are represented hovering in the air.

Functions. As the original Greek word indicates, the most important function of angels is to bring messages from God to men. In scenes from the life of Christ and the life of the Virgin, angels come to assist or to serve them (Fig. 12). Angels appear also in scenes of the martyrdom of saints to give them strength and to deliver them a palm branch or a crown as a symbol of their martyrdom. They are shown, like ancient muses, inspiring an Evangelist or a Church Father, such as St. Jerome, engaged in writing (Fig. 13). As the liturgical system developed and became more complex in the late Middle Ages, angels were regarded as participants in the heavenly liturgy, and many liturgical functions were attributed to them, such as those performed by deacons, acolytes, etc.

Fig. 6. Nike driving a two-horse chariot, Greek gold earring of the mid-4th century B.C.

Angelic Choir. The concept of a celestial hierarchy is derived from the order of Oriental monarchism. It was the *Hierarchia coelestis* by Pseudo-Dionysius the Areopagite that inspired the artistic representation of the heavenly hierarchy. Three orders are recognized, each order consisting of three choirs: seraphim, cherubim, and thrones (first order); dominations, virtues, and powers (second order); principalities, archangels, and angels (third order). Often the Virgin Mary is brought into the center of this hierarchy. Seraphim and cherubim are to be distinguished from other messenger angels in that they alone guard the thrones of the Holy of Holies, sometimes hiding them with their wings from human eyes. The seraph is characterized by six wings covered with eyes, whereas the cherub has only four wings. The former is represented in the red color of fire, the latter, in the blue color of sky. The origin of the type is Oriental, and the Biblical statement of the vision of Isaia (Is 6.21) provided the basis for the iconography. In scenes of the stigmatization of St. Francis, the crucifix appears in the guise of a Seraph.

Archangels. Among archangels, seven (and at times nine) are given names as well as various functions based on relevant Biblical testimony. Three of them, *Michael, *Gabriel, and Raphael, have been most popularly venerated. Among them Michael is the most popular as the militant angel and as the guard of the faithful—*Princeps militiae angelorum.* In Byzantine art he is represented in the purple chlamys or in the loro of the imperial court. In the West he is represented in a long tunic or in the coat of mail and helmet of a medieval knight. He appears in scenes of the Last Judgment combating the dragon of the Apocalypse (Ap 12.7) or battling the hordes of Satan (Fig. 14). This iconography is not to be confused with that of St. George. Michael is represented also weighing the souls of the dead. In the iconography of the heavenly hierarchy, he is shown as the guard of the celestial domain, hurling the rebellious angels, or demons, into the abyss. Gabriel is familiar to us as the bringer of glad tidings from God to men, as in the Annunciation to the Virgin and the annunciation to Zacharias. Raphael is represented most frequently in association with the story of Tobias.

Bibliography: G. STUHLFAUTH, *Die Engel in der altchristlichen Kunst* (Fribourg 1897). C. E. CLEMENT, *Angels in Art* (London 1901). Künstle Ikonog 1:239–264. H. LECLERCQ, DACL 1 (1907) 2080–2161. R. P. RÉGAMEY, *Anges* (Paris 1946). Réau IAC 2.1: 30–55. K. A. WIRTH, *Reallexikon zur deutschen Kunstgeschichte,* ed. O. SCHMITT (Stuttgart 1937–) 5:342–602. **Illustration credits:** Fig. 6, Courtesy, Museum of Fine Arts, Boston. Figs. 7, 9, and 11, Hirmer Verlag München. Figs. 8 and 13, National Gallery of Art, Washington, D.C., Samuel H. Kress Collection. Fig. 10, Alinari-Art Reference Bureau. Fig. 12, The Cleveland Museum of Art, Gift of Hanna Fund. Fig. 14, Courtesy of the Walters Art Gallery, Baltimore, Md.

[S. TSUJI]

ANGELS, GUARDIAN (IN THE BIBLE). Guardian angels are intelligent spiritual creatures divinely deputed to exercise individual care and protection over men on this earth and assist them in their

Fig. 7. Wingless angel in Roman armor, detail of a 4th-century reliquary in S. Nazaro Maggiore, Milan.

Fig. 9. Child's sarcophagus, second half of the 4th century, in the Archaeological Museum, Istanbul, Turkey.

Fig. 8. Infant angel, Tuscan relief, detail, c. 1500.

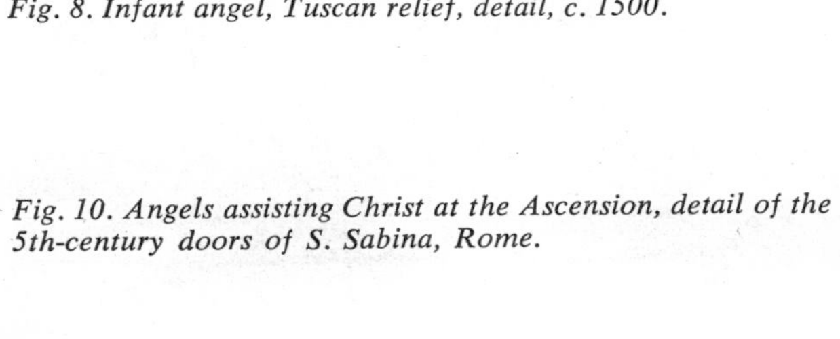

Fig. 10. Angels assisting Christ at the Ascension, detail of the 5th-century doors of S. Sabina, Rome.

Fig. 12. "Baptism of Christ," painting by the 16th-century Italian artist Tintoretto (Jacopo Robusti).

ICONOGRAPHY OF ANGELS

Fig. 11. Archangel Gabriel, 12th-century Byzantine steatite plaque, in the Museo Bandini, Fiesole, Italy.

Fig. 13. "Saint Jerome and the Angel," painting by the French artist Simon Vouet (1590–1649).

Fig. 14. St. Michael battling the hordes of Satan, miniature in a French Book of Hours, c. 1425 (Walters MS 281, fol. 230r).

attainment of eternal salvation. Most frequently, guardian angel is taken to mean a single angel assisting an individual man or groups of persons or a single nation, parish, etc.

The term *angel, as presently used in Catholic theology, indicates a spiritual minion of the divine court. Guardian indicates a protective function, not an entitative grade. The concept of guardian angel as a distinct spiritual being sent by God to protect every individual man is a development of Catholic theology and piety not literally contained in the Bible but fostered by it.

Scattered references to angelic guardianship of individuals or small groups in the OT [Gn 19.10–14, 16; 24.7, 40; 3 Kgs 19.5, 7; Tb 5.6 and *passim;* Dn 3.49–50, 95; Ps 33(34).8; 90(91).11–12] cannot be interpreted as presenting Israelite belief in a universal protective ministry of angels. The angelology of the OT is so unclear that it precludes any such well-defined conclusion. G. von Rad observes that the angels had little significance in the Israelite life of faith because their consciousness was of Yahweh's direct and pervasive action in nature and history without the help of intermediaries [*Genesis* (London 1961) 110]. Again, each instance of angelic custody (excluding those in the Psalms) is presented as special mission rather than customary office. Finally, the Israelites' pride in being Yahweh's chosen people and their concept of such exclusiveness would hardly be conducive to a universal extension of individual guardianship of angels over all men.

Nevertheless, the proximity of Israel to the extravagant Persian angelology and the increasingly emphasized transcendence of Yahweh in postexilic Judaism formed the consciousness into which God communicated deeper knowledge of the instruments of His government, as witnessed by the divine tenderness exercised by *Raphael in Tobit, the angel interpreter of Zacharia ch. 2 and 3, and the national tutelary angels of Daniel ch. 10. This led to an exaggerated proliferation of protecting angels' functions in intertestamental literature.

Two guardian angels protecting the Child Jesus as He is received in the Egyptian city of Sotinen—according to an Apocryphal Gospel. Mosaic of the 5th century on the apse of S. Maria Maggiore, Rome. St. Joseph is at right.

Thus, the way was prepared for the Christian angelology delineated in NT writings (see Gal 1.8; Acts 10.3–7; 12.15; Heb 1.13–14). Jesus's good news of the universality of God's love germinated the Catholic doctrine of the guardian angel from such sources as Jesus's saying, "See that you do not despise one of these little ones [members of His kingdom]; for I tell you their angels in heaven always behold the face of my Father in heaven" (Mt 18.10).

Bibliography: EncDictBibl 911–912. P. R. Régamey, *What Is an Angel?,* tr. M. Pontifex (New York 1960). P. Heinisch, *Theology of the Old Testament,* tr. W. G. Heidt (Collegeville, Minn. 1955). **Illustration credit:** Anderson-Art Reference Bureau.

[T. L. FALLON]

ANGELS OF THE CHURCHES, term used in the Book of *Apocalypse to designate the heavenly counterpart of the seven churches of the Roman province of *Asia. John sees the glorified Christ holding seven stars, perhaps in the form of a scepter, as He walks among the seven lampstands (Ap 1.20). His presence in the churches on earth is thus indicated. The stars are said to symbolize the "angels" of the churches; this is in keeping with the close relationship between stars and angels in ancient Semitic thought. Each of the seven letters that follow is addressed to its respective angel, who is praised, blamed, or warned, as the situation requires (2.1, 8, 12, 18; 3.1, 7, 14). Many Latin Fathers and modern commentators think that by angel here John means the bishop of the particular church. Nowhere in Apocalypse, however, or in the rest of the NT does "angel" mean anything but a superterrestrial being. St. Jerome, the Greek Fathers, and many other modern commentators think that the guardian angel of each church is the recipient of the letter. But can one suppose that John would be told to reprimand the guardian angel for disorders in the church? Here, as frequently in Apocalypse, the author depends upon the Book of *Daniel, where heavenly beings are called "princes" of the kingdoms of Persia, Greece, and Israel, respectively (Dn 10.13, 20, 21). From the context it is clear that they are not guardian angels, as one would now think of them. That they are called princes rather than angels suggests that they were regarded as a kind of heavenly corporate personality, summing up the characteristics and history of the earthly realm with which they were related. John calls them angels to underline their heavenly character, since the earthly reality was considered less real than its heavenly counterpart (see Heb 9.11, 23; 10.1). Because they are the heavenly reality of the respective church with, certainly, its bishop as the earthly corporate personality, they can be praised or reprimanded, as the case may be, for the merits or failings of their particular church.

Bibliography: J. Michl, *Die Engelvorstellungen in der Apokalypse des hl. Johannes* (Munich 1937). EncDictBibl 81–87.

[E. F. SIEGMAN]

ANGELUS CLARENUS, Franciscan author, cofounder of the Clareni; b. Peter, at Fossombrone (Pesaro), March of Ancona, Italy; d. S. Maria d'Aspro, Basilicata, Italy, June 15, 1337. After joining the *Franciscans at Cingoli, Italy, *c.* 1270, he became a partisan of the Franciscan *Spirituals, and after the Council of *Lyons (1274) was on this account condemned to life imprisonment in 1275. When freed *c.* 1289 by the minister general Raymond Gaufridi, he and other Franciscan Spirituals from Ancona went to Lesser Armenia, but the hostility of the Franciscans of the Syrian province forced the group back to Ancona (early 1294), where they were not welcome. Consequently, Friar Peter of Macerata, together with Peter, went to Pope *Celestine V and obtained permission for their group to leave the Franciscan First Order and become *Celestines. Peter of Macerata took the name of Liberatus: Peter of Fossombrone, that of Angelus (the Clarenus or Chiarino was added later). *Boniface VIII, however, voided the authorization granted these Franciscan Celestines, or more properly *Clareni, and they migrated to one of the islands of Achaia, to southern Thessaly, and back to Italy in 1304–05. When Liberatus died, Angelus succeeded him (1307) as head of the group. In 1311 he attempted to obtain papal recognition for the Clareni, but he was received by the Pope only in 1317. *John XXII acknowledged Angelus's personal innocence, but the Franciscan minister general, *Michael of Cesena, would not tolerate a separate group in the order, and Angelus agreed to receive the habit of the Benedictine Celestines—despite their opposition—under Abbot Bartholomew II of Subiaco. Angelus moved to the lands of Subiaco and devoted himself to his followers. His main writings date from this time. His extremist *Apologia* [ed. V. Doucet, ArchFrancHist 39 (1946) 63–200] reached Friar Alvaro Paez in October 1331 and on Nov. 22, John XXII ordered inquisitorial proceedings against Angelus, but the inquisitor died. In February 1334 came new pontifical orders; Angelus fled to Basilicata where he died. His cause for beatification was studied *c.* 1808 but rejected. His works included translations from the Greek of the Rule of St. Basil and of the *Scala* of John Climacus. He wrote an Expositio of the Franciscan Rule *c.* 1321 [ed. L. Oliger (1912)], *Historia septem tribulationum* in 1323 [1–2 ed. Tocco (1908); 3–7 ed. F. Ehrle, Denifle-Ehrle Arch 2 (1886) 308–309], and two ascetical treatises [ed. Mattioli (1898)]. His abundant correspondence, almost entirely unedited, is at Florence (B. N. Magliab. xxxix, 75). Edited sections, including the *Epistola excusatoria,* are in F. Ehrle, Denifle-Ehrle Arch 1 (1885) 543–569.

Bibliography: ActSS June 3:566–576. D. Douie, *The Nature and the Effect of the Heresy of the Fraticelli* (Manchester, Eng. 1932). A. Frugoni, *Celestiniana* (Rome 1954) ch. 4. DTC Tables générales 1:165–166. L. Bernardini, *Frate Angelo da Chiarino alla luce della storia* (Osimo 1964).

[J. CAMBELL]

ANGELUS DE SCARPETIS, BL., Augustinian; b. Borgo San Sepolcro (Umbria), date unknown; d. there, 1306 (feast, Oct. 1). The surname of Angelus has, in the past, been taken more often from his town (Angelus of Borgo San Sepolcro) or region (Angelus of Hetruria) than from his noble family. He became a Hermit of St. Augustine *c.* 1254. The virtues for which he was most noted were humility, a childlike innocence, the spirit of poverty, and apostolic zeal. He supposedly went to England and established a number of houses of his order there; but the source for this tradition cannot be ascertained. He reputedly worked miracles even during his lifetime. His cult was confirmed July 27, 1921.

Bibliography: F. Roth, *The English Austin Friars, 1249–1538,* 2 v. (New York 1961–), v.1 *History* (in progress), v.2 *Sources* (1961). ActApS 13 (1921) 443–446. J. Lanteri, *Postrema saecula sex religionis Augustinianae,* 3 v. (Tolentino-Rome 1858–60) 1:60–61. Butler Th Attw 1:345.

[J. E. BRESNAHAN]

ANGELUS SILESIUS

German mystic and religious poet of the baroque period; b. Breslau, December 1624; d. there, July 9, 1677. He was born Johannes Scheffler, the son of a Protestant landowner who had emigrated from Poland for religious reasons. Johannes studied philosophy and medicine at the Universities of Strassburg, Leyden, and Padua and was appointed court physician by Duke Sylvius Nimrod of Württemburg in 1649. Disgusted by the court chaplain's religious intolerance, Johannes resigned his post in 1652 and became a Catholic in 1653, taking the name Angelus Silesius; the conversion made him the target of vicious attacks and ridicule. After 6 years in Vienna, where he was court physician to Emperor Ferdinand III, he returned to Breslau, entered the Franciscans, and was ordained (1661). From 1664 until his retirement in 1671 he held high positions in the service of his friend Sebastian Rostock, the prince-bishop of Breslau. Angelus then lived in ascetic seclusion until his death at St. Matthias monastery.

While studying in Holland, Angelus had read and admired the writings of another Silesian mystic, Jakob *Böhme, the cobbler of Görlitz. But while Böhme, though uneducated, approached the object of his quest through intuition and an impressive poetic talent, Angelus founded his ideas on a continuation of early Christian *mysticism. In 1657 Angelus published the five-volume *Geistreiche Sinn- und Schlussreime*. For his aphorisms (1665) he used the verse form of the contemporary French drama, the Alexandrine, in which another Silesian, Daniel von Czepko (1605–60), had written his mystical-theosophical *Monodisticha sescenta sapientium.* With extraordinary creative power Angelus molded the experience of God in mystical absorption into the pointed and often paradoxical form of the epigram, in which he fused antitheses of *visio* and *ratio,* the mystical and the conceptual, since, to him, antithesis was the most significant expression of the deity who reconciles and resolves all contradictions. Angelus's theme was not meditation on or adoration of the suffering Christ or the ascent of the soul to God, but rather God's descent to the soul: "I am as great as God, He is as small as I am"; "I know that God cannot live a moment without me; if I perish, He must needs give up the ghost."

Such ambiguous expressions made Angelus suspect of pantheism, which probably accounts for the esteem in which he has been held by romantics and such moderns as R. M. *Rilke. But Angelus's spiritual-intellectual epigrams must be understood as a new variety of Christian mysticism, as the continuation of a tradition that cannot be interpreted by later modern concepts. His censor, the Jesuit N. Avancini, dean of the faculty of theology at the University of Vienna, not only gave permission for publication but wrote a highly commendatory preface to the work, which in its second edition (1674) and with the added sixth volume became known as *Cherubinischer Wandersmann. Heilige Seelenlust oder Geistliche Hirtenlieder der in ihren Jesum verliebten Psyche,* a collection of 205 songs (1657), revealed the zealous convert who, in the spirit of the Song of Songs and of contemporary bucolic poems, wanted to testify to his love for Jesus. Some of these poems are profoundly moving and have become favorites in both Protestant and Catholic churches.

Apart from a number of apologetic writings or "Lehrtraktätlein," as he called them, Angelus engaged also in spiteful religious polemics. Spurred on by his friend, the prince-bishop of Breslau, who was very active in the *Counter Reformation movement, and constantly provoked by his own detractors, Angelus published 55 pamphlets in which he battled with Protestant theologians, such as Chemnitz, Strauch, Scherzer, and Alberti. Two years before his death he published *Sinnliche Beschreibung der vier Letzten Dinge* (1675), a phantasmagoria on the four last things, meant to terrify men into abjuring sin. But he is best remembered for *Cherubinischer Wandersmann* and a few beautiful religious songs.

Bibliography: W. Kosch, *Deutsches Literatur-Lexikon,* v.3 (2d ed. Bern 1956) 2431, with bibliog. to date. H. Gies, "Ein Dichter und Mystiker des Barock," in *Literaturwissenschaftliches Jahrbuch der Görresgesellschaft* 4 (1929) 129–142. M. H. Godecker, *Angelus Silesius' Personality through His Ecclesiologia* (Washington, D.C. 1938). W. Stammler, *Von der Mystik zum Barock: 1400–1600* (Stuttgart 1927; 2d ed. 1950), with extensive bibliog.

[S. A. SCHULZ]

ANGELUS, the practice of commemorating the mystery of the Incarnation by reciting certain versicles, three Hail Marys, and a special prayer while a bell is being rung at 6 A.M., 12 noon, and 6 P.M. Although the origin is obscure, it is certain that the morning, midday, and evening Angelus did not develop simultaneously. While no direct connection can be claimed between the evening Angelus and the ringing of the curfew bell in the 11th century, Gregory IX is said to have prescribed the daily ringing of the evening bell to remind the faithful to pray for the Crusades. In 1269 St. Bonaventure admonished his friars to exhort the faithful to imitate the Franciscan custom of reciting three Hail Marys when the bell rang in the evening. John XXII attached an indulgence to this practice in 1318 and 1327. The morning Angelus again seems to be a 14th-century outgrowth of the monastic custom of reciting three Hail Marys at the sound of the bell during Prime. The noon Angelus originated in a devotion to the Passion that occasioned the ringing of the bell at noon on Fridays; it also came to be associated with praying for peace. The practice is first mentioned by the Synod of Prague in 1386 and was extended to the whole week when Callistus III in 1456 invited the whole world to pray for victory over the Turks. The 16th century saw a unification of the three customs. Benedict XIV, Leo XIII, and Pius XI indulgenced the practice: 10 years each time recited, and a plenary indulgence if recited daily for a month, whether or not a bell is sounded.

Bibliography: W. Henry, DACL 1:2069–78. H. Thurston, DictSpirAscMyst 1:1164–65. P. Paschini, EncCatt 1:1260–61.

[A. A. DE MARCO]

ANGER, the irascible emotion or emergency passion of the sensitive appetite directed toward a present evil with which one is confident he can cope successfully, though with difficulty, and against which one seeks vengeance. It is a general passion in that one is aroused to it only consequent to such other emotions as love, desire, hope, and sadness. Anger is excited by opposing obstacles, frustration of any desire or activity, restraint or coercion, pain, insult, or injury to self or to someone or something loved. Anger, therefore, has a twofold aspect: the quality of hatred directed toward the obstacle, insult or injury, the restraining or coercing force; and the quality of love directed toward the vindication of oneself or the thing or person loved.

As a passion or emotion, anger is psychosomatic. The visible physiological changes involved in the passion of anger are increased pulse, trembling, flushed face, knit eyebrows, tensed facial muscles, dilated and flashing eyes, and sometimes impaired speech. Internal changes are increased output of adrenalin, thus causing increased circulation, heartbeat, and blood pressure—which results in increased sugar in the blood and makes energy available faster to the brain and muscles; increased respiration and perspiration, change in skin temperature, and slowing down of stomach, gall bladder, kidney, and liver functions. The physiological changes accompanying anger are proportionate to the greater or lesser violence of the angry reaction. Physical indisposition caused by pain, fatigue or exhaustion, nervous tension, and insomnia can be a source of irascibility or anger.

Persons with choleric and melancholic temperaments are more easily inclined to vehement and longlasting anger (both just anger and sinful anger); the sanguine to quick, angry outbursts that do not last long. "Temper" usually designates that quality of a person who consistently and readily is excited to more or less violent anger in the face of obstacles, frustration, injury, or insult, even when such things, under ordinary circumstances, would not reasonably evoke it.

See also ANGER (MORAL ASPECT); EMOTION; APPETITE; FEELING; PASSION.

Bibliography: Hastings ERE 1:575–577. M. L. Falorni, Enc Fil 2:1548–49. Thomas Aquinas, ST 1a2ae, 46–48. P. V. O'Brien, *Emotions and Morals* (New York 1950).

[M. W. HOLLENBACH]

ANGER (IN THE BIBLE). Human anger is generally frowned upon in the Bible. Jacob curses the anger of Simeon and Levi (Gn 49.5–7; see also ch. 34). The wisdom literature sees anger as a source of harm for the one angered; it is folly, a source of sins, and a cause of discord [Ps 36(37).8; Prv 14.17, 29; 15.18; 29.22; see also 15.1; 19.11). To be the object of anger could be disastrous (Gn 4.5; 27.43–44; 1 Sm 18.8–9; Prv 16.14; 20.2; Eccl 10.4; see also Lk 4.28; Acts 7.54–58). The NT sees anger and its consequences as things to be avoided in the Christian community (Mt 5.21–22; 1 Cor 13.5; Eph 4.31; 6.4; Col 3.8; 1 Tm 2.8; Ti 1.7). "The wrath of man does not work the justice of God" (Jas 1.19–20). Ephesians 4.26 (cf. Ps 4.5) recognizes the uncontrollable movements of anger and admonishes the faithful not to remain in an angry state. Yet anger ordered to divine justice is just (Ex 16.20; 32.19–20; Is 13.5; 1 Sm 15.33). This is certainly true of Christ's anger (Mk 3.5; 10.14; Mt 12.34; 15.7; 16.23; 23.13–36; Jn 2.15–17.)

Divine anger in the Bible is an anthropomorphical expression of divine retributive justice. It brings out the personal element in God's dealings with men. His anger is provoked by Israel's unresponsiveness to divine love offered in the *covenant (Ex 32.1–10; Dt 11.16–17; Jgs 2.11–15; Is 65.1–7; Ez 7.1–27; Osee ch. 13). God's anger, however, is balanced by His love (Ex 32.12–14; Is 54.7–10; 63.9–15; Os 11.8–9; Mi 7.18–20). Divine anger is aroused by the wickedness of nations (Psalm 2) or by the rebellion of men against their Creator (Gn 4.10–14; 6.5–8; Sir 5.7). Often inexplicable, God's wrath is never satanical or a matter of divine caprice, though a few texts present difficulty in interpretation (Ex 4.24; 2 Sm 6.7; 24.1). Already an active force [Gn 6.17; Nm 11.33; 16.25–35; Ps 105(106).13–18; Is 30.30; 10.5–6; Jer 21.14; 22.1–6; Jgs 2.11–15; 1 Sm 5.9], it is being stored up for the *Day of the Lord (Am 5.18–20; Is 13.9; So 1.15–18). God's final wrath also is a prominent theme in the NT (Mt 3.7; 18.23–35; Lk 14.16–24; Rom 2.5; Col 3.5–6; 1 Pt 4.17–18; Jude 14–15). The last day is still the day of wrath, but the redeemed in Christ will be delivered from it (Jn 3.36; Rom 5.9; Eph 5.1–7; 1 Thes 1.9–10; 2 Tm 1.12, 18). Christ Himself will be the executor of divine anger (Mt 25.31–46; Jn 5.22; Ap 6.15–17; 22.12–13).

Bibliography: M. ALOYSIA, "The God of Wrath?" CathBibl Quart 8 (1946) 407–415. L. BOUYER, "The Servant of Yahveh," *The Paschal Mystery*, tr. M. BENOIT (Chicago 1950) 181–191. W. EICHRODT, *Theology of the O.T.*, tr. J. A. BAKER (Philadelphia 1961–) 1:250–258. A. RICHARDSON, *An Introduction to the Theology of the N.T.* (New York 1958) 75–79. W. EICHRODT and H. CONZELMANN, RGG³ 6:1930–32. EncDictBibl 90–91.

[J. A. FALLON]

ANGER (MORAL ASPECT)

A strong feeling of vexation, an antagonistic emotion usually aroused by a sense of injury. In animals this biological response serves the useful purpose of preservation. Among humans, anger is usually considered as capable of having an ethical rating inasmuch as it can lead to vengeful actions that are disproportionate to the injury suffered or simply unlawful, e.g., murdering a man for an insulting remark. From this point of view an excessive experience of wrath, the misguided discharge of vengeance, or the objectionable damage done in rage to persons or property could result in sins that would be seriously opposed to charity and justice.

"Christ Driving the Money Changers from the Temple," El Greco, Spanish, 16th century, canvas, 46 by 59 inches.

Obviously, the forementioned expressions of resentment might be of such inconsequential proportions as to be merely slightly sinful, or even not sinful at all if the subject has not yet reached an age at which the habitual control of his emotions is to be expected as part of human maturity. Even the most violent and disproportionate discharges of anger can be considered to be of little or no ethical import from the subjective point of view, if the outrageous assault is normally beyond ordinary human endurance, or if the psychological reaction is of such abrupt emergence that rational control becomes humanly improbable. Even in those who are of an age when emotional maturity is fairly well established, it is not uncommon that intense feelings of indignation will be experienced on the sense level, without in any way being made externally manifest in serious violations of justice and charity. Even from the most cautious and critical point of view, such feelings ought to be considered as of slight moral consequence.

Many vexations and the resultant expressions of emotion are entirely without moral objection, or are even morally laudable. Such a situation may occur when only a vigorous display of emotion will secure attention and obedience. Sometimes, as in the classical case of Jesus' driving the buyers and sellers from the Temple, deliberately achieved and discharged rage can be virtuous and worthy of praise.

Different personality types experience anger differently. Some find that the emotion arises quickly and subsides with equal rapidity; others find that anger is more slowly stimulated and only with difficulty dissipated. Accordingly, there are different approaches to the rational control of this human emotion. Granted that psychological understanding of self and others is a basic factor in conditioning one to bear vexations with tranquillity of spirit, various vicarious discharges of energy, e.g., golf or rail-splitting, frequently assist in the dissipation of pent-up rage. Some forms of entertainment that include a degree of violence also serve this same wholesome purpose.

Ancient Christian moralists incorporated anger along with the other six in their list of capital sins. This classification indicates merely that anger is related causally to other sins, and does not imply that it is per se grievous. The anger that St. Paul describes as excluding one from the kingdom of heaven would of necessity have to be seriously sinful.

See also: ANGER (IN THE BIBLE); HOSTILITY, FEELINGS OF; EMOTIONAL DISORDERS, TRANSIENT; EMOTION (MORAL ASPECT); SINS, CAPITAL.

Bibliography: THOMAS AQUINAS, ST 1a2ae, 74.3; 2a2ae, 157–158. Prümmer ManThMor 2:709–710. **Illustration credit:** The Minneapolis Institute of Arts.

[J. D. FEARON]

ANGERS

City of the Maine River near its confluence with the Loire, in west France. The Diocese of Angers (*Andegavensis*), suffragan of *Tours, comprises Maine-et-Loire Department (2,787 square miles), of which Angers is the capital. The Plantagenet kings of England were descended from the original counts of *Anjou; and from Charles of Anjou, brother of *Louis IX of France,

A panel of the "Apocalypse Tapestry," made in the 14th century and preserved at Angers.

descended a house that had ties with several European dynasties. In 1960 the diocese, for the most part rural, had 419 parishes, 922 secular and 140 religious priests, 220 men in 18 religious houses, 3,400 women in 127 convents, and 500,000 Catholics.

Caesar made the residence of the Gallic *Andes* or *Andegavi* a town (*Juliomagus*). Christianity was probably introduced rather early. After the first known bishop, Defensor (372), the episcopal succession is regular. The rebuilding of a circus in honor of Minerva in 347 showed pagan strength, but the evangelization of the countryside, especially along the Loire, made progress under Bishops SS. Maurilius (d. 453), *Albinus, *Licinius, and *Magnobod. In Merovingian times richly endowed abbeys flourished: Saint-Aubin (chapter founded *c.* 530, monastery in 966), Saint-Serge (in existence in the 7th century); *Saint-Maur-sur-Loire and *Saint-Florent-le-Vieil are near Angers. Angers was a strong point in *Charles Martel's time and a Carolingian frontier post against the Bretons. *Theodulf of Orléans, imprisoned in Angers, composed there his hymn **Gloria, laus et honor* to gain pardon from Louis the Pious (818). Bretons and Normans ruined ecclesiastical establish ments in the 9th century. Thereafter the bishops were dominated by the counts, who restored monasteries and built many churches and buildings in Plantagenet Gothic. Bishop Ulger (1125–48) defended episcopal rights, especially against monasteries such as *Fontevrault. His reorganization of the episcopal school (where *Berengarius of Tours, *Baudry of *Bourgueil-en-Vallée, *Marbod of Rennes, and *Robert of Arbrissel studied or taught) made it famous enough to attract an exodus of the English nation from the University of Paris in 1229 (when the University of *Toulouse was founded). Bulls of Urban V made the school a university (1366, 1373), which, however, was suppressed in 1793.

Henry II, Count of Anjou, became king of England and duke of Normandy in 1154, but *Louis VIII restored Anjou to France. Louis IX had the present castle built during an expedition against Brittany and gave Anjou as an appanage to his brother Charles (1246). The Hundred Years' War ruined Anjou, which Louis XI returned to France on the death of "King René" (1480), who had left Angevin Sicily to return to Anjou. Protestant pamphlets circulated from 1525, and Huguenots sacked the cathedral in 1562. The Edict of Nantes gave Protestants a refuge in Saumur, where they organized a university of sorts. Many religious houses were founded in the Counter Reformation. Jansenism gained influence under Bp. Henri *Arnauld (1649–92). In the French Revolution, Bp. Michel de Lorry (1782–1802) refused the oath of the *Civil Constitution of the Clergy, as did most of his clergy, 204 of whom were deported to Spain (1792) while others were drowned in the Loire at *Nantes. The Vendée rising broke out at Saint-Florent (1793). Revolutionary tribunals claimed at least 3,000 victims, including Bl. Noël *Pinot. Count Frédéric de *Falloux, from Angers, gave his name to the law of freedom of instruction passed in 1850. Bishop Charles

The Château d'Angers.

E. *Freppel (1870–91) restored many high schools and was responsible for the founding of the Catholic University of the West in Angers (1875). Bishop François *Mathieu (1893–95), of the French Academy, was transferred to Toulouse and then became a cardinal in the Curia.

The first cathedral was burned when Childeric's Franks sacked the town in 471. Originally dedicated to Our Lady, it was dedicated to St. Maurice after St. Martin supposedly gave it a vial of blood of the martyrs of Agaune in the 4th century. Bishop Ulger rebuilt it in Plantagenet Gothic with one nave; the choir is 13th-century. The church of Saint-Nicholas Abbey, founded by Fulk Nerra (1010–20), was consecrated by Urban II, who visited Angers in 1096. Fulk Nerra also added a convent of nuns to the 6th-century chapel at Ronceray. Angers had 6 collegiate chapters besides that of the cathedral. The abbots of the Augustinian Toussaint Abbey date from 1118; in 1635 it joined the reform of Sainte-Geneviève. The Dominican convent was one of the first in France (1219).

Angers' traditional procession (13th century) was a protest against Berengarius's heresy concerning the Real Presence even before the Feast of *Corpus Christi was instituted. Jehan Michel's beautiful dramatic *Passion* was performed in front of the cathedral (1486). The tapestry of the Apocalypse (1380), restored and retouched, still adorns the castle hall. Louis XIV founded a literary academy in Angers (1685). David of Angers was a painter and sculptor in the early 19th century. René Bazin (1853–1932), a novelist known for purity of language, freshness of feeling, and his vigorous Christian tradition, was from Angers.

Bibliography: F. Uzureau, DHGE 3:85–114. E. Jarry, *Catholicisme* 1:556–559. G. H. Forsyth, *The Church of St. Martin at Angers* (Princeton 1953). J. McManners, *French Ecclesiastical Society under the Old Régime: A Study of Angers in the 18th century* (Manchester, Eng. 1961). C. Port, *Dictionnaire historique et biographique de Maine-et-Loire et de l'ancienne provence d'Anjou,* ed. J. Levron and P. d'Herbécourt, v.1 (Angers 1965) 31–170. **Illustration credits:** Fig. 1, Archives Photographiques, Paris. Fig. 2, French Embassy Press and Information Division, New York City.

[E. CATTA]

ANGILBERT, ST., Carolingian poet and courtier, abbot; b. *c.* 750; d. Feb. 18, 814 (feast, Feb. 18). He was an official in the court of *Charlemagne for more than 20 years. He was a figure in the *Carolingian renaissance, a student of *Alcuin in the *Palace School, the head of the court chapel, and tutor of the young Pepin. He fathered two sons out of wedlock, *Nithard and Harnid, by Charles's daughter Bertha. Between 792 and 796, he took part in 3 embassies to Rome, taking the **Libri Carolini* to Adrian I in 794. He was present at Charlemagne's coronation in 800. In 811, he was one of the witnesses to Charlemagne's will. In 781, he was appointed lay abbot of *Saint-Riquier (Centula). Sometime between 796 and 802, he retired to his abbey to live an austere life. As abbot, he was an able administrator and builder. He wrote two treatises about his monastic work. He greatly increased the library holdings and introduced the uninterrupted recital of the Hours, the *laus perennis,* for his 300 monks. His poems have no exceptional literary merit; they do give us an interesting insight into life at Charlemagne's court. St. Angilbert's cult began at Saint-Riquier in the 12th century.

Bibliography: MGPoetae 1:355–381. MGS 15.1:173–190. ActSS Feb. 3:91–107. Hariulphe, *Chronique de l'abbaye de Saint-Riquier,* ed. F. Lot (Paris 1894). Wattenbach-Levison 2: 235–241. R. Aigrain, *Catholicisme* 1:559–560. Butler Th Attw 1:371. BiblSanct 1:1249–50. Manitius 1:543–547. P. Richard, DHGE 3:120–123.

[V. GELLHAUS]

ANGILRAMNUS OF METZ, bishop and canonist; d. 791. He was at one time abbot of the *Benedictine monastery of Sens and was consecrated bishop of *Metz on Sept. 25, 768. He was chaplain at the court of *Charlemagne from 784. Angilramnus seems to owe his place in history almost entirely to the accidental circumstance of being named author of that part of the pseudo-Isidorian decretals called the *Capitula* or *Capitularia Angilramni* (*see* FALSE DECRETALS). This collection of canons, which represents one stage in the gradual build-up of the celebrated *pseudo-corpus,* concerns itself chiefly with the defense of bishops against encroachments and molestations of civil tribunals and with establishment of the *privilegium fori.* Ostensibly Angilramnus sent the collection to Pope *Adrian II (*Capitularia Hadriani*) as part of his defense against accusations impugning his episcopal administration at Metz. Evidently, the sketchily known facts of his episcopate illustrate the evils that the pseudo-Isidorian decretals were designed to counter. The long-acclaimed text of P. Hinschius, *Decretals pseudo-Isidorianae et capitula Angilramni,* has recently come under severe criticism on scientific and paleographical grounds, but the continuing debate at least preserves for Angilramnus his anomalous place in history.

Bibliography: G. Hocquard, *Catholicisme* 1:560–561. A. Amanieu, DDC 1:522–526. Fournier-LaBras 1:142–145. *Decretales Pseudo-Isidorianae et Capitula Angilramni,* ed. P. Hinschius (Leipzig 1863; repr. 1963) 757–769. PL 96:1031–1102. Stickler 1:128. S. Williams, "The Pseudo-Isidorian Problem Today," *Speculum* 29 (1954) 702–707. A. Humbert, DHGE 3:125–127.

[P. L. HUG]

ANGLESEY, PRIORY OF, Cambridgeshire, England, Ely Diocese (patrons, SS. Mary and Nicholas). It was of unknown origin, served as a hospital in the 12th century, and was refounded for the *Canons Regular of St. Augustine, probably when it was endowed by Richard de Clare (*c.* 1212). It was further endowed and its buildings provided (1217–36) by Master Lawrence of St. Nicholas, papal chaplain. It undertook many chantry services for small benefactions in the 13th century. It was also enriched (1331–60) under the patronage of Elizabeth de Burgh, Lady Clare. The community numbered usually nine members. Its 1535 income was £125; it was suppressed in 1536.

Bibliography: *A Descriptive Catalogue of Ancient Deeds in the Public Records Office* (London 1890). No known chronicle or cartulary. Dugdale MonAngl 6:394–396. E. HAILSTONE, *The History and Antiquities of . . . the Priory of Anglesey* (Cambridge, Eng. 1873). *The Victoria History of the Counties of England: Cambridge and the Isle of Ely,* v.2 (London 1948) 229–234.

[S. WOOD]

ANGLICAN COMMUNION

Comprises the group of autonomous churches in communion with the See of Canterbury. A list of the members follows and a brief account of some major bodies.

The Church of England is the parent body, but there are also in the British Isles the Church of *Ireland, the Episcopal Church in Scotland, and the Church in Wales. Outside the British Isles are the Protestant *Episcopal Church in the U.S. (with its missionary dioceses in Latin America and the Philippines), the Church of India, Pakistan, Burma, and Ceylon, the Canadian Church, the Church of Australia, the separate Churches of the Provinces of New Zealand, South Africa, the West Indies, West Africa, Central Africa, and the Nippon Sei Ko Kwai (The Holy Catholic Church of Japan). In the Middle East Jerusalem has the status of an archbishopric with five dioceses in that region. A new Church of the Province of East Africa includes five dioceses in Kenya and Tanganyika. In Uganda, Ruanda, and Burundi a province has been formed with eight dioceses. In South East Asia the Anglican dioceses have formed a regional council that has a measure of autonomy. In addition, there remain a number of overseas dioceses under the jurisdiction of the archbishop of Canterbury.

Anglicanism was established in Wales in the 16th century by the English crown and fostered by the appointment of Welsh bishops and the use of the vernacular. In the 17th and 18th centuries pluralism, nepotism, and nonresidence among the Welsh clergy caused a great decay of Anglicanism and enabled *Methodism to capture most of the population. In 1920 the Anglican Church of Wales was disestablished. It had six dioceses. There were in 1960 about 200,000 Easter communicants.

The Anglican Church of Ireland was never widely accepted by the populace. Though officially established by the Irish Parliament of 1560 and supported by English governors, it was never notable for spiritual vigor. In 1871 it was disestablished. In 1964 it had 14 dioceses in Northern Ireland and in the Irish Republic and some 411,000 members.

In Scotland Anglicanism was established between 1612 and 1638 and again from the Restoration to 1690. Since that time the Episcopal Church of Scotland, after years of restricted influence because of its connections with the *Jacobites, has had a peaceful existence. It counted in 1964 some 108,000 members with 369 buildings in seven dioceses and had its own version of the Book of Common Prayer. In 1960 there were 57,000 Easter communicants.

In India the Church of England made its entry under the auspices of the East India Company as a consequence of the pressure of Evangelical missionary opinion in the early 19th century. An Anglican bishopric of Calcutta was founded in 1814. Other dioceses were eventually established, but ultimate authority lay with the English crown. In 1930 the Church of England in India became the Church of India, Burma, and Ceylon with full autonomy but with complete intercommunion with Canterbury. When both India and Pakistan gained independence in 1947, the name of Pakistan was also added to the Church's title (*see* SOUTH INDIA, CHURCH OF).

In Canada the Anglican Church had two dioceses in Nova Scotia and Newfoundland by 1800. When Upper Canada was created by the Constitutional Act of 1791, an unsuccessful attempt was made to set up an established Anglican Church. Vigorous Canadian bishops in the 19th century provided for the continuing life of the Canadian Church which also undertakes missions among the Indians and the Eskimos.

In those West Indian islands colonized by the British, the Anglican Church was established in the 17th century. Due to the hostility of the ruling planter class, the Negroes were not evangelized until the 19th century. Bishoprics were first set up in 1824 in Jamaica and Barbados. Outside the island of Barbados the Church was everywhere disestablished by 1900. The Province of the Church of the West Indies was established in 1883.

For England, *see* ANGLICANISM. For the U.S., *see* EPISCOPAL CHURCH.

Bibliography: J. W. C. WAND, *The Anglican Communion: A Survey* (London 1948). Cross ODCC 53–54.

[E. MC DERMOTT]

ANGLICAN ORDERS

In the judgment of the Catholic Church, declared by Leo XIII in the bull *Apostolicae Curae* of 1896, "ordinations performed according to the Anglican rite have been and are completely null and void." This decision of the Holy See has many practical repercussions throughout the world, and it is also a constant source of controversy. For the theological reasoning underlying the papal decision, *see* APOSTOLICAE CURAE. The question of Anglican orders is treated historically in this article, the theological issues being dealt with only insofar as they are relevant. This treatment considers in historical sequence the origins of the Anglican ordination rite; the Catholic rejection of Edwardine ordinations during the Marian restoration; the establishment of the Elizabethan hierarchy; significant events in the 17th, 18th, and 19th centuries; and developments since 1896.

Origins of the Anglican Ordination Rite. Until Henry VIII's death in 1547, and in the earlier years of the reign of his son Edward VI, the Catholic ordination rite continued in use. Then in 1550 a new rite, the Edwardine Ordinal, was officially substituted for the old. It was in use in England for the remaining 3 years of Edward's reign, with slight revisions made in 1552. Rejected during the Catholic restoration under Queen Mary, it was reintroduced in 1559 and used to institute the new Elizabethan hierarchy from which the succession of Anglican orders descends. It is this Ordinal, with some words added in 1662 but with substantially the same significance as when it was first composed, that is still used for ordination to the Anglican ministry. The Catholic Church has declared that this Ordinal was from the beginning, and still is, incapable of serving as a ritual formulary for the bestowing of her Sacrament of Holy Orders. In the bull *Apostolicae Curae* in which he settled the question, Leo XIII singled out one factor as being of decisive importance: "the native character and spirit" which the Edwardine Ordinal acquired from the circumstances of its origin. The Pope explained that it was this total signification of the rite, its unmistakable link with the Reformation protest against the Catholic doctrine of the priesthood, that made it certain that none of the phrases contained in the Ordinal, even if neutral in themselves, could signify the sense required for a Catholic sacramental form of ordination. The key to the understanding of the whole question of Anglican orders, therefore, lies in an accurate appreciation of the historical context in which the Ordinal was composed.

The chief architect of the Protestant Reformation in England during the years 1547–53 was Thomas *Cranmer, Archbishop of Canterbury, who carried through the change of religion with the support of a small but zealous band of like-minded churchmen, and in collaboration with the civil rulers. He also called in several foreign reformers to assist him in his task, among whom the most influential were Martin *Bucer, *Peter Martyr Vermigli, and John à Lasco. As appears clearly from their writings, Cranmer and his colleagues were in agreement with Martin *Luther, Ulrich *Zwingli, John *Calvin, and all the continental Reformers in their detestation of the Catholic doctrine of the Mass and of the sacrificing priesthood. Cranmer and his party also shared with the Swiss Reformers an additional reason for rejecting the Catholic belief about the powers of the priesthood, namely, their denial of any real objective presence of Christ in the Sacrament of the Eucharist.

As soon as the restraint of Henry VIII's doctrinal conservatism was ended by his death in 1547, there was an outburst of radical agitation, with a spate of printed and oral propaganda, against the Mass and the Real Presence. It was obvious to all that the new trend had the active favor of the men now in power, and books defending the old faith could not find a printer. Licenses to preach, controlled by Cranmer, were restricted to those who shared his aversion to the Catholic doctrine. In 1549 a Book of Common Prayer, to replace the Latin Missal and service books, was imposed by the reforming regime for use in public worship despite the reluctance of the Catholic-minded majority. In the new English Communion office several features were retained that outwardly resembled the Mass, but, as in the new Protestant liturgies on the Continent, there was a thorough expunging of all sacrificial language. After the popular risings that followed the imposition of the new form of worship had been crushed with great severity, the pace of the religious changes quickened. There followed the desecration and destruction of the altars.

Cranmer and his assistants were at work on a new code of ecclesiastical laws that was to include penal canons against any who should defend the Real Presence and the Mass. Their projected code denounced the "strange perversity" of those who "show forth their Masses, by which they think a sacrifice is offered to God the Father, namely the body and blood of our Lord Jesus Christ, truly and, as they say, really, in order to impetrate forgiveness of sins and welfare of souls, as well for the dead as for the living." At the same time a new confession of faith, the Articles of Religion, was composed and officially authorized. It included an article rejecting the Catholic doctrine of the Real Presence and another condemning "the sacrifices of Masses" as "forged fables and dangerous deceits." In 1552 the Second Prayer Book of Edward VI replaced that of 1549, which had been merely an interim measure. The structure of the Eucharistic rite was drastically rearranged in order to show, as Bucer put it, "that there is nothing in common between us and the Roman antichrists." Any ambiguities remaining in the 1549 rite were now removed, and the result was an accurate embodiment, in the dignified English of which Cranmer was a master, of the radical Protestant conception of the Eucharist as opposed to the Catholic doctrine of the Real Presence and the Eucharistic Sacrifice.

It was in the midst of this ferment of religious revolution that the Anglican Ordinal was composed and brought into use by Cranmer and his associates. It is this historical context that serves to determine the "native character and spirit" of their rite. Even though some traditional features were retained in the new formulary (and it even included a printed declaration of an "intent" to continue the apostolic ministry of bishops, priests, and deacons), nevertheless everything that in the pre-Reformation rite had expressed the essential consecrating and sacrificing function of the Catholic priesthood was now significantly omitted. It was plain to all parties that the new English rite was to make ministers in the sense of Reformation theology instead of bishops and priests in the sense of the Catholic Church.

Catholic Rejection of Edwardine Ordinations during the Marian Restoration. As soon as the Protestant regime fell from power at the accession of Queen Mary in 1553, there was a swift and general reaction against Cranmer's rites. Edwardine ordinations were now denounced as invalid and impious, for example, in Bishop Edmund *Bonner's homily ordered to be read in the churches (see Clark, *Eucharistic Sacrifice and the Reformation,* 203). Queen Mary, after seeking Cardinal Reginald *Pole's advice, sent a decree to the bishops in 1554 in which she charged them to be vigilant "touching such persons as were heretofore promoted to any Orders after the new sort and fashion of Order, considering they were not ordered in very deed." There is in fact plentiful evidence of a diligent policy on the part of the Catholic authorities to seek out such men and to disallow their orders. Only a few of the Edwardine clergy were eligible to enter the Catholic priesthood, and it is significant that these men were reordained, or rather, ordained absolutely according to the Catholic rite. Records of such reordinations survive from the registers of the dioceses of London, Oxford, Exeter, and York. There is much other evidence. For instance, in the heresy trials, degradation from Orders before punishment was prescribed for those bishops and priests who had been ordained according to the pre-Reformation rite, but not for those ordained with the Edwardine Ordinal, whose orders were treated as nonexistent. In the light of these and other similar facts it is not difficult to recognize the meaning of the bulls of Julius III in 1553 and 1554, of Paul IV in 1555, and the papal faculties communicated to the English bishops by the cardinal legate, which laid down the procedure for dealing with ex-Edwardine ministers. From the beginning, and consistently throughout the following centuries, the Holy See acted on the principle that Orders conferred with the Anglican Ordinal were invalid.

Establishment of the Elizabethan Hierarchy. The Catholic restoration lasted only 5 years, ending with Elizabeth's accession to the throne in 1558. The diocesan bishops, refusing with common accord to cooperate in the reintroduction of Protestantism, were then deprived of their sees and almost all imprisoned. None of them could be induced to consecrate Matthew * Parker, who was to be the first primate of the new Elizabethan hierarchy, but the government managed to bring together four other prelates of Protestant sympathies to perform the ceremony at Lambeth Palace, London, in December 1559. The presiding minister was William *Barlow, who had been made Bishop of St. Davids in the reign of Henry VIII, had been transferred to Bath and Wells under Edward VI, and had forfeited his see under Mary. Although all the normal documentary evidence is strangely lacking, it can reasonably be presumed that he had duly received episcopal consecration. The other ministers at Parker's consecration were John Hodgkin, suffragan bishop of Bedford who had been validly consecrated in 1537, and John Scory and Miles *Coverdale, made bishops merely by the Edwardine Ordinal.

For the consecration of the new archbishop of Canterbury, from whom the succession of Anglican orders is derived, the Edwardine Ordinal of 1552 was reintroduced. In the eyes of the Catholic Church, therefore, the ordination was invalid because of the use of that defective formulary. In addition to this primary and permanent defect of form, found also in all previous and subsequent ordinations in which the Anglican Ordinal was used, there was a second nullifying defect in the consecration of Parker, that is, defect of ministerial intention.

Significant Events of the 17th–19th Centuries. The invariable practices of the Catholic Church of treating Anglican orders as null and void and of reordaining converts from the Anglican ministry was continued during Elizabeth's reign and throughout the following centuries. The English government for a time kept secret all particulars of Parker's consecration, and as a result the "Nag's Head fable" began to gain currency at the beginning of the 17th century. According to this tale Parker had received no serious consecration at all but had been made archbishop in a frivolous manner in a tavern. There had in fact been a dinner and convivial gathering at the Nag's Head Inn in Cheapside, London, after the routine confirmation of Parker's appointment in Bow Church, and it seems that a garbled report of this event furnished the material for the later legend, which was widely repeated by Catholic controversialists. The official rejection of Anglican orders by the Catholic authorities in Rome and elsewhere was independent of this legend; it was based, as always, on theological objections to the Ordinal itself.

In 1661–62 some modifications were made to the Anglican rite. To the unspecific ordination "forms" in the 1552 Ordinal, "Receive the Holy Ghost . . . ," were now added the words, ". . . for the office and work of a priest," or "of a bishop." From the standpoint of Catholic theology, however, these additions did not remedy the abiding defect of form in the Anglican rite, which continues to this day. In the Ordinal such expressions, as Leo XIII explains, "cannot bear the same sense as they have in a Catholic rite."

From time to time particular cases concerning Anglican orders were referred to the Holy See, always with the same result. In 1684–85 the case of a young convert who had been first a French Calvinist and had later received ordination in the Church of England was submitted to Rome. At the command of Innocent XI a full investigation was undertaken. The decision of the Holy Office, based on a searching examination of the Anglican Ordinal and of the circumstances of its origin in the reign of Edward VI, was that it was invalid as a sacramental rite and that the succession of Anglican orders had been null from the beginning. Twenty years later another thorough investigation was undertaken at Rome into the case of John Gordon, converted Anglican bishop of Galloway, Scotland. Before pronouncing their verdict, which they did at a solemn session in 1704 in the presence of Clement XI, the cardinals of the Holy Office sought anew the opinion of leading theologians in Rome, Paris, and Douai, and also took careful cognizance of the facts and theological arguments brought forward in the inquiry of 1684–85. The decision of the Holy See was that none of the orders Gordon had received were valid. It added that since he had not even received the Sacrament of Confirmation (i.e. because there were no true bishops to confirm him), he was to be confirmed afresh before he could receive any Catholic Orders. This last point is significant in showing that the Roman judgment extended to the whole succession of Anglican episcopal orders. The decision was, as before, based on an objective examination of the origin and nature of the Edwardine Ordinal. The "Gordon case" became a classic precedent for the acts of the Holy See. Leo XIII wrote:

> It is important to notice that this papal decision applies in general to all Anglican ordinations; for although it refers to a particular case, yet the ground upon which it was based was not particular. This ground was the *defect of form*, a defect from which all Anglican ordinations suffer equally. And therefore whenever similar cases have subsequently come up for judgment this decree of Clement XI has been cited every time.

With the growth of the Anglo-Catholic party in the Church of England in the second half of the 19th century, the subject of Anglican orders became more and more discussed. For the events which culminated in the authoritative and public declaration of the invalidity of Anglican ordinations, delivered by Leo XIII in 1896, *see* APOSTOLICAE CURAE.

Developments since 1896. Since that time controversy about Anglican orders has continued, and there is extensive but rather confused literature on the subject. The attitude of the Eastern Orthodox Churches, which for a long time regarded Anglican orders as null, has varied in recent years. Some Orthodox Churches are now prepared to treat Anglican orders on the same footing as Roman Catholic Orders. Others, including the Moscow Patriarchate, still refuse to recognize in the Anglican rite anything that could avail for the Sacrament of Orders. The "Old Catholics," a small schismatical group whose theologians reported in 1894 against the validity of Anglican orders, have now recognized those orders and are in intercommunion with the Church of England.

A few Anglican clergymen have sought to allay doubt by obtaining ordination privately at the hands of *epis-*

copi vagantes, ecclesiastics of irregular position who claim to have received the apostolic succession of episcopal orders through some of the Middle Eastern rites or similar sources. The action of these eccentrics is not approved by the Anglican Church, which gives no recognition to any such clandestine ordinations. In any case, the credentials of these "free-lance bishops," the manner in which their ordination rites are performed, and even the written records relating to them are usually open to serious question.

Somewhat different is the case of the Dutch Old Catholic bishops who were officially asked by the Church of England to participate as co-consecrators in Anglican episcopal ordinations on four occasions in recent years. These Dutch prelates can be presumed to have been validly consecrated according to Catholic usage and to have intended to confer true Orders. Accordingly, some have thought that from this source a stream of valid orders has been introduced into the Anglican Church. Judged by the principles of Catholic theology, however, the episcopal consecrations performed on those occasions cannot be considered valid, since the Anglican Ordinal, with its permanent defect of sacramental signification, was employed for the ceremony as usual. There was one variation from the normal procedure. According to the Anglican rubrics, only the presiding archbishop normally pronounces the "form" and the assistant bishops merely lay hands on the candidate in silence; but it is related that on those occasions the Old Catholic prelates not only imposed hands but also pronounced the words, *Accipe Spiritum Sanctum* (Receive the Holy Spirit). These unspecific words by themselves would not suffice to confer the Catholic Sacrament of Orders. They could suffice only if the due specific significance accrued to them from the ritual context. Here the very contrary occurred. However orthodox may have been the subjective intentions of those Old Catholic prelates, the formula they used, insufficiently determinate in itself, was objectively determined to a defective sense by the ritual setting in which it was pronounced. The permanent antisacerdotal significance of the Ordinal—authoritatively declared to be such by the Holy See in 1896—remained decisive in those particular Anglican ordinations as in all others.

Bibliography: E. C. MESSENGER, *The Reformation, the Mass, and the Priesthood: A Documented History with Special Reference to the Question of Anglican Orders,* 2 v. (New York 1936–37). L. MARCHAL, DTC 11.2:1154–93. F. CLARK, *Anglican Orders and Defect of Intention* (New York 1956); *Eucharistic Sacrifice and the Reformation* (Westminster, Md. 1960); "Les Ordinations anglicanes: Problème aecuménique," Greg 45 (1964) 60–93. G. DIX, *The Question of Anglican Orders* (London 1944). F. CIRLOT, *Apostolic Succession and Anglicanism* (El Paso, Tex. 1946).

[F. CLARK]

ANGLICANISM

The religion professed by those Christians who are in communion with and acknowledge in some degree the leadership of the See of Canterbury. Of all the churches in the *Anglican Communion only the Church of England is still established by the State.

The other Anglican Churches within the British Isles are the Church of Ireland, the Episcopal Church in Scotland, and the Church in Wales. Outside the British Isles are the Protestant Episcopal Church in the United States of America (with its missionary dioceses in Latin America and the Philippines); the Church of India, Pakistan, Burma, and Ceylon; the Canadian Church; the Church of Australia, the separate Church of the Provinces of New Zealand, of South Africa, of the West Indies, of West Africa and of Central Africa; and the Nippon Sei Ko Kwai (the Holy Catholic Church of Japan). All these Churches are autonomous members of the Anglican Communion. In the Middle East, Jerusalem now has the status of an archbishopric with jurisdiction over five dioceses in the region. A new Church of the Province of East Africa, another in Uganda, Rwanda, and Burundi, a regional council of Anglican dioceses in South East Asia and a number of overseas dioceses under the jurisdiction of the archbishop of Canterbury complete the Communion.

This article deals with the origin, establishment, and history of the Church of England only; the parties existing at different periods within the Church; the Lambeth Conferences; the relationships with other Churches; ecumenical efforts; the position of the Church in modern English life; and its educational and missionary work, although its missionary work is to be found also in the existence and development of the Churches of the Anglican Communion.

Origins. The Church of England was set up and given its powers by the English crown in Parliament in 1559 and that authority still retains ultimate control of its beliefs and discipline. The first Parliament of Queen Elizabeth I during the Easter of that year promulgated two acts concerning religion: by the Act of Supremacy the Queen was declared to be "the only supreme governor of this realm . . . as well in all spiritual or ecclesiastical things or causes, as temporal," and the authority of the pope was wholly repudiated; by the Act of Uniformity, though all the bishops in the House of Lords voted against it, the Book of *Common Prayer was made the sole service book to be used in all English churches on and after the forthcoming feast day of St. John the Baptist. All existing service books, missals, pontificals, and the like, were henceforth forbidden to be used. Any priest, for example, who said Mass in England was to lose his income for 1 year and go to prison for 6 months. A second conviction was to bring 1 year's imprisonment and loss of his benefice and clerical dignities. A third conviction was to bring life imprisonment. An act passed later in Elizabeth's reign ordered all priests to leave the country within 40 days under pain of death for high treason.

The anti-Roman movement in England had been begun by Henry VIII, the father of Elizabeth I. It had been continued during the reign of his youthful successor, Edward VI, when Thomas *Cranmer, Archbishop of Canterbury, had produced his first edition of the Book of Common Prayer in 1549. This book contained an outline of the Mass service in English with Communion under both kinds. In 1552 Cranmer's second edition, showing the influence of Continental Protestants, had no such outline of the Mass. It was thoroughly Protestant in word and attitude. After Edward VI's death in 1553, his sister, Queen Mary, restored Catholicism; but her death and the accession of her sister, Elizabeth, ensured that England would once again repudiate the Roman allegiance. Elizabeth herself, or her ministers, wished to impose the first Book of Common Prayer as the standard text for all church services. Parliament, however, was dominated by a

The Archbishop of Canterbury about to place the crown of St. Edward upon the head of Queen Elizabeth II. At the coronation, the monarch becomes the head of both the State and the Established Church of the British Empire.

group of erstwhile Marian exiles and their sympathizers who were pressing hard to impose Calvinistic views on the English Church. The upshot was a compromise on the second Book of Common Prayer. This was further than Elizabeth's government had wished to go, but it was not Protestant enough for the agitators in Parliament. This Elizabethan settlement of religion, therefore, had no body of supporters for at least a generation, until those who had been brought up under its aegis gradually worked out its defense. Among the most notable of these was Richard *Hooker.

A series of *Thirty-Nine Articles of religion, similar to those of Cranmer in Edward VI's reign, were promulgated in 1563. These articles, while not a complete statement of Anglican belief, have remained authoritative to such an extent that all ordinands were henceforward required to subscribe to them and likewise all Oxford and Cambridge graduates until 1871. The articles contained many fundamental Christian teachings, an assertion of Elizabeth's power in Church and State, a statement that general councils of the Church were not necessarily infallible, a recognition of only two Sacraments, namely, Baptism and the Lord's Supper, and a declaration that what Catholics believed about the Mass was "a blasphemous fable and dangerous deceit." This last assertion was included in the 1571 edition of the Thirty-Nine Articles when it was clear that there could be no hope of reconciling convinced Catholics to the Elizabethan settlement of religion after the Pope's excommunication of the Queen (*Regnans in Excelsis*) and his order to her subjects (1570) to cease to obey her government. This decree encouraged on the one hand a more thorough persecution of Catholics on the ground that they must be traitors, and on the other, renewed efforts of many Catholics to overthrow Elizabeth's government; a few preferred exile. In contrast, the *Puritans, as the more extreme Protestants of Elizabeth's reign were called, sought to overthrow the compromise in favor of *Presbyterianism. While the government steadily opposed both Catholic and Puritan efforts to change the religious settlement, it did little or nothing to help the archbishop of Canterbury to foster Anglicanism. A major problem was to find Anglican preachers; another was to ensure uniformity of ritual. Puritanism, however, continued to grow both in numbers and in political influence by uniting itself with the increasing numbers of opponents to royal policy in the Elizabethan and Stuart Parliaments.

Historical Development. In 1604 the Hampton Court Conference set up by King James I emphasized the irreconcilability of Anglicanism and Puritanism. Meanwhile, a number of vigorous and intellectually gifted churchmen, generally known as the Caroline divines, among them Lancelot *Andrewes, Bishop of Winchester, and William *Laud, Archbishop of Canterbury, were giving an example of churchmanship that would have more than ensured Anglicanism's supremacy over Puritanism if the monarchy had not become financially dependent on Parliament. The political consequences of the Civil War and the events culminating in the *Revolution of 1688 made it clear that Puritanism, once divested of its political supporters, could not supplant Anglicanism as the established religion; that uniformity of religious belief and practice could not be enforced by the State; and that, as a consequence, England must accept the presence of numerous religious sects. As a result of the refusal of many Anglicans to recognize the supersession of the Stuart dynasty by the Hanoverian, and partly because of the close, political control exercised by the Whigs over Anglican prelates, the Established Church came, in the 18th century, to take on the appearance of a major department of state. One important group in the Church adopted a religious outlook known as Latitudinarianism. This group endeavored so to ally itself with what were thought to be the requirements of scientific thought as to accept beliefs that to many seemed non-Christian.

The general decline of the spiritual health of Anglicanism in the 18th century was partly halted by the rise of *Evangelicalism. This movement stressed the importance of personal religion and paid little heed to ritualism and church organization. Its greatest exponents were John *Wesley and George *Whitefield. Evangelicalism became a great influence for social reform, and one of its achievements was the abolition of slavery throughout the British Empire in the first half of the 19th century. One group of Evangelicals, however, left the Church of England and formed the various sects of Methodism that became a powerful religious and social force in the industrial areas of 19th-century England to which the Church of England was slow to penetrate.

Benthamism, which exerted so much power over the political, legal, and social life of England, was not without effect on the religious life of the nation. This was seen in the demands for reform of the financial structure of the Established Church and, chiefly, for the reduction of the immense incomes of prelates and an increase in the small stipends of the lower clergy. There was also much dissatisfaction with the notorious pluralism and nepotism. In 1827, for example, three-fifths of all Anglican incumbents were nonresident.

Tractarians. Contemporary with this reforming spirit appeared the Tractarian movement led by John *Keble, John Henry *Newman, and Edward *Pusey. These Tractarians, affected by the Romanticism of the time, with its idealization of the Gothic ages, took a growing interest in the Catholic, as distinguished from the Evangelical or Protestant, view of Anglicanism. That is, they stressed the Anglican links with the medieval Church in belief, ritual, and organization. Their ideas were spread in a long series of tracts published in the face of mounting opposition from Anglican Church leaders, who forbade the continuance of the tracts. One effect of this opposition was to cause many of the Tractarians, led by John Henry Newman, to enter the Catholic Church. The increasing campaign of the Anglican bishops against the ritualism of these High Churchmen, as the Tractarians were called, culminated in the passage by Parliament with the encouragement of Archbishop Archibald Tait of Canterbury, of the Public Worship Regulation Act of 1874, whereby those Anglican clergymen who in their services diverged too far from the prescriptions of the Book of Common Prayer could be more easily punished in the ecclesiastical courts. The High Church continued, however, its slow growth; and it now represents a major grouping in the Church of England, though the crown has shown a steady reluctance to advance its adherents to the episcopate. The other major group in the modern Church consists in the successors to the Evangelicals, Low Churchmen, whose outlook has not changed much in the last century, though some of them have continued the Latitudinarian ideas of a past age and have become known as Broad Churchmen. This last group became much infected by modernism at the end of the 19th century and is best represented by the Modern Churchmen's Union in the present-day Church of England. This Union is signalized by its rejection of belief in the miraculous and in the creeds of the early Church.

The Anglican Church has always taken pride in its comprehensiveness and has sought to make little inquiry into the beliefs of its members as long as they were prepared to worship publicly in the forms prescribed by the Book of Common Prayer. However, the growth of illegal ritualistic practices and the desire to modernize the Prayer Book led to the production of a new Book after 20 years of effort and with the authority of the bishops. Parliament, however, rejected it in 1927. A somewhat revised Book was submitted to Parliament in the following year and again vetoed. Much chagrined by its evident subjection to Parliament, many members of the Church of England make use of the illegal 1928 Book, though it is unlikely that any prosecutions will result from this infringement of the law.

Two 19th-century events had important consequences for the Church of England. In 1853 John William Colenso became the first bishop of the See of Natal. Biblical studies in which he denied traditional Christian doctrines concerning hell, the Sacraments, and the Pentateuch appeared under his name; and he was, in consequence, deposed by his metropolitan, Robert Gray of Capetown. Colenso repudiated Capetown's jurisdiction and appealed to the Judicial Committee of the Privy Council in England, which declared in his favor. Though his metropolitan consecrated another bishop of Natal, Colenso refused to yield and by means of the civil courts kept possession of his cathedral and his episcopal income. Backed by members of his diocese, Colenso never gave way and the schism continued long after his death, despite the efforts of successive archbishops of Canterbury to end it.

As a result of the publication in 1860 of *Essays and Reviews*, advocating freedom of inquiry into religious beliefs, two of the seven authors were officially condemned by the archbishop and bishops of the Province of Canterbury. However, the two defendants had the judgment quashed by the Judicial Committee of the Privy Council. The opposition to the book was so strong, nevertheless, that 11,000 clergymen of the Church of England joined in a declaration of their belief in the divine inspiration of the Bible and in the existence of hell. As a result of these events in the English Church, a synod of the Anglican Church in Canada in 1865 appealed for the holding of a general council of the Anglican Churches to issue an official statement of belief. Though agreement on such a statement proved impossible, such a council did meet at Lambeth Palace, the official home in London of the archbishop of Canterbury, under the archbishop's presidency. Similar meetings have been held at more or less 10-year intervals ever since. At the first Lambeth Conference in 1867, there were 76 bishops present; in 1908, there were 242; in 1920 there were 252; and in 1958 there were 310 bishops in attendance. The conferences have no executive authority and their resolutions have no binding force on Anglicans, but they enjoy great moral prestige and are obvious expressions of some contemporary Anglican thought and teaching.

Anglican Doctrine. In 1888 a series of four propositions, originally adopted at a general convention of the Protestant Episcopal Church in Chicago in 1886, were promulgated by the Lambeth Conference of that year as a statement of basic Anglican beliefs. These propositions subsequently known as the Lambeth Quadrilateral, represented an official declaration of fundamental Anglicanism. They were as follows: The Holy Scriptures of the Old and New Testaments contain all things necessary to salvation and are the rule and ultimate standard of faith. The Apostles' Creed and the Nicene Creed are a sufficient statement of the Christian faith. The two Sacraments ordained by Christ Himself, namely, Baptism and the Supper of the Lord, ministered with unfailing use of Christ's words of institution and of the elements ordained by Him are a necessary part of the Christian life. The historic episcopate, locally adapted in the methods of its administration to the varying needs of the nations and peoples called of God into the unity of His church is also a necessary part of Christian life.

This Lambeth Quadrilateral was issued primarily to provide a basis for discussion on reunion with the other Protestant Churches of England and elsewhere. In 1897 it was again declared to represent the mind of the Anglican Communion and to it was added the statement: "we believe that we have been Providentially entrusted with our part of the Catholic and Apostolic inheritance bequeathed by our Lord."

This Quadrilateral together with the report of the Archbishops' (of Canterbury and York) Committee on Doctrine in the Church of England, published in 1938, represent two major statements of Anglican belief in modern times.

Ecumenical Relations. There have been no official conversations with the Catholic Church in recent times with regard to reunion. In 1896 Pope Leo XIII declared Anglican clerical orders to be invalid. In 1922, after much negotiation with members of the Orthodox Churches, the ecumenical patriarch of Constantinople recognized the validity of Anglican orders, and other patriarchs did the same in later years. However, this recognition has never led to any extensive intercommunion between the Anglican and Orthodox Churches. The problem of union with nonepiscopal Protestant Churches has not generally surmounted the disagreement on church government, though the Church of South India has offered one solution to this difficulty. Intercommunion has been reached with the Old Catholics and to some extent with the Lutheran Churches of Sweden and Finland.

The Church of England has engaged in much discussion with other English Protestant bodies with a view to a general reunion of Christians. In 1942 the British Council of Churches was set up; it includes representatives from most of the Protestant Churches of England. It promotes common Christian action on public issues and engages in ecumenical discussions. There has been much talk between the Church of England, the Presbyterian Church in England, the Established (Presbyterian) Church of Scotland, the Methodist Church, and the Episcopal Church of Scotland with regard to reunion.

The Church of South India—which came into existence in 1947 as a result of a union of Anglicans and Methodists with a group originally composed of Presbyterians, Congregationalists, Lutherans, and others—has profoundly affected these ecumenical conversations. This new church of about 1 million members based itself on the Lambeth Quadrilateral and claimed to embody distinctive features of its component bodies. It was hoped that in about a generation all its ministers would have episcopal ordination. The Lambeth Conference of 1930 gave its blessing to the preliminary negotiations, and another Conference in 1948 gave the new Church a tentative approval. In 1955 the Convocations of Canterbury and York approved "a limited intercommunion" between the Church of England and the Church of South India. Despite these encouragements, a large group of Anglicans in South India refused to enter into this union, and very many Anglicans elsewhere were seriously disturbed by it, notably a number of Church of England clergymen who abandoned Anglicanism for the Catholic Church. *See* CONVOCATION OF THE ENGLISH CLERGY.

The fact of establishment has come to mean less and less in the effective religious life of England. The sovereign, who must be a member of the Church of England and must swear at the coronation ceremony to uphold it, receives the title of *Defender of the Faith, originally bestowed on Henry VIII by the Pope but assumed by subsequent monarchs by parliamentary grant. The archbishop of Canterbury has the right of anointing and crowning the monarch, and he takes precedence over all officers of state including the prime minister. All diocesan bishops are appointed by the sovereign on the advice of the prime minister and all clergymen take an oath of allegiance to the monarch. The bishops take precedence over the peerage and the 24 senior bishops and the two archbishops have a right to a seat in the House of Lords. (Anglican clergymen and Catholic priests are legally disqualified from sitting in the House of Commons.)

To many Anglicans the advantages of establishment are outweighed by the benefits that would follow a complete break with the State and it is likely that support for disestablishment will continue to grow. Many Anglicans regard their Church as continuing the ancient Catholic Church of England, differing only in a substitution of State authority for papal authority since the 16th century.

Ecclesiastical Organization. The Church of England with almost 15,500 ministers, is organized into 2 provinces, Canterbury and York, and 43 dioceses. Baptized members of the 2 provinces are about 27 million, i.e., about two-thirds of the population in those areas. In 1958, however, 2,073,000 communicated on Easter Day in the 14,500 parish churches; this represents a rate of 63 per 1,000 of the population over 15. Authority in matters of belief and practice is exercised, under the supreme jurisdiction of Parliament, by the Convocations of Canterbury and York. A convocation (made up of the archbishop, an upper house of bishops, and a lower house of representatives of each cathedral chapter, archdeacons, and elected clergy) meets not more than three times a year. There is also the Church Assembly established in 1919 at the request of the two Convocations and composed of three houses of bishops, clergy, and laity to propose ecclesiastical legislation for parliamentary approval. The Church Assembly has a general supervisory authority over the bodies dealing with the Church's work in education, the training of ministers and general Church work in England and abroad. It controls indirectly some 8,000 Church of England schools of all types, for approximately half of which the Church bears a quarter of the cost of improvements and repairs. The State pays most of the rest of these costs. There are 24 Church training colleges for school teachers, with nearly 5,000 students, and 26 theological colleges.

In 1921 parochial church councils were established to associate the laity with the government of the Church in the parish. In the 1960s the number of those Church members over 17 years of age who had applied for membership of the electoral roll of the parish was not quite 3 million. Each parish raises its own funds and sends a part to support the diocese. Each diocese contributes to the expenses of the Church Assembly. The State does not make any financial grant to the Church. In 1960 the income from 14,305 parochial church councils was more than 19 million pounds. Of this 7.5 per cent went to diocesan funds. In addition, the Church has an endowment fund, provided by its extensive landholdings dating from medieval times and administered by the Church commissioners who are responsible for the payment of clergy stipends and the financing of pensions, new churches, parsonages, and church schools. Only 6,000 of the Churches' livings are at the disposal of ecclesiastical authorities; the rest are bestowed by laymen and various public bodies such as the universities and the crown.

The Church of England has a system of ecclesiastical courts chiefly concerned with maintaining discipline among its clergy. Until the second half of the 19th century, the Church so dominated the ancient Oxford and Cambridge Universities that they were, in effect, Anglican seminaries. This atmosphere has gone and only certain professorships are still reserved to Anglican clerics.

Anglican Societies. In 1698 a group of Anglicans set up The *Society for Promoting Christian Knowledge, which has worked with much success to promote education and missionary work. It built many Church primary schools and teachers' training colleges both in

England and in missionary lands. It is also widely known for its extensive publishing of religious literature. While the Society for the Propagation of the Gospel was to share its work abroad, the National Society for the Education of the Poor in the Principles of the Established Church, founded in 1811, was a chief agent in the provision of primary schools in England and Wales before the State began its own national program in 1870. They received government grants from 1833 onward. The National Society also set up training colleges for teachers. After 1870 these Church schools remained independent, but they received State aid after 1902. As a consequence of the Act of 1944, the schools came increasingly under local government control though the teaching of Anglicanism was not interfered with.

The year 1701 saw the foundation of the *Society for the Propagation of the Gospel in Foreign Parts. This Anglican organization sought not only to evangelize native peoples but also to minister to British people living abroad. In the 1960s it gave financial support to more than 60 dioceses and about 1,000 European missionaries outside the British Isles.

Bibliography: H. H. Henson, *The Church of England* (Cambridge, Eng. 1939). C. M. Ady, *The English Church and How It Works* (London 1940). C. F. Garbett, *Church and State in England* (London 1950). S. L. Ollard et al., eds., *A Dictionary of English Church History* (3d ed. New York 1948). H. J. T. Johnson, *Anglicanism in Transition* (New York 1938). J. G. Lockhart, *Cosmo Gordon Lang* (London 1949). H. Davies, *Worship and Theology in England,* v.3 *From Watts and Wesley to Maurice, 1690–1850* (1961); v.4 *From Newman to Martineau, 1850–1900* (1962). Church of England National Assembly, *The Official Year-book of the Church of England* (London). P. E. More and F. L. Cross, eds., *Anglicanism* (Milwaukee 1935). J. K. Mozley, *Some Tendencies in British Theology* (London 1951). Y. Congar, *Catholicisme* 1:561–571. A. Gatard, DTC 1.1:1281–1302. P. Yelli, DTC 16.1:167–170. Cross ODCC. **Illustration credit:** British Information Service, London.

[E. MCDERMOTT]

ANGLIN, FRANCIS ALEXANDER, chief justice of Canada; b. St. John, New Brunswick, Canada, April 2, 1865; d. Ottawa, Ontario, Canada, March 2, 1933. He was the eldest son of Hon. Timothy Warren and Ellen (MacTavish) Anglin. After education at St. Mary's College, Montreal, the University of Ottawa (B.A. 1885), and the Ontario Law School, he was called to the Ontario bar in 1888 (king's counsel 1902). He set up practice in Toronto, and between 1896 and 1899 he served as clerk of the surrogate court. In 1904 he was appointed judge of the high court of Ontario, and in 1909 he was named to the Supreme Court of Canada, serving as chief justice from 1924 to 1933. Among the ablest judges of the Canadian bench, he was appointed an imperial privy councilor (1925) and named a knight commander of the Order of St. Gregory the Great. He married (1892) Harriet Isabel of Frazerfield, Glengarry, Ontario; they had two sons and three daughters.

Bibliography: *Canadian Who Was Who,* v.1.

[J. T. FLYNN]

ANGLIN, MARGARET MARY, American actress, Laetare medalist; b. Toronto, Canada, April 3, 1876; d. New York, N.Y., Jan. 7, 1958. Daughter of T. W. Anglin, Speaker of the Canadian House of Commons, Margaret was educated at Loretto Abbey in Toronto and at the Convent of the Sacred Heart in Montreal. She first appeared on the New York stage in *Shenandoah,* in September 1894, under the management of Charles Frohman. In 1898 she played Roxane to Richard Mansfield's Cyrano, and subsequently appeared with such leading actors as James O'Neill, E. H. Sothern, and Henry Miller, with whom she did *Camille* by Dumas *fils,* and *The Devil's Disciple* by G. B. Shaw. One of her greatest successes was scored in Henry Arthur Jones's *Mrs. Dane's Defence,* which opened in New York in 1900; another was in William Vaughan Moody's *The Great Divide,* which she introduced in 1906. During her varied career she was also seen as Phaedra, Antigone, Clytemnestra, Iphigenia, Medea, Rosalind, Kate, and Viola. She was married to Howard Hull, brother of actor Henry Hull. In 1927 the Laetare Medal of Notre Dame University was conferred upon her. Her last stage appearance was in a road company version of Lillian Hellman's *Watch on the Rhine* in 1943.

[J. MC G. CALLAN]

ANGLIN, TIMOTHY WARREN, journalist and politician; b. Clonakilty, County Cork, Ireland, Aug. 31, 1822; d. Toronto, Canada, May 4, 1896. He was the son of Francis Anglin, an officer in the service of the East India Company, and Joanne (Warren) Anglin. In 1849 he immigrated to Saint-John, New Brunswick, where he founded first the *Weekly Freeman* (1849) and then (1851) the *Morning Freeman,* a Liberal paper that became the organ of the Roman Catholics in that province. He was elected for Saint-John to the House of Assembly (1860), served as member of the House of Commons for Gloucester County (1867–82), and was twice (1874–77, 1878–79) chosen speaker of the House. During his last years in parliament (1879–82) he was a prominent member of the Liberal opposition under Edward Blake. In 1883 he moved to Toronto and became editor of the *Tribune.* He was married first in 1853 to Margaret O'Ryan, and in 1862 to Ellen MacTavish. Among his 10 children were Francis Alexander *Anglin, chief justice of the Supreme Court of Canada, and Margaret Mary *Anglin, actress.

Bibliography: J. C. Dent, *The Canadian Portrait Gallery,* 4 v. (Toronto 1880–81) v.4. W. S. Wallace, *The Macmillan Dictionary of Canadian Biography* (3d ed. New York 1963) 16.

[R. DUHAMEL]

ANGLO-CATHOLICS

Since the *Oxford Movement, this term has designated the more advanced element within the *High Church party in the Church of England. Somewhat ambiguously, the term's use covers two movements within modern *Anglicanism that, although evidently related, do not always coincide: the revival of Catholic dogmatic and sacramental tenets, and the Ritualist movement. The outstanding figures in the Oxford Movement were not liturgical innovators but faithful adherents of the prescriptions of the Book of *Common Prayer. Conversely, the use of Catholic forms of worship has not always been an infallible sign of orthodoxy in belief. However, in its origins, the Ritualist movement was the natural outgrowth of *Tractarianism. It was inevitable that the revival within the Church of England of Catholic doctrines concerning the Sacraments and public worship should lead men to express these beliefs outwardly through appropriate religious symbolism. This natural consequence was reinforced in the years immediately following the Oxford Movement by a growing appreciation of aesthetic values in England, a movement that, although not religious in its origins, led to a reaction against the Puritanism that characterized contemporary liturgical practice.

Doctrinal Positions and Ritualistic Practices. The basic doctrinal commitment of the Oxford Movement to the principle of *apostolic succession, besides constituting a protest against the Protestantizing of the Church of England and the inroads of religious *liberalism, was also, at least implicitly, an assertion of the Church's freedom from unwarranted interference by the State. As such, it encountered many challenges during the years immediately after the Oxford Movement. In 1850, in the Gorham case, the Privy Council decided in favor of a clergyman, whose views on Baptism had been found unorthodox by his bishop, and permitted him to teach that the doctrine of baptismal regeneration was an open question. In 1853 the Privy Council passed judgment on the Eucharist, sustaining the acquittal by the Court of Arches of Archdeacon George Denison of Taunton, who had denied the doctrine of the Real Presence.

In addition to such opposition to the doctrinal positions of Anglo-Catholicism, its Ritualist practices also came under fire. The ornaments rubric of the 1559 Book of Common Prayer was sufficiently ambiguous to permit the Anglo-Catholic clergy to introduce the use of Eucharistic vestments. After unsuccessful efforts to get the rubric changed, Abp. Archibald Tait obtained the passage of the Public Worship Regulation Act (1874), which was subsequently made more drastic by the amendments of Lord Anthony Shaftesbury. Four clergymen were imprisoned for contumacious violation of this act. The practice of confession by the Anglo-Catholic clergy also aroused bitter opposition. In this case, however, the practice had the explicit sanction of the Prayer Book, so that its opponents were forced to press for revision of the formula of absolution in the Visitation of the Sick.

By the second half of the 20th century, most of the practices for which the Anglo-Catholics suffered in the 19th century were taken as a matter of course, and the major concern of their spiritual descendants arose from the desire of Protestant elements within the Church of England to unite with Nonconformist bodies. The 1955 Convocations of Canterbury and York, concerned with relations between the Church of South India and the Church of England, produced a crisis of conscience for some Anglo-Catholics who believed that the Anglican episcopate, in declaring the orders of the new church to be equivalent to its own, had defined the intention of the Anglican ordination rite in a clearly heretical sense. Others took comfort in the fact that, although the principles on which the Church of South India was formed were regrettable, nevertheless the Church of England had stopped short of full communion with the new body, until such time as it should have an exclusively episcopally ordained ministry.

The sanctuary of the Episcopal church of the Ascension and St. Agnes, Washington, D.C. The setting is typical for the Sunday worship in an Anglo-Catholic parish.

The Ritualist movement within the Church of England has recently been affected by currents of change within the Catholic Church. The effort to be more Roman than the Romans, which has sometimes led Anglo-Catholics to adopt liturgical practices deplored by Catholic liturgists, has become rather pointless in the light of the constitution on the liturgy enacted by *Vatican Council II.

In the U.S. Although the Protestant *Episcopal Church in the U.S. anticipated the Oxford Movement in England, especially in the person of Bp. J. H. Hobart, whose *Tract on Episcopacy* appeared in 1807, the term Anglo-Catholic has never had the came currency in the U.S. as in England. In a church that since the American Revolution has been independent of the Church of England, the use of this hybrid expression has appeared somewhat anomalous. With the Episcopal Church (including many Catholic-minded clergy) now actively engaged in work among Negro and Spanish-speaking people, the "Anglo-" component of the term seems scarcely suitable; most of those to whom the designation might apply prefer to be known simply as Episcopalians.

Bibliography: Cross ODCC 55. P. M. DAWLEY, *The Episcopal Church and Its Work* (Greenwich, Conn. 1955). G. E. DEMILLE, *The Catholic Movement in the American Episcopal Church* (Philadelphia 1941). W. L. KNOX, *The Catholic Movement in the Church of England* (New York 1924). W. L. KNOX and A. R. VIDLER, *The Development of Modern Catholicism* (Milwaukee 1933). E. L. MASCALL, *The Convocations and South India* (London 1955). W. J. S. SIMPSON, *The History of the Anglo-Catholic Revival from 1845* (London 1932). D. STONE, *The Faith of the English Catholic* (London 1926). H. R. WILLIAMSON, *The Walled Garden* (London 1956). **Illustration credit:** Church of the Ascension and St. Agnes, Washington, D.C.

[S. BROWN]

ANGLO-NORMAN LITERATURE

The life of Anglo-Norman literature spans 4 centuries, from the conquest of Britain (1066) to the 15th century, with an extended afterlife as *Law French stretching well into the 18th century. The history of the literature can scarcely be separated from that of the language itself and from the political history of Anglo-French relations. The first period of the development of the language extends approximately to the middle of the 13th century, before the loss of the French provinces, during which time Anglo-Norman was a living speech, a dialect of French; after the mid-13th century the language continued to be spoken in England, but it was increasingly insularized and more and more a language that had to be taught. The early manifestation of conservatism and neologizing (there were many local differences), plus an accelerating freedom of analogical creation and other traits, very soon differentiated Anglo-Norman from Continental French; orthography was always a problem for Anglo-Norman scribes, and their MSS developed notable characteristics (e.g., a small

Gothic minuscule book hand usually in double columns, comparatively free from abbreviations). Many of the edited texts are unsatisfactory, and a great quantity of Anglo-Norman writing remains in MS.

Religious and Didactic Prevalence. If Anglo-Norman literature is viewed as a whole, a dominance of didactic religious writing is evident, probably a result of the emphasis of the Fourth Lateran Council (1215) on the instruction of the laity and on penance. There were many renderings and paraphrases of and commentaries on parts of the Bible, and a number of verse treatments of legends and saints' lives. Some of these were English saints (Edward the Confessor and Thomas Becket), but a considerable number were Celtic; the important writers here were Denis Piramus and Nicholas Bozon.

There is much "wisdom" literature, e.g., the Anglo-Norman translation of the Distichs of Cato; and much practical literature, treatises on falconry and the chase, on chess and medicine, lapidaries, and the like; and there are bestiaries, in which the fanciful, proverbial, and moral are rather forcefully mingled (*see* BESTIARY). There is much worth reading in narrative verse, in the drama, and even in the lyric.

High Point of the Literature. The peak of the writing (and of language development) was reached before 1250; at a time when literature in English was chiefly homiletic, Anglo-Norman literature was rich in quality and variety. (*See* SERMON LITERATURE, ENGLISH MEDIEVAL.) As late as the last quarter of the 14th century John *Gower wrote one of his three major poems in Anglo-Norman, the *Mirour de l'Omme,* a conventional yet sophisticated poem of 30,000 lines. In Vising's summary (p. 39), it appears that "the great religious literature, the most valuable translations of Biblical books, as well as the great epic literature, belong to the 12th century; that the smaller pieces, including sermons, are very numerous in the 13th century; that didactic and practical literature, such as works on natural science, philological works, laws and public documents, belong principally to the 13th and 14th centuries, and that, except for official documents and some very few works of other kinds, Anglo-Norman literature comes to an end in the 15th century."

Page from Wace's "Roman de Brut" in an Anglo-Norman manuscript, early 14th century (Add. MS 45103, fol. 13r).

Chronicle writing begins with Gaimar's *L'Estoire des Engleis* (recently dated not later than 1140, and therefore of philological as well as prosodic interest); matures with his contemporary Wace's *Roman de Brut* (*c.* 1155), the source for much of *Layamon and thus central to the development of Arthurian romance; and comes to an end with Nicholas Trivet (fl. 1300). *See* ARTHURIAN AND CAROLINGIAN LEGENDS. Two plays and two fragments are suggestive of a once-flourishing but now nearly lost dramatic tradition. As the most recent historian of Anglo-Norman literature comments, "the fragmentary character of these remnants of the Anglo-Norman drama must not be allowed to disguise the fact that the two early plays [*Le Mystère d'Adam* and *La Résurrection du Sauveur* are probably both 12th century] are works of considerable literary merit, besides being of capital importance for the history of the Western stage" (M. D. Legge, *Anglo-Norman in the Cloisters,* 331).

Much literary activity seems to have enjoyed the patronage of Henry I, the Conqueror's youngest son who acceded to the throne in 1100; Gaimar, Philippe de Thaün, and others wrote for his second wife, Adelaide of Louvain. Henry II and his famous queen, *Eleanor of Aquitaine, made the English court a center of cultural activity: to this patronage belongs the work of Wace, doubtless several lyric poets, and others. During the same period *Marie de France (fl. *c.* 1175) wrote for English patronage. Although her name is also attached to two rather mediocre religious collections and translations, she is justly famous only for the dozen *lais narratifs* (short narrative romances based on folk materials) attributed to her.

In a trilingual manuscript, such as Harley MS 2253 (*c.* 1320, now in the British Museum), there are some vigorous Anglo-Norman political songs, but few secular lyrics are extant. Anglo-Norman as a whole is particularly strong in narrative (perhaps because the two leading patrons of the writers were court and monastery); and *Horn* and *Tristan* are among the finest of medieval romances. (*See* ROMANCE, MEDIEVAL.) The great and versatile Bishop of Lincoln, *Robert Grosseteste (d. 1253), wrote an allegorical poem of some present-day interest and considerable historical importance, *Le Château d'Amour,* which includes many medieval conventions (the figurative castle, the debate of the Four Daughters of God, etc.) and had significant influence. There are many encyclopedic works: one is a still-unedited 20,000 line translation of and commentary on the Sunday Gospels by Robert of Gretham; another is the influential religious manual, *Le Manuel des péchés* of William of Wadington (translated into English verse in 1303 by Robert of Brunne with the title *Handlyng Synne*), which presents a lively portrayal of medieval life.

Significance of the Literature. Only as late as 1963 did Anglo-Norman literature receive its first separate and competent history in the work of M. D. Legge. There one sees it whole; its importance is clear. It had a great influence on both French and Middle English, for Anglo-Norman writers were creative from first to last and were often pioneers where Old French is concerned; they also left an extensive, rich *miroir de l'homme* of medieval England.

See also ENGLISH LITERATURE, 2.

Bibliography: There are three important early monographs. P. STUDER, *The Study of Anglo-Norman* (Oxford 1920). J. VISING, *Anglo-Norman Language and Literature* (London 1923). E. WALBERG, *Quelques aspects de la littérature anglo-normande* (Paris 1936). They are largely superseded by M. D. LEGGE, *Anglo-Norman in the Cloisters* (Edinburgh 1950); *Anglo-Norman Literature and Its Background* (Oxford 1963). Until the forthcoming list of MSS ed. Prof. RUTH J. DEAN appears, that of Vising is still a necessary tool; it lists, locates, and dates more than 400 MSS, and Vising's bibliog. is still the fullest available. Perhaps the best collection of Anglo-Norman texts will be found in P. STUDER and E. G. WATERS, eds., *Historical French Reader* (Oxford 1924). Since 1939, the publications of the Anglo-Norman Text Society have made available its definitive texts. M. K. POPE, *From Latin to Modern French* (2d ed. Manchester, Eng. 1952) pt. 5. *Year Books of Edward II. a. 1307–1309,* ed. F. MAITLAND (Selden Society Yearbook Ser. 17; London 1903). *Year Books of Edward II. a. 1316–1317,* ed. M. D. LEGGE and W. S. HOLDSWORTH, 2 v. (*Ibid.* 52, 54; London 1934–35), see "Introduction" to v.54. **Illustration credit:** Courtesy of the Trustees of the British Museum.

[R. J. SCHOECK]

ANGLO-SAXON ART

Anglo-Saxon art embraces both the pre-Christian idiom of Scandinavian and Germanic provenance, and, following the conversion of the British Isles, its Christian transformation. The Christian Anglo-Saxon style in turn pervaded Continental Europe by way of Irish and Anglo-Saxon missionary foundations, to enrich Carolingian art and constitute an essential element in the development of Romanesque and subsequent medieval art.

Pagan Period. Pagan Anglo-Saxon art (5th-7th centuries) is seen in the decoration of arms, jewelry, pottery, and other small belongings of the person or the home. There is nothing monumental, no large sculpture or painting. The metalwork, however, is often of great splendor, fashioned in gold, silver, or gilt, and boldly jeweled with garnets, colored glass, and shell. Where the cloisonné technique was used, Anglo-Saxon jewelers attained a skill unsurpassed in the pagan Germanic world, and made dexterous use of filigree and niello. Metalworkers of the pagan period produced accurate enameling in the Celtic style deriving from Celtic influences that preceded or existed alongside of Saxon conquests. (*See* CELTIC ART.)

The first Germanic invasions brought "chip-carving" metalwork preserving vestiges of foliate scrolls and animals that are Roman and naturalistic in origin; but the favorite Anglo-Saxon animal styles reject naturalism, and adopt rather a tightly jumbled pattern of separate heads, limbs, and bodies, covering the surface without background space (Style I), or a sinuous openwork treatment of an entire animal twisting itself into S's and loose knots (Ribbon Style). Occasionally the two styles are found in a single object, such as the rim of a 7th-century drinking horn from Taplow, Buckinghamshire (British Museum); but in general Style I, the earlier of the two, is characteristic of the 5th and 6th centuries. The fine polychrome jewelry with Ribbon Style animals dates from the 7th century, and the most spectacular examples are to be seen in the treasure of an East Anglian king found in a ship burial in 1939 at Sutton Hoo, near Woodbridge, Suffolk (British Museum).

Christian Period. The Anglo-Saxon conversion began with the arrival of St. Augustine at Kent (597), survived difficulties with the Irish at the Synod of Whitby (664), and after 669 found reorganization through a number of remarkable men, such as Theodore of Tarsus and *Benedict Biscop. The period yields illuminated manuscripts and sculpture in stone besides fine metalwork such as the golden "Alfred Jewel," which has an enameled portrait under crystal (Ashmolean Museum, Oxford). The earliest manuscript painting, from late 7th-century Northumbria, decorates the Book of *Durrow (Trinity College, Dublin); its style is hard and metallic, and embodies millefiori panels, Ribbon Style animals, and Celtic spiral scrolls. On the other hand, the Codex Amiatinus (Laurentian Library, Florence), a Northumbrian work of *c.* 700, has paintings of the Evangelists in a naturalistic Italian manner. The Lindisfarne Gospels (British Museum), also *c.* 700, has Evangelist portraits of Italian origin but changed in a hard, insular way, and magnificent full pages of minutely intricate, carpetlike abstract ornament of Celtic and Saxon origin. The 8th- and 9th-century manuscripts of the Canterbury School, though under Carolingian influence, are also of insular design imitating enameled or engraved metalwork.

In the early 10th century, Carolingian art of Byzantine origin is reflected in figures of Prophets and saints on the embroidered stole and maniple given to the shrine of St. Cuthbert by King Athelstan (Durham Cathedral Library). Under the Benedictines brought to Winchester by Bishop Aethelwold (963–984) a new style of illumination evolved with the introduction of the Carolingian minuscule. The Winchester school made figure drawings in Continental classical form, sometimes in the light, impressionistic style of the School of Rheims; but sometimes in more substantial form and appearing on daringly colored decorative pages with lavish scrollwork frames, figure and frame composing a single openwork design.

Anglo-Saxon sculpture has few works of merit, and the appeal of the stone crosses in churchyards and carvings in early churches lies chiefly in their settings. The Ruthwell cross in Dumfriesshire of *c.* 700 has rather heavy figure carving and a pretty, inhabited scroll; the Bewcastle cross in Cumberland has these same features treated in a harder, insular manner and combined with checker pattern and interlacings. There are many crosses in Northumbria, some later ones showing Viking influence; though the best known cross with Scandinavian elements is the round shaft at Gosforth, Cumberland, on which both Christian and pagan figure subjects appear. In the south there are some 20 carvings of the late Saxon period, with figure sculpture in the Winchester style. The "Harrowing of Hell" panel in Bristol Cathedral

Anglo-Saxon Art: (a) Fragment of the Cross of Easby, 8th or 9th century. (b) The "Fuller Brooch," c. 850, silver and niello. (c) Panel from a carved whalebone casket, 8th century, in the National Museum, Florence. (d) "The Second Coming," illumination in the "Benedictional of St. Ethelwold" (Add. MS 49598, fol. 9 v.), c. 971 to 984. (e) "Book of Lindau," back cover, 9th century, gold, silver, and enamels, possibly made at St. Gall.

and the angels at Bradford-on-Avon, Wiltshire, are the best known of these.

See also IRISH ART; CAROLINGIAN ART; MANUSCRIPT ILLUMINATION.

Bibliography: G. B. BROWN, *The Arts in Early England,* 6 v. in 7 (London 1903–37). T. KENDRICK, *Anglo-Saxon Art to A. D. 900* (London 1938); *Late Saxon and Viking Art* (London 1949). D. T. RICE, *English Art, 871–1100* (Oxford 1952). F. WORMALD, *English Drawings of the Tenth and Eleventh Centuries* (New York 1953). D. M. WILSON, *The Anglo-Saxons* (New York 1960). T. KENDRICK et al., eds., *Codex Lindisfarnensis,* 2 v. (Lausanne 1956–60). R. L. S. BRUCE-MITFORD, EncWA 1:446–463. **Illustration credits:** (*a*) Victoria and Albert Museum, Crown Copyright. (*b*) and (*d*) Courtesy of the Trustees of the British Museum. (*c*) Alinari-Art Reference Bureau. (*e*) The Pierpont Morgan Library, New York.

[T. KENDRICK]

ANGLO-SAXONS

Christianity came to Britain about A.D. 200. Britain was an ordinary part of the Church, organized on diocesan lines; it sent three bishops to the Council of Arles in 314, from London, York, and probably Lincoln. Between the middle of the 5th and the end of the 6th century, Christianity in eastern and southern England was almost completely wiped out by the invasion of the heathen Angles and Saxons. The remnant of British Christianity, centering in Devon and Cornwall, Wales, and Strathclyde, remained in isolation after Augustine of Canterbury failed to establish communication with them.

In A.D. 597 the Roman mission sent by Pope *Gregory I and led by Augustine landed in Kent, where it began the conversion of the English and the organization of the English Church according to the directions sent by the Pope in 601. The growth of the English mission is the story of the conversion of one heathen people after another and the establishment of dioceses for them. The earliest of these dioceses were Canterbury, London, Rochester, and York. The mission to York, under Paulinus, collapsed with the defeat of King Edwin at Hatfield in 632, but the work was begun again within a few years by Irish monks who came from Iona to *Lindisfarne on the coast of Northumbria. At the Synod of *Whitby in 663, King Oswiu settled in favor of Rome the conflict between the Irish and Roman missions over the date of Easter and certain ecclesiastical customs. In May of 669 Theodore of Tarsus, a Greek monk consecrated in Rome for the vacant see, arrived at Canterbury. Between then and his death in 690 he established dioceses, appointed bishops, held councils, founded monasteries for both men and women, and greatly fostered learning and culture.

Over the erection of new sees in Northumbria Theodore began a quarrel with Wilfrid, Bishop of York, that lasted for many years. However, in the days of Theodore's successor, Gregory's plan was virtually completed with the appointment of the 12th suffragan bishop for Canterbury. Although the projected 12 suffragans for York never materialized, the work begun by Augustine came to a successful conclusion in 735 with the conferral of the pallium on Egbert, Archbishop of York.

Monasticism had been a strong element in the Anglo-Saxon Church from the beginning. Canterbury, Glastonbury, Malmesbury, Melrose, Lindisfarne, Monkwearmouth, Jarrow, and the nunneries at Whitby, Ely, and Barking were but a few of the foundations. Augustine and his companions and Theodore and his companion Hadrian were monks; Aidan, Colman, Fursey, and countless others were Irish monks; SS. Cedd and Chad, brothers educated by Aidan at Lindisfarne, Cuthbert, Ceolfrith, Benedict Biscop, and Bede shed luster on Northumbria. No less famous were the Abbesses Hilda at Whitby, Ethelburga at Barking, and Etheldreda at Ely.

The monasteries provided a refuge where the holiness could grow that once made England an island of saints; but they did more. They spread civilization and learning, gathered books, provided schools, and produced literary works in both Latin and the vernacular. Though none of the monks reached the greatness of *Bede, who rose to a true conception of history and preserved much of what is known of early England, Aldhelm of Malmesbury, a great teacher and writer, at the beginning of the 8th century could claim that it was no longer necessary to go to Ireland to get an education.

Along with letters, art also flourished, especially in Northumbria; and in the 8th century, Anglo-Saxon monks, missionaries, and teachers went to the Continent in the footsteps of the Irish to advance the cause of religion and learning. The most famous of the teachers was *Alcuin of York; the greatest of the missionaries was St. *Boniface, the apostle of Germany, who returned to convert the land of his fathers.

With the burning of Lindisfarne in 793, the Viking raids began, causing great damage to the Church, especially in eastern England. King *Alfred began the work of recovery; the invaders accepted the faith, and in the 10th century, St. *Dunstan initiated a reform that eliminated abuses and brought the English Church into closer contact with the Continent. In 1066, with the

Fig. 1. "Christ with Mary and Martha," Anglo-Saxon relief thought to be from the cathedral at Selsey, now in the choir of the cathedral at Chichester.

Fig. 2. "The Evangelist Matthew," from the "Echternach Gospels," written in Northumbria, c. 700, possibly in the scriptorium at Lindisfarne, and now in the Bibliothèque Nationale at Paris (MS lat. 9389).

Fig. 3. Anglo-Saxons: (a) Church of St. John the Evangelist, 7th century, Escomb, County Durham. (b) Church of St. Lawrence, built by Aldhelm of Malmesbury in the late 7th or early 8th century, with 10th- and 19th-century restoration, Bradford-on-Avon, Wilts. (c) Church of All Saints, 10th century, Earl's Barton, Northants.

Fig. 4. Harold is offered the crown and is crowned the last Anglo-Saxon king of England, detail of the Bayeux Tapestry, c. 1070, preserved in the Musée Tapisserie at Bayeux, France. The textile is of Norman manufacture.

coming of the Normans, the Anglo-Saxon era came to a close.

Bibliography: F. Barlow, *The English Church, 1000–1066: A Constitutional History* (Hamden, Conn. 1963). C. J. Godfrey, *The Church in Anglo-Saxon England* (New York 1962). E. A. Fisher, *The Greater Anglo-Saxon Churches* (London 1962). M. Deanesly, *The Pre-Conquest Church in England* (New York 1961). D. M. Wilson, *The Anglo-Saxons* (New York 1960). P. H. Blair, *An Introduction to Anglo-Saxon England* (Cambridge, Eng. 1959). Bede, *A History of the English Church and People,* tr. L. Sherley-Price (Penguin Bks. Baltimore 1955). D. Whitelock, *The Beginnings of English Society* (Pelican Bks. Baltimore 1952). F. M. Stenton, *Anglo-Saxon England* (Ox HistEng 2; 2d ed. 1947). W. Levison, *England and the Continent in the Eighth Century* (Oxford 1946). **Illustration credits:** Fig. 2, Bibliothèque Nationale, Paris. Fig. 3, National Buildings Record, London. Fig. 1, Leo Herbert Felton. Fig. 4, From *The Bayeux Tapestry,* ed. F. M. Stenton, published by Phaidon Press, Ltd., London.

[C. P. LOUGHRAN]

ANGOLA

Country of southwestern *Africa, 481,350 square miles in area, bordering on the Atlantic Ocean, south of the *Congo-Léopoldville Republic, and north of *Southwest Africa. The Portuguese explored the coast toward the end of the 15th century, but their first permanent settlement was at Luanda in 1575. Dutch Calvinists occupied the coastal area from 1641 to 1648. Not until the late 19th century were the boundaries of this chiefly agricultural country defined by diplomatic agreements. The section along the coast provided large numbers of slaves for Brazil until 1875, when slavery was abolished. In 1951 Angola ceased being a colony and became an oversees province of Portugal. African nationalist sentiment arose in the 1950s and led to bitter fighting in 1961. The 1960 census recorded a population of 4,800,000, including about 200,000 Europeans. More than half the African population was pagan. Almost all the Europeans and about 40 per cent of the Africans were Christians. In 1957 Protestants reported 189,000 adherents (108,000 being full communicants).

Catholic missionary activity was inaugurated *c.* 1570 by Jesuits, Franciscans, Dominicans, and a few secular priests. Their efforts were seriously hampered by the slave trade. Early successes were less impressive than in the Congo; yet the region had about 20,000 Catholics in 1590. The Diocese of São Salvador, erected in 1596, was transferred to Luanda in 1676. In 1640 the Prefecture of the Congo was created and entrusted to Italian Capuchins, who labored in the interior of northern Angola. The mission was the most flourishing in Africa in the 17th and early 18th centuries; it then declined greatly for a century. Portugal expelled the Jesuits in 1759 and suppressed all orders in 1834. From 1826 to 1852 the diocese was without a bishop. Revival began in 1866 with the arrival of French Holy Ghost Fathers. Despite difficulties between the Portuguese government and the French missionaries, the Prefecture Apostolic of Cimbebasia was created in 1879, whose jurisdiction extended over the southern half of Angola and included southwestern Africa. Anticlerical governments in Portugal (1910–25) seriously hampered the mission. Thus religious were replaced by lay missions in 1910, to the detriment of the Church. Improvement became noticeable after the arrival of Benedictines in 1933. Since the concordat between Portugal and the Holy See (1940) progress has been notable.

In 1940 *Luanda became an archdiocese and metropolitan see for the country. Its suffragans in 1964 were the Dioceses of Luso (created in 1963), Malanje (1957), Nova Lisboa (1940), Sá da Bandeira (1955), and Silva Porto (1940). The archbishop of Luanda also administers the suffragan see comprising the islands of *São Tomé and Principe. Catholics, who numbered 220,000 in 1929, totaled 1,765,000 in 1963, when there were 285,000 catechumens, 188 parishes, 175 secular and 250 religious priests, 135 seminarians, 320 brothers, 460 sisters, and 95,000 students in 1,910 Catholic schools. Primary education has been entrusted to the missionaries as a result of the concordat.

Bibliography: F. de Almeida, *História da Igreja em Portugal,* v.3 (Coimbra 1912). E. A. da Silva Correia, *História de Angola,* 2 v. (Lisbon 1940). J. Alves Correia, *Les Missionnaires français en Angola* (Lisbon 1940). G. Lefebvre, *Angola: Son Histoire, son économie* (Liège 1947). M. de Oliveira, *História eclesiástica de Portugal* (2d ed. Lisbon 1948). R. Delgado, *História de Angola,* 3 v. (Benguela 1948–53). J. Cuvelier and L. Jadin, *L'Ancien Congo, d'après les archives romaines, 1518–1640* (Brussels 1954). A. Brásio, ed., *Monumenta missionária africana,* 8 v. (Lisbon 1952–55). B. J. Wenzel, *Portugal und der Heilige Stuhl* (Lisbon 1958). R. Pattee, *Portugal na África centemporânea* (Coimbra 1959), with full bibliog. J. Duffy,

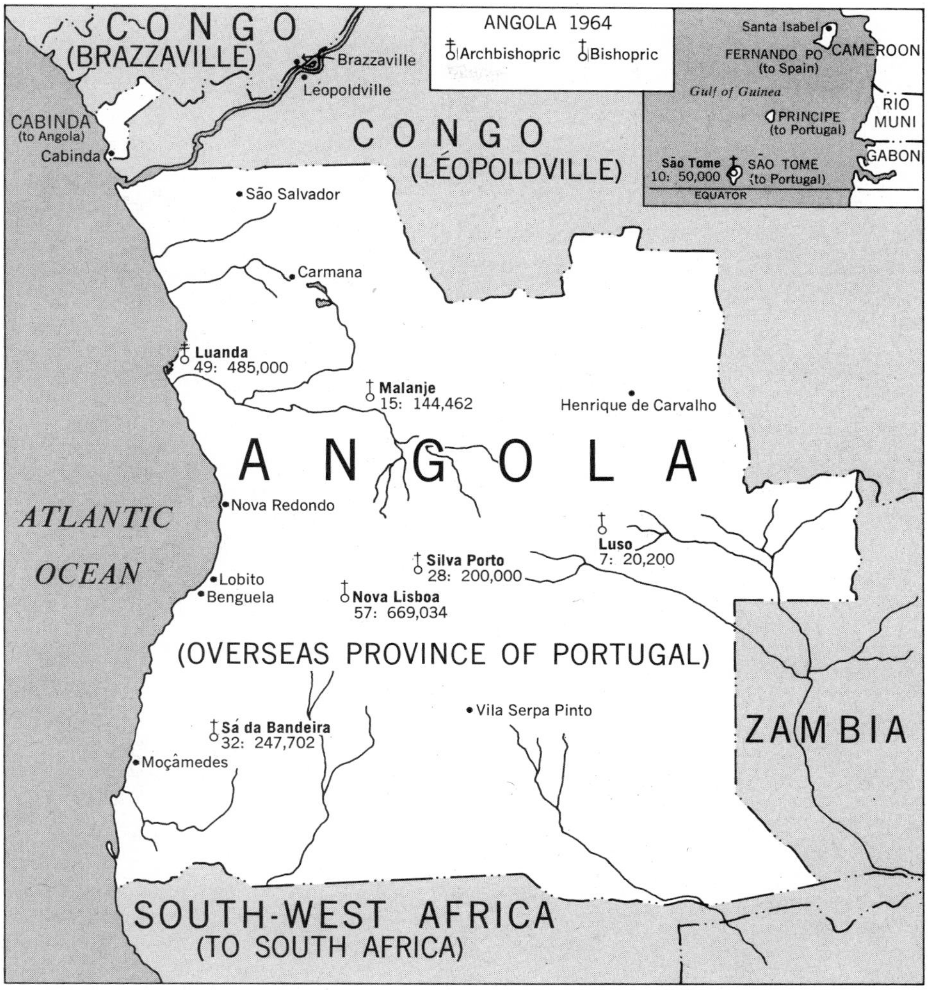

Portuguese Africa (Cambridge, Mass. 1959; *Portugal in Africa* (Cambridge, Mass. 1962; pa. 1963). A. DA SILVA REGO, *Lições de missionologia* (Estudos de ciências políticas e sociais 56; Lisbon 1961). A. MENDES PEDRO, *Anuário Católico do Ultramar Português (1960): Annuaire Catholique de l'Outre-Mer Portugais* (*ibid.* 57; 1962), Fr. and Port. on opposite pages. *Bilan du Monde* 2:71–77. Centro de Estudos Políticos e Sociais, Lisbon. Missão para o Estudo da Missionologia Africana, *Atlas missionário português* (Lisbon 1962). AnnPont has annual data on all dioceses. For further bibliography, *see* AFRICA.

[R. PATTEE]

ANGOULÊME, city on a promontory between the valleys Charente and Anguienne that commands vast horizons except eastward, where the plateau extends to the town Bussatte. Excavations in the 19th century uncovered ancient pagan and Christian sepulchres, engraved vessels, and *stelae.* A sarcophagus has carved upon it the Resurrection symbol of two peacocks facing each other drinking from a vessel from which springs the Eucharistic vine of immortality. Sunken spiraling columns soften its corners, and the shorter sides have parallel sets of chevrons.

The cathedral of St. Pierre (*c.* 1105; 19th-century restoration by Abadie) is distinctively Périgord-Romanesque; it has a single nave, and its massive piers are engaged to walls that carry four domes on pendentives. The north transept tower rises to a height of 195 feet. The extremely durable local stone determined its "oriental" silhouettes, which are peculiarly French and not Byzantine. A Christ in glory presides over the magnificent façade, which has 75 carvings in arcadings and medallions. In a garden beyond the chevet is the kneeling figure of Jean of Angoulême, grandfather of Francis I. (For illustration, see following page.)

The town hall (1858–68), built by Abadie in 13th-century style, incorporates two towers of the castle of the counts of Angoulême, Lusignan (13th century) and Valois (15th century). In the garden there is a statue of Marguerite of Valois, Francis I's sister, who was born at Angoulême in 1492. The Desaix rampart, facing a statue of Carnot (1897), overlooks the beautiful Anguienne Valley; the Beaulieu square commands the Jardin Vert and the Charente Valley. Other notable buildings in the town include the church of St. André with its 12th-century porch and 15th-century nave, and the Hotel St. Simon, dating from the Renaissance. Beyond Angoulême are the ruins of an Augustinian abbey (1122) and the Château La Rochefoucauld.

Bibliography: J. DE LA MARTINIÈRE, DHGE 3:242–257. H. SAALMAN, *Medieval Architecture* (New York 1962). Focillon ArtWMA, v.1. **Illustration credit:** Archives Photographiques, Paris.

[M. J. DALY]

ANI

Medieval Armenian city, 20 miles east of Kars, Turkey, the capital of Armenia under the Bagratuni

Christ in Glory, surrounded by angels and symbols of the Four Evangelists, detail of the central portion of the façade (begun in 1125, completed in 1150) of the Romanesque cathedral of St. Pierre at Angoulême, France.

dynasty (885–1079) and the seat of the Armenian patriarchs between 992 and 1072. The city, which is now in ruins, was built on a triangular promontory between mountain crags and surrounded by the Aladja-Tchaï (Akhourian) and Arpa-Tchaï Rivers. It was acquired by the satrap family of Kamsarakans from the King of Armenia, Ashot Mesaker (806–826); and its fortifications were built by Ashot III the Merciful (952–977), who transferred his residence there from Erazgavor. Smpat II (977–989) enlarged and beautified the city, had himself crowned there, and used it as his capital. Before his death the foundations for the cathedral were laid by the architect Tiridates.

A synod was held in Ani (*c.* 969) in which Bp. Ter Khatchik Archaruni and Abbot Stephen of Sevan, along with many bishops, abbots, and priests, condemned the legitimate catholicos, Vahan (967–969), and with the assent of the King replaced him with Stephen of Sevan (969–971). Vahan was accused of Western and Catholic sympathies in his attempt to achieve union with the Greeks by favoring the faith of the Council of Chalcedon.

Catholicos Ter Khatchik I Archaruni (971–992) prepared Ani to be the patriarchal see. He had been elected to replace Stephen in 971 and proved a strict Monophysite in controversy with Sion, the Armenian bishop of Sebaste, and John of Larissa. However, Khatchik I seems to have mitigated his Monophysite doctrine, despite his acerbity, in an exchange of controversial views with Theodore, the Greek metropolitan of Sebaste. His successor, Sargis I (992–1019), transported his residence from Arkina to Ani (993). He consecrated his successor, Peter Guetadartz (1019–54). Both Peter and Khatchik II of Ani (1054–60) resided there intermittently.

A second synod was held at Ani in 1039 under the leadership of Joseph, Catholicos of the Aghovans. He reestablished Peter Guetadartz in the Armenian Patriarchate and deposed the Abbot Dioscorus of Sanahin, whom King John Bagratuni had imposed on the see. Ani was used as a residence by Basil I (1105–13), the nephew and coadjutor of Catholicos Gregory II. Basil is considered to have been a legitimate catholicos in contradistinction to Basil II, who had proclaimed himself patriarch in 1195, when Gregory VI Apirat established his residence at Hromcla on the Euphrates. After the transfer of the catholicate from Ani, the resident priests and monks became intransigent opponents of the Chalcedonian doctrine and refused every effort at achieving religious unity.

After being sacked several times, Ani suffered an earthquake in 1319 and was practically abandoned. Although the city had been magnificently adorned, ancient descriptions of its beauty and the number of its inhabitants were greatly exaggerated; this is true likewise of the oath by which its citizens swore on its 1,001 churches (Matthew of Edessa, *Chron.* 2.88). However, excavations at the beginning of the 20th century revealed a splendid collection of monuments, particularly the royal palace and numerous chapels and churches. As a commercial center on the route between the Orient and Asia Minor, the city had achieved the height of prosperity under King Gagik I (989–1020) and was celebrated in legends and the chronicles of the Armenian historians.

The Armenian historians Agathangelus, Phaustus, and M. Khorenensis speak of a second Ani (Ani-Gamakh), the fortress situated to the southwest of Eriza on the Euphrates River, where Artaxias I collected his treasures and where many of the Arsacid kings were buried. *Gregory the Illuminator destroyed a statue of Jove there and burned many books connected with Armenian mythology. In 681 George the Bishop of Ani-Gamakh subscribed the acts of the Council of Constantinople III, and he also took part in the Council in Trullo (692).

Bibliography: F. Tournebize, *Histoire politique et religieuse de l'Arménie,* v.1 (Paris 1910) 126–139; DHGE 3:270–271. H. F. B. Lynch, *Armenia: Travels and Studies,* 2 v. (London 1901) 1:354–392. J. J. M. de Morgan, *Histoire du peuple arménien* (Paris 1919) 121–123. N. and M. Thierry, *Jardin des Arts* 65 (1960) 132–145. L. M. Alishan, *Description of Shirak* (Venice 1881), in Armenian. A. Vrouir, *The Labors and Excavations of Professor N. Mar in Ani, 1905–1906* (Houscharar 6; Tiflis). Stephanus of Taron, *Armenische Geschichte,* tr. H. Gelzer and A. Burckhardt (Leipzig 1907). A. Ter-Mikelian, *Die armenische Kirche in ihren Beziehungen zur Byzantinischen (vom IV. bis zum XIII. Jahrhundert)* (Leipzig 1892). S. Lyonnet, RechSc Rel 25 (1935) 170–187.

[N. M. SETIAN]

ANIANE, ABBEY OF, Benedictine abbey of the Holy Savior, in lower Languedoc, France; in the former Diocese of Maguelone (today Montpellier). It was founded by Witiza (*Benedict of Aniane), son of the Count of Maguelone, in 782 and was favored by Charlemagne, friend of Benedict, immunity being granted in 787. It soon prospered and spread the Benedictine rule to nearby Gellone (*Saint-Guilhem-du-Désert, founded in 806 by Duke William Short Nose, hero of *chansons de geste*), and also to Cormery (Touraine), Île-Barbe (Lyons), *Micy (Orléans), Sainte-Colombe-lès-Sens, and *Saint-Savin-sur-Gartempe (Poi-

Interior of the former abbey church of Aniane.

tou). The Council of Aachen (817) imposed Aniane's monastic customs on all monasteries of the Empire. Archbishop Rostaing of Arles occupied the rich abbey (890), leaving it to his successor; it later went to the bishops of Béziers. In the 11th century the Holy See recognized Gellone's independence, which was disputed by Aniane. Conflict with *Chaise-Dieu over a priory was settled by compromise (13th century). Aniane's abbots were important in general chapters, in *Narbonne province, and at the papal court in Avignon (14th century); several became bishops of Béziers, Nîmes, Saint-Papoul, and Montpellier. Decline in the 16th century (*commendation was begun in 1542) was followed by the pillaging of Calvinists, who burned the archives and furnishings and razed the church and buildings (1561–62). The Bonzi bishops of Béziers acquired the abbey's goods (1616–1703), redeeming the irregularity of their acquisition by charitable zeal. Clement de Bonzi (1621–59) instituted the *Maurist reform in 1633. His nephew, Cardinal Pierre de Bonzi (1660–1703), rebuilt (1679) and consecrated the church (1688). The 300 monks of 800 declined to 10 by 1768. Aniane was suppressed in the Revolution (1790); the abbey church became the parish church for the village of Aniane, and the buildings (now a house of detention) became a textile mill. Both Smaragdus Ardon (d. 843?), biographer of the founder (MGS 14.1:178–200), and an anonymous chronicler of Charlemagne's reign were monks of Aniane.

Bibliography: *Cartulaires des abbayes d'Aniane et de Gellone,* ed. P. ALAUS et al., 2 v. (Montpellier 1898–1910). R. THOMASSY, "Critique des deux chartes de fondation de l'abbaye de St-Guillem-du-Désert," BiblÉcChartes 2:177–187. A. DU BOURG, "L'Abbaye d'Aniane, son rôle, son influence, sa destinée," *Mélanges de littérature et d'histoire religieuses pour jubilé de Mgr de Cabrières (1874–1899)* (Paris 1899) 1:165–193. A. WILMART, "Le Lectionnaire d'Aniane," *Revue Mabillon* 13 (1923) 40–53, study of the only Visigothic liturgical text in France. R. GAZEAU, *Catholicisme* 1:573–574. A. RASTOUL, DHGE 3:277–279. Cottineau 1:115–117.

[P. COUSIN]

ANIANUS OF CHARTRES, ST., bishop of Chartres at the beginning of the 5th century (feast, Dec. 7). Medieval accounts name Anianus as the fifth bishop of *Chartres, but no early source mentions him. The church under his patronage and in which his relics are enshrined, burned in 1134. At Chartres his feast is commemorated on December 7, the date on which his relics were returned to the reconstructed church in 1136. A similar event in 1262 resulted in a second feast day, but this has not been retained.

Bibliography: BHL 1:80 suppl. 321. A. CLERVAL, "Translationes S. Aniani," AnalBoll 7 (1888) 321–335; DHGE 1:1111–14. Baudot-Chaussin 12:228.

[B. L. MARTHALER]

ANIANUS OF ORLÉANS, ST., bishop; b. Vienne; d. Orléans, *c.* 453 (feast, Nov. 17). In a letter to Bishop Prosper of Orléans, *Sidonius Apollinaris confirmed that Orléans was saved from Attila and his *Huns in 451 by the intervention of Anianus (MGAuct Ant 8:147). A century later *Gregory of Tours gave a more detailed and picturesque account (MGSrerMer 3:108–117). It seems that Anianus's contribution to saving Orléans lay in his organization of the defenses and in rallying the townsmen to resistance. The military defeat of Attila must be attributed to the Roman general, Aetius. The relics of Anianus are venerated in Orléans in the church that bears his name. F. *Dupanloup founded a teaching and nursing congregation in Orléans, the Sisters of St. Anianus, which was approved in 1852. It now has about 40 houses.

Bibliography: P. BARBIER, *Vie de S. Aignan* (1912). Baudot-Chaussin 11:559–562. Butler Th Attw 4:367. E. EWIG, LexThK[2] 1:561–562.

[B. L. MARTHALER]

ANIANUS AND MARINUS, SS., hermits of the 7th century (feast, Nov. 15). Anianus, a deacon, and Marinus, a bishop, established themselves as hermits at Wilparting in the Bavarian Alps. They were of either Irish or West Frankish origin, and their vita in two MSS (12th and 15th centuries) goes back to the work of Bp. Arbeo of Freising (8th century). They were martyred by a band of Vandals or Wends and their cult, which is still active, derives historical support from an entry in the Sacramentary of Emperor Henry II, the patron of Rott (on the Inn River) in the 12th century. Discoveries in the 18th century settled the dispute between Rott and Wilparting over who had the relics of the saints in favor of Wilparting.

Bibliography: B. SEPP, ed., *Vita SS. Marini et Anniani* (Regensburg 1892). R. BAUERREISS, "Die *Vita SS. M. et A.* und Bischof Arbeo von Freising," *Studien und Mitteilungen zur Geschichte des Benediktinerordens und seiner Zweige* 51 (1933) 37–49; *Kirchengeschichte Bayerns* (2d ed. Munich 1958–) 1:47–48. G. BAESECKE, "Bischof Arbeo von Freising," *Beiträge zur Geschichte der deutschen Sprache und Literatur* 68 (1945–46) 75–134. BHL 2:5531–35.

[C. P. LOUGHRAN]

ANICETUS, POPE, ST., pontificate 155–166 (feast, April 17). Eusebius says Anicetus ruled 11 years, placing his death in 168, the 8th year of Marcus Aurelius (*Hist.* 4.11, 14, 19, 22; 5.6, 24; Irenaeus 3.3). Jerome (*Chron.*) dates his accession in the 18th year of Antoninus Pius (155 or 156). *Polycarp came from Smyrna to discuss with Anicetus variations in the date of Easter according to the *Quartodeciman and Roman systems. The discussions ended amicably, but both Rome and the Orient continued their separate, traditional observance of the feast. Polycarp's martyrdom on his return to Smyrna in 155 fixes the beginning of Anicetus's episcopacy as 155 or earlier. Eusebius records that the Gnostic *Valentinus remained in Rome until Anicetus's pontificate and that the great Syrian scholar, *Hegesippus, and *Justin Martyr were there. The *Liber pontificalis* says Anicetus was from *Emesa (Homs) in Syria and that he was a martyr. It also reports that he forbade clerics to wear long hair and gives two accounts of his burial: one in the Vatican and the other in the cemetery of Calixtus, which did not exist, at least in name, until 50 years later. Its report that *Anacletus (79?–92?) built a sepulchral monument for Peter probably mistakes that Pope for Anicetus since it refers to the tropaion mentioned by the Roman priest Gaius in the 2nd century; recent excavations under St. Peter's have shown this monument to be a late-2nd-century structure.

Bibliography: EUSEBIUS, *Hist. Eccl.* 4.11, 14, 19. P. GOGGI, EncCatt 1:1288–89. E. KIRSCHBAUM, *Tombs of St. Peter and St. Paul,* tr. J. MURRAY (New York 1959).

[E. G. WELTIN]

ANIMA CHRISTI. The prayer *Anima Christi,* listed in the Missal and Breviary among prayers to be said after Mass, was commonly entitled *Aspirationes Sancti*

Ignatii. The 1964 edition of the Missal published in the U.S. includes the prayer but quite correctly omits this title. St. *Ignatius of Loyola frequently recommended the prayer in his *Spiritual Exercises* but, since he always quoted only the opening words, the *Anima Christi* must have been already quite well known in his time. That it was known as early as the 14th century is evident from several sources: a manuscript (now in the British Museum) written in England *c.* 1370 states that John XXII granted 3,000 days indulgence for the saying of this prayer under certain conditions; the text of the prayer is carved on the wall of the palace of the Alcazar in Andalusia, done probably about 1364; it is known that Margaret Ebner (d. 1351), a mystic of Swabia, was familiar with the prayer. That it was quite well known throughout Europe by the 15th century is evident from its frequent appearance in books of hours and other devotional books of that century (*see* PRAYER BOOKS). The author of the prayer is unknown. It has been attributed to Pope John XXII because of the many extraordinary indulgences he attached to it, and also to Bl. Bernardine of Fletre, OFM (1439–94), although the prayer was well known before his time. The suggestion that St. Thomas Aquinas composed the *Anima Christi* seems unlikely, since no 13th-century manuscript containing it has been found, and it has no special place in Dominican devotion, as has, for example, the *Lauda Sion* and the *Adoro te,* the former composed by St. Thomas and the latter frequently attributed to him. The existing manuscripts have interesting variations, the invocations *Sudor vultus Christi, defende me* and *Sapientia Christi, doce me* occurring in some. This prayer has been translated into practically all known languages.

Bibliography: H. THURSTON, "The *Anima Christi,*" *Month* 125 (1915) 493–505; DictSpirAscMyst 1:670–672. M. VILLER, "Aux Origines de la prière *Anima Christi,*" RevAscMyst 11 (1930) 208–209. P. SCHEPENS, "Pour l'histoire de la prière *Anima Christi,*" NouvRevTh 62 (1935) 699–710. I. CECCHETTI, EncCatt 1:1341–42.

[M. J. BARRY]

ANIMA NATURALITER CHRISTIANA, a phrase used by *Tertullian (*Apol.* 17.6; PL 1:377). Like Hellenistic philosophers, Tertullian looks for knowledge of God from the world outside of man and from the world within man's soul. Thus he appeals even to the witness of the pagan, a witness that he terms the "testimony of the soul naturally Christian" (*testimonium animae naturaliter christianae*). Even the pagan, he says, by different exclamations ("Great God!" "Good God!") spontaneously testifies to his knowledge of God (one and unique) and of those Christian truths which belong to the sphere of natural knowledge (*De test. animae*).

As used by theologians, this axiom can mean: (1) the possibility of a knowledge of God and of the natural moral law belongs to the very essence of man (Rom 1.20; 2.14–15) and predisposes him to Christianity; (2) a cult (even false and atheistic) is an essential anthropologic element; as a tendency towards transcendence it belongs necessarily to a real individual and collective human existence and thus witnesses to the *anima naturaliter christiana;* (3) man is naturally open to a possible divine word-revelation; (4) man as a creature of the Trinity and redeemed by Christ is a carrier of Trinitarian and Christologic seals and has an *obediential potency that is actualized by a *supernatural *grace in at least the lowest degree of intensity.

See also GOD, especially 1, 7, 8, 9; NATURAL LAW; SUPERNATURAL EXISTENTIAL.

Bibliography: K. RAHNER, LexThK[2] 1:564–565 with bibliog. Quasten Patr 2:264–266. Altaner 166–177 with bibliog. M. SCHMAUS and K. FORSTER, eds., *Der Kult und der heutige Mensch* (Munich 1961).

[P. B. T. BILANIUK]

ANIMAL LIFE

The type of vital activity that characterizes animals (including man) and serves to distinguish them from plants (*see* LIFE; PLANT LIFE). This article briefly summarizes the salient features of animal life as known to biological science and then discusses aspects of animal behavior that are of interest to philosophers.

SCIENTIFIC ACCOUNT

While plant and animal life exhibit basic similarities in the functions of reproduction, growth, and metabolism, animals are generally remarkably distinct from plants in the acuity, speed, and coordination of their responses to internal and external stimuli. The superior sensitivity of animals to slight variations in environmental conditions probably underlies the evolutionary proliferation of a much larger number of animal species.

Animal Behavior. In higher animals, behavior patterns exhibit a great degree of plasticity and coordination, even at the level of innate or unlearned activities. N. Tinbergen (1907–) has proposed a theory of the hierarchical organization of instinctive behavior to account for these features; e.g., the reproductive pattern of the Stickleback fish is variably expressed in a succession of subpatterns—fighting to establish territory, nest building, courting and mating, and care of offspring. Each subpattern has its own characteristic releaser, e.g., the appearance of another male fish in the vertical "fighting" posture, as well as its own characteristic subdivisions, e.g., chasing, biting, and threatening. Inasmuch as stimuli are regarded as releasers rather than forcers, the theory allows for the spontaneity of animal behavior, understood as a result of the characteristic neural and metabolic organization of the animal.

Other innate behavioral responses are taxes, oriented responses of a whole organism to a stimulus, and reflexes, usually involving only a specific part of the body. Learned behavior patterns, those more or less permanently modified by the history of the individual, are epitomized in man. There is questionable evidence of learning in protozoa. The first definite evidence is found with worms, but relatively stereotyped innate patterns predominate in invertebrates and lower vertebrates. General forms of learning include conditioning, trial and error, and insight.

Nervous System. Irritability and conductivity are basic properties of *protoplasm. While amoebae exhibit no distinct neural organelles, some ciliates do possess complex systems of receptors, and conducting and contracting organelles. In metazoa, the basic unit of neural organization is the neuron, typically composed of short, relatively numerous dendrites, a cell body, and a long axon. The neuron conducts the nerve impulse, a complex set of biochemical events involving the migration of sodium and potassium ions across the cell membrane, at speeds ranging from 1 to 100 meters per second. All impulses in a given axon are alike; variation in intensity of stimulation affects frequency rather than intensity of impulse transmission (all-or-none law). Synapses are commonly unidirectional; since they require a critical intensity for transmission, a spatial or temporal summation may be necessary for activation. Impulses arriving over certain fibers may inhibit the synapse. Summation and inhibition impose an elementary order upon neural transmission.

Centers of particular interest in the vertebrate nervous system are the spinal cord, the autonomic nervous system, and the *brain. The spinal cord functions to conduct sensory and motor impulses to and from the brain and is capable of coordinating some impulses in the absence of a functional brain. This so-called reflex coordination may involve sensory and motor areas of widely divergent areas of the body (as in the scratch reflex); it is capable of grading response to match the level of stimulation (clinical and postural manifestations of the stretch—"knee jerk" reflex); and it is complicated by the inhibitory relation of competing reflexes (stretch and flexor). The autonomic nervous system is composed of a sympathetic division (stimulation of which generally prepares the animal for vigorous performance: accelerating the heart rate, reducing visceral circulation, increasing the supply of blood to the muscles), and a parasympathetic division (generally of opposite effect).

Hormones. *Hormones are specific chemical substances, produced by endocrine glands, affecting metabolic and behavioral performance of the organism. Coordination by hormonal action is less rapid and specific than neural coordination. The rate of action is dependent upon the velocity of blood circulation, since the blood circulates the hormones, many of which have multiple effects, widely throughout the body. Nevertheless, the hormonal system has important functions in facilitating or inhibiting neuromuscular and general metabolic activity. The system can exhibit an oscillating periodicity of its own; e.g., an anterior pituitary hormone evokes a sex hormone that then represses its evocator. This may account for differential response to identical stimuli at different periods.

Circulation. Multicellular animals of any size require an efficient system of transport for the elements functioning in gaseous exchange, nutrient and waste materials, fluids, hormones, and inorganic ions. A closed circulatory system is found in annelid worms. An interesting feature of the circulatory system in vertebrates is the increasing separation of pulmonary and systemic circulation. In most fishes, the blood is returned to an undivided atrium and pumped by a single ventricle through the gills to the body. In birds and mammals, atria and ventricles are divided: the right ventricle pumps *blood through the lungs, it returns through the left atrium to the left ventricle, from which it is pumped to all parts of the body.

Musculature. The ability of animals to move about and to exert force upon obstacles or food objects is an effect of their muscular tissue. Musculature is inserted on skeletal or supporting tissue and, in contracting, changes skeletal orientation as one would change the position of a lever. Musculature functions also to maintain external bodily form and posture, to provide tone and constant diameter in various hollow organs, and to propel the blood around the body.

Skeletal musculature is striated, capable of rapid contraction; visceral musculature is nonstriated, capable of maintaining prolonged contraction. Muscle tissue generally contracts when attached nerve fibers are stimulated. Cardiac and some smooth musculature are capable of spontaneous contraction, the rate of which is under hormonal and autonomic nervous system control.

The energy for muscular contraction is derived from glycolosis, the controlled breakdown of glycogen to give lactic acid and adenosine triphosphate (ATP), a compound that stores energy in a form readily available for metabolic needs. The contractile tissue is made up primarily of two proteins, actin and myosin.

Classification. *Protozoa:* unicellular organisms, some colonial forms; complex social behavior exhibited by slime mold amoeba, Dictyostelium; reproduction by binary fission or budding, sexual activity (conjugation) may precede reproduction; includes amoeba, ciliates. *Porifera:* sponges; loosely organized cells, single layered skin, internal skeleton, some nerve cells. *Coelenterates:* jellyfish, hydra; two cell layers, an outer ectoderm, inner endoderm lining the digestive cavity; loosely organized neural net. *Echinoderms:* sea stars, sea urchins; three cell layers, adding mesodermal tissue; most adult forms exhibit pentaradial symmetry. *Platheminthes:* flatworms; parasitic; bilateral symmetry; incomplete digestive tract. *Nemata:* eelworms; parasitic; complete digestive tract. *Annelida:* segmented worms; coelom separating body wall and digestive tract. *Molluscs:* gastropods (snails), bivalves (clams), cephalopods (squid); neural system with specialized cerebral, pedal, and visceral ganglia; open circulatory system, blood sinuses without definite walls. *Arthropods:* arachnids (spiders), crustaceans, insects; bilateral symmetry; external skeleton; segmented appendages; increasing cephalization of nervous system; complex instinctive behavior patterns. *Chordates*: dorsal rodlike notochord; dorsal nerve cord; gill slits; includes urochordates (tunicates), cephalochordates (amphioxus), vertebrates. Vertebrates include Agnatha: jawless fishes; Chondrichthyes: cartilaginous fishes; Osteichthyes: bony fishes; Amphibians: frogs, toads, salamanders; Reptiles: snakes, lizards, turtles; Birds; and Mammals: primates, man.

See also LIFE; PLANT LIFE; INSTINCT; TROPISMS; METABOLISM.

Bibliography: J. T. BONNER, *Cells and Societies* (Princeton 1955). V. G. DETHIER and E. STELLAR, *Animal Behavior: Its Evolutionary and Neurological Basis* (2d ed. Englewood Cliffs, N.J. 1964). D. R. GRIFFIN, *Animal Structure and Function* (New York 1962).

PHILOSOPHICAL ASPECTS

While both plants and animals respond to finely graded differences of environmental stimulation, higher animal forms exhibit plastic behavior patterns that become increasingly adaptive with repetition; i.e., they learn by experience. Moreover, the behavior patterns of animals exhibit an affective tone (e.g., aggression, submission, and care of offspring) absent in plants. Since this distinction is discussed more fully in the articles on *life and *plant life, the present article focuses on the distinction between *man and the lower animals as it is considered to be of special philosophical relevance.

Descriptive Analysis. The description of animals and man can be profitably discussed in the context of three central topics: the use of language, the forms of learning, and the development of societies.

Use of Language. Animals clearly influence each other's behavior, not only by the production of specific sounds corresponding to particular situations (danger, food, mating), but also by emissions of similarly specific signals discernible by smell and sight (establishment of territorial boundaries by odorous deposits, the dance of the bees indicating the direction and distance of food). It is usually agreed, however, by linguists, biologists, and philosophers, that these communications are not properly linguistic in form.

Agreement concerning this distinction is somewhat implicit and is difficult to formulate in precise empirical terms. Some animal signals exhibit considerable complexity of spatial or temporal form: in bees, the "round dance" is a call to work close to the hive, whereas the pace of the "waggle dance" indicates the magnitude of distances of from 50 to 100 yards. These same dances make it clear that animal communication need not be a grossly stereotyped affair, but is capable of expressing rather fine differences of meaning. There is evidence from porpoises that flexibility in vocal communication increases with age and physical maturity. Much animal communication is instinctive in form and is not elicited in an automatic way by an isolated stimulus, requiring instead a balance of internal and environmental background stimulation as well as a specific releaser.

Forms of Learning. The distinction to be drawn between the various forms of animal communication on the one hand, and human *language on the other, is to a great extent dependent upon a close analysis of the forms of *learning exhibited in animals and men. The uniqueness of human language revolves around its employment of abstract terms and propositions, its continuing self-critical modification, and its elaboration (as in poetry) in forms considered beautiful because of the symmetry of meaning and auditory or visual characteristics to be found in them. Since human language is the medium of man's free, creative endeavor in art, morality, and science, it is not surprising that the uniqueness of man's language is difficult to express while abstracting from its total cultural significance.

Animals learn in a variety of ways: imprinting, habituation, various forms of conditioning, trial-and-error processes, and perhaps by insight—the more or less immediate apprehension of the solution to a complex problem. W. Köhler found it appropriate to attribute insight to the problem-solving, tool-using behavior of chimpanzees, but he also considered this insight to be confined by the animal's rather limited power of overcoming optical complications of the problem field. For example, sticks will not be used as probes to acquire food left outside the cage unless one happens to be visible when the animal is gazing directly at the food. Generalization is one of the properties of forms of animal learning as simple as conditioning: the conditioned response will usually be elicited by a range of stimuli approximately similar to the conditioned stimulus in at least one respect, e.g., tonal pitch, but differing in others, such as rhythm and intensity.

Development of Societies. The social behavior of some animal forms (notably insects) is remarkable for its complexity. The bees of a hive exhibit a division of labor that is in part rooted in fixed anatomical and physiological differences among workers, drones, and the queen, and in part based upon differences, e.g., of glandular development, that vary with the age and maturity of the insect. But studies have shown also that the artificial creation of the need for a particular function in a hive will itself induce the anatomical and physiological changes requisite for that function in a number of insects. Hence, the social behavior of animals, while rooted in their physical structure, cannot be regarded as grossly mechanical or stereotyped in form.

Evaluation. The various behavior patterns of animals exhibit spontaneity, complexity, and flexibility. Nevertheless, their form is determined by the concrete needs of the survival of a particular species in a definite environment.

In contrast, man's *freedom explains his commitment to goals and standards of his own choosing. His social organization and his scientific and artistic endeavors all establish that man's capacity for action is determined by principles higher than the expedient and the mundane. At their best, human societies do not blindly aim at group survival, but strive for a climate of peace and justice within which each individual is recognized as a value in himself and encouraged to realize his personal dignity. Similarly, human science and art seek significance and beauty transcending the utilitarian needs of the moment. Their advance is marked by a self-critical awareness of their present limitations and their eventual possibilities. The consequent restlessness of the human heart and mind marks man's transcendent dignity.

See also INSTINCT; SOUL; SOUL, HUMAN.

Bibliography: K. VON FRISCH, *The Dancing Bees,* tr. D. ILSE (New York 1955). J. J. DREHER and W. E. EVANS, "Cetacean Communication," *Marine Bio-Acoustics,* ed. W. N. TAVOLGA (New York 1964).

[A. E. MANIER]

ANIMALS, SYMBOLISM OF. In Christian symbolism, animals as well as plants, monograms, and other objects have often been used as religious symbols. The early Church preferred to use the animals mentioned in Sacred Scripture. In the Bible as well as in the liturgy, so-called clean animals are clearly distinguished from those that are unclean. As regards the virtues, the lion symbolizes courage, and the services of a powerful protector. The lamb represents Christ, and the meekness of the Christian. The bull represents strength; the dog, fidelity; the snake, caution and prudence; the dove, the Holy Spirit; the swallow, innocence; the lark, the singing of the praises of God; the deer, the longing of the Christian for salvation; the peacock, immortality. Certain animals are regularly used to represent the various vices. The chameleon symbolizes hypocrisy; the hyena, impurity; the wolf, greed; the fox, cunning; the owl, darkness; the ass, self-will; the serpent, the devil. In early Christian literature animals are borrowed also from the ancient fables together with their connotative symbolism. For example, the *pelican is used to represent redemption, and also Christ's giving of Himself in the Eucharist. The many-headed hydra is often used to represent heresy. The *fish is one of the earliest and most important of Christian symbols. The five letters of the word for fish in Greek form an acrostic, signifying Jesus, Christ, Son of God, Savior (*see* ICHTHUS). The fish is used also as a symbol of Baptism and of Christ in the Eucharist. The Church still encourages the use of animal symbols in her churches and schools as an easy means of symbolizing virtue and vice.

See also SYMBOLISM, EARLY CHRISTIAN; BESTIARY; PHYSIOLOGUS.

Bibliography: K. RATHE, EncCatt 1:1345–47. Künstle Ikonog 1:119–132. B. KÖTTING, "Tier und Heiligtum," in *Mullus: Festschrift Theodor Klauser,* ed. A. STUIBER and A. HERMANN (Jb AntChr suppl.1; 1964) 209–214. Réau IAC 1:76–132, bibliog. 138–140.

[T. J. ALLEN]

ANIMISM AND ANIMATISM

As opposed to the theory of E. B. Tylor (1832–1917) that religion began with belief in souls, R. R. Marett held that belief in the animation of nonphysiological things preceded the soul idea. A. E. Jensen maintains that Tylor's animism does not square at all with most of the evidence, which indicates that the idea of the human soul did not develop independently of the idea of God; and that it should be accepted as fundamental that the divinity, by giving origin to the soul by its "breath," contributed to the rise of the soul concept. The ideas of spirits of nature probably had other origins than dream experiences, to which Tylor traced the original concept of the soul. Jensen himself holds a theory of mythical origins and, in part, of divinities that had lost their earlier significance.

However, a careful analysis of the various concepts of the soul—and variety in this respect is characteristic of the nonliterate peoples—points in another direction, namely, to independent views of a different kind, even if dream experience should have led to the first idea of the soul.

The soul has been localized in various parts of the body, in the blood, in the heart, and in the bones. But much more important is the distinction—related to that made by C. G. Jung between *animus* and *anima*—between the earthly shadow-soul (Chinese *kuei*) and the heavenly spirit-soul (Chinese *shen*). Yet this differentiation does not coincide with the distinction, which is perhaps psychologically more significant, between breath and image-soul. The image-soul may be designated as the formative Gestalt principle for earthly rebirth. Insofar as spirits of the dead are thought of as having animal form and sex, and especially if they are conceived as restless and wandering ghosts, they are to be regarded as vestiges of the corporeal sphere. They cannot be brought to rest except through their complete freedom or destruction. In China, however, the revered ancestors are considered to be spirit-souls. The animal spirits of the early hunting cultures, according to Jensen, are at least in part survival forms of the "Lord of Animals." In the manner of Tylor, he traces the spirit-child idea of the Australian aborigines (the *rai* or *ratapa* concept) to dream experience. Animism, however, is more widespread and more precisely reported for Indonesia, South America, and Finland. It constitutes the basis for shamanism. J. R. Swanton maintained that Marett's animatism was a misconception [*American Anthropologist* (1917) 459–470]. The question arises whether the same is not true also of the *Dingbeseelung* (animation of material things), a concept held by numerous German scholars [see *Anthropos* 51 (1956) 864]. On the whole, belief in the soul is closer to the specifically religious sphere than is magic in the strict sense.

Bibliography: W. SCHMIDT, *The Origin and Growth of Religion,* tr. H. J. ROSE (2d ed. London 1935) 73–89. A. E. JENSEN, *Myth and Cult among Primitive Peoples,* tr. M. T. CHOLDIN and W. WEISSLEDER (Chicago 1963). O. FALSIROL, *Indagini sull'animismo primitivo* (Verona 1953) 220–231. H. NACHTIGALL, "Felsbilder und Animismus im frühzeitlichen Jägertum," *Studium Generale* 6 (1953) 256– . E. A. WORMS, "Der australische Seelenbegriff," ZMissRelw 43 (1959) 296–308. H. KREMSMAYER, "Schamanismus und Seelenvorstellungen im Alten China," *Archiv für Völkerkunde* 9 (1954) 66. C. HENTZE, *Das Haus als Weltort der Seele* (Stuttgart 1961).

[A. CLOSS]

ANIMUCCIA, GIOVANNI,

Renaissance church composer; b. Florence, *c.* 1500; d. Rome, March 25, 1571. His first publication (1547) consisted of madrigals; they are Florentine in both style and spirit and reveal the influence of Corteccia. In 1555 he succeeded *Palestrina as *maestro di cappella* at St. Peter's, and retained this position till his death, at which time Palestrina resumed it. During his tenure there, he was drawn into the circle of the newly founded Congregation of the Oratory (*see* ORATORIANS), and published some of the earliest Oratorian *laudi* (in two collections, 1563 and 1570). He became also a leading composer of Masses and other sacred works. Although he did not adhere rigidly to the chordal or simplified contrapuntal style employed by some composers after the Council of Trent, he strove to conform to the general aims laid down by the Council. Thus, in a collection of Masses for various voice groupings and based on plain-song melodies (1567), he stated in the preface that he had striven to embellish the texts with melody "which did not obscure the hearing of the words."

Bibliography: L. TORCHI, ed., *L'Arte musicale in Italia,* 7 v. (Milan 1897–1908) v.1–2, part of Mass *Conditor Alme,* Magnificat, and a five-part madrigal. K. G. FELLERER, MusGG 1: 483–485. A. EINSTEIN, *The Italian Madrigal,* tr. A. H. KRAPPE et al., 3 v. (Princeton 1949) v.1. Reese MusR.

[F. J. GUENTNER]

ANJOU, HOUSE OF

Princely French house whose history during the later Middle Ages became much involved with that of France, the papacy, Italy, Aragon, and Hungary.

Charles of Anjou (b. 1220), youngest brother of King *Louis IX of France, was granted the appanage of Anjou and Maine in 1246. After lengthy negotiations, the ambitious Charles was selected as papal champion to eliminate the Hohenstaufens from the Kingdom of the Two Sicilies. Successful in the crusade against *Manfred (Benevento 1266) and victorious over Conradin (Tagliacozzo 1268), he supplanted imperial authority in Italy with Angevin influence. On the death of Pope *Clement IV (1268), Charles delayed the papal election while he solidified his control in the peninsula and planned for the establishment of an Angevin empire in the eastern Mediterranean (e.g., his Crusades in Albania, 1270, 1272). He was checked in this ambition by Louis IX's Crusade, by Pope *Gregory X's interest in the reunion of the churches, by Pope *Nicholas III's Italian policy, and by Emperor *Michael VIII Palaeologus's diplomatic maneuvers, although Pope *John XXI did finally grant him the shadowy Kingdom of Jerusalem (1277).

Under the subservient Pope *Martin IV, Charles revived his eastern plans, but the *Sicilian Vespers (1282), which erupted against his French-dominated rule and extortionate taxes in *Sicily, ended his dream of conquest and brought him into conflict with the *Regnicoli* and *Peter III of Aragon (husband of Man-

Charles of Anjou, statue by Arnolfo di Cambio, Palazzo dei Conservatori on the Capitoline Hill, Rome.

fred's daughter, Constance), who seized the throne of Sicily. In 1285 Charles, capable but proud, died a failure. His son and successor, *Charles II* (1285–1309), supported by the papacy, especially Pope *Boniface VIII, carried on the struggle, which for 20 years involved France, Aragon, England, and the papacy in war and diplomatic maneuvering over their conflicting claims to Sicily and Aragon. Ultimately the Treaty of Caltabellotta (1302) recognized Frederick II of Aragon as King of Trinacria, and Sicily was lost to the House of Anjou. As part of the diplomatic solution, the counties of Anjou and Maine were granted to Charles of Valois in his marriage to Charles II's daughter, Margaret. However, the Anjou family remained influential, for Pope *Celestine V had created 12 cardinals favorable to the House, and Charles's eldest son, *Charles Martel* (d. 1295) and, later, his grandson *Carobert* were papal candidates for the Hungarian throne.

It was under Charles's third son and successor in Naples, *Robert the Wise* (1309–43) that the fortunes of the family reached their political peak. The *Avignon papacy and the untimely death of the Emperor *Henry VII (1313) left Italy a prey of local discord. Although Naples was reasonably well established and was the one center around which a turbulent Italy might unite, Robert, powerful yet vacillating, was too preoccupied with the chimerical reconquest of Sicily to assume the leadership. He was succeeded by his granddaughter, *Joanna I* (1343–82). This queen was four times wed: to Andrew of Hungary, a cousin, who was murdered; to Louis of Taranto, a French cousin; to James IV of Aragon; and to Otto of Brunswick. Joanna survived the war of vengeance (1345–50) waged by *King Louis I* of Hungary, of the Hungarian branch of the Anjou house, who twice occupied Naples. Restored to the throne with the assistance of Pope *Clement VI, to whom she sold *Avignon, Joanna, helped by her paramour, Niccolo Acciaiuoli, gave a decade of relative quiet to Naples, almost reconquered Sicily, and finally entered into a definite peace for the separate Kingdom of Trinacria with Frederick III of Aragon.

At the beginning of the *Western Schism, Joanna broke with Pope *Urban VI, despite the protests of the Neapolitans, and supported antipope *Clement VII. In retaliation Urban excommunicated her and bestowed Naples on her cousin, *Charles III, Duke of Durazzo* (1382–86), who successfully defended his claims against Joanna and Otto. As a countermove, Joanna, under the persuasion of Clement VII, named *Louis I,* Duke of Anjou (founder of the younger House of Anjou) and brother of Charles V of France, her heir. Louis, however, died (1384) in his unsuccessful attempt to dethrone Charles III. When Louis I the Great of Hungary died, Charles III successfully claimed the throne of Hungary also (1385), but he was murdered the following year. There followed a struggle for Naples between his widow, Margaret, and young son, *Ladislaus* (1386–1414), and an army sent by Clement VII on behalf of *Louis II* of Anjou. Although Ladislaus was crowned king of Naples by the Roman Pope *Boniface IX in 1390, he was not able to defeat Louis of Anjou and establish his authority until 1399. Ladislaus, alternately friend and foe of popes, astutely used the opportunity provided by the schism and the collapse of the *States of the Church to seek control of central Italy and the Kingdom of Hungary. Louis II of Anjou was recalled in a vain effort to stop Ladislaus, but the Pisan antipope *John XXIII was forced to accept Ladislaus.

In August 1414 death ended Ladislaus' ambitions. He was succeeded by his sister, *Joanna II* (1414–35). Naples suffered from the rule of this woman whose reign is infamous for her illicit loves and changing alliances. Popes *Martin V and *Eugene IV, the condottieri, Braccio and *Sforza, and her paramours, Alopo and Caracciolo, all played roles in courting her successor to the throne of Naples. Martin V and Sforza negotiated with *Louis III* of Anjou; Caracciolo and Joanna called in Alfonso V of Aragon. Alliances changed easily in a disquieted Italy. But Louis III died in 1434; and in the end Joanna, the last Angevin ruler, bequeathed Naples to Louis's brother, *René the Good.* Immediately a new Anjou-Aragon-papal struggle commenced with the *Visconti supporting Alfonso of Aragon and Eugene IV assisting René. However, in 1443 Alfonso was recognized by Pope Eugene, and the Kingdom of the Two Sicilies was reunited, this time under Aragonese rule. Alfonso the "Magnanimous" (1435–58) introduced Naples to a new era. On his death, he gave Naples to his illegitimate son, Ferdinand I, and Sicily to his brother, John. In 1495 King *Charles VIII of France conquered Naples, but the Spaniards victoriously reunited the Two Kingdoms in 1502 (*see* SPAIN, 2).

Charles Martel, eldest son of Charles II of Naples, had ruled Hungary successfully, being succeeded by King Carobert (1308–42) and King Louis I the Great (1342–82). The relationship between the Neapolitan and Hungarian branches of the family was seriously strained when Louis I fought his Neapolitan relative,

Joanna I, to avenge his brother's murder and when Charles III of Durazzo claimed the throne of Hungary. However, the Emperor Sigismund, who had married Louis's daughter, Margaret, prevented Ladislaus of Naples from duplicating the success of his father, Charles III.

Bibliography: É. JORDAN. *Les Origines de la domination angevine en Italie* (Paris 1909). J. R. TANNER et al., CMedH v.6, 7, 8 *passim.* L. BERRA, EncCatt 1:1266–1268. A. NITSCHKE, LexThK² 1:566–567. D. J. GEANAKOPLOS, *Emperor Michael Palaeologus and the West, 1258–1282* (Cambridge, Mass. 1959). S. RUNCIMAN, *Sicilian Vespers* (Cambridge, Eng. 1958). **Illustration credit:** Alinari-Art Reference Bureau.

[E. J. SMYTH]

ANKING, ARCHDIOCESE OF (NGANCHIMENSIS), metropolitan see since 1946, in Anhwei (An-hui) province, central *China. Statistics for 1950, the latest available, showed the See of Anking (An-ch'ing), 14,672 square miles in area, to have 25 parishes, 6 secular and 56 religious priests, 34 men in one religious house, 46 women in 3 convents, and 28,000 Catholics in a population of 7 million. Its two suffragans, Pang-fou and Wu-hu, both created in 1946, had 138 priests, 118 sisters, and 100,000 Catholics in a population of 14 million. A Franciscan mission in Anhwei in the late 17th century was short-lived. French Jesuits from *Nanking resumed missionary work after 1842 and established a residence at Anking in 1869, but progress was slow in the 19th century. From the Vicariate of Anhwei, which was separated from Nanking (1922) and called Wu-hu (1924), the Vicariate of Anking was detached (1929). The new vicariate was entrusted to Spanish Jesuits, who had arrived in 1913.

Bibliography: *Annuaire de l'Église catholique en Chine* (Shanghai 1950). MissCattol 344–346. A. PUCCI, EncCatt 1: 1357–58.

[J. KRAHL]

ANNA COMNENA, Byzantine princess, biographer of Emperor Alexius I; b. Constantinople, Dec. 1, 1083; d. after 1148. She was the daughter of Emperor *Alexius I Comnenus (1081–1118) and Irene Ducas, and is known chiefly for her biography of her father, called the *Alexiad.* As a child she was betrothed to her cousin Constantine Ducas, the son of Emperor *Michael VII, with whom Alexius had shared the imperial office. In 1091, however, Alexius deposed Constantine and raised his own son, John Comnenus, to the status of coemperor. Anna never forgave her brother John, despite the death of Constantine and her marriage (1097) to Nicephorus Bryennius Caesar. When Alexius died, Anna and her mother attempted to prevent the succession of John in favor of Bryennius, but they failed because of Bryennius's apathy, Alexius's earlier designation of his son, and John's energy. At his accession *John II Comnenus (1118–43) placed Irene and Anna in the convent of Cecharitomene, and it was here that Anna began the *Alexiad.* Her history of Alexius from 1069 to 1118 was based on her own carefully recalled memories as well as those of members of the court, verified as far as possible; for the period before 1069 Anna relied on the *Hyle* of her husband—which had been her original inspiration—and earlier Byzantine histories. Possibly she had access to the imperial archives. The *Alexiad* is the work of a highly educated woman and, though sympathetic to Alexius, it never becomes a mere panegyric. It suffers more from omission and confused chronology than from deliberate distortion. Anna knew little of events beyond the imperial frontiers and regarded all foreigners as barbarians. Despite its weaknesses, the *Alexiad* remains the best source for Alexius's reign and is of particular interest in presenting a Greek view of the First *Crusade.

Bibliography: ANNA COMNENA, *The Alexiad,* tr. E. DAWES (London 1928); *Alexiade,* tr. B. LEIB (Paris 1937). C. DIEHL, *Figures byzantines,* ser. 2 (2d ed. Paris 1908). G. BUCKLER, *Anna Comnena: A Study* (London 1929). J. M. HUSSEY, *Church and Learning in the Byzantine Empire, 867–1185* (Oxford 1937).

[J. FRANCE]

ANNA, CANTICLE OF, a messianic hymn praising God's concern for the poor and lowly and attributed to Samuel's mother, Anna, in 1 Sm 2.1–10. Later editors than the *Deuteronomists contributed to the final redaction of this canticle, which was probably inserted late in the monarchical period (2.10). Ascribed to Anna because of a reference to the fruitfulness of the barren in 2.5b, the hymn proclaims Yahweh to be the Lord of history and, hence, gives theological meaning to the events in the books of Samuel. The poetic insertion breaks into the middle of a sentence in the Hebrew text, in which its position differs from that in the *Septuagint (LXX). It is similar to Psalms 2, 17(18), and 112(113), uses a late word *ḥăsîdîm* for God's "faithful" in 2.9, and has a conception of the *Messiah in 2.10 that did not evolve until well after David. In 2.1 "horn" is a symbol of strength and victory, based on the image of a horned animal carrying its head high in triumph. The symbol occurs again in 2.10, forming an inclusion with 2.1. The scornful laughter of 2.1c was an ancient gesture of derision [Ps 34(35).21; Is 57.4]. Verse 2 extolls God's transcendence; He is completely other, the Holy One, but still the rock of refuge for those who trust in him (Lv 11.44–45; Os 11.9; Ez 20.41). Verse 2b is probably an inspired gloss on "holy," because it destroys the parallelism and, in LXX, occurs after 2c. The rock symbolizes that *Yahweh is eternal, reliable, immovable, and the source of stability and strength to men in need (2 Sm 22.2; 23.3). Verse 3 proclaims that Yahweh "tests hearts" (Prv 21.2; 24.12) and evaluates all human actions. Verses 4 and 5 teach that Yahweh, as a just judge, can reverse the fortunes of individuals and nations; the verses recall the basic themes of the Canticle of *Moses (Dt 32.1–43). Probably neither half of verse 6 refers to the resurrection of the dead; the verse simply emphasizes God's mastery over life and death. "Hell" (Douay) is a misleading translation of *Sheol, the abode of the dead (Jb 3.13–19), which was a symbol for death (Prv 5.5; 7.27). Verses 7 and 8 affirm that God will exalt the poor and the lowly just as surely as He has founded the earth on the pillars that support it [Ps 103(104).5]. The parallels in these verses to Ps 112(113).7–8 and to the *Magnificat (Lk 1.52–53) are quite apparent. The "saints" (Douay; Heb. *ḥăsîdîm*) are those who respond to the Lord's covenant with loving faithfulness. In 2.10 Yahweh's thundering recalls that, in Hebrew theological lore, severe storms often accompanied *theophanies or divine interventions (Ex 9.34; 19.16); the thunder symbolizes the powerful suddenness and terror of divine punishment (1 Sm 12.17–18). "King" and "Christ" of 2.10 are parallel terms; the verse signifies that God will finally triumph over all His enemies through the power He will give to an ideal son of David.

Bibliography: A. MÉDIEBELLE, *Le Livre de Samuel* in *La Sainte Bible*, ed. L. PIROT and A. CLAMER, 12 v. (Paris 1935–61) 3:355–357. R. DE VAUX, *Les Livres de Samuel* (BJ 8; 1953).

[S. D. RUEGG]

ANNA MARIA COLLEGE FOR WOMEN, a liberal arts college for women founded by the Sisters of St. Anne in 1946. It is situated on a 293-acre campus in Paxton, a suburb of Worcester, Mass. In 1963 there were six buildings, including two residence halls, which accommodated approximately 200 students. Full-time enrollment was more than 400. More than 200 students registered in a 1962 summer session.

The College was originally established in temporary quarters on the campus of St. Anne Academy in Marlborough, Mass., but moved to Paxton. It is under the patronage of the bishop of Worcester, who is honorary chairman of the College advisory board, which includes both clergymen and laymen. The board of trustees is composed of members of the religious community. Executive officers of the College include the president, dean of studies, registrar, treasurer, dean of students, and librarian. In 1964 the administrative and teaching staff consisted of 3 priests, 22 sisters, and 23 lay teachers. Faculty degrees included 9 doctoral, 2 professional, and 20 master's degrees.

Anna Maria College offers courses leading to a B.A. degree in art education, elementary and secondary education, liberal and fine arts, and natural and social sciences. It offers a premedical course, a B.S. degree in medical technology, and also a Mus.B. degree. Among campus facilities is a language laboratory for the study of French, Spanish, and German. The campus library in 1964 housed more than 18,700 volumes and received 220 periodicals. Students publish the *Word,* a literary quarterly; and *Veritas,* a newspaper. An honors seminar is offered to superior students in their junior or senior year. An effective student government has been functioning on campus since 1947. The College has also been active as a member of the National Federation of Catholic College students.

The College is accredited by the New England Association of Colleges and Secondary Schools. It is affiliated with The Catholic University of America and the National Catholic Educational Association. It is included in the list of approved colleges of arts and sciences compiled by the American Medical Association. Its curriculum leading to the degree of Bachelor of Arts is registered with the State Education Department of the University of the State of New York.

[M. R. I. EAGEN]

ANNALS AND CHRONICLES

Along with *hagiography, annals and chronicles constitute the typical forms of medieval historical literature. In practice, annals and chronicles often overlap in content and form, but they are theoretically distinct. Annals may be described as brief chronological listings of events regarded as important in the history of a kingdom, bishopric, or monastery, etc., by contemporary compilers who are usually anonymous. Chronicles list such events in chronological order also, but they furnish more detail, deal with the past, even the remote past, as well as with the contemporary period, and their authors are frequently known. Annals as described give way to chronicles in the later Middle Ages, but the term annals continues to be used to designate what may properly be considered chronicles, and the later chronicles themselves in part assume the character of "history" in the strict sense, since their authors tend to indicate causal relations between events and to inject formally their own judgments or evaluations.

Annals to the 7th Century A.D. As a literary genre, annals go back to the Hittites and Assyrians, who left records of their military campaigns in annalistic form. The Greeks apparently did not compose annals as distinct from chronicles. However, the early Roman historians were more properly annalists, as they presented historical events in a bald, annalistic fashion. The Romans adopted the practice also of recording contemporary historical events on their calendars, a procedure that anticipated the Christian usage, which is the foundation of all medieval annals.

The pattern for medieval annals was set by the **Chronographer of 354*. This work contains an official Roman calendar, a long list of consuls, Paschal Tables for 100 years beginning with the year 312, a list of popes from *Pontianus (230–235) to *Liberius, and a brief chronicle to the year 338. The Paschal Tables took on a new significance in *chronology in the West after the disintegration of the Western Roman Empire and the abandonment of the consular system of dating. The *Easter Controversy between the Irish and the Anglo-Saxons, which was finally settled at the Synod of *Whitby (664), indicates the special importance of the Paschal Tables in early Christian Britain. Anglo-Saxon missionaries carried their Paschal Tables to the Continent during the 7th century, and in the early 8th they were equipped with the invaluable *De temporum ratione* of *Bede, which, in addition to Paschal Tables, contained a brief chronicle of the Six Ages of the world from Creation to A.D. 729. It had already become customary in England to make marginal notes of historical or other events thought worthy of record opposite the given years in the Paschal Tables. These notes were at first very short, occupying not more than a single line, but as they necessarily had a chronological sequence, they were annals in embryo. The practice was likewise introduced on the Continent. Annals proper were created when the notations mentioned were detached from the Paschal Tables and assembled and circulated in an independent form. This final stage in the development of annals was reached in the course of the 7th century in Merovingian Gaul.

Chronicles to the 7th Century A.D. The so-called *Babylonian Chronicle* (a cuneiform document now in the British Museum, No. 21946) is an annalistic record rather than a chronicle in the strict sense. The chronicle proper was a creation of the Greeks. The *Atthis,* or *Chronicle of Athens,* and especially the *Marmor Parium,* or *Parian Chronicle,* covering a period from the 13th to the middle of the 3d century B.C., may be cited as typical examples. Pagan histories and chronicles could not satisfy the early Christians, preoccupied as they were with *salvation history as contained in the Old and New Testaments and as reflecting the universal power of God, the Father of all mankind. Furthermore, it was of the greatest importance for Christian apologetics to show that the history of the people of God, particularly their religious history, began long before that of the Greeks and Romans. Hence the Christian chronicle was created to meet a twofold Christian need by Sextus *Julius Africanus, whose *Chronicles* (preserved only in fragments) furnished a synchronized record of profane and Biblical events from Creation (5500 B.C.) to A.D. 221. A few years later (A.D. 234), *Hippolytus of Rome published a somewhat similar *Chronicle* of world history which is preserved only in fragments and in Latin translation. It was based in part on Africanus, but relied most heavily on the Bible itself. Africanus and, especially, Hippolytus were millenarians. *See* MILLENARIANISM.

The Chronicle of Eusebius-Jerome. The greatest and most influential of all Christian chronicles was compiled by *Eusebius of Caesarea. His *Chronicle* (first published in 303, but later brought down by him to 325) contains a brief survey of universal history as it was then known, followed by elaborate synchronistic tables of sacred and profane history. He begins his chronology with the birth of Abraham (2016–2015 B.C.), maintaining that no certain dates could be established for the period from Adam and the Fall to Abraham. He wished to demonstrate that the religion of the Hebrews was the oldest of all religions and that Christianity was its continuation and fulfillment. He used much better profane sources than his Christian predecessors and abandoned their millenarian ideas. The Greek original is lost except for fragments, but an Armenian translation of the whole work made in the 6th century is extant. The second part is preserved also in the free translation (*c.* 380) of St. *Jerome, who introduced much new material, especially from Roman history, and added a section covering the years from 325 to 378. The *Chronicle* of Eusebius or of Eusebius-Jerome became the immediate source of almost all subsequent universal Christian chronicles and histories in East and West until early modern times.

Post-Eusebian Chronicles. Among the other chronicles compiled before the 7th century, in part as supplements or continuations of Eusebius or Eusebius-Jerome, some in particular deserve mention. As already noted, the *Chronographer of 354* included a world chronicle to A.D. 334, which was essentially a Latin translation and continuation of the *Chronicle* of Hippolytus of Rome. The African Bishop Quintus Iulius Hilarianus (second half of the 4th century) compiled a chronicle, *De cursu temporum,* recounting events from Creation to A.D. 397. A pronounced chiliast, he set the end of the world for A.D. 470. The World Chronicle (*Chronicorum libri duo*) of *Sulpicius Severus, which runs from Creation to A.D. 400, is well organized and is especially valuable for the history of the 4th century A.D. Reference must be made also to St. *Augustine's *De civitate Dei* and to *Orosius's *Historiae adversus paganos*. In dealing with the past, and especially the remoter past, they present their material in chronicle fashion, and by their division of world history, beginning with Creation, into six and four periods respectively, both exercised an enormous influence on all later Western *historiography down to the 17th century. *Prosper of Aquitaine compiled a World Chronicle (*Epitoma chronicon*) from Creation to A.D. 455. For the period before 412, he took his material from Eusebius-Jerome and other sources, but the coverage of the years from 412 to 455 is his own. The *Chronicon* of the Spanish bishop *Hydatius may be described as a continuation of the *Chronicle* of Eusebius-Jerome to 468. *Marcellinus Comes compiled a *Chronicon* in Latin for the years 379 to 534. He restricted it almost exclusively to the Eastern Empire. The *Chronica* of *Cassiodorus, which goes down to 519, is based directly on Eusebius-Jerome and other sources, having independent value only for the last 20 years. Of the *Chronicle* of the African bishop *Victor of Tunnuna, only the second part, which covers the years 444 to 566, is extant. *Isidore of Seville compiled a short World Chronicle (*Chronicon*) from Julius Africanus, Eusebius-Jerome, and Victor of Tunnuna, continuing the work of the last to 615. He followed St. Augustine in dividing world history into six periods. The first book of the *Historia Francorum* of *Gregory of Tours must be included among the Latin chronicles of this period, because it is actually a brief chronicle of world history from Creation to the death of St. Martin of Tours (397).

Of the post-Eusebian chronicles compiled in the East and written in Greek or Syriac before the middle of the 7th century, it will suffice to mention the following. About 400 an anonymous Greek writer composed a World Chronicle down to the year 387. The work is extant only in a Latin translation made in the Merovingian period, the so-called *Excerpta Latina Barbari* (*see* TRANSLATION LITERATURE, GREEK AND ARABIC). *John Malalas (d. 577) compiled an elaborate and influential—but uncritical—*Chronographia* in 18 books. The extant text breaks off at the year 563. An anonymous Syrian writer composed, after 540, the *Chronicle of Edessa* covering the period from 133–132 B.C. to A.D. 540, in which he made good use of the archives of his native city. The most important and most valuable of the Eastern chronicles from this period is the so-called *Chronicon Paschale,* the name given to it by *Du Cange because of the preoccupation of its anonymous author with the dating of Easter. Written most probably at Constantinople before the middle of the 7th century, it runs from Adam to A.D. 629.

Annals and Chronicles, c. 650–1100. The period down to 900 was a golden age of annals; historical works of the high quality of Bede's *Ecclesiastical History* and *Einhard's *Life of Charlemagne* must be regarded as rare and isolated phenomena. The annals fall into two major categories, monastic and royal, although their authors were all monks or clerics. The older type of annals appearing as notes in Paschal Tables continued to flourish also, especially locally in monasteries somewhat removed from the main centers of ecclesiastical and political life. Chronicles became increasingly important in the 10th, 11th, and early 12th century. In this period one notes also the rise of a third type of historical work that is closely related to annals and chronicles and that was to have a wide development in the Middle Ages, namely, the *Gesta* of kings, bishops, abbots, etc., in which emphasis was placed on achievements and events rather than on biographical details. The *Liber pontificalis served as a model. The *Gesta episcoporum Mettensium* of *Paul the Deacon (*c.* 784) and the *Gesta abbatum Fontanellensium* (*c.* 833) may be cited as early and typical medieval examples. The gradual adoption of the birth of Christ as a starting point in chronologies is evident in both annals and chronicles. Finally, it is of interest that the *Anglo-Saxon Chronicle,* and the early Irish annals in part, were composed in the vernacular.

Annals. Among the earlier and rather sketchy annals produced in these 4 centuries may be mentioned the *Annales S. Amandi* (708–810), *Annales Mosellani* (703–798), *Annales Guelferbytani* (741–790), and the *Annales Mettenses priores* (late 7th and early 8th century). The *Royal Annals* are represented by the collection formerly called *Annales Laurissenses maiores* (741–829). Considering their central interest in the Carolingian kings, royal campaigns, and government, they could hardly have been composed at *Lorsch or any other monastery. The *Annales Bertiniani* continue the *Royal Annals* to 882. In this case it is certain that *Prudentius of Troyes compiled the section for 835 to 861, and *Hincmar of Reims, that for 862 to 882. For the 9th century, in part continuing the *Royal Annals,* of special note are the *Annales Xantenses* (831–873); the *Annales Fuldenses,* more properly called *Magontiacenses* (680–901, especially in its last sections); and the *Annales Vedastini,* or of **Saint-Vaast* (875–900). The so-called *Annales Einhardi* is merely a worked over and extended portion of the *Royal Annals.* After long controversy it has been almost definitely established that the *Royal Annals* derived some material from earlier and shorter annals and that the latter must be given priority.

Among the annals dealing with the Saxon House, particular value attaches to the *Annales* of *Flodoard of Reims for the years 919 to 968; the *Annales Quedlinburgenses,* beginning with Creation and exhibiting a fuller form from 708 on, and especially from 913 to 1025; and the *Annales Hildesheimenses,* likewise beginning with Creation, but becoming a valuable independent historical source for the years from 818 to 1137. The Salian House is better covered in the chronicles than in the annals. *Lambert of Hersfeld, for example, incorporated much material from the lost *Annales Altahenses maiores* and from other annals into his own *Annales,* which, despite the name, should be classified as a chronicle or even a history.

The annals compiled in Italy during this period were relatively few and poor in quality. Although England was the land of origin of annals based on the historical notations in Paschal Tables, no significant annals or chronicles in Latin—apart from the work of *Bede—were produced in that country before the Norman conquest. One collection provides an exception, namely, the *Annales Cambriae,* covering the years 444 to 954. The Irish were very fond of annals and compiled them in the vernacular as well as in Latin. The annalistic material from these early annals was incorporated into the much more elaborate Latin and Irish annals of the late Middle Ages and early modern times.

Chronicles. Although few chronicles were produced in the Carolingian Age and the decades immediately following, three are important because they are world chronicles modeled on Bede. Freculf, Bishop of Lisieux (d. *c.* 853), compiled a *Historia*—a chronicle, despite its name—beginning with Creation and coming down to his own time. The fifth and last book, especially, indicates an effort to write a connected narrative. *Ado, Bishop of Vienne (859–875), wrote a *Breviarium chronicorum,* beginning with Adam and closing with the year 869. In dealing with events of his own time, and especially with his own episcopal see, he did not scruple to introduce his own forgeries or falsifications. *Regino of Prüm, Abbot of Prüm in Lotharingia (892–899) and then of St. Martin's in Trier (to his death in 915), composed a chronicle, *Chronica,* beginning with the birth of Christ and ending at the year 905. Book 1 covers the period to 740, and book 2, from 741 through 905. He was interested primarily in the events of the western half of the Frankish Empire. Despite their shortcomings, these works reveal the awareness of their authors that they belonged to a new age and that it was important to have an understanding of the past and of its relation to the present.

In the 10th and 11th centuries numerous chronicles, universal, regional, or local, were composed on the Continent north of the Alps. Several were typical and at the same time of major importance. *Thietmar of Merseburg (975–1018) composed a *Chronicle of the Kings of Saxony.* Lambert of Hersfeld (d. 1077) wrote a work called *Annales,* which was really a world chronicle (see above). *Marianus Scotus (1028–83), one of the last of the significant Irish scholars on the Continent, compiled a *World Chronicle* exhibiting a number of personal ideas and contributions. *Hermanus Contractus (1013–54) produced a similar work, *Chronicon,* extending from the birth of Christ to 1054 and distinguished for its remarkable accuracy and objectivity. The *World Chronicle,* once assigned to Ekkehard of Aura (d. 1225), who revised and continued the work, was actually written by *Frutolf of Michelsberg. In content and arrangement it is one of the superior works of its kind. Much of its material for the period down to the middle of the 11th century was taken from the *Chronicon Wirziburgense* composed in 1045 or 1054. *Sigebert of Gembloux (1030–1112) produced a universal chronicle, *Chronographia,* which begins with the year 381. It is one of the best of the universal chronicles of the Middle Ages and probably the most influential of all such works in subsequent medieval historiography. *Hugh of Flavigny (d. after 1112) wrote a *Chronicon Virdunense seu Flaviniacense,* which begins with the birth of Christ and ends at 1102. It is not strictly a universal chronicle, although it is often so designated, for it is concerned almost exclusively with Church history and more specifically with northern France in the 10th and 11th centuries. Among the *Gesta*—which are closely related to chronicles—composed in the German area in this period, was the *Gesta Hammaburgensis ecclesiae pontificum* of *Adam of Bremen (d. 1076), one of the major historical works of the Middle Ages. All seven chronicles listed, especially those of the 11th century, reveal a greater concern for the immediate past and for contemporary events than do the earlier chronicles, and their writers often indicate their own convictions about events. This is true in particular in matters pertaining to the *investiture struggle.

Historical events of England in this period are recorded in the *Anglo-Saxon Chronicle,* more properly the *Old English Annals.* All extant versions stem from the compilation made in 891. Successive annalists carried the record down, in the E text, even to the middle of the 12th century (1154). These *Annals,* written in the vernacular, are of primary importance for the early history of England and for the history of the English language. Typical of Italy in the same period is the *Chronicon Salernitanum* (ed. U. Westerbergh, Stockholm 1956), which, after listing the Lombard kings from 574, begins its narrative in some detail with the year 775, ending at 964. This should, perhaps, be regarded as a history rather than as a chronicle in the strict sense.

Chronicles of the 12th Century. The distinction between annals and chronicles largely disappeared in the 12th century. The rather sparse, annalistic material was confined mainly to the earlier and unoriginal portions of chronicles as they became much more preoccupied with their own age and its immediate backgrounds. Their increasing fullness of treatment, and their interpretations, however embryonic, of historical events justify the classification of at least some chronicles as histories. The chronicles from the 12th century on, thanks to the Norman conquests, the Crusades, and the entry of northern Europe into the full life of Christendom, reveal much wider horizons of knowledge and interests. They exhibit the new intellectual depth and maturity and the greater mastery of Latin expression that are characteristic features of the renaissance of the 12th century. Furthermore, in the universal chronicles especially, alongside the traditional division of world history into six or four ages, a new tripartite division was introduced: *ante legem, sub lege, sub gratia* (before the Mosaic Law, under the Law, in the Age of Grace).

Universal Chronicles. The *Chronicon ex chronicis* of *Florence of Worcester (d. 1118) is the first attempt in England after the time of Bede to compile a universal chronicle. It is independent only from 1030 on, but is valuable for its record of events from that date to 1117. It was continued by John of Worcester to 1141, and by other writers to 1295. Five universal chronicles written on the Continent are more important. The Norman *Robert of Torigny, Abbot of Mont-Saint-Michel (d. 1186), continued the Chronicle of Sigebert of Gembloux. His work is especially valuable for the period from 1150 to 1186. It was continued by later chroniclers to 1272. Robert of Auxerre (1156–1212) composed a universal chronicle, *Chronologia,* divided according to the six ages of the world. Its geographical data, lists of rulers, the critical spirit displayed in the handling of legends, and the selection of material from the better earlier works ensured its success and its employment as a model by later chroniclers. It is one of the best historical contributions of the Middle Ages. *Vincent of Beauvais put it to good use in his *Speculum historiale.* *Guy of Bazoches (d. 1203) wrote a *Chronographia* in seven books, covering the time from Creation to 1199; this too has independent value for its contemporary age. *Hélinand of Froidmont (d. after 1230) was the author of a universal *Chronicle* (634–1204) in 49 books made up largely of extracts from other authors and arranged in the manner later adopted by Vincent of Beauvais. *Otto of Freising (*c.* 1112–58) shares with *John of Salisbury the distinction of being the most personal and original writer of the 12th century. His universal chronicle *Historia de duabus civitatibus* deliberately echoes in its title the *De civitate Dei* of Augustine. It is unique in that it is permeated throughout with philosophico-theological ideas and interpretations, which have as their immediate background, not paganism, but the history of the Christian centuries from Augustine to his own time. Romuald II of Salerno (d. *c.* 1182) compiled *Annales ab ortu Christi usque ad 1178,* for which sources now lost were employed; it has independent value especially for the years 1125 to 1178. Romuald compares the six ages of Augustine to the six ages of man, adding two others: a seventh, that of the elect before the Resurrection, and an eighth, that after the Last Judgment. In many respects the *Historia ecclesiastica* of *Ordericus Vitalis (1075–1142) is notable because, although the work was projected as a history of the Abbey of *Saint-Évroult, it was transformed in the course of composition into a kind of universal chronicle that is of the greatest value for the period from 1125 to 1140.

Regional and Local Chronicles Composed on the Continent. A few of the more important and typical regional chroniclers in France were: *Suger of Saint-Denis (d. 1151), *Liber de rebus in administratione sua gestis* (begun in 1144–45); *Rigord of Saint-Denis (d. *c.* 1209), *Gesta Philippi II Augusti*; Geoffrey of Vigeois, *Chronicon,* covering Limousin and La Marche (1184). Those from Italy were: Falco of Benevento, *Chronicon* (1140); Caffaro of Caschifelone (d. 1166) et al., *Annales Genuenses* (1099–1294); Bernard Marangon (fl. 1175) et al., *Annales Pisani* (1004–1178); *Leo Marsicanus (d. *c.* 1114–18) and *Peter the Deacon of Monte Cassino (1st half of 12th century), *Chronica monasterii Cassinensis* (1098–1138). Germany and the Low Countries had: *Annales Erphesfurdenses* (1125–57); Gislebert of Mons (2d half of 12th cent.), *Chronicon Hanoniense* (1050–1195); Reiner, monk of the Abbey of St. Lawrence at Liège (d. after 1182), *De ineptiis cuiusdam idiotae* (in part a history of important abbots and monks of his monastery). Eastern and northern Europe include: *Helmold of Bosau (*c.* 1120–77), *Chronica Slavorum* [to 1172; continued by *Arnold of Lübeck (d. *c.* 1211–14) to 1209]; *Chronica Polonorum* (written between 1109 and 1113); *Cosmas of Prague (1045–1125), *Chronica Bohemorum,* continued by successive writers to 1283; *Saxo Grammaticus (d. *c.* 1220), *Gesta Danorum,* in prose and verse; *Kaiserchronik,* a German chronicle in verse running from the time of Caesar to the Crusade of Conrad III in 1147. (It was written at Regensburg after 1160 by several ecclesiastics and continued in Bavaria to Frederick II, and in Swabia to Rudolph of Hapsburg).

Anglo-Norman Chronicles. The chronicles produced in the Anglo-Norman world deserve special attention. Through the Norman conquest of 1066 England was brought into the full current of European affairs and into active participation in religious reform, in the new intellectual movement of the 11th and 12th centuries, and in the Crusades. A series of Anglo-Norman writers produced a number of outstanding chronicles and related works in a fluent Latin style. The universal chronicle of Florence of Worcester was mentioned above. *William of Malmesbury (d. 1143) wrote *Gesta regum Anglorum* in 1125, *Historia novella* as a continuation to 1142, *Gesta pontificum Anglorum,* and *De antiquitate ecclesiae Glastoniensis.* He was much admired centuries later by Milton. *Henry of Huntingdon (1084–1159) wrote a *Historia Anglorum,* divided into four periods: Roman, Saxon, Danish, and Norman.

He revised the work five times. However, as a historian he was inferior to William of Malmesbury. John of Salisbury (d. 1180) wrote the *Historia pontificalis* (1162), preserved in part only, but an excellent work intended especially to correct Sigebert of Gembloux and his continuators. *Roger of Hoveden (d. 1201) compiled his *Chronica* in two parts, running from 732 to 1201. His chronicle was much read and used well into the 15th century. The Cistercian *Ralph of Coggeshall (d. *c.* 1228) compiled a *Chronicon Anglicanum* covering the years from 1066 to 1224. *Geoffrey of Monmouth (*c.* 1100–55), with his *Historia regum Britanniae,* produced a work of little historical value but one that from the first exercised an enormous influence on all the European literatures. Typical 12th-century monastic chronicles were: Jocelin of Brakelond (d. *c.* 1215), *Chronica,* recording the events in *Bury-St.-Edmunds for the years 1173 to 1202; *Gervase of Canterbury (d. 1210), *Chronica* of the Abbey of Christ Church, *Canterbury (1105–99).

Chronicles and Annals of the 13th, 14th, and 15th Centuries. The last years of the 12th century and all of the 13th were the golden age of monastic chronicles (often anonymous) and related works. The *Franciscans and *Dominicans gave a new impetus to the writing of such narratives. The universal chronicle enjoyed a revival, and the rise of towns encouraged the production of city-chronicles. The Crusades and the rapidly developing national literatures led to the composition of chronicles in vernacular prose and verse, as well as in Latin. The volume of chronicle literature from the early 13th century is especially large, and all parts of Europe are represented. Therefore, a few of the more important and typical chronicles are indicated here and further guidance is given in the bibliography to complete lists and detailed descriptions.

England and Ireland. *Roger of Wendover (d. 1236), a monk of *Saint Albans, compiled a universal chronicle, *Flores historiarum,* which has independent value only from 1188 and especially from 1202 to 1235. *Matthew Paris, his successor at Saint Albans, the greatest of the Anglo-Norman chroniclers, wrote an elaborate universal chronicle, *Chronica majora,* which depends essentially on Roger of Wendover up to 1235 but from then to 1259 is an independent work of special interest because of the author's personal outlook and observations; his *Historia Anglorum* (*Historia minor*) is his revision and abridgment of the larger work. Bartholomew Cotton, monk of Norwich (d. *c.* 1298), wrote a *Historia Anglicana* (449–1298); Geoffrey Baker (d. *c.* 1358–60), a *Chronicon* (1303–56) and a *Chroniculum* (from Creation to 1336); *Ralph Higden, a Benedictine monk (d. 1364), a universal chronicle, *Polychronicon,* to 1342 (translated by John *Trevisa in 1387, printed by Caxton in 1482, and by Wynkyn de Worde in 1495); *Nicholas Trevet (*c.* 1258–1328), *Annales sex regum Angliae* (1135–1328); Walter of Hemingburgh, prior of St. Mary's, Gisborn (d. after 1313), *Chronicon* (1048–1364); Thomas *Walsingham, monk of Saint Albans (d. 1422), *Chronicon Angliae* (1328–88); and William *Worcester (Botoner; d. *c.* 1480), *Annales rerum Anglicarum* (1324–1468).

Ireland exhibits among its chronicles: *Annals of Innisfallen* (to 1215, and later continued to 1318), in Irish and Latin; *Annals of Ulster* (from 444), compiled by Cathal *Maguire (d. 1498) and continued first to 1541 and then to 1604; *Annals of Boyle* (from earliest times to 1253), in Irish and Latin; *Annals of Clonmacnois* (to 1408), written originally in Irish but preserved only in the English translation of 1627.

France. The wide use of the vernacular in what may be regarded as national chronicles of France is noteworthy. The Dominican *Vincent of Beauvais (*c.* 1190–1264) wrote a universal chronicle on a vast scale with copious citations from his sources, the *Speculum historiale* (from the beginning of the world to 1250). *Albéric of Trois Fontaines, a Cistercian (d. after 1251), composed a universal chronicle, *Chronicon* (to 1251). The *Grandes chroniques de France,* or *Chronique de Saint-Denis* (from the beginnings of the monarchy to the end of the 15th century), is based in large part on earlier Latin chronicles and related works. *Les Gestes des Chiprois* is a collection of French chronicles written in the East in the 13th and 14th centuries. Jean *Froissart (d. after 1404) wrote *Chroniques de France, d'Angleterre, d'Ecosse, de Bretagne, de Gascogne, de Flandre et lieux circonvoisins* (1328–1400), one of the greatest of medieval historical works.

Germany and the Low Countries. Eike von Repkow wrote *Sächsische Weltchronik* (*c.* 1230), the first German historical work in prose; the Dominican *Martin of Troppau, or Polonus (d. 1278), the *Chronicon pontificum et imperatorum* (to 1277), one of the most widely disseminated historical works of the Middle Ages. The *Chronicon Austriacum* (973–1327) is very valuable from the last part of the 13th century; the *Chronica S. Petri Erfordensis moderna* (1–1334) has copious information on the early 14th century. C. Kuchimeister produced *Niiwe Casus Monasterii Sancti Galli* (1228–1329); John of Thilrode, a monk of Saint-Bavon in Ghent, a *Universal Chronicle* (to 1298); William Procurator, a monk of *Egmond in Holland from 1324 to 1333, *Chronicon* (647–1332).

Italy and Spain. The Franciscan *Salimbene of Parma (1221-*c.* 1289) wrote a *Chronica* (1167–1287), in which the record of historical events is spiced with anecdotes, satire, and humor; the Dominican *Bartholomew of Lucca (1236–1326), an *Annales* (1063–1303) of great value for the history of the Church in the 13th century. The *Chronicon Estense* is especially valuable for the period from 1241 to 1354. The *Historie Fiorentine,* or *Chronica universale* (from Creation to 1348) by Giovanni *Villani (*c.* 1275–1348) is a work of the greatest value for the history of Florence because of its exact and detailed information on all aspects of Florentine life; it is one of the best historical works of the Middle Ages. The *Chronicae* or *Summa historialis* of *Antoninus (1389–1459), Archbishop of Florence, is a universal chronicle that enjoyed a great vogue for 2 centuries, but which has independent value only for the late 13th and the 14th century. It should be remarked that Italy in the late Middle Ages is especially rich in city-chronicles.

Spain produced Lucas of Túy (d. 1249), *Chronicon mundi* (to 1236); Rodrigo-Jiménez de Rada (1170–1247), *Historia Gothica,* or *De rebus Hispaniae* (to 1212); *La crónica general,* a vast universal chronicle on the Spanish kings, inspired by *Alfonso X of Castile, the Wise (1252–84), covering history from the time of the Flood to his own time; Pero López de Ayala (1332–1407), compiler of chronicles of the reigns of Peter the

Cruel, Henry II, John I, and Henry III; Gutierre Díez de Games (1379–1450), *Crónica de Don Pedro Niño, o El victorial;* Bernat Dezcoll (d. *c.* 1390), *Crónica* of Pedro IV, King of Aragon (1336–87).

General Evaluation. Annals, chronicles, and the related genre, *gesta,* constitute a huge mass of historical source material from the end of antiquity to the beginning of modern times. They continued to exercise an influence on the form, at least, of 16th-century historiography, for *Baronius, the *Centuriators of Magdeburg, and, at a lower level, Holinshed reflect the annalistic or chronicle tradition. The medieval annals, chronicles, and *gesta* dealt with world history, secular rulers, popes, peoples, cities, bishops, abbots, and monasteries. In a large number of cases they are anonymous. In general, it may be said that all these works take on real historical value only as they approach periods contemporary with or immediately preceding those of their writers. Many of those extant have gone through repeated reworkings and enlargement by addition of later continuations, so that the original form is not always easy or even possible to establish. The material covering world history before the 5th century A.D. is based essentially on the Bible, Eusebius-Jerome, Augustine's *De civitate Dei,* and Orosius. This material is usually not taken directly from these sources in the later annals and chronicles, but is simply incorporated from earlier medieval works of the same kind.

The vast majority of the authors of annals, chronicles, and *gesta* were monks, friars, or members of the secular clergy. All regarded history in a religious sense, that is, as the working out of the history of salvation. With a small number of important exceptions, writers were more or less uncritical or even credulous in dealing with secular as well as religious themes. Furthermore, the horizons of writers of local or regional chronicles, and especially of annals, are very limited. Almost all are preoccupied not only with ecclesiastical affairs, but primarily with the special interests of the religious orders and the diocesan clergy. The monastic writers constituted the larger and more influential group.

Given the handicap that beset the obtaining, using, and disseminating of knowledge before the invention of printing, it is surprising to note that so many works, relatively speaking, were so widely known and employed. Latin was the international language, and French became a second international language in the course of the Norman expansion and the Crusades. The monks and friars played a very important role in the spread of annals and chronicles of a general nature. Medieval authors of annals, chronicles, and *gesta* were not trained historians nor could they be expected to be critical before the rise of genuine historical criticism centuries later. Their works contain precious metal, but the percentage shows wide variation, and the separation of the precious metal from the low grade ore is often a complicated and difficult process.

See also HISTORIOGRAPHY, ECCLESIASTICAL; BYZANTINE LITERATURE.

Bibliography: Altaner 278–284. R. L. POOLE, *Chronicles and Annals: A Brief Outline of Their Origin and Growth* (Oxford 1926). C. W. JONES, *Saints' Lives and Chronicles in Early England* (Ithaca 1947) 16–30. Laistner ThLett 261–265. Wattenbach-Levison 1:50–108. "Anhang: Quellenkunde für die Geschichte der europäischen Staaten während des Mittelalters," in Potthast Bibl 2:1647–1735, a comprehensive survey of each country or people of Europe with the names and dates of all annals and chronicles listed among the sources in each case. K. H. QUIRIN, *Einführung in das Studium der mittelalterlichen Geschichte* (2d ed. Braunschweig 1961) 251–264, annals and chronicles among the sources with dates and eds. "Die Chronisten," in Krumbacher 319–408, a comprehensive treatment of Byzantine chronicles to 1453. RepFontHistMA, annals and chronicles listed among the sources described in the analyses of the contents of the RollsS, Bouquet RGFS, Muratori RIS, Flórez EspSagr, and other collections. T. MOMMSEN, *Chronica Minora,* MGAuctAnt v.9, 11, 13. C. GROSS, "Chronicles and Royal Biographies," *Sources and Literature of English History* (2d ed. New York 1915; repr. 1952) 326–399, includes Ireland, Scotland, and Wales; "Collections Privately Edited: Chroniclers, etc.," *ibid.* 105–112, with lists of English chronicles printed in the RollsS, MGH, etc. Molinier SHF v.2–4, chronicles—including those outside of France that are pertinent—among the sources listed in the *Table de Matières* at the end of each v. Kenney 1–90, 103–104. Manitius v.1–3, treatment of annals, chronicles, and their writers when known, easily controlled through indexes under *Annales, Chronica, Chronicon,* and pertinent personal names. Ghellinck Essor 2:93–114, 135–163, with excellent bibliog. M. SCHULZ, *Die Lehre von der historischen Methode bei den Geschichtsschreibern des Mittelalters, 6.–13. Jahrhundert* (Berlin 1909). J. SPÖRL, *Grundformen hochmittelalterlicher Geschichtsanschauung: Studien zum Weltbild der Geschichtsschreiber des 12. Jahrhunderts* (Munich 1935). H. ZIMMERMANN, *Ecclesia als Objekt der Historiographie: Studien zur Kirchengeschichtsschreibung im Mittelalter und in der frühen Neuzeit* (Vienna 1960). A. D. VON DEN BRINCKEN, *Studien zur lateinischen Weltchronistik bis in das Zeitalter Ottos von Freising* (Düsseldorf 1957). V. H. GALBRAITH, *Historical Research in Medieval England* (London 1951). H. GRUNDMANN, "Geschichtsschreibung im Mittelalter," in *Deutsche Philologie im Aufriss,* ed. W. STAMMLER, v.3 (Berlin 1957) 1273–1335; v.3 (2d ed. 1961) 2221– . J. W. THOMPSON and B. J. HOLM, *A History of Historical Writing,* 2 v. (New York 1942) 1:143–469.

[M. R. P. MC GUIRE]

ANNAS, Jewish high priest, given his office by Coponius, Roman procurator of Judea (A.D. 6–9) while Quirinius was legate to Syria, according to Josephus. He continued as Jewish ethnarch until A.D. 15, when he was deposed by the procurator Valerius Gratus (15–26), who later appointed his son Eleazer and finally his son-in-law *Caiphas to the post. Gratus's successor, Pontius Pilate (26–36), retained Caiphas as high priest when he took office.

The expression "during the high priesthood of Annas and Caiphas" (Lk 3.2) does not mean that there were two high priests at the same time but that Annas continued to exercise power over Caiphas. That Annas was influential in Jerusalem is clear from the fact that besides Caiphas five of his sons and a grandson were high priests during or shortly after his lifetime. The NT also testifies to his power (Jn 18.13, 24). In Acts 4.6 inquiry into the Apostles' teaching is made before Annas and the high-priestly family. The reputation of Annas's clan was one of corruption and venality.

Bibliography: EncDictBibl 91–92. A. WIKENHAUSER, LexThK[2] 1:574. E. JACQUIER, DB 1.1:630–632.

[E. J. HODOUS]

ANNATES

A tax on the first year's income of an ecclesiastical benefice paid to the papal treasury. By the 11th century it had become customary for some bishops and ecclesiastical corporations to appropriate the income of a *benefice for a year or more after collation (*see* COLLATIO). This revenue, known as *fructus primi anni, annalia* or *annualia,* was sometimes collected with papal permission by bishops and kings in special need. Financially embarrassed in 1306, Pope *Clement V asserted a similar claim for the Holy See, appropriating the first fruits of all minor benefices in the British Isles for 3 years. The levy was repeated and extended to most of the Church by *John XXII in 1318. Beginning in 1326 the application of the tax became narrower but virtually continuous: it was paid on all minor benefices becoming vacant at the Holy See or reserved to it. As this was the period during which the number of papal collations and confirmations increased rapidly (*see* PROVISIONS), the income from the tax assumed considerable importance. Details touching *exemptions and the amount and manner of payment were worked out during the remainder of the century, a period that witnessed the first use of the word *annata* for this tax. John XXII had exempted benefices with an income less than 6 silver marks, but *Benedict IX set the minimum at 24 gold florins in 1389. The tax usually amounted to about one-half the gross annual income.

From the end of the 14th century the payment of annates received more and more opposition. Though it was defended in principle in the agreements between the papacy and the national churches after the Council of *Constance, income declined sharply because the papacy resigned many appointments and because payment was usually limited to 24 florins. The Council of *Basel (1435) sought to suppress annates entirely, and the Council of *Trent (sess. 24, c.13) restricted them considerably. In 1728 *Benedict XIII imposed a similar payment in favor of cathedral or capitular churches on minor benefices in Italy and adjacent islands not reserved to the Holy See. In the areas where this ruling continues as local custom the last vestige of annates survives (CIC c.1482). In the 15th and following centuries annates came to mean all taxes paid to the papacy on the reception of a benefice, whether major or minor. This is the usual meaning of the word in English; see the statutes of 23 and 26 Henry VIII, suppressing annates and then transferring them to the royal treasury.

See also FINANCE, ECCLESIASTICAL.

Bibliography: Sources. C. SAMARAN and G. MOLLAT, *La Fiscalité pontificale en France au XIVᵉ siècle* (Paris 1905) 23–34, 87–96. Studies. J. P. KIRSCH, ed., *Die päpstlichen Annaten in Deutschland während des XIV. Jahrhunderts* (Paderborn 1903). E. GÖLLER, *Die Einnahmen der apostolischen Kammer unter Johann XXII* (Paderborn 1910); *Die Einnahmen . . . Benedikt XII* (Paderborn 1920). W. E. LUNT, "The First Levy of Papal Annates," AmHistRev 18 (1912–13) 48–64; *Financial Relations of the Papacy with England to 1327* (Cambridge, Mass. 1939); *Financial Relations of England with the Papacy, 1327–1354* (Cambridge, Mass. 1962). A. PUGLIESE, *Annate e mezz'annate nel diritto canonico* (Milan 1939). J. P. KIRSCH, DHGE 3:307–315. S. GOYENÈCHE, EncCatt 1:1368–69. K. HONSELMANN, Lex ThK[2] 1:575. For a general orientation on papal finances, see G. LEBRAS, *Institutions ecclésiastiques de la chrétienté médiévale*, 2 pts. (Fliche-Martin 12; 1959–64) 2:351–353.

[M. M. SHEEHAN]

ANNE OF DENMARK

Queen consort of King James I of Great Britain; b. Skanderborg, Jutland, Dec. 12, 1574; d. Hampton Court, England, March 2, 1619. Anne, whose parents were King Frederick II of Denmark and Norway and Queen Sophia of Mecklenburg, was brought up in a traditional Lutheran household, and was the second of four daughters in a family of seven children. Anne was sought in marriage by James VI of Scotland as a means of settling in Scotland's favor a dispute with Denmark over the Orkney Islands. The marriage was solemnized at Oslo, Nov. 24, 1589. Of an indolent, but tolerant and amiable nature, the young bride showed little interest in anything more serious than rich clothes, court balls, and masques, which remained her chief delight throughout her life. She was the mother of six children: her eldest son, and favorite, Henry Frederick, was born at Stirling, Feb. 19, 1594, and his premature death in 1612 left her inconsolable; Elizabeth (b. 1596) became Princess of Bohemia; Margaret (b. 1598) died in infancy; Charles, the future King Charles I of England, was born in 1600; Robert (b. 1601) died in infancy, as did Mary (b. at Greenwich, England, 1605; d. 1607).

Anne of Denmark, miniature portrait painted in 1595.

Anne preferred Lutheranism to the Calvinism of Scotland. The deprivation of Lutheran services seems to have led to her interest in Catholicism. In 1600, at Holyroodhouse Palace, she received Robert *Abercromby, SJ: "After a long conversation with the father, she earnestly entreated him to stay with her three days that he might instruct her fully in Catholic doctrines and ceremonies. . . . On the fourth day, full of holy joy she made her general confession and having heard Mass twice, she received the most holy sacrament with joy in the presence of only a few persons of rank." Not only did James know of her conversion, he utilized it in negotiations with *Clement VIII for recognition of James's right to the throne of England at Elizabeth's death. The negotiations were carried on through Sir James Lindsay, the Pope's messenger.

During Anne's reign as Queen of England (1603–19), it is known that Alexander MacQuhirrie, SJ, was her chaplain and that Richard Blount, English Jesuit provincial, visited her secretly on a number of occasions before and after the birth of her daughter Mary at Greenwich. He reprimanded her severely for attending her infant daughter's baptism according to the Protestant form. Anne's light and frivolous nature has caused many historians to regard her Catholicism as a passing fancy and fad. Certainly her conversion seemingly did nothing to make her serious and devout, or to offer strength of character. Nonetheless, her refusal to receive the Sacrament according to the rites of the Church of England at her coronation with James, July 24, 1603, showed some courage and raised the hopes of Catholic England. She urged a Catholic marriage for Prince Henry and sought to obtain office for her coreligionists. She corresponded with the Spanish infanta and dared to employ Sir Anthony Standen, James's Ambassador to Italy, as her private agent in Rome. Undoubtedly the storm over the *Gunpowder Plot and the pressures of James, who then found his wife's Catholicism awkward for him, did much to weaken her resolution, at least publicly. Although James made a point of choosing only those favorites first accepted by his wife, it was always actually a manipulated affair, and Anne was known to have little political influence, as, e.g., in the case of Sir Walter Raleigh. Her correspondence with Ottaviano Lotti, the opinions of Philip III and Francisco Gómez de Sandoval y Rojas, Duke of Lerma, and ambassador's reports, all indicate continued knowledge and acceptance of her Catholicism throughout the years 1605 to 1618. Don Diego de Sarmiento de Acuna, Count Gondomar, Spanish Ambassador, attests to the fact that though Anne attended the services of the Church of England with James, she never took communion at these services, and that at Denmark House, her London residence, she frequently heard Mass secretly in the garret from recusant priests. At her country residence at Oatlands she had two priests and while there she heard Mass daily.

Anne, frustrated in any powerful public influence, seems to have resorted to extravagant expenditures for masques and building, utilizing the genius of Inigo Jones at Greenwich House and Denmark House especially. After 1612 Anne suffered for many years from dropsy, which eventually caused her mortal illness. She was attended at her deathbed by George Abbot, Archbishop of Canterbury, and the bishop of London. Her deathbed renunciation of "the mediation of all saints and her own merits" is taken as a denial of her Roman Catholicism, a position most recently accepted by Philip Caraman, SJ, who felt she was "persuaded vs. her true conviction." A virtuous wife, affectionate mother, and good friend, generous and compassionate, Anne was well liked by the English people.

Bibliography: D. H. Willson, *King James VI and I* (New York 1956). G. P. V. Akrigg, *Jacobean Pageant* (Cambridge, Mass. 1962). L. Hicks, "The Embassy of Sir Anthony Standen in 1603," *Recusant History* 5 (1959–60) 91–127, 194–222; 6 (1961–62) 163–194; 7 (1963–64) 50–81. A. W. Ward, DNB 1:431–441, bibliog. S. R. Gardiner, *History of England,* 10 v. (2d rev. ed. London 1883–84) v.1–3. A. Strickland, *Lives of the Queens of England,* 12 v. (London 1840–48) v.7. **Illustration credit:** National Galleries of Scotland.

[J. D. HANLON]

ANNE OF JESUS, VEN., Spanish Discalced Carmelite; b. Medina del Campo, Léon, Nov. 25, 1545; d. Brussels, March 4, 1621. Her parents, Diego de Lobera and Francisca de Torrès, were from prominent families of Spain. When 15 she rejected the prospect of a rich marriage because of a vow of chastity. She cut off her hair, wore a penitential gown, and under the guidance of a Jesuit, Pedro Rodriguez, sought admission into the reformed Carmel at Salamanca. There she took the habit, Aug. 1, 1570, and was professed Oct. 22, 1571. She assisted St. *Teresa of Avila in the foundation of convents in Andalusia (1575), where she was prioress for 3 years, and in Granada (1581). After the death of Teresa (1582), she became prioress in Madrid (1586) and began the edition of Teresa's writings. When Anne of Jesus obtained a brief from Sixtus V on June 5, 1590, confirming the constitutions of the Discalced Carmelites, she displeased the Carmelite Vicar-General, Nicolò Doria, and the *Consulta* (his 6 advisers), and was deprived of jurisdiction for 3 years (*see* CARMELITES, DISCALCED). In 1596 she was again prioress at Salamanca. At the invitation of Cardinal Pierre de Bérulle, she and *Anne of St. Bartholomew established houses at Paris (1604), and Pontoise (1605), but opposed the cardinal's aim to associate the Reformed Carmelites with his French Oratory. She left France, founded a convent at Brussels (1607), and then returned to Spain, where she worked on further editions of St. Teresa's works, translated them into Latin and Flemish, and wrote a biography of the saint. She also concurred in the establishment of communities in Cracow, Galicia, and Antwerp.

Bibliography: Berthold-Ignace de Sainte Anne, *Vie de la mère Anne de Jésus,* 2 v. (Mechlin, Belgium 1877–83). P. Marie Joseph, DHGE 3:340–343, bibliog. G. Marsot, *Catholicisme* 1:588. S. di Santa Teresa, EncCatt 1:1363.

[E. D. MC SHANE]

ANNE OF ST. BARTHOLOMEW, BL., Spanish Discalced Carmelite; b. Almendral, near Ávila, Oct. 1, 1549; d. Antwerp, June 7, 1626 (feast, June 7). Anne, the daughter of Ferdinand Garcia and Maria Manzanas, entered the Carmelite convent of St. Joseph at Ávila, Nov. 7, 1570, and was professed as the first lay sister of the Reform, Aug. 15, 1572. She was constantly with St. *Teresa until the latter's death in her arms, Oct. 4, 1582. She accompanied *Anne of Jesus in 1604, when the Reformed Carmelites were invited by Cardinal Pierre de Bérulle to found convents in France. There she was unwillingly promoted to a choir sister on Jan. 6, 1605, and became prioress at the convent of Pontoise, and then of Tours in 1608. Against the opposition of Bérulle, she left Paris on Oct. 5, 1611, to join Anne of Jesus in the Spanish Netherlands. She founded a convent at Antwerp (1612), and because of her prayers, she is credited with saving the city from the hands of the Calvinists (1622 and 1624). For this she is acclaimed "Liberator of Antwerp." There she wrote her autobiography and her instructions for superiors and mistresses of novices. She was declared venerable June 29, 1735, by Clement XII, and proclaimed blessed May 6, 1917, by Benedict XV.

Bibliography: M. Bouix, *Vie de la vén. mère Anne de Saint-Barthélemy* (2d ed. Paris 1872), the second edition is based on the autobiography. P. Marie-Joseph, DHGE 3:346–349, bibliog. ActApS 9:257–261. R. Aigrain, *Catholicisme* 1:589. Butler Th Attw 2:499–500.

[E. D. MC SHANE]

ANNE AND JOACHIM, SS.

Traditional names of the mother and father of the Blessed Virgin Mary. Since Sacred Scripture makes no mention of Mary's parents, one may rightly wonder about the basis for the devotion to St. Anne and St. Joachim. Does this devotion rest merely on a late invention of popular piety? Be that as it may, the Blessed Virgin surely had parents, no matter what their names may have been. The assumption that they were sanctified by God in view of their election by Him to bring the immaculate Mother of God into the world is entirely reasonable; otherwise it would be unreasonable to assume that Mary, Joseph, and John the Baptist had been sanctified in view of their participation in the Redemption.

There is not, however, a total lack of information about the lives of Mary's parents. The apocryphal Gospel known as the Protoevangelium Jacobi, written *c.* A.D. 170–180 [*see* BIBLE, III (CANON), 5], offers some interesting information on this matter. This work, which treats of Mary's infancy, is undoubtedly one of the most famous of the apocryphal writings, not only because of its antiquity and wide diffusion, but also because of the unparalleled influence that it had on devotion to Mary. It would be a sad mistake to class this work with the heretical writings that were circulated in the early Christian centuries, even though everything in it cannot be taken, without further ado, as historical. In any case, the story that it tells of Mary's parents is worth summarizing here.

Joachim and Anne According to the Protoevangelium. It happened one day that Joachim, who was rich and respected in Israel, met with reproaches because of his sterility. Feeling downcast, he left his wife Anne and retired to the desert to pray and fast. Meanwhile Anne too, now that she was left alone, wept and lamented before the Lord, bewailing her seeming widowhood and actual childlessness, which she regarded as a punishment from God. Finally, the prayers of both spouses were answered. An angel appeared to Anne and announced that she would conceive and bear a child who would become famous throughout the world. Anne thereupon promised to offer to the Lord the fruit of her womb. At the same time Joachim in the desert had a similar vision. Full of joy, he returned home. When his wife was told of his coming by messengers, she went out to meet him at the city gate. At the sight of Joachim, she ran and embraced him. "Now I know," she said, "that the Lord has wondrously heard my prayer. I who was a widow am a widow no longer; I who was once sterile have conceived in my womb."

The account of Mary's birth is then given, followed by the story of how the little girl was later presented to the Lord in the Temple by her parents (*see* PRESENTATION OF THE BLESSED VIRGIN MARY). In the rest of the account Mary's parents no longer appear.

Diffusion of the Story. The Christians of the early centuries were fascinated by the Protoevangelium. "In the original Greek text, or in the Latin, Syriac, Coptic, Armenian, Georgian, Arabic, and Ethiopic translations, or in more or less complete paraphrases in seven different languages, it spread at an early date in every part of Christendom. . . . It gave rise to a series of liturgical feasts: the feasts of Mary's Conception, her Nativity, and her Presentation in the Temple, as well as the feast of her parents, St. Joachim and St. Anne" (De Strycker, v). Numerous Fathers cited or commented on the story told in the Protoevangelium, among them St. Epiphanius, Andrew of Crete, the Patriarch Germanus I of Constantinople, St. John Damascene, Photius and his friend George of Nicomedia, St. Sophronius.

Popular Devotion. Churches in honor of St. Anne began to be erected in the 6th century. According to Procopius, there was a church dedicated to her in Constantinople *c.* A.D. 550. At about the same time a church in her honor was built in Jerusalem at the traditional site of her birthplace. These two churches were very influential in spreading the cult of Mary's parents, especially that of St. Anne. In the later Middle Ages, after her cult had spread to Europe, there were numerous churches, chapels, and confraternities dedicated to her.

The feast in honor of both St. Anne and St. Joachim on September 9, for which selections or paraphrases of the stories from the Protoevangelium were used as liturgical texts, was introduced first in the East, probably at the church of St. Anne in Constantinople or at her church in Jerusalem toward the end of the 6th century. In the West the cult of St. Anne was introduced at Rome in the 8th century; it was not until the 14th century that it became widespread in Europe. In 1584 Gregory XIII extended her feast, celebrated on July 26, to the whole Latin Church. Thereafter St. Anne became extraordinarily popular, especially in France. Her two greatest shrines are still those of Ste. Anne d'Auray in Brittany and Ste. Anne de Beaupré near Quebec in French-speaking Canada. The feast of St. Joachim was not introduced in the West until the 15th century. After being suppressed by St. Pius V, it was restored by Paul V (1621) and raised to a higher rank by Leo XIII. Its present date of August 16 was fixed only in 1913.

"The Embrace of Joachim and Anne at the Golden Gate," by the 16th-century German artist Albrecht Dürer.

One of the reasons for the popularity of the cult of SS. Joachim and Anne is its close connection with the cult of the Blessed Virgin Mary. At the same time, Christian married couples find in the parents of Mary a model of conjugal life such as they do not find in Joseph and Mary, at least on the level of conjugal relations. In this regard it is significant that, until the 16th century, the conception of Mary was represented in iconography by showing the meeting of Joachim and Anne at the Golden Gate of Jerusalem. The embrace (*osculum*) of the two spouses suggesting the conception of Mary is the sole example known in iconography. It seemed entirely normal that the faithful should see in this a glorification of Christian marriage.

Another reason for the popularity of their cult is the fact that the family, especially in former days, could not be thought of without the grandparents. If Mary is the mother of Jesus, her parents are His grandparents and belong, in a certain sense, to the "Holy Family." Finally,

St. Anne and the infant Virgin, tempera on pine panel, by an anonymous artist working in New Mexico, c. 1822.

Joachim and Anne are becoming symbols of the messianic expectations of the OT, while they introduce the NT. With Mary, they form the point in history where divinity entered into humanity.

Iconography. Christian iconography abounds in treatments of Mary's parents, especially in the cycles of the infancy of the Virgin. After Jesus and Mary, St. Anne is one of the subjects that appears most frequently in iconography, whether alone or with others in various scenes of her life. Extremely popular in the Middle Ages was the portrayal of Anne with the infant Jesus as well as the Blessed Virgin. She is represented most often as a venerable matron wearing a long robe, with cincture, mantle, and veil. Around A.D. 1500 artists added the headdress that was worn by the ladies of their time. St. Joachim is usually represented together with St. Anne. He is sometimes shown carrying the infant Mary or bringing two turtledoves (cf. Lk 2.24) as the offering for her presentation in the Temple.

Bibliography: É. AMANN, *Le Protévangile de Jacques et ses remainiements latins* (Paris 1910). É. DE STRYCKER, *La Forme la plus ancienne du Protévangile de Jacques* (Brussels 1961). B. KLEINSCHMIDT, *Die Heilige Anna: Ihre Verehrung in Geschichte, Kunst und Volkstum* (Düsseldorf 1930). P. V. CHARLAND, *Madame Saincte Anne et son culte au moyen âge,* 2 v. (Paris 1911–13); *Les Trois légendes de Madame Saincte Anne* (Montreal 1898). K. ALGERMISSEN et al., eds., *Lexicon der Marienkunde* (Regensburg 1957–) 1:230–257. H. LECLERCQ, DACL 1.2:2162–74. H. SCHAUERTE, LexThK² 1:570–571. B. KRAFT, *ibid.* 5:973. P. DE AMBROGGI, EncCatt 1:1360. A. AMORE, *ibid.* 6:403–404. Iconography. E. CAMPAGNA, "Iconografia dell' Immacolata," *Arte Cristiana* 15 (1915) 354–368. H. AURENHAMMER, *Lexikon der christlichen Ikonographie* (Vienna 1959–) 1:139–149. Künstle Ikonog 1:321–332. Réau IAC 2.2:155–161; 3.1:90–96; 3.2:751. K. RATHE, EncCatt 1:1360–61. **Illustration credits:** Fig. 1, The Baltimore Museum of Art, Carrett Collection. Fig. 2, Collection of Charles D. Carroll, Museum of International Folk Art, Santa Fe.

[J. P. ASSELIN]

ANNECY, MONASTERY OF, a priory of the Canons Regular of the Holy Sepulchre, founded in the 12th century in the town of Annecy, eastern France. Its members were authorized by Pope Celestine III (1191–98) to beg for their support and that of the pilgrims they received in their hospice; the surplus was to go for the Holy Land. In the 14th century, the monastery had 18 members. About mid-14th century the canons built a Gothic church, which still stands in great part, though invisible under later construction. Bl. Andrew of Antioch was probably prior of the community when the church was built, and his tomb was venerated there until 1792. In 1484 Innocent VIII united the houses of the Order in France and elsewhere to the Knights of Malta, but the monastery at Annecy was excluded from the decree. The priory was destroyed by fire in 1590 and was not rebuilt. The canons did not live in community thereafter, and the decline in religious spirit that had preceded this event continued its course and led to their secularization in the 17th century and their suppression in the 18th.

Bibliography: A. GAVARD, DHGE 3:363. G. LETONNELIER, *Annecy au XVe et XVIe siècles* (Annecy 1911).

[C. FALK]

ANNHURST COLLEGE. A Catholic liberal arts college for women located on a 200-acre campus in South Woodstock, Conn., Annhurst was founded in 1941 with the approval of Maurice McAuliffe, Bishop of Hartford. The College is conducted by the Daughters of the Holy Ghost (*see* HOLY GHOST, DAUGHTERS OF).

Chartered by the Legislature of the state of Connecticut, Annhurst is affiliated with The Catholic University of America and the National Catholic Educational Association. It is accredited by the Connecticut State Department of Education, the Board of Regents of the University of the State of New York, and the New England Association of Colleges and Secondary Schools. It holds membership in the American Council on Education, the American Medical Association, the American Association of Collegiate Registrars and Admissions Officers, the Association of American Colleges, the American Association of University Women, the College Entrance Examination Board, and the National Commission on Accrediting.

The board of trustees of Annhurst is composed of the mother provincial and the provincial council, the president of the College, the dean, and registrar. Administrative officers include the president, dean, registrar, librarian, and dean of women. In 1963 the faculty numbered 14 sisters, 3 priests, and 14 laymen. Faculty-held degrees included 9 doctorates and 18 master's degrees. Revenue accrues from tuition, fees, and the contributed services of the religious faculty. There is no monetary endowment of the College.

Annhurst College offers a 4-year course leading to the B.A. degree or the B.S. in business. Specialized study is offered in the liberal arts, mathematics, the social and natural sciences, and business. The Department of English for Foreign Students was established in 1964 to meet the needs of foreign students who come to the United States to continue their studies in English.

In 1964 the College library contained 20,500 volumes and received 230 periodicals. The natural sciences department was equipped with laboratories in chemistry, physics, and biology. A language laboratory was available for modern-language and foreign students.

One of three Catholic women's colleges in Connecticut, Annhurst has an average enrollment of 250 full-time resident and day students.

[H. BONIN]

ANNIBALE, GIUSEPPE D', cardinal, canonist, and moral theologian; b. Borbona (Aquila), Italy, Sept. 22, 1815; d. Rieti, July 18, 1892. Ordained at Rieti in 1839, he became professor of moral theology and Canon Law in the local seminary. Later he was named vicar-general of Rieti. In 1873 he published his commentary on the constitution *Apostolicae Sedis,* issued by Pius IX in 1869, abrogating, changing, and establishing a new list of censures. D'Annibale's commentary is renowned for its combination of conciseness and accuracy, and it won him the title *Commentator Reatinus.* Leo XIII named him titular bishop of Caristo Aug. 12, 1881, when he was appointed assessor of the Holy Office. And in 1889 Leo XIII created him a cardinal with the title of SS. Boniface and Alexis; he then became prefect of the Congregation of Indulgences. In addition to his commentary on the *Apostolicae Sedis,* he wrote a manual of moral theology, *Summula theologiae moralis* (3 v. Milan 1881–83).

Bibliography: P. DE SANCTIS, *Biografia del cardinale Giuseppe d'Annibale* (Rome 1898). J. J. A'BECKET, CE 1:540–541. A. BEUGNET, DTC 1.2:1322. T. ORTOLAN, DHGE 3:390–393. Hurter Nomencl[3] 5.2:1797.

[P. F. MULHERN]

ANNIHILATION

Hypothetically considered in theology, annihilation is the total reduction of the whole being from existence to nonexistence. Whereas *creation in the active causal sense is the act whereby the entire supposit (the individual being as such) is brought from nonexistence to existence, the act of annihilation is the reduction of the supposit in its entirety from existence to nonexistence (St. Thomas Aquinas, ST 1a, 41.3; 45.4, 8; 104.1, 3, 4; *De pot.* 3.3; 5.1, 4).

The term annihilation is used in physics not in the sense defined above but to characterize the conversion of mass into energy that occurs when a positron and an electron collide to produce two or more photons of gamma-radiation. In the corresponding fashion, the term creation is used in connection with pair production, in which the reverse of the above process occurs—a photon in collision with an atomic nucleus results in an electron-positron pair.

Comparison with Creation. Annihilation, theologically considered, is used in the proper sense and can be understood only by comparison with the concept of creation. God's causality of a being effects the production of the total creature from absolute nonexistence. The divine causality of the existence of being is not distinct as the principle of its being and as the principle of its conservation in being. Creation is the continuous conservation of the being in existence by the First Cause of its existence. The First Cause as the essential proper cause of being remains the proper direct cause as long as being, the proper effect, continues to exist (*see* CONSERVATION, DIVINE).

To say that God could create a being that would not need to be conserved in existence involves a contradiction in terms. Only that which has no proper cause needs not to be kept in existence by its proper cause. The withdrawal of the proper cause of existent being would constitute annihilation of being.

Possibility of Annihilation. While science, philosophy, and theology deny annihilation in the real order, speculative theology, nevertheless, asks the question whether or not God could annihilate creatures. Since God is the cause of all being by His absolute will and not by intrinsic or extrinsic necessity, He could withdraw His creative act and thereby annihilate created being (ST 1a, 9.2). As before He caused its existence, without prejudice to His goodness He could have abstained from bringing it into existence, so He could withdraw His act and as He did so creatures would cease to exist. An act may be said to be impossible to God either because the very act involves a contradiction, or because the opposite of the act would be necessary. But absolute nonexistence of creatures does not involve a contradiction, otherwise they would be necessary and not contingent. Moreover, God's power is not determined to the existence of creatures by any necessity. His goodness does not depend on their existence and gains nothing therefrom. He who is their First Cause is not necessitated to give them being unless He has divinely decreed their being. Therefore, it is not impossible for God to reduce being to nonexistence by the simple withdrawal of His conserving power.

Although God could annihilate creatures who sin against Him, yet it is more fitting that He conserve them in existence. Sin involves the rebellion of the will against the will of the Creator; it does not involve rebellion of the created nature as such; for despite the moral state of the sinner, his nature observes the order assigned it by God. Since sin is both aversion from the ultimate Good and conversion to an apparent, but not real, transient good, fitting punishment involves, therefore, the pain of loss proportionate to the sinner's aversion from the ultimate Good, and the pain of sense proportionate to the conversion to the apparent transient good. But if the sinner were annihilated, there could be no such fitting punishment, since the whole being would be reduced to nonexistence (ST 1a2ae, 87.4; 87.1).

Failing to find in reason or revelation any support for the erroneous supposition that there should be an ultimate conversion of all sinners, and considering immortality of the soul to be a grace rather than its natural attribute, some persons who came to be known as annihilationists proposed annihilation as the ultimate end of the finally impenitent, and maintained that God would be compelled thereby to confess failure of His purpose and His power.

In Eucharistic Theology. In the history of theological speculation relative to the nature and effects of the act of Consecration in the Holy Sacrifice of the Mass, certain theologians of the Scotist and nominalist schools came to advance the theory of annihilation as an explanation for what St. Thomas and his followers described to be "the disappearance" of the bread and wine after the words of the separate consecrations. As a result of long profound argumentation between the adherents of the respective positions, there gradually emerged the theological clarification of the doctrine of *transubstantiation. Ultimately, theologians came to distinguish the concept of *change* in which one of the two terms, the *terminus a quo,* or the *terminus ad quem,* may be expressed *negatively,* from that of *substantial conversion* in which two *positive extremes* are involved, each of which is related to the other by such an intimate connection that the last extreme (*terminus ad quem*) begins to exist only as the first extreme (*terminus a quo*) ceases to exist, while a third element (*commune tertium*) unites the two extremes with each other, and continues to exist after the conversion of the substances has taken place (*De ver.* 28.1; *De pot.* 3.2). This unique conversion was defined by the Council of Trent as transubstantiation (Denz 1642). In the use of the phrase, "disappearance of the bread and wine," St. Thomas had consistently refused to equate annihilation simply and properly; and while at first Scotus was inclined to accept annihilation as identified with "disappearance," the speculations that his position induced ultimately led to the clarification of the meaning of the Consecration of the Mass as the positive action of God effecting a total conversion of the *terminus a quo* into the *terminus ad quem* with the *commune tertium* of the accidents of the bread and wine remaining (ST 3a, 75.3; 77.5; Denz 1642, 1652).

See also CHANGE; ELEMENTARY PARTICLES; GENERATION-CORRUPTION.

Bibliography: K. JÜSSEN, LexThK² 1:576–577. A. MICHEL, DTC 15.1:1396–1406. P. RAYMOND, DTC 4.2:1916–18. A. PIOLANTI, *The Holy Eucharist,* tr. L. PENZO (New York 1961) 54–77. E. DORONZO, *De eucharistia* (Milwaukee 1947) 1:224–367.

[M. R. E. MASTERMAN]

ANNIUS, JOHN (NANNI), Dominican humanist; b. Viterbo, Italy, *c.* 1432; d. Rome, Nov. 13, 1502. He is noted also as a theologian, historian, archeologist, preacher, and student of Oriental languages. His fame led *Alexander VI to appoint him master of the sacred palace in 1499, for in the previous year Annius had begun his *Antiquitatum variarum volumina* (Rome 1498), later completed in 17 volumes. The work was designed to throw new light on ancient history by containing the writings and fragments of several pre-Christian Greek and Latin authors. Annius's work created an immediate controversy, especially among his contemporaries who questioned the authenticity of his texts of Berosus and Cato. Modern scholars regard Annius's work with some skepticism and charge him with naïveté in the acceptance of the authenticity of some of his sources. He is the author also of *De futuris Christianorum triumphis in Saracenos,* a commentary on the Apocalypse (Genoa 1480), *Tractatus de imperio Turcorum* (Genoa 1480), and *Chronologia nova* (unpub.), which was designed to correct the historical errors of *Eusebius of Caesarea.

Bibliography: Quétif-Échard 2.1:4–7. A. WALZ, EncCatt 1:1373–74; LexThK² 1:577. Pastor 6:491. L. BERRA, Mercati-Pelzer DE 1:157.

[C. L. HOHL, JR.]

ANNO OF COLOGNE, ST., archbishop of Cologne; b. Swabia, Germany, *c.* 1010; d. Abbey of Siegburg, Germany, Dec. 4, 1075 (feast, Dec. 4). He came of a noble Swabian family and was educated probably at Bamberg. He was named a canon of Goslar by Emperor *Henry III and became archbishop of *Cologne and chancellor of the Empire in 1056. To avoid confusion with an earlier archbishop, he is sometimes designated as Anno II. Dissatisfied with the regency of Agnes of Poitou (d. 1077), Anno connived in the kidnaping of the minor *Henry IV at Kaiserswerth and made himself guardian and regent for the boy in 1062. Because of his severe discipline, he was dismissed by Henry in 1063 in favor of the more lenient *Adalbert of Bremen, but was recalled in 1072. At Augsburg, in 1062, during the struggle between *Alexander II and the antipope Cadalus, Bishop of Parma (d. *c.* 1071), Anno supported Alexander. Despite his holy and penitential life, he was unpopular with the citizens of Cologne, who drove him from the city in 1074. Quickly restored through the help of the peasants, he retired shortly thereafter to the monastery of Siegburg, where he spent his last days, and where he was buried. He was canonized by Pope *Lucius III in 1183. His episcopacy was noteworthy both for the reform of existing monasteries and the establishment of new ones: Sankt George and Sankt Maria zu den Stufen (*ad gradus*), both in Cologne, as well as Saalfeld, Grafschaft, and Siegburg. The vita of Anno, composed about 1106 by a monk of Siegburg, is the basis of the Middle High German *Annolied* (MGS 11:462–464 and MG Dt Chron 1:2), but neither has historical value.

Bibliography: W. NEUSS, ed., *Geschichte des Erzbistums Köln* (Cologne 1964–) 1:184–200. P. RICHARD, DHGE 3:396–398. Hauck 3:712–730. T. LINDNER, *Anno II., der Heilige, Erzbischof von Köln, 1056–1075* (Leipzig 1869). G. BAUERNFEIND, *Anno II., Erzbischof von Köln* (Munich 1929).

[M. F. MC CARTHY]

ANNUNCIATION

The message by which God revealed to Mary that she would be the virgin mother of the Messiah; or, in a broader sense, the entire account of Lk 1.26–38, which contains later reflections upon the mystery of the Incarnation. The NT (in Mt 1.18–25) contains another account of an annunciation according to which Joseph is informed of Mary's virginal and miraculous conception of the Messiah. This latter section, however, seems to represent an official report of the Jerusalem church, for it is more concerned about scriptural fulfillment than Luke ch. 1–2 and more careful to present a summary of Christian beliefs, including the royal Davidic prerogatives of Jesus through His foster father Joseph. Interest here is limited to the Lucan account. After investigating the authorship of Luke ch. 1–2 this article considers some of the important doctrinal questions raised by the Annunciation narrative.

Authorship of the Account. The origin and literary style of the entire *infancy Gospel of Lk 1.5–2.52 must be appreciated in order to look with proper focus upon all other questions, such as those that inquire about the nature of the angel's appearance and the meaning of the message to Mary. In brief, according to the hypothesis proposed here, the Greek text of the Lucan infancy narrative reflects an earlier Hebrew form that circulated in a group dominated by St. *John the Apostle. John, in turn, derived the salient ideas from Mary herself in the early days after Pentecost. One must trace this development with more precision.

Hebrew Background. A Hebrew original frequently appears beneath the surface of the present Greek text, not only in the continual use of parallelism but also in many other literary details. Parallelism is a balancing of ideas, so that the second member repeats the first but with some new or different insight; such an ebb and flow of thought moves through almost every sentence of Luke ch. 1–2. A careful study of the Greek text reveals other Hebraic features, different from the classical Greek style of the prologue (Lk 1.1–4) and from the Septuagint form of Luke ch. 3–24. By translating the Greek back into Hebrew, one can discover examples of assonance, alliteration, and onomatopoeia, typical of Hebrew poetry: e.g., "He shall go before him [*lipnê*] . . . to prepare [*l^{e}pannôt*] for the Lord . . . (1.17; cf. Mal 3.1); "Mary remained [*wattēšeb*] . . . and returned [*wattāšob*] to her own house" (1.56).

Another indication of Hebrew background, evident in the larger development of these chapters, is the prevailing style of *haggadah. Whereas the midrashic style quotes Scripture and sees its interpretation in terms of present events (cf. Matthew ch. 1–2), the haggadic presentation simply alludes to Biblical passages and penetrates into a contemporary act of salvation by continual but indirect appeal to the ancient Scriptures. Later some of these allusions will be cited, but the following instances in Luke's Gospel can be noted at present: 1.12–13 (Dn 10.7, 12); 1.16–17 (Mal 3.1, 23); 1.19 (Dn 9.20–21); 1.28–32 (So 3.14–17); 1.35 (Ex 40.35). Haggadah, like *midrash, begins with history—with the great redemptive acts of God in the present as well as in the past—but it never delays over, nor is it primarily interested in, details of chronology, geography, or history. It seeks to bring the reader into close contact with the mysterious work of salvation contained within and beneath events and continuing into the present moment.

Marian and Johannine Influence. The first two chapters of Luke's Gospel, moreover, move in the quiet, rhythmic meter of personal reflection and humble simplicity. They reveal an intuitive, subjective, feminine approach. The heart in which these verses were originally formed seems to have been Mary's, for they reveal the secrets of her soul at that moment when God chose her to be His mother as well as during that long time afterward when she pondered God's goodness toward her. One also senses in the infancy narrative the calm, joyful spirit of the Christian assembly during the first years after Pentecost (Acts 2.42–47): the expectation of the messianic triumph any moment; the assiduous study and the careful observance of the Mosaic Law; Jerusalem as the center of hopes; the special place accorded the poor and lowly (Acts 1.12; 4.23–37; 1 and 2 Thessalonians). The atmosphere is not troubled by any of the controversies that soon began to disturb the Church: quarrels about the care of Hellenists and the reception of Gentiles (Acts 6.1; 11.1–3; Gal 2.11–14). During the first years of the Church Mary shared, especially with John, her contemplative appreciation of the Incarnation (cf. Jn 19.26–27; Acts 1.14).

John, for his part, made his own contribution to the infancy narrative, or at least one can say that, as Mary's story was sung or recited in the Johannine circle of Christians, ideas typical of John's theology acquired a

The Annunciation, detail of the mosaic executed c. 432–440 on the arch of the apse of the Basilica of S. Maria Maggiore at Rome.

prominent place in the narrative: e.g., the delight in number symbolism; the overarching presence of the Jerusalem Temple; the overshadowing of the divine presence; the analogies with the Book of Apocalypse in schematization, scenes, lyrics and OT imitation.

Diptych Arrangement. It is difficult to determine whether John or Luke was ultimately responsible for the carefully wrought literary structure of these chapters. They are arranged like a sacred drama in two diptychs: one of the annunciations of John the Baptist and of Jesus; the other, of their births. Each section is divided into a series of seven scenes, including: introduction of time and place; appearance of actors; canticle or dialogue; departure of actors. That the two annunciation scenes carefully follow a literary pattern becomes evident in the following outline, borrowed in part from René Laurentin's studies:

Annunication of John the Baptist (1.5–25)	Annunciation of Jesus (1.26–38)
Presentation of the parents	Presentation of the parents
Apparition of the angel	Entrance of the angel
Anxiety of Zachary	Anxiety of Mary
"Do not fear"	"Do not fear"
Announcement of the birth	Announcement of the birth
Question: "How shall I know this?"	Question: "How shall this happen?"
Answer: the angel's reprimand	Answer: the angel's revelation
Sign: "Behold, thou shalt be dumb"	Sign: "Behold, thy kinswoman has conceived"
Silence of Zachary	Response of Mary
Departure of Zachary	Departure of the angel

Luke, in any case, put the infancy narrative into final shape when he included it in his Gospel. This study of literary origins has important conclusions for the Annunciation account. In such an intricate, artificial arrangement as found in Luke ch. 1–2, one must admit that the author(s) took liberty with historical details

The Annunciation in a medieval setting, central panel of an altarpiece by Robert Campin (active 1406–44).

in order to highlight the religious significance of these details. The chapters contain far more than what Mary understood at the moment of the Annunciation; they are the fruit of her long, meditative prayer and the appreciation of her intuition by John, Luke, and others. Here, as elsewhere in the Gospels, God is not giving us a biography of Mary and Joseph, not even of Jesus, but the good news of salvation in Christ Jesus. Many details, therefore, which our curiosity finds important, are passed over in silence.

Doctrinal Question. Some doctrinal questions deserve attention. First, what, precisely, was God asking of Mary? In other words, did Mary understand that she was consenting to be the Mother of God or simply the Mother of the Messiah?

Mary's Knowledge of the Divinity of Her Son. From her OT background Mary had no clear reason to think that the Messiah would also be personally and substantially divine. The Scriptures spoke of a royal Messiah born of the family of David [2 Samuel ch. 7; Psalm 2; 88(89); 109(110); Isaia ch. 7–11; Mi 5.1–5], of some kind of priestly Messiah in the line of Aaron (Ez 44.15–31; Zacharia ch. 3–4; Dn 9.24–27; Joel), and possibly of a prophetic Messiah (Dt 18.15–19). Each of the messianic figures, though God's special representative, was expected to be thoroughly human. True, the Annunciation account describes Mary's child with Biblical phrases proclaiming God's presence among His people. Mary's child would be: great [Ps 47(48).1; 85(86).10; 95(96).4], the Son of the Most High (Gn 14.19–20; Sir 24.2), the Holy One (Is 1.4; 5.24; 41.14), the everlasting King of all the earth (Ex 15.18; Is 24.23; 40.10; Za 14.9); and the Savior, as implied in the name Jesus [Ps 23(24).5; Is 43.3; Dn 6.27]. In OT times, however, all these phrases were understood of God's personal intervention through human mediators but not of the mediators' being personally divine. From the Biblical texts woven into the Annunciation account, one can never establish a clear awareness on Mary's part of Jesus' divinity. If God accorded Mary a special revelation about the divine nature of her son, Mary's approach toward the Incarnation would have remained thoroughly Biblical, that is, more implicit than explicit, more experiential than notional, and more intuitive than rational.

Even Pentecost, which brought new light to Mary's understanding, did not direct attention primarily to the distinction of person and nature in Jesus but rather to God's presence in Jesus, dynamically saving His people in the Messiah, even to the extent of placing Him as an equal at His side in bestowing the Spirit (cf. Acts 2.32–36; 3.20–26; Rom 1.3–7). Mary certainly agreed to be the mother of the promised Messiah; how much more she knew about her son at the moment of the Annunciation cannot be clearly established from the Biblical text.

Mary's Resolution to Remain a Virgin. Another, perhaps insoluble, question centers on Mary's resolution to remain a virgin. When asked to be the mother of the Messiah, Mary replied: "How shall this happen, since I do not know man [as a wife does her husband for the procreation of children]?" (Lk 1.34; cf. Gn 4.1; Jgs 16.26; 1 Sm 1.19). Various interpretations are given to this answer: Mary is not yet married but only espoused to Joseph and therefore not able to conceive immediately (P. Gaechter); Mary is intending to be Joseph's wife and, therefore, unable to bear the Messiah who must be virginally conceived (J. P. Audet; T. W. Auer). The latter interpretation adds an elliptic phrase: "How can this be since I ought not to know man if I am to be mother of the Messiah, when, as a matter of fact, I am already bound to a man?" Both of these opinions seem to circumvent the obvious meaning of 1.34. Against the first, one can object that solemn espousals granted marital privileges, though at that time in Galilee it was considered improper to enjoy them; against the second opinion, the proposed interpretation cannot be supported by Greek grammar. The meaning, then, of Mary's words would seem to imply a resolve to maintain virginity and to follow a way of life intended to prepare one for the great eschatological victory of God. Such a vocation was known in the Bible (Jer 16.2) and especially among the members of the *Qumran community. Why, then, it is asked, did Mary consent to the solemn espousals with Joseph? Did she and Joseph have a private agreement between them? These confidences, understandably enough, remained locked within Mary's heart.

Mary's Holiness. The Annunciation account presents a rich theology of Mary's holiness. Aside from God, no one in the entire Bible is the recipient of such beautiful salutations as Mary: Lk 1.18, 30, 35, 45, 49; 2.19, 34. Mary is presented also as the new Temple and the new ark of the covenant, for God's spirit overshadows her (1.35) as it did Moses' Tent of Meeting and Solomon's Temple (Ex 40.35; 3 Kgs 8.10; Ag 2.6–9). She represents God's people at prayer, in pilgrimage to the Temple, struggling with the evil one and witnessing the promised salvation (1.35, 46–55; 2.21–50). Because of God's generosity in her regard, she already possesses what the rest of the world still anticipates. She receives in advance what other men will be given after the death and Resurrection of Jesus.

Appearance of the Angel. Finally, the question is asked, "Did an angel actually appear to Mary?" Some have raised a doubt because a number of OT passages actually refer to God under the metaphor of the *angel of the Lord (Gn 16.11–14; 48.15–16; Ex 3.2–4). There is little doubt, however, in late OT books, such as Daniel and Tobit, or in apocryphal works of the last century B.C., or in the NT that Palestinian Jews believed in angels and accorded them great veneration. In any case, the Annunciation account does not speak of any bodily appearance of the Angel. The best Greek MSS do not say that Mary saw the angel; even the words found in a few MSS, "when she heard him [the angel]" are not part of the original text. If God sent the angel Gabriel to communicate His message to Mary, the angel mediated some kind of interior locution within the silence of Mary's soul.

See also MARY, BLESSED VIRGIN, I (IN THE BIBLE).

Bibliography: E. BURROWS, *The Gospel of the Infancy, and Other Biblical Essays,* ed. E. F. SUTCLIFFE (London 1940). R. LAURENTIN, *Structure et théologie de Luc I–II* (ÉtBibl; 1957), with ample bibliog. A. MEDÉBIELLE, DBSuppl 1:262–297. I. CECCHETTI, EncCatt 1:1382–84. T. MAERTENS, *Le Messie est là: Lc 1–2* (Bruges 1954). P. GAECHTER, *Maria im Erdenleben* (Innsbruck 1953). M. J. LAGRANGE, "Le Récit de l'enfance de Jésus-Christ dans Saint-Luc," RevBibl 4 (1895) 160–185; "La Conception surnaturelle du Christ d'après Saint-Luc," *ibid.* 11 (1914) 60–71, 188–208. K. BORNHAUSER, *Die Geburts- und Kindheitsgeschichte Jesu* (Gütersloh 1930). H. SAHLIN, *Der Messias und das Gottesvolk: Studien zur proto-Lukanischen Theologie* (Uppsala 1945). **Illustration credits:** Fig. 1, Alinari-Art Reference Bureau. Fig. 2, The Metropolitan Museum of Art, The Cloisters Collection, Purchase.

[C. STUHLMUELLER]

ANOINTING

The smearing or pouring of an unctuous substance, especially olive oil, on a person, both as a utilitarian practice and as a symbolic ceremony. It was an ancient custom among various peoples, particularly in the Near East. Of special interest here is the custom of anointing as described in the Bible and the medieval ceremony of anointing high dignitaries in Church and State when they entered upon their offices. For the religious ceremony of anointing as an essential or a secondary part in the administration of the Christian Sacraments, *see* ANOINTING OF THE SICK, I, II; BAPTISM (LITURGY OF); CONFIRMATION, LITURGY OF; ORDINATION IN THE ROMAN RITE.

IN THE BIBLE

The anointing of persons and objects with oil or an unctuous substance was a frequent occurrence in the Bible. It had both a secular use and a religious use and significance.

Secular Use. Anointing had many uses in Biblical times. Its sanitary and therapeutic benefits were recognized at an early date. Palestine, with its semitropical and dry climate in the summer, made the smearing of oil on one's body almost a necessity, if not for health at least for comfort. Because of exposure to the sun and wind people used olive oil, sometimes scented, as a body lubricant after bathing [Ru 3.3; Ez 16.9; Dn 13.17; Ps 103(104).15]. Mourners abstained from ointment (2 Sm 14.2; Dn 10.3) since it was a sign of joy (Is 61.3; Mt 6.7). Oil bases were used for perfumed cosmetics (Dt 28.40; Jdt 10.3; 2 Sm 14.2). As a sign of respect a host anointed the head of a guest [Mt 26.7; Lk 7.46; Ps 22(23).5]. The anointing of the feet of a guest had a special significance of humble devotion and respect (Lk 7.28, 46; Jn 12.3). Released captives were clothed, fed, and anointed (2 Chr 28.15). Various ointments were used for curing wounds and bruises (Is 1.6; Mk 6.13; Lk 10.34). Corpses were anointed in preparation for burial (Mk 16.1; Lk 23.56; Jn 19.39; *see* BURIAL, II).

Religious Use. Both persons and objects were anointed for religious purposes. It would appear that the notion of a constitutive blessing was basic to this custom, which belonged to the process of setting apart either a person or thing for religious use. Jacob thus anointed the memorial pillar that he erected at Bethel [Gn 28.18; 35.14; *see* STONES, SACRED (IN THE BIBLE)]. The *Tent of Meeting and its sacred furniture and utensils were anointed with an expertly prepared ointment (Ex 30.22–33; 40.10–11). There seems, however, to be no reason to believe that implements of war were anointed with sacred oil, though they were apparently smeared with oil or fat as a preservative (2 Sm 1.21; Is 21.5).

The practice of anointing persons was a ceremony usually performed on only priests and kings. The consecration of priests was prescribed in the rather late texts of Ex 28.40–42; 29.1–46; 30.30–33, where the evidence points to the limitation of consecration by anointing to the class from which the high priests came, while there was no anointing for the ordinary members of the priestly tribe of *Levi. The anointing of prophets is generally interpreted as analogical to that of kings (3 Kgs 19.16; Is 61.1). In poetry the whole people are called Yahweh's anointed [Ps 104(105).15].

Among the lay people only the kings on their ascendance to the throne were consecrated by an anointing. A high priest or prophet anointed the head of the king, who henceforth was regarded as the anointed (*māšîāḥ*, whence Messiah) of the Lord (1 Sm 10.1; 16.13; 3 Kgs 1.39). The right of succession to the throne was assured by the ceremony of anointing (4 Kgs 9.3; 11.12; 23.30; 2 Chr 23.11). The consecration of Israelite kings was similar to that of their neighbors, but its significance rested in its particular Yahwistic religious meaning rather than in any borrowed elements of the rite. The kings of Israel were inviolable because they were the "anointed of Yahweh" (1 Sm 24.7; 26.9, 11, 16, 23; 2 Sm 1.14, 16; 9.22). *See* MESSIAH; MESSIANISM.

Religious Significance. The peculiar significance of the anointing of persons rested in their consecration to the service of the Lord. The Bible took this point for granted and did not dwell on it at length. The anointed was separated from others and placed directly under the authority of God. Among the few certain parallels in extra-Biblical literature, the *Amarna Letters (51.6–9; 34.51) record two ceremonies of religious investiture. The anointing of Hazael as king of Damascus by the prophet *Elisae might not have been a strictly religious rite despite the fact that the king became an instrument for the visitation of divine wrath upon unfaithful Israelites (3 Kgs 19.15). Although the enthronement of the king was a religious ceremony, the voice of, at least, the tribal leaders of the people had great weight in the selection or acceptance of a king (2 Sm 2.4, 7; 5.3; 3 Kgs 12.2–19; 4 Kgs 23.30). Some scholars have presumed that the original ceremony of the anointing of kings was at first secular in nature and then given a religious form. Israelite enthronement, however, always had a religious character. Its particular significance rested in the fact that the king became God's chosen one invested with His spirit and guarded by His special providence (1 Sm 10.1; 16.13). The king was thus a leader divinely endowed to carry out the wishes of Yahweh.

Samuel anointing David, Byzantine silver dish (c. 610–630), excavated on the island of Cyprus.

See also KINGSHIP IN THE ANCIENT NEAR EAST.

Bibliography: E. COTHENET, DBSuppl 6:701–732. E. KUTSCH and G. DELLING, RGG³ 5:1330–32. EncDictBibl 92–95. De Vaux AncIsr 103–106, 398–400. P. SIFFRIN, EncCatt 12:888–889. J. DE FRAINE, *L'Aspect religieux de la royauté Israélite* (Rome 1954). A. R. JOHNSON, *Sacral Kingship in Ancient Israel* (Cardiff 1955). D. LYS, "L'Onction dans la Bible," *Études théologiques et religieuses* 29 (1954) 3–54. C. R. NORTH, "The Religious Aspects of Hebrew Kingship," ZATWiss 50 (1932) 8–38. R. PATAI, *"Hebrew Installation Rites,"* HebUCAnn 20 (1947) 143–255. **Illustration credit:** The Metropolitan Museum of Art, Gift of J. Pierpont Morgan, 1917.

[G. T. KENNEDY]

ANOINTING IN THE MIDDLE AGES

The practice of anointing, derived from Biblical tradition (1 Sm 10.6), which was in turn perhaps inspired by Egyptian and Canaanite practices [E. Kutsch, *Salbung als Rechtsakt im alten Testament u. im alten Orient* (Berlin 1963)], became an integral part of the enthronement ceremonies of kings, popes, and emperors during the high Middle Ages. Anointing was in effect the traditional procedure for transferring a man or object from a profane to a sacred status. Used in the first centuries of Christianity for the confirmation of catechumens and for ordination of priests and bishops, it was employed by the *Visigoths [M. Ferotin, "Le liber ordinum en usage dans l'église wisigothique," *Monumenta ecclesiae liturgica,* 5 (1904)] and the *Franks in ceremonial relating to their sovereigns.

Anointing in France. When, with papal approval, *Pepin III superseded the *Merovingians and was elected king of the Franks in 751, he had himself anointed by St. *Boniface to set the seal of legitimacy on his rule; this anointing was renewed by Pope *Stephen II in 754 at *Saint-Denis. Pope *Leo III added coronation to this anointing for *Charlemagne in 800. Anointing and coronation were again combined in the ceremony performed at Reims in 816 for Emperor *Louis the Pious. The head of the Emperor was anointed with holy oil to indicate his status as protector of the Church. This rite was retained by the *Carolingians and was renewed by the *Capetians. As a consecrated person, *gratia Dei Rex,* the king of France exercised a thaumaturgic power; *Charles X in 1825 was the last to claim its use. The Plantagenets exercised an analogous power in England, patterned upon the French example. However, the author of the *Songe du Verger* was anxious to assert the independence of the king from the clergy and contended that the miracle-working power of kings was not derived from anointing. Anointing exalts the king above the laity and grants him status approximating that of priests [i.e., makes them *sacerdotalis ministerii participes,* said

Anointing of the King of France, miniature from the Coronation Book of Charles V, 14th century (London, Brit. Mus., Cotton MS Tiberius B viii, fol. 55v).

Guido of Osnabrück (*De controversia inter Hildebrandum et Heinricum,* MGLibLit 1:467)]. Enhanced as the custom was by legendary tales, it furnished a weighty argument in favor of the pretensions of the Capetians in Church affairs and bolstered the prestige of the French monarchy not only in France but even among foreign princes. For, according to legend, the holy oil used was of divine origin. Kept in the Abbey of *Saint-Remi in Reims, it assured this city the privilege of being the site of all royal anointing and coronation, with the exceptions of King *Henry IV at Chartres, and *Napoleon I at Paris. The ritual followed in the coronation ceremonies is known from liturgical manuals, the *Ordines ad consecrandum et coronandum regem.* One of these ceremonials, drawn up at Reims toward the end of the reign of King *Louis IX (*Ordo ad inungendum regem*) is particularly explicit (de Pange, *Le roi,* 374–378). The coronation book of Charles V (1364) likewise gives a detailed description. The unction took place during combined anointing-coronation ceremonies in the cathedral. The king knelt, and the archbishop of Reims anointed him on the head, breast, shoulders, and elbows. The *Traité du sacre,* drawn up by the Carmelite Jean Golein in the entourage of Charles V (extracts, M. Bloch, *Les rois,* 478–488), described the ritual and simultaneously explained its symbolism, stressing the religious character of royal power. The anointing ceremony in France generally enjoyed high political significance. It served to bolster the tenets of *Gallicanism, and even when critics challenged the basic concepts of anointing, it was to remain, as Etienne Pasquier stated, "most fitting for every good citizen to accept them, for the sake of the majesty of Empire." Anxious to stress the anointing of bishops as a rite superior to the anointing of princes, Pope *Innocent III, in a letter (PL 213:284) reproduced in the *Compilatio III* and in the Decretals of *Gregory IX (CorpIurCan X 1.15.1.5), declared that only bishops should be anointed on the head with chrism, while kings were to be anointed with holy oil only on shoulders and arms.

Anointing in England. The ritual dates at least from the time of King Egbert of Mercia at the Council of Chelsea (787). His anointing, doubtless patterned after the Frankish practice, became normal for the whole of Anglo-Saxon England and became part of the coronation ceremony [see the Egbert Pontifical, 9th century; ed. *Publications of the Surtees Society* 27 (1853)]. In the course of time certain variations were introduced into the rite. Thus, in the reign of King *Henry I only the head of the king was anointed. The unction of shoulders and arms appeared at the end of the 12th century, but already in 1154 *Henry II had been anointed on the head, breast, and arms. In the 13th century, *Henry III adopted the Reims ceremony as a pattern for the coronation of the English sovereign at *Westminster Abbey (Richardson, 136–150).

Anointing in the Empire. The Carolingian tradition was maintained both for the German king and for the emperor, and although both offices were most often held by one and the same person, a distinction was maintained between royal and imperial anointing.

Royal Anointing. In conformity with Biblical and Carolingian tradition the German king required anointing, the ceremony that conferred on him supernatural graces for the exercise of his functions, and that, according to the theology of the 12th century, possessed a sacramental character. The king was exalted above the laity; he was *rex et sacerdos.* Anointing imprinted upon the king a quasi-indelible character, which, during the *Investiture struggle, was set forward as the reason no king could be deposed. Although Henry I (919–936) refused anointing, his son *Otto I received it (936), and the tradition was respected thereafter (*Sachsenspiegel,* Ldr. III, 52.1). It was united to the coronation ceremony that was held at *Aachen. Until 1028 the archbishop of Mainz had the privilege of crowning and anointing; after this it became the right of the archbishop of Cologne, on whom the diocese of Aachen depended [C. Vogel, EphemLiturg (1960), 153, n.25, 155; *Pontifical romano-germanique,* 1:252–254]. After the Great Interregnum (1250–73) anointing and coronation of the king lost their importance.

Imperial Anointing. Imperial coronation and anointing were reintroduced when Otto I, already king of Germany (936), became emperor (962). From this time forward the two ceremonies were performed at St. Peter's in Rome, even during the period of the *Avignon Papacy, when Emperors Henry VII (1312) and Charles IV (1355) were anointed and crowned in Rome by cardinals. It was this twin ceremony that created the emperor and introduced him into the *ordo clericalis.* At first the imperial anointing closely imitated episcopal anointing, but the imperial ceremony was gradually modified to eliminate any confusion between the two and to circumvent any unfounded pretensions on the part of the emperor with respect to the Church. The 12th-century Roman *Pontifical (Andrieu, *Pontifical romain* 1:251, 253; 2:383, 389) describes the anointing ceremony thus: "using blessed oil, the bishop of Ostia is to anoint him on the right arm and between the shoulder blades." While performing the anointing the bishop is to recite the consecration prayer in which he declares that the emperor has been *constitutus ad regendam ecclesiam* (on the ritual, see Andrieu, *Ordines romani,* 4:459, 503; and C. Vogel, *Pontifical romano-germanique,* 1:263–266). The anointing between the shoulder blades instead of on the head, and with merely blessed oil instead of chrism, which was used for bishops, underscored the inferiority of the imperial anointing, while the increasing precision of sacramental theology denied sacramental character to imperial anointing. For their part, the theorists treating of imperial power were at pains to assert their independence of the pope and declared that imperial power was acquired prior to the coronation ceremony, that the anointing conferred only the name and not the imperial power (*Gerhoh of Reichersberg, *De investigatione Antechristi* 1:40; *Braunschweiger Reichsweistum* of 1252). However, the *Sachsenspiegel* (Ldr. III, 52.1) and the *Golden Bull of 1356 still made imperial power depend on pontifical anointing, and imperial coronations continued to be held in Rome until 1452.

Anointing and Consecration of the Pope. In the Middle Ages anointing was only one of the ceremonies marking the enthronement of a pope; in fact, it was required only in order to confer on him episcopal consecration. Consequently, anointing was part of the enthronement ceremonies only when the pope-elect was not already a bishop. This was the case with each new pope during the period in which the law, forbidding the transfer of bishops from one see to another, was strictly observed (Roman Synod of 769; *Ordo Romanus IX,* c.5). But from the 11th century the pope was usually chosen from among the bishops, and thus the episcopal consecration was rarely a necessary part of the enthronement.

However, it was the example of the episcopal consecration of the new pope that had inspired the imperial ritual, and the symmetry of imperial and papal enthronement was to symbolize and justify an equality of powers. The description of the papal rite given by the *Liber diurnus* (No. 57) probably goes back to the 6th century, and this text remained the basis of the *ordinatio pontificis* until the 13th century. The *Ordo Romanus IX,* c.5 [first half of 9th century, reproduced with slight variations in the Collection of *Deusdedit 2.13 (ed. W. von Glanvell, 240)], described a similar ceremony, and though it is not an official document, it probably represents the practice followed from the 10th to the 11th centuries. The *Romano-German Pontifical* No. 71, composed shortly after 950 by a monk of St. Alban in Mainz (cf. *Ordo XL* B in C. Vogel, *Pontifical romano-germanique* 1:245), kept the formula of the *Liber diurnus* 57, with a few additions. The Roman Pontifical of the 12th century, ch. 33 (Andrieu, *Pontifical romain* 1:249) remains faithful to that of the 10th century. The *Ordo Romanus XIV* (Andrieu, *Pontifical romain* 2:380–382) gives a description of the rite as it was observed between approximately the 7th and the end of the 13th century: prior to consecration the new pope was merely the *electus.* Consecration took place at St. Peter's the Sunday following the election. As was necessary prior to the 11th century, the new pope was consecrated bishop during the Mass, between the Kyrie and the Gloria, by the bishop of Ostia (Duchesne LP 1:202, 360; 2:175). After prostrating himself before the *confessio* of St. Peter and then at the altar, the pope-elect was helped to his feet by the consecrating bishops, who placed the open gospel book on his head and shoulders and then recited the prayer of consecration while laying their hands upon his head. The prayer preserved in the Romano-German Pontifical (Andrieu, *Pontifical romain* 1:147) refers to a "heavenly" anointing; but texts prior to the 10th-century fail to indicate a physical anointing of the pope-elect. The consecration was effected simply by the laying-on of hands and reciting the appropriate prayer.

The break between Rome and Byzantium and the concurrently growing influence of the Franks in the 9th and 10th centuries explain the introduction of anointing at Rome in the first half of the 10th century. Anointing was in fact unknown to the Oriental liturgy, while in the Frankish liturgy it was employed for bishops, priests, and princes. Inspired by imperial practice, papal anointing took place immediately after the consecration prayer, which had previously alluded to a celestial anointing. Holy chrism was used in anointing the head of the pope, whereas the emperor was thenceforth anointed only on the arms and neck with oil used in exorcism. The rite of papal consecration, however, never developed beyond this point, because the disappearance of the ban on episcopal translation in the 11th century generally brought an end to the rite of anointing in the ceremony of papal enthronement [see Duchesne LP 2:296- ; *Ordo Romanus XII* (*Censius,* c. 1192) in J. Mabillon, *Musaeum italicum* 2:165- ; and *Ordines Romani XIII* (1275) and *XIV* (1311)].

Bibliography: T. Godefroy, *Le Cérémonial de France,* 2 v. (Paris 1649). R. Poupardin, "L'Onction impériale," *Moyen-âge* 18 (1905) 113–126. M. Bloch, *Les Rois thaumaturges* (Strasbourg 1924). P. E. Schramm, "Die Krönung bei den Westfranken und Angelsachsen von 878 bis um 1000," ZSavRG Kan 23 (1934) 117–242; "Die Krönung in Deutschland bis zu Beginn des salischen Hauses (1028)," *ibid.* 24 (1935) 184–332; "Der König von Frankreich: Wahl, Krönung, Erbfolge und Königsidee vom Anfang der Kapetinger (987) bis zum Ausgang des MAs," *ibid.* 25 (1936) 222–354; 26 (1937) 161–284; *Der König von Frankreich,* 2 v. (2d ed. Weimar 1960). H. W. Klewitz, "Die Krönung des Papstes," ZSavRGKan 61 (1941) 96–130. J. de Pange, *Le Roi très chrétien* (Paris 1949). E. Eichmann, *Die Kaiserkrönung im Abendland,* 2 v. (Würzburg 1942); *Weihe und Krönung des Papstes im Mittelalter* (Munich 1951). C. A. Bouman, *Sacring and Crowning . . . Anointing of Kings and the Coronation of the Emperor before the 11th Century* (Groningen 1957). *Ordines coronationis imperialis,* ed. R. Elze, MGFontIurGerm NS 9 (1960). H. G. Richardson, "The Coronation in Medieval England," *Traditio* 16 (1960) 111–202. Andrieu OR. Andrieu Pont. C. Vogel, "Précisions sur la date et l'ordonnance primitive du Pontifical romano-germanique," EphemLiturg 74 (1960) 145–162. C. Vogel and R. Elze, eds., *Le Pontifical romano-germanique du dixième siècle,* 2 v. (StTest 226, 227; 1963). Also profitable are the articles in *The Sacral Kingship* (Studies in the History of Religions 4; Leiden 1959).
Illustration credit: Trustees of the British Museum.

[J. GAUDEMET]

ANOINTING OF THE SICK, I (THEOLOGY OF)

Formerly called Extreme Unction, this Sacrament is conferred upon Christians in serious illness or in old age. This article discusses the existence of the Sacrament; its history, effects, and administration; and the teaching and practice of separated Churches.

Existence of the Sacrament

That Jesus exercised a ministry of healing is recorded in Mt 9.35 and that He enjoined this ministry on the Apostles is recorded in Mt 10.1, Mk 6.7, and Lk 9.1. In speaking of their fulfillment of it, Mark alone adds the significant detail: "and they . . . anointed with oil many sick people, and healed them" (6.13). Mark does not explicitly state that the employment of this rite was at Jesus' command. There is certainly no question here of a Christian Sacrament, but the Council of Trent sees in the text a foreshadowing of the Sacrament of Anointing of the Sick (Denz 1695), and M.–J. Lagrange suggests that this rite of Mark may represent the real origins of this Sacrament [*Évangile selon S. Marc* (Paris 1929) 155].

Scriptural Evidence. In ch. 5 of his Epistle, St. James, in a context of counseling norms of Christian conduct in several life situations, recommends a special remedy in time of sickness. "Is any among you sick? Let him bring in the presbyters of the Church, and let them pray over him, anointing him with oil in the name of the Lord. And the prayer of faith will save the sick man, and the Lord will raise him up, and if he be in sins, they shall be forgiven him. Confess your sins, therefore, to one another, that you may be saved" (v. 14–16).

The subject of this rite described by James is a Christian who is not moribund, but seriously ill (ἀσθενεῖ; see Jn 4.46; 11.1–6; Acts 9.37). The presbyters of the Church are not the miracle-workers of 1 Cor 12.10, but the official rulers of the local Church, for the rite is not charismatic but hierarchic; the use of the plural need not designate that many presbyters be summoned, for it is a categorical plural. The rite itself is one of prayer accompanied, as the aorist participle ἀλείψαντες implies, by anointing with oil. This is performed "in the name of the Lord," an expression that scarcely implies a command of the Lord, but rather ascribed the efficacy of this rite to His power of healing (see Lk 10.17; Mk 9.38; Acts 3.6, 16; 4.7–10; 9.34). The Christian is anointed in the name in which he was baptized (see Acts 2.38; 8.16; 10.48). The explicit invocation of the powerful name of Jesus excludes any notion of a magical healing power.

The "prayer of faith" spoken in verse 15 may mean prayer said in confidence or prayer inspired by faith. In this second acceptation, which in the context is the more probable, the ritual prayer of the community is designated. The effect of this rite is expressed by three verbs, all in the future tense. There is a parallelism between the first two "will save" (σώσει) and "will raise up" (ἐγερεῖ). Though σώσει can refer to spiritual healing and does so in Jas 1.21; 2.14; 4.12; 5.20, it never in New Testament usage bears this meaning in contexts of sickness, death or their danger. Because of the above parallelism, it should be here accepted in the sense of restoration to bodily health, as the meaning of ἐγερεῖ suggests. The notion of spiritual healing need not be excluded; indeed it is expressly, although conditionally, stated as the third effect of this rite, but it is the physical effect that is emphasized. The purpose of the rite looks principally to the physical sickness that is certainly present and only secondarily to the sin that may possibly be present. ἁμαρτία implies grave sin, and the conditional reference to its forgiveness may be interpreted in three ways: (1) that not only those who are now in sin may receive this anointing; (2) that there is no necessary connection between sin and sickness; (3) that the eschatological effect of the rite is related to the forgiveness of sin.

The connective particle οὖν implies that the *exomologesis described in verse 16 is a correlative of the rite of anointing. Some Catholic commentators see here a reference to sacramental confession. The Council of Trent cites this verse when speaking of Penance (Denz 1679) but does not define the sense of the text. James certainly says that they are to confess their sins to one another and not to God alone. He does not say that it is a confession made to the presbyters, and the parallel verbs "confess" and "pray" indicate a confessing without implying a special function of the presbyters, although they may be included among those confessing and praying. This is a counsel addressed to all Christians, for the verbs pass from the singular to the plural. More likely the verse describes a public acknowledgment of sinfulness on the part of the bystanders, an acknowledgment that should precede prayer of intercession. The verb "may be saved" (ἰαθῆτε) signifies both bodily healing and the healing of the soul in the forgiveness of sin. Leviticus (14.10–31), in which the anointing of lepers with oil is related to the forgiveness of sin, may have influenced the arrangement of James.

Institution by Christ. One can discern the Sacrament of Anointing of the Sick in this rite described by James. In its authentic interpretation of the pericope (Jas 5.14–15), the Council of Trent states: "This holy anointing of the sick was instituted as a true and proper Sacrament of the New Testament by Christ our Lord; suggested, indeed, in Mark (6.13), but commended and promulgated to the faithful by James the Apostle and brother of the Lord" (Denz 1695). The Council appears to recognize that exegesis alone may not suffice to establish this, for it adds: "In these words [Jas 5.14–15], as the Church has learned from the apostolic tradition transmitted to her, he teaches the matter, the form, the proper minister and the effect of this salutary Sacrament" (*ibid.*).

In seeking to vindicate the institution of this Sacrament by Christ, one may appeal to the hypothesis that Christ did this in the Easter period when He spoke with His Apostles concerning the kingdom of God (Acts 1.3). Institution by Christ does not demand that He specified the sacramental sign (*signum tantum*) but only that He specified the sanctifying effect, the grace (*res tantum*), and that He commanded that it be annexed to a sign, the specification of that sign being left to the Apostles or the Church. Since anointing with oil had a recognized therapeutic value among the Jews, it is entirely plausible that the Apostles should have elected this as the sign ready-at-hand to signify the conferring of a special grace on those in a state of sickness just as an ablution was made a "new Baptism" when it was constituted a sign of Christian regeneration by the annexing to it of Christian grace. Karl Rahner [*The Church and the Sacraments* (New York 1963)], seeking to avoid what he considers an a priori historical hypothesis, proceeds from the position that the Church is the *Ursakrament,* the historical and eschatological presence of redemptive grace in the world. Any fundamental act of the Church in an individual's regard in situations decisive for salvation proceeds from the Church's nature as primal Sacrament and is *ipso facto* itself a Sacrament, even though no explicit promise of Jesus regarding it can be discovered in Sacred Scripture. The Christian, limited by mortality, is compelled by approaching death to decide about the ultimate meaning of his existence, a basic salvation situation that postulates an action from the Church. While the Eucharist, as Viaticum, is directly linked with that death in which true life comes to birth, there is room for another rite that more distinctly represents and so more abundantly confers a grace strengthening eschatological expectation and hope for eternity.

History

It evokes no surprise that clear references to this Sacrament are few in early Christian writings. This creates no prejudice against the sacramentality of this rite, but is a recognition of its subordinate importance as a means of grace in a particular situation as compared with the universal salvific necessity of Baptism and the Eucharist. Furthermore, since the rite was administered privately, it occasioned less opportunity for comment. The monuments of tradition witnessing to this Sacrament fall into three categories: patristic references to the ministry for the sick; texts of the liturgy employed in the blessing of the oil; mentions, in the biographies of saints, of the actual use of this oil.

The Fathers. Some of the earliest references to the ministry for the sick are so brief or their historical context so obscure that we cannot invoke them as certain witnesses to this Sacrament [Tertullian, *De praescriptione haereticorum* 41 (PL 2:56); Aphraates the Syrian, *Demonstrationes* 23.3 (PatrSyrG 2:6); Athanasius, *Epistola ad episcopos encyclica* 5 (PG 25:234)]. Other references imply a rite of anointing and invoke James as authority, but in a context suggesting penance and reconciliation rather than sickness [Origen, *Hom. 2 in Leviticum* 4 (PG 12:419); John Chrysostom, *De sacerdotio* 3.6 (PG 48:644)]. Still others speak clearly of anointing the sick in fulfillment of James' command [Cyril of Alexandria, *De adoratione et cultu in spiritu et veritate* 6 (PG 68:472); Victor of Antioch, *Catena in evang. S. Marcae* 6.13, ed. J. Cramer, *Catenae Graecorum Patrum* (Oxford 1840) 1:340]. A letter of Innocent I (d. 417) to Decentius (*Epist.* 25.8, PL 20: 559–60), however, is the first fully satisfactory witness to this Sacrament. Innocent authentically declares that the Epistle of James refers to this Sacrament; that the chrism employed in its administration must be blessed by a bishop; that priests as well as bishops are ministers of this rite; that this anointing is in some way a complement of Penance. He actually admits two anointings of the sick: one performed by the sick person himself or some relative, the other by the bishop or presbyters. As we would expect, since he is the author of the earliest extant commentary on James, Bede the Venerable (d. 735) discusses this rite at some length and affirms that the Apostle's recommendation to anoint the sick has been carried out in the Church since the time of the Apostles [*Super divi Jacobi epistolam* 5 (PL 93:39–40); *In Marci evangelium expositio* 6 (PL 92:188)]. He too recognizes lay anointing and cites Innocent as authority for it.

That pastors urged the practice of anointing the sick with oil we know [Caesarius of Arles, *Sermones* 50.1, 52.5 (CCL 103:225, 232); Eligius of Noyon, *De rectitudine Catholicae conversationis* 5 (among the works of Augustine, PL 40:1172–73)]. Possidius (d. after 437), the contemporary and first biographer of St. Augustine (d. 430), informs us that the saint "was accustomed to visit the sick who desired it in order to lay his hands on them and pray at their bedside" (*Vita S.* Aug. 27; PL 32:56). Since Augustine incorporated Jas 5.14–16 into his *Speculum* (PL 34:1036) as one of the counsels of Christian life, it is probable that on such occasions he personally anointed them with oil.

Liturgical Books. Significant witness to this Sacrament is found in the early rituals containing formulas for consecrating the oil for the sick. Their inclusion in these rituals manifests that the oil had to be blessed before it was used and offers the presumption that its use was widespread. The earliest extant formula that clearly applies to oil of the sick is found in the *Apostolic Tradition* of Hippolytus (5; Botte LFQ 18–19). It is noteworthy that in this liturgy the blessing of oil takes place toward the end of the Canon of the Mass, a position it retains in the present Roman liturgy of Holy Thursday. In the *Euchologian of Serapion* (d. after 362), we find a blessing entitled "Prayer for the Oil of the Sick or for Bread or for Water." Despite the ambiguity of the title, the prayer is almost exclusively concerned with oil, upon which God is entreated to bestow a curative power "so that it may become a means of removing every disease and sickness . . . unto health and soundness of soul and body and spirit, unto perfect will-being" (29 Funk DidConst 2:191–193). Another blessing is found in the *Gelasian Sacramentary* (1.40; ed. K. Mohlberg 61). This formula remains substantially unchanged in the present Roman Pontifical.

Biographies of Saints. In the *Dialogues* (3.3; PL 20: 213), Sulpicius Severus (d. 430?) tells of the wife of a certain Count Avitus who asked St. Martin of Tours to bless "as is the custom" a vessel of oil intended as a remedy in illness. A similar, but more revealing incident, is related of St. Genevieve (*Vita b. Genovefae;* MGSrerMer 3:236). She was accustomed to anoint with blessed oil the sick for whom she cared. One day, when the oil was urgently needed, the vessel containing it was found empty. The saint was deeply disturbed at this "because there was no bishop within reach to bless it [the oil]."

Lay Anointing. It was always the rule, although one does find exceptions, that the oil for this Sacrament had to be consecrated by a bishop. It is important to note that the intervention of the Church was indispensable in the blessing of this oil. The oil itself appears to have been regarded as a permanent Sacrament, in much the same way as the Eucharist today, and so its confection could be separated from the administration of the Sacrament. If this is so, the practice of lay anointing is easily understood. The problem, however, appears too complex to admit of so simple a solution. It would rather appear that, although the same oil was used, two disparate anointings existed side by side: the first, properly a Sacrament, was administered by a bishop or priest and was related to the forgiveness of sin as well as restoration to health; the second, a sacramental, administered by a layman, and looking only to the restoration to health. The practice of lay anointing gradually fell into disuse from about the beginning of the 8th century in the Frankish kingdom and probably at an earlier date in Celtic lands. The reform councils of the Carolingian era witness to this and in doing so witness even more clearly to the sacramentality of Anointing of the Sick.

Scholastic Era. With the rise of the scholastics in the 12th century, two views of the purpose of this Sacrament become evident. The first of these continues the early view and regards it as a Sacrament of the sick. The proper effect, therefore, is the cure of the body even though its more noble effect is the forgiveness of sins. This tradition is represented by Hugh of Saint-Victor (d. 1141), Roland Bandinelli (later Alexander III, d. 1181), Omnebene (d. 1185), and William of Auxerre (d. 1231). The second view stresses the spiritual effect of the anointing, the forgiveness of sin, and tends to see it as a Sacrament of the dying. This view is represented by the unknown author of the *Epitome theologiae christianae* and the author of the *Summa sententiarum.* It is the view adopted by Peter Lombard (d. 1160), who is among the first to employ the term Extreme Unction. The first to speak of this anointing as a preparation for the beatific vision is Master Simon, author of the *De septem sacramentis.* This opinion is further developed by William of Auvergne (d. 1249) and is the one adopted by the great scholastic doctors, including St. Albert the Great (d. 1280), St. Thomas Aquinas (d. 1274), St. Bonaventure (d. 1274), and Duns Scotus (d. 1308).

Although the Franciscan and Dominican schools agreed in viewing this Sacrament as a preparation for glory, the former saw this effected by the remission of venial sins, while the latter regarded the reality of this Sacrament as the purification of the soul of those remnants of sin that impeded its transit to glory. In either view, however, the sick person was only to be anointed when death was imminent and recovery despaired of. In this period, Anointing displaces Viaticum as the final Sacrament. In the older rituals the order of administering the Sacraments to the dying was Penance, Anointing, and Viaticum. The rituals of this period give the order as Penance, Viaticum, and Anointing. In our own time the Holy See has restored the earlier order of administration.

Responsible for this changed attitude toward the purpose of this Sacrament was an inability to appreciate how a physical effect, the recovery of health, could be the effect of a Sacrament. Sacraments are means of grace and grace is a supernatural perfection of man. Again, if Sacraments always produce their effect in a disposed subject, how could the recovery of health, an effect so seldom realized, be the effect of this Sacrament? These difficulties were obviated by concluding that the remission of sin was the Sacrament's principal effect. But since two Sacraments, Penance, and Baptism, already had this purpose, it was logical to see this one as destined for the removal of sin's last remnants, to delay its reception to the last moments of life, to see it as Extreme Unction. Several nontheological factors abetted the popular acceptance of the view that this Sacrament was to be delayed until life's final moments, e.g., that one who had received it and recovered could never again enjoy marriage.

Council of Trent. There is no evidence of change in the theological attitude toward the effect of this Sacrament in the period leading to the Council of Trent. Indeed the first draft of the schema on Extreme Unction presented at this Council might well stand as its epitome. It is to be administered "only to those who are in their final struggle and have come to grips with death and are about to go forth to the Lord" (*Acta genuina ss. oecumenici concilii Tridentini,* ed. Theiner 1:590). How different is the statement of the decree finally adopted: "this anointing is to be used for the sick, but especially for those who are dangerously ill as to seem at the point of departing this life" (Denz 1698). While this is not a forthright recapture of the primitive view, it is certainly an amelioration of the medieval position. Had Trent chosen to regard this as a Sacrament of the dying, it need only have approved the first statement. It is especially noteworthy that Trent did not demand danger of death as a condition for validity in the recepient of the Sacrament, even though this view was discussed.

Post-Tridentine Era. From Trent to the present one notes a progressive leniency in the theologians' interpretation of the danger of death required for anointing and a consequent reassertion of Extreme Unction as a Sacrament of the Sick. It may now be held that this danger need not be proximate, but remote; that a probable judgment of danger of death, even if an objective and real danger is not actually present, suffices for both validity and licitness. This view receives support from the Apostolic Letter *Explorata Res* of Feb. 2, 1923 [ActApS 15 (1923) 105], which says: "It is not necessary either for the validity or lawfulness of the Sacrament that death should be feared as something proximate; it is enough that there should be a prudent or probable judgment of danger." The action of Vatican Council II in changing the name of the Sacrament from Extreme Unction to Sacrament of the Anointing of the Sick is a harbinger of further reform that will probably come with the revision of the Code of Canon Law and even now authorizes a pastoral preaching that emphasizes this Sacrament as a Sacrament of the sick.

The thesis that regards this Sacrament as a preparation for glory was revived by Joseph Kerns in his famous work *De sacramento extremae unctionis* (Regensburg 1907). He regarded the Sacrament chiefly as a means of escaping purgatory and stresses its efficacy in remitting the total debt of temporal punishment. A modified reaffirmation of this view of the Sacrament as a preparation for glory by several able contemporary theologians has occasioned much of the writing that, by way of reaction to it, restores to us the view that this is a Sacrament, not of the dying, but of the sick. Three considerations are basic to this latter writing: the liturgy of the Sacrament, which gives no indication of imminent death; the history of the Sacrament in the first 10 centuries, when it was clearly a Sacrament of the sick; and pastoral needs.

Effects

The *Decree for the Armenians* states: "Extreme Unction heals us in spirit and in body as well, insofar as it is good for the soul" (Denz 1325). The teaching of the Council of Trent is more detailed. The effect of this Sacrament "is the grace of the Holy Spirit, whose anointing takes away sins, if there are any still to be expiated, as well as the remnants of sin; and it also comforts and strengthens the soul of the sick person by arousing in him great confidence in the divine mercy. Encouraged by this, the sick man more easily bears the inconvenience and trials of his illness and more easily resists the temptations of the devil. . . . This anointing occasionally restores health to the body if health would be of advantage to the salvation of the soul" (Denz 1696).

Remission of Sin. This statement of the Council is an explication of the two effects of the Sacrament, forgiveness of sin and some bodily effect, guaranteed to us by the Epistle of St. James. It is, therefore, certain that this Sacrament forgives sin, not merely venial but mortal sin as well. But Anointing of the Sick is primarily a Sacrament of the living; it presupposes grace and is ordered to its increase, as James indicates in the hypothetical statement "if he be in sins." This effect, therefore, is not the Sacrament's primary purpose. Nevertheless, it is a purpose of the Sacrament that directly pertains to it, however conditionally. In this it is unlike the other Sacraments of the living in which the forgiveness of sin is an indirect and accidental effect. If for any reason the subject of this Sacrament cannot confess his sins, whether mortal or venial, and have them forgiven by the Sacrament of Penance, they will be forgiven by this Sacrament provided he has at least habitual attrition for them.

Restoration of Health. The effect absolutely proper to this Sacrament is one related to bodily well-being. The history of Anointing of the Sick manifests that these two effects, one physical and one spiritual, bodily health and a grace that is the complement to the Sacrament of Penance, have all too often been viewed in isolation from each other. Actually they must be held in delicate tension and accounted for theologically in and through each other. The way to this synthesis is opened in a proper appreciation of the true nature of man, the subject of the Sacrament, as a corporal and spiritual unity in whom anatomical, physiological, psychological, and spiritual aspects exist in continuous relation and dynamic interaction. This Sacrament cannot affect the body as though it were separated from the soul, nor the soul as though it were separated from the body; it affects the person. If we are not again to be faced with the problem that confronted the scholastics, it must likewise be appreciated that the effect of this Sacrament, precisely because it is a Sacrament, is grace. This grace causes both the remission of sins and the alleviation of bodily infirmity. The former of these, an effect of grace, needs no elaboration here; but how the supernatural entity of grace can alleviate bodily infirmity requires some examination.

Through the Anointing the Church commends to God one of her sons burdened with infirmity and makes the very infirmity a source of grace to him. Infirmity is, of course, more than a physical aberration in the corporal organism; it is a profound alteration of the personality that renders difficult man's ascent toward God. Illness is not a good of man in either the natural or the supernatural order. It is an aspect of the disorder brought by sin, not actual sin, of course, but original. The very possibility of sickness unto death is the result of the loss of original integrity. Its actual presence in man evokes such a concentration of every vital energy upon the struggle to save the bodily organism, such a shrinking away from death, which nature sees only as dissolution, that it constitutes a powerful impediment to the surrender of the person to his spiritual fulfillment. The grace of this Anointing restores to man a portion of his lost gift of integrity sufficient for him to live an intensely supernatural life despite the special trials of illness. In the gift of integrity there were spiritual and corporal elements, both of them the fruit of grace. The grace of this Sacrament so permeates the sensitive faculties that they more facilely and promptly submit to the spirit. By the reestablishment of this harmony, grace gives comfort or relief to the body in order that it should no longer impede the soul but rather promote its spiritual freedom of action. In doing this it conquers in some measure the sad heritage of original sin remaining in us and it goes on to remove the remnants of actual sin, the pusillanimity in pursuing good, the depression and fear aroused by the memory of sin, wounds left in man by past sins and remaining even after the sin has been forgiven.

At times the strength and relief given, the restoration of hamony and spiritual freedom will bring about a cure of illness or at least accelerate recovery. It may well be, however, that the man is called upon to suffer this illness. Even here the primary effect of the Sacrament is realized, for it gives him such grace that physical debility does not impede the vigor and progress of his union with Christ. If death be the termination of this illness, this grace conforms him to the dying Christ in whom body was dominated by spirit even when He was in agony.

Administration

In the Latin Church the Sacrament of the Anointing of the Sick can be conferred only by a priest performing the prescribed rite upon a person who is suffering from a serious illness.

Essential Rite. This consists in the anointing with consecrated oil of the organs of the external senses and a form of prayer repeated at each unction with mention of the corresponding sense. The full number of these anointings is required for licitness, not validity. In case of necessity it is permissible to employ a single unction, usually on the forehead, and a correspondingly altered form. Until it was supressed by CIC c.447.2 and deleted from the Ritual in 1925, provision was made for anointing the loins. The same canon authorizes the omission of the anointing of the feet for any reasonable cause. In earlier times the number of anointings was more numerous and it was even the practice to anoint directly the part of the body that was the focal point of the disease or pain. The *Constitution on the Sacred Liturgy* 74, 75) calls for adaptation in the rite of administration of this Sacrament. *See* ANOINTING OF THE SICK, II (LITURGY OF).

The remote matter of this Sacrament is olive oil, which, according to the unanimous voice of tradition,

Anointing of a sick man, miniature in a Sacramentary from the Benedictine monastery at Fulda, Germany, c. 975 (Göttingen Univ. Bibl. MS 231, fol. 192 v.). At the left, the procession to the house of the sick man.

must be blessed before it may be validly employed. Indeed, as was noted earlier, at one time the Sacrament was considered to consist in the consecrated oil even independently of its use. In the Latin Church the blessing of this oil is reserved to bishops, although CIC c.945 provides that a priest, if duly authorized, may also bless it. In some of the Eastern rites, both the Orthodox and those in communion with Rome, the priest blesses this oil whenever he requires it for the administration of the Sacrament. In the West the blessing takes place on Holy Thursday. As for the proximate matter, one cannot claim that any specific number of anointings is required for validity, but only that there be a true unction with consecrated oil. Just as the number of unctions has varied over the centuries, so too has the form, and some of these variations are substantial. It is scarcely possible, in view of this history, even to enumerate the elements that must enter into a valid form. Theologians feel that it must be a prayer form in order to fulfill Jas 5.14.

Minister. James specifies the ministers of this Sacrament as "the presbyters of the Church" and the Council of Trent elaborates that these are the priests of the Church, that is, bishops or priests ordained by them (Denz 1719). Elsewhere mention has been made of lay anointing and the view sustained that such anointings did not constitute the Sacrament. Singular opinions maintaining the right of laymen or deacons to administer this Sacrament must be regarded as untenable in view of Trent's teaching. The administration of the Sacrament is a pastoral right and both the right and obligation to confer it fall upon the pastor within whose territory the sick person is staying. Not delegation, but simple permission either of the ordinary of the place or the pastor, is required for another priest licitly to confer this Sacrament. This permission may always be presumed in case of necessity.

Recipient. The subject of this Sacrament must, of course, be baptized, have attained the use of reason, and be here and now sick. These conditions are all necessary for the validity of the Sacrament. The limitation of this unction to those who have attained the use of reason reflects the constant theological tradition that this Sacrament is a complement of the Sacrament of Penance. Illness, not danger of death, is an intrinsically necessary requirement in the subject of this Sacrament for its valid reception. Canon Law stipulates that the subject must be constituted in danger of death from sickness or old age (CIC c.940.1). This condition, however, is a disciplinary norm of the Latin Church and, although it binds under pain of serious sin, it is only a condition for licitness. The norm of this canon is fulfilled if someone, either the subject himself or another interested person, reasonably judges from attendant circumstances that the sickness is sufficiently serious to offer real probability that death could follow from it. Danger, even certainty, of death from a cause other than sickness or old age does not entitle one to receive this Sacrament. Old age, however, even without specific illness does qualify one as a subject of the Sacrament.

To receive this Sacrament validly an adult possessing the use of reason must have an intention to receive it. This intention need not be actual or virtual; a habitual intention will suffice. The habitual intention required for the Sacrament of the Anointing of the Sick need never have been explicitly formulated, but may be implicitly contained in the desire to live and die as a Catholic or to employ all the means necessary or useful to gain salvation. Even if the subject should be unconscious, if it can be prudently judged that he had such an intention, he is to be anointed absolutely as CIC c.943 enjoins.

Today no theologian would so exclusively regard this unction as a Sacrament of the dying that he would delay its reception until the subject was in the last moments of life. In the present discipline, if the maximum benefit is to be realized, "as soon as any one of the faithful begins to be in danger of death from sickness or old age, the fitting time for him to receive this Sacrament has certainly arrived" (*Constitution on the Sacred Liturgy* 73). It may, of course, be received as many times as a person succumbs to serious illness. It may even be repeated within the same illness provided there should be a recurrence of the danger of death. It may never, however, be repeated in the same proximate danger of death no matter how long that crisis may last. There is no justification for anointing old people or those laboring under protracted illness at specified regular intervals as a matter of routine. But if there is any doubt as to whether any crisis is a new crisis, the patient may be reanointed. In her great desire that no one be deprived of any possible sacramental assistance and in her recognition that for an unconscious dying person the Sacrament of Anointing may be the only means of salvation, the Church directs that when a priest doubts whether one who is apparently dead is in fact dead, he should anoint him conditionally (CIC c.941). The fact of death is indeed a difficult one to adjudicate with certainty. But in the absence of such certainty a priest may, always avoiding scandal, anoint conditionally an apparently dead person.

Reviviscence. There is the possibilty that someone might validly receive this Sacrament because he had the requisite intention, but receive it unfruitfully because he was in sin and lacking the minimal requisite attrition for its remission. This obstacle to the efficacy of the Sacrament could be either inculpable or gravely culpable. In the latter case the reception of the Sacrament would be sacrilegious. Since the Sacrament was validly received and cannot be repeated in the same crisis, can its effects revive, i.e., can it later produce such effects as were impeded at the time of its reception? All theologians teach that it can. In the instance in which grave sin was committed in or since its reception, this sin must first be remitted by the Sacrament of Penance or an act of perfect contrition before the Sacrament of Anointing can produce it effects. If no sacrilege was committed in its reception or grave sin since then, all that is required is that that degree of attrition be actualized in the subject as would have sufficed to make it fruitful when first received. One important consequence follows from this doctrine of reviviscence: the minister of the Sacrament should always, regardless of doubts regarding the dispositions of a certainly valid subject, administer the Sacrament absolutely. To act otherwise would be to exclude the possibilty of reviviscence. The conditional administration of this Sacrament is to be reserved to those instances only where it is doubtful whether the subject of the Sacrament can receive it validly, viz, whether he is not already dead, whether he has been baptized, has reached the use of reason, has the requisite intention.

Obligation of Reception. Since Anointing of the Sick was instituted by Christ as a Sacrament, there is undoubtedly some obligation to receive it. This obligation is not in and of itself a grave one and only that neglect that proceeds from contempt for or disdain of the Sacrament intrinsically involves serious sin. Only in the instance in which neglect of the Sacrament without justifiable cause would give great scandal would there be a grave obligation to receive it. However, there is an obligation on those who have care of the sick "carefully and diligently" to see to it that the sick receive this Sacrament while they are still conscious (CIC c.944). While one cannot charge the unconscious with an obligation, it is well to emphasize that for one who is unconscious, if he is in serious sin and with only attrition for it, this Sacrament becomes a necessary means of salvation.

TEACHING AND PRACTICE OF SEPARATED CHURCHES

Among the Orthodox and Protestant churches a great variety exists in both theological understanding of this Sacrament and actual administration of it.

Orthodox Churches. All of the Eastern Orthodox Churches, with the exception of the Nestorians, recognize the Anointing of the Sick as a Sacrament. Their ritual usages for its administration differ from each other and from the Latin Church, and when fully implemented are elaborate. Before proceeding to note singular practices of particular churches, the following general observations appear justified: (1) The Orthodox Churches hold the principal effect of the Sacrament to be one related to bodily health. (2) The Churches have all had, and most still practice, a penitential anointing that appears to be a complement of Penance and might be regarded as an extension of the Sacrament of Anointing the Sick. There is reason to assert that they acknowledge, however implicitly, a difference between this anointing and that of the Sick similar to the distinction between a sacramental rite and a Sacrament admitted by Western theologians. (3) In most instances the subject of this Sacrament must be suffering from a serious illness, although danger of death is not a condition for its reception. (4) A plurality of ministers of the Sacrament is the ideal, but in the exigencies of the pastoral ministry, a single minister will suffice. (5) Where this Sacrament has fallen into desuetude, as among the Armenians and Nestorians, or where it is seldom conferred, as among the Ethiopians, the scarcity of olive oil is a partial factor in this lapse.

In the Greek Orthodox Church this Sacrament is administered not only to the sick but even to the well as a preventive against illness. The Russian Church has generally followed the Latin practice of administering it only to the seriously ill, but today one increasingly finds departures from this rule. Although the Copts administer the Sacrament to an individual suffering from serious illness, the practice of assembling the sick in the church on Monday of Holy Week to receive this anointing still survives. The liturgical books of the Ethiopian Church contain a rite for anointing the sick, but the Sacrament is rarely administered. One reads of the practice among the Syrian Jacobites of anointing the dead, a practice apparently still forming a part of the obsequies for bishops, priests, and deacons. This anointing is simply a burial ceremony and should not be confused, therefore, with the Sacrament of Anointing of the Sick.

In the dissident Armenian Church this Sacrament has fallen into desuetude since about the 15th century. Some vartapets seek to restore its use, but even among them some declare it should be administered only to bishops and priests. Possibly a remnant of the Sacrament can be found in the practice among the faithful of securing, for the healing of the sick, chrism or even the oil used in the lamps of a pilgrimage sanctuary. The situation among the Nestorians is shrouded in obscurity. There are indications of their having practiced some form of anointing of the sick until at least the 6th century, but the treatises on the Sacraments written in the early 14th century by Ebedjesus of Nisibis and Timothy II do not allude to this Sacrament. When the Chaldeans of Mesopotamia returned to Roman communion in the 16th century, they accepted the Roman liturgical formula translated into Syriac for administering this Sacrament.

Protestant Churches. All Protestants reject the Anointing of the Sick as a Sacrament instituted by Christ. Luther, in the *Babylonian Captivity,* would allow this anointing if one desired it, but insists that it be seen as "among those 'sacraments' which we ourselves have instituted" and emphatically asserts that the peace and forgiveness that it may indeed bring come from the faith that the rite stimulates and not from its being a Sacrament [*Luther's Works* 36 (Philadelphia 1959) 117–123]. Melanchthon speaks of it as a Sacrament recognized by the Fathers, but enjoying neither the command of Christ nor his promise of grace [*Apologia Confessionis Augustanae,* ed. H. Bindseil, *Corpus Reformatorum* 27 (Brunsvigae 1859) 570]. Calvin not only denies its Sacramentality but goes to the excess of designating it as "merely playacting" [*Institutes of the Christian Religion* 4.19.18, The Library of Christian Classics 21 (Philadelphia 1960) 1466]. Article 25 of the *Thirty-Nine Articles of Religion* ranks it among the "five commonly called sacraments . . . not to be counted as sacraments of the Gospel" [ed. J. Leith, *Creeds of the Churches* (Chicago 1963) 274–75].

A formula for anointing, if the sick person desired it, was provided in the first English *Book of Common Prayer* (1549), but it was deleted from the edition of 1552 and subsequent editions. In 1925, however, the Convocations of Canterbury and York approved a "Form of Unction and the Laying on of Hands" for provisional use subject to diocesan sanction. The revised Scottish and American Prayer Books (1929) make an optional provision for the rite of anointing the sick. It would seem that no other Protestant Church makes such a liturgical provision. One occasionally discovers in writing emanating from Protestant sources the view that the rite described in James 5.14 is a Sacrament or the suggestion that Protestants accept this anointing as a Sacrament [see e.g., B. Easton, *The Interpreter's Bible* 12 (Nashville 1957) 70–71; W. Anderson, "Sacramental Healing," *Christianity Today* 5 (1961) 348–49].

Bibliography: C. RUCH and L. GODEFROY, DTC 5.2:1897–2022. K. RAHNER AND M. FRAEYMAN, LexThK[2] 6:585–591. K. CONDON, "The Sacrament of Healing (Jas. 5:14–15)," *Scripture* 14 (1959) 33–42. C. KEARNS, "Christ and the Sick in the New Testament," *Furrow* 11 (1960) 557–571. A. CHAVASSE, *Étude sur l'onction des infirmes dans L'Église Latine du IIIe au XIe siècle,* v.1 *Du IIIe siècle à la Réforme Carolingienne* (Lyons 1942). P. MURRAY,

"The Liturgical History of Extreme Unction," *Furrow* 11 (1960) 572–593; this article has special importance because the author saw, in MS, the unpub. 2d v. of Chavasse. B. POSCHMANN, *Penance and the Anointing of the Sick,* tr. and rev. F. COURTNEY (New York 1964). Z. ALSZEGHY, "L'effeto corporale dell'Estrema Unzione," Greg 38 (1957) 385–405. C. DAVIS, "The Sacrament of the Sick," *Theology for Today* (New York 1962). P. DE LETTER, "The Meaning of Extreme Unction," BijdragenTijdFilTh 16 (1955) 258–270; "Anointing of the Sick and Danger of Death," IrTheolQ 29 (1962) 288–302. *Maison-Dieu* 15 (1948) entire issue. P. PALMER, "The Purpose of Anointing the Sick: A Reappraisal," ThSt 19 (1958) 309–344. C. RENATI, *The Recipient of Extreme Unction* (CUA CLS 419; Washington 1961). **Illustration credit:** Hirmer Verlag, Munich.

[J. P. MC CLAIN]

ANOINTING OF THE SICK, II (LITURGY OF)

Although several excellent studies of the liturgical rites for the Anointing of the Sick have been made, no adequate history of these rites has been written. That it is a complex history accounts for this, at least in part.

Scarcely anything is known about how this Sacrament was administered in early times. There is no known extant Ordinal for its administration that dates from earlier than the 9th century, but from the period between the 9th and the mid-10th century there is a rich proliferation of such books. It is certain that the ritual of Anointing used in the Roman rite evolved in the Frankish kingdom in the 9th century. The following factors influenced this evolution.

Historical Development. Prior to the 9th century, in addition to the sacramental anointing by a priest, there existed among the faithful the private practice of using the consecrated oil to anoint the sick. It was probably for this reason that the rites accompanying its use were unspecified. It has been suggested that the form employed was an adaptation of the form used in anointing catechumens or the newly baptized.

A decisive factor in the formulation of a fixed rite for the Sacrament was the transition from public to private Penance. Because of the severity of the penances imposed, it had become common to delay the reception of the Sacrament of Penance until the eve of death. Public Penance had had two stages, the admission to the ranks of penitents and the reconciliation, separated by a more or less lengthy interval. Each stage had had an appropriate liturgical rite. One of the rites that usually accompanied the reconciliation had been an anointing. As public Penance gave way to private Penance, some of the rites formerly annexed to the penitential anointing became attached to the Anointing of the Sick. By the early 9th century the practice of private Penance, introduced to the Continent from Ireland, had become common in the Frankish Kingdom. This rite was, of course, administered exclusively by a priest.

This was a period of great liturgical activity in the Frankish Kingdom when ritual observances were being given fixed formulation. One of the rites being liturgically organized was that of the Anointing of the Sick. The canonical legislation of the period shows that the practice of private anointing was condemned and that the sacramental Anointing reserved exclusively to priests was emphasized. This emerging rite was also being simultaneously integrated into the existing priestly functions of the visitation of the sick and administration of Penance and Viaticum. The conflation of these factors, which interacted upon one another, led to the administration of the Anointing of the Sick and deathbed Penance at the same time.

Ninth-century Rite. The Ritual of Theodulf of Orléans (d. *c.* 821) was long regarded as the prototype of the 9th- and 10th-century Ordinals for this Sacrament. It is now recognized that the rites for Penance and the dying contained in this Ritual represent a later period of liturgical history, probably the late 11th century. What is probably the earliest known liturgy for the Sacrament of Anointing that is of Roman origin—H. B. Porter calls it the Carolingian Unction Order—evolved in the Frankish Kingdom between 815 and 845. It can be found in H. Menard's edition of the Gregorian Sacramentary (PL 78:231–66). This rite, as it comes to us, is a developed one in which Roman, Frankish, and Mozarabic elements can be identified.

Basically this rite was a modified compilation of elements extracted from previously existing rites for the visitation of the sick into which the administration of the Anointing was inserted. The rite opened with the blessing of water and the sprinkling with it of the sick man and his house; this was followed by six prayers for the healing of the sick. All this was traditional Roman liturgical material, but in the form in which it appeared there it was taken from Alcuin's Ordinal for visiting the sick. The prayer *Domine Deus, qui per apostolum* that followed the prayers for healing is of contemporary Carolingian origin and still survives in the Roman Ritual. This prayer is a proclamation of the apostolic authority for the rite and a declaration of the effects for which it impetrates. Following this were three antiphons with their Psalms and a prayer. The anointing, accompanied by a form derived in part from the rite of exorcizing catechumens, followed these. The parts of the body anointed were the back of the neck, the throat, between the shoulders, the chest, and the focal point of the pain. Two prayers, both of Mozarabic origin, followed the anointing. Finally there was a rubric concerning the administration of Communion and the curious directive to repeat the entire rite, if there was need, for 7 days. In what appears to be a later addition to the rite, an alternative form was provided and the directive to anoint only the five senses was given.

Ceremonial Accretion. A comparison of this rite with the one provided in Theodulf's *Second Capitular* (PL 105:220–222) discloses the tendency of these rites to grow by ceremonial accretion as traditions merged. The influence of penitential anointing on this rite is also marked. The rite directed that Penance be administered first and that the sick man, if his infirmity would allow it, was to be washed, clothed in white garments, and carried to the church. There he was to be placed on sackcloth sprinkled with ashes. Three priests administered the Sacrament. While they recited the antiphon *Pax huic domui,* the sick man was sprinkled with holy water, and then ashes were imposed on his head and chest in the form of a cross. The seven Penitential Psalms and the litany were then recited. The anointing followed; 15 anointings were prescribed and the possibility of many more was approved. The sick man then recited the Our Father and the Creed. After this he was to recommend his soul to God, arm himself with the sign of the cross, and take leave of the living. The priest gave him the kiss of peace and administered Communion. The rite concluded with a directive to the priest to visit him, should he live, for 7 days.

With regard to the anointing, a trend developed not to anoint a part of the body that had been anointed in the reception of a previous Sacrament, but to anoint instead an adjacent part. These disputed anointings were later dropped and only the anointing of the five senses and the feet remained. The forms also manifested great divergence in length and manner of expression. Gradually, as the view that the Sacrament was one for the dying gained ascendancy, the forms ceased to speak of physical healing and stressed the forgiveness of sin. In the earlier Ordinals the accustomed order of the Sacraments was Penance, Anointing, and Viaticum; this order became Penance, Viaticum, and Anointing. [The earlier order was restored by Vatican Council II (*Constitution on the Sacred Liturgy* 74).]

The rite of Anointing had become such a lengthy one that, if the Sacrament was not to fall into desuetude, a reform of simplification was inevitable. This reform asserted itself in some areas while the rite was still developing in others. The rite adopted by the Benedictines of Cluny contributed greatly to the movement toward simplification. This rite appears to have influenced, at least indirectly, the *Ordo compendiosus,* an abridged rite of Anointing, found in the Pontifical of the Roman Curia in the 13th century. This Pontifical, itself influenced by the Romano-Germanic Pontifical of the 10th century, contained five rites connected with Christian death and burial. The first of these was a rite for the visitation of the sick, the second was the rite for Anointing (*Ordo compendiosus*). These two rites, joined and considerably abbreviated, appeared as the rite of Anointing in the Breviary of the Franciscans, a fact accounting for its wide diffusion. In this Breviary a threefold ritual for the last Sacraments is found: an order for Anointing, one for Viaticum, and an *Ordo commendationis animae.* With still further modifications, the *Ordo compendiosus* found its way into the *Liber sacerdotalis* of Alberto Castellani (d. *c.* 1522) and the Ritual of Cardinal Santorio (d. 1602). From this last Ritual it passed into the Ritual of Paul V (1614), the Roman Ritual still in use.

Modern Ritual. The existing rite for the Anointing of the Sick bears in itself the witness to its evolution. Its matrix was a rite for the visitation of the sick; the *Pax huic domui* of the present rite and the three prayers that follow it (*Introeat, Oremus et deprecemur, Exaudi nos*), none of which mentions anointing, manifest this origin. The first of these prayers is found in a 9th century Ordinal and the second, in Roman Ordinal 10; the third forms part of a prayer for the blessing of water in the Gelasian Sacramentary. The provision for Confession and the *Confiteor* that follows these prayers, and the mention of the Penitential Psalms and the litany that may be recited by the bystanders (rubric 7), show the imprint left on the rite by Penance. The prayer *In nomine Patris* was originally a formula for anointing the head. Later the anointing was dropped and replaced (in 1925) by an imposition of hands. The present Ritual admits two types of anointing: the usual one involves an unction of the five senses with a corresponding form for each sense; the second, to be used in necessity, calls for an anointing of the forehead and the same form without reference to any sense. The rite concludes with

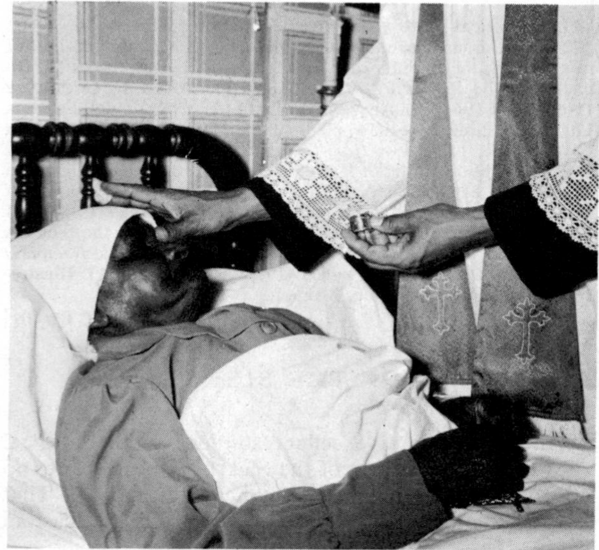

Anointing of a woman by a Divine Word Missionary on a sick call near Broissard, La.

three prayers, the first of which is found in the Gregorian Sacramentary, the second in the Hadrianum, and the third in the Gelasian Sacramentary.

The Commendatio Animae. For the Christian, the most important preparation for death is Viaticum. In addition to this, however, the Ritual provides a collection of prayers to be recited at the bedside of the dying. There are three groups of prayers in this ensemble: the Apostolic Blessing, the recommendation of the departing soul (*Commendatio animae*), and prayers at the hour of death.

Originally the term *Commendatio animae* referred to prayers for the dead, but in liturgical books beginning with the Carolingian period it designated prayers for the dying. Regardless of the designation, however, the practice of reciting prayers at the bedside of the dying Christian is an ancient one. The Gelasian Sacramentary contains a collection of such prayers, and there are indications of the practice from earlier times.

If the recommendation of the departing soul and the prayers at the hour of death are considered as one, there are 14 prayers (or groups of invocations) in the present collection. Two of these, the prayer to St. Joseph and the one to Our Lady, were added in the editions of the Ritual of 1913 and 1922 respectively. The prayer *Deus misericors* is found in an 8th-century Sacramentary as part of an absolution formula; the *Commendo te* is an extract from a letter of St. Peter Damian (*Epist.* 15; PL 144:497–98); the *Deus qui pro redemptione mundi* is attributed to St. Augustine. These, together with the three prayers at the conclusion of the *Commendatio,* first appeared as a collection in the Ritual of Paul V.

With the above exceptions, the remaining prayers appeared (and in the order treated) in the Roman Pontifical of the 12th century (51; Andrieu Pont 1:279–282). In this Pontifical, however, they were divided into two series. The first series followed immediately after Viaticum and included the reading of the Passion, the Psalms, and the litany. The Psalms and the litany form the oldest portion of the collection. The prayers in the second series, the *Commendatio* strictly so called, were to be recited when death was imminent. This series included: the *Subvenite* and the *Tibi, Domine, commendamus,* which are found in many Ordinals from the 9th and 10th centuries; the *Commendamus tibi,* which contains, at least in part, a prayer used at Arles in the 6th century; the *Suscipe Domine* and the 14 invocations introduced by it, which have their prototype in an 8th century Sacramentary; the *Delicta juventutis,* which, in the form found in the Ritual, comes from the Benedictional of Meissen (1512), although the portion invoking St. Michael is of an earlier origin; and the *Proficiscere anima,* which is found in two 8th-century Sacramentaries.

Although the practice of granting a plenary indulgence at the hour of death had existed for centuries, Benedict XIV in the bull *Pia Mater* of April 4, 1747, made available to all the faithful the Apostolic Blessing with a plenary indulgence. The rite by which the blessing is imparted was prescribed in the same bull.

Bibliography: A. CHAVASSE, *Étude sur l'onction des infirmes dans l'Église Latine du IIIe au XIe siècle,* v.1 *Du IIIe siècle à la Réforme Carolingienne* (Lyons 1942). F. W. PULLER, *The Anointing of the Sick in Scripture and Tradition* (London 1904). P. MURRAY, "The Liturgical History of Extreme Unction," *Furrow* 11 (1960) 572–593. H. B. PORTER, "The Origins of the Medieval Rite for Anointing the Sick or Dying," JThSt 7 (1956) 211–225; "The Rites for the Dying in the Early Middle Ages 1: St. Theodulf of Orleans," *ibid.* 10 (1959) 43–62; "The Rites for the Dying in the Early Middle Ages 2: the Legendary Sacramentary of Rheims," *ibid.* 299–307. L. GOUGAUD, "Étude sur les *Ordines commendationis animae,*" EphemLiturg 49 (1935) 3–27. Miller FundLit 468–473. A. G. MARTIMORT, *L'Église en prière* (Tournai 1961) 581–594. Righetti 4:186–203.

[J. P. MC CLAIN]

ANONYMITY AND PSEUDONYMITY

Many ancient literatures displayed a strong preference for anonymity and pseudonymity, literary techniques whereby a writer either withheld his identity or published under an assumed name. Authenticity (publication under the true author's name) was admittedly frequent in Chinese and Roman writing but gave way to anonymity and pseudonymity in the literatures of Egypt, Mesopotamia, Syria, Asia Minor, and Hellenistic Greece, at a time when these were providing literary models for the writers of the Jewish and Christian Scriptures.

Concealment of authorship could occur in a variety of ways, some of which were never exemplified in the Bible. For instance, many works of antiquity were anonymous only because the author's name, originally given, was later lost. Some pseudonymous productions appeared, not under the name of a celebrated personage of the past, but under a fictitious nom de plume. Still other pseudonyms were intended to deceive the reading public; thus, Jewish apologists in the Hellenistic Diaspora (*see* DIASPORA, JEWISH) published tracts purporting to be written by Sophocles, Euripides, Aristotle, etc., in praise of monotheism; again, heterodox Christian groups often put out their sectarian doctrines under the guise of apostolic authorship, e.g., the Gospel of Thomas and the Acts of John. But anonymity and pseudonymity in Scripture were neither accidental, nor casual, nor fraudulent.

In the Old Testament. The name of the author of only a single book of the OT is known with certainty—Jesus ben Elezar ben Sirach, whose *Wisdom* is commonly called the Book of *Sirach (for "ben Sirach"). Yet most of the books of prophecy, although later edited by others, are so integrally the work of the Prophets whose names they bear that they are best considered as authentic, e.g., Ezechiel and most of the *Minor Prophets. Some prophetic books, e.g., the Books of Isaia, Jeremia, and Zacharia, have basic nuclei of oracular sayings deriving from the titular authors, plus large blocks of supplemental material inserted later; they are thus partly authentic and partly pseudonymous. Books of historical or fictional narrative, on the contrary, tend to be uniformly anonymous.

However, not all anonymous works remained so. Since Solomon enjoyed the reputation of being a sage, many of the sapiential books came to be pseudonymously attributed to him, though they were compilations of materials originally anonymous (Proverbs, Ecclesiastes, Canticle of Canticles, and Wisdom). By a similar process Moses, the lawgiver, became in tradition (not in the text itself) the putative author of the *Pentateuch; David, the bard, was thought to have composed the entire collection of Psalms; and Lamentations passed as Jeremia's elegy over fallen Jerusalem. Finally, a few books alternated between anonymous passages in the third person and pseudonymous passages in the first person, e.g., Ezra, Tobit, and Daniel.

In the New Testament. The bulk of the Pauline corpus of letters is generally acknowledged as authentic. If one agrees that the hints in the Fourth Gospel point intentionally to John the Apostle as author, then this Gospel may be considered substantially authentic too. The Apocalypse claims to have been written by a certain John on Patmos, a claim one need not disallow despite later attempts to identify him with the Apostle. The authenticity of some NT books (Ephesians, Pastoral Epistles, and 1 Peter) is presently disputed. Eight were published anonymously (the three Synoptic Gospels, Acts, 1–3 John, and Hebrews). Nearly all critics agree that James, 2 Peter, and Jude are pseudonymous.

Most of the Biblical writings underwent considerable reediting and interpolation before final publication. Thus authorship was much more a group activity than was once thought. Yet among the hundreds of men who lent their pens to this literary endeavor, certain individuals—or, rather, classes—stood out clearly as direct spokesmen for God. The Prophets and the Apostles generally did not conceal themselves behind anonymity or pseudonymity but spoke or wrote in their own right and name. Other writers, on the contrary, conceived of themselves as collaborators in a group effort, rather than as men with a personal message to deliver. They compiled legal statutes, liturgical hymnody, moral aphorisms, royal chronicles, theological summaries of history, edifying fiction, homilies, and reinterpreted prophecy. They tended to publish these works anonymously, considering that they were transmitting, rather than shaping, a tradition. They sometimes pseudonymously attributed their own or others' writings to one or more of the recognized ancient, charismatic authors.

It has been conjectured that such pseudonymity was a device for endowing one's own works with authority, gaining for them a hearing they might otherwise not have enjoyed and lending them enough antiquity to have them classified as sacred books. Such motives may possibly have been behind pseudonymous heretical literature, but fails to account for Biblical pseudonymity.

Such intentions seem to be deceptive; and besides, a writer's contemporaries would likely be incredulous enough to reject such pious fraud. In actual fact, when unknown writers published under the names of Isaia, Ezra, or Paul, they were asserting their solidarity with the tradition that they traced back to their fathers in the faith. Just as they were anxious in their preaching to preserve the "faith once delivered to the saints," so in their writing they resorted to this accepted cachet of orthodoxy, pseudonymity (which was why the heretics so assiduously imitated it). Far from being a devious ploy to shore up an author's deficient personal authority, pseudonymity signified his intention to convey the same authoritative message of Isaia, Ezra, and Paul.

See also BIBLE, III (CANON), 4, 5.

Bibliography: J. A. SINT, *Pseudonymität in Altertum* (Innsbruck 1960); LexThK² 8:867. K. ALAND, "The Problem of Anonymity and Pseudonymity in Christian Literature of the First Two Centuries," JThSt 12 (1961) 39–49; et al., *The Authorship and Integrity of the NT* (London 1965). F. TORM, *Die Psychologie der Pseudonymität im Hinblick auf die Literatur des Urchristentums* (Gütersloh 1932). D. S. RUSSELL, *The Method and Message of Jewish Apocalyptic, 200 B.C. to 100 A.D.* (Philadelphia 1964). G. BARDY, "Faux et fraudes littéraires dans l'antiquité chrétienne," RHE 32 (1936) 5–23, 275–302.

[J. T. BURTCHAELL]

ANONYMOUS OF YORK, referred to also as the Norman Anonymous, is the title given by H. Böhmer to a series of 31 tractates found in the Cambridge, Corpus Christi, MS 415, written in several hands in the early 12th century. Some historians (H. Böhmer and N. F. Cantor) have proposed that they were composed by a single author, *viz,* the Norman Archbishop *Gerard of York (1101–08), and that York was the place of composition. Others have accepted the idea of single authorship but changed the person and location to Abp. William Bona Anima of Rouen (1079–1110). Multiple authorship also is suggested. Böhmer's thesis has generally prevailed. Although six tracts (nos. 8, 9, 10, 18, 21, and 31) present ideals of *Gregorian reform, the majority attack papal authority and defend royal and episcopal rights; canonical election is rejected, lay *investiture and clerical marriage are vindicated. The most important tract is no. 24a *De consecratione pontificum et regum* (MGLibLit 3:662–679) on lay investiture and theocratic monarchy. Apart from the novelty and extremism of its political and theological ideology, of interest to historians of political theory, the collection has had no influence. It probably was never published.

Bibliography: MGLibLit 3:642–687. H. BÖHMER, *Kirche und Staat in England und in der Normandie im XI. und XII. Jahrhundert* (Leipzig 1899). H. SCHERRINSKY, *Untersuchungen zum sogenannten Anonymus von York* (Würzburg 1940). G. H. WILLIAMS, *The Norman Anonymous of 1100 A.D.* (Cambridge, Mass. 1951). N. F. CANTOR, *Church, Kingship, and Lay Investiture in England, 1089–1135* (Princeton 1958).

[J. GILCHRIST]

ANOVULANTS (MORAL ASPECT)

A term used to signify drugs having a sterilizing effect that is achieved through the control of ovulation. Some earlier attempts to discover an effective drug for the control of conception did not aim at inhibiting ovulation as such, but when the investigation of the progestational steroids, which are synthetic forms of the female hormone, progesterone, revealed their influence on ovulation and hence on conception, the attention of investigators and those interested in the discovery of an effective contraceptive drug centered chiefly upon them. Consequently the debate among Catholic moralists about the morality of the control of conception by drugs has, since about 1957, been concerned almost exclusively with these specific pharmaceutical products.

Effect of the Drugs. The hormone progesterone is normally secreted by the female in the second half of each menstrual cycle and during pregnancy. Among the effects of the use of the progestational steroids appears to be the temporary suspension of ovulation. It has also been suggested that they have two other effects when taken in normal dosages. They seem to affect the physical consistency of the cervical mucus in such a way that it becomes hostile to sperms, and they seem also to render the endometrium, or inner lining of the uterus unfavorable to the implantation of the fertilized ovum. If pregnancy is avoided by means of this latter effect, the action of the steroids would be described by Catholic moralists as abortive. However, it has not been established that they actually have an abortive effect, and discussions of the morality of their use have generally been concerned only with their effect of suspending ovulation.

But in addition to their contraceptive effect, the steroids have also uses that are truly therapeutic, among which are the promotion of fertility in persons previously infertile, the supporting of pregnancy in women previously apt to suffer spontaneous abortions, the relief of painful menstruation and premenstrual tension, the regulation of menstrual bleeding, and the alleviation of endometriosis, to name but a few (see J. C. Ford and G. Kelly, 340).

Morality. The suppression of ovulation is a form of sterilization as defined by Catholic moralists. In any particular case, therefore, its morality depends on whether it is to be classified as a direct or an indirect sterilization. Indirect sterilization is allowable for a proportionately serious reason, but direct sterilization is considered illicit.

The directness or the indirectness of any mutilative procedure depends primarily on what is intended, and hence the distinction between direct and indirect sterilization in particular cases is to be determined by reference to its purpose. Pius XII, in his address to hematologists, Sept. 12, 1958, declared that the use of the medication not with a view to preventing conception, but as a necessary remedy for a malady of the uterus or of the organism can be considered an indirect sterilization, but the employment of the drug to prevent conception by preventing ovulation is a direct sterilization [ActApS 50 (1958) 735–736].

This general directive can be readily applied to two types of case. Some uses of the drugs are manifestly contraceptive, i.e., directly sterilizing and illicit, because they have no other immediate purpose than the suppression of ovulation in a fertile woman. Other uses are manifestly therapeutic, i.e., either not sterilizing at all, as when the drugs are taken to prevent miscarriage, or indirectly sterilizing only, as when they are taken for the immediate purpose of relieving some physical disorder. Between these two kinds of case there is a third in which the difference between direct and indirect sterilization is not so clear as to be beyond all question. There has been much discussion among theologians about the application of the general norms stated by Pius XII in certain types of situation falling under this heading. Opinion has been expressed favoring the classification of certain of these mooted uses of the drugs as indirectly sterilizing only. The positions that have been taken in this discussion enjoy varying degrees of probability, and not all can be regarded as sufficiently probable to be safely followed in practice.

The use of the steroid drugs in the so-called "rebound" therapy in which ovulation is suppressed in infertile women over a period of time in the hope that when the medication is discontinued the women will be able to become pregnant—an expectation that is realized in a significant number of cases—is commonly held to be licit. Indeed, it is doubtful whether the suppression of ovulation in an infertile woman can properly be considered sterilization. For similar reasons the use of the male hormone, testosterone, or even a progestational steroid, to reduce the sperm count in a treatment of infertility in a man has been regarded as allowable (J. C. Ford and G. Kelly, 348).

It is quite commonly held that the regulating of the menstrual cycle, at least in cases in which its variations are considerable enough to be accounted an abnormality, justifies the use of the steroids (*ibid.* 350–360). Opinion has taken less definite shape with regard to the use of the drugs to suppress ovulation during the period of lactation, or to suppress premature or extra ovulations so as to reduce abnormal fertility; and although these procedures have been defended, the probability of their licitness has not yet been satisfactorily established (*ibid.* 360–375).

It is evident that there is need for much discussion before all questions as to what is allowable and what is not in the use of these drugs can be fully answered. The matter is complicated by the fact that the available scientific information regarding ovulation and associated processes in the human organism is by no means complete. Neither is the precise manner in which the drugs produce their effect sufficiently understood. Moreover, final moral appraisal must await further research into the possibility of damaging side-effects of the use of the drugs, because this is not without relevance to the morality of their use. Moral judgment in a matter of this kind must always remain in some degree tentative and hypothetical until it is based upon complete physiological and medical information.

Nevertheless the desire for a solution to urgent individual and social problems has caused impatience with the slow course of scientific research and theological discussion. This impatience has expressed itself on the part of some in a call for revision of the confining general directives set forth by Pius XII. However, Pope Paul VI reaffirmed the directives of Pius XII in 1964 and declared them to be still in effect, but he added an assurance that the question of the pharmacological control of fertility was being investigated by the Holy See [ActApS 56 (1964) 588–589].

Bibliography: J. C. FORD and G. KELLY, *Contemporary Moral Theology*, 2 v. (Westminster, Md. 1958–63) v.2 *Marriage Questions*. J. J. LYNCH, "Moral Aspects of Pharmaceutical Fertility Control," CathThSoc 13 (1958) 127–135; "Progestational Steroids: Some Moral Problems," *Linacre Quarterly* 25 (1958) 93–99. F. J. CONNELL, "The Morality of Ovulation Rebound," AmEcclRev 143 (1960) 203–205. D. O'CALLAGHAN, "Fertility Control by Hormonal Medication," IrTheolQ 27 (1960) 1–5. M. THIÉFFRY, "Stérilisation hormonal et morale chrétienne," Nouv RevTh 83 (1961) 135–158. L. L. MCREAVY, "Use of Steroid Drugs to Regularize Menstrual Cycles," ClergyRev 46 (1961) 746–750. J. J. FARRAHER, "Notes on Moral Theology," ThSt 22 (1961) 610–651. C. DE KONINCK, "La Régulation des naissances," *Perspectives sociales* 19 (1964) 73–94. J. DEVANEY and P. REAVES, *The Truth about the New Birth Control Pills* (New York 1961). J. ROCK, *The Time Has Come* (New York 1963). J. T. NOONAN, *Contraception* (Cambridge, Mass. 1965) 460–475.

[P. K. MEAGHER]

ANQUETIL, LOUIS PIERRE, historical author; b. Paris, Jan. 20, 1723; d. Paris, Sept. 6, 1808. He was the older brother of A. *Anquetil-Duperron. In 1741 he became an Augustinian canon. He was director of the seminary at Reims and held ecclesiastical positions at La Roë, Senlis, Château-Renard, and La Villette. During the Reign of Terror, he was imprisoned but was released and in 1795 was attached to the archives of the Foreign Ministry, and remained there under Napoleon. Claim to authorship of his best work, the *Histoire de Reims* (3 v. 1756–59), was contested by Felix de la Salle. Two poorer works had great success also: his *L'Esprit de la Ligue* (3 v. 1767), and a *Histoire de France* from the Gauls to the end of the monarchy (14 v. 1805), undertaken at Napoleon's request. His other writings include a work on Louis XIV (4 v. 1789), and a *Précis de l'histoire universelle* (14 v. 1805).

Bibliography: C. GRANDJEAN, *La Grande encyclopédie* 3:121–122. P. CALENDINI, DHGE 3:422–423. R. CHALUMEAU, *Catholicisme* 1:611.

[J. E. HEALEY]

ANQUETIL-DUPERRON, ABRAHAM HYACINTHE, Orientalist; b. Paris, Dec. 7, 1731; d. Paris, Jan. 17, 1805. One of eight children, with two famous brothers, Anquetil distinguished himself in Hebrew, Arabic, and Persian at the Sorbonne and at Jansenist-inclined seminaries in Auxerre and Holland. Contact with a Parsee text in the Paris Royal Library prompted him to make their language and religion known to Europe, and he set off on his own for India, arriving in Pondichéry in August 1755. From Chandernagor, where he learned Bengali from Jesuit missionaries, he traveled on foot and on horseback almost the entire coast of India (Calcutta to Bombay), coming into contact with many archeological monuments not previously reported by Europeans. At the Indian Parsee center of Surat, north of Bombay, he spent 3 years transcribing and translating sacred texts into some 115 MSS (2,500 pages) under the direction of a Parsee destour, who also, according to Anquetil, introduced him into a Parsee temple. Barely 30 years old, Anquetil returned to Paris (1762) and spent the rest of his life as a somewhat controversial figure, living a life of voluntary poverty alone, publishing his *Zend-Avesta, ouvrage de Zoroastre* (3 v. Paris 1771) and a Latin translation of the Vedic Upanishads (2 v. Strasbourg 1801–02). His *Zend-Avesta,* studied by Schopenhauer, is, despite its errors, a monument in the history of erudition. Although Anquetil's Parsee and Vedic texts were not so ancient as he thought, but relatively modern, his labors served to open these fields to later scholars. As a member of the Académie des Inscriptions et Belles-Lettres (1763) he wrote several essays on Persia and India and published other works of interest: *Legislation orientale* (Amsterdam 1778), to prove that the despotism of Turkey, Persia, and India was not, as Montesquieu held, absolute; a study of the history and geography of India (Berlin and Paris 1786); a plan for the administration of India (Berlin 1788); and treatises on the dignity of commerce (Paris 1789) and on the political and commercial interests of India (Hamburg 1798). His MSS and his library are for the most part in the Paris Bibliothèque Nationale. Data about his remarkable life derive from his notes and writings.

Bibliography: R. SCHWAB, *Vie d'Anquetil-Duperron* (Paris 1934). G. SARTON, in *Osiris* 3 (1938) 193–223. A. Jaulme, Dict BiogFranc 2:1374–83.

[E. P. COLBERT]

ANSBALD, ST., abbot; d. July 12, 886 (feast, July 12). Very little is known about his early life, but after Eigil resigned as abbot of *Prüm (860), Ansbald was elected to succeed him. He is regarded as one of the outstanding men who held this office, and under his leadership the abbey gained great renown for its flourishing religious observance. From letters written by *Lupus of Ferrières, a close friend of the abbot of Prüm, it is clear that Ansbald was interested in collating the monastery's manuscripts of various classical authors, especially the MSS of the *Letters* of *Cicero. After the havoc wrought by the raids of the *Normans, Ansbald was able rapidly to restore the abbey to its once flourishing condition with the help of *Charles III the Fat. He died with a reputation for great sanctity, and his name was inserted in several monastic *martyrologies.

Bibliography: Mabillon AS 6:475–477. R. AIGRAIN, DHGE 3:429–430. Baudot-Chaussin 7:270–272. Zimmermann KalBen 2:439, 441. A. ZIMMERMANN, LexThK^2 1:583; BiblSanct 1:1336. LUPUS OF FERRIÈRES, *Correspondance*, ed. and tr. L. LEVILLAIN, 2 v. (Paris 1927–35) 2:4.

[H. DRESSLER]

ANSBERT OF ROUEN, ST., archbishop of Rouen; b. Chaussy, France, *c.* mid-7th century; d. Hautmont, France, Feb. 9, 693 (feast, Feb. 9). He came from a distinguished family of Chaussy and rose to be *referendarius* in the court of Chlotar III (d. 673). In 673 he entered the *Benedictine Order at *Fontenelle under Abbot *Wandrille, and in 679 he was himself made abbot. He succeeded *Ouen in the See of Rouen in 684. He had dedicated a poem to his saintly predecessor, and he promoted his cult. About 689 he secured for Fontenelle the right to elect its abbot free from royal and episcopal interference. Soon after, he was for political reasons confined by Pepin of Heristal (d. 714) to a monastery at Hautmont, where he died. His body was returned to Rouen and buried in the abbey church, where the translation of his relics took place early in the 8th century. He is mentioned in the Roman Martyrology, and his biography, written *c.* 800, is fairly trustworthy.

Bibliography: *Vita Ansberti*, MGSrerMer 5:613–643, critical ed. W. LEVISON; uncritical ed. ActSS 2 (1863) 348–357. His poem pub. by W. WATTENBACH, NeuesArch 14:171–172. According to S. LOEVENFELD, ed., *Gesta abbatum Fontenellensium*, MGSrerGerm 28 (1886) 48, A. wrote *Quaestiones ad Siwinum reclausum*, but this has been lost. E. VACANDARD, DHGE 3:431–433; "Les Deux vies de saint A.," RevQuestHist 67 (1900) 600–612. R. AIGRAIN, *Catholicisme* 1:611–612. Zimmermann KalBen 1:189–191.

[M. C. MC CARTHY]

ANSE, COUNCILS OF, a number of provincial councils held at the small town of Anse (Ansa, Asa) in the Diocese of Lyons.

In 994 the archbishops of Lyons, Vienne, and Tarantaise, meeting with many bishops and abbots, confirmed the possessions of the Abbey of *Cluny at the request of St. *Odilo, its abbot, and provided for canons in the church of Saint-Romain. Among other things, its nine disciplinary canons directed that consecrated hosts reserved in churches were to be renewed every Sunday, that only priests could and must take Viaticum to the sick, that there be no servile labor after 3 P.M. on Saturday.

In 1025 a council of prelates from the provinces of Lyons and Vienne heard the bishop of Mâcon protest against the archbishop of Vienne's having ordained monks at Cluny, an abbey located in the Diocese of Mâcon. Abbot Odilo exhibited a papal privilege exempting Cluny from diocesan authority, authorizing its abbot to choose any bishop to ordain his monks. Citing the ancient canons, notably canon 4 of the Council of *Chalcedon, which said that abbots and monks everywhere must be subject to their bishop, the council rejected any privilege to the contrary. Cluny's privilege was suspended, but restored when Odilo obtained a papal bull confirming it (Rome, 1027).

At a council in 1070, the bishop of Chalon-sur-Saône gave the cloister of Saint-Laurent to a monastery near Lyons.

In 1076 *Hugh of Die, the papal vicar, held at Anse one of the several councils called to promote *Gregory VII's reforms, especially the prohibition of lay *investitures.

In 1100 a council excommunicated those who broke their vow to go on the Crusade. The papal vicar, Hugh, now archbishop of Lyons, requested money for a trip to the Holy Land.

In 1112 the archbishop of Lyons, claiming primatial authority in France, tried unsuccessfully to convoke a national council concerning investitures. His authority was contested; a provincial synod, however, may have actually been held.

In 1300 the archbishop of Lyons held a synod in Anse designed to restore or modify ancient ordinances.

Bibliography: Hefele-Leclercq 4:871–872, 938–939, 1272; 5:219, 467, 535. Mansi 19:177–180, 423–424, 1077–80; 20:481–482, 1127–28; 21:77–84; 24:1217–32. A. REGNIER, DHGE 3:443.

[A. CONDIT]

ANSEGIS, ST., abbot, collector of Carolingian *capitularies; b. Lyonnais, France, *c.* 770; d. Fontenelle, July 20, 833 (feast, July 20). After being educated in a Lyonnaise monastery, he became a monk at *Fontenelle (Saint-Wandrille) in Normandy, as advised by *Benedict of Aniane. His abbot Gervold presented him to *Charlemagne, who entrusted him with various political missions. He was named abbot at Saint-Germer-de-Flay (Diocese of Beauvais), which he restored to prosperity. The Emperor called him to the imperial court at Aachen, and sent him to the Spanish March (Catalonia). He was a friend and correspondent of *Einhard. *Louis the Pious made him abbot of two more abbeys: *Luxeuil (817) and Fontenelle (823), where he restored the observance of the *Benedictine Rule, enriched the libraries, and encouraged education (at Luxeuil, Angelomus was his disciple). In 827, for the convenience of the emperors and in order to safeguard the goods of the Church, he undertook to make a collection of the imperial laws from 789 to 826, divided into four books: (1) *Capitularia Caroli Magni ad ordinem pertinentia ecclesiasticum,* 176 chapters; (2) *Capitularia Ludovici Pii ad ordinem pertinentia ecclesiasticum,* 46 chapters; (3) *Capitularia Caroli Magni ad mundanam pertinentia legem,* 90 chapters; (4) *Capitularia Ludovici Pii ad mundanum pertinentia legem,* 74 chapters. All these capitularies are authentic—even those that are preserved only in this collection of Ansegis. The collection (MGL 2: Capitularia regum Franc. 1:382–450) enjoyed great authority from the time it first appeared. Louis the Pious referred to it already in 829 (cf. the capitulary of Worms, 829). It was one of the principal sources for the similar work of *Benedict the Levite in 845. Several chapters passed into the *Decretum* of *Gratian, but through the intermediary of canonical collections. The collection is not without minor errors in chronological order, transcription of names, etc. (It was E. *Baluze who correctly reattributed this edition to Ansegis of Fontenelle rather than to the nonexistent "Ansegis of Lobbes.") Ansegis is inscribed in the catalogue of saints at Luxeuil.

Bibliography: *Gesta abbatum Fontanellensium,* MGS 2:293–300. GallChrist 11:173–174. M. BUCHNER, "Zum Briefwechsel Einhards und des hl. Ansegis von Fontanelle," *Historische Vierteljahrschrift* 18 (1918) 353–385. P. FOURNIER, DHGE 3: 447–448. A. AMANIEU, DDC 1:564–567. A. J. KLEINCLAUSZ, *Eginhard* (Paris 1942) 47, 160.

[P. COUSIN]

ANSELM OF CANTERBURY, ST.

Doctor of the Church; b. Aosta, Val d'Aosta (formerly Piedmont), *c.* 1033–34; d. (possibly in Canterbury), April 21, 1109. His parents were of the nobility. After the death of his mother, he went to France to further his education.

Life as a Churchman. In 1060 Anselm entered the newly formed Abbey of Bec in Normandy, and 3 years later he succeeded Lanfranc of Pavia as prior. Herluin, the founding abbot of Bec, died in 1078, and Anselm was unanimously elected abbot.

Although reluctant to accept this office, Anselm submitted to the wishes of the community and proved an excellent abbot. His skill as a teacher and his great virtue were assets in developing the abbey into a monastic school influential in philosophical and theological studies. At the behest of the community at Bec, Anselm began publishing his theological works, writings comparable to those of St. Augustine in quality and respected even in modern times.

In March 1093 Anselm was again called upon to succeed Lanfranc, this time as archbishop of Canterbury. The See of Canterbury, like many other bishoprics and abbeys, had been purposely left vacant after Lanfranc's death in 1089 so that the revenues might be appropriated by King William Rufus. Not until he was seriously ill did this King appoint Anselm archbishop. Anselm, realizing it would be impossible to cooperate with William Rufus, refused to accept the appointment; he was forced to yield, however, by moral pressure from all sides. The consecration took place on December 4.

As an energetic defender of Church reform, particularly that associated with Gregory VII, he foresaw the almost hopeless task with which he would be confronted because of Rufus's opposition. The King refused any cooperation in reforming morals or organizing a reform council. He denied Anselm permission to visit Rome to receive the pallium from Urban II (d. 1099) on the

St. Anselm of Canterbury's seal.

grounds that Urban had not been recognized in England as the rightful pope. Anselm, however, had recognized Urban, and now proposed a council of bishops and nobility to decide whether he could reconcile his obedience to the Holy See and his loyalty to the King. In the council, which met at Rockingham in March 1095, the bishops, fearing the King, sided against Anselm; it was the secular princes who prevented his immediate removal. The King's proposal after his recognition of Urban, to request the pallium himself in order to confer it on another, failed because the Cardinal-legate Walter, who had brought the pallium, would not consent to it. Finally, Anselm realized he must yield and leave England (Oct. 15, 1097); the King immediately took possession of the See of Canterbury.

The Pope received Anselm with dignity and declined to accept his proposed resignation from Canterbury. At Bari Anselm took part in the council (Oct. 1, 1098) that sought reunion with the Greek Church. Through his profound theological proof that the Holy Spirit also proceeds from the Son, Anselm played a prominent role in this council. Moreover, he effectively sought postponement of the council's planned excommunication of the English King. At the Easter Synod in the Lateran (April 24, 1099), he again participated, and again heard excommunication pronounced against kings and princes who awarded ecclesiastical offices through presentation of ring and crosier (lay-investiture), against recipients of such offices, and all who became vassals of laymen for the sake of ecclesiastical dignities. At the close of the council Anselm accepted the hospitality of the archbishop of Lyons. It was at Lyons that he received the news of the King of England's death in a hunting accident (Aug. 2, 1100).

Rufus's brother and successor, Henry I, immediately recalled Anselm to England. Even before Anselm called his council in London (1102), he had been in conflict with Henry, who, reluctant to relinquish his ancient "right," had insisted on Anselm's taking an oath of allegiance to the king. Anselm's refusal, based on the decree of the Council of Bari, led both sides to send envoys to Rome. When no solution to the difficulty was forthcoming, the King asked Anselm to go to Rome. This was tantamount to another 3 years in exile.

Finally, in 1106, an agreement was reached through compromise: the King renounced the right of investiture by means of ring and crosier; on the other hand, the archbishop would not refuse consecration to anyone who had taken the oath of allegiance. The last years of Anselm's life were saddened by York's claiming the primacy that had always belonged to Canterbury. Anselm died on Wednesday of Holy Week. He was canonized in 1163 and declared a Doctor of the Church in 1720.

Teaching. Before Anselm's time the study of theology had been a collecting and systematic arranging of the authorities (Sacred Scripture and Doctors of the Church). Anselm strove to analyze and prove the truths of faith by reason alone (*sola ratione*). His goal was to go beyond mere faith and arrive at an insight into faith. In the scale of values that he constructed, faith is in the lowest place; in the middle is the insight into faith that is attainable in this life, and that brings us closer to the beatific vision; the beatific vision is at the top of the scale. Anselm expected from insight into faith joy in the spiritual beauty of the truths of faith for the believer; furthermore, he believed that when he showed the reasonableness and necessity of truths of faith, he also defended them against all those who denied or argued against them.

In this, however, Anselm did not stop at the so-called natural truths, but extended his arguments to include specifically revealed doctrines, such as those of the Trinity, the Incarnation, and the Redemption. In so doing he went beyond the boundaries taken for granted by us today but not yet clearly defined in his time. Disregarding all authority in inquiry was for Anselm only a methodological means to demonstrate the reasonableness of faith. Subjectively, Anselm was far from being an un-Christian rationalist. In the event that Sacred Scripture and proofs from reason seemed to clash, he emphatically held the former to be correct; he submitted certain works to the judgment of the pope; he was prepared in every respect to retract anything in which he had been proven in error. Moreover, he was the most unyielding adversary of such rationalists of his time as Roscelin of Compiègne (d. *c.* 1120). Anselm demanded firmness in faith and philosophical preparation in everyone who approached theological issues. He himself had the best philosophical preparation of his time; he was a master of grammar, logic, and dialectics, although only a few writings on logic by Aristotle were known to him through Boethius. In addition he was well acquainted with the writings of the Fathers of the Church, especially St. Augustine. Anselm was rightfully called *"Augustinus redivivus."* However, the more or less generally held opinion that he accepted, without question, Augustine's Neoplatonic line of reasoning must be revised. He remained independent of Augustine and took issue with him on more than one occasion, e.g., in the definition of free will and the doctrine of Redemption. Anselm let himself be governed by principles of logic as well as by common sense. These simple tools never failed him in his explorations of new theological lands.

Writings. The works Anselm left behind [recent ed. F. S. Schmitt, 5 v. and index (Edinburgh 1942)] are divided into systematic works, prayers and meditations, and letters.

Systematic Works. The *Monologion* presents a kind of theodicy. Anselm, with precision and unprecedented skill in speculation, shows the existence of a Supreme Being to be the causal origin of everything good and great, and of all being and its essential properties. The word, love, and the Trinity are examined in their turn. Being is considered to be the object of reason, love, and future happiness. The last chapter states that this is what is signified by the name "God." Although in his speculation Anselm relies on Augustine, especially in what pertains to the analogy with the human psyche, he is independent in his method. Anselm is convinced that a nonbeliever could concede all this without the help of revelation.

The *Proslogion* is better known. In it Anselm seeks to replace the many proofs of the *Monologion* with a single argument. This argument consists in the concept of God as "that beyond which nothing greater can be conceived" (*id, quo maius cogitari nequit*). Here he seeks an a priori proof of the existence of God by analyzing the concept of God. He argues: such a being is greater when it exists in reality than when it exists merely in the mind. Consequently it must exist in reality, because if it were only in the mind it would not be that beyond which nothing greater can be conceived. Anselm's proof, known since the time of Kant as the "ontological proof" of the existence of God, had already been challenged by one of his contemporaries, Gaunilo of Marmoutiers, and later by Thomas Aquinas and others, on the grounds that it implied an invalid step from the sphere of logic to that of ontology. Others, such as Bonaventure, Descartes, Leibniz, and Hegel, incorporated this proof, with certain ramifications, into their systems. Today, men like Karl Barth, in attempting to explain the proof as a theological one, overlook the fact that it was designed for the benefit of atheists to whom revelation is meaningless. *See* ONTOLOGICAL ARGUMENT.

Following the proof are four dialogues between teacher and students. The first is an astute dialectical exercise on the question whether the word "grammarian" is a substance or a quality; *On Truth* and *On Free Will* give Anselm's own definitions of truth, free will, and justification; and *On the Fall of the Devil* goes deeply into the doctrine on the angels.

Because of Roscelin's tritheism (according to which Father, Son, and Holy Spirit are not the same from the standpoint of essence), Anselm wrote a letter dedicated to Urban II entitled "Letter on the Incarnation of the Word," in which he clearly presents and rationally defends the Catholic doctrine on the three Persons in one essence. His remarks on universal ideas are usually evaluated as expressions of extreme realism, which is perhaps an overstatement.

Anselm's main work is the dialogue *Cur Deus Homo* (Why God Became Man). In it he takes a stand in opposition to a theory of redemption widely held up to that time, namely, that the devil had a claim on man. Anselm denies any such right on Satan's part and works out the so-called "satisfaction doctrine." According to it, sin is an infinite offense against God, which demands

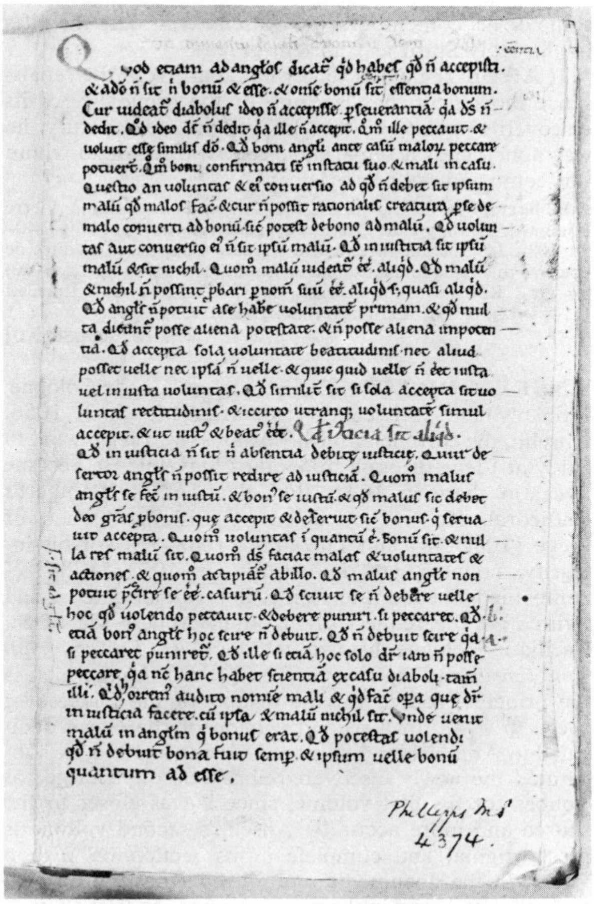

Page from St. Anselm's dialogue "On the Fall of the Devil"; late 12th-century French minuscule.

adequate atonement. Mere pardon cannot be reconciled with the justice of God. So the God-Man had to atone, since on the one hand man was obliged to do so, but on the other only God could do so adequately. From this situation, Anselm deduced the necessity of the Incarnation of God and the Redemption through Christ, and all other Christological dogmas so that God's plan for man—to make man happy—might not be frustrated. The main points of this theory were adopted by subsequent theologians, prescinding from the necessity of the Redemption's taking place exactly as it did. Anselm's partner in conversation here was a non-Christian, whom it was necessary to convince.

In the work *On the Virginal Conception and Original Sin* Anselm examines the question how Christ, although descended from the sinful mass (*massa damnatrix*), remained without sin. In this writing as well as in *Cur Deus Homo* it is evident that Anselm did not accept the Immaculate Conception of Mary. The work *On the Procession of the Holy Spirit* is a reworking of the speech Anselm delivered in Bari before the Fathers of the Council; it is an important advance in the doctrine on the Trinity. The last work of significance, *De concordia,* handles the difficult problem of reconciling God's prescience, predestination, and grace with the free will of man.

Although Anselm left behind no complete system of doctrine in the form of a *summa,* his individual treatises, complete in themselves, cover a large portion of Catholic doctrine. For his outstanding initiative in using reason for the examination of questions of faith he had earned the honorary title "Father of Scholasticism"; however, since he did not found a school, scholasticism cannot be regarded as a direct outgrowth of his work.

Prayers and Meditations. The 19 prayers and 3 meditations are creations of his own individual art. The prayers, written at special requests, are short, brilliantly executed rhetorical masterpieces, with the classical six parts of a discourse, in which God or a saint is to be moved to render help. The thing that is most striking in the artistic style employed is the use of parallelism in the sentences. *On the Redemption of Mankind* stands out above the rest of the meditations. In it Anselm summarizes the thought developed at greater length in his *Cur Deus Homo.* The meditation is not only shorter; it is in a purely theological form and has dispensed with the supplementary apologetics.

Letters. His correspondence (475 letters, 100 of which are from others) gives invaluable insight into Anselm's personality and is at the same time the most significant source for the history of the Church in England during his time. The addressees are popes, royalty, monks, nuns, and laity, living in all parts of the Christian world of that time. Anselm's letters to friends, particularly his early letters, illuminate his Germanic temperament and the richness of his spiritual character. In them the saint's views on Christian and monastic asceticism are aired.

Many ascetical works have been erroneously attributed to Anselm. Notes of his students concerning his oral method of teaching, based on parables from life, are available to us in *De similitudinibus* (PL 159:605–708). Eadmer recorded also Anselm's famous speech at Cluny on the 14 happinesses of heaven (*ibid.* 587–606).

Bibliography: M. Rule, *The Life and Times of St. Anselm,* 2 v. (London 1883). J. Clayton, *Saint Anselm* (Milwaukee 1933). R. W. Church, *Saint Anselm* (London 1937). J. Bainvel, DTC 1.2:1327–60. Ueberweg (1951) 2:192–203, 698–700. E. Gilson, "Sens et nature de l'argument de saint Anselme," ArchHistDoct LitMA 9 (1934) 5–51. J. Bayart, "The Concept of Mystery According to St. Anselm of Canterbury," RechThAm 9 (1937) 125–166. R. W. Southern, "St. Anselm and His English Pupils," MedRenSt 1 (1941–43) 3–34; *Saint Anselm and His Biographer* (New York 1963). Eadmer, *The Life of St. Anselm: Archbishop of Canterbury,* ed. and tr. R. W. Southern (New York 1962). J. McIntyre, *St. Anselm and His Critics: A Reinterpretation of the Cur Deus Homo* (Edinburgh 1954). **Illustration credits:** Fig. 1, Courtesy of The Trustees of The British Museum. Fig. 2, Rare Book Department, Free Library of Philadelphia.

[F. S. SCHMITT]

ANSELM OF HAVELBERG, archbishop, author, imperial envoy to the Greeks; d. Milan, Aug. 12, 1158. Almost nothing is known of Anselm's early life, but he was probably a *Premonstratensian canon before his consecration as bishop of the Brandenburg See of Havelberg in 1129. Anselm was active in the administration of Emperor *Lothair III, who sent him to Constantinople in 1136. There Anselm took part in friendly dialogues on the issues dividing the Greek and Latin Churches. During his absence, the Wends ravaged his diocese, and he was papal legate in the crusade against them (1147). He spent 1150–52 in pastoral work and writing. According to Anselm, the growth and development of the faith, both in understanding and in institutional expression, are the means of the Holy Spirit in His continuing reformation of the Church. This theology of history enabled Anselm to defend the Western Church against the charge of doctrinal novelty leveled by Eastern theologians and to defend the new *canons regular against attacks by some monastic authors. *Frederick I Barbarossa recalled Anselm to the service of the Empire, and in 1152 Anselm helped arrange the treaty with Pope *Eugene III. In 1154 he was again an emissary to the Byzantine court and once more debated with prelates of the *Byzantine Church. In 1155, the Emperor rewarded Anselm by making him archbishop and exarch of *Ravenna. He died suddenly while serving the Emperor at the siege of Milan.

Bibliography: ANSELM OF HAVELBERG, *Dialogorum adversus Graecos libri III,* PL 188:1139–1248; *Epistola apologetica pro ordine canonicorum regularium, ibid.* 1117–40. K. FINA, "Anselm von Havelberg: Untersuchungen zur Kirchen- und Geistesgeschichte des 12. Jahrhunderts," AnalPraem 32 (1956) 69–101, 193–227; 33 (1957) 5–39, 268–301; 34 (1958) 13–41. L. F. BARMANN, "Reform Ideology in the *Dialogi* of Anselm of Havelberg," ChHist 30 (1961) 379–395.

[J. R. SOMMERFELDT]

ANSELM OF LAON, theologian; b. Laon, date unknown; d. Laon, 1117. After receiving his training at the school of Bec, he sojourned in Paris in 1089. There he met Bernard of Chartres, who brought him to his city for a brief stay. On his return to Laon, he directed the illustrious school of *Laon with his brother Raoul. Anselm—his real name was Ansellus (Anseau)—was a brilliant teacher, the "Teacher of teachers," who attracted many pupils. Some of these became famous: *William of Champeaux (1068–1122), *Gilbert de la Porrée (d. 1154), Peter *Abelard (*c.* 1113). This last ridiculed him, comparing him to the fig tree of the Gospel that, while covered with leaves, remained fruitless. In reality, Anselm was one of the best teachers of the 12th century.

Works. Despite the fact that some works attributed to him remain doubtful, the *Sentences* are considered authentic. This is a particularly important work, for it is an example of the first attempts to systematize theological thought. Other works of the time manifested this tendency, which led to *Peter Lombard's *Book of Sentences,* and through it, to the great *Summas* of the end of the 12th and 13th centuries. Anselm's *Sentences* are collected according to a plan inspired—like many works of those times—by Scotus Erigena: creation, the Fall of the angels and of men (original sin), the necessity of Redemption, Redemption and the Sacraments. It is rather difficult to find texts that present Anselm's thought in continuity. More often than not, one must be content with small pieces or the *Liber Pancrisis de Troyes,* a neighbor if not a cousin of the *Sentences.* One of Anselm's innovations is to name the authors whom he quotes. Of his scriptural work, we possess commentaries on the Psalms, the Canticle of Canticles, the Apocalypse, fragments on Matthew's Gospel, lengthier ones on the Pauline Epistles, and Genesis.

Thought. It is impossible to give a complete exposition of Anselm's thought here. He is mainly attracted to problems connected with creation and original sin. His treatment is moral rather than dogmatic. Concerning the problem of the nature of the soul, however, he is more precise than others, i.e., for him the soul is less subject to the body, and even though it is weak like Adam toward Eve, its freedom is certain. Contrary to some of his contemporaries, Anselm considers the gifts of the Holy Spirit as transient graces.

If Anselm remained somewhat apart from the renaissance movement that, because of the originality of its discoveries, was to be the glory of the next century, he was nonetheless a remarkable school director to whom this century owed a great deal.

Bibliography: F. CAVALLERA, "D'Anselme de Laon à Pierre Lombard," *Bulletin de littérature ecclésiastique* 41 (1940) 40–54, 103–114. F. BLIEMETZRIEDER, "Trente-trois pièces inédites de l'oeuvre théologique d'Anselme de Laon," RechThAMéd 2 (1930) 54–79. P. ROUSSEAU, *Catholicisme* 1:619–621. A. MAIER, EncCatt 1:1417–18. A. M. LANDGRAF, LexThK[2] 1:595–596.

[P. ROUSSEAU]

ANSELM OF LIÈGE, chronicler; b. near Cologne, probably late 10th century; d. after March 3, 1056. Anselm, the chronicler of the bishops of *Liège, went to study at Liège through *Poppo of Stavelot. He became a canon there in 1041, then dean of St. Lambert's Cathedral. He was esteemed by Bishops *Wazo of Liège (1042–48) and Theoduin (1048–75) for his integrity, holiness, and knowledge. In 1053–54 he accompanied Theoduin to Rome. Before that date he had written, at the request of his aunt, Abbess Ida of St. Cecilia in Cologne, his two-volume *Gesta Episcoporum Tungrensium, Trajectensium et Leodiensium,* which is the principal source for the history of the Diocese of Liège to 1048. In a second version of the *Gesta* dedicated to Archbishop *Anno of Cologne in 1056, he substituted the newly discovered chronicle of *Heriger of Lobbes for his first volume, since it was closer to the source and more accurate. Anselm's second volume is most original and complete in its section on Bishop Wazo. In the documents reproduced (mostly liturgical and religious), and in the use of sources, Anselm showed himself to be well read and, by the standards of his age, critical.

Bibliography: Editions. MGS 7:161–234; 14:107–120. Martène VSM 4:837–911. PL 139:957–1102. Wattenbach-Holtzmann 1.1:143–148. Studies. R. GORGAS, *Über den kürzeren Text von Anselms "Gesta . . ."* (Halle 1890). J. DE GHELLINCK, DHGE 3:487–489. R. H. A. HUYSMANS, *Wazo van Luik* (Nijmegen 1932). F. J. SCHMALE, LexThK[2] 1:596–597.

[T. A. CARROLL]

ANSELM II OF LUCCA, ST.

Bishop; b. 1036; d. 1086; Anselm came from a noble Milanese family and was a nephew and successor of Anselm I, who became Pope Alexander II. Anselm, who was consecrated bishop in 1073, was a firm supporter of Pope St. *Gregory VII and of the movement to reform the Church. His efforts to reform the Diocese of Lucca, especially to force the cathedral canons to live the common life, caused opposition. He also opposed the Emperor Henry IV and the antipope Clement III. Having been forced to leave his see, he spent his last years as spiritual director to Countess Matilda of Tuscany, and vicar apostolic in Lombardy. His main works were the *Liber contra Wibertum* and the *Collectio canonum.*

The collection, compiled in about 1083 for Gregory VII, exists in two forms, called A and B. Form A is regarded as the original. The number of *capitula* varies from MS to MS but is between 1,150 and 1,281. These are divided into 13 books of unequal length, e.g., Bk. 8 has 34 capp.; Bk. 6 has 190. The contents of the books include the Roman primacy (1), appeals and clerical trials (2, 3), ecclesiastical privileges (4), status of churches (5), episcopal elections (6), the priesthood

(7), lapsed clergy (8), Sacraments (9), Marriage (10), Penance (11), excommunication (12), and lawful coercive power (13).

The main formal sources were the *Hadriana, Hispana, Pseudo-Isidore, Anselmo dicata,* Burchard, and especially the **Seventy-four Titles.* A number of other miscellaneous sources provided texts, e.g., of Roman law. The majority of the *capitula* were from papal decretals (false about 300, genuine about 420).

A rubric title introduces each *capitulum.* These enable us to determine the author's own views. Pre-Gratian collections had no glosses as such, and the texts were open to interpretation. Thus the rubrics play a part in bringing about the concordance of texts that triumphed with Gratian. (*See* GRATIAN, DECRETUM OF.)

As an instrument of papal reform Anselm's collection ranks with the *Seventy-four Titles* in importance. It was a carefully constructed collection that enjoyed wide popularity, being used in later collections as well as in polemical writings during the *investiture struggle. The main problems of the reform—simony, clerical celibacy, monastic freedom, lay investiture, the superiority of the spiritual power—inspired Anselm. Thus the collection is an important source for the history of the Gregorian reform, and as well for dogmatic and moral theology. Some 14 MSS of the collection are extant. Collections that used Anselm include the *Liber Tarraconensis, Caesaraugustana,* Alger of Liége, *Ashburnham,* and Gratian. The collection was also a main source through which the False Decretals were popularized in Italy and beyond.

Bibliography: ANSELM OF LUCCA, *Liber contra Wibertum,* ed. E. BERNHEIM, MGLibLit 1:517–528, PL 149:435–634, *Anselmi episcopi Lucensis collectio canonum una cum collectione minore,* ed. F. THANER 2 v. (Innsbruck 1906 and 1915). Fournier-LeBras 2:25–37. R. MONTANARI, *La "Collectio canonum" de S. Anselmo di Lucca e la riforma Gregoriana* (Mantua 1941). Stickler 1:170–172, 187. G. B. BORINO, "Il monacato e l'investitura di Anselmo vescovo di Lucca," StGreg 5 (1956) 361–374. F. KEMPF, LexThK² 1:596. ActSS March 2:647–663. Butler Th Attw 1:628–629.

[J. T. GILCHRIST]

ANSELM OF NONANTOLA, ST., duke, abbot; d. March 3, 803 (feast, March 3). Anselm, Duke of Friuli in the Lombard Kingdom, and brother of Giseltrudis, the wife of King *Aistulf, founded the Benedictine abbey of Fanano in 750 and that of *Nonantola *c.* 752. He withdrew from the world, entered Nonantola, and in 753 was appointed its first abbot by Pope Stephen II. In 756 the relics of Pope St. *Sylvester I were translated from Rome to Nonantola. Presumably, this was a "pious theft," because at the time King Aistulf was pillaging the Via Salaria, the former location of the relics. Anselm founded a number of hospices for the poor and for pilgrims. For a time he was *persona non grata* to Aistulf's successor, King *Desiderius, and spent several years in exile at Monte Cassino.

Bibliography: MGSrerLang 208–209, 503, 566–571. Kehr Ital Pont 5:330–362. R. AIGRAIN, DHGE 3:451–452. A. P. FRUTAZ, EncCatt 1:1419–20. Butler Th Attw 1:470.

[A. G. BIGGS]

ANSELMO DEDICATA, COLLECTIO. Toward the end of the 9th century in Milan, a canonical collection came to light, which the unknown author had dedicated to Anselm, Archbishop of Milan (II, 882–896), and which was to have considerable importance both in Italy and in Germany.

The scheme of this collection was new, since it was aimed at the distribution of a large number of matters, primarily but not exclusively of canonical origin, into a systematic form. However, this was done by using a method different from that which appeared in previous works—perhaps unknown to the author himself—such as the **Dacheriana Collectio.*

The subject matter was, in fact, divided into 12 books, of different lengths, containing three sections: works strictly canonical (canons and pontifical decretals); works derived from the letters of St. Gregory the Great; and, finally, works of Roman sources, from which came also the "Lex romana canonice compta" and the "Regulae ecclesiasticae" (called also "Excerpta bobiensia").

The contents of the work are as follows: book 1: high ecclesiastical hierarchy (pope, patriarchs, and metropolitans); book 2: bishops; book 3: councils; book 4: priests and deacons; book 5: minor clergy; book 6: regulars and widows; book 7: the laity; book 8: the practice of virtues; book 9: Baptism; book 10: worship, ecclesiastical benefices; book 11: feasts; book 12: heretics, schismatics, and non-Catholics.

A plan so formulated was suitable for placing at hand, in an organic form, a number of works that were not easy to consult otherwise. This explains the great diffusion of the work and its direct or indirect influence on all the canonical collections until the time of Gregory VII. The sources the author used included the *False Decretals, in the so-called A² edition. The part dealing with the conciliar canons and the post-Damasian authentic decretals was taken from the **Hadriana Collectio.* Many norms were taken also from the Collection of the manuscript of Novara (an edition of the *Hadriana Collectio* with many additions) and from other minor works of various origin.

Because of the form and scope of the *Anselmo Dedicata,* the texts are not always reproduced in their entirety but are split into several chapters and these are inserted into their proper places. Consequently, some texts are repeated more than once.

The diffusion of this collection was quite extensive for more than a century, and one may say that it governed the Italian as well as German canonical life until the publication of the *Decretum* of *Burchard of Worms. Indeed, some manuscripts in Germany prove that a certain influence was exercised by the collection until the first quarter of the 11th century, while in Italy its effects were felt until the time of *Anselm II of Lucca.

Bibliography: Fournier-LeBras 1:235–243. C. G. MOR, "Diritto romano e diritto canonico nell'età pregrazianea," in v.1 of *L'Europa e il diritto romano: Studi in memoria di Paolo Koschaker,* 2 v. (Milan 1954). A. AMANIEU, DDC 1:578–583.

[C. G. MOR]

ANSFRID, BL., Duke of Brabant, Benedictine, bishop of Utrecht; d. May 3, 1010 (feast, May 3). Ansfrid (Aufrid, Anfroi) was educated at the imperial school at Cologne. As duke, he vigorously suppressed brigandage. In 992 Ansfrid founded at Thorn a convent which his wife and daughter entered, and he himself became a monk at Heiligen, a monastery that he established. In 994 Emperor *Otto III persuaded the reluctant Ansfrid to accept the bishopric of Utrecht, where he served until 1006, when he became blind. He withdrew again to Heiligen. He died there but his relics were later stolen and now repose in St. Peter's Church in Utrecht.

Bibliography: ActSS May 1:433–435. THIETMAR VON MERSEBERG 4:31 in MGSrerGerm NS 9. A. M. ZIMMERMANN, LexThK² 1:597. Butler Th Attw 2:273.

[R. BALCH]

ANSGAR, ST.

Abbot, archbishop, "Apostle of the North;" b. near Corbie, *c.* 801; d. Bremen, Feb. 3, 865 (feast, Feb. 3). Ansgar (Anskar, Anschar) entered the *Benedictines (814?) at *Corbie, where he had been educated. After 823, he was a teacher and preacher at *Corvey. After the conversion of the Danish King Harold at the court of *Louis the Pious, Ansgar went to Denmark as a missionary; but 3 years later (829) he returned without having achieved any remarkable success. When a Swedish embassy asked for Christian missionaries, he immediately set out for that country with Witmar, another monk from Corvey. The ship on which they sailed fell into the hands of pirates, and only after great hardships did the two priests arrive at Björkö, where King Björn received them well. Among Ansgar's converts was Heriger, governor and councilor to the King. Emperor Louis recalled Ansgar 18 months later and designated him abbot of Corvey and bishop of Hamburg, a new diocese planned earlier by Charlemagne and decreed by the Reichstag at Thionville (Nov. 10, 831). Consecrated in 832 by *Drogo of Metz, Ansgar proceeded to Rome, where Pope *Gregory IV made him archbishop and the papal legate for the Scandinavian and remaining Slavic missions. In 834 Louis assigned Turholt monastery as Ansgar's training center and source of financial support for the Nordic mission, but Louis's death (840) and the Treaty of Verdun (843), which divided the Empire, deprived Ansgar of this source of income. After 13 years of work in Hamburg, Ansgar suffered his gravest setback when Northmen (845) burned Hamburg to the ground. Sweden and Denmark returned to paganism. In 847, Emperor *Louis the German appointed Ansgar to the vacant See of Bremen, which was to be united with Hamburg, although the Pope and the archbishop of Cologne actually refused to recognize this amalgamation. From his see in Bremen, Ansgar directed new missionary activities in the North. His associates, Gautbert, Bishop of Sweden, and Nithard, who had been working in Denmark and Sweden since 832, were caught in the pagan rebellion, and so it was Ansgar who traveled to Denmark, converted King Haarik, and, having obtained Louis the German's authorization and a letter of introduction from Haarik, set out for Sweden (852–853). There King Olaf cast lots to determine whether Christian missionaries should be allowed to return or not. The verdict was favorable, and the King himself was eventually won over to the Christian faith. Nithard had been killed during the persecutions, and Bishop Gautbert, a close friend, refused to return to his see. He was replaced by *Rembert, Ansgar's successor at *Bremen-Hamburg. Contrary to his wish, Ansgar was not to become a martyr; he died peacefully in Bremen and was buried in the cathedral. He was an extraordinary preacher, a modest, self-effacing priest and ascetic, a benefactor of the poor and sick, and a brilliant administrator, whom his biographer, Bishop Rembert, named a saint. Pope *Nicholas I confirmed the canonization. St. Ansgar is usually depicted with a fur collar on his episcopal robes and with a model church held in his hand.

Bibliography: MGS 2:683–725. MGSrerGerm v.51. REMBERT, *Anskar,* tr. C. H. ROBINSON (London 1921). W. LÜDTKE, "Die Verehrung des hl. Anschar," *Schriften des Vereins für Schleswigholsteinische Kirchengeschichte* 8.2 (1926) 123–162. É. DE MOREAU, *Saint Anschaire* (Louvain 1930). Zimmermann KalBen 1:159–165. Hauck 2:693–707. Baudot-Chaussin 2:73–78. Butler Th Attw 1:242–243. S. HILPISCH, LexThK² 1:597–598. ADAM OF BREMEN, *History of the Archbishops of Hamburg-Bremen,* tr. F. J. TSCHAN (New York 1959).

[S. A. SCHULZ]

ANSHELM, VALERIUS, Swiss chronicler; b. Rottweil, Württemberg, 1475; d. Bern, 1546 or 1547. Anshelm (Rued) studied at Cracow, Tübingen, and Lyons from 1492 to 1501. In Bern (1505) he taught school and in 1509 became the city doctor. Along with Berchtold Haller (1492–1536) and Niklaus Manuel (*c.* 1484–1530) he strove to spread Zwinglianism in Bern. His zeal and his wife's vocal anti-Catholicism caused his expulsion from Bern. At Rottweil he continued his reform efforts by word and letter, and in 1529 the victorious Reform party recalled him to Bern. He then revealed his desire to write chronicles of the city from 1477 to 1526 and obtained access to the archives and official requests for cooperation from neighboring cities. In the first part of the chronicles, Anshelm relied on previous writers, but added much new material from the archives and gave a broader treatment of the facts, using a popular, forceful style of writing. He is indeed biased, but his chronicles give a picture of the whole reform movement in and around Switzerland. They were published by E. Bloesch, *Die Berner Chronik der Valerius Anshelm* (6 v. 1884–1901) as part of the history of Bern.

Bibliography: F. MOSER, NDB 1:312–313. T. SCHWEGLER, LexThK² 1:598. Stern, ADB 1:483–484. A. BAYOL, DHGE 3: 502.

[D. MC ANDREWS]

ANSTRUDIS, ST.; b. *c.* 645; d. *c.* 709 (feast, Oct. 17). She was the daughter of SS. Blandinus and Salaberga. At the age of 12, when a certain Laudrannus claimed her in marriage, she sought refuge in the monastery of Notre Dame (later Saint-Jean) of Laon, where her mother was abbess (*c.* 657). At the age of 20 she succeeded her mother. The death of her brother Baldwin, deacon of Laon (*c.* 679), marked the beginning of serious difficulties in her life. She was accused of a liaison with the mayor of the palace, Ebroin, and the Bishop of Laon, Madelgarius, tried to take the abbey from her. More than once her life was in danger. At her death she was buried in one of seven churches built around her convent, and numerous miracles have been attributed to her. Her cult began soon after her death; her relics, transferred to Saint-Jean of Laon, were venerated there until the French Revolution.

Bibliography: ActSS Oct. 8:108–117. MGSrerMer 6:64–78. M. MELLEVILLE, *Histoire de la ville de Laon,* 2 v. (Laon 1846) v.2. P. FOURNIER, DHGE 5:798. J. BALTEAU, DictBiogFranc 2: 1460–61. G. JACQUEMET, *Catholicisme* 1:622. E. EWIG, LexThK² 1:601. Baudot-Chaussin 10:548–549. M. A. CALABRESE, Bibl Sanct 2:44–45.

[É. BROUETTE]

ANSUERUS, ST., abbot and martyr; b. Mecklenburg, Germany, *c.* 1040; d. Ratzeburg, Germany, July 15, 1066 (feast, July 15). He entered the *Benedictine monastery of Sankt Georg in Ratzeburg, where he was noted for his learning and piety and became abbot while still young. He devoted himself to the conversion of the *Slavs and preached the gospel to the pagans still living around Ratzeburg. Together with about 30 companions he was stoned in 1066 by pagan Wends. He begged his executioners to kill him last so that his companions would not apostatize and so that he could comfort them. His body was first interred in the crypt at Sankt Georg; but when a blind man was restored to sight at the tomb, Bishop Evermond (d. 1178) had the martyr's remains translated to the cathedral of Ratzeburg. The relics perished during the disorders of the Reformation period. Canonization was granted with papal approval by Abp. *Adalbert of Bremen. Ansuerus was included in the Schleswig and Ratzeburg Breviaries, but since the Reformation he is remembered only in monastic martyrologies. His memorials are a cross near Ratzeburg and a painting in the cathedral there.

Bibliography: ActSS July 4:97–108. Zimmermann KalBen 2:456–458. A. M. ZIMMERMANN, LexThK[2] 1:602. A. TAYLOR, DHGE 3:509.

[G. SPAHR]

ANTELAMI, BENEDETTO, greatest Romanesque sculptor in northern Italy; b. *c.* 1150; d. *c.* 1230. Antelami may have come from the region around Lake Como. There is no documentation for his work apart from his signature as sculptor on the marble "Deposition from the Cross" (Parma cathedral, 1178) and the architrave of the north portal of the Parma baptistery. The "Deposition," his earliest work, may originally have formed part of a pulpit or altar. In style and iconography the relief is dependent upon direct knowledge of Romanesque sculpture in Provence, e.g., S. Gilles and S. Trophime at Arles. Antelami's greatest work is the octagonal baptistery for the cathedral of Parma (begun 1196; dedicated 1270), for which he seems to have been architect as well as sculptor. The novel iconographic program of the three portals of the cathedral is the most complex one in Italy up to that time and includes on the west portal the first Italian sculptured "Last Judgment" tympanum. On the south portal are reliefs of the sun and moon derived from antique sources and also the legend of Barlaam and Josaphat, an allegory derived from Buddhist thought. A frieze with reliefs of animals surrounds the baptistery. The sculptural decoration is carried into the interior, with tympana, capitals, reliefs, and carved altar frontal. Personifications of the months, carved almost in the round and now placed between columns of the lower gallery, were perhaps originally in niches. Numerous assistants were required for the work, yet there is a unity of design that shows Antelami's close supervision. It is possible that Antelami traveled to France twice, the first time, early in his career, before executing the "Deposition"; and again, before the Parma baptistery program. There the sculpture is so closely integrated with the architecture that the influence of cathedral sculpture of the Ile-de-France is suggested. Three buildings have been attributed to him as architect: the baptistery at Parma; the cathedral of Borgo San Donnino (begun 1179); and S. Andrea, Vercelli (1219–27), the central tympanum of which is by Antelami.

Bibliography: G. DE FRANCOVICH, *Benedetto Antelami* (Milan 1952). **Illustration credit:** Alinari-Art Reference Bureau.

[M. M. SCHAEFER]

ANTENUPTIAL AGREEMENTS, U.S. LAW OF

The Catholic Church, as a condition precedent to marriage between a Catholic and a non-Catholic, once required that both parties execute in writing a promise that children born of the union will be reared as Catholics. The purpose of this article is to explore the extent to which civil courts enforced compliance with such a promise while this Church legislation prevailed.

Benedetto Antelami, "The Deposition from the Cross," façade of the cathedral at Parma, signed and dated 1178.

English Law. The issue first arose in the English courts during the latter half of the 19th century. In a series of decisions this rule was evolved: "As to the antenuptial contract that the children of the marriage should be brought up Roman Catholics, it has been decided over and over again that it is not in any legal sense binding," *In re Violet Nevins,* 60 L. J. Ch. 542 (1891); 2 Ch. 299; 6 5 L. T. 35. It has been suggested that anti-Catholicism was primarily responsible for this holding, but this is not tenable. The doctrine was grounded in the common law theory of the father's supremacy in all aspects of family life, which included the prerogative of deciding the religious affiliation of his children. In *Andrews v. Salt,* L. R. 8 Ch. App. 622 (1873), a leading case on the subject, it was said that "a father cannot bind himself conclusively by contract to exercise, in all events, in a particular way, rights which the law gives him for the benefit of his children." He may repudiate the antenuptial promise during life and it would not be binding after his death. Where it was clear that a non-Catholic father had desired his children reared in conformity with the antenuptial promise, the courts would enforce it after his death. This was evidenced in the case of *In re Clark,* 51 L. J. Ch. Div. 762, 47 L. T. 84 (1882). In that case the chancery court, over the objections of non-Catholic relatives, upheld the right of a Catholic widow to rear children as Catholics, the non-Catholic husband having, during his lifetime, clearly indicated his intent that the antenuptial promise be honored.

Parliament meanwhile abolished the ancient common law supremacy of the father [Guardianship of Infants Act (1925) 15 and 16 George V, c. 45]. It does not appear that any cases involving the antenuptial promise have come before the courts since that time.

American Law. In the United States, efforts to enforce the antenuptial promise have encountered different problems. The common law doctrine of the father's absolute supremacy had been abandoned in practically all American jurisdictions before the promise became a subject for litigation. Through statute and judicial decision the wife has attained legal equality, and American courts regard parents as "joint guardians of their children, with equal rights of custody and control" (39 *American Jurisprudence* 599, "Parent and Child"). Thus, the issue presented by differences over the promise becomes one requiring adjustment between parties who under the law have equal authority. Inasmuch as American decisions on the subject are framed against a background of principles applicable to custody and control of children in general, a very brief review of such principles will be helpful.

American courts will not interfere ordinarily in disputes between parents over the rearing of children. "Dispute between parents when it does not involve anything immoral or harmful to the welfare of the child is beyond the reach of the law. The vast majority of matters concerning the upbringing of children must be left to the conscience, patience and self-restraint of father and mother. No end of difficulties would arise should judges try to tell parents how to bring up their children" (*Sisson v. Sisson,* 271 N.Y. 285).

As a corollary, American courts generally hold that, when custody of children falls to one of the spouses through death or judicial award, the parent having custody is responsible for the rearing and education of the children. "The essence of custody is the companionship of the child and the right to make decisions regarding his care, control, education, health and *religion*" (17A *American Jurisprudence* 23, "Divorce and Separation"; italics added.) This is not a completely arbitrary rule, as courts, when awarding custody, will sometimes impose conditions relative to the rearing or education of the child; however, they do not like to do so. It is clear that the element of custody looms large in all cases involving the antenuptial promise. If custody is awarded to the Catholic spouse, there will be little difficulty about the child's rearing in that faith.

"Ordinarily the custody of an infant of tender years, or of a girl of more mature years, should be given to the mother if she is found to be fit to have custody and can supply a proper home" (17A *American Jurisprudence* 14, "Divorce and Separation"). In consequence, most American cases on the antenuptial promise, when in connection with divorce or separation, involve efforts by a Catholic husband to enforce it against a non-Catholic wife.

When one parent dies, the rule is equally strong that the surviving spouse is entitled to custody unless there are grave reasons to the contrary. Courts are not inclined to impose conditions on a surviving parent relative to the rearing of children.

American courts have differed in their attitude toward the antenuptial promise. The issue has been presented to courts, the decisions of which are preserved for record in at least 12 states (Connecticut, Delaware, Georgia, Illinois, Iowa, Kansas, Maine, Missouri, New Jersey, New York, Ohio, and Pennsylvania).

Cases indicate that it may come before the court in one of three fairly distinct patterns. The first occurs when, the Catholic spouse having died, efforts are made to compel an unwilling non-Catholic parent to honor the promise. The second occurs when, both parents having died, Catholic relatives seek to compel the child's Catholic rearing. The third, and most frequent, is in connection with divorce or separation proceedings where child custody is awarded to the non-Catholic.

Non-Catholic Surviving Spouse. The first pattern is undoubtedly the most difficult because of the reluctance of American courts to interfere in the domestic affairs of a home. There have been two cases involving this situation. In *Brewer v. Cary,* 148 Missouri Appeals 193 (1910) the Catholic mother had died and the non-Catholic father chose to rear the children as Protestants. The maternal grandfather sued in equity to compel the father to rear the children as Catholics in pursuance of his promise. The Missouri Supreme Court held that courts had no authority to interfere with the prerogative of a surviving parent to determine the rearing and education of a child in his care. "In no case have any of our courts directed a guardian remaining in control and custody of the ward, whether the guardian is the father or the mother, or one appointed by the court, as to what particular course of education or training, secular or religious, is to be pursued." This was determinative of the issue, but the court went on to say: "We might rest our decision on the above propositions, but for the fact that counsel have made a very strong appeal and able argument in support of the merits of the case, resting their contention on the enforceability of the antenuptial agreement between the defendant and his deceased wife." The court then cited the English cases, declaring that it could not "enforce a duty that is one of conscience. Nor in determining what is for the welfare of the infant, determine that on considerations of religion."

In *Denton v. James,* 107 Kan. 729 (1920), faced with a somewhat similar situation, the Kansas Supreme Court denied relief to petitioning Catholic relatives, saying in part: "The agreement of the child's father and mother that the child should be reared in the Catholic faith was a commendable compromise between the natural guardians, who under the statute of this state had equal authority. On the death of the mother, the father's right to educate his child became paramount and the agreement was merely persuasive upon him."

Catholic Relative. Again, there have been at least two recorded decisions involving the pattern where both spouses are dead. The first of these, and probably the earliest recorded American decision on the subject, was *In re Luck,* 10 Ohio Decisions 1 (1900), decided by an Ohio probate court. A non-Catholic father who had executed the promise survived his Catholic wife by 4 years, during which period two small children were cared for by non-Catholic relatives. On his death, Catholic relatives filed action in probate court seeking custody of the children, then aged 4 and 7, alleging moral responsibility to have them reared in conformity with the promise. The court spoke favorably of the promise itself: "As between the parties to this marital relation, when the wife was living, the binding force and inviolability of this compact would be recognized by all courts and sanctioned by the moral sense of mankind." However, it refused to take the children from the care of the Protestant relatives with whom they had made their home since the mother's death.

Commonwealth v. McClelland, 70 Pa. Sup. 273 (1913), involved a somewhat similar factual pattern, except that the widowed Catholic mother survived but was mentally incompetent (thus equating this pattern from a legal viewpoint) and the children had been in Protestant surroundings for an even longer period, 9 years. Again the court took a favorable view of the promise, as between the spouses, but judged it would be harmful to the children to change their custody.

These two decisions are indecisive on the question of the promise itself, as the issue of custody was paramount, with implications relative to the general welfare of the children. It is possible that, presented with a more favorable factual situation and lacking the element of long delay, the courts might have taken a different view.

Divorce or Separation. The two earliest American decisions involving the antenuptial promise in connection with separation proceedings were handed down by trial divisions of the New York Supreme Court, which held it legally enforceable. *Ramon v. Ramon,* 34 N.Y. Supp. 2d 100 (1942); *Shearer v. Shearer,* 73 N.Y. Supp. 337 (1947). In both, the custody of children was awarded to a Protestant wife, but subject to conditions that the children be reared as Catholics. In the Ramon opinion, it was said: "An antenuptial agreement providing for the Catholic faith and education of the children of the parties, in reliance upon which a Catholic has irrevocably changed the status of the Catholic party, is an enforceable contract having a valid consideration."

A similar decree in a later case was subsequently modified to permit the child to decide for himself what church to attend. The modification was sustained by the Court of Appeals, *Martin v. Martin,* 308 New York 136 (1954). This was not a reversal of the Ramon and Shearer decisions, because it was based on the court's view that the boy, then 12 years old, should be permitted to select his own religious affiliation. In *Miles v. Liebolt,* 230 N.Y. Supp. 2d 342 (1962), a trial court refused to order a wife having custody to rear the child in conformity with the promise on the ground that as her other children, by a subsequent marriage, were being reared as Protestants, "it would be confusing and, indeed, dangerous."

However, in *Gluckstern v. Gluckstern,* 220 N.Y. Supp. 623 (1961), another New York Court held a mother in contempt because she sought to induce her 12-year-old son to become a Christian Scientist in violation of a separation agreement, judicially ratified, which provided that he be reared in the Jewish faith. While this case did not involve an antenuptial promise, the applicable principles were similar.

The Court of Appeals, New York's highest tribunal, has not yet adjudicated directly on the issue; hence the antenuptial promise maintains a tenuous foothold in that jurisdiction.

In Illinois there has been no direct adjudication. In *Smith v. Smith,* 340 Ill. App. 636, an appellate court held that the action of a trial court in refusing to award custody to the Catholic husband "because of wife's alleged breach of agreement that child should be enrolled in a Catholic school . . . was not an abuse of discretion, in view of evidence . . . that wife in response to interrogation by Chancellor had agreed to enroll child in a Catholic parochial school."

In two subsequent cases, while there was no antenuptial promise involved, the Illinois Supreme Court held that decrees of trial courts, specifying the religious rearing of children, were legally enforceable (*Gottlieb v. Gottlieb,* 31 Illinois Appellate 2d 120; *Taylor v. Taylor,* 32 Illinois Appellate 2d 45.)

Outside of New York and Illinois the legal enforcement of the antenuptial promise has been denied in separation proceedings. The issue had been presented under various aspects. In all cases the husband was the Catholic party. Usually, he sought custody, alleging the promise as a ground thereof; in cases when the wife was awarded custody, the husband asked that she be required to rear the children as Catholics. Such applications were denied in *Boerger v. Boerger,* 26 New Jersey Superior Court 90 (1953); *Dumais v. Dumais,* 152 Maine 24 (1956); *Wojnarowicz v. Wojnarowicz,* 48 New Jersey Superior Courts 349 (1958); *Stanton v. Stanton,* 213 Georgia 545 (1957); *Wood v. Wood,* 168 A.2d 102 (Del. 1961).

Lynch v. Uhlenhopp, 248 Iowa 68 (1956), and *Hackett v. Hackett,* 4 Ohio Opinions 2d 245 168 Ohio State Reports 373 (1958), were cases in which the spouses, following initiation of divorce proceedings, entered into stipulations in connection with the divorce decree, conceding custody to the Protestant mother, but with proviso that the children be reared as Catholics in conformity with the antenuptial promise. In both cases, the wife having failed to observe this covenant, the husband filed action for contempt, and the appellate court denied relief. In *McLoughlin v. McLoughlin,* 20 Conn. Superior Court 274 (1957), a Catholic husband brought habeas corpus for custody of a small child being cared for by his wife, the couple having separated, alleging violation of the promise as one of his grounds. Relief was denied.

The reasoning by which courts have reached these conclusions has not been uniform. There was some formal reliance on the English precedents, but in general these were not a determining factor. As we have noted, American courts tend to award to the mother the custody of children of tender age, except in unusual circumstances. Courts, when so awarding custody, are reluctant to impose detailed conditions on the custodian. This was a factor in most cases. "The parent to whom custody is awarded must logically and naturally be the one who lawfully exercises the greatest control and influence over the child" (*Boerger v. Boerger, supra*). In *Lynch v. Uhlenhopp, supra,* a majority of the court felt that civil judges were not competent to supervise the details of a child's religious training. However, this was a 5 to 4 decision; the dissenting justices gave the opinion that the trial court's decree should have been enforced.

In addition, some courts have cited the Church-State issue. The Missouri Supreme Court in *Brewer v. Cary, supra,* said it could not make a "determination between religions." In several decisions the enforcement of the antenuptial promise is viewed as an unconstitutional establishment of religion, citing the doctrine of *McCollum v. Board of Education,* 333 U.S. 203, where it was held that released-time religious instruction might not be imparted on public school premises.

Religious Heritage. From these facts it is clear that the antenuptial promise has not been sustained in most jurisdictions. However, there are trends which might portend a more favorable attitude in certain situations. There is a strong doctrine, both statutory and judicial, that children should be reared in the faith of their parents. Adoption statutes of many states provide that a child be committed only to persons of its own faith or of the faith of its parents. Courts have construed such statutes as either highly persuasive or mandatory: *Ellis v. McCoy,* 332 Mass. 254 (1955).

In addition, there is a developing sentiment that a child baptized or otherwise inducted into a religious denomination acquires a status cognizable in court. "I find that no one, not even the parents, have the right to deny an immature child who has been baptized a Roman Catholic, the privilege of being reared in Catholicity" (Statement of Probate Court, *Pereira v. Pereira,* No. D-16741, Probate Court, Bristol County, Massachusetts, 1954).

In the *Matter of Dennis Glavis,* 121 N.Y.S. 2d 12 (1953), a domestic relations court held that when a child, adjudged as neglected, had been circumcised as a Jew, "It cannot be deprived of its Jewishness by an exposure to the culture of another religion prior to the age of reason." Consequently, the act of the father in having it subsequently baptized did not change the necessity of having it committed to a Jewish institution.

In *Gluckstern v. Gluckstern,* cited under the divorce pattern, the court, speaking of the mother's alleged proselytism, said: "I am of the opinion that this infant should not be permitted to abandon so easily the faith he was born in."

This doctrine is particularly applicable in situations where parents are deceased, but, as indicated in the Gluckstern case, it can be cited also in matrimonial proceedings. It is based on the status of the child, but the fact of parental consent, evidenced by the antenuptial promise, adds to its effectiveness.

The constitutional argument against recognition of the promise is of doubtful validity. It is difficult to understand how there can be any "establishment of religion" involved. With respect to an infringement of the "free exercise of religion" clause, it may be contended that the victim of any such violation is the child who is denied an opportunity to continue in the religion into which he was inducted with full parental consent.

To what extent courts would accept these views, or otherwise adhere to the doctrine of the Ramon and Shearer decisions, is problematical. For the present the issue is academic, since Church law no longer requires a written promise.

Bibliography: L. M. FRIEDMAN, "Parental right to control the religious education of a child," *Harvard Law Review* 29 (1916) 485–500. R. J. WHITE, *The Legal Effect of Ante-nuptial Promises in Mixed Marriages* (Washington 1932). L. PFEFFER, "Religion in the Upbringing of Children," *Boston University Law Review* 35 (1955) 333–393. "Parent's Right to Prescribe Religious Education of Children," *DePaul Law Review* 3 (1953) 83–89. J. F. SMITH, "Contracts for Religious Education of Children," *Cleveland Marshall Law Review* 7 (1958) 534–540.

[V. C. ALLRED]

ANTEPENDIUM, or frontal hanging (*pallium, paliotto*), a piece of precious material, richly ornamented, used to cover the entire front of an altar. With the three linen cloths it makes up the "clothing" of the altar. The use of the antependium is probably derived from the practice of the early Church of covering the table-altar with a colored fabric. The antependium has been an element in the decoration of the altar from the 4th century in the East and the 5th in the West. It is prescribed for altars by the Ceremonial of Bishops 1 (1.12.11.16). It used to be prescribed by a rubric of the Roman Missal, but the new Code of Rubrics (1960) no longer mentions it in dealing with the preparation of the altar for Mass (526). Until the 13th century the color for the antependium was not determined, but since then it has been fixed as the color of the office of the day. There are two exceptions to this rule: at an altar where the Blessed Sacrament is exposed the frontal must be white; for a Requiem Mass at an altar where the Blessed Sacrament is reserved the frontal should be violet, not black.

Bibliography: L. MORTARI, EncCatt 9:635–637. J. B. O'CONNELL, *Church Building and Furnishing* (Notre Dame, Ind. 1955) 192–196. J. BRAUN, *I Paramenti sacri,* tr. G. ALLIOD (Turin 1914) 171–176. P. RADÓ, *Enchiridion liturgicum,* 2 v. (Rome 1961) 2:1410.

Illustration credits: (*a*) R. V. Schoder, SJ. (*b*) Courtesy of the Walters Art Gallery, Baltimore. (*c*) Museum of New Mexico —Laura Gilpin.

[J. B. O'CONNELL]

ANTERUS, POPE, ST., *c.* 235 (feast, Jan. 3). The Liber pontificalis says he was a Greek, son of a Romulus, and that he was interested in collecting acts of martyrs. Its report that he was a martyr is untrustworthy. The *Liberian catalogue says that he "fell asleep," and he does not appear in lists of martyrs. He was the first pope buried in the bishops' crypt of the Cemetery of Callistus; apparently the body of *Pon-

(a)

(b)

(c)

Antependia: (a) of gold and precious stones, 9th century, in Sant' Ambrogio, Milan; (b) of painted and gilded wood, showing Christ in Majesty surrounded by scenes from the life of St. Martin, Catalonian, c. *1250; (c) of wool embroidery on cotton, Southwestern United States, 18th or 19th century.*

Inscription on the tomb of Pope Anterus, in the Cemetery of Callistus, Rome.

tianus, his predecessor, was buried there later. His feast does not appear in ancient calendars or Roman books of the liturgy before the 9th century.

Bibliography: EUSEBIUS, *Hist. Eccl.* 6.29. P. GOGGI, EncCatt 1:1428–29. G. SCHWAIGER, LexThK² 1:602–603. J. P. KIRSCH, DHGE 3:520–521. **Illustration credit:** Pontificia Commissione di Archeologia Sacra.

[E. G. WELTIN]

ANTHELM OF CHIGNIN, ST., Carthusian reformer; b. Chignin (Savoie), France, 1107; d. June 26, 1178 (feast, June 26). Having become a Carthusian at the charterhouse of Portes, 1136–37, he was sent to rebuild the recently damaged La Grande-*Chartreuse. He became its seventh prior (1139) and the first minister-general of the Carthusian Order (1142). He revived discipline and restored prosperity, creating five new charterhouses; but encountering difficulties with Pope Eugene III, he resigned in 1151. Anthelm served as prior at Portes from 1152 to 1154, and then was made bishop of Belley, France, in 1163 by *Alexander III, whom he had supported against the Emperor's papal candidate. He was appointed legate to *Henry II of England in the hope that he might reconcile the King with Thomas *Becket, but Anthelm was unable to go. In 1175 *Frederick Barbarossa bestowed on him and his bishop successors the title of Prince of the Holy Roman Empire. His cult has been observed by the *Carthusians since 1607. The elevation of his relics took place at Belley in 1630.

Bibliography: ActSS June 7:201–219. L. MARCHAL, *Vie de Saint Anthelme* (Paris 1878). S. AUTORE, DHGE 3:523–525. L. ALLOING, DictBiogFranc 2:1478–80. Baudot-Chaussin 6:444–447. R. AIGRAIN, *Catholicisme* 1:625–626. H. WOLTER, LexThK² 1:603. Butler Th Attw 2:650–652. Réau IAC 3.1:99–100. C. VENS, BiblSanct 2:48–50.

[É. BROUETTE]

ANTHELMI, JOSEPH, learned ecclesiastical historian, whose works are still highly regarded; b. Fréjus, France, July 27, 1648; d. there, June 21, 1697. A theology student of François de *La Chaise at Lyons, Anthelmi received his doctorate in theology in Paris (1688). After his ordination in Fréjus in 1673, he preferred the life of a scholar to that of church administrator. Accordingly, he devoted his life to the history of the Church, particularly of his province. Within a few years he published *De initiis ecclesiae Forojuliensis* (1680). His next few works were in local hagiography (St. Antiolus and St. Tropez). For the next few years he became involved in polemics with P. Quesnel over the authorship of several religious works, among which was the Athanasian Creed. In 1693 Anthelmi published a study of St. Martin of Tours. His scholarly activity was interrupted in 1694 by 3 years of fruitful conciliation as vicar-general of the Diocese of Pamiers. In 1697, exhausted by years of work and apparently ill from tuberculosis, Anthelmi returned to Fréjus. In addition to his many works, Anthelmi left manuscripts and notes, several of which were published as late as 1872.

Bibliography: R. D'AMAT, DictBiogFranc 2:1467. F. BONNARD, DHGE 3:515–516, contains list of works. Hurter Nomencl 2:540.

[R. J. MARION]

ANTHEMIUS

The name of many saints, ecclesiastics, and statesmen in the Church. The following are significant:

(1) Anthemius (Anthemus, Attenius, Aptemius) of Poitiers, St., is named as 13th in the Episcopal List, which according to L. Duchesne is subject to great caution during this period. Nothing is known of his life, but his feast has been celebrated in the Dioceses of Poitiers and Saintes since the 17th century. There is no authentic document supporting the claim that he died in Jonzac *c.* 400 (feast, Dec. 3).

(2) Anthemius, prefect of the Orient under Arcadius (fl. 400–414), undertook a successful embassy to the Persians, served as *magister officiorum* and patrician (406), and directed the government of the empire when Theodosius II became emperor in 408 at the age of 7. He was praised by St. *John Chrysostom for his rectitude (PG 52:699). He pushed the Huns beyond the Danube, organized a fleet, furnished Constantinople with a protective wall (413), and erected the Baths of Honorius and the church of St. Thomas. In 414 he ceded the government to Empress *Pulcheria and disappeared from history.

(3) Anthemius of Constantia, Cyprus (fl. end of 5th century), is renowned for having discovered the body of St. *Barnabas in 488. He used the occasion as a support for the claim of apostolicity, and therefore independence from Antioch, for the Church in Cyprus. The account of this miraculous event, written by Alexander, a 6th-century monk of Cyprus, in his encomium of St. Barnabas describes the finding as a result of a dream and states that a copy of the Gospel of Matthew was found on Barnabas's chest. Emperor *Zeno exempted Cyprus from the ecclesiastical jurisdiction of Antioch, and Anthemius built a basilica and established the feast of St. Barnabas on June 11.

Bibliography: (1) P. DE MONSABERT, DHGE 3:525. R. AIGRAIN, *Catholicisme* 1:626. (2) L. BRÉHIER, DHGE 3:525–526. (3) ActSS June 2:444–446. R. AIGRAIN, DHGE 3:526–527.

[F. X. MURPHY]

ANTHIMUS

The name of many saints, ecclesiastics, and statesmen in the Church. The following are significant:

(1) Anthimus, St., bishop of Nicomedia, martyr, beheaded in the Diocletian persecution of 303 (feast, April 27; Greek, Sept. 3). Emperor Justinian I built a church in his honor, and the legend of SS. Domna and Indes (PG 116:1073–76) credits him with a letter written to his community during the persecution of Diocletian.

(2) Anthimus, St., priest and martyr during the Diocletian persecution (feast, May 11). His *Acta* re-

count a series of conversions among Roman officials because of his courage.

(3) Anthimus of Tyana, 4th-century bishop, adversary and friend of St. *Basil of Caesarea, supported Basil's anti-Arian offensive, but opposed his jurisdictional arrangements, particularly in reference to the Church in *Armenia.

(4) Anthimus, St., hymnographer, member of a pious association of laymen called the Spoudaioi, was given to keeping vigils in the church of St. Irene in Constantinople. He became a priest (after 457) and the leader of the Chalcedonian party and was celebrated as the author of liturgical tropes or hymns for popular chanting (feast, Synaxary of Constantinople, June 7).

(5) Anthimus I, patriarch of Constantinople (535–536). Named bishop of Trebizond in 533, he was transferred to Constantinople at the instance of Empress *Theodora in June 535. Because of his Monophysite leanings and epistolary relations with *Severus of Antioch and *Theodosius of Alexandria, he was deposed by a synod of Constantinople under Pope *Agapetus I, and the decision was implemented by *Justinian I, who exiled him. His profession of faith is preserved by *Zachary the Rhetor (CSCO 2:96–117).

(6) Anthimus, a 14th-century anti-Latin Bulgarian archbishop, was a theologian.

(7) Anthimus II to VII were patriarchs of Constantinople. *Anthimus II* (June–October 1623) was supported by French policy in his opposition to Cyril Lucaris. He died at Mt. Athos, 1628. *Anthimus III* (1822–24); b. Naxos, *c.* 1760; d. Smyrna, 1842. He was exiled in 1824. *Anthimus IV,* Bambakis (1840–41 and 1848–52); b. Constantinople, *c.* 1788; d. Isle of Princes, 1878. He became metropolitan of Iconium (1825), of Larissa (1835), and of Nicomedia (1837). Elected patriarch in February 1840, he was deposed in 1841, but reelected in 1848 and deposed again, Nov. 11, 1852, when he retired to the Isle of Princes, where he died a nonagenarian. *Anthimus V* (1841–42); b. Neochorion, Turkey; d. Constantinople, June 1842. He was metropolitan of Agathopolis (1815), Anchialos (1821), and Cyzicus (1831) and was elected patriarch of Constantinople in May 1841. *Anthimus VI,* Joannides (1845–48; 1853–55; 1871–73); b. Isle of Koutali, *c.* 1790; d. Candili, 1878. A monk on Mt. Athos, he was elected and deposed three times. A decisive opponent of Bulgarian orthodoxy, he retired to Candili in 1873 and died there almost a nonagenarian. *Anthimus VII,* Tsatsos (1895–96); b. Janina, *c.* 1835; d. Halki, December 1913. He was a renowned preacher and theologian. Bishop of Paramythia (1869), metropolitan of Ainos (1878), then of Korytsa, Leros, and Kalymnos, he served 22 months as patriarch and retired to Halki. He rejected the ecumenical efforts of Pope Leo XIII's encyclical *Praeclara gratulationes* (June 20, 1894) in a letter published September 1895 (*see* BYZANTINE THEOLOGY, II).

Bibliography: (1) H. RAHNER, LexThK² 1:603–604. Altaner 248. R. JANIN, DHGE 3:530. G. MERCATI, StTest 5 (1901) 87–98. M. RICHARD, MélSciRel 6 (1949) 5–28. (2) R. JANIN, DHGE 3:529–530. ActSS May 2:612–614. (3) R. JANIN, DHGE 3:534. J. B. LIGHTFOOT, DCB 1:119. (4) S. PÉTRIDÈS, ÉchosOr 4 (1900) 228; 7 (1904) 341–342; DHGE 3:531. K. GROSS, LexThK² 1:604. (5) Stein-Palanque HistBEmp 2:381–388. R. JANIN, DHGE 3:531. H. RAHNER, LexThK² 1:603. (6) Krumbacher 110. S. SALAVILLE, DHGE 3:532. (7) R. JANIN, DHGE 3:532–534.

[F. X. MURPHY]

ANTHIMUS OF TREBIZOND

ANTHIMUS OF TREBIZOND, Monophysite bishop of Trebizond, named patriarch of Constantinople in 535, and deposed in 536; d. after 548. As bishop of Trebizond he participated in the Colloquy of Constantinople (532) in which *Justinian I attempted to achieve agreement between the orthodox and the Monophysite bishops. Although he participated on the Catholic side, Anthimus leaned toward the party of Severus of Antioch, and Empress *Theodora (1) had him named patriarch of Constantinople to succeed Epiphanius (d. June 5, 535) despite the canons that forbade transfer from one see to another. Anthimus promised to stay in communion with Rome, but sent an encyclical letter to the two Monophysite patriarchs, *Severus of Antioch in exile, and *Theodosius of Alexandria. Pope *Agapetus I, who arrived in Constantinople in early March 536, refused to communicate with Anthimus and demanded his deposition. In a synod held by the Pope, Anthimus was declared contumacious and deprived of his powers as priest and bishop. He was replaced by Mennas as patriarch on March 13, 536, and lived an ascetical life for at least 12 more years in Constantinople under the protection of Empress Theodora. Of his writings, fragments of a tract sent to Justinian I concerning the doctrine of one energy and one will in Christ and his synodal letter to Severus have been preserved. His profession of faith is recorded by Zachary Rhetor (*Hist. Eccl.* 9.21; 25: CSCO 2:96–117).

Bibliography: H. RAHNER, LexThK² 1:603. Caspar 2:222–223. Grill-Bacht Konz 2:159–162. Hefele-Leclercq 2.2:1142–55. Beck KTLBR 392–393. Stein-Palanque HistBEmp 2:381–385, 388.

[P. ROCHE]

ANTHONY, PATRIARCHS OF CONSTANTINOPLE (I–IV)

Anthony I, Kassimatas, iconoclast and patriarch, January 821 to *c.* Jan. 21, 837. As the son of a priest shoemaker, he became a teacher, then a monk, probably hegumen (abbot) of the Monastery of the Metropolitou in Petrion before 815, and later, apparently bishop of Sylaion. An iconoclast because of ambition, he aided Emperor *Leo V (813–820) against Patriarch *Nicephoras I, took part in the Iconoclastic Synod of 815 under Theodotus Melissenus, and became patriarch in 821. He excommunicated Job, Patriarch of Antioch, because he had crowned the usurping Emperor Thomas, who was supported by the Arab Emir Mamun.

Anthony II, Kauleas, patriarch, August 893 to Feb. 12, 901. At 12 he followed his father as a monk and later as hegumen in the Monastery of the Mother of God, whose title was later changed to Kalliou Kauleos (PG 117:308d). He instigated the canonization of the Athonite monk St. Blasius of Amorion (*c.* 894), and in the synod of September 899 received opponents of *Photius into communion with the Church in the presence of two papal legates. He also strengthened the power of the Byzantine patriarchate over the Church in Dalmatia.

Anthony III, the Studite, patriarch, March 974, to *c.* April 979; d. Studiu, Mt. Athos, 983. A monk in the Studiu monastery, he became Syncellus to Patriarch Basil I and after the latter's deposition by Emperor *John I Tzimisces, patriarch. He supported the antipope Boniface VII against Pope *Benedict VII and was forced into retirement (979), possibly for having sided with Bardas Sclerus in his conflict with Emperor Basil II.

He left a *Monitum* to his monks on confession and the monastic account of conscience, and fought against the simonaical activity connected with taxes for *Hagia Sophia.

Anthony IV, patriarch, 1389 to 1390, and 1391 to 1397; d. Constantinople, May 1397. Named patriarch in January 1389, he was deposed in July 1390, but he managed to regain imperial favor and returned to power in March 1391. He played a primary role in supporting the Byzantine sovereignty, despite the fact that Constantinople had become a vassal of the Turks under Bajezid. He controverted the statement of Basil I, Grand Duke of Russia, "We have a Church but no Emperor," with the claim that the Apostle Peter's admonition, "Fear God, honor the Emperor" (1 Pt 2.13) referred specifically to the ecumenical ruler of Byzantium. He tried to regulate the conflict between the various Byzantine-rite churches; held the Patriarchate of Alexandria in obedience to Constantinople despite the divisive efforts of the Sultan of Egypt; and not only wrote to King Jagellon of Poland (January 1397), the Hungarian Monarch, and the Metropolitan of Kiev, begging their assistance against the Turks, but encouraged Manual II to make a journey to the West in 1399 for this purpose. He also laid down regulations for the conduct of monks, particularly in regard to their novitiate and their clothing.

Bibliography: P. Joannou, LexThK² 1:669–670. V. Grumel, ed., *Les Regestes des Actes du Patriarcat de Constantinople* (Istanbul 1932–) 1.2:412, 594–597, 798–799; ÉchosOr 33 (1934) 257–288; 35 (1936) 5–42. R. Janin, *La Géographie ecclésiastique de l'Empire byzantin,* v.1.3 (Paris 1953); DHGE 3:746, 796–797. Beck KTLBR 584. F. Miklosich and J. Müller, eds., *Acta et diplomata graeca medii aevi,* 6 v. (Vienna 1860–90) 2:112–291. Ostrogorsky 181–186, 491–493.

[P. JOANNOU]

ANTHONY BONFADINI, BL., Franciscan preacher; b. Ferrara, Italy, *c.* 1402; d. Cotignola (Romagna), Dec. 1, 1482 (feast, Dec. 1, in Diocese of Faenza and among *Franciscans). He left a noble family, to become a Franciscan at the friary of the Holy Spirit, Ferrara, in 1439. Having obtained a doctorate in theology, he became a renowned preacher in Italy and a missionary in the Holy Land. On his return he preached at Cotignola, where he died at a pilgrim's hospice. Mariano of Florence praised his kindness and peacemaking spirit. One miracle was attributed to him during his lifetime, several others after his death. He protected Cotignola from calamities in 1630, 1688, and 1696. His body was transferred (1495) into the church of the Observant friary founded by Bl. *Angelo Carletti di Chivasso. A tomb (1631) and a special chapel were erected (1666). The diocesan process was held at Faenza (1894), and Leo XIII confirmed his cult (1901). The recognition of his intact body took place in 1902.

Bibliography: L. N. Cittadella, *Vita del beato Antonio Bonfadini da Ferrara* (Ferrara 1838). L. Oliger, DHGE 3:763. W. Forster, LexThK² 1:672. Butler ThAttw 4:460–461.

[J. CAMBELL]

ANTHONY OF EGYPT, ST., primitive Egyptian hermit; b. Comus, Egypt, 250; d. Egyptian Desert, 356. Anthony found school distasteful and shunned the companionship of other children. His well-to-do parents died when he was about 20, and he was left in charge of a younger sister. He gave himself over to prayer, and on hearing the Gospel message in church, he divided his property, keeping only enough to support his sister, whom he entrusted to a community of pious women. He practiced the religious life close to home and attached himself to an aged solitary, from whom he had the first lessons in the ascetic life. Later he went off in solitude to some empty tombs at a distance from the village. Here he remained some 12 or 15 years and was tempted by the devil. Then he moved to the desert and lived in an abandoned fort, where he was visited by people who had heard stories of his holiness and power over demons. He became their director in the spiritual life and gave them a long discourse, probably in the Coptic tongue since he knew no Greek.

This discourse on ascetic theology deals with the means of overcoming temptation and with the gift of the discernment of good and evil spirits. Later Anthony offered himself as a victim for martyrdom during the persecution of the Emperor Maximin Daja. He assisted the Christians in prison with material and spiritual solace, but was not called upon to suffer and recognized later that it took great spiritual courage to be a daily martyr to the flesh and one's own conscience.

He left his mountain retreat to combat the Arian heresy in Alexandria, and he spent his life partly in solitude, partly in journeys to his brethren to exhort them in the religious life. When he felt his end drawing near, he took two companions and retired into solitude. He died at the age of about 105 years.

"St. Anthony of Egypt Distributing His Wealth to the Poor," painting by the Sienese artist Sassetta (active 1423–50), tempera on wood, 18⅝ *by* 13⅝ *inches.*

The *Vita Antonii* was written by St. Athanasius one year after Anthony's death and influenced the whole Christian world. A Latin translation made by Evagrius, Bishop of Antioch (d. 392), spread through the Roman Empire, and both St. *Jerome and St. *Augustine knew of it. It was modeled on Greek biography, which had sought to idealize an important figure in public life.

Athanasius saw in Anthony the ideal monk, who could prove his divine vocation by discerning spirits and by performing miracles—which he never claimed for himself but always attributed to God. Though illustrated with preternatural and, to modern tastes, bizarre incidents, the biographical data appear authentic. This vita influenced subsequent hagiography and literary and pictorial art as well.

Bibliography: ATHANASIUS, *Vita Antonii,* PG 26:835–978; *The Life of Saint Anthony,* tr. and ed. R. T. MEYER (AncChrWr 10; 1950). A. KLAUS, LexThK² 1:667–669. L. BOUYER, *La Vie de Saint Antoine* (Paris 1950). Quasten Patr 3:39–45. H. DÖRRIES, "Die *Vita Antonii* als Geschichtsquelle," *Nachrichten der Akademie der Wissenschaften in Göttingen* 14 (1949) 359–410. G. BARDY, DictSpirAscMyst 1:702–708. **Illustration credit:** National Gallery of Art, Samuel H. Kress Collection.

[R. T. MEYER]

ANTHONY OF THE HOLY GHOST, Discalced Carmelite, moral theologian, canonist, spiritual writer, and bishop; b. Monte Moro Velho (Coimbra), Portugal, 1618 (baptismal date, June 20); d. Loandra, Jan. 27, 1674. He took the habit of the Discalced Carmelites in Lisbon, and after studying at the college of the order in Coimbra, he was ordained and became a lector in theology. He won some reputation for himself as a preacher, and held various offices of responsibility in his order, being successively prior of the Lisbon house, provincial definitor, and definitor for Spain. Nominated bishop of Angola by Peter II of Portugal, he took possession of his see Dec. 11, 1673, but died the following month. His works included: *Directorium regularium* (Lyons 1661), consisting of case studies in the law for regulars; *Directorium confessariorum* (Lyons 1668), a work for the guidance of confessors, with case studies on the Sacraments, censures, the Commandments, justice, law, and contracts; and *Directorium mysticum* (Lyons 1677, Paris 1904), a treatise on the spiritual life tracing the three ways in the Fathers, St. Thomas Aquinas, and St. Teresa of Avila.

Bibliography: *Bibliotheca carmelitico-Lusitana* (Rome 1754) 28–30. SILVERIO DI SANTA TERESA, *Historia del Carmen Descalzo en España, Portugal, y América,* 15 v. (Burgos 1935–52) 10: 665–666; EncCatt 1:1556. ELISÉE DE LA NATIVITÉ, DictSpirAsc Myst 1:717–718.

[B. CAVANAUGH]

ANTHONY NEYROT, BL., Dominican martyr; b. Rivoli, Italy; d. Tunis, April 10, 1460 (feast, April 10). Contrary to the advice of (St.) *Antoninus, under whom he had been professed several years earlier, Neyrot went to Sicily to preach; but growing tired of the island, he embarked for Naples. Pirates captured the ship (Aug. 1458) and took its passengers to Tunis. After a prison term Neyrot was released, but while waiting ransom he succumbed to temptation (April 1459), publicly denied Christ, became a Moslem, and contracted marriage. Four months later he repented, undertook a life of penance, and was reconciled to the Church. On Palm Sunday 1460 he publicly rejected *Islam, renounced his apostasy, and preached Christ before the Sultan, who had him executed. His body was sent to Genoa and thence to Rivoli (1469). Clement XIII beatified him on Feb. 21, 1767.

Bibliography: ActSS Aug. 6:530–541. Taurisano Cat 1:41. P. ALVAREZ, *Santos Bienaventurados venerables O.P.,* 4 v. (Vergara 1920–23) 2:195–200.

[F. C. RYAN]

ANTHONY OF PADUA, ST.

Franciscan Doctor of the Church; b. Lisbon, Portugal, Aug. 15?, 1195; d. Arcella, near Padua, Italy, June 13, 1231 (feast, June 13).

Life. At the age of 15, Anthony, the son of noble parents, entered the monastery of the *Canons Regular of São Vicente in Lisbon. After 2 years he came to S. Cruz in Coimbra, the study house of the Augustinian Canons, and there became expert in Sacred Scripture. Disappointed with the religious spirit of his monastery, which was under the patronage of the Portuguese court, and inspired by the news of the first Franciscan martyrs in Morocco, Anthony joined the *Franciscans at the friary of San Antonio in Coimbra (1220). At his own request, he was sent as a missionary to Morocco, but he was forced by illness to return; his boat, however, was driven off course, and he landed in Sicily. Arriving in Italy as an unknown, he took part in the famous chapter of the Mats at the Portiuncula (1221) and was affiliated to the Franciscan province of Romagna. For a time he resided in solitude and penance in the hermitage of Monte Paolo near Forlì. At his ordination he was recognized as an inspiring preacher and was commissioned to preach against the heretics in northern Italy (1222–24) and against the *Albigenses in southern France (1224). From 1227 to 1230 his preaching activity brought him back to Italy, and during the Lent of 1231 he preached daily in Padua.

In 1223 *Francis of Assisi appointed Anthony the first professor of theology for the friars; he is credited with introducing the theology of St. *Augustine into the Franciscan Order. During his brief career Anthony was guardian in Le Puy, custos in Limoges, and provincial in the Romagna. The furious pace of his activities completely ruined his feeble health; he died at the age of 36. At his canonization, May 30, 1232, Gregory IX declared him to be a "teacher of the Church," and Pius XII (Jan. 16, 1946) made him a Doctor of the Church with the title *Doctor evangelicus.*

Cultus. In popular devotion Anthony is venerated as the apostle of charity, invoked in both spiritual and temporal needs (the finder of lost objects; patron of lovers, of marriage, of women in confinement; as a helper against diabolic obsession, fever, animal diseases; as the patron of miners). The blessing of St. Anthony has become popular in all the above instances. His veneration as an effective preacher, added to his other titles of respect, have to a great extent caused the saint of Padua to displace St. *Anthony of Egypt in popular esteem. Special forms of veneration are the St. Anthony Bread (alms given to the poor in his name to beg his intercession) and the Prayer League of St. Anthony (both in vogue since the end of the 19th century); the Tuesday devotion to St. Anthony (since the 17th century), because his burial day (June 17, 1231) fell on a Tuesday; his veneration as an admiral by the

St. Anthony of Padua, fresco by Giovanni da Milano (working between 1349 and 1369), in the Medici Chapel, known also as the Chapel of the Novitiate, in the Church of S. Croce, Florence.

Feast of St. Anthony of Padua, Bica Quarter, Lisbon.

Portuguese (because of their victory over the French in 1710) and by the Spanish (because of the expulsion of the Moors from Oran in 1732).

In iconography he is variously symbolized according to his many activities: with book or cross for the teacher or preacher, a flame or a burning heart for the former Augustinian or the apostle of charity, and with a lily or the Christ Child for the saint. From the 13th century the liturgy for the Mass and Office of his feast was that of the common of a Doctor of the Church, still employed within the Franciscan Order. In the 16th-century liturgical reform of Pius V, the feast was suppressed, except within the order and in Portugal and Brazil. In 1585, however, Sixtus V restored the feast to the universal Church, with the liturgy taken from the common of a confessor.

Bibliography: Works. *Sermones dominicales et in solemnitatibus,* ed. A. M. LOCATELLI, 3 v. in 1 (Padua 1895–1913). S. CLASEN, ed., *Antonius Patavinus: Lehrer des Evangeliums* (Werl 1954), selected texts from the sermons of St. A. For other works attributed to him, see *ibid.* 29–69. Sources and literature. *Legenda secunda auctore valde antiquo* and *Liber miraculorum,* ActSS June 3:198–209, 216–231. A. M. JOSA, *Legenda seu vita et miracula S. Antonii de Padua* (Bologna 1883). F. M. D'ARAULES, *La vie de S. Antoine de Padoue par Jean Rigauld* (Bordeaux, Brive 1899). L. DE KERVAL, *S. Antonii de Padua vitae duae* (Paris 1904); *L'Évolution et le développement du merveilleux dans les légendes de S. Antoine de Padoue* (Opuscules de critique historique 2; Paris 1906) 221–286. *Dialogus de gestis ss. Fratrum Minorum,* ed. F. M. DELORME (Quarachi 1923). *La legenda fiorentina,* ed. E. PALANDRI, *Studi Franciscani* 4 (1932) 454–496. B. KLEINSCHMIDT, *Antonius von Padua in Leben und Kunst* (Düsseldorf 1931). H. FELDER, *Die Antoniuswunder nach den älteren Quellen* (Paderborn 1933). G. SCHREIBER, *S. Antonio, dottore della Chiesa* (Rome 1947). S. CLASEN, *St. Anthony, Doctor of the Gospel,* tr. I. BRADY (Chicago 1961). **Illustration credits:** Fig. 1, Alinari-Art Reference Bureau. Fig. 2, Casa de Portugal, New York.

[S. CLASEN]

ANTHONY PAVONIUS, BL., Dominican inquisitor and martyr; b. Savigliano (in Piedmont), *c.* 1326; d. Bricherasio, April 9, 1374 (feast, April 9). Born of noble stock, Anthony entered the Dominican priory at Savigliano in 1341 and made his novitiate there. In later years he was twice prior of this community. Ordained in 1351, he became a master in theology and in 1365 was appointed inquisitor general (*see* INQUISITION) for Liguria, Piedmont, and upper Lombardy. In the course of these duties he had to contend principally with the *Waldensians, some of whom became so infuriated with his persistence and success that they brutally murdered him as he left the church after preaching. He was beatified Dec. 4, 1856.

Bibliography: ActSS April 1:844–846. ArchStorIt, 3d ser., 1.2 (1865) 28–30. *Année dominicaine,* 23 v. (new ed. Lyons 1883–1909) April 1:295–301. Taurisano Cat 30.

[J. E. BRESNAHAN]

ANTHONY OF STRONCONE, BL., Franciscan laybrother; b. Stroncone (Umbria), Italy, 1381; d. *Assisi, Feb. 7, 1461, *not* 1471 (feast, Feb. 8). He was reared by fervent Franciscan tertiary (*see* THIRD ORDERS) parents of a prominent family that gave several outstanding priests to the *Franciscans. Anthony was only 12 when he joined the Observant Friars Minor. He served as assistant novicemaster in Fiesole (1411–20) under the saintly *Thomas Bellacci. From 1420 to 1435 he helped Bellacci convert and repress the *Fraticelli in Tuscany and Corsica. He spent his last decades as questing brother at the Carceri hermitage above Assisi and died in San Damiano friary there; he was revered for his humility, mortification, prophecies, and contemplative prayer. More than a score of major favors were reported at his tomb between the years 1461 and 1475. He was beatified by Pope *Innocent XI in 1687. In 1809 his well-preserved body was forcibly translated to Stroncone by 20 armed citizens.

Bibliography: G. ODDI, *La Franceschina,* ed. N. CAVANNA, 2 v. (Florence 1931) 1:397–410. Butler Th Attw 1:272–273. L. CANONICI, *Antonio Vici, principe conteso* (Assisi 1961), with extensive bibliog.

[R. BROWN]

ANTHROPOCENTRISM

This article discusses the notion and refers to historical forms of anthropocentrism in Christian thought.

Notion. As the name implies, anthropocentrism makes the dimensions of human existence (the supreme reality of the world of man's experience) a central term of reference in the orders of intelligibility and value. Anthropocentrism is only fully intelligible as a correlative of *theocentrism on the one hand and a dehumanized naturalism on the other.

Two basic tendencies have constantly manifested themselves in human culture. One is preoccupied with realities immanent to this world, and especially with the supreme among them, man. (Protagoras: "Man is the measure of all things.") The other is preoccupied with the Transcendent. (Plato: "God is the measure of all things.") The supreme achievement of human culture is an integration of what is valid in both of these insights. Such an integration is essential to Christianity, founded as it is upon the Divine Word's presence in the world in human flesh (*see* INCARNATION; CHRISTOCENTRISM). The Christ event at once canonizes anthropocentrism and subordinates it to theocentrism: the intelligibility and values of human existence are safeguarded by their subordination to the divine reality, through Christ.

Historical Review. The reconciliation of anthropocentrism with theocentrism cannot remove the tension that exists between these two terms of reference in man's world-view. It is with reference to this tension that historical forms of anthropocentrism within Christian thought should be understood. Broadly, it seems true to say that thought in the Western Church (which has its beginnings against the background of the anthropocentric world-view of Stoicism) has been characteristically anthropocentric, while that of Eastern Christianity (which developed in a confrontation with a theocentric Gnosticism) has been more markedly theocentric. Thus the great theological controversies of Western Christianity have concerned man's condition under God's grace (Pelagianism, Lutheranism); while those of the East have concerned the supreme mysteries of God (Trinity, Incarnation). In the theological traditions that are the background to the early councils, the anthropocentric tendency was most evident in the school of *Antioch. It provided a healthy corrective to the theocentric tendency of the school of *Alexandria.

In reaction to the unbalanced theocentrism of the early Middle Ages, the late medieval period in the West saw the emergence of a new anthropocentrism that progressively obscured the recognition of the Transcendent. It is typified in a concern with the human sufferings of Christ in the Passion that loses sight of the essentials of the Paschal mystery (*see* RESURRECTION OF CHRIST, 2). This tendency emerged as the humanism of the Renaissance and the modern period, more and more emancipated from religious connotations.

With *existentialism and *personalism a new form of anthropocentrism has emerged in Western thought in recent decades and has had a profound influence upon Christian theology. Its essential correlative is not theocentrism but a positivistic naturalism that would neglect the unique ontological status and value of the human person in a world of things. It has provided insights of great value in the theological revival of the mid-20th century.

Bibliography: C. H. DAWSON, *The Dynamics of World History,* ed. J. J. MULLOY (New York 1956) e.g., 458–459. K. RAHNER, LexThK[2] 1:632–634.

[J. THORNHILL]

ANTHROPOLOGY, CULTURAL

If anthropology is defined as the science of man and his works, then cultural anthropology is primarily concerned with man's works—his social behavior, beliefs, and languages, his shared ways of doing, thinking, and making things. Physical anthropology, the other main branch of the science, studies man as a biological organism (*see* ANTHROPOLOGY, PHYSICAL).

SCOPE, AIM, AND METHODS

Fundamental to an understanding of cultural anthropology is the notion of *culture. Despite the fact that anthropologists have used this term variously, and even with formally distinct meanings, it remains the basic and central concept of the science. Some attention must be given to its meaning before the several explanatory schools and the conventional divisions of the field are considered.

Nature of Culture. The core anthropological meaning of the word is that given by E. B. Tylor: "Culture or Civilization . . . is that complex whole which includes knowledge, belief, art, morals, law, custom, and any other capabilities and habits acquired by man as a member of society" [*Primitive Culture* (2 v. London 1871) 1:1]. Culture in this sense includes *all* learned and shared patterns of behavior, and not simply those that express good manners, sophistication, or a knowledge of the arts. For the anthropologist, to be human is to be cultured.

A more recent definition of the concept, which stresses that culture is not behavior itself or the products of behavior, but somehow an abstraction from behavior, is that of Clyde Kluckhohn and William H. Kelly, for whom culture means "all those historically created designs for living, explicit and implicit, rational, irrational, and nonrational, which exist at any given time as potential guides for the behavior of men." Here the term culture is taken in its widest sense, referring to the ways of all mankind at any one time in history. When reference is to a particular way of life, culture is defined descriptively as a "historically derived system of explicit and implicit designs for living, which tends to be shared by all or specially designated members of a group" ["The Concept of Culture" in *The Science of Man in the World Crisis,* ed. R. Linton (New York 1945) 97, 98]. It is with particular cultures or the comparison of several such cultures that most anthropological analysis is concerned.

Culture Patterns. The "designs for living" that compose a culture are often called culture patterns. Culture is not behavior or the products of behavior, but the plan, form, design, structure, or pattern that is shown forth in them both. These patterns are the distinctive ways of behaving of a *society. They exist primarily as habits, conscious or unconscious, mental, motor, or emotional, shared by all or some members of the society and manifested in their common way of action. They may also be approximated by the analyst insofar as he can "get inside people's heads" to discover the processes and products of their cognitive and other faculties. To attain this intimate knowledge by more accurate and testable means is a goal that is eagerly sought at least by those anthropologists who see this quest for the other's view as the basic ethnographic task.

When anthropologists speak of a way of behaving as characteristic of a society or some part of it, what they say is usually a generalization based on repeated observation within the society. It is not a description of individual behavior, but a kind of abstraction of the common denominator in the behavior of many. For the daily transactions of each individual in any society are in fact a unique compromise between what is expected of him, his understanding of these norms, and his ability and inclination to comply with them. Yet in any society there is a tendency to behave alike that attests to the existence of a pattern and makes abstraction both possible and legitimate.

Organization of Culture. The pattern that one abstracts from what people actually do or what they have made is a behavioral pattern. What they say should or must be done is called an ideal pattern. The importance of the distinction is this: when what people do is very frequently opposed to what they say ought to be done, a tension is often present and the observer is alerted to cultural change in process or prospect. Less obvious is the everyday strain for consistency that gives direction and character to a way of life. For by systematic selection and organization "the heterogeneous items of behavior take more and more congruous shape" [R. Benedict, *Patterns of Culture* (Boston 1934) 46]. This should not be understood to mean that each culture has a single motif, since few cultures can be seen as fully integrated systems. More generally acceptable is M. E. Opler's proposal that the content of a culture may best be organized around a number of summative principles, called themes.

Opler defines a theme as "a postulate or position, declared or implied, and usually controlling behavior or stimulating activity, which is tacitly approved or openly promoted in a society" ["Some Recently Developed Concepts Relating to Culture," *Southwestern Journal of Anthropology* 4 (1948) 120]. It is a pattern, or design for living, that is basic and central to a culture. However, its cardinal position does not preclude its being matched in importance by another theme that expresses a conflicting tendency. Thus Alexis de Tocqueville observed long ago that in the U.S. the principle of freedom inevitably contradicted the principle of equality. Free enterprise, for example, has a way of sifting and grading competitors, regardless of their equality before God and the law. Themes also tend to lie below the level of consciousness, controlling the players from behind the scenes, as it were. In fact, participants in the culture are often quite unaware of their existence. In this respect themes differ sharply from those patterns that are easily traced in the behavior or products they have shaped—a dress, a chair, a gesture, a word—but the difficulty in detection is rewarded by a correspondingly more basic understanding of the way of life that is being studied.

Transmission of Culture. To say that a culture is historically derived means that it is passed on from one generation to the next. It also means that a culture is subject to constant change by such factors as invention, outside contact, and its own adaptive drift. To speak of a culture as social heredity is misleading to a degree, for it makes the individual seem the passive recipient of an unchanging tradition. Nonetheless, it does highlight the fact that culture is transmitted by the processes of learning, informal and formal, largely, though not exclusively, through the symbolism of *language. Man's unique facility for language accounts for the continuity, stability, and growth of culture. Through language the experience of one generation or one part of the world can be transmitted with relative ease to another, making the learning process continuous and inventions and new ideas the starting points for further development.

Culture tends to be "shared by all or specially designated members of a group." As stated above, even when individuals have the same norms, they tend to act somewhat differently. There is also variation arising not from individual differences but from differences in the norms prescribed for the various subgroups within the society. These are the so-called restricted ideal patterns appropriate for the members of a particular *sect, *social class, age or occupational grouping, or other similarly defined segment. Although individuals can and do disregard these special rules on occasion, those who have the same position in a society or perform nearly the same roles tend nonetheless to share more culture patterns than do those in the same society who have different positions and roles.

Cultural Origins. This conception of culture, though agreeable to most anthropologists, has its opponents. Furthermore, it leaves untouched the question of culture's origin. Least happy with the conception are those who are impressed by the way culture seems to follow its own laws, independently of the men it influences. Leslie A. White (1900–) and A. L. Kroeber (1876–1961), American anthropologists, are considered the leading advocates of this position. In the final analysis the dispute very often, and perhaps inevitably, turns on a basic philosophical premise, human freedom. If man is without free will, culture can easily be assigned the determinant role in guiding the course of mankind. If man can choose, if he can take control, then his intervention must be reckoned with, and culture becomes, to some degree at least, the creature of his mind. Opler's pun is to the point when he suspects that "we have the impression that [culture] is autonomous only because it is anonymous" ["The Human Being in Culture Theory," *American Anthropologist* 66 (1964) 525].

Regardless of what and where culture is, a further question considers how it came to be. Culture is generally accepted as uniquely human, and anthropologists often speak of man as the tool-using or the culture-bearing animal. Associated with this definition is the critical-point theory of culture origin. According to this widely held view of human *evolution, a prehuman animal gradually approximated the human form and then, on the attainment of some final crucial feature, was abruptly over the line, empowered to speak and use tools—in short, a human being. Complete physical development preceded the sudden acquisition of culture.

This position is challenged by evidence that has been gathering since the first discovery of the fossil australopithecines in the middle 1920s. These South African man-apes apparently walked erect, made tools, and went hunting. They may even have had some simple system of communication. If they did, it would follow that most cortical development took place *after,* not before, the beginnings of culture, because the australopithecines had brains only one-third the human size. It would also follow, as Clifford Geertz has pointed out, that the fashioning of man was the joint accomplishment of this protoculture and the natural environment: "It is true that without men there would be no cultural forms. But it is also true that without cultural forms there would be no men" ("The Transition to Humanity" in S. Tax, ed., *Horizons of Anthropology,* 46). *See* ARCHEOLOGY, I (PREHISTORIC); EVOLUTION, CULTURAL AND SOCIAL.

Classical Evolutionism. Cultural anthropology first took shape as a recognizable enterprise in the second half of the 19th century. Until the beginning of the 20th century the principle most often invoked to explain cultural similarity and dissimilarity was one of cultural and social evolution. The essence of this position, expressed by Lewis Henry Morgan (1818–81), is that "savagery preceded barbarism in all the tribes of mankind, as barbarism is known to have preceded civilization. The history of the human race is one in source, one in experience, one in progress" [*Ancient Society* (New York 1877) v–vi]. Similarities were explained by stating that the cultures or patterns in question were at equivalent points on parallel lines of development. Differences were accounted for by unequal progress or local environment.

The basic difficulty with the classical evolutionist position is that, lacking proper chronological control, its so-called succession of stages, whether of culture in general or of some aspect of culture such as religion, becomes in fact the arrangement of cultural data according to a predetermined scheme. The primary emphasis accorded unilinear and parallel development led, moreover, to a deemphasis of the role played by cultural borrowing, or diffusion, in the formation of individual cultures. Furthermore, in the establishment of cross-cultural similarities, patterns were often considered out of context, so that forms superficially alike but functionally and in meaning quite different were taken as equivalent.

Despite their rejection of classical evolutionism, modern anthropologists are indebted to its exponents. These pioneers, aside from setting the basic goal of the discipline, pointed the way to its attainment by espousing systematic comparison as prerequisite to valid generalization. Beyond this, they also coined the concept of culture and established the principle that culture develops in continuous and orderly fashion. Theirs was the basic contribution to the science.

Diffusionism. Perhaps even more significant than early evolutionism was the reaction that followed closely on its heels. The explanatory concept of diffusionism tended to explain the similarity of cultures not by the evolutionary principle of parallel development but for the most part by the transmission, or diffusion, of ideas and techniques from one society to another. Two principal forms developed: the so-called historicalism that grew up with Franz Boas (1858–1942) and other anthropologists of the U.S., and the diffusionism of the German-Austrian school founded by F. Graebner (1877–1935) and fostered by Wilhelm *Schmidt (1868–1954).

American Historicalism. Central to the so-called American approach were two features: negatively, a distrust and avoidance of the kind of generalization that characterized the classical evolutionary schemes; positively, a rigorous attention to concrete phenomena. Information about individual cultures was not to be used, as it was by Sir James George *Frazer (1854–1941) in *The Golden Bough,* first published in 1890, to illustrate preconceived notions. Rather, for those with this "historical" or "natural history" orientation, understanding a culture in its own peculiar terms became, and still is, an end desirable in itself. This goal was to be attained by discovering the specific antecedents and context of each cultural form encountered, examined, and described. By appeal to marshaled evidence the typical American analyst made a case for the item's introduction or invention, thus explaining the actual distribution of cultural elements.

One reason for this empirical bent is found in the environment. Anthropologists of the U.S., unlike their European counterparts, were all more or less near neighbors of Indian peoples whose ways of life and origins begged for description and explanation. Furthermore, government and other agencies urged that concrete studies of this sort be undertaken, often providing the necessary means. It was in this atmosphere of sponsored curiosity that museum men such as F. W. Putnam (1839–1914) and academic field workers such as Boas made early 20th-century American anthropology almost synonymous with descriptive studies of North American Indians.

Dialogue between facts and theory was encouraged, but facts were allowed to speak more often and more at length than the low-level hypotheses to which they were related. Since it was felt that understanding of individual cultures had to precede propositions about culture in general and since this particular understanding involved painstaking descriptive labors, it happened that the dogged pursuit of the particular led quite often, and quite predictably, to a neglect of the general. Yet this was not counted as loss. It was expected that the new and rigorous criteria for probing cultural origins would make reconstructions and generalizations more difficult to achieve but, once made, less easy to disprove. This cautious spirit, introduced by Boas and others from the natural sciences, did much to shape anthropology as it is known today.

Single-minded concern for the origins of cultural elements led to a forgetting of the interplay that takes place among these various elements and of the individual's reaction to his cultural legacy. Boas himself has been accused of this oversight, but many of his colleagues and students (such as P. Radin, E. Sapir, M. Mead, R. Benedict, and A. I. Hallowell) progressed from concern for particular cultures to interest in the individual and, eventually, to exploring how the individual was formed by his culture and reacted with and against it to create his personality. This development led in the 1920s to the growth of one edge of anthropology outward toward psychology and psychiatry. Forces were joined, and fruitful cooperation has continued since that time.

German-Austrian School. This group set itself the same goal as the classical evolutionists, a worldwide synthesis of cultural history. Its basic strategy and hypothesis were derived from Graebner, a German ethnologist who fused historical and anthropological methods in an effort to replace the speculations of 19th-century evolutionism with sound proof of historicogenetic connections between cultures. Central to the school's explanation of cultural similarity and diversity was the postulate of a limited number of distinctive primeval cultures, or culture complexes. These original Kulturkreise, as they are sometimes called, diffused from a restricted territory, presumably Asia. Their surviving elements, in pure or blended form, were discerned in living cultures as the end-products of mankind's multilinear cultural development to date.

Graebner's scheme was modified and propagated by Schmidt, Austrian priest-ethnologist of the Society of the Divine Word and founder of the anthropological journal *Anthropos* (1906–). So great was Schmidt's influence on Catholic missionaries, especially those of his own congregation, that with his encouragement and assistance reports from the field filled volumes of *Anthropos* and other publications. The existence of a high-god, or monotheistic, concept among today's primitives, once disputed, was established as a fact, partly by Schmidt's monumental *Der Ursprung der Gottesidee,* 12 v. Münster 1912–54. (It should be noted that this is not the same as proving that early man was monotheistic; the minor premise of the argument, namely, that the beliefs of today's primitives are essentially those of the first men, remains unproved.)

Despite the changes made by Schmidt, the *Kulturkreis theory was found at variance with archeological fact and was generally abandoned, even in its homeland. Nonetheless, the comparative method evolved by Graebner and Schmidt continues to be used with effect, and their bold aims continue to inspire. Now, however, German, Austrian, and other Continental anthropologists are widening and deepening their study of culture history by absorbing additional viewpoints such as functionalism, social structural analysis, and the psychological approach [see J. Haekel, "Trends and Intellectual Interests in Current Austrian Ethnology," *American Anthropologist* 61 (1959) 865–874]. They move cautiously, with practical admission of the complexity that their predecessors theoretically never denied.

Heliocentrism. Caution of this kind never dampened the ardor of a third diffusionist grouping, sometimes termed the Pan-Egyptian or heliocentric school. Theirs was an extreme position that overemphasized the role of borrowing and reduced human inventiveness to a minimum. As proposed by the Englishman G. Elliott Smith (1871–1937) and elaborated by his countryman W. J. Perry (1887–1949) in *The Children of the Sun* (London 1923), it hypothesized that Egypt was the unique origin of many cultural parallels found from the Mediterranean, through Asia and Oceania, to the Americas. Rejected as farfetched, the heliocentric hypothesis had little or no influence on the mainstream of anthropological thought.

Functionalism. Scholars who used the early evolutionary and historical approaches were content that, given time, they could answer in depth the two questions of whence the elements of a culture came, and how. What made a culture hang together as it did, here and now, was a question they did not ask. In retrospect it seems clear that anthropology would inevitably have turned to this question in the 1920s, given the trend toward holism that was abroad in those years. In point of fact, however, it was as early as 1909 that at least one anthropologist was asking the question. A. R. Radcliffe-Brown (1881–1955) was moved to this less by some *Zeitgeist* than by his reading of Émile *Durkheim and Marcel Mauss. The impact of these French sociologists was so great, in fact, that he set aside what he had written on the Andaman Islands and reworked the material he had gathered. Although the original version was completed in 1914, *The Andaman Islanders* first appeared in 1922. What in the first writing had been a run-of-the-mill reconstruction of culture history was now a pioneering functional analysis of the interrelations of habitat, religion, and social organization.

Also published in London that year was *Argonauts of the Western Pacific,* by Bronislaw Malinowski (1884–1942), the first book-length report of the author's extended stay (1914–18) with the Trobriand Islanders of northeast Melanesia. With intimate detail he made the point that a culture had organic unity, its elements mutually adjusted to contribute to the functioning of the whole. This became a basic axiom of the functionalism promoted by both Malinowski and Radcliffe-Brown. The elements of a culture hung together not just because they had been put together, but because they belonged together. Beyond this, the whole culture was seen as having "functional unity" insofar as the interdependence of its parts was a means for the achievement of one or more ascendant ends, or functions, of that culture. It was characteristic of anthropological functionalism that such goals were posited for whole cultures and societies, not for individuals as such. Indeed the average member of a society would be completely unconscious of them. Yet it was the task of the anthropologist to discover what they were and to show the place of the culture's or society's several parts in the attainment of those ends.

In its relatively short career functionalism has been associated, justly or unjustly, with a number of features: intensive and problem-oriented field work; the postulate that every element of a culture has a function in that culture; and a shying away from history. As regards the last, one cannot deny that both founders of functionalism were in reaction against the conjecture that often passed for history in their day. But genuine history was always acceptable and, with the coming of interest in acculturation, indispensable. The tidy portrait of a culture with no loose ends was the work of Malinowski, for Radcliffe-Brown was quite ready to allow dysfunctions, as did Durkheim before him. Robert K. Merton (1910–), an American sociologist, subsequently wrote with insight on this subject and contributed, moreover, the very useful distinction between latent, or unapparent, function on the one hand and manifest function on the other.

From the beginning, fieldwork has been seen as the most effective means for testing and generating hypotheses about the inner workings of culture and society. Malinowski was the fieldworker par excellence; Radcliffe-Brown, a theoretician. But both, as integral functionalists, took their problems to the field for solving. So widespread among anthropologists has this alternation of office and fieldwork become that it can hardly be called an exclusively functionalist procedure.

In fact, the emergent role of functionalism is that of the other concepts that have been mentioned. It must become one part, one ingredient, of a more embracing approach to a fuller understanding of mankind. Among the formal syntheses that have been suggested, the method of controlled comparison employed by Fred Eggan (1906–) is notable for combining the best features of American historicalism and the British structural-functional approach ["Social Anthropology and the Method of Controlled Comparison," *American Anthropologist* 56 (1954) 743–763]. In this method several societies closely similar to one another in both structural and nonstructural features are selected for study. From the comparison of their social systems hypotheses are derived to explain whatever structural differences may have been noted, relating them to covariant characteristics, including history and ecology. In several comparative approaches to problems of cultural change (such as those of J. Steward, B. J. Meggers, and R. J. Braidwood and G. R. Willey), control of the environmental variable is essential, for ecology plays the dominant role. In fact this new emphasis on the interaction between culture and environment gives ecology its due while avoiding the excesses of geographical determinism on the one hand and mere possibilism on the other. Some conceptual frameworks (those of L. A. White, J. Steward, M. Sahlins, and E. R. Service) have an evolutionary perspective. However, the classical commitment to a predetermined scheme of stages has long since been discarded. Except for White, the neoevolutionists insist that cultures be studied in context, and in doing this they are more akin to functionalists than to their 19th-century namesakes.

Divisions and Specialties

Major and long-established subfields of cultural anthropology are archeology, ethnology, and linguistics. More ambiguous in status is social anthropology—some consider it the equivalent of cultural anthropology; others, a special part of it; still others take it to be the sociology of nonliterate societies.

Archeology. Like history, archeology is the study of man's past. What distinguishes the two is that the archeologist aims to trace the development of culture and portray bygone ways of life with or without the help of written inscriptions or documents. Unlike the historian and the historical archeologist, the prehistorian, or anthropological archeologist, has no such auxiliary texts. The peoples whose cultural remains he studies either had no knowledge of writing or left no evidence of it. Since writing first appeared less than 5,000 years ago and man's cultural history, reckoned conservatively, spans a half-million years, the prehistorian's scope includes all but the latest episodes in the human career.

His inferences must be based on the mute testimony of those signs of human passage that have survived the rigors of unrecorded time. The archeologist sees in these remains the possible makings of a reconstruction, always incomplete, of how men once lived. By adapting techniques of excavation, observation, and recording to the problem at hand and by seeking the help of specialists in the natural sciences, the skillful archeologist can elicit a remarkable amount of information from the material evidences, artifactual and environmental, with which he is confronted. But he is, for all that, limited. He can speak with confidence about technology in ancient times, and with reasonable assurance about subsistence economies. The lines of social and political institutions he will sketch with a hesitant hand, however; and he frankly takes religious forms and the spiritual life of prehistoric man as matters of conjecture. From the prehistorian's viewpoint, the more distinctly human the activity, the less intelligible it is [C. Hawkes, "Archeological Theory and Method: Some Suggestions from the Old World," *American Anthropologist* 56 (1954) 162].

Crucial to archeology are reliable means for dating the remains it discovers, since the satisfactory establishment of cultural connections across space or time demands that the terms of comparison be dated relative to each other. Improved techniques such as radiocarbon (C-14) dating have resulted in refined methods for estimating both absolute and relative chronology, but neither the archeologists nor their natural science colleagues are content with accomplishments to date. Archeologists agree that their contributions to the understanding of cultural form and process will multiply immeasurably with improved chronologies, sharpened concepts, and better constructed method and theory.

Ethnology. Ethnology takes up, in a sense, where archeology and prehistory leave off. Its concern is also with culture sequence and process, but it studies not cultures of the prehistoric past but ongoing cultures or those for which written records survive. In scope if not in fact, ethnology, like archeology, embraces total cultures. To understand its form and operation better, the modern ethnologist usually describes and analyzes the individual culture as a functioning whole composed of interrelated parts. This descriptive phase of his work, sometimes called ethnography, is preliminary to the comparative study of cultures, which is ethnology strictly so called. Here the aim is to account for the similarities and differences that a comparative inquiry reveals and to verify or disprove the existence of cultural contact through space and of cultural sequence through time. Some would have ethnology confine itself to a particularizing, historical approach that seeks no laws or regularities of cultural variation, continuity, or change. But ethnologists do as a matter of fact seek generalizations about culture as such, just as social anthropologists compare social structures and organizations "to formulate and validate statements about the conditions of existence of social systems . . . and the regularities that are observable in social change" [Radcliffe-Brown, *Method in Social Anthropology,* ed. M. N. Srinivas (Chicago 1958) 128].

Social Anthropology. If social systems are taken as part of the patterned behavior subsumed under culture (and this is the view of many Americans), then social anthropology, the comparative study of social systems, can be considered a subdivision of ethnology. But an important difference remains. The ethnologist, who is involved with culture in all its manifestations, tends traditionally to stay longer at the level of particular phenomena and to rise with difficulty to generalizations because of the very multiplicity of his historical concerns. The social anthropologist, on the other hand, tends to pay little attention to cultural details not directly related to social relations. He is less burdened, as it were, with concretized trivia, and so abstracts with fewer operations and greater ease. This advantage brings with it, however, a proclivity to portray social structures almost as closed systems impervious to outside influence and intolerant of individual deviation. The British social anthropologists R. Firth (1901–) and E. R. Leach (1910–) have led the way in correcting this tendency and adapting the structural-functional approach to the study of social change.

Culture-Personality Studies. A special branch of ethnology, developed since the 1920s, took as its first general problem the interplay between an individual's culture and his personality. The subsequent growth of this subdiscipline is briefly discussed below.

Linguistics. *Linguistics is the scientific study of language. From the viewpoint proper to the anthropological linguist, it is intimately related to the study of culture, not only because language is a part of culture and linguistics a part of ethnology, but because the satisfactory study of one must of necessity include the other. Like archeology and ethnology, linguistics has its descriptive and comparative aspects. Descriptive linguistics analyzes the sound systems, grammar, and vocabulary of languages at a particular point in time. The techniques of the descriptive linguist have been so successful in discovering the patterns in languages that students of other aspects of culture look to them with hope. They see them as a starting point for the development of similar techniques for the probing of nonlinguistic cultural phenomena.

One such advance in recent years has been that of componential analysis, an important movement away from ethnocentrism in fieldwork. Through the use of techniques borrowed from linguists two goals are sought: to be able at least to respond as members of the culture do in a given situation and, as closely as possible, to come to this appropriate behavior by the same cognitive processes as the people whose culture one studies [see A. K. Romney and R. G. D'Andrade, eds., "Transcultural Studies in Cognition," *American Anthropologist* 66 (1964) no. 3 pt. 2]. An earlier meeting point of ethnology and linguistics was the discussion of a hypothesis proposed by E. Sapir (1884–1939) and, later, by B. Whorf (1897–1941). Briefly, it stated that language defined experience for its speakers. Provocative and important as it was, the statement generated considerable enlightening research but was found unsuitable for genuinely experimental testing.

Historical, or comparative, linguistics studies historical relationships between languages. A fundamental assumption is that there is no necessary or natural connection between an idea and the sounds used to express it. Linguistic form and meaning are, in other words, arbitrarily related; and if the meaningful elements of several languages have significantly more form-meaning resemblances than can be accounted for by mere chance, they must be historically related. However, to pass from this conclusion to that of genetic relationship, the possibility of borrowing must be eliminated. A comparison of the retention over time of items in the basic vocabulary of several languages studied at known time depths led to the hypothesis that "the fundamental everyday vocabulary of any language—as against the specialized or 'cultural' vocabulary—changes at a relatively constant rate" [M. Swadesh, "Lexico-statistic Dating of Prehistoric Ethnic Contacts," *Proceedings of the American Philosophical Society* 96 (1952) 452]. Assuming the rate to be constant for "any language," at least for the span of 2 millenniums covered by the form-meaning resemblances in a lexical test list for two related languages, one can solve the equation for the time factor and estimate how long it is since the two languages began to develop separately. This new and special field of linguistics is called lexicostatistics or glottochronology [but see D. H. Hymes, "Lexicostatistics So Far," *Current Anthropology* 1 (1960) 4]. It is possible that through it anthropology may gain a much-needed tool for the reconstruction of culture history.

Applied Anthropology. The anthropologist is often consulted for the solution of practical problems, particularly those of a social, political, economic, or religious nature. He is called upon with increasing frequency to assist in implementing programs of change sponsored by government and private agencies in the fields of public health, resettlement, economic or technical assistance, and public administration. He advises on personnel management in business and industry and on advertising and mass communication. His help is also sought to achieve better interracial relations, and for the training and advising of those in foreign service, international relations, and mission work. Paradoxically, perhaps, the anthropologist's most valuable contribution is often a clarification of the problem rather than its solution.

Action anthropology, which is distinctively nondirective in approach, was developed by Sol Tax (1907–) and several coworkers at the University of Chicago. For the anthropologist who dislikes using his skills to implement governmental or other policies that may be contrary to the local will, action anthroplogy is one answer. The goal is ultimately ameliorative, but the path and the pace are the people's.

Growth of Specialization. The number of specialties encompassed by cultural anthropology is in actual fact very large and, in principle, almost infinite. For each and every aspect of culture is capable of becoming an area of intense study. Indeed, with so many varied interests under the heading of anthropology one can easily wonder whether anthropology is a unitary science (or humanity) or a federation of scholars. It is both. One analysis of this, which stresses the notion of federation, is that of Tax:

> Anthropology may be viewed as a tradition (or a subculture) founded by scholars with interests as diverse as those today.
>
> The founders shared a common passion for understanding and explaining the nature and origin of man and his works in all their rich variety.
>
> They self-consciously and explicitly joined together. . . .
>
> Anthropology is likely to exist as a discipline as long as linguists, folklorists, archeologists, biologists, geographers, historians, *and any other specialists* find meaning enough in the whole study of man to maintain their intercommunication. ["The Integration of Anthropology," *Yearbook of Anthropology,* ed. W. L. Thomas, Jr. (New York 1955) 315–316.]

Anthropology is, in other words, "the freest and most explorative of the sciences" (R. Redfield, "Relations of Anthropology to the Social Sciences and to the Humanities" in Kroeber et al., *Anthropology Today* 736). For cultural anthropology's proper object is culture in all its "rich variety": understanding the similarities and differences of cultural forms and laying out and explaining their sequence and process.

Relations with Other Disciplines

Anthropology relates itself easily to many disciplines. Only five of them are briefly considered here: *history, *sociology, *psychology, *economics, and *missiology.

History. According to Redfield, anthropology is "unclear as to whether it moves toward the writing of a science . . . or toward the writing of histories" (*ibid.*), but it seems in fact to do both. Insofar as anthropology strives to arrive at principles underlying the cultural development of man, it manifests the generalizing tendency of the natural sciences. In describing or reconstructing a particular culture, whether at one time level or several, it draws closer to the particularizing approach of history and the humanities. In searching for process, it is scientific; in delineating form and sequence, it is historical.

Anthropology has other common grounds with history, chief among them perhaps the use of records witnessing to change through time and space. If unwritten records such as oral traditions, archeological remains, and the forms and distributions of culture are accepted as legitimate sources of history broadly conceived, then much of what anthropologists do is historical in nature (W. D. Strong, "Historical Approach in Anthropology" in *Anthropology Today* 386). But even if history is taken in a limited sense and only written records admitted in evidence, anthropology and history nonetheless cross lines.

Written documents are often employed to extend knowledge of a culture backward in time, and particularly to establish a starting point for the study of culture contact and change. Thus in the Jesuit Relations of North America the ethnologist interested in Indian tribes of eastern Canada or northeastern U.S. finds an invaluable base line against which to compare present-day conditions. Use of these and similar historical sources is so common and effective that the procedure is well established as the ethnohistorical approach.

Sociology. Anthropology is sometimes distinguished from another discipline, sociology, on the grounds that sociologists study large, literate communities, especially of the Western world, whereas anthropologists are interested in small, nonliterate groups. This criterion has a basis in the history of the two disciplines, but it is true only as a statistical tendency, not as a matter of principle. Anthropologists are likely to set up shop in metropolis or village and feel quite at home in either setting. The comparative study of civilizations undertaken by Redfield and his colleagues, the many anthropological studies of American and European cities, and the national character studies of Japanese, Russians, English, and Americans make the size, location, and cultural attainment of the population studied unreliable clues to the professional identity of the fieldwork involved.

But differences do exist, and they can be summarized. Sociology is interested more in social behavior than in shared thoughts and thought patterns, more outside the group studied than inside it, more analytic than intuitive, more atomistic than holistic, more frequently quantitative than qualitative, more concerned with the present and future (to be bettered by ameliorative planning) than with the present in light of the past, and less inclined than anthropology to introduce cross-cultural comparisons on lower levels of theory. Sociology is teaching the anthropologist to sharpen his focus of inquiry. From anthropology the sociologist can learn to gamble on empathy now and then for the sake of insight.

Psychology. The blending of psychology and anthropology produced a subfield of ethnology concerned with the study of culture and personality. This union, clearly in evidence only since the 1920s, was given early and eloquent direction by Sapir. He pointed out that traditional anthropology, which conceived culture as patterns of behavior shared by all or most members of a group, had in practice neglected a fact revealed by studies of personality, namely, that these patterns were organized variously in individuals, for whom they have endlessly different meanings [C. Kluckhohn, "The Influence of Psychiatry on Anthropology in America during the Past One Hundred Years" in *Personal Character and Cultural Milieu,* ed. D. Haring (Syracuse 1956) 494–98]. In the concrete, culture is a personal matter.

The early exploration of the individual's relation to his society and culture was guided in great part by the psychology of personality, clinical psychology, and various kinds of psychoanalytic theory. Since the late 1950s there has been mounting interest in cognitive process and, where psychoanalytic theory is used, the ego is given prominence. Projective tests, especially the Rorschach ink blot series and the Thematic Apperception Test, proved profitable cross-culturally, especially for determining the range of personality types among the members of a society. However, both psychologists and anthropologists agree that these instruments need further refinement and validation. Direct observation and the interview remain the basic and most reliable techniques available for culture-personality studies.

Biological determinants of behavior, once taken as constants, are now taken as variables for both the group and the individual. Further, the various approaches to group character that once loomed so large in culture-personality studies (national character, basic personality structure, and the like) have in recent years been deemphasized in favor of studies of more restricted scope [A. F. C. Wallace, "The New Culture-and-Personality" in *Anthropology and Human Behavior,* ed. T. Gladwin and W. C. Sturtevant (Washington 1961) 5–6].

Studies of child rearing and development continue to be made cross-culturally, but Wallace notes that the maturation of the cognitive process claims more widespread attention than formerly. This same interest in the cognitive (and ego) processes has led to a new look at the function of cultural institutions relative to the individual personality. The distinction is clearly made between the consequences and the motive of an action, and it is now more generally accepted that in culturally organized behavior the consequence of the act need not also be the motive (conscious or unconscious). This is a significant new emphasis, for "once the principle of psychodynamic teleology is abandoned, the value of insisting on motivational uniformity is reduced, and culture may be seen as a mechanism for the organization of a diversity of individual motives and cognitions" (*ibid.* 7).

Economics. Like the subdiscipline of culture and personality, economic anthropology is a meeting place for the practitioners of several sciences. To date, however, few economists have chosen to appear. This reluctance cannot be traced to their being unaware that differences in social structure, value system, and other cultural features may have notable effects on general economic activity. Those who are professionally concerned with the economics of underdeveloped nations are keenly conscious of this fact. The reason is to be found elsewhere, in the lack of a common language, of a common focus of interest, and of the leisure to use the one to explore the other.

Anthropologists, like economists, tend to write for the members of their own profession. Even when the language they use is intelligible to outsiders, the premises they suppose and the concepts they employ may not be shared by the economist reader. Communication fails for want of a common tongue. Again, the economist and the anthropologist are generally interested in different spheres. When both are studying the economy of an underdeveloped nation, for example, the economist will be busy with the factors that relate the nation to the outside world, such as foreign trade. The anthropologist is often found at the village level, trying, for instance, to trace the effects of sharing mechanisms on the level of crop production. Each is typically interested in the work of the other and quite willing to admit that their common goal would be more quickly and surely attained if they worked together, or at least learned to talk with each other. Unfortunately, each is also typically hard-pressed by traditional duties and finds little or no time to pursue the alliance with the energy it demands.

Despite the problems that exist, economic anthropology has an unmistakable hybrid vigor. Publications appear with growing frequency, and the subfield seems clearly determined to meet "its greatest challenge," namely, "the fashioning of a theory encompassing both economic and noneconomic variables in a single explanatory system" (M. Nash, "The Organization of Economic Life" in *Horizons of Anthropology* 180).

Missiology. Missiology, the scientific study of missions, utilizes cultural anthropology as an auxiliary discipline. To begin with, anthropology can pave the way for a sympathetic understanding of the people to whom the missionary will be sent. It also illuminates and facilitates the process of innovation involved in missionary work. Most important, perhaps, the study of anthropology generates in the missionary a better knowledge of his own culture and enables him to recognize those elements of religious thought and practice that are his mainly because of his American, Belgian, French, or other cultural heritage. Armed with this awareness, the Christian missionary is less likely to confuse his homeland's religious customs with universal Church teaching. He is more apt to be true to the mandate that has been his since the earliest days of the Church, to preach Christ in such a manner as to retain and promote the good that is found in all cultures, everywhere.

Cultural Anthropology and Catholicism

This spirit of respect for other ways of life is at the heart of modern anthropology. It is also expected of one who professes to be a follower of Christ, whose hallmark is love. How is it, then, that Christianity seems hardly to have recognized this spiritual kinship? How is it that, at least until World War II, there was in the minds of many American Roman Catholics a suspicion—often a conviction—that anthropology was a godless and unchristian science best avoided or damned?

Causes of Antipathy. The feeling of antipathy was in part a heritage of the exaggerated claims and counterclaims hurled by churchmen and scientists in their debates on the origin of man and of religion, especially in the early post-Darwin days. This feeling was (and is) also supported by the observation that many anthropologists are, as a matter of fact, candidly agnostic and positivistic, and see religion as an evolutionary development. Furthermore, the anthropologist's doctrine of cultural relativism, when understood as meaning that one way of life is as good as another, seems clearly opposed to any absolute norm of morality. Despite the appearance of conflict, the Church and sound anthropology are closer than many people recognize.

To begin with, current Roman Catholic thinking on human organic *evolution accepts as possible anthropology's proposal that man evolved from a prehuman primate. To complete the explanation of man's origin it would, for philosophical and theological reasons, speak also of divine intervention in the process to account for the human soul. But grounds for basic agreement are present. Naturalistic theories of the origin of religion, once a favorite confection of the cultural anthropologist, were another source of annoyance to many believers in divine revelation. Now, however, the naturalistic origin of religion is more widely recognized as compatible with a divine revelation, and anthropologists have stopped claiming to know what the first religion was like. The beginnings of religious awareness are for the modern anthropologist a matter for conscious conjecture and speculation, not for definitive pronouncement.

Various reasons have been suggested to explain the preponderance of agnostics and atheists among professional anthropologists. Some of them were soured on religion by the intolerance and condescension of missionaries they encountered. But it seems likely that the phenomenon is more closely related to the peculiar distribution of centers of anthropological training. Until recently, professional training in anthropology was generally not offered in those institutions where students with explicitly religious backgrounds were likely to attend in large numbers. Thus recruitment into anthropology was heavily weighted to attract more than a chance percentage of nonbelievers. Indeed, for many students who came to college uncommitted to any religion or uninstructed or dissatisfied in that in which they had been reared, the relativistic humanism of anthropology offered a popular substitute and was often accepted as such.

As more religiously-committed students enroll at those nonsectarian colleges and universities that have long offered anthropological training, and as more church-sponsored institutions of learning add anthropology courses and programs to their curriculums, a growing number of men and women believers will make anthropology their career. In so doing, they will be in the tradition of such eminent anthropologists as Wilhelm Schmidt, Henri *Breuil, John M. *Cooper of The Catholic University of America, and the French Jesuit Pierre *Teilhard de Chardin.

Compatibility. A constant source of wonder to the nonanthropologist, and even to the anthropologist, if he has not thought the matter through, is the paradox of the Christian anthropologist. Is not cultural relativism, he may ask, part and parcel of the anthropologist's kit, and is it not, as well, incompatible with an absolute norm of morality? How, then, can a good Christian be a good anthropologist? Regardless of what place one assigns to cultural relativism in the essential scheme of anthropological values, close scrutiny suggests that it can be combined with an absolute norm of morality.

Some anthropologists have held otherwise, of course. They started from the fact that the view one has of reality, whether in the material or moral sphere, is shaped by the enculturative experience. On this basis they maintained that there could be no absolute norms for the evaluation of cultures other than one's own. "By whose standards shall we judge?" they asked.

Granted the knottiness of the problem, still it is solved on the practical level by the familiar distinction between tolerance and indifference. Even in matters closest to the heart a man can hold fast to his own conviction, believing his position to be absolutely correct (else why hold it?), while also accepting the fact that others take quite a different position (which is wrong, but theirs). This is tolerance, or "benign ethnocentrism" (D. Bidney, "The Concept of Value in Modern Anthropology" in *Anthropology Today* 690).

To say that two positions are equally valid is something else again. It is indifference. And as Redfield states, the doctrine of cultural relativism is not a doctrine of ethical indifference [*The Primitive World and Its Transformations* (Ithaca, N.Y. 1953) 146]. When pushed to it by the practical need to decide, even the staunchest defenders of cultural relativism will draw the line at racial discrimination and unprovoked armed conquest, appealing to underlying basic norms to justify their condemnation. In *The Quiet American,* Graham Greene's Mr. Heng puts it this way: "Sooner or later, one has to take sides—if one is to remain human."

Bibliography: Reference Works. R. S. and M. P. BECKHAM, comps., "A Basic List of Books and Periodicals for College Libraries," *Resources for the Teaching of Anthropology,* ed. D. G. MANDELBAUM et al. (Amer. Anthropological Assoc. Memoirs 95; Washington 1963) 77–316. M. J. HERSKOVITS, ed., *International Directory of Anthropologists* (3d ed. Washington 1950). W. L. THOMAS, JR. and A. M. PIKELIS, eds., *International Directory of Anthropological Institutions* (New York 1953), 2d ed. in *Current Anthropology* 5 (1964) 213–280. General Texts. R. L. BEALS and H. HOIJER, *An Introduction to Anthropology* (2d ed. New York 1959). P. BOHANNAN, *Social Anthropology* (New York 1963). F. M. KEESING, *Cultural Anthropology* (New York 1958). Substantive Inventories. A. L. KROEBER et al., *Anthropology Today* (Chicago 1953). B. J. SEIGEL, ed., *Biennial Review of Anthropology* (Stanford 1959–). S. TAX, ed., *Anthropology Today: Selections* (Chicago 1962); ed., *Horizons of Anthropology* (Chicago 1964). S. TAX et al., *An Appraisal of Anthropology Today* (Chicago 1953). W. L. THOMAS, JR., ed., *Current Anthropology* (Chicago 1956). History. R. H. LOWIE, *The History of Ethnological Theory* (New York 1937). T. K. PENNIMAN, *A Hundred Years of Anthropology* (2d ed. London 1952). Theory. D. BIDNEY, *Theoretical Anthropology* (New York 1953). A. L. KROEBER and C. KLUCKHOHN, "Culture, A Critical Review of Concepts and Definitions" in *Papers of the Peabody Museum of American Archeology and Ethnology* 47.1 (Cambridge, Mass. 1952; repr. pa. New York 1963).

[F. LYNCH]

ANTHROPOLOGY, PHYSICAL

A subdivision of anthropology concerned with certain aspects of the biology of man, having the study of human *evolution as its central interest. It is both broader and narrower than a strictly human biology—broader in that it traditionally includes the study of living and fossil nonhuman primates; narrower in that it touches only peripherally medicine and related sciences, such as psychology, physiology, biochemistry, and anatomy. In its earlier history it was largely anthropometric, and measurements of lengths and weights are still important in many anthropological studies. In recent years there has been an increasing tendency to utilize methods and techniques developed by other disciplines in trying to solve problems of physical anthropology; many studies that may properly be included within its range have been made by investigators who have not been primarily physical anthropologists. This wide range of interests and the relevance of so many kinds of information to the central problems of physical anthropology make for a certain amount of fragmentation in the field; but the main areas can be included under the following headings: (1) fossil and living primates, (2) fossil man, (3) human races, (4) evolution in living human populations, and (5) anthropometry. Research in each of these areas has provided greater detail and precision for the construction of theories of human evolution. This article illustrates methods and principles; it does not present a detailed account of the findings of physical anthropology.

HISTORY

Physical anthropology owes its origins to the applications of knowledge accumulated in post-Renaissance Europe, when taxonomic studies were stimulated by discoveries of many new plants and animals from distant lands. Classifications of new and different peoples were attempted as early as the 17th century, and were followed shortly by the first anatomical comparison of man and an anthropoid ape. J. F. Blumenbach (1752–

1840) is generally regarded as the founder of physical anthropology. He introduced measurements into the study of human variation and grouped living men into five great races. His anatomical orientation has been strongly and continuously represented in the development of the discipline.

Impact of the Theory of Evolution. The greatest influence in the development of modern physical anthropology has been that of Charles *Darwin (1809–82), who revolutionized biological thought in 1859 by presenting overwhelming evidence that evolution had taken place and by offering a plausible explanation of its most important basis, natural selection. Both Darwin and his close associate T. H. *Huxley (1825–95) wrote extensively on problems of human evolution and modern races of man. The greatest deficiency in Darwin's theory was lack of knowledge of biological inheritance. With the rediscovery in 1900 of the work of Gregor *Mendel (1822–84) and the prompt founding of the new science of *genetics, it became possible to clear away the last major restriction on the development of rational theories of evolution. The English biometrical school, founded by Francis *Galton (1822–1911) and the great statistician Karl Pearson (1857–1936), was at first skeptical of the general applicability of Mendelian genetics to the inheritance of continuously variable characteristics such as human stature; but as more was learned about the interactions of separate genes, it became possible to incorporate genetic theory into the analysis of traits involving an inheritance too complex to be determined by available techniques. Population genetics had its beginnings in 1908 with the mathematical demonstration by G. H. Hardy and Wilhelm Weinberg that gene frequencies remain stable from generation to generation in the absence of selection. By 1930 the biometrician R. A. Fisher had developed equations to show how long-term evolution could take place in spite of the enormous complexity of the genetic makeup of individuals and populations. In the ensuing decades S. Wright, J. B. S. Haldane, T. Dobzhansky, the paleontologist G. G. Simpson, and numerous others continued the development of the modern synthetic theory of evolution with mathematical formulations, experiments, and field observations of living and extinct populations.

Pioneers in the Development of Physical Anthropology. Much of this information was not simultaneously assimilated into the general body of anthropological theory. Physical anthropological research remained at first a continuation of traditional anthropometric and anatomical methods combined with evolutionary concepts that were developed by paleontologists of the late 19th century. The major figures in the early 20th century were Arthur Keith (1866–1955) in England, who developed the theory of the evolution of human upright posture from the locomotion of ancestral primates progressing through an arboreal environment by brachiating (swinging by the arms from overhead branches); Pierre Boule (1861–1942) in France, who described fossil Neanderthal men from French caves; Franz Boas (1858–1942) in the U.S., to whose influential position as a teacher and wide interests in cultural and physical anthropology is owed in large measure the American tradition that maintains the unity of physical anthropology with the other branches of the science (in contrast with the tendency toward their academic separation in Europe); and Aleš Hrdlička (1869–1943), who founded the *American Journal of Physical Anthropology* and was the chief organizer of the American Association of Physical Anthropologists. America is perhaps peculiar in that the great majority of the professional physical anthropologists of the mid-20th century were trained by a single great teacher, E. A. Hooton (1887–1954), or by his students. This reflects the relatively recent recognition of physical anthropology as an academic discipline and the late development of many scholarly specialties in North America. Contemporary trends in physical anthropology can be outlined best in the treatment of the various specialties within the field.

The Primates

In his *Systema Naturae* Carolus *Linnaeus (1707–78) placed man in the taxonomic order Primates; the name signifies the position of man at the head of the animal kingdom. The classification of man as a primate recognizes that he shows so many similarities of structure to the simian apes and monkeys that all may be classified together. Modern taxonomy continues the order Primates and uses the Linnaean genus and species name for man, Homo sapiens. The order has been expanded to include many forms, known collectively as prosimians, that are at a lower level of organization than the apes and monkeys; the bats, originally classified as primates, have been placed in a separate order. It is now recognized that the structural similarities used in grouping living forms are mainly a function of the inheritance of these characteristics from common ancestors. Both the similarities and differences among primates are results of evolutionary processes.

Living Primates. Physical anthropologists have focused much of their attention on the primates because these closest of human relatives are considered potentially to reveal more than other orders about the biology of man through comparative methods of study. The emphasis is on major features of evolution from prehuman to human stages of advancement and on better understanding of the biological processes involved. By using a variety of experimental and analytical techniques, comparisons can be made with primates that are similar to man but are frequently outside the normal human range of variation in structure, chemistry, physiology, or behavior.

The primate order is of special interest for another reason. It includes a very wide range of levels of biological organization, with a hierarchy that ranges from man through anthropoid apes, monkeys, and the prosimians. There are also definite connections with a group of small mammals called tree shrews, although some authorities do not believe that they should be regarded as primates. These authorities usually place the tree shrews in the order Insectivora, believed to be most similar in level of organization to ancestral placental mammals. Thus the primates show a series of graded connections from a complex to a relatively simple level of mammalian organization, down through animals that cannot even be considered primates. In addition, there are numerous sublevels of organization among the apes, monkeys, and prosimians.

The picture is not so simple and clear as one may be led to believe by this sketch, however. There are a great many primate species, each a product of long periods of evolution independent of the others. While each was establishing its own adaptation to the environment, many genetically controlled characteristics were altered from the common ancestral conditions by evolutionary processes. Thus no living primate is a precise counterpart of any human ancestor. Discovering and evaluating the characteristics of primates and their bearing on problems of human evolution is therefore an important but difficult part of anthropological research. Physical anthropologists and scientists from other disciplines have been accumulating knowledge and building theories for more than 100 years; but it is safe to state that, in relation to present knowledge, far more remains either unknown, imperfectly understood, or interpreted differently by different authorities. This is not essentially discouraging, however, because it indicates the vast amount of useful information that is available from the study of primates.

In addition, major evolutionary developments that allow higher stages of organization and at times entirely new ways of exploiting the environment are comparatively rare and often are readily distinguishable. Therefore, it is frequently possible to separate major features common to these organizational levels from those that represent special adaptations to a portion of the environment. For example, the two major groups of Old World monkeys have the same adaptation for stereoscopic color vision, but species of one subfamily have enlarged and sacculated stomachs that allow them to digest mature leaves, whereas those from the other subfamily have no such arrangement but do have cheek pouches that allow them to store seeds and fruits and to chew and swallow such food at leisure. These feeding adaptations, though very important to the species for survival, are probably not greatly significant in human evolution. In contrast, the visual apparatus of these monkeys is essentially the same as that of man; and if it had not been developed in the primate ancestors of man, it is unlikely that human evolution would have been possible.

Fossil Primates. The amount of biological data about living primates is far greater than could ever be accumulated from paleontological discoveries. Fossils, however, serve as essential guideposts in tracing the actual history of the primates and man and in evaluating characteristics of living primates for their evolutionary implications. On the other hand, knowledge of living animals allows many valid inferences to be made about the fleshy parts of fossils.

Fossil primates are somewhat few and fragmentary in comparison with fossil representatives of some of the other mammalian orders, probably because so many ancient primates lived in a forest environment, as is the case today. Forests generally provide poor conditions for fossilization. Nevertheless, the fossil record of primates is distributed among five continents and through vast stretches of time, and paleontologists have recovered an impressive variety of animals. The accompanying table is for easy reference in the placement of fossils in time. It gives an estimate of the beginning and the duration of each of the time periods of the age of mammals.

AGE OF MAMMALS

Period	Duration, in years	Time of beginning, in years before present
Pleistocene	1,000,000	1,000,000
Pliocene	11,000,000	12,000,000
Miocene	13,700,000	25,700,000
Oligocene	8,300,000	34,000,000
Eocene	21,000,000	55,000,000
Paleocene	23,000,000	78,000,000

Evolutionary Sequence of Levels of Organization. Parts of the picture on primates are fairly clear in their implications and yield a story of compelling interest. Primates are among the oldest of the orders of surviving mammals; the earliest specimens date from the middle Paleocene. In some Paleocene and Eocene deposits primates are among the most common of mammals. Their variety is astonishing; one authority lists fifty-eight genera, not all of which can definitely be included in a larger grouping into eight families. All were somewhat small animals, however, and all were probably at a prosimian level of organization. Many are known only from a few teeth and jaws, but in others the skull or skeleton is well preserved. Some show affinities with insectivores, and a rodentlike adaptation seems indicated in three separate families. Others, however, probably are closely related to modern lemurs and tarsiers and may be directly ancestral to them.

During the late Eocene a drastic reduction in number and variety of prosimian fossil primates took place, and after the early Oligocene they are almost completely absent from the fossil record until the Pleistocene. It is clear that a widespread extinction of the early prosimians occurred during this critical period. Their decline is coincident with the first evidence of higher primates during the early Oligocene and with the rise of the true rodents. It has been suggested that the early primates could not compete with rodents, and their near extinction followed directly. Furthermore, the evolution of the higher primates from prosimian ancestors may have been one consequence of this rigorous competition. The very survival of a few groups of primates may have depended on a shift to a more complex level of biological organization. This shift was most likely toward new adaptations for greater visual acuity and more complex behavior made possible by larger brains.

The early history of the primates thus corresponds very well to the inferences about their relationships drawn from comparative anatomy and behavior. The prosimian primates appear much earlier than the higher primates, and their origins go back nearly as far as the earliest placental mammals. Thus the implied evolutionary sequence of levels of organization approximates the actual historical one indicated by the early primate fossils.

Order of Appearance of Living Primates. The evolutionary sequence of monkey to ape, logically constructed from living forms, receives little or no support from paleontological evidence, however. The earliest simian primates recovered in the Old World date from the early Oligocene. Once more the bulk of the specimens are teeth and jaws, and these resemble those of modern anthropoid apes more closely than they do the Old World monkeys. The similarities to the small living anthropoid apes, the gibbons, are especially noteworthy. There is indirect evidence that a simian level of visual acuity had been attained by this time, but that the brain was still small by present-day higher primate standards. From the evidence of later forms it now seems probable that at least some (and possibly all) of these early apes progressed quadrupedally (on all four limbs) rather than in a semiupright, or brachiating, manner as do living anthropoid apes. They would thus be equivalent to modern monkeys in their general locomotor adaptation. The first clear evidence of Old World monkeys is quite late, in the Pliocene, and the specimens seem to be fully modern in structure. The possibility thus appears strong that Old World monkeys are descended from primates genetically similar to anthropoid apes, rather than the reverse.

Larger apes appear in the Miocene. They have definite resemblances in tooth structure to the modern African chimpanzees and gorillas, but the few specimens for which more than the skull is preserved indicate that they were either quadrupedal or were somewhat poor brachiators. Probably ancestors of the gibbons were also much less well adapted to brachiation than the living forms, the most adept of all primate brachiators.

A few very fragmentary lower jaws with teeth have been recovered from very late Miocene and early Pliocene deposits that show similarities to man. It is thus possible that the line leading to the hominids was developing throughout the Pliocene. No other skeletal evidence is available; so the nature of the evolutionary history of human ancestors remains unknown for the epoch before the transitional period between the Pliocene and Pleistocene. By this time the separation between hominids (man and his immediate evolutionary predecessors) and pongids (the anthropoid apes) had quite clearly taken place.

The living primates of the New World can only be mentioned here. They show many parallels with Old World monkeys and include various levels of organization, from the marmoset, not much higher in scale than prosimians, to monkeys as intelligent as any in the Old World. They may have reached their higher level of organization independently of African and Asian counterparts. The fossil record indicates a very long separation from all other primates. They provide very interesting parallel data for testing evolutionary theories based mainly on Old World forms.

Contemporary Primate Studies. As more precise knowledge of human biology is needed, the nonhuman experimental animals used have to have greater genetic similarity to man, and the nature of the differences has to be evaluated in order to understand the significance of results of the research. From the above account of the history of the primate order, it is clear that the primates offer by far the best chance for fitting these specifications. Species from other mammalian orders have evolved separately from human ancestors for more than 50 million years. The nature of their common ancestry with primates is lost in obscurity, and every major evolutionary change has probably tended to separate them genetically even further from man.

It is the principal task of physical anthropologists concentrating on nonhuman primates to evaluate the significant similarities to and differences from man and to relate them to the evolutionary picture. It is a formidable undertaking. Some of the more strictly biological approaches used are (1) anatomical studies of bones, muscles, and joints, in analyzing human and primate posture and locomotion; (2) studies of special features of the skeleton and teeth that promise to show genetic relationships of both living and extinct primates; (3) immunological investigations of body fluids and tissues, the amounts of cross reactions indicating degrees of relationship of different species; (4) separation of molecular components of tissues by such techniques as chromatography and electrophoresis, which can often be used along with immunological techniques; (5) analysis of chromosome numbers and morphology; and (6) examination of parasites and susceptibility to diseases. New methods are being developed, and more can be expected in the future.

The behavior of primates is as revealing as their structure. Many features of primates may be regarded as laying the groundwork for the evolution to the human state: their basic grasping adaptation, emphasis on vision, slow development, long life, and in higher primates their social gregariousness and high learning capacity. These have led to profitable research on the distribution, ecology, and social organization of primates in their natural habitats, and this research is contributing much to anthropological theories of the primate foundations of the human cultural way of life. These are supplemented by studies of captive groups of animals, for which conditions can be controlled more closely. Finally, the primates have been essential experimental animals in the development of theories of the nature of human learning, because of their high intelligence and adaptability.

These and other kinds of primate studies are being pursued vigorously, more often than not by scientists who are not physical anthropologists. However, the emphasis of anthropologists on evolutionary and ecological approaches to the study of man and their broad overview of the entire primate order make it certain that they can advance understanding of the significance of the new information as it is revealed.

Fossil Man

The record of early fossil man is confined to the Old World, as is that of all fossil apes. The earliest finds are the Australopithecine man-apes, which have been recovered almost entirely from Africa.

Discoveries. The Australopithecines are recorded from the transitional period between the Pliocene and Pleistocene, which was the time of the earliest toolmaking traditions, and some may have survived into the middle Pleistocene, when more advanced men had already evolved. They had brains that were not much larger than those of living anthropoid apes, but their teeth were basically human in structure, and they certainly walked upright. These features suggest that their teeth were not primarily weapons and that the hands were free to manipulate tools. They manufactured tools, or at least one species did.

Human fossils from the middle Pleistocene are scarce and widely spread. By this time the upright posture was fully established (it may have been with the man-apes also) and the group called Peking man were using fire. The molar teeth had become reduced in size and the brain was considerably larger, but still well below average size for modern man. Another specimen (Steinheim), probably later in the middle Pleistocene, was approaching the skull structure of modern man. Later human populations, which probably preceded the advent of modern man by a relatively short period of time, are large-brained but differ markedly from modern man and from each other in appearance (European Neanderthal, Rhodesian). All later fossil populations are fully modern in form.

Interpretation. The overall picture seems consistent, and was summarized by Franz Weidenreich (1873–1948), who described the Peking fossils as a progressive increase in size of the brain accompanying a decrease in size of the face. The archeological record indicates that the human adaptation of culture was developing during the same period. The sequence beyond the ape stage was probably (1) upright posture, (2) use of tools, (3) manufacture of tools accompanying the development of symbolic language, (4) increase in brain size as an adaptation to the cultural way of life. The selection for more intelligent individuals and populations was probably intense during the Pleistocene, since they would be much better able to exploit the developing uses of language and culture. This view of the basic factor in explicitly human evolution is the most important concept uniting physical anthropology with the other branches of anthropology; yet it is almost entirely a product of theoretical advances since 1950.

Although the broad outlines seem clear, there are many unsolved smaller problems of great importance in understanding the causes and course of human evolution from primate ancestors to modern man. The present trend in attacking these problems is to use a wide variety of techniques of analysis. It received its greatest impetus when K. P. Oakley in 1949 revived the fluorine method of determining whether a particular specimen was from the same general time period as the other fossils in a deposit. An early application of the method led relatively soon to the suspicion that the fragmentary Piltdown skull, probably the most famous and controversial of all, was actually a hoax. This was quickly established by microscopic examinations and various chemical analyses, which subsequently revealed that associated tools and animal fossils were also placed at the sites by the forger. The elimination of Piltdown cleared the way for rational and consistent interpretations of the human fossil record. From that time forward, objective techniques have been used increasingly in fossil studies, fortunately without any other such spectacular discoveries.

Human Races

Anthropologists are interested in the physical characteristics of peoples in different parts of the world, particularly with reference to differences that are the result of separate evolutionary processes. The study of races is thus another phase of the central problem of human evolution. Racial studies differ somewhat from those of fossil and living primates in that they deal only with a single species. They also differ from studies of fossil man, because the latter are concerned with individuals and groups that are usually not contemporaneous, making questions concerning the existence of more than one species of man at any single moment in time difficult to answer.

Present-day man fits quite precisely the modern definition of a species of higher animals: a population in which exchange of genes is taking place or has recently taken place throughout its geographical range. This implies that representatives of different subpopulations are able to interbreed, as has been demonstrated repeatedly in man.

Evolutionary Diversification. Partial isolation of different human groups because of geographical or other barriers has allowed local evolutionary diversification to take place. Some of this diversification is readily apparent in the averages of such features as skin color, hair form, and a variety of facial structures. Others are characterized by smaller differences revealed only by relatively small mean differences in bodily measurements, and still others are indicated by different frequencies of traits that can be inferred only from physiological, biochemical, or immunological data. Where enough average differences are found between groups of people, anthropologists usually call these groups races. Opinions differ widely as to what constitute "enough average differences." One recent classification lists five races; another describes 32, with others, not readily defined, that are presumed to exist. (*See* RACE.)

Such differences of opinion suggest that the delimitation of human races can become a taxonomic exercise rather than an advance in genuine knowledge. They also tend to reflect the kinds of problems the individual anthropologist is trying to solve. Few have been content with classifying alone. They have attempted also to discover the degree of biological relationship among differing human groups and to trace the broad outlines of their historical connections. Unfortunately, the genetic basis for many of the characteristics used in race studies is at present unknown and probably too complex for analysis by existing methods. In addition, many of the human traits controlled by variants of a single gene (alleles), such as the blood groups, are now believed to have selective value at times for one or another of the different effects of the alleles. This is likely to cause such rapid changes in the percentage of alleles of a gene in the differing environmental circumstances of separate geographical areas that many anthropologists think that these single gene effects are extremely unreliable as indicators of the amount of time human populations have been isolated from each other, and that they may be misleading as measures of the amount of remaining genetic similarity of separate races, in the present state of knowledge.

Trends in Studies of Race. Attempts to classify living races as a function of recency of common descent from ancestral groups extend the principles of post-Darwinian taxonomy to populations within a single species. This is inherently difficult to accomplish because very precise biological information is necessary to make a satisfactory analysis of the traits used in assessing relationships, because the extent of genetic modification resulting from different adaptive requirements of separate environments is difficult to measure, and because there has probably been a great deal of migration and consequent genetic exchange between different populations throughout much of the history of mankind. It is a task not often attempted by taxonomists examining nonhuman species, where the difficulties are probably less than with man.

As a result of increased awareness of these difficulties and greater knowledge of the processes of population stability and change, there has been a trend away from classifications that try to assess degrees of relationship, such as the classic division of mankind into Caucasoid, Mongoloid, and Negroid primary races, with subgroups presumed to result from later differentiation or from hybridization between representative populations within the major groups. Present-day anthropologists also usually reject the "racial type" and "pure race" concepts, which are holdovers from taxonomic procedures devised before population genetics became a central part of evolutionary theory. For example, it is highly improbable that individuals with the darkest skin, the most tightly curled hair, and the greatest lip dimensions represent survivals of the original "African type" or that there was ever a "Nordic race" consisting entirely of tall, blond individuals with blue eyes and long heads.

Social implications of race and studies of interactions of racial groups, aside from their genetic consequences, are not a primary concern of physical anthropology. These subjects are frequently so explosive in their implications, however, that it becomes a task of the physical anthropologists to make sure that the measurement and analysis of racial differences are based on the most accurate and complete information available. (*See* RACE DIFFERENCES.)

Evolution in Living Human Populations

The difficulties in classifying human races and tracing their histories have led to a decrease in the amount of effort expended by anthropologists along these lines. A developing trend is to use the different populations of the world as subjects for the study of those processes of human evolution that are actively taking place or did so recently enough to allow good estimates of some of the genetics of the situation. Different racial groups are found in differing environments; so the study of races and the causes of their formation (as well as change or possible disappearance) usually enters into such investigations. This research overlaps with the work of human geneticists, but the concern with human evolution places it legitimately within the realm of physical anthropology.

Evolutionary Processes. Evolution may be defined objectively as change of gene frequency in a population through time. Significant alterations come about from four processes: mutation, migration, selection, and genetic drift. Mutation gives the basic material for evolution, changes within the hereditary materials of chromosomes and genes. All alleles are the result of mutation. In some cases it has been possible to calculate the actual rate of mutation for particular alleles in human populations. Migration, referred to also as "gene flow" or "hybridization," consists of exchanges of genes by interbreeding, either from actual invasions or from mating between individuals of contiguous populations. Selection is the most important of all processes of gene frequency change, and results largely from differential survival and breeding of individuals. These individuals are usually better adapted to the particular environment and transmit some of their genetic characteristics to their larger number of offspring. Genetic drift refers to fluctuations in gene frequencies in the absence of selection. It is more likely to occur in small populations, where accidents alone may result in the elimination or reduction of the numbers of some alleles and increases of others.

A study of possible effects of migration is that of P. B. Candela, who has compiled evidence that the long-observed tendency for blood group B to increase in frequency in Europe as one goes farther east is a result of invasions by Asiatic peoples, such as the Huns, Tartars, and Hungarians. There are some European populations that do not fit this scheme too well, but on the whole the evidence is fairly convincing.

Selective Effects: the Sickle-cell Phenomenon. More significant for recent trends in the research of physical anthropologists are studies indicating that natural selection can have very profound effects on the genetic differences between living human populations. It has long been known that a phenomenon called "sickling" was very common in red blood cells of people of African origins and that some of the people with this characteristic developed a severe and often fatal anemia, whereas others did not. It was finally established that individuals with the sickle-cell anemia had inherited both of the alleles giving rise to the sickle-cell characteristic, whereas those who had the sickle cells but not the disease had inherited one allele for normal red blood cells and one allele for the sickling characteristic. Since individuals with sickle-cell anemia more often than not died without producing offspring, the following question arose: Why was the allele for the sickle characteristic not eliminated from the population? When human populations in tropical Africa were examined, many of them were found to have much higher percentages of people with the sickle-cell characteristic than percentages among American Negroes, ranging as high as 45 per cent in one area. The probable solution to the puzzle was provided by A. C. Allison, who showed that the high percentages of sickling were in areas with high incidence of a particularly deadly form of malaria. Individuals with the sickle-cell trait showed much greater resistance to this malaria parasite than those with only normal red blood cells (Allison actually demonstrated this by experimentally injecting volunteers with the parasites). A clear case of balanced polymorphism is indicated. Individuals with alleles only for normal cells tend to die of malaria; those with alleles only for sickle cells tend to die from the anemia. The best fitted to survive in areas heavily infested with malaria are those with one allele for each type of cell ("heterozygotes," in genetic terminology). They resist malaria and do not have the anemia.

This demonstration of a selective advantage in one geographical area for an allele that is deleterious in another helped bring about a revolution in thinking about the selective advantages of many other single gene effects that had formerly been thought to be neutral in value. Investigations have shown that some blood groups are associated with higher incidence of particular diseases. It has also been shown theoretically that a high frequency of any allele in a population is evidence of a selective advantage, either at present or during some time in the past. Unraveling these supposed selective effects will probably be an expanding task of physical anthropologists for some time to come.

Anthropometry

Anthropometry, literally "the measurement of man," was at one time virtually synonymous with physical anthropology. Although the field now encompasses techniques that are not measurements in the conventional sense of length, weight, or volume, the main anthropological purposes of determining quantifiable units that can be used in problems related to human evolution remain a function of newer genetic approaches. At the same time, conventional measurements remain essential and are being extended by photography, X rays, and other devices to allow measurements not otherwise possible with calipers and scales.

Evolutionary Studies. In the description and comparison of fossils, measurements are essential for evaluating the significance of such features as gross size of different parts of the skeleton, limb proportions, tooth morphology, and cranial capacity. The measurements of living individuals often show average differences of one kind or another between local populations or larger racial groups that may not be readily apparent from observations alone, sometimes indicating the nature of the evolutionary processes operating. In cross-species comparisons measurements aid in the analysis of locomotion in man and living nonhuman primates in seeking answers to questions about the evolutionary development of the unique upright human posture and gait. Measurements are especially important in the study of growth when changes in body proportions accompany increases in size and when the additional measurement of time is a function of the determination of rates of growth.

Applications. Besides its being frequently essential in evolutionary studies, the analysis of growth also has many medical applications. Growth abnormalities can aid physicians in diagnosing some diseases, and slow growth rates may be indicators of nutritional deficiencies. Other applications of anthropometry to practical problems include studies to aid in the design of military clothing, airplane cockpits and passenger accommodations, space capsules, and the fitting of industrial machines to the people who must attend them.

Relationship to Other Branches of Anthropology

There has been an increase of interest in social, cultural, and other behavioral factors that may contribute to past or present human evolution. Virtually concurrently, there has been a growing awareness among cultural anthropologists that many aspects of primate and human evolution need to be clarified if general theories of behavior of present-day man are to be considered valid. Thus, while the physical anthropologists have been drawing more and more upon new biological techniques and concepts developed by other fields of study, the interdependence of physical anthropology with other specialties in anthropology has increased. Some of the interrelationships are mentioned below.

Archeology. Estimating the antiquity of a fossil skeleton is often critically important for interpreting its significance for human evolution. Archeologists have much the same chronological problem with cultural remains, and they are often better trained and equipped than human paleontologists to analyze the geological sequences and to use the various methods of absolute or relative dating. On the other hand, archeologists are greatly interested in the evolutionary status of the people associated with the cultures they are attempting to recover and analyze. The physical anthropologists and archeologists therefore often work quite closely together, or one person may be forced to assume both roles.

Association of Hominid Fossils and Tools. The archeological record is virtually the only tangible evidence of the human status of the early hominid fossils. The cranial capacity and what little can be deduced about the structure of the brain of the early men give no positive clues about their cultural capacity. The discovery that the Australopithecine man-apes must have been erect bipedal walkers, and therefore were probably closely related to modern man, led to renewed interest in their possible use and manufacture of tools. With the hands and arms freed, it seems fairly certain that they used tools of a simple kind, but the early discoveries indicated that they lived at a time earlier than any worked stone tools. It is one thing to use tools (many animals do) and quite another thing to manufacture spears, knives, or scrapers. However, R. A. Dart in South Africa found more and more evidence that animal bones were being made into cutting tools by these creatures, and later finds indicated that there were stone tools in layers contemporaneous with Australopithecine deposits. Finally, L. S. B. Leakey in Tanganyika discovered a man-ape skull in direct association with stone tools of a crude but well-established tradition that was already known in Africa. There is some dispute as to whether or not more advanced men were also present in Africa at the same time, but the evidence for this view is quite sketchy and subject to other possible interpretations.

Authorities also disagree on the significance of tool manufacture as an indicator of the power of speech in these creatures, some believing that tool traditions are not possible without symbolic communication and others leaning toward the idea that tool manufacture could be accomplished at the level of imitation and may actually have helped in achieving true speech, by favoring social groups with better communicating methods. Here the problems of physical anthropology impinge not only upon archeology but also upon linguistic and social anthropological theory. It is possible that positive evidence to settle the question can be derived from several sources in the future. In any case, the evidence for incipient human culture is strong, indicating the interrelationship between evolving man and developing culture.

Ecological Aspects of Human Evolution. Other questions in which archeology relates closely to human evolution concern the extent to which fossil men in some regions evolved separately from other human populations and whether recognizable cultural zones have distinctive human populations. These problems are too numerous and detailed to describe here. For present-day anthropology one of these is quite important and requires mention. Skeletons of men who are anatomically modern (within the normal range of variation of present populations) first appeared relatively recently, perhaps within the past 40,000 years, except for a few fragmentary specimens whose ancient date or modern status are disputed. Similarly, evidence for human populations that differ noticeably from modern men and from each other has been uncovered in deposits that are nearly as late in time and may actually overlap the date of appearance of modern man. The famous Neanderthal men of Europe represent an example of one such population. Did these local premodern human populations evolve into modern man in their own regions, or were most of them replaced by modern men who had evolved in one locality and spread out from there? If these questions can ever be answered, it is likely that the archeological record will provide the evidence, since it is so much more complete than the fossil sequences.

Archeological sites from later horizons, where bone need not be fossilized to be preserved, often have so many skeletons that the structure of the human population can be analyzed with some confidence by physical anthropologists. It is possible to determine the racial composition in some cases, but in general it must be admitted that differences between archeological populations of modern men are too small for present methods to show many genetic and historical relationships with real assurance of their validity. A newer and more practical trend is to obtain inferences about the ecology of the people and to use such varied information as population size and age composition of burials, nutritional status, and probable causes of death. In some cases it has been possible to record stability or changes in populations through periods of time that often extend for centuries. *See* ARCHEOLOGY I (PREHISTORIC).

Ethnology and Social Anthropology. Although some anthropologists use the terms interchangeably, in this article ethnology is defined as the study of the historical relationships between contemporary peoples, usually nonliterate ones at the time of discovery by Europeans; social anthropology concerns the comparison of ways of life of different human groups and generalizations that can be made about human behavior from such comparisons. The concept of *culture is central to both types of study.

Physical Anthropology and Ethnology. Ethnology in this definition is an extension of archeology, although there is frequently little or no archeological record to aid the ethnologists. The physical anthropologists can in some cases aid ethnologists by giving measurements of the amount of biological similarity or divergence of different peoples, and there is more and better material to work with in examining living populations than with skeletons. The analysis is usually on surer ground with peoples in the same geographical area; it is often possible to state that different peoples with similar cultures were either originally part of a common tribe or that they have similar ways of life because one or both groups entered an area and adopted new methods and attitudes. A classic example of the latter is that of the many distinct American Indian groups that entered the plains of the west only after the introduction of horses by Europeans made it possible to hunt bison effectively. Linguistic evidence is often even more important for this kind of problem; but the presence of castelike groups, such as the pygmies in parts of Africa, who use the same language as surrounding peoples but are quite distinct physically, indicates that previous languages can be abandoned entirely and that the biological differences either result from an original historical separation or from reproductive isolation based on caste barriers. Both possibilities come within the area of problems in human evolution.

Physical Anthropology and Social Anthropology. The relationship between physical anthropology and social anthropology is somewhat more indirect. The things the individual person learns as a part of society are so important and the instinctive aspects of human behavior are so minimal or altogether lacking that it is sometimes convenient to ignore the biological basis for man's culture. This attitude has been exacerbated by unfortunate attempts of some scholars (and nonscholars) to make oversimplified correlations of behavior with race, body build, or head shape, to mention some of the most persistent categories.

The theory of human evolution that has become the orthodox view among anthropologists serves as the main bridge between physical and social anthropology. This postulates that culture, a way of life emphasizing behavior learned mainly through the symbolic method of communication, language, is the most important human adaptation to the environment and that the evolution of man from his immediate nonhuman ancestors was primarily the story of a species progressively improving this cultural adaptation. The numerous ramifications of the theory now occupy many social anthropologists and linguists as well as physical anthropologists. There has also been an increasing awareness that cultural practices of human groups can have important consequences for small-scale evolution.

The social structures of human societies are part of their adaptations to particular environments, though not always especially effective ones. The resurgence of ecological approaches, even when the evolutionary consequences may be extremely obscure and of no immediate concern to social anthropologists, is an application of biological concepts to problems of human behavior that will inevitably bring about closer relationships with physical anthropologists. (*See* ANTHROPOLOGY, CULTURAL.)

Linguistics. Human *language is a structured method of communication that must be learned by each individual. It is the most important method for transmitting human culture, and it gives human societies an enormously important tool for adapting to both familiar and unfamiliar situations. It is certain that language has had an important role in human evolution; but as mentioned previously, authorities disagree on the nature of that role and the period of time in which speech began to play a part in the human story.

Anatomical and physiological studies of the brain and nervous system of man and other primates continue to give information on the biological correlates of human speech and primate communication. The brain is one of the areas where direct experimentation is possible in humans as well as in animals, and new techniques of electrical recording and stimulation and of drug injections in tiny amounts at defined locations in the brain have increased the pace at which new knowledge has been acquired. Studies of primate communication by sounds, gestures, and facial expressions in laboratories and in the field and their correlations with social behavior give some idea of the primate bases from which human speech developed and may eventually lead to adequate theories of the method by which the transition took place. Studies of the vocal apparatus itself need to be expanded. The author of one study has concluded that chimpanzees could never reproduce the majority of human sounds, and attempts to teach these animals to speak have certainly been notable for meager results. Many investigators think that the failure lies more in the inadequacy of the ape nervous system; there is probably not enough brain power there to adapt to anything so complex as speech.

Bibliography: J. BUETTNER-JANUSCH, ed., *Evolutionary and Genetic Biology of Primates,* 2 v. (New York 1963–64). P. B. CANDELA, "The Introduction of Blood-group B into Europe," *Human Biology* 14 (1942) 413–443. W. E. LE GROS CLARK, *The Antecedents of Man* (Chicago 1960); *The Fossil Evidence for Human Evolution* (2d ed. Chicago 1964). C. S. COON, *The Origin of Races* (New York 1962). R. A. DART, "The Bone-tool Manufacturing Ability of Australopithecus Prometheus," *American Anthropologist* 62 (1960) 134–143. S. M. GARN, *Human Races* (Philadelphia 1961). R. F. HEIZER and S. F. COOK, eds., *The Application of Quantitative Methods in Archaeology* (Chicago 1960). W. C. O. HILL, *Primates* (Edinburgh 1953–). A. HRDLIČKA, *Practical Anthropometry,* ed. T. D. STEWART (4th ed. Philadelphia 1952). A. L. KROEBER, ed., *Anthropology Today* (Chicago 1953). L. S. B. LEAKEY, "A New Fossil Skull from Olduvai," *Nature* 184 (1959) 491–493. F. B. LIVINGSTONE, "Anthropological Implications of Sickle Cell Gene Distribution in West Africa," *American Anthropologist* 60 (1958) 533–562. M.

F. A. MONTAGU, ed., *Culture and the Evolution of Man* (New York 1962). H. L. SHAPIRO, "The History and Development of Physical Anthropology," *American Anthropologist* 61 (1959) 371–379. F. WEIDENREICH, *The Skull of Sinanthropus Pekinensis: A Comparative Study on a Primitive Hominid Skull* (Palaeontologia Sinica NS 10; Pehpei-Chungking 1943). J. S. WEINER, *The Piltdown Forgery* (New York 1955).

[N. TAPPEN]

ANTHROPOLOGY, THEOLOGICAL. In this sector of theology *man is considered not alone but in his relation to *God. A study of his being-in-relation shows him to be dependent upon God for his origin, nature, condition, dignity, and destiny.

Man was created by God in His image and likeness (Gn 1.26–27). The area of likeness is especially the spirit, although at its origin the human spirit has only an approximate likeness to God (*see* IMAGE OF GOD).

The three chief elements constituting man in the Biblical concept are flesh, soul, and spirit, yet they are unified into one living reality. *See* FLESH (IN THE BIBLE); SOUL (IN THE BIBLE); SPIRIT (IN THE BIBLE). Man is entirely flesh and entirely spirit; in the former he feels his frailty in contrast with the strength of his spirit. The Hebrew term for soul, *nepeš,* denotes breath; only one who breathes, who has the principle of life in him, is a living being (Gn 2.7). Biblical writers play upon the idea of spirit, suggesting that God put something of His own spirit into man and gifted him with intelligence and free will. *Salvation history reveals how man passes from one covenantal stage to another, from the people of God to the Mystical Body. His spirit enables man to participate in divine life.

The name *Adam, used in Genesis to designate the first man, is ambivalent. It may mean one man or many. Adamic man is given woman for a helpmate, and the two are to be fruitful and multiply (Gn 1.27–28).Originally man is placed in a condition of innocence, where he has free access to and *friendship with God (Gn 2.25; 3.8). Through a mysterious primordial sin he involves himself and his offspring in a condition of estrangement from God. The sin mars but does not destroy the human image of God; sin deprives it of some of its pristine gifts. With the *Incarnation of Christ, who Himself is the Image of the Father, the marred image of man is re-created (2 Cor 5.17; 3.18; Eph 4.24; Gal 6.15; Col 3.10).

Eventually man attains to the fullness of Christ in His Mystical Body (Eph 1.23; 3.19). The ultimate dignity and destiny of man is to return to his Maker. Man synthesizes, individually and socially, the stuff of the universe, but at present he is "the most mobile point of the stuff in the course of transformation" [Pierre Teilhard de Chardin, *The Phenomenon of Man,* tr. B. Wall (New York 1959) 281].

See also CREATION; CREATION OF MAN; CREATION STORY; ORIGINAL JUSTICE; ELEVATION OF MAN; SUPERNATURAL; REDEMPTION, ARTICLES ON; GRACE; MYSTICAL BODY OF CHRIST.

Bibliography: J. SCHMID, LexThK² 1:604–615. K. RAHNER, *ibid.* 1:618–627. DTC Tables générales 2:2100–06. O. WEBER and R. PRENTER, RGG³ 1:414–424. J. FICHTNER, *Theological Anthropology* (Notre Dame, Ind. 1963). G. C. BERKOUWER, *Man: The Image of God,* tr. D. W. JELLEMA (Grand Rapids 1962). W. G. KÜMMEL, *Man in the New Testament,* tr. J. J. VINCENT (rev. and enl. Philadelphia 1963).

[J. A. FICHTNER]

ANTHROPOMORPHISM

The representation of God or gods under human form and with human attributes. In a broader sense it may be applied to the practice of assigning human characteristics or attributes to nonhuman beings or objects. It is a common phenomenon in primitive religion and has a practically worldwide distribution. The two forms of anthropomorphism are well illustrated by Greek and early Roman religion, respectively.

In Greek religion, the Sky and Earth are represented as gods, Οὐρανός and Γαῖα, and creation as a generation and a birth (cf. Hesiod, *Theog.*). The Greeks always sought to get closer to their gods or to bring their gods closer to themselves. However, when Homer calls Zeus "father of gods and men," he does not mean necessarily that he considers the two races identical. The distinction is clear, e.g., in the *Iliad* 5.441–442, where Apollo in addressing Diomedes says: "since in no wise of the same kind is the race of immortal gods and that of men who walk upon the earth." Pindar uses almost identical language: "One is the race of men, one is the race of gods" (*Nem.* 6.1). Divine power is especially manifest in Apollo, but most of the other gods in Homer are almost too human to be gods in a strict sense. This "humanization" of the gods made man familiar with them. The Greek, accordingly, was without fear of his gods, and opposed to any magical conception of terror or restraint; he was able to study the nature and order of the world and to create science.

But "humanization" had other results also. In its extreme form, it set up a contrast between the gods fashioned in the image of man, with all their weaknesses and even their crimes, and the sublimity and omnipotence attributed to them by earlier faith. This contrast was exploited by the comic poets, and, in particular, by Aristophanes (*Clouds, Birds, Frogs*), yet he remained strongly attached to traditional beliefs. The logic of anthropomorphism finally worked against religion. The philosophers repeatedly protested against

Zeus shown in human form. Greek coin (after Phidias).

such a gross anthropomorphic conception of the gods; e.g., Xenophon of Colophon in the 6th century, the philosopher and dramatist Euripides in the 5th, and Plato in the 4th century.

Animism, the second form of anthropomorphism, peopled all nature with *numina* (powers) or *daemones* (spirits). A formula, although one too brief perhaps, has been proposed for the religion of the Greeks, namely, that it was the resultant of a clash between two attitudes or outlooks: the dynamic animism of the Indo-Europeans, which might be defined as "anthropopsychic," and the "Aegean" and subsequent Hellenic demand for divine generating presences, which was anthropomorphism proper.

If this formula is applied to the Romans, it must be recognized that "anthropopsychism" lasted much longer among them than among the Greeks. In fact, it left marked traces of its vitality in the course of an evolution spread over 1,000 years, and exercised an influence on the concept of the anthropomorphic gods themselves. The history of Vesta is a case in point. She was not given anthropomorphic form until late in Roman religion.

Anthropomorphism did not spare the basic cult of the Mother-Goddess and her male companion, whether husband or son. Even in the case of Mithras, who personified Heaven, and later the Sun and Light, personification signified the progress of anthropomorphism at the same time, for Mithras thus becomes an intermediary (μεσίτης) between man and the Supreme Being.

See also GREEK RELIGION; ROMAN RELIGION; NEMESIS.

Bibliography: F. B. JEVONS, Hastings ERE 1:573–578. G. VAN DER LEEUW, "Anthropomorphismus, nichtchristlich," Reallex AntChr 1:446–448. G. MENSCHING, RGG³ 1:424. PRÜMM, Rel Hdbh, esp. 42–46. C. BAILEY, "Roman Religion," CAH 8:423–453. J. BAYET, *Histoire politique et psychologique de la religion romaine* (Paris 1957). **Illustration credit:** Courtesy of the Trustees of the British Museum.

[É. DES PLACES]

ANTHROPOMORPHISM (IN THE BIBLE),

the attribution of human characteristics, emotions, and situations to God. Israel's faith in God found concrete expression in anthropomorphic language. Anthropomorphisms occur in all parts of the OT. God is described as having eyes (Am 9.3; Sir 11.12), ears (Dn 9.18), hands (Is 5.25), and feet (Gn 3.8; Is 63.3). He molds man out of the dust, plants a garden, takes His rest (Gn 2.3, 7–8). He speaks (Gn 1.3; Lv 4.1), listens (Ex 16.12), and closes the door of Noe's ark (Gn 7.16); He even whistles (Is 7.18). Other expressions credit God with human emotions: He laughs (Ps 2.4), rejoices (So 3.17), becomes angry (1 Chr 13.10), disgusted (Lv 20.23), regretful (Jer 42.10), and revengeful (Is 1.24). Very frequently He is declared to be a jealous God (Ex 20.5; Dt 5.9).

Such language reflects the Semitic belief that the spiritual and physical realms are not mutually exclusive. The Hebrews, little inclined toward philosophical abstraction, were helped by anthropomorphisms better to understand God's living presence among them.

To speak so familiarly of God entailed some risk, but no widespread misunderstanding of the bold imagery of anthropomorphic language seems to have arisen. Periodically, however (Os 11.9; Jb 10.4; Nm 23.19), warnings were issued lest anyone take the graphic images literally. Yahweh was consistently understood to be divine, holy, entirely different from creatures, and utterly unique. No man-made image of Him was ever permitted (Dt 4.12; 5.8), lest it be thought to imprison Him or to place Him under man's control. Unlike the pagan gods, Yahweh had no visible shape or form, and was clearly known to be all-holy, transcendent, self-sufficient, and spiritual.

Bibliography: W. EICHRODT, *Theology of the Old Testament,* tr. J. A. BAKER (London 1961–). P. VAN IMSCHOOT, *Théologie de l'Ancien Testament,* 2 v. (Tournai 1954–56). E. JACOB, *Theology of the Old Testament,* tr. A. W. HEATHCOTE and P. J. ALLCOCK (New York 1958).

[R. T. A. MURPHY]

ANTHROPOMORPHISM (IN THEOLOGY)

From the two Greek words ἄνθρωπος (man) and μορφή (form). The term designates in *theology the tendency to conceive God in human terms. To think of God, for instance, as literally shaking His fist, would be anthropomorphic. For God is pure spirit; before His Incarnation, even the Son, the eternal Word, was exclusively spirit. Since God as God, then, is pure spirit, He has no body, and so no fist.

Such an example may be quite obvious. A much more subtle and problematical anthropomorphism, however, has lain at the base of some of theology's greatest controversies. Thus, to cite a single but very important ex-

The Trinity, 18th-century New Mexican cottonwood-root statue, gesso and tempera pigments. Such anthropomorphic artistic renderings of God are commonplace throughout the history of Christian art.

ample, the various attempts to explain Christ's sacrificial death on the cross as satisfying the Father's vindictiveness have been motivated, at least in part, by a subconscious anthropomorphism. For, in the final analysis, they picture the heavenly Father as subject to a strictly human sort of passion and reaction.

In a brief article, it is possible to touch only on selected aspects of this total question: first, the pedagogical anthropomorphism of which God Himself made use; second, the successful elimination of anthropomorphism through theological analogy; and, third, the psychological inevitability of at least an element and degree of anthropomorphism in theology despite man's best efforts.

Any reader of the OT is aware of the extent to which God tolerated provisionally anthropomorphic ideas about Himself in His slow, step-by-step instruction of His chosen people. He had walked with Adam in the garden, spoken with him as one man with another. He was moved to anger and then placated, all in a manner that sounded very much human.

But in the same divine plan, there would come a time, in the new dispensation, when theological understanding—the effort of human intelligence illuminated by faith—would see rather clearly that nothing material can be said of God, unless in metaphor, but only what is purely spiritual. More than this, not even what is purely spiritual can be said of God, unless by *analogy. If God is called a lion, this is metaphor. If God is said to see, and hear, and vent emotion, this also is metaphor. On the other hand, when God is said to know and, in the strictly spiritual sense, to love, this is not metaphor. For God really does know and love—just as human beings do; *just as,* yet *differently.* And this is analogy. Man's knowing and loving is imperfect; God's is infinite. What separates analogy from metaphor is the dropping out of the "as it were." One says that God shouts, "as it were." For God cannot really shout. To take out the "as it were" at this point is anthropomorphism. But one says that God knows—period. The "as it were" drops out, and must drop out; because God really does know, even though His knowing is infinitely more perfect than man's.

There is still, however, a psychological problem. Under the influence of imagination, even the sharpest theological mind can avoid only with difficulty the almost inevitable inclination to invest the divine object, which in this life man can know but dimly, with the qualities of the human object, which man knows quite well, and upon which he bases his analogical understanding of the infinite. Unless attention to the true nature of analogical predication along with exercise of theological judgment supply, so to speak, a constant corrective, an element or degree of unsuspected anthropomorphism will always be just around the corner.

See also ACCOMMODATION; ANALOGY, THEOLOGICAL USE OF; METHODOLOGY (THEOLOGY); REASONING, THEOLOGICAL; THEOLOGICAL TERMINOLOGY.

Bibliography: A serious study of anthropomorphism, and in the context of theological analogy, courses through several of the writings of B. LONERGAN, e.g., *Insight: A Study of Human Understanding* (New York 1957), ch. 17 and 19, nos. 9, 10; *De Deo trino,* 2 v. (v.1 2d ed., v.2 3d ed. Rome 1964) 1:15–112; 2:7–64. Cognate ideas are reflected also by J. C. MURRAY, *The Problem of God* (New Haven 1964), pt. 2. There are likewise the excellent studies, with more attention to linguistics, of E. L. MASCALL, *Words and Images: A Study in Theological Discourse* (New York 1957); *Existence and Analogy* (New York 1949); *He Who Is* (New York 1948). **Illustration credit:** Museum of New Mexico Collections.

[R. L. RICHARD]

ANTHROPOSOPHY

A religious system developed by Rudolf *Steiner (1861–1925) from *Theosophy as a means of arriving at true knowledge and of final liberation from enslavement to the material world. Anthroposophy, as a theory of knowledge, claims that man originally shared in the spiritual consciousness of the cosmos and that his present mode of knowledge is only a dreamlike vestige of a primordial cognitive state. Through various disciplines it is possible to regain more or less of this innate intuition. In its metaphysical aspect, Anthroposophy holds to the existence of spiritual worlds that are more real than matter and knowable through direct vision by the higher but latent powers of man.

As the name implies, Anthroposophy postulates a "wisdom of man" that calls for two selves in each person: a lower self that knows and a higher ego that is known. In this sense, it is not unlike philosophic *Hinduism, in which Brahman, or the impersonal Absolute, is identified with Athman, or the inner Self; and all human striving after the divine is a quest for self-knowledge in the deepest ontological terms. Similar to Hinduism, Anthroposophy requires certain physical, mental, and spiritual exercises to arrive at final wisdom. The enlightened one thus becomes a *Hellscher,* or master of clear vision, gaining supersensible means of perception that are familiar in Buddhist psychology.

Theosophy teaches that besides the material world there are six invisible worlds of subtle matter, which interpenetrate the visible world as water permeates a sponge. Man possesses three bodies, a physical body of motion, an astral body of feeling, and a mental body of thought. Anthroposophy adopts the same premises, but considers the invisible world immaterial and gives man seven corporeities in addition to body, soul, and spirit that correspond to the common triad of the physical, astral, and mental Theosophy. The seer of Anthroposophy gradually comes to understand these seven "bodies" and especially the most intimate "I" that forms the human personality. The same septet obtains in the world outside man. There are seven colors to the spectrum and seven planets to the universe—Saturn, Sun, Moon, Earth, Jupiter, Venus, and Vulcan. As the clairvoyant penetrates into the recesses of his own ego, he also learns the secrets of the world around him, always in greater depth as one after another the elements of the cosmic septet unfold.

Steiner elaborated on this higher knowledge in all his major writings, but mainly in the *Akaska Chronicle.* He differed further from the Theosophists in assigning a leading role to Christ in his system. Whereas Theosophy makes Christ to be merely one of many *arhats* (master teachers) or *avatars* (incarnations), Anthroposophy holds that Christ is the one *avatar,* or divine manifestation, yet only in the sense of a greater solar being who appeared among men to rescue the human race from its own destruction. The merger of Christianity and Anthroposophy was due largely to the efforts of Friedrich Rittelmeyer (1872–1938), former Evangelical pastor, who organized the existing societies into Christian Fellowships and promoted the establishment of a sacerdotal class of priests and priestesses to care for the ritual aspect of the movement.

Furthermore, Christ is claimed to possess the full revelation of the supersensible world. Contact with him affords deeper penetration into his own profound vision of reality. Accordingly, celebration of the Sacrament of the Eucharist is considered the highest act of worship in the Christian religion. Anthroposophy teaches that the bread and wine are changed with the spirit and body of Christ, through which the communicant becomes truly human, whereas before he was only an image distorted by hostile powers. The service is called Act of Consecration of Man, and has a liturgy filled with Steiner's teachings, yet modeled on the Catholic Mass.

Anthroposophists are found mainly in Germany, Britain, and the U.S., especially among those in search of religious experience outside the normal channels of church life. Anthroposophy was condemned by the Roman Catholic Church in 1919.

Bibliography: G. A. KAUFMANN, comp. and ed., *Fruits of Anthroposophy* (London 1922). R. STEINER, *The Story of My Life,* ed. A. FREEMAN (London 1928); *World History in the Light of Anthroposophy,* tr. G. and M. ADAMS (New York 1951). F. RITTELMEYER, *Reincarnation* (New York n.d.).

[J. A. HARDON]

ANTICHRIST

One opposed to the work of God, especially that accomplished in Jesus the Messiah (Christ).

IN THE BIBLE

Some passages suggest that this hostile figure attempts to work by usurping divine and messianic prerogatives, and thus winning over followers by deceiving them concerning his (or its) true nature. The Greek prefix ἀντί, the first element of ἀντίχριστος, can express the idea of substitution or replacement, as well as that of hostility. The term Antichrist is found only in 1 Jn 2.18, 22; 4.3; 2 Jn 7; but the concept is present in 2 Thes 2.3–12, in certain passages in the Apocalypse, and possibly in other NT texts. In some of these passages the figure is referred to in personal terms, and Christian interpretation has traditionally regarded the Antichrist as a person; it is, however, far from certain that the personification is intended to point to an individual at all, much less to any specific person. Before attempting to appraise the NT teaching, it will be useful to look for the roots of this idea in the OT.

Old Testament Roots of Antichrist Concept. In certain OT passages, largely apocalyptic in nature, there is the expectation of a final great struggle between the forces of good and evil, between those faithful to God (the true Israel) and those hostile to Him (mainly identified with the pagan nations). The struggle is to culminate in the eschatological battle in which the victory will be won by God Himself intervening on behalf of His people to the accompaniment of cosmic signs and disturbances.

The clearest example of this picture is found in Ez 38.1–39.29, a passage usually conceded to be later than Ezechiel himself. The nations of the earth assemble under the leadership of Gog, chief prince of Mosoch and Thubal, in order to attack and plunder the land of Israel. But God will strike the bow and arrows from their hands, the invaders will be slaughtered on the mountains of Israel, and the birds and beasts will feast on their flesh (39.3–5, 17–20). It is to be noted that, while Gog is an individual, he is not a historical figure but simply the embodiment of the leadership of those forces hostile to God's people [*see* EZECHIEL (EZEKIEL), BOOK OF].

The four beasts of Daniel ch. 7 represent the great world kingdoms; special attention is given to the fourth beast, which represents the Greek Empire, under which the Israelites were suffering at the time of the composition of Daniel. The "little horn" (v. 8, 21–22, 24) of the fourth beast represents *Antiochus IV Epiphanes, desecrator of the Temple and dreaded persecutor. The vision describes God's intervention in the form of judgment upon the beasts and the end of their power to harm. Antiochus IV is given special attention again in 11.21–45, where his campaigns and victories are described; but the section concludes with the note that "he shall come to his end with none to help him." There is little doubt that the author of this apocalyptic composition expected that God's intervention to end this crisis would be the definitive intervention and would usher in the final age. But the final struggle had not yet come. History was to vindicate the author's expectation of God's delivering intervention, but other crises would be known. Antiochus IV, so closely connected with a particular persecution, was to become a type of those who lead the anti-God forces, and elements of the descriptions of him in Daniel are to be found in later writings. (*See* DANIEL, BOOK OF.)

Antichrist in the New Testament. The closest link between the OT passages just reviewed and the NT is found in the Apocalypse. Imagery taken from Daniel is freely used, and the struggle between the Church and the wicked persecutors is an important part of the concern of the book. Chapter 13 describes a "beast of the sea," which is a composite of the four beasts of Daniel ch. 7. Many commentators identify it with the Roman Empire, the power persecuting the Christian Church during much of the late 1st century; at any rate, it is an instrument of Satan (the Dragon of 12.3–18) in his war against the Church. The beast of the sea is also aided by the "beast of the earth" (13.11–17), possibly to be identified with the pagan priesthood of Rome. These two together sum up, in this section of the book, the forces on earth utilized by Satan in the struggle against the people of God. Elements of these visions have been referred to historical Roman emperors, but the personal aspect is not stressed. God's victory over the forces hostile to Him is described in the latter part of the book; see especially ch. 17–18, where the beast described is probably the same as the beast of the sea; see also 19.17–21, where Christ effortlessly overcomes the beast and the false prophet (probably the beast of the earth) and their armies, and the birds of the air are invited to feast on their flesh. Although the term Antichrist does not appear, the concept is present. The struggle now has specifically Christian features, not only in that it is the Christian Church that is being persecuted and Christ who overcomes, but also in that the hostile forces are in many ways a blasphemous parody of elements in the Christian dispensation (note the "unholy trinity" in 12.3–13.17; and cf. 7.3 with 13.16–17, and 5.9–10 with 13.7). *See* APOCALYPSE, BOOK OF.

The same picture of the final violent struggle of the anti-God forces with the people of God lies at the base of St. Paul's thought in 2 Thes 2.3–12. Paul is attempting to allay the fears of the Thessalonians, who seem to believe that the final day has already arrived, by insisting on certain recognizable signs, not yet in evidence, that must precede it. The principal one of these is the ἀποστασία (apostasy, rebellion), which probably refers to the eschatological struggle. St. Paul sees the hostile forces led by "the man of sin . . . the son of perdition . . . the wicked one," whom "the Lord Jesus will slay with the breath of his mouth." Again there is the parody of true religion: the adversary will "be revealed," will assume divine prerogatives, and his coming is connected with the "mystery of iniquity" that is already at work.

Certainly the manner of speaking in this passage seems highly personalistic, but it must be remembered that St. Paul is using apocalyptic language; the details need not be considered to have been revealed to him, for obscure events of the last day are habitually presented in stereotyped imagery. Some of the descriptive details of the "man of sin" are taken from earlier presentations of the wicked men (Ez 28.2; Dn 11.36). The fact that the "man of sin" is presented as already in existence but held in check by someone or something (the Thessalonians knew what Paul was referring to, but the modern reader can only guess) tells against a specific person. Yet it would not be false to Paul's thought to see here an expectation that, when the final assault of evil does materialize, it will be headed by an individual who incarnates, so to speak, the power of evil in his person.

There is no clear reference to the cosmic struggle in the allusions to Antichrist in St. John's Epistles, although the evidences of Antichrist's activity are seen to indicate that the "last hour" is at hand (1 Jn 2.18). Yet St. John can also speak of "many antichrists," referring to apostate Christians, and can label as "the liar . . . the Antichrist" the one who denies that "Jesus is the Christ" (v. 22; see also 2 Jn 7). Thus the author thinks of a person or a power hostile to God whose influence and activity are seen in and inferred from the rejection of God's revelation in Christ by some.

Bibliography: D. BUZY, DBSuppl 1:297–305. EncDictBibl 96–98. E. B. ALLO, *L'Apocalypse* (Paris 1921) cxi–cxxi. W. BOUSSET, *Der Antichrist in der Überlieferung des Judentums, des N.T. und der alten Kirche* (Göttingen 1895). P. H. FURFEY, "The Mystery of Lawlessness," CathBiblQuart 8 (1946) 179–191.

[M. RODRIGUEZ]

COMMENT OF FATHERS, THEOLOGIANS

Like other prophecies, that of the Antichrist will be clearly understood only in its fulfillment. Understandably, then, there is little on the subject in the documents of the Church's magisterium other than in its condemnations of Wyclif and the Fraticelli (Denz 916, 1156, 1180). This section, therefore, confines itself to a sketch of the patristic and theological speculation that has surrounded the Antichrist.

Patrology. The comment of the Fathers on the Antichrist, which begins with the *Didache, is complete in all its essential features by the First Council of Nicaea (325). According to the Didache, the final days of the world will be marked by the advent of the "world-tempter," appearing as though he were the Son of God and doing "signs and wonders." The earth, it is said, will be given into his hands (Didache 16.3–5).

Preceded by false prophets speaking in the name of Christ, he will appear with the whole panoply of diabolic power (Justin, *Dial.* 51, 110). "Sinner, murderer, robber," says Irenaeus, he will make incarnate in himself the entire diabolic apostasy. Of Jewish origin, sprung from the tribe of Dan, he will establish himself in Jerusalem and reign for 3½ years (*Haer.* 5.30.2; 5.25.3; 5.30.4). The unhappy privilege of fathering the Antichrist is assigned to the tribe of Dan by many of the ancient writers, who deduce it from Gn 49.17 and from the omission of the name of Dan in Ap 7.5–8.

The antithetic character of "the man of sin" is developed by Hippolytus, who sees in the Antichrist a perfect caricature of Christ Himself. Like Christ, he will be of Jewish ancestry; as Christ is from the tribe of Juda, his adversary will be from Dan. Claiming the scriptural titles of lion, lamb, and man, the Antichrist will have his own apostles and will dedicate himself to the persecution of the saints; his assault on the work of Christ will culminate in an apotheosis of himself (*Antichr.* 5–19; 29–41; 48–58). Commenting on Daniel's prophecy of the four kingdoms, Hippolytus says that the Antichrist will appear at the *end of the world after the Babylonian, Persian, Greek, and Roman empires (*Com. in Dan.* 4.1–10).

Tertullian added a new dimension to patristic thought when he applied the term Antichrist to any heretic or rebel against Christ (*Adv. Marcion.* 5.16; *De praescr. haer.* 4.4). The African author, however, clearly distinguished these forerunners of the Antichrist from the eschatological personality who would appear at the end of time.

Neither Cyprian nor Origen denied the eschatological character of the Antichrist, but, like Tertullian, they found an application of the idea in their own times. Origen described what might be termed the principle of the Antichrist: "Invenimus omnes veras virtutes esse Christum, et omnes simulatas virtutes esse Antichristum" (*Comm. ser.* 33 *in Mt.*). The principle of the Antichrist, he said, has many proponents, but from among these many antichrists, there will come one who will deserve the name in its proper sense, one whose types and forerunners the others are. This true Antichrist will appear at the end of the world, while the others, in some measure, are already in the world (*Comm. ser. 47 in Mt.*; *Cels.* 6.79). Among the antichrists already present Cyprian lists the heretics and schismatics (*Ep.* 69.5, 70.3). They deserve the name, he says, because they are imbued with the spirit of the Antichrist who will be the complete antithesis of Christ (*Ep.* 73.15; 71.2).

The figure of the Antichrist, as it emerges from patristic speculation, has both a contemporary and an eschatological dimension. There is, first of all, the individual who will appear at time's end to launch a final assault on the work of Christ. In a second, but by no means contradictory, perspective, the Antichrist is seen to be embodied in the archenemies of God and his Church. This dual dimensionality of the patristic Antichrist seems an adequate premise for K. Rahner's remark in this regard that Christians have the right not only to abhor ungodly ideas but to recognize and to flee from the individual men who champion evil (LexThk[2] 1:635).

Extension of Term. The patristic license to concretize unholy ideas and forces in individuals and organizations and to label them Antichrist has been exercised by innumerable writers over the centuries. Countless political figures and institutions from Nero to Stalin have been identified with the "man of sin" (see W. Bornemann). Indeed, the popular interest in the Antichrist and the "signs of the times" that were to precede his coming was so played upon by the preachers of the 14th and 15th centuries that Lateran Council V forbade preachers to describe as imminent the coming of the Antichrist.

The polemic possibilities of the Antichrist idea escaped neither the Church's friends nor its foes. Thus it became quite common in the Middle Ages for opponents—popes and emperors, Guelfs and Ghibellines—to hurl this epithet at one another. While Catholic writers denounced as Antichrist those who dissented from the doctrines of the Church or attacked its liberty, their antagonists saw the Antichrist in the institution of the papacy itself. As Cardinal J. H. Newman observed, the papal Antichrist theory was developed gradually from the 11th to 16th centuries by the *Albigenses, the *Waldenses, and the *Fraticelli ["The Protestant Idea of Antichrist," *Essays Critical and Historical,* v.2 (London 1897)]. A terrifying weapon during the great religious controversies of the 16th century, the idea of the papal Antichrist had been used effectively by John Wyclif in England and John Hus in Bohemia. One of the dynamisms of Martin Luther's thinking, the idea was even incorporated into the Schmalkaldic Articles. St. Robert Bellarmine refuted the exegesis by which the beast of the Apocalypse was identified with the papacy; and it was also rejected by the Protestant H. Grotius. Nevertheless, papal Antichrist theory persisted into the 19th century and accounted for Newman's two essays on the subject, "The Protestant Idea of the Antichrist" and "The Patristic Idea of the Antichrist," the latter in *Discussions and Arguments on Various Subjects* (London 1899).

Theologians. Catholic theologians have been nearly unanimous in maintaining that the Antichrist will be an individual person. Those, however, who prefer a collective interpretation can point out quite correctly, it seems, that in this matter there is no real doctrinal tradition. And even in this latter interpretation, the eschatological character of the Antichrist is preserved, for the "last times" commence with the first coming of Christ and extend to the *Parousia.

Bibliography: A. GELIN, DTC, Tables générales 1:179–180. R. SCHÜTZ et al., RGG[3] 1:431–436. W. BOUSSET, Hastings ERE 1:578–581. L. ATZBERGER, *Geschichte der christlichen Eschatologie* (Freiburg 1896). W. BORNEMANN, *Die Thessalonicherbriefe,* v.10 of *Kritisch-exegetischer Kommentar über das Neue Testament,* ed. H. A. MEYER (Göttingen 1891–). V. DECHAMPS, *Christus und die Antichristen nach dem Zeugnisse der Schrift, der Geschichte und des Gewissens* (Mainz 1859). T. MALVENDA, *De antichristo libri undecim* (Rome 1604). B. RIGAUX, *L'Antéchrist et l'opposition au royaume messianique dans l'Ancien et le Nouveau Testament* (Gembloux 1932).

[G. J. DYER]

ANTICLERICALISM

This is a term whose prefix and suffix render it equivocal. "Anti" indicates that the word is the contrary of *clericalism. Clericalism, however, has two principal meanings very different from one another; sometimes it is considered as an abuse and is reproved by the ecclesiastical magisterium; at other times it is identified with the Church itself. "Ism," the suffix, intimates that the term deals with a doctrine. But the best-known type of anticlericalism, that which is opposed to the Church and generally to other religions, is much less a doctrine than a practical attitude, whose aims and themes vary according to circumstances. To avoid confusion it is preferable to distinguish two kinds of anticlericalism. The first is that of Catholics, anxious to maintain the dignity of the clergy and the abstention of the Church from state affairs. The second is that of adversaries of religion, which is sometimes so ardent that it resembles a religious faith that revolves around belief in humanity, in reason, and in liberty.

Catholic Anticlericalism. An anticlericalism that seeks to remain Catholic obviously cannot be destructive of the Church's hierarchical order. Theories claiming to suppress differences between clerics and laymen pertain, properly speaking, to *laicism. Catholic anticlericalism presents itself under a double guise in two epochs far distant from one another.

Medieval. During the Middle Ages secular and regular clergy were very numerous in western Europe, but their quality was much inferior to their quantity. Clerics were recruited from all classes of society and mixed intimately with all classes. When clerics deviated from their obligations, their ecclesiastical confreres, and laymen too, constituted themselves censors and thereby practiced a kind of fraternal correction. Not all of them were as severe in criticism as St. Bernard; many preferred a comic tone: *Castigat ridendo mores.* Pleasantries against lazy, greedy, ribald monks developed into almost a literary genre, in which the Latin language in particular ventured to defy what is nowadays regarded as propriety. *Erasmus in his *Praise of Folly* and *Rabelais in *Gargantua* and *Pantagruel* prolonged a medieval tradition into the Renaissance with a sense of opportuneness that was, to say the least, questionable. Critics who practiced this rather smirking type of anticlericalism did not do so without peril, even in the Middle Ages. No doubt they acted from a praiseworthy desire to possess a clergy worthy of its vocation and of its ministry; but they risked scandalizing the weak, who inclined to form generalizations as hasty as they were unjust.

Contemporary. Nowadays Catholics run the same risk by openly calling themselves anticlerical. They often prefer to take this stance in another fashion, by posing as adversaries of a certain type of clericalism and by repeating with Cardinal Saliège that "the Church is not clerical." They experience some mistrust of the distinction between a country that is supposedly unanimous in its Catholic belief and a religiously divided (pluralistic) country in which the State must allow each citizen to practice his religion freely. These Catholics are aware of the unwarranted conclusion drawn from this distinction, namely, that wherever Catholics are in the majority their consciences oblige them to oppress those who disagree with them, but wherever Catholics are relatively few and powerless to impose their doctrines, only there do they consent to religious liberty. These anticlerical Catholics ask themselves if unanimity of belief is not a figment of the imagination, and if any Catholic country exists without free thinkers. It is not by religious indifference, they say, but by respect for persons and for the complete liberty of the act of faith (CIC c.1351) that the Church must preserve itself from becoming servile to the State, which will be more tempted to promote its own interests than to serve the Church. Fear of clericalism does not lead necessarily to a regime of separation of Church from State; it is compatible with a concordat such as that of Portugal (see Maritain, 140–149).

Antireligious Anticlericalism. This type of anticlericalism, as the words indicate clearly, is aggressive. It is not to be confused with simple irreligion, which sceptics, atheists, and merely tolerant persons can profess. Antireligious anticlericalism regards religion as an error and an evil, something that must be extirpated. Nothing prevents it from sparing the faithful in order to strike harder at the clergy who guide them, or from flattering the secular clergy by picturing the regular clergy as competitors who are harmful to the influence and wellbeing of the seculars. This kind of anticlericalism gives little heed to religions with few adherents and directs its blows at the strongest, particularly at the Catholic Church in countries where the majority is Catholic. It has preceded, prepared, and accompanied laicism. Since the 19th century anticlericals of this type have venerated as their ancestors the rationalists of the 16th century, the libertines of the 17th, and especially the philosophers of the Enlightenment of the 18th, whose actions and writings continue to inspire them. Although the term "anticlericalism" was not part of the 18th-century vocabulary, it was then that the phenomenon took shape.

The 18th Century. The 16th and 17th centuries supplied the themes destined to undermine religion, but it was the 18th century that discovered the art of popularizing them and placing them within reach of wide circles of readers, even those deprived of philosophical formation. The 18th century began by using irony to sow doubts; it imagined Chinese, Persians, Congolese, Hurons, and other "good savages" who came to Europe, only to meet there Christians who massacred in the name of religion, while recommending to others charity and pardon for injuries. Another tactic was to mock at mysteries as offensive to reason and at Biblical accounts as contrary to scientific discoveries. Still another strategy was to interpret current events in a manner injurious to religion. Thus divine providence was denied because Lisbon, with all its churches and convents, was leveled by an earthquake (Nov. 1, 1755). Suspicion was directed at the faith of priests, because a pastor who had been very exact in the fulfilment of his ministry had left a will that was a profession of atheism. *Voltaire declared war *c.* 1760 on the infamous thing (*l'infâme*), by which he meant Christianity. St. Francis of Assisi and Dante, as he pictured them, were fools. From Voltaire's literary mill in Ferney flowed an endless stream of pamphlets that were more dangerous to believers than the productions of Amsterdam, London, Paris, or Berlin. The same negation appeared under a thousand guises, according to Paul Hazard. This century prided itself on being the age of light (*Enlightenment, *Aufklärung*), in which experience and reason would expel faith and its obscurities. To speed this process *Diderot launched a voluminous *Encyclopédie,* among whose mass of notions about history, geography, physics, and other subjects the essential concept, a "firm, audacious philosophy," was adroitly distributed, a tactic that Diderot himself admitted in a letter to his publisher (1764). After sowing the wind, these men reaped the whirlwind. During the *French Revolution, *c.* 1793, everything that tended to discredit priests and religion became acceptable, including the filth in which the journal *Le Père Duchesne,* published by Jacques *Hébert, specialized. Despite the Reign of Terror, the faithful churchgoers (*calotins*) and the "papists" were not annihilated. In vain did the Directory attack "the infernal empire of priests." For many decades afterward, however, this style remained in fashion among anticlericals.

The 19th Century. *Napoleon I, although a freethinker, ended this odious and sterile combat by concluding with Pius VII the *Concordat of 1801. Priests were placed on the payroll of the State and were directed to teach Frenchmen their duties toward their emperor (*see* CATECHISM, IMPERIAL). It sufficed, however, for the clergy to be "grenadiers in long vestments and short ideas"; a role that was anything but enviable. After Napoleon's downfall, the *bourgeoisie,* which remained Voltairean, profited from its liberty to ridicule the clergy, who were rendered still more unpopular by the royal government's maladroit measures, such as the law regarding sacrileges (1825). Caricatures, songs, novels, and theatrical productions did not spare clerics. Anticlericalism of the most violent type was at times furnished with weapons by Catholics such as Count François de Montlosier, whose famous *Mémoire* (1826; placed on the Index June 12, 1826) denounced Jesuitism, *ultramontanism, and the "priest party," which was "composed of those who will brave any risk or peril to hand over society to the priesthood." The "tyranny" of the *Jesuits became, between 1830 and 1848, the theme preferred by anticlericalism. At the Collège de France in Paris, Edgar *Quinet and Jules *Michelet presented the Revolution of 1789 as the new revelation, denigrated the Church, and thundered against the Jesuits. The publication of a collaborative work, *Des Jésuites* (1843), did nothing to moderate the irritation of these two professors against the Society of Jesus, according to the testimony of a student who audited their lectures [M. Minghetti, *Miei ricordi* (2d ed. Turin n.d.) 2:131–132]. Eugène *Sue increased the circulation of the journal *Le Constitutionnel* by publishing in serial form *The Wandering Jew* (*Le Juif errant*). When these episodes were collected, they formed a 10-volume novel, which went through many editions and translations into English and several other languages; it concentrated on the dark intrigues and infamies attributed to the sons of Loyola.

In Italy, the struggle for political unification provoked a rash of anticlericalism that supposedly revealed the imprisonments, hangings, and other atrocities practiced by the clergy in collusion with the Austrian army (see V. Gorresio, *Risorgimento scomunicato,* Florence 1958). Francesco Crispi, president of the Chamber of Deputies (1876) and premier (1887–91, 1893–96), was considered the "high priest of anticlericalism" in Italy and in Europe. At a meeting in 1877 with Léon *Gambetta and Otto von *Bismarck, the inaugurator of the *Kulturkampf, Crispi persuaded them that the peace of Europe was menaced by only one man, the Pope, who aspired to the reestablishment of the States of the Church. The renewal of the Senate in 1879 permitted French anticlerical opinion to take root in a body of laic laws. Until World War I, anticlericalism permeated the government of the Third Republic.

The 20th Century. Other countries copied France and Italy, notably *Portugal (1910–18) and *Mexico (1911–20). In the *Union of Soviet Socialist Republics the government forbade all religious propaganda and established the Union of the Militant Godless, which claimed in 1930 a membership exceeding 2 million. *National Socialism in Germany combined anticlericalism with anti-Semitism. In *Spain during the civil war (1936–39), 4,184 priests or seminarians were executed, along with 2,635 religious. In most Latin countries, anticlericals have not put aside their arms; they carry on their struggle by means of associations, periodicals, and conferences, supported generally by *Freemasonry.

Bibliography: G. DE BERTIER DE SAUVIGNY, "French Anticlericalism since the Great Revolution: A Tentative Interpretation," HistRecStud 42 (1954) 3–21 L. L. RUMMEL, "The Anticlerical Program as a Disruptive Factor in the Solidarity of the Late French Republics," CathHistRev 34 (1948–49) 1–19. C. A. WHITTUCK, Hastings ERE 3:689–693. C. J. H. HAYES, *A Generation of Materialism, 1871–1900* (New York 1941). P. HAZARD, *European Thought in the Eighteenth Century: From Montesquieu to Lessing*, tr. J. L. MAY (New Haven 1954). J. MARITAIN, *Man and the State* (Chicago 1951; repr. 1956). V. GIRAUD, *Anticléricalisme et catholicisme* (Paris 1906). É. FAGUET, *L'Anticléricalisme* (Paris 1906), liberal viewpoint by an agnostic. B. EMONET, DictApolFoiCath 2:1771–81. J. LECLER, "Origines et évolution de l'anticléricalisme," *Études* 253 (1947) 145–164; *Catholicisme* 1:633–638. L. CAPÉRAN, *L'Anticléricalisme et l'affaire Dreyfus, 1897–1899* (Toulouse 1948); *Histoire contemporaine de la laïcité française*, 3 v. (Paris 1957–61). *Dictionnaire de sociologie*, ed. G. JACQUEMET (Paris 1933–) 1:936–951. I. MARTÍN MARTINEZ, *El desarrollo de la Iglesia Española y sus relaciones con el Estado* (Madrid 1963). B. DUHR, *Jesuiten-Fabeln* (4th ed. Freiburg 1904). A. BROU, *Les Jésuites de la légende*, 2 v. (Paris 1906–07). E. M. ACOMB, *The French Laic Laws, 1879–1889* (New York 1941).

[C. BERTHELOT DU CHESNAY]

ANTIGONISH MOVEMENT

An integrated program of social reconstruction developed by priests and people of the Diocese of Antigonish in eastern Nova Scotia. It is a self-help program aimed specifically at improving social and economic conditions in economically disadvantaged areas. To that end it employs in new and imaginative ways the time-tried techniques of *adult education and *cooperatives. The standard method is to awaken people to a recognition of their needs and possibilities through adult education and then to present the cooperative as an instrument for group action.

History. Education preceded action in the development of the movement. About the time of World War I, Rev. James J. *Tompkins, vice president and professor at *St. Francis Xavier University, a diocesan college, began to plead that the university should be brought to the people. He was responsible for organizing people's schools in the early 1920s. Although considered successful, they were discontinued for reasons unrelated to adult education, and Tompkins took up parish work in the diocese. Even as a pastor, however, he continued his campaign for education for the common people.

His ambitions for adult education were ultimately realized in a way that surpassed his expectations, in large measure because of the vision, energy, and organizing genius of Rev. Moses M. *Coady, a member of the faculty of St. Francis Xavier University. Urged on by parish priests, whose people were suffering from the depression even before 1929, and aided by priests, sisters, and laymen of extraordinary ability, Coady organized in 1930 an extension department for the specific purpose of bringing the university to the people. This department developed the set of techniques for which the movement is known.

Approach. The techniques consist normally in awakening in depressed communities of farmers, fishermen, or industrial workers a burning desire to better their condition, then guiding the people in an intensive study of their needs and potentialities, and finally organizing cooperatives to carry out undertakings considered most feasible and necessary. There are many variations, depending upon local circumstances, but the usual way of arousing enthusiasm in a community is to hold a mass meeting at which a speaker from the extension department gives a stirring address, outlining in forceful language how the people can help themselves by intelligent conmmunity action. Once their interest is aroused, he issues a warning note, pointing out that a too hastily formed organization may fail before getting started, and emphasizing the necessity of study. The audience normally consists of adults with jobs and family responsibilities who would find it impractical to return to school, but there is at hand the study club, an educational device that was growing in popularity during the 1920s.

Study Clubs. If the community has caught fire as a result of the appeal of the speaker, he may consider the time ripe to issue a call for study club leaders. Candidates are usually acclaimed by the crowd right then and there; and with the selection of a topic for study, the program for the community is under way. Theoretically, any topic of interest to the community may be chosen for study; but since the movement is essentially one of self-help, it has been natural for most of the communities to study toward an end issuing in some form of concrete action. Local needs may suggest studying toward the formation of a lobster cannery or marketing organization, for example; but as the extension leaders gained experience, they normally advised communities to begin their rehabilitation with the formation of *credit unions.

Credit Unions. There were several reasons for this. During the depressed 1930s, people were usually in debt and often burdened with high interest rates; so a method of systematic saving and a ready source of loans at moderate rates of interest were excellent preludes to further achievement. Second, the credit union is an ideal training ground to give people experience in managing their own affairs. It is practically foolproof. It is easy to understand and simple to organize; and if the rules are followed, it can hardly fail. By studying the theory and operation of a credit union for 10 or 12 months and then taking an active part in its operation, members become acquainted with legal terms, learn to conduct affairs in a formal manner, and acquire some knowledge of the theory and practice of cooperation. The almost certain success of the credit union then whets their appetites for further action.

Cooperative Stores. This may take the form of any project from marketing blueberries to managing the farm woodlot, but very often the second step is the organization of a cooperative store. In industrial areas the store provides an ideal way to stretch the weekly wage and to carry on a program of consumer education. In rural areas and fishing villages the store serves as a purchasing agency not only for consumer goods, but also for supplies used in production. Frequently it serves also as an agency for marketing farm and sometimes marine products. Since a cooperative store is a much more complex undertaking than a credit union and requires a larger membership and more capital, it is desirable to spend at least 2 years in preliminary study, during which time the members save in order to purchase shares (usually one share of share capital at $5 and five shares of loan capital at $5 each).

Community Projects. The third step in the program can be any project that meets community needs. In fishing villages there may be a need for cooperative fish processing; in farming areas the greatest need may be for an agency to market farm products; in cities it may be a group health program or a cooperative housing project. The latter type of undertaking is unique in Nova Scotia as an example of cooperation between a private educational institution, the provincial unit of government, and local cooperative groups formed to build (through supply of much of the labor as down payment by individuals) and to own homes cooperatively. By 1963 there were 170 cooperative housing groups in Nova Scotia, which had built homes for 1,530 families.

Organizational Development. Once a series of projects has been studied and brought to fruition, many further developments are possible, such as federation of the local units into regional or national bodies to carry on educational and organizational activities or to provide large-scale services such as wholesaling, manufacturing or processing, and marketing for the local units. Once an area has established as many credit unions and cooperatives as conditions warrant, the extension department directs study and action to the perfecting of existing organizations and the adapting of these to serve new needs. It is here that it meets its greatest challenge. Once the organizations are going concerns, is becomes more and more difficult to arouse enthusiasm and to promote study for such routine activities as day-to-day operation. However, the study habit is being kept alive through scheduled educational programs on radio and television and through community development activities sponsored by the extension department.

Influence. The Antigonish movement has had worldwide repercussions and has served as a training ground in social action for community leaders from a large number of countries. Ever since its beginning, visitors have toured the area and observed the cooperatives in action. Since the end of World War II, students from various countries have come for more formal training and have remained for longer periods. It is estimated that from 1946 to 1960, 312 students from 55 countries visited Antigonish, received formal training in the techniques of the movement, and then returned to carry its message to some three-quarters of a million people in their native lands. This type of training was expanded and further formalized in 1960 by the establishment at St. Francis Xavier University of the Coady International Institute, which offers a 9-month program of courses in social theory and action for students from all over the world.

While the movement has had great success in the maritime provinces of Canada and has achieved worldwide acclaim, including special recognition on three occasions from the Holy See, its leaders recognize that it cannot work miracles. As in the case of any form of economic development, improvements in productivity in primary industries such as agriculture and fishing normally require the movement of workers released

A typical graduating class of Coady International Institute, St. Francis Xavier University, Antigonish, Nova Scotia.

through technological advance to some type of industrial employment. If, however, the resources for industrial development are lacking or inferior in the region or area, the only solution may be migration or, failing that, the development of low-wage industries that can compete with those of areas more liberally endowed with resources. Even in the latter eventuality, however, the movement has a role to play in directing its educational program to facilitate the required adjustments.

Bibliography: M. M. Coady, *Masters of Their Own Destiny: The Story of the Antigonish Movement of Adult Education through Economic Cooperation* (New York 1939). A. F. Laidlaw, *The Campus and the Community: The Global Impact of the Antigonish Movement* (Montreal 1961). G. Boyle, *Democracy's Second Chance: Land, Work, and Cooperation* (New York 1941); *Father Tompkins of Nova Scotia* (New York 1953). D. M. Connor, *The Cross-Cultural Diffusion of a Social Movement* (unpub. MS, Cornell U. library 1962). M. E. Schirber, "Study Clubs: Democracy in Action," *Land Policy Review* 4.5 (1941) 13–17. J. T. Croteau, *The Economics of the Credit Union* (Detroit 1963). **Illustration credit:** Buckley Studios, Antigonish, Nova Scotia.

[M. E. SCHIRBER]

ANTINOMY

An antinomy is a real or apparent contradiction between equally well-based assumptions or conclusions. Contradiction is a generic term for both paradox and antinomy, which are roughly synonymous. However, many recent writers employ *paradox as an informal catchall for interesting contradictions of any sort, and antinomy as a technical term for contradictions derivable by sound rules of reasoning from accepted axioms within a science. Antinomies may for convenience be gathered under three headings, depending on whether they arise: (1) in ordinary language; (2) in metaphysics or cosmology; or (3) in logic, mathematics, and kindred formal disciplines.

Ordinary Language. Paradoxes arising in ordinary language have been pondered from early Greek times (cf. Plato, *Parm.*). The Megaric philosophers about 400 B.C. studied the well-known Liar Paradox, one version of which runs as follows: If a man says "I always lie," how are we to understand his statement? In a puzzling way it seems to be both true and false, since the truth of his confession conflicts with the fact that it is a confession of never telling the truth. Among the main suggestions offered to resolve the Liar Paradox are: (1) that the man's remark can be called both true and false, but in different respects (*Aristotle); (2) that it makes no sense at all (Chrysippus); (3) that in a covert manner it embodies two statements having different levels of reference, and when these are kept separate no paradox arises (Bertrand *Russell); and (4) that the offending sentence would normally be used as an outpouring of remorse or self-disgust, not as an occasion for drawing inferences, and its paradoxical aspect troubles us only when we fail to notice its normal use (Ludwig *Wittgenstein). The Liar Paradox and numerous other *insolubilia,* i.e., statements whose assertion or denial leads to the opposite, were discussed in great detail by medieval logicians (*see* LOGIC, HISTORY OF).

Kantian Antinomies. In his *Critique of Pure Reason* Immanuel *Kant claimed to expose four serious antinomies in the then prevailing *cosmology. Using valid steps of reasoning, he said, a philosopher can demonstrate on the one hand that the universe is infinite in size and duration, and on the other that it is finite. He constructed similar pairs of rival proofs for and against the infinite divisibility of matter, the possibility of freedom, and the world's ultimate dependence upon a necessary being. The scandal of these antinomies, Kant believed, spelled the doom of metaphysics as a science. He regarded them as a species of "transcendental illusion," the result of a natural and unavoidable human urge to apply the categories of the understanding beyond their safe reach, the realm of sensible experience.

Kant's notion that nature should have built into man a disposition toward illusion has tended to strain his readers' comprehension as much as the antinomies themselves. Part, at least, of the blame can be laid to an obscurity in the tradition Kant criticized, dominated by the philosophy of *Leibniz and C. *Wolff. That tradition spoke of the physical universe and everything in it "as appearance," i.e., in terms of the perceiver's mental content. This habit of thought, shared by Kant himself, left unsettled the primary issue between *idealism and *realism: whether what we call the material world is mind-dependent, like the domain of mathematical inventions, or exists independently of minds. Where that issue is unresolved, the inadvertent risk of thinking about the world in both ways at once is also left open, and with it the possibility of antinomous proofs.

Antinomies in Formal Systems. At the turn of the 20th century, antinomies of a different sort forced logicians and mathematicians to reconsider certain accepted fundamentals, chiefly in the foundations of arithmetic. Russell's antinomy, discovered in 1901, was derived from the efforts of Gottlob * Frege to develop number theory in terms of the theory of classes. It can be paraphrased in nontechnical terms as follows: The class of all classes is itself a class, but the class of all lions is not a lion. Some classes, then, appear to be members of themselves while others do not. Now consider the whole class of classes which are not members of themselves. Call it C. Is C a member of itself or not? Let us suppose that it is. That would make C a member of a class that is by definition made up of classes that are not members of themselves. Therefore C is not a member of itself, which contradicts the original supposition. On the other hand, if we now suppose it is not, then on second look C must be included in the membership it was defined as having, and so must be counted a member of itself. Whether we call C a member of itself or not, the result leads to the opposite position.

At one time Russell suggested that expressions of the form "C is either a member of itself or not" be struck out of the theory of classes as meaningless. A more popular solution, his "simple theory of types," instead lays down restrictions on the ways in which references to classes of different levels may be combined in a single assertion. Alternative solutions pioneered by Ernst Zermelo in 1904 can be found in certain axiomatizations of set theory.

Semantical Antinomies. It is now common practice to distinguish between antinomies containing reference to natural language, and those involving no metalinguistic expressions. The first kind are called semantical, the second logical. One example of the former, called Grelling's paradox, runs as follows: Work up two lists of adjectives, the first titled self-describing and containing words that apply to themselves, such as "mispelled," "short," "four-syllabled"; the second titled non-self-describing and containing words that do not, such as "long," "misspelled," "five-syllabled." Into which list shall we put the term "non-self-describing"? If it is a non-self-describing word, as "short" is a short word, then it belongs under self-describing. But in order to go there, "non-self-describing" would have to be non-self-describing, as "short" is short. Put into either list, it switches into the other. This antinomy, like that of Russell, can be solved by employing suitable type restrictions.

Logical Antinomies. Among the second group are certain contradictions arising in theories of ordinal and cardinal number series. In the years from 1895 to 1897, Georg *Cantor and C. Burali-Forti independently hit upon a contradiction involving ordinals, i.e., numbers defined in terms of their relations to neighbors in a series. If we suppose the series to be well ordered, which roughly means surveyable in the way that segments of it are, then we can speak of the type of the greatest ordinal. At the same time, as we know, any ordinal can be increased by adding one, so there can be no greatest. As a result of holding to both claims, one is forced to allow the possibility of two different ordinals neither of which is greater. This runs counter to the accepted role of "greater than" in numerical relations. The question of removing this contradiction turns upon the permissibility of assuming that the whole series resembles well-ordered classes within itself.

About 1900, Russell pointed out contradictions arising in connection with Cantor's proofs that there is no greatest cardinal number. Cantor argues, for example, that the number of classes in any class is larger than the number of terms in the class. The contradictions appear, according to Russell, when we assume that Cantor's proofs hold good for nonnumerical classes, such as the class of propositions. If we correlate every class of propositions with its own logical product, and then apply Cantor's argument, we notice something wrong with the phrase "every class" as used here. It fails to include the class of propositions that are logical products but are not members of the class they are products of. Where does the product of that excluded class belong? It can be shown, by the kind of reasoning used in Russell's antinomy above, to be both a member and not a member of the excluded class.

See also LOGIC, SYMBOLIC; MATHEMATICS, PHILOSOPHY OF; NUMBER.

Bibliography: I. M. BOCHEŃSKI, *A History of Formal Logic,* tr. I. THOMAS (Notre Dame, Ind. 1961). B. RUSSELL, *Introduction to Mathematical Philosophy* (London 1919); *Principles of Mathematics* (2d ed. New York 1938). A. N. WHITEHEAD and B. RUSSELL, *Principia Mathematica,* 3 v. (2d ed. Cambridge, Eng. 1925) v.1.

[H. A. NIELSEN]

ANTIOCH

The ancient city situated on the Orontes in what is now Syria. The word comes from the Greek Ἀντιόχεια (Lat. *Antiochia*). It was "the first place in which the disciples were called Christians" (Acts 11.26), and was especially fitted to be the center of the mission to the Gentiles.

The Apostles. Founded in 300 B.C. by Seleucus, a general of Alexander the Great, Antioch was a center of communications by land and also by sea through its port, Seleucia Pieria. The population was cosmopolitan and *Judaism was familiar to some of the people because of the presence of an important Jewish colony, which provided an opportunity for Gentiles to hear the Old Testament read in Greek at synagogue services. Nicholas, one of the seven deacons in Jerusalem, was a proselyte from Antioch (Acts 6.5). Thus when some Greek-speaking Christians fled to Antioch from persecution in Jerusalem, they were able to preach to Greeks (Acts 11.19–21), some of whom may have already been acquainted with Judaism. Barnabas and Paul converted "a great multitude," and there were five "prophets and teachers" at the head of the local community—Barnabas, Simon Niger, Lucius of Cyrene, Manahen, and Paul (Acts 13.1). The presence of both Jewish and Gentile Christians raised the question of whether the Jewish law (e.g., concerning food and circumcision) should be extended to Gentile converts. The famous dispute between Peter and Paul (Gal 2) resulted, and Paul devoted himself to the Gentile mission, using Antioch as the base for his journeys. The ultimate fate of the Jewish Christian community is not known. According to tradition, Peter was the founder of the Church at Antioch and its first bishop. Luke the Evangelist was said to be from Antioch. The Gnostic teachers Menander, Basilides, and Satornilus were active there.

Pagans and Arians. The first figure in the post-Apostolic Church at Antioch known in any detail is Bishop *Ignatius of Antioch, martyred at Rome under Trajan (98–117). His letters are important evidence for the early development of the episcopate, showing the function and authority of the bishop at the head of the threefold ministry of bishop, presbyters, and deacons. Prominent figures in the early Church at Antioch were Babylas, a bishop martyred in the persecution of Decius (249–251), and *Paul of Samosata (260–272), a heretical bishop deposed by a local council for his Christological doctrine. By the time of the persecution of Diocletian, the Christian community at Antioch was sufficiently large to have a number of martyrs, including St. *Romanus, one of the most important local saints. In the Arian controversy, local councils (325, 341) formulated anti-Arian creeds, but Antiochene theologians were inclined to accept Arian ideas; Arian or crypto-Arian bishops came into power and a council in 361 issued an extreme Arian creed. Often during this period there were two rival bishops of Antioch: one Arian, supported by the local congregation; the other orthodox, supported by the imperial government. In addition, there was for a time a schism within the orthodox, "Nicene," party, so that at times there were two "Nicene" bishops.

The Emperor *Julian the Apostate (361–363) made Antioch the headquarters of his campaign to suppress Christianity and restore paganism, and a number of Christians, especially in the army, were martyred at Antioch. Julian's efforts, though unsuccessful, made such an impression on the Christians that they joined to seek a solution of their doctrinal differences. The Arian Emperor Valens in 365 inaugurated a persecution of the orthodox Christians at Antioch which continued until 376. Peace was made within the Church at Antioch when Valens's successor, Gratianus, in 378 issued a rescript of toleration. The restoration of orthodoxy was celebrated by a council in 379 and by the construction of the cruciform church of St. Babylas, which was found in the excavations. St. Jerome visited Antioch in 374–375. After a period of retirement in the desert east of Chalcis, he returned to Antioch and was ordained there. The latter part of the 4th century is one of the best-known periods of the Christian history of Antioch, thanks to the writings of St. John Chrysostom, a leading figure in the local community from his ordination as deacon in 381 until his departure in 398 to become archbishop of Constantinople. Like many Christians, Chrysostom studied Greek literature and rhetoric under Libanius, the celebrated pagan teacher who at this time was the leading citizen of the city. The simultaneous careers of teacher and pupil exemplify the interaction between paganism and Christianity at Antioch at this period.

Liturgy. The extant evidence for the liturgical usages of the latter part of the 4th century, including allusions in homilies of Chrysostom and *Theodore of Mopsuestia (d. 428), show that this was the time when the characteristic rite of Antioch was taking mature form. The Liturgy of St. John Chrysostom, in the form preserved today, was certainly not composed by him, and one can only speculate as to its origin. The Liturgy of St. James is a close relative of the Antiochene rite but the history of its evolution is not clear. It became the principal rite of the Syrian Jacobites, who during the Monophysite controversy controlled the Church at Antioch and in Syria. The peculiar Antiochene usage of Confirmation prior to Baptism has recently received new documentation in eight baptismal homilies of Chrysostom discovered on Mt. Athos in 1955.

Patriarchate Rivalry, Nestorius. The status of Antioch among the great churches was altered by the Council of Constantinople in 381. Since Nicaea (325) Antioch and Alexandria had been recognized as preeminent in the East. Now Constantinople sought recognition for its see corresponding to its political prestige as imperial capital, and in 381 the Church of Constantinople was given first place after that of Rome. One purpose of the pronouncement was to put down the pretensions of Alexandria, but it also had the effect of reducing the prestige of Antioch.

In the time of Chrysostom, Christians were being attracted to the Jewish cult at Antioch. The ceremonial, the fasts, the monotheistic teaching, and the reputed healing powers of the relics of Jewish martyrs, all drew Christians, especially women, to the synagogues. During the reign of Theodosius II (408–450) St. Simeon Stylites was a popular and influential figure in all the region of Antioch. On his death (459) his body was buried in a church built for the purpose at Antioch. Under Theodosius a council at Antioch (424) condemned Pelagius (*see* PELAGIUS AND PELAGIANISM). Theodore of Mopsuestia, who had been trained at Antioch, continued his important Christological studies along the lines indicated by *Diodore of Tarsus. Theodore's pupil at Antioch, *Nestorius, who became archbishop of Constantinople, carried the same line of investigation further, and a major controversy was precipitated, in which Antioch, supporting Nestorius's views that there were two separate Persons in the Incarnate Christ, came into conflict with *Alexandria, whose patriarch *Cyril became Nestorius's chief opponent. A council at Antioch in 430 warned Nestorius to avoid excess. At the Council of Ephesus in 431 Nestorius was deposed, the Antiochene party was defeated by Cyril of Alexandria, and the territorial jurisdiction of the Antiochene See was reduced in favor of the See of Jerusalem. At the end of the council Nestorius by imperial order was confined in his old monastery outside Antioch. Two synods were later held at Antioch at which peace with Alexandria was restored. The Nestorians remained influential in Syria and another council at Ephesus in 449 took such measures against them that it became known as the Latrocinium or Robber Council. Though the Council of Chalcedon (451) convened in order to undo the injustices of the Latrocinium, its definition of the faith only produced further dissension. Syria and Egypt, in reaction against the Chalcedonian formula for the nature of Christ, became predominantly Monophysite.

Monophysitism. The whole history of Antioch until the Arab conquest was colored by its being one of the strongholds of *Monophysitism. Some scholars have considered that the Monophysite heresy combined with Syrian and Egyptian nationalism to produce a heightened opposition to the imperial government as the representative of Chalcedonian orthodoxy. This hostility developed into a separatist movement which in time facilitated the conquest of Syria and Egypt by the Persians and the Arabs, who were welcomed by the dissident Monophysites as being less oppressive than the Constantinopolitan government.

The story of the remainder of the 5th and 6th century is dominated by the struggle between Chalcedonians and Monophysites for control of the Church at Antioch and in the rest of Syria. One of the prominent Monophysites, Peter the Fuller, was bishop of Antioch on four separate occasions. In 488 he brought to a head the old dispute about the ecclesiastical supremacy of Antioch over Cyprus. Antioch, as an apostolic foundation, claimed ecclesiastical jurisdiction over Cyprus, whose Church (Antioch asserted) was not of apostolic origin. However, the alleged discovery in Cyprus of the perfectly preserved body of St. *Barnabas, holding on his chest a copy of the Gospel of Matthew written in Barnabas's own hand, was taken as proof that the Church in Cyprus was apostolic, and the Emperor Zeno pronounced it to be ecclesiastically autonomous. The accession of the Emperor Anastasius (491–518), who favored the Monophysites, brought heightened disorders in Antioch, culminating in the election of the prominent Monophysite Severus as bishop. In addition to a permanent resident synod which Severus established, special synods convened at Antioch in 513 and 515 to enforce Severus's policies; but he had to flee when the orthodox Justin I (518–527) succeeded Anastasius. The ecclesiastical fortunes of the Monophysites were reversed. The circus factions, which had become powerful political influences in all large cities, continued the street fighting which kept cities such as Antioch and Constantinople in continual unrest. The Green faction had been Monophysite; the Blue faction, orthodox. The government began a veritable persecution of the Monophysites, which continued with increased severity under Justinian (527–565). All this time, however, the Monophysites managed to maintain an organized church, with a complete hierarchy, throughout Syria. This was a national Syrian church, known as the Jacobite Church from its leader, James *Baradai. Justinian's reign witnessed the remarkable series of disasters which marked the end of ancient Antioch. A devastating fire (525) was followed by two severe earthquakes (526, 528), all resulting in serious losses in population and economic activity. The culmination was the capture and sack of the city by the Persians (540). Antioch continued to exist until it was taken by the Persians (611) and the Arabs (638), but it never recovered its ancient greatness. Under the Arabs it soon shrank to a village.

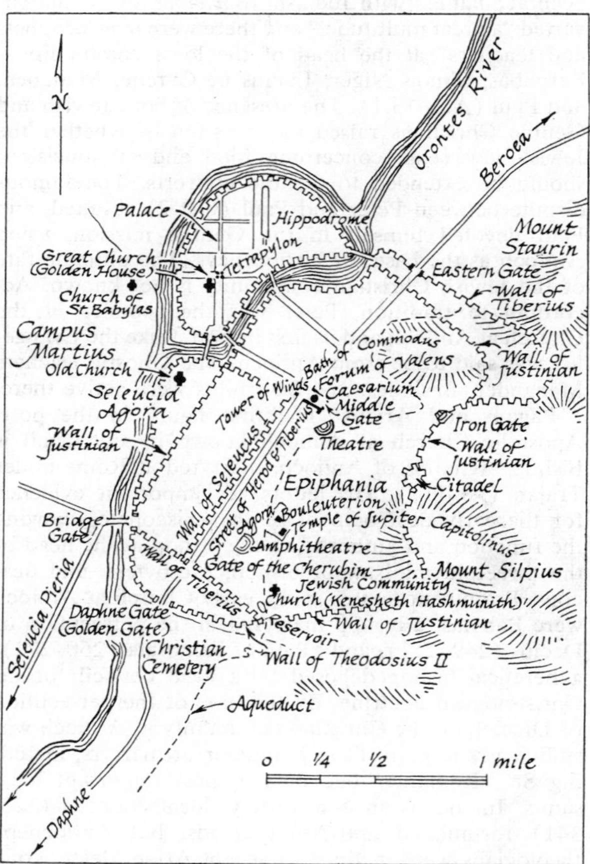

Fig. 1. Restored plan of ancient Antioch, based on literary evidence, archeological excavations, and monuments preserved above ground.

HIRMER FOTOARCHIV, MUNICH

Fifth-century mosaics in the dome of the Baptistery of the Orthodox at Ravenna. The central motif is the Baptism of Christ. Around it, in two zones, are the Twelve Apostles with their crowns of martyrdom, and a design of thrones and Gospel Books upon altars, symbols of the *etimasia*.

Fig. 2. Detail from a topographical border frieze in mosaic from a villa floor in Daphne, near Antioch. Extreme right, the octagonal silhouette of the Great Church of Antioch dating from the 4th century. Mosaic, c. end of 5th century.

Pagan Survivals. Reports of Justinian's vigorous persecution of pagans and heretics indicate that paganism survived to some extent at Antioch, as at other old pagan centers, such as Athens. Even after Justinian's death a number of pagan priests were discovered in Antioch and in 578 a bishop of Antioch was accused of taking part, with another Christian priest, in the sacrifice of a boy. He was able to clear himself before a court in Constantinople, but the fact that the charge could be made is significant of the strength of paganism.

Theological School. As an ancient center of Greek learning, Antioch offered excellent facilities for the study of Greek philosophy and rhetoric, and the terms of Greek philosophy and the methods of Greek speculation had an important influence on the thought of the Antiochene theologians. A regular "school" of theology was flourishing under *Lucian of Antioch (martyred 312), if not earlier. Theologians trained in this school followed Aristotelian, historical, and philological methods, in contrast to the Platonic, mystical approach of the great rival school of Alexandria. Lucian's scientific study of the text of the Bible was the examplar of the famous Antiochene Biblical scholarship, which combined meticulous textual criticism with literal exegesis, as against the allegorical method popular at Alexandria. Prominent representatives of Antiochene theology were *Marcellus of Ancyra; Chrysostom; Diodore, later bishop of Tarsus; Theodore of Mopsuestia; Nestorius; and *Theodoret of Cyr. Beginning with the heretical teaching of Paul of Samosata on the Person of Christ, Antioch tended toward an insistence on the oneness of God, which in time made the city a stronghold of Arianism. In the Christological controversies of the 5th century, the Antiochene emphasis on the humanity of Christ clashed with the Alexandrian tendency to stress the Divine Nature of the Incarnate Christ.

Art and Archeology. Excavations conducted at Antioch, the suburb Daphne, and the seaport Seleucia Pieria (1932–39) obtained important results, but time did not allow extensive exploration and much remains to be excavated. Objects found in the excavations are preserved in the museum at Antioch, in the Louvre, and in museums in the U.S. The city plan (Fig. 1) can be restored in its main features from surface indications, archeological evidence, literary testimonia, and air photography. Along with topographical evidence, many fine mosaic floors were found in houses, public baths, churches, and luxurious suburban villas. A unique discovery was the topographical border of a large mosaic floor (Fig. 2) in a villa at Daphne depicting a tour of Antioch and Daphne (late 5th century). The route illustrated corresponds with the itinerary described by Libanius in his encomium of Antioch (356). The scenes in the border are a precious source for contemporary architecture and daily life, illustrating dress, food, occupations, social life, recreations, and worship. This mosaic and Libanius's description of Antioch offer a view of Antiochene life that is not available for other cities in this epoch.

The city having suffered from frequent natural disasters and pillage, Christian archeological remains found in the excavations were not extensive, but the style of the local church architecture and liturgical silver is known from discoveries made elsewhere. Antioch and Constantinople were centers for the manufacture of gold and silver liturgical vessels and church ornaments, and numerous examples of silversmith work, both secular and religious, found in Syria illustrate the style and craftsmanship of the Antiochene workshops. The celebrated Chalice of Antioch (cf. Fig. 3) is a fine example of 4th-century work.

No early house churches such as those at *Ostia and *Dura-Europos were found, but later Antiochene structures had an important influence on church architecture. The famous octagonal church of Constantine the Great, the Domus Aurea or Golden House, was the prototype of the great pilgrimage church of St. Simeon Stylites in the mountains east of Antioch, and the Church of St. Babylas was an important early example of the cruciform plan. Names of a number of churches are preserved in literary texts and the topographical border at Daphne illustrates "the *ergasterion* of the martyrium," evidently the workshop at the shrine of St. Babylas at Daphne where religious objects and souvenirs for pilgrims were manufactured. The Greek and Latin inscriptions of Antioch and its vicinity contain a number of Christian texts recording the building of churches, dedications and offerings, and names of bishops, priests,

Fig. 3. Ivory pyx showing Christ and Disciples. Eastern Mediterranean, c. 400. The composition of this piece is almost identical with that of the Great Chalice of Antioch.

and church officials. A number of Christian epitaphs also have been found.

Bibliography: G. DOWNEY, *A History of Antioch in Syria from Seleucus to the Arab Conquest* (Princeton 1961), bibliography; *Ancient Antioch* (Princeton 1963). C. KARALEVSKIJ, DHGE 3:563–703. H. LECLERCQ, DACL 1.2:2359–2439. S. VAILHÉ and V. ERMONI, DTC 1.2:1399–1439. G. M. PERELLA et al., EncCatt 1:1455–75. L. A. JALABERT and R. MOUTERDE, eds., *Inscriptions grecques et latines de la Syrie* (Paris 1929–), v.3 contains the inscriptions from Antioch, Daphne, and vicinity. C. H. KRAELING, "The Jewish Community at Antioch," JBiblLit 51 (1932) 130–160. G. DOWNEY, tr., "Libanius' Oration in Praise of Antioch (Oration XI)," ProcAmPhilS 103 (1959) 652–686. A. J. FESTUGIÈRE, *Antioche païenne et chrétienne* (Paris 1959). R. DEVREESSE, *Le Patriarcat d'Antioche* (Paris 1945). M. H. SHEPERD, JR., "The Formation and Influence of the Antiochene Liturgy," DumbOaksP 15 (1961) 25–44. *Antioch-on-the-Orontes,* v.1–4 (Princeton 1934–52), reports on the excavations. D. LEVI, *Antioch Mosaic Pavements* (Princeton 1947), complete publication and study of all floors discovered. H. H. ARNASON, "The History of the Chalice of Antioch," BiblArchaeol 4 (1941) 49–64; 5 (1942) 10–16. G. DOWNEY, *Antioch in the Age of Theodosius the Great* (Norman, Okla. 1962). B. M. METZGER, "The Lucianic Recension of the Greek Bible," *Chapters in the History of New Testament Textual Criticism* (Leiden 1963). E. C. DODD, *Byzantine Silver Stamps* (Washington 1961), on hallmarks used at Antioch and elsewhere. **Illustration credits:** Fig. 1, Courtesy of University of Oklahoma Press. Fig. 2, Kunsthistorisch Instituut, Nijmegen, Netherlands. Fig. 3, Photo Archives—Maria Laach.

[G. DOWNEY]

ANTIOCH, PATRIARCHATE OF

According to ancient tradition, the Christian community of *Antioch had been founded by St. Peter, and with the destruction of Jerusalem in A.D. 70 it became the chief radial point of Christianity in the East. Its authority spread over Syria, Phoenicia, Arabia, Palestine, Cilicia, Cyprus, and Mesopotamia.

Formation of the Patriarchate. In the Ecumenical Council of *Nicaea I (325), Antioch was recognized after Rome and Alexandria as one of the ancient apostolic patriarchates. However, its authority was gradually decentralized in the 5th century. In the Council of *Ephesus (431), the Antiochene Patriarch of Constantinople, *Nestorius, was condemned, and his followers separated from Antioch to form the East Syrian Nestorian Church. *See* CHALDEAN RITE. Cyprus obtained its autonomy in this council. At the Council of *Chalcedon (451) the Patriarchate of Antioch suffered even greater losses by the formation of the Patriarchate of Jerusalem with 58 bishoprics formerly under Antiochene jurisdiction. The council condemned the heresy of Eutyches (*see* MONOPHYSITISM), and the Patriarchate of Antioch split into two factions concerned with this Christological dogma. Orthodox Catholics predominated in the Hellenized cities along the coast, while the Monophysites occupied the country and the towns of inner Syria, such as Edessa and northern Mesopotamia, where the Jacobite Syrian Church got its start (*see* SYRIAN CHURCH; SYRIAN RITE). The Christians faithful to the Christology taught in the Council of Chalcedon were called Melchites (*see* MELCHITE RITE).

Melchites and Jacobites. The first Monophysite to rule as patriarch of Antioch was Peter the Fuller (468–470; 485–488), but *Severus of Antioch (512–518), as a theological writer, was the true founder of Monophysitism, although his doctrine was heterodox more by expression than in fact. He was deposed by the Byzantine Emperor, and under *Justinian I, Catholics prevailed. When Severus died in exile (538), his followers were unable to elect a successor. However, James *Baradai (*c.* 543), with the cooperation of Empress *Theodora (1), consecrated a Monophysite hierarchy, whose members were called *Jacobites in his honor. From 550 onward the Patriarchate of Antioch was split between the Melchites, faithful to Chalcedon, and the Jacobites.

The Melchite Church remained powerful even after the Arab invasion. The Moslems preserved the *status quo* as regards the Church's position, while the Melchite patriarch had his see (at first Monothelite; *see* MONOTHELITISM) in the imperial court at Constantinople until the end of the 7th century. From 702 to 742 the Antiochene patriarchal see remained without recognition from the Arabs, and the monks of the monastery of St. Maro, in opposition to the Melchite followers of *Maximus Confessor, took advantage of this disturbance to establish their own Maronite patriarchate (*see* MARONITE RITE).

Break with Rome. When the Byzantines recaptured part of Syria in 960, the Melchite patriarchs in Antioch gradually accepted the Byzantine rite and Church law, thus becoming more dependent upon the Patriarchate of Constantinople. Until then the Melchites had used the West Syrian rite in both the Antioch and Jerusalem patriarchates. Between the 10th and 12th centuries the Antiochene rite was completely substituted for the Byzantine rite of Constantinople, and the Melchite Patriarchate of Antioch followed *Michael Cerularius, Patriarch of Constantinople, into schism (*c.* 1054). The exact date of the break with Rome is not clear.

The Latin Crusaders fomented division by regarding the Melchites of Antioch as schismatics and heretics. Latin patriarchates were set up in Antioch and Jerusalem. During the Latin occupation the Melchite patriarch of Antioch resided in Constantinople, thus increasing his dependence on the Byzantine Church. After the fall of the Crusaders' kingdom of Antioch in 1268, the Melchite patriarch returned to his native see, and from then on the Antioch Patriarchate was considered inimical to Rome. But the city of Antioch had suffered greatly under the siege of the Mameluke Turks; its glory was gone; hence the Melchite patriarch changed his see to Damascus (1366). This patriarchate was more strictly controlled by the Moslems than was that of the Maronites, and the sultans of Egypt, on whom Syria depended during this time, forbade all contact with the West.

Catholic Patriarchate. Work for union began in the Patriarchate of Antioch with the arrival of the Capuchins, Jesuits, and Carmelites after the foundation of the Congregation for the Propagation of the Faith in Rome in 1622. These missionaries slowly infiltrated a community with Catholic elements so that eventually a Catholic hierarchy could be introduced, in the beginning allowing Catholics to receive the Sacraments from the Orthodox clergy. For a time no true distinction was made between Catholic and Orthodox communities. Gradually one or another patriarch or bishop and many faithful were reconciled with Rome. The amalgamation of the entire patriarchate, however, was premature. The two rival patriarchs, Athanasius III (1686–1724) and Cyril V (1672–1720), were recognized as Catholics by Rome at different times but still governed mixed Catholic and Orthodox communities. Archbishop Euthymius Saifi of Tyre and Sidon played an important role in the reunion when in 1701 he was accepted by Rome as bishop of all the Melchite Catholics who did not have their own bishop.

Cyril Tanus. On the death of Athanasius III (*c.* 1724, as a Catholic), it seemed to the Catholics of Antioch that the moment had come to make the patriarchate unmistakably Catholic, and they chose an unequivocal Catholic for the patriarchal see. This was *Cyril (Seraphim) of Turiv, the nephew of Archbishop Euthymius, who took the name of Cyril VI. His election, in which the Orthodox also participated, was made according to ancient custom by the clergy and people of Damascus. The intention of the voters to give the whole patriarchate a Catholic bishop was nullified when Sylvester of Cyprus, consecrated by Jeremias III, Patriarch of Constantinople, obtained the support of the Sultan and Cyrus VI had to flee into exile. He took up residence in the mountainous monastery of the Redeemer near Sidon. The patriarch of Constantinople excommunicated Cyril Tanus as an apostate. The Holy See at first delayed its recognition since Cyril, like his uncle, had been denounced in Rome for his tendency to change customs, and also because there were doubts concerning the validity of his election. In 1729 he received recognition, and in 1744, the pallium.

With the election of Cyril, the Antiochene Patriarchate was actually, but against Rome's intention, split into two communities: one was unmistakably Catholic, while the other was acknowledged as schismatic. In 1759 Cyril VI retired and named his young nephew Ignatius Gohar as his successor; this led to complications, because some of the bishops rejected the nephew and appealed to Rome. Rome named Archbishop Maximus Hakim of Alep as patriarch. This was a difficult test for the still new union, but it soon proved a happy solution.

Melchite Catholics. At first the authority of the Catholic patriarch was confined to Antioch, but on July 13, 1772, the Holy See gave the patriarch jurisdiction over the Catholic Melchites in the territories of Jerusalem and Alexandria (Mansi 46.581–582).

There have been conflicts in the course of history between the Holy See and the Melchite hierarchy caused by an assertion of rights claimed by each side. The Synods of Qarqafel (1806) and of Jerusalem (1849), whose aim was to make of the Melchite community an independent law-making body, were not acknowledged by Rome. The renowned Patriarch *Maximos III Mazlūm (1833–55) had many difficulties with Rome, but in 1838 the Holy See gave him as a personal privilege the right to assume the threefold title of patriarch of Antioch, Alexandria, and Jerusalem; this right has been uninterruptedly renewed by all his successors. Maximos was able to set up a residence in Damascus in 1834, and he received full civil recognition from the Sultan in 1848.

Gregory II Jusof (1864–97) appeared at *Vatican Council I as an opponent of the definition of the Primacy because he saw in it an obstacle to reunion. He accepted the definition only on condition of the acknowledgement of the rights accorded the patriarchs by a clause in the acts of the Council of *Florence (1439), which Pius IX took amiss. Under Leo XIII, who valued him greatly, Gregory played a leading role in the Conference of Oriental Patriarchs held under the presidency of the Pope in 1894. Patriarch Maximos IV Saigh proved himself an energetic assertor of the traditions of the Oriental Churches and the rights of the patriarchs at Vatican Council II.

In 1662 Andrew Akidgean was consecrated Syrian Catholic Patriarch of Antioch, thus creating the confused picture of an ancient apostolic patriarchate broken up into five distinct patriarchates. Today there are two patriarchs of the Byzantine rite who claim the ancient patriarchal See of Antioch as their legitimate heritage: the Orthodox and the Catholic Melchite. The Catholic Maronite patriarch also claims Antioch as his rightful patriarchal see. As a result of Monophysitism the Jacobite Syrians broke from the Church, yet they still claim Antioch for their patriarchal lineage, while the Syrian Catholics do the same.

Bibliography: D. Attwater, *The Christian Churches of the East,* 2 v. (rev. ed. Milwaukee 1961–62). R. Devreesse, *Le Patriarcat d'Antioche* (Paris 1945). C. Karalevskij (Charon), DHGE 3:563–703; *Histoire des Patriarcats Melkites,* 3 v. in 2 (Rome 1909–10). A. A. King, *The Rites of Eastern Christendom,* 2 v. (London 1950). J. Nasrallah, *Sa Beatitude Maximos IV et la succession apostolique* (Paris 1963). OrientCatt. M. Théarvic, ÉchosOr 3 (1899–1900) 143–147, hierarchy. S. Vailhé, DTC 1.2:1399–1433. W. de Vries et al., eds., *Rom und die Patriarchate des Ostens* (Freiburg 1963).

[G. A. MALONEY]

ANTIOCH, SCHOOL OF

The common doctrinal tendencies particularly in exegesis and Christology that characterized the theological thinkers and writers who represented the Antiochian tradition. There is no record of a formal school such as apparently existed at *Alexandria, although *Lucian of Antioch directed his *didascalion* and Diodore of Tarsus his *asceterion* in Antioch. The school of

Antioch represented a group of theologians exhibiting common doctrinal characteristics; these theologians were not necessarily from Antioch, although they had undergone the influence of Antiochene masters. The problems posed to the theologians of Antioch in the 3d century and at the beginning of the 4th century differed from those dealt with at the end of the 4th century and during the 5th century. Hence there were two distinct periods in the history of the school of Antioch.

First Period. Eusebius of Caesarea mentioned the literary activity of Bishop Serapion of Antioch at the beginning of the 3d century; and Jerome spoke of a priest, Geminus of Antioch (d. *c.* 230), as a writer of theology. At the Synod of Antioch in 268, two Antiochene theologians, *Paul of Samosata and the Sophist Malchion, held discussions on the Trinity and Christ. But the true founder of the school was Lucian of Antioch. From about 270 he conducted an important *didascalion*; he died a martyr in 312. During this time a certain Dorotheus also served as a theologian and exegete. The relationship between him and Lucian, as between the latter and Paul of Samosata, is not clear. Little is known of the doctine of Lucian himself. He labored at scriptural exegesis and composed a version of the text after the example of *Origen. He had many disciples, who were called Collucianites or followers of Lucian, among whom *Philostorgius named: Eusebius of Nicomedia, Maris of Chalcedon, Theognis of Nicaea, Leontius of Antioch, Anthony of Tarsus, Menophantes of Ephesus, Noominus, Eudoxius, Alexander, and *Asterius the Sophist.

These authors defended *Arius, who was also a disciple of Lucian. Lucian is, as a consequence, properly considered the father of *Arianism. This does not exclude the possibility that Lucian actually found inspiration in the thought of Origen. One of Arius's most rabid opponents was *Eustathius, Bishop of Antioch. He made a clear distinction between the divinity and the humanity of Christ. This caused him to be considered a precursor of the Christology defended against the school of Alexandria by the theologians of the school of Antioch in its second period. With them, he attacked the allegorical exegesis of Origen.

Second Period. The problem of *Christology dominated the controversies that began with *Apollinaris of Laodicea (fl. *c.* 362). This period was inaugurated with *Diodore of Tarsus, who was primarily an exegete; but Diodore developed a dualistic Christology that remained characteristic of the school of Antioch. As disciples, Diodore had *John Chrysostom and *Theodore of Mopsuestia; *Nestorius and *Theodoret of Cyr also belonged to this lineage. Finally, the school of *Edessa was influenced by Antioch. It is through this school that Theodore of Mopsuestia became the official exegete of the Persian Church. The consequence of this was the "Nestorianization" of Mesopotamian Christianity.

Doctrine. Opposition between the school of Antioch and the school of Alexandria developed in the spheres of exegesis and Christology. In an explicit manner, the teachers of Antioch opposed their own literal understanding of Scripture to the allegorical interpretation given by their Egyptian colleagues. They did not repudiate typology as such, when the employment of it was justified by the text. But they were opposed to the arbitrary manner in which the Alexandrian exegetes discovered typological meaning in the Bible.

Opposition to the school of Alexandria was more marked in the approach to Christology and dominated the controversies of the 5th century. Against Apollinaris, who was regarded as a representative of Alexandria, Diodore strongly defended the immutability and eternity of the Logos. This led him to insist on the duality of the natures in Christ, as Eustathius of Antioch had already done. But Diodore did not succeed in explaining the unity in the person of Christ with the same exactitude. He spoke of Him as at once "Son of God" and "Son of Mary," a distinction that was too readily accepted as stemming from a doctrine of two persons in Christ. Diodore preferred to speak of the indwelling of the Word in the Flesh, rather than of the Incarnation. Mary, he said, is the mother of a man (*anthropotokos*); she is not the mother of God (*theotokos*); and he cautioned against saying that God suffered. The Word of God and the Son of Mary are both Sons of God; the one by nature, the other by grace. These are characteristic formulas of the Antiochene Christology and can be found in the writings of Theodore of Mopsuestia, Theodoret of Cyr, and other theologians of the Antiochene Patriarchate, who rallied to the defense of Nestorius.

Bibliography: G. BARDY, *Recherches sur S. Lucien d'Antioche et son école* (Paris 1936). H. DE RIEDMATTEN, *Les Actes du procès de Paul de Samosate* (Fribourg 1952). L. ABRAMOWSKI, DHGE 14:496–504; "Zur Theologie Theodors von Mopsuestia," ZKirchgesch 72 (1961) 263–293. F. A. SULLIVAN, *The Christology of Theodore of Mopsuestia* (AnalGreg 82; 1956); "Further Notes on Theodore of Mopsuestia," ThSt 20 (1959) 264–279. J. L. MCKENZIE, "Annotations on the Christology of Theodore of Mopsuestia," *ibid.* 19 (1958) 345–373. R. V. SELLERS, *Two Ancient Christologies* (London 1940). J. GUILLET, "Les Exégètes d'Alexandrie et d'Antioche," RechScRel 34 (1947) 257–302. V. ERMONI, DTC 1.2:1435–39. Cross ODCC 63–64. H. RAHNER, LexThK[2] 1:650–652. W. ELTESTER, RGG[3] 1:452–453.

[A. VAN ROEY]

ANTIOCH IN PISIDIA, Greco-Roman city located in the border zone of Pisidia and Phrygia in Asia Minor. The site of the ancient city lies 2 miles east of modern Yalvaç, southwest of Aksehir in modern Turkey. It is to be distinguished from the more famous *Antioch, the one on the Orontes in Syria (Acts 13.1; 14.26; 15.22; etc.). The former is referred to in Acts 13.14 as Ἀντιόχεια τῆς Πισιδίας (Antioch of Pisidia). Despite this appellation, it was really a Phrygian city belonging to Galatia. Strabo (*Geography* 12.6.4; 12.8. 14) describes it as ἡ πρὸς τῇ Πισιδίᾳ [the (city) near Pisidia] and ἡ πρὸς Πισιδίᾳ καλουμένη [the (city) called (Antioch) near Pisidia]. The shorter term Ἀντιόχεια ἡ Πισιδία (Pisidian Antioch) later came into general use. The Hellenistic city as such was founded by Seleucus I of Syria (312 or 311–292 B.C.), declared free of Pontus by the Romans in 188 B.C., and made a Roman colony (*Colonia Caesarea Antiochia*) as part of the province of Galatia by the Emperor Augustus (27 B.C.–A.D. 14). At the time of St. Paul, therefore, its inhabitants could be called Galatians (*see* GALATIANS, EPISTLE TO THE). In the course of his first missionary journey the Apostle preached the gospel in the synagogue of this city; when the Jews saw that many of their coreligionists, especially among the *proselytes, were accepting the new religion, they incited a persecution against Paul and Barnabas that drove them away (Acts 13.14–51;

2 Tm 3.11). Later, however, Paul visited the city at least twice, though no details are given (Acts 14.24; 16.6).

Bibliography: InterDictBibl 1:144–145. A. WIKENHAUSER, LexThK[2] 1:650. A. ROMEO, EncCatt 1:1454–55. O. HIRSCHFELD AND E. KORNEMANN, Pauly-Wiss RE 1.2:2446; 4.1:531–532. W. M. RAMSAY, *The Cities of St. Paul* (London 1907) 245–314. D. M. ROBINSON, "Roman Sculptures from Colonia Caesarea (Pisidian Antioch)," ArtBull 9 (1926–27) 5–69. H. METZGER, *St. Paul's Journeys in the Greek Orient,* tr. S. H. HOOKE (New York 1955) 25–27.

[P. P. SAYDON]

ANTIOCHENE RITE, LITURGY OF

The manner of celebrating Christ's redemptive mystery in the Patriarchate of Antioch and, in a modified form, among some Syrians today.

Origins. The tradition is that the liturgical formula of "offering thanks" as observed at Antioch of Syria, an important early Christian community (Acts 8 to 11), spread to Jerusalem, where it was translated from Greek to Aramaic. The Antioch usage, further modified at Jerusalem, thereafter became the model of almost all the other Eastern rites.

Liturgical customs radiating from Antioch left their mark on the Church life of the surrounding area. The rapid growth of Christianity in this region (Antioch itself counted 150 suffragan bishops at Nicaea in 325) demanded a close surveillance over the prayers of the liturgy lest nonapproved forms be adopted. As a consequence, prayer texts came to be written, and in this manner, rather than orally, they were transmitted from one community to another; the smaller communities of Christians borrowed the written texts from those that were larger and more influential. In due time, then, the liturgical practices carried out in the city of Antioch were found in use throughout the area known as the Patriarchate of *Antioch. Thus, the Antiochene Liturgy came into existence.

It is not surprising to discern in the somewhat fixed 4th-century Antioch usage described below the outlines of various other Eastern rites. Such a resemblance was inevitable in the Liturgy of Byzantium or Constantinople, universally acknowledged as the handiwork of St. John Chrysostom, who before he became bishop of Constantinople (370–397) was a priest of the city of Antioch. At a much earlier date, St. Mark is said to have introduced the Antiochene usage into Egypt, where it developed into the Alexandrian rite (*see* ALEXANDRIAN RITE, LITURGY OF).

Order of Mass. There follows in outline form, based on quotations taken from book eight of the *Apostolic Constitutions,* a 4th-century Syrian Christian writing, a description of the early Antioch usage: (1) reading from the Old Testament, (2) reading from the Epistles and Acts and the Gospels, (3) homily by the bishop, (4) dismissal of nonmembers, those preparing for Baptism, and public penitents, (5) prayer for all the faithful, (6) kiss of peace and greetings by the bishop, (7) washing of hands, (8) bringing in of the gifts, (9) Eucharistic Prayer, Preface, Sanctus, (10) words of institution, (11) Anamnesis, (12) Epiclesis, (13) intercessory prayers for the Church, the living, the dead, (14) prayers in preparation for Communion ("Holy things for the holy"), (15) Communion, (16) post-Communion prayer of thanks, and (17) final blessing by the bishop. Of note in this usage at this time are: (1) the prominent role played by the deacon as intermediary between bishop and people; (2) the frequent petitions made in litany form by the deacons to which the faithful responded "Kyrie eleison," (3) the position of the Epiclesis after the Consecration (see Quasten MonE 198–233).

Later Developments. From the time of the Council of Chalcedon (451) until the 7th-century Arab conquest of Syria, the Antiochene rite was used by both Catholic and Monophysite Syrians. However, with the rise of Constantinople to a position of ecclesiastical supremacy in the East came the widespread use of the *Byzantine rite. The Antiochene rite, except for its use in a modified form by the Jacobites, simply ceased to exist. *See* JACOBITES (SYRIAN).

The Antiochene rite is sometimes called the West Syrian rite to distinguish it from the East Syrian rite, a liturgy usually identified with the Christian churches of Mesopotamia and Chaldea. These Christians, originally dependent on Antioch, dwelt beyond the borders of the Roman Empire, where because of their isolated position they gradually acquired an ecclesiastical semi-independent status, a condition that favored the development of a distinct liturgical rite. The liturgy that evolved in that region is the one we know today as the East Syrian rite. Christians of this rite who have reestablished full union with Rome, having set aside their Nestorianism, are today known as members of the *Chaldean rite.

Parts of India are thought to have received Christianity from Antioch, for the Christians of the *Malankar rite claim West Syrian origins; on the other hand, *Malabar-rite Christians acknowledge East Syrian origins. Today, the Antiochene rite survives only in a small body of Christians, numbering about 150,000 divided almost equally between Catholics and Jacobites, living in Iraq and Syria. Among the Catholics, the Antiochene rite is commonly called the *Syrian rite.

Bibliography: D. ATTWATER, *The Christian Churches of the East,* 2 v. (Milwaukee 1961). J. A. JUNGMANN, *The Mass of the Roman Rite* (New York 1959). N. LIESEL, *The Eucharistic Liturgies of the Eastern Churches,* tr. D. HEIMANN (Collegeville, Minn. 1963). Miller FundLit 48–50.

[E. E. FINN]

ANTIOCHUS IV EPIPHANES

King of the Seleucian Kingdom of Syria (175–163 B.C.). He pursued a policy aimed at Hellenizing the Jewish religion that brought on the Machabean revolt; occupied by revolts in the eastern part of his empire and strongly opposed by the nationalism and religion of the Jews, Antiochus IV was unable to implement his Hellenizing decrees in Palestine.

Aggressive Hellenism of Antiochus IV. After the Battle of Magnesia (190 B.C.) Epiphanes was taken hostage and held in Rome for about 15 years. Upon his release, though not in a position to succeed immediately to the throne, he was able to eliminate his older brother's rightful heir, Demetrius. Antiochus made extravagant efforts to live up to his surname Epiphanes, which means "(God) Manifest"; his enemies punned on it, calling him Epimanes, "crazy." His relationship with the Jews and Jerusalem was unhappy and turbulent. Early in his reign he intervened to settle the dispute between the high priest *Onias III and his brother Jason. Since Jason showed Hellenizing sympathies and came forward with a substantial bribe, Antiochus de-

Antiochus IV Epiphanes, portrait on the obverse of a coin of his reign.

posed Onias and made Jason high priest. Three years later one Menelaus, not of the lineage of the high priests, successfully bribed Antiochus to depose Jason and make him high priest. A subsequent, ill-advised revolt led by Jason in the absence of Antiochus was severely punished; Antiochus stripped the Temple of its treasures and put Jerusalem under a despotic governor named Philip (1 Mc 1.21–29). Frustrated in Egypt by Roman interference, Antiochus vented his anger on the Jews. His edict (1 Mc 1.43–53) that all peoples within his kingdom must be one in law, custom, and religion brought his relationship with the Jews to the worst possible climax, that of general persecution. Antiochus decreed the sternest measures against the Sabbath observance, circumcision, and food laws (1 Mc 1.48, 51). Any Jew discovered in possession of a copy of the Law was executed. The unforgiveable desecration, however, was the erection of an altar to the Olympian Zeus in the Temple, the "horrible abomination" (Dn 11.31; 1 Mc 1.57; *see* ABOMINATION OF DESOLATION).

Machabean Revolt. In 167 B.C. Antiochus's policy, aimed at Hellenizing the Jews, brought open revolt, first under the leadership of the priest Mattathias (1 Mc 2.1–2.69), and then under his famous son *Judas Machabee. The latter, aided by the Jews faithful to the Law, especially the *Hasidaeans (1 Mc 2.42), drove the Syrians out of Judea through a swift succession of victories (3.1–4.35). The enraged Antiochus was powerless to do anything about it. He was distracted and concerned by serious insurrections in Parthia and Armenia. Eventually he lost his life in leading an expedition against the Parthians (1 Mc 6.1–16). Tradition adds the ironic note of tragedy that, shortly before his death, Antiochus really became insane. The Book of Daniel, in its last four chapters, tells in veiled symbolism the story of Antiochus IV.

See also DANIEL, BOOK OF; MACHABEES (MACCABEES), HISTORY OF THE; SELEUCID DYNASTY.

Bibliography: F. M. ABEL, "Antiochus Épiphane," RevBibl 50 (1941) 231–254. A. AYMARD, "Autour de l'avènement d'Antiochos IV," *Historia* 2 (Wiesbaden 1953–54) 49–73. M. NOTH, *The History of Israel,* tr. P. R. ACKROYD (2d ed. New York 1960). J. BRIGHT, *A History of Israel* (Philadelphia 1959) 401–412. G. DOWNEY, *A History of Antioch in Syria from Seleucus to the Arab Conquest* (Princeton 1961) 95–111. M. WELLMANN, Pauly-Wiss RE 1.2 (1894) 2470–76. **Illustration credit:** American Numismatic Society.

[J. F. DEVINE]

ANTIPATER, the son of Alexander Jannaeus's governor in *Idumea and the father of *Herod the Great. (On Alexander Jannaeus and his successors, *see* HASMONAEANS.) The marriage of Antipater to Cyprus of Petra joined his Idumean line with a leading *Nabataean family as the first step in a lifelong pursuit of power. He was able to manipulate for his own ends the weak Hyrcanus II, legitimate heir to Jannaeus's widow, Queen Alexandra. After Alexandra's death in 67 B.C., Hyrcanus's younger brother Aristobulus usurped the throne and high priesthood. Though Hyrcanus was satisfied with possession of his life and estates, Antipater finally prevailed on him to try to regain his rightful position, with the assurance of support from the legitimist party of Pharisees and aristocrats in Jerusalem and from the Nabataean King Aretas III (65 B.C.). Pompey's sudden intervention in the dispute indicated to Antipater that Roman influence would thenceforth be decisive in Syrian affairs, and in representing Hyrcanus's interests before Pompey he made it his aim to be recognized as a friend of Rome. Aristobulus's defiance ensured his own defeat, but Hyrcanus was restored only the office of high priest, with loss of secular power and of much territory. Antipater, continuing to ingratiate himself with the Romans, in 62 B.C. aided Pompey's legate Scaurus against the Nabataeans; arranged an alliance between Aretas and Rome; helped Gabinius, one of Scaurus's successors, put down successive revolts by Aristobulus and his sons (57–55 B.C.); and joined Gabinius's campaign in Egypt (55 B.C.). He was rewarded with an appointment as governor of Jerusalem. After Pompey's death, Antipater gave aid in the Alexandrian campaign of Caesar, who therefore gave him Roman citizenship and immunity from taxation and made him procurator of Judea under Hyrcanus as ethnarch; Antipater appointed his son Phasael governor of Jerusalem, and Herod, governor of Galilee (47 B.C.). His dominance over the ineffectual Hyrcanus aroused the resentment of leading Jews against the Idumean Antipater and his sons, but to little effect. His protective association with Rome continued with support of C. Cassius after Caesar's assassination. In 43 B.C. a rival for power, Malichus, had him poisoned by Hyrcanus's butler. Herod in turn avenged his father by instigating Malichus's murder. The line of Antipatrids continued in power, from Herod through *Agrippa II.

Bibliography: U. WILCKEN, Pauly-Wiss RE 1.1 (1894) 2509–11. A. H. M. JONES, *The Herods of Judaea* (Oxford 1938) 15–34. H. WILLRICH, *Das Haus des Herodes: Zwischen Jerusalem und Rom* (Heidelberg 1929) 4–33.

[J. P. M. WALSH]

ANTIPATHY, an emotional reaction of an individual who experiences aversion, repugnance, or dislike. It is a fixed attitude and may be based on either rational or irrational foundations. In the former case, the individual is usually aware of his feelings and the reason for them; in the latter case, he simply experiences an

Antiphons for the distribution of palms on Palm Sunday, in a "Graduale," Italy c. 1039 (Ang. MS 123).

aversion for the object or person without any recognized justifiable reason. Whenever he finds himself confronted with the object, he involuntarily shrinks from it. Antipathy usually includes some degree of hostility, inasmuch as it involves feelings of opposition. For the moral evaluation of antipathy *see* HOSTILITY, FEELINGS OF.

[R. P. VAUGHAN]

ANTIPHON, in Western liturgical practice, a refrain sung before and after a Psalm or canticle. In Byzantine liturgical usage it means several verses of a Psalm, a complete Psalm, or even several Psalms followed by a doxology. Although the original meaning seems to have referred to an alternation of groups in Psalm singing (*see* PSALMODY), by the 6th century it had come to mean in the West a refrain that accompanied such alternation. It forms the largest category of chants found in the Office (*see* DIVINE OFFICE, ROMAN, CHANTS OF) and in the Mass (*see* MASS, ROMAN, MUSIC OF). Later medieval pieces with alternating choruses but not with accompanying psalmody are also called antiphons (processional antiphons and *Marian antiphons).

Bibliography: O. STRUNK, "The Antiphons of the Oktoechos," JAmMusSoc 13 (1960) 50–67. A. GEVAERT, *Le Mélopée antique dans le chant de l'église latine* (Gand 1895). Apel GregCh 392–404, 217–228. B. STÄBLEIN, MusGG 1:523–545. **Illustration credit:** Biblioteca Angelica, Rome.

[R. G. WEAKLAND]

ANTIPODES

This term was used to designate either the opposite sides of the earth or the people who dwelt there. The problem of whether there were people living on the opposite sides of the earth was of great interest to ancient and medieval scientists, philosophers, and theologians. While the question was mainly a geographical one, and the Fathers of the Church considered it open as regards the faith, St. Augustine questioned whether such inhabitants, if they existed, would be descendants of Adam. He concluded they would not be. This gave a theological cast to the problem and led to a situation frequently cited by the enemies of the Church as a conflict between the Church and science.

Following the Augustinian line of thought, Pope Zachary on May 1, 748, asked St. Boniface to inquire about Virgilius (or Fergal), who perhaps believed in another world and other men existing beneath the earth, or in another sun and moon there, and to excommunicate him if he held these "perverse" tenets (PL 89:946). Virgilius was an Irish monk who had become abbot of St. Peter's in Salzburg and who for many years (746–784) administered that episcopal see, though he was not consecrated bishop until 767. He was also a geographer and, as Lowe has proved, he wrote (under the pseudonym of Ethicus Istes) a *Cosmographia* (Clavis

Patrum; no. 2548), a mixture of ancient geographical doctrines and curious stories. He did not mention the antipodes in this book, but perhaps in another he had quoted or commented on *Martianus Capella.

The outcome of this case is not known, but surely Virgilius was not condemned since he remained abbot-bishop of Salzburg. *See* VIRGILIUS OF SALZBURG (FERGAL), ST. Because of the subsequent furor, it is important to emphasize that the Pope did not pass canonical sentence. Further, the Pope was interested in the question from a theological point of view and, following Augustine, objected to the antipodes on account of the unity of mankind. Once writers began postulating the ability of reaching the antipodes by navigation, the theological aspect of the problem disappeared.

By the 13th century writers were beginning to see the antipodes as a scientific question, and many argued that it could be settled only by experiment—that all that transpired before experimental verifications was pure speculation and no more. There is a possibility that Christopher Columbus had read *Peter of Ailly's *Imago Mundi* before his voyage and was influenced by its insistence on experimental inquiry.

The conflict with Virgilius and the letter of Pope Zachary were used by Kepler and Descartes against the theologians who did not accept the Copernician system, while the Encyclopedists employed the incident to attack the Church and the papacy. These objections were answered by the Jesuits in the *Mémoires de Trévoux* (1708).

Bibliography: F. S. BETTEN, *St. Boniface and St. Virgil* (Washington 1927). G. BOFFITO, "Cosmografia primitiva: Classica e patristica," *Pontifica accademia delle scienze: Memorie* 19 (1901) 301–353; 20 (1902) 113–146. P. DELHAYE, "La Théorie des antipodes et ses incidences théologiques," in *Le Microcosmus de Godefroy de St-Victor: Étude théologique,* ed. P. DELHAYE (Lille 1951). H. LÖWE, *Ein literarischer Widersacher des Bonifatius: Virgil von Salsburg und die Kosmographie des Aethicus Ister* (Wiesbaden 1952). G. MARINELLI, "La Geografia ed i Padri della Chiesa," *Scritti minori* (Florence 1908–) 1:281–381. J. O. THOMSON, *History of Ancient Geography* (Cambridge, Eng. 1948).

[P. DELHAYE]

ANTIPOPE

One who uncanonically claims or exercises the office of Roman pontiff. Historically, this situation has occurred as the result of various causes, not all of which imply bad faith. Antipopes have risen by violent usurpation (Constantine, 767); by election following a prior selection falsely judged as invalid (Clement VII, 1378); accession after an unwarranted deposition or deportation of the previous pope (Felix II, 355); double election (Anacletus II, Innocent II, 1130); or confusion as to the requirements for a valid choice (Benedict X, 1058). Such confusion may have been due to the lack of a readily accessible electoral code (*see* POPES, ELECTION OF). Instances occurred where a pontificate, uncanonical in its beginnings, was validated by subsequent acceptance on the part of the electors (Vigilius, after Silverius's resignation or death, 537). But it must be frankly admitted that bias or deficiencies in the sources make it impossible to determine in certain cases whether the claimants were popes or antipopes.

The term "antipope" can be traced to *c.* 1192 [J. H. Baxter and C. Johnson *Medieval Latin Word-List* (1950) 22], though other names appear earlier, e.g., *perturbator* (370; CSEL 35:52), *pervasor* (506; Thiel, *Epist. Rom. pont.* 1:697). Authors variously calculate the number of antipopes: Baümer counts 33 with three others bracketed with legitimate popes: Amanieu, 34; Frutaz, 36 plus 7 doubtful and 9 improperly designated; Moroni, 39. Since 1947 the Vatican *Annuario Pontificio* has printed Mercati's list of popes which includes 37 antipopes in the text (with additional possibilities in the notes), as follows:

Hippolytus	217–235	Honorius II	1061–1072
Novatian	251	Clement III	1080–1100
Felix II	355–365	Theodoric	1100
Ursinus	366–367	Albert	1102
Eulalius	418–419	Sylvester IV	1105–1111
Lawrence	498–505	Gregory VIII	1118–1121
Dioscorus	530	Celestine II	1124
Theodore	687	Anacletus II	1130–1138
Paschal	687	Victor IV	1138
Constantine	767–769	Victor IV	1159–1164
Philip	768	Paschal III	1164–1168
John	844	Callistus III	1168–1178
Anastasius	855	Innocent III	1179–1180
Christopher	903–904	Nicholas V	1328–1330
Boniface VII	974	Clement VII	1378–1394
Boniface VII	984–985	Benedict XIII	1394–1423
John XVI	997–998	Alexander V	1409–1410
Gregory	1012	John XXIII	1410–1415
Benedict X	1058–1059	Felix V	1439–1449

All lists are subject to reservations, and the Mercati catalogue occasions the following dissent: *Eusebius of Caesarea (*Hist. Eccl.* 5.28:8–12) gives reason for considering Natalius, contemporary of Victor I (189–199) or Zephyrinus (199–217), as the first antipope. That Hippolytus (217–235) falls in this classification is questionable in the light of J. M. Hanssens [*La liturgie d'Hippolyte* (Rome 1959) 313–316]. From Duchesne (LP 1:282), it seems that Dioscorus (530) was an authentic pope so that only after his death, Oct. 14, 530, does the pontificate of Boniface II (Sept. 22, 530–Oct. 17, 532) become canonical. Duchesne (LP 1:290) further implies that the beginnings of Silverius's reign [June 1, 536–Nov. 11 (Dec. 2), 537] were illegitimate, though rectified later; because of this subsequent validation, Vigilius's pontificate (March 29, 537–June 7, 555) was probably canonical only after Silverius's resignation or death (537). The legalization of the reign of Eugene I (Aug. 10, 654–June 2, 657), before the death of the exiled Martin I (July 649–Sept. 16, 655), seems clear from Martin's *Epist.* 17 (PL 87:204), but how much before is not evident.

The elections of Conon (Oct. 21, 686–Sept. 21, 687) and Sergius I (Dec. 15, 687–Sept. 8, 701) as described in Duchesne (LP 1:368–372), exclude the considering of the mild Theodore and the aggressive Paschal as other than disappointed candidates for the papacy in 686 and 687. So also, in the cases of John in January 844 (LP 2:87) and of Anastasius in August–September 855 (LP 2:142–143), though there is proof of violence, no real evidence points to their usurpation of papal authority. Sergius III (898?; Jan. 29, 904–April 14, 911), according to his epitaph (LP 2:238; cf. Flodoard, PL 135:831), may have been the true pope in early 898, thus making antipopes of John IX (898–900), Benedict IV (900–903), Leo V (903), and Christopher (903–904). If the epitaph is tendentious, then Sergius himself was an antipope in 898. (Christopher was certainly antipapal from LP 2:234–235.) The deposition of John XII (Dec. 16, 955–May 14, 964) by a synod dominated by the Emperor *Otto I, Dec. 4, 963 (Liutprand, *Hist. Ottonis,* 15, 16; MGS 3:345) raises serious question about the canonicity of his imperial replacement, Leo VIII. However the authentic nature of the following imperial pontiff, John XIII, seems vindicated inasmuch as his Roman rival, Benedict V (d. July 4, 966), had accepted deposition, June 23, 964 (*Hist. Otton.* 22).

The complication of the expulsions and resignation (?) of Benedict IX (1033–44; March 10–May 1, 1045; Nov. 8, 1047–July 17, 1048), as recorded in the *Annales Romani* (MGS 5:468–469), precludes certitude regarding the end of his pontificate and the question whether his competitors, Sylvester III (1045), Gregory VI (1045–46), and Clement II (1046–47) are to be counted as popes or antipopes. Celestine II (1124) is presented by Pandulph (*Vita Honorii,* ed. J. M. Watterich, *Pont. Rom. vitae* 2:157–58) not as an antipope but as a canonically elected pope who withdrew in favor of Honorius II (1124–30). The double election of Feb. 14, 1130 is so difficult to appraise [cf. Fliche-Martin 9 (1946) 51–52] that the historian cannot say whether from 1130 to 1138 legitimacy lay with Innocent II (1130–43) or with his rivals Anacletus II (1130–38) and his successor Victor IV (1138), although Victor's resignation, May 29, 1138, either gave or confirmed Innocent's canonicity thereafter.

W. Ullmann [*The Origins of the Great Schism* (London 1948)] and Fliche-Martin [14 (1962) 3–17] provide grounds for considering the Roman succession as the true papal line after 1378. Mercati is thus warranted in treating the Avignon (Clement VII, Benedict XIII) and the Pisan (Alexander V, John XXIII) lines as antipapal, yet consistency requires that he place the two additional Avignon claimants, Clement VIII and Benedict XIV, in the text of his catalogue rather than in the footnotes.

As a curiosity, the interdicted Michel Collin [Act ApS 43 (1951) 477; 53 (1961) 107] may someday be listed as an antipope without any canonical claim other than a mystical experience of Oct. 7, 1950. On this basis he was designated Clement XV, "servant of Pius XII [1939–58] and John XXIII" (1958–63), and since Pope Paul VI the "only true pope who was chosen by heaven."

Bibliography: AnnPont (1964) 7*–22*, cf. A. MERCATI, "The New List of the Popes," MedSt 9 (1947) 71–80. Duchesne LP. Jaffé E, K, and L. L. A. ANASTASIO, *Istoria degli antipapi,* 2 v. (Naples 1754). Moroni 2:181–215. A. AMANIEU, DDC 1:598–622. G. JACQUEMET, *Catholicisme* 1:653–658. A. P. FRUTAZ, EncCatt 1:1483–89; LexThK² 4:583–585. R. BÄUMER, LexThK² 8:54–59.

[H. G. J. BECK]

ANTI-SEMITISM

A term first used in 1879 by W. Marr, a German racist (*see* RACISM), to designate antipathy to Jews on racial, pseudoscientific, and often political grounds. Since then, however, it has become idiomatic and signifies anti-Jewish attitudes or activities of all kinds and eras. It is a misnomer, because it confuses the Semitic with the modern Judaic categories, which, if comparable at all, contrast as much as they coincide. In modern scholarship the term Semitic refers to a family of languages (*see* SEMITIC LANGUAGES) more than to a race of men, and the theory of pure Aryan and Semitic races existent in the present has been repudiated. It is recognized also that the Jews do not constitute a race; from earliest times they have commingled with other peoples. The complex phenomenon of anti-Semitism derives its energies from many areas of human experience—theological, social, political, and psychological. But it is primarily a historical development in which these energies have been combined anew in each succeeding era to produce differing anti-Semitic reactions fairly continuously from the 3d century B.C. to the present. The Church, though its relations with Judaism have at times appeared ambiguous, has always condemned every form of hatred and injustice. Its part in the history of anti-Semitism must be carefully distinguished among the several factors that make up the complex etiology of anti-Semitism.

HISTORY

The history of anti-Semitism is usually divided into three periods: ancient, medieval, and modern. The ancient period, however, should be subdivided into classical and Christian antiquity, for the latter was a crucial time when the Church and Synagogue confronted each other for a moment on equal terms, a period indispensable for an understanding of the subsequent course of events.

Classical Antiquity. As long as Jews inhabited a homeland of their own, they experienced the normal hostility of rival powers but nothing that could be strictly considered anti-Semitism, whose beginnings were reserved for the Dispersion (*see* DIASPORA, JEWISH). As the Jews grew numerous in many lands, and Hellenism spread everywhere following Alexander the Great's conquests, they stirred reactions. Their refusal to become part of the surrounding cultures, their dedication to their Torah (Mosaic Law) and Holy City, their social exclusivism, and their proselytism aroused resentment. *See* PROSELYTES (BIBLICAL). Some of it was expressed as popular fanaticism, principally in Alexandria and Antioch, where fierce economic rivalry affected Jews and their neighbors and where outbreaks and massacres were frequent. But the chief impetus of classical anti-Semitism came from literary and intellectual circles alienated by the Jewish refusal to conform with the religious and cultural traditions. Among Greek authors, Manethon and Apollonius Molon took the lead in propagating humiliating fables about Jewish origins and elaborating upon Jewish "unsociability," "misanthropy," and "vice." Apion, whose attitude represented the apogee of Greek anti-Semitism, laid down a barrage of complaints referring mainly to the Jews' exclusivism, "hatred of mankind," and "superstition." Roman anti-Semitism, less harsh than the Greek, took up most of the same themes. The masses resented the privileges granted the Jews by the Caesars, but again it was the intellectuals who spearheaded the opposition. Cicero, Seneca, Ovid, Pliny, Suetonius, Juvenal, and others, were unfriendly; but Tacitus surpassed all in bitterness, working over all the charges made before. The emperors were generally favorable, especially Julius Caesar; but Caligula, Tiberius, and Hadrian were hostile. Classical anti-Semitism, in sum, was mostly the work of a group of conservative intellectuals fearful of the threat Judaism posed to religious and national unity. One may agree with Salo Baron who found in ancient anti-Semitism "almost every note sounded in the cacophony of medieval and modern anti-Semitism."

Christian Antiquity. As the nascent Christian Church drew upon itself many of the old charges leveled against Judaism, pagan anti-Semitism declined. But a new conflict was already in the making. For a moment the Church and Synagogue were at peace, and the Church was regarded by the latter merely as a dissident Judaic sect. As it grew clearer that the Jews as a group were to remain outside the Church, and as St. Paul clarified the doctrine of universal Redemption through Christ, the necessary severance took place, and before long it led to serious tensions on both sides. To the Synagogue the new Church was now an apostasy; to the Church all forms of Judaizing (*see* JUDAIZERS) were heresies.

Jewish Hostility. The Synagogue struck the first blow. Examples of Jewish hostility in the 1st century are numerous: the Apostles and their converts were severely harassed, as the Acts and St. Paul's Epistles amply show; Stephen, James, Polycarp, and Simeon were martyred by Jewish hands; a malediction against Jewish converts to the Church (*Minim*) was inserted in the *Shemone Esre,* daily prayer of the Jews (*c.* 80); and at Jabneh (Jamnia) the Sanhedrin banned all associations with them. The 2d century saw little change. St. *Justin Martyr, complaining in his *Dialogue with Tryphon* that the Jews cursed Jesus and boasted of killing Him, confronted Tryphon with the charge, "You hate us" (*Dial.* 133); and again, "You allow no Christian to live" (*Dial.* 110). Jewish apologists often calumniated Jesus as an imposter and a magician, and some claimed that He was the illegitimate son of a Roman soldier—charges to be repeated many times later and elaborated in the infamous *Toledot Jeshu* of the Middle Ages. During *Bar Kokhba's uprising (132–135) many Jewish converts to the Church were massacred at Pella in Transjordan. The probability is strong that during the persecutions of the Christians, Jews conspired with the empire against them. In the 3d century *Tertullian called synagogues "fonts of persecution" (*Scorp.* 10). For fuller documentation of Jewish behavior, see Vernet, Dict ApolFoiCath 2:1654–63; Wilde, 141–147; for another view, see Parkes ch. 2–4.

Christian Reaction. In face of this hostility the attitude of Christians toward Judaism hardened, and the Synagogue now took on the visage of an enemy of the gospel and chief obstacle to the conversion of paganism. Early Christian writers, for the greater part, were content to prove against the Jews the messiahship of Jesus and the insufficiency of the Old Law, but several were contemptuous of Jewish interpretation of the Scriptures and ritual observances, and complained of Jewish hostility. Foremost in this literature was St. Justin's *Dialogue with Tryphon,* an irenic piece of polemic that served as a model for the many such dialogues thereafter. The *Epistle of Pseudo-Barnabas* and the *Letter of Diognetus* continued these themes but adopted a sharper tone. In the writings of St. *Irenaeus and Tertullian traces can be found of the already emerging view that the Jews were a people cursed and dispersed in punishment for their deicide. In the 4th century this view grew stronger, as relations between Christians and Jews rapidly deteriorated. Many factors entered into the change of atmosphere. An active Jewish proselytism and strong Judaizing tendencies among Christians alarmed the Fathers and bishops; and the lowering status of the Jews, without homeland or Temple, lent further credence to the belief that the Dispersion was a punishment for unbelief and deicide. In the light of the current situation, some of the Fathers reinterpreted certain scriptural texts, so as to endow the view with divine authority. SS. Ephraim, Jerome, and Cyril of Alexandria were hostile, and St. Ambrose even countenanced the burning of a synagogue. But above all others St. *John Chrysostom towers in polemical vehemence. In eight sermons at Antioch, where Jewish proselytism was strong, he excoriated the Jews, in language shocking to modern ears, as an accursed and deicidal people, full of every depravity. St. Augustine, adhering to the Pauline tradition of love for the old Israel but impressed by the continued Dispersion, propounded the theory that the Jews were outcasts of Christian society in witness to the Redemption, a theory that was to wield great influence in the years to come.

Middle Ages. In the wake of Christianity's triumph under *Constantine I, the Great, anti-Judaism, hitherto theological and pastoral, took a political and legislative turn. The Theodosian and Justinian codes (*see* THEODOSIUS II, BYZANTINE EMPEROR; JUSTINIAN I, BYZANTINE EMPEROR), which made Christianity the official religion of the empire and conceded to Judaism a merely tolerated position, favored Christian but curbed Jewish proselytism. Jews were forbidden to circumcise slaves, own Christian slaves, marry Christian women, disinherit children who had become Christians, or to stone converts from Judaism; construction of synagogues and Sabbath worship were regulated; and Jews were barred from public office. Direct action by the Church took the form of canonical legislation of the councils, principally those of Elvira, Nicaea, Vannes, and Orleans, which as a whole forbade the mingling of Jews and Christians, separated the celebration of Easter from the Jewish calendar, and prohibited participation in Jewish banquets. The great churchman of the epoch, Pope St. *Gregory I (the Great), enunciated the principle: "Just as Jews should not be accorded liberties not permitted by law, they should suffer no prejudice to whatever is conceded them by law" (*Epist.* 7.25), thus setting Church policy for centuries to come. Moreover, he laid down the norm, not always followed in practice, that the Jews should suffer no injustice, violence, or interference in worship, and should not have Baptism forced upon them, but should be won to Christ by persuasion and kindness.

Repressive Measures. The Byzantine Emperor *Heraclius applied the policies of the Theodosian and Justinian codes and added his own contribution in the form of an edict (632) of compulsory Baptism for all Jews, an action in which he was emulated by the Emperors *Leo III in the 8th century, *Basil I in the 9th, and Romanus I (920–944) in the 10th. The mass conversions resulting from these edicts commenced a strain of crypto-Judaism in Christendom that was rarely absent in subsequent centuries. The barbarian kings in the West accepted the imperial codes but, while still Arian, applied their anti-Jewish measures mildly. Chilperic (d. 584) and Dagobert I (d. 639) in the Frankish Empire offered the Jews the alternative of Baptism or banishment. In Visigothic Spain, from the conversion of Reccared in 586 (or 587) until the Moslem occupation in 711, the Jews were subject to grave oppressions. King Sisebut (d. 621) imposed the choice of Baptism or exile. Numerous councils, hard pressed to deal with backsliding converts, imposed oaths of fidelity and even ordered Jewish children withdrawn from their families for Christian education. *Charlemagne, indulgent to Jews, had a special Jewish oath composed for judicial cases. His successor *Louis I, who also was well-disposed, granted the Jews letters of protection. This leniency of the crown was strongly opposed by two leading churchmen of the time who, fearing the Jews as sources of apostasy, insisted on the rigors of the statutes. Bishop *Agobard of Lyons wrote his *De Insolentia Judaeorum,* a veritable summa of accusations against the Jews, and fought the regal policy bitterly; Bishop Amolo (d. 852), his successor, prolonged this effort, chiefly by this *Liber Contra Judaeos.* The Councils of Meaux (845) and Paris (853) called for reinstatement of the Theodosian legislation. Throughout this period anti-Jewish customs were practiced in several communities, such as, slapping the chief rabbi on Good Friday, striking the synagogue with a mallet, and stoning synagogues.

Reaction to Jewish Moneylenders. From the 8th century anti-Judaism added to its theological and legal aspects an economic coloring, which was to aggravate it. Jews betook themselves increasingly into commerce. Their success in this field won them the further ill will of the Christian population. As the Middle Ages advanced, the Jews turned more and more to moneylending, and before long the Jew and usurer became synonymous in the medieval mind, an identification fraught with grave consequences for all of Jewry.

Several causes led to Jewish involvement in trade and usury. Although a cultivator of the land in the past, the Jew was less inclined to be so in his precarious exile, while, on the other hand, his connections with the Diaspora turned him naturally to trade. Moreover, the *guilds, which controlled access to other occupations, were semireligious organizations and remained closed to him. The Church's ban on Christian practice of *usury, which was understood at the time as any lending of money on interest, meanwhile left the moneylending field open to him. He found further reason for his calling in his constant need of liquid assets, a need caused by the special taxes and confiscations to which he was ever subject. On the other hand, he set himself to his new vocation with a will. Even Jewish chroniclers criticized the riches some Jews accumulated and the high rate of interest they charged. At all events, this traffic in usury exerted a noxious degrading influence on him and created in the popular mind a still less flattering image of the Jew. In the medieval mind he was now not only an insincere disbeliever but a sort of archfiend, rapacious and merciless as well.

Massacres. From the end of the 11th century almost to modern times the history of Judaism comprises for its major part an unrelieved succession of massacres, pillages, banishments, and harassments. The *Crusades precipitated the onslaught. Determined to exterminate the "infidel at home," the crusaders offered Jews the option of Baptism or death. Massacres, large and small, struck Jewish communities along the Rhine Valley and in Hungary and Jerusalem in the first Crusade; in northern France and Germany in the second; and in England in the third. Most were popularly inspired, with the exception of those of the second, which were incited by an irregular monk named Radulph, against whom St. *Bernard of Clairvaux and the Pope himself inveighed. Few Jews became Christians, but their suicides were numerous. In all the Crusades many bishops strove to restrain the mobs and harbor the Jews, but with small success. In the town of Norwich, England, in 1144, Jews were accused of murdering a Christian boy for ritual purposes. The accusation gained little credence at the time, but during the Third Crusade, some 50 years later, they were massacred for the alleged crime. This was the first of numerous so-called blood accusations in the Christian era that was to continue the shedding of Jewish blood even into the 20th century. The accusation, without foundation in the Bible or the Talmud, was condemned by several popes, and again after a complete, official investigation by Cardinal Ganganelli in 1758. Other charges of a delusional nature born at this time included Jewish desecration of the Sacred Host, about which many miraculous legends sprang up and for which many innocent lives were lost. The poisoning of wells, another crime frequently laid to Jews, created such a hysteria on the occasion of the Black Death in 1348 that Jewish communities all over Europe were decimated by gruesome massacres. The efforts of Pope *Clement VI and Emperor *Charles IV to terminate both the charge and the massacres were vain.

Expulsions. The great expulsions that occurred in England, France, Germany, Spain, and Portugal between the 13th and 15th centuries were motivated by both religious and economic considerations. Since the Jews were considered an alien and dangerous growth in Christian society, and their involvement in finance and tax collecting—a role imposed by the crown—was resented, both clergy and laity were anxious to be rid of them. The crown, chief gainer from Jewish money, regarded the Jews as personal serfs (*servi camerae*) and often protected them, but it always sacrificed them whenever their usefulness ended or the anger of the people made itself felt. The expulsions of the Jews from Spain and Portugal were the most extraordinary. A class of Jews baptized under duress during the massacres of 1391 in Spain adhered secretly to Judaism while openly practicing Christianity. These converts, called *Marranos, became very prosperous and incensed the people, who, under the goading of a fanatical archdeacon, Martinez, rose up and killed many of them. The *Inquisition was introduced to deal with the problem, but it encountered difficulty in coping with it. The difficulty was attributed to the close ties the Marranos maintained with their Jewish brethren who were not subject to the jurisdiction of the Inquisition. To remove the tie, the permanent expulsion of all Jews from Spain was ordered by the Spanish crown in 1492. Seven years later a similar expulsion took place in Portugal.

Agitation against the Jews continued off and on to the end of the Middle Ages. Troubles of any kind—a famine, an epidemic, a disappearance—were often signals for a pillage or a massacre of the Jewish quarter. The persecutions by the Crusade of the *Pastoureaux in France and by the mobs led by Rindfleisch (1298) and Armleder (1336–39) in Germany exemplify on a large scale what occurred frequently in local Jewish communities throughout Europe. Of another kind were the campaigns led by religious, such as St. *Vincent Ferrer, St. *John Capistran, and Bl. *Bernardine of Feltre, whose importunings of the Jews, though motivated by zeal for their conversion, often resulted in direst consequences for them.

Policy of the Church. Papal policy varied with individual popes, though in general the popes were the Jews' best recourse; the Jews in Rome and the papal territories fared better than elsewhere in Europe. Numerous papal bulls and briefs were issued from Rome on occasion to condemn forced Baptisms, the "blood accusation," pillages, massacres, and other injustices; but they were seldom effective against the popular fanaticism.

The councils were more severe. The fourth Lateran Council (*see* LATERAN COUNCILS) prescribed the badge, and the Council of *Basel enforced confinement to a Jewish quarter, eventually called the *ghetto, into which the Jews had long since betaken themselves for self-protection and in virtue of their social exclusivism. Examinations of the Talmud and public theological disputations with Jews, often instigated by converts from Judaism, were staged, and the banning or burning of the Talmud was the usual outcome. Sermons to which the Jews were obliged to listen, such as had been preached by the Dominicans in England in the 13th century, were imposed by Emperor *Charles V, by Popes *Benedict XIII and *Gregory XIII, and by the Council of Basel.

Modern Era. The modern era arrived late for the Jews. The *Renaissance and its wake, which for the rest of Europe was a period of scientific, philosophical, and religious revolution, was for the Jews one of wandering and stagnation. The great expulsions had set them adrift and forced upon them a precarious existence wherever they went. It was the age of the ghetto also. A distinct and pathetic Jewish type was created both in reality and in literature. The unfortunate effect of this age upon Jewish personality lent all too much substance to the caricature that the literature of the time concocted: that of a stooped and frightened usurer, the Shylock whom Shakespeare immortalized.

Partial Improvement. Yet a certain softening of the lot of the Jews was under way. Massacres were fewer, and in many of them the Jews now suffered in common with other classes. Exceptional was the horrible massacre inflicted in the Ukraine at the hands of the revolutionary Chmielnycki (1648–49), who cruelly murdered more than 100,000 Jews. The causes of the softening were several. Interest in Hebraic studies among Christian scholars [*see* HEBREW STUDIES (IN THE CHRISTIAN CHURCH)], a new humanism and spirit of inquiry, and the gradual displacement of the Jew as the main source of capital tended to lessen traditional anti-Judaism. The Reformation had little direct effect on the Jews. Although he was at first indulgent toward Jews in order to win them, Martin *Luther later turned violently against them, and in his *Lies of the Jews* urged their expulsion in the vilest terms. Indirectly, however, Protestantism aided their cause by emphasis on the OT and the theory of private interpretation. The papacy of the 16th century was favorable and granted privileges to the Jews; but with Paul IV, when the Church was now menaced by Protestantism, a reaction set in, and restrictive statutes and customs were reinvoked. As the 18th century opened, the Jews' social and economic situation improved, and some of them grew in wealth, but most occupations remained closed to them.

Political Emancipation. After it was furthered by *Joseph II's Edict of Toleration and *Louis XVI's emancipation project, political emancipation of the Jews became a reality with the American and French Revolutions. Thereafter emancipation spread rapidly. *Napoleon I accorded Jews the rights of Frenchmen but at the price of his infamous laws of 1808, which attempted to de-Judaize them. The post-Napoleonic era witnessed a reaction, and old restrictive practices reappeared everywhere. But by 1870 emancipation was finally established throughout Europe—with the exceptions of Russia and Rumania, where the Jews' plight remained extreme until the dawn of the 20th century.

New Kind of Anti-Judaism. Anti-Semitism, in the strict, racial sense, first appeared in the 1870s in Germany. This new brand of anti-Judaism, now less religious than ideological and political, was erected on a theory of race evolved from Hegelian philosophy (*see* HEGELIANISM AND NEO-HEGELIANISM) and linguistic studies. The Jews were categorized as a Semitic people, inferior, corrupting, and unassimilable. A new nationalist spirit could tolerate neither their religioethnic independence nor their business prowess. Social unrest, which stemmed from the financial crisis of 1870, sought a scapegoat for Germany's woes. In 1870 appeared Marr's famous pamphlet, *Victory of Judaism over Germanism,* which set off a wave of anti-Semitic reaction at court, in Parliament, in the universities, and on the street. Anti-Jewish debates and congresses proliferated until the 1890s, when the fever abated. The Catholic organ *Germania* was one of the first to condemn the Jew-baiting.

In France. France, depressed by the loss of the war of 1870, political scandals, and economic difficulties, was soon infected by the epidemic raging across her border. Edouard Drumont denounced the Jews as corruptors of France in his *La France Juive,* which reached 100 editions. The famous Dreyfus case followed in which the Jewish captain, accused of treason, suffered 12 years of legal hardships and ignominy before he was exonerated (*see* DREYFUS, ALFRED). In 1905 the *Protocols of the Elders of Zion* appeared, a pamphlet that was to become a bible for anti-Semites of the future. Although it was proved spurious many times, it continued to be used by anti-Semites and their dupes to prove the existence of an international Jewish conspiracy aimed at the subversion of Christian civilization—a charge that played a counterpoint to the older one of the Jews as founders of capitalism and of a worldwide financial oligarchy.

In Russia and Germany. Critical for the destiny of Judaism was the Communist victory of 1917. The Bolshevik constitutional ban on anti-Semitism and the presence of a few prominent Jews (who were later liquidated) in the original leadership gave new vigor to the suspicion of Jewry as an international conspiracy. It was soon to become plain, however, that the constitutional guarantee in Russia was no more than a device to wrest the Jew from his Judaism, to save his body in order to kill his soul.

Adolf *Hitler's rise to power in Germany dominates the history of anti-Semitism. This prince of anti-Semites skillfully exploited popular discontent over the Versailles treaty, reparations, and inflation in his campaign against the "Jewish" Weimar Republic. In *Mein Kampf* he warned darkly of the Jewish threat, and his associates flooded the country with tracts against the Jews, "the enemy within." After his election as chancellor in 1933, Hitler increased the propaganda, and a purge of Jews from all phases of German life was begun. In 1935 came the well-known Nuremberg laws that stripped German Jews of their citizenship. Two years later the yellow badge was decreed. A cultural attack was launched to eliminate Jews from teaching, journalism, the theater, and labor organizations. Jews were forbidden to marry Germans, to hold office, or to vote. A great pogrom, sanctioned by the government, took place in November 1938. The systematic nature of the arrests and plunder of synagogues and Jewish homes showed clearly the hand of the government. The "final solution of the Jewish problem"—annihilation—appears to have been decided by Hitler and a few of his closest associates in 1941. From this point, concentration camps began to receive Jews in growing numbers, and before the end of the war these camps, equipped with gas chambers, crematoria, experimental medical programs, and starvation units, functioned as full scale *genocide factories, in which most of the 6 million Jewish war casualties died. The program was carried to all parts of *Festung Europa.* Jewish resistance was scant, with the exception of the Warsaw ghetto uprising, in which 25,000 Jews perished.

Hitler's persecution did not enjoy full popular backing, and examples of heroic Christian charity abounded. Strong resistance came from all the Churches, which fought bravely against the new racial paganism and at great risk formed an underground to save Jewish refugees from the Gestapo. Protests from bishops and Church leaders were heard in most countries. In Rome *Pius XI denounced racism in his encyclical *Mit Brennender Sorge,* and *Pius XII used Rome and his chancelleries to assist hunted Jews. Yet, on balance, the record of the Churches—especially in Germany—as well as that of the secular governments and agencies left much to be desired.

After the war, in 1949, revivals of anti-Semitism occurred in Germany when Jewish cemeteries were desecrated and familiar accusations heard, but such actions were strongly opposed by the Adenauer government. A "swastika epidemic" occurred in 1960 and spread to many countries.

The most serious postwar resurgence was in Soviet Russia and her satellites, where the plight of Jews has been described as "without precedent" in Jewish history. Under J. *Stalin Hebrew publications were suppressed and Zionism considered treasonable. Jews were spied upon and discriminated against in government posts. In 1948 the Yiddish language was suppressed, most of the Jewish writers were imprisoned, and many of them were killed without trial under Beria in 1952. The same year the famous "doctors' trial" was staged, in which the accused, almost all Jews, "confessed" in the usual Communist style. Reports of the rising numbers of Jews in concentration camps filtered out of Russia, and the estimates were given at 600,000. N. Khrushchev did little to change things. To allay world opinion he reinstated one Yiddish journal, which retained clear marks of censorship. Jews, looked upon as cosmopolitans or Zionist spies, were denied the rights of other minorities. The practice of Judaism was rendered extremely difficult, particularly by a ban on matzoth (unleavened bread eaten at the *Passover).

In the United States. Anti-Semitism never gained a foothold in the U.S. except for a mild or "polite" type of discrimination. A few rabble-rousers, such as W. Pelley, Rev. G. Winrod, R. Deathridge, C. McWilliams, Gerald K. Smith, and George Lincoln Rockwell; publications, such as *Commonsense* and *Thunderbolt;* and such movements as the Christian Fronters and the Christian Mobilizers failed to attract wide or lasting popular support. Henry Ford, influenced by the *Protocols,* indulged in an anti-Semitic line for a while but later repudiated it. The charges made against Jews by Rev. Charles Coughlin of Royal Oak, Mich., and his mouthpiece, *Social Justice,* were repudiated by responsible Catholics. German Bunds were active here and there during World War II. In 1962 an extensive survey produced evidence of a widespread furtive discrimination against Jews in social life, education, housing, and employment.

Nature and Causes

Scant agreement exists among inquirers on the nature and causes of anti-Semitism. Some attempt to reduce the phenomenon to common forms of prejudice; others discuss it entirely in economic and sociological terms.

Complex Nature. Most inquirers agree that such analyses fail to account for the unique persistence and intensity of the anti-Semitic animus or to appreciate the exceptional complexity of anti-Semitic motivation that, as the course of its history shows, leads the inquirer into the provinces of theology, economics, politics, and sociology, and to a consideration of the recesses of human irrationality. So complex does this motivation appear that the question has been raised whether anti-Semitism can be considered a homogeneous development at all. Can the racial anti-Semitism of the Hitlerian variety be compared with the anti-Judaism or Jew-hate of earlier epochs? Two opposing answers have been given. One opinion, represented mainly by Jewish observers, such as Theodore Reinach, Heinrich Graetz, Jules Isaacs, but also some non-Jews, such as James Parkes and Rev. Paul Demann, regard the modern outburst as merely a new phase of an age-old demonry that has fed off Christian teaching concerning Jewish culpability for the Crucifixion. The other opinion, held mostly by Christians but also by Hannah Arendt and Maurice Samuel, sharply distinguishes the modern genocide from the earlier anti-Judaism and considers anti-Semitism in its strict sense to be as anti-Christian as it is anti-Jewish. These two opinions are not mutually exclusive. A comprehensive answer requires an understanding both of the deeply anti-Christian nature of anti-Semitism and of the importance of the historical contribution. To kill a Jew as a Christ-killer or merely as a Semite are not totally dissimilar actions.

Jewish Self-isolation. Search for the primary cause of anti-Semitism begins with the Jew. For the question arises: Why is it the Jew who perennially remains in such exceptional circumstances? Why, from classical Greece to the Soviet and Nazi dictatorships, have the Jews been persecuted by pagans, Christians, Moslems, atheists, and even Jews? Obviously, a necessary—but not necessarily fully adequate—cause resides in that which isolates the Jew in every culture. This isolation stems from his dedication to his Law, to his sense of divine election by the one true God, and to his cult of Yahweh. From this religious commitment has flowed not only the Jew's religious but also his social and psychological differences, which have provided the ground for the many varying and often contradictory Gentile reactions to him. In a remarkable article, Karl Thieme (7–14) has demonstrated how from the Jew's dedication to the Law the principal forms of anti-Semitic motivation have sprung: the motives of "foreignness," by which the Jew's nonconformism is resented; the motive of "exploitation," by which he is made a scapegoat; the motive of "corruption," which makes him feared as an underminer of the established order; the motive of "antisociability," which embitters those who aspire after a monolithic national culture. Bernard Lazare (1:48), a Jew, likewise roots anti-Semitism in Jewish attachment to the Law and its resultant separatism.

Deeper Reasons. Other observers, impressed by the irrational quality of anti-Semitism, depart from historical considerations altogether. Freudian psychologists trace it to displaced, unconscious, hostile forces, whose original object was either the repressing force itself (superego) or the unaccepted instinctual urges (id), but which the Jew for certain sociological reasons attracts by virtue of an unconscious displacement. Somewhat along this level of analysis is the theory proposed by Sigmund Freud, Maurice Samuel, and Jacques Maritain, who, independently, reduce anti-Semitism to a "Christophobia," an unconscious hatred of Christianity, which is projected on the Jews as cognates of Christianity's Founder. In an extension of this theory to include pagan and neopagan anti-Semites, anti-Semitism may also be seen as a "nomophobia," or unconscious and displaced resentment of all law or restraint. This extension is strengthened by Hitler's remark quoted by Hermann Rauschning: "Conscience—that Jewish invention."

The Church and Anti-Semitism

The relations of the Church toward anti-Semitism should be considered first from a historical and theological viewpoint and then from the viewpoint of the official stand of the papacy.

Historical Considerations. It is customary for some historians to lay the blame for the growth of anti-Semitism in the Christian era entirely at the door of the Church. According to Jules Isaacs (17–18), "Christian anti-Semitism is the powerful, millenary, and strongly rooted trunk upon which [in the Christian world] all other varieties of anti-Semitism are grafted, even those of a most anti-Christian nature." J. Darmesteter wrote: "The hatred of the people against the Jews is the work of the Church. And yet it is the Church that protects him against the furies she has unleashed" [*Les prophètes d'Israel* (Paris 1892) 183]. The Catholic apologist is faced with the question: What was the role of the Church in the development of anti-Semitism?

At the outset, there can be no question on the part of the Christian apologist of pious dissimulation or defensive minimizing of the magnitude of the crime committed against the Jews in the Christian era. It is permitted, from the modern vantage point, to regret that the Church was associated, closely or remotely, with oppressive forces in the Jewish tragedy and to deplore the complicity of many clerics and laymen who, in the name of Christian truth, often sank to the depths of calumny, greed, and violence in their dealings with God-fearing, as well as less worthy, Jews. This said, historical and ethical standards demand that the role of the Church be accurately assessed and that all realities and necessary distinctions be respected. Some of the Church's critics err doubly by minimizing the Jewish contribution to the conflict and by succumbing to the temptation peculiar to many non-Catholic scholars of identifying the Church with whatever develops within its confines no matter how heterogeneous.

Partial Jewish Culpability. The Jewish contribution to the conflict was real, particularly in the first Christian centuries. J. Isaacs himself admits that "The Jews were the first persecutors" [*Has Anti-Semitism Christian Roots?* (New York 1961) 40]; and Lazare (1:3) admits as much. One may assume that a certain inevitability affected the conflict that developed between the two faiths laying claim to exclusive election by the one true God and using the same source of revelation to uphold their claim. But over and beyond this, the hostility of the Synagogue toward the Christian converts, its active proselytism, its occasional complicity with the enemies of both Church and the Christian state, these and other irritants aroused the fears of many of the Fathers, bishops, and civil rulers of the Jewish threat to the faith and the faithful. This threat, moreover, was measured in an age when the rabbinate was often superior intellectually, particularly in scriptural matters, to Gentile Christians, who were often summarily Christianized. It is permissible to speculate whether the lot of the Jews in Christendom would not have been easier had they reacted less bitterly to the fact of Christianity's existence. It was the layman Constantine who said, "Let us have nothing to do with the most hostile crowd of Jews" (Eusebius, *Vita Constantii* 3.18).

Political Structure and Religious Bias of Christendom. A determination of the Church's involvement in Israel's fate demands an acknowledgment of multiple factors. Rigorously, only that can be attributed to the Church which the Church as a whole has accepted and taught, if not by formal definition, at least by universal, dogmatic tradition. Rulings of individual bishops, regional councils, or even popes dealing in *ad hoc* applications of principle, elements emanating from minority traditions, political and social structures peculiar to an epoch, or from human weakness—none of these active factors in the growth of anti-Semitism can be considered strictly the policy or work of the Church. Two factors in particular, the secondary tradition concerning Jewish deicidal guilt and the temporal political structures, though intimately bound up with the life of the Church, should not be considered fruits of the Church's essential teaching.

The secondary theological tradition, as mentioned above, stemmed mostly from the 4th century, when certain Fathers, particularly Chrysostom, influenced by the deteriorating status of Judaism, reinterpreted scriptural texts in the sense of a divine punishment for Israel's sin. Chrysostom, moreover, was strongly impressed by the dramatic failure of Julian the Apostate to rebuild the Temple of Jerusalem (see Flannery, "Theological Aspects . . .," 308). Although this secondary tradition never attained the status of a universal dogmatic tradition, to it, not to Catholic doctrine or policy, must be attributed the high incidence of oppressors of the Jews among churchmen and religious people.

The political structure prevailing from the age of Constantine to the end of the Middle Ages was modeled on the theory of the Christian state, a "sacral" form of governance in which all institutions were impregnated with Christian concepts. In such a society, the Jews, regarded as obstinate negators of Christ and a threat to social and political unity, were conceded a second-class civil status, and anti-Jewish codes were deemed essential. The Catholic apologist is under no obligation either to defend this sacral arrangement, which he can regard as a provisional and imperfect historical compromise, or, for like reasons, to defend its anti-Jewish laws and policies. [See C. Journet, *The Church of the Incarnate Word,* tr. A. H. C. Downes (4 v. London and New York 1955) 1:300.] Nor can he defend those anti-Jewish vexations and violences that, though often performed in the name of religion, stand only as lapses from Christian teachings and morals.

True, a certain ambiguity appears to affect even the authentic social policy of the Church toward the Jews. At the same time it both protects their basic rights and restricts their activities. The dualism is more apparent than real. A single standard guided the Church: the salvation of souls, Christian and Jewish. Christians must be protected from apostasy and Jews must be given the liberty to arrive at their salvation. Thus did the Church consider herself the solicitous mother, anxious for the health of her family, desirous of its growth, and saddened by the defection of her eldest.

True Christian Attitude toward the Jews. The true position of the Church toward Israel is rooted in Christ's love for His people, manifest in the Gospels and formulated in theological terms by St. Paul. In the Pauline view, the Law gave way to the grace of Christ and was fulfilled in the gospel. If Judaism was repudiated as a church, "God has not cast off His people" (Rom 11.2). "Most dear for the sake of the fathers" (11.28), they are still a people of election, for God's promises are "without repentance" (11.29). They are predestined in Christian hope, and their redintegration will be for the Church as a coming to "life from the dead" (11.15). It is for the Christian to "be not high-minded, but fear" (11.20) and to "provoke to jealousy" (11.14) the old Israel by his Christian patrimony.

Theological Considerations. Catholic theology leaves no room for equivocation concerning anti-Semitism, which it condemns in both its dogmatic and moral parts.

Dogmatic Considerations. Essential articles of Catholic dogma on the unity of the human race and the universality of Christ's Redemption preclude denial of natural or supernatural rights to any person or group. By virtue of creation in God's image, every man by his nature is possessed of a dignity beyond the reach of all earthly jurisdiction; and by virtue of God's universal, salvific will, made efficacious by Christ's redeeming death and Resurrection, man acquires an infinite dignity. From these doctrines it follows that all men, even those outside the Church, are brothers. Every type of racism that violates these doctrines is heretical.

Moral Considerations. Catholic moral theology, deriving its norm from the nature of man and his final end, which it conceives of as essentially social or corporate, is basically other-oriented. Dynamically conceived, Christian morality is seen as a growth from primitive egocentrism to an all embracing altruism. Its fundamental virtues are universal justice and charity. Charity is accorded primacy and considered the soul and crown of all the virtues and the distinguishing mark of the Christian. Jews are included in it without distinction or reserve. Moreover, in St. Paul's perspective, because of their kinship with Christ and the patriarchs, their contribution to the Church, and their predestination in Christian hope, the Jews are entitled to a special love and respect.

The Papacy. In recent years, as in centuries past, the Church's opposition to anti-Semitism has been best expressed through the papacy. Leo XIII strongly urged that offensive accusations of the Jews be avoided, and he repudiated anti-Semitism as opposed to the spirit of Christ [*Etsi Nos,* ActSS 14 (1882)]. Benedict XV, through his secretary of state, assured the American Jewish Committee that the "principles of natural law must be respected in the case of the children of Israel . . ." [CivCatt 2 (1916) 358–359]. In 1928 the Holy Office stated: "As every kind of envy and jealousy among nations must be disapproved of, so in an especial manner must be that hatred that is generally termed anti-Semitism" [ActSS 20 (1921) 104]. Pius XI on many occasions condemned racism and exaggerated nationalism, calling the first "a curse" and the second "a myth," and proclaimed that there is no distinction in Christianity of blood or race. His also are the memorable words: "Anti-Semitism is a movement in which we Christians can have no part whatsoever . . .. Spiritually we are Semites" (*To the directors of the Belgium Catholic Radio Agency,* 1938). Pius XII condemned racism, and during World War II he opened his hand to Jewish refugees in Rome and elsewhere through his representatives. He restored the genuflection to the prayer for the Jews on Good Friday, which alone among the others prescribed had been omitted since the Middle Ages. Pope John XXIII struck out the Latin word *perfidia* from the liturgy where it applied to Jews, because of the regrettable custom of rendering it as "perfidious" instead of "disbelieving" in the vernaculars. He likewise suppressed a section of the Consecration to the Sacred Heart and of the Ritual of Baptism of Adults that Jews might consider offensive. In the "Declaration on the Relation of the Church to Non-Christian Religions" promulgated by Vatican Council II (1965) it is stated: ". . . The Church, mindful of the patrimony she shares with the Jews and moved not by political reasons but by the Gospel's spiritual love, decries hatred, persecutions, displays of anti-Semitism, directed against Jews at any time and by anyone" (official English translation).

Papal leadership spurred efforts in the Church. Revisions of Christian teaching were undertaken in Europe and America in order to expunge false or misleading references to Jewish guilt or aspersions on Jewish character. Catholic scholarship took up the cause with vigor, as such personages as Jacques Maritain, Msgr. Charles Journet, Fathers Demann and Congar, Karl Thieme, and Eric Petersen provided Christian answers to anti-Semitism. In Germany the *Freiburger Rundbrief* and in France the *Cahiers Sioniens,* scholarly Catholic journals, devoted themselves to the problem; and in the U.S. the Archconfraternity of Prayer for Israel, sponsored by the Sisters of the *Congregation of Notre Dame de Sion, devoted itself to prayer for the conversion of Israel. Particularly notable on both the intellectual and practical levels is the work of Msgr. John Oesterreicher, founder of the Institute of Judaeo-Christian Studies, but the fullest official statement of the Church's position is to be found in the *Declaration of the Relationship of the Church to Non-Christian Religions* (*Nostra aetate*) of *Vatican Council II.

See also JEWS, POST-BIBLICAL HISTORY OF THE.

Bibliography: Classical antiquity. I. HEINEMANN, Pauly-Wiss RE suppl. 5 (1931) 3–43. J. LEIPOLDT, ReallexAntChr 1:469–476. Christian antiquity. R. WILDE, *The Treatment of the Jews in the Greek Writers of the First Three Centuries* (CUA PatrSt 81; 1949). G. F. MOORE, *Judaism in the First Centuries of the Christian Era,* 3 v. (Cambridge, Eng. 1927–30). H. I. BELL and W. E. CRUM, eds., *Jews and Christians in Egypt* (London 1924).

J. PARKES, *The Conflict of the Church and the Synagogue: A Study in the Origins of Antisemitism* (London 1934; pa. Philadelphia 1961). J. JUSTER, *Les Juifs dans l'Empire romain,* 2 v. (Paris 1914). Middle Ages. F. MURAWSKI, *Die Juden bei den Kirchenvätern und Scholastikern* (Berlin 1925). A. L. WILLIAMS, *Adversus Iudaeos* (Cambridge, Eng. 1935). Modern Period and General Studies. A. ROMEO, EncCatt 1:1494–1505, with extensive bibliog. K. THIEME, LexThK[2] 1:658–659; "Der religiöse Aspekt der Judenfeindschaft," *Freiburger Rundbrief* 10 (1957) 37–38. F. VERNET, DictApolFoiCath 2:1651–1764; DTC 8.2:1870–1914. J. OESTERREICHER, *Racisme, antisémitisme, antichristianisme, documents et critique* (New York 1943). B. LAZARE, *L'Antisémitisme,* 2 v. (Paris 1934). M. SAMUEL, *The Great Hatred* (New York 1940; repr. 1948). L. POLIAKOV, *Du Christ aux Juifs du Cour* (Paris 1955). J. ISAAC, *Genèse de l'antisémitisme* (Paris 1956). G. BAUM, *The Jew and the Gospel* (Westminster, Md. 1961). J. MARITAIN, *Ransoming the Time,* tr. H. L. BINSSE (New York 1941). C. JOURNET, "The Mysterious Destinies of Israel," *The Bridge* 2 (1956) 35–90. E. H. FLANNERY, *The Anguish of the Jews* (New York 1965); "Theological Aspects of the State of Israel," *The Bridge* 3 (1958) 301–324. S. W. BARON, *A Social and Religious History of the Jews,* 8 v. (2d ed. New York 1952–58). H. H. GRAETZ, *History of the Jews,* ed. and tr. B. LÖWY, 6 v. (Philadelphia 1945).

[E. H. FLANNERY]

ANTITRUST POLICY

A policy enforced through a variety of Federal laws and administrative rules and directed toward the maintenance of open markets that function spontaneously to regulate but not inhibit the dynamic thrusts of private enterprise. Freedom of enterprise within a market system—distinguishable from an insistence on atomized markets—is the hallmark of the policy. Encouragement of competition and suppression of monopolistic tendencies are judged to produce the maximum productive use of resources, achievement of a high rate of innovation with lowered prices for better products, an equitable distribution of real income, and stability of economic growth and employment. Beyond strictly economic considerations, political and social values are sometimes cited as supporting justifications of a free-enterprise policy.

Statutes. The legal cornerstone of the national antitrust policy is the Sherman Act of 1890, which sweepingly condemns "every contract, combination in the form of trust or otherwise, or conspiracy, in restraint of trade or commerce among the several states, or with foreign nations. . . ." Another provision renders illegal monopolizing and attempts to monopolize, whether performed singly or in combination with others. This statute was provoked by post–Civil War industrialization, agrarian discontent, popular indignation with the power of railroads, and the establishment of such giants as the Standard Oil, sugar, and whiskey trusts. Although the Sherman Act remained the basic expression of antitrust philosophy, it was supplemented in 1914 by the Federal Trade Commission Act and the Clayton Act. The former established the Federal Trade Commission, charged with eliminating "unfair methods of competition in commerce" and, by subsequent amendment, "unfair or deceptive acts or practices." The Clayton Act imposed stricter standards than those of the Sherman Act upon such economic phenomena as mergers, exclusive-dealing arrangements, and price discrimination.

Since 1914, major legislative action has been restricted to refinements of the Clayton Act. In 1950, section 7 of the act, dealing with mergers, was amended to cover asset as well as stock acquisitions, and to clarify the application of the law to vertical as well as horizontal combinations. In 1936, section 2 was drastically overhauled by the Robinson-Patman amendments to meet the problem posed by mass purchasing by chain stores that demanded preferential pricing from sellers. This latter revision, which represents comprehensive legal regulation of pricing and which imposes difficult statutory burdens of justification on business firms deviating from uniform pricing, has been roundly criticized as promoting anticompetitive rigidity in the market.

Enforcement. Both criminal fines and imprisonment and civil sanctions may be imposed for some violations of the laws, but in practice, defendants are rarely jailed. The laws are enforced by the Department of Justice, the trade commission, and private litigants, who may recover treble damages for injuries to their business or property as a result of violations. Because of the flexibility and breadth of the laws, the role of the courts in interpreting and applying them has been crucial.

Judicial interpretation has shown a gradual and long-range tendency to strictness. Business agreements embracing price-fixing, division of markets, boycotts, and tying arrangements have been condemned as per se violations, requiring no extensive analysis of their economic effect. On other matters, a close study of the economic setting of a challenged practice may be necessary to determine if the effects are reasonable.

Exemptions from the Policy. The identification of the American economy with a policy of antitrust, as described in preceding paragraphs, is a relative judgment. The patent and copyright laws are obvious examples of enclaves of legal privilege that are judged to be in the public interest. The National Industrial Recovery Act of 1933, in which codes of fair competition were formulated by whole industries and officially sponsored by the government, represents a significant historical gloss on the ambivalence of attitude toward rigorous competition, at least in time of economic depression.

American polity, despite the breadth of coverage of the antitrust laws, is honeycombed with exemptions from and modifications of market competition. On the Federal level, the Miller-Tydings and McGuire Acts exempt from the national antitrust laws private agreements among producers and distributors regulating the price at which branded products are resold in those states having *fair-trade laws. Specific exemptions are given to agricultural, horticultural, and labor organizations. Special laws have been written for some industries that curtail in varying degrees the requirement of competition, often under the protective supervision of an administrative agency. These agencies may be given the power to exempt types of business conduct from the antitrust laws, or to apply *ad hoc* standards tailored by Congress for these industries, or to decide (subject to judicial review) the appropriateness of antitrust policy in a given instance. Some of the industries affected by these special laws are banking, communications, exporting, fishery associations, importing, insurance, meat packing, power transmission, and transportation.

Effectiveness of Policy. There is no simple way to measure accurately the effectiveness of the antitrust law in maintaining a competitive economy in the U.S. Price-fixing conspiracies are uncovered often enough to raise doubts about the degree to which competition governs. Further, the existing statutes are generally unable to reach anticompetitive effects achieved through parallel actions by oligopolists, such as the phenomenon of price leadership. A common charge is that, while the laws deal with isolated transactions, the basic structure of American industry remains anticompetitive. On the other hand, diligent enforcement methods should work to reduce the number of deviations from market competition. By erecting barriers to the progress of monopolistic tendencies, moreover, the laws provide time for market forces themselves to break down restraints. The material prosperity of the mass of American people itself argues in favor of the judgment that the laws have been workably effective.

Bibliography: H. B. THORELLI, *The Federal Antitrust Policy* (Baltimore 1955). M. S. MASSEL, *Competition and Monopoly* (Washington 1962). S. C. OPPENHEIM and R. W. POGUE eds., *Federal Antitrust Laws: Cases and Comments* (2d ed. St. Paul, Minn. 1959). C. KAYSEN and D. F. TURNER. *Antitrust Policy* (Cambridge, Mass. 1959).

[J. E. DUNSFORD]

ANTOINE, CHARLES, economist, teacher; b. Fumay, France, Dec. 16, 1847; d. Le Dorat, April 24, 1921. After graduating as an engineer from the École des Mines in Paris and studying chemistry at the Collège de France, Antoine entered the Society of Jesus in 1869; he left it in 1913. He taught theology in Jesuit seminaries and at the Facultés Catholiques of Angers, from 1887 to 1906. His *Cours d'Economie Sociale,* published in 1896, was the first work of its kind in France since Villeneuve-Bargemont (Jean Paul Alban vicomte de Villeneuve-Bargemont) and A. Ott to be based on natural law and theology as well as on economics. Despite its lack of genuinely original ideas, this work was an excellent and successful textbook; its sixth edition was brought out by Rev. H. du Passage in 1921. Through the *Cours,* Antoine became widely known. He lectured at the Semaines Sociales of France from 1905 to 1913. His other writings on economics consisted of brochures and numerous articles in the *Dictionnaire de Théologie Catholique* and in various periodicals, especially *L'Association Catholique* and *Études*. For this last he wrote the "Social Chronicle" from 1897 to 1906.

[J. VILLAIN]

ANTOINE, PAUL GABRIEL, Jesuit theologian; b. Lunéville, Lorraine, Jan. 10, 1678; d. Pont-à-Mousson, Jan. 22, 1743. He entered the Jesuits on Oct. 9, 1693, and after his studies he taught humanities for several years. He became professor of philosophy at Pont-à-Mousson and then professor of theology. Eventually he became rector of the college there.

His *Theologia universa, speculativa et dogmatica,* published in 1723, immediately established his reputation as one of the foremost theologians of his time and went through 9 editions during his lifetime and 10 editions after his death. His *Theologia moralis universa* (1726) brought him even greater acclaim and was published in 60 editions in different countries. In the judgment of St. Alphonsus Liguori and also of Jean Pierre Gury, Antoine's doctrine was overly severe, but its excellence as a textbook in moral theology recommended its wide use. The Roman edition of 1746, published with several additions by Philip Carbognano, was prescribed by Benedict XIV for use by the students of the College of Propaganda and was widely encouraged also by many bishops in France and Italy.

Bibliography: Sommervogel 1:419–427. Hurter Nomencl 4: 1351–52.

[J. C. WILLKE]

ANTOLÍNEZ, AGUSTÍN, Augustinian theologian; b. Valladolid, Castile, Dec. 6, 1554; d. June 19, 1626. Antolínez was a professor of theology at Valladolid and at Salamanca and became bishop-elect of Ciudad Rodrigo in 1623 and archbishop of Santiago de Compostela in 1624. He left a number of theological treatises in manuscript and published lives of St. John of Sahagún and St. Clare of Montefalco. His pious commentary on the strophes of the *Spiritual Canticle* of St. John of the Cross—*Amores de Dios y el Alma*—has in recent times emerged from oblivion because of its bearing on the critical problem of the works of the Mystical Doctor.

In 1922 P. Chevallier, OSB, arguing against the authenticity of the second redaction of the *Spiritual Canticle,* stated that it made use of the commentary by Antolínez. In 1948 J. Krynen published a voluminous study in support of this position. Neither author, however, established the contention, for a careful comparison of the two redactions of the *Spiritual Canticle* with the *Amores* provides evidence that Antolínez had before his eyes the text of the second *Canticle* in the form of a transcription revised by John of the Cross himself. It is probable that this text had been left to Antolínez by his equally distinguished confrere Luis de León.

The possession by the Augustinians of an unquestionably authentic text of St. John of the Cross, quite different from that which the Carmelites, for good reasons, intended to edit, and the transmission to the Carmelites of this text and that of the *Amores* after the death of Antolínez suggest answers to a number of vexing questions in the history of the works of John of the Cross. In particular this helps to explain why Antolínez and later the Carmelites did not wish the *Amores* to be published and why the Augustinians were willing to make no claim on behalf of Antolínez.

Bibliography: A. C. VEGA, *Fray A. Antolínez: Amores de Dios y el Alma* (Madrid 1956), with app. by M. LEDRUS, "L'Incidence de l'*Exposición* d'Antolínez sur le problème textuel johannicrucien." P. CHEVALLIER, "Le Cantique spirituel a-t-il été interpolé?" *Bulletin Hispanique* 24 (1922) 307–342. J. KRYNEN, *Le Cantique spirituel de s. Jean de la Croix commenté et refondu au XVIIe siècle* (Salamanca 1948). JUAN DE JESÚS-MARIA, "El 'Cantico espiritual' de San Juan de la Cruz y 'Amores de Dios y el Alma' de A. Antolinez, O.S.A.," *Ephemerides Carmeliticae* 3 (1949) 443–542.

[M. LEDRUS]

ANTONELLI, GIACOMO

Cardinal, secretary of state to Pius IX; b. Sonnino, near Terracina (Latium), Italy, April 2, 1806; d. Rome, Nov. 6, 1876. His sharp mind, practical sense, and elegant manners favored his rapid progress in the papal administration, despite his lowly birth. After being attached to a tribunal from 1830 he became successively delegate to Orvieto (1835), Viterbo (1837), and Macerata (1839). He returned to Rome (December 1840) as assistant to Cardinal Mattei in the department of the interior (*dicastero dell' interno*). At this time he received the diaconate; he never advanced to the priesthood. As head of the financial administration (1845), he proved very capable.

*Pius IX (1846–78) named him cardinal (June 11, 1847). During the first 2 years of this pontificate Antonelli pleased the moderate liberals by favoring a policy less reliant on alliance with Austria. He became president of the *Consulta di Stato* (November 1847) and played an important role in the elaboration of the new constitution (*Statuto*). Antonelli's first term as secretary of state lasted from March 10 to May 3, 1848. At this

Giacomo Antonelli.

time Pius IX placed him at the head of the first ministry charged with applying the new constitution. When this ministry resigned after the papal allocution of April 29, Antonelli temporarily receded into obscurity, although he remained a highly regarded counselor of the Pope. He returned as prosecretary of state (Dec. 6, 1848) and as secretary (March 18, 1852), holding office until death. Largely because of him Pius IX decided first to flee Rome (Nov. 24, 1848) and then to remain at Gaeta, despite the contrary advice of *Rosmini-Serbati, whose influence Antonelli knew well how to undermine. Antonelli was made head of the papal government in exile (November 26). Convinced that it would be impossible to make the government of the *States of the Church partially a lay one, he decided to practice a severe policy toward the Roman liberals by refusing all contact with them and appealing to the Catholic powers to restore papal temporal power by arms. After the fall of the Roman Republic, Antonelli was the source of the motu proprio (Sept. 12, 1849) that promised administrative and judicial reforms and immunities to municipalities, but no specific political liberty. As secretary of state he was the one mainly responsible for putting it into effect. Although his policy had become frankly reactionary, his government, which lasted until 1870, did not lack merit, but neither did it progress beyond the outlook characteristic of 18th-century enlightened despotism.

The Roman question came to the forefront with the war in Italy (1859). Antonelli had no faith in direct negotiations with Piedmont and regarded the policy of armed independence advocated by Monsignor de *Merode as chimerical. Instead he relied, as in 1849, on the support of the conservative powers to save the States of the Church, not realizing how much ideas and political conditions had changed in the interim. Believing that the young kingdom of Italy would soon disintegrate, he supported the Neapolitan guerrillas. Monsignor de Merode could not support the concessions to the France of *Napoleon III implicit in this policy of passive resistance and sought to utilize his ascendancy over Pius IX to undermine the influence of Antonelli, who was also being attacked by all who reproached him with replacing the nepotism of the popes with the nepotism of the secretary of state. The Pope, however, judged Antonelli "without equal for the defense" and refused to part with his secretary, who, moreover, was conscious that he had no title to involve himself in the spiritual government of the Church and very carefully refrained from doing so. After 1870 Antonelli, who had advised the Pontiff against leaving Rome, as some wished, successfully reorganized the new situation of the Holy See on solid financial bases.

Antonelli was severely criticized as a morally lax man, avid for money, who strove by authoritarian means to concentrate all power in his own hands, and did not hesitate to break those who opposed him. Although his concepts were lacking in breadth and his actions in grandeur, he possessed admirable qualities. He was diligent and competent in economic and administrative matters, energetic, invariably amiable, and master of himself. His clear, subtle mind permitted him to adapt himself to circumstances with dexterity and to find a ready solution to difficulties that arose daily. His defects and limitations were undeniable; yet he was a conscientious servant of Pius IX and managed affairs with great skill under the circumstances, whatever the exalted ultramontanes grouped around Monsignor de Merode may have thought.

Bibliography: R. Aubert, DizBiogItal 3:484–493. M. Rosi in *Dizionario del Risorgimento nazionale,* ed. M. Rosi et al., 4 v. (Milan 1930–37) 2:85–87. P. Richard, DHGE 3:832–837. E. Soderini, EncIt 3:547–548. P. Dalla Torre, EncCatt 1:1514–17. P. Pirri, "Il cardinale Antonelli tra il mito e la storia," Riv StorChIt 12 (1958) 81–120; ed., *Pio IX e Vittorio Emanuele dal loro carteggio privato,* 5 v. (Rome 1944–61). A. Lodolini, "Un archivo segreto del cardinale Antonelli," *Studi romani* 1 (1953) 410–424, 510–520. A. Omodeo, *Rassegna storica del Risorgimento* 47 (1960) 319–324. A. M. Ghisalberti, *Roma da Mazzini a Pio IX* (Milan 1958). F. Engel-Janosi, *Österreich und der Vatikan, 1846–1918,* 2 v. (Graz 1958–60) v.1. *The Roman Question: Extracts from the Despatches of Odo Russell from Rome, 1858–1870,* ed. N. Blakiston (London 1962). M. Gabriele, *Il carteggio Antonelli-Sacconi, 1858–1860,* 2 v. (Rome 1962). N. Miko, *Das Ende des Kirchenstaates* v.2 (Vienna 1961). R. Aubert, *Le Pontificat die Pie IX* (Fliche-Martin 21; 2d ed. 1964). E. E. Y. Hales, *Pio Nono* (New York 1954). **Illustration credit:** Museo del Risorgimento, Rome.

[R. AUBERT]

ANTONELLO DA MESSINA, Italian painter; b. Messina, 1430; d. Messina, February 1479. He received his training in the cosmopolitan city of Naples under Colantonio, a practitioner of the Flemish style, which was popular at the time in Naples. Antonello's early works include a "Madonna," which shows considerable Spanish influence, the "Salvator Mundi," "St. Jerome in His Study" (all in the National Gallery, London), and the "Crucifixion" (in Sibiu, Romania). Before leaving for Venice in 1475, he painted several very realistic portraits and the famous "Annunciata" (Museum of Palermo). The most important work of his Venetian period (1475–78) is the large "Altarpiece of S. Cassiano," fragments of which only recently were discovered in Vienna. In its style, this influential painting exhibits a perfect synthesis of Flemish realism, Tuscan formal composition, and the qualities of geometrically abstracted form best observed in the paintings of *Piero della Francesca and the sculpture of Francesco da *Laurana. Antonello had seen their works at Messina and Naples. From this period came also the "Pieta" (Correr Museum, Venice); "St. Sebastian" (Dresden Gallery); several portraits, especially the "Trivulzio"

Antonello da Messina, "Christ Crucified," oil on panel, 16½ *by* 10 *inches, signed and dated* 1475.

(Turin), and two Crucifixions (Antwerp Museum; National Gallery, London).

Bibliography: S. BOTTARI, *Antonello da Messina,* tr. G. SCAGLIA (New York 1955), with bibliog. **Illustration credit:** Courtesy of the Trustees of the National Gallery, London.

[I. GALANTIC]

ANTONIA, a tower fortress overlooking the Temple area in Jerusalem in Biblical times. Situated at the northwest corner of the Temple at a height of some 75 feet, it fortified the area at its least defensible point and held a commanding position overlooking Temple and city.

In its remote origins the Antonia may date back to a tower fortification of Solomon, which defended Jerusalem on its north side. During the divided monarchy it would have been destroyed in frequent depredations "from the north" and as often repaired. Nehemia 2.8 calls the Antonia the "fortress (*bîrâ*) of the Temple." According to Josephus (*Ant.* 15.14, 4; 18.4, 3), Hasmonaean rulers rebuilt the fortified tower (called the "acropolis, citadel" in 2 Mc 4.12, 27) and dwelt there. Huge 5- to 10-ton blocks of stone were used in the foundations. Herod the Great later enlarged and embellished it as part of his building program (*Bell. Jud.* 1.21, 1; 5.5, 8), named it Antonia to honor Marcus Antonius, and made the fortress his residence from 35 to 23 B.C.

Under the Roman procurators the main function of the Antonia (called the "barracks" in Acts) was to keep a watch over the Temple area, especially during the great feasts when Jerusalem was thronged with visiting Jews. Stairways from the fortress provided quick access to the Temple area. Josephus asserts that a Roman legion was quartered in the Antonia (*Bell. Jud.* 5.5, 8; cf. Acts 23.23–24). The Antonia figured in Paul's arrest (Acts 21.31–36) and his Jerusalem imprisonment (Acts 22.24; 23.16). When Jewish elements revolted against Rome in A.D. 66, they first captured the Antonia. Titus regained control of the tower, used it as a command post against Temple and city, and destroyed it with them in A.D. 70 (cf. Tacitus, *History* 5.11–12). On the Antonia as the possible scene of the Roman trial of Christ, *see* PRAETORIUM.

Bibliography: G. E. WRIGHT, *Biblical Archeology* (rev. ed. Philadelphia 1962) 233–226. J. FINEGAN, *Light from the Ancient Past* (2d ed. Princeton 1959). H. VINCENT and A. M. STÈVE, *Jérusalem de l'Ancien Testament,* 3 v. in 2 (Paris 1954–56) 1:193–221. **Illustration credit:** The Matson Photo Service, Los Angeles.

[E. MAY]

ANTONIA OF FLORENCE, BL., Poor Clare; d. Aquila, Italy, Feb. 29, 1472 (feast, Feb. 28). As a young widow she entered the convent of Third Order sisters founded in Florence by *Angelina of Marsciano (1429), and later went on to Foligno. In 1432 she was made prioress at Aquila, an office she held for 13 years. Moved by the desire for a stricter rule of life, she consulted (St.) *John Capistran, and through his intercession was placed in charge of a cloister of *Poor Clares. She was an example of patience under the trials of long, painful illness and of family difficulties, caused by a

Northwest corner of the Haram esh-Sherif (courtyard of Herod's Temple) in Jerusalem; the buildings are of medieval or modern construction, but the man-made escarpment at the right was part of fortifications of the Antonia.

spendthrift son and other relatives. Her cult was approved in 1847.

Bibliography: LÉON DE CLARY, *Lives of the Saints and Blessed of the Three Orders of St. Francis,* 4 v. (Taunton, Eng. 1885–87) v.2. Butler Th Attw 1:446–447.

[N. G. WOLF]

ANTONIĬ (ALEKSEĬ PAVLOVICH KHRAPOVITSKIĬ), outstanding metropolitan and controversial theologian of the Russian Orthodox Church; b. March 17, 1863; d. Karlovci, Yugoslavia, Aug. 10, 1936. He graduated from St. Petersburg Theological Academy, entered a monastery, and was ordained in 1885. He was a professor at St. Petersburg Academy and Kholm Seminary, and rector of theological academies in Moscow and Kazan and of St. Petersburg Seminary. Consecrated in 1897 and appointed bishop of Volhynia, Ukraine, in 1902, he suppressed remnants of the Ukrainian Catholic Church and national aspirations of the Ukrainian Orthodox Church. He was archbishop of Kharkiv (1914–17) and in 1918 became metropolitan of Kiev. When the Ukraine won its independence, he was exiled to Buczacz because of his anti-Ukrainian activities. The Bolshevik occupation of the Ukraine forced him to flee to Yugoslavia, where he became head of the Russian Synod. He was strongly anti-Catholic and very radical in his dogmatic teachings, which caused conservative Orthodox theologians to accuse him of heresy. He wrote many ascetic and dogmatic works, the most controversial of which are *Dogma of Redemption* (Kharkiv 1917) and *Catechism* (Karlovci 1924).

Bibliography: *Opera,* 4 v. (St. Petersburg 1911; v.4, 2d ed. Kharkiv 1917). NIKON RKLIT͡SKIĬ, *Biography of His Beatitude Antony Metropolitan of Kiev and Halych,* 10 v. (New York 1956–), in Russ. A. M. AMMANN, *Abriss der ostslawischen Kirchengeschichte* (Vienna 1950). Jugie TheolDogm v.1, 3–4. M. D'HERBIGNY and A. DEUBNER, *Evêques Russes en exil, 1918–1930* (Orientalia Christiana 21; Rome 1931).

[W. LENCYK]

ANTONIL, ANDRÉ JOÃO, Jesuit author and teacher in Brazil; b. Lucca, Tuscany, Italy, Feb. 8, 1649; d. Bahia, March 13, 1716. His real name was João António Andreoni. He studied civil law at the University of Perugia for 3 years and entered the Society of Jesus in Rome May 20, 1667. After teaching for some years in the seminary at Rome, he went to Brazil with António Vieira, in 1681. He made his solemn profession of vows in Bahia Aug. 15, 1683. In Bahia he was professor of rhetoric, director of students, and secretary to Visitor General Vieira, who later sent him to Pernambuco as local visitor. He was a preacher, novice master, rector of the Colégio of Bahia twice, and provincial. He was a good religious and an able administrator. In 1711 he wrote *Cultura e opulência do Brasil* in Portuguese under the pseudonym André João Antonil. The book did not have the approval of the society, but, in spite of the anagrammatic name, it was known that Andreoni was its author. The book is still considered a source of great value on the economic and social aspects of Brazil at the beginning of the 18th century. It deals very precisely with medicinal plants, gold and silver mines, the production of sugar, the planting and useful purposes of tobacco, etc. He dedicated his work to the venerable Father *Anchieta.

[C. STELLFELD]

ANTONINES (ANTONÍANS)

Under this title are included several religious orders of Oriental rite that have taken as their guide and inspiration St. *Anthony of Egypt. Anthony did not leave a written rule; his followers were united only by a common spirit and the observance of similar ascetic practices. What is known as the Rule of St. Anthony is of later origin and was published in Arabic (1646) by *Abraham Ecchellensis and in Latin (1661) by Lukas Holste (Holstenius); it is based on the life of Anthony, his authentic and apocryphal writings, and a compilation known as the *Apophthegmata patrum.* The influence of Anthony over Oriental monachism is universally recognized, but the systematic application of his rule to a religious order dates only from 1695, when it was adopted by a group of Maronite monks. Only the first part of their monastic legislation was based on the Rule of St. Anthony; the second part was patterned according to the constitutions of the Order of St. Paul the First Hermit, a community founded in Hungary in 1250 (*see* HERMITS OF ST. PAUL). Following the occupation of Hungary by the Turks and the subsequent decline of the order, a thorough reform was made in the 17th century by means of new constitutions that were devised at Rome in 1643. These constitutions became the prototype not only for the Antonines, but also for other Oriental orders.

Lebanese Maronite Order of St. Anthony. Monasticism flourished among the Maronite people who lived in the neighborhood of the great monastery of St.

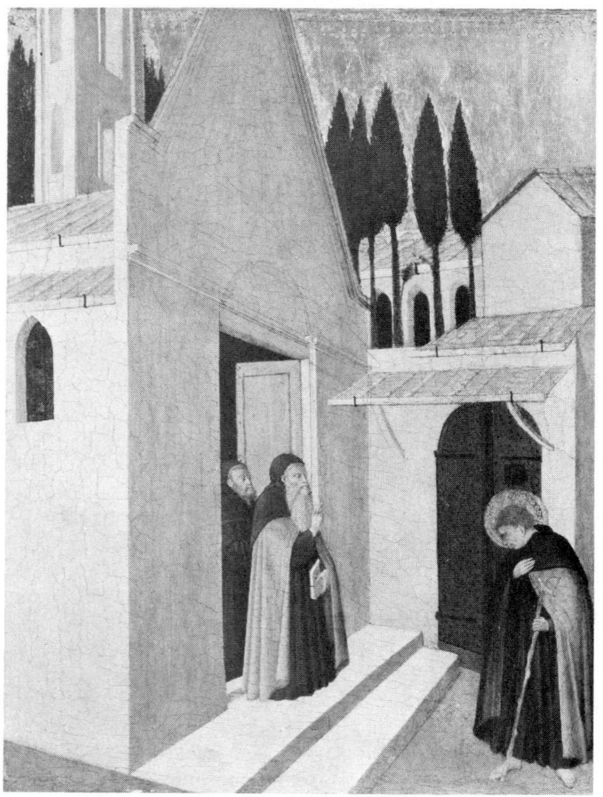

"Saint Anthony Leaving His Monastery," painting by the Sienese artist Sassetta (active 1423–50) and assistants.

Maro, located near the source of the Orontes River (*see* MARO OF CYR, ST.). When the monks of St. Maro migrated to Lebanon, they were already accustomed to the cenobitic life, but they were forced, by lack of means for building monasteries, to return to a more heremitic form of monastic life. The valley called Qadisha, with its numerous natural caves, lent itself to this type of life and became for centuries the abode of holy hermits. At that time there were no explicit vows made in a juridical form. According to the traditional custom of the East, the embracing of the religious life was manifested by the taking of a religious habit and by the celebration of a special rite.

Patriarch Stephan Al-Douaihi (1671–1704), who had studied at Rome, introduced among the Maronite monks the Western system of religious congregations in order to unite the separate and independent monasteries. He began with three young men from Aleppo who, on Nov. 10, 1695, received from his hands the monastic habit. Soon a group of disciples gathered around them. In 1698 a first draft of constitutions was adopted along with the Rule of St. Anthony. The constitutions, approved by the patriarch in 1700, were later revised and approved by Clement XII in 1732.

The new order was known at first as the Aleppian congregation after the name of the city of the founders. This name was changed to that of Lebanese in 1706. At certain periods the Lebanese monks were known also as Baladites, that is, "natives," from the Arabic word *balad.* At first the contemplative life prevailed in the congregation, but in time the monks began to dedicate themselves to parish work and teaching. This new role was officially recognized by the Holy See in the motu proprio *Postquam apostolicis litteris* (1952), and on Dec. 16, 1955, the Lebanese Antonine congregation was declared a nonmonastic (active) order. In 1962 the congregation, whose headquarters are in Beirut, had 465 professed members and 53 houses, most of them located in Lebanon. They conducted 17 schools and 110 parishes. Associated with the order is a branch for religious women, comprising five autonomous monasteries of ancient origin. The nuns, who are contemplatives, had some 95 professed members in 1962.

Aleppian Maronite Order of St. Anthony. Tensions that existed in the original Maronite congregation between the Aleppian and Lebanese (Baladite) factions were not resolved. At a meeting held at Louaizé, Lebanon, on April 1, 1758, the order split into two independent congregations, one called Aleppian, and the other Lebanese. The successive attempts of Rome to reconcile the two groups failed. Finally Clement XIV, in the brief *Ex iniuncto* (July 19, 1770), approved officially the split in the order. The Aleppian congregation retained the same constitutions and the same form of government as the Lebanese. It too was declared a nonmonastic order in 1955. In 1962 the superior general, who resides at Louaizé, governed 80 professed members who conducted 2 schools, 26 parishes, and 6 missions. These were located in Lebanon, Egypt, Ghana, and South America.

Maronite Antonine Order of St. Isaia. In 1700 the Maronite bishop of Aleppo, Gabriel Blouzawi, gathered some of the remaining independent monasteries, those that had not joined the Lebanese congregation, to form the Antonine Order of St. Isaia, named after the principal monastery, Mar Isaya. He gave them the Rule of St. Anthony and constitutions that were approved by Patriarch Al-Douaihi in 1703. Clement XII granted papal approval in the brief *Misericordiarum Pater* (Jan. 17, 1740). The constitutions and way of life are practically identical to those of the other Antonines, and, like them, the congregation of St. Isaia also was declared a nonmonastic order in 1955. The headquarters are located near Beirut. In 1962 there were 79 professed members who cared for 9 parishes and 7 schools in Lebanon. From the beginning there existed also a feminine branch of the order, dedicated to the contemplative life. In 1953 the religious women of the Antonine Order of St. Isaia were constituted as an independent congregation with an active apostolate. They had about 140 professed members and 19 houses, including 17 schools (1962).

"The Death of Saint Anthony," painting by the 15th-century Sienese artist Sassetta and his assistants.

Chaldean Antonines of St. Hormisdas. The ancient Chaldean monachism, which flourished in Persia from early Christian times until the invasion of the Mongols (12th century), became extinct at the beginning of the 19th century. Around that time a Catholic Chaldean merchant, Gabriel Dembo, founded the Chaldean Antonines. He embraced the monastic life in the novitiate of the Maronite Antonines in Lebanon. After returning to his own country (Iraq), he established a monastery on the ruins of the ancient monastery of Rabban Hormizd (7th century) near Alqosh in 1808. There he gathered a few followers to whom he gave the Rule of St. Anthony and constitutions borrowed from the Maronite Lebanese Antonines. These constitutions, with some modifications, were approved by Rome in 1830 and 1845. Dembo spent the rest of his life working for the conversion of the Nestorians (*see* NESTORIAN CHURCH). He was assassinated by the pasha of Ravanduz in 1834. The Chaldean Antonines, who numbered 51 in three houses in 1962, had the care of 15 parishes, 17 mission centers, and several schools, all in Iraq (*see* CHALDEAN RITE).

Other Antonines. Several groups that no longer exist, some of them Oriental and others Latin, are included under the term Antonines.

Armenian Antonines. Four brothers, Armenian Catholics who lived in Aleppo, established a monastic institute in 1705 and founded the monastery of St. Salvator at Creim, near Beirut, Lebanon. An attempt to join their group to the *Mechitarists of Venice failed, and the congregation adopted (1752) the Rule of St. Anthony after the manner of the Maronite Antonines. Clement XIII approved the constitutions in 1761 and transferred the novitiate to Rome. The monks never exceeded 60, and their number declined after they went into schism during the politico-religious troubles (1869–80) under the rule of the Armenian Patriarch and Cardinal Anthony Hassoun (1809–84). The former library of these Antonines is conserved in the Armenian institute at Bzommar, Lebanon.

Ethiopian-Coptic Antonines. Although there has never been a congregation of Antonines among the Ethiopians of either the Monophysite or the Catholic tradition, there is a fictional "Order of St. Anthony" associated with the hospice San Stefano dei Mori in Vatican City. San Stefano was designated for the use of Ethiopian pilgrim monks by Sixtus IV in the 15th century. The so-called rule of the hospice dates from 1551, but it is only a set of regulations for the discipline of the house. In a brief of Clement XII (Jan. 15, 1731) the care of the hospice was handed over to the Coptic and Ethiopian monks of the "Order of St. Anthony," although no such order existed. Much later, in 1919, San Stefano dei Mori was converted into the Ethiopian College and placed under the direction of the Capuchins.

Antonines of the Latin Rite. The Antonine Hospitallers, or Canons Regular of St. Anthony of Vienne, began in France in 1095, and the Antonines of Flanders, founded in 1615, did not follow the Rule of St. Anthony, but rather that of St. Augustine. Neither group is extant.

See also MONASTICISM, 4.

Bibliography: OrientCatt 560–565, 606–608. P. J. KHAIRALLAH, *Histoire résumée de l'ordre Antonin Maronite de la Congrégation de s. Isaie* (Beirut 1939). C. KARALEVSKIJ and F. TOURNEBIZE, DHGE 3:861–873. R. JANIN and K. HOFMANN, LexThK[2] 1:676–677. Heimbucher 1:67–76. V. ADVIELLE, *Histoire de l'ordre hospitalier de s. Antoine* (Paris 1883). M. SCADUTO et al., EncCatt 1:1521–25. **Illustration credit:** National Gallery of Art, Washington, D.C., Samuel H. Kress Collection.

[E. EL-HAYEK]

ANTONINUS, ST.

Archbishop of Florence, founder of the Convent of San Marco in that city, 15th-century reformer, pastoral theologian, economist, sociologist, historian; b. Florence, March 1389; d. May 2, 1459 (feast, May 10).

Life. When but a delicate youth of 15 years, he was inspired by the preaching of Bl. John Dominici to apply for admission to the Dominican Order. For several years Dominici had been the idol of his native Florence and for 15 years the leader in Italy of the reform movement within his Order initiated by Bl. Raymond of Capua, Master General (1380–99) and former director of St. Catherine of Siena (d. 1380). Dominici accepted the frail youth a year later and sent him to Cortona for his novitiate. There Antoninus made profession in February 1406. In that same year he became the first religious to

St. Antoninus. Bust in church of S. Maria Novella, Florence.

be assigned to a convent of strict observance, dedicated to St. Dominic and erected by Dominici in Fiesole.

In his formative years Antoninus was grievously troubled by the general corruption in the Church and society, but especially by the turbulent events in the closing years of the Western Schism. Dominici was called to Rome shortly after the election of Gregory XII (1406) to become cardinal archbishop of Ragusa. Then the friars at Fiesole lost their convent and fled to Foligno because they refused obedience to Alexander V elected in the pseudo-Council of Pisa (1409). In consequence of these disturbances, Antoninus had a teacher for but a short time and in logic only. He was dependent upon his own inclinations and industry in pursuing his studies. He was ordained at Cortona in 1413.

He quickly became prominent. He was prior at Cortona in 1418, at Fiesole in 1421 when the friars there recovered their convent, at Naples in 1428, and at the Convent of S. Maria sopra Minerva in Rome in 1430. After the election of Eugene IV (1431) Antoninus became auditor general of the Rota, a tribunal that in his day had jurisdiction over all ecclesiastical trials in Christendom and all civil cases in the Papal States. He was also vicar-general of Dominican convents of strict observance in Italy from 1432 to 1445. Since this office was under the immediate jurisdiction of the master general of the Order, it served a twofold purpose: it gave protection and sanction to the reform, and it preserved the unity of the Order.

Antoninus returned to Florence in 1436 or 1437, and with the aid of the despotic but munificent Cosimo di Medici, he established the Convent of San Marco. Even after the lapse of centuries, San Marco is one of the artistic glories of Florence. As theologian, Antoninus took part in the Council of Florence (1439), and as prior conjointly of San Marco's and of San Domenico's in Fiesole, he was host to other Dominican theologians summoned to the council by Eugene IV. As a token of esteem, the Pope with the whole college of cardinals assisted at the consecration of the Church of San Marco in 1443. The following year the famed library of San Marco was made available to scholars. It was probably the first public library in Europe.

The austere simplicity of the buildings, illuminated by the delicate frescoes of Fra Angelico in the convent, is a fitting monument to the spirit of Antoninus and his influence on Florentine society. He had no interest in the new learning, but by word and example he raised the hearts of his brethren to the heights of the Dominican ideal. The office of preaching raised him above and beyond the narrow horizons of those immersed in the study of ancient pagan lore. He deserved to be called "Antoninus the Counselor," for he was sought by all classes as confessor and director of souls. Though a simple friar, he was commissioned by Eugene IV to supervise the creation of societies to bring children together for instruction in Christian doctrine. His compassion for the degraded poor, for the victims of political strife, of the forces of nature, of plague, and of pestilence, inspired him to form an association of charitable citizens, known as the *Buonomini di San Martino*. It was somewhat similar to the Society of St. Vincent de Paul in modern times but had a more extensive field of action. It is still in existence.

Antoninus's nomination by Eugene IV to the archiepiscopal See of Florence brought joy to his native city. He was consecrated in the Church of San Domenico in Fiesole on March 12, 1446, and took possession of his see the next day in utmost simplicity. From the episcopal palace he removed all that smacked of luxury and pomp, for he was determined to continue living as a poor friar. The revenues of his see were spent upon the poor. By his visitation of parishes, he remedied abuses of long standing: he insisted upon the preaching of the Gospel, services in the churches, ministrations to the faithful, observance of Canon Law. He had the churches repaired and made worthy of divine worship. His reputation for prudence and justice made him arbiter in party strife, and his tact brought him papal commissions to institute reforms in religious communities canonically exempt from his jurisdiction.

His pastoral labors were frequently interrupted. He was summoned to Rome by Eugene IV to take part in the negotiations terminating in the Concordat of Princes, and he assisted at the deathbed of that Pontiff. In the conclave that followed, in which the humanist Tommaso Parentucelli was elected, Antoninus received several votes. The new Pope, Nicholas V, desired to retain him in the Roman Curia, but Antoninus was able to evade what might have led to the cardinalate. He headed the Florentine embassies to the papal court of Calixtus III and Pius II, and by the latter Pontiff he was appointed to serve on the committee of cardinals charged with the proposed reform of the Roman Court. When Antoninus died, May 2, 1459, Pius II, then in the vicinity, came to Florence to preside at the obsequies. His native city gave testimony of the veneration in which he was held by placing his statue in her exclusive hall of fame—the only statue of a priest in the Uffizi Palace.

Writings. Reform had been the keynote of his life and labors; it was also the motive that inspired him to write. He humbly claimed to be only a compiler, not an author; yet he was proclaimed to be among the Doctors of the Church in the bull of his canonization, though the title has never been conferred upon him.

His first work, which really consists of three distinct treatises, has been called the *Confessionale* (1472, 1473, 1475). The 102 incunabula editions attest its importance and practicality. The *Omnium mortalium cura* (1475), written in Italian to help the faithful in approaching the tribunal of Penance, was a guide to Christian living. The *Defecerunt* (1473) and the *Curam illius habe* (1472) constituted manuals for priests in the administration of the Sacrament of Penance.

The *Summa Theologica* (1477), more properly called the *Summa Moralis,* is the work upon which his theological fame chiefly rests. There were no less than 20 complete editions in four large folio volumes, excluding the reprint in 1958 of the 1740 Verona edition. The first part, reflecting the doctrine of St. Thomas, treats of the soul and its faculties, the passions, sin, law; the second deals with the various kinds of sin; the third is concerned with the different states and professions in life whether social, political, religious, or ecclesiastical; and it has added treatises on the pope, the councils, and censures. The fourth part is devoted to the cardinal and theological virtues and to the gifts of the Holy Spirit. This *Summa* is probably the first—certainly the most comprehensive—treatment from a practical point of view of Christian ethics, asceticism, and sociology in the Middle Ages. It gives to Antoninus the place of honor in moral theology between St. Thomas and St. Alphonsus Ligouri.

The *Chronicon* (1440–59)—an episodical history of the world in three folio volumes—was designed to illustrate from the past how men should live in this world. It is filled with borrowings from the Scriptures, lives of the saints, extracts from the writings of the Fathers and Doctors of the Church, and decrees of popes and councils—the whole forming a practical library for preachers and pastors of souls.

The *Sermones* of Antoninus remain unpublished. The *Opera a ben vivere,* a treatise on the Christian life, was not printed until 1858.

Bibliography: R. Morçay, *Saint Antonin, fondateur du Couvent de Saint-Marc, archevêque de Florence, 1389–1459* (Paris 1914). B. Jarrett, *S. Antonino and Medieval Economics* (St. Louis 1914). J. B. Walker, *The "Chronicles" of Saint Antoninus: A Study in Historiography* (CUA Stud. in Med. Hist. 6; Washington 1933). W. T. Gaughan, *Social Theories of Saint Antoninus from His Summa Theologica* (CUA Stud. in Sociol. 35; Washington 1951). **Illustration credit:** Alinari-Art Reference Bureau.

[J. B. WALKER]

ANTONIUS ANDREAS, Franciscan scholastic, known as *Doctor dulcifluus* and *Scotellus;* b. Tauste, Saragossa, *c.* 1280; d. *c.* 1320. A member of the province of Aragon, he studied at the newly founded University of Lérida, then under *Duns Scotus at Paris. An ardent advocate of the Subtle Doctor, he promulgated his master's teaching in numerous writings, notably commentaries. Although he wrote a commentary on the *Sentences* (ed. Venice 1572), it is not certain that he ever became a master in theology. Nevertheless his works were widely read and frequently printed in the 15th and 16th centuries. Although not an original thinker, he substantially influenced the development of *Scotism. The *Quaestiones de anima* commonly attributed to Scotus were probably written by him. Among his better-known writings are *Tractatus formalitatum ad mentem Scoti* (ed. Padua 1475); *Quaestiones super libros 12 metaphysicae* (ed. Venice *c.* 1475); *Expositio* *in libros metaphysicae* (ed. Venice 1482); *De tribus principiis rerum naturalium* (ed. Padua 1475); *Commentaria in artem veterem* (ed. Bologna 1481); and the *Compendiosum principium in libros sententiarum* (ed. Strassburg 1495), formerly attributed to St. Bonaventure.

Bibliography: Gilson HistChrPhil 466, 765, 768. M. BIHL, DHGE 2:1633–34. Hurter Nomencl 2:466–467. L. AMORÓS, LexThK² 1:671–672. T. CARRERAS ARTAU, *Historia de la filosofía española,* v.2 (Madrid 1943) 458–571. MARTÍ DE BARCELONA in *Criterion* 5 (1929) 321–346.

[M. J. GRAJEWSKI]

ANTONIUS DE BUTRIO, lay canonist, decretalist, and teacher; b. Butrio, near Bologna, 1338; d. Bologna, October 4, 1408. He received his degrees in civil law (1384) and Canon Law (1387) in Bologna. He periodically taught in Bologna, Florence, Ferrara, and Perugia. In 1407 he was sent by Gregory XII to Marseilles to negotiate the end of the schism with Benedict XIII. After helping bring about the treaty of April 21, 1407, he returned to Bologna where he died. His works, which were noted for their practicality and wide diffusion, included: *Commentaria in quinque libris Decretalium* (2 v. Rome 1473, 1474; Milan 1488, etc.), *Commentaria in Sextum* (Venice 1479, 1575), *Consilia* (Rome 1472, 1744; Pavia 1492; Venice 1493, etc.). He also produced other works designed to remedy the evils in the Church and to bring about Christian unity.

Bibliography: A. AMANIEU, DDC 1:630–631. Hurter Nomencl 2:771–772. Van Hove 1:496–497. Schulte 2:289–294.

[H. A. LARROQUE]

ANTWERP

Capital of Antwerp province, *Belgium, on the Schelde River, 55 miles from the North Sea. It revived as a port when France reopened the Schelde to navigation (1795), closed since the Peace of *Westphalia (1648). In 1964 the city had 237,000 Catholics in a population of 258,000, 244 secular and 181 religious priests, 13 religious houses of men, and 68 convents with 1,154 sisters. In Catholic schools there were 4,972 children (3 to 6 years old), 13,251 pupils (6 to 12), and 7,193 humanities and 8,464 technology students (12 to 18). In Greater Antwerp there were 12 Catholic clinics (1,661 beds), 16 homes for the aged (666 beds), 3 medical-pedagogical institutes caring for 470 children, 11 family homes with 496 orphans, and 2 psychiatric institutes (845 beds). The Diocese of Antwerp (created 1559, suppressed 1801–1961), suffragan to *Mechelen-Brussels, is 985 square miles in area.

History. Christianity was first preached there by SS. *Eligius (647), *Amandus (650), and *Willibrord (697 and after). From the 7th to the 11th centuries there was a parish inside the bourg of Antwerp, which was part of the See of *Cambrai. The chapter of canons moved to the Church of Our Lady and left St. Michael Church, Antwerp's first church, to St. *Norbert's Premonstratensians (1124).

In the 13th century the port of Antwerp began to develop; but annexation by the county of Flanders, which favored the port of *Bruges, hampered its growth. Only in the late 15th century could Antwerp develop commercially to become the largest Atlantic port and the most important banking center of Europe in the 16th century. New parishes were added: St. Willibrord (1441), St. George (1477), St. *Walburga and St. James (1477–79), and St. Andrew (1529).

This international commercial center, with an important German colony, was the first Lutheran center in the Low Countries. The first Protestants to be burned at the stake in the Low Countries were two Augustinians of Antwerp (1523). In vain did Charles V issue condemnations of heretics; Antwerp, concerned only with commercial prosperity, was quite tolerant in religion and invariably moderated governmental intervention in religious matters and the enforcement of Charles' condemnations. After Lutherans and Anabaptists, Calvinists became the important religious group in Antwerp (from 1560).

In 1559 Paul IV made Antwerp a see suffragan to Mechelen; but Antwerp, not wishing an Inquisitor bishop inside its walls, sent an embassy to Philip II in Madrid and the installation of a bishop was suspended *sine die.* Only under the Duke of *Alva could the first bishop obtain his see (1570). After the Spanish Fury, which destroyed 600 houses and massacred thousands of people in Antwerp (1576), Protestants held the city until they were expelled by Alexander *Farnese (1585). The city of 100,000 (14,000 foreigners) was cut off from the sea by the Sea Beggars for more than 200 years, not until the 19th century did Antwerp revive as a world port. Its first bishops, F. Sonnius (1570–76), L. Torrentius (1586–95), and J. Miraeus (1603–11), with the aid of Jesuits and Capuchins especially, obtained the triumph of the Catholic Reformation. Its last bishop, C. F. Nelis (1785–98), opposed *Josephinism. The *Concordat of 1801 suppressed the see, which was not restored until 1961.

Art. Antwerp was a center of famous painters. In the 16th century Quinten Massys and the Brueghels prepared the way for the great school of Peter Paul Rubens,

Antwerp, the Gothic Cathedral of Our Lady (1352 to 1606).

Antwerp, St. James Church, site of Rubens' tomb.

which included Anthony Van Dyck, Caspar de Crayer, Jacob Jordaens, Adriaen Brouwer, and others, almost all of whom endowed churches with magnificent religious paintings. The Cathedral of Our Lady (1352–1606), with 7 naves, is 384 feet long and 213 feet wide and has a tower 403 feet high; it is the largest church in Belgium. Although it was badly damaged by iconoclasts in 1566, it still has famous paintings by Rubens (Crucifixion, Descent from the Cross, the Assumption) and statues by Artus Quellinus (1609–68). St. James Church (1491–1656), with many artistic masterpieces, and St. Paul Church (1533–1621), with paintings by Rubens, Jordaens, and David Teniers (1582–1649), are Gothic. The Jesuit St. Charles, a famous baroque church with many paintings by Rubens, suffered from fire (1718). The hôtel de ville by Cornelius Floris de Vriendt stands on one side of the main square, which is bordered by other admirable buildings dating from the 16th century.

Monasteries. The Norbertine Abbey of St. Michael (1124), a double monastery for 30 years, was ruined by iconoclasts (1566, 1576) but flourished under J. C. Van der Sterre (d. 1652); confiscated by *Joseph II (1789) and suppressed (1796), it was sold and demolished (1831). It founded other famous abbeys, such as *Tongerloo (*c.* 1130) and Averbode (1134–35). Antwerp also had a Victorine priory (Sainte-Margrietendal), a Charterhouse for men (Sainte-Cathérine-au-Mont-Sinaï, 1320), the Cistercian Peeter-Pots or St. Salvator (1446, an abbey in 1652), a *Beguine house (*c.* 1250), and other religious houses. The *Bollandist editors of the *Acta Sanctorum* lived in Antwerp from *c.* 1650 until the suppression of the Jesuits (1773).

Bibliography: P. F. X. DE RAM, *Synopsis actorum ecclesiae Antverpiensis* (Brussels 1856); *Synodicum belgicum* 3 (Louvain 1858). J. DE WIT, *De kerken van Antwerpen* (Antwerp 1910). É. DE MOREAU, DHGE 3:885–908; *Histoire de l'Église en Belgique,* 5 v. (Brussels 1945–52; 2 suppl.). J. A. GORIS, *Lof van Antwerpen* (Brussels 1940). A. VAN DE VELDE, *Antwerpen de Stoute* (Bruges 1942). F. PRIMS, *Antwerpen door de eeuwen heen* (Antwerp 1951); *Antwerpen in de XVIIIe eeuw* (Antwerp 1951); *Bouwstoffen voor de geschiedenis van Antwerpen in de nouveaux diocèses aux Pays-Bas, 1559–1570* (Brussels 1966). *XIXe eeuw* (Antwerp 1964). M. DIERICKX, *L'Érection des* AnnPont (1965) 34. **Illustration credits:** Belgian Government Information Center, New York City.

[M. DIERICKX]

ANUNCIACIÓN, DOMINGO DE LA, Dominican missionary and explorer; b. Fuente-Ojejuna (Vejuna), Estremadura, Spain, 1510; d. Mexico City, 1591. He was baptized Juan de Paz. His father, Ferdinando de Ecija, had five other sons and three daughters. In 1528 Juan and Alonso, his oldest brother, went to Mexico. Juan entered the Dominican Order in 1531 or 1532. He received a brief education in the Dominican convent and was ordained in 1534, sometime before October, by Julian Garcés, the Dominican bishop of Tlaxcala. He then apparently did missionary work among the Indians, probably at Tepetloaxtac, and learned Indian dialects. As a result, in 1544 or 1545 he wrote a *Doctrina Cristiana* for use in Indian catechetic work. (*See* CATECHISMS IN COLONIAL SPANISH AMERICA.) The history of his province, begun by Andrés de Moguer, was continued by Domingo de la Anunciación down to 1580, and later completed by *Dávila y Padilla. During a number of epidemics among the Indians, particularly in 1545 and again in 1577, Fray Domingo worked among the sick and dying. This may help to explain the fact that over 100,000 Indian baptisms are attributed to him. He accompanied Governor Tristán de Luna y Arellano on the expedition of 1559–61 to the port of Ochuse (Pensacola Bay) and northwest Florida. He went out with scouting parties, which, in search of food, explored parts of Alabama. The hardships he underwent on these expeditions undermined his health, but it improved after his return to Mexico. The last years of his life were spent in missionary work in Mexico.

Bibliography: V. F. O'DANIEL, *Dominicans in Early Florida* (New York 1930). H. I. PRIESTLEY, ed. and tr., *The Luna Papers,* 2 v. (De Land, Fla., 1928).

[A. B. NIESER]

ANXIETY

An emotional state of fearfulness or of uneasiness. The concept has recurred throughout the history of philosophy but has taken on special meaning in existentialist thought; it has been discussed also in traditional psychology, and here too has received new emphasis owing to developments in psychiatry. This article is thus divided into two parts: the first considers anxiety in philosophy; the second, anxiety in psychiatry.

ANXIETY IN PHILOSOPHY

The notions of anxiety, fear, and dread are as old as human nature itself. Not only did Homer and Vergil dramatize them in the lives of their heroes, but both Plato and Aristotle gave their genius to an analysis of their basic meanings. Summarizing what the important philosophers and theologians had written, St. *Thomas Aquinas defines *fear as the sadness that arises in man from his awareness of an approaching misfortune, evil, or suffering (see APPETITE). But for modern thought, especially that of the existential variety, fear, anxiety, and dread have taken on added significance.

Kierkegaard. S. A. *Kierkegaard is the source of this contemporary interest. In his work *The Concept of Dread,* Kierkegaard distinguishes between ordinary fear and dread (the usual translation of his term *Angst*). The various fears of men have determinate and specifiable objects, whereas dread is an apprehension that, though very real, is an anxiety about "nothing in particular," since one cannot indicate just what it is that is making him so profoundly uneasy and alarmed. What is at the root of this deep-seated uneasiness, according to Kierkegaard, is the note of possibility that is inherent in human *freedom. One is in the grip of dread because he is beginning to appreciate the awesome expanse of the *possibility that is the meaning of human freedom. It is beginning to dawn on him that freedom entails the possibility of willing an infinity of things in an infinity of ways, and he is both fascinated and horrified at the prospect. Hence Kierkegaard sees dread as an antipathetic sympathy in relation to the good and as sympathetic antipathy as regards evil. In either case the individual undergoes a dialectic of contrary emotions, for he loves the possibility of freedom and yet flees from it. This profound uneasiness, this elemental disquietude at the alarming possibility of "being able" is what Kierkegaard calls dread.

Since dread arises from the awareness of freedom, it is the mark of a man who is beginning to exist as a true human being. In the past it has manifested itself in the thoughtful Greek as dread of fate; in the observant Jew it is a dread of guilt before the Law; in the Christian context it can appear as the dread of sin. It is this dread that, according to Kierkegaard, is the only true way to faith in Christ. But dread in any case is the sign of the awakening spirit in man.

Heidegger. Aware of Kierkegaard's distinction between fear and dread, M. Heidegger in his *Being and Time* carries on the analysis, but he uses the term dread or anxiety (both are used in translating his term *Angst*) with a somewhat different meaning (*see* EXISTENTIALISM, 2). Fear again designates the feeling that is aroused by the approach of a determinate threatening object, and anxiety still signifies an apprehensiveness brought about by an object that is indeterminate, indefinite, and "nothing in particular." But this "nothing in particular" is not so much the possibility that is inherent in freedom as it is the possibility of a human being to become himself in all his unique individuality, that is, the possibility to become his true and authentic self. Man, or *Dasein* as he is called by Heidegger, easily becomes involved in a mode of existence that, although less demanding of him, is not truly his own. This happens when *Dasein,* forgetting its own individuality and selfhood, allows itself to become absorbed into the many, into "the crowd." Accepting the judgment of "they say" and conforming all its activity to the pattern of "they all do," *Dasein* has not yet achieved its true selfhood; anxiety can be the means by which this might be attained.

While in anxiety, *Dasein* feels threatened, not in any particular and relative facet of its existence as happens in fear, but in the very roots of its being, its very possibility of being. Because *Dasein* has been existing in an inauthentic mode, it has been fleeing from its innermost self to find shelter in "the many." But while in the state of anxiety, this inauthentic existence begins to disintegrate. *Dasein* can find no help in the various entities in the world that until now have absorbed its attention, nor can it receive support in the clichés of the "they say." *Dasein* is thus thrown back upon its own resources. For the first time it is face to face with itself; it can recognize itself in its own unique individuality; it can now see that it must depend upon itself.

Anxiety thus opens up to a man the possibility of becoming what he should be; for it takes away all the extrinsic props on which he has been leaning. *Dasein* can now become really free; for it can turn to its innermost, or in Heidegger's terms, its "ownmost" possibility: the possibility of becoming its own self. This possibility of becoming his authentic self means that man must choose himself in all his individualized being. As in Kierkegaard, so in Heidegger, anxiety or dread can bring man to his true being; for it makes man aware of his freedom, which is his only authentic existence.

Sartre and Others. In this question as in many others, J. P. Sartre has been greatly influenced by Heidegger (*see* EXISTENTIALISM, 3). Sartre teaches that man's existence becomes truly human only when he freely begins to make himself the man he has freely decided to become; for Sartre maintains that each man forms his own essence by the morality he pursues. Since there is no God, in Sartre's opinion, he insists that there are no objective standards of morality, so that each individual man becomes the supreme arbiter of values. This total and complete responsibility for creating goods and values brings with it the feeling of anguish (*angoisse*). A man can run away from this anguish or try to conceal it, but the existential man, the man of good faith, is the man who recognizes that anguish is the very quality of human freedom. Sartre's work *Being and Nothingness* examines in great detail the meaning and responsibility of human freedom, and his many plays are concerned with portrayals of men either accepting or shirking the anguish of freedom's responsibility. In all his writings Sartre makes it clear that though the anguish of responsibility is burdensome, it is the crowning point of human existence; for freedom means that each man is the supreme legislator of morality—man is the being whose existence is to make his own essence.

Similar to Sartre's position is that of the artists of the nonobjective school, the authors of the literature of despair, and the dramatists of the theater of the absurd, all of whom depict man as struggling in anguish and dread to grasp at some semblance of freedom in a world that has no God, is without any ultimate truth, and lacks any objective moral standard (*see* ABSURDITY).

The concept of dread has thus taken a full and complete turn in its meaning. Kierkegaard saw in it a fruitful theme that could recall men to a rich existence lived in the presence of God thanks to their faith in Christ. Because they lack belief in Christ, many contemporary thinkers use the concept to remind men of the agony of existence in a world from which God is absent. *See also* EXISTENTIALISM, 1.

Bibliography: F. BERTHOLD, *The Fear of God: The Role of Anxiety in Contemporary Thought* (New York 1959). M. HEIDEGGER, *Being and Time,* tr. J. MACQUARRIE and E. ROBINSON

(New York 1962). S. KIERKEGAARD, *The Concept of Dread,* tr. W. LOWRIE (Princeton 1944). J. P. SARTRE, *Being and Nothingness,* tr. H. E. BARNES (New York 1956); *Existentialism and Humanism,* tr. P. MAIRET (London 1948).

[V. M. MARTIN]

ANXIETY IN PSYCHIATRY

Psychiatrically, anxiety is used to designate those fears whose source is within the psychic makeup of the individual, e.g., fear of one's own sex impulses, and is largely unknown or unrecognized. Anxiety is considered pathologic when it is intense enough to interfere with effective and satisfying living. Anxiety is a general characteristic of neuroses (*see* PSYCHONEUROTIC DISORDERS).

Freud's Theories. Sigmund *Freud developed two theories of anxiety, the later of which has become of great importance in contemporary psychiatry.

Before 1926. There exists a neurotic and a real anxiety. The distinction is not only descriptive, but also causal and etiological. Real anxiety arises from the perception of real danger. The neurotic form is indistinguishable by its qualities from the real; it is differentiated only by its cause, being produced by an insufficient discharge of libidinal energy. Through some unknown process, this undischarged libido becomes directly transformed into anxiety. The relation between the psychological conflict and the anxiety is, however, indirect. An existing conflict may repress the libido, which sometimes remains kept in check and at other times becomes transformed into anxiety. This is what occurs in neurosis. As the amount of repressed libido increases, the possibility that the repression will fail and that neurotic symptoms and anxiety will develop becomes greater. These cases constituted "actual neurosis" in contrast with "psychoneurosis" insofar as the libidinal conflict was due to repression. To summarize, neurotic anxiety was libido transformed and not, as in real anxiety, a fear of danger. It was produced by unsuccessful repression or unsatisfied sexual desires. It did not cause psychological conflict, but was its consequence.

After 1926. In his later thought Freud abandoned his theory of anxiety as transformed libido. The relation between anxiety and repression reversed itself. Previously anxiety originated in repression; now anxiety caused or motivated the repression. Later Freud formulated the hypothesis that anxiety appears when stimuli reaching the psychic apparatus are too large to be absorbed or incorporated in it. Thus, anxiety is an adaptive response to a situation. Anxiety is a reaction that brings on hyperactivity in the face of danger. Between neurasthenia and hysteria Freud located a new form of neurosis that he first called the hysteria of anxiety and later anxiety neurosis. Only sometime afterward did he conclude that the dynamics of neurosis set up both anxiety and the mechanisms used to combat it.

Neurotic and Real Anxiety. It is important to know whether neurotic and real anxiety are the same. To the degree that neurosis manifests itself in abnormal reactions or in psychic conflicts, the subject suffers from a psychic impact (trauma) that cannot be worked out or diverted. This resistance to integration into the psychic life is what gives it the imprint of abnormality. The trauma disturbs the normal flow of psychic life. It is difficult to explain why psychic experiences that are assigned the role of traumatization are incapable of being assimilated. Many human experiences are considered anxiety-provoking, and yet do not produce these effects. Anxiety, fear, sorrow, boredom, anger, resentment, guilt, vengeance—none of these are in themselves pathological. They pertain to the normal play of the emotional life. The question then becomes: when do these vibrations of the emotional life take on a pathological character?

The first and most frequently attempted solution is to calibrate the intensity of the response in relation to its stimulus; an inadequate response to a strong stimulus is called pathological. But this interpretation is insufficient. A stimulus does not produce an abnormal reaction because it is strong or violent, but because it surpasses the individual's capacity to support it. The stimulus overwhelms him; little stimuli may produce disproportionately great effects. The important thing is that the traumatizing character comes not from the emotion but from the subject's inability to sustain it. This inability to integrate is called abnormal anxiety. And this incapacity is shown by the subject in the face of a pathological emotion of fear, boredom, vengeance, or sadness. All these emotions have a common structure, which consists in their impossibility of being digested and in disruptions they cause on the flow of the psychic life. In anxiety the impossibility of absorbing traumatized emotion becomes apparent.

Clinical experience demonstrates that an emotion cannot be worked out effectively when the traumatizing experience has a special meaning to the individual. The traumatizing character comes, then, not from its violence but from its meaning. In other words, the problem of quantity becomes translated into quality.

Meaning of Anxiety. But what is the meaning of this imprinting traumatizing phenomenon? Psychoanalysis answers that it is those traumas that occurred in infancy and that have disturbed the development of the libido. Being repressed or forgotten, they occur a second time. They were repressed or forgotten precisely because they could not be incorporated. The inability to incorporate the trauma sets off a defense mechanism that may extend much further than that which caused the organism to summon it. The organism does not care that in defending itself against a disease it uses a mechanism that at times constitutes a "second illness." In a certain sense, all neurosis becomes a second illness. In biology, the impact of sickly matter that cannot be fitted into the organism disorganizes it. All illnesses contain a process of disorganization. The same thing occurs in psychology and psychopathology. And the experience of a psychological stress is what is called *Angst,* or anxiety, depending on its intensity.

Anxiety's most important meaning is in relation to life itself, i.e., the meaning of life. It is concerned not with what life contains, but with what life is, precisely because a specific experience tears away the veil hiding what life is not. It is a veiled threat of death or of personal disintegration, of lunacy or of emptiness, the phantasm of nothingness that appears materialized, that constitutes anxiety. Before it the individual can be nothing. The phantasm does no more than appear, but the threat forces one to feel the bottomlessness of his position. The feeling of being overwhelmed by the trauma is an active form of this substructure. The experiences that make evident these depths are those that cannot be incorporated psychologically. Their threat is not the threat of a particular individual, but one that reaches the bottom of life itself and is man's essential frustration. All men are frustrated to a greater or less degree; neurotic frustration is a transcription of this essential frustration of a life threatened by *nonbeing, by the infiltration of nothingness.

See also PSYCHOANALYSIS.

Bibliography: S. FREUD, "Anxiety and Instinctual Life," *New Introductory Lectures* (1933) in *The Standard Edition of the Complete Psychological Works,* ed. J. STRACHEY, 24 v. (London 1953–) v.22. F. J. BRACELAND and M. STOCK, *Modern Psychiatry* (New York 1963). J. J. LOPEZ IBOR, "The Existential Crisis," *Faith, Reason, and Modern Psychiatry,* ed. F. J. BRACELAND (New York 1955); "Angoisse, existence et vitalité," *L'Évolution psychiatrique* 15 (1950); *Angustia vital: Patologia general psicosomática* (Madrid 1950).

[J. J. LOPEZ IBOR]

APAMEA, name of several ancient cities. Modern Mudanya was once the bishopric of Apamea in Bithynia originally called Myrleia and located in southeast Propontis on the Sea of Marmara. The city was founded by colonists from Colophon, and taken by Philip V of Macedonia (221–179 B.C.) and given to Prusias I of Bithynia (230?–183 B.C.), who changed its name to Apamea in honor of his wife. Julius Caesar called it colonia Julia Concordia Augusta Apamea. There were many Christians in Bithynia in the early 2d century as a letter of Pliny the Younger (A.D. 62–113) to Trajan proves; but there is little information on the early bishops of Apamea. It was a suffragan see of Nicomedia; but by 536 it had become a metropolitan see. Since the middle of the 14th century it has been only a titular see.

Apamea in Phrygia is known to have had a bishop during the 4th or 5th century; but the exact site is not known, and it is not mentioned in the Byzantine lists of bishoprics.

Apamea in Pisidia is known from the ruins found near modern Dinar at the source of the Maeander River. The original city, built on a hill, was called Kelainai. At the foot of this hill the Syrian King Antiochus III (223–187 B.C.) built a new town and gave it the name of his mother, Apamea. It was known in history as Apamea ad Meandrum, Apamea Kelainai, and Apamea of the Ark (Cibotus), since legend made it the landing site of Noe's ark. After Ephesus, it was the most renowned see in Asia Minor. Under the Romans it was a trade center, but it was destroyed in the 11th century by the Seljuk Turks.

Apamea, metropolitan see in Syria, was first called Pharnake, and then Pella by the Macedonians. Seleucus I Nicator named it Apamea for his wife. It was sacked under the Persian Chosroes II in 611 and, though rebuilt, was destroyed in an earthquake in 1152. Its ruins can be seen near modern Qal'at al-Mudiq northeast of Hama. It is possible that Apamea in Syria had a bishop in apostolic times. Under Theodosius II (408–450) it was a metropolitan see that disappeared under Arab occupation after 650. Tancred captured it in 1111 and erected a Latin archbishopric that continued in existence till 1238; since then it has served merely as a titular archbishopric.

Bibliography: R. JANIN, DHGE 3:916–920. R. NORTH, Lex ThK[2] 1:684. W. M. RAMSAY, *Cities and Bishoprics of Phrygia,* 2 v. (Oxford 1895–97) 2:396–483. V. SCHULTZE, *Altchristliche Städte* 4 v. (Leipzig 1913–37). 2.1:450–461. R. DUSSAUD, *Topographie de la Syrie* (Paris 1927) 194–198. F. MAYENCE, *L'Antiquite classique* 1 (1932) 233–242; 4 (1935) 199–204; 5 (1936) 405–411.

[A. NEUWIRTH]

APARECIDA, ARCHDIOCESE OF (APPARITIOPOLITANUS), located in the state of São Paulo, Brazil: it was never a diocese but was created an archdiocese in the division of the ecclesiastical province of São Paulo in 1958. In 1964 it had as suffragan sees Taubaté (1908) and Lorena (1937).

1964 STATISTICS

Area	Population	Parishes	Clergy	
			Sec.	Reg.
Aparecida	*67,450	6	8	51
Taubaté	*348,950	31	55	53
Lorena	150,000	15	11	28

*This figure represents Catholics only.

In 1717 fishermen found in the Rio Paraiba an image of the Blessed Virgin that lacked a head. Sometime later they found the head also. The image became an object of veneration among the faithful and was called the "Aparecida." In 1745 a chapel was built for it and ultimately a large church was constructed and finished in 1888. German Redemptorists were put in charge of the church in 1894 and the next year it was raised to an episcopal sanctuary. Pilgrimages to the shrine increased steadily. In 1908 it was made a minor basilica and in 1930 Nossa Senhora Aparecida was proclaimed the patron of Brazil. In 1952 the construction of a national basilica was begun. When it is completed, it will be the largest Marian church in the world and be exceeded in size only by St. Peter's in Rome and St. Paul's in London. The square in front of the basilica will accommodate 300,000 persons. Cardinal Carlos Carmelo de Vasconcellos Motta of São Paulo supplied the impetus for this building and the erection of the archdiocese. Cardinal Motta was named administrator of the archdiocese but he left its government to Auxiliary Bishop Antônio Ferreira de Macedo. In April 1964 Cardinal Motta secured his own transfer to Aparecida.

The Diocese of Taubaté, which once was a place for exploration and conquest, has become, as a result of its good climate, a center for hospitals, sanatoriums, and rest homes, particularly for the clergy and religious orders. In 1904 the first Trappist monastery in Brazil was founded in Tremembé and it lasted for about 20 years. A similar monastery for women failed for lack of vocations. Among the religious orders working in the province in 1964 were Redemptorists, Franciscans, Salesians, Conventual Franciscans, Capuchins, Servites, Fathers of the Sacred Heart, and about 600 sisters of various congregations.

Bibliography: *Nossa Senhora Aparecida. Seu Santuário, sua história* (Aparecida 1962). L. CASTANHO DE ALMEIDA, *São Paulo, filho da Igreja* (Petrópolis 1955). A. BRANDÃO, *Dom Epaminondas* (São Paulo 1941).

[O. VAN DER VAT]

APARICIO, SEBASTIÁN DE, BL., pioneer colonist in New Spain; b. Gudiña, Galicia, Spain, Jan. 20, 1502; d. Puebla, Feb. 25, 1600. The son of poor peasants, he worked as a field hand during his adolescent years. In 1533 he sailed to Mexico and established his residence in Puebla de los Angeles. He worked there as a farmer, a road builder, and a trainer of young bulls; and he taught all those trades to the Indians. In 1542 he started the construction of the highway that later linked Mexico City and Zacatecas. He was married twice, but neither marriage was consummated. When his second wife died, he sold all his possessions and gave the proceeds to the poor.

At the age of 72 he received the friar's habit at the convent of San Francisco in Mexico City. He made his profession in 1575 and was assigned by his superiors to procure the daily bread by asking for charity at various convents. He carried out this task, a burdensome one for his old age, with great efficiency. He was noted for his extraordinary health and strong will; his humility and charity were outstanding. He was assigned to serve at the Franciscan house of studies in the convent of Puebla, and for 20 consecutive years he provided it with all the needed material goods. In like manner, he gave extensive help to all sorts of poor and needy people. Granted the grace to work miracles, he performed so many toward the end of his life that the Bishop of Puebla, Diego Romano, determined to begin at once the canonical process for his beatification. Despite the fact that his miracles continued after his death, the process lasted for 2 centuries; among the main causes for the delay were his two marriages. Finally he was solemnly beatified by Pius VI on May 17, 1789.

Bibliography: E. ESCOBAR, *Vida del B. Sebastián de Aparicio* (Mexico City 1958). C. ESPINOSA, *Fray Sebastián de Aparicio* (Mexico City 1959).

[F. DE J. CHAUVET]

APARISI Y GUIJARRO, ANTONIO, Spanish poet and journalist; b. Valencia, May 22, 1815, d. Madrid, Nov. 8, 1872. He was a brilliant student, although he had to struggle for an education because his father died deeply in debt and his mother worked to reimburse the creditors. He first became known when he won a prize for poetry at the age of 12. He started his professional life as a lawyer in Valencia and founded the journals *La Restauración* (1843) and *El Pensamiento de Valencia* (1855). After moving to Madrid, he continued to practice law and founded *La Regeneración* (1862), which he edited for 10 years. He became a deputy to parliament and a leader of public opinion; he was a traditionalist in politics, which were at that time in a state of considerable unrest. He spoke in favor of the temporal power of the papacy and for Catholic unity, and worked for a conciliation between Queen Isabel and Don Carlos of Bourbon. He was one of the founders of the Carlist party. Aparisi died as he left Parliament House in Madrid after making a speech. During his life he published several volumes of verse, including *A San Vicente Ferrer, España y Africa, La Batalla de Bailén,* and a number of political pamphlets. He was elected to the Academia Española on Nov. 5, 1872, and a year after his death his admirers published five volumes of his works, including *Pensamientos filosoficas religiosas,* and his political speeches. His profound religious convictions impregnated all of his writing.

Bibliography: A. APARISI Y GUIJARRO, *Antología,* ed. V. GENOVÉS (Madrid 1940). R. OLIVAR-BERTRAND, *Aparisi y Guijarro* (Madrid 1962), with comprehensive bibliog.

[S. LOWNDES]

APATHY, a mental state in which a person is disinclined to intellectual, volitional, or physical activity. Specifically, the apathetic will seeks to avoid the effort required in choosing and in carrying out decisions. At times this is a morbid disposition resulting from poor health. More seriously it can be a disease of the will that tries to escape all effort. Apathy is also a moral state that disinclines a person to fulfill his religious duties. An individual can be morally responsible for permitting himself to fall into this state; furthermore, he has an obligation to use means to free himself. Apathy in its moral aspect is usually called sloth (*see* ACEDIA). When a slothful person is so lazy as to neglect his essential religious duties and the important duties of his state of life, he can be guilty of grave sin [*see* SIN (THEOLOGY OF)]. Ordinarily, however, laziness is only venially sinful. Yet torpor in one's religious life is debilitating and militates against the *zeal needed for a full and joyous Christian life. To overcome apathy one should begin with a conviction that effort and work are necessary and that indolence cannot bring a sense of life's fulfillment. To carry out this conviction, the individual must first set tasks for himself that are possible in his debilitated state, and gradually quicken the pace. For the mature person, listing things that need doing and checking them off as they are performed can aid in overcoming apathy.

See also WILL POWER.

[J. A. BURROUGHS]

APER (EVRE) OF TOUL, ST., bishop; b. Trancault, Diocese of Troyes, in the 5th century; d. *c.* 507 (feast, Sept. 15). Aper was the seventh bishop of Toul. A late, formalized vita gives his birthplace and states that he served 7 years as bishop. The only positive information furnished by this life (aside from the account of his miraculous liberation of three prisoners of the common law of Chalon-sur-Saône) is his construction of a basilica in honor of St. Maurice at the gates of Toul. Aper was buried in this basilica, which bore his name as early as 626 or 627 and which later became famous as the Abbey of Saint-Aper. The cult of the bishop is widespread in the ancient See of *Toul and in several neighboring dioceses.

Bibliography: BHL 1:616–618. ActSS Sept. 5:55–79. MGS 4: 515–520. E. MARTIN, *Histoire des diocèses de Toul, de Nancy et de Saint-Dié,* 3 v. (Nancy 1900–03) v.1. Duchesne FÉ 3:62.

[J. CHOUX]

APHRAATES, the earliest-known Christian writer in Persia; fl. first half of the 4th century. He was an ascetic and high-ranking cleric, but it is not clear whether he was a bishop. Manuscripts of the 5th and 6th centuries preserve 23 of his sermons or homilies, the first 10 composed in 337, the following 12 in 344, the last in 345, at the beginning of the persecution of Sapor II. The homilies are preceded by a letter falsely ascribed to Gregory the Illuminator.

Sermons 1 to 10 are hortatory and ascetical in tone and content: 1, on faith, contains an ancient Trinitarian creed; 2 to 4 deal with charity, fasting, and prayer; 5, written when war was imminent, hopes subtly for Roman victory in the interests of Christianity; 6 to 10 cover Christian perfection, Penance (against rigorism in forgiving sins), resurrection of the dead, humility, and the shepherds of souls. The remainder are frequently polemics against the Jews, who were numerous and learned in Northern Mesopotamia, and treat of circumcision, Easter, the Sabbath, distinction of foods, Gentiles supplanting the chosen people, Jesus' divine sonship, virginity, impossibility of restoring the kingdom of the Jews, and the saving blessing that lay hidden on the vine of Israel and came to flower in the Gentiles. Sermon 14 castigates clerical morals; 20 is concerned with the poor and needy; 21, with impending persecution; 22, with the last things.

Doctrinal elements in Aphraates include a profession of the Trinity, salvation through Christ-God, who invaded Sheol and conquered the devil in his own domain, and the Real Presence. His works bear no trace of Hellenistic influence; rather, he reveals a mentality discoverable in contemporary rabbinic literature and Judeo-Christian thought. His grasp of Scripture is remarkable, his use of it felicitous, especially in his constant recourse to the Old Testament, which he regards as intimately linked to the New. His theology, while genuinely Christian, is quite primitive; the Bible may well have been his only written source.

Bibliography: J. PARISOT, ed., *Demonstrationes* (PatrSyrG 1–2; 1894–1907). PatrSyrO 43–47, with bibliog. E. J. DUNCAN, *Baptism in the Demonstrations of Aphraates, the Persian Sage* (Washington 1945). A. VÖÖBUS, "Methodologisches zum Studium der Anweisungen Aphrahats," OrChr 46 (1962) 25–32. E. BECK, "Symbolum-Mysterium bei Aphraat und Ephräm," *ibid.* 42 (1958) 19–40.

[I. ORTIZ DE URBINA]

APOCALYPSE, BOOK OF

The NT writing generally found in the last place in our Bibles, named from its superscription, "The revelation [ἀποκάλυψις, apocalypse] of Jesus Christ . . ." (1.1). This article treats the book's authorship and canonicity, occasion, date of composition, contents, unity, the character of the visions and their literary form, and methods of interpretation.

Authorship and Canonicity. The author of Apocalypse gives his name as John (1.1, 4, 9; 22.8) and identifies himself as a Christian prophet (22.6, 9; see also 1.3; 10.11). Nowhere does he claim to be St. *John the Apostle. An early and persistent tradition, however, has made this identification: the Gnostic *Apocryphon of John* (*c.* A.D. 150 or earlier), Justin Martyr (*c.* 160), Irenaeus (*c.* 175), the *Muratorian Canon (*c.* 200), Tertullian (*c.* 200), and Clement of Alexandria (*c.* 200). About this time the *Alogoi, led by the Roman priest Caius, in reaction to the abuse of Apocalypse by the Montanists, ascribed both the Gospel according to St. *John and Apocalypse to the heretic Cerinthus and denied their canonicity. Though St. *Dionysius of Alexandria (d. 264) considered Apocalypse an inspired writing, he questioned its apostolic authorship because of literary and theological considerations similar to those that prompt most modern scholars to posit different authors for the Fourth Gospel and Apocalypse. Dionysius' arguments are reproduced by Eusebius (*Hist. eccl.* 7.25; SourcesChr 41:204–210), who also credits John the Presbyter with the writing of Apocalypse (*ibid.,* 3.39.5; SourcesChr 31:154–155). Between A.D. 300 and 450 a number of the Fathers of the Church in the East, especially of the Antiochian School, excluded Apocalypse from the Canon. *See* BIBLE, III (CANON), 3. During the same period, however, it was accepted in the West and in the East by Athanasius, Cyril of Alexandria, Basil, Gregory of Nyssa, and others, all of whom assumed apostolic authorship of the book.

Today this question is far less important than it was when apologetic considerations emphasized the apostolic authorship of the NT writings. Throughout the Biblical period conception of authorship was not so rigid as it is today. The work of a disciple could easily be ascribed to his master. At present it is widely recognized that the author of Apocalypse was a Christian prophet named John who enjoyed authority in Christian circles about Ephesus. If he was not the Apostle John, he was certainly one of his disciples. It is hardly probable that both the Fourth Gospel and Apocalypse were authored by the same person.

Occasion. Like other *apocalyptic writings, John's was occasioned by a religious crisis. He wrote to encourage Christians, in the first instance those of Asia Minor, to be steadfast even to martyrdom in the face of the social, economic, and legal pressures that made it increasingly difficult to avoid taking part in pagan religious practices, especially emperor worship. Many had become disheartened and disillusioned because the glorious return of Christ, His *Parousia, which they had been eagerly expecting, seemed to recede farther and farther from the horizon of their hope.

John himself had been exiled to the penal island of Patmos for having borne witness to the word of God (Ap 1.9–10), probably for preaching Christianity and refusing to participate in the state religion. Intensely worried over the fate of the churches (5.4), he was caught up in rapture on a certain Sunday and received supernatural assurances from the glorified Jesus, whom he saw; these he was commanded to write on a scroll and send to seven important churches of Asia Minor (1.10–20). The visions and auditions granted him reminded the Christians that Jesus is Lord of all history, both as Son of God and as Redeemer; He is as truly present in the churches even now, though invisibly, as He will be in His Parousia, which is certain to come. The trials that Jesus' followers are suffering have been foreseen and foreordained; many more will be called to suffer martyrdom before the end. Pagan Rome, however, is doomed to destruction, and a glorious future of unending happiness awaits all those who suffer with patient endurance.

Date of Composition. Most commentators, ancient and modern, think that Apocalypse received its present form in the last years of the reign of Domitian (81–96). Internal evidence can be adduced that confirms this external consensus. Some scholars, however, believe that the historical background of Apocalypse was the reign of either Nero [54–68; the cryptograph 666 in Ap 13.18 is probably the name Nero by gematria; *see* NUMBERS AND NUMBER SYMBOLISM (IN THE BIBLE)] or Vespasian (69–79). The simplest explanation of the enigmatic statement in 17.9 that "five [emperors] have fallen" indicates the reign of Vespasian.

A combination of both views is proposed by several authors: either the present Apocalypse resulted from the fusion of two earlier apocalypses (see below), or John resorted to the popular apocalyptic device of antedating his work, i.e., though writing under Domitian he adopted the standpoint of the time of Nero or Vespasian.

Contents. The introduction (1.1–20) includes a superscription (1.1–3); an epistolary introduction (1. 4–6), like those of the Pauline Epistles; a solemn assurance of the Parousia (1.7–8); and the historical occasion of the work; the first prophetic investiture of John (1.9–20). The body of the book contains two main sections of unequal length: (1) the Apocalypse of the Present (ch. 2–3): the letters to the seven churches of Ephesus, Smyrna, Pergamum, Thyatira, Sardis, Philadelphia, and Laodicea and, (2) the Apocalypse of the Future (ch. 4–22). The visions of this main section are partly parallel and fall into two clearly defined sections—the Church and Judaism, and the Church and the *antichrists, followed by a conclusion—the consummation.

The Church and Judaism (*ch. 4-11*). The preparatory vision in heaven (ch. 4–5) serves as a second prophetic investiture for the revelation of God's interventions from the Resurrection of Christ to the fall of Jerusalem, including the rejection of the Jews and assurance of their ultimate conversion. Transported to the heavenly temple, John sees in God's hand a seven-sealed scroll, containing the divine decrees that govern all history. Only Christ as Redeemer can open and disclose the contents of the scroll. As the first four seals are successively broken (ch. 6), four horsemen appear —white [representing either the victory of the Gospel (cf. Mk 13.10) or imperialism], red (war), black (famine), and pale green (pestilence and death); the scene is like that in Jesus' apocalyptic discourse (Mk 13.5–8 and parallels, especially Lk 21.8–11). The opening of the fifth seal discloses the martyrs praying for a hastening of divine judgment and vengeance upon their persecutors, while the sixth introduces upheavals in nature, described in current apocalyptic clichés. An intermediate vision (ch. 7) shows how the elect, both Jewish and Gentile Christians, are preserved from the punitive aspect of the plagues.

The seventh seal, silence in heaven (8.1), ushers in the seven apocalyptic trumpets, introduced by a vision that depicts them as the answer to the prayers of Christians (8.2–6). The first four trumpets (8.7–12) herald calamities reminiscent of the *plagues of Egypt, though it is futile to ask what specific realities the seer had in mind. An eagle (8.13) warns that the last three trumpet blasts are to be special woes. The fifth shows a huge infernal invasion, while the sixth summons a vast demonic horde from the Euphrates to destroy a third of mankind (9.1–20). S. Giet here finds apocalyptic allusion to different phases of the Jewish War of A.D. 66–70.

A second intermediate vision (10.1–11) prepares for the universal character of the revelations to follow and includes a third prophetic investiture of John, that to the Gentiles, symbolized by the eating of a small scroll (10.8–11). This vision, however, anticipates (as frequently in Apocalypse), since John has not yet finished his predictions regarding Judaism.

The measuring of the Temple and the preaching, death, and resurrection of the two witnesses (11.1–14) depict parabolically the temporary rejection of the Jews, the witness of the Church through "Moses and the Prophets" to Christ in the face of Jewish opposition to Him, and the final conversion of the *remnant of Israel, referred to also in Romans ch. 9–11, especially 11.25–29. The seventh trumpet depicts the culmination of the covenant in the opening of heaven (11.15–19).

The Church and the Antichrists (*ch. 12-19*). Seven "signs" seen by John portray various aspects of the conflict between the Church and anti-God forces, as incarnate initially in pagan, emperor-worshiping Rome. The Church is presented as the *woman clothed with the sun, who gives birth to the Messiah, whom the great red dragon, Satan (cf. Gn 3.15), tries in vain to destroy; the Church is driven underground (12.1–6). The heavenly counterpart of this battle shows Michael casting Satan to earth (12.7–12), where he pursues the woman, divinely protected in the desert (12.13–18). Satan calls up two lieutenants: the "beast from the sea," the political antichrist, the Roman Empire with its emperor worship (13.1–10); and the "beast of the earth," the philosophical and theological antichrist (13. 11–18).

As in 7.1–17, an intermediate vision portrays the heavenly security of the faithful with the Lamb (Christ) on Mount Sion (14.1–5). Three angels successively warn all mankind to fear God, predict the fall of Babylon-Rome, and threaten eternal damnation (14. 6–11). A heavenly voice proclaims that the faithful who have died even now enjoy their reward (14.12–13). An anticipatory vision shows the Last Judgment, the reprobation of the wicked, and the ingathering of the elect (14.14–20).

After a brief introductory scene (15.1–8), the final septenary of plagues is hurriedly described as the outpouring of the wrath of God from seven bowls. The effects that follow remind the reader, though in heightened form, of the Egyptian plagues and the first four trumpets (16.1–12). Probably they create a dramatic effect rather than specify concrete happenings of the future. Between the sixth and seventh bowls three frog-like evil spirits summon the kings of the earth for the great final battle with the forces of God (16.14–16). After the last bowl, Babylon-Rome falls amid great upheavals in nature (16.17–21).

Once more the fall of Babylon is depicted, now under the image of the great harlot who leads the world astray and persecutes the Christians (17.1–18). Her destruction is dwelt upon with relish (18.1–24) and hailed by heavenly songs of triumph (19.1–10). Seated upon a white horse, Christ appears, His garments red with His own blood, or, according to many interpreters, with the blood of His enemies (19.11–16). Again the destruction of the beasts is proclaimed (19.17–21).

Next Satan is chained, the millennium (*see* MILLENARIANISM) is rapidly mentioned, and Satan is unloosed but summarily defeated along with his followers and cast into hell after the judgment (20.1–15).

The Consummation (21.1–22.5). The new heaven and the new earth (21.1–8) and the heavenly Jerusalem, of which God and the Lamb are temple and sun, with the river and tree of life, are the figures used to disclose final glory, which the elect enjoy for all eternity.

An epilogue (22.6–21) confirms in Christ's words what has been previously promised.

Unity. The inconsistencies and repetitions in Apocalypse have often raised the question: Is this a single composition or a conflation of more than one writing? Impressed by the uniformity of style and vocabulary and the closely knit character of the work, most scholars judge that Apocalypse is the work of one author. M. E. Boismard has revived and modified the opinion of R. Charles that both divergences and unity of style can be accounted for by distinguishing two apocalypses, both written by the same disciple of John the Apostle. Boismard dates what he calls Text 1 from a time toward the end of Vespasian's reign; Text 2, the

Fig. 1. The 24 elders cast their crowns before the throne (Apocalypse, ch. 4), miniature in the "Bamberg Apocalypse" written at Reichenau, c. 1020, and preserved in the Staatliche Bibliothek, Bamberg (MS Bibl. 140, fol. 11v).

nam. sciens quod modicum tempus habet.

Fig. 2. Michael's battle with the dragon (Apocalypse, ch. 12), miniature in the "Bamberg Apocalypse" written at Reichenau, c. 1020, and preserved in the Staatliche Bibliothek, Bamberg (MS Bibl. 140, fol. 30v).

Fig. 3. The second, third, and fourth bowls are poured (Apocalypse, ch. 16), miniature in the 9th-century "Trier Apocalypse" preserved in the Stadtbibliothek, Trier (MS 31, fol. 50r).

reign of Nero; the letters of ch. 2–3, that of Domitian. The fusion of the three parts was made by another writer, who slightly retouched his sources [*see* M. E. Boismard, "L'Apocalypse ou les Apocalypses de saint Jean?" RevBibl 56 (1949) 507–541].

Character of the Visions and Literary Form. Do the visions of Apocalypse purport to be a precise description of what John actually saw and heard? Or are they merely a literary device, as in the case of the noncanonical apocalyptic writings and probably also of the Book of *Daniel? The first alternative must be ruled out because of the inconsistencies and contradictions, the improbable images that this would involve. The second alternative, while it would not militate against the admittedly inspired nature of the book, yet fails to account for the realism of the descriptions and the impression conveyed that the writer seriously intended to report a supernatural mystical experience.

Accordingly, many students of Apocalypse today hold that John actually had a supernatural vision (or visions) with accompanying revelations from Christ that he was told to write down. When he carried out this order, he naturally resorted to the apocalyptic literary form, because it was the best-known vehicle, using symbols and imagery of every kind, to report as best he could experiences that defied the limitations of human speech.

One characteristic of Apocalypse must be stressed, its use of the OT. It has been computed that in the 404 verses of Apocalypse, 518 OT citations and allusions are found, 88 of them from Daniel; 278 of the 404 verses are made up of reminiscences of Scripture, especially (besides Daniel) Isaia, Jeremia, Ezechiel, Zacharia, Psalms, and Exodus. Apocalypse is, then, a rereading of the OT in the light of the Christian event. There is also good reason to surmise, with Origen, that the scroll that John saw (5.1–8) is the OT. Christ alone could open it because it finds in Him its ultimate meaning. The Christological reading of the Scriptures is, in the last analysis, the answer to the anguished questions and problems that faced the churches in John's day and in all times.

Methods of Interpretation. Here it is possible merely to summarize the systems of interpretation relevant to this study. For a complete history and evaluation the reader is referred to the more extensive commentaries, introductions, and the article of A. Feuillet, "Les diverses méthodes d'interprétation de l'Apocalypse . . .," AmiDuCl 71 (April 27, 1961) 257–270. The labels attached to the five different systems summarized here indicate emphasis; obviously, these systems have much in common.

Recapitulation. This method goes back to *Victorinus of Pettau (martyred under Diocletian); it was adopted by Tyconius, Augustine, and other commentators, medieval and modern. In its most developed form, that of E. B. *Allo, it may be summarized thus: the septenaries of the seals (6.1–8.1) and the trumpets (8.2–9.21) describe the future of the world from the glorification of Christ to the Last Judgment, mentioned as early as 11.15–18, with emphasis upon world events. The section 12.1–21.8 covers the same period, but centering on the role of the Church. The millennium describes the same period from another viewpoint (20. 1–15), and even the description of the heavenly Jerusalem (21.1–22.5), though it offers a transcendent image of the Church, takes in the Church both on earth and in heaven, under the regime of grace as well as of glory.

While there is much truth in this reading of Apocalypse, the evidence of chronological progression rules out the sweeping nature of Allo's parallelism. It seems true, nevertheless, that while alluding to specific events of his time and of the past and predicting the future to the end of the world, John has in mind some succession of events, which he sees, perhaps, less as individual facts than as "laws" that mark God's dealing with mankind and the Church through all ages.

World History. *Joachim of Fiore (d. 1201) popularized the system that sees in the septenaries of Apocalypse seven periods in the history of the Church; *Nicholas of Lyra (d. 1340) systematized this exegesis and gave it a stricter chronology. Again and again, in various forms, it has been proposed, even in modern times, especially in popularizations. Because it was based upon a misunderstanding of prophecy and of the apocalyptic genre, it has had to be revised and corrected whenever events belied previous conclusions drawn from it.

Eschatological. The originator of this interpretation was Francisco de *Ribera, whose commentary appeared in 1591; it has been called the beginning of scientific study of Apocalypse. Ribera held that only the first five seals refer to the primitive Church down to the reign of Trajan. The last seals and the rest of the book have to do with the end-time. Since then this system has been favored by many commentators, some of whom assume that John thought the Parousia near and did not reckon with the possibility of a long future for the Church.

Historicizing. To some extent this method is at opposite poles from the eschatological. Inaugurated by J. Henten in the middle of the 16th century, it holds that at least part of Apocalypse refers to contemporary or past events. Henten interpreted ch. 6–11 as referring to the abrogation of Judaism, ch. 12–19 as referring to the destruction of paganism. Modern proponents of this view differ in regard to the amount of contemporary or past material they find in Apocalypse.

Liturgical. John intended his work to be read in the liturgical service of the churches (1.3). Apocalypse is admittedly full of references and allusions both to the liturgy of the OT and to the Christian Eucharistic service. John receives his inaugural vision on a Sunday, possibly during the liturgical service. He is invited up to heaven (ch. 4), where a cosmic service of praise and adoration takes place that is reminiscent of OT inaugural visions (cf. Isaia ch. 6, where the vision takes place in the Temple, and Ezechiel ch. 1–3) as well as the Christian service (the throne of the bishop surrounded by the 24 elders suggesting the sanctuary setting of the ancient Eucharistic service). The description of the heavenly Jerusalem (ch. 20–21) is also cast in liturgical forms. Again, the hymns scattered throughout Apocalypse are probably echoes of Christian hymns at the seer's time. That the structure of Apocalypse itself was modeled upon the early liturgy has been argued by M. H. Shepherd, *The Paschal Liturgy and the Apocalypse, Ecumenical Studies in Worship* 6 (Richmond, Va. 1960).

Bibliography: A. FEUILLET, *L'Apocalypse: État de la question* (Bruges 1963), introductory problems to date and thorough bibliog. E. B. ALLO, *Saint Jean: L'Apocalypse* (3d ed. Paris 1933); DBSuppl 1:306–325. R. H. CHARLES, *A Critical and Exegetical Commentary on the Revelation of St. John,* 2 v. (ICC; New York 1920). E. LOHSE, *Die Offenbarung des Johannes* (Das Neue Testament Deutsch 11; 8th ed. Göttingen 1960). S. GIET, *L'Apocalypse et l'histoire* (Paris 1957). A. ROMEO, EncCatt 1:1600–14. J. MICHL, LexThK[2] 1:690–696. O. A. PIPER et al., RGG[3] 3:822–836. EncDictBibl 104–110. **Illustration credits:** Figs. 1 and 2, Hirmer Verlag München.

[E. F. SIEGMAN]

APOCALYPSE, ICONOGRAPHY OF

The Apocalypse of St. John the Apostle, last book of the New Testament, has been a rich source of subjects for art, especially in the early Christian and medieval periods. The abundant symbolism has yielded, through commentary and interpretation, such major themes as the Christ in Majesty (*Majestas Domini*) and the Adoration of the Lamb in addition to a large number of other figural subjects. Verse by verse, the Apocalypse is one of the most thoroughly illustrated books of the Bible.

Early Christian. The visions of the Apocalypse appeared on the triumphal arches of the basilicas of Rome to exalt the triumph of Christ and His Church after the persecutions (432–440, S. Maria Maggiore). The theophany of the adoration of the Lamb by the 24 Elders was represented (5th-century mosaic, St. Paul-Outside-the-Walls), as well as that of the Lamb enthroned between the seven lamps "which are the seven Spirits of God" (Ap 4.5). These important themes were repeated in Carolingian illumination (the Elders in the Evangeliary of St-Médard of Soissons and the Codex aureus of 870) and in later periods of Christian art. The Venerable Bede tells in the *Lives of the Abbots* (ch. 6) that Benedict Biscop brought back from Rome images from the Apocalypse of St. John for the decoration of the abbey church of St. Peter at Wearmouth. These images were copies made after Roman frescoes.

Early Medieval. In North Africa the visions of St. John found early commentators, such as Tertullian and St. Cyprian. The enthusiasm for the Apocalypse, rendered more pathetic by the persecutions of the Christians under the Vandal occupation, reached Visigothic Spain. There it became sanctioned by the 17th canon of the Council of Toledo (633). The 12 books of commentaries on the Apocalypse written by Beatus of Liébana (d. 798) were recopied until the 15th century. Twenty-four manuscripts of the illustrated text still bear witness to their fame (MSS 429 and 644; Pierpont Morgan Library, New York City). Three capitals in the church of St. Mary at Fleury were inspired by Spanish models in an illuminated Beatus commentary. They show the Son of Man in the midst of the seven candlesticks, the Four Horsemen, and the Dragon put in chains and thrust down to the abyss.

Romanesque. The influence of the Beatus manuscripts is detectible on Romanesque sculpture of southern France. In the tympanum of the porch of St. Peter at Moissac, the 24 Elders raise their crowned heads toward the vision of a colossal Christ. He is crowned (Ap 12.10) and enthroned amidst a complex pattern of the Four Animals and two six-winged Seraphs. The tympanum of Moissac represents essentially the diffusion of the *Majestas Domini.* The theophany of the *Majestas,* a theme first created for the decoration of the apses, was transferred in the 11th century to the front of the churches, as a sign of holiness and salvation. The façade of the church, being turned toward the setting sun, designated the place where the assize of the Last Judgment was anticipated.

As a revival of the Carolingian style within a Romanesque environment, an outstanding series of frescoes was painted at the end of the 11th century in

Fig. 1. The Lamb enthroned between the seven candlesticks and angels, detail of the 6th-century mosaic on the face of the arch of the apse of the basilica of SS. Cosmas and Damian, Rome.

Fig. 2. The Dragon and his angels are overcome by Michael and his angels (Ap 12), two-page illumination in a MS of Beatus of Liébana written and illuminated in Spain in 1220 (Morgan MS 429, fol. 31v and 32r).

ICONOGRAPHY OF THE APOCALYPSE

Fig. 3. Miniature illustrating Ap 6.9–11 in the 13th-century "Dublin Apocalypse" at Trinity College, Dublin.

Fig. 4. St. John seeing a vision of the Son of Man (Ap 1.13–16), fresco, c. 1350, in the Papal Palace, Avignon.

the porch under the western tower of the church of Saint-Savin-sur-Gartempe. These frescoes illustrate the Second Coming of Christ, accompanied by the Apostles and adored by angels, who bend in the attitude of the proskynesis. Twelve scenes encompass the *Majestas,* illustrating: the swarm of locusts appearing like battle horses (Ap 9.7); the release of the four angels imprisoned by the Euphrates (9.14–15); the Woman attacked by the Dragon; the war fought by Michael and the Angels against the Dragon (12); and the new Jerusalem sent down by God from heaven, clothed like a bride adorned to meet her husband (21.2).

In the *Hortus Deliciarum* of Herrade de Landsberg (*c.* 1180) we find the unique representation of God wiping away the tears from the eyes of His own people and emphasis laid on the deeds of antichrist in nine illustrations, an emphasis derived from St. Augustine's *De Civitate Dei.* The influence of the Byzantine iconography of the Last Judgment and of Greek art is obvious in the *Hortus Deliciarum.* The dragon with seven heads is named *eptazephalus* after the Greek. The throne prepared for the Judgment—the Etimasia of Byzantine art—was interpreted as the altar above "the souls of those who had been slain for the word of God" (6.9).

Gothic. In the monumental art of the High Gothic period, the representations of the Apocalypse disappeared from the tympanum of the portals. The radiant vision of the 24 Elders occupies the rose window in the south transept of Chartres cathedral. Apocalyptic cycles were carved in the voussoirs of the archivolts of the Last Judgment portals of the cathedrals of Paris and Amiens, where the Four Horsemen and the torments in hell are prominent.

The inexhaustible attraction that the Apocalypse exerted as a source of grandiose imagery is exemplified in a series of English or Franco-English manuscripts of the 13th and the early 14th century. They continue the early Christian tradition of manuscript illustration that was transmitted by Italy to Gaul. The earliest and perhaps most beautiful English Gothic Apocalypse is that of Trinity College, illustrated around 1230 at St. Albans. This and other manuscripts of its type were decorated splendidly for royal and aristocratic patrons, most of them English. A few are only picture books, with legends in Latin or French accompanying the illuminations; they incorporate the life of St. John at the beginning and his death at the end, both series of episodes being based on the 2d-century apocryphal Acts of John. They include a sequence of illustrations picturing the miracles and final overthrow of the antichrist. The importance granted to the antichrist was later to be echoed in the frescoes of the Last Judgment with apocalyptic overtones, painted after 1500 by Signorelli in the cathedral of Orvieto.

The monumentality inherent in the Apocalyptic visions was fully realized in the tapestries woven in Paris on the looms of Nicolas Bataille from 1375 to 1381 for Duke Louis of Anjou. The cartoons provided by Jean Bondol of Bruges copied the illuminations of various manuscripts of the Channel school. The original tapestry for the château of Angers was made up of 7 pieces, each divided into 14 subjects arranged in 7 pairs, with backgrounds alternately blue and red and introduced by an enraptured reader, sitting under a canopy. The 7 readers, who are as tall as the height of the tapestry, may symbolize the seven Churches of Asia (1.11). The gigantic cycle of Angers included 98 scenes and was 800 square meters when intact.

Only faded remains of Cimabue's frescoes—the opening of the seals, the angels holding the winds, and the fall of Babylon—remain in the upper church at Assisi. But the Apocalyptic frescoes incorporated by Giusto de' Menabuoi in the encyclopedic program of paintings in the baptistery at Padua (1375–78) are particularly important because they are related to the Pentecost in the choir and also to the "great multitude which no man could number" (7.9) displayed in the cupola, illustrating the theme of All Saints. In the oldest Italian tradition, Ap 7.9 was read on Pentecost, but the evocation of the Great Multitude was shifted to All Saints' Day. The immense east window in the choir of York Minster was filled by John Thornton of Coventry (1405–08) with 1,700 square feet of painted glass that developed a program second in scope only to that of Padua, since it includes 27 panels illustrating the Old Testament and 81 depicting 90 scenes of the Apocalypse.

In the polyptych by Jan and Hubert van *Eyck at St. Bavon, Ghent (1432), the vision of the Heavenly Jerusalem descended in the form of a reredos upon the altar itself. Open, it shows in the upper section the world of transcendence: a Deesis, in which the Virgin and St. John are enthroned in glory as Christ's first elect, and musicians, who are symbols of the 44,000, singing and playing on their harps (Apocalypse, ch. 14). Below, a flowering meadow introduces the world of immanence in the Adoration of the Lamb. Around the Lamb, who sheds His blood on the altar amidst angels proffering the trophies of the death and Resurrection of Christ, are assembled eight groups: the martyrs and the virgins nearest to the altar; in the foreground, the patriarchs and Prophets, the Apostles and confessors, to the left and right of the fountain of life; on the wings, the just judges, the knights, the hermits and, finally, the pilgrims. These eight groups represent the Beatitudes, in keeping with the Gospel read on All Saints' Day. The core of the iconography, which is the "choir of the blessed in the sacrifice of the Lamb," as the painting is entitled in a document of 1458, corresponds to the reading of Ap 9.2–12 on November 1. The adoration of the Lamb by all the saints received its visual expression as a result of the liturgy adopted in 835 for All Saints' Day.

Renaissance and Modern. From the 15th century on, the chief medium of the illustration of the Apocalypse was the woodcut. *Dürer published his Apocalypse himself, both in Latin and German, in 1498. This great artist condensed the Apocalypse into 14 woodcuts. What was fundamentally new in Dürer's Apocalypse was the individual and polemical approach, the material aspect of the pamphlet that he conveyed through his work. This was soon to inspire the Protestant iconography of the Apocalypse originated in Wittenberg by Luther and Cranach in 1522. Through the Wittenberg New Testament the imagery of Dürer was carried to Lutheran Bibles illustrated by Burgkmair, Schaüfelein, Hans *Holbein the Younger (1523), Erhard Altdorfer (1533–34), and Martin Schaffner (1534). On the Catholic side, his influence was felt in Bibles edited by Martin l'Empereur (Antwerp 1530) and Sebastian Gryphius (Lyons 1541). The woodcuts

Fig. 5. Sounding the second trumpet (Ap 8.8), detail of the "Angers Tapestry," c. 1375–81, Town Hall, Angers, France.

ICONOGRAPHY OF THE APOCALYPSE

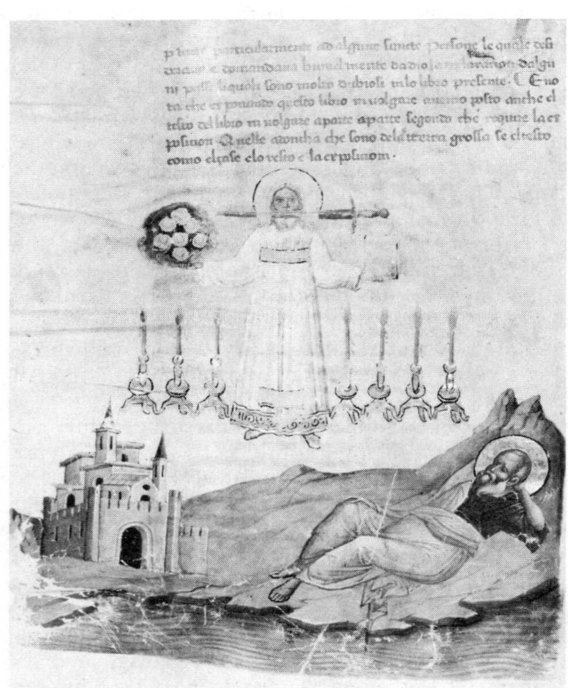

Fig. 6. St. John's vision of the Son of Man (Ap. 1.13), miniature in a MS of Federicus de Venetus's "Literalis expositio super Apocalypsim," written on Crete, Oct. 10, 1415 (Walters MS 335, fol. 1v).

Fig. 7. Satan cast into the abyss (Ap 20.3), woodcut by the German artist Albrecht Dürer, 1498.

of Dürer, reinterpreted in the formal idiom of the school of Fontainebleau, gave birth to the magnificent series of Apocalyptic windows in the chapel of the château of Vincennes (1558).

Paradoxically enough, Dürer's Apocalypse, or a set of illustrations inspired by him, was used as a model book in the first apocalyptic cycle painted in Byzantine art at the Dionysiou monastery on Mt. Athos in 1547. In Byzantium the Apocalypse was not accepted as a canonical book before the 12th century. The contribution of Byzantine art to the iconography of the Apocalypse is late and remained derivative. The Elizabeth Day McCormick Apocalypse in Chicago illustrates 69 subjects of an early 17th-century translation of the Apocalypse into vernacular Greek.

The tragic events of the mid-20th century surrounding World War II have inspired moving interpretations of the Apocalypse in the graphic arts by E. Georg (1943), G. de Pogedaïeff (1947–50), A. Collot (1952), G. de Chirico (1952), and H. de Waroquier (1955). The medieval cycle of Angers was emulated by Jean Lurçat in the great tapestry that decorates the apse of Notre-Dame-de-Toute-Grâce at *Assy (1947–48), showing the vision of the Dragon pursuing the "Woman that wore the sun for her mantel" and bore a Son (Apocalypse, ch. 12).

Bibliography: For an essential treatment see F. Van der Meer, *Maiestas Domini: Théophanies de l'Apocalypse dans l'art chrétien* (Paris 1938), extensive bibliog. H. L. Ramsay, "Manuscripts of the Commentary of Beatus of Liébana on the Apocalypse," *Revue des bibliothèques* 12 (1902) 74–103. C. Schelenberg, *Dürers Apokalypse* (Munich 1923). H. C. Hoskier, *Concerning the Text of the Apocalypse,* 2 v. (London 1929). M. R. James, ed., *The Dublin Apocalypse* (Cambridge, Mass. 1932). I. Yoshikawa, *L'Apocalypse de Saint-Savin* (Paris 1939). H. R. Willoughby and E. C. Colwell, *The Elizabeth Day McCormick Apocalypse,* 2 v. (Chicago 1940). E. A. Van Moé, *L'Apocalypse de Saint-Sever* (Paris 1943). J. Croquison, "Une Vision eschatologique carolingienne," *Cahiers archéologiques* 4 (1949) 105–129. R. Planchenault, "L'Apocalypse d'Angers: Éléments pour un nouvel essai de restitution," *Bulletin monumental* 111 (1953) 209–262. P. Coremans, *Van Eyck: L'Adoration de l'Agneau* (new ed. Anvers 1951). J. Lurçat, *L'Apocalypse d'Angers* (Angers 1955). Réau IAC 2.2:663–726. Aurenhammer LexChrist Ikon. **Illustration credit:** Fig. 1, Anderson-Art Reference Bureau. Fig. 2, The Pierpont Morgan Library, New York City. Fig. 3, Green Studio Limited, Dublin. Figs. 4 and 5, Archives Photographiques, Paris. Fig. 6, Courtesy of the Walters Art Gallery, Baltimore. Fig. 7, National Gallery of Art, Washington, D.C., Rosenwald Collection.

[P. VERDIER]

APOCALYPTIC

A Biblical style of writing that developed during the Exile (587–538 B.C.) and especially the postexilic age. The term is derived from the Greek verb ἀποκαλύπτω, meaning to unveil. The apocalyptists wrote as though they had received a vision involving God's cosmic kingdom and His eschatological battle to establish it. Almost every earthly element acquired symbolic value: parts of the human body, animals, colors, clothing, and numbers; for God was utilizing everything for His world triumph. Angels acted as mediators not only of the revelation, but particularly of its explanation. Finally, the authors usually wrote in the name of personages of the distant past; thus, under the literary form of a vision granted centuries earlier, they actually described contemporary scenes.

Apocalyptic evolved out of an earlier prophetic style of preaching. A historical study of the development of prophecy into apocalyptic not only explains the origin but also the dominant features of apocalyptic. The development can be observed in the three periods of OT history: (1) the late preexilic, (2) the exilic, and (3) the postexilic age.

Late Preexilic Age. The weird symbolism of apocalyptic had its roots in the events and reactions of the last 60 years before the Babylonian exile, which began in 587 B.C. The colossal Assyrian empire was collapsing. In 22 years it plunged from a peak of extravagant glory and terrifying ruthlessness to the depths of total destruction. Nations shuddered at such swift reversals. They began to write official documents, as in Babylon, in ancient scripts and long-forgotten languages, and in many ways people revived religious traditions and practices of hoary origin.

This almost haunting return to ancient customs and accounts showed up in Jerusalem in the *Deuteronomic reform of King Josia (*c.* 640–609 B.C.). The Biblical books of Josue, Judges, Samuel, and Kings were redacted, and their Deuteronomist author recognized in the accumulation of early stories, folklore, and liturgy a pattern of action repeated over and over again in history: sin brings suffering; suffering induces compunction; compunction moves God to send deliverance (Jgs 2.6–3.6). Deuteronomy used these early traditions to actualize faith in the present moment (Dt 5.1–5).

In a somewhat different way the Prophets of this final period before the exile thundered doom and destruction upon sin. Sophonia (Zephaniah) and Nahum both cried out that a *Day of the Lord was to strike Israel with almost annihilating force (Sophonia) and to sweep aside all opposition from foreigners (Nahum). The Prophet *Jeremia stressed the cosmic impact of Israel's sins (Jer 2.12; 4.23–36; 5.22–23). In this account of preexilic Israel only those details are highlighted that later become united in apocalyptic: reappearance of ancient personages and events; cosmic and agonizing battles between God and wickedness; and victory's emerging out of the sorrowful effects of sin.

Exilic Age. The Babylonian Exile (587–538 B.C.) destroyed all the external forms of religious and civil life, almost everything that seemed of utmost importance to Israel. Two prophets—*Ezechiel (Ezekiel) and Deutero-Isaia (author of Isaia ch. 40–55)—then pointed out what was truly at the heart of existence: faith in God, who is personally interested in His chosen people, who is adamant against evil, and who will secure His world kingdom.

Ezechiel is of special interest here in the development of prophecy into apocalyptic. He made a free, extravagant use of symbolism (ch. 1–3; 40–48); his word pictures defy imagination just as the explosive destruction of the Exile did. *See* EZECHIEL (EZEKIEL), BOOK OF. The mystery of God's promised kingdom breaks the bonds of reasoning and picturing. Ezechiel not only spoke but acted apocalyptically (5.1–5; 12.6, 11; 24.24, 27). By his concern over the priestly traditions within the Pentateuch (*see* PRIESTLY WRITERS, PENTATEUCHAL) Ezechiel may have been responsible for preserving accounts that later apocalyptists generously used, such as the creation story, Henoch and other patriarchal figures, and Noe (Noah) and the Flood.

Postexilic Age. During the postexilic age, from the return of the first Jewish exiles to the first half of the 2d Christian century, apocalyptic writing completely replaced the older prophetic style. There are only a few exceptions, such as parts of Zacharia (ch. 7–8) and of Malachia [*see* ZACHARIA (ZECHARIAH), BOOK OF; MALACHIA (MALACHI), BOOK OF]; but even in these cases the Prophets were subservient to the priest, a situation that had hardly been true of the preexilic Prophets. In Joel, for instance, trumpet blasts and locust plague proclaim the Day of the Lord, but the writer calls not for social reform but for fasting and liturgical prayer (ch. 1–2; *see* JOEL, BOOK OF). The liturgy suddenly expands into the outpouring of the Spirit with "blood, fire and columns of smoke" (ch. 3) and a terrifying judgment upon the nations of the world (ch. 4).

The great persecution of 167 to 164 B.C., when *Antiochus IV Epiphanes, the Seleucid king of Antioch, attempted to suppress Jewish national identity in Palestine, brought forth the most complete form of OT apocalyptic, the Book of *Daniel. The first six chapters of the book are probably a haggadic reediting of early stories (*see* HAGGADAH), some of which originated as far back as the Exile. Chapters 7 to 12 show all the major trends of apocalyptic: visions explained by the angel Gabriel; a pseudonym of a hero of the Babylonian Exile; a flamboyant concoction of clashing and fearful images; catastrophic suffering; and the sudden appearance of a glorious cosmic victory for Yahweh. The author seeks to sustain the faith of his persecuted coreligionists by assuring them that God will quickly reverse their sorrows with eschatological triumph.

Apocalyptic continued in Judaism among the *Pharisees and the members of the *Qumran community. It seems, however, that after the devastation of Jerusalem in A.D. 70 and again after the suppression of the revolt of *Bar Kokhba in A.D. 136, *Judaism gave up its apocalyptic hopes and settled down as the people of the Torah, devoted to the careful study and punctilious fulfillment of the Law.

Christianity inherited the apocalyptic; and, in fact, the last NT book, the Book of *Apocalypse, like the Book of Daniel, is one of the finest examples of this literary form. Jesus used the apocalyptic style (Mark ch. 15), and the Apostles after the Resurrection did likewise (1 and 2 Thessalonians). Soon, however, the tendency set in of seeing apocalyptic hopes already realized in Jesus' presence, in the gift of the Spirit, and in the liturgy (Romans and Gospel of St. John). Christians, however, still looked forward to a new heaven and a new earth (2 Peter), when sorrow would be totally removed (Romans ch. 8) and the fullness of the Godhead revealed (Ephesians and Colossians). Then would apocalyptic hopes be satisfied, and vision and symbol be turned into reality.

See also FORM CRITICISM, BIBLICAL.

Bibliography: S. B. FROST, *O.T. Apocalyptic: Its Origin and Growth* (London 1952). H. H. ROWLEY, *The Relevance of Apocalyptic* (3d ed. New York 1964). R. H. CHARLES et al., eds., *The Apocrypha and Pseudepigrapha of the O.T. in English,* 2 v. (Oxford 1913); *Religious Development Between the Old and the New Testaments* (New York 1914). M. J. LAGRANGE, *Le Judaïsme avant Jésus-Christ* (ÉtBibl; 1931). D. S. RUSSELL, *Between the Testaments* (Philadelphia 1960). O. PLÖGER, *Theokratie und Eschatologie* (2d ed. Neukirchen 1962). J. BLOCH, *On the Apocalyptic in Judaism* (Philadelphia 1952). J. B. FREY, DBSuppl 1:326–354. F. J. SCHIERSE, LexThK² 1:704–705. A. ROMEO, EncCatt 1:1615–26. H. RINGGREN and R. SCHÜTZ, RGG³ 1:464–469. J. SICKENBERGER, ReallexAntChr 1:504–510. EncDict Bibl 110–111.

[C. STUHLMUELLER]

APOCALYPTIC MOVEMENTS

Trends toward revolutionary eschatology, which foresee the return of Christ as imminent. Deriving sustenance from Ezechiel, Daniel, and the Book of Revelation, these movements keep alive messianic hopes and emphasize the prophetic note. Often vigorously individualistic in character, they attempt to identify the *Antichrist, prepare through militant asceticism for the impending end of the world and the *Parousia, or second coming of Christ, and indulge in visionary expectation. Socioeconomic grievances may often guide such chiliastic exaltation (*see* CHILIASM) and sharpen an ethic built on penitence and voluntary poverty.

It is convenient to treat these movements in three periods: early Christian, high and late Middle Ages, and modern. The emergence of the visible church was accompanied by the formation of such Judeo-Christian sects as the *Ebionites (poor men). As a protest against growing institutionalism and secularization of the Church, the *Montanists appeared in Phrygia in the second half of the 2d century and spread to North Africa, where they attracted the sympathetic attention of *Tertullian. While reaction to relaxed discipline and externalism fostered the primitivism of the apostolic Church, political failure fed millenarian hopes (*see* MILLENARIANISM). By the 4th century this eschatological and chiliastic stream receded, only to reappear in periods of religious and social unrest. In the medieval period crusades, war, pestilence, social instability, and clerical delinquency created the environment from which the flagellants (*see* FLAGELLATION) sprang in the 13th and 14th centuries. Apocalyptic literature was given fresh impetus by *Joachim of Fiore (*c.* 1130–1202), Cistercian abbot, hermit, and founder of the stricter Cistercian monastery of S. Giovanni in Fiore (Calabria). He proclaimed the imminent coming of the kingdom of the Spirit. Essential to Joachimism was the unfolding of history through three successive stages: the Age of the Father (OT), the Age of the Son (NT to 1260), and the Age of the Holy Spirit (since 1260). This ascent leads to a vision that can be identified with the "everlasting gospel" to be preached to all peoples in the Last Days. Although hierarchy and Sacraments will disappear, monasticism as the essence of the primitive Church will become the vehicle of the new age. Such ideas were especially potent among the Franciscan *Spirituals, the **Fraticelli,* and the disciples of Fra *Dolcino. In 1254 Gerard of Borgo San Donnino completed Joachim's blueprint by proclaiming the *Evangelium aeternum* which would supersede both Testaments. If Emperor *Frederick II served as the object of eschatological expectation in the 13th century, this apocalyptic literature found, in the political and religious scene, conditions congenial to the later visions of *Cola di Rienzo, the Bohemian *Taborites, and *Savonarola. Since the 16th century the apocalyptic stream has been represented chiefly by a segment of the Radical Reformation: *Anabaptists and *Seventh-day Adventists. In the English civil war of the mid-17th century, Fifth Monarchy Men kept alive chiliastic dreams.

Bibliography: N. R. C. COHN, *The Pursuit of the Millenium* (London 1957). A. DEMPF, *Sacrum Imperium* (2d ed. Darmstadt 1954). D. L. DOUIE, *The Nature and the Effect of the Heresy of the Fraticelli* (Manchester, Eng. 1932). H. GRUNDMANN, *Studien* *über Joachim von Floris* (Leipzig 1927). R. M. JONES, *Spiritual Reformers in the 16th and 17th Centuries* (Boston 1914; repr. pa. 1959). E. ANAGNINE, *Dolcino e il movimento ereticale all'inizio del trecento* (Florence 1964).

[E. W. MC DONNELL]

APOCATASTASIS, name from the Greek of Acts 3.21 (ἀποκατάστασις) given to the doctrine of the ultimate salvation of all rational creatures. As it is expounded in the *De Principiis* by Origen, its most influential early exponent, it is the claim that all punishment, whether in this world or in the next, is educative and is therefore not eternal. Apocatastasis was condemned by the Synod of Constantinople in 543 (Denz 411). Numbered among its early adherents were St. Gregory of Nyssa, Didymus of Alexandria, and Evagrius of Ponticus. Since the Reformation it has had supporters among Anabaptists, Moravians, Christadelphians, and Universalists. Followers of Friedrich *Schleiermacher (1768–1834), who based religion on feeling, gave a renewed emphasis to the doctrine in modern times.

Bibliography: Cross ODCC 67. J. LOOSEN, LexThK² 1:708–712. C. ANDRESEN and P. ALTHAUS, RGG³ 6:1693–96. J. DANIÉLOU, *Origen,* tr. W. MITCHELL (New York 1955).

[A. D. TURNEY]

APOCRISIARIUS, a Byzantine diplomatic term for the representative of a civil, military, or ecclesiastical governor at another headquarters or court. The Latin term was *responsalis,* or one bringing an answer; and the word referred primarily to the representatives of the pope, metropolitan bishoprics, or monasteries in Constantinople, although it was employed also of ecclesiastical representatives at other patriarchates or metropolitan sees. Bishop Julian of Cos served as an *apocrisiarius,* at Constantinople, for Pope *Leo I (440–461); while the patriarch of Alexandria had had an official representative there since the beginning of the 5th century. *Anatolius became patriarch of Constantinople (449–458) after serving as the Alexandrian *apocrisiarius* for the Patriarch Dioscorus. John the Scholastic had served as *apocrisiarius* for Antioch before being selected patriarch of Constantinople (565–577) by Justinian I. Rome recalled its *apocrisiarius* from Constantinople at the beginning of the Acacian Schism (484), but was represented intermittently during the reign of Emperor *Anastasius I. A permanent *apocrisiarius* seems to have taken office with the appointment of the deacon (543), later Pope Pelagius I. Pope *Gregory I, while a deacon, had served in Constantinople as the papal *apocrisiarius* (579–585). The representative of the patriarch at the imperial court in Constantinople was known as the *referendarius.* At the court of *Charlemagne, the term was applied to the ecclesiastic who served as spiritual adviser to the king, and not infrequently it was applied also to the papal representative.

Bibliography: J. PARGOIRE, DACL 1.2:2537–55. A. EMEREAU, ÉchosOr 17 (1914) 289–297, 542–548. R. GUILLAND, RevÉtByz 5 (1947) 90–100. Beck KTLBR 103. A. BAUS, LexThK² 1:712. O. TREITINGER, ReallexAntChr 1:501–504. M. JUGIE, *Catholicisme* 1:694.

[F. X. MURPHY]

APOCRYPHA, ICONOGRAPHY OF THE. From late Hellenistic times through the medieval period, apocryphal literature constantly provided artists with rich sources of iconography. As a source of iconography the apocrypha of the New Testament is of much greater importance than that of the Old Testament. Of the Old Testament apocrypha, *Ascensio Jesaiae* is the only book known today to have been used as an iconographical source. It is assumed that there existed a certain number of narrative cycles on deuterocanonical literature of Hellenistic Jewish origin from the late Hellenistic period.

In early Christianity artists used the apocryphal New Testament literature to complete narrative cycles of the lives of Christ, the Virgin Mary, the Apostles and other saints, since canonical books gave artists only imperfect information about the lives of these important figures. The influence of apocryphal New Testament literature is most conspicuous in the following cycles: (1) The life of Christ. For the Nativity and the Infancy, the *Protoevangelium Jacobi* and the *Evangelium Pseudo-Matthaei* are the main sources for themes such as the Birth in the Mountain Cave, Two Midwives, the Animals by the Manger, etc. The *Evangelium Infantiae Salvatoris arabicum* as well as the *Gospel of St. Thomas* provides supplementary information about the Nativity and the Infancy, such as the Star of Angels and the occurrence of early miracles. The Bathing of the Infant Christ in the Nativity scene is a borrowing from pagan birth scenes. There are two sources for the apocryphal details of the Passion and the *Descent of Christ into Hell: the *Gospel of Bartholomew* and the *Gospel of Nicodemus* (*Acta Pilati*). (2) The life of the Virgin. The *Protoevangelium Jacobi* is again the most important source for the life of the Virgin in reference to Joachim and Anna, the Nativity of the Virgin, the Presentation of the Virgin, the Engagement, and the Annunciation. For the last part of her life, the *De transitu Beatae Mariae Virginis* attributed to Melito of Sardis is the main source. (3) The lives of Apostles. There are several apocryphal books of the Acts of the Apostles, e.g., *Acts of Paul, Acts of Peter, Acts of Andreas,* etc. They are the principal sources of the miraculous deeds and martyrdoms of the Apostles as well as the source of their portraits [Peter and Simon Magnus, Martyrdom of Peter (*Quo vadis, Domine*), etc.]. Illus., following page.

See also BIBLE, III (CANON) 4, 5.

Bibliography: E. B. SMITH, *Early Christian Iconography* (Princeton 1918). *Reallexikon zur deutschen Kunstgeschichte,* ed. O. SCHMITT, v.1 (Stuttgart 1937) 781–801. K. WESSEL, ed., *Reallexikon zur byzantinischen Kunst,* v.1 (Stuttgart 1963) 1: 209–218. **Illustration credit:** The University of Glasgow, Scotland.

[S. TSUJI]

APOLLINARIANISM

A 4th-century Christological heresy that denied the human soul in Christ. It received its name from Apollinaris, Bishop of Laodicea, who had been a champion of Nicene orthodoxy and a friend of St. *Athanasius of Alexandria. Apollinarianism signalized the point of transition from the Trinitarian to the Christological heresies.

Its principal thesis was a result of the anti-Arian polemic of Apollinaris, but in attempting to defend the divinity of the Word, he actually accepted the Arian postulate minimizing the human nature in Christ (*c.* 352). In his zeal to preserve the humanity of Christ, and his lack of a distinction between the concept of nature and person, Apollinaris relied on the Platonic trichotomy of the human being: body, sensitive soul, and rationality (σάρξ, ψυχὴ σαρκική, and ψυχὴ λογική).

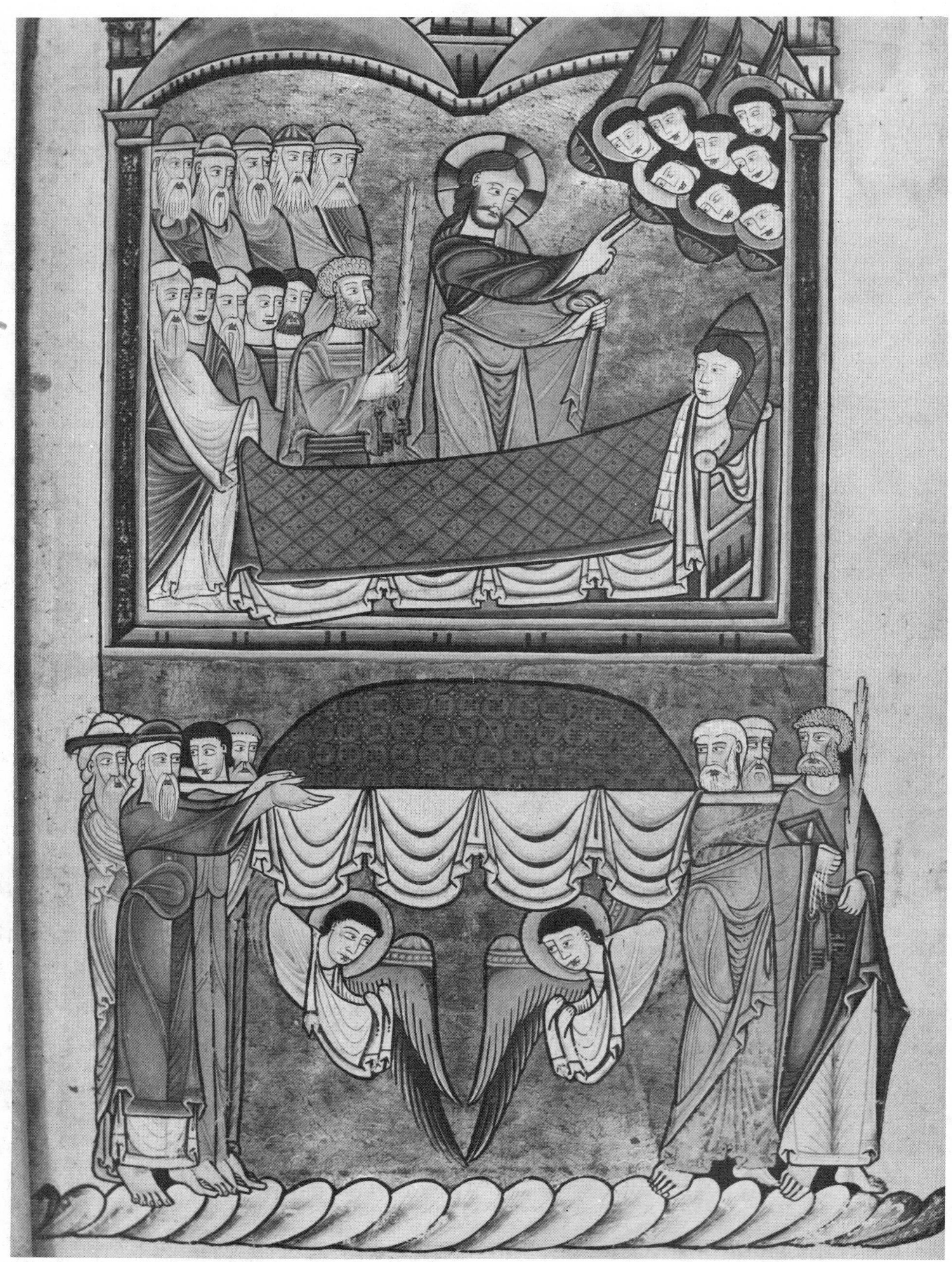

The death and funeral procession of the Virgin, miniature illustrating a portion of the "De transitu Beatae Mariae Virginis," in the 12th-century "York Psalter" preserved in the library of the Hunterian Museum, Glasgow.

In his literal interpretation of the Johannine text "The Word became Flesh," Apollinaris believed that he had found the key to the solution of the Christological problem. He taught that (1) if one does not admit a diminution of the human nature in Christ, the unity of Christ cannot be explained, since two complete natures cannot constitute one unique entity; (2) where there exists a complete man, sin exists, since sin resides in the will, that is, in man's spirit, for free will and sin are interdependent; hence Christ's being exempt from sin cannot be explained if he had a human spirit in the Incarnate Word; and (3) the Word of God did not assume a complete human nature, but only a body (σάρξ) and what is strictly connected with the body, the sensitive soul. The Word itself has taken the part of the spirit of man, or the rational soul (νοῦς). Only thus can one speak of "one sole nature incarnate of the Word of God" (μία φύσις τοῦ λόγου τοῦ θεοῦ σεσαρκωμένη). This formula is found in Apollinaris' *Incarnation of the Word of God,* which is frequently interpolated among the works of St. Athanasius.

As intended by Apollinaris, the sentence cannot have an orthodox meaning, but since it was reputedly accepted by St. Athanasius, St. *Cyril of Alexandria, in his polemic against *Nestorianism, gave it an orthodox interpretation. After the Council of *Ephesus, however, it was accepted by *Eutyches and *Dioscorus of Alexandria in a strictly Monophysitic sense, and by Sergius of Constantinople with a Monoenergetic and Monothelite meaning. Apollinarianism appears in the history of Christian dogma as a heresy more disturbing in its consequences in the long perspective than in its immediate effects.

Examined first in the Synod of Alexandria in 362, the doctrine of Apollinaris was condemned on the principle common in Oriental theology that "that which is not assumed [by the Divine word] is not healed." Hence if the Logos had not assumed a rational soul, the redemption would be inefficacious as regards human souls. This condemnation was formulated in a delicate manner, not mentioning the name of Apollinaris. But his position was definitively compromised when his disciple Vitalis, after the *Meletian schism (362), founded an Apollinarian party at Antioch (375). Vitalis at first deceived Pope *Damasus I, but in a Synod of 377, on the basis of further information, the Pope admonished Vitalis to reject Apollinarianism and called for the deposition of Apollinaris and the bishops infected with his heresy.

Apollinaris gave final definition to his ideas in his *Demonstration of the Divine Incarnation* (376), answered the papal condemnation by consecrating Vitalis a bishop for his sect in Antioch, and helped his follower Timotheus to become bishop of Berytus. But neither these measures nor the attempt to spread his teaching among the Egyptian bishops exiled by the Emperor Valens to Diocaesarea succeeded.

The Roman Synod's decision was confirmed by Synods of Alexandria (378), and Antioch (379), and the General Council of *Constantinople I (381). It was reconfirmed by Damasus' Roman Council in 382. Thereupon the Emperor *Theodosius I intervened with decrees in 383, 384, and 388, outlawing the Apollinarists and sending their major representatives into exile. But the imperial decrees did not succeed, and the heresy was well received among many Orientals. However, it did not long survive its originator who died in 390.

Toward 420 the schismatic community was reabsorbed into the Catholic Church, although a group of intransigents, called Sinusiati, finished later by joining the Monophysite movement, with whom they had a theological affinity.

The dogmatic writings in which Apollinaris exposed his doctrine have been handed down as having other authorship than his: *Profession of Faith,* among the works of St. Athanasius, and a letter to the presbyter Dionysius, under the name of Pope *Julius I. His principal work *Demonstratio Incarnationis divinae* is known mainly through its refutation in the writings of St. *Gregory of Nyssa (*Antirrheticus adv. Apollinarem*). St. *Gregory of Nazianzus, *Diodore of Tarsus, and *Theodoret of Cyr also wrote against Apollinarianism, but their works have not been preserved. The work *Adv. fraudes Apollinaristarum* is probably to be attributed to *Leontius of Byzantium.

Bibliography: H. LIETZMANN, *Apollinaris von Laodicea und seine Schule* (Tübingen 1904). G. VOISIN, *L'Apollinarisme* (Louvain 1901). C. E. RAVEN, *Apollinarianism* (Cambridge, Eng. 1923). H. DE RIEDMATTEN, "Some Neglected Aspects of Apollinarist Christology," *Dominican Studies* 1 (1948) 239–260; Grill-Bacht Konz 1:102–117, 203–212. Altaner 363–365. Quasten Patr 3:377–383. A. GESCHÉ, RHE 54 (1959) 403–406.

[F. CHIOVARO]

APOLLINARIS OF HIERAPOLIS, ST., bishop in Phrygia who received his see in the second half of the 2d century during the reign of Marcus Aurelius (161–180). In the early days of *Montanism Apollinaris was an outstanding champion of orthodoxy whose writings served to counteract the heresy. Though none of his works is extant, he wrote much, including an apology of the Christian faith addressed to the Emperor Marcus Aurelius. Apollinaris wrote also five books *Against the Greeks,* two *On the Truth,* and two *Against the Jews.* There is no serious reason to attribute to Apollinaris the *Cohortatio ad Graecos,* nor is he the author of the long anti-Montanist fragments cited by Eusebius (*Hist. Eccl.* 5.16–19). Since Apollinaris wrote against the early Montanists and these fragments were written 14 years after Maximilla's death, they could not have been written by Apollinaris.

Bibliography: P. DE LABRIOLLE, DHGE 3:959–960. A. FERRUA, EncCatt 1:1635. Quasten Patr 1:228–229. H. RAHNER, LexThK[2] 1:713–714.

[E. DAY]

APOLLINARIS OF LAODICEA, the Younger, 4th-century theologian and heretic; b. Laodicea in Syria, *c.* 300; d. *c.* 390. He was the son of Apollinaris the elder, a grammarian and priest. The Younger Apollinaris received an excellent profane and religious education. He served as lector in the church of Laodicea under Bishop Theodotus (d. 333) and also taught rhetoric; yet he was excommunicated by the bishop for participating in a pagan ceremony conducted by the rhetorician Epiphanius, but was subsequently readmitted to communion. He was excommunicated a second time by the Arian Bishop George in 346 for giving hospitality to *Athanasius of Alexandria, but was elected bishop (*c.* 361) by the Nicene community of Laodicea. He lectured at Antioch (*c.* 374), where St. Jerome was one of his auditors (Jerome, *Epist.,* 84.3), and was renowned for his support of Trinitarian doctrine against the Arians, his opposition to Julian the Apostate, and his logical mind and knowledge of Hebrew.

He had opposed the doctrine of *Diodore of Tarsus, who apparently taught that in Christ the union of the divine and human natures was purely moral. In his opposition, Apollinaris denied that Christ had a soul, thinking that His divine personality supplied the assumed human nature with that function. This error was condemned at a synod of Alexandria, which did not mention Apollinaris by name because of his strong opposition to Arianism, and he modified his teaching. Accepting the Semitic trichotomy of body-soul-spirit, he admitted that Christ had a soul but denied He had a human spirit. This doctrine was opposed in 374 by *Basil of Caesarea, who asked Pope *Damasus I to condemn it as heresy. In 377 Rome censured Apollinaris's teaching, and he was condemned at the Council of *Constantinople I (381). In 385 *Gregory of Nyssa wrote a refutation of Apollinaris called the *Antirrheticus contra Apollinarem,* which was directed against Apollinaris's *Proof of the Incarnation.*

Most of the writings of Apollinaris have disappeared. However, his disciples camouflaged several under pseudonyms, such as the letter of the Pseudo-Athanasius to the Emperor Jovian; letters under the name of Pope Julius; and a *Profession of Faith in Detail,* attributed to *Gregory Thaumaturgus. Fragments of his writings have been discovered also in Gregory of Nyssa's *Antirrheticus* and in the *Contra fraudes Apollinaristarum* attributed to Anastasius of Sinai. The 30 books against Porphyry of Apollinaris, his *De veritate* against Julian the Apostate, and his Biblical commentaries are represented in citations in the scriptural chains or testimonia. The full extent of Apollinarist frauds and interpolations came to be understood only in the 6th century, during the later Monophysite controversy. However, early orthodox writers were aware that St. *Cyril's famous phrase "one nature of the Logos incarnate" was actually a definition created by Apollinaris.

Bibliography: H. LIETZMANN, *Apollinaris von Laodicea und seine Schule* (Tübingen 1904). H. DE RIEDMATTEN, Grill-Bacht Konz 1:203–212, fragments; LexThK² 1:714. C. RAVEN, *Apollinarianism* (Cambridge, Eng. 1923). A. AIGRAIN, DHGE 3:962–982. G. L. PRESTIGE, *St. Basil the Great and Apollinaris of Laodicea,* ed. H. CHADWICK (SPCK: 1956). R. WEIJENBERG, *Antonianum* 33 (1958) 197–240, 371–414; 34 (1959) 246–298, Basil. Quasten Patr 3:377–383. Altaner 363–365.

[J. BENTIVEGNA]

APOLLINARIS OF MONTE CASSINO, ST., Benedictine abbot; d. Nov. 27, 828 (feast, Nov. 27). Having been given as an oblate to Monte Cassino by his parents when he was still very young, he was ordained deacon and priest under Abbot Gisulfus, whom he succeeded (817–828). During his reign, the monastery received many endowments. He was famous for the sanctity of his life, and he is said to have crossed the Liri River dryshod. His remains were interred first near the church of St. John and were translated by Abbot Desiderius (*Victor III) to the same church and honored with an epitaph in verse. In 1592 the relics of Apollinaris were placed under an altar in the chapel dedicated to him, decorated with paintings by Luca Giordano. The relics survived the destruction of World War II and were replaced in the same chapel after its restoration.

Bibliography: BHL 1:622. DESIDERIUS, *Dialogi* 1.1–2, MGS 30.2:1118. *Chronicon Casinense* 1.19–21, MGS 7:594–596. PETER THE DEACON, *De ortu et obitu iustorum Casinensium,* ch. 26 in PL 173:1081–90. L. TOSTI, *Storia della badia di Montecassino,* 4 v. (Rome 1880–90) 1:46. G. FALCO, "Lineamenti di storia cassinese . . .," *Casinensia* (Monte Cassino 1929) 2:510. Zimmermann KalBen 3:363–365.

[A. LENTINI]

APOLLINARIS OF VALENCE, ST., bishop; b. Vienne, *c.* 453; d. Valence, *c.* 520 (feast, Oct. 5). He was the son of (St.) Hesychius (Isicius) and the brother of (St.) *Avitus, successively bishops of Vienne. When elected to the See of Valence (*c.* 490), vacant for some years and in dire need of reform, Apollinaris successfully labored to reestablish discipline in his diocese and to restore the Catholic faith to the Burgundian kingdom, which had fallen into *Arianism. He assisted at the Synods of Epaon (517) and Lyons (516–523). Shortly after Epaon he was exiled by King Sigismund, angered (according to a vita of questionable historical value) by the excommunication of a royal official on charges of incest, but he was restored to his see the following year. His correspondence with Avitus, together with the acts of the councils, are the best sources for his biography.

Bibliography: MGSrerMer 3:197–203. Correspondence with Avitus, PL 59:231–232, 273. MGConc 1:29, 32–34. P. CHAPUIS, *S. Apollinaire, évêque, principal patron de tout le diocèse de Valence* (Paris 1898). R. AIGRAIN, DHGE 3:982–986; *Catholicisme* 1:705–706. H. LECLERCQ, DACL 15.2:2901. Butler Th Attw 4:36. G. MATHON, BiblSanct 2:249–250.

[G. M. COOK]

APOLLONIA OF ALEXANDRIA, ST., virgin and martyr, died in a popular uprising preceding the persecution of *Decius (feast, Feb. 9). Her martyrdom is described in a letter of Dionysius, Bishop of Alexandria, to Fabius, Bishop of Antioch (Eusebius, *Eccl. Hist.* 6.41.7). According to Dionysius, a mob seized "the marvelous aged virgin Apollonia," broke her teeth, and threatened to burn her alive. Having been given a brief respite, she leaped into a fire and was consumed. The morality of such acts was discussed by St. Augus-

St. Apollonia of Alexandria, portion of predella, early 16th century, by Andrea del Sarto.

tine (*Civ.* 1.26). Despite the fact that Dionysius explicitly mentions her age, Apollonia is usually represented in the late Middle Ages and Renaissance as a young woman, generally holding a forceps and a tooth. She is venerated as the patroness of dentists.

Bibliography: M. SCADUTO, EncCatt 1:1645–47. G. D. GORDINI, BiblSanct 2:258–262. **Illustration credit:** National Gallery of Ireland, Dublin.

[M. J. COSTELLOE]

APOLLONIUS OF TYANA, Neopythagorean philosopher and alleged wonderworker; b. Tyana in Cappadocia; fl. 1st century A.D. The chief source for his career is the *Life of Apollonius,* written in Greek, by Philostratus II (b. *c.* A.D. 170), a typical representative of the *Second Sophistic, who enjoyed the patronage of the Emperor Septimius Severus (A.D. 193–211) and his wife Julia Domna. Apollonius is described as a wandering ascetic and teacher, a miracle-worker, who traveled as far East as India and who barely escaped death under Nero and Domitian. As a clairvoyant he foretold the death of the latter. Philostratus apparently wished to present his hero as an ideal representative of Pythagoreanism and to refute charges that Apollonius was a common magician or charlatan. It is quite possible, as De Labriolle suggests, that Philostratus became acquainted with the Gospel narrative and utilized some of its elements to transform Apollonius into a kind of pagan Christ.

In spite of the unreliability of the *Life,* Apollonius should be regarded as a historical person and as a Neopythagorean teacher, although there is no precise information extant on his doctrine. The *Life* was very popular among pagans in the 3d and 4th centuries. Sossianus Hierocles, a high official under Diocletian, wrote a book against the Christians in which he employed the work of Philostratus to make an unfavorable comparison between the life and miracles of Christ and those of Apollonius. The great Church historian, Eusebius, refuted this attack on Christianity in his *Contra Hieraclem.*

Bibliography: A. BIGELMAIR, LexThK² 1:718–720. K. GROSS, ReallexAntChr 1:529–533, with bibliography. P. DE LABRIOLLE, *La Réaction paiënne: Étude sur la polémique antichrétienne du Ier au VIe siècle* (6th ed. Paris 1942) 175–189.

[M. R. P. MC GUIRE]

APOLLOS, a pious Jew whose name (Gk. Ἀπολλῶς) is a contracted form of Apollonius (of Apollo), mentioned by St. Paul and in Acts. Expert in Scripture, eloquent and with an ardent temperament, he was perhaps a traveling lecturer or professional orator. Apollos was a native of Alexandria, the center of Jewish Hellenism, which boasted of its exegetical Scripture schools and also of the Jewish philosopher *Philo Judaeus. While not yet fully instructed in Christianity, Apollos met *Aquila and Priscilla in Ephesus; they completed his instruction, baptized him, and sent him with recommendations to Achaia and Corinth (Acts 18.24–27). A clever apologist, he refuted the Jews at Corinth and deeply impressed Jews and Christians by his eloquence (Acts 18.28). One of the cliques formed at Corinth gave him special allegiance (1 Cor 1.10–13). He joined Paul in Ephesus and did not want to return to Corinth (1 Cor 16.12). The only other mention of this loyal friend of Paul is in Ti 3.13. A tradition (*Menolog. Graec.* 2b.17) places him later as bishop of Caesarea. He has been suggested as the author of Hebrews (*see* HEBREWS, EPISTLE TO THE).

Bibliography: E. B. ALLO, *Saint Paul: Première épître aux Corinthiens* (ÉtBibl; 2d ed. 1956) xix–xxi. EncDictBibl 114–115.

[R. G. BOUCHER]

APOLOGETICS, ARTICLES ON

The principal articles are: APOLOGETICS (scientific apologetics); APOLOGETICS, PRACTICAL. Related articles are: REVELATION, THEOLOGY OF; MIRACLES, THEOLOGY OF; MYSTERY (IN THEOLOGY). Where appropriate, the theological aspects are supplemented by philosophical and scriptural treatment under separate headings. Particular orientations, discussions, and concepts in the area of apologetics also receive individual articles: e.g., IMMANENCE APOLOGETICS; SYMBOL IN REVELATION; ACCOMMODATION; FAITH.

See also CHURCH, ARTICLES ON.

[E. A. WEIS]

APOLOGETICS

The following dimensions give an adequate understanding of apologetics: (1) the history of apologetics; (2) apologetics as a discipline; (3) the theological nature of apologetics; (4) the method of apologetics.

1. History of Apologetics

The term apologetics is an almost exact transliteration of the adjective ἀπολογητικός used substantively. The root verb, ἀπολογεῖσθαι, meaning to answer, to account for, to defend, or to justify, gives an indication of what apologetics has actually been and what one may expect it to be, no matter what the technical definition. In the large sense of giving an answer, accounting for, or defending, the Judeo-Christian tradition has a rich apologetic history reaching back to the very earliest records of God's intervention in human history.

Old Testament. To give an account of Yahweh's great deeds is the purpose of the Old Testament itself. As has been so often noted, the narration is not simply the detached recital of past acts, though the Old Testament is sometimes this, but rather the theologically interpreted account of Yahweh's activity in relation to His chosen people. Thus there is, in the broad sense of the term, an "accounting for" God's actions, or what might be described as an apologetic concern. To cite an instance, Yahweh's covenant relation with the Israelites is central to the OT experience. ". . . I will be your God and you shall be my people" (Jer 7.23). This covenant bond literally founds the religious experience of Israel. *See* COVENANT (IN THE BIBLE). Obedience to the Mosaic *Law, loyalty to the covenant relationship, is always related to the history of Yahweh's choice of Israel. The apologetic element that one finds in most of the OT and especially in covenant history is precisely the attempt of the authors and of those who stood behind the tradition to render Yahweh's activity in history both comprehensible and credible. The activity and demands of Yahweh are not presented primarily for study but for acceptance. Thus when the Israelites find themselves in exile and their temple destroyed, the Deuteronomist explores various explanations—the *Word of God as a promise to the Patriarchs, the Word considered in the covenant, which allows the possibility of a curse, the Word as prophetic and therefore giving hope for the future. In 4 Kings ch. 17 the Deuteronomist reflects mournfully on the exile, for he has not solved the problem of the exile except to affirm that the ways of Yahweh toward men are just. He is thus giving "an account of," or "answering for," or "justifying" Yahweh's activity in history, an activity that man is to embrace and accept in faith. In this type of event and in its portrayal by the Deuteronomist one sees an essential demand for *faith.

New Testament. The historical evidence of the NT indicates that Jesus worked miracles and that His words and deeds led His disciples to believe that He was the Christ, the Son of God. *See* MIRACLES (OF CHRIST). Hardly anyone would deny that the tradition of the above occurrence was formed and written with some, in the large sense of the term, apologetic intent. Hence the very structure of the gospel may be considered to be apologetic in the sense that the thinking from within faith from which the Holy *Gospels emerged was again a thinking and a witnessing that directed itself to religious persuasion, to giving an account of God's activity in Christ. *See* WITNESS TO THE FAITH. Very clear indications of apologetic intent can be seen in Mark—probably the least apologetic of the four Gospels—which apparently intends to answer evident questions that would occur to early Christian readers. If Jesus performed so very many miracles, how is it that the Jews refused to believe in Him? If Jesus were the Son of God, could He not have saved Himself from the Crucifixion? To these questions Mark proposes the fact that people in general did accept Jesus, and in Jerusalem people listened gladly to Jesus. In fact, Mark narrates, it is this very success with the people that induced the leaders to arrest Jesus by stealth and have Him crucified very shortly after. And in ch. 8, 9, and 10 Mark gives the three prophecies of the Passion, death, and Resurrection in which Jesus affirmed the necessity of His suffering and dying. Thus the Passion and death did not come on Jesus by surprise but rather as part of His redemptive task.

This same general notion of apologetics in the NT is found in 1 Pt 3.15, where the writer asks that the believer be able to give a reason for the faith that is in him, a procedure that is exemplified in the Lukan accounts of the very first preaching. In an analysis of this first preaching in Acts, one sees OT quotations used apologetically. An analysis of Acts on the basis of form criticism discloses a further apologetic intent in the very structure of the speeches and of the narrative material, e.g., the account of Cornelius. Thus an apologetic concern is deeply involved in the intention, the structure, and the contents of the NT.

Early Apologetics. The Greek *apologists of the 2d century defended Christianity through four arguments. The first argument was from the moral effects of Christianity, especially from the exercise of Christian charity. Justin Martyr, writing about 150, pointed out how Christianity made men change from the practice of magic to the worship of the good God, changed a craving after wealth to a common possession of goods and a sharing of wealth with the poor and needy, altered hatred to charity, self-gratification to self-restraint, selfishness to generosity. Second, the apologists argued from the predictions of both Christ and the Prophets. The third argument was the proof from antiquity. This argument emphasized the coherence and unity of the Old and New Testaments, for the prophetical books of the OT received their highest fulfillment in the NT. Thus Christianity was not a new religion, one that had come on the scene only lately, but a religion that went back to Moses, who lived before the Greek poets and sages. The fourth argument, the one least used, was the proof from the miracles of Christ. Miracles were not widely used as apologetic proofs because at that time there were wandering magicians and pseudo-Christs who seemed able to perform wonders, apparently through demonic assistance.

The high point of 2d- and 3d-century apologetics was probably reached by Origen (*c.* 185–*c.* 254) in his *Contra Celsum* (246–248). Origen used all the four arguments listed above. But he went on to point out that the greatest miracle is that of the Resurrection, and he stressed the demonstration of the Spirit, the power of the Spirit to demonstrate and persuade one of the credibility of Scripture and its contents. In general, the highly gifted Origen employed a tremendous variety of arguments sufficient to answer the individual difficulties brought up by Celsus. Particular arguments for Christianity were virtually unlimited, especially in the hands of skillful dialecticians. Tertullian, for example, on occasion used the argument that Christian teachings were quite similar to those of pagan poets and philosophers. The effort was to relate the Christian demand for faith to the concrete man as he existed in a well-determined set of historical circumstances.

Medieval Period. In the *Summa contra gentiles* Aquinas began with principles that he knew his opponents would acknowledge, the principles of Aristotelian philosophy. In the light of these mutually acknowledged principles Aquinas sought to answer objections to the faith. Aquinas further evolved the argument of the superiority of Christianity over another religion that would win its adherents by promising carnal delights, for instead of carnal delights Christianity offered only spiritual benefits and, indeed, suffering. Thus the enigmatic fact that Christianity existed at all was a proof, really, that miracles did take place and did, therefore, guarantee the truth of Christian revelation. On the other hand, a fully developed apologetic in the modern sense of the term did not really exist in the medieval period because people born into a Christian community assumed that faith was the normal status of man and was a communal possession. Thus the medievals did not grapple with the problem of the nonbeliever coming to the faith, for the medieval community was a social entity in which it was connatural to believe.

Reformation. The Reformation generated a polemic apologetics largely limited to an apologetic of the Church. Bellarmine, de Sales, and others explained the necessity of the Church in opposition to the reformers, who believed in Scripture but not in the external Church as it existed in the 16th century. The treatise on the Church that emerged at the end of the 16th and the beginning of the 17th century proceeded from the marks of the Church to a proof that the Roman Catholic Church was the true Church, and as the true Church had the right and the authority to judge controversies. The 16th century was the period when apologies abounded. Religious divisions and the antipathies aroused among the contenders turned the apologetic arguments into a form of attack and counterattack. The argument from authority remained basic. Scripture was a quarry from which theologians and apologists could hew quotations to use against each other. In general, because of the climate of controversy, polemic intruded into the area of theological understanding.

After the Reformation. *Descartes (1596–1650) greatly, though unintentionally and unknowingly, influenced apologetics. His scientific criterion of not accepting anything as true unless it is perceived to be evident by the knowing subject was transferred to theology. And Descartes's basic principle was that all nature is intelligible through a disciplined scientific method and the proper use of reason. True in itself, this principle was incorporated into a book, *Forma verae religionis quaerendae et inveniendae* (Naples 1662), written by Miguel de Elizalde. [Some writers find the beginning of the manual form of apologetics in Hugo Grotius (1583–1645) and his book *De veritate religionis christianae,* published in 1627.] The basic premise of the work was that Christian faith should be justified by a speculative, articulated, and antecedent knowledge of the fact of divine revelation. At this point a new factor enters Christian apologetics—some anterior certification for the future commitment and knowledge of faith. After de Elizalde, treatises on *De vera religione* multiplied and were dominated by the Cartesian mentality, viz, that there must be a clear, precise, and ascertainable reason for everything, as is so in mathematical procedure.

*Deism, which began with J. Toland in 1696, is largely a consequence of the use of Cartesian method in the sphere of the religious. The 18th-century *Encyclopedists in France, the *Aufklärung* in Germany, and an atmosphere somewhat less acrimonious than that of Reformation days continued and developed an increasingly rationalistic apologetic.

In the 19th century, Christian apologetics was directed to the defense of the supernatural and the historical reliability of Scripture against those who denied the supernatural and held that both the Bible and tradition were unreliable sources of historical truth. When David F. Strauss (1808–74) said Scripture was predominantly myth, and Joseph Ernest Renan (1823–92) sought to diminish the mysterious and supernatural element in Christianity, apologists directed their attention to showing that supernatural revelation was possible, suitable, necessary (if God destines man for a supernatural end), and actually took place. The same emphasis was placed on showing that the Gospels are true historical documents and thus are to be believed. In the mid-19th century the general form of apologetics as it would be known for the next 100 years became fairly well settled. The pattern appeared in G. Perrone's *Praelectiones theologicae* (1835–42), a series that went through 30 editions. His tract *De vera religione* determined the tone, content, and method of nearly all Catholic apologetics for the next century. From Perrone's time on, apologetic treatises began with the possibility of revelation, the necessity of revelation, the criteria of revelation, and the existence of revelation in the OT, in Christ, and in the Church.

In the latter half of the 19th century Christian apologetics centered about the historical reliability of the Gospels, especially their testimony to the Resurrection and divinity of Christ. The divinity of Christ was, at times, established from the OT. After verifying the authenticity and veracity of the canonical Gospels in the historicist sense, the divinity of Christ was attested by His preaching, His miracles, and His prophecies.

During exactly this same period John Henry Newman (1801–90) was writing about the primacy of conscience and its first principle that the world is governed by a providential Creator. From providence and creation Newman proceeded to the fact that all nature manifests both the intention and design of God. From this Newman went to the principle of analogy, primarily to refute objections to the supernatural. The accumulation of probabilities and the use of the illative sense made Newman's apologetic different from the one common in his day. Because Newman was well aware of the depths of the human mind, and the tortuous route it follows to religious truth, Newman's writings treat the human mind with great reverence. Nonetheless, Newman continually proposed the perennial problems: the existence of God, the relation of God to contemporary man, the development of *doctrine, the identification of the Church of his time with the apostolic Church.

M. Blondel (1861–1949) based his immanentist apologetic on the theory that Christianity does not come exclusively from the outside. *See* IMMANENCE APOLOGETICS. Some few other apologists paralleled the apologetic of Newman, as, for example, Jean Guitton, who considered the divinity of Jesus and the Resurrection of Jesus in the light of the rationalist, Protestant, and Catholic approaches and asked which opinion best explains all the data.

Modern apologetics is in a state of flux and tends toward versatility of approach. Most Catholic apologists feel that the modern option is between belief or nonbelief. Thus apologetics is tending to ask questions about the basic orientation involved in either position. Modern apologetics is also attempting to formulate an ontology of the principles of natural and supernatural revelation. Theologians such as Karl Rahner have attempted to exploit the openness of man, since he is spirit, to all being. Because revelation is essentially relational, both terms in the relation are undergoing scrutiny, and apologetics is becoming more subjective to offset the overly objective and extrinsicist apologetics of a generation ago. Apologists are likewise tending to view Scripture in the light of the latest research and as religious witness and testimony. Modern apologetics is emphasizing that since man exists in the temporal order, the apologetic approach must be in categories and patterns taken from that order. Because man is open to all being, the transcendent God can perpetually and permanently give stability within a very variable and volatile temporal order.

2. The Discipline

As a discipline apologetics must continuously investigate the relation of the Christian to the Judeo-Christian revelation and the relation of every man to God revealing naturally and supernaturally (*see* REVELATION, THEOLOGY OF). Thus apologetics will deal with the principal facts in Christianity: God's self-disclosure transmitted in a Church to believers in the contemporary world.

As a discipline, apologetics in its objective aspects will consider the nature of revelation in general and the Judeo-Christian revelation in particular, the fonts of *revelation, the fact of revelation, the media of revelation, the large and general structure of revelation, the need of revelation, the possibility of revelation, and the meaning of revelation. The subjective dimensions of apologetics will involve the believer standing before the transcendent and free God revealing Himself in history, and will thus unfold the metaphysics of belief in its personal and social dimensions. Inevitably, therefore, apologetics must concern itself with the relationship between *faith and reason; it is in Christian apologetics that faith and reason have their meeting point.

While it is true that apologetics may be taught as an independent discipline since it deals with the fundamentals of Christianity, it is necessary that Christian apologetics be a factor in every theological treatise as well as in the entire theological synthesis. Thus there should be an apologetic of the preached word, an apologetic of the Trinity, an apologetic of the Word Incarnate, of the Sacraments, and of the liturgy.

3. Theological Exposition

In mid-20th century the name apologetics had unpleasant connotations, so much so that some wished to drop apologetics as a theological category or substitute for apologetics something else, for example, ecumenism. Further, manuals of theology were divided in their very definitions of apologetics. Critics said it would be presumptuous for man to make human judgments about the Word of God. The function of the Christian witness, it was maintained, is to confront the world with the Word of God. In answer to such criticism and in the midst of such confusion it might have been said that since apologetics is undeniably present in Scripture, and is likewise part of the great theological tradition, and presumably can illuminate the relationship of faith and reason, apologetics has a necessary place in theology.

Apologetics, a Use of Theology. A random selection of authors indicates diversity of definition. One author claims that apologetics should prove that the mysteries of the faith are credible and are to be believed; the method is not from the authority of revelation but rather through strictly rational procedure. Another claims that apologetics performs the work of *theology but is not theology. J. Kleutgen said apologetics is a necessary condition for theology. A. Knoll and others see it as the very foundation of theology. L. Maisonneuve says that apologetics embraces a theory of knowledge, a theodicy, elements related to religion and the supernatural, general and particular introduction to Scripture, treatise on the Church, etc. A. Gardeil pointed out years ago that if there were any area where the object and method remained a problem for theologians, it was surely the field of apologetics. If there is hope of a definition, it will come from an examination of the history of apologetics, a consideration of what is consistent and fruitful in this history and therefore deserving of perpetuation, and an investigation of what the total history indicates needs evolution and development.

It is rather commonly admitted today that the sacred writers and those who stood behind the scriptural traditions were theologians—some of higher talent and insight than others. When the Deuteronomist attempted to reconcile the destruction of the Temple and the exile with the covenant relation, this reconciliation that issued in a finished written document presumed a prior theological understanding. So too in the Gospels. Mark, for example, writes from faith, to arouse faith, about an object faith. The apologists of the 2d and 3d century were theologians first and then from their habit of theologizing brought forth apologetic arguments and even systematized these arguments. So too the medieval theologians and the apologists after the Reformation were first of all theologians. After the Reformation period apologetics was a part of *fundamental theology, which proves the divine origin of Jesus and the Church. The aim of this apologetic has always been the credibility and "credendity" of the Catholic faith. Thus here, despite a possible conflict and confusion of definition, in practice all the apologists actually did utilize their theological understanding to construct a systematic apologetics. Vatican I has indicated that theological activity takes place when man, through his human reason transformed by faith, seeks an understanding of the Word of God transmitted in the Church. Empirically, therefore, apologetics has always proceeded from theology, i.e., it has always been a form of theological activity. More exactly, apologetics is a use of the habit of theology.

Purpose of the Use. In every instance of what would legitimately be called apologetics one finds that the use of theology was directed to religious persuasion, some type of relevant explanation. The apologetic attempt is an effort to persuade, to translate, in the literal sense, the Christian demand for faith. The attempt may be quite systematic and argumentative, as in a work such as the *Contra Celsum.* Or the attempt may be purely pragmatic and empirical, as appears to be the case in 1 Cor 14.23–25, where Paul stresses the importance of the gift of prophecy and indicates that the visible activity of the Spirit in the liturgical gatherings of the early Church will bring the visitor or unbeliever to acknowledge God in adoration and confession. Persuasion, as the purpose of apologetics, is primarily directed to the will, that the individual may respond to God. Thus Scripture is direct address challenging a response. The beautiful Pauline prayers present Christ as an object of adoration, even though in the letters Paul may go on to another type of persuasion, the intellectual. Even the highly polemic apologetic sought to persuade, though some of the means used were perhaps undesirable from a modern standpoint. The apologetic effort to persuade is directed to the full man, and in an age of intellect the rational argumentation tends to dominate. Yet the letters of Paul indicate that persuasion is a comprehensive effort, embracing the total man. The Pauline letters make it clear that he sensed the reality of God, of Christ, of freedom from sin, of trust, of hope, and of faith as pure gift of God in opposition to the works of the Law. His letters are the effort to communicate what he himself felt and experienced. Paul was well aware of the fact that man is so constituted that he can understand without approving. Apologetics goes beyond understanding to acceptance of what is understood.

Because the use of the habit of theology that one calls apologetics is an effort at religious persuasion and because this type of persuasion is a major factor in Scripture, one must include the direction of the Holy Spirit in any definition of apologetics. For the attempt to persuade man of the Christian revelation is an effort to intrude into the depths of the man's being. Because the message is *supernatural and the mode of accepting the message comes as a free gift of God, the apologist must always seek to be under the direction of the Holy Spirit. Theological activity is made possible by the divine action in history. If theological thinking is thinking in faith, and this faith is a gift of God, then the use of theology directed to religious persuasion cannot simply be defined as a profane activity, though all the competence and means used to achieve this competence in profane activities must also find their place in apologetics. One might urge as another reason for affirming that apologetics should be under the direction of the Holy Spirit the fact that the apologist must respect the freedom, the dignity, the conscience of the individual for whose benefit he is attempting to translate the demand for faith, as well as the freedom of God Himself to act beyond categories systematically established by the apologist. Further, acrimonious polemic will tend to be eliminated as an essential part of apologetics if the use of this particular habit of theology is consigned on principle to the direction of the Spirit.

Object of the Use of the Habit. Revelation is essentially free divine self-disclosure in history. When Yahweh chooses to act in history, He becomes God-with-us. In the NT Christ becomes the Lord-with-us. This divine self-disclosure constitutes a demand for faith, for God the eternal enters time, the invisible becomes visible; but the mystery, the transcendence, the otherness of God remains. Thus the entrance of God into time is a call, a demand upon man, precisely a demand for faith, which is, paradoxically enough, likewise the gift of God. The demand for faith may also be expressed by the more common terms, credibility and "credendity." But the personal dimensions of apologetics seem to be better served by the phrase, "demand for faith."

"Demand for faith" is correlative to Paul's use of the term mystery, which summed up God's entire plan of salvation for man. This plan of salvation, the mystery, was revealed in the Person of Jesus Christ, and it was a drama of human Redemption that began in God. The great mystery was manifested in Jesus and in the Church. It is through faith that man is capable of apprehending the great mystery of salvation. Yet though the great mystery is revealed both in Christ and in the Church, the mystery remains beyond complete human understanding. Precisely because the great mystery of salvation is secret it must be apprehended by faith. Yet the mystery is revealed because salvation took place in Jesus and is announced to all. To present this mystery precisely in its faith-demanding aspect is the object of the use of theology called apologetics.

It is quite clear that the demand for faith has an objective and a subjective dimension. The objective pole is God Himself and the means of self-disclosure in themselves, that is, the content of revelation expressed in human language. The subjective pole is intelligent and willing man subject to the influence and light of grace. This subject exists in a *supernatural order. But history is the meeting point of the objective and subjective poles.

Apologetics and Theology. Without prejudicing other concepts of theology, it may be said that positive theology is theology as it actually unfolds in the theological sources. The relation between revelation and theology as it exists in Scripture is a technical problem of no concern here. It is safe to affirm that there is positive theology in Scripture, in the Fathers, and in the teaching of the Church. Put another way, positive theology may be called the unfolding of theological questions and the immediate and apt answers given in the theological context. Speculative theology, however, begins from the articles of faith and from the data of positive theology. In general, the articles of faith as announced in the Word of God and taught by the Spirit through the Church answer the first theological question: Is this the case or not? The fact that Jesus is both God and man is affirmed by the Church. Speculative theology asks the question of understanding: What do you mean when you say that Jesus is both God and man? The goal of speculative theology is theological understanding on the systematic level by an objective consideration of objects as they are in themselves. Apologetics is a mean between positive and speculative theology. For apologetics asks the question: What does this fact mean to man in terms of acceptance? The goal of this use of the habit of theology is the relation of the total Christian synthesis or one or other Christian fact to the concrete individual in terms of a truth to be accepted by belief.

A comparison of the habit of theology with the use of this habit that is called apologetics might be helpful. The habit of theology is in the speculative intellect, and it is a good of this intellect. The use of the habit would be the work of the practical intellect, and it is directed to the good of the will. The habit of theology seeks intelligibility, an answer to the question: What is the thing in itself? The emphasis is on the objective. Apologetics seeks credibility. What is this in relation to man as a believer? The emphasis is on the subjective. Speculative theology is an upward movement to the world of system, the world of theory, the atemporal, the abstract, the transcendent. Apologetics, on the other hand, is the descending movement whereby one relates to the singular, the thing, the real, the temporal, the concrete, the individual. The actual use of the habit pertains much more to the world of intersubjectivity than to the world of theory. Speculative theology seeks a notional assent and is religious by context. Apologetics seeks a real assent in the world of decision, the world of the practical judgment, and it is religious in itself. Speculative theology seeks to understand the divine-human encounter or dialogue with the movement being primarily *ad intra.* Apologetics seeks to occasion, stimulate, facilitate the divine-human encounter and is primarily a motion *ad extra.* Hence apologetics is theology. There is no diversity of formal objects, for speculative theology and a use of the habit of theology. It would appear that the formal object *quod* of apologetics is revealed religion under the aspect of credibility and "credendity"; the formal object *quo* is the same as theology, the light of faith or, in the concrete, the human reason transformed by faith.

Subjective Pole of Apologetics. The history of apologetics indicates that the religious persuasion characteristic of all apologetics in all ages is directed to the existential man in the historical now. The demand for faith is directed to man here and now, man in his present human situation, in his own culture, his own ethos, and with his own personal and unique orientation. This is man in the concrete, not man as an abstraction. In the broad sense man is historical, because he may think, choose, will, elect, and so to a large extent determine his own existence. This is the world of history as opposed to the world of nature. Man is historical in a particular sense because he lives in an historical moment diverse from any other historical moment. Apologetics relates the demand for faith to man in the relevant religious, historical context. It is true to say that apologetics becomes a dialogue conditioned by the apologist, by the man to whom he is speaking, and the concrete history in which all of this takes place. Apologetics, therefore, will possess a contemporaneity that is more than an updating; it will possess an awareness of the personal and social ethos, attitude, culture, and climate.

Definition. In the light of what has been said, apologetics may be defined as a use of the habit of theology, under the direction of the Holy Spirit, to render the Christian demand for faith persuasive to the existential man in the historical now.

Conclusion. Since Vatican I (Denz 3020) notes that understanding, knowledge, and wisdom are to increase in the theology both of the individual and of the community, then apologetics should evolve and develop to meet the needs of each age. Apologetics of its nature will have to be versatile. It is likewise true that if apologetics is a use of the habit of theology, then all branches of theology have a possible apologetic. Though apologetics will afford a certain primacy to the two great and principal Christian facts—God has revealed and has founded a Church—still apologetics is a far broader subject than that included in the two basic Christian facts.

4. Method of Apologetics

Apologetic method will depend upon two things: the concept of theology, and the concept of the relation between theology and apologetics. Granted the definition here proposed, apologetics will begin within theological thinking. Only when one is a theologian, when he is able to move about in the area of theological question and answer with a certain amount of facility, only then can he become apologist. Once one acquires some understanding of the Christian mysteries, he is then in a position to use the habit of theology in attempting to render the Christian demand for faith persuasive to the existential man in the concrete now. This use of the habit of theology will first of all be a systematic scientific effort, the attempt to formulate an apologetic in terms of the objective and subjective poles, the first moment of apologetics. The theoretical formulation of an apologetic is quite different from the concrete application of the apologetic, or the second moment of apologetics. The two moments of apologetics will constitute a self-correcting hermeneutic circle.

Since apologetics depends on theological understanding, the nature of the case implies a certain diversity of apologetic and apologetic method. There can be a metaphysical apologetic in which one formulates the ontology of the principles of natural and supernatural revelation. There can be a sacramental apologetic analyzing the connaturality of the presence of God to man in and through matter and gesture and symbol. There can be an apologetic of natural revelation and the historical response to natural revelation in the various forms of religion. This apologetic can move into the OT revelation and the historical response, the NT revelation and the religious response, and the Judeo-Christian revelation and the current religious response. Such a procedure would show how Christianity is the historical determination of the relation of man to the Absolute (Bouillard). Further development of this general apologetic would examine the relation of present-day Christianity to the Christianity of the gospel, a procedure that has actually taken place in Vatican II.

There can further be a Biblical, an existential, and a liturgical form of apologetic. Because of the contextual bipolarity of apologetics, apologetics is stable and unified insofar as it always relates mystery to man. On the other hand, because understanding of God should grow and because of the variability of man in history, apologetics will be protean. All, therefore, that can be said about method is that there are no mechanical rules and that apologetics will proceed from the habit of theology and relate the Christian demand for faith to the concrete existing man.

See also APOLOGETICS, ARTICLES ON; APOLOGETICS, PRACTICAL.

Bibliography: L. Maisonneuve, DTC 1.2:1511–80. A. Michel, DTC, Tables générales 1:196–206. H. Lais and W. Lohff, Lex ThK[2] 1:723–731. J. H. Crehan, Davis CDT 1:113–122. R. Aubert, *Le Problème de l'acte de foi* (3d ed. Louvain 1958); "Le Caractère raisonnable de l'acte de foi," RHE 39 (1943) 22–99. A. Dulles, *Apologetics and the Biblical Christ* (Westminster, Md. 1963). C. Donahue, "Roman Catholicism," in *Patterns of Faith in America Today,* ed. F. E. Johnson (New York 1957). R. Knox, *In Soft Garments* (2d ed. New York 1953). J. Levie, *Sous les yeux de l'incroyant* (2d ed. Paris 1946). B. Lindars, *N.T. Apologetic* (Philadelphia 1961). A. Richardson, *Christian Apologetics* (London 1947; repr. 1960). H. Bouillard et al., "Le Christ envoyé de Dieu," *Bulletin du Comité des Études* 35 (1961) 303–456. J. M. Le Blond, "Le Chrétien devant l'athéisme actuel," *Études* 231 (1954) 289–304, condensed in TheolDig 3 (1955) 139–143. R. X. Redmond, "How Should *De Ecclesia* Be Treated in Scientific Theology," CathThSoc 17 (1962) 139–160. F. Taymans, "Le Miracle, signe du surnaturel," NouvRevTh 77 (1955) 225–245, condensed in TheolDig 5 (1957) 18–23.

[P. J. CAHILL]

APOLOGETICS, PRACTICAL

In speaking of practical apologetics, one uses the term in the meaning closest to its etymological derivation, that of an apology, or defense, of the Catholic Church. It refers properly not to a science, but to the art of defending or explaining the Church to the nonbeliever, of preparing him for an act of *faith. While one may speak of scientific Protestant or Orthodox apologetics, the art of practical apologetics is for all useful purposes a peculiarly Catholic one. The discussion here is restricted accordingly. Since through the centuries nonbelievers have been of many different sorts, practical apologetics has assumed a diversity of postures. This article indicates the nature of this practical art, observes some of its historical postures, and discusses the challenges faced by the practical apologist today.

Nature and Scope. Considered in the concrete, apologetics includes two areas of endeavor, which differ in purpose and method. The first, scientific apologetics, strives to demonstrate the rationale of Catholic faith, that the *teaching authority of the Roman Catholic Church is the *rule of faith intended by God. The second area, a more general one sometimes called practical, or pastoral, apologetics, ordinarily refers to the practical application of the principles established by the scientific apologist. It may even be extended to include defense of any truth whatsoever of Christian revelation. Taken in its proper sense, scientific apologetics need not consider demonstrations of the existence and attributes of God, of the relation of the world to God, or of the nature of religion, for these propositions are validly assumed to have been established by the philosopher. However, practical apologetics must concern itself with them insofar as such truths are related to a person's "motives of credibility," or reasons for judging that a reasonable assent of the mind can be given to truths proposed as revealed.

Thus it is that practical apologetics deals with the pastoral use of scientific principles and demonstrations insofar as one's pastoral experience and prudent judgment indicate their adaptation and accommodation. Just as it is the task of the scientific apologist to ascertain and to formulate the objective rational grounds for faith, so must the practical apologist present these motives of *credibility in a way most suited to the needs of his own time and country.

Hence the practical apologist considers not only abstract principles, but the psychology of *conversion as well. He judges which type of scientific demonstration will be most effective according to the moods and needs of the individual or the group. Thus he will discuss the claims of Christianity in one way with a group opposed to the Christian message, as did Justin with the Jews and the pagans. He will speak in another way with atheists, in yet another with Protestants, and in still another with the Orthodox. A Pascal is not a Blondel; nor is Newman a contemporary apologist. He will adopt one approach with the young and vigorous, another with the old and infirm; one approach with the scholarly and the educated, another with the ignorant and unschooled. The missionary more than any other individual understands this need for constant adaptation.

In fact, adaptation has always been one of the primary principles of the practical apologist in his efforts to present the demonstrations of scientific apologetics more meaningfully to his listeners. In his sermon to the Areopagites St. Paul set the earliest tone of adaptation, speaking to them of the "unknown God" and relating his preaching to what was already accepted and admitted by his pagan listeners. Justin Martyr attempted to give a rational foundation to this manner of procedure by developing his concept of the *λόγοι σπερματικοί*; according to him truths taught by the Greek philosophers were "seeds" of the Logos, or Word of God. Jerome and Augustine refined this notion even further, developing the twin themes of the *captiva gentilis* and the *spoliatio aegyptiorum,* both of which compared Old Testament narratives with the desired attitude of the Christian toward truths taught by pagan philosophers. The *captiva gentilis* theme dealt with the custom of purifying captive pagan women by shaving their heads and paring their nails before marrying Israelites (Dt 21.10–13). The *spoliatio aegyptiorum* dealt with God permitting the Israelites to take with them in their exodus from Egypt gold and silver trinkets of the Egyptians (Ex 12.35–36). In like manner, the Fathers reasoned, the Christian can and should purify the truths contained in pagan writings and use them for expressing the truths of Christianity. Such writing led finally to the two classic instances of intellectual adaptation executed by Augustine and St. Thomas Aquinas with truths contained in the writings of Plato and Aristotle. On the more practical level, one must mention the work of Matteo *Ricci and the famous *Chinese rites controversy. And today (1965), representing adaptation of value to the modern practical apologist, one may note the celebrated labors of P. Johanns and G. Dandoy with Hindu philosophical and religious thought.

Historical Postures. In presenting the motives of credibility the practical apologist has through the centuries come to rely upon three so-called traditional approaches: the *via primatus,* the *via notarum,* and the *via empirica.* In the *via primatus* (way of the primacy) he attempts to demonstrate that the Gospels are reliable historical documents, that Christ claimed to be a divine legate, that this claim was proven by miracles, that His work of mission was to be continued by a Church, and that this Church is today identified with the Roman Catholic by reason of the *primacy bestowed upon Peter and continued through his successors, the bishops of Rome. The *via notarum* (way of the marks) proceeds from the assumption that the Church of Christ would possess certain qualities, readily discernible in practice and found in their fullness only in the Roman Catholic Church. Those qualities most frequently cited were four in number—unity, holiness, catholicity (or universality), and apostolicity. Other sets of notes were also given, such as those based upon the writings of Augustine—perfect wisdom, accord in faith, miracles, pastoral succession, and the name catholic—and those derived from the writings of Vincent of Lérins—universality, antiquity, and universal accord. In the third and final traditional approach, developed in the 19th century by Cardinal V. Dechamps, great stress was laid upon the Church as an empirical fact. This *via empirica* (empirical way), developed from the concept that the Church itself studied historically bore certain incontestable signs of its divine origin, proceeds from considering the Church in its historical reality—its strengths and weaknesses, its successes and failures—to a conclusion of its divine origin.

The practical application of these three methods in the U.S., where the 19th-century Church grew so rapidly, deserves special attention. When one considers the minority status of Roman Catholics in the earliest days of American independence, it is not surprising to observe the defensive nature of the first American apologetical writings. The earliest American apologists, men such as John *Carroll and Demetrius *Gallitzin, wrote when the American Church was in what amounted to a state of siege. Their writings, frequently harsh in tone and historical rather than doctrinal, were directed not so much toward conversion as toward diminishing prejudice and righting erroneous conceptions of Catholicism. Later in the 19th century Francis Kenrick and Martin Spalding discarded this earlier defensive posture and concentrated upon demonstrating the truth of Catholicism in a positive, albeit traditional, manner. It remained for the distinguished lay convert Orestes *Brownson to develop a practical apologetics peculiar to America, one that was, however, more original in its manner of presentation than in its content. For more than 30 years Brownson defended Catholicism in his voluminous writings, using not only the primacy approach and that of the notes, but also employing that of Cardinal Dechamps and devising an approach of his own based upon the teachings of the French socialist Pierre Leroux. It was, however, under the influence of Isaac *Hecker and the Paulists that organized techniques of mass instruction and conversion finally began to be developed.

Practical Apologetics Today. But over the years, as the apologist presented and adapted these demonstrations for the nonbeliever, certain objections arose against them. Although the solution of these problems often rested with the scientific apologist, the problems themselves confronted the practitioner in his work. Against the *via primatus* it was objected that modern critical historical method could not establish with sufficient certainty an adequately clear and definite picture of what Jesus Christ had said and done; moreover, that even if it could, history could not affirm apodictically that Christ was truly a divine legate, the promised messiah. Along these same lines it was also objected that the Gospels themselves could not be established for the nonbeliever as scientifically accurate historical documents. Even prescinding from the validity of such objections, the apologist nevertheless found himself arguing from a much less firm historical foundation.

Against the *via notarum* it was argued that such an approach was, on the one hand, entirely too provincial and, on the other, not entirely accurate in its reasoning. The four notes most frequently cited were, it was argued, agreeable only to those who professed the Nicene-Constantinopolitan Creed, upon which they were based, and thus were of their very nature limited in their effectiveness. Moreover, it was asserted, the reasoning was a fallacious one founded upon a distorted interpretation of data, namely, that the fullness of these qualities could not be found in any of the Protestant or Orthodox communions. Again prescinding from the validity of such objections, the practical apologist found the *via notarum* less and less useful, since it too often tended to irritate and to alienate his Protestant and Orthodox listeners on purely personal grounds.

Finally, against the *via empirica* it was objected that this approach really demonstrated nothing in a truly scientific manner. Even bearing in mind the words of Vatican Council I that the Church itself is a "great and perpetual motive of credibility and an unquestionably valid witness of its own divine legation" (Denz 3013), the practical apologist frequently found the approach championed by Dechamps more useful as a suasive device than as a truly convincing one.

In such a context the modern apologist, striving to adapt principles to listeners disquieted by these and similar objections, reaches out for new approaches. One such approach emphasizes the concept of the Gospels as *salvation history, the account of God's dealings with His specially chosen people. It asserts that clarification of this peculiar literary genre as well as of the nature and spirit of the Gospel message would act as the strongest possible apologetic. A more specific, newer approach advocated by A. Dulles is to regard the Gospels and other New Testament writings as the religious testimony, embracing both factual memories and spiritual insights, proferred by the primitive Church. The practical apologist will then build upon the various good qualities of this primitive Christian witness—its intrinsic sublimity, its inner coherence, and its profound adaptation to man's spiritual needs.

It thus becomes clear that the principal relation between scientific and practical apologetics today is found in their common need for the presentation of truth. It is up to the scientific apologist to determine where truth is to be found in establishing the motives of credibility and of credendity, and also what degree of certitude can be expected in arriving at this truth. And thus the scientific apologist will depend upon many other disciplines for the raw material of his investigations. He will depend upon the scholar competent in the area of comparative religion to supply him with data about the beliefs and practices of primitive pagans and Jews. He will depend upon the Scripture scholar for data about the precise meaning of certain words and expressions in both Old and New Testaments. He will depend upon the Church historian for data regarding the beliefs and witness of the Christian community down through the ages. He will depend upon the epistemologist and the logician for conclusions about the validity of his reasoning and the degree of certitude to be obtained from historical study. Perusing this mass of data and observations precisely in the light of formulating valid motives of credibility, he turns his findings over to the practical apologist for adaptation and presentation.

In this presentation the practical apologist must go even deeper into these and other related questions. Frequently he must present a negative defense of various doctrines or practices of the Catholic insofar as these may offer an obstacle to the motives of credibility. Again he must often descend to the purely natural philosophical level in attempting to demonstrate the existence of God, the immortality of the soul, and the freedom of human will. While such questions pertain more specifically to the areas of dogmatic theology, natural theology, or rational psychology, they are extended to the domain of the practical apologist in the exercise of his art.

Indeed it is perhaps in this area of related topics that the modern practical apologist faces his greatest challenge. His work of presentation and adaptation depends of its very nature upon the listeners to whom he addresses his words. Now with the growing sophistication of the educated classes and their greater dependence upon automation with the concomitant advent of the "computer age," greater stress than ever before is being placed upon precision in thought, the nature of truth, and the criteria for discerning certitude. With an evergrowing class of computer analysts and programmers, such fundamental epistemological questions will underlie much of the apologist's labors tomorrow.

Along these same lines, another specific difficulty facing the practical apologist today is found in the conflicting theological views about the very nature of the act of faith and its proper object. While this divergence of opinion is hardly new, its current agitation causes the apologist many problems. In his own presentations the apologist must answer first for himself this question: is the *fact* of divine revelation itself an object of faith or is it a truth that must be naturally known? For if the fact of revelation can be naturally known, it becomes the task of the apologist to convince his listeners of this fact. On the other hand, if the fact of divine revelation is itself an object of faith, then the most a practical apologist can do is assay a demonstration of its reasonableness. He realizes, therefore, that there are many today, even among devout practicing Christians, who regard his art as not only unnecessary, but even in a certain sense destructive of true faith. Such, he understands, is the attitude of many existentially minded theologians, who regard faith in its essence as a blind personal encounter between the soul and God, one eventually reduced to obscurity and total risk. For such theologians, to seek a rational foundation for faith is actually to suppress it. Such, he is aware, is also the attitude of those who would see in faith a subjective reality, simply the encounter in which God speaks His Word to man and in which man recognizes and discerns the Word of God in Scripture. For these also a practical apologetics would be at the very least useless.

But even among those who would admit the validity and necessity of apologetical science and art, new questions are raised precisely upon the epistemological level. The phenomenological analysis of consciousness proposed by E. Brunner has won a certain following in Germany, with a consequent emphasis upon preconceptual intuition, rather than the concept or the judgment, as the focal point leading to the placing of an act of faith. While such speculations pertain more properly to the scientific apologist, the practical apologist can ill afford to ignore their presence and their possible implications for him.

In his search for vital, meaningful, and relevant ways of presenting the motives of credibility, the practical apologist is ever mindful of Catholic teaching that faith is truly the work of God, that no man can come to Christ unless he be drawn unto Him. On the purely natural level he understands that one will not believe unless one wishes to believe. He thus realizes most clearly that he cannot force a man by purely logical reasons to place an act of supernatural faith, any more than Christ Himself could do so by making claims and actually proving them by miracles. His, in short, remains the task of offering the rational foundation for a supernatural, superrational edifice.

See also APOLOGETICS; ACCOMMODATION; MARKS OF THE CHURCH (PROPERTIES); MIRACLE, MORAL (THE CHURCH); IMMANENCE APOLOGETICS; APOLOGETICS, ARTICLES ON.

Bibliography: DTC, Tables générales 1:196–206. H. LAIS and W. LOHFF, LexThK² 1:723–731. M. BECQUÉ, *L'Apologétique du cardinal Dechamps* (Paris 1949). A. DULLES, *Apologetics and the Biblical Christ* (Westminster, Md. 1963). R. GORMAN, *Catholic Apologetical Literature in the U.S. 1784–1858* (pa. Washington 1939). J. J. HEANEY, ed., *Faith, Reason, and the Gospels* (Westminster, Md. 1961). G. K. MALONE, *The True Church: A Study in the Apologetics of Orestes Augustus Brownson* (Diss. St. Mary of the Lake; pa. Mundelein 1957). A. A. MICEK, *The Apologetics of Martin John Spalding* (Washington 1951). J. R. QUINN, *The Recognition of the True Church according to John Henry Newman* (Washington 1954). G. A. MCCOOL, "The Primacy of Intuition," *Thought* 37 (1962) 57–73.

[G. K. MALONE]

APOLOGIES, LITURGICAL

An apology is an acknowledgment of personal unworthiness, generally on the part of the celebrant, to take part in the holy Sacrifice of the Mass. An apology evinces therefore, at least implicitly, a consciousness of personal sin; and it is often conjoined to a prayer begging God's merciful forgiveness. The Confiteor recited by the celebrant at the beginning of the Roman Mass is such an apology.

The apology was not much employed in the ancient Christian liturgy. However, for various reasons, apologies began to appear with greater frequency within the *Gallican rites in the 6th and 7th centuries (cf. the Mone Masses, PL 138:863–882, *passim*); and they reached the peak of their development between the 9th and 11th centuries, finding their way into numerous Mass formulas. The *Missa Illyrica* (*c.* 1030), for example, contains apologies after vesting, before entering the house of God, after kissing the altar, during the Gloria and the chants between the readings, during the Offertory singing and the preparation of the offerings, after the Orate fratres, during the Sanctus, and during the Communion of the faithful (Martène AER 1.4.4: 490–518). In the Orient, apologies that serve as prayers of preparation for the priest are found in the 6th century.

Some authors maintain that apologies were adopted in the Celtic–Gallican liturgical tradition in imitation of Eastern practices (Eisenhofer Lit 83). Others attribute the apologies in the East and West to a common cause, namely, the fact that the concept of the mediatorship of Christ had receded into the background as a result of the Arian controversy. In opposition to * Arianism, the Catholic camp stressed the divinity of Christ rather than His humanity and mediatorship. Such a tendency impressed upon sinful man the awesome majesty of the Almighty, without reminding him of the Mediator between God and man. Thus the celebrant was led to insert into the liturgy admissions of his own unworthiness to celebrate the divine mysteries. Moreover, until the 11th century, sacramental Penance was an infrequent matter, and greater emphasis was placed upon extrasacramental confession of sins as a means of forgiveness; hence the celebrant lessened his unworthiness by frequent apologies in the course of the liturgical service.

In the modern Roman rite, the Confiteor and the two prayers that follow it, the *Aufer a nobis* and the *Oramus,* are apologies that serve to prepare the celebrant for the celebration of Mass. These began as silent prayers recited by the celebrant as he approached the altar. They became obligatory on all churches following the Roman rite only with the Missal of Pius V in 1570. The *Munda cor meum* is an apology that prepares the minister for the reading or chanting of the Gospel, and the *Per evangelica dicta* is a plea for forgiveness through the efficacy of the Gospel. Apologies also accompany the Offertory of the Roman Mass. Under Innocent III (d. 1216), the Offertory rite in Rome was accomplished in silence on the part of the celebrant (*De sacro altaris mysterio* 29; PL 217:831), but in 1570 the current Offertory prayers were sanctioned by Pius V. The two apologies *Domine Jesu Christe* and *Perceptio Corporis tui* prepare the celebrant for the reception of Communion. The *Placeat* which precedes the blessing was found in the Sacramentary of Amiens in the 9th century [V. Leroquais, "Ordo Missae du sacramentaire d'Amiens," EphemLiturg 41 (1927) 444]. It is a final appeal for God's acceptance of the Sacrifice despite the unworthiness of the celebrant.

Bibliography: F. CABROL, DACL 1.2:2591–2601. J. A. JUNGMANN, *The Mass of the Roman Rite,* tr. F. BRUNNER, 2 v. (New York 1951–55) 1:78–80; *Die Stellung Christi im Liturgischen Gebet* (Liturgiegeschichtliche Forschungen 19; Münster 1925) 223–225. Eisenhofer Lit. Miller FundLit 175–176.

[E. J. GRATSCH]

APOLOGISTS, GREEK, Greek Christian writers of the 2d century who presented an account of their faith for outsiders. The term is not ancient, for the

Greek word *apologia* meant a speech from the dock made by one about to suffer martyrdom. *Justin Martyr was an apologist who suffered martyrdom, but not all the apologists did. After the close of the apostolic age Christians became conscious that they were a third race, neither Jewish nor Hellene, and two kinds of apology began to appear, aimed at either of these groups. Justin's *Dialogue with Trypho* and the dialogues of Jason and Papiscus, of Timothy and Aquila, of Athanasius and Zacchaeus, or of Simon and Theophilus are specimens of the dialogue with Jews. The better-known works addressed to Greeks, and most educated Romans had some Greek, were prompted mainly by the desire to remove from Christianity what the Emperor *Trajan had called the *flagitia cohaerentia nomini,* i.e., crimes associated with the (Christian) name; these were cannibalism, promiscuity, and the worship of many gods, including animals (*see* ATHENAGORAS). The spur to the writing of apologies was the knowledge that it was imperial policy to give Christians a fair hearing. A rescript of *Hadrian, now generally accepted as genuine, to Minucius Fundanus in 124–125 had ordered governors not to listen to popular clamor against Christians but only to evidence of crimes. *Quadratus, the first apologist, was contemporary with this rescript, and he was soon followed by *Aristides, Aristo of Pella, and in midcentury by Justin. *Melito of Sardes is credited with an apology (now lost) presented to Marcus Aurelius. The *Embassy* of Athenagoras to the same Emperor (*c.* 176–180) is fortunately preserved. *Clement of Alexandria's *Protrepticus* and Origen's reply to Celsus are apologies; and the *Logos alethes* of Celsus (*c.* 178) and satire of Lucian on the *Death of Peregrinus* (*c.* 167) show that a pagan reaction was beginning. The only apology that is a speech from the dock is that of Apollonius, delivered *c.* 180–185; it is extant in an Armenian version, having been recovered by F. C. Conybeare in 1894, and part of a Greek version has survived also. Attacks on Greek culture, such as those of *Tatian and Hermias, cannot be considered apologies for Christianity. Knowledge of the apologies is in large part attributable to Bishop *Arethas, who in 914 had a copy made of many of them. It is from this codex that present texts are derived.

Bibliography: Quasten Patr 1:186–252. M. PELLEGRINO, *Studi sul'antica apologetica* (Rome 1947). P. C. DE LABRIOLLE, *La Réaction païenne: Étude sur la polémique antichrétienne du Ier au VIe siècle* (6th ed. Paris 1942). A. L. WILLIAMS, *Adversus Iudaeos* (Cambridge, Eng. 1935). E. J. GOODSPEED, *Die ältesten Apologeten* (Leipzig 1914); *Index Apologeticus* (Leipzig 1912). F. C. CONYBEARE, ed. and tr., *The Apology and Acts of Apollonius* (New York 1894). E. GROAG, Pauly-Wiss RE 13.1 (1926) 461–462, rescript of Hadrian.

[J. H. CREHAN]

APOPHTHEGMATA PATRUM. In its primitive state an *apophthegma* is a terse reply or statement made by an elderly monk to a young candidate whom he is instructing in the ways and principles of the monastic life. The word is based on the Greek ἀποφθέγγομαι—I speak my mind plainly, I make a statement—and the axiomatic type of counseling, whether spontaneous or requested, could develop into a short dialogue, a parable in words or actions, or more rarely, into the discussion of a Scripture passage. Eventually collections of such axioms were called in monastic circles "The Sayings of the Fathers."

Such an utterance was looked upon as inspired, a charism, and was treasured by the recipient as a gift from heaven. In terse and vivid terms, without rhetorical development or philosophical grounding, it set forth some principle of the spiritual life or its application from the elementary repelling of vice to the highest type of contemplation.

The second stage of the *apophthegma* came when the saying was repeated by the monks and commented upon. The point at issue was noted and the name of the author preserved as the saying became common property.

Eventually some literate monk wrote these statements down, and they became material for the collections of later days.

The *apophthegmata* of the fathers first appeared at the beginning of the 4th century among the monks and solitaries of Egypt, seemingly in Nitria, the Cellia, and especially in the Scetis Valley. The gift belonged mainly to the unlettered Copts, and it was in their language that the oral tradition was active. The written recording was done for the most part in Greek by educated Hellenes from the Greek settlements in Egypt. Yet much of the vigor of the popular tongue was kept in the Greek translations, and the form of life presented is the semianchoritic. After the mid-5th century, with the spread of education and monastic rules, the authentic type of *apophthegmata* disappeared, although new forms of expression came under this name: excerpts from the lives of the saints and from homilies, miracle stories, and so on.

The *apophthegmata patrum* are of importance for understanding the beginnings of monastic life and the development of religious centers. In the opinion of W. Bousset, they can be compared to the primitive Life of St. *Pachomius and his Rule as a source for the history of Christian piety.

Bibliography: F. CAVALLERA, DictSpirAscMyst 1:766–770. W. BOUSSET, *Apophthegmata: Studien zur Geschichte des ältesten Mönchtums,* ed. T. HERMANN and G. KRÜGER (Tübingen 1923); J. C. GUY, *Recherches sur la tradition grecque des Apophthegmata Patrum* (Brussels 1962). Quasten Patr 3:187–189.

[A. C. WAND]

APORIA, a transliteration of the Greek ἀπορία, meaning without passage, is used to signify the mental state of *doubt arising from consideration of a vexing problem or difficulty that causes anxiety and is apt to urge further inquiry or investigation. Aporia or mental impasse can arise from any set of difficult circumstances or considerations regarding either thought or action. It can also be aroused artfully by the dialectician who desires to make someone aware of a problem and perhaps help toward solving it. The Socratic method of question and answer, of argument and counter argument, was aimed at bringing attention to bear on a problem so that an aporia would result, which would stimulate further inquiry and lead to clarification. An aporia is thus a kind of methodical doubt that may be both real and positive, with probable arguments pro and con.

*Aristotle approved and regularly employed the method of raising aporia while teaching. In the *Metaphysics,* he says that philosophical investigation should begin with consideration of the aporias that arise from the conflicting statements of other philosophers or from matters they have not treated (995a 22). An aporia does not spring from nowhere, but from imperfect knowledge of things and from the natural curiosity or drive of the mind. It urges one to consider carefully what is doubtful and what is not doubtful, and to find out why it is or is not so. Just as a hard knot can be untied only after one knows how it was tied in the first place, so also in the investigation of truth it is necessary to know beforehand the various reasons or causes of aporia. Otherwise in study or research one would not know what to look for and whether to stop or to continue the investigation. But this is manifest to one who knows his previous doubts and the reasons for them; he is thus better able to judge of the *truth when it appears.

Thus aporia is not a skeptical doubt, nor does it lead to *skepticism, because it presupposes that one already knows something and hopes to know something more or better. It does not take away all *certitude, nor does it commit one to an aimless search; rather it urges him to proceed hopefully in the light of what he already knows toward the solution of a clearly formulated question or problem.

See also EPISTEMOLOGY; KNOWLEDGE.

Bibliography: Eisler 1:77. G. FAGGIN, EncFil 1:302. L. M. RÉGIS, *Epistemology,* tr. I. C. BRYNE (New York 1959) 21–26.

[W. H. KANE]

APOSTASY, in the strict, traditional sense of the word, is the gravely sinful act by which one totally abandons, inwardly and outwardly (both *corde* and *ore,* in a kind of perversion of Rom 10.10), the Catholic faith in which he has been baptized and which he has heretofore professed (see St. Thomas Aquinas, ST 2a2ae, 12.1; 10.1; 10.5; CIC c.1325.2; 188.4; 646.1; 1065.1). Complete and massive disbelief is the immediate term of such an apostasy from the Christian faith. In order to have the sin of apostasy it is not required that the defector find a surrogate for the Christian faith, which he has entirely forsworn, in a non-Christian religion, such as Judaism, Islam, or paganism, much less that he start a new non-Christian religion of his own devising. Even if he remain alienated from religious belief of any kind, and lead a wholly areligious life, he is an apostate from the faith.

It is commonly held that the sin of apostasy differs not in kind but only in degree from the sin of *heresy, with apostasy accidentally aggravating heresy's malice by the totality of its rupture with God's word and of its rebellion against His authority (St 2a2ae, 12.1 ad 3). However, in the concrete pastoral sense, an apostate differs notably from a heretic in that (1) unlike the heretic who "retains the name of Christian" (CIC c.1325.2), he abjures and discards that name completely; and (2) while he may pass over to a non-Christian religion, he does not form a rival Christian communion, as heretics often have done.

See also EXCOMMUNICATION; FAITH, LOSS OF; FAITHFUL; INFIDEL; MEMBERSHIP IN THE CHURCH; SCHISM; UNITY OF FAITH.

Bibliography: A. BEUGNET, DTC 1.2:1602–12. J. BOUCHÉ, DDC 1:640–652. P. DE LABRIOLLE, ReallexAntChr 1:550–551. G. W. H. LAMPE, ed., *A Patristic Greek Lexikon* (Oxford 1961–) fasc. 1:208.

[F. X. LAWLOR]

APOSTLE

One of the 12 intimate followers of Jesus who were commissioned by Him to preach His gospel. This article will first treat of the Biblical data on the Apostles and then consider the theological significance of their office in the Church that Christ founded.

1. IN THE BIBLE

In classical Greek the word ἀπόστολος (from the verb ἀποστέλλω, to send away, to send out) is used several times in the meaning of a naval "expedition," but seldom in the meaning of "one sent," a messenger, an envoy. In the Greek NT, besides being used to designate a messenger in general (Jn 13.16; 2 Cor 8.23; Phil 2.25) and a messenger from God in particular (Lk 11.49; Heb 3.1—in this case of Christ as God's messenger), it is most frequently used in a special sense to designate the *Twelve whom Jesus chose from among His *Disciples to assist Him in His earthly mission and to be its continuators under the leadership of St. *Peter, His vicar.

The Greek word as used in the NT is no doubt a translation of the Aramaic word *šᵉlîḥā',* "one sent." But its change of meaning from a term connoting a temporary function of anyone sent on any mission to a title of a permanent office is strictly a NT development. The Talmudic use of the Hebrew word *šᵉlîaḥ* in a similar sense for the Jewish officials who acted as contact men between the Jews of Palestine and those of the Diaspora is post-Christian and perhaps due to Christian influence. In the NT the broader usage that includes any Christian missionary (e.g., Barnabas in Acts 14.13; 1 Cor 9.6) is older than its technical usage as limited to the Twelve and Paul, who puts himself on a par with them. In the latter sense it is used only once in Matthew (10.2) and Mark (6.30) and never in John, but it is common in the Epistles, Acts, and Luke, who ascribes to Jesus Himself the attribution of this title to the Twelve: "He chose twelve, whom he also named apostles" (Lk 6.13). Treatment will be made here of the call of the Apostles by Jesus, the lists of their names, and their office.

Call of the Apostles. Andrew, John, Simon (Peter), Philip, and Nathaniel (Bartholomew) were on intimate terms with Jesus before He formally chose the Twelve. They first met Him at the Jordan, where they had been disciples of John the Baptist (Jn 1.35–51). They were witnesses of His first public miracle at Cana (Jn 2.1–11), and they stayed in His company when He made His headquarters at Capharnaum (Jn 2.12). Where the other Apostles first met Jesus is not known, except for Matthew (Levi), who, as he was sitting in his tax collector's place, received from Jesus the simple call, "Follow me" (Mk 2.13–14 and parallels).

Later, after spending a night in prayer, Jesus summoned all His Disciples and from among them selected twelve (Mt 10.1; Mk 3.13–14; Lk 6.12–13). Mark and Luke situate the event on "a mountain," but Matthew does not connect it with his *Sermon on the Mount. From then on the Twelve formed a special inner circle within the general group of Jesus' Disciples, preparing for an unexampled work, to be Christ's envoys as He was the envoy of His Father (Jn 17.18; 20.21).

Scriptural Lists of the Apostles. The names of the twelve Apostles are listed four times in the NT, once in each of the three Synoptic Gospels and once in Acts. The relatively fixed nature of the lists, with minor variations in each one, shows that they represent four variant forms of a single early oral tradition. The need that was felt for a knowledge of the names of the Twelve among the early Christians is an indication of the reverence in which the early Church held them.

Christ among His Twelve Apostles, a fresco of the 4th century from the catacomb of the Giordani at Rome, Italy.

In each of the four lists the names fall into three groups of four names each, the first name in each group being constant. On the assumption that Jude, the brother of James, is the same as Thaddeus, the same men are mentioned in each of the three groups of the four lists (*see* JUDE THADDEUS, ST.). But the order of the names varies somewhat in each group, with the exception that Judas Iscariot is named last by all three Synoptics (and naturally is missing from the list of Acts). The greatest variation occurs in the third group, where the lists distinguish between an Apostle already mentioned and another with a similar name. (For the epithet of St. *Simon the Apostle, *see* ZEALOTS.)

Apostolic Office. The essence of the apostolic office lies in the sending or commission of the Apostles by Christ. As one who is sent (the meaning of the Greek term for Apostle), an Apostle is Christ's envoy, ambassador, or vicar, with full power to act in His name. Hence the stress that is laid in the NT on the sending by Christ of His Apostles (Mt 28.19; Mk 3.14 and parallels); He sends them just as He has been sent by His Father (Mt 10.40; Jn 13.20). Matthias cannot take the place of Judas among the Apostles until God has designated him by lot for this commission (Acts 1.21–26). The Apostles do not receive their commission from the Church (Gal 1.1), and therefore they are

APOSTLES LISTED IN SCRIPTURE

Mt 10.2–4	Mk 2.16–19	Lk 6.14–16	Acts 1.13
Simon Peter	Simon Peter	Simon Peter	Peter
Andrew	James, son of Zebedee	Andrew	John
James, son of Zebedee	John	James	James
John	Andrew	John	Andrew
Philip	Philip	Philip	Philip
Bartholomew	Bartholomew	Bartholomew	Thomas
Thomas	Matthew	Matthew	Bartholomew
Matthew	Thomas	Thomas	Matthew
James, son of Alpheus	James, son of Alpheus	James, son of Alpheus	James, son of Alpheus
Thaddeus	Thaddeus	Simon, the Zealot	Simon, the Zealot
Simon the Cananean	Simon the Cananean	Jude, brother of James	Jude, brother of James
Judas Iscariot	Judas Iscariot	Judas Iscariot	

above the Church and not subject to its tribunal (1 Cor 4.3). They are the official witnesses of Christ, especially of His Resurrection (Lk 24.48; Acts 1.8, 21–22; 13.31); Paul can rank as Apostle because he too saw the risen Lord (Acts 9.3–5; 1 Cor 15.8). Yet the mere fact of having seen Christ risen from the dead does not make a man an Apostle (1 Cor 15.5–6).

As God's envoys and spokesmen, the Apostles have the right to be heard (2 Cor 5.20; 1 Thes 2.13) and to be received as if they were Christ Himself (Gal 4.14). In the same capacity they perform the liturgical functions of the Church—baptizing (Acts 2.41), celebrating the Eucharist (Acts 20.7–11), and laying their hands on other men in Confirmation and Ordination (Acts 6.6; 8.15–17). In God's name they can forgive sins (Mt 18.18; Jn 20.23). With the fullness of Christ's power they can work miracles (Mk 3.15; 6.7 and parallels; Acts 2.43; 5.12; Rom 15.19; 2 Cor 12.12; Heb 2.4).

The Apostles are thus the ministers and fellow workers of God and of Christ (Rom 1.9; 15.15–16; 1 Cor 3.9; 2 Cor 6.1; Col 1.23; 1 Thes 3.2). As such, they can demand the obedience of the community (Rom 15.18; 1 Cor 14.37; 2 Cor 10.8; 13.1–3). Yet they must be willing to forego their personal privileges (1 Cor 9.12–19; 1 Thes 2.7), for they are not the lords but the servants of the Church (Mk 10.42–45; Mt 24.45–51; 2 Cor 1.24; 4.5), its shepherds or pastors (Jn 21.15–17; Acts 20.28; Eph 4.11; 1 Pt 5.2–4), and its fathers (1 Cor 4.15). Theirs is a ministry of service (Acts 20.24; Rom 11.13; 12.7). They preside over the faithful, not as rulers over subjects, but as fellow members of the same community (Acts 15.22; 1 Cor 5.4; 2 Cor 2.5–10). They serve as models for them (1 Cor 4.16; 1 Thes 1.6; 2 Thes 3.9; 1 Pt 5.3), and the Church is built upon the Apostles as an edifice on its foundation (Mt 16.18; Eph 2.20; Ap 21.14).

Bibliography: A. Médebielle, DBSuppl 1:533–588. EncDict Bibl 115–120. K. H. Rengstorf, Kittel ThW 1:397–448. K. E. Kirk, ed., *The Apostolic Ministry* (London 1957). K. H. Schelkle, *Jüngerschaft und Apostelamt* (Freiburg 1957).

[M. L. HELD]

2. In Theology

In this second, theological, part of the article the sense of the word Apostle will first be discussed in its stricter scope and then in its wider meaning.

The Twelve. According to Catholic tradition the college of the Twelve is an institution of Jesus historically significant in the economy of *salvation for the *Church, for office in the Church, and for the *deposit of faith entrusted to the Church.

Meaning for the Church. While alive the Twelve were first witnesses of the *Resurrection of Christ (Acts 1.21–22; 10.41; Lk 1.2; 24.36–43; Jn 20.24–29; 1 Jn 1.1–3) and guarantors of "the continuity between the risen and historical Jesus" (O. Cullmann), who authorized them (Acts 1.8, 24–26; Mt 28.18–20; Mk 16.15–18; Lk 24.47–49; Jn 21.15–17). They were the nucleus of the primitive Church in Jerusalem under the guidance of Peter (Acts 1–6; 9–12; 15; 1 Cor 15.5; Gal 1.18–19). Their missionary activity hardly extended beyond Judea, Galilee, and Samaria according to Acts 8–11. Because of persecution Peter "went into another place" (Acts 12.17). After the "council of *Jerusalem" (Acts 15.30; 16.4) further details are lacking. The first mention of the missionary journeys is in the apocrypha.

Even after death the Twelve, apart from their eschatological significance (Mt 19.28; Lk 22.30; Ap 7.4–8; 21.12–14), are "the foundation and origin of the Church" (P. Gaechter; cf. Eph 2.20; Ap 21.14; Denz 468–469, 2886–88). From the Apostles it receives doctrine and fundamental structure (Acts 2.42; 5.28; Gal 2.2); to them are referred *creeds (Apostles' Creed; cf. Rufinus, *Expositio symb.* 2.10–15, Corp Christ 20:134) and Church regulations; even heretics appeal to them. Hence the care for reliable apostolic *tradition (2 Thes 2.15) and the κοινωνία of the Churches among themselves.

It is thus that the Twelve stand between Jesus and the Church. They preach what they have received from the Lord by *revelation, not by tradition; the Church preaches what has been entrusted to it by the preaching of the Apostles (1 Tm 6.20; 2 Tm 1.12, 14; 2.2; 3.14; Ti 2.1). Despite the difference between "Age of the Apostles" and "Age of the Church," between apostolic and postapostolic (ecclesiastical) tradition, the latter tradition also can be normative, even infallible, because of the presence of the Lord (Mt 28.20; Jn 16.8–15; cf. Cullmann).

Meaning for Office in the Church. The *apostolicity of the Church means (H. Küng) "continuity in the apostolic faith and creed" (*traditio apostolica*) and "in the apostolic office" (properly *successio apostolica*). Even the activity of the Twelve (Acts 1.25) was not merely a spiritual *charism or a passing assignment (A. v. Harnack; R. Sohm), but a spiritual office to continue the *mission of Jesus (Jn 20.21–23; 13.20; 17.18; 21.15–17; Mt 4.19; 10.40; 18.18; Lk 10.16).

The Twelve could not have successors as witnesses of the Resurrection and as the foundation of the Church, but only as Apostles (Mt 28.20). As a matter of fact the office was handed on from the beginning by the *imposition of hands (Acts 6.6; 13.1–13; 14.22; 20.28; 1 Tm 4.14; 2 Tm 1.6; Ti 1.5) to missionaries and *elders, and they were sometimes called apostles (Acts 14.4, 13; 1 Cor 15.7; 2 Cor 8.23; Phil 2.25), as *Paul who was already "a man of the second generation in the line of tradition and transmitted authority to rule" (Gaechter). And so to the horizontal line of intercommunication between the Churches there is added the vertical line ordained by the Founder of the Church of ordination to office and mission. The line, God-Christ-Apostle-bishops-deacons (1 Clem. 42.1–5), is already vouched for by Scripture. True, the Churches cooperate in the continuation of the line, but the authority never came from them (Acts 1.15–26; 6.1–6; 1 Tm 3.2; *Did.* 15.1; 1 Clem. 44.2–3).

Traditio and *successio apostolica* are intimately connected: the former is person-bound, the latter connected with the service of the word (J. Ratzinger; cf. Irenaeus, *Adv. haer.* 3.3.1, PG 7:849). Hence in the arguments with the Gnostics the succession element was stressed (H. von Campenhausen) and the most important Churches were shown to have derived from the Twelve (Tertullian, *De praescr. haer.* 32; CSEL 70:39–41).

Therefore not all of the prerogatives were passed on to the bishops as successors of the Twelve; moreover, they are successors only as a part of "the one, undivided college of *bishops" (Cyprian, *De cath. eccl. unit.* 5; CSEL 3.1:213), which as a whole succeeds the college of Apostles (T. Zapelena, K. Rahner) and which with the *pope as head is the recipient of the highest

Jesus Christ, the Redeemer, in glory, attended by His 12 Apostles and 2 angels, detail of the 9th-century mosaic commissioned by Pope Paschal I, on the arch of the apse of the Church of S. Maria in Domnica, Rome.

power in the Church [see Vatican II, *Lumen gentium* 22; ActApS 57 (1965) 25–27]. Only the pope is the successor of a definite Apostle. It is controverted whether or not one must admit two supreme guiding authorities in the Church; whether or not the pope, when acting "alone," acts as the head of the college of bishops (Rahner).

Significance for Revelation. The postapostolic preaching and tradition of the Church is tied to the deposit of revelation transmitted by the Apostles (Denz 3069–70, 1501). Therefore it is theologically certain that public revelation closed as to content (Denz 3421) with the "Age of the Apostles," with the "first generation of the Church" (Rahner), but this does not exclude a "subjective development of dogmas" (H. Bacht; *see* DOCTRINE, DEVELOPMENT OF).

Other "Apostles." As the word apostle is used variously in Scripture (see above), so it is used also in noncanonical writings. At first Jesus (Heb 3.1), the Twelve, Paul, missionaries, and itinerant preachers are called apostles; soon the term refers also to the immediate disciples and successors of the Twelve, the *viri apostolici* and founders of the *ecclesiae apostolicae* (Tertullian, *De praescr. haer.* 32; CSEL 70.39–41). The concept is extended as early as the 3d century to bishops and, from the 5th and 6th centuries, progressively more exclusively to popes. As a characterization of their function the name apostle is soon given to Christians who serve those who are officially apostles, who live after the manner of apostles (Lk 9.3; 10.3; 18.22), whose apostolic activity has its source in charisms or even in *Baptism alone. Pseudoapostles are also mentioned (2 Cor 11.13).

In judging this extension of the word apostle one must consider that its limitation to the Twelve and Paul, perhaps even its limitation to the Twelve (despite Lk 6.13) already belongs to a second phase (K. Schelkle, G. Klein, W. Schmithals), so that the apostles of 1 Cor 12.28 and Eph 4.11 are charismatics (J. Brosch), those of Rom 16.7 simply coworkers of Paul, and those of 1 Cor 15.7 the whole circle of disciples. Through the outpouring of the Spirit and by Baptism all Christians also have the faculty and duty to continue the work of Christ (1 Pt 2.9; Acts 4.31). Thus the wide use of the word apostle expresses the thought that the whole Church is a college, a "council of divine calling" (Küng) and must be apostolic even in the active sense.

See also APOSTOLIC SUCCESSION; AUTHORITY, ECCLESIASTICAL; HIERARCHY; MARKS OF THE CHURCH; OFFICE, ECCLESIASTICAL.

Bibliography: A. MICHEL, DTC 16:216–218. H. BACHT, LexThK[2] 1:736–738. E. M. KREDEL, *Bibeltheologisches Wörterbuch,* ed. J. B. BAUER, 2 v. (2d ed. enl. Graz 1962) 1:61–69. A. KOLPING, Fries HbThGrdbgr 1:68–74. J. BROSCH, *Charismen und Ämter in der Urkirche* (Bonn 1951). G. SÖHNGEN, *Die Einheit in der Theologie* (Munich 1952) 305–322. H. VON CAMPENHAUSEN, *Kirchliches Amt und geistliche Vollmacht in den ersten drei Jahrhunderten* (Tübingen 1953), bibliog. O. CULLMANN, *Die Tradition als exegetisches, historisches und theologisches Problem,* tr. P. SCHÖNENBERGER (Zürich 1954). T. ZAPELENA, *De ecclesia Christi,* 2 v. (5th ed. Rome 1950–54). P. GAECHTER, *Petrus und seine Zeit* (Innsbruck 1958). G. KLEIN, *Die zwölf Apostel* (Göttingen 1961), bibliog. K. RAHNER and J. RATZINGER, *The Episcopate and the Primacy,* tr. K. BARKER et al. (New York 1962). W. SCHMITHALS, *Das kirchliche Apostelamt* (Göttingen 1961), bibliog. F. KLOSTERMANN, *Das Christliche Apostolat* (Innsbruck 1962), bibliog. H. KÜNG, *Strukturen der Kirche* (Freiburg 1962), bibliog. **Illustration credits:** Fig. 1, Pontifical Commission of Sacred Archeology. Fig. 2, Alinari-Art Reference Bureau.

[F. KLOSTERMANN]

APOSTLES, ICONOGRAPHY OF

The 12 disciples of Christ were called "apostles," because they were sent out (Gr. ἀποστέλλειν, to send forth) by Him to spread the gospel through the world. Thus one of the characteristics of the Church is its apostolicity; an indispensable element in its foundation was the preaching, holiness, and martyrdom of the Apostles. This article treats the development in Christian art of the full group, or college of the Apostles, in symbolic representations and in narrative scenes from the New Testament. For additional information on the

Apostles in art, *see* LAST SUPPER, ICONOGRAPHY OF; PENTECOST, ICONOGRAPHY OF; and SAINTS, ICONOGRAPHY OF.

Traditio Legis. The establishment of the Church is shown in early Christian art by the seating of the Apostles to the left and right of Christ. The idea of the *Traditio Legis* or expansion of the Church is conveyed by standing Apostles converging in a double line toward Christ (4th-century sarcophagus; S. Ambrogio, Milan). The establishment of the Church by the teaching of Christ to the Apostles was painted in the Roman catacombs. In the fresco of the "cripta dei fornai" (Domitilla), St. Peter and St. Paul are sitting on folding stools, while the other 10 Apostles are standing. Christ was shown enthroned twice amidst 10 Apostles making the gesture of "adclamatio" (5th-century silver chalice from Antioch, The Cloisters, New York). He appears as the teaching Logos and as the Apocalyptic Christ, accompanied by the lamb.

The hillock represented in the early Christian sarcophagi, on which Christ teaches, sitting, or delivers the Law, standing, was interpreted as Mt. Zion on which Jerusalem is built. The mountain in Galilee where Christ appointed the "eleven disciples" to meet him before He delegated to them His authority and vanished from their view (Mt 28.16–20) was equated by St. Jerome with the mountain, exalted above the mountaintops, toward which a multitude of people will climb to hear the teaching of the Lord (Is 2.2–3). Thus, Christ stands on the mountain, "giving the law" to the Apostles and presenting St. Peter with the rotulus of the New Dispensation (Borghese sarcophagus, probably of the 4th century, Louvre).

Sometimes the college of the Apostles is gathered around Christ resurrected and holding the victorious "crux gemmata" (Probus sarcophagus, Museo Petriano). In a "star and wreath" sarcophagus in the Museum of Arles, the Resurrection was rendered symbolically present by a cross topped by a wreath of victory encompassing the monogram of Christ. On a beautiful fragment of a sarcophagus in the S. Sebastiano catacomb, the crowns, which in the Arles sarcophagus are held by the hand of God above the head of each Apostle against a starry sky, are now presented by the Apostles to Christ. The latter theme was taken from the Roman practice of having the provinces send the *aurum coronarium* to the head of state and according to which on solemn occasions the senators offered to the emperor the *aurum oblaticium.*

The key motif of the *Traditio Legis* was made explicit by the words "Dominus legem dat" inscribed on the rotulus proffered by Christ to Peter (sarcophagus, Arles Museum). According to St. Irenaeus and to the Fathers, the *Traditio Legis* consisted in the authority delegated to the Apostles to redeem through Baptism (Mk 16.16; Mt 28.19). That connection is made manifest in the mosaics of the early Christian baptisteries (S. Giovanni in Fonte and Baptistery of the Arians, Ravenna).

The *Traditio Legis* received its official recognition at the Roman synod of 382. Christ stands on the mountain, Mt. Zion and Paradise, uplifting His right hand with the gesture of *Sol Salutis* (Sun of Salvation), inherited from the Roman monuments of *Sol Invictus.* St. Paul hails Him and St. Peter takes in his veiled hands the rotulus of the new law. In this way the doctrine of the priority of the See of Rome, based on the double apostolicity of Peter and Paul in Rome and their martyrdom there, was confirmed in the circle of Pope Damasus. In the apse of the Cluniac priory of Berzé-la-Ville, the early 12th-century fresco developing the theme of the *Traditio Legis,* complete with 12 Apostles, signified the direct allegiance of the order of Cluny to the Holy See under the patronage of St. Peter and St. Paul, whose relics had been deposited in the main altar of the abbey church consecrated in 1095. In Rome the tradition of the modified *Traditio Legis* was continued until the 9th century (mosaics in SS. Cosmas and Damian, S. Prassede, and S. Cecilia).

Animal Symbols. As early as the time of Pope Damasus the *Traditio Legis* theme developed into the introduction into Paradise of saints whom St. Peter and St. Paul presented to Christ. After the saints, a new symbol appears. Twelve lambs representing the Apostles are shown going out of the symbolical cities of Bethlehem and Jerusalem; they converge toward the *Agnus Dei* standing on the mount. The Apostles are symbolized by lambs also in the presence of the Transfiguration (mid-6th-century mosaic, S. Apollinare in Classe, Ravenna).

In the apse of the 5th-century baptistery at Albenga, 12 doves, symbolizing the 12 Apostles, surround a triple halo bearing the triple monogram of Christ as well as the letters alpha and omega repeated three times, which is a threefold anti-Arian reference to the Trinity.

Narrative Scenes. In the primitive liturgy the Ascension was celebrated on the afternoon of the Feast of the Pentecost. In the church of the Apostles in Constantinople, as it had been rebuilt by Justinian I (546), the cupola with the mosaic of the Ascension was located above the southern arm of the cross-shaped building—a plan that was copied in the church of the Apostles in Milan—and the cupola with the mosaic of the Pentecost was located above the western arm. The Ascension cupola was separated from the central cupola, reserved to the Pantocrator, by an arch the mosaics of which illustrated the appearance of Christ before His Disciples in the cenacle before the Ascension. The Pentecost cupola was separated from the Pantocrator cupola by an arch illustrating the mission of the Apostles. Mosaics on the three wall arches supporting the Pentecost cupola showed the Apostles administering Baptism. In a 9th-century manuscript of the sermons of St. Gregory of Nazianzus, the scene of the mission given to the 11 Apostles (Mt 28.19) tops a composition divided into 12 compartments in each of which an Apostle is painted performing the rite of Baptism. Together with the 46 illuminations representing the Passions of the Apostles, they constitute a cycle illustrating the common feast of the Apostles which, in the Greek East, was celebrated on June 13. The Greek iconography of the Apostles' Passion, revived in the 9th century after pre-iconoclastic models, was transmitted to the illustrators of the Western medieval Passionalia; their works, in their own turn, were used as the sources of the martyrdom of the Apostles in Gothic sculpture (portals of the cathedral of Strasbourg, Holy Cross in Gmünd, and Saint-Thiébaut in Thann).

Although the feast of the *Divisio Apostolorum,* which in the West occurs on July 15, was not celebrated

Fig. 1. Christ as the teaching Logos with two Apostles, detail of the chalice from Antioch, 5th century.

Fig. 4. Christ Pantocrator with angels, Apostles and the Virgin, 9th-century mosaic in the dome of Hagia Sophia, Salonika, Greece.

ICONOGRAPHY OF THE APOSTLES

Fig. 2. Procession of Apostles, 5th-century mosaic in the dome of the baptistery of the Arians, Ravenna.

Fig. 5. "Death of Ananias," drawing by Raphael.

Fig. 3. Apostles as sheep proceeding from Bethlehem, detail, 12th-century mosaic, S. Maria in Trastevere, Rome.

Fig. 6. Column carved with images of three Apostles, 12th century, from Santiago de Compostela, Spain.

Fig. 7. Bust, 5th century, from a mausoleum in the church of the Apostles, Constantinople.

Fig. 8. Baptismal font carved with Apostles on the shoulders of Prophets, 12th century, in the cathedral at Merseburg, Germany.

until the end of the 11th century, a long tradition prepared it. It was initiated by Eusebius's *Historia Ecclesiastica* (PG 20:213–216) and the apocryphal Acts of the Apostles and iconographically anticipated in illuminated codices of the commentary on the Apocalypse by Beatus of Liébana (*c.* 776). The names of the nations allotted to the Apostles are written above the head of each, that of "Spania," inscribed above St. James, bearing testimony to the belief in the apostolicity of his mission in Spain and to the fame of the pilgrimage to Santiago de Compostela. The separation of the Apostles, departing toward their respective assignments, appears in the lunettes of the 12th-century façade of the cathedral of Angoulême. Peculiar to Byzantine iconography is the blessing of His Apostles by Christ in Bethany, before "He parted from them and was carried up into heaven" (Lk 24.50–51). The ceremonious bowing down of the Apostles worshiping Christ is treated in an awe-inspiring way in a splendid mural painting in the choir of Hagia Sophia at Trebizund (13th century).

Romanesque art, with its propensity for synthesis, achieved the fusion of the iconography of the mission of the Apostles and that of Pentecost. In the Pentecost image in a lectionary from Cluny, Christ proffers a scroll with the inscription: "Ecce mitto promissum Patris mei in vos." The first word "Et" of Lk 24.49 was significantly changed to "Ecce." On the main tympanum of the Magdalene church at Vézelay, a gigantic Christ, flattened against the mandorla that circumscribes Him, darts shafts of light onto the Apostles. On His proper right the clear sky and the books held open by the Apostles proclaim in the words of Mk 16.16: "He who believes and is baptized shall be saved." On the left side the closed books and the waves of thunder, billowing above the Apostles, warn that "he who does not believe shall be condemned."

The renewal of the early Christian and Byzantine association between the Ascension and the mission of the Apostles is exemplified in a relief by *Donatello (*c.* 1427). Christ enthroned on a mountain between clouds beyond which He is about to vanish, gives the keys to St. Peter in the presence of the Virgin and the other Apostles. The tapestry cartoons designed by Raphael in 1514, however, broke with every allegorizing trend as well as with the apocryphal tradition. Following the literal straightforwardness first exhibited by *Giotto in the Arena Chapel of Padua, *Raphael conceived his cycle of the life of the Apostles as "istorie" in the sense of *Alberti. The first series of the tapestries for the Sistine Chapel was begun in Brussels in 1516 (cartoons, Victoria and Albert Museum).

The Mystical Mill. At the opposite aesthetic and intellectual pole of the compositions by Raphael, the dying spirit of the Middle Ages invented the mystical mill or host mill. The theme assumed an extraordinary development in the visionary and surrealistic art of the end of the Middle Ages and was used for the purpose of putting double emphasis on the "Corpus Mysticum" both as the Eucharist and as the Church. In a miniature of a Gradual, the Apostles turn the crank of the host mill, *molendarium hostiae* (Zentralbibliothek, Lucerne).

Apocalyptic Themes. The Apostles embody the walls of the heavenly Jerusalem in keeping with Ap 21.14: "The wall of the city has twelve foundation stones, and on them twelve names of the twelve apostles of the Lamb" (Romanesque fresco; San Pietro al Monte, Civate). The 24 Elders (Ap 4.4) are interpreted as the double college of the Prophets and Apostles in early medieval illustrated apocalypses and in Romanesque portals. As a rule, the 24 Elders accompany the *Majestas Domini,* but in the transept of the cathedral of Lausanne (13th century) they gyrate around the coronation of the Virgin. In the final phase of Romanesque art, the theophany of the Last Judgment according to Matthew (24.27–31) progressively replaced the Apocalyptic *Majestas Domini.* In an intermediate period, the *Majestas Domini* became more and more imbued with connotations of the Last Judgment. The Apostles, enthroned on globes, accompany Christ enthroned as a judge (Mt 19.28): "You shall sit on twelve thrones and shall be judges over the twelve tribes of Israel" (early 12th-century fresco, church of Saint-Savin-sur-Gartempe).

Architectural Symbolism. On account of the very number 12, the college of the Apostles sustained a special relationship with architectural symbolism. Realizing the will of Emperor Constantine the Great, Emperor Constantius II (337–361) buried him in a mausoleum joining the church of the Apostles. Because of relics deposited there of St. Peter, St. Paul, St. John, and St. Thomas, with those of St. Timothy added in 356 and those of St. Andrew and St. Luke in 357, the church became the shrine of the apostolic founders of the church. The mausoleum was in the form of a rotunda surrounded on the inside by 12 columns which were surmounted by as many bust reliefs of the Apostles as *imagines clipeatae* (Medallions of the Apostles, Ottoman Museum, Istanbul). As we see on an ivory plaque representing the Resurrection (*c.* 400, Bayerisches Nationalmuseum, Munich), the rotunda built above the tomb of Christ in the Anastasis church in Jerusalem was decorated with similar busts of the Apostles. The formula of the college of Apostles, carved on both sides in the splays of a Last Judgment portal, prevailed in the cathedrals of Chartres and Amiens between 1215 and 1230. There, as "bases" and "columns" of the church of which Christ standing against the trumeau of the portal is the "doorway," they continued the tradition of statue-columns of the ancestors of Christ on façades of cathedrals and abbey churches of western and northern France of the mid-12th century. Apostle portals descended from French models are found in the German Gothic cathedrals at Strasbourg, Münster, Erfurt, and Augsburg.

Symbol of the Creed. According to early tradition, before they scattered toward the countries assigned to them (Rufinus, PL 21:337), on the very day of the Pentecost (Pseudo-Augustine, PL 39:2188–91), the Holy Spirit inspired the Apostles to speak, each in his turn, one article of the creed. Ottonian art seized upon that tradition and dramatized it by building the concordance of the articles of faith and the prophecies, perching the Apostles on the shoulders of the Prophets (fresco, S. Sebastiano in Pallara, Rome). This caryatidal pattern of concordance struck deep roots in Germany (12th-century baptismal font, cathedral of Merseburg; 13th-century "Fürstenportal," Bamberg Cathedral). The iconographical scheme of the concordance of the Prophets and Apostles became very popular in the 12th century in the Cologne and Mosan workshops (enameled portable altar, made by Eilbertus of

Cologne, *c.* 1130, Berlin Museum). In France, Suger had laid out symbolically the choir of his abbey church—"raised aloft by columns representing the number of the twelve Apostles and, on the second hand, by as many columns in the ambulatory that signified the number of the prophets" (*De Consecratione* 5, with reference to Eph 2.20). From the end of 14th to the 16th century the credo tapestries continued the tradition of presenting the Apostles and Prophets in pairs.

Apostle Glasses and Spoons. Some early Christian sense of the mysterium of the Church embodied in the college of the Apostles was salvaged in the decorative arts of the Renaissance and 17th century, illustrating the Apostles. On enameled glasses produced in Silesia, Franconia, and Bohemia, the 12 Apostles distributed into two tiers under arches surround the *Salvator Mundi.* The Apostle silver spoons were first made as separate baptism gifts, and later ordered as complete iconographical series. They are recorded from 1494 to 1686 in England, Holland, Germany, Switzerland, and Italy.

Bibliography: D. T. B. Wood, "Credo Tapestries," *Burlington Magazine* 24 (1914) 247–254, 309–316. A. Fabre, "L'Iconographie de la Pentecôte," *Gazette des beaux-arts,* 5th ser., 8 (1923) 33–42. C. G. Rupert, *Apostle Spoons* (New York 1929). A. Katzenellenbogen, in *Reallexikon zur deutschen Kunstgeschichte,* ed. O. Schmitt (Stuttgart 1937–) 1:811–829, bibliog.; "The Separation of the Apostles," *Gazette des beaux-arts,* 6th ser. 35 (1949) 81–98. J. Pope-Hennessy, *Donatello's Relief of the Ascension with Christ Giving the Keys to Saint Peter* (London 1949). G. Downey, "The Builder of the Original Church of the Apostles at Constantinople," DumbOaksP 6 (1951) 53–82. F. Salet, "Les Statues d'apôtres de la Sainte Chapelle conservées au musée de Cluny," *Bulletin monumental* 109 (1951) 135–156; 112 (1954) 357–363. E. Mâle, *Les Saints compagnons du Christ* (Paris 1958), iconography of individual apostles. C. David-Weyer, "Das Tradito Legis und seine Nachfolge," *Münchner Jahrbuch der bildenden Kunst,* 3d ser., 12 (1961) 7–45. A. E. M. Katzenellenbogen, "The Sarcophagus in S. Ambrogio and St. Ambrose," ArtBull 29 (1947) 249–259. **Illustration credits:** Fig. 1, The Metropolitan Museum of Art, The Cloisters Collection, Purchase, 1950. Fig. 2, Anderson-Art Reference Bureau. Fig. 3, Alinari-Art Reference Bureau. Fig. 4, R. V. Schoder, SJ. Fig. 5, Courtesy of the Victoria and Albert Museum, London. Copyright reserved. Fig. 6, Courtesy of the Fogg Art Museum, Harvard University, Gift, The Republic of Spain through the Museo Arqueologico Nacional and Prof. A. Kingsley Porter. Fig. 7, Hirmer Verlag München. Fig. 8, Marburg-Art Reference Bureau.

[P. VERDIER]

APOSTLESHIP OF PRAYER, a spiritual association of Catholics who are not only concerned for their own salvation but also intent on spreading the Kingdom of Christ. They work for this by prayer and sacrifice in the spirit of apostles, mainly through three practices: (1) The daily offering of all their prayers, works, joys, and sufferings to the Sacred Heart of Jesus, or to God the Father through Him, (2) The uniting of their offering with the sacrifice of Christ renewed in the Mass and reception of Communion in reparation at least once a month, (3) The daily recitation of the Rosary, or at least one decade of it.

Although it was started in 1844 by Francis X. Gautrelet, SJ, in Vals, France, Henri Ramière, SJ, is credited with making it a world movement by giving it a definite structure; by publishing in 1861 his book, *The Apostleship of Prayer, the Holy League of Hearts United to the Heart of Jesus;* and by the *Messenger of the Sacred Heart,* which has become the monthly organ of the Apostleship in many countries and languages. There were 51 *Messengers* in 1963. The statutes of the Apostleship, first approved by the bishop of LePuy, were revised in 1866, 1879, 1896, and 1951, the last with the approval of Pius XII.

Theological Basis. Only abundant grace can save millions of souls. Ordinarily only prayer, liturgical and private, can secure this grace. Too many forget this. Therefore the Apostleship of Prayer strives to enroll and continually remind all Catholics, as members of Christ's Mystical Body enjoined to love others as He has loved them, that they should make everything they do every day a prayer and sacrifice for the salvation of souls. It promotes devotion to the Sacred Heart, the soul of the Apostleship, through consecration, reparation, and other practices.

Organization. The Apostleship of Prayer is not a sodality or confraternity, but a richly indulgenced spiritual association of approximately 38 million members in 140,000 centers (1964). Its general director is the father general of the Society of Jesus. His delegate directs it from Rome with the assistance of national, regional, and diocesan directors. He appoints the diocesan directors nominated by their bishops. Diocesan directors establish local centers in parishes, schools, institutions, and societies and appoint pastors, chaplains, or other priests to serve as local directors of these centers. The faithful who have the intention, not binding under sin, of making the daily offering, may become members for life by enrolling in any center. Members appointed by directors to help spread the Apostleship are called promoters. There are sections, like the Eucharistic Crusade for children and the League of the Sacred Heart for men, and a radio and television program. The Confraternity of Christian Doctrine in the U.S. has adopted the Apostleship of Prayer for the spiritual formation of its members. The national office of the Apostleship is in New York. Principal publications are the *Handbook of the Apostleship of Prayer,* the *Sacred Heart Messenger,* monthly *League Leaflets,* and Eucharistic Crusade literature.

[F. SCHOBERG]

APOSTLESHIP OF THE SEA (Opus Apostolatus Maris), an international association for the spiritual care of seafarers, was founded by a group of laymen in Glasgow, Scotland, in 1920. Two years later Archbishop Mackintosh of Glasgow secured the blessing of Pius XI and a letter of approval for the society dedicated to prayer and good works for seamen. By 1927 200 churches in various ports of the world were designated as centers for seamen. In 1942 the Consistorial Congregation assumed jurisdiction over both the port and ship chaplains, and in 1952 the apostolic constitution *Exsul familia* established the General Secretariate in Rome. In 1957 Pius XII promulgated a series of laws and statutes for the organization and guidance of the movement. John XXIII granted special supplementary faculties to chaplains in 1961. In the U.S. the office of episcopal moderator of the Apostleship of the Sea was established in 1951. In 1962 there were 66 chaplains in U.S. ports and 6 seamen's clubs in Mobile, New Orleans, San Pedro, Wilmington, Seattle, and San Francisco. The apostleship chaplain has the care of souls of maritime personnel both ashore and at sea. He serves seafarers aboard ship and in port, at navigational academies and in maritime hospitals; he is responsible for arrangements necessary for the proper liturgical celebration of Mass by all priests making a sea voyage. His faculties include the administration of Confirmation to seamen under special conditions, the privilege of the portable altar, the use of the antimension for Mass and the appointment of substitute chaplains for single voyages. Traditionally the Apostleship of the Sea ministers to all seafarers, with special concern for foreign seamen of all faiths.

Bibliography: PIUS XII, "Exsul familia" (Apostolic Constitution, Aug. 1, 1952) ActApS 44 (1952) 649–704.

[M. F. CONNOLLY]

APOSTOLATE, from the Greek ἀποστολή, a sending, commission, or expedition. The Greek term is more indefinite than the Latin *apostolatus,* which refers more to the condition and office of the messenger than to his action. The Koine (NT) is of course greatly influenced by the Latin.

In the NT [Rom 1.5; 1 Cor 9.2 (cf. 2 Cor 12.12 Vulg); Gal 2.8; Acts 1.25] ἀποστολή is the *apostolic office of Paul, of Peter, and the *Twelve. Its limitation to the Twelve (Acts 1.25) is a later development. The apostolic office of the Twelve consists of a nontransferable commission as witnesses of the *Resurrection of Christ and as foundation of the Church; it is transmittable by the imposition of hands and mission, the apostolate proper. This is exercised collegially and individually so that the successors of the Apostles bring to the present the *mission of Jesus (Jn 20.21) and of the college of the Twelve. Protestant research questions the nature of the official character of the apostolate and its original connection with the institution of the Twelve ("a connection of post-Pauline origin"); the Twelve-Apostle concept itself is termed "a product of ecclesiastical reflection" (Klein).

The infrequent post-Biblical use follows hesitantly the wider sense of "apostle" already used in the Bible (*see* APOSTLE); its extension to the office of bishops follows two centuries later; its restriction to the papacy later still; the apostolic activity of lay people is called apostolate only in the middle of the 19th century. Its use for organizations and apostolic media renders it meaningless.

Apostolate is the mission of Christ (1 Cor 1.1) and participation in it: by ordination and mission—hierarchical apostolate; by Baptism and Confirmation (Jn 4.14; 7.38; Rom 6.1–12; Gal 3.26–29; 1 Pt 2.5–9; Ap 1.5–6; 5.10; 20.6; 22.3–5), by charism (1 Cor 12.1–31), by marriage (1 Cor 7.7, 14), by vocation and special gifts (1 Cor 7.17, 20, 24)—apostolate of Christians; by general supplementary mandate of the hierarchy (Catholic Action) and by particular mandate (*missio canonica*)—the specific apostolate of lay people; by close imitation of Christ (1 Cor 7.32–34)—apostolate of the counsels.

For bibliography, *see* APOSTLE.

[F. KLOSTERMANN]

APOSTOLATE AND SPIRITUAL LIFE

The normal relationship between the apostolate and the spiritual life is a mean standing between the various species of activism, on the one hand, and another extreme less easily denominated, the main feature of which would be solicitude about the "disturbances" consequent upon the exercise of the apostolate, on the other. This article can provide only the briefest introduction to the question of how the two complement one another and how, under some conditions, the apostolate is apparently opposed to the spiritual life.

The Church has been in a mission status from the very beginning of its existence. Those who first constituted the new people of God were given the title, "apostles." The community founded upon them is essentially apostolic, not merely in the sense of being in historical continuity with that small group through the apostolic succession of episcopal consecration but also in the sense of having the mission, at the present time, of preaching the gospel to the whole of creation (Mk 16.15).

The Church, however, is a community in whose members the word of the Gospel has borne fruit in various degrees, and it is also a community that is organized hierarchically. Both these factors determine the exercise of the apostolate: the former because it is assumed that apostolic works are somewhat the overflow of communion with God in the Church, the latter because the whole apostolate of the Church is under the direction of the episcopal hierarchy, who stand in place of the Apostles.

The exercise of the apostolate, by those who share in this mission of the Church, normally bears fruit in the interior life of the apostle himself. Experience witnesses to the fact, and that it should be so is to be expected because such activity is in the likeness of trinitarian life. In God, the Father unceasingly generates the Son without losing anything of Himself. Rather, the Son abides in the bosom of the Father and gives Himself to Him in love, so that from their mutual embrace proceeds the Holy Spirit. The apostle exercises, in one degree or another, a spiritual paternity, through which real relations are established between himself and those to whom he is sent. "I became your Father in Christ Jesus through the Gospel," says St. Paul (1 Cor 4.15b). This does not mean that the persons brought forth "in Christ Jesus" remain in some infantile way dependent upon the Father-Apostle, for "through the Gospel" they receive a share not in his life but in God's. Nonetheless, if the exercise of the apostolate is authentic, those who are spiritually engendered thereby, as they grow up in Christ Jesus, remain united to their apostle-father by love and piety. The communion thus established must obviously bear fruit in his interior life.

What, then, in this context, is an authentic apostolate? Reference here is not primarily to the so-called "canonical mission," which gives a certain juridical authenticity to the work of the apostle who receives such a mandate, even though the "canonical mission" should normally be the sign and guarantee of the overall authenticity of a given work. Here the word "authentic" refers more to the moral quality of the apostolate, its genuineness as an exterior and visible expression of the apostle's interior life.

St. John provides the best possible description of this authenticity: ". . . that which we have seen and heard we proclaim also to you, so that you may have fellowship with us; and our fellowship is with the Father and with his Son, Jesus Christ" (1 Jn 1.3). The order is clear: seeing and hearing come first, then proclamation, and this in turn is for the sake of fellowship, i.e., deeper communion with God in the Church. An authentic apostolate, therefore, in terms of the spiritual life, is one that is based upon a measure of "seeing and hearing" and is motivated by a desire for sharing. Of course, St. John refers to an experience wherein Jesus was physically present to those whom he chose as Apostles, but the sensible contact scarcely exhausts what he means. The Apostles saw and heard by faith what the Father revealed in Jesus, especially through his "enactment" of the paschal mysteries. Living faith, then, is the heart of the apostolate, together with that work of charity called mercy. The interior life of any apostle is constituted by an acceptance and assimilation of the living truth of God's love for mankind in Christ Jesus, together with the urge to share the joy that is the normal fruit of being "in the truth." "The love of Christ urges us on" (2 Cor 5.14a).

Bibliography: J. B. CHAUTARD, *The Soul of the Apostolate,* tr. J. A. MORAN (Trappist, Ky. 1941). F. CUTTAZ, DictSpirAscMyst 1:773–790, with bibliog. to 1937. THOMAS AQUINAS, ST 2a2ae, 32.2–3; 182, 188.2.

[M. B. SCHEPERS]

APOSTOLIC, the adjective affirming a relation of people, activities, or objects to the *Apostles, their mission, their actions. It is first found in Ignatius of Antioch (*Trall.*) and the *Martyrdom of Polycarp*. In the patristic age the word serves to represent the relation of origin and similarity of the *Church to the *Twelve and Paul (apostolicity). It is applied to the immediate disciples and successors of the Twelve and Paul; from the 3d and 4th centuries to *bishops; from the Middle Ages, religious, missionaries, priests, and lay people are called *viri apostolici. Ecclesia apostolica* is a Church established by one of the Twelve or their immediate successors; from the 4th century it designates every episcopal see and the whole Church (Denz 3, 43—as a property and a note). In the 6th century, particularly in the West, apostolic is restricted to the papal sphere (cf. CIC cc.3, 4, 7 etc.). *Vita apostolica* is, from the 2d and 3d centuries on, a life like that of the Apostles, i.e., an ascetic life (Nilus of Ancyra, *Ep.* 3.26; PG 79:384), the monastic life (Socrates, *Hist. eccl.* 4.23; PG 67:512), from the 6th century on rather the active pastoral life; so also among the sects.

As a noun *apostolicus* means bishop (Tertullian), in the 6th century *pope, and later the receiver of certain papal letters. As early as the 4th and 5th centuries *apostolici* are heretics; *apostolicum,* the word of an Apostle (Augustine); later the designation was connected with a creed, a lectionary, letters and decrees of the popes. *Apostolica* were the official vestments of bishops.

See also APOSTOLATE.

Bibliography: H. BACHT, LexThK² 1:758–759, bibliog. K. G. STECK, RGG³ 1:516, bibliog. W. NAGEL, *Der Begriff des Apostolischen in der christlichen Frühzeit bis zur Kanonsbildung* (Habilitationsschrift, typescript; Leipzig 1958).

[F. KLOSTERMANN]

APOSTOLIC BLESSING. A blessing was usually given at Mass by a bishop, in the Gallican rite after the fraction, but in the Roman rite at the end. When the pope gave this blessing, it was known as an apostolic blessing. The custom developed of its being given solemnly after Mass on certain occasions, e.g., at St. Peter's on Maundy Thursday and Easter Sunday, at St. John Lateran's on Ascension Thursday, at St. Mary Major's on the Assumption. A plenary indulgence was attached to it. Sometimes it was also given outside Mass, as the blessing *Urbi et orbi* from the balcony of St. Peter's after the election of a new pope. All bishops are empowered to give the apostolic blessing twice a year, and all priests to the dying.

[B. FORSHAW]

APOSTOLIC CHURCH ORDER, a small treatise that claims to have been written at the command of the Lord by the 12 Apostles. The first half (4–14) sets forth moral precepts in the form of a description of the two ways, that of good and that of evil, based on *Didache (1–4). The author adapts the two-way device to the more developed ecclesiastical situation of the 4th century. The second part (15–29) contains canonical legislation and issues regulations for the election of a bishop, priests, readers, deacons, and widows and for the subordination of the laymen. The author, and the time and place of origin are unknown. There are indications that it might have been composed in Egypt *c.* 300; but some scholars point to Syria as its place of origin. The high authority in which it was held in Egypt speaks perhaps more for Egyptian provenance.

J. Bickel was the first to publish (1843) the Greek original from a 12th-century Vienna manuscript, the only one containing the entire text. He named it the *Apostolic Church Order.* There is reason to assume that its real title was *Ecclesiastical Canons of the Holy Apostles.* These canons are attributed to the various Apostles who spoke at a reputed council at which Mary and Martha were present. The ignorant compiler ranked Peter and Cephas as two different Apostles. The extant Latin, Syriac, Coptic, Arabic, and Ethiopic versions testify to the reputation this *Church Order* enjoyed.

Bibliography: J. W. BICKEL, *Geschichte des Kirchenrechts,* 2 v. in 1 (Giessen 1843–49) 1:107–132, Gr. text. T. SCHERMANN, *Die allgemeine Kirchenordnung,* v.1 (Paderborn 1914) 12–34. G. HORNER, ed. and tr., *The Statutes of the Apostles or Canones ecclesiastici* (London 1904), gives Eng. tr. of the Coptic-Sahidic version and the Arabic and Ethiopic text with Eng. tr. E. HAULER, ed., *Didascaliae apostolorum fragmenta Veronensia Latina* (Leipzig 1900) 92–101, fragment of Lat. version. A. HARNACK, TU 2.5 (1886). Funk DidConst. Quasten Patr 2:119–120.

[J. QUASTEN]

APOSTOLIC CONSTITUTION, a form of papal decree dealing with matters of faith and affairs of the universal Church or a sizable portion of it. It is usually written according to the formal style of a papal bull, beginning with the words *Constitutio Apostolica,* followed by a statement of the subject matter. Then is inscribed the name of the pope, to which is added the title *Episcopus, Servus Servorum Dei* and the expression *Ad perpetuam rei memoriam.* If the apostolic constitution deals with a dogmatic definition it is signed only by the pope as the Bishop of the Catholic Church. Otherwise, this kind of letter is signed by the cardinal chancellor, the prefect or secretary of that Congregation to whose jurisdiction the subject matter pertains, and then the protonotaries. Apostolic constitutions are published in the **Acta apostolicae sedis.*

See also DOCUMENTS, PAPAL.

Bibliography: A. BRIDE, *Catholicisme* 3:117.

[J. A. FORGAC]

APOSTOLIC CONSTITUTIONS, a large collection of ecclesiastical law, written in Syria about 380. The full title, *Ordinances of the Holy Apostles through Clement,* suggests that these canons had been drawn up by the Apostles and transmitted to the Church by *Clement I of Rome. In reality they are the work of an Arian, who seems to be identical with the 4th-century interpolator of the Epistles of St. *Ignatius. The first six of its eight books are an adaptation of the **Didascalia*

Apostolorum, a Church Order composed in the first half of the 3d century in Syria.

The Constitutions contain canonical legislation for the clergy and deal with Christian ethics, the penitential discipline and Eucharistic Liturgy, fasts and feasts, schism, heresy, and Christian burial. Book 7, 1–32, is based on the *Didache; book 7, 33–38, contains a very interesting collection of Jewish prayers; 39–45, the Antiochene rites of Baptism and Confirmation; and 46–49, other liturgical material, especially (47) the *Gloria in excelsis* as the liturgical morning prayer.

Book 8 is the most important. Its first two chapters probably used a lost work of *Hippolytus of Rome, *Concerning Spiritual Gifts;* ch. 3–22 adapt the same author's *Apostolic Tradition,* formerly called the **Egyptian Church Order*. Book 8, 3–27, is an elaborate version of the Antiochene Liturgy. This section contains (5–15) the so-called Clementine Liturgy for use in the consecration of a bishop. Its completeness renders it a valuable source for the history of the Mass. Chapters 16 to 46 describe the duties of the members of the community. Chapter 47 comprises the so-called Apostolic Canons, a collection of 85 canons, derived in part from the preceding Constitutions, in part from the canons of the Councils of Antioch (341) and Laodicea (363). The first 50 of these were transmitted by *Dionysius Exiguus, and were used in later canonical collections of the West. The last of the 85 canons contains a list of Biblical books that omits the Apocalypse but adds the Apostolic Constitutions and the two epistles of Clement to the canon of Scripture.

An "Epitome" of book 8 of the Constitutions draws independently on the *Apostolic Tradition* of Hippolytus. The title "Epitome" is misleading because it is not an abbreviation or condensation, but a series of excerpts. In some of the manuscripts this "Epitome" is called "Constitutions through Hippolytus." Time and place of origin are unknown and difficult to determine but the excellence of its readings suggests that these extracts must have been made at a fairly early date after the composition of the Constitutions.

Bibliography: PG 1:555–1156. Funk DidConst. Quasten MonE 178–233, liturgical texts. F. E. BRIGHTMAN, *Liturgies Eastern and Western,* 2 v. (Oxford 1896) 1:3–30. F. NAU, DTC 3.2:1520–1537. H. LECLERCQ, DACL 3.2:2732–95. Quasten Patr 2:183–185, bibliog. D. VAN DEN EYNDE, RechScRel 27 (1937) 196–212. J. QUASTEN, ThSt 7 (1946) 309–313, baptismal font. J. A. JUNGMANN, *Missarum sollemnia* (4th ed. Freiburg 1962). W. E. PITT, JEcclHist 9 (1958) 1–7, Anamnesis.

[J. QUASTEN]

APOSTOLIC DELEGATION IN THE U.S.

Although the Holy See prefers to be represented in most countries by an apostolic nuncio (accredited to the civil government as well as to the episcopate) rather than by an apostolic delegate (having only an internal or religious and not also an external or political mission), an apostolic delegation was established in the U.S. because a nunciature was found to be impossible.

Preliminary Steps. In 1853, five years after Pius IX had received an American minister in Rome, he sent Gaetano *Bedini, titular Archbishop of Thebes and Apostolic Nuncio to Brazil, to the U.S. in the hope of preparing the way for a nuncio at Washington and of solving certain purely ecclesiastical problems. When John Hughes, Archbishop of New York, addressed an inquiry to a Catholic in the Cabinet, James Campbell, Postmaster General, the reply stated that the President, Franklin Pierce, would receive a chargé or minister but only as the pope's political representative, and would prefer a layman. The U.S. government, under pressure from nativists and European exiles, did not deem it opportune to increase its diplomatic relations with the reactionary Papal States (*see* NATIVISM, AMERICAN). Nevertheless, Bedini's July 12, 1854, report advised the Holy See to establish a nunciature in Washington at once: to effect complete unity among the U.S. bishops, to ensure uniformity of discipline, to safeguard the Church's interests in the newly acquired lands of Texas and New Mexico, and to provide a substitute for the primate desired by the First Plenary Council of Baltimore (1852). The U.S. bishops, however, feared that if diplomatic representatives were exchanged mutually, the government might meddle in spiritual affairs and that *Know-Nothingism might assail the Church even more violently. In view of the riots and demonstrations staged against Bedini in Cincinnati, Ohio; Wheeling, W.Va.; and elsewhere and of the government's failure to accord him the promised protection, the Holy See wisely declined to risk the possibly disastrous consequences involved in any such unilateral action as Bedini recommended. If the U.S. government refused to receive a nuncio, who would be an ecclesiastic, at this time, it would be even less likely to agree to such a proposal after it ceased, in 1868, to maintain its own minister in Rome and after the pope ceased, in 1870, to be *de facto* a temporal sovereign. Overtures were still made occasionally and secretly, however, on the part of the Holy See; for example, a minor Roman prelate, Paolo Mori, on a visit to the U.S. in 1886, tried to persuade the government to accredit an envoy to the Holy See, and the bishop of Fort Wayne, Ind., Joseph Dwenger, apparently used his insufficient influence both in Rome and in Washington to have himself appointed first nuncio or delegate.

Apostolic Visitators and Temporary Delegates. In the course of the 19th century several ecclesiastics were commissioned by the Holy See to act as apostolic visitators or delegates to the U.S. for specific purposes. In 1820 Joseph Octave Plessis, Bishop of Quebec, Canada, at the request of the Congregation of the Propagation of the Faith, investigated the troubles caused by obstreperous trustees in New York. In 1852, 1866, and 1884 the successive archbishops of Baltimore, Francis Patrick Kenrick, Martin John Spalding, and James *Gibbons, were appointed apostolic delegates by the Holy See to preside over the First, Second, and Third Plenary Councils of Baltimore, respectively. From time to time, moreover, foreign churchmen were sent to the U.S. to handle particular cases.

Petitions and Recommendations for a Permanent Delegation. Petitions for an apostolic delegate were sent to Rome mainly by priests who looked to the Holy See for support in their quarrels with their bishops. Thus around 1819, Robert Browne, OSA, who had resisted the legitimate authority of the archbishop of Baltimore, Ambrose Maréchal (and his two predecessors), in his undated report to the Propaganda concerning the Church in the U.S., requested the establishment of an apostolic delegation in Washington for the purpose of settling the controversies existing in many U.S. dioceses. Similarly, in 1883 Rev. William Mahoney in a 385-page book entitled *Jura Sacerdotum Vindicata. The*

Rights of the Clergy Vindicated; or, A Plea for Canon Law in the United States, which he published anonymously in New York, asserted with moderation and respect that the necessary remedy for the widespread abuse and "monstrous evil" "of priests being uncanonically dismissed from their dioceses and thrown helplessly on the world, to the infinite degradation of the sacerdotal character . . . and to the great scandal of the faithful" was the appointment by the Holy See of an apostolic delegate who would enforce a just and uniform discipline and insist on the observance of the then unheeded laws. Furthermore, Rev. Edward *McGlynn, who had been suspended in 1886 by Michael Corrigan, Archbishop of New York, for supporting Henry George and had been excommunicated for not obeying a summons to Rome, publicly welcomed and vaunted the report of the Holy See's endeavors to send a representative to Washington.

Advice of a similar nature was first offered to the Holy See in 1817, when Jean Lefebvre de Cheverus, Bishop of Boston, suggested to the Propaganda that Archbishop Maréchal be appointed apostolic delegate for the U.S. with power to settle in the first instance all conflicts between the lay trustees and the bishops.

After the First Plenary Council of Baltimore Rev. Thomas Heyden, of Bedford, Pa., wrote to the Propaganda (Nov. 12, 1852): "What we need is not more bishops and more councils but an Apostolic Nuncio so that we may speak more often with the Holy Father." In 1857 the Propaganda asked Pius IX to appoint an apostolic delegate to the U.S. without diplomatic character in order to promote uniformity in the petitions presented to the Holy See and to provide a source of information; the cardinals of the congregation proposed to give the office to a resident American, Archbishop Kenrick of Baltimore, who was practically serving in that capacity already. But the Pope feared that the appointment would revive the desire for an American primate and preferred to choose a non-American. In the end nothing was done during his pontificate.

In 1878 George Conroy, Bishop of Ardagh, Ireland, and temporary Apostolic Delegate to Canada, after visiting the U.S., expressed the opinion that a delegate should be appointed for that country too, but only for a time, according to need; and not with residence in Washington, where he might be slighted by the U.S. government and the foreign diplomatic corps, but rather in New York. In the same year Francis X. Weninger, the famous Jesuit missionary among the German immigrants, urged the Propaganda to appoint a permanent delegate—"a solid and moderate Italian," not an Irishman—in view of the serious disorders in the U.S. Church and of the caprice with which so many bishops treated their clergy.

Reasons For and Against a Delegation. In the last quarter of the 19th century more and more priests turned to the Holy See for the redress of their real or imagined grievances against their ecclesiastical superiors. On the whole, both bishops and priests were extremely ignorant of Canon Law and, consequently, unaware of their respective and reciprocal rights and duties. Most of the dioceses lacked a regularly organized tribunal or court or even a regularly appointed quasi-judicial counsel; hence, the cases were not properly handled in the first instance, and this lack of a proper trial often made it difficult in Rome to evaluate the conflicting testimony and to render a definitive judgment. In a considerable number of cases the Holy See gave a decision favorable to the priest, because the bishop had failed to furnish the requisite evidence. Some bishops maintained that they were not bound by various provisions of the general law of the Church because of the missionary status of this country. Some priests, acting in good faith, availed themselves of Roman justice and impartiality in order to protect themselves against the arbitrary dispositions of their bishops; others, acting in bad faith, took advantage of Roman leniency and slowness in order to evade due punishment and to prolong their refractory conduct. The Holy See believed that a delegate with his auditor could hear such appeals much nearer the scene of the disagreement, weigh the arguments on either side more judiciously, and pronounce a verdict more promptly.

Another reason for establishing an apostolic delegation was the Holy See's desire to bring the U.S. episcopate into closer union and greater concord with itself. Roman officials had the impression that the Americans were jealous and distrustful of them, were eager to remain as independent as possible in administrative affairs, and were suspicious of a highly centralized government of the Church. The proximate reason, however, was the need to restore harmony among the American bishops themselves. In the last 2 decades of the 19th century they were divided on several vital issues—on the rights of national groups, especially of the German-Americans; on the founding, location, and support of The Catholic University of America; on the toleration of secret societies that were essentially benevolent associations; and most of all, on the question of parochial or public schools. Only a disinterested observer on the scene could ascertain which of the contrary views were objectively based on fact.

All the bishops, however, with the single exception of John *Ireland, Archbishop of St. Paul, who expected a delegate to sustain his singular position in the school controversy, were as united in their rejection of the proposal of establishing an apostolic delegation in the U.S. as their predecessors had been in regard to a nunciature. Probably the chief motive for their opposition was the fear that the presence of a delegate (or nuncio) would limit the power and diminish the dignity of the individual bishops and decrease the esteem with which the faithful regarded them. The bishops resented the prospect of having their actions reported to Rome; moreover, they had been annoyed by minor Roman prelates who had visited the U.S. from time to time without any particular mission but had conducted themselves in an imprudent and officious manner, especially by commenting for the newspapers on problems they did not understand. Not unnaturally, the bishops dreaded the thought of there coming to this country a stranger who would immediately be besieged by a crowd of malcontents and would be unable to appreciate the circumstances or implications of the cases laid before him. They believed that the appointment of a delegate would harm their precarious relations with non-Catholics by confirming their enemies' allegation that the Catholic Church was a foreign religion and paid homage to a foreign power; that it would arouse latent prejudices; and, especially in the 1890s, would pour fuel on the flames of bigotry being fanned by the *American Protective Association (APA). In the political sphere, the sending of a delegate, they felt, would embarrass the Democratic party, to which a majority of the Catholics belonged, and thus would help the Republicans. They knew that there was no apostolic delegate in the United Kingdom and perceived no greater need of one in the U.S.; in fact, there were only seven apostolic delegates in the whole world at that time, and all of them were in predominantly Orthodox or Moslem countries. Hence, the American bishops, individually and collectively, repeatedly endeavored, up to the last minute, to dissuade the pope and his officials from sending a delegate to this country.

As an alternative, many of the American bishops favored the proposal of engaging an American prelate who would reside in Rome and represent them before the Holy See. Such an agent, they believed, could wield more influence on behalf of the U.S. Church than any individual bishop in his own diocese; moreover, he could supply authentic information on American problems and prevent inept legislation. The Roman officials, however, thought that the American bishops envisioned a plenipotentiary such as no other national episcopate had and desired to tie Rome's hands. Hence, when in 1882, Gibbons in his own name and in that of other bishops requested of the Propaganda that an American prelate be established in Rome, no affirmative response was given. Then, after Denis J. *O'Connell was named rector of the American College in Rome in 1885, he was employed by the bishops who trusted him as an intermediary with the Holy See, but he never received an official appointment from the American episcopate as a whole or any official recognition from the Holy See even though Gibbons formally asked Leo XIII to appoint him a counselor of the Propaganda. The greatest concession that the American bishops would willingly have made was that one of their own number be appointed delegate, although they could not easily have agreed on the choice of the individual; if the appointee were an American, said Gibbons, the principal objection would be removed. The Holy See, nevertheless, thought that only an Italian could be impartial among the rival national factions in the American Church.

Establishment of the Delegation. At last Leo XIII decided to overrule the objections of the American hierarchy. He found a convenient occasion for sending the future delegate when the Holy See was invited by the U.S. government to lend some 15th-century maps from the Vatican Library for the World's Columbian Exposition at Chicago. The Pope not only complied with this request but also appointed a personal representative to bring the historic materials for the exhibit. This was Francesco *Satolli, titular Archbishop of Lepanto, who had been ablegate also at the celebrations for the centennial of the American hierarchy and the opening of The Catholic University of America, Washington, D.C., in November 1889, and who had afterward told the Pope that more direct means of communication between the Holy See and the U.S. Church were desirable. He arrived in New York on Oct. 12, 1892, and in the following month announced to the archbishops assembled in that city the Pope's desire to establish with their concurrence a permanent apostolic delegation in the U.S. All the archbishops but Ireland were unwilling to give their consent because of the "serious difficulties connected with the subject." Throughout that autumn Satolli was not only attacked mendaciously in the APA press but also treated disrespectfully in certain Catholic quarters. On Jan. 3, 1893, Gibbons in the name of the archbishops signed a letter to Leo XIII in which he declared that a permanent delegate "would not serve the best interests of the Church." In the next few days many U.S. newspapers carried false reports about the ablegate's mission and sensational stories of ecclesiastical intrigue and conspiracy, and the journalists were abetted in creating this confusion by deplorable breaches of confidence among the bishops themselves. Satolli believed that the Jesuits were also opposed to him because of his approval of Ireland's plan for elementary education (*see* FARIBAULT PLAN).

On January 10, in the midst of all this discord, the Pope ordered the establishment of the delegation and appointed Satolli first delegate; the official documents were dated a fortnight later. On January 21 the Prefect of the Propaganda, Cardinal Miecislaus Ledochowski, informed the bishops in a circular letter that the decision was made both because it was customary to provide a delegate for countries in which the Church had reached a certain stage of maturity and because the peculiar situation in the U.S. required special attention. In the instructions drawn up for Satolli, the chief purpose of the delegation was said to be the fostering of a more intimate union of the American bishops among themselves and with the Holy See. He was also directed to see to the organization of episcopal courts and the due observances of juridical procedure in the various dioceses, to settle disputes between bishops and priests in the second or third instance without the right of further appeal, to study the reasons for the existence of so many "tramp-priests" in the U.S., to induce the bishops to adopt uniform regulations regarding schools, and to gather information on episcopal candidates.

Confronted with this *fait accompli,* the American bishops for the most part acquiesced in the Pope's will; some even wrote letters of thanks to the Pope for the great joy and immense benefit just conferred on the U.S. Church. James Ryan, Bishop of Alton, Ill., however, sent three cablegrams of vehement protest to Cardinal Ledochowski, who in reply sternly rebuked him for his "irreverence" toward the Pope and demanded "condign satisfaction" under threat of canonical penalties; the bishop made adequate amends but did not change his mind. Gradually the bishops reconciled themselves to the presence of the delegate in the U.S. Nevertheless, in the following year John Lancaster Spalding, Bishop of Peoria, Ill., published an article entitled "Catholicism and Apaism" in the *North American Review* [159 (September 1894) 278–287], in which he asserted that the delegate was "a source of strength to the Apaists," because this so-called "American Pope . . . though a foreigner, with no intention of becoming a citizen, ignorant alike of our language and our traditions, was supposed to have supreme authority in the church in America." Thereupon Satolli not only reprimanded Spalding directly but also reported him to Rome, and Leo XIII ordered the cardinal prefect to remonstrate with him for his hostile attitude toward the apostolic delegation.

In the apostolic letter *Longinqua oceani* of Jan. 6, 1895, Leo XIII averred that the apostolic delegation fittingly crowned the work of the Third Plenary Council of Baltimore, denied that the powers conferred on the delegate would be an obstacle to the authority of the bishops, and asserted that the ultimate aim of the delegation was to strengthen and perfect the constitution of the Church in the U.S.

Functions and Residences. In addition to the functions mentioned in Satolli's original instructions, he and his successors have discharged all the usual duties of an apostolic delegate, including the furnishing of advice to the Holy See on the division of existing dioceses and the erection of new ones, the oversight of religious orders, and the granting of dispensations, and they have exercised certain special powers (faculties) bestowed on them by the pope. *See* DELEGATION (CANON LAW). They have also consecrated many bishops of American birth and for American sees. Until 1908 the successive delegates were dependent upon the Propaganda; since that year they have been dependent upon the *Consistorial Congregation, but have dealt directly with all the proper organs of the Roman Curia; at all times they have remained in close contact with the papal secretariate of state. As the representative of the Consistorial Congregation, the delegate is the ordinary of the Pontifical College Josephinum at Worthington (near Columbus), Ohio, and he assigns its students to the various dioceses at the request of the bishops. The first delegate was assisted by one auditor and one secretary, both Italians; in 1964 the delegate had a staff of five Italian and three American priests.

Satolli was ordered to fix his residence in the national capital. At first he resided at The Catholic University of America, and then on Nov. 16, 1893, he removed to a house in northwest Washington, which had been purchased with money collected by the American bishops and priests. In 1906–07 a new building was erected for the delegation, again through the generosity of U.S. Catholics. The next home of the delegation, a stately edifice on Massachusetts Avenue, N.W., was paid for with similar contributions and was occupied in the spring of 1939.

List of Delegates. By 1964 seven ecclesiastics had served as apostolic delegates to the U.S. All titular archbishops during their term of office, the first six were created cardinals at the end of it, and were appointed to various offices in the Roman Curia. (Thus the delegation is practically equivalent to a first-class nunciature in the Vatican diplomatic service.) From the date of their elevation to the Sacred College until their departure the incumbents are called pro-delegates. The seven delegates included: Francesco Satolli (1839–1910), delegate from 1893 to 1896; Sebastiano Martinelli, OSA (1848–1918), delegate from 1896 to 1902; Diomede Falconio, OFM (1842–1917), delegate from 1902 to 1911, who had been ordained in the U.S. in 1866, had been rector of the seminary of Allegany, N.Y., and had been naturalized as a citizen; Giovanni Bonzano (1867–1927), delegate from 1911 to 1922, who returned as papal legate to the International Eucharistic Congress held at Chicago in 1926; Pietro Fumasoni-Biondi (1872–1960), delegate from 1922 to 1933; Amleto Cicognani (1883–), delegate from 1933 to 1958, who returned as papal legate to the Inter-American Congress of the Confraternity of Christian Doctrine held at Dallas in 1961; Egidio Vagnozzi (1906–), delegate from 1958, who was secretary and then auditor of the delegation from 1932 to 1942. Several of the other auditors and secretaries eventually became cardinals, e.g., Donato Sbarretti, Francesco Marchetti-Selvaggiani, and Paolo Marella.

Bibliography: J. T. ELLIS, *Life of James Cardinal Gibbons: Archbishop of Baltimore, 1834–1921,* 2 v. (Milwaukee 1952). W. J. LALLOU, *The Fifty Years of the Apostolic Delegation, Washington, D.C.* (Paterson 1943); "The Apostolic Delegation at Washington," AmEcclRev 65 (1921) 447–462; rev. *ibid.* 95 (1936) 576–592. T. T. MCAVOY, *The Great Crisis in American Catholic History, 1895–1900* (Chicago 1957). F. J. ZWIERLEIN, *The Life and Letters of Bishop McQuaid* 3 v. (Rochester 1925–27).

[R. TRISCO]

APOSTOLIC FATHERS

The term employed for a collection of the earliest Christian writings contemporary with and succeeding the later New Testament documents. It was already used by Monophysites, but its precise denotation is still disputed. In 1672 J. B. Cotelier published as *Patres aevi apostolici* works by Pseudo-Barnabas, the Shepherd of Hermas, Clement I of Rome, Ignatius of Antioch, and Polycarp of Smyrna. In a second edition in 1698, J. Clericus used the expression Apostolic Fathers (*Patres apostolici*); but L. Ittig restricted the term to Clement, Ignatius, and Polycarp in 1699. However the name was extended later to include the *Ad Diognetum,* fragments of Papias of Hierapolis, Quadratus, the Presbyter fragments in Irenaeus, and the Didache.

Apostolic Tradition. Pieces of different types and times of composition were thus bound together as a whole, but the term Apostolic in a strict sense used as a historical and traditional qualification was not applicable to each of the authors included. It would seem proper to limit the term Apostolic Fathers to those non-New Testament early Christian authors who were disciples or hearers of the Apostles (in a strict sense) or, even though without personal contact with the Apostles, demonstrate their particular respect for them, and in a comparatively truer sense are carriers and witnesses of Apostolic tradition.

Inclusion. These attributes belong to St. Clement of Rome's letter to the Corinthians, the seven letters of St. Ignatius of Antioch, and two of St. Polycarp of Smyrna; and Quadratus, though actually an apologist, should be added (Eusebius *Hist. eccl.* 4.3). All writings falsely attributed to these men, such as the so-called Second Letter of Clement, should be excluded, as well as the reports of their martyrdom, which do not come from their works. Neither the so-called Letter of Barnabas nor the work of the Shepherd of Hermas, qualify as Apostolic Fathers under the criteria in the sense described above. The *Ad Diognetum* was scarcely written by Quadratus and is of later authorship, while Papias was probably not an immediate disciple of the Apostles, but hands down an at least partially confused tradition. The Didache, recently studied as a collection of instructions given by Apostles in a generic sense, probably stands closest in time and content to the Twelve and thus could be added as an appendix to the Apostolic Fathers. Finally there are sayings of the Apostolic Fathers in the Presbyter sections of *Irenaeus.

Literary Form. With regard to literary form, the Apostolic Fathers imitate the Epistles of the Apostles. Their language, in general the Greek *Koine,* is influenced by the Septuagint and gives signs of the formation of a Christian *Sondersprache* or idiom. Yet there are stylistic differences among them: they extend from simple and uncontrived narrative as in Polycarp, through changes of format (Clement of Rome), to the passionately mystic expressions of Ignatius of Antioch. The classical rules of rhetoric and letter writing were not unknown to the Apostolic Fathers, and the authors are related to one another in literary dependence.

Theological Witness. In the ancient Church these writings received a high, partially canonical evaluation. As oldest testimonies to the development of the *Christian way of life alongside and after the New Testament, they possess an uncommon significance.

For Biblical theology they show the way from an extraordinary consideration of the Old Testament (Clement of Rome and partly the Didache) to the formation of the New Testament canon; and in Polycarp there is all but clear certification of the Pauline Corpus.

The scriptural inspiration of the Holy Spirit is clearly taught, and doctrinally the Apostolic Fathers are the oldest witnesses for the *Creed tradition. Their declarations concerning the three divine Persons, and particularly their witnesses to Christology and the Redemption as the midpoint of the new faith, are a reflective and clarifying theology, in part mystical, particularly in Ignatius, and based primarily on the foundation of the Scripture and the earlier Apostolic preaching.

The concept of the church exhibited by the Apostolic Fathers is stamped with the battle against schisms and primitive heresies. Hence the essential and necessary oneness of the Catholic Church (καθολικὴ ἐκκλεσία, first used by Ignatius: *Smyr.* 8.2), as an organism and the Body of Christ, is signified by a unified community whose character is demonstrated in unity with the bishop and in a common celebration of the liturgy.

In Ignatius there is a development of the theology and mystique of ecclesiastical offices, particularly that of the bishop. Besides the idea of spiritual unity, a God-willed hierarchy differentiated into clergy and laity (λαϊκός is first used by Clement 40.5) is given prominence. The Didache describes a collegial hierarchy in the community, and a definite teaching authority of the charismatically gifted; meanwhile there is evidence in the other documents for a transition from a collegiate to a monarchical episcopate without loss of the benefit of extraordinary charisms. Ignatius is the first witness to the threefold order: bishop, priests, and deacons; and the commanding position of the Roman church is early indicated (Clement of Rome and Ignatius). There is likewise evidence for the ecclesiastical position of widows and virgins. In the contribution of Ignatius one finds beginnings of patristic sacramental theology (particularly in regard to the Eucharist).

The writings of the Apostolic Fathers state the faith with regard to sin, justification, and grace, as well as the possibility of cooperation in salvation, and they offer numerous examples for it. Abstracting from the "one Penance" doctrine of the Shepherd of Hermas, who does not properly belong to the Apostolic Fathers, the theology and practice of Penance is developed beyond the foundation appearing in the New Testament.

In eschatological thought the authentic Apostolic Fathers are sober, but filled with the hope of the nearness of the Lord. Finally, the letter of Clement affords an insight into contemporary preaching on the resurrection of the flesh (ch. 24–26).

In their writings, the Apostolic Fathers desire above all else to serve the divinely willed order in the Church, and directions in moral, ascetical, and pastoral theology play an important role. The call to the faith, fraternal charity, and ecclesiastical obedience is clear and notable. Whereas in the letter of Clement and the Didache great Old Testament influence appears, in Ignatius the imitation of and union with Christ becomes an essential motive. Stimulated also by his mysticism, Ignatius likewise elaborates an early Christian theology of martyrdom. The Apostolic Fathers approach the pagan state with express loyalty. Finally these writings are sources for the Church history of their time, especially for the history of the liturgy: the Didache records the earliest texts for the performance of Baptism and the celebration of the Eucharist; the letter of Clement gives the oldest form of prayer of the community (Ch. 59–61); and Ignatius' letters are likewise rich in liturgical allusions.

Certain Hellenistic elements from philosophy, Gnosticism, and an insight into the mystery religions in the writings of the Apostolic Fathers attest the education and spiritual predilection of the authors; an example of this is the obvious Stoic influence on the letter of Clement.

Bibliography: Editions and translations. K. BIHLMEYER and W. SCHNEEMELCHER, *Die Apostolischen Väter* (Tübingen 1956–). J. A. FISCHER, *Die Apostolischen Väter* (Munich 1956). L. T. LEFORT, *Les Pères Apostoliques en copte,* 2 v. (CSCO 135–136, Scriptores Coptici 17–18; 1952). E. J. GOODSPEED, *The Apostolic Fathers* (New York 1950). J. A. KLEIST, AncChrWr 1 (1946); 6 (1948). Literature. H. KRAFT, *Clavis Patrum Apostolicorum* (Munich 1964). Altaner 50–54, 80–88, 97–113, 117–118. Quasten Patr 1:29–105. G. JOUASSARD, "Le Groupement des Pères dits Apostoliques," MélSciRel 14 (1957) 129–134. H. PIESIK, *Bildersprache der Apostolischen Väter* (Bonn 1961). J. LAWSON, *A Theological and Historical Introduction to the Apostolic Fathers* (New York 1961). G. KITTEL, "Der Jakobusbrief und die Apostolischen Väter," ZNTWiss 43 (1950–51) 54–112. F. X. GOKEY, *The Terminology for the Devil and Evil Spirits in the Apostolic Fathers* (Washington 1961). R. M. GRANT, ed., *The Apostolic Fathers,* v.1 (New York 1964).

[J. A. FISCHER]

APOSTOLIC SEE

The noun see, meaning seat, is now used only of the seat of a bishop, in the sense of the place where he presides, or the Church over which he rules. In early Christian literature the term *apostolic was applied to those Churches that had been founded by one of the *Apostles and hence were looked upon as primary witnesses of the apostolic tradition, agreement with which was a norm of orthodoxy for the other Churches. In this sense, Tertullian appealed to Corinth, Philippi, Ephesus, and Rome as "apostolic Churches, in which the seats of the Apostles still preside" (*De praescr. haer.* 36; CorpChrist 1:216). While in the eastern part of the Roman Empire there were many apostolic sees, the most prominent of which were Jerusalem, Antioch, and Alexandria, the only Church in the West recognized as an apostolic see was Rome.

See of Rome. One finds Rome referred to as the "see of Peter" in the writings of St. Cyprian (*Epist.* 59.14; CSEL 3.2:683), Optatus (*Contra Parm.* 2.2; CSEL 26: 36), and St. Jerome (*Epist.* 15.2; CSEL 54:63–64), as also in the synodical letter of the Council of Sardica to Pope Julius (Denz 136). It is in the writings of Pope Damasus I (366–384) that one first finds the term Apostolic See used consistently of Rome. From his time onward it was a characteristic of papal letters, and it was similarly used in the acts of Western synods and in the writings of the Latin Fathers, for whom Rome was *the* Apostolic See. While the Greek Fathers recognized Rome to be the see of Peter, and thus the first among apostolic sees, examples are rare of their adopting the Latin usage of referring to Rome simply as *the* Apostolic See.

See also APOSTOLIC SUCCESSION; APOSTOLICITY; CHAIR OF PETER; HOLY SEE.

Bibliography: H. LECLERCQ, DACL 15.1:1427–31. P. BATIFFOL, "Papa, sedes apostolica, apostolatus," RivArchCrist 2 (1925) 99–116; *Cathedra Petri* (Paris 1938) 151–168.

[F. A. SULLIVAN]

Canon Law. The Code gives a working definition of Apostolic See in these words: "By the term 'Apostolic See' or 'Holy See,' wherever it occurs in the Code, is meant not only the Roman Pontiff, but also unless a different meaning follows from the nature of the matter or the context, the Sacred Congregations and the Roman Tribunals and Offices through which the Roman Pontiff habitually transacts the affairs of the Universal Church" (CIC c.7; PostApost c.302).

The term Apostolic See was in constant use during the Middle Ages to designate the pope together with his Curia. However, such a concept only gradually entered the written law, and the designation given in the Code is the most general and absolute use of this term. In international diplomacy the term Holy See, and not Vatican City, is the proper nomenclature. Since 1957 the United Nations, as a result of an agreement with the Holy See, has discontinued the use of the term Vatican City in international conferences.

It is evident that when the Code speaks of matters that are proper to the Apostolic See by divine law (CIC cc.100.1; 241; 268.1), this term does not include the Roman Curia, since that body is of ecclesiastical origin. Likewise the context may demand the restrictive sense, as in CIC c.220, which speaks of cases reserved to the Roman pontiff alone.

Canons 246 through 257 of CIC (ClerSanc cc.192–203) list 11 Congregations through which the pope habitually exercises his administrative and executive powers. His judicial power is exercised through the use of three tribunals, the Sacred Penitentiary for matters of the internal forum, or forum of conscience; and the Roman Rota and the Supreme Tribunal of the Apostolic Signatura for cases within their competence (CIC cc. 258–259; ClerSanc cc.204–205). There are mentioned five offices (CIC cc.260–264; ClerSanc cc.206–210); the best known of which is the Secretariate of State.

Bibliography: R. A. GRAHAM, *Vatican Diplomacy* (Princeton 1959) 346, n. 11. A. G. CICOGNANI, *Canon Law* (2d ed. rev. Westminster, Md. 1947). Abbo 1:7, 246–264.

[J. F. DEDE]

APOSTOLIC SUCCESSION

The doctrine of apostolic succession means that the mission and sacred power to teach, rule, and sanctify that Christ conferred on His *Apostles is, in accordance with Christ's intentions, perpetuated in the Church's college of bishops. This doctrine in no sense denies the uniqueness of the role that the Apostles had as eyewitnesses, personally chosen and sent by Christ to proclaim the new revelation and lay the first foundations of His Church (*see* WITNESS TO THE FAITH). The fact that these prerogatives of the Apostles could not be passed on to the postapostolic generation does not mean that the Apostles could have no successors in their pastoral mission to preach, baptize, forgive sin, and teach men to observe all that Christ had commanded. For, in giving them this mission, Christ promised that He would be with them "all days, even unto the consummation of the world" (Mt 28.20). This promise of abiding divine assistance, given in the context of the apostolic mandate, implies that the mandate itself was to endure, even though the original recipients of the mandate were mortal men.

While one does not find in the New Testament any words of Christ indicating how the apostolic mandate was to be handed on, one does see how the Apostles understood that this was to be done. Following the example of Jesus, who had chosen and prepared them and then sent them out to continue His work, the Apostles in turn chose other men and shared with them their mission and apostolic authority. Thus, for example, St. Paul took *Timothy and *Titus as two of his fellow workers in the *apostolate. In the case of Timothy it is narrated that he received the grace of his ministry by the "laying on of hands" (1 Tm 4.14; cf. 2 Tm 1.6), a rite that the infant Church had very early adopted as a symbol of the conferring of a spiritual grace of office (Acts 6.6; *see* IMPOSITION OF HANDS). While Timothy and Titus are nowhere called Apostles, they did receive from St. Paul the mandate to exercise the apostolic ministry of teaching (1 Tm 4.6, 11–16; 6.2, 20; 2 Tm 1.13–14; 2.2, 14; 4.1–5); of governing the Churches to which Paul sent them (1 Tm 5; Ti 1.5, 10–14; 2.1–15); of selecting *deacons, *presbyters, and bishops (1 Tm 3.1–13; Ti 1.5–9) and ordaining them by the laying on of their hands (1 Tm 5.22). In the earlier years, when St. Paul still expected to survive to the *Parousia, it is likely that he looked on these men rather as coworkers than as future successors. But when he realized that his own death was near (2 Tm 4.6), he addressed Timothy as one who was to carry on his apostolic mission, guarding the *deposit of the faith and handing it on to trustworthy men who would be competent in their turn to teach others (2 Tm 2.2). One can hardly understand 2 Timothy except in the supposition that Paul intended that after his own death his younger collaborators would carry on as his successors. Indeed, it would be surprising if the Apostles had not thought of passing on their ministry to successors, since this idea was so clearly found in the Old Testament, where Aaron was succeeded by Eleazar (Nm 20.22–29) and Moses by Josue (Nm 27.15–23).

The Epistle of Clement of Rome to the Corinthians witnesses to the belief of the Church, in the last decade of the 1st century, that the Apostles had made provision for a succession in their ministry. Clement says that the Apostles installed bishops and then laid down the rule that when these men passed on, other proven men should take over their ministry. He speaks of these bishops as having been constituted either by the Apostles themselves, or subsequently by "other eminent men" (*1 Clem.* 44; Funk 1:154–156). While the exact sense of this passage is disputed, the most likely explanation is that these "eminent men" were the coworkers of the Apostles, who inherited the apostolic function of installing the local clergy. Although it seems that at the end of the 1st century some Churches were presided over by a college of men called either presbyters or bishops, the letters of Ignatius of Antioch show that the "monarchical" episcopate was already firmly established in Syria and Asia Minor in the first decade of the 2d century. In the latter half of this century, the "monarchical" bishops were universally acknowledged to be the successors of the Apostles, as is shown by the testimony of Hegesippus (cited by Eusebius, *Hist. eccl.* 4.22.1–3), of Tertullian (*De praesc. haer.* 32, 36; Corp Christ 1:212–213, 216), and of Irenaeus, who even gives the names of the 12 bishops of Rome from the time of Peter and Paul to his own day (*Adv. haer.* 3.3.1–3; Harvey 2:8–11).

While the scarcity of documents leaves much that is obscure about the early development of the episcopate, there is no doubt about the fact that from the 2d century to the Protestant Reformation Christianity unanimously recognized in its bishops the divinely-established successors of the Apostles. It was on the basis of this constant tradition that the Councils of Trent (Denz 1768), Vatican I (Denz 3061), and Vatican II [*Dogmatic Constitution on the Church, Lumen gentium* 20; ActApS 57 (1965) 23–24] declared the bishops to be by divine right the successors of the Apostles. Vatican II further explains that it is the episcopal college that succeeds to the apostolic college; individual bishops therefore share in the apostolic succession by their membership in the episcopal body, which is had by virtue of sacramental consecration and hierarchical communion with the head and other members [*ibid.* 22; ActApS 57 (1965) 27]. Where valid consecration is had without hierarchical communion, apostolic succession is only imperfectly realized.

See also APOSTOLIC; APOSTOLIC SEE; AUTHORITY, ECCLESIASTICAL; BISHOP (IN THE BIBLE); BISHOP (IN THE CHURCH); HIERARCHY; JURISDICTION, POWER OF; OFFICE, ECCLESIASTICAL; PONTIFF.

Bibliography: W. BREUNING, LexThK² 9:1140–44. Semana Española de Teologia, 16, 1956, *Problemas de actualidad sobre la sucesión apostolica* (Madrid 1957). P. ETIENNE et al., *Verbum Caro* 15 (1961) 129–198. A. EHRHARDT, *The Apostolic Succession in the First Two Centuries of the Church* (London 1953). A. M. JAVIERRE, *El tema literario de la sucesión* (Rome 1963). K. E. KIRK, ed., *The Apostolic Ministry* (London 1946; repr. 1957). C. H. TURNER, in *Essays on the Early History of the Church and the Ministry,* ed. H. B. SWETE (London 1918) 93–214.

[F. A. SULLIVAN]

APOSTOLICAE CURAE

The title of the papal bull of 1896 by which Leo XIII declared Anglican ordinations invalid. This account of the bull (which should be read in conjunction with another article, *see* ANGLICAN ORDERS) is divided as follows: the preliminary discussions and the final decision, the defect of form, the defect of intention, the dogmatic force of the bull.

Preliminary Discussions and Final Decision. Between 1892 and 1896 there was renewed discussion of the question of Anglican orders, and hopes were expressed that the Holy See might reconsider its fixed practice of treating those orders as null and void. Fernand Portal—a close friend of Lord Halifax, the leading Anglo-Catholic layman—championed the Anglican claims and enlisted the sympathetic interest of a number of eminent Catholic ecclesiastics. Leo XIII decided to set up a preliminary commission of inquiry in 1896 under the presidency of Cardinal Camillo Mazzella. Several of the consultors chosen were men known to be favorable to the Anglican case, and these were provided with further information and advice by two Anglo-Catholic divines, Timothy Puller and Thomas Lacey, who were in Rome for that purpose. After several meetings, the reports of the consultors were presented to Leo and to the commission of cardinals of the Holy Office appointed to judge the question. The cardinals' deliberations continued for 6 weeks, after which they held a plenary session in the Pope's presence on July 16th. They gave their unanimous verdict that the invalidity of Anglican orders had previously been decided by the Holy See after full and proper inquiry and that the recent reinvestigation had served to vindicate this decision as just and wise. The Pope himself had reached the same conclusion after long study of the evidence. He gave a public and authoritative judgment in the apostolic constitution *Apostolicae Curae* of Sept. 13, 1896. After setting out the relevant historical facts and theological reasons, he gave his decision in these terms:

> Wherefore adhering entirely to the decrees of the Pontiffs our predecessors on this subject, and fully ratifying and renewing them by our own authority, on Our own initiative and with certain knowledge, We pronounce and declare that ordinations performed according to the Anglican rite have been and are completely null and void.

Unfortunately, mistaken interpretations of the Pope's reasoning led from the start to much irrelevant argument. The critics have failed to interpret its condensed and carefully chosen language in the wider context of Catholic sacramental theology needed to appreciate its precise meaning.

In the preliminary historical section of the bull, Leo stresses the importance of the previous decisions and practice of the Church, in particular, the rejection of Anglican orders by the Catholic authorities in Queen Mary's reign (1553–58), the inquiry into the case of a French ex-Calvinist in 1684, and the judgment of Clement XI in the John Clement Gordon case of 1704. However, it is the following section of the bull, stating the theological reasons for the invalidity of Anglican ordinations, that had been most widely misunderstood. An analysis of these reasons follows (see Clark, *Anglican Orders*).

Defect of Form. A sacrament must signify outwardly what it effects inwardly. In the Sacrament of Holy Orders it is primarily the "form" that must convey this essential signification, that is, the spoken words which combine with the "matter" (here, the laying on of hands by the bishop) to determine the sacramental meaning of what is to be done. What the Sacrament of Orders does principally and essentially is to confer the priestly powers of consecrating the true Body and Blood of Jesus Christ and of offering the trust sacrifice of the Eucharist. Thus, for an ordination rite to be valid, the ritual form must sufficiently signify, *in one way or another,* the bestowal of this priestly power. The decisive theological objection against the rite used for Anglican ordinations is that it in no way conveys this essential sacramental signification, and indeed it cannot, because it equivalently signifies the contrary. Since this is the crux of the whole question, it is well to concentrate attention on Leo XIII's treatment of this defect of form.

Determination of Form. Some Catholic authors held the opinion that for an ordination rite to be valid, the order to be conferred, or at least its essential grace and power, must be expressly mentioned in the actual wording of the "operative formula." But, as Leo was well aware, this restrictive opinion was proposed only by a minority. There was a more probable opinion, explained by Pietro Gasparri and other leading theologians and canonists of the time, that an ordination rite is not necessarily invalid if, in the actual wording of the "operative formula," it does not make express mention of the order to be conferred or of its essential grace and power. Rather, the wording of an ordination form, even if not specifically determinate in itself, can be given the required determination from its setting, that is, from the other prayers and actions of the rite, or even from the connotation of the ceremony as a whole in the religious context of the age. This principle of sacramental theology was commonly accepted in the schools at the time of *Apostolicae Curae* and had been given full weight in the Roman inquiry of 1896. Some were urging it in defense of the Anglican ordination forms. Even if not sufficiently specific in themselves, it was suggested, those forms might acquire the necessary specification from the other accompanying prayers, exhortations, and rubrics of the Ordinal, or even from the printed preface.

Application to Edwardine Ordinal. In *Apostolicae Curae* the Pope takes judicious account of the two alternative opinions among Catholic theologians. He begins by pointing out that the words, "Receive the Holy Ghost," etc., which were usually claimed as the "operative" forms in the Ordinal published in 1550 and in 1552 during Edward VI's reign, certainly did not contain (at any rate until amended in 1662) any express mention of the order to be conferred, or of the essential sacerdotal power. Thus if the first and more restrictive opinion held by some Catholic authors is followed, those forms were obviously defective, at least during the vital first century of the Church of England's history, and consequently the succession of orders was extinguished. Leo is not content, however, to base his judgment merely on this reasoning. He goes on to take due account of the wider and more solid opinion common among Catholic theologians, who allow that a determinate significance may accrue to a sacramental form from its environment. He applies it with rigorous accuracy to the case of the Anglican rite. It is here that consideration of the historical circumstances in which Thomas Cranmer's Ordinal was composed is seen to be of decisive importance. What Leo calls "the native character and spirit of the Ordinal" colors and determines its total meaning. It originated as an instrument of the Reformation doctrine of the Christian ministry. Hence, with its significant alterations and omissions, it connotes the rejection of the Catholic consecrating and sacrificing priesthood. "It is impossible," the Pope points out, "for a form to be suitable and sufficient for a Sacrament when it suppresses that which it ought distinctively to signify." When the rite is judged in its total context, historical and theological, it is plain that none of the formulas it contains, even those which expressly include the words "priest" or "bishop," can serve to convey the essential sacramental signification required for transmitting the Catholic priesthood. Leo XIII elaborated this cardinal argument as follows:

> For a just and adequate appraisal of the Anglican Ordinal it is above all important, besides considering what has been said about some of its parts, rightly to appreciate the circumstances in which it originated and was publicly instituted. A detailed account would be tedious as well as unnecessary: the history of the period tells us clearly enough what were the sentiments of the authors of the Ordinal towards the Catholic Church, who were the heterodox associates whose help they invoked, to what end they directed their designs. They knew only too well the intimate bond which unites faith and worship, *lex credendi* and *lex supplicandi;* and so, under the pretext of restoring the order of the liturgy to its primitive form, they corrupted it in many ways to bring it into accord with the errors of the [Protestant] innovators. Hence not only is there in the whole Ordinal no clear mention of sacrifice, of consecration, of priesthood, of the power to consecrate and offer sacrifice, but, as We have already indicated, every trace of these and similar things remaining in such prayers of the Catholic rite as were not completely rejected, was purposely removed and obliterated. The native character and spirit of the Ordinal, as one might say, is thus objectively evident. Moreover, incapable as it was of conferring valid orders by reason of its original defectiveness, and remaining as it did in that condition, there was no prospect that with the passage of time it would become capable of conferring them. . . .
>
> Even though some words of the Anglican Ordinal as it now stands may present the possibility of ambiguity, they cannot bear the same sense as they have in a Catholic rite. For, as we have seen, when once a new rite has been introduced denying or corrupting the sacrament of Order and repudiating any notion of consecration and sacrifice, then the formula, "Receive the Holy Ghost" (that is, the Spirit who is infused into the soul with the grace of the sacrament), is deprived of its force; nor have the words "for the office and work of a priest" or "bishop," etc., any longer their validity, being now mere names, voided of the reality which Christ instituted.

Defect of Intention. It is clear that the paramount reason for judging all Anglican ordinations invalid is the original and abiding defect of form, or of sacramental signification, in the English Ordinal. It is a reason that is fundamentally simple and wholly conclusive, once the key principle has been grasped. Almost the whole of the doctrinal exposition in the bull is accordingly devoted to showing the decisive importance of the defect of form. Having done that, Leo XIII mentions briefly an additional and distinct reason for judging Anglican orders invalid: defect of ministerial intention. This reason had been urged by noted theologians in the discussions of 1895 to 1896. The Pope gives this additional reason due weight as a supplementary consideration, but he does not elaborate upon it.

Misinterpretation of Defect of Intention. Although Leo XIII devotes only a brief paragraph to it, the question of intention now demands fuller explanation, since it has been made the chief source of misunderstanding about the bull's meaning. Not a few commentators have mistakenly supposed that when he spoke of "defect of intention" the Pope was referring again to the "native character and spirit of the Ordinal," which, as we have seen, is the decisive factor in determining the defect of form. Consequently some have obscured the real issues by attempting to apply to one defect the terms and principles that apply properly only to the other. Many critics, likewise, have too readily assumed that the intention in question here was that of the authors of the Ordinal, or that of the rite itself, or the intention, or corporate faith, of the Church of England. These misinterpretations arose through failure to realize that Leo XIII used the term *intention* here in the fixed technical sense it bears in Catholic sacramental theology, namely, to refer solely to the ministerial intention of the person who actually administers a Sacrament. To avoid what seems to be otherwise inevitable confusion in this connection, it is well to follow the Pope's example and never to use the term intention when discussing the defect of *form.*

Defect of Intention Applied to Anglican Orders. What then is meant by the defect of intention in connection with Anglican orders? For a valid Sacrament of the Catholic Church there is required, in addition to the essential form and matter, a due intention in the minister. He must intend "at least to do what the Church does" (Denz 1312, 1611). It is true that this ministerial intention may be very vague and minimal, and can be presumed sufficient even in one who does not understand or believe the Church's sacramental doctrine, provided he continues to use the accustomed matter and form of the Church's Sacrament. Indeed, even if he openly denies the Catholic doctrine he can still have an intention sufficient for validity, since it is presumed (unless the contrary is proved) that his intellectual error is merely concomitant and is not carried into his will in such a way as to nullify his general intention of doing what Christ requires. If, however, the minister has not merely concomitant intellectual error, but there is, while he performs the rite, *a positive act or movement of his will* against something which is—whether he realizes it or not—essential to Christ's Sacrament, then this positive contrary intention necessarily vitiates and nullifies his whole ministerial intention. Sometimes such a defect is outwardly manifest from the circumstances of a particular case, and consequently the Church is able to pass certain judgment on it. This "principle of positive exclusion," which must be presupposed for a fuller understanding of *Apostolicae Curae,* was already solidly established in Catholic theology and canonical practice by the time of Leo XIII.

It need not be thought that *Apostolicae Curae* declared defective the ministerial intention of all those who have administered the Anglican ordination rite even to our own day. Such a rigid opinion would be logically held only by those few theologians who favor a return to the theory of "external intention" associated with the name of Catharinus, according to which the ministerial intention is invariably tied to the due outward performance of the sacramental rite. They would naturally conclude that all who administer the defective Anglican rite must be judged automatically to have defective intention. What is relevant here is the personal intention of those who acted as the ministers of the early Anglican ordinations in the 16th century. In particular, the question of the ministerial intention in the episcopal consecration in 1559 of Matthew Parker, first archbishop of Canterbury in the new Elizabethan hierarchy, is of special relevance, since it is from Parker that the whole subsequent succession of Anglican orders derives. In the debates preceding *Apostolicae Curae* there had been much discussion of the intention of Bishop William Barlow, who acted as chief consecrator at that ceremony, assisted by three other prelates. These men, who were open supporters of the Reformation doctrines, agreed to the change of the ordination rite for the consecration of Parker, deliberately reintroducing Cranmer's Ordinal, with its known antisacerdotal significance, in substitution for the Catholic Pontifical in use during Queen Mary's reign. It is this manifest act that provided evidence sufficient for the Holy See to judge that they had not merely concomitant intellectual heresy, but positive intention of the will directed against the Catholic doctrine of the consecrating and sacrificing power of the priesthood, a power which is essential to the Sacrament as Christ instituted it. It is against this background, taking into account both the canonical "principle of positive exclusion" and the circumstances of Parker's consecration, that Pope Leo's brief reference to defect of ministerial intention must be interpreted. In summation of his position, he concludes:

> If the rite is changed with the manifest purpose of introducing another rite which is not accepted by the Church, and of repudiating that which the Church does and which by Christ's institution belongs to the nature of the Sacrament, then it is evident that this is not merely a case in which the intention necessary for a Sacrament is absent, but one, indeed, in which an intention is present adverse to and incompatible with the Sacrament.

Dogmatic Force of the Bull. The dogmatic force of the papal decision in *Apostolicae Curae* should be mentioned. In a letter to Cardinal Francis Richard, Archbishop of Paris, dated Nov. 5, 1896, Leo XIII declared: "It was our intention to deliver a final judgment and to settle the question completely. . . . All Catholics are bound to receive the decision with the utmost respect, as being fixed, ratified, and irrevocable." In papal documents of this kind, of course, the explanatory sections leading up to the final decision do not share the same absolute authority as the decision itself. Whether that decision, which in any case is binding and certain for Catholics, was delivered with infallible authority is a point on which theologians are not agreed. However, as many of them point out, there are strong reasons for concluding that the matter does come within the category of what is called the "secondary object" of papal infallibility. Not only was the Pope pronouncing on a matter which concerns the Church's world-wide mission, but his decision was an exercise of the Church's divinely committed office as guardian of the Sacraments, which must include the power to determine with final certainty what does and what does not constitute a true sacramental rite.

Bibliography: LEO XIII, "Apostolicae Curae," ActaSS 29 (1869–97) 193–203; tr. AmCathQRev 21 (1896) 846–857. S. M. BRANDI, *La condanna delle ordinazioni anglicane* (4th ed. Rome 1908); *A Last Word on Anglican Ordinations,* tr. S. F. SMITH (New York 1897); *Rome et Cantorbéry,* tr. A. BOUDINHON (Paris 1898). H. VAUGHAN, *A Vindication of the Bull 'Apostolicae Curae'* (London 1898). S. F. SMITH, CE 1:491–498; Dict ApolFoiCath 3:1162–1227. E. YARNOLD, "Gli ordini anglicani," *Il problema ecumenico oggi,* ed. C. BOYER (Brescia 1960). F. CLARK, *Anglican Orders and Defect of Intention* (New York 1956); "A 'Reopening' of the Question of Anglican Orders?" ClergyRev 47 (1962) 555–560; "Les Ordinations anglicanes, problème oecuménique," Greg 45 (1964) 60–93. F. TEMPLE, *Answer of the Archbishops of England to the Apostolic Letter of Leo XIII on English Ordinations* (London 1897). A. E. G. LOWNDES, *Vindication of the Anglican Orders,* 2 v. (New York 1911). E. L. MASCALL, "Intention and Form in Anglican Orders," ChQuartRev 158 (1957) 4–20.

[F. CLARK]

APOSTOLICI, term applied at various periods, generally in a pejorative sense, to reformers wishing to return to the primitive Church, poor, humble, simple, and penitential, through close imitation of the Apostles. Some Gnostic communities (*see* GNOSTICISM) in Asia Minor from the 2d to the 4th centuries were called "*apostolici*" by *Epiphanius (*Panarion* 2.1,61; PG 41: 1040–52). Extremely austere, they renounced property, marriage, and religious practices, which they considered mere outward forms. In the 12th century, alongside such *Wanderprediger* as *Robert of Arbrissel and *Norbert of Xanten, whose orthodoxy was never impugned, were other itinerant barefoot preachers, near Cologne, in Périgueux, and in Brittany, who were infected with the spreading Manichaeism. Their presence in the Rhineland about 1143 induced Everwin, prior of Steinfeld (PL 182:676–680), to enlist the services of *Bernard of Clairvaux in combatting them. In refutation Bernard wrote his *Sermones in Canticum Can-*

ticorum 65–66 (PL 183:1088–1102). Sharper identification may be found in the sect begun at Parma in 1260 by Gerard Segarelli, who emphasized penance and apostolic poverty (*see* POVERTY MOVEMENT), and was indebted to Joachimite ideas (*see* JOACHIM OF FIORE) and Franciscan example. These *apostolici* (*ordo apostolorum*), described by contemporaries as pseudo-apostles or hypocrites, were condemned by Pope Honorius IV in 1286 (Potthast Reg 22391) and by Nicholas IV in 1291 for violating the decree of the Second Council of *Lyons (1274) regulating the mendicant orders. In 1287 the council of Würzburg proscribed them as vagabonds (c.34; Mansi 24:863). But shortly after Segarelli was sent to the stake in 1300, the movement was revived by Fra *Dolcino, who elaborated apocalyptic doctrines (*see* APOCALYPTIC MOVEMENTS) and a theology of history derived from Joachimism. Imitation of apostolic life and absolute poverty, mitigated only by alms, constituted the basis of the new order. In the early modern period the term was assigned to branches of *Anabaptists who observed poverty and interpreted Scripture literally.

Bibliography: SALIMBENE, *Cronica fratris Salimbene de Adam,* ed. O. HOLDER-EGGER in MGS 32 (1905–13) 255–293, 389, 563, 619. *Historia fratris Dulcini haeresiarchae,* in Muratori RIS 9:427–460. B. GUI, *Manuel de l'inquisiteur,* ed. and tr. G. MOLLAT, 2 v. (Paris 1926–27). E. VACANDARD, *Vie de saint Bernard* (4th ed. Paris 1910). M. BODET and J. M. VIDAL, DHGE 3:1037–48. A. MENS, *Oorsprong en betekenis van de Nederlandse Begijnen en Begardenbeweging* (Louvain 1947) 23–36. L. SPÄTLING, *De apostolicis, pseudoapostolicis, apostolinis* (Munich 1947). E. ANAGNINE, *Dolcino e il movimento ereticale all'inizio del trecento* (Florence 1964).

[E. W. MC DONNELL]

APOSTOLICI REGIMINIS, a bull published Dec. 19, 1513, by Leo X in the eighth session of the Fifth Lateran Council. Three propositions were designated heretical; that the soul is mortal; that all humanity shares a common soul; and that truth may be double, i.e., that a certain proposition may be true in terms of rationalistic philosophy even if it is not in accord with truth as disclosed by revelation. The bull expressly affirms that each man has an individual and immortal soul. The condemned propositions concerning the soul were conspicuously defended by Pietro *Pomponazzi in his *De immortalitate animi* in 1516. The notion of a *double truth, associated with nominalism, had been suggested by *Nicholas of Cusa in his *De docta ignorantia* in 1440. To offset paganistic ideas derived from classical studies, the bull stipulated that clergy intending to pursue advanced philosophical and literary studies should first devote 5 years to theology and Canon Law.

Bibliography: W. BETZENDÖRFER, *Die Lehre von der zweifachen Wahrheit* (Tübingen 1924). F. VERNET, DTC 8.2:2681–83.

[D. R. CAMPBELL]

APOSTOLICITY

The Church of Christ was founded "super fundamentum apostolorum et prophetarum" (Eph 2.20). It is and ought to be, in all the meanings this expression can have, in perfect reference to the *Apostles: *apostolic by the spirit that animates it, in the doctrine it proclaims, in its sacramental and hierarchical structure.

A Property of the Church. Apostolicity denotes the Church itself insofar as it represents, conserves, and develops from the beginning the spirit, doctrine, and structure that its founders, the Apostles of Christ, gave it. The Church is apostolic because the Apostles are its founders; this principal element involves all the others. The *Twelve are founders in that they make present in a moment of history the Body of Christ already formed in its head resurrected by the power of the Spirit, for it is the Lord Himself who has received all authority in heaven and on earth. The group of the Twelve, the college of Apostles, received the ministry of founding and governing the Church to exercise it *in nomine Domini.* Apostolicity, rooted in the Trinity and the divine *missions, extends to the visible and social structures of the ecclesial community.

Three aspects can be distinguished in this apostolicity. First of all, it is a likeness of spirit, of spirituality: the Church should be, like the Apostles, a minister, humble and poor, at the service of all. It is in this sense that one speaks of the "apostolic life." It is an identity of doctrine: the Church must preach the message of which the Apostles were the first heralds; and no matter what ripening and development this message may undergo throughout the centuries, it must nevertheless remain *in eodem sensu,* according to the classic phrase used by St. Vincent of Lérins. Finally, it involves continuity in the episcopal succession. The Twelve not only chose assistants during their lifetime but, in order that the mission entrusted to them might continue after their death, gave their collaborators the mandate to continue their work and to tend the Church of God, and so arranged that afterward other approved men should receive this ministry. The episcopate is the crown of the ministries transmitted since the Apostles. Of course, it is true to say that in a certain sense the Apostles do not have successors. Actually, only the Apostles are the founders of the Church; they alone are the "sent" par excellence. But the exercise of authority that is bound to the choice and to the mission of the Apostles must continue by succession.

Apostolicity, moreover, is simultaneously "institution and event," or "succession and mediation." For all that has been said regarding spirit, doctrine, and episcopal succession is to be found at the level of the Church. One must look beyond, nevertheless, toward Christ and His Spirit, who play the primordial role in the very reality and vital substance of apostolicity. The apostolic spirit and mentality spring up in the heart of God's people by the power of the Spirit of God, who in them manifests the fruits of charity, humility, and patience. The apostolic doctrine is preserved pure by the vigilance of the Spirit, who also leads His people toward all truth. The apostolic succession of the episcopate is as it were permanently suspended in the Act of the God-Man, who remains eternally the *auctor sacramentorum* and the one to whom all power has been given in heaven and on earth. Not to consider apostolicity in all its dimensions would be to impoverish it indeed.

Note of the Church. The early Fathers based their great proof of the truth of Christianity on the accord that the Churches maintained, by means of the continuity of hierarchical succession, with the Churches founded by the Apostles or at least founded in the time of the Apostles; hence the concrete importance of the episcopal lists drawn up by Irenaeus, by Tertullian, and by St. Augustine. [See D. van den Eynde, *Les Normes de l'enseignement chrétien dans la littérature patristique des trois premiers siècles* (Paris 1933).] All these elements were to be analyzed, classified, and minted in the great

Christ (represented by the "Etimasia," an enthroned cross) attended by 12 sheep representing the Apostles. Byzantine relief, probably of the 12th or 13th century, on the Basilica of San Marco at Venice.

controversy that arose in the 15th and 16th centuries.

At the beginning of the Reformation, the mark of apostolicity appeared under the most varied names, names that indicate its different aspects: *perpetuitas, firmitas, antiquitas, successio, duratio.* Three major elements were proposed as distinctive of the true Church: the apostolic origin, i.e., the Church was founded *on* the Apostles and, especially, *by* the Apostles; the apostolic doctrine, i.e., the continuity of the Christian faith throughout history, or also the identity of the faith of the 16th century with that preached by the Twelve; finally, the apostolic succession, i.e., the uninterrupted train of legitimate pastors who link the early Church with that of the modern epoch.

In the following centuries these three aspects of apostolicity were to undergo some changes. The apostolicity of origin, always considered as necessary, lost its prominence when the controversialists, instead of addressing themselves merely to the communions inspired by the Reformation, also took the Eastern Church into consideration. The apostolicity of doctrine, too, suffered a certain decline, at least within the *via notarum;* for it took an amazing flight into those monumental histories of the faith or of the Church that the controversy between Catholics and reformers were to give us in the most debated realms, such as the Eucharist, the ministry, etc. As regards the apostolicity of the ministerial succession, it always maintained its weight; nevertheless, to assure the decisive value of this argument in the discussions that they carried on with the Churches of apostolic origin, the apologists finally identified, in practice, the legitimacy of the pastors and communion with the apostolic see in Rome. [See G. Thils, *Les Notes de l'Église dans l'apologétique catholique depuis la Réforme* (Gembloux 1937) 255–286.]

After 1870 the theme of apostolicity was often completed by that of the *invicta stabilitas* that Vatican Council I presented as an aspect of the moral *miracle that the Church itself constituted. By this is understood the constancy and the unshakable stability in the faith and in the essential structures of Christianity.

Apostolicity and Ecumenism. The question of apostolic ministry is perhaps the most delicate among all the subjects in ecumenical dialogue. The universal assemblies of the World Council of Churches have always had to recognize their profound disagreements in this domain. This is evident when one reads in the different reports of these assemblies what is said about the ministry. Since the Faith and Order Conference at Lund (1952), the World Council of Churches accords a greater importance to the παράδοσις (tradition), and the Faith and Order Conference at Montreal (1963) revealed how much progress the idea of tradition has made in their minds. By this shift of position, they return to a sector of apostolicity. However, on the question of the ministry, in its origin and legitimacy, they do not seem to have made any notable progress.

See also MARKS OF THE CHURCH (PROPERTIES); APOSTOLIC SUCCESSION; MIRACLE, MORAL (THE CHURCH); CHURCH, ARTICLES ON.

Bibliography: O. KARRER, LexThK² 1:765–766. A. MÉDEBIELLE, DBSuppl 1:533–588. Y. M. J. CONGAR, *Catholicisme* 1:728–730. A. M. JAVIERRE, *El tema literario de la sucesión* (Zurich 1963). C. JOURNET, *L'Église du Verbe Incarné,* v.1 *La Hiérarchie apostolique* (2d ed. Bruges 1954). H. HOLSTEIN, "L'Évolution du mot apostolique au cours de l'histoire de l'Église," in A. HAMMAN et al., *L'Apostolat* (Paris 1957) 41–61. **Illustration credit:** Alinari-Art Reference Bureau.

[G. THILS]

APOSTOLIS, ARSENIOS, Byzantine humanist in the West; b. Candia (Herakleion), Crete, 1468–69; d. Venice, 1535. Son of the Byzantine copyist and scholar Michael *Apostolis, Arsenios is best known for his philological work and for teaching Greek in Renaissance Florence and Rome. The early life of this cleric was spent in Crete, where he copied manuscripts and taught; his pupils included John Gregoropoulos and Marcus *Musurus. In 1492 Arsenios became a copyist in Florence and 2 years later, was employed in Venice at the press of *Manutius, where his name appears as an editor for one of the very first Aldine editions. From 1497 to 1504 Arsenios was again in Crete, employed as copyist and teacher. It was during this period that he conceived the idea of gaining the archiepiscopal See of Monemvasia, a Venetian-held Greek city on the eastern Peloponnesus, and much of the remainder of his life was spent in scheming to achieve this end. At various times he was installed as Orthodox archbishop there and later, even as a prelate of the Latin Church. In 1519 Arsenios taught at the papal

Greek institute in Rome, and later he acted as director of the papal Greek school of Florence (1520–21). He devoted the last years of his life to seeking papal and Venetian aid for Monemvasia, which was constantly in danger of Turkish attack.

He edited a number of Greek works important for the *Renaissance. He contributed to the *Thesaurus cornucopiae et horti Adonidis* (published in 1496 by Aldus), a work containing fragments of ancient Greek poets that cannot be located elsewhere. In Rome in 1519 he edited the important *Apophthegmata,* a collection of aphorisms drawn up originally by his father Michael from ancient Greek authors. His edition of the scholia on Euripides (1534) is fundamental for subsequent Euripidean scholarship. Arsenios's importance for Renaissance Greek scholarship lies in his editions of classical and Byzantine authors, in his pupils, and in his copying of manuscripts.

Bibliography: E. L. J. LEGRAND, *Bibliographie hellénique,* 4 v. (Paris 1885–1906; repr. Brussels 1963) 1:clxv–clxxiv, for his life; 2:337–346, 418, for his letters. M. MANOUSAKAS, "Arsenios Monemvasia . . . Unedited Letters" (in Gr.), *Epeteris tou Mesaionikou Archeiou,* 8–9 (1961) 5–56, for his letters. D. J. GEANAKOPLOS, *Greek Scholars in Venice: Studies in the Dissemination of Greek Learning from Byzantium to Western Europe* (Cambridge, Mass. 1962) 167–200, with bibliog., most complete and recent account of his life.

[D. J. GEANAKOPLOS]

APOSTOLIS, MICHAEL, Byzantine scholar on Crete; b. Constantinople, *c.* 1422; d. *c.* 1486. Though born in Byzantine Constantinople, Michael fled that city after the Turkish capture in 1453 and settled in Candia, Venetian capital of *Crete. This city subsequently became an important center of Greek manuscript copying and a halfway point in the transmission of Greek learning from Byzantium to Italy. In 1454 Michael traveled to Italy for the first time and met the great Byzantine scholar and cardinal of the Roman Church, *Bessarion, who commissioned Michael to return to Crete and search out Greek manuscripts for him in the old Byzantine East. Michael supplemented his income by teaching; among his pupils were Laonikos, later editor of the first book entirely in Greek to be published in Venice, and the young Emmanuel Adramyttenos, tutor of Greek to *Manutius and *Pico della Mirandola. In the controversy between Aristotelians and Platonists after the Council of *Florence in 1439, Michael composed a polemic against the Aristotelian Theodore of Gaza. Because of the scurrilous tone of the work, however, Michael was severely reprimanded by Bessarion (1462). Michael also compiled a large collection of aphorisms (*Ionia*), extracted from classical Greek authors. This work, published in part after his death by his son Arsenios *Apostolis (1519), was to have considerable influence on subsequent Greek scholarship of this type. It is possible that Michael was still alive in 1486, since in that year his verses appear in the *Batrachomyomachia,* published by his pupil Laonikos in Venice.

Michael is representative of the large number of lesser-known Greek *émigré* scholars who fled Byzantium in the years immediately following 1453. Always overshadowed by more successful compatriots such as Bessarion, he nevertheless deserves attention as an important connecting link between the Byzantine Hellenism in Crete and the rising interest in Greek studies in *Renaissance Italy. Greek manuscripts copied by him are to be found in virtually all major libraries of western Europe.

Bibliography: *Lettres inédites,* ed. H. NOIRET (Paris 1889), for his correspondence. E. L. J. LEGRAND, *Bibliographie hellénique,* 4 v. (Paris 1885–1906; repr. Brussels 1963) 1:lxvi–lxx; 2:234–259. D. J. GEANAKOPLOS, *Greek Scholars in Venice: Studies in the Dissemination of Greek Learning from Byzantium to Western Europe* (Cambridge, Mass. 1962) 73–110, only monograph.

[D. J. GEANAKOPLOS]

APOTHEOSIS

In the ancient Greek world it was believed that divinity was everywhere, but in a special way in great men. The legendary founders of cities were thought to have been gods in disguise or at least the offspring of gods. They were worshiped by the official cult of the city. Contrasting with this "descending" theology was an "ascending" point of view expressed in the idea that exceptional men escaped the common fate of mortals and were transported beyond the stars to share in the eternal blessedness of the gods. Hercules is the classical case in mythology of the hero who by his exploits on earth achieved divine status. Within historical times Alexander the Great and later Hellenistic kings were apotheosized. An Athenian memorial to the heroes fallen at Potidaea (432 B.C.) goes so far as to ascribe this blessedness even to ordinary soldiers: "The ether has received their souls, the earth their bodies" (Cumont, 146). The apotheosis of the first two Caesars may be said to have been, to some extent at least, the result of a genuine religious feeling that a divine hand was at work in the reestablishment of peace and order in a ravaged world. In accordance with the scientific picture of the world at that time, apotheosis was conceived of in strictly spatial terms. A Roman relief represents Julius Caesar standing in a chariot that four winged horses are carrying toward the heavens.

Some historians of the early 20th century tried to explain Christianity's faith in the divinity of Christ as a derivation from the apotheosis of heroes and emperors. W. Bousset, in his *Kyrios Christos* (Göttingen 1913), advanced the hypothesis that the title *Lord was first given to Jesus by gentile converts at Antioch and other centers of gentile Christianity under the in-

The apotheosis of Antoninus and Faustina, relief on the base of the Antonine Column (A.D. 161–169) in the Cortile della Pigna of the Vatican.

fluence of the mystery cults (*see* MYSTERY RELIGIONS, GRECO-ORIENTAL). St. Paul would have introduced the title and the divine worship paid to Christ into the Judeo-Christian Churches. E. Lohmeyer [*Christuskult und Kaiserkult* (Tübingen 1919)] held that the title *Son of God was a commonplace in ancient times and expressed man's need for a concrete embodiment of the divine on earth. The term was used of political saviors and of religious saviors. It was given, according to Lohmeyer, to Jesus under the influence of the apotheosis of Augustus some decades earlier.

Contemporary scholars are agreed that these titles arose, not within gentile Christianity, but in the Judeo-Christian Churches. The title Lord is found in the oldest passages of the New Testament (e.g., Mk 12.35–37; Acts 2.36; Gal 4.1), and the passage in which Christ is given the divine "name that is above every name" (Phil 2.9) is clearly inspired by passages in Isaia. The title Son of God probably originated with, or at least was popularized by, St. Paul, for whose gentile hearers Our Lord's own designation of Himself, Son of Man, would be meaningless.

See also RULER-CULT.

Bibliography: K. PRÜMM, LexThK[2] 1:766–767. L. CERFAUX, *Christ in the Theology of St. Paul,* tr. G. WEBB and A. WALKER (New York 1959). O. CULLMANN, *The Christology of the New Testament,* tr. S. C. GUTHRIE and C. A. M. HALL (rev. ed. Philadelphia 1963). F. CUMONT, *Lux perpetua* (Paris 1949) 171– . G. DIX, *Jew and Greek* (Westminster, Eng. 1953). **Illustration credit:** Anderson-Art Reference Bureau.

[J. M. CARMODY]

APPEAL AS FROM AN ABUSE (APPEL COMME D'ABUS)

This term referred at one time to a recourse to secular justice to complain about a decision of an official or about an act of ecclesiastical authority; at another time, to an intervention by secular justice to reprimand something in the Church that seemed contrary to the rights of the State. The repression of abuses committed by clerics who exercised the functions of royal judges or by officials (e.g., arrest and condemnation of innocent persons, sentencing of clerics who married or practiced commerce or offended against common law) was handled by secular jurisdictions before the institution of the *appel comme d'abus.* When this appeal was entered against a sentence by an official, the secular tribunal competent to handle the appeal was supposed to pronounce only on the fact (the existence or nonexistence of the abuse) and then to designate the tribunal, ecclesiastical or lay, competent to judge the case. In practice the judges of the *appel comme d'abus* generally reserved to themselves judgment on cases submitted to them. The intervention of the public minister helped to restrict the activity of ecclesiastical tribunals and to extend the interference of the State in Church matters. Thus a bull that was printed without an *exequatur was considered abusive and was suppressed; those responsible for printing it were fined. Likewise a bishop's pastoral instruction, if judged contrary to the State's traditional "liberties," was regarded as unauthorized and was suppressed. The punishment inflicted on the bishop could consist of the seizure of his temporal possessions. (*See* GALLICANISM.)

Most medieval states placed some limitations on the competence of ecclesiastical judges. England did so in the statutes of *praemunire (1353 and 1393). But the *appel comme d'abus* originated in France, where it first appeared in 1448 after an infraction of the *Pragmatic Sanction of Bourges (1438), and in 1449 in an affair unrelated to this Pragmatic Sanction. Between 1539 and 1695 the royal power was forced to define this appeal and to restrict its use because of continual complaints from bishops and officials. Bishops claimed that their ministry was impeded because *parlements were too ready to heed complaints from subordinates and to take action against episcopal instructions. Officials protested that they were deprived more and more of their business. (By 1600 they had lost five-sixths of their cases.) German principalities followed the example of France and in the 15th century established the *recursus ad principem* (recourse to the prince). Spain under Charles V began in 1525 the *recurso de fuerza* (forced recourse), which was used also in Spanish territories in Italy (Duchy of Milan, Kingdom of Naples). The *appel comme d'abus* was retained in Flanders and also in Savoy, where Emmanuel Philibert in 1560 had only to regulate what the French had introduced in 1542. During the 19th century, France, Italy, and Germany during the *Kulturkampf sometimes utilized *appels comme d'abus* as weapons against the Church itself rather than against abuses.

Archbishop François Fénelon in 1711 denounced "the enormous abuses of the *appel comme d'abus.*" King Louis XV was so much alarmed by the actions of his parlements in the quarrel concerning the refusal of the Sacraments that he nullified several arrests made by his council; but this did not prevent his procurators-general from appealing "from abuses of bulls, briefs, apostolic letters and *viva voce* responses" concerning the Jesuits, in order to place the Society of Jesus on trial and to destroy it. The bulls *In Coena Domini* of Paul III (April 13, 1536) and of Gregory XIII (April 4, 1583) condemned *appels comme d'abus,* but they remained dead letters, because they were not "received." The concordats of the 19th and 20th centuries were more efficacious. The *appel comme d'abus* was condemned in 1864 in the *Syllabus of Errors (Denz 1741). Both aspects of the appeal as from an abuse incurred the penalties enacted by the *Code of Canon Law (cc.2334n2, 2333).

Bibliography: D. AFFRE, *De l'appel comme d'abus* (Paris 1845). A. M. J. J. DUPIN, *Libertés de l'église gallicane: Manuel de droit public français* (Paris 1860). R. F. JAHAN, *Étude historique de l'appel comme d'abus* (Laval 1888). P. GODARD, *La Querelle des refus de sacrements 1730–1765* (Paris 1937). R. GÉNESTAL, *Les Origines de l'appel comme d'abus* (Paris 1951). P. G. CARON, *L'appello per abuso* (Milan 1954), important. J. CAPTIER, DHGE 3:1049–54. F. LIUZZI, EncCatt 1:1708–09. R. NAZ, DDC 1:818–827.

[C. BERTHELOT DU CHESNAY]

APPEAL TO A FUTURE COUNCIL

A complaint by a physical or moral person against a papal act, in order to have this act examined by the next ecumenical council (*see* COUNCILS, GENERAL). An appeal of this kind implies a belief in the superiority of a general council over the pope. Two opinions are current concerning the origin of this appeal. However, according to Victor *Martin this term did not always have the above significance. After studying the earliest of these appeals—those made by the Colonna cardinals (1297), by King *Philip IV of France and his counselors (1303), and by Emperor *Louis IV the Bavarian (1334)—Martin concluded that these early appeals were based on two traditional principles: (1) the pope cannot be judged by anyone (CorpIurCan C.9 q.3, c.16) and (2) a heretical pope, by deviating from the faith, is already judged and lacks authority (CorpIurCan D.40 c.6). Martin was all the more certain that these first appellants were orthodox, because, in his view, the doctrine of the superiority of a council over a pope arose between 1409 and 1415 and not before. Brian Tierney, on the other hand, has found it curious that a pope could be already judged without the existence of a judge to pronounce on his culpability. He has established that from the end of the 12th century different opinions existed among canonists and that one of these opinions asserted the superiority of a council over a pope (*see* CONCILIARISM). According to Tierney, when the Council of *Constance in its fifth session issued the decree *Sacrosancta* (April 6, 1415) it was not ratifying a recently formed opinion but one that had been in existence for more than 2 centuries without being condemned. Whatever may be said of Martin's and Tierney's interpretations, it is certain that appeals to a future council were numerous in France, especially during the 15th century. The supporters of *Gallicanism claimed constantly that one could appeal from a pope to a council; they affirmed this claim in the *Pragmatic Sanction of Bourges (1438), in the quasi-official book in 1594 by Pierre *Pithou, *Les Libertez de l'Église gallicane* (art. 78), and in the *Declaration of the French Clergy in 1682 (art. 2). *Louis XIV appealed to a future council in 1688, and the French Jansenists did so in 1717.

Pius II (1458–64) was the first pope to denounce this appeal as an "execrable abuse" and ridiculed it by asking how anyone could appeal "to a tribunal that does not yet exist, and, for all anyone knows, may never sit." The same Pope also excommunicated appellants (*Execrabilis,* Jan. 18, 1460) and later repeated his condemnation (Nov. 2, 1460). His example was followed by Sixtus IV (1483), Julius II (1509), Leo X (1520), Benedict XIV (1745), and Pius IX (1869). The present *Code of Canon Law condemns even an appeal to a council already in session (c.228.1). Also, it excommunicates physical persons and threatens with the interdict moral persons who make such appeals (c.2332).

Bibliography: V. MARTIN, *Les Origines du gallicanisme,* 2 v. (Paris 1939). B. TIERNEY, *Foundations of the Conciliar Theory* (Cambridge, Eng. 1955); "Pope and Council: Some New Decretist Texts," MedSt 19 (1957) 197–218. P. G. CARON, *L'Appello per abuso* (Milan 1954). A. AMANIEU, DDC 1:807–818. H. KÜNG, *Structures of the Church,* tr. S. ATTANASIO (New York 1964).

[C. BERTHELOT DU CHESNAY]

APPELLANTS, a name given to opponents of the bull **Unigenitus,* who appealed against the papal decree to a general council; they thus logically applied the Gallican doctrine of the Four Articles of 1682, which affirmed the superiority of a general council over a pope. The first act of appeal was presented under the form of a notarized act lodged at the Sorbonne on the morning of March 5, 1717 by four bishops: Jean Soanen, of Senez; Joachim Colbert, of Montpellier; Pierre de la Broue, of Mirepoix; and Pierre de Langle, of Boulogne. Many members of the secular and regular clergy, an important segment of the faithful, as well as several corporate societies, among them the Sorbonne, adhered to the Appeal, which finally united 12 bishops and a little more than 3,000 priests and religious of the approximately 100,000 that made up the French clergy. The Appellants thought that the bull condemned some authentic Christian truths, and that consequently the Pope had erred in faith and that only a general council could remedy the situation. On Sept. 8, 1718 (day of publication), by the brief *Pastoralis officii,* Clement XI excommunicated the Appellants. In view of the opposition from the Gallican parliamentaries, this measure produced no practical effect. In order to guarantee the failure of any attempt at a compromise, the four bishops renewed their appeal on Sept. 10, 1720, and the "Reappellants" who joined them were numerous. The regent then embarked on a veritable campaign of police persecution against the Appellants, and their number decreased year by year; many of them, however, maintained their attitude until death.

See also JANSENISM; ACCEPTANTS.

Bibliography: The most complete selection of the acts of appeal is that of G. N. NIVELLE, *La Constitution "Unigenitus" déférée à l'église universelle,* 3 v. in 4 (Cologne 1757).

[L. J. COGNET]

APPETITE

In normal usage the term appetite designates a desire for food and the capacity to enjoy it. Without straining its meaning, however, it can signify almost any desire, e.g., an appetite for hard work or for pleasure. The word derives from the Latin *appetitus,* which means a seeking for something. As used in scholastic philosophy, appetite is defined as an inclination and an order of a thing toward the *good, and designates the element in the nature of things whereby they have or develop tendencies toward objects that benefit them.

THOMISTIC CONCEPT OF APPETITE

In Thomistic philosophy, appetite in the strict sense specifies the capacity of a thing to seek its good; when used more broadly, it includes the actual seeking as well. Appetite thus is both the fundamental power to seek and the actual exercise of that power. Psychologically, this concept is closely connected with a number of other concepts, for example, orexis, conation, urge, drive, feeling, emotion, affectivity, and passion. Orexis is the Aristotelian term for appetite, sometimes signifying appetite in general and at other times the power of the will. Conation, urge, and drive are terms that are used almost interchangeably to indicate the forceful or impulsive aspect of appetites (*see* DRIVES AND MOTIVES). *Feeling and affectivity are generally used to indicate the felt quality connected with appetitive activity. Emotion and passion can be used for both the feeling aspect and the drive aspect of appetites. Passion in current usage often signifies a more intense emotion; in scholastic use, it did not have this connotation.

In the philosophy of St. *Thomas Aquinas, and among scholastics generally, appetite is attributed to all beings, from God, who has Will, to primary matter, which has an appetite for substantial form. The classical expression of this idea is: An inclination follows every form (ST 1a2ae, 8.1), for everything is either on account of itself or on account of another, and what is on account of itself seeks itself, while what is on account of another seeks that other. Otherwise the parts of the universe are absurd, as being ordered to purposes but not effectively equipped to attain them (*see* FINAL CAUSALITY; TELEOLOGY).

Division of Appetite. The first division of appetite is into natural and elicited appetites. Because things exist as they are and tend to continue in existence for a while, and because they operate as they ought to operate, they are said to have a natural appetite to exist and to operate. Such a natural appetite is not conceived as a reality in a thing distinct from its *nature; it is rather the nature itself conceived in terms of tendency to be and to operate.

Elicited appetites are the appetites aroused by cognitive acts, and they are considered to be distinct parts of the nature of a cognitive being. The evidence for elicited appetites is, first, our human experience, and secondly our observation of other animals. We feel impulses and affects aroused in ourselves by cognitive acts toward various objects, and these impel us to action toward these objects; we see, moreover, that animals seem to act the same way and are furnished with the same kind of organs that serve us. We conclude, then, that cognitive beings are in fact equipped with appetites. Moreover, it would be absurd if the case were otherwise, for a knowing being who was absolutely unable to be moved by what he came to know would be frustrated; his knowledge would be futile. Therefore knowing beings ought to have the capacity to be moved by objects as known, and such a capacity would be, by definition, an elicited appetite.

Since, therefore, there are appetites aroused by cognitive acts, there will be at least as many distinct kinds of elicited appetite as there are distinct orders of *knowledge (ST 1a, 80.1). Scholastics, dividing knowledge basically into *sense knowledge and intellectual knowledge, divide appetite into sensitive appetites and the will, which is the appetite of the intellective part.

Sensitive Appetites. By definition, a sensitive appetite is a capacity to be aroused by a concrete object perceived through the *senses. It is, therefore, an operative power, i.e., a power to respond and react. This response or reaction on the part of the possessor of the appetite has a twofold moment. First of all, it is a kind of passivity, by which the possessor is changed or moved by the impact of the object sensed. Secondly, since this change is of the nature of a tension produced in the possessor, an inclination to action follows, for the purpose of relieving the tension. Hence appetites tend to provoke action. The actions are designed to obtain or avoid the object that originally aroused the appetite: to obtain it if it is good, or to avoid it if it is evil. Since avoiding evil is itself good, one can define the appetite as ordered simply to the good, either directly or indirectly.

Organic Changes. Hence the sense appetites arise from the sense knowledge that elicits them, involve a physical change in the organism, and result in action. The physical change may be greater or less, but it is always present. Medieval scholastics spoke of such changes as the rising of the blood around the heart in anger, the withdrawal of the blood toward the bowels in fear, and so on. Modern physiology recognizes changes in the circulatory, respiratory, glandular, etc., systems, as component parts of emotional changes. The basic organs of appetitive movement seem to be the hypothalamus in the brain and perhaps parts of the rhinencephalon, for experiments stimulating these organs of the brain with electric currents result in reaction patterns of the emotive or motivational order [see J. Olds, "Pleasure Centers in the Brain," *Scientific American* 195 (October 1956) 105–116]. The autonomic nervous system that stimulates visceral, glandular, and other somatic changes in emotional reactions is the connecting link between the brain centers of sensitive appetite and the other corporeal reactions involved.

Concupiscible vs. Irascible Appetites. Thomistic psychology posits two sensitive appetites, the concupiscible and the irascible. The arguments for this division run thus: Some passions in the organism are aroused on the basis of simple *pleasure and *pain, as it seeks out what is pleasing physically and avoids what feels injurious. These reactions constitute the operations of one appetite, the concupiscible, whose ultimate object is defined as the simple, sensitive good. But other emotional reactions are based not simply on pleasure and pain. Thus we experience inclinations impelling us toward things that are hard or difficult to attain, or we find emotional responses impelling us to reject or despair of good objects. These appetitive activities are assigned to a second sensitive appetite, called the irascible appetite, whose object is the difficult or arduous sense good.

Of the two, the basic appetite is the concupiscible. The irascible appetite is an emergency appetite, aroused when simple movements toward a sensible good or away from a sensible evil are impeded by some obstacle. The irascible appetite is aroused precisely to overcome the obstacle. When it is overcome, the irascible appetite subsides, and the simple concupiscible appetite functions alone. For example, love is a simple concupiscible movement toward a good or pleasant object, and when the object is here and now attainable, the love for it generates an actual desire. If the object can be obtained, the desire comes to fruition in joy or delight. This all occurs in the concupiscible appetite. But if, when desire is aroused, a sudden obstacle impedes the attainment of the good, then anger, an irascible passion, will perhaps be stirred up against the impediment. Anger urges toward overcoming or destroying it; once this is done, nothing prevents obtaining the object, and so there is a return to delight or joy. Or again, one might be faced with an object he dislikes, feel an aversion toward it, and hence avoid it—all movements of the concupiscible appetite. If he can avoid it, he feels contentment or joy. But if some circumstance suddenly appears making it seem impossible to avoid the disliked object, his aversion takes on an emergency quality; it turns into fear, another irascible passion, and under the stimulus of fear he reacts more energetically to escape the evil. If he does escape it, he again feels joy.

Acts of the Sense Appetites. The various actions of the sense appetites, which are called the *passions or *emotions, are divided in Thomistic psychology into 11 general categories, 6 in the concupiscible appetite and 5 in the irascible appetite. *Love, the first passion of the concupiscible appetite, is the fundamental passion underlying all others. Love is defined, in an abstract way, as the simple tendency toward a good thing. *Desire, which arises from love, is a tendency toward a good thing that is not yet possessed but is presently possessible. *Joy follows from desire when the good thing is actually possessed. Hate, the opposite of love, is the turning away from an evil thing. Aversion arises from hate, as an actual repugnance to an evil thing presenting itself. Sorrow follows after aversion, if the evil thing actually afflicts us. *Hope is the name given to the first of the irascible appetites. It is the vehement seeking for a good object that is hard to obtain. *Courage is the energetic attack on an evil that is hard to overcome. *Despair is the giving up of a good object because of difficulties, and *fear is the urgent avoidance of an evil that is hard to escape. *Anger, finally, is the movement toward an evil that is hard to overcome for the sake of destroying it. All movements of passion, with their various modalities and mixtures and shades of difference, can be comprised without great difficulty under these eleven basic categories.

Human Will. The *will is the rational or intellectual appetite in man, i.e., the appetite that seeks goods as they are perceived by the power of *intellect. As the intellect is the supreme cognitive power in man, so the will is the supreme appetite in man, controlling all human behavior; and as the intellect is a spiritual power, so also is the will. Thus all purely spiritual or rational goods are sought by the will alone, and rational and spiritual evils are rejected by the will. It is the will that desires justice, truth, order, immortality, the service of God, and the like, and hates injustice, deceit, chaos, and death. However, the will's objects are not limited to spiritual things—it seeks also to obtain or avoid physical goods sought by the sensitive appetites; but when the will acts in this sphere, it is because it sees reasonableness in these physical goods. Thus, the sight of food might arouse a person's concupiscible appetite because food is pleasant to eat, but he wills to eat it only if he sees that it is reasonable here and now to do so. Hence a man can also starve himself in spite of a contrary urging from the sensitive appetites, if in the circumstances he judges this is a reasonable thing to do. The will ultimately controls all behavior, as long as man is conscious and sane; even behavior motivated primarily by the sense appetites is not carried out unless the will consents.

Free Will. The will is a free power in man, because it is the appetite that follows reason (*see* FREE WILL). Because reason can see several alternatives equally feasible as means of reaching one end, the will has freedom to elect from among them.

Acts of the Will. The acts of the will are often called by the same name as the passions of the sense appetites, namely, love, hate, desire, fear, anger, and so on. These, however, are not the names of the will's proper acts. The principal proper acts of the will are to intend an end or purpose, to elect the means to accomplish it, to command the actions that execute it, and to rest content in the purpose accomplished (*see* HUMAN ACT). If the purpose is to attain a good, we call the acts of intention, election, and command acts of love; if they are aimed at destroying evil, we call them anger; if at escaping an evil, we call them fear, and so on.

Relationship to Sense Appetites. The relationships between the will and the sense appetites are complex. One can arouse the sensitive appetites deliberately by willing to think about and imagine the objects that stir them. Moreover, it often happens that a particularly strong act of the will produces a similar passion in the sense appetites, by a kind of overflow or redundance. So, for instance, some people feel fright physically when called on suddenly to address a large audience, although there is nothing physically threatening. In their turn, the sense appetites can exert considerable influence on the will. The freedom of the will, for instance, depends on the power of reason to judge a situation calmly, taking into account all possibilities. But when the passions are strongly aroused, the power of reason often fails to judge carefully, and a man is precipitated into actions he would not otherwise have performed. The passions fix the attention of the mind on the things that stir them and limit its capacity to reflect, and thus indirectly limit the freedom of the will. Moreover, to act contrary to strong passions produces strong feelings of pain and sorrow, and rather than endure these, men often consent to things they would otherwise reject. Thus, although the will is free and in supreme command in theory, in practice it is often limited by the sense appetites.

Other Theories of Appetition

Many philosophers and psychologists have disagreed with one element or another of the theory of appetition outlined above. Some have denied that appetition is a force consequent and subordinate to cognition. Others have questioned its precise relationship to action. Still others deny the distinction between sense appetites and will, or introduce a dichotomy between affectivity and conation or drive. A summary of representative views along these lines follows.

Scotus, Schopenhauer, and Freud. John *Duns Scotus in the 14th century placed appetite above cognition in the ordering of faculties, arguing that the will is the supreme power in man, against the Thomistic position that intellect is the highest power, eliciting, governing, and regulating the acts of the will (*see* VOLUNTARISM; INTELLECTUALISM).

Arthur *Schopenhauer (1788–1860) made will not only the supreme power in man's psychological equipment, but the fundamental reality in all of nature. He argued that the will leads the intellect to its judgments; governs memory, imagination, logic, and reflection; drives men in all their actions; and, in short, constitutes the essence of man. Moreover, will governs all movements in nature, in animals, in plants, and in inanimate bodies—will is the ultimate reality. "The world is wide in space and old in time and of an inexhaustible multiplicity of forms. Yet all this is only the manifestation of the will to live" [*The World as Will and Idea,* tr. R. B. Haldane and J. Kemp (London 1906) 3:379].

Sigmund *Freud (1856–1939) made drive the major element in human nature and denied that it was elicited by cognition. For him, the drives are basically the psychological manifestations of biological processes, arise spontaneously and inexorably in the mind, and only subsequently attach themselves to cognitive elements or objects that represent actions and things peculiarly fitted to provide satisfaction ["Instincts and their Vicissitudes," *Collected Papers* (London 1956) 4:60–67].

Leibniz, James, and Dewey. Other theories of appetition differ regarding its relation to action. G. W. *Leibniz (1644–1716) gave his monads two basic activities, perception and appetition, but appetition did not give rise to action, it merely effected the transition from one perception to another within the *monad. Since Leibniz did not hold that the mind could efficiently move the physical world, he could not make appetition the cause of action. In higher organisms, appetition is called will, which is an effort or tendency toward good and away from evil. Will results from consciousness of good and evil, and is guided by reason, which propose images of the greater goods and evils that will follow from different courses of action [*New Essays Concerning Human Understanding,* tr. A. G. Langley (La Salle, Ill. 1916) 177, 195].

The so-called James-Lange theory of emotions, proposed by William *James in 1884 and Carl *Lange in 1885, also realigns emotion and action. According to this theory, objects arouse instinctive reactions that in turn produce bodily changes, which are then perceived as emotions. The instinctive reaction results directly from the perception of the exciting fact, whereas the emotion is the felt result of the bodily alteration. "Common-sense says, we lose our fortune and weep . . . the more rational statement is that we feel sorry because we cry" [James, *Principles of Psychology* (New York 1913) 2:449–450]. Experimental evidence does not give unqualified support to this theory, but the element of truth it expresses may perhaps be accounted for by the fact that man becomes conscious of his emotions as a consequence of feeling the bodily commotions they cause [M. Stock, "Sense Consciousness according to St. Thomas," *The Thomist,* 21 (1958) 460–466].

John *Dewey (1859–1952) proposed a theory of emotions that made them the effects of impeded action rather than a spur to effective action. He held that emotions are felt as physical disturbances that arise when a strong urge to act is impeded; as long as actions are carried out uninhibitedly, emotions do not occur.

Materialist Views. Philosophers of materialist schools deny the scholastic distinction between sense appetites and will. Herbert *Spencer (1820–1903) thought of the will and all the higher powers in man as products of materialistic evolution, whereby simpler psychic responses such as reflexes and tropisms are gradually developed into the more complex operative patterns we name intelligence and will [*Principles of Psychology* (New York 1883) 1:495].

Freud also denied the will as a distinct and higher faculty in man, and attributed all drive in human nature to instinctual urges. He did, however, believe that men could control their drives reasonably, and contemporary *psychoanalysis often accepts will as a power in man distinct from instinctual drives [e.g., H. Hartmann, tr. D. Rapaport, *Ego Psychology and the Problem of Adaptation* (New York 1958) 74–75].

Hamilton, Lotze, and Cannon. Modern psychological theory, both philosophical and empirical, usually makes a dichotomy between affectivity, or the felt quality of emotion, and conation or drive. This distinction is at least as old as William *Hamilton (1788–1856) who posits cognition, feeling, and conation as the three elemental phenomena of consciousness.

R. H. *Lotze (1817–1881) makes the division of ideation, feeling, and volition. Feelings arise from pleasure and pain, which are caused by circumstances that are either harmonious to or disturbing to the body. Impulses arise from these feelings, but as distinct from them. Volition also is distinct from impulse [*Microcosmus,* tr. E. Jones and E. Hamilton (Edinburgh 1888) 1.2.2.3]. Although there is a basis in felt experience and in functional role for a distinction between affect and drive, the intimate connection between these two aspects of appetitive activity is lost by positing two distinct powers or capacities. An affect, e.g., guilt feeling, can motivate a conation, e.g., the urge to confess. An action motivated by a drive, e.g., eating when hungry, terminates in an affect, namely, contentment. The interplay of drive and feeling is obscured and rendered difficult to explain if the two aspects of appetite are not seen in their organic relationship.

The physiological researches of W. B. Cannon (1871–1945) have contributed useful information to theories of appetite. Cannon investigated the physiological changes produced in the body by situations that demand vigorous action. He traced the patterns of discharge in the involuntary nervous system, the glandular reactions and the alterations in respiration, circulation, and muscular tension, etc., and noted how they were all ordained to the exigencies of a body about to be engaged in violent action. These patterns of response did not correlate with specific emotional categories, but were generalized reactions to an emergency. In a scholastic theory of appetite, they would suggest the physiological changes involved in the arousing of the irascible appetite [see *Bodily Changes in Pain, Hunger, Fear and Rage* (New York 1929)].

See also EMOTION; FEELING; PASSION; WILL.

Bibliography: G. P. KLUBERTANZ, *The Philosophy of Human Nature* (New York 1953). T. V. MOORE, *The Driving Forces of Human Nature* (New York 1948). J. WILD, *Introduction to Realistic Philosophy* (New York 1948). J. F. DASHIELL, *Fundamentals of General Psychology* (New York 1937). R. S. WOODWORTH, *Experimental Psychology* (rev. ed. New York 1954). W. MCDOUGALL, *Body and Mind* (7th ed. London 1928).

[E. M. STOCK]

APPREHENSION, SIMPLE

The operation by which the *intellect apprehends a *quiddity without affirming or denying anything of it. In this operation the intellect simply grasps what a thing is, i.e., its *essence, without attributing any predicate to it. *Thomas Aquinas described this activity as an *indivisibilium intelligentia,* understanding of indivisibles or of essences (*In 1 perih.* 3.3).

Explanation. Three things should be noted in the definition of simple apprehension. (1) It is an operation, i.e., the second act or activity of an operative power. As in most creatural activities, four really distinct factors must be recognized: the operative power itself, its operation, its internal product, and the external *sign of that product. The operative power or faculty involved in simple apprehension is the possible intellect; the first activity the possible intellect performs is that of simply apprehending a quiddity; its internal product is a formal *concept or mental word; the external sign of that concept is an oral or written *term. (2) It apprehends a quiddity, an essence. Simple apprehension knows merely what man, or white, or learned is. Such "whatnesses" or quiddities are called indivisibles in the sense that a definite group of notes is required for their comprehension—if any of these is missing, the quiddity is not attained. For example, the quiddity of man requires the inclusion of the notes of substance, body, living, sentient, and rational; none can be eliminated and still leave as remainder the quiddity of man. Furthermore, simple apprehension is not limited to merely substantial and accidental essences, formal acts; even when it knows something that is not itself a quiddity, it knows this as if it were one (*per modum quidditatis*). (3) It does so without affirming or denying. This feature distinguishes simple apprehension from *judgment. This first act rests in the knowledge of what man, or white, or learned is; it does not go on, as judgment does, to assert the existential identity or non-identity of two notions, such as "man *is* white" or "this man *is not* learned."

The act of simple apprehension is not simple, for it involves three prerequisite steps and then the act itself. The first step is the operation of the external *senses, since nothing comes to be in the intellect that was not first in some way in the senses. The external senses supply various unrelated bits of information about the external thing and thus supply the material for intellection and its bridge of contact with extramental reality. The second step involves the activities of the internal senses. The *central sense combines the data received from the external senses into a common sensible image or percept (*see* PERCEPTION). The other internal senses either estimate the thing thus perceived or reproduce the thing's image in its absence. The common sensible image of the internal senses is, in general, called a *phantasm. Then begins the third step in the process, the functioning of the active intellect; this gives a dematerializing illumination to the phantasm, rather like an X ray. Using the phantasm as its instrument, the active intellect produces a determinate immaterial impression on the possible intellect, called the impressed intelligible species (*see* SPECIES, INTENTIONAL). At this stage comes the act of simple apprehension itself. Thus determined and specified by the reception of the impressed species, the possible intellect actually knows by producing an expressed species or mental *word in which it attains its abstracted object (*see* ABSTRACTION).

When the possible intellect moves on to its second type of operation, forming judgments, simple apprehension is required to present the concepts of the possible subject and predicate. Likewise, simple apprehension is required in *reasoning, which basically is only a special coordination of judgments.

How Effected. The perfection of human knowledge is a gradual process; it is not fully accomplished in one swoop. Simple apprehension does not grasp an object in all its richness at first thrust. It attains it first in its most general aspects, then gradually proceeds through the more proximate genera and differences, down to its most special species, and finally its individuality. St. Thomas illustrates this by an analogy: "When a thing is seen afar off it is seen to be a body before it is seen to be an animal; and to be an animal before it is seen to be a man; and to be a man before it is seen to be Socrates or Plato" (ST 1a, 85.3). Similarly, human knowledge proceeds from confused notions, wherein an object is known only generically, to distinct notions, wherein it is known in its proper and specific features. It must be recognized, however, that even if man does succeed in attaining an explicit knowledge of the inmost constitution of some few things, in most instances he has to be content with imperfect knowledge through external signs.

Apprehension of Singulars. The above description of the process of simple apprehension indicates that the human intellect directly proceeds by abstracting from the individuating conditions with which an object is represented in the phantasm. Consequently, in its state of union with the body the intellect directly knows only *universals. However, since the universal has been drawn from the sensed singular, the intellect can, as it were, retrace its steps and through reflection see an essence as it is individualized in the phantasm. This dependence of intellect on phantasm precludes the possibility of *imageless thought in such knowledge. Yet the intellect is only one of the instruments by which man knows. As Aquinas observes, "Man knows singulars through the imagination and sense; and therefore he can apply the universal knowledge which is in the intellect, to the particular: for, properly speaking, it is not the senses or the intellect that know, but man through both" (*De ver.* 2.6 ad 3). Ordinarily, human knowledge of a singular material thing is, therefore, a complex of contributions: man's knowing through what is contributed by both the intellect and the senses.

Apprehension of Self. In the light of the abstractive process, how does man know himself and his spiritual aspects? First of all, he knows himself and his acts through the act of knowing something other than himself. When, in signified act (*in actu signato*), he knows something extramental, such as a tree, he is concomitantly aware of himself and of his activity in knowing the tree. Such concomitant knowledge is called by scholastics exercised knowledge (*in actu exercito*) and, by psychoanalysts, coconsciousness.

Likewise, man knows the existence of his soul experimentally and immediately through its activities. When he perceives that he is exercising any vital operation, such as intellection or sensation, he vaguely perceives that he has a principle of intellection, of sensation, etc., which is his soul. In knowing the existence of the soul, he has an obscure and confused knowledge of its essence. However, a clear and distinct knowledge of the essence of the soul is arrived at only after a careful and diligent inquiry based on the objects and acts of the vital principle (*see* SOUL, HUMAN, 4).

Moreover, man has a rational appetite called a *will. He is vaguely aware of its existence and essence in the exercise of its acts. This knowledge becomes clarified and perfected by inferences from activities that indicate the nature of the principle from which they spring. It is in the same manner that man gains a knowledge of habits, for these are but further determinations of operative powers, disposing them to act easily and stably in a certain manner.

Apprehension of Spiritual Entities. The proper object of the human intellect while united to the body is the abstracted essences of material things as represented in a phantasm. Since pure spirits, such as angels and God, are by definition immaterial beings, man can rise to a knowledge of them only by *analogy. He affirms of such spirits some positive perfections (called pure perfections) noticed in inferior beings; these perfections he affirms of them in a higher degree, while denying the imperfections involved in "mixed" perfections. Thus the presence of intellection is affirmed of such spirits in an eminent degree, for this involves no imperfection in its proper concept. On the other hand, sensation is denied of pure spirits, for this is a mixed perfection that involves organicity, an imperfection, in its proper concept.

Relation to Intuition. Some contemporary thinkers, especially under the influence of H. *Bergson, tend to devaluate conceptual knowledge as gained through simple apprehension in comparison with that gained through *intuition. Such antipathy is better directed against Kant than Aquinas. Aquinas frequently used intuition in the broad sense of understanding anything whatsoever. He also used the term analogously with reference to the omniscience of God, the nonabstractive knowledge of angels, and human abstractive knowledge. Concepts arrived at through abstraction are called intuitive if they represent a thing that is present precisely as it is present. Conceptual knowledge gained through abstraction does not necessarily distort or falsify; it can well be thoroughly accurate as far as it goes, even though it does not grasp the full richness of the object. In this regard St. Thomas noted that "the understanding of mathematical notions is not false, although no line is abstracted from matter in reality" (*In 1 sent.* 30, 1.3 ad 1). Abstraction and conceptualization is simply the lot of a human intellect while united to a body.

See also KNOWLEDGE, PROCESS OF; UNDERSTANDING; INSIGHT.

Bibliography: J. MARITAIN, *The Degrees of Knowledge,* tr. G. B. PHELAN et al. (New York 1959); *Bergsonian Philosophy and Thomism,* tr. M. L. and J. G. ANDISON (New York 1955). J. F. PEIFER, *The Concept in Thomism* (New York 1952); *The Mystery of Knowledge* (Albany 1964). É. H. GILSON, *The Christian Philosophy of St. Thomas Aquinas,* tr. L. K. SHOOK (New York 1956); *Réalisme thomiste et critique de la connaissance* (Paris 1947). G. P. KLUBERTANZ, *The Philosophy of Human Nature* (New York 1953). J. DE TONQUÉDEC, *La Critique de la connaissance* (3d ed. Paris 1961). R. GARRIGOU-LAGRANGE, *God: His Existence and His Nature,* tr. B. ROSE, 2 v. (St. Louis 1934–36). R. ALLERS, "On Intellectual Operations," NewSchol 26 (1952) 1–36. B. J. F. LONERGAN, "The Concept of *Verbum* in the Writings of St. Thomas Aquinas," ThSt 10 (1949) 3–40, 359–393. M. DE MUNNYNCK, "Notes on Intuition," *Thomist* 1 (1939) 143–168.

[J. F. PEIFER]

APPROPRIATION

Appropriation is a more or less spontaneous way of thinking and speaking about the Triune God relative to creatures. In appropriation some divine characteristic, activity, or effect that belongs equally to all three Persons is thought and spoken of as belonging to one of the three. This manner of thinking and speaking is not merely an invention of men but is sanctioned by God Himself, who inspired the writers of the New Testament in their use of appropriation, and who providentially safeguards the creeds and liturgy of the Church in their use of appropriation. By means of appropriation God reveals to men the otherwise unknowable depths of the divine being and life and the truly distinct characters of the Father, the Son, and the Holy Spirit, who live it.

Scripture, Creeds, Liturgy. St. Paul offers an example of appropriation in the New Testament. He sometimes speaks of God (and by God, Paul generally means the Father) dwelling in the Christian community: ". . . in him [the Lord] you too are being built together into a dwelling place for God in the Spirit" (Eph 2.22). Another time he says the Holy Spirit dwells in the community: "Or do you not know that your members are the temple of the Holy Spirit, who is in you, whom you have from God, and that you are not your own?" (1 Cor 6.19). It should be noted that "you" in this passage is, in the Greek, plural, referring to the Corinthian community. Thus the divine presence in the Christian community is appropriated in one instance to the Father, in another to the Holy Spirit; yet one knows that wherever one of the Divine Persons is present, the other two must also be present as well.

The early creeds also use appropriation. One professes belief, for example, in God, the Father almighty, creator of heaven and earth . . ., in the Holy Ghost, the holy Catholic Church, the communion of saints, etc. Thus creative power and activity are attributed to the Father and the effects of unifying Christian love, forgiveness of sins, resurrection, eternal life—in a word, sanctification—are attributed to the Holy Spirit.

A similar manner of expression is found in the liturgy, where prayers are usually addressed to the Father, who is considered as having the power to grant man's request, through the Son (though the mediation of the Son in virtue of His human nature is not appropriation, but truly the unique possession of the Word incarnate), and in the Holy Spirit, who is conceived as the source of the love that binds Christians together with one another and with Christ and God in the liturgical assembly.

Theology of Appropriation. In the Scriptures the Father is associated with creation and power (Mt 3.9; Acts 4.24). Thus one begins to see the Father more clearly as the source of all and realizes more what is implied in His fatherhood within the Trinity, e.g., His being without a principle. The Son is viewed as the Word of God through whom God creates (Jn 1.3; Col 1.15–17); He gives meaning, order, and intelligibility to chaos. Hence the Son is associated with wisdom, and is understood to proceed from the Father by a generation akin to the generation of an idea in knowing. The Holy Spirit is given to Christians as a gift to sanctify, to aid, to comfort them (Rom 5.5; 2 Cor 1.22; Jn 14.26; 16.13); thus one is led to understand His position in the Trinity as the bond of love between Father and Son.

The basis for attribution usually is a similarity between a divine perfection, action, or effect and a characteristic proper to one of the Persons. Something in the Person Himself calls for the appropriation. The appropriations fall into a pattern with certain things seen usually in relation to one Person, as, for example, goodness, peace, joy to the Holy Spirit. There should be a mutual clarification between the quality, action, or effect appropriated and the Divine Person. Gradually one discovers in these relationships what God wishes to tell man about Himself, not so much with regard to His absolute nature as in His Trinitarian being—the character of the Persons involved and their intra-Trinitarian dialogue.

The divine nature, however, is one and possessed completely by all three Persons, so that what is not relatively opposed in the Trinity is really something belonging to all three Persons (*see* TRINITY, HOLY; PERSON, DIVINE). Because divine power, divine wisdom, divine love, mercy, etc. are associated with one Person, it does not mean that they belong exclusively to that Person. Divine power, for example, is connected with the Father, but not only the Father is powerful. The various divine qualities and activities do not cease to be essential and common by the fact of appropriation. All of God's external works proceed from divine omnipotence under the direction of His wisdom inspired by love, and are actions of the Trinity as a whole, not of this or that Person. Although Sacred Scripture does associate creation with the Father, wisdom with the Son, sanctification with the Holy Spirit, nevertheless, as exercises of the divine power these activities and their effects have their effective source in all three Divine Persons functioning through the one power and the one activity.

This does not mean that appropriation is useless or a mere playing with words. It is one of the ways for God to reveal His inner self and the uniqueness of Persons. Furthermore, there is a basis in the Trinity itself for appropriation, in the proper characteristics of each Person; that is, creation is associated with the Father as generator of the Word; the unity of the soul with God and of Christians with one another is associated with the Holy Spirit as bond of unity. That which is common to all, at least as one conceives it, has a greater likeness to what is proper to one Person than to what is proper to another.

Insofar as any one of the Divine Persons can be considered from several aspects, a number of things may be appropriated to Him. For example, depending on the aspect considered, eternity, power, or unity may be seen in relationship to the Father; or wisdom, beauty, or truth to the Son; or goodness, love, or joy to the Holy Spirit. Furthermore, one and the same divine quality or action might be associated with different Persons depending on the aspect of the Person or quality considered. The revelation of the mysteries of God to men might be connected with the Son as the Word of God and with the Holy Spirit as manifesting or communicating goodness or aiding men (Heb 1.1–4; Jn 16.12–14).

See also TRINITY, HOLY, ARTICLES ON.

Bibliography: A. CHOLLET, DTC 1.2:1708–17. M. SCHMAUS, LexThK² 1:773–775. I. M. DALMAU, SacTheolSumma BAC 2.1: 544–553.

[J. B. ENDRES]

APTITUDES

Individuals' potentials for learning or for acquiring a pattern of behavior. Degree of aptitude indicates an individual's capacity to acquire proficiency with a given amount of training. Aptitude tests, sometimes called prognostic tests, differ from ability or achievement tests, which measure performance, that is, what a person can do now. Aptitude tests measure potential ability not yet formally trained. They predict probable ability to profit from training.

Aptitude is the product of inborn capacity interacting with and developed by a stimulating environment. Educational opportunity has much to do with the amount of aptitude one manifests, but inborn capacity determines the kind of aptitude one can express. While psychologists do not agree as to the relative importance of heredity, environmental experience, or motivation, they seemingly tend to credit increasing importance to the effect of environment on the development of an individual's inherent potentialities (*see* HEREDITY AND ENVIRONMENT, INFLUENCE OF).

Aptitude tests measure general capacity to learn, such as intelligence or scholastic aptitude, as well as capacity to learn and succeed in specific areas such as music, art, mechanical engineering, etc.

Louis L. Thurstone, in applying multiple factor analysis to intelligence scores, identified such primary mental abilities as verbal comprehension, rote memory, number facility, word fluency, ability to visualize spatial relations, perceptual speed, and inductive and deductive reasoning.

Differential aptitude tests are of two broad types: pencil and paper, and manipulatory or performance. The latter measure manual dexterity, eye-hand coordination, or similar capacity. Scholastic aptitude tests include in the main two types of items: verbal—measuring linguistic ability such as word fluency in reading, and quantitative—measuring numerical ability and spatial relations.

Tests of general scholastic aptitude are of two types: group and individually administered. The Stanford revision of the Binet Scale and the Wechsler Scales (WAIS and WISC) have no serious competitors among individually administered general ability predictors.

Among the commonly used group tests of general aptitude are the Army General Classification Test (AGCT), Ohio State, Terman-McNemar, Pintner-Patterson, Primary Mental Abilities, California Test of Mental Maturity, and Kuhlmann-Anderson Test.

Specific aptitude tests have been developed for determining ability to acquire skill in art, music, clerical or mechanical work, mathematics, foreign language, reading, engineering, medicine, aviation, etc.

Aptitude tests cannot predict success or failure since opportunity and desire to learn are essential additional factors. Aptitude scores indicate merely the extent to which the subject has the ability to learn and succeed if he tries. Aptitude tests are used for two purposes: (1) to counsel youth in educational programs and (2) to select personnel best fitted for particular jobs, thus preventing frustration and waste of time and personnel.

Since it is no longer tenable to expect an individual with high academic aptitude to obtain high scores in all other aptitudes (although there is a tendency toward positive correlation among abilities), educational experiences must be realistically planned for the diversity of human abilities capable of development.

See also INTELLIGENCE; MEASUREMENT; EDUCATIONAL MEASUREMENT.

Bibliography: D. WECHSLER, *Measurement and Appraisal of Adult Intelligence* (4th ed. Baltimore 1958). R. L. THORNDIKE and E. P. HAGEN, *Measurement and Evaluation in Psychology and Education* (2d ed. New York 1961). W. B. KOLESNIK, *Educational Psychology* (New York 1963), ch. 7. R. E. RIPPLE, ed., *Readings in Learning and Human Abilities* (New York 1964).

[U. H. FLEEGE]

APULEIUS OF MADAURA, pagan Latin writer, rhetorician, and philosopher; b. Madaura (modern M'daourouch, in Algeria), *c.* 124; date and place of death unknown, but probably after 170. He was a typical representative of the Latin Second Sophistic. Proud of his virtuosity, he wrote and spoke on a wide variety of subjects and enjoyed a great reputation, especially in Africa, for several centuries. His culture and training were bilingual. Hence, while exhibiting a natural creative talent, he was able to draw heavily on Greek sources for his works. His *Apología* (or *Pro se de Magia*) is a refutation of the charge of employing magic that was made against him and is valuable for the information it furnishes on ancient magic. His most famous work is the rambling novel called the *Metamorphoses* or the *Golden Ass.* It relates the adventures of a certain Lucius who was turned into an ass by magic. Its full description of the mysteries of Isis and Osiris may be based on Apuleius's own initiation into this religion. At any rate, it is important as a source for the ancient mystery religions. Among many tales found in the work is the beautiful little story of Cupid and Psyche. The *Florida* is a collection, diverse in character, of the author's declamations.

Apuleius was a rhetorician rather than a philosopher, but the following philosophical works have had considerable influence: (1) *De Platone et eius dogmate* (On the Teaching of Plato), in 3 books, of which the third is lost; (2) *De deo Socratis* (On the *daimon* of Socrates); (3) *De Mundo* (On the Universe), a Latin translation of the Pseudo-Aristotelian Περὶ κόσμου. A large number of other works by Apuleius are known by title only. The style of Apuleius is luxuriant and highly artificial. It is no longer classified as peculiarly African (*Africitas*), but is identified as a Latin form of Asianism. St. Augustine used Apuleius as a source on demons in *De Civitate Dei* (bks. 8–9), and he bore witness to his fame, especially as a magician (*Epist.* 136, and *Epist.* 138).

Bibliography: H. E. BUTLER, OxClDict 173–174. R. HELM, "Apuleius von Madaura," ReallexAntChr 1:573–574. SchHos Krüg GeschRL 3:100–136. M. BERNHARD, *Der Stil des Apuleius von Madaura* (Stuttgart 1927).

[M. R. P. MC GUIRE]

AQUARIUS, MATTIA DEI GIBBONI, theologian; b. Aquaro (near Eboli), date unknown; d. Naples, 1591. He entered the Dominican Order at Naples. In 1558, he was a student at Bologna; in 1562 he was prefect of studies, and in 1569, regent at Milan. He was professor at the Universities of Turin (1569), Naples (1572), and Rome (1575). Besides his opening lectures at Turin and Naples, *De excellentia theologiae* (Turin 1569; Naples 1572), he published *Adnotationes super IV libros sententiarum Joannis Capreoli* (Venice 1589), *Controversiae inter Divum Thomam et caeteros theologos et philosophos* (Venice 1589), and the *Formalitates iuxta doctrinam Divi Thomae* (Naples 1605), edited posthumously by A. de Marcho, OP.

[A. DUVAL]

AQUILA, ARCHDIOCESE OF (AQUILANUS), archbishopric located in the Apennines in central Italy since Jan. 23, 1876; immediately subject to the Holy See. In 1964 it had 104,612 Catholics in 148 parishes, 110 secular and 95 religious priests, 154 men in 15 religious houses, and 419 women in 46 convents; it is 1,004 square miles in area. Alexander IV made it a bishopric Feb. 20, 1257, transferring there the See of Furcona, which, dating from the 7th century, had incorporated the See of Amiternum. In 1818 Città Ducale was suppressed and united to Aquila. Already a mountain fortress for refugees during the barbarian invasions, Aquila was built in 1254 as a republican outpost for the kingdom of Naples. *Manfred destroyed it, but Charles of Anjou rebuilt it in 1265. In the Middle Ages it had more than 120 churches, 50 squares, and 32 public fountains. Under Spanish rule the city declined and after the earthquake of 1703 had to be almost entirely rebuilt. Among the abbeys of note in Aquila are Bominaco Santa Maria e San Pellegrino, built in 1001 and suppressed in 1762; San Giovanni di Collimento, founded after 1100 and suppressed in 1461; the architectural monument, Santa Maria di Collemaggio, founded in 1287, where Celestine V became pope and where he is buried; the Cistercian Santa Maria della Riviera, founded before 1303; and the Olivetan Santa Maria di Soccorso (1472). The churches of Aquila, despite later modifications, have preserved elements of a distinctive Romanesque-Gothic style. Most of them were built between 1256 and 1350. Renaissance and baroque art are also represented in the city. The episcopal and cathedral archives have been despoiled of their oldest documents.

Bibliography: Gams. Eubel HierCath. F. BONNARD, DHGE 3:1105–08. S. PRETE and G. CARANDENTE, EncCatt 7:913–917. G. EQUIZI, *Storia de L'Aquila e della sua diocesi* (Turin 1957). AnnPont (1964) 230.

[G. A. PAPA]

AQUILA AND PRISCILLA, a *Judaeo-Christian couple, originally from Pontus in northern Asia Minor, who had become Christians, probably in Rome. They had to leave Rome in A.D. 49 or 50, when the Emperor Claudius issued his edict of expulsion against the Jews (Acts 18.1–2). Despite the Greek spellings, their names are Latin: that of the man, Aquila (Ἀκύλας), meaning eagle; and that of the woman, Priscilla (Πρίσκιλλα), diminutive of Prisca (Πρίσκα—Paul's usage), meaning venerable. Paul met them and stayed with them in Corinth and worked with them at their common trade of "tent makers" or, rather, canvas weavers (Acts 18.3). They later accompanied Paul to Ephesus, where, in Paul's absence, they instructed *Apollos in the faith (Acts 18.24–26). They were still living in Ephesus when Paul wrote his First Epistle to the Corinthians (1 Cor 16.19). If Rom 16.3–16 is an original part of the Epistle to the *Romans, they were in Rome again when Paul wrote this Epistle (probably in A.D. 57); yet at a later date they were apparently in Ephesus (2 Tm 4.19). Priscilla is usually named before her husband, which may imply that she had a stronger personality or was the more active of the two. As dedicated friends of Paul, for him they "risked their own necks" (Rom 16.3)—how or when is unknown. The local Christian community met in their home (1 Cor 16.19; Rom 16.5). According to a tradition, Aquila later became bishop of Heraclea in Pontus. The Roman Martyrology lists them on July 8.

Bibliography: A. WIKENHAUSER, LexThK[2] 1:779–780. F. SOLE, EncCatt 1:1721–22. EncDictBibl 121, 1927.

[R. G. BOUCHER]

AQUILEIA

Former patriarchate and metropolitan see on the Natissa River in Friuli (Udine), Italy. Having been founded as a Roman military colony *c.* 180 B.C., Aquileia was greatly prized by the Caesars as a port and bastion against the Illyrians. A 5th-century legend traces its Christianity to St. Mark and names St. Hermagoras its first bishop, though its beginnings were in the mid-3d century. In the 5th century it exercised metropolitan rights over Venice, Istria, West Illyricum, Rhaetia, and Noricum; and its bishops claimed the title of patriarch in the mid-6th century (Pelagius I, *Epist.*). When the Huns destroyed Sirmium in 452, they besieged Aquileia, which thereafter extended its jurisdictional claims to the Pannonian borderlands.

After the condemnation of the *Three Chapters in 553 by the Council of *Constantinople II and Pope *Vigilius, Patriarch Paulinus I rejected the condemnation in a provincial council (554); the schism thus created lasted until 607, when Bishop Candidianus restored communion. However, Paulinus had fled to the isle of Grado in Byzantine territory before the Lombards in 568; hence the Lombards elected their own

Aquileia, 4th-century mosaic of the Good Shepherd (detail).

patriarch for ancient Aquileia with its see at Cividale, and this territory remained in schism until Patriarch Peter, with the consent of King Cunibert, made peace with Rome in a synod at Pavia (*c.* 700).

In 716 two dioceses were recognized: Aquileia and Grado. Grado's line of patriarchs continued until the 15th century. Under Paulinus II (*c.* 785–804), a friend of *Charlemagne, missioners were sent among the Avars and Slovenes, and the Drava River was made the boundary between Aquileia and the See of Salzburg in 811. Patriarch Maxentius attempted vainly to reunite Aquileia with Grado in a synod at Mantua (827), when the patriarchate was granted *immunity and free election.

The present cathedral was begun by Poppo (1019–42), and in 1077 Henry IV granted suzerainty to Patriarch Sigehard (1068–77) as Count of Friuli and Istria. Berthold of Andechs changed the see to Udine in 1238, and Gregory of Montelongo (1251–69) was the first Italian to become patriarch. Beset by its neighbors, particularly Venice, the patriarchate functioned only partially; but Marquard of Randech (1365–81) issued a civil and penal code (*Constitutiones patriae Foriiulii*) with the consent of the city's parliament. Louis of Tech (1412–39) joined the King of Hungary in war against Venice, and the territory was then taken over by the Venetians. When the Hapsburgs assumed jurisdiction over Aquileia, the patriarchate was absorbed by Venice; leaders such as Marco Barbo (1465–91), Ermolao Barbaro (1491–93), Giovanni and Daniello Delfino (1658–99, 1734–51) subsequently ruled as patriarchs.

Under Austrian pressure, *Benedict XIV suppressed the Patriarchate of Aquileia (July 6, 1751) and erected the archbishoprics of Udine and Gorizia, and the former patriarchate was made a parish church depending immediately on the Holy See.

Archeological excavations have uncovered an imperial villa under the foundations of the ancient church, which after the peace of Constantine was enlarged and decorated with mosaics of the Good Shepherd, Jonas, etc. A stone pavement (lithostratos) was uncovered. The baptistery was on one side and surrounded an octagonal basin. In the 5th century a large basilica with three naves and a decorated pavement was destroyed by fire. New constructions were made under *Justinian I and at that time a polygonal baptistery was added. The present campanile tower dates from the patriarchate of Poppo.

Bibliography: P. Paschini, *Storia del Friuli,* 3 v. (Udine 1934–36). P. Paschini and C. Cecchelli, EncCatt 1:1722–27. H. Schmidinger, LexThK² 1:780–781; *Patriarch und Landescherr* (Graz 1954). G. Brusin, *Aquileia e Grado* (2d ed. Padua 1952).
Illustration credit: Museo Archeologico, Aquileia.

[F. X. MURPHY]

AQUILEIA, RITE OF. Little is known of the primitive rite of Aquileia, but it was used in such distant places as Verona, Trent, and Pola. The oldest extant document pertaining to the rite is a fragmentary 7th- or 8th-century Lectionary (*Capitulare evangeliorum*), added by a Lombard hand to the earlier Codex Richdigeranus; its characteristics resemble the *Milanese more than the Roman rite. In evidence of this, Advent has five Sundays, with the Gospel *Missus est,* commemorating the Annunciation, for the fifth Sunday; Septuagesima is excluded, and there are three baptismal scrutinies and the *Traditio Symboli* on the Sunday before Easter. The feast of St. Stephen is kept on the Antiochene date, December 27. Milanese usages are found in the marginal notes of the Codex Forojuliensis of the Gospels, in which the rubric "In triduanas" precedes the Rogation Days (P. Borella, "L'anno liturgico Ambrosiano," Righetti 2:288). On the strength of a statement in a letter of the Council of Aquileia (381) to the Emperor Theodosius, "In all things we always hold the order and arrangement of the Church of Alexandria" (Mansi 3:624), R. Buchwald claims that Aquileia owed its liturgy to Alexandria ["Die Epiklese in der römischen Messe," *Weidenauer Studien* 1 (1906) 47]. But this theory remains untenable.

Whatever form this primitive rite may have taken, it was superseded in the Carolingian period by some kind of Roman variant, which throughout the Middle Ages appears to have been increasingly approximated to the standard Roman rite. The last Aquileian Missal (1519) had retained few distinctive characteristics. The rite, such as it was, was suppressed at Trieste (1586), Monza (1578), Aquileia (1596) and Como (1596 or 1597).

Bibliography: F. Cabrol, DACL 1.2:2683–91. A. F. Frisi, *Memorie storiche di Monza e sua corte* (Milan 1794). A. A. King, *Liturgies of the Past* (Milwaukee 1959). A. Fortescue, *The Mass* (New York 1912). B. M. de Rubeis, *De sacris Forojuliensium ritibus* (Venice 1754).

[A. A. KING]

AQUILINUS, ST., martyr; b. Würzburg, Germany, *c.* 970; d. Milan, Italy, *c.* 1015 (feast, Jan. 29). He went to Cologne in order to pursue his studies but left when his fellow canons attempted to make him bishop. Leaving Paris for the same reason, he crossed the Alps, stayed a short while at Pavia, and finally joined the canons of the church of S. Lorenzo at Milan. Early in the 11th century he was martyred because of his outspoken opposition to the spread of *Manichaeism. His body rests in a chapel of the church of S. Lorenzo that bears his name and is decorated with 24 scenes from his life. He seems to have enjoyed a continuous cult, and he is honored by the churches of Cologne, Würzburg, and Milan and by the canons of the *Lateran. Ancient Breviary lessons, the martyrologies, and the Bollandist critique of the sources all indicate that he was martyred in conflict with *Arianism and lived probably during the 6th century.

Bibliography: ActSS Jan. 3:585–586. G. Dorio, *Memoria sul culto del martire Santo Aquilino* (Milan 1856), basic study. G. Allmang, DHGE 3:1147–48. A. Wendehorst, LexThK² 1:782.

[N. M. RIEHLE]

AQUINAS, PHILIPPUS, Hebrew scholar and convert to Christianity; b. Carpentras, southern France, *c.* 1575; d. Paris, 1650. His Jewish name was Juda Mordechai. Little is known of his early years, but while occupying the position of rabbi at Avignon he showed great sympathy for Christianity. Because of this, he was forced to resign his position in 1610. He subsequently entered the Church at Aquino in the Kingdom of Naples, taking the name Philip Aquinas (of Aquin). In later years he was engaged in teaching Hebrew at Paris, where he was named professor at the College of France by Louis XIII. Some indication of his position in French court life may be drawn from the fact that his grandson, Anthony of Aquin (d. 1696), became the chief physician of Louis XIV. Philippus worked on the Paris Polyglot (*see* POLYGLOT BIBLES), but his principal publications were *Radices breves linguae Sanctae* (Paris 1620) and *Dictionarium Hebraeo-Chaldaeo-talmudico-rabbinicum* (Paris 1629), in which he made the Hebrew dictionaries of Nathan ben Jehiel of Rome (d. 1106) and J. *Buxtorf more complete.

Bibliography: A. Strobel, LexThK² 1:782. *Nouvelle biographie générale,* ed. J. C. Hoefer, v.2 (Paris 1859) 946.

[S. M. POLAN]

AQUINAS COLLEGE, a fully accredited Catholic, coeducational, liberal arts college in Grand Rapids, Mich., empowered to grant both bachelor's and master's degrees. The College was originally founded as a novitiate normal school in 1886 by the Dominican Sisters of Marywood. In 1923, the normal school merged with the College for laywomen that was founded that year and incorporated by the Michigan State Legislature with full power to grant degrees. In 1931 the College transferred to a downtown location as a coeducational junior college. In 1940 the need for advanced training caused the congregation to reorganize the College as a 4-year institution called Aquinas College. In 1945 the College purchased the 65-acre Edward Lowe estate in eastern Grand Rapids. Use was made of buildings already located on the property. Between 1955 and 1964 a series of five new buildings was planned and completed to provide additional classroom and residential facilities.

In 1923 the College received its charter from the State of Michigan, which further recognized it as a standard teacher training institution. It is accredited by the North Central Association of Colleges and Secondary Schools and is affiliated with The Catholic University of America. Degrees conferred in the undergraduate program are the B.A., B.S., B.S. in Business Administration, B.S. in Education, and Mus.B. In the graduate program degrees conferred are the M.A. and M.A. in Education. Aquinas also offers preprofessional courses in dentistry, law, medicine, medical technology, social work, journalism, government service, and engineering.

Governed by a board of trustees composed of members of the religious community, the College also has a lay board of trustees empowered to advise and assist in the planned expansion. In 1964 the 87-member faculty was made up of 9 Dominican priests, 31 sisters, and 47 laymen. The staff held 11 doctorates and 70 master's degrees. Enrollment was 1,200 students with expansion planned to accommodate 3,000.

The College is organized on a two-semester plan with an evening college and a summer session which offers special intensive language courses. Majors and minors are offered in 20 different fields with seminars and research studies included in the course for advanced students.

In addition to the modern science hall, electronic language laboratories and closed-circuit TV are also used on campus. The College operates its own FM radio station, WXTO, in conjunction with the Diocese of Grand Rapids, and provides in-service training in journalism and speech. In 1964 the library housed 45,500 volumes and received 350 periodicals.

[M. CLAPP]

AQUINAS JUNIOR COLLEGE, a coeducational junior college in Nashville, Tenn., founded in 1928 for training of student sisters, and expanded in 1961 to include lay students. It is conducted by the Dominican Sisters of St. Cecilia Congregation who originally came to Nashville in 1860 at the invitation of the bishop to establish an academy for girls. In 1883 a state charter empowered the congregation to confer academic honors and collegiate degrees. In 1929 the institution became the first religious normal school to receive affiliation with The Catholic University of America. In September 1961 Aquinas College enrolled 68 lay students.

The administration of Aquinas is vested in a board of trustees, the officers of the College, and various committees. These standing committees include administration, admissions and scholarships, library, guidance, public relations, budget, and curriculum. The corporate powers of the College lie in the board of trustees, consisting of 6 members of the community, the prioress general, the 4 members of the general council, and the bursar general. The advisory board, initially composed of 1 priest and 6 laymen, assists the president and the trustees. Officers of the College include a president, a dean of studies, a registrar, a treasurer, and a chaplain.

The faculty is composed of 15 members, including a priest, 10 sisters, and 4 laymen. Four are engaged full time in college instruction, others in both high school and college instruction. Faculty degrees include 2 doctoral and 10 master's degrees. Full-time enrollment averages about 65 students.

Courses sufficiently broad to satisfy the need of either the terminal or the transfer student are offered in liberal arts, fine arts, science, and business. In 1964 a library on the 86-acre campus housed approximately 5,000 volumes and received 42 periodicals.

Aquinas Junior College is affiliated with The Catholic University of America and is a member of the Dominican Educational Association.

[D. GOBEL]

ARABA, Hebrew name (*hā'ărābâ,* "the steppe, desert, plain") for all or part of the Great Rift Valley extending south from the Sea of Galilee in Palestine to the Gulf of Aqaba (*see* GALILEE, SEA OF). In the Bible it comprises three main sections: the 50-mile-long Jordan Valley (el-Ghôr), e.g., Dt 4.49; the 50-mile stretch of the Dead Sea area, the "Salt Sea of the Araba," e.g., Dt 3.17; Ez 47.8; and the 100 miles of wilderness from the Dead Sea to the Gulf of Aqaba (modern Wâdī el-'Arabah), e.g., Dt 2.8 and probably Am 6.14. The width of the Biblical Araba varies from 5 to 25 miles. Some 700 feet below sea level at the Sea of Galilee, it descends to 1,286 feet below sea level at the Dead Sea and rises above sea level farther south. Quite fertile north of the Dead Sea, it is mud, sand, and gravel to the south. The term Araba today is reserved for the southern section. In ancient times this section was a north-south travel route; it was used by at least some of the Israelites during the Exodus from Egypt (Dt 2.8). Explorations by Glueck indicate that the south Araba sustained a civilization as early as the 4th millenium B.C. Phinon (Nm 33.42; modern Feinan) and other sites in the Araba testify to intensive copper- and iron-mining activities that reached their peak under King Solomon. Excavations at Tell el-Kheleifeh near Asiongaber/Elath, Solomon's port city and industrial center at the head of the Gulf of Aqaba (3 Kgs 9.26,28), turned up remains of a huge ore refinery. In the OT era, control of the south Araba fluctuated between Israelites and Edomites. The Nabateans possessed it after the 3d century B.C.

Bibliography: N. GLUECK, *Rivers in the Desert* (New York 1959). G. E. WRIGHT, "More on King Solomon's Mines," Bibl Archaeol 24 (1961) 59–62. D. BALY, *The Geography of the Bible* (New York 1957) 198–217.

[E. MAY]

ARABIA

A large triangular peninsula lying between Asia and Africa. Classified by geographers as a part of Asia, although connected to Africa by the Sinai Peninsula and in many respects more properly a part of the African land mass, its size of approximately one million square miles entitles it to be considered as a subcontinent.

1. HISTORY

Before treating of the Islamic and pre-Islamic history of Arabia, this article will give a brief description of the geography and ethnology of the Arabian peninsula.

Geography. Arabia is bounded on three sides by water (the Red Sea on the west, the Gulf of Aden and the Arabian Sea on the south, the Gulf of Oman and the Persian Gulf on the east) and has from early times been called *Jazīrat al-'Arab* (Island of the Arabs) by its inhabitants. There is no natural northern boundary; a vast steppe leads into Jordan, Iraq, and Syria. There are many islands off the southern coasts and a few shallow bays along those coasts. A chain of mountains (in some regions two chains) called al-Sarah runs close and parallel to the coastline of the Red Sea, with many plateaus along their eastern slopes. The mountains are highest in the Yemen and reappear again in the south-east in Dhufar and Oman. There are coastal plains and hills, mesas, and buttes, especially in the north. Most of the peninsula, however, is a sandy desert. The principal desert areas are the Great Nufud and the Empty Quarter (*al-Rub' al-Khâlī*), the latter constituting the largest continuous body of sand in the world.

Climate and Rainfall. Arabia, bisected by the Tropic of Cancer, generally enjoys a temperate climate, although the lowlands are semitropical. The summer heat is intense, with temperatures as high as 122° F, but winter in the highlands can be proportionately bitter. The inlands are dry and subject to severe sandstorms. Limited eastern parts are affected by the monsoons, but, in general, rainfall is scarce throughout the peninsula. In the desert regions, in fact, no rain may fall for periods of 8 or 10 years, though in some places sudden torrential rains caught in a stream channel (*wâdī*) cause flash-floods. There are no large rivers (a few small ones flow along the southern and eastern coasts) and no lakes. In fact, human life is made possible in much of the peninsula only by the presence of springs, pools, and wells, around which oasis settlements have grown up. Some of these oases are hundreds of square miles in area, large enough to permit several separate villages and large camping areas within them; others are merely watering places where the water is too salty for human consumption but generally satisfactory for camels. There is some evidence of ancient irrigation systems and dams, which very probably made fertile some regions that are no longer so.

Produce. Since there are no prairies or forests and many inimical migrating dunes, cultivation in Arabia is necessarily limited and requires much skill. The date palm is the principal tree and is put to many uses. Some wheat, barley, and alfalfa are grown, as well as coffee, introduced by Europeans, and qat, with its slightly narcotic leaves, in Yemen and the south. Plants yielding frankincense, myrrh, and other aromatics, as well as dyes such as indigo, have been grown there since ancient times. In a few isolated regions roses, pomegranates, mangoes, figs, grapes, peaches, and bananas can be grown. In general, milk and dates provide the staple foods, supplemented by bush fruit and truffles, for man and beast alike. The camel is the most important animal, since it is well adapted to desert conditions, and there are many sheep and goats. Arabian horses and gazelles are rapidly dying out. There is a wide variety of small animals, birds, and insects.

Ethnology. Much more archeological and anthropological research will have to be done before the ethnology of Arabia is reliably clear. Tribal traditions are mostly legendary and unreliable, although they are not to be dismissed for more recent Arabian history. The size of the population is uncertain, but it is surely less than 10 million. Nearly all Arabians are of the Mediterranean race, but there is a distinct Veddoid strain in the south. The modern Arabs themselves accept a descent from two ancestors, Qahtan and Adnan, the descendants of the former being supposed to be the southern Arabs and those of the latter the northern Arabs. Naturally such a scheme is open to serious question. There are strong indications that the earliest southern Arabians had migrated from the northern and central parts of the peninsula. Many tribes retain no tradition of ever having belonged to either group, while others are known to have moved or changed their allegiance

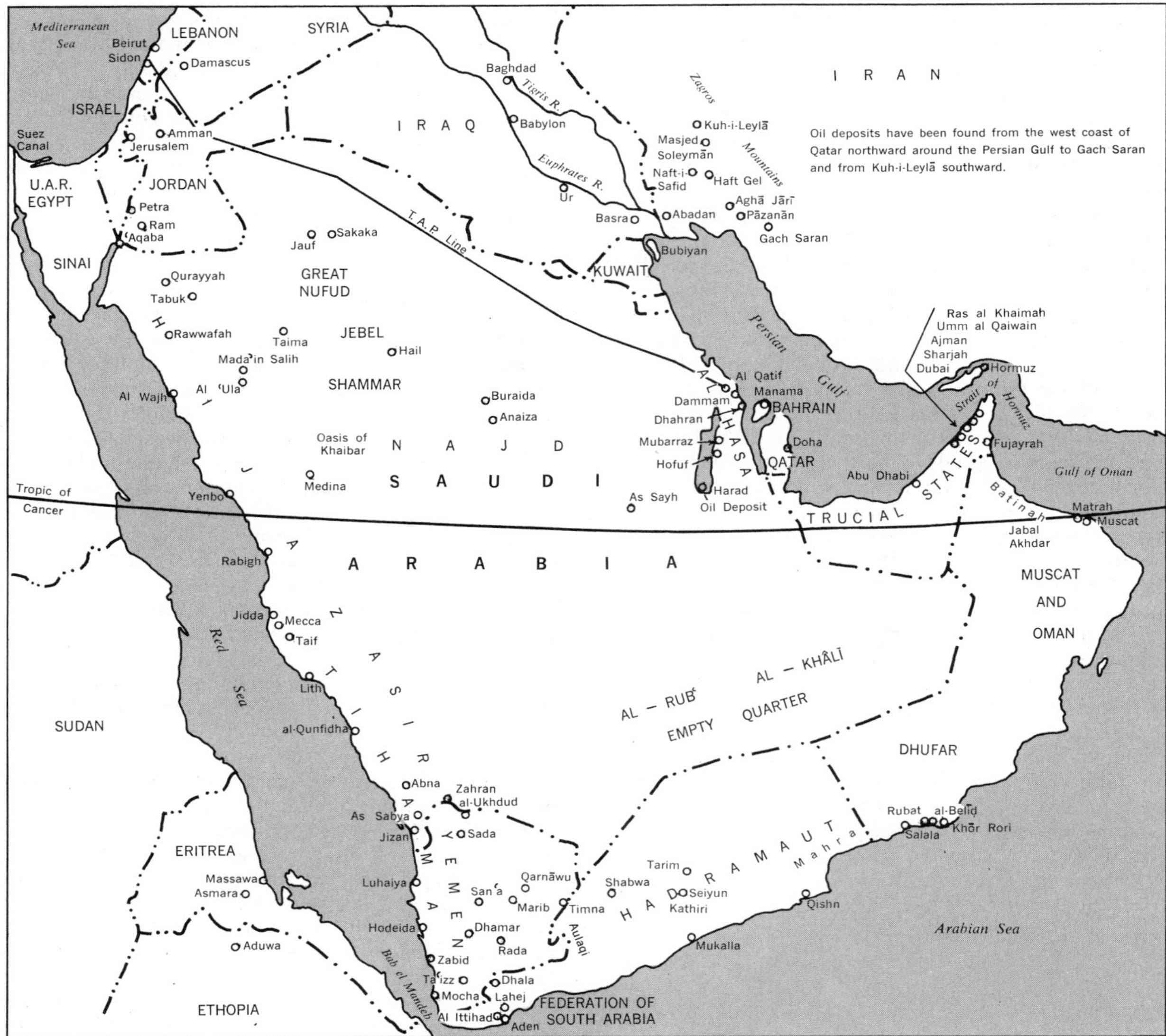

by alliances. Nevertheless, the tradition expresses something utterly real: a cultural difference and a spirit of rivalry between northern and southern Arabians, which remained a factor of notable importance in Islamic history well into modern times and as far away from Arabia as Spain and Transoxiana. Today there are a few immigrants, mostly in the coastal regions. Slavery of Africans apparently still exists, although it is said to be minimal. There has been no type of color bar in Arabia since Islamic times. Significant migrations of peoples have taken place within the peninsula in recent times, but few Arabians have emigrated, and those few to adjacent Iran, India, and East Africa.

Pre-Islamic history. Arabia is still one of the lesser-known parts of the world, and a great amount of basic scientific exploration remains to be done before its history can be made precise.

Modern Exploration. Such investigation began with Carsten Niebuhr and the Danish expedition of 1761 to 1764. A century later Joseph Halevy and Eduard Glaser explored several south Arabian sites and were able to copy many Sabaean inscriptions. *See* SABA (SHEBA). The interior of Arabia was penetrated during the 19th century by J. L. Burckhardt, Richard Burton, and W. G. Palgrave; British officers of the Indian government completed technical surveys of the southeastern regions, and Charles Doughty wrote his invaluable study of northern Arabia. The studies preparatory to the building of the Hejaz railway and the more recent work of Alois Musil, K. S. Twitchell, and H. St. John B. Philby have added immeasurably to knowledge of the peninsula. The Empty Quarter was crossed and documented by Bertram Thomas in 1931 and 1932. More recently oil companies have sponsored illuminating surveys of eastern Arabian territories.

Dawn of History in Arabia. Future investigations will doubtless improve the state of knowledge of early Arabia, but as yet it has only the most shadowy history before the 1st millennium B.C. A few chance finds have proved that the peninsula was inhabited in Palaeolithic and Neolithic times. Some of those who believe in the existence of a Semitic race have speculated that Arabia might have been the original home of that race. It is quite solidly established, at any rate, that nomads from the Arabian deserts began infiltrating the Iraqi and Syrian portions of the Fertile Crescent about the middle of the 4th millennium B.C. and made substantial incursions thereafter at intervals of approximately a millennium until the Moslem conquest. Early in the 2d millennium B.C. a system of alphabetic writing was invented and about the same time the camel was domesticated. Soon afterward there were considerable migrations of peoples within Arabia, perhaps originating the traditional division between northern and southern tribes, and about 1500 B.C. the Aramaeans entered the Fertile Crescent in large numbers.

Assyro-Babylonian, Egyptian, and Hebrew (notably Gn 10.26–30; see under 2. below) records mention some place names and tribes that are almost certainly to be identified within Arabia. The "Aribi" in Assyro-Babylonian texts are thought by some scholars to denote the Arabs. Strong organized states came into being in South Arabia during the second half of the first millennium B.C., while in North Arabia the Persians were succeeding the Assyrians and Neo-Babylonians in bringing substantial portions of that area under their influence. Evidently there was a rapid development of commerce and trade at this time, and Arabia—particularly South Arabia—emerged and flourished on that account. The Neo-Babylonian King *Nabu-na'id (Nabonidus; 556–539 B.C.), as a recent discovery indicates, had extended his influence as far south as Yathrib, and the presence of Jewish colonies in Arabia may date from this time.

Early Kingdoms. The kingdom of Ma'in existed in Yemen from about 1200 to 650 B.C. Scholars are at variance as to how long it continued to coexist with the Sabaean kingdom, which was newly founded, after a 3-century rule of priest-kings, about 650. A queen of the Sabaeans (the Queen of Sheba) is reported in 3 Kgs 10.1–13 to have visited Solomon. Saba was more or less constantly at war with the younger kingdoms of Hadramaut and Qataban, but appears to have maintained the upper hand. Its rule lasted until 115 B.C., when it was conquered by the Himyarites. Qataban fell at about the same time. The Himyarite kingdom lasted until A.D. 525. In the meantime the Nabataean kingdom rose in the north, from its famous capital at Petra, and prospered as an entrepot and from later cooperation with the Romans (*see* NABATAEANS). Rome launched its single attempt to conquer Arabia in 24 B.C. under Aelius Gallus, but the expedition ended in failure. The height of Nabataean influence occurred during the reign of Harithath (or Aretas) IV, who ruled from 9 B.C. to A.D. 40. In 106 the Emperor Trajan incorporated the state into the Roman Empire.

There is mention of Arabs at Pentecost (Acts 2.11) and St. Paul visited Arabia, although that may only mean some region south of Damascus, after his conversion (Gal 1.17). Some Arab *shaykhs* whose identity is now impossible to determine are known to have accepted the Christian faith in the 3d century, and Arab bishoprics are noted thereafter by historians of the times (see under 5. below). In the mid-4th century the (Christian, later Monophysite) Abyssinians succeeded in occupying Himyarite territory in South Arabia. The ensuing struggle became an open quarrel between Judaism, accepted by the Himyarites, and Christianity. Abyssinia, supported by Byzantium, assumed a spacious colony in Arabia in 525, but 50 years later was effectively defeated by Persian forces. In the meantime the political arrangements in North Arabia had come to reflect this important power-struggle. Client kingdoms had been established: Ḥīra, the Lakhmids, dependent upon Persia, and the Ghassanids, dependent upon Byzantium. After 583 the Ghassanids themselves split, and in the later years of the century the tribe of Kindah began to assume power in Central Arabia as a type of vassal state of Yemen. There was thus a condition of political confusion on the eve of the foundation of Islam.

Islamic History. About 570 Mohammed was born in *Mecca, a center of trade and religious pilgrimage in west Central Arabia. His career as founder of the religion of *Islam fundamentally changed the entire course of Arabian history. In his youth Mohammed was a poor orphan, but later he married a wealthy woman. About the age of 40 he received his "prophetic call" to unite the Arabs under a monotheism, which he came to insist was a reaffirmation of pure Judaism and Christianity. His "revelations" were collected after his death in the *Koran. But the Meccans did not welcome Mohammed's message, and he was obliged to flee with his followers to Yathrib (known thereafter as *Medina) in 622, the *Hegira (Arabic *hijrah,* "flight") from which Moslems date their era. At Medina Mohammed's fortunes took a sharp turn for the better and he found himself directing a political community, which gradually gained ascendancy in Central Arabia and was ready, at the time of his death in 632, to consolidate its territories and prepare to conquer other lands.

In the Middle Ages. Mohammed's immediate successors, the "Orthodox" caliphs, superintended a series of successful invasions to the north, east, and west of the Arabian peninsula. During the reign of the caliph Ali, Mohammed's cousin and son-in-law, there ensued a dispute over the caliphate that resulted in the establishment of the dynasty of the *Umayyads, which ruled over the still-expanding Islamic empire for almost a century (661–750) from its capital in *Damascus, but resulted also in the most important and enduring division among Moslems, that between the *Sunnites and the *Shiïtes. A carefully planned revolution put the dynasty of the *'Abbāsids in power in 750, and the capital of the empire was moved to *Baghdad. The 'Abbāsid caliphs continued nominally to rule the Islamic empire until the capture of Baghdad by the *Mongols in 1258, though in point of fact the empire was already hopelessly fragmented after the first century of their rule. Arabia, in particular, provided favorable conditions for the further growth of Shiism, and by the end of the 9th century two revolutionary branches of Shiïtes, the *Ismailis and the Carmathians held large portions of the peninsula. The success of the Ismaili Fatimid caliphate in Egypt prolonged the dominance of Shiïte rule of Arabia, but Salah-al-Din (*Saladin) restored Sunnite control toward the end of the 12th century.

Arabia generally shared the fortunes and misfortunes of neighboring Egypt and Syria during the period of the *Mamelukes (1250–1517), but in some respects and more particularly in its southern and eastern regions was able to follow an independent course. Early in the 16th century Portuguese explorers reached Arabia, and at the same time the *Ottoman Turks wrested Egypt from Mameluke rule. Under the impact of European trading activity in south and east Asia, *Yemen, Hadramaut, and Oman in South Arabia entered upon a new period of prosperity. In the 18th century the reforming movement of the *Wahhābis took root in Najd and won over the Saud tribe to its tenets. But its expanding state ran into powerful opposition from the sherifs of Mecca and the newly vitalized Sayyid dynasty in Oman, which eventually extended its authority to the coastal areas of East Africa. Later technological advances enabled the Ottomans to strengthen their hold over parts of Arabia.

In Modern Times. The Arab Revolt under Sharif Husayn of Mecca, with British assistance, brought about the end of Ottoman rule during World War I. Sharif Husayn was recognized as king of Arabia (and later, briefly, as *caliph), but was soon at war with the Saud tribal confederacy under Abd-al-Aziz ibn-Saud. Ibn-Saud defeated Husayn, conquered the Hejaz, and proceeded to unify the peninsula under his own rule; in 1932 he assumed the title of king of *Saudi Arabia. His conquest stopped short at the boundaries that have been maintained since, separating Saudi Arabia from the imamate of Yemen and the so-called Trucial states. The discovery of enormous deposits of oil in eastern Arabia and their subsequent exploitation have very markedly changed the fortunes of this country and brought it increasingly forward into world affairs; but Christianity remains forbidden (except for diplomats and other authorized foreigners) within it.

Bibliography: D. G. Hogarth, *Arabia* (Oxford 1922). C. M. Doughty, *Travels in Arabia Deserts,* 2 v. (new ed. New York 1937). A. Musil, *In the Arabian Desert* (New York 1930). B. Thomas, *Arabia Felix* (New York 1932). J. A. Montgomery, *Arabia and the Bible* (Philadelphia 1934). H. R. P. Dickson, *The Arab of the Desert* (London 1949). R. H. Sanger, *The Arabian Peninsula* (Ithaca 1954). H. St. J. B. Philby, *Saudi Arabia* (London 1955). P. K. Hitti, *History of the Arabs* (6th ed. New York 1956). K. S. Twitchell, *Saudi Arabia* (3d ed. Princeton 1958). G. A. Lipsky et al., *Saudi Arabia* (New Haven 1959).

[J. KRITZECK]

2. Arabia in the Bible

The Hebrew word *'ărab* is used in Is 21.13 to designate the steppe countries where the nomads, the desert dwellers (Jer 25.24), lived, regardless of the dialect spoken by each individual ethnic group. Therefore, Arabia (in the contemporary meaning of the Arabian peninsula inhabited by Arabic speaking populations) is an entity foreign to the Israelites of the OT period. The generic name, Arabian(s) (Heb. collective *'ărab;* gentilic *'ărābî,* pl. *'ărābîm;* the *Aribu* of the cuneiform inscriptions), refers to the tent-dwelling (Is 13.20) Bedouins of the desert (Jer 3.2) east of Palestine; hence they are known also as the Cedemites or Easterners (*bᵉnê-qedem,* the children of the East, e.g., in Is 11.14). The generic name, however, is used rather seldom compared with the proper names of the various Arabian populations neighboring Palestine, as they are found, for instance, in the ethnic genealogical lists of Genesis ch. 10, 11, and 25. Although the ancestors of the Israelites originated (about the 19th century B.C.) in northwestern Mesopotamia, where they had been in contact with and influenced by Semitic as well as non-Semitic populations, their conviction of being close kinsfolk of the peoples living in northern and southern Arabia is stressed in these lists. Among the descendants of Eber (Heb. *'ēber*), a descendant of Sem, several names are mentioned in Gn 10.25–29 that are similar to those of peoples in South Arabia, such as, *yoqṭān* = Qaḥṭân [mentioned in Jamme 635.27 (about 60 B.C.) as forming a kingdom along with Kindat]; *ḥăsarmāwet* = Ḥaḍramawt; *šᵉbā'* = Saba'; and *ḥăwîlâ* = Ḫawlân. It is noteworthy that the names of Ma'în and Qatabân are not found, and that Saba' is listed as the brother of Dedan in the Bible (in Gn 10.7 as a grandson *kûs*—Chus; in Gn 25.3 as a grandson of Abraham and *qᵉtûrâ*—Cetura; see also Ez 38.13). The city of Dedan, at the present time al-'Ulá, was an important Minaean (not Sabaean) trading center. The mention of faraway Ḥaḍramawt is explained by actual commercial contacts, as illustrated by the Ḥaḍrami clay stamp (probably of the 9th century B.C.) discovered by J. L. Kelso during the 1957 excavations at Beitin, Biblical Bethel. The Sabaeans, whose country is said to be far off (Jl 4.8), are described as merchants (Ez 25.23; 27.22–23) trading in gold, frankincense [Is 60.6; Jer 6.20; Ps 71(72).15], the best spices, and precious stones (Ez 27.22), but also as raiders (Jb 1.15) and slave traders (Jl 4.8).

During the monarchical period of the Israelite history, the Arabians intervened in Jewish affairs on several occasions. For instance, the Queen of *Saba (Sheba) visited Solomon; King Josaphat of Juda received a large tribute of sheep and goats from the Arabians (2 Chr 17.11); South Arabians raided the realm and even the capital of Juda at the time of King Joram (2 Chr 21.16–17; 22.1). After the return from exile, Gossem (Geshem) the Arabian (Neh 2.19) and his band of Arabs (Neh 4.1) joined the coalition that tried unsuccessfully to prevent the reconstruction of the walls of Jerusalem.

Among the descendants of *Ismael (Ishmael), the son of Abraham and *Agar (Hagar) the Egyptian (Gn 25.12), the most famous were the *Nabataeans, known also as Arabians (2 Mc 5.8; Acts 2.11). Finally, it was in the northern end of Arabia, i.e., in the Syro-Arabian desert east of Damascus, that Paul withdrew after his conversion to Christianity (Gal 1.17).

Bibliography: R. P. Dougherty, *The Sealand of Ancient Arabia* (New Haven 1932). J. A. Montgomery, *Arabia and the Bible* (Philadelphia 1934). A. Jamme and G. W. Van Beek, "The South-Arabian Clay Stamp from Bethel Again," BullAm SchOrRes 163 (1961) 15–18. EncDictBibl 122. J. Assfalg, Lex ThK² 1:786–787. G. Finnegan, EncCatt 1:1742–43.

[A. JAMME]

3. Paganism in North Arabia

The following summarizes the pantheons and the cult of Arabs in the central and northern portions of the Arabian Peninsula before Islam and the religious beliefs of the Nabataeans and Palmyrenes, among whom Arabic influences assumed growing importance. Being more or less nomadic, these tribes retained certain primitive traits found also in the religion of the Hebrews of the patriarchal era.

Early North Arabians. The earliest firsthand information on North Arabia is from Assyrian annals. For the Neo-Babylonian period we have a few proto-Arabic graffiti. Their consonant script is related to that of South Arabic inscriptions. The most ancient are those of Dedan (Is 21.13–14); but those of Tema follow closely and constitute Thamudic A (6th and 5th centuries B.C.). The tribe of Thamud was already mentioned in the annals of Sargon II for the year 714 B.C.; but in the proto-Arabic graffiti its name does not appear until the end of the Persian era and during the Hellenistic era. (Thamudic B, in the Nejd). At Dedan the tribe of Liḥyan was in control during this time. Its script (Liḥyanite A and B) derives from Dedanite. At the Roman epoch and in the early Byzantine era, the proto-Arabic alphabet continued to be used, with increasingly cursive forms: Thamudic C and D in the Dedan region, E in the regions of Tebuq and Petra, and the so-called Ṣafaitic script in the eastern and southeastern Hauran̈. The most recent explorations of H. St. John B. Philby and of G. and J. Ryckmans show that the more southerly routes also, which lead from *Mecca or Ryad to *Yemen, are covered with proto-Arabic graffiti. Current studies of these indicate that they should not be attributed to the Thamudeans, inasmuch as classical and Arabic sources situate this tribe only in the northwestern portion of the Peninsula. The Aramaean sources are represented by the famous stele of Tema (6th century B.C.), by the Nabataean and Palmyrene inscriptions (1st century B.C. to 3d century A.D.), and by a few passages of Syriac literature. It has been possible to glean precious information from Greek Byzantine writings and Arabic authors. In fact, the Book of Idols of Ibn al-Kalbi (*c.* A.D. 800) deals exclusively with this subject.

The Pantheon. A description of the gods of ancient North Arabia can best be made by considering separately the inscriptions, according to their provenance, that mention these gods.

The Cuneiform Texts. The annals of Esarhaddon (680–669) contain a list of the Arabic gods of Adumatu, the Duma of Gn 25.14 (Pritchard ANET 291b). At the head of the list is Atar-samain, i.e., Atar-of-the-heavens. It is the god 'Athtar of Ugarit (15th century) and of the southern Arabs. But here it is a goddess, like the Babylonian Ishtar and the Phoenician Astarte (3 Kgs 11.5). 'Athtar (this seems to be the primitive form of these four names) is above all the personification of the planet Venus, whence the vagueness in the attribution of sex. The brilliant star of morning and evening, so familiar to the nomad, thus supplemented El, the ancestral deity of the Semites. ("El" appears also under the augmentative form "Ilah," whose plural of majesty is the Hebrew "Elohim.") The fourth god in the list is Ruldaiu, who is also mentioned by Ibn al-Kalbi under the form of Ruḍa. The corresponding root signifies to satisfy, and various indices lead one to think that Ruḍa is the name of Mercury, the beneficent planet.

Dedan and *Liḥyan, Thamud* and *Ṣafa.* The proto-Arabic inscriptions of Dedan give little information on the autochthonous gods of the Neo-Babylonian era. The name of the supreme god El is found only in personal names. Thus a "king of Dedan" was named Kabir'el, son of Mati'el. The names ending in *'ēl* and in *'ilah* are more numerous in the various proto-Arabic dialects than those in honor of any other deity. Taken as a whole, they are to be considered as survivals, for it has been proved that they were preponderant in ancient Akkadian and in proto-Aramaic. Since the word *'ēl* corresponds to the word god, it has been rightly concluded that the proto-Semites invoked only El. In fact, if the word god had applied to various deities, the personal names in *'ēl* would have had an equivocal meaning. It is legitimate to translate El as God, but this practical monotheism does not imply a clear awareness that the gods adored by neighboring peoples did not exist. The reason that the primitive Dedanite and Thamudic texts now known contain no direct invocation to El or Ilah is perhaps because of the rarity of these graffiti. In Thamudic B several examples have been found that cannot be interpreted as innovations or said to have been borrowed. The authors of the graffiti in Thamudic A gave first place to Ṣalam. His name, which signifies Image, was actually accompanied by the image of the oxhead; in South Arabia this was generally the symbol of the lunar god, who was almost as important as the god 'Athtar. The Aramaic stele of Tema also names Ṣalam, with the same representation of an oxhead. The moon regularly accompanies Venus; 20 kilometers east of Tema, Philby discovered a Thamudic graffito in which a "king of Duma" invokes " 'Atarsam and Ṣalam." The first name is a shortened form of Atar-samain. Venus seems also to have been designated by the appellation al-Ilat, the Goddess, in a contemporary graffito, an appellation that was afterward widely accepted. We find this name also in Herodotus in the mid-5th century. The Arabs of Sinai invoked Orotal and Alilat in their oath, names they gave to Dionysus and heavenly Aphrodite (*Histories,* 3.8; 1.131). The form Orotal is the approximate pronounciation of Ruḍa by a Greek, the *ḍ* giving rise to a light "l" sound. Ruḍa was identified with Dionysus as the god of renewed vegetation. The explorations of N. Glueck have shown that the Sinai Peninsula has almost always been partly under cultivation. As for the heavenly Goddess, she is also attested to by the Aramaic dedication of a silver bowl "offered by Qainu, son of Geshem, king of Qedar [see Is 21.16] to han-Ilat" (*han* is an ancient form of the Arabic article *al*). The tribe of Qedar lived nomadically in the north of Dedan, and our Geshem was doubtless the same "Geshem the Arab" of Nehemia 2.19, thus bringing us back to the mid-5th century B.C. At Dedan the Liḥyanites also adored Ilat, and this goddess first appeared under the name of 'Uzzai, the very strong one, in a text in Liḥyanite A. In South Arabia 'Athtar was given similar epithets, no doubt as the Morning Star. Other inscriptions in Liḥyanite A name han-Aktab, i.e., the scribe, the Arabic counterpart of the god-scribe Nebo, whose planet was Mercury. Thus han-Aktab could very well be identical with Ruḍa, frequently invoked in the Thamudic B graffiti, which were in part contemporaneous. The Liḥyanite texts name Dhu-Ghabat even oftener, i.e., the One from Ghabat, an oasis north of Medina. Dhu-Ghabat is an anonymous appellation in truly Arabic manner, referring perhaps to han-Aktab himself. The Thamudic B graffiti are addressed also to 'Atarsam. Thus in the Persian era, the North Arabic pantheon is consistently astral. One qualification to this must be made by those who agree that the mysterious NHY (Nahay), the divine name that appears most frequently in Thamudic B, is merely a phonetic variation of LHY or 'LHY (Lahay, Ilahay), elongated forms of Ilah. In this case, the important tribe of Thamud would have reserved first place for the ancestral deity. But if we come down to the Greco-Roman era, we see that Ilah (sometimes elided to Lah) is mentioned far less often than Ruḍa, and especially than Ilat (or Lat).

The Nabataeans. At the end of the Persian era the Nabataeans, who had come from central or southern Arabia, displaced the Qedarites in the area extending from Dedan to Petra. They soon controlled all of Transjordania and even southern Syria. At Gaia (modern Wadi Musa), a village close to which flowed the spring that also watered Petra, a god of anonymous appellation was venerated: Dushara, the One of the Shara. This

Arabic word signifies region and even to this day designates the mountain range on whose western slopes Gaia was nestled. Two inscriptions described Dushara as the "god of Gaia." According to the Alexandrian lexicographer Hesychios, Dusares (the Greek form of Dushara) was identified with Dionysus, as the god of vegetation and vineyards. The equation Orotal-Dionysus (made by Herodotus) thus suggests that the real Master of the Shara was none other than Ruḍa, which would explain the curious absence of this divine name in Nabataean texts. Besides, several dedications lend support to this identification, as well as to that of Ruḍa with the scribe-god Mercury. Thus the chief gods of the Nabataeans appear to have been Venus and Mercury. Venus was invoked also under the name of Allatu (the Goddess), in particular at Iram (modern Ramm) and Boṣra. Among the other Arabic deities named in the Nabataean inscriptions, the mysterious Hubalu and the goddess of fate Manawatu may be cited; both were invoked at Hegra.

Palmyra. Allat, Shamash (Shams), and Raḥim (the Merciful, likewise discovered in the Safaitic graffiti) are Arabic gods who were adopted at Palmyra. To these may be added Arṣu, whose name represents another form of Ruḍa and who seems to have been invoked in a special way by the caravaneers. One relief shows him mounted on a camel before 'Azizu on horseback. The latter name is simply a masculine form of 'Uzza. Pairs of masculine deities are characteristic of the Palmyrene pantheon. Ma'an and Sha'ar, or Shalman and Abgal, should also be mentioned. They are the "Ginnaye" (whence the Arabic word *jinn*), i.e., "protective" gods. The name Gad, Fortune, expresses the same need of protection. Veneration was given the Gad of the village, the Gad of the gardens or of the olive tree, the Gad of Palmyra, the Gad of Taimay (the ancestor of a tribe). But the Arabic deities had been preceded by those of Babylon. The largest temple of the city was dedicated to Bel, the Master, whom Greek dedications called Zeus. He replaced the indigenous god Bol, whose goddess-consort was called 'Ashtor, the local pronunciation of 'Athtar (just as Bol equates with Bel, or rather with Baal). Bel was the great cosmic god, and by virtue of this title, the Sun and the Moon were associated with him, they being represented by Yarḥi-Bol and 'Agli-Bol. The second divine name signifies Bull-of-Bol, the horns symbolizing the crescent. Originally Yarḥi-Bol, i.e., Moon-of-Bol, also was represented by the crescent, but he was later transmuted into a solar god. 'Agli-Bol is often paired with another solar deity, Malak-Bel, and these two represent the two heavenly luminaries in the second triad, the triad of Be'el-Shemin, the Master-of-the-heavens, dispenser of fecundating rain. The inscriptions describe him as "master of the world," and as the "kind and remunerating" god. In the 2d and 3d Christian centuries the cult of Be'el-Shemin became anonymous. The many pyres dedicated to him were then offered "to the one whose name is blessed forever, the kind and remunerating one," a formula that translated an almost monotheistic attitude. The Jewish colony that resided in Palmyra or the philosophers who had been attracted to the princely court influenced this movement, but its origins were Semitic. The name of Ilahay is attested to on a relief in the Palmyrene region, the name of El or Ilah has been preserved in the onomastic (Rabbel, Zabdilah). Finally, several inscriptions attest to the cult of El-qōne-ra', i.e., of El-Creator-of-the-Earth, one of the Phoenician aspects of El. In the Nabataean region, there was no analogous purification of worship, but the numerous personal names ending in El or in Ilahay, e.g., Wahbilahay, "God has given," reveal an ancient heritage that was certainly related to the cult of Ilah among the Thamudeans.

The Arabs on the Eve of Islam. In the 7th century of our era, Thamud had disappeared, but the preaching of Mohammed assumed faith in Ilah on the part of the Meccans, or rather faith in Allah (al-Ilah), the Creator of heaven and earth, the provider of fecundating rain and the savior from danger. When they were out in their boats they all prayed to Allah, but once back on land they "associated" other gods to him (Koran, 29. 61–65). To the mind of Ibn al-Kalbi, the principal god of the Ka'ba, the sanctuary of Mecca, was Hubal, an anthropomorphous idol who was consulted by means of arrows. The Prophet first set up Allah in opposition to him and then substituted Allah for him, holding Allah to be the Lord of the Ka'ba, which had been founded by Abraham and his son Ismael (Koran, 96.3, and 2.121).

The Jewish colonies of Tema, Khaibar, and Medina, as well as the colony of San'a in South Arabia, and the Christian community of Najran on the borders of Yemen, had created a climate of opinion favorable to the *ḥanifs,* or devout Arabs who were becoming aware of the impossibility of associating other gods to the supreme deity Ilah. Before the triumph of Mohammed's efforts, there were certainly many idols on the Peninsula. Ibn al-Kalbi enumerates 24; but most of these belonged to a particular ethnic group. In addition to Hubal, the Qoraish invoked al-Lat, al-'Uzza and Manāt (Manawat), a triad that is likewise mentioned in the Koran. The cult of the goddess 'Uzza persisted even after the coming of Islam, for the ritual of abjuration dating from the 9th century anathematized "worshippers of the Morning Star, i.e., Lucifer and Aphrodite, who is called Chabar in Arabic, i.e., the Great One." This ritual mentions also the great stone of the Ka'ba, "bearing a representation of Aphrodite." Is this betyl of 'Uzza the famous Black Stone of the Ka'ba, through which certain poorly Islamized Arabs continued to venerate Venus?

Cult. Pagan religion in ancient North Arabia had its own kind of idols and sanctuaries, its proper priests and rites, and its special funeral customs.

Betyls and Sanctuaries. The idols of the Arabs were often sacred *stones, considered as abodes of the gods, whence the word betyl (*bet-'el,* "house of the god"). The idol of Atar-samain mentioned by Esarhaddon as having a golden star adorned with precious stones, the symbol of Venus-Ishtar (Pritchard ANET 301a), was probably a betyl. Several South Arabic texts describe 'Athtar as Ḥagar, i.e., stone. We know other betyls of the goddess, under the name of 'Uzza, Allat, or Kokabta (Star). The betyl of Dushara was "a black stone, quadrangular and aniconic, four feet high and two feet wide, resting on a gold base" (Suidas, s.v. "Theusares"). Philo of Byblos says that the betyls were "animates," and the Arabs did not escape the danger of litholatry. The people who lived on the banks of the Orontes River venerated a "Zeus-Betyl, ancestral god," and the North Syrians venerated "the ancestral gods Symbetylos and Leōn" (the associated gods Betyl and Lion). Another degradation of the divine was the worship of the "seat" of the deity, i.e., of the throne or base beneath the betyl, sometimes even when the betyl was not there. The Nabataean inscriptions introduce us to the god Motaba (seat). An analogous phenomenon was the deification of the altar. In North Syria, which was strongly Arabized, dedications to Zeus-Altar have been found; and the Nabataean stone pyres, which the inscriptions call *masgida,* might first have been betyl altars. Porphyry says likewise that the Arabs of Duma used their altars as if they were idols (*De Abstinentia,* 2.56). By extension, the word *masgida* designates the sanctuary and has been borrowed by Islam with this particular signification (*mosque).

The cult of betyls did not exclude the cult of divine effigies. In Palmyra the sacred stones of the Arabs never supplanted cultural beliefs. And temples in the strict sense were not unknown in Arabia, especially in Palmyra, where the temples of Bel and of Be'el-shemin are still standing. Within the cella of the temple of Bel two large cult niches face each other, both described by the name "Holy" in an inscription (cf. the Holy of Holies of the Temple of Jerusalem). The rear of the principal temple of Petra has three compartments, according to a plan well known in Syria; the central one was no doubt occupied by the betyl of Dushara described by Suidas. In the Nabataean region, there are also sanctuaries with small cellae, sometimes designated by the word *rab'ata* (square), which corresponds to the Arabic *ka'ba,* "cubic" chapel. The Black Stone, of volcanic origin, is immured in the Ka'ba of Mecca. Nabataean chapels were sometimes encased inside a second wall, with a stairway between the two. This is the plan of the Iranian fire temples. The *ḥammana* mentioned in certain Palmyrene and Nabataean dedications is perhaps a fire temple.

Priests and Rites. Priests were designated by various terms, such as the Aramaic *kumra* (in the Bible: priest of the idols); the Akkadian *apkal,* which signifies wise man in that language, but which in the Arabic cults alludes to a category of priests; or the Arabic *kāhin,* diviner. This last was used in Hebrew also, but to refer to Jewish priests. In the Assyrian era there were priestesses as well (*kumirtu, apkalatu*). And even at the time of the birth of Islam, women could be guardians of the *qobba* (the betyl tent). Divination with arrows (Ez 21.21) played an important role, and Ibn al-Kalbi mentions an idol who was consulted by means of three arrows: the imperative, the prohibitive, and the expectative. The Arabs had communion sacrifices (1 Sm 20.4–6), but the Palmyrenes had holocausts as well. The essential rite was the pouring of the victim's blood against the altar (Ex 24.6) or against the betyl. At Boṣra the god A'ra was venerated, whose name signifies betyl "anointed" with blood. He was identified with Dushara. The sacrifice was followed by a sacred *meal, in which the deity was supposed to take part. The existence of cult associations is attested to also by Nabataean inscriptions (the term is *marzeḥa,* cf. Jer 16.5). The ceremony of sacrifice was often preceded by processions or, more precisely, by circumambulations: the one around the Ka'ba of Mecca is still observed, obviously with a new significance. There are no Arabic liturgical anthologies in existence, but the proto-Arabic graffiti give us ample information on what the nomads asked of their gods. Thus Lat was invoked for security, but also for vengeance. There is little evidence of prayers of thanksgiving except those that are found in the Palmyrene dedications to the unnamed god.

The Dead. The Arabs shared the Semitic belief in the survival of the *nepeš* (i.e., the vital principle), which, being deprived of its body, was thought to lead a very reduced existence. The stone or stele erected on the tomb was supposed to localize the presence of the deceased one; in funerary texts it too is called *nepeš,* a term that was ultimately applied even to mausoleums. At Palmyra the *nepeš* was often a tower with several stories of sepulchers. The funerary temples and the hypogea were equally common. Elsewhere, and in particular in Petra, the word *nepeš* referred above all to the monument built of a square block of stone and surmounted with a pyramid. However, the majority of tombs in this city were hewn out of the rock, the façade being sculpted in the form of an edifice with merlons. The central room of these hypogea was sometimes used for the funeral banquet. According to a Hellenistic custom, the kings of the Nabataeans were divinized after their death. We know of a festival of Obodat the god. And on the Petra-Gaza route, the city of Eboda (modern Avdat) owed its name to the same Obodat I of the early 1st century, where the deceased king had his mausoleum (Stephen of Byzantium). We do not know how widely the Greek concept of the immortality of the soul had penetrated Arabia. Funerary paintings attest to such a belief in Palmyra, where a few inscriptions have been found that envisaged the survival of the soul in the Sun, in the Pythagorean manner. On the eve of the coming of Islam, Judaism and Christianity had made great inroads against Saracen paganism. certain tribes having even been converted to one or the other of these religions. But it is established that the Arabs in all epochs invoked Ilah (God), even when they associated idols with Him.

See also NABATAEANS; PALMYRA; PETRA, ANCIENT.

Bibliography: G. RYCKMANS, "Les Religions arabes préislamiques" in M. GORCE and R. MORTIER, *Histoire générale des religions,* 4 v. (rev. ed. Paris 1960) 4:201–228, 593–605. J. STARCKY, "Palmyréniens, Nabatéens et Arabes du Nord avant l'Islam," *Histoire des religions,* ed. M. BRILLIANT and R. AIGRAIN, 5 v. (Paris 1953–56) v.4. DB Suppl 6:1088–1101; 7:951–1016. R. DUSSAUD, *La Pénétration des Arabes en Syrie avant l'Islam* (Paris 1955). H. LAMMENS, *L'Arabic occidentale avant l'Hégire* (Beirut 1928). H. SEYRIG, *Antiquités syriennes,* ser. 1–5 (Paris 1934–58) offprints from *Syria* (1931–57). M. HÖFNER, "Nord- und Centralarabien," in *Wörterbuch der Mythologie,* ed. H. W. HAUSSIG (Stuttgart 1961–) 1.1:407–481.

[J. STARCKY]

4. PAGANISM IN SOUTH ARABIA

South Arabic pre-Islamic religions are still in a rudimentary stage of investigation; no mythological or ritual text or important temple has been discovered, and the inscriptions that have been found need further study. Many interpretations offered by the Dane D. Nielsen, are definitive; others, though inaccurate, survive, viz, the identification of *'Il* with the moon-god, the restriction of the South Arabic pantheon to the three astral deities, and the primacy of *'Aṯtar* in the pantheon (this last was maintained especially by J. Plessis).

Deities. The three great deities are the astral triad composed of the moon, Venus (*'Aṯtar*), and the sun. Only these had official cults in the several kingdoms.

The Moon-god. The most important of the three great deities is the moon-god. His name as the national god varies in each kingdom, and the populations call themselves his children: the children of *Wadd* (Minaeans), of *'Ilumquh* (Sabaeans), and of *'Amm* (Qatabanians). The moon-god is also the protective deity of the main cities, where his most important temples existed, and he is represented as the owner of Qataban and Saba. In Saba, his chief name is *'Ilumquh* (*'Il* is power), often qualified by *Ṯahwan* [he who speaks (through his oracle)]; three other names allude to the phases of the moon. In Ḥadhramaut his principal name is *Sin*. In *Ma'īn* his national name is *Wadd* (love). In Qataban his principal designation is *'Amman* or *'Ammum* (uncle); the epithets *ray'an* or *ray'um* (he who grows) and *ray'an waśaḥrum* (he who grows and rises), as well as the two names *Waraḫ* (month) and *Rub' Šahr* (the lunar quarter), refer to the phases of *Wadd*.

The Stellar God. The name of *'Aṯtar* seems best explained by the Arabic adjective *'attār* (strong, brave, courageous); the name is often accompanied by the epithet *'izzān* or *'izzum* (strength). Other names of the stellar god mentioned in Sabaean texts are *Ḥagar* (stone), *Mutibnaṭiyan* [he who secures humidity (?)], *Nawraw* (light), and *Saḥar* (dawn).

The Sun-goddess. Unique in some ways is the sun-goddess. Like *'Aṯtar*, she has a proper name, *Šams*, which is used in all the kingdoms, though sometimes treated as a dual, *Šamsay*, or plural, *'Ašams*. Like the moon-god, she also has diverse names. These are ordinarily given in antithetic pairs and do not characterize the sun-goddess as a national deity. In Saba, the two antithetic names *Ḏāt-Ḥimyām* (she who darts forth her rays) and *Ḏāt-Ba'dān* (she who is remote) refer respectively to the summer and winter sun. Other names are *Samayhat* (celestial), *Tadūn* (despised), and *Tanūf* (sublime). She is also described as *'Umm 'Aṯtar* (the mother of *'Aṯtar*). In Qataban, she is called *Ḏāt-Ẓahrān* (she who appears in her splendor) and *Ḏāt-Ṣantim* (she who fixes); a third name, *Ḏāt-Raḥbān* (she who is broad), is sometimes added. The main phases of the sun's course are given in the names *Mašraqītān* (she who rises), *'Aṯirat* (bright), and *Maḥrudāwu* (she who declines). In *Ma'īn*, the most common name is *Nakraḥ*. In Ḥadhramaut, her antithetic names are *Ḏāt-Ḥusūl* (she who is rejected) and *Ḏāt-Ḥimyām* as in Saba. In a few cases in the inscriptions all three of the deities are mentioned together, under an aspect of kindness or strength.

Lesser Gods. Minor deities protect persons, clans, families, and places; they are often referred to under the titles *'l* (god of . . .) and *b'l* (patron of . . .). We know of *Warafu*, the Qatabanian god of boundaries, and *Munḏiḥ*, the god of irrigation. Other gods are named only by their attributes. Such in *Ma'īn* are *Ḏū-'Awdān* (he who preserves), *Madhuwāwū* (he who brings calamity), and *Muṯībqabṯ* (he who secures the harvest). In Saba there are *Balw*, a god connected with burial who is known also in Qataban; *Bašīr* (announcer of good tidings); *Ḥalīm* (kind); *Ḥalfān* (the oath); *Yiṯa'um* (savior); *Mutībmaḏgad* (he who guards the house); *Nasrum* (eagle); *Q̱aynān* (artisan); *Raḥīm* (gentle); *Rā'at* (frightening); and *Ta'lab* (he who collects, that is, the clouds). Several North Arabic, Syrian (*Rummān*), and Egyptian (*Osarapis*) deities also appear. Four deified persons also known are the Sabaean *'Azizlat, Hawf'il,* and *Yada'sumhu,* and the Awsanite King *Yaṣduq'il*.

Divine Attributes and Activities. Attributes and activities of the deities are described in detail in theophonic names. The divinity in general (*'il*, god) is generous, jealous, large of stature, and handsome; he speaks, orders, helps, and rewards; he also overwhelms and lacerates. He is considered as father, brother, king, lord, savior, protector, and lover of justice. Individuals are called his sons, servants, friends, etc. Theophoric names related to the three principal deities describe these same relationships. *'Ilumquh* is attested only once, in the name *'Amat'ilumquh* (the maid-servant of *'Ilumquh*); it is usually replaced by *'Awwām*, the name of the great moon temple near Mārib. Known inscriptions abound in data on the relations of the deities with one another, with men, and with things. Gods are sometimes represented as unequal and sometimes as equal to one another. *Wadd* orders sacrifices to be offered to *'Aṯtar*, who commands the Sabaeans to build a temple for *'Ilumquh*. At times, offerings are presented to two different deities (e.g., *Tadūn* and *Sin*), or to three (e.g., *'Aṯtar, Nakraḥ,* and *Wadd*), or to several (e.g., *'Amm, Ḏāt-Raḥbān,* and the deities of the clan Rawyān); similarly, temples and altars are built and sacrifices offered to several deities at once. The deities command men to undertake particular work and sometimes help them to accomplish it. The gods are invoked as witnesses, guarantee possessions, and are owners of land.

Cult. Places of worship are both public and private. The exteriors of five of the larger temples have been described by travelers. Excavations have been made in five less important temples: in Yeḥa, Ethiopia; at Ḥureiḍa and Ḫōr Rōrī, both in Ḥadhramaut; at Ḥeid bin 'Aqīl, Qataban; and at Hugga in Saba. At each site the three requirements for a temple were found: a cella with an altar, a reservoir or well with a drainage canal, and one additional room. The principal temples, such as *'Awwām* in Mārib, doubtless were more complicated and included the *mḏqnt* (oratory for prostrations), the *mśwd* (place for burning incense), and the *mhtn/mlkn* (ceremonial place of the king). In addition to these, there probably was at least another place where either the originals or copies of various juridical protocols were kept under the protection of a god. There was a great variety of altars for incense (*mśwd* and *mqṭr*), libations (*mslm*), burnt offerings (*mṣrb*), and sacrifices (*mḏbḥt*). Idols were doubtless used in the temples. The location of the idols in a temple is probably indicated by the inscriptions *ṯbt/'l'ltn* (the seat of the deities). Ceremonial utensils are probably indicated by the noun *ṣrf* in a text from *al-'Amāyid* at Mārib, and benches were discovered in the temple at Ḫōr Rōrī.

Temple Personnel. There were three classes of temple personnel: priests, superintendents, and assistants. The common noun for priest is *ršw* (fem. *ršwt*). While the specific difference between *ršw, šw',* and *'fkl* (a loanword from Sumerian) is unknown, the *śhr* was probably a kind of priest-magician who gyrated around the altar or offering. The Qatabanian temple was administered by a group (*'rby;* sing. *rby*) of which a priest might eventually become a member. They had charge of the temple and the gifts it received, whether in money or in kind. There were also regular revenues from estates and properties, first fruits of the harvest, and tithes on individuals and clans. Some persons were oblates for various reasons; they probably assisted the priests in the maintenance of the temple. There is no evidence of the existence of sacred prostitution; expressions such as "son of *Wadd*" and "firstborn of *'Amm* and *Ḥawkum*," referring to an Awsanite king and a Qatabanian *mukarrib* respectively, are to be understood as metaphorical. The existence of private sanctuaries for household gods is indicated by expressions such as "his god," "his patron," and "the patron of their house." A sanctuary where incense was burned is represented as belonging to three courtiers of a Sabaean king.

Religious Customs. Private devotions included the use of a geometric symbol or of a symbolic animal along with an inscription, astral worship on the terraces of homes, and the cult rendered to the household gods. On the other hand, observances during pilgrimage were a part of the public cult. Religious solemnities are known only through ritual prescriptions for public worship: an ordinance prescribing purity for the feast of *Ḥalfān,* stipulations for offerings and ritual purity during pilgrimages, etc. Sexual relations were forbidden during certain periods of the year. Known texts do not establish the existence of a ritual hunt. Ablutions were required before entering the temple, and during ceremonies or acts of devotion it was forbidden to sit. For sacrificial banquets in the temple, however, when devotees partook of an animal victim cooked, as in *'Awwām,* with "onions and stinking herbs," they sat on benches, sometimes before a statue representing a deceased associate. Offerings to the deities frequently were outright gifts: persons made slaves or oblates, temple buildings and their appurtenances, statues, animals, all kinds of incense and spices, libations, and other tangible objects.

The texts commemorating these offerings ordinarily specify the reasons for the ritual act, the petitions addressed to the deities, and the occasions for thanksgiving. Personal, public, military, and historical considerations were involved, and the material dealing with these makes up the most detailed section of the inscriptions. Several texts refer to faults and sanctions of an unknown nature. Other acts of expiation were performed to atone for transgressions or precepts imposed by a god, violations of regulations on sexual purity, and violations of a god's property or of the immunity of the temple and of the documents it contained. Consultation of the deities doubtless took many forms. Only a few of them are known, among which are dice (*m'rb,* pl. *m'rbt*) and sorcery (*rqt*). The divine answer was immediate in the first case. In the second, however, the divinity had to make his decision known in some way; the texts speak of oracles (*ms'l*), dreams (*ḥlm*), and omens (*r'y* and *hr'yt*). The wearing of *amulets was a common practice; many of them were inscribed with the magic formula "*Waddum* is father." Incantations (*'r'b*) were probably connected with the hunt, and there are indications of bewitching through an image (*ḫṯṯ*). The invocation *'ynm/n'm* concerns the "good eye"; however, *šsy,* which is commonly translated "evil eye," means "wickedness." Geometric and quasi-alphabetic forms in rock carvings are most probably emblems of clans, caravans, or individuals.

The astral character of the three main divinities must be seen as connected with the importance of the stars to communities whose wealth depended to a large extent on the caravan trade. Moreover, the rigors of the climate helped to produce an acute sense of helplessness and an anxiety for divine aid. The great diversity of deities matches a complexity of needs, and the frequency of recourse to the gods shows the people's desire to involve the divinity in every aspect of their lives; yet their devotion is strongly characterized by materialistic egocentricity.

Incipient Monotheism. None of the inscriptions tell us about the beginnings of monotheism in South Arabia; the so-called "Sabaean era," mentioned only in monotheistic texts, began roughly about 110 B.C. The texts with the monotheistic name of God number about 20 and date from the 4th or 5th centuries A.D. Their vocabulary, phraseology, and contents do not in any way differ from those of the polytheistic texts. In some inscriptions the use of a symbol and two monograms intimately connected with the moon-god suggests that the authors of these monotheistic texts indulged in syncretism. The one God is called *'lhn* (the God), *mr'* (Lord), or more often *rḥmnn* (the Merciful); and His name is normally followed by the epithet *b'l/smyn* or *smyn/w'rḍn* [Patron of heaven (and of earth)]. One expression is certainly Jewish: *rḥmn/ḏbsmyn/ . . . / w'/lhhmw/rbyd* [the Merciful, He (who is) in heaven . . . and their God, master of Juda]; two others are Christian: *rḥmnn/wmsḥhw/wrḥqds* (the Merciful and His Messiah and the Holy Spirit) and *rḥmnn/wbnhw/krśtś/ġbln* (the Merciful and His Son Christ the Victorious).

Bibliography: A. JAMME, "Le Panthéon sud-arabe préislamique d'après sources épigraphiques," *Muséon* 60 (1947) 57–147; "La Religion sud-arabe pré-islamique," *Histoire des religions,* ed. M. BRILLANT and R. AIGRAIN, 5 v. (Paris 1953–56) 4:239–307. D. NIELSEN, "Zur altarabischen Religion," *Handbuch der altarabischen Altertumskunde* (Copenhagen 1927) 1:177–250. G. RYCKMANS, "Les Religions arabes préislamiques," *Histoire générale des religions,* v.2 (Paris 1960) 200–228, 593–605.

[A. J. JAMME]

5. CHRISTIANITY IN ARABIA

Arabia here is taken to include the Arabian peninsula and, to the north of it, the desert and sown land adjacent to the territories of Rome and Persia. The period studied runs from the 1st to the 7th Christian century. Sources of evidence include lists of bishops at Church councils and inscriptions and writings in Greek, Syriac, Arabic, and South Arabic.

Northwest. The origins of Christianity in the northwest sector of this area are obscure. Among its bearers may have been "Arabs" of Pentecost (Acts 2.11) and Jewish Christians of Pella. Christian development here can be followed only partially. In the 3d century mention must be made of Origen, who intervened so fruitfully; of Philip the Arab, the officially pagan and privately Christian Roman Emperor; and of the martyrs of Philadelphia. Church organization in the region was marked by many small sees. The change from the patriarchate of Antioch to that of Jerusalem was evidenced at Chalcedon (451). It is interesting to note that, in the mounting conflict with the Monophysites, the Chalcedonians seemed to have clung to the churches of the small towns and villages. Arab phylarchs emerged from legend in the 4th century, but the first Ghassanid phylarch belonged to the early 6th century. Al-Ḥārith ibn Jabala (528–569), the second of this line, was something of a pious Monophysite Constantine. The picture of this late Arab Christianity includes the traits of monastic zeal and austerity; of rulers at times polygamous, who protected the Church, visited shrines, and yet projected through the pagan Arabic poetry the image of the pleasant life of wine, flowers, music, and women. The vigorous persecution of the Monophysites by the Melchites and the imperial distrust and treachery have their part in explaining the warm reception given by these Arab Christians to their Moslem blood brothers.

Northeast. Christian origins in the northeast sector also are poorly known. At Pentecost "Parthians, and Medes, and Elamites, and inhabitants of Mesopotamia" (Acts 2.9) were present. Toward the middle of the 3d century there were Christians in Hatra, and toward the end of the century Roman Christian captives in Babylonia. Ḥīra, the Lakhmid capital and a settled Arab town, was the earliest but not the only see among the Christian Arabs of this territory. Other sees lay north along the Euphrates and south along the western shore of the Persian Gulf. Even in Ḥīra not all the Arabs were Christian. The bishops of the Arab sees had their part in cutting the Persian Church off from Antioch (424) and orienting it into the path of Nestorianism (486). In the 6th century, Monophysites from the Roman zone were active and initiated the continuing Monophysite-Nestorian conflict. Lakhmid phylarchs, like their Ghassanid counterparts, emerge from legend in the 4th century. Of the 15 Lakhmid rulers, one was married to a Christian; two may have been Christian; one, al-Nu'mān, the last of the line (d. 602), became a Christian. The quality of his Christianity, however, has to be appreciated in the light of his polygamy, his marriage to his stepmother, and his imprisonment and execution of the Christian to whom he owed his throne. Ḥīra was the principal center of the wine trade and naturally an inspiration of Bacchic poetry. The Christians of Ḥīra and al-Anbār (to the north on the Euphrates), through their Syriac alphabet, shared in creating the Arabic alphabet (early 6th century). The Arab Christians of this zone exercised a religious influence through the work of certain pagan and Christian poets. The extent of that influence is felt to have been reduced by the fact that Syriac, not Arabic, was their religious language, and also by a certain weakness in their Christian life.

Southwest. In the southwest or Ḥimyarite sector the rulers were polytheistic pagans until the late 4th century. Monotheistic terms, particularly *al-raḥmān* (the merciful), then began to be found in inscriptions. Far though this region was from Persia and Byzantium, both these empires sought to dominate it. Christianity came from Alexandria and directly from the emperor. The account of Christian origins mentions the names of SS. Bartholomew and Pantaenus. There was an Arian mission in the mid-4th century. A more influential mission was sent under Emperor Anastasius (491–518). It resulted in conversions and the ordination of a bishop. There were churches at Taphar, Aden, and Najrān. In 523, probably after an Abyssinian conquest and more conversions, Christianity was felt to wear the appearance of something protected by foreigners. A persecution followed under Masruḳ *Dhū Nuwās (Dunaan of the Roman Martyrology), a member of the old ruling family and a Jew by religion. After the persecution the Abyssinians returned. Abraha, a governor of the Abyssinian viceroy, revolted and achieved independence. Under his reign the number of priests dwindled while he vainly insisted that the Emperor Justinian should send a Monophysite bishop to ordain more. Abraha's expedition in the late 6th century against the *Hejaz (al-Ḥijāz) may have been due to rivalry between his church at Ṣan'ā' and the Ka'ba of *Mecca or to the desire to move against Persophile Jews in the Hejaz.

The Hejaz. In speaking of Christians in the Hejaz one must limit the term to mean Mecca, Taymā', Khaibar, al-Ṭā'if, and *Medina. The existing evidence refers to the time just before or during the lifetime of Mohammed. The Hejaz had not been touched by Christian preaching. Hence organization of a Christian church was neither to be expected nor found. What Christians resided there were principally individuals from other countries who retained some Christianity. Such were African (mainly Coptic) slaves; tradespeople who came to the fairs from Syria, from Yemen, and from among the Christian Arabs under the Ghassanids or Lakhmids; Abyssinian mercenary soldiers; and miscellaneous others whose Christianity was evidenced only by their names. The few native Christians whose names have come down to us furnish us with more questions than answers. This Christianity had the marks that go with want of organization. It lacked instruction and fervor. It is therefore not surprising that it offered no opposition to Islam. Finally it is to be borne in mind that it was the Christianity in Arabia, here briefly sketched, that projected the image of Christianity seen in the Koran.

Bibliography: R. AIGRAIN, DHGE 3:1158–1339, with detailed bibliog.; scholars still find the essentials on this subject in this masterly study. G. OUSSANI, CE 1:666–674. J. ASSFALG, LexThK[2] 1:788–789. P. GOUBERT, *Byzance avant l'Islam,* 2 v. (Paris 1951–55) v.1. G. RENTZ, EncIslam[2] 1:533–556. S. SMITH, "Events in Arabia in the 6th Century A.D.," *Bulletin of the School of Oriental and African Studies* 16 (1954) 425–468; facing 426, detailed and helpful map. J. RYCKMANS, *La Persécution des chrétiens himyarites au sixième siècle* (Istanbul 1956).

[J. A. DEVENNY]

ARABIAN PHILOSOPHY

"Arabian philosophy" usually denotes the philosophical thought of those inhabitants of the Islamic world who were influenced by Greek learning but used the Arabic language as their medium of expression. An Arabian philosopher, therefore, was not necessarily a native of the Arabian peninsula but perhaps a native of Persia, like Avicenna, or of Spain, like Averroës, or of any of the lands conquered by the followers of Mohammed. Since the Arabic word for philosopher, *failasūf,* referred to one who made use of Greek learning, this account of Arabian philosophy begins with the transmission of Greek culture to the Arabic-speaking world, continues with an introduction to the thought of the major Arabian philosophers and the problems they discuss, and concludes with an indication of their influence on the Christian philosophers of the Middle Ages.

Greek and Arab Background. The Arab world was introduced to Greek culture between the 8th and 10th centuries by the Syrian Christians. Having learned Greek to read theological works, the Syrians had also studied philosophical and scientific writings of the Greeks. They translated some of these into Syriac and, for the caliphs who employed them, especially for al-Mansur and al-Mamun, made Arabic translations either directly from the Greek or by way of Syriac translations. Notable among the Syrian Christian translators were Ḥunayn ibn Isḥāq (*Johannitius) of Baghdad (809–

Mid-16th-century miniature of Alexander the Great approaching the circle of Plato and the philosophers, illustrating that even in legend the influence of ancient Greek philosophy on Arabian and Islamic philosophy was documented in the Middle Ages. (Leaf from a Khamsah of Nizāmī in Freer Gallery of Art.)

873) and *Costa ben Luca (864–923), author of a work translated into Latin in the 12th century as *De differentia spiritus et animae.* Among the works that the translators made available in Arabic were: Plato's *Republic, Laws, Timaeus, Sophist;* Aristotle's *Organon, Physics, Metaphysics, De anima, Nicomachean Ethics;* and two pseudo-Aristotelian treatises with a Neoplatonic content, the so-called *Theology of Aristotle* and the **Liber de Causis.*

Some of the theologians of Islam saw in Greek thought a danger to their religion. Influenced by the Jews and the Christians, whom he respected as "People of the Scripture," the Prophet Mohammed had taught the unity of God, creation, the divine knowledge of individual things, and the resurrection of the body. These and other teachings expressed in the holy book of Islam, the *Koran, seemed to be challenged by the views of Greek thinkers.

Among the theologians, one group—the * Mu'tazilites, the so-called "people of unity and justice" who were known as opponents of fatalism—began to use reason and argument, **kalām,* in their work as apologists of the Koranic teachings. Although they were regarded as too liberal and rationalistic by orthodox theologians, the latter group also began to use *kalām* against the *kalām* of the Mu'tazilites. Thus the orthodox theologians became the *Mutakallimun* (*Loquentes,* to the Latins), and the scholastic theology of Islam was founded.

One of the most influential of the early theologians was a man who renounced the Mu'tazilite views and became a Mutakallim, al-*Ash'arī (873–935). In an effort to exalt the power and the arbitrary will of God, he taught a cosmology of atomism. He held that matter was composed of separate and distinct atoms continually being recreated by God, with their accidents, in each instant of time. According to his view, fire does not cause burning, but God creates a being that is burned when fire touches a body. There are no secondary causes; the sole cause of all change is God.

A contrast to this attempt at a rational defense of a dogmatic position was the movement of *Sufism or Islamic mysticism. The Sufis, or those clothed in wool (*ṣūf*), sought to achieve union with God through asceticism and prayer, first singly, and in the later history of the movement, through religious communities. Their early stress on religious practices was later combined with more speculative interests. Among the more famous Sufis was Rabi'a, the woman mystic of Basra (d. 801); al-Hallaj, a Persian who was tortured and executed for heresy in 922; and *Jalāl al-Dīn al-Rūmī (d. 1273), a Persian mystical poet.

Arabian Philosophers in the East. The religious movements of Islam influenced Arabian thinkers, but the first outstanding Arabian philosopher, the only one of Arabic descent, undertook the task of presenting Greek thought to the Muslims. Abū Yūsuf al-*Kindī (*c.* 805–873), called "the first Peripatetic in Islam," translated and commented on some of Aristotle's works. His acceptance as a genuine work of Aristotle of the so-called *Theology of Aristotle,* an abridged paraphrase of the last three books of the *Enneads* of *Plotinus, was to give a Neoplatonic tinge to the Arabs' interpretation of Aristotle. A prolific writer with a wide range of interests, al-Kindī wrote more than 260 treatises on such varied subjects as mathematics, music, astronomy, optics, meteorology, medicine, politics, logic, and psychology. His treatise on the intellect, circulated in Latin translation during the Middle Ages, shows his interest in the problems of Aristotle's *De anima* and the influence of Alexander of Aphrodisias, the Greek commentator on Aristotle. al-Kindī's teachings concerning the "first intelligence that is always in act," distinct from and superior to the soul, marks the beginning of the Arabian doctrine of one agent intellect for all men.

*Alfarabi (*c.* 870–950) was born in Turkistan and studied at Baghdad. Known as "the second master" (Aristotle being the first), he wrote commentaries on Aristotle, and in his treatise *The Harmonization of the Opinions of Plato and Aristotle* tried to show a basic agreement in the thought of "the two founders of philosophy." Platonic influences are evident in his works on political theory, which include *Political Regime* and *Aphorisms of the Statesman.* Regarded as the founder of political philosophy among the Arabs, Alfarabi also had a great interest in metaphysics and anticipated Avicenna in the presentation of a Neoplatonic doctrine of emanation together with a distinction of essence and existence in creatures. His treatise on the intellect, known to medieval Europe in Latin translation, posits, like the treatise of al-Kindī, an agent intellect or intelligence that is a separated spiritual substance. This agent intelligence, by abstracting sensible forms, enables man's possible intellect to pass from potency to act and become first an "intellect in act" and, when in possession of knowledge, an "acquired intellect" (*intellectus adeptus*). When the human intellect has acquired almost every abstracted intelligible, then the intelligible forms that never did, do not, and never will exist in matter can become objects of direct human intellection. On man's abstractive knowledge of sensible being, Alfarabi thus seems to superimpose a non-Aristotelian intuitive knowledge of separated intelligible forms. His theory of intellect has been described as Aristotelian at its base and Neoplatonic at its summit.

Ibn Sina or, to the Latins, *Avicenna (980–1037) was born in Persia. Of his many works, one of the best known is his *Canon of Medicine;* its Latin translation was used as a standard textbook of medicine through the 17th century. His chief philosophical work was the *al-Shifa* (*The Cure*), which included sections on logic, mathematics, physics, and metaphysics. The last section sets forth a theory of emanation similar to that of Alfarabi. At the summit of Avicenna's universe is a Necessary Being, who is one, incorporeal, and the source of all other beings. Through this Being's act of self-reflection, the first effect, a Pure Intelligence, necessarily proceeds. This effect must be one, for from one simple thing, only one can proceed. When this First Intelligence thinks of the Necessary Being, it gives rise to a Second Intelligence. When the First Intelligence thinks of itself as necessary by the First Being, it gives rise to the soul of the outermost celestial sphere; when it thinks of itself as possible in itself, it gives rise to the body of this same sphere. Then the Second Intelligence, in similar fashion, gives rise to a Third Intelligence, and to the soul and body of the second sphere. This emanation of intelligences is halted only with the production of the sphere of the moon and the tenth or last intelligence, which is called the agent intellect. The agent intellect, instead of begetting the soul and body of a sphere, begets human souls and the four elements (*Meta.* 9.4, fol. 104v–105r).

This theory is primarily a description, in temporal imagery, of the eternal relation of the world to God. It is meant to safeguard the unity of the Necessary Being and to stress that creatures that are "possible in themselves but necessary through another" depend for their actual existence upon that Being. In addition to its metaphysical implications, as for example, the real distinction of essence and existence, the theory also has implications for a doctrine of intellect and the nature of man. Here the agent intellect, the last of the separated intelligences, is a spiritual substance and one for all men. From it intelligible forms or species are infused into the possible intellects belonging to individual human souls (*De anima* 5.5–6). Each human soul, although a form in its function of animating the body, is in itself an immortal spiritual substance, for a man could know himself to be, even without knowing whether he had a body (*De anima* 1.1, 5.4 and 7). Some of the views expressed by Avicenna seem consistent with the teachings of Islam, but an eminent theologian, Algazel, opposed him.

Al-Ghazzālī or *Algazel (1058–1111), a Persian, is regarded as one of the great theologians of Islam for his work, the *Iḥyā' 'Ulūm ad-Dīn,* on the renewal of religious knowledge. Called "the Muslim St. Augustine," he tells in his spiritual autobiography, *Deliverance from Error,* about his painful doubts concerning the basis of certitude, his search for truth among the theologians and philosophers, and his surrender of wealth and position to lead for 10 years the life of a Sufi. One of his later achievements was to incorporate the values of Sufism into the orthodox Muslim tradition. Although he knew the positions of the philosophers, as is clear from his summary in the *Maqāṣid al-falāsifah* of the views of Alfarabi and Avicenna, he strongly opposed them. In his *Tahāfut al-Falācifah* he tried to show the limits of reason by exposing incoherence in the philosophers' handling of 20 important problems. Because many medieval Christians, including Albert the Great and Thomas Aquinas, knew only the *Maqāṣid* in Latin translation, and not the *Tahāfut,* they thought Algazel was a follower rather than an opponent of Avicenna.

Thought in the West. The Arabian philosophers mentioned so far belonged to the eastern part of the Arabian empire, but after the Arab conquest of Spain there was also an Arabian philosophy of the west. Ibn Baddja or, to the Latins, *Avempace (d. 1138), one of the first outstanding philosophers among the Arabs in Spain, wrote commentaries on Aristotle and some original works. In his *Regime of the Solitary* he discussed the philosophical means by which man could achieve union with the agent intellect. A younger contemporary, Abū Bakr ibn Ṭufail or, to the Latins, Abubacer (*c.* 1105–85), is famous for his novel, *Hayy ibn-Yaqẓan,* an allegorical statement of the author's position on faith and reason. It was also Ibn Ṭufail who introduced Ibn Rushd at the court of the caliphs in Spain.

Ibn Rushd or, to the Latins, *Averroës (1126–98), was born at Cordova, Spain. He studied theology, law, medicine, and philosophy. He wrote a work on medicine that was known to Christian thinkers as *Colliget* and used by them as a textbook. He wrote a paraphrase of Plato's *Republic* and commentaries on many of the works of Aristotle, including the *Metaphysics, Physics, On Generation and Corruption, Nicomachean Ethics,* and *De anima.* For him, Aristotle was "the Master," and any attack on him or his followers had to be answered. In the *Tahāfut al-Tahāfut* (*The Incoherence of the Incoherence*), Averroës attempts to destroy Algazel's "destruction" of the philosophers. Averroës implies, in *The Accord between Religion and Philosophy,* that the philosopher sees truth as it is; the ordinary believer attains only a symbolic representation of the truth. The troublemakers of Islam are not the philosophers, he claimed, but the theologians who arouse the people against each other by openly teaching different interpretations of the Koran.

On the question of the world's relation to God, philosophy might seem to oppose religion. Religion teaches that the world had a beginning and was created *ex nihilo;* for Aristotle and Averroës the world existed necessarily and eternally. Averroës rejected Avicenna's "concessions" to the theologians (*In 4 meta.* 3). He rejected the principle that from one only one can proceed, the type of emanation theory that Avicenna developed from that principle, and the Avicennian distinction between existence and essence (*Tahāfut al-Tahāfut,* disp. 3.182; *In 4 meta.* 2–3). For Averroës being is substance, and God may be called a cause of being insofar as "the bestower of the conjunction of matter and form is the bestower of existence" (*In 4 meta.* 3; *Tahāfut al-Tahāfut,* disp. 3.180). Thus both the philosopher and the simple believer may say that the world is dependent upon an eternal "Creator," but the philosopher, in Averroës's view, gives a more exact statement of this truth.

On the intellect Averroës held not only that the agent intellect is a separated substance and one for all men, but that this is true also of the possible intellect. The highest powers of the individual human soul are the *cogitative power, *imagination, and *memory, and their task is to prepare phantasms for the separated intellects to use. When the separated agent intellect has made the intelligible species potentially present in these phantasms actually intelligible, the separated possible intellect is put in act (*In 3 de anima,* comm. 4–6, 32–33). Averroës's doctrine was meant to ensure the spirituality of the possible intellect and the universality of its knowledge, but by denying to man a spiritual power of knowing, it seemed to destroy the philosophical basis for maintaining the immortality of the individual human soul.

The intellect and knowledge, the relation of the world to God, and the relation of philosophy and religion are topics that were often discussed by Arabian philosophers. They were also interested in science, but for the Arabs' accomplishments in this field one would have to consult the work of such astronomers as al-Battani (Albatani, *c.* 900), al-Farghani (Alfraganus, *c.* 860), al-Biṭrūjī (Alpetragius, *c.* 1180), and such mathematicians as Alkwarizmi (*c.* 830) and Alhazen (*c.* 1000). All these men were known to medieval Christians through Latin translations of some of their writings.

Influence on Christian Philosophy. One of the main channels by which Arabian works were transmitted to Christian Europe was the school of translators founded during the first half of the 12th century by Archbishop Raymond at Toledo, Spain. As these works became available in Latin translation, the names of their authors began to be cited by Christian thinkers. The influence of Avicenna and Averroës on Christian thought is especially notable. *Dominic Gundisalvi, *Roger Bacon, and *John Peckham identified Avicenna's agent intelligence with the Christian God. Other thinkers, including *William of Auvergne, *Henry of Ghent, *Duns Scotus, and *Thomas Aquinas, although critical of Avicenna's teachings, were favorably impressed by some aspects of his metaphysics.

Averroës was known to Christian thinkers as "the Commentator" on Aristotle. Those who, like *Siger of Brabant, had read his commentaries in Latin translation and accepted as necessary conclusions of human reason such teachings as the eternity of the world and unity of the intellect for all men, were called Latin Averroists (*see* AVERROISM, LATIN). Because they refrained from asserting that these teachings were true, they thought they could still be good Christians. But seeing in such views a source of error, Bishop Tempier of Paris condemned these and related propositions in 1270 and 1277. Three of the leading thinkers of the 13th century attacked the errors of Averroës: St. Albert in *De unitate intellectus contra Averroem;* St. Bonaventure, especially in the *Collationes in Hexaemeron,* Sermo VI; St. Thomas Aquinas, especially in *De aeternitate mundi contra murmurantes* and *De unitate intellectus contra Averroistas.* Because these refutations were not always understood or accepted, Averroism continued to flourish, especially in Italy, during the 14th, 15th, and 16th centuries. The history of western philosophy from the 12th to the 16th centuries is, in part, an account of the influence of Arabian thought on Christian philosophers.

See also DOUBLE TRUTH, THEORY OF; INTELLECT, UNITY OF; NEOPLATONISM; SCHOLASTICISM; ISLAM.

Bibliography: Gilson, HistChrPhil. W. M. WATT, *Islamic Philosophy and Theology* (Edinburgh 1962). T. J. DE BOER, *The History of Philosophy in Islam,* tr. E. R. JONES (London 1933).

M. FAKHRY, *Islamic Occasionalism and Its Critique by Averroës and Aquinas* (London 1958). D. O'LEARY, *How Greek Science Passed to the Arabs* (London 1949); *Arabic Thought and Its Place in History* (New York 1939). É. H. GILSON, "Les Sources gréco-arabes de l'augustinisme avicennisant," ArchHistDoctLit MA 4 (1929) 5–149. **Illustration credit:** Freer Gallery of Art, Washington, D.C.

[B. H. ZEDLER]

ARABIC CHRISTIAN LITERATURE

Christian writers played a significant role in the history of Arabic belles-lettres chiefly in three periods: the pre-Islamic and early Islamic, the classical, and the modern.

Pre-Islamic and Early Islamic Period. Louis Cheikho, SJ, contended that most of the poets of pre-Islamic *Arabia were Christians. But apart from the fact that authorship in pre-Islamic Arabic literature in general poses a difficult problem that is not yet fully solved, the religious elements in it are not sufficient to let one recognize the religious affiliations of even the most famous writers of the period (see Pellat, 67–68). However, the Christian 'Adī ibn Zayd is commonly regarded as a master of Bacchic poetry (drinking songs) and a skilled portrayer of human weakness. As a poet of the Lakhmid court of the Nestorian kingdom of Ḥīra (in opposition to the Ghassanid court, which, despite its Monophysitism, owed allegiance to Constantinople), 'Adī symbolized the presence of Christianity and the influence that it exercised, even though rather feebly, in central Arabia on the linguistic and literary tradition of the Arab world.

In the entourage of *Mohammed were several poets who were more or less sincere in their acceptance of the new religion (see the *Koran* 36.68; 21.5; 52.30; 69.41; 25.224). But it seems that none of them mixed any religious note in their panegyrics or satires. "Only the poet A'sha [d. *c.* A.D. 629], although not a convert to Islam, knew how, in his praise of Mohammed, to find allusions for the Prophet's religious position, since he was familiar with the fine points of the faith through his converse with the Christians of Ḥīra" (Pellat, 76). This is a rather typical indication of the presence and influence of Christianity within Arabic literature in its early period. Feeble and diffuse though it was, it seems to have produced a marked effect on Islamic religious sensibilities.

Classical Period. During the second or classical period of Arabic belles-lettres the great Akhṭal (d. *c.* 710) of the Christian tribe of Taghlib, who is known as "the bard of the Umayyads," was distinguished as one of the celebrated trio composed of himself, Farazdaq (d. *c.* 732), and Jarīr (d. *c.* 729) and noted for the correctness and purity of his language, which can truly be called Christian. After the time of Akhṭal there was no outstanding Christian literary work of notable extent until the *World Chronicle* of Makīn (1205–73) and the *General History* of *Bar-Hebraeus (1226–86). The latter, a convert from Judaism to Christianity who eventually became a Jacobite bishop, translated some of his Syriac works into Arabic. For lesser writers, see the interesting monograph of K. Salibi, *Maronite Historians of Medieval Lebanon* (Beirut 1960). The term literature is used here in the limited sense of belles-lettres. But some mention might be made also of Christian authors who wrote doctrinal, though not strictly literary, works in Arabic, such as the Melchites *Theōdūrus Abū Qurra (d. 825, the first openly Christian writer to use Arabic), *Agapios of Hierapolis (who wrote his history *c.* 942), and *Eutychios of Alexandria (d. 940); the Nestorians 'Abd al-Masiḥ al-*Kindī (10th century), *Abū 'l-Faraj 'Abdallāh ibn aṭ-Ṭayyib (d. 1043), and the *Bukhtīshū' family (8th to 11th centuries); and the Copt *Abū 'l-Barakāt (d. 1324).

Although the names of Christians in medieval Arabic belles-lettres are relatively few, Christianity left its mark in a certain way on this literature inasmuch as its two main themes were wine and love. On the one hand, the development of these themes among Moslems was hindered by the religious nature and the canonical legislation of the Koran; on the other hand, in keeping with their pre-Islamic origin, which had been mainly among Christians, these themes continued, during the Umayyad and 'Abbāsid periods, to be cultivated by Christians and even in Christian monasteries, where the monks were always industrious cultivators of the grape vine. Abū Nuwās (d. *c.* 810), the most famous of the Bacchic poets and a familiar figure at the high places of Oriental hospitality, showed in this respect the most original evolution in Arabic letters. Since he was a Moslem of less than mediocre fervor and not very "Arabic" as far as descent from natives of the Arabic peninsula was concerned, one can argue that he made capital of Christian inspiration gone astray. Arabic letters, like orthodox Islam, lay at the time near the border of Christianity; but the quasi connaturality was greater in the case of poetry than in that of religion.

It seems that even the ascetic, gnomic, and sapiential types of literature were paradoxically developed by this debauchee—after a dubious "conversion" to the demands of Islam—in his *zuhdiyyāt* (religious poems), probably not without some connection with the same Christian, especially monastic milieu. Similarly, the *ḥubbu 'udhrī* (Platonic love) poetry, which had been developed by certain poets who were in touch with primitive Bedouin life and its erotic poetry that sometimes bordered on the obscene, is related, in its later developments among the mystics and in its adoption by the troubadours of the West, with a certain Christian spiritual phenomenon.

Finally, one must remember that in the field of ideas Christians served as intermediaries between Islam and Hellenistic thought, which was first translated into Syriac before it was translated from this language into Arabic, particularly by the Nestorians *Johannitius (Ḥunayn ibn Isḥāq; d. 873) and Qusṭa ibn Lūqa (d. *c.* 923) and the Jacobite Yaḥya ibn 'Adī (11th century).

Modern Period. In the third period of Arabic literature, the period of the modern renaissance that has arisen in the Near East, the number of Christian authors who are worthy of special mention is quite impressive. (1) In the field of linguistics, after Germānus Farhāt, Maronite bishop of the 18th century, whose Arabic grammar was still used in schools in the beginning of the 20th century, there were the famous families of the Yāzigī (Nāssif, Khalīl, Ibrahīm, and Warda) and the Bustānī (Boutrus, Sulaymān, 'Abdallah, Amīn, and, in the second half of the 20th century, Boutrus and Fu'ad). (2) Among important journalists were Adīb Isḥāq and the Taqla (Aḥrām) brothers, Sarrūf, Nimr, and Gemayel. (Mention should be made also of Father Cheikho and his periodical *Mashriq* and Father Anastase of St. Elias and his periodical *Lughat al-'Arab.*) (3) The writers of novels, especially historical novels, include Zaydān, Medawwar, 'Abd el-Masiḥ Haddād, and Farah Antūn. (4) In drama were playwrights Marūn Naqqāsh, Nagīb Haddād, and Tannūs Hurr, and the actor George Abyad. (5) Notable in the field of poetry were: in Egypt, the famous Khalīl Mutrān and the very original Bishr Fāris [see his *Jabhat al-Ghayb* (Beirut 1961), with a bibliography of the author]; in Lebanon and among the Lebanese in the Americas (New York, Rio de Janeiro, and Buenos Aires), a pleiad of poets, including those of the Yāzigī and Ma'lūf families.

In regard more particularly to the field of poetry, Charles Pellat wrote: "Under the influence of the Western poets the Lebanese school and especially its American branch is freeing itself of the classical disciplines and adopting free verse, the strophe, and even a typographical arrangement that gives a poem a pictorial value" (193).

This appraisal contains a deeper judgment, which is valid for the whole Christian contribution to the Arabic renaissance. Paralleling the line of purists that seems to have reached its climax in the Baghdad Carmelite Anastase of St. Elias, the last of those with a "mania for lexicography" and the last of the *ansār al-gharīb* ["travelers' helpers"; see L. Massignon, *Opera minora* (Beirut 1963) 3:402], is the school of the innovators, who are not less competent linguistically. At present (1965) their leader, who is at the same time a highly controversial figure, is the Lebanese poet Sa'īd 'Aql. In regard to the form as well as the themes that characterize the Arabic renaissance in as far as it is Christian, he seems to be making a commendable effort to render both the grammatical structure of the Arabic language and the traditional Arabic manner of writing more supple and responsive for following the contemporaneous movements in ideas and expressions and to make them better adapted for addressing the mass of the Arabic-speaking peoples, as well as the cultured elite of the international circles.

Although the loyalty in general of the Christian Arabs of the renaissance from the 18th century to the present cannot be questioned, one should not for that reason underestimate the endeavors of many of them (which are significative of the general effort) to graft a foreign, particularly Western, branch on the Arabic trunk for the sake of revitalizing the tree and making it bear more abundant and more savory fruit. In this respect the bilingualism of the Oriental Christian communities, as of certain well-known authors (Gibrān, 'Aql, Fāris, and others), is as typical as the role of "broker" between the Arab East and the Latin West that devolved on the best of the Uniate Christians since the 16th century [see J. Hajjar, *Les chrétiens uniates du Proche-Orient* (Paris 1962)].

The future of Christian Arabic literature depends on the development of ecumenical Christianity in the Near East, and it is to be hoped that, as this ecumenicism grows, it will not be in any way exclusive or negative in regard to anyone. The recent translations of the Psalms made from the original Hebrew into Arabic by 'Afīf 'Osseyran in collaboration with Maḥmūd Marḥaba in Lebanon and by the Dominicans in collaboration with Muḥammad al-Ṣādiq Ḥusayn in Egypt constitute a very happy example of what can be done in the future in the field of Arabic letters through a free, loyal, and truly ecumenical collaboration between Moslems and Christians.

Bibliography: Graf GeschChArabLit. A. Baumstark, *Die christlichen Literaturen des Orients,* 2 v. (Leipzig 1911) 2:7–36. C. Pellat, *Langue et littérature arabes* (Paris 1952). J. M. Abd-el-Jalil, *Brève histoire de la littérature arabe* (Paris 1947). J. Assfalg, LexThK² 1:789–790. L. Cheikho, *An-Naṣrāniyya wa-ādābuhā bayn 'Arab al-Jāhiliyya,* 2 v. (Beirut 1912–13). J. Berque, "L'Inquiétude arabe des temps modernes," *Revue des études islamiques* 1 (1958) 87–107. V. Monteil, *Les Grands courants de la littérature arabe contemporaine* (Beirut 1959); *Anthologie bilingue de la littérature arabe contemporaine* (Beirut 1961).

[Y. MOUBARAC]

ARABIC LANGUAGE AND LITERATURE

Arabic belongs to the southern branch of the Semitic language family, which includes also South Arabic and Ethiopic. Hebrew, Ugaritic, and Aramaic belong to the northwestern, and Akkadian to the northeastern branches of this family; Arabic shares certain linguistic traits with Northwest Semitic.

Arabic Language. The most common characteristic of the *Semitic languages is the triliteral root, three consonants representing the basis of a word at its notional stage. By the addition of vowels, long or short, to these radical consonants, by the use of prefixes, infixes, and suffixes, and by the doubling of the second radical, definite words may be formed. Arabic dictionaries are etymological. To find a word in the dictionary, one must strip it of all its accretions, taking it back to its primitive form. Thus an ordinary Arabic dictionary yields its information only to those who have the knowledge of Arabic forms necessary to recognize the primitive root of the word. Moreover, a knowledge of syntax also is necessary even for the simple purpose of reading a text because the vocalization is usually omitted. Even with a knowledge of syntax, the reader has the perennial problem that in order to begin reading the text he must understand it, and in order to understand it he must read it. Therefore, the reader is forced to interpret while he reads.

Consonantal Script. The root word *ktb* may be used to illustrate this. As it stands, this root word conveys the notion of writing. The play of vowels on its three radical letters produces several derivative words: *kataba* (he wrote), *kutiba* (it was written), *katb* (a writing), *kattaba* [he caused (another) to write], *kutub* (books). But all of these words would appear written in their consonantal form only, *ktb,* and the reader would have to supply the vowels. Special exceptions to this general rule of unvocalized texts are textbooks and dictionaries, sacred texts, and (though not always) poetry. Any other Arabic text is quiescent and comes to life only when recited. It is significant that the meaning of *Koran, the sacred text of the Moslems, is "recitation," not merely silent reading.

Local Dialects. From pre-Islamic times to the present, Arabic has been characterized by bilingualism. In pre-Islamic Arabic there were several dialects and one common language understood by all. Today it is the same, a language with two aspects, literary and dialectal.

The literary language is used for expressing oneself through such media as lectures, conferences, and newspapers, and also among Arabic-speaking people who do not understand one another's dialect. The dialectal language is used in daily converse. This bilingualism presents difficulties to the foreigner because, while literary Arabic is common to all Arabic-speaking countries, ordinary conversational Arabic is divided into several dialectal groups, each of which is subdivided into numerous local dialects. The dialectal groups are divided into eastern ones, including Iraqi, Syrian, and Egyptian, and those of the west, including African and North-African.

Literary Language. In its literary form, Arabic is the liturgical language of nearly 400 million Moslems throughout the world. In its dialectal forms, it is spoken by 60 million people in Asia and Africa: Iraq, Syria, Lebanon, Jordan, Saudi Arabia, Egypt, Sudan, Libya, Tunisia, Algeria, Morocco, Mauritania, French West Sudan, the northern Sahara, Djibouti, and Zanzibar. Arabic is still spoken in Malta, and by the Syro-Lebanese diaspora in North and South America and French West Africa. It was spoken in Spain until the 15th century and in the Balearic Islands, Sicily, and Pantellaria until the 18th century. Literary Arabic is taught in the Koranic schools in Liberia, northern Nigeria, and Senegal.

The Arabic alphabet is used in the writing of Persian, Pashtô, and Tamil, and for a number of non-Arabic local languages in the Senegal, the Niger, Liberia, and northern Nigeria. In Yugoslavia, the Moslems of Bosnia use Serbian written with the Arabic alphabet.

History of the Language. The earliest texts in Arabic are three graffiti found in the temple of Ramm in Sinai, dating from about A.D. 300. At Zabad, there are Christian inscriptions dated A.D. 512, and at Ḥarrān, some dated A.D. 568. Christian inscriptions suggest that the Arabic script was invented by Christian missionaries, probably at Ḥīra or Anbār in Mesopotamia. Some parts of the Koran recall the style of the Old and New Testaments, and it is probable that the Bible was translated into Arabic, at least in part, before the advent of *Islam.

With the advent of Islam and the Moslem conquests of the first Islamic century, Arabic, which had been confined to Arabia and its environs, followed the Moslem conquerors throughout the Arab empire in Asia, Africa, and Europe. The Koran gave rise to the study of grammar, to which the Persians contributed in great measure. By the 10th century, literary Arabic had become standardized as a written language. With the advent of the *Seljuks in the 11th century, Persian was used with Arabic in both the political and the literary field in the lands of the eastern Caliphate, especially from Khurasan to the frontiers of Syria. With the advent of the *Mongols and the destruction of *Baghdad in the 13th century, the center of Islamic culture shifted to Egypt and Syria where the language flourished for 2 centuries until the coming of the Ottoman Turks in the early part of the 16th century. The period from the 16th to the 19th century has been characterized as a period of slumbering in the history of the Arabs. Little is known concerning it, linguistically as well as politically.

Modern Arabic. Napoleon's expedition to Egypt in 1798 ushers in the period of Modern Arabic. The reforms of Muḥammad 'Alī of Egypt were inspired chiefly by French culture. The impact of the West on the Near East had a far-reaching influence on the development of the language. Besides the inevitable borrowing of foreign words to express foreign concepts, neologisms of pure Arabic origin were coined. By the second half of the 19th century, a counter-movement of purism developed in Syria and Lebanon, leading ultimately to the foundation of language academies: one was founded in Damascus (*al-Majma' al-'Ilmī al-'Arabī*) in 1919; one in Cairo (*Majma' al-Lugha al-'Arabīya*) in 1932; and another in Baghdad (*al-Majma' al-'Ilmī al-'Irāqī*) in 1947. As far as the language is concerned, the chief function of these academies is to regulate and expand the modern vocabulary on a scientific basis.

The work of these academies has been concentrated on terminology. Medieval works in print and in manuscript are studied for words of purely Arabic origin that may be used to replace so-called "foreign-origin loan words." There has been a considerable measure of success in this endeavor, to which the richness of the vocabulary of classical Arabic has greatly contributed. On the other hand, the phraseology and style of the press and radio are greatly influenced by French and English. The bulk of articles in the newspapers are translations of dispatches from Western news agencies, the English or French originals of which appear in the newspapers of these languages sold at the same newsstands. Such phraseology and style are perpetuated by writers unfamiliar with the classical traditions of the language. Yet the syntax and the morphology of the written language have remained generally constant to the present day throughout all the Arab world from Iraq to Morocco. Thus, though the spoken language may differ from country to country, there is little reason to believe that the dialects will eventually replace the written language, as the Romance languages replaced Latin.

Arabic Literature. For 2½ centuries, from about A.D. 500 in pre-Islamic times to the end of the Umayyad dynasty (A.D. 750), poetry was the undisputed vehicle of Arabic literature. Prose, as a sustained literary production, was virtually nonexistent until the appearance of the Koran, the sacred book of Islam.

Poetic Conventions of Arabic. The principal genre of poetry is the ode, called *qaṣīda*, an artistic form peculiar to Arabic literature, and particularly suited to the desert life of the Arab Bedouins. The *qaṣīda* is composed of a journey theme (*raḥīl*) introduced by an erotic prelude (*nasīb*) and followed by the main theme of the poem, which is either boasting (*fakhr*) or panegyric (*madīḥ*). The poet eulogizes his tribe or a patron from whom he expects a rich reward, and the virtues he extols are those held in high regard by the Bedouins: bravery in battle, loyalty to the tribe, courage and patience in the face of adversity, the spirit of tribal vendetta, and generosity and hospitality. The following is a successful translation of the beginning of a famous early poem by Imru'l-Qays (Gibb, 18).

> Stay! let us weep, while memory tries to trace
> The long-lost fair one's sand-girt dwelling place;
> Though the rude winds have swept the sandy plain,
> Still some faint traces of that spot remain.
> My comrades reined their coursers by my side,
> And "Yield not, yield not to despair" they cried.
> (Tears were my sole reply; yet what avail
> Tears shed on sands, or sighs upon the gale?)

The poet, after such a beginning, goes on to a description of his beloved, whose memory is recalled by the sight of the deserted encampment. This leads him to a journey theme, in which he describes and praises his mount, a camel or horse. After this introduction, the main theme is entered upon and elaborated by scenes of Bedouin life, extolling its virtues and the virtues of the patron for whom the ode is being composed and satirizing rivals of the tribe or patron. Such is the framework within which poets did their creative work. The usual length of an ode is between 50 and 100 verses. Each verse (*bayt*) is divided in halves, the first verse having the same rhyme at the end of each hemistich, which rhyme is then repeated at the end of each verse throughout the poem.

Pre-Islamic Poetry. The authenticity of pre-Islamic poetry has long been the subject of lively dispute. The problem arises from the oral transmission of this poetry for 2 or 3 centuries before it was committed to writing. However good the memory of the early transmitters (*rāwī*), modifications of all sorts were bound to develop and to increase with the passage of time. Added to this were the deliberate modifications made by rival philologists, who used pre-Islamic poetry as proof of their respective theories. Although this procedure led to a certain amount of deliberate tampering as well as unintentional modifications due to the fallibility of human memory, nothing warrants the hypercritical thesis that all pre-Islamic poetry is forged.

This ancient Arabic poetry was rescued from oblivion by the philologists of Basra and Kūfa (in Iraq). One of the chief collections is entitled the *Mu'allaqāt,* or *Suspended Poems,* so-called according to the legend that they were hung up in the Ka'ba because of their high merit. However, it is generally believed that a compiler who died about A.D. 772 first brought them together. The number of poets whose writings were collected in this manner varies from 6 to 10. They are Imru'l-Qays, Ṭarafa, 'Amr ibn Kulthūm, Ḥārith ibn Hilliza, 'Antara, Zuhair, Labīd, Nābigha of Dhubyān, A'shā, and 'Alqama. Other collections are the *Mufaḍḍalīyāt* compiled by Mufaḍḍal al-Ḍabbī (d. *c.* A.D. 786), the *Ḥamāsa* of Abū Tammām (d. *c.* 850), the *Ḥamāsa* of Buḥturī (d. 897), and *Jamharat Ash'ār al-'Arab* of Abū Zaid al-Qurashī (d. *c.* 1000). In addition to the ode, there were shorter poems: elegies (*marthīya*), praises or boasts of courage (*ḥamāsa*), satire (*hijā'*), and taunts of poets of rival tribes (*mufākhara*). Besides the early poets already named, mention is due to two excellent robber-poets, Shanfara and Ṭa'abbaṭa Sharran, and a famous poetess, al-Khanṣā'.

Umayyad Poetry. The poetry after the advent of Islam, during the period of the *Umayyads (till A.D. 750), is a continuation of pre-Islamic poetry with little change in its general character. New subjects were added, however, to the old ones. Love poetry, virtually nonexistent in the previous period except for the amatory prelude of the *qaṣīda,* now became established with 'Umar ibn Abī Rabī'a as its most representative exponent. There was also a more sublimated Platonic love, called *'Udhrite,* after the name of the tribe of Banū 'Udhra, whose love was celebrated for its purity and sincerity. This love is illustrated in the famous poetic romance of Majnūn and Laila. The 'Udhrite poets' names are coupled with those of their beloved, for instance, the Majnūn of Laila (Majnūn who loved Laila), Jamīl of Buthaina, and Kuthaiyir of 'Azzah. On the political scene, three rival poets distinguished themselves; Akhṭal (d. *c.* 710), Farazdaq (d. *c.* 732), and Jarīr (d. *c.* 729). Their controversy brought into existence a collection of satirical poems exchanged among them and known as the *Naqā'iḍ* (pl. of *naqīḍa,* "contradiction") in which each aims at undoing the poetry of another.

'Abbāsid Poetry. The Umayyad period was still predominantly Arab; not so that of the *'Abbāsids with its Persian atmosphere whose influence somewhat widened the horizons of poetry. The period is known for the quarrel between the traditionalists and the modernists. Among the modernists may be mentioned Abū Nuwās (d. *c.* 810), celebrated for his love poetry; Abū 'l-'Atāhiya (d. *c.* 828), known for his ascetic and moralizing poetry; and Ibn al-Mu'tazz (d. 869), the Caliph, author of a long epic poem. For the most part, however, poetry remained within the framework of the classical tradition. The celebrated Mutanabbī, who belongs to this tradition, was nevertheless able to express himself in a highly personal way and has perhaps contributed more than any other poet to the literary taste of the Arabs. The evaluation of his poetry has given rise to a controversy among European Orientalists as well as among the Arabs themselves, a controversy that began in his own period. Another poet of high merit was Abū 'l-'Alā' al-Ma'arrī, at first a follower of Mutanabbī, but later striking out in a direction of his own. In this period there is also the mystical poetry of Ḥallāj (d. 922), Ibn Fāriḍ (d. 1235), and *Ibn 'Arabī (d. 1240).

Western Poetry. Though the poetry of the Islamic West remained bound for the most part to the conventions of the East, it developed two types of folksongs, the *zajal* and the *muwashshaḥ*. The *muwashshaḥ* was a strophic verse that came into being in Spain. It was confined to erotic compositions, had a strong influence on Provençal poetry in Europe, and also became established in Egypt. *Zajal* was another form of strophic verse, using colloquial language. This verse form, which ignored the rules of classical poetry, had the troubador Ibn Quzmān (d. 1160) as its foremost exponent. Ibn Hānī of Seville, who died in the latter part of the 10th century (973), had been the principal representative of the traditional poetry. Western poetry did not flourish until the 11th century; among its chief poets are Mu'taḍid (d. 1042), King of Seville, and his son Mu'tamid (d. 1091), Ibn Rashīq of Qairawān (d. 1070), Ibn Zaidūn (d. 1071), Ibn 'Ammār (d. 1084) of Seville, and Ibn Hamdīs (d. 1132) of Sicily.

Early Prose Literature. At first prose was confined to certain forms of artistic speech: the concise proverbial phrase (*mathal*), elaborate oratory in rhymed prose (*saj'*), and elements of folk literature exemplified in the riddle and the fable. There are also some fragmentary remains of literature in oracular style used by preachers at the Arab fairs. The early Mekkan suras of the Koran are reminiscent of this type of prose.

The Koran, sacred book of Islam, is considered by the Moslems as the word of God, divine and inimitable. Its influence has been great on the language and literature of the Arabs, as on all phases of Islamic culture. The Koran became the object of linguistic research from which Arabic grammar came into being, and thus contributed to the crystallizing of the forms. The flexibility of its language also helped prose to break out of its confines at a time when the Islamic conquests were bringing the newly converted Arabs out of their geographical confines. The time was ripe for the development of the language in the service of a more advanced civilization. The Koran also exercised a literary influence on the oratory of the early Islamic period. The language of the Koran is a rhythmic rhyming prose of an ardent religious and social reformer with the unmistakable gifts of a great poet.

The first essays in prose are due to the chancery secretaries (*kātib,* pl. *kuttāb*), whose earliest representative was 'Abd al-Ḥamīd ibn Yaḥyā (d. 749), author of *The Art of the Secretary.* At this period the influence of translations from Pahlavi literature, combined with the flexibility brought by the Koran, contributed to the creation of a "belles-lettres." The first prose masterpiece of Arabic literature is a translation of the Bidpai fables from Pahlavi by Ibn al-Muqaffa' (d. 759). But the most representative writer of belles-lettres is Jāḥiz (d. 869), a man of vast and varied culture and a prolific writer.

The 8th and 9th centuries witnessed the development of prose in other fields of literature, first in philology, law, history, and Koranic studies, followed by the natural and mathematical sciences of geography, philosophy, theology, and mysticism. Among the great names in these fields may be mentioned: Ibn Qutaiba (d. 889), philology; Tabarī (d. 922), history; Qustā ibn Lūqā (d. 835), Ḥunayn ibn Isḥāq (d. 873; *see* JOHANNITIUS), and Isḥāq ibn Ḥunayn, the latter's son (d. 910), translators of Greek works; Rāzī (d. 923), the physician known to medieval Latin literature as *Rhazes; al-*Kindī (abū Yūsuf Ya'qūb ibn-Isḥāq, d. *c.* 873), *Alfarabi (Fārābī, al-, d. 950), *Avicenna (Ibn-Sīnā, d. 1037), and *Averroës (Ibn Rushd, d. 1198), in philosophy; the founders of the four schools of law, Abū Ḥanīfa (d. 767), Mālik (d. 799), Shāfi 'ī (d. 820), and Ibn Ḥanbal (d. 855); and in the field of mysticism, Muḥāsibī (d. 857) and Ḥallāj (d. 922).

Under the later 'Abbāsids, the most important development was that of the "Assemblies" (*maqāmāt*), a literary genre of the narrative type written in rhymed prose; this genre of dramatic anecdotes, created by Hamadhānī (d. 1007), who was called the "Wonder of the Age" (*Badī 'al-zamān*), was given its classical form by Ḥarīrī (d. 1122). This period also produced its great theologians and jurisconsults, among whom was the well-known *Algazel (Ghazzālī, al-, d. 1111). Spain also gave great writers in these fields, including: the bellettrist Ibn 'Abd Rabbihi (d. 940), author of the famous *Unique Necklace* (*al-'Iqd al-farīd*), important as a literary work as well as a source of citations from early Islamic poetry; the theologian and jurisconsult Ibn Hazm (d. 1064), author also of a delicate literary work on love, *The Dove's Necklace;* and the abovementioned Averroës, commentator on Aristotle, antagonist of Ghazzālī, and eponym of the Western medieval school of philosophy, Latin *Averroism.

Medieval and Modern Literature. From the end of the 'Abbāsid period (mid-13th century) to the 19th century, Arabic literature appears to have slumbered. Yet it was not without great personalities such as *Ibn Khaldūn (d. 1406), author of a universal history, the introduction ("Prolegomena," *Muqaddima*) to which is one of the most original works of all time in the fields of social philosophy and the philosophy of history. Ibn Khaldūn's work is all the more remarkable for having appeared in a period mainly concerned with the compilation of the literary labors of the previous periods. Suyūṭī (d. 1505), the most intelligent compiler, was a prolific writer in philology, history, and the religious sciences.

The "awakening" (*nahḍa*) of Arabic literary activity in the 19th century began with the revival of classical traditions. Among its representatives was Nāṣīf Yāzijī (d. 1871), author of *Majma' al-Baḥrayn,* a continuation of the "Assemblies" made famous by Ḥarīrī. Soon, the influence of Western literature, through translation, introduced new literary forms such as free verse, the novel, and the drama. After a period of experimentation, a new, original Arabic literature began in the first part of the 20th century. Its representatives have reflected the social, religious, intellectual, and cultural interests of the Arabs. Noteworthy in the field of the novel and drama are the Egyptians Muḥammad Taymūr (d. 1921), his brother Maḥmūd (b. 1894), and Tawfīq Ḥakīm (b. 1898). Ṭāhā Ḥusayn (b. 1899) became prominent in the field of literary criticism. In the America's, the most important literary movement took place in the United States with the famous Lebanese trio Jibrān Khalīl Jibrān (d. 1931), Amīn Rīhānī (b. 1879), and Mikhā'īl Nu'ayma (b. 1889). In poetry, two Iraqīs distinguished themselves, Jamīl Zahāwī (d. 1936) and Ma'rūf Ruṣāfī (d. 1945).

Bibliography: H. FLEISCH, *Introduction à l'étude des langues sémitiques: Eléments de bibliographie* (Paris 1952). C. PELLAT, *Langue et littérature arabe* (Paris 1952). L. MASSIGNON, ed., *Annuaire du monde musulman* (4th ed. Paris 1955). J. FÜCK, *Arabiya, Untersuchungen zur arabischen Sprach- und Stilgeschichte* (Berlin 1950), French translation by C. DENIZEAU (Paris 1955).

Grammars—classical. C. P. CASPARI, *A Grammar of the Arabic Language,* tr. W. WRIGHT, 2 v. (3d ed. Cambridge, Eng. 1896–98; reissued 1951). M. GAUDEFROY-DEMOMBYNES and R. BLACHÈRE, *Grammaire de l'arabe classique* (3d ed. Paris 1952). Modern. C. PELLAT, *Introduction à l'arabe moderne* (Paris 1956). F. J. ZIADEH and R. B. WINDER, *An Introduction to Modern Arabic* (Princeton 1955).

Dictionaries—classical. E. W. LANE, *Arabic-English Lexicon* (London 1863–93, bk. 1 reissued New York 1955). A. DE BIBERSTEIN-KAZIMIRSKI, *Dictionnaire arabe-français,* 4 v. (Cairo 1875). R. DOZY, *Supplément aux dictionnaires arabes,* 2 v. (Leiden 1927). Modern. H. WEHR, *A Dictionary of Modern Written Arabic,* ed. J. M. COWAN (Ithaca, N.Y. 1961). C. PELLAT, *L'Arabe vivant* (Paris 1952), a useful vocabulary list, arranged according to subject.

For a general bibliography, see the very important biobibliographical work by C. BROCKELMANN, *Geschichte der arabischen Literatur,* 2 v. (2d ed. Leiden 1943–49) suppl. 3 v. (1937–42). For good surveys, see H. A. R. GIBB, *Arabic Literature* (London 1926) new ed. forthcoming. R. A. NICHOLSON, *Literary History of the Arabs* (2d ed. Cambridge, Eng. 1930). J. M. ABD-EL-JALIL, *Brève histoire de la littérature arabe* (Paris 1947). F. GABRIELI, *Storia della letteratura araba* (Milan 1956). For the modern period, H. A. R. GIBB, "Studies in Contemporary Arabic Literature," *Bulletin of the School of Oriental and African Studies* (London Univ. 1928, 1929, 1933).

[G. MAKDISI]

ARABS, HISTORY OF THE

The Arabs, like the Assyrians, the Aramaeans, and the Hebrews, came originally from the Semitic-speaking tribal peoples of the Arabian Peninsula. While not all Arabs are Moslems, their history has been intimately involved with the larger history of Islam. The Islamic Arab conquests of the 7th and 8th centuries entailed vast folk migrations of Arab tribesmen into other lands. With time, Arabs passed their blood and their language to a host of other peoples. Today the word has lost any proper racial significance and, outside the Arabian Peninsula, is used to mean almost anyone whose ancestral language (however recently) was Arabic and who feels that he is an Arab.

Origins. The identity of the Arabs is a complex question closely related to the broader one of the origins of the Semites and Hamites and involving the Arab genealogical legends. Arab genealogists divide all their tribes into the "Northern," sprung from 'Adnān, descendant of Isma'īl (Ishmael, son of Abraham), and the "Southern," descended from Qaḥṭān or Jectan the descendant of Sem (Gn 10.25). The tribes of Qaḥṭānid descent were looked upon as having the "purest" origin, but the Northern tribes have claimed to be themselves more noble, since the Quraysh, tribe of the prophet *Mohammed, was Northern. The debate continued through many bitter tribal wars (*see* UMAYYADS) and still lingers in rural Syria and Jordan. Even among Arabs, the word Arab has not always had the same meaning. In the first book set down in Arabic, the *Koran, "Arab" always means "Bedouin," as distinguished from town and oasis dwellers. Thus God is represented as saying, "The Arabs are most stubborn in unbelief and hypocrisy, and least likely to know the limits of what God has revealed to His apostle [Mohammed]."

The Arabs before Islam. Until archeological investigations are possible in the Arabian Peninsula, most of our early information about the Arabs must come from the accounts of peoples who had contacts with them. The name first appears with reference to camel nomads. Camels, however, were not domesticated until quite late, the earliest mention of them occurring in the Book of Judges about 1000 B.C. Shortly after 854 B.C., an Assyrian inscription refers to the Aribi, a kingdom of camel nomads in the North Arabian desert. At about the same time, in the highlands of South Arabia, the *Yemen (*Arabia Felix*), rose the first Arab civilization, founded on irrigation-agriculture and commerce, monopolizing the trade in incense, so vital to the temples of the ancient world. The southern kingdoms—*Saba (Sheba), Ma'īn, Qatabān, and Ḥadramawt—established trading colonies in the oases of the North and sea trade with India and East Africa, and colonized Abyssinia across the Red Sea. Late in the 1st millennium B.C. the Arab state of the *Nabataeans, with its capital at *Petra (fl. 312 B.C. to A.D. 105), rose south of the Dead Sea at the north end of the caravan route from Yemen and the Indian Ocean trade. Steady Arab immigration into the Fertile Crescent was going on at the beginning of the Christian Era, and Arabs rose in the armies of Rome and Persia. Philip the Arab (reigned 243–249) was perhaps the first Christian to become a Roman Emperor. *Palmyra, an Arab merchant kingdom based on the oasis of Tadmor in Syria, flourished from A.D. 130 to 270 and, under its energetic Queen Zaynab (Zenobia), nearly conquered the eastern provinces of the Roman Empire. In the 6th century A.D., Transjordan and the Ḥawrān were a Byzantine vassal kingdom of Christian Arabs under the Ghassānid kings—a buffer between Byzantine Syria, the desert tribes, and Persia. The Ghassānids championed the Monophysite creed. A similar Arab kingdom, that of the Lakhmids of Ḥīra, was set up in Iraq as a buffer state of the Sassanid Empire. Most of its people embraced the Nestorian heresy. Both these Arab states ended in the early 7th century, while Byzantium and Sussanid Persia exhausted themselves in eruptions of their ancient war.

South Arabian civilization was in a state of collapse following the fall of the Himyar kingdom *c.* A.D. 525, and Abyssinia, now Christianized from Egypt, had invaded its parent culture from across the Red Sea. Christianity and Judaism were making some converts in the peninsula, and there was a large Christian community at Najran in South Arabia; but the great majority of the tribesmen clung conservatively to the star gods, fertility gods, and fetishes of their ancestors. They raided each other in incessant tribal wars and bloodfeuds, which they celebrated in a heroic oral literature of high quality (e.g., the *Mu'allaqāt*). The shrunken caravan trade of the incense road was controlled chiefly by the tribe of Quraysh, residing in a well-watered station, Mecca, also the site of the Ka'ba, one of the chief pagan cult-centers. It was here, in A.D. 570, that Mohammed was born.

The Islamic Period. By the time of Mohammed's death at Medina in 632, most of the peninsular tribes had been briefly brought into a confederation under Medina, in which *Islam had a special and protected status, and within which warfare was outlawed. The Ka'ba, as the temple of Abraham and Ishmael, was now the center of a monotheist religion. One of the problems created by Mohammed's death (*see* ALI) was that many tribesmen now felt that their allegiance to Medina should end; the leader was dead. Some of them turned to new prophets who claimed to have inherited his authority. It was then necessary for the first successor, or *caliph, Abū Bakr, to reimpose the authority of Medina on the tribes. Their subjugation in the so-called wars of apostasy took the better part of 2 years, but it was decided that Islam was to remain one community, with one leader. The decision was imposed only by force, however, and only sullenly accepted.

The Arab Empire. For several years Arabs had already been raiding towns on the borders of Syria and Iraq, and Mohammed had himself sent several war parties to the North. To reunite the spirit of the people and demonstrate the advantages of unity under the Islamic state, Medina now organized raids on a larger scale. The results astonished even the caliphs. The weakened empires of Byzantium and Persia were unable to meet the Arab camel cavalry. The Arab vassals who might once have helped them were alienated and made common cause with the invaders. In 636 the Byzantines under Heraclius withdrew from Syria, and in 637 the Persian capital Ctesiphon-Seleucia in Iraq fell and its court fled. In 641 the Byzantine garrison of Egypt, hampered by the hostility of the native Copts under their monophysite clergy, capitulated to an Arab army. Persia and Armenia were subjugated by 652. From 647 to 667 Arab war parties were raiding Byzantine North Africa, and by 670 the Arabs had established a permanent base in Tunisia. In 711 the armies of Visigoth Spain were shattered.

The Christian, Jewish, and Zoroastrian inhabitants of the conquered lands were expected to retain their own religions, languages, and property; to pay taxes; and to keep the peace. Arab contingents were maintained in new garrison-towns built between the deserts and the sown land, such as Kūfa and Basra in Iraq, Fusṭaṭ in Egypt, and Qayrawān in Tunisia. Each of these cantonments was later to become an important diffusion center of the Arabic language and the new

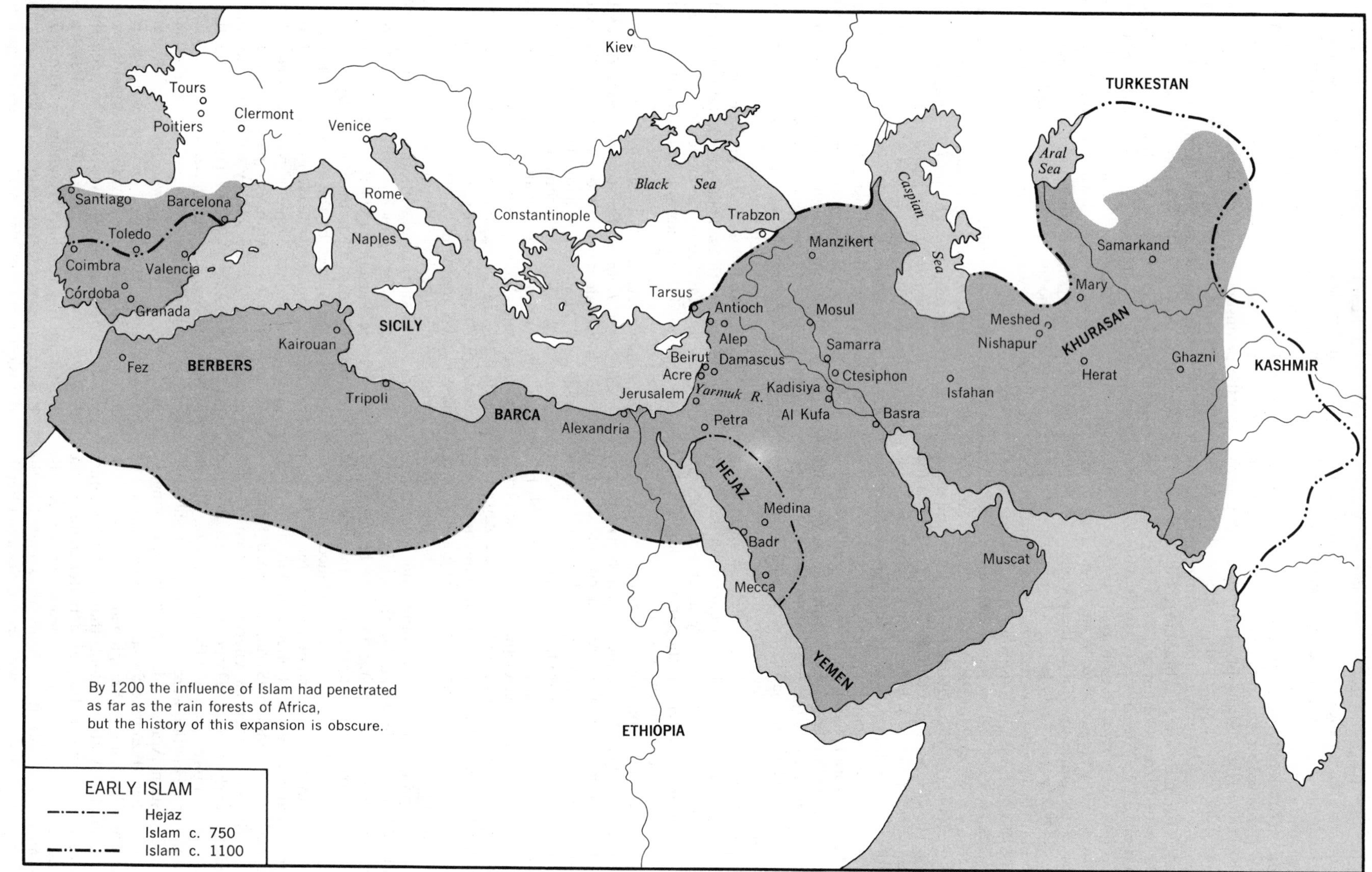
Kiev
Tours
Poitiers
Clermont
Venice
TURKESTAN
Aral Sea
Black Sea
Caspian Sea
Santiago
Barcelona
Rome
Constantinople
Trabzon
Toledo
Naples
Manzikert
Samarkand
Coimbra
Valencia
Córdoba
Granada
Tarsus
Mary
SICILY
Antioch
Mosul
Meshed
Alep
KHURASAN
Nishapur
Kairouan
Samarra
Ghazni
Fez
BERBERS
Beirut
Damascus
KASHMIR
Acre
Ctesiphon
Herat
Isfahan
Jerusalem
Yarmuk R.
Kadisiya
Tripoli
Al Kufa
BARCA
Basra
Petra
Alexandria
HEJAZ
Medina
Badr
Muscat
Mecca
YEMEN
By 1200 the influence of Islam had penetrated
as far as the rain forests of Africa,
but the history of this expansion is obscure.
ETHIOPIA
EARLY ISLAM
Hejaz
Islam c. 750
Islam c. 1100

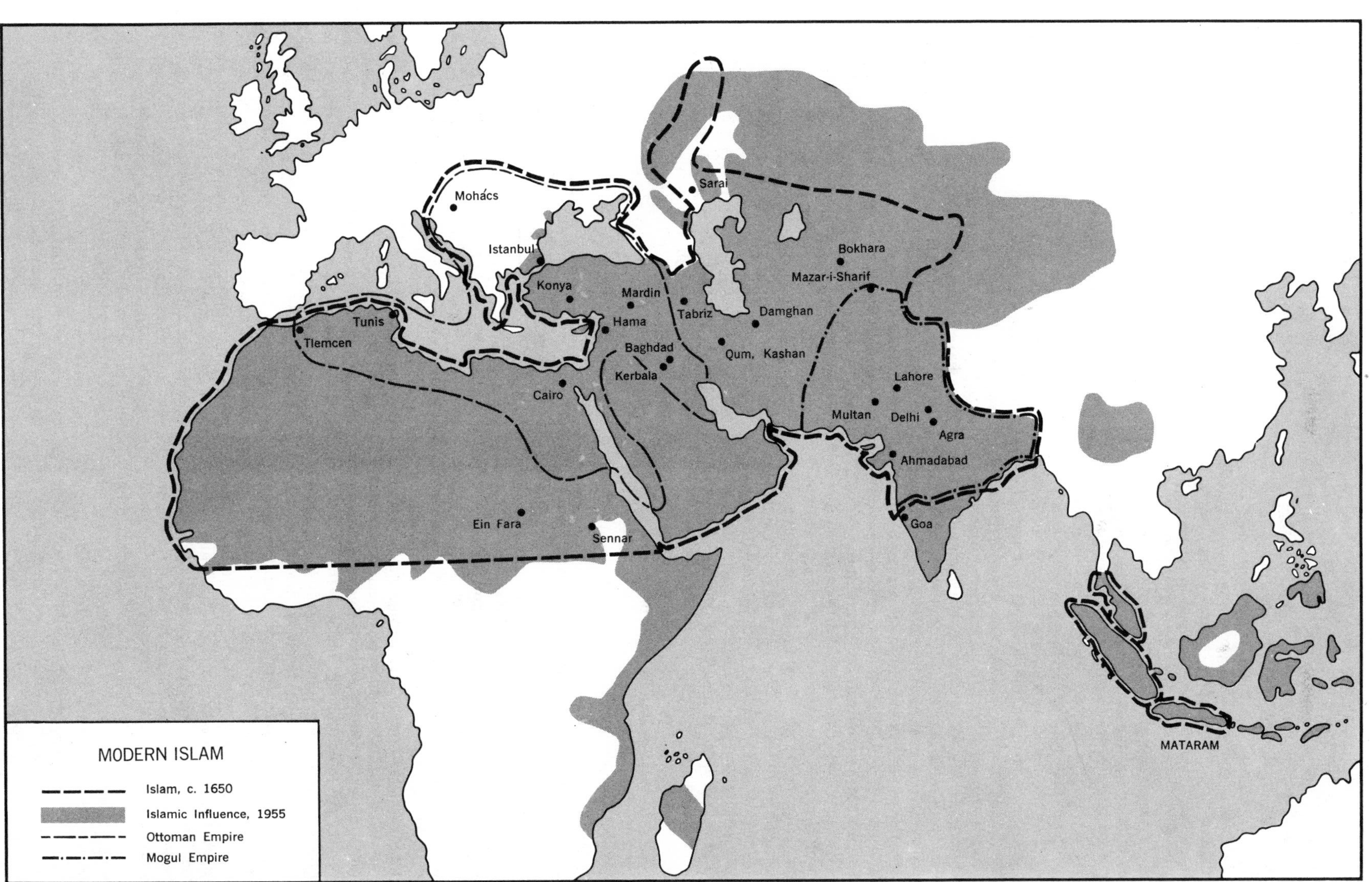

Countries where Arabs spread Islam. Apart from Sicily, Spain is the only important region that was once (8th to 15th century) but is no longer Moslem.

religion. Each Arab Moslem—man, woman, and child—was given an allowance of cash and kind from the tribute money. There was continual movement into the camps by individuals and groups, as well as large-scale migration with flocks and herds into new territory. The empire as envisaged by 'Umar, the second caliph, was an Arab-Moslem military elite governing with a certain aloofness the lands of peaceful, taxpaying non-Moslem cultivators and artisans. This remained in broad outline the theory of empire under the dynasty of the Umayyads, but it was increasingly difficult to maintain. One reason for this was that the Prophet had tolerated the old Arabian custom of making concubines of women captured in warfare, but had given their children equal rights with those of freeborn Arab women. Thus, as a result of the conquests, thousands of children of mixed parentage were born and the numbers of the ruling class greatly enlarged. Moreover, the general tendency of the Arabs, who believed their religion to be a new dispensation, was to proselytize. As yet Islamic theology had developed none of its later subtleties, and little more seems to have been required of a convert than an admission that God was one and that Mohammed was one of His prophets. The advantages of conversion were such that large numbers of the conquered people, particularly those with warrior traditions (such as the Berbers of North Africa and the peoples of the eastern frontiers), quickly embraced Islam. This was especially true from 717 to 720 under the pious caliph 'Umar ibn 'Abd al-'Aziz, who stopped the costly wars with Byzantium, abolished the taxes (except on land) of all his subjects who accepted Islam, and gave them equal status with Arabs.

Arabs in a Divided Islam. 'Umar's predecessors, not wishing to see their revenues diminished, had made even converts pay the tribute, and his successors returned to this system. Pious Moslems, Arab and non-Arab, regarded such discrimination as an example of un-Islamic injustice, and this discontent was exploited by the sectarian forms of Islam in a growing number of religious rebellions. Thus predominantly Islamic groupings and loyalties supplanted the older Arab and tribal consciousness in most areas and necessitated, under the *'Abbāsids, new principles of political organization. Within an empire and civilization now Islamic rather than Arab, the Arabs could move with a considerable degree of freedom as one people among many. The Arabic language remained the official language of government, as well as the cult language of Islam, and in many areas Arabic dialects became the speech of the people. This was especially true where Semitic languages had been used, as in Syria; Iraq; Palestine, where Syriac dialects were spoken; and the Roman province of Africa (Tunisia and Constantine), where Carthaginian Punic still lingered in the country districts. In Spain, Arabic was the language of Moslems, but the Romance language was retained as a household and vulgar language. In Aryan-speaking Persia, Transoxania, and Sind, wherever the Arabs settled and intermarried with local population, they gave up their language. Exceptions occurred only where natural conditions forced Arab immigrants to retain the isolation of a nomadic way of life. This has been the case in the southern coasts of Persia and some small areas in Central Asia. Along with the Islamization of non-Moslems, movement of Arab tribes into new areas continued through the Middle Ages. In North Africa, the tribal migrations of the "Northern" tribes of Banu Hilal and Banu Sulaym after the end of the 11th century destroyed the bases of the economy, nearly causing the extinction of urban life. This led the great North African historian, *Ibn Khaldūn, to regard Arabs as the enemies of civilization. In the upper Nile valley, pressure of Beduin tribes from upper Egypt in the 13th and 14th centuries brought about the destruction of the Christian kingdoms of Maqurra (*c.* 1340) and 'Alwa (*c.* 1500), and the Islamization of the Sudan.

With the importation of the modern ideology of nationalism in the 19th and 20th centuries, Arabic-speaking areas of the world have come to identify themselves as Arabs and to look upon the cultural achievements of medieval Islamic civilization as "Arab." Since Arabophone Christians can with equal justice claim to have had Arab ancestors (particularly in Greater Syria and Iraq) and to have contributed to Islamic civilization, they have often participated vigorously in Arab nationalist causes, partly from real convictions, partly in the hope of building a social structure that will offer them equality with Moslem Arabs.

Bibliography: M. GUIDI, *Storia e cultura degli Arabi fino alla morte di Maometto* (Florence 1951). P. K. HITTI, *History of the Arabs* (5th ed. London 1952). I. KHALDŪN, *The Muqaddimah*, tr. F. ROSENTHAL, 3 v. (New York 1958) 1:302–308. B. LEWIS, *The Arabs in History* (New York 1950). S. MOSCATI, *Storia e civiltà dei Semiti* (Bari 1949). G. MARÇAIS, EncIslam² 1:524–533.

[J. A. WILLIAMS]

ARACAJU, ARCHDIOCESE OF (ARACAJUENSIS), located in the state of Sergipe, Brazil; created a diocese in 1910; raised to an archdiocese in 1960, the same year in which its two suffragan sees, Propriá and Estância, were created.

1965 STATISTICS

Area	Population	Parishes	Clergy	
			Sec.	Reg.
Aracaju	368,876	26	32	19
Propriá	*163,307			7
Estância	*223,800	12	10	3

*This figure includes Catholics only.

In 1575 the Jesuits founded three Indian missions in this area, but these were shortly destroyed by the whites. Colonization began in 1589 with the foundation of the town and parish of São Cristóvão. Jesuits continued with missionary work and in 1631 founded a small house. The Carmelites founded a convent there in 1600. After the Dutch occupation (1630–45) the city had to be rebuilt. The Jesuits founded three *aldeias*, and the Carmelites established two residences and a mission. In 1693 the Franciscans founded a small convent and soon thereafter two missions. Since 1843 the Capuchins have been charged with pastoral visits and popular missions. The first bishop, José Tomás Gomes da Silva (1911–48), organized the diocese, founded the seminary, and energetically defended the reputation of his clergy. Bishop Fernando dos Santos (1949–57) promoted various social works, while his successor, José Vicente Távora, began the agrarian apostolate and organized the workers of the interior into syndicates.

This type of activity is also underway in the Diocese of Propriá. In 1964 among the religious orders working in the province were Franciscans, Salesians, Redemptorists, Marianists, and about 150 sisters of various congregations.

Bibliography: S. LEITE, *História da Companhia de Jesús no Brasil,* 10 v. (Lisbon–Rio de Janeiro 1938–50). B. ROEWER, *A Ordem Franciscana no Brasil* (Petrópolis 1942). F. M. DE PRIMERIO, *Capuchinhos em terras de Santa Cruz . . .* (São Paulo 1942). A. NÓBREGA, *Dioceses e bispos do Brasil* (Rio de Janeiro 1954).

[O. VAN DER VAT]

ARAMAEANS

An ancient northwest Semitic people who inhabited the area between the Taurus Mountains and the Arabian Peninsula, east of the Lebanon and principally in Upper Mesopotamia about the Tigris, Euphrates, Ḥabur, and Baliḥ Rivers. This region was called Aram, or Paddan-Aram, or Aram-Naharaim ("Aram of the two rivers"). This article will discuss the folkloric origins and historical emergence of this ancient people, the development of the Aramaean states, their religion and language, and the Nabataean and Palmyrene kingdoms.

Folkloric Origins and Historical Emergence. The OT made Aram, the descendant of Sem (Gn 10.22–23; 1 Par 1.17), the son of Noah, the progenitor of the Aramaeans, thus relating them to the Semitic peoples. Camuel, "the father of Aram" (Gn 22.21), was born to Nahor, brother of Abraham; Laban, Rebecca's brother, was "the son of the Aramean Bathuel," another son of Camuel (Gn 28.5). Israel thus remembered that its patriarchs were Aramaeans (Dt 26.5) who first learned Hebrew, the language of Canaan, when they arrived in Palestine. According to Am 9.7 the Aramaeans came from Kir (see also Am 1.5), a place not identified with certainty, but associated with Elam in Is 22.6.

Unsuccessful attempts have been made to trace the Aramaeans back to the beginning of the 3d millennium; the first certain appearance of this people is found in historical records of the 12th century B.C. From the early 2d millennium B.C., however, there is evidence of a people in northern Mesopotamia with west-Semitic names who may be the forebears of the Aramaeans later found in Syria and Palestine. Moreover, a nomadic people, called Aḫlame, appear in Assyrian records [of the time of King Arikden-ilu (1325–1311 B.C.)], emerging from the Syrian-Arabian Desert, attacking Assyrian lands and towns, and gradually settling down in the northern Mesopotamian area. The specific "Aramaean" type of Aḫlame appears only in the late 12th century. In the 4th regnal year of Tiglath-Pileser I (1115–1076 B.C.) a major campaign was first recorded against "Aramaean Aḫlame" in the area about the confluence of the Ḥabur and Euphrates Rivers. Their invasion of Assyrian territory was persistent and Tiglath-Pileser I eventually had to conduct 28 campaigns against them. Soon thereafter an Aramaean usurper, Adad-apil-iddin (1079–1058 B.C.), mounted the throne of Babylon. To this wave of Aramaean invaders belongs also the origin of the Chaldeans, who settled in southern Babylonia probably in the 10th century. But the most important area penetrated by the Aramaeans was Syria, on both sides of the Upper Euphrates; it became known as Aram (Nm 23.7; 22.5). The Aramaeans never formed one great empire to rival the empires of the Assyrians or the Babylonians, but lived, instead, in small federated states.

Aramaean States. Although historical data about the Aramaean states at the beginning of the 1st millennium B.C. are scarce, the eventual emergence of these must have been the result of their importance, which fluctuated constantly as certain areas were dominated now by one, now by another of their more powerful neighbors. Eleventh-century cuneiform texts reveal Bit-Adini (Beth-Eden in Am 1.5) in north Syria, with its capital at Til-Barsip, as the most important Aramaean state of that time. In the 9th and 8th centuries B.C. the prominent states were Arpad (Arphad: 4 Kgs 18.34) in northern Syria, with such places as Aleppo and Neirab its vassal kingdoms; *Hamath (4 Kgs 18.34) in central Syria, with 19 vassal districts; and *Damascus in southern Syria. Damascus (often called simply Aram) figured prominently in the history of Israel. Rasin I, who had rebelled against Hadadezar, King of Soba (3 Kgs 11.23–25), set up the Damascene dynasty during Solomon's reign.

Four other Aramaean states are mentioned in the OT. Soba (2 Sm 8.3–8) was a state north of Damascus in the Beqa', rich in silver and copper. At a time when it outranked Damascus, David defeated its King, Hadadezer, son of Rehob. Beth-Rohob (2 Sm 10.6) was a small state east of the Jordan and north of Ammon, whose armies the *Ammonites hired to fight David. Maacha (2 Sm 10.6), a small state at the southern ends of the Lebanon and Anti-Lebanon ranges, west of Dan, had once belonged to Israel, but was conquered by *Ben-Adad (Ben-Hadad) I of Damascus. Gessur (2 Sm 3.3; 13.37–38) was a small state east of the Sea of Galilee. Other Aramaean states are known from inscriptions, such as Sam'al (Ya'di), 'Umq, Lu'ath.

Ben-Adad I had 32 vassal kings in his Damascene army (3 Kgs 20.1, 24)—an indication of the multiplicity of Aramaean states in his time. The independence of these states came to an end with the campaigns of *Tiglath-Pileser III, who subjugated most of them between 740 and 732 B.C. Little is known about the political history of the Aramaeans after they were incorporated into the Persian Empire in the 6th century. They continued to appear as traders and traveling merchants. Aramaean ethnic groups were found throughout the empire, even at Elephantine in Egypt where they served along with Jews in a 5th-century military colony.

Religion and Language. The Aramaeans were not monotheistic, but rather venerated a pantheon headed by Hadad, the storm god, whose principal temple was in Aleppo (Ḥalab). His consort was apparently 'Attar (Ishtar—but 'Attar sometimes appears as a god!). In 4 Kgs 5.18 Hadad is mentioned under the local Damascene epithet Remmon ("Thunderer"; Za 12.11); he was apparently also called *Ilu-wer* ("the god Wer") and *Be'elshamayn* ("Lord of the heavens") in the states of Hamath and Lu'ath (Zakir inscription a1, b20, 23; see Pritchard ANET[2] 501–502). The Sefîre treaty between Bar-Ga'yah, King of *Ktk,* and Mati'el, King of the Aramaean state of Arpad (see Pritchard ANET[2] 504), reveals that the Aramaeans admitted many Babylonian and Canaanite deities to their pantheon. Among the gods who are called to bear witness to the treaty are *Marduk and Zarpanit, Nabu (*see* NEBO) and Tashmet, *Nergal and Laṣ, Shamash and Nur, Sin and Nikkal, Sibitti, El and 'Elyân (these last two Canaanite names eventually became epithets of the OT Yahweh in Gn 14.22), Heaven and Earth, Abyss and Springs, and Day and Night (the last three pairs are personifications).

The early Aramaeans spoke a northwest Semitic language called Aramaic, cognate to the Hebrew and Canaanite dialects. Though derived from a common Proto-Semitic parent stock, it developed independently as a sister language of Hebrew and Phoenician, and constantly underwent influence from the languages spoken by the peoples who adopted it as a secondary language. It was widely used for international communication from *c.* 700 to 300 B.C., until it was superseded by Greek. (*See* ARAMAIC LANGUAGE, 2.)

Nabataeans and Palmyrenes. Two later Aramaean kingdoms came to prominence at *Petra in southern Transjordan and at *Palmyra in the Syrian Desert. The *Nabataeans were originally nomads of obscure origins, perhaps connected with Nabaioth, the first-born of Ismael (Gn 25.13; Is 60.7), or with the Nabate of 8th- to 7th-century Assyrian inscriptions (see Pritchard ANET[2] 298). They first clearly emerged near Petra *c.* 312 B.C., when they refused allegiance to Antigonus, a successor of Alexander the Great. As prosperous caravan traders, they conducted a flourishing commerce along the caravan route from the Persian Gulf across the Arabian Desert to the Palestinian and Syrian coasts. Though they spoke Aramaic, it was influenced by early Arabic, as was their religion and culture; indeed, their rulers sometimes bore the title, "King of the Arabs" (ὁ τῶν Ἀράβων τύραννος). Some of the chief names of the Nabataean dynasty are: Aretas I (*c.* 169 B.C.), associated with the flight of the Jewish high priest Jason (2 Mc 5.8); Aretas III, the conqueror of Damascus *c.* 85 B.C.; Aretas IV (9 B.C. to A.D. 40), whose daughter was married to Herod Antipas, but was later repudiated by him in favor of Herodias (Mt 14.3–4). The ethnarch of Aretas IV controlled Damascus at the time of Paul's escape (2 Cor 11.32). The Nabataeans were conquered by the Romans in A.D. 106, and the Nabataean town, Bostra, became the capital of the Roman province, Arabia.

With the decline of the Nabataeans the rich caravan trade passed into the hands of the Palmyrene Aramaeans. Palmyra was the Greek name used by the Romans for ancient Tadmor, a fertile oasis in the Syrian Desert. An amalgamation of Aramaean tribes settled there and dominated the caravan route from Babylon to Damascus. Though Tadmor had been inhabited much earlier (built by Solomon according to 2 Chr 8.4), it emerged into political importance only in the 1st century as a somewhat Hellenized kingdom. From that day until its final defeat in A.D. 272 by the Emperor Aurelian, it passed through various periods of Roman colonization and independent rule, a fact which reflected the unstable conditions of Mesopotamia in those centuries. The Aramaeans who settled there were considerably influenced by the spread of Hellenistic and Roman culture to that part of the world; many bilingual inscriptions (Aramaic and Greek) witness to this influence. Palmyra's heyday, which occurred during the reign of Odaenathus and Queen Zenobia (*c.* A.D. 260), immediately preceded its downfall.

Bibliography: R. T. O'CALLAGHAN, *Aram Naharaim: A Contribution to the History of Upper Mesopotamia in the Second Millennium B.C.* (Rome 1948). J. STARCKY, "The Nabateans: A Historical Sketch," BiblArchaeol 18 (1955) 84–106; "Palmyre," DBSuppl 6:1066–1103; *Palmyre* (Paris 1952). M. F. UNGER, *Israel and the Aramaeans of Damascus* (London 1957). Inter DictBibl 1:190–193. EncDictBibl 123–127. A. DUPONT-SOMMER, *Les Araméens* (Paris 1949). E. FORRER, "Aramu," ReallexAssyr 1 (1928) 130–139. A. ALT, "Die syrische Staatenwelt vor dem Einbruch der Assyrer," *Kleine Schriften zur Geschichte des Volkes Israel,* 3 v. (Munich 1953–59) 3:214–232.

[J. A. FITZMYER]

ARAMAIC LANGUAGE

One of the *Semitic languages, belonging, together with Ugaritic, *Hebrew, and other Canaanite dialects, to the Northwest Semitic group. Originally spoken by *Aramaeans in northern Syria and Mesopotamia, it gradually became the lingua franca of the ancient Near East from India to Egypt. In importance it rivaled Phoenician and far surpassed Hebrew. It is the general name for various dialects often difficult to classify. Here, after treating of the various phases of ancient Aramaic in general, special consideration is given to Biblical Aramaic because of its importance in Biblical studies.

1. ANCIENT

Four main phases of ancient Aramaic are distinguishable: Old Aramaic, Official Aramaic, Middle Aramaic, and Late Aramaic. For the sake of completeness, a few words will be added concerning its survival in the dialects of Modern Aramaic.

One of the features that make Aramaic distinct from all the other Semitic languages is the phonetic shift whereby the Proto-Semitic fricative interdentals, which were largely retained in Arabic and South Arabic and which became sibilants in Akkadian and Canaanite (Hebrew), became simple dentals in Aramaic; thus, Proto-Semitic *ḏ, ṯ, ṯ̣* became respectively *z, š, ṣ* in Akkadian and Canaanite, but *d, t, ṭ* in Aramaic. But in Old Aramaic this shift had apparently not yet taken place in all local dialects. Old Aramaic was written in a script borrowed from the Phoenician script of only 22 consonants, which had no letters for fricative interdentals. The indiscriminate writing of the demonstrative particle as both *d* and *z* in Official Aramaic documents seems to show that this particle was still pronounced as *ḏ* (as in Proto-Semitic). The phoneme that was *ḏ̣* in Proto-Semitic (voiced emphatic interdental), which shifted to *ṣ* in Canaanite, became in Aramaic first *q* and then ʿ.

Another characteristic of Aramaic is its means of expressing determination (the definite article). Proto-Semitic had no article; Akkadian did not develop one. In Canaanite (e.g., Hebrew) the article was expressed by prefixing *ha-* to the substantive; in Aramaic it was expressed by suffixing *-a* at the end of the substantive. Finally, at least in the later periods of the language, Aramaic reduced to zero grade unaccented short vowels much more than the other Semitic languages did.

Old Aramaic. The earliest attested phase of Aramaic extends from *c.* 925 to *c.* 700 B.C. Inscriptions from northern Syria, written in the borrowed Canaanite (Phoenician) alphabet, preserve dedications and treaties in a language that is basically Aramaic, but distinct from later phases by the retention of Canaanite phonetic and syntactic features. Probably not many centuries earlier both Aramaic and Canaanite developed from a common mother-language (Proto-Northwest-Semitic). Except for two inscriptions from Zinjirli, *Hadad* and *Panammu,* the rest (e.g., *Ben-Hadad, Zakir, Sefire I-II-III, Nerab I-II;* see Pritchard ANET, 501–505) present a fairly homogeneous picture of this early Aramaic.

Official Aramaic. During the Assyrian domination of the 7th century, Aramaic developed a characteristic form and came to be used widely in the Levant as a means of international communication, probably due to traveling Aramaean merchants. The name "Imperial" was given to this form of Aramaic, which lasted from *c.* 700 to *c.* 300 B.C., in the belief that its standardization was due to the Persian imperial chanceries' use of it for communication in their far-flung administration. Though its international use clearly antedated that empire (see 4 Kgs 18.26; Asshur Ostracon, dated *c.* 650, in which an Assyrian official writes to a colleague in Aramaic), the Persian imperial administration certainly furthered its use and standardization. Documents from 5th-century Egypt show how it was used for contracts, letters, and notes about household affairs between Jews and Egyptians or other Jews (Pritchard ANET, 427–430, 491–492). The largest group of Official-Aramaic texts has come from Egypt (*Elephantine, Saqqarah, Hermopolis West, etc.). The correspondence of the satrap, Arsames, was found in Egypt, but written apparently in Babylon. To this phase also belongs Biblical Aramaic (see below).

Likewise from this period come the Aramaic ideographs in Middle Persian (i.e., words written as Aramaic but read as Persian) and inscriptions from such places as Arabia, Persia, Asia Minor, India, and Afghanistan. It is also during this period that Aramaic gradually supplanted Hebrew in Palestine, although small areas always remained where Hebrew too was used. With the fall of the Persian Empire, Aramaic was replaced by Greek as the international language, but it persisted in wide use among Semitic peoples.

Middle Aramaic. This phase of Aramaic is a slight development of the former, when Aramaic, lacking the normative control of the royal chanceries, began to break down into dialects. To be grouped here is the Aramaic used between roughly 300 B.C. and A.D. 200. To this phase belong (1) in Palestine: the Nabataean inscriptions of *Petra (Aramaic with early Arabic influence), Qumran Aramaic, Murabba'at Aramaic (*see* DEAD SEA SCROLLS), the beginnings of Rabbinical literature, inscriptions on Jewish *ossuaries and tombstones, the Aramaic words in the NT and Josephus; and (2) in Syria and Mesopotamia: the inscriptions found at *Palmyra, Hatra, etc. Local dialects now appear, especially Palestinian, Nabataean, and Palmyrene, but they are still closely related to Official Aramaic. The important discovery of Qumran-Aramaic texts fills in a gap in our knowledge of Palestinian Aramaic that previously existed between the final redaction of Daniel (*c.* 165 B.C.) and the first of the Rabbinical writings (**Megillat Ta'anit* or "Scroll of Fasting," *c.* A.D. 100). Whereas Palestinian Aramaic of this period was previously known almost exclusively from tombstone inscriptions, there are now many literary texts, which reveal the type of Aramaic in use in Palestine at the time of Christ. Moreover, several scraps of Targums have also been found there, which suggest that possibly some of the Targums that are extant only from a later date (Yerushalmi II, Neofiti) may actually preserve older translations belonging to this period. *See* BIBLE, IV (TEXTS AND VERSIONS), 11.

Late Aramaic. In this phase, which extends from about A.D. 200 to 700 mainly, but in certain areas lasted even longer, a clear distinction can be made between Western Aramaic, which includes Syro-Palestinian Christian Aramaic, Samaritan Aramaic, and Palestinian Jewish Aramaic on the one hand, and Syriac, Babylonian Talmudic Aramaic, and Mandaic on the other. (Mandaic is the language of the Gnostic sect of Mandaeans in southern Mesopotamia; *see* MANDAEAN RELIGION.)

Syriac, the dialect of Edessa (modern Urfa in Turkey), became the most important dialect of Late Aramaic; it developed two chief forms, Eastern or Nestorian at Nisibis, Western or Jacobite at Edessa. It is this form of Aramaic, Syriac, that persists as the liturgical language of several Eastern churches, among them the Chaldean, Malabar, Malankarese, Maronite, and Syrian Jacobite churches. (*See* SYRIAC LANGUAGE AND LITERATURE.)

Modern Aramaic. Aramaic has persisted into modern times, being spoken in the west in isolated villages of the Anti-Lebanon regions north of Damascus in Syria (by Christians in Ma'lūla, by Moslems in Jubba'dīn and Bakh'a); and in the east in three areas [by Jacobite Christians in Ṭur 'Abdīn, by Jews and Nestorian Christians ("Assyrians") between the Lakes Urmia and Van in Kurdistan and Azerbaijan, by Chaldean Christians in the region north of Mosul]. Modern Aramaic is quite corrupt, having been heavily influenced by Kurdish, Turkish, and Arabic.

Bibliography: F. ROSENTHAL, *Die aramaistische Forschung seit Th. Nöldekes Veröffentlichungen* (Leiden 1939), basic. C. BROCKELMANN et al., "Aramäisch und Syrisch," *Handbuch der Orientalistik,* 3.2–3 (Leiden 1954) 135–204. W. BAUMGARTNER, "An Introduction to the Aramaic Part," *Lexicon in Veteris Testamenti Libros,* ed. L. H. KÖHLER (Grand Rapids 1958) 2: xxxiv–xlix. M. BLACK, "The Recovery of the Language of Jesus," NTSt 3 (1956–57) 305–313. A. DUPONT-SOMMER, *Les Araméens* (Paris 1949). H. FLEISCH, *Introduction à l'étude des langues sémitiques: Éléments de bibliographie* (Paris 1952) 67–87. H. L. GINSBERG, "Aramaic Dialect Problems," AmJSemLang 50 (1933–34) 1–9; 52 (1935–36) 95–103; "Aramaic Studies Today," JAm OrSoc 62 (1942) 229–238. F. ALTHEIM and R. STIEHL, *Die aramäische Sprache unter den Achaimeniden* (Frankfurt a. M. 1959–). G. GARBINI, "L'Aramaico antico," *Accad. N. dei Lincei, Memorie, scienze morale, ser.* 8, v.7, fasc. 1 (Rome 1956) 235–285.

[J. A. FITZMYER]

2. BIBLICAL

By the term Biblical Aramaic is meant the form of Aramaic, once called Chaldaic, that is used in certain passages of the original text of the OT. These passages, written in general between the second half of the 5th century B.C. (if the Ezra passages were composed at that time, as is commonly accepted) and the second quarter of the 2d century B.C. (the Daniel passages), are: Gn 31.47 (two words); Jer 10.11; Ezr 4.8–6.18; 7.12–26; and Dn 2.44–7.28.

Older Term. It had been the custom to speak of the Aramaic of the Bible and the Targums as "Chaldaic." Strictly speaking, this would be the correct term for the Aramaic used in the 1st millennium B.C. by the Chaldeans of Mesopotamia. *See* CHALDEANS (IN THE BIBLE). St. Jerome used it for the Aramaic of the Bible and the Targums, partly because it is said to be the language used by the "Chaldeans" in Dn 2.5 (where, however, the word Chaldeans means merely soothsayers) and partly because he thought that the Jews who returned to Palestine from the Babylonian Exile had brought this language back with them from Mesopotamia, which was at that time largely inhabited by

Aramaic-speaking Chaldeans. Actually, the fact that certain passages of the OT are composed in Aramaic is merely a manifestation of the widespread process whereby in the second half of the 1st millennium B.C. Aramaic supplanted, not only Hebrew in Palestine, but also the remnants of other older languages in Syria and Mesopotamia, while it was used as the lingua franca throughout the ancient Near East and the official chancery language of the Persian Empire. Biblical Aramaic, however, represents a somewhat late stage of this Official or Imperial Aramaic, as it is called, standing in general about midway between the Aramaic of the Elephantine papyri of the late 5th century B.C. and the Aramaic of the Dead Sea Scrolls from about the time of Christ.

Characteristics. There are some slight differences between the Aramaic of the Book of Ezra and that of the Book of Daniel. The former is more archaic and closer to the language of the Elephantine papyri, while the latter has traits in common with Middle Aramaic. Thus, with one exception, the suffix of the second person masculine plural is *-kōm* (as in the Elephantine papyri), whereas it is *-kōn* in Daniel (as in the Targums). The suffix of the third person masculine plural, *-hōm,* is found in Ezra, as it is in older Aramaic, but it is no longer used in Daniel.

The Aramaic passages of the OT are important from a linguistic viewpoint, inasmuch as their traditional vocalization, as preserved in the Masoretic Text, casts light on the pronunciation of the unvocalized texts written in Official Aramaic. Some of the more striking features of Biblical Aramaic, as contrasted with Biblical Hebrew, are: the absence of the reflexive-passive form of the verb, *nif'al,* for which a *hithpᵉ'ēl* form is substituted; the existence of a verbal form *hithpa'al* in place of the passive *pu'al;* the absence, on the other hand, of the *hithpa'ēl* form; and traces of a causative form of the verb in *š*- (in a few words borrowed from Akkadian), which is used in both an active and a passive sense. The normal causative form appears both as an *'af'ēl* (the later form) and as a *haf'el* (the older form, corresponding to the Hebrew *hif'îl*). The active participle is used very frequently in Biblical Aramaic, where it is employed to form both an imperfect and a present tense. Finally, the preposition *l*- is used not only to express the dative relationship, but also as the so-called sign of the accusative.

As distinct from general Official Aramaic, Biblical Aramaic has been considerably affected by Biblical Hebrew, not only in its vocabulary (particularly in religious terminology), but also, to some extent, in its vocalization. Together with general Official Aramaic, it contains many words borrowed from Akkadian and Persian (particularly terms used in political and legal administration) and a few words from Greek (names of musical instruments).

Bibliography: F. ROSENTHAL, *A Grammar of Biblical Aramaic* (Wiesbaden 1961). L. PALACIOS, *Grammatica aramaico-biblica* (Rome 1953). H. BAUER and P. LEANDER, *Grammatik des Biblisch-Aramäischen* (Halle 1927); *Kurzgefasste biblisch-aramäische Grammatik* (Halle 1929). H. L. STRACK, *Grammatik des Biblisch-Aramäischen* (6th ed. Munich 1921). H. H. ROWLEY, *The Aramaic of the O.T.* (Oxford 1929). G. R. DRIVER, "The Aramaic of the Book of Daniel," JBiblLit 45 (1926) 110–119, 323–325. H. L. GINSBERG, *Studies in Daniel* (New York 1948).

[J. M. SOLA-SOLE]

ARANY, JÁNOS, Hungary's greatest epic poet; b. Nagyszalonta, March 2, 1817; d. Budapest, Oct. 24, 1882. He was the son of a noble but impoverished Calvinist family with "a broken coat of arms." His pious father was his first teacher and destined his hymn-loving, gentle son for the ministry. From 1833 to 1836, with interruptions, Arany studied at the College of Debrecen and tried to make a living as a teacher, then as a traveling actor, but remorse and despair drove him home to his almost blind father, carrying all his property tied up in a handkerchief. In 1840 he was appointed notary in his home town and married Juliana Ercsey, the orphan daughter of a lawyer. His first epic poem, *Az elveszett alkotmány* (The Lost Constitution), written in hexameters, was a bitter satire on Hungary's outmoded feudal system and won him the prize of the Kisfaludy Society in 1846. Arany's most popular work, *Toldi* (1847), the first part of a trilogy, is a national epic based on the legends of a Herculean youth. The second part, *Toldi Szerelme* (1879, Toldi's Love), was written after the concluding part, *Toldi Estéje* (1854, Toldi's Eve). *Petőfi, the great lyric poet, was the first to recognize Arany's talent for treating national themes with great artistry in typically Hungarian form. Arany was elected to the Hungarian Parliament (1848), but after the failure of the revolution of 1848–49, he returned to his native town and, though depressed by the loss of his friend Petőfi and the collapse of his country, wrote the dramatic ballads that earned him the title of "the Shakespeare of the ballad." *Bolond Istók* (1850, Istok the Fool) is a poetic autobiography. Of his projected trilogy on Hun and Hungarian history, only the first part, *Buda halála* (Buda's Death), was completed. He was elected a member of the Hungarian Academy (1858), and from 1865 to 1877 he was its secretary. In this position he edited a translation of Shakespeare's works, to which he contributed *Midsummer Night's Dream, Hamlet,* and *King John.* The poems of his last years strike a most serene note; in form and concept they rival the finest lyric poetry of world literature. They are typically Hungarian and yet deeply rooted in the ideals of Western civilization.

Bibliography: A. JÁNOS, *Összes munkái,* 13 v. (Budapest 1900). F. RIEDL, *Arany János* (Budapest 1957). D. KERESZTURY, *Arany János* (Budapest 1937).

[O. J. EGRES]

ARATOR, a 6th-century Christian poet; b. Liguria, before 500; d. *c.* 550. He was an orphan, and was educated by Bp. Lawrence of Milan and the poet *Ennodius. He studied classical literature and rhetoric with Parthenius and became an advocate and careerist at the court of *Theodoric the Great in Ravenna. With the collapse of the Ostrogothic Kingdom in Italy *c.* 540, Arator retired and was ordained subdeacon in Rome under Pope *Vigilius. In 544 he published an epic poem *De Actibus Apostolorum* in 2,326 hexameters, modeled on the *Carmen Paschale* of *Sedulius, with three metric letters of dedication to Vigilius, an Abbot Florian, and his friend Parthenius, respectively. The poem was originally read to an audience in St. Peter-in-Chains and was popular during the Middle Ages; it is an amalgam of faulty prosody, uninspired rhetoric, excessive allegory, and the mystical interpretation of numbers. There are editions in PL 68:45–252 and in CSEL 72 (1951) by A. P. McKinlay.

Bibliography: P. DE LABRIOLLE, DHGE 3:1443–45. Raby ChrLP 117–120. Altaner 600–601. Dekkers CPL 1504–05.

[V. C. DE CLERCQ]

ARAÚJO, ANTÔNIO DE, Jesuit missionary in Brazil, linguist, and historian; b. São Miguel, Azores, 1566; d. Espíritu Santo, Brazil, 1632. He had already obtained the master's degree when in 1582 he entered the novitiate of the Society of Jesus at Bahia, Brazil. After ordination, he taught briefly in Bahia and was then assigned to missionary work among the Tupí Indians. Noteworthy were Araújo's apostolic zeal and his ability to master the Indian tongue to a point of perfection equal to that with which he used his native Portuguese. He was admired by his contemporaries also for the facility with which he adapted himself to living conditions among the Indians. In spite of an extremely active apostolic life, he found time to write his famed *Catecismo na lingoa brasilica no qual se contem a summa da doctrina christã* (Lisbon 1618; 2d ed. 1686; new ed. Leipzig, 1898), a catechetical work written in Tupí and later translated into other native languages. Araújo wrote also two historical treatises. The *Informação da entrada que se pode fazer da vila de São Paulo ao Grande Rio Pará* treats of one of the *bandeirante* expeditions led by Pero Domingues out of São Paulo through Brazil's northern hinterland to the Pará River. Written about 1625, it is considered one of the period's valuable historiographical works. A few years later, Araújo wrote the shorter *Relação dada perlo mesmo [Pero Domingues] sobre a viagem que de São Paulo fez ao Rio de S. Francisco* describing with more precision the route of the expedition and certain ethnographical details. These were first published in Brazil in 1937 by Serafim Leite.

Bibliography: S. LEITE, *Páginas da historía do Brasil* (São Paulo 1937).

[N. F. MARTIN]

ARAÚJO, FRANCISCO DE, Dominican bishop and theologian; b. Vérin, Spain, 1580; d. Madrid, March 19, 1664. Born of a noble family, he entered the Order of Friars Preachers at Salamanca and was professed in 1601. He taught in various houses of the order, including that of Burgos until 1617, when he became assistant to Pedro de Herrera at the University of Salamanca. In 1623 he succeeded Herrera in the chair of moral theology, a position that he held for 25 years. In 1648 he was consecrated bishop of Segovia, and he governed the see until 1656, when he retired to a Dominican house in Madrid. His writings include: *Commentarii in universam Aristotelis metaphysicam* (2 v. Burgos 1617; Salamanca 1631); *Opuscula tripartita* (Douai 1633); *Commentarii in primam, secundam et tertiam partem d. Thomae* (7 v. Salamanca 1635–47); and *Variae et selectae decisiones morales ad statum ecclesiasticum et civilem pertinentes* (Lyons 1664).

Bibliography: Quétif-Échard 2:609–611. Hurter Nomencl 2:5–7. P. MANDONNET, DTC 1.2:1729–30.

[J. C. WILLKE]

ARAUJO, JUAN DE, South American composer; b. Villafranca, Spain, *c.* 1648; d. Sucre, Bolivia, late 1714. As a boy he was brought to Lima, Peru, by his father, a civil functionary. There he studied music (probably with the cathedral chapelmaster) and prepared for the priesthood. While enrolled at San Marcos University he was banished from the city by the Count of Lemos (viceroy, 1667–72). He served briefly as chapelmaster at Panama but returned to Lima in the same post upon the Count's death. In both Panama and Lima, where he remained until 1676, he was "much applauded for the consummate distinction of his compositions." In 1680 he became chapelmaster at La Plata (now Sucre), Bolivia, seat of the archbishopric of Charcas. In his eventful 34 years there, he brought music to the highest point ever known in inland South America, bequeathing more than 200 compositions to the cathedral archive, most of them for eight, nine, or ten voices, frequently with the accompaniment of harp, organ, and other instruments. Examples of his genius survive also in the seminary library at Cuzco, Peru.

See also LATIN AMERICA, MUSIC IN.

Bibliography: R. M. STEVENSON, *The Music of Peru: Aboriginal and Viceroyal Epochs* (Washington 1960).

[R. M. STEVENSON]

ARAÚJO LIMA, PEDRO DE, viscount and marquis of Olinda, minister in the first empire of Brazil, and four times head of the Brazilian government in the second empire; b. Engenho Antas, Serinhaém, Pernambuco, Dec. 22, 1793; d. Rio de Janeiro, June 7, 1870. He received a degree in Canon Law in 1819 at the University of Coimbra. After returning to Brazil in 1821, he was elected deputy for Pernambuco to the Cortes in Lisbon, which he attended until the separation of Brazil in 1822. He was elected deputy to the general constitutional assembly of the new empire of Brazil and distinguished himself for his moderate attitudes as a member of the commission on the constitution. He served in the legislature of the first empire and held various ministerial positions under it and during the period of the regency. He was elected senator for his province on Sept. 5, 1837. On September 18 he was appointed minister of the empire and when Diogo Antônio *Feijó resigned as regent, on the following day, Araújo Lima temporarily took over the position. Working with Bernardo Pereira de *Vasconcelos, Minister of the Empire and of Justice, he created the Imperial Colégio de Pedro II and the Public Archive, now the National Archive. His regency had to put down the Farroupilha revolt in Rio Grande do Sul and also revolts in Bahia and Grão-Pará. When the great political parties of the empire, the conservative and the liberal, were organized Araújo Lima became one of the most respected leaders of the conservatives. During the second empire he was head of the government in 1848–49, 1857–58, 1862–64, and 1865–1866. In the last period, at the start of the War of the Triple Alliance against Paraguay, he supervised the repelling of the invaders from Rio Grande do Sul and the successful beginning of the invasion of enemy territory. As a member of the council of state to which he had been appointed in 1842, Araújo Lima continued to serve the empire until his death.

Bibliography: L. DA CÂMARA CASCUDO, *O Marquês de Olinda e seu tempo 1793–1870* (São Paulo 1938).

[H. VIANNA]

ARAÚJO VIANA, CÂNDIDO JOSÉ DE, Viscount and Marquis of Sapucaí, Brazilian professor, and imperial politician; b. Congonhas do Sabará (now Nova Lima), Minas Gerais, Sept. 15, 1793; d. Rio de Janeiro, Jan. 23, 1875. His real name was Cândido Cardoso Canuto da Cunha. He studied law at the University of Coimbra, receiving his degree in 1821. Upon returning to Brazil, he was appointed judge in the episcopal city of Mariana. As president of its municipal chamber, he participated in the acclamation of Emperor Pedro I in Minas, 1822. During the first empire he served in the legislature and held a number of administrative and judicial positions. In 1839 he was named professor of literature and science for the imperial family, becoming a friend of Emperor Pedro II, who later made him professor of literature, Portuguese, and Latin for his daughters. From 1841 to 1843 Araújo Viana was chief minister of the empire and as such countersigned the creation of the new Council of State, of which he was a member after 1850. Although he belonged to the Conservative party, he held no other posts as minister, owing to his well-known friendship with the Emperor. He was founding member of the Brazilian Historical and Geographical Institute and was its president from 1847 to 1875. On Dec. 2, 1854, he was made Viscount of Sapucaí; and on Oct. 15, 1872, promoted to marquis. Although he never collected his verses in book form, his poems "Violetas," written in 1861 on the death of his daughter, the godchild of the Emperor, is well known.

Bibliography: J. M. DE MACEDO, *Ano biográfico brasileiro,* 3 v. (Rio de Janeiro 1876) 1:103–113.

[H. VIANNA]

ARBELA, CHRONICLE OF. The ancient city of Arbela in Mesopotamia was renowned for its temple to Astarte, which became world famous after Alexander's victory over the Persian Darius in 331 B.C. Having been converted to Christianity under the martyrs Bps. John (d. November 343) and (St.) Abraham II (martyred Feb. 4, or 7 or 8, according to the Armenians, 344), its Christians were savagely persecuted by the Persian King Shapur II (309–379). It was originally the metropolitan See of Adiabene, but was united to *Nisibis and Mosul in the late 4th century and became a Nestorian center before the Arab domination.

The *Chronicle of Arbela* is a Syrian Acts of the Martyrs discovered and published by A. Mingana in 1907. It was written by Mĕšiḥā-Zĕkā, probably at Adiabene in the mid-6th century and covers the history of Christianity in Persia between 100 and 550. Recent scholarly investigation indicates that much of its information is legendary.

Bibliography: A. MINGANA, ed. and tr., *Sources syriaques* (Leipzig 1908) v.1. F. ZORELL, ed., "Chronica ecclesiae Arbelensis," *Orientalia Christiana* 8 (1926–27) 145–204, Lat. tr. E. SACHAU, *Die Chronik von Arbela* (AbhBerlAk 6; 1915). I. ORTIZ DE URBINA, "Intorno al valore storico della cronaca di Arbela," OrChr Per 2 (1936) 5–32. E. STOMMEL, LexThK² 1:820.

[F. X. MURPHY]

ARBIOL Y DIEZ, ANTONIO, Franciscan spiritual writer; b. Torellas (Spain), 1651; d. Saragossa, Jan. 31, 1726. Arbiol, who entered the Franciscans at Saragossa, was a brilliant teacher of philosophy and of theology, a celebrated preacher, and a prolific writer. He held various offices within as well as outside the order. In 1720 Philip V offered him the bishopric of Ciudad Rodrigo, but he refused. He died with a reputation for holiness. His writings are in the fields of theology, homiletics, asceticism, and mysticism. He defended the Ven. Mary of *Agreda, but was a strenuous adversary of the *Alumbrados and of Miguel de *Molinos. The list of his published works includes 33 items, some of which had as many as 10 editions, e.g., *Desengaños misticos* (Saragossa 1706), *Novenarios espirituales* (published posthumously, Saragossa 1928), *La familia regulada* (Saragossa 1715). Other works worth mentioning are: *Manuale sacerdotum* (Saragossa 1693), *Certamen Marianum Parisiense* (Saragossa 1698), *Mistica Fundamental* (Saragossa 1723). Some of his works, such as *Contra insanias de Molinos,* have never been edited. His mystical theology was inspired by SS. Bonaventure, Teresa of Avila, and especially John of the Cross.

Bibliography: J. HEERINCKX, "Les Écrits d'Antoine Arbiol, O.F.M.," ArchFrancHist 26 (1933) 315–342; DictSpirAscMyst 1:834–836.

[G. GÁL]

ARBOGAST OF STRASBOURG, ST., bishop; b. probably Aquitaine; d. near Strasbourg, mid-6th century (feast, July 21). It was his original intention to live as a hermit, and to that end he settled in a forest in Alsace. According to a later tradition, he was made bishop of *Strasbourg *c.* 673 through the influence of King *Dagobert II, who seems to have been his patron. As bishop, Arbogast was known for his simplicity and humility, and before his death he asked to be buried in a cemetery where only criminals had previously been interred. In the 11th century a magnificent church was erected on the site: but it was destroyed in the 16th century, and the relics of the saint were lost. He is the patron of the Diocese of Strasbourg. It should be noted that the ancient episcopal catalogues of the diocese, as well as inscriptions on parts of the cathedral built in the 6th century, assign his episcopate to *c.* 550.

Bibliography: ActSS July 5:168–179. UTO III, *Vita* in A. POSTINA, *Sankt Arbogast, Bischof von Strassburg* (2d ed. Strasbourg 1929). Butler Th Attw 3:158–159. Mercati-Pelzer DE 1:203. G. ALLMANG, DHGE 3:1462–63. Zimmermann KalBen 2:484–485.

[J. F. FAHEY]

ARBROATH, ABBEY OF, former Benedictine abbey of the Tironian congregation (*see* TIRON) situated in Angus, Scotland, within the ancient Diocese of Brechin, and now a ruin. It was founded by King William the Lion, Aug. 9, 1178, from the Abbey of Kelso, and dedicated to St. Thomas *Becket, whom the King may well have known in his younger days. Arbroath was richly endowed at its foundation, and later it became one of the wealthiest abbeys in Scotland. Among its many distinguished abbots were Bernard de Linton, who may have drafted the Scottish Declaration of Independence dispatched to Pope *John XXII from Arbroath, April 1320; John Gedy (1370–95); and Cardinal David Beaton, its last resident abbot (1524–36). After a series of commendatory abbots (*see* COMMENDATION) Arbroath was erected into a temporal lordship for the Marquis of Hamilton in 1608.

Bibliography: C. INNES and P. CHALMERS, eds., *Liber S. Thome de Aberbrothoc,* 2 v. (Edinburgh 1848–56). R. L. MACKIE and S. CRUDEN, *Arbroath Abbey* (Edinburgh 1954). Easson 58.

[L. MACFARLANE]

ARCADELT, JAKOB, Renaissance composer, master of the madrigal (also Arkadelt, Archadet, Harcadelt); b. Liège?, Belgium, *c.* 1504; d. Paris?, between 1562 and 1572. His Flemish nationality is attested in the 1539 records of the Julian Chapel at the Vatican (*Jacobus Flandrus magister Capellae*). By 1540 he was appointed to the Sistine Chapel, and he remained there until at least 1549. During the 1550s he was perhaps in Paris, where his chansons, earlier published only sporadically, were issued as collections after 1553. In his book of Masses (1557) he is called choirmaster of Cardinal Charles Lorraine (Duc de Guise), as well as *regius musicus* to the King of France. Since he is in the royal chapel records for 1562, but not in the next extant list, 1572, he probably died between these dates. Although Arcadelt composed motets, Lamentations, and Masses, his greatest importance rests with his chansons and madrigals, whose four-part species he brought to perfection. The madrigals are essentially diatonic works, displaying a sensitive awareness of the text, and are written in a judicious alternation of imitative and note-against-note polyphony. In them he first successfully infused the simple Italian forms with the artistic polyphony of his homeland.

Bibliography: A. EINSTEIN, *The Italian Madrigal,* tr. A. H. KRAPPE et al., 3 v. (Princeton 1949). W. KLEFISCH, *Arcadelt als Madrigalist* (Cologne 1938). Reese MusR.

[E. R. LERNER]

ARCADIANISM

A term applied in literature and art to genres in which shepherds (or persons impersonating them) are depicted as leading happy, carefree lives in lovely bucolic settings. The obvious nostalgia for a "lost" world of innocent joy relates Arcadianism to the literary search for Utopias (*see* UTOPIAN LITERATURE).

The word itself derives from the region of Arcady, the mountainous central part of the Greek Peloponnesus, inhabited in ancient times by shepherds and hunters, worshipers of the god Pan. The least intellectual part of Greece, Arcadia came to be identified with rustic simplicity. Almost indistinguishable from Arcadian literature is the pastoral, which is somewhat stylized; the bucolic is allied to these, but is more realistic. Arcadian literature began with the Greco-Sicilian poet Theocritus in the 3d century B.C. and was continued by Vergil, among others, in his *Eclogues* and *Georgics*.

The theme of the shepherd has roots far back in the past. Paris, son of Priam, King of Troy, had been brought up as a shepherd boy on Mt. Ida, and in his famous "judgment" had awarded the prize to Aphrodite, the goddess of Love. Aphrodite herself, in the guise of a shepherdess, seduced Anchises, King of Dardanus, and became the mother of Aeneas. Thus the shepherd motif figures in the origin of the Trojan War and in the legend of the founding of Rome, and the significance of this carried over from the ancient world into the Middle Ages; medieval knights earnestly traced their ancestry back to Trojan warriors.

Judaism and Christianity also made their contribution. Isaiah's prophecy, so strangely like Vergil's fourth *Eclogue*, of the Messiah who would feed his flock like a shepherd; Psalm 22(23); the shepherds at Bethlehem; Christ, the Good Shepherd; the Christian Pastor with his crozier—all gave a Christian flavor to the cult of the shepherd. Northern Italy, Spain, France, and England had a long medieval tradition of bucolic verse, which competed with the chivalric epics and romances, tales of war and *courtly love (*see* CHIVALRY; ROMANCE, MEDIEVAL). At the Renaissance, classical impulses softened the somewhat cruder bucolics into Arcadianism and the pastoral, and more sophisticated societies turned avidly to mock rusticity.

The first vernacular work in the Arcadian-pastoral convention was *Boccaccio's *Ameto* (1341), a mingling of poetry and allegory. Politian's *Favola di Orfeo* (1472) was the first dramatic pastoral. Before 1481 Sannazaro wrote the first pastoral romance, *Arcadia.* *Tasso's *Aminta* (1580) is a charming pastoral idyll. The *Pléiade, led by Ronsard, introduced Arcadian themes into France in the 16th century; Montemayor did the same in Spain with his pastoral novel *Diana* (*c.* 1559); and *Cervantes and Lope de *Vega both wrote in this genre.

Following *Sidney's *Arcadia* (1580), England produced a wealth of Arcadian and pastoral literature in the forms of novel, poetry, and drama. *Spenser made important allegorical use of the convention in *The Faerie Queen* (1589–96). In *Daphnaida* (1591), Spenser introduced the pastoral elegy, a form developed in some of the finest poetry of Milton, Shelley, and Arnold. Shakespeare delicately satirized Arcadianism in *As You Like It*.

Arcadianism had strong vogue in music and painting. Lully, Handel, and Gluck, among others, wrote operas on Arcadian themes, while Poussin, Watteau, and others popularized it in painting. The Arcadian dream played a role even in political thought, as is evident in the theories of Jean Jacques *Rousseau on the "golden age" and the "return to Nature." An inverted Arcadianism can be discerned in many sociological novels of rural life.

Bibliography: J. M. EDMONDS, tr., *Greek Bucolic Poets* (Loeb ClLib; New York 1928). E. K. CHAMBERS, "The English Pastoral," *Sir Thomas Wyatt and Some Collected Studies* (London 1933). G. HIGHET, *The Classical Tradition* (New York 1949). W. W. GREG, *Pastoral Poetry and Pastoral Drama* (London 1906; repr. New York 1959). J. E. Congleton, *Theories of Pastoral Poetry in England, 1684–1798* (Gainesville, Fla. 1952). W. EMPSON, *Some Versions of Pastoral* (New York 1960).

[A. M. CAVE]

ARCADIUS, ROMAN EMPEROR, from 383 to 408; b. *c.* 377; d. Constantinople, 408. Flavius Arcadius was the eldest son of Emperor *Theodosius I and Aelia Flaccilla. Proclaimed Augustus by his father in 383, he was left in Constantinople as sole ruler in the East in 394. Upon the death of Theodosius I (395), the administration of the empire was shared by Arcadius, who retained the East, and his younger brother, *Honorius I, in the West. Lacking both energy and judgment, Arcadius submitted to the schemes of his wife, Eudoxia (d. 404), whom he had married in 395, and those of two ministers, the prefect Rufinus (murdered in 395) and the eunuch Eutropius (executed in 399). Growing friction with the Western imperial administration and increasing difficulties with the barbarians troubled his reign. From 395 to 396 the Visigoth Alaric devastated Greece, while Gothic troops led by Gainas were in open revolt from 399 to 400 in support of the Arians in Constantinople.

Orthodox in his ecclesiastical policies, Arcadius prohibited assemblies of heretics, ordered the confiscation of pagan temples, and banished *Apollinarians; however, his religious zeal was motivated by caesaropapism. When the Patriarch of Constantinople, *John Chrysostom, denounced the frivolity of the court and of the Empress, the quarrel led to the disgrace and banishment of the patriarch and to a temporary success of Eudoxia's Arian policies. The banishment furthered the subordination of the patriarch to the emperor in the East. Arcadius was succeeded by his only son, *Theodosius II.

Bibliography: Stein-Palanque HistBEmp 1:225–253. Fliche-Martin 4:145–159. J. B. BURY, *A History of the Later Roman Empire,* 2 v. (London 1923; repr. pa. New York 1957) v.1. E. DEMOUGEOT, *De l'unité à la division de l'Empire romain, 395–410* (Paris 1950). C. BAUR, *John Chrysostom and His Time,* tr. M. GONZAGA, 2 v. (Westminster, Md. 1960–61).

[J. BRÜCKMANN]

ARCANUM, an encyclical letter of Leo XIII (Feb. 10, 1880) occasioned by the increasingly vehement demands that civil legislation be enacted even in Christian countries to loosen the bond of marriage. This Pope restated the Church's position that by divine law marriage is one and indissoluble, as manifested by the design of the Creator in uniting the first man and woman "in one flesh" (Gn 2.24). These necessary properties of the marriage bond were reaffirmed by Christ in all their pristine vigor. Men had always recognized the sacred and religious character of matrimony by reason of its divine institution. Christ not only deepened this conviction by blessing this union, but elevated it to the supernatural order by making of it a Sacrament of the New Covenant. Since it is the very contract between man and woman that constitutes the Sacrament, only the religious authority established by Christ to continue His mission, the Church, has a right to enact laws regulating marriage. Civil authority may issue only such decrees as affect the civil order without prejudice to the nuptial bond, and even in these limited areas the State must bow to the prior rights of the Church in the event of conflict. While their marital status grants the partners many privileges, it imposes corresponding duties—to each other and to the fruit of their union. Relations between husband and wife must ever be founded upon true conjugal love that will never deprive their children of the love and care that is their right. Children will in turn be moved to render their duties of filial respect and obedience gladly. The Church's marriage laws have ever been intended to be and have in fact been a boon to both the individual and to society. She has always safeguarded the sanctity of marriage despite all opposition. It is clear that all bishops must instruct the faithful committed to their care, concerning the sacredness of the marriage bond. Moreover the faithful must be warned of the dangers inherent in mixed marriages. Lastly, no pastor of souls may abandon those involved in illicit unions but should encourage them to obtain the graces of the Sacrament.

Bibliography: LEO XIII, "Arcanum" (Encyclical, Feb. 10, 1880) ActSSed 12 (1879) 385–402, Eng. *The Church Speaks to the Modern World,* ed. É. H. GILSON (Garden City, N.Y. 1954) 86–113. J. HUSSLEIN, comp., *Social Wellsprings,* 2 v. (Milwaukee 1940–42) 1:24–46.

[S. KARDOS]

ARCHANGEL OF PEMBROKE, Capuchin Friar Minor, one of the first directors of Angélique *Arnauld; b. William Barlow, Slebech, Pembrokeshire, *c.* 1568; d. Paris, Aug. 24, 1632. He was the second son of John Barlow, a prominent Catholic in Wales, and the grandson of Roger Barlow, a noted discoverer, whose brother Bp. William *Barlow was one of the leaders of the English Reformation. Since William wished to practice religion freely, he escaped to France and there joined the Capuchins on April 4, 1587. He was in Flanders after his ordination, but returned to France *c.* 1594, and was appointed successively novice-master, guardian, and definitor. He was well known in religious circles in Paris, and he worked effectively for the reform of convent life, notably at Port-Royal. In 1607, Maffeo Barberini, nuncio in Paris (later *Urban VIII), included Archangel's name on a list of candidates considered suitable for the office of bishop in England. In 1614 Archangel led a contingent of Capuchins on a missionary enterprise to Brazil. In 1624, his help was enlisted in an effort to convert Hugo *Grotius.

Bibliography: J. M. CLEARY, *The Catholic Recusancy of the Barlow Family of Slebech in Pembrokeshire in the XVI and XVII Centuries* (Cardiff 1956). L. COGNET, *La Réforme de Port-Royal* (Paris 1950). *Lexicon Capuccinum* (Rome 1951) 120–121 where a standard bibliog. is given. CASSIAN [REEL] OF STANLEY, *Fr. Archangel of Pembroke and the Conversion of Grotius* (Rome 1964).

[C. REEL]

ARCHANGELA GIRLANI, BL., Carmelite; b. Eleanora, at Trino, 1460; d. Mantua, Jan. 25, 1494 (feast, Feb. 13). Her father resisted her desire to become a religious but finally agreed to allow her to enter a Benedictine convent of relaxed observance near Trino. This plan having been thwarted, she eventually joined the *Carmelites at Parma (1477), who led the stricter life she desired. Soon after she was made prioress, the *Gonzaga family requested that she be sent to Mantua to found a new convent. She was noted for her austerity, charity, and spirit of prayer and for reputed mystical experiences. Her body was found to be incorrupt 3 years after her death. Her cult was confirmed in 1864.

Bibliography: ALBAREI, *Notice sur la vie de la bse. Archangela Girlani* (Poitiers 1865). Butler Th ATTw 1:327–328.

[N. G. WOLF]

ARCHANGELO OF CALATAFIMI, BL., hermit, Franciscan observant, b. Archangelo Placenza, Calatafimi, Sicily, 1380; d. Alcamo, July 26, 1460 (feast, July 30). Desirous of a hermit's life, he sought solitude as a young man but his reputation for sanctity and the miracles attributed to him attracted many seeking advice. He fled to Alcamo where he revived and organized a hospice for the poor. When *Martin V required all hermits in Sicily to return to the world or to accept religious life in an approved order he became a Franciscan of the Observance at Palermo. He was sent back to the hospice at Alcamo to make it a house of his order, and later was made provincial of the Sicilian Observants. His cult was approved in 1836.

Bibliography: A. GIOIA, *Il beato Arcangelo Placenza da Calatafimi* (Palermo 1926). LÉON DE CLARY, *Lives of the Saints and Blessed of the Three Orders of St. Francis,* 4 v. (Taunton, Eng. 1885–87) v.2. Butler Th Attw 3:214–215.

[N. G. WOLF]

ARCHBISHOP

This ancient designation for certain major ecclesiastics has undergone, in the course of centuries, changes of meaning in the East and West that make it difficult to explain. Originally, as its etymology suggests, it designated a superior or chief bishop and was applied to bishops who presided over the greater sees. It was not infrequently in the East a title for those who later were called more technically *patriarchs.

In the West (Latin Patriarchate) at the present time the title is closely allied to that of metropolitan, the head of an ecclesiastical *province (or regional group of dioceses), and it may be said that today in the West every metropolitan is an archbishop. This basic correlation seems to be insinuated in the wording of CIC c.272, which declares that "a metropolitan or archbishop presides over an ecclesiastical province," and by CIC c.275, which provides that a metropolitan within a period of 3 months from his appointment must ask for the *pallium, "which signifies archiepiscopal power."

It is by no means true, however, that everyone with the title of archbishop is a metropolitan. We may distinguish three other uses of the term. It is used (1) for the ordinary of a diocese that is outside any ecclesiastical province but itself is not a metropolitan center and hence has no suffragan dioceses. Such for instance was the Archdiocese of Washington, D.C., from 1947, when it was severed from the Province of Baltimore, to 1965, when it was made a metropolitan center. The reason for this somewhat unusual disposition is sought in the civil importance of the place or in its former ecclesiastical prestige. The term is used (2) for an ordinary who personally has merited the honor and is so designated by the Holy See. In this case the diocese itself does not change its ecclesiastical status; i.e., it remains within the province to which it already belongs and the successors in that see do not succeed to the title of archbishop. For example, in the U.S. in 1964 the ordinaries of Cleveland, of Mobile-Birmingham, and of Erie, Pa., all had been named by the Holy See "personal archbishops" (*ad personam*). Finally, the term is used (3) for nonresidential bishops ("titulars") who are raised to the dignity because of their special functions as members of the Roman *Curia or of the papal diplomatic corps (e.g., apostolic delegates) or because of exceptional service as coadjutor or auxiliary bishops.

With regard to the powers and rights of an archbishop who is a metropolitan *see* ARCHDIOCESE. For archbishops who head archdioceses that are not metropolitan centers, the dignity is one of a certain immediate dependence on the Holy See. In the case of ordinaries who are "personal" archbishops and of titular archbishops, the title confers a special honor (the title itself, precedence in ecclesiastical gatherings and liturgical functions, generally the possession of the pallium and the right to the metropolitan cross), rather than any ecclesiastical power.

See also BISHOP (IN THE BIBLE); BISHOP (IN THE CHURCH); BISHOP, AUXILIARY; BISHOP, COADJUTOR; METROPOLITAN (CANON LAW); ORDINARIES, ECCLESIASTICAL.

Bibliography: E. RÖSSER, LexThK² 3:1066–67. K. MÖRSDORF, *ibid.* 7:373–375. E. VALTON, DTC 5.2:1704–05. A. S. POPEK, *The Rights and Obligations of Metropolitans* (CUA CLS 260; Washington 1947). **Illustration credit:** Photo Archives Maria Laach.

[S. E. DONLON]

Archbishop, detail of an ivory panel, c. 980, in Fitzwilliam Museum, Cambridge. The pallium, symbol of his archiepiscopal authority, is clearly visible over his chasuble.

ARCHBISHOP (ORIENTAL RITES)

The title of archbishop is given in the Eastern Churches to several degrees of the hierarchy: archbishops to whom metropolitans are subject, the heads of archdioceses that have no subject suffragan bishop, and bishops upon whom this title has been conferred as an honorific distinction. Metropolitans in the Eastern rites are generally not styled archbishops (although among Catholics the Latin-rite usage has often been followed), but they are included in the canonical norms governing archbishops and other metropolitans (ClerSanc cc.315–339). The principal holders of the title archbishop in the Eastern Churches are: Archbishop Major (ClerSanc cc.324–339), Catholicos (ClerSanc c.335.1), Maphrian (ClerSanc c.335.2), and Metropolitan (cc.215–324).

Archbishop Major. All bishops to whom other bishops were subject were originally called archbishops. Later the title was given to all patriarchs and also to the heads of some other Churches that did not acquire the patriarchal title but possessed quasi-patriarchal jurisdiction (*see* PATRIARCH). There is one such archbishop in the Catholic Church, the Byzantine-rite Ukrainian archbishop of Lvov and metropolitan of Galicia (Western Ukraine), recognized as such by Pope Paul VI in 1963. Among the dissident Orientals there are the archbishops of Greece and Cyprus. The Byzantine-rite dissident patriarchs grant this title to the heads of their semi-independent exarchies in North and South America, Western Europe, and South Africa (*see* EXARCHY).

Archbishops major enjoy patriarchial rights in nearly all respects, the privileges that are an immediate reflection of the patriarchal dignity. The archbishop is elected by a synod of the bishops of his territory, and after confirmation by the pope, he is enthroned. Besides the jurisdiction he enjoys as metropolitan over one of the provinces of his territory, he presides at all gatherings of his bishops. *See* JURISDICTION (CANON LAW). The archbishop consecrates and enthrones the metropolitans, who in turn consecrate the bishops of their respective provinces. He supervises metropolitans in the fulfillment of their duties, admonishes them, and perhaps denounces them to the Roman pontiff if stricter measures are to be taken. The archbishop addresses encyclical letters to all bishops and other hierarchs (ordinaries) of his Church, who are obliged to have them read and explained to the faithful. He promulgates and authentically interprets the laws of the synods. His power of granting matrimonial dispensations is the same as that of patriarchs. In the government of his territory he is assisted by a permanent synod of four bishops, or at least by a council of two bishops, whose consent he needs in all matters of importance. Affairs that are of greater consequence are resolved by the archbishop in a synod of all the bishops.

The archbishop has an ecclesiastical tribunal that accepts appeals from metropolitan tribunals. While patriarchs can erect eparchies (dioceses) and exarchies, an archbishop can establish, change, or suppress only exarchies, having obtained the prior approval of the Roman pontiff.

Catholicos. The chief bishops of certain Eastern Churches received the title of *catholicos because they made use of the universal (*katholikos*) jurisdiction of a patriarch and were considered delegates of a patriarch for all matters whatsoever. The title of patriarch was later assumed by them when the bond with the mother Church was severed. Such was the case with the head of the Nestorian Church in Persia when his subjection to the patriarch of Antioch was set aside (544). The chief bishop of the Armenian Church was styled catholicos even earlier. The Syrian (Monophysite) metropolitan of Mossul, the representative of the Syrian patriarch of Antioch in Persia, was titled catholicos of the East.

Today there is no Catholic prelate with this title who is not also a patriarch, e.g., the catholicos-patriarch of Cilicia of the Armenians and the catholicos-patriarch of Babylonia of the Chaldeans. They all enjoy patriarchal rights and prerogatives. Among the dissidents, this title is given to the catholicos-patriarch of the Byzantine rite in Georgia (U.S.S.R.); to the three Armenian catholicoses of Echmiadzin (Soviet Armenia), Constantinople, and Jerusalem; and to the Nestorian catholicos-patriarch of Babylonia (Seleucia-Ctesiphon), now residing in the U.S.

Catholicoses who do not enjoy the dignity of patriarchs are equal in their rights and duties to the archbishops major.

Maphrian. The title of maphrian is a degree in the ecclesiastical hierarchy developed in the West Syrian Church. When the Monophysite (Jacobite) Church was divided into two parts—one within the Byzantine Empire, the other in the empire of the Sassanides in Persia—the Syrian patriarch of Antioch appointed the foremost metropolitan of Persia as his delegate, to whom he ceded the right to appoint and consecrate metropolitans and bishops and to bless the holy chrism, and who was therefore called the maphrian, the source of ecclesiastical authority. Being the chief hierarch of his Church after the patriarch, the maphrian was entitled to consecrate and enthrone the patriarch of Antioch. The title is conferred today only among the dissidents on the catholicos or maphrian of India, the chief bishop of the Monophysite (Jacobite) Christians in south India.

The maphrian is equal to an archbishop major but remains subject to the authority of the patriarch.

Metropolitan. The bishops of the Eastern Catholic Churches who head ecclesiastical provinces enjoy rights and duties identical with those of *metropolitans of the Latin rite, with one exception: the metropolitans of the Western Church have no official right to consecrate the bishops of their province, since they are directly appointed by the pope, who designates the consecrating bishop. The consecration of Oriental-rite bishops is reserved to the metropolitan. In patriarchates in which ecclesiastical provinces do not exist, the patriarch is the consecrating prelate. The Catholic Eastern patriarchates are too small to be divided into provinces. There exist resident metropolitans and archbishops but without suffragan bishops, and all bishops, regardless of hierarchical rank, are under the immediate and direct authority of the patriarch. The patriarchs therefore exercise all metropolitan rights until ecclesiastical provinces can be reestablished.

While the CIC accords the same rank to archbishop-metropolitans and archbishops without suffragan bishops and does not grant precedence to resident archbishops or metropolitans over titular archbishops, Oriental Canon Law assigns resident metropolitans precedence over other metropolitans and archbishops, whether they are resident bishops without suffragans or only titular ones.

Among Oriental dissidents the title of metropolitan is sometimes the style for resident bishops, or it is given to the bishops of some cities, or it is the title of the head of an autonomous Church, as the metropolitan of Warsaw (Poland), Tirana (Albania), and Prague (Czechoslovakia). Ecclesiastical provinces under metropolitans are in existence today only in the Rumanian Orthodox Patriarchate.

Bibliography: A. COUSSA, *Epitome praelectionum de iure ecclesiastico orientali* (Grottaferrata 1948) suppl. (1958) 1:187–196, 287–291. Pospishil PersOr 152–160. M. RIZZI, "De personis iuxta novum ius orientale," *Apollinaris* 31 (1958) 89–101. M. WOJNAR, "The Code of Oriental Canon Law De Ritibus Orientalibus and De Personis," *Jurist* 19 (1959) 427–437. A. WUYTS, "Il diritto delle persone nella nuova legislazione per la Chiesa Orientale," OrChrPer 24 (1958) 175–201. *Oriente Cattolico* (Rome 1962).

[V. J. POSPISHIL]

ARCHCHANCELLOR, the title given in the Middle Ages to a high ecclesiastical official who also directed the royal chancery. The Merovingian Franks continued the late Roman practice of having lay persons, *referendarii,* prepare royal documents and letters. In Carolingian times, when the educated were predominantly clerics and when civil and religious administration were closely related, priest members of the court chapel also prepared the royal documents. At their head was the first chaplain, called (after 825) archchaplain, who was the highest church dignitary at the court of the Franks. At the time of *Charlemagne and *Louis the Pious, an untitled chief chancellor oversaw the actual writing of documents. In 856 *Louis the German put the document-preparing organization directly under the archchaplain. The combined office was given to Abp. Liudhard of Mainz in 870. Under the Ottonian emperors, the office was attached to the see of *Mainz and the title archchancellor commonly applied to it. After 1031 the archchancellor was the archbishop of Cologne, who also fulfilled this office for the Roman Church during the 11th century. Under *Henry III (1039–56) the archbishop of Besançon was archchancellor; after 1157 under the Hohenstaufen, the archbishop of Vienne; after 1308, the archbishop of Trier. As the office of archchaplain disappeared in the 11th century, a distinction was made between the chancellor, who directed the work of chancery personnel, and the chaplain, who directed clerics attached to the royal *chapel in their spiritual functions. In the 12th century the chancery became an independent institution. As archchancellor in the 9th century, the archbishop of Mainz had a definite influence on chancery procedure, as did the archbishop of Cologne to some extent during the 11th and 12th centuries. The title archchancellor was applied analogously to a position established for the three spiritual electors of the empire by *Charles IV in the *Golden Bull of 1356. The abbot of Fulda was designated archchancellor of the empress. The position remained in later years only as a title that accorded its possessor certain honors in court ceremonial.

Bibliography: L. PERRICHET, *La Grande chancellerie de France des origines à 1328* (Paris 1912). P. F. KEHR, "Die Kanzlei Ludwigs des Deutschen," AbhBerlAk (1932) fasc. 1. L. GROSS, *Die Geschichte der Reichshofkanzlei von 1559 bis 1806* (Vienna 1933). H. W. KLEWITZ, "Cancellaria," DeutschArch 1 (1937) 44–79. F. HAUSMANN, *Reichskanzlei und Hofkapelle unter Heinrich V und Konrad III* (Stuttgart 1956). J. FLECKENSTEIN, *Die Hofkapelle der deutschen Könige* (Stuttgart 1959–).

[W. H. WALLAIK]

ARCHCONFRATERNITY OF PRAYER FOR ISRAEL, a spiritual association established by the *Congregation of Notre Dame de Sion at the request of the laity who wished to join their prayers formally with those of the sisters for the intention of promoting a better understanding between Jews and Christians. The association was founded in 1905 and raised to the status of an archconfraternity by Pius X in 1909. Its canonical headquarters are in Jerusalem, and branch confraternity centers are located in many countries. These centers work with the local Jewish community and organize documentary libraries specializing in Biblical studies: Judeo-Christian relations; Jewish history, religion, and culture; material on social problems such as anti-Semitism; as well as Catholic information for non-Catholics. The centers also provide lectures by Catholic and Jewish speakers who discuss problems from both viewpoints and seek to bring about mutual understanding of liturgy, rites, religious feasts, etc. In addition, educators conduct scholastic courses in many parts of the world.

In the U.S. 55,390 members have been enrolled in the archconfraternity since 1934. The U.S. center is in Kansas City, Mo., and is called Ratisbonne Center after the founders of the Congregation of Notre Dame de Sion, the brothers Marie Alphonse *Ratisbonne and Marie Théodore *Ratisbonne, French Jewish converts of the 19th century. *At the Crossroads* is the quarterly publication of the Ratisbonne Center.

There is a connection between the Catholic Guild of Israel and the Archconfraternity of Prayer for Israel. During World War I, Catholic publications pointed out the need in Britain for a society of some kind sponsored by Catholics for the purpose of aiding the Jewish people. Bede *Jarrett, OP, indicated that such a group was, in fact, already in existence, namely, the London center of the archconfraternity. With this center at the core, priests, laymen, and the sisters of the Congregation of Our Lady of Sion worked together, organizing meetings, street preaching, and founding a library. This activity was carried on under the name of the Catholic Guild of Israel. World War II scattered the members of the guild. There have been recent attempts made by the sisters to reorganize it, and in 1962 a center for Biblical and Jewish Studies was established in London by the sisters of Our Lady of Sion in the name of the Catholic Guild of Israel.

[M. MC DONNELL]

ARCHDEACON. Although the title of archdeacon is first referred to by St. Optatus of Milevis (4th century), from the 3d century the bishop would select one of the deacons (not necessarily the senior) to assist him in both the liturgy and administration of the diocese. The office grew in importance as the amount of administration grew, so that by the 5th century the archdeacon was next in importance to the bishop, whom he frequently succeeded. Although at first there was only one, from the 9th century additional archdeacons were appointed (first in France, later elsewhere) within a diocese; they were delegates of the bishop in the areas into which the diocese was divided for administrative purposes. They gradually increased in power and obtained first a share in the bishop's jurisdiction, then independent jurisdiction in courts of their own. Their heyday was in the 12th century; thereafter a succession of councils, culminating in Trent, restricted their power, while as a counterblast to it, bishops appointed their own vicars-general. After the Reformation the English Church did not revive this institution, although it continues to exist in the Anglican Church. In Ireland archdeacon is the honorific title of the second dignitary of the diocesan chapter.

See also DEACON.

Bibliography: A. AMANIEU, DDC 1:948–1004. G. W. O. ADDLESHAW, *The Beginnings of the Parochial System* (St. Anthony's Hall Publications 3; London 1953); *The Development of the Parochial System from Charlemagne (768–814) to Urban II (1088–1099)* (*ibid.* 6; London 1954).

[B. FORSHAW]

ARCHDIOCESE

In the Latin Patriarchate the archdiocese is a *diocese whose bishop is immediately dependent upon the Roman pontiff. Generally such a diocese is the center of a province or metropolitan area, which is composed of the archdiocese and several suffragan dioceses: occasionally such a diocese stands by itself outside the provincial structure. Thus in the U.S. in 1964 there were 28 archdioceses, 27 of which were provincial centers (Atlanta, Baltimore, Boston, Chicago, Cincinnati, Denver, Detroit, Dubuque, Hartford, Indianapolis, Kansas City, Kans., Los Angeles, Louisville, Milwaukee, Newark, New Orleans, New York City, Omaha, Philadelphia, Portland, Ore., St. Louis, St. Paul, San Antonio, San Francisco, Santa Fe, Seattle, and the Byzantine Rite Province of Philadelphia). Only one, the Archdiocese of Washington, D.C., was not a metropolitan center. This diocese was separated in 1947 from the Province of Baltimore and made immediately dependent upon the Holy See; in 1965 it became a provincial center.

This article confines its attention to the metropolitan center in its relationship to the province and to the suffragan dioceses, and to the reasons for this structural form in the Church.

The relationship to the province and to the individual suffragan dioceses is most easily treated by citing the rights and duties that the *archbishop has in the present Canon Law. It may be noted that there is no uniformity in the number of dioceses grouped within a province; thus, in the U.S., the number of suffragan dioceses within a province varies from nine (in the Province of St. Paul) to one (in the Province of Washington, D.C.).

In regard to the province as a whole, the archbishop's principal duties are found in CIC cc.284 and 292. Canon 284 directs that the metropolitan, after hearing all who may attend the provincial council with deliberative vote, choose the place for its sessions. It is the archbishop's right also to convoke the council, which is to be held at least every 20 years (CIC c.283), and to preside at its sessions. Canon 292 places on the metropolitan the obligation of arranging every 5th year a conference of the ordinaries of the province to discuss the problems of the Church in their region and to prepare the agenda for the next provincial council.

In regard to the individual dioceses and bishops of his province, the archbishop's functions are listed in CIC c.274. The principal ones are: (1) to observe the doctrine and discipline of the suffragan dioceses and in case he notes any abuses to report these to the Holy See; (2) if the local ordinary has neglected to do so, to conduct a canonical *visitation of the suffragan diocese after receiving approval from the Holy See. During such visitation he is empowered to preach, hear confessions, absolve from reserved cases, make inquiries into the life and conduct of clerics, delate to the ordinary for correction reprehensible clerics, punish very grave crimes or insults against his person or his retinue. Other rights are: (3) to celebrate pontifical functions (i.e., liturgical functions in which the insignia of crosier and miter are required) in all churches of a suffragan diocese, to bless the people, to have the metropolitan cross carried before him; (4) to receive appeals from definitive and certain interlocutory decrees of the courts in the suffragan diocese.

From this enumeration it is clear that the archdiocese and its bishop have little right to interfere in the ordinary pastoral direction of the local bishop; in fact there is little that the archbishop can do ex officio except report abuses to the Holy See. Outside the time of a visitation, which is in each instance to be approved by the pope, he cannot exercise doctrinal or disciplinary functions within the territory of a suffragan. This very limited surveillance is considered by most theologians a regular and permanent participation of the powers of the Holy See and derived not from any immediately divine law but from ecclesiastical law. The Church has for centuries found this grouping of dioceses within provinces under the leadership of one designated archdiocese a useful instrument for safeguarding order and preventing fragmentation that might ensue were all dioceses subjected only and immediately to the Holy See.

In the Eastern patriarchates the prestige of the *patriarch throughout the region subject to him has tended to absorb the metropolitan structure, though in recent times there appears to be a tendency to restore the province as a functioning unit. In these patriarchates the metropolitan is subject to his patriarch and does not, as in the Western Patriarchate, immediately depend on one who is at the same time Western patriarch and supreme pontiff.

The origins of the archdiocese and the metropolitan arrangement are hard to fix in time. It would seem that such intermediate groupings—between the individual local Churches or dioceses and the Church universal—emerged as recognized units at least in the 3d century, and many trace the metropolitan (as well as the patriarchal) divisions back to the special prestige enjoyed by certain Churches from the first postapostolic generations. Thus the grouping arises out of a combination of factors: some embedded in the Church's own nature, some in the historical development from apostolic times of the Church in a given area, some in the politico-geographical conditions that prevailed in the world in which the Church began its corporate life.

See also BISHOP (IN THE BIBLE); BISHOP (IN THE CHURCH); COUNCILS, CANON LAW OF; METROPOLITAN (CANON LAW); ORDINARIES, ECCLESIASTICAL.

Bibliograhpy: K. MÖRSDORF, LexThK² 7:373–375. E. RÖSSER, *ibid.* 3:1066–67. E. VALTON, DTC 5.2:1704–05. A. S. POPEK, *The Rights and Obligations of Metropolitans* (CUA CLS 260; Washington 1947).

[S. E. DONLON]

ARCHELAUS, the son of *Herod the Great and Malthace of Samaria. Archelaus ruled as ethnarch of Judea from 4 B.C. to A.D. 6. Herod's last will had named him king, with his younger brother *Herod Antipas and his half brother *Philip as tetrarchs subordinate to him. Immediately after Herod's death, however, Archelaus had taken certain actions that suggested he was anticipating Augustus's required confirmation and thus usurping the royal power, and he was therefore challenged before Augustus by rival factions of his family, by the Roman procurator of Syria, by the Jews, and by the Greek cities of the kingdom. Augustus divided the kingdom among the three sons of Herod; Archelaus was made ethnarch of Judea, Samaritis, and Idumea. He was ruler of Judea when the Holy Family returned from Egypt (Mt 2.22). Archelaus divorced his first wife, Mariamme, to marry his half brother Alexander's widow, Glaphyra. In A.D. 6, in response to grievances represented by Jewish and Samaritan leaders, Augustus deposed him and entrusted his territory to a procurator. Archelaus died in exile in Vienne, probably before A.D. 18.

Bibliography: J. BLINZLER, LexThK² 1:822–823. V. CAVALLO, EncCatt 1:1798. EncDictBibl 128–129. A. H. M. JONES, *The Herods of Judaea* (Oxford 1938) 156–168. W. OTTO, "Herodes," Pauly-Wiss RE suppl.2 (1913) 191–200; sep. pub. (Stuttgart 1913) 165–174.

[J. P. M. WALSH]

ARCHEOLOGY, I (PREHISTORIC)

The science and art of the reclamation and interpretation of material traces of man's cultural activities in the past. These material traces are usually understood to consist of artifacts—the things men made—but they include also the so-called nonartifactual materials or things directly consumed or utilized by men. By accepted but not very logical practice, prehistoric archeology deals with the artifactual and nonartifactual remains of preliterate men, leaving concern with materials from the literate levels of culture history to "historic" archeology. The analysis and interpretation of the immediate biological traces of men themselves, usually in the form of fossilized human bones, is the business of physical *anthropology or human paleontology rather than of archeology.

This article presents first a brief history of the development of prehistoric archeology and a consideration of its locus within general scholarly interests. A second concern is the natural world in which preliterate men lived, the span of time involved, and the means used to establish a chronology of prehistoric time. Third, the factors of discovery and preservation, along with some aspects of field procedure and laboratory analysis, are considered. Finally, there is a brief account of what the now available evidence appears to reveal of human history before the beginnings of writing.

History and Locus of Prehistoric Archeology

There has been a conventional but overgeneralized and too facile tendency to see two distinct streams in the history of archeological development (sometimes this more apparent than real dichotomy is marked by the variant spellings, "archeology" vs. "archaeology").

Humanist Background. The older stream ("archaeology"?) arose within the intellectual milieu of the later Renaissance, and reflected a concern with the high cultural achievements of Greece, Rome, and the Bible lands. The proponents of this kind of archeology came to flourish within university departments of classics and Biblical history and within fine arts museums. A few spectacular but non-Western artistic manifestations, such as ancient Chinese bronzes, vases, and paintings, were given attention also.

Evolutionist Impetus. The second stream arose within the great burst of evolutionary interest of the 19th century. There were, to be sure, the germs of fascination with the pre-Roman histories of supposed national ancestors (such as the Celts, Gauls, and Germans) even before the time of Darwin and his contemporaries. Nevertheless, the worldwide concerns of this second stream were set primarily by social evolutionists such as Herbert *Spencer, Lewis Henry Morgan, and Friedrich *Engels. The ideas of these men developed within a milieu of increasing anthropogeographical and ethnographical interest and at a time when such geologist-naturalists as Louis *Agassiz and Charles *Lyell had already laid the foundations of geological and paleontological understandings.

To the degree in which the two intellectual foundations of archeology were ever distinct and separate, which of course they were actually not, there was useful complementation. The "humanists" of the first stream were little interested in preliterate or "peripheral" societies; the "scientists" of the second stream were fascinated with them. Even today, prehistoric archeologists are most likely to be found in university departments of anthropology and in natural history museums.

Development of Classification. Already in 1819, in an attempt to bring order to the vastly increasing collections of the Danish National Museum, Christian Thomsen formulated the famous three-age system of prehistoric classification on typological grounds alone, distinguishing (1) the old stone age, characterized by chipped stone tools, (2) the new stone age, characterized by tools of ground stone and by pottery, and (3) the metal age, characterized by the appearance of copper, bronze, and presently iron tools. Thomsen's first two ages were subsequently given more pretentious neoGrecized names, paleolithic and neolithic (which some present authorities believe have outlived their usefulness). It was in 1859, however, the same year as the publication of Darwin's *The Origin of Species,* that the British Royal Society accepted Boucher de Perthes's claim to have found prediluvian chipped stone tools in association with the fossils of now extinct animals. From that date onward, prehistoric archeology continued to develop in conjunction with increasing sophistication of understanding of the geological and paleontological record. It is now known that Thomsen's typologically based and partly intuitive arrangement corresponds with the real sequence as established by geological stratigraphy. Chipped stone tools were made and used by men for hundreds of thousands of years before ground stone tools and pottery were devised. The use of metal came later, although not by too many thousands of years.

In its formative years, prehistoric archeology remained primarily a western European or North American preoccupation. Because of the great activity of prehistorians in certain regions of France, many type-tool names have French place-name derivations. Following the first quarter of the 20th century, however, prehistoric archeologists began to turn their attention somewhat more to Africa and Asia. For reasons of convenience and economy of operations, western Europe and parts of the U.S. remain most carefully investigated, but it is at last becoming possible to have a world view—however incomplete—of mankind's preliterate past.

Changing Environments and Time

The title of Reginald Daly's classic account of the Pleistocene period is *The Changing World of the Ice Age.* From new evidence briefly noted below, there is reason to believe that the Pleistocene began almost 2,000,000 years ago (*see* EARTH). Furthermore, the fluctuating climatic and environmental nature of this last geological period may not yet be ended. The Pleistocene has been marked so far by at least three major phases of extended continental glaciation in the northern latitudes (with at least four major phases—named Günz, Mindel, Riss, and Würm—evidenced in the Alps). Each of these glacial phases brought about marked changes in the world's climatic and environmental patterns, while the interglacial phases (or in-between-times), which may have been of longer cumulative duration than were the glacial phases, witnessed other types of climatic and environmental patterns. During some of the interglacial phases, a given region in, for example, the middle latitudes might be warmer and perhaps drier than at present. During the glacial phases, the same region might be colder and wetter. During a glacial phase, huge quantities of the world's water balance were tied up in the ice sheets; during the maxima of the interglacial phases, the sea level stood much higher than it does today. Climates and environments responded to these great changes, and the natural ranges of plants and animals were distributed and often completely destroyed. Some species—mastodons, cave bears, saber-toothed tigers, giant elks—eventually became extinct during the course of the Pleistocene. There has recently been a marked increase in knowledge of the changing climatic and environmental phases of the Pleistocene based on borings made of the ocean bottoms and of the beds of lakes and swamps. These borings yield a record, in stratigraphic order, of the fossil remains of aquatic animals and plant pollen as these changed or fluctuated in time.

Whatever his definition of a hominid, or however far back to a primitive manlike form in the fossil record he may have chosen to go, no human paleontologist or prehistoric archeologist has suggested that "man" existed in pre-Pleistocene times (*see* EVOLUTION, HUMAN). Hence the whole drama of hominid and human history has been played on a stage upon which the properties were constantly being moved. Nevertheless, the time duration of any event within the Pleistocene seems to have been so long, the pace so slow, that no individual or immediate sequence of generations of individuals can have been conscious of the changes. The post-factum view of most of mankind's cultural history in the Pleistocene may be to see early culture primarily as an extrasomatic means of adaptation to ever changing environments. Certainly, however, the predecessors of modern man who achieved these adaptations were not conscious of what they were doing or of why they were doing so, in modern terms.

Stratigraphic Succession. The grand scale changing phenomena of the Pleistocene period have also provided the geologists, paleobotanists, paleontologists, and—importantly, through the aid of these natural scientists—the prehistoric archeologists with marks on their yardsticks of time. The fronts of advancing glaciers acted like gigantic bulldozers providing the raw materials for new beds in the stratigraphic succession. The raw materials were carried farther south by the action of swift-running streams and rivers or as wind-borne dust that was redeposited as loess. New layers of sediments were formed on the ocean floors. New marine shore lines or new river terraces were formed also. Geologists have been able to arrange most of the pieces of the world's stratigraphic picture puzzle into a complete and orderly sequence, and they know which beds either precede or follow which other beds. At the same time, the plant and animal fossils characteristic of most of these beds have been identified. The places of the different types of fossil men and even of the artifacts made by these men have been fixed within the ascending stratigraphic record.

Thus the marks on the yardstick of time have been provided, but stratigraphy does not give the real time value of any of its units. It is certain that one bed in a given sequence is older than a second that covers it, that this second is in turn older than a third by which it is covered, and so on; but in each case, older by how much real time? Stratigraphy gives only a relative chronology. How, then, to determine a real chronology?

Techniques for Determination of Age. Since World War II several methods of real chronological reckoning have been developed that are based on measurements of radioactive residues in organic material or in rocks (*see* ISOTOPES, 3). The best-known of these is based on measuring the residual amounts of a carbon isotope, C^{14}, in organic materials (e.g., charcoal, shell, burned bone). During its lifetime, any plant or animal receives, through cosmic rays in the atmosphere, a fixed amount of C^{14}. After death, the C^{14} is no longer ingested and begins to disappear at a predictable rate. Suppose, then, that the find is a hearth where prehistoric men once built fires. An assay of the charcoal from this hearth will reveal how long ago the wood ceased to live. The radioactive carbon method of age determination leads back to approximately 75,000 years ago.

A still newer method, based on measurement of the potassium-argon balance in certain volcanic rocks, leads back much further. Here it must be assumed that it is possible to find a stratum containing the fossil and artifactual remains of prehistoric men (ideally also with the fossils of plants and animals associated with the prehistoric men) and subsequently covered by a lava flow. The potassium-argon method will allow at least fixing the real time of the lava flow, and it is known that the underlying stratum must be at least somewhat older. It will be readily apparent that not every find-spot of interest has been sealed in by a lava flow. Nevertheless, this method has provided a "date" of at least 1,750,000 years ago for Bed I at Olduvai in Tanzania, which contains specimens of the most primitive tool-making hominids now known, the *Australopithecinae*. This new method has also already provided several other real time points for the marks on the relative yardstick of early and middle Pleistocene events.

Some of the older means of establishing real chronology depended on so-called annual increment counts. Thus in the U.S. Southwest, it has been possible to make a master chart of the rings of certain species of trees, which leads back to about the time of the birth of Christ. These trees formed thicker or thinner tree rings, depending on the rainfall and temperature of any given year, and—given a sequence of a dozen or more rings on a fragment of charcoal—the varying pattern of this

Fig. 1. The "main dig" before removal of balk, Bed I, at Olduvai, Tanzania.

succession of ring widths is unique. Thus once the master chart was constructed, it became possible to "date" a fist-sized lump of charcoal from an ancient fireplace. In Scandinavia a similar method has been devised that depends on varves, the yearly layers of sediment laid down on the bottom of lakes.

For a time span back to almost 3000 B.C. in southwestern Asia and Egypt, it has been possible to reckon real time on the basis of contemporary written accounts, lists of kings, lengths of dynasties, and especially through remarks concerning astronomical events that may be independently checked. Not all authorities agree on the details of this "real historical" chronology, especially for the earliest thousand years or so of its span (for example, whether the reign of the Babylonian lawgiver king, Hammurabi, began in 1792 B.C., or some 60 years earlier or 60 years later, is still a matter of dispute). Nevertheless, given a more or less real chronology in one region, it is possible to base reckonings upon it for events in surrounding regions, sometimes quite distant. For a century or so after *c.* 1500 B.C., a certain type of segmented frit bead seems to have been exported from Egypt in considerable numbers. Examples of these Egyptian beads have been found in Britain and along the Baltic. They are said to "date" the archeological inventories that yield them to soon after 1500 B.C.

For the many hundreds of thousands of years of more remote Pleistocene time, however, one must depend upon the relative yardstick of changing geological, climatic, and environmental events and upon the aid of the natural scientists to provide "real" dates. Since the radioactive carbon and potassium-argon methods have come into use, it appears that hominid evolution and the course of cultural development has taken a considerably longer time than was once anticipated.

Discovery, Preservation, and Method

One hundred years ago, almost every archeological discovery—save such exposed monuments as those of Egypt, Greece, and Rome—was made accidentally. Gradually, however, and especially since World War II—as an all-embracing curiosity about the past has come to be replaced with "problem-oriented" concern for some particular phase or aspect of culture history—methods have been developed that lead to archeological discovery. For example, if one's concern happens to be with early Pleistocene hominids, a first reference would be to geological maps showing the places in the world where early Pleistocene geological beds were exposed. Reports of these beds would be studied to see which fossils occurred in them (marine sediment beds would be of no use, since no hominid could have lived under water), and an assessment made of the probable environmental circumstances that obtained. Such studies would be followed by on-the-spot survey. With luck, discovery would follow.

If the problem were the recovery of evidence for early plant and animal domestication and the first village farming communities, again the first step would require maps of vegetation zones, of animal communities, and of rainfall and climate. Since enough is already known to reckon that the event in question followed the last major phase of Pleistocene glaciation, the climatic and environmental situation cannot have been too different from that of today. Where would there still be found modern wild counterparts for the plant and animal forms that were the first domesticates, for example, wild wheat and barley, wild sheep, goats, and pigs? Once the most likely regions are located on the maps, and after accounts of what has already been found in a given region have been studied, the next step is surface survey in the region itself.

Field Surveys. It will be obvious how (already before he leaves for the field in the first instance) the archeologist must depend on the advice and cooperation of his colleagues in the natural sciences. Although the archeologist is trained to deal primarily with the cultural manifestations of man's past, he must inform himself and be able to comprehend the environmental factors bearing on the phase of cultural history that is his concern.

Field survey involves covering a countryside—by jeeplike vehicles or horseback, or best of all on foot—with respect to topography that would have supported one or another level of human settlement, and also with respect to water supply, drainage patterns, and even soil types. Unless they have been completely covered over by subsequent geological strata, archeological sites almost always yield surface traces due to soil wash on slopes, animal burrowing, or such human disturbance of the surface as plowing or well digging. Sites cut by river banks or gorges may also show exposures of deep-lying strata; the good surface surveyor is a persistent "wadi-walker" (*wadi* being the Arabic word for gully). Provided with a topographic map, compass, and cloth sacks and tags to contain and label the surface materials he picks up, the surveyor keeps his eyes to the ground as he walks. Surface scatters of flint tools, bits of bone, shreds of pottery, and almost buried alignments of stone indicate a site for him. He collects as much of the surface scatter as he can carry in his cloth sacks, labels them, and locates their position on his topographic map. The yield goes back to his base camp for identification and analysis.

It is the well-trained archeologist's business to know the contents of the Sears Roebuck catalogues of the past, especially for the region of his immediate concern. To continue the modern analogy, spark plugs suggest one period and way of life to him, horseshoes another. He will have informed himself of the inventories or assemblages of artifacts characteristic of each known phase of his region's cultural history. On this basis, he identifies and analyzes the contents of the various sacks of his surface collections. However, if little previous archeological work has gone on in the region of his concern, his surface collection may yield many unknowns. These he must assess as best he can, in terms of resemblances to artifacts from adjoining and better known regions, or even by a sort of dead reckoning based on his general sense of the overall typological development of human tool-making.

Once the surface survey of a given region has been completed, the phase of initial discovery is (in theory, if the survey was really exhaustive) at an end. The next step is excavation of the most promising site located in the survey, judged by the culture-historical phase and problem of the archeologist's interest. As the above account reads, there is the suggestion that all discovery now results from careful planning. This is far from the case. Few surveys are completely exhaustive, many sites that once existed may have been completely eroded, many important finds are still made completely by ac-

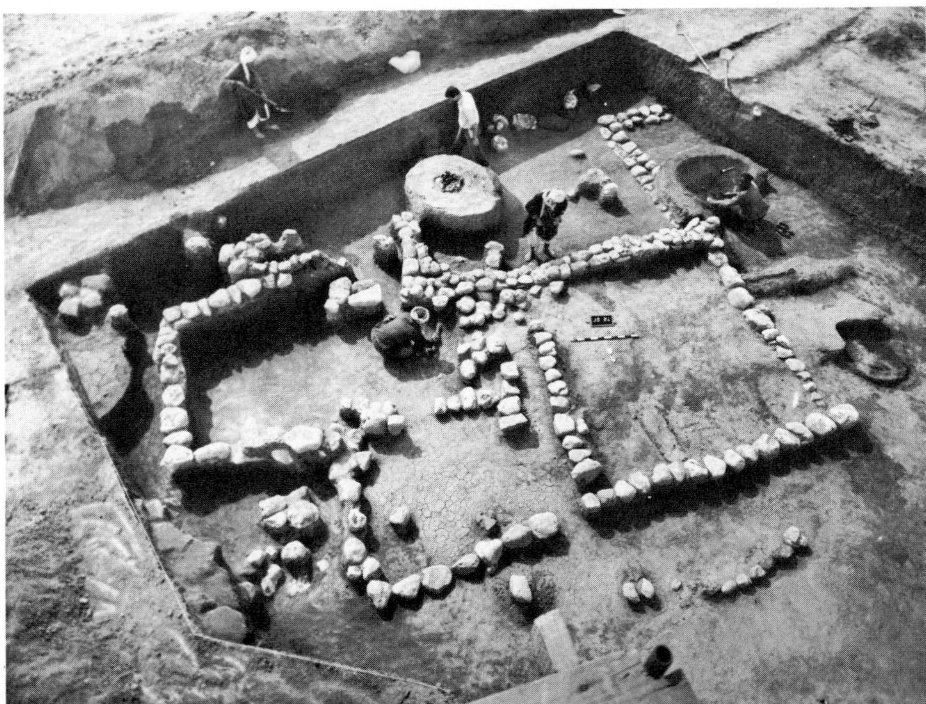

Fig. 2. View of a digging at Jarmo, in the hill country of Iraqi Kurdistan.

cident. A contractor's excavation for a building foundation or an expressway may turn up artifacts and fossils of great significance—if the contractor informs the archeologists of their discovery.

Let us return to the analogy of the mail-order catalogue. Suppose one takes an old copy of a catalogue and tears out all the pages with materials that would not last for several thousand years in the soil of the climate of a given place. Suppose he were concerned with a level of culture that had not yet achieved metal tools or pottery; all those pages would have to be torn out too. The remainder would be a dramatic representation of what the factor of preservation means to an archeologist. It is his business to "construct a sort of history" from what remains.

Very dry soils and climatic situations, such as those in Egypt and along the coastal desert of Peru, have very high preservation factors. Certain very wet waterlogged conditions, such as the bogs of northern Europe, also have high preservation factors. But in most places in the world, preservation would probably be listed as poor or bad, in terms of what must have been the total original inventory or assemblage. Furthermore, the farther back in time one moves, the less complex the original assemblage must have been; hence there is less to find.

Method. The limitations just mentioned underline the necessity for archeological attention to the *totality* of what remains of an assemblage. To return to an earlier analogy, if one would want to understand the cultural ways of late 19th-century America by archeological means alone, he would need more than simply its horseshoes. He would want as much of its Sears Roebuck catalogue as he could possibly recover. He would need also to be sure that what he recovered had perfect togetherness or association, that everything belonged to one culture and one moment of time. This analogy illustrates the importance of the principle of context in archeology—what artifacts have context with what other artifacts or other forms of evidence? It also illustrates what would be the archeologists' level of exasperation if the excavating contractor brought in one pot, but said, "The rest of the stuff got all broken up, so we threw it away."

Archeological excavation in the field is little more than hard work, applied with horse sense, in order to uncover all possible evidence of some moment of men's activities, in relation to its full context. Whether the site be a shallow open-air encampment, a cave, or one of the many-layered mounds of the Near East, the prime problem is to remove the overburden in such a careful way that what belongs together is exposed together, and can be photographed and mapped and recorded together. A layman could, with no difficulty, list the artifacts that, if found together, would identify an American kitchen or an American service station or an American church. This hints at how the modern archeologist tries to excavate his site with respect to context—he is not simply after gasoline pumps, however beautiful they might be in themselves.

The lay public's notion of archeology (firmly reinforced by Sunday newspaper supplements and Hollywood) is that the real excitement comes during field excavation. In prehistoric archeology at least, the excavator and his staff are usually so busy with the painstaking pace of the work, the various means of recording all materials in order to preserve their context, and with their cleaning and preservation, that there is little time for reflection on their significance. Samples for radioactive carbon age determination are taken, to be measured well after the field season is completed. Samples of plant materials and animal bones are secured for the excavator's botanical or zoological colleagues. Soil samples are taken for analysis in home laboratories. Hundreds of thousands of chipped flint tools need labels, classification as to type, and analysis of types (perhaps even with the aid of electronic computers) with respect to circumscribed find-spots that may suggest their original uses. By analogy, what else goes with paring knives and what else with screw drivers? This all adds up to the fact that the full comprehension of, and excitement about, what was achieved by an excavation may not be apparent until the laboratory analysis is completed.

When Howard Carter and Lord Carnarvon found and opened the tomb of Tutankhamen in Egypt in 1922, they knew almost immediately what they had. This almost never happens in current prehistoric archeology, but it does not seem to dim the enthusiasm of prehistoric archeologists. The "sort of history" they are able to construct is a different kind of intellectual adventure, done at a different pace and demanding the cooperation of many collaborators.

World Prehistory

Any history is an idiosyncratic reflection of the historian who writes it, the more so if it be so highly compressed as the following attempt to describe the culture history of the preliterate world. Up to the beginnings of literate history at least, a major theme appears to have been the changing relationship between men and nature, through time. It is granted at the outset that there may have been other major themes, but the incomplete nature of the archeological record blurs the ability to see them from the evidence now in hand. The theme that is visible (already hinted at above) is the gradual development of *culture through time and mankind's increasing ability to adapt its ways of life to an ever increasing variety of environments by means of culture. Culture, to repeat, consists of the ways of life that, persisting through tradition and manifest in art and artifact, characterize any human group.

Australopithecene Finds. Even the immediate prehominids, of which there is as yet no fossil record, must have been gregarious and social beings. The recently mounting interest in the behavior patterns of various primates in-the-wild assures this proposition. Allowing that the australopithecines of 1,750,000 years ago were already early hominids, it is possible to note the probability of their gregariousness and of small social groups, and to note also the presence of the earliest known stone (and probably bone) tool-making. Some authorities would even allow that the australopithecines had begun, in an elementary way, to standardize their stone tool forms and that several types, presumably for different purposes, were being made persistently. At the very least, the australopithecines were fashioning tools, even if their tool types had not yet become standardized through tradition.

The find-spots of australopithecine fossils spread from South Africa up through East Africa and as far as Lake Chad, and there is a hint that a southeastern Asiatic fossil may conform to australopithecine type. The coarse trimmed pebble tools, which have context with the australopithecine fossils in several reliable exposures, have been found from South Africa to Northwest Africa, recently in Palestine and Syria, and also in eastern Asia. This hints at a very broad and reasonably uniform environmental belt, probably then mainly of savannah grassland, through which early hominid forms could range. Each individual social group would, one may suppose, have had its own territory within this vast and generally uniform range. Each group must have lived in very immediate balance with its given territory, but given the uniformity of the whole range and thousands upon thousands of years, the vast area of distribution of the fossils and of the characteristic pebble tools is understandable.

The cultural level of the australopithecines—if it is granted that they possessed an elemental culture—must have been very low. It may be assumed that they had no technological or other extrasomatic means of coping with environments other than their vast range of savannah grassland. They were bound to stay within their single range, broad as it was.

Standardization of Stone Tools. Potassium-argon age determination of Bed II at Olduvai assures the archeologist that by 500,000 years ago a still more manlike fossil form than *Australopithecus* had appeared, also that standardized types of stone tools were certainly present. These tool forms included both the core-biface and the flake types, and require consideration of two major forms of standardization.

A core-biface, or hand axe, was made by removing chips from both faces of an original chunk (the core) of flint or other hard stone, in such a way as to yield a sharp cutting edge about the margin of the tool. A good core-biface has a pear-shaped profile, and the similar obverse and reverse faces (hence biface) are rather flatly sloped to the surrounding cutting edge. They were first recognized in France; an earlier generalized category of core-bifaces is called Abbevillian or Chellean, a later generalized category Acheulian.

A flake-tool was made by removing a broad flake from an original core in such a way as to yield a sharp ready-made broad cutting edge. There are many categories of flake-tools; one, which involved a certain careful preparation and trimming of the core before the flaketool was struck off, is called Levalloisian.

Core-bifaces and flake-tools appear to have resulted from the establishment of two different sets of persisting habits or traditions for the production of tools for different uses. Many different subtypes were developed within each generalized category, and different combinations of these subtypes and categories appear in different contexts. Some of the differences were certainly due to time and to improvement of technique as time went on. Other differences reflect the varying uses called for by different environmental situations. A distribution map of all the find-spots of core-biface and flake-tools in the Old World (men had not yet inhabited the New World) would show how mankind had begun to spread out beyond the old generalized savannah grassland range of the australopithecines. Life in new, and sometimes more rigorous, environments was being attempted, although many groups certainly remained within the old range as well.

Another interesting thing is that a third tradition, or persistent set of habits in the preparation of stone tools, had appeared in eastern and southeastern Asia. This was the so-called chopper-chopping tool complex. Furthermore, tools of the core-biface and flake-tool traditions seem not to have been made east of India. Taking this distributional fact along with that of the regional differences in the makeup of industries (all of the tools of a given material from any one context) for

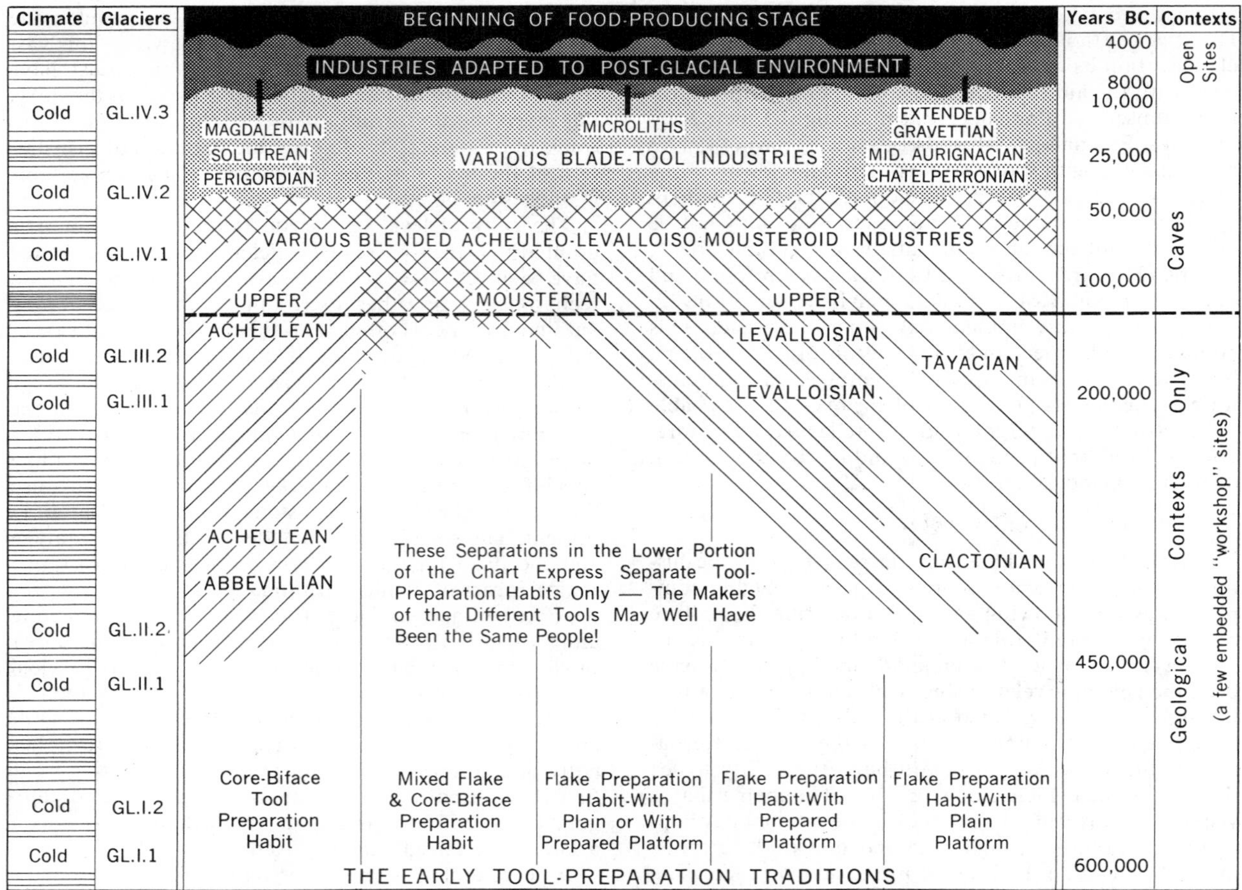

Fig. 3. Chart of present understanding of relationships and succession of tool-preparation traditions, industries, and assemblages of west central Europe. Wavy lines indicate transitions in industrial habits that are not yet understood in detail. [From R. J. Braidwood, "Prehistoric Men" (6th ed. 1963) 65.]

each of the three traditions, the trend the major theme is taking begins to be apparent. Mankind's ability, through culture, was beginning to allow adaptation to a variety of somewhat different environments. At the same time, there appears to have been the beginnings of concentration upon the ways of life necessary within any given environment.

Paleolithic Cultures. Sometime between 100,000 and 50,000 years ago, the way of life of the world's people who made core-biface and flake-tools reached its culmination. By this time, the trend of the theme is unmistakable. There are a welter of names, some of French and some of given local derivations, used to name the different tool types and different industries that have been recovered from this span of time. There are industries called "Acheuleo-Levalloisian," "Mousterian of Levalloisian tradition," and "Acheuleo-Mousterian," as well as "diminutive Levalloisian," "Khargan," "Aterian," and so on. The details are not of concern here, but what does matter is mankind's increased ability to adapt to an ever increasing number of regional and even subregional environments.

The time span in question covers the flourishing of classic Neanderthal man in western Europe and of less extreme forms of "Neanderthalism" elsewhere. By this time, almost without question although it cannot be proved, language had appeared. Also apparent are first traces of other dimensions of cultural activity. Intentional burial of the dead was practiced. Deep in certain caves in Italy and Switzerland, traces of a so-called bear cult have been found. By now, is not the archeologist dealing with men as men?

Next, about 40,000 years ago, two new and remarkable bits of evidence appear in the record. Fossils of a completely modern type of man, anatomically speaking, are first evidenced. More or less coincidentally (not necessarily connectedly) in both Europe and southwestern Asia, the old core-biface and flake-tool traditions were gradually replaced by a new, more complicated, and more efficient tradition for the preparation of flint tools—the blade-tool tradition. Another yet unanswered question is whether either or both of these appearances were occasioned by one of the marked world climatic changes that occurred early in the last major glacial phase. One cannot make environmental change a directly causative factor here, or it would be hard to explain why these appearances did not come during one of the many earlier climatic swings of the Pleistocene.

A blade of flint is a long parallel-sided flake, struck from a specially and painstakingly prepared core. The blade was either utilized as it came off the core, with its useful long cutting edges, or it was further dressed into a great variety of other tool types. There were, for the first time, special tools to make other tools, often of wood, bone, antler, or shell. Needles, with their implications of sewn skin clothing, appeared. Artifacts of bone and antler were now decorated in one way or another, the mother-goddess (or Venus) figurines were carved, and the great Franco-Cantabrian cave art began (*see* ART, PREHISTORIC). At last, the prehistoric archeologist begins to have a respectable Sears Roebuck catalogue to deal with.

Rise of Agriculture. The trend of the major theme was now nearing its culmination. The record clearly shows the abilities of various groups of men to adapt themselves to all the world's environmental niches where human occupation was possible (without modern technological resources). The New World was occupied, and a spread into Oceania had certainly begun. By about 10,000 B.C., the process of filling all major portions of the world had been completed by peoples capable of more or less developed levels of a hunting and collecting way of life. This culmination of the trend toward ever more specialized adaptations to ever more specialized environments—this increasing ability of separate groups of men to "live into" a given environmental niche—can be seen as the first great cultural achievement of mankind.

The next step in the record may be identified as one result of the culmination of living into a particular niche. About 9,000 B.C. in southwestern Asia and perhaps about 7,000 B.C. in Mesoamerica, groups of people living on a reasonably intensified level of food collection began to domesticate food plants and animals or, in Mesoamerica, food plants alone. In the sense in which the great British prehistorian V. Gordon Childe used the expression, this "food-producing revolution" was the real culmination of the trend of the major theme.

There is a logical possibility, but not yet archeological evidence, that independent achievements of food production may also have been made somewhere in eastern or southeastern Asia or in sub-Saharan Africa. As yet, only the bare outlines of the beginnings of food production in southwestern Asia and in Mesoamerica are known. In both these regions, the first step appears to have been a level of incipience and experimentation, during which the major portion of the food supply was doubtless still due to collection. This incipient level appears to have had a duration of about 2,000 or 3,000 years. About 7000 B.C. in southwestern Asia and about 5000 B.C. in Mesoamerica, a settled village farming community way of life gradually supplanted the earlier level of incipience.

In southwestern Asia, at least two aspects of the level of incipient cultivation and domestication have been identified. One of these aspects, the Natufian of Palestine, with extensions northward perhaps even to southern coastal Turkey, appears to have been generally adapted to the country along the hill slopes and narrow coastal plains of the eastern Mediterranean littoral. The second known aspect, named Karim Shahirian after a site in Iraqi Kurdistan, appears to have been adapted to the upper piedmont and intermontane valley hill

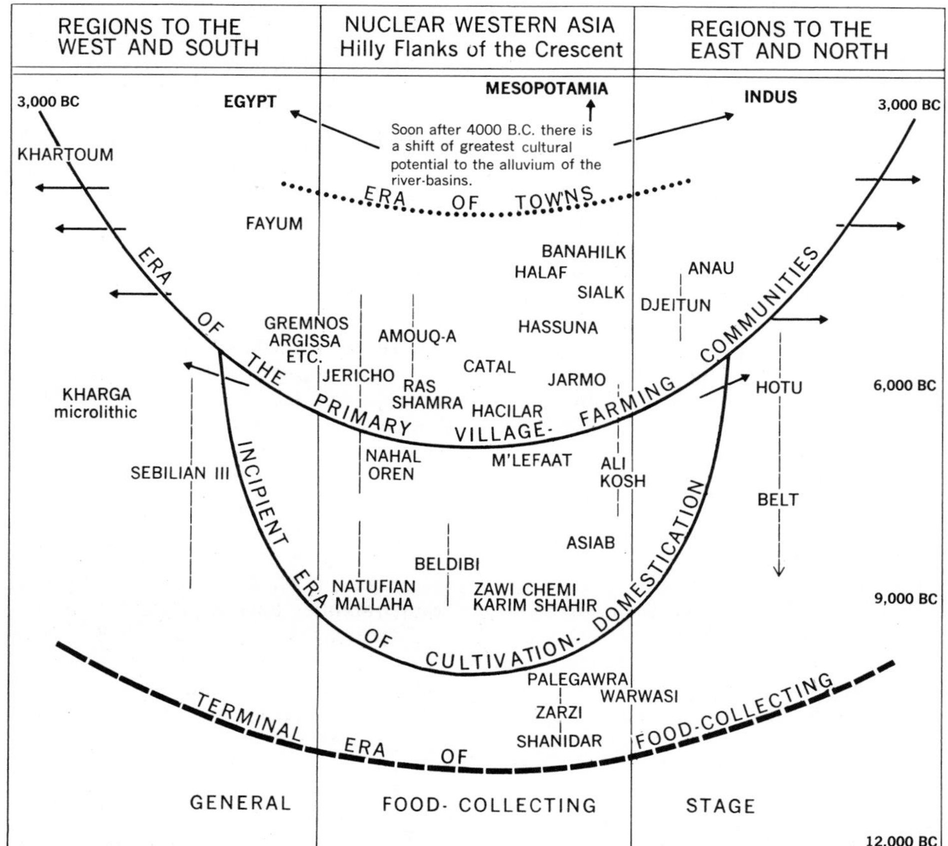

Fig. 4. Possible relationships of stages and eras in agricultural development in western Asia and northeastern Africa. [From R. J. Braidwood, "Prehistoric Men" (6th ed. 1963) 111.]

Fig. 5. A black clay figurine of the mother-goddess type, 3d to 2d millennium, B.C., from Tureng Tepe, near Asterabad, Iran.

flanks of the Zagros mountains in Iraq and Iran. It is anticipated that a third aspect may yet be identified along the hill flanks of the Tauros mountains in southern Turkey and perhaps toward the north and west, in propitious intermontane valleys of the Anatolian plateau. This environmental zone still yields most of the wild counterparts of the food complex that characterized the early Western cultural tradition—wheat, barley, certain legumes, sheep, goats, cattle, pigs, and a half-ass. It is doubtful whether the level of incipient cultivation and domestication was viable outside the natural habitat zone of these potential domesticates.

In Mesoamerica, the environmental situation appears to have been rather comparable; a topography of subarid piedmonts or intermontane valley plains (such as those of Tehuacan, southeast of Mexico City, or Tamaulipas to the northeast). Like that in southwestern Asia, the level of incipience in Mesoamerica seems to have arisen out of a level of food collection that was only reasonably intensified and effective, and based more heavily on collection and the taking of smaller animals than upon big game. Squash, peppers, and beans appear to have been the first cultivated plants, with small pod maize following later, after 5000 B.C. Again, although there is still very much to learn of this level, the assemblages implying incipience do not seem to spread beyond the apparent natural habitat zone of the potential domesticates. Also, as in southwestern Asia, this zone is one of considerable subregional diversity, where minor fluctuations of climate would have been compensated for, by modest upslope or downslope movements both of plant and animal communities, as well as of men.

In southwestern Asia, the succeeding level of primary village farming communities is also best known, at its beginnings (*c.* 7000 to 6000 B.C.), along the east Mediterranean littoral, along the Zagros flanks and in certain intermontane valley plains of Anatolia. There even seem to have been fingerings out of the new way of life toward Cyprus, Crete, northern Greece, and Macedonia by the end of this phase, although strains of the plant and animal domesticates that would tolerate the rich but hot and relatively rainless river valleys of southern Mesopotamia and Egypt had not yet appeared. An early phase of this primary village farming community level is seen at the site of Jarmo in the hill country of Iraqi Kurdistan. Here a small cluster of mud-walled, several-room houses yielded two strains of domesticated wheat as well as traces of barley, a form of pea, and the bones of domesticated goats, probably of sheep and dogs, and of pigs in the latest levels. Pottery vessels also appeared, but only in the upper levels. Clay figurines, many of which were of the mother-goddess or fertility spirit type, appeared throughout the sequence. The best-known, although somewhat enigmatic, site in the littoral regions is Tell es-Sultan (the mound identified as later Jericho), where a much larger and more elaborate architectural manifestation is exposed. So far, however, little direct trace of its food producing bases has been reported. A northern littoral variant is to be seen at two sites in south central Anatolia, Hacilar and Catal Hüyük.

The primary village farming community level is, unfortunately, still only poorly known in Mesoamerica. This may be in part because a somewhat more scattered open farmstead type of settlement pattern was eventually favored. Nevertheless it is known that new and more effective strains of maize, beans, and squash presently appeared, that so-called ceremonial centers seem to have been built at a relatively earlier phase in the New World developmental sequence than was the case in its Old World counterpart, and that at such sites as Zacatenco there was great emphasis on the making of figurines of an evidently sacred nature.

It seems probable that the appearance of effective agriculture along the Andean coast of South America came slightly later than did that of Mesoamerica, although there is no direct evidence that the South American experiment depended on stimulation from the north. Evidence for the cultivation of lima beans on the Peruvian coast as early as 3750 B.C. has been reported. The succession of Sears Roebuck catalogues of the Andean region always remained essentially distinct from those of Mesoamerica, although certain intriguing comparabilities have been noted.

To return for a moment to what was happening (in terms of the major theme) to the rest of the world after 10,000 B.C., it seems that most of the world's cultural patterns survived the climatic and environmental changes that, especially in the temperate and subarctic latitudes, attended the end of the last major glaciation. However, these cultures survived by renovation rather than by real change; they "changed just enough so that they did not need to change." They remained on a food-collecting basis, at however intensified a level in one given region or another. The so-called Mesolithic cultures of northwestern Europe, such as the Maglemosian of Scandinavia, were direct cultural readaptations, still on a food collecting level, to the postglacial forested environments.

The world's preliterate history, from this point onward, has been that of increasingly more specialized cultural adaptations to increasingly more specialized natural environments (the persistence of the major theme) until, at various times and places the cultures based on food collection were captured by the spread of food production. A few relics of the old theme, in its elemental form, remain, such as the Eskimo, the Kalahari Bushmen, the Australian aborigines, but all have already been touched by newer ways of life.

The Beginning of History. The end of prehistory, in both the Old and New Worlds, followed the same general pattern. There was both consolidation and intensification of food production adjacent to, or within, the nuclear regions where the village farming community had its start, and a spreading outward of the new way of life from the nuclear regions. In dealing with the immediately preliterate, preurban, and precivilized phases in the nuclear regions, the prehistorian faces new problems of interpretation for which his conventional training may not have prepared him. Because of the increasing complexity of the artifactual manifestations of cultures, because the available Sears Roebuck catalogues now become much more complete, new vistas of broader dimensions of culture begin to appear. Some prehistorians, notably V. Gordon Childe, have attempted to continue their culture-historical interpretation of the latest preliterate and early literate societies, writing still from the essentially technological-economic or predominantly materialistic baseline of the old major theme. Others now feel uncomfortable with this single theme alone. It served well when the evidence was restricted, but now prehistorians look for aid to colleagues who deal with what is conventionally called ancient history, and are sensitive to their attempts to extrapolate backward from the written accounts and myths of early literate times. Purely materialistic interpretations for the building of a Great Pyramid or a Stonehenge now ring hollow.

The impingement of food-producing ways of life upon those of older food-collecting cultures provides opportunities for fascinating studies of the mechanics of cultural change. Radioactive carbon age determinations now relate that by 4200 B.C., the new way of life had spread from southwestern Asia to the Low Countries of Atlantic Europe; by 3500 B.C. it had reached Britain and southern Scandinavia. But Childe rightly insisted that the inhabitants of Europe were not slavish imitators and that they adapted the "gifts from the East" in ways that were distinctly European. Much less is known of the spread of things and of ideas into sub-Saharan Africa or what may have been the indigenous adaptations or independent developments there. The same is true regarding more remote Asia. The great Harappan civilization of the Indus Valley may have been in some fair part a response to stimulation from Mesopotamia and Persia, but the case for the real origins of Chinese civilization is not so clear. New and rather remarkably early radiocarbon age determinations for the Jomon settlements in Japan (approaching 7000 B.C.) make one ever more sensitive to the possibility of an independent origin of food production in eastern

Fig. 6. Clay figurine, 2d to 1st millennium, B.C., from the Jomon excavations of Japan.

or southeastern Asia, with a still unprobed sequence following from it.

The same story of impingement of the new way of life, spreading outward from the nuclear regions of Mesoamerica and the Andes, and of the various cultural adaptations and changes which resulted, may be told for the New World. In some instances there was surprisingly steadfast resistance to change, but in most cases the new food crops, especially maize, and the new ways of life their cultivation and utilization allowed or demanded presently superseded the ways of food collectors. In this sense, the cultural historian is sorry that this great independent instance was truncated by the Conquistadores.

Thus as history began, the major theme that may be seen in prehistory had already passed its culmination—in the basic culture vs. nature sense. Nature is of course still with us, and always will be. Men still fish and enjoy wild strawberries on occasion, or cringe before tornadoes or earthquakes. On pain of creating dust bowls, they gradually learn to treat nature with respect. With the passage of time, however, cultural achievements have freed men from painful dependence on one given type of environment. It is only rather recently—in the long view of the hominid span of time—that increasing sociocultural complexity has tended to mitigate the necessity that all men stay within an immediate balance with nature. New dimensions of culture, although perhaps some may be older than the available record shows, have arisen in the course of cultural history, as man has become more fully man.

See also ANTHROPOLOGY, CULTURAL; ANTHROPOLOGY, PHYSICAL; CULTURE; EVOLUTION, CULTURAL AND SOCIAL.

Bibliography: G. E. DANIEL, *A Hundred Years of Archaeology* (London 1950); *The Idea of Prehistory* (Cleveland 1963). J. C. GREENE, *Darwin and the Modern World View* (Baton Rouge, La. 1961). R. J. BRAIDWOOD, *Archeologists and What They Do* (New York 1960); *Prehistoric Men* (6th ed. Chicago 1963). R. J. BRAIDWOOD and G. R. WILLEY, eds., *Courses Toward Urban Life* (Chicago 1962). R. E. M. WHEELER, *Archaeology From the Earth* (Oxford 1954). G. CLARK, *Archaeology and Society* (New York 1961). R. A. DALY, *The Changing World of the Ice Age* (New Haven 1934). R. F. FLINT, *Glacial and Pleistocene Geology* (New York 1957). *American Journal of Science, Radiocarbon Supplement* (New Haven 1959–). R. L. HAY, "Stratigraphy of Beds I Through IV, Olduvai Gorge, Tanganyika," *Science* 139 (March 1, 1963) 829–833. V. G. CHILDE, *Man Makes Himself* (rev. ed. New York 1955). G. CLARK, *World Prehistory* (New York 1962). R. REDFIELD, *The Primitive World and Its Transformations* (Ithaca, N.Y. 1953). **Illustration credits:** Fig. 1, Photograph by J. S. B. Leakey. Fig. 2, Courtesy of The Oriental Institute, University of Chicago. Figs. 3 and 4, Chicago Natural History Museum. Fig. 5, The University Museum of the University of Pennsylvania. Fig. 6, Musée Guimet, Paris.

[R. J. BRAIDWOOD]

ARCHEOLOGY, II (BIBLICAL)

Etymologically, archeology is the study of antiquity; more specifically, it is the study of the material remains of the past. As applied to the Bible, it is that of the life, culture, and even the beliefs of peoples associated with the Bible, as these are discoverable through the excavation of ancient sites, through the examination of artifacts and ruins and through inscriptions and other written documents. While epigraphy is, strictly speaking, a science in itself, it has become almost inextricably bound up with Biblical archeology—to such a degree that nearly all books on Biblical or Near Eastern archeology discuss inscriptions, documents, and even philology. Similarly, archeology easily associates to itself and lends itself to history, numismatics, ceramics, architecture, and other subjects that can be studied apart from any Biblical frame of reference. From this one may gather what an exacting science Biblical archeology is, and what care it demands from its practitioners. This is one reason why women have done some of the finest work.

Methods. The methods of archeology have developed steadily during the past 150 years from the roughest type of spadework—at times destroying forever evidence that was actually present—to the highly technical methods of modern times. A few archeologists, e.g., Nelson Glueck, do surface exploration—simply examin-

Fig. 1. "Step-trench" excavating of a typical tell (Tell Judaidah, near Alalakh, Syria). The drawings at the right symbolize artifacts of 14 different settlements dating from 4500 B.C. to A.D. 800, one above the other.

ing materials that lie open for appraisal; but the majority are excavators, systematically uncovering sites, e.g., of ancient cities. At times the sites do not rise appreciably above the surrounding ground level; but more often they have taken on the form of a mound (called a *tell* in Arabic) within which, as a rule, lie the ruins of a number of different civilization levels. Since the sites of cities were generally chosen for strategic (defensive) or commercial reasons (often close to ancient caravan routes), with fairly easy access to water supplies (springs), they were used over and over, new cities being built on the ruins of older ones. Excavators may either attempt a strata-type investigation, "peeling off" one stratum at a time, as the Americans did at *Mageddo (Megiddo), or they may simply run deep vertical trenches into various parts of the *tell,* thus getting a good cross-section view of what is there. The latter system was used with great success at Tell es-Sulṭân (OT *Jericho) by Miss K. Kenyon. While several of these mounds (Arabic plural *tulûl*) have been excavated in whole or in part, most of them await examination and hold rich promise within. Stratification, as is revealed by vertical trenches, is highly irregular, and the excavator must use the utmost care in completing one stratum and not confounding it with another. For this reason balks with straight vertical sides are now generally left across a trench at regular intervals. The highly erroneous and deceptive reports by John Garstang on Jericho are a clear example of such confusion of strata.

Sites are selected because they are commonly identified with important Biblical locations; or because they seem full of promise, even though their identification is unknown; or because of some accidental discovery at the site; or simply because of convenience. Khirbet ("ruins of") Qumrân would probably not have been excavated (1951–56) had it not been for the discovery of the *Dead Sea Scrolls in the immediate vicinity. Excavations of the City of David (Sion, Zion), immediately south of the walled city of Jerusalem, along the southeastern slope that leads down toward the conjunction of the Cedron (Kidron) and Hinnom valleys, were undertaken despite the misplaced attachment of *Sion (Zion) to the southwestern slope and despite the present low altitude of the site. Excavations are no longer private affairs, for each site is visited by experts of different background. This, together with the obligation to publish the results, very nearly precludes archeological caprice or prejudice.

Palestinian Archeology. Individual articles in this encyclopedia deal with the more important Palestinian sites (for a detailed account of Palestinian archeology, *see* PALESTINE, 7). Here it is sufficient to say that although much has been accomplished, much more remains to be done. Some of the larger, more promising sites, e.g., Mageddo and *Beth-San (-Shan), were excavated before modern scientific methods had been fully developed. Excavations have been left incomplete for various reasons, usually for lack of funds, and even on account of the murder of the excavator, as happened at Lakish when J. L. Starckey was stabbed to death in 1938. The operations were suspended until some years later, when they were resumed by Olga Tufnell.

Chronology has been a constant problem, especially in regard to the nonliterate Palestine of the 3d–2d millennia B.C. Where calendars, king lists, and other fixed forms of chronological data are lacking, the archeologist

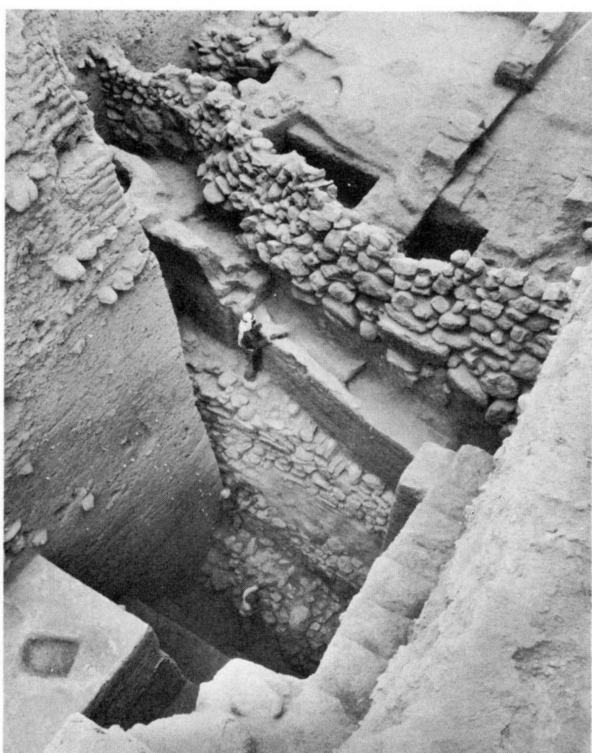

Fig. 2. The excavation of the site of ancient Jericho. The lowest section of stone wall visible in the photo is the town wall of the oldest Jericho.

must begin with what is termed "sequence dating"—carefully noting the styles of artifacts, such as flints (in the preceramic times) and especially pottery, as these appear on the various levels of an excavation. Each site provides its own sequence of styles, and these in turn may be linked to other sites and to some date, known through comparative study, e.g., the time of the destruction of a city as recorded in the annals of the enemy. As far as flints are concerned, a rather reliable chronology has been worked out for Palestine by Miss Dorothy Garrod, through her studies of the Mt. Carmel caves (1929–34). The pottery sequence is still in progress. It was falteringly begun by Sir Flinders Petrie at Tell el-Ḥesi (probably ancient Eglon) in 1890. Although his conclusions were wrong, he established a sound method, and by the concerted effort of many archeologists the margin of error has gradually been reduced. At the present time there is reasonably accurate dating of Palestinian sites and levels, by means of pottery, from 3000 B.C. on. For earlier dates the margin of error is much greater. It may be noted that Palestinian archeologists speak, not so much in terms of years (though these are implied), as in terms of cultural levels. Thus the Stone Age (divided into Paleolithic, Mesolithic, and Neolithic) in Palestine came to an end roughly around 3000 B.C., at about which time the Bronze Age began. This in turn is variously divided by archeologists into Early, Middle, and Late, with even further subdivisions in some cases, e.g., EB I [Early Bronze I (*c.* 3100 to 2900 B.C.), based on Egyptian chronology and similarity of ceramics]. Finally, there is the Iron Age, which began about 1200 B.C. in Palestine.

Fig. 3. Biblical archeology: the excavation of Beth-San. (a) View of the south side of the tell. (b) Two stele of Ramses II as they were being excavated and (c) one of them as exhibited in the Palestine Archaeological Museum. (d) Pedestal of an offering altar with a figure of a worshiper about to sacrifice two birds to a serpent.

Fig. 4. Biblical archeology: (a) The pool at the site of the ancient city of Gabaon. (b) Excavation of an industrial area at Gabaon. (c) Pottery jars excavated at Gabaon, after mending and cleaning. (d) The 14th-century B.C. "King's Gate" at the ancient Hittite capital of Boghazköy. (e) Underground stairway to the water supply at Gabaon.

In recent times Carbon-14 dating has been developed. This is especially valuable on older materials, containing radioactive carbon, where the margin of error makes less difference. The method is being constantly perfected with an ever-decreasing margin of error. It was used both at Jericho and on the linen wrappers in which the major Dead Sea Scrolls were found, and in both instances it has given invaluable guidance.

Near Eastern Archeology outside Palestine. A large part of Biblical archeology has been carried on outside of Palestinian soil. Yet this has supplemented Palestinian archeology and has, in its own way, thrown immense light on the background of the Bible. Mistakes have been made, but these were inevitable and not due to anything, in most cases, other than a science in its infancy and experimental stage.

Mesopotamia. The land lying between the Tigris and Euphrates rivers has undergone countless excavations, and the results have stocked many a museum with highly valuable statues, reliefs, figurines and other artifacts. But, most important of all, ancient *Mesopotamia has yielded up enormous amounts of cuneiform tablets, including such famous documents as the **Enuma Elish,* the **Gilgamesh Epic,* and various *Law Codes* (*see* LAW, ANCIENT NEAR-EASTERN), all of which have thrown valuable light on the Biblical narratives, especially on the Book of *Genesis and the Mosaic *Law. (*See* SUMERIAN LANGUAGE AND LITERATURE; AKKADIAN LANGUAGE AND LITERATURE.) This does not mean that the Biblical writers were mere borrowers; but it does mean that accounts roughly paralleling theirs existed in very ancient times, and these, at least in part, must have been known to the inspired writers. Whatever information they may have used in common with these cuneiform documents was purified of polytheism, was placed upon a much higher theological plane, and was often set forth in a strikingly different manner. Yet one cannot deny the points of contact. The Sumerian lists of prehistoric kings, with their eight or ten entries before, and several entries after the Flood, and especially with the astronomical figures of their regnal years—running as high as 36,000 years (Pritchard ANET[2] 265; for illustration, *see* CHRONOLOGY, ANCIENT, 2)—alert scholars to the significance of the longevity of the 10 pre-Flood and the 10 post-Flood Patriarchs in the narrative of the Pentateuchal *priestly writers (Gn 5.1–28, 30–32; 11.10–27, 31–32). Here, too, one sees the overlapping of archeology with other sciences. Interesting, too, is the work of Leonard Wooley, with his overhasty statement of his "Flood" discoveries at Ur—and the ensuing correction demanded by more careful analysis. The documents of ancient Mesopotamia have made numerous important linguistic contributions toward our understanding of Biblical Hebrew. These are exploited, with exceptionally good judgment, by Ephraim Speiser, in his commentary on Genesis (New York 1964).

Egypt. This country, too, has furnished rich rewards to the efforts of archeologists. Important king lists have been turned up; the building projects of *Ramses II have thrown light on the early chapters of Exodus; the writing known as the Wisdom of *Amen-em-Ope shows a relationship to the Book of Proverbs (esp. Prv 22.17–24.22). Many men have contributed to the archeological explorations of Egypt and the science of *Egyptology, not the least of whom was the decipherer of the Rosetta Stone, J. F. *Champollion (1822). His work led to the understanding of the countless hieroglyphic inscriptions in ancient Egyptian (*see* EGYPT, ANCIENT, 3). While Israel is mentioned only once in the known Egyptian inscriptions, viz, on the Stele of Mer-ne-Ptah, where (*c.* 1219 B.C.) it is written: "Israel is destroyed, its seed does not exist," there are many points of contact between Egypt and Palestine established through archeology, e.g., in the *Amarna Letters. The discovery (1947) of the Gnostic texts of *Chenoboskion (Nag Hammâdi), important for NT studies, equals the earlier discoveries of various papyri, one of them (P52) very close to the autograph copy of the Gospel according to St. John (*see* PAPYROLOGY). Egypt's climate has made possible the survival of literary works obtainable through archeological investigations, though its claims are not isolated in this regard.

Ugarit. The discoveries at Ras Shamra (ancient *Ugarit), beginning in 1929, have led to the reconstruction of an important Semitic dialect and to the gradual assemblage of an alphabetical cuneiform literature, much of which is highly useful to Biblical studies. In less than 40 years Ugaritic grammars and lexica have been assembled, and countless word parallels with Biblical Hebrew have been established or suggested. Apart from linguistics, the religion of Ugarit, with its emphasis on Baal and El and on the goddess of fertility, etc., throws light on the type of religion encountered by the Israelites as they entered Canaan around the beginning of the Iron Age, and to some extent on the patriarchal narratives in Genesis ch. 12–50. With many of the tablets still unpublished, Ugaritic holds out even greater promise for the future.

Boghazköy. Excavations beginning in 1906 at Boghazköy, about 100 miles east of Ankara, Turkey, under the direction of H. Winckler, gradually revealed the ancient capital of the powerful Hittite Empire. The discoveries here, besides architecture and cultural objects, include the archives of this once important kingdom. Winckler found more than 20,000 clay tablets, written both in Akkadian and Hittite, and by 1915 B. Hrozný had made the initial decipherment of the Hittite language; soon grammars and lexica began to appear (*see* HITTITE LANGUAGE AND LITERATURE). Relationships of the *Hittites with the Bible are indirect but important. Thus, the downfall of the Hittite Empire seems to be connected with the invasion of the Sea Peoples (*c.* 1200 B.C.), of whom the *Philistines were a part. The Hittites were widespread, and are frequently mentioned in the OT before and long after the destruction of their kingdom (Gn 15.20; Nm 13.29; Jos 1.4; 2 Sm 11.3; 3 Kgs 10.29; 11.1; 4 Kgs 7.6; Ez 16.3.45). The Hittite Laws are helpful in clarifying Biblical narratives, e.g., that of the transaction of Abraham with Ephron the *Hethite (Hittite) at Mamre (Gn 23.3–20); see M. R. Lehmann, BullAmSchOrRes 129 (1953) 15–18.

Value of Archeology for Biblical Studies. With good reason Pius XII in 1943 spoke of the great "light that has been derived from these explorations for the more correct and fuller understanding of the Sacred Books . . ." and referred to ". . . the discovery from time to time of written documents that help much towards the knowledge of the languages, letters, events, customs, and forms of worship of most ancient times" (**Divino affante Spiritu*). With archeological help, knowledge of ancient Palestine may be extended back, though with qualifications, to nearly 8000 B.C. It is now possible to write such a thing as an archeological commentary on the whole of Biblical history, including the "prehistory" of Genesis ch. 1–11; the story of Israel's neighbors and their influence on Israel; and the influence of the Near East on the NT. Many ancient problems have been solved, and new ones have been created through archeology. This archeological knowledge of the ancient Near East is useful also for the understanding of the literary forms of the Bible (*see* FORM CRITICISM, BIBLICAL) and for the evidence it gives of the chief preoccupations, methods, and modes of thinking and writing of the sacred writers, thus clarifying Biblical inerrancy also. All of this leads to truth—whether it confirms or runs counter to the traditional way of thinking. So valuable a service can only promote the true good.

Bibliography: G. E. WRIGHT, *Biblical Archaeology* (2d ed. Philadelphia 1962). W. F. ALBRIGHT, *The Archaeology of Palestine* (rev. ed. Pelican Bks; Baltimore 1960). J. B. PRITCHARD, *Archaeology and the O. T.* (Princeton 1958). M. BURROWS, *What Mean These Stones?* (New Haven 1941; pa. New York 1957). J. FINEGAN, *Light from the Ancient Past* (2d ed. Princeton 1959). H. J. FRANKEN and C. A. FRANKEN-BATTERSHILL, *A Primer of O.T. Archaeology* (Leiden 1963). J. GRAY, *Archeology and the Old Testament World* (New York 1962). A. ROLLA, *La Bibbia di fronte alle ultime scoperte* (3d ed. Rome 1959). **Illustration credits:** Fig. 1, Courtesy of the Oriental Institute, University of Chicago. Fig. 2, British School of Archaeology, Jerusalem. Figs. 3 and 4*a*, 4*b*, 4*c*, 4*e*, The University Museum of the University of Pennsylvania. Fig. 4*d*, Hirmer Verlag München.

[I. HUNT]

ARCHEOLOGY, III (CHRISTIAN)

The study of ancient Christian monuments to ascertain all that is knowable concerning the life and thought of the early Christians. It supplements in an important degree the literary sources of information consisting of the remains of early Christian literature, but does not include them. Christian archeology is dealt with as a concept; then its history, organization, research, and excavations are described.

Concept. The objects dealt with in Christian archeology are the various classes of existing monuments produced for or by Christians: monuments of architecture; painting; mosaics; miniatures; sculpture; products of the minor arts, such as lamps, rings, medals, gems; inscriptions or *epigraphy; and papyri. The study of these monuments presupposes the search for them by trained archeologists in systematic excavations. Thus the science of Christian archeology comprises two tasks: (1) the search for the monuments, and reliable reports on the excavations, including photographic reproductions of the monuments *in situ;* and (2) a critical study of the discoveries. The latter includes the duty of ascertaining the authenticity, the date of origin, the style, and the purpose of the monument.

Archeological research must be based on reliable historical methods. Christian archeology is not identical with the history of early Christian art but must be considered a branch of historical theology, free from all apologetic tendencies, and following the laws and rules of historical and philological studies. It represents a part of the history of the sources of theology. As such it has become indispensable for ecclesiastical history, the history of religions, and the history of art and liturgy. As to the chronological limits to be assigned to it, opinions differ, since the concept of Christian antiquity is extended further in the East than in the West, where the death of Gregory the Great (604) marks the end of the ancient and the beginning of the medieval period. In the East the transition from Christian antiquity to the Byzantine Period is gradual and extends far beyond the 7th century.

History. The beginnings of Christian archeology go back to the 16th century and are a result of the lively theological discussion devoted to the character and practices of the early Church that followed the Reformation. In 1554 the Augustinian Onofrio *Panvinio (d. 1568) published an important work on the basilicas of Rome (*De praecipuis urbis Romae sanctioribus basilicis*), and in 1568, another on the cemeteries and sepulchral rites of the early Christians (*De ritu sepeliendi mortuos apud veteres Christianos et de eorum coemeteriis*).

Antonio Bosio. This inauguration of the study of Christian antiquity was followed by a systematic exploration of the ancient Roman cemeteries or catacombs by Antonio Bosio. Born at Malta in 1575, Bosio began his studies with excavations in the Eternal City in 1593; these resulted in the publication of his main work, *Roma Sotterranea,* 3 years after his death (1629), in an edition by the Oratorian Giovanni Severano. Though the copies of catacomb paintings in this work have often been found inaccurate, the detailed description of its 200 paintings testify to the critical judgment and the scholarly method of its author. A Latin translation published in two volumes by Paolo Aringhi in 1651 at Rome, with reprints (1671) at Cologne and Paris, made Bosio's work known to the world of scholars. As a result, even Protestant circles began to show interest in the Roman catacombs.

E. S. Cyprian wrote his *De ecclesia subterranea liber* (Helmsted 1699), P. Zorn his *De catacombis seu cryptis sepulchralibus* (Leipzig 1703), and A. G. Femel his *De catacombis* (Leipzig 1710–1713), all highly polemical and without sufficient scientific approach. About the same time the Anglican theologian Joseph Bingham published his important work on the hierarchy, organisation, discipline, liturgy, and calendar of the early Church, *Origines ecclesiasticae or Antiquities of the Christian Church* (London 1708–22, 2d ed. 1726), which also appeared in a Latin version by J. H. Grischow (Halle 1724–28, 2d ed. 1751–61). Though Bingham dealt with early Christian monuments, baptisteries, churches, and cemeteries, he failed to use Bosio's *Roma Sotterranea,* one of the great shortcomings of his otherwise fundamental work.

During the entire 18th century Christian archeology remained mainly an occupation of Italian scholars. Marc Antonio Boldetti's *Osservazioni sopra i cimiteri dei santi martiri e antichi cristiani di Roma* (Rome 1720) deals not only with the ancient cemeteries of Rome, as the title suggests, but also with many outside the Eternal City, including those of Naples, Malta, Cologne, and Trier. His work remains a valuable source of information, though the author lacked critical sense. The epigraphical parts are often unreliable. The three volumes *Sculture e pitture sacre estratte da i cimiteri di Roma* (Rome 1737–54) by Giovanni Bottari are based on Bosio's work.

G. B. de Rossi. A new epoch in archeological studies began with the first half of the 19th century. The Jesuit Giuseppe Marchi (1795–1860) published (1841) the first volume of a work on early Christian art. Though he was unable to complete this undertaking, he deserves great credit in the history of Christian archeology because he had associated with him a young man, only 20 years of age, who was destined to elevate Christian archeology to a science. This was Giovanni Battista de Rossi, born in Rome, Feb. 22, 1822. After successful studies in law, he dedicated his life to the exploration of the Roman catacombs.

Following in the footsteps of Bosio, De Rossi introduced a critical method in Christian archeology that made extensive use of such sources as the *Itineraria of the 7th and 8th centuries, early Christian inscriptions, and martyrologies to ascertain historical dates. As a result he made important discoveries, including the tomb of Pope Cornelius in 1852, the crypt of the popes of the 3d century in S. Callisto in 1854, the basilica of Nereus and Achilleus in the catacomb of Domitilla in 1873, and the tomb of the antipope and martyr Hippolytus in 1882. These excavations enabled him to reconstruct the topography of the ancient Christian cemeteries, which he described in his monumental work *Roma sotterranea cristiana* (3 v. Rome 1864–77). In 1863 he began the publication of his *Bullettino di archeologia cristiana,* and in 1861 and 1888 he edited the first two volumes of the *Inscriptiones christianae urbis Romae septimo saeculo antiquiores,* important for all epigraphical studies of Christian antiquity.

De Rossi's efforts led to a complete rebirth of Christian archeology in many countries. Among the archeologists who followed in his footsteps in Italy were: R. Garrucci, M. Armellini, O. Marucchi, E. Stevenson, C. Stornaiolo, and G. Gatti; in Germany: F. Piper, F. X. Kraus, N. Müller, J. P. *Kirsch, A. de *Waal, J. *Wilpert, J. Sauer, V. Schultze, J. Ficker, J. *Strzygowski, C. M. Kaufmann; in France: J. A. Martigny, E. LeBlant, L. *Duchesne, C. de Vogüe, C. Rohault de Fleury, S. Gsell; in England: S. Northcote, O. M. Dalton, C. W. King; and in Russia: N. P. *Kondakov, D. *Aĭnalov, J. Smirnow.

Organization. The 20th century has seen a remarkable progress in Christian archeology. It was of great advantage that international congresses contributed toward organizing efforts for systematic excavations and for the publication of dictionaries, periodicals, and series of monographs. So far seven such international congresses have taken place: in Spalato-Salona (1894), Rome (1900), Ravenna (1932), Vatican City (1938), Aix-en-Provence (1954), Ravenna (1962), and Trier (1965).

Academies and Professorship. The increased interest in Christian archeology has led to the founding of academies and the establishing of chairs at the universities. Rome has a Pontificia Accademia Romana di Archeologia, the Pontificia Commissione di Archeologia Sacra, and the Istituto Pontificio di Archeologia Cristiana, this last opened by Pope Pius XI in 1926. Departments for Christian archeology exist in Rome, Vatican City, Paris, Arles, Carthage, Cairo, Athens, Istanbul, Berlin, London, and Washington (Dumbarton Oaks); there are institutes and seminars in Heidelberg, Freiburg (Breisgau), Erlangen, Göttingen, Kiel, Marburg, Würzburg, Bonn (F. J. Dölger Institute), Rome, Nijmegen, and Princeton University (U.S.A.).

Index of Christian Art. The head of the Department of Christian Art at Princeton University, Charles Rufus *Morey, organized an important tool for studies in Christian archeology, the so-called *Index of Christian Art.* It began in 1917 as a listing of all subjects and objects of early Christian art down to *c.* A.D. 700. At present (1965) it contains more than 120,000 photographs and 500,000 cards comprising the subject entries. The aim of the index, according to Morey, was "to catalogue by subject the picture-type of all the known (published) monuments of Christian art dated before the year 1400, to record briefly the history of the objects, to assemble the important bibliography relative to each monument, and finally, when the literature of art history now available has been searched and exhausted, to maintain the catalogue by an annual edition of the newly published material and all of the pertinent bibliographical references." The index is supplemented by a monument file or collection of photographs of the objects and monuments described in the subject file. The photographs are arranged by material and filed geographically by name of place rather than subject. So far there are four complete copies of the Princeton index, namely, in the Dumbarton Oaks Research Library and Collection of Harvard University in Washington, D.C., in the University of California, in the Bibliotheca Vaticana, and in the Kunsthistorisch Instituut of the Rijksuniversiteit at Utrecht (Holland).

Research. The 20th century has contributed to a better understanding of the origin of Christian art. Excavations in the Christian East have brought an increasing amount of material to light that led to a reexamination of questions concerning the beginnings of Christian art. It had been customary to regard Rome as the center and the place of origin, until Strzygowski (1901) pointed to Asia Minor, Antioch, and especially Alexandria as the places of origin of the first Christian art. While some of his conclusions were exaggerated, he found many followers, e.g., Wulff, Diehl, and Dalton. Since then the isolated, exclusively Rome-centered study of early Christian art that had little regard for the Oriental monuments has been abandoned. The results of the excavations at *Dura-Europos in Syria have proved again that Christian art began in the East at an early date.

Classical and Christian Art. The question "Rome or Orient" cannot be solved without a comparative study of late classical art. Christian art in both the East and the West is only a branch or offshoot of late classical art, and must be regarded as such. Since 1930 comparative studies have led to a new approach. The style of early Christian art is now regarded as a part of the late classical development. As such it is recognized by classical archeologists as well and has become an object of their studies. At the same time, progress made in the comparative study of the history of religions has resulted in such studies as the monumental investigation of the fish symbol by F. J. *Dölger (IXΘYC, 5 v. 1910–43) and the interesting study EIS THEOS (1926) by E. *Peterson.

Dating Monuments. In addition, considerable progress has been made in the 20th century in the solution of the difficult problem of determining the dates of early Christian monuments, cemeteries, paintings, and art in general. For a long time Christian archeologists were convinced that Christian art was as old as Christianity itself. The opinion prevailed that from the beginning, Christians renounced pagan art and substituted Christian decorations for hitherto pagan paintings, sculpture, and ornaments in their homes, in their liturgical meeting places, and in their cemeteries. Following this idea, they were convinced that the great treasure house of art, the Roman catacombs, contained paintings that originated with the beginnings of the Christian community of Rome, in the second half of the 1st century. Since there were Christian members in the families of the Flavii and Acilii of the 1st century, the catacombs of Domitilla and Priscilla were thought to have commenced with the time of the Apostles.

O. Marucchi did not hesitate to claim in his *Roma sotteranea* and his *Manual of Christian Archeology* that both catacombs contained bodies of persons baptized by the Apostles themselves. Even G. B. de Rossi [*Bullettino di archeologia cristiana* 3 (1865) 34] shared this view for the dating of the catacomb of Domitilla. He called a part of it *Sepulchrum Flaviorum* and believed that it originated between the reigns of Nero and Domitian. The legendary Acts of Cecilia of the 5th century served J. *Wilpert as a basis for attributing the founding of the Crypt of the Popes in S. Callisto on the Via Appia to the Christian family of the Caecilii [*La cripta dei papi* (Rome 1910) 11]. According to B. Armellini [*Gli antichi cimiteri cristiani* (Rome 1903) 249] the cemetery of Nicomedes on the Via Nomentana was begun in Apostolic times.

The Roman Catacombs. Since 1928, however, all these opinions have been proved erroneous. A thorough investigation of the structure of the so-called Hypogaeum Flaviorum in the cemetery of Domitilla by A. M. Schneider convinced him that it could not have originated before the middle of the 2d century. Shortly afterward P. Styger examined the chronology of the Roman catacombs. The structural history of these cemeteries led him to the conclusion that none of the Roman catacombs was built before the middle of the 2d century. As a result none of their paintings can be older than this date. Several studies on the style of early Christian art proved that there are no known Christian paintings that belong to the 2d century.

Fig. 1. The Crypt of the Popes as it appeared at the time of its discovery, 19th-century lithograph.

F. Wirth compared the style of the paintings in the Roman catacombs with contemporary pagan paintings and found that the oldest Christian products belong to the 3d century. G. Rodenwaldt, H. U. von Schoenebeck, and F. Gerke came to the same conclusion soon after by studying the style of the oldest Christian sarcophagi. The earliest of these originated *c.* A.D. 220. J. De Wit, in a careful study of the style of the catacomb paintings, proved most of Wirth's dating to be correct. A. M. Schneider in 1951 was able to prove that none of the Roman catacombs are earlier than 200. Thus the early dates that Wilpert assigned to a great number of Christian monuments, paintings, and sculptures must be regarded as antiquated. The same can be said about the chronology on which C. R. Morey based his *Early Christian Art* (Princeton 1942).

The oldest paintings of the Roman catacombs of a definitely Christian character and the oldest Christian sarcophagi date from about 220, not earlier. The excavations of Yale University at Dura-Europos have added proof for this date. The frescoes discovered in 1932 in this earliest known Christian church are from about 240. Hence in the East as well as in the West the first half of the 3d century witnessed the origin of a truly Christian art, i.e., an art based on Christian thought. A chronology of pagan and Christian sarcophagi up to A.D. 400 has been established by F. Gerke, G. M. A. Hanfmann, and F. Matz. J. Kollwitz and F. W. Deichmann deserve credit for having given a chronological order to Christian sculpture in the East between the 4th and 6th centuries.

Excavations. Remarkable progress has been made in this century in excavations in the East and West. Rome has seen new discoveries of great importance. The excavations of A. de Waal and P. Styger, begun in 1915 in San Sebastiano, have led to the rediscovery of the famous *Memoria Apostolorum,* and several hundreds of graffiti and inscriptions with invocations of the Apostles Peter and Paul. The examination of these monuments continues, and the literature grows from year to year. Several new catacombs have been found: in 1920 the cemetery of S. Panfilo near the Via Salaria vetus, in 1921 that of the Giordani on the Via Salaria nova; in 1926 an anonymous catacomb on the Via Tiburtina; and the new Viale Regina Margherita, with its highly decorated tomb of a single martyr, Novatian.

Rome and St. Peter. The excavations in the Lateran Baptistery initiated by Pope Benedict XV and finished in 1924 have brought to light the Constantinian Baptistery decorated by *Sixtus III (432–440). Those conducted under the Lateran Basilica between 1934 and 1938 discovered the *castra nova* of the imperial bodyguard, over which Constantine had built this church. The most important excavations in Rome are those below St. Peter's Basilica on the *Vatican between 1939 and 1949, which led to the discovery of an entire early

Fig. 2. Christ as teacher, mid-4th-century sculpture from the catacombs, now in the Museo dell Terme, Rome.

Fig. 4. Coin of Lucius Verus embedded in the plaster of a 3d-century tomb in the cemetery of S. Panfilo, Rome.

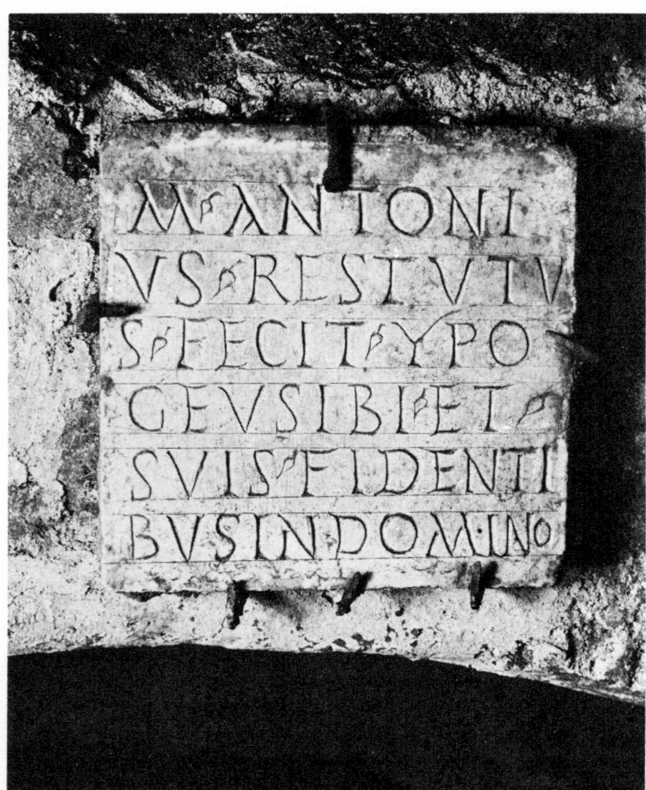

Fig. 3. Inscription of Marcus Antonius. 3d century, in situ in the catacomb of Domitilla, Rome.

CHRISTIAN ARCHEOLOGY

Fig. 5. Mosaic from a North African catacomb, now in the museum at Sousse, Tunisia.

Christian and pagan necropolis with a series of highly decorated mausoleums of pre-Constantinian times, and the memorial of the Apostle (*tropaion*) mentioned by the priest Caius in A.D. 180 at the burial place of St. Peter.

One of the latest Roman discoveries is the catacomb found in 1955 on the Via Latina. Forty-eight meters long and twenty-seven meters wide (157.4 by 88.6 feet) at the broadest point, it is of small size in comparison with other catacombs. But it contains the finest collection of murals depicting Old and New Testament and pagan scenes in perfect condition. The cemetery belonged most probably to a pagan family among whom were several converts to Christianity. The murals include subjects from the Old Testament—expulsion of Adam and Eve from Paradise, Cain and Abel, the Flood, the drunkenness of Noah, and Lot's wife turned into a pillar of salt. The New Testament murals represent Jesus and the Twelve Apostles, the Sermon on the Mount, the soldiers casting lots for Christ's garments, and Lazarus rising from the dead in the presence of 83 witnesses. Among the pagan subjects are Cleopatra and the Asp and scenes from the life of Hercules. Since the catacomb had no famous martyr, it escaped the attention of other Roman burial places. Thus it was spared the looting and destruction that befell well-known catacombs.

Italy, Spain, and France. The discovery of the so-called heretical *hypogaeum* of the Aurelii near Viale Manzoni in 1919 was important for the study of the borderlines between pagan and Christian ideas as they appear in art. The excavations in S. Maria Maggiore and S. Pudentiana brought important results for the history of the ecclesiastical edifices in Rome. Knowledge of the cult of the martyrs at Rome in Constantinian times was enriched by the excavations after World War II conducted in S. Lorenzo fuori le mura by R. Krautheimer and E. Josi and in the original church of St. Agnes near St. Costanza by R. Perrotti, and by the discovery of the church of Marcellinus and Peter connected with the Mausoleum of St. *Helena by A. Tschira and F. W. Deichmann.

For the rest of Italy, A. Belucci rediscovered (1931) in Naples the catacomb of St. Eusebius and new zones in the catacomb of St. Gaudiosus. H. Achelis published a valuable work on the catacombs of Naples in 1936 with 60 plates. C. Mercurelli found catacombs at Agrigentum, and A. Agnello made excavations in the catacombs of Syracuse. A. de Capitani d'Arzago excavated the church of St. Thecla, and E. Viola that of the Apostles at Milan. Other excavations that deserve to be mentioned are those of St. Apollinare in Classe, at Ravenna, by M. Mazotti, of the Basilica Tullio and the Monastero at Aquileia by G. Brusin, of the necropolis of Julia Concordia by P. L. Zovatto, of the cathedral of Grado by M. Mirabella Roberti, and of St. Giusto in Trieste and the basilica of Ancona.

In Spain excavations between 1924 and 1934 near Tarragona have brought a large early Christian necropolis to light with more than 2,000 graves from the 3d to the end of the 5th century, with six *mensae* for funeral repasts. The remains of the basilica found in the center of the area are those of the early bishop's church of Tarragona and not those of a cemetery chapel, since a baptistery with a rectangular font once formed part of the church. The basilica belongs to the 4th century. France saw the reconstruction of the three baptisteries of Riez, Aix, and *Fréjus in their original early Christian forms and the excavations of the crypt of St. Victor at Marseille, the oldest known liturgical building in France.

Germany, the Balkans, and Greece. Interesting discoveries were made in Germany, especially in the Rhineland, between 1932 and 1934. The excavations below the church of St. Victor at Xanten in 1933 proved the existence of a pagan and Christian cemetery. The tomb of two martyrs and a *mensa* for the cult of the dead belonging to the 4th century were found, together with a church erected above these martyr graves in the 5th century. Similar cemeterial churches located in originally pagan cemeteries were discovered below St. Alban at Mainz, St. Severin in Cologne, and the cathedral of Bonn. Excavations in 1943 and 1945–57 below the cathedral of Trier have led to the discovery of the early Christian bishop's church of the 4th century.

At Salona in Dalmatia, a lively center of archeological research, F. Bulic obtained important results in excavations conducted before World War I. He rediscovered the cemeterial basilicas of Manastirine, Marusinac, Crikvine, and the five (*quinque*) martyrs at Kapljuc. These excavations were resumed in 1928 by the Danish scholars Weilbach, Brönsted, and Dyggve and by the Austrian archeologists Gerber and Egger. Their investigations threw new light on the origin of this Christian city and its cult of the martyrs. Excavations in Stobi, Butrinto, and Bulgaria contributed to a more complete picture of the beginnings of Christianity in the Balkans.

Those in Greece and on the Greek islands, in Epirus, Thessalonika, Attica, Peloponnese, and Macedonia by A. Orlandos, G. Soteriu, and P. Lemerle gave a survey of early Greek Christian architecture. The excavations at Thasos, Nikopolis, Branson, Corinth, and Athens by A. Orlandos, G. Travlos, G. Soteriu and E. Stikas round out the picture of this development.

North Africa and Egypt. Mention must be made of the results achieved in the excavations of North Africa in the 20th century. In Algeria two basilicas and the cemetery of St. Salsa were discovered at Tipasa; two basilicas and a baptistery, at Djemila; a pagan basilica from the time of Alexander Severus converted to a Christian church in the 4th or 5th century, at Madaura; a basilica and a monastery excavated in 1927, at Ain-Tamda; a basilica at Henchi-el-Ateuch; the famous basilica, built before 415 at Thebessa, that was erected above the *memoria* with the tomb of St. Crispina from 313; the basilica of five naves with an Eastern and Western apse at Orléansville, the ancient *castellum Tingitanum;* and a basilica of Donatists, between Thebessa and Khenchela in Kasr-el-Kelb (Numidia).

The greatest and most numerous Christian cemeteries of all Africa Romana were excavated at Sousse, the ancient Hadrumetum. They are similar to the catacombs of Rome. Six basilicas were excavated at Carthage. Excavations at Carthage, Thibiuca, Bulla Regia, Maktar, Junca, Sbeitla, Thebessa, Thebessa Kalia, Hippo, Timgad, and Tigzirt have had interesting results. In Tripolitania the excavations of the Italian government at Sabratha brought four Christian basilicas with baptisteries and precious mosaics to light. R. Bartoccini, P. Romanelli, and B. Apollonij-Ghetti discovered churches in Leptis Magna, Ptolemais, and Apollonia, among them two basilicas at Leptis Magna with a bap-

Fig. 6. Christian archeology: (a) Third-century wall paintings in the "Heretical hypogaeum" on the Via Manzoni, Rome. (b) Adam, Eve, Abel, and Cain, detail of the wall paintings in a catacomb on the Via Latina, Rome.

tistery that had a cruciform font. J. B. Ward Perkins has recently resumed the excavations at Sabratha and Leptis Magna. The investigations of Monneret de Villards unearthed the monuments of ancient Christian Nubia.

In Egypt C. M. Kaufmann discovered (1905) in the Mareotis Desert the great Christian pilgrimage place of St. Menas with the burial church of this saint consecrated under Emperor *Theodosius I (379–395), a basilica 125 feet long and 74 feet wide with nave and aisles, each terminating in an apse, and the altar directly above the martyr's crypt. To accommodate the increasing masses of pilgrims, a much larger basilica was built under Emperor Arcadius (395–408) on the eastern end of the first church, with a large transept, 164 feet long and 66 feet wide. At the western end a monumental baptistery was erected. Other basilicas, baths, and guesthouses for the pilgrims were built under *Zeno (474–491).

J. B. Ward Perkins excavated recently the crypt church of St. Menas. The F. J. Dölger Institute of Bonn is now preparing (1965) a continuation of Kaufmann's excavation. While Kaufmann was making his discoveries, T. Cledat excavated Bawit, and T. E. Quibell, Saggaria. In 1946 a jar was found near Nag-Hammadi in the vicinity of the ancient Chenoboskion, 30 miles north of Luxor on the east bank of the Nile. It proved to be one of the greatest discoveries of the century because it contained 12 volumes, or more than 1,000 pages, of Gnostic texts in Coptic, amounting to 37 complete treatises and 5 in fragmentary condition, hitherto totally unknown. Only a few of them have been published so far, e.g., the Gospel of St. Thomas. The rediscovered treatises are casting a flood of light on the history of Gnosticism and the beginnings of Christian theology.

Palestine and Syria. In Palestine a great number of early Christian basilicas were excavated with important results for the history of Christianity's holy places. R. W. Hamilton's excavations under the basilica of the Nativity in Bethlehem brought the original structure of the Constantinian basilica and an earlier church to light. A. E. Mader excavated the church of Mamre, A. M. Schneider, that of Garizim. Both Mader and Schneider in 1932 near el-Tabga on the Lake of Galilee excavated the ancient basilica of the "Multiplication of Loaves" in the traditional place of the miracle. It is a large building with three naves, a transept, and marvelous floor mosaics. Shortly afterward B. Bagatti discovered the remains of the church of the Beatitudes of the 4th century. H. Vincent and F. Abel excavated the basilica at Emmaus, which originated in the 3d century.

A joint expedition of Yale University and the American Schools of Oriental Research achieved successful excavations at Gerasa, the city of the Decapolis. Eleven churches built between the second half of the 4th century and the year 611 were brought to light. A number of Christian buildings were discovered at Mount Nebo by S. J. Saller and Bagatti and at Sbeita in Negeb by C. Baly. At Mount Nebo they found the church of the 4th century where pilgrims venerated the tomb of Moses. New excavations in Bethania at the tomb of Lazarus, at the Mount of Olives, Susith-Hippos, Chirbet el-Kerak, Shikmona, and Bethsean must be mentioned also. In Syria the expeditions of Marquis M. de Vogüe, paralleling in time those of G. B. de Rossi and Princeton

(a)

(b)

(c)

Fig. 7. Christian archeology: (a) Partially restored ruins of the basilica of St. John, Ephesus. (b) Excavation of Romanesque structures under a parish church in the Netherlands. (c) Uncovering and cleaning of the mosaics of the north tympanum of Hagia Sophia, Istanbul.

University, had brought a great number of churches to light. After excavations at Brad, Quirk Bize, J. Lassus and G. Tschalenko were able to answer many questions regarding the interior of Syrian Churches and the influence of the liturgy on the structure. The greatest martyrion of Syria, that of Qalat Seman, was unearthed through excavations conducted by D. Krenker, R. Naumann, and G. Tschalenko. The excavations at Antioch in the years 1933–36 conducted by Princeton University deserve special mention because they make possible a reconstruction of the past of this important city. But the most startling results were obtained at Dura-Europos, the ancient city in the Syrian Desert, where since 1928 a series of archeological expeditions has been conducted by Yale University and the French Academy of Inscriptions and Letters under the general supervision of M. I. Rostovtzeff. In the season of 1931–32 a Christian house church was discovered with a baptistery and wall paintings from the first part of the 3d century. This represents the first example of a pre-Constantinian house church, whereas the mural paintings of the discovered synagogue contributed important material for the question of the relations between Jewish and Christian art.

J. Kollwitz began in 1952 his excavations of Rusafa-Sergiopolis in Syria. At Ephesus the Austrian Archaeological Institute excavated the great basilica of St. John the Apostle with the tomb of the saint, constructed at the time of Justinian I. The expedition began in 1921 and led, in addition, to the discovery of the cemetery of the Seven Sleepers. The excavations were under the supervision of G. Soteriu, J. Keil, H. Hörmann, E. Reisch, and F. Knoll. The church of the Seven Sleepers was built between the 5th and 6th centuries, with a catacomb of 10 family tombs. The Austrian scholars discovered, moreover, the great church of the Mother of God, where the Council of Ephesus (431) took place, and a number of smaller churches. At Smyrna a number of liturgical buildings of the 5th and 6th centuries, among them a baptistery, were brought to light. G. De Jerphanion produced an interesting study on the churches of Cappadocia.

Asia Minor. The American Society for Archeological Research in Asia Minor undertook a series of excavations in Cilicia and discovered at Meriamlik the church of Tekla, two basilicas, one of them built by Emperor Zeno (d. 491), and the remains of a third, and at Koryls three large churches. A. M. Schneider and W. Karnapp excavated the city walls of Nicaea (Iznik). At Istanbul the Hagia Sophia became the object of very important archeological studies in 1934, after the building ceased to be a house of actual worship. The excavations contributed to knowledge of the history of the pre-Justinian church of Hagia Sophia and the architecture of the present edifice. T. Whittemore of the Byzantine Institute of America began in 1932 his search for the ancient mosaics of the Hagia Sophia, which resulted in an astonishing discovery of the finest mural decorations in the narthex and the southern vestibule. A. M. Schneider discovered the Martyrion of St. Euphemia; and A. Müfid Mansel, several churches in the IXth region; Rice and Perkins continued the excavations near the great palace.

Bibliography: C. M. Kaufmann, *Handbuch der christlichen Archäologie* (3d ed. Paderborn 1922). P. Testini, *Archeologia cristiana* (Rome 1958). B. Bagatti, *L'archeologia cristiana in Palestina* (Florence 1962).

Dictionaries. W. Smith and S. Cheetham, *Dictionary of Christian Antiquities,* 2 v. (Hartford 1880). F. X. Kraus, ed., *Real-Encyclopädie der christlichen Altertümer,* 2 v. (Freiburg 1882–86). DACL. ReallexAntChr. K. Wessel, ed., *Reallexikon zur byzantinischen Kunst* (Stuttgart 1963).

Journals. *Bullettino di archeologia cristiana* (Rome 1863–94). *Nuovo bullettino di archeologia cristiana* (Rome 1895–1922). RivArchCrist, with bibliog. RömQuartalsch. BullAmSchOrRes. *American Schools of Oriental Research: Annual* (New Haven 1919–). DumbOaksP.

Epigraphy. J. B. de Rossi, ed., *Inscriptiones christianae urbis Romae,* 2 v. (Rome 1857–87), suppl. to v.1 ed. J. Gatti (Rome 1915); new ser. ed. A. Silvagni and A. Ferrua, 3 v. (Rome 1922–57). Diehl ICLV.

Architecture. R. Krautheimer, *Corpus basilicarum christianarum Romae* (Vatican City 1937–), cf. J. Quasten, Röm Quartalsch 46 (1938) 66–67. J. G. Davies, *The Origin and Development of Early Christian Architecture* (SPCK; 1952), cf. J. Quasten, ThSt 14 (1953) 313–317.

Art. H. Woodruff, *The Index of Christian Art at Princeton University* (Princeton 1942). O. M. Dalton, *East Christian Art* (Oxford 1925). Morey EChArt. D. T. Rice, *The Beginnings of Christian Art* (London 1957). Wilpert MosMal. Wilpert Sarc. J. Strzygowski, *Origin of Christian Church Art* (Oxford 1923). A. M. Schneider, "Der Eingang zum *Hypogaeum Flaviorum,*" *Mitteilungen des Deutschen Archäologischen Instituts. Römische Abteilung* 43 (1928) 1–12. H. U. von Schoenebeck, "Die christliche Sarkophagplastik unter Konstantin," *ibid.* 51 (1936) 238–336; "Die christlichen Paradeisos-Sarkophage," RivArchCrist 14 (1937) 289–343. P. Styger, *Die römischen Katakomben* (Berlin 1933); *Römische Märtyrergrüfte* (Berlin 1935). F. Wirth, *Römische Wandmalerei* (Berlin 1934). J. de Wit, *Spätrömische Bildnismalerei* (Berlin 1938). F. Gerke, "Indeengeschichte der ältesten christlichen Kunst," ZKirchgesch 59 (1940) 1–102; *Die Zeitbestimmung der Passionssarkophage* (Berlin 1940). A. M. Schneider, "Die ältesten Denkmäler der römischen Kirche," *Festschrift der Akademie der Wissenschaften in Göttingen* (1951) 166–198. A. von Gerkan, RömQuartalsch 42 (1934) 219–232, Dura. M. I. Rostovtzeff, *Dura-Europos and Its Art* (Oxford 1938). J. Quasten, "The Painting of the Good Shepherd at Dura Europos," MedSt 9 (1947) 1–18. G. M. A. Hanfmann, *The Season Sarcophagus in Dumbarton Oaks,* 2 v. (Cambridge, Mass. 1951). G. Bovini, *I sarcofagi paleo-cristiani* (Rome 1949); *Sarcofagi paleocristiani di Ravenna* (Vatican City 1954). J. Kollwitz, *Die Sarkophage Ravennas* (Freiburg 1956). F. Matz, *Ein römisches Meisterwerk: Der Jahreszeitensarkophag* (Berlin 1958).

Survey of reports. J. Quasten, "Beziehungen zur christlichen Archaeologie," JbLiturgwiss 14 (1938) 396–418; 15 (1941) 405–440.

Congresses. *Atti del III. Congresso internazionale di archeologia cristiana* (Rome 1934). *Atti del IV. Congresso internazionale di archeologia cristiana,* 2 v. (Rome 1940–48). *Actes du Ve Congrès international d'archéologie chrétienne* (Rome 1957).

Illustration credits: Fig. 1, Anderson-Art Reference Bureau. Fig. 2, Leonard Von Matt. Figs. 3, 4, and 6, Pontificia Commissione di Archeologia, Sacra. Fig. 5, German Archaeological Institute, Rome. Fig. 7*a,* National Council of Catholic Men. Fig. 7*b,* Enciclopedia Cattolica, Vatican City. Fig. 7*c,* The Byzantine Institute of America, Dumbarton Oaks, Washington, D.C.

[J. QUASTEN]

ARCHES, COURT OF, the ecclesiastical court of appeal for the Archdiocese or Province of *Canterbury. From as early as the end of the 13th century it sat in St. Mary of the Arches (*de arcubus*), so called from its arched crypt. St. Mary was an exempt deanery within the city of London. This court dealt with the provincial appeals of the archbishop, and presiding over its sessions was the archbishop's Official, who later frequently combined that office with the deanship of the Arches. The Court continued after the Reformation and has also been known as the Arches Court. It is still the Provincial Court of the Archbishop of Canterbury, the corresponding institution for York being the Chancery Court of York. Woodcock has an illuminating discussion of the medieval practice; there is much further material in the *Black Books of the Arches* (partially printed in D. Wilkins, *Concilia,* 2, London

1737, and described by Churchill, 2:206). A study of the customs of the Court was in preparation (1964) by F. Donald Logan.

Bibliography: W. LYNDWOOD, *Provinciale* (Oxford 1679). J. AYCLIFFE, *Parergon juris canonici anglicani* (London 1726). Holdsworth HEL 3 (1903) 369– . I. J. CHURCHILL, *Canterbury Administration,* 2 v. (New York 1933) 1:422. *Canon Law of the Church of England* (London 1947) 48, 89, 198. B. L. WOODCOCK, *Medieval Ecclesiastical Courts in the Diocese of Canterbury* (New York 1952). Cross ODCC 79.

[R. J. SCHOECK]

ARCHIEREUS, Greek, ἀρχιερεύς, equivalent of the Russian *arkhierei,* term for bishop in its theological and liturgical meaning: one possessing the fullness of the power of the priesthood. It is applicable to any consecrated bishop. The term is frequently used in the liturgical books of the Greek Orthodox, Greek Catholic, and Byzantine churches. Without any special jurisdiction, his position was to represent the hierarchy of Order in solemnizing divine services. The title enhanced the dignity of those holding the office of rector of certain theological establishments or of archpriest of historic basilicas and was a mark of personal privilege. Conferred frequently on major religious superiors, it was a mark of special honor to their communities. This term is not to be confused with *protoiereus*—archpriest—the highest rank to which married clergy could aspire, in contrast to the celibate episcopacy. In the rubrics of the Byzantine liturgies, a bishop is frequently referred to as archpriest, but he is distinguished as *archiereus* from the *protoiereus,* or protopriest, as above indicated.

Bibliography: J. BJERRING, *Offices of the Oriental Church* (New York 1884). A. MICHIELS, *Les Origines de l'épiscopat* (Louvain 1900). N. MILASH, *Pravoslavno Crkveno pravo* (3d ed. Belgrade 1926). R. JANIN, *Les églises orientales et les rites orienteaux* (Paris 1955).

[L. NEMEC]

ARCHIVES

Ecclesiastical archives are as old as the organization of the earliest churches, for these congregations produced records that required preservation and storage. In large cities that were seats of metropolitans, as well as in the major cities of the imperial dioceses, ecclesiastical archives were most probably modeled on the parallel archival practices of the Roman Empire. In the Middle Ages episcopal sees, collegiate and cathedral chapters, and monasteries continued to be important archival centers, preserving not only records of their own land holdings, contracts, etc., but also important documents that lay officials might want to deposit there.

At the beginning of the modern era the Council of *Trent promulgated brief regulations on the preservation of important documents. Subsequently Popes *Sixtus V (who planned a central Roman Archives and the Notarial Archives for the States of the Church), *Clement VIII, and *Paul V initiated important archival reforms. Consequently, Pope *Benedict XIII issued his constitution on Italian ecclesiastical archives *Maxima vigilantia,* dated June 14, 1727 [BullRom 12 (Rome 1736) 221–225, entitled: "A constitution on archives to be erected in Italy for the preservation of legal papers and documents pertaining to cathedral churches both collegiate and noncollegiate, to seminaries, monasteries of both men and of women, guilds, confraternities, hospitals and to all other pious institutions legally instituted. To this is added an instruction in Italian concerning the documents which are to be preserved therein"]. *Maxima vigilantia* consists of 34 chapters in Latin plus 7 chapters of instruction in Italian. To a large extent it is upon this constitution that the archival regulations of modern Canon Law (CIC cc.375–384) are based. They state that each diocese must have an archives and describe how its inventory must be made. They treat of the recovery of lost archival holdings, of precautions against loss of archival documents through loans, and of the manner in which such materials should be used. Beyond this, every bishop is to have a secret archives or at least a secret safe under double lock. A duplicate of the inventory of each ecclesiastical archives in the diocese is to be deposited in the episcopal archives.

Furthermore, every parish must have an archives (CIC c.470) for the storage of the *libri paroeciales* (the registers of those baptized, confirmed, married, deceased, and the register of the spiritual condition of the members of the parish). The same canon provides that in this same archives shall be kept all pastoral letters from the bishop, other important documents, and valuable papers.

The content and importance of ecclesiastical archives vary greatly from country to country. Those of Italy and Spain are of special historical importance. The Holy See sent instructions pertaining to archives to all Italian bishops in 1902 (*Forma di regolamento per la custodia e l'uso degli archivi e delle biblioteche ecclesiastiche*), again in 1907 (on the creation of an archives commission in every diocese), and in 1923 (on preserving and putting in order Italian ecclesiastical archives). But during World War II Italy's archives were severely damaged, despite rigorous measures taken by the Vatican. Immediately after the outbreak of the war Cardinal Giovanni *Mercati issued a questionnaire (*Censimento*) to all ecclesiastical archives asking for a summary of their holdings. After the war this project was further pursued and brought up to date. From these efforts grew (1955) the Pontifical Commission for the Ecclesiastical Archives of Italy. Its constitution, dated Feb. 29, 1960, is printed in ActApS 52 (1960) 997–1000; its instructions to the local ordinaries, dated Dec. 5, 1960, are in Act ApS 52 (1960) 1022–25. It is currently planned to extend this commission to all ecclesiastical archives throughout the world.

To further and coordinate archival activities in the Church, the Associazione Archivistica Ecclesiastica was founded in Rome in 1956. Membership is open to all ecclesiastical archivists, although, in fact, Italy provides most of its members. Since 1958 it has published *Archiva Ecclesiae,* with important articles on church archives in all countries. It holds congresses (e.g., its sixth congress met in Rome in 1964), initiates courses in the auxiliary sciences, and promotes registration in the Vatican Archives' Pontifical School of Paleography, Diplomatics, and Archives. Its constitution appears in *Archiva Ecclesiae* 1 (1958) 9–10.

See also ARCHIVES, ECCLESIASTICAL; ARCHIVES, U.S. CATHOLIC; VATICAN ARCHIVES.

Bibliography: E. LOEVINSON, "La costituzione di papa Benedetto XIII sugli archivi ecclesiastici: Un papa archivista," *Gli archivi Italiani* 3 (1916) 159–206. G. BATTELLI, "Il censimento degli archivi ecclesiastici d'Italia e la loro tutela durante la guerra," RivStorChIt 1:113–116; "Gli archivi ecclesiastici d'Italia danneggiati dalla guerra," *ibid.* 306–308. H. L. HOFFMANN, *De archivis ecclesiasticis, imprimis dioecesanis secundum iuris ca-*

nonici codicem (Rome 1962). J. GRISAR, "Notare und Notariatsarchive im Kirchenstaat des 16. Jahrhunderts," StTest 234 (1964) 251–300.

[K. A. FINK]

ARCHIVES, ECCLESIASTICAL

The necessity of archives was recognized very early in history and we find them in use among the most ancient peoples. Assyria, Babylon, Israel, Phoenicia, Egypt, Greece, and Rome appreciated the value of preserving important documents and usually reserved a part of the temple for the archives. The sacredness of the holy place was expected to be an additional guarantee against violation.

History. The Liber pontificalis claims that Pope St. Clement (*c.* 88–97) divided the Church at Rome into seven regions, and assigned to these regions notaries who were to compile accurate and diligent accounts of the history of the martyrs. Most likely the procedure followed by these notaries was patterned after that of the civil government except that the Liber pontificalis adds that these accounts were kept "in ecclesias," that is, in the church itself or one of its buildings. Pope St. Fabian (236–250) is said to have appointed seven subdeacons who were to supervise the notaries and transcribe the *acta* in full from the *notae* or shorthand methods of the notaries.

As early as 367 B.C. Roman law saw the need of an archivist. The norms of Roman law undoubtedly served as guides in the development of administrative procedures of the early Christian Church.

Cardinal Amleto Cicognani cites the writings of Pope St. Damasus (366–384) to prove that the old archives (*Cartharium*) of the Holy See were housed on the same spot where they are now located, the present Apostolic *Chancery.

Before the 16th century there seems to have been an almost total lack of ecclesiastical legislation dealing with archives. A few references to the contents and custody of church archives indicate that their existence was taken for granted by the legislators.

Common and Secret Archives. The rules for the erection, contents, custody, and use of both common and secret archives is contained in CIC cc.375–384. The residential bishop must erect archives in a safe and suitable place (CIC c.375); this canon expresses a grave precept. If possible, a separate room ought to be used for the archives. It is impossible to give an exhaustive list of all the documents that should be kept in the archives but the Code of Canon Law gives ample indication of what type of material ought to be preserved there: authentic copies of parochial books (CIC c.470.3), records of ordinations (CIC c.1010.1), authentic documents regarding church property ownership and rights (CIC 1523n6), documents of completed ecclesiastical trials that should remain with the tribunal (CIC c.1645.2).

The obligation of some practical and orderly arrangement of the archives is required by CIC c.375. A chronological filing may be preferable for certain types of documents whereas an alphabetical system might be more practical for other types. The diocesan *chancellor is the legal custodian of the archives (CIC c.372) and therefore he, together with the bishop, should determine their arrangement.

Custody of the archives is a serious matter (CIC c.375.2) and even an inventory of archive documents is required as a safeguard (CIC c.376.1). The bishop is instructed to seek out documents that were borrowed (e.g., for microfilming or for historical research) and replace them in the archives (CIC c.376.2). The law requires also that permission be obtained to enter the archives (CIC c.377) and to borrow or remove any document (CIC c.378).

The secret archives are governed by similar norms (CIC cc.379–384). The Code of Canon Law made universal laws regarding secret archives for the first time, although such archives were in existence in many areas prior to the Code. The contents of this special archive are cited in various canons, e.g., notations of marriages of conscience (CIC c.1107), documents of tribunal cases that demand secrecy (CIC c.1645.2), and the transcript of an inquiry that precedes a criminal trial (CIC c.1946). The custody of these secret archives is particularly important if the see is vacant and therefore detailed rules of custody are cited in Canon Law (CIC c.380–382). The use of secret archive material also is carefully legislated with penalties cited for abuses (CIC cc.382–384).

Identical legislation on these archives for the Oriental Churches is found in ClerSanc cc.439–451. These canons vary from the Latin Code only in terminology and in more exact expressions.

Bibliography: R. NAZ, DDC 1:1026–36. A. CICOGNANI, *Canon Law* (2d ed. rev. Westminster, Md. 1947) 141. H. J. WOLFF, *Roman Law* (Norman, Okla. 1951) 34. A. TOSO, *Ad codicem iuris canonici commentaria minora* (Rome 1925) 2.3.1:22. W. F. LOUIS, *Diocesan Archives* (CUA CLS 137; Washington 1941). J. E. PRINCE, The Diocesan Chancellor (CUA CLS 167; Washington 1942). C. A. KEKUMANO, *The Secret Archives of the Diocesan Curia* (CUA CLS 350; Washington 1954). H. HOFFMANN, "De codificatione iuris archivistici per jus novissimum Codicis Iuris Canonici," PeriodicaMorCanLiturg 49 (1960) 204–236.

[C. A. KEKUMANO]

ARCHIVES, U.S. CATHOLIC

Catholic manuscript centers in the U.S., varying widely in extent and value, include those connected with archdiocesan and diocesan sees, educational institutions, and religious orders and congregations.

Early Beginnings. During the latter part of the 19th century, Prof. James Farnham Edwards of the University of Notre Dame, Ind., initiated a project that he named the Catholic Archives of America. Edwards' ambition was to create an archival depository at the University of Notre Dame for all the Catholic material of the nation. The result of these efforts was the bringing to Notre Dame of papers of the Archdiocese of Detroit, Mich., 1785–1870; the major portion of the Archives of New Orleans, La., 1785–1897; and of the Archdiocese of Cincinnati, Ohio, 1821–1881; as well as the papers of many outstanding Catholics, such as Charles Warren Stoddard, James A. McMaster, Orestes Brownson, and William J. Onahan, and collections relative to the activities of priests and nuns during the Civil War. This collection has been enhanced recently by microfilm copies of the available U.S. material in the archives of the Congregation for the Propagation of the Faith, in Rome. Although the Catholic Archives of America never became a national depository, the work of Edwards stimulated interest in archival preservation.

Archdiocesan and Diocesan Collections. The Archdiocesan Archives of Baltimore, Md., more commonly known as the Baltimore Cathedral Archives, constitute the foremost collection of documentary material for the history of the Church in the U.S. Of the four dioceses created from Baltimore in 1808—Philadelphia, Pa., New York, N.Y., Boston, Mass., and Bardstown, Ky.—the largest extant archival collection is that of New York. From the administration of the first three bishops, nothing has survived, but from 1838, when John Hughes was appointed coadjutor to the aging Bp. John DuBois, the archival collections of the diocese and subsequent archdiocese have been built up. The dynamic personality of Hughes and his commanding position among the Catholic prelates during the Civil War make the records of his administration of particular interest. The later administration of Abp. Michael A. Corrigan covered one of the most significant eras of the history of American Catholicism, and the material of this period is essential to any study of theological *Americanism. Of the other three suffragan sees erected in 1808, only Boston possesses any sizable archival collection from the early period. Much of the material of the early archives of the Archdiocese of Philadelphia has been gone since mid-19th century. Of the early records of the pioneer Diocese of Bardstown-Louisville, there remains only a fraction of the diary of its first bishop, Benedict Joseph Flaget.

In 1793 Spanish Louisiana was erected into the Diocese of Louisiana and the Floridas. After the Louisiana Purchase, Bp. John Carroll of Baltimore was authorized by Rome to assume jurisdiction over the newly acquired American territory. In 1826 the northern section was made a separate diocese with the see city at St. Louis, Mo. Because of the residence of Bp. L. W. DuBourg in St. Louis from 1818, much of the early archival material is in the archives of the Archdiocese of St. Louis. Though they are particularly fortunate in the DuBourg and J. Rosati papers, there is a tremendous lacuna for the long administration of Abp. Peter Richard Kenrick. The collection is housed in excellent quarters in the new chancery building.

One of the richest sources for the history of the Church in the Pacific Northwest is the archives of the Archdiocese of Portland, Ore., which contains the correspondence of F. N. Blanchet with Bps. J. Signay and P. F. Turgeon of Quebec, Canada, and other members of the hierarchy of the U.S. and Canada.

Archbishop Rudolph A. Gerkin of Santa Fe, N.Mex., made a major effort to gather the original records of the churches and missions of New Mexico. This collection has been organized in a system of year-by-year files, a serious violation of the archival principle of provenance. The collection lacks many essential documents for the late 19th century, particularly concerning the administration of Abp. J. B. Salpointe. For the story of the Church in the Southwest, the Catholic Archives of Texas, located in Austin, Tex., are essential. This collection was begun under the direction and inspiration of Paul J. Foik, CSC, and later greatly enhanced by the activity of the late Bp. Laurence J. Fitzsimon of Amarillo, Tex., who obtained many photostats and transcripts from European sources.

Among the major tragedies befalling American Catholic archives was the loss of considerable portions of the collections of the Archdiocese of Chicago, Ill., and St. Paul, Minn. The former suffered the first of several misfortunes in the great fire of 1871, and a large block of the St. Paul collection concerning Abp. John Ireland was destroyed in another catastrophe. There seems to be, however, a large collection of Ireland papers still in private hands.

The activities of Bp. Bernard J. McQuaid while he was governing the Diocese of Rochester, N.Y., from 1868 to 1909 make that collection of great interest and value. McQuaid's correspondence provides the researcher with a unique cross-sectional view of American Catholic life and development during the crucial closing decades of the 19th century, particularly because McQuaid failed to see eye to eye with many of the more prominent members of the hierarchy of his time.

One of the archival problems is the failure of conservation on the parish level. The decentralization of record keeping resulting from the administrative structure of the Catholic Church is compensated to a certain extent by the policy of microfilming parish records for deposit in the diocesan archives. Probably no diocese or archdiocese has centralized records equal to those of Los Angeles, Calif., since the administration of Cardinal J. F. McIntyre. There all business of the quarterly sessions of the archdiocesan consultors is preserved in regularly numbered bound volumes.

Institutional Archives. In addition to the holdings of the parishes and dioceses, there is much essential archival material in the various educational institutions and the records of the various religious orders. Prominent among the institutional archives are those of Georgetown University, Washington, D.C., where the transcripts acquired by B. U. Campbell and John Gilmary Shea are of particular interest. Regis College in Denver, Colo., is the repository of the diaries and other manuscript materials of the educational and missionary activities of the Neapolitan Jesuits who in 1867 began their work throughout Colorado, New Mexico, and western Texas. This collection is particularly valuable in view of the destruction of a large number of papers when the move was made from the old to the new cathedral in Denver, Colo.

At Kenrick Seminary, St. Louis, Mo., the late Charles L. Souvay, CM, assembled an extensive collection of transcripts and photostats covering the work of the Vincentian fathers in the U.S. This collection is particularly valuable for the early 19th-century ministry to the whites in the Mississippi Valley and Texas. Similarly Victor F. O'Daniel, OP, has gathered at the Dominican House of Studies at The Catholic University of America, Washington, D.C., a large collection of transcripts, photostats, and original documents concerning the history of the Dominican Order in the U.S.

There is much material, unexploited and somewhat difficult of access, to be found in the archives of the various religious orders of women, particularly those of American origin, such as the Sisters of Charity of Nazareth, the Sisters of Loretto of Kentucky, and the Sisters of Charity of Leavenworth.

Essential for study of the Indian missions are the archives of the various provinces of the Society of Jesus in America. The archives of the Jesuit Missouri province at St. Louis University contains the Pierre DeSmet letter books and other DeSmetiana, but is almost totally lacking in letters written *to* DeSmet. The papers of P. Ponziglione, which contain accounts of missionary work among the Osages and early white settlers of southeastern Kansas are included in the St. Louis collection. The recent divisions into new provinces have somewhat complicated the location of Jesuit archival material. The St. Louis collection could probably be more accurately described as a collection of memorabilia. The best-organized archives are those of the Jesuit Oregon province at Gonzaga University, Spokane, Wash.; this collection contains a wealth of material on the Pacific Northwest and Alaska.

As a result of the efforts of Wilfrid Schoenberg, SJ, the papers of the Italian Jesuits of the Turin province, who staffed the Rocky Mountain Mission, have been gathered and preserved. Because Alaska is a mission of the Oregon province, much primary documentation of that area is included. An excellent collection of dictionaries and grammars of various Indian languages and an extensive collection of books on the Church and the American Indian make this center one of the most important in the West. An inadequate calendar of the holdings was published some years ago.

Zephyrin Engelhardt, OFM, assembled at Santa Barbara Mission, Calif., either in the original or in copy, the records of the old Franciscan missions of California. This work has been ably continued by his successors and the Academy of American Franciscan History, in Bethesda, Md. The Santa Barbara collection is divided into three sections: the Junipero Serra Collection, the California Mission Documents from 1769 to 1853, and the Archives of the Apostolic College of Our Lady of Sorrows of Santa Barbara from 1853 to 1885.

Monsignor Peter Guilday during 3 decades at The Catholic University of America assembled at that institution an unusually significant collection of transcripts and photostats gathered from throughout Europe and America pertaining to the Catholic history of the U.S. from the 18th to the 20th century.

During the 1930s an attempt was made to found a Jesuit Institute of History at Loyola University, Chicago, Ill. The purpose was to gather transcripts, photostats, and microfilm records of Jesuit educational and religious endeavor in the Americas, but the death and transfer of key personnel ended this project. In the 1960s St. Louis University inaugurated a western branch of the Roman Jesuit Institute of History. The members of this organization are actively engaged in microfilming American Jesuit records for deposit at St. Louis.

Other Collections. Among the source materials of American history acquired, either in original or in copies by American universities, libraries, and historical societies, there is much of paramount importance to the student of American Catholic history. Prominent among these collections are those of the Library of Congress, the Newberry, John Carter Brown, and Huntington libraries, the Bancroft Library at Berkeley, the Santa Fe Historical Society, the Stetson Collection of the Florida State Historical Society, and the Latin American Library of the University of Texas.

It is still necessary for the American Church history scholar to use European archives. In view of the fact that the U.S. was under the Congregation of Propaganda until 1908, it could reasonably be expected that these archives should be a rich source of information. Until recently, access to this material was difficult. Moreover, the scholar will be disappointed by the paucity of material. It seems the American bishops were not voluminous correspondents, at least with Rome. Another major archival source in Rome is the archives of the various religious orders. Because of the requirement of regular periodical reports from each institution, the archives of the generalate of the Society of Jesus contain much useful material, some of it duplicates of reports no longer extant in America. The great handicap of using the material in Rome is the standard rule of not releasing documents less than 100 years old.

In England, the Westminster Archdiocesan Archives and those of Stonyhurst College contain matter relating to the English-speaking ministry of colonial America. Essential for the story of the Church in the Ohio-Mississippi Valley are the Archdiocesan Archives of Quebec and the archives in Laval University in the same city.

Training Programs. No specific course in training for church archivists is yet available, but an increasing number are profiting by the short summer course offered by the National Archives and by several state programs. The greatest need of Catholic archives still is for trained personnel, with the time necessary to do the essential work of organization and then publication. Although the awakening of interest in Church history has had repercussions in the archival field, it remains for some American university to offer a genuine program in Church history and thus help to provide the stimulus necessary for adequate buildings and personnel for Catholic archives.

[E. R. VOLLMAR]

ARCHPOET, THE, the grandiose pseudonym of the author of the Latin poems that represent the high point of medieval satire; b. *c.* 1130; d. *c.* 1164. Apparently he was a German. He was the protégé of *Rainald of Dassel, Archbishop of Cologne, and accompanied him to Italy, where he wrote much of his surviving poetry, that is, 10 poems, which total about 850 lines. In these he flattered his patron, complained of his poverty and sickness, and begged for assistance, all in a humorous or ironic tone, displaying magnificent virtuosity in rhyme and meter. The masterpiece of medieval secular Latin verse is the Archpoet's *Confessio Goliae,* in which he defended himself against charges of venery, gambling, and frequenting taverns. It is this last section that contains the famous stanzas beginning, "Meum est propositum in taberna mori. . . ." The poem has a remarkable excursus on the role of the artist in society, and turns out to be a mocking justification of the poet's life rather than a confession. It found its way into the **Carmina Burana,* and was largely responsible for the subsequent vogue of the metrical form now called the Goliardic strophe (*see* GOLIARDIC POETRY). Probably the Archpoet, the most famous of the Goliards, did not long survive his last datable poems, 1164.

Bibliography: Manitius 3:978–984. M. MANITIUS, *Die Gedichte des Archipoeta* (2d ed. Munich 1929). Raby SecLP 2. H. WATENPHUL, *Die Gedichte des Archipoeta,* ed. H. KREFELD (Heidelberg 1958), with superb introduction, text, and commentary.

[P. PASCAL]

ARCHPRIEST. This title dates from the 4th century; it was given, usually, to the senior priest attached to a cathedral. He was empowered to take the bishop's place at liturgical functions. Later, rural archpriests also were appointed who were superior to the local clergy as was the cathedral archpriest to the cathedral clergy. The cathedral archpriest became known as the dean; his rural counterparts, as rural deans; vicars forane are the modern equivalent of rural archpriests. Today the title archpriest, as at St. Peter's, Rome, Notre Dame, Paris, and elsewhere is honorific. In England from 1598 to 1623 the Church was ruled by an archpriest as superior of the English mission; when in 1623 persecution had abated sufficiently to make it probable that the presence there of a bishop would not provoke worse persecution, the third and last archpriest was replaced by a vicar apostolic.

Bibliography: A. AMANIEU, DDC 1:1004–26. P. HUGHES, *Rome and the Counter-Reformation in England* (London 1942) 287–306. CIC c.217.

[B. FORSHAW]

ARCHPRIEST CONTROVERSY

The archpriest controversy (1598–1602) grew out of the opposition of a few English seminary priests to the institution of the archpriest and to the authority of George *Blackwell, first to be appointed to this office in March 1598. During Cardinal William *Allen's lifetime the weakness of having no superior over the clergy in England was obscured by his own great prestige and by that of Henry *Garnet, the Jesuit superior, who dealt with urgent practical problems.

After Allen's death in October 1594, Clement VIII, thinking the time yet unripe for a bishop, appointed Blackwell through Cajetan, the Cardinal Protector, as archpriest with 12 assistants to rule the seminary priests on the mission. Over Blackwell with appellate powers was the papal nuncio to Flanders. For years there had been a combined move on the part of the rebellious students in the English College, the faction in Flanders, and a few priests in England, mostly prisoners in Wisbech Castle, to have the Jesuits recalled from England and removed from the government of the seminaries. One clause of the Protector's Instructions to Blackwell provided for consultation with the Jesuits. This later caused contention. The new appointment was warmly welcomed in England by more than 300 priests. Some 15, however, at first refused to recognize their new superior. Two of them, William Bishop and Robert Charnock, left for Rome in late summer 1598 to appeal, while those remaining enlisted the support of the persecuting government, a ploy later so characteristic of the group. Blackwell's appointment, however, was but the occasion for the journey, for the trouble-makers in England and abroad had been planning an embassy to Rome some months before it had been made; they now pursued these plans, adding thereto dislike of the new office and personal complaints against Blackwell.

Their embassy caused great displeasure in Rome. They were examined individually, and a papal brief on April 6, 1599, confirmed both the institution of archpriest and the appointment of Blackwell. Hostilities against Blackwell were resumed, and for 2 years letters, manifestoes, and polemical pamphlets, printed with the connivance of the bishop of London, developed the grievances of the dissidents. They alleged canonical objections to Blackwell and his office, and even questioned the Pope's power to make such an appointment. The appellants charged that Blackwell was a tool of the Jesuits, who, according to the appellants, were interested chiefly in their own aggrandizement on the English mission. Exasperation at their insolent tone and their protection by the persecutors drove Blackwell to denounce them in sharp language and to issue edicts and suspensions against them somewhat indiscriminately, thus providing ostensible justification for their second appeal, Nov. 17, 1600. A second brief reconfirmed the appointment and forbade prosecution of the appeal, but the appellants, having left England late in 1601, with passports and covert government backing, saw the brief in Flanders and ignored it. In France they were favorably received by the court, for reasons of its anti-Spanish policy, and in Rome they were protected by the French ambassador. The documents reveal the latter's skillful intervention, as well as the impudence and inveracity of the appellants.

Hearings were terminated by a brief, Oct. 5, 1602, addressed to Blackwell, *ipso facto* confirming his authority, but severely reproving aspects of his conduct. It restricted his powers and ordered him to appoint appellants among his assistants. Though the Jesuits were praised, all official consultation with them was, with their agreement, forbidden. All controversial writings, and collusion with heretics *in praejudicium Catholicorum,* were forbidden under censures. Because it broke unity among mission workers, the brief was a disastrous turning point for English Catholicism.

Very extensive unpublished MSS material, now being collected, has been drawn on for this sketch. Traditional accounts of the controversy have been based largely on appellant assertions, e.g., H. Tootell, *Dodd's Church History of England . . .,* ed. M. A. Tierney (5 v. London 1839–43) volume 3, with documentary appendixes.

Bibliography: T. G. LAW, ed., *The Archpriest Controversy,* 2 v. (Camden Society 56, 58; London 1896–98). J. H. POLLEN, *The Institution of the Archpriest Blackwell* (New York 1916). R. PERSONS, *A Briefe Apologie . . .* (London 1602). P. RENOLD, ed., *The Wisbech Stirs, 1595–1598* (CathRecSoc 51; 1958).

[P. RENOLD]

ARCIMBOLDI, GIOVANNANGELO, archbishop of Milan and papal nuncio to the Scandinavian countries; b. in Milan, 1485; d. there, April 6, 1555. After traveling in the Low Lands and Germany, he purchased (for 1,100 guldens) the right to preach in Scandinavia the indulgence for the building of St. Peters. When he arrived in Denmark in 1516, he was well received by King Christian II. Two years later Arcimboldi went to Sweden to preach, and while there he associated and sympathized with those forces plotting rebellion against Denmark. He even negotiated with Sten Sture on behalf of Pope Leo X, implying papal sympathy with the rebel cause. Christian II, who believed the papal nuncio was working on his behalf in Sweden, was furious upon learning the contrary. He immediately confiscated all of the property and money Arcimboldi had left in Denmark and imprisoned his brother and servants. The nuncio fled to Lübeck, from whence he was recalled by Leo X as soon as news of his activities reached Rome. However, the damage was done, and Christian II invited Lutheran theologians to the Danish court—thus paving the way for the conversion of Scandinavia to Lutheranism. In 1522 Arcimboldi was sent to Spain to meet the pope-elect, Adrian VI. In 1526 he was named bishop of Novara by Clement VII. In 1550 he became archbishop of Milan.

Bibliography: E. SANTOVITO, EncCatt 1:1840–41. G. M. MAZZUCHELLI, *Gli scrittori d'Italia,* 2 v. (Brescia 1753–63). C. M. BUTLER, *The Reformation in Sweden* (New York 1883). Pastor v.7. J. LENZENWEGER, LexThK² 1:827–828.

[J. G. GALLAHER]

ARCOSOLIUM, an elaborate *loculus,* or catacomb grave. The word may owe its origin to *arcus* (arch) or *arca* (coffin) and *solium* (throne). The processional litter used in antiquity in the burial rites of important personages was called a *solium.* By extension, the tomb itself came to be called a *solium,* and the term was used in this sense by certain ancient writers (Curtius, *Hist.* 10.10; Suetonius, *Nero.* 50). The *arcosolium* was formed by excavating in the wall a space similar to that of an ordinary *loculus* and surmounting the space by an arch. The arch facilitated the opening of the downward cavity where the corpse was to be laid. *Arcosolia* differed from *loculi* in elegance and in the mode of closing. *Loculi* were closed vertically by a marble slab fixed to the wall, whereas *arcosolia* were closed horizontally. Above the horizontal slab was an arch or vault of stucco, frequently ornamented with frescoes. A more ancient form of *arcosolium* was the arched niche excavated to floor level; sarcophagi were placed in this earlier type. Although some *arcosolia* are found along the passages of the catacombs, the greater number are located in the *cubicula. Arcosolia* were used everywhere in Rome during the 3d century, and many later martyrs were interred in them.

Bibliography: Centre de Pastorale Liturgique, *Le Mystère de la mort et sa célébration* (Le Orandi 12; Paris 1956). H. LECLERCQ, DACL 1.2:2774–87. O. MARUCCHI, *Le Catacombe romane* (Rome 1932) 312–336. J. KOLLWITZ, ReallexAntChr 1: 643–645; 3:231–235. P. TESTINI, *Archeologia cristiana* (Rome 1958) 75–326. F. DE VISSCHER, AnalBoll 69 (1951) 39–54.

[M. C. HILFERTY]

ARCOVERDE DE ALBUQUERQUE CAVALCANTI, JOAQUIM, first cardinal of Rio de Janeiro and of Latin America; b. Pernambuco, Jan. 17, 1850; d. Rio de Janeiro, April 18, 1930. He was ordained on April 4, 1874. Although elected bishop of Goias in 1890 and consecrated in Rome, he renounced that office before taking power and was named coadjutor bishop of the Diocese of São Paulo in 1892. In 1894 he became bishop of São Paulo, and then strove to stimulate the rather lifeless Brazilian Catholicism of the period, coordinating the labors of Catholic associations and attracting to the diocese such religious congregations as that of the Immaculate Heart of Mary, the Premonstratensians, and the Redemptorists.

In 1897 he was transferred to Rio de Janeiro as the second archbishop of the archdiocese created there in 1892. In this position Dom Joaquim gave his greatest contribution to the Church of Brazil, which at the time not only failed to influence national life—though Catholics formed an absolute majority—but also lacked sufficient organized political support. He actively participated in the Latin American Plenary Council held in Rome in 1899. The better to put the decisions of the council into practice, he assembled his suffragan bishops annually after 1901. The fruits of these reunions were published in *Pastorais colectivas* (1901, 1909, 1915). These episcopal meetings were necessary antecedents for the important Brazilian Plenary Council held in Rio de Janeiro in June 1939.

In Rio de Janeiro Dom Joaquim constructed the Palácio S. Joaquim, the archiepiscopal headquarters. A series of difficulties forced him to close the diocesan seminary in 1907, but he sent his more intelligent clerical students to Europe to complete their studies. He reaped the fruits of closer contact between the Church and the new republic when in 1905 he was named cardinal of Rio de Janeiro, the first Latin American cardinal in history. In 1921 D. Arcoverde's mental and physical health began to fail. From that date until his death, he was merely a figurehead as the archdiocese was administered by coadjutor Abp. D. Sebastião *Leme de Silveira Cintra, who succeeded the cardinal in 1930.

Bibliography: M. ALVARENGA, *O Episcopado Brasileiro* (São Paulo 1915). L. CASTANHO DE ALMEIDA, *São Paulo, filho da Igreja* (Petrópolis, Brazil 1955). G. SCHUBERT, ed., *A província eclesiástica do Rio de Janeiro* (Rio de Janeiro 1948).

[I. SILVEIRA]

ARDBRACCAN, ABBEY OF, former Celtic monastery of Áird Breccáin near Navan, in Meath, Ireland. It was distinguished by its bishop and abbot, Ultan moccu Conchobuir, who seems to have been the first scholar to collect, or have collected, into one volume the historical material dealing with the work of St. *Patrick in Ireland. It was this *Liber apud Ultanum* that was used by Bishop Tírechán *c.* 670, when he compiled the Memoir, which is the earliest account now extant of St. Patrick's life. The deaths of various abbots who headed this abbey were recorded in the Irish annals of the 8th, 9th, and 10th centuries. Maelruba, e.g., anchorite, bishop and abbot of Ardbraccan died in 825. Like every other Irish monastery, it was plundered and burnt on many occasions by the Northmen: as late as 1031 its chief church was set on fire by the Norse of Dublin, and the 200 people who had taken refuge within its walls were burned to death. Maelbrigte, head of the monastic school, died in 1054. By the end of the 12th century the monastery had ceased to function, and its lands had passed to the bishopric of east Meath.

Bibliography: *The Annals of Ulster,* ed. and tr. W. M. HENNESSY and B. MACCARTHY, 4 v. (Dublin 1887–1901). *The Annals of Inisfallen,* ed. and tr. S. MACAIRT (Dublin 1951). *Chronicum Scotorum,* ed. W. M. HENNESSY (RollsS 46; 1866). "Annals of Tigernach," ed. W. STOKES, *Revue celtique* 17–18 (1896–97). *Annals of the Four Masters,* ed. and tr. J. O'DONOVAN, 7 v. (Dublin 1851). *The Martyrology of Tallaght,* ed. R. I. BEST and H. J. LAWLOR (HBradshSoc 68; 1931). *The Martyrology of Oengus the Culdee,* ed. W. STOKES (*ibid.* 29; 1905). *The Martyrology of Gorman,* ed. W. STOKES (*ibid.* 9; 1895). Kenney, *passim.*

[J. RYAN]

ARDCHATTAN, PRIORY OF, a former *Valliscaulian house on the shores of Loch Etive, Argyllshire, Scotland, founded by Duncan Mackoull, or Macdougall, in 1230, and dedicated to St. Mary and St. John the Baptist. Its name was derived from the Gaelic, meaning "hill of Cattan," which probably refers to Cailtan, an early Scottish saint of the district. The priory's early history is obscure: it is known to have sworn fealty to Edward I in 1296, although Robert the Bruce held a parliament there in 1308. In 1506 James, the prior general of the order, commissioned the prior of Beauly to visit Ardchattan and to make such reform regulations as he should find necessary. By 1538 only six monks appear to have been left at Ardchattan, and in 1602 James VI dissolved the monastery and erected it into a temporal lordship for Alexander Campbell, its former prior. It is now a ruin.

Bibliography: Edinburgh Bannatyne Club, *Origines parochiales Scotiae,* ed. C. Innes, 2 v. (Edinburgh 1850–55) v.2.1. M. Barrett, *The Scottish Monasteries of Old* (Edinburgh 1913). Easson 70. S. Cruden, *Scottish Abbeys* (Edinburgh 1960).

[L. MACFARLANE]

ARDEN, EDWARD, high sheriff of Warwickshire; b. Warwickshire, 1542?; d. Smithfield, Dec. 30, 1583. Arden succeeded as heir to his grandfather Thomas's estates in 1563. A devout Catholic, he maintained a priest disguised as a gardener at Park Hall, his residence. Under the influence of Father Hugh Hall, members of the Arden household, especially John Somerville, Arden's son-in-law, began to conspire and intrigue against Queen Elizabeth I. Somerville's recklessness soon led to his arrest. Under torture, Somerville implicated Hall and the Arden family. Unfortunately, Arden had also cast aspersions on the character of Robert Dudley, Earl of Leicester, who soon took a personal hand in prosecuting Arden. Hall, Somerville, and Arden were tried, convicted, and sentenced to death. Somerville strangled himself in his cell, Mrs. Arden and Hall, who aided the prosecution, were pardoned; but Arden was hanged for treason, protesting until the end that his only crimes were those of being a devout Catholic and of having incurred Leicester's wrath.

Bibliography: R. Harrison, DNB 1:546; DictEngCath 1:57–58.

[P. S. MC GARRY]

ARDENNE, MONASTERY OF, abbey of *Premonstratensians near Caen, *Normandy, Diocese of *Bayeux, dedicated to the Blessed Virgin. Founded as a cell of hermits by a certain Gilbert (1138) and endowed by Aiulph du Four, it was traded to the Premonstratensian abbey of La Luzerne by Bp. Philip de Harcourt of Bayeux (1144). In 1150 it became an abbey, with 16 churches and chapels eventually, receiving papal confirmation in 1161. One of the richest Premonstratensian houses in France, it received, after 1507, commendatory abbots. Wars and the rapacity of abbots afflicted it in the 17th century, when its annual revenue was 17,800 livres. In 1629 it joined the Reformed Congregation of Lorraine. When it was suppressed (1790), its abbot was an Englishman, Edward Booth. Its many buildings were standing a century ago, but the destruction of World War II has left only the Gothic church (14th-15th century), a 13th-century tithe barn, a Gothic gatehouse, and parts of the monastery. The church, which was used as a barn in 1944, is in the process of being restored.

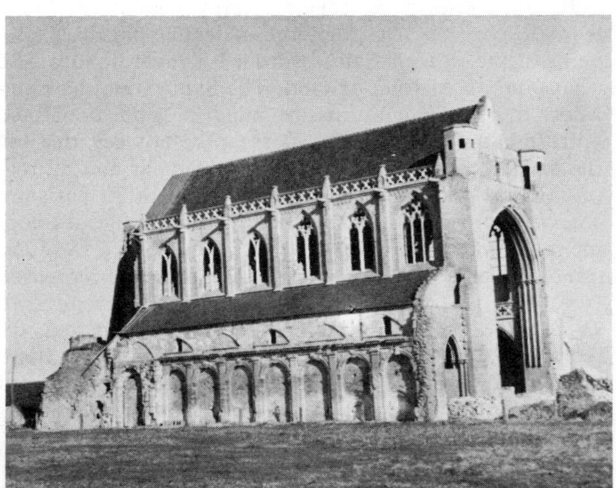

The Gothic church of the abbey of Ardenne.

Bibliography: E. Ringard, "Les Origines de l'Ordre de Prémontré en Normandie: Recherches sur la filiation des abbayes de la Luzerne et d'Ardenne," AnalPraem 2 (1926) 159–177. Cottineau 1:893. M. Prevost, DHGE 3:1602–04. Backmund Mon Praem 3:33–36.

[N. BACKMUND]

AREDIUS, ST., abbot, also known as Aridius, Arigius, Yrieix; b. Limoges, France, early 6th century; d. Aug. 25, 591 (feast, Aug. 25). He came from an important family and grew up at the court of King *Theudebert I. Attracted by the sanctity and eloquence of Bishop *Nicetius of Trier, he went to study under him, subsequently becoming one of his clergy and showing signs of holiness. He returned to Limoges after the death of his father and used his patrimony to build churches and, some time before 572, to found the Abbey of Attane, later named St. Yrieix in his honor. Aredius became first abbot, and he and his monks followed the teachings of the monastic fathers, especially those of *Basil and John *Cassian. He was also a friend of the poet *Fortunatus, who mentions him in his poems. He was buried in the abbey, and his relics were translated when a new church was built *c.* 1180. *Gregory of Tours reported many miracles worked through his intercession.

Bibliography: Gregory of Tours, *Historia Francorum* 10.29, MGSrerMer 1:440–442. BHL 1:664–668, lists other refs. in Gregory. *Vita,* ActSS Aug. 5:178–194 and MGSrerMer 3:581–609. F. Arbellot, *Vie de saint Yrieix* (Limoges 1900). R. Aigrain, DHGE 3:1632–36; *Catholicisme* 1:806. Baudot-Chaussin 8:475–478. Zimmermann KalBen 2:622–623.

[M. C. MC CARTHY]

AREMBERG, CHARLES D', Prince, Capuchin polemicist, iconographer in the early period of reproductive engraving; b. Brussels, Spanish Netherlands (birthdate unknown), 1593; d. Brussels, June 5, 1669. This scion of a princely Flemish family entered the Capuchin Order at Ghent in 1616, and subsequently served as definitor general in Rome and as provincial in his native Flanders. He was also an ardent patriot and earned a place in the history of Belgium's long quest for independence. His published writings are chiefly of an historico-ascetical character, occasioned by the celebrated controversy in which the Capuchins defended their usages, and, above all, their claim to be authentic Friars Minor, against the opposing claims of Observant and Conventual Franciscans. D'Aremberg was one of the chief protagonists for his order. His best known works are the *Flores Seraphici* (Cologne 1640), a sequence of vignettes of early Capuchin life; *Epilogus totius Ordinis Seraphici* (Antwerp 1650), an iconographical table of the Franciscan saints and branches; and the *Icones antiquae* (Brussels 1666), a collection of engravings depicting the primitive Franciscan habit and the order's early adoption of the beard and sandals. The *Epilogus* and the 100 illustrations for *Flores Seraphici,* engraved under the author's directions, won popular acclaim.

Bibliography: *Lexicon Capuccinum* (Rome 1951) 348–349.

[T. MAC VICAR]

AREOPAGUS

A rocky height in Athens west of the Acropolis, from which it is separated by a narrow depression; it bore the name Areopagus [hill of Ares (Mars)]. In antiquity it was the meeting place of the oldest Council of Athens, also called the Areopagus, made up of the king's chief men and having special authority to try murder cases. Its competence varied with the times, but its authority was very great until the democratic reforms of the early 5th century B.C. Thereafter it remained an honorable remnant of antiquity but without political power. At the time St. Paul was summoned before this Council it probably met in the agora and no longer on Mars Hill.

Paul's Arraignment before the Areopagus. When Paul arrived in *Athens, although he had been fleeing from the Jews in Thessalonica and Boroea, he nevertheless first went to the synagogue of the Jews and to others favorable to monotheism. He also preached in the market place every day, debating with Epicurean and Stoic philosophers without much success. His audience either did not understand him at all or they misinterpreted his teaching as propaganda for two new gods, Jesus and Anastasis (Resurrection). This confusion led to a more formal inquiry about his doctrine before the Areopagus. There was nothing particularly hostile about the hearing as some have thought; it was called to gather information about a doctrine new to the Athenians' jaded ears. Something entirely new and unheard of had come to the center of human wisdom and learning (Acts 17.16–21).

Paul's Speech before the Areopagus. A literary problem is connected with Paul's exposition of his new doctrine (Acts 17.22–31). Is it really Paul's speech or St. Luke's invention put into Paul's mouth to break the narrative's monotony and add greater vividness? It is universally agreed that Greek and Roman historians invented speeches that they attributed to various historical persons. Furthermore, Luke did not accompany Paul from Philippi and he rejoined him only during his last journey, as may be surmised from the long hiatus between the "we sections" of the Acts (16:17; 20.5). Apart from the possibility of a written source, then, Luke had to rely on only Paul himself for knowledge of the Athenian sojourn and the discourse—unless Timothy had not yet returned to Thessalonica (1 Thes 3.1–2). Whatever his source, the author of the Acts had ample means to learn of the substance of Paul's discourse; and there is no need to demand a verbatim account of it. The speech has an authentic ring to it, when one considers that it is a type of Paul's customary *kerygma to polytheistic pagans. Moreover, the citation of a Greek poet and philosopher (Acts 17.28) to an Athenian audience is especially appropriate. The judgment of the world by Jesus—established as judge by His Resurrection—brings out the specifically Christian character of this kerygma (Acts 17.31). Finally, if the writer were a forger, he would certainly have represented the result of the speech quite differently (Acts 17.32–34).

Areopagus, on Mars Hill, viewed from the Acropolis.

Paul's mission in Athens, although it was apparently frustrated, fulfilled nevertheless his principle: he became all things to all men, even a poet-quoting Greek, that he might save at least some (1 Cor 9.22, in the Greek text). Later, however, in Corinth, having learned his lesson from the Athenians' scorn, he would no longer speak in the words of human wisdom but in those of divine wisdom and the Cross—and with much more success (1 Cor 1.17–31).

See also AGNOSTOS THEOS.

Bibliography: EncDictBibl 129–130. OxClDict 85. A. WIKENHAUSER, LexThK[2] 1:830–831. I. C. T. HILL, *The Ancient City of Athens: Its Topography and Monuments* (Cambridge, Mass. 1953). **Illustration credit:** Matson Photo Service, Los Angeles, Calif.

[P. P. SAYDON]

AREQUIPA, ARCHDIOCESE OF (AREQUIPENSIS)

Located in southern Peru; created a diocese 1577; raised to an archbishopric May 23, 1943. In 1964 it included the suffragan Dioceses of Puno (1861) and Tacna (1944) and the prelatures *nullius* of Juli (1957), Caravelí (1957), Ayaviri (1958), and Chuquibamba (1962).

After the first erection that remained without effect, the diocese was established by Paul V on July 20, 1609, as a suffragan of Lima. Pedro de Perea, the first bishop to enter the diocese (1619), made his visitation, founded the seminary, and began the cathedral. His immediate successor, Pedro de Villagómez, celebrated the first synod (1638) and stamped out the remnants of idolatry among the Indians, leaving only a few very isolated nuclei, which were evangelized several years later. In 1680 the number of secular clergy in the diocese exceeded 100, and those in the regular clergy kept pace. There were 56 parishes (36 in charge of secular priests), convents of the four mendicant orders, a Jesuit school, and a hospital of St. John of God. The Santa Catalina monastery of Dominican nuns, founded in 1559, flourished with 75 choir nuns, 17 lay sisters, and 5 novices. In 1964 the archdiocese had 137 priests (50 secular and 87 regular) for a population of 306,000 souls in 39 parishes. The religious institutes had had a remarkable development, tripling their numbers in 15 years. Since 1955 the establishments of learning of the Church had increased from 8 to 11 for boys and from 14 to 21 for girls. In 1962 St. Mary's Catholic University was opened, directed by the North American Marianists, with three faculties and several schools. Women religious directed the state normal school for women, and the Brothers of the Christian Schools the normal school for men.

The works of social welfare have increased in proportion to the needs of the population. In addition to the archdiocesan "Caritas," there are seven institutions un-

Façade of the Jesuit church at Arequipa, Peru, 1698.

der the exclusive jurisdiction of the Church, plus nine others sponsored by the State but administered by women religious. The Church also collaborates in extensive social and educational action among the poor people in urban and rural areas, especially by means of television schools and free schools, frequently initiating and bearing the principal weight of the work. The Telescuelas Populares de Arequipa (TEPA), founded in 1960 by the Society of Catholic Educators, is accomplishing much in parishes, markets, and urban areas.

In the suffragan Diocese of Puno, the Maryknoll Fathers conduct a school, founded in 1956 by Thomas Verhoeven, for training Indian catechists to teach Christian doctrine and assist or substitute for the priest in the religious care of the towns that lack a parish church. Instruction is given there to voluntary catechists recruited from the Indians among whom they will work. Some receive special training and then serve as salaried catechetical directors. The Maryknoll Fathers have opened similar schools in Cuzco and Huancayo. At the request of the bishop of the diocese, Julio González Ruiz, they have also organized radio schools for the education and social advancement of 700,000 Quechua-speaking and 500,000 Aymara-speaking rural dwellers over *Radio Onda Azul* of Puno. The pupils hear the programs on transistor radios, which serve groups of four families or 15 pupils. In the city of Puno the interdiocesan minor seminary of St. Martin de Porres was inaugurated on May 2, 1964, with 60 pupils from the Dioceses of Puno and Abancay and the prelatures *nullius* of Ayaviri, Juli, and Sicuani, as well as several seminarians from the Dioceses of La Paz and Pando in Bolivia.

Bibliography: S. Martínez, *La diócesis de Arequipa y sus obispos* (Arequipa 1933). R. Vargas Ugarte, *Historia de la Iglesia en el Perú,* 5 v. (Lima 1953–62). J. J. Rodríguez, *Pueblos y parroquias del Perú,* 3 v. (Lima 1950–56). **Illustration credit:** Abraham Guillén M.

[E. T. BARTRA]

ARETAS IV, King 9 B.C. to A.D. 40 of the *Nabataeans, a people of Arabian origin who lived in the region to the south, east, and northeast of the Jews in Palestine and Trans-Jordan. The name Aretas comes from the Greek transliteration Ἀρέτας of the Nabataean name Ḥāriṭat. The Nabataeans controlled important trade routes to Arabia, Syria, and Egypt. A daughter of Aretas IV was married to *Herod Antipas, who divorced her to marry *Herodias, his brother's wife. This fact, along with a border dispute, provoked a war between the two kings in which Antipas was defeated (Josephus, *Ant.* 18.5.1–2).

According to the NT, an "ethnarch" of King Aretas guarded the gates of Damascus to capture Paul, who escaped by being lowered over the walls in a basket (2 Cor 11.32–33; Acts 9.22–25). Paul himself relates (Gal 1.17) that, after his conversion, he retired into "Arabia," probably the Hauran region. At the time (between A.D. 36 and 39) Damascus did not belong to Aretas. The ethnarch there was probably the head of the Nabataean colony in Damascus.

Bibliography: G. Priero, EncCatt 1:1856–57. J. Blinzler, LexThK[2] 1:831–832. W. Schmauch, RGG[3] 1:590. EncDictBibl 130.

[J. A. GRASSI]

ARETHAS, ARCHBISHOP OF CAESAREA, b. Patras, *c.* 850; d. *c.* 944. Possibly he was a pupil of the Patriarch of Constantinople *Photius; Arethas was prominent in the revival of classical and patristic letters at Constantinople during the latter part of the 9th century. He procured several classical MSS, of which the *Cod. Clarkianus* of Plato is the best-known survivor, and he is responsible for the preservation of many excerpts from the works of the early Church Fathers, particularly the Greek text of the Apologists. The Arethas codex (Paris gk. 451) testifies to his scholarship. He was ordained deacon *c.* 895 and became court orator to the Byzantine Emperor *Leo VI in 900. After his appointment to the See of Caesarea (*c.* 903), he produced a series of tracts and letters in opposition to the Emperor Leo's fourth marriage, for which the Patriarch of Constantinople *Nicholas I wished to grant a dispensation (906–907). Arethas wrote a treatise on polygamy, quoting patristic authors; a diatribe; and an elenchus against Nicholas's position. But later he seems to have acquiesced in the dispensation granted by the next Patriarch, *Euthymius I. The most famous of Arethas's exegetical writings is his commentary on the Johannine Apocalypse (*c.* 913) based on that of Andrew of Caesarea (between 563 and 614). He wrote a commentary and gloss on the Pauline letters, attempted to complete the homilies of St. Basil of Caesarea on the Old Testament, and provided scholia for the writings of the earliest Church Fathers, such as *Clement of Alexandria and *Justin. He fought for the right of asylum and against the translation of bishops. His pastoral interests brought him into contact with the theological problems of the day, and he wrote letters and sermons for the consecration of bishops and churches. Many of his writings are still unpublished.

Bibliography: Beck KTLBR 591–595. U. Riedinger, LexThK[2] 1:832. O. von Gebhardt, "Der Arethascodex, Paris Gr. 451,"

TU 1.3 (1883) 154–196. F. DIEKAMP, *Analecta patristica* (OrChr Anal 117; 1938) 230–236. G. HEINRICI, Herzog-Hauck PRE 2:1–5. R. J. JENKINS and B. LAOURDAS, "Eight Letters of Arethas," *Hellenika* 14 (1956) 293–372. R. J. JENKINS et al., ByzZ 47 (1954) 1–40, Photius Scholia. J. SCHMID, BiblZ 19 (1931) 228–254, Apocalypse. J. COMPERNASS, *Studi bizantine* 1–44, psalms; 4 (1935) 87–125, translation of bishops.

[F. X. MURPHY]

ARETINO, PIETRO, Italian man of letters; b. Arezzo, 1492; d. Venice, 1556. The son of a poor cobbler, he went to Rome and by 1516 was in the service of the noted banker, Agostino Chigi. Here he became

Pietro Aretino, by Titian.

notorious for his slanderous pasquinades. For 7 years (1517–24), he served in the employ of Leo X and Clement VII. Aretino left Rome for Fano where he was welcomed by the famed *condottiere,* Giovanni de' Medici. Shortly after Giovanni's death in 1526, he made his permanent residence at Venice. His income was derived from his adulatory, libelous, or threatening writings. His reputation as libelist and satirist grew in Venice; he was named by Ludovico Ariosto *il divino* and by others the "Scourge of Princes." Pensions, honors, and gifts were heaped upon him by famous personages, including Francis I, Charles V and his son Philip, Duke of Urbino, and Julius III. His universal popularity and esteem continued throughout his life.

Among Aretino's many works the most important are his letters, his comedies, and his *Ragionamenti.* His letters, which fill volumes, constitute a valuable source for the history of Renaissance mores and for the character, tastes, and inconsistencies of the author. His prose comedies, *Il Marescalco, La Cortigiana, La Talanta, L'Ipocrito,* and *Il Filosofo* are classified among the finest of Renaissance literature. The *Ragionamenti* or *Dialoghi* are largely a reflection of Aretino's life and character, and contemporary immoralities.

Bibliography: C. BERTANI, *Pietro Aretino e le sue opere, secondo nuove indagni* (Sondrio 1901). P. ARETINO, *Il primo (-secondo) libro delle lettere,* ed. F. NICOLINI, (Bari 1913–16). E. HUTTON, *Pietro Aretino: The Scourge of Princes* (Boston 1922). T. C. CHUBB, *Aretino: Scourge of Princes* (New York 1940). G. PETROCCHI, *Pietro Aretino, tra Rinascimento e Contrariforma* (Milan 1948). A. DEL VITA, *L'Arentino* (Arezzo 1954). A. FOSCHINI, *L'Aretino* (Milān 1931). **Illustration credit:**

[V. LUCIANI]

ARÉVALO, RODRIGO SÁNCHEZ DE, Spanish bishop and canonist-theologian; b. Santa María de Nieva?, 1404; d. Rome, Oct. 4, 1470. His diplomatic career as well as his writings defended the papacy against conciliarist attacks after the Council of *Constance, promoted supreme spiritual and temporal papal primacy, and urged ecclesiastical reforms. Arévalo graduated from Salamanca, 1428–29, with doctorates in civil and Canon Law. Between 1434 and 1439 he served as a member of the Castilian delegation to the Council of *Basel. By June 16, 1439, when that delegation under the leadership of Alfonso of Cartagena withdrew from Basel in protest over the council's attempt to depose Pope Eugene IV, Arévalo's anticonciliarist ideas had fully matured (*see* CONCILIARISM). These he expressed in his *De remediis schismatis,* a tract resulting from diplomatic missions undertaken for his sovereign John II of Castile. The tract promoted adherence to Eugene IV (d. 1447) in the courts of France, Germany, and Italy. Four similar works, written between 1447 and 1470, apply his basic attitudes to recurring instances of conciliarist agitation. On April 22, 1457, Pope Callistus III raised Arévalo to the Spanish bishopric of Oviedo. Later Pope Paul II made him bishop successively of Zamora, Calahorra, and Palencia. As royal procurator for King Henry IV, and then as adviser to Paul II, he resided in Rome, from 1460 to 1470, serving also as papal castellan of Castel San Angelo.

¶ Der ſcolaſticus verſicht die ſchůl·

DAs ampt der ſchůlmeyſterey iſt nit allein wirdig vnd eerlich· Sunder auch notturftig in der kirchen gots Wann als Honorius ſpricht ·die meyſter der ſchůlē·gieſſent dz liecht der ler als die ſtern in ewige ewigkeyt· Darumb werdent ſy billich· von der kirchen geeret·vnd mit pfrůnden vnd gültē belonet vñ gereichet·das ſy in ieder tům kirchen·die prieſter vnd ander arm ſchůler vmb ſunſt lerent· Vñ wirt inen darumb bas wann andern fürſehen·dz den lernenden·der weg zů der ler bas werde geöffnet·aber höre kurtz die beſchwärd·arbeyt ·vnnd kummernuß des ſelben amptes· Vnd merck von erſt·Dz der ſchůl meyſter den namen hat von der ſchůl der weyßheyt· Vnd ich mein ·er freüwe ſich des loblichen namens nitt vil·wo er mit rechter weyßheyt begabet wäre· Wañ als der poet petrarcha ſpricht gefeſtigete weißheyt bedarff nit loblichs namens · Wann ſy iſt fürſich ſelber gelobet vnnd ſcheynbar· Wann es wäre

Page from a German translation of Arévalo's "Speculum vitae humane," printed at Augsburg between 1475 and 1478.

His ideas on the *primacy of the pope were best formulated in his *Libellus de libera et irrefragabili auctoritate Romani Pontificis* and *De monarchia orbis;* his ideas on *reform in the Church, in *Defensorium ecclesiae et status ecclesiastici.* His Latin letters to contemporary Italian humanists place Arévalo among Spain's foremost humanists (*see* HUMANISM); his Castilian essays rank him first among his country's 15th-century writers in the vernacular. His writings are mostly unedited.

Bibliography: T. TONI, *Don Rodrigo Sánchez de Arévalo . . . su personalidad y actividades . . .* (Madrid 1941). R. H. TRAME, *R. S. de A., 1404–1470* (Washington 1958). R. B. TATE, "R. S. de A. (1404–1470) and his *Compendiosa Historia Hispanica,*" *Nottingham Mediaeval Studies* 4 (1960) 58–80. **Illustration credit:** Library of Congress, Rosenwald Collection.

[R. H. TRAME]

AREZZO

A Tuscan city and diocese immediately subject to the Holy See. Of Etruscan origin, Arezzo (Arretium) was an important military station on the Via Cassia under the Romans and was occupied successively by the *Lombards and the Franks. As part of the Marquisate of Tuscany, in 1098 it was organized as an independent commune. Caught in the struggles between Guelfs and Ghibellines, at enmity with Siena and Florence (Dante participated in the Battle of Campaldino between Arezzo and Florence: *Purg.* 5.92), it became subject to Florence in 1336 and followed this political line until the formation of the Kingdom of Italy.

Christianity came to Arezzo early, since it was on a main route north, but the organization of a church with a bishop can be traced back only to the 4th century; St. Satyrus is the first known bishop. The diocese was cut back in the 14th century, losing Cortona under *John XXII (1325); Pienza and Montalcino, under *Pius II (1462); Borgo San Sepolcro, under *Leo X (1520); and Montepulciano, under *Pius IV (1561). It is still, however, the largest diocese in Tuscany.

In the Etruscan period Arezzo was famous for its school of sculpture and plastic art (*vasi aretini*). In the 13th century it had a law school that seems to have begun with the migration of professors and students from Bologna. Its studium became famous and taught, besides law, medicine and the arts (statute of 1255). After a period of decadence owing to civil discord, the studium was reinvigorated under Charles IV who made it a *studium generale* (diploma of May 5, 1355). Frederick III attempted a second reinvigoration (1456), but it had to be abandoned in 1470. Arezzo's more important cultural institutions now include an Accademia Francesco Petrarca that publishes a weekly review *Atti e Memorie*. The library has 79,000 volumes, 160 incunabula, and 354 MSS. Arezzo has one of the more notable ecclesiastical archives in Italy, a museum founded in 1822, and a painting gallery established in 1810. Its cathedral is Romano-Gothic of the 13th century; the church of St. Francis (14th century) has the famous frescoes by Piero della Francesca. The diocese contains numerous monasteries and abbeys, of which the most notable are the monastery of the Camaldoli founded by St. *Romuald; that of Verna, on the site where St. *Francis of Assisi received the stigmata; and the original abbey of the Olivetani fathers.

The see is occupied by an archbishop through the concession of Pope Clement XII. The diocese covers

"Exaltation of the Holy Cross," 14th-century fresco by Piero della Francesca, church of St. Francis, Arezzo.

3,500 sq. kilometers, has 235,500 Catholic inhabitants in 350 parishes with 317 secular priests, 16 religious houses of men with 150 priests, and 76 convents with 530 nuns (1964).

Bibliography: F. ANTONELLI and I. CECCHETTI, EncCatt 1: 1860–67. C. HÜLSEN, Pauly-Wiss RE 2.1 (1895) 1227–28. U. PASQUI, *Documenti per la storia della città di Arezzo nel medio evo,* 4 v. (Arezzo 1899–1929). M. FALCIAI, *Storia di Arezzo* (Arezzo 1928). A. MORETTI, *Atti e Memorie della R. Accademia Petrarca* NS 15.2 (1933) 289–319; 16–17 (1934) 105–150, with documents. H. RASHDALL, *The Universities of Europe in the Middle Ages,* ed. F. M. POWICKE and A. B. EMDEN, 3 v. (new ed. Oxford 1936). **Illustration credit:** Alinari-Art Reference Bureau.

[F. CHIOVARO]

ARGENTEUIL, ABBEY OF, Benedictine monastery near Versailles, founded for religious women, between 650 and 675, by Erminric and his wife, Numana, courtiers at the Neustrian court. Its early history is obscure. In the 9th century Theotrade, a daughter of Charlemagne, and Judith, a daughter of Charles the Bald, were abbesses; but their role was probably limited to receiving the revenues and giving protection from afar. It was destroyed *c.* 1000 by the Normans and restored again under Robert the Pious. Heloise made her first studies there *c.* 1115 before becoming a pupil of *Abelard in Paris and took the veil there (1118–20) after the tragic sequel to her marriage. She became superior soon afterward. In 1129 she and the nuns were replaced by monks, and the monastery became a dependent priory of St. Denis. A very austere regime was introduced, but a gradual decline set in. A reform took place in 1646 under the Maurists. Of the four monks living there at its suppression in 1791, only one left the religious life. The holy cloak of Argenteuil, thought to be the seamless garment woven for Christ by his mother, was venerated at the priory; it is first mentioned in a 12th-century document of uncertain value.

Bibliography: A. LESORT, DHGE 4:22–39. Cottineau v.1. H. GLASER, LexThK[2] 1:833–834.

[C. FALK]

ARGENTINA

South American republic with an area of 1,079,965 square miles and an estimated population of 22 million. It is bounded on the north by Bolivia, on the northeast by Paraguay, on the east by Brazil, Uruguay, and the

Fig. 1. The ecclesiastical divisions of the Republic of Argentina in 1964.

Atlantic Ocean, and on the west by Chile. Buenos Aires is the capital, and the population is concentrated in that province and northward to Córdoba. Argentina's population is largely of Spanish or Italian origin with very few Negroes, Indians, and mestizos. It has a larger Jewish population than other Spanish American countries; in 1963 this was estimated at 450,000. While the republic is highly urbanized, it still derives much of its national income from agriculture.

Early Christianization. Several priests arrived in Argentina with Magellan's expedition (1519–20); on April 1, 1519, in San Julián, Patagonia, the explorers landed and raised a cross. One of the priests said a Mass, which was attended by the members of the expedition and, probably out of curiosity, by some natives. In February 1536 the colonizing expedition of Pedro de Mendoza arrived at the site of Buenos Aires. Three churches or provisional chapels were built, and the same was done a few months later in Asunción, Paraguay. One of the priests, Juan Gabriel de Lezcano, after resigning from a chaplaincy that he held, opened a school for the Indians. He taught them catechism, chant, reading, and writing, and at the same time tried to train them not to tatoo themselves, to kill each other, or to eat human flesh.

The first settlement at Buenos Aires was soon depopulated, but its inhabitants increased the populations of recently established towns, such as Corpus Christi (1536) and Asunción, Paraguay (1537). Years later, settlers from Chile founded the city of Mendoza in 1560, and San Juan in 1561; others coming from Peru founded Tucumán in 1565, Córdoba in 1579, Santa Fe in 1578, and again Buenos Aires in 1583. All of these settlements and most of the military expeditions were attended by regular or secular clergy, Franciscans and Dominicans predominating at first. For the Spaniards at that time, founding a city meant establishing a cabildo, and a church and school entrusted to the priest. The *conquistadores were predominantly men of profound and deep-rooted faith, loyal to religious and pious practices, even if the habits of some were not always in accordance with moral standards. Some priests, fleeing from the peninsular Inquisition or in search of freedom for their licentiousness, went to Río de la Plata and were a corrupting influence.

Diocesan Organization. On July 1, 1547, Paul III created the Diocese of Río de la Plata, which included all of present-day Argentina, Uruguay, Paraguay north to the Paranapanema River, and the southern part of present-day Brazil, Rio Grande do Sul and adjacent states. The see was in Asunción, and the first bishop appointed was the Franciscan Juan de Barrios Toledo, who never took over the position. Pedro Fernández de la Torre, another Franciscan, was actually the first bishop in these regions of America (1555–73). With the creation of the Diocese of Tucumán (sometimes called Córdoba de Tucumán) in 1570, including the central and northwest sections of the country, and the appointment of Francisco de Victoria as bishop, effective episcopal action began. While that bishop had difficulties because of his mercantilist enterprises and because of a pro-Portuguese attitude (he was a native of Portugal), to him is owed the ecclesiastical organization of the Argentine territory. His successor, Fernando de *Trejo y Sanabria, did incomparably more. Both made much use, not of the few inefficient secular clergy, but of the religious orders, especially the Jesuits, brought in by Bishop Victoria.

The Diocese of Buenos Aires, created by Paul V on March 30, 1620, was suffragan of Charcas, or La Plata, as was the Diocese of Tucumán. These two dioceses were the only ones that existed until Salta was created in 1806. Salta included all the area belonging up to that time to Tucumán, except for Córdoba, where the bishopric of Tucumán had its see after 1699.

In 1834 the three provinces of Cuyo (now Mendoza), San Juan, and San Luis came to form the Diocese of San Juan de Cuyo. Its first bishop, Justo Santa Mariá de Oro, of the Order of St. Dominic, was a man as wise as he was saintly and he actively worked for the independence of the country. In 1859 Pius IX created the Diocese of Paraná, separating it from that of Buenos Aires; it included the coastal Provinces of Entre Rios, Corrientes, Santa Fe, and Misiones. In 1897 Leo XIII created the Dioceses of La Plata, Santa Fe, and Santiago del Estero and on Feb. 3, 1910, those of Corrientes and Catamarca.

In 1934 Pius XI created the Dioceses of Azul, Bahía-Blanca, Jujuy, La Rioja, Mendoza, Mercedes, Río Cuarto, Rosario, San Luis, San Nicolás, and Viedma, to which was added that of Resistencia in 1939; in 1957 were added Comodoro Rivadavia, Santa Rosa, Morón, Nueve de Julio, San Isidro, Villa María, Posadas, Formosa, Lomas de Zamora, Mar del Plata, Gualeguaychú, and Reconquista; in 1961, those of Anatuya, Avellaneda, Concordia, Goya, Neuquén, Orán, Rafaela, Rio Gallegos, San Francisco, San Martín, and San Rafael; and in 1963, those of Concepción in Tucumán, Presidencia Roque Sáenz Peña in Chaco, Cruz del Eje in Córdoba, and Venado Tuerto in Santa Fe.

Missionary Work. This increase in the number of dioceses between 1570 and 1963 is an external proof of the slow but constant progress of Catholicism in Argentina and is evidence of the success of the conversion of the Indians in the Franciscan and Jesuit missions. The Franciscan fathers, among them Alonso de San Buenaventura and Luis de *Bolaños, from 1578 or 1579, and the Jesuit Fathers, among them Alonso Barzana and Pedro de Añasco, from 1586, began the conversion of the Indian in an organized and systematic manner. The Franciscans worked in the prosperous Reductions in present-day Paraguay and in what are now the Provinces of Buenos Aires and Santa Fe, such as San José del Bagual, Santiago del Baradero, Isla de Santiago, and Tumbichaminí; the Jesuits worked in the 30 Reductions they established, beginning in 1610, in what is now the Province of Misiones and in adjacent regions, both Paraguayan and Brazilian. In addition to these Reductions the Jesuits founded in the 18th century those of Abipones in the Chaco, the Mocobíes in Santa Fe, the Vilelas in Salta, the Lules in Tucumán, and those of the Pampas in the Province of Buenos Aires.

After the expulsion of the Jesuits in 1767, they were replaced in their 30 towns of Guaraní Indians by Franciscans, Dominicans, and Mercedarians. These towns were destroyed in the battles that took place between 1810 and 1818 by Paraguayans, Uruguayans, and Brazilians. The other Jesuit Reductions ceased to exist after the expulsion of the order. At the end of the 18th century Franciscan fathers from the Propaganda Fide, and after 1876 the Salesians, again undertook the conversion of the few uncivilized Indians still left in the extreme north and the extreme south of the country. Their numbers did not exceed 30,000.

Education. Fernando de Trejo y Sanabria, second bishop of Tucumán (1595–1614), through several synods, organized his diocesan church in conformity with the decisions of the Council of Trent and set up cultural centers for the better preparation of his clergy. To achieve this objective he established in Santiago del Estero the Colegio Seminario de Santa Catalina, which was afterward moved to Córdoba and was called Loreto. Later he founded the Colegio Convictorio de San Javier in Córdoba, and in 1613 he took the first steps toward the creation of the University of Córdoba, founded in 1622. At the end of the 17th century this initial work, implemented by the Jesuits, was completed by Ignacio Duarte y Quirós with the foundation of the Convictorio de Monserrat, which fostered many priestly vocations.

Although the Jesuits in the University of Córdoba and in Monserrat, from the beginning of the 18th century to 1767, were Cartesian, as were the Franciscans who succeeded them in the university professorships and in the direction of Monserrat, Catholic doctrine suffered no impairment, nor was it affected by the liberal ideas dominant in Spain. This was not the case at the Colegio de San Ignacio in Buenos Aires, directed by the secular clergy since 1773, among them Julián Fernández de Agüero, a priest of agnostic doctrines and lax morality.

Independence Period. Since the more radical ideas of the Enlightenment were not widespread in the area, the Revolution of 1810, which broke the ties with Spain, was completely Catholic and orthodox. Cornelio Saavedra, leader of the revolt, was a thorough and

Fig. 2. The basilica of S. Francisco at Buenos Aires.

even pious Catholic, as was the priest Manuel Alberti, who was one of the spokesmen of the revolutionary government. The three bishops, those of Buenos Aires, Córdoba, and Salta, did not sympathize with the separatist movement, but 95 per cent of the clergy and 60 per cent of the members of the religious orders supported the new political regime. Almost all of the Mercedarian fathers did so, and almost all of the Franciscans were against or only tolerated what had happened. Since ties between religious orders and their superiors in Europe were broken, the government created the Commission for Religious, an illegitimate instrument of the antireligious assembly. The nature of the revolution changed under the leadership of misguided and immoral men, such as Juan José Castelli and Bernardo Monteagudo. However, the movement was corrected at the Congress of Tucumán, which proclaimed independence on July 9, 1816. Eleven of the 29 representatives who signed this declaration were priests.

While independence had been declared, the form of government for La Plata was a matter of dispute. Buenos Aires wanted to hold control of all the provinces, and this attitude provoked a civil war that lasted from 1818 to 1820. The prolongation of this conflict necessitated a strong government, as General San Martín had foreseen. *Rivadavia aspired to be that government. However, he could count on the support only of the Province of Buenos Aires, and even there he had committed serious errors. A presumptuous man, dazzled by what he had seen in France, he wished to civilize through decree. Influenced by enlightened priests who were his friends and who wished to put an end to their completely Christian preaching, Rivadavia tried to carry out the ill-named Reform of the Clergy. He was imbued with the ideas of Joseph of Austria and Febronius, encouraged by the concept of patronage that both the national and the provincial governments felt they had inherited from Spain, and so he wanted to legislate ecclesiastical as well as civil affairs. His government was disastrous for Argentina. In 1824, when the papal delegate *Muzi arrived in Buenos Aires on his way to Chile, Rivadavia refused to let him administer the Sacrament of Confirmation and ordered him to leave the city as soon as possible. In this Rivadavia was supported by the high clergy in Buenos Aires. The next year Rivadavia made a treaty with England by which Protestantism was officially permitted and with it toleration of all religions.

In 1829, during one of many short-lived governments, the Governor of Buenos Aires, Juan José Viamonte, took the first steps to restore relations with Rome, which had been suspended since 1810. Pius VII appointed Mariano *Medrano bishop of Buenos Aires, where there had been none since the death of Benito Lue in 1812. He served as bishop until July 2, 1832, to the great satisfaction of the Argentine people and the great opposition of some jurists and many priests.

Rosas and the Liberal Reaction. Juan Manuel *Rosas governed the Province of Buenos Aires and the whole country from 1835 to 1852. Through force he brought a measure of peace and order to the country. A firm supporter of patronage, he interfered in clearly ecclesiastical matters, supporting the Church in spiritual and apostolic work but expelling from the country priests and religious whom he considered too involved in politics. His relations with Bishop Medrano were always of a very cordial nature.

After Rosas was overthrown in February 1852, the government was headed by men of heterodox views, such as Juan María Gutiérrez; or of ambition, such as Bartolomé Mitre; or of flexible ideology, such as Domingo *Sarmiento. They were the dominant influences in the preparation of the Constitution of 1853, a document little in keeping with the doctrine and spirit of Catholicism. Among the members of the congress that drew up the constitution was a priest, Benjamín Lavaisse; and another, Mamerto *Esquiú, spoke in favor of its adoption.

Catholicism waned appreciably among intellectuals during the period 1853 to 1880. At the same time Masonry became more and more active, believing that the time had arrived to do away with the decadent Argentine Church. By the decade 1880–90 the effects of the Constitution of 1853 upon the Church were evident, some resulting from the specific content of its articles, others resulting from erroneous interpretation. President Julio A. Roca, detested in Buenos Aires because he was from Tucumán, allowed Masonry to attack the Church openly and thus began a struggle that lasted throughout his term of office (1880–86). In and out of parliament the struggle was fought over education and civil marriage, the enemies of the Church winning on both counts.

To oppose these tendencies, José Manuel Estrada, militant Catholic, once a liberal, formed the Unión Católica and was the moving force of the First Argentine Catholic Assembly, which met in 1884. He founded the daily *La Unión,* and, above all, inspired others with his heroic spirit, among them Pedro Goyena, Tristán Achaval Rodríguez, Emilio de Alvear, Aureliano Argento, Mariano Demaría, Emilio Lamarca, Dámaso Centeno, and many others who fought boldly for the interests of Christ. If the ecclesiastical authority of Buenos Aires proved less than valiant, the Franciscan Bishop of Salta, Buenaventura Risso Patron and the vicars of Córdoba (Jerónimo Clara), Santiago del Estero (Reinerio Lugones), and Jujuy (Demetrio Cau) acted so decisively and so valiantly that they were either arrested and jailed or removed from ecclesiastical posts. In 1902 it was believed that the de-Christianizing process begun in 1880 could be completed by introducing divorce. It seemed that everything favored this project in the Argentine Congress, but the calm and effective speech of a young deputy from Tucumán, Ernesto E. Padilla, brought about its spectacular failure.

The Church in the 20th Century. This victory in 1902 strengthened the Catholics, shaken by the earlier persecutions and alert to the leftist forces that were gaining ground. Outstanding in the work of revival was the German Redemptorist Federico *Grote. His work was, above all, in accordance with the necessities of the age. He started the Workingmen's Groups, founded the Catholic newspaper *El Pueblo,* and inspired a new generation of men, among them Emilio Lamarca, Miguel de Andrea, Alejandro Bunge, Gustavo J. *Franceschi, José M. Samperio, and many others.

At the death of Mariano A. Espinosa, Archbishop of Buenos Aires from 1900 to April 8, 1923, President Marcelo T. de Alvear proposed as his successor Miguel *de Andrea, who was only a titular bishop. Since the Holy See did not accept the recommendation, the liberal press and not a few Catholics who sympathized with the prelate undertook a campaign against the Papal Nuncio, Beda Cardenali, and against the religious orders and faithful Catholics who, in one way or another, sided with the Holy See. It was a national scandal, for it divided the Catholic community into two camps, and both sides committed lamentable errors. The election of the Franciscan José María Bottaro in 1926 put an end to this unpleasant situation.

The International Eucharistic Congress of 1934 was a success that exceeded even the hopes of the most optimistic. The entire nation took part. The ceremonies one night attracted over half a million people; and that night there were a great number of Confessions, and all available ciboria were used. Many conversions or returns to God resulted. In 1943 the government of Gen. Pedro Pablo Ramírez placed in the public school curriculum elective courses in religion or morals; 92 per cent elected religion, and only 8 per cent, morals. In some provinces the figure was higher: 99.5 per cent in Catamarca, 99.1 per cent in La Rioja, 98.6 per cent in Corrientes, and 98.5 per cent in San Luis. Even in cosmopolitan cities, e.g., Buenos Aires, the majority remained Catholics, the census of 1936 showing 1,935,125 out of a total population of 2,415,142, or 81 per cent of the total. In 1947, in Buenos Aires, it was verified that 85.4 per cent of the children born that year were baptized as Catholics and 68.8 per cent of the marriages were blessed by the Church.

From 1934 to 1964 the Church advanced in many areas: the increase in the number of dioceses; the foundation of the Argentine Catholic Action Movement

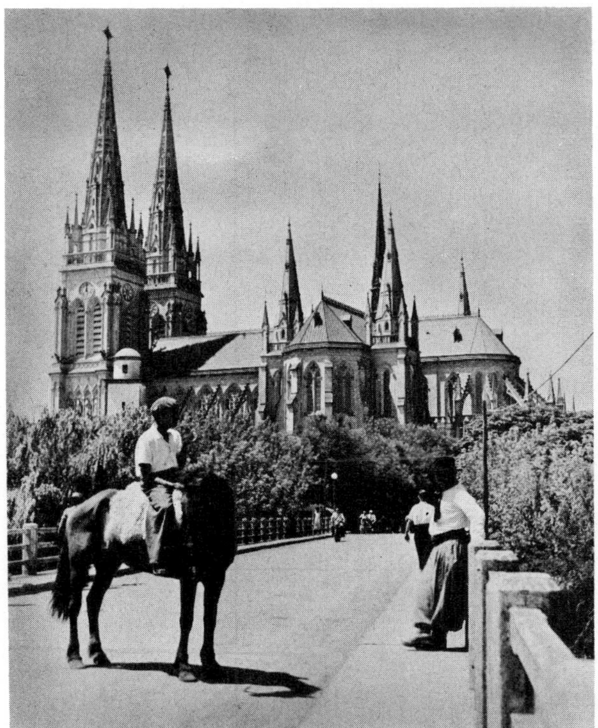

Fig. 3. The cathedral of Our Lady of Luján, Argentina. Four weeks after Easter many Argentines make a pilgrimage to this church, the site of a 17th-century shrine to the Virgin, the first dedicated in Argentina.

in 1931; the multiplication of parishes and of parochial schools; the work done in secondary schools founded and directed by the Jesuits, the Missionaries of Our Lady of Lourdes, the Betharram Fathers, Salesians, Order of the Divine Word, Brothers of the Pious Schools, Christian Brothers, and Marist Brothers, as well as other male and female congregations.

Perón Era. When the government of Perón stressed its totalitarian tendencies in 1952, a serious conflict with the Church was provoked. The official press began to mock everything Catholic; Catholic gatherings were prohibited; Catholic organizations, such as the university athenaeums of Santa Fe and of Córdoba, were abolished; crucifixes were removed from government offices; religious teaching in schools was suppressed; the divorce law was approved; and houses of prostitution were again authorized. The entire episcopate remained firm and energetic, and the faithful supported their pastors. Priests and laymen were jailed and mistreated on many occasions, and every expedient was used to harass Catholics. Persecution reached its high point on the afternoon of June 11, 1955, when a huge crowd gathered in the cathedral and in the adjacent plaza to hear Mass and afterward, in absolute silence, passed through the center of the city to the congressional building. On June 16, after an attempt to overthrow the government had been thwarted, the government instigated mobs to take revenge by burning churches (S. Francisco, S. Roque, Sto. Domingo, S. Miguel, S. Nicolás, etc.) and also the episcopal curia, the contents of which, including the historical archives, were reduced to ashes. The sacking and burning of churches raised a great reaction throughout the country and even abroad. Never had anything like this occurred in Argentina.

After the fall of the government in September 1955 the revolutionary junta began to reestablish justice and return to each one that which was his. Soon this government was infiltrated by anti-Catholic elements, and although the divorce law passed in the time of Perón was suspended, the pre-Perón religious education law was not reinstated. During Frondizi's presidency the educational freedom law, muzzled by liberalism and Masonry since 1853, was passed, and immediately Catholic universities were founded in Buenos Aires, Córdoba, and Santa Fe.

Conclusion. In 1963, with the establishment of more new bishoprics and archbishoprics (Aug. 14), the ecclesiastical hierarchy in the Argentine Republic came to number 12 archdioceses (Bahía Blanca, Buenos Aires, Córdoba, Corrientes, La Plata, Mendoza, Paraná, Rosario, Salta, San Juan de Cuyo, Santa Fe, and Tucumán) and 38 dioceses. For a population of 22,000,000 there were only 5,000 clergymen; in 1960 there were 1,295

Fig. 4. The blessing of the vines and the "new wine" at an annual wine festival in the state of Mendoza.

parishes and 3,324 churches, chapels, and oratories. There were in the entire country that same year 605 male and 1,413 female religious houses. The latter were in charge of almost all Catholic education, both primary and secondary, in 112 academies and 215 schools for boys and in 285 academies and 670 schools for girls.

The Spanish religious heritage, institutional and traditional, received in 1810 by the Republic of Argentina, was already losing its greatest value, its true spirituality. The deficiencies of this anemic Catholicism were increased through the abuses of the governments and the weaknesses of some bishops. In accepting the 1853 Constitution, the clergy were short-sighted and in large part infected with false liberalism. Between 1880 and 1930 lay leadership was not lacking, but ecclesiastical leadership was, and in large part it counteracted the lay activity. Since 1930, in spite of the work of Catholic Action and a few clergy, static and centralizing leadership has tended to stifle initiative and any attempts to adapt the Church to new situations in a changing society. A small number of dynamic leaders, chiefly laymen, have tried to encourage sound movements toward modernization, but they have clashed with the traditionalists, who have hesitated to confront the present, to say nothing of the future.

See also CHURCH AND STATE IN LATIN AMERICA: SPANISH SOUTH AMERICA; LATIN AMERICA, CHURCH AND INDEPENDENCE IN.

Bibliography: J. C. ZURETTI, *Historia eclesiástica argentina* (Buenos Aires 1945). G. FURLONG, *Diócesis y obispos de la iglesia argentina, 1570–1942* (Buenos Aires 1942). *Anuario eclesiástico de la República Argentina* (Buenos Aires 1961–). A. DONINI, "Un análisis para el futuro del catolicismo argentino," *Estudios* 549 (Buenos Aires 1963) 651–657. A. P. WHITAKER, *Argentina* (Englewood Cliffs, N.J. 1964). **Illustration credits:** Figs. 2, 3, and 4, Pan American Airways.

[G. FURLONG]

ARGENTINA, CATHOLIC UNIVERSITY OF

A private institution of higher learning, officially founded in Buenos Aires on March 7, 1958, following a 1956 decree of the Argentine bishops. In November 1958 the Argentine government recognized the University in keeping with a 1958 law that authorizes the freedom of university education and directs private universities. The Congregations of Seminaries and Universities canonically erected the institution as a pontifical university on July 16, 1960.

The University, also known as St. Mary of Buenos Aires, is governed by a commission of three bishops, headed by the archbishop of Buenos Aires, who is also chancellor. The rector, named for 5 years by the Holy See on the advice of the bishops, exercises executive authority. Legislative authority is reserved to the supreme council, of which the rector is president. The council comprises the deans of faculties, directors of institutes, and six professors who represent various departments and are elected by their colleagues for 3-year terms. The deans are chosen for 4-year terms by the commission of bishops from among three names presented by the professors. The University is financed through an annual nationwide church collection, subscriptions from friends of the University, gifts and legacies, and tuition.

The administration building and other buildings of the University are located in Buenos Aires, while extension Faculties and Institutes are maintained in various parts of the country, including Rosario, Mendoza, La Plata, and Paraná.

The Catholic University grants a licentiate after 6 years of study in a chosen field and the doctorate upon completion of a 7th year. In addition to these the University confers the professional titles of lawyer and engineer. State examinations validate the academic degrees and give graduates the right to practice their respective professions.

The University comprises the Faculties of Philosophy; Letters; Law and Political Science; Economics and Social Science, including Business Administration; Law and Social Science (located at Rosario); Musical Arts and Sciences; Theology; Physical Sciences, Mathematics, and Engineering; the Institutes of Theology; Culture and University Extension; Social and Family Education; Modern Language Teaching; and at Rosario, a Polytechnic Institute; the Schools of Human Relations; Social Service; Sacred Science; Modern Languages; and a department of biological research.

In each faculty the related disciplines are grouped into departments as centers of research. The University also includes independent departments of culture and extension education; a biological laboratory for research relating to gastroenterology and metabolism; libraries; and a publications department.

Closely related to the Catholic University are incorporated Faculties and Institutes that are academically dependent on it but administratively and economically autonomous. They include Law and Social Sciences; Educational Psychology (both in San Juan); Law (Mar del Plata); and Psychology. The Institutes comprise the Schools of Human Relations; Social Service; Sacred Sciences; Family Education; and a secondary school of modern languages.

The curriculum of the University includes experimental and practical programs in preparation for all the professions, especially engineering, economics, law, teaching, and sociology. Research is an important activity of every department and particularly in biology, technology (in which the Center for Technical Research is used), the Marxist Institute, and the sociology section. In 1964 the Emilio Lamarca Library housed 60,000 volumes. Individual Institutes and Faculties maintain special libraries.

Each sequence of studies includes an established number of subjects for a 6-year period. Each chair is held by a professor aided by several assistant professors and instructors. Classes are theoretical and practical and number approximately 20 a week. There are two examination periods during each semester as well as a final examination. The school year begins on March 15 and ends on November 15. In 1963 University enrollment totaled 2,438 students, and the staff included 422 professors.

The Catholic University publishes books written by its professors and numbers among its publications: *Teología*, a semiannual review of theology; *El Derecho*, a law daily that forms three volumes a year; *Sapientia*, a quarterly philosophical review; and the *Boletín de la Pontificia Universidad Católica Argentina*, which is published quarterly.

[O. N. DERISI]

ARGENTINE LITERATURE

The literature of the Argentine is one of the most important in the Spanish-speaking world. It has grown particularly in the 19th and 20th centuries, after a rather fruitless period of historical writing dealing with the Spanish Conquest, and a humanist movement of more social than literary consequence during the 18th century.

Early Chroniclers and Missionaries. The history of the Conquest has come to us in narratives of official recorders and in one or two poems of doubtful merit. The chronicle of the first attempt to conquer the River Plate country was written by a Bavarian adventurer, Ulrich Schmidl, around 1554, and first published in Frankfurt in 1567: it is known in Spanish as *Viaje al Río de la Plata.* Alvar Núñez Cabeza de Vaca, who gained his reputation as an adventurer and *cronista* with his fabulous *Naufragios* (1542), participated in the conquest of the River Plate region but left no literary testimony of his exploits. His secretary, Pedro Hernandez, wrote in 1554 a detailed account of what they saw and did, under the title *Comentarios.* Two other *cronistas* might be mentioned: Fray Reginaldo de Lizárraga (1539–1609), author of *Descripción breve de toda la tierra del Perú, Tucumán, Río de la Plata y Chile,* known also as *Descripción y población de las Indias* (Lima 1908); and Ruy Díaz de Guzmán (1554–1629), whose *La Argentina* should not be confused with Martín Barco de Centenera's epic poem *La Argentina* (1602), a modest imitation of Ercilla's *La araucana.*

Most of the literary activity during the 16th and 17th centuries was connected with the work of the missionaries—Franciscan, Dominican, and Jesuit—and was concerned with the different aspects of teaching the natives. The organization of the Jesuit missions in Argentina and Paraguay was a model of progressive social thought (*see* REDUCTIONS OF PARAGUAY). Collective rural work, education in arts and crafts, and a liberal attitude toward relations between Spaniards and Indians brought about an era of general welfare, which, however, came to an abrupt end with the expulsion of the Jesuits in 1767 [*cf.* G. Furlong, *Los jesuítas y la cultura rioplatense* (Buenos Aires 1946)]. Theater in its most primitive form tried to glorify religious festivities.

Bartolomé Mitre, by Raimundo de Madrazo y Garreta.

Scientific work was also of interest to the missionaries. Two names should be remembered in this connection: Buenaventura Suárez, SJ (1670–1750), an astronomer who kept in active correspondence with the Swede Celsius, and whose *Lunario de un siglo* was published in 1744; and Fray Pedro Montenegro (1663–1728), author of *Materia medica misionera* (1710). In addition to grammars, dictionaries, and glossaries, a number of sacred biographies were written by Jesuits based on the *Cartas anuas,* and some of these had true literary significance: *Insignes misioneros de la Compañía de Jesús en la Provincia del Paraguay* (1687), by Francisco Xarque (1601–91); *Siete estrellas de la mano de Jesús* (1732), by Antonio Machoni (1671–1753); *De vita et moribus sex sacerdotum paraguaycorum* (1791) and *De vita et moribus tredecim sacerdotum paraguaycorum* (1793), by José Manuel Peramás.

The first Argentine poet of the Colonial period was Luis José de Tejeda (1604–80), who wrote religious poetry (e.g., "Canción sáfica a Santa Teresa"), and parables in which he followed the Gongoristic trend: *Romance de su vida, El peregrino en Babilonia,* and *Soledades* (*see* GONGORISM). The most significant literary production in Argentina during the 18th century, however, was not related to poetry but to works of scientific nature written by the exiled Jesuits after 1767. Some of these treatises had great stylistic distinction; for instance, the *Historia de la conquista,* by Pedro Lozano (1697–1752).

The Romantic Movement. The war of independence (1810–17) inspired few writers of merit: most of the poetry was pedestrian, and the prose (essays, sermons) was primarily didactic. Nevertheless, the political struggle originated an intense nationalistic feeling that soon found its literary expression in the romantic movement. Juan Cruz de la Varela (1794–1839) was a precursor, and Esteban Echeverría (1805–51) the leader, of Argentine romanticism. Echeverría lived for a time in France and was able to absorb directly the ideas of French romanticism. He returned to Argentina in 1830 and founded the *Asociación de Mayo,* a secret organization, to combat the dictatorship of José Manuel Rosas (1793–1877). After the revolution of 1839, Echeverría fled to Montevideo and there spent the rest of his life. His poetry is eloquent in the romantic tradition, as in "La cautiva" (1837), but his fame rests on one short story, *El Matadero,* in which he combined brutal realism with political allegory and created a masterpiece of social satire.

The dictatorship of Rosas had an unexpected effect on Argentine letters: writers of different political tendencies joined forces to fight him and thereby started an intellectual movement that left a deep imprint not only in Argentina but also in Uruguay and Chile. The leaders of this movement were Bartolomé Mitre (1821–

1906) and Domingo Faustino Sarmiento (1811–88). Mitre was a poet (*Rimas,* 1846), a novelist (*Soledad,* 1847), a distinguished scholar (*Historia de Belgrano,* 1858), and the first constitutional president of Argentina (1862). Sarmiento was a highly effective social reformer and educator; his *Civilización y barbarie: Vida de Juan Facundo Quiroga* (1845) had a profound influence on several generations of Latin Americans. Rosas was also opposed by José Mármol (1817–71), a brilliant poet and novelist, best remembered for *Amalia* (1851–55), a romantic tale of political adventure. Three other writers should also be mentioned because their work illustrates the development of romanticism in Argentina: Olegario Andrade (1841–82), Ricardo Gutiérrez (1836–96), and Rafael Obligado (1851–1920).

An interesting phenomenon that might be considered an offspring of romanticism was the development of a popular form of poetry dealing with the life and adventures of the *gaucho.* The first of the *gaucho* poets was Hilario Ascásubi (1807–75), who collected his works under the title *Paulino Lucero,* and then wrote a novel in verse form, *Santos Vega o los mellizos de la Flor,* full of folklore and descriptions of Argentine country life. Ascásubi was followed by Estanislao del Campo (1834–80), author of *Fausto,* a parody of Gounod's opera. But the greatest of the *gaucho* poets was José Hernández (1834–86) whose *Martín Fierro* (1872) has become a Latin American classic.

Modernismo and Vanguardismo. Rubén *Darío arrived in Buenos Aires in 1893 and soon gathered around him a group of poets who became the leaders of Argentine modernism, among them Leopoldo Lugones (1874–1938), Leopoldo Díaz (1862–1947), and Angel de Estrada (1872–1923). *See* MODERNISMO. Lugones is the most important of these early modernists. He reflects in his poetry all the major trends in the literature of the turn of the century. Lugones is remembered for his *Odas seculares,* (1910), *Romancero* (1924), and *Poemas solariegos* (1928), all rooted in regional tradition and revealing a deep love for the people and the land. With Enrique Banchs (1888–), Evaristo Carriego (1883–1912), and Baldomero Fernández Moreno (1886–1950), Argentine poetry began to move away from the rhetoric of modernism. A new generation turned its attention to the experimental writing of the French avant-garde. There was a transitional period, however, during which poets such as Arturo Capdevila (1889–), Arturo Marasso (1890–), and Ezequiel Martínez Estrada (1895–) prolonged the Spanish tradition in a manner reminiscent of the Generation of 1898 (*see* SPANISH LITERATURE, 5). Perhaps the most significant poetry of this period was written by a woman, Alfonsina Storni (1892–1938), who shocked and amazed her readers with her passionate themes and the bold imagery of her love poetry.

In the initial moments of *vanguardismo,* when French influences clearly set the course for Latin American poetry, three Argentine writers assumed leading roles: Ricardo Güiraldes (1886–1927), Jorge Luis Borges (1899–), and Francisco Luis Bernárdez (1900–). The first two are unquestionably the most significant and made for themselves an international reputation as poets and fiction writers. Guiraldes wrote a classic in *gaucho* literature: *Don Segundo Sombra* (1926), in which he attempted to bring together all the mythical qualities of the land and of the man who personifies it. His style is lyrical without ever being rhetorical. Borges used the imagery of *ultraísmo* to evoke intimate visions of Buenos Aires and project them into a limitless time, (e.g., *Fervor de Buenos Aires,* 1923). He was also a fascinating storyteller and essayist in *Ficciones* (1944), *El Aleph* (1949), *Historia de la eternidad* (1936), and *Otras inquisiciones* (1952). Bernárdez is a religious poet of delicate expression notably in *Poemas elementales* (1942), his best-known book.

Under the guidance of Borges, the new poets combined a sentimental adherence to regionalism with sophisticated imagery, and used the term *martínfierristas* to indicate their Argentine roots. Eduardo González Lanuza (1900–) excelled in this type of poetry, as did Conrado Nalé Roxlo (1898–). More baroque in their expression were Ricardo E. Molinari (1898–) and Leopoldo Marechal (1900–). Raúl González Tuñón (1905–) and Alvaro Yunke (1890–), on the other hand, emphasized social and political elements. Mid-century poets tend toward a neosymbolism in which traces of Rilke, Eliot, Jiménez, and Neruda can be detected. They have mastered the traditional forms of Spanish poetry and avoid the free play of metaphors so characteristic of early *vanguardismo.* Some of them have already attained a firm reputation, among them, Daniel Devoto (1916–), Mario Rinetti (1916–), César Fernández Moreno (1919–), and Alfredo Roggiano (1919–).

Realism in the Novel. From the historical trend predominant during the romantic period, Argentine novelists evolved toward a form of realism and naturalism in which social significance was the main concern (*see* NATURALISM, LITERARY). Eugenio Cambaceres (1843–88) can be considered the most typical novelist of this period. In his books, as in those of Paul Groussac (1848–1929), Julián Martel (pen name of José Miró, 1867–96), and Carlos María Ocantos (1860–1949), vast social panoramas are described in a style at times reminiscent of *Pérez Galdós, and at other times of Balzac and Zola. From this preoccupation with social problems and the fate of the Argentine nation came a powerful literary expression in which elements of the essay and the novel were blended. Manuel Gálvez (1882–1962), at first influenced by Zola (e.g., in *Nacha Regules,* 1918), gradually moved away from naturalism and began to use his characters as symbols of his own spiritual conflicts.

This subjective motivation within a concept of social realism is found also in other Argentine novelists of the 20th century: in Leonidas Barletta (1902–), Elías Castelnuovo (1893–), Max Dickman (1902–), and in more recent writers, such as Ernesto L. Castro and Alfredo Varela. One important group of novelists has given Gálvez's speculation an even more profound turn: Eduardo Mallea (1902–) in *La bahía del silencio* (1940), Juan Goyanarte (1900–) in *Lunes de carnaval* (1952), Juan Carlos Onetti (1909–) in *La vida breve* (1950), and José Bianco (1911–) in *Las ratas* (1943) analyze contemporary life in Argentina with a sense of personal and universal anguish that may be of existentialist origin (*see* EXISTENTIALISM IN LITERATURE). Apart from these novelists, who have certain features in common, one should mention Roberto Arlt (1900–42), a strange, Dostoievskian writer whose *Los siete locos* (1929), *Los lanzallamas* (1931), and *El jorobadito* (1933) have been rediscovered by the younger generations.

Parallel to this social trend, a form of novel dealing particularly with country life developed at the end of the 19th century and continued to be popular during the first half of the 20th. Roberto J. Payró (1867–1928) was for several years the best-known representative of the *gaucho* novel and excelled in the use of the popular idiom. Some of his novels [e.g., *Pago chico* (1908), and *Las divertidas aventuras de Juan Moreira* (1910)] belong in the picaresque tradition and were written almost completely in dialogue form. Enrique Larreta (1875–), famous for his modernist novel *La gloria de don Ramiro* (1908), also wrote stories on the *gaucho* theme [e.g., *Zogoibí* (1926)]. But the two greatest interpreters of *gaucho* life were Ricardo Guiraldes (already mentioned) and Benito Lynch (1880–1951). Lynch, more realistic than Guiraldes, analyzed the psychological and social problems of the *gaucho* in relation to his modern environment, for example, in *El inglés de los huesos* (1924). Other novelists who wrote on country life in Argentina are: Eduardo Acevedo Díaz (1887–), Carlos B. Quiroga (1890–), Juan Carlos Dávalos (1887–), and Pablo Rojas Paz (1896–1957).

Ernesto Sabato (1911–) and Marco Denevi (1922–) deserve special mention because they seem to be setting new trends for the writers who appeared after 1950. Sabato is a novelist of great intellectual power and deep feeling; his *Sobre héroes y tumbas* (1961) can be described as a neoromantic Argentine epic in which the life of a people and a nation is scrutinized through the experiences of a young man growing up in Buenos Aires. Denevi is a master of the psychological fantasy: he has written two mystery novels, *Rosaura a las diez* (1955) and *Ceremonia secreta* (1962), in which he surprises with all kinds of technical devices that successfully maintain an atmosphere both poetic and satirical.

Theater. Argentine theater is important because its playwrights, directors, and actors worked together to elaborate a popular style combining folklore with a strong element of social satire, and created characters that have become typical. The foundations for this type of theater were laid in the works of an Uruguayan writer, Florencio Sánchez (1875–1910), whose plays *M'hijo el dotor* (1903), *La gringa* (1904), and *Los muertos* (1905) contained powerful criticism of local conventions, and strong characterization. Francisco Defilippis Novoa (1891–1930) and José González Castillo (1885–1937) also contributed to the growth of the Argentine *sainete*. The outstanding playwright of the first half of the 20th century was Samuel Eichelbaum (1894–), noted for his sharp realism and psychological analysis; his best-known plays are *Pájaro de barro* (1940) and *Un guapo del 900* (1940).

Recent Essayists and Critics. Among the many brilliant essayists and literary critics of Argentina, the following should be particularly remembered: Calixto Oyuela (1857–1934); Alejandro Korn (1860–1936); José Ingenieros (1877–1925), whose *Evolución de las ideas en la Argentina* (1918) is still an indispensable reference book; Ricardo Rojas (1882–1957); Jorge Max Rhode (1890–); Alfredo Bianchi and Roberto Giusti, cofounders of the magazine *Nosotros;* Ezequiel Martínez Estrada (1895–); Rafael Alberto Arrieta (1888–); Alberto Gerchunoff (1884–1950); Manuel Ugarte (1875–1954); and Victoria Ocampo (1893–). Other essayists who have distinguished themselves in the mid-century period are: Luis Emilio Soto (1902–), Raimundo Lida (1908–), María Rosa Lida de Malkiel (1910–), E. Anderson-Imbert (1910–), Aníbal Sánchez Reulet (1910–), and Alfredo Roggiano (1919–).

Bibliography: E. Anderson-Imbert, *Spanish-American Literature: A History,* tr. J. V. Falconieri (Detroit 1963). P. Henríquez-Ureña, *Literary Currents in Hispanic America* (New York 1963). R. A. Arrieta, ed., *Historia de la literatura Argentina,* 6 v. (Buenos Aires 1958–60). R. F. Giusti, "Las letras Argentinas en el siglo actual y sus antecedentes en el XIX," *Panorama das literaturas das Américas de 1900 à actualidad,* 3 v. (Angola 1959) 3:831–921. G. García, *La novela Argentina: Un itinerario* (Buenos Aires 1952). J. C. Ghiano, *Poesía Argentina del siglo XX* (Mexico City 1957). E. Morales, *Historia del teatro Argentino* (Buenos Aires 1944). Pan American Union, Letters Section, *Diccionario de la literatura latinoamericana* (Washington 1958–) v.1 and 2 *Argentina.* **Illustration credit:** Courtesy, The Hispanic Society of America.

[F. ALEGRIA]

ARGENTRÉ, CHARLES DU PLESSIS D', theologian; b. near Vitré, France, May 16, 1673; d. Tulle, Nov. 27, 1740. After he became a socius of the Sorbonne in 1698, he was ordained in 1699 and obtained the doctorate in theology the next year. In 1707 he was named vicar-general of Tréguiers and in 1725 was consecrated bishop of Tulle. Among his scholarly works are the anonymous *Apologie de l'amour* (Amsterdam 1698) written against F. *Fénelon in the controversy over *quietism, and his edition of *Martini Grandini opera theologica* (6 v. Paris 1710–12), to which he added some valuable works of his own as appendices. His most important contribution is, however, his *Collectio de novis erroribus* (3 v. Paris 1724–36). This work contains many documents (decisions of Roman congregations, papal *acta,* judgments of famous universities) on erroneous doctrines and controverted theological questions from the 12th century onward.

Bibliography: J. Balteau, DictBiogFranc 3:575–576. F. Stegmüller, LexThK[2] 1:837.

[M. A. ROCHE]

ARGIMIR, ST., matryr; b. *c.* 785, Cabra, Spain; d. June 28, 856, Córdoba (feast: July 7). Argimir was an elderly nobleman who had earlier held the office of *censor* in the Moslem government of Córdoba. He had retired from the administration of justice and withdrawn to a monastery when certain Moslems accused him of scurrilous derision of their prophet and profession of the divinity of Christ. Argimir admitted the charges before the cadi and was hung on the *eculeus* while still alive and finally slain by the sword. Christians buried his relics in the basilica of St. Acisclus in Córdoba. He was included in the Roman martyrology in 1586.

Bibliography: Eulogius, *Memoriale sanctorum,* PL 115:815–818. E. P. Colbert, *The Martyrs of Córdoba, 850–859* (Washington 1962) 262–264.

[E. P. COLBERT]

ARGUMENTATION

An argumentation is defined as an expression signifying the inference of one *truth from another truth. Just as a *term is the *sign of a *concept, and a *proposition the sign of a *judgment, so argumentation is the sign of the act of the mind known as *reasoning. As a sign, it is expressed primarily in spoken words and secondarily in written words. An example of the latter would be: "Everything white reflects light, and snow is white; hence snow reflects light."

Elements of Argumentation. Every argumentation consists of three elements: the antecedent, the conclusion, and the inference. The antecedent is the truth or truths already known as a starting point; the conclusion, sometimes called the consequent, is the truth newly arrived at; the inference, also called the illation or consequence, is the mental act involved in drawing the conclusion from the antecedent. The first two elements are found explicitly in an argumentation, while the third is indicated implicitly by a "therefore," "so," or "hence." Of the three inference is the most important element, because it gives unity and meaning to the other two, fashioning them into a logical unit. Thus, an argumentation is not merely a list of truths connected by a "therefore"; rather it signifies a growth of truth. And just as a growing organism has parts that are unified by its soul or vital principle, so argumentation has parts that are unified by the act of inference.

One difficulty in understanding argumentation comes from the inadequacy of examples. A teacher can communicate antecedent and conclusion to a student, but he cannot communicate or exemplify the inference. The act of inferring must take place in the student's mind, and there alone. As a result, examples of argumentation given in standard logic texts can be meaningless to the reader. Unless he proceeds step by step and sees the conclusion as a new truth drawn from the old, there is for him no argumentation. Inference, therefore, is not to be confused with mere succession. In argumentation one truth does not follow another; rather it follows *from* another. There must be a causal dependence of the conclusion on the antecedent, and precisely this is difficult to convey by means of examples.

Valid Inference. The rules or laws of argumentation are phrased as follows: (1) from a true antecedent there always follows a true conclusion; (2) from a false antecedent there sometimes follows a true conclusion; and (3) the conclusion always follows the weaker part, i.e., if the antecedent is negative or particular, the conclusion will correspondingly be negative or particular. These rules govern the inferences made in a reasoning process.

Another type of inference is found in judgment, when, from the truth or falsity of a given proposition, one infers the truth and falsity of related propositions. This is done in the matrices of symbolic *logic and in the traditional square of *opposition. Such a procedure is improperly called immediate inference by some writers. Mediate inference, which is said to be employed in argumentation, requires, on the other hand, that the conclusion be a new truth and not merely the rephrasing of a truth already known.

Because of the role of inference, argumentation is not said to be true or false (although obviously the conclusion can be so called), but rather argumentation is valid if it observes the necessary dependence of the conclusion on the antecedent, and invalid if it does not. Some authors speak of good and bad argumentation. Thus a geometrical proof that leads to a true conclusion through the observance of proper method is known as a good or valid argumentation.

Kinds of Argumentation. Argumentation can be divided on the basis of either its form or its matter. The division on the basis of form or structure has two principal members: argumentation that is good, and argumentation that is only apparently good. The latter is called *fallacy or sophistry. Although it has the appearance, at least to the neophyte, of valid argumentation, some fault hidden in its structure or content renders it invalid.

Argumentations that are good or valid are of two types: inductive and deductive (*see* INDUCTION; DEDUCTION). The inductive process is one whose antecedent is less general than the conclusion; the deductive process, on the other hand, is one whose antecedent is more general than its conclusion. Both induction and deduction are equally argumentations. When arranged artificially by the logician, deduction is formulated in the *syllogism. The argumentation already given as an example can be cast in syllogistic form as follows:

Everything white reflects light.
But snow is white.
Therefore snow reflects light.

Another division is that on the basis of matter or content. Argumentation is apodictic when the matter involved is necessary, i.e., the various terms of the antecedent cannot be related other than they are. When this obtains within the deductive process the argumentation is a *demonstration. When the matter is only contingent or probable, the argumentation is dialectical (*see* DIALECTICS). When the matter is such that it involves the emotions, but in a hidden way, the argumentation is rhetorical (*see* RHETORIC). Finally, when open appeal is made to the emotions, the argumentation may be called poetic [*see* POETICS (ARISTOTELIAN)]. Thus argumentation can express a reasoning process in a variety of ways, ranging from the strictest scientific reasoning to the subtle intimations of poetry. It embraces inductive and deductive processes, and often combines both.

The universal scope of argumentation is often lost on the rationalist, who overemphasizes deduction, and on the empiricist, who stresses induction to an extreme. Neither the rationalist nor the empiricist considers rhetorical and poetical forms of argument as legitimate forms of reasoning. This is in sharp contrast to the cultural and scientific appreciation accorded this means of attaining truth by the ancient Greeks and medieval schoolmen.

See also LOGIC; PROOF.

Bibliography: S. J. HARTMAN, *Fundamentals of Logic* (St. Louis 1949). J. A. OESTERLE, *Logic: The Art of Defining and Reasoning* (2d ed. Englewood Cliffs, N.J. 1963). V. E. SMITH, *The Elements of Logic* (Milwaukee 1957). E. D. SIMMONS, *The Scientific Art of Logic* (Milwaukee 1961).

[E. BONDI]

ARGYROPOULOS, JOHN, Byzantine scholar teaching in the West; b. Constantinople, 1415; d. Rome, June 26, 1487. One of the most celebrated Byzantine scholars to appear in Italy during the years immediately preceding and following the fall of Constantinople to the Turks in 1453, Argyropoulos was a member of the Greek delegation to the Council of *Florence (1438–39) and seems to have remained in Italy after the close of the council, studying and subsequently teaching Greek privately at Venice and Padua. After returning to Byzantium a few years later, he taught Greek literature at Constantinople's higher school, the Mouseion of Xenon, and took the side of the pro-unionists in the conflict over the union with Rome. Upon the capture of Constantinople by the Turks, he fled to the Peloponnesus, whence, in 1456, he was summoned to Florence by Cosimo de' *Medici to occupy *Chrysoloras's old chair of Greek studies at the University of Florence. During the epidemic of 1471 he moved to Rome, where he continued teaching Greek until his death.

Argyropoulos made major contributions to the transmission of Greek learning to the West, particularly of Aristotelianism. His translations of many of the works of Aristotle (among them the *Physics,* the *Metaphysics,* and the *Nicomachean Ethics*) facilitated the study of that author among Western humanists. Equally important, Argyropoulos numbered among his students in Florence and Rome some of the most influential Western intellectuals of the age: Politian, *Reuchlin, Palla *Strozzi, Donato *Acciaioli, and even Lorenzo de' *Medici. Lorenzo the Magnificent and Acciajuoli were later to become admirers of Plato. However, Argyropoulos's translations and teaching were signally to help in the diffusion of the philosophy of Aristotle, especially north of the Alps, at a time when it appeared that Aristotelianism might be completely overshadowed by the Quattrocento's concentration on Platonism.

See also TRANSLATION LITERATURE, GREEK AND ARABIC.

Bibliography: S. LAMPROS, *Argyropouleia* (in Greek) (Athens 1910), for his minor works. G. CAMMELLI, *Giovanni Argiropulo,* v.2 of *I dotti bizantini e le origini dell'umanesimo* (Florence 1941–), for biog. and writings. D. J. GEANAKOPLOS, *Greek Scholars in Venice: Studies in the Dissemination of Greek Learning from Byzantium to Western Europe* (Cambridge, Mass. 1962), for the problem of the transmission of Greek learning to the West.

[D. J. GEANAKOPLOS]

ARGYROS, ISAAC, antipalamite, Greek monk, theologian, and astronomer; d. *c.* 1375. Although Argyros followed the inspiration of Theodore Metochites and Gregoras in pursuit of astronomy and mathematics, he also proved himself to be a theologian and powerful polemist. Argyros ranged himself with Nicephorus *Gregoras against Gregory *Palamas and Emperor *John VI Cantacuzenus in the controversy over *Hesychasm. He seems to have accepted the theological method of *Barlaam of Calabria in his principal treatise against Palamism, written probably after 1360. He is also credited with a monograph on the teaching of Barlaam against Theodore *Dexios and is probably the author of a tome published by the patriarch of Antioch (*c.* 1370). Two further opuscules against Palamism are also attributed to him.

Besides theological treatises, Argyros wrote numerous scientific tracts that are still in MS: *Apparatus astrolabii* (Vatican), *De reducendis triangulis* (Oxford), *De reducendo calculo astronomicorum* (Vienna), *Methodus Geodesiae* (Escorial), *Methodus solarium et lunarium* (Leyden), and *Geometriae aliquot problemata* (Paris). His chief scientific works concern the sun and the moon cycles and the 12 winds. It is probable that Argyros wrote a short commentary on the works of Ptolemy relating in particular to the defective chapter of the *Harmonics,* a work to which Nicephorus had also given attention.

Bibliography: G. MERCATI, *Notizie di Procoro e Demetrio Cidone* (StTest 56; 1931) 229–242, 270–275. J. F. MOUNTFORD, "The Harmonics of Ptolemy and the Lacuna in II, 14," *Transaction and Proceedings of the American Philological Association* 57 (1926) 71–95, esp. 95. Beck KTLBR 729–730. M. CANDAL, "Un escrito trinitario de Isaac Argiro en la contienda palamítica del siglo XIV," OrChrPer 22 (1956) 92–137; "Argiro contra Dexio," *ibid.* 23 (1957) 80–113. M. JUGIE, DTC 11.2:1806. E. VON IVÁNKA, "Die philosophische und geistesgeschichtliche Bedeutung des Palamismus," *Studi bizantini* 7 (1953) 124–129.

[G. LUZNYCKY]

ARGYRUS, MARIANUS, Byzantine *Dux Italiae;* b. Bari, Italy, *c.* 1005; d. *c.* 1068. The son of the Lombard Melo, held in Constantinople as a hostage following his father's rebellion in 1009, Argyrus returned to Italy in 1029. In 1040 he rebelled against Byzantium, and in 1042 the Normans of Troja chose him as their chief. Reconciled to Byzantium soon afterward, Argyrus went to Constantinople and returned in 1051 as governor of Byzantine Italy. In this post, Argyrus, who was passionately attached to the Latin Church, favored cooperation between *Leo IX and Constantine IX against the *Normans. This aroused the fear of the Patriarch *Michael Cerullarius who as a consequence launched his attack on the Latins, which led to the *Eastern schism of 1054. Argyrus was active until 1058.

Bibliography: C. J. C. WILL, *Acta et scripta* (Leipzig 1861). L. BRÉHIER, DHGE 4:93–95. A. MICHEL, *Humbert und Kerullarios,* 2 v. (Paderborn 1924–30). GUILELMUS APULIENSIS, *La Geste de Robert Guiscard,* ed. and tr. M. MATHIEU (Palermo 1961).

[P. CHARANIS]

ARI THORGILSSON, Icelandic historian, called the father of Icelandic historical writing; b. 1067; d. 1148. He was a descendant of an aristocratic family in Breiðifjörður that traced its genealogy back to the kings of Dublin. He was educated at the important seat of learning at Haukadalr on the south coast and was ordained. Details of his life are almost unknown, and only one of his historical works has survived, the *Islendingabók,* which in 10 short chapters tells the history of Iceland from the Norwegian settlements (*c.* 870) to 1120. The example of his predecessor, *Sæmund Sigfússon, probably occasioned his concern for accurate chronology. Ari based his chronology upon the series of *lögsögumenn* (lawspeakers) elected for 3 years to recite the unwritten law to the public at the *allþing* (assembly). The lawspeakers' dates are correlated with those of the Norwegian kings, occasionally with those of the popes and continental royalty.

Ari consistently refers to his oral sources whom he chooses with great concern for their learning and trustworthiness. Despite these efforts to be accurate, he does not properly date the Norwegian kings. With some narrative power and sense of historic causality, Ari blends factual information with the description of the development of Iceland from the establishment of the *allþing* and the changes consequent upon the introduction and development of the Church. It has been suggested that Ari intended to write his history in connection with the establishment of ecclesiastical law in 1125. Only Ari's last version of the *Islendingabók* is extant; from its prologue we gather that he had written an earlier version containing an account of the Icelandic families and their genealogies together with the list of the kings of Norway. Ari's work on Icelandic families is now considered basic to the *Landnámabók* (Book of Settlements); and his list of the kings of Norway was the chief source for later historians, especially *Snorri

Sturluson. Ari was the first to use Icelandic for scholarly purposes.

See also OLD NORSE LITERATURE.

Bibliography: ARI THORGILSSON, *The Book of the Icelanders,* ed. and tr. H. HERMANSSON (Ithaca, N.Y. 1930); *Islendingabók,* ed. F. JÓNSSON (Copenhagen 1930). E. ARNÓRSSON, *Ari Froði* (Reykjavik 1942).

[A. SALVESEN]

ARIALDO, ST., reformer and martyr; b. Cantu, Italy, *c.* 1000; d. on an island in Lake Maggiore, Italy, June 27, 1066 (feast, June 27). Although he had never been elevated beyond the rank of deacon, he was chosen by *Henry III to lead the reform of the Milanese clergy, a movement assisted by the Milanese Cardinal *Anselm II of Lucca and the noted clerical historian Landulph Cotta (fl. 1085). Reform was already a leading demand of the *Patarines, but Guido of Velate (d. 1071), Archbishop of *Milan, led the forces that opposed it. Soon after Arialdo began preaching at Varese, a provincial synod with Guido presiding excommunicated Arialdo and Landulph, both of whom appealed to Rome. Thereupon the Roman legates, Anselm of Baggio and Hildebrand, who became popes as *Alexander II and *Gregory VII respectively, reached Milan and encouraged the reformers to persevere. When Landulph died, his brother *Erlembald led the cause, associating his name and sanctity with Arialdo, whose feast he shares. A bull of excommunication against Guido prompted his associates to capture Arialdo and isolate him on an island in Lake Maggiore. There he was assassinated by two priests; his body was later brought to Milan by Erlembald. In 1068 Alexander II declared Arialdo a martyr, and his ancient cult was confirmed by *Pius X in 1904.

Bibliography: ActSS June 7:250–272. C. PELLEGRINI, *I santi Arialdo ed Erlembaldo* (Milan 1897). C. CASTIGLIONI, EncCatt 1:1882–83; *I santi Arialdo ed Erlembaldo e la Pataria* (Milan 1944).

[N. M. RIEHLE]

ARIANISM

Major 4th-century Trinitarian heresy, originated by the teachings of the Alexandrian priest *Arius (d. 336). The basic tenet of Arianism was a negation of the divinity of Christ and, subsequently, of the Holy Spirit. Arius reduced the Christian Trinity to a descending triad, of whom the Father alone is true God.

The key to the theology of Arius is the doctrine of *agennèsia* (the unbegotten) as the essential attribute of the Godhead: God is by necessity not only uncreated, but unbegotten and unoriginate. Hence God is absolutely incommunicable and unique. As a result the Logos, whom the Scriptures designate clearly as begotten from the Father, cannot be true God. Even though He is adored by all Christians, He is God and Son of God only by participation in grace or by adoption. Since the Godhead is indivisible and incommunicable and the Logos has His being from the Father, there remains but the affirmation that He is a creature, "alien and dissimilar in all things from the Father"; a perfect creature and immensely above all other created beings, but a creature nevertheless.

Since Arius did not accept the opinion of *Origen, which postulated an eternal creation, he asserted that the Son had a beginning: "There was when He was not." This assertion was considered blasphemous by the faithful, and it was condemned as such by the Council of *Nicaea I (325). Since He was not true God, the Logos had but an imperfect knowledge of the Father; He was also subject to change and peccable by nature, if not in fact.

The main arguments used by the Arians were scriptural texts such as "The Lord created me a beginning of his ways" (Prv 8:22); "The Father is greater than I" (Jn 14.28); "the first-born of all creation" (Col 1.15). Moreover, all through the controversy with the defenders of the Nicene Creed, the Arians consistently rejected nonscriptural words and expressions.

Part of the Arian system was the Word-flesh *Christology, which denied the existence of a human soul in the Incarnate Word; its place was taken by the Logos Himself. Although Arius said little about the Holy Spirit, his followers, true to the logic of their system, considered the third person, or hypostasis, of the Trinity as the highest creature produced by the Son, but inferior to and dissimilar from both the Father and the Son.

Doctrinal Antecedents. The problem of the doctrinal antecedents of Arianism has not yet been fully elucidated. Although Arius claimed to be a disciple of *Lucian of Antioch, much of his theology points to the Origenistic tradition, which was dominant in Alexandrian circles: an insistence on the Father as the only God; an emphasis on distinction rather than unity in the Trinity; and the subordinate position of the Son and the Spirit. But neither Origen nor any other pre-Nicene writer offered support for Arius's teaching that the Logos had a beginning of existence. The influence of Aristotle, for which Arians were often blamed by their adversaries, seems to have consisted more in the rationalistic method of argument than in the ideas themselves. Certainly, the cosmological conception of the Logos as a demigod, produced by the Father of all as an intermediary being between the Godhead and the universe, appeared as an adaptation of Christianity to the Hellenistic philosophy of the time. As H. Gwatkin justly remarked, Arianism, scarcely disguised by the traditional terminology and the addition of scriptural quotations, was pagan to the core.

Historically, the controversy concerning the theology of Arius broke into the open in Alexandria about 320, when a local synod under Bishop *Alexander condemned his views. When he refused to submit and gained more followers, Alexander summoned a council of the entire Egyptian episcopate, which again condemned Arius and excommunicated him. As a result he left Alexandria and journeyed through Palestine, Syria, and Asia Minor, gaining support from such influential bishops as *Eusebius of Caesarea and *Eusebius of Nicomedia. They sent out numerous letters to fellow bishops and organized synods to uphold Arius's position, while Alexander, in turn, wrote to Eastern and Western bishops to express the true nature of the conflict. Thus, what started as a local dispute soon caused division in the entire Eastern Church.

Constantinian Intervention. When *Constantine I conquered the East in 324, he sent his ecclesiastical adviser Bishop *Hosius of Córdoba (more properly Ossius) to Alexandria with a letter to Bishop Alexander and Arius exhorting them to make peace. But this mission failed; and Hosius on his return to the court presided at a Council of the Orient in Antioch (early 325). Arianism was condemned, and a profession of faith was promulgated that closely resembled the Alexandrian creed. Three bishops were provisorily excommunicated

The priest Arius of Alexandria prostrate before the Emperor and the archbishops at the Council of Nicaea I, miniature in the 10th-century Menologion of Emperor Basil II, Vatican Library (Cod. Vat. gr. 1613, fol. 108).

for their refusal to sign it. Meanwhile Constantine, probably at the suggestion of Hosius, had summoned a general council of the Church, first at Ancyra in Galatia, then at Nicaea in Bithynia for the summer of 325.

Council of Nicaea I. Having heard an exposition of the teachings of Arius, the Council of Nicaea I condemned them as blasphemous; from this condemnation radical Arianism never recovered. The Council, apparently led by Hosius, also promulgated the famous *Nicene Creed, defining once and for all the true relation of the Son to the Father as **homoousios*.

Eusebius of Caesarea, *Athanasius of Alexandria, and *Philostorgius have given divergent accounts of how this creed was drafted; what follows is only the most probable reconstruction of events at Nicaea. Some bishops, Hosius and probably Alexander among others, persuaded Constantine that the promulgation of a unique creed would be the surest way to achieve lasting unity in the Church. They selected a local creed, probably that of Syro-Palestinian origin, and inserted into it several clauses intended to exclude the typically Arian opinions. Thus they added "from the substance of the Father"; "true God from true God, begotten not made"; and the key word of the creed, which was to become so controversial for many decades, *homoousion tōi Patri,* that is, "of one substance with the Father." In the end the redactors added the anathemas and explicitly rejected the shocking Arian expression "there was when He was not." Significant in this connection was the fact that *hypostasis* (person) was identified with *ousia* (substance), against the dominant Origenist tradition in the East that affirmed three *hypostaseis* in the Godhead. But Constantine crushed the opposition among the bishops and demanded the signature of all present under the penalty of banishment. Only two bishops from Libya refused; together with Arius and the priests who remained faithful to him, they were exiled to Illyricum.

Anti-Nicene Reaction. Ostensibly, the Arian crisis had been resolved, and unity had been restored among the churches. But a few years later a strong anti-Nicene reaction arose, in which two tendencies seem to have been at work. There was a small but active group of Arian sympathizers who had signed the Nicene Creed for fear of exile but had renounced none of their convictions. The other group comprised a large number of Eastern bishops whose beliefs were basically orthodox but whose fear of *Monarchianism inspired them with a marked distrust of the *homoousios.* These sentiments were shrewdly exploited by the first group, to which the real leaders of the reaction belonged, including both Eusebius of Nicomedia and Eusebius of Caesarea, Paulinus of Tyre, and Menophantes of Ephesus. Knowing how strongly Constantine was attached to the Nicene faith, they at first avoided a direct attack against it and concentrated their efforts on eliminating the most influential defenders of the *homoousios.* Thus, from 328 on Eustathius of Antioch, Marcellus of Ancyra, Asclepas of Gaza, and finally the foremost leader of all, Athanasius of Alexandria, fell victim to this war of persons: all were deposed by synodical sentence and replaced by members of the anti-Nicene party. After the death of Constantine (337) all exiled bishops were allowed to return to their sees; but the division of the Empire between Constans, who ruled in the West and favored the Nicene party, and Constantius II, who ruled the East and favored the anti-Nicene reaction, soon was reflected on the ecclesiastical level.

Athanasius, Marcellus, and others were recognized as legitimate bishops by the West at the Council in Rome (340–341) but were considered deposed and excommunicated by the East at the Dedication Council of Antioch (341). At the Antioch meeting Eusebius of Nicomedia and his supporters for the first time dared to attack the Nicene faith directly: they promulgated the so-called Second Creed of Antioch, known also as the creed of Lucian of Antioch, which, while condemning several Arian doctrines, omitted the characteristic Nicene phrases "from the essence of the Father" and *homoousios.*

Synods at Sardica and Sirmium. The Council of *Sardica, summoned in 343 by both Emperors to restore unity, failed to heal the breach between the Eastern and Western episcopates, as the former refused to sit in a joint meeting with Athanasius and his fellow exiles. Nevertheless the dominant position of Emperor Constans and a general desire for *rapprochement* produced a precarious peace; Athanasius returned to Alexandria in 346 and remained in possession of his see until 356. But the deaths of Constans in 350 and Pope *Julius I in 352, and the accession of Constantius II as sole ruler of the Empire, gave rise to a renewed offensive on the part of the Arians.

As early as the winter of 351 a group of Eastern bishops held a synod in the imperial residence at *Sirmium. After deposing the local bishop, Photinus, a disciple of *Marcellus of Ancyra, they promulgated what is known as the First Formulary of Sirmium, consisting of the Fourth Creed of Antioch and a series of anathemas directed partly against radical Arianism and partly against the doctrines of Marcellus and Photinus. Except for the omission of *homoousios* and a few traces of subordinationism, this formulary was susceptible of an orthodox interpretation. The leaders of the anti-Nicene party, especially two Arian court bishops, Valens of Mursa and Ursacius of Singidunum, then staged an all-out attack against the undisputed leader of Nicene orthodoxy, Athanasius. Under strong pressure by Emperor Constantius, two Western councils agreed to the condemnation of Athanasius: Arles in October 353 and Milan in the spring of 355. The few bishops who refused, including Pope Liberius and *Hilary of Poitiers, were exiled to the East, and the centenarian Hosius of Cordova was detained for a year at the court of Sirmium.

Arian Triumph and Downfall. Having forced the Western churches into submission, Constantius and his Arianizing counselors then turned to the East. In February 356 Athanasius was forced to flee to the desert, where he hid for 6 years; and an Arian intruder, George of Cappadocia, was installed in his place. Thus all voices raised in defense of the Nicene faith were silenced, and all bishoprics were occupied by the opposition.

This apparent triumph caused the downfall of the anti-Nicene coalition: united in the battle against Athanasius and the faith of Nicaea, they fell out with each other when trying to impose a definitive substitute for the *Nicaenum.* Three main factions emerged, vying for the favor of Constantius and supremacy in the Church. Each had its own formulary; each held a council dominated by its leaders; each knew its hour of triumph. Since the doctrinal position of each was characterized by a proposed substitute for the Nicene *homoousios,* they have been named after their favorite theological expression: the radical Anomoeans, who held that the Son was *anomoios* (unlike) the Father; the moderate Homoeousians, who preferred the term *homoiousios* (of like substance) with the Father; and the devious Homoeans, whose password *homoios* (similar to, like) covered any and all opinions.

The first to bid for power were the radical Arians, led by Valens and Ursacius in the West and by Eudoxius and Eunomius in the East. In the summer of 357 they held a synod at Sirmium that, with the approval of Constantius, promulgated the Second Formulary of Sirmium. This stressed the inferiority of the Son to the Father; and since their doctrine was of unmistakingly Arian inspiration, it provoked violent indignation both in the West and in the East. *Basil of Ancyra and George of Laodicea organized the opposition among the moderates of the anti-Nicene party. In the Synods of Ancyra (spring 358) and Sirmium (summer 358) they strongly condemned anomoeism and defined their own position in the Third Formulary of Sirmium, the key word of which was *homoiousios,* that is, "the Son is of like substance with the Father." Basil of Ancyra even planned another general council to be held at Nicomedia, but an earthquake forced postponement and gave his enemies time to gain the Emperor's favor for a third group, the Homoeans, led by *Acacius of Caesarea. He persuaded Constantius to summon not one but two meetings, one for the West at Rimini and the other for the East at Seleucia.

To prepare for these meetings, Marcus of Arethusa drew up yet another creed, the Fourth Formulary of Sirmium, better known as the Dated Creed, which proclaimed the Son *homoios,* like the Father in all things that the Scriptures declare. With a few variations—the most important of which was the final omission from the text of the clause "in all things"—this creed was forced on the bishopric of the entire Church at the Councils of Rimini (October 359), Seleucia (winter 359), and Constantinople (January 360).

This triumph of homoeism was deceptive, however, since it was based solely on imperial support: it collapsed immediately after the death of Constantius in 361. Moreover, by persecuting Homoousians and Homoeousians alike, it brought about better understanding and, ultimately, reconciliation between the two groups. Beneficial in this aspect were also the wise decisions of Athanasius at the Synod of Alexandria in 362; the peacemaking efforts of *Basil of Caesarea; and the theological writings of all three Cappadocian Fathers.

Under *Valens (364–378) homoeism regained imperial favor in the East; but it collapsed again after his death. Both Gratianus and *Theodosius I were strong defenders of the Nicene faith: by official decrees of 380 and 381 Catholic orthodoxy was imposed on all Christians and the Arians were deprived of their offices and churches. In 381 the Council of *Constantinople I for the East and that of Aquileia for the West sealed the final adoption of the faith of Nicaea by the entire Church and completed it by proclaiming the full divinity of the Holy Spirit against the so-called *Macedonians, or Semi-Arians as they are known also.

Later Revival. Utterly defeated in the Roman Empire, Arianism received new life through its implantation among the Germanic tribes and, with them, reentered the Western Empire. The conversion of these peoples was initiated by the missionary activity of Wulfila, apostle of the Goths, who were established on both banks of the lower Danube. This grandson of Christian captives from Cappadocia had been consecrated bishop by Eusebius of Nicomedia at the Dedication Council of Antioch in 341; and upon his return north, he succeeded in converting a good many of his people. He invented a Gothic alphabet and translated the Bible; but the creed he gave his people was the Homoean Creed of the Council of Constantinople of 360, at which he was present. Thus the Germanic Christians were known as Arians. Despite some persecution, Christianity in this form spread with remarkable vigor from the Goths to the neighboring tribes, such as the Gepides, Herules, Vandals, Suevi, Alamanni, and Burgundians. When they invaded the West and established the various Germanic kingdoms, most of these tribes professed homoeism as their national religion and in some instances persecuted those among the Roman population who professed Catholic orthodoxy.

This religious division, added to the ethnic antagonism, retarded the unification of the Roman and barbarian peoples; but gradually the Catholic Church succeeded in eliminating Arianism. In some instances this was achieved by military action that all but wiped out the Germanic element: in 553 the *Vandals in Africa were utterly destroyed by the armies of Justinian I; and in 552 the Ostrogothic kingdom of Italy suffered a similar fate. By peaceful means and through the action of Bp. *Avitus of Vienne, the *Burgundians in southwestern Gaul had accepted Catholicism in 517, under King Sigismund.

In Spain the *Suevi turned to Catholicism *c.* 450 but were soon afterward absorbed by the strong Visigothic kingdom, which remained Arian until 587, when its King, Reccared, became Catholic under the guidance of *Leander of Seville. The *Lombards, the last tribe to enter the former Roman Empire, were partly pagan and partly Arian. Their conversion to Catholicism, prepared by Queens Theodolinda and Gondeberga, took place under Kings Aribert and Perctarit toward the end of the 7th century.

Bibliography: J. R. PALANQUE et al., *The Church in the Christian Roman Empire,* tr. E. C. MESSENGER, 2 v. in 1 (New York 1953) 396–408. Quasten Patr 3:7–13. *Bibliographia Patristica* (Berlin 1956–), for all studies pub. after 1955. A. D'ALÈS, *Le Dogme de Nicée* (Paris 1926). X. LE BACHELET, DTC 1.2: 1779–1863. J. N. D. KELLY, *Early Christian Creeds* (2d ed. New York 1960); *Early Christian Doctrines* (2d ed. New York 1960) 223–279. G. L. PRESTIGE, *God in Patristic Thought* (SPCK; 1935; repr. 1959). T. E. POLLARD, "The Origins of Arianism," JThSt NS 9 (1958) 103–111. H. A. WOLFSON, DumbOaksP 12 (1958) 3–28. W. HAUGAARD, "Arius Twice a Heretic?" ChHist 29 (1960) 251–263. H. GWATKIN, *Studies of Arianism* (2d ed. Cambridge, 1900). E. SCHWARTZ, *Zur Geschichte des Athanasius* (Gesammelte Schriften 3; Berlin 1959); "Zur Kirchengeschichte des 4. Jahrhunderts," ZNTWiss 34 (1935) 129–213. H. G. OPITZ, ed., *Urkunden zur Geschichte des arianischen Streites* (Athanasius' Werke v.3.1; Berlin 1934). V. C. DE CLERCQ, *Ossius of Cordova* (Washington 1954) 189– . J. ZEILLER, *Les Origines chrétiennes dans les provinces danubiennes* (Paris 1918). K. D. SCHMIDT, *Die Bekehrung der Germanen zum Christentum,* 2 v. (Göttingen 1939–40). P. DE LABRIOLLE, Fliche-Martin 4:353–396. **Illustration credit:** Biblioteca Apostolica Vaticana.

[V. C. DE CLERCQ]

ARIAS, FRANCIS, Jesuit theologian and spiritual writer; b. Seville, 1533; d. there, May 15, 1605. His work as a Jesuit included a 4-year professorship in theology at the University of Cordoba and two successive terms as rector of the colleges at Triguero and Cadiz. Among his contemporaries Arias was known for his rigorous discipline and observance. In a letter to C. *Acquaviva in 1594, a fellow Jesuit described him as a holy man, exemplary, devout, and spiritual. Renown has come to him primarily because of his spiritual writings. In 1588 he wrote *Exhortación al aprovechamiento espiritual,* in which he discussed spiritual progress, mistrust of self, and mental prayer. The work was later translated into other tongues. *Libro de la imitación de Cristo nuestro Señor* and *Contemptus Mundi,* among his other works, gave him a reputation as another Thomas à Kempis, despite the fact that his style lacked the simplicity and brevity of à Kempis. St. Francis de Sales admired his works.

Bibliography: A. ASTRAIN, *Historia de la Compañía de Jesús en la Asistencia de España,* 7 v. (Madrid 1902–25) v.4. J. DE GUIBERT, DictSpirAscMyst 1:844–855. Sommervogel 1:540–549. Espasa 6:174.

[D. M. BARRY]

ARIBO OF MAINZ, archbishop of Mainz, a member of the noble Aribo family; b. *c.* 990; d. Como, April 6, 1031. He was buried in the Mainz cathedral, which he rebuilt. He founded (1020) the Styrian convent of Göss and later the church at Hasungen. Already an imperial chaplain, he became in 1021 archbishop of Mainz and thereby archchaplain of the Empire. In 1025, through *Conrad II, whose imperial election he had effected, he became also the chancellor of Italy. Gifted, learned, and a prodigious writer, he succeeded in obtaining *Ekkehard IV of Sankt Gallen as director of the cathedral school at Mainz. In several synods he strengthened the ecclesiastical discipline of his province. His domineering character and intolerance of the rights of others involved him in numerous disputes. He revived the controversy regarding metropolitan jurisdiction over *Gandersheim with Bp. Godehard of Hildesheim, a struggle that the latter's tact and goodness brought to an end in 1030. His harsh attitude toward Otto and Irmgard of Hammerstein, whose marriage had already been contested by his predecessor, became so offensive that *Benedict VIII withdrew his faculties when he rejected Irmgard's appeal to the Holy See (Synod of Seligenstadt, in 1023; cc.16, 18; Hefele-Leclercq 4:921–924). Thus he is said, though unjustly, to have been an opponent of the *Cluniac reform. Because, among other reasons, he doubted the validity of Conrad's marriage, he refused to permit the coronation of the Empress Gisela in Mainz and thus relinquished an ancient privilege of his see. In 1027 he attended the coronation of Conrad II and also a Lateran council in Rome. He died returning from a later trip to Rome.

Bibliography: MGSrerGerm 11:684. N. BISCHOFF, MitteilIÖG 58 (1950) 285–309. P. ACHT, NDB 1:351. Hauck v.3, *passim.* A. BRÜCK, LexThK² 1:849–850.

[H. WOLFRAM]

ARIDITY, SPIRITUAL, a condition of soul in which a person derives no consolation or satisfaction from prayer. This absence of spiritual gratification makes it very difficult for one to produce the intellectual and affective acts of prayer. According to spiritual writers, aridity may be due to different causes. It may be caused by such infidelity to God's grace as lukewarmness in the service of God, habitual venial sin, habits of sensuality, vain curiosity, inconstancy, superficiality, lack of esteem for spiritual goods, or excessive activism.

Aridity may result also from the physical discomfort caused by sickness, by heat or cold, or by the lack of sufficient sleep. Or it may be the effect of the mental uneasiness caused by worry, family problems, absorbing occupations, overwork, or a lack of the natural ability for a particular method of prayer. Certain mental or emotional problems also may cause aridity in the spiritual life.

Finally, aridity may be sent by God to humble the soul and purify it of its excessive attachment to consolation in prayer. But if this aridity is accompanied by the signs of purgative contemplation, by an inability to meditate upon the things of God, a disinclination to fix the mind on other objects, and an anxious solicitude about backsliding and not serving the Lord, then the dryness is an indication of a more accentuated divine influence. In this case, aridity manifests a divine call to enter upon a new, more simplified form of prayer, a contemplative loving attentiveness to God.

When the aridity is caused by infidelity, a person may find the remedy in a greater diligence in his practices of the spiritual life and in a more careful effort to correct his defects. In the case of the aridity caused by physical discomfort or mental uneasiness, a person should seek the means for alleviating the causes of these ills. If this alleviation is not attainable, the endurance of the aridity can then be the occasion for the practice of greater virtue, especially patience. When purgative contemplation is the cause of the dryness, a person should not continue to try to meditate or force particular acts, but he should remain at peace, in a simple, loving attentiveness to God in pure faith and love, without the desire to experience or feel anything.

See also PURIFICATION, SPIRITUAL.

Bibliography: FRANCIS DE SALES, *Introduction to the Devout Life,* ed. and tr. J. K. RYAN (New York 1950) 2.9; 4.14–15. JOHN OF THE CROSS, *The Dark Night of the Soul* in *Collected Works,* tr. K. KAVANAUGH and O. RODRIGUEZ (Garden City, N.Y. 1964). A. F. POULAIN, *The Graces of Interior Prayer,* tr. L. L. YORKE SMITH, ed. J. V. BAINVEL (St. Louis 1950). J. DE GUIBERT, *The Theology of the Spiritual Life,* tr. P. BARRETT (New York 1953). R. DAESCHLER, DictSpirAscMyst 1:845–855.

[K. KAVANAUGH]

ARIEL (JERUSALEM). The term Ariel (Heb. *'ărî'ēl*) can mean etymologically either "lion of God" or "hearth of God." It occurs as a clan name in Gn 46.16; Nm 26.17 and as a personal name in 2 Sm 23.20; 1 Chr 11.22; Ezr 8.16. Ezechiel uses the term to designate the "hearth" of the altar in the Temple of Jerusalem (Ez 43.15–16). Isaia, however, uses the term as a poetic synonym for the city of Jerusalem (Is 29.1–2, 7; see also the emended text of 33.7). The most likely explanation of this is that the original reading in Isaia was *'ŭrû'ēl* (*'rw'l* in IQIs[a]) and that *'ēl* (God) was substituted by the Israelites for the name of the Canaanite god Shalem (*šălim*) in the ancient name of Jerusalem, *urušalem,* which is known from Egyptian and Akkadian documents. Rabbinical speculation, understanding "the messengers of Salem" (*mal'ăkîm šălôm,* messengers of peace) in Is 33.7 as angels, arrived at the notion that Ariel was the name of an angel.

Bibliography: A. ROMEO, EncCatt 1:1897–98. V. HAMP, Lex ThK[2] 1:850–851. EncDictBibl 131. A. VACCARI, StAnselm 27 (1951) 256–259.

[W. F. CUMMINGS]

ARINTERO, JUAN GONZÁLEZ, spiritual writer; b. Lugueros (Province of León), Spain, June 24, 1860; d. Salamanca, Feb. 20, 1928. He entered the Dominican Order at Corias in 1875. From 1881 to 1886 he studied at Salamanca. As a specialist in the natural sciences, he taught at colleges in Vergara, Corias, and Valladolid from 1886 to 1898. During this period he published works on topics of scientific and religious interest. In 1900 he inaugurated at Valladolid the Academía de Santo Tomás, dedicated to the study of natural science in relation to philosophy and theology. In 1903 he was recalled to Salamanca as professor of apologetics, and except for one year (1909–10), which he spent as a professor at the Angelicum in Rome, he remained for the rest of his life in that city. The title of master in sacred theology was conferred upon him in 1908. At this period, he abandoned the study of the natural sciences and apologetics in order to give himself completely to ascetical and mystical theology. At the age of 45 Arintero projected the four-volume work that was to be his masterpiece, *Desenvolvimiento y vitalidad de la Iglesia.* As a result of his teaching regarding the call of all Christians to perfection and the normal development of the life of grace into contemplative prayer, and as a result of his denial of such a thing as acquired contemplation, Arintero became embroiled in controversies with Jesuits and Carmelites and with some of his Dominican brethren. In 1920 he founded the Spanish Dominican review of spirituality, *La Vida sobrenatural,* after having collaborated with the French Dominicans the previous year in the inauguration of *La Vie spirituelle.*

Bibliography: *The Mystical Evolution in the Development and Vitality of the Church,* tr. J. AUMANN, 2 v. (St. Louis 1949–51); *Stages in Prayer,* tr. K. POND (St. Louis 1957); *Cuestiones místicas* (BiblAutCrist 154; 1956). A. SUÁREZ, *Vida del M. R. P. Juan de Arintero . . .* (Cádiz 1936). J. AUMANN, "Mystic of San Esteban," CrossCrown 1 (1949) 198–207. J. L. CALLAHAN, "Fire on Earth," *ibid.,* 225–234. M. M. GORCE, DictSpirAscMyst 1: 855–859.

[J. AUMANN]

ARIOSTO, LODOVICO

A poet of the Italian Renaissance; b. Reggio Emilia, Sept. 8, 1474; d. Ferrara, July 16, 1533. In his early years he accompanied his father Niccolò, a captain in the service of Ercole d'Este, to Rovigo, Modena, Lugo, and finally to Ferrara, where he received most of his education. After the death of Niccolò in 1500, Lodovico entered the service of the Este family. In 1501 he was made captain of the Canossa citadel and in 1503 became private secretary to Cardinal Ippolito d'Este. Subsequently, he traveled to Rome, Florence, Mantua, and many other cities for the Cardinal and the Este family. When Ippolito was made Bishop of Buda, Hungary, in 1517, Ariosto refused to follow him, so as not to be separated from Alessandra Benucci-Strozzi, a beautiful Florentine widow with whom he had fallen in love and whom he was to marry secretly only after 1528. From

IL NEGROMANTE.
COMEDIA DI MES
SER LODOVICO
ARIOSTO.
Nessuno ardisca imprimerlo, ne venderlo per
Anni diece, sotto le pene contenute nel
Priuilegio concesso dal Sena/
to di questa Citta.
M D XXXV.

Title page of "Il Negromante" (1535 edition) with woodcut portrait of Lodovico Ariosto.

1522 to 1525 he served, on behalf of Duke Alfonso, as governor of the newly acquired district of Garfagnana. On his return to Ferrara, he built a modest house, where he lived until his death.

Early Work. Ariosto's first poems were in Latin, in accordance with the established humanistic tradition. In them he showed a superb mastery of expression, but no great originality. Other lyric poems, written in Italian at various stages of his life, closely followed Petrarchan models. More important are his comedies, composed for the court of Ferrara, where theatrical representations were then given and encouraged far more than in other Renaissance courts. By taking the plays of Plautus and Terence as models and integrating them with themes and motives drawn from contemporary life, Ariosto was able to create that Renaissance theater which was to exert so great an influence in the development of the European drama. (*See* DRAMA.) His *Cassaria* and *Suppositi,* performed in 1508 and 1509, respectively, must be considered the first regular Italian plays of any significance. But *Negromante* (1520) and *Lena* (1530) are more original and mature: the former is a remarkable satire of human gullibility, and the latter a picture of certain aspects of life in Renaissance Ferrara. A fifth comedy, *Studenti,* left unfinished, was completed by his brother Gabriele, who retitled it *Scolastica.*

Between 1517 and 1525 Ariosto also wrote *Satire,* or seven poetic epistles, in which he recreated in Italian the Latin style and tone of Horace's poems of the same kind. They are generally considered the best of Ariosto's minor works, because they combine preceptive portrayals of the customs of the time with reflections on life and on social conduct in general, and, still more interesting, with the author's reactions to events that touched him closely. The man revealed in the *Satire* is a moralist of solid common sense, one who can look on the virtues and vices of his contemporaries with an aloof yet sympathetic view.

Orlando Furioso. The vast epic, *Orlando Furioso,* to which he devoted almost 30 years, is the work that ranks Ariosto with the great poets. He began it *c.* 1503 with the intention of completing Matteo M. Boiardo's (1441–94) *Orlando Innamorato.* In 1516 he published the first edition in 40 cantos, in 1521 a minutely revised second edition, and in 1532 the final version in 46 cantos, brought to structural, rhytmical, and expressive perfection. It is considered the greatest work of the Italian Renaissance, the poem that synthesizes and symbolizes the ideals of the period, beginning with the cult of beauty and the recognition of the importance of life on earth.

Orlando, the Roland of the Carolingian *Chansons de Gestes,* had already become a man in love in Boiardo's story; in that of Ariosto he keeps pursuing Angelica through all kinds of adventures, and when he discovers that she has married a common man, he becomes mad with love. His madness is necessarily woven with the story of Angelica, who is constantly wanted by the various knights and who constantly flees from them, or, when her fleeing is temporarily postponed, exploits their feelings to her advantage. An additional main plot tells the story of Ruggero and Bradamente, who are destined to marry and originate the Este family—a device to thank his employers and protectors; however, Ariosto was to be disappointed with Cardinal Ippolito's cold reception of his great work.

The many subplots—some concerned with the Christian-Saracen war in the Pyrenees, some with the vicissitudes of numerous other characters—are all so deftly managed that the result is like a series of concentric circles. The reader is given a vision of an extremely complex and fascinating world, a sort of suprareality, into which Ariosto transports his characters, with their desires, passions, and frustrations, and watches them move and act. He succeeds, moreover, in maintaining a mastery of every situation: he views the people he has created with such detachment that he can smile at their actions and reactions. But his smile always implies an understanding and acceptance of human frailties, and a fine irony emerges as the consistent tone within the poem.

A marvelous world of fantasy and the understanding smile of Ariosto find superb expression in the perfection of the epic's stanzas, the purity of its language, and the music of its lines. These many hallmarks of greatness have assured its popularity and influence throughout the centuries.

Bibliography: *Opere minori,* ed. C. SEGRE, and *Orlando Furioso,* ed. L. CARETTI (La Letteratura italiana: storia e testi: 19–20; Milan 1954) one of the best editions; *Orlando Furioso,* tr. J. HARINGTON (London 1591; reprint 1963), and tr. W. S. ROSE, 8 v. (London 1823–31); *Supposes,* tr. G. GASCOIGNE (London 1566; reprint Boston 1906). R. RAMAT, *La critica ariostesca dal secolo XVI ad oggi* (Florence 1954). G. FATINI, *Bibliografia della critica ariostesca, 1510–1956* (Florence 1958). E. G. GARDNER, *The King of Court Poets* (London 1906). B. CROCE, *Ariosto, Shakespeare, and Corneille,* tr. D. AINSLIE (New York 1920). A. MOMIGLIANO, *Saggio sull' "Orlando Furioso"*

(2d ed. Bari 1932). W. BINNI, *Metodo e poesia di Ludovico Ariosto* (2d ed. Florence 1961). **Illustration Credit:** Folger Shakespeare Library, Washington, D.C.

[G. CECCHETTI]

ARISHIMA, TAKEO

Japanese novelist, playwright, essayist; b. Tokyo, Feb. 4, 1878; d. Karuizawa, June 9, 1923. He was the first son of a high government official and was educated at the Peers' School in Tokyo and at Sapporo University Agricultural School, Hokkaido. At Sapporo, he was taught by the outstanding Japanese Christian leader Inazō Nitobe. Through Nitobe he met the founder of the so-called non-church group, Kanzō Uchimura. In the Sapporo Independent Church at Hokkaido in 1900, Arishima, the Buddhist, accepted Christianity. Indicative of the quality of his new faith is a diary entry wherein he agrees with Carlyle that nature is the "living garment of God."

In memory of his graduation from the Sapporo school he coauthored the *Life of David Livingston.* After a year's army service, where he began to doubt his Christian faith, he studied history and economics at Haverford College (Haverford, Pa.) and Harvard University (1903–08). His doubt was deepened by the grandiose, empty formality of some American churches. In the U.S. he discovered *Whitman's poems and was lastingly influenced by their views on religion.

In Japan again, he taught English at his alma mater, and also served as Sunday school superintendent; but, unable to bear the church's "hypocrisy," he formally left it in 1911. He became a staff writer for the humanitarian literary magazine *Shirakaba* (White Birch), left his teaching position, and moved to Tokyo to devote himself to writing.

During the next few years he produced such major works as the novels *Aru Onna* (1919, A Certain Woman), *Kain no Matsuei,* (1917, The Descendant of Cain) and *Meiro* (1918, The Maze); the play *Shi to Sono Zengo* (1917, Death: Before and After); and the essays *Oshiminaku Ai wa Ubau* (1920, Love Demands Everything), *Ibusen Kenkyū* (1920, A Study of Ibsen), and *Hoittoman ni Tsuite* (1919, On Whitman). He also translated Whitman's poetic works under the title *Hoittoman Shishū* (1919–23). *Aru Onna,* depicting the newly independent woman of the 20th century, is regarded as the first realistic novel in Japanese literature.

Takeo Arishima.

Although Arishima has been thought a heretic, he wrote to a friend that despite leaving the church he considered himself a Christian. If he detested institutional Christianity, he had a love for Christ and read the Bible faithfully. His plays based on Biblical stories, such as *Daikozui no Mae* (1916, Before the Great Flood), *Samuson to Derira* (1915, Samson and Delilah), and *Seisan* (1919, The Last Supper), are unique in Japanese literature. His idea of "impulsive life," advocated in *Oshiminaku Ai wa Ubau,* is traceable to an odd combination of Christian love and Whitman's idea of loafing.

See also JAPANESE LITERATURE.

Bibliography: T. ARISHIMA, *Arishima Takeo zenshū,* (Tokyo 1929–30).

[K. KODAMA]

ARISTEAS, LETTER OF

A Hellenistic Jewish apologetic treatise composed at Alexandria in the 2d century B.C. As to whether early or late in the 2d century there is no agreement. Superficially, it has the form of a letter addressed by a Hellenic pagan at the court of Ptolemy II Philadelphus (285–246 B.C.) to a certain Philocrates, a visitor from some island, possibly Cyprus. This framework is fictional; and the author, a Jew writing in the first instance for fellow Jews, remains anonymous. His work describes the production of the Greek translation of the Hebrew Torah (the five books of Moses). This description also is fictional, but the number of 72 translators alleged by "Aristeas" has become standardized in the name Septuagint (Latin for 70), loosely applied to the entire Greek OT produced and partly revised during the whole period from the early 3d century B.C. to the early 2d Christian century.

As "Aristeas" tells the story, Demetrius of Phaleron, a known statesman and philosopher, is the librarian of Philadelphus. He is engaged in building up the famous library at Alexandria, and for this purpose he desires copies of the Jewish Law. The King prepares an embassy to Eleazar, high priest in Jerusalem, requesting such copies for translation into Greek; Aristeas persuades the King, as a good-will gesture, to free certain slaves brought as captives from Judea by Ptolemy I; and the King attaches Aristeas to the embassy. The letter goes on to cite a correspondence between the King and the high priest, and to describe gifts sent by the King for ritual use in Jerusalem. There follow descriptions of Jerusalem, first the Temple, then the city as a whole. Eleazar selects translators, 6 from each of the 12 tribes [!], to accompany the books of the Law to Egypt; and Aristeas records the high priest's demonstration of the probity and the reasonableness of the Mosaic code. The translators are welcomed to Alexandria in a 7-day symposium (or banquet), at which the King presides. This becomes for the author a device to introduce a long round of discussions on kingship, which shrewdly blend Stoic principles on the subject with Jewish ideals for royal conduct and the common good. After this, the translators accomplish their work in 72 days, to the satisfaction of the Jews of Alexandria, Demetrius, and the King. They are sent home in honor, with appropriate gifts for themselves and for the high priest.

All the action embodied in this narrative is fiction out of whole cloth. Told and retold by Philo, Josephus, Justin, Irenaeus, and a long line of Jewish and Christian writers, the story took on such absurdities as that the 72 (or 70) translators worked each in isolation, and yet all produced an identical complete result. This feature of the story was scornfully repudiated by St. Jerome (*Praef. in Pentateuchum,* repeated in *Apol. adv. Rufin.* 2.25) on the authority of the *Letter* itself and of Josephus; for the rest, he says of the supposed 70, "They interpreted before the coming of Christ and put forth in hesitant statements the things of which they were ignorant" (*ibid.*).

In our day, the *Letter of Aristeas* has been treated by P. E. *Kahle as a piece of propaganda for an officially revised late 2d-century B.C. form of a previously fluid and variable assortment of Greek renderings of the Mosaic books. Propaganda it certainly is, but Kahle's construct depends on a particular theory of Septuagint origins that overrides the existing evidence; it also postulates a historical development of revision work in a specified place and time for which no acceptable data can be adduced.

Bibliography: H. B. SWETE, *An Introduction to the O.T. in Greek* (rev. ed. Cambridge, Eng. 1914), with the Greek text only of *Aristeas,* as an appendix. R. H. CHARLES et al., eds., *The Apocrypha and Pseudepigrapha of the O.T. in English,* 2 v. (Oxford 1913) 2:83–122, with tr. and nn. H. G. MEECHAM, ed., *The Letter of Aristeas* (Manchester, Eng. 1935), critical study. M. HADAS, ed. and tr., *Aristeas to Philocrates* (New York 1951). S. JELLICOE, "Aristeas, Philo, and the Septuagint *Vorlage,*" JThSt NS 12 (1961) 261–271. A. PELLETIER, ed. and tr., *Lettre d'Aristée à Philocrate* (SourcesChr 89; 1962).

[P. W. SKEHAN]

ARISTIDES, 2d-century Athenian philosopher and Christian apologist. Aristides, known primarily through a notice in Eusebius (*Hist. Eccl.* 4.3.2), was the author of an Apology for the Christian faith addressed to the Emperor Hadrian (117–138). In 1878 the Mechitarist monks of San Lazzaro in Venice published an Armenian fragment of an Apology discovered in their monastery. Its title indicated that it was the lost Apology of Aristides. The authenticity of this claim was substantiated by J. R. Harris, who found a 4th-century Syrian version of the full text at Mt. Sinai in 1889. This discovery led J. A. Robinson to conclude that most of the Greek text was embodied in the legendary vita of *Barlaam and Joasaph (ch. 26–27) found among the writings of *John Damascene. In the vita, the author presents the Apology as made by a pagan philosopher in favor of Christianity. Papyri in the British Museum also contain several chapters of the Greek text (5.4; 6.1–2; 15.6–16.1).

The Apology begins with a discussion of the harmony in creation, using stoic concepts. This harmony, the author claims, led him to a knowledge of the Divine Being who created and preserves the universe (ch. 1). The author divides mankind into three categories in accordance with their religious beliefs: the barbarians, the Greeks, and the Jews. He describes as inadequate the barbarian (Chaldean) worship of the elements of the universe (ch. 3–7); the Greek cult of anthropomorphic deities, including Egyptian animal worship (ch. 8–13) and the Jewish devotion to angels and external ceremonies, instead of adoration of the true God whom their prophets served. He acknowledges, however, a nobility in the Jewish concept of spirituality (ch. 14).

The Christians as a "new nation" alone have a true idea of God who is the creator of all things in His only begotten Son and in the Holy Spirit. Their worship of God consists in purity of life based upon the commandments of the Lord Jesus Christ, to whom they look for the resurrection of the dead and life in the world to come (ch. 15–17). Together with a well-developed Christology (2.6–9), Aristides stressed the charity of the Christian community (15.7–9) and insisted that it is due to the supplications of the Christians that God continues the world in existence. His Apology is close in sentiment to that of *Quadratus and the letter to *Diognetus. While he acknowledged the fewness of the Christian faithful, he believed that as a new people they were to reanimate the world and save it from the corruption of contemporary immorality. The claim that Aristides is the author of the letter to Diognetus and possibly also identical with Quadratus has not met with the assent of most patristic scholars.

Bibliography: J. R. HARRIS and J. A. ROBINSON, eds., *The Apology of Aristides* (Texts and Studies 1; 2d ed. Cambridge, Eng. 1893). R. SEEBERG, ed., *Der Apologet Aristides* (Erlangen 1894). J. R. HARRIS, *The Newly Recovered Apology of Aristides* (London 1891). J. GEFFCKEN, *Zwei griechische Apologeten* (Leipzig 1907). B. ALTANER, ReallexAntChr 1:652–654. P. FRIEDRICH, ZKathTh 43 (1919) 31–77, doctrine. Altaner 118–119. K. RAHNER, LexThK² 1:852–853. Quasten Patr 1:191–195, 247–248.

[F. X. MURPHY]

ARISTOCRACY

The rule by a few by reason of their wealth, nobility, or virtue.

Early Concepts. For *Plato (*c.* 427–347 B.C.) the perfect state was the aristocratic state. This ideal was given its best expression in the *Republic:* "Unless philosophers become kings, or those now called kings become philosophers, there will be no end of evils for mankind" (473). Plato describes a state in which social justice would be fully realized as embracing three classes of men: the king-philosophers, or the ruling class, who constitute the legislative and executive power; the soldiers or guardians of the state; and the workers. The rulers must be intensely trained to become true philosopher-kings and must be subjected to a rigid process of selection that will bring the best philosophic minds to the top. Rulers and soldiers must be supported by the state; they cannot hold private property or enjoy normal family life because these are incompatible with full devotion to their duties. This system is proposed as a "model fixed in the heavens for human imitations, but not attainment" (592). *Aristotle (384–322) attempted to describe the existent state. To discover an ideal state, he observed in the *Politics,* it is necessary to begin by examining both the best states of history and the best that the theorists have imagined. The best practical policy is aristocracy, the rule of the informed and capable few; this is nowhere described realistically, however.

St. *Thomas Aquinas (*c.* 1225–74) also insisted that the state should be governed by the ablest. Right order among men demands naturally that the more intelligent should rule (*C. gent.* 3.81). Later St. Thomas *More (1478–1535) revived Plato's conception in his *Utopia,* describing an imaginary communist state so governed as to secure universal happiness. *The City of the Sun* of Tommaso *Campanella (1568–1639) substituted wise priests to rule instead of philosophers. In the *New Atlantis,* Francis *Bacon (1561–1626) placed scientists at the head of the state.

Modern Forms. An imitation of an aristocracy might have been the appropriate political form under *feudalism, in which ownership of land was accompanied by special duties of armed defense. In modern circumstances, aristocracy can be described as the dominance of a single, well-organized interest group over other community groupings. Perhaps the most obvious examples are the hereditary aristocracies that alternated in power with absolute monarchies in European history until the time of the French Revolution and even later. Also, merchant groups ruled many prosperous European states, such as Venice and the states of the Hanseatic League.

Plato's *Republic* has also been the source of inspiration for modern and contemporary theorists, such as Charles de *Montesquieu, G. W. F. *Hegel, J. F. *Renan, Thomas *Carlyle, Ralph Waldo *Emerson, Edmund *Burke, Friedrich *Nietzsche, and George *Santanyana. These theorists generally claim that men have always been governed by aristocratic institutions; that political power has changed its shape but not its nature; that every people is governed by an *elite, by a chosen element in the population; that aristocracies have been more favorable to literature, arts, and sciences; and, in a phrase that summarizes their theory, that all civilization is the work of aristocracies.

The managerial aristocracy of business corporations corresponds to the members of a mediocre state *bureaucracy. It is an aristocracy of wealth. In 1933 Pres. F. D. Roosevelt enlisted a so-called brain trust to cure national ills. Some theorists advocate an aristocracy of talent and the reconstruction of the federal and state system to arm the executive branch with great and immediate power. They find traditional *democracy dangerously unworkable when faced by the challenge of the cold war. They fear collapse and defeat by default for the democratic Western world unless something along this line is attempted.

Democratic theorists, on the other hand, such as K. R. Popper or D. Spitz, deny the above allegations, and indict Plato and his followers as forerunners of modern *totalitarianism. Plato's ideal state is not regarded as a means to an end, but becomes an end in itself. Such a view militates against sound philosophy and Christian belief. Plato held that each individual and family exists for the state; Christianity holds that each individual and family possesses certain natural rights that every government must respect and protect. Among these rights are the right to life and to a reasonable amount of liberty of movement, of self-assertion, and association.

See also GOVERNMENT; STATE, THE.

Bibliography: R. H. CROSSMAN, *Plato Today* (London 1937). H. W. ELDREDGE, *The Second American Revolution* (New York 1964). *The Works of Plato,* tr. B. JOWETT (New York 1936). D. GRENE, *Man in His Pride* (Chicago 1950). K. R. POPPER, *The Open Society* (Princeton 1963). B. F. SKINNER, *Walden Two* (New York 1948). D. SPITZ, *Patterns of Anti-democratic Thought* (New York 1949). J. WILD, *Plato's Theory of Man* (Cambridge, Mass. 1946).

[A. J. OSGNIACH]

ARISTOTELIANISM

The effect of the philosophical and scientific teachings of *Aristotle upon subsequent intellectual history through the transmission of his writings, terminology, ideas, and influence. To trace the history of Aristotelianism is to unravel one of the major strands in the evolution of Western and Near Eastern civilization. Especially in the ancient and medieval periods its history has been intimately bound up with that of *Platonism, *Neoplatonism, and *Stoicism, and with the theological development of the three monotheistic religions, Christianity, Islam, and Judaism.

GREEK ARISTOTELIANISM

Beginning with the death of Aristotle (322 B.C.), this section discusses the Aristotelianism of the early peripatetic, the Hellenistic, and the Byzantine periods.

Peripatetic Period. After Aristotle's death, his disciple Theophrastus of Eresos (d. *c.* 288 B.C.) became scholarch or head of his school, called the Peripatos or the Lyceum. The older representatives of this school were of varying fidelity to the balanced synthesis of the empirical and the ideal that had been achieved by their founder; most tended toward more empirical researches in the natural sciences, popular considerations in psychology, ethics, and politics, philosophical doxography, studies in the history of literature and institutions stemming from Aristotle's *Rhetoric, Poetics,* and *Politics,* and constitutional researches. Theophrastus was exceptional in that, besides researches in biology and characterology (the latter of relevance to rhetoric), he wrote a small treatise of *Metaphysica* that seems to be an introduction to a more complete work (ed. W. D. Ross and F. H. Fobes, Oxford 1929). His most significant contribution to theoretical thought, his logic, has been reconstructed from fragments by I. M. Bocheński. Developing modal argument and propositional logic, it shows an effort at a higher synthesis of Megaric and peripatetic logic. His Opinions of the Philosophers of Nature was the source for much of the doxography concerning the first centuries of Greek thought. For the most part the writings of the early Peripatos survive only in fragments.

Dicaearchus of Sicilian Messene (b. before 341) and Aristoxenus of Tarentum, immediate followers of Aristotle, were associated in their theory of the soul as a mortal harmony of the elements but as sharing in the divine. Dicaearchus is typical of this early school. He held the eternity of the human species (a dubious point in Aristotle; cf. *Pol.* 1269a 5) and a cyclical theory of history that he attempted to reconcile with a doctrine of cultural development. Besides a treatise On the Soul, he wrote on prophecy, on the cultural history of Greece, on geography, and on Homeric literary problems. Aristoxenus, who wrote a life of Plato, made lasting contributions to the theory of music.

Eudemus of Rhodes seems to have edited Aristotle's *Physics.* He devoted attention to the history of mathematics and astronomy and worked with Theophrastus in logic. Substantial parts of his history of geometry were transmitted by Proclus in his commentary on Euclid. Demetrius of Phaleron was engaged mainly in the study of politics. He brought the Aristotelian spirit of empirical research to Alexandria. Strato of Lampsacus (d. 269), who followed Theophrastus as scholarch, was interested chiefly in the philosophy of nature; his views are quite materialist. The *De coloribus* and *De lineis insecabilibus,* included in the *Corpus Aristotelicum,* can be ascribed to him or to Theophrastus; the *De audibilibus* is Strato's; and the *Mechanica* comes from him or his school. In the *Mechanica* and *On Motion* he discussed the acceleration of falling bodies, the law of the lever, inertia, and the parallelogram of velocities, and controverted Aristotle's theory of projectile motion. His mathematical formulations are accurate but his ultimate explanations are more qualitative, i.e., physical. One of his students was the astronomer Aristarchus of Samos (fl. 280), who anticipated the Copernican system. Strato's brother Lyco (d. 225) succeeded him in the Lyceum and made contributions to pedagogy and *paideia* (general education; cf. *Part. animal.* 639a 1–15). Other early members of the school are of importance mainly for their doxographical or biographical contributions, largely fragmentary, e.g., Hieronymus of Rhodes, Aristo of Ceos, and Hermippus.

Hellenistic Period. Philosophical polemics with the Skeptics and with other doctrinal schools (*c.* 100 B.C.–A.D. 100) resulted in the widespread use of Aristotelian dialectic and logic in the clarification of their positions and their absorption of Aristotelian natural philosophy and psychology, e.g., Carneades' mastery of the *Topics* and the Stoic discussions on the internal senses. By the same process, the materialistic tendency of the Peripatetics was reinforced by Middle Stoicism, though in a strangely theological way. The Middle Stoic school centering on Rhodes—Panaetius, Posidonius, and especially the Stoic-Platonist Antiochus of Ascalon—seems to have reinforced the immanentist factor present in Aristotle's dialogue *On Philosophy,* where stars and souls are said to be both of aether, and in parts of the *De caelo* (e.g., 279a 30–b 3), where the God seems to be the immanent form of the outermost heaven. The apocryphal *De mundo* included in the *Corpus Aristotelicum* bespeaks this tendency. In reaction to the polemics of the other schools, this group, and Antiochus in particular, began the harmonization of Aristotle with Stoicism and, especially, with Platonism. (Only the Epicurean tradition remained obdurately anti-Aristotelian.) Through Cicero it is known that Antiochus considered the difference between Plato and Aristotle to be one merely of vocabulary.

The peripatetic historico-philological interest continued with Diodorus of Tyre and eventually effected its own cure with the edition of Aristotle's works by Andronicus of Rhodes (fl. 50–40 B.C.) and his collaborator Boethus of Sidon. This invited the first extensive philosophical commentary, the paraphrases On The Philosophy of Aristotle in five books by Nicolaus of Damascus, fragments of which survived among the Arabians along with his *De Plantis,* falsely ascribed to Aristotle and included in the *Corpus Aristotelicum.* Though Boethus insisted on the Aristotelian methodic dictum that one must proceed from the more familiar toward the more intelligible in itself, which would indicate starting with natural philosophy, Andronicus seems to have organized the philosophical works of his edition in a descending order: God, the world, the celestial phenomena; the soul, nature, and the natural phenomena (I. Düring). He probably coined the term metaphysics, which first appears in Nicolaus, and, certainly, assigned the term Organon to Aristotle's collected logical treatises. He prefaced the whole with a critical essay On Aristotle's Writings, parts of which were cited by later commentators, particularly Simplicius.

2d to 4th Centuries. There is a gap until the 2d century A.D. and Aspasius, who commented on the *Ethics* and is said to have taught Galen's teacher. Both *Ptolemy (fl. 150) and *Galen (129–*c.* 199) must be loosely accounted, by their education and participation in the peripatetic logical and scientific interest, as Aristotelian. Ptolemy attempted a brilliant mediation between Eudoxus and Aristotle, but the element of the Academy dominates that of the Lyceum in his work. His astronomy thus stood somewhat in opposition to the physico-theological astronomy of Aristotle and was a remote prototype of mathematical physics. Galen wrote an important Introduction to Logic that combined Aristotelian and Stoic elements.

Herminus (*c.* 130–190), a highly independent commentator on the *Prior Analytics,* taught Alexander of Aphrodisias (*c.* 160–220), the first commentator whose stature is evident, since many of his works survive. He directed the Peripatos at Athens and was called by later generations the Exegete, or Commentator, and the Second Aristotle. He had a sharp awareness of the distinction between the form and the matter of the logical art and appears to have been the first to comment extensively on the *Posterior Analytics,* an indication of his intention to proceed throughout his expositions in accordance with the scientific canons of Aristotle. He commented on nearly all of Aristotle's major works and in addition wrote important Questions on problems arising from his philosophy. (As a literary form this is a remote ancestor of the scholastic *quaestiones.*) There are Platonic elements in his interpretation, but he does not intentionally attempt harmonization of Aristotle with Plato. On the contrary, he is materialistic in his psychology, reducing the individual human intellect to little more than an especially gifted animal imagination (νοῦς ὑλικός, the scholastic *intellectus materialis,* or *intellectus passivus*) and exalting the separate agent intellect by identifying it as the First Cause. Aristotle had expressed his noetic theory, both human and divine, somewhat indeterminately (*Anim.* 424b 20–435b 26; *Meta.* 1074b 15–1075a 11), but its problems as focused by Alexander's commentary were to remain central to Aristotelian interpretation down through the Renaissance. Alexander's work is essential for understanding the original texts and also contains precious fragments taken from Aristotle's youthful exoteric writings. His treatise On Fate was used in Mohammedan debates on determinism and free will.

In this late Hellenistic period the attempt to systematize the Aristotelian corpus was paralleled by the efforts of Plotinus and Porphyry to give a unified exegesis of the Platonic writings. *Plotinus opposed as two extremes the current *gnosticism and the naturalism of the Aristotelian materialists and advanced his combination of rationalism and his own private mysticism. He severely attacked the Aristotelian categories, yet he incorporated Aristotle's act and potency and the separate intellect. He freed act and potency from confinement within the physical principles of matter and form and developed the doctrine of the limitation of act by potency, harmonizing it with Platonic participation theory; and he attempted a unified metaphysics of knowledge by locating the Platonic Ideas in the Aristotelian separate Intellect. He was able to take these steps by drawing upon that element in Aristotle himself that had always remained Platonist, the ultimate primacy of *final causality.

*Porphyry moved closer to Aristotle with a commentary on the *Ethics* and his important harmonization, On the Unity of the Doctrine (αἵρεσιν) of Plato and Aristotle, works known through Arabic channels but lost in the original. He developed the theme that their apparent disharmony stems from the fact that Aristotle began with sense knowledge and physics, whereas Plato started higher, with the mind of man, and went further in divine matters. In weakened form this harmonization became a commonplace of the tradition of *philosophia perennis,* e.g., the prologues of Aquinas and Albert the Great to their commentaries *In de divinis nominibus* (and, recently, J. Wild's defenses of classical philosophy against K. Popper). Porphyry regarded the Aristotelian categories more favorably than had Plotinus. His chief legacy to the Aristotelian tradition was his treatise On the Five Predicables, or the *Isagoge.* It was later used as an integral part of the Organon, though some avowed Aristotelian logical purists, notably William of Ockham, have claimed that it obscures the realistic beginnings in the matter of Aristotelian logic by substituting as initial the Neoplatonic dialectical form—i.e., the context of logical relations, the *predicables, which are second intentions—for the original starting point in first intentions, the *categories of being.

In the 4th century, *Iamblichus preserved most of Aristotle's early introduction to philosophy, the *Protrepticus,* by quoting almost all of it in his own work of the same name. Themistius (fl. *c.* 387), who wrote incisive paraphrases of most of Aristotle's chief theoretical works, enkindled Aristotelian studies in Constantinople. His commentary on the *De anima* was of great value to Thomas Aquinas in arguing against its Averroist interpretation.

5th and 6th Centuries. Members of the 5th-century Neoplatonic school at Athens stemming from Porphyry and Iamblichus were *Proclus and Syrianus (fl. *c.* 430); Syrianus is often cited by Boethius. Among them Platonic convictions replaced Aristotle's critical suspension of judgment on certain transcendental matters, e.g., life after death, prophecy, and divine inspiration. In contrast the more economical Alexandrian school of the late 5th and the 6th centuries advocated rationalism in natural theology and regarded the various religious revelations as symbolic manifestations of the one transcendent truth evidentially accessible only through the rigors of philosophical discipline. This notion of levels of communication was articulated by considerable reflection upon the so-called Aristotelian modes of discourse: demonstrative, dialectical, rhetorical, and poetic. The *Rhetoric* and *Poetics* were relocated as extensions of the *Topics* and *Sophistical Refutations* and therefore as parts of the Organon. Simplicius explained them Neoplatonically as degrees of participation in the maximal type, absolute demonstration. This Alexandrian idea of an expanded Organon, passing westward via the Arabs, became another commonplace of perennial philosophy (see Thomas Aquinas, *In 1 perih.* 1, *In 1 anal. post.* 1). This development of a theory of symbolic forms was an important work of the Alexandrian philosophers. Alfarabi continued this line of inquiry among the Arabs.

The moving spirit of this late Alexandrian school was the Aristotelian commentator Ammonius Hermeae (fl. 485), who is said to have studied under Proclus in the Athenian Academy. Upon returning to Alexandria, he taught John Philoponus, Simplicius (fl. *c.* 533), and Olympiodorus (fl. *c.* 535). Simplicius, in his prologues and his commentaries on the *Physics* and the *De caelo,* shows himself the master doxographer of this school. He followed courses in the Academy of Athens and taught there until it was closed in 529 by decree of the Emperor Justinian. Then he and the scholarch Damascius sought refuge at the court of the Persian Emperor Chosroes, bringing with them the teachings of the Alexandrian school.

Some of Ammonius's disciples had become Christian, notably *John Philoponus, who holds a central place in the long history of the interpenetration of Christianity and Aristotelianism. Upon his conversion, Philoponus took independent positions against the Aristotelian doctrine of the eternity of the world and Alexander's doctrine of a separate agent intellect, and he taught the creation of matter and the immortality of the personal soul. His commentary on the *Physics* advanced, in dynamics, the theory of *impetus, which was destined to play an important role among the Latins of the 14th century. Remotely preparing the way for both the Mohammedan dialectical theologians and the Latin scholastics, John entered the Christological dispute. Though his solution tended to *Monophysitism, theological controversy was henceforth inseparable from the technical equipment of Aristotelian logic and metaphysics.

Byzantine Period. The Latin Church Fathers generally distrusted Aristotle, of whom they knew little more than the *Categories.* Typically, Jerome said that it is characteristic of heretics to quote Aristotle. Laymen such as *Marius Victorinus and Boethius were exceptions. But in the East the theologians were forced by the learned climate of controversy to use Aristotle more and more. This tendency is already present in *Nemesius (fl. 400), Bishop of Emesa, whose treatment of the soul and human acts shows study of the *De anima* and *Ethics.* But it was the full theology of St. *John Damascene that became a channel for the importation of Aristotelian ideas and terms into Latin theology, counterbalancing the earlier importation of theological Neoplatonism via *Pseudo-Dionysius. In the Byzantine Church the tradition of a sort of Aristotelian scholasticism, side by side with a stronger Platonism, continued, following the authority of the Damascene and the educational reform of the patriarchal academy by *Photius, through Michael *Psellus and his pupil Michael of Ephesus (fl. 1090), down to the controversies at the Council of Florence, and during the Renaissance. During these centuries the defensive military position of the Byzantines against the Mohammedan advance did not dispose them to be receptive to developments in Islamic Aristotelianism; the openness of the West explains in large part the superior growth of Latin scholasticism. (*See* GREEK PHILOSOPHY; PLATONISM; NEOPLATONISM.)

SEMITIC ARISTOTELIANISM

This section discusses the influence of the ideas of Aristotle on Syrian, Arabian, and Hebrew philosophies.

Syriac Translation. The relatively small but formative Roman absorption of Greek philosophical literature and thought, particularly Stoic, in the late Republic and the Augustan empire was far exceeded by the Syriac, which took place from the 5th to the 8th century. It divided itself along religious and linguistic lines into the East Syriac and Armenian absorption by the Nestorian academic centers of Mesopotamia and northward, chief among them Edessa and Jundi-Shapur (Gandisapora); and the West Syriac and Coptic absorption by the Jacobite and smaller Orthodox or Catholic centers in the great cities of the Levant and Egypt. When Simplicius and Damascius were at the court of the Emperor Chosroes, *c.* 529, the Persians, and the Syrians within their empire, had shown considerable interest in Greek philosophy, and their school at Jundi-Shapur was already in existence. The Nestorian Probus (fl. 480) and the Monophysite physician Sergei of Reshaina (fl. 530) had done early translations and commentaries on Aristotle in Syriac. Sergei, along with many other early Syrian scholars, had studied in Alexandria. Paul of Persia (fl. 570) dedicated to the same Emperor Chosroes a still extant treatise on the Organon. Thus the entire Syriac tradition bears the impress of Ammonius and his Alexandrian disciples at the end of the pagan period.

But with the fall of this whole area to Islam the Arab reception of Greek philosophy took place on a scale dwarfing both of the earlier cultural absorptions and unsurpassed, at least in range and quantity, even by the Latin West of the 12th and 13th centuries. The beginnings of the reception of Greek philosophy can be traced back to as early as 150 years after the *Hegira (622); it took place full scale between 800 and 1000. It bears three features: (1) a motivation that is strongly theoretical and scientific, but even more strongly political and religious; (2) a powerful Neoplatonic impetus toward the One—toward seeing Aristotle as the thoroughly methodic teacher of a nearly complete system, which yet is open at the top and in doctrinal continuity with the transcendental philosophy of Plato and Plotinus; (3) the order in which the books of Aristotle came into Arabic: (*a*) what the Latins were to call the *logica vetus,* viz, the *Categories, On Interpretation,* and schematic digests of the beginning of the *Prior Analytics,* appeared first; (*b*) next was the *logica nova,* the full *Prior Analytics* and the books on the degrees of proof as grouped together by the Alexandrians, viz, *Posterior Analytics* through *Poetics;* (*c*) the translation of the rest of Aristotle did not begin until the founding of the Beit al-Hikma, or House of Wisdom, in 830 under the Caliph of Baghdad, al-Mamun. Here certain scientific and theoretical works seem to precede the practical.

Arabian Development. The medical, astrological, and transcendental interests of the first major Moslem philosopher, al-*Kindi, ibn-Ishāq, court philosopher of the Baghdad caliphate, are shown by the works made available to him in Arabic: the main zoological writings, *On the Heavens, Meteorology, Metaphysics,* and the so-called *Theology of Aristotle,* the last two works expressly translated for his use. The last is one of two mistaken ascriptions that bedeviled the medieval philosophical interpretation of Aristotle in both Islam and Christendom. The Arabs generally so take for granted the Neoplatonic harmonization of the Stagirite with Plato that they credit him with Neoplatonic works. The *Theology of Aristotle* is a reedited selection from Proclus's *Elements of Theology.* (The other false ascription, a paraphrase of Plotinus's *Enneads,* is the **Liber de causis,* whose authority was not questioned until St. Thomas Aquinas.)

The work of translating became highly organized under the Nestorian Hunayn ibn-Ishāq (the scholastic *Johannitius) and his son Ishaq ibn-Hunayn. They showed a scholarly prudence by their care to establish critical Greek and Syriac texts before translating into Arabic.

*Alfarabi began his studies with Nestorians in Khorasan, then continued in Baghdad with teachers in filiation from the Alexandrian academy. He taught in Baghdad and Aleppo. His propaedeutic works, the Introduction to the Philosophy of Plato and Aristotle and the Enumeration of the Sciences, were the highroads to philosophy for generations in Islam. He was a master of the liberal arts in the broad sense, ranging from Arabic grammar to the mode of communication of divine law, all seen in the light of the Aristotelian modes of discourse. He was accomplished even in the quadrivial arts, having written a major commentary on the *Almagest* of Ptolemy. He was more Aristotelian than Platonic, except in the domain of political philosophy. His scholastic associates Abu Bishr Matta ibn-Yunus (*c.* 870–940) and the Jacobite Yahya ibn-'Adi also are interesting. The former did treatises on the *Prior Analytics* and on conditional syllogisms. The latter proposed a rationalistic Aristotelian "trinity" as the philosophical way of stating what Christians express symbolically as the Triune God.

In regard to his sources in practical philosophy, Alfarabi is typical of the Islamic philosophers. Though there are occasional references and even quotations from the *Politics,* no Arab ever wrote a commentary on it. In the late 12th century, Averroës sought in vain for a copy. All this points to the likelihood that the Arabs had only a digest of its chief sentences. In this respect Islam was in just the reverse position to that of Latin Christendom, which possessed the *Politics* but lacked the *Republic* and the *Laws* until the Renaissance. The Arab world lacked also the *Eudemian Ethics,* the *Magna Moralia,* and the dialogues, except for fragments cited mainly by Alexander, Iamblichus, and Simplicius.

The two greatest Islamic philosophers, who became most thoroughly known to the Latin West, were the Persian Avicenna and the Spanish Moor Averroës. The logic of *Avicenna is like that of Alkindi, i.e., it shows the Stoic preference for the hypothetical syllogism. Avicenna attempted a systematic harmonization of Aristotle, Neoplatonism, and Moslem belief. He made substantial contributions to psychology and wrote a *Metaphysics* that is both Neoplatonic and Aristotelian in inspiration but is not a commentary on Aristotle's *Metaphysics.* He accepted the Aristotelian definition of the soul as first act and form of the body but maintained also that the individual human soul is an incorporeal substance and hence, as the Koran teaches, immortal. He anticipated Descartes with his mental experiment of the "flying man," i.e., thinking away one's body until one is simply thinking that one is thinking. He elaborated a theory of the internal senses that was in large part taken over by St. Albert the Great and Aquinas, and that culminated in his theory of imagination as elevated by prophetic inspiration.

In metaphysics Avicenna is more the Platonist, and *Averroës, the Aristotelian, although Averroës rejected Avicenna's distinction between the *forma partis* and *forma totius,* thus making it necessary to affirm that the soul of man and the species man are one and the same (*see* QUIDDITY). Moreover, Avicenna tried to balance necessary and contingent aspects of the natural world, preparing the way for the Thomistic real distinction between *essence and existence; whereas Averroës is more immanentist and necessitarian in his view of the relationship between God and the world. Their metaphysical influence increased with the Renaissance, when they were frequently reprinted.

With respect to the agent intellect, Avicenna maintained a separate agent intellect less than God, and identifiable more with the demiurge of the *Timaeus,* and a personal possible intellect proper to each individual man; Averroës maintained a separate agent intellect that is, in a sense, a separate possible intellect as well. This is the human species, identified as the intelligence of the lunar sphere. Such a doctrine seems to leave individual men with nothing more than acutely receptive animal imaginations. It appeared again in the late Latin *Averroism of Italy. Avicenna favored a hypothetico-mathematical astronomy in the tradition of Eudoxus, the *Timaeus,* and Ptolemy, which Averroës rejected for a physical astronomy that is a celestial physics and a star theology, similar to that of the *De caelo.* Echoes of this controversy were heard in the opposition between Adelard of Bath and the Mertonians at Oxford, on the one hand, and the Parisian Aristotelians, on the other; and later in the Galileo-Bellarmine controversy.

In logic Averroës emphasized the *Posterior Analytics* and, accordingly, attacked Avicenna's preference for the hypothetical syllogism. This was a renewal of Alfarabi's criticism of al-Kindi and the Stoic logic of the Kalam: unlike Aristotelian demonstration the hypothetical syllogism lacks terminal resolution since it fails to display through an explicitly defined middle term the causal force of the nature under discussion.

Like Alexander and Alfarabi, Averroës also was known as the Commentator and became a model for the scholastic art of commenting. He brought to perfection three types of exposition that reflect forms of teaching current in the late Hellenistic Empire. The short commentary, or epitome, seeks to give the student guidance to an intelligent first reading of the text. The middle commentary is a paraphrase, a close second reading and reexpression of the text, accompanied by fresh and effective examples. The long commentary is a thorough reading of the text, which has been broken down into small passages, each of which is thoroughly analyzed and related structurally to the whole of the work. Other texts of the author are correlated with it; controversies over special passages are examined and solutions proposed. This last is the genre in which Thomas Aquinas wrote his commentaries on Aristotle.

Other notable Arabian thinkers of Aristotelian inspiration were the sociological philosophers al-Baruni, who analyzed Indian religion and culture, and *Ibn Khaldun, who analyzed world culture. *Algazel objectively summarized philosophical views, particularly those of Alfarabi and Avicenna, in On the Intentions of the Philosophers. As doxography this had wide circulation among the Latins; however, they lacked his sequel of refutation, the Destruction of the Philosophers. Averroës's Spanish predecessors, *Avempace and Ibn Tufail, also are significant. (*See* ARABIAN PHILOSOPHY.)

Hebrew Philosophy. Medieval Hebrew philosophy benefited from both Islamic and Christian speculation, but even more it benefited Christian philosophy by serving as the conveyor of texts and ideas. *Crescas was a strong critic of Aristotelian physics; of more significance to the West was *Avicebron, whose *Fons Vitae,* translated at Toledo by *Dominic Gundisalvi with either Abraham ibn Daoud or *John of Spain or both, was influential especially among the 13th-century Franciscans. It is important for its anti-Aristotelian doctrines of spiritual matter and plurality of forms, and for the scriptural inspiration of its assigning a powerful role of efficient causality to these forms and their divine author. Most important was *Maimonides, whose *Guide for the Perplexed* influenced Albert the Great and Thomas Aquinas. (*See* JEWISH PHILOSOPHY; FORMS, UNICITY AND PLURALITY OF.)

LATIN ARISTOTELIANISM

The absorption of the Aristotelian corpus by the Latins extended over a much longer period than that of the Arabs, i.e., from the 4th to the 13th century.

The Classical Period. The Romans of the first centuries B.C. and A.D., e.g., *Cicero, *Varro, and *Seneca, read Aristotle in the original, mainly his exoteric writings; their understanding of him was colored by the syncretism of the Middle Stoa. Cicero is significant for his enrichment of Latin philosophical language through his invention of Latin parallels to Greek technical terms and for his *Topics,* destined to play a central role in the long and confusing history of rhetoric and dialectic in the Latin West.

With the decline of Greek cultural dominance at the extremities of the Roman Empire a period of translation into Latin set in, from the 4th to the 6th century. *Marius Victorinus, who had become a Christian *c.* 355, translated the *Categories* (lost) and Porphyry's *Isagoge* (partly preserved). Adaptations into Latin of Themistius's paraphrases of the *Analytics* (also lost) were made by Agorius *Praetextatus at Rome. *Augustine mentions having studied the *Categories*; and a paraphrase of it, made also about this time, was later incorrectly ascribed to him. Toward the close of the 4th century, *Martianus Capella digested the *Categories* and *On Interpretation* in book 4 of his *De nuptiis philologiae et mercurii.* A hundred years later *Boethius set himself the task of rendering all of Plato and Aristotle into Latin, of interpreting them, and, in the spirit of Porphyry, of showing their continuity with each other.

Of these four early translators, the two Christians, Victorinus and Boethius, were Aristotelianizing Neoplatonists in the more intellectual tradition of Porphyry and Proclus, rather than in the mystical tradition of

Iamblichus. Boethius's ambitious project, far from finished at his death, was well begun with the *Isagoge* and *Categories,* each with a commentary, *On Interpretation* with two large commentaries, *Prior Analytics, Posterior Analytics, Topics,* and *Sophistical Refutations.* All this he completed with a highly significant personal treatment of argument in three works: *De categoricis syllogismis, De hypotheticis syllogismis,* and *De differentiis topicis.* In them the Aristotelian syllogistic laws are reformulated in Stoic rules; the treatment of the hypothetical syllogism shows the influence of Theophrastus and the Stoics; and the *Topics* shows study of both Cicero's and Aristotle's *Topics.* His posing of the problem of *universals in his commentary on Porphyry's *Isagoge* is the *locus classicus* for the many-sided medieval debate on their ontological status.

Though laymen, Victorinus and Boethius each wrote a *De Trinitate* against the Arian heresy. In Boethius's treatise, his combination of Aristotelian and Neoplatonic terminology and definitions became a source within Latin Christian theology for Aristotelian theorizing. Noteworthy in this regard are his definitions of *eternity and *person, his definitions and divisions of *nature, and his briefly sketched division and methodology of the sciences commented on by Thomas Aquinas (*In Boeth. de Trin.* 5, 6) and later scholastics. On the whole, however, Boethius's influence in theology was that of a dialectical theologian, one who seeks to clarify and show the implications of theological positions but does not demonstrate.

12th Century. The Latin aspiration toward scientific theology became possible of fulfillment with the translation of the *Posterior Analytics* by James of Venice. The *Physics, De anima, Metaphysics* 1–4, and the *Parva Naturalia* first came to the Latins through his hands. His translations, though revised in the next century by William of Moerbeke, remained the received texts until the Renaissance.

Besides putting into Latin two of the three Platonic dialogues known to the scholastics, the *Meno* and the *Phaedo* (the *Timaeus* had been done by Calcidius *c.* 300 and revived at Chartres), *Henricus Aristippus translated book 4 of the *Meteorologica* and possibly the *De generatione et corruptione.* About this time anonymous renditions were made from Greek of the *De generatione et corruptione, De sensu et sensato,* and the *Nicomachean Ethics*; the *Posterior Analytics* and *Physics* were retranslated.

Translation of Aristotle from Arabic began slightly later, in Spain and in England. *Gerard of Cremona at Toledo put into Latin the *Physics, De caelo, De Generatione et Corruptione, Meteorologica, Metaphysics* 1–3, and the *Posterior Analytics* accompanied by Themistius's paraphrase. *Alfred of Sareshel commented on the *Meteorologica*; he translated from Arabic and commented on the *De plantis* of Nicolaus of Damascus, believed then to be by Aristotle. Associated with Alfred was *Adelard of Bath, the translator of Euclid, first among the scholastics to make current the Arabian commonplace that Aristotle represents science while Plato represents wisdom. At this time the works of the Arabian philosophers, largely commentaries on Aristotle, began to come into Europe through the Spanish translation centers.

13th Century. The frequent retranslation of the *Posterior Analytics* testifies to the intellectual effort being made during the course of the 12th century to capture the spirit of Aristotelian scientific explanation. At the beginning of the 13th century this key work received its first major Latin commentary from the hand of *Robert Grosseteste; his was a somewhat Neoplatonizing interpretation influential throughout the Middle Ages, which continued to be reprinted even in the Renaissance. He gathered and translated from Greek the erroneously ascribed *De mundo* and the *De caelo* and *Nicomachean Ethics.* Chronologically, the scholastics distinguished among the Greco-Latin translations between an *Ethica vetus,* comprising books 2 and 3, and the first complete *Ethics,* that of Grosseteste. Likewise they spoke of a *Metaphysica vetustissima,* comprising books 1 to 4, the work of James of Venice; a *Metaphysica media,* comprising all but book 11; and finally the complete *Metaphysics,* done at Thomas Aquinas's request by William of Moerbeke.

An event of major importance for the subsequent evolution of philosophical thought was the introduction of Averroës into the Latin West in the second quarter of the 13th century. *William of Auvergne and *Philip the Chancellor were the first to quote the Arabian Commentator. Albert the Great used him about equally with Avicenna, being more Averroist in logic and natural philosophy but more Avicennian on the deeper problems of human psychology and metaphysics. St. Thomas was exposed to Averroës at the University of Naples. The principal translator of Averroës was *Michael Scot at the court of Frederick II in Sicily between 1228 and 1235. Averroës's infiltration into the Western world was virtually complete by 1240, and the extent of his challenge to Christian faith had become evident. The chief points of conflict were three: (1) his doctrine of the eternity and necessity of the world opposed the Christian doctrine of creation; (2) the unity of the separate intellect, both agent and possible, conflicted with the immortality of the personal soul; and (3) his Latin interpreters' understanding that he taught a theory of *double truth and the primacy of the philosophical over the theological mode of knowledge ran counter to the primacy accorded revelation by Christianity.

The vigor and originality of the scholastic intellectual response was in proportion to the profundity of the Averroist challenge. Members of the arts faculty at Paris, such as *Siger of Brabant and *Boethius of Sweden, favored the Commentator's interpretations, whereas champions of theology, chiefly *Albert the Great and *Thomas Aquinas, advanced their own resolutions of the problems. The challenge forced them to acquire more accurate translations of Aristotle, which were provided by their confrere *William of Moerbeke. He translated in their entirety and for the first time the *Poetics, Rhetoric,* and zoölogical books, though the first two works were almost totally neglected by scholastics. He translated also books 3 and 4 of the *De caelo;* books 1 to 3 of the *Meteorologica,* and retranslated book 4; books 3 to 8 of the *Politics;* and the theretofore missing book 11 of the *Metaphysics.* He did anew the *Categories* and *On Interpretation* and thoroughly revised the existing Greco-Latin translations, chiefly those of James of Venice.

During the 13th century, Aristotelianism was the object of several prohibitions by ecclesiastical authorities. But in 1255 a statute was enacted for the University of Paris legalizing the study of all the known works of Aristotle. Then in 1270 E. *Tempier, Bishop of Paris, condemned the chief doctrines of Averroist Aristotelianism; on March 7, 1277, he summed up in brutal, haphazard, pell-mell fashion (F. van Steenberghen) under 219 headings the doctrines to be rejected. Similar but less rash prohibitions were imposed on the philosophy of Aristotle at Oxford by *Robert Kilwardby and *John Peckham. With the more mature study of Thomas Aquinas's writings, the difficult but successful defense of Thomas by the early Thomistic school, notably by *John (Quidort) of Paris, and the canonization of St. Thomas (1323), the cause of Christian Aristotelianism was assured. Then the pendulous weight of authority swung the other way. The inceptor in arts at Paris was sworn during the 14th century to teach nothing inconsistent with Aristotle, and as late as 1624 the French Parlement threatened with death all who taught anything contrary to his doctrines. This was renewed by the University of Paris in 1687. Among the colleges of the New World there were some restrictions against Copernican astronomy and in support of the traditions of Aristotle and *Ptolemy. The surviving Dominican oath to teach according to the mind of St. Thomas is in this paradoxically voluntaristic tradition.

Thomas Aquinas distinguished between theology and philosophy, according to both the dignity of science; and in analogous fashion he distinguished between Church and State, according to each the dignity of being a perfect society. His commentaries on the *Ethics* and *Politics* won a lasting place for them in civil and ecclesiastical governmental theory. John of Paris, in *De potestate regia et papali,* championed the Aristotelian and Thomistic principles of natural law and the integrity and natural character of the State against the theory of absolute papal monarchy in temporal matters propounded by *Giles of Rome. The relevance of the *Ethics* and *Politics* to civil life was sufficiently appreciated by the middle of the 14th century for *Nicholas Oresme, Bishop of Lisieux, to translate them into the vernacular. On the opposite side from Giles of Rome there soon appeared the *De Monarchia* of *Dante, who insisted on a world-state centering in the independent and supreme power of the emperor against the claims of the pope, and capable of achieving human happiness on earth. The imperial unity and world-state theme seems to owe something to the Arabian interpretations of Aristotle regarding the common agent and possible intellect.

Both the 13th and the 14th centuries saw advances in the empirical scientific side of Aristotelianism made principally at Merton College, Oxford, in the tradition of Robert Grosseteste; in France by *John Buridan, Oresme, and others; and by the German Dominicans, e.g., *Theodoric of Freiberg, in the tradition of St. Albert. (*See* THOMISM, 1; SCHOLASTICISM, 1.)

The Renaissance, Reformation, and Enlightenment

The 14th to the 18th century was a period characterized by four developments respecting the authority of Aristotle: (1) the humanist movement, (2) psychological and methodological controversies, (3) naturalistic and scientific movements, and (4) development of political theory. The first and third are understood to be largely revolts against the Aristotle of scholasticism, the second is, by intention at least, in part pro-Aristotelian, and the third and fourth have both aspects. They began or centered in Italy.

Humanism, Platonism, and Second Averroism. The humanist revolt was a vengeance taken on the demonstrative logic and dialectic of the late scholastics by the practitioners of the so-called lesser modes of discourse, rhetoric and poetics, for scholasticism's neglect since the 12th century of these modes of communication in favor of what appeared to be the sterility of Aristotelian logic and methods. Though a late expression, Stefano Guazzo's *La Civil Conversazione* (Venice 1586) sums up this reaction. Already in the 14th century the humanist followers of the medieval *ars dictaminis* had begun to unearth unsuspected treasures of classical Roman history and literature, and the mid-15th century saw Greek letters come alive again in Italy. That the humanists were not unfriendly to Aristotle as such is shown by their continued interest in the ethical writings and the *Politics,* and by their studies and editions of the long neglected *Rhetoric* and *Poetics,* which the famous Aldine press in Venice first published in 1498 in the *Rhetores Graeci,* edited by Giorgio Valla. The influence of the *Poetics,* rightly or wrongly understood, is a whole chapter in early modern literature, culminating in the French classical theater.

Closely associated with humanism was the Platonic revival. A Christian Platonism flourished in the Platonic Academy at Florence. Its founder, Marsilio *Ficino, was particularly concerned to defend the immortality of the soul against the Averroist Aristotelians. The humanists underestimated the degree to which Aquinas was able to master Aristotle while remaining, in a profound sense, a good Augustinian theologian. On substantive matters such as defense of the natural freedom of man, which had been attacked by *Luther, *Erasmus quickly fell back upon the moral theology of St. Thomas and its philosophical base in the Aristotelian *Ethics.*

The humanist movement took place to a large extent outside the university framework. The revived Averroist tradition that began early in the 14th century was scholastic in the broad sense of the term. It arose within, and came to dominate, the Italian universities, chiefly Bologna in the early period and Padua later. Remote inspiration came from the natural philosopher *John of Jandun and the political theorist *Marsilius of Padua at the court of Ludwig of Bavaria. At Bologna were Gentile da Cingoli, his pupil Angelo of Arezzo, and Thaddeus of Parma, who worked in the allied fields, for an Averroist, of astronomy and psychology. At Padua, Peter of Abano was more of a Galenian medical methodologist than an Averroist. In the 15th century the distinguished logician Paolo *Veneto, an Averroist, taught at Padua. Sharing the scholarship of the Paduan school, and well acquainted with its Averroism, was the celebrated Thomist philosopher and theologian Tommaso de Vio *Cajetan, who also commented on Aristotle.

The humanist appetite for belles-lettres and the university study of Aristotle were the primary and secondary conditions preparing the ground for the reception of Byzantine learning. The 15th-century Greek contribution to Aristotelian scholarship was a substantial and permanent acquisition for all subsequent ages. The Council of Florence and the fall of Constantinople (1453) brought to Italy many learned Greeks, among them George of *Trebizond, who, in a comparative study of Plato and Aristotle, opts for the latter; Theodore of Gaza; John *Argyropoulos, Bishop of Florence, who commented on the *Ethics* and translated Aquinas's *De ente et essentia* into Greek; and Cardinal *Bessarion, who translated the *Metaphysics* into Latin, moderated Gemistos Plethon's criticisms of Aristotle, and attempted anew the conciliation of Aristotle with Plato. Philosophical Greek was taught, new translations were made, and many theretofore unknown Greek commentaries were printed and translated; finally in 1495 the Aldine press produced the *Editio princeps* of most of the Aristotelian works. Textual criticism, developed first by Lorenzo *Valla on historical documents, began to be applied to Aristotle and his commentators. Robertellus produced in 1549 the important second edition of the *Poetics* with Latin translation and commentary, and Fasolo translated Simplicius's commentary on the *De anima*.

Psychological and Methodological Controversies. All this sharpened the quest for an authentic interpretation of Aristotle and led to controversy in two chief areas: (1) psychology, centering on *De anima* 3, *Metaphysics* 12, and *De caelo;* and (2) methodology, centering on the opening chapters of the natural works and the prologue literature of the Greek and Arabian commentators.

The first controversy involved rival supporters of the interpretations of Alexander of Aphrodisias and Averroës, who differed over whether the separate agent intellect discussed in the *De anima* is in any sense human. According to the Averroists an impersonal but human immortality is attached to the separate intelligence of the species man, a sort of immortal overmind, or "noosphere"; the Alexandrists denied human immortality, holding that the only overmind, or separate intellect, was God. Some historians regard the Averroists as attempting to de-Christianize the Aristotle of Thomistic interpretation, and the Alexandrists as attempting to demetaphysicize Aristotle in himself.

In 1516 Pietro *Pomponazzi, drawing support from Alexander, wrote a treatise against the immortality of the soul. The more important of the Averroists were Nicoletto Vernia, who taught at Padua from 1471 to 1499, Agostino *Nifo, Leonicus Thomaeus, Alexander Achillini, and Marco Antonio *Zimara. J. *Zabarella, who had studied Greek with Robertellus, developed Pomponazzi's position in psychology but in other parts of philosophy was much influenced by Averroës, as well as by Themistius and Simplicius. He made his chief contribution in methodology where, as a logician and natural philosopher, he opposed the moralist and metaphysician Francesco Piccolomini (1520–1604). His works and commentaries and those of his student Julius Pacius continue to influence modern scholarship on Aristotle. Pacius (1550–1635) edited and translated Aristotle's Organon and *Physics* (Frankfurt 1592, 1596) and edited the whole *Corpus Aristotelicum* (Lyons 1597). His *Institutiones logicae* (Sedan 1595) marks him as an extreme methodological pluralist, a humanist inclined to see the differences in texts, whereas Zabarella, a logician, had seen their structural similarities.

In the Protestant north, particularly in Calvinist circles, the anti-Aristotelian logic and methodology of the Huguenot martyr Peter *Ramus had great vogue. In his *Dialecticae institutiones* and *Aristotelicae animadversiones* (Paris 1543) and his two books on the *Posterior Analytics* (1553) he fused logic and rhetoric and reduced all methods to one. Historical Aristotelianism had begun in France with J. Lefèvre d'Étaples and was carried on after Ramus's attacks by Pacius. Ramus was opposed by J. Carpentarius (or Charpentier, 1524–74), a student of Greek mathematics who wrote a Comparison of Plato and Aristotle (Paris 1573) in the ancient tradition of their harmonization.

The controversy between Aristotelians and Ramists was continued in England and Germany. Oxford tended to be more Aristotelian, Cambridge more Ramist, and later, Platonist. At Oxford the study of Aristotle remained an integral part of the university curriculum until the middle of the 17th century; particular attention was given to the reading and explication of the logical, ethical, and political works. Thomas *Hobbes wrote a digest of the *Rhetoric* and was a keen student of its theory of the passions. Of varying strength among the representatives of declining Aristotelianism in this period were John Sanderson, John Case (d. 1600), whose Roman Catholic leanings forced him to teach privately, Richard Crackenthorpe, Thomas Wilson, Ralph Lever, Jacobus Martinus Scotus, and the extraordinary Everard *Digby. In 1620 Francis *Bacon published his *Novum Organum,* a work stressing induction and intended to replace the Organon of Aristotle. Nonetheless, an impressive strand of Aristotelian and Thomistic learning, tempered with humanism, continued in the clergy of the Anglican Church, particulary in matters of logic, ethics, and politics. It flowered in Richard *Hooker (1554–1600), author of *Ecclesiastical Polity;* in the 18th century, in the ethics and natural theology of Joseph *Butler (1692–1752), Bishop of Durham; as late as the 19th century in the logic of H. L. Mansel (1820–71); and in the 20th-century metaphysics of E. L. Mascall (1905–). Especially worthy of mention is a member of the dissenting ministry, Thomas Taylor (1758–1835), who singlehandedly translated nearly the whole Aristotelian corpus between the years 1801 (*Metaphysics*) and 1818 (*Nicomachean Ethics*). To these he added *Copious Elucidations from the Best of his Greek Commentators.* He was devoted to a Neoplatonism that, in the Alexandrian fashion, he regarded as capable of taking into its higher synthesis of wisdom all that is scientifically positive in Aristotle.

In Germany, despite Luther's opposition, the scholarly conciliator P. *Melanchthon worked to insure the continuance of Aristotelian learning, particularly the logic, where his authority prevailed over that of Ramus. However, the Aristotelianism he had in mind contained Stoic elements. A branch of early Lutheran theology, following Melanchthon, has been called Lutheran scholasticism. Jacob Schegk (1511–87), professor of logic and medicine at Tübingen, was an able Greek scholar and student of the *Analytics* who refuted Ramus. Others undergoing Aristotelian influence were J. Jungius, his student G. W. *Leibniz, who corrected the excessive attacks of the Italian Renaissance rhetorician M. Nizolio (1498–1576) on Aristotelian logic and theoretical philosophy, and the systematizer Christian *Wolff. The decisive critic of Ramus was the progressive Aristotelian Bartholomew Keckermann (*c.* 1572–1609), whose work gained wide circulation on the Continent and in England. With the Germans must be mentioned the Dutch professor of theology at Utrecht, G. Voëtius, who, though Calvinist, was far from being a Ramist. He based himself on Aristotle in order to attack the new methodical monist R. *Descartes. The German universities began in the 16th and 17th centuries the double tradition of metaphysical and philological penetration of Aristotle that was to flower in the 19th-century work of the Berlin Academy.

Second Scholasticism. This movement began mainly in Italy with the Dominican resurgence prior to and during the Council of Trent. The expositors of Aquinas commented also on Aristotle, e.g., *Dominic of Flanders wrote on the *Metaphysics;* *Ferrariensis on the *Posterior Analytics, Physics,* and *De anima;* G. C. *Javelli on Aristotle's chief works (he also refuted Pomponazzi); and Cajetan on the *Categories, Posterior Analytics,* and *De anima,* and on Porphyry's *Praedicabilia.*

Soon the center of the second scholasticism became Spain and Portugal. At Salamanca F. de *Vitoria revived and developed the Aristotelian-Stoic heritage of natural law, and Domingo de *Soto commented on the Organon, *Physics,* and *De anima.* The *Complutenses, Carmelite professors at Alcalá, and the Conimbricenses, the Jesuits of Coimbra, did collective works on Aristotle's logic and physical philosophy. F. de *Toledo, who had studied under Soto at Salamanca, taught there and in Rome and commented on Aristotle. Benedict Pereira in 1585 wrote a vast and free commentary on the *Physics,* showing study of contemporary Italian humanist and naturalist work as well as a slight Scotist influence. The chief scholarly contributions to Aristotelian studies were made on the *Metaphysics* by P. da *Fonseca and F. *Suárez. Fonseca's work is considered the first erudite edition of the *Metaphysics* in the modern age by reason of its vast critical apparatus: collation of codices, discussion of authenticity of texts, evaluation of variants, and comparison of translations. Suárez' *Disputationes metaphysicae* (1597), not a commentary as such, develops according to his own outline but is doxographically helpful for all prior, particularly scholastic, views on Aristotelian metaphysics. To these should be added the useful paraphrases of Sylvester *Maurus on the chief works of Aristotle (1668). As a whole, however, the second scholasticism has been judged to have been too drawn in upon itself, too exclusively clerical, and to have lacked the dialectical engagement with contemporary thought and science and the appreciation for empirical research that characterized the historical Aristotle and marks vital philosophizing in any age (F. Copleston).

Naturalism and Science. In Italy there arose a kind of natural philosophy, which conceived of nature as a more or less self-sufficient system, either independent of God once it had been created (*see* DEISM), or tending to be identified with God (*see* IMMANENTISM; PANTHEISM). To the Aristotelian *hylomorphism it opposed *atomism and *hylozoism; to the Aristotelian *intentionality of cognition, a mechanical theory of perception and even of intellection; to the Aristotelian view of the universe as finite, its extensive infinity. From the Aristotle of Averroës and Alexander it took a necessitarian view of the existence of the universe. Chief among these natural philosophers were G. Fracastoro (1478–1553), G. *Cardano, B. *Telesio, G. *Bruno, and T. *Campanella. Using Aristotelian terms to oppose Aristotle, Bruno revived David of Dinant's identification of pure matter with pure act. G. C. Vanini (1584–1619), much influenced by Pomponazzi, also used Aristotelian language to maintain that Nature, which he divinized, is the prime mover and needs no prime moving principle outside itself. Two thinkers loosely associated with the Italian natural philosophy who explicitly attacked Aristotle were F. *Patrizi, in *Discussionum Peripateticarum Libri XV* (1571), and P. *Gassendi, in *Exercitationes Paradoxicae adversus Aristoteleos* . . . (1624).

The influence of these philosophers on the development of modern science was overshadowed by that of the Aristotelian methodologists of Padua. However, it was chiefly the revival of pure Greek mathematics, mathematical physics, and the tradition of hypothetico-mathematical astronomy, which in the Alexandrian and Arabic worlds had constantly rivaled Aristotle's *De caelo,* that set the stage for classical modern physics and astronomy. This revival began the refutation of Aristotle on falling bodies, the movement of the planets, the aether, or so-called crystalline quintessence, the speed of light, etc. Among its chief figures were *Copernicus, G. *Galilei, and S. *Stevin.

Modern and Contemporary Aristotelianism

Aristotelian scholarship declined in the 18th century, was revived in the 19th century under the influence of the Berlin Academy, and flourished with the third scholasticism of the 20th century.

18th Century. There was little activity in Aristotelian studies during this period, so crushing had the victory of classical modern physics been interpreted to be. In epistemology some idea of the Aristotelian-scholastic theory of intentionality managed, through B. *Bolzano, to survive the Enlightenment and the rise of idealism. Only logic and, to a greater degree, political philosophy received much attention.

No part of Aristotle's writings has a more extensive history of study than the *Politics*. From Aquinas and Moerbeke there is a continuous line through John of Paris, Cajetan, Bellarmine, Suárez, the founders of *international law, Vitoria and *Grotius, and the English common and natural law traditions of Blackstone (1723–80) and others to the 20th century. The idea of division of powers found in Montesquieu (1689–1755) is traceable to Aristotle, and it appeared also in Thomas Jefferson (1743–1826). The direct influence of Aristotle and Aquinas on R. *Hooker, of Aristotle and Hooker on J. *Locke, and of all these on E. *Burke, J. *Acton, and J. Bryce (1838–1922) is certain. The discovery in 1890 of Aristotle's *Constitution of Athens* intensified interest in his philosophy of the state.

19th Century. During the 19th century in France, Italy, and especially Germany, the philosophical climate of *nationalism and *idealism and the consequent interest in philology and the history of ideas and institutions combined with the continuity, maintained chiefly in England, of Aristotelian philosophical studies and a more traditional humanistic philology to bring about a revival of Aristotelian scholarship, with emphasis on the literary style of the treatises, their chronological order, the youthful fragments, and the evolution of Aristotle's thought. The Berlin Academy sponsored a definitive edition of the *Corpus Aristotelicum* (1831) under the supervision of J. Bekker, who edited Aristotle's treatises (v.1, 2) and the Latin versions of the Renaissance (v.3); C. A. Brandis and H. Usener edited the scholia (v.4); and H. Bonitz edited the *Index Aristotelicus* (v.5, 1870). V. Rose's edition of the fragments in the *Corpus* was superseded by his third edition, *Aristotelis qui ferebantur librorum fragmenta* (Teubner 1886). Theodor Waitz edited the Organon with commentary in 1844–46. Also by the Berlin Academy is the *Commentaria in Aristotelem Graeca,* completed in 1909, and a *Supplementum Aristotelicum* (1882–1903).

A. Trendelenburg, his students C. Heider and F. Brentano, and R. Eucken placed Aristotle at the base of their philosophical teaching as a result of their researches showing his formative role through Roman and scholastic translators in the whole history of Western philosophical vocabulary. Trained in scholasticism and by Trendelenburg, *Brentano maintained that the true method of philosophizing is continuous with that of the science of nature, meaning by the latter to include both the Aristotelian organic and the modern positive approaches to nature. He tried to demonstrate this in the field of psychology, to which he introduced the Aristotelian and scholastic notion of *intentionality. This was continued in various ways by his followers in *phenomenology, C. *Ehrenfels, A. *Meinong, E. *Husserl, and M. *Scheler, and their existentialist successors. Other Germans who have studied the thought of Aristotle are H. *Driesch, E. Zeller, and H. Maier.

Aristotle's reception in France was less sympathetic. F. Ravaisson-Mollien (1813–1900) found that the Aristotelian characterization of being as *act complemented his dynamic spiritualism. He influenced a whole generation of French philosophers, e.g., L. *Brunschvicg, O. Hamelin (1856–1907), and L. Robin (1866–1947), but their idealist and rationalist positions caused them to regard Aristotle merely as a rather prosaic follower of Plato. However, the appreciative work of the great French historians of science, P. Tannery (1843–1904) and especially P. *Duhem, is indispensable for an understanding of the scientific role of Aristotle and his successors. A Platonic and idealistic judgment of Aristotle is present also in the work of the Englishmen J. Burnet, A. E. Taylor, and A. N. *Whitehead, though less sharply than in that of their French counterparts.

20th Century. The neoscholastic movement, or, preferably, the third scholasticism, was already underway at the time of Leo XIII's encyclical *Aeterni Patris* (1879), formally directed to revitalizing the teaching of Thomas Aquinas. But, by its admonition to return to the sources of Aquinas's teaching, the encyclical did much to direct the attention of scholars to Aristotle and to the problems of Aristotelian transmission, especially in the Latin, Arabic, and Syriac periods. Especially noteworthy in this regard is the ambitious project of editing and publishing, with studies, the whole corpus of extant Latin translations of Aristotle made during the Middle Ages—*Aristoteles Latinus.*

The dominant problem of 20th-century Aristotelian studies, however, is not the place of Aristotle in the grand scale of development of human thought, but the personal evolution of his doctrines. W. Jaeger, in his monumental *Aristotle*: *Fundamentals of the History of His Development* (1923, Eng. tr. 1934), offered a creative solution and formulated problems for subsequent students. He concluded that Aristotle's development was a sort of fall from grace: from a wholly transcendental young Platonist, an extreme realist committed to the existence of the Forms and the immortality of the soul, through a stage of abandonment of the Forms and divinization of the visible heavens, to an old naturalist, empiricist, and nominalist who regarded astral theology and metaphysics as "conjecture" (*τὸ φαινόμενον ἡμῖν*, *Part. animal.* 645a 5). The developmental hypotheses of the Jaeger school were received cordially but critically by the more conservative Oxford scholars, e.g., W. D. Ross, G. R. Mure, E. Barker, and in general the group that, under the general editorship of Ross and J. A. Smith, has succeeded in translating the whole of the *Corpus Aristotelicum* into English. The difference between the Jaeger and the Oxford schools is not unlike that in English literature between the historical critics and the new or Aristotelian critics of the Chicago school.

The work of I. Düring has indicated that after an early and brief adherence to Plato's doctrine of Forms, Aristotle opposed his master with the thesis that *οὐσία* (substance, entity) is concrete; then, through the biological, psychological, and astronomical researches of his middle period, he found his way to a philosophical position much nearer to Plato's metaphysical doctrine, but on his own terms and out of, rather than in place of, his own sense of concretion and immanent final causality. The later works of the *Metaphysics,* particularly books 7 to 9, belong to this last period.

A recent characteristic of 20th-century textual study of Aristotle has been teamwork. The central organ of this is the *Symposium Aristotelicum.* One was held at Oxford in August 1957, and its papers were published by the University of Göteborg, *Aristotle and Plato in the Mid-Fourth Century,* ed. I. Düring and G. E. L. Owen (1960); the work of the second symposium, held at Louvain in August 1960, was published there in 1961, *Aristotle et les problèmes de méthode,* ed. S. Mansion.

See also PLATONISM; NEOPLATONISM; SCHOLASTICISM, 1, 2, 3; THOMISM, 1; NEOSCHOLASTICISM AND NEOTHOMISM.

Bibliography: General. L. MINIO-PALUELLO, in *A Catholic Dictionary of Theology* 1 (1962) 142–145. R. WALZER, EncIslam² 1:630–633. G. DI NAPOLI, EncFil 1:369–375. G. PATZIG, RGG³ 1:602–606. Gilson HistChrPhil. Copleston v.3. K. O. BRINK, Pauly-Wiss RE Suppl 7 (1940).

Special. E. ZELLER, *Aristotle and the Earlier Peripatetics,* tr. B. F. C. COSTELLOE and J. H. MUIRHEAD, 2 v. (New York 1897). F. R. WEHRLI, ed., *Die Schule des Aristoteles,* 10 v. (Basel 1944–59), texts and notes. P. MORAUX, *Alexandre d'Aphrodise: Exégète de la noétique d'Aristote* (Paris 1942). E. F. CRANZ, *Alexander of Aphrodisias: Genuine and Spurious Works and Their Translations, History, Description, Bibliography,* v.1 of *Catalogus translationum et commentariorum: Mediaeval and Renaissance Latin Translations and Commentaries: Annotated Lists and Guides,* ed. P. O. KRISTELLER et al. (Washington 1960–). R. WALZER, *Greek into Arabic: Essays on Islamic Philosophy* (Oriental Studies 1; Cambridge, Mass. 1962). M. GRABMANN, *Methoden und Hilfsmittel des Aristotelesstudiums im Mittelalter* (Munich 1939). G. LACOMBE and M. DULONG, *Aristoteles Latinus,* cod. 1 (Rome 1939). L. MINIO-PALUELLO, ed., *Aristoteles Latinus,* cod. 2– (Cambridge, Eng. 1953). F. VAN STEENBERGHEN, *Aristotle in the West* (Louvain 1955); *Siger dans l'histoire de l'aristotelisme* (Louvain 1942). R. P. MCKEON, *Aristotelianism in Western Christianity* (Chicago 1939). S. D. WINGATE, *The Mediaeval Latin Versions of the Aristotelian Scientific Corpus*

(London 1931). D. A. CALLUS, "Introduction of Aristotelian Learning to Oxford," *Proceedings of the British Academy* 29 (1943). P. MORAUX et al., *Aristote et Saint Thomas d'Aquin* (Paris 1957). R. LERNER and M. MAHDI, eds., *Medieval Political Philosophy: A Sourcebook* (New York 1963). N. W. GILBERT, *Renaissance Concepts of Method* (New York 1960). J. H. RANDALL, *The School of Padua and the Emergence of Modern Science* (Padua 1961), repr., with original texts added, of "The Development of Scientific Method in the School of Padua," JHistIdeas 1 (1940) 177–206. P. PETERSEN, *Geschichte der aristotelischen Philosophie im protestantischen Deutschland* (Leipzig 1921). I. DÜRING, *Aristotle in the Ancient Biographical Tradition* (Göteborg 1957); "Von Aristoteles bis Leibniz," *Antike und Abendland* 4 (1954) 118–154.

[J. J. GLANVILLE]

ARISTOTLE

Philosopher of Stagira, a Greek colony in the Chalcidic Peninsula, and hence referred to as the Stagirite; b. summer of 384 B.C.; d. Chalcis in Euboea, autumn of 322 B.C. For 20 years a student of *Plato, Aristotle broke with Plato's successors in the Academy and founded his own school, later known as the Peripatetics. Very influential in the whole of Western philosophy, especially with the scholastics of the 13th century, his thought is notable for its development of logic; its elucidation of the four causes and the related doctrines of matter and form, and potency and act; its ethical teaching on the moral virtues; and the political notion of the common good. His writings are important also in the history of literature and of the natural sciences.

BIOGRAPHY

Nothing is known directly of Aristotle's boyhood, though his ancestry was thoroughly Greek. His father, Nicomachus, was described as a descendant of the Machaon Asclepiadae, thus indicating aristocratic birth and medical interests. As physician and personal friend of Amyntas (II or III), father of Philip of Macedon, Nicomachus lived at the Macedonian court. Aristotle's mother, Phaestis, of a colonizing family from Chalcis in Euboea, was also represented as of Aesculapian lineage.

Early Life. Both parents died while Aristotle was a minor, and the charge of his education devolved upon a certain Proxenus, probably a close relative. At about 17 Aristotle arrived at Athens. During the next 20 years, his "first Athenian period," he associated with the great philosopher Plato, head of the already highly organized and well-known Academy. His writings show that he acquired a deep and solid background in Platonic philosophy during his formative days. He engaged in teaching, and at a certain time he is reported to have suddenly changed his method of instruction to emphasize rhetorical training, in order to compete with the rival school of Isocrates. His prolific career as a writer began with *Gryllus,* a work on rhetoric named after Xenophon's son, which may be dated about 361 B.C., when Aristotle was about 23. Another work, *Eudemus,* suggests dating about 353, when he was about 30.

Early in 347, possibly before Plato's death in the first half of that year, Aristotle left Athens, perhaps because of a surge of anti-Macedonian sentiment, and spent the next 3 years at the court of Hermias, ruler of Atarneus and Assos, coastal towns of Asia Minor facing the island of Lesbos. Hermias had been interested in Plato's work and was most cordial in his hospitality to Aristotle, giving him in marriage Pythias, his niece and adopted daughter. Of this marriage was born a daughter, named Pythias. Aristotle had a son also, called Nicomachus. In his will the two children are viewed in the same legal status. A later report, claiming that Nicomachus was Aristotle's son by Herpyllis, one of his domestics, was taken from the noted but adversely disposed historian Timaeus and has the earmarks of a calumny circulated in a program of defamation after the Stagirite's death. Sometime during 345–344 B.C. Aristotle left the court of Hermias for Mytilene on nearby Lesbos. In 343–342 he was summoned to Macedon to tutor Alexander. His stay there lasted until a short time after Alexander's succession to the throne at about 20 in the summer of 336. Geographical indications suggest that Aristotle conducted his extensive research in natural history mainly during these years in Asia Minor and Macedon.

Aristotle's School. In 335–334, probably in the spring of 334, Aristotle returned to Athens and remained there until near the end of 323 or early 322. These years are known as his "second Athenian period," or *Meisterjahre*. During this remarkably short span of about 12 years he gave definite shape to a philosophical tradition that was to carry his name and intellectual seal through the subsequent centuries. While absent in Macedon, he had been proposed for election as head of the Platonic school after the death of its second scholarch, Speusippus, but Xenocrates received a plurality of votes over two other members. The two withdrew from the Platonic circle, and Aristotle, on his return to Athens, began to teach in the Lyceum, another public park. From the Lyceum gatherings an organized philosophical school developed. By the next century it was known as the *peripatos;* its adherents, as Peripatetics. The original force of *peripatos* as its designation is obscure. Etymologically signifying a "walking about," the word had come to mean a place for walking about, a discussion carried on during a stroll, school discussions or lectures in general, or a place in which school activity was conducted. As applied to the Peripatetic school, it most likely came from the place where the gatherings were held. Theophrastus, Aristotle's successor, left in his will "the garden and the *peripatos,*" with houses adjoining the garden, to the common possession of a group of associates for use in philosophic pursuits. He likewise provided for the upkeep of the *peripatos,* showing that a place was meant. Theophrastus had drawn exceptionally large numbers of hearers to his own discussions, so it is not surprising that the place in which his discussions were conducted should have become known as "the" *peripatos,* outstanding among centers referred to at Athens as *peripatoi*. Privately owned by Theophrastus, it could hardly have been located in the Lyceum. The explanation that Aristotle and his associates walked up and down while engaged in philosophical discussions, though circulated about 200 B.C., appears in an unreliable context and seems to have been a guess based on the etymology of the term Peripatetic. Though connection with a *peripatos* is traceable to Theophrastus rather than to Aristotle, a comparison of the writings of the two men shows that the structure and methods of thought and the teachings characteristic of the Peripatetics are attributable to Aristotle himself. The immense amount of work that he accomplished and the influence apparent in his followers mark these years as a period of indefatigable, penetrating, well-organized intellectual labor carried on in common with a closely associated group of companions and disciples.

Retirement. After the death of Alexander in June 323 B.C., Aristotle was exposed to a wave of anti-Macedonian feeling, possibly for a second time. A charge of impiety, reported to have been based on a hymn and inscription written in memory of his deceased father-in-law, Hermias, was laid against him. By the early spring of 322 he had retired to Chalcis; and by October, just past 62, he had died of what was vaguely called a stomach illness. In his will, Aristotle makes arrangements for disposing of slaves and goods that imply considerable family wealth, making possible his life of cultural and scholarly pursuits. The warm, high-minded, urbane, and understanding personality manifested in the will shines on occasion through his usually objective writings. Derogatory views of his character stem from a deliberate campaign to belittle his reputation during the decades following his death. Some later reports about unattractiveness in physical appearance, though handed down only as hearsay, possibly stem from reliable sources. Other adverse reports, for instance that he spoke with a lisp, that he was ungrateful and disloyal to his teacher, that he was profligate, that he turned to philosophy too late in life, and that he ended his life by drinking poison, have by careful criticism of their origins been shown to be without foundation.

PHILOSOPHICAL TEACHING

Philosophy had for Aristotle a much wider ambit than it has today. It included rhetoric, poetics, mathematics, natural science, and political science, as well as *logic, *philosophy of nature, *metaphysics, and *ethics. Aristotle himself was a pioneer in making a systematic classification of all fields of knowledge. Though he called logic a science, Aristotle did not list it in his formal classification but regarded it as a preparation and instrument for science proper. *Science (*scientia*) itself meant for Aristotle universal and necessary knowledge through causes. Metaphysics, natural philosophy, and ethics were accordingly sciences as he understood the term. His division of the sciences was based on their purposes and starting points (*see* SCIENCES, CLASSIFICATION OF). One broad type, proceeding from starting points in the things known, aimed at knowledge alone. As a scrutiny or contemplation (*theoria*) of things it was called theoretical science, either natural, mathematical, or theological. The other type had its starting point in the knower, and aimed at action or at production. If the starting point was free choice, the aim was confined to human conduct and Aristotle called the science practical. If the starting point was a conception of something to be made, the aim was a product different from the action itself, and he called the science productive. Practical and productive sciences, accordingly, aimed at something over and above knowledge.

Logic. Aristotle may be called the founder of logic, as logic was handed down to later Christian culture, although the Megarians before him had already inaugurated a tradition in logic (*see* LOGIC, HISTORY OF). One of their leaders, Eubulides of Miletus, is reported to have kept up controversial attacks on the Stagirite. In such a milieu, against the background of Platonic dialectic, a scientific logic achieved full development in Aristotle. He called it "analytics"—an unraveling, as it were, of the complicated processes of human thought. It regarded particular sensible things, in which all human cognition originates, as knowable under universal aspects. The proximate universal is the *species. Continually widening generic aspects follow, until the most universal, those that cannot be divided into further genera, are reached. Individual horses, for instance, are seen; they are known specifically as horses, generically as animals, and so on to wider generalizations. Aristotle called this process *induction (ἐπαγωγή), meaning that by a consideration of particulars the mind is "led to" the universal content present in the particular or the less general. Under each supreme *genus the inferior genera are arranged in columns named categories. As supreme logical genera Aristotle lists substance and nine accidents (*see* CATEGORIES OF BEING). He also catalogues some features that are not confined to any one category. Often a notion appears as belonging immediately to a subject and is at once predicated of it, for instance that an ox is an animal or that a man is running. In this immediate intuition (*nous*) the basic premises for reasoning are grasped.

Because of their relatively increasing degrees of universality, two notions that do not immediately show connection may each be seen as related to a third in a way that involves relationships with each other. Three such notions form the basis of reasoning, or the *syllogism. The three notions, called the terms, are arranged in three propositions, two of which are known as the premises and the third as the conclusion. Exact rules are elaborated for arranging the terms so that their varying degrees of universality allow a conclusion to be drawn. Affirmative and negative premises make possible different types of reasoning, or figures of the syllogism. Particular premises, and the notes of possibility or necessity, add complications. If reasoning proceeds according to a correct figure from true and immediately known premises, it is called *demonstration and yields scientific knowledge. If demonstrative reasoning is based on the proximate cause of what is concluded, it gives the most perfect type of science, "knowledge of the reasoned fact" (Gr. ἐπιστήμη διότι, Lat. *scientia propter quid*). If demonstrative reasoning is based on an effect, or in negative demonstration upon a remote cause (e.g., a wall does not breathe because it is not an animal), it gives only "knowledge of the fact" (Gr. επιστήμη ὅτι, Lat. *scientia quia*). If reasoning proceeds from premises that are merely probable, it is called dialectical. *Dialectics is important for the inductive process by which the mind gradually focuses attention on universal aspects of things and so comes to grasp the immediate indemonstrable premises of scientific reasoning. All truths cannot be demonstrated, since demonstration itself requires indemonstrable premises.

This logic, very evidently, has as its operative unit the universal (*see* UNIVERSALS). It is therefore labeled today a "class logic," in contrast to propositional logics. It was consistently viewed by Aristotle not as self-sufficient but as meant to guarantee scientific procedure in other branches of knowledge. Although pedagogically it came before the other sciences, it was not given any commanding rank over them. Their proper intelligibility was already constituted in priority to any logical activity of the human mind.

Philosophy of Nature. One type of theoretical science deals with things that are mobile and that have their intelligible content or *form inseparable from *matter. These things constitute the sensible universe. They may be approached from the standpoint of their changeableness, or mobility. *Change, or *motion, requires a subject that loses one form (understood as an intelligible aspect) and acquires another. If the forms lost and acquired are accidents, such as *quantity, *quality, or *place, the change is accidental. Change in the category of *substance, called *substantial change or *generation-corruption, correspondingly involves a subject that loses one form and acquires another. Since form in the category of substance is the basic form in the thing, its subject as such has no form or intelligibility whatever. This subject, because able to receive form, is potency, or primary matter (*see* MATTER AND FORM). In contrast, the intelligible aspect, or form, is actuality (ἐνέργεια) and perfection, or *entelechy (ἐντελέχεια). Change, or motion, is defined as the actuality of something existent in potency precisely as it is in potency. The actuality, or intelligible aspect, present in the changing thing is there in the status of *potency to further *act. The notions of potency and act, taken originally from analysis of change, run through all of Aristotelian philosophy (*see* POTENCY AND ACT).

Nature. Since sensible things are changeable, they are composed of matter and form. Each of these components is called *nature, and things formed by their composition are natural. Nature is itself defined, from the viewpoint of sensible change, as a primary principle of motion and rest. Matter and form are two of a natural thing's causes. The other two causes are the *agent and the *end, or purpose. In later Peripatetic tradition the four causes are named, respectively, material, formal, efficient, and final. On the basis of these causes Aristotle investigates themes such as *chance, place, *time, the *void, and the infinite. Motion and time emerge as eternal of their very nature. They exist in an indivisible, but are unable to start or end in an indivisible, and so always require both previous and subsequent parts. An examination of the nature of motion and a survey of its instances show that everything in motion is being moved by something else; therefore an infinite regress in moved movers cannot account for any motion (*see* MOTION, FIRST CAUSE OF). In a self-mover, one part has to remain unmoved while moving the whole. Most unmoved movers are perishable; but since motion is eternal, the primary mover of the sensible universe will have to be eternal. Located at the circumference of the universe, such a mover imparts rotatory motion only, the one motion that is unchangeable in direction. The heavens are regarded as animated. They are imperishable, because their one observable motion, the circular, leaves no room for alteration or perishing. Their matter is accordingly distinguished from the traditional sublunar elements (earth, water, air, and fire) and is characterized as a further nature called ether (αἰθήρ).

Soul. *Soul is the basic actuality of a natural organic body. In sentient things soul is the principle not only of movement and growth, but also of *sensation and *appetite. In man it is also the principle of intellection and volition. Actual *knowledge, both of sense and of *intellect, consists in a peculiarly cognitional identity of knowing subject and thing known. From this viewpoint "the soul is in a certain way all things." In man the intellect is called a part of the soul and is divided into passive intellect and agent intellect, or intellect that produces. The passive intellect perishes in death. The agent intellect is not only imperishable but is "separate" from matter; as a form separate from matter it is not a subject for natural philosophy. Such teaching on the human soul is brief and somewhat obscure. It does not seem to allow the imperishable intellect, after death, any recollection of happenings in the body, and if so, precludes personal immortality.

Other Sciences. For Aristotle, natural philosophy included qualitative procedures that are now assigned to botany, zoology, experimental psychology, and other such studies. These qualitative procedures he regarded as giving only "knowledge of the fact." Knowledge through the basic causes, matter and form, was in contrast the most scientific of physical knowledge. If there were no immaterial beings, it would constitute for Aristotle the absolutely highest type of science, higher than any mathematical procedure.

Mathematics. Mathematics in the Aristotelian explanation was a theoretical science dealing with objects immobile but not existent outside mobile things, for instance numbers, lines, surfaces, and mathematical solids. By a process called *abstraction, the mathematician may, without falsification, consider these as though they had existence separate from sensible bodies. Since there could be many individual instances of the same mathematical form, some kind of matter was required to explain the multiplicity. It was called intelligible matter, in contradistinction to sensible matter in real bodies. Sciences such as optics, harmonics, astronomy, and mechanics he regarded as essentially mathematical sciences, though as the "more physical" of those sciences. In contrast to qualitative procedures, they explained bodies through "knowledge of the reasoned fact." For further details of Aristotle's teaching on mathematics, see H. G. Apostle, *Aristotle's Philosophy of Mathematics* (Chicago 1952).

Metaphysics. Things entirely immobile and in their existence completely separate from matter Aristotle regarded as divine, hence coming under theological science. He based his proof of their real existence on the eternity of motion established in natural philosophy. Since the unmoved physical movers impart motion eternally, the ultimate ground of that eternity must be a substance entirely actual and so without matter. Any potency in it would mean that motion could in some way cease to be. Such substance is real form without matter, real actuality without potency. It causes motion only by being desired. It is so completely self-contained that it cannot know anything outside itself, since any dependence whatsoever on something outside itself would mean imperfection and so potentiality. It is a plurality, because there has to be one such substance for every original astronomical movement. It is a thinking that has itself as its object, and so may be described as a "thinking on thinking." It is the highest and most divine life. The science treating of it is "first philosophy," and so is universal in scope, the science of being

Personifications of reason conversing with personifications of the virtues and vices, miniature in a manuscript of Aristotle's "Ethics" written in 1376 for the personal use of Charles V of France (MS 10 C 1, fol. 126).

as being. Accidents are beings only in reference to prior, relatively permanent substance, while in sensible substance itself form is primary substance and the cause of being to both matter and composite. But the primary instance of substance without qualification is simple substance. According to the movement of Aristotle's metaphysics in relating secondary to primary instances, and against a background in which being meant permanence in contrast to becoming, theological science as first philosophy could readily be understood as the science that treats universally of beings as beings. Among modern commentators, however, there is much disagreement on the way Aristotle conceived metaphysics and on the nature of the unmoved movers dealt with respectively in natural and first philosophy.

The title "metaphysics" does not appear in Aristotle's writings, but seems to date back to his immediate disciples. In the Aristotelian setting it meant that the things "beyond" the physical were investigated "after" natural philosophy (Reiner). The proposal that the term metaphysics was merely editorial in origin (Buhle) is an unsupported conjecture of the late 18th century.

Ethics and Politics. Moral philosophy is called political by Aristotle on the ground that the supreme human good is the same for individual and for city-state. Its subject matter is human conduct, and its aim is to achieve the *good. This good, continually fluctuating, always consists in a mean between two ever-varying extremes of excess and defect. The mean is determined in each individual case by a judgment of the prudent man. Since the good is always a mean, it can serve as a universal that makes possible the type of reasoning proper to practical science. To be prudent, a man needs the moral virtues, of which the three basic are temperance, fortitude, and justice. Yet to have these one must have the intellectual virtue of prudence (*φρόνησις*) for determining their mean.

These four virtues have to be inculcated simultaneously by correct education from earliest youth. Good laws and customs are therefore all-important in the formation of the correct ethical starting points. If accompanied by bodily welfare, good fortune, sufficient riches, and friends—all spread through a complete lifetime—the virtues make possible a life of contemplation. Contemplation is the highest human activity, thinking on the highest knowable objects. It is felicity (*εὐδαιμονία*), the chief good (*see* EUDAEMONISM). To its attainment all other activity, individual and social, is to be orientated. It is self-sufficient and in its own way divine, and gives the greatest of pleasure. Other ways of virtuous living give only secondary degrees of happiness. Some men are fashioned by nature itself to work with their bodies, as instruments under the guidance of others; slavery for such men is therefore natural. True forms of government aim at the *common good, instead of at the good of a particular class. (*See* POLITICAL PHILOSOPHY.)

Poetics and Rhetoric. Aristotle develops the "productive" sciences in his treatises on poetics and *rhetoric. *See* POETICS (ARISTOTELIAN). In his poetics he makes "re-presenting" (*mimesis*) the basis of fine art. Concentrating on tragedy, he exploits this view especially in regard to the elaboration of plot. To tragedy he assigns the much-debated function of catharsis, variously interpreted as a purification either of the tragic events (G. F. Else) or of the spectators' emotions. In his rhetoric he investigates persuasive arguments and their use through proper delivery, style, and composition.

Development, Works, and Influence

In Aristotle's philosophy a number of items may easily be characterized as Platonic, in contrast to distinctively Peripatetic thought. In the 19th century Platonic passages were at times excised as unauthentic or labeled as inherent contradictions in Aristotle's basic thought. In the first half of the 20th century a development theory, outlined by Thomas Case and elaborated in detail by Werner Jaeger, represented the Stagirite's thought as noticeably Platonic in the earliest writings, then gradually changing until it culminated during his mature period in a philosophy characteristically his own. Shadings and changes were added to this theory by other interpreters. It was carried to its extreme in the stand that Aristotle's own thought always remained Platonic, with all the characteristically Peripatetic philosophy coming from Theophrastus (Zürcher). A later reaction has explained the development in the opposite direction—Aristotle began strongly in his own characteristic way of thinking, then strove through the years to become a Platonist (I. Düring). No development theory has proved satisfactory, nor has any adherence of Aristotle to Platonic elements inconsistent with his own proper thought been sufficiently established.

Writings. In later antiquity Aristotle's writings, filling several hundred rolls, were distinguished in three broad classes: hypomnematic, exoteric, and acroamatic. The hypomnematic were notes to aid the memory and prepare for further work. The exoteric, written in dialogue and other current literary forms, were meant for the general reading public. Only fragments of them are extant. No reason why they ceased to be copied has been handed down in Greek tradition. Outstanding titles were *On Philosophy, Protrepticus, Eudemus, On Justice,* and *On Ideas.* The third class consisted of treatises (λόγοι, μέθοδοι, πραγματεῖαι) meant for school use and written in a concise style peculiar to their own literary genre. To this class belong the surviving works of Aristotle.

The *Categories, On Interpretation, Prior Analytics, Posterior Analytics, Topics,* and *Sophistical Refutations* contain the Aristotelian logic. In later Greek tradition they became known as the *Organon,* or instrument for learning. The general topics of natural philosophy are investigated in the *Physics,* and more particular phases in *On the Heavens, On Generation and Corruption, Meteorology, On the Soul,* and in a group of shorter treatises known since the Middle Ages as *Parva Naturalia.* The animal kingdom is studied in five works: *History of Animals, Parts of Animals, Generation of Animals, Progression of Animals,* and *Movement of Animals.* The collection later known as the *Metaphysics* contains the treatises on first philosophy. The Aristotelian ethics has come down in three redactions, the *Nicomachean Ethics* (seemingly named from some unknown connection with Aristotle's son, Nicomachus), the *Eudemian Ethics* (seemingly named from Eudemus of Rhodes or, as Dirlmeier suggests, from Eudemus of Cyprus), and though of still disputed authenticity, the *Magna Moralia.* The treatment in the *Nicomachean Ethics* is continued in the *Politics.* A study of constitutions of various cities intervened; of these only the *Constitution of Athens,* recovered from Egyptian papyruses during the last quarter of the 19th century, is extant. The *Rhetoric* and the *Poetics* round out the list of surviving works.

A number of these treatises, missing in the earliest catalogue, seem to have been recovered only with the finding of Theophrastus's personal library, buried for nearly 200 years in a cellar at Scepsis in Asia Minor. A few works that would come under Aristotle's notion of mathematics were listed in the ancient catalogues, but none has survived.

Since the acroamatic writings were school λόγοι, they were open to additions and to change in arrangement as long as Aristotle continued his teaching career. This circumstance renders dating difficult and uncertain. As yet no satisfactory overall chronology has been established. For scholarly use the fragments, edited traditionally according to the order given them by Rose under the pseudepigrapha, should be divided into three classes: (1) those ascribed with sufficient certainty to a definite work, followed by fragments that may be attached to these; (2) those attributed with sufficient certainty to Aristotle but not to any definite work; and (3) those whose attribution to Aristotle has been alleged but remains doubtful (Wilpert).

Influence. Aristotle's philosophy continued to be taught at Athens under a succession of scholarchs that can be traced quite definitely into the 1st century B.C., and nebulously into the 3d century A.D. After the death of Theophrastus the school seems to have had less widespread influence than its rivals. Upon the edition of the Stagirite's works by Andronicus of Rhodes in the 1st century B.C., the extensive Greek commentaries began; and they continued down to the 14th century A.D. Among the Christian Church Fathers, the attitude toward Aristotle was not favorable. His logic became influential in the early Middle Ages through *Boethius. His metaphysics and natural philosophy (in spite of several ecclesiastical prohibitions) and his ethical and political doctrines came to provide the framework for philosophical thought during the 13th century. They earned for Aristotle his rank as "The Philosopher," and with Dante the title of "the master of those who know." His doctrines were made to fit into various Christian interpretations. The Renaissance and the Reformation reacted violently against the scholastic Aristotle, although since the Renaissance the *Poetics* has served as a fundamental text in literary criticism. The rapidly developing quantitative physics and chemistry struggled bitterly to throw off the yoke of qualitative methods that had become traditional in the wake of Aristotelian doctrine, even though the Stagirite's teaching, if it had been rightly understood, could have provided a welcome abode for these new sciences under its

Page of a manuscript of Aristotle's "Politics" written in England in the 14th century (Garrett MS 102, fol. 72r). As is usual with study manuscripts of the Middle Ages, the margins are filled with copious notes.

mathematical divisions, as it had done for the ancient astronomy, optics, harmonics, and mechanics. Early in the 19th century a keen philological interest in Aristotle took hold, and it has developed increasingly in the 20th century. Along with the revival of interest in scholasticism this has led to renewed philosophical appreciation of the Stagirite's doctrines, giving assurance that Aristotle's wisdom will continue to be digested with increasing profit by Western culture. Its outstanding importance for the Church lies in the help its fundamental principles can give to the structure of Christian philosophy and theology, even though Aristotle himself developed these principles in a thoroughly pagan atmosphere.

See also ARISTOTELIANISM; GREEK PHILOSOPHY; SCHOLASTICISM.

Bibliography: Sources. *Opera,* ed. I. BEKKER, 5 v. (Berlin 1831–70); in scholarly works Aristotle is cited by page, column, and line of v.1–2; v.5 contains the invaluable *Index Aristotelicus* by H. BONITZ. There are more recent critical texts of most individual treatises. *The Works of Aristotle Translated into English,* ed. W. D. ROSS, 12 v. (Oxford 1908–52), standard Eng. tr. T. W. ORGAN, *An Index to Aristotle in English Translation* (Princeton 1949). For translations of individual works see LoebClLib and others. F. R. WEHRLI, ed., *Die Schule des Aristoteles,* 10 v. (Basel 1944–59), fragments of the Peripatetics up to the beginning of the 1st century B.C. Preussische Akademie der Wissenschaften, *Commentaria in Aristotelem Graeca,* 23 v. (Berlin 1882–1909); *Supplementum Aristotelicum,* 3 v. (Berlin 1885–1903), Greek commentaries.

Literature. I. DÜRING, *Aristotle in the Ancient Biographical Tradition* (Göteborg 1957). I. DÜRING and G. E. L. OWEN, eds., *Aristotle and Plato in the Mid-Fourth Century* (Göteborg 1960). M. SCHWAB, *Bibliographie d'Aristote* (Paris 1896). M. D. PHILIPPE, *Aristoteles* (Bern 1948), a bibliographical study. A. H. ARMSTRONG, *An Introduction to Ancient Philosophy* (3d ed. London 1957). W. W. JAEGER, *Aristotle: Fundamentals of the History of His Development,* tr. R. ROBINSON (2d ed. New York 1948). W. D. ROSS, *Aristotle* (5th rev. ed. New York 1953). G. R. G. MURE, *Aristotle* (London 1932). J. H. RANDALL, JR., *Aristotle* (New York 1960). D. J. ALLAN, *The Philosophy of Aristotle* (New York 1952). J. OWENS, *The Doctrine of Being in the Aristotelian Metaphysics* (Toronto 1951). C. DIANO, Enc Catt 1:1912–35. C. GIACON, EncFil 1:339–365. Copleston v.1.

Illustration credits: Fig. 1, Museo Meermanno-Westreenianum, The Hague, Netherlands. Fig. 2, Princeton University Library, Robert Garrett Collection.

[J. OWENS]

ARIUS, KING OF SPARTA, mentioned in 1 Mc 12.7 as the king of Sparta who in times past sent a letter to the Jewish high priest Onias broaching a conventional diplomatic treaty of friendship. The letter is given in 1 Mc 12.19–23, where it is appended to a letter of Jonathan Machabee [*see* MACHABEES (MACCABEES), HISTORY OF THE], who in 143 B.C. referred to it in offering a renewal of the ancient treaty entered into between Arius ['Αρεῖος, "belonging to Ares (Mars)"] and Onias. From the Hebraic Greek in 1 Machabees it is obvious that the author of Machabees had only the Hebrew translation and not the original letter [*see* MACHABEES (MACCABEES), BOOKS OF THE]. Since Arius II (264–256 B.C.) died as a boy of 8 years, it is reasonably certain that Arius I (309–265) is indicated. Of the three high priests by the name of Onias (Onias I, d. *c.* 300 B.C.; Onias II, d. *c.* 227 B.C.; and *Onias III, d. *c.* 170 B.C.), it is obviously Onias I to whom the letter was written—sometime between 309, the beginning of the reign of Arius I, and 300 B.C., the death of Onias I. Arius I belonged to the family of the Agiades and was a son of Acrotatos. On two occasions he allied himself with Egypt against Antigonus Gonatas of Macedonia; the first time in 280 B.C. with Ptolemy Ceraunos (*see* PTOLEMIES), the second time in 267 B.C. with Ptolemy Philadelphus. In 272 B.C., while Arius was occupied with an expedition to Crete, Pyrrhus, King of Epirus, invaded Sparta. Arius hurried home, and the ensuing war ended when Pyrrhus died. Arius himself died in 265 B.C. in a battle against the Macedonians.

Bibliography: EncDictBibl 132. J. C. SWAIM, InterDictBibl 1:222.

[P. F. ELLIS]

ARIUS, Alexandrian priest and heresiarch; b. Libya, *c.* 250; d. 336. Arius probably studied under *Lucian of Antioch and joined the Alexandrian clergy. While still a minor cleric, he took part in the *Meletian schism against Bp. Peter of Alexandria, but afterward he made his peace and was promoted to deacon and priest. Bishop Alexander held him in high repute and gave him charge of the important parish of Baucalis. His learning, grave manners, and ascetical life gained him a large following, but his unorthodox views on the divinity of Christ came under attack; *c.* 318—or 323, according to others—the conflict with Alexander broke into the open.

Arius was first rebuked at a local synod, and when he refused to submit he was excommunicated by a provincial council of all Egypt. He went to Palestine and Bithynia, where he received support from *Eusebius of Caesarea and *Eusebius of Nicomedia, who sent out numerous letters to fellow bishops and convened synods in his defense. Macarius of Jerusalem and Marcellus of Ancyra opposed his doctrine and, as a result, the Church in the East was divided on his account. This caused the intervention of *Constantine I, who conquered the East in 324. He sent *Hosius of Córdoba with a letter to Alexander and Arius, urging them to cease fighting over what he called "a trifling and foolish verbal difference." Hosius' efforts to restore peace failed and, upon his recommendation, Constantine then summoned a general council of the Church.

Hosius presided at a council of Antioch (324) that condemned Arius's doctrine. At the Council of *Nicaea I (325), some of his writings were read and rejected as blasphemous by a vast majority of the fathers. The *Nicene Creed, with the *homoousios and the anathemas, was drawn up to exclude his errors. After the council Arius was banished to Illyricum. When and how he was recalled and rehabilitated is a matter of dispute. Some historians connect this with an alleged second session of the Nicene Council in 327; others, with the Council of Tyre and Jerusalem in 335. It is certain that the assembly of Jerusalem (335) decided to readmit him into the Church. Constantine ordered a solemn reinstatement in Constantinople, but Arius died suddenly on the eve of the appointed day, early in 336. Of his writings there exist only three letters and fragments of the *Thalia,* or versified condensation of his teaching chanted by his followers in the church and streets.

See also ARIANISM.

Bibliography: H. G. OPITZ, ed., *Athanasius' Werke,* v.3.1 (Berlin 1934) 1–3, 12–13, 64, letters. G. BARDY, *Recherches sur St. Lucien d'Antioche et son école* (Paris 1936) 246–274, Thalia. H. GWATKIN, *Studies of Arianism* (2d ed. Cambridge, Eng. 1900). X. LE BACHELET, DTC 1.2:1779–1806. E. SCHWARTZ, *Zur Geschichte des Athanasius* (Gesammelte Schriften 3; Berlin 1959); *Kaiser Constantin und die christliche Kirche* (2d ed. Leipzig 1936). N. H. BAYNES, *Constantine the Great and the Christian Church* (London 1930). G. BARDY in J. R. PALANQUE et al., *The*

Church in the Christian Roman Empire, tr. E. C. MESSENGER, 2 v. in 1 (New York 1953) 1:73–132. Quasten Patr 3:7–13. E. BOULARAND, "Les Débuts d'Arius," *Bulletin de littérature ecclésiastique* 75 (1964) 175–203.

[V. C. DE CLERCQ]

ARIZONA

A state in southwest U.S., one of the Rocky Mountain states, admitted (1912) to the Union as the 48th state. It has an area of 113,810 square miles and is bounded on the north by Utah; on the west by the Colorado River, Nevada, and California; on the south by Mexico; and on the east by New Mexico. The capital and largest city is Phoenix.

History. The first European to enter Arizona was Fray Marcos de *Niza, who went north from Mexico City in 1539 and returned to Viceroy Antonio Mendoza with exaggerated reports of the wealthy cities to the north. In 1540 Francisco Vasquez de Coronado searched in vain for the fabled "Seven Cities of Cibola"; after this failure, Arizona was neglected by the Spanish except for a brief visit (1581) by Antonio Espijo and expeditions sent out from New Mexico by Juan de Oñate (1598–1604). The most influential and significant colonizer of the late 17th and early 18th centuries was Eusebio *Kino, SJ, who established missions among the agricultural Indians of the Pimería Alta south of the Gila and west of the San Pedro Rivers. After Kino's death in 1711 the Arizona Pimería was neglected until the arrival (1768) of Fray Francisco Garces, who was active in the same area until his death at the hands of the Yuma Indians in 1781.

From 1781 to 1868 Arizona was virtually without Catholic clergy. But in 1868 Arizona was made a vicariate apostolic, and Jean B. Salpointe became its first bishop. The Diocese of *Tucson was created on May 8, 1897; on Dec. 16, 1939, *Gallup was erected as a suffragan of the Archdiocese of Santa Fe, comprising the five northern counties of Arizona and an area in western New Mexico. In 1952 the state population totaled 749,587, of whom 26.4 per cent were Catholics; 19 per cent, Protestants; 1.3 per cent, Jews; all others constituted 55.1 per cent (*see* CHURCH MEMBERSHIP, U.S.). In 1960 the estimated total for Catholics was 435,000 in the state's population of 1,302,101. Within the Diocese of Tucson there were (1963) 45 parish schools, 9 Catholic high schools, 3 hospitals, a home and school for girls, 75 parishes, and 240 priests. In the five northern counties there were two high schools, a home and school for girls, and six parish schools.

Church-State Relations. References to and provisions affecting religion are incorporated in the state constitution and in acts of the legislature and the judiciary.

Constitution. Arizona is governed by the Constitution of 1912, as amended. The preamble states that the people, "grateful to Almighty God for our liberties, do ordain this Constitution." Article 2, sec. 12, provides for liberty of conscience but does not "excuse acts of licentiousness, or justify practices inconsistent with the peace and safety of the State." Appropriations for religious purposes are prohibited. "No religious qualification shall be required for any public office or employment, nor shall any person be incompetent as a witness or juror in consequence of his opinion on matters of religion, nor be questioned touching his religious belief in any court of justice to affect the weight of his testimony."

Justices, judges, and justices of the peace must take an oath of office (art. 6, sec. 26).

"Property of educational, charitable, and religious associations or institutions not used or held for profit may be exempt from taxation" (art. 9, sec. 2).

"No tax shall be laid or appropriation of public money made in aid of any church, or private or sec-

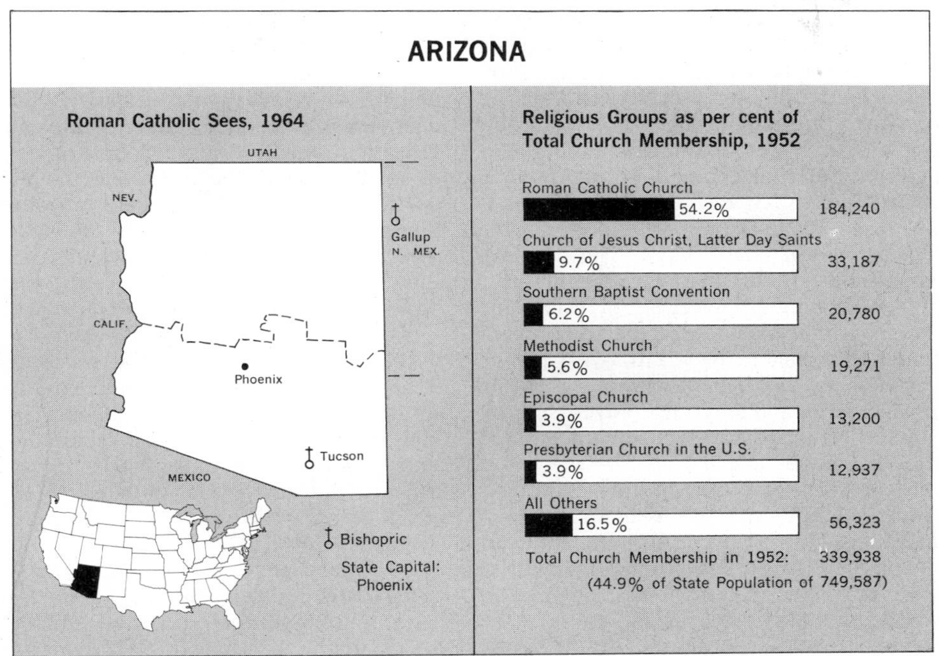

Church-membership statistics were compiled by the Bureau of Research and Survey of the National Council of the Churches of Christ in the U.S.A.

tarian school, or any public service corporation" (art. 9, sec. 10).

"No sectarian instruction shall be imparted in any school or state educational institution that may be established under this constitution, and no religious or political test or qualification shall ever be required as a condition of admission into any public educational institution of the State. . . . but the liberty of conscience hereby secured shall not be so construed as to justify practices or conduct inconsistent with the good order, peace, morality, or safety of the State, or with the rights of others" (art. 11, sec. 7).

Article 20, first ordinance, provides that "perfect toleration of religious sentiment shall be secured to every inhabitant of this state, and no inhabitant of this state shall ever be molested in person or property on account of his or her mode of religious worship, or lack of the same."

Marriage and Divorce. Marriages of men under 18 and women under 16 are forbidden. The consent of a parent is needed for men under 21 and women under 18. A license and blood test are required. Certain public officials and clergy may perform the ceremony. Common-law marriages are not recognized.

Marriages are void if the parties are related by blood in any degree of the direct line, and up to and including first cousins; or if contracted between white persons and Negroes, Hindus, Malays, and Mongolians. Marriages may be annulled when an impediment renders the marriage contract void. The common-law rule of age 14 for males and 12 for females determines nonage.

The grounds for absolute divorce are: adultery; physical incompetency at the time of marriage and continuing to the time of suit; conviction and imprisonment for a felony, but not until 1 year after the conviction and not if convicted on the plaintiff's testimony; willful desertion for 1 year; habitual intemperance; extreme cruelty; inexcusable failure to provide; conviction of a felony before marriage when the fact in unknown to the other party at the time of marriage; wife's pregnancy at the time of marriage by another man and unknown to the husband; noncohabitation for 5 years or more for any reason. Either party may remarry 1 year after the judgment unless there are proceedings to set aside the judgment. The wife may get a limited divorce. The Uniform Reciprocal Enforcement of Support Act is in force. *See* MARRIAGE, U.S. LAW OF; DIVORCE, (U.S. LAW OF).

Abortion, Birth Control, Sterilization. The law forbids *abortion unless it is necessary to save the mother's life. Providing, supplying, administering, or using any instruments or means whatever to procure the miscarriage of a woman is punishable by a 2- to 5-year prison sentence. The use of any instrument with the intent to produce a miscarriage is a felony. The advertising of medicine or any other means for producing a miscarriage or abortion is a misdemeanor.

The law restricts *birth control. It is a misdemeanor to advertise any means or medicine used for the prevention of conception. Doctors may distribute literature on this subject and the Planned Parenthood Association may also distribute it if the information is sought (*see* CONTRACEPTION; ANOVULANTS).

The superintendent of the state hospital may authorize *sterilization in certain cases when the inmate-patient is afflicted with hereditary, recurrent insanity, idiocy, imbecility, feeble-mindedness, or epilepsy. The patient may have a hearing and appeal. Therapeutic sterilization is permitted when it is incidental to medical or surgical treatment.

Property and Taxation. Religious societies may incorporate either under the nonprofit corporation statute or as a corporation sole. Charities may incorporate under the nonprofit corporation statute. A person vested with legal title to the property of a church or religious society may form the corporation sole with the title to property vested in him.

Real and personal property of religious societies and charities not run for profit is exempt from taxation. The statute is construed against granting the exemption whenever possible.

There are no mortmain statutes or fund-raising statutes.

Prisons and Reformatories. The superintendent of the state prison appoints a Protestant and a Catholic chaplain. The chaplains devote their time to giving the prisoners moral and religious instruction. The have access at all times, with the superintendent's permission, to the prisoners for that reason. The chaplains hold services at the state prison at least twice each month.

Holidays and Sunday Observance. Sunday, Christmas and New Year's Days, Labor Day, and general election day, Thanksgiving Day, February 12, February 14, February 22, May 30, and July 4 are legal holidays. When a holiday falls on Sunday, the next day is observed. Public offices may not be open and judicial business is not allowed on holidays. There is a fine and possible imprisonment for barbering on Sunday.

Morality, Public Health, and Safety. No state condones polygamy. Willful disturbance of a meeting assembled for religious worship is a misdemeanor. The general provisions for "The Regulation of Hospitals and other Health Centers," do not apply to the "remedial care or treatment of residents or patients in any home or institution conducted for those who rely upon treatment by prayer or spiritual means in accordance with the creed or tenents of any well recognized church or religious denomination." Compulsory vaccination is prohibited, but a minor child may be prohibited from attending a public school in the state if a smallpox epidemic is prevalent, unless he has been vaccinated. The Tuberculosis Control Statute does not impose on any person against his will, or contrary to his religious concepts, any mode of treatment, provided that sanitary or preventive measures and quarantine laws and regulations are complied with by any such person.

Various Constitutional Freedoms. An ordinance of Casa Grande, Ariz., imposing license taxes on the sale of printed matter and vesting no discretionary power in public authorities to refuse a license to anyone wanting to sell religious literature was found to be not invalid since it did not abridge freedom of speech, press, or religion, as applied to members of Jehovah's Witnesses (*Jones v. City of Opelika, Ala.* 316 U.S. 584).

A general revenue ordinance of a city imposing a license on peddlers, as applied to a minister of the Jehovah's Witnesses who was peddling printed books and pamphlets setting forth his views on the meaning of the Bible, was found not unconstitutional since it did not violate the right of free speech [*State v. Jobin* 118 P (2) 97].

Bibliography: H. H. BANCROFT, *History of Arizona and New Mexico, 1530–1888* (San Francisco 1889). H. E. BOLTON, *Rim of Christendom: A Biography of Eusebio Francisco Kino* (New York 1936). H. C. HODGE, *Arizona As It Is: Or, the Coming Country* (Boston 1887). R. WYLLYS, *Arizona, the History of a Frontier State* (Phoenix 1950). H. E. BOLTON, ed., *Spanish Exploration in the Southwest, 1542–1706* (New York 1952), a reprint of *Original Narratives of Early American History* (New York 1916). *Arizona Revised Statutes Annotated* (St. Paul 1956–). *Arizona Digest, 1866 to Date* (St. Paul 1937–).

[P. C. HENDERSON]

ARK OF THE COVENANT

The sacred chest of ancient Israel. The ark (Heb. *'ărôn*) of the covenant is described in Ex 25.10–22; 37.1–9 as a chest of acacia wood, about 4 feet long, 2½ feet wide and 2½ feet high; it was covered with gold plates and fitted with rings, through which poles for carrying it could be passed. Over the ark was a gold plate, the same size as the ark, called in Hebrew the *kappōret*. This word is usually translated either as propitiatory (DV, CCD, through the Vulgate's *propitiatorium* from the Septuagint's ἱλαστήριον—means or place of propitiation) or as mercy seat (AV, RSV, from the influence of Luther's rendering, *Gnadenstuhl*) in accordance with the meaning of the Hebrew root *kpr* (to cover) in the transferred sense "to atone" (*kippēr*) and with the role of the *kappōret* in certain ceremonies (Leviticus ch. 16) on the Day of *Atonement (Yom Kippur). Two golden *cherubim rested on the *kappōret,* one at one end and one at the other, and covered it with their outspread wings. According to Ex 25.16; 40.20; Dt 10.1–5, the tablets on which the Ten Commandments were written were placed in the ark. In Dt 31.25; Ex 16.33; and Nm 17.10, mention is made of other objects beside or in front of it.

In Dt 10.8 it is stated that the ark was carried by Levites; and in Nm 10.33–36, that when the Israelites left Sinai, it went before them and indicated the resting places. In these desert wanderings the ark was probably sheltered in the tent sanctuary, called the *Tent of Meeting by the Pentateuchal *Priestly Writers. At the Jordan the ark led the way into the Promised Land (Josue ch. 3–6). Then the ark, without the tent sanctuary of the desert, stood in the camp at Gilgal (Jos 7.6). It is next mentioned at *Bethel (Jgs 20.27) and then in a more permanent sanctuary at *Silo (Shiloh; 1 Sm 3.3). In 1 Sm 4.3–7.2 it is stated that it was carried into battle at Aphec, captured by the Philistines, and then returned to the Israelites at *Beth-Sames (Beth-shemesh) and housed for a while at *Cariath-Jarim. David finally brought it to Jerusalem and installed it in a tent (2 Samuel ch. 6). After Solomon built the Temple, the ark was placed in its Holy of Holies (3 Kgs 6.19; 8.1–9). It was probably destroyed with the Temple in 587 B.C. (despite 2 Mc 2.4–5).

Of all the aspects about the ark, the one most easily understood is that of a container for the stone tablets from Sinai, which explains why the ark was called "the ark of the covenant." But it is also the visible sign or extension or even the embodiment of the presence of God, as can be seen in Nm 10.35–36; 1 Samuel ch. 4–6; 2 Samuel ch. 6; and 3 Kings ch. 8. Many extra-Biblical parallels show that there is no contradiction between the idea of the ark symbolizing God's presence and of the ark as a receptacle. (*See* SHEKINAH.) It is also a war palladium according to Nm 10.35–36; 1 Samuel ch. 4; and 2 Sm 11.11. Its formidable power is seen also in 1 Sm ch. 5; 6.19; and 2 Sm 6.7. From the period at Silo onward the ark was called "the ark of Yahweh Sabaoth who sits above the Cherubim." This idea of the ark as the throne of God is not necessarily contradicted by references to the ark as the "footstool" of God in 1 Chr 28.2; the ark, the cherubim, and eventually even the *kappōret* were all symbols of God's providential presence with His chosen people. Posture hardly makes a difference in symbolic presence. In this as well as in the various explanations of the purpose of the ark, there are several ideas that overlap to some extent, and different aspects are emphasized in different traditions.

The late tradition of Leviticus ch. 16, confirmed by 1 Chr 28.11, indicates that after the Exile the *kappōret* had been substituted for the ark. As for the antiquity

Medieval interpretation of the Ark of the Covenant carried on the shoulders of the Israelites of the Exodus, detail of a miniature in a 12th-century Bible from S. Maria ad Martyres, Rome (Cod. Vat. lat. 12958, fol. 60v).

of the ark itself, it seems from the old tradition of Nm 10.35–36 to extend in some form back into the desert period. In fact, the conception of a deity standing or enthroned on an animal or mythical creature was common in the Near East for centuries before the Exodus. It is not strange to find Israel using a similar symbol—but without an image of Yahweh Himself. (*See* IMAGES, BIBLICAL PROHIBITION OF.)

Bibliography: De Vaux AncIsr 297–302, 540. A. MILLER, Lex ThK² 2:780. G. RINALDI, EncCatt 1:1783–85. EncDictBibl 133–136. T. WORDEN, "The Ark of the Covenant," *Scripture* 5 (1952) 82–90. M. HARAN, "The Ark and the Cherubim: Their Symbolic Significance in Biblical Ritual," IsrExplorJ 9 (1959) 30–38. E. NIELSEN, "Some Reflections on the History of the Ark," *Congress Volume, Oxford 1959,* VetTest Suppl. 7 (1960) 61–74. **Illustration credit:** Biblioteca Apostolica Vaticana.

[E. J. CROWLEY]

ARKANSAS

A state in central and southwest U.S., admitted (1836) to the Union as the 25th state. It is bounded on the north by Missouri, on the west by Oklahoma and part of Texas, and on the south by Louisiana; it is separated on the east from Tennessee and Mississippi by the Mississippi River. The capital and largest city is Little Rock; other centers of population include Fort Smith, Pine Bluff, and Hot Springs.

History. The area comprised a portion of the Louisiana Territory purchased from France in 1803. It was visited by H. De Soto, J. *Marquette, and R. C. de *La Salle, who through his lieutenant Henri de Tonti established the first settlement, Arkansas Post (1685). Most of the early missionary work was carried on by the Jesuits; later, priests of the Congregation of the Missions (Vincentians) labored in the area. Ecclesiastical jurisdiction was often transferred as the territory passed from French to Spanish and again to French possession, but with the Louisiana Purchase it was placed under the administration of Bp. John *Carroll of Baltimore, Md. In 1816 the Diocese of Louisiana and the Floridas was established but was split 10 years later, with Arkansas going to the new Diocese of St. Louis, Mo. The Diocese of *Little Rock was established in 1843, headed by Bp. Andrew *Byrne. After his death in 1862 there was a 5-year interregnum occasioned by the difficulties of the Civil War and the early Reconstruction days. Bishop Edward *Fitzgerald, who was appointed in 1867, was succeeded in 1907 by John B. Morris, his coadjutor. Morris led the diocese through its period of greatest development until his death in 1946, when Albert L. Fletcher, a native of Arkansas who had been auxiliary bishop since 1940, was made ordinary.

When Bishop Byrne first arrived in Arkansas there were fewer than 1,000 Catholics. In 1952 they constituted 1.4 per cent of the state population of 1,909,511; Protestants accounted for 29.8 per cent; Jews 0.1 per cent; and all others, 68.7 per cent (*see* CHURCH MEMBERSHIP, U.S.). In 1964 Catholics numbered 48,305 in the state total of 1,823,329. In that year there were 11 high schools (2,471 students) and 52 elementary schools (8,497 students) under Catholic auspices; an additional 2,645 students received religious instruction under released-time programs.

Church-State Relations. References to and provisions affecting religion are incorporated in the state constitution and in acts of the legislature and the judiciary.

Constitution. Arkansas in governed by the Constitution of 1874, as amended. The preamble states that the people are "grateful to Almighty God for . . . religious liberty."

"All men have a natural and indefeasible right to worship Almighty God according to the dictates of their

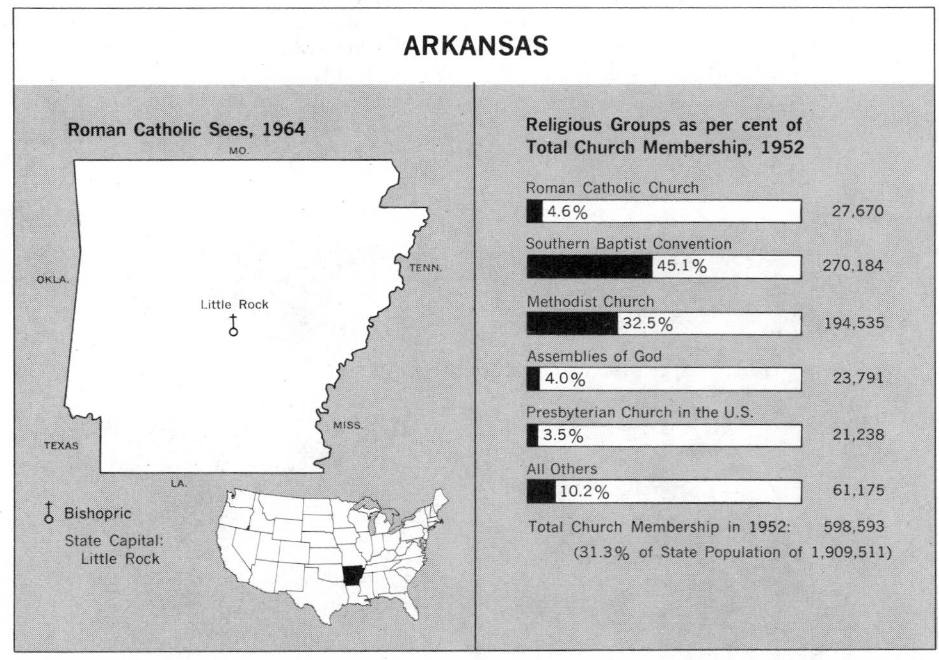

Church-membership statistics were compiled by the Bureau of Research and Survey of the National Council of the Churches of Christ in the U.S.A.

own consciences; no man can, of right, be compelled to attend, erect or support any place of worship; or to maintain any ministry against his consent. No human authority can . . . control or interfere with the right of conscience; and no preference shall ever be given, by law, to any religious establishment, denomination or mode of worship above any other" (art. 2, sec. 24). Article 2, sec. 25, provides for the protection of every religious denomination in the enjoyment of its own religion; sec. 26 states that no religious test may be a requirement to hold office and that one cannot be rendered incompetent to be a witness because of religious belief; "but nothing herein shall be construed to dispense with oaths or affirmations."

Justices of the peace must take an oath (art. 7, sec. 38).

Property exempt from taxation includes "churches used as such; school buildings and apparatus; libraries and grounds used exclusively for school purposes, and buildings and grounds and materials used exclusively for public charity" (art. 16, sec. 5).

"No person who denies the being of a God shall hold any office in the civil departments of this State nor be competent to testify as a witness in any court" (art. 19, sec. 1).

Article 19, sec. 20, provides for an oath of office by various civil and military officers.

Marriage and Divorce. Marriages of men under 18 and women under 16 are forbidden except in certain cases of pregnancy. The consent of parents is needed for men under 21 and women under 18. A license and blood test are required. Certain public officials and clergy may perform the ceremony. Common-law marriages are not recognized.

Marriages are void if the parties are related by blood in any degree of the direct line, and up to and including first cousins; between a white person and a Negro or mulatto. Marriages may be annulled on the grounds of nonage, force, or fraud, lack of understanding, or physical causes. A 5-year abandonment, without knowledge of whether the spouse is living, gives rise to a presumption that the spouse is dead, and the remarriage of the abandoned spouse is valid.

The grounds for absolute divorce are: adultery, impotency at time of marriage continuing to the action, unreasonable desertion for 1 year, bigamy, conviction of a felony or infamous crime, habitual drunkenness for 1 year, cruel treatment endangering life, intolerable indignities, willful nonsupport, living apart for 3 consecutive years without cohabitation, insanity for 3 years or confinement in an asylum for that period. A husband suing an incurably insane wife must provide for her for the rest of her life. The court may restore the maiden name of the wife at the request of either party. There are no statutory restrictions on remarriage. *See* MARRIAGE, U.S. LAW OF; DIVORCE (U.S. LAW OF).

Abortion, Birth Control, Sterilization. The law forbids *abortion unless it is necessary to save the life of the mother. "It is unlawful for anyone to administer or prescribe any medicine or drugs to any woman with child, with the intent to produce an abortion, or premature delivery of any foetus before or after the period of quickening, or to produce or attempt to produce such abortion by any other means." The penalty is up to $1,000 and 1 to 5 years in prison. The advertising of means or methods of producing an abortion is prohibited by state law.

The law restricts *birth control (*see* CONTRACEPTION; ANOVULANTS). Drugs or appliances for the prevention of conception or venereal disease may not be advertised, displayed, sold, or otherwise disposed of without a license. This does not apply to advertising in periodicals whose circulation is substantially limited to physicians and the drug trade. These laws do not apply to physicians and regularly licensed medical practitioners.

There is no reference to sterilization in the state code.

Property and Taxation. Religious societies may incorporate under the nonprofit corporation statute. Charities may incorporate under the nonprofit corporation statute or the charitable organizations act. The real property of religious societies is held by the trustee or trustees who have been elected or appointed according to the society's rules.

A statute restricts to 40 acres the amount of land that may be conveyed to a trustee for the use of a religious society.

A professional fund raiser is a person who for consideration solicits funds in behalf of a charitable organization. He must register and post bond; contracts must be in writing and filed. None of the above rules apply to any solicitation made by or on behalf of any church, missionary, or religious organization or by bona fide officers and employees of a charitable organization.

Prisons and Reformatories. All clergymen of every denomination are admitted free to prison, or may visit any convict confined therein, subject to the rules necessary for the good government and discipline of the penitentiary, and may administer the rites and ceremonies of the church to which they belong if such convict desires it. The superintendent and physician must afford every facility to the clergymen to visit the convicts and to administer such rites, ceremonies, and spiritual consolation to such convicts not inconsistent with the rules of the prison.

Holidays and Sunday Observance. Sunday, Christmas and New Year's Day, Thanksgiving Day, Labor Day, statewide election days, January 19, February 22, May 30, July 4, and November 11 are legal holidays. Transactions on legal holidays are valid, but a contract made on Sunday is void unless it is ratified on a subsequent weekday. When a legal holiday falls on Sunday, the next day is observed. Any city or town may regulate business on Sunday by ordinance. Horse racing, cockfighting, card playing, and operating a store or saloon on the Sabbath are all punishable by fine.

Various Constitutional Freedoms. An ordinance of Fort Smith, Ark., imposing a license tax on the sale of printed matter and vesting no discretionary power in public authorities to refuse a license to anyone desirous of selling religious literature was found not invalid as abridging the freedoms of speech, press, or religion as applied to members of Jehovah's Witnesses (*Jones v. City of Opelika* 316 U.S. 584). Freedom of speech and of peaceful assembly are protected by the Federal constitution not only against heavy-handed frontal attack but also from being stifled by more subtle interference from agencies of government (*Bates v. City of Little Rock* 361 U.S. 516).

The imposition of a license tax on persons selling

and delivering religious books was held not to be an infringement of religious liberty [*Cook v. City of Harrison* 215. W (2) 966.]

Bibliography: D. T. HERNDON, ed., *Annals of Arkansas,* 4 v. (Hopkinsville, Ky. 1947). J. G. FLETCHER, *Arkansas* (Chapel Hill, N.C. 1947). Historical Commission of Diocese of Little Rock, *The History of Catholicity in Arkansas* (Little Rock 1925). *Arkansas Statutes, 1947* (Indianapolis 1947–). *Arkansas Digest, 1820 to Date* (St. Paul 1937–).

[J. E. O'CONNELL]

ARLEGUI, JOSÉ, Franciscan chronicler; b. Laguardia, Navarre, Spain, 1685; d. place unknown, 1750? He was the son of José Arleguiz and Ana San Martín and joined the Franciscans at San Francisco de Vitoria in 1701. He taught arts and theology at the convent of Aránzazu. Then he went to Zacatecas, Mexico, where he was lector in theology, regent of studies, guardian (1721), provincial (1725), and chronicler of the province. He was also an officer and commissary of the Inquisition. As an administrator he walked 900 miles visiting his provincial area. He promoted education and built (and actively helped build—since he himself cut trees in the sierra to get wood for church floors) convents and churches. He was a noted preacher, and many of his sermons were printed in Mexico City, Guatemala, and Madrid; they have been catalogued by the bibliographer Beristain. Arlegui's most important work is *Crónica de la santa provincia de nuestro P. San Francisco de Zacatecas* (Mexico City 1737; repr. 1851). It is divided into five parts: part one, the origin of the custody of Zacatecas; part two, the founding of monasteries; part three, Indian customs and the conflicts with Indians; part four, biographies of martyred friars; part five, biographies of famous Franciscans. The chronicle is inaccurate for the early period but becomes more exact for the late 17th and the early 18th century. It closes with 1733. Arlegui stated that his order then had in New Spain 10 provinces with 3,200 religious, 397 convents, 122 missionary centers among the pagans, 4 apostolic colleges, and 187 professorships of theology, grammar, rhetoric, and the various native languages.

Bibliography: J. M. BERISTAIN DE SOUZA, *Biblioteca hispanoamericana septentrional,* 5 v. in 2 (3d ed. Mexico City 1947).

[E. GÓMEZ-TAGLE]

ARLES

A city on the Rhône, department of Bouches-du-Rhône, France, 55 miles northwest of Marseilles, formerly the seat of an archbishopric, with a population in 1962 of 42,353.

Secular History. There is no knowledge of a settlement on the site by the native Ligurians, but by the 6th century B.C. Ionians from Marseilles had established a trading post there called Theline, and by the 4th century B.C. the port was being designated as Arelate. In 46 B.C. Julius Caesar gave his name to the community of veterans located there as the *colonia Julia Paterna Arelate Sextanorum.* The Romans, under Caius Marius *c.* 104 B.C. had linked Arles to the Mediterranean by canal, and the city came to exercise a monopoly over the river traffic of lower Provence. Impressive ruins—an amphitheater, forum, and theater (all of the Augustan Age), baths (Constantinian), and the city walls (late Empire)—witness to Arles's splendor in this period. After A.D. 353 the city was named *Constantia* in honor of Constantius II (350–361) who resided there. The prefecture of the Gauls was transferred from Trier to Arles *c.* 395, and in 418 the city was made the seat of the assembly of the seven Gallic provinces.

Arles was controlled by the Visigoths from *c.* 480 to 508–510, then by the Ostrogoths to 536, and thereafter by the Franks. When the Carolingian empire broke up, the city in 879 was incorporated into the kingdom of Provence-Vienne. In 947 the kingdom of Burgundy-Provence was constituted, and this in turn passed under the titular control of the Holy Roman Empire in 1032. Arles was held by the counts of Barcelona from 1113 to 1245 and, through marriage, by the house of Anjou-Naples from 1246 to 1481. On the death of Charles III of Anjou, Dec. 11, 1481, Arles and Provence were ceded to Louis XI of France.

Church History. The presence of Christianity at Arles before the middle of the 3d century cannot be documented. *Gregory of Tours (*Franc.* 1.30) attributes its evangelization to Bishop Trophimus in 250. A see was soon established, for about 254 Bishop Marcianus of Arles had embraced the teachings of *Novatian (Cyprian, *Epist.* 68). In connection with the Donatist question (*see* DONATISM) a council of Western bishops was held at Arles in 314 under the presidency of its bishop, Marinus. In the long list of Arles's prelates (probably 94 in all) eminent names appear: SS. *Honoratus (d. 429?), *Hilary (d. 449), *Caesarius (d. 542), and *Aurelian (d. 551); Archbishops Rotlandus, (d. 869) and Rostagnus (d. after 904); Bl. *Louis d'Aleman (d. 1450) and its last archbishop, Jean Marie Dulau, a victim of the Paris massacre of Sept. 2, 1792.

The council of Turin *c.* 398 (can. 2) was prepared to recognize Arles' metropolitan authority over neighboring dioceses within the civil *provincia Viennensis.* March 22, 417, Pope *Zosimus extended Arles' prerogative to all the sees of the civil provinces of Vienne and Narbonne I and II (Jaffé K 328), but in 422 Boniface I withdrew Narbonne I from the metropolitan authority of Arles (Jaffé K 362). *Leo I abolished this metropolitanate altogether on July 8, 445, only to reestablish it in 450 over all but four of the dioceses in the Vienne province, as well as over the dioceses of Narbonne II and, probably, of Alpes-Maritime (Jaffé K 407, 450). The erection of Aix and Embrun as archdioceses in 794 limited Arles' jurisdiction to eight sees stretching from Marseilles to Trois-Châteaux, though by the 10th or 11th century the Dioceses of Antibes and Vence were also subject to Arles. The erection of Avignon as an archbishopric in 1475 withdrew four suffragans from Arles, which itself was abolished as an episcopal see by the Concordat of 1801. Today Arles is an archdeanery in the Archdiocese of Aix-en-Provence (whose ordinary adds Arles and Embrun to his title) with the parishes of Saint-Trophime, Saint-Césaire, Saint-Julien, and Notre Dame de La Major within the city proper, and that of Trinquetaille on the west bank of the Rhône.

Arles has been the scene of numerous diocesan synods (the series between 1410 and 1570 is unique in its documentation) and of many broader councils: in 314, 353, 443–452, 451, 455, 475–480, 524, 554, 813, 1211, 1234, 1263, 1275. The archbishop of Arles has several times served as papal vicar for France, a dignity that can be documented for 417, 514, 545, 546, 557, 595, and

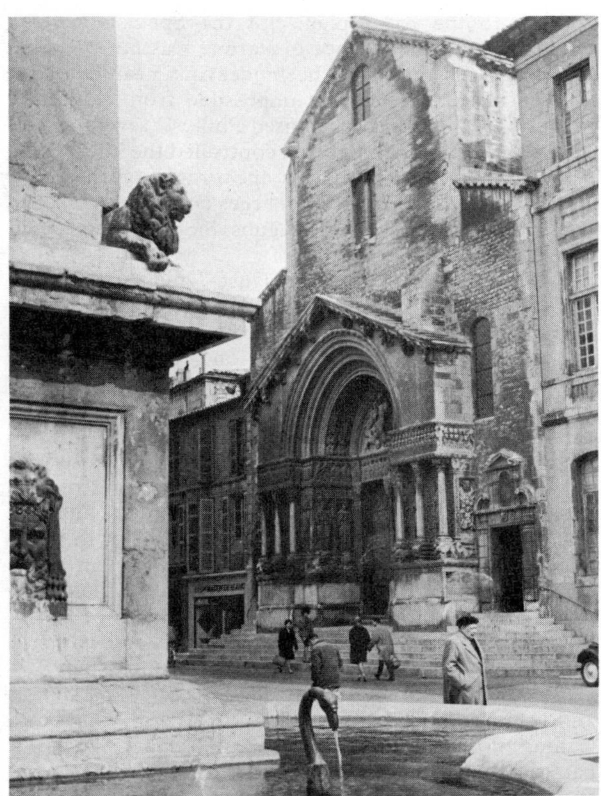

Church of Saint-Trophime at Arles.

878 (Jaffé 328, 769, 913, 918, 944, 1374, and 3148).

Architecture. The paleochristian archeology of the city is not without difficulties. That the cathedral (probably the site of the council of 314) was known as St. Stephen's by 449 appears from the *Vita s. Hilarii* (28). Originally it seems to have stood at the inner angle of the southeast corner of the city walls, where the Asile de Saint-Césaire now stands on the Rue Vauban. During the pontificate of St. Caesarius (502–542) the female monastery of St. John was transferred to this place from its first site at Aliscamps and by 524 had been provided with the basilica S. Mariae. It is the contention of F. Benoît (*Villes,* 18) that this monastic church was but a reworking of the ancient cathedral and that this latter had already (before 449) been relocated at the center of the city, site of today's Saint-Trophime's on the Place de la Republique. The present writer has argued against this view, contending that the cathedral continued at the original location all through the episcopate of St. Caesarius and that the nuns' church was thus a flanking edifice (Beck, 363–368); and that the ancient pavement underlying Saint-Trophime's (the oldest portions of the present church date from the 8th century) probably belonged to the basilica Constantia, mentioned in the *Vita s. Hilarii* (13).

There is no contemporary evidence for the claim made by an inscription in the vestibule of the church of Notre Dame de La Major that it was dedicated in 453. Its most ancient sections date from the 12th century, yet it does stand on the site of a pagan temple. The basilica Apostolorum et Martyrum connected with the men's monastery founded by St. *Aurelian in 546 or 548 (*Regula ad monachos,* PL 68:395) is later localized by *Gregory I (*Reg.* 9.216) as within the city walls. This cannot, therefore, be identified with the basilica SS. Petri et Pauli, founded by 530, which corresponds with the actual S. Pierre des Mouleirés, just to the east of the city's modern cemetery (see Benoît, *Provence historique,* Jan.–March 1957, 8–21). However, the basilica S. Crucis to which the Abbot Florentinus's remains were removed *c.* 588 (CIL 12.944) would seem to fit the church of Sainte-Croix on the Rue de la Roquette.

There are two ancient Arlesian cemeteries: that on the west bank of the Rhône at Trinquetaille, attached to the 12th century church of Saint-Genest de la Colonne, which probably marks the site of the martyrdom of St. *Genesius (d. 303?); and the famed Aliscamps (southeast of Arles) with its avenue of Merovingian stone sepulchres and the church of St. Honoratus, which, though rebuilt in the 9th and 12th centuries, still contains a monolithic threshold of the basilica Beati Genesii where St. Honoratus was interred in 429 or 430.

Bibliography: L. Royer, DHGE 4:231–243. J. Gilbert, *Arles gréco-romaine* (Aix-en-Provence 1949). H. G. J. Beck, *The Pastoral Care of Souls in South-East France During the Sixth Century* (AnalGreg 51; Rome 1950). *Villes episcopales de Provence,* ed. F. Benoît et al. (Paris 1954). R. Busquet, *Histoire de Provence* (Monaco 1955). G. Baader, LexThK² 1:864–865. M. C. McCarthy, *The Rule for Nuns of St. Caesarius of Arles* (Washington 1960). **Illustration credit:** Arthur O'Leary.

[H. G. J. BECK]

ARMADA, THE SPANISH

A naval expedition sent in 1588 by King Philip II to rendezvous with the Spanish army in the Netherlands and to escort it across the English Channel in order to effect the conquest of England. Philip II embarked on this enterprise against Queen Elizabeth I after the execution of Mary, Queen of Scots, on Feb. 18, 1587. Mary's failure to accede to the English throne had removed the threat of strong alliance between England and France that might have effectively closed the English Channel to Spain, thereby rendering Philip's position in the Spanish Netherlands intolerable. Until 1587 many cogent economic, strategic, and diplomatic reasons favored peace between Philip and Elizabeth. Since 1567, however, seamen such as John Hawkins and Francis Drake had encroached on Spain's trade monopoly with her American colonies, and had acted as privateers against Spanish ports and shipping. Elizabeth, moreover, fearing the effects that a victorious Spanish suppression of the Dutch revolt would have on the Protestant cause and on England's national security and commerce, had supplied the Dutch with men, money, and material.

Preparation of the Fleet. In 1587 Philip II began to fit out the expedition against England, but was delayed by Drake's pillaging of Cadiz harbor and his blockading operations off the Portuguese coast. His destruction of available supplies of seasoned barrel staves destined for the preservation of the Armada's provisions further jeopardized its success. In February 1588, Philip II placed Alonzo Pérez de Guzmán, Duke of Medina Sidonia, in command. Although he was inexperienced as an admiral, Medina Sidonia nevertheless quickly organized the fleet; by May 30 there were 130 assorted ships carrying 30,000 men at Lisbon, led by a fighting core of 20 galleons. It was forced by storms to put into

Coruña for refitting and reprovisioning. On July 22 a fair wind for England blew the Armada northward, forcing at the same time the providential turnabout of an English fleet that had been sailing to engage the Spaniards in their home waters.

To prevent any landing on the English coast and to destroy the Armada were the objectives of the English fleet, comprising 21 of the fastest, most modern, and best-armed galleons in Europe, equal to and often larger than their Spanish counterparts. These warships, commanded by the experienced Admirals John Hawkins, Martin Frobisher, and Francis Drake under First Lord Howard of Effingham, were supported by 151 other armed vessels.

The Encounter. As the Armada, arrayed in an impregnable crescentlike formation slowly plodded up the Channel between July 31 and August 6, two concepts of naval warfare clashed in the greatest sea battle in history to that time. The Spanish with their high forecastled and pooped galleons filled with soldiers strove to lure the English ships within grappling distance and capture them. The English with their more seaworthy and faster galleons hoped to sink their opponents with long-range culverin cannon. When the Armada anchored at Calais roads, both sides had practically exhausted their supply of shot without having inflicted significant damage on each other.

Medina Sidonia had up to this point succeeded according to the royal plan, but the Spanish general, Alexander Farnese, Prince of Parma, was not prepared to embark his troops at the rendezvous near Dunkirk. He considered the venture impossible from a military point of view and had so advised Philip II several times. Heavily armed Dutch flyboats controlled the intervening waters between the Armada's anchorage and the coast, so that before Parma's troop barges could have reached the protection of the galleons' guns, these flyboats would have decimated them.

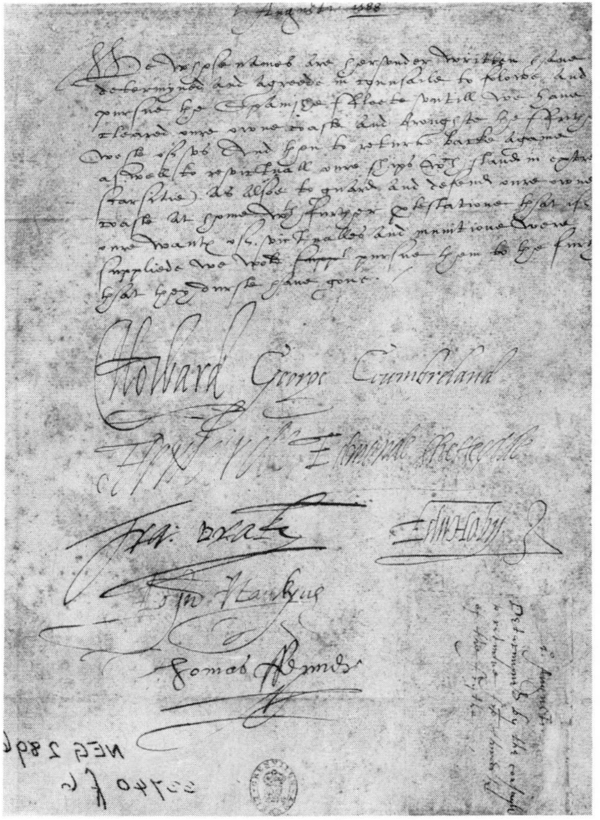

Original draft, dated Aug. 1, 1588 (O.S.), of an English council of war held immediately after the defeat of the Spanish Armada. Signatures include the Earls of Cumberland and Sheffield, Francis Drake, and John Hawkins.

Defeat. On the night of August 7 five English fireships threw the anchored Spaniards into a panic, causing them to slip their cables and scatter. Medina Sidonia again reassembled his fleet and on August 8 the last battle began. The English finally realized that if they were to destroy the enemy they must move in close to deliver really damaging broadsides. Having exhausted their supply of large shot, the Spanish sustained serious damage, which ended short of complete destruction when the English also ran out of cannon balls. On August 9 after escaping destruction again on the Zeeland sandbars, the Armada sailed into the North Sea. The English pursued the Spanish northward until on August 12 they turned wearily into the Firth of Forth, satisfied that the immediate danger of invasion was past.

Medina Sidonia now issued orders that the desperate fleet would sail north around the Shetland Islands and southward into the Atlantic, giving wide berth to the inhospitable western coast of Ireland. Sixty-four battered hulks, which had followed the Admiral's instructions, limped into northern Spanish ports at the end of September carrying 9,000 sick and dying men.

Bibliography: G. MATTINGLY, *The Armada* (Boston 1959); *The "Invincible" Armada and Elizabethan England* (Ithaca, N.Y. 1963). M. A. LEWIS, *Armada Guns, A Comparative Study of English and Spanish Armaments* (London 1961). T. WOODROOFFE, *The Enterprise of England* (London 1958). J. A. WILLIAMSON, *The Age of Drake* (London 1938); *Hawkins of Plymouth* (London 1949). J. S. CORBETT, *Drake and the Tudor Navy,* 2 v. (New York 1898). A. L. ROWSE, *The Expansion of Elizabethan England* (New York 1955). R. B. MERRIMAN, *The Rise of the Spanish Empire in the Old World and in the New,* 4 v. (New York 1934). L. VAN DER ESSEN, *Alexandre Farnèse,* 5 v. (Brussels 1933–37). A. MCKEE, *From Merciless Invaders: An Eye-Witness Account of the Spanish Armada* (London 1963).
Illustration credit: Courtesy of the Trustees of the British Museum.

[R. H. TRAME]

ARMADIUM, a derivative form of the Latin word *armarium* (closet, chest, or cupboard). In Italian it became *armadio* and in English *ambry or aumbry. In medieval churches the armarium was a small chest suspended near the altar or a recess in the wall where the sacred vessels were kept. In the great Benedictine abbeys of the Middle Ages, such as Cluny, the word referred most often to the library or the room where the books were kept. In the 11th-century Anglo-Saxon glossary compiled by Aelfric, the word "bochard" or book-hoard, meaning library, is interpreted by *bibliotheca vel armarium;* and a monastic proverb maintains that *claustrum sine armadio est quasi castrum sine armentario* (a monastery without a library is like a fortress without an arsenal). In another form, almery, confused with almonry, it refers to a chest or room in which the alms were kept that were to be distributed to the poor. In some monasteries and churches, particularly in Germany, the word armarium was used with reference to

An armadium housing manuscripts of the four Gospels; detail of a mosaic of the 5th century in the Mausoleum of Galla Placidia at Ravenna.

the sacristy, probably because the precious books and manuscripts were often preserved there. Roman Canon Law forbade the reservation of the Blessed Sacrament in the armadium, but the practice is common in Anglican churches.

Bibliography: H. Thurston, CE 2:107. Cross ODCC 110, s.v. aumbry. H. Held, LexThK² 1:867. G. Matthiae, EncCatt 1: 1952. F. A. Gasquet, *English Monastic Life* (London 1904) 51–55. E. Maffei, *La Réservation eucharistique jusqu'à la Renaissance* (Brussels 1942). S. J. P. van Dijk and J. H. Walker, *The Myth of the Aumbry* (London 1957). F. Cognass and P. Toesca, EncIt 4:404–405. **Illustration credit:** Anderson-Art Reference Bureau.

[E. E. MALONE]

ARMAGEDDON, the place where, according to Ap 16.16, the devil and his two *antichrists will summon the kings of the earth for the final battle with the forces of good (similarly in 19.11–21, before the millennium; in 20.7–10, after the millennium). The name Armageddon (or Armagedo) was doubtless suggested by Za 12.11, which localizes the great mourning for Adadremmon "in the plain of Mageddon." Since the author of the Book of *Apocalypse states that Armageddon [ʽΑρμαγεδ(δ)ών] is a Hebrew name, he no doubt had in mind Hebrew *har* m^{e}*giddô* [the mountain(s) of Mageddo]. But *Mageddo (Megiddo), the scene of the defeat of the Canaanite kings (Jgs 5.19) and of the tragic death of Josia (4 Kgs 23.29; 2 Chr 35.22–25), although close to the Carmel Range, is on the Plain of *Esdraelon and therefore not a "mountain." Moreover, apocalyptic tradition makes the environs of Jerusalem the stage for the last great conflict (Za 12.2–9; 14.2; Jl 4.1–2; Is 29.1–8; 4 Esdras 13.1–38; Ap 20.7–10). None of the proposed explanations for this crux has won appreciable acceptance.

Bibliography: C. C. Torrey, HarvThRev 31 (1938) 237–248. J. Jeremias, ZNTWiss 31 (1932) 73–77; Kittel ThW 1:467–468. J. Michl, LexThK² 5:14. A. Romeo, EncCatt 1:1952–53. Enc DictBibl 137.

[E. F. SIEGMAN]

ARMAGH, ARCHDIOCESE OF (ARMACHANUS)

Metropolitan see, which, with *Cashel and Emly, *Dublin, and *Tuam, since 1152, has been the primatial see of "all Ireland"; Armagh is situated in the southern part of Northern Ireland. In 1963 it had 55 parishes, 183 secular and 121 religious priests, 199 men in 18 religious houses, 603 women in 20 convents, and 144,500 Catholics in a population of 215,240. It is 1,305 square miles in area. Its eight suffragans, which had 1,100 secular and 270 religious priests, 2,558 sisters, and 812,800 Catholics, were: Ardagh and Clonmacnois (united in 1729), Clogher, Derry, Down and Connor (united in 1439), Dromore, Kilmore, Meath, and Raphoe.

Founded by St. *Patrick *c.* 450, Armagh developed on Irish monastic lines; and its abbots were also bishops until *c.* 750. The school was famous both in Great Britain and on the Continent. Armagh's ecclesiastical preeminence appears in documents from 640 and in periodic visitations of other provinces carried on from the 8th century by its head, a cleric who bore the title of *Comharba Phádraig* (successor of Patrick). Despite a *Culdee foundation (8th-16th century), Ar-

"The Cross of Muiredach," at Monasterboice, in the Archdiocese of Armagh. This early 10th-century monument is considered the finest surviving example of the Irish carved medieval crosses.

magh declined with the coming of Danish raids and local warfare (9th–10th centuries). The way was thus opened for the intrusion of lay abbots from a local family, the Clann Sínaigh (965–1129), one of whom, Ceallach (St. Celsus), ended the abuse by having himself consecrated bishop (1106). At the Synod of Rathbreasail (1111), which assigned jurisdictions to Irish sees, Armagh received what is roughly its present territory in the Counties of Armagh, Tyrone, and Derry (Northern Ireland) and in Louth and Meath (Irish Republic). Ceallach chose as his successor St. *Malachy, who resigned the see after much opposition. Gelasius (1137–74) received the pallium at the Synod of Kells (1152); Concord (1174–75) is still venerated at *Chambéry, where he died.

The Anglo-Norman invasion brought a struggle between Irish and English for the see and prepared the ground for conflicts with Dublin about the primacy. Maolpadraig O'Scanlan (1261–70) built a larger cathedral, of which the present Protestant cathedral is an 18th-century rebuilding. Nicholas Mac Maolíosa (1272–1303) was the last Irish prelate till the Reformation. Of the Norman prelates, the most noteworthy was *Richard Fitzralph (1346–60), known for his contests with the mendicant orders. In these years the see was virtually partitioned between the Irish in Armagh, Tyrone, and Derry under an Irish dean and the English in Louth, where the archbishop resided. At the Reformation, George Cromer (1521–42) and George *Dowdall (1553–58) opposed doctrinal changes but failed to provide the leadership of their successors.

Outstanding prelates under the *penal laws were Richard Creagh (1564–85), who spent 18 years in the Tower of London before his death, Hugh O'Reilly (1628–53), who played a prominent part in the Confederation of Kilkenny, Edmund *O'Reilly (1657–69), Oliver *Plunket (1669–81), and Hugh McMahon (1714–37), who defended Armagh's primatial rights against Dublin. Peter Lombard (1601–25) and Hugh McCaughwell (1626), two of Armagh's distinguished scholars, spent their lives in exile. In 1731 the see still had 26 places of worship served by 77 secular priests and 22 friars.

The cathedral of St. Patrick at Armagh, Ireland.

The easing of persecution in the late 18th century allowed many small churches to be built. Discipline was restored by Richard O'Reilly (1787–1818). William Crolly (1835–49) took up residence in Armagh and began the building of the neo-Gothic St. Patrick Cathedral (dedicated in 1873). Paul *Cullen (1849–52) transferred to Dublin after the national synod of Thurles (1850). Under Joseph Dixon (1852–66) the diocesan chapter was reconstituted; it now numbers 16 members. Michael Logue (1887–1924) and his successors, Patrick O'Donnell (1924–27), Joseph *MacRory (1928–45), John D'Alton (1946–63), and William Conway (1963–), have been cardinals of Armagh. The minor seminary has been staffed by Vincentians since 1861. Religious houses in the archdiocese included the Cistercian Abbey of *Mellifont. The archdiocese has 228 primary, 16 secondary, and 5 technical schools. The shrines of St. *Brigid (Faughart) and Bl. Oliver Plunket (Drogheda) attract many pilgrims.

Bibliography: J. STUART, *Historical Memoirs of . . . Armagh*, ed. A. COLEMAN (Dublin 1900). H. J. LAWLOR and R. I. BEST, *The Ancient List of the Coarbs of Patrick* (Dublin 1919). J. B. LESLIE, *Armagh Clergy and Parishes* (Dundalk 1911; suppl. 1948). A. GWYNN, *The Medieval Province of Armagh, 1470–1545* (Dundalk 1946). *Seanchas Ardmhacha* (Armagh 1954–), annual journal of the Armagh Diocesan Historical Society, ed. T. Ó FIAICH. *Irish Catholic Directory*, annual. *Catholic Directory for Archdiocese of Armagh* (1964). AnnPont (1964) 38.

[T. Ó FIAICH]

ARMAGNAC, GEORGES D', French cardinal, diplomat, and humanist; b. *c.* 1500; d. Avignon, June 5, 1585. He was the natural son of the Baron de Caussade, and became, through the favor of his patroness Marguerite of Angoulême, bishop of Rodez and governor of Armagnac and Rouergue in 1530. As the ambassador of Francis I to Venice (1536 to 1538) to prevent an alliance between Venice and Charles V, he gained skill in diplomacy. He was ambassador to Rome, 1540 to 1545, with a similar mission, and received the cardinal's hat in 1544. After his recovery from a serious illness he became archbishop of Tours (1545–51), and in 1552 archbishop of Toulouse and lieutenant-general of Languedoc. Tolerant by nature, he worked against heresy and civil war in the south of France. In 1561 he participated in the Conference of *Poissy. His most difficult task was to govern the papal state of Avignon in the name of the king of France, 1565 to 1585. From his youth he was a patron and enthusiast of letters and had one of the best libraries of his time. His correspondence contains more than 1,000 letters, and his dispatches in archives of France and Italy, though unstudied, are very important historical sources.

Bibliography: C. SAMARAN, DHGE 4:263–267. E. LEDOS, DictBiogFranc 3:667–679. J. GRISAR, LexThK[2] 1:866–867.

[F. D. S. BORAN]

ARMAND DE BELVÉZER, or de Beauvoir, Dominican theologian; b. near Milau (Aveyron), 2d half of 13th century; place and date of death unknown. In 1313 he was sent on a mission to Emperor Henry VII by Clement V. He taught theology in the priory at Montpellier and was regent of studies there in 1326. He was master of the sacred palace at Avignon from 1328 to 1334. He took part in the discussions stimulated by John XXII's sermon on the beatific vision, and lost favor with the Pope because of his opposed position. His commentary on the *De ente et essentia* shows him to be closer to St. Thomas than to the *via moderna.* His *declaratio difficiliorum dictorum et dictionum in theologia* (Lyons 1495) is interesting for the history of the Thomist school. His *Collationes* on the Psalter, as well as most of his works, have remained unedited. His letters concerning the beatific vision and his responses written as master of the sacred palace may be found in the public library of Cambridge, Ji. 3.10, fol. 10–38; 95.

Bibliography: A. DUVAL, *Catholicisme* 1:840–841. P. MANDONNET, DTC 1.2:1887–88. F. PUGLIESE, EncCatt 1:1954–55. Quétif-Echard 1.2:583–585. P. M. SCHAFF, DHGE 4: 274–275. A. THOMAS, HistLittFranc 36:265–295. M. H. LAURENT, "Armand de Belvézer et son commentaire sur le *De ente et essentia,*" RevThom 35 (1930) 426–436.

[A. DUVAL]

ARMELLINI, MARIANO, Benedictine historian; b. Ancona, Dec. 10, 1662; d. Foligno, May 4, 1737. He entered the monastery of St. Paul in Rome in 1682. After completing his studies at Monte Cassino, he taught at various Cassinese monasteries from 1687 to 1695. He preached with great success throughout Italy and was appointed abbot of the monastery at Siena by Pope Innocent XIII (1722). He was sent to the monastery of St. Peter at Assisi (1729) and to the monastery of St. Felician, near Foligno (1734). He is an eminent historian of the Cassinese congregation and wrote the well-known *Bibliotheca Benedictino-Cassinesis* (2 v. Assisi 1731–32), *Appendix de viris literis illustribus a congregatione Casinensi* (Foligno 1732), *Additiones et correctiones bibliothecae Benedictino-Casinensis* (Foligno 1735–36), *Catologi tres episcoporum, reformatorum et virorum sanctitate illustrium e congregatione Casinensi* (Assisi 1755).

Bibliography: Hurter Nomencl 2:1212. M. ZIEGELBAUER, *Historia rei literariae ordinis S. Benedicti . . .* , 4 v. (Augsburg 1754) v.3. T. LECCISOTTI, EncCatt 1:1956–57. A. PRÉVOST, DHGE 4: 283. Kapsner BenBibl 1:29.

[N. R. SKVARLA]

ARMENIA

Greater Armenia comprised the land bordered on the north by the Kura River, on the east by the Caspian Sea, on the south by Mesopotamia, and on the west by the Euphrates River. It was inhabited in the 13th century B.C., as both Assyrian and Urartian cuneiform monuments indicate. The identity of the Urartian people is preserved by association with the Ararat of the Bible (Gen 8.4; Is 37.38; Jer 51.27). Between 612 and 582 B.C. Indogermanic tribes from Armenia, apparently coming from the Thrasic-Phrygian Tsaph, invaded the country and eventually blended with the Urartian people; but they fell under the domination of the Medes and Persians.

Early History. Artaxias, or Artashēs, was appointed governor by Antiochus the Great (223–187) and is said to have founded Artaxata, or Artashat, on the advice of Hannibal. Tigranes II, after extending his reign over the whole of Armenia, was defeated by Lucullus and Pompey (66 B.C.). Tiridates was crowned in Rome

Fig. 1. King Tigranes II, the Great, obverse of a tetradrachma struck during his reign.

by Nero (A.D. 66), and a pact with the Romans made the Armenian kings dependent on the Parthians. Under Marcus Aurelius (161–180) Artaxata was destroyed and a new capital erected at *Valarshapat. Tiridates III of the Arsacid dynasty was recognized by Rome (*c.* 296), and Armenia became a Roman protectorate.

The historian Strabo (11.14.6) spoke of an early cult of Ma and of Cybele Attis in Armenia. Under the Persians the god Aramazd, his son Mihr, and two daughters, Anahid and Nane, entered the ancient Armenian mythology. The goddess Astghik corresponded to the Assyrian Ishtar and was honored at Ashtishat; and the god Vahagn was the popular patron of virility, both physical and moral. A well-organized pagan priesthood presided over the nation's religion.

Christianity. There is no evidence of the presence of Christian missionaries in Armenia before the 3d century. Legend attributed a 1st-century evangelization to the Apostles Thaddeus and Bartholomew, and the false history of *Abgar and Addai had its setting there. The earliest known Christianization of the country begins with the missionary efforts of *Gregory the Illuminator (Lusaworitsch), who received episcopal consecration in Cappadocia and converted King Tiridates III at the end of the 3d century. *Athanasius of Alexandria mentions the presence of Christianity in Armenia *c.* 274 (*De Incarn.* PG 25:118), and under King Chosroes III (330–339) efforts were made to evangelize the Georgians and Albanians. The Church with its see at Valarshapat was considered a suffragan of Cappadocia, but the bishopric remained in the possession of Gregory's family. His son Aristaces took part in the Council of Nicaea (325). The new religion was greatly opposed by the pagan priests who were aided by some of the princes, and several of the bishops were put to death for opposing the King's conduct. Bishop Isaac signed a letter to Emperor Jovian (363–364) from the Council of Antioch (Socrates, *Hist. eccl.* 3.25), and King Arsaces (Arshak) II (350–367) selected *Nerses the Great as bishop in 353. Consecrated in

Cappadocia, he held a synod at Ashtishat, which legislated regarding matrimonial impediments for the nobles (Nakharars), the abolition of pagan funeral customs, and the establishment of hospitals and leprosaria. Under King Pap (367–374) Nerses signed the letter sent by *Basil of Cappadocia to the bishops of Italy and Gaul in 372 (Basil, *Epist.* 82); but a short while later he was assassinated by the King, and Basil of Caesarea had to intervene in subsequent affairs (*Epist.* 120, 122).

The Church was persecuted under King Yazdgard I (399–420), but through the intervention of Emperor Theodosius II Christians obtained toleration from King Vahrām V (*c.* 421–439). King Chosroes selected *Isaac the Great as bishop (*c.* 390–438), and with the aid of *Mesrop, the calligrapher Rufinus, and a group of young monks educated in the West established an alphabet and translated the Bible and the Greek and Syrian works of the Church Fathers, thereby originating an *Armenian Christian literature. When the see was brought under the control of Constantinople, Byzantine aid was given to the bishops for schools and missionary enterprises. After the Council of *Ephesus (431) the Armenian bishops requested information regarding Nestorianism and received the renowned Tome of Proclus to the Armenians. A council was held at Ashtishat (435) accepting the *Theotokos.

In the 5th century the term catholicos came into use as the official title for the metropolitan. Catholicos Joseph (441–453) held a synod of 20 bishops that condemned the Messalians, or *Paulicians, in 444; and in 450 at Artashat 17 bishops refused the invitation of the Persian King to embrace the cult of the god Aramazd. A persecution followed, and, after a revolt under the noble military leader *Vardan Mamikonian, Archbishop Gevund and a number of clerics were martyred (454). Vahan, nephew of Vardan, persuaded King Kavâdh I (488–551) to remove the fire symbol from Armenia, and with Byzantine assistance peace was restored in 506.

Prevented from attending the Council of Chalcedon (451) by internal troubles, the Armenian bishops had a faulty knowledge of the problems posed by *Monophysitism, and in 506 at a synod in *Dwin they accepted the *Henoticon of Zeno. Catholicos Nerses II (548–557) and 17 bishops came under the influence of followers of *Julian of Halicarnassus and repudiated the doctrines of the Council of Chalcedon.

In 572 Catholicos John II fled to Constantinople after the revolt against the Persians by Vardan II and rallied to the Chalcedonian doctrine. Emperor *Maurice obtained western Armenia to the river Ozal from King Chosroes Abharvēz II (590–628) and held a council in Constantinople for its 21 bishops. But Catholicos Moses II (574–604) of Dwin refused to attend and was replaced by John III (592–610). The Iberian Catholics had accepted the teachings of the Council of Chalcedon as a result of a letter of *John of Jerusalem (575–593); and Kyrion, Archbishop of Mts'khet'a, entered into communion with Pope Gregory I (590–604). The Syro-Armenian Synod at Ctesiphon (*c.* 614) rejected Chalcedon, but the synod held by Catholicos Eger under Emperor *Heraclius (632) at Karin (Erzurum) accepted it. Despite the intervention of the philosopher David, the third Council of Dwin in 649 accepted Monophysitism under Catholicos Nerses II at the insistence of the Arab conquerors, who were anxious to separate the Armenians from the Byzantines. When Emperor Constans II (653) dominated the land, the catholicos returned to Dyophysite doctrine. However, the council in Trullo (692) accused the Armenians of using wine unmixed with water in the liturgy and of sacrificing animals (cc. 32, 33, 81, 99).

Arab Rule. Although the Arab conquerors at first dealt leniently with the Catholics, they soon turned to intimidating and persecuting them for their revolts. They appointed governors in Dwin from among the Armenian nobles: Theodorus (654–662), Gregor Mamikonian (662–685), and Ashot Bagratuni (686–696). But after the rebellion of the nobles at Vardanakert the government was put into the hands of Mohammedan rulers. An uprising in 772 resulted in a cruel suppression with the burning of churches, convents, and the wiping out of a large portion of the aristocracy.

Several 8th-century synods at Manzikert dealt with the Christological doctrines in dispute in Byzantium, and the catholicos found it necessary to leave the see of Dwin because of the hostility of the Moslems. Under the 'Abbāsids the lot of the Christians became almost intolerable, and frequent revolts were put down with intensified persecutions.

In 859, however, the Caliph Motawakel-Billah named Ashot Bagratuni governor with the title prince of princes, and for 2 centuries this dynasty managed to pursue a policy of rebuilding the country and Church despite continual wars with the Byzantines, the Mohammedans, and the Armenian dynasty of the Artsruni. Under the rulers Ashot I (V) the Great (855–890), Ashot III (VII) the Merciful (952–977), Sembat II (977–989), and Gagik I, (989–1020) the capital at *Ani became one of the principal cities of the Orient; commerce and literature flourished. Vahan, Bishop of Siunia, elected catholicos at Ani (967–971), was in sympathy with the doctrines of the Council of Chalcedon and was opposed by a synod (970) called by King Ashot the Merciful. He was supported by the poet Gregory of Narek. Catholicos Sargis I changed his see to Ani, and Gagik I built a cathedral with the aid of Queen Katramite. The successor of Sargis, Peter I (1019–54), was suspected of treason for his voyages among the Greeks and in 1045 delivered the city of Ani to Emperor Constantine Monomachus, who tried to force Chalcedonian doctrine on the Armenian clergy. However, King Gagik II (d. 1079) repudiated this doctrine and broke the agreement reached with the Byzantines. He was imprisoned and deposed. Catholicos Gregory (Vahrām Pahlav), however, communicated with Pope Gregory VII (1073–85) and received the pallium as well as instructions to subscribe to the Council of Chalcedon.

Internal conflict among the noble families, the Vaspurakan, Agvan, Lori, and Kars, prevented the unification of the country. The Seljuk caliph, Tougrul Bey invaded the Euphrates Valley (1048–54) and sacked Sebaste (1059). His nephew Alp-Arslan destroyed Ani (1064), and with the defeat of the Byzantine emperor Romanus IV at Manzikert (1071) the Seljuks were free to conquer Armenia. Many of the aristocracy emigrated to Constantinople and Europe; a large group of nobles and other people fled to the Taurus Mountains.

The Kingdom of Cilicia. During the Sassanian persecutions of the 4th century a number of Armenians had taken refuge in Cilicia; they were joined during the centuries by other of their compatriots. After the assassination of Gagik II (1079), the Armenian prince Ruben (1080–1095) took the fortress of Partzpert and proclaimed the independence of Cilicia (1080). His son Constantine (1095–99) enlarged the territory and made contact with the leaders of the Second *Crusade.

In 1113 Catholicos Basil was succeeded by Gregory III (1113–66), who took part in the Latin Synod at Antioch and was called by *William of Tyre a *doctor eximius.* Pope Innocent II sent him the pallium, and he in turn assured Eugene III of his willingness to accept Roman stipulations regarding the sacrifice of the Mass (Otto of Freising, *Chron.* 1.7.21–33). Catholicos Nersēs IV (1166–73) wrote an elegy on the sacking of Edessa and was called the Gracious (*Šnorhali*) for his theological disquisitions. He entered discussions with the representatives of the Greek Church at Hromcla, and his successor Gregory IV pursued reunion efforts with the Greek Church at the synod of Hromcla in 1179. Gregory was in contact also with Pope Lucius III, whom he assured of his filial submission in 1184 and from whom he received the pallium with a miter and ring.

Prince Thoros I (1100–29) had defeated the army of Malek Shiah, but his brother Leo (1129–38) was defeated by Emperor *John II Comnenus. Thoros II (1145–69) reached an accord with the Byzantine rulers, and the aid given the Third Crusade was rewarded by Pope Celestine III, who acknowledged Leo I the Magnificent (1196–1219) as the monarch of the Armenians. Leo adopted many Western customs and confided the custody of his principal fortresses to the Knights *Templars. Het'um I (1226–70) personally visited the court of the Mongol Khan Mangou and arranged a treaty of peace. However, the *Mamelukes of Egypt invaded Cilicia, and Het'um retired to a monastery in 1270. Under Leo II (1270–89) the kingdom enjoyed a minor renaissance of culture, commerce, and religious life, despite a temporary alienation from Rome over the Templars. Leo's successor Het'um II (1289–1305) and Catholicos Constantine I protested to Pope Gregory IX against the crusaders' attempt to extend the jurisdiction of the Latin Patriarchate of Antioch over Armenia. A synod at Sis (1243) attacked the vices of simony, divorce, and the ordination of children; and the synod of 1251 accepted a decree of Innocent IV on Extreme Unction.

King Het'um II sent John of Montecorvino to Pope Nicholas IV with his testimony of submission (1289), and despite the Pope's attempt to send aid, the Mamelukes captured Hromcla (1292), took Catholicos Stephen prisoner, and carried off the relic of the right arm of Gregory the Illuminator. A synod in Sis (1307) undertook dogmatic and disciplinary reforms in accord with Roman prescriptions, and despite violent opposition from a part of the clergy King Oshin held a council at Adana (1316) that received encouragement from Pope *John XXII (1316–34). The Pope established a college of Dominicans at Aïas and sent 37,722 florins by way of aid. In 1356, Innocent IV approved the constitution of an order of Friars Unifiers, who exercised a fruitful apostolate near Nakhichevan (1440–1766).

Despite the appeals of the popes, the Western princes failed to aid the kingdom of Cilicia; its last king, Leo of Lusignan, was captured by the Emir Ischqtimur, and on being ransomed from the Caliph of Egypt became the guest of Charles VI of France until he died and was buried in the Abbey of St. Denis outside Paris (1393). Cilicia fell under the power of the Tartars and was given up to persecution and plunder. Despite the disarray of the Armenian church its catholicos Constantine VI was represented at the Council of Ferrara-Florence and on Nov. 22, 1439, accepted decrees of the council. Pope Eugene IV sent a letter of gratitude that was received by the Catholicos Gregory IX (1440–53).

Fig. 2. Kings Sembat and Gagik I as donors of the church, relief on the east façade of the main church at the monastery of Haghbat, A.D. 991.

However, opposition to the Council of Florence came from the monks of Oriental Armenia. Four bishops demanded the change of the catholicate to Echmiadzin (Valarshapat) and were excommunicated by Gregory X. In a synod at Echmiadzin 12 bishops elected the monk Cyriacos, who immediately won the support of 12 other bishops and their people. After the fall of Constantinople (1453) Muḥammad II recognized the Armenian bishop Joachim (Hovakim) as patriarch with his palace at Psammathia (1461), and entrusted him with ruling the domestic affairs of all the Armenians in his vast realm.

The catholicos of Sis was restricted to spiritual functions; the city itself (1587) had 12 chapels and the catholicate counted 24 dioceses, 300 priests, 20 convents, and hundreds of monks. Catholicos Khach'atur (1560–84) wrote to Pope Gregory XIII; and his suc-

Fig. 3. Armenia: (a) 1910 photograph (from the southeast) of the basilica at Ereruk, built 6th and 7th centuries. (b) Pre-1906 photograph (from the southwest) of the cathedral at Ani, built between 989 and 1001.

Fig. 4. Reliefs of the early 10th century on the façade of the domed church on the island Aght'amar in Lake Van.

cessor, Catholicos Azaria accepted a profession of Catholic faith. In 1683 another Azaria died in Rome, where he had taken refuge; so too did his successor Gregory Pidzak (1683–91).

Catholicos Stephen V had made a profession of faith in Rome (1548–50), and his successor Michael sent an envoy to the court of Paul IV, who helped found an Armenian printing press in Rome. Pius V gave the Armenians the church of St. Mary of Egypt, and Gregory XIII in his bull *Romana Ecclesia* praised the faith of the Armenians. But Armenia itself was racked between the Turks and the Persians so that the bishops and people were in continual ferment, at times in union with Rome, and at times in schism.

In 1583 the Dominicans had established a province in Trans-Caucasia; and in 1626 the Jesuits opened a house in Alep. They started a mission at Isfahan in 1653 and carried on successful work at Erzurum (1685–91) and Erevan (Yerevan) toward the end of the century despite the outbreak of persecution. The Capuchins arrived in Alep in 1627; and the Carmelites were sent into Persia in 1705. Augustinians and Theatines also worked in Turkey and Georgia. Between 1694 and 1764 the constant struggle between Catholics and Orthodox Armenians for predominence was encouraged by the civil rulers, although Catholicos Moses III, Philip, and James IV of Sis attempted reunion with Rome. Pope Clement XI was in touch with Catholicos Alexander of Dzhulfa (1706–14).

The Armenian order of Antonites and the *Mechitarists sent clerical students to the Urban College in Rome for theological training, thus preserving the secular clergy; and an Armenian archbishopric was established at Lvov in Poland in the 17th century. In the early 18th century the Catholic Patriarchate of Sis was settled in Lebanon and cared for Catholics in Cilicia, Syria, Palestine, Mesopotamia, and Egypt. In 1830 an archbishop-primate was established at *Istanbul; and in 1866 the two branches of the Catholic Church were united under Patriarch Peter IX Hassun. This led to difficulties that were renewed in 1911. A synod was held in Rome (1911) to deal with the reorganization of the Church's governance. But the Ottoman persecutions during and after World War I reduced the clergy by more than half and exterminated up to 2 million of the Christian inhabitants.

Russian Rule. In the late 18th century Russia occupied the territory of Armenia that had formerly been controlled by the Persians and began a systematic attempt to incorporate the Armenians into the Russian state and Orthodox church. Toward the close of the 19th century young Armenian intellectuals educated in the West attempted to found resistance groups: the Hintchak (1889), the Dashnak (1890), and the Ramgavar-Azadakan (1908). They hoped to enlist the aid of the Western powers against Ottoman oppression. They combined with the Young Turks in revolt against the ruler Abdul Hamid II (1897–1909), but were soon repudiated by the Mohammedans.

After World War I Armenia declared its independence (May 28, 1918), but in 1923 the Treaty of Lausanne recognized the incorporation of Armenia in the U.S.S.R. With Yerevan as its capital, it is now one of the 15 Soviet republics. Some 150,000 Armenians returned to the country in 1946 and 1947; but still more than half live in other parts of the world. About 1,200,000 live in other parts of Russia; 630,000, in the Near East, France, and South America; and 250,000, in the United States.

The Orthodox Armenian Church counts 3,500,000

Fig. 5. Obverse of the gold seal of King Leo I of Armenia on a letter concerning the royal succession, dated 1207.

faithful in two catholicates, Echmiadzin and Sis, and two patriarchates, Jerusalem and Istanbul. The Catholicos of Echmiadzin is considered the head of the national Church; the Catholicos of Sis has his residence in Antelias in Lebanon. Bishops are elected by delegates of the clergy and laity; they consecrate vardapet, priests, and deacons, for preaching and teaching. There is both a married and a celibate clergy; the latter usually live in clerical communities and are selected as vardepet and bishops.

For Armenian Catholic Church, *see* ARMENIAN RITE.

Bibliography: V. INGLISIAN, *Armenien in der Bibel* (Vienna 1935). F. KÖNIG, *Handbuch der chaldischen Inschriften,* v.1 (Graz 1955). H. F. TOURNEBIZE, *Histoire politique et religieuse de l'Arménie* (Paris 1910); DHGE 4:290–391. M. ORMANIAN, *The Church of Amenia,* ed. T. POLADIAN, tr. G. M. GREGORY (2d Eng. ed. London 1955). W. DE VRIES, *Der christliche Osten in Geschichte und Gegenwart* (Würzburg 1951). M. J. TERZIAN, *Le Patriarcat de Cilicie et les Arméniens cath.* (Beirut 1955). M. VAN DEN OUDENRIJN, OrChr 40 (1956) 94–112; LexThK[2] 1:869–873. N. ADONTZ, *Histoire de l'Arménie* (Paris 1946). J. SANDALGIAN, *Les Inscriptions cunéiforms urartiques* (Venice 1900). R. KHERUMIAN, *Les Arméniens* (Paris 1941). S. WEBER, *Die katholische Kirche in Armenien* (Freiburg 1903). H. HAGOPIAN, *The Relations of the Armenians and the Franks* (Boston 1905). **Illustration credits:** Fig. 1, Courtesy of the Trustees of the British Museum. Figs. 2, 3*a*, 3*b*, and 4, Istituto per la Collaborazione Culturale. Fig. 5, Archivio Segreto Vaticano.

[N. M. SETIAN]

ARMENIAN ART

*Armenia adopted Christianity from the end of the 3d century when the country became a protectorate of the Roman Empire; the monuments inspired by the new religion occupy an important place in the history of medieval art.

The oldest surviving churches (e.g., Ereruk, Kasakh) are vaulted basilicas, but recent excavations at the Cathedral of Echmiadzin reveal that already in the 5th century the square with four salient apses and free-standing piers supporting a dome were used. The 6th and 7th centuries produced variations of the centralized-dome plan: the niche-buttressed square of different types (e.g., St. Hrip'simé, Artik, Bagaran); the cross inscribed in a square (e.g., Mren, St. Gayane); trefoils and quatrefoils (e.g., T'alin, Zvart'nots); and more complex polygonal forms (e.g., Eghvard). The massive walls sometimes hide the inner divisions which are merely indicated by triangular slits on the outer walls. From the 9th to 13th centuries these types were revived with modifications, and new forms were initiated. At the Cathedral of Ani (A.D. 1001), the masterpiece of the architect Trdat, clustered piers support the dome and the slightly pointed arches and vaults are ribbed. Other buildings exhibit various systems of ribbed vaults to support a stone web—antedating Gothic architecture's somewhat different solutions of the same problem.

Stone architecture lent itself to carved decoration, and from an early period onward relief sculpture appears on the façades. Images of Christ and of saints, portraits of donors, and floral and geometric motifs decorate the lintels and the lunettes of the doors and are carved around the windows (e.g., Mren, Ptghni). The Church of Aght'amar, on Lake Van (10th century), is the outstanding and earliest medieval example of a church entirely covered with relief sculpture. Funerary steles with figured representations (5th to 7th centuries), and later cross-stones decorated with intricate interlaces, are noteworthy too.

There are but few remnants of wall paintings, and the painter's art can best be studied in illuminated manuscripts. In many manuscripts of the 10th and 11th centuries (e.g., Gospels of Queen Mlk'e and of Trebizond) the rich ornamental designs and figure compositions, painted in vivid colors on a gold ground, have a monumental character. In the iconography of the Gospel scenes one finds, together with schemes derived from early Christian and Byzantine art, original interpretations that show a more realistic approach. This is true of the manuscripts executed in Great Armenia, and even more so of those which were illustrated in the kingdom of Cilicia, where important schools of miniaturists flourished in the 13th and 14th centuries. Works were produced there that rank in artistic quality with the highest achievements of medieval painting.

Bibliography: J. STRZYGOWSKI, *Die Baukunst der Armenier und Europa,* 2 v. (Vienna 1918). J. BALTRUSAITIS, *Études sur l'art médiéval en Géorgie et en Arménie* (Paris 1929); *Le Problème de l'Ogive et l'Arménie* (Paris 1936). K. WEITZMANN, *Die armenische Buchmalerei des 10. und beginnenden 11. Jahrhunderts* (Bamberg 1933). S. DER NERSESSIAN, *Manuscrits arméniens illustrés des XIIe, XIIIe et XIVe siècles de la Bibliothèque des Pères Mekhitharistes de Venise,* 2 v. (Paris 1938); *Armenia and the Byzantine Empire* (Cambridge, Mass. 1945). L. DURNOVO, *Armenian Miniatures,* tr. I. J. UNDERWOOD (New York 1961). G. TSCHUBINASCHWILI, EncWA 1:716–728.

[S. DER NERSESSIAN]

ARMENIAN CHRISTIAN LITERATURE

Spiritual, poetic, doctrinal, didactic, and romantic works written since the advent of Christianity in Armenia (298). Cuneiform inscriptions on rock or tablets throughout the Armenian plateau and the testimony of classical authors witness to the fact that Armenian literature is one of the most ancient in the world. Older historiographers recognized the existence of a high culture and rich literature during the 1st century B.C.,

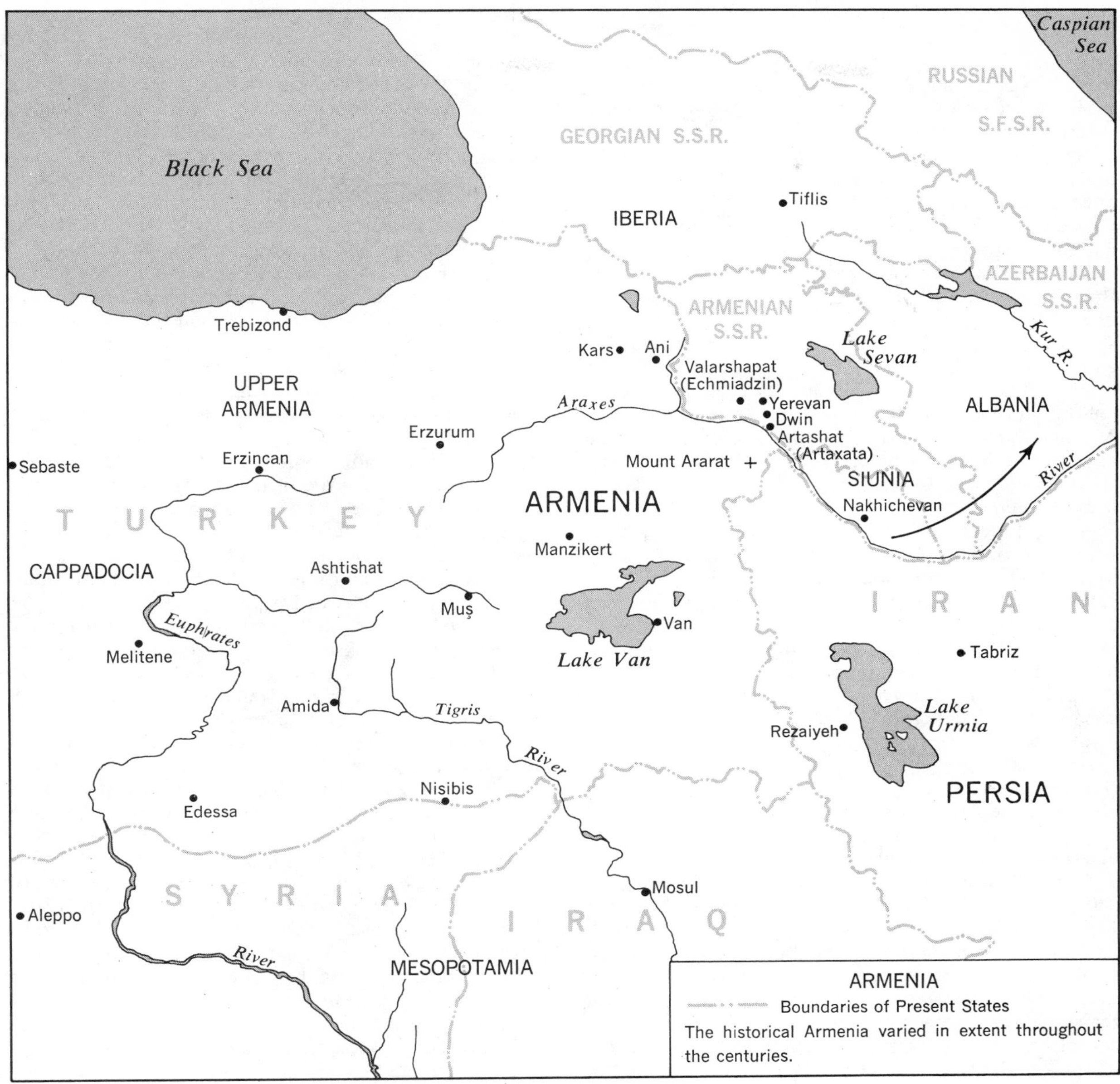

Map of Armenia showing sites important in the development of Christianity in the area.

particularly in drama and playwriting. Plutarch wrote that in that century there were theaters in a number of Armenian cities, the largest of which, built in 69 B.C., was located in Tigranocerta, the capital. King Artavazdus II (94–31), the son and successor of Tigranes the Great, was a talented playwright and director. Literature flourished until A.D. 298, when, inspired by his kinsman, *Gregory the Illuminator, the Arsacid King Tiridates, is said to have denounced it as heathen and destroyed all traces of it, except for some stone inscriptions. These literary monuments were to be replaced by an Armenian Christian literature and culture that had its onset at this time (*c.* 298).

From the Rise of Christian Literature to the Arab Domination. A valuable work of the early Christian period is the story of the founder and first catholicos (patriarch or supreme pontiff) of the Armenian Church, Gregory the Illuminator; its author is unknown. The narrative, based on authentic historical data, although deftly interwoven with vivid human interrelationships and legendary material, describes the martyrdom of the Apostles Thaddeus and Bartholomew, as well as the maidens Gayanē, Ripsimē, and Shołakat' in pre-Christian Armenia; it depicts also the internal political upheavals in which Gregory spent the earlier years of his life, his conversion to Christianity, which apparently was followed by long years of imprisonment in an underground dungeon because of his faith, and his ultimate victory.

According to the testimony of the historian Moses of Khorēn, it was during this period that the earlier versions of the folk epic concerning David of Sasun began to take shape and to harmonize with Christian life and spirit. This epic was to achieve its final form later, in the 8th and 9th centuries, and become one of the great poems of world literature, both in scope and stylistic perfection, but above all by the ideals of universal humanity and the Christian spirit that it evokes.

In a relatively short time the Armenian Church, through sanctuaries, schools, and vast landholdings combined with her moral and spiritual authority, grew, tended to overshadow the Royal House itself, and became an even more powerful force in the internal and external policies of the nation. It was natural that the Church with her spiritual influence should tend to be independent in her external relations. As a consequence, after the Council of *Nicaea I (325) the Church of Armenia was transformed into an individual, national institution and embarked on the task of Armenianizing the nation's entire spiritual culture. In 393 Bp. *Mesrop Mashtots', one of the great scholars and linguists of his time, with the cooperation and sponsorship of the Catholicos Sahak Part'ew, perfected and completed the Armenian alphabet, which is used in its original form to this day. The golden age of Armenian culture and literature began with the translation of the Old and New Testaments for the Armenian Church and people. Earlier scholars considered the Armenian translation of the Gospel so perfect that they named it the "queen of translations."

Meanwhile, Sahak Part'ew and Mesrop Mashtots', who have been canonized by the Armenian Church, founded schools throughout Armenia and established the first Christian college in Ejmiatsin (*Echmiadzin), next to the episcopal palace; and their students became writers, scholars, and translators, many of whom are still held in high esteem as authoritative sources. Classical Armenian, or *Grabar,* became the language of divine service, of instruction in schools, of statesmanship and literature.

Armenian historiography flourished. The books of this category represent the authentic contemporary history of the Armenians and their neighboring nations; in addition, the historical narratives present an artistic and vivid picture of contemporary life.

The chroniclers of the early period include Agathangelus, Koriwn (Koriun), Faustus of Buzanda, Moses of Khorēn, and Lazarus of P'arpi. They provide the primary sources for the history of the Armenians and insight into the customs, culture, viewpoints, and lives of the peoples of Caucasia and the Near East. Along with their own creative works, Armenian writers and scholars of the 5th century produced translations of the works of nearly every outstanding Greek and Latin author, thereby preserving in Armenian versions many works whose original texts have been lost. Eznik of Kołb, a distinguished philosopher of the 5th century, in a series of treatises (notably his *Refutation of the Sects* [*De Deo*]), made a profound and logical criticism—from the Christian standpoint—of the theories and thoughts of the Greek and other writers, authors, and philosophers. Eznik's work is a complete encyclopedia of the culture of his epoch, as well as a synthesis of Christian thought.

Since the Armenian people were situated in the farthest and most sensitive outpost of Christendom, they were frequently forced to wage a life and death struggle against anti-Christian forces of assaults coming from the east and the south, which threatened their Christian faith and culture.

The first and most significant of these battles took place on May 26, 451, when the great King of Persia, Yazdgard II, profiting by the conflict between Armenia and the East Roman Empire, invaded Armenia, demanding that the Armenians renounce Christianity and accept Mazdaism. Armenian laymen and clergy alike, led by the commander in chief *Vardan Mamikonian and the priest Leontius, rose with cross and sword in hand to defend their faith in the Battle of Awarayr on the banks of the River Tłmut, fighting against the numerically far superior forces of the Persian army. Many were martyred, including Vardan and Leontius, but the Armenians won a great moral victory and saved their faith and culture.

The Vardapet Eliseus, who had personally taken part in the war, wrote his *History of Awarayr and the War of the Vardanians* to describe not only the heroism of the soldiers fighting on the battlefield but also the conflict of the rival faiths; he defended the supremacy of the Christian faith over that of Mazdaism. This *History,* many passages of which are quoted to this day as inspired expressions of wisdom, is one of the great masterpieces of Armenian literature.

From the Arab Domination to the Invasion of Tamberlane. During the troubled times through which the Armenians lived under Arab domination, historiography practically ceased to exist. It was replaced by the religio-mystical literature of such authors as Theodore Krtenawor and John of Mayravank' and the liturgical poetry of Sahak of Dzorap'or, Komitas, etc.

In 859 King Ashot I restored the independence of Armenia and established the Bagratid kingdom, which ruled Armenia until 1046. Soon afterward Ruben I, a kinsman of the Bagratids, founded the Rubenid kingdom of Cilicia, which lasted until 1375. During the reign of these two dynasties the country's economic and intellectual life prospered; the arts and sciences flourished, bringing about a renaissance of Armenian literature and culture. The 10th century brought forth a number of gifted historians, such as John of Draskhanakert, Thomas Artsruni, Stephen Asołik of Tarōn, and Aristakēs of Lastivert (10th and 11th centuries). New types of literature were developed and perfected, including the lyric poetry of Constantine of Erznka (13th century), John Bluz (13th century), and others, and the fables of Mkhit'ar Gosh (12th century) and Vardan of Aygek (13th century). The most outstanding figures of the Armenian renaissance were unquestionably Bp. Gregory of Narek and Catholicos Nersēs of Kla (surnamed the Gracious). Gregory's *Book of Lamentations* is a poetic masterpiece, and the collection of his religious treatises and prayers, called *Narek* after the author, is to this day a revered book found side by side with the Bible in the home of every devout Armenian. The prayers, sermons, and hymns of the 12th-century Nersēs the Gracious enjoy nationwide esteem also.

End of the 14th Century to Mid-19th Century. In 1375 the Armenian kingdom of Cilicia came to an end following the invasions of Tamerlane. Partitioned between Persia and the Ottoman Empire, the land of Armenia was the scene of continuous devastations during the succeeding centuries, and the Armenians were subjected to repeated massacres and exploitation, under which the country's economy and civilization suffered a serious decline. Schools and colleges were demolished. A large portion of the Armenian heritage in priceless manuscripts was destroyed. The fields of intellectual and cultural life were made desolate. *Grabar* ceased to be the language of the people and became solely the liturgical language. The art of writing took shelter within the walls of the few surviving monasteries and abbeys. Monastic life took hold, and the dominant literary style became monastic versification, as in the works of Khach'atur of Kech'ar (14th century) and Aṙakēl of Siunia (15th century).

Among the general public the ballads of minstrels written in the so-called Middle Armenian dialect gained popularity. The names of more than 300 minstrels are known; many of them were renowned poets, such as Nahapet K'uch'ak (16th century), Jonathan Nałash (18th century), Balthazar Dpir (18th century), and Sayat Nova (1712–95). The towering stature of Sayat Nova rises above the others. He was martyred in 1795 by the soldiers of the Persian Agha Mahmud Khan in St. George's (Armenian) Church at Tiflis when he categorically refused to renounce his Christian faith. Sayat Nova could compose with equal skill in Armenian, Georgian, and Azerbaijani, and he has remained the greatest and the best-loved minstrel of these three trans-Caucasian nations.

Armenian secular and ecclesiastical intellectuals, fleeing from the stagnation of the homeland, went abroad and established centers of Armenian culture in India, Italy, and other countries of Europe. The most famous of these centers is the *Mechitarist Congregation, founded in September 1717 by Abbot Mkhit'ar of Sebastea. This congregation and its affiliate in Vienna have for 2½ centuries rendered invaluable service to Armenian culture and Christian literature. The Mechitarist Fathers Michael Tchamtchian (1738–1823), Mkrtich' Auguerian (1762–1854), Arsen Pakraduni (1790–1866), Arsen Aydinian (1824–1902), Leontius Alishan (1820–1901), and countless others have been the pillars of Armenology and Armenian literature.

In the early 19th century the Russian Empire expanded southward. reached the frontiers of Armenia, and engaged in a war with Persia and the Ottoman Empire. After the signing of the treaty of Turkmenchai on Feb. 10, 1828, and of Adrianople on Sept. 14, 1829, Armenia was partitioned between Russia, Persia, and Turkey; this placed Echmiadzin, the Holy See of the Armenian Church, in the Russian sector. Russia, although a colonial power, was a Christian country. This circumstance enabled the Armenian Church and communities to resume their cultural and educational activities with renewed vigor. Churches, monasteries, schools, and printing presses were restored. Seminaries and theological colleges were opened, including the Nersesian College in Tiflis, the diocesan schools of Erevan, Shusha, and Nor Nakhijevan (Nakhichevan), the Georgian College in Echmiadzin, and the Lazarian Institute in Moscow. Armenian youth could now enroll in Russian universities and, by way of Russia, in other European universities. During the next 2 or 3 decades several Armenians returned from the University of Dorpat or Tartu, in Estonia, to this native cultural fold, including the brilliant publicist Stephen Nazaryants' (1814–79), the illustrious "father" of modern Armenian literature, Khach'atur Abovyan (1809–48), the great national poet Gamaṙ-K'atipa (1830–92), the author of the celebrated song *Tsitseṙnak* (The Swallow), George Dodokhyan (1830–1908), and many others.

Mid-19th Century to Mid-20th Century. The publication in 1858 of Abovyan's book *The Wound of Armenia*, written in the Erevan dialect, which is the literary and official language of Armenia today, opened a new era of Armenian Christian literature and brought in its wake a steady stream of followers. Through his influence an abundant literature was created, not only in Russian-occupied Armenia but also in Constantinople, where Armenian intellectuals from the provinces under Ottoman domination had taken refuge. In the impressive Armenian Christian literary output at the end of the century, the following authors achieved predominance: the poets Smbat Shahaziz (1841–1907), Bedros Tourian (1852–72), Hovannes Hovhannesyan (1864–1929), Lazarus Aghayan (1840–1911), Hovannes Toumanyan (1869–1923), and Avetik' Isahakyan (1875–1957); the philosopher Michael Nalbandyan (1830–66); the novelists Perch Proshyan (1837–1907), Raffi (1835–88), Tserents' (1822–88), Murats'an (1854–1908); the playwright Gabriel Sundukyan (1825–1912); and the humorist Hagop Baronian (1843–91). In this rich literary heritage there are books dealing with the glorious deeds of the religious life, such as *The Mysterious Nun* by Murats'an or *The Man of the Black Mountain* by Matt'eos Mamourian (1830–1901).

Before World War I, Armenian Christian literature and culture had reached a high degree of growth and prosperity and brought forth another generation of creative talent. But the war came, and the flower of Armenian intellectual life was ruthlessly destroyed. The Turkish government decimated the population of Armenian territories under Turkish rule. One and a half million Armenian men, women, and children were murdered. Among the large number of intellectuals who fell victim to Turkish atrocities, which began in April 1915, were the poets Daniel Varoujean (1884–1915) and Siamanto (1878–1915), the novelist Grigor Zohrab (1861–1915), and the authors Yeroukhan (1870–1915), Roupen Zartarian (1874–1915), and Roupen Sevag (1885–1915).

As the German explorer Kurt Faber wrote, this massacre was the most shocking crime ever directed against Christendom, as a result of which a country with an ancient civilization was denuded of its native population and was turned into an economic and cultural wilderness.

Despite this tragedy, Armenian Christian literature endured and began to grow once more. During the interwar period, Armenian writers who found asylum in the U.S., in France, and in the countries of the Near East made a significant contribution to Armenian literature away from the homeland, or in the diaspora, as it has come to be called. These include Avetis Aharonyan (1866–1948), Leon Shanth (1869–1951), Arshag Tchobanian (1872–1959), Vahan Tekeyan (1877–1945), Roupen Vorperian (1874–1931), Hamasdegh (b. 1895), and others who continued the traditions of the ancient Armenian Christian literature. Their work is now carried on by a new generation of writers.

Meanwhile, in Caucasian Armenia, which as an autonomous republic had been a part of the Soviet Union since Dec. 2, 1920, the following have adorned the field of contemporary Armenian literature: the dramatist Shirvanzadē (1858–1935), the novelist Derenik Demirchyan (1877–1964), the lyric poet Vahan Teryan (1885–1920), the prose writer Step'an Zoryan (b. 1890), the luminary of the Soviet era and the most eminent Armenian writer Ełishē Tcharents' (1897–1937), and novelist Aksel Bakunts' (1900–37).

In the darkest days of the Stalin regime (1936–38) the intellectual elite of Soviet Armenia, especially the writers, were subjected to severe persecution and oppression. Many of them, notably Tcharents' and Bakunts', were executed or purged in 1937. Others, after being held in Siberian concentration camps for 10 to 15 years, were freed as unfit and disabled, among them the poet Alazan (b. 1903), who has been bedridden in his Yerevan home since 1957. Nevertheless, after the death of Stalin there were signs of new literary activity, with Hovhannes Shiraz, Paruyr Sevak, Sero Khanzadyan, Bakhshi Hovsēpyan, Khach'ik Dashtents', and others promising a rebirth of Armenian literature.

Bibliography: *Archives of Armenian History* (Tiflis 1899), in Armenian. E. Kolb, *Refutation of the Sects: De Deo* (Tiflis 1914), in Armen. Koriwn, ed., *History of the Life and Death of the Vardapet Saint Mesrop* (Tiflis 1913), in Armen. Moses of Khoren, ed., *History of the Armenians* (Tiflis 1913), in Armen. M. Abeghyan, *History of Classical Armenian Literature* (Yerevan 1946), in Armen. S. Agontz, *History of the Life of Lord Mkhit'ar of Sebastea* (Venice 1810). H. Ajarian, *Literary and Philological Studies* (Yerevan 1945), in Armen. A. Arakelyan, *History of the Intellectual Development of the Armenian People* (Yerevan 1964). M. Gianaschian, *History of Modern Armenian Literature* (Venice 1953). N. Adontz, *Dionysius of Thrace and the Armenian Commentators* (St. Petersburg 1915), in Russ. K. Faber, *Mit dem Rücksack nach Indien* (Tübingen 1927). C. Goyen, *The 200th Anniversary of the Armenian Theatre* (Moscow 1952), in Russ. M. van den Oudenrijn, LexThK[2] 1:872–873. A. Baumstark, *Die christliche Literatur des Orients,* v.2 (Berlin 1911) 62–99. V. Inglisian, *Das armenische Schrifttum* (Linz 1929). H. Thorossian, *Histoire de la littérature Arménienne* (Paris 1951).

[G. SAHARUNI]

ARMENIAN RITE

Within the Catholic Church there are 18 canonical *rites that are of equal dignity, enjoy the same rights and are under the same obligations. Although the particular Churches possess their own hierarchy, differ in liturgical and ecclesiastical discipline, and possess their own spiritual heritage, they are all entrusted to the pastoral government of the pope, the divinely appointed successor of St. Peter in the primacy. The Armenian rite is followed by both Orthodox and Catholics.

History. Although an ancient national tradition places the origins of Christianity in Armenia as far back as apostolic times, it is certain that until the end of the 3d century the doctrine of Christ had made little progress and the country had no ecclesiastical hierarchy in the strict sense. Christianity became the state religion *c.* A.D. 300, when the great apostle of Armenia, St. *Gregory the Illuminator preached the gospel there. This noble descendant of the royal family, who had been trained in Christian doctrine from childhood and was consecrated by the bishop of Caesarea in Cappadocia, quickly won over King Tiridates II to Christianity, as well as a large portion of the population. He was helped in his work of evangelization by Greek and Syrian missionaries whom he had invited to Armenia from Asia Minor (Cappadocia) and Syria (Edessa), respectively. There are a few traces of the influence of the Byzantine Church in the formation of the Armenian liturgy (*see* ARMENIAN RITE, LITURGY OF).

The invention of the Armenian alphabet at the beginning of the 5th century by St. Mesrop (d. 439), Doctor of the Armenian Church, resulted in the substitution of the national language for two foreign languages, Greek and Syrian. Holy Scripture and the most important works of the Fathers of the above-mentioned Churches, as well as the liturgies then in existence in Armenia, were translated into the Armenian language. This was done during the reign of the Catholicos Sahag the Great (387–438).

The Armenian Church inherited the heresy, at least nominally, of *Monophysitism by unfortunate political circumstances. Caught as a political pawn between the opposing armies of the Byzantine and Persian Empires, the Armenians were unable to attend the Councils of *Ephesus (431) and *Chalcedon (451). The decrees were translated into their new but undeveloped national language, and they saw only heretical teachings as the result of the Councils' acts. It was an easy step for the Synod of Dvin (506–507) to accept the *Henoticon* of Emperor *Zeno and condemn formally the Council of Chalcedon in order to receive political protection from the Monophysite-tainted Byzantine Emperor. From this time on the Armenian Church persisted in rejecting the Council of Chalcedon. Attempts were made by the Byzantine Church under the Emperors Heraclius (610–641) and Justinian II (685–695, 705–711), but the Armenians remained staunch in their type of Monophysitism.

The kingdom of Armenia had been for centuries the victim of attacks by the Byzantines, the Persians, and later by the Turks. It dissolved with the destruction of its capital, Ani. The catholicoi (comparable to a patriarch) moved their see of residence first to Ashtishat, then finally in 1293 to Sis, *Cilicia (Turkey), to set up New Armenia. Here, near the Holy Lands fought for by the Latin Crusaders, the Armenians came into close contact with Roman Catholicism and a reunion with Rome was actually effected that lasted from 1198 until 1375. Internal strifes within the Armenian Church of Cilicia then split the Church into many factions and dissolved the union with Rome. From the 15th century it had four competitors for the legitimate Armenian lineage. In 1113 the bishop of Aghtamar, on an island in Lake Van (Armenia), declared himself the legitimate successor of the ancient See of Echmiadzin and took the title of catholicos. An Armenian bishop of Jerusalem in 1311 took the title of patriarch. A dissenting group in 1441 moved back to former Armenia from Cilicia and set up the seat of a catholicate at Echmiadzin while the legitimate catholicos remained in the See of Sis in Cilicia. In 1461 Mohammed II recognized at Constantinople a new Armenian patriarchate. Thus in the 15th century there were three catholicates: the one at Echmiadzin enjoying the greatest authority and largest following, and two others at Sis and Aghtamar. Two other patriarchates split the Armenian Church further, one at Constantinople and the other at Jerusalem.

Organization of the Monophysite Armenians. Today the Armenian Monophysite Church is split into the various jurisdictions already mentioned. The chief catholicate in dignity and jurisdiction is that of Echmiadzin in the Republic of Armenia, U.S.S.R. Its 26 dioceses are scattered throughout Russia, Iraq, Iran, Egypt, Europe, and North and South America. The small catholicate of Aghtamar was dissolved in 1915 and exists no more. The other catholicate of the ancient See of Sis is today (1965) located in Antelias, a suburb of Beirut, Lebanon. This catholicos of ancient Cilicia has jurisdiction over four dioceses in Lebanon, Syria, and Cyprus with 125,000 faithful. The Patriarchate of Jerusalem numbers only 6,400 faithful. The Patriarchate of Constantinople has been extremely reduced since World War I, from approximately 1,350,000 faithful to its present 60,000. Many of these migrants moved to Bulgaria, where they formed an independent archbishopric that was approved as autonomous by the catholicos of Echmiadzin in 1928. They number about 25,000.

Among these different jurisdictions of so-called Gregorian Armenians it is difficult to understand exactly the degree of intercommunion of one with another. In spite of five independent ecclesiastical organizations, the Gregorian Church is theoretically one and depends on the Catholicate of Echmiadzin. The catholicos of Echmiadzin has a primacy of honor over the other ruling prelates but jurisdiction only in his own catholicate. There are about 1,600,000 Gregorian Armenians in the world, and about 1 million of these are in the U.S.S.R.

Doctrinal Differences. Their chief difference from Roman Catholicism is generally considered to be in their teaching on the two natures of Christ. For centuries they have held a Monophysitism at least in words, clinging to the pre-Chalcedon terminology of St. Cyril of Alexandria, "one nature in Christ after the union." Today there is very little interest in this theological problem; hence it is difficult to know what their common teaching is. In the meeting of Orthodox and Monophysites (represented by the Armenians, Jacobites, Copts, and Ethiopians) in 1964 in Aarhus, Denmark, there was a common agreement on the Chalcedon teaching that made the Monophysitism of the Armenians seem now to be merely nominal. Under the late Byzantine influence the procession of the Holy Spirit from the Father and Son, filioque, was suppressed from the Symbol of Faith. Up to the 13th century it was accepted in the Creed sung in the liturgy. The doctrine of the existence of purgatory is denied; yet the Gregorian Armenians pray for the dead and set aside five days of special petition for the repose of the souls of the departed. Their ecclesiology is a loose expression of their own decentralized organization. The Church as founded by Jesus Christ is one in essence; yet in actual existence there are as many different churches with different rites, disciplines, usages as there are different patriarchs. No one church is to be subordinated to another; yet all are to be coordinated and submitted to the rule of Christ. Hence the Armenians vigorously deny jurisdiction of the pope over other patriarchates. The pope enjoys a primacy of honor only because this has been time-honored by the early ecumenical councils.

Catholic Armenians. The reunion with Rome of the Armenians in Cilicia, lasting from 1198 until 1375, has already been mentioned. The Dominican Order was engaged in keeping alive the union when it began to flounder in the 14th century. A native Armenian order, the Friars of Unity, founded in 1320, was a peculiar adaptation of Armenian monasticism to the Dominican rule, but was gradually absorbed entirely into the Dominican Order. The bull of reunion of the Council of Florence (1439), *Exsultate Deo,* did not effect a lasting union but did lay down norms of discipline and liturgical practices that later were put into effect by the Catholic Armenians. There had always been an occasional catholicos united with Rome; but after the union of 1375 was dissolved, there was no Catholic Armenian Church until the Catholic Armenian bishop of Alep, Abraham Ardzivean, was elected catholicos of Sis. However, he was unable to return as catholicos to Sis after Benedict XIV confirmed him in Rome in 1742 because of a dissident catholicos rival in Syria. He moved his seat to Kraim in Lebanon, and his successor transferred the see to Bzommar, which then became the center for the Armenian Catholics, who were scattered throughout Syria, Mesopotamia, Palestine, and Egypt.

The Armenian Catholics in various parts of the Ottoman Empire were subject to the Latin apostolic vicar, but under the Moslem civil law they were regarded as subjects of the Monophysite Armenian patriarch of Constantinople. This caused friction and even bitter persecution of the Catholics from 1700 until 1830. The Moslem government, through French insistence, granted the Catholics in Turkey civil and religious freedom under the single leadership of the Catholic archbishop of Constantinople, whom the Turks wanted as patriarch. Since there could hardly be two simultaneous Catholic Armenian patriarchs, the problem was solved in the Synod of Bzommar through the election of the primate of Constantinople as catholicos of Cilicia in 1867. Pope Pius IX confirmed the union of the two Catholic Armenian sees in his bull *Reversurus,* but this only led to a schism of several bishops and many monks of St. Anthony under the leadership of Father Malachy Ormanian. Further internal disputes and persecutions by the Turks almost completely dissolved the Catholic Armenian Church. A decree from Rome in 1928 transferred the patriarchal seat from Constantinople to Beirut, and Constantinople (Istanbul) became an archbishopric.

From the 14th century there had already existed an Armenian bishopric in Galicia (Ukraine) with residence at Lvov. In 1635 Abp. Nicholas Torosowicz became a Catholic, and thus this archbishopric continued to be Catholic until 1944. During World War II the faithful were dispersed, many having gone to Silesia, in East Germany.

Canonical Sources. After the monk Mesrop invented the Armenian written language, scholars busied themselves in the 5th century translating the Bible and liturgical and canonical books into Armenian. The acts of the Councils of *Nicaea I (325) and Ephesus (431) were thus introduced as a basic canonical source for the growing Armenian Church. A series of early canons proper to the Armenian Church is attributed to Sahag the Great, a 4th-century catholicos; in it attention is given to the office of chorbishop, an inspector sent by the bishop to visit the far-distant places of the diocese. Two important, early councils, Chahapivan (447) and Vagarshapat (491), are to be remembered. The first legislated 20 canons setting the catholicate on a solid foundation of independence, and the second rejected the Council of Chalcedon (451) and made the rift from the Byzantine Church definitive. Gradually the canons of Council of *Constantinople I (381) and those of the local synods accepted by the Byzantine Church in general, such as Ancyra, Neocaesarea, Antioch, Gangres, Sardis, and Laodicea, were translated from the Greek and incorporated as a basis of the Armenian canon law. (*See* GREEK RITE.) Other traditional sources, such as the *85 Canons of the Apostles,* the *90 Canons of St. Athanasius,* and the *50 Canons of St. Basil,* were incorporated; so also were certain canons proper to the

Armenian Church, such as the *39 Canons* attributed to the catholicos Narses Achtarak (548–577), those of the Councils of Dvin (645) (719), and those of Partav (771).

Byzantine influence was felt in the field of canonical sources, depending on the political events at any given period. At one time even the canons of the Council of Chalcedon were accepted along with the 22 canons of *Nicaea II (787). Historians claim that Catholicos John Otznetzi (717–728) was the first to collect all the canons then in force into one volume. It is certain at least that these became fixed in some sort of a compendium in the 8th century. The canonical sources from then until the Crusades did not change radically.

Influence from the Crusades. With the establishment of New Armenia in Cilicia (Turkey) and the arrival of the Latin Crusaders in the Holy Land, new contact was made with Rome and a new influence entered into the canonical legislation of the Armenian Church. An important work at this time was compiled by the monk Mechitar Goch at the end of the 12th century. He strove to compile a book on jurisprudence, but succeeded only in collecting and commenting on canonical texts that seemed to him useful. His *Book of Judicial Cases* was a standard work for all Armenian canonists. In 1198, when Rome recognized the Catholicos Gregory VI, the door was opened both to a religious renaissance and to radical changes in canonical legislation. The Councils of Sis (1204, 1246, 1307, 1342) and of Adana (1316) inaugurated many Latinizations into the liturgy (*see* ARMENIAN RITE, LITURGY OF). This was the basic reason for the hostility of the Armenian monks of Jerusalem, who elected their own patriarch in 1311. After the schism in 1441, when a group left Sis to establish a seat at Echmiadzin and the two principal catholicates and two patriarchates were formed, no new canonical additions were added to the ancient sources.

Canonical Sources for Catholics. Pius IX in 1867 fixed the residence of the fused two Catholic patriarchates at Constantinople. A council at Constantinople (1869) and another at Chalcedon (1890), although not approved by Rome, nevertheless formed the basis for the later council called in Rome by Pius X in 1911. Its acts were approved officially by the Congregation for the Propagation of the Faith in 1913. These 1,009 canons under 12 chapters form the basis for the canonical legislation of the Catholic Armenians. However, the outbreak of World War I made it impossible to put them into effect immediately.

Armenian Catholic Statistics. The Armenian Catholic Church suffered severe losses during World War I, especially in the dioceses of Turkey, where great numbers of Catholics were put to death for the faith by the Turks. The Church was reorganized in 1928 through a synod held in Rome. The seat of the patriarchate was placed in Beirut, and Constantinople (Istanbul) became a simple archbishopric. The patriarch bears the title of patriarch of the Catholic Armenians and Catholicos of Cilicia and resides in the suburb of Ashrafieh, outside Beirut. He takes the name of Peter. An outstanding recent patriarch, known to Western Catholics, was Gregory Peter XV Agagianian, elected in 1937 and made a cardinal in 1945. He resigned as patriarch in 1962 because of his many activities as head of the Congregation for the Propagation of the Faith. He was succeeded by Ignatius Peter XVI Batanian.

Of the 18 dioceses that existed before World War I, there are now (1965) seven: Beirut, Constantinople, Alexandria in Egypt, Alep, Isfahan, Baghdad, and Kamechlie. The faithful in the Patriarchate of Cilicia number 52,100. Outside of the patriarchate the Armenian Catholics number about 45,000. The seat of Lvov (in the Ukraine) has had no resident bishop since 1943. In France an apostolic exarch administers to the 20,000 Catholics. For the 600 Catholics in Greece and the 5,000 in Rumania, apostolic administrators have been appointed. In Argentina (5,000 Catholics) and in Brazil (2,000), the Armenians are under the jurisdiction of the bishop appointed for all of the Oriental rites in the respective countries. In the U.S., 8,000 Armenians and their priests are under the jurisdiction of the local Latin bishops.

Religious Institutes. The Congregation of the Mechitarist fathers was founded in Constantinople in 1701 by Mechitar of Sivas (1676–1749). As a result of persecutions and war, the congregation was transferred to Venice, where it established itself on the Isola S. Lazzaro on Sept. 8, 1717. As a result of dissensions, there are now two distinct congregations bearing the same name: one in Venice, Italy, and the other in Vienna, Austria. Each congregation is governed by an abbot general, who is often a bishop. In 1963 there were 80 Mechitarist fathers, known also as Armenian Benedictines. For more than 2 centuries they have been the guiding light to the Armenian people, thanks to their publications, their literary, historical, scientific, and archeological works, as well as their many schools providing instruction to Armenian youth, including those of the dissident Church.

The Congregation of Bzommar was founded in Beirut in 1749 by Patriarch James Peter II Hovsepian. In 1963 it had 40 members. It is a pious association of priests belonging to the patriarchal clergy. The members of this congregation devote themselves to the care of souls in the missions and parishes of the patriarchate.

The Congregation of the Armenian Sisters of the Immaculate Conception was founded in Constantinople in 1847 by Cardinal Anthony Peter IX Hassoun. In 1963 it had more than 150 members. Since 1922 the motherhouse and novitiate have been located in Rome. The sisters dedicate themselves to the training and education of young Armenian girls. They direct many high schools and elementary schools in Turkey, Iraq, Syria, Egypt, Iran, and France.

Seminaries. In 1963 there were seven seminaries for the formation of the regular and secular clergy. Three of these were in Lebanon, four in Europe. The European seminaries are located in Vienna, Austria; Venice and Rome, Italy; and Le Pec, France. The Armenian Pontifical College of Rome was founded by Pope Leo XIII.

Bibliography: *Acta et decreta concilii nationalis Armenorum Romae habiti anno Domini MDCCCCXI* (Rome 1914). A. BALGY, *Historia doctrinae catholicae inter Armenos . . .* (Vienna 1878), in Armenian and Lat. V. HATZUNI, *Cenno storico e culturale sulla nazione Armena* (Venice 1940). R. JANIN, *Les Églises Orientales et les Rites Orientaux* (Paris 1955). A. A. KING, *The Rites of Eastern Christendom,* 2 v. (London 1950). G. ZANANIRI, *Pape et patriarches* (Paris 1962). G. AMADUNI, ed., *Disciplina Armena: Testi vari di diritto canonico armeno* (Fonti CICO, ser. 1, fasc. 7; 1932). P. HATZUNI, "Disciplina Armena" in *Studi storici sulle fonti del diritto canonico orientale* (*ibid.* fasc. 8; 1932) 139–168. C. DE CLERCQ, "Notae historicae circa fontes iuris particularis Orientalium Catholicorum," *Apol-*

linaris 4 (1931) 409–427; DDC 1:1043–47. T. E. DOWLING, *The Armenian Church* (SPCK; 1910).

[J. KAFTANDJIAN]

ARMENIAN RITE, LITURGY OF

The way of celebrating the mysteries of salvation in the Armenian Church. This article treats its history; characteristics of the Liturgy; and the church building, vessels, vestments, and books.

History. The history of this Liturgy, as seen from its title, "The Liturgy of our Blessed Father Saint Gregory the Illuminator revised and augmented by the Holy Patriarchs and Doctors, Sahag, Mesrob, Kud and John Mandakuni" has undergone many and diverse influences. It seems to derive from a modification of the Liturgy of St. Basil with Latin interpolations, although S. Salaville claims the Armenian Liturgy developed as a compilation from the Greek Liturgy of St. James and that of St. John Chyrsostom.

Reforms. Armenian Liturgy received innovations in the council of Dvin under Katholikos Nerses II (*c.* 524) and other enactments of councils in the 7th and 8th centuries. When the Armenian kingdom came to an end with the destruction of its capital, Ani, the katholikoi (patriarchs) moved about and finally settled in Sis, Cilicia (1293), to found New Armenia. Here the Monophysite Armenians came into contact with Latin Crusaders and missionaries of the Roman rite. A union with Rome from 1198 until 1375 brought also many Latinizations into the Liturgy that were sanctioned in various synods of Sis during the 13th and 14th centuries. The Liturgy for the Armenian Catholics was corrected by Basil Barsegh and John Agop, both educated in the Latin traditions, who introduced still more "hybridisms" from the Latin rite. However, at the beginning of the 19th century, under the leadership of Catholic Mekhitarists, especially Gabriel Avedikian (d. 1827), a movement to expurgate glaring Latinisms from the Liturgy was begun.

Churches Using Rite. Today both the Gregorian (Orthodox) and Catholic Armenians use this rite. The Gregorians (so called because Christianization of Armenia is credited to St. Gregory the Illuminator, d. 325) are divided into various jurisdictions. Besides the supreme katholikos of Echmiadzin in the Armenian Republic of the U.S.S.R., there is one inferior katholikos, governing the ancient katholikate of Sis, now centered in Antelias, Lebanon, and independent of the supreme katholikos of Echmiadzin. There are also two patriarchs in Jerusalem and Constantinople, while an independent Armenian Church has been set up in Bulgaria since 1927. The total of Gregorian Armenians of this rite is about 1,600,000 with nearly a million of these in the Soviet Union. The Catholic patriarch has his residence in Beirut and governs a total of 97,100 faithful. There are in the U.S. about 8,000 Catholic Armenians who are under the jurisdiction of the local Latin ordinaries.

Sources. Besides the unknown translators and compilers of the Liturgy, history has honored Patriarch Sahag of the 4th century as the one who introduced the new Armenian language into the Liturgy. John Mandakuni (d. 490?) and Moses of Khoren (d. 458?) added several prayers and hymns. Two leading commentators of the Liturgy were Chosroes the Great, Bishop of Andzevatzentz (d. *c.* 972), and Nerses of Lampron (d. 1198). Katholikos Nerses IV (1166–73) added his poetic gifts to the Liturgy by many hymns still used today. The Gregorian Liturgy has been edited several times, first at Venice (1686), then at Constantinople (1706, 1823, 1844), at Jerusalem (1841, 1876, 1884), and at Echmiadzin (1873). The Catholic Liturgy has been edited several times also, but today the editions depend mostly on the editions of the Mechitarists of Venice (1895) and of Vienna (1884).

Characteristics of the Liturgy. The general lines of the Armenian Liturgy are quite simple; the outline of the Byzantine Liturgy is ever in evidence (*see* BYZANTINE RITE). Unlike other Eastern rites the Armenian has only one Anaphora. The great variety allowed in vestments, along with the haunting melodies of choir and the steady beat of cymbals and gong, tends to create a joyful, yet solemn, atmosphere. The five principal parts are: (1) the preparation prayers said in the sacristy; (2) the preparation prayers said in the sanctuary; (3) the preparation of the gifts at the altar of preparation; (4) the Mass of the Catechumens; and (5) the Mass of the Faithful. After having prayed to be worthy to offer the Sacrifice and having vested, the priest blesses the people and then kneels before them as he makes a public confession. A prayer of absolution is given and the priest approaches the main altar reciting the Psalms "Judge me, O God" and "I will go unto the altar of God," as is done in the Roman Mass. He moves to a side altar, the *prothesis,* where the bread and wine are prepared and incensed. The Mass of the Catechumens consists primarily in the singing of the Trisagion (directed to Christ with the insertion "Who was crucified for us"), the Epistle, and the Gospel. The Athanasian Creed is sung while the deacon holds the Gospel book over the priest's head. Litanies for peace and pardon of sins are climaxed with the blessing of the people by the priest and the dismissal of the Catechumens. From this point on, the proper Anaphora, until the close, follows very closely the Byzantine Liturgy. The priest removes his crown (among the Gregorians, his sandals also) and makes the Great Entrance, followed by litanies and the kiss of peace, which is given from priest to deacon to congregation. The choir sings the Sanctus while the priest reads in a low voice the Anaphora, raising his voice aloud for the singing of the words of Consecration.

Chanting of Gospel by a bishop priest in Armenian Liturgy.

Holy Communion is given under two species by dipping part of the consecrated azyme bread (unleavened bread, a great exception to the majority of Oriental Liturgies) into the Precious Blood. The Catholics, however, give Holy Communion under the one species of unleavened bread, similar to the Roman rite. The priest blesses the congregation with the Gospel book and then reads the prologue of St. John's Gospel, facing them.

Church Building. Armenian churches are usually rectangular in form and always face east. The interior is divided into a vestibule, the nave, the choir (*bem*), and the raised sanctuary (*srbaran*). Over the nave there is usually a cupola covered with a conical or pyramidal roof. The altar has several tiers upon which a cross, relics, candelabras, flowers, liturgical fans, etc., are placed. A double curtain is stretched across the sanctuary, and when it is pulled, it conceals the priest and the altar from the people during various parts of the Liturgy. Another curtain directly in front of the altar hides the priest during his reception of Holy Communion. Usually side altars where other Masses can be said abound. The Catholics reserve the Blessed Sacrament in a tabernacle on the main altar, while the Gregorians reserve it usually in a niche in the north wall. Except in the West, benches or seats are not usually found in the churches. The clergy and people stand or sit on rugs or pillows, which they bring to church with them. The fact that few pictures or icons are found in the churches, stems perhaps from a distrust of icons due to Monophysite tendencies in the past history of the Armenians.

Vessels. There are fewer sacred vessels than in the Byzantine rite; there is no asterisk (star) over the paten and no spoon. The priest blesses the faithful with a small hand cross consecrated with chrism, bearing no figure, but usually containing a relic. This is adorned with a small silk streamer. Both Gregorians and Catholics use unleavened bread, a carry-over from their bitter hate for the Greeks and Syrians. This bread resembles the Latin hosts except that in general it is softer and thicker. Bells are attached to fans that are waved over the consecrated gifts by deacons, and cymbals are used to mark the tempo for the choir. No water is added to the wine in the preparation or before Communion as in the Byzantine rite.

Vestments. Simple clerics functioning as lectors wear a long robe of any color and no cincture, with a cape, usually red and marked with two crosses on the front and one on the back, over the shoulders. The deacon wears the same vestments as the deacon of the Byzantine rite except that the orarion (*ourar*) is usually much longer and falls to the ground in front and behind. The priest wears an alb (*chapik*) of no fixed color or material, along with the wide stole (*porurar,* corresponding to the Byzantine *epitrachelion*), an embroidered cincture (*goti*), cuffs, and a full-flowing cope in place of the chasuble or *phelon.* This cope is topped by a tall, stiff collar (*vakas*). The ordinary priest wears a crown on his head similar to that worn in the Byzantine rite only by bishops. The Armenian bishop wears fundamentally the same vestments as the priest, but replaces the crown with a miter similar to that worn by a Latin bishop. As among the Greeks, the bishop also wears the *omophorion,* a very wide cloth covering the shoulders and falling down the front, as well as the pectoral cross (similar to that worn by a Latin bishop) and the picture of Our Lady (*panague*). He wears also a ring, but only on his little finger, while the katholikos wears it on his ring finger.

Books. Only four books are used in the actual celebration of the Liturgy. *Donatzouitz* indicates the order to be observed in celebrating either the Liturgy or the Divine Office. It corresponds to the Latin *Ordo Celebrationis. Badarakamadouitz* (Book of the Sacrament) contains all the prayers that the priest recites or chants in the Liturgy. The Epistle and Gospel for each day are found in the *Giaschotz* (Book of midday). The chants and hymns for the choir are found in the *Terbroutiun.*

Bibliography: L. ARAKELIAN, *The Armenian Liturgy* (Watertown, Mass. 1951). D. ATTWATER, *The Christian Churches of the East,* 2 v. (rev. ed. Milwaukee 1961–62). A. A. KING, *The Rites of Eastern Christendom,* 2 v. (London 1950) v.2. J. MÉCÉRIAN, "Un Tableau de la diaspora arménienne," *Proche Orient Chrétien* 6 (1956) 333–345; 7 (1957) 119–138, 229–249, 310–327; 8 (1958) 340–366; 9 (1959) 308–329; 11 (1961) 137–168. S. SALAVILLE, *An Introduction to the Study of Eastern Liturgies,* tr. J. M. T. BARTON (London 1938).

[G. A. MALONEY]

ARMENIANS, DECREE FOR

The decree *Exsultate Deo,* published in the Council of Florence on Nov. 22, 1439, by Pope Eugene IV, in an attempt to bring about the reunion of the Armenian Church with the Catholic Church. The decree constitutes a compendium of Christian doctrine concerning especially the unity of the divine essence and the Trinity of Divine Persons, the humanity of Christ, and the nature of the seven Sacraments, because of the errors of the Armenians on these points. It contains the Constantinople Creed, the definitions made at the Council of Chalcedon about the two natures in Christ and at Constantinople III about the two wills and operations of Christ, a decree about accepting the authority of Chalcedon and the Letter of Pope Leo I, an instruction concerning the Sacraments, the Athanasian Creed, the decree of union with the Greeks, and a decree about the common celebration of certain feasts.

It is best known for the lengthy instruction on the Sacraments that constitutes its fifth section, taken almost verbatim from the opusculum of St. Thomas Aquinas entitled *De articulis fidei et ecclesiae sacramentis.* This instruction enumerates the seven Sacraments and indicates how they differ from the sacraments of the Old Law. The distinction between Sacraments for the individual and social Sacraments is made, and the essential elements of matter, form, and intention in the Sacraments are treated. Mention is made of the indelible character of the Sacraments of Baptism, Confirmation, and Orders. Each Sacrament is then taken up in particular, with a consideration of its form, matter, and minister.

Concerning the authority of this instruction on the Sacraments there has been some question in the past. It was raised anew by the constitution *Sacramentum ordinis* of Pope Pius XII, issued Nov. 30, 1947, because Pius XII no longer considered the tradition of instruments mentioned in the Decree for Armenians as necessary for the validity of the Sacrament of Orders. Some scholars assert that this instruction enjoys infallible authority because the purpose of the decree is to instruct the Armenians in the "rectitude of the faith" and it was issued in a solemn way with the approbation of the Council of Florence. Others maintain that the instruction is of a disciplinary character only, since it was not made for the whole Church and was based on the practice then prevailing in the Latin Church.

Bibliography: Mansi 31A:1047–62. Denz 1310–28; 3857–61. J. GILL, *Eugenius IV: Pope of Christian Union* (Westminster, Md. 1961); *The Council of Florence* (Cambridge, Eng. 1959). N. VALOIS, *Le Pape et le concile, 1418–1450,* 2 v. (Paris 1909). Cappello Sac 4:141–148. Hefele-Leclercq 7.2. G. D. SMITH, "The Church and Her Sacraments," ClergyRev NS 33 (1950) 217–231; NS 34 (1950) 432.

[W. F. HOGAN]

ARMENTIĄ, NICOLÁS, Franciscan missionary, explorer, and bishop; b. in a small town in the Spanish Basque country, 1845; d. La Paz, Bolivia, November 1909. He entered the Franciscan Order while still a boy and was sent to La Recoleta in La Paz where he was ordained. Between 1870 and 1883 he worked in the missions of Covendo, Ixiamas, and Tumupasa, on the western shore of the Beni River. In addition to serving the neophytes there, he made many expeditions through the neighboring jungles in search of aborigines to attract to the missions. He explored unknown regions, with the idea of converting new groups of the forest tribes and founding new missions.

During 1884 and 1885 he made an expedition down the Beni River to the Madre de Dios River, at the behest of the national government. He toured the hinterland of both rivers extensively, establishing relations with the Araona and Toromona tribes, among which he founded a mission. The following year he entered those regions again and reached the Purus River and later the Amazon. As a result of these and other travels he wrote several books, among which were *Exploración del Madre de Dios, Diario de viaje a las tribus comprendidas entre el río Beni y el arroyo Ibon, Límite de Bolivia con el Perú por la parte de Caupolicán,* and *Navegación del Madre de Dios.* The last-mentioned work contains valuable information for ethnography and observations of the flora and fauna of the area that reveal the soundness of his knowledge of zoology and botany. He wrote also a grammar and vocabulary of the Chipibo language spoken by a jungle tribe of the High Beni. He translated and published the curious work of the Jesuit Father Eder, *Descripción de los Moxos.*

He was consecrated Bishop of La Paz in Sucre early in 1902. As prelate he was distinguished by his dedication in instructing the infidels, his careful attention to religious services, and, principally, his reorganization of the seminary.

[H. SANABRIA FERNÁNDEZ]

ARMINIANISM

A system of belief that takes its name from *Arminius (Jacobus Hermandszoon). During the 16th century much theological discussion centered in Holland. In their efforts toward attaining national independence, the people of Holland had been attracted to *Calvinism. Although they eventually accepted it as their national religion, in those early days many expressed dissatisfaction with rigid Calvinist principles, especially the teaching that God had predestined some to be saved and others to be lost even before the Fall (*supralapsarians). These held the milder doctrine that while God foresaw the Fall, the formal decree was not made until after Adam's transgression (*infralapsarians). Some professors at Leyden University who were opposed to strict Calvinism sought for tolerance of all religions, believing that persuasion, not persecution, should be the policy; they met with strong opposition.

Jacobus Arminius.

It was in such an atmosphere that Arminius made his studies. After he began his ministry he defended the strict Calvinist doctrine, but was later repelled by its harshness, and participated in a number of discussions that resulted in the formulation of his own doctrine. Appointed at Leyden, he found himself involved in controversy, especially with a fellow professor, Franciscus *Gomarus, who upheld the rigid Calvinist principles of absolute predestination with strong feelings and bitter antipathy toward his adversaries.

As a religious system, the teaching of Arminius was stated in the Remonstrance of 1610. The major points of departure from stricter Calvinism were contained there: (1) atonement was intended for all men, (2) man needs grace, yet is able to resist it and can even lose it. This denial of absolute predestination and admission of the concurrence of free will and grace were strongly condemned by Gomarus, who feared that such a view would undermine the Protestant teaching on salvation. Dutch Protestants were divided; the general populace inclined toward Gomarus, while many of the learned and a number of high public officials favored Arminius. The discussions became so heated that there was fear of a civil war in some of the Dutch provinces. The professors debated even before the States General in 1608 and 1609. Though Arminius seemingly won the arguments and appeared in a favorable light to those who followed the discussions, Gomarus gave the impression that Arminian doctrines would disrupt the national unity that was being accomplished through strict Calvinist belief. Maurice of Orange, impressed with Gomarus's argument, and believing that the Arminians favored the pro-Spanish party in politics, attacked the group. After their condemnation at the Synod of Dort (1618–19), they were persecuted and banished by the prince. Arminianism was tolerated in Holland after the death of its founder, but it was not until 1795 that it was able to gain official recognition (*see* CONFESSIONS OF FAITH, PROTESTANT).

The Arminians are one of the smaller religious sects in Holland. Yet their teachings have been taken over by some Methodists, by many individuals who belong to churches that are Calvinist in name, by some Baptists, and by members of other religions.

Bibliography: G. O. McCulloh, ed., *Man's Faith and Freedom* (New York 1962), contains addresses of the Arminius symposium held in Holland 1960. R. L. Colie, *Light and Enlightenment: A Study of the Cambridge Platonists and the Dutch Arminians* (Cambridge, Eng. 1957). F. A. Christie, "The Beginnings of Arminianism in New England," *American Society of Church History. Papers,* Ser. 2, v.3 (1912) 151–172. W. F. Dankbaar, RGG³ 1:620–622. Y. Congar, *Catholicisme* 1:845.

[L. RUSKOWSKI]

ARMINIUS, JACOBUS, called also Jakob Hermandszoon, Dutch Reformed theologian; b. Oudewater, South Holland, Oct. 10, 1560; d. Leiden, Oct. 19, 1609. Aided by friends, Arminius, after his father's death, studied at Utrecht and at Marburg (only briefly, since he was called home when most of his family was slain during the Spanish siege of Oudewater); he later attended the University of Leiden to study theology (1576–82). He went to Geneva, at that time under Theodore Beza, where he studied for 3 years (interrupted by a brief stay in Basel); he then went to the University of Padua, made a short visit to Rome, and spent a few more months in Geneva. In 1587 he was called to Amsterdam and in the following year became a minister. For 15 years he served as a kind and devoted pastor, showing his love for his people especially at the time that the plague struck so devastatingly (1602). He was a gifted preacher who possessed a thorough knowledge of the Scriptures. A few years after his arrival in Amsterdam he married and became the father of nine children. In 1603 he was invited to become professor of theology at the University of Leiden, where he remained until his death. By nature a peace-loving man, Arminius nevertheless became involved in many disputes over the Calvinist teaching of unconditional predestination, since his studies in St. Paul's Epistle to the Romans had led him to doubt so harsh a doctrine and inspired him to promote the milder form of a conditional predestination. The disputes continued till the time of his death.

Bibliography: *Opera theologica* (Leiden 1629); Eng. ed. and tr. J. and W. Nichols, 3 v. (London 1825–75). C. Brandt, *The Life of James Arminius,* tr. J. Guthrie (Glasgow 1854). N. Bangs, *Life of James Arminius,* ed. J. Nichols (New York 1843). J. H. Maronier, *Jacobus Arminius,* (Amsterdam 1905). A. H. W. Harrison, *The Beginnings of Arminianism to the Synod of Dort* (London 1926); *Arminianism* (London 1937). W. F. Dankbaar, RGG³ 1:622.

[L. F. RUSKOWSKI]

ARNALDUS AMALRICI, or Arnaud-Amaury, archbishop of Narbonne; b. southern France, *c.* 1160; d. Cistercian abbey of Fontfroide, Sept. 26, 1225. He was from Languedoc nobility, and his cousin was vice count of Narbonne; he was buried at *Cîteaux. He entered the monastery of Cîteaux, became abbot of Poblet, in Catalonia (GallChrist 6:61); and, in 1199, of Grandselve, in Languedoc. Finally, in 1201 at Cîteaux, he was elected abbot general of the order, which, since the days of St. *Bernard, had been involved in the intellectual controversy with the *Albigenses. Toward the end of 1203, Pope *Innocent III appointed the Fontfroide monks Raoul and *Peter of Castelnau as missionaries and papal legates for Languedoc, which was threatened by heresy. On May 31, 1204, Arnaldus was commissioned to join them (Potthast n.2229), but he could not begin his mission until March 1207, after the general chapter of 1206 at Cîteaux, in which his order gave the enterprise its strong support. The failure of their efforts because of the opposition of the southern clergy and the nobility, led by *Raymond VI of Toulouse, culminated in the murder of Peter of Castelnau on Jan. 14, 1208, for which Raymond was believed to have been responsible. With a papal commission, Arnaldus began a crusade against the Albigenses, mustering an army at Lyons in June 1209; they captured Béziers on July 22 and perpetrated a bloody massacre. It was there that Arnaldus is said to have uttered the infamous words: "Kill them all. God knows his children." The authenticity of this statement is questionable; none of the chroniclers (e.g., Pierre de Vaux-Cernay) or accounts (*Chanson de la Croisade*) mention it, although they did not shrink from horrors (e.g., they report a genuine statement of Arnaldus, encouraging the crusaders with: "Do not worry. I believe very few will be converted."). Pope Innocent tried to change the course of events by reprimanding his legate and by negotiating personally with Raymond VI in 1209; but ultimately (1211) Innocent excommunicated Raymond. On March 12, 1212, Arnaldus replaced Archbishop Berenger II of Narbonne (who either resigned or was deposed); but then, because he also ruled the duchy of Narbonne, Arnaldus came into conflict with *Simon de Montfort l'Amaury, who claimed Narbonne on March 21, 1215. Against Simon's bid for power Arnaldus defended even his former enemy Raymond VI at the *Lateran Council of 1215 and excommunicated Montfort in 1216. As papal legate, Arnaldus had led the French troops into the battle of Navas de Tolosa, in which the three united Spanish kings defeated the Moors (July 16, 1212). He succeeded in separating Raymond VII and his knights from the Albigenses at the Synod of Montpellier (Aug. 25, 1224); nevertheless, under pressure by the French King, the agreements resulting from the negotiations were rejected by Honorius III.

Bibliography: Sources. Petrus de Vaulx-Cernay, *Hystoria Albigensis,* ed. P. Guébin and E. Lyon, 3 v. (Paris 1926–39). Literature. A. Luchaire, *Innocent III: La Croisade des Albigeois* (3d ed. Paris 1911). Hefele-Leclercq 5.2:1260–1303. P. Belperron, *La Croisade contre les Albigeois* (Paris 1942). A. Borst, *Die Katharer* (Stuttgart 1953). F. Niel, *Albigeois et Cathares* (Paris 1956). A. Sabarthès, DHGE 4:420. A. Posch, LexThK² 1:888.

[H. WOLFRAM]

ARNAULD

The name of a family whose members practically created the Jansenist party of 17th-century France. The Arnaulds (Arnaut, Arnault) came of middle-class stock from Herment in Auvergne. Their rise to political power began with *Henri Arnauld* (1485–1564), who served Pierre de Bourbon and his nephew the constable, who owed much, possibly his life, to Henri's loyalty. This connection assisted the brilliant career of his son, *Antoine de la Mothe-Arnauld* (?–1585), who moved to Paris, where he reached high legal office at the Parlement and was ennobled in 1577. His son, *Antoine II* (1560–1619), surpassed his father's reputation at the bar, while leaving his descendants the so-called "original sin of the Arnaulds." This was the *Plaidoyer pour l'Université de Paris contre les jesuites* (Paris 1594–95), which started the quarrel with the Jesuits that Jansenist theologians, particularly his own children, continued with untiring relish. Antoine is remembered chiefly as

Mother Catherine Agnès Arnauld (Mother Agnès de Saint-Paul) and Sister Catherine of St. Susan (daughter of the artist), votive painting by Philippe de Champaigne, 1662, painted upon his daughter's recovery from illness, now in the Musée du Louvre, Paris.

the father of almost all the first leaders of the French Jansenist party. Ten of the twenty children whom he had by Catherine Marion, his wife, reached maturity. The six girls entered the Cistercian convent of *Port-Royal. Jacqueline (Mother Angélique) and Jeanne Catherine Ágnès (Mother Agnès) were most prominent in making Port-Royal the center of French Jansenism. Their eldest sister, *Catherine* (1590–1651), as the wife of Antoine Le Maistre before entering Port-Royal, bore two famous Jansenist theologians, Antoine Le Maistre and Le Maistre de Saci (*see* LE MAISTRE). The three other sisters were *Anne de Sainte Eugénie de l'Incarnation* (1594–1653), *Madeleine de Sainte-Christine* (1607–49), and *Marie de Sainte-Claire* (1600–42), who for a short time threatened to upset the peace of Port-Royal by heading an opposition to Jean *Duvergier de Hauranne, Abbé St. Cyran. The sons, apart from *Simon* (1603–39), a lieutenant in the army, were distinguished in the story of Jansenism: Antoine, the "Great Arnauld," became the chief theologian of the sect in France; Henri was bishop of Angers; Robert Arnauld d'Andilly was the fashionable *solitaire*.

Whatever the individual importance of the five Arnaulds whose biographies follow, the family's formative influence on French Jansenism transcends the bounds of a few biographies. The Arnaulds did more than provide it with many gifted theologians. Family background and temperament welded the Arnaulds together, so that they seem to have branded their family outlook on the sect itself. This distinguished legal family continued to produce several lawyers during the 17th century, and there is much to suggest that some of the theologians and ascetics in the family remained lawyers at heart. For a sect whose avowed concerns were the cosmic issues of grace and salvation, there was an incredible amount of legal speechifying and debate about theological niceties. This is apparent particularly in the "Great Arnauld's" distinction between "law" and "fact," by which French Jansenists claimed that certain propositions, although legally condemned by the Pope, did not in fact exist in the writings of Jansen. With their legalistic outlook the Arnaulds seemed to thrive on controversy. If the Jansenists often squandered their religious zeal in crusades against the Jesuits, the example of the Arnauld family was partly to blame. The Arnaulds' very prominence as theologians and spiritual leaders hurt the young Jansenist party by making it seem the possession of a family clique.

Jacqueline Marie Angélique. Mother Angélique, abbess and reformer of Port-Royal; b. Paris, Sept. 8, 1591; d. Port-Royal, Aug. 6, 1661. At the age of 7 she was named coadjutrix with the right of succession to Jeanne Boulehart, Abbess of Port-Royal, and she assumed government of the convent at Jeanne's death in 1602. She shared the worldly life of her spiritual charges until converted by a Capuchin friar in 1608. Ruthless reforms followed, culminating in the famous "day of the grating," when her father and brothers were turned away from the convent cloister. Reform was carried to many other foundations, beginning with Maubuisson, where Mother Angélique spent 5 years from 1618. The following year St. *Francis de Sales influenced her so strongly that she tried impetuously, but unsuccessfully, to join his Visitation nuns. Her imperious will was again thwarted when the community at Port-Royal replaced her as abbess in 1630. Nonetheless, she remained influential and was instrumental in introducing Saint-Cyran as the convent's spiritual director from about 1636. In 1633, under the guidance of Sebastian Zamet, Bishop of Langres, she established the Institute of the Blessed Sacrament, whose orthodoxy was questioned because of the writings of Mother Agnès. As abbess from 1642 to 1655, Mother Angélique ensured the permanence of Saint-Cyran's work. The *Fronde,* which brought more than 200 religious as refugees to Port-Royal, helped her to disseminate Jansenist ideas still more widely. Mother Angélique's spiritual teaching can be studied in papers that were written either by her or under her immediate inspiration. They include: *Mémoires pour servir à l'histoire de Port-Royal . . .*, 3 v. (Utrecht 1742–44); *Entretiens ou conférences de la Révérende Mère Angélique Arnauld . . .*, 3 v. (Utrecht 1757); *Mémoire et relations sur ce qui s'est passé à Port-Royal des Champs . . .* (Utrecht 1716); and *Lettres de la Rév. Mère Marie-Angélique,* 3 v. (Utrecht 1742).

Jeanne Catherine Agnès. Mother Agnès de Saint-Paul, abbess of Port-Royal; b. Paris, Dec. 31, 1593; d. Port-Royal, Feb. 19, 1672. At the age of 6 she was nominated abbess of Saint-Cyr. In 1608 she joined her sister, Mother Angélique, at Port-Royal, where she gave valuable help in carrying out reforms. She was abbess of Tard at Dijon from 1630 to 1636, of Port-Royal from 1636 to 1642, and again at Port-Royal from 1658 to 1661. After refusing repeatedly to accept the "Formulary" of Alexander VII against Jansenism, she was banished to the Visitation Convent in 1664, but returned to Port-Royal the next year. Although Agnès lived in the shadow of her sister Angélique, her own deep spirituality greatly impressed contemporaries. Her manuscript work of 1627, *Le Chaplet secret du Saint Sacrement,* which was championed by Saint-Cyran in a lively controversy, was one of the sect's most important writings. It interjected into traditional Augustinianism what Jean Orcibal in *Les Origins . . .* described as "the negative theology of the mystics" (2.311). Many other of her spiritual writings, mainly in manuscript, are summarized in C. J. Goujet's *Mémoires* (3.241–250). Her *Lettres* (ed. A. P. Faugère, 2 v. Paris 1858) are a useful source for the history of Port-Royal.

Antoine. Called the "Great Arnauld"; b. Feb. 5, 1612; d. Brussels, Aug. 2, 1694. He came increasingly

Antoine Arnauld, engraving by Edelinck after a portrait by Philippe de Champaigne.

under the influence of his mother after his father's death (1619), and through her, of Saint-Cyran. After studying law, he entered the Sorbonne and in 1635 presented his bachelor's thesis on the doctrine of grace. Force of argument and lyrical eloquence, together with the fortuitous attendance of many bishops, gave it a brilliant success. This success, despite the fact that Arnauld's views were essentially those that Jansen developed 5 years later in his *Augustinus,* shows the prevalence of Augustinianism among French theologians. That Jansenist ideas had already made headway before they were branded as heretical explains much of the bitterness and confusion of Jansenist controversy.

A new phase in Arnauld's life began in 1638 when he put himself completely under the spiritual direction of Saint-Cyran, who insisted on his ordination in 1641 and inspired him to write *De la Fréquente communion* (Paris 1643). Judging from the amount of controversy it provoked and St. Vincent de Paul's belief that it kept at least 10,000 people from receiving the Sacrament, this was, in France, probably the most influential of all the Jansenist writings. It established Arnauld after Saint-Cyran's death (1643) as the undisputed head of the Jansenist sect in France. While Jansen himself had written almost exclusively about predestination and grace, Arnauld elaborated the Jansenist position on the Sacraments, particularly Penance and the Eucharist, on the ecclesiastical hierarchy, and on papal infallibility. Yet, although Arnauld was a brilliant theologian and polemicist, he injured French Jansenism by infusing into it his own love of bitter controversy. The turbulent events of Arnauld's private life, his degradation by the Sorbonne in 1656, reinstatement by Louis XIV in 1669, and self-imposed exile from 1679, permeate his writings and, together with his literary feuds, obscure the inner message of Jansenism. Arnauld's biography is really comprised in his 320 works, which are analyzed acutely by J. Carrèyre (DHGE 4:454–482). Most of his writings are collected in *Oeuvres de Messire Antoine Arnauld* (43 tomes, ed. G. Dupac and J. Hautefage, 38 v. Lausanne 1775–83). These show that, although Arnauld's chief interest lay in theology, he wrote also important works on mathematics, science, and philosophy.

Henri. Bishop of Angers; b. Paris, October 1597; d. Angers, June 8, 1692. To please his father, Henri practiced at the bar until his parent's death in 1619. The papal nuncio Cardinal Guido Bentivoglio took Henri with him to Rome in 1621. Meanwhile, Louis XIII appointed Henri abbot of Saint-Nicolas d'Angers in 1622; later, Henri was ordained in 1624. On his return from Rome in 1625, Henri would certainly have had a fine career but for Richelieu's implacable hostility toward the Arnauld family. For about 20 years Henri lived in retirement, following a life of prayer and austerity in the shadow of Port-Royal, while taking a leading part at the literary *salons* of the Hôtel Rambouillet. In 1645 Mazarin charged him with the delicate task of reconciling the Barberini, clients of France, with Clement X. His great skill as a diplomat emerges from his *Négotiations à la cour de Rome* (1645–48; 5 v. Paris 1748). In 1649 he was rewarded for his services by nomination to the See of Angers. Henri was a devoted pastor, tireless in carrying out visitations and in raising standards among the clergy. His codified *Statuts de l'évêché d'Angers* (1680) became a model for the French episcopate. Henri's position made him one of the most prominent French Jansenists. He was among the 11 bishops to protest that the five propositions condemned by Innocent X in the bull *Cum occasione* (1653) were not in the works of Jansen. Together with Bishops Caulet of Pamiers, Buzenval of Beauvais, and Pavillon of Alet, he refused for several years to accept the "Formulary." Henri's Jansenist sympathies involved him in protracted disputes, particularly with the University of Angers. Nonetheless, this saint of the Jansenist calendar disliked controversy and, with age, cooled in his affections toward Jansenism.

Robert Arnauld d'Andilly. Celebrated *solitaire* of Port-Royal; b. Paris, 1588; d. Port-Royal, Sept. 17, 1674. Andilly married Catherine Le Fèvre de la Boderie (1613). Of his 15 children the most famous were: *Mother Angélique de Saint-Jean* (1624–84), Abbess of Port-Royal, and considered by Sainte-Beuve the most brilliant after Pascal of Port-Royal's second generation; and *Simon, Marquis de Pomponne* (1618–99), who was secretary of state for foreign affairs to Louis XIV at the height of his power. Five others, *Catherine de Sainte-Agnès* (1615–43); *Marie Charlotte de Sainte-Claire* (1627–78); *Marie Angélique de Sainte-Thérèse* (1630–1700); *Anne Marie* (1631–60); and *Charles Henri* (1623–84), a *solitaire* under the name of M. de Luzancy, were associated with Port-Royal. Andilly's own political career under Gaston d'Orleans was ended by Richelieu's rise to power. Nonetheless, his likeable nature won him many influential friends, including the Queen Mother (Anne of Austria) and Mazarin. It appears that only his Jansenistic connections decided them against making him tutor to Louis XIV. In 1643, after much indecision, Andilly went into semiretirement at Port-Royal. The "courtly anchorite," as Cécile Gazier called him, helped make Jansenism fashionable while using his influence to protect the sect. This courtier, who chose the farcical role of "superintendant" of the convent's gardens, was an industrious and talented writer. Besides his chief writings that appear in the three folio volumes of *Oeuvres diverses . . .* (Paris 1675) are several translations that include *The Confessions of Saint Augustine, The Lives of the Desert Fathers, The Meditations of Saint Teresa,* and Josephus's *History of the Jews.*

Bibliography: J. BRUCKER, DTC 1.2:1978–83. J. OSWALD, Lex ThK[2] 1:889–890. Cross ODCC 88–89. B. MATTEUCCI, EncCatt 1:2005–08. R. P. DU PAGE, DictBiogFranc 1:760–764. J. DEDIEU, *ibid.* 2:1061–71. J. BALTEAU et al., *ibid.* 3:849–897. L. PICHARD et al., DictLetFranc 2:64; 84–85; 98–103. A. VOGT et al., DHGE 4:444–500. J. ORCIBAL, *Les Origines du jansénisme,* 5 v. (Louvain 1947–62). P. J. VARIN, *La Vérité sur les Arnaulds,* 2 v. (Paris 1847). J. LAPORTE, *La Doctrine de Port-Royal,* 2 v. in 4 (Paris 1923–51). C. A. SAINTE-BEUVE, *Port-Royal,* ed. M. LEROY, 3 v. (Bibliothèque de la Pléiade 98, 99, 107; Paris 1952–55). A. DE MEYER, *Les Premières controverses Jansénistes en France, 1640–1649* (Louvain 1919). A. GAZIER, *Histoire générale du mouvement janséniste . . .,* 2 v. (Paris 1922); *Jeanne de Chantal et Angélique Arnauld d'après leur correspondance, 1620–1641* (Paris 1915). C. GAZIER, *Ces messieurs de Port-Royal* (Paris 1932); *Histoire du monastère de Port-Royal* (Paris 1929). C. P. GOUJET, ed., *Mémoires pour servir à l'histoire de Port-Royal,* 3 v. (n.p. 1734–37). H. BRÉMOND, *Histoire littéraire du sentiment religieux en France,* 11 v. (Paris 1916–33) v.4. J. FRENCKEN, *Agnès Arnauld* (Nijmegen 1932). J. PANNIER, *. . . La Mère Angélique* (Issy-les-Moulineaux 1930). L. COGNET, *La Mère Angélique et saint François de Sales, 1618–1626* (Paris 1951). C. COCHIN, *Henry Arnauld, évêque d'Angers* (Paris 1921). **Illustration credits:** Fig. 1, Alinari-Art Reference Bureau. Fig. 2, Archives Photographiques, Paris.

[J. Q. C. MACKRELL]

ARNDT, ERNST MORITZ, German poet, historian, and Protestant theologian; b. Schoritz, Isle of Rügen, Germany, Dec. 26, 1769; d. Bonn, Jan. 29, 1860. After studying history, philosophy, theology, and science at the universities of Greifswald and Jena, he became professor of history and philosophy at Greifswald (1805) and at Bonn (1818). The first edition of his *Geist der Zeit* (1806) urged the Germans to resist the French, and consequently he was forced to flee to Sweden (1807–09). The fourth part of the same book (1818), which criticized the reactionary policies of the German princes, precipitated his dismissal from the university (1820). He was not rehabilitated until 1840. Arndt was one of the Prussian royalist representatives to the *Paulskirchen* Assembly in Frankfurt (1848). His numerous books, patriotic and religious poems, and hymns revealed his political and social ideals. Under the influence of the Swede Thomas Thorild, Rousseau, and Luther (whom he interpreted in strange fashion), Arndt developed and applied the ideas of Johann Friedrich von *Schiller and the ideals of classical antiquity by advocating a romantic Germanic-Christian notion of the national personality. Much of Arndt's thought was formulated as a reaction to anti-Christian feeling in France after the French Revolution. Arndt made concrete proposals for the political structuring of Germany that would exclude Austria, but his nationalistic ideas conflicted with his original notion of a Germany mediating between nations. His suggestions for church unity between Protestants and Catholics were founded on political considerations that lacked a theological basis.

Ernst Moritz Arndt.

Bibliography: *Ausgewählte Werke,* ed. H. RÖSCH et al., 14 v. (Leipzig and Magdeburg 1892–1909). E. MÜSEBECK, Herzog-Hauck PRE 23:117–123; *Ernst Moritz Arndt* (Gotha 1914). G. LANGE, *Der Dichter Arndt* (Berlin 1910). E. CREMER, *E. M. Arndt als Geschichtsschreiber* (Potsdam 1926). W. VON EICHHORN, *E. M. Arndt und das deutsche Nationalbewusstsein* (Berlin 1932). A. G. PUNDT, *Arndt and the Nationalist Awakening in Germany* (New York 1935). Cross ODCC 89. E. WOLF, RGG[3] 1:630–631. **Illustration credit:** Ernst Moritz Arndt Haus, Bonn.

[D. RITSCHL]

ARNOBIUS, THE ELDER, 4th-century Christian apologist; d. *c.* 327. According to St. *Jerome (*Chron.* ad ann. A.D. 253–327), Arnobius, a distinguished rhetorician at Sicca in proconsular Africa, who numbered Lactantius among his pupils (*De vir. ill.* 80), was a pagan who vigorously combated Christianity. Arnobius, however, was converted by dreams (*Chron. loc. cit.*), although he himself did not mention his motives. To prove his sincerity, he composed the *Adversus nationes* sometime before 311. More an attack on paganism than a defense of Christianity, the *Adversus nationes* is classed among the apologies on the strength of the first two of its seven books. In the 4th century only Jerome knew of it; by the 6th century it was grouped with the apocrypha. It is extant in only one 9th-century manuscript. The work was greatly influenced by non-Christian writers, although it gives evidence that Arnobius was familiar with Clement of Alexandria, Tertullian, and Minucius Felix. Arnobius made no use of the New Testament, and openly repudiated the Old (*Adv. nat.* 3.12). Though a poor source for Christian teaching, the work is useful for information about contemporary pagan religions. Book 1 defends Christianity against the calumnies of the pagans. Book 2 treats Christ's salvific acts, the final destiny of mankind, and the essence of Christianity. Books 3 to 5 attack the pagans, their deification of abstractions, and the mystery cults. Books 6 to 7 demonstrate that the pagans offend the divinity by their false cults and pagan sacrifices.

Bibliography: A. REIFFERSCHEID, ed., CSEL v.4 (1875). PL 5:350–1372. Bardenhewer 2:517–525. P. MONCEAUX, *Histoire* *littéraire de l'Afrique chrétienne,* 7 v. (Paris 1901–23; repr. Brussels 1963) 2:135–197. E. RAPISARDA, *Arnobio* (Catania 1946). Quasten Patr 2:383–392. M. NICCOLI, EncCatt 1:2011. J. MARTIN, LexThK² 1:891–892.

[R. K. POETZEL]

ARNOBIUS THE YOUNGER, 5th-century Christian writer; d. after 451. Arnobius was probably an African who lived as a monk in Rome. The list of his writings is equally uncertain, but modern critics, especially Dom G. *Morin, have tried to establish them.

Arnobius wrote *Commentarii in Psalmos* (PL 53: 486–552), which contains brief and pointed, but uncritical comments on the Psalms as well as an attack on the Augustinian theory of predestination. He probably wrote also *Expositiunculae in Evangelium,* a poorly constructed commentary on the Gospels of Matthew, Luke, and John, and *Conflictus Arnobii catholici cum Serapione Aegyptio* (PL 73:569–580), a dialogue attacking the Monophysites (*see* MONOPHYSITISM). Morin attributed two other works to him: *Liber ad Gregoriam,* a spiritual treatise addressed to an unhappily married woman, formerly attributed to *John Chrysostom; and *Praedestinatus* (PL 73:587–672), a tract in three books that surveys the heresies listed in Augustine's *De haeresibus,* outlines the doctrine on grace and predestination wrongly attributed to Augustine, and refutes these latter doctrines.

In Morin's attribution of these works to Arnobius, one problem remains unexplained: how can the man who attacked Augustinian teachings in both *Commentarii* and *Praedestinatus* be also the author of *Conflictus,* which defends Augustine's writings on Pelagianism almost as if they were the writings of an Apostle. Arnobius is considered a semi-Pelagian who approached orthodoxy in *Commentarii* with his recognition of the evils that befell mankind as a result of original sin.

Bibliography: G. MORIN, *Anecdota maredsolana,* v.3.3 (Maredsous 1903) 129–151; *Études, textes, découvertes,* v.1 (Maredsous 1913) 383–439. P. DE LABRIOLLE, DHGE 4:547–549. M. NICCOLI, EncCatt 1:2010–11. H. KEYSER, *Die Schriften des sogenannten Arnobius* (Gütersloh 1912). M. MONACHESI, *Bolletino del circolo universitario di studi storico-religiosi,* 1 (1921) 96– ; 2 (1922) 18– . A. PINCHERLE, EncIt 4:551.

[R. K. POETZEL]

ARNOLD OF BONNEVAL (MARMOUTIER), abbot, writer, and friend and biographer of St. Bernard of Clairvaux; d. after 1156. Few facts about his life are available, but he is known by his writings and for the esteem in which he was held by St. Bernard. He was a monk of Marmoutier in 1138 and was made abbot of Bonneval in the Diocese of Chartres, probably *c.* 1144. Because of internal troubles in his monastery, he journeyed to Rome, where he received papal approval for his policies. He resigned his abbatial office sometime before 1156 and possibly died at Marmoutier. He was recognized for his learning and piety, and many important personages were numbered among his friends and correspondents. At the request of the monks of Clairvaux, he undertook the writing of the life of St. Bernard begun by *William of Saint-Thierry. His writings include discourses on the gifts of the Holy Spirit, on the seven last words of Our Lord, a sermon in praise of Our Lady, a commentary on Psalm 132, and a variety of meditations and spiritual treatises.

Bibliography: A. PRÉVOST, DHGE 4:421–423. P. POURRAT, *Catholicisme* 1:849. I. CECCHETTI, EncCatt 1:2000–01.

[J. C. WILLKE]

ARNOLD OF BRESCIA, radical Church reformer; b. Brescia, Italy, *c.* 1100; d. Rome, 1155. Arnold studied at Paris under Peter *Abelard and later joined the *Canons Regular of St. Augustine, becoming prior of the monastery in Brescia. There he advocated a radical reform of the Church, emphasizing the necessity of absolute clerical poverty and the abandonment of wealth and temporal power by the Church. In 1139, when his reform proposals were condemned by the Second *Lateran Council, Arnold was banished from Italy. He took refuge in France and helped his former master, Abelard, defend himself at the Council of Sens in 1141. They were unsuccessful, for by a decree of July 16, 1141, *Innocent II upheld the Council's condemnation of Arnold and Abelard and ordered them to be confined in separate monasteries. Soon after this, however, Arnold was teaching in the schools of Mont Sainte-Geneviève in Paris. When *Bernard of Clairvaux persuaded the French King to expel him from France, Arnold took refuge in Zurich and later in Bohemia. In 1145 he was reconciled with Pope *Eugene III, but the reconciliation was short-lived. Arnold soon broke with the Pope and allied himself with a rebel political party in Rome that sought to abolish the Pope's *temporal power. Arnold was excommunicated once more on July 15, 1148. Pope *Adrian IV continued the struggle against Arnold and his allies. In 1155 Arnold was finally expelled from Rome and fell into the hands of the Emperor *Frederick I Barbarossa, who committed him to the prefect of Rome for trial as a rebel. The prefect condemned Arnold to be hanged, his body to be burned, and his ashes to be thrown into the Tiber. Arnold was executed in 1155.

The Arnoldist movement, which survived Arnold's death and which became overtly heretical, stressed apostolic poverty for the clergy, as did other heretical movements of the 12th century. The Arnoldists went further, however, and repudiated the power of the hierarchy entirely, denied the jurisdictional powers of the Church, and held as invalid the Sacraments administered by clerics possessed of any worldly goods. They were condemned by the Council of Verona in 1184.

Bibliography: OTTO OF FREISING, *The Deeds of Frederick Barbarossa,* ed. and tr. C. C. MIEROW and R. EMERY (New York 1953). JOHN OF SALISBURY, *Memoirs of the Papal Court,* ed. and tr. M. CHIBNALL (New York 1956). A. FRUGONI, *Arnaldo da Brescia nelle fonti del secolo XII.* (Rome 1954). A. FLICHE, *Catholicisme* 1:849–850.

[J. A. BRUNDAGE]

ARNOLD OF HILTENSWEILER, BL., monastic founder; fl. first quarter of the 12th century (feast, May 1). He was a layman who founded a convent at Langnau, near Bern. Few details of his life are known. He appears to have been a member of the First *Crusade from 1099 to 1100 and is usually represented with a banner on which there is a cross inscribed. Although married, he was childless, and in 1122, by a grant confirmed by the Emperor *Henry V, he left all his property to the house of All Saints at Schaffhausen on the Rhine. The date of his death is unknown but was after 1127, when his name last appears in the records. He was buried in the oratory that he had founded at Hiltensweiler.

Bibliography: W. MÜLLER, LexThK² 1:893. P. VOLK, DHGE 4:565. *Schriften des Vereins für Geschichte des Bodensees* 13 (1884) 133–148.

[J. L. GRASSI]

ARNOLD OF LÜBECK, abbot, chronicler; d. between 1211 and 1214. He was educated at *Hildesheim or Brunswick, and he became the first abbot of the Benedictine monastery of St. John in *Lübeck. In the conflict between the papacy and the Hohenstaufen, he championed the papacy. He compiled the *Chronica Slavorum* for the years 1172 to 1209. The title of this work, written by Arnold between 1204 and 1209, does not adequately describe its contents. It is a continuation of the chronicle of *Helmold, to whom the author was inferior as a historian. Nevertheless, the *Chronica* was based on letters and documents as well as information received orally from Bp. Henry of Lübeck. Despite exaggerations, errors, and interpolations, the chronicle is an important source of information about many events of the era in which *Henry the Lion, *Henry VI, Philip of Swabia, and *Otto IV were active. At the request of William of Lüneberg, younger brother of Otto IV, Arnold translated the *Gregorius* of Hartmann of Aue into Latin verse.

Bibliography: MGSrerGerm v.14. R. DAMUS, *Die Slavenchronik Arnolds von Lübeck* (Lübeck 1872). Wattenbach 2:343–345. L. BOITEUX, DHGE 4:567–568.

[M. F. MC CARTHY]

ARNOLD OF VILLANOVA, medical doctor, lay theologian, Church reformer; b. Diocese of Valencia, Spain, *c.* 1240; d. near Genoa, en route from Sicily to *Avignon, September 1311. He was born of a Provençal family, and he studied theology under the *Dominicans in Montpellier (*c.* 1260) and later (1281–85) Hebrew as well as Talmudic and rabbinic literature in the missionary college for Oriental languages in Barcelona, directed by the Dominican *Raymond Martini. His medical studies, begun likewise in Montpellier (*c.* 1260), were continued in Naples and with Arabic physicians in Valencia. From 1289 to 1299 Arnold taught medicine at the new University of *Montpellier. He was the physician of popes (Boniface VIII, Benedict XI, and Clement V) and kings (Peter III and James II of Aragon and Frederick III of Sicily). Frederick III frequently sent him on diplomatic missions, and Arnold used his prestige to spread his ideas on theology and reform. Apocalyptic and eschatological treatises such as the *Expositio super Apocalypsi* and *Tractatus de tempore adventus Antichristi et fine mundi* gave way in his last years to works favoring the Franciscan *Spirituals, the *Beguines, and to royally directed evangelical reform. Arnold's religious works, written in Latin and Catalan, never became well known, because of inquisitorial condemnation on 14 counts in Tarragona (1316). However, his 70 scientific works written in Latin were popular and were printed in incomplete editions at Lyons (1504), Paris (1509), Venice (1514), and Basel (1585). They include translations of Arabic works, commentaries on classical medical texts, aphorisms, *summae* of medical science (e.g., *Breviarium practicae capite usque ad plantam pedis*), treatises on hygiene (*regimina*), and tracts on alchemy (e.g., *Rosarius philosophorum*) and on other occult sciences (*see* TRANSLATION LITERATURE, GREEK AND ARABIC).

Bibliography: ARNOLD OF VILLANOVA, *Obres catalanes,* v.1 *Escrits religiosos;* v.2 *Escrits mèdics,* ed. M. BATLLORI (Barcelona 1947). B. HAURÉAU, HistLittFranc 28:26–126, 487–490. M. MENÉNDEZ Y PELAYO, *Historia de los heterodoxos españoles,* 7 v. (2d ed. Madrid 1911–32), ed. E. SÁNCHEZ REYES, 8 v. (*Edición nacional* 35–42; Santander 1946–48) 2:247–292. Thorndike 2:841–861. Sarton 2:893–900. M. BATLLORI, "Orientaciones bibliográficas para el estudio de A. de V.," *Pensamiento* 10 (1954) 311–323. Edition of Latin religious writings in preparation, *Corpus philosophorum medii aevi* (Desclée).

[F. GORMLY]

ARNOLD, GOTTFRIED, evangelical mystic and Church historian; b. Annaberg, Saxony, Sept. 5, 1666; d. Perleberg, May 30, 1714. After absorbing *Pietism from Philipp *Spener in Dresden, he drifted toward radical spiritualism. In line with the teaching of Abbot Joachim of Floris and Sebastian Franck, his *Die erste Liebe* (1696) depicted the early Church as a golden period from which subsequent ages fell. His controversial, richly documented *Unpartheyischen Kirchen- und Ketzerhistorie* (1699), though announcing the principle of impartiality, virtually presented the heretics, especially the mystics, as the true Christians. In it Church and piety, dogma and experience are considered incompatible; Church history becomes the history of regenerate men. This subjective emphasis anticipated the idealistic principle that history is the education of mankind; it influenced the historiography of the Enlightenment (Johann Semler, Johann Lorenz von Mosheim), of Johann Gottfried von Herder, Johann Wolfgang von Goethe, Wilhelm Dilthey, and Walther Koehler. Subsequently moderating his religious views, he settled down as a pastor in Allstedt (1702) and Werben (1704), and as superintendent in Perleberg (1707). He was a prolific author of historical works, devotional treatises, and hymns; translator of Miguel de Molinos and Mme. Jeanne Guyon; and editor of Angelus Silesius.

Bibliography: *Gottfried Arnold,* ed. E. SEEBERG (Munich 1934), excerpts. E. SEEBERG, *G. Arnold, die Wissenschaft und die Mystik seiner Zeit* (Meerane, Ger. 1923). W. NIGG, *Das Buch der Ketzer* (Zurich 1949). E. HIRSCH, *Geschichte der neuern evangelischen Theologie,* 5 v. (Gütersloh 1949–54; reprint 1960) v.2. B. HEURTEBIZE, DTC 1.2:1987. M. SCHMIDT, RGG[3] 1:633–634. E. W. ZEEDEN, LexThK[2] 1:896.

[R. H. FISCHER]

ARNOLD, MATTHEW

Poet and critic; b. Laleham, Middlesex, Dec. 24, 1822; d. Liverpool, April 15, 1888. He was the eldest son of Thomas Arnold, England's most famous schoolmaster ("Arnold of Rugby"). He attended Rugby School and Oxford, where he earned second-class honors (1844), and was elected a fellow of Oriel College (1845). In 1847 he became private secretary to Lord Lansdowne, and from 1851 to 1886 worked as an inspector of schools. He was professor of poetry at Oxford from 1857 to 1867; this entailed only an occasional lecture but gave him a platform for his critical ideas. He visited the U.S. twice, in 1883 and 1886.

During the 1840s and 1850s Arnold devoted his talent to poetry; during the 1860s, to literary criticism and to commentary on politics and society; during the 1870s, to the search for a viable basis for Christianity in the modern world; and during the 1880s, again to literary and social criticism.

Arnold was a minor poet; the final impression left by his relatively small output of verse is pleasant but fragmentary. But although minor, Arnold was definitely modern. Using the plain, or "pure," idiom learned from Wordsworth, he applied his poetic insight to the dilemma of contemporary man: his isolation, his alienation from himself and from his fellow man, and his loneliness. In his prose, too, Arnold saw himself as a modern spirit, that is, one of the "dissolvents of the old European system of dominant ideas and facts." His whole effort was to remove "the want of correspondence between the forms of modern Europe and its spirit, between the new

Matthew Arnold, portrait by G. F. Watts.

wine of the eighteenth and nineteenth centuries, and the old bottles of the eleventh and twelfth centuries, or even of the sixteenth and seventeenth." This effort is all-pervasive and all-controlling in Arnold's thought on literature, on society, on religion. Like Goethe, Wordsworth, and Newman—from each of whom he learned much—he felt that "the sky over his head [was] of brass and iron" and that humanity was about to go into "the drab of the earnest, prosaic, practical, austerely literal future." Against this disturbing prospect, Arnold set culture, a knowledge of the best that has been thought and said in the world, and the "social idea" of culture, the attempt to make the best prevail.

Though himself a liberal Protestant, Arnold saw in Catholicism superiority "in its charm for the imagination, its poetry." "I persist in thinking," he said in *Mixed Essays* (1879), "that Catholicism has, from this superiority, a great future before it; that it will endure while all the Protestant sects (amongst which I do not include the Church of England) dissolve and perish. I persist in thinking that the prevailing form of Christianity of the future will be the form of Catholicism. . . ."

Arnold's first volume of poetry, *The Strayed Reveller, and Other Poems,* appeared in 1849; the first collected edition in 1869. Among his principal prose works are: *On Translating Homer* (1861); *Essays in Criticism,* First Series (1865); *On the Study of Celtic Literature* (1867); *Culture and Anarchy* (1869); *St. Paul and Protestantism* (1870); *Literature and Dogma* (1873); *Last Essays on Church and Religion* (1877); *Irish Essays, and Others* (1882); *Discourses in America* (1885); and *Essays in Criticism,* Second Series (1888).

Bibliography: *Works,* ed. G. W. RUSSELL, 15 v. (London 1903–04); *The Poetical Works,* ed. C. B. TINKER and H. F. LOWRY (3d ed. London 1950). G. E. SAINTSBURY, *Matthew Arnold* (New York 1899). H. W. PAUL, *Matthew Arnold* (London 1902). G. W. RUSSELL, *Matthew Arnold* (New York 1904). L. TRILLING, *Matthew Arnold* (New York 1939). E. K. BROWN, *Matthew Arnold: A Study in Conflict* (Chicago 1948). **Illustration credit:** National Portrait Gallery, London.

[W. BUCKLER]

ARNOLDI, BARTHOLOMAEUS, Augustinian, Luther's teacher, later opponent; b. Usingen near Frankfort, 1465; d. Würzburg, Sept. 9, 1532. Arnoldi (commonly called Usingen) entered the University of Erfurt in 1484 and received a master of arts (1491) and a doctorate in theology (1514). As a professor of philosophy there he expounded the nominalist viewpoint (*via moderna*) of Ockham and Biel, which Luther (studying there, 1501–05) later reflected in his theology. Around 1512 Luther persuaded him to join the Augustinians, for whom Usingen later taught theology. Always firmly Catholic, although he attacked abuses, Usingen rejected Luther's 95 theses and broke with him in 1520. He feared the consequences of the new doctrines, especially that on good works. Luther tried persuasion, but after Usingen's sermons at Erfurt in 1521, his violent reply provoked a war of letters. Although weak as theologian and Latinist, Usingen answered Luther's ideas on their own ground after thorough study. He believed that Luther had gone wrong in theology by rejecting philosophy. In 1526 he left Erfurt to join the Augustinians at Würzburg. There he assisted the bishop (Conrad von Thungen), took charge of several monasteries, and preached against Luther. At the diet of Augsburg (1530) he helped examine the Augsburg Confession.

Bibliography: N. PAULUS, *Der Augustiner Bartholomäus Arnoldi von Usingen* (Freiburg 1893). N. HÄRING, *Die Theologie des . . . B. A. v. Usingen* (Limburg 1939). C. BERTOLA, EncCatt 1:2013. L. BOITEUX, DHGE 4:583–586. A. ZUMKELLER, LexThK² 1:896–897.

[J. T. GRAHAM]

ARNOLFO DI CAMBIO, Italian Gothic sculptor and architect, the most important pupil of Niccolò *Pisano; b. Colle di Val d'Elsa, *c.* 1245; d. Florence, *c.* 1302. Arnolfo is first mentioned as chief assistant to Niccolò Pisano in the pulpit for Siena cathedral (1265–68); he also seems to have taken an important part in the work on the tomb of St. Dominic (1265–67, S. Domenico, Bologna). After his early training in Niccolò's classicizing style, Arnolfo began to work independently about 1268. His funeral monuments had a lasting influence on medieval tomb ensembles. The most important of these is the signed monument of Cardinal Guglielmo de Bray (1282; San Domenico, Orvieto), in which the two angels drawing back the curtains on either side of the recumbent effigy show the new Gothic naturalism that is most apparent in Arnolfo's early works.

Arnolfo di Cambio, monument of Cardinal Guglielmo de Bray, in the church of San Domenico, Orvieto, 1282.

Still debatable is the extent of his direct participation in the designing of two signed ciboria in Rome (1285, St. Paul-Outside-the-Walls; 1293, S. Cecilia in Trastevere). In 1296 Arnolfo was called to Florence for his most important architectural commission, the cathedral. Perhaps influenced by the Baptistery nearby, his project for the façade stresses a balance between horizontals and verticals that led *Vasari to call him the first "modern" architect. His plan, including a trefoil-shaped east end and providing for great spaciousness, was retained in the later construction. Some of the sculptures from his workshop for the façade are extant; these show Etruscan influence in the heavy forms with their angularly stylized drapery. His Virgin and Child for the main portal (Museo dell'Opera, Florence) is done in a severely classic, monumental style.

Bibliography: J. Pope-Hennessy, *Italian Gothic Sculpture* (his *Introduction to Italian Sculpture* 1; New York 1958). M. Salmi, "Una precisazione su Arnolfo architetto," *Palladio* NS 7 (1957) 92–94. **Illustration credit:** Anderson-Art Reference Bureau.

[M. M. SCHAEFER]

ARNON, Hebrew name (*'arnôn*) of an important wadi (Heb. *naḥal*) in *Transjordan now called Wâdī el-Môjib. It was first formed geologically by an east-west side-faulting at the time of the great north-south faulting that caused the Jordan-Araba depression. The torrential rains that here accompanied the periods of Pleistocene glaciation in the north cut this side-fault down into a deep canyon. The Arnon, which is fed by side streams about 50 miles east of the Dead Sea, runs almost due west through deep ravines with high rugged sides until it empties into the Dead Sea. The gorge is more than 2 miles wide at one place where the river bed is 1,650 feet below the top of the cliffs. In its lower half flows a perennial stream. At the time of the conquest of the Promised Land, when the upper Arnon was crossed by the Israelites, it formed the boundary between the Amorrite kingdom of Sehon to the north and *Moab to the south. Later, the land north of the Arnon was temporarily occupied by the Israelite tribe of *Ruben. The account of these events, with its mention of the Arnon, is related in Nm 21.13, 24; 22.36; Dt 2.24; 3.8, 12, 16; 4.48; Jos 12.1–2; Jgs 11.13, 18. Also, the *Mesha Inscription (*c.* 845 B.C.) from Dhībân, which recounts Moab's taking of the territory of Ruben in the 9th century by Mesha, King of Moab (4 Kgs 3.4), mentions the valley: "I built Aroer, and I made the highway in the Arnon [Valley]" (see Pritchard ANET[2] 320). The new highway to Petra now crosses the Arnon.

Bibliography: L. H. Grollenberg, *Atlas of the Bible,* tr. J. M. Reid and H. H. Rowley (New York 1956) 16, 54, 80. D. Baly, *The Geography of the Bible* (New York 1957) 227, 236. EncDictBibl 138. Abel GéogrPal 1:177, 487–489.

[C. F. DE VINE]

ARNOUX, JEAN, French preacher and confessor of Louis XIII; b. Riom, Jan. 19, 1576; d. Toulouse, May 19, 1636. He entered the Jesuits in 1594 and began his career as a teacher of philosophy and theology. His talent for preaching led to a number of assignments in eastern France and then in Paris where he gained the attention of *Louis XIII. From 1617 to 1621 he acted as confessor to Louis XIII. During his years as royal confessor Arnoux was involved in a doctrinal controversy with the Huguenots. He also played an important role in the reconciliation of Louis XIII and *Marie de Médicis in 1619 and 1620. After his dismissal as confessor Arnoux preached throughout France and in Rome, and died while he was serving as the provincial of the Jesuits of Toulouse.

Bibliography: H. Fouqueray, *Histoire de la compagnie de Jésus en France: Des origines à la suppression, 1528–1762,* 5 v. (Paris 1910–25) 3:420–474. Sommervogel 1:566–572. E. Lamalle, DHGE 4:627.

[J. M. HAYDEN]

ARNULF, GERMAN EMPEROR, Feb. 22, 896, to Dec. 8, 899, last Carolingian emperor; b. the natural son of Carloman, King of Bavaria, and the noblewoman Liutswind, *c.* 850; d. Regensburg. As margrave of Carinthia and Pannonia from 876 he distinguished himself for ability and valor. In 887 he led a successful uprising against *Charles III the Fat and was proclaimed King of the East Franks. His defeat of the Northmen in the battle of the Dyle in 891 helped to drive them westward from Germany. He was less successful in his struggle with the Slavic kingdom of Greater Moravia, against which he invoked the aid of the Hungarians. Summoned by Pope *Formosus to protect the Holy See from *Guido III of Spoleto (d. 894), he made two expeditions to Italy. In 895 he captured Rome from Guido's widow, Agiltrude, and was crowned Emperor by Formosus. While attempting to follow up his victory, he was stricken by paralysis and carried on a litter back to Germany, where he died after securing the succession in that country to his legitimate son, Louis the Child. He had previously appointed his natural son, Zwentibold, King of Lorraine (895). Arnulf was the last representative of the Carolingian imperial tradition. He recognized the monarchs chosen by France, Burgundy, and Italy but claimed the same kind of preeminence over them that *Lothair I had claimed over his brothers. An able and vigorous ruler, he fought a losing battle against the growing forces of particularism. He is buried in the abbey of *Sankt Emmeram in Regensburg.

Bibliography: Regino of Prüm, *Chronicon,* ed. G. H. Pertz, MGS 1:537–612. Liutprand of Cremona, *Antapodosis,* ed. G. H. Pertz, MGS 3:273–339; tr. F. A. Wright, in *The Works of Liutprand of Cremona* (London 1930) 1–123. *Arnolfi Diplomata,* ed. P. F. Kehr, MGD 3 (2d. ed. Berlin 1955). G. Tellenbach, "Zur Geschichte Kaiser Arnulfs," HistZ 165 (1942) 229–245. C. G. Mor, *L'Età feudale,* 2 v. (Milan 1952–53) 1:2–42. Gebhardt-Grundmann 1:155–159, with bibliog. T. Schieffer, LexThK[2] 1:900.

[C. E. BOYD]

ARNULF OF GAP, ST., bishop; b. Vendôme, France; d. Sept. 19, 1070–79 (feast, Sept. 19). Only fragments of information about Arnulf have been preserved. While a monk of Sainte-Trinité at Vendôme, he accompanied his abbot, Oderic, to Rome (*c.* 1061) to secure for Sainte-Trinité papal confirmation of the Roman church of St. Prisca and for its abbot the dignity of cardinal priest. Pope *Alexander II detained Arnulf as an adviser until *c.* 1066, when he consecrated him and installed him as bishop of Gap in France. There he was an able administrator and defender of the Church during the tumultuous *Gregorian Reform of the late 11th century.

Bibliography: ActSS Sept. 6:95–101. Zimmermann KalBen 3:77–79. A. M. Zimmermann, LexThK[2] 1:899–900. R. Aigrain, *Catholicisme* 1:855.

[S. WILLIAMS]

ARNULF OF LISIEUX, bishop; b. possibly Rouen, Normandy, France; d. monastery of Saint-Victor, Paris, France, Oct. 31, 1184. He was born of a well-known family in Normandy, and under the tutelage of his uncle John (fl. *c.* 1150), who was bishop of Sées, he began intensive literary studies. He became an archdeacon and subsequently went to Rome, where he remained for some time engaged in the study of *Canon Law. While in Rome he was a witness to the difficulties caused by the antipope Anacletus II (*see* PIERLEONI), who opposed the election of *Innocent II, and in 1134 he wrote a violent letter in defense of the Pope against Gerard, Bishop of Angoulême (d. 1136). Elected bishop of *Lisieux in 1141, he was for some time prevented from taking possession of his see until *Bernard of Clairvaux interceded with Pope Innocent to prevail upon Geoffrey, Count of Anjou (d. 1151), to withdraw his objections. In 1147 he accompanied *Louis VII on his crusade. Arnulf was an important figure and was deeply involved in the political events of his time. In the schism that followed the election of Pope *Alexander III he was faithful to the Pope and encouraged his fellow bishops in France, as well as *Henry II and the English bishops, to remain loyal. Arnulf became involved in the Thomas *Becket affair and attempted to arbitrate the difficulties although he has often been accused of being motivated by personal interests. In spite of serving the cause of the Plantagenet kings he was disgraced by the King but successfully defended himself against his charges. He resigned his episcopacy in 1181 and spent his final years in the monastery of *Saint-Victor in Paris. His works included the treatise on the schism of Anacletus and 130 letters to important personages of his time, as well as a collection of sermons and poems (PL 201:5–200).

Bibliography: H. WOLTER, LexThK² 1:900. A. NOYON, DHGE 4:609–611. Manitius 3:59–60, 903–905. HistLittFranc 14:304–334; 16:655–679.

[V. A. SCHAFER]

ARNULF OF METZ, ST., bishop; b. near Nancy, France, *c.* 582; d. Remiremont (*Habendum*), July 18, *c.* 641 (feast, Aug. 16 or 19). A member of a prominent Austrasian family, Arnulf was reared at the court of Metz and entered the administration of King Theodebert II (d. 612), possibly as mayor of the palace. He was the father of two sons, Ansegis (Ansegisellus; d. *c.* 685) and (St.) *Chlodulf (Cloud), the first of whom married (St.) *Begga, the daughter of Pepin of Landen (d. 640), and became the father of Pepin of Heristal (d. 714). Arnulf was thus the progenitor of the *Carolingian dynasty. The second son, Chlodulf, became his father's third successor in the See of *Metz. After the fall of *Brunhilde in 613, Arnulf assisted Pepin of Landen in reuniting the Frankish kingdoms; the following year his wife entered a convent in Trier, and Arnulf, still a layman, was promoted to the bishopric of Metz. He took part in the Synods of Clichy (626–27) and Reims (627–30), and after serving both Church and State for 15 years, he retired with his friend St. Romaric (d. 653) to the solitude of *Habendum* (*Remiremont), where he passed his remaining years. His successor, Goeric (d. 642), brought Arnulf's relics back to Metz.

Bibliography: *Vita,* ed. B. KRUSCH, MGSrerMer 2:426–446. PSEUDO-FREDEGARIUS, *Chronicon* (*ibid.* 2:140, 146–147, 150). PAUL THE DEACON, *Liber de episcopis Mettensibus,* MGS 2:264–265. M. PREVOST, DictBiogFranc 3:944–945. E. HATTON, DHGE 4:612–615. R. AIGRAIN, *Catholicisme* 1:855–857. J. DEPOIN, "Grandes figures monacales des temps mérovingiens: Saint Arnoul de Metz," *Revue Mabillon* 11 (1921) 245–258; 12 (1922) 13–25, 105–118.

[O. J. BLUM]

ARNULF OF MILAN, historian of the archbishops of *Milan; d. 1077. He was the great-grandson of the brother of and earlier archbishop of Milan, Arnulf I (d. 974), but very little is known of his life; what is known about him is derived from his writings. He was a member of the aristocratic class of the Capitani and was a notable person in his day. He was probably a cleric and perhaps even a subdeacon, for his writings contain many Biblical allusions and his style is Biblical. In the struggle for supremacy, in spite of his aristocratic background, he remained faithful to the discipline of the Church and to Pope *Gregory VII, although he frequently spoke out sharply against other ecclesiastics for their fraud and deceit, and he even resisted the appointment of Abp. *Atto of Milan. After the submission of *Henry IV at Canossa (*see* INVESTITURE STRUGGLE), Arnulf submitted to Atto and was a member of the diplomatic mission sent by the Milanese to promise loyalty to the archbishop. Arnulf is famed for his authorship of the *Gesta archiepiscoporum Mediolanensium*. In his history he related the events in which he participated, or based his account on the testimony of those whom he considered credible. The chronicle begins with King Hugo of Italy (d. 947) in 925 and concludes with the election of Rudolf of Rheinfelden (d. 1080) as king through the year 1077, though without a formal conclusion. The work is a source of first rank, and it is of great value for the study of the period.

Bibliography: PL 147:279–332. MGS 8:1–13. L. BOEHM, LexThK² 1:900–901. Manitius 3:507–509. A. FLICHE, DHGE 4:599; *La Réforme grégorienne,* 3 v. (Louvain 1924–37) v.2, *passim.*

[V. A. SCHAEFER]

ARNULF OF SOISSONS, ST., reforming bishop; b. Pamel, Brabant, Belgium, *c.* 1040; d. Oudenbourg, Belgium, Aug. 15, 1087 (feast, Aug. 15). His life admirably illustrates both the piety and the irregularity of ecclesiastical life in Europe before the *Gregorian Reform. He devoted himself to personal asceticism and to an unsuccessful effort at ecclesiastical reform. After a brief military career, Arnulf entered the monastery of Saint-Médard at *Soissons *c.* 1020. His rigorous asceticism won the admiration of his fellow monks, and they elected him to replace Raymond, then abbot of the monastery, a worldly man and guilty of *simony. In the year 1080 or 1081 he was elected bishop of Soissons, again to replace an ecclesiastic of bad repute, Bishop Ursio. However, Arnulf's efforts to reform the diocesan clergy were stoutly and successfully resisted, and within a few years he was compelled to leave the diocese. He resigned the bishopric and again took up the monastic life, this time at Oudenbourg in Flanders, where he founded a monastery and lived out his days. He was buried in the church there, and in 1121 his body was translated and a public cult was declared. His life was written by Lizard, Bishop of Soissons, in the same century. Another life was written by Hariulf (d. 1143), who was abbot of Saint-Médard at Oudenbourg.

Bibliography: BHL 1:703–705a. MGS 15.2:872–904. A. PRÉVOST, DHGE 4:617–618. Zimmermann Kal Ben 2:576–578. É. DE MOREAU, *Histoire de l'Église en Belgique* (2d ed. Brussels 1945–). O. ENGLEBERT, *The Lives of the Saints,* tr. C. and A. FREMANTLE (New York 1951). Butler Th Attw 3:335–336. A. M. ZIMMERMANN, LexThK² 1:901.

[H. MAC KINNON]

AROSEMENA, MARIANO, Panamanian historian and politician; b. Panama City, July 26, 1794; d. there July 31, 1868. He was educated in accord with the social position of his family, which contributed many notable men to Panama. During the monarchial regime in Panama, Arosemena held such posts as agent of public credit, political head of tax administration, treasurer, and general administrator of plantations. He contributed to the success of Panamanian independence, which came on Nov. 28, 1821. The republican government of Colombia entrusted him with important and sensitive posts. He was deputy to the legislature, senator in the national congress, counselor of state, secretary of plantations and foreign relations of the state of the Isthmus, and minister plenipotentiary to Peru. The Republic of El Salvador honored him as its representative to the American International Congress of Lima in 1864. He had a strong bent for journalism and was editor of the first newspaper published in Panama (1820), *La Miscelánea del Istmo de Panamá*. He was also Panamanian correspondent for reputable foreign newspapers. In 1860 he wrote a book entitled *Apuntamientos históricos* (not published by the national government, however, until 1949); it is the first full account of political events in the isthmus during the first 40 years of the 19th century. [E. J. CASTILLERO]

ARRAS, COUNCILS OF. Episcopal succession at Arras (*Atrebatum*) dates from St. *Vedast (Vaast), *c.* 500–*c.* 540, though in the pontificate of either St. Vedulph (*c.* 545–*c.* 580) or St. *Géry (Gaugericus, 584 or 590–624 or 627) the diocesan seat was moved to Cambrai, where it remained until Pope Urban II (Dec. 2, 1092, and March 23, 1094; see Jaffé L 5472, 5512) decreed that Arras be a diocese distinct from Cambrai. On a Sunday early in 1025 the first known synod at Arras was summoned by Bp. *Gerard of Cambrai (1013–51). The extant acts (Mansi 19:423–460) show it to have dealt with the disciples of an Italian Manichee, Gundulph, who relied upon works for justification and rejected Baptism, the Eucharist, Matrimony, Penance, and Holy Orders, as well as sacred images and ecclesiastical burial. Gerard expounded a solid theology of the Church, of the Sacraments, and of justification and won a recantation from the heretics. Subsequent to Arras's reestablishment as a see, Bishop Lambert (1094–1115) held two synods in the city, one on Feb. 5, the other on Oct. 21, 1097 (Mansi 20:941–948). In February he granted a privilege to St. Denis monastery, Rheims; and in October, exemptions to religious houses at Saint-Amand-les-Eaux, Mont-Saint-Eloi, and Arrouaise. One of these assemblies threatened the chatelain Gonfrid with excommunication for his occupancy of church lands. A provincial council at Arras on May 10, 1128 (Mansi 21:371–374), transferred the church of the Virgin and St. John, Laon, from the control of canonesses who were in poor repute to that of monks. Later synods took place at Arras in 1442, 1490, and 1501 (Hefele-Leclercq 7:1151; 8:142, 219). In 1570 at Arras Bp. Francis Richardot (1561–74) published a collection of synodal statutes; between 1604 and 1616 eight diocesan synods were held, and another was convened in 1678 (Lestocquoy, 102, 130, 147).

Bibliography: Sources. T. M. J. GOUSSET, *Les Actes de la province ecclésiastique de Reims,* 4 v. (Reims 1842–44). Literature. R. RODIÈRE, DHGE 4:688–706. F. VERCAUTEREN, *Étude sur les civitates de la Belgique seconde* (Brussels 1934). H. LANCELIN, *Histoire du diocèse de Cambrai* (Valenciennes 1946). S. RUNCIMAN, *The Medieval Manichee* (Cambridge, Eng. 1947). J. LESTOCQUOY, *La Vie religieuse d'une province: Le Diocèse d'Arras* (Arras 1949). O. ENGELS, LexThK² 1:903.

[H. G. J. BECK]

ARRAS, MARTYRS OF, a group of four beatified Daughters of *Charity of St. Vincent de Paul who were martyred in 1794 during the *French Revolution (feast, June 26). They were Marie Madeleine Fontaine (b. 1723), superior of the community in Arras (Pas-de-Calais), Marie Françoise Lanel (b. 1745), Marie Thérèse Fontou (b. 1747), and Jeanne Gérard (b. 1752). The Daughters of Charity, who had been in Arras since 1656, were conducting a school for girls and aiding the sick in the town in 1789 and had 7 sisters in their convent. Their work continued as usual until 1793 when Joseph Lebon, an apostate priest and government official, imposed a lay director on the house, whose name was changed to *La Maison de l'Humanité,* and seized the community's goods, but permitted the sisters to remain and care for the sick, while dressed in secular attire. At this time the superior sent the two youngest sisters to Belgium, disguised as peasants, to preserve them from danger. A third sister returned to her family when her temporary vows expired (July 1792). When the four remaining sisters persisted in their refusal to take the oath of *Liberté-Égalité,* they were imprisoned (Feb. 14, 1794). On June 26 they were brought to Cambrai, placed on trial, condemned, and guillotined. They were beatified, together with the Martyrs of *Valenciennes, June 13, 1920.

Bibliography: A. LOVAT, *The Sisters of Charity Martyred at Arras in 1794* (London 1920). Baudot-Chaussin 6:448–455.

[M. LAWLOR]

ARREGUI, ANTONIO MARÍA, Spanish Jesuit theologian; b. Pamplona, Navarre, Jan. 17, 1863; d. Barcelona, Oct. 10, 1942. After teaching for 13 years before World War I in the Jesuit theologate at Oña, he published *Summarium theologiae moralis* (Bilbao 1918), a convenient handbook of moral theology used by Jesuit students of theology ever since. His 20 years as tertian master at Manresa brought him fame as an expert director in Jesuit spirituality. His second major work was on the constitution and rules of the Society of Jesus, *Annotationes ad epitomen Instituti Societatis Jesu* (Rome 1934).

Bibliography: M. ZALBA, "Un moralista español de nuestros días," *Estudios eclesiásticos* 19 (1945) 247–257. E. LAMALLE, EncCatt 2:21.

[J. M. UPTON]

ARREGUI, DOMINGO LÁZARO DE, 17th-century Mexican writer; place and date of birth and death unknown. Little is known about this author of *Descripción de la Nueva Galicia* except what can be gleaned from his writings. He was a native of Tepic, then an Indian village in which a few Spaniards lived. From his references to Spain, it may be that he was a Peninsular and not a Creole. The first positive date is 1607, when he served as sponsor for some Indians being baptized by the Jesuits at Atotonilco in Sinaloa. Apparently he knew Nahuatl well. At the beginning of the 17th century he went on a series of expeditions into the northeast, probably along the coast of Sinaloa. In 1621 he had already lived some time in New Galicia judging from the details of his description of it. It is not clear whether he was a layman or a cleric, but in any event he must have held some position under the bishop. According to documents in the Archivo General de Indias, the description of New Galicia was needed on the occasion of the division of the bishopric of Guadalajara so that justifiable boundaries could be made. A royal cedula of June 14, 1621, directed the president of the *audiencia* of Guadalajara, Pedro de Otalora, to have it done. Probably Arregui had an earlier unofficial order, for the report was ready Dec. 24, 1621. It was well organized and clearly presented, though the author was poor in literary style. The information was almost all based on observation and on the archives of the *audiencia;* there is little historical perspective and no critical spirit. However, the author clearly had no thesis he was trying to support in his writing, and therefore he produced a valuable historical document.

Bibliography: D. L. DE ARREGUI, *Descripción de la Nueva Galicia,* ed. F. CHEVALIER (Seville 1946).

[J. HERRICK]

ARRIAGA, PABLO JOSÉ DE, Jesuit missionary and author; b. Vergara, Guipúzcoa, Spain, 1564; d. in a shipwreck near Cuba, Sept. 6, 1622. Arriaga had been a student in Madrid before he entered the Jesuit novitiate at Ocaña Feb. 24, 1579. He taught rhetoric there and at Belmonte before going to Peru in 1585. He became a professor of rhetoric in Lima and made his profession in the society March 19, 1594. With the exception of a few intervals, he served as rector of the Colegio de San Martin in Lima and the Colegio in Arequipa for 24 years. He made a trip to Spain in 1601 and was on his way there again as a representative of his province when he died. Arriaga was a man of action as well as of study. Much concerned with the apostleship to the unfortunate Indians in both urban and rural areas of Peru, he worked particularly in the cities where they were mixed with Europeans. In Lima he supervised the building of a school for the children of the neighboring caciques. He was the author and translator of many spiritual books, including *La retórica cristiana* and some works of Mariology. His experiences as official visitor of the Indians resulted in his most important work, *Extirpación de la idolatría del Perú* (Lima 1621). José Toribio Medina felt that this volume, of all such books printed in Lima in colonial times, was worthy of being reprinted because of the information it contained on the history and ethnology of the Quechua area and especially of the Inca religion.

Bibliography: J. E. DE URIARTE and M. LECINA, *Biblioteca de escritores de la Compañía de Jesús pertenecientes a la antigua asistencia de España desde sus orígenes hasta el año de 1773,* 2 v. (Madrid 1925–30).

[A. DE EGAÑA]

ARRIAGA, RODRIGO DE, Spanish Jesuit philosopher and theologian; b. Logroño, Spain, Jan. 17, 1592; d. Prague, June 7, 1667. He entered the Society of Jesus in 1606 and taught philosophy at Valladolid and theology at Salamanca. In 1625 he was sent to the University of Prague, where he remained for the rest of his life. There he became professor of theology, then chancellor, and finally prefect of studies. His important works were *Cursus philosophicus* (Antwerp 1632, and other editions) and *Disputationes theologicae* (8 v. Antwerp 1643–55) based on St. Thomas Aquinas. He is known as one of the foremost Spanish Jesuits of his day and as a leading representative of the school of Suárez.

Bibliography: A. ASTRAIN, *Historia de la Compañía de Jesús en la Asistencia de España,* 7 v. (Madrid 1902–25) 6:4–5, 49–53. E. LAMALLE, EncCatt 2:22. Sommervogel 1:578–581.

[J. C. WILLKE]

ARRICIVITA, JUAN DOMINGO, Franciscan missionary and historian; b. Toluca, Mexico, 1720; d. Querétaro, Mexico, April 16, 1794. He entered the Franciscan Order at the Mission College of the Holy Cross in Querétaro in 1735. A reliable friar and a good priest, he spent most of his years in posts of secondary importance: as missionary in the San Sabá region of Texas (1748–50) and procurator of the missions of his college from 1757 to 1767, when he helped make arrangements for the Franciscans to replace the expelled Jesuits in their former missions in Sonora and lower Arizona. As part of this plan, he went to Spain in 1768 to recruit more missionaries. In 1770 the Inquisition named him censor of books for the Querétaro region and in 1778 his friend, Juan Ignacio de la Rocha, Bishop of Michoacán, requested him to head a group of friars to give missions in Colima and its environs. On Oct. 29, 1787, Arricivita was named official historian of Querétaro College to continue the work of Isidro *Espinosa, who had published the first part of the history of the college in 1746. The work had been neglected by the official historians in favor of other books, so Querétaro's achievements were sometimes bypassed as the chroniclers of the other colleges in Mexico published their accounts. Arricivita worked rapidly and his *Crónica seráfica y apostólica del colegio de Propaganda fide de la Santa Cruz de Querétaro* was sent to the press in 1791. Historians have generally considered Arricivita's work inferior to that of Espinosa even though its merits are substantial, chiefly because Arricivita knew the mission area so well and had taken an active part in many of the enterprises he described.

[L. G. CANEDO]

ARRIETA, FRANCISCO SALES DE, Peruvian Franciscan, archbishop of Lima; b. Lima, Jan. 29, 1768; d. there, May 4, 1843. He joined the Discalced Franciscans in Lima. He was named director of the Franciscan house of exercises in 1813, and later served as inspector of convents of the Lima province and as rector of the Third Order. In 1839 President Gamarra nominated him for archiepiscopal See of Lima. Arrieta's secret letter to Gregory XVI asking that he be excused from serving in this post was to no avail. On Jan. 24, 1841, he was consecrated archbishop. Arrieta worked to reform monastic life in Peru, becoming the confessor of many of the regular clergy. Owing to the reorganization he initiated in 1842, the Seminary of San Toribio began gradually to reacquire intellectual influence. Arrieta was indefatigable in his efforts to improve the religious instruction of children. The most serious challenge to Archbishop Arrieta was the shifting attack of Peruvian liberalism against the Church, manifested particularly in the actions of Manuel Lorenzo Vidaurre (1773–1841). As a young man Vidaurre showed a tendency to dismiss the spiritual beliefs of Catholicism, boasting deism and confidence in reason and science. In 1839 he published the *Vidaurre contra Vidaurre,* allegedly disavowing his own theological errors. The book, however, reflected the new position of Peruvian liberalism, insisting that the Church democratize its organizational structure, questioning papal supremacy, arguing that councils represented the voice of ultimate truth in Church affairs, demanding the suppression of ecclesiastical privileges such as private law courts, and affirming the absolute right of the State to supervise the Church in all temporal activities. Archbishop Arrieta condemned the widely read book. Thus were clearly established the main battle lines that Peruvian churchmen and anticlerical liberals defended for the next half century.

Bibliography: J. A. DE LAVALLE, *Galería de retratos de los arzobispos de Lima* (Lima 1892).

[F. B. PIKE]

ARRILLAGA, BASILIO, Jesuit defender of the Church in Mexico; b. Mexico City, June 1, 1791; d. there, July 28, 1867. After completing his studies in the humanities, philosophy, and law, and being ordained, Arrillaga joined the Jesuits (July 28, 1816). He was first appointed assistant to the master of novices, and from then on he held various important offices in the order, including dean of the college in Puebla and in Mexico City and later Jesuit provincial. During much of his life the Jesuits lived a precarious existence in Mexico, for the order was dissolved on occasion and persecuted frequently. Arrillaga was a dynamic and competent protagonist in the political-religious debates between the Church and the State. In 1821 he was named an alternate deputy to the Cortes and in December of that year he was one of the supporters of *Iturbide. From 1822 to 1825 he was rector of the Colegio Carolino in Puebla, but left there to go to Mexico City. He served briefly as a pastor, but even while carrying on pastoral duties he engaged actively in political discussion. He represented the Federal District in the congress in the mid-1830s and was president of the congress several times. He worked on a commission to plan a new educational system and was one of the founders of the Academia Mexicana de la Lengua and the Academia Nacional de la Historia. Santa Anna included him in a national legislative junta in 1842. From 1844 to 1849 he was rector of the University of Mexico. He was an honorary councilor of state under Maximilian, for which he was briefly imprisoned on the restoration of the republic. Arrillaga was a militant defender of the Church against liberal Catholicism and against the antireligious actions of those in charge of the government. He spoke and wrote vehemently and frequently, publishing in books and periodicals. He collected a library of thousands of volumes principally in philosophy, law, and history, which he used in writing his books, refuting his critics, and preparing his polemics.

Bibliography: G. DECORME, *Historia de la Compañía de Jesús en la República mexicana durante el siglo XIX,* 3 v. (Guadalajara, Mex. 1914–21; Chihuahua City 1959). E. VALVERDE TÉLLEZ, *Biobibliografía eclesiástica mexicana, 1821–1943,* 3 v. (Mexico City 1949).

[F. ZUBILLAGA]

ARROWSMITH, EDMUND, BL., Jesuit priest and martyr; b. Haydock, near St. Helens, 1585; d. Lancaster, Aug. 28, 1628 (feast, Aug. 28). This son of Robert Arrowsmith, a yeoman farmer of Lancashire, and Margery Gerard of Bryn, both of whom had been imprisoned for their faith, was christened Brian and in Confirmation took the name Edmund, by which he was henceforth known. After his father's death he was educated by an old priest, who in December 1605 sent him to the English College, Douai. There, after delays caused by ill health, he was ordained in 1612; the following year he returned to Lancashire. His forthright speech and fearlessness put his life in such constant danger that a friend recommended in jest that he should always carry salt in his pocket to season his actions. About 1622 he was caught and examined before the Anglican bishop of Chester, but was released; for at this time James I, interested in a Spanish match for his son, was anxious that his officials should show clemency to Catholics. Later Arrowsmith entered the Society of Jesus in the London novitiate at Clerkenwell, where his name appears on the lists of the house when it was raided in 1628. Shortly after his return to Lancashire he was betrayed by Holden, a young man whom he had reproved for his immoral life. At Lancaster assizes in August 1628 Arrowsmith came before Sir Henry Yelverton and was indicted for being a priest. Although the evidence against him was inadequate, he was sentenced to death and for 2 days was left without food and heavily manacled in a cell so narrow that he was unable to lie down. In the prison yard on his way to execution he received absolution from Bl. John *Southworth, who was also confined in Lancaster castle. Until his last moment Arrowsmith was heckled by ministers with the promise of his life if he would renounce his faith. He pleaded: "Tempt me no more. I will not do it, in no case, on no condition." His last words were "Bone Jesu." He was beatified by Pius XI on Dec. 15, 1929. His hand is preserved in the Catholic Church of St. Oswald at Ashton-in-Makerfield, near Wigan, and has been the source of many remarkable cures.

Bl. Edmund Arrowsmith.

Bibliography: *A True and Exact Relation of Two Catholicks Who Suffered for Their Religion at Lancaster in 1628* (London 1737), repr. and modernized in *Bl. Edmund Arrowsmith* (Postulation pamphlet; London 1960). B. CAMM, *Forgotten Shrines* (St. Louis 1910). H. FOLEY, ed., *Records of the English Province of the Society of Jesus,* 7 v. (London 1877–82) 7.1:18–19. R. CHALLONER, *Memoirs of Missionary Priests,* ed. J. H. POLLEN (rev. ed. London 1924). Butler Th Attw 3:439–440.

[G. FITZ HERBERT]

ARS DICTAMINIS

The medieval art of epistolary composition, which played an important part in the revival of studies in the 11th and 12th centuries. It began at *Monte Cassino when the monk *Alberic of Monte Cassino (d. *c.* 1105) taught *dictamen* (from Lat. *dictare,* dictate, draft, compose; hence Ger. *dichten, Dichter*) as a part of Ciceronian rhetoric in the classical tradition then prevailing in liberal arts schools. At *Bologna (*c.* 1115) teachers such as Adalbert of Samaria and *Hugh of Bologna began to teach *ars dictaminis* for clergy and laity alike. They also created the pattern for treatises on the art, the *Artes dictaminis* (or *dictandi*), which from then on consisted of two parts. The first treated of the theory of the style and structure of the letter, i.e., the salutation formulary and the "five parts"; the second contained models or examples for the letter and its parts.

Letter collections of a private, literary character as well as those of official character had long been used at the cathedral schools of Germany and France for the purpose of instruction. The chancellor of the chapter, who drafted the official documents, was also the teacher. Under the influence of Bologna, more and more fictitious material, such as that found in style exercises and models for student letters, was mingled with historical letters. Large collections of this type were composed in the schools of *ars dictandi* at Orleans, Meung, and Tours by such resident and itinerant teachers as Bernard of Meung, Pontius of Provence, *John of Garland, and Lawrence of Aquileia.

In Italy (*c.* 1200) at the Roman Curia, *Thomas of Capua took the lead with his *Summa dictamis;* at Bologna Buoncompagno, Guido Faba, Magister Bene, and Bonus of Lucca adapted the instruction in the art of letter writing to the needs of law students. Their new collections of *dictamina* provided models of letters for all classes and groups of society, including the citizens of the Italian communes. Here *ars dictaminis* was taught as a prerequisite for notatries, scribes, and schoolmasters. Moreover, since it also included rules and models for public oratory (*ars arengandi*), it served for the average citizen preparing for a public career.

Instruction in *ars dictaminis,* although barren of content and inferior to the training in classical literature of the preceding and the following centuries, nevertheless taught the elements of a style considered the highest literary fashion of the day. It was the *stilus altus* of the Sicilian court of Frederic II known from the *dictamina* of his famous chancellor, *Peter of Vinea. *Ars dictaminis* proved its training value not only for the Latin rhetoricians and *dictatores* but also for the Italian *rimatori* and *prosatori* from Guittone of Arezzo to *Dante. Because of their preoccupation with formal style and with secular oratory, the *dictatores* were forerunners of the humanists.

See also CURSUS.

Bibliography: L. VON ROCKINGER, ed., *Briefsteller und Formelbücher des elften bis vierzehnten Jahrhunderts* (Munich 1863). C. V. LANGLOIS, ed., *Formulaires de lettres* (Paris 1890–97). A. GAUDENZI, "Sulla cronologia delle opere dei dettatori Bolognesi," *Bullettino dell'Istituto Storico Italiano* 14 (1895) 85–174. C. S. BALDWIN, *Medieval Rhetoric and Poetic* (New York 1928). C. H. HASKINS, *Studies in Mediaeval Culture* (Oxford 1929). E. H. KANTOROWICZ, "An 'Autobiography' of Guido Faba," Med RenSt 1 (1941–43) 253–280. H. WIERUSZOWSKI, "'Ars Dictaminis' in the Time of Dante," MedHum 1 (1943) 95–108. H. M. SCHALLER, "Die Kanzlei Kaiser Friedrichs II," *Archiv für Diplomatik* 4 (1958) 264–327. G. VECCHI, *Il magistero delle artes latine a Bologna nel medioevo* (Bologna 1958). ADALBERTUS SAMARITANUS, *Praecepta dictaminum,* ed. F. J. SCHMALE (Weimar 1961). F. J. SCHMALE, LexThK² 2:693–694. A. SCHIAFFINI, *Tradizione e poesia* (Genoa 1934). P. O. KRISTELLER, "Humanism and Scholasticism in the Italian Renaissance," *Byzantion* 17 (1944–45) 346–374. E. R. CURTIUS, *European Literature and the Latin Middle Ages,* tr. W. R. TRASK (New York 1953). R. WEISS, *Il primo secolo dell'umanesimo* (Rome 1949).

[H. WIERUSZOWSKI]

ARS MORIENDI, a term that means the art of dying, refers to the whole collection of devotional books of the late Middle Ages containing thoughts of pastoral and ascetical value on death and dying. They were influenced by the reform movements of the high Middle Ages and the *Admonitio morienti,* attributed to *Anselm of Canterbury. The texts had a wide dissemination in the 14th and 15th centuries in the general anxiety attending the sociological, economic, and religious crises of the period. Numerous manuscripts as well as block-printed and hand-pressed books (there were 65 editions by 1500) are known to us. They first served to instruct the clergy in assisting the dying; then they appeared as illustrated block books, and once translated into the vernacular European languages, came into the possession of numerous laymen. They constitute an important source for study of the pastoral work and popular devotion of the late Middle Ages.

Especially well-known texts are those of Jean *Gerson [*Opus tripartitum de praeceptis decalogi, de confessione et de arte moriendi; Opera omnia,* v.1 (Antwerp 1726)], *Nicholas of Dinkelsbühl (who wrote the *Speculum artis bene moriendi,* previously attributed to

The "last agony of the dying man," woodcut from an "Ars Moriendi" block book printed in Germany c. 1470.

Dominic de *Capranica), Thomas Peuntner, and *Geiler von Kaisersberg. The most famous *Ars moriendi* is the block-book, originating probably in the Netherlands between 1430 and 1440 (a unique copy in the British Museum); it was frequently reprinted. The struggle of the angels and devils over the final destiny of man is represented in five pairs of pictures; in an 11th and final illustration the happy death of the Christian is depicted.

Bibliography: Editions. *The Ars moriendi . . . A Reproduction of the Copy in the British Museum,* ed. W. H. Rylands (London 1881). T. Peuntner, *Kunst des heilsamen Sterbens,* ed. R. Rudolf (Berlin 1958). Literature. F. Falk, *Die deutschen Sterbebüchlein* (Cologne 1890). W. L. Schreiber, *Manuel de l'amateur de la gravure sur bois et sur métal au XVe siècle,* v.4 (Leipzig 1902) 253–314. GesamtkW 2:2571–2635. J. Huizinga, *The Waning of the Middle Ages,* tr. F. J. Hopman (London 1924). A. Romeo, EncCatt 2:28–30. R. Rainer, *Ars moriendi* (Cologne 1957). **Illustration credit:** National Gallery of Art, Washington, D.C., Rosenwald Collection.

[F. DRESSLER]

ARS PRAEDICANDI

A literary genre comprising manuals on the art of preaching. In the period from 1200 to 1500, with the rise of the great preaching orders and the spread of scholasticism, preaching flourished both in practice and in theory. Special manuals proliferated; well over 200 are known, although most of them are still in manuscript form, unpublished. Many are anonymous. These systematic treatises are quite different from the sketchy and rudimentary attempts of the earlier period to give outline to the art, a period when the direct and uncomplicated *homily was the common type of preaching.

The professed aim of the preacher was to win souls to God, to provide instruction in faith and morals. He was advised to feed the mind rather than charm the ear, to confer profit rather than delight, and not to make a vainglorious display of his powers. Yet eloquence could be the handmaid of Christian truth and secular learning could be made use of by the preacher. Several of the best treatises on the *ars praedicandi* were devoted to sermons to be delivered to the clergy and students in the theological schools of the great universities, and they therefore reflect the taste of learned audiences.

The influence of classical rhetoric on the *ars praedicandi* is in some degree apparent, but the scholastic foundation goes even deeper—dialectical *topoi* abound in the method of developing the sermon. The most common method of sermon development in this period was the thematic, and this embraced a variety of types.

The thematic sermon was generally constructed of the following parts: the theme, drawn from the Bible; the protheme (or antetheme), likewise from the Bible, which should render the hearers attentive, receptive, and well-disposed, and lead to a prayer invoking God's aid; the reintroduction of the theme, beginning with a citation from Scripture, the Fathers, or a moral philosopher, and then proving by scriptural authorities the terms present in the theme, employing for the purpose argument, narration, example, or other means of explication; finally, the development, in which the parts of the theme are divided and subdivided and the process is carried out with application of a great variety of hermeneutical principles. Recourse to the concordant points in the authorities is constant. The sermon was often compared to a tree, the theme corresponding to the root, the protheme to the trunk, the main divisions to the larger branches, the subdivisions to the smaller, and the development to the rich foliage, flowers, and fruit.

Development by expansion was an important feature of preaching theory. Among the numerous means are maxims, the **exemplum,* etymology, the four senses of scriptural interpretation, rhythm, metrical consonance, and cadence (the last three serving also a mnemonic purpose), multiplication of synonyms, interpretation of a name, the logical categories, cause and effect, syllogisms and enthymemes, and opportune humor. The preacher's ethical qualities, personality, and deportment, and the psychology of many different kinds of audience are often considered, and advice of practical value is offered for the delivery of the sermon. Occasionally homiletical aids are recommended, such as Biblical commentaries, glosses, concordances, tracts on vices and virtues, collections of *exempla,* homiletic lexica, and text-materials—all storehouses on which the preacher could draw.

The highly schematized nature of the *artes,* with their serrated tissue of texts and divisions and their tendency to encourage mechanical artifice, verbal dexterity, and often false subtleties, induced an adverse reaction on the part of some critics both at the time and later. Others, however, praised the ingenuity of the inventional scheme, the adherence to good order, the firm foundation in Scripture, and the shrewd and sound observations. When allied to talent, the rules doubtless trained many effective preachers in their day.

See also PREACHING, I (HISTORY OF); PREACHING, II (HOMILETIC THEORY).

Bibliography: É. Gilson, "Michel Menot et la technique du sermon médiéval," *Revue d'histoire franciscaine* 2 (1925) 301–350. G. R. Owst, *Preaching in Medieval England* (Cambridge, Eng. 1926). T. M. Charland, *Artes praedicandi* (Ottawa 1936). W. O. Ross, ed., *Middle English Sermons* (London 1940). C. H. E. Smyth, *The Art of Preaching: A Practical Survey of Preaching in the Church of England, 747–1939* (New York 1940) 19–98. D. Roth, *Die mittelalterliche Predigttheorie und das Manuale Curatorum des Johann Ulrich Surgant* (Basel 1956). H. Caplan, "Classical Rhetoric and the Mediaeval Theory of Preaching," in *Historical Studies of Rhetoric and Rhetoricians,* ed. R. F. Howes (Ithaca 1961) 71–89, 387–391; "Rhetorical Invention in Some Mediaeval Tractates on Preaching," *Speculum* 2 (1927) 284–295; "The Four Senses of Scriptural Interpretation and the Medieval Theory of Preaching," *ibid.* 4 (1929) 282–290; *Mediaeval Artes praedicandi: A Hand-List* (Ithaca 1934); *Mediaeval Artes praedicandi: A Supplementary Hand-List* (Ithaca 1936).

[H. CAPLAN]

ARSENIUS AUTORIANUS, PATRIARCH OF CONSTANTINOPLE, 1255 to 1259 and 1261 to 1266, surnamed Autoreianos; b. probably Constantinople, *c.* 1200; d. 1273. He was baptized George, but changed his name to Gennadius as a monk; he became abbot of the monastery of Oxeia on the Island of Prinkipo. As Arsenius he was chosen by Theodore II Lascaris as an emissary to Rome (1254) and on his return was named patriarch of Nicaea (1255). Despite his distrust of the Emperor, he permitted himself to be used by the latter to crown (1259) *Michael VIII Palaeologus Emperor of Byzantium disregarding claims of the legitimate heir to the throne, John IV Lascaris. Tormented by his conscience, he resigned as patriarch of Nicaea; but under the prompting of Michael VIII he accepted the patriarchate of Constantinople (1261). When Michael VIII had John IV, the legitimate heir to the throne, blinded, Arsenius excommunicated the Emperor; and when Michael refused to abdicate, Arsenius was dethroned and exiled to the island of Proconnesus.

Arsenius declared his deposition and the nomination of the new Patriarch Joseph (1267–75) misdeeds that were bringing about the ruin of the Church. His many followers among the clergy and laity caused a crisis in the Byzantine Church by provoking the Schism of the Arsenites. Arsenius was exonerated and given a pension of 300 byzants, but he spent the remaining years of his life in exile on Proconnesus. Of his writing a number of Patriarchal Acts and a Testament have been preserved. He is credited with a Euchelaion Liturgy (last anointing), which is probably the result of a MS misunderstanding. He seems to have been the author of an Easter Sunday song and several poetic canons.

Bibliography: Beck KTLBR 702–703. Ostrogorsky 395, 411, 435. L. PETIT, DTC 1.2:1992–94. L. BRÉHIER, DHGE 4:750–751. A. A. VASILIEV, *History of the Byzantine Empire* (2d Eng. ed. Madison 1952) 544–661. V. LAURENT, ByzZ 30 (1929–30) 489–496. M. JUGIE, ÉchosOr 26 (1927) 416–419, Extreme Unction. V. GRUMEL, *ibid.* 33 (1934) 269–270.

[G. LUZNYCKY]

ART, ARTICLES ON

This article discusses the organization, scope, and types of articles covering the visual arts, including church architecture, in the NCE.

Art of Non-Christian Peoples. Surveys of the artistic production of cultures outside of predominantly Christian influence or those preceding Christianity have been limited to what is directly relevant to or impinges on Christianity. For the art and archeology of prehistory, *see* ARCHEOLOGY, I (PREHISTORIC); ART, PREHISTORIC. For the relevance of ancient art to the milieu of Biblical times and its influence on early Christian culture, *see* HITTITE AND HURRIAN ART; MESOPOTAMIA, ANCIENT, 2; ISLAMIC ART; EGYPT, ANCIENT, 2. For Biblical archeology *see* ARCHEOLOGY, II (BIBLICAL); PALESTINE, 7. Several articles discuss the formative influences of the classical world on Christian art; *see* HELLENISTIC ART; ART, EARLY CHRISTIAN; BYZANTINE ART; CHURCH ARCHITECTURE, 1, 2, 3; ARCHEOLOGY, III (CHRISTIAN). For Christian missionary art and architecture in such areas as Japan, India, and China, *see* MISSIONARY ART.

Early Christian to Modern. The vast amount of material on early Christian art and architecture and their development to the present is covered in a variety of articles.

Period Surveys. Systematic surveys by historical periods concentrate on painting, sculpture, and the minor arts; *see* ART, EARLY CHRISTIAN, 1, 2, 3; ART, MODERN EUROPEAN, 1, 2, 3. This last article begins with the 18th century. For the period from medieval to baroque, *see* MEROVINGIAN ART; CAROLINGIAN ART; OTTONIAN ART; ROMANESQUE ART; GOTHIC ART; RENAISSANCE ART; and BAROQUE ART. For the same period in Eastern Christianity, *see* BYZANTINE ART. For a systematic survey of ecclesiastical building by periods, *see* CHURCH ARCHITECTURE.

National and Geographic. Period surveys tend to follow a core of stylistic development concentrated in western Europe. More specialized articles treat of art and architecture in areas peripheral to this development but with important traditions of their own; *see* AMERICAN ART; ARMENIAN ART; CATALAN ART; COPTIC ART; GEORGIAN LITERATURE AND ART; HUNGARIAN ART; IRISH ART; LATIN AMERICA, ART AND ARCHITECTURE IN; etc. For art in the Slavic countries, *see* SLAVIC ART.

Styles, Schools, and Movements. Many articles deal with specific art styles and movements, not only those that originated with a decided Christian orientation, but also the modern movements that have an important bearing on problems of contemporary art and the Church. For example, *see* INTERNATIONAL GOTHIC; MANNERISM; NAZARENES (BROTHERHOOD OF ST. LUKE); BEURONESE ART; CUBISM; DADA; BAUHAUS; ABSTRACT EXPRESSIONISM; CHICAGO SCHOOL (ARCHITECTURE).

Monuments, Places, and Objects. Outstanding architectural monuments and works of art are discussed in individual articles; *see* SISTINE CHAPEL; HAGIA SOPHIA; KELLS, BOOK OF; DOORS, CHURCH; ASSISI; RONCHAMP, NOTRE-DAME DU HAUT; ASSY, NOTRE-DAME-DE-TOUTE-GRÂCE; etc.

Biographies. Important artists, architects, art historians, and critics, including modern artists and architects whose works have indirectly influenced the modern renewal in religious art, are discussed in biographical articles or in articles of broader scope. The index volume provides useful direction to discussions of individual names.

Specific Arts. Articles on the general development of specific arts and crafts are necessarily select; *see* FRESCO; GRAPHIC ART; IVORY CARVING; MOSAIC; PHOTOGRAPHY, THE ART OF; STAINED GLASS; etc.

Iconography. The general subject of iconography and its relationship to iconology in the light of important modern studies appears in the article ICONOLOGY AND ICONOGRAPHY. Articles on motifs and subjects of particular importance in the development of Christian art may be found under proper names or categories of persons (e.g., JESUS CHRIST, ICONOGRAPHY OF; MARY, BLESSED VIRGIN, ICONOGRAPHY OF; EVANGELISTS, ICONOGRAPHY OF; APOSTLES, ICONOGRAPHY OF; SAINTS, ICONOGRAPHY OF), theological subjects (e.g., GOD THE FATHER, ICONOGRAPHY OF; TRINITY, HOLY, ICONOGRAPHY OF; DESCENT OF CHRIST INTO HELL; SACRAMENTS, ICONOGRAPHY OF), and narrative or descriptive subjects—e.g., CRUCIFIXION (IN ART); PIETÀ; LAST SUPPER, ICONOGRAPHY OF. For the influence of the Bible and Apocryphal literature, *see* BIBLE CYCLES IN ART; APOCRYPHA, ICONOGRAPHY OF THE. The icon and iconostasis of Eastern Christianity are under ICON.

Art and the Church. For aspects of the relationship of art to religion in general and Christianity specifically, and for the problems of art and morality, *see* ART, 1, 2, 4. For the controversies and theological problems surrounding the use of image art for devotional purposes, *see* IMAGES, VENERATION OF; ICONOCLASM. The modern development of abstract art is considered in ABSTRACT ART AND THE CHURCH. For a discussion of aspects of art in the service of Christianity, including considerations on art in the Eastern liturgies and in the Protestant Church, *see* LITURGICAL ART.

See also MUSIC, ARTICLES ON; LITERATURE, ARTICLES ON.

[R. J. VEROSTKO]

ART

This article discusses art and religion, art and Christianity, art criticism, and art and morality.

1. ART AND RELIGION

The historic beginnings of religion, magic, and art are irrevocably lost, although it may be assumed that all three belong to the cultural heritage of Homo sapiens from the earliest times of his existence. Prehistoric finds clearly demonstrate the existence of art in paleolithic times. There is no such incontrovertible evidence for the very early existence of religion and magic, although this existence can be deduced with a fair degree of probability from certain prehistoric data. However, it must be noted at once that our knowledge of religion and magic in prehistoric times never goes further than more or less plausible conclusions based on analogy. Direct knowledge concerning the manifestations of the human spirit begins from the invention and development of writing, that is, from the last part of the 4th millennium B.C. Hence, while the history of art may well start with paleolithic art, as long as it is confined to stylistic and aesthetic studies and does not attempt to interpret the spiritual content of prehistoric art forms, a comparable history of prehistoric religion and magic is not possible. Prehistoric finds furnish at best only indirect knowledge of prehistoric religion and magic, as all finds have to be interpreted in the light of religions known through history or modern observation.

The foregoing preliminary remarks must be kept in mind in discussing the connections between art, religion, and magic. In this section, magic and religion will be considered as one complex whole. There is no sharp dividing line between magic and religion, although a progressive differentiation in both directions may be observed. There is, however, a clear difference between religion and sorcery in its many forms, but the facts do not justify the view that primitive or archaic religions are made up wholly or mainly of elements of magic—the word magic being taken here in its usual and popular sense.

Distinction between Art and Religion. In most cultures art and religion are closely connected. Nevertheless, unlike religion and magic, which are interwoven and interdependent, art and religion form two clearly differentiated manifestations of the human spirit. Both transcend the rational limits of the human mind, and both depend heavily on the possibilities of symbolic representation of a spiritual reality envisioned in, behind, or above the material world of the senses. Without the possibility of symbolic representation, art can be nothing more than a duplication of material forms, and religion has to be silent. In both art and religion man can feel himself to be in communication with the inexpressible infinite. In both, man tries to break through the frontiers of his own existence.

Art, however, even though in recent times it has more than once been proposed as a substitute for religion, can never replace religion—except perhaps in the case of a few exceptional individuals. Art, even when it serves religion, is essentially concerned with beauty and with beauty only. It is self-evident that beauty in this context is not meant to be identified with any historic ideal of beauty, as, e.g., the Greek, but is meant to express the specific concern of art, the truth of art. Art as such is autonomous. Religion, on the contrary, in one way or another, always offers a coherent whole on which man can base his present existence and, if necessary, his hereafter.

Although there may be ethics without religion, there is certainly no religion without ethics. A work of art may be completely without ethics, for instance, a landscape, a flower piece, a still life. The quest of art is the quest for beauty; religion is always concerned with God or gods and the reality of the divine in whatever form this conception may be symbolized. Looked at in this way, religion is autonomous. Although art and religion may collaborate, and have done so extensively in fact, both are to be regarded as autonomous fields of human spiritual endeavor. A work of art as such is not to be judged by any religious or ethical standards, nor is religion to be judged by criteria of beauty. It is clear, in practice, that other considerations may intervene, since art and religion both must function in a community and in a society that cannot be atomized or divided into a number of watertight compartments. The secondary character of such considerations, however, ought to be clearly understood. (See section 4, below.)

Art and Magic. Many elements of religion have been misinterpreted as magic. Elements such as hunting rites, fertility ceremonies, and many others, are here considered to be religious and not magical. With this in mind, it may be said that the relations between art and magic are far less close than those between art and religion. This is not difficult to understand, for, while religion is a social as well as an individual phenomenon, magic is in nearly all instances strictly personal, or at the most is practiced by a small minority group. It may perhaps be better described by the terms sorcery and witchcraft. On this point E. Durkheim is right in his sociological distinction between religion and magic: there is no *église magique*.

In every culture art is produced by artists—even though they need not be professional artists—and they often serve their society by serving religion. In many cultures, in fact, the production of art is connected mainly with religious purposes. Artists seldom have reason, however, for putting their gifts at the service of magic. Hence, the paraphernalia of sorcery are usually the home products of the performers of magic themselves, irrespective of their artistic talents, as can be demonstrated in any ethnographic or folkloristic museum. The waxen images of European sorcery, to mention one convincing instance, were not fashioned by professional sculptors but by sorcerers, lay or professional, themselves. Moreover, art is generally meant to be seen, and art in the service of religion can, as a rule, be seen by the religious group as a whole and not merely by a restricted number of persons. Magical art, on the other hand, is not meant to be observed and inspected but is often kept hidden or secret. Hence, magical figurines, for example, are usually much poorer artistically than religious ones. All great art in primitive cultures is religious art; or, if it is not religious in the full sense of the word, it has a social function as a mark of status. In any case, it may be considered as participating in religious values.

Religion and Art in Primitive Cultures. In primitive societies most art has either a religious or a social function. Art for art's sake does not exist. When a work of art has a social function, there may be indirect connections with religion. Accordingly, royal insignia are more than merely symbols of status; they belong to the sphere of religion as participating in the sacred position of the king. Other insignia, too, may have a religious value, e.g., the ceremonial adzes from Mangaia (Polynesia), which are shaped in such a way that they are useless for any real work, but serve to indicate the special place of the skilled craftsman in the service of the god Tane. Among the Dan tribes (West Africa) masks have a religious function, but masks may be used also to implement the power of a chief. Utensils, weapons, and other objects may be ornamented with sacred motives that remind the user of religious concepts. Most utensils from the Geelvinkbay area (northwest New Guinea) are ornamented, in the local Korwar style, with a small human figure representing an ancestor and, in this way, rendering the ancestor present in the daily life of his descendants. Practically everything made by the Dogon (western Sudan) and related tribes bears an ornamentation consisting of religious symbols. A zigzag line signifies the principle of duality that pervades the whole universe and is, at the same time, a reminder of the spiral movement of the unfolding of creation. By such ornamentation even the humble tools of everyday life are placed in the context of the sacred.

In primitive art there is no clear dividing line between the sacred and the profane. Only a few objects, if any, are completely free from connections with religion. This should not be interpreted to mean, as is often done, that all primitive art is religious art.

Art Objects in Their Functional Relations. For a better understanding of the religious art of the nonliterate peoples it is necessary to study the function and significance of the individual objects in the context of their own cultures. While it is possible to arrive at an aesthetic appreciation of primitive art without possessing specialized knowledge, it is clear that religious understanding is not possible without a thorough study of the whole cultural background. A people of hunters has a type of religion that differs from that of an agricultural tribe; the culture of an island in Melanesia is far different from that of an Eskimo tribe in the high North or from that of a West African monarchical state. All these differences in cultures and religions are reflected in their art. It is impossible to mistake a mask from New Ireland (Melanesia) for one of the Yoruba (Nigeria) or to confuse it with an Eskimo mask from Alaska. Nor is the function and significance of the mask in all three cases exactly the same.

Within a given culture it is of importance to know whether an object may be part of anyone's private possessions, such as an amulet or some kinds of oracles; or whether it belongs to the sacred possessions of the whole community, as is, for instance, a mask used and shown in a ceremony that is generally accessible to all; or whether it is the prerogative of some person or group of persons to have and use such objects, as is the case with the paraphernalia of the priest and of the shaman and objects that are the exclusive possession of a secret society. Among the Azande (southern Sudan) the rubbing oracle is generally in use, but only their Mani secret society possesses the small figurines, called *yanda,* that preside over the oracles of this society.

It is important, too, to know whether a given object is meant to be used and kept for as long a time as possible, as, e.g., the image of a deity, often made from stone or hardwood for that purpose, or whether it has been produced to serve only for a short period. In that case it is often made of more perishable material, such as light wood or even less permanent materials. This is true of many masks, dance ornaments, and other ceremonial paraphernalia that are made for use in one ceremony and must be replaced by new ones the next time the same ceremony is to be performed. In some cases the term of life is not fixed in advance. The Korwar ancestor figures from the Geelvinkbay area (northwest New Guinea) are used and preserved as long as the ancestor represented through the medium of the Korwar manifests himself as helpful, but may be thrown away or sold without much ado as soon as the ancestor shows himself unwilling to help his descendants.

It is likewise important to know under what kind of conditions a work of sacred art is shown and observed. It makes a difference whether a statue or mask is meant to be seen clearly in the full light of day or only vaguely in the flickering light of the fire, or whether it is meant to be seen from nearby, to be touched, perhaps, or to be viewed only from afar. To judge a mask, it is necessary to know to what kind of full costume it belongs. The form of some statues can be understood only if it is known that they are kept partly wrapped up and that the shape is adapted to that purpose.

Importance of Attitudes and Attributes. Knowledge of attitudes, attributes, and symbolic ornamentation is indispensable for the understanding of primitive religious art. The Dogon have figures with the hands raised to indicate the attitude of praying to the powers of heaven. Many African statues show a woman pressing her breasts, a gesture of loving motherhood. One type of canoe ornament of the Solomon Islands (Melanesia) consists of a prognathic head and a pair of arms. Such figures, which were fastened to the prow of the large war canoes, represent the protecting spirit of the headhunting expedition. These figures sometimes hold a head in their hands. This signifies that the head they go out to hunt has already been cut off by the protecting spirit of the expedition. In a few cases, the figure holds a bird instead of a head, but the meaning is the same, for the bird is the soul bird and can thus substitute for the head. A few statues from the Bapende (Kwango region, Congo) have been found that represent a woman, the so-called "woman of power," and were originally placed on the hut of the chief of the village. They represent the first wife of the chief. In her right hand the woman holds an ax, in the left one, a bowl. The ax is a deviation from the original meaning, as it is the misrepresentation of an agricultural tool for hacking open the ground, an attribute serving as a symbol of the fertility of the fields. This change probably took place under the influence of the significance of the bowl. At the ceremony of the installation of a new chief a human sacrifice was made and the bowl was used for holding the blood.

Significance of Symbolism. Symbolism is one of the most prominent features of primitive religious art, and it can be present in various ways. In some instances it is indicated by a combination of heterogeneous elements that are held together by an underlying idea. Knowledge of the religious conceptions behind such combinations—which are often strange to us—is the only key to their understanding. There is a type of mask from the Eskimo of Alaska representing an animal and its *inua* (soul). A seal and its *inua,* for instance, are represented by the combination of a recognizably realistic figure of a seal combined with a human face because the *inua* of a seal, being a spirit, is thought to be of a more or less anthropomorphic shape. There are comparable masks of other animals, of birds, and even fish, such as the salmon. A large type of mask in use among the Senufo (Ivory Coast) is often called a "firespitter" because burning tinder may be placed in the open mouth. It is emphasized in the ceremonies of the Korubla antisorcery society and combines the characteristics of various animals, such as the hyena, wart hog, antelope, and sometimes other elements. All species represented in this type of mask are of importance in the mythology of the Senufo.

Symbolism in Morphological Characteristics. Symbolism may be found in morphological characteristics. A type of mask in use among the Bambara (western Sudan) during the initiation ceremonies for boys of the Ndomo society has a very large nose and an extremely small mouth or no mouth at all. In the symbolism of this people the nose is the organ of social contact. A large nose symbolizes full participation in the social life of the community. The mouth, the organ of speaking, on the contrary, is made as small as possible, for in the mouth lies danger for a man: "The mouth is the enemy of the man," is an utterance found in a Bambara sacred chant.

Symbolism in Ornamentation. Many examples from the North American Indians have been collected by F. Boas in his well-known book *Primitive Art.* He describes, e.g., the hood of a cradle board of the Cheyenne Indians on which, in various colors and ornamental forms, the life of the child has been symbolically expressed. The white background designates the sky and life. A strip, bounded by blue lines, running down the middle of the hood is meant to represent the path of life of the child lying in the cradle. Here, again, use is made of color symbolism: green for growth and development; yellow for maturity and perfection; red for blood, life, and good fortune.

The Eskimo of Alaska have masks surrounded by a number of rings, each of which designates one of the spheres of the universe that encompass our world.

A very rich symbolism is connected with masks of the Dogon. One type, the *kanaga* mask, is characterized by a double-armed cross (Lorraine cross) on the top, the symbolism of which is explained by M. Griaule in

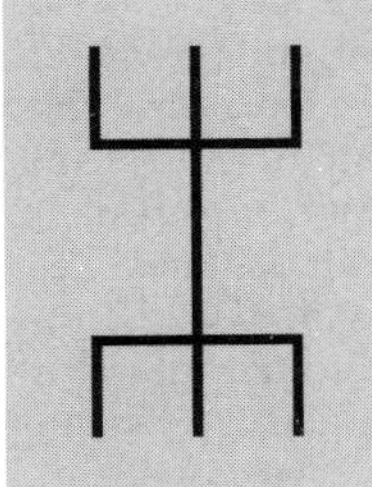

The Lorraine double-armed cross.

a number of publications. The exoteric meaning is that it represents a species of bird in flight, and this is what is told to the young members of the *Awa,* the community of all those who are entitled to wear a mask and to participate in the masked ceremonies. In the esoteric meaning the double-armed cross is connected with the myths of creation that play a prominent role in all religious speculations of the Dogon. This symbolism is explained to the members of the *Awa* only in a later stage of their membership. They are then told that the double-armed cross is derived from a half swastika, which symbolizes the creator pointing upward to heaven with one arm and downward to earth with the other, thus indicating that he has created heaven and earth. The statues from this tribe exhibiting the same attitude ought perhaps to be interpreted in the same way. The half swastika is still at rest, but to bring forth order out of chaos the creator had to move. This movement is conceived as rotary, the spiral movement described in another version of the creation myth. Thus the half swastika is duplicated and now assumes a completed form, the symbol of a rotary or spiral movement.

The development of the swastika into the Lorraine double-armed cross remains unexplained, but it may be surmised that the resemblance to a human being in the fully developed form is the main source of this development. The supposition is supported by the further symbolism connected with this type of mask, for the double-armed cross is interpreted also as a representation of the world. The world, according to the religious philosophy of the Dogon, is said to be in the shape of a man, as is made clear in another part of their myths of creation.

Symbolism of Numbers. Number symbolism is also present in primitive religious art. Among the Bambara (western Sudan) horned masks are in use during ceremonies of initiation. The horns themselves, as in African art generally, symbolize force and fertility. Horns may be compared to vegetation: they push up from the head as the vegetation rises from the earth. The growth of plants and trees is a sign of the forces of fertility residing in the earth; in the same way, horns demonstrate the force innate in many animals. In the Ndomo society of the Bambara D. Zahan has found masks with two to eight horns. Two is the number of duality. It also reminds man of his dual nature: in body he is an animal, but he possesses also reason and intelligence. Three is the number of masculinity, spirit, activity, etc. Four is that of femininity, the material nature of man, passivity, and suffering. Five reminds man, because of the five fingers of the hand, of his need to work if he wants to live. Six is the symbolic number of knowledge and instruction. According to the Bambara, man has six senses: hearing, sight, smell, taste, feeling, and the sense of orientation. Seven designates the integrity of the human personality: man is partly male and partly female (the same conception and the same symbolism is found among the Dogon), but he is integrated into one indivisible whole. Seven symbolizes man also as created to live in community in a society, and the smallest cell of society, marriage, is symbolized by this number as well. Eight, the highest number employed in this series of symbolic numbers, expresses the principle of renewal embodied in man: man as an individual is destined to die, but he may rise immortal from death, as is taught by the Kore society and represented dramatically in its rites.

Arbitrary Character of Symbols. Some symbols in primitive religions and art can best be explained psychologically, as has been shown by the researches of S. Freud, C. G. Jung, and many others; but most of these symbols can be understood only as more or less arbitrarily chosen or invented signs. They must be interpreted in the context of the religion and culture of which they constitute a part. A symbol of the first type, to give one instance, is that of the mother goddess among the Ibo (southern Nigeria); it consists of a pot filled with water. Symbols of the second type, consciously chosen images, are often combined into complexes of interrelated symbols that can be read, once one possesses the necessary data, in a way comparable to that in which the solution of an allegory, or sometimes even a rebus, is worked out. This can be demonstrated convincingly by a concrete example from the culture of the Asmat Papuans (southwest New Guinea).

The Papuans of the Asmat area live in a country of extensive swamps. Their world consists mainly of water and mud, and of trees. In their religious world view, man and tree are closely related: a man is a tree, and a tree is a man. Man and tree are not completely identified, but they are so closely related that they can stand as symbols, the one for the other. If one now starts by comparing a man to a tree, it is reasonable to compare the fruit of a tree to the head of a man; the shape of the coconut especially is well adapted for this comparison. Then, again, one can compare the eating of fruit to the ritual act of head-hunting as practiced among these tribes. When the comparison has gone as far as this, one may employ also the black, fruit-eating birds, like the black cockatoo and the hornbill, as symbols of the Asmat head-hunters, who are black as well, and this is what is actually done.

Rules Governing the Production of Religious Objects. The person who fashions the objects for religious purposes must often submit to special rules. He may have to practice sexual abstinence for a time, and certain kinds of food may be prohibited. The rule is practically universal that sacred objects must be made in secret. On the Ivory Coast the sculptor retires into the bush when making a mask, because women and uninitiated children are strictly prohibited from seeing his work—in any case before it has been finished. Their viewing of his work would cause failure on his part or would be an evil omen generally.

Other rites, too, may be performed. Small sacrifices are offered and ceremonies performed when cutting down a tree. In Hawaii a human being was sacrificed when a divine image was to be made. Special values may be attached to certain materials, and special demands may be made concerning the materials used. In West Africa gold was sacred. Certain species of trees may be regarded as sacred, as, e.g., in Indonesia, and their wood may be considered as especially well adapted for religious purposes. Among the Iroquois (colonial New York) masks were worn for certain ceremonies. The wood for these masks had to be cut out of a living tree in such a way that the tree did not die afterward. Thus, the vital force of the wood was kept intact.

Religion and Art in Myths. The close connections between religion and art may receive explicit mention in myths regarding the origins of sculpturing, painting, or other forms or techniques of art. As a rule, the myth tells that some divine being was the first to practice the particular art and that he then taught it to human beings or, in the case of a deified ancestor, to his descendants. A myth of the Baluba (Katanga, Congo) narrates how Nkulu teaches the making of the small figurines in use in this tribe to ward off illness and other kinds of ill luck.

In summary it may be stated that any view of the relations between religion and art in prehistoric times rests on assumptions, some rather plausible, some very tenuous. The theories on the relation of prehistoric religion and art reflect for the most part the theories on primitive religion and art in force at the same time and in the same school. Recent research has tried to find new methods of approaching prehistoric art (for example, A. Leroi-Gourhan), but it is still too early to judge the results.

Separation of Religion and Art in the Higher Cultures. The close relations between religion and art in primitive cultures, and they may be found also in the more archaic forms of Oriental and European cultures, show a tendency to become less close as the progressive differentiation within a culture takes place. In primitive and archaic cultures religion is the main client of the artist. Chiefs and other persons of authority come second, but their power and dignity are still intimately connected with religious values. Utensils, tools, weapons, and other objects of everyday life may attain the beauty of an object of art, and this beauty may be considered very important, but no need is felt, in either the house or the village, for objects serving merely the purpose of decoration. The situation changes when further development results in social and economic changes through which religion as patron of the arts becomes less important. Religious changes, too, may have the same result, as in those parts of Europe that became Protestant. (*See* LITURGICAL ART, 10.) Authority, too, became gradually more secularized.

Art under New Patronage. On the other hand, a new class of patrons comes forward, demanding the services of the artist to decorate its houses, gardens, cities, etc. While some of this decoration may still be of a religious character, much of it is bound to be completely secular: portraits painted or carved, sculptures and paintings commemorating special events of family life or of the life of the nation, etc. Through this development the purpose of a work of art becomes less clearly circumscribed than it once was, and the way is opened to a purely aesthetic appreciation of art for art's sake. This aesthetic tendency is evidenced, for example, in the collecting of art objects, first the pastime of princes, then that of the rich, and now in part an activity of the state. In a collection or museum the objects of art are completely divorced from their original practical purposes. Except for some forms of modern art, they are completely divorced also from their original function and stripped of all values except the aesthetic. The process described is in the main still a typical feature of Western civilizations, but it is now spreading very quickly throughout the world. In a comparable way religion has been driven away or excluded from many fields that in the past it could consider its own, and it has been compelled to concentrate more on its own specific values and categories.

Opposition between Art and Religion. While usually art and religion go together, history reveals instances also of enmity between art and religion, as, on the one hand, *iconoclasm, and on the other, the propagation of art and beauty, as such, as rivals of religion. These clashes, however, are of less real significance than the relations between both. They are not so much conflicts between art and religion as such but are based rather on disagreement between a specific type of religion and a specific type of art.

See also RELIGION; MAGIC; MYTH AND MYTHOLOGY.

Bibliography: C. H. RATSCHOW, RGG[3] 4:126–131. K. DITTMER et al., *ibid.* 131–161. H. G. GEYER, *ibid.* 161–165. A. HALDER et al., LexThK[2] 6:682–687, with bibliog. F. BOAS, *Primitive Art* (new ed. pa. New York 1955). G. VAN DER LEEUW, *Sacred and Profane Beauty: The Holy in Art,* tr. D. E. GREEN (New York 1963), with bibliog. H. READ, *Icon and Idea* (Cambridge, Mass. 1955). A. LEROI-GOURHAN, "Préhistoire," *Histoire de l'art* 1 (Encyclopédie de la Pléiade; Paris 1961) 1–92. J. GUIART, "Océanie," *ibid.* 1587–1635. G. BALANDIER, "Afrique noire et Madagascar," *ibid.* 1743–1829. M. GRIAULE, *Folk Art of Black Africa,* tr. M. HERON (New York 1950); *Masques dogons* (Paris 1938), with bibliog. D. ZAHAN, *Sociétés d'initiation Bombara* (Paris 1960). T. P. VAN BAAREN, *Bezielend Beelden: Inleiding tot de beeldende Kunst der primitieve Volken* (Amsterdam 1962). A. MALRAUX, *Psychology of Art,* tr. S. GILBERT, 2 v. (Bollingen Ser. 24; New York 1949–51).

[T. P. VAN BAAREN]

2. ART AND CHRISTIANITY

The relationship between art and Christianity has had profound influences on the development of painting, architecture, sculpture, and the minor arts. It has produced a vast deposit of iconographic schemes and influenced both the theories of aesthetics and the artistic procedures of artists themselves. For the history of art in Western Christian cultures, *see* ART, ARTICLES ON. This article considers only the general relationship of Christianity to the artist and his artistic production; it attempts to present some of the more important ways in which Christianity is related to the arts.

Christianity and Art in General. The artistic production of man preceded Christianity by many thousands of years, and, since the beginnings of Christianity, it has existed alongside of and, for the most part, independent of Christian influence in large geographic areas of the world, e.g., countries of the Far East, such as China, Japan, India, and Malaya; all the regions of North and South America up to the time of modern history; and the larger parts of Africa. The first Christian influences on art occurred during the early Christian period in northern Egypt, and in and around Rome and Constantinople. During the Middle Ages this influence gradually spread throughout Byzantium, western and central Europe, and the British Isles. A high sophistication of art under Christian influence was achieved in Europe during the late Middle Ages and the Renaissance; following the Counter Reformation and baroque art this influence gradually waned and, by the 19th century, had lost its inner vitality. Modern efforts at renewal on the part of Christians began in the late 19th century in Europe and spread to North America in the 20th century.

In order to examine the relationship of Christianity to art as manifested in this development, art is taken first in its most general meaning in Western thought as an intellectual virtue directive of the skilled making of things. *See* ART (PHILOSOPHY). The influence of Christianity on the practice of art may be examined then under two aspects: the actual making and the maker himself.

The Making of Things. Human making (both of tools and of things) is rooted in the desire to satisfy human needs, which are determined by the urge to survive and by the will toward perfection. Such needs are dictated and evaluated by the aims that man consciously sets for himself and that give meaning to human existence. The virtue of art is the developed aptitude of making things properly; and, insofar as human existence is recognized as being dependent on God and ordered to union with Him, art is at once endowed with religious significance.

Christianity with its clear teaching on creation and on the ultimate purpose of human activity as the glory of God, as well as on the immortal destiny of man, emphasized the intimate and natural relation of art to religion. In common with other religions it helped man to see nature as the language and instrument of God, as full of His presence and as sharing in His power and beauty. To this it added the realization that man was, by the work of his hands, participating in the work of creation and enabling it to attain its end. Art could thus be seen as endowed with cosmic purpose and with a dignity exceeding that of the object made.

The Maker or Artist. The sense of dependence on and of union with God, which is so central to the great world religions, was presented by Christianity as a dependence based on creation rather than myth; this implied that at every moment all things and all actions continue to depend on God for their existence. The Christian could view all productive activity as a certain cooperating with God "in whom we live and move and have our being" (Acts 17.28). Human making could thus be seen as sacred and significant not only in its object and end but in its source, the human person as sustained and moved by God. However, the artist's view of himself in Christianity may not be isolated to a single concept; it was colored in the East and the West with shifting theological and philosophical speculation. By the time of the Renaissance art was profoundly influenced by the Christian insistence on the dignity of man. Man was seen as a creature, made in the image of God, intellectual and free, with an immortal soul directly created by God and destined for eternal union with Him. Thus Renaissance man was able to produce an image of the Christian world and of his belief that was permeated with the light of reason and carried the imprint of his dignity as a Christian.

Christianity and the Concept of Art. Concepts of art emerge reflectively through the interest of philosophers, artists themselves, and in modern times through the work of art historians and critics. Contemporary concepts of art in Western thought vary considerably and often bear the influence of concepts inherited from Christian tradition. In order to examine some influences Christianity has wielded on theories of art, considerations are presented here first under the aspect of beauty and then under the aspect of the art process.

Beauty. A Christian synthesis of Jewish thought and of Greek thought from Plato to Plotinus on beauty in relation to God is already found in St. Augustine and the Pseudo-Dionysius. It formed a tradition that had a profound influence on the art of the Middle Ages and was clearly formulated in the 12th-century school of Chartres (see de Bruyne). Its speculation on number, light, proportion, and order was realized especially in the Gothic cathedral. This tradition saw beauty, in its formal elements, as verified most fully in God, and as shared from God to creatures, so that the beauty of finite things was seen as stemming from God and as apt to raise the mind of the beholder to the contemplation of God. To see beauty as a divine perfection is to stress its spiritual nature, or at least to ensure that it will not be identified entirely with its sensible forms. The transcendent character of beauty was thus strongly affirmed by Christian thought, all the more so since created beauty was seen as sharing in the perfection of the Creator.

The humanity of Christ was, moreover, exalted as the supreme beauty of the created order, and that beauty was regarded as shared and manifest to varying degrees in the sensible realities of the world. Beauty was thus more closely linked with God and valued because of that link. The Incarnation was seen as an exemplar that elevated all created and visible forms of beauty.

This Christian teaching on beauty strengthened and helped deepen the vision and enhance the function of the artist. It implied that to make a beautiful thing is to make something sacred; "every good painting is noble and devout of itself, for it is nothing more than a copy of the perfections of God and reminiscence of His own painting" (Michelangelo, as recorded by Francis of Holland in his *Four Dialogues on Painting;* Fr. tr. L. Rouanet, 1911, 29–30).

The Art Process. The Greek and Neoplatonic notion of the formation of things from an eternal matter by a demiurge looked to subsistent ideas as prototypes to serve as an illustration of the human process of artistic making. The demiurge, however, was conceived as being inferior to God, to whom action could not be attributed. It was St. Augustine who, on lines suggested by Philo and Plotinus, identified the eternal exemplars with ideas in the divine mind, and thus conceived of God's activity as supremely artistic. It was possible to conceive of God in this way only when the notion of creation had been accepted from revelation.

The Christian concept of God's creative activity, while affirming a great difference between divine creation and human making, drew attention to the intellectual side of the artistic process, to the stage now known as conception or idealization. By attributing art in its supreme form to the creation of the universe by God it ennobled and enhanced the analogous human activity of artistic creation and the status of those who exercised it.

Speculation on intra-Trinitarian life and the Incarnation also served to deepen the analogy between God as Creator and artist as creator. The Son of God was seen as the revealed word, the Idea born from all eternity in the mind of the Father, by which and in which all things were created. He was thus seen as the Supreme Art or the Perfect Image of the Father, the Idea by which all things were made (Aquinas, *In 2 sent.* 16.1. ad 2; *De ver.* 1.7). The Incarnation gave a supreme exemplar of what the work of art can be. Not only is the Word made flesh, the Idea given a visible form, but the flesh is spiritualized and made the outward sign of the invisible Godhead. From this point of view the art process was seen as analogous to the Incarnation, and at the same time the symbolical character of art was thrown into relief. Considerations such as these permitted Dante to sum up the Christian notion of art in his immortal words: "sì che vostr' arte a Dio quasi è nipote" (so that your art is to God, as it were, a grandchild, *Inferno* 11.105).

Christianity and the Content of Art. In any consideration of content in art it is important to distinguish between the subject matter and the content of a work. A subject treated by an artist in the Renaissance may be quite the same as that treated by a Byzantine artist. However, the manner of conception deriving from different social, theological, geographical, and technical factors produces a content in one somewhat different from that in the other. Thus the person of Christ may be conceived by the Byzantine artist theocentrically in terms of hieratic power and executed in an otherworldly planal structure with a strict symbolical hierarchy of organization. The Renaissance artist, on other hand, may interest himself more in the humanity of Christ divinized through dramatic heroic power and thus present Him as a believable figure in a rationalized space displaying active moral concern and emotional force. The manner of conceptualization employed by the artist enters the content of the work. Throughout Christian cultures in different geographic areas and at different times, shifting theological emphases have colored the content of Christian themes as they are presented in Christian art.

That Christianity has provided art with new and specific subjects is obvious in the vast deposit of Christian iconography. The primary source of such subjects was the Bible, especially the Gospels, in the presentation of the life, death, and Resurrection of Christ. The events of the life of Mary, her sorrows and her assumption and glorification, were favorite subjects of art in all its forms; so too were the lives, and especially the miracles and martyrdoms, of the saints; the Church herself, usually through some symbol; the Sacraments; the Last Judgment; heaven; and hell. (*See* MARY, BLESSED VIRGIN, ICONOGRAPHY OF; JESUS CHRIST, ICONOGRAPHY OF; SAINTS, ICONOGRAPHY OF.)

Christian art represented man himself in the light of his supernatural destiny, showing his life as guided by the New Law and as consisting essentially in the exercise of the virtues. The various states of life and the different vocations of man in the Christian order were frequent subjects for artistic presentation, just as the main human activities were shown in their religious significance, usually through connection with a patron saint.

This does not imply that visible nature was excluded from Christian art, as though such art were concerned with a spiritual reality divorced from the sensible world. The Augustinian tendency in theology, with its Neoplatonic heritage, invited man to turn away from bodily manifestations of beauty in order to gaze on spiritual beauty and thus to gain almost an intuition of God (see St. Augustine, *Trin.,* PL 42:949, 950; St. Anselm, *Proslogion,* PL 158:225). But the insistence of Christian realism, as formulated by St. Thomas on the ground of Aristotelian thought, on the sense origin of all knowledge, taught men rather to find beauty first among finite things and then to rise to a purified knowledge of the beauty of the spirit and of God. The more severe and purely symbolic forms of early Christian art gradually gave way to more realistic and naturalistic forms (e.g., the introduction of landscape into painting), which opened up the whole of nature for artistic use.

Christian Art. Art within Christianity has been a vital part of the mainstream of culture and, like other areas of human endeavor, is in process. As such, its characterizing qualities and its aims are subject to continuing discussion. Questions of whether or not there is a Christian art in a strict and proper sense of the term have been raised recently in the context of the modern renewal in sacred art. The problem has been sharpened by the use within the Church of purely abstract art that is not distinguishable from certain works one might see in museums far removed from the immediate interests of formal religion (*see* ABSTRACT ART AND THE CHURCH). The attitude one takes in regard to the nature of Christian art depends largely on the angle from which one approaches the question and on the philosophical framework within which it is considered.

The scholastic philosopher will presumably approach the question of Christian art by asking first of all whether there is any such thing, for it can well be maintained that art remains just art whoever may happen to practice it, whether he be Jew or Hindu or Christian or pagan. It can be argued that art is essentially the same, whatever the beliefs or conduct of the artist. One does not speak of a Christian mathematics or medicine. The arts and sciences have their own laws and standards; to qualify them or restrict them in any way would seem to interfere with their essence, to spoil their purity and to limit their freedom.

On the other hand we do in fact speak of Christian art, though not of Christian geometry. We speak of a Christian literature, of Christian painting, sculpture, architecture, and music that are recognized as such.

The common assumption that art can be called specifically Christian when its subject matter is drawn from Christianity is narrow and derives from an inadequate understanding of content in art. On this assumption, the difference between Christian and other forms of art would be purely external (iconographic). Much less can one define Christian art in terms of technique or style, except perhaps in the historical sense that certain styles have in fact evolved in a Christian context. To limit Christian art to fixed forms, as *Pugin, who would lodge the Christian ideal only in a Gothic-styled architecture, is to stifle art and to relegate it to stylism.

If we regard art, insofar as it is art, in the scholastic sense of a naturally acquired intellectual virtue of the practical order, it is one and the same in all men whatever their creed or culture. Art, in its formal constituents, is as unaffected by one's belief as it is by one's conduct.

Art, however, should not be viewed only in relation to its own proper object and in its formal elements, but as placed in the stream of activity issuing from the person of the artist, as a vital power at the service of that person, and as affected by the status or manner of being of the artist. Art is more affected than philosophy and the sciences by this influence. The sciences, in search of truth, are determined by their object, and seek to conform to things as they are; hence they are predetermined in their very nature. Art is practical, and rather than conform itself to what is, it seeks to mold reality to its inner form. Art begets its own form, which it molds in conjunction with existing elements; its object is partly within the artist himself so that art is much more free than science. It will, to a far greater extent, be the expression of the inner life of the artist, communicate his vision, glow with his feeling and embody his ideals. Where art and architecture have been molded from a Christian vision of the world as distinct, for example, from a primitive vision of the world, we can speak of that art as Christian. The science of iconology, which attempts to interpret the meanings underlying structure and iconographic motifs, is best equipped to determine the formative Christian elements in a specific work (*see* ICONOLOGY AND ICONOGRAPHY).

Insofar then as art bears the imprint and shows the influence of its existential Christian setting it can be regarded as a distinctive kind of art with a modality proper to itself. The question has been raised whether this Christian modality may be present in the work of the non-Christian artist who executes a work of art for specific Christian use, or who selects Christian themes. One thinks, for instance, of *Matisse and the Stations of the Cross in the chapel at *Vence. To the extent that such artists effect the Christian conceptions attempted in such works one can speak of their art as Christian.

See also LITURGICAL ART, 1; CHURCH ARCHITECTURE, 1.

Bibliography: General. For a list of sources see R. ASSUNTO and C. CECCHELLI, EncWA 3:605–606. F. A. R. DE CHATEAUBRIAND, *Génie du christianisme,* 2 v. (new ed. Paris 1885; repr. 1936), Eng. *Genius of Christianity,* tr. C. I. WHITE (7th ed. Philadelphia 1868). A. GHIGNONI, *Il pensiero cristiano nell' arte* (Rome 1903). A. FABRE, *Pages d'art chrétien* (new ed. Paris 1920). J. SAUER, *Wesen und Wollen der christlichen Kunst* (Freiburg 1926). P. GARDNER, *The Principles of Christian Art* (London 1928). L. BRÉHIER, *L'Art chrétien* (2d ed. Paris 1928). E. GILL, "Christianity and Art," in *Art-Nonsense* (London 1929). M. S. GILLET, *Le Credo des artistes* (Paris 1929). *Atti delle Settimana d'arte sacra per il clero,* 5 v. (Vatican City 1933–38). C. COSTANTINI, *L'istruzione del S. uffizio sull' arte sacra* (Vatican City 1952). E. I. WATKIN, *Catholic Art and Culture* (rev. ed. London 1947). B. CHAMPIGNEULLE et al., *Problèmes de l'art sacré* (Paris 1951). J. MONCHANIN, *De l'esthétique à la mystique* (Tournai 1955). M. A. COUTURIER, *Se garder libre: Journal, 1947–54* (Paris 1962). For periodicals see bibliography under LITURGICAL ART, 3.

Particular. J. AUMANN, *De pulchritudine, inquisitio philosophico-theologica* (Valencia 1951). J. CAMÓN AZNAR, *El tiempo en el arte* (Madrid 1958). C. BELL, *Art* (New York 1958). W. G. COLLINGWOOD, *The Art Teaching of John Ruskin* (London 1900). E. DE BRUYNE, *Étude d'esthétique médiévale,* 3 v. (Bruges 1946); *L'Esthétique du Moyen Âge* (Louvain 1947). M. ELIADE, *The Sacred and the Profane,* tr. W. R. TRASK (New York 1959). É. H. GILSON, *Painting and Reality* (Bollingen Ser. 35.4; New York 1957). A. LITTLE, *The Nature of Art* (New York 1946). J. B. LOTZ, "Christliche Inkarnation und heidnischer Mythos als Wurzel sakraler Kunst," *Archivio di filosofia* 3 (1957) 55–78. J. MARITAIN, *Art and Scholasticism,* tr. J. W. EVANS (New York 1962); *Creative Intuition in Art and Poetry* (Bollingen Ser. 35.1; New York 1953); *The Responsibility of the Artist* (New York 1960). A. M. MONETTE, *La Beauté de Dieu* (Montreal 1950). F. PIEMONTESE, *Problemi di filosofia dell'arte* (Turin 1962). F. VON SCHLEGEL, *Ansichten und Ideen von der christlichen Kunst,* v.6 of *Sämtliche Werke,* 15 v. (2d ed. Vienna 1846).

[A. MC NICHOLL]

3. ART CRITICISM

The question of what constitutes a valid and meaningful art criticism is complicated by the equally perplexing question of what constitutes art, *aesthetics, and art history. Intelligent, sensitive, and discriminating critics differ in their concepts of the key terms, art and criticism, and are unable to agree on a terminology that best elucidates their concepts. Thus any generic consideration of art criticism will be complex and controversial. This section treats questions about the nature of and discusses the main functions and types of art criticism.

It is necessary at the outset to indicate and to distinguish between fundamental approaches in art criticism. Critics have at times asserted that their work should deal with experiences and that the chief task of the critic is to define, to clarify, and to evaluate his own experience of the work of art. A more objective view sees criticism as an instrument for revealing the meaning of a work of art in its totality. This view of criticism is the one accepted for the ensuing discussion.

The concept of a work of art that is most satisfactory as a basis for criticism permits art objects to be analyzed in terms of three organically related categories: matter (i.e., materials and subject matter or theme), form (i.e., structure or formal organization), and content (i.e., artistic expression). Many writers reject this analysis—notably by ignoring the importance of content or by confusing it with subject matter. Clearly, however, one subject, e.g., the Crucifixion, can be expressed in countless different ways.

Criticism, Philosophy, and Experience. Before discussing and illustrating the chief functions and methods of art criticism, two other questions require mention: (1) the relation between art criticism and philosophy of criticism; (2) the relation between criticism and artistic experience.

First, although criticism and philosophy are different intellectual pursuits, the work of a particular critic is based on one or another philosophical position. Three such positions constitute an important determining factor in critical statements: absolutism, subjectivism, and objective relativism. Although an analysis of these doctrines is beyond the scope of this discussion, the central difference between them may be summarized. An absolutist has strict standards of judgment and contends that there is only one correct evaluation of a work of art. A subjectivist relies on his unreasoned, intuitive preferences; and his evaluations are a matter of individual taste that is at once self-justifying and incapable of justification. And an objective relativist holds that evaluations are conditioned, to a degree, by deliberation and reflection, and maintains that differing, competent interpretations and evaluations of art may be equally convincing. The last position admits the need for intelligent appreciation of a work of art without requiring a scientifically exact judgment on it.

Second, the experience of "feeling" a work of art, though an essential condition of the critic's job, is by no means his function except, perhaps, in criticism that is highly emotive and impressionistic. Criticism does not deal with artistic experience but with the formulation of statements that are made after the experience and in relation to it. Whereas artistic experience is concerned with valuing, criticism deals with the process of evaluation. Unlike artistic experience, moreover, the critical attitude is essentially one of analysis, of detachment or "distancing," and of commitment to defend one's value judgments.

Evaluative Criticism. The making of value judgments in criticism has been severely criticized in the 20th century. For example, it has been argued that critics, rather than attempting to evaluate painting, should help people to see painting. Literary critics have expressed special disdain for evaluative criticism, denying that such criticism has ever helped the reader to understand or appreciate a great work (*see* LITERARY CRITICISM, HISTORY OF). Further, it is maintained that since values cannot be imparted by the critic to the reader, value judgments must be abandoned forthwith. The kind of art history and of criticism (the two disciplines are closely linked) that eschews valuations and consists primarily of biographical, descriptive, and other informative kinds of material has been declared by some to be the most useful. This sort of criticism is valuable and can be practiced with great results, but the view that it is the most useful kind is open to serious question. There is little doubt, however, that exclusively evaluative criticism, especially when it is dogmatic, unreasoned, and condemnatory, is useless, if not downright harmful.

Though thus disparaged in theory and in practice by some writers, a large majority of critics find that evaluative, or judicial, criticism is of great importance. They take the determination of values to be the primary function of art criticism, the rendering of a judgment the principal reason for the critic's being. It is pointed out in this connection that the cataloguer, after all, does not list all plastic objects but only those that the critics have distinguished from the mass through the process of evaluation. Certainly appraisals have been a major concern of the most famous English art critics. Sir Joshua *Reynolds insisted that both in "invention" and in "expression" artists must deal with the general, not with the particular; and in saying this he was enunciating a criterion, he believed, not only for himself but for all men of good taste. In the 19th century John *Ruskin endlessly pointed out which paintings were bad, mediocre, good, excellent, and supreme, and propounded his verdicts with a conviction that never wavered. Even Roger Fry, who was usually far less dogmatic than Reynolds and Ruskin, flatly asserted the supremacy of late over early Greek sculpture and of Italian over Flemish painting.

Even if there is now disagreement with some of the judgments of these and other famous critics—and it is certain that there is often disagreement—their assessments have been valuable because the reasons for them have been given either implicitly or explicitly. Thus Bernard *Berenson's analyses of tactile values, of movement, and of space in Italian painting are the major reasons for his appraisals. Not only are his analyses descriptively relevant to individual works of art, but they serve to establish his main normative requirement of art, namely, that it be "life-enhancing." Even if critics avoid specific judgments, evaluations are implied either by the tone of the criticism or by the subjects selected for discussion. The very fact, for example, that Sir Kenneth Clark wrote his book *Landscape Painting* shows his love of this kind of art.

Normative Criticism. Some critics find useful the primarily normative concepts of artistic truth, perfection, and greatness. Concepts of artistic truth appear to be of questionable value in art criticism. The distinction, however, between artistic perfection and greatness—though it is often blurred, misunderstood, or denied—seems helpful. If, for example, two works of art are being compared by the critic, the "more perfect" one would usually be more flawless in its "aesthetic surface," in its form, and in its content; yet it would have a less complex structure and be less expressive. The "greatness" of the other work would depend, to a degree, on the richness of its formal organization and on the profundity and scope of its content. One might in this way usefully compare "perfect" water colors of Delacroix with his "great" oil paintings or the "perfect" prints of Daumier with his "great" pictures.

Another normative distinction that some critics find useful differentiates liking, which is an immediate sensuous response, from approbation, which is essentially rational and reflective. The distinction may be described also by contrasting the emotional spontaneity of the activity of "taste" with the more intellectual, thoughtful activity of "judgment." Here it is frequently a question of a critic's making the distinction within himself between professional responsibility and individual preference. Presumably all critics have experienced the phenomenon of liking works of art more than they genuinely admire them and of genuinely admiring ones that they do not much like. It is obviously valuable for a critic to recognize this distinction, for he is most serviceable to others when he is evaluating that of which he approves.

A salient problem in normative criticism is the difficulty of evaluating contemporary art. Judicial criticism of modern art, though undoubtedly necessary, is a perilous undertaking in that opinions pro and con are usually so extreme that anything approaching an objective judgment is nearly impossible. The voices that defend the *avant-garde* of the 20th century are manifold and vociferous. The liberation of abstract art from the duty to represent recognizable objects has led many critics to declare the products of this new freedom uniformly beautiful and immediately appealing. Not only do these critics extol the aesthetic merit of most of modern art; they also praise its "heroic creativity" in successfully presenting various aspects of present-day culture—notably its social and scientific trends.

Although contemporary art critics generally agree in their high assessments of 20th-century art, some eminent voices have been raised in protest. Cubist art, for example, has been declared not beautiful and utterly lacking in the capacity to give pleasure to the beholder. It is argued further that, though its artistic forms are valid, nonobjective art must not be considered art at all, because the otherwise valid forms bear no relationship to the world of common visual experience. A slightly more charitable, but equally negative, critical position grants to the best of abstract painting the status of being "decorative." To generalize, then, one can say that what he finds in criticism of modern art is the liveliest kind of reaction to the force of that art's most radical innovations. Indeed, the critics have chosen sides and entrenched themselves in camps. It is entirely possible, however, that later critics will come to more balanced judgments of modern art, lessening the present enthusiasm for the *avant-garde* movements and perhaps manifesting more appreciation of the "traditional" schools.

Interpretive Criticism. Whatever importance a critic may attach to judicial criticism, he values highly another critical function, namely, the "interpretive." Although "interpretation" has been rejected by some critics in favor of "description" and "elucidation," most critics agree that the meanings of these and other terms—vague and imprecise as they often are—are closely related and that interpretation is the most inclusive way of referring to a number of aspects of the critic's job: describing, explaining, explicating, and the like. As splendid examples of art criticism that is preeminently interpretive, the sensitive, imaginative analyses by Meyer Schapiro and D. C. Rich may be cited.

There are many schools, kinds, and types of art criticism involved in evaluating and in interpreting. While considering three of these, one should keep in mind two basic ideas. First, the best art critics combine a variety of approaches or methods and thus avoid what Dewey calls "the reductive fallacy" of criticism. Unless the critic is enamoured of oneness, he should adopt a pluralistic view of criticism that accords him a free choice among different methods. Those he selects will depend largely on the kind of art with which he is dealing. Second, what finally matters is the quality of mind that the critic brings to his work. There is, in other words, no method that can substitute for the alert intelligence and good sense required of a true critic.

Impressionist Criticism. Impressionist criticism, which generally implies a subjective theory of criticism, is currently disparaged because it is a record of personal enjoyments that largely precludes the "distancing," already mentioned, that is basic to the critical act. Impressionist art criticism had its heyday in England in the late 19th century. Walter Pater, protagonist of "art for art's sake," brilliantly expressed his highly subjective feelings about works of art; and Ruskin wrote criticism that, though usually acute and persuasive, is in the main intensely emotive. In the 20th century there have been at least a few prominent art critics, now usually looked down upon, who have written stimulating impressionist criticism, notably Elie Faure and Frank Jewett Mather, Jr., whose brief account of Italian painting remains, in this writer's opinion, the best introduction to the subject. A work of art exists to be enjoyed, and good impressionist criticism can, after all, greatly increase one's appreciation of works of art by imbuing him with enthusiasm for art. For the impressionist critic it is often a matter of communicating this enthusiasm in such a way that the criticism does not serve as a replacement for direct experience of the work of art but rather as an incitement to going out and viewing it firsthand.

Contextual Criticism. Another major type of art criticism is historical, or contextual. Unlike impressionist criticism, which stresses the personal preferences of the critic, contextual criticism deals with the origins and interpretation of works of art in the light of biographical, sociological, and other types of evidence. The value of this criticism has been much disputed. Those critics (e.g., *Taine and Arnold Hauser) who find a close link between artistic style and the cultural milieu of the artist naturally stress the importance of historical criticism. This position has been challenged by other, more numerous, critics who believe that the genesis of works of art is irrelevant to both interpretation and appraisal. Both views, when stated in the extreme, are questionable. For although psychological, cultural, and other genetic aspects of criticism are indeed often irrelevant, more often still they may be fruitful, if used with caution, as a guide to comprehension, and hence to appreciation, of works of art. Even the intention of the artist—the feature most emphatically decried by opponents of historical criticism—may help the critic to interpret and evaluate more effectively. A knowledge that *Bernini was genuinely devout, for example, gives an important clue to what he wished to express in the St. Teresa group. (There is general consent that Bernini succeeded in carrying out his aims.) If this knowledge is combined with information about the religious background of the 17th century and about the account of the ecstasy by the saint herself, it then seems absurd to interpret the work, as many critics have done, as profane and lascivious. Or again, the explanation of the symbolic significance of baroque churches has clarified the intentions of the Catholic patrons (and thus implicitly those of the artists) and so enabled unbiased percipients to understand and enjoy these buildings in a new light. Erwin Panofsky's *Studies in Iconology* and his analysis of Titian's "Allegory of Prudence" admirably show how contextual material can illuminate works of art. Panofsky's studies are intensive and masterful historical explications in which great learning is brought to bear with skill and taste on the elucidation of enigmatic older works of art. More modest utilization of historical material also can be of benefit in criticism. The observation by Kenneth Clark that "nips of information" not only increase understanding of works of art, but are an important means of helping one to experience them more fully, gives concrete backing to historical criticism from perhaps the foremost living art critic.

Formal Criticism. Formal, or intrinsic, art criticism is analogous to the "new criticism" in literature. The attention of the rigorous formalistic critic is devoted almost exclusively to the structure of form of works of art. He is concerned with the interrelationship of the parts and component elements that make up the work of art as an organic whole. The conscientious formalist has great care for the aesthetic integrity of the work of art and, hence, carries his investigation into the work rather than into ancillary areas of inquiry. This critical approach is congruent with the statements of many modern artists on the nature of their creative works. The rise of formalist criticism may reflect a reaction against the emotional overflow of impressionist criticism and the overemphasis on context by the historical critics. Heinrich *Wölfflin and Roger Fry, both of whom stressed formal analysis, nonetheless wrote great art criticism because they were aware that purely formal criticism is too narrow. Wölfflin confessed that art cannot be separated from the total historical situation, though he believed that the latter remains peripheral to the work of art and that the benefits of the formalist approach in criticism outweigh the danger.

Conclusion. The answers of critics and artists to the question of the value of art criticism show, as do nearly all matters considered in this discussion, wide diversity. There are some who make lofty claims for criticism, others who consider it a much overrated activity, and still others who take a position between these extremes.

For some, criticism is the indispensable auxiliary of art, without which the understanding of art would be barely possible. The further claim is made that criticism is of the utmost importance for society, since it preserves the quality of a steadily accruing cultural inheritance. The critic makes a contribution to civilization that complements the work of the artist. Others maintain that the overestimation by the public of critics and criticism in the contemporary age has contributed to the neglect of the works of art themselves. As is well known, artists in particular tend to distrust critics and have a low estimate of their importance. The balanced view is that all aspects of criticism have decided merit insofar as they contribute to the understanding and enjoyment of works of art. It is not criticism that counts in the long run, but the increase of knowledge, the sharpening of the ability to discriminate, and the further education of perception that criticism makes possible. After it has served its function of enhancing the experience of art, its importance ceases. "The great art of criticism," wrote Matthew Arnold, "is to get oneself out of the way and let humanity decide."

See also AESTHETICS; ART (PHILOSOPHY); LITERARY CRITICISM.

Bibliography: The best general introduction to art criticism is J. STOLNITZ, *Aesthetics and Philosophy of Art Criticism* (Boston 1960).

Critical theory. W. ABELL, *Representation and Form* (New York 1936). G. BOAS, *A Primer for Critics* (Baltimore 1937). F. P. CHAMBERS, *The History of Taste* (New York 1932). A. DRESDNER, *Die Kunstkritik* (Munich 1915). H. FOCILLON, *The Life of Forms in Art*, rev. tr. C. B. HOGAN and G. KUBLER (2nd ed. New York 1948). A. FONTAINE, *Les Doctrines d'art en France* (Paris 1909). H. GARDNER, *The Business of Criticism* (Oxford 1959). T. M. GREENE, *The Arts and the Art of Criticism* (Princeton 1940). A. HAUSER, *The Social History of Art*, tr. S. GOODMAN, 2 v. (New York 1951). B. C. HEYL, *New Bearings in Esthetics and Art Criticism* (New Haven 1943). J. HOSPERS, *Meaning and Truth in the Arts* (Chapel Hill 1946; repr. Hamden, Conn. 1964). C. S. LEWIS, *An Experiment in Criticism* (Cambridge, Eng. 1961). D. A. STAUFFER, ed., *The Intent of the Critic* (Princeton 1941). L. VENTURI, *History of Art Criticism* (New York 1936; pa. 1964); *Art Criticism Now* (Baltimore 1941).

Critical practice. J. RUSKIN, *Modern Painters*, 5 v. (New York 1929–35); *Stones of Venice*, 3 v. (New York 1921–27); Berenson ItPaint; *The Drawings of the Florentine Painters*, 3 v. (Chicago 1938). J. C. BURCKHARDT, *Der Cicerone* (Cologne 1953); Eng. *The Cicerone*, tr. A. H. CLOUGH (New York 1908). K. M. CLARK, *Landscape Painting* (New York 1950); *The Nude* (New York 1956); *Looking at Pictures* (New York 1960). M. J. FRIEDLÄNDER, *Landscape, Portrait, Still-Life*, tr. R. F. C. HULL (New York 1950; repr. pa. 1963). R. FRY, *Vision and Design* (London 1920; repr. pa. New York 1956); *Transformations* (London 1926); *Last Lectures* (Cambridge, Eng. 1939; pa. Boston 1962). R. JANSSENS, *Les Maîtres de la critique d'art* (Brussels 1935). F. J. MATHER, *Venetian Painters* (New York 1936). E. PANOFSKY, *Studies in Iconology* (New York 1939). H. E. READ, *Art Now* (new ed. New York 1948). D. C. RICH, *Degas* (New York 1952). M. SCHAPIRO, ed., *Cézanne* (New York 1952).

[B. C. HEYL]

4. ART AND MORALITY

This section presents considerations on the more common moral problems that may arise in connection with the visual arts and literature. Questions relating to art in its broad scholastic sense as the *recta ratio factibilium* (right reason in making things) belong to the theology of work (*see* WORK, THEOLOGY OF). For consideration of moral problems related to pornography, *see* EROTIC LITERATURE.

The problem of art and morals is usually stated in terms such as the following: "If a genuine work of art is truly beautiful and attains to perfection in its own order, how can it be considered immoral?"; or conversely, "If a work of art is immoral, how can it be considered beautiful, and consequently, how can it be perfect in its own order?" Stated in these terms the problem may invite oversimplified and therefore erroneous solutions. One is apt to conclude that: "From the moment a work of art is genuinely beautiful its morality is irrelevant"; or, "From the moment that a work of art seems morally dubious its beauty is irrelevant." The artist and art critic have a tendency to adopt the former; the cleric, the public official, and the censor usually adopt the latter. Most problems of morality and art result from a failure of communication between these two positions and from misunderstandings that follow that failure.

This section examines briefly the traditional relationship between art and prudence, and reviews familiar theories and principles in the light of recent developments that have occurred in art.

Art and Prudence. Scholastic philosophy, following Aristotle, regards both art and prudence as virtues of the practical intellect. Both are concerned with man's active life. Art regards man's activity as a maker in relation to the things he makes. On the one hand, the virtue of art is ordered to the perfection of the work of art itself (*bonum operis*), irrespective of the good of the worker (*bonum operantis*). On the other hand, prudence is concerned with the good of the worker and with his ultimate end as a person, that is to say, with his happiness and his salvation.

The artist as artist is concerned exclusively with the perfection of his work, and that perfection in its turn does not depend essentially on the moral and spiritual condition of the artist. An uncharitable man may still produce a genuine work of art. Yet a great artist can be imprudent in his use of the work of art. He may fail to fulfill the deeper demands of the virtue and gift of art (for example, by unduly subordinating his talent to the acquisition of immediate material success or the approval of critics). There is the further possibility that the practice of an art can lead to the deviation of the artist's entire life, becoming an end in itself to which all other goods, including happiness and personal integrity, are sacrificed.

Art as Virtue and Experience. Ideally speaking, in a fully successful exercise of the gift and virtue of art, the good of the work, the good of the worker, and the good of the spectator are all achieved together on a transcendent artistic and spiritual level. That is to say, the artist and spectator share together an intellectual and spiritual experience in the creative enjoyment of the work of art. The artist, by reason of his intellectual *virtus* and his skill and also by reason of his inspired creative response to his artistic *kairos* (providential time), seizes upon and manifests to the spectator something profoundly alive in the world that could not be expressed or conveyed in any other way. The discovery of this unique view of reality is the source of aesthetic enjoyment. In this creative act, which the spectator shares (as he experiences the work of art), there occurs an aesthetic revelation of being and of life, not in the sense of philosophic or religious exhortation but in the sense that the work of art itself is an inscrutable sign of a deep and hidden reality. This sign has an eternal and universal significance. *See* SIGN; SYMBOL.

J. Maritain appraises the spiritual fruitfulness of artistic and creative perception by stating that "the virtue of art which resides in the intellect must not only overflow into the sense faculties and the imagination, but it requires that the whole appetitive power of the artist, his passion and will, tend straightly to the end of his art" (*Art and Scholasticism,* 47). This applies also to the serious viewer of the work of art. The work of art tends to elevate and clarify the intelligence and heart both of the artist and of the spectator. The art experience thus approaches something analogous to the purity of religious contemplation.

Consequently the work of art has spiritual and moral resonances in the sense that it tends to the self-transcendence of the artist and of the viewer in God's light and thus orients them to their final end. The harmonization of art and prudence is necessary then for the fulfillment of man; disharmony between the two gives rise to questions of artistic excellence on the one side and moral integrity on the other. Hence the problems of morality and art are lodged in the perfection of relationship between art and prudence.

Beauty and Sin. The fear of art often arises because art is unashamedly concerned with an intellectual pleasure, which St. Thomas approvingly called *delectatio*. Art is for the delight of the intelligence and heart of man; but it reaches him through the delight of the senses. Art presents objects that the eye, the creative imagination, and the spiritual intelligence all together apprehend as delightful and beautiful. Together they love to engage in tireless contemplation of these forms. Very often the artist begets aesthetic pleasure by the creation of forms borrowed from what is most attractive and pleasing to man's senses: the beauty of the human being.

This raises, in some minds, the question of whether there may be certain subjects that the artist cannot treat even with extreme care because these subjects may turn out to be sinful by their very nature. Moral judgments in this case need to be drawn in the light of several considerations: (1) Evil and immorality in a work of art usually derive not so much from the subject matter or from the art itself as from the way in which the subject matter is treated by the artist or from the way in which it is viewed by the spectator. (2) A moral problem may accidentally arise for the spectator who is not able to view a genuine work of art in its artistic integrity by reason of his immaturity, his lack of education, or his moral or psychological disposition. This does not necessarily create a problem of prudence for the artist as such. The responsibility may fall to the viewer himself, or to those in charge of his formation, as well as to those who market and display the work. (3) A moral problem may arise in the case of an artist who is deficient in his artistic responses and does not possess the gift of detachment that enables him to transcend his subject matter and express its formal perfections. If the artist's talent is deflected from its true purpose, i.e., the artistic perfection of his work, and becomes obsessed with some other secondary end, he may sin against his art as well as against prudence. But this need not be confined to cases where the artist becomes absorbed in connivance with carnal inclinations. It may occur also when he subjects his talent in a servile way to the requirements of commercial or political propaganda or even to jejune editorializing in the area of social, ethical, or religious platitudes.

Art Censorship. Since all art is not perfect in its own order and since both artist and viewer may suffer from certain deficiencies, censorship may be required in unusual situations, as St. Thomas points out, following Plato (ST 2a2ae, 169.2 ad 4). However, prudence avoids excesses of censorship that lead to puritanical sterilities and tend to censure the experience of any art touching the senses. A wholesome Christian view enjoys the artistic eye that Yves Simon called "a privilege of aloofness, a privilege directly opposed to whatever evil may be connected with desire." Rather than censor works of art, a balanced moral judgment seeks to develop a spirit of cultured and reasonable sublimation. Both aesthetic illiteracy and Jansenist types of morality may conspire to put the unsophisticated Christian into a moral quandary about entering art galleries and reading modern novels. Under such conditions it has been thought best by some to stay away from art and avoid all but the most innocuous novels and plays on the ground that all others constitute a possible moral danger. This scruple does not protect the Christian against the climate of vulgar and obvious immorality that pervades the popular communication media but rather deprives him of the formation that would enable him to rise above his milieu and seek his *delectatio* on a higher level. Man deprived for a long time of properly ordered *delectatio* may go over to the carnal (see ST 2a2ae, 35.4 ad 2). It is the function of the virtue of art to provide man with the intelligent *delectatio* that he needs and that is an important element in the Christian life. *See* CENSORSHIP; CENSORSHIP OF BOOKS (CANON LAW); FREEDOM OF SPEECH.

Art and the Role of the Church. In an address to artists on May 7, 1964, Pope Paul VI publicly lamented the estrangement that had developed between the Church and the art world. Artists, he said, no longer felt at home in the Vatican, which was once the home and workshop of the greatest talents. It is true that artists have wandered far from the Church in search of inspiration. The Pope wondered whether this was because the Church itself had failed to provide inspiration. The Church had demanded that artists conform to certain canons of style and confine their efforts to imitation of the past. It had perhaps not understood the aspirations and vision of the present. "Forgive us for having placed on you a cloak of lead! And then we abandoned you, we too," said Pope Paul to the artists. He continued candidly "to confess the whole truth . . . we resorted to oleographs and works of little artistic or real value, our only justification that we have not had the means of understanding great things, beautiful things, new things, things worthy of being seen. We have walked along crooked paths where art and beauty and, even worse, the worship of God have been badly served" (*Ci premerebbe,* May 7, 1964, *Pope Speaks* 9:390–395).

The Godless Artist. A tragic result of the divorce between art and prudence, and between art and the Church, has been that in modern times the cult of art as an end in itself has been substituted for religion and even for morality. The romantic quest for aesthetic experience has tended to become an end in itself. For many artists and viewers the quest for new experience is the whole of life. Morality is considered irrelevant to this quest. Thus the poet Rimbaud wrote in a letter:

> I say one must be a *seer.* One must make himself into a *seer.* The poet makes himself into a *seer* by a long, unbounded and reasoned *disordering* of *all the senses.* All the forms of love, of suffering, of madness he himself seeks out, and he drains in himself all poisons, keeping only their quintessences. It is an inexpressible torture in which he requires all faith, all superhuman strength, in which he becomes the great sick one, the great criminal, the great accursed and the supreme Wise man among all other men. [Letter to Paul Demeny, May 15, 1871.]

Thus the *poète maudit* (the accursed poet) or saint in reverse lives as an outcast and delivers himself up unresistingly to every passion and new experiment. Refusing no drug or perversion, he makes it a point of honor to shun nothing except conventional morality and becomes the hero of decadent romanticism. He becomes the symbol and embodiment of the desire to be without limitation, to escape from the tyranny of norms and rules. However, artists themselves have realized that preaching a gospel of experience as an end in itself leads the preacher and his hearers alike into deeper despair.

Beyond Art. Statements such as that of Rimbaud represent a deliberate revolutionary attack on the traditional aesthetic (and moral) consciousness of man. But this does not form a substantial basis for the dismissal of all modern art as a gratuitous sin against both art and prudence or an impious revolt against all that is good, beautiful, true, and Christian. The ideology of the artist as "satanic saint" is recognized by artists themselves as a dead end and is not to be taken as the statement of a definite irreversible program. Neither can it be a pretext for the rejection of modern expressions, whether they be surrealistic, nonrepresentational, or nonfigurative. The basis of artistic judgments ultimately rests on the inner logic and precision or excellence of the work itself.

Setting aside obvious deordinations and extremes, the attempt of modern *expressionism to explore the frontiers of the human consciousness is basically valid. The work of major 20th-century artists such as *Kandinsky, *Matisse, *Klee, Miro, Chagall, *Pollock, and others constitutes a real and necessary development in art that is not arbitrary and irresponsible. The validity of aesthetic communication in recent art forms depends on the energy, economy, honesty, and precision with which these "images of vitality" (Herbert Read) are organized. (*See* ABSTRACT ART AND THE CHURCH.)

Beyond expressionism, which concerns itself with the frontiers of a subjective self where the individual rejoins the collective subconscious in archetypal symbols, there is another important direction in abstract art: the impersonal, objective, "constructivist" effort of men such as *Mondrian, Arp, Calder, Le Corbusier, Naum Gabo, and *Malevich. In spite of all their differences these artists look beyond subjective feeling, personal intuition, and contemplative concentration to a world of logical necessity, free from personal limitations as well as from utilitarian programs. Their work is objective not in the sense that it creates images or forms as pure objects but rather in the sense that it strives to integrate image and life in one reality, liberated from the human and accidental, a "pure reality," which is apprehended without "particularities of form and natural color" [P. Mondrian, *Plastic Art and Pure Plastic Art* (DocModArt 2; New York 1945)], not in the personal and subjective apprehension of beauty but in a more universal intuition like that of the mathematician or of the Zen master. Here the encounter is not with the work of art in the mode of the traditional aesthetic experience but (it is claimed) with expressions of "pure harmony" that liberate one's vision from the limitations of personal attractions. This art attempts to transcend the demand for subjective pleasure even of the highest spiritual order and assumes the development of a new consciousness indifferent to the canons of that Greek and European humanism that is essentially individualistic. Its futuristic vision requires a new dimension of life in which the total environment and ambiance of human existence is itself penetrated with clean and impersonal aesthetic harmony. Here artistic meaning is no longer sought from the individual work of art appropriated by the connoisseur or enshrined in the museum but from the very environment in which all live and move together. Mondrian has been called a "modest and saint-like pioneer" toward this new futurist world that will, it is hoped, be different from a disorganized and troubled one. Such aspirations are not immoral but rather bear resonances that are profoundly Catholic, as they strive for the perfect marriage of art and life, and art and prudence. However, in embracing the whole ot reality art cannot exclude the legitimate expression of personal feeling, specifically human experience and spiritual aspiration (*see* LITERATURE, NATURE AND FUNCTION OF).

Bibliography: J. MARITAIN, *Art and Scholasticism and the Frontiers of Poetry,* tr. J. W. EVANS (New York 1962). H. E. READ, *Art and Society* (2d ed. New York 1950). Y. R. SIMON, "Art and Morality," NewSchol 35 (1961) 338–341. A. G. SERTILLANGES, *L'Art et la morale* (Paris 1899). É. H. GILSON, *Painting and Reality* (Bollingen Ser. 35.4; New York 1957), *passim.* Gilson Arts, *passim.* A. DE PROPRIS, EncCatt 8:1400–03. G. JACQUEMET, *Catholicisme* 1:869–878.

[T. MERTON]

ART (PHILOSOPHY)

There is no simple yet comprehensive definition of art; the word has in fact many meanings. The Greek and Latin equivalents (*τέχνη, ars*) can include broadly everything customarily grouped under the label of fine art, and servile and liberal arts as well. Even when narrowed to fine art, the word retains ambiguity in at least two important respects. First, whatever community of meaning the various fine arts share, distinctive differences among them prevent the name's remaining exactly the same in meaning; poetry and painting, for example, are not art in a wholly identical sense. Current usage tends to limit the meaning of art to painting and sculpturing. Second, within the context of fine art, art may signify the product of art, the creative process itself, or the experience of appreciating a work of art, sometimes referred to as the aesthetic experience.

This article deals with art from a broad, philosophical point of view, considering its definition and division, the notion of fine art, and problems associated with the latter's finality.

Notion of Art. In the Western tradition, the original meaning of art is skill in making; the word was used by the ancient Greeks to refer, first of all, to the crafts that satisfy basic human needs. Throughout the dialogues of *Plato and the writings of *Aristotle, this meaning of art is the basic one employed to explain all other skills, whether physical or mental. Art was also early recognized as a sign of a certain excellence, testifying to man's progress beyond what nature can provide. Aristotle accordingly points out that he who invented any art was naturally admired by men as being wise and superior to the rest. "But as more arts were invented, and some were directed to the needs of life, others to recreation, the inventors of the latter were naturally always regarded as wiser than those of the former, because their branches of knowledge did not aim at mere utility" (*Meta.* 981b 16–19). Art as "the capacity to make, according to sound reason" (*Eth. Nic.* 1140a 20) was accordingly extended to what we now call liberal and fine art. The history of the meaning of art is the history of man's progress from making products immediately necessary for living to making things ordered to knowledge or enjoyment. This Greek conception of art dominated the Middle Ages and persists in modern times.

Art and Nature. Craftsmanship enabled man to attain a grasp of the operations of nature, for he soon noted strong resemblances between the way he produces something and the way in which nature works. Much of Plato's *Timaeus* seeks to render the pattern of the universe intelligible by comparison with man's own making, while still viewing nature as a work of divine art. In the *Physics,* Aristotle appeals to the making of a statue or a bed to help understand how natural *change takes place. It is in this context of making as resembling natural processes that Aristotle's often misunderstood dictum, "art imitates nature," should first be grasped before it is applied to fine art. In another area, medicine, the understanding of nature in terms of art has been fruitfully pursued, as the writings of *Galen and *Harvey show. Nevertheless, however much art and nature resemble each other, and however much the understanding of one leads to an understanding of the other, they remain quite distinct. The likeness of the work of art exists first in the mind of the maker; the *form of a living natural object, existing independently of the human mind, preexists in some other natural object. A chair comes from a man's mind, but the man himself comes from another man, from nature.

Art and Science. The common notion of art as skill also distinguishes art from *science, even though both arise from the human mind. Both art and science are *knowledge, but art is ordered to something apart from knowledge itself, namely, the work produced. In art, therefore, knowing is for the sake of producing. In science, we seek to understand that something is so or why it is so. This distinction does not prevent some disciplines from being both art and science. For example, figures are constructed in *mathematics, and thus there is both knowledge and production; at the same time what is produced is a subject of *demonstration, and thus pertains to a science.

Art and Prudence. Art also differs from prudence or practical wisdom, for although both involve reason, they are concerned with distinct kinds of activity: work and behavior. Art uses knowledge to produce a work; prudence uses knowledge to deliberate well and to arrive at decisions regarding what is to be done to ensure right behavior. Prudence therefore involves the moral order in a way that art does not; consequently, prudence is a moral as well as an intellectual quality in man.

Art and Aesthetics. The narrowing of the meaning of art to fine art, and the corresponding resolution of a theory of art to *aesthetics is a relatively modern contribution. The development of art in the Renaissance undoubtedly accelerated this tendency. Alexander Baumgarten, in the middle of the 18th century, is generally regarded as the first to try to construct a systematic aesthetics in the modern sense. True enough, Plato and Aristotle in ancient times, and various writers in the Middle Ages, made major contributions to what is now regarded as a philosophy of fine art. But in the last 200 years the fine arts have been approached in a quite different spirit, emphasizing an association of art with *beauty and stressing the autonomy of fine art. In such a view, there is a distinct world of fine art and aesthetic experience; a special *creative imagination and sensibility are thus required to appreciate the distinctive values found in such works.

Kinds of Art. Art has been traditionally divided into liberal and servile. This division is basic, referring as it does to a difference in the work to be made. The most obvious type of makeable object is one that exists in external physical matter, for such matter is susceptible to receiving an artificial form; wood, for example, readily lends itself to being shaped into a table, a chair or a bed. It is equally evident that such making, initially at least, is the result of bodily effort on the part of the maker, and this feature characterizes such art as servile. Further, the action involved in such making is transitive, that is, an activity which, though originating in an agent, terminates outside the agent in some product that comes to exist in physical matter. These characteristics of servile art indicate, as suggested earlier, that the name "art" refers primarily to servile art; this priority is in the order of naming, not a priority of perfection.

Liberal Art. Liberal art, therefore, is art in a less obvious sense. We are nonetheless familiar with the extension of the name to liberal art; we are familiar also with the traditional division of the liberal arts into the *trivium* (logic, grammar, and rhetoric) and the *quadrivium* (arithmetic, geometry, music, and astronomy). Liberal art is less evidently art because the making involved is not a transitive action, but immanent, activity that both originates and terminates within the agent, forming the agent rather than some external physical object. The object of a wholly liberal art, therefore, is immaterial, found primarily in the mind or imagination of the artist. Such an object does not involve making in the original sense, yet proportionally, there is an indetermination in the mind of man requiring that he set in order his means of knowing; for example, order is brought into man's thinking when he establishes what a *proposition is or how we reason in a valid way. A *syllogism, for example, is something we construct deliberately, in the manner of a mathematical figure, and not just spontaneously. Such constructions enjoy existence in the mind and imagination. We thus see the reason for calling such arts liberal, since the subjects and purposes of these arts pertain to the mind of man whereby he is set free from lack of *order. We see also that although the name "art" first signifies manual craft, nevertheless, considering the work produced, liberal art is primary. (*See* LIBERAL ARTS.)

Fine Art. Though the distinction of servile and liberal is basic, it is not particularly revealing in regard to fine art which, in fact, cuts across that division. Some fine arts are liberal; poetry and music, for example, would fall within the liberal division, for the poet and the composer produce their works primarily by immanent action, and their works exist chiefly in the imagination. Other fine arts are servile in the sense that the objects made require external physical matter and labor for their existence; thus the painting is embodied on canvas and paint, the statue in stone, and the church in stone or brick. To appreciate the distinctive character of fine art, another division must be considered.

From the standpoint of purpose, art is further divided into useful and fine. The useful arts produce things to be enjoyed not in and for themselves, but for some other good. The servile arts would here be classed as useful. Liberal arts such as *logic, grammar, and *rhetoric could be termed useful in the sense they are not ends in themselves but are sought as indispensable aids for bringing about knowledge, adequate expression, or persuasion.

The productions of fine art are contemplated and enjoyed for their own sake (which does not preclude their also being ordered to another extrinsic end). The reason for this division can be shown in a painting, for example, that has a kind of significance inciting enjoyment of a form wholly lacking to a merely useful product, such as a shovel. The painting is viewed primarily for itself; any functional value it might have, e.g., its location in a particular area, is secondary. There is, moreover, a distinctive and unique type of enjoyment that arises in the viewing or hearing of a work of fine art consequent upon the equally distinctive type of *contemplation realized in appreciating the work. Some prefer to make this point by saying that the end sought in the work of fine art is the contemplation and enjoyment of beauty, provided that beauty is taken in a properly aesthetic sense.

It is worth noting that man's preoccupation with beauty, pleasing form, design, and so on, carries over into many useful products of art, and hence the division into useful and fine should not be understood too rigidly. A shoe is clearly a product of useful art, yet we find it both necessary and desirable that a shoe look good. As human beings, we project our desire for beauty of form into objects around us as much as possible; in fact, very few products of human art, no matter how utilitarian they are, escape our passion for artistic enjoyment. We humanize our environment in precisely this way.

Analysis of Fine Art. From an Aristotelian point of view, what sets off fine art from either liberal or servile is imitation. We have already noted that in a sense all art imitates nature, sometimes in appearance, sometimes in operation. What is peculiar to fine art is that imitation (and delight in the imitation) is the immediate end sought in fine art, whereas imitation serves only as a means in liberal or servile art.

The word "imitation" is subject to easy misunderstanding ("representation" might serve better for a modern reader). In any event, it is not to be identified with more or less literal copying. The tendency to identify them may originate in the fact that the most evident instances of artistic imitation occur in the visual arts, where imitation is associated too readily with natural or photographic likeness. Artistic imitation by no means rests upon a complete dependence of the image upon some original in nature from which it proceeds. It always involves some degree of abstraction. There is equal, if not more, dependence of the image upon man's creative imagination and understanding. Such imitation should therefore be understood as creative. It is imitative in the sense that a work of art represents something other than itself, being some sort of *sign or *symbol; it thus has reference to some aspect of reality as we experience it. It is creative as well, for the mind and *imagination of the artist is also a source, and indeed a more significant one. Hence no artist merely reproduces some aspect of reality; on the other hand, no matter how "abstract" or "non-objective" the work of art, it cannot wholly escape reference to human experience of reality.

Artistic imitation, therefore, is a broad notion ranging from the one extreme of approaching a somewhat literal representation of reality to the opposite extreme of retaining only a tenuous but still significant representation of some quality detected in reality. The history of painting and sculpturing reflects this movement within these extremes. It is realized also in proportionately different ways in other arts. In the poetic arts the object of imitation is the action and passion of men as reflected variously in the poem, the novel or the drama. One could say that the common object of all fine art is human action and passion; the differences among the fine arts come from the manner and means of imitation. Though music is sometimes regarded as a non-imitative art, the facts of musical history belie this observation. Music, of course, does not represent in a visual manner nor is it imitative in the sense that it copies natural sounds. Music represents the flow of passion, originally expressed in the intonation of the human voice, by means of tonal and properly musical progressions. The use of music to accompany drama or motion pictures obviously manifests this; more serious works, even the most "abstract" forms of musical composition, do so more subtly and with more elaborate technique. Even 20th-century music bears witness to such primal representational principles as tension and release, the expected and the unexpected, arousal and resolution. *See* MUSIC (PHILOSOPHY).

Finality of Art. Finality refers to a good or purpose; in art, this refers both to the purpose of the artist and to the work of art itself. The two may coincide, but the artist can also order the work of art to something extrinsic to the work itself. Thus the artist can intend the work for propaganda or some other foreign end. The artist then acts as man rather than as artist, and this is one way art and morality may be related. In other words, over and beyond the good of art itself, the artist may be working for a morally good or bad cause; this consideration falls under the scope of prudence.

Morality of Art. Art and morality may also be related within the work itself. Any work of art is an idea expressed by an image in the artist's mind and in an appropriate sense medium. The power of art lies in its simultaneous appeal to *senses and *understanding. What is universal in art is realized in this sense medium; the tragic hero, for example, is a type of man exemplified individually by his action, and with whom the spectators can identify themselves. Such a work of art images human nature in its various manifestations, and chiefly in its moral character. The artistic image, while not itself of a moral nature, can thus express man in some way acting as a moral agent. This is primarily so in poetic art and proportionately so in other arts.

Consequently, an intrinsic relation between art and morality is evident in the following way. Whenever the work of art creatively represents something of human action and passion, the moral order enters into the work of art as a formal constituent, for human action and passion are voluntary, and voluntary acts are moral acts. Moreover, the moral order contributes to the delight, intelligibility, and beauty of much art. For example, the intelligibility and delight we find in a tragedy depend in great measure on grasping some moral grandeur in the action of the hero; the development of a musical composition images in tonal progression the movement of human passion at its finest, whether noble, tragic, or joyful. Hence it can be maintained that when a moral dimension enters into the construction of a work of art, the artist, as artist, has an obligation to represent as morally right what is morally right or what is morally wrong as morally wrong. As far as the relation of art and the moral order is concerned, then, what should be excluded from good art is the artist's representing what is morally good as evil and what is morally evil as good; otherwise, he will be unconvincing as an artist and will fail to move us in the manner that is appropriate to art.

At the same time, the intrinsic end of art cannot be overtly moral; art suffers when used merely to propagandize morality. It is one thing for a moral dimension to enter into the artistic representation; it is quite another to make the work of art specifically moral in its aim. We are thus led to recognize a finality of art which, in fact, is twofold. One end is the arousal and release of the emotions wherein lies the great appeal art has for man, for art represents the flow of emotional tension and release more skillfully than our normal experience usually permits. Aristotle's notion of catharsis manifests this point in relation to tragedy. The cathartic end in art is instrumental, however, in that it disposes us for the ulterior end of artistic contemplation and delight. *See* POETICS (ARISTOTELIAN).

Art and Contemplation. Artistic contemplation is a distinct kind of knowing, accompanied by a distinct type of delight, realized proportionately in the different arts. So far as this can be summarized generally, it is a knowledge of what need not be, rather than of what must be, and yet the work has its self-contained inevitability; it is an imaginative reconstruction of some aspect of reality and life we are familiar with; it is more intuitive than discursive; it bears on the singular, but in such a way that something universal is realized in it; it must be both concrete and abstract. It is knowledge especially appropriate to the human mode of knowing: an intimate union of sense and intellect, image and concept, imagination and understanding. Therein lies the source of the special delight that accompanies this contemplation, which is at once an action of sense and intellectual *appetite. There is the initial sense delight accompanying the grasp of such qualities as color, tone, line, and sound. There is the intellectual delight attendant upon the grasp of the order entering into the rhythmic, melodic, and harmonic construction of a musical composition, or of the order of elements in a work of sculpture or a drama. Most of all, however, such delight arises from seeing in a work of creative representation an object that is more expressly formed and more intelligible than the original referent. The action of the play is more intelligible and more significant than human action ordinarily is. The sound of music is better formed and more discerning than the sound of speech as normally expressive of passion.

Artistic contemplation, constantly fluctuating between an image and an original, never exhausts the significance set in motion by the initial experience of the work of art. The unterminating character of this contemplation is the main reason we enjoy over and over again the same work, for new significance and vitality always emerge in enduring works of art, tantalizing the mind with promises of hidden meaning waiting to be uncovered. Such artistic finality, contemplation with its ensuing delight, constitutes the primary worth of art. For in the final analysis, the work of art is simply the worth of man himself as mirrored in his creative representations.

See also ART; LIBERAL ARTS; AESTHETICS; BEAUTY; SYMBOL; PRUDENCE.

Bibliography: J. DEWEY, *Art as Experience* (New York 1934). E. GILL, *Art* (New York 1950). T. M. GREENE, *The Arts and the Art of Criticism* (Princeton 1940). S. K. LANGER, *Philosophy in a New Key* (3rd ed. Cambridge, Mass. 1957). J. MARITAIN, *Art and Scholasticism and The Frontiers of Poetry,* tr. J. W. EVANS (New York 1962). T. MUNRO, *The Arts and Their Interrelations* (New York 1949). R. WELLEK and A. WARREN, *Theory of Literature* (New York 1956). H. READ, *Meaning of Art* (new ed. London 1956).

[J. A. OESTERLE]

ART, EARLY CHRISTIAN

Early Christian art comprises the architecture, painting and mosaic, sculpture, and minor arts of the first 4 centuries of Christianity. After the 5th century, it was replaced by Byzantine art. In this article early Christian art is treated under its three geographical manifestations: (1) in the West, (2) in the East, and, because of special conditions prevailing there, (3) in Egypt.

See CHURCH ARCHITECTURE, 2; COPTIC ART; BYZANTINE ART; ARCHEOLOGY, III (CHRISTIAN); SYMBOLISM, EARLY CHRISTIAN.

1. In the West

The limits in time and space of early Christian art in the West are somewhat a matter of convention. Nevertheless, as far as time is concerned, the flowering of Byzantine art in the 6th century at Constantinople under Justinian establishes a convenient *terminus ad quem* for all early Christian art. With regard to extent in space, the works of Christian art produced in the areas under Roman domination can be considered as belonging to early Christian art of the West. However, the monuments and objects produced in the Byzantine enclaves in the West, notably at *Ravenna, and above all the monuments that were direct forerunners of Byzantine art, must be excluded. With its limits thus defined, early Christian art in the West is seen to be the continuation of Roman art under new social conditions as well as in a new spirit, that of Christianity.

Actually, one cannot speak of a Christian art in a strict sense. The essential of any art is not the subjects it treats so much as the forms in which they are clothed, the latter issuing on one hand from the physical and social milieu and on the other hand from the moral climate, which is often even religious and mystical. It is in this sense that one can speak of an art that is Christian. Situated within the orbit of imperial Rome, the Christian ideal was clothed from its very beginnings in the forms offered to it by Roman art.

From the technical point of view, the West offered unusually propitious conditions for the formation of a Christian art. Among these was a certain richness of means available even to the less wealthy classes. These means included: solid and varied materials for construction, architectural knowledge that was constantly employed, a pictorial tradition inherited from the Etruscans, a craft that handled the difficulties of sculpture with great ease, and a whole range of possibilities in the minor arts, including mosaic work. Because of these factors, it is easier to follow the various stages of early Christian art in the West than in the East. Moreover, it is quite possible that the West furnished to Christian art as a whole its first expressive forms.

The evolution of early Christian art is not, however, an unbroken progression. A definite date—the official recognition of Christianity by the Edict of Milan in 313—separates it into two stages. Before 313, Christian art was clandestine; after that date, it was openly established.

Clandestine Period. Christianity is in large part rooted in Judaism, but unlike Judaism it is not hostile to the use of images. Even though Christianity emphasizes the importance of the invisible, it is nevertheless the religion of an incarnate God and consequently recognizes the full value of the visible. The use of works of art is therefore in complete accord with its teaching. But Christianity was born in a milieu and in circumstances far from favorable to this concept.

In early apostolic times, those who preached did so in the synagogues. At that period, and especially throughout the regions of the Diaspora, the synagogues were less rigid in their opposition to the representation of sacred objects. This is borne out particularly by the presence of the paintings at *Dura-Europos and of others in Palestine itself. The evidence, however, dates from a period later than the beginning of the 3d century and is scanty. In Rome the decoration of Jewish catacombs is confined almost exclusively to ornamental motifs or reproductions of liturgical furnishings. It is therefore quite probable that at first in the Christian communities the converts from paganism had to combat a current of opinion somewhat opposed to the representation of religious scenes. But the doctrine of the Church was on the side of the converted pagans, and they won their case.

Very soon both in Rome and throughout the empire, Christianity was faced with persecution. The Jewish communities were accused of atheism, exclusiveness, and hatred of the human race. The Christian faith aroused the same prejudices, since it appeared to be linked with the Jewish faith. A decree of Nero after the burning of Rome made the profession of Christianity a legal offence. Under Decius the profession of Christianity was counted as an attack against the Roman religion (which in fact it was) and by that very fact, an attack against the imperial authority. Persecution was undertaken as a measure of public safety and would often be cruel and violent, except under the reign of tolerant emperors such as Alexander Severus, Philip the Arab, and Gallienus. Throughout this whole period, therefore, the Christians were forced into the practice of covert worship.

They nevertheless took advantage of all the available possibilities to construct and decorate what they needed for worship or for the burial of their dead. Under these conditions Christian art began, and the circumstances and milieu of the time played a large role in shaping it.

Architecture. The first Christian churches were modest and unobtrusive. As the Acts of the Apostles indicate, the first churches were in private homes. It is probable that, especially in Rome, the richer Christians offered their palaces for the reunions of the faithful, since these were buildings particularly suited to the celebration of divine services. Doubtless the first churches in the real sense of the term were constructed under the reign of Alexander Severus (222–235); at least, according to Origen, his successor Maximinus had them burned. In any case, at the beginning of the 3d century, Pope Callistus arranged for the purchase of meeting places (*tituli*) in the different quarters of Rome. In 260 Gallienus issued a decree ordering the restitution to the Christians of their places of worship. During the period of peace lasting from that date until 300, churches were permitted to be built.

These churches were in the form of *basilicas, a type of structure whose origin is uncertain. Unlike the ceremonies in the pagan temples or in the Temple of Jerusalem, in the Christian ceremonies the faithful participated in the drama taking place in the sanctuary. The Roman civil basilica, like the *tablinum* adjoined by the *triclinium* in the palaces, permitted this participation,

Fig. 1. The Multiplication of the Loaves, fresco of the 4th century in the catacomb of the Giordani, Rome.

though there were other possible architectural arrangements that could have been used.

The *catacombs also formed part of Christian architecture; they represent an authentic Christian innovation. In various sections of Rome, taking advantage of the laws applicable to groups, the Christians acquired ground for burial and then used it to dig catacombs. Such burial places are most numerous in Rome, but they exist also in Naples, Syracuse, and even outside of Italy.

Roman underground burial areas (hypogeums) consisted of only two or three subterranean rooms containing tombs (sarcophagi) or cinerary urns. Cremation was rejected by the first Christians as a practice opposed to the preservation of the body for the resurrection and lacking in respect for those sanctified members whose fidelity to Christ had been carried often to the point of martyrdom. To find sufficient space for the burial of the constantly increasing number of Christians became a problem. It was resolved by constructing something resembling the modern skyscraper in reverse. Subterranean galleries at various levels were dug out. In the walls of the galleries, niches were hollowed out to serve as tombs, either in the form of an arch (**arcosolium*) or cubicles that were placed one above the other (**loculus*).

One must classify also as catacombs the underground burial places (hypogeums) of such families as the Aurelii, who were heretical Christians of Rome. The catacomb on which the basilica of St. Peter now stands is one of the most ancient. It is the probable burial place of Peter the Apostle and is surrounded by a number of pagan and Christian tombs, all of which are decorated like the catacombs.

Painting. In the hypogeums, the walls and the *arcosolia* were decorated with paintings. In the catacombs, such paintings are scattered. At regular intervals along the passageways of the catacombs, either *arcosolia* or square rooms were dug out and sometimes provided with *loculi.* The walls of the rooms were further excavated to form *arcosolia;* it is there that the paintings are found on each side of the arch or vault: at the back of the *arcosolium,* on the area below the *arcosolium,* or on the ceilings of the rooms. In these rooms, squares and lozenges in imitation of marble designs cover the lower part of the walls, while the ceilings are divided into sections by geometric lines. In these sections there are decorative motifs taken from Roman art (heads, busts, and animals) and especially figures of people either singly or in groups. The latter adorn also the various parts of the *arcosolia.*

In general, the subjects in the catacomb paintings are taken from the Bible, and the same ones occur repeatedly. The subjects most frequently treated include: the Good Shepherd or Orpheus with the animals, the story of Jona, the resurrection of Lazarus, Daniel in the lions' den, the Multiplication of the Loaves, Noe's ark, the sacrifice of Abraham, the paralytic of Bethsaida, the three youths in the fiery furnace, Adam and Eve, the Adoration of the Magi, the story of Job, the Baptism of Jesus, the man born blind, Moses and the burning bush, Susanna and the elders, the Good Samaritan, and the Wedding Feast of Cana. To these may be added a few mythological subjects, such as Eros and Psyche and the seasons. It is remarkable that Christ is shown only under the symbol of the Good Shepherd or Orpheus, or in the working of a miracle, but never in a scene showing His Crucifixion or His Resurrection.

Various hypotheses have been offered to explain the choice of these subjects. J. *Wilpert has tried to link them with the Christian idea of death and, in particular, to the episodes from the Old Testament and the Gospels mentioned in the ancient prayer commending a soul to God. The archeologist P. Styger believes that these subjects were used to adorn both the catacombs and the Christian homes, and that they have therefore no symbolical value. Neither of these theories takes into account all the facts. The symbolism of these subjects cannot be denied, as the painting showing Susanna as a lamb between two wolves proves, but the symbolism is more general than Wilpert believes. The symbolism may also be related to the *catechesis and the liturgy of the period, though it is safer to say that it is related to the ancient Jewish rituals and to Jewish and early Christian "summaries." The latter were canonical or apocryphal enumerations of outstanding deeds of the heroes of the faith and of the miracles worked by God. In any event, the symbolism is essentially related to the general idea of the economy of the salvation of men's souls.

The oldest examples of these paintings date from the beginning of the 3d century. In this first period of early Christian art, the paintings either express a certain blitheness to be found in pagan art, or they are symbolical in nature and in accord with millennialist, otherworldly ideas. The earliest style closely resembled the elegant Roman style, as in the catacomb of Domitilla, but it later became more impressionistic. At the end of the 3d century, relief was replaced by contrasting tones, as in the group of Adam and Eve in the catacomb of SS. Peter and Marcellus (*see* ARCHEOLOGY, III). These changes in style indicate an acceptance of the contemporary tendencies toward allegory and symbolism, and an evolutionary process in which classical naturalism was gradually replaced by abstraction and simplification.

Sculpture. In the 3d century the wealthier pagans and Christians interred their dead in tombs, and the walls of the tombs were decorated with reliefs. On the Christian tombs frequent use was made of decorative motifs, particularly strigils and other motifs carrying Christian symbolism, e.g., the fish (*see* FISH, SYMBOLISM OF). But quite early other decorative motifs, such as the masks employed in ancient art, were combined with these.

The decorated lamps used in the catacombs to light the passageways and the places of burial first appeared probably in this period. The subjects used on them are in most cases conventional; fish, laurel leaves, cross, shell, and rosette (*see* LAMPS AND LIGHTING, EARLY CHRISTIAN).

In the beginning, different Christian subjects were juxtaposed or combined with others of pagan origin without much concern for blending the subjects into a unified whole. This can be seen in the tomb of Livia Primitiva (Fig. 2), where the Good Shepherd with his sheep is seen between strigils, flanked by a fish and an anchor; or in the tomb at La Gayolle in Provence, where the Good Shepherd is shown with a fisherman, an orante, and a seated figure. A fragment depicting the story of Jona (Fig. 5) shows the attempt to use the classical style to express Christian content. As the century progresses, the Christian subject becomes the central or dominant element of the whole composition,

Fig. 2. "The Good Shepherd," detail of the sarcophagus of Livia Primitiva, 3d century.

EARLY CHRISTIAN ART

Fig. 4. "The Good Shepherd," bone, late 3d century, height 6 inches, Musée du Louvre, Paris.

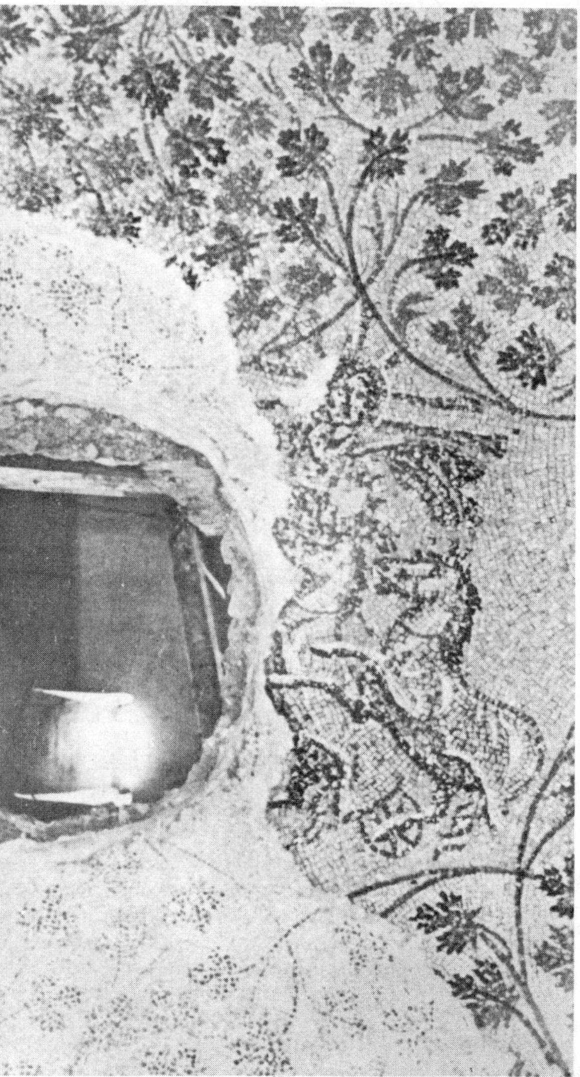

Fig. 3. "Christ the Sun," mosaic, in a mausoleum of the Vatican necropolis, late 3d century.

Fig. 5. "Jona under the Arbor," fragment of a sarcophagus, late 3d century.

Fig. 6. The baptistery of the Lateran, Rome, 4th and 5th century with later decoration, view from entrance.

which is generally pastoral in nature. Though derived from pagan sources, the Good Shepherd is represented in the light of the imagination of Christian artists intent on their own religious symbolism.

In this first period, then, Christian art developed by borrowing forms, by introducing new themes into them, and by transforming the whole in the direction of symbolic abstraction. The tendency toward symbolic abstraction is evident in all the art of the time, but Christian inspiration was one of the most active forces producing it.

Period of Open Development. The ordinance of 313 issued by Licinius in agreement with Constantine granted official recognition to Christianity and, by so doing, afforded conditions favorable to the fuller development of Christian art. The support given to religion by the emperors—except during the brief reign of Julian the Apostate (361–363)—improved these conditions still further. As a result, the erection of religious edifices became widespread. The art of mosaic, used to decorate the buildings, received new impetus, as increasingly its use in the catacombs was abandoned. The spirit of artistic productions also changed. The gracious charm of the classical style gave way to a more serious tone, eventually yielding a hieratic style more suited to the exaltation of the Supreme Sovereign, and modeled after the respectful images demanded by the emperor.

Church Architecture. The number of churches increased, and from the very beginning they were of large dimensions. The form most frequently employed was that of the basilica. Constantine probably took an active part in the erection of the following churches of this type in Rome: St. John Lateran, St. Peter, St. Paul-Outside-the-Walls, SS. Peter and Marcellinus, and St. Agnes. The basilicas of St. Pudentiana and St. Mary Major were also begun in the 4th century, and St. Sabina in the 5th. St. John Lateran is evidently the prototype of the Christian basilica; it is the first church mentioned in the records of the Holy See and the one in which the heads of St. Peter and St. Paul were deposited. It seems to have been the first official church of the bishops of Rome and was without doubt built at the same period as the triumphal arch of Constantine (315).

In Rome the basilica of the period of Constantine had five naves, with a projecting transept and apse at the east end of the building; in the provinces it was built with one or three naves without a transept and with a recessed apse. Unlike the ancient temples, which did not provide for the participation of the faithful in the important ceremonies, the Christian churches had their chief decorative work on the interior. The high-pitched wooden roof of the principal nave was gilded; the effect of depth was accentuated by the long rows of columns and by the austere appearance of the walls, relieved only by mosaics of a didactic nature. In addition, bays or bay windows in the walls lit the major interior area. Attention was thus drawn toward the altar, the center of worship. The transept itself was a passageway that permitted the faithful to approach directly. On the exterior there were no longer any of the groups of pillars typical of ancient buildings. On the façade the pediment remained to emphasize the sacred character of the edifice. In North Africa the Western type of basilica grew more complicated, as at Damus el-Carita, where it is divided into nine naves, or at Orléansville, where a new apse was added facing the west.

The circular plan of construction was taken from the Eastern basilica. It was employed particularly for commemorative monuments and persisted in the West in the form of *baptisteries (Fig. 6). The circular plan was used for the octagonal church of St. Constance (Fig. 7), which was built in the first third of the 4th century and transformed into a baptistery in the 5th.

Painting. Painting was confined almost entirely to the decoration of the catacombs, where it served the cause of decoration along with mosaics. In the 4th century the character of painting remained the same as before until 350, when there was a sudden shift to the classic style. This can be seen in the decoration of the New Catacomb on the Via Latina (Fig. 8*b; see* ARCHEOLOGY, III). However, the quality of painting declined increasingly, and in the 5th century it wavered between conventionalism and mechanical execution. The decline of painting in the catacombs was due to the fact that the attention of artists was turned to the decoration of the buildings in which Christian life was then being carried on. At the same time, the subjects assumed a less symbolical and more profane aspect as the life of the Christians became more involved in the temporal world (e.g., tomb of Maximus and hypogeum of Trebius Justus).

Mosaics. As a result of the exuberance of this period of open development, wall surfaces blazed with the beauty of a technique richer than painting. Mosaic work took on a new life, which would reach its highest peak of expression in the Byzantine world. (*See* MOSAICS.) Up to this point, mosaic work had been confined to the vaulting, to the apses, and to the upper friezes. In the 4th century in St. Constance it was still strongly classic in style with a mixture of picturesque tendencies. The ceiling of the vaulted aisles of this church is divided into eight sections, on either side of which there are agricultural scenes related to the Eucharist, geometric and natural motifs, and portraits. In the 5th century the style changed. It evolved toward the hieratic Byzantine style, as in the representation of Christ enthroned among Apostles and holy women in the apse of St. Pudentiana. Narrative cycles with a didactic content appear also, as on the upper frieze of the nave of St. Mary Major, where in 44 panels the whole story of Genesis is told in a very compact and rigid style. See Figs. 9–11.

In 5th-century North Africa, mosaic work still retained many of its classical tendencies, as in the decoration of a tomb in a church near Kelibia in which birds and flowers are depicted near the plaque bearing the name of the deceased. Mosaic work also took on a more popular and abstract aspect, as on the tomb stones of Tabarka (see Fig. 12), where the deceased is represented in a full-face portrait with the features greatly simplified.

Certain features of the evolution that affected both mosaic and painting can be seen in the reliefs on tombs. Orderly structuring in composition disappears; different episodes are ranged next to one another in little pictures, sometimes in a disorderly fashion, in an effort to use all the available space. Artistry was still very flexible and strong in the 4th century, as is demonstrated by the tomb of Junius Bassus in 359 (*see* SARCOPHAGUS); but it became increasingly less skillful in the handling of planes and of figures. The human body became thicker and postures more stiff. Symbolism, such as the representation of the faithful by sheep, was progressively replaced by the use of historical figures in hieratic poses.

Minor Arts. In this period the minor arts assume more importance than they had during the period of clandestine Christian life. Notable examples of work in glass, gold, silver, and ivory survive. (*See* GOLD GLASS; GOLD AND SILVER WORK; IVORY CARVING.) There is a 5th-century cup of engraved glass in the Louvre Museum that shows the monogram of Christ surrounded by scenes from the Old Testament. Fine examples of goldsmith's work include a gold buckle bearing portraits of saints and another in filigreed gold showing birds facing each other. A silver box for liturgical use bears scenes from the Scriptures: the three youths in the fiery furnace, the Adoration of the Magi, and the resurrection of Lazarus. Numerous examples of an art peculiar to this period have been found, especially in the catacombs. Glasses depicting Biblical scenes similar to those on the walls of the catacombs were made by placing a sheet of cut gold between two layers of glass. Another art form that developed and became more widespread was that of ivory carving, in the round or, more commonly, on diptychs, pyxes, and combs. Christian subjects are used along with profane subjects from mythology. Classical forms are employed, as on a diptych from the north of Italy (Brescia Museum) that depicts Diana and Endymion and on a panel showing Christ's Ascension (Munich Museum; *see* ASCENSION OF JESUS CHRIST). There occur forms tightly compressed within the frames, as on the diptych of Boethius in the Brescia Museum (Fig. 20). Several ivory statuettes of the Good Shepherd are still in existence; one is in the Louvre.

Early Christian art in the West thus shows two fundamental tendencies, one toward mysticism and the other toward an acceptance of the secular. Their respective force depends on the circumstances, but between them an equilibrium is established in accord with Christian ideas. In the first period, mystical symbolism is preponderant and closely corresponds to the tendency of the time. It is expressed in the choice of subjects and in its spiritual overtone, even though it does not at first reject the classical style. In the second period, when Christianity became more involved in daily life, the use of symbolism diminishes to permit a more direct representation of the divine. However, the divine is exalted so that the world in which Christianity is henceforth involved may be submitted to it.

2. In the East

Early Christian art of the East, like that of the West, consists in general of the Christian art previous to the appearance of Byzantine art. Actually, only a few examples remain, and those are too scattered to permit the formation of an idea of the whole.

In no city of the East are there Christian funerary monuments comparable to those of Rome. As in the West, persecution in the East was intermittent; but the religious edifices built during the lulls in persecution were either destroyed by wars and invasions or replaced by Byzantine style churches. Because of the paucity of exemplars, the major tendencies of the period cannot be easily discerned. The difficulty is increased by the fact that each center of art was quite different from the others and by the fact that the influence of Roman art

Fig. 7. The church of St. Constance, Rome, 4th century, interior view showing the circular gallery.

Fig. 8. Early Christian art (in the West): (a) "Moses Striking the Rock," fresco, 4th century, catacomb of Callistus, Rome. (b) "The Sermon on the Mount," fresco, 4th century, in the "New Catacomb" on the Via Latina.

Fig. 9. "The Vintage," detail of vault mosaics, 4th century, St. Constance, Rome.

Fig. 10. "Enthroned Christ," detail of the mosaic, c. 401–417, in the apse of St. Pudentiana, Rome.

EARLY CHRISTIAN ART

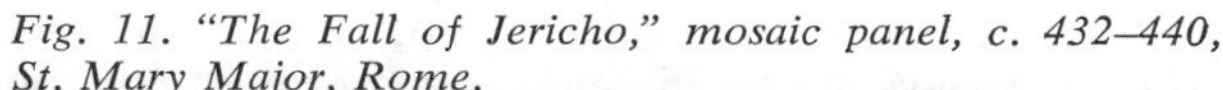

Fig. 11. "The Fall of Jericho," mosaic panel, c. 432–440, St. Mary Major, Rome.

Fig. 12. Orant, mosaic, 5th century, found at Tabarka, Tunisia, now in the Musée du Bardo, Tunis.

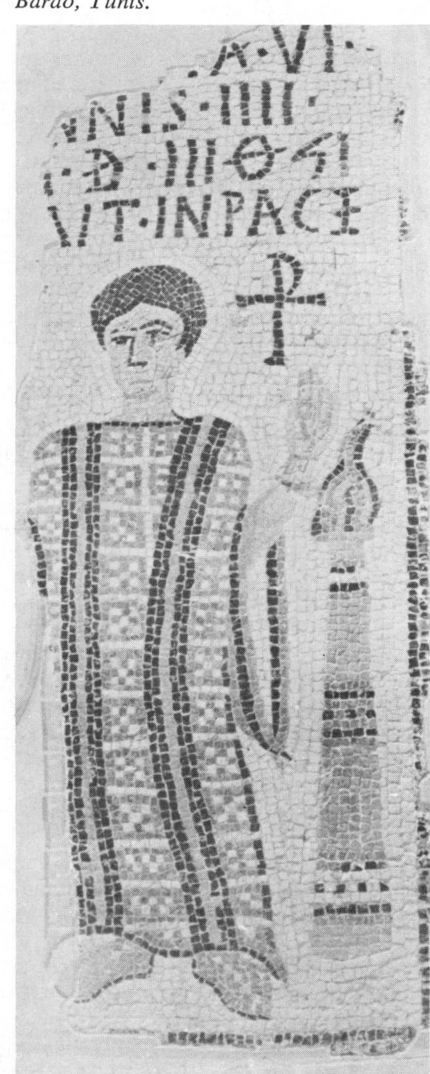

entered subtly into local art. Documentation on the subject is too incomplete to permit tracing a systematic picture of early Christian art in the East. To supplement the lack of objects and monuments, one is forced to draw up instead a sort of nomenclature and to have recourse to contemporary or later written documents.

Early Christian art in the East reached a dividing point at the beginning of the 4th century, as had Christian art during the imperial era in the West. Just as in the West, two periods are apparent: a period of semiclandestine activity and a period of open, officially sanctioned life.

Period of Semiclandestine Activity. The use of private homes for gatherings of the faithful, following the example of Christ in the Cenacle, is attested to from apostolic times. As proof of this one need only refer to the Acts of the Apostles (8.3) and to the Acts of the Martyrs. This custom continued for quite a long time and resulted in the transformation of private homes into "church homes." This was the case at Dura-Europos, a caravan stop between northern Syria and Mesopotamia, dating beyond any doubt from the first third of the 3d century.

The house at Dura-Europos was built around a court and consisted of several rooms, one of which was arranged and decorated as a chapel, probably with the additional use of one or two other rooms as the community grew. At the back of the chapel was a sort of receptacle in front of which there was an arch on two columns; the back wall was ornamented with two superimposed frescoes. The upper fresco depicted the Good Shepherd and the lower one Adam and Eve in the Garden of Eden. On the walls beginning at the north side of the arch were the story of Peter saved from the waters of Genesareth, followed by the episode of the paralytic of Capharnaum, and underneath that the three Marys at the sepulcher; on the south side, the story of David and Goliath; on the west, the Good Samaritan.

The first two paintings show clear evidence of Roman influence. The others bear traces of Roman influence, yet something of the Oriental style is also apparent, notably in the hieratic quality of certain poses. The style is more marked in numerous paintings depicting scenes from the Old Testament that adorn a synagogue (of a slightly later date), which is located quite close to the chapel.

According to the Chronicle of Edessa, the great flood of 201 destroyed a church of Edessa, and if it is recalled that under Abgar IX the Great, Christianity was established in 202 as the state religion, there is every reason to suppose that numerous churches were then constructed in this independent kingdom. In Apamea in Phrygia, traces of a small, square church with an apse, called the church of the Ark, can still be seen in the location of the acropolis of Celaenae. The church was doubtless anterior to the persecution of Diocletian in 303.

The numerous square churches in Asia Minor, notably the group known under the name of Bin-bir-Kilissé (the thousand and one churches) and the basilicas of central Syria built in the 4th century, lead one to believe that they had been preceded by churches of the same style, especially if one reads the letter of St. Irenaeus to Florinus (190) in which he speaks of Polycarp of Smyrna teaching in a *Basilichê aulê*. In the middle of the 3d century, because of his crimes, the Emperor Philip was forbidden access to the *Palaia Ecclesia* (Ancient Church) of Antioch.

It seems quite certain that there were numerous Constantinian churches in Palestine and Syria. This can be surmised from several works written in the 4th century by Gregory of Nyssa, and also from the writings of Origen. According to the latter, in the middle of the 3d century the churches of Caesarea of Palestine were burned by the pagans. Eusebius also recorded that a large number of churches were destroyed by the persecution of Diocletian, though they had been officially tolerated by Gallienus.

Very little can be learned either from literature or archeology about the funerary architecture. Dating certainly from this period are tombs in Palestine and Arabia (Khefa Amer, Haifa, Nâblus, and Nazareth), in Mesopotamia (Edessa and Dara), and in Asia Minor (Ephesus, Seleucia, and Sardis). On the whole, except for Dura-Europos, whose Western characteristics have been noted, recourse must be had to written documentation for information about this period. It is from texts that one learns of the transformation of the "church home" into a church in the real sense of the word.

Period of Open Development. When they had received full liberty to practice their religion, the first concern of the Eastern Christians, like those of the West, was to erect places of worship. The destroyed churches were rebuilt; the written records of about the same date, and in particular the *Ecclesiastical History* of Eusebius, are explicit on this point. A great number of new churches were built. Starting in the 4th century, the greater part of them were built on the plan of a basilica, which was so common in the 5th century; but the octagonal plan was used also, as described in a letter of St. Gregory of Nyssa to Amphilochus, Bishop of Iconium. Among the various forms of decoration, painting was frequently employed; at the end of the 4th century St. Nilus wrote a letter about a church that an eparch wished to have decorated with hunting scenes. Relief work on the capitals and friezes was certainly employed, since a link must have been established in this period between the elongated and pointed acanthus leaves of Leptis Magna of the 3d century in North Africa and those of the same type used in the 6th century throughout the East.

The birth of Byzantine art may be attributed to a new spirit that substituted aulic directions for local initiative and provided an environment of Oriental richness. Artistic techniques, however, had developed before the 6th century and later were only transformed.

Influences on Church Architecture. The art of the early Christian period, especially in regard to the basilicas, can be distinguished by geographical areas, i.e., Constantinople, Greece and the Balkans, Palestine, and Syria and Asia Minor; and by influences, i.e., Roman, Hellenistic, Constantinopolitan, and Oriental.

The Roman influence is seen in the basilica type of construction with its three or five naves, transept, apse to the east, wooden roof, and preference for brick. The Roman influence was evident in Constantinople in the first church of Hagia Sophia (415) and the church of John Studios (463); in Greece at Epidaurus (end of the 4th century), Nicopolis (end of the 5th century), Corinth (5th century), and at Salonika in the basilica of Demetrius, which in its original state dates from 412; in northern Syria, in the church of Kalat Siman (end of

Fig. 13. The "Jona Sarcophagus," late 3d century, in the Lateran Museum, Rome.

Fig. 14. The "Sarcophagus of Adelphia," c. 340, in the National Museum at Syracuse, Italy.

Fig. 15. Sarcophagus, catacomb of Praetextatus, second half of the 4th century, Lateran Museum.

Fig. 16. "St. Agnes," gold glass, from the catacomb of Panfilus, Rome, 4th century, in the Vatican Museum.

Fig. 17. "Adoration of the Magi," panel of the wood doors of St. Sabina, Rome, c. 432, panel height 11 in.

Fig. 18. Silver box, 5th century, length 4¾ inches, found in Lombardy, now in the Musée du Louvre.

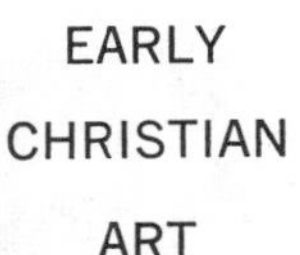

EARLY
CHRISTIAN
ART

Fig. 19. Ivory casket, c. 360–370, height 8⅝ inches, church of St. Giulia (now the Museo Civico), Brescia.

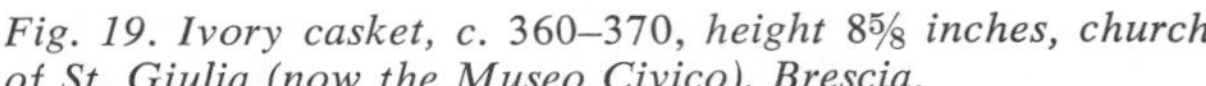

Fig. 20. The "Diptych of Boethius," ivory, 5th century, height 13⁷⁄₁₀ inches, Museo Civico, Brescia.

the 5th century) and at Tafna in the Hauran, where the buildings were close to the square type; and in Asia Minor in the group of churches known as the Bin-bir-Kilissé (5th–6th centuries). The Hellenistic influence contributed the ornamental arcades on the façade and along the interior walls, as well as the arches with ceiling beams on the inside, to the church of Kalat Siman and the buildings at Tafna. Constantinople's main architectural contribution was to provide Asia Minor with the Roman type of construction, to which was added the façade with columns, but without any decoration in relief which was forbidden by the formal austerity of Constantinople. Examples can be seen at Perga, at Sagalassos, and in the group of Bin-bir-Kilissé.

The Oriental tendencies appear under four combined or separate aspects: the absence of the transept or the prolongation of the naves into the transept with a widening of the choir, the commemorative function of the sanctuary, and the triumphal arches on the pillars. Basilicas without a transept are found also in Greece at Salona (early 5th century), in Palestine in the basilica of the Nativity at Bethlehem (326), and in the basilica of the Holy Sepulcher at Jerusalem (323–335).

The prolongation of the naves into the transept together with the broadening of the choir to meet the needs of the liturgy can be seen in Greece in the basilica of Demetrius at Salonika. The sanctuary is most frequently octagonal in form and honors a monument of sacred history: in Palestine, the basilica of the Nativity at Bethlehem and the basilica of the Holy Sepulcher at Jerusalem; and in Asia Minor, the original church of St. John at Ephesus, which consisted of four basilicas adjoining the *martyrium of the saint. This latter type of construction on a larger scale is found at Kalat Siman. There four buildings of the basilica type, one of which has an apse at its east end, are arranged in a cross around an octagonal court whose center is occupied by the pillar of St. Simeon.

The triumphal arches with pillars originated in central Syria at the end of the 4th century at Idjaz in the church of the Apostles. They appeared again in the same region at the end of the 5th century at Kalb Lauzeh and Ruweha, and in Hauran at Umm Idj-Djimal in the churches of Julianos and of Masechot.

In ancient Mesopotamia the use of unfired brick as well as a fondness for display resulted in the technique of applying facings to buildings. The Christian Orient shared the same tastes, joined with a predilection for fired brick, which, though not used in Syria, was the most commonly employed material in Roman architecture. Under the reign of Constantine, several churches were decorated at Constantinople, and doubtless also at Bethlehem, with facings of marble and mosaic. Where mural paintings existed, they were repeated in the floor mosaics, as St. Gregory of Nyssa attested in his description of the representation of the martyrdom of St. Theodore. The same sumptuous technique was used also in secular edifices. The mosaics of the pavement of the Grand Palace or those found while the foundations were being dug for the City Hall at Constantinople, all dating from the 5th century, are justly celebrated.

Mosaic and Minor Arts. In the 5th century, mosaic work covered the walls of churches and apses and appeared in the ornamentation of the cupolas; regrettably, very few examples remain. There is outstanding work in several churches in Palestine, especially in the church of the Multiplication of the Loaves at Et-Tabgah on Lake Genesareth. In Syria, the celebrated mosaic of the Phoenix of Antioch (Fig. 22) was probably Christian in origin.

Some famous buildings and important objects can be dated from the 4th and 5th centuries: the baptistery of the Orthodox or the mausoleum of Galla Placidia at Ravenna (5th century); the Rothschild Cameo (middle of the 4th century); the numerous consular diptychs or pyxes in ivory; golden objects such as buckles, of which one bearing the name of Constantine is in the Louvre; illuminated manuscripts such as the Itala (Berlin), Homer's *Iliad* (Ambrosian Library, Milan), and the Vaticanus and Romanus Virgils (Vatican Library). All these are objects belonging to court art and therefore essentially pre-Byzantine. For this reason they perhaps should not be assigned to the period of early Christian art.

Sculpture. The same holds true for sculpture in Byzantium, where statues of the emperors and functionaries and the triumphal columns were erected by imperial or official order. Unlike the West, tombs with figures are rare and of the triumphal type, such as the tomb found at Constantinople (now in Berlin) on which Christ is shown between two Apostles.

Objects that sprang from individual or local initiative are also of considerable interest. There is, for example, a head of the 4th or 5th century (Louvre), which came from Tartus in Syria. It shows some Oriental characteristics in the treatment of the eyes and hair, and there is a Greek cast to the outline of the face, indicating that studios were set up in the vicinity of the court. A Syrian relief depicts St. Simeon Stylites praying on his pillar (Fig. 21). Its decidedly local origin is indicated by the stiff style employed. A fragment of a parapet from Crimea (4th or 5th century; Fig. 23) has a clearly designed and finely cut picture of Christ. There is also a small gold box of the 5th century from Syria, decorated with repoussé work of a rather primitive style. The fragment remaining bears two medallions, one of which contains a picture of the Virgin and the other a figure who perhaps is Christ. The eyes, the stylization of the hair, and the beard of the male figure are all of a very definite Oriental style (Fig. 24).

It is regrettable for the history of early Christian art that examples are so rare in the East. The few that do remain illustrate some of the techniques adopted by Byzantine art, but they can give no true notion of the interpenetration of ancient aesthetics and Christian ideas, which must have been greater in the East than in the West.

3. In Egypt

During the Christian period and long after the country came under Moslem domination, Egypt had an indigenous Christian art, known as Coptic art. Before the distinguishing characteristics of Coptic art developed, and parallel to its development up to the 6th century, there was a certain amount of artistic production that cannot be called Coptic and belongs to an early Christian art linked to the art that appeared in the area covered by the expansion of Christianity. Much of this art has disappeared, and nothing is known of some works but the bare mention by contemporary or later writers. Celsus speaks of the "great church" of Alexan-

Fig. 21. "St. Simeon Stylites on his Pillar," basalt relief, end of the 5th century, height 48 inches, from Djibrin, Syria, now in the Musée du Louvre.

Fig. 22. "Phoenix," detail of a 5th-century mosaic from Antioch, now in the Musée du Louvre.

Fig. 23. Fragment with head of Christ, marble, 4th or 5th century, height of fragment 17⅘ inches, from Crimea, now in the Musée du Louvre.

EARLY

CHRISTIAN

ART

Fig. 24. Fragment of a gold box, 5th century, height of fragment 1⅕ inches, from Antioch, now in the Louvre.

Fig. 25. Christ blessing, bronze, 5th or 6th century, Syrian, Musée du Louvre.

Fig. 26. Early Christian art (in Egypt): (a) "The Exodus," 5th-century fresco in the chapel of the Exodus at the oasis of Khargeh. (b) "SS. Thecla and Paul," 5th-century fresco in the chapel of Peace at Khargeh.

Fig. 27. Metal ampoule decorated with a figure of St. Mena, 6th century, Egyptian, Musée du Louvre.

dria, ruled by Bishop Demetrius (189–231). A papyrus of Oxyrhyncus (3d century) mentions churches located in the upper and lower valleys of the Nile, which undoubtedly were destroyed during the persecution of Diocletian. In Alexandria, before the peace of Constantine, a martyrium of St. Mark and a church built by the bishop Theonas are known to have existed. It is also possible that during this period the back portion of the columned agora of Ashmunein in Middle Egypt was transformed into a trefoiled apse.

Catacombs. The catacombs of Abu el-Akhem, Mustapha, and Qabbary, all near Alexandria, belong also to this first period. To these must be added the hypogeums of Qabbary, of Kom al-Kugafa, and of the eastern necropolis. There are *loculi,* or small chambers, hollowed out in their rooms. The inscriptions and the ampullae found there prove they are Christian. At some distance, but unfortunately destroyed, is the subterranean cemetery of Karmuz, behind the Serapeum; the arrangement would lead one to believe that it originally served as a sanctuary. The gallery containing the *loculi* was entered through a square chamber lengthened by an apse, and on the side was another square chamber in which *arcosolia* were dug. The frieze of the apse, from the 3d century but altered during the Byzantine period, presented successively the Wedding Feast of Cana, the Multiplication of the Loaves and Fishes, and a Eucharistic banquet. It is possible that this painting should be listed among the very rare examples of the union of a Biblical scene and its symbolical interpretation. Some of its details were unusual: the presence in the farthest scenes of a half-nude seated woman seen from the back; the movement of the Apostle Andrew carrying the fish to Christ; and especially the triangular composition formed by Christ between the Apostles Peter and Andrew. The *arcosolia* of the lateral room were also decorated with paintings: angels standing erect, the Marys at the Tomb, Christ with a lion and a dragon under His feet, the Apostles, St. John the Baptist, and others.

Churches. Of the churches erected by imperial order in Egypt, the best known are the four basilicas that constituted the center of pilgrimage of Apa Menas, near Lake Mariut, west of Alexandria. The basilica of the crypt, with three naves, a projecting apse, and a baptistery, was constructed probably by Constantine. The basilica was intended for pilgrims, but it proved too small. At the end of the 4th century, therefore, Arcadius constructed a longer basilica with a protruding transept. The sick gathered in the basilica of the Baths (5th century); this basilica terminated in two facing apses. A funerary basilica with two apses, an atrium, a baptistery, and funeral chapels on the sides (5th century) was joined to the north cemetery. These basilicas are in ruins, but enough remains to indicate how rich they were in decoration: marble columns, marble facings, beautiful capitals, and sometimes mosaics.

At the other extreme of Egypt, as far south as Luxor, a group of 10th-century chapels is found in the oasis of Khargeh, where Nestorius died in exile (*c.* 451). In the midst of the chapels are two little sanctuaries in the form of square mausoleums (4th and 5th centuries). One is called the chapel of the Exodus because the principal painting on the ceiling, which is in the form of a cupola, depicts soldiers pursuing the Hebrews (Fig. 26*a*). Other figures and scenes from the Old and New Testaments include: Adam and Eve, Noe, Jona, Job and his friends, Daniel in the lions' den, the sacrifice of Isaac, St. Thecla and her followers, a shepherd with his flock, the suffering of Isaia, and Susanna and the elders. Some subjects are of special interest because they are unknown in other early Christian monuments: Jeremia weeping over the ruin of Jerusalem, Jethro rejoining Moses on Sinai, and the meeting of Rebecca and Eliezer. The painting in the other chapel, called the chapel of Peace, contains several hieratic figures grouped around a center decorated with plant motifs: Adam and Eve, the sacrifice of Isaac, an allegory of peace, Daniel in the lions' den, allegories of justice and of prayer, Jacob, Noe's ark, the Annunciation, and St. Paul with his disciple St. Thecla (Fig. 26*b*). Certain elements are clearly Egyptian, notably the costumes in the allegory of peace and the shape of the boat representing the ark.

These are the principal Egyptian early Christian monuments that are not typically Coptic. Unlike the products of Coptic art, on the whole these monuments show a direct Alexandrian or imperial influence.

Bibliography: DACL. R. GARRUCCI, *Storia dell'arte cristiana,* 6 v. (Prato 1872–81). Wilpert MalKatakomb. H. LECLERCQ, *Manuel d'archéologie chrétienne,* 2 v. (Paris 1907). W. LOWRIE, *Monuments of the Early Church* (New York 1923). P. STYGER, *Die römischen Katakomben* (Berlin 1933). E. W. ANTHONY, *A History of Mosaic* (Boston 1935). Walters Art Gallery, *Early Christian and Byzantine Art* (Baltimore 1947). F. W. DEICHMANN, *Frühchristliche Kirchen im Rom* (Basel 1948). E. H. SWIFT, *Roman Sources of Christian Art* (New York 1951). Morey EChArt. L. HERTLING and E. KIRSCHBAUM, *The Roman Catacombs and Their Martyrs,* tr. M. J. COSTELLOE (2d ed. London 1960). D. T. RICE, *The Beginnings of Christian Art* (Nashville 1957). E. COCHE DE LA FORTÉ, *L'Antiquité chrétienne au Musée du Louvre* (Paris 1958). W. F. VOLBACH, *Early Chris-*

tian Art, tr. C. LIGOTA (New York 1962). W. SAS-ZALOZIECKY, *L'Art paléochrétien* (Paris 1964). P. DU BOURGUET, *La Peinture paléochrétienne* (Paris 1965). R. KRAUTHEIMER, *Early Christian and Byzantine Architecture* (PelHArt Z24; 1965), a good survey in English. **Illustration credits:** Figs. 1, 13, and 17, Leonard Von Matt. Figs. 2, 4, 5, 23, 24, and 27, Maurice Chuzeville, Vanves. Figs. 3, 8*b*, and 16, Pontificia Commissione di Archaeologia Sacra. Figs. 6, 7, 8*a*, 9, 10, 14, 15, 18, and 19, Hirmer Verlag München. Figs. 11 and 20, Alinari-Art Reference Bureau. Figs. 12, 22, and 26, André Held. Fig. 21, Archives Photographiques, Paris.

[P. DU BOURGUET]

ART, MODERN EUROPEAN

The 18th century provides a convenient point of departure for initiating a presentation of the modern movements that were to occur in European art following the demise of Renaissance art. This article presents a summary of modern developments from the beginning of the 18th century to the present day. This summary is divided into three parts covering the 18th, 19th and 20th centuries respectively. For considerations on the art of the baroque period preceding the 18th century *see* BAROQUE ART; CHURCH ARCHITECTURE, 7.

1. 18TH CENTURY

The general pattern of European culture during the 18th century is that of movement from the late baroque style of the previous era into a rococo phase and finally into neoclassicism. Adding variety and complexity to this pattern is the emergence, especially in England, of Romantic trends, which find their fulfillment in the 19th century.

At the opening of the 18th century, France, still under the rule of Louis XIV (1643–1715), was politically and culturally the leading power in Europe. This article, accordingly, begins with French painting and sculpture. English art is treated next, since in the course of the century England assumed leadership and produced the most progressive art of the age. Then the arts of the Germanic countries, of Italy, and of Spain and Portugal are discussed. French and Italian taste dominated the other geographical areas of European art productivity during the 18th century. *See* CHURCH ARCHITECTURE, 8; NEOCLASSICISM (IN ART); ROCOCO ART; SCULPTURE, 2.

France. In France the baroque style of the period of Louis XIV was superseded by rococo art of the Regency (1714–23) and of Louis XV's mature reign (1723–74). Late in this period, due to enthusiasm for the classical art recovered in Italy and Greece, a turn of taste toward stricter imitation of antique models occurred and was to characterize also the style of Louis XVI's reign (1774–92), foreshadowing the neoclassicism of the Napoleonic era. The sequence of styles is most clearly marked in the decorative arts. Indeed, the term rococo derives from a style of interior decoration and only by extension of meaning has it come to be applied to painting and sculpture. The term probably evolved from the word *rocaille,* meaning an irregular, asymmetrical shell-like decoration on carved wall panels, painted ceilings, mirror frames, etc.

Painting. While the beginnings of rococo decorative art can be found in the period of Louis XIV in motifs at Versailles and designs by Jean Bérain with adaptations of Oriental designs known as *chinoiserie,* the first radical break with baroque tradition in French painting was made by Antoine Watteau (1684–1721). He reflected the aspirations of a new aristocratic and wealthy bourgeois life, which arose after the death of Louis XIV and

Fig. 1. Antoine Watteau, "The Embarkation for Cythera," 1717, oil on canvas, 51 *by* 75½ *inches.*

the abandonment of formal court life at Versailles. Watteau's paintings suggest a world quite unimaginable under the old regime. His heroes and heroines are no longer the grand idealized figures of classical and Biblical history; they are elegantly dressed young lovers of the contemporary world, whose spirits respond not to heroic deeds or lofty thoughts, but are tinged with a gentle melancholy born of introspection and the plights of love (Fig. 1). In contrast with the grand style of the academy, Watteau's figures have shrunk in scale until they no longer dominate nature but sympathetically form a part of it. They exist in a dream world inherited from the pastoral poets of antiquity, a modern Arcadia invested with a mood of gentle reverie. An interest in actual human feelings, which replaced the codification of emotions by Descartes and LeBrun in the previous century, may have led Watteau to paint the Italian and French comedians frequently; their spontaneous performances must have been veritable "abstracts and brief chronicles of the time." His rare portraits, too, have a new intimacy of scale and a new psychological penetration, qualities pursued in the portraits by the Drouais family and excelled by the brilliant pastels of Maurice Quentin de la Tour (1704–88). Watteau's followers in figure composition, Nicolas Lancret (1690–1743) and Jean Baptiste Pater (1695–1736, Fig. 3) lacked his precision in draftsmanship and his emotional depth; they transformed his style into a decorative genre of appealing dexterity and extroverted feeling. The same trend, but on a grander scale, is exemplified in the work of François Boucher (1703–70) who diverted academic classicism into erotic forms, the *mythologie galante,* acceptable to a taste dominated by Madame de Pompadour, mistress of Louis XV. Boucher epitomized the developed rococo style as Watteau had that of the Regency. His draftsmanship rendered figures into graceful, curvilinear patterns, and his opalescent coloring is infinitely sensuous (Fig. 4).

During the same period Jean Baptiste Siméon *Chardin (1699–1779) illustrated the life of the *petite bourgeoisie* and painted many still-lifes, derived from Dutch tradition. Jean Honoré Fragonard (1732–1806) was his pupil and worked also with Boucher. He drew heavily upon the baroque style in his conception of forms summarized in planes of light and shade; in fact he owed much to Rembrandt, but his sparkling colors, small, mobile figures, and glamorized vistas are as much a part of his age as is his frequent eroticism and sentimentality. In these latter qualities he was rivaled by Jean Baptiste *Greuze (1725–1805), whose style, however, was more in conformity with neoclassic ideals.

Rococo art should not be criticized as having been subservient to a decadent aristocracy. Many of its themes are understandable in terms of J. J. *Rousseau's paradoxical philosophy; love for the innocence of childhood and youth above the complexities of civilized life often explains the preference for apparently trivial subject matter.

Sculpture. Sculpture in 18th-century France was more conservative than painting. It carried on the two main trends of late baroque style that existed in Rome, where most French sculptors studied. On the one hand was the baroque animation of pose and swirl of drapery; on the other, the restraint of classical example. At the opening of the period in France the baroque manner of Antoine Coysevox (1640–1720) was followed by that of Nicolas and Guillaume Coustou. Edmé Bouchardon (1698–1762), however, derived an admiration for classical art from his nine years of study in Rome (Fig. 2). Many sculptors of the time were extremely versatile and accommodated their styles to the purposes of their commissions. Jean Baptiste Pigalle (1714–85) and Étienne Maurice Falconet (1716–91) could produce monumental sculpture in a baroque-realist style or could turn out small figurines for table decoration in rococo rooms. Claude Michel, called *Clodion (1738–1814), paralleled the themes of Fragonard's pictures. The most famous French sculptor of the late 18th century was Jean Antoine *Houdon (1741–1828), whose portraits blend realistic effects with neoclassical dignity and simplicity (Fig. 5).

England. During the 18th century, England, which had previously brought in foreign painters, developed an impressive number of native artists. Sculptors continued to be imported, L. F. Roubiliac (1702 or 1705–62), a Frenchman, being the best; but at the end of the century John Flaxman (1755–1826), an English neoclassicist, rose to prominence, and Josiah Wedgwood (1730–95) was producing handsome neo-Greek reliefs on his pottery.

In painting, the tradition of Sir Anthony *van Dyck dominated English portraiture at the opening of the century. Sir Godfrey Kneller (1646–1723) carried on this style of flattering society portraiture but gave it a new directness and intimacy. Decorative figure painting in a grand baroque manner was at first dominated by foreign artists. Yet as early as 1708 the Englishman James Thornhill (1675 or 1676–1734) overcame foreign competition by winning the commission to paint the ceilings at Greenwich naval hospital (completed 1727). Thornhill also decorated the dome of St. Paul's Cathedral with two murals that stimulated Hogarth.

William *Hogarth (1697–1764) was the outstanding early 18th-century English artist. Apprenticed to a silverplate engraver, he sought wider fields to express his interest in human nature and studied in an academy run by Thornhill. Book illustrations and small, almost rococo, family group portraits were followed by his famous moral pictorial dramas: "The Harlot's Progress" (1732), "The Rake's Progress" (1735, Fig. 6), and 10 years later "Marriage à la Mode." These, and other series, were made into prints for popular sale. Hogarth is to be admired for his draftsmanship, painterly ability, and perceptive social satire.

There was considerable French influence upon English painting, and portraits in the rococo style were done by Francis Hayman (1708–76) and Thomas Hudson (1701–79), the teacher of Reynolds. Sir Joshua *Reynolds (1723–92), however, raised the status of British painting by incorporating the Italian grand manner into portraiture (Fig. 8). His effort was unfortunately forced and his draftsmanship poor, but his reputation was so considerable that he became first president of the Royal Academy, founded in 1768. The "Discourses" he gave annually to the students of the academy are a restatement of baroque academicism, redeemed by Reynold's personal sensitivity to art. His style was carried on by John Hoppner (1758–1810) and, with neoclassic modifications, by George Romney (1734–1802). Of far greater interest to modern sensibility is the remarkable talent of Thomas Gainsborough (1727–88), who, unlike Reynolds, did not travel to Italy but absorbed

Fig. 2. Edmé Bouchardon, "Cupid," 1744, marble, height 29 inches.

Fig. 3. Jean Baptiste Pater, "Fête Champêtre," c. 1730, oil on canvas, 29⅜ by 36½ inches.

MODERN EUROPEAN ART 18TH CENTURY

Fig. 4. François Boucher, "Allegory of Painting," 1765, canvas, 40 by 51 inches.

Fig. 5. Jean Antoine Houdon, "Voltaire," 1778, marble, height 20½ inches.

Fig. 6. William Hogarth, "The Rake's Progress," plate number 3, 1735, engraving and etching.

Fig. 7. Thomas Gainsborough, "The Honorable Mrs. Graham," probably 1775, canvas, 36 by 28 inches.

MODERN EUROPEAN ART 18TH CENTURY

Fig. 9. John Singleton Copley, "Watson and the Shark," 1778, canvas, 71¾ by 90½ inches.

Fig. 8. Sir Joshua Reynolds, "Lady Elizabeth Delmé and Her Children," 1777–80, canvas, 94 by 58 inches.

the grace of Van Dyck into his portraits together with a French influence from Hubert Gravelot, who worked in London (1732–45). Better than any other English painter, Gainsborough incorporated the feeling of his age in lively portraits (Fig. 7) and landscapes, which combine the growing interest in "picturesque" and "sublime" themes that herald Romanticism. His rhythmic, sketchy brushwork is highly individual and effective. The Scottish painters Allan Ramsay (1713–84) and Sir Henry Raeburn (1756–1823) also did notable portraits, blending realism and idealism in a typically 18th-century compromise. Richard Wilson (1713–82) painted splendid landscapes, departing from the realism of Samuel Scott (1702?–72), who followed the style of *Canaletto's London scenes.

In the mainstream of academic painting, Reynolds's successor as president of the Royal Academy was Benjamin West (1738–1820), an American-born painter, who had phenomenal success in continuing the tradition of the "history piece," the most highly esteemed type of painting, but one which had outlived its purpose. After studying in Rome, he anticipated the neoclassicism of J. L. *David by about 20 years, and his painting of themes dictated by Burke's "terrible sublime" was important in the formation of early Romanticism. Another important American followed him to Italy and to England, John Singleton Copley (1738–1815), who was a far more talented painter. Copley anticipated Romanticism in his "Watson and the Shark" (1778), which dramatically treated a contemporary event (Fig. 9). Much of the mature work of William *Blake (1757–1827) was done in the 18th century. A prophetic mystic, Blake put his talent, both in poetry and in painting, to the service of his personal religious and ethical revelations. Rejecting reason, the 18th-century idol, he preferred unqualified love as the source of man's salvation and poured forth symbolic poems, lavishly illustrated, to celebrate it.

The Germanic Countries and Central Europe. In contrast with the central monarchy of France, the Germanic countries were divided into small principalities during the 18th century. Palaces, castles, and great monastic establishments were lavishly decorated. The style, a brilliant blend of late Italian baroque and French rococo, is often termed German Baroque.

The great number of artists employed on these projects are relatively unknown, but outstanding work was done by several native German masters. Cosmas Damian Asam (1686–1739) painted illusionistic ceilings, derived from such great examples as the Gesù in Rome, and his brother Egid Quirin Asam (1692–1750) was a sculptor. Their aim, which was to blend the two arts and achieve a union of real and visionary elements in ecstatic expression, is well exemplified in the pilgrimage church at Rohr (1717–25). Easel painting in Germany closely followed French style. Anton Raphael Mengs (1728–79), although of German origin, developed his art in Rome and later in Madrid.

Italy. The style of Giovanni Lorenzo *Bernini (1598–1680), the greatest of Italian baroque masters, dominated the opening of the 18th century as it had the last part of the previous century. The naturalism of his sculpture was pursued further by the Neapolitans, Francisco Queirolo (1704–62) and Giuseppe Sammartino (1720?–93?). Antonio *Canova (1757–1822) won international fame for his neoclassic statues.

In painting, Bologna remained an important school, chiefly because of Giuseppe Maria Crespi (1665–1747), who carried on the tenebrist, or shadowy, style of Caravaggio's school, revealing realistic detail in sharp contrasts of light and dark. The work of Alessandro Magnasco (1667–1749) is notable too for its macabre quality and original *al tocco* (separate touches) style (Fig. 10). The baroque was carried on in wall and ceiling decorations of striking facility and power by Francesco Solimena (1657–1747), chiefly active in Naples, and by the great Venetians Giovanni Battista Piazzetta (1682–1754) and *Tiepolo (1696–1770), whose masterpieces are the ceilings over the staircase in the prince-bishop's residence at Würzburg and in the throne room of the royal palace at Madrid. Tiepolo brings to a climax the long tradition of deep spatial illusionism that began with *Mantegna in the early Renaissance, but his facility and light coloring render his work comparable to the rococo in style. Besides Tiepolo, Venice produced the Ricci brothers, Sebastiano (1659–1734) and Marco (1679–1729), who first adopted rococo coloring in Italy, and Antonio Canaletto (1697–1768), all of whom were active also in England. Francesco *Guardi (1712–93), Tiepolo's son-in-law, painted the views of Venice and the *capriccios,* or imaginative views, which appeal most to modern eyes. Rome, on the other hand, although nominally still the cultural center of the world, produced rather dull painting. Giovanni Paolo Panini (1691 or 1692–1765), whose views of Roman monuments delighted tourists (Fig. 11), should not be overlooked, although he was surpassed by the etcher Giovanni Battista *Piranesi (1720–78). Piranesi's prints of ancient Roman ruins are among the most imaginatively stimulating works of the age (Fig. 13). Pompeo Batoni (1708–87) and Anton Raphael Mengs, a Bohemian in Rome, reflected *Winckelmann's ideas about ancient art and began, though humbly, the neoclassic style with simplified compositions and a closer imitation of ancient sculptures.

Spain and Portugal. In 1701 Philip V, grandson of the French Louis XIV, introduced the rule of the Bourbon dynasty into Spain and with it a taste for French art. His second queen was Isabella Farnese, who favored her native Italian art. For these reasons, Spanish artists were out of favor at court and local schools of art diminished. An echo of baroque grandeur was sustained in the early years of the 18th century by Antonio Palomino (1653–1726), who fluently executed huge, complex church murals and ceiling paintings as well as easel pictures. He was noted also as a writer on art and has left invaluable information about the lives of many Spanish painters.

After the accession of Charles III in 1759, the work of Mengs and Tiepolo exercised a powerful influence on Spanish taste. Tiepolo's art was officially overshadowed by the harsh, academic style of Mengs, which especially influenced portrait painting such as that of Francisco Bayeu (1734–95). In the long run, however, Tiepolo's more painterly and luminous style had a greater effect; Bayeu, Goya, and Luis Paret (1746–99), the best painters of the latter half-century, followed it in their figure compositions. Francisco *Goya (1746–1828) is the only native Spanish artist of worldwide fame in this period. His early works are typically rococo, but he retained a pleasing naïveté of vision, which lent originality to every picture he painted. His official portraits of the

Fig. 10. Alessandro Magnasco, "The Baptism of Christ," c. 1740, canvas, 46¼ by 57¾ inches.

Fig. 11. Giovanni Paolo Panini, "The Interior of the Pantheon," c. 1740, canvas, 50½ by 39 inches.

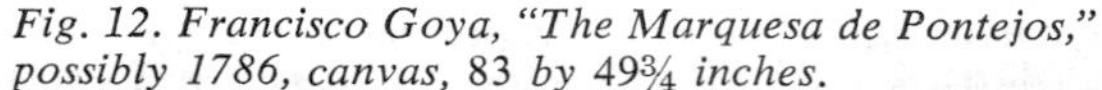

Fig. 12. Francisco Goya, "The Marquesa de Pontejos," possibly 1786, canvas, 83 by 49¾ inches.

MODERN EUROPEAN ART
18TH CENTURY

Fig. 13. Giovanni Battista Piranesi, "The Basilica of Constantine," c. 1774, etching.

court and of Madrid's nobility are redeemed by a painter's joy in the sparkle of fashionable costumes and a surprising penetration into character (Fig. 12). His tapestry cartoons are tellingly simplified into handsome designs, and his genre scenes are admirably direct in conveying an experience of the event. His work done after the turn of the century is marked by introspection, fascination with the weird and supernatural, and psychological penetration.

In sculpture, in areas distant from court influence, Spain offered splendid patronage for the carvers of the remarkable altarpieces that are so prominent in Spanish churches. The most famous example is Narciso Tomé's "Transparente" (1721–32) in the Toledo Cathedral. It is unusual in being behind the altar and lighted theatrically by a window high above the ambulatory. The light falls upon a dazzling array of swirling figures surrounding a central Madonna and Child and interspersed between decorative columns. Multicolored jasper, glass, marble, and bronze are unified by illusionistic perspective, which enhances the size of the work.

In Portugal, liberal artistic patronage was offered by King John V (1706–50), who imported the French rococo style in the paintings of Pierre Antoine Quillard (1701–33). As court painter he was succeeded by Vieira Lusitano (1699–1783), a painter trained in Rome. The Portuguese artist of greatest importance, however, was Domingos António de Sequeira (1768–1837). A near contemporary of Goya, he rivaled that painter in versatility but was more academic. French rococo decoration was extensively imitated also by Portuguese sculptors, especially at Oporto. The great Lisbon earthquake in 1755 necessitated the rebuilding of much of the city and thus hastened the development of the neoclassical style.

Bibliography: G. BAZIN, *Baroque and Rococo,* tr. J. GRIFFIN (New York 1964). A. HAUSER, *The Social History of Art,* tr. S. GODMAN, 4 v. (New York 1958) v.3. S. F. KIMBALL, *The Creation of the Rococo* (Philadelphia 1943). G. KUBLER and M. SORIA, *Art and Architecture in Spain and Portugal and Their American Dominions, 1500–1800* (PelHArt Z17; 1959). N. POWELL, *From Baroque to Rococo* (New York 1959). A. SCHÖNBERGER and H. SOEHNER, *The Rococo Age,* tr. D. WOODWARD (New York 1960). W. SYPHER, *Rococo to Cubism in Art and Literature* (New York 1960). E. WATERHOUSE, *Painting in Britain, 1530 to 1790* (2d ed. PelHArt Z1; 1962). R. WITTKOWER, *Art and Architecture in Italy, 1600–1750* (PelHArt Z16; 1958). **Illustration credits:** Fig. 1, Musée du Louvre, Cliché des Musées Nationaux. Figs. 2, 3, 4, 10 and 11, National Gallery of Art, Washington, D.C., Samuel H. Kress Collection. Figs. 5 and 7, National Gallery of Art, Washington, D.C., Widener Collection. Figs. 6 and 13, National Gallery of Art, Washington, D.C., Rosenwald Collection. Figs. 8 and 12, National Gallery of Art, Washington, D.C., Andrew Mellon Collection. Fig. 9, National Gallery of Art, Washington, D.C., Ferdinand Lammot Belin Fund.

[G. EVANS]

2. NINETEENTH CENTURY

The 19th century had no clear boundaries in the area of the arts. Stylistically, it began with neoclassicism or Romantic classicism, as it is now often called, which seems to have developed gradually in Europe between 1760 and 1780. This was the last style to be manifested in sculpture and architecture as well as painting, which thereafter became the leading art form. Although it had lost its vitality by the middle of the century, neoclassicism remained in the hands of lesser artists the universal idiom of artistic conservatism until 1900 and even later. Romanticism, diametrically opposed to neoclassicism in form, was its exact contemporary and often shared with it the desire to re-create a lost past. Neoclassicism and Romanticism thus ran parallel in the first half of the 19th century, and are in many ways comparable to the styles of *Poussin and *Rubens in the 17th.

By 1850 Romantic sentiment had gradually declined in intensity and painters were turning to a more objective presentation of life about them. Thus, toward the middle of the century the Realists, under the leadership of Courbet, replaced the Romantics as the strongest opponents of the continually weakening neoclassic tradition. France was by now acknowledged as the artistic leader of Europe. In the 1870s a group of Parisian painters known as the Impressionists developed a style of landscape and genre painting of great brilliance; it was actually a late phase of the Realist movement. By 1885, however, this group was clearly beginning to disintegrate.

The collapse of Impressionism was accompanied by a renewed interest in the spiritual and intellectual values that the Realists had ignored. The term Postimpressionism is generally used for a rather heterogeneous group of painters who, between 1885 and 1900, managed to adapt the style of the Impressionists to their own interests. On the one hand, Seurat and Cézanne tried to impose a formal, geometrical order on the Impressionists' intuitive techniques of color and composition. Others, such as Van Gogh, Gauguin, and a host of minor painters throughout Europe, attempted to use Impressionism as the vehicle of an intense personal symbolism.

The basic motive underlying these diverse styles was the desire for an art that would be valid and at the same time capable of reflecting change. Neoclassicism had attempted to adapt the symbols of antiquity to current issues, first the radical political ideals of the French Revolution, later the conservative programs of established institutions. The Romantics had sought to escape to the Middle Ages, to exotic lands, to the landscape surrounding Europe's rapidly growing cities. The Realists, in their attempt to mirror life about them, had often called implicitly or explicitly for social reform. The hedonistic outlook of the Impressionists seemed to reveal the oppressed city-dweller's growing need for relaxation and escape. Finally, many of the Symbolists, for example, Gauguin, sought to fuse orthodox Catholicism with personal forms of mystical experience.

In general, however, it is clear that the 19th century was not a period of great sacred art. Virtually every major artist painted some traditional Catholic pictures, for example, Ingres' "Vow of Louis XIII" (1824; Cathedral, Montauban), Delacroix's "Good Samaritan" (1850; Philadelphia Museum of Art), Manet's "Christ Scourged" (1865; Chicago Art Institute), and Gauguin's so-called "Yellow Christ" (1889; Albright-Knox Art Gallery, Buffalo). Yet these were not always their most typical or most popular paintings. Christian sentiments were more often presented in new and unconventional forms. These may be elaborate and ingenious (Fig. 17) or simple and moving (Fig. 18). With the Symbolists in the 1890s, they were often the personal expression of an individual's unorthodox mystical experience.

Neoclassicism. After 1750 a new interest in the antique, based upon the careful gathering and imaginative reinterpretation of archeological evidence, became evident throughout Europe. The German J. J. *Winckel-

Fig. 14. Jacques Louis David, "The Oath of the Horatii, canvas, 50 by 65 inches, 1785.

Fig. 15. Eugène Delacroix, "Liberty Leading the People," canvas, 102 by 128 inches, 1830.

MODERN EUROPEAN ART 19TH CENTURY

Fig. 16. Gustave Courbet, "The Stonebreakers," canvas, 63 by 102 inches, 1849, destroyed 1945.

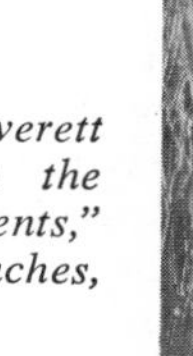

Fig. 17. John Everett Millais, "Christ in the House of His Parents," canvas, 33½ by 54 inches, 1850.

mann, in his *Thoughts on the Imitation of Greek Art Works* (1755), repudiated both Dutch realism and rococo sensuality, maintaining that only an inspired imitation of the antique could lead to truly great art. Accurate drawings of Greek architecture were published, and excavations at Pompeii aroused great interest. This new attitude toward the antique was immediately noticeable in art. Though many features of the neoclassical aesthetic first appeared in the works of the Anglo-American Benjamin West (1738–1820), the major exponent of the style was the Frenchman Jacques Louis *David (1748–1825).

David. David began as a rococo artist. He then spent the years 1780 to 1785 in Rome, in the company of sculptors and avidly studying the antique. These two influences appear in his first major painting, "The Oath of the Horatii" of 1785 (Fig. 14). The subject is from Roman legend, and the theme is the sacrifice of personal interests to political duty. Stylistically, the picture exhibits a concentration of form that satisfied the most rigorous demands of neoclassic theory: the few figures are clearly posed, the unambiguous space is constructed by means of parallel planes arranged one behind another, the use of sensual color is suppressed in favor of sculptural form and hard, sharp outline. David drew heavily upon Poussin and the High Renaissance in his effort to recreate the antique. Nevertheless he fused these sources together well, and skillfully placed form at the service of his narrative. The crucial action is clearly legible, as the three determined sons take their swords from their aged father; the weeping women at the right constitute a decisive contrast. On the eve of the French Revolution, this antique scene was clearly interpreted as a call to arms, which helps explain its enormous popular success. It is both a document of political ideals and a paragon of neoclassical aesthetics —a search for moral and political regeneration in the resurrection of antique forms and ideals.

David was very active in both politics and art education, and his influence in promoting the neoclassicist aesthetic through the French Academy can hardly be exaggerated. His vitality, together with his ability to express ethical and political issues in appropriate forms, was the secret of his greatness, both as an artist and a teacher. Because of its attempt to re-create a lost past, *neoclassicism is now often considered one aspect of the larger Romantic movement; this point of view seems more comprehensive than the previous tendency to regard neoclassicism as the disciplined antithesis of Romantic excess.

Ingres. David's most important pupil, and perhaps the last great academic, was Jean Auguste Dominique *Ingres (1780–1867). His early portraits, such as "Mme. Rivière" of 1806 (Louvre), had a stylized, archaizing flatness derived largely from Greek vase painting and the Quattrocento masters. The refined curvilinear pattern reveals Ingres' supreme ability as a draftsman. In 1806 he went to Italy, where his tendency to favor flatness and decorativeness diminished under the influence of Raphael. There he remained until 1824, when his "Vow of Louis XIII" (Cathedral, Montauban) was immediately recognized as the neoclassic alternative to Delacroix's Romantic "Massacre of Scio" (Louvre) at the Salon of that year. Ingres then returned to France to accept the leadership of the artistic conservatives. His "Apotheosis of Homer" of 1827 is perhaps the best example of his own modification of David's neoclassic style. The composition is more centralized, the forms are crisper and more linear, and the references to the antique are even more obvious: the Greek temple, the winged Victory, the portrait of Homer from a well-known Hellenistic bust. In the foreground can be distinguished portraits of famous Frenchmen such as Poussin, Voltaire, and Louis XIV. The picture is actually a pantheon of academic heroes and an attempt to legitimize neoclassical art by grafting it onto the tradition that Ingres saw extending from ancient Greece through Raphael to his own work. But a certain stiffness has replaced the masculine vitality of David's Roman heroes, and the whole scheme seems rather stilted and contrived.

Ingres, like David, became professor at the École des Beaux-Arts and devoted his best energies to defending his linear style and the cult of Raphael against the growing competition of Delacroix's more painterly manner. Ingres had intellectual limitations, however, and his refusal to compromise with his opponents drove him further into dogmatic conservatism. His attempts to preserve the classic ideal caused it rather to petrify. Ingres' large figure paintings now seem cold and empty; his portraits retain their appeal for the 20th century, however, because of their masterful draftsmanship and their evidence of the artist's penetrating grasp of the intimate personality of the subject.

Romanticism. The Romantic movement was characterized, in general, by a preference for intuition rather than logic and analysis; for the miraculous rather than the rational and predictable; for legend and myth rather than precise historical fact. A dissatisfaction with the present state of things often led Romantic artists to seek escape in the past, in exotic lands and cultures, or simply in nature unspoiled by the presence of man. Its love for the ancient past linked neoclassicism to Romanticism; yet the truly Romantic temperament usually preferred the spiritual fervor of Shakespeare and the Middle Ages to the order of Greek and Roman antiquity, and the color and chiaroscuro of Rubens and Caravaggio to the balanced composition of Poussin and Raphael. Exotic scenes of North Africa and the Near East attracted Delacroix, as well as many other painters of his generation. Moreover, the Romantics' love for unspoiled nature established landscape as a major genre of painting for the remainder of the 19th century.

Romanticism did not encourage collective artistic endeavor; indeed, it was an individualistic mode of creation. The cult of genius and of the hero was an important Romantic theme. The most prominent political figure of the time was Napoleon, and various contemporary artists left diverse images of the French Emperor. Antonio *Canova (1757–1822), the leading neoclassicist sculptor, chose to depict him in the guise of a Roman emperor (1808; Brera, Milan). Ingres showed Napoleon in his study, surrounded by the symbols of political administration (1804; Musée des Beaux-Arts, Liège). These visions of the leader as the abstract personification of the state contrasted sharply with the Romantic conception of Baron Gros (1771–1835) in his "Napoleon Visiting the Plague-Stricken at Jaffa" (1804; Louvre). Gros saw the great leader as a deeply human individual, showing compassion for the plague victims in this exotic setting. Moreover, he employed a traditionally Christian iconographic image, that of Christ and the doubting St. Thomas, for the figure of Napoleon reaching out to touch a sick man's wound.

Goya. The Spaniard Francisco *Goya (1746–1828) defies classification. His earliest works, influenced by *Tiepolo, were tapestry designs for the royal factories. He later became first painter to the Spanish King, though his portraits of the royal family (1800; Prado, Madrid) are seldom flattering. He is perhaps most famous for his etchings: *Los Caprichos* (1796–1803), satirical attacks on contemporary manners and abuses within the Church; and "The Disasters of War" (1810–13), based on the French invasion of Spain in 1808. Like his compatriot Velazquez, he was especially influential on Manet and the Realists of the mid-19th century.

Delacroix. The greatest and perhaps the most typical Romantic painter was Eugène *Delacroix (1798–1863). His journals reveal him to be broadly and deeply learned in literature and music as well as art. His earliest works, e.g., "Dante and Virgil in Hell" (1822; Louvre), show him reviving the painterly and coloristic manner of Rubens, the artist he most admired. His "Massacre of Scio" (1824; Louvre), depicting scenes from the contemporary Greek struggle for independence against the Turks, left no doubt that a powerful style of color and movement had arisen to oppose Ingres' neoclassicism. No subject could have better suited the Romantic temper: passion and exoticism were united with the themes of political freedom and the persecution of Christians by infidels. Delacroix turned to French politics in his "Liberty Leading the People" of 1830 (Fig. 15). Géricault's "Raft of the Medusa" (1819; Louvre) had established the contemporary catastrophe as an acceptable heroic subject. The female figure appearing in the midst of the charging revolutionaries, however, is Delacroix's own original adaptation of a classical draped nude—she represents Marianne, symbol of the French Republic. Strong movement along diagonals, rich application of paint, and the flicker of light and shade recall the 17th-century baroque. The intensity of Delacroix's patriotism obscures the improbability of the scene and sweeps the viewer into the picture as Ingres never could have done. A trip to North Africa from 1830 to 1832 supplied Delacroix with exotic motifs for the rest of his life. His other subjects included scenes from the Old Testament ("The Abduction of Rebecca" 1858; Metropolitan, New York); the New Testament ("The Good Samaritan," 1850; Philadelphia Museum of Art); or history and myth, always Romantic in conception and baroque in style. By the middle of the century he was acknowledged, especially by the younger painters, as equal to, if not greater than, the aging Ingres.

Landscape Painting. Romantic landscape painting flourished in Britain and Germany as well as in France. John Constable (1776–1837) was praised in Paris when his paintings appeared at the Salon of 1824, though his influence on French artists has usually been exaggerated. His "Stoke-by-Nayland" (1836; Art Institute, Chicago) emphasizes the unity of man and Gothic church with the landscape of which they are a part. Joseph M. W. Turner (1775–1851) developed a freedom of brushwork and color that was equaled only much later by the Impressionists. His "Fighting Temeraire" (1838; Tate Gallery, London) shows a wooden man-o'-war being towed away for dismantling by a new steam tug, the symbol of the industrial revolution that many 19th-century artists realized was thoroughly changing the basic organization of society. Caspar David Friedrich (1774–1840) was the greatest German landscape painter. In his pantheistic mountain idyls a lone tree can serve almost as a devotional shrine for the wanderer, demonstrating the Romantics' ability to sense God's presence in nature.

In France a loosely organized group of landscape painters left the city of Paris for the Barbizon forest nearby. Among these was J. B. C. Corot (1796–1875), whose misty forest scenes became extremely popular in the later 19th century and can now be found in virtually every major American museum. Jean-François Millet (1814–75) concentrated on the peasant himself rather than his rural habitat. For Millet the French farmer embodied the virtues of honesty, simplicity, and piety that his urban compatriot lacked. "The Angelus" of 1859 (Fig. 18) represents two field workers in prayer at evening, pausing in their labor as they hear the bells of the church, which is barely visible on the horizon. The enormous popularity of this picture suggests that Millet's nostalgia for the land was and still is shared by millions of people.

Daumier. While most Romantics were expressing dissatisfaction with the present by avoiding it, other artists turned instead to life around them. Honoré *Daumier (1808–75) made his living as a political cartoonist, creating lithographs that now rank as great works of 19th-century Realism. In a painting such as "The Third-Class Carriage" (*c.* 1862; Metropolitan, New York) he employed a style of line and chiaroscuro that was based partly on his lithographic technique and partly on Rembrandt. By showing the boredom and loneliness of a group of passengers in a railway carriage, Daumier evidently expressed a critical attitude toward the machine that accidentally brought them together.

Mid-century Shift of Attitude. By the 1840s a change in painters' attitudes as well as their subject matter was evident in France, now the acknowledged artistic leader of Europe. Typical subjects were no longer the deeds of antique or modern heroes, but rather events of a more popular character. Romantic escape from present reality was yielding to a search for meaningful themes in the daily life of the modern world. The painter's attitude was correspondingly less dramatic, sometimes mildly nostalgic, often overtly critical. The rise of the popular press, the extension of political rights, and the development of new techniques such as lithography contributed greatly to the expansion of the art public and helped spread the belief that art should concern itself with contemporary issues.

Courbet and Realism. These trends ultimately crystallized in the work of Gustave *Courbet (1819–77), whose "Stonebreakers" (Fig. 16) and "Burial at Ornans" (Louvre) caused a sensation at the Salon of 1850. Courbet maintained that painting should consist of a direct, critical observation of contemporary life, with the implied goal of social improvement. Often explicitly socialist ideas were intertwined with Realist art theory, as in the writings of Courbet's close friend Pierre Joseph Proudhon (1809–65). Though the goal of Realism was thus to mirror contemporary society, it is clear that painters like Courbet and Daumier, on a more spiritual level, were also engaged in a search for new and valid symbols. Dissatisfied, as it were, with the images of antique myth and traditional Christian iconography, they sought artistic themes that embodied the spiritual characteristics of their age as directly as traditional subjects

MODERN EUROPEAN ART 19TH CENTURY

Fig. 18. Jean François Millet, "The Angelus," canvas, 22 by 26 inches, 1859.

Fig. 19. Édouard Manet, "Luncheon on the Grass," canvas, 84 by 106 inches, 1863.

Fig. 20. Claude Monet, "The River," canvas, 31⅞ *by* 39½ *inches, 1868.*

Fig. 21. Edgar Degas, "Carriages at the Races," canvas, 14 by 22 inches, 1873.

had expressed the thoughts and feelings that had been a part of previous centuries.

To the Salon of 1844 Courbet had sent a self-portrait entitled "The Man with the Leather Belt" (Louvre), which earned the critics' praise for his obvious adaptation of a 16th-century Venetian prototype. "The Stonebreakers" of 5 years later marked a decisive change in his outlook. The subject itself was not revolutionary, for Romantic landscapists such as Millet had often included peasants in their pictures. Courbet's manner, however, was more precise and objective, and may have owed something to the then recently invented technique of photography. Moreover, his object was to depict not the honest virtues of the peasant, but the "complete expression of misery" that struck him in those two laborers. His "Burial at Ornans" was a poetic panorama of a village funeral, with a precise enumeration of all the persons present. Needless to say, such uncompromising views of contemporary life aroused a good deal of critical controversy, which the artist exploited for the sake of publicity. His many forest landscapes (Metropolitan, New York) and hunting scenes (Museum of Fine Arts, Boston) of the 1860s show Courbet's compositional and technical skill in pictures devoid of social meaning.

Mid-century Controversies. The neoclassicists, now more conservative than ever, still dominated the official academies; by the 1850s they rightly regarded Courbet, rather than Delacroix, as their most powerful opponent. Courbet's intentionally brutal manners and his love of publicity aggravated their opposition. The critics, for their part, tended to associate themselves with the different schools (neoclassicism, Romanticism, Realism) or took various intermediate positions. Vigorous controversies abounded. Twentieth-century criticism, in its eagerness to vindicate modern art, has often tended to see the nineteenth century as a battle of progressives against philistines; this interpretation now seems too extreme. Courbet's ability as a craftsman, for example, was universally acknowledged; it was rather his undignified conceptions that the neoclassicists condemned. Moreover, the Realists and the Impressionists, like all artists, were neither willing nor able to cut themselves off from previous tradition. Just as David and Ingres had relied upon Poussin and Raphael, so too had Delacroix revived the baroque manner of Rubens. Thereafter artists chose instead the Venetians, the Spanish masters, and especially the painters of 17th-century Holland as their models. The Barbizon painters had looked a great deal at Dutch landscape, and the importance of Rembrandt for Millet and Daumier is undeniable. Many of Courbet's pictures show the influence of the Venetians and the Spanish, and his "Burial at Ornans" obviously recalls the 17th-century Dutch tradition of group portraiture. So, too, do Degas's early group portraits ("Bellelli Family," *c.* 1858; Louvre). A close look at Courbet and the Impressionists, therefore, will show that they were not intent upon breaking all links with the past; they were concerned rather with adapting certain European traditions that the classicists had ignored, reviving them to suit the needs of their own time.

The Pre-Raphaelites. A curious group of painters and writers in England, unaffected by events in France, flourished in the 1850s. They called themselves Pre-Raphaelites because they wished to avoid the affected, contrived styles that they associated with Raphael and the academies, and return to a simpler, more natural art (*see* PRE-RAPHAELITISM). The leading painters of the circle were D. G. Rossetti (1828–82), William Holman Hunt (1827–1910), and J. E. Millais (1829–96). Though the aesthetics of the group and of their critical mouthpiece, John *Ruskin (1819–1900), were complex and sometimes confused, these artists are especially interesting because their rejection of the academic tradition was parallel to, though independent of, that of their French contemporaries. They deliberately abandoned the painting of history and myth and sought to transform genre painting into a monumental Christian art. In "Christ in the House of His Parents" of 1850 (Fig. 17) Millais has filled a simple genre scene with the most profound symbolic meaning. The child Jesus has wounded his palm, the Virgin comforts Him, John the Baptist brings water, and the carpenter's tools have been carefully chosen to represent the instruments of the Passion. The artist has presented the traditional Christian symbols in a new and ingenious manner, hoping that they might thus appeal to a generation that preferred genre painting to more monumental art forms.

The Salon of the Rejected: The Impressionists. The French Salon had meanwhile become a hotbed of controversy. The extreme strictness of the official jury in 1863 had led the rejected artists to demand an exhibition of their own, the famous "Salon des Refusés." The most controversial picture at that exhibition was the "Luncheon on the Grass" (Fig. 19) by Édouard *Manet (1832–83). It was clearly a modernization of Giorgione's "Fête Champêtre" (Louvre) of the early 16th century. The picture was viciously attacked on two grounds: not only was the spatial recession incorrectly executed, but the representation of nude and clothed figures together was obviously indecent. As for Manet's space, it seems that the artist, in his concentration upon the picture's two-dimensional design, preferred to tolerate or even encourage an ambiguous third dimension. Whatever Manet's exact intentions, this picture clearly made an issue of the relationship between the flat canvas and the illusory picture space; and this was to become a major concern of the Impressionists.

Monet. Chief among these was Claude Monet (1840–1926), whose landscape "The River" of 1868 (Fig. 20) is a good example of the Impressionist style. The palette is very bright, and colors are applied in large, flat patches. There is consequently little detail and great interest in paint texture. The field of vision seems relatively narrow and the picture space is considerably flatter than that of Barbizon landscape. The artist has conceived of the picture as a flat, shimmering surface of brilliant color. This style was perfected by Monet and his colleagues in the 1870s and proved very influential on French and foreign artists during the succeeding decades.

Renoir, Degas, and Whistler. Another Impressionist was August Renoir (1841–1919), whose "Dance at Bougival" of 1883 (Museum of Fine Arts, Boston) depicted the exuberance of Parisian café life in a technique similar to Monet's. Edgar Degas (1834–1917) concentrated on studies of motion and asymmetrical composition based largely on Japanese prints. In his "Carriage at the Races" of 1873 (Fig. 21) he allows the picture frame to slice off foreground objects in a novel

MODERN
EUROPEAN ART
19TH CENTURY

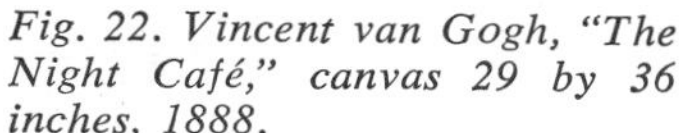

Fig. 22. Vincent van Gogh, "The Night Café," canvas 29 by 36 inches, 1888.

Fig. 23. Paul Cézanne, "Mont Sainte-Victoire Seen from Bibemus Quarry," canvas, 25½ by 32 inches, c. 1898–1900.

Fig. 24. Paul Gauguin, "Where Do We Come From? What Are We? Where Do We Go?" canvas, 67 by 177 inches, 1898.

and exciting way. The effect of this sort of composition on modern painting and, indirectly, on all modern design, can hardly be exaggerated. His many pastels of dancers and bathers reveal Degas's genius at capturing motion in a seemingly unpremeditated format, while his portraits are among the most revealing character studies of the 19th century ("Morbilli Family," *c.* 1865; Museum of Fine Arts, Boston). A landscape style related to Impressionism was developed in England by the American-born James *Whistler (1834–1903). His portrait of his mother of 1871 (Louvre), which he subtitled "Arrangement in Grey and Black," demonstrated his skill at constructing abstract harmonies of form and color.

Although the Impressionists were not consciously concerned with symbolism, their choice of subject (landscape, the horserace, the café) indirectly revealed the city-dweller's flight to places of relaxation and amusement. Moreover, their attempt to represent on canvas their fleeting optical sensations, rather than the external scene before them, deprived painting of all purpose other than formal beauty. Their hedonistic attitude toward art soon proved inadequate.

The Postimpressionists. By 1885 Impressionism was disintegrating, and younger artists began seeking ways of placing its brilliant technical accomplishments at the service of some higher goal. French painting between 1885 and 1900, therefore, is usually called "Postimpressionism" because it followed Impressionism and sought to modify it in various ways. At the risk of oversimplification, two basic attitudes might be distinguished among the various Postimpressionists. On the one hand Seurat and *Cézanne sought to submit Impressionism to formal discipline and thus make of it a more classic, permanent art form. On the other hand Van Gogh and Gauguin used it to express intense spiritual meanings, generally of a very personal sort.

Seurat. Georges Seurat (1859–91) was a child prodigy thoroughly trained at the academies. His first and greatest major composition, "A Sunday Afternoon on the Grande Jatte" (1885; Chicago Art Institute) was a product of long preparation and many preliminary sketches. It represented a typically Impressionist subject, a public park, with a bright Impressionist palette. Seurat, however, refined Monet's patches of color and covered the surface of his canvas with tiny dots, carefully arranged according to scientific principles of color harmony. His figures, constructed with infinite care, seem stiff and wooden compared with those of the Impressionists. In an attempt to bring their technique into agreement with his own tendency toward discipline, Seurat lost much of their brilliance and spontaneity.

Cézanne. Paul Cézanne (1839–1906) left his native Provence to study in Paris, where in the 1870s he acquired the bright palette of the Impressionists but seemed unable to shake off a certain clumsiness of form. By the late 1870s he had returned to the south of France for good, where he devoted himself to painting landscapes, still lifes, and occasional portraits. He sought, as he himself said, "to make of Impressionism something solid and durable, like the art of the museums." His preoccupation was the interaction of the two-dimensional painted surface with the scene it represents, and his goal was to manipulate patches of color so as to create the illusion of solid form. A more specific explanation of his theory is difficult, for his many remarks on art are seldom clear. Nevertheless, his late landscapes such as "Mont Sainte-Victoire Seen from Bibemus Quarry" (Fig. 23) served as a major inspiration for the Cubists, thus indirectly linking Impressionism with the abstract art of the 20th century. Although he was a powerful and turbulent person, Cézanne sought and ultimately attained discipline in his painting.

Van Gogh. Vincent van *Gogh (1853–90) employed art rather as a vehicle for the expression of his intense personal feelings. After exploring various occupations in his youth, he came to Paris from his native Holland in 1886. His palette immediately lightened, and he quickly attained the vigorous, almost primitive style of brilliant color and violent brushwork so typical of his mature work. In 1888 he moved to southern France, where he produced a profusion of landscapes, portraits, and still lifes charged with enormous emotional intensity. In each picture Van Gogh expressed as directly and intuitively as he could the emotional reaction aroused in him by the object represented. His portrait of Mme. Roulin (1889; Museum of Fine Arts, Boston) was intended to evoke the idea of motherhood in the heart of the viewer. In "The Night Café" of 1888 (Fig. 22) he sought by contrasts of color "to express the terrible passions of humanity" as he said in one of his many letters to his brother. Still, Vincent's art was not a sufficient outlet for the passions that raged within him. After some very eccentric behavior and voluntary commitment to psychiatric care, he feared that recurring madness would eventually prevent him from painting. For this reason, at the age of 47, he killed himself.

Gauguin. Perhaps the most complex personality among the Postimpressionists was Paul *Gauguin (1848–1903). Like Van Gogh, he was engaged in a continual search for spiritual experience; yet unlike the Dutchman, his experience took strange and mysterious forms. Finding civilized life too complicated, Gauguin left his wife and children to paint with a group of neoprimitives in Brittany. Here he executed a crucifixion, his so-called "Yellow Christ" (1889; Albright-Knox Art Gallery, Buffalo), in which a traditional Catholic theme is mixed with arbitrary formal devices and a very ambiguous personal mysticism. His departure for Tahiti in 1891 was the last stage of his search for primitive simplicity. His large painting "Where Do We Come From? What Are We? Where Do We Go?" of 1898 (Fig. 24) is a vast panorama involving Christian and primitive religious symbols in an inextricable tangle. Its meaning was unclear even to the painter, who preferred suggestion, rather than description, in his art. Gauguin's Christian symbolism is incomprehensible, and his personal behavior indicates that he was not genuinely devout. Yet his example shows that the most original painting of the 19th century was no longer the usual vehicle of Catholic ideas, and that, in the absence of a viable pictorial tradition, the religious artist was forced to seek his own mode of expression.

Gauguin was a friend of the poet Mallarmé and was associated with a group called the "Synthetists," some of whom can be considered constituents of that universal European phenomenon known as *art nouveau. Thus the expressionist branch of Postimpressionism merged gradually with various other symbolist movements of the *fin-de-siècle*. Odilon *Redon (1840–1916), Émile

*Bernard (1868–1941), and Gustave Moreau (1826–98) were representative of symbolism in painting, each in his own way. In their great diversity, the symbolist artists and writers of the 1890s demonstrated the poverty of materialism and the consequent dissatisfaction of a generation that knew that spiritual values are as essential as formal ones for true art.

See also CHURCH ARCHITECTURE 9; IMPRESSIONISM; NEOCLASSICISM (IN ART).

Bibliography: F. NOWOTNY, *Painting and Sculpture in Europe, 1780–1880* (PelHArt Z20; 1960). W. FRIEDLAENDER, *David to Delacroix,* tr. R. GOLDWATER (Cambridge, Mass. 1952). R. HERBERT, *Barbizon Revisited* (New York 1962). R. IRONSIDE, *Pre-Raphaelite Painters* (New York 1948). J. SLOANE, *French Painting Between the Past and the Present* (Princeton 1951). Rewald HistImpr. Rewald Post-Impr. M. SCHAPIRO, ed., *Cézanne* (New York 1952). **Illustration credits:** Fig. 14, The Toledo Museum of Art, Gift of Edward Drummond Libbey. Figs. 15, 18 and 19, Musée du Louvre. Fig. 16, Bruckmann—Art Reference Bureau. Fig. 17, Reproduced by Courtesy of the Trustees of the Tate Gallery, London. Fig. 20, Courtesy of the Art Institute of Chicago, Potter Palmer Collection. Figs. 21 and 24, Courtesy, Museum of Fine Arts, Boston. Figs. 22, Yale University Art Gallery, Bequest of Stephen Carlton Clark. Fig. 23, The Baltimore Museum of Art, The Cone Collection.

[J. SANDBERG]

3. Twentieth Century

European art of the 20th century is characterized by a succession of avant-garde movements originating in a demand for a total renewal of artistic principles. From a historical point of view, the avant-garde movements from which the art of the 20th century was born began in the 19th century with the realism of Gustave *Courbet (1819–77). The article he published in connection with his exhibition of 1855 can be considered a veritable manifesto against preceding art and in favor of new content and new artistic forms. From that point on, the development of European art was conditioned by a series of movements that affected not only figurative art but also architecture and the applied arts.

Beginnings to World War I. European art of the 20th century began with two avant-garde manifestations, namely Fauvism in France and the expressionism of the Brücke in Germany. These were followed by other movements, all of which had influences on each other; after cubism began, historical sequences are so intermixed that a strict sequence of events is difficult to determine. The various movements presented here often overlap in time.

The Fauves. Fauvism was a product of the temporary union of a group of artists whose ideas sprang from the postimpressionist experiments of the group known as the *Nabis consisting of P. *Bonnard, E. Vuillard, M. *Denis, P. Ranson (1862–1909), F. Vallotton (1865–1925), and especially from the art of P. *Gauguin and V. van *Gogh. The main characteristic of Fauvism is the use of pure colors. The official birth of Fauvism occurred in 1905 when almost all the members of the group exhibited together for the first time in the Salon d'Automne: H. *Matisse, A. Derain (1880–1954), M. de Vlaminck (1876–1958), A. Marquet (1875–1947), H. Manguin (1874–1943), L. Valtat (b. 1869), E. Camoin (b. 1879), and J. Puy (b. 1876). The term Fauves originated during this exhibition, and is attributed to the art critic Louis Vauxcelles who, when entering the room in which the paintings were displayed and seeing the wild explosion of colors in the paintings hanging near a statue of a young boy done in the Florentine style by the sculptor Marquet, is said to have exclaimed, "Donatello parmi les fauves" (Donatello among the wild beasts). The leader of the group was Matisse, around whom a cluster of artists had formed in the years immediately preceding this exhibition; among these were G. *Braque, R. Dufy (1877–1953), O. Friesz (1879–1949), K. van Dongen (b. 1877), and G. *Rouault. They were artists of widely diverse tendencies, but all tended to paint with either violent or warm and sensual colors (*see* FAUVES).

The Brücke. At the same time that the vividly colorful paintings of the Fauves appeared in France, the artistic movement known as the Brücke began in Germany. This was an association of artists founded in Dresden in 1905 by the painters E. L. *Kirchner, Erich Heckel (b. 1883), and Karl Schmidt-Rottluff (b. 1884), with the aim of bringing together (the term Brücke means bridge or something that joins separated points) all the avant-garde tendencies and artists of the period. Although the movement had no precise program, it strove to establish a form of art that would constitute a reevaluation of the creative subjectivity of the artist and an instrument for the expression and liberation of the inner forces of the individual as opposed to the constraints and conventions of society.

"We will use all the colors which, directly or indirectly, express the pure creative impulse," wrote Kirchner in 1913, thus emphasizing the liberating function of color. From this point of view, the German expressionists reveal more than one point of contact with the Fauves, with whom they shared, in addition to the discovery and appreciation of Negro art, a preference for pure and strong color and for a free representation of external reality. The painting of the Fauves was violent in color but clearly showed a striving for formal equilibrium; the works of expressionists allied with the Brücke, like those of E. *Nolde and M. Pechstein (1881–1955), displayed a marked inclination toward a symbolical expression revealing a mysterious relation between the interior life of the artist and nature. The artists also laid great stress on social content, which constituted, even after the group was dissolved, one of the dominant aspects of German expressionism, especially in the first years after World War I.

Cubism. The artistic movement that brought about a radical innovation of artistic expression and opened new avenues to modern art was cubism, which originated in France in the first decade of the 20th century. The term cubism was used for the first time in 1908, when Matisse, looking at Braque's painting "Maisons à l'Estaque," spoke of "little cubes." Matisse's remark was taken up by Vauxcelles, who wrote that the paintings of Braque were "reduced to cubes."

Cubism began between 1905 and 1906, when Pablo Picasso abandoned the painting of strolling actors and acrobats of his "blue" and "pink" periods, which had been characterized by a symbolical use of line and a subtle, refined use of color, and began to show a growing interest in more solid forms and a simplification of natural appearances. This period in Picasso's artistic development was marked by a series of canvases painted in 1906, among which is the famous portrait of the American writer Gertrude Stein. In this painting the sense of monumental composition and the incipient

Fig. 25. Kazimir Malevich, "Scissors Grinder," 1912–13, canvas, 31⅜ by 31⅜ inches.

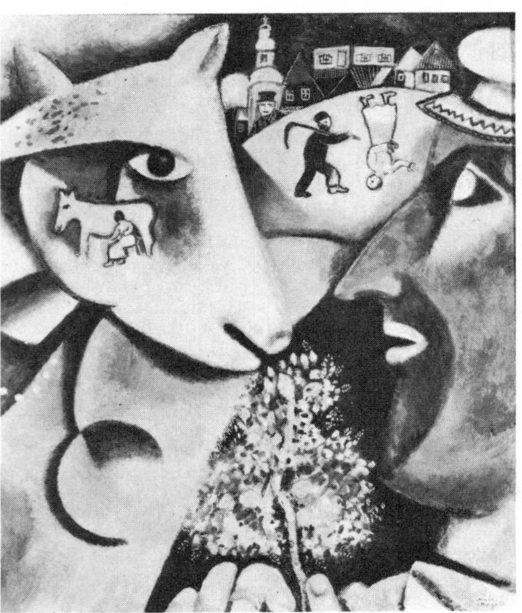

Fig. 26. Marc Chagall, "I and My Village," 1911, canvas, 20 by 18 inches.

Fig. 27. Umberto Boccioni, "States of Mind I: The Farewells," 1911, canvas, 27¾ by 37⅞ inches.

Fig. 28. Franz Marc, "Blue Horses," 1911, canvas, 41¼ by 71½ inches.

MODERN EUROPEAN ART
20TH CENTURY

Fig. 29. Pablo Picasso, "Dancer," 1907, canvas, 59 by 39¼ inches.

Fig. 30. Marcel Duchamp, "Nude Descending a Staircase, No. 2," 1912, canvas, 58 by 35 inches.

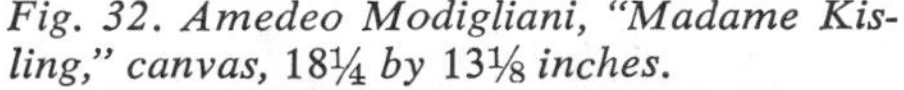

Fig. 32. Amedeo Modigliani, "Madame Kisling," canvas, 18¼ by 13⅛ inches.

Fig. 31. Juan Gris, "Still Life," 1914, collage with charcoal, 28¾ by 36¼ inches.

Fig. 33. Henri Matisse, "Nasturtiums and 'The Dance' II," canvas, 75⅛ by 45⅛ inches.

geometrical treatment of the forms clearly reveal the influence of Paul *Cézanne. In that same year Braque also discovered in the work of Cézanne the inspiration for a more solid type of painting based on a firm geometric structure.

Both Picasso and Braque were deeply interested in the paintings of Cézanne and were trying to apply the lessons of order and expressive clarity that Cézanne had explicitly stated in a letter to his friend Émile Bernard: "Let me repeat what I said to you: to present nature by means of the cylinder, the sphere, the cone." The first phase of cubism, which is generally called "analytical cubism," sprang from the effort of Cézanne to present reality as visually analyzed in terms of geometric structure.

In addition to the influence of Cézanne, that of Negro sculpture and primitive art played important roles in the origin of cubism and particularly in the cubist painting of Picasso. In his search for construction and simplification of forms, Picasso was inspired by the plastic qualities of Negro sculpture, an element that is clearly evident in his "Les Demoiselles d'Avignon" (1906–07). Both Picasso and Braque painted a series of canvases in which the analytical breaking down of the forms was accompanied by an extremely restrained use of color. Another more important aspect of their work, which became even more marked in succeeding phases of cubism, was elimination of tridimensional representation and reduction of the painting elements to the two dimensions of the pictorial surface.

Beginning in 1912, the links with external reality became looser, and the movement turned toward an increasingly abstract pictorial representation. The subject of the painting was no longer analyzed into its structural components but became the occasion employed by the artist to construct an ensemble of signs and colors more and more removed from external reality. This new phase was accompanied by the inclusion in the structure of the painting of objects or fragments of objects. Thus the "synthetic" phase of cubism began, characterized by the tendency to consider the work of art as an organism that obeys aesthetic laws only, with no reference to external reality.

In the meantime, beginning in 1910, a group of artists became actively interested in cubism. Two among them, Juan Gris (1887–1927) and Fernand *Léger, attracted attention through the original quality of their work. Gris, Spanish in origin like Picasso, produced a series of remarkable still life paintings constructed on severely geometric lines and with an ascetic renunciation of the representation of natural appearances. Léger, on the other hand, added to cubist themes motifs taken from modern industrialism and mechanization; the figures in his paintings were transformed into bright colored planes, strongly modeled and resembling human robots.

Along with Gris and Léger, many other artists shared in the cubist movement, with the result that it was divided into diverse tendencies. The most important of these were the "orphic cubism" of Robert Delaunay (1885–1941), the group known as "Section d'Or," and the so-called "group of Puteau" gathered around the prestigious personality of Marcel Duchamp (b. 1887) and including Raymond Duchamp-Villon (1876–1918). When World War I broke out, the leaders of the movement dispersed, but cubism had already taken its place in the history of art. It generated new forces that exercised a determining influence on later movements.

During the years immediately preceding World War I, a community of artists from all parts of the world gathered in Paris. The center of this cosmopolitan, bohemian community was the quarter of Montparnasse. The artists, each very different from the other, all found the artistic culture of the French capitol an ideal terrain for the development of their art. Although they had come from widely varied countries they merged into the so-called "École-de-Paris" or "School of Paris." The painters Marc Chagall (b. 1889) and Chaim Soutine (1894–1943), and the sculptors Alexander Archipenko (b. 1887), Jacques Lipchitz (b. 1891), and Ossip Zadkine (b. 1890) were from eastern Europe. The latter, with the French sculptor Henri Laurens (1885–1954), carried out cubist principles in sculpture. Moise Kisling (1891–1953) and Louis Marcoussis (1883–1941) were from Poland; the sculptor Constantin *Brancusi, from Roumania; Amedeo Modigliani (1884–1920) from Italy; Franz Kupka (1871–1957), from Czechoslovakia; Jules Pascin (1885–1930), from Bulgaria; and the sculptor Julio González, from Spain.

Futurism. In the same period in which the analytical phase of cubism developed, futurism began in Italy. Futurism embodied the typical manner and characteristics of the artistic avant-garde; in direct opposition to tradition, it offered a program for the creation of art that was to be a faithful expression of the modern era, which is characterized by the advent of the machine and of industrial technology. The basic principle of futurism was expressed by the poet F. T. Marinetti in a manifesto published in French in *Figaro* on Feb. 20, 1909, under the title "Foundation and Manifesto of Futurism." The author predicted the destruction of museums, libraries, and academies; he praised, in their place, the beauty of speed and the machine. Among other things, Marinetti said in this manifesto, "A racing car, with its hood adorned with huge tubes like serpents breathing forth flames, a roaring automobile that seems to be running like a machine-gun, is more beautiful than the Victory of Samothrace."

At this time Marinetti met a group of artists, among whom were U. *Boccioni, C. Carrà (b. 1881), and L. Russolo (1885–1917). They signed the "Manifesto of the Futuristic Painters" and later the "Technical Manifesto of Futuristic Painting" to which G. Balla (b. 1871) and G. Severini (b. 1883) also subscribed. Following the principles set forth by Marinetti, the artists took up the problem of dynamism and its application to works of art. They opposed the prevalent acceptance of static cubist painting. Their difficulty was in presenting the interpretation of an image with its environment as well as the simultaneity of plastic states of mind. The futurist artists attempted, by as many different methods as there were artists, to resolve this problem by having recourse to a dynamic analysis of plastic forms.

Boccioni started from previously undeveloped symbolist premises (in his series of the "Addi," for example) and developed a type of vigorous plastic expression reminiscent of the art of Cézanne; he produced important works of sculpture as well. Severini used the color of the French postimpressionists, in particular that of G. Seurat (1859–1891), but added to it the dynamic and whirling rhythms of futurism. Carrà showed a more marked plastic sense and a tendency toward the neutral color of the first stages of cubism. Balla executed a series of studies of movement ending in completely abstract paintings. Russolo, on the other hand, showed an inclination toward symbolism and allusive evocation that can be called presurrealistic.

The interest of the futurists was not confined solely to painting and sculpture; they displayed also a keen interest in architecture, applied arts, theater, cinema, and music. They introduced innovations that would condition rayonism (or lucism) in Russia and vorticism in England.

After the death of Boccioni in 1916, the group lost several of its leaders, such as Carrà and Severini who turned to other types of art. But the movement begun by Boccioni was carried on, especially in the work of Balla, Enrico Prampolini (1896–1956), and Fortunato Depero. These last opposed the movement of cultural restoration that had developed in Italy immediately after World War I and that turned later into a conflict between the classicists and naturalists of the "Novecento" resulting finally in the adoption of the official art of the Fascist regime.

Metaphysical Painting. Metaphysical painting represents, though in original ways and with original results, one of the components of the shift toward classicism that appeared in Italy after the death of Boccioni. Unlike futurism, which accepted modern life and made it the dominant theme of its philosophy, metaphysical painting rejected the present to turn nostalgically to the past, to the classic tradition. Instead of being an artistic movement in the sense that futurism was, metaphysical painting, as exemplified in the work of Giorgio de Chirico (b. 1888), Carrà, and Giorgio Morandi (1890–1964), was an introverted art, founded on the memory of the past, on the symbolical and enigmatic value of images, and on the interpretation of dreams. De Chirico's first metaphysical paintings date from 1910 and 1911, even though the theoretical definition of this type of painting, made with the aid of his brother Alberto Savinio (1891–1952), was issued only in 1919 in an article published by the artist in the magazine *Valori Plastici* under the title "Metaphysical Esthetics."

Blaue Reiter. In the meantime, the artistic movement known as Blaue Reiter (the Blue Rider) began in Germany. It was related to the expressionist movement but had its own individual characteristics. The title of the movement was taken from that of a painting by Wassily *Kandinsky, the most important artist of the group and its leader. Like the Brücke, the Blaue Reiter also started as a movement of the avant-garde. The group's activity began in Moscow in December 1911, with an exhibition of contemporary art organized at the Tannhäuser Gallery by Kandinsky, Alfred Kubin (1877–1959), Franz *Marc, and Gabrielle Münter (b. 1877) and with the publication of an almanac bearing the title *Blaue Reiter* dedicated to the new artistic and musical currents. The artists of the group, which included August Macke (1887–1914) and Paul *Klee, did not proclaim any precise program or demand any definite form of art but appealed, like the expressionists of the Brücke, to the individuality of the artist and to "interior necessity." The artist was to express his own interior spiritual state through purely pictorial means, renouncing the representation of external forms of nature.

With these principles as a base, the Blaue Reiter represents one of the first abstract art movements equipped both with theory and with works that expressed it. The Blaue Reiter did not intend to break all contact with the external world but called upon the interior forces of the artist as a means of finding a way to reach a closer link with nature.

Kandinsky, who in 1910 had painted the first abstract watercolor, wrote, "With the passage of time it will be fully shown that *abstract* art does not exclude a connection with nature, but that instead this connection is greater and more intense than has ever been the case in recent times. Abstract art discards the *skin* of nature, but not its laws. Permit me to use the great word: cosmic laws."

Kandinsky's thought, in which it is not difficult to discern more than one component of a romantic origin, was shared by the other artists of the group and in particular by Klee, for whom art does not reproduce the visible but renders visible that which is invisible. Franz Marc expressed in his work a pantheistic love of nature, which he strove to represent in its essence: "We will no longer paint the woods or a horse as people like to see them or as they appear, but as they really are, as the woods or the horse themselves feel they are, their absolute essence which exists behind the appearances we see."

Rayonism. The influence of futurism was apparent particularly in Russia. There it spread through the direct efforts of Marinetti. In 1913 the painters Michael Larionov (b. 1881) and Natalia Gontcharova (b. 1881) published the manifesto of rayonism, which was defined by its creators as a synthesis of cubism, futurism, or orphism. The rayonist paintings of Larionov and of Gontcharova, produced in 1911 and 1912, represent abstract forms by the intersecting of strips of color.

Suprematism and Constructivism. After an initial Fauve period, Kazimir *Malevich turned toward abstract art. In 1913 he produced the state settings for a production of the futuristic comedy *Victory over the Sun* by Kruchenikh, one of which consisted of a black and white painting. This began his nonfigurative phase, characterized by geometrical forms such as the square, circle, and cross in black on white backgrounds, which he defined as "suprematist." In the *Manifesto of Suprematism* published in 1915 and prepared by Malevich in collaboration with the poet V. Mayakovsky, the artist set forth a theoretical explanation of his first abstract works, affirming the superiority of the artistic sensibility over the external world.

At the same time, the painter Vladimir Tatlin (b. 1875) executed a series of abstract compositions entitled "counter-reliefs." They were constructions that employed real materials (tin, wood, iron, glass, and plaster), arranged in a three dimensional space. Tatlin's "counter-reliefs" started another current in Russian contemporary art. Constructivism developed in the years immediately following the October Revolution, with the work of El Lissitsky (1890–1941), Naum Gabo (Nahum Pevsner, b. 1890), and Anton Pevsner (b. 1886), authors of the manifesto of the "New Realism." Alexander Rodchenko (Rodzenko, b. 1891), in accord

Fig. 34. Kazimir Malevich, "Suprematist Composition: White on White," 1918?, canvas, 31¼ by 31¼ inches.

Fig. 35. Theo van Doesburg, "Interior," 1919, canvas, 26 by 21¾ inches.

MODERN EUROPEAN ART 20TH CENTURY

Fig. 36. Wassily Kandinsky, "Composition VIII," 1923, canvas, 55½ by 79⅛ inches.

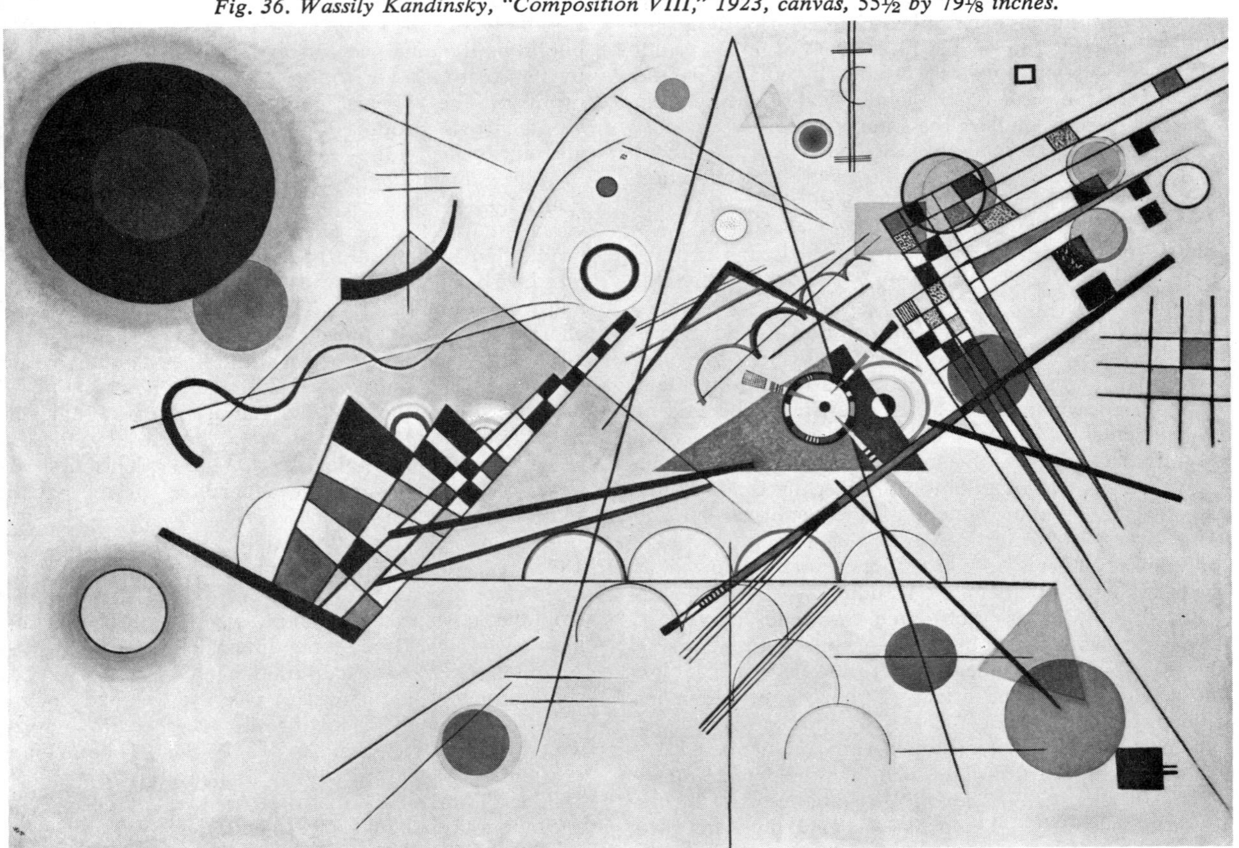

with the philosophy of "productivism," advocated incorporating art into collective life through the processes of industrial technology.

In Russia of the 1920s, an identification of art with the Revolution was effected by avant-garde movements. In fact, the artists looked forward to being fully integrated with the process of social formation, an event no longer to be relegated to the utopia of the future. They hoped to realize the aspiration, typical of all avant-garde artistic movements, of making art and life one and the same experience, in which liberty and imagination would serve not as an escape and a personal contemplation but as the organizer and transforming agent of reality. However, in the following years, the development of Russian art slowed down and then stopped as a result of the bureaucratic liquidation officially ordered by the state.

Reactions during and after World War I. The need for reuniting art and life and for turning artistic work into an instrument for renewing existence was a fundamental demand, above all, of French culture in the second half of the century. This need was expressed by the philosophy of the artistic avant-garde of the first part of the 20th century. But the optimistic positivism and the faith in progress inherited by European culture from the 19th century suffered a shock with the outbreak of World War I, which seemed to prove that the 19th-century myth of the "magnificent destiny and progress" of society was false. From this realization and the consequent necessity of establishing new bases for the relation between the individual and society, art and collective life, two artistic movements sprang up during World War I, Dadaism and de Stijl. These represent opposite poles of the same fundamental effort that had already been made by Rimbaud, to use art as a means to change life (*see* DADA and STIJL, DE).

Dada. Dadaism was an artistic and literary movement of anarchistic revolt and opposition to bourgeois society, which was accused of having unloosed the greatest disaster of history. It is not suprising that the movement originated in a neutral country like Switzerland, in Zurich, which became the gathering point for political refugees, anarchists, and intellectuals of all countries. The first Dadaist group was formed there in the Cabaret Voltaire, in 1916, by the Roumanian poet Tristan Tzara, the German writers Hugo Ball and Richard Huelsenbeck, and the artist Jean Arp (1887–1943). The term Dada was found by chance in the pages of the Larousse dictionary (it is a term taken from baby talk). Dadaism rapidly spread through all of Europe and had repercussions in the U.S. through the exhibitions of the work of Marcel Duchamp and Francis Picabia (1878–1953).

Rather than an artistic movement, Dadaism was primarily a rejection and condemnation of shallow cultural manifestations in bourgeois society. The Dadaists were deliberately blasphemous. The mustache drawn on the "Mona Lisa" and Duchamp's gesture in sending a urinal to a 1917 New York exhibition with the title "Fountain" (and with the signature of a noted dealer in sanitary articles) were both accurate expressions of the anarchistic spirit of Dadaism.

In Germany the movement acquired the more frankly political aspect of revolt against the classes responsible for having led the country into defeat and crisis. In 1917 Huelsenbeck founded the Dadaist group in Berlin, which later included the satirist George *Grosz. This prepared the way for the satire and aggressive realism of the "Neue Sachlichkeit," whose outstanding results were the art of Grosz and of Otto Dix (b. 1891). In Cologne, Dadaism expressed itself in the political activity of Baargeld and the more strictly artistic activity of Max Ernst (b. 1891), while in Hanover it acquired a more formal structure in the collages of Kurt Schwitters (1887–1948).

De Stijl. Almost contemporaneously with Dadaism, de Stijl began in Holland, another country that had remained neutral during the war. The movement sprang up around a review of the same name founded in 1917 by the painter and architect Theo van Doesburg (C. E. M. Küpper, 1883–1931) in collaboration with the painters Piet *Mondrian, Bart van der Leck (b. 1876), and Vilmos Huszar; the sculptor Georges Vantongerloo (b. 1886); and the architects Pieter Oud (b. 1890), Robert van't Hoff, and Jan Wils. Other artists who joined the group were the architects Gerrit Rietveld and Van Eesteren and the poet Antony Kok. Their aim was to heal the rupture between art and technology and art and society created by the rise of industrialism. They paid particular attention to architecture, which could combine beauty and general usefulness. Because architecture is essentially a social collective art, it seemed to them the most effective artistic tool for rebuilding life on a rational basis. The members of de Stijl proclaimed that art offered the remedy for the inconsistencies and contradictions of the age in which they were working, namely, that of World War I. They vigorously rejected all interpretations of art that would perpetuate the disagreement between the rights of the individual and those of society. Thus they were the immediate precursors of the ideological position of Walter Gropius (b. 1883) and the program of the *Bauhaus.

The Dutch group proposed to act on two fronts: to create, on the one hand, a new kind of art; and on the other hand to instill in the public a new aesthetic sense. The preface of the first manifesto of the group stated, "The truly modern artist has a double mission: first, he must create purely plastic works of art; second, he must help the public acquire an understanding of an esthetic of pure plastic art." This "pure plastic art," which the members of de Stijl termed neoplasticism, was based on simple and clear expression, capable of assimilating the exactitude of industrial technology. It aimed at setting up a dialogue with the public that would be as clear and elementary as possible. However, the artists of de Stijl gradually abandoned the representation of natural appearances in favor of an abstract geometrical style based on straight lines and primary colors—yellow, red, and blue—placed on neutral backgrounds of white or gray. The simplicity and rationality of neoplasticism influenced contemporary arts of painting, sculpture, architecture, industrial design, typography, and advertising.

De Stijl and Dadaism therefore shared in common the desire to establish a basis for the relations between the individual and society. As Van Doesburg observed they sought the same end though with different means.

Surrealism. Van Doesburg saw a generic relation between Dadaism and surrealism. Actually, surrealism grew out of the Parisian Dadaist movement when the

Fig. 37. Joan Miro, "Dog Barking at the Moon," 1926, canvas, 28¾ by 36¼ inches.

MODERN EUROPEAN ART 20TH CENTURY

Fig. 38. Max Beckmann, "Departure," 1932–35, canvas, triptych, 84¾ by 124⅛ inches overall.

Fig. 39. Paul Klee, "Traveling Circus," 1937, canvas, 15½ by 19¾ inches.

Fig. 40. Fernand Léger, "Divers on a Yellow Background," 1941, canvas, 75¾ by 87½ inches.

Fig. 41. Ben Nicholson, "St. Ives, Version 2," 1940, oil and pencil on masonite, 9¾ by 12¾ inches.

Fig. 42. Pierre Soulages, "10 Juillet 1950," canvas, 51¼ by 63¾ inches.

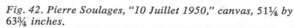

Fig. 43. Francis Bacon, "Cardinal No. 5," 1953, canvas, 60 by 66 inches.

Fig. 44. Morandi, "Still Life," 1953, canvas, 8 by 15⅝ inches.

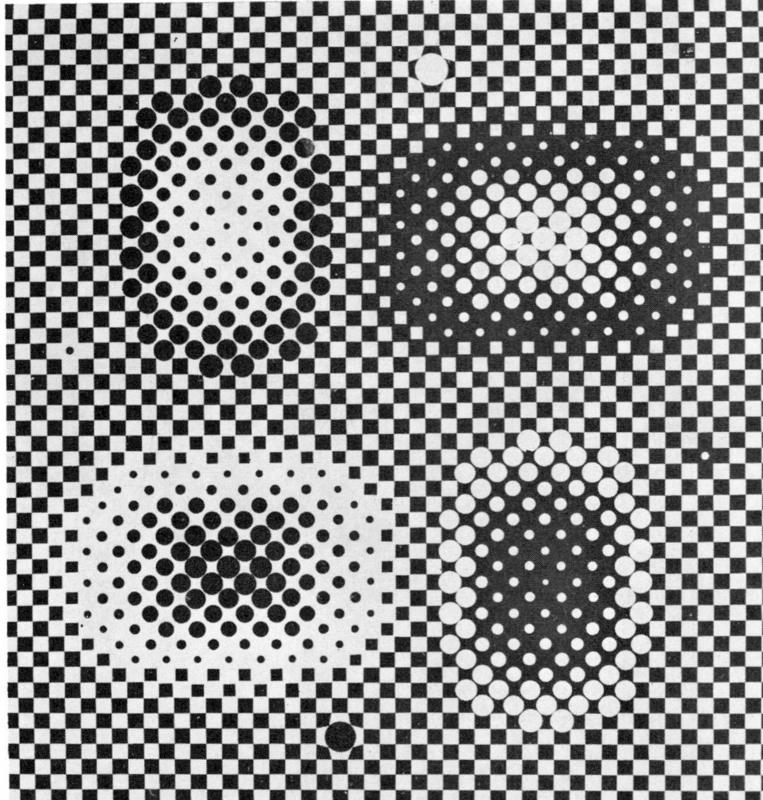

Fig. 45. Victor Vasarely, "Metagalaxie," 1959, canvas, 31¾ by 29½ inches.

MODERN
EUROPEAN ART
20TH CENTURY

Fig. 46. Alfred Manessier, "Du Fond des Ténèbres," 1963, canvas, 29 by 36 inches.

artists began to realize the necessity of substituting for the destructive and anarchistic spirit of Dadaism a methodical and positive exploration of the unconscious and the irrational. They aimed to found a new art and a new society on these two elements, both of which would be free of the rule of conventional rationality that prevented them from producing any real sense of existence. André Breton, Louis Aragon (b. 1897), Paul Eluard (1895–1952), Philippe Soupault (b. 1897), and Max Ernst are the most significant as the artists who prepared the way for the birth of surrealism. The first official act of the surrealist movement dates from 1924, when Breton published his *First Manifesto of Surrealism;* it was followed the next year by the first surrealist exhibition in the Galerie Pierre in Paris.

Like Dadaism, the surrealist movement embraced all fields of artistic activity, from literature to the theater and the figurative arts. Surrealist painters such as Max Ernst, Salvator Dalí (b. 1904), Yves Tanguy (1900–55), Joan Miro (b. 1893), André Masson (b. 1896), Man Ray (b. 1890), René Magritte (b. 1898), Jean Arp, Victor Brauner (b. 1903), and Alberto Giacometti (b. 1901) all rejected traditional plastic means. Their use of the unconscious and the unforeseen led to an art in which the images are lifted out of their habitual context to such a point that the ensemble has a new and startling effect. Breton had written that the best surrealist paintings were those that had the greatest degree of arbitrariness; a logical consequence of that statement is the frequent combination of heterogeneous images used by these artists for the purpose of creating an astounding and magical atmosphere.

The creative process as formerly understood was repudiated, and the work of the surrealists was founded on automatic processes of execution freed, as far as possible, from the control of reason. The results were widely diverse. Rather frequently they produced art that was substantially illustrative, in which rational control was only apparently avoided, and in reality the work was executed with conscious technique. This limitation is especially evident in the work of Dalí, of Paul Delvaux (b. 1897), and Magritte. It was overcome by artists like Arp, Miro, and Masson, who employed spontaneous automatism, a creative factor later found in *abstract expressionism and in informal art (*l'art informal*).

But surrealism was not confined to the field of figurative arts and literature. It touched not only aesthetics but political problems and the relations of the artist with the revolutionary movements for which it had always demonstrated its sympathy.

The relationship between art and revolution from the viewpoint of the surrealist movement gave rise to disputes and strong differences of opinion, especially between Breton and Pierre Naville. Breton claimed that revolution should be carried on not only in practical action but in the techniques of art. According to Breton, an artist of the left should "justify his *advanced* technique by the very fact that he is at the service of the mentality of the left"; the autonomy of the artist's character should be expressed through revolutionary behavior. For Naville, it was chiefly a matter of abolishing bourgeois materialism; he attached somewhat less importance to the problem of the total liberation of the spirit.

From 1930 to World War II. The ascendancy of surrealism resulted, especially in France, in a momentary eclipse of abstract art, which had begun between 1910 and 1920, and it was only around 1930 that there was any considerable resumption of work and of exhibitions in the field of nonfigurative art. The first sign of its reappearance was the exhibition "Cercle et Carré" presented in Paris in 1930, showing the works of Mondrian, Kandinsky, Vantongerloo, Sophie Taeuber, Arp, Vordemberge-Gildewart (b. 1899), A. Pevsner, E. Prampolini, and others. Van Doesburg did not share in this exhibition. He established a separate group that published one number of a review entitled *Art Concret* and thus launched a new denomination for nonfigurative art in place of the term abstract. This new title of "concrete art" was preferred also by other artists, such as Kandinsky, Arp, and later on, Max Bill (b. 1908).

The artistic nonfigurative tendencies gathered in 1931 in a movement directed by Vantongerloo and Auguste Herbin (b. 1882) called *Abstraction-Création;* its members published a review bearing the same name, of which the first number appeared in 1932.

Between 1930 and the beginning of World War II, abstract geometric art spread throughout Europe and America, where its original vigor was reproduced.

Italy. In Italy from 1930 to 1940 there was a resumption of avant-garde artistic activity. The second generation of futurists was represented by Prampolini, Depero, Giulio Evola, Gerardo Dottori, Mino Rosso, Pippo Oriani, Fillia, Nicola Diulgheroff, and Ivo Pannaggi; activity went on in Turin, Milan, and Rome. Opposition to a return to the classicism and naturalism of the "Novecento" was furnished also by the abstractionists united in Milan around the Milione Gallery and those who formed the group of Como. Atanasio Soldati (1896–1953), Mauro Reggiani (b. 1897), Mario Radice (b. 1900), Manli Rho (v. 1901), Luigi Veronesi (b. 1908), Lucio Fontana (b. 1899), and Bruno Munari (b. 1907) were the most significant artists of the movement. To these must be added Alberto Magnelli (b. 1888), who worked mainly in Paris, and Osvaldo Licini (1894–1958), who had withdrawn to the provinces.

The reaction against the official culture of the Fascist regime was carried on during the same period by other groups such as the "Six of Turin," consisting of Levi, F. Menzio (b. 1899), Paulucci, Chessa, Galante, and Boswell; the "Roman School" of Scipione (Gino Bonichi, 1904–33) and M. Mafai (b. 1902); and, later on (*c.* 1940), by the group of "Corrente," whose art took on a clearer, political anti-Fascist aspect: R. Birolli (1906–59), B. Cassinari (b. 1912), R. Guttuso (b. 1912), E. Morlotti (b. 1910), and E. Vedova (b. 1919).

During the same period, outside of these groups and currents, the artists of the preceding generation continued to work: Carrà, G. Morandi, M. Sironi (b. 1885), O. Rosai (1895–1957), F. de Pisis (1896–1956), M. Campigli (b. 1895), and F. Casorati (b. 1886), and the sculptors Arturo Martini (1889–1947), Marino Marini (b. 1901), and Giacomo Manzù (b. 1908).

Germany. In Germany between 1930 and 1940 the Nazi regime sought to eradicate avant-garde art, which was categorized as "degenerate." Artists emigrated or worked in absolute secrecy. In 1928 Walter Gropius left the Bauhaus, which in 1932 was transferred to

Berlin and the following year suppressed by the Nazis as a "den of Bolshevist culture." Gropius, Mies van der Rohe (b. 1886), Laszló Moholy-Nagy (1895–1946), Herbert Bayer (b. 1900), and Marcel Breuer (b. 1902) left for the U.S.; Kandinsky went to Paris, and Klee returned to Berne; Oskar Schlemmer (1888–1943) and Willi Baumeister (1889–1955) continued to work in Germany in almost total clandestineness; Otto Freundlich (1878–1943) was deported in 1943 to a concentration camp; Vordemberge-Gildewart left the country a little before war broke out and established himself in Holland.

Russia. In Russia the destruction of the avant-garde was carried out by Stalinist officialdom; the only artists given sanction were those who worked in the jejune manner of socialist realism.

France, Belgium, Holland. In France and in Belgium the most important accomplishments were realized in the ambience of the two dominant currents of surrealism and geometric abstraction, while in Holland the abstract influence of de Stijl predominated.

England. In Great Britain the period from 1930 to 1940 was marked by a radical break with tradition. In 1930, a group of artists, among whom were Henry Moore (b. 1898), Ben Nicholson (b. 1894), and Barbara Hepworth (b. 1903), began to live and work together in Hampstead as an integrated community. In 1934 the critic Herbert Read, who had been a member of the group, published a volume entitled *Unit One* in which he discussed the most significant artists working in Great Britain at that time. Along with Moore, Nicholson, Hepworth, and Paul Nash (1889–1946), the names of John Armstrong (b. 1893), John Bigge, Edward Burra (b. 1905), Tristram Hillier, and Edward Wadsworth (1889–1949) and of the architects Wells Coates and Colin Lucas appeared. In the meantime, several Continental artists arrived in England: Gropius in 1934, Moholy-Nagy and Naum Gabo in 1935, and Mondrian in 1938. Moholy-Nagy and Gabo diffused the philosophy of the art of constructivism in Great Britain and in 1937 published the volume *Circle,* which constituted a manifesto. The influence of constructivism was accompanied during these years by the spread of surrealism, which also exercised a significant influence on Moore, Nash, Bigge, Burra, S. W. Hayter (b. 1901), and Victor Pasmore (b. 1908).

World War II to the Present. The period of World War II and the enormous human and material ruin resulting from the conflict had a decisive effect on the art of the 20th century, both in Europe and in America. From 1945 on, artists rejected not only traditional figuration but also the rigorous structures of geometric abstraction and the ideology of constructivism, which had believed it possible to entrust the renewal of society to art, whether pure or combined with technology.

Abstract Expressionism. Recent art movements have continued the protest against rationalist optimism, retaining from surrealism a reliance on the unconscious and on chance. Artists employed methods based on automatism, on violent action, and on signs understood as an immediate and unreflecting transcription of the existentialist situation of the artist. "Generalized automatism, spasms of sign or of style," wrote Jaroslav Serpan, "were so many returns to the profound sources of the psyche. Never had a more radical effort been furnished by the painter to transcribe on canvas the primordial sincerity of the living being." But the pure expression of interior life pursued by the adherents of abstract expressionism, or informal art, is understood as the means by which the individual can reach a more profound and authentic unity with the external world. Nature and the unconscious, for the abstract expressionist, are two aspects of one reality. (*See* ABSTRACT EXPRESSIONISM).

In informal works, the pictorial material and with it the fragments of reality, along with the gesture and sign, assumed a role of prime importance; the artist, to the degree in which he sought a rapport with the external world, gave primacy to the materials in the making of a work. According to Jean Dubuffet (b. 1901), one of the major informal artists, "Art should be born from the material and from the tool and should preserve the mark of the tool and of the struggle with the material. Man should speak, but the material and the tool should speak also."

In the years immediately following World War II, the first informal exhibitions appeared almost simultaneously in the U.S. and in Europe: in America (*see* AMERICAN ART) with the work of Hans Hofmann (d. 1966), Arshile Gorky (1905–48), Willem de Kooning (b. 1904), Jackson *Pollock, Mark Tobey (b. 1890), Franz Kline (1910–59), Sam Francis (b. 1923), Philip Guston (b. 1912), and the Canadian Jean Paul Riopelle (b. 1924); in Europe with the French artists Alfred Manessier (b. 1911), Jean Dubuffet, Jean Fautrier (b. 1898), Camille Byren, Pierre Soulages (b. 1919), César (C. Baldacinni, b. 1921), Étienne Martin, Georges Mathieu (b. 1921), and Hans Hartung (b. 1904); the English artists Francis Bacon (b. 1909), Graham Sutherland (b. 1903), Kenneth Armitage (b. 1916), Reg Butter (b. 1913), and Lynn Chadwick (b. 1914); the Italian artists Alberto Burri (b. 1915), Lucio Fontana (b. 1899), Giuseppe Capogrossi (b. 1900), Emilio Vedova (b. 1919), Mattia Moreni (b. 1920) Edgardo Mannucci, Leoncillo Leonardi, Ennio Morlotti (b. 1910), Antonio Corpora (b. 1909), and Afro (Basaldella, b. 1912); the Spanish artists Antonio Tapiès (b. 1923), Antonio Saura (b. 1930), Rafael Canogar, and Luis Feito (b. 1929); the Jugoslav Edo Murtic; the Germans E. W. Nay (b. 1902) and Wols (Wolfgang Schulze, 1913–51), K. R. H. Sonderborg (b. 1923), Winfred Gaul (b. 1928), Gerard Hoehme, Emil Schumacher, Bernard Schultze (b. 1915) and K. O. Götz (b. 1914).

European art of the decade 1955–1965 can be schematically divided into three large currents: the so-called new figuration, *art de reportage* (neo-Dada and pop art), and programmed art or visual and optical art.

The New Figuration. To the informal style the new figuration adds themes and modes derived from expressionism. It originated with a group of artists of Copenhagen, Brussels, and Amsterdam, called the "Cobra" group from the initials of the cities: Asger Jorn (b. 1914), Karel Appel (b. 1921), Guillaume Corneille (b. 1922), C. H. Pedersen, and Pierre Alechinsky (b. 1927). Starting in 1950, the Milanese artists Enrico Baj (b. 1924), Sergio D'Angelo, Gianni Dova (b. 1925), and Cesare Peverelli, were in contact with the "Cobra" group. The so-called West Coast School in the U.S. represented a strong American current of the new figuration.

Neo-Dada and Programmed Art. In 1965 the tendencies of art were toward neo-Dada or pop art, and programmed or optical art. These two artistic currents are based on a concept of the human condition as one increasingly determined by technological development in its fundamental manifestations as industrial production and mass consumption. Faced with the character of urban life today with its accent on industry and advertising, the artists of these groups provided two lines of artistic response. The neo-Dadaist or pop artist accepted the challenge of his environment and sought to demystify the products of consumption and the media of mass communication (advertising, television, newspapers, etc.) He used the products of industrialized society as elements in works of art. In the mid-1960s the American neo-Dadaists were R. Rauschenberg (b. 1925) and J. Johns (b. 1930); pop art was associated with C. Oldenburg (b. 1929), J. Dine (b. 1935), R. Lichtenstein, A. Warhol, T. Wesselmann, and J. Rosenquist. In Europe a similar direction was assumed by artists like David Hockney (b. 1937), R. B. Kitaj, Mimmo Rotella, and Martial Raysse (*see* POP ART).

The artists working along the lines of programmed art and optical art (called "op" in the U.S.) did not attempt to demystify mass-consumption products by grotesque amplification or ironical emphasis. They sought rather to restore clarity and vigor to the physical structure of the image by establishing a new rapport between the individual and his environment on purely optical-psychological bases. Hence the importance these artists attributed to optical perception and rational programming. Often on the basis of group work, they studied and attempted to program objects and structures capable of arousing in the spectator an aesthetically satisfying vision. Programmed art tended to exceed the domain of figurative art and to shift to architectural and urban design as well as to new instruments of visual communication. The artists included Victor Vasarely (b. 1908), Nicolas Schoffer, and the Parisian group of "Visual Research"; the "Group 57" in Spain; the Jugoslavs Voijn Bakic, Vjenceslav Richter, and Aleksandr Srnec; the Italians Bruno Munari, Enzo Mari (b. 1932), Getulio Alviani (b. 1939), the "Group T" of Milan, and the "Group N" of Padua; and the Germans of the "Group O" of Düsseldorf. Joseph Albers (b. 1888) is considered the father of op in the U.S. An exhibition, "The Responsive Eye," representing programmed work in more than 15 countries, was presented at the Museum of Modern Art, New York City, early in 1965. This show revealed important and varied activity in programmed art.

Bibliography: Dictionaries. Vollmer AllgLex. C. LAKE and R. MAILLARD, eds., *Dictionary of Modern Painting,* tr. A. BIRD (New York 1955). Seuphor DictAbstPaint. *Encyclopédie de l'art international contemporain,* ed. W. GEORGE et al. (Paris 1958). *Dictionnaire de la sculpture moderne* (Paris 1960).

General. EncWA 5:251–254. H. FOCILLON, *La Peinture aux XIXe et XXe siècles du réalisme à nos jours* (Paris 1928). R. HUYGHE, ed., *Histoire de l'art contemporain: La peinture* (Paris 1935), bibliog. Barr Cubism. Venturi ModPaint. M. RAYNAL, *History of Modern Painting,* tr. S. GILBERT and D. COOPER, 3 v. (Geneva 1949–50). B. S. MYERS, *Modern Art in the Making* (New York 1950). A. C. RITCHIE, *Sculpture of the Twentieth Century* (New York 1952), bibliog. A. H. BARR, ed., *Masters of Modern Art* (New York 1954). C. GIEDION-WELCKER, *Contemporary Sculpture: An Evolution in Volume and Space* (3d ed. New York 1961). C. HEISE, ed., *Die Kunst des 20. Jahrhunderts,* 3 v. (Munich 1957). C. MCCURDY, ed., *Modern Art: A Pictorial Anthology* (New York 1958). J. E. CANADAY, *Mainstreams of Modern Art* (New York 1959). E. LANGUI, ed., *Fifty Years of Modern Art,* tr. G. SAINTSBURY (New York 1959). H. E. READ, *A Concise History of Modern Painting* (New York 1959; repr. pa. 1962); *A Concise History of Modern Sculpture* (New York 1964). W. HAFTMAN, *Painting in the Twentieth Century,* tr. R. MANHEIM, 2 v. (New York 1960). N. PONENTE, *Modern Painting: Contemporary Trends,* tr. J. EMMONS (New York 1960), bibliog. M. SEUPHOR, *The Sculpture of This Century,* tr. H. CHEVALIER (New York 1960). E. TRIER, *Figur und Raum: Die Skulptur des 20. Jahrhunderts* (Berlin 1960). W. SANDBERG and H. L. C. JAFFÉ, eds., *Pioneers of Modern Art,* tr. I. F. FINLAY (New York 1961).

Interpretation and Theory. R. J. GOLDWATER, *Primitivism in Modern Painting* (New York 1938). P. MONDRIAN, *Plastic Art and Pure Plastic Art* (DocModArt 2; 1945). W. KANDINSKY, *Concerning the Spiritual in Art* (DocModArt 5; 1963). S. GIEDION, *Space, Time and Architecture* (3d ed. Cambridge, Mass. 1954). *Three Lectures on Modern Art* by J. J. SWEENEY et al. (New York 1949). J. CASSOU, *Situation de l'art moderne* (Paris 1950). B. CHAMPIGNEULLE, *L'Inquiétude dans l'art d'aujourd'hui* (Paris 1952), introd. R. HUYGHE. S. K. LANGER, *Feeling and Form* (New York 1953). M. BRION, *Art abstrait* (Paris 1956). G. KEPES, *The New Landscape in Art and Science* (Chicago 1956). L. MOHOLY-NAGY, *Vision in Motion* (Chicago 1956). E. H. GOMBRICH, *Art and Illusion* (New York 1960). Cassou Gateway.

Movements. G. DUTHUIT, *The Fauvist Painters,* tr. R. MANHEIM (DocModArt 11; 1950), bibliog. by B. KARPEL. J. LEYMARIE, *Fauvism: Biographical and Critical Study,* tr. J. EMMONS (New York 1959), bibliog. J. P. CRESPELLE, *The Fauves,* tr. A. BROOKNER (New York 1962). B. S. MYERS, *The German Expressionists: A Generation in Revolt* (New York 1957), bibliog. P. SELZ, *German Expressionist Painting* (Berkeley 1957), bibliog. *The Blue Rider Group* introd. H. K. RÖTHEL (London 1960). J. GOLDING, *Cubism: A History and Analysis* (New York 1959), bibliog. Rosenblum Cubism, bibliog. R. T. CLOUGH, *Looking Back at Futurism* (New York 1942), bibliog. J. C. TAYLOR, *Futurism* (New York 1961). L. LOZOWICK, *Modern Russian Art* (New York 1925). K. S. MALEVICH, *The Non-objective World,* tr. H. DEARSTYNE (Chicago 1959). N. GABO, *Constructions, Sculpture, Paintings, Drawings, Engravings* (London 1957). A. OZENFANT, *Foundations of Modern Art,* tr. J. RODKER (New York 1952). A. H. BARR, ed., *Fantastic Art, Dada and Surrealism* (3d ed. New York 1947), bibliog. R. MOTHERWELL, *The Dada Painters and Poets: An Anthology* (New York 1951), bibliog. M. JEAN, *History of Surrealist Painting,* tr. S. W. TAYLOR (New York 1960). W. C. SEITZ, *The Responsive Eye* (New York 1965).

Illustration credits: Fig. 29, From the Collection of Walter P. Chrysler, Jr. Fig. 28, Collection Walker Art Center, Minneapolis. Fig. 27, Nelson A. Rockefeller Collection, New York City. Fig. 26, Philadelphia Museum of Art. Fig. 25, Yale University Art Gallery, Collection of Société Anonyme. Fig. 30, Philadelphia Museum of Art, the Louise and Walter Arensburg Collection. Figs. 31 and 37, Philadelphia Museum of Art, A. E. Gallatin Collection. Fig. 32, National Gallery of Art, Washington, D.C., Chester Dale Collection, 1962. Fig. 33, The Dial Collection, Worcester Art Museum, Worcester, Mass. Figs. 34 and 38, Collection, The Museum of Modern Art, New York City. Figs. 35 and 39, The Baltimore Museum of Art, Saidie A. May Collection. Fig. 36, The Solomon R. Guggenheim Museum Collection. Fig. 40, Courtesy of the Art Institute of Chicago, gift of Mr. and Mrs. Maurice E. Culberg. Figs. 41, 42, 44, and 46, The Phillips Collection, Washington, D.C. Fig. 43, The Joseph H. Hirshhorn Foundation, Inc. Fig. 45, Courtesy of Pace Gallery, New York City, collection of Mr. Richard Zeisler.

[F. MENNA]

ART, PREHISTORIC

This article surveys Paleolithic art discovered in various world regions and outlines the development of Neolithic and protohistoric art.

Franco-Cantabrian Art. The art of the Upper Paleolithic caves of France and of the Cantabrian Mountains of Spain evolved during the 30,000 to 40,000 years preceding 8,000 B.C., between the Aurignacian-Perigordian and the Solutrean-Magdalenian culture periods (*see* ARCHEOLOGY, I). It represents, by engravings or paintings in naturalistic style, the fauna of the glacial period of southwestern Europe (mammoth, wooly

(c)

Prehistoric art: (a) Ivory "Venus," figure found at Lespugue, Haute-Garonne, France, Aurignacian-Perigordian sculpture, upper Paleolithic period. (b) Elk, with indications of internal details, rock engraving at Askollen, Drammen, Vestfold, Norway. (c) Deer, paintings in the cave at Lascaux, France, c. 15,000 to 10,000 B.C.

rhinoceros, bison, reindeer, bear, horse). Its original purpose was presumably to exercise magical influence over game animals. There are also imprints of hands. This art covers the walls of caves, sometimes in almost inaccessible chambers used for ceremonial purposes. It exemplifies the first climax of human artistic development.

The evolution is from simple silhouettes in one color or traced by the human hand to polychrome paintings or finely engraved figures (Magdalenian). There are also carved rock sculptures (the horses of Cap Blanc or the nude women of Laussel, probably related to fertility rituals) and clay sculptures (the bison of Tuc d'Audoubert). In Les Trois Frères a painted "sorcerer" is disguised with animal hide and horned mask; in Lascaux (final Perigordian) a painted bison is shown threatening a man. Henri *Breuil considered as the "six giants" the caves of Altamira (with its polychrome ceiling of bison), Font-de-Gaume, Les Combarelles (with its elephant frieze), Lascaux, Les Trois Frères, and Niaux. In Spain this art infiltrates to the extreme south (La Pileta). In Italy it reaches the south (Romanelli) and Sicily (the engravings of Levanzo and Addaura). It exists also in central Europe and in the southern Urals (Cave Kapova) and the Lake Baikal region in Siberia.

Decorated movable objects include pebbles or stone plates with engraved animals and horn or bone with reliefs or engravings. Especially remarkable are the Aurignacian "Venus" statuettes, such as those of Brassempouy, Savignano, Vistonice, Willendorf, Kostienki, and M'alta in Siberia.

Franco-Cantabrian art did not continue beyond Paleolithic times because the glacial fauna became extinct or retired to the extreme north as a result of climatic change. There are, however, engravings on bone of the Maglemosian Mesolithic culture of Denmark, and there are paintings and engravings on the rocks of the Norwegian fjords and even in Carelia and West Siberia, continuing into the Neolithic period.

Levant Art in Spain. In eastern Spain the paintings are not in caves but in rock shelters in the open air. The oldest are linked with the Franco-Cantabrian animal representations (Minateda), but later paintings show the evolution of a different style, called "expressionistic"; if the animals are still naturalistic, the movement and attitudes of the human figures are stressed and even exaggerated. In contrast to the Franco-Cantabrian art, in which there are generally no scenes, in Levant scenes are the rule, as in the hunting parties at Val del Charco del Agua Amarga, Valltorta, Tormón, Alpera, Minateda; battles at Morella and Valltorta; the collection of honey at Araña, and a fecundity dance of women around an ithyphallic personage at Cogul.

Some scholars date Levant art in the Mesolithic period, because there is no association with archeological layers and because its fauna is not specifically Pleistocene. Others hold to the Paleolithic date since there are horses identified with species of Franco-Cantabrian art. Also, resemblances with the engraved or painted Aurignacian and Solutrean plaquettes of the Parpalló cave are evident, and some frustrated attempts at polychromy in Cogul and Minateda—pointing to a Magdalenian influence—seem to be arguments for a Paleolithic date.

In the Mesolithic and Neolithic periods, Levant art was diffused to central and south Spain, which show a seminaturalistic phase, with hunting and domestication scenes, followed by another schematic phase, using mostly human figures only. The sequence is evident in the Laguna de la Janda rocks. This art is associated with *ancestor worship and appears on the slabs of megalithic tombs. In the Bronze Age it follows a phase with concentric circles, labyrinths, and other geometric signs (Portugal, Galicia, and the megalithic graves of Brittany and Ireland).

Africa. The Spanish Levant art has parallels in Africa to the extreme south. Some representations are still Paleolithic and Mesolithic, associated with layers of the Stillbay and Wilton cultures. In the North, engravings resembling those of Sicily may also be Paleolithic, but others (finely engraved goats with sun disks between their horns) are certainly Neolithic. The paintings reveal a Neolithic phase (bovine period) with herds of oxen. In the Tassili des Ajjers there are many other styles difficult to date (small figures of "diablotins," "Martians" or men with round heads, nude women, scenes in Egyptian style). Chariots with horses belong to the 2d millennium B.C., since horses were introduced into Africa through the *Hyksos invasion of Egypt. Paintings continued in the Sahara until Roman times, as evidenced by their being associated with the Lybian tifinagh alphabet. In South Africa there are also later styles showing white women, supposed by some to be of European or Arabian influence, and fights between Negroes and Bushmen.

Asia, Oceania, and America. There are rock paintings of types similar to the African styles in Asia (Palestine, South Anatolia, India) as well as in the Celebes and Australia, and also in central Asia. In the Lake Baikal region they are associated with Neolithic layers.

In Patagonia, hand and feet impressions like those of western Europe, dated by association with an archeological layer (Los Toldos), are Paleolithic. There follow naturalistic or seminaturalistic phases with hunting scenes and others that are schematic or geometric, continuing to very recent times. The same evolution is observed in Mexico and in southeastern U.S. Alaska had a schematic art in the protoeskimo cultures.

Neolithic and Protohistoric Art. The Neolithic revolution in the Near East beginning in the 7th millennium B.C. gave rise to a new art, preceding that of the historical high cultures. This was characterized by paintings in houses in the tradition of rock paintings and by clay and stone figurines representing fertility divinities as well as by painted pottery.

In Europe, the megalithic architecture developed after the 5th millennium B.C. with dolmens, passage graves, covered galleries, and stone cists (Portugal, Brittany, the Nordic circle). The evolution continues until the beginning of the 2d millennium with "tholoi" with corbelled chambers. In Brittany and England, upright stones (menhirs), single or in circles (cromlechs) or in parallel rows (alignments), had religious significance (Carnac in Brittany with alignments interrupted by cromlechs). Stonehenge in England was from the middle of the 3d to the middle of the 2d millennium a sanctuary for sun worship, consisting of several concentric cromlechs opening on an avenue directed toward the dawn. In France, there are menhirs in human figure and in the Marne caves carved representations of a god with an ax as a power symbol and a fertility deity. It has been assumed that the megaliths were diffused from the Near East with a new religion, but it is more likely that they are of indigenous and independent origin both in Portugal and in Scandinavia, although trade relations in the Chalcolithic may have introduced new building techniques. In the Balkan and Danubian countries or in the Ukraine agriculturalists in their villages evolved a primitive sculpture with clay figurines of the Oriental fertility goddesses.

The pottery of Europe was decorated. In the Mediterranean countries there are reliefs and incised or impressed patterns, sometimes with a cardium shell. The bell beaker pottery of Spanish origin was diffused to the eastern Mediterranean, to France and central Europe up to Poland and from Holland to Great Britain. In central Europe, the pottery was decorated with spiral and meander designs. In Rumania (Cucuteni) and in the Ukraine (Tripolye culture), the designs are painted. The megalithic pottery of northern Europe had incised designs, and at the end of the Chalcolithic the peoples of the steppes of eastern Europe diffused cord-impressed pottery. Impressed pottery evolved in the Siberian Neolithic with resemblances to the Jomon culture of Japan, in which pottery is connected with an evolved clay plastic. It has been assumed that the Siberian pottery was diffused also to North America in the Woodland culture, beginning at the end of the 2d millennium B.C. and continuing until recent times.

In the Bronze Age (2d millennium), pottery became plain and the artistic instinct was concentrated mostly in the decoration of bronze implements (swords, axes, fibulae, etc.) with spiral ornaments in the Nordic, South German, and Hungarian cultures. Pottery also had spiral decoration in Hungary. The Bronze Age was contemporary with the Minoan and Mycenean high civilizations in the Aegean.

In the Iron Age of central Europe, the Urnfield culture was related with the Villanovan of Italy. It flourished in the Hallstatt culture, also related with Italy (Etruscan orientalizing culture). The Celtic urnfields, beginning in the Hallstatt culture, expanded to the West (*see* CELTIC ART). In southwestern France and in the Iberian Peninsula the post-Hallstatt culture continued its traditions into the second Iron Age, the time of the transformation of the Hallstatt culture in the La Tène culture, in whose art Greek and Scythian influences are present. The Greek influence in Spain originated the Iberian high culture with its remarkable sculpture (statues of the Cerro de los Santos and the Dama de Elche), votive bronzes, and painted pottery. The Iberian influence in the post-Hallstatt pottery of Numantia produced a Celt-Iberian art of special character.

Bronze figures, probably of god and goddesses of a fertility cult; excavated at Faardal and Grevensvaenge, Denmark; late Bronze Age.

Bibliography: S. GIEDION, *The Eternal Present: The Beginnings of Art* (New York 1962). S. PIGOTT, ed., *The Dawn of Civilization* (New York 1961). H. BREUIL, *Four Hundred Centuries of Cave Art*, tr. M. E. BOYLE (Paris 1952). P. GRAZIOSI, *L'arte dell' antiea età della pietra* (Florence 1956). H. G. BANDI and J. MARINGER, *Art in the Ice Age*, tr. R. ALLEN (New York 1953). H. G. BANDI et al., *The Art of the Stone Age*, tr. A. E. KEEP (New York 1961). P. BOSCH-GIMPERA, "The Chronology of Rock Paintings in Spain and North America," *Art Bulletin* 32 (1950) 71–76; "El arte rupestre americano," *Anales de antropología* 1 (1964) 29–45; *El poblamiento antiguo y la formacíon de los pueblos de Espana* (Mexico City 1944). H. ALIMEN, *Préhistoire de l'Afrique* (Paris 1955). J. D. LAJOUX, *The Rock Paintings of Tassili* (London 1963). MENGHIN, "Las pinturas rupestres de Patagonia," *Runa* 5 (Buenos Aires, May 1921). G. E. DANIEL, *Megalith Builders of Western Europe* (New York 1959). ReallexVorgesch. D. R. MACIVER, *Villanovans and Early Etruscans* (Oxford 1924). M. PALLOTTINO, *Etruscologia* (3d ed. Milan 1955); Eng. tr. J. CREMONA (pa. Baltimore 1955). T. G. E. POWELL, *The Celts* (New York 1958). T. T. RICE, *The Scythians* (New York 1957). A. ARRIBAS, *The Iberians* (New York 1964). L. PERICOT GARCÍA and E. RIPOLL PERELLO, *Prehistoric Art of the Western Mediterranean and the Sahara* (New York 1964). F. MORI, *Tadrart Acacus: Arte rupestre e culture del Sahara preistorico* (Turin 1965). **Illustration credits:** Fig. 1*a*, Museé de l'Homme. Fig. 1*b*, Universitetets Oldsaksamling, Oslo. Fig. 1*c*, Archives Photographiques. Fig. 2, The Danish National Museum, photo by Lennart Larsen.

[P. BOSCH-GIMPERA]

ART EDUCATION

The term art education refers to the teaching of graphic and plastic art within the framework of an established school system. Arts and crafts as taught in shops or technical and professional art schools and art as therapy in hospitals, and as recreation in camps and clubs are not included in this term.

Objectives. Like all other phases of Catholic education, art education is focused on the development of the human person in all his capacities. Everything in the curriculum finds its place in the scale of importance in relation to this primary objective. Placing its stress on process rather than on product in earlier stages of the elementary school, the teaching of art gradually moves toward the adult concept of right making. From mere correctness it advances to creative achievement in the later stages of the secondary and college levels. Since there is no distinction between Catholic and non-Catholic art principles and techniques, the general teaching objectives of art in the Catholic educational system are much the same as those in secular or state-conducted schools. The difference lies mainly in the accepted philosophic background, in the recognition of the power of religious ideas as motivation or subject matter, and in the greater freedom to use the latter whenever students and teachers choose. An incidental difference in Catholic schools stems from the homogeneous religious background in which creative art expression naturally turns toward interpretation of common interests, and religious subjects and events are freely intermingled and integrated with family life, social events, and individual experiences of the students.

Far more than the learning of facts or principles, the end of art teaching is enrichment. Whatever content there is deals with relationships and subjective experiences: basic aesthetic ideas of unity, balance, harmony, variety, contrast, movement; and the elements of line, shape, texture, value, and color. The skills are learned by actual manipulation.

As development takes place, there is growth in natural sensibilities, alertness, observation, empathy, and understanding. The pupils' experimental or experienced environment increases in depth. The sense of security and personal worth grows almost perceptibly. Psychological balance and development of creative potential are other incidental byproducts. In fact, the most valuable results of art education redound from the nature of these immeasurable and intangible benefits.

Old Concept of Art Education. This concept of art education is of comparatively recent origin. Around the turn of the century, in the schools of both Europe and America, art was considered a refined accomplishment. Young ladies in "female institutes" and finishing schools painted in water colors, did needlework, and decorated china as incidentals to the curriculum. For the average art teacher there was a certain stolid respectability in the immutable laws of linear perspective, the Prang color theory, and the precise exercises of the Augsburg drawing books. The ordinary classroom teacher hectographed patterns and the children colored them.

On the higher levels, students drew still life and "antique cast" in a meticulous charcoal or crayon technique, copied the masters in oils or water colors, and executed crayon portraits from life or from daguerreotypes. Assignments in appreciation and history of art consisted mostly of writing essays on the lives and works of the old masters illustrated by small black-and-white prints. These studies were frequently oriented toward a projected future tour of Europe where such information would presumably be an invaluable background.

Just before World War I, there was a perceptible movement toward freedom, further emphasized during the interwar period. Although some Catholic parochial schools adopted the new art methods, there was not a widespread revolution until after 1947. In that year the English edition of Viktor Lowenfeld's book *Creative and Mental Growth* appeared. With this clear and well-documented analysis of the psychology underlying children's creative expression at various age levels, a new era dawned in art education—the child's art was no longer "small adult" art, but an evidence of his mental state. The Catholic schools shared in the awakening.

New Concepts of Art Education. In developing man's natural capacities, a balance should be established between the literary modes of knowing and expressing, and the nonliterary, but equally important, ways of contacting the external visible world and the other intuitional world within. The value of art education is its power to develop these more direct, sensory, but nonliterary ways of registering experience, and to provide tactile and visual expression for the emotional reactions generated by them. It is toward this end, rather than toward producing artists, that general art courses in elementary and secondary schools are oriented. In senior high schools the advanced classes tend to isolate the more gifted students and to direct them into specialized fields of achievement. This specialization continues in colleges and graduate schools.

Courses in the history and appreciation of art also serve the personal development aim. Because works of art are products of sensitive minds capable of imaginative and ordered expression in a visual medium, study and appreciation of them are cited by Pius XII as a source of enrichment and depth of soul. In April of 1952 he said to a group of artists: "Souls ennobled, elevated, and prepared by art are better disposed to receive religious truth and the graces of Jesus Christ." The instruction to the Catholic bishops, issued by the Holy Office in June 1952, specifically states: "Care should be taken that aspirants to sacred orders in schools of philosophy and theology be educated in sacred art and formed to its appreciation. . . ."

Theoretically the art program has well-defined and clearly justifiable objectives. There is a legitimate question, however, as to whether the actual courses are ordered as means to such ends. A study involving Catholic schools in England, France, Germany, Italy, Scotland, Japan, North and South America, India, Africa, and Formosa indicates that methods and courses follow about the same pattern as those of local government-conducted schools.

In missionary schools, the methods of the home country are dominant, with greater modernity evident in areas influenced by Germany and North America. Many missionaries, however, have not as yet assimilated the ethnic cultural expression of the people to whom they minister. Although efforts to revive native crafts and traditional art forms were evident at the mission exhibit in Rome in the Holy Year of 1950, 14 years later they continue to be the exception rather than the general trend.

In the U.S. the pattern has become somewhat uniform—ideally, if not always practically. A few superintendents of schools continue to maintain that they see no need for art in their schools, and therefore, make no provisions for it in their schedules. More progressive systems, particularly in thickly populated areas, prescribe an average minimum of 60 minutes per week for each elementary grade, a 250-minute minimum for high schools in the first year, with full credit electives in the following years, and in some cases specialized advanced courses for gifted students.

Colleges differ in the scope of their art curricula. Some have elective courses in appreciation or history of art and major studio programs of approximately 40 hours in the bachelor of arts or of science programs. Others give the bachelor of fine arts degree for 60 or more semester hours in art. Most women's colleges have art departments, some strong, others weak. The requirements for state certification have been a determining factor in influencing both the content and the quality of art courses in teacher training departments of sisters' colleges. Although they are difficult to evaluate, the *Sister Formation Movement's recommendations for art activities as a part of the psychological, professional, and cultural training of young religious have given still another dimension to Catholic art education.

Most of the men's colleges either have no art, or occasionally offer a lecture course in the general history or appreciation of art. A few Catholic graduate schools have good art departments that offer courses comparable with those in similar secular schools. After the instruction to bishops quoted above, many seminaries introduced art lecture courses, but others did not. In regard

Class in printmaking in the "Studio Angelico" of Siena Heights College, Adrian, Michigan.

to equipment and teacher proficiency, there is still a noticeable unevenness on all levels.

Bibliography: V. LOWENFELD, *Creative and Mental Growth* (3d ed. New York 1957). M. HELENA, *Art Syllabus and Manual for Catholic Elementary Schools* (Morristown, N.J. 1962). Catholic University of America, *Workshop on New Trends in Catholic Art Education, 1958,* ed. E. NEWPORT (Washington 1959); *Workshop on Re-evaluating Art in Education, 1959,* ed. E. NEWPORT (Washington 1960). NCEA, Sister Formation Conferences, *Report of Everett Curriculum Workshop* (Seattle 1956).

[E. NEWPORT]

ART MUSEUMS (U.S.)

The art museum as such is mainly the creation of modern, that is, 19th- and 20th-century, man; it is a collection of art objects, sensitively displayed to a public more or less consciously seeking the knowledge or experience of aesthetic values.

History. Ptolemy I founded at Alexandria in Egypt a library and university called the *Musaion,* or temple of the muses. In it were not only sculptures and paintings but a collection of books of the combined wisdom of Greece. In the late Middle Ages, monarchs such as the Hapsburgs collected works of art, curiosities of nature, and other interesting objects worthy of study. The Hapsburg collection was called the *Schatzkammer,* or treasure house. The *Medici, in 15th-century Florence, brought antique statues to the gardens in the rear of their palace on the Via Larga and encouraged artists to study them there. Throughout the 16th and 17th centuries other monarchs and the great nobility emulated the Hapsburgs and the Medici. In the 1740s the Vatican Museum was formally established under Pope Benedict XIV (1740–50). This includes, besides Roman antiquities and medieval treasures, the works of some of the finest Renaissance artists. All these museums and gallaries were to a great extent private ventures, open only to a few, the aristocracy of birth and scholarship.

In contrast, an art museum in the modern sense is usually a public institution founded with the express purpose of enlightening the widest number of people as to the meaning and uses of art. Museums in the U.S. are as old as the country. In 1773 the first museum, that of the Literary Society of Charleston, S.C., was founded. It was primarily a museum of natural history. When Congress vacated Independence Hall in Philadelphia, the painter Charles Wilson Peale set up (1802) a museum of art and science in that building. A few years later (1805) the Pennsylvania Academy of Fine Arts opened its doors to the public—the first museum in America devoted exclusively to the exhibition and study of art. In 1832 Yale University built the first college art museum, the Trumbull Gallery, with paintings donated and hung by John Trumbull. The Wadsworth Atheneum at Hartford, Conn. (1842), and the Smithsonian Institution, Washington, D.C. (1855), both had art collections. Next in order came the National Academy of Design in New York (1865) and Memorial Hall at the Philadelphia Centennial Exposition of 1876. From these beginnings, since 1870, when the Metropolitan Museum in New York and the Museum of Fine Arts in Boston were organized, by 1939 the country had seen the growth of 96 civic art galleries and museums and 27 additional art galleries in colleges and universities.

The greatest growth in the number of art museums, according to figures furnished in 1964 by the American Association of Museums, took place between 1939 and 1961. In those years the total number grew to 381 art museums and galleries serving the public. At the same time 386 municipal art associations, most of them sponsoring exhibitions, had been formed for the study and enjoyment of art. Leading art museums are: the Metropolitan Museum of Art, New York, with its attendant museum of medieval art, the Cloisters, and a children's museum; next, according to the number of visitors in 1963, was the National Gallery of Art, Washington, D.C.; and then, also in order of attendance, came the Chicago Art Institute, the H. M. de Young Museum of San Francisco, the Philadelphia Museum, the Boston Museum of Fine Arts, the Brooklyn Museum, the Detroit Institute of Arts, and the Cleveland Musuem of Art. An important museum devoted exclusively to modern art is the Museum of Modern Art in New York City. Other municipal museums whose holdings are rich in works of religious content are the City Art Museum, St. Louis; Toledo Museum of Art, Ohio; Kansas City Museum; and the Dayton Art Institute Museum.

Auxiliary Services and Character. All these museums offer considerably more than mere collections of pictures exhibited in galleries. Almost every one has, besides its curatorial staff organized primarily for research, publication, and the preparation of exhibitions, an educational department providing interpretation and introductory lectures, tours, motion pictures, and in many cases television shows and concerts for the public. These auxiliary functions of providing cultural experience and education in the arts follow the example set by Peale in his Independence Hall museum. In this respect most American museums have had a democratic touch from their very inception, differing from the more aristocratic approaches of the many European museums based formerly on various royal collections. Unlike European galleries and museums that (almost without exception) charge for admission the American museums are free to the public. Also mostly an American innovation are extension services, the lending of traveling exhibitions of fine works to smaller institutions in different parts of the country.

Bibliography: *International Directory of Arts,* ed. H. RAUSCHENBUSCH (Berlin 1953–), international directory of museums, galleries, schools, artists, collectors, etc., 7th ed. 1963–64. *Museum* (Paris 1948–), a quarterly review, text in Eng. and Fr. L. V. COLEMAN, *The Museum in America,* 3 v. (Washington 1939). E. SPAETH, *American Art Museums and Galleries* (New

York 1960). L. POWEL, *The Art Museum Comes to the School* (New York 1944). G. CART et al., *Musées et Jeunesse* (Paris 1952).

[R. S. STITES]

ART NOUVEAU, the art style that prevailed in the applied arts between 1892 and 1905 and imposed its language to a certain degree on painting, sculpture, and architecture, as well as on the graphic arts. It derives its name from the Paris gallery "Maison de l'Art Nouveau," opened by S. Bing in 1896. The movement was directed against the machine-made imitations of historical styles, typical of the Victorian period, and emphasized handicrafts executed with a sympathetic understanding for the employed materials.

The designs of *art nouveau* were derived from two sources: undulating lines in natural things, such as water and bending grass. Japanese art, with its asymmetrical character and curvilinear design, also provided inspiration. The apparent mannerism of *art nouveau* springs from the conflict between the genuine shape of an object and its subordination to nature-derived serpentine forms.

Historically, *art nouveau* was the outgrowth of the anti-industrialist movement that originated in England with William *Morris (1834–1898) in the 1860s and developed in the 1880s in the "Arts and Crafts" movement. The illustrations of Aubrey Beardsley (1872–98) were particularly influential in spreading the style. In France the tendency toward languid decorative patterns and linear abstraction made an appearance among some of the pioneers of modern painting. This was manifest in the late paintings of G. Seurat (1859–91), in the draftsmanship of Henri de Toulouse-Lautrec (1864–1901), in the work of É. *Bernard, and especially in that of P. *Gauguin after the 1880s. In architecture and design, *art nouveau* developed first in Belgium (after 1892) with Henri van de Velde (1863–1957) and Victor Horta (1861–1947). In France the new style was represented by E. Gallé (1846–1904) and H. Guimard (1867–1942); in England, by A. H. Mackmurdo (1851–1942) and C. R. Mackintosh (1868–1928); in Holland, by J. *Toorop; in Germany by H. Obrist (1863–1927) and R. Riemerschmid (1868–1957); in Austria, by J. Olbrich (1867–1908) and J. Hoffman (1870–1956); in Spain, by A. *Gaudí; and in America, by C. Tiffany (1848–1933). The spirit and form of *art nouveau* were expressed in a decade of graphic work by E. *Munch, sculpture and tapestries by A. Maillol

Antonio Gaudí, Casa Mila apartment house, Barcelona (1905–07).

Henri van de Velde, "Guardian Angels," appliqué and embroidery (1893).

(1861–1944), and works by the German Max Klinger (1857–1920).

Art nouveau represents a curious blend of *fin de siècle* decadence and hopeful contemporaneity. In the latter aspect it is paralleled by H. Bergson's *élan vital* philosophy and its equivalent manifestations in the social and ethical reform movements of the period.

Bibliography: P. SELZ and M. CONSTANTINE, eds., *Art and Design at the Turn of the Century* (New York 1959), best introd. with bibliog. S. T. MADSEN, *Sources of Art Nouveau* (New York 1956). N. PEVSNER, *Pioneers of Modern Design: From William Morris to Walter Gropius* (2d ed. New York 1949); EncWA 1: 811–814. H. VAN DE VELDE, *Zum neuen Stil,* ed. H. CURJEL (Munich 1955). H. SELING, ed., *Jugendstil: Der Weg ins 20. Jahrhundert* (Heidelberg 1959). H. H. HOFSTÄTTER, *Geschichte der europäischen Jugendstilmalerei* (Cologne 1963). R. SCHMUTZLER, *Art Nouveau,* tr. E. RODITI (New York 1962). **Illustration credits:** Fig. 1, MAS Barcelona. Fig. 2, Kunstgewerbemuseum, Zürich.

[A. NEUMEYER]

ARTAUD DE MONTOR, JEAN ALEXIS FRANÇOIS, diplomat and historian; b. Paris, July 21, 1772; d. Paris, Nov. 12, 1849. He was an attaché at the French Embassy in Sweden (1792), and afterward served the exiled Bourbons. Upon returning to France (1800), he took part in the negotiations preceding the *Concordat of 1801, and became attaché of the Embassy in Rome, chargé d'affaires in Tuscany (1806), and imperial censor (1807). His publications include: *Considérations sur l'état de la peinture en Italie dans les quatre siècles qui ont précédé celui de Raphaël* (1808); *Voyage dans les catacombes de Rome* (1810); a translation of Dante's *Divine Comedy* (3 v., 1811–13). In 1814 he returned to diplomacy and was secretary at the embassies in Rome, in Vienna (1816), in Madrid (1818), and again in Rome (1819–30). He then resumed his literary work. His more important publications are: *Machiavel, son génie et ses erreurs* (1833); *Histoire de Dante Alighieri* (1841); *Histoire du Pape Pie VII* (2 v., 1836), his best work; *Histoire du Pape Pie VIII* (1844); and *Histoire des Souverains Pontifes romains* (8 v., 1847). In 1830 he became a member of the Académie des Inscriptions et Belles Lettres.

Bibliography: E. G. Ledos, DictBiogFranc 3:1132–35.

[R. LIMOUZIN-LAMOTHE]

ARTAXERXES I AND II, the first two of three Achaemenid kings of the Persian Empire.

Artaxerxes I Longimanus (464–423 B.C.) became king upon the assassination of his father and elder brother. It was the misfortune of Artaxerxes (Old Persian *artaḫšatrā,* Hebrew *'artaḥšastā',* Greek 'Αρταξέρξης) to be one of the rulers who presided over the dissolution of the Persian Empire. The early years of his reign were marked by insurrection, especially in Egypt. Although most revolts were suppressed, some of the eastern provinces were lost. At the same time, the Greeks were a problem in the West. With a combination of Median diplomacy and Grecian disunity and intrigue, Artaxerxes was able to end the war with Athens in 448. He was a benevolent ruler regarding Juda, probably due in part to the fact that Juda did not revolt. Moreover, a peaceful, friendly, stable Juda provided military routes necessary in dealing with rebellious Egypt. In his 20th year (445) he appointed his Jewish cup-bearer *Nehemia governor of Juda and authorized him to rebuild the walls of Jerusalem and thus protect the inhabitants from the hostile neighboring peoples (Neh 2.1–8).

Artaxerxes II Mnemon (404–358) was the son of Darius II (423–404) and grandson of Artaxerxes I. During his reign, the still vast Persian empire was subject to internal rebellion and harrassment from the Greeks. He crushed a rebellion led by his brother Cyrus in 401 at the battle of Cunaxa (the beginning of Xenophon's *Anabasis*). However, he lost Egypt; and during the last decade of his reign, all satrapies of Asia Minor, allied with the Greeks, were in revolt. Although Persian authority had been restored in the satrapies by the end of his reign, this was due not to Artaxerxes, but rather to the suspicion and treachery of the rebels among themselves. If the text (Ezr 7.1, 7–8) is correct, it was probably in the 7th year of this Artaxerxes (i.e., 396) that *Ezra came to Jerusalem. Artaxerxes III Ochus (358–337), the son of Artaxerxes II, was an energetic monarch, but his attempts to subdue the rebellious provinces had no lasting success. He is not mentioned in the Bible, but Josephus (*Ant.* 11.7.1) speaks of a revolt of the Jews in his (rather than his father's) reign that was crushed with great severity by the Persian general Bagoses (Bagoas).

See also PERSIA.

Bibliography: NÖLDEKE, Pauly-Wiss RE 2.1 (1895) 1311–18. J. B. GRAY and M. CARY, CAH 4:185–210. A. T. E. OLMSTEAD, *History of the Persian Empire: Achaemenid Period* (Chicago 1948). H. LESÊTRE, DB 1.2:1038–43. F. SALVONI and A. ROMEO, EncCatt 2:32–33. EncDictBibl 140.

[E. A. BALLMANN]

ARTHURIAN AND CAROLINGIAN LEGENDS

Of all the legends that flourished in the Middle Ages, the two major cycles clustered around the figures of Arthur and Charlemagne. Both cycles were widely known throughout Western Christendom, and their literary influence has extended even into modern times. Arthur and Charlemagne were historical personages, though Arthur is known almost exclusively through the legendary material. Reliable historical sources tell us much more about *Charlemagne (742–814), his conquests, his interests in education and government and the revival of learning he fostered in an age of barbarism. The legends of Arthur and Charlemagne, in the course of time, followed paths of development so different that in spirit they seem to have little in common. The romances about Arthur and his knights of the Round Table deal with a world of chivalry, love, and adventure, in which marvels occur with astonishing frequency. The *chansons de geste* about Charlemagne and his paladins, on the other hand, exalt French nationalism in the struggle against the infidel and stress the conflicts arising between feudal obligations to the suzerain and personal concepts of honor. (*See* ROMANCE, MEDIEVAL; FRENCH LITERATURE, 1.)

ARTHURIAN LEGENDS

Historically, Arthur is the earlier figure. During the Saxon invasions of Britain in the late 5th century, Arthur led the British forces in a series of battles that ended with a decisive victory at Mt. Badon, somewhere in southern England, about A.D. 500. Despite the eventual triumph of the Saxons, Arthur's fame lived long in the memory of the defeated British and their descendants. St. *Gildas, a Briton, writes (*c.* 540) about the battle of Mt. Badon as a British victory that halted the advance of the Saxons and initiated a period of peace, although he does not mention Arthur. The earliest extant reference to Arthur by name occurs in a Welsh poem, *The Gododdin* (*c.* 600), which extols the valor of a fallen warrior by comparing him with Arthur. About 800, the Welsh priest *Nennius, in the *Historia Britonum,* lists Arthur's 12 victories over the Saxons, concluding with that at Mt. Badon, and in an account of the natural wonders of Britain, he records two local legends connected with Arthur. The *Annales Cambriae,* another Latin compilation of Welsh origin (*c.* 950), also mentions the victory at Badon and another battle at Camlann, in which Arthur and Medraut (Modred) fell.

Early Welsh literature independent of the chronicles and historical annals presents Arthur as the hero of adventures derived from Celtic myth and the leader of a company endowed with preternatural powers. In a Welsh poem of the 10th century, *The Spoils of Annwn,* Arthur sets out with three shiploads of men to capture the magic cauldron of Annwn, the Celtic Otherworld. Although the vessel is taken, only seven men, including Arthur, return from the disastrous raid. In another early Welsh poem, a fragmentary dialogue between Arthur and a gatekeeper, Arthur lists among his companions not only Kay and Bedivere but also many figures derived from Welsh myth, with references to their accomplishments as slayers of monsters. The Welsh prose romance *Kulhwch and Olwen* (*c.* 1100) includes a rationalized version of Arthur's raid upon the Otherworld and recounts his hunting of a preternatural boar.

Origin and Diffusion. The legend of Arthur, according to the earliest documents, originated in Wales, where the memory of the historic military leader was preserved and later drawn into the orbit of native Welsh mythological tradition. Arthur's fame was cultivated also among the Cornish and the Bretons, linguistically and culturally allied with the Welsh. Traditions of Arthur's birth and death were localized in Cornwall, and the Cornish, like the Bretons, believed in the survival of Arthur and his inevitable return to his people. The wide diffusion of the Arthurian legends on the Continent, beginning in the 11th century, was chiefly the work of the Bretons, whose fluency in French and whose professional skill in exploiting their Celtic heritage of legend to entertain French-speaking patrons spread the stories wherever the language was understood—not only in France, but also in England, Italy, and the crusader states.

Another major contribution to Arthur's international fame was the appearance about 1136 of *Geoffrey of Monmouth's Latin *Historia Regum Britanniae,* a work intended to give the British a full-scale history like those of the Normans, the Saxons, and the French. Geoffrey purports to be merely a translator of an ancient book in the British tongue, but no trace of such a source has ever been discovered. Geoffrey's book is primarily his own invention, based upon material derived from Nennius, Welsh genealogies, and the usual historical sources accessible to a cleric. Geoffrey's history begins with the first king of Britain, Brutus, who, as a descendant of Aeneas, links Britain with Rome. Among the early figures are King Lear, Cymbeline, and Sabrina, whose legends later influenced Shakespeare, Spenser, and Milton.

Arthur as Central Interest. The Arthurian story is naturally the center of interest. Arthur in his youth was supervised and protected by the wizard Merlin. After his coronation and marriage, he subjugated not only the Saxons but other Continental peoples and established his empire even over Gaul. When the Roman Emperor challenged him, he set out to conquer Rome, leaving his kingdom in charge of his nephew Modred. Modred's attempt to usurp the throne and to seize Arthur's queen brought the King home before he could complete the conquest. At a battle on the River Camel in Cornwall, Modred was slain and Arthur, though mortally wounded, was borne to the isle of Avalon to be healed. After the reign of Arthur, the British kingdom declined until it was finally overwhelmed by the Saxons in the 7th century.

Geoffrey presents Arthur as a 12th-century king presiding over a magnificent court and accepting the homage of royal vassals. The emphasis upon the theme of empire and the independence of Britain agrees with the political aspirations of the Anglo-Norman kings of the time. Although some of Geoffrey's contemporaries doubted his veracity, the *Historia* was generally accepted as the standard history of early Britain until the 16th century, when historical scholarship revealed it to be largely fiction.

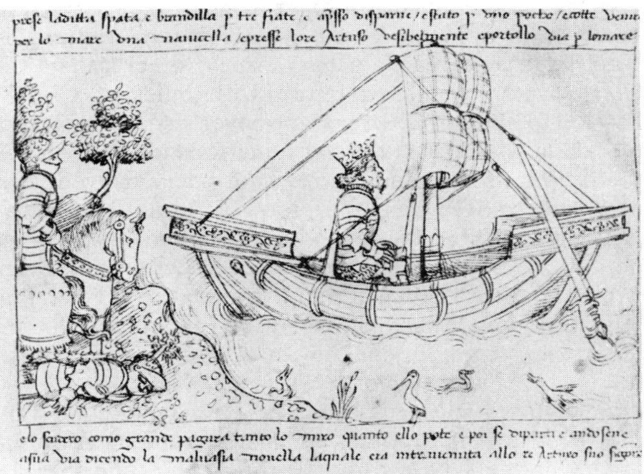

King Arthur sails to Avalon; drawing attributed to Bonifacio Bembro of Cremona in a manuscript of the "History of Lancelot of the Lake" written in 1446 by Zuliano di Anzoli (MS Pal. 556, fol. 171a).

In 1155 the *Historia* was translated into French as *Le Roman de Brut* by the Norman poet Wace, evidently in response to a demand from courtly patrons. Wace follows his original faithfully and adapts the story to courtly interests chiefly by expanding descriptive passages. His most significant addition is the story of Arthur's Round Table, of which, he writes, Bretons tell many tales, and which was founded to prevent quarrels over precedence. (*See* ANGLO-NORMAN LITERATURE.) About 1200, the first English version was composed by a parish priest in Worcestershire named *Layamon. Although an expanded paraphrase of Wace, Layamon's *Brut* is a re-creation of the story in the alliterative meter and style typical of the Old English epic, ironically the literary style of Arthur's historic foes, the Saxons.

The account of Arthur's career in Geoffrey's *Historia* remains substantially unchanged in these and later versions, but its influence is negligible on the French Arthurian romances that began to appear in the second half of the 12th century. These stories were derived from the oral legends circulated by Breton storytellers, and they deal with a variety of heroes unknown in the pseudohistorical tradition of Geoffrey. Many of these tales, though originally independent, were absorbed into the Arthurian legend because of the great King's prestige. Sometimes the process began before the story reached the Continent. When the Tristan legend, for example, migrated from northern Scotland to Wales, the Welsh linked Arthur to the originally Pictish hero, and in some Continental versions of the Tristan legend, Arthur plays a minor role that is evidently derived from this tradition.

Heroes other than Arthur; the Grail. In general, Arthur and his court become in the French romances of the 12th century the background for the adventures of the hero of the story. In the four romances of *Chrétien de Troyes that are based on traditional sources, the interest is centered not on Arthur himself but on the individual heroes—Erec, Yvain, Lancelot, and Perceval—and the role of Arthur varies according to the story. In *Erec* and *Yvain,* in which Chrétien delicately balances the claims of love and chivalry, the hero's adventures begin at Arthur's court and the happy outcome of his trials and suffering in each romance is explicitly connected with Arthur and his knights. In the unfinished *Lancelot,* on the contrary, Arthur's role is ignominious: he allows his queen to be abducted, and her rescue is accomplished by her devoted but adulterous lover Lancelot. In the story of Perceval (*Li Contes del Graal*), which Chrétien also left unfinished, the hero is at first an uncouth lad whose gradual education in chivalry prepares him for the adventures of the Grail; Arthur's court clearly represents the standards of chivalry that test the hero's worth, although the King himself suffers without resistance a humiliating insult that is avenged by the young Perceval.

Other French romancers attempted to continue Chrétien's unfinished works, especially the *Graal;* and his influence penetrated fruitfully into Germany, where Hartmann von Aue adapted *Erec* and *Yvain,* and where *Wolfram von Eschenbach composed *Parzival,* a profoundly spiritual yet realistic reworking and expansion of Chrétien's story, stressing humility and compassion as the noblest virtues of chivalry (*see* GERMAN LITERATURE, 2).

Prose Cycles. Although the Grail stories were derived from the same reservoir of Celtic tradition as other parts of the Arthurian legend, the mysterious vessel called the Grail inevitably suggested Christian interpretation, which became a prominent feature of 13th-century versions (*see* HOLY GRAIL, THE). Two other major trends distinguish the development of the French Arthurian legends in the 13th century: the use of prose rather than verse and the effort to assemble all the legends into one immense compilation. The so-called Vulgate prose cycle consists of five long romances, written at various times and by different authors whose identity remains unknown. The earliest part, composed between 1215 and 1230, is the trilogy of the prose *Lancelot, La Queste del Saint Graal,* and *La Mort Artu.* The prose *Lancelot* is a long biographical romance about Lancelot, his devotion to the Queen, his supremacy as a knight, and his begetting of Galahad, the destined Grail hero. The *Queste* is a religious allegory, the work of a Cistercian, the hero of which is the sinless Galahad, who achieves the perfect mystical vision of the Grail denied to his father Lancelot because of adultery with Guenevere. Inexorable doom dominates the *Mort Artu,* causing the sequence of disasters resulting from that sin: Arthur's discovery of his queen's infidelity with Lancelot, the feud between Gawain and Lancelot, and the final battle between Arthur and his incestuously begotten son Modred. To this trilogy two other romances were added: the *Estoire del Saint Graal,* a prelude relating the early history of the Grail and its role in the evangelization of Britain, and the prose *Merlin,* which carries the narrative through the period of the pre-Arthurian kings to the coronation of Arthur, the establishment of the Round Table, and the Saxon wars.

The Vulgate cycle spread the concept of *chivalry as a noble, ideal way of life through its powerful influence upon later romances in France, Italy, Spain, the Netherlands, Ireland, Wales, and England. It was the principal source of Sir Thomas Malory's *Le Morte Darthur* (1469–70). Although Malory used other sources, French and English, he followed the Vulgate in presenting Lancelot as the embodiment of chivalry and the hero of the Arthuriad. Malory condensed and abridged freely; and he deliberately unraveled stories that were carefully interwoven in his French sources, narrating them as self-contained units. *Caxton edited and printed (1485) Malory's work and gave it the title by which it is generally known.

In the English Renaissance, the Arthurian legend became the center of political controversy over the authenticity of Geoffrey's *Historia,* which was used to support Tudor claims to the throne; and moralists like Roger *Ascham condemned Malory's tales for their bawdry and manslaughter. Yet Caxton's edition of Malory was reprinted five times before the 18th century, and such poets as Spenser and Milton were attracted to the legends. As a result of the renewed interest in medieval legends during the Romantic revival, Arthurian themes became important in the 19th century. The most notable achievements are *Tennyson's *Idylls of the King* and Richard *Wagner's music dramas *Tristan und Isolde* and *Parsifal.* (*See* ROMANTICISM; ENGLISH LITERATURE, 7; GERMAN LITERATURE, 5.)

CAROLINGIAN LEGENDS

If the romance is the characteristic genre of the Arthurian legend, the epic, or *chanson de geste,* is the natural form for the legends about Charlemagne. Unlike Arthur, there was never any question about Charlemagne's historicity, and his conquests of most of western Europe were real, not fictional. The actual Charlemagne was a Frank, whose native language was German, and whose principal residence was Aix-la-Chapelle, the German Aachen. Yet he became the national hero of the French, who developed the earliest epics about his exploits.

Legends about Charlemagne seem to have circulated even in his lifetime. Court poets composed Latin panegyrics about him in a rhetorical style that made him a majestic, almost superhuman figure, and even *Einhard's generally trustworthy biography, modeled upon Suetonius's life of Augustus, contributed to this idealization by associating him with the great Roman Emperor and by recording the preternatural portents that preceded his death. Oral traditions about Charlemagne were compiled by a monk of St. Gall about 885, for example, the anecdote about King Desiderius of Lombardy and Otker the Frank awaiting Charles's arrival at Pavia, and Otker's swoon at the awesome sight of the Iron Emperor. Charlemagne's glorious memory was fostered by the clergy partly because from the beginning he was regarded as the defender of Christendom against its enemies and partly because of his benefactions to numerous churches. There can be little doubt that the clerical tradition encouraged the spread of the Carolingian legends along the great pilgrimage routes of the Middle Ages, but there is also evidence of a vigorous vernacular tradition of songs and tales about Charlemagne that prepared the way for the later epics.

Transformation of the Historical Figure. The legendary Charlemagne differs, of course, from the historic original. Although the historic Charlemagne waged long and successful wars against the Saxons, the Slavs, the Huns, and the Danes, legend made his chief enemy the Saracens, transforming a minor engagement in Spain into a major threat to Christian civilization. Another legend recounts his journey to Jerusalem and Constantinople and his return with relics of Christ's Passion. Although Charlemagne never visited the Orient, his friendly relations with Harun al-Rashid (764?–809), the Caliph of Baghdad, with whom he exchanged gifts, and with the Greek emperors of Constantinople may well have inspired the invention of such a legend. Since no historical records survive of Charlemagne's childhood and youth, a legend was invented to fill the gap, relating his exile in Spain to escape from his two evil bastard brothers. Under the assumed name of Mainet, he offers his services to the Saracen King and delivers him from a dangerous foe. The King's daughter falls in love with him, becomes a Christian, and marries him after Charlemagne regains his throne and punishes the wicked brothers. Although Charlemagne is a youth in this story, he is usually depicted as an aged man with a flowing white beard, yet vigorous and commanding—a majestic, patriarchal figure.

Charlemagne mourning knights killed in battle; detail of 13th-century shrine of Charlemagne in the cathedral, Aachen, Germany.

Defender of Christendom. So he is presented in the stories dealing with the wars against the infidel. In this cycle he is the leader of France, the people chosen by God to defend all of Christendom. The mutation of history into legend can be observed in the *Song of Roland* (*c.* 1100), the earliest, the best, and the most famous of these epics. Earlier versions seem to have been reshaped under the powerful impetus of the Crusades to emphasize the urgency of military action against the infidel and the spiritual rewards awaiting those martyred for the faith.

The only defeat of Charlemagne recorded by Einhard was the result of a surprise attack by Basques in a pass of the Pyrenees on the rearguard of Charlemagne's army, an assault that destroyed all the men, among them Roland, Count of Brittany. The Basques plundered the baggage train and fled under cover of nightfall. Their dispersal, we are told, made immediate vengeance impossible. The event, dated in 778, was an interruption of the Saxon wars that Charlemagne undertook to assist Saracen princes in Spain who had appealed for his aid against foes of their faith. The defeat occurred after Charlemagne's recall from Spain to meet a renewed attack by the Saxons.

At the time Charlemagne was 38, but in the *Song of Roland* he is 200 years old; the Basques are metamorphosed into a horde of treacherous Saracens, greatly outnumbering the French rearguard; and Charlemagne exacts a mighty vengeance (although the historical sources are careful to explain why he could not do so). The ambush in the poem is initiated by a conspiracy between Roland's stepfather Ganelon and the Saracens in order to destroy Roland, who is here represented as Charlemagne's nephew and the mightiest of the 12 peers. The central episode is the heroic defense led by Roland and the peers in the Battle of Roncevaux, ending in death for them and the 20,000 who would never again see France. Charlemagne himself is the hero of the rest of the poem, destroying the infidels, leveling Saragossa, and converting the Queen to Christianity. Ganelon's fate is decided not by Charlemagne but by God in a judicial combat. His terrible punishment for his treason follows, and the poem ends, not with a celebration of victory but with Charlemagne's weary acceptance of the angel Gabriel's summons to yet another war in defense of Christendom.

The wars in Spain became the center of the early Carolingian legend since they presented Charlemagne as the divinely ordained defender of Christianity against the infidel and as a king of justice and piety. A far smaller number of *chansons de geste* deal with Charlemagne's wars against foes in Italy and against the Saxons, though historically these conquests were more significant than the Spanish expedition. Later, other legends developed about his relationship with his vassals and these offer a less idealized image of Charlemagne. Since the narrator's sympathy is usually with the rebellious vassal, Charlemagne is often presented as harsh, vindictive, and cruel in stories that probably reflect the struggles in the 9th and 10th centuries between the ruling monarchs who succeeded Charlemagne and their recalcitrant but powerful vassals. Even in the *Song of Roland* there is a hint of this theme in the hostile attitudes and actions of Ganelon, which, though directed against Roland rather than Charlemagne, nevertheless endanger the Emperor's cause. Such *chansons de geste* as *Ogier the Dane, The Four Sons of Aimon,* and *Doon de Mayence* relate at great length the feuds between the rebel vassals, aided by their families and allies, against the authority of Charlemagne. There were intermittent reconciliations and renewals of hostilities, but the foes generally united if Christendom was threatened.

In the 13th century the Carolingian legends, like the Arthurian, were combined into cycles, but there was no influential re-creation of the stories comparable to the Arthurian Vulgate. Such Carolingian compilations as those of Philippe Mouskés and the monk *Alberic of Trois-Fontaines are valuable because they preserve legendary material that has since disappeared from the extant versions; and the Old Norse prose *Karlamagnús saga* is important because its compilers had access to texts that are often superior to those that have survived (*see* OLD NORSE LITERATURE).

Spread of the Legends. The legendary fame of Charlemagne spread into Germany, the Low Countries, Scandinavia, England, Italy, and Spain. Knowledge of Carolingian legends can be documented in England over a long period. One of the earliest allusions tells of the minstrel Taillefer at the Battle of Hastings in 1066 who sang of Charlemagne, Roland, and those who died at Roncevaux. Though his song could not have been the extant epic, it is significant that the earliest MS was written in Anglo-Norman about 1170 and that it was preserved at Oxford. The Carolingian legends in Middle English are late and inferior versions, but in the 15th century interest was still strong enough to persuade Caxton to publish *Charles the Great* in 1485 and 4 years later *The Four Sons of Aymon.*

In the Italian Renaissance, the Carolingian legends experienced a literary rebirth in the narrative poems of L. Pulci (1432–84), M. Boiardo (1441–94), and *Ariosto. The work of their 14th-century predecessors, the Franco-Italian compilations and the Italian prose *Reali di Francia* (*c.* 1400), by Andrea da Barberino (*c.* 1370–*c.* 1432), had already established the distinctive features of the Italian tradition: the reduction of the complicated relationships into a feud between two great families, the houses of Clermont and Mayence. Charlemagne became a background figure, and the heroes of Clermont were Roland (Orlando) and Renaud de Montauban (Rinaldo). The head of the enemy house, of course, was Ganelon.

Professional minstrels popularized these stories orally in the streets of Italian cities and along the pilgrimage routes to Rome. They reached literary eminence when Pulci, poet of the household of Lorenzo de' *Medici, used them as the basis of his comic epic *Il Morgante Maggiore* (1482). Boiardo's *Orland Innamorato* (1494) inaugurated a new phase with the introduction into the Carolingian epic of chivalric and romantic themes derived from the Arthurian cycle. The invincible Roland of earlier tradition becomes Orlando, vanquished by love for a pagan princess who plans to destroy Christendom by seducing Charlemagne's paladins. In this romantic epic, Boiardo invents a world of knight-errantry, surprises, enchantments, and magic, blended with the wars of Christian against Saracen. With a spirit of ironic detachment, Ariosto continued Boiardo's unfinished poem in *Orlando Furioso,* the central theme of which is Orlando's madness induced by love and jealousy. Thus transformed, the old Carolingian tradition contributed to one of the most brillant and polished narrative poems of the Italian Renaissance.

Except for the influence of Ariosto's masterpiece on *Spenser's *Faerie Queen* in the 16th century in England and Byron's delighted discovery of Pulci in the 19th, the Carolingian legends have been less important in modern times than the Arthurian. In different ways, however, the two cycles of legends have significantly enriched the culture of western Europe.

See also COURTLY LOVE; LEGENDS, MEDIEVAL.

Bibliography: R. S. LOOMIS, ed., *Arthurian Literature in the Middle Ages* (Oxford 1959); *The Development of Arthurian Romance* (London 1963); *The Grail: From Celtic Myth to Christian Symbol* (New York 1963). J. S. P. TATLOCK, *The Legendary History of Britain: Geoffrey of Monmouth's Historia Regum Britanniae and Its Early Vernacular Versions* (Berkeley 1950). J. FRAPPIER, *Chrétien de Troyes: L'Homme et l'oeuvre* (Paris 1957); *Étude sur La Mort le Roi Artu* (2d ed. Paris 1961). T. MALORY, *Works,* ed. E. VINAVER, 3 v. (Oxford 1947). J. A. BENNETT, ed., *Essays on Malory* (Oxford 1963). R. S. and L. A. H. LOOMIS, *Arthurian Legends in Medieval Art* (New York 1938). G. PARIS, *Histoire poétique de Charlemagne,* ed. P. MEYER (new ed. Paris 1905). J. BÉDIER, *Les Légendes épiques,* 4 v. (2d ed. Paris 1914–21). H. G. LEACH, *Angevin Britain and Scandinavia* (Cambridge, Mass. 1921). J. E. WELLS, *A Manual of the Writings in Middle English, 1050–1400* (New Haven 1916; 9 suppl. 1919–52). J. B. FLETCHER, *Literature of the Italian Renaissance* (New York 1934). L. A. H. LOOMIS, *Adventures in the Middle Ages* (New York 1962). **Illustration credits:** Fig. 1, Biblioteca Nazionale Centrale, Florence. Fig. 2, Marburg-Art Reference Bureau.

[H. NEWSTEAD]

ARTICLE OF FAITH. The term was unknown in the age of the Fathers. Though it came into use before the time of St. Thomas Aquinas, it was he who apparently first gave it precise meaning. For him an article of faith has three qualities: it is a formally revealed doctrine (that is, its meaning is made known by God in a *supernatural way) conceptually distinct from other doctrines; it embodies a truth of salvific importance; and it is incorporated into an official Church *creed.

The articles of faith are the basic expressions of Christian belief. They are interrelated in the organically unified body of Church teaching. Some are more fundamental than others, the less fundamental being amplifications of the more fundamental. Thus, the articles of faith are the building blocks of *theology, which is the science of first revealed principles. In the course of the centuries the Church makes explicit the doctrines implicitly contained in them, and it strives to show ever more clearly the interrelationships existing among them, and between them and the doctrines derived from them.

See also DEPOSIT OF FAITH; DOGMA; FUNDAMENTAL ARTICLES OF BELIEF.

Bibliography: R. RUCH, DTC 1.2:2023–25. H. BACHT, LexThK[2] 4:934–935.

[P. F. CHIRICO]

ARTIFICIAL INSEMINATION (MORAL ASPECT)

Artificial insemination among humans can refer either to an act or to an entire procedure. The act of artificial insemination is the placing of semen into the female genital tract, not by sexual intercourse, but through the use of an instrument, usually a syringe. The procedure of artificial insemination embraces not only the act of insemination but also the obtaining of semen for the purpose of insemination. The procedure, therefore, is subject to moral evaluation from two points of view: (1) the method used to obtain the semen and (2) the act of insemination itself.

This article will discuss first the morality of homologous artificial insemination (AIH), or the insemination that is effected with semen derived from the husband of the woman inseminated; second, the morality of heterologous artificial insemination (AID), or that which is effected with semen obtained from a donor who is not the husband of the woman inseminated; and third, the morality of using certain means to facilitate the natural act of intercourse to achieve its purpose of fecundation.

Homologous Artificial Insemination. The purpose of insemination of this kind is to make a marriage fruitful when, because of some physical condition in husband or wife, issue has not been forthcoming as desired. The morality of AIH could be questioned either because of the methods used to obtain the semen or because of the act of insemination itself.

Methods Used to Obtain the Semen. Artificial insemination was successfully used on animals at the end of the 18th century. Not until the end of the 19th century did widespread human experimentation occur. The first experiments took place with semen obtained from the woman's husband. Dissatisfied with an ejaculate obtained from real or attempted intercourse, many physicians came to prefer an ejaculate obtained from masturbation. The first serious moral evaluation, therefore, of artificial insemination took place within this context.

Almost all Catholic moral theologians condemned the procedure of AIH when masturbation was the means for obtaining semen. Two 19th-century theologians, E. Berardi and D. Palmieri, dissented largely because they were inclined to regard the ejaculation in these circumstances not as real masturbation but rather as an act that preserved a fundamental orientation toward a procreative objective. They retracted their view when, in 1897, the Holy Office declared that artificial insemination was immoral (Denz 3323). Despite the direct language of the Holy Office's statement, most theologians considered the statement to be condemnation not of artificial insemination itself, but rather of artificial insemination when masturbation formed part of the procedure. As a consequence, further discussion on the subject continued.

A small number of influential Catholic moralists suggested that if a licit way could be found to obtain semen, such a product could be used for AIH. The examples commonly given of licit ways to obtain semen were anal massage of the prostate or direct puncture of the epididymis. Although a semen specimen could be obtained by these procedures, the amount would never be sufficient for employment in artificial insemination. Nevertheless, the examples did afford a basis for continued discussion of principle.

It must be noted parenthetically that the problem of licitly obtaining semen arose also in another area of medical practice. Physicians desiring to determine and treat causes of male sterility faced the moral problem of obtaining semen specimens for examination. (*See* STERILITY AND STERILITY TESTS.)

In a discourse to the Fourth International Congress of Catholic Doctors, Pius XII declared that semen can never be procured licitly through acts that are contrary to nature. Among such acts the following must certainly be enumerated: masturbation, condomistic intercourse, and interrupted intercourse. When, therefore, AIH uses any of these methods to obtain semen, the entire procedure is morally objectionable from the beginning.

There are other methods of obtaining semen, however, that are either clearly, or at least probably, licit. (1) Clearly licit: removal of semen about an hour after normal coitus from the genital tract of the wife; the use of a vaginal cup, that is, of a rubber cup that is inserted into the vagina after coitus and that will catch semen that would otherwise be lost. (For these and other examples, see G. Kelly, SJ, *Medico-Moral Problems,* 224–225.) (2) Probably licit: anal massage and puncture of the epididymis; use of a perforated condom during intercourse; and the use of the so-called cervical spoon, when the spoon and its contents are removed immediately after intercourse.

The procedures in (2) have been termed "probably licit" because each one is the subject of controversy among moralists. Precisely because they are probably licit, however, their use may not be forbidden. (*See* PROBABILISM.)

However, the moral problem of AIH is not solved merely by the discovery of methods of obtaining semen that do not violate the moral law. This leads to the second point in the moral evaluation of AIH.

The Act of Artificial Insemination. It is one thing to maintain that there are legitimate ways of obtaining semen apart from the marital act, and another to suggest that the product of such a legitimate procedure may then be used for the purpose of homologous insemination. One must establish that the act of insemination itself is licit.

Before 1949 most Catholic moralists rejected AIH, even though semen could be obtained licitly. They reasoned that the transmission of the lifegiving element of generation had to take place in a marital act. Only the marital act is capable of expressing the unity of persons signified by marriage; only the marital act unifies the couple as one coprinciple of procreation. The marriage contract furthermore gives the right to only those acts that are of themselves fitted for generation; it does not give or establish the right to artificial insemination.

As mentioned above, some theologians expressed a view contrary to the majority. In the 1949 allocution of Pius XII, referred to above, the Holy Father officially adopted the majority view. He repeated his teaching in a subsequent address to the Italian Catholic Midwives in October of 1951 (*see* VEGLIARE CON SOLLECITUDINE). In the former document Pius XII stated unequivocally that artificial insemination is "absolutely to be rejected." In the latter he amplified the reasons for his condemnation. He stated

> To reduce the cohabitation of married persons and the conjugal act to a mere organic function for the transmission of the germ of life would be to convert the domestic hearth, sanctuary of the family, into nothing more than a biological laboratory. Hence in Our Allocution of 29 September 1949, to the International Congress of Catholic Doctors, We formally excluded artificial insemination from marriage. The conjugal act in its natural structure is a personal action, a simultaneous and immediate cooperation of the parties, which, by the very nature of the actors and the peculiar character of the act, is the expression of that mutual self-giving which, in the words of Holy Scripture, effects the union "in one flesh. . . ."
>
> This is much more than the mere union of two life-germs, which can be effected also artificially, that is, without the natural action of the spouses. The conjugal act, as it is ordained and willed by nature, is a personal cooperation, the right to which the parties have mutually conferred upon

each other in contracting marriage. [Tr. from Bousc-O'Connor 3:434.]

In summary, even if semen can be obtained licitly, it is immoral to use such a product for artificial insemination. The Pope also noted that if the natural act of intercourse is permanently impossible to a couple, the marriage must be considered invalid. Having a child by artificial insemination would not make such a marriage valid.

Heterologous Artificial Insemination. In the case of AID, since the semen is obtained from a donor other than the husband of the woman inseminated, the woman can be married or unmarried. Heterologous artificial insemination is immoral for the same basic reasons as those used in the evaluation of AIH, but there are also additional grounds for holding AID to be morally objectionable. In the above-cited 1949 document Pius XII made the following statement: "Artificial fecundation outside of marriage is to be condemned purely and simply as immoral." And again: "Artificial fecundation in marriage, but produced with the active element taken from a third party, is equally immoral and as such is to be condemned without reserve." The reasons for judging AID to be immoral also center about the methods used to obtain the semen, and the act of insemination itself.

Methods Used to Obtain Semen. The usual method for obtaining donor semen is masturbation, which is obviously immoral. For purposes of speculative elucidation, it may be pointed out that the following methods of obtaining semen, possible though not feasible in the situation, would also be immoral: condomistic intercourse, interrupted intercourse, fornicative and adulterous intercourse. Other methods for obtaining semen that are in themselves morally legitimate are immoral if the donor intends the product to be used for artificial insemination.

The Act of Artificial Insemination. Here, as in AIH, the very act of artificial insemination is immoral. This act, however, takes on an additional note of immorality precisely because the woman is not married to the donor. Hence, if either the man or the woman is married, the act of insemination takes on the note of injustice that characterizes *adultery. This is true whether the partner of the married person consents or not. If both donor and recipient are unmarried, the act of insemination is vitiated by the element of injustice involved in *fornication.

Assisted Insemination. Pius XII in his allocution of Sept. 29, 1949, stated explicitly that his condemnation of artificial insemination did not necessarily "proscribe the use of certain artificial means designed only to facilitate the natural act or to enable that act, done in the normal way, to attain its end."

The Pope gave no examples of procedures that might come within the meaning of these words. His thought seems adequately expressed in the term "assisted insemination." Theologians have suggested various techniques that would come within the meaning of "assisted insemination." They postulate in every example that the true marital act take place. This is obviously what Pius XII meant by "normal." For instance, if the husband were suffering from hypospadia, making ejaculation into the vagina impossible, the semen resulting from orgasm could not licitly be used for insemination. The same would be true of semen resulting from attempted but nonconsummated intercourse.

Once, however, a true marital act is postulated, various techniques may be used, either before the act or after it, that will assist fecundation. The use of a device by the wife to assist sperm migration through the *os cervicis* would be one example. The cervical spoon, when used to protect the spermatozoa from deleterious matter in the vagina, would be another. This latter would serve merely to conduct the sperm through an area of the female genital tract that is potentially dangerous to the life or the strength of the sperm.

Is it permissible to aspirate semen from the vagina into a syringe immediately after marital intercourse in order to place it deeper into the wife's vagina? Many moralists respond negatively. Others will permit it as long as the syringe is not removed from the vagina. Still others will allow the procedure even if the syringe is temporarily removed. Both of these procedures may be regarded as probably licit, and therefore permissible in practice.

Mention was made above of the probable opinion that a couple may have intercourse with a perforated condom in order to obtain a semen specimen. Would it be licit to take the content of the condom and use it for insemination? Among the few who discuss this question Alfred Boschi, SJ, emphatically rejects the permissibility of such a procedure. He argues that the semen to be inseminated never reposed in the vagina and therefore could not form part of the substance of the marital act (*Problemi Morali Del Matrimonio,* 289). A French moralist, P. Tiberghien, would apparently permit the procedure (*Médecine et Morale,* 191–192). It could be argued that the semen reposing in the condom did actually form part of the substance of the act and could therefore be used for subsequent insemination. While preferring Boschi's view, the author of this article would hesitate to deny that the contrary view may be followed at the present time.

Bibliography: Congregation of the Holy Office, "Dubium quoad artificialem foecundationem," (Decree, March 26, 1897) Act SSed 29 (1896–97) 704. PIUS XII, "Votre présence autour," (Address, Sept. 29, 1949) ActApS 41 (1949) 557–561. PIUS XII, "Vegliare con sollecitudine," (Address, Oct. 29, 1951) ActApS 43 (1951) 835–854. A. BOSCHI, *Problemi morali del matrimonio* (Turin 1953). H. DAVIS, *Artifical Human Fecundation* (London 1951). W. H. GLOVER, *Artificial Insemination among Human Beings* (Washington 1948). E. F. HEALY, *Medical Ethics* (Chicago 1956). H. HERING, *De Fecundatione artificiali* (Rome 1952). G. KELLY, *Medico-Moral Problems* (St. Louis 1961). C. P. TIBERGHIEN, *Médicine et morale* (Paris 1953).

[P. E. MC KEEVER]

ARTIFICIAL INSEMINATION (U.S. LAW OF)

Artificial insemination has been defined as "an attempt to further the chances of and facilitate the encounter between the female germ-cells, the ova, and the male seed, the semen, by artificial means." Artificial insemination is either homologous when the semen used is that of the husband of the inseminated woman (usually abbreviated to AIH), or heterologous in which case the semen is that of a third party donor (AID).

History and Early Cases. Although exact knowledge of the historical development of artificial insemination is lacking, it is generally conceded that the Arabs used this method as early as the 14th century to inseminate horses. The first recorded instance of human application is attributed to the English clinician, John Hunter, about 1799. Thereafter, the practice spread and gradually was adopted in many countries. The first recorded case, in 1883, was of an action by a doctor to collect medical fees for the insemination of the defendant, the husband being the donor. The Tribunal of Bordeaux, France, ruled against the doctor. In 1905, in Coblenz, Germany, a husband repudiated a child on the grounds of no cohabitation; the wife alleged artificial insemination with her husband's semen but without his knowledge. The courts affirmed the legitimacy of the child.

No court has ever found difficulty with AIH; the succeeding cases have to do with AID. The most quoted of legal precedents is the Canadian case, *Orford v. Orford,* 58 D.L.R. 251 (1921). Of special notice was not the holding of the case, which was one of ordinary adultery, but the dicta, which constituted a sharp indictment of AID. The essence of the offense of adultery, stated the court, consists not in the moral turpitude of the act of sexual intercourse but in the voluntary surrender to another person of the reproductive powers or faculties; and any act on the part of the wife that involves the possibility of introducing into the family of the husband a false strain of blood would be adulterous. This position was strengthened in the English case of *Russell v. Russell* [*Law Rep. A.C.* 687 (1924)], which held that the essence of adultery was not intercourse but fecundation *ab extra.* This thinking was modified in the Scottish case of *Maclennan v. Maclennan,* Scot Law Times (1958) 12, in which the court reasoned that the true test of adultery was *conjunctio corporum,* carnal connection.

U.S. Cases. The first U.S. case, *Hock v. Hock* (unreported) did not arise until 1945. This was an action for divorce in which AID was alleged, but the court found adultery in the ordinary sense and granted the plaintiff husband a divorce on that ground. As dicta the court ventured the opinion that artificial insemination, if proved, would not be adultery such as to constitute grounds for divorce. An unreported case in Chicago held AID not to be adulterous since the definition of adultery does not take AID into account. In the New York case, *Strnad v. Strnad,* 78 N.Y.S. 2d 390 (1948), the wife, contesting her husband's rights of visitation, alleged AID with the husband's consent. The court ruled in favor of the husband's rights in the best interests of the child. The child, explained the court, had been "potentially adopted or semi-adopted by the defendant," and hence defendant was "entitled to the same rights as those acquired by a foster parent who has formally adopted a child." Obviously, the court's sympathies were involved, since the New York statutes acknowledge adoption after a legal proceeding only. The legal position of AID was radically reformulated in *Doornbos v. Doornbos* (unreported). In a declaratory judgment, the court held that AID, with or without the consent of the husband, is contrary to public policy and good morals, and constitutes adultery on the part of the mother; a child so conceived is not a child born in wedlock and therefore illegitimate; as such, it is the child of the mother, and the father has no right or interest in said child. As for AIH, the court continued, it is not contrary to public policy and good morals and does not present any difficulty from the legal point of view. This constitutes, therefore, the first case in the U.S. in which AID was placed in the same category as adultery, and the AID child was declared illegitimate. Like the Orford case, with which it was substantially in agreement, this case provoked severe criticism.

Both the Orford and the Doornbos cases achieved new force with the most recent cases of *Gursky v. Gursky,* 242 N.Y.S. 2d 406 (1963), and *Anonymous v. Anonymous,* 246 N.Y.S. 2d 835 (1964), both of New York. The latter case is based squarely on the Gursky case as to the issue of support of an AID child. The Gursky case resolved itself to two issues, the legitimacy of the AID child and the husband's duty to support the issue of AID. As to legitimacy, the concept, said the court, "which historically is deeply imbedded in the law is that a child who is begotten through a father who is not the mother's husband is deemed to be illegitimate." The legislature of the state has confirmed this doctrine. Regarding the child's support, the court held that it did not follow from the determination of illegitimacy that the husband was thereby free of obligation to support the child. The husband's conduct and consent, said the court, implied a promise on his part to furnish support for the child and precluded any defense on the theory of equitable estoppel.

Summary. Based on relatively few cases, U.S. law on artificial insemination holds that the AID child is illegitimate, and with or without the consent of the husband, AID constitutes adultery on the part of the mother. The husband of the wife with an AID child stands in a dubious position. Possibly he may have rights of visitation if this is in the best interests of the child, and, practically without doubt, he must support the child. The third-party donor has had very little said about him; the Doornbos case held that the donor-father has no right or interest in his issue.

The courts have indicated that, other than relief obtainable under traditional theories of law, the remedy lies with the Legislature. To date, bills have been proposed in several states, but none has been enacted into law. The need for legislative intervention, however, grows by the day as such new facets as liability of physician and donor manifest themselves; entire areas have been untouched, such as property rights and rights of inheritance. There is also the new area of scientific experiment, with transplantation of ovaries and of the fertilized ovum, and the fertilization of the ovum outside the human organism.

As for the Church, the address of Pope Pius XII to the Second World Congress on Fertility and Sterility, on May 19, 1956, sets forth Catholic doctrine very clearly. The Holy Father rejected categorically the practice of AID; regarding AIH, the Holy Father sanctioned, as consistent with natural law, only those artificial methods intended simply either to facilitate the natural act or to enable the natural act, carried out in the natural manner, to attain its end. This has been referred to by some Catholic theologians as "assisted insemination."

Bibliography: A. M. SCHELLEN, *Artificial Insemination in the Human,* tr. M. E. HOLLANDER (Amsterdam, N.Y. 1957). A. F. LOGATTO, "Artificial Insemination," *Catholic Lawyer* 1 (1955) 172–184, 267–280; 2 (1956) 352–355, a brief, practical résumé of the legal, ethical, and psychiatric aspects. W. H. GLOVER, *Artificial Insemination among Human Beings* (Washington 1948). N. ST. JOHN-STEVAS, *Life, Death and the Law* (Bloomington, Ind. 1961).

[A. F. LO GATTO]

ARTIGAS, JOSÉ GERVASIO

Uruguayan revolutionary leader; b. Montevideo, June 19, 1764; d. Asunción, Paraguay, Sept. 23, 1850. Artigas, a descendant of one of the first settlers of Montevideo, was educated at the Colegio de San Francisco there. For some years he lived and worked as a gaucho. In 1797 he joined the regiment of *Blandengues,* a frontier guard for Montevideo, as a lieutenant. When the revolution of 1810 took place, he was a captain and

José Gervasio Artigas.

company commander. During this period, in which the foundation of his popular prestige was laid, he was in the service of the Spanish officer and naturalist Félix Azara, from whom he learned much. When the revolution of May 25, 1810, occurred in Buenos Aires, Artigas left his post in the Spanish forces and offered his services to the revolutionary junta early in 1811. Backed by its authority, he returned to his native region, organized the forces scattered through the countryside, and called the Banda Oriental to arms against the Spanish forces that held Montevideo. After several successful battles (Paso del Rey and San José), on May 18, 1811, he met a Spanish army under the command of José de Posadas at Las Piedras, and, with a maneuver that military historians consider very astute, defeated it. The battle of Las Piedras was of great political importance in fostering the spirit of revolution. Three days later Artigas besieged Montevideo. At the request of the Spanish viceroy Elío in Montevideo, a Portuguese army invaded the Banda Oriental and raised the siege. In these circumstances Artigas was proclaimed "Jefe de los orientales," and with his people, civilians as well as the army, he withdrew north of the Uruguay River in what has been called the Exodus of the Oriental People. After serious differences with the representative of the Buenos Aires government, Manuel Sarratea, Artigas broke with Buenos Aires and returned to military action in 1813 as the head of an independent state. On April 5 he called a congress to select representatives to the General Constituent Assembly of the United Provinces of Río de la Plata, which was meeting in Buenos Aires. This congress drew up the "Instructions" of 1813, the bases of the political and institutional ideology of Artigas. This document, influenced by the Articles of Confederation and the Federal Constitution of the U.S., defended the declaration of independence and provincial autonomy, the federal system of government, the division of powers, individual guarantees of civil and religious liberty, freedom of trade and navigation. The representatives bearing these instructions were not admitted to the Constituent Assembly, and this intensified the alienation of Artigas.

In June 1814 the royalist forces of Montevideo turned the city over to Buenos Aires, and the city had a brief period of Argentine government, but the next year Montevideo and the whole province came under control of Artigas. He consolidated his power in five provinces (Banda Oriental, Córdoba, Santa Fé, Entre Ríos, and Corrientes) and set up his capital in Purificación. In 1816 there was another Portuguese invasion, and Montevideo fell in January 1817. After his forces had suffered a number of defeats and all resistance was useless, Artigas withdrew into Paraguay in September 1820. There he remained the rest of his life. As a national hero of his country, he holds the universal admiration of Uruguayans.

Bibliography: J. STREET, *Artigas and the Emancipation of Uruguay* (Cambridge, Eng. 1959). E. ACEVEDO, *José Artigas; Su obra cívica: Alegato histórico,* 3 v. (Montevideo 1950). A. D. GONZÁLEZ, *Las primeras fórmulas constitucionales de los países del Plata, 1810–1814* (new ed. Montevideo 1962). **Illustration credit:** Pan American Union, Washington, D.C.

[A. D. GONZÁLEZ]

ARTUSI, GIOVANNI MARIA, music theorist of the Roman conservative circle; b. Bologna, Italy, 1540 (1545?); d. Bologna, 1613. By 1562 he was a canon of the Congregation of the Saviour. Though his polemics against *Monteverdi put him in the early Italian baroque, it is difficult not to classify him with the Renaissance. He took exception not only to the *seconda prattica* of Monteverdi, but also wrote against *Gesualdo, Vincentino, *Rore, and A. *Gabrieli, showing how they had strayed from classical Renaissance traditions. In *L'Arte del contrapunto* (1586–89; microprint, Rochester, N.Y. 1954) he showed himself a conservative student of Zarlino, but later attacked even him. Other writings were *L'Artusi, overo delle imperfettioni della moderna musica* (1600) and *Considerazioni musicali* (1603). He remained a defender of the old styles until the end, but in later life he softened with regard to Monteverdi's music, which he even professed to admire. Of his compositions a book of four-voiced *Canzonette* is well known (1598).

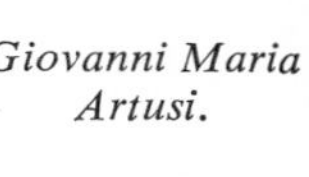

Giovanni Maria Artusi.

See also MUSIC, SACRED, HISTORY OF, 5.

Bibliography: Strunk SourceR. H. F. REDLICH, MusGG 1:747–749. Reese MusR. L. SCHRADE, *Monteverdi: Creator of Modern Music* (New York 1950). G. GASPARI, *Dei musicisti bolognesi al XVI secolo* (Bologna 1876). G. B. MARTINI, *Esemplare ossia saggio fondamentale di contrapunto,* 2 v. (Bologna 1774–75). **Illustration credit:** Antonio Bonavera.

[F. J. SMITH]

ARUNDEL, JOHN, bishop and physician; b. Cornwall, England; d. Oct. 18, 1477. He held a fellowship at Exeter College, Oxford, from 1420 until 1431. During that time he served as principal of a hall, possibly St. Mildred's, in 1424 and as junior proctor of the university in 1426–27. He was a master of arts and a doctor of medicine by 1457. Having been ordained in 1432, he was serving as chaplain and physician to King *Henry VI by 1453 and retained this office until at least 1456. A medical work, *Medicamenta contra sciaticam passionem,* has been attributed to him. In 1457 he was a commissioner appointed to conclude a peace with Scotland. He held prebendaries at numerous cathedrals before 1457, in which year he became archdeacon of Richmond. In 1459 he was made bishop of *Chichester by papal *provision. Since his register is no longer extant, it is impossible to judge his 18 years of episcopal administration. He may have built the screen across the west end of the choir in his cathedral church (since removed to a nearby campanile); the cathedral still contains his tomb.

Bibliography: J. H. BAXTER, DHGE 4:846. Emden 1:49–50; 2:ix–x. LeNeve FastEcclAngli v.7.

[H. S. REINMUTH, JR.]

ARUNDEL, JOHN, bishop; d. at the episcopal palace, London, March 15, 1504. He was the third son of Sir Renfrey and Lady Jane Arundel of Lanherne, Cornwall, of one of the foremost families in the west country, and he was educated at Oxford (B.A. 1457, M.A. by 1461, and bachelor of theology by 1473). His family connections doubtless assisted his ecclesiastical promotion: he was dean of Exeter (1483–96) and bishop of Lichfield and Coventry by papal provision (1496), until his translation to Exeter (1502). As a curialist he was chaplain to Edward IV in 1479 and diplomatic representative on missions in 1485 and 1488 for Henry VII, who also made him chancellor to Arthur, Prince of Wales, in 1493. During his brief episcopate at Exeter he continued his family's tradition of generous hospitality by daily almsgiving at the palace gate; he was noted also for his love of learning.

Bibliography: Emden 1:50–51. A. L. ROWSE, *Tudor Cornwall* (London 1941).

[H. S. REINMUTH, JR.]

ARUNDEL, THOMAS

Archbishop, chancellor of England, foe of Lollards; b. 1352; d. Feb. 19, 1414. He was the son of Richard Fitzalan, Earl of Arundel, whose title he used as a surname; his mother, Eleanor, his father's second wife, was daughter and coheiress of Henry, Earl of Lancaster. His studies at Oriel College, Oxford, were terminated by his exceptionally early promotion to the bishopric of *Ely, to which he was provided by the Pope (Aug. 13, 1373) in opposition to both King *Edward III and the cathedral chapter. On the same day that he was consecrated bishop (April 9, 1374) he was ordained both deacon and priest. During the turbulent reign of *Richard II, Arundel joined his brother Richard, Earl of Arundel, in opposition to the King. He supported the Lords' Appellant (1386–88) and served as Lord Chancellor (1386–89). When Abp. *Alexander Neville of York was translated *in partibus* to the schismatic See of *Saint Andrews, Scotland (*see* WESTERN SCHISM), Arundel was translated to *York (April 3, 1388). In May 1389 he relinquished the great seal to William of *Wykeham, but he resumed the chancellorship in 1391 and held it until his translation to the Archbishopric of *Canterbury (Sept. 25, 1397). However, the Commons impeached and banished him as Richard II's former adversary at the same time that his brother, the Earl of Arundel, was appealed of treason, summarily condemned, and executed (Sept. 1397). Arundel fled to Rome, but Richard II's will prevailed, and Pope *Boniface IX translated him, as his predecessor at York, Neville, *in partibus* to Saint Andrews. After he had traveled widely on the Continent, visiting among others the great Florentine humanist Coluccio *Salutati, Arundel joined Henry Plantagenet, with whom he returned to England in July 1399; restored to his see, he crowned Henry IV (Oct. 13, 1399). Subsequently Arundel proved an efficient and vigorous administrator: he made a *visitation of his entire province, successfully maintained his right to visit Oxford University, and provided new statutes for the Court of *Arches. Most important he became a vigorous opponent of *Lollards, whom he fought through provincial councils at London (1397) and at Oxford (1408) and through constitutions regulating preaching and forbidding the translation of the Bible into the vernacular; above all he worked in cooperation with the secular authority through parliament. In 1401 he was instrumental in securing the passage of the statute *De heretico comburendo,* after which he presided at the trials of Lollard sympathizers John *Purvey and William Sawtry (1401), John Badby (1410), and Sir John *Oldcastle (1413). In addition, he vigorously opposed the Commons's demand for disendowment of the Church, especially in 1404 and 1410. He served Henry IV as chancellor (1407–10 and 1412–13). Because of his exercise of authority during Henry's illness, he earned the resentment of Henry V, who replaced Arundel as chancellor with Henry *Beaufort upon his accession in 1413. Arundel was buried in a tomb, since destroyed, in Canterbury cathedral.

Bibliography: Arundel's registers are extant in MS: Ely at the Ely Diocesan Registry; York, Borthwick Institute of Historical Research; Canterbury, Lambeth Palace Library, London. J. GAIRDNER, DNB 1:609–613. A. STEEL, *Richard II* (Cambridge, Eng. 1941; repr. 1963). K. B. MCFARLANE, *John Wycliffe and the Beginnings of English Nonconformity* (New York 1953). Emden 1:51–53. LeNeve FastEcclAngli 4:4, 14 for Canterbury and Ely; 6:4.

[H. S. REINMUTH, JR.]

ARUNDELL, THOMAS, first Baron Arundell of Wardour, soldier and statesman; b. 1560; d. Wardour, Nov. 7, 1639. He was of probable Norman descent, the great grandson of Sir John Arundell of Lanherne and the son of Sir Matthew (d. 1598), who resettled this branch of the family at Wardour (1570). With Queen Elizabeth's commendatory letters (1579–80), Sir Thomas served the Emperor, Rudolph II. For seizing the Ottoman standard at Gran (1595), he was created Count of the Holy Roman Empire by letters patent (Dec. 14, 1595). In England again in 1596, he unwisely claimed precedence as Imperial Count over certain English peers, and was imprisoned in the Tower. In spite of Arundell's apologetic letter to Lord Burghley, Elizabeth protested to the Emperor (March 13, 1595 O.S.; 1596 N.S.) against this honor given and received without her consent. Arundell was pardoned under the Great Seal (Nov. 17, 1603), and created Baron Arundell of Wardour (May 4, 1605). He undertook with Henry

Thomas Arundell, oil on panel, 4 by 5¼ inches, by an unknown 17th-century English artist.

Wriothesley, Earl of Southampton, to equip a voyage of discovery to America, and in the summer of 1605, became commander of the English regiment serving Archduke Albert in Flanders against the Dutch. Arundell maintained a good understanding with the English government through the ambassador, Sir Thomas Edmondes. Active in the parliament of 1605 to 1611, he sat on several committees, and took the oath of allegiance in 1610. In 1614, he was on a committee to consider a bill "for the preservation and increase of wood and timber," as in the previous parliament. He was too ill to attend the parliament of 1621, and at Charles I's accession (1625) was disarmed as a recusant, later receiving a pardon (Feb. 10, 1626).

Bibliography: G. OLIVER, *Collections Illustrating the History of the Catholic Religion in the Counties . . .* (London 1857) 75–80. W. H. TREGELLAS, DNB 1:620–621. DictEngCath 1:71–72. **Illustration credit:** National Portrait Gallery, London.

[F. EDWARDS]

ARVAD, a Phoenician city mentioned in Ez 27.8–9; 1 Mc 15.23 (see also Gn 10.18; 1 Chr 1.16). It was built on a practically impregnable rocky island off Ṭarṭūs (Tortosa) on the coast of Syria, at the mouth of the Eleutherus River (Nahr el-Kebīr). It was referred to in the *Amarna Letters (14th century B.C.) and in the annals of Tiglath-Pileser I (1116–1078 B.C.). Long independent, Arvad was eventually conquered by the Persians, whence it passed to Alexander the Great and the Ptolemies. The island and its town are now called Erwâd or Ruâd. Phoenician ruins, particularly a gigantic wall, are still visible on three sides of the island.

Bibliography: J. BENZINGER, Pauly-Wiss RE 2.1 (1895) 371–372. F. M. ABEL, DBSuppl 1:597–598. Abel GéorgPal 2:251–252. R. NORTH, LexThK² 1:912. A. ROMEO, EncCatt 1:1754–55. R. JANIN, DHGE 3:1345–46. J. D. DAVIS and H. S. GEHMAN, *The Westminster Dictionary of the Bible* (Philadelphia 1944) 43, 481–482. A. S. KAPELRUD, InterDictBibl 1:242–243.

[I. J. MAUSOLF]

ÅS (ASYLUM), ABBEY OF, a former *Cistercian monastery located at the mouth of the Viska River, Halland, Sweden, in the former Archdiocese of *Lund (also known as *Aos, Aas, Asylum*). It was founded in 1194, probably by Waldemar (d. *c.* 1237), a son of King Canute V of Denmark and Bishop of Schleswig, and placed in the care of Cistercian monks who had been encouraged to come to the area by Abp. *Eskil of Lund. It was affiliated to the abbey of Sorö, near Copenhagen, which was in turn a daughterhouse of Esrom, founded directly from *Clairvaux. Very little is known of the history of the abbey. Two daughters of the Swedish king Magnus Eriksson were buried there *c.* 1340, and Queen Margaret of Denmark gave the monastery a gilded table with relics, asking the community for remembrance in its prayers; in return, her deceased father, King Waldemar, was affiliated with the order. During the last decades of the 14th century two of the abbots later became abbots of Sorö. The records show that the abbey was devastated by fire in 1397, and a document of 1441 notes that the church of the monastery was damaged and had no roof. In 1535 the last abbot, Mats Eriksson, was appointed as the first Protestant rector of the parishes of Veddige and Ås. The abbey was later destroyed.

Bibliography: P. VON MÖLLER, *Bidrag till Hallands historia* (Lund 1874), v.1. J. M. CANIVEZ, DHGE 4:865–867. Cottineau 1:168–169.

[O. ODENIUS]

ASA, KING OF JUDA, *c.* 913 to *c.* 873, son of Abia (*c.* 915–*c.* 913). The reign of Asa (Heb. *'āsā'*) is recounted in 3 Kgs 15.9–24; 2 Chr 14.1–16.14. He is praised for his vigorous action against sacred prostitution [*see* PROSTITUTION (IN THE BIBLE)] and idolatry, in which he even went so far as to destroy an idol worshiped by his mother Maacha. The praise of the Deuteronomistic editor of Kings (*see* DEUTERONOMISTS) is somewhat modified, however, by the usual complaint that he "did not destroy the *high places." The Book of Kings records that "there was war between Asa and King Baasa of Israel [*c.* 900–*c.* 877] all their days" (3 Kgs 15.16). That Asa was largely successful against Baasa (Heb. *ba'šâ* or *ba'śâ*) was due in large part to the help he had from *Ben-Adad (Ben-Hadad) I of Damascus, whom he bribed with gifts from the treasures of the Temple and the royal palace.

Bibliography: M. RHEM, LexThK² 1:915. G. PRIERO, EncCatt 2:74–75. R. RENARD, DB 1.2:1051–54. EncDictBibl 141–142.

[B. MC GRATH]

ASARHADDON (ESARHADDON), KING OF ASSYRIA (680–669 B.C.). The third oldest son of *Sennacherib (705–682), Asarhaddon (Assyrian *Aššûr-aḫa-iddin,* the god "Assur has given a brother"; Heb. *'ēsarḥaddōn*) was appointed crown prince in 681 at the insistence of his Aramaean mother Naqiya. He succeeded his father on the throne after putting down the revolt of his parricidal brothers (4 Kgs 19.37; Is 37.38). He engaged in only a few large-scale military campaigns, such as those in Phoenicia and Egypt. With the power of his army he was able to keep his vassals in submission. For the construction of his large palace at Ninive he received tribute from his vassal kings, including *Manasse of Juda (*c.* 687–*c.* 642; see Pritchard ANET[2] 291a). To protect his supply line for a projected invasion of Egypt, he neutralized the Phoenician city-states, controlled the Arabian tribes, and resettled Samaria (Ezr 4.2). After launching an unsuccessful attack on Egypt in 673, Asarhaddon, urged by the queen mother Naqiya, appointed an older son, Shamash-shum-ukin, king of Babylon and designated another son, Assurbanipal, crown prince of Assyria. In the Egyptian campaign of 671 the Assyrian troops overran the delta and took *Memphis (Noph). When Pharao Theraca (Tirhakah) of the Ethiopian Dynasty of Upper Egypt revolted in 670, Asarhaddon, though ailing, prepared to conduct a new expedition in person. He died at *Haran en route to Egypt in the fall of 669 and was succeeded by *Assurbanipal.

Bibliography: A. T. E. Olmstead, *History of Assyria* (New York 1923) 337–385. H. Schmökel, *Geschichte des alten Vorderasien* (Handbuch der Orientalistik Abt. 1, v.2.3; Leiden 1957) 274–278. R. Borger, *Die Inschriften Asarhaddons* (ArchOr; Graz 1956). D. Wiseman, "The Vassal Treaties of Esarhaddon," *Iraq* 20 (1958) 1–99. ReallexAssyr 1:198–203. F. Gössmann, LexThK[2] 1:96. G. Boson, EncCatt 2:78. EncDictBibl 142–143. Pritchard ANET[2] 289–294.

[M. A. HOFER]

ASBURY, FRANCIS, first Methodist bishop in America; b. Handsworth, England, Aug. 21, 1745; d. Spotsylvania, Va., March 31, 1816. His parents were poor, and after a scanty common school education he was apprenticed to a blacksmith. In 1763 he was converted and became a lay preacher, while continuing to work at the forge. In 1766 he was asked to take the place of an ailing Methodist itinerant and thereafter

Francis Asbury.

devoted himself entirely to preaching. At the Bristol Conference in 1771 he volunteered for America; he arrived at Philadelphia, Pa., on Oct. 27, 1771. He set out at once on a preaching tour of New Jersey and southern New York, forming new congregations and strengthening old ones. Devoted to John *Wesley's principle of itinerancy, he never again had a home and, with one brief exception, continued these missionary journeys until his death. Between 1772 and 1776 he preached in Pennsylvania, Maryland, Virginia, and West Virginia. Because of war conditions, he was in partial retirement in Maryland and Delaware until 1780; in the ensuing years he continued preaching from North Carolina to New York.

In November 1784 Thomas Coke and Richard Whatcoat arrived from England to discuss proposals for the organization of an independent Episcopal Church. At the Christmas conference in Baltimore, Asbury was chosen superintendent with Dr. Coke and on three successive days was ordained deacon, elder, and finally superintendent on Dec. 27, 1784. Asbury later used the title bishop, although this was repugnant to Wesley. The *Form of Discipline* was adopted in 1785 and the *Arminian Magazine* begun in 1789. Throughout this period, Asbury continued his itinerant ministry, visiting existing congregations and penetrating South Carolina (1785), Georgia and Tennessee (1788), and New England (1791). He was able to block Coke's efforts at reunion with the Protestant Episcopal Church in 1791; his insistence on itinerancy made the remarkable growth of Methodism possible. He was less successful in his efforts against slavery. In 1785 he petitioned the Virginia Assembly in favor of general emancipation and sought to make abolitionism a principle of the Methodist Church. He ordained Richard Allen as the first Negro Methodist minister in 1799 but was unable to prevent the change from separate Negro congregations (1793–95) to a wholly independent African Methodist Episcopal Church. He was an early advocate of camp meetings and made them a fixture of American Methodism. Despite his continual journeys, his health was always precarious, and in 1800 Bishop Whatcoat was chosen to assist him. He continued his missionary labors, however, and died on a preaching tour.

Bibliography: F. Asbury, *Journal and Letters,* ed. E. T. Clark et al., 3 v. (Nashville 1958). H. K. Carroll, *Francis Asbury in the Making of American Methodism* (New York 1923). W. L. Duren, *Francis Asbury* (New York 1928). W. C. Larrabee, *Asbury and His Coadjutors,* ed. D. W. Clark, 2 v. (Cincinnati 1853). W. P. Strickland, *The Pioneer Bishop* (New York 1858). E. S. Tipple, *Francis Asbury: The Prophet of the Long Road* (New York 1916).

[R. K. MAC MASTER]

ASCALON, ancient city located on the seacoast between *Gaza and *Azotus (Ashdod). It was mentioned in Egyptian writings of the Middle Kingdom and in the *Amarna Letters. About 1285 B.C. *Ramses II conquered the city after it had revolted from Egypt. His conquest is depicted on the temple wall at Karnak. In turn the *Philistines took the city (*c.* 1200 B.C.) and made it one of their five principal cities.

Although Ascalon (Heb. *'ašqᵉlon*) is mentioned in Jgs 1.18 as conquered by Juda, other Biblical passages show that this was not the case and that it remained a Philistine city during the times of the Judges and David (Jos 13.3; 1 Sm 6.7; 2 Sm 1.20). The Prophet Amos predicted ruin for the city and its ruler (Am 1.8). This did in fact prove true under the conquering might of *Tiglath-Pileser III in 734–732. In the following century, internal and external difficulties kept Ascalon in an unsettled situation. When *Nabuchodonosor demanded submission and payment of tribute from Ascalon, the city refused and was decisively punished and destroyed (Jer 47.5–7), and many of its inhabitants were deported to Babylon.

During the Persian period, Ascalon suffered under the yoke of Tyre. After the conquest of Alexander the Great it became Hellenistic and a center of anti-Jewish activity (1 Mc 10.86). Under the Romans, Ascalon became a free city in 104 B.C., and *Herod the Great, though he did not rule the city, constructed baths and other public buildings there. In A.D. 66 it was partly destroyed by the Jews. Later Ascalon recovered, and eventually it became a Christian city. During the Crusades it changed several times between Moslem and Christian masters. Excavations have revealed extensive remains from the Hellenistic and Roman periods and traces from the Philistinian and earlier periods.

Bibliography: F. M. ABEL, DBSuppl 1:621–628. Abel Géogr Pal 2:252–253. L. GROLLENBERG, LexThK² 1:927–928. G. M. PERRELLA, EncCatt 2:81–82. W. F. STINESPRING, InterDictBibl 1:252–254. EncDictBibl 144. R. JANIN, DHGE 4:875–876.

[D. A. PANELLA]

ASCELLINO (Asselino, Anselmo), Dominican from Lombardy; papal envoy to the Tartars. His antecedents and the dates of his birth and death are not known. In 1245 he headed one of four missions that Innocent IV sent by different routes to the Tartars, who were exhorted to cease their depredations and become Christians. Apparently, he was also commissioned to treat with the dissidents and Moslem sultans of the Near East with regard to reunion and conversion. These tasks occupied him and his Dominican staff of four until the fall of 1246. Going from Acre, the friars contacted the Tartar general Batschu in the Transcaucasus (or middle Persia) on May 24, 1247, 59 days after leaving Tiflis. Ascellino's undiplomatic refusal to follow Oriental protocol endangered the lives of the envoys and led to great discomfort, hunger, and insults. Finally Batschu accepted the papal letters but forced Ascellino to await a reply from the Grand Khan. He departed for Europe on July 25, 1247, accompanied by two Tartar envoys to the pope. The letters from the Khan and Batschu were arrogant, demanding papal submission to the Tartars. Ascellino reached Lyons in the autumn of 1248. His later career is unknown. The story of his martyrdom in Asia is pure speculation.

Bibliography: B. ALTANER, *Die Dominikanermissionen des 13. Jh.: Forschungen zur Geschichte der kirchlichen Unionen unter den Mohammedanern* (Breslauer Studien zur historischen Theologie 3; Habelschwerdt 1924). P. PELLIOT, "Les Mongols et le papauté," *Revue de l'Orient Chrétien* 24 (1924) 265–335.

[W. A. HINNEBUSCH]

ASCENSION ISLAND, volcanic island in the South Atlantic, 35 square miles in area, 703 miles northwest of *Saint Helena and 1,770 miles west of Angola in Africa. It was discovered by the Portuguese on Ascension Day, 1501, and occupied by the British in 1815. Since 1922 it has been part of the British colony of Saint Helena. Before the construction of the Suez Canal it had some military importance protecting trade routes to the East. The island now serves as a cable station and as a missile tracking station for the U.S. In 1964 its population was estimated at 500. Among the predominantly Protestant inhabitants there were about 30 Catholics, served by an occasional visiting priest. Ecclesiastically Ascension Island is subject to the Archdiocese of *Cape Town.

[J. E. BRADY]

ASCENSION OF JESUS CHRIST

The Church believes that the risen Jesus "ascended into heaven" in body and soul (Denz 11, and in the creeds generally).

BIBLICAL

In its widest sense the Ascension includes three moments: the final historical departure of Jesus from His disciples, the metahistorical passage and entry into heaven, and the exaltation, also metahistorical, "at the right hand of the Father." Three groups of NT texts describe these three moments: those that narrate the visible departure of Jesus as a *terminus a quo;* those that treat of the Ascension from a primarily theological aspect, more or less explicitly referring to the witnessed departure while concentrating on the metahistorical victory; and, finally, those texts that refer to the *exaltation of Jesus as a *terminus ad quem* without explicit mention of the previous moments. This article under the heading "Biblical" treats the first two moments.

Visible Departure. The primitive kerygma recorded in 1 Cor 15.3–8 mentions no final leave-taking of the risen Jesus. The early Jerusalem preaching (see below) refers to Jesus' departure only in as far as it is theologically significant and never turns to the material details of when, where, and how that are the indispensable data for the historian. The early preaching, for which the continual presence of the risen Jesus with believers (Mt 28.20) was the all important datum, may well have considered such details irrelevant. The departure of Jesus did not alter essentially the relation of the believer to his Lord. He had been seen, and He would be seen again—soon, they hoped; meanwhile, His invisible presence perdured.

As years lengthened into decades and fervent hope for the *Parousia was tempered by the full realization that no one knew the exact time of the future return (Mk 13.32; Acts 1.6–7, 11), the second generation of Christians desired to know further details about the final visible departure of Jesus. Luke responded by gleaning from the first-generation preaching and its documentary precipitate (Lk 1.1–4) such details as he could concerning the when, where, and how of Jesus' departure.

The final chapter of St. Luke's Gospel describes appearances of the risen Jesus to the disciples at *Emmaus (24.13–33, 35), to Peter (24.34), and to the Eleven (24.36–43). The narrative seems to place these events on the day of the Resurrection (24.13), and the following discourse (24.44–49) is not distinguished in time from the preceding meal. The notice of the Ascension then occurs with no indication of its being separated from the preceding materials. "He then [Gr. δέ] led them out towards Bethany, and lifting up his hands, he blessed them. While he blessed them, he parted [aorist] from them *and was carried up* [imperfect] *into heaven*" (24.50–51). The italicized words are found in P⁷⁵, B, A, W, and Θ, but they are omitted by S, D, and the Western tradition, perhaps because of the difficulty of harmonizing these verses with Acts 1.1–12. The form and the language of this notice are filled with cultic connotations. Certain data are, however, of a primarily historical nature. At first glance, since the day of the Resurrection frames all the other events in this chapter, it seems that Luke has placed the Ascen-

Fig. 1. The three Marys at the tomb and the Ascension of Jesus, ivory plaque, carved probably in north Italy, c. 400; in the Bavarian National Museum, Munich. Christ, in the sight of two of His Apostles, ascends to heaven, grasping the hand of God the Father.

sion during Easter night (see 24.29). Yet there are no indications of time in this chapter after 24.33, and their absence might well be deliberate and theologically motivated. Luke depicts Jesus' departure as occurring after He had led His disciples out of Jerusalem up the western slope and over the crest of Mt. Olivet to Bethany (15 stadia from Jerusalem, according to Jn 11.18, or about 1⅝ miles). There, in the very act of blessing them, He made His final departure (verb in the aorist). The next action is presented as a progressive movement that takes time (verb in the imperfect), as the risen Jesus is borne into the sky. Even here the simply physical movement is described with the theologically evocative ἀναφέρειν, usually used in the NT for an offering of sacrifice.

The Ascension also figures in the canonical conclusion of Mark (Mk 16.19), which is the Gospel reading for the Feast of the Ascension in the Roman rite. The text is certainly canonical and inspired (Denz 1502), and the verse in question may even belong to a very archaic creed, but historically speaking the notice is dependent upon the traditions recorded in Luke and John and thus cannot be treated as a primary witness.

The only lengthy description of Jesus' Ascension in the NT is Acts 1.1–11 (the epistle for the feast in the Roman Missal). Luke begins by recapitulating his Gospel, noting that his first volume had extended "until the day that . . . [Jesus] was taken up . . ." (Acts 1.2—the original Western tradition may have omitted the verb). The events that were framed as a miniature within the "day" of the Resurrection Luke now sketches on a broader temporal canvas. The appearances of the risen Lord are now said to have occurred "during 40 days" (1.3), a number that need not be taken as exact (cf. Acts 13.30–31; Mk 1.13) but simply as referring to a rather lengthy period. After noting Jesus' final instructions (1.4–5, 7–8; cf. Lk 24.47–49), Luke begins his description of the Ascension itself with the words, "he was lifted up before their eyes, and a cloud took him from their sight" (1.9). The narrative unmistakably emphasizes that the departure had been witnessed. The language, however, is highly charged theologically. The verb of v. 9a is usually used in the NT of gestures associated with prayer and hope (cf. Lk 18.13; 21.28; 24.50); in v. 9b the cloud (cf. Lk 9.34–35) is represented as bearing Jesus off as on a chariot [cf. 4 Kgs 2.10–12; Ps 103(104).3]. The witnesses did not grasp the full significance of this leave-taking. But while "they were still staring after him into the sky," a revelation given by "two men in white garments" (1.10; cf. Lk 24.4) enabled them to begin to penetrate what they had seen. This last glimpse of the risen Jesus borne into heaven on a cloud was a sign and promise of how He would appear again (cf. Mk 13.26; 14.62 and parallels). Luke's narrative then closes with a reference to Mt. Olivet as the scene of the departure (cf. Lk 24.50).

Entrance into Glory. The next question concerning the Ascension moves from the area of the historically verifiable to the metahistorical. No passage says that the disciples understood that this was the last appearance of Jesus to them in their lifetime. Ever since His Resurrection His visible presence had not been continuous, but He had appeared to His disciples only to vanish again (Lk 24.31). Where was He at other times? The answer (implicit in the arrangement of the materials in Luke ch. 24) is explicit in Jn 20.17. On the morning of the Resurrection, Jesus, appearing to Mary Magdalene, says: "Do not cling to me, for I have not yet ascended to the Father. Rather go to my brothers and tell them 'I am ascending to my Father and your Father, to my God and your God.' " The disciples first saw Jesus on that evening (Jn 20.19). Evidently, in John's thought, when the risen Jesus left Mary Magdalene, He ascended to heaven. Thence He returned for each later appearance. Thus an "ascension," a return to the Father's glory [*see* GLORY (IN THE BIBLE)], is implied after every appearance of the risen Jesus. He was no longer earthbound, and the Ascension was linked immediately with His Resurrection as part of a single movement from the grave to glory. Eventually the term Ascension was reserved for what had proved to be the final leave-taking of Jesus.

What happened to Jesus after His departure? An answer to this can be had only from revelation. The archaic Jerusalem kerygma presumed the fact of the Ascension (Acts 5.30–31) and probed its metahistorical aspect by applying the words and concepts of the OT to what the disciples had witnessed [Acts 2.33–35, using Ps 109(110).1]. The Pauline didache of Eph 4.7–10, in like fashion, uses Ps 67(68).19 to show that "he ascended far above all the heavens, that he might fill all things." Thus the Ascension brought everything in the universe into contact with the risen Jesus. The ancient Christian hymn quoted in 1 Tm 3.16 links "taken up in glory" with "seen by angels" and thus specifies those who witnessed the Ascension victory. The baptismal didache of 1 Pt 3.18–22 specifies still further that "the spirits that were in prison" (i.e., fallen angels, conceived as imprisoned in the lower "heavens"; cf. Eph 1.20–21; 2.2; Col 2.15) became subject to the risen Jesus as He ascended. The Ascension is used in the Epistle to the *Hebrews as a theological fact linked to the priesthood of Jesus, who passed through the heavens as a great high priest (Heb 4.14) to enter the heavenly sanctuary (6.19–20; 9.24).

Ascension in Early Christian Literature. The writings of the Apostolic Fathers contain no reference to the Ascension, but Judeo-Christian literature, with its distinctive theological methodology, exploited it fully. These writers added Psalm 23(24) to those already used in the NT as loci for the Ascension. Their central interest was the manifestation of Jesus' victory in the realm of the angels, both good and bad; but the details they give are patently nonhistorical.

In the writings of Justin the perils inherent in using the Jewish Ascension imagery appear, for he was compelled to defend the fact of Jesus' Ascension (1 *Apol.* 50) as something quite different from the "ascensions" of Dionysus, Bellerophon (1 *Apol.* 54), and Heracles (*Dial.* 69). Irenaeus reaffirmed the basic fact of the Ascension (*Dem.* 83–85), evidently depending upon Acts 1.9–12, and he used Psalms 23(24) and 67(68) to develop the theological aspects of the event.

The centrality of the Ascension in the faith of the Church is witnessed not only by the most archaic creeds but also by the Roman Canon, where it figures with the Passion and Resurrection in a summary of Jesus' whole redemptive work.

Bibliography: EncDictBibl 144–150. F. J. SCHIERSE, LexThK[2] 5:358–360. E. LUCCHESI-PALLI, *ibid.* 362–363. P. BENOIT, "L'Ascension," RevBibl 56 (1949) 161–203, repr. in *Exégèse et*

Fig. 2. The Ascension of Jesus, early 14th-century fresco by Giotto in the Scrovegni Chapel at Padua, Italy.

théologie, 2 v. (Paris 1961) 1:363–411. J. DANIÉLOU, *The Theology of Jewish Christianity,* ed. and tr. J. A. BAKER (Chicago 1964) 248–263. E. H. SCHILLEBEECKX, "Ascension and Pentecost," *Worship* 35 (1961) 336–363.

[J. D. QUINN]

THEOLOGICAL

The Ascension of Jesus Christ, theologically speaking, is first a mystery of faith; second, it is an event that has a meaning in God's plan to save mankind because it concerns the human nature of Christ; and, third, it has, as an essential element in the mystery of salvation, a meaning in the life of each Christian now and for eternity.

Mystery of Faith. As an object of *faith the Ascension is not something the contemporary believer can see or sense in any way [*see* MYSTERY (IN THEOLOGY)]. The reality one believes is that the human nature of the risen Christ has been taken into the sphere of divine life with the Father, Son, and Holy Spirit in power and majesty. This reality of Christ's bodily entry into a new order of existence transcends the experience of one's human senses and imagination and as a result can only be inadequately represented in the human expressions used to describe it. One must be careful, therefore, not to mistake the total reality of faith with the presentation that is used in Scripture to express it. The inspired writers and the Creed speak of Christ as "going up" and "sitting" at the "right hand" of the Father. Certainly the presentation here, as far as the total reality of faith is concerned, is anthropomorphic, and the total meaning conveyed is in a sphere beyond its quite human idiom of communication. Biblical scholars (especially P. Benoit, OP, and P. Miquel, OSB), in their awareness of this difference, have distinguished two aspects of the Ascension: (1) the invisible aspect, or theological fact of Christ's exaltation and glorification with the Father in heaven that in this area is the principal object of faith; and (2) the visible aspect, or historical fact (also object of faith) of Christ's manifestation of His glory that was incorporated in His last farewell on Mt. Olivet (Acts

1.3, 9–11). One uses the word Ascension for either of these or both, but the latter is also a sign of the divine reality contained in the former.

Salvation Event. The role of theology is to investigate the meaning of this event, as an object of faith, and to examine and elucidate its meaning in relation to the other mysteries of faith and the final goal of mankind. What then is the theological significance of this exaltation of Christ's manhood? The dogmatic definition of Chalcedon, that Christ is one Person in two natures, implies that one and the same Person, the Son of God, also took on a visible human nature. In His humanity Christ is the Son of God. Therefore Christ is God in a human way and man in a divine way. Everything Christ does as man is therefore an act of the Son of God; His acts then are a penetration of a divine activity into a human activity (*see* THEANDRIC ACTS OF CHRIST). His human love is the embodiment of the redeeming love of God. Now it is precisely because the human acts of Christ are divine acts of the Son of God that He can fulfill God's promise of *salvation in the concrete way intended by God. As divine acts in visible human form they possess a divine saving power and are therefore causes of man's salvation, accomplished in time and space but transcending the limits of time and space. Although this is true of every human action of Christ, it is especially true of those actions that, though enacted in His human nature, are by nature acts of God (because actions are done by persons) bringing man back to Himself. This truth is realized in a special way in the great mysteries of Christ's life: His Passion, death, Resurrection, and exaltation to the side of His Father.

Fig. 3. The Ascension, detail, German woodcut, 1485.

St. John and St. Paul (each in his own way) link the Ascension with Christ's death and Resurrection and point out its relationship in the total picture of salvation. John's Gospel gives a central place to the redemptive work of Christ in His death and Resurrection. However, it must be remembered that for John "glory" and "lifted up" refer to all the aspects of salvation: Passion, Resurrection, and Ascension (Jn 12.32–33; 3.13; 6.63). For John the Resurrection and Ascension are but two aspects of the same mystery (Jn 13.1). Exalted in glory at the right hand of the Father (Jn 12.23; 17.5), Christ sends the Holy Spirit (Jn 7.39) and through Him extends His dominion over the world (Jn 16.14).

For Paul the Ascension takes on a value in terms of man's salvation because Jesus was not only a man among men, but a new Adam (Rom 5.18). Hence each event of Christ's life modifies the condition of our own life to the very depths of our being. The mystery of man's salvation, accomplished by Christ, is not simply paying a debt or a buying back, but rather it is a mysterious but very real transformation of mankind in Christ. Salvation, in its most profound reality, is for Paul the God-Man in the Person of the Son incarnate, agreeing to succumb to the power of death but soon snatching His victory from it by His Resurrection. His Ascension renders this victory definitive. Mankind thus enters into the sphere of the Trinity once and for all in the Person of the Word incarnate as the Epistle to the Hebrews insists (Heb 9.26; 10.10). Nothing henceforth will be able to separate from God the human nature that has entered into heaven. The Ascension of Christ, then, is the ascension of man, united to the divinity, arriving substantially at its goal, substantially saved forever. "But God . . . even when we were dead by reason of our sins, brought us to life together with Christ . . . and raised us up together, and seated us together in heaven in Christ Jesus" (Eph 2.4–6). This passage is especially interesting because it shows how the mysteries of Christ's death, Resurrection, and Ascension were linked in Paul's mind as one great mystery of salvation. For the formulas used here—"to be given life together with Christ," "to be raised up from death together with Christ," and "to be seated together with Christ in heaven"—have the same meaning in Paul's mind, the salvation of mankind in Christ Jesus Our Lord.

Christian Meaning. The fact that Christ's Ascension has vital meaning for each Christian was forcefully pointed out in Christ's words: "It is expedient for you that I depart. For if I do not go, the Advocate will not come to you; but if I go, I will send him to you" (Jn 16.7). Hence the departure of Christ in His physical humanity was to be the inauguration of a new presence of Jesus, more profound and fruitful, for the Father, Son, and Holy Spirit would now come to live in a new way in the individual Christian. St. Paul makes it clear in the above text from the Ephesians that Christ's exaltation was the beginning of our own glory by reason of the mysterious living unity that we have with the physi-

Fig. 4. The Ascension of Jesus Christ, pen and brown-ink drawing, by the German artist Albrecht Dürer, c. 1510.

cal Christ, who is now with the Father. St. Thomas, following Paul, maintains that our contact with Christ in glory is not merely something in the future, but now, in the present, and is indeed a marvelous basis for hope (ST 3a, 57.6 and ad 2; cf. 2 Cor 5.16–18).

Though Christ possessed the fullness of the Spirit throughout His life, He could only communicate it to others by His death, that is, by His death, glorification, and Ascension, which taken together form the unity of mysteries that conditioned the coming of the Holy Spirit. In departing physically by His Ascension, Christ promises a far richer presence in the Spirit. In promising His Apostles that He would not leave them orphans, Christ indicates that only after His return to the Father would they discover His enduring presence with them that is modeled after the presence of the Father and the Son to one another in the Trinity (Jn 14.18–21). St. Augustine compares the presence of Christ with us after His Ascension to His presence with the Father after His Incarnation. Pope St. Leo says that Christ became more fully present as God on the day He became less present as man. *See* JESUS CHRIST, III (SPECIAL QUESTIONS), 11.

As a pledge of our own glory, the mystery of the Ascension points out clearly that human nature in its totality, the embodied human person, is now glorified with Christ. In Christ Jesus the final effect of our grace of adoption is attained, the Redemption of our body. In Him, too, the yearning of all creation toward its full achievement is resolved at the same time. What this means for the Christian in his practical everyday life is beautifully expressed in ch. 4 of St. Paul's Epistle to the Ephesians. By means of Christ's Ascension the individual Christian is enabled to mature to the full stature of Christ his head. He is drawn by the gift of the Spirit toward his own personal fulfillment, and that of the whole universe, in Christ in one simultaneous movement of faith, hope, and love.

Benoit, in the conclusion of his article on the Ascension, neatly sums up the meaning of this truth in these words:

> The essential teaching of Scripture . . . is that Christ, by the triumph of His Resurrection and Ascension, has departed from this present world that is corrupted by sin and destined for destruction in order to enter a new world . . . much more real than our present world because it alone possesses true Life; however, it is vain to seek "where" it is, just as it is wrong to imagine it as "far away." This new world, where Christ reigns and awaits us, is not far from us; it is not outside our world, but transcends it. It is of another order . . . and we have access to it by faith and the Sacraments in a contact that is mysterious but more real and close than any of our contacts with this world can be. And we are convinced . . . that He inaugurated this new world . . . when He was exalted at the side of His Father.

See also RESURRECTION OF CHRIST, 2; PASSION OF CHRIST, II (THEOLOGY OF); REDEMPTION, ARTICLES ON.

Bibliography: B. VAWTER and J. HEUSCHEN, "Ascension of Jesus," EncDictBibl 144–150. G. ROTUREAU, *Catholicisme* 1:887–888. J. H. BERNARD, Hastings ERE 2:151–157. L. CERFAUX, *Christ in the Theology of St. Paul,* tr. G. WEBB and A. WALKER (New York 1959). F. X. DURRWELL, *The Resurrection: A Biblical Study,* tr. R. SHEED (New York 1960). W. K. M. GROSSOUW, *Revelation and Redemption,* ed. and tr. M. W. SCHOENBERG (Westminster, Md. 1955). E. H. SCHILLEBEECKX, *Christ: The Sacrament of the Encounter with God,* tr. P. BARRETT et al. (New York 1963); "Ascension and Pentecost," *Worship* 35 (May 1961) 336–363. R. SCHNACKENBURG, *New Testament Theology Today,* tr. D. ASKEW (New York 1963). P. BENOIT, L'Ascension," RevBibl 56 (1949) 161–203, repr. in *Exégèse et théologie,* 2 v. (Paris 1961) 1:363–411. C. DAVIS, *Theology for Today* (New York 1962) P. MIQUEL, "Christ's Ascension and Our Glorification," TheolDig 9 (1961) 67–73. **Illustration credits:** Fig. 1, Hirmer Verlag München. Fig. 2, Anderson-Art Reference Bureau. Fig. 3, The Metropolitan Museum of Art, The Elisha J. Whittelsey Collection, 1956. Fig. 4, Courtesy, The Cleveland Museum of Art.

[JOHN CLIFFORD MURRAY]

ASCETICISM (EARLY CHRISTIAN)

Early Christianity retained from Judaism the basic practices of prayer, fasting, and works of charity, but with varied motivation and form. Fasting became an ascetical means for growth in holiness rather than a ritual purification. Charitable works, drawing new meaning from Christ's command to love "as I have loved you" (Jn 15.12), were developed into a major aspect of communal pastoral action. The basic truths reiterated in the central prayer, the Eucharist, brought a fuller meaning to other forms of prayer, public or private, such as the recitation of the Psalms. New ascetical attitudes prevailed regarding martyrdom and virginity. Martyrdom, seen as the culmination of perfection in the following of Christ, was a meaningful ideal even for those who would not attain it. The daily dying with Christ, inculcated in the baptismal rite as a radical demand of the Christian vocation, was represented as a constant preparation for actual martyrdom, always more or less imminent. Exaggerations of this essential self-denial, however, resulting in large part from the influence of Oriental dualism, took heretical form in the excessive asceticism of Gnostics, Montanists, and Manichaeans. Contempt for the material world, a negative or even condemnatory attitude toward marriage, abstention from flesh meat, and a severe moralism denying all forgiveness for certain sins were characteristic of this trend.

Asceticism and the Counsels of Perfection. Lifelong virginity attracted increasing numbers as the Church expanded. It inspired a literature that, by elucidating both the ideal and its safeguard, enriched the development of ascetical teaching and practice. Virgins and ascetics were generally part of the local Christian communities until, inspired by pioneers such as St. *Anthony of Egypt in the latter part of the 3d century, they began to move in increasing numbers to the deserts of Syria, Palestine, and especially Egypt, where they lived a life of seclusion, self-denial, and prayer, striving toward *apatheia,* a complete subduing of the passions, so that the soul could rise untrammeled to God. Mortification was practiced by maximum retrenchment in food, sleep, clothing, and lodging rather than by the self-inflicted penances of the later Celtic monachism.

In the earlier asceticism there were but seminal indications of the medieval notion of suffering in mystic union with Christ or of the ideal of reparation. Paradoxically, after the Peace of Constantine (313), many Christians spurned life in the Christianized empire as compromise rather than conflict with the world and chose the severe life of the desert as a substitute for martyrdom and the embodiment of pure Christianity. This new exodus gained additional impetus when, in the same period, *Pachomius instituted cenobitic monachism in Egypt. This life in common according to a written rule, with a single superior and a daily order of prayer and assigned tasks, was monastic life much as it is known today, though the threefold practice of poverty, chastity, and obedience had not yet become a matter of formal, public vow in the early Church.

Distortions. Though this whole movement made an incalculable contribution because of the saintly lives and the classics of spiritual literature it inspired, it was not without its deficiencies. Greco-Roman and even Buddhist influences introduced dualistic attitudes difficult to reconcile with traditional values. The Stoic ideal of *apatheia,* even though Christian ascetics sought it not as an end but as a means, tended to oversimplify the scriptural opposition between spirit and flesh into a mere conflict against the body. Neoplatonist ideas, with characteristic Greek stress on intellectual quest of the transcendent, brought new significance to *gnosis* (inner spiritual enlightenment) and *theoria* (contemplation), but often at the expense of the more radical Christian truth that perfection is primarily a matter of the will, i.e., love expressed in active charity. These ideas taken together not infrequently resulted in a pessimistic contempt for the material world in place of traditional Eucharistic optimism and in an individualistic preoccupation with one's own salvation to the detriment of the communitarian values of the New Testament. Such nonecclesial spirituality was reflected also in an emphasis on private asceticism that often left little or no place for the corporate life of the liturgy and in a withdrawal from worldly involvement to the extent that the apostolate itself became suspect as an inferior occupation and even as an occasion of sin.

The forms of monachism initiated by St. Basil (d. 379) and advocated by St. John Chrysostom (d. 407) were in part conscious reactions against these deficiencies. Both saints encouraged monastic retirement but only as a preparation for the apostolate. For Basil, habitual retirement hindered growth in numerous virtues, especially charity, that should aim above all at communicating to others the greatest of gifts, grace and knowledge. Chrysostom organized his monks to cover a vast missionary field reaching from Palestine to beyond the Danube. In the West, Benedictine monasticism reflected a similar shift of values. For though its rule was not primarily apostolic, it strongly inculcated an active charity grounded in the liturgy that became a major factor in the evangelization of Europe.

Lay Asceticism. Lay spirituality, though influenced by the early monastic movement, contemporaneously had a most significant development of its own. Because of numerous defections during the persecutions of Decius and Valerian in the middle of the 3d century, the catechumenate evolved as a more thorough program for the instruction of converts. Based on the scriptural history of salvation and coming to a climax in the sacramental initiation rites of the Easter Vigil, it graphically represented the Christian life as a conflict between Christ's kingdom and the realm of the Prince of Darkness. As such, it can be seen as the elaboration of the simple moral catechesis of the "two ways" of the *Didache* (1.1–2.7) and *Pseudo-Barnabas* (18.1–20.2). In the mature development of the classic 4th-century catecheses of Cyril of Jerusalem, Chrysostom, and Ambrose, the ritual renunciation of Satan and all his pomps and works was the liturgical climax to a comprehensive 3-year ascetical formation. Sacramental life, prayer, penance, discernment of spirits, and the practice of charity received detailed treatment that was intensified during the final weeks of training. Since by this time these final instructions were usually attended also by the baptized, the pre-Easter season had become a period of renewal for the Church as a whole, and the paschal rites recapitulated the central, traditional truths in a dramatic liturgical setting.

In the history of asceticism the importance of this far-reaching pastoral development has perhaps been overshadowed by the striking phenomena and abundant literature associated with early monachism. Though the catechumenate waned as an institution during the 6th century when adult Baptism became the exception rather than the rule, the Lenten season and the structure of the Holy Week services are abiding evidence of its influence on the life of the early Church.

Bibliography: P. POURRAT, *Christian Spirituality,* tr. W. H. MITCHELL et al., 4 v. (Westminster, Md. 1953–55) v.1. L. BOUYER, *The Spirituality of the New Testament and the Fathers,* tr. M. P. RYAN (New York 1964). G. BARDY, *La Vie spirituelle d'après les pères des trois premiers siècles* (Paris 1935); *En lisant les Pères* (new ed. Paris 1933). M. VILLER, *Aszese und Mystik in der Väterzeit,* rev. and tr. K. RAHNER (Freiburg 1939). J. DE GHELLINCK, *Lectures spirituelles dans les écrits des pères* (Paris 1935). G. B. LADNER, *The Idea of Reform* (Cambridge, Mass. 1959). H. VON CAMPENHAUSEN, *Die Askese im Urchristentum* (Tübingen 1949). C. BUTLER, *Western Mysticism* (2d ed. London 1927). J. R. PALANQUE et al., *The Church in the Christian Roman Empire,* tr. E. C. MESSENGER, 2 v. in 1 (New York 1953). Quasten Patr v.1–3. Anthologies. F. CAYRÉ, *Spiritual Writers of the Early Church,* tr. W. W. WILSON (New York 1959). Ench Ascet. EnchPatr. J. DE GUIBERT, ed., *Documenta ecclesiastica Christianae perfectionis studium spectantia* (Rome 1931). E. C. WHITAKER, ed., *Documents of the Baptismal Liturgy* (SPCK; 1960). *L'Initiation chrétienne: Textes recueillis et présentés par A. Hamman* (Paris 1963), introd. J. DANIÉLOU. Studies. J. DANIÉLOU, *Platonisme et théologie mystique* (new rev. ed. Paris 1954). P. COUSIN, *Précis d'histoire monastique* (Paris 1956). P. RESCH, *La Doctrine ascétique des premiers maîtres Égyptiens du quatrième siècle* (Paris 1931). IVO AUF DER MAUR, *Mönchtum und Glaubensverkündigung in den Schriften des hl. Johannes Chrysostomos* (Fribourg 1959). V. LOSSKY, *The Mystical Theology of the Eastern Church* (London 1957). T. MAERTENS, *Histoire et pastorale du rituel du catéchuménat et du baptême* (Bruges 1962). A. STENZEL, *Die Taufe* (Innsbruck 1958). J. JUNGMANN, "History of Catechesis" in *Handing on the Faith,* tr. and rev. A. N. FUERST (New York 1959), with bibliog. L. BOUYER, *The Paschal Mystery: Meditations on the Last Three Days of Holy Week,* tr. M. BENOIT (Chicago 1950). DictSpir AscMyst. See also studies listed in Quasten Patr 3:147–148.

[T. R. O'CONNOR]

ASCETICISM (IN THE NEW TESTAMENT)

In the Gospels asceticism is presented under the concrete theme of following the historical Christ and thus sharing the hardships, dangers, and penalties that loyal discipleship to Him exact; in the Epistles of St. Paul asceticism is described principally in the image of the spiritual athlete who consciously and constantly disciplines himself in a strong effort to live more fully in docile obedience to the Spirit of Christ, to attain not only his own salvation but also that of the community.

In the Gospels. The relationship between the disciples and Jesus, described in the Gospels as following Jesus, implies an ascetic self-renunciation by the disciple. Those invited by Jesus to follow Him must sacrifice their feelings and former ties, give absolute priority to the work of the kingdom, and be animated by a singleness of purpose. His call was: "If any man wishes to come after me, let him deny himself and take up his cross and follow me. For whoever would save his life will lose it; and whosoever loses his life for my sake and the gospel's will save it" (Mk 8.34–35; Mt 16.24–

25; Lk 9.23–24). Following Jesus is difficult for human nature because it requires total self-commitment and entails contempt and danger from others. Yet following the historical Christ is a special gift of God (Jn 6.65), not granted the wise of this world (Mt 11.25). In the Gospels, following Christ does not mean merely imitating what Jesus does, but actually sharing His experiences with Him. It means discipleship and participation in His fate. For later Christians the lesson of the Gospels is that they, as Jesus' disciples, must deny themselves all that separates them from Christ and be ready to sacrifice even their life in loyalty to Him. Another ascetic theme of the Gospels is that of humility, so well exemplified in the poor of spirit (*'ănāwîm;* Mt 5.3; cf. Lk 6.20). The *'ănāwîm* are those pious and humble persons who, conscious of their spiritual need, look to God for strength and help. Often enough they are also the economically poor, oppressed and trodden upon by the rich and powerful. To them Christ addresses the first beatitude, "Blessed are the poor in spirit for theirs is the kingdom of heaven" (Mt 5.3). Christ, in describing Himself as "meek and humble of heart" (Mt 11.29), is probably referring to Himself as an *'ănāw* (a poor one).

In the Epistles of St. Paul. In St. Paul the asceticism necessary for the Christian life is expressed by diverse images, especially that of the spiritual athlete: the Christian is like the athlete who must constantly train and practice self-control in order to win the race (1 Cor 9.24–27; 1 Tm 4.7); his fight is against the old man (Eph 4.22), the flesh and its weaknesses (Rom 8.12–13; Eph 6.8), and the demonic world rulers (Eph 6.12). The Christian thus must practice humility and self-discipline in emptying himself of selfishness (Phil 2.5–8) in order to live in communion with Christ (Rom 6.1–3, 12–14). St. Paul himself has made strenuous efforts in the manner of the disciplined athlete in striving for the goal (Acts 24.16; see also Heb 5.14; 12.11; 2 Pt 2.14), and he is aware that he must strive to the end (Phil 3.13).

Another prominent feature of Paul's asceticism is its corporate significance. The Christian lives and acts in and with his glorified Lord and His Spirit. He has a mystical relationship to Christ (Gal 2.19–20) and to all who are baptized into Christ (Rom 6.3–14); thus what he does either helps or hurts the total body of Christ. The individual's strivings, like those of Paul, have communal significance; he "fills up what is lacking in the sufferings of Christ for His body, which is the Church" (Col 1.24).

See also FAST AND ABSTINENCE (IN THE BIBLE); FOLLOWING OF CHRIST (IN THE BIBLE).

Bibliography: R. SCHNACKENBURG, LexThK² 1:930–932. T. W. MANSON, "The Sayings of Jesus," *The Mission and Message of Jesus,* ed. H. D. A. MAJOR and C. J. WRIGHT (New York 1938) 301–639. G. T. MONTAGUE, *Growth in Christ: A Study in Saint Paul's Theology of Progress* (Kirkwood, Mo. 1961). L. BOUYER, *Introduction to Spirituality,* tr. M. P. RYAN (New York 1961). A. GELIN, *Les Pauvres de Yahvé* (Paris 1953). J. KREMER, *Was an den Leiden Christi noch mangelt* (Bonn 1956).

[J. LACHOWSKI]

ASCETICISM (NON-CHRISTIAN)

The Greek noun ἄσκησις from which "asceticism" is derived means "exercise," "practice," or "training" for the purpose of obtaining something that is worth aspiring to, that represents an ideal.

TERMINOLOGY AND CONCEPT

Displaying an extraordinary flexibility in their application, ἄσκησις and its cognates (the verb ἀσκεῖν, "to practice," and the noun ἀσκητής, "one who practices") are related to a fourfold ideal in ancient literature.

Association with Training. In connection with the ideal of bodily excellence, the word and its cognates denote the strenuous training and the whole mode of life that leads to the highest possible degree of physical fitness either of the athlete (Aristophanes, *Plut.* 585; Plato, *Rep.* 403E–; Xenophon, *Mem.* 1.2.24; Plutarch, *De gen. Socr.* 24.593D) or the soldier (Thucydides, 2.39; 5.67; Xenophon, *Cyr.* 8.1.34). The ἀσκητής, "the man who is trained," is contrasted with the ἰδιώτης, "the one who is untrained" (Xenophon, *Mem.* 3.7.7; Eq. *Mag.* 8.1).

With the development of philosophy came the training of the mind. To the ideal of the athlete and soldier there was added the ideal of the man who by exercising his intellectual faculties acquired wisdom. Heraclitus [Frg. 129 (Diels FrgVorsokr)] says that Pythagoras "practiced research" (ἱστορίην ἤσκησεν) and, by using an eclectic method, "created for himself a wisdom that was his own." Isocrates (*Bus.* 22) points to the benefit derived from "philosophy's training," namely, its power "to establish laws and to inquire into the nature of the universe." He contrasts the training of the mind with that of the body and recommends a liberal education and "a training of this sort" (τὴν ἄσκησιν τὴν τοιαύτην) for young men (*Antid.* 302; 304). Elsewhere (*Ad. Demon.* 40) he gives the advice: "But above all train (ἄσκει) your intellect; for the greatest thing in the smallest compass is a good mind in a human body." With this the word ἄσκησις and its synonym μελετή entered the field of education and, together with two other terms—φύσις (natural endowment) and μάθησις (acquisition of knowledge), or ἐπιστήμη (knowledge)—has an important place in Greek philosophical thought, but especially in the pedagogical system of the Sophists. The three terms occur frequently in ancient literature. They are mentioned by Plato (*Phaedrus* 269D) as the necessary requirements for a good orator.

Association with Ethics. The idea of the body's requiring strenuous training in preparation for an athletic contest or for warfare was easily extended to the areas of mental culture and ethics. The ideal aspired to was that of καλὸς κἀγαθός, the "good and worthy man." As early as Herodotus (1.96; 7.209) the verb ἀσκεῖν is found in such combinations as "to practice justice" or "veracity." In the sense of a systematic and comprehensive training as a self-preparation for a virtuous course of conduct it is used by Xenophon (*Mem.* 1.2.19–). Comparing those who do not "train" the body with those who neglect the "training" of the soul, he observes that, as the former cannot perform the functions proper to the body, so the latter cannot perform those proper to the soul, because they are not able to control their will with regard to what they ought and ought not to do. Hence one should cultivate the association with good men, because it is an ἄσκησις τῆς ἀρετῆς, a "training for virtue" (cf. same idea in Aristotle, *Eth. Nic.* 1170a 11). The training for virtue is then expounded especially by Epictetus. A chapter in his *Dissertationes* (3.12), entitled περὶ ἀσκήσεως, is devoted to this subject. The object of this training, according to Epictetus, is the freedom of the sage who acts without hindrance in choice and in refusal. It is, therefore, principally a training of the will. If one is fond of pleasure, loath to work, or hot-tempered, he must, "to train himself" (ἀσκήσεως ἕνεκα), turn to a behavior directly contrary to the dictates of those urges. Similarly indulgence in drinking, eating, and sensual love must be counteracted by a training in the opposite direction (*Diss.* 3.12.7–12). Moreover, whatever is outside the moral purpose—be it women's beauty, compassion, or fame—is of no concern to the sage (*ibid.* 3.3.14–19; cf. 4.1.81).

Association with Religion. With the growth of a stronger sense of personal religion, in the history of Greek religious life, ἄσκησις assumed a final meaning, denoting an act of religious devotion or an exercise of piety. In this sense ἄσκησις is probably first used by Isocrates (*Bus.* 26) who describes Busiris, a legendary king of Egypt, as establishing for his subjects "numerous and varied exercises of piety" (ἀσκήσεις τῆς ὁσιότητος), convinced that this would accustom them to obeying the commands of those in authority. Religious asceticism, in the form of purificatory observances such as fasting and refraining from sexual intercourse, was practiced especially by sects of a religio-mystic temper like the Orphics and Pythagoreans. It continued to gain ground with the spread of the Oriental mystery religions, especially those of Attis-Cybele and Isis, that followed an elaborate system of ascetical exercises as cathartic measures before certain celebrations, and, through the proselytizing efforts of mendicant preachers of the Cynic school, it exhorted men to combat their appetites and to practice virtue.

In Cynic-Stoic popular philosophy the concept of ἄσκησις grew narrower and assumed a negative character, not in the sense that the ideal aspired to had ceased to be positive, but in that the main stress was laid on a complete detachment from the comforts and enticements of the world, on a radical suppression of the appetites, and on a predisposition to accept every hardship in the pursuit of this ideal, in accordance with the Epictetian precept: ἀνέχου καὶ ἀπέχου, "endure and renounce" (Favorinus *ap.* Gell., *Noct. Att.* 17.19.6). This negative attitude is prominent also in Orphic-Pythagorean asceticism: the soul was to be purified by the denial and inhibition of the body and its impulses. Because of this strong negative emphasis, the notion of ἄσκησις as "practice" or "training" receded into the background. The influence of Cynic-Stoic philosophy and Orphic-Pythagorean thought is still discernible in the notion of the modern word "asceticism," which has eluded a generally accepted definition. In common usage it refers ordinarily to all those phenomena in the history of religion that are characterized by a methodical, and often minutely regulated, practice of a varied amount of austerities, ranging from the denial of comforts, emotions, desires, and activities to the actual self-infliction of pain.

Most frequently asceticism is conceived as the product of a more or less developed system of dualism, its basic motive being the endeavor to free the spiritual part of man from the defiling corruption of the body. This one-sided conception is no doubt too narrow. Although dualism is most conducive to asceticism, not all asceticism is dualistic. The two weekly fasts of the Pharisee (Lk 18.12) can unhesitatingly be termed ascetical practices. Yet, in observing them, the Pharisee was not motivated by any kind of dualistic speculation but considered them simply an especially meritorious work and a self-understood expression of his piety. Dualistic ideas no doubt were a powerful impulse toward asceticism, but, besides them, many other factors were active in its birth and development: the fear of hostile influences from demons, the conception of asceticism as a potent means to enter into communion with the supernatural, the sense of sin with the concomitant urge for atonement, the idea of earning salvation by merit, a radical otherworldliness of interest in view of the instability and transitoriness of all things earthly, and an ethical rigorism provoked by weariness with exaggerated cultural refinement and hope for a realization of the ascetic ideal in simple social environments.

Means and Methods

Both may be grouped into acts of self-discipline passing over into the outward life on the one hand and exercises of an inward kind on the other. To the former belong fasting, sexual continence, renunciation of bodily comforts, and actual infliction of pain.

Fasting. The history of religion reveals a widespread belief among primitive peoples that taking food is dangerous because demoniac forces may enter and harm the body. As a precaution, primitive man fasted or avoided certain foods that he considered dangerous because they were attractive to such pernicious forces. This originally negative aim to avert evil can, by the natural development of the same idea, be changed into a positive one. To be free from disturbing demoniac influences means also to be in a state of ritual purity, a necessary condition, it seems, for one who wants to enter into communion with the supernatural. This purity is supposed to bring man nearer to the divine, to endow him with extraordinary, superhuman powers. It is, therefore, required in the sacred rites of initiation. It is demanded also of the seer or prophet, to free his soul from any possible obstruction so that the god can take full possession of him during the ecstasy. In the same sense, the ascetic of religio-mystic temper hopes that such a state of purity will aid him in surmounting the barrier separating man from god, lift him up into the spiritual, and lead him to his final goal, the union with the divine. Finally, fasting is practiced as an act of devotion and morality. In its religio-ethical aspect it aims especially at controlling the lower appetites and promoting the cultivation of virtues.

Sexual Continence. As in fasting, the aim of sexual continence originally is apotropaic, or evil-averting. Cohabitation is regarded as producing ceremonial uncleanness. Ritual purity, on the other hand, is considered a necessary condition for approaching the divine. Hence Greek inscriptions, dealing with regulations concerning the ritual purity of lay worshippers entering sacred precincts, put great stress on their freedom from the defilements of sexual intercourse. Continence was a requisite also for participation in certain religious celebrations such as the Eleusinian Mysteries or the festival of the Thesmophoria. Connected with the same idea was a custom according to which a number of ancient Greek priesthoods were held by a boy or a girl until the age of puberty, but not after, or by old women. Sometimes priestly functions were performed by priestesses who were obliged to remain virgins during their tenure of office, either for a certain period or for life.

Chastity was made one of the rules also of Buddhist monasticism.

Isolation and Self-infliction of Pain. Other external acts of self-discipline, practiced especially among primitive peoples in the training preparatory to admission to the mysteries of their tribal religions, and practiced also by Buddhist monks, include retirement from the world or solitary confinement, utmost simplicity in dwelling and clothing, sleeping on the bare ground or in an uncomfortable position, privation of sleep, and general neglect of the body. These austerities are sometimes increased by the infliction of pain, a method used by the fakirs of India. To this category belong immobility in diverse postures of the body, self-laceration, and other kinds of self-torture. The highest expression of non-Christian asceticism is found in spiritual exercises. They include such observances as silence, the examination of conscience, the study of sacred writings, prayer, mental concentration, and meditation. Buddhism provides remarkable examples of this kind.

Asceticism in the History of Religion

Hardly any religion is without at least some traces of asceticism. Ascetical practices, rooted in magical or crude religious beliefs and belonging to a rigorously enforced set of purificatory rites for males at the age of puberty, or at a time previous to their admission to the tribal community, are found among the more advanced agricultural, herding, and higher hunting tribes that constitute most of the uncivilized population of the world. While the boys undergoing initiation are introduced into the religious lore and the moral code of the tribe, they must live in seclusion, submit to a harsh discipline with regard to the quantity and quality of their food, and bear with fortitude tests of endurance and actual torment. The purificatory rites to be observed by pubescent girls correspond in character to those imposed on boys at initiation. Moreover, in the mind of primitive man childbirth and death are phenomena that, because of their mysteriousness and therefore dangerousness, require certain precautions and abstentions such as seclusion, fasting, and cessation of customary activities. The medicine man also must be an ascetic, lean from fasting, because it is only through severe and constant self-discipline that he is able to acquire and retain occult powers.

Primitive Survivals in Higher Religions. Survivals of this primitive asceticism, which aims simply at averting a polluting evil that might threaten man from without, occur even in such highly developed religions as that of the Hebrews. Thus the rule requiring sexual abstinence of priests as preparation for liturgical functions is rooted ultimately in the belief that sexual phenomena, especially intercourse, produce ceremonial uncleanness and thus disqualify for worship (cf. Ex 19.15; Lv 15. 16–18; 1 Sm 21.5–; 2 Sm 11.5–13). A similar notion is at the root of the widespread custom in later Judaism to abstain from sexual intercourse on the Sabbath. To the same category belongs, apart from the extraordinarily complicated system of dietary laws, the abstention from wine observed by the priest before offering sacrifice (Lv 10.9; Ez 44.21), by the Nazirite for the period of his vow (Nm 6.3–; Am 2.11–; cf. Jgs 13.4, 7, 14), and by the Rechabites for life (Ez 35). The traditional ritual of mourning after a death also included restrictions such as fasting, abstaining from sexual intercourse, and avoidance of bathing and anointing.

Ascetical Aspects of Hebrew Practices. There are religions in which asceticism does not figure as an essential feature. Among the Hebrews the OT concept of man and the world as the handiwork of an infinitely perfect God, precludes a dualistic view of the world. Married life and earthly possessions are thought of as having their foundation in a divine order and being God's gifts to man. What God in turn demands of man is not renunciation of these gifts, but the fulfillment of certain obligations laid down by the Mosaic Law in cult and in the moral and social spheres. Despite its essentially nonascetic character, however, the religion of the Hebrews contained seeds from which ascetical practices in the strict sense of the word could later develop.

The doctrine of reconciliation or atonement, always set forth by the teachers of Israel as their peculiar faith, led to the custom of penitential fasting. While at first the only fast day strictly enjoined in the Law (Lv 16.29–; 23.27–; Nm 29.7) was the Day of Atonement (Tishri 10), 4 more fast days were introduced into the Jewish calendar of the 4th, 5th, 7th, and 10th months during the Babylonian Exile (Za 7.3, 5; 8.19) to commemorate disasters in the history of the Jewish people. How long the fast days of the 4th, 7th, and 10th months were kept after Zacharias, was no longer known in later rabbinic tradition. Only the fast day of the 5th month (Ab 9) seems to have continued as a national day of mourning in the post-Exilic period; it grew in importance after the Romans captured Jerusalem A.D. 70, since on this day, according to rabbinic tradition, both the first and the second temple were destroyed by fire.

On what day the so-called Fast of Esther (Est 9.31), now kept on the eve (Adar 13) of the Feast of Purim, was observed in antiquity, is not known. Many other fast days were later introduced; the *Megillat Ta'anit* (Scroll of Fasting) lists as many as 24. They were, however, not considered obligatory and were never accepted universally. In times of national emergencies, such as war, and imminent danger of extermination or public calamities, such as drought or locusts devouring the harvest, extraordinary general fasts were ordered by the authorities (Jgs 20.26; 1 Sm 7.6; 2 Chr 20.3; Jdt 4.9; Est 4.16; Jer 14.12; 36.6; Jl 1.14; 2.12, 15; Jon 3.5–; 1 Mc 3.47; 2 Mc 13.12; *Syr. Bar Ap* 86.1–; Josephus, *Ant. Jud.* 11, 134; *id., Vita* 290).

The more vigorous way of fasting consisted in abstaining from food and drink and in avoiding other physical pleasures such as bathing, anointing, and sexual intercourse; and in donning penitential garments, sprinkling the head with dust and ashes, and performing acts of self-humiliation. Since fasting on these days was accompanied by prayer and almsgiving, it was considered meritorious and pleasing to God. A certain measure of asceticism was then generally regarded as a sign of virtuous and holy living (Jdt 8.6; *Testament of Joseph* 9; *Henoch* 108.7; Lk 2.36–; 18.12; Josephus *Vita* 2). Fasting was used also to strengthen the prayer of the prophet and to prepare him for the reception of divine revelations (Dn 9.3; 10.2, 3, 12). As with other ascetical exercises, it is characteristic of the prophet in a number of late Jewish apocalypses (4 Ezr 5.13, 19f–; 6.31, 35; 9.23–25; 12.51; *Syriac Apocalypse of Baruch* 9.2; 12.5; 20.5; 21.1–; 43.3; 47.2; cf. *Apocalypse of Abraham* 9.7; *Ascension of Isaia* 2.7–11).

A fully developed ascetical system, however, remained a foreign thing in Jewish thought. As in ancient Greece, it found a home only in such closed and exclusive societies of spiritualistic enthusiasts as the Essenes who lived outside of the broad current of Jewish piety and formed a kind of religious order, following an established mode of life with vows of celibacy, poverty, and obedience. An idealized picture of asceticism is given by Philo of Alexandria in his treatise *De vita contemplativa*, in which he describes the mystic-contemplative life of the Therapeutae, a colony of Jewish ascetics in Egypt.

Non-Christian asceticism reached its fullest development in India where it was established in the ancient Vedic religion, and continued to play an extraordinary part in the later forms of Hinduism, Jainism, and Buddhism.

See also RELIGION (IN PRIMITIVE CULTURE); BUDDHISM; HINDUISM; JAINISM; YOGA; MYSTERY RELIGIONS, GRECO-ORIENTAL.

Bibliography: E. D'ASCOLI, *La spiritualità precristiana* (Brescia 1952). G. VAN DER LEEUW, *Phänomenologie der Religion* (2d ed. Tübingen 1956). F. PFISTER, "Lanx Satura," no. 2, Ἄσκησις, *Festgabe für A. Deissmann* (Tübingen 1927) 76–81. H. STRATHMANN, *Geschichte der frühchristlichen Askese,* v.1 *Die Askese in der Umgebung des werdenden Christentums* (Leipzig 1914). J. DE GUIBERT and M. OLPHE-GALLARD, DictSpirAscMyst 1:936–960. Hastings ERE 1:63–111, introduction and separate articles by a number of specialists on Buddhist, Greek, Hindu, Japanese, Jewish, Mohammedan, Persian, Roman, Semitic and Egyptian asceticism. H. WINDISCH, KittelThW 1:492–494. R. MOHR and R. SCHNACKENBURG, LexThK[2] 1:928–932. H. STRATHMANN, ReallexAntChr 1:749–758. R. MENSCHING et al., RGG[3] 1:639–642. H. DRESSLER, *The Usage of ἀσκέω and Its Cognates in Greek Documents to 100 A.D.* (Washington 1947).

[R. ARBESMANN]

ASCETICISM (PSYCHOLOGY OF)

Religion is a relationship between man and God. Advances in the knowledge of man deepen man's understanding of both terms of this relationship—he understands himself better and, since the closest analogue to God is man, he understands God better. Religious asceticism is the means of improving man's relationship with God; it is a means to perfection. Taken in a broad sense, it refers to any practices that lead to religious perfection; taken in a more restricted sense, it refers to the voluntary denial or frustration of legitimate human inclinations or impulses or the bearing of self-inflicted pain in order to attain religious perfection. It has behind it various conscious motivations such as training, self-discipline, the liberation of the spiritual faculties for prayer and union with God, the atonement for sin and guilt, solidarity through communal penance with other members of the religious group, a sacrificial offering made to God out of love, and, finally, identification with the suffering Savior. It is allied with such terms as penance, mortification, and self-denial. The rationale for these depends on one's perception of the nature of his relationship to God and Christ.

What used to be the accepted values of asceticism do not readily harmonize with mid-20th-century knowledge of man and of God. New emphases and developments in doctrine clarify the nature of the ideal relationship between the Christian and Christ. Hence they clarify the status of asceticism as a means of attaining this end. Trends within theology itself, undoubtedly influenced by new understandings of man, challenge the goals of asceticism or question the conscious motivations or rationale for it. Psychology, since it deepens man's insights into the nature of Christian perfection, influences the goals toward which man consciously strives. Beyond this it offers profound understanding of the unconscious dynamisms with which man must contend as he struggles for his conscious goals.

Historical Perspective. The attitude of man toward asceticism is part of his whole outlook and can be expected to vary in different cultures and to evolve with increased understanding of himself and of his relation to the universe. Asceticism may thus be seen as the way man goes about perfecting himself in the context of his own culture.

Severe bodily penances and mortifications had a vogue in the early ages of Christianity and were meaningful in an era characterized by deep mistrust of the human body. Since the Middle Ages, perhaps connected with the change from a rural to an urban culture, the character of these practices has undergone a notable transformation, from a putting to death of the flesh to a denial of the self. The trend has been from bodily to psychological self-denial, with an emphasis on the victory of will over the lower appetites. During this period, mental and emotional disorder was looked upon as diabolical possession, as having its roots outside the individual. Man was viewed either mechanistically or rationalistically, and no solid connection was seen between man's spiritual side and his feelings and emotions. The postmedieval development was thus accompanied by a distrust not of the body alone but of man's affective life as well.

With the growing respect for the whole person that has characterized recent thought, however, the term asceticism has come to symbolize man's evolving quest for the means to spiritual perfection—his search for *virtue. There has also been a growing awareness that man's perfection is not to be found in a denial, but rather in the acceptance, of what is most deeply human, viz, the interdependence of body and spirit in an organic unity. A psychology of asceticism can thus be viewed as a step or stage in the search for a psychology of human holiness and spiritual perfection.

It is illuminating to see when the term asceticism is currently employed and when it is passed over. William *James dealt at some length with asceticism in *The Varieties of Religious Experience* (1902). The term is hardly to be found in contemporary works on the psychology of religion. Its use is confined to manuals of theology and of spiritual formation and, even there, spiritual literature influenced by the new psychology places less emphasis on asceticism and more on response and relationship. Hand in hand with this goes the gradual waning of "will training," which often disguised a mistrust for the affective side of man.

The Contemporary Position. The psychology of religion is the science that treats of the psychology of religious asceticism (*see* RELIGION, PSYCHOLOGY OF). It is a branch of the scientific disciplines of psychology and psychiatry, which came on the scene in the last quarter of the 19th century. These differ from earlier forms of religious psychology of a philosophical, observational, and casual sort, largely because of their distinctive methodologies.

The psychology of asceticism is either positive or negative. The former analyzes the constructive effects on religious personality of various ascetical practices; the latter focuses on the immature and pathological aspects of it. Up to the 1960s there were little or no experimental or clinical data on the positive aspects of asceticism. The scientific data that exist emphasize the negative aspects and are based on the clinical experience of psychotherapists who report on the pathology of asceticism. They point out striking parallels between ascetical behavior in known neurotic and psychotic patients and ascetical practices as described in religious biographies. Such students of psychopathology warn about the phenomenon of masochism, which is a perversion by which pain and suffering are sources of sexual pleasure or of thinly disguised substitutes for this. They ask whether the asceticism they see and read about is motivated by the self-destructive urges of hostility, hatred, and guilt or whether it emanates from attitudes of respect, value, and worth toward the *self.

One of the substantial contributions of modern personality theory has been the concept of *repression. Feelings and emotions that are driven under the surface by denial or distortion still exert their influence on the person, e.g., psychosomatically. Dealing exclusively with symptoms is often not effective, for one symptom is replaced by another; rather the dynamic roots of the symptoms that lie deep in the emotional life of the individual must be coped with. An asceticism that concentrates merely on the elimination of symptoms is of little value for removing such roots.

Asceticism can also be used as an unconscious mechanism for defending against unacceptable feelings and impulses. An attraction to ascetical practices is known to coincide with the dawning sexuality of adolescence. On the other hand, ascetic practices can ferret out defenses of which the individual was previously unaware and thus serve as a test of where defenses lie. More appropriate procedures may then be used for the elimination of the defenses.

The present psychological climate has a healthy respect for *feeling and *emotion as an integral part of the *person. Man should integrate his feelings with his values, not repress them. Overeating, lack of punctuality, excessive sleeping, difficulties with authorities, and sexual problems are not treated by forms of therapy akin to traditional ascetical practice. Rather, methods are preferred that rely on a relationship and that penetrate to such roots of selfishness as the need for affection. It has been pointed out how the growing child learns to handle frustration by forgoing instinctive desires when he perceives that these are incompatible with the love he has for a parent. Within the framework of a warm relationship one accepts the frustration of impulses and desire in order to achieve other goals that are more important.

Many areas of contemporary psychology are relevant for developing a true scientific psychology of asceticism. Under the social psychology of asceticism should be considered the process by which ascetic practices tend to become formalized, institutionalized, and depersonalized, as in the use of the *discipline. This makes such practices difficult to change and increasingly likely to be used as a defense, since they lose their personal meaning. Penances also have their fads. Other relevant areas are *abnormal psychology, puritanism, sensory deprivation, conditioning, frustration, pain, conflict, defense, and repression.

Critique. An evaluation of asceticism depends on the validity of the conscious values and awareness of the unconscious mechanisms. Practical guides for asceticism based on psychological principles are more easily expressed negatively than positively. A healthy asceticism does not proceed out of mistrust or contempt for the body, on the one hand, or for feeling and emotion, on the other. It is not a process to facilitate repression by serving as a defense against unacceptable feelings. It is not a training procedure or therapy. The motives from which it proceeds should be healthy. It is the mature act of an adult who, for religious motives, renounces his personal impulses and desires; this renunciation he has accepted and healthily integrated into his life. For those in the active life a full dedication to the needs of others automatically entails the curbing of one's own desires and inclinations. For those in the contemplative life, a voluntary asceticism is more necessary.

See also ASCETICISM (THEOLOGICAL ASPECT); PERSONALITY; SPIRITUAL THEOLOGY.

Bibliography: K. MENNINGER, *Man Against Himself* (New York 1938). J. LINDWORSKY, *The Psychology of Asceticism,* tr. E. A. HEIRING (London 1936). *Christian Asceticism and Modern Man,* tr. W. MITCHELL et al. (New York 1955).

[P. F. D'ARCY]

ASCETICISM (THEOLOGICAL ASPECT)

For the Christian, asceticism is an aspect of the following of Christ, the price that must be paid daily for increasing assimilation to Christ. Certainly, asceticism is not itself the aim and substance of the following of Christ but only a means thereto, an expression for resoluteness of will. Asceticism means conscious self-control and systematic exercise of the Christian life.

Eschatological View. Asceticism is not merely an exercise of self-mastery or a struggle against the passions; neither is it a mere subjection of the body to the spirit. Granted, the struggle is against human weakness and instability; yet when the Scriptures speak of the war against "the flesh" (σάρξ) they do not mean against bodiliness, but against the existential condition of fallen man, proud and self-centered. Implied in this are all the forces of perdition: original sin, the burden of personal sins for which one is still insufficiently repentant and for which he has not yet sufficiently atoned, the social milieu formed by one's sins and the sins of others that tends to draw one downward, and the fallen angels, who exercise their powers in the world. "For our wrestling is not against flesh and blood, but against the Principalities and the Powers, against the world-rulers of this darkness, against the spiritual forces of wickedness on high. Therefore take up the armor of God . . ." (Eph 6.12–18). On the opposite side stand Christ and the community of saints.

When Christian asceticism is considered thus at the level of the history of salvation and the sacred-social order, it is clear that the important thing should not be a rigidly patterned routine. Asceticism must rather be—and this above all—*true to life,* suited to the necessities and contingencies of the battle. The Apostle admonishes us to this effect when he says, "therein be

"St. Francis in the Wilderness," oil on panel, 49 by 55⅞ inches, by the Italian artist Giovanni Bellini (c. 1430–1516). The scene is thought to represent the saint during his retreat into the Apennines in 1224.

vigilant in all perseverance" (Eph 6.18). Vigilance is one of the typical Christian eschatological virtues. When Paul claims that "he chastises his body" he actually refers to the notion taken from boxing jargon (ὑποπιάζειν), to strike decisively at the right moment. The context makes this still clearer: "I, therefore, so run as not without a purpose; I so fight as not beating the air . . ." (1 Cor 9.26–27). Here the chief enemy is not the inertia of the body but pride of spirit and ambition, which are responsible for the disorder of the passions. The driving power of the passions ought not be weakened, but must be systematically guided toward the good—above all through attention to purity of motive.

Asceticism within the Order of Love. Asceticism must help to overcome all that stands in the way of fulfilling the chief commandment: love of God and love of neighbor. From this point of view it is likewise clear that Catholic moral theology—no less than evangelical theology—must reject that form of asceticism that is chosen for motives of vainglory. Asceticism ought never be practiced at the expense of service to the kingdom of God and to one's neighbor; for the central notion of Christian morality is not self-perfection—definitely not self-perfection conceived egoistically—but true fulfillment of the general and particular call received from God. An asceticism that is true to life is thus a conscious exercise of service. In case of doubt, mere exercise must yield to the service of love. Augustine says of the virtue of temperance that "discipline and moderation is that love which keeps itself unsullied and undiminished for God" (*Mor. Eccl.;* PL 32:1322). This is true also of asceticism, which is allied with the Christian virtue of temperance.

Legal Prescription as Secondary. A Catholic understanding of asceticism ought not to lay emphasis onesidedly on legally prescribed action, as if, for example, the purely external fulfillment of abstaining from meat on Friday implied ascetical perfection. The intent of the law is rather education to genuine abstinence, indeed likewise to humble obedience through which pride is put in check. More important than the exact fulfillment of an act positively prescribed by the Church is the fulfillment of the intent of the law. Still more important—and this is the ultimate purpose of the Church—is the ever-ready submission to every renunciation and sacrifice imposed by divine providence (the best school of suffering) and demanded by the love of neighbor.

For the most part, asceticism is a "work of supererogation." Actually, that implies no arbitrary selfrighteousness. It means only that most forms and exercises of asceticism are not universal legal impositions to which all can and should conform. It implies a call suited to the situation, a call of service for the kingdom of God and for neighbor, a call that goes beyond the legal obligations affecting all men.

It is a responsive fulfillment of the call of grace. Christian asceticism is distinguished from most non-Christian forms precisely by this humble openness for the καιρός for each individual opportunity with its offer of grace.

Asceticism as a Universal Requirement. Asceticism is not a concern peculiar to the monastic state. It belongs to the Christian living in the midst of the world as well as to the monk, though the forms and emphases differ. The monks—sometimes simply called ascetics—should bear witness through their state and their example to the fact that "this world as we see it is passing away" (1 Cor 7.32). Yet if the entire people of God (and especially the laity living in the midst of the world) must attempt that brave encounter with the world of which Vatican II speaks in the schema *On the Church and the World Today,* then the spirit of evangelical poverty, i.e., renunciation of the egoistic desire to possess and to rule, is an absolute prerequisite. The Christian who is aware of the groaning of creation, of its longing to partake more and more in the blessed freedom of the children of God (cf. Rom 8.19–23), must follow this admonition: " . . . it remains that . . . those who use this world [be] as though not using it, for this world as we see it is passing away" (1 Cor 7.29–31). Without a definite, though flexible, measure of self-control, discipline and systematic struggle, the Christian cannot attain to this freedom.

Asceticism: A Way of the Joyful to Joy. Christian asceticism must be ultimately understood in terms of the paschal mystery. It is an affirmation of the cross as the path to resurrection. The ability to bear the cross, of which asceticism is indeed only one aspect, comes from the joy of being redeemed. "Joy in the Lord is your strength" (Neh 8.10): this is true also with regard to asceticism. The aim of the exercise that at times is found painful is a purified love of God, of neighbor, and of the whole of creation. But that also means an increase of joy.

Bibliography: *Christian Asceticism and Modern Man,* tr. W. MITCHELL and the CARISBROOKE DOMINICANS (New York 1955). R. EGENTER, *Die Aszese des Christen in der Welt* (Ettal 1956). H. FICHTENAU, *Askese und Laster in der Anschauung des Mittelalters* (Vienna 1948). B. HÄRING, *The Law of Christ: Moral Theology for Priests and Laity,* tr. E. G. KAISER (Westminster, Md. 1961–) 1:528–562. H. E. HENGSTENBERG, *Christliche Askese* (Regensburg 1936). J. LINDWORSKY, *The Psychology of Asceticism,* tr. E. A. HEIRING (London 1936). H. SCHMIDT, *Organische Aszese* (6th ed. Paderborn 1952). **Illustration credit:** The Frick Collection, New York.

[B. HÄRING]

ASCH, SHOLEM, Yiddish novelist and dramatist; b. Kutno, Poland, Nov. 1, 1880; d. London, July 10, 1957. His novelistic portraits of Jesus, Mary His Mother, and St. Paul made him a controversial figure to Christians and Jews alike. Reared in an Orthodox Jewish environment, Asch first encountered Western European, especially German, literature and culture in Warsaw (1899). In 1901 he married Mathilda Spira, who bore him one daughter and three sons. His first stories, written in Hebrew, were followed by lyric dramas in Yiddish. *The Days of the Messiah* (1906) and *The God of Vengeance* (1907) portrayed characters suffering from deep conflicts and yearning for a religious faith. *The God of Vengeance,* produced by Max Reinhardt in Berlin in 1910, introduced Asch to the non-Yiddish world.

At the outbreak of World War I Asch brought his family to New York City, where he was naturalized in

Sholem Asch.

1920. The freshness of his style, his humor, and his epic conceptions brought his Yiddish literature onto the international literary scene. The desire to lift the tragic barrier between Judaism and Christianity absorbed him after a visit to Palestine in 1906. "I have never thought of Judaism or Christianity separately since that time," he wrote. "For me it is one culture and one civilization on which all our peace, security and freedom are dependent." *The Nazarene* (1939), the first volume of a trilogy, set forth a Jewish portrait of Jesus. The second novel, *The Apostle* (1943), portrayed St. Paul. The trilogy was completed (1949) with *Mary.* Despite many theological and historical errors, it is remarkable for its warmth of appreciation of some great Christian figures. Although Asch spoke of Christ as "the fulfillment," "the Torah," and the "true Sabbath," he did not trust "organized religion" and was vehement in his criticism of both Church and Synagogue.

Bibliography: A. A. ROBACK, *The Story of Yiddish Literature* (New York 1940). J. M. OESTERREICHER, "An Epistle to Sholem Asch," *Catholic World* 162 (1946) 438–442. **Illustration credit:** E. H. Emanuel.

[I. AND C. SÜSSMAN]

ASCHAM, ROGER, English humanist, scholar, and educational writer; b. Kirby Wiske, Yorkshire, England, *c.* 1515; d. London, Dec. 30, 1568. Typical of his age, Ascham combined the careers of scholar, court official, and, most successfully, author and developer of English prose. After receiving his B.A. (1534) and his M.A. (1537) at Cambridge where he was strongly influenced by Sir John Cheke, he pursued an academic career there as reader in Greek and public orator until his parents' deaths and his own failing health obliged him to seek achievement elsewhere.

His first and only completed work, *Toxophilus* (1545), an instruction in archery and a persuasive argument in favor of recreation and physical exercise, especially for the scholar, succeeded far beyond his expectations. It was accepted not only as a work of literature and a standard authority on physical training as essential to education but also as a model of prose used in schools. It also helped to further his career by winning the favor of the crown. After tutoring Elizabeth briefly and serving as secretary to Sir Richard Moryson, English ambassador to Emperor Charles V, Ascham was made secretary to Queen Mary (despite his earlier outspoken support of the Protestant view while a student at Cambridge), and continued in that post for Queen Elizabeth until his death.

Final evidence of his lifelong interest in scholarship and learning is found in his last and best known work, *The Schoolmaster,* published by his widow in 1570. Admittedly a popularizer of traditional ideas rather than an original thinker, Ascham produced a typical humanistic treatise on education, showing the strong influence of his correspondence with J. Sturm, his reading of T. Elyot (whom he never mentions), and Quintilian. His advocacy of Ciceronian imitation and the method of double translation also had predecessors in both classical and Renaissance authors. However derivative, *The Schoolmaster* nevertheless influenced the works of such later English writers on education as R. Mulcaster and J. Locke.

Bibliography: R. ASCHAM, *Toxophilus,* ed. E. ARBER (London 1869); *The Schoolmaster,* ed. D. C. WHIMSTER (London 1934). L. V. RYAN, *Roger Ascham* (Stanford 1963).

[J. C. BRONARS]

ASEITY (ASEITAS)

A term used in scholastic philosophy and theology to express one of the primary attributes of God. Aseity comes from the Latin *a se* (*aseitas*), and signifies the attribute of God whereby He possesses His existence of or from Himself, in virtue of His own essence, and not from any other being outside Himself as cause. It is best understood by contrast with its opposite, i.e., the attribute whereby a being receives its existence from another (*ab alio*) or is a caused or contingent being. It is thus one of the primary marks distinguishing God from creatures.

Meaning. Aseity has two aspects, one positive and the other negative. In its negative meaning, which emerged first in the history of thought, it affirms that God is uncaused, depending on no other being for the source of His existence. In its positive meaning, it affirms that God is completely self-sufficient, having within Himself the sufficient reason for His own existence. The technical analysis of this in terms of essence and existence, which took longer to develop in Christian thought, affirms that God possesses existence per se, i.e., through, or in virtue of, His own essence. This does not mean that God is literally the cause of Himself in the strict sense of cause, since this would imply some kind of real distinction between God as causing and God as effect. Such a teaching, as St. Thomas Aquinas has pointed out (*C. gent.* 1.22), would be absurd. What it does mean is that God's existence is absolutely identical with His essence, that His essence necessarily includes existence itself, so that God cannot not exist: He is the Necessary Being par excellence.

This identity of essence and existence, although held by all Christian thinkers, has been explained in different ways. The following account traces the development of the notion in Catholic thought from the Greek and Latin Fathers to the late scholastics, and then concludes with some observations on the meaning of aseity as understood by certain modern philosophers.

Patristic Writers. The notion appears first clearly in the Apologists of the 2d century, expressed in the negative terms ἀγένητος (uncaused, unoriginated) and ἀγέννητος (ungenerated). St. *Justin Martyr is a typical witness: "For God alone is unoriginated and incorruptible, and it is for this reason that He is God. Everything else after Him is originated and corruptible" (*Dialogue with Trypho,* 5.4–6). The same idea, in one form or another, quickly became the primary attribute of God among the Greek Fathers: He alone is uncaused, unoriginated, underived, and ultimate.

The early Latin writers repeated this doctrine. But *Lactantius (early 4th century) adds a more positive analysis of his own, describing God as "self-originated [*ex se ipso est*] and therefore of such a nature as He wanted Himself to be" (*Div. instit.* 2.8, CSEL 19:137). At times he slips into such philosophically unsound and theologically unorthodox language as the following: "Since it is impossible for anything that exists not to have at some time begun to exist, it follows that, when nothing else existed before Him, He was procreated from Himself before all things [*ex se ipso sit procreatus*]," and again, repeating the words of *Seneca; "God made Himself [*Deus ipse se fecit*]"—*Div. instit.,* 1.7, CSEL, 19:28. The same positive notion of self-causality, but without the note of temporal beginning, appears in *Marius Victorinus, the convert who so deeply influenced St. Augustine. He speaks of God in one place as "*a se, per se,* without any beginning of existence" (*Contra Arium* 4.5 ed. P. Henry and P. Hadot, SourcesChr 68). In another context, not very consistently, he says that God is "the original cause both of Himself and all others," who "makes Himself to be [*se esse efficit*]"—*ibid.,* 1.3; 4.27. This incautious interpretation of *a se* as self-caused, taken over from pagan philosophers like Seneca or *Plotinus (God "made Himself . . . is cause of Himself"—*Enneads* 6.8.13–14), was later rejected by Latin Fathers such as St. *Augustine (*Trin.* 1.1.1). Neither Lactantius nor Marius Victorinus, it should be noted, is a Father of the Church.

SS. Hilary and Jerome. The next important step is the linking of the notion of God as *a se* with the Biblical text in which God declares His name to Moses: "I am who am" (Ex 3.14). The result is the identification of being itself with the very essence of God. This appears first in St. *Hilary of Poitiers, who describes his sudden realization, while meditating on the text of Exodus, that the essential nature of God and the source of all his attributes was revealed therein (*Trin.* 1.5–6, PL 10:28; cf. *In psalm.* 2.13, CSEL 22:46).

St. *Jerome also appeals to the Exodus text. The strong expressions he uses to explain it, such as God is "the origin of Himself and cause of His own substance," he interprets quite traditionally as meaning that God has no cause or origin outside of Himself (*In Eph.* 2.3.14; PL 26:488).

From Hilary on, the text of Ex 3.14 is central in the West for the analysis of the essence and attributes of God. The official Vulgate translation of St. Jerome, commonly used in the Latin Church, was: *"Ego sum qui sum"* (I am Who am). This was universally interpreted as identifying the very essence of God (since the name for the Hebrews signified the essence) with being itself. This interpretation endured, and continued to nourish deeply the thought of Christian theologians and philosophers, until the revival of Biblical scholarship in the 20th century. Contemporary Biblical studies have shown, however, that the original Hebrew text does not in fact offer any positive metaphysical description of the essence of God, but most probably means simply, "I am Who I am," that is, My name (and therefore My essence) is My own secret, hidden from men. It is an affirmation of the mystery, incomprehensibility, and ineffability of the divine nature with respect to the human mind. Another possible but less favored meaning is: "I am the one Who gives, or is the source of, being." Thus theologians no longer hold that the identity of God's essence and existence is directly revealed in this text. This does not alter the fact that the older interpretation exerted a decisive influence on Christian thought about God for many centuries, especially on St. Thomas Aquinas and the whole tradition of *scholasticism in the West.

St. Anselm. St. *Anselm of Canterbury is responsible for firmly imbedding the notion of aseity in the rising scholastic tradition as a primary attribute of God, thus summing up the whole patristic tradition. He expresses the negative aspect by *a se,* the positive by *per se* (*Monologion* 6). Anselm also introduces a more technical analysis of the identity of essence and existence. He explains existence as an attribute or perfection flowing necessarily from the very concept of the divine essence as the infinitely perfect Being; thus, for him, it is impossible even to think of God, i.e., of "that than which nothing greater can be conceived," save as actually existing. This notion is basic to his famous *ontological argument (*Proslogion* 1–4).

St. Thomas. The next decisive step, marking a new orientation in the interpretation of the identity of the divine essence and existence, was taken by St. *Thomas Aquinas. In terms of his central thesis of existence as act, the fundamental perfection of all things that is participated only in limited modes by finite essences, Aquinas teaches that the very essence of God is a pure subsistent act of existence (*Ipsum Esse Subsistens*). This has no admixture of potency or limit of any kind, and thus contains within it the plenitude of all possible perfection (*C. gent.* 1.26, 28; ST 1a, 3.4; 8.1). The Exodus text is his central authority from revelation (ST 1a, 13.11). In view of his radical reduction of essence to existence in the divine nature, St. Thomas carefully avoids the Anselmian way of speaking of the divine existence as though it were an attribute flowing necessarily from the divine essence, with its hint of a conceptual priority of essence. In fact, the term itself, *a se* (or *aseitas*), traditional though it be, is never actually used by Aquinas in speaking of God, possibly because of its faintly ambiguous suggestion of some causal relation between the divine essence and its existence. The closest he comes is when he speaks of God as the per se necessary being (ST 1a, 2.3; *C. gent.* 1.15), or as being by essence (*ens per essentiam*), in contrast to creatures, which are beings by participation (ST 1a, 3.4; 6.3). Later Thomists resume the use of the older term aseity, but continue to explain the identity between essence and existence in the same way as St. Thomas.

Franciscan School. The Franciscan school parted company with St. Thomas on his doctrine of existence as the basic perfection of all things, limited by essence, and preferred to explain the perfection of things as rooted in their essences or forms. In agreement on this point with all non-Thomist scholastics, they analyzed all the attributes of God, including existence itself, in terms of His infinitely perfect essence, to which, precisely because of its infinite perfection, existence necessarily belongs. Hence it is not surprising that in all these schools aseity should retain a central place among the divine attributes.

Not yet clear-cut in St. *Bonaventure (*Itinerarium* 5.5), the difference of approach becomes fully explicit in the teaching of John *Duns Scotus. For him, though the divine existence is, of course, absolutely identical with the divine essence, it is conceived by man as an intrinsic mode of the latter following logically after the primary mode of infinity. This, for Scotus, is the proper defining note of the metaphysical essence of God (*Opus Oxon.* 1.2.1–2.1.4; 1.8.3.3.28; for God as *ex se,* see *De primo principio* 3).

Suárez. Founder of the school of Suarezian Thomism that had been widely influential, F. *Suárez sought to make a synthesis of Thomism and Scotism. His *Disputationes Metaphysicae,* the first systematic treatise of metaphysics in the West, did much to render classic the primary division of all beings into *ens a se* (God) and *ens ab alio* (creatures), and to establish aseity as the primary attribute of God. Although in explaining the positive meaning of aseity Suárez often uses the Thomistic description of the divine essence as the subsistent act of existence, his own metaphysical doctrine of existence led to a more Scotistic interpretation. For Suárez, existence is reducible to actual essence—hence his denial of their real distinction in creatures; this made it inevitable that he should interpret God's existence more as a necessary attribute of the infinitely perfect divine essence than as the very core of all its perfection. (*Disp. Meta.* 28.1.6–7; 30.1.2–23; *Tract. de Div. Subst.* 1.2; 1.3.1; 1.5–9.) In Suárez's teaching, *ens a se* becomes practically synonymous with Necessary Being.

Modern Philosophy. The Suarezian notion of aseity seems to have passed into modern philosophy through the teaching of C. *Wolff and there influenced the development of the branch of philosophy known as *theodicy. Other thinkers gave different interpretations of aseity in the modern period, notably R. *Descartes and certain rationalist, idealist, and spiritualist philosophers.

Descartes initiated the rationalist tradition that restored to honor Anselm's ontological argument and deduced the existence of God from the concept of His essence as an infinitely perfect being (*Medit.* 3 and 5). He also revived the ancient term *causa sui,* abandoned since Augustine. When taken to task for this, he explained that he did not mean cause in the strict sense of producing an effect distinct from itself. But he insisted that it did mean some positive power in God that is responsible for constantly maintaining Him in existence. This is none other than the infinite power of God's essence, conceived as eternally positing His own existence (*Resp. to 1st and 4th Obj.*).

The same basic conception, understood in an even more rigorously rationalistic way, is found in the notion of God as *causa sui* advanced by B. *Spinoza (*Eth.* 1, Def. 1). A similar notion of God as somehow self-causing keeps recurring in various forms down through the German idealist philosophers, as, for example, in F. W. J. Schelling's conception of a procession of the conscious divine being from a deep, irrational, groundless abyss within Himself, or in A. Schopenhauer's notion of an autogenesis of God by absolute will, or in the self-positing, self-unfolding Absolute Spirit of G. W. F. *Hegel. The primary defect in all these positions, when they are to be taken literally, is that they all imply either some ultimate priority of essence, or will, or power over actual existence, or some kind of distinction (contrary to the absolute divine simplicity) between the ultimate source or ground of God and His actual completed being.

A more subtly qualified and acceptable notion of God as *causa sui* has reappeared among some French spiritualist philosophers of the 20th century, such as M. *Blondel (*L'Etre et les êtres,* Paris 1935, 176–181, 342, 520) and L. *Lavelle (*De l'Acte,* Paris 1937, 111–126). Despite their sometimes obscure and ambiguous language, especially Lavelle's, there is a profound and mysterious truth hidden behind their descriptions of God as pure spiritual act, pure "cause" without effect, as though somehow giving Himself to Himself in a pure spontaneous eternal act of consciously loving self-position or self-affirmation.

See also GOD; ESSENCE AND EXISTENCE; PURE ACT; SUFFICIENT REASON, PRINCIPLE OF.

Bibliography: G. L. PRESTIGE, *God in Patristic Thought* (SPCK; London 1959). C. TOUSSAINT, DTC 1.2:2077–80, 2223–35. M. CHOSSAT et al., DTC 4.1:756–1300. P. DESCOQS, *Praelectiones theologiae naturalis,* 2 v. (Paris 1932–38). R. GARRIGOU-LAGRANGE, *God, His Existence and His Nature,* 2 v. (St. Louis 1934–36). J. D. COLLINS, *God in Modern Philosophy* (Chicago 1959). M. BOURKE, "Yahweh the Divine Name," *The Bridge* 3 (1958–59) 271–287. J. ÉCOLE, "La Notion de 'Deus causa sui' dans la philosophie française contemporaine," RevThom 54 (1954) 374–384. S. CARAMELLA, EncFil 1:393–394.

[W. N. CLARKE]

ASER, eighth son of *Jacob, full brother of Gad; his mother was Zelpha, Lia's maid (Gn 30.10–13). He had four sons and one daughter (Gn 46.17). The Bible regards the tribe of Aser as being descended from him.

In the *priestly writers the tribe of Aser, led by Phagiel, numbered 41,500 warriors (Nm 1.13, 40–41). During the *desert journey of the Israelites, flanked by *Dan and *Nephthali, its position was to the north of the *Tent of Meeting (Nm 2.25–30), and it later served as rear guard when Israel left Mt. *Sinai (Nm 10.26). Of its ranks, Sathur acted as scout in Canaan (Nm 13.13). In the second census the tribe's male population is given as 53,400 (Nm 26.47).

To Ahiud, the new leader, fell the task of allotting the territory of the Aserites (Nm 34.27), who, as poetically indicated in *Jacob's oracles (Gn 49.20) and in *Moses' oracles (Dt 33.24–25), were allotted the narrow coastal plain along the Mediterranean from the tip of the Carmel ridge to the outskirts of the Phoenician town of Sidon (Jos 19.24–31), a fertile land that included some of the finest orchards and olive groves in the country. Lack of positive identification of most of its towns and uncertainty as to the extent of land adjoining the identified towns precludes accurate determination of its boundaries. To the south the Carmel range served as the common border with *Manasse, which was awarded the Aserite cities of Thaanach and Mageddo (Jos 17.7, 11). The Galilean hill country separated Aser on its southeastern side from Zabulon, and on its northeastern side from Nephthali as far as Tyre.

Egyptian inscriptions of Seti I (1303–1290 B.C.) and Ramses II (1290–1224 B.C.) mention a vanquished Asaru nation in the central Phoenician hinterland corresponding vaguely to the zone later assigned by Josue to Aser. This indicates that elements of the tribe were established there before the Exodus.

Since it contributes neither judge nor leader to Israel, Aser is not prominent in Biblical history. Inability to control its coastal cities (Jgs 1.31–32) suggests that Aser never overcame Phoenician dominance. This explains its failure to join in the battle led by Debora and Barac (Jgs 5.17) against Sisara, the general of Jabin who ruled the neighboring territory to the east (Jgs 4.2). At a later date we see the tribe aiding Gedeon against the Madianites (Jgs 6.35; 7.23).

Their subsequent history is obscure. Forty thousand warriors were present at David's coronation at Hebron according to 1 Chr 12.36, but Aser's name is missing from later tribal lists of his reign (1 Chr 27.16–22). Solomon's administration of Aser under Baana (3 Kgs 4.16) was probably limited, and this King was later to cede much of this region to the Phoenicians (3 Kgs 9.11–13), who controlled it until the Assyrian conquests of the 8th century B.C. In Ezechia's reign Aser is represented at the Passover in Jerusalem (2 Chr 30.11). The lone Aserite of any significance was the prophetess Anna, who praised God at the presentation of Jesus in the Temple (Lk 2.36).

Bibliography: EncDictBibl 150–151.

[R. BARRETT]

ASERA (ASHERAH), a goddess of the Canaanite pantheon, whose cult was adopted by many Israelites. In the texts found at *Ugarit Asera is called the wife of the supreme God *El; in practical worship, however, she was often confused with the goddesses of fertility, Ishtar (*Astarte) and Anath. Thus, Asera appears in the Bible as the consort of *Baal (Jgs 3.7). There were 400 prophets of Asera in Israel under *Jezabel (3 Kgs 18.19); her cult was popular in Jerusalem (3 Kgs 15.13); and Manasse set up her idol in the Temple (4 Kgs 21.7). Her worship was connected with cultic prostitution (4 Kgs 23.7). Her name (Heb. *'ăšērâ*) was used also for her symbol, a wooden post, probably a stylized tree, which was set up in a cultic *high place beside an image of Baal (Dt 7.5; 12.3; Jgs 6.25; 4 Kgs 18.4; etc.). The ancient versions rendered this wrongly as grove. Her cult was associated also with incense altars (Is 17.8) and stone pillars (2 Par 34.4). The plural of Asera refers to her many sanctuaries and images, not to many goddesses.

Bibliography: EncDictBibl 151. R. MAYER, LexThK[2] 1:918–919. O. EISSFELDT, RGG[3] 1:637–638. W. L. REED, *The Asherah in the O.T.* (Fort Worth, Tex. 1949).

[H. MUELLER]

ASH'ARĪ, AL- (ABŪ AL-ḤASAN 'ALĪ)

Eponym of the Ash'arite school of Islamic theology; b. Basra, 873; d. Baghdad, *c.* 924.

Life. Very little is certain about al-Ash'arī's life. For a long time he was a pupil of the famous Mu'tazilite, Abū 'Alī al-Jubbā'ī. Tradition gives six different accounts of his conversion from the *Mu'tazilites to "orthodoxy," i.e., to traditional Islamic doctrine. After his conversion, al-Ash'arī championed the traditionist approach, which was finally to triumph over Mu'tazilism. Later in life he moved to Baghdad, where he lectured and wrote until his death. More than 100 titles are attributed to him in the various sources. With the exception of a few short treatises, only three important works seem to be extant: *Kitāb al-Luma', al-Ibāna 'an Uṣūl al-Diyāna*, and *Maqālāt al-Islāmiyyīn*. The first two are dogmatic treatises and exist in English translations. The third is an objective and immensely important heresiography, edited by H. Ritter in 1929.

Doctrine. Al-Ash'arī owed much to his Mu'tazilite training. It is difficult from the extant sources to form a clear and complete synthesis of his own teaching. Much of the doctrine attributed to him by subsequent writers may well have been the work of later Ash'arites.

It has been affirmed that al-Ash'arī's chief contribution to Islamic theology was his introduction of a *via media* between the two extremes of the Mu'tazilites (and others) and the traditionists. But I. Goldziher insists that Ash'arism, not al-Ash'arī, was the *via media*. Some idea of his teaching may be had from his *Ibāna* written from an extremely traditionist point of view with an admixture of rational argument, and from the *Luma'*, which contains more rational argument, but remains quite traditionist. It seems to have been intended as a brief handbook of polemics for use against the Mu'tazilites, and its structure follows the five basic Mu'tazilite principles.

Al-Ash'arī's doctrines are presumably those summed up in the creeds inserted in the *Maqālāt* and the *Ibāna*, both strongly traditionist. On the problem of man's responsibility for his acts, al-Ash'arī is quite deterministic. He made some effort to save free will by the doctrine of acquisition (*kasb*), but this doctrine was not originated by him, and it is not clear precisely what he, or anyone else, meant by it.

Among the works attributed to al-Ash'arī is a short treatise containing a vindication of *kalām*, i.e., of the use of rational argument in dogmatic discussions. While it may not be the actual work of al-Ash'arī, it is an interesting document which underlines a certain tension that was long felt in Moslem theological circles. It appears that al-Ash'arī himself was rather reserved in this use of rational argument. Certainly he was far removed from the long and subtle philosophical discussions of the much later theologians who were called Ash'arites.

Influence. Whatever the immediate personal influence of al-Ash'arī may have been, his name is associated with the theological synthesis that ultimately came to be the "orthodox" theology of the vast majority of Moslems. Yet it is not clear why al-Ash'arī came to be regarded as its founder; sources close to his time give no indication of the prominence his name was to enjoy. Nevertheless, the work of al-Ash'arī himself, and of those whom he did influence, may well have given rise to the currents developed and enriched by the genius of later "Ash'arite" theologians.

The earliest complete Ash'arite treatise at our disposal is the *Tamhīd* of al-Bāqillānī (d. 1013). In this dogmatic and apologetic compendium are discussed, or at least adumbrated, practically all the questions with which Moslem theology would ever deal. It is possible that much of what al-Bāqillānī wrote was simply a restatement of views and arguments already put forth by al-Ash'arī. The next important Ash'arite theologian was al-Juwaynī (d. 1085). His work shows considerable advance in reasoning over that of al-Bāqillānī. *Algazel (Ghazzālī, al-; d. 1111) was a disciple of al-Juwaynī and an Ash'arite, but his work marked a new departure in theology, and his *Iqtiṣād* is far removed from al-Ash'arī's *Luma'*. Ibn Khaldūn calls him the first of the "modern" theologians.

The most prominent Ash'arites after Algazel were Shahrastānī (d. 1153), Fakhr al-Dīn al-Rāzī (d. 1210), Iṣfahānī (d. 1348), Ījī (d. 1355), and Jurjānī (d. 1413). But no real theological advances were made. More emphasis was given to questions now regarded as purely philosophical. Ash'arism as a theology was no longer a living system, but a kind of fixed dogmatic conservatism. It ended, as W. M. Watt put it aptly, in a blaze of philosophy. This was a consummation very far from the essentially religious spirit of its eponym.

See also KALĀM.

Bibliography: AL-ASH'ARĪ, *Al-Ibānah 'an Uṣūl ad-Diyānah* (*The Elucidation of Islam's Foundation*) tr. W. C. KLEIN (American Oriental Series 19, New Haven 1940); *The Theology of al-Ash'arī*, ed. R. J. MCCARTHY (Beirut 1953), the *Luma'*, the vindication of Kalām, and other texts in Arabic and English. G. MAKDISI, "Ash'ari and the Ash'arites in Islamic Religious History," *Studia Islamica*, 17 (1962) 37–80; 18 (1963) 19–39.

[R. J. MC CARTHY]

ASHES, LITURGICAL USE OF. The ashes of burned objects (plants, animals, human bodies) and dust are commonly found in use among ancient peoples for religious, magical, and medical purposes; opinions regarding the import of these uses are diverse (cf. Cabrol and Schneider). The two principal meanings are that certain ashes have a sacred character and power and that dust and ashes signify mortality, mourning, and penance. In the OT one finds ashes (*'ēper*) and dust (*'āpār*) used only as signs of mortality and worthlessness, sorrow and repentance. One finds such practices as sprinkling them on the head, covering the body, sitting or lying in them, and eating them. A sacrificed cow's ashes mixed with water are used with a purificatory significance (Nm 19.9). Christian liturgical usage and symbolism seem clearly to have been taken from the Jewish tradition.

Presently the Roman liturgy uses ashes only on Ash Wednesday and in the rite for the dedication of a church. The practice of all the faithful receiving ashes on their heads has been universal since the Synod of Benevento in 1091 (Mansi 20:739); however, this was known by the Anglo-Saxons a century earlier (Jungmann, 58–60). The first prayer for the blessing of the ashes gives them a sacred character as sacramentals for healing from sin ("healing remedy"); the other three prayers and the formula of imposition express their symbolism of mortality. Originally ashes were used as signs of private penance; then they became a part of the official ritual for public penitents and were given to them only. Another important dimension of this action is that the ashes on the penitent were to arouse prayerful sympathy for him within his fellow Christians.

Ashes are employed in two ways in the dedication of a church. The so-called Gregorian water used for sprinkling the interior of the church is a mixture of water, wine, salt, and ashes; the addition of salt and ashes is already found in the 8th-century Roman Ordinal 41, perhaps a biblicism from Nm 19.9. After the bishop enters the church, he writes in ashes strewn on the floor with the Latin and Greek alphabets crossing each other diagonally to form the Greek letter "chi" (X for Christ). The symbolism seems to indicate that Christ, the beginning and the end, has taken possession of the new church. This seems to be an Irish custom, which came through Ordinal 41 (Andrieu OR 4:319–320).

Formerly, in some places, ashes were imposed on Rogation days as well as on Ash Wednesday. They were used also for catechumens. In the Middle Ages one finds the custom of laying a dying person in ashes before he was anointed. Popular, nonliturgical uses also arose attributing special powers to the ashes of the Easter fire and to the dust of saints' remains (see Cabrol, 3043–44, 3039).

Bibliography: F. Cabrol, DACL 2.2:3037–44. M. A. Canney, Hastings ERE 2:112–114. C. Schneider, ReallexAntChr 1:725–730. V. Hamp and B. Löwenberg, LexThK² 1:917–918. J. A. Jungmann, *Die lateinischen Bussriten in ihrer geschichtlichen Entwicklung* (Innsbruck 1932).

[E. J. JOHNSON]

ASIA

This article treats first the geographical, ethnological, cultural, and political conditions of central and far eastern Asia insofar as they concern the background for the rise, progress, and mid-20th century status of the Catholic Church; it then summarizes the development of the Catholic Church and gives the 20th century status of other religions in Asia. Separate articles describe in more detail the history and current status of the Catholic Church in this area. *See* AFGHANISTAN; BHUTAN; BURMA; CAMBODIA; CEYLON; CHINA; HONG KONG; INDIA; INDONESIA; JAPAN; KOREA; LAOS; MALDIVE ISLANDS; MALAYSIA; MONGOLIA; NEPAL; PAKISTAN; PHILIPPINES; TAIWAN (FORMOSA); THAILAND; TIBET; TIMOR, PORTUGUESE; VIETNAM.

For Asia Minor and the Near East, *see* CYPRUS; IRAN; IRAQ; ISRAEL; PALESTINE; JORDAN, HASHEMITE KINGDOM OF; LEBANON; SAUDI ARABIA; SYRIA; TURKEY.

Land and People

Great diversity exists in the topography and climate of Asia, and its peoples are both ancient and numerous.

Discovery of the Continent. Asia, the vastest of continents (23,965,621 square miles), was crossed and recrossed by traders, missionaries, explorers, and surveyors for centuries. In early times the Greeks first heard about the Asian continent from Phoenician traders who brought salt from Northern India to the coasts of the Mediterranean Sea (14th century B.C.). Alexander the Great passed the Indus River in 326 B.C. During the last centuries B.C., Chinese silks were conveyed across the Asian continent to Cos in Anatolia and the Chinese general Chang Ch'ien crossed the Pamir region and subdued Sogdiana (136–123 B.C.). The Chinese travelers Fa Hsien (A.D. 403), Sung Yüng (A.D. 519), Hsüan Tsang (A.D. 642), and Wu K'ung (A.D. 572) journeyed into innermost Asia. The Nestorian Alopen, with Syrian priests, traveled over the Asian continent from Persia to China. Arabs conquered the towns of Sogdiana and East Turkestan. The conquering advance of the *Mongols westward occasioned the diplomatic missions of *John da Pian del Carpine (1245–47); *William of Ruisbroek (1253–55); Niccolò, Matteo, and *Marco Polo (1271–95); *Odoric of Pordenone (1318); and Ibn Battoeta (1325–49). These journeys contributed much to Western knowledge of Asia and to hearsay descriptions of Japan.

After the destruction of the Mongol Empire by the Chinese (1368), Tamerlane's conquest of central Asia (1403) and the expansion of the *Ottoman Turks (1453) cut off relations between Asia and Europe. But as soon as the Portuguese Vasco da *Gama discovered (1497–98) a new sea route to India via the Cape of Good Hope, and Ferdinand *Magellan found (1521) a way to the Philippines via South America and the Pacific, knowledge about Asia developed rapidly. Early *Jesuits settled in several south Asian countries, surveyed them scientifically, and journeyed through the heart of the continent. Notable among them were B. Goës (1602–07) and H. I. Desideri (1714). Russians explored northern Asia, crossed the Gobi Desert (1654) to the Great Wall, and discovered the Bering Strait (1648). The Dane, Vitus Bering (d. 1741), explored the straits for Peter the Great. In the 19th and 20th centuries Asia was further explored and surveyed. In the mid-20th century more attention was paid to the conquest of the Himalayan peaks, such as Mt. Everest (1953) and the Manaslu (1956). The map of Asia had by 1965 almost no unknown territory.

Geography and Climate. Much of Asia consists of an almost endless plain rising out of the Arctic Ocean in the north, the Pacific in the east, and the Indian Ocean in the south. The western fringe of the continent is separated from the great lowland of northern Europe by the Ural Range (5535 ft), and the Caspian, Black, and Mediterranean Seas, and from Africa by the Red Sea. In the middle of the continent a tableland rises above the plain; its cyclopean walls are the highest mountains in the world; they enclose the deserts of Mongolia, Taklamakan, and Tibet. The marches of Amdo (24,900 ft) which give birth to rivers, such as the Mekong, Salween, Yangtze, Yaling, and Huang ho, are spurs of the world's highest mountains: the Himalayan (29,002 ft), the Karakoram (28,250 ft), and the Indukush (25,260 ft) chains, in which the Brahmaputra, the Ganges, and the Indus find their source. To the south of this great fortress lies the Indian triangle of about a million square miles, the Burma-Malayan fan, and to the east, China, with island-arcs to the east (the Philippines, Ryukyu, Japan, Sakhalin, and the Kuriles) and to the south (Indonesia and New Guinea).

The climate of Asia depends on many factors, such as the vastness of the continent and the many high mountain ranges. Three-twentieths of Asia lies in the Arctic zone, one-twentieth in the Tropical, and four-fifths in the Temperate. In winter, cooling of the air is very intensive above the hinterland, producing a movement of air to the sea; a contrary movement takes place in the summer. These winds are called monsoons (from the Arabic *mausim* meaning season) and are very important climatic agents in Asia. Winter monsoons are cold and dry and are charged with polar Siberian air; they carry cold weather and prevent precipitation. (In northeastern Siberia a temperature of −90° was recorded in 1892). Summer monsoons are warm and provide great quantities of moisture. The monsoon and the high ranges of innermost Asia cause great differences in precipitation. Jacobad (West Pakistan) has 7.6 rainy days per year with 4 inches annual

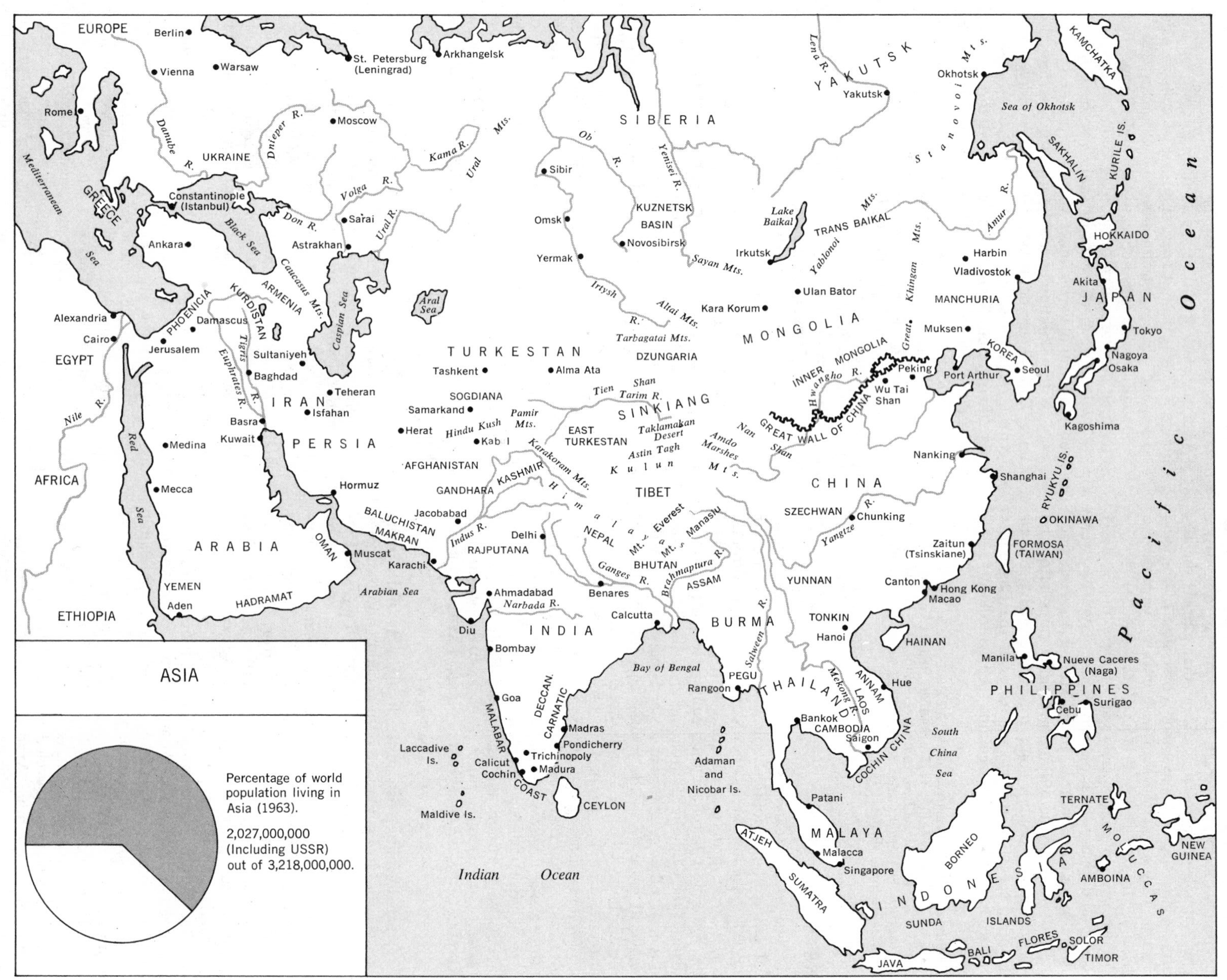

Reference map for the Church history of Asia from the early missionary period to the present (see the separate articles on each archdiocese).

rainfall, while Krangan (Indonesia) has 228 rainy days with 321 inches of precipitation.

Peoples and Cultures. The population of Asia is very sparse in both the Arctic regions and the central deserts, but very dense in the Chinese and Indian plains, as well as on the south and southeast islands of Japan and Java. Asia formerly was considered to be the cradle of mankind (Africa probably deserves this honor), and many races occupy the continent. In the northwest Ugrian people live east of the Urals, in central north Asia Altaic people wander near the Altai ranges, and Tungusic races occupy the Amur Basin in northeast Siberia. In central middle Asia Turkish people are numerous, but in the south the Semitic Indo-Iranian, the Tibeto-Chinese, and the Malayan people make up the bulk of Asia's millions. Of all these races, the Mongolian (yellow) race constitutes two-thirds. The white race living south of the Caspian Sea and around the delta of the Ganges includes Hindus, Persians, Armenians, and Kurds. More primitive races are found in several countries: Negritos in Indonesia and the Philippines, Weddas in Ceylon, Dravidians in Deccan (India), Mon-Khmers in Pegu-Cambodia, Lolos in China, and Ainus in Japan. Asia's population has grown from 330 million in 1650 to 1,759,000,000 in 1960 (700 million of whom are Chinese).

Chinese culture exerted the most widespread influence on Asia's peoples. It not only molded the civilization of countries such as Japan, Korea, and Annam (central Vietnam), but it also affected deeply the culture of Tibetans, Siamese, Mongols, Cambodians, and Burmese by introducing Chinese script, a distinctive style of art, and Confucian thought. Second in influence to the Chinese is the Indian culture (more specifically, Hinduism and Indo-Buddhism) which diffused Indian art and literature throughout India, Ceylon, Tibet, Indonesia (Java and Bali), and Cambodia. The Romano-Buddhist culture, originating in Gandhara, northwest India, is an adaptation of Romanized Hellenistic culture to Indian types and Buddhist thought. It especially affected the Iranian people of the Tarim Basin of the Taklamakan Desert (now western China). Its innumerable relics fill the museums of Europe and the U.S. *Islamic art and thought spread into western and central Asia and thence to India (especially Pakistan). In southern Asia it conquered the Malay Archipelago and the southern islands of the Philippines. From central Asia it affected especially the western provinces of China, but could not gain a foothold in Japan, the Ryukyus, or Formosa. Buddhist culture got a firm foothold in East Asia, spreading a typical art into Indochina, China, Japan, Korea, and Okinawa.

The Catholic Church in Asia

Although Christianity, like every other world religion, originated in Asia, its growth on that continent (except in Asia Minor and adjoining areas) was slow and late. The main reasons for this are the vastness of the continent, the lack of easy communication, and chiefly, the high cultural development of its large nations.

Medieval Period: 13th to 15th Centuries. The assertion that the Apostle *Thomas spread the Catholic faith in China can hardly be accepted. Even his presence in India cannot be established historically, though Catholics certainly existed in India from early times. The Moslem conquest of central and east Asia ended absolutely every connection of the eastern world with the West until the Mongol conquerors became interested in Christianity through Franciscan and Dominican embassies (1245) and that of Ruisbroek (1253). Later, Rome dispatched numerous missionaries, such as *John of Monte Corvino (1291), in order to propagate the Catholic faith in the East. The Asian Church was hierarchically organized in two ecclesiastical provinces: the Archdiocese of Khanbaliq (1307), with the suffragan See of Zaitun, and the Archdiocese of Sultaniyeh, with the suffragan Sees of Alimaliq, Tana, Kumuk, and Sarai. In the late Middle Ages more than 100,000 Catholics were scattered over the Asian continent, but few of their names have come down to us. The ruins of the first Catholic church of Mongolia, the oldest remains of the Church in Asia, were discovered by N. Enami's excavations (1938–41). The Chinese recovered their political independence by a nationalistic uprising against the Mongols in 1368. The Turkish people of central Asia, headed by Tamerlane, united in 1404 into one mighty empire. The primitive races and Hindus of Indonesia and the Malays of the Philippines were gradually subdued by Arabic conquerors and became partly Moslem. Meanwhile, the *Black Death (1346–1353) killed 25 million Europeans and 23 million Asians, decimating the clergy at home and abroad. Almost every missionary community of the *peregrinantes pro Christo* was wiped out, and the two ecclesiastical provinces of Asia ceased to exist (1482).

Missions under European Patronage: 16th and 17th Centuries. Extensive missionary activity was carried out in this period under the supervision of the governments of Portugal and Spain.

Portuguese Patronage. In 1493 Pope Alexander VI assigned one-half of the unknown world to Portugal and the other half to Spain. The Holy See entrusted the spreading of the Catholic Church in the newly discovered countries to the *Order of Christ in Portugal and to the crown of Spain (*see* PATRONATO REAL). An intense evangelization of the pagan world in the 16th century resulted from this right of patronage. Once Da Gama's new route to Asia (1497) opened up, the Portuguese began to make their power felt in the politics of the Asian continent; they founded trading centers in India (*Goa), Sunda (Ternate, Amboina, Solor), Malacca, and *Macao (China), and brought Franciscans, Dominicans, and secular priests, who took care of the spiritual needs of the Portuguese established in these colonies and made a few converts among the natives. The Thomas Christians of India were discovered and partially incorporated into the Catholic Church (*see* MALABAR RITE). Franciscans evangelized Ceylon and the Malayan Peninsula, after A. de Albuquerque took Malacca (1511) from the Moslems. There were few converts from Hinduism and Islam, because Christianization meant adopting Portuguese customs. Only among the ordinary people and the outcasts in Goa and Cochin did conversions take place.

The Church was strengthened when Goa was erected into a diocese (1533) that included all of Africa and the Far East. When Francis *Xavier went to India with the Jesuits (1542), mission work was extended to the Malabar coast, where Xavier baptized 30,000 Paravers. He conceived a great mission plan in order to win

Asia for Christ. In 1546 he journeyed to the Moluccas, where he founded a mission (Amboina). Acquaintance with a Japanese sailor in Malacca aroused his interest in a journey to Japan. Notwithstanding many dangers and hardships, Xavier went ashore in Kagoshima in 1549 and laid the foundations of the Catholic Church of Japan. Here he learned from the Japanese bonzes that, if he could convert the Chinese to the Catholic Faith, every Japanese Buddhist would become a Christian. Thereupon Xavier left Japan to enter China. A Portuguese ship put him on the shore of the island of Sancian near the delta of the Pearl River of Canton, where he died before entering China (1552). Soon after his death, the Portuguese got a foothold in Macao, threshold of the Chinese Empire.

Rome erected a new ecclesiastical province in Asia in 1557 by making Goa an archdiocese, with the suffragan Dioceses of Cochin (1557), Malacca (1557), Macao-China-Japan (1576), Funay (Japan; 1588), Angamale or Malabar (1599), Cranganore (1600), and Meliapore (1606). The Dioceses of Peking and Nanking were separated from Macao in 1690. These countries were not conquests of Portugal, yet Rome put the newly erected dioceses under Portuguese *padroado*. The Portuguese usually limited their colonial action to maintaining a few bases for trade, while apostolic action extended far behind the area under Portuguese control. Such was the case in the Moluccas and in India. The Jesuits started missions in the Mogul Empire (1580) and Roberto de *Nobili adopted a new method of conversion among the Brahmans of Madura (1614), while Desideri vainly endeavered to convert the Tibetans. In China, where Matteo *Ricci and the Jesuits constructed a flourishing church under Portuguese patronage, the arrival of rival orders of Spanish origin, Franciscans and Dominicans, gave rise to the *Chinese rites controversy. The intransigence of the new missionaries caused a fierce persecution that almost destroyed the Church in China.

Spanish Patronage. The Spanish, led by Ferdinand Magellan, discovered the Philippines (1521), and even before M. López de Legazpe had subdued the population of Manila in 1570, *Augustinians already had settled in Cebù (1565). The kings of Spain were aware of their obligations toward the conquered people. They sent missionaries of all religious orders: Franciscans, Dominicans, Jesuits, and Recollects, as well as Augustinians. Manila, erected as a diocese in 1579, was suffragan to Mexico; but in 1595 it became an archdiocese, the second of Asia, with three suffragan sees: Nueva Segovia, Nueva Cáceres and Cebù. Spain favored the Christianization of the Philippines and, notwithstanding some resistance in a few areas, conversion was rapid. At the end of the 19th century more than 7 out of almost 8 million Filipinos were Catholics; only half a million Moros remained Moslems. From the Philippines the Spanish missionaries advanced to the northern part of Formosa (*Taiwan) in 1626; they founded several missions there and made 4000 converts.

Although the political autonomy of Asia was threatened by the Portuguese and the Spanish, actual conquest was prevented by the rivalries among the Western powers. The arrival of Dutch Protestants in southern Asia (1595) was tantamount to a struggle to the death for the Catholic Church in many countries of Asia. They evicted the Portuguese first from Amboina (1605) and Ceylon, took Java and Malacca, and expelled the Spanish from Formosa, which they themselves lost to the Chinese (1668). When the Dutch settled in Japan (1620), the Portuguese and the Spanish trade passed into their hands and the Catholic Church in Japan was destroyed (1637). The Dutch attacked the Spanish also in Manila, but were defeated. In the 17th and the 18th centuries the British captured most of the Portuguese possessions in India and limited the arrival of new missionaries. They seized Ceylon from the Dutch and overthrew the Mogul Empire (1803), thus extending their domination to the Himalayas.

Missions under the Congregation for the Propagation of the Faith: 17th Century. The deterioration of the Portuguese power had a bad effect on Catholic missions in Asia. This fact induced the Holy See to erect (1622) the Congregation for the *Propagation of the Faith (Propaganda). Many problems arose between Portugal and Spain on one side and the Holy See on the other. Portugal could no longer provide priests for all its missions, but obstinately refused to permit evangelization by priests of other nations. The Catholic Church in Asia declined rapidly. Rome considered the *patronato real* of Portugal and Spain a unilateral contract, a privilege which she had granted. Jurisdiction under this privilege extended only to territories in Spain's and Portugal's possession, but *patronato* dioceses in Asia actually extended far beyond these territories. Although Portugal opposed the Holy See's decisions, she had to yield in the end. The main aim of the new Congregation was to entrust missionary work to native clergy in dioceses not under Portuguese patronage. This plan was achieved by erecting the Vicariate Apostolic of Idalcan (1637) and entrusting it to Matteo de *Castro, a former Brahman; a second apostolic vicariate was established at Malabar. The *Paris Foreign Mission Society was begun in 1663 and approved by Rome (1664). Its founders were consecrated by Rome as bishops *in partibus infidelium:* François *Pallu became apostolic vicar of Tonkin; P. *Lambert de la Motte, of Cochinchina (1659); and I. Cottolendi, of Nanking (1660). The main purpose of their mission was to train native clergy and form a native episcopate.

The innumerable, painful conflicts that arose between missionaries of the Propaganda and those of the patronage system impeded the progress of mission work in Asia. Besides the French missionaries of the Foreign Mission Society, the Propaganda sent also to China Italian Franciscans and *Vincentians. Spain's most powerful antagonist, the King of France, dispatched to Peking a group of French Jesuits who were pledged to undertake the mission work free from Spanish-Portuguese patronage. Propaganda erected new apostolic vicariates in China (1696), in Tibet (1704), and one entrusted to the *Theatines in Borneo (1692). As a result of the vigorous action of Propaganda a new spirit was injected into the missionary activities in Asia, principally in India and China. Despite this revival, however, organized Catholic life completely disappeared from Japan and Formosa, and almost totally from Indonesia, except for a few stations in Flores and Timor.

Opposition and Decline: 18th Century. At the dawn of the 18th century, the rationalistic climate of the *Enlightenment brought a sharp decline in vocations to the religious orders and a consequent decline in mission personnel. Following the suppression of the Jesuits (1773), most of their missionaries had to leave Asia. Rome tried to fill the gap by sending French Vincentians, Capuchins, and Carmelites. At the close of the century the French Revolution struck the Paris Foreign Mission Society and the Vincentians an almost mortal blow. Italian Franciscans, Portuguese Vincentians, and native priests, struggling against poverty, persecutions, and official annoyances, saved the Catholic Church in Asia from extinction. Even in India the churches erected under Portuguese patronage deteriorated seriously when Portugal broke off diplomatic relations with Rome in 1833. The Catholic Church in Asia was at its lowest ebb.

Revival of the Missions: 19th Century. Napoleon's defeat ushered in a period of political stability (1815–1914). The French clergy increased rapidly, and new missionary institutions were established. Pope Gregory XVI, by his encyclical *Probe nostis* (1840), encouraged missionary work, and new life was poured into the Catholic Church of Asia. Apostolic vicariates were erected in India: Calcutta and Madras (1834), Ceylon and Pondicherry (1836), and Trichinopoly (1846). The territories still under Portuguese patronage were correspondingly reduced; three of the four *padroado* dioceses in India were abolished by the Holy See (1838). Although this measure was indispensable if the Church was to develop, a schism broke out in Goa. It was not settled until agreements were reached between the Holy See and Portugal in 1886 and 1928, reducing Portuguese patronage to the Archdiocese of Goa, and the Dioceses of Meliapore and Macao.

When the Western powers, by their colonial policy in Asia, opened a new approach to the pagan world, the missionary activities of the Church were closely linked to them. Britain extended her power to the whole of Asia, establishing a ring of bastions in North Borneo (1816), Straits Settlements and Singapore (1819), Burma (1824), Aden (1839), *Persia and Basra (1872), and Arabia and *Kuwait (1899). She forced China to open some ports and took Hong Kong (1842). But the Chinese mainland, notwithstanding many treaties with the Western powers, remained politically independent, as did Japan, although the latter was forced to give up its isolationist policy. The French, through the negotiations of T. Lagrené (1844) with China, induced its government to grant religious freedom to Chinese Catholics and laid the basis of a French protectorate of the Catholic Church in China (completed by the agreements of 1858 and 1860). The spread of the Church was intensified. New religious congregations sent missionaries and sisters to China. Each congregation had charge of a territory that was set up as an apostolic vicariate or prefecture. The number of converts rose from 50,000 (1815) to 700,000 (1900) and the number of ecclesiastical territories from 7 to 41, while the two *padroado* dioceses, Nanking and Peking, were abolished in 1856. The reopening of Japan permitted the "hidden Christians," a community that had survived 2 centuries of harsh persecution, to emerge. They were discovered on March 17, 1865.

The French, evicted from India, cut for themselves a sphere of influence out of the five states of Indochina and consolidated them into a union dominated by France: Tonkin, Annam, and Cochinchina in 1862, and Cambodia and Laos in 1867. The mission work, taken over by the French from the Portuguese, was hindered by fierce persecutions, until the French regulated agreements with the emperor of Annam in 1883 and 1887. From then on, the Catholic Church developed quickly into a strong community, better organized than the Buddhist church. When the Western powers reached agreements with Korea in 1882, new mission fields were opened in an area where earlier attempts by French missionaries had met with bloody persecutions. While British tolerance allowed the Catholic Church to proselytize in Ceylon and Burma, Russian policy prevented missionary activity in northern and central Asia where the Russians extended their influence by military expeditions and colonization, from the Urals to the Pacific coast, including the Kuriles and Sakhalin (1875). The Chinese under the Manchu rulers founded a colonial empire on China's border by establishing their sovereignty over Manchuria (1626), Inner Mongolia (1635), Formosa (1682), Outer Mongolia (1679), Tibet (1720), and Dzungaria-Turkestan (1746). Japan, drawn out of its isolation policy by the U.S. in 1854, was the first nation of Asia to react to the impact of the Western nations. It made an energetic decision to match their superior forces and deliberately raised itself to the rank of a colonial power by annexing the Kuriles (1875), the Ryukyus (1879), Formosa (after the defeat of China in 1895), South Sakhalin (1905), and Korea (1910). The Dutch East-India Company was dissolved by the government of the Netherlands (1799), which assumed the control of the Dutch East Indies. Catholic priests were again allowed to stay in the colony (1807) and to rebuild the churches. The Church revived also in Flores and Timor (islands in the Malay Archipelago), when the Jesuits resumed missionary work there in 1859.

Recent History: 20th Century. New vitality appeared in the Catholic Church in Asia, when Pope Benedict XV by his encyclical *Maximum illud* (1919) and Pope Pius XI by *Rerum Ecclesiae* (1926) placed responsibility for the missions on the whole Catholic world and stressed the need for an indigenous *clergy to make the Catholic Church in Asia entirely independent (*see* MISSIONS, PAPAL LETTERS ON). In the 19th century seminaries had been founded in Asia and native priests ordained, but they were considered by foreigners to be on a lower plane. Pius XI himself consecrated the first Chinese bishops in 1926. From this date to the end of World War II, scores of native bishops ruled the Church along with foreigners, in every nation of Asia.

The imperialistic policy of the Western powers gave way in the 20th century before nationalistic aspirations (*see* COLONIALISM). Asia recognized the strength resulting from the scientific and industrial revolution of the West and tried to emulate it by establishing political and economic institutions on Western patterns, but independent of Western political entanglements. The Japanese freed themselves from their treaties in 1899 and China attempted by the Boxer Rebellion (1901) to withdraw the commerical and political privileges that it had yielded to the Western powers. Only after the revolution against the weakened Manchu Dynasty gave birth to the republic (1911) did the Chinese people succeed in recovering the privileges wrested from them. In the same struggle, however, China lost her sense of political unity, until a firm government was established by the Nationalists (1927). Ultimately, totalitarian Communist rulers, in close cooperation with the *Union of Soviet Socialist Republics, broke entirely with the past (1949) and destroyed the Catholic Church, at least externally. Meanwhile, Outer Mongolia, through a Pan-Mongolian movement, revolted against imperialist China and became an independent nation (1911) that finally fell into the hands of Communist rulers and became a satellite of the Soviet Union (1922). The Japanese prepared a "new order" in Asia, where they were to be the leading nation (1931).

British India, revolutionized by Mohandas *Gandhi, won its independence in 1947, but was partitioned into the states of Pakistan, the Indian Union, Burma, and Ceylon. The Dutch yielded to the nationalists of Indonesia on Dec. 28, 1949, and the Japanese lost their colonial empire in 1945. Korea became independent and Formosa was returned to China. The Chinese and Russian policy of spreading Communism by means of war inflamed Korea with civil war; American help to democratic Korea prevented a Communist victory, though Korea north of the 38th parallel is still under Communist control. In Indochina, however, the French were expelled from Tonkin by combined Communist forces. Four states of the union were set free (1954). The Philippines obtained independence in 1947. But the Communists strengthened their grip on the conquered peoples of north and central Asia by establishing republics on a Communist pattern, strongly united to the Soviet Union. Communist China dominated Tibet (1951) and demonstrated its imperialist policies in south and southeast Asia. The Portuguese withdrew from Goa in 1961; the British, from Singapore and the Straits Settlements (1957) and North Borneo (1963); and the Dutch, from West New Guinea (1963).

Throughout these political developments the Catholic Church in Asia after World War II showed a remarkable ability to adapt herself to every nation and people. Free from the strain of the colonial era, the Church in 1965 prospered in every free nation of Asia. Ecumenical dialogue was attempted with other Christian and non-Christian Churches. Eight Asian nations had diplomatic relations with the Holy See and papal representatives resided in 11 nations. Communism was the principal active enemy of the Church in Asia. Its aim was the total annihilation of every religion. In China, which had about 4 million Catholics in 1949, those of the faithful who were not put to death or imprisoned, were forbidden to worship publicly, except in a few centers left open for propaganda purposes. The Catholic Church in North Korea and North Vietnam fell victim to Communist persecution.

Statistics reveal a steady numerical growth of the Catholic Church in Asia. Of the approximately 37 million baptized Catholics in 1963, some 21 million were in the Philippines, 6 million in India, and 345,000 in Pakistan, 4 million in China (as of 1949), 246,000 in Taiwan and 205,000 in Hong Kong, 1.5 million in Indonesia, 1.3 million in Vietnam, 800,000 in Ceylon, 625,000 in Korea, 300,000 in Japan, 260,000 in Malaysia, 215,000 in Burma, 120,000 in Thailand, 54,000 in Cambodia, and 27,000 in Laos. In other Asiatic countries the Catholic population was much less; in Afghanistan, Bhutan, Mongolia, and Tibet it was almost nonexistent. Catechumens totaled another half million (*see* CATECHUMEN; CATECHUMENATE).

The Church conducted an active educational, charitable, social, and literary apostolate (*see* CATHOLIC PRESS, WORLD SURVEY, 2, 8, 13; LAY APOSTOLATE; MISSIONS, CATHOLIC; MISSIONS, SOCIAL ACTION OF).

Other Religions in Asia

As in other respects, the peoples of Asia are greatly diversified also in respect to religion.

Christian Religions. There are in Asia, in addition to the Protestant Churches, several other groups of Christians.

Nestorianism. After the definitive settlement at Seleucia-Ctesiphon (Persia), *Nestorianism spread not only into Asia Minor, but also into India, central Asia, and even in China (635), where it prospered until 845. Proscribed by the Chinese emperor, Nestorianism found a new field among the nomadic tribes of central Asia. It flourished under the Mongol Yüan Dynasty (1260–1368) in China, but almost disappeared at the rise of the Ming Dynasty. It survived in Persia, Iraq, and India, where a group of 175,000 believers was excluded from the Jacobite community in 1875 (*see* NESTORIAN CHURCH).

Jacobites. They are members of a sect founded by James (Jacobus) *Baradai, a bishop of Antioch in the 6th century. He taught that Christ possessed only a divine nature (*see* MONOPHYSITISM). Some 800,000 of his followers survive in India.

Orthodox. The Russian conquerors of Siberia introduced the Orthodox Church into their Asian territories. In every town along the southern Siberian border Orthodox churches were built. Russian Orthodoxy spread into China in 1727, where it had 6,587 adherents. In 1861 it was propagated in Japan and in 1900 in Korea (*see* MISSIONS, ORTHODOX). Some 40,000 Orthodox Christians survive in those areas, but in China and Siberia they disappeared almost entirely (*see* EASTERN CHURCHES; ORTHODOX CHURCHES).

Protestantism. The Dutch were the first Protestants to introduce their Church into Asian countries: the Moluccas and Batavia (1606), Formosa (1624), and Ceylon (1656). The British, more tolerant than the Dutch, allowed the Catholic Church to stay in their possessions while at the same time they gave Protestant missionaries entire freedom to introduce their churches. Protestant Christianity developed quickly in the 19th century in India, in Burma and Siam, and especially in China, Formosa, Japan, and the Dutch Indies. When the U.S. occupied the Philippines (1898), Protestantism was introduced but without great success. Protestant churches were built also in Malaya, Singapore, and every British colony. Protestants numbered about 10 million in 1964 (*see* MISSIONS, PROTESTANT).

Non-Christian Religions. By far the greater portion of Asia's population belongs to the numerous non-Christian sects, or, in the case of the Communists, to no religion at all. The principal Asiatic religions are treated in the articles on *Buddhism, *Confucius and Confucianism, *Hinduism, *Islam, *Jainism, *Parsees,

*Shintoism, and *Taoism. *Animism is practiced by about 16 million people among the peoples found in Indonesia, the Philippines, Taiwan, Cambodia, etc. Jews also are found in many countries of Asia; in 1964 there were 80,000 in Iran; 21,000 in India; 6,000 in Lebanon; 6,000 in Iraq; 3,000 in Syria; 4,000 in Afghanistan; etc. The total number of Jews in Asia was 1,753,296 (1957), about 10 per cent of the world Jewish population (*see* JUDAISM). Communists in China and elsewhere have attempted to suppress all religion. There are, therefore, many people in Asia who might be listed as unbelievers.

Bibliography: Streit-Dindinger v.4–14. J. ROMMERSKIRCHEN and J. DINDINGER, *Bibliografia missionaria* (Rome 1936), annual. Delacroix HistMissCath. Mulders. G. BARDY and J. B. AUFHAUSER, DHGE 4:940–1035. Latourette v.1–3, 6–7. Latourette Christ19th–20thCent v.3, 5. R. GROUSSET, *Histoire de l'Asie,* 3 v. (Paris 1921–22); *Histoire de l'Extrême-Orient,* 2 v. (Paris 1929). G. B. CRESSEY, *Asia's Land and Peoples* (3d ed. New York 1963). D. F. LACH, *Asia in the Making of Europe* (Chicago 1965–), v.1 *The Century of Discovery.* T. OHM, *Die Religionen in Asien* (Cologne 1954). J. BECKMANN, *Weltkirche und Weltreligionen* (Freiburg 1960); *La Congrégation de la propagation de la foi face à la politique internationale* (Schöneck, Ger. 1964). E. B. HARPER, ed., "Aspects of Religion in South Asia," *Journal of Asian Studies* 23 (June 1964) 3–197. H. EMMERICH, *Atlas missionum* (Vatican City 1958), to be used with L. SCHORER'S *Data statistica* (Vatican City 1959). A. FREITAG et al., *The Twentieth Century Atlas of the Christian World* (New York 1964). MissCattol. *Bilan du Monde.* J. B. AUFHAUSER et al., LexThK[2] 1:923–927. AnnPont has annual statistics on all dioceses, vicariates, and prefectures.

[J. VAN HECKEN]

ASIA, ROMAN PROVINCE OF, the region comprising the western section of Asia Minor (modern *Turkey) that constituted a Roman province in the late 2d century B.C. During the Apostolic period it included the territory from *Galatia to the sea, with the offshore islands of Ionia, and was bounded on the north by Bithynia and on the south by Lycia. A senatorial province, it was governed by a proconsul who resided at Ephesus. It was a rich agricultural and pastoral land, famous for the fabrication of colorful woolen cloth and was much subject to the exploitation of Roman capitalists. Its ports connected the hinterland of Asia Minor and the East with Greece and Rome through the opulent Hermus and Maeander valleys. Besides Ephesus the most important ports were Cos, *Miletus, Smyrna, *Pergamum, and Troas, while farther inland, along the valley routes, were Thyatira, *Sardis, Philadelphia on the Hermus, and Laodicea, *Colossae, and Hierapolis on the Maeander.

St. *Paul first passed through Asia on his second missionary journey when he traveled through Mysia and set sail from Troas for Neopolis in the Roman Province of *Macedonia (Acts 16.6–10). He spent most of his third missionary journey in Ephesus (Acts 19.1–20.1), whence his disciples evangelized the hinterland and where he could have easy access to his churches in the Roman Province of *Achaia. He gave his pastoral sermon to the elders of the Church of Ephesus at Miletus on his last trip to Jerusalem with the collection for the poor from the Greek communities (Acts 20.17–38). Two of his so-called *Captivity Epistles were sent to the churches of Asia to combat the incipient heresies that were taking root there. (*See* COLOSSIANS, EPISTLE TO THE; EPHESIANS, EPISTLE TO THE.) That such heresies were commonplace in this region at the crossroads of the Eastern and Western worlds is clear also from the letters sent by John, the author of the book of *Apocalypse, to the seven churches of Asia from his exile on the island of Patmos (Ap 1.9–3.22).

In the books of the *Machabees the term Asia (e.g., 1 Mc 8.6) refers to the empire of the *Seleucid Dynasty, which included, at the time of its greatest expansion, the modern countries of Turkey, Syria, Iraq, Iran, and Afghanistan. By the Machabean period, however, the Seleucids had forfeited Asia Minor to the Romans at the battle of Magnesia, near Ephesus, a fact that led them to concentrate their military efforts on holding their eastern territories (1 Mc 6.1–5).

Bibliography: EncDictBibl 152. F. DÖLGER, LexThK[2] 6:327–329. G. BARDY, DHGE 4:966–989. G. M. PERELLA, EncCatt 2: 121–122.

[P. P. SAYDON]

ASIA MINOR, EARLY CHURCH IN

In extant documents the 5th-century author *Orosius (PL 31:679A) is the first to use the term Asia Minor. The name Asia occurred earlier and designated the Roman Province that developed from the kingdom of Pergamum bequeathed to Rome by Attalus III (d. 133 B.C.). To the Attalid legacy were subsequently added Mysia, Lydia, Caria, Phrygia, Cappadocia, Bithynia, Galatia, and Pontus. At the beginning of the Christian era the territory thus augmented was coextensive with the Asiatic peninsula of which Ephesus was the administrative center. In the late 3d century, Diocletian and his immediate successors reorganized the territory into the Diocese of Asia in seven separate provinces along the lines of the older boundaries: Proconsular Asia, the islands of Lesbos, Chios, Rhodes, and Cyprus, the Hellespont and Cyzicus, Lydia, Caria, Phrygia I Pacatiana, and Phrygia II Salutaris. To the Byzantines this area was known as *mikrà Asía* or *Anatolé,* and still later it was called the Levant.

Culture and Religion. Asia Minor, the bridge between East and West, felt the impact of many cultures, some dating back to the 3d millennium B.C. More important, however, for the early Church were the contacts established there with Hellenistic civilization, the Hellenized Jews of the Diaspora, the Roman imperial administration, and the mystery religions. The great temple of Diana at Ephesus and the cult image of the Mother Goddess and her mysteries were factors that left traces of influence on the manner in which the Christian gospel was proclaimed. Well-organized Jewish communities in all the large cities, though frequently hostile to Christianity (see Acts 13.45; 14.2), disposed many for accepting its message. The presence of diverse ethnic groups seems to have minimized any national resistance to Christianity, such as the Syro-Phoenician sun-worship at Emesa.

Knowledge of the spread of Christianity in apostolic times is limited to the information gathered from the books of the New Testament. The record of Paul's activity in Asia Minor is found in Acts ch. 13–16 and 18 or can be inferred from his Epistles to the Ephesians, Colossians, and Galatians. The messages directed by John to the seven Churches in Asia (Apoc 1.11; ch. 2, 3), each located in a capital city with a *conventus juridicus*—Ephesus, the largest market west of the Taurus, Smyrna, Pergamum, Thyatira, Sardis, Philadelphia, Laodicea—all point to an urban-centered

Map locating the early Christian foundations in Asia Minor.

Church in the region that was to become the land of Christianity par excellence.

The Post-apostolic Age. Evidence of the growth of Christianity centers in important places, as is indicated by the letters of *Ignatius of Antioch to the Churches in Asia Minor. It tends to become slightly more detailed in regard to specific persons. Smyrna gained renown through its Bishop Polycarp, the spokesman with Pope Anicetus for the Church in Asia Minor in the *Easter controversy. The account of his martyrdom (*Martyrium Polycarpi*), written, in its earliest form, immediately after his death, continued to focus attention on the Church of that city. Laodicea is known for its Bishop Sagaris, who died as a martyr (Eusebius, *Hist. eccl.* 4.26.3), and Eumenia in Phrygia is famous for its martyr Bishop Thraseas (*ibid.* 5.24.4). Ephesus took on a preeminence that it held for many years; it is known in this period for its Bishop Polycrates, who presided at a synod *c.* 190 attended by numerous bishops (*ibid.* 5.24). Hierapolis in Phrygia is especially remembered for two of its bishops, Papias, author of an *Explanation of the Sayings of the Lord,* and Apollinaris, an apologist and strenuous opponent of *Montanism. Sardis merits specific mention because its Bishop Melito was distinguished as an apologist and author of numerous treatises (*ibid.* 5.28.5).

The Church in Asia Minor was disturbed by the rigoristic errors and the so-called "new prophecy" of Montanus in Phrygia and by the Monarchian teachings of Noëtus of Smyrna. From the closing years of this period comes the earliest extant nonliterary evidence concerning the spread of Christianity, recorded in the inscription of *Abercius, Bishop of Hierapolis in Phrygia Salutaris.

Only a few place names are known as early centers of Christianity. *Caesarea in Cappadocia, under the leadership of its Bishop *Firmilian, was a thriving center of missionary activity. Between 230 and 235 two important councils were held, one at Iconium, the other at Synnada, attended by bishops from Galatia, Phrygia, Cappadocia, and Cilicia. On both occasions the bishops of Asia Minor denied the validity of heretical baptism, thus anticipating the decision of the African bishops in the Council of *Carthage of 256 under the leadership of *Cyprian (*Epistula* 75.7).

The tragic event for the Church in this period was the Decian persecution and the serious problem it caused in dealing with **lapsi*. Only two authentic contemporary accounts of the martyrs in Asia Minor are extant. The *Acta Pionii* relate the martyrdom of the presbyter Pionius of Smyrna and the apostasy of his bishop, Euctemon, a successor of Polycarp (*Acta Pionii* 15; 16). The *Passio SS. Carpi et sociorum* gives the details of the trial and death of Carpus, Papylus, and Agathonice at Pergamum [see *Analecta Bollandiana* 58 (1940) 142–176]. Later information coming from Gregory of Nyssa (PG 46:944–953) tells of the ravages of this persecution in Pontus and the flight of Gregory Thaumaturgus. Legendary accounts of martyrdoms purporting to date from this persecution are numerous; among them is the account of the *Seven Sleepers of Ephesus walled up in a cave during the Decian persecution; their alleged tomb was a famous place of pilgrimage till the days of the Turkish conquest of Asia Minor. Toward the end of the 3d century, *Methodius of Olympus, an early opponent of Origen, defended Christianity against the attacks of Porphyry. Of his voluminous writings, only one, the *Symposium* or *Banquet of the Ten Virgins,* has survived in its entirety.

The Diocletian Persecution. While the Church in Asia Minor suffered greatly during this period, surviving documents yield little detailed information. It is recorded that "armed soldiers surrounded a little town in Phrygia, of which the inhabitants were all Christians, every man of them, and setting fire to it burnt them all, along with young children and women" (Eusebius, *Hist. eccl.* 8.11.1). The little town is probably Eumeneia. Pontus felt the terror of persecution in which judges are said to have vied with one another, "ever inventing novel tortures, as if contending for prizes in a contest" (*ibid.* 8.12.1). A third place in Asia Minor afflicted by this persecution was Cappadocia (*ibid.* 8.12.1).

With the accession of Constantine I a new era began for the Church. Local councils dealing with doctrinal and disciplinary matters became frequent, and great ecumenical councils met in this region to deal with fundamental Christian teachings. From the great urban centers, Christianity spread to the outlying districts, thus increasing the number of the chorepiscopi or bishops (*see* CHORBISHOP) of rural areas, 50 of whom are said to have been assisting the bishop of Caesarea by the end of the 4th century. The pattern for the administrative organization of the Church into metropolitan sees with suffragan bishops was set in Asia Minor.

Bibliography: W. M. RAMSAY, *The Historical Geography of Asia Minor* (London 1890). C. BRANDIS, *Pauly-Wiss* RE 2 (1896) 1533–62. H. LECLERCQ, DACL 5.1:1013. H. GELZER, "Ungedruckte und ungenügend veröffentlichte Texte der *Notitiae Episcopatuum,*" *Abhandlungen der Bayerischen Akademie der Wissenschaften. Philosophisch-philologische Klasse* 21 (1901) 529–641. G. BARDY, DHGE 4:966–988; *Catholicisme* 1:896. J. KEIL, ReallexAntChr 1:740–750. B. KÖTTING, *ibid.* 2:1144–47. E. KIRSTEN, *ibid.* 2:1105–14. Jedin HbKirchgesch. Daniélou-Marrou ChrCent. A. VON HARNACK, *The Mission and Expansion of Christianity in the First Three Centuries,* ed. and tr. J. MOFFATT, 2 v. (2d ed. New York 1908). J. LEBRETON and J. ZEILLER, *The History of the Primitive Church,* tr. E. C. MESSENGER, 2 v. (New York 1949).

[H. DRESSLER]

ASÍN PALACIOS, MIGUEL, Arabist; b. Saragossa, Spain, July 5, 1871; d. San Sebastián, Spain, Aug. 12, 1944. After obtaining the doctorate in theology at the Conciliar Seminary of Saragossa, Asín Palacios studied Arabic under Julián Ribera at the University of Madrid. Soon he was given the chair of Arabic studies there, which he held for almost 40 years. Later he also became the director of the Royal Spanish Academy. During all these years, he was the leading scholar of Spanish-Arabic studies. His research was primarily in the field of Islamic philosophy and mysticism (*see* SUFISM) and their relationship to their Christian counterparts. He demonstrated the Christian origins of the theology of *Algazel (al-Ghazzālī) and the practical mysticism of the school of Abenmassara and Abentofail. Other works of Asín Palacios tend to make evident the influence of Islamic thought on the scholasticism of the 13th century. In the field of literary studies, Asín Palacios is best known for his work, *La escatología musulmana de la Divina Comedia* (Madrid 1919), in which he showed that a good part of the ultraterrestrial voyage of Dante had its origin in the Islamic legend of Mohammed's ascent to heaven; there were numerous European versions of this story that must have been known to the Italian poet. Although the point was much disputed, certain later finds have confirmed the thesis of Asín Palacios.

Miguel Asín Palacios.

Bibliography: E. GARCÍA-GÓMEZ, "Don Miguel Asín (1871–1944): Esquema de una biograffí," *Al-Andalus* 9 (1944) 267–291. **Illustration credit:** MAS, Barcelona.

[J. M. SOLA-SOLE]

ASIONGABER (EZIONGEBER), port at the northern end of the Gulf of Aqaba from which King *Solomon and some of his successors conducted trade with Arabia, and where Solomon built an extensive copper refinery; it has been identified with modern Tel el-Kheleifeh. Nelson Glueck, the excavator of the site, believes that Elath (distinguished from Asiongaber in some texts—see Dt 2.8; 3 Kgs 9.26) is the name given to the same site at a later time (see 4 Kgs 14.22), although this is not certain. Earlier references to Asiongaber (Nm 33.34–35; Dt 2.8) probably refer to some small settlement in the neighborhood that later disappeared, for Solomon's complex was founded on virgin soil.

Solomon's refinery, a truly magnificent accomplishment, is not mentioned in the Bible. The location was chosen because of the strong, steady wind from the north (for the smelting process) and because it was near the mineral deposits of the *Araba and on the seashore. It was here that Solomon built ships to carry the copper products to Arabia to exchange for spice, ivory, gold, and other products (3 Kgs 9.26–27). The trade with Arabia was carried on by his successors, but not always with the same success (3 Kgs 22.49). Between 1938 and 1940, the American School of Oriental Research in Jerusalem carried on extensive excavations at Asiongaber under the direction of Nelson Glueck. This archeological project brought to light, not only the plant for smelting and refining copper, but also such objects as fishhooks, arrowheads, nails, fragments of safety pins, all of which were most probably manufactured there. Glueck called Asiongaber the Pittsburgh of ancient Palestine. The tell was formed by four or possibly five settlements, for the town was destroyed and rebuilt several times.

Bibliography: EncDictBibl 153, 639. H. HAAG, LexThK[2] 3:1103–04. Abel GéogrPal 2:320. N. GLUECK, BullAmSchOrRes 71 (1938) 3–17; 72 (1938) 2–13; 75 (1939) 8–22; 79 (1940) 2–18; BiblArchaeol 1 (1938) 13–16; 2 (1939) 37–41; 3 (1940) 51–55; *The Other Side of the Jordan* (New Haven 1940) 89–113.

[C. CORCORAN]

ASKE, ROBERT, leader in Yorkshire insurrection, during the *Pilgrimage of Grace, 1536–37; b. place and date unknown; d. York, England, (June-July?) 1537. Little is known of his early life, except that he was a lawyer with a good London practice. Restrictive enactments of Parliament (1536) brought about an uprising of squires, knights, and commons in Lincolnshire. By October 30,000 Yorkshiremen, wearing the badge of the "Five Wounds," also were in arms; Aske was their leader. Objectives of the pilgrimage were complex; the pilgrims' motives were not always clear and distinct; and religious and social elements were inextricably combined in the revolt. Aske issued a proclamation opposing Thomas Cromwell and "other evil counsellors" of Henry VIII, demanding repeal of the Statute of Uses, and calling for an end to the suppression of monasteries. The pilgrims proclaimed loyalty "to Holy Church militant . . . and to the preservation of the King's person and his issue." Aske advocated moderation and restraint. Only if all petitions to the King failed was the sword to be used. Under the command of Thomas Howard, Earl of Surrey and second Duke of *Norfolk, a royal force of some 8,000 was sent to quell the revolt. On December 5 Aske, falling on his knees, confronted Norfolk at Doncaster and petitioned the King's pardon. Invited to court, Aske received Henry's promises of pardon and assurance that a parliament would shortly be held at York. In January 1537 a new outbreak in East Yorkshire provided Henry with a pretext for breaking his pledge. Treachery and brutality marked his treatment of the leading insurgents. Aske, again summoned to London, was imprisoned in the Tower. He insisted that the Supremacy Act "could not stand with God's law," and that belief in the pope's authority was the touchstone of orthodoxy; he maintained that Thomas Cranmer and other bishops were heretics because they had been the cause of the breach of unity in the Church and were supporters of the new learning and of the opinions of Luther and Tyndale. Aske was sentenced and condemned to be drawn on a hurdle through the city of York and hanged in chains.

Bibliography: M. H. and R. DODDS, *The Pilgrimage of Grace, 1536–1537, and the Exeter Conspiracy, 1538,* 2 v. (Cambridge, Eng. 1915). Hughes RE. A. TAYLOR, DHGE 4:1048–49. J. GAIRDNER, DNB 1:661–664.

[J. G. DWYER]

ASMODAEUS, in the Book of Tobit, a demon who successively killed seven husbands of Sara, Raguel's daughter, on their wedding nights (Tb 3.8). Following the instructions of the angel *Raphael, the young man Tobias, on his own wedding night with Sara, burned the heart and liver of a fish he had caught in the Tigris, and the smoke drove Asmodaeus to the desert of upper Egypt, where Raphael kept him in bonds (Tb 6.8; 8.2–3). This story is not to be judged historically, but in keeping with the folklore incorporated in the Book of Tobit.

The name of Asmodaeus (Greek, Ἀσμοδαῖος) is no doubt to be connected with that of Aēšma Daeva (literally, wrath demon) of the *Avesta, the Persian demon of destruction, the one "with the bloody bludgeon." However, because of the pure monotheism and complete lack of Iranian *dualism in the Book of Tobit, it seems probable that merely the name was borrowed from Iranian mythology. The concept of a "destroying angel" had deep roots in ancient Israel (Ex 12.23; Wis 18.25; 2 Chr 21.15). In Ap 9.11 the prince of the nether world, *Abaddon, is likewise called the destroyer. Perhaps by popular etymology the Jews of the last pre-Christian centuries connected the name Asmodaeus with the Hebrew verb *hišmîd* (to destroy). In the apocryphal and rabbinical literature the same demon appears under the Hebrew name Ashmedai (*'ašmēdai*), especially in legends about King Solomon.

Bibliography: B. BRODMANN, LexThK[2] 1:940. G. MESSINA, EncCatt 1:358–359. EncDictBibl 153–154. C. H. HUNZINGER, RGG[3] 1:649. A. KAMINKA, "The Origin of the Ashmedai Legend in the Babylonian Talmud," Jewish QuartRev 13 (1922–23) 221–224.

[M. R. RYAN]

ASOLA, GIOVANNI MATTEO, Italian composer of the late Renaissance Venetian school; b. Verona, *c.* 1540; d. Venice, Oct. 1, 1609. He was educated at the *collegio* of the Canonici Regolari on the small island of Alga, near Venice. From *c.* 1569 to 1577 he was in Venice, where his publications first appeared, beginning with two sets of Masses in 1570. In late 1577 he accepted the position of maestro at Treviso, and a year later, the same function at Vicenza. In 1588 he returned to Venice as one of the chaplains at the church of San Severo; he remained there until his death.

Asola was an assiduous composer. Although he produced some madrigals, his main efforts were devoted to about 40 Masses for from three to eight voices, psalms for Vespers, numerous motets for various voice combinations, etc. Notable was his dedication to a volume entitled *Psalmodia vespertina* containing works of various Venetian composers and published in honor of Palestrina in 1592. His psalms are usually set in a simple harmonic fashion, while his motets and Masses reveal the composer as a deft handler of all the polyphonic techniques of the late 16th century.

Bibliography: G. ASOLA, *Sixteen Liturgical Works,* ed. D. M. FOUSE (New Haven 1964). G. D'ALESSI, *La Cappella musicale del Duomo di Treviso, 1300–1633* (Treviso 1954). Reese MusR.

[F. J. GUENTNER]

ASPERGER, SEGISMUNDO (APERGER), missionary and doctor; b. Innsbruck, Oct. 20, 1687; d. Guaraní Reduction of Apóstoles, Nov. 23, 1772. He was the only Jesuit who did not leave in the expulsion of 1767–68 because he was physically disabled. He was a missionary among the Guaraní Indians from 1719 until his death. Although he was not a doctor by profession, he acquired considerable prestige because of his medical knowledge and his cures. He was a stanch advocate of the balm that is obtained from the leaves of the Aguaraybai, of the family of the *Teribintáceas,* which was commonly called balm of missions and was formerly used as a cure-all. In the British Museum there is an unpublished volume, "Medicinal Prescriptions, the chief ingredients of which are the medicinal herbs of Paraguay," by the Rev. Segismundo Asperger, Jesuit and missionary. The volume, which consists of 166 pages, lists 88 diseases and their respective remedies. In 1802 several of Asperger's studies were published in Buenos Aires, one on dragon's blood, Paraguayan maté, nutmeg, and wild vicereine (*virreina silvestre*). Asperger also contributed to the *Manuale ad usum sacerdotum* (Loreto 1721).

Bibliography: G. FURLONG, "Un médico colonial," *Estudios* (Academia Literaria del Plata) 54 (1936) 117–148.

[G. FURLONG]

ASPILCUETA, MARTIN (DOCTOR NAVARRUS), canonist and moral theologian; b. Barasoain, Navarre, May 13, 1493; d. Rome, June 21, 1586. A cousin of St. Francis Xavier, he became a doctor of Canon Law and taught at the Universities of Toulouse,

Salamanca, and Coimbra (1524–38). Three popes, Pius V, Gregory XIII, and Sixtus V, honored him with their friendship and made him consultor to the Sacred Penitentiary. The high point of his juridical career was his acting as lawyer for the defense of the Dominican Archbishop of Toledo, Bartolomé de *Carranza. Because of Spanish prejudice, he demanded that the case be transferred to Rome and thus incurred the enmity of King Philip II, who later prevented his becoming a cardinal. His chief work, *Manuale sive Enchiridion confessariorum et paenitentium* (Rome 1588), was long considered a classic. The best complete edition of his numerous writings is *Doctoris Navarri . . . opera* (5 v. Cologne 1609).

Bibliography: L. SIMEONE, EncCatt 8:219–220. A. LAMBERT, DHGE 5:1368–74, with extensive bibliog.; DDC 1:1579–83. Hurter Nomencl[3] 3:344–348.

[M. J. BARRY]

ASSAULT, understood in moral theology as the unjust infliction of bodily harm on another. It is equivalent not to simple assault but to the assault-and-battery of civil law, for in civil law simple assault may be committed by menacing words and actions, even though no physical harm is actually done. Assault as here understood is distinguished from the "criminal assault" of newspaper euphemism, which is assault with the specific injury of sexual violation. It also differs from the infliction of bodily harm in legitimate *self-defense and from the reasonable infliction of punishment by one having the authority to do so.

In inflicting bodily injury and pain on another, the assailant usurps to himself an unlawful control over another, thus affronting his victim's human dignity and autonomy and depriving him of his well-being, comfort, and security—goods of which presumably he is reasonably and seriously unwilling to be dispossessed. Assault is therefore a violation of commutative *justice, and as such it is per se gravely sinful, although subjective considerations such as imperfect responsibility or the triviality of the injury can make it less than a grave sin in particular cases. In sports involving physical contact and in good-natured roughhouse and horseplay among the young, actions that would in other circumstances constitute assault may be free of any moral fault whatever.

As an offense against commutative justice, assault subjects the assailant to an obligation to *restitution for the damage he has done. Evidently he is bound in justice to make amends for what the victim is out of pocket by reason of medical expenses, loss of income, etc., in consequence of injuries received. What restitution is owed for other elements in the injury is more difficult to estimate. Strictly speaking there is no equivalence between monetary damages and the pain or humiliation the victim may have suffered, but if legitimate authority imposes indemnification of this kind, justice demands that it be made.

See also INJURY, MORAL.

Bibliography: THOMAS AQUINAS, ST 2a2ae, 65. J. A. MCHUGH and C. J. CALLAN, *Moral Theology*, rev. E. P. FARRELL, 2 v. (New York 1958).

[T. J. HAYES]

ASSEMANI, JOSEPH ALOYSIUS, theologian and canonist; b. Syria, 1710; d. Rome, 1782; one of the pioneers in modern Oriental studies. Following his theological studies at Rome under his uncle, Joseph Simon *Assemani, he was appointed by the Pope as professor of Syriac at the Sapienza in Rome. Benedict XIV named him professor of liturgy at the same institute and a member of the newly formed academy of research. His principal works are the *Codex liturgicus ecclesiae universae in XV libros distributus* (Rome 1749–66); *De sacris ritibus dissertatio* (Rome 1757); *Commentarius theologicocanonicus criticus de ecclesiis, earum reverentia et asylo atque concordia Sacerdotii et Imperii* (Rome 1766); *Dissertatio de unione et communione ecclesastica* (Rome 1770); *Dissertatio de canonibus poenitentialibus* (Rome 1770); *De Catholicis seu Patriarchis Chaldaeorum et Nestorianorum commentarius historico-chronologicus* (Rome 1775); and the *De Synodo Diocesana dissertatio* (Rome 1776); a Latin version of Ebedjesus' *Collectio Canonum,* published by Cardinal Mai.

Bibliography: Mai SVNC. Van Hove 1:563.

[T. F. DONOVAN]

ASSEMANI, JOSEPH SIMON, Orientalist; b. Tripoli, Lebanon, July 27, 1687; d. Rome, Jan. 3, 1768. His was an illustrious family. He was ordained after study at the Maronite college in Rome, and in 1710 was appointed scriptor in the Vatican Library to catalogue 40 MSS, mostly Syriac, then recently received from Egyptian monasteries, and the first large acquisition of such MSS by a library in the West. Assemani himself on later trips to the Near East brought back almost 150 MSS. In 1736 he presided as papal legate over the Maronite synod convoked by Clement XII in Lebanon. From the many MSS that had become available in the Vatican he published four volumes of the *Bibliotheca Orientalis* (1719–28); many copies of these, along with his MS for the 8 other volumes planned, were destroyed by a fire in his private library in 1768. He also published the *Menologium Graecorum* (6 v. 1727), the *Chronicon Orientale* of Ibn ar-Rāhib (1731), the works of *Ephrem the Syrian (6 v. 1732–46), 6 of the planned 12 volumes of the *Kalendaria ecclesiae universalis* (1750–55)—Greco-Slavic liturgy only—and the *Bibliotheca iuris orientalis canonici et civilis* (5 v. 1762–66). The editing of MSS was continued by his nephews, Stephen Evodius Assemani and Joseph Aloysius Assemani, and by his grandnephew Simon Assemani. Some of his works were published by A. *Mai, *Nova collectio* (v.4–5, 1831), and G. Notain edited his list of the patriarchs of Antioch (1881). He was a canon of St. Peter's, vice prefect and prefect of the Vatican Library, and in 1766 became titular archbishop of Tyre.

Bibliography: G. LEVI DELLA VIDA, *Ricerche . . . dei manoscritti orientali della Biblioteca Vaticana* (StTest 92; 1939). J. PARISOT, DTC 1.1:2120–22. L. PETIT, DACL 1:2973–78. P. SFAIR, EncCatt 2:159–160. A. SCHALL, LexThK[2] 1:942–943.

[L. F. HARTMAN]

ASSEMBLIES OF FRENCH CLERGY

Convocations of representatives of the clergy called by the French king during the 16th, 17th, and 18th centuries.

Origins. The first such assembly is usually considered to have been the Colloquy of Poissy convened in 1561 by Michel de *l'Hôpital, Chancellor for Charles IX. Catholic and Protestant theologians were invited to attend in an effort to work out a formula for religious agreement that would satisfy both reformers and Catholics. The Protestant reformer Theodore *Beza attended and refused to accept the doctrine of the Real Presence in the Eucharist. On the other side, the Catholic leaders refused to accept any form of compromise, insisting that only the pope had authority to arbitrate on such religious matters. From the time of the Assembly of Melun (1579) the assemblies became an established institution, and eventually they met every 5 years. In due time procedures for representation and the conduct of business were developed. Each French province was represented by two bishops and two members of the inferior clergy, usually abbots and canons. A president was elected and members were divided into committees to carry on the detailed business of the meeting.

Evolution. One of the regular features of the assemblies, introduced at Poissy, was the approval of the *don gratuit,* an annual free gift to the king. In 1561 the amount of the *don gratuit* was fixed at 1,600,000 livres per year for 6 years. Additional grants were made on special occasions. In 1641, for example, the assembly was virtually coerced into approving an additional 4,000,000 livres to be contributed within 3 years. The regular annual grant was gradually increased to a maximum of 16,000,000 livres by 1755. Attempts by the crown to make the *don gratuit* compulsory were successfully resisted.

One of the most famous of the assemblies was held in 1682. It was called by Louis XIV as a means of resisting papal pressure to end the *régale,* the right of the French kings to appropriate the revenues of a vacant see and to make appointments to its benefices. It was at this time that Jacques *Bossuet, Bishop of Meaux, delivered an eloquent oration at the opening of the session, emphasizing the unity of the Church. The assembly supported the position of the King on the *régale* and also approved the Four Articles: (1) the temporal sovereignty of monarchs is independent of the pope; (2) the supremacy of the General Council over the pope as affirmed at the Council of *Constance is to be upheld; (3) the ancient liberties of the Gallican church are inviolate; (4) the infallibility of the *magisterium* belongs to pope and bishop jointly. These had been drawn up by Bossuet and represented an expression of *Gallicanism. Although Innocent XI was offended by the Four Articles, he took no action against them. He did, however, demonstrate his opposition by refusing to approve members of this assembly as appointees for vacant sees. In 1693 the Four Articles were withdrawn on the insistence of Innocent XII and with the approval of Louis XIV.

The last struggle between the Assembly of French Clergy and the government occurred in 1785 when the finance minister, Charles de Calonne, demanded an increase in the *don gratuit.* The clergy refused, and no further action was taken.

The meetings were concerned as much with religious as with temporal matters. In many of the sessions the question of Protestantism was considered. One of the important issues was *Jansenism. In general, the clergy supported the proclamations of the popes against Jansenism. In effect, the assemblies assigned the French clergy an important role in maintaining the purity of French Catholicism and a voice in determining the extent of secular influence in the Church.

The beginning of the French Revolution brought the institution of the assemblies to an end. To a significant degree they had represented the independence of the French clergy in their relations with the crown. Unlike the nobles who had lost most of their rights and privileges, the clergy had maintained their immunities and privileges; the institution through which this was successfully accomplished had been the Assembly of French Clergy.

Bibliography: R. CHALUMEAU, *Catholicisme* 1:916–918. L. SERBAT, *Les Assemblées du clergé de France . . . 1561–1615* (Paris 1906). P. BLET, *Le Clergé de France et la monarchie: Étude sur les assemblées générales du clergé de 1615 à 1666,* 2 v. (Rome 1959). A. SICARD, *L'Ancien clergé de France,* 3 v. (Paris 1893–1903). I. BOURLON, *Les Assemblées du clergé sous l'ancien régime,* 2 v. (Paris 1907).

[W. J. STEINER]

ASSEMBLIES OF GOD

The largest organized church in the pentecostal movement. Its origins may be found in the holiness revival within the Methodist Church in the decades immediately following the Civil War. The main distinction between the pentecostal groups and the other denominations that grew from the same source lies in their belief that, after the religious experience of conversion and of the baptism by the Holy Spirit that sanctifies and cleanses from inner sin, it is part of the divine dispensation that the same charismatic signs that marked the Apostles after the first Pentecost should reappear in the Christian community. Thus, the "second blessing" of the holiness sects is made manifest among the pentecostals by the healing of the sick and speaking with tongues.

The Apostolic Faith Movement, the immediate precursor of the Assemblies of God, began (1901) at Bethel Bible College, Topeka, Kans. Charles F. Parham, a holiness revival preacher, had organized this small institution the previous year to offer courses in Scripture study and to prepare men and women for the evangelistic ministry. Speaking in unknown tongues became common among the Topeka students, and this form of the "second blessing" began to manifest itself in revival meetings. Pentecostal congregations developed in Kansas, Missouri, and Oklahoma in a loose fellowship. William J. Seymour experienced a similar outpouring of the Spirit in Texas and founded a holiness mission (1906) in Los Angeles, Calif. One of his converts, G. B. Cashwell, conducted similar revivals in North Carolina. The same type of pentecostal movement sprang up elsewhere, with such leaders as A. J. Tomlinson gathering (1908) the Church of God at Cleveland, Tenn., and Elder C. H. Mason forming the Church of God in Christ the same year. In 1914 a general convention of Pentecostal Saints and Churches of God in Christ was held at Hot Springs, Ark. Endorus N. Bell, pastor of a Baptist church in Texas and editor of the pentecostal *Word and Witness,* and J. Roswell Flower, editor of the *Christian Evangel,* were the prime movers of the meeting. Its aim was to recognize the need for a standard in the ministry and preaching of the pentecostal movement, for fellowship between the congregations, and for a centralized agency for foreign missionary work. A missionary board, the Home and Foreign Mission Committee, was set up and a general council incorporated legally. The highly democratic movement had little interest in denominational machinery, loosely organizing itself under an annual general council, with state and district councils, and local assemblies. The ministry of women was recognized and a central publishing house set up in St. Louis, Mo.

The loose organization of the Assemblies of God was scarcely completed when doctrinal division threatened to dissolve it in 1915. The question of rebaptism in the name of the Lord Jesus arose in Tennessee and spread throughout the movement, winning the adherence of Bell and other leaders. Some began to drop Trinitarian formulas altogether and to preach an identity of Persons in the Trinity. The 1916 convention condemned these excesses, adopting a Trinitarian faith and disapproving of any tendency to make no distinction between the Father and Son and Holy Spirit. The following years marked a steady growth of the denomination, with the number of assemblies and adherents more than doubled between 1928 and 1935. Foreign missionary efforts began in South Africa (1913) and the Congo (1921); by 1958 there were 1,467 local assemblies in Africa. Extensive missionary work has also been carried on in Italy, Latin America, and the Philippines; in 1965 the denomination was supporting more than 800 overseas missionaries.

The Assemblies of God are avowedly fundamentalist in their theological views, emphasizing the unity and Trinity of God, the Incarnation and atoning death of Christ, man's fallen nature, his need for repentance and sanctification by faith, and the inspiration and sufficiency of the Scriptures. They stress the work of the Holy Spirit in the process of conversion and the outpouring of the Spirit cleansing from inner sins. The movement known as the New Order of the Latter Rain, beginning in 1947, placed even greater stress on pentecostal manifestations, but has gradually died out. In addition, the Assemblies condemn the use of liquor, tobacco, cosmetics, and worldly adornment. A great deal of freedom is allowed in both worship and evangelistic services for spontaneous demonstrations of praise or zeal. Services center on sermons and hymns and are often of long duration. Local assemblies among minority groups use the vernacular of the immigrant groups, and Spanish-, Italian-, and Ukrainian-speaking congregations are numerous in the U.S.

Bibliography: C. BRUMBACK, *Suddenly From Heaven* (Springfield, Mo. 1961). I. WINEHOUSE, *The Assemblies of God* (New York 1959). R. M. RIGGS, *We Believe* (Springfield, Mo. 1954).

[R. K. MAC MASTER]

ASSER, JOHN (ASKER), English chronicler; b. Menevia, Wales; d. England, 909. He was a kinsman of Nobis, Bishop of *Saint Davids (d. 873), and was reared, educated, and ordained at Saint Davids monastery in western Wales. After the treaty of 878, when *Alfred the Great could turn to peacetime activities, Asser was recruited along with other scholars, such as *Plegmund, later archbishop of *Canterbury, Werferth, later bishop of *Worcester (d. 915), John the Old Saxon and *Grimbald from the Continent, to assist the King to educate himself, his priests, and his nobles. Alfred summoned him to Dene in Sussex *c.* 884–885 to invite him to his court. Unwilling to cut his ties in Wales, Asser consented to seek leave to spend one half of each year at court. On his way home he fell ill, possibly at Caerwent, and was delayed over a year. The monks of Saint Davids consented to the arrangement as they sought Alfred's protection against Hemeid, King of Dyfed, one of the independent rulers in Wales. Asser records that he began to read and interpret with Alfred at Martinmas (878), and Alfred acknowledges his aid in the preface to the *Pastoral Care* (ed. H. Sweet for EEngTSoc, 1871–72). *William of Malmesbury credits Asser with assisting Alfred with the difficult passages of *Boethius's *De consolatione philosophiae.* In return for his assistance the King conferred on the scholar the monasteries of Congresbury and Banwell. Later, possibly for relinquishing his half-year sojourn in Wales, Alfred granted him the Diocese of Exeter, and before 900 Asser became bishop of Sherborne. His unique achievement was a life of King Alfred, *De rebus gestis Aelfredi,* the sole source of much information about both men. Although its authenticity was impugned in 1841 by Thomas Wright, scholars are now agreed that it is genuine. Since this work, the first part of which was written in chronicle form, was transcribed almost entirely and without credit to Asser in the chronicles of *Florence of Worcester and *Simeon of Durham and thence passed into later chronicles, the original was long neglected. The provenance of the only known manuscript (Otho A xii) is not clear, and even though none of the editions is without serious flaws, fortunately the manuscript was transcribed and printed three times (Archbishop Parker, 1574; William Camden, 1602–03; Frances Wise, 1722) before it was destroyed by fire in 1731. The manuscript version was free of the legends that were later interpolated into the Life, such as that of the burning oat cakes or the early foundation of the University of Oxford. As Stevenson notes, Asser's life is unique in its literary interest, as the first biography of an English layman and as a source of English history.

Bibliography: *Annales rerum gestarum Aelfredi Magni,* ed. F. WISE (Oxford 1722); *Asser's Life of King Alfred,* ed. W. H. STEVENSON (Oxford 1904). R. H. HODGKIN, *A History of the Anglo-Saxons,* 2 v. (3d ed. New York 1952) v.2. DNB 1:670–671. B. HEURTEBIZE, DHGE 4:1115–16. V. REDLICH, LexThK[2] 1:944.

[M. E. COLLINS]

ASSISI

Town with 10,800 inhabitants in Umbria, central Italy. It was the home of SS. *Francis and *Clare and is now a major spiritual and artistic center. The Diocese of Assisi (*Assisiensis*), immediately subject to the Holy See, in 1963 had 40 secular and 120 religious priests, 180 men in 11 religious houses, 430 women in 26 convents, and 42,400 Catholics; it is 136 square miles in area.

History. Assisi was originally a village of the *Umbri,* with Etruscan ties, and then a Roman *municipium* where the poet Propertius was born (*c.* 50 B.C.). It became a diocese probably in the 3d century. The passions of SS. Victorinus, Felicianus, Sabinus, and Rufinus (early martyr bishops) are late and unreliable; but St. Rufinus, whose cult is mentioned by St. *Peter Damian, became Assisi's first patron. The first recorded bishop, Aventius, was a legate of the Ostrogoths of Justinian after Totila took Assisi (*c.* 545).

From the late 8th to the 12th century, Assisi belonged to the Lombard Duchy of *Spoleto. Bishop Ugo (1036–52) was a civic leader of the newly independent Ghibelline commune (*see* GUELFS AND GHIBELLINES). The first of Assisi's numerous wars with its belligerent Guelf neighbor *Perugia occurred in 1054. Under the Hohenstaufen, Assisi was ruled by German counts (1160–98). In 1198 the citizens revolted against the German ruler and razed his fortress (rebuilt by Cardinal *Albornoz in 1367). Under the litigious Bishop Guido II (1204–28), who approved the foundation of the first and second orders of Franciscans, the prosperous diocese owned half the area of the commune. All extant archival documents of the 13th century (Assisi's greatest) were published in 1959 by A. Fortini; they shed considerable light on the social, political, and economic background of the era. In the 14th and 15th centuries Assisi fell under the *Visconti, Montefeltro, and *Sforza families, suffered internal conflicts, was sacked several times, and gradually lapsed into three relatively uneventful centuries (1535–1860) as part of the *States of the Church. St. Gabriel *Possenti was born there in 1838.

In the 20th century Assisi has become again one of the spiritual capitals of Christendom. For many years it was the second home of the writers Paul *Sabatier, Jens Johannes *Jorgensen, and Nesta de Robeck, and of the American artist William Congdon. In 1926 two million pilgrims came to celebrate the 700th anniversary of the death of St. Francis. At the request of the Holy See, in 1944 the Germans designated Assisi a hospital town, and it escaped damage.

The communal library is rich in medieval MSS from religious houses suppressed in 1866. Assisi has been since 1902 the headquarters of the International Society of Franciscan Studies and since 1939 of the pious society *Pro Civitate Christiana. The First International Congress on Pastoral Liturgy met there in 1956. A Church-affiliated University of St. Paul was founded in 1964.

Architecture. Classical Roman remains include an amphitheater and the hexastyle Corinthian pronaos of the 1st century B.C. Temple of Minerva (praised by Goethe). Notable medieval secular buildings on the Piazza del Comune are the Palazzo del Capitano del Popolo (1212–1305) and the Palazzo dei Priori (1337). But Assisi's architectural glories are its eight major Romanesque and Gothic churches: (1) S. Maria Maggiore, or Vescovado, the first cathedral, rebuilt in 1163 by Giovanni da Gubbio, who also enlarged (2) the second cathedral, S. Rufino, with its striking Lombard-Romanesque façade; (3) the Benedictine Abbey of S. Pietro, rebuilt in 1253; (4) the Basilica of S. Chiara, erected in 1257 in place of the earlier S. Giorgio over the tomb of St. Clare; and (5) the Gothic Basilica of S. Francesco designed by Brother *Elias of Cortona, which includes the single-naved upper and lower churches, the crypt tomb of St. Francis (reopened in 1818 and restored in 1925), a sacristy rich in the saint's relics, and the vast Sacro Convento and papal residence, with portico (1300), cloister (1476), and 18th-century refectory. Outside the city are (6) the modest 11th-century oratory of S. Damiano and 13th-century convent where St. Clare lived; (7) the hillside Carceri Hermitage, enlarged by St. *Bernardine of Siena; and (8) the *Portiuncula Chapel [enclosed in the massive Basilica of S. Maria degli Angeli (1569–1676, rebuilt in 1836)].

Basilica and convent of S. Francesco, Assisi.

Bibliography: L. Duff-Gordon, *The Story of Assisi* (London 1901). F. Lanzoni, *Le diocesi d'Italia dalle origini al principio del secolo VII (an. 604),* 2 v. (2d ed. Faenza 1927) 1:461–480. R. Riccardi et al., EncIt 5:40–46. A. Fortini, *Assisi nel medio evo* (Rome 1940). F. S. Attal, "Assisi città santa: Come fu salvata dagli orrori della guerra," *Miscellanea francescana* 48 (1948) 3–32. A. Bertini Calosso, EncCatt 2:170–176. Touring Club Italiano, *Guida d'Italia: Umbria* (3d ed. Milan 1950). S. Chierichetti, *Assisi: An Illustrated Guidebook* (Milan 1957). A. Cristofani, *Le storie di Assisi* (4th ed. Venice 1959). A. Fortini, *Nova vita di San Francesco,* 4 v. in 5 (Assisi 1959). EncWA 8:647–649. M. Adams, *Umbria* (London 1964). Ann Pont (1965) 40. Englebert-Brady-Brown, with extensive bibliog. and app.

[R. BROWN]

Painting. The frescoes in the upper and lower churches of the Basilica of S. Francesco (1228–53) are the paintings of greatest significance in Assisi. Each level of the basilica consists of a simple nave, transept, and a sanctuary; during the 14th century, chapels were added to the nave of the lower church. Since the most prominent contemporary painters were employed for this decoration, there has remained for posterity an invaluable record of the fresco styles of the 13th and 14th centuries in central Italy.

In the nave of the lower church are the faded remnants of the earliest frescoes: episodes from the life of Christ and of St. Francis, painted by the 13th-century Master of St. Francis, pupil of Giunta Pisano. In the right transept, an enthroned Madonna with St. Francis by *Cimabue is hemmed in closely by later frescoes of the 14th century. This suggests the possibility of other 13th-century frescoes having been here originally. In these later frescoes of the transepts and the crossing vault, the work of Giotto's workshop and of Pietro Lorenzetti, the juxtaposition of Christ and St. Francis occurs again, but in more elaborate fashion: in the crossing vault are four allegories glorifying the saint, and in the right and left transepts, respectively, are scenes from the early life of Christ and of His Passion. There are two Crucifixions, one on each transept wall. The frescoes in the St. Nicholas and the Magdalen chapels, added in the 14th century, are the work of pupils of Giotto. The St. Martin chapel was decorated by Simone *Martini.

The entire wall surface of the upper church is covered with frescoes begun during the late 13th century, presumably with the support of Nicholas III (1277–80) and Nicholas IV (1288–92), the latter a Franciscan. The earliest frescoes, in the sanctuary and transepts, are by Cimabue and assistants. The subject cycle in which the Virgin, SS. Peter and Paul, many angels, and St. Michael figure seems to support the assertion of St. *Bonaventure that these were all subjects close to the

"Crucifixion," fresco by Cimabue and his assistants, lower church, Basilica of S. Francesco, Assisi.

heart of St. Francis. As evidence also of the saint's fervor for the Crucified, there are two huge Crucifixion frescoes in the transepts with Francis kneeling at the foot of the cross.

On the upper half of the nave walls in two registers are stories from the Old and New Testaments. These are chiefly the work of artists of the Roman school, Torriti and Rusuti and their assistants, and the anonymous Isaac Master, but also in part of the young Giotto.

In the lowest register of the nave walls, 28 scenes from the life of St. Francis, set under a painted colonnade simulating a *stoa pictile,* are the climax of the whole decoration of the upper church. These have been variously attributed to Giotto and assistants, to the St. Cecilia Master, and to a 14th-century Umbrian master.

Bibliography: B. KLEINSCHMIDT, *Die Basilika San Francesco in Assisi,* 3 v. (Berlin 1915–28); *Die Wandmalereien der Basilika San Francesco in Assisi* (Berlin 1930). I. B. SUPINO, *La Basilica di Can Francesco d'Assisi* (Bologna 1924). F. J. MATHER, *The Isaac Master* (New York 1932). M. MEISS, *Giotto and Assisi* (New York 1960). L. TINTORI and M. MEISS, *The Painting of the Life of St. Francis in Assisi* (New York 1962). **Illustration credit:** Fig. 2, Alinari-Art Reference Bureau.

[E. T. DE WALD]

ASSISTANTS AT THE PONTIFICAL THRONE. There are two kinds of assistants at the pontifical throne, clerical and lay.

The clerics are high prelates with the episcopal character and precede all others, except cardinals. They form a college composed of three ranks, viz, patriarch (all *de jure*) assistants, archbishop assistants, and bishop assistants (who ceremonially outrank archbishop nonassistants), each created for life by the sovereign pontiff as a special sign of benevolence. No distinction is made between titular or residential assistants, and they rank *inter se* according to date of creation, and not according to date of episcopal election or promotion, as nonassistants do. If they are not already *domestic prelates, they become so, and formerly they were simultaneously created Roman counts as well. Bishop assistants become automatically archbishop assistants if promoted to an archbishopric, while keeping their original date of precedence and without having to have their diploma, the document that officially notifies them of their assumption into the college, renewed. Among the requisites for eligibility (since 1960) is either 25 years in the episcopacy or 50 in the priesthood. There are a very few exceptions to this rule, e.g., the pope's private almoner, the papal sacristan, and the bishop of Pescia, Italy, who are always assistants. Although several popes have given different privileges to assistants, only a few of these privileges have remained so specifically, since most have been gradually extended to all bishops. But only assistants may wear non-moire violet silk robes (cassock, mantelletta, mozetta, and *cappa magna*). Assistants do, as a matter of course, enjoy a special place in the *capella papalis,* between the pope and the cardinals. This recalls the historic origin of the distinction, the Holy Father inviting especially meritorious bishops to sit close by the papal throne as far back as the 11th century. In 1964 the college was composed of about 300 members.

Representing the Church's laity at the sovereign pontiff's right hand, performing ceremonial duties, and also *veluti custodes sacrae personae vicarii Christi,* some high-ranking laymen have for many centuries been appointed to the privileged office of assistants. They are called prince assistants at the throne. The heads of the Roman Orsini and Colonna families for many generations served the Holy Father in this capacity. In 1964 Prince Torlonia of Fucino was also given the honor in question.

[P. C. VAN LIERDE]

ASSIZES OF JERUSALEM

A collection of laws and legal treatises pertaining to the Kingdom of *Jerusalem compiled during the 13th century. According to a 13th-century tradition, *Godfrey of Bouillon (d. 1100) had ordered a compilation of the existing usages of his day, the so-called *Lettres du Sépulcre.* These were revised and amended during the succeeding decades, but they were entirely lost in 1187 at the fall of Jerusalem. Since, for various reasons, those whose memories might have been adequate to the task did not prepare a new edition immediately after the fall of Jerusalem, much of the legal tradition of the 12th century was handed down only in an attenuated or altered form. Jerusalem law, therefore, remained customary until the compilation of the *Assizes* in their present form. Since the researches of Grandclaude, this tradition, including the attribution of the *Lettres* to Godfrey, has been largely discredited. But recent studies have traced the origin of certain laws to the 12th century. The *Livre au roi,* for example, which has been dated between 1197 and 1205, presumably reflects to some degree the legal practices of the earlier period. And the *Livre des assises de la cour de bourgeois,* dating probably after 1215, is also thought to mirror earlier usages.

The other books, *Livre de Philippe de Novare, Livre de Jean d'Ibelin, Livre de Geoffroi le Tort, Livre de Jacques d'Ibelin,* and *La Clef des assises de la haute cour du royaume de Jérusalem et de Chypre,* were compiled about the middle of the 13th century or after and reflect the conditions of those later days. At that time, the kingdom was reduced to a small coastal area around Acre and included the island of Cyprus. For a number of years (1229–43) following the crusade of Emperor *Frederick II, the local barons, including the jurists Philippe de Novare, Jean d'Ibelin, and Geoffroi le Tort, were engaged in a struggle to preserve their liberties against the centralizing tendencies of Frederick's regents. The *Assizes,* therefore, unduly emphasize the rights and privileges of the *Haute Cour,* the high court of the barons. As a consequence, they represent what has been described as an "ideal" baronial feudalism, but certainly not one that faithfully mirrors the monarchical institutions of the preceding century. As edited by M. Beugnot in the *Recueil des historiens des croisades,* Lois (2 v. Paris 1841–43), the collection includes, in addition to the works mentioned above, documents pertaining to Cyprus, genealogies, miscellaneous charters, etc.

Bibliography: M. GRANDCLAUDE, *Étude critique sur les Livres des Assises de Jérusalem* (Paris 1923). J. L. LA MONTE, *Feudal Monarchy in . . . Jerusalem . . .* (Cambridge, Mass. 1932); "Three Questions concerning the Assises de Jérusalem," *Byzantina-Metabyzantina* 1 (1946) 201–211. J. RICHARD, *Le Royaume latin de Jérusalem* (Paris 1953). J. PRAWER, "The *Assise de teneure* and the *Assise de vente . . . ,*" *Economic History Review,* ser. 2.4 (1951–52) 77–87; "L'Établissement des coutumes . . . et la date de composition du *Livre des Assises des Bourgeois,*" RevHistDrFranÉtr 28 (1951) 329–351; "Étude préliminaire sur les sources et la composition du *Livre des Assises* des Bourgeois," *ibid.* 31 (1954) 198–227, 358–382; *Toldot mamlekhet ha-Tsalbanim,* 2 v. (Jerusalem 1963) v.1. A. WAAS, *Geschichte der Kreuzzüge,* 2 v. (Freiburg 1956).

[M. W. BALDWIN]

ASSMAYER, IGNAZ, late classical composer; b. Salzburg, Austria, Feb. 11, 1790; d. Vienna, Aug. 31, 1862. A student of Michael *Haydn, he became organist at St. Peter's in Salzburg when he was 18. After moving to Vienna in 1815, he studied with Joseph von *Eybler. He was named court organist in 1825 and assistant director of music in the court chapel in 1846. His concern with symphonic form reflects his study with Eybler, although his general style with its lighter texture is more reminiscent of the Salzburg school. A direct tie with Haydn's liturgical propriety can be seen in his Graduals and Offertories. Among his compositions are two published oratorios, *The Death of Saul* and *David and Saul;* 15 Masses (only one published), 2 Requiems, and other sacred writings, in addition to more than 60 instrumental compositions.

See also CAECILIAN MOVEMENT.

Bibliography: Wiessenbäck. Riemann. C. F. POHL, Grove DMM 1:244. E. TITTEL, *Österreichische Kirchenmusik* (Vienna 1961). Fellerer CathChMus.

[F. J. MOLECK]

ASSOCIATION

As a social entity, an association is a durable union between men to attain a common goal. It is thus an expression of the human sociality that is manifested in many ways, from occasional and fortuitous encounters or more or less stable interrelations between persons to lasting structures that can extend from the family or clan to worldwide pluralities. In every time and place men have lived in *society; human existence is social coexistence. Human personality cannot develop or express itself except within and through society; personal life has a social end just as social life has a personal end. The "life within the self" of the human person cannot be conceived without "living for others." Thus, human sociality is commonly expressed in the formation of an association to attain a *common good that is beyond individual capabilities. In short, since man cannot live adequately or attain the goals of his life outside of society, his sociality must be regarded as a requisite of his human nature and the right of association must be respected as a right based on the natural law (*see* RIGHT AND RIGHTS).

Classification. Given the complexity of human life and its needs, human sociality gives rise to a great variety of groupings whose names are to be found in all modern languages; one needs only to peruse any dictionary to note the richness of terminology that points to the fundamental tendency of man to associate with others. Scholastic philosophers customarily distinguish the different forms of associations according to their (1) end, (2) origin, (3) legal status, and (4) degree of perfection. According to their end associations are religious, scientific, cultural, social, sporting, commercial, etc. They are further classified as natural or voluntary in origin. Thus natural societies are those that are indispensable for the attainment of man's existential ends. Traditionally these have been regarded as the *family (or clan) and the *state in the natural order and the Church in the supernatural order (*see* CHURCH, II), but the international society must now be included among the former. Societies that are not necessary to attain human existential ends are called voluntary or free. Reminiscent of this distinction are sociological typologies such as that of Ferdinand Tönnies, for whom *Gemeinschaft* (community) is based on a common love arising from natural affinity; and *Gesellschaft* (association), on a common interest pursued by deliberate choice. According to their legal status, public societies, regulated by public law, are distinguished from private societies arising from private rights. Last, social philosophy distinguishes between perfect and imperfect societies. Perfect societies are those possessing all the necessary means to procure their final good for their members. Traditionally the sovereign state in the natural order and the Church in the supernatural order have been regarded as perfect societies.

The development of international society makes necessary some modification of this view of the state. As Pope John XXIII remarked in **Pacem in terris,* "at the present day no political community is able to pursue its own interests and develop itself in isolation, because the degree of its prosperity and development is a reflection and a component part of the degree of prosperity and development of all the other political communities" [ActApS 55 (1963) 292; cf. *Mater et Magistra, ibid.* 53 (1961) 449]. It follows that no contemporary state can be considered a perfect society in the scholastic sense of the word. The inclusion of the international community, politically organized, is necessary to ensure to men the totality of temporal goods to which they may quite rightly aspire.

Recognition of the Right of Association. Although it is a natural right, the right of association is not absolute, nor has it been or is it now guaranteed by law everywhere. In the history of ideas this right is associated with individual rights, but in fact it safeguards collective interests as well; moreover, it is intimately linked with other *civil liberties, such as *freedom of religion, *freedom of the press, *freedom of speech, and the right of petition. The Bill of Rights added to the Constitution of the U.S. in 1791 was one of the first guarantees of the right of association as well as of other liberties. In the same year in France the Le Chapelier law forbade the reestablishment under any pretext or form of the corporations (or guilds) that were dissolved by its provisions. Interestingly, it was in the name of individual liberty that the right of association and of coalition was outlawed. In the mind of the law's authors an association, as the organ and voice of a collective interest, had no reason for existence; for it was believed that there was no interest intermediate between the particular interest of the individual and the general interest of the state. Freedom to associate, by grouping collective interests, was held to constitute a hindrance to individual goals as well as a menace to the general welfare of the state, the trustee of individual welfare. In other nations also certain forms of association were forbidden in the name of the public interest. Otto von Bismarck's *Kulturkampf in Germany, for example, excluded the Society of Jesus (1871) and socialist groups (1878); later, the right of association recognized by the Weimar constitution of 1918 was abolished by the National Socialist regime in 1933 and reestablished in the constitution of the Federal Republic in 1952.

It is impossible to summarize the varied legal provisions dealing with the right of association in individual countries. In general this right is recognized in most and is usually made explicit as one of the personal rights of citizens. It is legally acknowledged even in Communist countries, where it is sometimes more clearly formulated statutorily than in democratic nations. But there exists always some discrepancy between the law and the spirit, between theory and practice. The right of association is required in the name of liberty; yet in every instance it is limited by the needs of the public order and the public good. To understand its real meaning one must understand the meaning of freedom and of the public interest in each case. Thus the right of association in the "peoples' democracies" is not seen as the guarantee of personal or collective liberty but as the right of a so-called socialist personality at the service of the Communist system in force.

The right of association has been affirmed constantly by the popes since Leo XIII, who insisted in particular on the right of workers to form unions at a time when this right was often denied. In **Rerum novarum* he wrote: "Although private societies exist within the state and are, as it were, so many parts of it, still it is not within the authority of the state universally and *per se* to forbid them to exist as such. For man is permitted by a right of nature to form private societies; the state, on the other hand, has been instituted to protect and not to destroy natural right, and if it should forbid its citizens to enter into associations, it would clearly do something contradictory to itself because both the state itself and private associations are begotten of one and the same principle, namely, that men are by nature inclined to associate" [ActSSed 23 (1891) 665; cf. Pius XII, *Sertum laetitiae,* ActApS 31 (1939) 643]. In **Mater et Magistra* John XXIII stressed the importance of associations or intermediary bodies between the state and individuals (*loc. cit.* 417). In *Pacem in terris* he declared: "From the fact that human beings are by nature social, there arises the right of assembly and association. They have also the right to give the societies of which they are members the form they consider most suitable for the aim they have in view, and to act within such societies on their own initiative and on their own responsibility in order to achieve their desired objectives" (*loc. cit.* 262–263).

The Declaration of the Rights of Man of 1948 includes the right of association (art. 20), as does the European Convention of the Rights of Man of 1950 (art. 11). *See* HUMAN RIGHTS.

Moral Right of Association. It is natural for every being to seek its good. Man also has a natural tendency toward his own good, toward the development of his being. This development can be realized only with the help of his fellows and by collaboration with others. To attain his own good, man not only has the right but also the duty to associate with others for common purposes that are genuine and useful. This right and duty extend to association not only with contemporaries but also with successive generations, since human progress is a sacred task confided to all men and transmitted from age to age.

Man must seek in social life not only an individual profit that supplies for his personal deficiencies, but a field of action for his devotion to the common good; to fulfill himself he must surpass himself. Society is not an agglomeration of individual egos but a cluster of reciprocal attachments. To live for himself alone is one of the worst sins that man can commit. Moreover, his personal good can be realized only in and by the common good. It is necessary therefore to keep in mind the duty as well as the right to associate.

This duty, however, is not absolute and unlimited. Although there exists among all men a community of nature, of origin, and of natural and supernatural destiny, one cannot conclude that a given man is bound to associate with all men. He has this duty only toward those with whom he interacts in concrete situations of life and with whom he can collaborate for common goals. Similarly, the right of association is neither absolute nor unlimited. It proceeds from human nature and provides for the normal development of man. It follows that this right exists only to serve man's true welfare, that is, a personal or common good. It is the prerogative of public authority to recognize the right of association within the limits of the common good and to respect the autonomy of associations and enact statutes permitting them to survive and develop.

Associations in Contemporary Society. Responding to their needs, men of all ages have united with others to form associations. Primitive man lives in such intimate dependence on his social group that his own personality is often submerged or at least diminished; he is above all a member of the clan or tribe. The modern era, beginning with the Renaissance, has given rise to the cult of the individual and of the rights of the individual and of the human person. It is the era of both individualism and *personalism, the latter transcending the limitations of the former. Personalism, while proclaiming the primacy of the human person, recognizes his social dimension and social end. "One of the principal characteristics of our times is the multiplication of social relationships," wrote John XXIII in *Mater et Magistra,* referring to "a daily more complex interdependence of citizens, introducing into their lives and activities many and varied forms of association, recognized for the most part in private and even in public law" (*loc. cit.* 415–416). The increase in number and influence of associations is at the same time a cause and an effect of the *socialization to which Pope John referred. It is explained by scientific and technical progress, the proliferation of needs, the increase of productivity, and the growth of civilization; it is at the same time the index and the cause of increasing government intervention, even in the intimate spheres of personal life.

In the last analysis the phenomenon of increasing social complexity is traceable to natural human sociality and is therefore almost irresistible. In effect "men are impelled voluntarily to enter into association in order to attain objectives which each one desires, but which exceed the capacity of single individuals. This tendency has given rise, especially in recent years, to organizations and institutes on both national and international levels, which relate to economic and social goals, to cultural and recreational activities, to athletics, to various professions, and to political affairs" (*ibid.* 416). The benefits derived from associations are incontestable: they facilitate the realization of a great number of personal rights, especially those dealing with the means of subsistence, medical care, cultural values, professional formation, lodging, work, and recreation. They permit individuals and groups to defend and promote their particular interests, which, although subordinate to the public good, constitute an important part of it. They contribute to the maintenance among their members of a sense of social responsibility, a spirit of devotion, and a willingness to collaborate with public authority and other groups. They contribute also to the structuring of society by creating intermediary groups between the state and the individual, thus avoiding the two extremes of social atomism and state collectivism.

Unfortunately the proliferation of social bonds also presents problems, such as the restriction of individual liberty, the diminution of initiative and personal responsibility—in one word, depersonalization. To prevent these problems from arising or at least to ameliorate them and attain the maximum advantages from the development of social bonds in associations, it is necessary (1) that public authority be guided by a precise notion of the common good that consists in the creation of that ensemble of social conditions necessary to promote the full development of the human person, for in the last analysis the common good is the personal good of each member of the collectivity (*Mater et Magistra, loc. cit.* 417; *Pacem in terris, loc. cit.* 262); (2) that the associations or intermediary bodies enjoy real autonomy and instead of hindering or replacing the personal activity of their members associate them with the organized action and treat them as responsible persons; and (3) that every effort be made through education to form men convinced of their dignity and their personal responsibility as well as of their social duty.

Bibliography: L. JANSSENS, *Personne et société: Théories actuelles et essai doctrinal* (Gembloux 1939). J. LECLERCQ, *Leçons de droit naturel,* v.1 *Le Fondement du droit et de la société* (3d ed. Namur 1947). W. MALLMAN, StL 8:106–109. A. VERDOODT, *Naissance et signification de la Déclaration universelle des droits de l'homme* (Doctoral diss. Louvain 1964). E. WELTY, *Gemeinschaft und Einzelmensch . . . nach Thomas v. Aquin* (Salzburg 1935). M. WULLAERT, *Maatschappelijke Ordening en Toegang tot het beroepsen bedrijfsleven* (*Organization sociale et accès à la vie professionnelle et industrielle*) (Doctoral diss. Louvain 1964). "L'État et les associations" in Union internationale d'études sociales, *Code de morale politique: Synthèse doctrinale* (Paris 1957) 124–130. D. FELLMAN, *The Constitutional Right of Association* (Chicago 1963).

[C. VAN GESTEL]

ASSOCIATION, MENTAL

A technique used in the fields of *psychiatry, *psychoanalysis, and psychology to obtain information regarding *unconscious thoughts and feelings, and certain sensitivities, attitudes, and complexes of individuals. In the medical disciplines of psychiatry and psychoanalysis, the term "association" is used without the qualifying word "mental."

Types. Associations may be free or induced; in the former instance, the subject is requested to allow his thoughts to wander without the imposition of any restrictions or direction, and to verbalize the mental content without any censorship or selection. Induced associations refer to the mental content that immediately follows the giving of a stimulus word, phrase, theme, or image to the subject by the test observer. Cognizance may be taken not only of the content of the associations, but also of the time interval between the stimulus and the first reported associations. If the interval has been of relatively long duration, the stimulus may have had powerful emotional associations of a conscious or even unconscious nature, and may be related to a complex or certain sensitivities. In experimental work, some tests of association incorporate specific time limitations, or give the test-subject a choice of certain answers, or provide other restrictions in the experiment. The types of responses in these test situations may give a clue as to certain general personality orientations or attitudes of the subject, but do not provide as much information about the unconscious mental content as does free association when performed in relationship to a competent observer. Induced associations are used generally by the experimental or clinical psychologist, but infrequently used by the psychiatrist or psychoanalyst.

Free association, commonly used in psychiatry, is the fundamental exploratory and therapeutic tool in psychoanalysis. Its effective employment requires the full cooperation of the patient or subject and the concentrated attention of the therapist. Another factor must operate, namely, the complete confidence of the patient in the discretion of the therapist, that all information expressed will be used exclusively for the benefit of the patient and never divulged to anyone else. Otherwise, inhibitions and selective censorship will interfere with the verbal productions.

Evidence indicates that the free association technique provides access to unconscious thought, perceptions, imagery, and emotions that play a significant role in the behavior of the individual without his being aware of their effects upon his conscious mentation and activities. Freud first became aware of the importance of mental association in the understanding and treatment of the deeper roots of certain cases of mental illness in connection with his early studies on the use of *hypnosis. He discovered that careful listening to the trends of thought of the patient gave him more information about the unconscious than he could obtain by hypnosis, and at the same time was more effective therapeutically than hypnosis.

In free association, the subject is usually requested to lie on a couch in order to be as fully relaxed as possible. The therapist may be seated behind the patient in order to reduce to a minimum any distractions or embarrassments caused by confronting the therapist, especially when the subject is expressing material of strong emotional content.

Relation to the Unconscious. There are two questions that are of vital importance concerning free association and the unconscious: (1) Why does unconscious thought and feeling appear in conscious verbal productions? (2) How is the unconscious mental content manifested or detected in free association?

The answer to the first question lies in what is termed the therapeutic alliance between patient and therapist, and the automatic development of *transference phenomena. The patient engages in free association with a general goal in mind, namely, relief of mental symptoms; the therapist is present for the sole purpose of helping him. This collaboration, called the therapeutic alliance, stimulates a transference development, in which many old and unconscious patterns of relationship in the mind of the patient are displaced onto the therapist without the full awareness of the patient. Because these patterns are involved in a person's neurosis and symptoms, his associations, if properly understood, will also incorporate elements of his neurosis, the unconscious conflicts and problems as they involve emotions and attitudes toward the therapist. As the unconscious meanings of the associations become understood, they are interpreted to the subject by the therapist in order to resolve the patient's conflicts and infantile patterns of behavior. Both P. Greenacre and L. Stone have emphasized that the child-mother relationship is the ultimate paradigm that the patient is driven to repeat by transferring it onto the therapist in the analytic situation, in which the free association technique dominates the therapeutic procedure. It is to be noted that there are nonverbal forms of free association in which the patient indicates by his movement, posture, or expressions the various transference feelings and attitudes toward the therapist, including his primitive longings for dependency, maternal solicitousness, and support.

Free associations are therefore influenced by the upward-driving effects of the instincts or drives seeking to make themselves conscious in the form of derivative wishes, feelings, and thoughts, and frequently centering about the person of the analyst. It must be evident that free association is significantly different from daydreaming, or so-called stream of consciousness activity, or productive thought, since free association involves a highly unique relationship with another person, the therapist.

Free association cannot easily be conducted without an observer present, since the subject cannot easily remember the associations; and once he makes notations, the process of association is disrupted. If he attempts to direct his associations, they are no longer "free" and become characterized more by the logical sequence of reason and rationalization.

A variety of factors interfere with the free flow of mental association or make themselves evident in the content of free association; these are called resistances and are classified according to their origins from the divisions of the mental structure. Thus there are *id, *ego, and *superego resistances. Excessively powerful instinctual drives that the patient directs to the person of the therapist may cause the patient to censor his remarks because of embarrassment or his desire to be in the good favor of the therapist. His ego resistance may derive from the unconscious *mental mechanisms, while superego resistances may stem from self-punitive tendencies. Some persons have a tendency to be extremely obsessive and repetitious, others may be extremely circumstantial; some use language excessively to hide specific thoughts, others merely hesitate and use too few words to avoid the full expression of thoughts.

The detection of unconscious meanings involves the psychiatrist's training, experience, and sensitivity to the patient's mental productions. A few examples may be useful. In free association an individual spoke of the great intellectual qualities of his father, but at the same time indicated that his father never understood him and was never close to him; *unconsciously,* he was expressing the fear that the therapist might not understand him and was not giving him enough attention. Another simple instance is the person who spoke about his superior performance in one area of endeavor and then almost immediately spoke of his childhood fear of teachers who he believed considered him inferior. He was unconsciously telling the therapist of his basic fears of inadequacy all his life that he had to overcome by constant superior performance, thereby creating a constant tension and anxiety in his mind. He also was conveying to the therapist his need to be accepted by an authority figure and his fear of any failure whatsoever. In clinical practice, the therapist deals with many more complex instances of unconscious material in free association.

*Dream interpretation is substantially dependent upon free association in relationship to the manifest content of the dream, and dreams really cannot be adequately understood without the spontaneous verbalizations of the person on the day of the dream or the day after. Attempts to interpret the dreams of a subject by the method of interpreting symbolic meanings of objects or actions in the dream or by the associations only of the observer are of little clinical value.

Although some form of association is present in all mental content and behavior from one moment to the next, the action of the conscious will in directing the topic and the path of introspections and preoccupations places it under the aegis of what is called secondary process thinking. This type of thinking is characterized by sensitivity to external realities, the maintenance of logical thought, and a consideration of sequence and time relationships. On the other hand, free association is in closer communication with primary process thinking, a more primitive type of mental functioning, more influenced by the unconscious wishes and drives, not necessarily following the laws of logic and time relationships, and not under the direction of immediate conscious goals.

Since in free association a thought or mental image is always influenced by or linked somehow to its predecessor, it is said to be deterministic. This determinism can be interrupted or attenuated by the takeover of consciously directed thought; but here again, one may not completely disestablish mental content at any particular time from what went on before in the mind.

There is an economic principle governing the operations of the mind that gives it an inherent tendency to function with the minimum expenditure of energy; thus one mental image will be more prone to elicit a succeeding mental image that has a familiarity to it, rather than expend the energy to seek out an entirely new mental image. If this tendency is allowed free play (free association), it will tend to scan automatically the past for succeeding related mental images and thus be a factor in directing the flow of associations. The less the direction from the will or the outside, the stronger the linkage from the unconscious.

Bibliography: S. Freud, *The Standard Edition of the Complete Psychological Works,* ed. J. Strachey, 24 v. (London 1953–), v.4, *The Interpretation of Dreams* (1900–01) 100–106; v.15, *Introductory Lectures on Psychoanalysis* (1916) 106–112; v.23, *An Outline of Psychoanalysis* (1940); v.18, *Beyond the Pleasure Principle* (1920) 7–64. A. Freud, *The Ego and the Mechanisms of Defence,* tr. C. Baines (New York, 1946). R. M. Loewenstein, "Some Considerations on Free Association," *Journal of the American Psychoanalytic Association* 11.3 (1963) 451–473. P. Greenacre, "The Role of Transference: Practical Considerations in Relation to Psychoanalytic Therapy," *ibid.* 2 (1954) 671–684. E. Jones, *The Life and Work of Sigmund Freud,* 3 v. (New York 1953–55), v.1. L. Bellak, "Free Association: Conceptual and Clinical Aspects," *International Journal of Psychoanalysis* 42 (1961) 9–20. G. Zilboorg, "Some Sidelights on Free Associations," *ibid.* 33 (1952) 489–495. L. Stone, *The Psychoanalytic Situation: An Examination of Its Development and Essential Nature* (New York 1962).

[B. PACELLA]

ASSOCIATION FOR INTERNATIONAL DEVELOPMENT, an organization of Catholic men and women engaged in the international social apostolate. It was founded May 1, 1957, by Gerald F. Mische and John S. Connor at the request of the Mission Secretariat, with headquarters at Paterson, N.J. A.I.D. volunteers collaborate with local leaders in the emerging nations of Africa, Asia, and Latin America in programs for social, economic, cultural, and educational development, and leadership formation. A.I.D. recruits professionally competent and highly motivated single men and families willing to serve a minimum of 3 years after completion of 8 months of training. Three allied domestic operations include: leadership training for foreign students and visitors; courses in world affairs, notably a 6-week Summer Institute for International Service, conducted at Seton Hall University; and press and public informational services, including a monthly publication, *A.I.D. Dialogue.* A.I.D. cooperates with other international development programs without discrimination based on race, religion, or nationality. From 1957 to 1961 the post of director was filled by the cofounder Gerald F. Mische, who was succeeded by James J. Lamb for a 3-year term.

See also LAY MISSIONARIES.

[G. F. MISCHE]

ASSOCIATION OF CATHOLIC TRADE UNIONISTS, a national association founded in New York City in 1937 to give practical effect to Catholic social teaching as it concerns workingmen in home, school, factory, and community. The founding group included professional persons, trade unionists, and students. Martin Wersing was the first president, John P. *Monaghan the first chaplain. A publication, the *Labor Leader,* was inaugurated in 1938. During 1938 chapters were established in Boston, Detroit, and Pittsburgh; there were 11 in all by late 1941 and about the same number 15 years later, but by 1964 only 3 remained active.

In purpose, ACTU was not intended as a Catholic labor union on a European model. Rather, it took its inspiration from the advice of Pius XI: "Side by side with . . . unions there should always be associations zealously engaged in imbuing and forming their members in the teaching of religion and morality so that they in turn may be able to permeate the unions with that good spirit which should direct them in all their activities" (*Quadragesimo anno,* par. 35). In brief, ACTU helped nonunion men to organize, advised rank-and-file members on procedures for choosing union officers, and assisted unions in collective-bargaining negotiations. Recognizing that some aspects of trade unionism are of broader scope, it initiated and staffed labor schools to educate workingmen in parliamentary procedure, legal rights, and the like. It has appeared before congressional committees and compiled reports on such problems as racketeering in unions and sweatshops, in an effort to build and maintain the high ideals outlined in the social encyclicals.

[D. C. BAUER]

ASSOCIATIONISM

A theory contending that the entire conscious life of man can be explained on the basis of associative processes. It teaches that the mind consists of mental elements and compounds thereof. When one perceives an object, he has a sensation; but even when the object is no longer actually present, he may retain an idea, meaning by this a faint copy of a sensation or sensory image. Sensations and their copies are the sole elements of mind, and they are compounded or synthesized into larger mental structures, like complex perceptions and thoughts, by the mechanism of association. Conversely, any complex mental content can be reduced into its elemental components by mental analysis.

Hence the assumptions underlying associationistic psychology are those of elementarism and *sensism. Since its method is introspective, it is a form of mentalism. It has also been called content psychology, because of its concerning itself solely with contents that the mind passively receives; strictly speaking, its advocates maintained that there is no mind apart from its contents. At times associationism was referred to as the "brick-and-mortar theory," the bricks being the sensory impressions and their copies, and the mortar the associations connecting them.

Historical Development. Associationist theory, being a continuation of British *empiricism, has as its forerunners John *Locke and David *Hume. Its founder, however, was David *Hartley (1705–57), a physician, who gave the theory a physiological reference. For him, sensations occur parallel with vibrations in the nerves, and ideas run parallel with minute vibrations in the brain. When the vibratiuncles form clusters, the corresponding simple ideas coalesce into complex ideas by means of simultaneous association.

British Associationists. James *Mill (1773–1836) further elucidated the process of coalescence: the mental elements are connected by mechanical synthesis but remain what they are in the associative whole. This is the brick-and-mortar theory in its purest form. His son, John Stuart *Mill (1806–73), tempered the explanation by replacing mental mechanics with the concept of mental chemistry: the whole is not merely the sum of its elements, but something new, just as water is more than the sum of hydrogen and oxygen.

Other British associationists were Alexander *Bain (1818–1903), who combined associationism with *physiological psychology, and Herbert *Spencer (1820–1903), who introduced a new class of mental elements—feelings—previously thought of as mere attributes of sensations. Spencer also taught evolutionary associationism: when associations are often repeated, they create a hereditary predisposition. The last orthodox British associationist was E. B. *Titchener (1867–1927), who brought the theory to the U.S. via Germany.

German Associationists. The outstanding proponent of associationism in Germany was Wilhelm *Wundt (1832–1920), whose doctrine of content psychology was mitigated from the British form in two ways. First, Wundt introduced the concept of apperception: whereas association is passive, apperception is an active process that focuses attention upon certain features of a perception. Secondly, Wundt's system broke with the mentalist method underlying other types of associationism. According to Wundt, introspection and mental analysis can be applied only to lower mental processes, viz, sensory perceptions and feelings; the method is inadequate for the study of higher processes of mind, such as thinking, reasoning, and problem solving. These can be studied only by examining what Wundt called the natural history of mankind, i.e., by observing what these higher processes have produced: languages; customs; moral habits; works of science, art, and culture; social and economic systems; and religion. These cultural goods are objectivations of the human mind and, therefore, reveal its abilities. Wundt called this branch of psychology *Völkerpsychologie* (ethnic psychology).

Other psychologists, especially George Elias Müller (1850–1934) and his school, continued the associationist trend, but the movement has faltered in more recent times under the attacks of its critics.

Critique. The crux of associationist psychology has always been the problem of meaning. Many associationists attempted to solve the problem with what Titchener named the context theory: one perception or idea has no meaning, at least in the case of new ideas, but meaning arises from the context of related images that gather about the original presentation. How this came about was never satisfactorily explained. Since, according to the fundamental presupposition of associationism, there is no other mental mechanism, meaning presumably becomes attached to a perception or image by association. But if this is so, is meaning to be considered another mental element or a free-floating entity?

Another objection to associationist psychology was its limitations. Though it claimed to cover the whole of mental life, it confined itself to cognitive aspects alone, and was deficient in its consideration of the dynamic, motivational features of psychology. The Würzburg school, dissatisfied with the associationist contention that all conscious data of a cognitive order could be reduced to sensations and images, introduced a new kind of mental element, namely, imageless thought—a position strongly criticized by Titchener, who maintained that even thought processes are of a sensory and imaginal nature (*see* IMAGELESS THOUGHT, THEORY OF).

The act psychology of F. *Brentano and his followers was a partial return to Aristotelian-scholastic psychology; it taught that the mind is not simply a kind of receptacle passively receiving impressions, but is itself active in reacting to the presentations of sense.

The Gestalt school—preceded, if not influenced, by the Graz school with its form qualities—denied the very notion of mental elements and mental analysis. Perception, in *Gestalt psychology, is not a mosaic of elementary sensations and feelings, but the resultant of the total sensory impression: one perceives a unitary whole immediately, and not as a sum of its parts. Phenomenological psychology also rejected *introspection, in the sense of mental analysis, and insisted upon the total description of immediate experience.

The most radical opposition to associationist and content psychology came from American functionalists, who were no longer interested in the theoretical problem posed by *consciousness and concentrated on the practical question of its use. Finally, *behaviorism gave associationism the *coup de grâce* by repudiating all mentalism as irrelevant or useless, and by concentrating exclusively on the observation of human behavior.

See also PSYCHOLOGY, HISTORY OF; MEMORY; IDEA; CONCEPT.

Bibliography: H. C. WARREN, *A History of the Association Psychology* (New York 1921). E. G. BORING, *History of Experimental Psychology* (2d ed. New York 1950). W. DENNIS, ed., *Readings in the History of Psychology* (New York 1948). A. MARZI, EncFil 1:402–405.

[J. H. VAN DER VELDT]

ASSUMPTION, CONGREGATION OF THE, a congregation of teaching sisters with papal approbation (1888), founded in 1839 by Mother Marie Eugénie de Jésus (Anne Eugénie Milleret de Brou, d. 1898) at Paris, France, where the motherhouse is still located (*Religieuses de l'Assomption,* RA). The religious, who profess simple perpetual vows, wear a simple, violet habit with a white veil. The congregation is ruled by a superior general and five councilors, all of whom are elected in a general chapter, the superior for a term of 12 years, the councilors for 6 years. Each province is governed by a provincial and three councilors, elected for 6 years by the general council. Local superiors are appointed by the general council according to the recommendation of the provincial concerned.

The congregation is semicontemplative, combining elements of a rather intensive prayer life (recitation of the Divine Office in common, meditation, and adoration of the Blessed Sacrament), with an active apostolate that embraces teaching and mission work. The sisters are engaged principally in education; they teach in day and boarding schools and in colleges; they conduct orphanages and do catechetical work. In the lifetime of the foundress, who was declared venerable in 1961, the community established itself in France, England, Spain, Italy, the Philippines, Nicaragua, and El Salvador. Between 1954 and 1964, 41 new foundations were made, 31 of them in mission lands. In 1964 the congregation counted more than 1,800 sisters in 83 houses in 22 countries and provided education for 40,000 students. Nearly half the houses (38) were in mission territories. In the U.S., where the sisters arrived in 1919, there were 80 professed members (1964), teaching in four schools in Pennsylvania and Florida.

Bibliography: G. BERNOVILLE, *Les Religieuses de l'Assomption* (Paris 1948). C. C. MARTINDALE, *The Foundress of the Sisters of the Assumption* (London 1936). A. M. F. LOVAT, *Life of Mère Marie Eugénie Milleret de Brou* (London 1925).

[M. D. BLACHÈRE]

ASSUMPTION, SISTERS OF THE, a congregation whose full title is Sisters of the Assumption of the Blessed Virgin Mary (ASV). It was founded in 1853 by Rev. J. Harper, pastor of Saint-Grégoire, Quebec, Canada, to provide teachers for his school. The community was canonically erected as a diocesan institute in 1856, received the decree of praise from the Holy See in 1923, and became a pontifical institute in 1944, with final approbation of the constitutions in 1957. The motherhouse and novitiate were transferred to Nicolet, Quebec, in 1872. A foundation in Western Canada and one in the U.S. at Southbridge, Mass., were made in 1891. Missions were begun in Japan in 1934 and in Brazil in 1956.

In 1963 the community numbered more than 2,600 religious in 7 provinces. The U.S. province, established in 1946 with headquarters in Petersham, Mass., maintained 24 convents, with 315 sisters staffing 5 high schools, 21 elementary schools, and 1 private school, in the archdioceses of Boston and Hartford, and in the dioceses of Albany, Burlington, Manchester, Providence, Springfield (Mass.), and Worcester.

The purpose of the congregation is to extend God's kingdom through teaching and auxiliary services, at home and in mission fields. Besides the educating of students in 4 countries, these services include the training of future organists; promotion of children's church choirs and of sacred music; organization of Confraternity of Christian Doctrine classes, study and mission clubs, and Catholic Action movements; and the conducting of dispensaries and home and hospital visits. The sisters, who make simple vows of poverty, chastity, and obedience, have a 6-month postulancy and a 2-year novitiate, with temporary profession for 5 years before perpetual vows are pronounced. They wear a simple black costume that was modified in 1959, in conformity with the pope's wishes. As members of a Marian congregation, the sisters look to the Blessed Mother as their guide in community living and apostolic endeavors.

[A. O. BAILLARGEON]

ASSUMPTION COLLEGE (RICHARDTON, N.DAK.). North Dakota's only Catholic institution of higher learning for men is a 2-year liberal arts college. Together with Assumption Abbey and the Abbey Preparatory School, it is located on a 2,000-acre campus near Richardton in the Diocese of Bismarck. The College is conducted by the Benedictine Fathers of Assumption Abbey, which is a member of the American Cassinese Congregation (*see* BENEDICTINES, AMERICAN CASSINESE).

The history of Assumption College and of Assumption Abbey began in the early 1880s when Vincent de Paul *Wehrle, OSB (later first bishop of Bismarck), left the ancient Swiss Abbey of Einsiedeln to do missionary work in central U.S. In 1893 he established a priory near Devils Lake in northeastern North Dakota. Six years later he moved his small community of monks across the state to Richardton, where he established a monastery and St. Mary's College for the training of young men for the priesthood. In 1930 the name of the College was changed to Assumption Abbey College. It was not until 1960 that the community decided to expand the school's facilities to include lay students. A residence hall and student union were completed in 1962, and the name of the institution was shortened to Assumption College. The 1964 faculty numbered 15 priests and 2 laymen. Courses offered included the liberal arts, sciences, and the preprofessional fields.

An outstanding feature of the College is the library, which in 1964 housed approximately 60,000 volumes and subscribed to more than 100 periodicals. It contained many rare first editions of American frontier history and of American literature. In addition to an extensive theology-philosophy section, the library held a large classical language section and adequate science and literature sections.

One of the landmarks of the Dakotas, the Abbey Church, called the "Cathedral of the Northwest" at the time of its consecration in 1910, serves as Assumption College chapel.

Assumption College is affiliated with both the University of North Dakota and The Catholic University of America.

[L. PFALLER]

ASSUMPTION COLLEGE (WORCESTER, MASS.)

A Catholic college for men established at Worcester, Mass., in 1904, by the Congregation of the Augustinians of the Assumption, better known as the Assumptionist Fathers (*see* ASSUMPTIONISTS). Early known as Le Collège de l'Assomption, it was at first a secondary school and was later expanded into a 4-year liberal arts college. In 1917 it was authorized by the Commonwealth of Massachusetts to confer the degree of Bachelor of Arts, and in 1950 the legislature granted the College a university charter to confer both the master's degree and the doctorate. The evening college and the graduate school were instituted in 1951; the summer sessions, in 1952; the adult education program, in 1955; and the programs of foreign affairs and of education, in 1958.

On June 9, 1953, the original Assumption campus was almost totally destroyed by a tornado. What remained was rebuilt as the Assumption Preparatory School. In September 1953, Assumption College moved to a temporary campus, a 6-acre estate in south Worcester; in 1956 it occupied the new buildings of the present campus.

Assumption College is accredited by the New England Association of Colleges and Secondary Schools and the State Department of Education of Massachusetts. It is affiliated with The Catholic University of America and with the Institute of Augustinian Studies and the Institute of Byzantine Studies, both located in Paris, France. It holds membership in the National Catholic Educational Association, the American Council on Education, the Association of American Colleges, the National Commission on Accrediting, and the College Entrance Examination Board.

Assumption College is incorporated under the laws of the Commonwealth of Massachusetts and administered by a board of trustees made up of Assumptionist Fathers. The advisory board, whose membership rotates every 6 years, acts as a consulting body only. The administrative officers are all those who are heads of offices in the College organizations. The president's board and the dean's council govern policy in general and academic matters, respectively. In 1964 the 55-member staff was composed of 18 priests and 37 laymen who held 16 doctoral and 30 master's degrees. The College is not subsidized in any way. It is endowed with more than $300,000, most of which is allocated to scholarship aid.

The College is divided into four academic divisions: theology and philosophy, natural sciences, languages and literatures, and social sciences. To ensure both basic liberal education and the development of a given intellectual virtue in a field of primary interest, a concentration-integration system is employed. The first 2 years are devoted exclusively to the acquisition of general knowledge and of basic skills; training in independent study is initiated in two courses, English and humanities. The last 2 years are focused on extensive study in a selected area with continued emphasis on a liberal education. In the junior year the equivalent of a 1-year course is devoted to independent study in the area of concentration. In the senior year the student enrolls in one of three seminars depending upon his area of concentration. These are offered in economics, English, foreign affairs, French, history, mathematics, modern languages, natural sciences (including premedical and predental), and philosophy.

The campus of Assumption College, Worcester, Mass.

In 1964 the College library held about 57,000 volumes and subscribed to 437 periodicals. Special emphasis is placed upon Canadiana and foreign affairs. It has an extensive audio-visual collection, including an excellent section on fine arts. Its microfilm facilities include the only complete file on the North American continent of *La Croix,* a French Catholic daily newspaper. All the science laboratories are located in the Lt. Joseph P. Kennedy, Jr., Memorial Science Hall.

All undergraduate courses lead to the B.A. degree. The graduate school offers the M.A. and the M.A.T. degrees. In 1964 enrollment numbered 305 full-time students in the day college, 130 in the graduate school, 100 in the St. Augustine Institute (adult B.A. program), 170 in the Center for Continuing Education, and 90 in the PEP program (preparatory program) for high school students.

Assumption recognizes that beyond its normal role of education, it has an obligation to both the local and world community. Many programs and projects have been inaugurated, including the annual Institute on the Person and the Common Good; Management Training Institutes; and lecture series on foreign affairs, French culture, and the humanities.

Bibliography: P. GUISSARD, *Un Siècle d'histoire assomptioniste* (Worcester, Mass. 1950).

[C. E. GRADY]

ASSUMPTION OF MARY

"The Immaculate Mother of God, the ever-Virgin Mary, having completed the course of her earthly life, was assumed body and soul into heavenly glory." In these words of the apostolic constitution **Munificentissimus Deus* (MD) Pope Pius XII, on Nov. 1, 1950, most solemnly described the crowning event of the life of the Blessed Virgin. Thus defining the dogma of Mary's Assumption, he wrote the final chapter of the centuries-long tradition of belief in this mystery.

This article considers mainly the scriptural basis, taking as its guide the apostolic constitution, the theological explanation of the Assumption, and, finally, the question of the death of Mary.

Scripture. There is no explicit reference to the Assumption in the Bible, yet the Pope insists in the decree of promulgation that the Scriptures are the ultimate foundation of this truth. Our Lord Himself, the Evangelists, and the Fathers repeatedly emphasize the capital importance of the Resurrection of Christ as proof of His divinity, as promise of man's victory over sin, Satan, and death. "If Christ has not risen," wrote St. Paul (1 Cor 15.14–22), "vain then is our preaching, vain too is your faith. . . . For if the dead do not rise, neither has Christ risen. . . . If with this life only in view we have had hope in Christ, we are of all men the most to be pitied. But as it is, Christ has risen from the dead, the first-fruits of those who have fallen asleep. For since by a man came death, by a man also comes resurrection of the dead. For as in Adam all die, so in Christ all will be made to live." The new life brought by Christ is a life transforming man totally, body and soul, so that man's body too is meant to share in the victory of Christ over death, just as the whole of man, body and soul, suffers the consequences of Adam's sin. "When this mortal body puts on immortality, then . . . 'Death is swallowed up in victory.' . . . Now the sting of death is sin. . . . But thanks be to God who has given us the victory through our Lord Jesus Christ" (1 Cor 15.53–57). If these texts are part of the scriptural basis for the resurrection of the Christian, there remains the need to justify the anticipated resurrection that he attributes to the Virgin Mary. Pius XII himself extends the relevance of Lk 1.28 and 42 (which Pius IX had carefully analyzed in the bull of definition of the Immaculate Conception, *Ineffabilis Deus,* in 1854) to the Assumption: "Hail, [thou who art] full of grace, the Lord is with thee. Blessed art thou among women." That fulness of grace bestowed on the Blessed Virgin was, according to Pius XII, only achieved by her Assumption (MD 27).

Fig. 1. The Assumption of Mary, detail of a fresco in the subterranean basilica of St. Clement at Rome, 9th century. This is one of the earliest known clearly identifiable representations of the Assumption.

It is not theology but the evidence of Scripture that shows Mary "as most intimately joined to her divine Son and as always sharing His lot" (MD 38). St. Paul assures the Romans (6.4–13) that through Baptism they are joined to Christ and share in His victory over sin. Mary's unique similarity to Christ began with her conception. Since it is sin and its consequent punishment in death and corruption that delay the final triumph of the ordinary Christian, it is implicit that anyone perfectly free from sin, like Christ, would be free from the deferment of the resurrection of the body, as Christ was. Mary is surely an exception to the rule (MD 5), portrayed perhaps (MD 27) in the Apocalypse (12.1) as the great sign in the heavens, a woman clothed with the sun, the moon under her feet, her head crowned with 12 stars. That St. John was primarily here describing the Church in ultimate victory is generally agreed, but that he was also describing the personification of the Church in Mary, the eschatological image of the Church, a prototype already enjoying the glory that the Church will eventually share, has been seriously proposed and defended.

New Eve. But the most pregnant idea, implied in Scripture and specific already in patristic writings, for accepting and understanding something of the mystery of the Assumption, is that of Mary as the New Eve. Three times in the bull of definition (MD 27, 30, 39) the Holy Father alludes to this telling comparison, without defending or explaining it, accepting it as an obvious deduction from Scripture and a logical development of tradition. Holy Writ says that "as from the offense of the one man the result was unto condemnation to all men, so from the justice of the one the result is unto justification of life to all men. For just as by the disobedience of the one man the many were constituted sinners, so also by the obedience of the one the many will be constituted just" (Rom 5.18–19). The first Eve proved not to be the helpmate God had intended her to be for Adam, proved not to be the "mother of the living" but rather, in a sense, mother of the dead, for she had led Adam into sin and thus been his accomplice in bringing all men to the punishment of death and the dominion of Satan. In contrast, Mary, the New Eve, by her obedience to the Annunciation of the angel brought life to men in having conceived the person of the New Adam and in having united herself to the principal acts of His redemptive mission. Just as Eve cooperated not only in the original sin but also shared with Adam his subsequent life, parenthood, and the sufferings that were sin's punishment, so Mary cooperated with Christ not only in giving Him birth, but she cooperated with Him, evidently in a secondary and unessential—but actually necessary and important—role, in the significant events of His life, the Presentation, one of His first miracles, the Crucifixion, the Ascension, and, later, in the beginnings of His Church (His members) at Pentecost. More truly than Eve ever would have been, Mary became—at Nazareth, at Bethlehem, at Calvary—in an ever fuller sense, the mother of all the members of the Mystical Body. Hence as things said of Adam apply also, but proportionately, to Eve, so things said of Christ apply also, but proportionately, to Mary. The author of the Epistle to the Hebrews (2.14) had said "that through death He [Christ] might destroy him who had the empire of death, that is, the devil." Chris-

Fig. 2. The death of the Virgin and the carrying of her soul to heaven, 12th-century mosaic in the church of the Martorana at Palermo. This motif is the typical Eastern counterpart of the Western iconography of the Assumption.

tian intuition, guided by the Holy Spirit, gradually came to see that Mary's share in Christ's victory over sin began with her conception in a state free from all sin (the state in which Eve was created), and ended with her miraculous Assumption (an immunity from death and corruption which Eve enjoyed until the Fall).

The union of Mary with Jesus, so obvious in the scriptural record of their earthly lives, is just as true of their respective roles in the Redemption. Holy Scripture, the Fathers, the medieval theologians, and Pius XII in this most solemn pronouncement, tell of one enmity between God and the devil; one evil—embodied in Adam, Eve, Satan, and his seed—confronting one power of good—God, the Woman, and her Seed; an enmity that will end in a single triumph—of the Woman and her Seed; and of the New Adam one with the New Eve. As Adam's love for Eve led him into sin, so Christ's love for Mary led Him to have her "share in the conflict [and] share in its conclusion" (MD 39)—like Him, a complete victory in body and soul over sin and death.

Mother of God. Pius XII repeatedly refers to Mary's being the Mother of God as the theological reason (for Christ's unique love for and union with Mary and) for the Assumption (MD 6, 14, 21, 22, 25), like a superlative application of the text, "His father's honor is a man's glory; disgrace for her children, a mother's shame" (Sir 3.11). For Mary was united to all three Persons of the Blessed Trinity in a unique relationship—as privileged daughter, mother, and spouse, privileges that involved her body and soul, that implicated her in extraordinary sufferings and joys (MD 14). From earliest times the Fathers defended her perpetual virginity as a proof of the divinity of her offspring, as evidence of her exemption from painful parturition, which is the punishment for sin (cf. Gn 3.16), as the effect of a sinlessness that, negatively, preempts her from the curse of death and that, positively, merits for her the immediate contemplation (after this life), in body and soul, of God. God's justice would not inflict punishment (pain, death, corruption) on one innocent of the crime (sin) being punished: "For all lives are mine; the life of the father is like the life of the son, both are mine; only the one who sins shall die" (Ez 18.4). Briefly—and less weightily than the two previous explanations—the propriety of the Assumption is indicated: The fact that Christ loved Mary and united her in His mysteries makes it proper that the woman He had created sinless, that the virgin whom He had chosen for His mother, be, like Him, completely triumphant over death in her Assumption as He had triumphed over sin and death in His Resurrection.

Death of the Virgin. One final question: Did the Blessed Virgin die? In the climactic paragraph of definition, the Pope chose to say, "Mary, having completed the course of her earthly life, was assumed body and soul into heavenly glory" (MD 44). The crucial phrase *expleto terrestris vitae cursu* offers support neither to those who argue that Mary died (the "mortalists") nor to those who say that she did not die (the "immor-

Fig. 3. Boss in the vault of the porch of the cathedral at Peterborough, England, carved to represent the Assumption, 13th century. The choice of an overhead location for the sculpture must have seemed very fitting to the medieval sculptor.

Fig. 4. The Assumption of Mary, Nicolas Poussin, French school. On the basis of style it has been dated c. 1637.

talists"). While most of the faithful and most of the writers on the subject accept without debate the fact of the death of Mary, it is a subject of controversy among theologians.

Patristic writers cannot be called as support for either side. Before the Council of Nicaea (325) the only overt reference to the close of Mary's life is a phrase attributed to Origen: "With respect to the brethren of Jesus, there are many who ask how He had them, seeing that Mary remained a virgin until her death." But this and a phrase in a hymn of St. Ephraem are praises of the perpetual virginity of Mary; her death is taken for granted, affirmed but not explained. The only writer before the Council of Ephesus (431) to treat the problem *ex professo* was St. Epiphanius, and he concludes that Mary could have enjoyed immortality or could have suffered either martyrdom or natural death. The ambiguity of SS. Augustine, Ambrose, and Jerome point rather to the assumption by Christians that Mary had died than that she was an exception to the law of death to which even Christ had submitted. As history, the apocryphal accounts of *transitus Mariae* are ambivalent, but they are respectable evidence of a conviction among Christians of the 5th century that Mary had died. And the feast of the Dormition of Mary, documented from the second half of the 6th century in the East (Syrian Jacobite Church) and from the 7th century in the West (in Rome under Pope Sergius I), was in its beginnings a tribute to the anniversary of the death of Mary—only later to become a commemoration of the Assumption as such. For patristic writers the reasons for Mary's death were: (1) she belonged to a fallen human nature (even though sinless herself) and inherited a mortal human body; and (2) she was conformable in all things to Christ, who had chosen the humiliation of death despite His divine holiness.

Scholastic theologians, e.g., St. Bonaventure, were to accept these explanations for Mary's death and add: (1) the pertinence of virginity, i.e., that Mary's body, which had maintained its integrity even in childbirth, and which was always in harmony with reason and grace, would have merited assumption after death (e.g., St. Bernardine of Siena); (2) the advantage of Mary's meriting herself, by her own death, the resurrection and glorification, as Christ had done (e.g., St. Thomas Aquinas and Dun Scotus).

Most theologians of our day are mortalists and find that the Holy Father, while not taking an ex officio position on the question of the death of Mary, repeatedly used texts from tradition that refer to or imply Mary's death. But a few writers (Balić, Carol, Coyle, Filograssi) have expressed the opinion that the Pope's not favoring either side has left the question in the same state as it was before the definition.

See also MARY, BLESSED VIRGIN I, II; MARIAN FEASTS; DORMITION OF THE VIRGIN.

Bibliography: PIUS XIII, "Munificentissimus Deus" (Apostolic Constitution, Nov. 1, 1950) ActApS 42 (1950) 753–771. *Catholic Mind* (Eng.) 49 (Jan. 1951) 65–78. *Thomist* 14.1 (1951); the entire issue is on the Assumption. W. BURGHARDT, "The Testimony of the Patristic Age Concerning Mary's Death," *Marian Studies* 8 (1957) 58–99. J. M. EGAN, "The Doctrine of Mary's Death During the Scholastic Period," *ibid.*, 100–124. T. W. COYLE, "The Thesis of Mary's Death in the Light of *Munificentissimus Deus*," *ibid.*, 143–166. Carol Mariol 2:461–492. F. M. BRAUN, *La Mère des fidèles: Essai de théologie johannique* (Tournai 1953) 134–176. C. X. FRIETHOFF, *A Complete Mariology*, tr. Religious of the Retreat of the Sacred Heart (Westminster, Md. 1958) 143–164. M. JUGIE, "Assomption de la Sainte Vierge," *Maria*, ed. H. DU MANOIR (Paris 1959) 1:621–658. R. LAURENTIN, *Queen of Heaven*, tr. G. SMITH (London 1956) 114–125. S. MATHEWS, ed., *Queen of the Universe* (St. Meinrad, Ind. 1957). K. RAHNER, "The Interpretation of the Dogma of the Assumption," *Theological Investigations*, tr. C. ERNST (Baltimore 1961) 215–227. **Illustration credits:** Figs. 1 and 2, Alinari-Art Reference Bureau. Fig. 3, National Buildings Record, London. Fig. 4, National Gallery of Art, Washington, D.C., gift of Mrs. Mellon Bruce.

[J. W. LANGLINAIS]

ASSUMPTIONISTS

Augustinians of the Assumption (AA), a congregation of religious priests with simple vows founded in 1845 by Emmanuel Daudé d'*Alzon, vicar-general of the Diocese of Nîmes, France. The first five members pronounced their vows on Christmas Day 1850. Although a pontifical brief of Nov. 26, 1864, encouraged the foundation, the constitutions were not formally approved until Jan. 30, 1923.

The founder, a staunch supporter of *ultramontanism, was strongly influenced by the 19th-century school of *traditionalism and by the ideas of Hugues Félicité de *Lamennais before his condemnation (1832). The purpose assigned to the institute was "to restore higher education according to the mind of St. Augustine and St. Thomas; to fight the Church's enemies enlisted in secret societies under the revolutionary flag; to fight for the unity of the Church. . . ." D'Alzon's spiritual doctrine was essentially Trinitarian, tending to a contemplation of the Three Divine Persons and a participation in the mysteries of Jesus, in the spirit of the French school of spirituality of the 17th century. This spirituality was expressed in the congregation's *Spiritual Directory* (1859–65), *Instructions* and *Circular Letters* (1868–75), and *Meditations* (1879–80). Publication of D'Alzon's writings began in 1952 (*Les Cahiers d'Alzon*, Paris). Besides the *Constitutions* and a *Customary*, the Assumption fathers officially follow the *Spiritual Directory*, although in fact their spirit was shaped mainly by the second superior general, François Picard (1880–1903), who influenced them through his *Circular Letters*.

Under Emmanuel d'Alzon, the Assumption fathers, in keeping with the threefold purpose of the institute, established three kinds of activities: teaching, the Catholic press, and the conducting of Byzantine-rite residences in Eastern Europe. Under Picard and Emmanuel Bailly (1903–17) the congregation broadened its aims, and the organization of pilgrimages and parish work became features of its life.

Expelled from France in 1900 by the anticlerical government of that time, the congregation temporarily closed most of its houses there, and migrated to Spain, the Netherlands, Belgium, England, the U.S., and South America. One of their first American settlements was in Louisiana, where they stayed only a short time. In 1891 the Assumption Fathers settled permanently in New York City, where they opened the oldest Spanish-language parish, Our Lady of Guadalupe. In 1903 they went to Worcester, Mass., where they founded Assumption Preparatory School. In the meantime, they also consolidated their work in Eastern Europe and opened several houses in Russia, where one of their members, Pie Neveu, remained as bishop after the Soviet Revolution.

Under Gervais Quenard, fourth superior general (1923–51), the congregation increased from 700 to 1,800 members; three provinces were established in France and one in Belgium, as well as one each in the Netherlands, England, the U.S., and South America; Chile is the center of the South American province. The congregation is governed by a superior general (resident in Rome) elected for 12 years by the general chapter, which is composed of the major superiors and two delegates from each province. Rev. Wilfred Dufault, an American, was elected superior general in 1951 and reelected in 1964.

Before 1939 Assumption missionaries were in the Belgian Congo, Brazil, Tunisia, and Manchuria. After 1945 they entered the Ivory Coast, Madagascar, Algeria, and New Zealand. In Europe, they have greatly suffered from the Communist regimes which reduced their houses in Bulgaria and Rumania to inactivity, and also drove them out of Manchuria.

The Assumption fathers maintain their founder's ideal of an intellectual apostolate by two institutions: the Institute for Byzantine Studies, established in 1897 and successively located in Istanbul, Bucharest, and Paris, where it publishes the *Revue des Études Byzantines* (formerly, *Les Echos d'Orient*); and the Institute for Augustinian Studies, founded in Paris in 1939, which publishes the *Revue des Études Augustiniennes.* Concern for the unity of the Church inspired the foundation of one of the first reviews devoted to ecumenical questions, *L'Union des Églises* (published from 1922 to 1938, in Lyons, France). Since 1948, a quarterly dealing with the Eastern Churches has been published in Nijmegen, Holland: *Het Christelijk Oosten en Herenining.*

The American province, with headquarters in New York City, maintains houses in New York State and in Massachusetts; the Province of Quebec, Canada; and Mexico City, Mexico. It has fewer than 100 members and is best known for *Assumption College in Worcester, Mass., and for its presence in Moscow, U.S.S.R., where, since 1935, it has provided chaplains to the American Catholics in the Soviet capital.

Several congregations of sisters are connected, by their origin, with the Augustinians of the Assumption: the Ladies of the Assumption, the Oblates of the Assumption, the Little Sisters of the Assumption, and the Orantes of the Assumption.

Bibliography: S. Vailhé, *Vie du Père Emmanuel d'Alzon,* (Paris 1926–34). G. H. Tavard, "The Assumptionists and the Work for Christian Unity," EChurchQ 8 (1950) 482–494. A. Sage, *Un Maître spirituel du XIXe siècle* (Rome 1958). A. Pépin, *L'Ame d'un grand apôtre, le père d'Alzon* (Paris 1950).

[G. H. TAVARD]

ASSUMPTUS-HOMO THEOLOGY. To bring out the completeness of the Redemption (*quod non est assumptum non est sanatum*), many of the Fathers described the *Incarnation in terms of the *Word assuming manhood in its entirety. But the term they used, *assumptus homo,* could be read as "the man the Word assumed to Himself," and there is a danger of this being understood in a Nestorian or adoptionist sense (*see* NESTORIANISM; ADOPTIONISM). While one admits the individuality of Christ's humanity, the Word did not assume an already-existing man and unite him to the Godhead.

In *Liber sententiarum* 3.6 Peter Lombard referred to the view of theologians in his day who, following certain patristic authorities, spoke of Christ as *quidam homo,* a man that was assumed and united to the Word. This view was never condemned, but was criticized by St. Thomas, Scotus, and other scholastics as being liable to misunderstanding in a Nestorian sense.

In recent years there has been an attempt to return to this way of speaking, especially among those who wish to give Christ a fully human psychological autonomy. D. M. de Basly (d. 1937) claimed that his view was in the tradition of the *Antioch school and of Scotus. L. Seiller went so far as to say that Christ in His manhood was a "somebody," and this opinion was condemned by the Holy Office [ActApS 43 (1951) 561]. The encyclical *Sempiternus rex* (Denz 3905) does not reject the term *assumptus homo,* but says it has to be used with discernment as it can easily lead to adoptionism.

See also HYPOSTATIC UNION; JESUS CHRIST, II (IN DOGMATIC THEOLOGY); JESUS CHRIST, III (SPECIAL QUESTIONS), 13; CHRISTOLOGY; INCARNATION, ARTICLES ON; JESUS CHRIST, ARTICLES ON.

Bibliography: DTC, Tables générales 2:2647–48. Landgraf Doggesch 2.1:116–137. H. M. Diepen, LexThK² 1:948–949; *Douze dialogues de christologie ancienne* (Rome 1960); *La Théologie de l'Emmanuel* (Bruges 1960); "L'*Assumptus Homo* patristique," RevThom 63 (1963) 225–245, 363–388; 64 (1964) 32–52, 364–386. Crisóstomo de Pamplona, "El *Assumptus Homo* y el *Yo* humano de Christo a la luz de la doctrina de Escoto y de Basly," *Estudios Franciscanos* 63 (1962) 161–194.

[M. E. WILLIAMS]

ASSUR (ASSHUR), CITY OF, first capital of Assyria, situated on the west bank of the Tigris (as rightly stated in Gn 2.14), 60 miles south of Ninive and 37 miles south of the junction of the Great Zab with the Tigris. The Assyrian capital was moved from Assur to Kalḫu (Chale, Heb. *kelaḥ;* modern Nimrud) *c.* 1330 B.C., and to *Ninive (Nineveh) in 860 B.C. The site of ancient Assur is now called Qal'āt Sherqāṭ. Though discovered in 1821, it was not systematically excavated until 1903, when a German expedition under W. Andrae began work there that lasted until 1914. The excavations disclosed that the site was occupied from the 2d half of the 4th millennium B.C., when its culture was north Sumerian, to the middle of the 2d Christian century, when there was a large Parthian palace there. Tukulti-Ninurta I (1233–1199 B.C.) built a vast palace at Assur; *Sargon II (721–705) and *Sennacherib (705–680) fortified it with walls and moats and enriched and restored its numerous temples. Various temples of the gods Assur, Ishtar, Nabu, Sin, and Shamash, as well as various city walls, gates, and palaces, have been identified by the excavators. A very large collection of cuneiform tablets from Assur has been published, including many important historical, literary, and religious texts.

The history of the city is closely connected with the general history of Assyria (*see* MESOPOTAMIA, ANCIENT, 2). The earliest-known inhabitants of the site bore non-Semitic, non-Sumerian names. The place was settled by the Semitic Akkadians probably in the 1st half of the 3d millennium B.C. It was subject to the Dynasty of Akkad (2360–2180) and the Third Dynasty of Ur (2060–1950). Like the kings of the First Dynasty of Babylon (1830–1531), its contemporary kings were Semitic Amorrites. (*See* AMORRITES.)

In the Hebrew Bible the frequent mention of *'aššur* (except in Gn 2.14) refers to the land and the people of *Assyria.

Bibliography: ReallexAssyr 1:170–198. W. ANDRAE, *Das wiedererstandene Assur* (Leipzig 1938). S. A. PALLIS, *The Antiquity of Iraq* (Copenhagen 1956).

[L. A. BUSHINSKI]

ASSURBANIPAL (ASHURBANIPAL), KING OF ASSYRIA

Son and successor of *Asarhaddon (Esarhaddon). He reigned from 668–627 B.C. Assurbanipal (Assyrian, *Aššur-bāni-apal,* the god "Assur creates an heir"), who was known to the Greeks and Romans as a semilegendary Sardanapalus, was the last great ruler of the Assyrian Empire. His first task was to complete the conquest of Egypt that his father had begun. In 667 he put down the revolt of Pharao Theraca (Tirhakah) in *Memphis (Noph). A new Egyptian revolt in 663 led to the Assyrian conquest of *Thebes (No-Amon) in Upper Egypt (Na 3.8–10). In the course of these campaigns, Tyre was besieged and captured by the Assyrians, while the kings of the neighboring states, including *Manasse of Juda (*c.* 687–*c.* 642; see Pritchard ANET[2] 294a), sent Assurbanipal their tribute. After reducing southern Armenia to vassalage, the Assyrian repulsed the attacks on Babylonia by the Elamite King Teumman and then in a series of campaigns overran Elam, captured Teumman, and installed Humbanigash as satellite king over the country. Teumman's head was sent as a gruesome trophy to Ninive (*c.* 653). In 652 Assurbanipal's brother Shamash-shum-ukin, vassal King of Babylonia, with the aid of Humbanigash and several Arabian chieftains, rebelled against Assurbanipal. In a series of costly campaigns Babylon was finally captured and Shamash-shum-ukin burned to death in his palace (648); *Susa, the Elamite capital, was sacked, and all of *Elam utterly devastated.

Although Assyria was then at the height of its power and ruled over a larger empire than the world had ever known before, it had exhausted itself in wars of conquest, and its collapse was imminent. As early as 656 Psamettichus, whom Assurbanipal had installed as vassal king of Egypt, could with impunity declare himself an independent ally of Assyria. King Gyges of Lydia in western Asia Minor could break his treaty with Assyria, and Assurbanipal could do nothing but pray the gods to send the *Cimmerians to punish him. By destroying Elam, Assyria removed the barrier between itself and the young, vigorous nation of the *Medes. In a little more than a decade after the death of the great Assyrian King, his capital *Ninive was captured and destroyed by the Medes (614), and a few years later (*c.* 607) the last remnant of Assyrian power disappeared at Haran.

Although in his numerous inscriptions Assurbanipal speaks of himself (in the standard style of Assyrian royal inscriptions) as personally leading his armies in battle and inflicting the usual atrocities on his captured foes, he was apparently a mild-mannered man, who preferred to stay in his palace and commit the conduct of his armies to his generals. As a generous patron of the fine arts, he had his palace at Ninive adorned with magnificent bas-reliefs (*see* MESOPOTAMIA, ANCIENT, 4). He boasted of his ability to read and write the complex cuneiform script—a difficult art ordinarily reserved to professional scribes—and he had his secretaries collect and copy numerous Sumerian and Akkadian tablets in the ancient towns of Babylonia; these copies he then placed in his great library at Ninive, which contained tens of thousands of cuneiform tablets (now mostly in the British Museum). Modern scholars are indebted primarily to the scholarly interests of this learned king for their knowledge of Assyrian and Babylonian literature (*see* AKKADIAN LANGUAGE AND LITERATURE; SUMERIAN LANGUAGE AND LITERATURE).

Bibliography: S. SMITH, CAH 3:88–127. A. T. E. OLMSTEAD, *History of Assyria* (New York 1923). H. R. HALL, *The Ancient History of the Near East* (8th ed. New York 1935) 500–512. W. F. VON SODEN, *Herrscher im alten Orient* (Berlin 1954) 127–138. D. D. LUCKENBILL, ed., *Ancient Records of Assyria and Babylonia,* 2 v. (Chicago 1926–27) 2:290–407. Pritchard ANET[2] 294–301. F. SCHMIDTKE, LexThK[2] 1:949–950. G. BOSON and A. ROMEO, EncCatt 2:213–214. **Illustration credit:** Courtesy of the Trustees of the British Museum.

[R. H. PUNKE]

Assurbanipal feasting with his queen in the royal garden after the defeat of Teumman (c. 653 B.C.), whose severed head hangs from a tree on the left; bas-relief from the Upper Chambers, North Palace, Ninive.

ASSURNASIRPAL II, King of Assyria (884–860 B.C.), son and successor of Tukulti-Ninurta II (891–885). Continuing the conquests of his father, he established his rule over the neighboring *Hurrians and *Aramaeans. In 876 his armies reached the Mediterranean. The Phoenician cities Tyre, Sidon, and Byblos paid him tribute. He did not, however, attempt to attack the strong Aramaean city of Damascus. His inscriptions record the tortures he inflicted on the conquered and the terror he inspired. His highly mobile army, to which he introduced cavalry for the first time, explains his successes. In 880 he removed his capital from *Ninive (Nineveh) to Chale (Calah; Heb. *kalaḥ;* Assyrian *kalḫu*), now a mound of ruins known as Nimrud, about 20 miles southeast of modern Mosul. Here excavators found extensive bas-reliefs of the King at worship and at war. One of the finest available examples of free-standing Assyrian sculpture is a statuette of Assurnasirpal in which, as in the bas-relief, stiff hieratic form predominates. Though his name is not mentioned in the Bible, Assurnasirpal II was a contemporary of Kings Asa and Josaphat of Juda and of Kings Amri (Omri) and Achab of Israel. He passed on to his son *Salmanasar (Shalmaneser) III the powerful army with which the latter made Israel under *Jehu his tributary.

Bibliography: Pritchard ANET[2] 275–276. D. D. Luckenbill ed., *Ancient Records of Assyria and Babylonia,* 2 v. (Chicago 1926–27) 1:138–199. **Illustration credit:** Courtesy of the Trustees of the British Museum.

[J. F. MATTINGLY]

ASSY, NOTRE-DAME-DE-TOUTE-GRÂCE

A parish church, consecrated in August 1950 to service Catholics in the French Alps where tubercular patients and sanatoria convalescent services increased considerably between 1930 and 1950. The church, designed by Maurice Novarina, is not particularly distinguished architecturally; however, the appointment of its decoration served as a focal point of the postwar controversies surrounding the Dominican-led *art sacré* movement in France.

In March 1939, at the request of the Canon Jean Devémy and the architect M. Novarina, Pierre M. A. *Couturier, OP, agreed to assist in the planning and execution of the church. The subsequent evolution of this plan in its iconographic program and its relationship to the specific convictions and abilities of the artists engaged, as well as the kind and quality of contemporary art employed, served to sharpen questions on contemporary religious art. The problems posed were consequent to the employment of outstanding artists from the secular art world in an effort to initiate a notable renascence within the area of religious art. The majority of artists engaged were chosen not on the basis of their faith but on the basis of the quality of their work; most were non-Catholics. The art work itself was, for that time, unusually advanced and seemed foreign to what was considered religious art by reactionary Catholics in France and elsewhere.

Assurnasirpal II, King of Assyria (884–860 B.C.). Sandstone figure, 3 ft, 8½ in., from Nimrud. In his right hand the King has a mace, in his left a weapon usually carried by a god; an inscription is carved on his breast.

Fig. 1. Main façade and the belfry.

ASSY

Fig. 2. Nave of the church looking toward the sanctuary with the Jean Lurçat "Apocalypse."

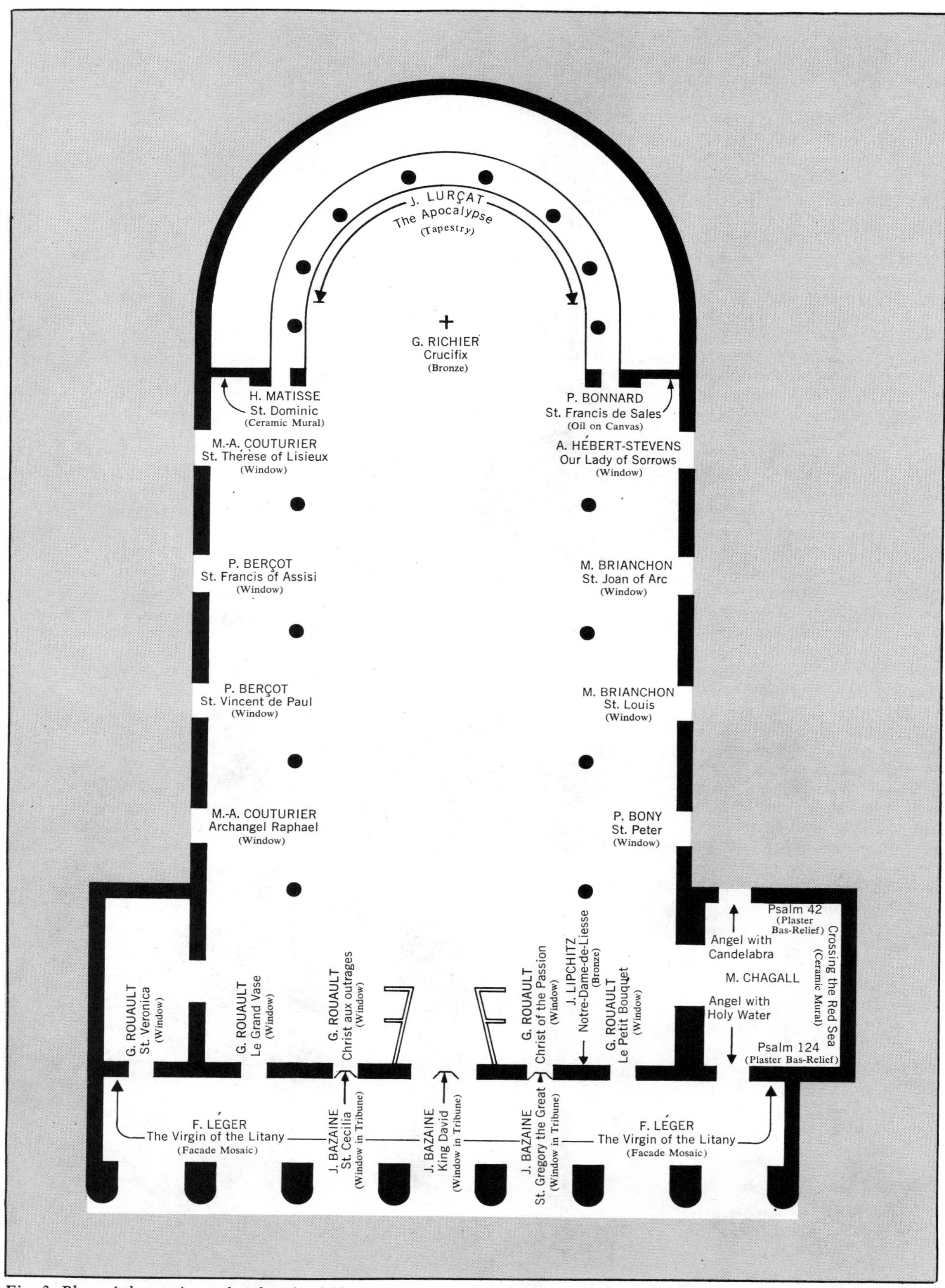

Fig. 3. Plan of decorations, the church of Notre-Dame-de-Toute-Grâce at Assy.

The iconographic program unfolded gradually and was partly adjusted to afford a suitable conjunction of the temperament and ability of a particular artist with the subject and its location in relation to the sanctuary. Works for the church included: a façade mosaic by F. *Léger, "Virgin of the Litany"; baptistery mosaic and reliefs by Marc Chagall, "Crossing of the Red Sea," "Psalm 42," and "Psalm 124"; stained glass designed by G. *Rouault, notably his "Christ aux outrages"; a large tapestry based on Apocalypse, ch. 12, by Jean Lurçat; altarpieces representing St. Dominic (ceramic tile) by H. *Matisse and St. Francis de Sales (oil) by P. *Bonnard; a bronze statue by J. Lipchitz, "Notre-Dame-de-Liesse"; tabernacle door relief by G. *Braque; and stained-glass windows by J. Bazaine, P. Bony, P. Berçot, M. Brianchon, A. Hébert-Stevens, and Father Couturier. The controversial bronze crucifix was designed by Germaine Richier for placement on the main altar.

Though brilliant in individual qualities and somewhat appropriately appointed iconographically, the works as an artistic ensemble show a disparity of styles that has been criticized as an exhibition of talent more suitable for a museum. The controversies that followed the dedication of the church were precipitated by the wide attention given to the church through illustrated articles in magazines such as *France Illustration* and *Life*. A public lecture given by the Canon Devémy on Jan. 4, 1951, for the Friends of Art at Angers received cries of "insult" and "outrage" from a band of Integrists when the crucifix by Germaine Richier appeared in the slides. The Integrists distributed a tract (known as "The Tract of Angers"), which attacked the Richier crucifix. It indicted artists belonging to a "school" led by the "communist Picasso" and asserted that it was time to "unmask the trickery of this spurious art." During February and March the bishop of Annecy was pressured by letters and by a drive led by Charles du Mont in the *Observateur de Genève;* in April Bishop Cesbron ordered that the crucifix be removed. Reactions to this move were rapid and received wide attention in the press. The art critics Jean Cassou and Bernard Dorival defended the Richier work and saw the move as an imposition on what is properly the domain of art; G. Marcel responded to Dorival noting that an art critic may not contest ecclesiastical authority. F. Mauriac asked whether art can be heretical, and Gaston Bardet answered by proposing that there be created an "index" for artistic works. Celso *Costantini issued the most provoking censure in the *Osservatore Romano* (June 10, 1951) in an article *"Dell'arte sacra deformatrice,"* which referred to the crucifix as an "indecent (*sconcio*) pastiche" and attacked the so-called modern movement in art as a Protestant plot against figurative art.

The debates over sacred art were met by an official 11-point directive issued in May 1952 by an episcopal commission for pastoral and liturgical matters and approved by the cardinals and archbishops of France. The document avoided mentioning any specific works and provided a sufficiently general basis to pacify both sides. The first article recognized that sacred art like all other art is a living art and must correspond to the spirit of its times in its techniques as well as in its use of available materials.

The Assy controversies, by sharpening questions surrounding contemporary art, the artist, and the Church, provided practical precedents and a spirit of inquiry that contributed considerably to the growing modern renewal in liturgical art.

See also CHURCH ARCHITECTURE, 10; LITURGICAL ART, 3.

Bibliography: W. S. RUBIN, *Modern Sacred Art and the Church of Assy* (New York 1961), illus., extensive bibliog.; for critical evaluation see R. SOWERS, *Stained Glass: An Architectural Art* (New York 1965), n. 39, p. 126–127, *passim.* A. CHRIST-JANER and M. M. FOLEY, *Modern Church Architecture* (New York 1962). **Illustration credits:** Figs. 1 and 2, Helga Schmidt-Glassner.

[R. J. VEROSTKO]

ASSYRIA, ancient country in northeastern Mesopotamia (*see* MESOPOTAMIA, ANCIENT, 1). Its heartland was the area of the middle Tigris, the site of the cities of *Assur (from which the land takes its name), *Ninive, and Calah (see Gn 10.11). Shut off by mountain ranges on the north and east, the land has a rugged aspect throughout much of its extent; this factor encouraged the yearly military campaigns by which, from the 14th century B.C., the kings of Assyria sought to gain control of neighboring and more richly endowed lands. Their greatest successes were obtained from the 9th to the 7th centuries B.C., with the subjugation of Syria, northern Palestine, and parts of Egypt and Asia Minor (see 4 Kgs 15.27; 17.3–6; 18.13–19.37). At the zenith of its power, Assyria was overcome by a coalition of its Chaldean and Median enemies, who captured the capital city of Ninive in 612 B.C. (see Na 2.2–14). For a more detailed account of the history of Assyria, *see* MESOPOTAMIA, ANCIENT, 2. On the Assyrian language, *see* AKKADIAN LANGUAGE AND LITERATURE.

Bibliography: B. MEISSNER, *Babylonien und Assyrien,* 2 v. (Heidelberg 1920–25). ReallexAssyr 228–303. M. A. BEEK, *Atlas of Mesopotamia,* tr. D. R. WELSH (London 1962).

[R. I. CAPLICE]

ASSYRIOLOGY

In the widest sense, Assyriology is the study of the civilization and culture of ancient Assyria and Babylonia (including especially the history, language, and antiquities of these lands). In a narrower but more usual sense, Assyriology is generally restricted to the study of texts written in the Akkadian (i.e., Assyro-Babylonian) language. (*See* AKKADIAN LANGUAGE AND LITERATURE.)

Discovery of the Cuneiform Texts. Although medieval and Renaissance travelers, such as *Benjamin ben Jonah of Tudela (12th century) and Pietro della Valle (17th century), mentioned the ancient ruins of Mesopotamia in their writings, it was only in the early 19th century that serious efforts were made at excavating these ruins and deciphering their curious cuneiform script. (*See* WRITING, ANCIENT SYSTEMS OF.) The first excavations were conducted in Assyria (hence the origin of the term Assyriology for Mesopotamian studies in general) and were begun by P. É. Botta at Kuyunjik (ancient *Ninive) in December 1842. In March 1843, he shifted to Khorsabad, where he quickly discovered the palace of *Sargon II (721–705 B.C.) with its mammoth halls, numerous stone reliefs, and stone and clay inscriptions. In November 1845, A. H. Layard started digging at Nimrud (ancient Calah),

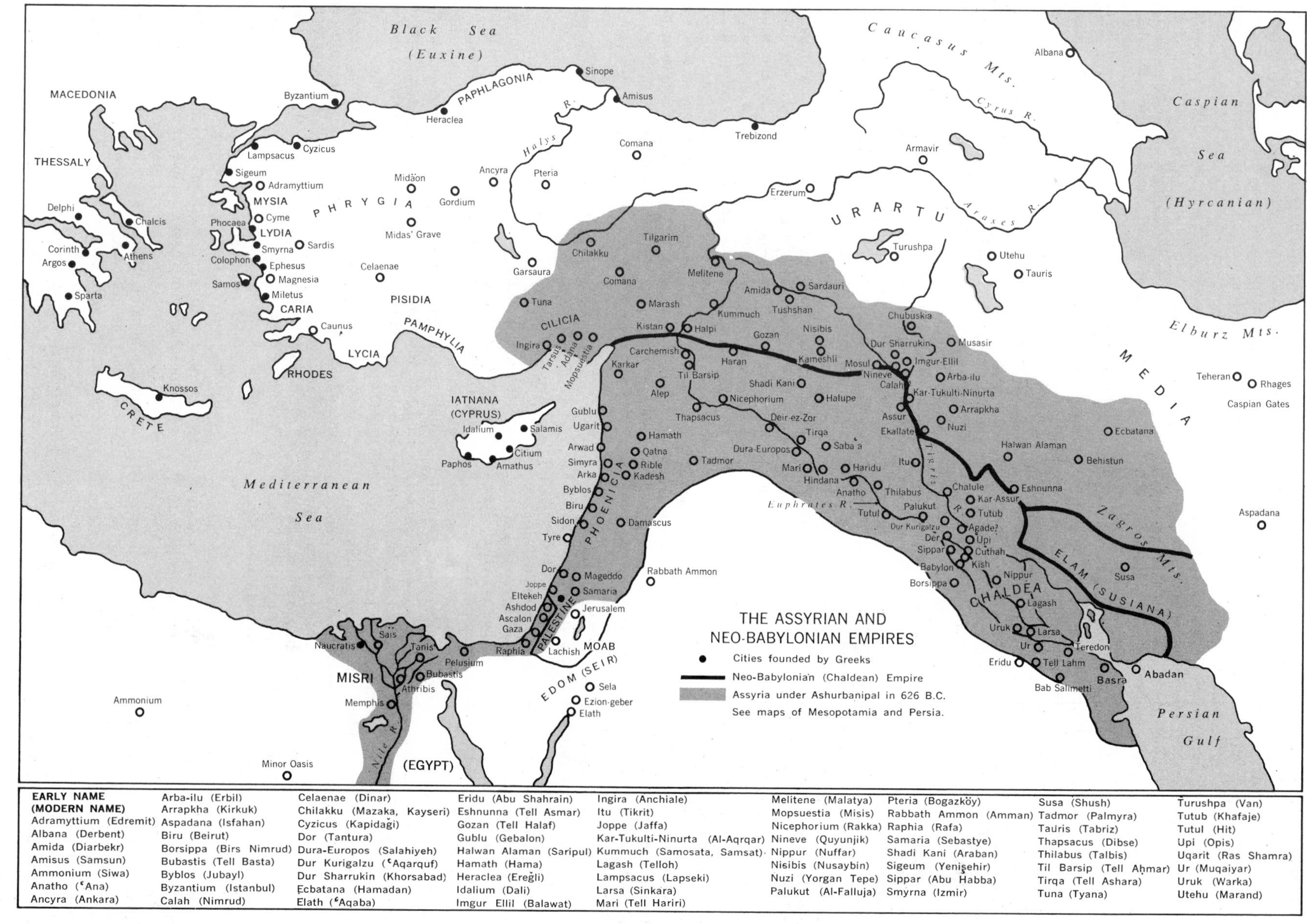

EARLY NAME (MODERN NAME)				
Adramyttium (Edremit)	Arba-ilu (Erbil)	Celaenae (Dinar)	Eridu (Abu Shahrain)	Ingira (Anchiale)
Albana (Derbent)	Arrapkha (Kirkuk)	Chilakku (Mazaka, Kayseri)	Eshnunna (Tell Asmar)	Itu (Tikrit)
Amida (Diarbekr)	Aspadana (Isfahan)	Cyzicus (Kapidaği)	Gozan (Tell Halaf)	Joppe (Jaffa)
Amisus (Samsun)	Biru (Beirut)	Dor (Tantura)	Gublu (Gebalon)	Kar-Tukulti-Ninurta (Al-Aqrqar)
Ammonium (Siwa)	Borsippa (Birs Nimrud)	Dura-Europos (Salahiyeh)	Halwan Alaman (Saripul)	Kummuch (Samosata, Samsat)
Anatho (ʿAna)	Bubastis (Tell Basta)	Dur Kurigalzu (ʿAqarquf)	Hamath (Hama)	Lagash (Telloh)
Ancyra (Ankara)	Byblos (Jubayl)	Dur Sharrukin (Khorsabad)	Heraclea (Ereğli)	Lampsacus (Lapseki)
	Byzantium (Istanbul)	Ecbatana (Hamadan)	Idalium (Dali)	Larsa (Sinkara)
	Calah (Nimrud)	Elath (ʿAqaba)	Imgur Ellil (Balawat)	Mari (Tell Hariri)

Melitene (Malatya)	Pteria (Bogazköy)	Susa (Shush)	Turushpa (Van)
Mopsuestia (Misis)	Rabbath Ammon (Amman)	Tadmor (Palmyra)	Tutub (Khafaje)
Nicephorium (Rakka)	Raphia (Rafa)	Tauris (Tabriz)	Tutul (Hit)
Nineve (Quyunjik)	Samaria (Sebastye)	Thapsacus (Dibse)	Upi (Opis)
Nippur (Nuffar)	Shadi Kani (Araban)	Thilabus (Talbis)	Uqarit (Ras Shamra)
Nisibis (Nusaybin)	Sigeum (Yenişehir)	Til Barsip (Tell Aḥmar)	Ur (Muqaiyar)
Nuzi (Yorgan Tepe)	Sippar (Abu Habba)	Tirqa (Tell Ashara)	Uruk (Warka)
Palukut (Al-Falluja)	Smyrna (Izmir)	Tuna (Tyana)	Utehu (Marand)

where he uncovered several Assyrian royal palaces. Later he also turned his attention to Kuyunjik, where he came upon a section of the famous library of *Assurbanipal (668–627 B.C.), one of the most precious literary hoards of Assyriology. After the news of the discoveries of Botta and Layard had reached Europe and America, the next 50 years witnessed many new archeological expeditions to Mesopotamia—most of them, unfortunately, assuming the character of undignified scrambles for spectacular antiquities. During this time, old sites as well as new (e.g., Lagash, Sippar, Larsa) were dug; and thousands of cuneiform inscriptions poured into the museums in Istanbul and in western Europe. The age of scientific excavations of Mesopotamian sites was ushered in by R. Koldewey at *Babylon (1899–1917) and by W. Andrae at *Assur (1903–14); and most 20th-century excavations in Iraq [e.g., the Germans at Samaria and Warka (*Uruk); the English at *Ur and Nimrud; the Americans in the Diyala region and at *Nippur] have achieved similar high standards. Despite the great mass of already excavated materials awaiting publication, major excavations are still carried out each year in Iraq and the surrounding countries; and there seems little likelihood that the publication gap will ever narrow.

Decipherment and Study of the Cuneiform Texts. The remote starting point for the decipherment of Akkadian cuneiform was the work of G. F. Grotefend, who by 1815 had established the names of certain Persian kings in the trilingual (Old Persian-Elamite-Babylonian) inscriptions of Persepolis and had distinguished between Assyrian and Babylonian cuneiform script (though not by name). In 1847–48, Botta published a detailed study of the writing of inscriptions he had unearthed at Khorsabad in Assyria and proposed the correct meaning of several common Assyrian logograms (word signs). Between 1846 and 1849, E. Hincks delivered a series of five papers (subsequently issued in the *Transactions of the Royal Irish Academy,* 1848–50), in which he laid the real basis for the decipherment of Akkadian cuneiform, including a perceptive analysis of the syllabic character of the script and the correct identification of about 80 cuneiform signs. On the basis of his publication of the *Behistun Inscription, H. C. Rawlinson in his *Memoir on the Babylonian and Assyrian Inscriptions* (1851) made the final step forward by establishing the principle of polyphony (one sign being able to express several dissimilar phonetic values) and by translating and analyzing a complete Babylonian inscription. By 1857, the decipherment was an accomplished fact—as shown by the celebrated test in which Hincks, Rawlinson, W. H. Fox Talbot, and J. Oppert independently made substantially the same translation of a unilingual Babylonian text.

In the subsequent period of systematization of the knowledge of the language, Oppert contributed significantly to the young science through his thorough investigation of the syllabary texts (the scientific dictionaries of the Assyrians and Babylonians themselves), which enabled him to produce more accurate translations than his predecessors, and through his publication of the first Assyrian grammar (1860). E. Norris issued the first extensive *Assyrian Dictionary* (1868–72), and R. E. Brünnow (1889) compiled a comprehensive classified list of the then known cuneiform signs and logograms. Subsequent grammars worthy of note have been those of A. H. Sayce (1872), Friedrich *Delitzsch (1889), A. Ungnad (1906; 4th ed. 1964), and the now standard work of Von Soden: *Grundriss der akkadischen Grammatik* (1952). Further significant dictionaries have been those of J. N. *Strassmaier (1886), Delitzsch (1896), W. Muss-Arnolt (1894–1905), Carl Bezold (1926); two definitive Akkadian lexica are now being issued: the *Assyrian Dictionary* of the University of Chicago (1956–) and the smaller *Akkadisches Handwörterbuch* (1959–) of Von Soden. Other important sign lists and syllabaries have been those of J. G. F. *Thureau-Dangin (1898, 1926, 1929), A. *Deimel (1928–33), R. Labat (1948), and Von Soden (1948). Despite the many text publications, especially by the staffs of large museums, the majority of excavated cuneiform texts are still unpublished; and new inscriptions continue to be brought to light each year.

Areas of Assyriology less exclusively concerned with language have also been explored. Men such as M. San Nicolò and P. Koschaker have written extensively on Assyro-Babylonian legal institutions. O. Neugebauer, Thureau-Dangin, and A. J. Sachs have investigated Babylonian mathematics and astronomy. Fields such as the political history, chronology, economics, sociology, religion, literature, medicine, technology, art, and architecture of ancient Mesopotamia have likewise been the subject of treatment by numerous authors. An annual bibliography of publications pertaining to the realm of Assyriology appears regularly in the periodical *Orientalia;* and the encyclopedic *Reallexikon der Assyriologie,* begun by E. Ebeling and B. Meissner in 1928 to provide a reference work for all phases of Assyriology, is still in the course of publication.

Bibliography: S. A. PALLIS, *The Antiquity of Iraq* (Copenhagen 1956). A. PARROT, *Archéologie mésopotamienne,* 2 v. (Paris 1946–53) v.1. S. LLOYD, *Foundations in the Dust* (London 1947; pa. Baltimore 1955). A. L. OPPENHEIM, "Assyriology—Why and How?" *Current Anthropology* 1 (1960) 409–423.

[J. A. BRINKMAN]

ASTARTE, a Canaanite goddess. In the texts of *Ugarit she plays the subordinate role of introducing adorers to *Baal. In the OT, however, she is interchanged repeatedly with *Asera (Asherah), frequently associated with Baal, and is probably taken to be Baal's wife. There is no agreement as to which goddess—Asera, Anath, or Astarte—was Baal's consort. Astarte is the Greek form of the Hebrew *'aštōret* (see below), often used in the plural *'aštārōt* as referring to her various local manifestations. She was called Ištar in Babylonia, where her cult originated and where she was identified with the planet Venus. Venerated as the goddess of fertility and war throughout the ancient Semitic world, she began to be worshiped by the Israelites after their arrival in Palestine (Jgs 2.13; 10.6). Although Samuel opposed her cult (1 Sm 7.3–4; 12.10), King *Solomon adopted it and erected in Jerusalem an altar in her honor, which was later destroyed by Josia (3 Kgs 11.1–13; 4 Kgs 23.13). That her cult was popular is shown by numerous statues and plaques of the "naked goddess" type found even in Israelite levels of archeological sites. The deliberate misvocalization in the Hebrew OT of original *'aštart* into *'aštōret*

A figurine used in the worship of Astarte, the ancient Semitic goddess of fertility, found in southern Syria, 9th to 6th century B.C. *Although many such figurines have been found in the Near Eastern archeological explorations, it is difficult to determine whether they were cultic objects or amulets for successful childbirth.*

by taking the vowels from the word *bōšet* (shame), indicates a later attempt to ridicule the cult.

Bibliography: EncDictBibl 162–163. T. KLAUSER, ReallexAnt Chr 1:806–810. J. B. PRITCHARD, *Palestinian Figurines in Relation to Certain Goddesses Known through Literature* (Philadelphia 1943). **Illustration credit:** Cincinnati Art Museum.

[H. MUELLER]

ASTERIUS OF AMASEA, bishop, preacher, and saint; b. Cappadocia, *c.* 350; d. Amasea, *c.* 410 (feast, Oct. 30). Asterius, having specialized in rhetoric and the practice of law, abandoned this profession to enter the clergy, and subsequently became metropolitan of Amasea in Pontus between 380 and 390. His extant writings consist of 16 homilies and panegyrics of the martyrs (PG 40:155–480). *Photius supplies quotations from 10 other sermons that have disappeared (PG 104:201–204). Some works formerly attributed to him belong to his namesake, *Asterius the Sophist (d. 341). His style is elegant, vigorous, and vivid, as in his description of a hunting scene in a sermon on Lazarus. His sermons show the high esteem in which the martyrs were held and throw light upon contemporary events, such as the persecution under *Julian the Apostate and the pagan customs still in vogue at the beginning of the year. A sermon on St. *Euphemia is important in the history of art, because a painting of this saint is compared with the works of Euphranor and Timomachus. The Second Council of *Nicaea (787) twice referred to this picture as a proof that sacred images were venerated in the ancient Church. This Council also speaks of Asterius as a saint, and he is honored as such by the Greek church.

Bibliography: ASTERIUS OF AMASEA, *Ancient Sermons for Modern Times,* tr. G. ANDERSON and E. J. GOODSPEED (New York 1904). Quasten Patr 3:300–301. M. RAUER, LexThK² 1:958.

[S. J. MC KENNA]

ASTERIUS THE SOPHIST, b. Cappadocia; d. *c.* A.D. 341. He was a pupil of Lucian of Antioch, but unlike his teacher, who died a martyr, Asterius apostatized in the persecution of Maximinus. St. *Athanasius, who is the chief source for his life, calls him the "sacrificer" because of his apostasy, and, on his return to the faith, the "advocate" of Arian doctrines. As a well-trained sophist—St. Athanasius calls him "the many-headed sophist"—he was a persuasive speaker and a voluminous writer. He exercised considerable influence as he traveled from place to place, participating even in synodal discussions. He has been characterized as perhaps the first Arian writer. At any rate, Arius employed his works in his polemic against the Nicene teachings, and by his own example encouraged their circulation. The *Syntagmation* of Asterius, known only through excerpts quoted by Athanasius and Marcellus of Ancyra, is Arian in its treatment of the Son. According to Marcellus, Asterius drew copiously on the writings or official pronouncements of Eusebius of Nicomedia and other Arian-minded bishops to support his position. His *Refutation of Marcellus* is lost. The church historian Socrates (*Hist. eccl.* 1.36) stated that Asterius accused Marcellus of *Sabellianism; St. Jerome (*De vir. ill.* 94), that he wrote commentaries on the Epistle to the Romans, on the Gospels, and on the Psalms, and many other works, all of which were long regarded as lost. Since the 1930s, however, M. Richard and E. Skard have discovered 31 homilies, of which 29 are on the Psalms, and 27 fairly large fragments of the Commentary on the Psalms. Nine of the homilies were preached in Easter Week. These finds not only reveal the ability of Asterius as a preacher and theologian, but also furnish valuable information on Antiochene exegesis. It is now clear that Asterius represented a moderate form of Arianism.

Bibliography: Quasten Patr 3:194–197, with copious bibliog. G. BARDY, *Recherches sur St. Lucien d'Antioche et son école* (Paris 1936). E. SKARD, "Asterios von Amaseia und Amasios der Sophist," *Symbolae Osloenses* 20 (1940) 86–132.

[M. R. P. MC GUIRE]

ASTRAIN, ANTONIO, Spanish Jesuit historian; b. Undiano, Navarre, Nov. 17, 1857; d. Loyola, Spain, Jan. 4, 1928. After joining the *Jesuits (1871) and completing his priestly studies, he taught humanities and history to Jesuit scholastics for several years. In 1891 he became editor of the *Mensajero del Sagrado Corazón.* During his editorship he contributed important historical and literary studies to the *Mensajero* on the Spain of Loyola, Spaniards at the Council of Trent, the works of Menéndez y Pelayo and other such topics. Next he joined the staff of the *Monumenta historica*

Societatis Iesu. This labor oriented him toward the great work that preoccupied his life after 1895, the principal one on which his scholarly reputation stands, *Historia de la Compañia de Jesús en la asistencia de España*. Seven volumes appeared (1902–25) detailing the Spanish Jesuit story from its origins to mid-18th century. Illness and death prevented him from completing the history to the Jesuit expulsion from Spanish dominions (1767). The first volume is largely a life of St. *Ignatius of Loyola, later reworked and published separately. The last four volumes devote half their pages to the work of Spanish Jesuits in the Americas, the Pacific Islands, and the Philippines. Astrain was greatly aided in preparing these sections by the prodigious archival researches of his fellow Jesuit, Pablo Pastells, although Astrain was no stranger in the great document depositories of Spain and Mexico.

[J. F. BANNON]

ASTRAL RELIGION

Worship of the stars, which long antedated *astrology. It was an underlying element in many ancient cults, more conspicuously in some than in others. The observable combination of change and variety with fixed and undeviating regularity (i.e., the motions of the sun, moon, and planets as contrasted with that of the "fixed" stars and constellations) deeply impressed even the profoundest thinkers, e.g., Aristotle (see *Frag.* 10, found in Sextus Empiricus, *Adv. Mathematicos* 3.20–22), Plato (*Phaedrus* 246F), the Stoics, Immanuel Kant (*Critique of Practical Reason ad fin.*), and even the Biblical poet (Psalm 19). Some writers, both ancient and modern, have held that astral religion was the beginning of true worship as distinct from magic, and have interpreted the Greek and Egyptian mythology as parables or allegories of the heavenly constellations. More probably, however, the constellations were interpreted from current mythology, and so received their names. One cannot fail to see here the poetic instinct at work, endeavoring to describe the harmony of the heavens in personal terms. Some of this poetry was religious, some merely secular—as Plutarch assumed in his meteorological interpretation of Isis and Osiris.

Babylonian Star Worship. The ancient Babylonian religion was the classic development of star worship. Here the stars were all gods, i.e., animate beings of a divine or at least supernatural rank. The earliest cuneiform sign for "god" was a star (*). Thus the sun, moon, and planet Venus were identified with Shamash, Sin, and Ishtar; Jupiter was Marduk; Saturn (not Mars) was the war god; Mercury was Nebo, the herald; Mars was Nergal, god of the dead. This system of identification was taken over and modified by the Greeks and Romans, using the names of their own deities.

Among Other Peoples. "Primitive" peoples, like the East African Masai and some of the Canadian Indians, as well as peoples of higher cultures like the Aztecs, worshipped the stars. Often the sun was the chief god of the pantheon, and the other heavenly bodies were his family of servants. This primeval cult not only influenced many others, both Semitic and Western as well as Egyptian, but even survived them, as when the cult of *Sol Invictus* (the Unconquerable Sun) supplanted many others under the dynasty of the Severi in the Roman Empire of the 3d century. The god Mithras, originally a friend of the Sun, was finally identified with him. The Egyptian Pharoah Akhnaton (Amenhotep IV) tried to establish the Sun God (Aton) at Heliopolis as the center of the whole Egyptian cult, but he was unsuccessful; the entrenched priesthoods of the old deities rejected this revolution in the direction of monotheism. In pre-Islamic Arabia there was a whole pantheon of astral deities; astral rites and beliefs were found also in ancient China, so widespread was this primitive cult. Among the Indo-Iranian peoples the same phenomenon was found, but in a modified form. The "Heaven God" (or gods) was only the personification of heaven—a usage still reflected, in reverse, in the Jewish religion (e.g., "Let the fear of Heaven [i.e., God] be upon you," Mishnah, Pirke Aboth 1.3). The immense influence of this ancient terminology survived in the Roman imperial and early Christian designation of the first day of the week as "Sun-day" (the very earliest Christian designation was "first day of the week," as in 1 Cor 16.2, or "the Lord's day," Ap 1.10).

Stars in the Bible. Among the Greeks, even in Plato's later writings (*Tim.* 40B), the stars were thought to be animate beings or "visible gods." But among the Hebrews and the Biblical writers generally, the references to stars either were figurative or stressed the sovereignty of the one and only God, their Creator (Is 14.12; Sir 50.6; Ap 22.16; and see Gn 1 and Ps 19). The "seven stars" in Am 5.8 are the Pleiades; in Ap 1.20 they are the seven churches in the Province of Asia. Only in connection with pagan religion and rites are the stars referred to as deities (Am 5.26; cf. Jer 7.18; 19.13; 44.17, 19, 25; Acts 7.43).

Relation of Star Worship and Astrology. It is easy to see how the Greek and Roman inheritance of astral worship led directly to astrology. It had originated in Babylonia and was combined with Iranian influence to

Boundary stone of Meli-Shipak, found at Susa, c. 12th century B.C. *Under the symbols of Ishtar, Sin, and Shamash, the goddess Nanna receives the King and his daughter.*

enter the West during the 2 centuries of the Persian Empire (538–330 B.C.) and later. Eudoxus and Theophrastus were the first to show acquaintance with it, and both rejected it (Cicero, *Div.* 2.87; Proclus, *In Tim.* 285f). But with Eudemus of Rhodes a contrast began to be drawn between the baleful and the beneficent stellar beings—a theory derived from Zoroastrian dualism (Damascius, *De princ.* 125). The rest followed easily; star worship had opened the gate to astrology, and even some of the best minds cultivated it henceforth, for it was regarded as a science. *Fata regunt orbem, certa stant omnia lege,* "Fates rule the world, and everything stands firm by law" (Manilius, *Astronomicon* 4.14). Any religious sentiments retained by astrology were derived from the earlier star worship; however, many later writers viewed astrology exclusively as a science with no reference to religion. Thus Melanchthon the German reformer was an expert astrologer, but would have denied *in toto* astral religion. In passing on the torch to astrology, astral religion met its end, and thus itself reflected the further principle of Manilius (4.16): *Nascentes morimur; finisque ab origine pendet,* "Being born, we begin to die; and the end depends upon the beginning."

In Christian theology and philosophy the Biblical conception naturally prevailed: the stars are "divine" only in a poetic or figurative sense; they are God's creation, His "handiwork," and manifest His glory. Yet they shall fade, or fall from heaven, or be supplanted by other stars in a new heaven, after the Judgment. Nevertheless, the old usage still survived. In the Roman catacombs there are inscriptions that imply that the Christian soul is now *super astra* ("above the stars"), and the beautiful passage in Dn 12.3 is not forgotten: "They shall shine as the stars for ever and ever."

See also MESOPOTAMIA, ANCIENT, 4; ASTROLOGY.

Bibliography: F. VON OEFELE et al., Hastings ERE 12:48–101, a series of 12 articles. W. GUNDEL, ReallexAntChr 1:810–817. G. R. DRIVER, Hastings DB[2] (1963) 936–938. F. J. BOLL, *Kleine Schriften zur Sternkunde des Altertums,* ed. V. STEGMANN (Leipzig 1950). H. GRESSMANN, *Die hellenistische Gestirnreligion* (Leipzig 1925). E. W. MAUNDER, *The Astronomy of the Bible* (4th ed. London 1923). O. RÜHLE, *Sonne und Mond im primitiven Mythus* (Tübingen 1925); RGG[3] 1:662–664. E. ZINNER, *Sternglaube und Sternforschung* (Freiburg 1953). **Illustration credit:** Musée du Louvre.

[F. C. GRANT]

ASTROLOGY

Although the study of astrology has been pursued in many cultures and continues to have an important role in the Far East, this article deals only with Babylonian astrology and its subsequent development in the Greco-Roman world and in Europe. It is important to note that astrology, in many aspects at least, was recognized as a science—not as a pseudoscience—until the 18th century.

Babylonian Astrology. The chief source for information about Babylonian astrology is the library of King Assurbanipal (668–626 B.C.) at Nineveh, from which many thousands of astrological documents and fragments, embodying a simple type of astrology that did not distinguish celestial from terrestrial phenomena, have been recovered. Babylonian *horoscopes were applied to the royal family and the land; the earliest known prediction for a private person dates from 263 B.C. The following example is typical: "If an eclipse of the moon occurs on 14 Sivan and the fourth [east] wind is blowing, enmity will prevail; there will be deaths."

It is not surprising that astrology arose in Mesopotamia, with its extremely clear atmosphere and a religion that identified various gods with particular heavenly bodies. Babylonian astrology rests ultimately on a single large work of unknown date written in about 70 large tablets, fragmentarily preserved in several recensions. This system, unlike that of the Greeks later, made the moon more important than the sun (probably because of its easy observability and conspicuous phases) and arranged the planets in the so-called Babylonian order: moon, sun, Jupiter, Venus, Saturn, Mercury, Mars. More than 200 constellations were distinguished, as well as 12 signs of the zodiac, and attention was paid also to comets, meteors, winds, storms, earthquakes, clouds, thunder, and lightning. Although the documents are in Old Babylonian and Assyrian, traces of Sumerian usage suggest that some of this material is earlier than 2000 B.C.

In Classical Greece. Though the early Greeks practiced various forms of *divination, they had no astrology. Minoan art shows little concern with the heavens, and few early Greek myths deal with the stars. Even an author as late as Aristophanes (*Peace* 406–413; 421 B.C.) can refer to the sun and moon as barbarian gods. Zeus, despite the etymology of his name, was far more to the Greeks than a sky-god; and this broader conception accords with the fact that the major Greek gods, unlike the Semitic, were not closely bound to nature. The stars were observed for purposes of navigation, but there is hardly a trace of astral religion. Thales of

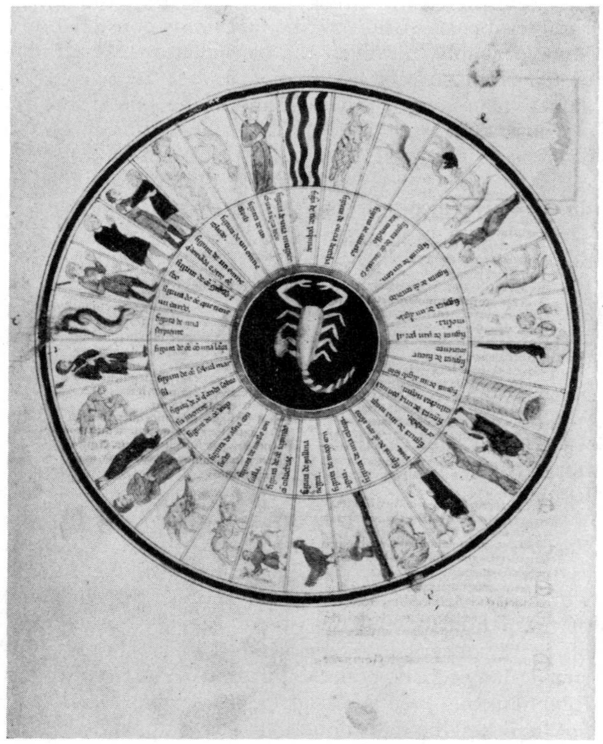

Scorpion page from an astrological manuscript written in Spain in the mid-13th century (Cod. Vat. Reg. 1283, fol. 7v), probably by someone in the circle of Alfonso X.

Miletus (6th century B.C.) and his successors derived much, directly or indirectly, from Babylonian sources (e.g., the rough prediction of solar eclipses, celestial equator, ecliptic, planets, constellations, the 12-hour day), but they used these data to construct a scientific cosmology. Typical of classical Greek rationalism is the story of Pericles (Plutarch, *Pericles* 35), who calmed a frightened sailor by holding up his cloak to show how an eclipse occurs. Among the classical Greeks prophecy based on such phenomena as eclipses and lightning was on the same footing as prophecy from the flight of birds, the entrails of sacrificial animals, and dreams. There were no special astrological techniques.

Greek reason, however, provided a potentially hospitable environment for the introduction of astrology: if the world is governed by unchanging (scientific) laws, then fatalism becomes easy. The early Pythagoreans illustrate the possibilities. They discovered the oldest known scientific laws by experiments with the strings of musical instruments, but they also developed numerical and geometrical symbolisms involving astral elements, such as the harmony of the spheres.

Plato and even Aristotle (who was no mystic) believed the stars to be divine, no doubt under Oriental influence. The planets play an important role in the myth of Er, son of Armenius (an Oriental name), at the end of the *Republic,* and Plato emphasizes the relationship between souls and stars in *Timaeus* (41D). The appendix to the *Laws* by Plato's nephew and successor, Philip of Opus, is full of astral lore. Such developments prepared the way for astrology, though so distinguished an astronomer as Eudoxus of Cnidus (*c.* 350 B.C.) was opposed to it.

Rise of Astrology in the Hellenistic Age. Between Alexander and Augustus the Greek world was altered by world-shaking political, economic, and cultural upheavals. Reason (*logos*) gave way to esoteric knowledge (*gnosis*). Imperturbability (*ataraxia*) before the buffetings of *Fortune became the great desideratum, and chance was deified (*see* FATE AND FATALISM). Carneades (214–128 B.C.) and Panaetius (*c.* 185–109 B.C.) might oppose astrology, but Posidonius (*c.* 135–50 B.C.) and Hipparchus of Nicaea (*c.* 190–*c.* 126 B.C.), the greatest Greek astronomer, both accepted its validity.

It was in Hellenistic Egypt, where all races and cultures mingled, that Greek astrology finally developed. There is no evidence of astrology in Egypt under the old Kingdom, but Babylonian lore reached there under the Ptolemies and was combined with the exact data of Greek astronomy to produce the strange two-headed monster of astrology, partly religious and mystical and partly scientific. There can be no doubt about the importance of Greek astronomy in this development, for the standard order of the planets was the so-called Greek, which is based on the observed periods of revolution: moon, Mercury, Venus, sun, Mars, Jupiter, Saturn. The sun was most important, not the moon as in Babylonian astrology. Some Egyptian star lore also entered the system: for example, the decans, a series of 36 constellations, each ruled a 10-day week. The earliest authoritative handbook now known, called *Nechepso-Petosiris* (*c.* 170–150 B.C.) after the names of its supposed authors, remained the astrological bible until the publication of Ptolemy's *Tetrabiblos*.

"The Victory of Christendom over Heathen Stargazing," woodcut from an edition of Paul of Middleburg's "De recta Paschae celebratione," published in 1513.

Dominance of Astrology in the Greco-Roman World. Astrology swept the Greco-Roman world, reaching all races, nations, and types of men: rulers, scholars (such as Varro), philosophers (*see* NEO-PYTHAGOREANISM), and also the well-to-do, both aristocrats and *nouveaux riches* (such as Trimalchio in Petronius's *Cena Trimalchionis* 39, 77). It invaded the sciences of medicine, botany, chemistry (via alchemy), and mineralogy. It had a central place also in the mystery religions, especially that of Mithras, whose votaries invoked the planet ruling the day of the week. In the end, only the skeptics and Epicureans held out against astrology.

At first it was available only to the rich; the necessary computations were complicated and difficult, and consequently astrologers were often called *mathematici.* But the Julian calendar reform of 46 B.C., introduced later in outlying parts of the Empire, changed this. The sun now entered a new sign of the zodiac, usually on the 25th of the month, the moon was easily observable, and the planets were assigned each to a day of the week (first evidence is found in Tibullus, 1.3.18). With the new calendar the poorest persons, even slaves, could afford astrology, and its use became almost universal. The popularity of talismans and amulets shows that astrology was often combined with belief in *magic, while the educated resorted to it because it contributed to apathy by removing the unexpected. Stoicism was its natural home. The final, complete victory of astrology is well illustrated by the Emperor Aurelian's introduction of the worship of *Sol invictus* into the state cult after his victory over Palmyra in the year A.D. 273.

Astrology's success is hard for the Western mind to comprehend, but it doubtless came about because astrology offered a causal explanation, based on the most advanced science, of everything that occurs. Since people of antiquity often thought "in myths," no one attacked the mythological foundation of astrology. It could, and sometimes did, lead to atheism, as in the case of the Emperor Tiberius; but to most men it was a cosmology that was also a religion, and a universal religion in contrast with belief in the Greek and Roman gods, who were essentially local.

Astrology and Christianity. Christianity is fundamentally opposed to astrology; yet the earliest Christian documents contain references to it, partly in opposition (Gal 4.9–11; Rom 8.38; Col 1.16; 2.8, 20), but partly because astrology permeated the entire culture. The Church, by calling Christ "the sun of justice" (a phrase derived from Mal 3.20), substituted Him for Sol; and in the 4th century it deliberately put His Nativity on December 25, the birthday of the sun, when "lux crescit." Christ was now "the light of the world" in a symbolic sense, but His day was still called *dies solis* (Sunday) in the West, as contrasted with *Kyriake* (the Lord's Day) in the East. The Gospels speak of the eclipse at Christ's death and of the wonderful star seen by the Magi, a phenomenon that Christian defenders of astrology always cited. Astrology must have continued or even begun to revive among Christians, for Tertullian found it necessary to state that God tolerated it only until Christ's birth. Lactantius and St. Augustine believed that demons were at work in the stars and in astrology, but that their influence could be overcome through God's grace. It should be observed that astrology is logically compatible with a belief in predestination.

Astrology among the Byzantines and in Islam. The Church Fathers were not completely successful in rooting astrology out, since it pervaded all ancient culture, and it revived during the Byzantine renaissance of the 9th century along with Greek astronomy, which was rediscovered partly in original Greek documents and partly in Arabic translations. The Byzantine Emperor Manuel Comnenus (A.D. 1143–80) relied on astrology and defended it on the basis of natural science, the Gospels, and the Fathers. Greek translations of Arabic and Persian astrological treatises became common, though some leading Byzantine astronomers and Churchmen condemned the art. The revived Greek doctrines spread from Byzantium to the West long before the fall of Constantinople.

Astrology flourished under Arabic influence, for Islam is essentially fatalistic, and it spread to the West from Arabic sources as well as from the Greek East. While Avicenna and ibn-Khaldun condemned it, such influential thinkers as al-Kindi and Averroës supported it. As late as 1909 the Sultan Abdul-Hamid II still had a court astrologer. Christians came in contact with Arabs not only during the Crusades but also in Spain and Sicily, so that scholastic philosophy was brought face to face with the problem of astrology. The scholastic philosopher, Michael Scotus (d. *c.* 1235) was court astrologer to Frederick II of Sicily, whose son-in-law Ezzelino also kept astrologers about him, including some Saracens. Roger Bacon also recognized astrology as a science. Many Italian cities, dynasties, and prelates resorted to astrologers; and since medieval culture was international, astrology spread rapidly throughout Europe as early as the 13th century.

Astrology in the Renaissance and Later. Astrology was used by Pope Julius II to set the day of his coronation and by Paul III to determine the proper hour for every Consistory. Leo X founded a chair of astrology at the Sapienza, for by that time no respectable university could ignore the subject. Down to the 18th century many literary works, buildings, and works of plastic art were unintelligible without a knowledge of astrological doctrines.

Astrology pervaded European culture just as it had the culture of the Roman Empire, and, though official Church doctrine opposed it, no one attacked the whole manner of thinking that lay behind it. Even St. Thomas Aquinas had attributed physique, sex, and general character to the stars, and was followed by Dante ("Purg." 17.73). "Inclinant astra, non necessitant" (the stars influence, they do not compel) was the most that Christian thinkers would allow. The humanists, inspired by later antiquity, only strengthened the movement, and the Reformation made no difference. Melanchthon, for example, lectured on astrology at Wittenberg and published a standard Latin translation of Ptolemy's *Tetrabiblos*. The leading astronomers, including Kepler, Tycho Brahe, and (later) Newton, were usually astrologers also.

The invention of the telescope damaged astrology seriously. The seven Pleiades, of which most people can see but six, were discovered to include scores. Two more planets, Uranus and Neptune, were presently discovered, as well as hundreds of planetoids between Mars and Jupiter, and thousands of stars whose very existence destroyed the apparent primacy of the traditional constellations. Astrology's neat system, which had never been really neat or systematic, broke down. As a pseudoscience astrology survives only among the uneducated and the credulous, while the influence of the heavenly bodies upon the earth and man has become the subject of various strictly scientific studies without occult implication.

See also HOROSCOPES; ASTRAL RELIGION.

Bibliography: M. VERENO and J. C. PILZ, LexThK² 1:964–967. J. H. CREHAN, Davis CDT 1:179–182, with bibliog. F. VON OEFELE et al., Hastings ERE 12:48–103, a comprehensive world coverage. F. J. BOLL, *Sternglaube und Sterndeutung*, ed. W. GUNDEL (4th ed. Leipzig 1931). **Illustration credit:** Fig. 1, Biblioteca Apostolica Vaticana.

[H. S. LONG]

ASTRONOMY

The astronomer is primarily an observer. Whether he is concerned with the mapping of the stars, the motions of the planets, or the analysis of the light from the stars, he requires the most accurate record of position, of brightness, and of spectrum that he can obtain with the instruments he builds.

Recent History. One of the first astronomers to emphasize the precision of observation was Tycho *Brahe (1546–1601), who designed instruments without optical parts that gave accuracies of position good to one-half minute of arc. His observations of the planets were accurate enough to enable J. *Kepler to discover his three laws of planetary motion. These were not verified by application of the law of gravity until Isaac *Newton

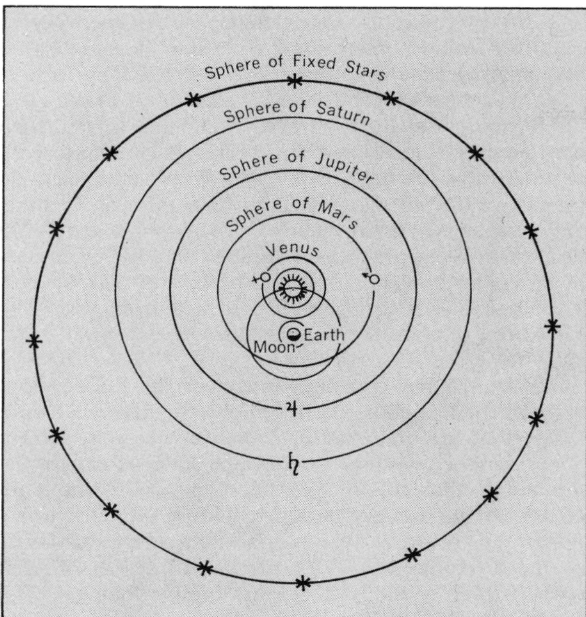

Fig. 1. The Universe according to Tycho Brahe.

(1642–1727) showed that all three of Kepler's laws depended on his law of gravity. Newton himself almost repudiated his law of gravity because his first effort to test its application on the moon failed. The cause of his failure was poor observational material on the dimensions of the earth, which he used in his test.

Following the discovery of optical telescopes by Galileo (1564–1642), observations began to accumulate at a great rate (*see* GALELEI, GALILEO). Positional astronomy grew to such accuracy in the next century that the first parallax of a star was measured by F. W. Bessel (1784–1846) with a heliometer. Although Galileo had suggested the procedure used by Bessel, he did not possess an instrument of sufficient accuracy to measure the very small angle required for the parallax of a star. At the same time visual observers such as the Herschels undertook extensive surveys of the sky with large-aperture telescopes. These men concentrated on the stars and nebulosities invisible to the naked eye, and their classifications provided modern astronomy with catalogue titles that are still used for these objects. William *Herschel (1738–1822) was the first to suggest that certain types of faint nebulosities were actually "island universes" or galaxies outside the Milky Way.

Other astronomers who relied only on visual astronomy designed elaborate photometers for the measurement of the magnitudes of stars. Such photometric catalogues were essential for the proper identification of stars. A system of magnitudes was adopted in the middle of the 19th century after the scale suggested by N. R. Pogson (1809–91). It was based on the fact that the difference between first- and sixth-magnitude stars is approximately 100 times in brightness, so that one magnitude interval amounts to the fifth root of 100 or 2.512 times the brightness of a star one magnitude fainter. This scale has never been changed, and all magnitudes are still based upon it. With an exact scale, the photometric work in astronomy advanced in studies of variable stars that show changes in brightness or magnitude due to intrinsic or extrinsic causes.

The use of the spectroscope as an observational tool developed rapidly after J. *Fraunhofer (1814) introduced a slit before the prism and discovered the absorption lines in the solar spectrum, and R. Bunsen and G. Kirchhoff (1860) showed that the lines were due to chemical elements. Angelo *Secchi (1818–78), the Jesuit astronomer in Rome, was the first to classify stars according to the type of spectrum. His original 4 classes were extended later to embrace a sequence of at least 10 classes with many subclasses. Because he introduced this field of astronomy, Secchi has been known as the father of modern astronomy, or astrophysics, as distinguished from the older astronomy, which concerned itself principally with the motions and positions of stars. Secchi's work was done by visual observations with the spectroscope, whereas the later work of spectral classification of stars was done photographically at Harvard Observatory by Miss A. C. Maury (1866–1952) and Miss A. J. Cannon (1863–1941) with stellar spectra obtained with an objective prism.

Photographic Methods. The application of photography to all phases of astronomical observation began shortly after the discovery of the photographic process. The first photograph of a star, Vega, was made at Harvard Observatory in 1849, and before 1858 the Harvard astronomers had demonstrated the usefulness of the photographic plate for determining an exact scale of magnitudes. While the visual estimates of the brightness of a star depended upon the response of the eye to light stimuli, the results were never precise because of the different response of the eye to slight changes in color or brightness. The use of a standard light source

Fig. 2. Detail from Callot etching, "The Fan," 1619, with the earliest known representation of a telescope. Callot was reputedly a friend of Galileo.

at the eyepiece of the telescope was also difficult because the individual stars vary in color. The peculiar feature of point source images, which is characteristic of stars in a telescope, is the spreading of the image with intensity. Hence the images of bright stars not only appear brighter in a telescope, but they also appear larger due to the spurious disk produced by the optical system. Brightness on a photographic plate was measured by the diameter of the photographic image. This criterion had to be supplemented later with the measurement of the density of the image as well, in order to obtain the greatest accuracy.

Once photographic methods for stellar magnitudes had been adopted and controlled by use of filters for a uniform color range, a reliable system of stellar magnitudes was established among certain groups of stars, particularly those around the north pole of the sky. The stars comprising the North Polar Sequence were studied both at Harvard and at Mt. Wilson observatories for many years until the best scale and zero point of the sequence of magnitudes had been determined. In order to preserve uniformity, the photographic and visual scales for these stars were adopted as international standards in 1922. All magnitude measurements were to be referred to these stars for any part of the sky. The need for two separate scales became apparent as more precise photometric methods were used. The photographic plates used were generally most sensitive to blue light while the naked eye is more sensitive to light in the yellow region of the spectrum. Hence the photographic magnitudes represented the blue light of the stars while the visual represented the yellow (*see* COLOR).

The color characteristics of stellar magnitudes have become more pronounced in recent years with the introduction of photographic materials that are sensitive to colors other than blue. It is now possible to take photographs in blue, yellow, or red light; in fact, any desired range of the spectrum may be studied. Since stellar magnitudes still represent a certain effective wavelength, or band, in the spectrum, it is essential in photometry to specify the type of magnitude when referring to the brightness of stars. The increase in the wavelength range of photographic materials has also widened the area of the spectrum in which astronomical cameras can be used.

Instrumentation. The instruments selected by an astronomer are tools designed for specific purposes. Telescopes of long focal length are used primarily for observing individual objects, while those of short focal length are best suited for photographing large areas of the sky. The larger the aperture of the telescope, the more light is gathered by the instrument, and the fainter the objects that can be seen. Large apertures also permit photography with shorter exposures, and they give a finer resolution of detail. When designing an instrument, aperture and focal length are adjusted according to the use intended for the instrument. Examples of this can be seen in the two large instruments on Mount Palomar. The 200-inch reflector, having both long focal length and large aperture, is suited to the study of very faint objects, such as external galaxies or individual stars; the 48-inch Schmidt telescope has a rather short focal length, and its contribution has been the photographic atlas of the sky, including stars down to the 19th apparent magnitude.

Many of the long-focus telescopes, designed before 1900 for visual observations, have now become useful for photoelectric photometry of stars. The photomultiplier tubes currently used in astronomy are capable of detecting the light of very faint stars faster than photographic plates, and accuracies of one-hundredth of a magnitude in their readings have revived a scientific interest in the variations in brightness of variable stars, and of stars which are members of dynamic groupings or clusters. Very precise measurements of the brightness of these cluster stars at selected regions of their spectra provide the astronomer with evidence from which he can learn the surface temperature, the spectral class, and the age of the entire cluster.

Electronics has also been introduced in the development of the image orthicon, or light amplifier, to obtain a direct image of a star field on a fluorescent screen. Such image converters, as they are called, increase the luminous efficiency of the telescope from one-tenth of 1 per cent usually obtained with the photographic plate to 30 or 40 per cent of the light energy gathered by the objective lens. For example, the 200-inch telescope, which cannot detect stars fainter than the 21st magnitude because of the low efficiency of the eye or the photographic emulsion, may reach as faint a magnitude as the 26th with an image converter.

Limits of Visual Astronomy. The limiting factor for the telescope in this instance is the brightness of the night sky. The sky is not perfectly dark because of permanent luminescence from solar ion streams, reflected sunlight from small particles in space, and other causes of airglow. There is, therefore, a magnitude limit beyond which telescopes on the surface of the earth cannot reach because of natural brightness of the atmosphere.

The earth's atmosphere also imposes a definite limit on the wavelengths over which any type of optical astronomy can be done. For example, observational work in the ultraviolet is impractical below 3000 A because the atmosphere becomes opaque at that point. Ordinary crown and flint glass lenses become opaque before that wavelength, usually around 3500 A, so that reflectors or fused quartz lenses must be used. In the same way the atmosphere again becomes quite opaque in the infrared due to the absorption of these wavelengths by water vapor.

For these reasons, telescopes designed for use on the surface of the earth have reached the limit of their efficiency for resolving power and spectral range for present apertures, and for focal lengths. Recent ultraviolet studies of the stars and the sun have been carried out with rockets by astronomers at the United States Naval Research Laboratory with some success. Despite the spinning and yawing of the rocket, astronomers have identified photoelectric scannings of about 60 stars at wavelengths deep in the ultraviolet. This sort of observation will be carried out much more efficiently from a stabilized platform in space, whether on a satellite or in the gondola of a balloon. In the same way the surface details of the moon, sun, and planets can be observed with a degree of resolution unobtainable at present because of the unsteadiness of an optical path through the lower layers of the earth's atmosphere.

Radio Astronomy. At the longer wavelengths an entirely new field of observational astronomy has developed. In the early 1930s K. G. Jansky observed

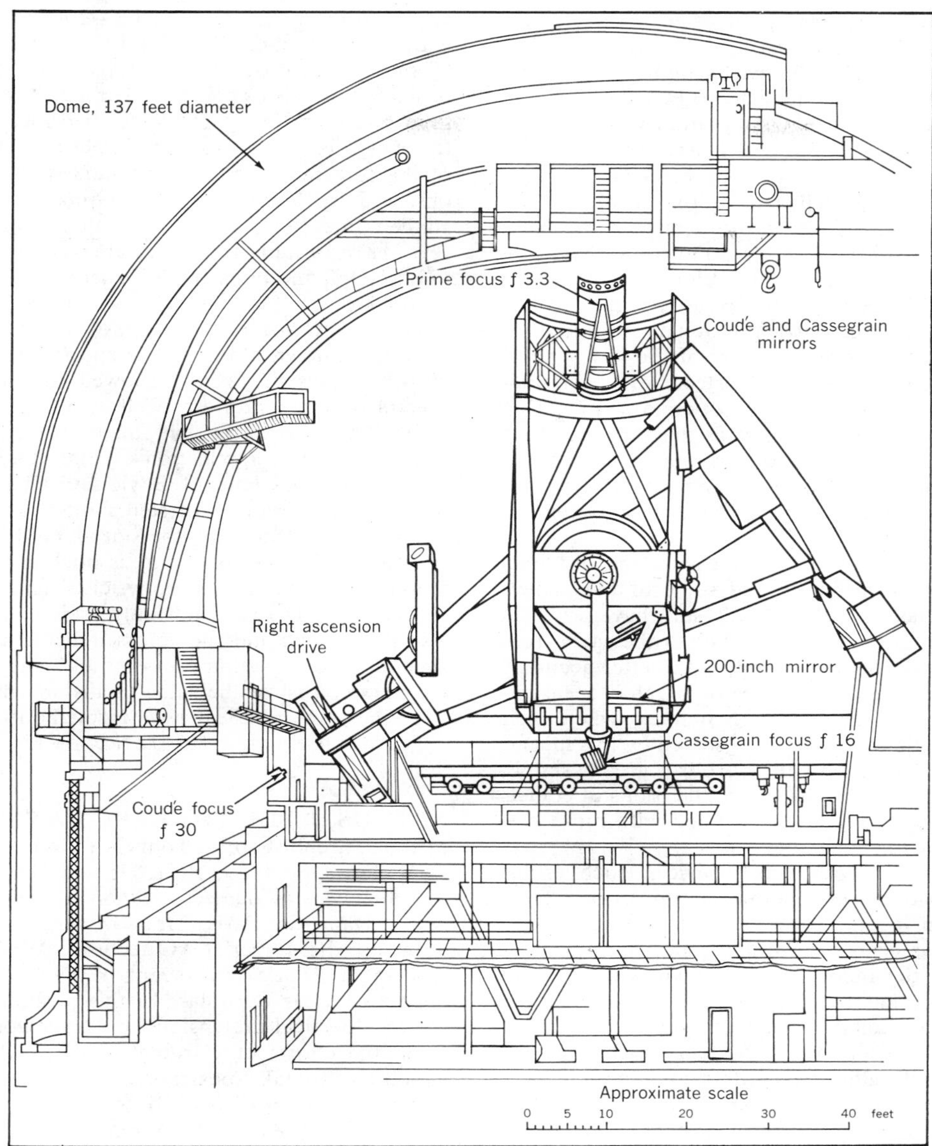

Fig. 3. The 200-inch Hale telescope, at Mt. Palomar, California. Sectional view through dome.

radiation at wavelengths common to radar or short-wave radio coming from both the sun and from the Milky Way. The early pioneers in this field, which is now known as radio astronomy, set up large antenna arrays for use as interferometers or parabolic reflectors of large aperture to collect this radiation, which they detected as an increase in the noise level of very sensitive radio receivers. With the development of receivers of higher sensitivity for use with radar during World War II, the field of radio astronomy revealed many previously unsuspected features of the Milky Way and other objects in space.

Certain sources of radio frequency, sometimes called "radio stars," have been distinguished against the general background of the galaxy or Milky Way. A few of these, such as the Crab nebula in the constellation of Taurus, correspond with objects that can be seen with optical telescopes, but most of them defy detection with even long exposures of the 200-inch reflector at Mount Palomar. Some of these discrete sources of radio-frequency energy apparently come from very distant galaxies that lie hidden behind the dust clouds of our Milky Way. The energy from such sources is so small on reaching the earth and the areas of the sky whence it comes so minute, that parabolic antennas of extremely great apertures are required to locate and detect them. A parabola of about 50 feet in aperture has a resolving power for radio frequencies equivalent to the naked eye for visual light. Hence, efforts to construct radio telescopes of apertures of several hundred feet have produced the huge reflectors at Jodrell Bank, England; Green Bank, W.Va.; Mount Stromlo, Australia; and in Puerto Rico.

Aside from a search for discrete sources of radio-frequency energy, many observatories now use parabolas of apertures from 20 to 80 feet for studies of certain definite frequencies. Most important in this specialized field of radio astronomy is the investigation of the distribution of an absorption of energy at a wavelength of 21 cm due to neutral hydrogen in interstellar space. The absorption at this wavelength by hydrogen atoms was predicted by H. C. van der Hulst in Holland, and the first verification by observation was made by E. M. Purcell and H. I. Ewen at Harvard in 1951.

Since radio frequencies are not blocked by intervening clouds of interstellar dust, the absorption by clouds of interstellar hydrogen in interstellar space has been traced almost completely around the galaxy. The results show the outline of these clouds of hydrogen sufficiently well to confirm the spiral structure of our galaxy and the highly eccentric position of our sun.

It has not been possible, because of the low level of this radio frequency energy, to detect any other individual star except our sun. The discrete sources that have been identified are not stars as they are seen with visual telescopes. Hence, radio astronomy is paralleling optical astronomy in that one concentrates on stars and the other on the hydrogen clouds in between the stars.

The use of radar pulsing to measure the distances from the earth to the moon and some of the planets has been introduced successfully. Results have provided a determination of the mean distance of the earth from the sun, or the astronomical unit, with better accuracy than obtained hitherto by means of parallax measurements. In the case of artificial satellites, when their distances from the earth can be observed by this means, the problem of determining their orbits is greatly simplified. It is possible that in the future the orbits of comets and minor planets may be determined with more precision by use of this technique.

The adaptation of other new devices, such as the laser in observational astronomy, may open new fields of investigation in the near future. The beam of light from a laser has been successfully reflected back from the surface of the moon. No other known source of luminous energy has been useful for the same experiment. It may be possible to use lasers for tracking interplanetary probes after they have gone out beyond the range of the small radio transmitters contained in them.

See also ASTROPHYSICS; SUN AND STARS (for the history of astronomy before Tycho Brahe, see articles on science, or refer to the biographies of astronomers, e.g., Copernicus, Ptolemy).

Bibliography: G. DE VAUCOULEURS, *Discovery of the Universe* (London 1957). F. BECKER, *Histoire de l'astronomie* (Paris 1955). G. BIGOURDAN, *L'Astronomie: Évolution des idées et des méthodes* (Paris 1911). H. MACPHERSON, *Makers of Astronomy* (Oxford 1933). H. SHAPLEY and H. E. HOWARTH, *Source Book in Astronomy* (New York 1929). G. ABETTI, *The History of Astronomy,* tr. B. B. ABETTI (New York 1952). A. M. CLERKE, *A Popular History of Astronomy during the Nineteenth Century* (4th ed. London 1902). R. L. WATERFIELD, *A Hundred Years of Astronomy* (London 1938). A. ARMITAGE, *A Century of Astronomy* (London 1950). H. C. KING, *The History of the Telescope* (Cambridge, Mass. 1955). **Illustration credits:** Fig. 2, National Gallery of Art, Washington, D.C. Fig. 3, Mt. Wilson and Palomar Laboratories.

[F. J. HEYDEN]

ASTROPHYSICS. The study of the composition and properties of the stars and nebulae, and of the physical phenomena taking place within them, by analysis of the radiations they emit. Such radiations include the energy of the entire electromagnetic spectrum, from the cosmic rays detected by special photographic materials and Geiger counters, through the luminous region visible to the naked eye, to the frequencies observable with radiotelescopes. This emitted energy is analyzed by measurement of its intensity, such as the brightness or magnitude; of its color in the ranges from ultraviolet to infrared; or, finally, of the detailed spectrum showing the energy levels of atoms and molecules. The spectrum of the sun, the nearest of the stars, was first carefully observed by Isaac *Newton (*Optiks,* 1675) but not studied intensively until *Fraunhofer (1814). Many features of Fraunhofer's spectrum were unexplained until Kirchhoff and Bunsen (1859) demonstrated the meaning of spectra. During the next decade P. A. *Secchi classified stars according to type of spectra, and Huggins identified known atoms in the spectra of the stars. Sir Norman Lockyer (1868) showed the dependence of spectra on temperature as well as on chemical composition. This opened the way finally to the advances that have come from application of Planck's law of radiation and the gas laws of Boyle and Charles. The tremendous temperatures of stellar interiors and the ages of stars as evidenced by the sun alone, have led to the realization that stellar energy is nuclear in origin. The findings of modern astrophysicists indicate that the spectra of stars reveal not only their temperatures but also their sizes; and the colors indicate age as well as spectral type. Most important of all is the evidence that the stars consist of the same atoms and molecules that obey the same physical laws throughout the universe.

See also SUN AND STARS; ASTRONOMY.

[F. J. HEYDEN]

ASTROS, PAUL THÉRÈSE DAVID D', French cardinal, archbishop; b. Tourvès (Var), Oct. 15, 1772; d. Toulouse, Sept. 29, 1851. He was ordained in 1797. In 1802 he was named a canon in the Cathedral of Notre Dame in Paris. He was assigned in 1806 to draw up the Imperial *Catechism. When the Archdiocese of *Paris fell vacant in 1808, D'Astros was appointed vicar capitular. In this position he opposed the ecclesiastical pretensions of *Napoleon I and withstood the efforts of Cardinal *Maury, the Emperor's appointee, to take possession of the see without the approval of Pope *Pius VII. As a result D'Astros was imprisoned (1811–14). While bishop of Bayonne (1820–30) and archbishop of Toulouse (1830–51) and cardinal (1850) he was a zealous and capable pastor and administrator. D'Astros, a conservative, was a supporter of *Gallicanism. He denounced Hugues Félicité de *Lamennais to Rome and composed a censure of 56 propositions drawn from the latter's writings. The archbishop asserted his independence of the July Monarchy and upheld vigorously liberty of education for Catholic schools. As a champion of the diversities in the traditional Gallican liturgy he opposed Dom Prosper *Guéranger.

Bibliography: P. DROULERS, *Action pastorale et problèmes sociaux . . . chez Mgr. d'Astros* (Paris 1954). J. BELLAMY, DTC 1.2:2142–43. J. DEDIEU, DHGE 4:1253–55. G. LAZARE, Dict BiogFranc 3:1383–88. R. CHALUMEAU, *Catholicisme* 1:970–971.

[M. H. QUINLAN]

ASTRUC, JEAN, French physician of the 18th century who played an important role in the history of Biblical criticism; b. Suave (Tarn), France, March 19, 1684; d. Paris, May 5, 1766. Though his father was a Protestant at the time of Jean's birth, and though the latter was baptized in the Protestant church at

Suave, the elder Astruc was soon after converted to Catholicism, and his son was raised and always lived as a Catholic. Jean Astruc received his higher education at Montpellier, France, where he became a doctor of medicine in 1703. He succeeded his former master, Pierre Chirac, in teaching medicine at Montpellier (1707–10) and then obtained the chair of anatomy at the University of Toulouse. After a year in Paris and a year as physician to King Augustus II of Poland, he was appointed medical consultant to Louis XV of France and later (1731) professor at the College of France. Besides publishing several works on medical topics, he took a side interest in philosophy, theology, and Biblical exegesis. He is best known for a work that he published anonymously, *Conjectures sur les mémoires originaux dont il paraît que Moise s'est servi pour composer le livre de la Genèse* (Brussels 1753). Noticing that in certain parts of Genesis God is designated by the Hebrew word Elohim, and in other parts by the Hebrew word Yahweh, he strung the Elohim parts together and the Yahweh parts together and thus obtained two fairly coherent parallel accounts. From this he concluded that Moses had used two principal documents, an Elohistic one and a Yahwistic one, in addition to 10 smaller documents (from Moab, Edom, etc.); Moses would have placed the documents one parallel to the other, but later copyists jumbled them together. Thus was born the so-called documentary hypothesis, which Astruc proposed as merely probable and expressly subject to the judgment of the Church. This hypothesis as applied to the other books of the *Pentateuch by J. G. Eichhorn and K. D. Ilgen won favor, especially in Germany. Although Astruc was not correct in most of the points of his theory about the composition of Genesis, his acute observation about the Elohistic and the Yahwistic documents used in the composition of this book laid the foundation for the modern, much more elaborated documentary hypothesis on the composition of the Pentateuch.

Bibliography: A. LODS and P. ALPHANDÉRY, *Jean Astruc et la critique biblique au XVIIIe siècle* (Paris 1924). A. M. LAUTOUR, DictBiogFranc 3:1391–94. E. O'DOHERTY, "The Conjectures of Jean Astruc, 1753," CathBiblQuart 15 (1953) 300–304. J. DE SAVIGNAC, "L'Oeuvre et la personnalité de Jean Astruc," *La Nouvelle Clio* 5 (1953) 138–147. A. STROBEL, LexThK[2] 1:967. E. KUTSCH, RGG[3] 1:666. P. AUVRAY, *Catholicisme* 1:971. V. CAVALLA, EncCatt 2:251.

[A. M. MALO]

ASUNCIÓN, ARCHDIOCESE OF (ASSUMPTIONIS), the ecclesiastical province of Paraguay, created a diocese July 1, 1547; raised to an archdiocese May 1, 1929. In 1964 it included also the Apostolic Vicariates of Pilcomayo (1950) and of Paraguayan Chaco (1948) and the Prelatures *Nullius* of Encarnación y Alto Paraná (1957), Caacupé (1960), Caaguazu (1961), and Coronel Oviedo (1961), and the three dioceses: San Juan Bautista de las Misiones (1957), Concepción (1929), and Villarrica (1929). The bull of Pius XI creating the archdiocese was put into effect by the decree of Sept. 8, 1929, signed by the apostolic nuncio in Asunción Felipe Cortesi. The first archbishop, Juan Sinforiano *Bogarín, was consecrated in the metropolitan cathedral the following August. Juan José Aníbal Mena Porta was appointed auxiliary bishop of Asunción in 1936 and 5 years later coadjutor with the right of succession. On the death of Archbishop Bogarín, Feb. 25, 1949, Mena Porta took charge and was installed formally in June. He also became chancellor in 1960 of the newly founded Catholic University of Nuestra Señora Santa María de la Asunción. Oblates of Mary Immaculate are in charge of the apostolic vicariate of Pilcomayo, Salesians of Chaco Paraguayo. Of the prelatures, Encarnación y Alto Paraná is the mission territory of the Fathers of the Divine Word, Caacupé of the Salesians, and Coronel Oviedo of Franciscans.

The church and plaza of San Roque, Asunción, Paraguay.

See also PARAGUAY.

Bibliography: C. R. CENTURIÓN, *Síntesis histórica del obispado de la Asunción* (Asunción 1963). **Illustration credit:** Pan American Union, Washington, D.C.

[C. R. CENTURIÓN]

ASYLUM, CITIES OF, designated sanctuary cities in Israel that took the place of local altars in offering protection to the involuntary manslayer who fled for his life from the blood avenger. Among many ancient peoples, the inviolable right of asylum at a designated sanctuary for the fugitive was a common institution (Tacitus, *Ann.* 3.60; Strabo, 16.2.6; 1 Mc 10.43; 2 Mc 4.33). As part of their culture, the Israelites inherited the ancient nomadic custom of *blood vengeance, imposed as a duty on the nearest of kin, the *gō'ēl*. He was held responsible to execute the capital punishment by killing the murderer in retribution and avenging the blood of his slain kinsman. (*See* COLLECTIVE RESPONSIBILITY.) As a means of preventing undue blood vengeance, the law provided six cities of refuge to be administered by the Levites (Nm 35.6). The place of refuge took the manslayer from the personal police action of the avenger (*gō'ēl*) and gave him an opportunity for an orderly trial. Such a sanctuary was meant only for the unintentional or accidental manslayer (Dt 4.42; 19.4). He was safe in the city of refuge as long as he stayed there, but outside of it, he could be put to death by the avenger. Once the prevailing high priest died, the manslayer could return home and have no further anxieties (Nm 35.25–28).

Of these six cities, Deuteronomy represents Moses himself selecting three in Transjordan, namely, Bosor in the tribe of Reuben, *Ramoth in the tribe of Gad, and Golan in the tribe of eastern Manasse (Dt 4.43). On the western side of the Jordan, three other cities were chosen, namely, Cedes in Nephthali, *Sichem in Ephraim, and *Hebron in Juda (Jos 20.1–9).

Bibliography: De Vaux AncIsr 160–163, 276, 414. EncDictBibl 164–165. N. M. NICOLSKY, "Das Asylrecht in Israel," ZATWiss 48 (1930) 146–175. J. P. E. PEDERSEN, *Israel: Its Life and Culture,* 4 v. in 2 (New York 1926–40; repr. 1959) 1:396–397, 425. M. GREENBERG, "City of Refuge," InterDictBibl 1:638–639; "The Biblical Conception of Asylum," JBiblLit 78 (1959) 125–132. M. HARAN, "Studies in the Account of the Levitical Cities," *ibid.* 80 (1961) 45–54.

[J. E. STEINMUELLER]

ASYLUM, RIGHT OF, the custom or privilege by which certain inviolable places become a recognized refuge for persons in danger. Asylum may take a secular form, such as an immunity granted to a locality, i.e., a city of refuge, a franchise, an embassy with extraterritorial rights, or a religious form, when it is attached to a consecrated place.

Religious asylum, or "sanctuary," with which the present article is concerned, is found at some stage in the history of most religions. It assumes special prominence when the maintenance of justice by public authority is weak, for it limits the excesses of private vengeance. Asylum was honored by the Jews (Ex 21.12–14; Nm 35.11–29; Dt 19.1–13), by the Egyptians, by the Greeks, and to a lesser extent by the Romans. As Christianity became the religion of the Roman Empire, a right of asylum became attached to churches, though at first it was simply a delay of pursuit while the clergy made intercession for the refugee.

In medieval Europe asylum attached to a sacred place was usually independent of intercession. It assumed an important place in the peace movement of the 11th century, protecting not only those accused of crime, but also peasants, merchants, and others threatened by the violence of the time (*see* PEACE OF GOD). During the 12th century the Canon Law of asylum was elaborated (e.g., CorpIurCan c.17 q.4).

As civil society extended its authority late in the Middle Ages, asylum declined in importance, a fact recognized by the popes since Gregory XIV (*Cum alias,* May 24, 1591), though the present Code maintains asylum in principle (CIC cc.1160–79). It still plays a role in some pagan areas of Africa and Asia.

Bibliography: J. C. COX, *The Sanctuary and Sanctuary Seekers of Medieval England* (London 1911). P. TIMBAL DUCLAUX DE MARTIN, *Le Droit d'aisle* (Paris 1939). L. R. MISSEREY, DDC 1:1084–1104. J. LECLER, *Catholicisme* 1:909–913. N. C. SCIPIONI, EncCatt 2:136–139.

[M. M. SHEEHAN]

ATENEO DE MANILA

A complex of educational institutions including lower division and secondary schools and the University in Manila, P.I., administered by the Philippine Province of the Society of Jesus. Although the Jesuits operated San Ignacio, a small university in Manila from 1623 until their suppression in the Philippines in 1768, they did not establish the Ateneo until their return to the Islands in 1859. The Ateneo opened as a primary school subsidized by the Manila City Council, and in 1865 under the Spanish government developed into a secondary-level European-style *colegio* of national prominence. In 1885, to the 5-year baccalaureate curriculum, which formed the principal program of instruction, the Ateneo added three shorter curricula leading to a title of *perito* (expert) in commerce, engineering, and agriculture. Of the 823 graduated between 1870 and 1900 more than 40 per cent took one or another of the *perito* diplomas. Chief among distinguished alumni of this period is Dr. José Rizal, national hero of the Philippines, who in 1877 received his B.A. with high honors.

In 1898 upon the transfer of political jurisdiction over the Islands from Madrid to Washington, the Ateneo became a private institution. It did not lose its predominantly Spanish character, however, until 1921 when Jesuits from the New York–Maryland Province replaced those from Barcelona as its administrators. In 1958 management passed to the newly constituted Philippine Province, and the following year the Ateneo attained legal status as a university.

The Ateneo is administered by the rector president generally appointed for 6 years and assisted in matters concerning the Jesuit community by two officials called respectively the superior and the minister. An academic council composed of the vice presidents, deans, and department chairmen, for the most part laymen, aid the rector in executive and advisory affairs. In 1964 the total academic staff of all divisions comprised 48 Jesuits and 187 laymen, of whom 25 per cent held doctoral and 75 per cent master's degrees. Total enrollment numbered approximately 5,000, with 1,650 on the college and university levels. Financial support derives largely from student fees, gifts, concessions, and investment income. Scholarships are limited in number and in value. The combined holdings of the graduate school, law school, college, faculty, and Rizal Room libraries total approximately 50,000 volumes.

The Ateneo de Manila University consists of the college of law; college of arts and science; graduate school of arts and science, including education; graduate school of economics and business administration; institute of social order; institute of Philippine culture; and a central guidance center. It offers a bachelor's program in law, and B.A. and B.S. programs in more than a dozen fields of concentration, including physics, chemistry, and mathematics. Eight departments provide master's degree courses, which in 1963 enrolled about 400 students who were largely part time. The Ateneo does not offer doctoral programs but encourages and helps those so interested to study abroad. All applicants to the Ateneo University must take standardized tests and, in general, be interviewed as well. About 60 per cent of the liberal arts college students and 10 per cent of the master's level students actually receive a degree, and only the graduate school accepts women.

In 1964 the University was engaged in two experimental projects significant for educational purposes: (1) a language-learning and language-teaching program designed and conducted by the Language Center; and (2) a closed-circuit educational television program made possible by a 1963 Ford Foundation grant of $100,000. While the Manila Observatory, an affiliated institution on campus, devotes practically all of its energies to research in solar physics, sound in space, and seismic phenomena in cooperation with the U.S. Bureau of

Standards and the U.S. National Aeronautics and Space Administration, instructional units of the University proper allot only a minor portion of their attention to professional research. In 1963 these projects included studies in Philippine history, Filipino psychology, and Philippine culture as a whole. The University publishes a quarterly, *Philippine Studies,* containing research reports as well as articles of fact and opinion.

Bibliography: Ateneo de Manila, *The Ateneo Report 1963* (Manila 1963). M. RAVAGO, ed., *Reseña histórica de las fiestas jubilares del Ateneo de Manila celebradas con motivo del 50° aniversario de su fundacióm* (Manila 1910). P. PASTELLS, *Misión de la Compañía de Jesús de Filipinas en el siglo XIX,* 3 v. (Barcelona 1916–17).

[F. FOX]

ATHALA OF BOBBIO, ST., abbot; b. Burgundy, *c.* 570; d. March 10, 627 (feast, March 10). His life was written by his contemporary *Jonas of Bobbio. After having been educated at Lyons and having become a monk at *Lérins, he sought the stricter observance of *Luxeuil. Though nominated to replace *Columban, who had been exiled by *Brunhilde (610), he followed the Irish ascetic into northern Italy, where they established the monastery of *Bobbio. Here he succeeded Columban as abbot (*c.* 615), combatted *Arianism among the *Lombards, and sided with the Pope in the schism of Aquileia over the condemnation of the *Three Chapters.

Bibliography: B. KRUSCH, MGSrerMer 4:113–119. BHL 1:742–744. Baudot-Chaussin 3:232–233. Butler Th Attw 1:547–548. BiblSanct 2:565–567.

[J. E. LYNCH]

ATHANASIAN CREED

Called also the *Quicumque* or *Quicumque-vult* from its opening words; a profession of the Christian faith in 40 rhythmical sentences. Although originally private and nonliturgical, it gradually found its way into the liturgy of the Western Church in the early Middle Ages. It achieved quasi-ecumenical standing in Carolingian times, and the scholastics of the 13th century placed it on a par with the Apostles' and Nicene Creeds. The Reformers accepted it unreservedly, and it still has a place in the liturgy of the Church of England.

Content. The Athanasian Creed deals mainly with the Trinity and the Incarnation. It reflects a doctrinal development corresponding at least to the era of the Council of *Chalcedon (451). The divine nature is expressed by the term substance, and the term person is used to describe the three in the Trinity. Hypostasis is not used. The distinction of the Persons and their equality are strongly emphasized. The unity of the three Persons in common attributes, such as eternity and omnipotence, is expressed by stating that there is "one omnipotent"—*unus omnipotens non tres omnipotentes*—a usage that St. Thomas Aquinas justifies but does not prefer (ST 1a, 39.3). The Holy Spirit is said to be "from" the Father "and" the Son.

In the theology of the Incarnation, Christ's full and perfect divinity and full and perfect humanity are vindicated. Christ was born by eternal generation from the substance of the Father, by temporal generation from the substance of Mary. Christ's humanity is composed of a rational soul and human flesh. In a characteristically Western expression, Christ is said to be equal to the Father in His divinity and less than the Father according to His humanity. *Eutychianism is excluded by the denial of any conversion or confusion of natures and by the affirmation of the assumption of a human nature in the divine Person. The comparison of union of body and soul is used to illustrate the union of the divine and human natures in the person of Christ. The concluding portion of the Athanasian Creed deals with the Passion of Christ, his descent into hell, Resurrection, Ascension, enthronement at the right hand of the Father, the Second Coming, general resurrection, Judgment, and the sanctions of eternal life and eternal fire. The Creed begins and ends with the necessity of so believing for salvation under pain of eternal loss.

Problem of Authorship. Attribution of the Creed to Athanasius seems to have been a gradual process beginning in the 7th century and continuing uncontested till the 17th. This attribution is now generally abandoned. It is widely held now that the original language of the Creed was Latin and that the Greek forms are later translations. Only a few Eastern scholars refuse to accept this last conclusion. The content and style of expression as well as the documentary evidence indicate that Athanasius was not its author. The first manuscripts in which it occurs are from the 7th and 8th centuries. The first certain witness to its existence as a creed is *Caesarius of Arles (*c.* 542). The area of its first appearance and influence was southern Gaul or, more exactly, the region around Arles. From there it seems to have spread to Spain and to the Carolingian Empire. A document of Autun (670) obliging clerics to memorize it attests to its penetration into the liturgy and clerical training.

The identity of the author is still unknown. It may be that the Creed is the work of several authors and is perhaps a compilation of the decrees of several synods. The time of composition may be placed sometime between 434 and 440 (date of *Excerpta Vincentii Lirinensis,* discovered in 1940, which suggest a source for some of the expressions in the Creed), with a terminal date of 542, the year of the death of Caesarius of Arles. Among the suggested authors of the Creed are St. *Ambrose, St. *Vincent of Lérins, St. Caesarius of Arles, *Fulgentius of Ruspe, *Nicetas of Remesiana, and even St. *Hilary of Poitiers.

Liturgical Use. In Germany the *Quicumque* had penetrated into the liturgy by the 9th century. It was recited on Sunday after the sermon. Later it was used in the Office at Prime. It entered the Roman liturgy somewhat later. Until 1955 it formed part of the ordinary Sunday Office for Prime in the Roman liturgy. Since 1955 it has occurred only at Prime on the feast of the Most Blessed Trinity.

Quicumque in the Eastern Church. The earliest manuscripts are from the 14th century, but it seems that the Western monks in Jerusalem in the 9th century confronted the Eastern monks with the *Quicumque* in support of the filioque, since it read "from the Father and the Son." The Eastern theologians at first paid no attention to the claim that attributed the Creed to Athanasius and simply rejected its authority in the matter of the filioque. At a later date, when manuscript evidence showed that the Creed enjoyed some support in Eastern tradition, the filioque text was regarded as an interpolation and deleted. The *Quicumque* has been used in the Russian liturgy since the 17th century. It was adopted into the Greek liturgy in 1780 for a relatively short

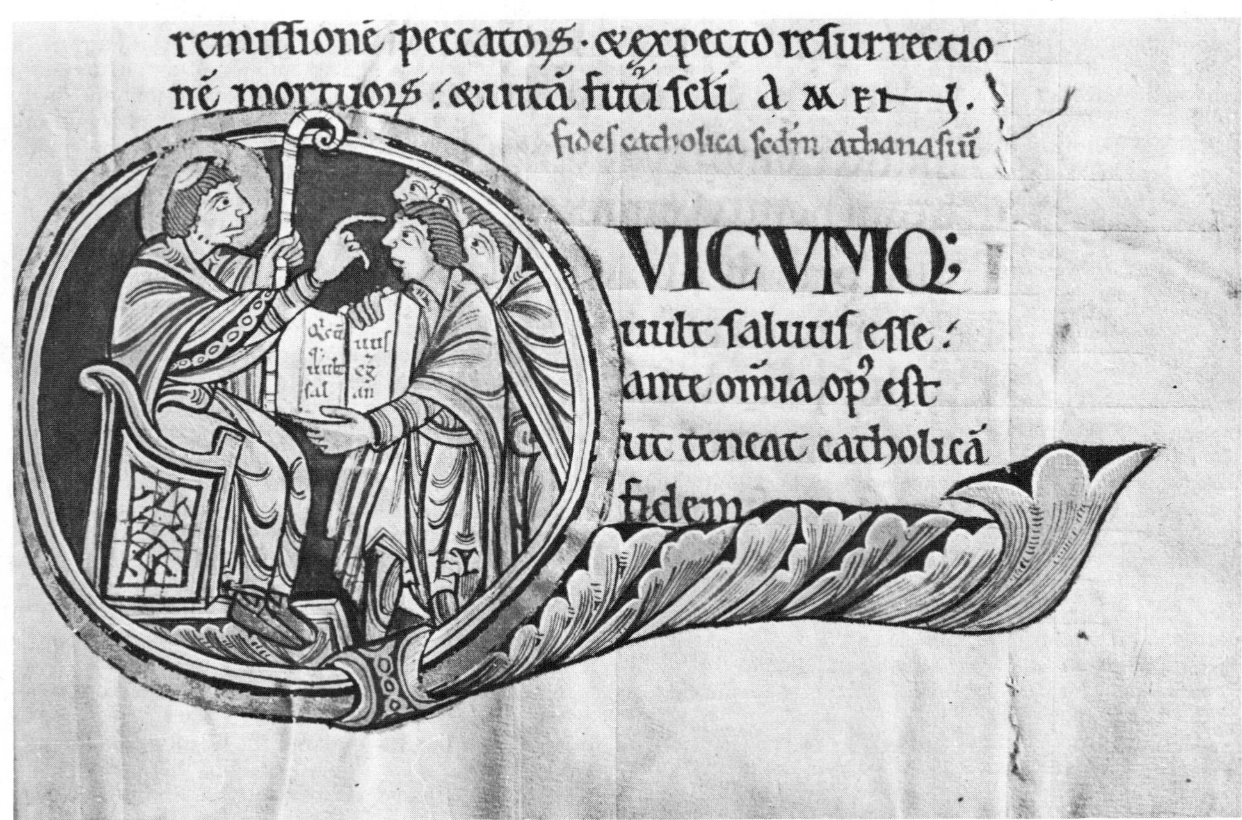

The beginning of the Athanasian Creed in the 12th-century English "St. Alban Psalter" now at Hildesheim, Germany.

period but was later abandoned even though many Eastern writers had no hesitation in accepting the Athanasian authorship of the Creed once the filioque was deleted.

Bibliography: Quasten Patr 3:32–33. Altaner 319–323. J. TIXERONT, DTC 1.2:2178–87. Denz 40–42. L. OTT, Grill-Bacht Konz 2:895–912. **Illustration credit:** The Warburg Institute, University of London.

[G. OWENS]

ATHANASIUS, ST.

Bishop of Alexandria from 328 to 373, dominant 4th-century churchman, and theologian in the battle for orthodoxy against *Arianism; b. Alexandria, *c.* 295; d. Alexandria, May 2, 373 (feast, May 2).

Life. Athanasius was born apparently of a Christian family and received a good classical education that was followed by a solid scriptural and theological formation. At an early age (*c.* 312) he entered the ranks of the Alexandrian clergy and was ordained a deacon (*c.* 318) by Bishop Alexander, whom he served as secretary. Contemporary sources say little about his role in the earliest stages of the Arian dispute; undoubtedly not he but Bishop Alexander was the leading figure. Athanasius accompanied Alexander to the Council of *Nicaea I (325) and supported his actions but did not occupy the predominant position in this assembly attributed to him in later panegyrics.

Before his death in 328, Alexander designated Athanasius as his successor, and this choice was confirmed by the Egyptian bishops, despite the opposition on the part of Arians and Meletians. Athanasius first made extensive pastoral visits to the entire Egyptian province, but soon had to face vicious attacks from various enemies. In 331, the partisans of the *Meletian schism accused him at the court of Constantine I, but Athanasius was able to vindicate himself, and on his return to Alexandria he took severe measures against the Meletians. Next, he became the target of the anti-Nicene reaction, led by the Arian-minded *Eusebius of Nicomedia, who had already succeeded in deposing *Eustathius of Antioch and other bishops for their pro-Nicene stand.

First Exile and Exoneration. With the approval of Constantine, Athanasius was summoned to the Council of Tyre (335), composed almost exclusively of his enemies. Seeing no hope of obtaining a fair judgment, he left for the imperial court to present his case directly to the emperor. There are conflicting reports on what happened in Constantinople; however, Constantine exiled him to Treves in Northern Gaul. On the Emperor's death (May 337), his son Constantine II gave Athanasius permission to resume his episcopal duties. Soon afterward, however, the Eusebian bishops deposed him again at the Synod of Antioch (337 or 338) and established first Pistus, then Gregory as bishop in Alexandria. Athanasius protested this violence in an encyclical letter to all Catholic bishops and took his case to Rome, where he found *Marcellus of Ancyra, Asclepas of Gaza, and other victims of the anti-Nicene reaction. Pope Julius I (337–352) convened a Roman synod attended by some 50 bishops in the fall of 340 or spring of 341. The charges brought forth at the Council of Tyre were fully examined, and Athanasius and Marcellus were declared innocent.

The Eastern bishops refused to accept this verdict, and Athanasius remained in the West, where he promoted the monastic ideal in his travels through Italy and Gaul. With Bishop *Hosius of Córdoba he traveled to *Sardica, where a general council had been summoned by the Emperors Constans and Constantius II (343). The council proved a failure because the Eastern bishops refused to sit in joint session with their Western colleagues, who had Athanasius and Marcellus in their midst. The Western assembly proceeded to examine anew the case of the accused bishops and again fully exonerated them. On the death of the Alexandrian usurper Gregory of Cappadocia, Constantius allowed Athanasius to return to his see, where he arrived in October 346. There followed 10 years of relative peace, which he used to renew Christian life in Egypt, to promote monasticism, and to compose some of his writings, including his *On the Decrees of the Nicene Synod* and *On the Opinion of Dionysius of Alexandria.*

Subsequent Exiles. On the death of Constans in 350, Constantius became sole emperor, and the enemies of Athanasius resumed their agitation against him. Concentrating their efforts in the West, they had him condemned at the Council of Arles in 353 and at the Council of Milan in 355. Later, imperial emissaries were sent to collect signatures from the bishops absent from these councils; the few who resisted, among whom were Pope *Liberius (352–366) and *Hilary of Poitiers, were banished to the East, while the centenarian Hosius of Córdoba was detained for a year in the imperial court at Sirmium. Abandoned by the West, Athanasius was attacked at home. In February 356 a military detachment invaded the church where he was celebrating a vigil service; he managed to escape and went into hiding in the Libyan Desert, while an Arian bishop, George of Cappadocia (357–361), was installed in his place. For the next 6 years, eluding pursuit by moving from one hiding place to another and supported by the loyalty of his clergy and monks, Athanasius managed to govern his flock and even made several secret visits to Alexandria. During this period he composed some of his major writings, including the three *Discourses against the Arians,* the *Life of St. Antony,* the *History of the Arians,* and the *Letters to Serapion* and *to Epictetus.* He kept himself well informed about events in the Christian world, and particularly about the many synods held during these years, each of which proclaimed a different creed according to the faction of the anti-Nicene coalition enjoying the momentary favor of Emperor Constantius. Like Hilary of Poitiers exiled in Phrygia, Athanasius in his *De Synodis* ridiculed this multiplication of creeds and, powerless, watched the defeat of orthodoxy at the councils of Rimini, Seleucia, and Constantinople.

A reaction set in with the death of Constantius, on Nov. 3, 361. George of Cappadocia was murdered by the rabble (Dec. 24, 361), and the new emperor, *Julian the Apostate, set the exiled bishops free. In February 362 Athanasius made his triumphant reentry into Alexandria. Immediately he convened a synod, attended mostly by bishops who had suffered for the orthodox faith. Its decisions, contained in the *Tomus ad Antiochenos,* had far-reaching effects and contributed greatly to the restoration of unity in the Eastern Church. The Synod anathematized Arianism and made special note of the heresy's application to the Holy Spirit (so-called Semi-Arianism), and also condemned the first traces of the Christological heresies. It dealt leniently with bishops who had signed the Arian, Homoean formulary under duress, provided they now adhered to the Nicene Creed. By admitting that the Origenistic formula of "three hypostases" could have an orthodox meaning, it paved the way for the reconciliation of many Homoiousians. Julian, however, who promoted a revival of paganism, did not desire a strong and united Christianity. In October 362 Athanasius was exiled once more, but the death of the Emperor in June 363 set him free. Before regaining his see, Athanasius tried without success to solve the Antiochian schism.

On the death of Jovian in February 364, the new emperor, Valentinian, made his brother Valens coemperor and entrusted him with the government of the Eastern Empire. Valens favored a return to the Homoean (Arian) formulary and resumed the persecution of all who rejected it. For the fifth time, Athanasius went into hiding. Four months later the mutinous attitude of the Alexandrians forced Valens to rescind the exile. Athanasius spent the last years of his life in peace, continuing by his actions and writings to prepare the ultimate triumph of orthodoxy. Before his death, he designated his brother Peter as his successor.

Writings. Athanasius was a prolific author whose literary production was intimately linked with his life and, as such, part of his unceasing battle against the enemies of Christ, as he designated Arianism in any form. This explains the predominantly polemical nature of most of his dogmatic works, the biased selection of documents in his historical compositions, the lack of serenity in his argumentation, and the public character

St. Athanasius, 8th-century fresco in the church of Santa Maria Antiqua at Rome.

of his letters. Even the *Life of St. Antony* contains an attack against Arianism. For the same reason he cared more for clarity and persuasiveness than for literary excellence.

Dogmatic Writings. The major work in this section is constituted by his three *Discourses against the Arians;* they contain a summary of the Arian doctrine, a defense of the Nicene definition, and a comprehensive discussion of scriptural arguments. The discourses were written, in all probability, during his third exile (*c.* 358). A fourth *Discourse,* added in the Benedictine and Migne editions, is now considered as definitely spurious. The *Oration against the Pagans* and the *Oration on the Incarnation of the Word,* although often edited as separate works, are one treatise mentioned by Jerome as the *Two Books against the Pagans.* Since this work contains no reference to Arianism or to Nicaea, the date of composition is commonly assigned to *c.* 318. A third work *On the Incarnation and against the Arians* deals with the divinity of Christ and of the Holy Spirit. It dates probably from a later period of his life; but its authenticity has been challenged. To this category belong also several letters that are, in fact, short dogmatic treatises: the *Four Letters to Serapion,* written between 359 and 360, in which Athanasius set forth his admirable doctrine on the divinity and procession of the Holy Spirit; the *Letter to Epictetus,* often quoted in later Christological controversies; the *Letter to Adelphus,* on the same theme; and the *Letter to Maximus the Philosopher.* His *Letter concerning the Decrees of the Nicene Council* (*c.* 350 or 351) presents a defense from Scripture and the Fathers of the nonscriptural expressions in the Nicene Creed. The *Letter on the Teaching of Dionysius the Alexandrian* is probably a later addition to the letter on the decrees of Nicaea. Among the dogmatic writings attributed to Athanasius but definitely spurious, the following should be mentioned: *On the Incarnation against Apollinaris;* the *Sermo Maior de Fide;* the *Expositio Fidei;* and the *Athanasian Creed* called the *Quicumque,* the date and authorship of which is still debated.

Historical-Polemical Writings. Athanasius composed several apologies during his third exile from 356 to 362; they include: the *Apology against the Arians,* particularly valuable for its collection of documents pertaining to the councils of Tyre and Sardica; the *Apology to Constantius,* important for its doctrine on Church and State; the *Apology for His Flight;* and the *History of the Arians,* written at the request of the monks with whom he was living in 358. This last book covers events from 335 to 357. To this category belong also his *Letter on the Synods of Rimini and Seleucia* of 359, which contains valuable data on the texts of the various Arian creeds; the *Encyclical Letter to the Bishops,* protesting his expulsion from Alexandria in 339; and the *Encyclical Letter to the Bishops of Egypt and Libya,* written on his expulsion in 356.

Ascetical Writings. Of paramount importance is the *Life of St. Antony,* founder of Christian monasticism. Written *c.* 357 at the request of the Egyptian monks and intended to provide "an ideal pattern of the ascetical life," it enjoyed astonishing popularity and was soon translated into various languages. Particularly in the Latin translation of Evagrius of Antioch, this biographical tract contributed greatly to the establishment of monastic life throughout the Western Christian world. From the literary point of view, it created a new, Christian genre, and set the pattern for countless later lives of monks and saints. The *Letter to the Monk Amun* and the *Letter to Dracontius* also belong in this category. According to Jerome, Athanasius wrote several treatises on virginity; because of this statement, many similar treatises have been attributed to him, creating problems of authenticity that contemporary scholars have only begun to solve. The treatise *On Virginity,* for example, edited among his works (PG 28:251–282), is defended as authentic by E. von der Goltz but rejected by M. Aubineau. In recent years several other treatises and fragments of works on virginity have been discovered and edited, some in the original Greek, others in Coptic, Syriac, or Armenian translations. Not all of these are genuine writings of Athanasius, but some of them will undoubtedly in time be recognized as his. Noteworthy among these is a *Letter on Love and Self-control* that may well be an original Athanasian Coptic writing.

Homiletic and Exegetical Works. Much remains to be done to determine the authenticity of sermons attributed to Athanasius, either in the collection published in PG v.28 or in newly discovered Syriac and Coptic MSS. As to his Biblical commentaries, none have survived in full, but numerous fragments are found in ancient *catenae. Many of these pertain to a *Commentary on the Psalms,* a few, to Genesis or to Ecclesiastes and the Canticle of Canticles. There is also a *Letter to Marcellinus on the Interpretation of the Psalms* that serves as a general introduction on their meaning and use.

Letters. Besides the letters mentioned in the preceding groups, there is a collection of annual Lenten messages, the so-called *Festal Letters.* Thirteen of these have been preserved in a Syriac translation; 17 others, in a recently published Coptic MS. Of major importance among these is the festal letter of 367 for its enumeration of the canonical books of the Old and New Testaments. Three other letters were written at the request of Alexandrian synods: *Tome to the Antiochians* (362), *To the Emperor Jovian* (363), and *To the African Bishops* (369). The *Letter to Bishop Rufianus* gives directives for the reconciliation of the Arians; while the *Letter to the Monks* contains a warning against the heretics.

Doctrine. Because Athanasius's life and writings were one long battle against Arianism, his doctrinal horizon is dominated by Trinitarian and Christological controversies; there is little to glean in his writings on other tenets of the Christian faith. His doctrine is eminently traditional; he created no new synthesis of his own, but clarified and defended the central mysteries of the Trinity and the Incarnation by means of revealed concepts rather than philosophical constructions. While not opposed to philosophy in principle, Athanasius had little use for it. The key to his theological thinking is the dogma of Redemption. Like Justin Martyr and Irenaeus of Lyon, he stressed the identity of the Logos with the Son of God become man. He saw the Logos as the mediator of divine salvation rather than as the agent of divine creativity; hence the predominantly soteriological nature of his argumentation.

Against the Arians, Athanasius argued that if Christ were not truly God, He could not have imparted divine life and resemblance to man. Similarly, against the Pneumatomachians, he argued that, since men are divinized and sanctified by partaking of the Holy Spirit, He must have the nature of God. Again, against the incipient Christological errors, Athanasius stressed the reality of the Incarnation and the personal unity of Christ as indispensable conditions for the effectiveness of His redeeming death. In his spiritual doctrine, asceticism and virginity are but means to achieve in man the divine image through the Divine Word, who is the substantial image of the Father.

Bibliography: PG v.25–28. H. G. OPITZ, *Untersuchungen zur Überlieferung der Schriften des Athanasius* (Berlin 1935). G. MÜLLER, *Lexicon Athanasianum,* 10 pts. (Berlin 1944–52). X. LE BACHELET, DTC 1.2:2143–78. Quasten Patr 3:20–79, editions and bibliog. *Bibliographia patristica,* ed. W. SCHNEEMELCHER (Berlin 1956–). H. M. GWATKIN, *Studies in Arianism* (2d ed. Cambridge, Eng. 1900). E. SCHWARTZ, *Zur Geschichte des Athanasius* (Gesammelte Schriften 3; Berlin 1959). K. F. HAGEL, *Kirche und Kaisertum in Lehre und Leben des Athanasius* (doctoral diss.; Giessen 1933). G. BARDY, DHGE 4:1313–40. J. R. PALANQUE et al., *The Church in the Christian Roman Empire,* tr. E. C. MESSENGER, 2 v. in 1 (New York 1953) v.1. H. VON CAMPENHAUSEN, *The Fathers of the Greek Church,* tr. S. GODMAN (New York 1959) 67–79. H. MUSURILLO, EncBrit (1965) 2:664–667.

Doctrine. F. LAUCHERT, *Der Lehre des hl. Athanasius* (Leipzig 1895). E. WEIGL, *Untersuchungen zur Christologie des hl. Athanasius* (Mainz 1914). A. GAUDEL, "La Théorie du Logos chez S. Athanase," RevScRel 9 (1929) 524–539; 11 (1931) 1–26. C. HAURET, *Comment le "Défenseur de Nicée" a-t-il compris le dogme de Nicée?* (Rome 1936). L. BOUYER, *L'Incarnation et l'Église-Corps du Christ dans la théologie de S. Athanase* (Paris 1943). F. L. CROSS, *The Study of St. Athanasius* (Oxford 1945). M. RICHARD, "S. Athanase et la psychologie du Christ selon les Ariens," MélSciRel 4 (1947) 5–54. A. GRILLMEIER, Grill-Bacht Konz 1:77–102. J. LEBON, "Le Sort du 'consubstantiel' nicéen," RHE 48 (1953) 632–682. R. BERNARD, *L'Image de Dieu d'après S. Athanase* (Paris 1952). P. GALTIER, "S. Athanase et l'âme humaine du Christ," Greg 36 (1955) 553–589. T. E. POLLARD, "Logos and Son in Origen, Arius and Athanasius," *Studia patristica* 2 (TU 64; 1957) 282–287. G. FLOROVSKY, "The Concept of Creation in Saint Athanasius," *ibid.* 6 (TU 81; 1962) 36–57. J. N. D. KELLY, *Early Christian Doctrines* (2d ed. New York 1960) 243–258, 284–295. **Illustration credit:** Gabinetto Fotografico Nazionale, Rome.

[V. C. DE CLERCQ]

ATHANASIUS I, PATRIARCH OF CONSTANTINOPLE, 1289 to 1293, 1304 to 1310; b. Adrianople, 1230; d. Constantinople, Oct. 28, 1310. He was baptized Alexius and took the name Athanasius on becoming a monk at Thessalonica, whence he emigrated to the monastery of Esphigmenou on Mt. *Athos. He undertook a journey to the Holy Land and became a hermit at St. Lazarus on Mt. Galesios, but he soon returned to Mt. Athos. His opposition to the reunion Council of *Lyons (1274) and to John Beccus forced him to return to Mt. Galesios and later to go to Ganos in Thrace, where he founded a monastery. Probably during his stay at Mt. Galesios he was ordained; he was selected patriarch of Constantinople by Emperor *Andronicus II (1289), and set about stabilizing ecclesiastical discipline. He passed severe measures for the reform of the clergy; despite his own travels, he restrained wandering monks and bound the bishops to residence in their own dioceses. In 1293 reaction against the severity of Athanasius was such that the Emperor had to accept his resignation (October 13). Athanasius retired to a monastery of Xerolophus, but he had to be recalled because of the demands of the people. He expelled the Franciscans from Constantinople in 1307 and early in 1310 resigned a second time. He died a short while later in the monastery of Xerolophos. Most of the writings of Athanasius are unedited; 126 letters concerned with the ecclesiastical discipline are known, and he is credited with two catechetical lectures and a canon or hymn in honor of the Mother of God (*Theotokaria*).

Bibliography: PG 142:471–528. ActSS Aug 1:169–175. Beck KTLBR 692. K. BAUS, LexThK[2] 1:981. H. DELEHAYE, *Mélanges d'archéologie et d'histoire* 17 (1897) 47–74. R. GUILLAND, *Études sur l'histoire et sur l'art de Byzance. Mélanges Charles Diehl,* v.1 (Paris 1930) 121–140.

[F. CHIOVARO]

ATHANASIUS THE ATHONITE, ST., Byzantine founder of cenobitic monasticism on Mt. *Athos; b. Trebizond, *c.* 920; d. Mt. Athos, *c.* 1000. His well-to-do family had him baptized Abraham. He studied at Constantinople and became a monk at Mount Kiminas under Abbot Michael Maleinos, uncle of *Nicephorus Phocas (later emperor). While still a general, Nicephorus employed Abraham as his spiritual director. Abraham changed his name to Athanasius and retired to Mt. Athos as a hermit to escape court honors; however, he was persuaded to accompany the general during his campaign against the Saracens in *Crete. With imperial support he founded the Great Lavra on Mt. Athos in 963 and introduced a *Typicon,* or rule, for cenobites based on the common-life ideals of St. *Basil the Great and *Theodore the Studite. Opposition to this innovation developed on the death of the Emperor (969) and was combined with the accusation that the success of Athanasius's experiment was a result of imperial influence. But the new Emperor, *John I Tzimisces, rallied in favor of Athanasius, who had fled to Cyprus. Strengthened by a vision as well as by financial support, Athanasius returned to Mt. Athos, where he was killed *c.* 1000 when the masonry collapsed as he was laying the keystone of a dome. The Athanasian *Hypotyposis* was based upon the Studite rule but shows strong traces of Benedictine influence. A third document, the *Diatyposis,* deals with the succession and station of superiors and the rights of the *epitropos,* or adminstrator, and provides a directory for the Easter Liturgy and other rites. A factual life of Athanasius was written by a younger Athanasius who seems to have obtained most of his information from the founder's disciple, Anthony, and a John Hexapteryos. A second anonymous *Bios,* or life, seems to have been based on the first.

Bibliography: K. BAUS, LexThK[2] 1:976. P. MEYER, *Die Haupturkunden für die Geschichte der Athosklöster* (Leipzig 1894). L. PETIT, "Vie de Saint Athanase l'Athonite," AnalBoll 25 (1906) 5–89. J. LEROY, "S. Athanase L'Athonite et la règle S. Benoît," RevAscMyst 29 (1953) 108–122. E. AMAND DE MENDIETA, *La Presqu'île des Caloyers: Le Mont-Athos* (Paris 1955). Beck KTLBR 578, 588–589. P. LEMERLE, "La Vie ancienne de S. Athanase l'Athonite," *Le Millénaire du Mont Athos* (Chevetogne 1963–) 1:59–100.

[G. A. MALONEY]

ATHANASIUS OF NAPLES, ST., bishop; b. 832; d. Veroli, Italy, July 15, 872 (feast, July 15). He was a pastor of great compassion for the needs of his flock, a competent administrator, and a stanch champion of the Church against the political freebooters of the age. Rather precise details of his life may be gathered from two contemporary works: a vita by *John the Deacon of Naples and another more complete version by an anonymous Neapolitan, who provides also an account of the translation of his remains. His father, Sergius, came of a powerful Neapolitan family, and as defender of his city against Lombard incursions, was elected duke by his fellow citizens; Athanasius' mother was Drusa, a noble lady. Athanasius, destined for the clerical life from early youth, came under the tutelage of priests at the church of Santa Maria and of the saintly bishop John IV (d. 849). After the death of John, Athanasius, a deacon only 18 years of age, was elected bishop and consecrated in Rome by Pope *Gregory IV. Personally austere of life, he poured himself out in service to his flock, especially the poor, orphans, and Saracen prisoners. He rebuilt churches, reunited communities of priests and monks, and represented the interests of Naples before the Emperor, who esteemed him both for holiness and for his practical conduct of affairs. After the death of his father and his brother, Duke Gregory, Athanasius suffered the relentless persecution of his ambitious nephew, the younger Duke Sergius, who held Athanasius and other relatives prisoner despite courageous protests of the clergy of both the Latin and the Greek rites. Sergius tried to force him to renounce his episcopacy and retire into a monastery, but, rescued by *Louis I the Pious, Athanasius came with honor to Benevento. Sergius's pillaging of Church property and the rebellion of the people against their bishop brought down upon the city of Naples the *excommunication of *Adrian II. From 867 to 872 Athanasius sought refuge with his brother Stephen, Bishop of Sorrento, and worked indefatigably for a lifting of the ban on Naples and a return to his see. To this end he traveled to Rome and approached the Emperor, who was then engaged in freeing southern Italy from Saracen incursions, but on the return trip he died at Veroli, near *Monte Cassino. He was 40 years old and had governed the Church of Naples for 22 years. First buried at Monte Cassino, his body was translated to Naples 5 years later by his nephew Bishop Athanasius II (d. 895) and interred at the church of San Gennaro. Later, probably during the 13th century, his relics were translated into the cathedral church, where they are venerated in Saint Savior's chapel.

Bibliography: ActSS July 4 (1867) 72–89. MGSrerLang 433–435, 439–452, 1065–76. F. BONNARD, DHGE 4:1388–90. A. P. FRUTAZ, EncCatt 2:263–264. BHL 1:734–739.

[P. L. HUG]

ATHEISM

An atheist is a man who lives without God. If he persists in this state for any length of time—say, for several years—atheism truly becomes his way of life. It is not possible to formulate a single, comprehensive definition of atheism that will cover all cases equally and adequately. The very term is analogical and the notion is realized in actual historical instances only with important variations. In view of this, the treatment here is divided into two parts, the first entitled the structure of atheism and discussing the analogy involved in atheism as a way of life and as an intellectual position; the second entitled the dynamics of atheism and discussing the problems of identifying atheists and their place in the history of human thought.

STRUCTURE OF ATHEISM

If atheism is a way of life, for some men at any rate, then it must also be a mental attitude, an intellectual position, for man lives by art and reason, as Aristotle noted. Yet atheism is more than an idea, far more than a set of ideas, however complex: by reason of its object, which is ultimately the meaning and purpose of life, atheism involves what is called a world outlook, a total view of life.

Atheism as a Way of Life. The man for whom atheism is a way of life may be found to (1) deny in fact, by the way he lives, the God in whom he professes to believe, or (2) believe, in spite of himself, in the God in whom he thinks he does not believe, or (3) deny, knowingly and in reality, the true God. These three types may, in J. Maritain's terminology, be designated respectively as (1) the practical atheist, (2) the pseudo-atheist, and (3) the absolute atheist.

Practical Atheism. The practical atheist is perhaps the most common and certainly the most curious, because he is not only unaware of his atheism but would almost infallibly deny it if it were called to his attention. For this type of atheism is his very style of life: it is as significant of his character and personality as any other single physical or mental trait. What is true of every atheist as such—that he lives without God—is verified in a striking manner of the practical atheist. Practical atheism evidently entails a set of moral standards, a code of ethics that flatly ignores the force of the precepts of the divine and natural moral law. A completely naturalistic moral code guides the practical atheist in his actions only to the extent that he finds in the code a ready justification. Every sinner lives without God, in a real sense, but the sinner may be acutely and even painfully aware of this terrible isolation. The practical atheist is neither conscious of, nor disturbed by, the absence of God from his life.

Pseudo-Atheism. The pseudo-atheist is willing to be called an atheist because he denies and repudiates the gods he knows other men worship. He knows of no other god, none he finds understandable or is willing to love and serve. Yet in his heart he yearns for the presence of the God of life; he may even—without realizing what he is actually doing—search for years, drawing ever closer to the Unknown God, while continuing to proclaim his unbelief in the ghosts and shadows other men take for God. Life must be lived without God, because God is nowhere to be found. At least He is unrecognizable in these absurd substitutes and surrogates that men falsely endow with His sacred name. The pseudo-atheist has never sufficiently known the true God, whereas the practical atheist has chosen to ignore his God and to eject Him effectively from his thoughts and his way of life. In his contacts with the practical atheist, the pseudo-atheist may be chagrined and scandalized by the contradiction between lip service to divinity and the flouting of standards of human decency.

Absolute Atheism. Radical and absolute atheism, that of a life from which God has been consciously and consistently excluded, is not only possible, it is actual, and in the present age more than in any other. For the absolute atheist the denial of God is the natural and indispensable corollary of the positive affirmation of himself, of humanity focused and concentrated in his own person as his solitary concern and ultimate end. The absolute atheist has much in common with the practical atheist, but the two types should not be confused. The practical atheist almost never thinks of God, and when he does, his thoughts are characteristically fleeting and vague, without personal impact. The absolute atheist, however, may think of God often, but only the more firmly and resolutely to shut him out of his life and to deepen his attachment to the values that have usurped the place of God. Militant atheists, in whom aversion for God has become a hatred, are recruited from the camp of absolute atheists.

Atheism as an Intellectual Position. As a philosophy, atheism is a view of the universe as a closed and self-contained system, existing and intelligible in and of itself. Theoretical atheism may be negative or positive, depending on whether or not there is a lack of sufficient reflection on the question of God.

Negative Atheism. The negative atheist is similar to what has been called the practical atheist in that neither gives any serious or prolonged thought to God. The practical atheist lives without reference to the God he has known and in whose supernatural revelation he may believe or have believed at one time. By definition, however, the negative atheist does not know God: his denial is the result of ignorance rather than of indifference. This ignorance may be complete, if the thought of God has never been entertained in any meaningful way, or it may be partial, if the atheist has heard about God but has not sufficiently reflected on all that is implied in the concept of God as Supreme Being.

Complete negative atheism involves a lack of any conscious or reflective knowledge of God as infinitely superior to man and requiring man's total obedience, love, and devotion. In itself atheism is not formally or intrinsically a kind of ignorance; it is a denial of God, but in the case of negative atheism the denial is the result, at least in part, of ignorance. There is no contradiction in this, for it is never a question of branding atheism as the mere absence of a knowledge of God. Complete negative atheism is conceivable, being a logical possibility; whether and in what way it is a fact is a question not easily resolved.

Negative atheism is partial when the ignorance that sustains it is relative and more or less under the domination of affective factors. The will settles the issue: the question of God is to be dismissed and man refuses to seek a rational solution to the problems of theology and religion. In general this type of atheism is skeptical and tinged with *agnosticism, *subjectivism, and *relativism. Far from being a revolutionist, the negative atheist is usually concerned only with living as comfortably as possible, with freedom to do exactly as he pleases. The idea of God, supreme law-giver and judge, is rejected as incompatible with the unfettered exercise of human freedom. Atheism thus lays waste the inner world of thought and striving and becomes an obsession that cannot be surrendered.

Positive Atheism. Positive atheism involves the rejection of the reality of God by one who has reflected sufficiently on the evidence of His existence. His denial of God becomes an affirmation and even the ground of all affirmation: an entirely original set of values and the positing of man's complete autonomy. The negation of God releases in one's innermost being the uninterrupted dialectic in which the denial must be constantly reaffirmed in face of recurrent doubt and faltering conviction. On this basis it is possible to distinguish various degrees of positive atheism and these may be described as, respectively, self-confident, uneasy, and uncritical.

The self-confident atheist is utterly convinced of the truth of his position, which rests chiefly on two arguments. The first of these is that there is no direct evidence of God, nor can His reality be inferred from anything in the world of experience. The universe is intelligible—so far as man has succeeded in deciphering it—without any need of positing a divine Being as first Cause, Creator, etc. The second argument is based on the presence of *evil in the world, especially in the form of the suffering of the innocent and the prosperity of the wicked. The atheist claims that evil makes the assertion of a good and provident God outrageous and perverse. The first argument supposes the capacity of the human mind to account for the data delivered by the senses within the limits of these same data, entirely and exclusively. The second line of reasoning, more popular and more emotionally charged, is put forth as the heart's refusal to recognize an all-wise and infinitely good God in the face of the world's frustration and sorrow.

Uneasy atheism is still a conscious, intellectual repudiation of God, but not unmixed with occasional doubts and perhaps fears. The predominant attitude is positive unbelief, pierced by the sharp point of a doubt too unsettling to ignore altogether, but not strong enough to penetrate deeply or leave an open wound. The atheist must then commit himself more resolutely than before to the rejection of *transcendence and the embracing of a radical *immanence, to reassure himself that the universe of experience is totally self-contained and self-explanatory. When confronted with theistic arguments of a Kantian or nominalist stamp, the atheist is able to reduce them to an illogical shambles and thereby stave off the attacks of doubt to which his own reasoning is increasingly liable.

The uncritical atheist hardly bothers to subject the theoretic foundations of atheism to serious thought or analysis. The price that must be paid for this intellectual carelessness is one of doubt and of confusion, neither of which can be suppressed because its real causes are not understood. In order to sustain his dogmatic denial of transcendence, the atheist brands mystery and belief in God as errors of the imagination, mistakes of what Hegel called man's "unhappy consciousness." For the uncritical atheist God is absent because His presence is unthinkable and unbearable, not because he has succeeded, through mature reflection, in refuting the evidence and the arguments for His existence.

Dynamics of Atheism

In order to identify precisely the type of atheism involved in a philosophical system, once the presence of atheism has been determined, it is necessary to examine the implications of the system's fundamental premises. Atheism as a full-blown phenomenon presupposes a sufficiently elaborated *theism: the atheist in the fullest sense should have at least some knowledge of the concept of the God whom he denies. The key to the recognition of atheism is the idea of, and the attitude toward, the divine order that may be discovered in a given historical context. Atheism, psychologically as well as logically, has no firm meaning apart from theism.

Identifying Atheists. Where God is denied or the divine reality is rejected, whatever the reason or the circumstances, there is atheism. It used to be said that men were horrified and ashamed to be branded as atheists. This may have been true at one time in the past, but for the past 200 years atheists have shown scant trace of embarrassment or indignation at the charge. The atheist label has sometimes been unjustly affixed out of spite or hatred, but still more often it has been attributed mistakenly, out of a misunderstanding of the nature of atheism or an erroneous judgment in a particular instance. In the ancient world *Anaxagoras, *Socrates, and *Plato were compelled undeservedly to endure the accusation of atheism, and in recent centuries the charge has been leveled against *Descartes, *Malebranche, *Locke, and *Kant, among others.

Related Positions. The theistic criterion will not of itself suffice to prevent the confusing of unorthodox and otherwise untenable beliefs and attitudes with authentic atheism. Other positions besides atheism fail to attain a clear and unambiguous concept of God as creator and lord of the universe, perfectly distinct from it, unique, all holy, the ultimate end of man. To the extent that these positions (agnosticism, polytheism, *pantheism, *deism) deviate from, or imperfectly sustain, the commitments of theism, they may be in danger of degenerating into something more or less akin to atheism. One of the serious difficulties of historical analysis is the commingling of several theoretical strains in a single given author or school of thought.

Principle of Discrimination. Theism represents the human mind's most successful effort, prescinding from the influx of grace, to formulate its knowledge of the Reality that surpasses all comprehension. As such, theism may serve as a measure against which every less adequate and every positively distorted attempt to conceptualize the Divine must be evaluated. It is thus the standard of reference in a historical survey of man's variously successful endeavors to deny God. If what are essentially contradictories may be regarded as extreme limits of a continuum, the atheist stands at the farthest opposite end from the theist. In more concrete terms, the extremes are believer and unbeliever: the one lives in the knowledge of God, whatever his moral shortcomings; the other rejects that knowledge. Theism is thus a maximum; strictly speaking, any falling away from the theistic position is in some degree a falling short of man's capacity for natural knowledge of God.

It is conceivable that a man may not have received, or may even have rejected, the gift of *faith and still preserve the essentials of theism. Theistic truth is eminently included in the higher wisdom of faith, in which it is immeasurably purified and elevated to a perfection to which reason unaided by grace could not attain. A lack of faith, even apostasy from the faith, does not, of itself, entail an unequivocal abandonment of theism. It is another question whether, without faith, a pure, uncontaminated theism can be attained or preserved by a given individual. The necessity of grace to avoid or overcome the attraction of atheism is also a problem, but outside the scope of the present article.

An unbeliever is an atheist insofar as he rejects God and lives without Him. By this same standard the heretic is not an atheist, nor is the man who, while lacking the Christian faith, acknowledges the existence of God as, in the words of the Vatican Council I, "Creator and Lord of heaven and earth." One's conception of the divine Being may be gross and vague, but as long as it is not positively distorted he may be a theist. All deformed positions, falling short of recognition of the Living God, are the counterparts of atheism, which simply denies Him.

Historical Survey. A logical and abstract analysis of the meaning of concepts and their inferential relations is by no means an exhaustive account of the problem of atheism. It must be completed by a more concrete determination of the forms that atheism has taken and the areas it has infected. After 4 or 5 centuries of intellectual confusion and religious defection, there are large gaps in man's philosophical and spiritual fiber that many have sought to fill with atheism of one sort or another. Atheism is more than a problem in historical terms; at a deeper level it is a mystery, one of the most disturbing manifestations of the mystery of evil. Statements of an atheistic character are traceable as far back as the pre-Socratic philosophers, while there are indications of at least a practical atheism in primitive tribes discovered by European explorers in Brazil in the 16th century. It was not until the 18th century, however, that explicit and energetic formulations of atheistic doctrine were attempted, as part of a general attack on Christianity and the sociocultural order with which it had become identified.

Greco-Roman Antiquity. If there were expressions of atheism in Greco-Roman antiquity, these were for the most part directed against the prevailing civic religions or the popular polytheistic superstitions of the masses. The earliest philosophers did not clearly distinguish matter and spirit, so that it is somewhat inappropriate to accuse them of a *materialism that would be incompatible with belief in divinity, in unequivocal terms. After Socrates it was not uncommon for philosophers, and especially poets, to be suspected of atheism and impiety, but this generally meant a skeptical or critical attitude toward the debased religious practices and fantastic myths on which the populace thrived. Alongside a proliferation of magical and superstitious creeds and rites, there actually developed among the Stoics a purer and more refined notion of a supreme Deity. Pantheism was prominent well into the imperial era of Rome, but there were some signs of a personal approach to a God who was regarded as benign and providential.

It seems clear that ancient proponents of atheism were more concerned with overthrowing moral principles and conventional ideas of right and wrong based on a belief in the gods than with denying absolutely the reality of the divine. The Epicureans in particular, who are most commonly regarded as atheists, did not reject the gods as nonexistent, but taught that men should not fear them and that moral standards must be derived from considerations of human welfare and happiness and not from the alleged decrees of divine beings. Lucretius' *De rerum natura* may be atheistic in tone and inspiration, but it was intended to be primarily a treatise of a new, radically immanentist humanism. The note struck at this early date, many centuries later signaled the arrival of an unabashed atheism, the sweeping away of every vestige of belief in an order not imposed or controlled by and for man himself.

Sources of Modern Atheism. The traces of atheism in the Middle Ages are too faint and uncertain to merit consideration; it may be noted that as early as the 13th century forces of irreligion were in evidence in the intellectual as well as in the political and social orders. When atheism made its unequivocal appearance, it had behind it several centuries of a falling away from the Christian faith and the gradual construction of a way of life from which religion was increasingly excluded. The 16th century witnessed for the first time in the history of Christendom men who openly professed contempt for the faith of Jesus Christ and still maintained positions of public respect and trust, at least in some parts of Europe. Contemporary documents, including citizens' petitions and reports of official commissions, indicate that the 17th century saw the diffusion of anti-Christian ideas and irreligious movements and societies in England, France, the territories of Spain, and Italy. It was not until the 19th century that atheism managed to capture the allegiance of leaders in public life as well as in the arts and sciences. For this full-blown atheism the way was cleared in three stages: (1) libertinism or freethinking, in the 17th century; (2) deistic and anti-Christian naturalism, in the 18th century; and (3) materialistic scientism, after 1750 and well into the 19th century.

The self-styled *freethinkers or *libertins* appeared first in France, hard upon a period of ideological strife and chaos that covered the closing decades of the 16th century with a pall of *skepticism. There was a concrete effort to "liberate" reason from faith and morals from the influence of religion. In England the freethinkers were even more outspoken and published numerous works calculated to undermine Christian belief and to substitute for it a cult of humanity and a thoroughly laicized social order. Throughout the 18th century, atheism attracted adherents and fervent supporters among the *philosophes* and advocates of revolutionary upheaval, as well as the champions of a materialistic view of man and of the universe. The French *encyclopedists counted several atheists in their number; but in some instances it is not easy to distinguish outright atheism from other positions, ranging from virulent rejection of the supernatural to pantheism, deism, and agnosticism. The 18th century closed with Kant's massive attack on metaphysics and the power of natural reason to attain an objective and certain knowledge of God. Concomitant with this, there developed a heightened sensitivity to the misery and suffering of mankind and a corresponding desire for man to find, by his own efforts and here in this life, satisfaction of all his needs and an existence free of all pain and want.

Modern Atheists. At the head of the 19th century stands the figure of G. W. F. *Hegel, towering over an era and casting before him a shadow from which many even at the present time have not escaped. To his intellectual posterity Hegel bequeathed a vision of human history caught in the snares of an impersonal *Absolute that would subsequently be misapprehended as the Living God of Christianity. The vision was intolerable, and, to some, atheism seemed the only viable alternative. They were trapped in this impasse by their isolation from a genuine, theistic metaphysics and their rejection of Christian faith. Henceforth atheism was embraced as the only way to preserve the rights and liberties of man: enlightenment had to be godless, in opposition to the forces of reaction and ignorance in league with the old religion. (*See* HEGELIANISM AND NEO-HEGELIANISM.)

In the mid-19th century Karl *Marx declared religion to be the opium of the people, and proposed atheism as the cornerstone of a brave new edifice of humanity transformed by total revolution. His was a war cry, in the name of the downtrodden proletariat, against belief in a God who provides for His creatures and in behalf of a new order in which man alone would provide for himself (*see* MATERIALISM, DIALECTICAL AND HISTORICAL).

Marx's atheism was scientistic, at least in part, and materialistic; Nietzsche's was lyrical and romantic, a paean of praise of the superman of the future. F. W. *Nietzsche lashed out against the "slave morality" of Christianity and exhorted whoever could to go beyond the distinction between good and evil and to decide his own future for himself in complete autonomy. Nietzsche left to the 20th century the twofold boast that God is dead and that hereafter man is completely free; for him, the possibilities for human achievement were unlimited.

Both scientistic and romantic atheism continue in the 20th century, but a new and profoundly disturbing voice is heard in the camp of the godless. J. P. Sartre is representative of a new brand of atheism that is deeply skeptical and pessimistic and at times collapses into sheer *nihilism. Existentialist atheism agrees that God is dead, but doubts seriously that this liberates man in any sense other than that of leaving him alone and overwhelmed in an absurd universe filled with peril and dread (*see* EXISTENTIALISM).

Critique. Atheism stands refuted both by reason and by the witness of the faith of Christ: human reason is doubly assured that God is not dead but lives eternally, but the work of metaphysical theism and basic apologetics lies outside the province of this article. Arguments that meet the difficulties of atheists will center on an analysis of reality as man experiences it, compounded of potency and act, contingent, and in flux, and also on evil as it is found, especially in the areas of human wickedness and suffering.

See also GOD; GOD, PROOFS FOR THE EXISTENCE OF; GOD AND MODERN SCIENCE; HUMANISM, SECULAR; ATHEISTIC ORGANIZATIONS; EVIL.

Bibliography: C. TOUSSAINT, DTC 1.2:2190–2210. M. SCHULIEN, EncCatt 2:265–284. E. BORNE, *Atheism,* tr. S. J. TESTER (New York 1961). H. DE LUBAC, *The Drama of Atheist Humanism,* tr. E. M. RILEY (New York 1949). I. LEPP, *Atheism in Our Time,* tr. B. MURCHLAND (New York 1963). J. MARITAIN, *The Range of Reason* (New York 1952) 103–117. J. D. COLLINS, *God in Modern Philosophy* (Chicago 1959). A. J. FESTUGIÈRE, *Epicurus and His Gods,* tr. C. W. CHILTON (Cambridge, Mass. 1956).

[J. P. REID]

ATHEISTIC ORGANIZATIONS

Associations for the purpose of: promoting godless tenets; eliminating governmental support for, or toleration of, religious activities; providing legal aid in cases of religious discrimination and minority rights.

Atheistic organizations accept the assumption of modern atheism that full liberty of man of necessity implies denial of God: atheism alone is the direct and concrete affirmation of humanity by man. Since belief in God is alleged to limit, destroy, or invert man's development in the temporal sphere, these organizations are also antitheistic. Organized state atheism is antireligious; e.g., the Soviet Constitution (art. 124) provides for "freedom of antireligious propaganda," which in context has turned out to mean strong antireligious pressure from the government. Organized religion becomes professedly a threat to established public order for these groups.

Combining theory and practice, atheistic organizations in the U.S. perpetuate the doctrines of such alleged atheists as Thomas Paine, Voltaire, and R. Ingersoll and frequently initiate court cases involving civil liberties and social religious traditions. The American Association for the Advancement of Atheism (founded 1925 in New York) proposes the following manifesto: (1) matter constitutes the reality of the universe; (2) all ideas come only from experience, from which man can form no conception of God; (3) organisms have evolved mechanically through natural selection; (4) no beneficent, omnipotent being offers provident care of man; (5) happiness of this life alone should be the motive of conduct. Its practical demands, as well as those of related associations [e.g., Freethinkers of America (1925), National Liberal League (1946), American Secular Union and Free Thought Federation (1876)], emphasize separation of Church and State by advocating repeal of all laws that restrict rights of atheists and that enforce Christian morals and practices (e.g., oaths in courts of law and at inaugurations; chaplains on public payroll; recognition of religious marriage ceremonies; teaching of religion in public schools).

In extolling the philosophy of Paine, Voltaire, and Ingersoll, these societies perpetuate attitudes that challenged the Judeo-Christian traditions in the U.S. Deists rather than atheists, Paine and Voltaire attempted to rid society of established religion that tended to encourage superstitious practices and clerical abuses, and to establish political freedom through a democracy that would guarantee behavior based on one's own convictions. Although Voltaire was militantly anti-atheistic, his rationalistic principles logically concluded in the scientific atheism of P. H. d'Holbach and Diderot. Paine's anti-Christian polemic (i.e., the word of God is not to be found in any written or spoken expression—namely, supernatural revelation—but in the creation itself) was developed in order to combat atheism. Deism, the religion of Nature—not Christianity—would supplant ascendant atheism. R. Ingersoll, on the contrary, was so impressed with the universe ("substance") that he held it to be eternal. Revealed truth, omnipotent person, supernatural activity, eternal life are all superstitions. Even the positivist theory of Auguste Comte did not satisfy Ingersoll, in spite of his declaration that the agnostic and the positivist "have the same end in view—both believe in living for this world." The anti-Christian enthusiasm of Paine, the acerbic denunciations of Voltaire, and the penetrating questions of Ingersoll still provide atheistic organizations with material for development.

In 1965 Pope Paul VI created the Secretariate for Relations with Non-Believers to coordinate cultural, spiritual, and pastoral efforts for understanding the phenomenon of atheism based on scientific research in its historical-doctrinal, sociological (cultural), and psychological perspectives. With social and political moves toward atheists beyond its scope, the secretariate will, nonetheless, investigate the types of atheism—practical atheism (e.g., moral evil and godlessness of action), doctrinal atheism (e.g., Marxism), and state-supported atheism (e.g., communism). Although the large number of variations of atheism preclude initiating a dialogue, the facilities of the secretariate provide the means of contact with atheists that may ultimately lead to dialogue with the Church [cf. *Ecclesiam suam* 99–106; ActApS 46 (1964) 650–654]. Its objective is not polemic but peaceful; its end is to contribute to the intellectual peace of the world.

See also ATHEISM; DEISM; NON-BELIEVERS, SECRETARIATE FOR.

Bibliography: *The Works of Robert G. Ingersoll,* ed. C. P. FARRELL, 12 v. (New York 1900). Gale Research Co., *Encyclopedia of Associations* (4th ed. Detroit 1964–) v.1 *National Organizations of the U.S.*

[T. F. MC MAHON; A. J. SHANLEY]

ATHELNEY, ABBEY OF, former Benedictine monastery established by King *Alfred in 888, on an island site amid marshes in the county of Somerset and in the ancient Diocese of *Bath and Wells, England. The original foundation, made by foreign monks under John the Scot, was a failure. It was refounded *c.* 960 with a Saxon community under the *Benedictine rule. There were insufficient resources for great development and the house was little more than a satellite of *Glastonbury. The monks were few and poor, but content with their poverty and solitude. The church, dedicated to SS. Peter and Paul, rested on piles and was built on the round continental plan. It was rebuilt in 1321. The abbey was dissolved in 1539 when the abbot and six monks were pensioned. Chancellor Audley sold the buildings.

Bibliography: Somerset Record Society, *Two Cartularies of the Benedictine Abbeys of Muchelney and Athelney in the County of Somerset,* ed. E. H. BATES (London 1899). *The Victoria History of the County of Somerset,* ed. W. PAGE (London 1906–) v. 2. Knowles MOE. Knowles-Hadcock.

[F. R. JOHNSTON]

ATHENAGORAS

Apologist of the 2d century and perhaps a native of Athens. By the report of *Philip Sidetes (who is here probably reliable) he was founder of a Christian philosophical school at Alexandria, in which he was followed by Pantaenus and Clement. Between 176 and 180 he wrote an *Embassy for the Christians* for presentation, either real or imaginary, to Marcus Aurelius, and he followed it with a treatise on *Resurrection of the Dead.* Before his conversion to the Christian faith he was a Platonist, and he used Plato's strictures on the ancient poets for their immoral tales about the gods with great effect in his attack on paganism. The wealth of detail that Athenagoras supplied concerning pagan worship makes him a principal source for knowledge of ancient Greek cults and for the sculpture and painting that was used to adorn them. He defended Christians against the three charges of atheism, cannibalism, and promiscuity, which, originally coupled in classical anti-Semitism for use against the Jews, had already been by the 2d century transferred to the Christians. In answering the first charge he had to show that the doctrine of the Trinity does not involve Christians in polytheism, and thus he became one of the first Christian writers to philosophize about the Trinity. Athenagoras explained the prodigies claimed by pagan cults as the work of the devil. Christians are not atheists, even though they do not take part in the civic sacrifices of paganism, for they raise holy hands to God, bringing forth a bloodless sacrifice. In reply to the third charge, Athenagoras set out contemporary Christian teaching on sexual morality in these words: "The begetting of children is the limit of our indulging our passions." He has been accused of having favored *Montanism in his dislike of second marriages, but this seems to result from his literal interpretation of what Scripture says about the unity of the flesh. He may also have been influenced by Stoic ideas.

To answer the charge of cannibalism, Athenagoras appealed to the fact that Christians were not allowed to be present at public shows involving loss of human lives; hence they could certainly not be guilty of eating human flesh. Furthermore, Christians had their own slaves, and these had never accused their masters; he was thus the first author to advert to the widespread ownership of slaves by Christians. In concluding his *Embassy* Athenagoras hinted at the need for an exposition of his next topic, the *Resurrection of the Dead*.

The two works have survived in a single manuscript; and though the second work is in slightly more formal language, since it is a public lecture, there is no reason for assigning the two works to different authors. To clear away difficulties from his theme of resurrection Athenagoras undertook to show that God does not lack the knowledge or the power to bring about a resurrection of the dead, nor is He unwilling to effect it. He faced the objection based on the fact of cannibalism and utilizes considerable detail of physiological argument to refute it. His positive exposition starts from God's purpose in creating; not for His own need but to image forth His own likeness for all eternity. Athenagoras parted company with Plato when he came to the argument from the nature of man. This he called a natural compounding of body and soul, not an imprisoning of soul in matter. Sleep and death are interruptions in man's completeness of living; but interruption does not imply permanent dissolution. He also abandoned the threefold Platonic division of the nature of man in favor of a twofold, for which he provided a new term of his own. He brought in the argument from the need for rewards and penalties for both body and soul in a life after death, but did not regard it as a equal value with his more philosophical reasons.

The quality of the work of Athenagoras is higher than that of the other 2d-century apologists. He was better versed in Greek philosophy, and more moderate in tone, and he tried to find new technical terms in which to express the concepts of his faith. Without him, Clement of Alexandria would not have been able to write what he did.

Bibliography: ATHENAGORAS, *Libellus pro christianis* and *Oratio de resurrectione cadaverum*, ed. E. SCHWARTZ (TU 4.2; 1891), Gr.; Eng. tr. J. H. CREHAN, ed. and tr., AncChrWr 23 (1956); *Zwei griechische Apologeten*, ed. J. GEFFCKEN (Leipzig 1907), Eng. tr. C. C. RICHARDSON in *Early Christian Fathers*, ed. and tr. C. C. RICHARDSON et al. (Philadelphia 1953) 290–340. Quasten Patr 1:229–236. Altaner 130–131. H. H. LUCKS, *The Philosophy of Athenagoras* (Washington 1936). R. M. GRANT, HarvThRev 47 (1954) 121–129. P. KESELING, ReallexAntChr 1:881–888.

[J. H. CREHAN]

ATHENS

The most important cultural center of ancient Greece, with access to the Aegean Sea through the port of Piraeus. In the late Roman Empire it retained academic importance until Justinian closed its pagan schools of philosophy (529). Byzantine Athens was overshadowed in all ways by Constantinople. Some commercial importance was regained under Latin rule (Franks 1204–1311, Catalans 1311–88, and the Florentine Acciaiuoli 1388–1456). It declined under Turkish rule (1456–1833), when exploding magazines ruined the Propylaea (1645) and the Parthenon (1687). As capital of the Kingdom of Greece, its importance has again increased.

Apostolic Times. A detailed, though confused, description of Athens in the 1st century A.D. was given by Pausanias a century later. Very probably Paul entered the city by the gate of Piraeus and walked by the road leading to the agora. It was on this road that the altar to the Unknown God (*see* AGNOSTOS THEOS) and the innumerable shrines and statues that attracted Paul's attention were erected (Acts 17.16–17, 22–23). He passed by the Ceramicus, a burial ground, and entered the agora close by the Acropolis. Here, where philosophers once discussed and perorated, where sellers had booths for the sale of the world's merchandise, and idle Athenians came to spend their leisure and pick up the latest news (Acts 17.21), Paul disputed every day with the Epicurean and Stoic philosophers (Acts 17.18).

Christianity was thus brought to Athens by Paul during his second missionary journey. Compelled to leave *Philippi, he came to *Thessalonica, whence again he had to flee to Beroea and finally to Athens (Acts 16.34–17.15). Paul's ministry in Athens yielded scanty results. Although no persecution is recorded, only a few accepted the Christian faith, among whom were a woman called Damaris and Dionysius, a member of the *Areopagus, who is mentioned by Dionysius of Corinth as the first bishop of Athens.

The Church in Athens was never prominent, although it boasts some famous names. Dionysius mentions Bishop Quadratus as the successor of Publius. The apologist Aristides came from Athens, as did Athenagoras, who defended Christianity in a letter to Marcus Aurelius. Clement of Alexandria probably came from Athens. There were several Athenian martyrs. Among the signatories of the Council of Nicaea was Bp. Pistus of Athens.

Bibliography: EncDictBibl 166–167. Pauly-Wiss RE Suppl 1: 159–219. A. W. GOMME, OxClDict 114–116. G. HOFMANN, Enc Catt 2:287–299. G. STADTMÜLLER and H. PAULUS, LexThK² 1:993–995. I. C. T. HILL, *The Ancient City of Athens: Its Topography and Monuments* (Cambridge, Mass. 1953). R. JANIN, DHGE 5:15–42.

[P. P. SAYDON]

Medieval Period. SS. *Basil and *Gregory of Nazianzus studied in a pagan Athens. Christianity competed successfully with paganism only after the decree of *Theodosius II making temples Christian (426) and after Justinian's decree (529). In 421 Theodosius failed to attach *Illyricum Oriens* (Thessalonica), of which Athens was part, to the Patriarchate of *Constantinople; but during the Iconoclast controversy under Emperor *Leo III the area was detached from the Patriarchate of Rome *c.* 733, after an abortive attempt by an Athenian to become emperor (727). Athens, the home of Empress *Irene (797–802), remained iconodule. By 810 Athens was a Greek metropolitanate, whose prelates took part in the controversy over *Photius; in the 10th century it had 10 suffragans. Archbishop Michael I Syncellus (d. 1030) was a canonist; Leo I Syncellus (d. 1069) supported *Michael Cerularius. Prelates of the 12th century were distinguished, especially the zealous and learned Michael III Choniates (1182–1204, d. *c.* 1220), whom the Latins replaced in 1204. *Constans II

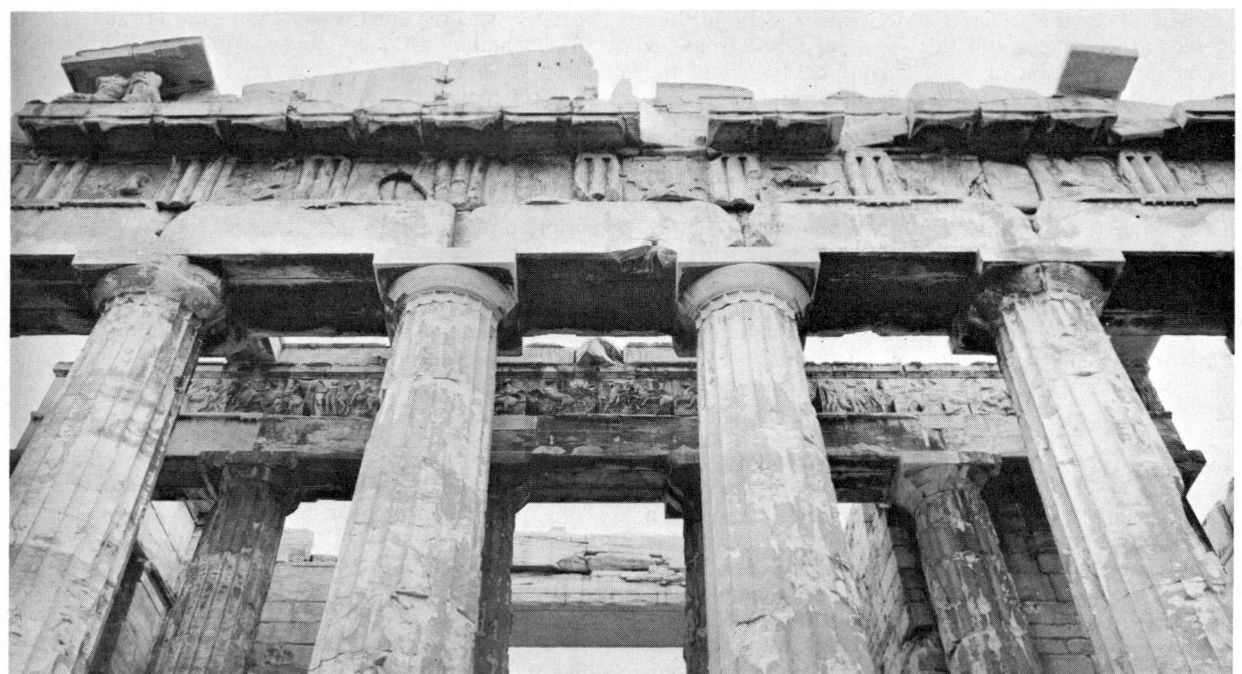

Fig. 1. Detail of the western entrance of the Parthenon, built 448 to 432 B.C., on the Acropolis at Athens.

ATHENS

Fig. 2. The church at Daphni, near Athens.

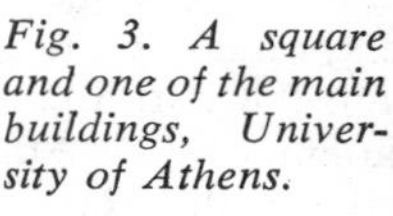

Fig. 3. A square and one of the main buildings, University of Athens.

wintered in Athens (662) on his way to the West, and *Basil II gave thanks in the Parthenon for his victory over the Bulgars (1019). Many churches were built in the city (900–1200).

Latin crusaders pillaged churches and monasteries, despite the protection of Innocent III; and a Latin archbishop (with 11 suffragan bishops) and clergy under papal supervision were installed in the Parthenon (1206) under the ecclesiastical constitution of *Paris. The lower clergy and people, however, continued in the Greek rite. Abandoned Greek monasteries were taken over by the Latins, especially Cistercians, who were replaced by Franciscans *c.* 1250. Cistercians continued in the monastery of Daphni (founded probably in the 5th century and restored in the 11th) from 1208 until the Turkish conquest (1456). Relations between Latin and Greek clergy were not good, especially after the Byzantine Empire was restored (1261). Peter IV's extension of the ecclesiastical privileges of Aragon and Catalonia to Latin and Greek clergy of Athens was authorized in one of the last documents pertaining to the Latin Church there. The last medieval Latin archbishop, Nicholas Protimus, died in 1482; and the see became a titular bishopric until 1875. Capuchins worked in Athens from 1665 to end the schism.

After 1204 Constantinople named titular Greek metropolitans to the See of Athens, usually the metropolitans of other Greek sees. In 1387 the Florentine Acciaiuoli allowed the Greek metropolitan Dorotheos (1371–93) to return to Athens beside the Latin archbishop, but Dorotheos called in the Turks. Venice drove them out, but Florence used Turkish aid to regain the city (1402), recognizing it as a Turkish fief after 1435. Dorotheos's successor, Macarius, was imprisoned in Venice (1395–1405) for conspiring with the Turks. The union of the Council of *Florence (1438) was promulgated in Athens, which had a unionist metropolitan.

Modern History. The Turks, few in number, made mosques of all the churches but one; but in the 17th century there were, according to travelers, 52 Greek Orthodox parish churches in Athens and some 100 in the outskirts. The metropolitans, with civil and ecclesiastical authority, were national representatives of the Greeks. Few of the more than 30 under Turkish rule continued long in office because of the large sums that had to be paid to the patriarch of Constantinople and to the Turks, leaving the metropolitanate constantly in debt. Several metropolitans of Athens became patriarchs of Constantinople, and Athens provided a patriarch of Alexandria *c.* 1500 and two patriarchs of Jerusalem (1737–71). Most of the monasteries of 1456 continued under the Turks, responsible directly to the patriarch of Constantinople, and some new ones were founded. Regilla Venizelos, who founded the convent of St. Andrew with a school for girls, was beaten to death by Turks for saving four girls from Islam (1589) and was venerated as a saint. Many monasteries disappeared in Turkish persecutions of the 18th century, especially that of the Vaivode Hasséki (1773–95). There was an intellectual decline under the Turks; but efforts in education continued, and Greek libraries were maintained, three perishing in the war of independence (1826).

After the rebellion of Greece (1821), the Orthodox national Church of Greece (10 sees) proclaimed its independence of the patriarch of Constantinople (1833). The first metropolitans, recognized by the patriarch in 1850, were liberal and Protestant-minded and became involved in domestic politics. After 1871 the government, which was expropriating religious property, came into conflict with the metropolitans, especially Germanos II Calligas (1889–96). His successor, Procopius II Economides, who had studied theology in Moscow, Geneva, and Heidelberg and taught at the University of Athens, had to resign (1901) because of approval given to a vernacular translation of the New Testament. Under Chrysostomos *Papadopoulos (1923–38) the regulations of 1852 were replaced by a constitution more in accord with Canon Law, whereby the Church of Greece is governed by a holy synod of 13 bishops, and an assembly of bishops that meets every 3 years. Apart from Rhizarios seminary (1844), there is a faculty of Orthodox theology at the University of Athens.

University of Athens. The state university, founded in 1837 by the Catholic King Otto of Bavaria, has faculties of Orthodox theology, law, philosophy, medicine, and physics-mathematics; buildings were erected (1839–57). Since the University of Thessalonica opened (1925), enrollment has declined. About one-seventh of some 750 students of theology (1955–56) are women, who go on to teach religion in schools. The importance of the Faculty of Theology, almost all of whom have studied in German universities, extends to all the Orthodox Church. Noteworthy professors include Christos Androutsos (1911–35), Grigorios Papamichail (1918–56), Dimitrios Balanos (1923–48), Hamilkar Alivisatos (1919–), and Panagiotis Bratsiotis (1925–).

Modern Archdiocese (Atheniensis). The Latin Archdiocese of Athens is an archbishopric without suffragans, restored in 1875. With the Vicariate Apostolic of Thessalonica (created in 1926) it comprises the Latin hierarchy of continental *Greece. In 1962 it had 12 parishes, 13 secular and 27 religious priests, 41 men in nine religious houses, 83 women in seven convents, 4,360 pupils in 10 schools, and 26,000 Catholics (mostly foreigners or persons of foreign descent) in a population of 4 million; it is 15,444 square miles in area. Thessalonica, 11,583 square miles in area, had 2,100 Catholics in a population of 2 million.

Bibliography: F. A. GREGOROVIUS, *Geschichte der Stadt Athen im Mittelalter von der Zeit Justinians bis zur türkischen Eroberung,* 2 v. (3d ed. Stuttgart 1889; repr. Basel 1962). S. M. SOPHOCLES, *A History of Greece* (Thessalonica 1961); *The Religion of Modern Greece* (Thessalonica 1961). D. SICILIANOS, *Old and New Athens,* tr. R. LIDDELL (New York 1960). H. LECLERCQ, DACL 1.2:3039–3104. G. MOCKEL, RGG[3] 1:678–679. AnnPont (1965) 42. **Illustration credits:** Fig. 1, Alinari-Art Reference Bureau. Fig. 2, The National Tourist Organization of Greece, Athens. Fig. 3, Royal Greek Embassy Information Service, Washington, D.C.

[E. P. COLBERT]

ATHENS, UNIVERSITY OF. The Athenian schools in the early Christian period never formed a corporate university. However, from the time of the Antonine emperors (A.D. 86–180) there were imperial endowments for chairs in each of the four schools of philosophy, and one for Sophism. During the 2d- to 4th-century sophistic revival (*see* SECOND SOPHISTIC) several Christians came to Athens. *Clement of Alexandria may have received an Athenian education; *Basil of Caesarea and *Gregory of Nazianzus studied rhetoric there (A.D. 351–357); and *Diodore of Tarsus imbibed the wisdom of Athens. When *Synesius of Cyrene visited the city, the schools were dormant, for the Goths had overrun the city's outer precincts in 396. The founding of the Neoplatonic school by Plutarch of Athens (*c.* 400) made the city again a famous center. *Boethius studied the systematic curriculum of this school (*c.* 500). Striking evidence of the later school's influence on a Christian appears in the works of *Pseudo-Dionysius the Areopagite. An edict of *Justinian I forbidding the "teaching of philosophy and interpretation of law at Athens" caused the Athenian schools to close in A.D. 529.

Bibliography: J. W. H. WALDEN, *The Universities of Ancient Greece* (New York 1909). T. WHITTAKER, *The Neo-Platonists* (2d ed. Cambridge, Eng. 1928). F. SCHEMMEL, "Die Hochschule von Athens im IV. und V. Jahrhundert," *Neue Jahrbücher für Pädagogik* 22 (1908) 494–513. L. G. WESTERINK, ed. and tr., *Anonymous Prolegomena to Platonic Philosophy* (Amsterdam 1962) xxv–xli, curriculum. E. ÉVRARD, "Le Maitre de Plutarque d'Athènes et les origines du néoplatonisme athénien," *L'Antiquité classique* 29 (1960) 108–133, 391–406. H. D. SAFFREY, RevÉtGr 67 (1954) 396–410, curriculum. F. FUCHS, *Die höheren Schulen von Konstantinopel im Mittelalter* (Leipzig 1926).

[R. F. HATHAWAY]

ATHOS, MOUNT

The outside promontory of the three-pronged peninsula in northern Greece called Chalcidice. It extends about 35 miles into the Aegean Sea and is named after a pyramidlike peak that rises to 6,760 feet. It is unique in being a theocratic republic whose main inhabitants are Orthodox monks, living under the suzerainty of Greece but allowed a certain amount of autonomous rule.

History. Before the advent of Christian monks the site contained several cities dating from pre-Christian antiquity. Legend places a sanctuary of Zeus or Jupiter on the peninsula. Even today the traces can be seen of the canal, 3,950 feet long, that Xerxes constructed on the isthmus in his attempt to invade Greece in 480 B.C. without having to undergo the dangers of rounding the cape of the peninsula.

Although there were individual hermits inhabiting the Holy Mountain earlier, the first documentary records of Christian hermitages are from the 9th century when fugitives from the persecutions of *Iconoclasm increased the hermit population. Organized monastic life began there in 963, when St. *Athanasius the Athonite built the first cenobitic monastery, known as the Great Lavra. His Rule derived chiefly from that of St. *Basil the Great and St. *Theodore the Studite. Despite opposition to the innovations of organized community monasticism on Mount Athos, and with the support of the Byzantine Emperors *Nicephorus Phocas and *John I Tzimisces, the Rule of St. Athanasius was accepted as a model; cenobitic life was imposed upon the hermits and Athanasius became the abbot, ruling 58 monasteries.

Fig. 1. Dionysiou Monastery on Mount Athos.

Under the constitution approved by the Emperor *Constantine Monomachus, the famous law excluding women and female animals from the holy mount was enacted in 1045. In the 11th century other Christian nations began to send representatives to Mount Athos, and princes of the Balkan peninsula and of the northern Slav countries (especially Russia) endowed monasteries, thus making the peninsula pan-Orthodox in its representation. Even after the Eastern Schism (*c.* 1054), Benedictine monks of Amalfi, Italy, maintained a Catholic monastery there.

The monks turned to Pope *Innocent III for protection against the Latin Crusaders and Catalan invaders in the 13th century; but when the Turks captured Salonica in 1430, the monks broke off all contact with Rome and submitted to their Turkish rulers.

Government and Monasteries. Today Mount Athos exists as a republic under the Greek government, but enjoys self-rule, which is centered in the holy *Koinotis* (central governing body) made up of 20 members chosen from the 20 large monasteries that have the sole voting power. From these 20 members, a committee of 4 called the *epistatae* is chosen to form the executive branch. A president elected for 1 year presides over the sessions, which are held in the capital of Karyes, the seat of government since the 10th century. Of the 20 monasteries with voting power, 17 are Greek, 1 Bulgarian, 1 Russian, and 1 Serbian; these are: the Great Lavra (the oldest), Vatopedi, St. Panteleimon (Russian), Hilandari (Serbian), Xeropotamou, Xenophontos, Docheiariou, Kastamonitou, Zographou (Bulgarian), Esphigmenou, Pantokratoros, Iviron, Koutlomousiou, Philotheou, Karakallou, St. Paul's, Dionysiou, Gregoriou, Simopetra, and Stavroniketa (the last built, in 1545). Today nine of these follow the cenobitic rule. They give a great degree of obedience to an abbot (*higoumenos*) chosen for life, perform all liturgical services in common, and submit to a stricter discipline in regard to food and property. The other 11, called idiorrhythmic, allow the individual monk to set his own pace (literally, one's own rhythm). The larger and more wealthy monasteries are idiorrhythmic. This type of loose rule is said to occasion abuses and a slackening in religious fervor.

Besides the 20 main monasteries, there are others, called sketes, some of which are even larger than the 20 main monasteries. These sketes, or clusters of ascetics living together, are also divided into the cenobitic and idiorrhythmic types. The cenobitic sketes differ externally from the main cenobitic monasteries, only in that rather than an abbot, a superior (*dikaios*) rules and is subject to the abbot of the main monastery to which the skete belongs. The idorrhythmic sketes are groups of small huts with three of four monks living together in each hut. In the midst of these clusters of huts there is the central church (*kyriakon*), so called because the monks come to common liturgical services only on Sunday, the day of the Lord (*Kyrios*). An elder rules the hut or hermitage, while the whole group of huts comes under the rule of a superior chosen by the main mon-

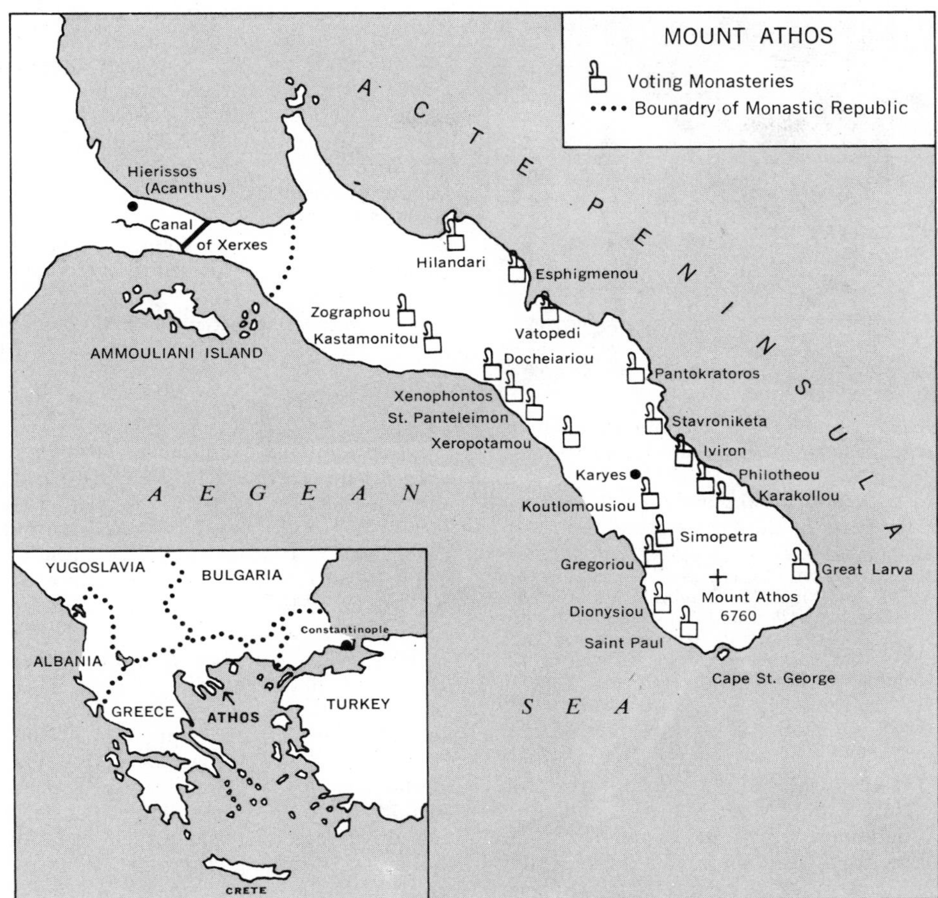

Fig. 2. Mount Athos, showing the principal foundations of the monastic community.

astery to which the skete is attached. Observance in the idiorrhythmic skete, unlike the idiorrhythmic life in the main monasteries, is usually conducive to strict discipline and fervor in religious life.

Scattered throughout the rugged terrain of Mount Athos there are independent hermitages, called *kalyves.* The hermits who inhabit the southernmost tip of the peninsula (called *Karoulia* meaning pulleys), live one to a hut or in very small groups; each hermitage is independent and directly under one of the main monasteries. There are also *kellia,* separated houses ruled by an elder and dependent only upon the main monasteries, but in which the ascetical rule is not so austere as that practiced in the *kalyves.* Thus one finds a great deal of variety in monastic rule and observance, with much left to individual preference.

The peninsula has resisted the encroachment of modernization in avoiding electric lights, radios, newspapers, automobiles, and so forth. All the monasteries but two still use the Byzantine monastic measure of time; 12 o'clock is at sunset.

Architecture, Art, Libraries. Because of the ravages of time, earthquakes, plundering by pirates and the coming of Latin Crusaders, little of the architecture and art work dates back further than the 16th century; yet because of the utter conservatism, all that is found exactly reflects the Byzantine architecture and art of the 10th to 14th centuries. All the large monasteries follow an identical architectural plan and have fortified walls on the outside and on the inside a quadrangle, where the central church (*katholikon*) is found. The walls of the church and the numerous cupolas are frescoed; along with the art work of icons painted on wood, the metal work, and the *iconastasis,* the frescoes reflect very well the style of medieval Byzantine religious art.

Many of the libraries, such as those in the monasteries of St. Paul and Simopetra, have been destroyed by fire; some were ravaged by the Turks during the War of Greek Independence (1821–29); and others were depleted by the neglect or even the vandalism of monks. Many ancient manuscripts were sold to libraries and museums in Russia and France; but about 11,000 remain, dealing mostly with theological and ecclesiastical subjects. Since contemplation rather than intellectual culture has characterized the monks of Mount Athos, little research has been done on these manuscripts. There has been a steady movement to give the monks a better education, and aspirants now spend 5 years training at the Athonias school in Karyes before they are attached to a monastery.

Mount Athos is unique as the last outpost where Byzantine religious culture and the spirituality of *Hesychasm are preserved in modern times. Today a crisis in religious vocations threatens the effectiveness of these monks in the Orthodox world. Whereas there were over 9,000 monks (with Russians in the majority) before 1917, today there are only 1,580 monks on the

Fig. 3. Sixteenth-century mural, Vatopedi Monastery, Mount Athos; apocalyptic scene of martyrs, priests, prophets.

Holy Mountain, with 800 monks assigned to pastoral ministry in various parts of the Greek mainland.

Bibliography: *Le Millénaire du mont Athos, 963–1963,* 2 v. (Chevetogne, Belg. 1963–64) v.1. C. CAVARNOS, *Anchored in God* (Athens 1959). R. M. DAWKINS, *The Monks of Athos* (New York 1936). F. W. HASLUCK, *Athos and Its Monasteries* (New York 1924). S. LOCH, *Athos: The Holy Mountain* (New York 1959). P. MEYER, *Die Haupturkunden für die Geschichte der Athosklöster* (Leipzig 1894). **Illustration credit:** Figs. 1 and 3, R. V. Schoder, SJ.

[G. A. MALONEY]

ATIENZA, JUAN DE, Jesuit educator and collaborator with Toribio de *Mogrovejo; b. Valladolid or possibly Tordehumos, 1544; d. Lima, 1592. He studied Canon Law for 2 years and entered the Society of Jesus at Salamanca on May 1, 1564. He made his profession of three vows on Sept. 14, 1570, and of four vows on June 5, 1580. He was professor of philosophy in Avila, rector of San Ambrosio at Valladolid, and rector and master of novices at Villagarcía de Campos (Valladolid). In 1581 he went to Peru, where he founded the Colegio de San Martín in Lima and wrote its constitution. He was rector of the major seminary of San Pablo in Lima and participated in the third and fourth provincial councils of Lima. During his term as provincial, beginning in 1585, the society spread itself through Tucumán, the Chaco, and Paraguay. The Archbishop of Lima, Toribio de Mogrovejo, greatly esteemed him for his prudence and his knowledge of ecclesiastical law. Atienza was concerned during his term as provincial with two main questions of government: the internal discipline of the province, and the organization of the missions already established and expansion to new areas. Acting little for public acclaim, he concentrated on creating and directing significant works, guided by his knowledge and his experience of the South American situation.

Bibliography: A. ASTRAIN, *Historia de la Compañía de Jesús en la asistencia de España,* 7 v. (Madrid 1902–25).

[A. DE EGAÑA]

ATKINSON, MATTHEW (PAUL OF ST. FRANCIS), English Franciscan who was imprisoned for more than 30 years under the anti-Catholic penal laws of his time; b. Yorkshire, 1656; d. Hurst Castle, Hampshire, 1729. Father Paul, who had served for 12 years on the English mission and was at one time definitor of the English province of Franciscans, was betrayed to the authorities for £100. In 1698 he was condemned to life imprisonment for the offense of being a Catholic priest, and most of the long years of his incarceration were spent at the prison of Hurst Castle on the Solent. Gentle and amiable, he soon gained the trust and regard of his keeper, and was allowed for a time to walk outside the prison walls and to enter into friendly relations with many of the people of the area. Eventually, however, a complaint was made about his warder's leniency, and for the last 30 years of his life he voluntarily confined himself to the narrow limits of his cell to avoid causing difficulties for his keeper.

Bibliography: DictEngCath 1:84. J. COOPER, DNB 1:697.

[H. F. GRETSCH]

ATLANTA, ARCHDIOCESE OF (ATLANTENSIS)

Metropolitan see embracing 71 counties in the northern part of Georgia. The area was part of the Diocese of *Savannah (1850–1937), then Savannah-Atlanta (1937–56), and was established as an independent diocese July 2, 1956. Created an archdiocese Feb. 21, 1962, its suffragans included the Dioceses of Charleston, S.C., Miami, Fla., Raleigh, N.C., St. Augustine, Fla., Savannah, Ga., and the Abbatia Nullius of Belmont Abbey, N.C. Atlanta's first bishop was Francis E. Hyland, a native of Philadelphia, Pa., and auxiliary bishop of the Savannah-Atlanta diocese since 1949. In 1956 the Catholic population of the diocese numbered about 23,000 in a total population of 1,800,000. Catholicity in the area centered principally in the vicinity of the city of Atlanta, where in 1963, 12 of the archdiocese's 29 parishes were situated.

The first teaching sisters in Atlanta were the Sisters of Mercy who arrived in 1886 and were followed 6 years later by the Sisters of St. Joseph. The Dominican sisters maintain Our Lady of Perpetual Help Free Can-

The Cathedral of Christ the King, Atlanta.

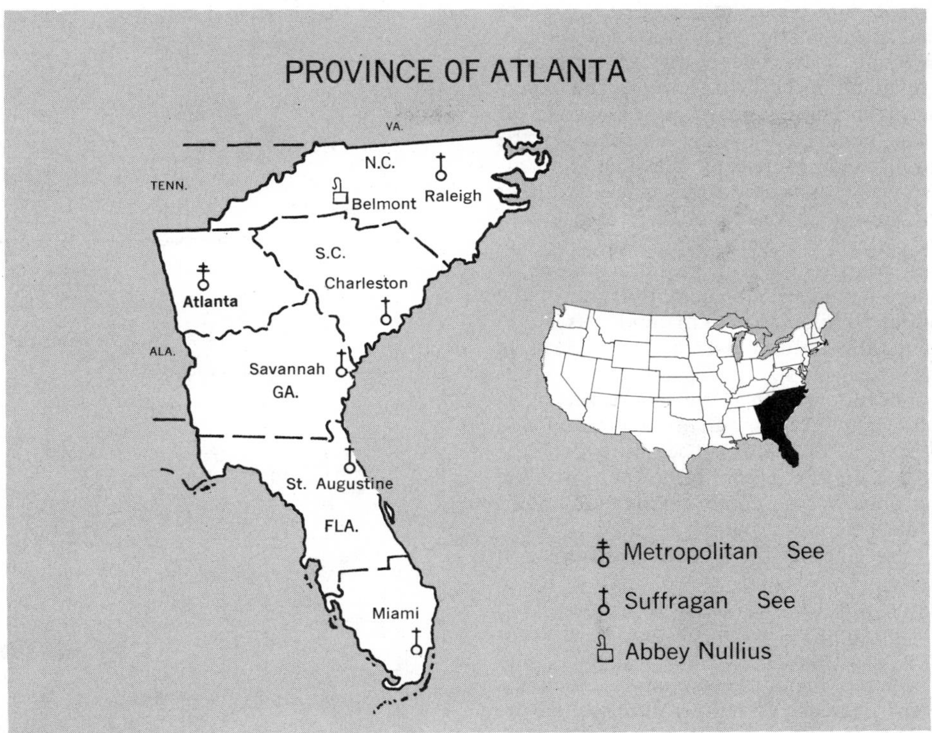

Province of Atlanta, comprising the Archdiocese of Atlanta, known as the metropolitan see, and six suffragans. The archbishop has metropolitan jurisdiction over the province.

cer Home in Atlanta. Marist School, operated by the Marist fathers, was for years the only Catholic high school for boys in Atlanta. Later St. Pius X (1958), St. Joseph's (1960), and Drexel (1962) were established as coeducational diocesan high schools. In 1944 the Trappist monks established the Abbey of Our Lady of the Holy Ghost near Atlanta at Conyers, Ga. Other religious communities of men serving in the diocese include the Redemptorists, who staff missions in the northwestern part of the diocese, centering their activities in Dalton; the Franciscan fathers, who conduct the Catholic Students' Center at the University of Georgia, Athens, as well as the Diocesan Shrine of the Immaculate Conception, Atlanta; and the Jesuits, who have been active in Georgia for many years and in 1960 were in Augusta and Atlanta, conducting a retreat house in the latter city. Because of the lack of Catholic schools of higher learning, Newman Clubs operated at Agnes Scott College, Decatur; Emory University, Georgia Institute of Technology, and Oglethorpe University, all in Atlanta; Brenau College, Gainesville; and three state colleges. The Catholic Laymen's Association, founded in 1916, was active until about 1940 defending the faith by means of writings, distribution of literature, and participation in civic affairs. In the 1960s the association published the diocesan newspaper, the *Bulletin.* In addition to the well-established Councils of Catholic Women and the Confraternities of Christian Doctrine, such groups as the Catholic Youth Organization, Serra International, and Knights of Columbus were active in the archdiocese.

When Hyland resigned, Oct. 11, 1961, he was named titular bishop of Bisica and retired to St. Charles Seminary, Philadelphia. The following February, Atlanta was created an archdiocese and Bp. Paul J. Hallinan, of Charleston, S.C., was named first archbishop and installed in his see city, March 29, 1962. Although the industrialization of the diocese in the post-World War II years had attracted many Catholics, they still constituted only a small percentage in 1963, numbering about 43,340 in a total population of 2,204,635. They were served by 33 secular and 91 religious priests, including Passionists, Redemptorists, Franciscans, Jesuits, Marists, Glenmary Home Missioners, and Sacred Heart fathers. There were 33 brothers, and 204 sisters from 14 religious communities of women, helping to staff the institutions of the archdiocese, including 5 high schools, 19 elementary schools, 3 hospitals, and 1 orphanage.

Bibliography: J. J. O'Connell, *Catholicity in the Carolinas and Georgia 1820–1878* (New York 1879).

[A. PLAISANCE]

ATMOSPHERE, PHYSICS OF

The two broad subareas of atmospheric science are: (1) Meteorology—which deals with the atmosphere in a general manner, and particularly with the motion and weather systems. Emphasis in meteorology has traditionally been on the processes in the troposphere and the stratosphere. (2) Aeronomy—which deals with the atmosphere above the stratosphere including the mesosphere and the thermosphere and reaching out to the interplanetary medium. The direct influences of solar activity, cosmic rays and electron streams, are increasingly important at these high altitudes.

Progress of Concepts of the Atmosphere. The primary properties of the atmosphere are its density, temperature, pressure, composition, and motion. Motion was perhaps the first of these to be studied, through the use of wind vanes that gave the direction of the motion. Such vanes date from the time of the ancient Greeks, but the speed of the wind was not reliably measured until much later. The barometer and thermometer were invented in the 17th century. The expectation that the air pressure measures the weight of overlying air was confirmed by the decrease in the barometer reading with increasing altitude. The air temperature also was measured on mountains and later on balloons and kites, and was found to decrease with increasing height. At first it was thought that this decrease continued to the "top" of the atmosphere. If so, the atmosphere would have a limited height, of the order of only about 50 kilometers (km) and thus would form an aerial mantle around the earth of relatively small thickness.

This simple conception of the atmosphere was overthrown (*c.* 1900) when recording thermometers carried on kites found that the temperature ceases to decrease at a height of about 10 km. There, rather abruptly, the temperature was observed to remain relatively constant through some distance with increasing height. Convenient names were given to the level of this transition and to the regions below and above it. The lower region of changing weather was called the troposphere (*tropos,* turn); the upper region of nearly uniform temperature, the stratosphere (*stratus,* spread); and the boundary between them, the tropopause (*pausis,* end). The upward decrease of temperature, called the lapse rate, amounts to about 6°C per km in the troposphere.

Progress in the atmospheric sciences depends upon advances in the physical sciences and upon technological developments. The development of the electronic computer, high-level balloons, aircraft, rockets, satellites, tracer techniques, and a number of indirect means of probing the atmosphere make it possible, for the first time in history, to keep the whole atmosphere under constant surveillance and to process vast columns of data. It is now possible to formulate and solve fundamental problems concerning the motion of the atmosphere, to make realistic mathematical models of the atmosphere, and to estimate the rate at which these advances may lead to progress in weather forecasting and related services. Further, advances in physics and a better understanding of the atmospheric response to energy sources point toward the possibilities of modification and control of large-scale weather and climatic processes.

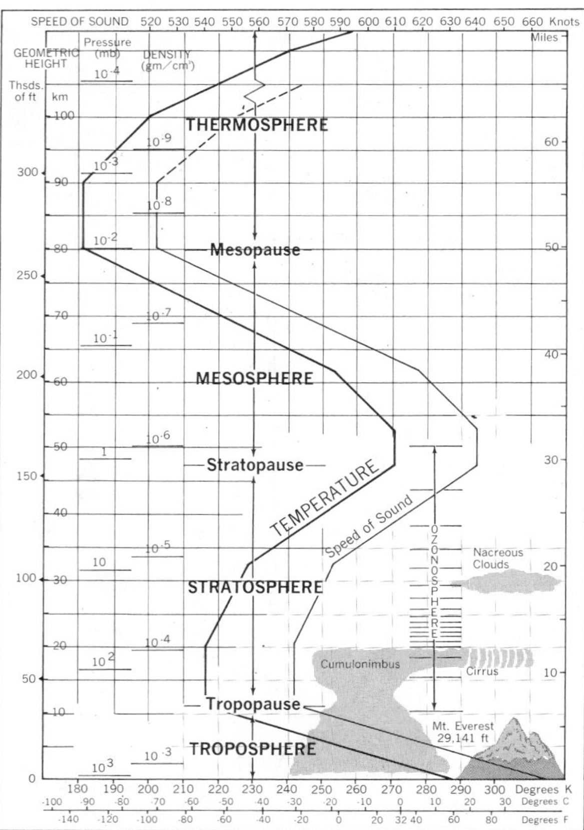

Variation of pressure, density, speed of sound, and temperature in the atmosphere as a function of altitude.

Composition. In a discussion of its composition, the atmosphere may be separated into two parts: homosphere, a region of substantially constant mean molecular weight extending to about 85 km above the earth's surface; and the heterosphere, a region of significantly varying composition above the homosphere, which extends indefinitely outward. The homosphere is essentially constant in composition and consists of the following principal substances, according to percentage: nitrogen 78, oxygen 20, argon 0.9, carbon dioxide 0.03, and water vapor 1.0. In addition, the homosphere contains very small amounts of neon, helium, krypton, xenon, hydrogen, methane, nitrous oxide, and ozone.

In the heterosphere, molecular oxygen and nitrogen dissociate into their monatomic forms due to photochemical action of the sun's ultraviolet radiation. Above 200 km, diffusive separation occurs—a tendency of the heavier molecules to settle out from the others due to the greater pull of gravity on them. This leads to a gradual increase in the proportion of oxygen to nitrogen as the atmosphere thins out, until at about 300 km oxygen predominates. At some height above 1,000 km, the even lighter-weight hydrogen begins to predominate over oxygen as the prime constituent of the atmosphere.

Lower Atmosphere

Within the lower atmosphere physical and dynamical phenomena dominate and produce the winds, clouds, and the migratory weather systems. This is the conventional realm of meteorology.

Part of the incoming radiation from the sun is reflected back into space by the atmosphere; however, the great bulk of the radiation is converted into sensible heat at the earth's surface and redistributed back to the atmosphere through long-wave radiation, eddy motion, evaporation, and condensation. The processes at the earth-atmosphere interface are exceedingly important in determining the energy budgets of the troposphere and lower stratosphere, and they are intimately related to the physical properties of the earth's surface. Thus the expanses of oceans, continents, mountains, forests, grasslands, and deserts have marked influences on climate. They affect the local weather, the migratory weather systems, and even the circulation of the atmosphere as a whole. The processes associated with earth-atmosphere interactions translate themselves into problems of air pollution, health, agriculture, water supply, and soil conservation.

Motion. From a mechanical point of view, the atmospheric shell responds to certain impulses with rhythmic signals, the characteristics of which depend upon the dimensions of the earth and the rate of its rotation. The semidiurnal, diurnal, annual, and other oscillations of the atmosphere are of this type.

The atmosphere also responds in an irregular manner and produces upheavals associated with internal instabilities. These upheavals are often violent and tend to overshadow the cyclic motions. Common examples are showers, thunderstorms, and squalls. More complicated forms of instability are associated with the large migratory weather systems that dominate the mid-latitude belt.

An essentially different type of motion manifests itself in the irregular small-scale and rapid changes called turbulence. Rapid fluctuations, brought about by small and short-lived eddies, play an important part in the transfer of energy and water vapor and in dispersing the many air particulates.

It is typical of the atmosphere motions that they are complex, in the sense that they exist in superimposition, and that energy is shuttled back and forth, as the case may be, between the larger and smaller systems. All these interwoven motions and physical processes on different life spans and space scales integrate themselves into what is commonly called weather. On a time scale of about 30 years the weather processes integrate themselves into the climate; and on a time scale of centuries climatic changes must be considered.

Of the physical sciences only atmospheric sciences consider phenomena that are so markedly varied. The time scales reach from zero to a day, a year, and very much longer periods, and the space scales range from almost molecular dimensions to distances comparable with the circumference of the earth.

Weather Prediction. Traditionally, weather forecasting has developed along empirical lines, but advances along theoretical lines have been made and progress in weather prediction is being greatly accelerated. The most promising results are coming from experiments with nonlinear physical and statistical models of the atmosphere and solutions obtained by electronic computers. Further development of nonlinear models will open the way to an understanding of the sequence in which important events occur in the atmosphere, and this should lead to techniques of prediction for extended periods of time. Parallel laboratory research with rotating tanks is adding to the general knowledge of the large-scale weather circulation patterns.

Weather Modification. With the work of Langmuir, Schaefer, and Vonnegut in Project Cirrus (mid-1940s) fundamental studies on the problem of weather and climate control received new emphasis and support. Significant results in this field include:

1. Artificial modification of clouds; for example, certain kinds of super-cooled fog and cloud can be dissipated over areas large enough to be of practical importance.
2. Artificial augmentation of rainfall under special conditions.
3. Alteration of evaporation processes to some extent over water surfaces, and the possibility of artificial interference with the transpiration processes over vegetation-covered land. The significance of such interruption in one phase of the hydrologic cycle is not yet known, but the fact that it can be done points to the importance of further research.
4. Artificial modification of the electrical space charge in the lower part of the atmosphere, with the resulting modification of the electrical properties of cumulus clouds leading to possible effect upon precipitation.
5. Exploration of the possible release of energy stored in the upper atmosphere in the form of atomic oxygen and free radicals through the use of suitable catalysts.
6. Appreciation of the serious results of altering the atmosphere by polluting it with wastes from industry, homes, and transportation vehicles.
7. Study of the as yet undetermined effects on meteorological processes of using the atmosphere as the site for testing nuclear weapons (*see* RADIATION AND SOCIAL ETHICS).
8. Conduction of preliminary cloud-seeding experiments on hurricanes in an attempt to explore further the energetics of these severe storms.
9. Scientific speculations on the possible consequences of filling in or deepening the Strait of Gibraltar; of damming the Bering Strait, and pumping water from the Arctic Ocean into the Pacific to stimulate warm currents from the Atlantic into the Arctic Ocean; of opening up passes in the Sierra Nevadas to permit the passage of moist air into the Nevada desert; of creating an ice crystal fog over the Arctic to interfere with the radiation balance; and of modifying the distribution of heat in the upper atmosphere by using new space technology to produce and maintain artificial clouds over large areas.

All these speculations are issuing from man's interest in arriving at effective control of his climate.

Upper Atmosphere

The task of the aeronomist is to describe, understand, and integrate the behavior of the upper atmosphere, from the stratosphere out to the interplanetary medium. Solar-terrestrial relationships, airglow and aurora, the atmospheric effects of energetic particles, magnetic fields, the Van Allen belt, and meteoric dust all lie within the broad scope of his work. Advancing technology since World War II has expanded and accelerated the field. For example, observation with high-altitude balloons, rockets, and satellites has permitted new types of experiments and has opened up new areas of investigation.

The structure and composition of the earth's upper atmosphere constitute a major problem in aeronomy. The chemical composition changes with height under the influences of dissociation, diffusive separation, and mixing. Furthermore, the upper atmosphere is partially ionized, the degree of ionization being a complicated function of height, time, and geographical position. Information on the density, temperature, pressure, chemical constituents, and ionization as a function of height exists to heights of about 5,000 km. None of these parameters are known in detail over this height range, however, and their diurnal, seasonal, and geographical variations are largely unknown. The minor constituents, such as atomic oxygen, methane, carbon dioxide, nitric oxide, and meteoric dust, are often of great importance in the behavior of the upper atmosphere.

Fields. The gravitational field of the earth is the primary terrestrial factor determining the structure of the upper atmosphere. Its influence is well understood and is invariant. However, due to the rotation of the earth and its atmosphere, the gravitational fields exerted by the sun and the moon are cyclical and lead to tidal effects in the upper atmosphere. These tidal effects provide the driving force for the electrical currents that flow in the lower ionosphere and cause small systematic variations in the magnetic field. (*See* GRAVITATION.)

The magnetic field in the upper atmosphere has two components. One is believed to be due to electrical currents flowing in the interior of the earth. These vary slowly with time and produce a dipole magnetic field, which decays approximately as the cube of the distance from the center of the earth. In addition to this essentially static field, variable magnetic fields are produced by changing electric currents that flow in the lower ionosphere. The magnitude of the static magnetic field is well known out to distances of several earth radii; however, the time variations of the variable components are not well known or understood. At the greater heights the variable magnetic fields increase in relative importance. The earth's magnetic field acts as a barrier to the solar wind, and determines the impact region of auroral particles and most of the cosmic rays. It also controls the motions of electrically charged particles in such a way as to inhibit gross movement of the particles transverse to the field. (*See* GEOMAGNETISM.)

The electric fields in the upper atmosphere, their existence, origin, locations, and magnitude, together with their time variation, are largely unknown. These must be understood before many phenomena at ionospheric heights can be correctly interpreted.

Solar Photons. The principle input of energy into the upper atmosphere is the absorption of solar photons. The temperature, pressure, density, and chemical constituents of the upper atmosphere are greatly influenced by this absorption. A broad spectrum of solar photons bombards the outer atmosphere, ranging from gamma and X rays through the ultraviolet and visual wavelengths to infrared radiation. In the visible and near-ultraviolet spectrum the sun is a relatively well-defined and constant source of radiation, but the extreme ultraviolet and X-ray regions remain to be explored in detail. Such information can be obtained only from outside the earth's atmosphere; therefore a continuing series of observing satellites throughout the sunspot cycle is required. (*See* ELECTROMAGNETIC RADIATION.)

Electrical Phenomena. Visual evidence of electrical activity in the upper atmosphere is provided by the sporadic aurora, the spectacular northern lights of high latitudes. The luminescent airglow, which is the source of about two-fifths of the light of the sky over middle and low latitudes on a clear moonless night, is observed also. Both the aurora and the airglow are produced by emissions of radiant energy from electrically excited chemical constituents of the upper atmosphere.

Whistle-like sounds (whistlers) of descending pitch are recorded on radio receivers. These have been identified as electromagnetic disturbances, produced by lightning discharges, that follow the magnetic lines of force out to many earth radii from one hemisphere to the other, often reflecting back and forth several times.

Perhaps the most important of the electrical phenomena of the upper atmosphere is the ionized region called the ionosphere, which extends from about 70 km to an indefinite height. At these altitudes the density of the air and the unfiltered rays of the sun are favorable for the ionization of many of the air molecules. This produces a great many free electrons that can reflect radio waves.

Energetic Particles. Since the discovery of the Van Allen belt (1958) there has been considerable progress in the understanding of energetic particles trapped by the earth's magnetic field. The first concept of two or more Van Allen belts has been replaced by that of a single, doughnut-shaped region with its plane in the plane of the magnetic equator. At the inner surface of the belt there is a steady loss of the trapped particles to the upper atmosphere due to collisions; the outer surface is defined as the interface between the terrestrial atmosphere and the solar wind. Within the belt there exists an assortment of electrons and protons with energies ranging up to several million electron volts for the electrons and several hundred million electron volts for the protons. The origin of these particles remains a mystery, as does their life history in terms of acceleration, deceleration, and ultimate decay due to collision and absorption in the upper atmosphere. Other problems include the possible presence of ions heavier than protons, and the relationship between the energetic particles and observed electrical currents.

Two other types of energetic particles interact with the upper atmosphere: cosmic rays and the solar-wind particles. Most of the cosmic rays are absorbed in the upper atmosphere and only the most energetic reach the lower atmosphere. The energy spectrum of cosmic rays, particularly those emitted by the sun during so-called solar proton events, is of considerable concern to the man-in-space program. Solar cosmic rays also are of significance because they can interrupt radio communications in the polar latitudes by producing radio-wave absorption in the ionosphere.

The solar-wind particles are much more numerous and much less energetic than the cosmic rays. The particles of the solar wind may create a turbulent boundary region between the earth's outermost atmosphere and the interplanetary medium. It is thought that these particles may be the principal source of the trapped radiation in the Van Allen belt. Little quantitative information exists on the density of the solar-wind particles and on the details of their interaction with the upper atmosphere.

Bibliography: H. R. BYERS, *General Meteorology* (3d ed. New York 1959). J. A. RATCLIFFE, ed., *Physics of the Upper Atmosphere* (New York 1960). N. H. FLETCHER, *The Physics of Rainclouds* (Cambridge, Eng. 1962). U.S. Air Force, Cambridge Research Laboratories, Geophysics Research Directorate, *Handbook of Geophysics* (rev. ed. New York 1960). National Academy of Sciences, *The Atmospheric Sciences, 1961–1971,* 3 v. (Publication 946; Washington 1962). American Meteorological Society, *Journal of the Atmospheric Sciences.* American Geophysical Union, *Journal of Geophysical Research.*

[E. G. DROESSLER]

ATOMIC THEORY

The assumption that matter is not infinitely divisible but is composed of ultimate particles called atoms dates back to the Greek philosophers Democritus and Epicurus, but was first put on a quantitative basis by John

*Dalton at the beginning of the 19th century. Dalton's laws of definite and multiple proportions governing chemical reactions agreed well with the existing experimental evidence and found their simplest explanation in the combining of atoms of chemical elements to form molecules. During the 19th century considerable additional evidence on the structure of atoms was collected from experiments on the passage of electric currents through solutions (M. *Faraday, 1834) and through gases (W. Crookes, 1879). These experiments indicated clearly the existence in all atoms of a fundamental unit of electrical charge that G. J. Stoney (1826–1911) in 1874 named the electron. J. J. Thomson (1856–1940) studied the properties of the so-called cathode rays that occur in electrical discharges in evacuated tubes and concluded that they were negatively charged particles expelled from the cathode with a high velocity and identical in every way with Stoney's electrons. Thomson measured the charge-to-mass ratio, e/m, and showed that it was the same for all electrons, independent of the electrode material from which they came. He thus concluded that electrons are a universal constituent of all matter. Later measurements of the charge of the electron (R. *Millikan, 1909), together with Thomson's value for e/m, showed that the mass of the electron was 9.1×10^{-28} grams. This small mass is responsible for many of the most important physical properties of electrons and atoms. The electron is not visible even with the largest electron microscope, since its radius is of the order of 10^{-13} cm. One of the most striking accomplishments of modern physics is the wealth of detailed information available on electrons and other atomic particles even though they cannot be perceived directly by man's senses. The physicist has gotten this information by studying the consequences on the macroscopic level of the microscopic structure of atoms.

Thomson's work on the electron led him to propose in 1904 a model for the atom consisting of a continuous, spherical distribution of positively charged matter in which were embedded negatively charged electrons. For normal atoms, which have no net charge, the number of electrons was such as to cancel the amount of positive charge present. Experiments on the scattering of α particles (helium nuclei) by E. *Rutherford in 1911 proved, however, that Thomson's model could not be correct. Rutherford shot α particles from radioactive elements at thin foils and found that while most of the α particles passed through the foil without any deflection, some bounced back directly toward the source from which they came. As Rutherford later expressed it, "It was quite the most incredible thing that ever happened to me in my life. It was almost as incredible as if you had fired a fifteen-inch shell at a piece of tissue paper and it came back and hit you." The only explanation of Rutherford's experiments was that the positive charge and the mass of the atom were concentrated in a very small region of space now called the *nucleus and that the greater portion of the space surrounding this nucleus was empty except for the electrons that moved in orbits about the nucleus. Since the mass of the lightest of all nuclei, the hydrogen nucleus, is 1,840 times the electron mass, it is clear that most of the mass is concentrated in the nucleus.

This so-called Rutherford atom or nuclear atom has proved to be a most fruitful physical concept. The nucleus is made up of protons and neutrons. These have very nearly the same mass, but the proton is positively charged, while the neutron has no charge. The number of protons in the nucleus determines the so-called atomic number of the atom, whereas the number of protons and neutrons together determines the atomic mass of the atom. Elements are distinguished by their atomic numbers, whereas *isotopes of the same element have the same number of protons but different numbers of neutrons. Isotopes are often distinguished by a notation indicating the atomic number as a subscript and the mass number as a superscript. Thus the common uranium isotopes are ${}_{92}U^{235}$ and ${}_{92}U^{238}$. All uncharged atoms have a number of electrons outside the nucleus exactly equal to the number of protons in the nucleus. Since electrons and protons carry charges that are numerically the same but of opposite sign, the total atom is electrically neutral.

Though the nuclear atom was proposed by Rutherford in 1911, it did not at first receive much attention. It was only in 1913, when Niels *Bohr, after working in Rutherford's laboratory in Manchester, was able to explain the spectrum of the hydrogen atom on the basis of the nuclear atom and a few additional postulates, that Rutherford's model was accepted by physicists.

During the 18th and 19th centuries physicists had measured the wavelengths of the spectral lines of many elements. It was well known that the wavelengths, and hence the *colors, that occur in the spectrum of an element are characteristic of all samples of the same element, but no one was able to relate these spectra to the structure of the atoms involved. The frequencies occurring in an individual spectrum were not harmonics one of the other, as with *sound waves, and no other reasonable explanation of the observed frequencies could be found. Bohr solved this problem by employing some concepts from quantum theory, the development of which will now be traced.

Old Quantum Theory

The old *quantum theory embraces the development of concepts in physics associated with the quantum, from its introduction by M. *Planck in 1900 to the achievement of the new, more consistent quantum mechanics by W. Heisenberg (1901–) and E. *Schrödinger some 25 years later. The main steps in this effort are associated with the names, besides Planck, of A. *Einstein and Bohr.

That *energy, even on an atomic scale, could occur only in discrete units was foreign to previous physics. In Newton's *mechanics and Maxwell's theory of *electromagnetic radiation successful in so many explanations of macroscopic phenomena, energy and other related quantities were always continuous variables. It seemed natural to extend these notions to the realm of atomic dimensions. The physical properties of matter were treated by the statistical mechanics of L. *Boltzmann and W. *Gibbs as averages of the behavior of large aggregates of atoms undergoing energy exchanges in arbitrarily small units. There were, however, unsatisfactory consequences to this theory, now generally called classical theory, which were recognized by Maxwell, *Kelvin, and others, probably first in connection with the theory of specific heats. On the one hand, as the properties of the atom were revealed, the list of unexplained phenomena grew. Quantum theory, on the other hand, gradually succeeded in giving an account of most of these, albeit in the *ad hoc* manner.

initially, of putting discrete restrictions upon a basically continuous classical theory. Thus Planck derived a correct formula for heat radiation; Einstein was able to account for the photoelectric effect and related phenomena and to point the way to a proper handling of specific heats; and Bohr provided the key to the explanation of atomic spectra, as well as giving a rationale for the stability and basic structure of atoms and molecules. Although superseded in conceptual basis by the newer theory, most of the principal formulas of the old theory remain correct today.

Planck's Quantum. Planck introduced the concept of the quantum in his work on the theory of heat radiation. Although it was a phenomenon of everyday experience (for example, in the change of color of a hot metal with change in its temperature), classical physics seemed unable to account for it. In a precise form the problem was the distribution in frequency, or the spectrum, of electromagnetic energy at thermodynamic equilibrium within a hollow enclosure with opaque walls at constant temperature. Thermodynamics and Maxwell's theory could account successfully for several facts: (1) the properties of equilibrium radiation depended only on the absolute temperature T, independent of the material constitution of the walls, being equivalent to the radiation from a perfectly black body (Kirchhoff's law); (2) the total radiation energy was proportional to T^4 (Stefan-Boltzmann law); (3) the frequency ν_{max} at which the energy was maximum (corresponding to the dominant color) was proportional to the temperature, $\nu_{max} \sim T$; and, more generally, the energy in a unit volume of radiation at frequency ν, E_ν, obeyed the relation $E_\nu/\nu^3 = f(\nu/T)$ where $f(\nu/T)$ was some unspecified function of only the quantity ν/T (Wien's law). However, thermodynamics did not lead further toward determining the function itself.

Planck turned to statistical mechanics. He began by imagining an enclosure with walls made of model atoms, electrical oscillators, for which the emission and absorption of radiation could be calculated by Maxwell's theory. Equilibrium of energy exchange then led to a relation between E_ν and the mean energy of the atomic oscillators at the same frequency, U_ν: $E_\nu = (8\pi\nu^2/c^3)U_\nu$, where c is the velocity of light. The general equipartition principle of classical statistical mechanics could then be applied to the oscillators. This stated that, assuming energy could be exchanged in arbitrarily small units, each square term in an expression for the energy had at equilibrium the mean value $kT/2$, where k is Boltzmann's constant. Since U_ν could be expressed as the sum of two square terms corresponding to the potential energy of displacement and the kinetic energy proportional to the square of the momentum, this gave $U_\nu = kT$ and $E_\nu = (8\pi\nu^2/c^3)kT$, known as the Rayleigh-Jeans formula. This result seemed unavoidable assuming the principles of classical physics, yet it agreed with experiment only at low frequencies, predicting no dominant color but an indefinite increase of energy with frequency. At high frequencies, a relation put forward by W. Wien (1864–1928) on somewhat unsatisfactory grounds, $E_\nu = \Phi_0 \exp(-\Phi_0/kT)$, where $\Phi_0 \sim \nu$ seemed to fit the experimental measurements.

Planck then looked into the possibility that there might be some intrinsic irreversibility in the exchange of energy between matter and radiation. Although he abandoned this view, it served to bring out relations between the thermodynamic entropy of his oscillators and their energy and temperature. This assisted him in finding an interpolation formula that fitted the Rayleigh-Jeans expression at low frequencies and Wien's at high:

$$E_\nu = \frac{8\pi\nu^2}{c^3}\,\frac{h\nu}{e^{h\nu/kT} - 1}$$

where h is Planck's constant. This expression, the black-body radiation formula, agreed with experiment extraordinarily well at all frequencies, indicating that he had hit upon the correct one. Planck found he could derive it only on the assumption that the oscillators' energies were not continuous but composed of an integral number of discrete units ϵ_ν, which he called quanta. The equipartition principle could no longer be used. Planck had to proceed more directly, and he calculated the *probability P of the distribution of a given amount of energy among a large number of oscillators, and thereby their *entropy S_ν, giving Boltzmann's relations, $S_\nu = \log P +$ const., the definite form $S_\nu = k \log P$. This allowed the first calculation of an absolute value of entropy for an arbitrary configuration of a thermodynamic system. Then following his previous relations of entropy to energy and temperature, he obtained $U_\nu = \epsilon_\nu(e^{\epsilon_\nu/kT} - 1)^{-1}$, which led to his black-body formula if $\epsilon_\nu = h\nu$. The constant $h = 6.7 \times 10^{-27}$ erg-sec now had a universal physical significance.

By using the values of the constants h and k obtained from fitting the experimental data, along with the equation of state of a perfect gas and Faraday's law of electrochemical equivalence, Planck was able to derive values of Avogadro's number and the charge on the electron that were remarkably accurate.

In his later work, seeking a deeper understanding of the significance of the quantum, Planck emphasized that h was a measure of the smallest element of probability (or phase volume) of statistical mechanics. This had the dimensions of action J; and in the case of an oscillator of momentum p and coordinate q, the smallest element of probability $\Delta J = dp\,dq = \epsilon_\nu/\nu = h$. (It was more fundamental, therefore, to regard action as quantized in units h rather than energy in units $h\nu$). This indicated how entropy might be calculated for any atomic system; later, when it became possible to do so, there was a marked influence on the theory of chemical equilibria (*see* STATISTICAL PHYSICS).

Light Quanta. In Planck's theory the electromagnetic energy of radiation was continuous, as in classical theory. Einstein put forward in 1905 the theory that radiation itself must occur in finite parcels, which he called light quanta. His first argument for this was statistical, using the relation $S_\nu = k \log P$ to find the probability P that an amount of radiation energy E_ν would occupy a given small volume at temperature T, with S_ν calculated from Planck's formula for E_ν and the thermodynamic relation between energy and entropy $dE_\nu = TdS_\nu$. For the high frequency part of the spectrum, the result for P was the same as the probability, according to the statistical theory of gases, that a number of independent particles equal to $E_\nu/k\nu$ would be found in the same volume (*see* KINETIC THEORY). This led Einstein to seek other manifestations of particle-like behavior of light. He found he could explain in this way the hitherto puzzling threshold phenomena, which required radiation above a minimum threshold frequency ν_{min}. Of these, one of the most important was the photoelectric effect, the liberation of electrons from matter by light. Experiments had shown that the kinetic energy of these electrons depended only on the frequency and was otherwise independent of the light intensity. The number of electrons, however, did increase with light intensity. Also, there was no measurable time lag between arrival of light and appearance of electrons. All these features could be accounted for if the effect took place by the direct interaction of a light quantum of energy $h\nu$ with a single electron. The kinetic energy of the electron when free would be $W_2 = h\nu - W_1$, where the threshold energy W_1 (the minimum work required to extract the electron from the particular material) was related to the threshold frequency by $W_1 = h\nu_{min}$. In classical theory, however, electromagnetic energy was distributed continuously over a wave front and depended on both wave amplitude and frequency. On this basis it seemed inexplicable that the electron's kinetic energy would depend only on frequency and that the very small electron could accumulate enough energy to escape in the short times observed.

Einstein's propositions raised in a new form the old arguments between wave and particle theories of light, which went back to Newton and Christian *Huygens and had seemed settled in favor of the wave theory by the phenomena of interference. Einstein simply acknowledged, at this point, that this was a problem that would require deeper insights before it could be resolved.

Specific Heats. In 1907 Einstein suggested that not only atomic electrical oscillators and radiation but also purely mechanical atomic oscillations should have quantized energies. He developed this into a theory of specific heats of solids, adopting the simple model that a solid is composed of N atoms, all vibrating at a single frequency in three dimensions. According to the classical equipartition principle, the energy at temperature T was $U = 3NkT$ and the specific heat $C = dU/dT = 3Nk \simeq 6$ calories/deg.-mole in agreement with the empirical law of Dulong and Petit. It was known, however, that C decreased for all solids at low temperatures; in fact, the third law of thermodynamics stated that C approached zero with the temperature. Even where the Dulong-Petit law held, however, it was not possible to explain why the electrons known to be present in the solid were not counted in N, the total number of oscillators. Einstein pointed out that the mean energy of N quantized three-dimensional atomic mechanical oscillators would be given just by Planck's expression. Then the specific heat $C = 3Nk\, x^2 e^x\, (e^x\text{-}1)^{-2}$, where $x = h\nu/kT$, would exhibit qualitatively at least the correct behavior, decreasing to zero with T. To assume that all atoms of a solid vibrate as independent oscillators with the same frequency was an oversimplification. Rather, the vibrations of a solid are more like those of a coupled set of particles, describable as modes of oscillation of the system of particles as a whole. Using approximate theories of these modes advanced by (among others) P. Debye (1884–) and assuming that each mode could be quantized as an independent oscillator, values of specific heats were obtained in good quantitative agreement with experiment. It could be understood, also, that electrons, acting as high-frequency oscillators, do not contribute appreciably to the specific heat at ordinary temperatures.

Bohr's Atomic Theory

In 1913 N. Bohr achieved a synthesis of these quantum ideas with the Rutherford model of the atom described above. According to classical physics, this model led to a number of fundamental difficulties. It was possible to describe, at least approximately, the displacement of the electrons from the nucleus as a Fourier series of contributions from a fundamental frequency and its harmonics. Since, according to Maxwell's theory, a charge radiated proportional to the square of its acceleration, the electrons should lose energy continuously by radiation at all the harmonically related frequencies. Because of this continual loss the frequencies would be expected to change, and in a short time the electrons would fall into the nucleus. The difficulty in reconciling this with the concept of an atom as a stable entity was obvious. Also, it was known that relatively isolated atoms radiated at sharply defined frequencies, producing discrete spectral lines, which were not harmonically related but were steady in time and obeyed the Rydberg-Ritz combination rules: characteristic of an atom there were sets of numbers T_1, T_2, . . ., called "terms," which could be arranged so that the frequencies of the spectral lines of the atom were included among the differences between the term values, e.g., $\nu_{12} = T_2 - T_1$, $\nu_{23} = T_3 - T_2$, ... For hydrogen atoms, the terms were given empirically by the Balmer formula $T_n = R/n^2$, where R was the Rydberg constant and n an integer.

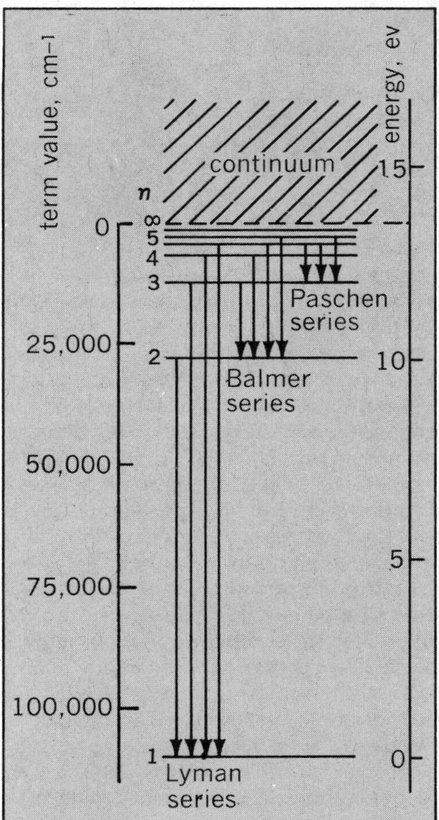

Fig. 1. Terms and transitions for the hydrogen atom according to Bohr theory.

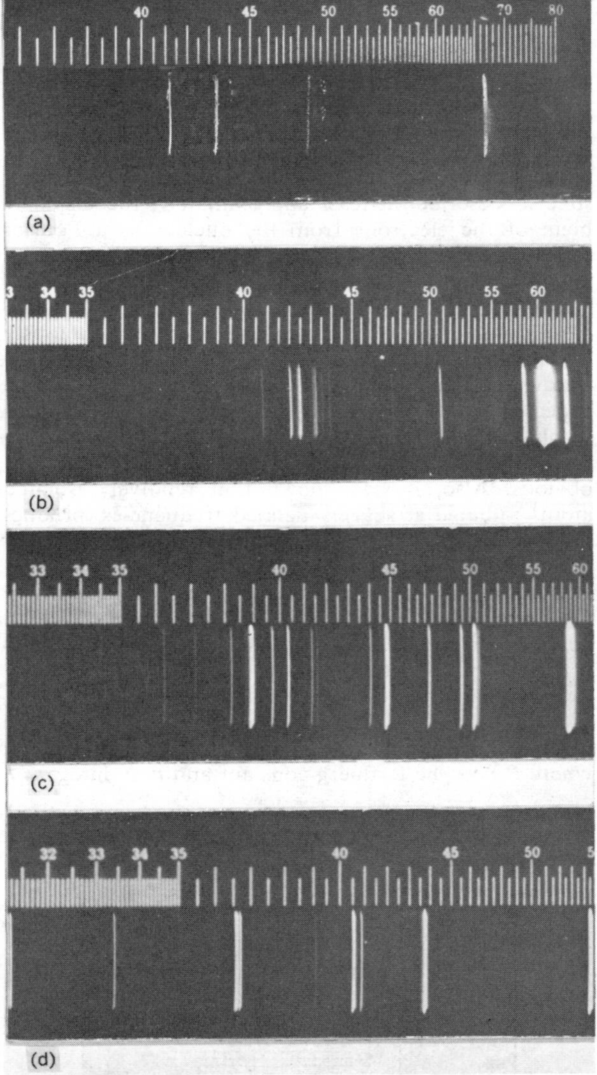

Fig. 2. The Balmer series in hydrogen. The scale gives the wavelengths in millionths of a centimeter (that is, in hundreds of angstroms).

Bohr then postulated that an isolated atom (or molecule) can exist only in one of a set of quantized, characteristic, nonradiating stationary states, having energy values, or levels, W_1, W_2, ... There is a state of lowest energy W_1 called the ground state; stability of the atom follows since there is no state of lower energy. Changes of energy can take place only in discrete amounts equal to the differences $W_2 - W_1$, etc. Emission and absorption of radiation of frequency ν obeyed the relation $h\nu = W_2 - W_1$, the so-called Bohr-Einstein frequency condition, one light quantum being involved at a time in a transition between the typical states 1 and 2. (Clearly the interpretation of the Rydberg-Ritz terms T_n could now be given by their association with energy levels $W_n = h\,T_n$.) According to Bohr it was not possible in classical physics to show how the atom did not radiate in a stationary state or how the atom did radiate in a transition. This was in spite of the fact that values of the energy levels W_1, W_2, . . ., were first obtained by imposing quantum conditions on classical orbits of the electrons.

Hydrogen Spectrum. Bohr made immediate application of his postulates to explain the spectrum of atomic hydrogen. To calculate the quantized energies W_n for a single electron and nucleus, he assumed the simplest circular orbits and proceeded by supposing that if the electron were sufficiently far from the nucleus its behavior should correspond to that of classical physics. The single frequency of rotation of the electron would then be also the frequency of its radiation, and disregarding the energy loss by radiation as small compared to the electrons kinetic and potential energies, the classical (Kepler) laws of planetary motion could be used. Bohr therefore first obtained the frequency of rotation ν, in terms of nuclear charge Ze, mass m, and energy W of the orbital electron, $\nu = W^{3/2}(2/\pi^2 me^4)^{\frac{1}{2}}$, from the Kepler laws. This he equated to the frequency difference of successive energy levels given by the Balmer formula for large n, $\nu = 2R/n^3 = 2(Wn/h)^{3/2}\,R^{-\frac{1}{2}}$, thus deriving an expression for the Rydberg constant $R = 2\pi^2 me^4\,Z^2/h^3$ in remarkably good agreement with experiment. Bohr also noted that his result could be obtained more rapidly from a simple rule of quantization for the stationary circular orbits: the electron's angular momentum, calculated according to classical physics, was to be equated to integral multiples of $h/2\pi$. The approach followed first—that quantum and classical results should correspond for relatively small changes of action, i.e., small changes in large quantum numbers (Bohr's correspondence principle)—proved a valuable guide for the development of the quantum theory. The energies of the states of the hydrogen atom calculated in this way are shown in Fig. 1. The lines in the spectrum of hydrogen, differences between these energies, are indicated in Fig. 2 for the Balmer series in hydrogen; the frequencies of these lines are predicted quite closely in Bohr's theory.

There are many defects in Bohr's theory: it introduces seemingly arbitrary postulates; it does not take account of the spin of the electron, of relativistic effects, of the wave properties of matter, and of other subtleties now known to be required in any adequate theory. It also does not apply quantitatively to atoms with more than one electron. But it represents a giant step forward in understanding atomic structure and is still the best pictorial description physicists have of what goes on inside atoms. Although the new quantum mechanics has replaced the Bohr model for calculational purposes, quantum mechanics confirms and builds on the energy-level concept that Bohr introduced.

The next most complicated element after hydrogen is helium, which is formed of a doubly charged nucleus and two planetary electrons. If a helium atom loses one electron, a singly ionized helium atom results. This helium ion resembles a hydrogen atom except that the nuclear charge and mass are different. Hence the spectrum of singly ionized helium should be very similar to that of hydrogen, except that $Z = 2$ in Bohr's expression for the Rydberg constant, so that the main effect of the doubly charged nucleus was to multiply the frequency of the spectral lines by four. This led Bohr to attribute to ionized helium the so-called Pickering series discovered in the spectra of certain stars, and which had wrongly been attributed to hydrogen. This was another triumph for the Bohr theory.

Experimental Verification. There is a wealth of experimental evidence for the existence of discrete energy states or levels within atoms. Thus atoms can be changed from one energy state to the other by bombarding them with electron beams of controlled energy or by shining on them electromagnetic radiation of the proper frequency. It is also possible to remove electrons completely from atoms (ionization) by using light of a sufficiently high frequency. Starting with a series of important experiments in 1914 by J. Franck (1882–) and G. Hertz (1887–), many experiments on excitation and ionization energies have been performed and all corroborate both qualitatively and quantitatively the basic ideas of the Bohr theory.

The energy-level structure of atoms is actually much more complicated than is indicated above. The energy levels shift in electric and magnetic fields; there are energy shifts introduced by interactions among the electrons and interactions between the electrons and the nucleus. These effects can be measured to very high precision by optical and electronic techniques that cover the whole electromagnetic spectrum. Thus the old data of optical spectroscopy, which are limited to the visible portion of the spectrum, have been supplemented by a wealth of results from the fields of radio-frequency spectroscopy, microwave spectroscopy, infrared and ultraviolet spectroscopy, gamma-ray spectroscopy, and nuclear magnetic resonance. The last two reveal also the applicability of Bohr's concept of energy levels to the structure of the nucleus. In a certain sense it is true to say that the work of the great majority of physicists today consists in measuring to high precision the energy levels of atoms and nuclei and understanding these energies in terms of the interactions that go on within the atom and the nucleus.

X Rays. The spectroscopic and chemical properties of atoms are determined chiefly by the outer electrons in the atom, i.e., those outside completely filled shells. The inner-shell electrons are also the key to an understanding of X rays. These rays, which were first discovered by W. Roentgen (1845–1923) in 1896, are nothing but extremely energetic bundles of electromagnetic energy (quanta) and differ from light quanta only in possessing a much higher frequency and hence a much greater energy, since $E = h\nu$. One would therefore expect X rays to originate in a fashion similar to that in which light quanta arise in the Bohr theory when an atom jumps from one energy level to the other. The essential difference is that X rays arise from transitions involving the inner energy levels of the atom, and hence the energy changes are much greater than in the case of transitions involving the outer-shell electrons only. This is illustrated in Fig. 3, which shows the types of transitions involved in the production of X rays. The energies involved in the K and L series shown in this diagram are orders of magnitude greater than the 2 to 5 electron volts (ev) typically involved in optical transitions.

If a heavy atom, e.g., lead, is bombarded with high-energy electrons in an X-ray tube, electrons can be knocked out of the inner shells of the lead atoms. Outer-shell electrons, seeking the lowest allowable energy states, can then fall into the empty inner shells and radiate away their excess energy as X rays, with a frequency satisfying the Bohr-Einstein frequency condition. This is the characteristic X-ray spectrum. Normally it appears superimposed on a continuous spectrum due to the direct conversion of the electrons' kinetic energy into radiation as they are slowed down by crashing into the target of the X-ray tube. The continuous spectrum yields no information about the structure of the target material and hence is of no further concern here. Because of their high energies X rays are exceedingly penetrating. The higher the atomic weight of the bombarded material, the greater the absorption of X rays by atoms; hence the possibility of obtaining X-ray photographs of the bones, which contain a much greater proportion of heavy metallic atoms than the surrounding flesh.

Experiments on X rays have also given further insights into the structure of atoms. Thus H. Moseley (1887–1915) in 1913 was able to show that as atoms increased in atomic number, the X-ray lines associated with the innermost shell (K series) increased in frequency proportionately to the square of the atomic number, or $\nu = a(Z - b)^2$, where ν is the frequency, Z the atomic number, and a and b are constants. In this way he was able to point out where missing elements should appear in the *periodic table, and these were later found to exist and to have precisely the properties predicted from the place Moseley's law assigned to them. The physical reason for the dependence of frequency on the square of the atomic number is that the atomic number determines the number of positive charges on the nucleus. The larger the number of positive charges, the more tightly bound the inner electrons, and hence the higher the frequency of the X rays emitted when elec-

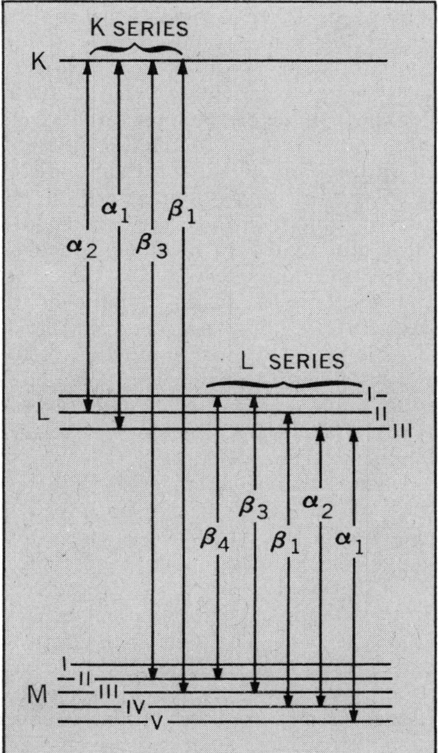

Fig. 3. Typical arrangement of the higher X-ray energy levels of an atom. The vertical lines indicate the transitions or jumps between pairs of these levels, which account for some of the stronger X-ray spectral lines as designated. Only some K and L series lines are shown (not to scale).

trons fall into this shell. This increase in the tightness of the binding of the electrons with atomic number ensures that atoms with many electrons have more of them close to the nucleus. As a result all atoms are of approximately the same size, approximately 1 to 3 $\times 10^{-8}$ cm in diameter.

Philosophical Implications. The knowledge of the structure of matter acquired by physicists since 1900 is of great importance to philosophers who are interested in the ultimate principles of matter. Thus the question, "Is an atom in an excited state a different atom than in its normal ground state?" can be answered on the basis of the known physical fact that an excited state differs from the ground state only in a change in the configuration of the outer-shell electrons. Hence as regards the nucleus and the inner-shell electrons the atom is essentially unchanged. But the excitation has added energy to the atom and has changed the configuration of one or more outer-shell electrons (more precisely, has changed the wave function representing the outer-shell electrons). Now the chemical reactivity, light absorption, and many electric and magnetic properties of atoms depend only on the outer-shell electrons. Hence a change in the outer-shell electron configuration can radically change the observable properties of atoms. If philosophers desire to say that atoms with greatly different properties are different atoms in a philosophical sense, then an excited-state atom is radically different from a ground-state atom of the same element.

There is a difficulty here, however. There is theoretically an infinite number of excited states for any one atom. Most of these are extremely difficult to produce and observe in the laboratory, but from a fundamental point of view they are just as real as the ground state. These excited states would correspond, for example, to the excitation of one outer-shell electron to higher energy states, culminating finally in the removal of the electron completely and the production of an ionized atom. Such ions are completely different chemically and spectroscopically from their parent atoms. Thus the spectra of singly ionized helium He^{+} and doubly ionized lithium Li^{++} are very similar to that of the hydrogen atom and bear no resemblance whatever to the spectra of atomic He or Li. Hence for each chemical element there is an infinity of different atoms depending on the state to which the atom is excited. This is an example of a situation often occurring in physics, where a small quantitative change (in this case the addition of a small amount of energy to the atom) can produce large qualitative effects (changes in spectra, chemical reactivity, etc.).

A somewhat similar situation exists with respect to the question of how elements are contained in compounds. The nuclei and inner-shell electrons are essentially (though not perfectly) unchanged. This is clear from the fact that X-ray spectra remain unchanged and that nuclear scattering cross sections and other nuclear properties are the same. The outer-shell electrons, however, are radically changed. They are now in energy states that are peculiar to the whole molecule, not to the individual atoms; as a result the chemical and spectroscopic properties observed are those of the molecule and not those of the constituent atoms. Hence these atoms have changed precisely insofar as they combine to form a compound. The individual atoms are still there virtually, however, since the molecule can be again broken up to give back the atoms out of which it was constituted.

The chemical and spectroscopic properties of compounds depend more on how atoms combine to form a molecule than on the properties of the constituent atoms. A good example is the two types of structure in which carbon atoms can combine in the solid state, diamond and graphite. Both of these are formed out of carbon atoms and nothing else. But diamond is a very hard, transparent, crystalline substance, whereas graphite is a black, soft, flaky material. The electrical conductivity of graphite is 100 billion times greater than that of diamond. Hence the identical carbon atoms must be modified in some way depending on whether they unite to form diamond or graphite. This modification consists of the way the outer-shell carbon electrons bond together to form the compound. The energy states are quite different in graphite and diamond, even though they are formed from identical atoms. This seems clear proof that elements are not present actually, but only virtually, in compounds.

Bibliography: E. T. WHITTAKER, *History of the Theories of Aether and Electricity,* 2 v. (rev. and enl. New York 1952–54). A. RUBINOWICZ, "Ursprung und Entwicklung der älteren Quantentheorie," in *Handbuch der Physik,* v.24.1 *Quantentheorie* (Berlin 1933) 1–82. S. TOMONAGA, *Quantum Mechanics,* v.1, tr. KOSHIBA (New York 1962). M. PLANCK, *A Survey of Physical Theory,* tr. R. JONES and D. H. WILLIAMS (New York 1960). P. A. SCHILPP, ed., *Albert Einstein, Philosopher-Scientist,* 2 v. (Torchbks. 502–503; New York 1959). N. BOHR, *Atomic Theory and the Description of Nature* (New York 1934; repr. 1962). M. BORN, *The Mechanics of the Atom,* ed. D. R. HARTREE, tr. J. W. FISCHER (New York 1960); *Atomic Physics,* rev. R. J. BLIN-STOYLE, tr. J. DOUGALL (7th rev. ed. New York 1962). J. C. SLATER, *Modern Physics* (New York 1955). F. O. RICE and E. TELLER, *Structure of Matter* (New York 1949). R. B. LEIGHTON, *Principles of Modern Physics* (New York 1959).

[J. F. MULLIGAN; S. G. REED, JR.]

ATOMISM

A term deriving from the Greek ἄτομον, meaning indivisible, and usually applied to systems maintaining that everything is composed of unchanging and indivisible elements or atoms, whose movements and arrangements account for the changing appearances of reality. In a broader sense, the term is applied also to any systematic explanation that attempts to reduce complex phenomena to invariant unit factors. Thus one may speak of logical atomism, as elaborated in the philosophy of Bertrand *Russell, which regards the logical proposition as an ultimate unit; psychological atomism, which attempts to reduce all mental phenomena to combinations of simple elements, along lines proposed by J. *Locke, D. *Hume, and the advocates of *associationism; and biological atomism, which attempts to explain vital phenomena in terms of discrete units such as genes, cells, etc. (*see* MECHANISM, BIOLOGICAL). The historically more important type of atomism may be described as physical atomism to distinguish it from these other forms. From its beginnings in Greek philosophy it has consistently lent its support to the philosophies of *materialism and *mechanism, and has been used by proponents of *atheism to combat belief in the world of *spirit. Physical atomism is not to be completely identified with materialism, however, for many thinkers have subscribed to atomistic hypotheses without regarding atoms as the sole reality and while admitting the existence of spiritual entities. Again, physical atomism permits of many different views regarding the nature of the ultimate units, ranging from the mathematical points of the Pythagoreans, the force centers of R. Boscovich, and the monads of G. W. Leibniz to the solid particles of Democritus and the qualitatively similar parts (Gr. ὁμοιομερῆ) of Anaxagoras. Yet most forms of atomism maintain that there is a quantitative limit to the division of bodies, that small ultimate units exist, and that all large-scale phenomena are to be accounted for in terms of these.

This article treats of physical atomism chronologically under the headings of Greek atomism, other early forms, medieval conceptions, developments from the Renaissance to the 17th century, the classical atomism of the 18th and 19th centuries, and the status of atomism in the 20th century.

Greek Atomism. The first atomistic theories to arise among the Greeks were speculative in nature. The forerunners of Greek atomist concepts are to be found among the Milesian naturalists, such as Thales, Anaximenes, and *Heraclitus, who successively conceived water, air, and fire as the primary matter of which all things are made. The solutions these thinkers proferred to the problem of change prompted *Parmenides, a philosopher of the Eleatic school in Italy, to argue that change itself is an illusion: in his view, being is one and unchangeable, for apart from it there is only nothing. The metaphysical speculations of Parmenides gave birth to the first atomist school at Abdera in Thrace, where atomism was proposed by Leucippus (fl. 450 B.C.) and his pupil *Democritus. Democritus argued against Parmenides that being is not one but is divided into a number of beings, themselves unchangeable and indivisible, which he called atoms (Gr. ἄτομα). He also conceived nothing differently from Parmenides, assigning it a type of reality that he described as the *void. By admitting the void Democritus thought he could explain the motion of atoms, and through this motion all types of change. He postulated that atoms were infinite in number, qualitatively identical, and distinct only in shape and size; he endowed his atoms also with motion, which he conceived as ceaseless and eternal like the atoms themselves. (*See* MATERIALISM.)

At approximately the same time as Democritus was elaborating his atomic theory, rival theories were being proposed by *Empedocles and *Anaxagoras. According to Empedocles, the primordial beings are four qualitatively different elements, viz, fire, air, water, and earth; he explained change in terms of the commingling and separation of these four elements, which themselves remain unchanged. Anaxagoras accented Empedocles's notion of commingling, but held that the primitive constituents of matter are an unlimited number of qualitatively different substances, themselves eternal and incorruptible, which he referred to as seeds (Gr. σπέρματα). In his view, every composed substance contains all possible kinds of seeds and is named after the type of seed that predominates in it.

In the classical period of Greek philosophy, *Plato, influenced by the ideas of *Pythagoras and the Pythagoreans, who held that *number is the essence of things, and likewise influenced by Democritus, proposed a geometrical theory of the basic particles of the universe. He regarded these as fire, earth, air, and water, and associated them with the four regular solids, viz, the tetrahedron, the cube, the octahedron, and the icosahedron. *Aristotle, less partial to Democritean ideas than his teacher, explained change by a fourfold causal analysis that placed accent on substance and primary matter as substrates underlying accidental and *substantial change respectively (*see* MATTER AND FORM). In this context, he adapted Empedocles's theory of the four elements and taught that all bodies are continuous but composed of natural *minima,* i.e., smallest particles of various kinds (*see* CONTINUUM).

Later Greek thought centered on the theories of Democritus and of Aristotle, and thereby provided two influential currents that have persisted down to recent times. The notions of Democritus were taken up by *Epicurus, who reformulated them and used them as a method of inference from the visible to the invisible. The school of *Epicureanism that he founded kept atomistic notions alive long after the decline of Greek philosophy, and can be said to have laid the remote foundations for the atomic theories of modern chemistry. The views of Aristotle, on the other hand, were taken up by his Greek commentators, Alexander of Aphrodisias, Themistius, and *John Philoponus, all of whom contributed to a more systematic explanation of Aristotle's theory of natural *minima.* They spoke of the smallest particles of particular kinds of matter as ἐλάχιστα, a term with somewhat the same connotation as the modern word molecule. The concept was further developed in the Middle Ages and in the Renaissance; it was eclipsed somewhat with the rise of modern chemistry, only to take on new significance in 20th-century discussions of elementary particles.

Other Early Forms. A type of atomism is to be found also in *Indian philosophy, where it is associated with the system of Vaisésika Sūtra, attributed to a mythical Kanāda but probably recorded during the first 2 centuries A.D. Little is known of its origins, although it is possible that it was influenced by Greek thought. Indian atomism is relativistic; both the small (*anu*) and the very small (*paramānu*) are denied any absolute value. In the system of Vaisésika the very small is described as an elementary form; in an earlier type of atomism associated with *Jainism, it is regarded as lacking in any forms that would make it perceptible but still as endowed with qualities. Both systems deny the existence of a void and do not regard the atom as the unique principle of reality, admitting that the soul is a spiritual substance and not atomic in character. Where materialism does appear in Indian philosophy, it does not assume an atomistic form.

In Rome, the Greek physician Asclepiades (*c.* 124–40 B.C.) ascribed diseases to alterations in the size, arrangement, and motion of the atoms that make up the human body. More influential was the teaching of the Roman poet and philosopher *Lucretius, who gave eloquent expression to the ideas of Democritus in his poem *De rerum natura.* This was a systematic account of an atomist theory of nature, describing in detail the formation of the universe, the origins of life and of thought, the nature of human sensation and of sexual attraction, and the development of human society. Preserved in monastic libraries during the Dark Ages, this became the principal channel through which interest in Greek atomism was preserved to modern times.

Largely because of the materialistic atheism endorsed by Lucretius, Christian writers, such as *Dionysius of Alexandria, attacked the atomists' doctrine as being based on *chance and denying a principle of order within the universe (*see* UNIVERSE, ORDER OF). The Fathers of the Church were likewise unfavorable to atomistic concepts because these seemed to form the basis for a materialistic Epicurean ethics. Through their polemics and through the efforts of encyclopedists such as *Isidore of Seville, basic atomic concepts continued to be discussed. Isidore likened atoms to points, since they were indivisible, and distinguished atoms of matter, of time, of number, and of language (*Etymol.* 13.3; PL 82: 472–473).

Medieval Conceptions. Atomistic theories did not enjoy great popularity during the Middle Ages, the main line of development taking place in a thought context that was predominantly Aristotelian. In the 9th century, an Arab alchemist and physician named Rhazes (al-Rāzī, 865?–924) taught a type of atomism, and other Islamic thinkers developed atomic ideas not unlike the earlier Indian concepts (*see* ARABIAN PHILOSOPHY). In the 14th century *Nicholas of Autrecourt defended a Democritean type of atomism, speculating over the motions of atoms and their mutual attractions. Some historians list *William of Conches, *Hugh of Saint-Victor, and *Adelard of Bath as atomists also, but the basis for this ascription is debatable (Van Melsen, 77).

The main concern in the Middle Ages regarding theories of matter was one of reconciling how material substance could be composed (*compositum*) of primary matter and substantial form and at the same time be a compound (*mixtum*) formed from the four elements. The problem this posed is referred to as that of the presence of elements in compounds; this was strenuously debated because of its intimate connection with the problem of the unicity of substantial forms (*see* FORMS, UNICITY AND PLURALITY OF). *Avicenna taught that the essential form of the element remains unchanged in the compound, although the qualities that characterize the element there undergo a remission of intensity. *Averroës disagreed with this teaching, maintaining that not only the qualities of the element, but also its substantial form, undergo remission, and thus the element is not present in all its perfection within the compound. St. *Albert the Great minimized the differences between Avicenna and Averroës, while associating the minimum elemental parts present in a compound with the atoms of Democritus (*In 1 de gen.* 1.12; ed. Borgnet, 4:354b). A different solution was that of St. *Thomas Aquinas, who rejected Avicenna's view that the elements are present in compounds actually and Averroës's views that they are present only potentially, to propose an intermediate position, viz, that elements are virtually present in compounds in the sense that their forces, or powers (*virtutes*), are there conserved. Most other medieval thinkers, as A. Maier has shown, adopted either the Averroist solution (*Roger Bacon, *Henry of Ghent, *Peter John Olivi, *Theodoric of Freiberg, *John of Jandun) or that proposed by Aquinas (*Peter of Auvergne, *Giles of Rome, *Duns Scotus, *William of Ockham, *John Buridan, *Nicholas Oresme).

The controversy over the presence of elements in compounds was related to Aristotle's theory of natural *minima.* Fourteenth-century thinkers generally did not identify such *minima* with atoms, as Albert the Great had been tempted to do. They distinguished between *minima inexistentia,* i.e., as these might exist within a body, and *minima per se existentia,* i.e., as these exist when separated from a body. It was generally taught that separated *minima* could exist, but that *minima inexistentia* were not present within a body. The elaboration of a theory of natural *minima* that could be reconciled with atomistic concepts had thus to await the developments of later centuries.

Renaissance to 17th Century. The Italian Averroist movement of the 16th century, in the person of such thinkers as A. *Nifo, continued to develop Aristotelian doctrine and to apply this to speculation concerning the physical universe. Natural *minima* were conceived as parts of substance with a more independent existence than heretofore, and were ascribed certain functions in physical and chemical processes. A. Achillini (1463–1512) spoke of the *minima* as reacting upon each other, and J. *Zabarella worked out a more explicit theory concerning the forms of the *minima* and that of the bodies constituted from them. Perhaps the most complete theory of natural *minima* that shows affinities with atomic theories was that of J. C. *Scaliger, who taught that the *minima* of different substances vary in size and who used this to explain their different properties, such as density. Scaliger defined chemical composition as "the motion of *minima* toward mutual contact so that a union is effected."

Other Renaissance thinkers, such as G. *Bruno and F. Bacon, revived the notions of Democritus as transmitted through Lucretius, and began to explain physical phenomena in terms of the motion of the ultimate particles of bodies. From about 1550 onward, increased interest manifested itself in Greek atomism and in the relation of atomic concepts to the newly forming sciences of mechanics and chemistry. In 1575 F. Commandino published a translation of the writings of Hero of Alexandria (1st century A.D.), who emphasized the importance of the size and shape of the empty space between the particles of bodies. G. *Galilei read Democritus and Hero, and used their notions to propose a distinction between primary and secondary qualities: the first are those associated with the motions of atoms and are objectively real; the second are sensations produced in a knowing subject and are merely subjective (*see* QUALITY).

The first systematic application of atomic notions to chemistry was made by a German physician, D. Sennert (1572–1644), who developed the ideas of Scaliger and attempted to reconcile the *minima* theory with Democritean concepts. He taught that in chemical compositions the reagents are divided into their smallest parts, which subsequently unite through their *minima* and then act upon each other through their contrary properties. Perhaps the most influential atomist of the early 17th century was P. *Gassendi, a French priest and mathematician, who expurgated materialistic connotations from Democritean atomism. According to Gassendi, atoms are not eternal but are created by God; they are not infinite in number; and their motion is not eternal but has been impressed upon them by God for a definite purpose. R. *Descartes rejected the Democritean concept of the void and conceived all physical processes as taking place in a medium composed of infinitely small particles in motion. Although not an atomist in the strict sense, Descartes contributed to the growth of atomism by his highly influential mechanical philosophy. T. *Hobbes, the English mechanist, held for the existence of atoms but taught that the spaces between them were filled with some kind of fluid. Rejection of empty space in this and later periods was usually prompted by a philosophical recognition of the impossibility of *action at a distance.

The most influential atomists of the later 17th century were R. *Boyle, R. *Hooke, C. *Huygens, and I. *Newton. Boyle made use of both medieval and modern concepts to clarify the notion of a chemical element. He regarded heat as a type of atomic vibration and explained alteration as well as generation and corruption mechanically, i.e., in terms of the motions and rearrangements of atoms. Boyle proposed a complex hierarchy of particles (primary, secondary, etc.), but shared the alchemists' conviction of the unity of matter and the transformability of one type of atoms into another. Hooke suggested that the regular forms of bodies, particularly of crystals, could be explained in terms of arrangements of "globular particles." He taught that all particles are in vibration and explained heat as an oscillatory motion of the smaller particles. Huygens further developed Gassendi's notions while attempting to work out a consistent kinetic theory that would explain the phenomena of gravitation, atmospheric pressure, light, and cohesion. Newton also subscribed to the atomistic views of Gassendi, as well as those of Lucretius, and attempted to elaborate these quantitatively in terms of his laws of mechanics. He showed that Boyle's law for gases could be derived on the assumption that these consist of hard particles repelling each other inversely as the distance. He also considered both attractive and repulsive forces and used them to replace the hooks postulated in more naïve explanations of atomic combination. From optical studies of the thickness of soap bubbles, he calculated an upper limit of about 10^{-5} cm for the size of soap particles.

Classical Atomism. Quantitative atomism thus had its tentative beginnings in the second half of the 17th century. The 18th century saw an accumulation of experimental data and the proposal of theoretical concepts that would lay the groundwork for the full-blown development of classical atomism in the 19th century.

18th Century. G. W. *Leibniz, G. *Vico, E. *Swedenborg, R. G. *Boscovich, J. *Priestley, R. J. *Haüy, and J. L. Proust figured most prominently in this period. At first a materialistic atomist, Leibniz later developed his theory of the *monad, which he conceived as a simple substance without extension, shape, position, or movement but with the power of perception. Somewhat similar was the view of Vico, who held that the universe is constituted of point centers of action; unlike Leibniz's "metaphysical points," however, these had location and a tendency to movement and were not endowed with perception. Swedenborg proposed a theory of natural points similar to Vico's to explain all geometrical and mechanical phenomena.

These dynamistic notions reached their culmination in the mathematical theory of atomism proposed by the Jesuit mathematician Boscovich. This theory postulated the existence of a finite number of quasi-material point centers of action, all with identical properties and all obeying an alternately repulsive and attractive force of interaction whose magnitude depended on the distance between each pair. In proposing it, Boscovich substituted a monism of special relations for the earlier dualism of occupied vs. empty space, and gave meaning to the concept of physical structure in terms of a three-dimensional array of point centers. His ideas were viewed favorably by I. *Kant, who developed a similar theory shortly after Boscovich. Priestley also was aware of Boscovich's theory and called it to the attention of English scientists. (*See* DYNAMISM.)

While these theoretical considerations were being proposed, the French chemist Proust was gathering proof that true compounds contain chemical elements in constant proportions. His countryman C. A. Coulomb at about the same time established his law of the attraction and repulsion of electrical charges; and Haüy, a French priest and mineralogist, proposed that a crystal of any type could be subdivided into ultimate solid units of the same shape as the crystal.

19th Century. Such contributions prepared for the serious experimental work that provided the empirical base for 19th-century theories of classical atomism. Although many distinguished scientists collaborated in this development, J. *Dalton, J. L. Gay-Lussac, A. *Avogadro, D. I. *Mendeleev, and M. *Faraday may be singled out for comment.

Dalton is generally credited with having placed the atomic theory, for the first time, on an exact quantitative basis. Building on the experimental findings of A. L. *Lavoisier and assuming the law of conservation of weight in chemical reactions, he first formulated the law of multiple proportions. With its aid, and using measurements of the weights in which chemical elements combine, he was able to calculate the relative weights of their constituent atoms; in this way he reasoned to the existence of about 20 kinds of atoms or elements. Gay-Lussac, experimenting with gases entering into chemical combination, concluded that gases combine in very simple ratios by volume; in his analysis, the law of combining volumes was more accurate than the law of combining weights proposed by Dalton. The oversimplified conceptual schemes used by both Dalton and Gay-Lussac in analyzing their data thereupon led Avogadro to adumbrate the distinction between atoms and molecules. Avogadro assumed that the constituent molecules of any simple gas are made up of half-molecules or third-molecules, etc., later identified with atoms, and proposed as a hypothesis that the number of integral molecules in any gas is always the same for equal volumes, or is always proportional to the volumes. With the aid of this hypothesis, he was able to reconcile apparently contradictory experimental data obtained by Dalton and Gay-Lussac.

Building on the work of Avogadro and of S. *Cannizzaro, Mendeleev noted regularities in the properties of the then-known elements, by this time 63 in number. He argued that since the mass of a substance is its most fundamental property, a periodicity of its other properties should be expected when the elements are arranged in the order of their atomic weights. He then proposed conclusions following from the periodic law that would be useful for discovering and correcting data on the elements (*see* PERIODIC TABLE). Meanwhile, Faraday's work on electrolysis led directly to the conception of units of electricity and to estimates of the value of charge that were later to be identified with the electron.

Despite vocal opposition from the empiricist E. *Mach and from the energeticist W. Ostwald, the cumulative effect of these discoveries convinced most scientists, toward the close of the 19th century, of the atomic structure of matter. Almost all of the data of chemistry were then capable of explanation in terms of atomic concepts. It seemed only a matter of time that the more complex electromagnetic phenomena of physics would yield to their explanatory power.

20th-century Status. Such confidence, however, was doomed to be short-lived. The even more rapid development of atomic physics in the first part of the 20th century led quickly to the abandonment of attempts to explain all physical phenomena in terms of the mechanical motion of Democritean atoms. The details of this development are quite complex and are treated elsewhere (*see* ATOMIC THEORY). For present purposes, it suffices to mention only the major conceptual developments as these are relevant to the present state of atomistic thought.

No sooner had fairly conclusive evidence for the existence of atoms and molecules been made available than a series of investigators, including J. J. Thomson, E. *Rutherford, F. W. Aston, and G. H. J. Moseley, produced a theory of atomic structure that viewed the atom as composed of subatomic particles. In the process, it was shown that the atom was divisible, i.e., that electrons could be removed from it and that its *nucleus could be disintegrated. Attempts to explain electromagnetic radiation and absorption in terms of this atomic structure led to the development of *quantum theory but produced no clear-cut mechanical conception of the motion of atomic parts. L. de Broglie, noting parallels between the dynamics of bodies and wave propagation, showed how electrons and other subatomic particles have also a wave or undulatory aspect. This led to the introduction of wave mechanics by E. Schrödinger and others, wherein the planetary motion of electrons was replaced by the interference of systems of stationary waves. More elaborate mathematical theories were then developed, which have been subjected to various physical interpretations but provide no easily imaginable picture of the structure of the atom. W. Heisenberg has pointed out how these conceptual advances forced physicists to adopt the *uncertainty principle, to abandon their commitment to physical *determinism, and to seek only statistical laws when investigating the microcosm. In 1958 he suggested that "all particles are basically nothing but different stationary states of one and the same stuff" (*The Physicist's Concept of Nature,* 46), and urged the return to the Aristotelian concept of potency as an ontological basis for the *indeterminism that seems to characterize the realm of the very small (*Physics and Philosophy,* 41, 53, 59–62, 69–72, 160, 166).

The status of atomism in 20th-century thought must be evaluated in the context of continuing research in the theory of *elementary particles. While atomistic concepts have proved most fruitful in exploring the structure of matter, physicists have generally abandoned hope of attaining the indivisibles Democritus regarded as the ultimate building blocks of the universe. Their researches have accented, rather, elements of truth in competing theories, such as those of Aristotle and his medieval commentators. At the same time, philosophers of science have become more critical of conceptual schemes elaborated by physicists, and are more prone to question the ontological status of theoretical entities than heretofore (*see* SCIENCE, PHILOSOPHY OF).

In light of these trends, atomism has ceased to play the central role in speculation about the physical universe that it played in the 19th century. This notwithstanding, and granted the oversimplifications that it involves when attempting to account for the wealth of detail in the microcosm, it still stands as one of the most fruitful conceptualizations in the history of scientific thought.

See also HYLOSYSTEMISM; ELEMENT; ETHER (PHYSICS); SPACE; VACUUM.

Bibliography: L. L. WHYTE, *Essay on Atomism* (New York 1960). A. G. VAN MELSEN, *From Atomos to Atom,* tr. H. J. KOREN (Pittsburgh 1952; Torchbk 1960). K. LASSWITZ, *Geschichte der Atomistik vom Mittelalter bis Newton* (Hamburg 1890). Eisler 1:132–137. V. E. ALFIERI, EncFil 1:447–455. Copleston v.1. S. SAMBURSKY, *The Physical World of the Greeks,* tr. M. DAGUT (New York 1962). C. BAILEY, *The Greek Atomists and Epicurus* (Oxford 1928). A. MAIER, *Die Vorläufer Galileis im 14. Jahrhundert* (Rome 1949); *An der Grenze von Scholastik und Naturwissenschaft* (2d ed. Rome 1952). W. C. and M. D. DAMPIER, eds., *Readings in the Literature of Science* (Cambridge, Eng. 1924; Torchbk 1959), classical contributions to atomic theory. L. K. NASH, "The Atomic Molecular Theory" in *Harvard Case Histories in Experimental Science,* ed. J. B. CONANT, 2 v. (Cambridge, Mass. 1957) 1:215–321. M. BOAS, "The Establishment of the Mechanical Philosophy," *Osiris* 10 (1952) 412–541. Chen Ning Yang, *Elementary Particles* (Princeton 1962). W. HEISENBERG, *The Physicist's Concept of Nature,* tr. A. J. POMERANS (New York 1958); *Physics and Philosophy* (New York 1958). P. SOCCORSI, *Quaestiones scientificae cum philosophia coniunctae: De vi cognitionis humanae in scientia physica* (Rome 1958); *Quaestiones scientificae cum philosophia coniunctae: De physica quantica* (Rome 1956). W. A. WALLACE, "The Reality of Elementary Particles," ProcAmCathPhilAs 38 (1964) 154–166.

[W. A. WALLACE]

ATONEMENT

The word atonement is of special interest in the fields of philology, literature, theology, and Scripture. It is the only word of Anglo-Saxon origin that signifies a theological doctrine. It indicates a setting "at one" of two parties that were estranged.

History of the Word. The verb "atone" existed in Middle English prior to the substantive "atonement." "Atone" was coined from "at" and "one" and signifies to set at one, to reconcile. It originated in the phrase "to be at one," a translation of the Anglo-French phrase *être à un,* to agree. In *Le Livre de reis* we read of Henry II and St. Thomas Becket: "Ils ne peusent être à un"—They could not agree.

Wyclif already used the noun "onement" for reconciliation. From frequent use of the phrases "set at one" or "at onement," the combined *atonement* began to take the place of *onement* early in the 16th century. St. Thomas More is the earliest known author to use the word atonement, in his English work the *History of King Richard III.* William Rastell, More's nephew, edited a strictly correct text in 1557. Rastell claimed that More wrote this incomplete history in 1513. Referring to the discord of the nobles at the time of Richard's coronation, More observed their lack of regard for their new atonement. *Atonement* was used here to signify reconciliation.

The Anglican Bibles—Tyndale (1525 or 1526), Coverdale (1535), Matthew (1537), Taverner (1539), Geneva (1557). King James (1611)—made ample use of the word atonement in the sense of reconciliation and expiation. C. S. Lewis, an Oxford authority on Tudor English, observed that the use of this word of Anglo-Saxon origin was probably no more than a case of stylistic preference. The King James Version was substantially Tyndale corrected and improved by Coverdale,

WYCLIF—1380.	TYNDALE—1534 ed.	CRANMER—1539.
11 and not oonli this: but also we glorien in god, bi oure lord ihesus crist: bi whom we han resceyued now recounceilvnge,	11 Not only so, but we also ioye in God by the meanes of oure Lorde Iesus Christ, by whom we have receavyd the attonment.	11 Not onely this, but we also ioye in God by the meanes of oure Lord Iesus Chryst, by whom we haue now optayned the attonment.
GENEVA—1557.	**RHEIMS—1582.**	**KING JAMES—1611.**
11 And not only so, but we also reioyse in God by the meanes of our Lord Iesus Christe, by whom we haue now receaued the atonement.	11 And not only this: but also vve glorie in God through our Lord Iesvs Christ, by vvhom novv vve haue receiued reconciliation.	11 And not onely so, but we also ioy in God, through our Lord Iesus Christ, by whom we haue now receiued the atonement.

Geneva, Rheims, and Cranmer, almost in collaboration [C. S. Lewis, *English Literature in the Sixteenth Century, Excluding Drama* (Oxford 1954) 214]. This was reflected in the use of the word atonement to translate καταλλαγή in Rom 5.11, as evidenced in the English Hexapla (Bodleian Library, Oxford MS Mason H H. 168, p. 88), which used later editions of the Tyndale and Geneva Bibles. (See table above.)

Theology. Since reconciliation is generally between one who has been offended and one who offends, atonement receives the ordinary meaning of satisfactory reparation or expiation for an offense. In the OT atonement is the reestablishment of Yahweh's communion with His people, who had offended Him by sin. It is a work of mercy on the part of God and on the part of man the fulfilling of certain things prescribed by God.

The Hebrew verb *kippēr,* pi'el of the root *kpr,* is translated as atone. It probably meant to cover, especially with a liquid. In the priestly documents it signifies mainly "to make atonement for sin by an expiatory rite" (Lv 4.31–35; 6.17–23). The LXX regularly translates *kippēr* by ἐξιλάσκομαι, which means to

¶ theyr destruccion, hauyng more regarde to their olde variaunce, then their newe attonement. For whiche cause thei shoulde assemble on the other partie muche people agayne for their defence, whose power she wyste wel farre stretched. And thus should all the realme fall on a rore. And of al the hurte that therof should ensue, which was likely not to be litle, and the most harme there like to fal wher she lest would, all the worlde woulde put her and her kinred in the wyght, and say that thei had unwyselye and untrewlye also, broken the amitie and peace that the kyng her husband so prudentelye made, betwene hys kinne and hers in his death bed, and whiche the other party faithfully obserued.

Detail of page from "Thomas More's English Works," edited by William Rastell, 1557 (BM MS C11, b14.41). The word "atonement" appears in the third line.

propitiate, also to atone. The highest spiritual sense of atonement in the OT is found in Is 52.13–53.12. The placation concept of atonement seems to have disappeared, and the passage concentrates on expiation. Sin is atoned for with a life, the life of the Suffering Servant of Yahweh, as a guilt offering. The personal deeds of this innocent mediator take the place of sinners. He suffers for them and effects atonement with a personal God moved by pity for them. The ideas of reconciliation and vicarious expiation permeate the passage (*see* SERVANT OF THE LORD ORACLES).

In the NT atonement does not play a primary role. In Heb 2.17 Christ has "become a merciful and faithful high priest before God to expiate [ἱλάσκεσθαι] the sins of the people." Paul presents atonement as an act of divine love that effects a new state of things, the peaceful relationship between God and man. Man is reconciled to God (2 Cor 5.18–19; Eph 2.15–16). In the second phase man acts: "be reconciled to God" (2 Cor 5.20). Paul develops these ideas out of the OT background: e.g., the OT notion of sacrifice, when he speaks of the *sacrifice of the cross, of which atonement is an effect. Thus atonement is effected through the blood of the cross (Rom 5.9; Eph 2.13–16). The Pauline concept of atonement is related to the idea of *justification, which forms the basis of atonement. Man is placed in a new relation to God. We live with God in peace (Rom 5.1–2; Eph 2.17–18).

Among the Christian writers atonement in the sense of satisfaction for sin, as applied to Christ's work, is found in its early development in the works of SS. Irenaeus, Ambrose, and Peter Damien. It assumed greater importance in the *Cur Deus Homo* of St. Anselm of Canterbury. Anselm made the atonement the basis of his explanation of the *Incarnation and the Redemption, in place of earlier notions of sacrifice and payment for sin. The great scholastic theologians of the 13th century, notably, St. Thomas Aquinas, perfected the Anselmian doctrine. In place of Anselm's teaching on the quasi-necessity of the atonement, St. Thomas holds that it was a work of the free choice of God that vicarious satisfaction for sin was effected by the God-Man.

While the Council of Trent treats of the all-sufficient atonement of Our Lord, it also takes into account man's personal cooperation in the work of satisfaction for sin under the influence of Christ's grace. Trends in contemporary Lutheran theology of justification show remarkable agreement with this position. Excessive stress on man's personal cooperation in the work of atonement is evidenced in the long and arduous penances for remission of sin demanded by the Jansenists.

In the present stance of Catholic and Protestant Biblical studies, there is a common stress on the atonement as a work of divine mercy rather than a juridical placation of divine wrath.

See also EXPIATION (IN THEOLOGY); PASSION OF CHRIST, II (THEOLOGY OF); RECONCILIATION WITH GOD; REDEMPTION, ARTICLES ON; REPARATION, THEOLOGY OF; SATISFACTION OF CHRIST.

Bibliography: A. C. BAUGH, *A History of the English Language* (2d ed. New York 1957) 245. W. W. SKEAT, *Principles of English Etymology* (2d ed. Oxford 1892) 56. A. MÉDEBIELLE, DB Suppl 3:1–262. Kittel ThW 1:252–260; 3:301–318; 4:330–337. H. F. DAVIS, CDT 1:189–198. J. BONSIRVEN, "Le Péché et son expiation selon la théologie du judaisme palestinien au temps de Jésus-Christ," *Biblica* 15 (1934) 213–236. S. LYONNET, *De peccato et redemptione* (Rome 1957–), 4 v. planned. J. DUPONT, *La Réconciliation dans la théologie de St. Paul* (Paris 1953).
Illustration credit: Courtesy of the Trustees of The British Museum.

[K. F. DOUGHERTY]

ATONEMENT, DAY OF (YOM KIPPUR)

An annual fast and day of expiation, observed on 10 Tishri (September or October), the most widely observed of all Jewish holy days. The term *yôm kippûr* is late rabbinical Hebrew for Biblical Hebrew *yôm hakkippûrîm,* both terms meaning Day of Atonement.

In the Bible. The only explicit references to this day in the OT are found in the most recent stratum of the Pentateuch: Lv 16.1–34; 23.26–32; 25.9; Nm 29.7–11. In this source the prescriptions for Temple worship are projected historically to the *Tent of Meeting in the desert where Aaron ministered. The day is described as one of most solemn rest from work as on the Sabbath. There is a convocation at the Temple and special sacrifices are ordained. All must "afflict themselves," i.e., fast and perform acts of penance for their sins and those of the whole nation. The *Jubilee year is to be heralded by the blowing of the ceremonial ram's horn, the Shofar, on the Day of Atonement.

The unusual Temple ceremonies are described in detail in Lv 16.1–34. The high priest, wearing special vestments, first sacrificed a bull for his own sins and those of the priests. On this occasion only, he was permitted to enter the Holy of Holies, behind the sanctuary veil, with incense and the blood of the sacrificial animal to sprinkle the mercy seat as an act of expiation. Then he repeated this ritual, the second time sacrificing a male goat in expiation for the sins of the people and for the sanctuary itself. Finally the priest made atonement also for the outer sanctuary by sprinkling blood upon the altar (Ex 30.10).

In addition there was quite a different kind of rite often referred to as that of the *scapegoat. The high priest selected two goats and cast lots upon them, "one lot for Yahweh and one lot for *Azazel" (Lv 16.8). The goat "for Yahweh" was sacrificed as described above; the other had all the sins of the people placed upon its head by the symbolic imposition of the high priest's hands and was released in the wilderness to carry away the burden of guilt. The name scapegoat (Lat. *caper emissarius*) reflects a misunderstanding of some of the ancient versions in translating the phrase "for Azazel." A modern theory, that the word identifies the place where the goat was released, is not generally accepted. Azazel was in fact thought by the Jews to be an evil spirit or devil that dwelt in the wilderness (a fallen angel according to 1 Enoch 10.4–8). The Israelites did not sacrifice a goat to him, but they presented it before Yahweh and then sent it and their sins "into the wilderness to Azazel" (Lv 16.10). A number of parallels to this ritual have been pointed out in Babylonian and other ancient religions, and it is very probable that the Israelites here adopted an ancient popular custom and interpreted it in the light of their own religious observance.

"Yom Kippur in the Synagogue," by B. Picard, 1723.

The origin of the Day of Atonement itself remains obscure. The fact that it is not mentioned in any preexilic text of the OT, nor even in the oldest postexilic texts, establishes a probability that it was instituted very late, but more precise information is not available. It is possible, however, that the practice of expiatory rites among the Hebrews was itself very ancient. The ritual of the Day of Atonement is alluded to in the NT (e.g., Heb 6.19; 9.7), but it did not persist in Christian observance. A tractate of the Mishnah (*Yômâ,* The Day) is devoted to details of the ritual.

Modern Customs. After the destruction of the Temple, prayers and synagogue services replaced the sacrifices and rites described above, but the essential motifs of self-affliction, confession, and expiation have always remained the heart of Yom Kippur observance. In the modern celebration there is a preliminary ritual on the eve, for which tradition prescribes a festive meal before sundown, the kindling of the festival lights, the settling of debts and disputes, and reconciliation with relatives and neighbors. The evening penitential services that follow in the synagogue begin with the *Kol Nidrê* (All vows . . .), a formula of absolution from all ceremonial or ritual vows intended to provide the worshiper with a new beginning and release him from any unfulfilled or forgotten promises of cult or custom. In the Ashkenazic (German-Jewish) ritual the *Kol Nidrê* is adapted to a distinctive and beautiful melody characteristic of the emotions of Yom Kippur. Since in history this formula has been the occasion of much misunderstanding outside Judaism, Jewish writers have been careful to insist that it does not refer to obligations to one's fellowmen or one's country.

On the Day of Atonement itself observance prohibits, even more solemnly than on the Sabbath, not only all business transactions or manual labor, but also, throughout the holy day, eating and drinking, bathing and anointing, the wearing of shoes, especially during services, and sexual relations. Custom has also associated almsgiving with Yom Kippur, and also the burning of candles in the synagogue in memory of the deceased, and the visiting of their graves. In keeping with the ancient idea of substitution or transference, it was once customary for an individual to swing a fowl over his head in symbolic sacrifice for some other person deserving of death for his sins. Other men, as an additional form of self-affliction, submitted to 39 lashes to be administered in the synagogue.

The essence, however, of the observance is the series of synagogue services, consisting of prayers, hymns, readings, and the confession of sins, which have been so much expanded that from sunrise to sunset on Yom Kippur they constitute one continual service. The Morning Service (*šaḥărît*) contains a memorial ceremony for the dead, including the prayer *yizkōr* (may he remember). The passages of Lv 16.1–34, Nm 29.7–11, and Is 57.15–58.14 are read at this time. In the Additional Service (*mûsāp*), there is a long description of the Temple ceremony on the Day of Atonement. The Afternoon Service (*minḥâ*) contains the reading of Leviticus ch. 18 and the Book of Jona. In the evening again there is a service peculiar to this day called the Neilah (*n*ᵉ*ʿîlâ*, conclusion), which concludes with the recital of the liturgical prayer *Shema* (Hear, O Israel . . .) and a single blast on the Shofar. The public confession of sins, which recurs throughout the day, is a general formula recited in unison, and not an individual confession. In the Ashkenazic, Sephardic (Spanish-Jewish), and other rituals there are many more prayers and readings that have been adopted into the liturgy. These rituals also contain many minor variations in the services themselves.

Bibliography: EncDictBibl 175–178. De Vaux AncIsr 507–510. E. ZOLLI, EncCatt 5:607–608. H. DANBY, tr., "Yoma," *The Mishnah* (Oxford 1933). K. KOHLER and M. L. MARGOLIS, JewishEnc 2:275–289. G. F. MOORE, *Judaism in the First Centuries of the Christian Era: The Age of the Tannaim,* 3 v. (Cambridge, Mass. 1927–30) v.2. S. LANDERSDORFER, *Studien zum biblischen Versöhnungstag* (*Alttestamentliche Abhandlungen* 10.1; Münster 1924). J. MORGENSTERN, "Two Prophecies of the 4th Century B.C. and the Evolution of Yom Kippur," HebUCAnn 24 (1952–53) 1–74. A. Z. IDELSOHN, *Jewish Liturgy and Its Development* (New York 1932) 223–248. **Illustration credit:** Photo Archive of the Jewish Theological Seminary of America, New York. Frank J. Darmstaedter.

[G. W. MAC RAE]

ATONEMENT, SOCIETY OF THE

This branch of the Third Order Regular of St. Francis of Assisi, founded in 1898 by Lewis Thomas *Wattson (Father Paul, SA), is composed of priests and brothers engaged in pastoral, missionary, and charitable work in the U.S., Canada, Japan, England, Brazil, and Rome. They are popularly known as Graymoor or Atonement friars; their motherhouse is at Graymoor, Garrison, N.Y., where the community originated.

Foundation. Wattson, who, as an Episcopalian clergyman, held pastorates in Kingston, N.Y., and Omaha, Nebr., wished to begin "a preaching order like the Paulists," based on the ideas of St. Francis, especially in the observance of religious poverty. On July 9, 1893, while reading from St. Paul, he found the word "atonement" and chose it as the name for his proposed community. Several years later he met Lurana Mary White (1870–1935), who, as Mother Lurana, SA, subsequently founded the *Franciscan Sisters of the Atonement. On Oct. 7, 1898, they pledged themselves to God to establish the Society of the Atonement.

The foundation was made that December when Mother Lurana went to Graymoor. Father Paul arrived the following October and spent the first winter in an abandoned paint shack. In 1900 the first small building was erected on the friars' property, the Mount of the Atonement. For the next several years the two communities struggled to survive against the threats posed by paucity of numbers, poverty, and the ostracism by their fellow Anglicans.

On Oct. 30, 1909, in the sisters' chapel at Graymoor, Father Paul, Mother Lurana, and 15 followers were received into the Catholic Church. Permission for this singular event was granted by Pius X through the apostolic delegate to the U.S., Diomede Falconi, OFM. Shortly after, the group was received into the Franciscan Order. Father Paul was ordained on July 16, 1910, at St. Joseph's Seminary, Yonkers, N.Y., by Abp. John Farley of New York. During the next 30 years, Father Paul's efforts were expended for the Church, for Graymoor, and for Christian unity.

Chair of Unity Octave. In 1908, he instituted the Chair of Unity Octave, a prayer crusade for religious unity from January 18 to 25. Pius X approved the practice in 1909; in 1916, Benedict XV extended it to the universal Church and granted indulgences. Pius XII renewed the indulgences in 1946 and in a letter (Nov. 1, 1957) urged the octave's observance to be spread as widely as possible. In 1959 John XXIII recommended it to all the faithful. The U.S. hierarchy in 1921 agreed to observe the octave in each diocese; this resolution was renewed in 1957 at the annual bishops' meeting in Washington, D.C.

The Chair of Unity Apostolate office at Graymoor is the center of various activities for promoting Christian unity. As a development of the octave, the friars direct the League of Prayer for Unity under the patronage of Our Lady of the Atonement. Its purpose is to inspire the faithful to pray, to work, and to offer sacrifices daily for Christian unity. The league, with headquarters at Graymoor, has a membership of 250,000. Formed in 1949, it received papal approval in 1956.

Other Activities. Graymoor friars also maintain a mission band to conduct parish missions, novenas, and other exercises. They direct St. Christopher's Inn at Graymoor (opened in 1909), a hospice for homeless

Chapel at Graymoor where Father Paul, Mother Lurana, and 15 followers were received into the Catholic Church.

and jobless men. In 1935 they introduced the Ave Maria Hour, a transcribed radio program on the lives of the saints. They publish the *Lamp,* a monthly periodical devoted to Christian unity and the missions; an English edition of *Unitas,* a quarterly on reunion; and books and literature directed to the same cause. The friars are particularly devoted to Our Lady of the Atonement, a title that originated with Father Paul and Mother Lurana; they celebrate this feast on July 9.

In 1951, the friars received their *decretum laudis* from the Holy See; the decree of final approbation was granted in 1960. The constitutions agree substantially with those of the Friars Minor, with whom the Graymoor friars have a decree of aggregation (1932). The priests and clerics recite the Divine Office in choir each day. All members wear the grayish-brown habit fastened at the waist by a cord to which is attached the Franciscan rosary of the Joys of Our Lady; and a crucifix is worn about the neck. The motto of the community is "All for Christ and the Salvation of Men." The friars have houses of study at Graymoor and Montour Falls, N.Y., and at Washington, D.C.; their novitiates are at Saranac Lake, N.Y., and Cumberland, R.I., where there is also a brother's training school. They work among the Negroes in North Carolina, the Mexicans in Texas, and the Japanese and Indians of western Canada. Since 1949 they have had a mission territory in the Diocese of Yokohama, Japan. In prayer and work they seek the ideal of Father Paul, "that all be one."

Bibliography: D. GANNON, *Father Paul of Graymoor* (New York 1951). T. CRANNY, *Father Paul: Apostle of Unity* (Peekskill 1955). E. F. HANAHOE, ed., *One Fold* (Garrison, N.Y. 1959).

[T. CRANNY]

ATTENDANCE AT NON-CATHOLIC SERVICES

The general legislation of CIC c.1258, forbidding active participation in non-Catholic religious services and tolerating passive presence, is supplemented by numerous decisions of the Holy Office. These decisions are particular ones, arrived at in view of circumstances peculiar to particular localities; hence they are not to be applied without reservation. As precedents they may be applied with these conditions in mind.

Active and Formal Participation. Catholics are forbidden to take any active part in non-Catholic services because it implies a profession of a false religion and, consequently, the denial of the Catholic faith. Active participation in these services is prohibited precisely because they are authorized by a religious group separated from the Catholic Church and represent its particular form of belief and worship. Although a person dissociates his mind from all intention of worshiping in these services, he is under grave obligation to abstain from taking active part in them. There remains some danger of perversion for the one participating, of scandal for the faithful, and of an external approbation of a false belief, all of which the natural law forbids. Granted that certain rites of non-Catholics, such as the Mass of the dissident Orthodox and the Baptism of heretics, are not wrong in themselves, participation is forbidden in these rites because it would at least imply an external approbation of schism or heresy. Active participation consists either in being a recipient of a rite, as the Sacraments or blessings, or in being a participant in their services, as praying or singing with them.

Sacraments. Catholics may not, under pain of excommunication, present themselves or their children to non-Catholic ministers for baptism, or attempt marriage before a non-Catholic minister. Especially because of its theological implications, Catholics are most gravely forbidden to receive Holy Communion at non-Catholic services. Catholics are not allowed to act as sponsors at non-Catholic baptisms. In the hour of death a Catholic should ordinarily be discouraged from seeking the administrations of the Sacraments from a schismatic priest, when no Catholic priest is available. Because of the danger of perversion, the dying Catholic should be induced to rely on the mercy of God and His grace to make an act of perfect contrition.

Sacramentals and Services. The Catholic faithful are not allowed to receive candles, palms, the blessing of ashes, or any other such blessing at non-Catholic services, or with exceptions indicated below, to join non-Catholics in the recitation of prayers or in the singing of hymns at non-Catholic religious services. Nor may a Catholic assume a role as cross-bearer, acolyte, or chorister in a non-Catholic religious procession. Since it is difficult to concede that playing the organ may be merely material cooperation, a Catholic may not be an organist in a non-Catholic church.

Passive and Material Presence. Even passive attendance of Catholics at non-Catholic services is ordinarily forbidden, but given certain conditions, the Code of Canon Law tolerates it. Passive and merely material presence at funerals, weddings, or any other such solemnities of non-Catholics may be tolerated for the sake of civil duty or honor for a grave reason, which in case of doubt should be approved by the bishop, provided there is no danger of perversion and scandal (CIC c.1258.2). It is for the bishop to decide in case of doubt whether a reason based on one's duty as an official, citizen, or servant, or on one's respect due to relationship or friendship warrants such an exception. Passive attendance consists in being merely present and observing what is being done. It need not imply inertness and inactivity. One assists passively as long as the action engaged in does not form a part of the sacred function. To uncover the head, to stand, to sit are considered usual marks of courtesy bearing civil signification. Some authors forbid kneeling because it may imply a religious attitude.

Funerals and Weddings. A grave reason permits passive attendance at these and other such solemnities as a baptismal ceremony, the giving of thanks for a civil reason, or the inauguration of a public official. No matter how cogent the reasons, a Catholic may not go beyond being witness or an honorary member at a non-Catholic baptismal ceremony. If a baccalaureate program is held in a Protestant church and includes denominational worship, Catholic students should object. If they will not be given their diplomas unless they attend, they may be present, but must refrain from taking any active part in the services.

With conditions prevailing in the U.S. in mind, and for reasons greater than mere friendship, a Catholic may be a bridesmaid or best man at a non-Catholic marriage in church. At an invalid marriage of a Catholic (or Catholics) before a non-Catholic minister, even Catholic parents and relatives with special reasons would seldom be permitted to attend the marriage ceremony. Custom has made it permissible for Catholic laymen to act as pallbearers at a non-Catholic funeral.

Visiting Churches. To visit a non-Catholic church as a sightseer is not forbidden. Ordinarily Catholics should avoid entering such churches when services or sermons are being conducted. A maid may accompany her non-Catholic employer to non-Catholic services if required to do so; but if done frequently, extraordinary care to safeguard her faith and to offset scandal must be taken. Sisters and nurses should honor the request of a non-Catholic who calls for a minister or rabbi (*Ethical and Religious Directives for Catholic Hospitals* 58).

Ecumenical Influence. Formerly any participation with non-Catholics in an activity of a religious character was forbidden. But the present ecumenical view that best harmonizes theory and practice does not regard all religious participation as intrinsically wrong. Granted the safeguards against scandal and loss of faith, it is permissible to pray with non-Catholics on certain occasions. This was clearly indicated by Vatican Council II in the *Decree on Ecumenism* (ch. 2.8), which declared that "in certain circumstances, such as in prayer services 'for unity' and during ecumenical gatherings, it is allowable, indeed desirable that Catholics should join in prayer with their separated brethren." It was also stated that it belongs to local episcopal authority to make decisions regarding concrete courses of action to be adopted with regard to such joining in prayer in varying circumstances of time, place, and persons, unless the Bishops' Conference or the Holy See should determine otherwise (*ibid.*).

The Interim Guidelines. The U.S. Bishops' Commission on Ecumenical Affairs issued on June 18, 1965, a document containing recommendations intended to be helpful to bishops in their supervision of ecumenical activity. This was entitled "Interim Guidelines for Prayer in Common and *Communicatio in Sacris*." A distinction was drawn between prayer in common at ecumenical gatherings that is not a part of the official liturgies of any of the participants and *communicatio in sacris,* which was understood as participation in services that pertain to the official liturgy of a specific church.

Prayer in Common. Subject to the guidance of local bishops, the participation of Catholics in nondenominational or "ecumenical services" when such services are held for the cause of promoting Christian unity is to be encouraged. This was understood according to the spirit of the *Decree on Ecumenism* to include participation of Catholics in nondenominational services held for some other immediate purpose such as peace, public need, mourning, or thanksgiving. Priests, with the approval of the local bishop, might be encouraged to take an active part in the conducting of such services, for example, by reading Scripture lessons, preaching homilies, offering prayers, and giving blessings, using for the occasion the form of dress the bishop judges to be suitable. Members of the laity, if qualified, might also be permitted by the local bishop to take an active part in services of this kind.

Communicatio in Sacris. The attendance of Christians of other communions at Catholic liturgical celebrations is to be welcomed, although caution is recommended in the issuance of general invitations in order to avoid giving offense to other ecclesial bodies or evoking invitations in return that it would be undesirable for Catholics to accept. Non-Catholics are not to be invited to act as sponsors at Catholic Baptism or Confirmation, nor to partake of the Eucharist, although some exception may be permitted in the case of members of the Eastern Churches, with whom "some worship in common [*communicatio in sacris*], given suitable circumstances and the approval of church authority, is not merely possible but is encouraged" (*Decree on Ecumenism,* ch. 3.15; cf. *Decree on the Catholic Churches of the Eastern Rite,* 26–29). Christians of other denominations present at Mass may be invited to join in the dialogue, in the recitation of prayers and in singing hymns, but not to assume roles of leadership within the assembly or to give the homily. It is recommended that public prayers for Christians of other communions be admitted within the liturgical celebrations. They may be invited to be present at the conferral of Holy Orders, but not to take leading roles; they may be admitted as witnesses and attendants at the celebration of Matrimony within the Catholic Church, but it is not recommended that clergymen of other communions be invited to take an active part in the ceremony. It is recommended that at funerals, when requested by the family of the deceased, priests be permitted to conduct funeral services and to lead prayers at wakes for those not of the Church, with the local bishop determining what rite is to be used on such an occasion.

Some participation by Catholics, under the supervision of the local bishop, in the official worship of other communions is envisaged in the *Decree on Ecumenism.* Such participation, according to the "Guidelines," would include attendance at official services of other churches that have special civic or social significance, especially weddings and funerals. However, Catholics are not to act as sponsors at non-Catholic Baptisms or Confirmations, although their presence for reasons of friendship or courtesy at such events may be permitted. Priests may not accept invitations to preach during Eucharistic celebrations in non-Catholic churches, nor may they take an active role in ordination services in such churches, although, with the approval of the local bishop an invitation to be present may be accepted. With the approval and under the guidance of the local bishop, Catholics may be permitted to serve as witnesses at marriages celebrated in churches of other communions.

The supervision of the new conciliatory policy established by the *Decree on the Catholic Churches of the Eastern Rite* with regard to *communicatio in sacris* with the brethren of the separated Eastern churches was put in the care and control of local bishops. The delicate question as to the manner in which this policy is to be implemented was declared to be under study.

Bibliography: J. R. Bancroft, *Communication in Religious Worship with Non-Catholics* (Washington 1943). F. J. Connell, "Communication of Non-Catholics in Sacred Rites," AmEcclRev 111 (1944) 176–188. H. Davis, *Moral and Pastoral Theology,* 4 v. rev. and enl. L. W. Geddes (New York 1958) 1:282–286. R. Naz, DDC 3:1091–95. H. Schauf, LexThK[2] 3:24–26. Text of "Interim Guidelines," in *Jurist* 15 (1965) 362–370.

[J. PRAH]

ATTENTION

The directing and focusing of consciousness upon some particular matter. It is a function of the cognitive powers, whereas intention pertains to the will. It is opposed to distraction, which is the withdrawal of advertence from some object upon which a person should, or would like to, keep his thought engaged. Attention is of moral significance because it is required for the proper performance of certain actions.

Attention is said to be internal when the action is performed with a mind free from distraction and intent upon what is being done. It is external when the action is performed with a distracted mind that does not fix itself upon what is being done, although there is sufficient awareness to permit the continuation of the intended action. Attention of this kind is not called external because an internal act is lacking (since all attention is cognitive and therefore of its nature internal), but because such attention as exists is directed only to the performance of the external act without thought of its significance.

In the administration and reception of the Sacraments greater attention is required on the part of the minister than on the part of the recipient. In Baptism, for example, pouring the water and saying the words demand more attention from the minister than reception of the Sacrament demands from the person baptized. For the valid administration of Baptism, the minister must be aware that he is applying water to the person baptized and that he is pronouncing the necessary words. For the validity of his act it is not necessary that he give attention to the meaning nor understand the significance of what he does, provided that he intends to do what the Church requires for the baptismal rite. Even voluntary distractions on his part would not invalidate the Sacrament, though he is under obligation to avoid them out of reverence for the sacred rite.

What has been said in general about Baptism applies also to the other Sacraments, but in the case of certain of them special observations are necessary. Because of the peculiar nature of the Holy Eucharist, the recipient with no attention to his action really receives the Body and Blood of Christ, but he receives more fruitfully if he gives more actual attention to the sacramental Presence. In Penance, unless there is danger of death, that attention is required which suffices for the three acts of the penitent, namely, contrition, confession, and purpose of satisfaction. In Matrimony the spouses, who are the ministers as well as the recipients, must have sufficient advertence to the offering and acceptance of matrimonial consent to enable them to make a valid contract.

Attention has a particular relevance to prayer, for the asking of becoming things from God can hardly take place without the petitioner's adverting in some way to the fact that he is speaking to God and making requests of Him. This advertence need not always be internal so far as the meritorious value of prayer is concerned, since all merit depends on at least persevering intention. The same can be said of prayer's second effect, the obtaining of the things asked for, since God is believed to hear those prayers from which all voluntary distractions have been banished. But the spiritual sweetness resulting from prayerful union with God will be obtained to the extent that attention is actual and internal.

Attention in vocal prayer can be directed to three different objects: (1) to the words only, with the purpose of orderly and correct pronunciation; (2) to the sense of the words, concentrating on the meaning of what is said; and (3) to the end of prayer, namely, God or the favor sought.

Obviously, some external or internal attention is necessary for any kind of prayer since it is a human act of speaking to God. For mental prayer it seems that even internal attention must be present, for meditation by its nature is a thinking about God.

Bibliography: V. Oblet, DTC 1.2:2215–20. J. A. McHugh and C. J. Callan, *Moral Theology,* 2 v. (New York 1958) 2: 2164–69. H. Davis, *Moral and Pastoral Theology,* 4 v. (rev. ed. New York 1958) 3:20–21.

[C. I. LITZINGER]

ATTICUS OF CONSTANTINOPLE, ST., patriarch 406 to 425; b. Sebaste, Armenia; d. Constantinople, Oct. 10, 425 (feast, Oct. 11 and Jan. 8). Atticus became a monk and an admirer of *Eustathius of Sebaste, and "though of mediocre talent, was endowed with sagacity" (Sozomen, *Hist. eccl.* 8.27). After his ordination in Constantinople, although not a great orator, he gained a reputation as a facile speaker despite his Armenian accent. He served as one of the seven accusers of St. *John Chrysostom at the Synod of the *Oak (Palladius, *Vita John Chrysos.* 11), and succeeded Arsacius as patriarch in 406. He increased the episcopal authority of his see through a law, sanctioned by *Theodosius II, that prohibited episcopal consecrations in Hellespont, Bithynia, and Asia Minor without his consent (Nicephorus Callistus, *Hist. eccl.* 14.29). An imperial decree of 421 directing appeals from Illyricum to Constantinople instead of Rome, although canceled because of the protest of Pope Boniface I, was incorporated in the Justinian code. Atticus's orthodoxy was acknowledged by the Councils of Ephesus (431) and Chalcedon (451). Having avenged himself on the followers of John Chrysostom, he sought reunion with Rome, inscribed Chrysostom's name in the diptychs, forcing St. Cyril of Alexandria to do likewise (Grumel Reg 1.1:37, 40, 41), and attacked the Pelagian Celestius and the Messalians. His sanctity was acknowledged by the Bollandists but challenged by L. de *Tillemont. Of his writings, letters to St. Cyril, Bishop Sahak of Armenia, Calliopes of Nicaea, and others, and fragments of a *Treatise against Nestorius* have been preserved. The Latin version of the Canons of Nicaea, which he sent to the Synod of Carthage (419), is preserved under his name.

Bibliography: A. Bigelmair, LexThK[2] 1:1016–17. Bardenhewer 3:361–363. M. T. Disdier, DHGE 5:161–166. G. Bardy, Fliche-Martin 4:149–162. Grumel Reg 1.1:35–48. M. Brière, "Une Homélie inédite d'Atticus," *Revue de l'orient chrétien* 34 (1933–34) 160–186. J. Lebon, "Discours d'Atticus de Constantinople," *Muséon* 46 (1933) 167–202. Turner EOMIA 1.1:104–142.

[P. JOANNOU]

ATTIGNY, COUNCILS OF, a number of Church councils held at Attigny, near Vouziers, France, in the Diocese of Reims, where there were both an episcopal residence and an important residence of the Carolingian kings.

In 765 about 25 bishops, 17 abbots, and other clerics met there; all that is now known of their transactions is that they promised that when one of them died the others would offer as suffrages a certain number of Masses and Psalms.

In 785 or 786, *Charlemagne attended the council at which two conquered Saxon princes, *Widukind and Albuin, were baptized.

In 822, at an assembly of bishops and princes, Emperor *Louis the Pious was reconciled with his three brothers, including *Drogo of Metz, and did public penance for blinding his nephew Bernard, King of

Italy. He promised to correct abuses and to restore ecclesiastical and civil order. He commended the Rule of St. *Chrodegang of Metz for every chapter of *canons. The bishops promised a program of reform, including the foundation and improvement of schools for future clerics.

At a council held in 834, Louis again promised to correct abuses and ordered his son Pepin to return certain Church properties.

There may have been a council at Attigny in 847, confirming decisions of the council of Paris of 846 or 847, which denied the claims of *Ebbo of Reims and confirmed the nomination of *Hincmar as archbishop of Reims.

In 865 a council decreed that King *Lothair II must leave his concubine and take back his wife. The papal legate promulgated two papal excommunications.

In 870, 30 bishops from 10 provinces and 6 archbishops participated in a council that found Carloman guilty of conspiracy against his father, Emperor *Charles II the Bald. *Hincmar, Bishop of Laon, had to promise obedience to Charles and to his metropolitan.

Bibliography: Hefele-Leclercq 3:951–952, 994; 4:34–36, 88–89, 363–364, 1306–07, 1344. A. Prévost, DHGE 5:168.

[A. CONDIT]

ATTILANUS, ST., patron and probably first bishop of Zamora; place and date of birth unknown; d. Zamora(?), 916 (feast, Oct. 5). He was the colleague of St. *Froilán in the organizing of monastic life in northwestern Spain. His name appears in the cartularies of Sahagun and Santiago. Zamora was destroyed by the Moors at the end of the 10th century, but, when the diocese was restored in the 12th, the cult of St. Attilanus spread widely. In 1260, thanks to a miraculous revelation, a shepherd discovered his relics in Zamora; his head was later stolen and taken to Toledo. A 12th-century vita that ascribes his origin to Tarragona, where his feast is celebrated August 28, lacks authenticity; and the claim that Urban II canonized him is false. He was included in the Roman martyrology in 1583.

Bibliography: A. Lambert, DHGE 5:169–173. B. de Gaiffier, "Les Notices hispaniques du martyrologe romain," AnalBoll 58 (1940) 80–89.

[E. P. COLBERT]

ATTITUDES

Predispositions to react in a certain way in response to certain kinds of stimuli. Attitudes are accompanied by positive or negative feelings associated with a specific psychological object, i.e., a habitual way of thinking and feeling about a group, person, situation, or object.

Attitudes are complex; they are composed of elements that fall into three categories—cognitive, affective, and behavioral. Attitude structure tends to be hierarchical; specific attitudes tend to be subsidiary to general attitudes; for example, one prejudiced against a religious minority group will more than likely be found prejudiced against other minority groups whether religious, racial, or national.

In most adults attitudes are moderately well integrated and generally resistant to change. People tend to seek out persons and situations reflecting attitudes consistent with their own. It is unclear, however, as to whether consistency or attitudes is a cause or a reflection of certain personality characteristics.

Social environment is the principal determinant of the kinds of attitudes acquired and held. A child tends to acquire the attitudes he sees and hears expressed within the home. Where there is attitude uniformity in the environment, attitudes take shape readily. Generally accepted attitudes become stable and enduring. They can be changed through altering a person's perception of the significance of the attitude object as a means for obtaining cherished goals.

In principle, an attitude cannot be measured directly but rather by inference from what a person says or does. In general, what one says is the more direct measure of attitude since what is said is affected principally by one's habitual way of thinking and feeling about a given object or situation.

Attitude scales, consisting of 15 to 25 statements, fairly equally spaced along the continuum from very favorable to very unfavorable, ask the respondent for expressions of opinion on specifics of a given attitude. Each attitude statement is assigned by a group of "judges" a value on a 1-to-11 point scale according to degree of attitude expressed. An individual's score is the median value of items checked.

Attitude measures can evaluate the extent to which educational aims are achieved, e.g., the effect of a school program in achieving attitudinal objectives. Attitude evaluation likewise assists in the understanding of the dynamics of behavior.

Attitudes are effective determinants of behavior that can be influenced through education and measured. Current techniques, while being improved, are sufficiently valid and reliable to warrant their use.

See also INTEREST; INTERESTS AND ACADEMIC ACHIEVEMENT; MOTIVATION.

Bibliography: H. J. Klausmeier, *Learning and Human Abilities* (New York 1961). R. E. Ripple, ed., *Readings in Learning and Human Abilities* (New York 1964). L. L. Thurstone, *The Measurement of Values* (Chicago 1959), pt. 3; *Multiple Factor Analysis* (Chicago 1947). M. J. Rosenberg et al., *Attitude, Organization and Change* (New Haven 1960). B. F. Green, "Attitude Measurement," in *Handbook of Social Psychology,* ed. G. Lindzey, 2 v. (Reading, Mass. 1954).

[U. H. FLEEGE]

ATTO OF MILAN, cardinal and canonist; b. place and date unknown; d. 1085 or 1086. A Milanese cleric of noble birth, he was elected to succeed Archbishop Wido on Jan. 6, 1072, in the presence of Pope Alexander II's legate and with the support of the *Patarine reformers. Ensuing disorders prevented enthronement, and Atto took refuge in Rome under Pope Gregory VII when a rival candidate was consecrated with King Henry IV's approval. Despite recognition of Atto as bishop-elect by Roman synods in 1072 and 1074 and efforts to secure his rights by Pope Gregory (*Registrum* 2.30; 3.8, 9), he never occupied the see. He was created cardinal priest of the title of St. Mark, but little is known of his Roman career. He was among those who deserted Gregory in 1084, as Cardinal Beno and Hugh of Lyons both testify, and he was eulogized after death by the moderate Pope Victor III. His fame rests on his *Breviarium* (*see* ATTO, COLLECTION OF). The title cardinal of Milan is a modern misnomer.

Bibliography: Bonzio of Sutri, *Liber ad amicum,* lib. 6, MG LibLit 1:599–600. Arnulf of Milan, *Gesta archiepiscoporum Mediolanensium,* lib. 3–4, MGS 8:22–31. A. Fliche, DHGE 5:184–185.

[J. J. RYAN]

ATTO OF VERCELLI, bishop, theologian, and canonist; b. *c.* 885; d. Dec. 31, 961. He is called also Atto II, to distinguish him from an earlier bishop of *Vercelli of the same name who lived about the middle of the 8th century. Born of a distinguished Lombard family, the son of the Viscount Aldegarius, he became a figure of outstanding importance in the Church and state of his day. Details of his education are not known, but it must have been considerable, for his works indicate a knowledge of Greek. The year 924 was the turning point in his career; the Hungarians, during their incursion into Italy, ravaged the city of Pavia on March 12, and Ragembert, Bishop of Vercelli, died in the attack. Atto was made his successor, and his office brought him into association with the leading figures of his day: Hugh of Provence, King of Italy (d. 947), whose grand chancellor he became; *Lothair II (d. 950), Hugh's son, whom he served in a like capacity; and the Margrave Berengar II (d. 966). Yet his activities did not prevent him from devoting considerable time to writing. The three books of his *De pressuris ecclesiasticis* (*c.* 940) are the earliest of his major works and deal with such subjects as the refutation of charges against the clergy, the filling of clerical posts (especially bishoprics), and the unjust seizure of church property by the laity after the death of the bishop. His *Commentary on the Epistles of Paul* considered the question of why the Roman Epistles stand first. There are also *Letters* and *Sermons,* as well as a work entitled *Canones statutaque Vercellensis ecclesiae,* which is a recapitulation of past ecclesiastical legislation in the diocese and includes the *False Decretals. His somewhat remarkable *Polipticum* (*Polypticum, Perpendiculum*), an abridgment of moral philosophy (ed. G. Goetz, AbhSächsAk 1922, 37.2), seems to have been completed in the last months of Atto's life and to have been sent to a friend, who in turn composed a foreword to the work, using the same distinctive Latinity that Atto had employed. Atto himself stands as a valuable index to his age and as a person of notable endowments and achievements.

Bibliography: Works. PL 134:9–916. C. BURONZO DEL SIGNORE, ed., 2 v. (Vercelli 1768). Literature. J. SCHULTZ, *Atto von Vercelli* (Göttingen 1885). E. PASTERIS, *Attone di Vercelli ossia il più grande vescovo e scrittore italiano del secolo X* (Milan 1925). P. PIRRI, "Attone di Vercelli," CivCatt 1 (1927) 27–42. A. FLICHE, *La Réforme grégorienne,* v.1 (Paris 1924) 61–74. Manitius 2:27–34. Wattenbach-Holtzmann 1.2:317. M. MACCARRONE, EncCatt 2:361–362. P. MIKAT, LexThK² 1:1019.

[W. C. KORFMACHER]

ATTO, COLLECTION OF, a compendium of Canon Law, *Breviarium,* in 500 unnumbered chapters compiled in Rome *c.* 1075 by *Atto of Milan, cardinal priest of St. Mark, to supply the needs of the clergy of his titular church. It stands among the first such works inspired by the program of Pope Gregory VII, to which the author was devoted, at least in its early stage. He aimed to present in brief the norms of law and morality that represented the discipline of the Roman Church, as found in the ancient papal decretals and conciliar canons, and constituted the basis of the *Gregorian reform. His chief sources were the *False Decretals, *Dionysius Exiguus (for Oriental and African councils), and Pope Gregory I's letters (more than 100 excerpts). Material not previously in circulation came notably from Pope Gelasius I. The first series of texts embraces the decretals; the second, the councils—each in chronological order. Its influence was very limited, but it was used in the Collection of *Deusdedit and by *Anselm of Lucca. The title *Capitulare* is a modern misnomer.

See also CANONICAL COLLECTIONS BEFORE GRATIAN.

Bibliography: Mai SVNC 6.2:60–120, from the one known MS, now identified as Codex Vaticanus latinus 586. Fournier-LeBras 2:20–25. P. FOURNIER, "Les Collections canoniques romaines de l'époque de Grégoire VII," *Mémoires de l'Académie des inscriptions et belles-lettres* 41 (1918) 271–395, also pub. sep. (Paris 1918). Stickler 166–167. R. NAZ, DDC 1:1330–31.

[J. J. RYAN]

ATTRITION AND ATTRITIONISM

Attrition or imperfect contrition is sorrow and detestation of sin motivated by sin's malice or the fear of hell and God's punishments. The term is first employed by Alan of Lille (d. 1202) to express a certain displeasure for sin but one not deep enough to prompt the sinner to a firm purpose of amendment. According to Alan, those who are attrite "become less evil, but they do not cease to be evil until they are perfectly contrite" [*Regulae de sacra theologia, 85* (PL 210:665)]. A more positive approach to attrition was taken by William of Auvergne (d. 1249). Having more regard for the etymology of the word (Latin *attero,* p. part. *attritus,* to wear away by rubbing), William regarded attrition as the first step in the removal of sin. Attrition is not merely the natural displeasure that is consequent upon sin, it is the result of God's gratuitous grace (*gratia gratis data*) by which the destruction of sin is begun, whereas *contrition is the result of God's sanctifying grace (*gratia gratum faciens*) by which the process is completed. Hence, contrition presupposes the gift of charity, whereas attrition is a preparation for the grace of charity that elicits the act of contrition. Although William is not the author of the adage *"ex attrito fit contritus"* (a person who is attrite becomes contrite), William regarded attrition as a sufficient preparation for the Sacrament of Penance, in and through which the sinner becomes contrite [cf. *De sacramento paenitentiae,* 4; *Opera Omnia* (Venice 1591) 441].

William of Auvergne's distinction between attrition and contrition became the common property of the great scholastic doctors of the 13th century, including St. Bonaventure and St. Thomas Aquinas. Out of deference, however, to Peter Lombard (d. *c.* 1160), the Master of the *Sentences,* who held that sorrow prompted by perfect love of God was the only proper disposition for the remission of sins, both Thomas and Bonaventure held that contrition informed by charity should be the normal disposition in one approaching the power of the keys. Both admitted, however, that putative contrition (actually attrition), when informed by the priest's absolution, would result in perfect contrition and the remission of sins, the position of William of Auvergne (cf. Bonaventure, *In 4 Sent.* 17.2.2.3; Thomas, ST Suppl 3a, 18.1).

Council of Trent. In the 14th session of the Council of Trent (1551) attrition was distinguished from contrition not so much by the eliciting principle, the virtue of charity, but by the motive that prompted the act. Thus, against Luther, who held that attrition made man a hypocrite and a greater sinner, Trent defined attrition as a gift of God and a prompting of the Holy Spirit, since "it is ordinarily conceived from a consideration of sin's malice or from fear of hell and punishment" [Sess. 14, ch. 4 (Denz 1678)]. True, such attrition does not of itself justify the sinner apart from the Sacrament of Penance, "yet it disposes him for the attainment of God's grace in the Sacrament" (*ibid.*). Trent also insists that such attrition must exclude the will to sin and be accompanied by hope of pardon (*ibid.*).

Controversies after Trent. The basic issue after Trent concerned attrition from the motive of fear (*attritio formidolosa*). According to the Jansenists "fear of hell is not supernatural" nor a sufficient motive for attrition [cf. *Propositions,* 14, 15, condemned by Alexander VIII, 1690 (Denz 2314, 2315)]. According to the Jansenist Quesnel, "Fear merely restrains the hand, while the heart is attached to sin so long as one is not motivated by love of justice" [*Proposition* 61, condemned by Clement XI, 1713 (Denz 2461)]. The Jansenist Synod of Pistoia (1794) insisted that sorrow for sin even in the Sacrament of Penance must be prompted by the most perfect love of God, the "fervor of charity" (cf. Denz 2636). Against the Jansenists, Catholic theologians appealed to the Old and the New Testament to show that God repeatedly urges the motive of fear as the first step in the repentance of the sinner and as an incentive for avoiding sin in the future. Typical of such exhortations is Christ's own warning: "And do not be afraid of those who kill the body but cannot kill the soul. But rather be afraid of him who is able to destroy both soul and body in hell" (Mt 10.28). Again, to demand perfect contrition as the motive of sorrow in the Sacrament of Penance is to deny that the priest's absolution is in any way directed to the remission of sin.

Unlike the Jansenists, the Contritionists of the 17th century admitted that fear of God was both good and salutary. They denied that attrition from the motive of fear was a sufficient preparation for obtaining pardon in the Sacrament of Penance. Without going to the extremes of the Jansenists who demanded the fervor of charity, the Contritionists demanded some love of God or love of benevolence for pardon even in the Sacrament of Penance. Attrition from the motive of fear disposes the sinner for the grace of pardon in the Sacrament of Penance, but only remotely. The proximate disposition must be love or charity towards God.

The Attritionists, many of whom were Jesuits and suspicious of anything that seemed to be Jansenistic, insisted that attrition from the motive of fear, so long as it was coupled with hope of divine pardon, was a proximate disposition for forgiveness in and through the Sacrament of Penance. For Attritionists, love of God for His own sake, no matter at what state of development, or how lacking in emotional fervor, was sufficient of itself to justify the sinner even before the actual reception of the Sacrament of Penance. Hence, it could not be demanded in the Sacrament of Penance without undermining the sacramental efficacy of the priest's absolution. Many Attritionists, however, did speak of "love," but it was a love of concupiscence or the love of hope (*amor concupiscentiae vel spei*), an initial love of God as the source of all justice, of which Trent speaks in its decree on justification (cf. Denz 1526).

The controversy between the Contritionists and the Attritionists waxed so warm, particularly in Belgium, the homeland of Jansenism, that Alexander VII sponsored a decree of the Holy Office which warned both parties to the controversy under the severest of penalties "not to dare to affix a note of theological censure" to either opinion. The decree, however, does note in passing that the view of the Attritionists "appears to be more common among scholastics" [*Decree of the Holy Office,* May 6, 1667 (Denz 2070)].

See also PENANCE, SACRAMENT OF.

Bibliography: P. F. PALMER, ed., *Sacraments and Forgiveness* (Sources of Christian Theology 2; Westminster, Md. 1960). J. PÉRINELLE, *L'Attrition d'après le Concile de Trente et d'après Saint Thomas d'Aquin* (Kain, Belg. 1927). H. DONDAINE, *L'Attrition suffisante* (Paris 1943).

[P. F. PALMER]

ATWATER, WILLIAM, bishop of Lincoln; b. according to his epitaph *c.* 1440; d. Feb. 4, 1520 or 1521. He was probably a fellow of Magdalen College, Oxford, in 1480. In 1492–93 he took the degree doctor of theology and in 1497 became vice chancellor of the university. He held this office in conjunction with others until 1502, for a time filling the post of chancellor left vacant by the death of Abp. John Morton. On June 21, 1504, he became canon of Windsor and registrar of the Order of the Garter. From 1506 to 1512 he was chancellor of the cathedral of Lincoln, exchanging the chancellorship on Oct. 30, 1512, for a prebend in the cathedral. In July 1509 Atwater secured the prebendary of Ruscomb in Salisbury cathedral along with a coat of arms, and in September of the same year he obtained the appointment of dean of Salisbury. For a short time from 1509 to 1512 he was archdeacon of Lewes. From June 3 until November of 1514 he was archdeacon of Huntington. He was elevated to the bishopric of Lincoln in September 1514 in succession to Wolsey and was consecrated at Lambeth on Nov. 12, 1514. His rise in the Church was due probably to the favor of Wolsey. On Oct. 22, 1514, he resigned the canonry of Windsor, but continued in the deanery of the chapel royal. He was buried in Lincoln Cathedral; an inscription above his grave states that at the time of his death he was 81 years old.

Bibliography: Emden 1:73–74. Gams 192. S. LEE, DNB 1:713. R. VAN DOREN, DHGE 5:199.

[V. PONKO, JR.]

AUBARÈDE, JEAN MICHEL D'ASTORG D', French ecclesiastic; b. Tarbes, 1639; d. Bayeux, 1692. His was an old and prominent noble family. He became a cleric in the Diocese of Tarbes until he moved to Pamiers as canon. There he became involved in the fateful issue of the *régale.* A staunch supporter of François *Caulet, bishop of the diocese, he was consequently deprived of his benefice by the royal agents, as were the bishop and all other opponents of Louis XIV's policy. Upon the death of Caulet, Aubarède was elected capitular vicar, but the King annulled the election and imposed his own choice (a man who had earlier been excommunicated by Caulet) by means of the armed strength of the notorious intendant, Nicholas Foucault. When appeals by the chapter to Innocent XI and the archbishop of Toulouse failed, Aubarède humbly accepted the sentence of exile, changed suddenly by royal whim to imprisonment in the Bastille. There he is said to have been offered a bishopric by Pontchartrain if he would submit. On his refusal he was transferred to a prison in Caen where he remained until the eve of his death.

Bibliography: N. J. FOUCAULT, *Mémoires,* ed. F. BAUDRY (Paris 1862). L. DE ROUVROY SAINT-SIMON, *The Memoirs of the Duke of Saint-Simon on the Reign of Louis XIV and the Re-*

gency, tr. B. ST. JOHN, 4 v. in 2 (New York 1936). G. DOUBLET, *Un Prélat janséniste* (Paris 1895). J. CARREYRE, DHGE 5:201–202.

[L. L. BERNARD]

AUBENAS, MARTYRS OF, Jesuits slain Feb. 7, 1593, by Huguenots in Aubenas, Diocese of Viviers, France (feast, Feb. 7). They were beatified June 6, 1926, and are honored as "Martyrs of the Eucharist." James Salès, b. Lezoux in Auvergne, March 21, 1556; studied at Billom and Paris. He entered the novitiate at Verdun and taught philosophy at Pont-à-Mousson and theology in Tournon. Ordained in 1585, he preached in Lorraine. In Nov. 1592 on the request of the mayor for a Jesuit to preach the Advent series, he was sent to Aubenas, recently retaken from the Huguenots. A lay brother, William Saultemouche, b. St. Germain d'Herm, Clermont, 1556, was his companion. On Feb. 6, 1593, the Huguenots attacked Aubenas and seized the Jesuits. Salès defended the faith at length before a court of Calvinists. When he refused to renounce articles of the faith, especially with regard to the Eucharist, he was shot, stabbed, and beaten. Saultemouche remained with him rather than attempt to escape. Their relics are in Avignon.

Bibliography: C. TESTORE, EncCatt 2:382–383. G. WAGNER, *Catholicisme* 1:1008–09. B. SCHNEIDER, LexThK² 1:1022.

[F. D. S. BORAN]

AUBERT OF AVRANCHES, ST., bishop; d. Avranches, 725 (feast, Sept. 10). According to the accounts of the foundation of *Mont-Saint-Michel, Aubert, Bishop of Avranches (704?–725), had retreated to Mont Tombe to pray. Having fallen asleep, he was told three times in a dream to build a church on the site and dedicate it to St. Michael the Archangel. The records report that the church was so dedicated on Oct. 16, 709. Aubert is supposed also to be the founder of the pilgrimage to the famous spot, henceforth called Mont-Saint-Michel. The chapter of canons was later replaced by *Benedictines; Aubert's body was translated to the abbey June 18, probably 1009. Since the French Revolution, the only relic extant is in Saint-Gervais in Avranches. A 15th-century vita of St. Aubert is of little value.

Bibliography: ActSS Sept. 8:76–78. BHL 1:858–860; 2:5951. E. DUPONT, DHGE 5:222. R. AIGRAIN, *Catholicisme* 1:1009–10. Butler Th Attw 3:533.

[G. J. DONNELLY]

AUBIGNÉ, JEAN HENRI MERLE D', Swiss Protestant ecclesiastical historian, preacher, and founder of the College of Geneva, whose thinking and achievement influenced Genevan Calvinism, b. Eaux Vives, Geneva, Aug. 8, 1794; d. there, Oct. 21, 1872. D'Aubigné's paternal ancestors were French Huguenot refugees, the name *d'Aubigné* being added to the family name of *Merle* by his maternal grandmother. He was educated in Geneva, where he imbibed the influence of the Scottish missionary preacher, Robert Haldane, and in Berlin, where he profited from the scholarship of William Neander and W. M. L. de Wette. After ordination he was appointed in 1819 pastor of the Protestant French church in Hamburg. From 1823 to 1830 he served as court preacher to King William I of the Netherlands in Brussels and also became president of the consistory of the French and German Protestant churches. The Belgian revolution of 1830 decided his return to Geneva, where he served as professor of church history until his death. He became an outstanding promoter of "evangelical alliance," founding, with others, the Evangelical Society for the promotion of evangelical Christianity. Calvinistic in its main doctrines, under D'Aubigné's guidance this society staunchly opposed Church-State union and aimed boldly at establishing an all-Protestant church relationship. Thus he helped to break that inflexible exclusiveness hitherto characteristic of Genevan Calvinism. As a counterpoise to the Genevan Academy, and to meet the need for theologically trained ministers capable of pursuing the necessary Protestant colloquy and union, as well as to encourage a missionary spirit, he founded the College of Geneva and was its president. He remained very anti-Catholic.

In addition to preaching and instructing, he labored indefatigably in writing ecclesiastical history. His most notable works are: *Histoire de la réformation du XVIe siècle* (5 v. Paris 1835–53, tr. into most European languages), *Histoire de la réformation en Europe du temps de Calvin* (8 v. Paris 1862–77, tr. into English), and a historical monograph on Oliver Cromwell. He visited Britain frequently and was honored both by Oxford University and by the city of Edinburgh.

Bibliography: V. ROSSEL, *Histoire littéraire de la Suisse romande des origines à nos jours,* 2 v. (Geneva 1889–91), v.2. C. CRIVELLI, EncCatt 2:383–384. H. HOHLWEIN, RGG³ 4:879.

[F. D. S. BORAN]

AUBIGNÉ, THÉODORE AGRIPPA D'

Soldier, poet, and historian; b. Saint-Maury, France, Feb. 8, 1552; d. Geneva, Switzerland, May 9, 1630. The soldier began his career of combat at the age of 16 when he crept from his tutor's house to join the Huguenot armies fighting the third Religious War (1568). His services to Henry of Navarre (later *Henry IV) obtained for him the military grade of *maréchal de camp* (brigadier-general) and the civil office of governor of Maillezais, an important fortress in Poitou. After Henry IV's assassination (1610), D'Aubigné's Protestant intransigence implicated him in plots against the strongly pro-Catholic regency of Marie de Médici. He was condemned for treason and fled to Geneva (1620), where he took up the task of renovating the fortifications. D'Aubigné's presence at the Valois court in the 1570s and his occasional visits to Henry IV in Paris after the pacification of France in 1593 give his writings a political framework that makes them more than a record of military exploits. This sense of the political and social significance of religious conflicts also allowed him to transcend, at least in part, the distortions of Protestant partisanship in his two major works, the poem *Les Tragiques* and the *Histoire universelle.* Hardly universal, the latter records the battles of the French Religious Wars and their relationship to France's foreign policy. True to the canons of humanist historiography, D'Aubigné avoided all partiality in style; only the selection of the facts to be related, not the manner of his narration, betrays his Protestantism. D'Aubigné's intention was to record the misery of a great nation suffering from internecine conflict as well as to vindicate the struggle of the Huguenot minority.

The intensity of D'Aubigné's moral revulsion at the suffering of France and at the selfish indifference of her aristocratic rulers in *Les Tragiques* liberates the Protestant from dogmatism in a manner analogous to his humanist coolness in the *Histoire universelle.* The poem, however, passes beyond the sphere of social, historical reality to end on the plane of religious vision: D'Aubigné's seventh and last book portrays God's rectification of the sufferings of the elect on earth at the Last Judgment. Here too his moral fervor carries him beyond the limitations of his Protestant creed: the mystic surrender to Deity of the souls "washed by pardon," which D'Aubigné portrays at the end of his poem, expresses with rare lyric force an aspiration familiar to every variety of believer.

D'Aubigné's *Mémoires* might be said to reveal his central artistic gift: the ability to compress the varied aspects of experience into an explosive image, the power to reduce the events and issues of an age to the dimensions of a single personality. D'Aubigné compressed by eliminating: his world is black and white, and the elimination of mediating shades of gray condemns his world to unceasing conflict.

D'Aubigné's other major works are: *Le Printemps* (love lyrics) and *La Confession catholique du sieur de Sancy* and *Les Aventures du baron de Faeneste* (religio-political satires in prose). His many short poems on men and events of the day cut and thrust like his soldier's sword and are perhaps his most finished productions. D'Aubigné's writings on political theory, science, and theology, as well as his paraphrases of Genesis and the Psalms, are of less interest.

Bibliography: *Oeuvres complètes*, ed. E. RÉAUME et al., 6 v. (Paris 1873–92), incomplete, poorly ed.; *Pages inédites*, ed. P. PLAN (Geneva 1945); *L'Histoire universelle*, ed. A. DE RUBLE, 10 v. (Paris 1886–1909); *Supplément à l'Histoire universelle*, ed. J. PLATTARD (Paris 1925). Other works by d'Aubigné have been pub. in the *Bulletin de la Société de l'histoire du protestantisme français* (1885–1927), *passim* and in StPhilol (1966); still others will undoubtedly be discovered. The only satisfactory eds. of his works have been pub. by PLATTARD (*Supplément:* see above), A. GARNIER and J. PLATTARD, eds., *Les Tragiques*, 4 v. (Paris 1932–33), and H. WEBER *Le Printemps* (Paris 1960).

Secondary works. C. A. SAINTE-BEUVE, *Tableau de la poésie française au XVIe siècle*, 2 v. (Paris 1876); *Causeries du lundi*, v.10 (Paris 1855) 312–342. A. GARNIER, *Agrippa d'Aubigné et le parti protestant*, 3 v. (Paris 1928), definitive biog. J. PLATTARD, *Une Figure de premier plan dans nos lettres de la renaissance, Agrippa d'Aubigné* (Paris 1931), important for D'Aubigné as historian and satirist. H. A. SAUERWEIN, *Agrippa d'Aubigné's Les Tragiques* (Baltimore 1953), structural and linguistic criticism. C. BAUDOUIN, "La Tentation d'Agrippa d'Aubigné," *Psyché* (1955) 521–529, suggestive psychoanalytic study. H. WEBER, *La Création poétique au XVIe siécle en France*, 2 v. (Paris 1956), excellent synthesis of all preceding criticism of D'Aubigné's *Tragiques*.

[S. KINSER]

AUBRAC, ORDER OF, community of hospitallers founded in 1120 by Adalard, Viscount of Flanders, as he was returning from *Santiago de Compostela. At the same time he established the hospital (*see* HOSPITALS, HISTORY OF) of Sainte-Marie at Aubrac, on a mountain in Rouergue, 22 km from Espalion, France. In 1162, Peter II, Bishop of Rodez, gave the community a rule based on the Rule of St. *Augustine; it was confirmed by Pope Alexander III. The community was composed of five groups: priests, knights, lay brothers, oblates, and the women assistants of high birth. Aubrac founded a number of dependent hospitals. Attempts to amalgamate with the Order of St. John of Jerusalem (*Knights of Malta) or with the *Templars were unsuccessful. In 1477 the monastery was placed in *commendation. By 1697 such laxity had set in that the Congregation of France (canons of *Sainte-Geneviève of Paris) was sent to take over the hospital. The harsh climate forced the canons to withdraw, and in 1699 they were replaced by the Reformed Canons of Chancelade. Aubrac was suppressed by the French Revolution. The religious at Aubrac wore a black cassock with an eight-pointed blue cross at the left side; in choir, they wore a black cowl that bore the same cross.

Bibliography: C. DE VIC and J. VAISSETE, *Histoire générale de Languedoc*, ed. E. DULAURIER et al., 16 v. in 17 (2d ed. Toulouse 1872–1904) 4:888–898. P. HÉLYOT. *Histoire des ordres monastiques, religieux et militaires*, 8 v. (Paris 1714–19) 3:169–174. C. BELMON, DHGE 5:256–258. R. CHALUMEAU, *Catholicisme* 1:1013–14. Archives of Department of Aveyron, ser. G. and H.; Collection Doat.

[J. CAMBELL]

AUBRY, PIERRE, musicologist whose studies, editions, and bibliographies are of importance in medieval music scholarship; b. Paris, Feb. 14, 1874; d. Dieppe, France, Aug. 31, 1910. After studies in philology and law, in 1898 Aubry received the degree Archiviste-paléographe from the École de chartes in Paris. Armed also with a diploma in the Armenian language, he undertook researches on Armenian music. His prime interest, however, was medieval music, and after 1904 he concentrated on polyphony and the monophonic music of the trouvères. His editions, *Cent motets du XIIIe siècle* (1908), *Le Roman de Fauvel* (1907), *Le Chansonnier de l'Arsenal* (1909), and his book *Trouvères et Troubadours* (2d ed. 1910; Eng. ed. 1914) all have lasting value. His earlier work on the religious background of medieval music, such as the four-volume *Mélanges de Musicologie critique* (1899–1903) and his edition (1901) of the proses of *Adam of Saint-Victor, are also important, although his treatment of tonic rhythm (1903) has now been superseded. In addition to his scholarly publishing, Aubry lectured at the Institut catholique, Schola cantorum, and École des hautes études sociales. He survived a bitter controversy over authorship of one of his theories but died prematurely of an accidental fencing injury.

Bibliography: É. DACIER, in BiblÉcChartes 71 (1910) 701–704. H. BESSELER, MusGG 1:778–780. H. G. FARMER, Grove DMM 1:256–257. Baker 57–58.

[K. G. FELLERER]

AUBUSSON, PIERRE D', cardinal and grand master of the Order of St. John of Jerusalem; b. 1423; d. July 3, 1503. He belonged to the noble family who ruled the town of Aubusson, the Viscounts de la Marche. He served with Emperor *Sigismund and with Albert VI, Archduke of Austria (d. 1463), before joining the Order of St. John (*see* KNIGHTS OF MALTA), where he rose rapidly through the various offices until he was selected grand master, June 8, 1476. The main problem during his administration was to prevent the Turks from conquering *Rhodes. The knights fought off an all-out attempt in 1480 in an engagement in which Aubusson was wounded. His success against the Turks made him widely known in Europe. The island was temporarily saved from further attack by the death in 1481 of Mohammad II, the Turkish leader. During the struggle for succession, one of Mohammad's sons, Jem, sought asylum with the grand master. Aubusson sent him to France and then, for reasons that are not exactly clear, accepted an annuity of 45,000 ducats from Sultan Bajazet (d. 1513), the captive's brother, on condition that he prevent Jem from appealing to Christian Europe for aid. Jem, in effect, became a prisoner of the knights in France until 1489, when he was handed over to Pope *Innocent VIII. In that same year Aubusson was made a cardinal and given the power to confer all benefices connected with the order without the sanction of the papacy. The knights received also the wealth of the suppressed orders of the Holy Sepulcher and the *Hospitallers of St. Lazarus. Aubusson spent the last years of his life trying to organize a crusade against the Turks, but the death of Jem in 1495 removed the most formidable weapon that could be used against the Sultan. Aubusson's last efforts were handicapped also by dissension among his own troops. Aubusson was an able soldier and an effective diplomat, but his reputation has been somewhat clouded by his acceptance of money from the Sultan for the neutralization of Jem and his efforts, in his last years, at stamping out *Judaism on Rhodes by expelling all adult Jews and forcibly baptizing their children. The letters and documents of Aubusson are to be found in the second volume of the *Codice diplomatico del sacro militaire ordine Gerosolimitano,* ed. S. Paoli (Lucca 1737).

Bibliography: R. A. DE VERTOT, *Histoire des chevaliers hospitaliers de S. Jean de Jerusalem,* 7 v. (Paris 1778) v.3. D. BAUHOURS, *Histoire de P. d'Aubusson* (4th ed. Paris 1806). G. E. STRECK, *Pierre d'Aubusson* (Chemnitz 1872). A. GABRIEL, *La Cité de Rhodes, 1310–1522* (Paris 1923). G. MOLLAT, DHGE 5:270–274.

[V. L. BULLOUGH]

AUCH, ARCHDIOCESE OF (AUXITANUS), metropolitan see since *c.* 850, corresponding to Gers department, southwest France. The city of Auch, on the right bank of the Gers River, was the capital of medieval Armagnac and of 18th-century Gascony. In 1963 the archdiocese, completely rural with an area of 2,417 square miles, had 507 parishes, 251 secular and 13 religious priests, 10 men in 2 religious houses, 424 women in 49 convents, and 179,000 Catholics. Its three suffragans, which had 1,339 parishes, 1,767 priests, 2,483 sisters, and 880,000 Catholics, were: (1) Aire and Dax (created *c.* 100), (2) Bayonne (8th century), (3) and Tarbes (medieval Bigorre) and *Lourdes (4th century).

In the 9th century Auch absorbed Eauze (Elusa), then a metropolitan, which the Normans had burned. Auch's archbishop holds the titles of the former Sees of Condom, Lectoure, and Lombez, whose areas are now included in that of Auch. The archbishop, who *c.* 1650 called himself primate of *Novempopulana* and the Two Navarres, before the French Revolution had as suffragans, Aire, Bazas, Béarn (Lescar), Bigorre, Comminges (Saint-Bernard), Couserans (Saint-Lizier), Labourd (Bayonne), Lectoure, and Oloron. The See of Auch was suppressed by the *Concordat of 1801, but was restored in 1822.

Eauze, capital of *Novempopulana,* had a bishop at the Council of *Arles (314). Auch's first bishop appeared in the German invasions of 407. Until *c.* 1000 the history of the region is poorly known; it suffered from Visigoths, Gascons, and Normans. Thirteen synodal statutes are known (1304–1770). The provincial council of 551 dealt with penitential discipline, clerical celibacy, pagan superstititions, the promotion of clerics to Holy Orders, and slaves of the Church. The report of a council in 1068 is a forgery; in 1280 feudal problems were treated; in 1304 the Fourth Lateran Council was promulgated; the council of 1851 lacked interest.

St. Orentius, Auch's first bishop, in a *Commonitorium*

The Gothic cathedral at Auch, France.

described the miseries of the German invasions of 407. Under St. Austinde (1042–68; feast, Sept. 25), a reform bishop who presided over the council of Jaca in Aragon (1060), the abbeys of Saint-Orens and Saint-Mont became Cluniac. Leonard de Trapes (1597–1629) attended the council of *Bordeaux (1624), which was inspired by St. Charles *Borromeo, and applied its decisions (synodal statutes of 1624). Jean François de Montillet (1742–75), vigorous opponent of the *Enlightenment, published a catechism and liturgical books and introduced devotion to the Sacred Heart.

Auch once had a number of abbeys for men and women (some founded by *Fontevrault). Its monuments include the three-nave Gothic cathedral of Auch (1489–1548) and the former cathedrals of Condom, Lectoure, and Lombez. Throughout the archdiocese there are several shrines of Our Lady to which pilgrimages are made.

Bibliography: *GallChrist* v.1. F. LOT, *Études sur le règne de Hugues Capet et la fin du Xe siècle* (Paris 1903). A. ARTONNE et al., *Répertoire des statuts synodaux des diocèses de l'ancienne France* (Paris 1964). A. DEGERT, DHGE 5:276–285. E. JARRY, *Catholicisme* 1:1016–18; 3:1223–24. AnnPont (1965) 42. *Annuaire catholique de France* (Paris 1964). **Illustration credit:** Archives Photographiques, Paris.

[E. JARRY]

AUCTOR OF METZ, ST., bishop; fl. *c.* 451 (feast, Aug. 10). Auctor, 13th bishop of Metz, was apparently a contemporary of Attila the Hun, who ravaged the region in 451. In the time of *Louis the Pious, Bp. *Drogo of Metz transferred the relics of Auctor to Maursmünster, where his feast is kept on August 10. Although there are distinct traditions surrounding an Auctor, bishop of Trier, whose feast was formerly kept on August 20, he is an unhistorical personage whose vita (ActSS Aug. 4:37–53) perhaps derives from that of Auctor of Metz (ActSS Aug. 2:536–538). There is extant a life of Auctor of Metz written by *Paul the Deacon.

Bibliography: BHL 1:746 (A. of Metz); 747–749 (A. of Trier). A. M. BURG and A. HEINTZ, LexThK^2 1:1024–25.

[W. A. JURGENS]

AUCTOREM FIDEI, a bull of Pius VI, dated Aug. 28, 1794, condemning the errors of the Synod of *Pistoia. This synod was held in the autumn of 1786 on the initiative of Scipione de' *Ricci, Bishop of Pistoia-Prato, a protégé of Peter Leopold, the Grand Duke of Tuscany and brother of Emperor Joseph II. Ricci, imbued with the Gallican, Richerist, and Jansenist ideas of the French *Appellants, which at the time were widespread in Italy, from 1780 on attempted to introduce these ideas into his diocese. The decrees of the synod that he held at Pistoia clearly reflect his thought, but at the same time they give evidence of a very real concern for the moral improvement of the faithful and the formation of the clergy. The council held at Florence in April-June 1787 sharply criticized a number of the decisions made at Pistoia. The acts of the synod were nevertheless published in October 1788. Pius VI had them examined by a commission, and Ricci had to resign in June 1791. Numerous translations of the acts, however, spread his ideas everywhere, particularly among the constitutional French clergy. The bull *Auctorem fidei* condemned the 85 propositions extracted exactly from the acts of Pistoia, while giving to each one a formal theological note. The condemned errors referred mainly to the Church and the hierarchy, grace, the Sacraments, and the liturgy. Appearing during the troubled times of the Revolution, the bull *Auctorem fidei,* although remarkably well drawn up, did not produce the reaction that one could expect. Ricci, who died in January 1810, never seemed sincerely to have accepted it.

See also JANSENISM.

Bibliography: Denz 2600–2700. A. C. JEMOLO, *Il giansenismo in Italia prima della rivoluzione* (Bari 1928). E. CODIGNOLA, *Illuministi, giansenisti e giacobini nell'Italia del settecento* (Florence 1947).

[L. J. COGNET]

AUDI BENIGNE CONDITOR, a Lenten hymn formerly attributed to Pope Gregory the Great (Migne), but now dated as late as the early 9th century (Szövérffy). It was composed either in Italy (Raby) or in Gaul (Blume) and appears in many 10th-century MSS from those areas, as well as in numerous German and English MSS of the following century. The hymn consists of five strophes of octosyllabic iambic dimeter. Half of its 20 lines are rhymed, in the unschematic manner characteristic of pre-Carolingian prosody. The first four strophes each contain a reference to human infirmity and a request for divine assistance; the fifth concludes this simple theme with a prayer that the Trinity will make our fasting fruitful. Assigned in the Roman *Breviary of 1632 to Vespers between the Saturday after Ash Wednesday and Passiontide, it had been sung also at Lauds in many places before the Reformation. Its English translators include W. Drummond ("O merciful Creator! hear our prayer," 1619), J. M. Neale ("O Maker of the world, give ear," 1852), and E. Caswall ("Thou loving Maker of mankind," *Lyra Catholica,* 1849).

Bibliography: AnalHymn 51:53–55. PL 78:849–850. A. S. WALPOLE, ed., *Early Latin Hymns* (Cambridge, Eng. 1922) 320–321. M. BRITT, ed., *The Hymns of the Breviary and Missal* (new ed. New York 1948). Connelly Hymns. Raby ChrLP 124. Julian DictHym 91.

[J. DU Q. ADAMS]

AUDIENCE, PAPAL

The Vatican being the home of the father of all, as the popes so often recall, anybody wishing to pay homage to the successor of St. Peter and obtain the blessing of the vicar of Christ may be received in audience. The great multitudes availing themselves of this privilege have necessitated the organization of these audiences into the following kinds.

General audiences, accessible to all, are held for the most part on Wednesdays in St. Peter's Basilica, the Hall of Benedictions, and the Consistorial and Clementine Halls. During the summer when the pope is in residence in Castel Gandolfo he also receives there. When audiences are held in St. Peter's, the pope is carried in on the *sedia gestatoria,* or portable throne, so as to be visible to all (the number of persons present always running into thousands). After greeting those acclaiming him, the pope gives from the throne a short address, which is immediately repeated in different languages either by the Holy Father himself or by a member of his household in those languages the pope does not speak fluently. Before the end of the audience the supreme pontiff allows the leaders of groups and others to kiss his ring. The audience ends with the recitation of the Angelus and the *apostolic blessing.

Group audiences are granted to parties of pilgrims and others who have come to Rome for a definite purpose, to groups traveling through Rome to the missions, etc. Often the Holy Father gives a special address on an important subject that concerns the group in question. This entails the pope's possibly asking to see beforehand the speech that the leader of the group will address to him, so that he may give an appropriate answer.

Semiprivate, or *baciamano,* audiences are granted to small groups of especially deserving persons, who may kiss the pope's ring and exchange a few words with him.

Private audiences are granted almost exclusively to those who have the most urgent or important business with the vicar of Christ: bishops, heads of state, ambassadors, etc. They generally take place in the pope's private library.

Official audiences are the colorful state audiences, given to kings, presidents, and heads of government who officially visit the pope. For reasons of courtesy and appreciation Vatican protocol during the visits of such representatives of nations is very elaborate. When these occasions involve non-Catholic heads of state, they are received by the pope dressed in the mozetta; when they involve Catholic heads of state, the pope also wears the papal stole, sign of his jurisdiction. The last audience given to a Spanish king has remained memorable, Pius XI receiving the monarch in *manto papale* and miter.

Tabèlla, or scheduled, audiences are granted to the high officials of the Roman *Curia. At regular intervals, according to a special calendar, the cardinals who head sacred Congregations and other important prelates are received to attend to the current affairs of the Church's central government. The only person to be received every day is the cardinal secretary of state, who acts, in a very true sense, as the pope's right hand.

All audiences are regulated by the office of the *maestro di camera* (equivalent to the lord high chamberlain in most courts), but Americans may address their petition to be received by His Holiness through the Pontifical *North American College in Rome.

[P. C. VAN LIERDE]

AUDIO-VISUAL MEDIA

The Church has always used visual materials, e.g., frescoes, statues, stained glass, carvings, paintings, and marionettes, to bring its religious message to the people. Not until 1644, however, was the most powerful aid of all developed—the projected image. When the German Jesuit Athanasius *Kircher, "Doctor of a Hundred Arts," professor of mathematics and Oriental languages at the Roman College, showed a set of slides mounted in the rim of a revolving disc, which told the story of the life of Christ, his first viewers saw it as black magic, and the demonstration ended in a riot.

Secular educators fared no better, for although they had the way opened by John Amos *Comenius's *Orbis Pictus* (1658), it was not until 1898 that Henry C. Bristel's *The Use of the Stereopticon in Teaching* structured the educational use of photographic materials. With the turn of the century, visual aids of different kinds were emphasized, and school systems (e.g., in Boston, New York, Philadelphia, and Chicago) began to organize specific means of use and distribution. Not until 1937 was a truly definitive compilation of audio-visual research in education attempted by Edgar Dale and his collaborators. Since 1940 numerous syntheses of research have appeared, especially Monroe's *Encyclopedia of Educational Research* and the *National Society for the Study of Educational Research: 48th Yearbook,* pt. 1. The works of McClusky, Hoban, and Van Ormer are both critical and highly scientific.

Films, filmstrips, and other teaching aids developed for the public school curriculum are usually acceptable in Catholic education, except in the field of religion and such subjects as history or guidance; material in these areas must be carefully evaluated. Since the classroom teacher rarely has time to do a critical evaluation, a national group, the Catholic Audio-Visual Educators Association (CAVE, Box 618, Church St. P.O., New York 8, N.Y.), undertook the task in 1956. Materials are reviewed by committees, and the evaluations are published monthly in *The Catholic Educator*. CAVE's four-volume *Audio-Visual Evaluations and Directory* is the most current religious and catechetical film review.

Experimental research has shown not only that the audio-visual approach provides the concrete experiences essential to sound learning, but also that more accurate communication of ideas results in less verbalization, that desirable attitudes develop through arousal of the emotions and feelings, that classroom discussion more easily develops, and that individual pursuit of subject matter follows. Catholic schools and parishes, however, have been slow to employ audio-visual methods save where required for certification or accreditation. In 1964, 1 out of 10 Catholic school classrooms was equipped to handle projected visuals, and only 1 out of 50 parishes used slides or motion pictures with any regularity for religious education. A concerted national effort by the hierarchy and Catholic educators would seem to be indicated to better this state of affairs.

Bibliography: American Council on Education, Committee on Motion Pictures in Education, *Motion Pictures in Education,* comp. E. DALE et al. (New York 1937). F. D. MCCLUSKY, *The A-V Bibliography* (rev. ed. Dubuque 1955). C. F. HOBAN and E. B. VAN ORMER, *Rapid Mass Learning 1918–1950,* Pa. State College, Instructional Film Research Program (Port Washington, N.Y. 1950). J. P. LUCID, *Classification and Evaluation of Films, Filmstrips, and Slides in Teaching Religion* (Master's diss. unpub. De Paul U. 1957).

[R. F. VALLE]

AUENBRUGGER, LEOPOLD, Austrian physician, inventor of percussion in physical diagnosis; b. Graz, Nov. 19, 1722; d. Vienna, May 17, 1807. His early education was received at Graz and his university training at Vienna, where he received his medical degree in 1744. He then served at the Spanish military hospital where he spent 10 years and had ample opportunity for clinical study. The university frequently used interesting ward cases for demonstration to students. This type of work developed in Auenbrugger habits of careful investigation. His case histories were published in the work *A New Discovery that Enables the Physician, from the Percussion of the Human Thorax, to Detect the Diseases Hidden within the Chest.* Josef Skoda (1805–81) considered this discovery the beginning of modern diagnosis and Auenbrugger himself as the founder of the new science. His percussion experiments are treated in detail by Walsh. Some biographers said that he died during the typhus epidemic of 1798, but the parish church register in Vienna shows that he died in 1807.

Bibliography: J. J. WALSH, *Makers of Modern Medicine* (New York 1907). W. LIBBY, *The History of Medicine in Its Salient Features* (Boston 1922).

[M. A. STRATMAN]

AUGER, EDMOND, Jesuit preacher, confessor of Henry III, effective in stemming Calvinist influence; b. Alleman, near Sézanne in Champagne in 1530; d. Como, Lombardy, Jan. 19, 1591. In 1550 St. Ignatius himself admitted Auger to the novitiate and formed him in the religious life. Auger was made professor of Latin, first at the Roman College and then at Perugia and Padua. Even before his ordination he began to manifest great talent for preaching. In 1559 Auger returned to France where with others he founded a college at Pamier and later another college at Toulouse. He taught at Pamier and Tournon. He preached with great naturalness, vigorously and cheerfully, in the most varied circumstances. He was hailed as the "Chrysostom of France," and was so able and gracious a preacher that he attracted even the Calvinists, whose heresy was then spreading in southern France. He had ardently and successfully devoted himself to counteract their influence. Having been captured by the Huguenots in Valence in 1562 and sentenced to death by burning, he addressed the onlookers while standing at what was intended to be his pyre and so won them that they demanded his release. To his preaching he added works of charity, visiting the sick, and comforting the prisoners. He was tireless in administering the Sacraments.

His French catechisms earned him the title of the "French Canisius." The first, a larger work, a summary of Catholic doctrine, appeared in 1563; the second, a smaller catechism published in 1568, was translated even into Greek. Both catechisms were reprinted and translated several times. Since they were written in the form of a dialogue and showed less erudition than the Canisius Catechism, they were useful for instructing children and uneducated adults. The catechisms confuted Calvinist doctrine without entering into polemics.

Auger became the first provincial of Aquitaine in 1564. He preached to King Charles. He became the chaplain of the Duke of Anjou. In 1574 when the Duke became Henry III, Auger was made his confessor and preacher. Henry III appealed to the Pope to have Auger remain at court, and only in 1587 was Auger authorized to leave. His attachment to Henry III aroused the hostility of the Leaguists. After the assassination of the King, Auger had to take refuge in Lyons and Tournon before leaving for Como where he died.

Bibliography: J. DORIGNY, *La Vie du P. Emond Auger* (new ed. Avignon 1828). F. J. BRAND, *P. Edmundus Augerius, S.J.* (Cleve 1903); *Die Katechismen des Edmundus Augerius* (Freiburg 1917). Sommervogel 1:632–642; 8:1706. P. DESLANDRES, "Le Père Emond Auger," *Revue des Études Historiques* 104 (1937) 28–38. H. JOLY, DictBiogFranc 4:504–511. J. DUTILLEUL, DHGE 5:378–383.

[R. B. MEAGHER]

AUGSBURG

City in Swabia, Bavaria, German Federal Republic, at the confluence of the Wertach and Lech Rivers. In 1964 156,000 Catholics comprised 75 per cent of the city's population; there were 102 secular and 61 religious priests, 48 Catholic schools with 10,359 students, and many Catholic social and charitable institutions. The diocese, *Augustanus Vindelicorum,* suffragan to *Munich and Freising, in 1963 had 1,385,803 Catholics in 951 parishes, 1,240 secular and 357 religious priests, 337 men in 37 religious houses, and 5,195 women in 291 convents; it is 5,310 square miles in area.

Founded by Rome *c.* A.D. 30, Augsburg, as the capital of Raetia, thrived culturally and economically. The martyrdom of St. *Afra (*c.* 304) and archeological findings show that Christians were there before the time of Constantine, and in such an important city there was probably a bishop. The Romans withdrew *c.* 400 and Alamanni destroyed the city *c.* 450, but Christianity survived, the tomb and chapel of St. Afra being a pilgrimage center in the 6th century. In 536 the Franks took Augsburg, which became a bishopric *c.* 600. Wikterp (738) is the first bishop known with certainty. Invested by the Carolingians as counts, the bishops were able to encompass merchant settlements south of Augsburg as late as the 12th century. In the 10th century Bishop *Ulric (923–973) defended the city against the Magyars until Otto I won the battle of the Lechfeld in 955. An episcopal schism (1077–88) followed the investiture struggle. In the 11th and 12th centuries the burghers, abetted by the German kings, began to seek independence of the bishop. In 1316 Emperor *Louis IV made Augsburg an imperial city, and in the 15th century the split between bishop and city became so bad that the chancery and at times the bishop moved to Dillingen. Jews were banned from Augsburg from 1439 to 1805, while from the late 15th century the city became world famous for its extensive trade and riches, which did not benefit the lower classes.

Humanism, introduced to Augsburg through trade relations with Italy, was taken up in ecclesiastical circles. The split between bishop and city, social agitation, and the worldliness of the higher clergy prepared for the Reformation of Luther, who was in Augsburg in 1518. Zwinglianism replaced Lutheranism in 1526, and even Anabaptists became prominent. In 1537 Catholic services were banned by law, images were forbidden, and the clergy was forced to leave the city. After Charles V's victory over the Schmalkaldic League in 1547, the city had to agree in the Interim of Augsburg

Nave of the church of St. Ulrich, Augsburg.

(1548) to the return of the clergy, the restoration of church goods, and the continuation of Catholic services. In 1555 the Peace of *Augsburg, ratified by the Augsburg Diet, specified the equality of Catholicism and Lutheranism in Augsburg; apart from passing disturbances, it was strictly observed, as the Peace of Westphalia (1648) witnesses. The restoration of Catholicism after 1548 was the work of the bishops, especially Cardinal Otto *Truchsess von Waldburg and Heinrich von Knöringen, with the help of the *Fuggers and new religious houses.

In 1809, when Augsburg ceased to be an imperial city, it was again predominantly Catholic (16,944 Catholics and 11,534 Evangelicals). The secularization of 1802–03 suppressed religious institutions (12 men's and 5 women's), deprived the bishop of his principality and chapter, and incorporated the city into Bavaria (1805). Romanticism in the early 19th century favored the Catholic revival. Religious orders returned after 1820. Rapid industrialization after 1835, with increases in population density and the incorporation of heavily Catholic fringe communities, posed difficult problems for the Church. New parishes were built, social and charitable institutions founded, and associations developed. World War II destroyed several churches, but Bp. Joseph Freundorfer (d. 1963) and the city, with help from abroad, repaired the damages and overcame post-war problems.

Augsburg has had noteworthy ecclesiastics: David of Augsburg (*c.* 1200–72); Johannes *Fabri (1504–58); St. *Peter Canisius (1521–97); Placidus *Braun (1756–1829); canon Antonius Steichele (1816–89), historian and archbishop of Munich-Freising; and Bp. Pancratius von Dinkel (1858–94).

The 11th-century Romanesque cathedral was modified with Gothic in the early 14th century. St. Gall

Church dates from the 11th, and St. Peter am Perlach from the 12th century. Several churches were built in the 15th and 16th centuries. In the Middle Ages there were 3 collegiate cloisters (founded 1020, 1060, 1071) apart from the cathedral chapter, 2 Augustinian cloisters (1135, 1160), a Benedictine (1012), a Dominican (1225), a Conventual Franciscan (1221), and a Carmelite (1321); a cloister of canonesses (968) and a Benedictine (1262); 3 Franciscan (1258?, *c.* 1315, before 1366) and 3 Dominican (1235, *c.* 1250, 1298) convents. A number of others were founded during and after the Reformation, including the Jesuits (1579), the Capuchins (1601), and the English Ladies (1662), who dedicated themselves to educating young girls.

Augsburg has been famous for religious art and artists, including Burkhard Engelberger, Gregor Erhardt, Hans Holbein the Elder, Hans Burgkmair, Johann Georg Bergmüller, Matthew Günther, Christopher Thomas Scheffler, Francis Xavier and Johann Michael Feuchtmayr. Goldsmiths Jörg Seld, Johann Zeckel, Franz Ignaz Berthold, and others supplied liturgical equipment far and wide from the 15th to the 18th century. The holy pictures of the Klauber press in the 18th century had worldwide distribution. Erhard Ratdolt printed liturgical books (1486–1528), and the Benedictines of St. Ulrich managed a press (1472–74). The cathedral choir was known for its music and organists (Jacobus de *Kerle, Gregor *Aichinger, and Christian Erbach).

The Latin schools of the cathedral chapter and 4 cloisters, suspended 1537–48, were surpassed by the Jesuit school founded in 1582. The cloister schools were suppressed with the secularization of 1802–03, but in 1828 the state opened a Catholic *Gymnasium* under the Benedictines.

In the 10th century Bishop Ulrich founded a hospital (*hospitium*) for the poor. Another appeared in 1143, and a third by 1239. A house for lepers was founded *c.* 1250. St. Jacob's Hospital (1348) also cared for pilgrims. In 1514 the Fuggers built a model settlement for poor families that still exists.

Bibliography: W. ZORN, *Augsburg: Geschichte einer Stadt* (Munich 1955). C. BAUER et al., *Augusta 955–1955* (Munich 1955). T. BREUER, *Die Stadt Augsburg* (Munich 1958). A. HORN, *Dome, Kirchen, und Klöster in Bayr. Schwaben* (Frankfurt a.M. 1963). F. ZOEPFL, *Das Bistum Augsburg und seine Bischöfe im Mittelalter* (Munich 1956); LexThK[2] 1:1076–79. A. SCHRÖDER, DHGE 5:389–406. AnnPont (1964) 43. **Illustration credit:** German Information Center, New York.

[F. ZOEPFL]

AUGSBURG, PEACE OF, an agreement between the Catholics and Lutherans of Germany giving recognition in imperial law to the *Augsburg Confession (1530) as well as to the Catholic faith. Embodied in a decree delivered at the Diet of Augsburg on Sept. 25, 1555, it definitively registered the failure of Emperor *Charles V's efforts to repair the broken religious unity of Germany (*see* INTERIMS). The Emperor's military pacification of Germany was wrecked by the political ambitions of the princes who rose in rebellion under Maurice of Saxony in 1552. This second Schmalkaldic war resulted in the defeat of Charles V by Maurice, who was aided by his French allies (*see* SCHMALKALDIC LEAGUE). Charles's subsequent failure to recapture Metz after his treaty with Maurice completed his discouragement. Charles appointed his brother Ferdinand (later Emperor Ferdinand I) to preside over the negotiations that arranged a political settlement of the religious strife. It stipulated that the religion of the ruler was to determine whether a state was to be exclusively Catholic or Lutheran (*cujus regio, ejus religio*). Lutherans were confirmed in their title to all ecclesiastical property that they had appropriated before 1552. A private declaration of Ferdinand conceded religious freedom to certain subjects of ecclesiastical princes. Ecclesiastical princes who turned Protestant were obliged to resign their sees according to a clause inserted by Ferdinand. The treaty began a new era in the religious history of Germany that lasted until the Peace of *Westphalia (1648).

Bibliography: M. SIMON, *Der Augsburger Religionsfriede* (Augsburg 1955). H. HOLBORN, *A History of Modern Germany* (New York 1959–) v.1 *The Reformation.* J. HECKEL RGG[3] 1:736–737. E. W. ZEEDEN, LexThK[2] 1:1081–83.

[T. S. BOKENKOTTER]

AUGSBURG CONFESSION

So called from its presentation (in slightly divergent but equally authoritative German and Latin versions) at the Diet of Augsburg on June 25, 1530, to Holy Roman Emperor *Charles V in response to his invitation to the parties in the theological debate to present their "opinions and views." The Augsburg Confession (*Confessio Augustana*) is the primary particular symbol of the Lutheran Church. Although signed by seven imperial princes and representatives of two imperial free cities, it is primarily the work of Philipp *Melanchthon, who drew it up in its present form (chiefly on the basis of the Schwabach, Marburg, and Torgau Articles) to counter the charge of Johann *Eck in his *404 Articles* that the Lutheran party was reviving ancient heresies.

Deliberately irenic in character, it consists of 21 articles (on God, original sin, Christ, justification through faith, the sacred ministry and the channels of the Holy Spirit; the new obedience, the Church, the Sacraments, ecclesiastical order, humanly instituted rites, civil affairs, Christ's return to Judgment, free will, the cause of sin, faith and good works, and the veneration of the saints) explicitly designed to show that the Lutherans did not depart at any point from Scripture, the Catholic Church, or the Roman Church (Epilogue to pt. 1.1), plus 7 concluding articles on Communion under both species, the marriage of priests, the abrogation of private Masses, confession, humanly instituted traditions, monastic vows, and the authority of bishops. The imperial reply, commonly called the Papalist Confutation because it was drawn up by a panel of theologians at the Diet, approved nine articles without exception, approved six with qualifications or in part, and condemned thirteen. The Lutheran theologians under Melanchthon's leadership readied the first draft of a Defense (Apology) and submitted it on September 22, but the Emperor refused to receive it. Back at Wittenberg, Melanchthon reworked it into the Apology of the Augsburg Confession, first printed (along with the *editio princeps* of the Confession itself) in 1531. It repeats and defends the positions taken by the Confession, but goes beyond it in its definition of the Sacraments and in its exposition of the sacrificial aspects of the Holy Eucharist. The official German version of the Apology is a paraphrase by Justus *Jonas. The Apology formally received symbolical status as a commentary on the Augsburg Confession in 1537. A revised edition (Variata) of the Augsburg Confession, which Melanchthon published in 1540, was less explicit in its Eucharistic doctrine than the 1530 edition and gained extensive acceptance in German Reformed circles; the Lutherans rejected it in the Preface to the Book of Concord (1580) and committed themselves to the 1530 edition (*see* CONCORD, FORMULA AND BOOK OF).

In varying degrees the Augsburg Confession influenced other 16th-century confessions, including the *Thirty-Nine Articles of the Church of England and through them John *Wesley's Methodist Articles of Religion. An effort of Samuel S. Schmucker (1799–1873) to accommodate the Augsburg Confession to the prevailing Protestantism of the U.S. in the *Definite Platform* (1855), by omitting all characteristically Lutheran elements, was vigorously rejected. The original manuscripts of the Augsburg Confession submitted to Charles V appear to have perished in the 16th century, but 54 copies surviving from 1530 alone adequately secure the text of both the Latin and the German version.

See also CONFESSIONS OF FAITH, PROTESTANT.

Bibliography: H. LIETZMANN, ed., *Die Bekenntnisschriften der evangelisch-lutherischen Kirche,* 5th ed. by E. WOLF (Göttingen 1963) 44–404, critical Lat. and Ger. text of both documents. Eng. T. G. TAPPERT, ed. and tr., *The Book of Concord: The Confessions of the Evangelical Lutheran Church* (Philadelphia 1959) 24–285. Text of the Papalist Confutation in CorpRef 27 (1859) 81–244. J. M. REU, *The Augsburg Confession* (Chicago 1930), contains Eng. tr. of many of the pertinent documents. W. D. ALLBECK, *Studies in the Lutheran Confessions* (Philadelphia 1952). M. LACKMANN, *The Augsburg Confession and Catholic Unity,* tr. W. R. BOUMAN (New York 1963).

[A. C. PIEPKORN]

AUGURY, a term deriving its name from the fact that the officials of the Roman state who were legally and constitutionally empowered to practice the art of divination for official purposes were called Augurs. The Roman College of Augurs, consisting eventually of 16 members, had as its function not to foretell the future but to discover by observation of signs (the flight of birds, the behavior of chickens, etc.) whether the gods did or did not approve a proposed action. Such signs could be accidental, such as the flight or cry of birds, or could be carefully studied, such as the manner in which domestic fowls pecked at their food.

See also DIVINATION.

Bibliography: H. J. ROSE, OxClDict 120. F. MÜLLER, Reallex AntChr 1:975–980.

[T. A. BRADY]

AUGUSTINE, ST.

Bishop, theologian, and Doctor of the Church; b. Tagaste, in Numidia, Africa, Nov. 13, 354; d. Hippo, Aug. 28, 430 (feast, Aug. 28). By the greatness of his achievement as thinker and theologian, Augustine dominates the Christian tradition of the West, of which he may be considered the founder. His genius and personal history, which recapitulates man's experience of sin, grace, and charity, provide a basis for understanding his thought and for coping with the immeasurable influence he has had on the Western world. This article deals with Augustine's life and works, his ideas, and his influence. The key to his thought, as well as to his influence, must be discovered within his life.

LIFE

Aurelius Augustine was born of a Christian mother, St. *Monica, and a pagan father, Patricius. Patricius, though a provincial of some importance, was not able, despite considerable sacrifices, to provide of his own resources for the boy's full education. Although not baptized as a child, Augustine was inscribed as a catechumen in his youth (*Conf.* 1.11.17) and was reared as a Christian (*Conf.* 3.4.8). He attended the local school and went to nearby Madaura for further schooling. But at 16 he had to interrupt his studies for lack of funds (*Conf.* 2.3.5). This year of forced leisure coincided with the most difficult period of his adolescence and seems to have involved him in a life of sensual pleasure. The following year, thanks to the benefactions of a certain Romanianus, he was able to resume his studies at Carthage (*C. acad.* 2.2.3), and he engaged in a gay student life, frequented the theater, and formed a liaison with a concubine who bore him a son, Adeodatus (*Conf.* 9.6.14).

Philosopher and Manichaean. Although in his *Confessions* Augustine gives the impression that he pursued a life of debauchery and anarchy, he was in fact a serious student and, on reading Cicero's *Hortensius,* was enthralled by the ideal of wisdom, in which he recognized from that moment a call from Christ (*Conf.* 3.4.7–8). He attempted to read the Sacred Scriptures; but, repelled by their literary style and anthropomorphism, he quickly abandoned this venture (*Conf.* 3.5.9). Attracted at this point by the preaching of the Manichees (*see* MANICHAEISM), who in their discussion of gnosis promised to provide him with a comprehension of all that exists (*Util. cred.* 1.2), Augustine joined the sect and remained a member for 9 years, during his career as teacher at Tagaste (1 yr) and Carthage (8 yrs).

He seems to have placed all his intellectual hopes in Manichaeism and, behind the Manichaean myths, he kept expecting a secret revelation or some type of illumination (*Beat. vit.* 1.4). He did not, however, abandon other intellectual pursuits, as is attested by his interest in astrology, his composition of a treatise *De pulchro et apto* (unfortunately lost), and his reading of the *Categories* of Aristotle and a number of other philosophical works (*Conf.* 4).

After a disappointing encounter with the Manichaean Bishop Faustus, who could not give satisfactory answers to his searching queries, Augustine abandoned the sect (*Conf.* 5.6.11–5.7.13). By this time he had already worked out a personal philosophy, composed of *Stoicism, Pythagoreanism (*see* PYTHAGORAS AND PYTHAGOREANS), and Ciceronian skepticism. Gradually the dualistic explanation of the universe that had initially captured his interest gave way before a conception, with a Stoic tinge, of an infinite God disseminated everywhere in space (*Conf.* 7.1.1–2).

Conversion. Augustine left Carthage for Rome in 383 and taught rhetoric there for a year; then, thanks to the assistance of influential Manichees, he obtained a chair as professor at Milan. It was there that he encountered the three principal factors that led to his conversion: his meeting with Bp. *Ambrose of Milan, his introduction to *Neoplatonism, and his reading of St. Paul.

St. Ambrose. In Milan, Augustine was attracted by the eloquence of Ambrose, followed his preaching assidu-

Fig. 1. The earliest known portrait of St. Augustine, fresco, c. 600, in the Lateran.

ously, and was gradually affected by his teaching. Three discoveries prepared his conversion. Ambrose was the first to give him an idea of the spiritual interpretation of Scripture; as an immediate consequence, Augustine broke completely with Manichaeism and was inscribed in the catechumenate of the Catholic Church (*Conf.* 5.14.24–25). This exegesis likewise gave him an understanding of man as made in the image of God, not by a corporeal resemblance, but according to the spirit (*Conf.* 6.3.4). While fear of being deceived prevented his commitment to the Catholic faith, he began to understand the role of belief in human life; and by means of a probabilistic intellectual technique, he gradually came to see the part that authority could play in coming to the aid of human reason (*Conf.* 6.5.7–8.11.18). The bishop of Milan introduced him to a Christian Neoplatonism that, in its spiritual exegesis, depended primarily on *Origen and the great Alexandrian teachers, and only secondarily, by frequent and often literal quotations of Plato and *Plotinus, revealed its connection with Neoplatonic philosophy.

Meanwhile Augustine's mother, Monica, joined him in Milan and insisted that he prepare for a good marriage, first of all by sending the mother of his son, Adeodatus, back to Africa. The young woman she selected was not of legal age for matrimony; faced with a 2-year delay, Augustine took another concubine (*Conf.* 6.13.23–6.15.25).

Neoplatonism. Ambrose's preaching brought all of Augustine's problems into focus; yet he hesitated to join the Church. Although Ambrose had given him a spiritual concept of God and man, Augustine lacked a true interior experience and could not conceive of something spiritual by nature (*Conf.* 7.1.1–2). As time went on, he did discover man's personal responsibility for evil, and this became for him no longer a speculative question, but an agonizing personal problem (*Conf.* 7.7.11–7.8.12).

It was at this point that "certain Platonic books" translated into Latin by *Marius Victorinus were placed in his hands; in reading them, Augustine went through a spiritual, perhaps even a mystical, experience that completely changed his vision of the world. This experience revealed to him the spiritual within himself and the transcendence of God above and beyond his own internal, spiritual experiences, and led to the notion of the Divine Trinity, which he identified with the three hypostases of Plotinus (*Conf.* 7.9.13–7.10.16).

Research into his Cassiciacum *Dialogues,* written several months later, leads to the conclusion that these "Platonic books" were some dozen treatises of Plotinus accompanied perhaps by the *Sentences* of *Porphyry. But proper consideration must be given also to the direct influence of a whole atmosphere permeated by Neoplatonism in which Augustine found himself in Milan. In particular Simplicianus, the intimate friend of Marius Victorinus, who had instructed Ambrose in ecclesiastical sciences and succeeded him as bishop of Milan, played a part; for Augustine visited him and apparently received from him a further initiation into Christian Neoplatonism (*Conf.* 8.2.3). Finally, it is perhaps necessary to consider the influence of the works of Porphyry as an explanation of certain changes that appear in the general tone of Augustine's Neoplatonism toward the end of his stay at Cassiciacum, or at the moment of his return to Milan for Baptism. His thought turned in the direction of a creationist metaphysic in the consideration of being and nonbeing, as well as of the degrees of being.

St. Paul and Conversion. The mystical experience occasioned by his Platonist readings, however, proved a deception. While they stimulated him to the point of pride, they likewise caused him anguish when he found that he could not sustain himself on that high level. Moreover, he began to feel more than ever torn and oppressed by the weight of his sensual habits. He affirmed (*Conf.* 6.18.24; 6.20.26) that at this point he had not yet found Christ or understood the salvific role of the Incarnation. It was then that he took up the Epistles of St. Paul (*Conf.* 7.21.27) and seems to have continued reading them all through this moral crisis (*Conf.* 8.6.14), which he expressed elsewhere in the very language of the Epistles to the Galatians and to the Romans (*Conf.* 8.5.11–12).

Little by little, Paul's writings gave him an understanding of the grace of Christ that comes to man in his weakness, to show the way to a homeland indistinctly glimpsed (*Conf.* 8.21.27). Finally, by reading a text of St. Paul (Rom 13.13–14) at the moment of crisis when he heard "tolle, lege" in the garden with *Alipius, he was filled "with a light of certainty, and all shadow of doubt disappeared" (*Conf.* 8.12.29).

Interiority and Transcendence. These events and discoveries had a decisive effect on the essential structures of Augustine's thought. On the philosophical level, his Neoplatonic experience of interiority and transcendence, having saved him at once from the materialism of a sense-dominated imagination and from the skepticism that resulted from his Manichaean experiences, would remain for him, with its twin movements of conversion and transcendence, the model of man's approach to spiritual reality.

On the theological level, his discovery of divine transcendence and of a trinity in Neoplatonism was attributable mainly to an unconscious projection induced by the Christian Neoplatonic adaptations of St. Ambrose. Before his discovery of grace and the incarnate Christ, this was to condition all his understanding of the Christian Trinity. In his view, the philosophers were able to know the Trinity, but only confusedly and to their detriment, for it led them to a false pride. But they did not know Christ, who is the only one to save man from this pride.

Finally, on the spiritual or moral level, the fact that his intellectual conversion preceded his moral conversion would occasion a profound dichotomy between these two phases of his personality. Later it would cause him to conceive of grace as an interior assistance strengthening the will, a concept that strongly influenced Western theology. The experience of his conversion, that is in the first place the experience of inefficacious light, convinced him that there could be an efficacious grace necessary to break the bonds of habit and the slavery of sin (*Conf.* 7–8; *In psalm.* 106.4–5).

Cassiciacum. At the beginning of August 386, having read the Platonic books during the spring, Augustine decided to abandon his teaching career and his proposed marriage. With some friends and students he retired to an estate at Cassiciacum, near Milan, to live a life of prayer and studious leisure. He wrote four works describing his philosophic discussions with his companions in this retreat. These tracts give evidence of a decided adhesion to the Catholic faith (*C. acad.* 3.20.43) and so daring an effort to grasp intellectually the gifts of faith that it might appear to be a gnosis (*Beat. vit.* 4.34). For this reason, some critics maintain that Augustine was converted to Neoplatonism, while others claim that with his experience at Cassiciacum he accepted an authentic Christian faith in full.

Although neither possibility should be minimized, a certain play, or even an imbalance or time lag, between his faith and his understanding of this faith must not be excluded. The account of his conversion demonstrates the serious risk he ran of being overcome by the illumination of Neoplatonism. But his submission to the authority of Christ is nonetheless decisive, even though it needed more time to impregnate and transform his understanding in this regard. In actual fact, full comprehension came only with his accession to the episcopate and the exercise of his pastoral office.

Baptism. Augustine returned to Milan at the beginning of Lent in 387 and inscribed his name together with that of Alipius and that of his son, Adeodatus, among the candidates preparing for Baptism; he was baptized in the course of the Paschal Vigil. He remained several months in Milan, living in community with his friends and his mother, who took care of their needs. In search of a suitable site for their life of prayer and retreat, they decided to return to Africa (*Conf.* 9.8.17); but Monica died at *Ostia when they were about to embark (*Conf.* 9.11.27–28).

Postponing the return to Africa, Augustine spent a year in Rome during which he began two philosophical dialogues and his first treatise against the Manichees. In the autumn of 388 he left for Carthage, then returned to Tagaste, where he sold his property, gave the money to the poor, and retired with his friends to a monastic way of life. He wrote several books that have a philosophic cast, among them his *De magistro,* which is a dialogue with his 16-year-old son, who died soon afterward (*Conf.* 9.6.14).

Priest at Hippo. Following the practice of the older monks, Augustine carefully avoided involvement in ecclesiastical functions to the point of staying away from cities whose episcopal sees were vacant (*Serm.* 355.1.2). But one day in *Hippo he attended a sermon by Bishop Valerius, who spoke to his people of the necessity of choosing and ordaining a priest for services in the city. The congregation, on recognizing Augustine, seized him and presented him to the bishop as their candidate for ordination (*ibid.;* Possidius, *Vita Aug.,* 4). Valerius raised him to the priesthood, but permitted him to continue his monastic way of life, providing him with a house and a garden near the church (*Serm.* 355.1.2). Contrary to African custom, the bishop, who was of Oriental origin, entrusted Augustine with the task of preaching in the church in his presence (Poss., *Vita* 5). Augustine quickly became aware of how poorly he knew the Scriptures. Hence he requested of Valerius a period of leisure to complete his education (*Epist.* 21).

Of these early sermons, besides certain *Enarrationes in Psalmos,* only three or four have been preserved (*Serm.* 1; 12; 50; perhaps 2). They have an anti-Manichaean orientation that corresponds to the contents of most of his other works written at this time, although he had already begun his campaign against the Donatists. *See* DONATISM. Augustine was asked to speak on the faith and the Creed before the African bishops gathered in Council at Hippo, and afterward he wrote out the discourse at the request of several of the bishops (*Retract.* 1.17). Since Valerius was growing old and feared that Augustine might be chosen bishop for another see, he obtained permission from the metropolitan of Carthage, Aurelius, to consecrate Augustine as bishop so that he could be associated with him in the See of Hippo. It was apparently in the summer of 395 that Augustine was consecrated, and Valerius died a short while later (Poss., *Vita* 8).

Bishop of Hippo. Augustine served about 35 years as bishop of Hippo, the city second in Africa in ecclesiastical importance. Upon becoming bishop, he took up residence in the episcopal palace in order to be at the disposal of visitors, but grouped his clerics around him in a sort of clerical monastery, based on a community of goods in imitation of the Apostles. At first optional, this arrangement was soon made obligatory for all his ecclesiastics (*Serm.* 355; 356). But Augustine the bishop could hardly live a life of silence and retirement, for he was rapidly inundated with visitors; nor could he remain tranquilly at Hippo. He was frequently called to preside at synods and councils; to preach; to take part in controversies; to visit his friends among the bishops, so that much of his time was consumed in travel.

Evidence points to between 40 and 50 journeys during his episcopate, and this represents absences from Hippo of from a few days to 4 or 5 months at a time. It took about 9 days to make the trip to Carthage, and he went there at least 20 or 30 times. It is in the context of this busy life that his immense literary production should be seen: almost 100 treatises, some 200 letters, and an enormous number of sermons, more than 500 of which are intact, besides the *Tractatus* on the Gospel of St. John and the *Enarrationes in Psalmos.*

Manichaeism. Until 399, Augustine found it necessary to struggle against Manichaeism. He wrote four tracts against this heresy at the beginning of his episcopate. On Dec. 7 and 8, 398 (or 404), he engaged in a public discussion with the Manichaean Felix in the church at Hippo. The official acts of this dialogue have been preserved, and they testify to the conversion of his opponent at the close of the discussion (*C. Felic.*). Augustine had subsequently to oppose similar doctrines spread by the Priscillianists and the Marcionites. (*See* PRISCILLIANISM; MARCION.)

Donatism and Use of Civil Power. When Augustine was ordained a priest, *Donatism had been in existence for 80 years and had caused great difficulties for the Church in Africa. In Hippo the Donatists were in the majority (*C. Petil.* 2.83.184), and their church had been enriched with numerous legacies (*In evang. Ioh.* 6.25); they were even more powerful in the neighboring countryside. After the Council of Hippo in 393, Augustine began a campaign against them with the composition in 396 of a *Psalm against the Donatist Party,* destined to be chanted by the faithful. He then published (394) the tract *Contra epistulam Donati,* which, along with a number of other anti-Donatist writings, has been lost. The position he adopted then in their regard was astonishingly ecumenical in the modern sense of the term, as his letters testify (*Epist.* 23).

Little by little, however, he found himself forced to enlarge the field of these activities and change his methods. He preached against the Donatists at Carthage, corresponded with schismatic bishops in other cities, took part in open discussions, made careful investigation

Fig. 2. "St. Augustine Listening to St. Ambrose," by the 16th-century artist Bernard van Orley.

of the origin and history of the problem, and inquired into local incidents. It was particularly the violence engaged in by the Circumcellions that forced him to admit the legitimacy of appeal to the civil authorities and the use of legal constraint. In 396 or 397 he rejected recourse to coercion (*Retract.* 2.5); but in 400 he began to justify this practice (*C. Parm.* 1.18.13), and he finished by making an apology for the appeal to the secular arm in 405 (*C. Cresc.* 3.43.47–59.65) and again in 417 (*Epist.* 185).

From 400 onward, Augustine devoted himself to combating the Donatists without regard to the consequences. He published some controversial tracts and preached at Carthage, at Hippo, and in nearby villages. He opened a path for the return of schismatic clergy by permitting them as Catholics to exercise the same offices they held as Donatists. But he also appealed to the civil authority. He complained against the misdeeds of the Circumcellions and obtained the condemnation of the Donatist bishop of Calama, who was declared a heretic and fined 6 pounds of gold in 403–404. The Council of *Carthage (404) requested the Emperor to make this punishment general by applying the Theodosian Code on heresy wherever violence had been perpetrated; but the Emperor went much further and published an edict of union depriving the Donatists of their sanctuaries.

After experiments with rigor (408) and indulgence (410) on the part of the civil authorities, the Council of Carthage (410), apparently influenced by Augustine, persuaded Emperor *Honorius to convoke a public confrontation of Catholic and Donatist bishops. In 411, on June 1, 3, and 8, 286 Catholic and 279 Donatists bishops held discussions in the presence of the imperial commissioner Marcellinus. Augustine and Aurelius of Carthage served as the Catholic spokesmen; victory was accorded to the Catholic position, and a new edict of repression was directed against the Donatists.

Augustine used a stenographic report of these discussions in his further anti-Donatist efforts and had it read yearly in the churches of his diocese during Lent. The summary he wrote of it formed the basis of his final anti-Donatist works. He continued preaching against the sect and engaged in two more public controversies with the Donatist bishops. Not till 420 could he relinquish this struggle to devote himself totally to the problem of Pelagianism (*see* PELAGIUS AND PELAGIANISM).

Personal Approach. Augustine was fully conscious of his change of position regarding the use of civil power to restrain heretics (*Epist.* 93.5.17); but he felt it justified by the violence committed by the Circumcellions, the social pressure that kept good people in schism, and the refusal of many Donatist bishops to engage in the intelligent dialogue that Augustine preferred. His personal approach and sensitive charity in controversy, evident from his very first encounter with the Donatist bishop of Hippo, marked all his dealings with his opponents. It reached its culmination when the Catholic bishops in the conference of 411 offered to resign and allow the Donatist bishops to retain their sees if they would acknowledge their errors (*C. Emer.* 5–7).

It is easy to see how this immense pastoral enterprise and responsibility for Church unity transformed Augustine from the Christian Neoplatonist he had been when ordained to the priesthood. This pastoral experience guided by charity and the demands of unity affected the structure of his thought and modified the natural bent of his mind that appears, however, each time he paused in his episcopal activity to indulge in speculation. This wedding of the pastoral and the speculative stamped his charity with an uncommonly profound personal quality.

Pelagianism. Once or twice during the conference of 411, Augustine caught a glimpse of Pelagius (*C. Pelag.* 22.46); it was the first and only time these future adversaries met. Pelagius had arrived in Africa from Rome during the winter of 410–411 and debarked at Hippo during Augustine's absence. They exchanged letters of courtesy (*Epist.* 146). But since Augustine was alarmed at the doctrines of Pelagius, he dealt with him reservedly, and Pelagius soon departed for Palestine. A council at Carthage in July and August 411 condemned Celestius, a disciple of Pelagius, but Augustine was not present. However, he soon took note of the council's decisions, and at the request of Governor Marcellinus, he wrote in 411–412 his first anti-Pelagian work, *De peccatorum meritis et remissione*. He did not incriminate Pelagius by name, except in a letter that accompanied the work. This attitude toward the man he preserved until 415, although he attacked the doctrine vigorously (*De spiritu et littera; De fide et operibus*).

In 415 he sent *Orosius to Jerusalem to aid St. *Jerome in combating Pelagius, after Pelagius had gained the good will of Bp. *John of Jerusalem. A council held at Diospolis justified Pelagius; and when Orosius reported this news in Carthage in 416, the synod of that year renewed the condemnation of 411 and sent a letter to Pope *Innocent I denouncing the errors of Pelagius and Celestius and requesting a formal condemnation by Rome (*Epist.* 175). The Synod of Milevis, in which Augustine took part, did the same (*Epist.* 176); and on Jan. 27, 417, the Pope confirmed the excommunication of the two heretics (*Epist.* 181–183). At the beginning of the same year, Augustine obtained the acts of the Synod of Diospolis and used them in composing his *De gestis Pelagii.*

Pope Zosimus. In March 417 *Zosimus succeeded Innocent as pope; and on receiving an apparently irreproachable profession of faith from Pelagius, as well as a personal visit from Celestius with a similar profession, he convoked a synod that cleared Pelagius and demanded that the accusers of Celestius present themselves in Rome before the Pope.

The bishops of Africa, however, gathered in a synod at Carthage and conjured the Pope to maintain the decisions of Innocent. A number of them, including Augustine, appealed to influential people in Rome to intercede in the matter (*Epist.* 186; 191; 192). On May 1, 418, they renewed their condemnation of Pelagian doctrine. In Rome, meanwhile, the Pelagians provoked difficulties that prejudiced their cause; and when the Pope called Celestius for a hearing, Celestius fled. An edict of Emperor Honorius ordered the expulsion of the Pelagian leaders, the deportation of their followers, and the confiscation of their goods. Zosimus's *Tractoria,* or encyclical letter (418), then confirmed the position of his predecessor and approved the decrees of the Synod of Carthage.

After this condemnation by Zosimus, Augustine had to wage a 10-year campaign against *Julian of Eclanum, an exiled Pelagian bishop, the champion of the heresy from 421 on. He proved an ambitious and arrogant polemicist who had neither the moral stature of Pelagius nor the dialectical subtlety of Celestius, but was never-

Fig. 3. Tomb of St. Augustine, by the sculptor Benino da Campione, 1362, in the cathedral at Pavia, Italy.

theless a person of intelligence who had mastered the naturalist rationalism contained germinally in the doctrine. Augustine wrote four tracts against Julian; the last of these was unfinished at his death in 430.

Semi-Pelagianism. Beginning in 425 Augustine had to defend his doctrine on grace against a group of monks designated as Semi-Pelagians by the 17th-century theologians. These ascetics were scandalized by Augustine's blunt formulas, in which they detected an attack on ascetical efforts. The problem concentrated on the *initium fidei,* or the beginning of the faith in the soul. Was it the result of grace or of an act of the free will? Augustine wrote numerous treatises in response to the monks of *Hadrumetum (*Grat. et lib. arb.; Corrept.*), to Vitalis of Carthage (*Epist.* 217), and finally to the monks of Provence in France (*Praed. sanct.; Persev.*).

The anti-Pelagian controversy gave Augustine the occasion to grasp two implications of his experience of grace and to consolidate his comprehension of the Pauline message. From the hour of his conversion he had lived this primacy of grace in the light of the Epistles to the Galatians and Romans (*Conf.* 8). At the beginning of his episcopate, commenting on Romans for Simplicius, he understood in a more definite fashion the words of the Apostle, "What have you that you have not received?" (*Quaest. Simpl.* 2), and the notion of the salvation of grace (1 Cor 4.7). The controversy provided him with the opportunity to draw out the consequences of this doctrine with a logical rigor in which at times the pastor yields place to the polemical theologian.

Arianism. Although before the last decade of his life Augustine had little conflict with *Arianism, he often insisted in his sermons on the equality of the Father and the Son; and his *De Trinitate,* on which he worked intermittently for more than 20 years, combines a synthesis of the anti-Arian controversies with the elaboration of a highly original formulation of Trinitarian doctrine that he achieved with the help of Aristotle's *Categories* (bks. 5–7). It is difficult to decide whether or not this exposition was aimed at a concrete Arian danger. It is known, however, that the Semi-Arians had sought an alignment with the Donatists (*Epist.* 44.6).

Augustine dealt on several occasions with Arians who wrote to him (*Epist.* 242.1), or who provoked him to a public discussion in Carthage (*Epist.* 238–241; Poss., *Vita,* 17), or whom he converted by his preaching (*Epist.* 170–171). It is not known when these individual encounters took place, but it is known that before 418–420 there were no known Arians (or almost none) in Africa—at least in Hippo (*Serm.* 46.18; *In evang. Ioh.* 40.7); but in 418 he received an Arian tract and refuted it point by point in his response (*C. Arrian.; Retract.* 2.52.79). The *Goths who were sent to northern Africa in 427 by the Empress to quell the revolt of Count Boniface were Arians, and they brought with them to Hippo an Arian bishop whom Augustine had to refute publicly (*Coll. c. Max.*).

Augustine's Death. In 426, at the age of 72, Augustine had the people acclaim his choice for successor, the priest Heraclius, to whom he confided much of his pastoral affairs. Heraclius was not consecrated, however, before Augustine's death (*Epist.* 213), and the aged bishop continued to work to the end. In 426–427 he undertook the revision of all his writings (*Retractationum*); and in 430, while the *Vandals were besieging Hippo, Augustine was working on a refutation of *Julian of Eclanum when death claimed him at age 76 (Poss., *Vita* 29–31).

Augustine the Man. St. Augustine was a rhetorician of the Later Empire and a late Neoplatonist, but he was a man of brilliant genius, whose profound humanity transformed the already declining rhetoric and philosophy into something new and distinctive and made him a precursor of modern times. In philosophy, he is often eclectic as regards his sources, but he is always personal in the crucible treatment whereby he amalgamates them into new schemata of striking power and freshness. He marks all that he treats with that personal quality that is the product of a nature that is exceptionally sensitive, of an experience that is exceptionally lucid, and, above all, of a love that is exceptionally profound. This personal consciousness is perhaps the most striking trait of his genius and the most decisive source of his influence upon our history.

Works

Although Augustine's writings have been edited in several collections (see below), eventually all his works will be edited also in CorpChrist. To date (1965) the following works have appeared in CorpChrist: *De civitate Dei* (v.33), *Locutiones in Heptateuchum* (v.33), *Quaestiones in Heptateuchum* (v.33), *De VIII quaestiones ex Vetere Testamento* (v.33), *Sermones* (v.41), *Tractatus in Iohannis Evangelium* (v.36), and *Enarrationes in Psalmos* (v.38–40).

Augustine's works are listed below (see table) chronologically, following the *Retractationum,* so development of his thought may be seen. The editions given in the table are the following: Maurists, *Opera Augustini;* PL; CSEL; and *Bibliothèque Augustinenne,* with a French translation (Paris 1936–).

Philosophy and Theology

In characterizing Augustine's philosophical and theological thought, an attempt is made here to describe its fundamental structures and the lines of force in which his mobility and incessant creativity tend to balance their impulse. Augustine described man's human situation in the form of a dramatic tension such as he himself had lived. His discovery of Neoplatonism, and then of St. Paul, had rescued him from the snares of materialism by introducing him to a true spirituality that he experienced in a sincerely interior conversion, from skepticism, that helped him to recognize the certitude of Truth, the source of all certitude. Finally it freed him from sensuality, by revealing to him the victorious attraction of grace. This conversion is the beginning and the center of his whole vision of the world.

Man between World and God. Man can lose himself through his external desires or enter into himself and find the light of Truth that created him (*Vera relig.* 39.72; *Conf.* 10.34.53). Man is in a middle position. "You who are in the soul, are in the center; if you look below, there is the body; if you look above, there is God. Withdraw from the body, rise above yourself" (*In evang. Ioh.* 20.11). From one to the other of these directions, there is a reversal: if the soul turns from the interior light, it tends to vanish into nothingness; if it returns to its own interior self, it is established in true being. To abandon God is to lose oneself; to find oneself is to rediscover God by rising above oneself (*Serm.*

Date	Works	Editions and volume numbers			
		Maurists	PL	CSEL	Bbli. Aug.
	Before Baptism				
386 (Nov.)	Contra academicos	1	32	63	4
386	De beata vita	1	32	63	4
386	De ordine	1	32	63	4
386–387 (winter)	Soliloquiorum	1	32		5
387	De immortalitate animae	1	32		5
387	Disciplinarum (lost, except De musica)				
	From Baptism to Priesthood				
388; 389–390	De moribus ecclesiae catholicae et Manichaeorum	1	32		1
388	De quantitate animae	1	32		5
388; 391	De libero arbitrio	1	32	74	6
388 or 389	De genesi contra Manichaeos	3.1	34		
389	De musica	1	32		7
389	De magistro	1	32	77	6
390	De vera religione	3.1	34	77	8
	From Priesthood to Episcopate				
391	De utilitate credendi	8	42	25.1	8
392	De duabus animabus	8	42	25.1	17
392 (Aug. 28–29)	Disputatio contra Fortunatum Manichaeum	8	42	25.1	17
393 (Oct. 8)	De fide et symbolo	6	40	41	9
393; 426	De genesi ad litteram imperfectus	3.1	34	28.1	
394	De sermone Domini in monte	3.1	34		
394	Psalmus contra partem Donati	9	43	51	28
394	Contra epistulam Donati (lost)				
394	Contra Adimantum Manichaeum	8	42	25.1	17
394–395	Expositio quar. propos. in Epistula ad Romanos	3.2	35		
394–395	Expositio in Epistulam ad Galatas	3.2	35		
394–395	Epistulae ad Romanos inchoata expositio	3.2	35		
388; 395	De diversis quaestionibus	6	40		10
394–395	De mendacio	6	40	41	2
	Episcopate, Donatist Controversy				
395 or 396	De diversis quaestionibus ad Simplicianum	6	40		10
396	Contra epistulam, quam vocant Fundamenti	8	42	25.1	17
396	De agone christiano	6	40	41	1
396; 426	De doctrina christiana	3.1	34		11
396	Contra partem Donati (lost)				
397–401	Confessionum	1	32	33	13–14
397–398	Contra Faustum Manichaeum	8	42	25.1	
397–398 or 404	Contra Felicem Manichaeum	8	42	25.2	17
398?	De disciplina christiana	6	40		
399	De natura boni contra Manichaeos	8	42	25.2	1
399	Contra Secundinum Manichaeum	8	42	25.2	17
399	Contra Hilarum (lost)				
399–	Quaestiones Evangelicarum	3.2	35		
399	Adnotationum in Iob	3.1	34	28.3	
399	De catechizandis rudibus	6	40		11
399–422	De Trinitate	8	42		15–16
400–	De consensu evangelistarum	3.1	34	43	
400	Contra epistulam Parmeniani	9	43	51	28
401	De baptismo contra Donatistas	9	43	51	29
401	Contra quod attulit Centurius a Donatistis (lost)				
c. 400	Ad inquisitiones Ianuarii (*Epist.* 54–55)	2	33	34	
401	De opere monachorum	6	40	41	3
401	De bono coniugali	6	40	41	2
401	De sancta virginitate	6	40	41	3
401–414	De Genesi ad litteram	3.1	34	28.1	
401; 402; 405	Contra litteras Petiliani	9	43	52	

Date	Works	Editions and volume numbers			
		Maurists	PL	CSEL	Bbli. Aug.
405	Epistula ad Catholicos de secta Donatistarum (De unitate ecclesiae)	9	43	52	28
405–406	Contra Cresconium grammaticum Donatistam	9	43	52	
406 or 408	Probationum et Testimoniorum contra Donatistas (lost)				
406 or 408	Contra Donatistam nescio quem (lost)				
406 or 408	Admonitio Donatistarum contra Maximianistas (lost)				
406	De divinatione daemonum	6	40	41	10
408	Quaestiones vi contra Paganos (Epist. 102)	2	33	34	
410 (end)	De urbis excidio	6	40		
410–420 or 430	De fide rerum, quae non videntur	6	40		8
from 411	Expositio epistulam Iacobi (lost)				
411–412	De utilitate ieiunii	6	40		2
411–412	De peccatorum meritis et remissione	10.1	44	60	
from 411 (June)	De unico baptismo contra Petilianum	9	43	53	
411 or 412	De Maximianistis contra Donatistas (lost)				
	Episcopate, Anti-Pelagian Controversy				
412	De gratia novi Testam. (Epist. 140)	2	33	44	
412	De spiritu et littera	10.1	44	60	
412–413	De fide et operibus	6	40	41	8
411–412 (winter)	Breviculus collationis contra Donatistas	9	43	53	
411–412 (winter)	Post collationem contra Donatistas liber unus (Ad partem Donati post gesta)	9	43	53	
413?	De videndo Deo (Epist. 147)	2	33	44	
413?	Commonitorium ad Fortunatianum (Epist. 148)	2	33	44	
414	De bono viduitatis	6	40	41	3
415	De natura et gratia	10.1	44	60	
415?	De perfectione iustitiae hominis	10.1	44	42	
413–427	De civitate Dei	7	41	40	32–36
415	Ad Orosium contra Priscillianistas et Origenistas	8	42		
415	Ad Hier., De origine animae (Epist. 166)	2	33	44	
415	Ad Hier., De sententia Iacobi	2	33	44	
416	Ad Emeritum Donatistam post collationem (lost)				
416–426	De continentia	6	40	41	3
417	De gestis Pelagii	10.1	44	42	
417	De correctione Donatistarum (Epist. 185)	2	33	57	
417	De praesentia Dei (Epist. 187)	2	33	57	
from 418	De patientia	6	40	41	
418	De gratia Christi et de peccato originali	10.1	44	42	
418 (Sept. 18)	Sermo ad Caesareensis ecclesiae plebem	9	43	53	
418 (Sept. 20)	De gestis cum Emerito Donatista	9	43	53	
418	Contra sermonem Arrianorum	8	42	26	
418–420	De nuptiis et concupiscentiis	10.1	44	42	
419–	Locutionum in heptateuchum lib. VII	3.1	34	28.2	
419	Quaestionum in heptateuchum lib. VII	3.1	34	28.3	
419 (end)	De anima et eius origine	10.1	44	60	
419	De adulterinis coniugiis	6	40	41	2
419	Contra adversarium legis et prophetarum	8	42		
419; 420	Contra Gaudentium Donatistarum episcopum	9	43	53	
419	Contra mendacium ad Consentium	6	40	41	2
419–420	Contra duas epistulas Pelagianorum ad Bonifatium	10.1	44	60	
421 or 422	Contra Iulianum	10.1	44		
421	De cura pro mortuis gerenda	6	40	41	2
422–423	Enchiridion	6	40		9
422	De octo Dulcitii quaestionibus	6	40		10
425	De gratia et libero arbitrio	10.1	44		24
426	De correptione et gratia	10.1	44		24

Date	Works	Editions and volume numbers			
		Maurists	PL	CSEL	Bbli. Aug.
426–427	Retractationum	1	32	36	12
	Works Written after the Retractations				
427	Collatio cum Maximino	8	42		
427	Ad Firmum de civitate Dei [RevBén 51 (1939) 109–121]				
428	Contra Maximinum Arrianum	8	42		
428–429	De haeresibus ad Quodvuldeum	8	42		
429 or 430?	Tractatus adversus Iudaeos	8	42		
429	De praedestinatione sanctorum	10.1	44		24
429	De dono perseverantiae	10.2	45		24
428–430	Contra Iuliani responsionem opus imperfectum	10.2	45		
	De symbolo ad cathechumenos	6	40		
	Quaestiones XVII in Evangelium	3.2	35		
	De VIII quaestionibus ex Vetere Testamento	3.2	35		
	Regula	1	32		
	Speculum	3.1	34	12	
	Works of Uncertain Date or Composed over Many Years				
386–429	Epistulae	2	33	34.44 57.58	
391–430	Sermones post Maurinos reperti (ed. G. Morin, 1930)	5	38–39		
406–407; 419–424	In Evangelium Iohannis tractatus	3.2	35	36	
406–407 or 416	In Epistulam ad Parthos tractatus	3.2	35		
392–420	Enarrationes in Psalmos	4	36–37		

96.2.2). This situation and the levels of human existence that it defines cannot be understood except as the steps in an ascension. In this regard, Augustine is essentially a Neoplatonist. His metaphysics cannot be described from the exterior: it is primarily a symbolical history (*Confessions*); it is essentially an *itinerarium mentis ad Deum,* a journey of the mind to God.

Ascent to God. The first phase of this ascent consists in drawing back from the senses that drive man to the outer world, and bind him to the body. Man must discover the activation of his inner sense, which judges the external senses (*Lib. arb.* 2.3.8), or also that of the memory, which preserves the images of the body, but stripped of their spatiality (*Conf.* 8.10.13). However, if a man enters into himself and remains at this stage, he can fall into an illusion worse than that of the senses by accepting the mere figments of the creative memory (*Conf.* 8.10.14) as the spiritual or the divine (*Vera relig.* 20.40). It is not the image but the ideas that represent genuine spirituality within man (*Trin.* 8.6.9). Through them man judges all things, for they are the radiants of the Truth that is the rule of all judgment and that no one can judge (*Lib. arb.* 2.12.34).

This ascent can be described as a double movement: the return within oneself, and the rising above oneself. For Augustine this is the key to all access to the transcendent: the design of conversion (*In evang. Ioh.* 18.10; *In psalm.* 41.7–8).

Trinitarian Structure of Creation. At the end of these ascensions Augustine thought that he would discover the Triune God. From the illumination of 386, following his reading of Plotinus, he believed that he had attained his desire (*Conf.* 7.9.13; 7.10.16). In his early writings, every anagoge ends with an evocation of the Trinity (*Beat. vit.* 4.34–35; *Musica* 6.17.56). This is understandable, if it is recalled that he assimilated the Three Persons of the Trinity to the three Hypostases of Plotinian anagoge.

But the difficulties of this assimilation soon forced him to seek a different perspective. He turned to a Trinitarian vision of creation with which he tried to organize his knowledge of the faith. The Father is the principle of all existence. But a being derived from nothingness tends toward nothingness, that is, to complete dispersion, unless it is formed and converted to its principle. The function of the Word is to form and convert, while the Spirit urges toward unity, bringing about the harmony and mutual agreement of all creatures (*Epist.* 11; *Vera relig.* 43.80; 55.113; *Gen. ad litt.* 4.3.7–).

This Trinitarian economy of creation in which the Three Persons cooperate (*Serm.* 71.16.27) brings conversion once more into the center of his vision of the world. This conversion is the decisive moment of creation in which the creature is, as it were, a second time snatched from nothingness and returned by the Word toward its Principle. The creature is formed by Him who is indefectibly turned toward the Father, and is the Form of every creature (*Gen. ad litt.* 1.4.9–1.5.10).

The creature with free will, whether angel or man, is a privileged case in this double or even triple creation. Taken from nothing, it remains essentially capable of turning toward nothingness, i.e., of committing sin. Its nature is good, for it is constituted in its very freedom through a first turning toward God (*Gen. ad litt.* 4.22.39), and it is ordered toward unity by the Spirit who is the bond of unity. Creation and conversion or illumination are two simultaneous moments that offer the possibility of liberty. This explains how the angels were able to commit sin, whatever may have been the difficulties Augustine experienced in fitting them into this pattern (*Civ.* 11.11). Liberty is thus, as it were, enveloped by a grace of conversion that is its constitutive element. Sin is the choice of nothingness. It entails the "deformation" of the created being, which, however, cannot go so far as causing it to lose its form, i.e., the nature that makes it what it is.

This deformation, resulting from aversion to the good, calls for a "reformation" by a new conversion that is again the work of the Word become incarnate, to bring man back to the Father in the Spirit (*Vera relig.* 12.24; *Trin.* 14.16.22). This Trinitarian vision of creation and of Redemption culminates in what has been improperly called the "psychological analogies" of the Trinity. It is not an analogy, because it is a true history of salvation by which the human soul takes cognizance of itself within the frame of a creative ascendancy of the Trinity, and is thus reformed to its image. Nor is it psychological, since it is an actual Trinitarian metaphysic that expresses itself interiorly in a triple recognition: I am, I know myself, and I love myself. It thus opens itself to the very life of the Trinity, of which it is the created image (*Trin.* 8–15). This Trinitarian dialectic in which St. Augustine's effort to comprehend his faith culminates is, as it were, the final synthesis, although incomplete, of his anagogic and Trinitarian vision of creation, the interrelated elements of which have been indicated here.

Understanding and Mysticism. It is impossible to describe the coherence of Augustine's thought without grasping it at the profound level at which it means "understanding of the faith," or even mysticism. It is to be recalled how the Manichaean gnosis had attracted him, and how again Neoplatonic illumination had been the portal for his return to the faith. Theology was for him a contemplative understanding of the mysteries held by faith; an understanding that situates these mysteries within an ascendant and Trinitarian perspective.

It can be asked whether Augustine was a mystic in the same sense as the great Spanish mystics. In using expressions such as "intellectual mysticism" or "mysticism of wisdom," numerous nuances must be made before applying them to Augustinian thought. For him, mystical passivity coincides with the highest degree of interior activity, since this interiority coincides with the fullest dispossession of self. "He is more intimate to me, than I am to myself," he says of God.

The experience of a radical dependence at the heart of the most creative liberty is the source of the whole Augustinian theology of grace. Mystical experience is nought else than a flowering of a presence constitutive of the self, and is made manifest by recalling into the self one's consciousness preoccupied with the cares of the world. The gratuity of this mystical presence is but the grace of this conversion, and not this presence itself, which is constitutive of the human mind. This mysticism is but the understanding of the faith carried to its term. This method of understanding, i.e., of reflection, is borrowed from Neoplatonism. It is animated by the sense of a personal God, a concept that goes beyond the perspectives of that philosophy. It borrows from it, however, its movement as a whole; for faith is present only to regulate its use and to furnish moral preparations. Thus mystical experience is always deceptive, as Augustine's first experience of illumination (in 386) seems to have been (*Conf.* 7.17.23; *Soliloq.* 1.10.17; *Quant. anim.* 15.25; *Trin.* 8.2.3; *In evang. Ioh.* 18.11; etc.).

This alternation between a mystic and almost gnostic audacity, with a submission to the humble rule of faith that he never desired to forego, supplies the fundamental structure of Augustinian thought. In form it is the dialectic of reason and authority; in substance, it is the dialectic of the eternal home and the way that leads to it, that is, the Trinity and the Incarnation.

Authority and Reason. The authority to which one renders faith precedes the understanding in leading the soul to the light; but it follows it in restraining intellectual presumption. This double aspect played its part in Augustine's conversion. Brought from skepticism to a consideration of the Scriptures by the authority of Ambrose (*Conf.* 6.4.5–6.5.8), then brought back to himself by the books of the Platonists (*Conf.* 7.10.16), he relied finally on the authority of Christ incarnate to cure him of the presumption of the philosophers (*Conf.* 7.18.24). Faith is first of all that indispensable adhesion without which nothing can be apprehended. All certitude begins with faith, even certainty regarding human origins (*Util. cred.* 12.26). But it is likewise faith that causes one to live in an obedience that renders him open to teaching (*De ord.* 2.9.26; *In evang. Ioh.* 29.6). Hence the role of authority is to demand faith and prepare for reason (*Vera relig.* 24.45).

Reason leads to understanding. But it does not thereby free itself from all relation to authority; it rather points out what deserves faith, and submits itself to the supreme authority of Truth (*ibid.*). In fact, authority has only a temporal priority; reason actually enjoys a primacy by right (*De ord.* 2.9.26), and even a certain priority in the order of time, since to believe one must understand the words of the speaker (*Serm.* 43.9). There is a reciprocal relation between authority and reason when the one is connected with the other: particularly in the process of admonishing (*admonere*) and of teaching (*docere*). The sinner needs to be admonished from the outside and alerted thereby to reenter into himself. There are two types of knowledge: (1) science or faith, which concerns history, words, external realities; (2) reason, which is an interior illumination and is concerned with eternal truths (*Trin.* 4.18.24). The first type brings light only when it turns the soul to the source of all light, the Truth, that is, man's interior Master (*Divers. quaest.* 9; *Epist.* 13.4; *Mag.* 11.38).

The Redemption in action usually is conceived in this fashion: Christ appeared in the exterior world to bring man back within himself where He can teach him as God and as Truth (*Lib. arb.* 3.10.30). He who is the Truth is also the Way; the Word made flesh leads to God the Word (*Serm.* 141.1.4). Thus the gnosiological schemata of authority and reason are combined completely with the theological schemata of the Incarnation and the Trinity.

The Heavenly Country and Its Way. The structure of Augustine's theology is likewise governed by the experience of his conversion. In the seventh book of his *Confessions,* Augustine explained at length how he discovered the Trinity (God and Word) in the books of the Platonists, but that he had not found in them the Incarnation or the humility of Christ. He thanked God for having had this experience, since he was thus able to gauge how the knowledge of God could lead to presumption and pride, without the humility of Christ incarnate.

The philosophers knew the truth, even that of the Trinity. But they saw it from afar; they knew it as their true country; but they did not know the road that leads others to Christ (*Conf.* 7.20.26–7.21.27). This pattern became a fundamental articulation of his theology (*Doctr. christ.* 1.10–12). Christ is the way of humility; His cross is the ship that leads to the true country that is still only glimpsed (*In evang. Ioh.* 2.3–4).

God and the Trinity. Augustine recognized that the philosophers had a kind of knowledge of the Trinity (*Civ.* 10.29; *Trin.* 13.19.24). He himself certainly sought an understanding of this mystery in an anagoge of the Neoplatonic type. Hence it is not Christ who reveals the Trinity by his Incarnation; He is solely the way that purifies man's heart and prepares it thus for the vision of God. Augustine's whole theology of the Trinity and the Incarnation is fitted into this frame. It is an oversimplification to say that Augustine put the consideration of God's nature before that of the divine Persons. His theological speculation, it is true, evolved along this line, as is testified by the *De Trinitate,* whose composition was spread over 20 years. While he frequently spoke of God without further precision, he did so to orient the thought of his faithful in a direction away from that of creatures, to lead them to a spiritual concept of God, to present them with a Being neither mobile nor extended, yet "in all things everywhere" (*Conf.* 6.3.4; *Serm.* 277.13.19).

He wished likewise to affirm that this God alone exists truly and that all creatures take their being and goodness primarily from Him (*In psalm.* 101; *Serm.* 2.10–14). This being, sovereign good because He possesses being in a sovereign manner, is the Trinity of the Father, Son, and Holy Spirit, the One and Only God (*Serm.* 156.6). It is to be noted that when the *Confessions* mention God, it is always the Father who is addressed; Truth always designates the Son; and Charity, the Holy Spirit. The attribution of illumination to the Word, and of sanctification, or the effusion of charity, to the Spirit are not merely simple appropriations. They must be seen in the perspective of this Trinitarian metaphysics of creation (*Civ.* 11.23–28) and the anagoge modeled on it (*Trin.* 8–14).

It is only in bk. 15 of *De Trinitate* that the further aspect of these appropriations begins to be emphasized. This results from the problems that Augustine had to face in his attempt to understand the Trinity through creation rather than through Redemption. Furthermore, a double influence, the Johannine theology of the Spirit and the Neoplatonic pattern of procession, conversion, and union, which made him think of the life in the Trinity, led him to place the Spirit between the Father and the Son as their mutual love (*Trin.* 6.5.7). His Trinitarian theology is characterized by the gradual abandoning of traditional patterns to which he still adhered in 389–390 and in which the Spirit leads to the Son through whom the Father himself is known (*Mor. eccl.* 1.17.31). The anagoge through the interior life of the spirit, which gradually becomes simply analogy in the *De Trinitate,* forced him through his penchant for introspection to think of the life of the Trinity as that of a God who knows Himself and loves Himself (*Trin.* 9).

Augustine's initial experience, the mental and theological structures that determined it, and the evolution of his Trinitarian doctrine flowing therefrom give that doctrine three characteristic features that have been decisive for Western tradition: (1) the psychological concept of the processions, conceived by analogy with the production of the mental word and with love of self, as the circular pattern in the life of the Trinity turned back upon itself; (2) the systematic use of the Aristotelian category of relation to express what each divine Person has proper to Himself, namely, His own proper relation to the other Persons (Father, Son, and Holy Spirit), and what each has in common with the other Persons namely, what He is in Himself (God, eternity, immutability, etc.; see *Trin.* 5–7; *Civ.* 11.10; *In evang. Ioh.* 39.3–4); (3) a tendency already accentuated by the Cappadocian Fathers to consider theophanies as the appearances of the whole Trinity, not only that of the Word (*Trin.* 1–4), and the exterior works of the Trinity, as the undifferentiated operations of all three Persons. But this last point needs careful nuance; for with Augustine, there can be question only of a tendency in this direction, since the Trinitarian economy of creation occupied so considerable a place in his thought.

Mediator and His Humility. In Christ incarnate, Augustine had found Him who by His humiliation saved him from pride, and by His mediation rescued him from the despair of ever attaining his true destiny (*Conf.* 7.18.24). His Christology and soteriology represent a thousand variations on this fundamental theme: pride has precipitated man into despair; the humility of the Word-made-man lifts man up.

Christ actually became man to teach man humility (*Serm.* 117.17; *Epist.* 118.4.23). Augustine's insistence on the humility of Christ crucified is not merely a moral exhortation; it is the very source of his Christology. Man must hold to his faith in Christ incarnate; he must let himself be nourished on the milk of Christ's humanity to become capable of digesting the solid nourishment of his divinity (*In psalm.* 130.9–12). Man must be purified by faith in the Incarnation, so that, renovated and healed, he can then contemplate the immutable light of the Word (*Civ.* 11.2). Every prideful elevation of man toward God is fatal to him, for he is quickly rejected, blinded, and given over to despair.

Hope. Despair characterizes the situation of man as a sinner: despair of finding the Truth, of attaining and enjoying what has only been glimpsed here in the world (*In epist. Ioh.* 1.5). But Christ assumed man's mortality, thus abdicating His power; with His Resurrection He has taken away man's impotence. He has taught man to renounce his desire for power by searching for what is his due and, while spiritually impotent, to await the fulfillment of his desires. He has thus taught man to renounce his will to power and to begin by desiring what it is meet that he should desire, although he is still in the state of impotence for attaining what he desires. Through His Resurrection Christ has promised man a share in His power (*Trin.* 13.4.7–13.16.21), since death and the Resurrection are integral parts of Augustine's soteriology (*Trin.* 4.19.25). Often, furthermore, the last word on the Redemption seems to be God's love for man. To save man, God had to convince him of how much He loved him in order that he should not become puffed up with pride (*Trin.* 4.1.2). He came then to give proof of His love and to enkindle man's love in return (*Catech. rud.* 1.4.7–8; *In epist. Ioh.* 7.6; 8.10–11).

Mediation. For it is His love also that accounts for His meditation (*In epist. Ioh.* 6.13). Christ came to participate in man's life, to make man part of His possession. He took on man's mortality to make him part of His immortality (*Civ.* 21.15–16). In contrasting this mediation of Christ with that assigned to the daimonic powers by the Neoplatonists such as Porphyry, Augustine represented the God-Man as He who truly connects the lower with the higher regions (*Civ.* 9.15–17; *Cons. Evang.* 1.35.53; *Epist.* 137.3.12). To be the perfect mediator, He must be, therefore, perfect God and perfect man. He cannot be changed into man, abandoning that which He was. It is man who is changed in Him, assuming that which he was not (*Serm.* 97.11.20–97.12.21; *In psalm.* 130.10). The Augustinian stamp of these formulas passed through St. Leo I into the definition of Chalcedon.

Identification of Christological Errors. For Augustine, three Christological heresies summed up all possible positions outside Catholicism: the Manichaean denial of the humanity of Christ; the Photinian denial of His divinity; and the Apollinarist denial of Christ's full humanity (*Perserv.* 24.67; *In evang. Ioh,* 47.9; *Serm.* 92.3.3). But as Mediator, perfect God and perfect man, Christ is one sole person, the Word made flesh; otherwise, there would be a quaternity instead of a trinity of persons in God (*In evang. Ioh.* 27.4; *Epist.* 140.4.12; *Serm.* 186.1.1; *Praed. sanct.* 15.31).

But the assumed humanity is not only an individual human nature; it is also all humanity in an unbroken chain beginning with Adam (*Civ.* 21.15; *Epist.* 137.2.8; *In psalm.* 74.5.85.1; *In evang. Ioh.* 3.12). This is why the new humanity that is born on the cross, that is the Church, is the total Christ. It is necessary to see how the Christology and soteriology of Augustine are inserted both (1) into his personal experience, namely, that of salvation by grace, and of a God who sought man before man sought Him (*Conf.* 11.2.4); and (2) into the Platonic vision of a world with higher regions to which man aspires without being able to attain them and with a lower region where he has fallen by sin. It is the Christian synthesis of these two elements that gives the key to the Augustinian theology: the true country on high and the way of humility.

Scriptural Thought. Augustine's thought is interwoven with Biblical quotations. This was the result of grace, for his first contact with the Scriptures had provoked in him a disdain for its anthropomorphisms (*Conf.* 3.5.9; 3.7.12). In Milan, Ambrose's spiritual exegesis proved a revelation to Augustine. He understood that these writings had been placed at the service of all through their humble appearance. The key to this secret was expressed by St. Paul: "The letter kills, the spirit gives life" (2 Cor 3.6). Augustine thus read the Scriptures according to the exegetical tradition of the Alexandrians, as it was transmitted to him by St. Ambrose.

Textual Research. Nevertheless, Augustine did not neglect textual research or the need to seek and establish the literal sense. He was convinced of the inspired value of the Septuagint translation, however (*Doctr. christ.* 1.15.22; *Civ.* 18.43), and asked St. Jerome to undertake its translation into Latin (*Epist.* 71.4.6). But since Jerome then favored the *hebraica veritas,* the truth of the Hebrew original, Augustine had to attempt this task himself. He seems to have revised his text according to the Greek whenever he could, but there is no evidence that he published his revisions. In the end he admitted the inspiration of the Hebrew text, and explained the divergences in the Septuagint text as due to the prophetic translation (*Cons. Evang.* 2.66.128; *Civ.* 18.43). It has been established that he refers to the Vulgate more and more frequently for the Old Testament; but his text remained the old African, Latin version, strongly Europeanized and revised on the basis of the Greek.

New Testament. For the New Testament after revising an older Latin version, to which the *Freysing Fragments* are very close, Augustine adopted the Vulgate text (*Cons. Evang.*), beginning *c.* 400. For the Psalter he employed at first a text very close to the Verona and Sinai Psalter. Beginning in 415, in his *Enarrationes in Psalmos*, which he composed by dictation, he used the *hexapla* version of St. Jerome with known corrections.

Literal and Spiritual Sense. The literal, historical meaning remained fundamental for him (*Serm.* 2.7). But incoherence or obscurity in this meaning was an incentive for his adoption of the spiritual sense (*In psalm.* 103; *Serm.* 1.18). The Scripture thus seemed to him frequently to be speaking in figures and to contain mysteries (*sacramenta*). For him too, the whole Old Testament is a prefiguration of the New; and not only the Scripture, but the Hebrew people themselves were prophetic (*Civ.* 10.32.2) in both their history (*In psalm.* 63.2) and their rites (*Civ.* 7.32). The New Testament is hidden in the Old; and the Old is revealed in the New (*Civ.* 16.26; *Quaest. hept.* 2.73). Since the Old Testament speaks only of Christ (*C. Faust.* 16.9), it is only properly understood when one finds Christ in it (*In psalm.* 96.2). Finally, the whole of Scripture teaches nothing more than the two commandments that contain all the Law and the Prophets (*Retract.* 1.22.2; *Catech. rud.* 26.50; *Civ.* 10.5). Augustine found a multiplicity of widespread meanings possible (*Doctr. christ.* 3.27.38), because, even when he found a meaning that has not been envisioned by the author, but that is in conformity with charity (*Conf.* 12.18.27), he felt that in so doing he did not depart from Truth (*Doct. christ.* 1.33.39–1.35.41). It is by means of interior Truth that we judge that Moses spoke the truth (*Conf.* 12.25.34–12.26.36). Now this Truth is Charity and therefore cannot be questioned. It is found only in unity; and it leads one to believe that it includes all true opinion (*Conf.* 12.25.34–12.26.36). This is the core of the remarkable Augustinian synthesis: the truth is within, but it is not subjective because it is inseparable from charity. Augustine became more and more "Christianized" through the reading of the Word and in the light of his pastoral experience, where charity, that is, the Spirit, revealed its meaning to him.

The Church and the Sacraments. Augustine's ecclesiology was elaborated in the course of his painful experience with *Donatism. Affronted by a sect that claimed to be the Church of the pure, the Church of the martyrs, he refused to identify the Church in its present state with the chaff sown amid the good seed, and the Church purified of evil by the Last Judgment (*C. Parm.* 3.3.17–19). But the Church of the saints is not merely to come; it is already in existence, although it cannot be assigned definite limits, for it has sheep outside and wolves within (*In evang. Ioh.* 45.12). The Church is not solely eschatological; it is also transcendent and spiritual. It is the City of God, mingled here below with the terrestrial city, but already spiritually differentiated. The Church is, then, more than it appears to be; it is the Spouse without stain. Its name is that of the Dove (*Bapt.* 3.18.23) because it is the Dove spoken of in the Canticle of Canticles: "Unique is my dove" (5.2; 6.8) and also because it is gathered and united by the Holy Spirit, the Dove who descended upon Christ in the Jordan (Jn 1.32–33). And yet one cannot be a participant in the Church if one destroys; for it is necessary to "preserve the unity of the Spirit in the bond of peace" (Eph 4.2–3).

Ecclesiastical Charity. It is charity again that forms the bond between the visible and invisible. It is the sign that one belongs to the society of the saints, and it demands that the bond of unity be kept intact through adherence to the one Church, spread throughout the world. Catholicity and unity go hand in hand.

In his sixth *Tract on the Gospel of St. John,* Augustine discusses all these themes. He uses the ecclesiology of St. *Cyprian, which was employed by the Donatists, to refute them. But Augustine had a more vivid and stronger consciousness of the transcendence of the Church than did Cyprian. This appears in precise form in his sacramental theology, where he introduces a new distinction between the Sacrament and its spiritual effect, between the mere reception of the Sacrament and the useful or salutary possession of the Sacrament (*Bapt.* 4.17.24; *C. Cresc.* 1.29.34).

Whatever the condition of the minister of Baptism, whether he be unworthy, or in heresy, or in schism, it is Christ who baptizes: "If Judas baptizes, it is Christ who baptizes" (*C. Petil.* 1.9.10; *In evang. Ioh.* 6.8). However, although Baptism is found even among the heretics, in their case it does not produce its salutary effect, the remission of sins, since this can be granted only by the Spirit of unity in the one Church (*In evang. Ioh.* 121.4; *Bapt.* 3.18.2.3; *Serm.* 71.17.28). Augustine channeled this distinction into the categories of his philosophy. He distinguished inchoative being from completed being by his insistence on a return to unity. The Sacrament is constituted by the word of Christ (*Bapt.* 3.10.15), who produces the character or mark of Baptism (*C. Parm.* 2.13.29). The Spirit completes this work by integrating it in unity (*Serm.* 269.2). Augustine extended to the other Sacraments the same distinctions that he was forced to elaborate for Baptism and Holy Orders (*C. Parm.* 2.13.28) by the Donatist controversy. The same controversy forced him to deal more fully also with Confirmation (*C. Petil.* 2.104.238) and the Eucharist (*Serm.* 57.7; *Civ.* 21.25). The useful reception of the Eucharist realizes the unity of the Christian people.

The Eucharist. In the reading of Augustine in the perspective of later problems, an attempt has been made to oppose his realistic and symbolic affirmations regarding the Eucharist. But, in fact, his realism and symbolism are not in opposition. The reality of the Eucharist is expressed in the Sacrament, which is essentially a sign (*C. Adim.* 12.2): the reality (*res*) of the Eucharistic bread and wine is the body of Christ, the whole Christ, the Church (*Serm.* 272; *In evang. Ioh.* 21.25.4; 26.15). But without pausing over what has since been termed the *res et sacramentum,* Augustine most often stressed (*Serm.* 37; 131.1) the ultimate reality of this Sacrament of unity (*Serm.* 227). All his theology of the Church and of the Sacraments is thus centered on unity, which is the ultimate reality, because "God is love."

Grace. Augustine had discovered and corrected certain Semi-Pelagian formulas in his earlier writings (*Retract.* 1.23; 26.16). Nevertheless it is certain that his understanding of grace goes back to the period of his conversion, as his first writings demonstrate (*Soliloq.* 1.1.2). Between 395 and 398, hence 15 years before the anti-Pelagian controversy (*Quaest. Simpl.*), his theology of grace was entirely developed and clear in his mind.

No two spiritual experiences could be more opposed than those of Augustine and *Pelagius. Pelagius, a solid Breton monk, of an irreproachable past and of a juridical, logical mentality, claimed that God cannot demand the impossible of man (*Nat. et grat.* 69.83)—an assertion that Celestius expressed in even stronger terms: "If one must do something, he can; if he cannot, he simply ought not be bound to do so" (*Perf. iust.* 3.5). Nothing could be more revolting to Augustine, who had had so tragic an experience of the powerlessness of the will to move toward the good when it is entangled in sin (*Conf.* 8.8.20–8.11.27). This was equivalent in his thinking to an elimination of the mercy of the Savior, the doctor of souls, and to a reduction of the Redemption to a matter of good example and salutary exhortation.

Contrary to the Pelagian assertion that God's assistance remains outside the human will, Augustine himself experienced that grace is "poured into our hearts by the Holy Spirit" (Rom 5.5), by a God closer to us than our very selves. As a result of this spiritual experience, his philosophy professed a creation that makes God not only the source of man's being, but also of the conversion that makes man free. This doubling of the divine gratuity in creation and in man's formation is shown again in the accomplishment of a good will: He from whom man has received gratuitously existence has also given man goodness (*In psalm.* 58; *Serm.* 2.11; 26.2–4). In directly opposing Pelagius, Augustine made this even more explicit by stating that God also gives man capability, desire, and action (*Pecc. orig.* 1.4.5) and even final perseverance (*Corrept.* 12.38).

Freedom of the Will. This theology is governed by Augustine's idea of the primacy of grace and of his experience of the wound caused by sin. The will exists in a state of ignorance and trouble (*Lib. arb.* 3.18.51–52); it is enslaved by concupiscence. The Augustinian concept of freedom is astonishingly existential in its perception of the inner disposition of the self (*Lib. arb.* 2.19.51; *Conf.* 8), and even more by its emphasis on the impossibility of the will's remaining neutral. The will is always a love, i.e., a pleasure and a pressure (*Conf.* 13.9.10; *Epist.* 55.18). Accordingly, grace, far from being reduced to a light, moves the liberty within by a love and a pleasure (*Spir. et litt.* 14.26). God does not order without giving man what he ordains (*ibid.* 29.51; *Conf.* 10.19.40). But how is man free under the impress of this ascendancy? Augustine holds both ends of the chain, not only in the darkness of the faith, but also in the inchoative understanding of the mystery: "Show me someone who loves, he will understand what I mean" (*In evang. Ioh.* 26.5).

This tendency on grace is introduced into the whole theological structure that was challenged by Pelagius and that Augustine vigorously defended. Man's state of ignorance and difficulty is the result of original sin, which is transmitted through heredity, since man, he admitted, is conceived in concupiscence (*Nupt. et concup.* 2.21.36; *Pecc. mer.* 2.9.11). He thus insisted on the necessity of infant Baptism and concluded that infants who die without Baptism are damned (*Persev.* 12.30).

Predestination. Finally, on the subject of predestination, Augustine took an extreme position, drawing what seems to be too logical a conclusion from his insistence on the infallible efficacy of grace. It follows that God does not give efficacious grace to all and that only a number, decided in advance, are predestined for glory (*Epist.* 186.25), whereas others are simply left to their just damnation (*Epist.* 204.2; *Perf. iust.* 13.32). Augustine's preoccupation with mystery, however much he tried to reconcile freedom and grace—for this fell within the domain of his spiritual and pastoral experience—led him, apparently, from mystery into pure incomprehensibility. He appears to have let himself be drawn by his opponents onto dangerous terrain and to think of divine governance in terms of human temporality that comprises a before and an after. Might he not have been contaminated, however unconsciously, by Pelagian rationalism? It is to be noted in any event that his theology of grace is completely individual and subjective, rather than ecclesial and sacramental.

Morality and Charity. Augustine's moral thought is at once a morality of obligation and of goodness: "Happy is he who has all that he desires, and desires nothing evil" (*Trin.* 13.8.11). Following Varro, he distinguished between enjoyment and usefulness. A thing is enjoyed for itself; it is used for a purpose other than itself (*Doctr. christ.* 1.3.3–1.4.4). Morality consists in ordering what is merely a means toward what can be sought for itself. This synthesis of happiness and usefulness is possible only because it tends to go beyond the perspectives of each word and to pass into a morality of charity. Then it is no longer proper to speak of the enjoyment or usefulness that is sought, but of Him whom man loves, since He has first loved man (*Catech. rud.* 4.7–8). This love requires a forgetting of oneself (*Serm.* 142.3.3), for God is to be loved freely (*In epist. Ioh.* 2.11; *In psalm.* 55.17).

For Augustine, the principle of morality consists in converting self-love into love of God (*Civ.* 14.28); in changing from cupidity to charity (*Doctr. christ.* 3.10.16); in abandoning one's own well-being for the good of all (*Conf.* 3.8.16). It is only thus that love of self and of one's neighbor becomes truly possible according to a properly ordered charity (*In evang. Ioh.* 83.3; *Doctr. christ.* 1.27.28–1.30.31). Rooted in charity, the Christian has nothing to fear, for he can do no evil (*In epist. Ioh.* 8.9–10.7). This is the origin of the famous axiom: "Love, and do what you will" (*ibid.* 7.8; *Serm.* Frang. 5.3).

It is impossible here to touch on all the moral questions that Augustine discussed in his writings. He wrote two tracts on lying, condemning the practice absolutely and in all instances. He wrote two treatises on marriage, and frequently returned to that topic during his Pelagian controversies. He affirmed the goodness of marriage against the Manichees (*C. Faust.* 6.3) and distinguished three purposes in marriage: children, mutual fidelity, and the Sacrament (*Bon. coniug.* 24.32). Conjugal relations not directed to procreation, but solely to the appeasement of concupiscence, constitute a venial fault. However, the couple may not refuse each other, since they are bound by mutual fidelity; yet they can renounce their rights by common agreement (*ibid.* 6.5).

This pessimistic attitude toward sexuality has been corrected by later tradition; but nonetheless it has left its mark on Christian conjugal morality. Although Augustine praises virginity highly, he does not forget the superior value of obedience and humility. He says frankly that he prefers a humble married woman to a proud virgin (*Serm.* 354.8.9) and an obedient wife to an indocile virgin (*Bon. coniug.* 23.28–29). He was likewise often concerned with the problem of riches. He preached frequently on the necessity of giving alms (*Serm.* 38.7.9). But reacting against the attack of the Manichees on wealth (*C. Faust.* 5.10.11), and against certain Pelagian theories, he affirmed that true poverty is in the heart. A poor person can be rich in thought and in the desires of his heart (*Serm.* 345.1; *In psalm.* 51.14).

Augustine's moral teaching is summed up in the requirements of charity, where all is brought into a synthesis, including even the two great commandments, for "God is love." Even when Scripture is silent on the need to love God, it is probably to be implied that man finds God in fraternal love (*Trin.* 8.8.12; *In epist. Ioh.* 7.10).

INFLUENCE

Augustine's influence in the West has been compared to that of Origen in the East. But just as in the case of Origen, two levels of influence have to be distinguished for Augustine. There is, first, his direct influence, accessible to the simple inquiry of the historian: the influence of his thought and his formulation of doctrine on the greatest of the Latin Fathers who came after him, such as Leo I and Gregory I, as well as on the whole Middle Ages; the influence of his preaching on preachers of his own age and of the following century, such as Quodvultdeus, *Fulgentius of Ruspe, and *Caesarius of Arles; the influence of his spirituality on medieval piety and on canonical institutions, in particular through his Rule and his sermons *De vita et moribus clericorum suorum* (*Serm.* 355; 356); finally, the influence he exerted on the whole history of the Christian West through the medium of the "system" called Augustinianism, which was more a point of view or a turn of mind, though it furnished background for all the later, great religious controversies, from Semi-Pelagianism, Predestinationism, the Protestant Reformation, Baianism (*see* BAIUS AND BAIANISM), and the quarrel over grace called *de auxiliis* (*see* GRACE, CONTROVERSIES ON) to *Jansenism and Ontologism.

But these waves and tempests were only peripheral as compared with a main current flowing from the depths of Augustinian thought, a profound Augustinian influence that produced a new intellectual problematic, a new type of man, and a new consciousness. For the study of this influence, which is still to be undertaken, a so-called objective inquiry cannot suffice, for man is implicated in the subject of his research, and it is the question of understanding oneself that is at issue here.

Structure and Problematic of Western Theology. The Augustinian experience and its consequences in the structuring of his thought have been the source of the problematic framework within which Western Christian theology had developed down to the 19th- and 20th-century rediscovery of the Bible and the Eastern Fathers. Augustine influenced this theology in two major instances. In the first place, he gave priority to the study of the Trinity over that of Christ and the Incarnation. This had the important consequence of introducing into theology a philosophical problem regarding the Trinity, thereby dampering the development of a Trinitarian theology and turning Western piety away from the life of the Trinity. Secondly, it gave rise to the attempt to comprehend the Trinity within the realm of human reflection, an attempt that frequently (e.g., with G. W. F. Hegel) went beyond the bounds of orthodoxy.

The Augustinian theology has likewise directed the order in the Western teaching of dogma, for the tract on the Triune God (*De Deo Trino*) precedes that on the Word Incarnate (*De Verbo Incarnato*), or that on Christ, the Redeemer (*De Christo Redemptore*), even though the Incarnation is the revelation in action of the Trinity. Trinitarian theology has thus lost the character of an "economy" that in ancient tradition gave meaning to the history of salvation itself. But what theology lost, one can almost say, has been recovered by philosophy, yet not without risk, but certainly with the promise of a new fecundity, when theology will once more take over its own domain and give up being shaped by what transpired outside of it.

Religious Thought. A second essential structure of the Augustinian experience has fashioned Western religious thought. This is the experience of grace in an individual reflectively conscious of himself. It is a reenactment of the Pauline experience in part, but also with its individualization somewhat introverted. The whole modern problematic of grace and liberty flows from this source. Beyond this conflict, Christians are now beginning to see the primacy of the communion of consciences above the confrontation of freedoms—a primacy lived by Augustine in his charity, but a primacy that his Neoplatonic intellectuality was not able to accept formally. But this sharp conflict has given to Western consciousness a personal depth that it never would have attained without Augustine.

The New Human Consciousness. The Platonic experience in which the world disappeared before the light of self-consciousness and that became an experience of an irreplaceable subjectivity—"what am I in your eyes, that you should love me" (*Conf.* 1.5.5)—and of an existence in a world given new values by the Incarnation is the novelty of the Augustinian experience. It has brought forth a type of individual whose most striking traits are doubtless exemplified by Martin Luther and S. Kierkegaard or, in another spiritual family, by B. Pascal and J. H. Newman. But Christians now recognize this consciousness of self and this sense of personal individuality in certain spiritual beings only because Christians themselves are impregnated with the same ideas. The most revealing fact in this regard is the immense popularity of the *Confessions,* which has been read, meditated upon, and imitated by so many generations. Thus it can be said that Western man has become aware of Augustine in this mirror. A whole current of modern thought, from Cartesianism and Kantianism to phenomenology, existentialism, and personalism, have germinated in this ground plowed and seeded by the man who remains the Doctor of the West.

Bibliography: General. E. PORTALIÉ, DTC 1.2:2268–2472, tr. R. J. BASTIAN as *A Guide to the Thought of Saint Augustine* (Chicago 1960). Altaner 487–534. Dekkers CPL. H. POPE, *St. Augustine of Hippo* (Westminster, Md. 1949). G. BONNER, *St. Augustine of Hippo* (Philadelphia 1964). H. I. MARROU, *St. Augustine and His Influence through the Ages,* tr. P. HEPBURNE SCOTT (Torchbks; New York 1958). É. H. GILSON, *The Christian Philosophy of St. Augustine,* tr. L. E. M. LYNCH (New York 1960). G. BARDY, *Les Revisions* (Paris 1950). E. NEBREDA, *Bibliographia Augustiniana* (Rome 1928). T. J. VAN BAVEL and F. VAN DER ZANDE, *Répertoire bibliographique de saint Augustin* (Louvain 1954). A. M. LA BONNARDIÈRE, *Recherches de chronologie augustinienne* (Paris 1965). *Bulletin Augustinien* in Rev ÉtAug. *Augustinus magister,* 3 v. (Congrès international augustinien; Paris 1954). *Recherches augustiniennes* (Paris 1958–).

Life. POSSIDIUS, *Vita sancti Augustini,* PL 32:33–66, ed. M. PELLEGRINO, (Alba 1955). M. PELLEGRINO, *Le "Confessioni" di sant'Agostino* (Rome 1956). J. J. O'MEARA, *The Young Augustine* (London 1954). P. COURCELLE, *Recherches sur les "Confessions" de Saint Augustin* (Paris 1950). J. M. LE BLOND, *Les Conversions de saint Augustin* (Paris 1950). F. VAN DER MEER, *Augustine the Bishop,* tr. B. BATTERSHAW and G. R. LAMB (New York 1962). P. MONCEAUX, *Histoire littéraire de l'Afrique chrétienne,* v.7 (Paris 1923; repr. Brussels 1963). G. G. WILLIS, *Saint Augustine and the Donatist Controversy* (London 1950). W. H. C. FREND, *The Donatist Church* (Oxford 1952). G. DE PLINVAL, *Pélage: Ses écrits, sa vie et sa réforme* (Lausanne 1943).

Thought. H. I. MARROU, *Saint Augustin et la fin de la culture antique* (4th ed. Paris 1958). F. CAYRÉ, *La Contemplation augustinienne* (Bruges 1954). C. BOYER, DictSpirAscMyst 1:1101–26. P. HENRY, *La Vision d'Ostie* (Paris 1938). E. DINKLER, *Die Anthropologie Augustins* (Stuttgart 1934). J. HESSEN, *Augustins Metaphysik der Erkenntnis* (2d ed. Leiden 1960). M. SCHMAUS, *Die psychologische Trinitätslehre des hl. Augustinus* (Münster i. W. 1927). I. CHEVALIER, *S. Augustin et la pensée grecque* (Fribourg 1940). O. J.-B. DU ROY, *L'Intelligence de la foi en la Trinité selon saint Augustin* (Paris 1966).

Theology. T. J. VAN BAVEL, *Recherches sur la christologie de saint Augustin* (Fribourg 1954). J. RIVIÈRE, *Le Dogme de la Rédemption chez saint Augustin* (Paris 1933). A. M. LA BONNARDIÈRE, *Biblia Augustiniana* (Paris 1960–). M. PONTET, *L'Exégèse de saint Augustin prédicateur* (Paris 1946). E. LAMIRANDE, *Un siècle et demi d'études sur l'ecclésiologie de saint Augustin* (Paris 1962). Y. M. J. CONGAR, "Introduction" to *Traités anti-donatistes,* v.28 of *Oeuvres* of Augustine (Paris 1963). G. LECORDIER, *La Doctrine de l'Eucharistie chez saint Augustin* (Paris 1930). P. T. CAMELOT, RevScPhilTh 31 (1947) 394–410, Eucharistic symbolism. A. NIEBERGALL, *Augustins Anschauung von der Gnade* (Göttingen 1951). H. RONDET, *Gratia Christi* (Paris 1948); *Essais sur la théologie de la grâce* (Paris 1963). G. NYGREN, *Das Prädestinationsproblem in der Theologie Augustins* (Lund 1951). A. SOLIGNAC, "La Condition de l'homme pécheur d'après saint Augustin," NouvRevTh 78 (1956) 359–387. J. MAUSBACH, *Die Ethik des hl. Augustinus,* 2 v. (2d ed. Freiburg 1929). B. ROLAND-GOSSELIN, *La Morale de saint Augustin* (Paris 1925). H. J. BURNABY, *Amor Dei: A Study of the Religion of Saint Augustine* (London 1938; repr. 1960). F. CAYRÉ, "Great Augustinism," TheolDig 2 (1954) 169–173. P. VIGNAUX, "Influence augustinienne," *Augustinus magister,* v.3 (Paris 1954) 265–273. J. GUITTON, *The Modernity of St. Augustine,* tr. A. V. LITTLEDALE (Baltimore 1959). C. FABRO, "S. Agostino e l'esistenzialismo" in *S. Agostino e le grandi cor-*

renti della filosofia contemporanea (Tolentino 1956) 141–166. P. COURCELLE, *Les Confessions de saint Augustin dans la tradition littéraire* (Paris 1963). J. COURCELLE-LADMIRANT and P. COURCELLE, *Iconographie de Saint Augustin* (Paris 1965). **Illustration credits:** Fig. 1, Pontificia Commissione di Archeologia Sacra. Fig. 3, Brogi-Art Reference Bureau. Fig. 2, Bayerische Staatsgemäldesammlungen, Munich.

[O. J.-B. DU ROY]

AUGUSTINE (TRIUMPHUS) OF ANCONA, Augustinian philosopher; b. Ancona, *c.* 1241; d. Naples, April 2, 1328. In 1297 he was made lector in his order. He read the *Sentences* for 2 years in Paris and became master of theology *c.* 1314. Assigned to Naples in 1321, he served also as counselor to King Robert. In 1326 Augustine published his celebrated treatise *Summa de ecclesiastica potestate,* reputed to be the earliest work of its kind on the Roman pontiff. He was called "the most encyclopedic and prolific theologian of the school of Giles" (M. Grabmann), though many of his works, including treatises on philosophy, Scripture, and Canon Law, remain unpublished. He undertook the earliest concordance of the writings of St. *Augustine, the *Milleloquium veritatis,* which was completed by his pupil *Bartholomew of Urbino. Although medieval historians acknowledge his merits as an exegete and Aristotelian commentator, Augustine remains best known for his political doctrines on the nature and extent of papal authority. Carrying the theocratic principles of his predecessors, *Giles of Rome and *James of Viterbo, to their extreme conclusions, Augustine contended that all power, spiritual and temporal, resides in the pope, and that through him alone (*mediante ipso*) other rulers, both religious and lay, derive their authority. Thus, e.g., the grant of Constantine to Pope Silverius was in no sense a donation but rather the restoration of alienated property to its lawful possessor.

See also AUGUSTINIANISM.

Bibliography: Works. *Summa de potestate ecclesiastica* (Rome 1584); *Tractatus brevis de duplici potestate praelatarum et laicorum,* ed. N. SCHOLZ in *Die Publizistik zur Zeit Philipps des Schönen und Bonifaz VIII* (Stuttgart 1903) 486–501. Literature. B. MINISTERI, "De A. de A. vita et operibus," *Analecta Augustiniana* 7 (1952) 7–56, the only modern critical study on Augustine's life and works. M. J. WILKS, *The Problem of Sovereignty in the Latin Middle Ages: The Papal Monarchy with Augustinus Triumphus and the Publicists* (New York 1963). U. MARIANI, *Chiesa e Stato nei teologi Agostiniani del secolo XIV* (Rome 1957). J. RIVIÈRE, "Une Première 'Somme' du pouvoir pontifical: Le Pape chez Augustin d'Ancone," RevScRel 18 (1938) 149–183.

[R. P. RUSSELL]

AUGUSTINE OF CANTERBURY, ST.

Apostle of England, first archbishop of Canterbury; d. May 26, 604 (feast, May 26 and 28). He was prior at St. Andrew's on the Coelian Hill, Rome, when *Gregory I (the Great) sent him with 30 monks to evangelize the *Anglo-Saxons. After difficulties in Gaul and his return to Rome, he was consecrated bishop and landed at Ebbsfleet in 597. There the King, *Ethelbert of Kent, who was married to a Christian, allowed the monks to preach, giving them a house and an old church in Canterbury. Eventually Ethelbert and many of his people became Christian. In 601, reinforcements of personnel, books, relics, and sacred vessels arrived from Rome.

Augustine was given a *pallium and made a metropolitan, independent of the bishops in Gaul but without authority over them. Surviving letters from Gregory instructed him on principles and procedure: he was left free to adopt Gallican or other liturgical uses; he was to live a common life with his monks, although married clerks in minor orders also had a place in his household. He was not to destroy pagan temples, only the idols. Pagan rites, if innocent, could be taken over for the Christian feasts. Relying on Roman documents, Gregory decided that he should establish his see at London, with 12 suffragans, and another see at *York, also with 12. Instead, Augustine founded his see at *Canterbury, the capital of Kent, the most cultured and the only Christian Anglo-Saxon kingdom. There he built the Cathedral of Christ Church, and just outside the city wall Ethelbert erected the abbey of SS. Peter and Paul, later called *St. Augustine. Augustine established a bishoporic at London, with *Mellitus as its bishop, having already set up Rochester as a kind of suburban see to Canterbury. *See* LONDON, ANCIENT SEE OF; ROCHESTER, ANCIENT SEE OF. Shortly before his death he consecrated *Lawrence of Canterbury as his successor.

In his 7-year apostolate, Augustine failed to win any cooperation from the Christian Britons in the West Country because of their hatred for the Anglo-Saxon race and their attachment to provincial Celtic customs. Meeting with real but limited success in his lifetime, Augustine's mission bore fruit long after in the conversion of the rest of England, in the Synod of Whitby, and in the missionary work of Anglo-Saxons on the Continent (*see* WHITBY, ABBEY OF). He was buried at SS. Peter and Paul, Canterbury.

Bibliography: *Gregorii I Papae registrum expistolarum,* ed. P. EWALD and L. M. HARTMANN, MGEp v.1, 2. BEDE, *Historia ecclesiastica,* ed. C. PLUMMER (Oxford 1896; reprint 1956) 1:23; 2:3. A. BROU, *St. Augustine and His Companions,* tr. from the French (London 1897). F. A. GASQUET, *Mission of St. Augustine* (London 1924). F. M. STENTON, *Anglo-Saxon England* (Oxford History of England 2; Oxford 1943) 103–112. S. BRECHTER, *Die Quellen zur Angelsachsenmission Gregors des Grossen* (Münster 1941). P. MEYVAERT, "Les 'Responsiones' de S. Gregoire le Grand a S. A. de Cantorbéry," RHE 54 (1959) 879–894.

[H. FARMER]

AUGUSTINE KAŽOTIĆ, BL., Dominican bishop; b. Trogir, Dalmatia, *c.* 1260; d. Lucera, Apulia, Aug. 3, 1323 (feast, Aug. 8). He entered the Order of Preachers at an early age and in 1286 was studying at the University of Paris. On returning to Dalmatia he founded several convents and undertook missions in Italy, Bosnia, and Hungary. *Benedict XI consecrated him bishop of Zagreb, Croatia (1303). He restored discipline in his diocese and fostered learning, particularly in Biblical studies. Miladin, Governor of Dalmatia, against whose tyranny he had protested, defied and persecuted him. In 1317 *John XXII transferred him to the See of Lucera in Apulia, where he died in the Dominican convent he had founded. He was venerated for his charity to the poor and for his gift of healing, and was accorded public honor soon after his death; in 1702 Clement XI confirmed his cult.

Bibliography: Quétif-Échard 1.2:553. Butler Th Attw 3:255–256. A. WALZ, LexThK[2] 1:1103.

[M. J. FINNEGAN]

AUGUSTINE NOVELLUS, BL., jurist and Augustinian prior general; b. Tarano, in Sabina, Italy, date unknown; d. near Siena, May 19, 1309 (feast, May 19).

He studied law at the University of *Bologna and became chancellor to King *Manfred of Sicily. After the death of the King (1266) he entered the *Augustinian Order as a brother and took the name Augustine. According to the traditional account, he was ordained a priest after his identity as a famed jurist became known among his fellow religious. He was appointed papal confessor by *Nicholas IV and served as papal legate in Siena under *Boniface VIII. Together with Bl. Clement of Sant' Elpidio (d. 1291) he revised the early constitutions of his order and in 1298 was elected prior general. After resigning in 1300, he retired to the hermitage of San Leonardo near Siena. The designation "Novellus" was added in the 15th century, when his cult became widespread, in order to distinguish him from St. *Augustine of Hippo. The cult was confirmed by *Clement XIII in 1759, and his relics are preserved in a church dedicated to him at Siena, where there is also an early 14th-century portrait.

Bibliography: ActSS May 4:614–626. *Analecta augustiniana* 6 (1915–16) 120–133. A. Corrao, *Sopra la patria del beato Agostino Novello* (3d ed. Palermo 1922). Jordan of Quedlinburg, *Liber vitasfratrum*, ed. R. Arbesmann and W. Hümpfner (New York 1943), *passim*. W. Hümpfner, LexThK² 1:1103. V. Cambiaso, EncCatt 1:517–518.

[A. J. ENNIS]

AUGUSTINE, RULE OF ST.

Several documents have been known as the Rule of St. *Augustine: (1) *Regula consensoria* (RC), today considered by no one to belong to Augustine, probably coming from Spain (6th to 8th century). (2) *Disciplina monasterii* (DM), a rule of 11 brief sections, beginning: *Ante omnia, fratres carissimi;* ending: *et nobis non parva erit laetitia de vestra salute. Amen.* (3) A rule for men (RV) in 12 chapters, beginning: *Haec sunt quae ut observetis praecipimus;* ending: *et in temptationem non inducatur. Amen.* Recent studies indicate this to be the original rule of Augustine, written for his first monastery of Hippo. (4) Regula puellarum (RP), a feminine rule, corresponding today to sections 5–16 of *Epist. 211,* and preceded by four sections (*Obiurgatio*) in which Augustine rebukes sisters of Hippo who had rebelled against their *praeposita.* As early as 1156 it was contended that the *Prologus* (*Obiurgatio*) proves that *Epist. 211* is the original text. Erasmus used weak internal arguments to prove this claim, and up to our century, his view was considered correct. Hence, A. Goldbacher in 1911 published *Obiurgatio* and RP together as *Epist. 211.* But in 1927 B. Capelle showed that Goldbacher's use of the MSS was insufficient. Today the opinion of Erasmus is no longer considered indisputable, as appears from the reasons in favor of the authenticity of RV, of which RP seems to be a later adaptation (perhaps from 6th-century Spain). For the following reasons RV seems to be the original text.

Manuscript Tradition. RV is found in the oldest and best MSS. DM and RV are found in Paris B.N. Lat. 12634 (dated by Lowe, 6th–7th century) and in MS Laon 328 bis (9th century, unknown to Goldbacher). RV, without DM, is found in Munich Clm 28118 (9th–10th century). The false notion that the last manuscript has RP, and not RV, comes from Holste(nius), who in his *Codex regularum* substituted *Epist. 211* for RV. W. Hümpfner left at his death in 1961 a new text of RV (unpublished), based upon 18 MSS of RV before 1100, and 21 of DM, of which 9 antedate 1100 and 12 are from the 12th century. His list of MSS of RV before 1200 amounted to about 80, of which nearly 30 have DM. The latter are of the so-called central European group, whereas the Spanish family lacks DM. On the contrary, RP has much weaker MS evidence, not appearing until the 9th century in Escorial aI13, with a mutilated and abbreviated text, but also with parts of RV, as well as other monastic texts, and DM in feminine form. C. Lambot, who considers *Epist. 211* as alone authentic, admits that only a few MSS of late date (12th century) have its text. Besides, the oldest MSS of *Epist. 211* have an *explicit* after the *Obiurgatio,* so that the latest study of the MSS concludes that any future editions should end after section 4, that is, should contain merely the *Obiurgatio,* while RP should be published merely as an adaptation of RV.

Citations. RV is cited as early as *Caesarius of Arles, who *c.* 512, though writing for nuns, used not RP but RV; the latter was cited also by *Benedict, the *Regula Tarnatensis,* the *Regula Pauli et Stephani,* Eutropius, *Isidore of Seville, the *Gelasian Sacramentary,* and *Benedict of Aniane. *Abelard evidently believed that only RV existed (PL 178:213–217). Possibly *Ildefonsus refers to the bringing of RV to Spain from Africa *c.* 570 by Abbot Donatus (*De viris ill.* 4; PL 96: 200), and in fact Eutropius (who cites the rule) was Donatus's successor as abbot. The earliest citations of a feminine form of the rule are found in *Leander and Isidore, who cite DM and RP, but with adaptations to the Spanish background.

It is sometimes said that *Possidius makes no mention of a rule, in spite of his reference to a *regula* according to which Augustine's monks lived in his first monastery of Hippo, founded in 391 (PL 32:37). Such a denial must prove that this reference cannot be to a written rule. Further, M. Verheijen has found that the reference here made by Possidius to Acts 4.32–34 is the combination of 4.32b–32c–35b, and that this sequence of the *Vetus Latina* is found in only two places: in this text of Possidius and in RV.

Comparison with Augustine's Other Works. Recent philological comparisons of RV with undoubted works of Augustine strengthen the belief that this is a genuine work. In addition, a comparison of RV with other sources that speak of the monastic life of Augustine yields positive results, without contradictions. It is probable that Augustine himself quotes RV in various other works.

The authorship of DM is not easy to determine. P. Mandonnet considered it the rule written by Augustine for his monastery of Tagaste, founded in 388, and claimed that RV was Augustine's ascetical commentary, written for his first monastery of Hippo, before he personally adapted RV to RP *c.* 425. But this last part is not borne out by MS evidence cited above. *Gelasius II in 1118 dispensed the canons of Springirsbach from outdated precepts of DM and, according to Mandonnet, on this occasion the first sentence of DM was placed before RV, and the rest of DM was ignored. This is not exact, for many copies of DM were subsequently made. The oldest MSS of RV, preceded by only the first sentence of DM, come from France and England, which suggests that this combination derives from canons of these two countries in the 11th and 12th centuries, perhaps from *Ivo of Chartres. But does DM come from Augustine, himself, as the oldest citations suggest, or was it later added to RV, as early as the 5th century? Internal arguments brought against its authenticity are inconclusive and so it seems wiser to leave this point undecided.

The combination of *Obiurgatio* and RP seems to have originated in Spain. C. Lambot, however, claims that RP (preceded by *Obiurgatio*) is the genuine work of Augustine. He reaches this conclusion by a study of the masculine and feminine texts, and claims that the characteristics of the masculine text do not correspond to the clear style of Augustine.

Content and Use. The Rule's chief teachings are love of God and neighbor, common life and the necessary virtues therefor, abstinence and care of the sick, authority (a *praepositus* and *presbyter* are mentioned), and weekly reading for free followers of divine grace. It is found in several early medieval *Codices regularum,* and was used extensively by canons in various countries from the 11th century onward. The Fourth *Lateran Council considered it an approved rule, and it was adopted by St. *Dominic for his friars. In 1256 it was employed (preceded by the first sentence of DM) by *Alexander IV for the groups of hermits united into the mendicant order, the *Augustinians. Its Augustinian characteristics of charity and discretion have commended it to many communities, of which more than 150 follow it today.

Bibliography: Editions. Of RC, PL 32:1447–50. JORDAN OF QUEDLINBURG, *Liber vitasfratrum,* ed. R. ARBESMANN and W. HÜMPFNER (New York 1943) 484–488. Of DM, PL 32:1449–52. ARBESMANN-HÜMPFNER, op. cit. 490–493. RevBén 42 (1930) 318–319. Of RV, PL 32:1377–84. RevBén 42 (1930) 320–326. ARBESMANN-HÜMPFNER, *op. cit.* 494–504. Of *Epist. 211,* PL 33:958–965. CSEL 57:356–371. Manuscripts. C. DEREINE, "Enquête sur la Règle de Saint Augustin," *Scriptorium* 2 (1948) 28–36. A. ZUMKELLER, "Zur handschriftlichen Überlieferung und ursprünglichen Textgestalt der Augustinusregel," *Augustiniana* 11 (1961) 425–433. L. VERHEIJEN, "Les Manuscrits de la lettre CCXI de Saint Augustin," RevMALat 8 (1952) 97–122. Literature. A. C. VEGA, *Notas histórico-críticas en torno a los orígenes de la Regla de San Agustín* (Madrid 1963). C. LAMBOT, "La Règle de S. Augustin et S. Césaire," RevBén 41 (1929) 333–341; "Saint Augustin, a-t-il rédige la Régle pour moines qui porte son nom?" *ibid.* 53 (1941) 41–58. W. HÜMPFNER, Lex ThK[2] 1:1104–05. T. VAN BAVEL, "Parallèles, vocabulaire et citations bibliques de la *Regula sancti Augustini,*" *Augustiniana* 9 (1959) 12–77. A. MANRIQUE, *La vida monástica en S. Augustín* (Salamanca 1959). J. J. GAVIGAN, *De vita monastica in Africa Septentrionali inde a temporibus S. Augustini usque ad invasiones Arabum* (Turin 1962). G. B. LADNER, *The Idea of Reform* (Cambridge, Mass. 1959). A. CHAVASSE, *Le Sacramentaire gélasien* (Strasbourg 1958). L. VERHEIJEN, "La Règle de S. Augustin: L'État actuel des faits," *Augustinianum* 4 (1964) 109–122. J. MOIS, *Augustiner-Chorherren und Augustiner-Regel* (Munich 1953). M. C. MCCARTHY, *The Rule for Nuns of St. Caesarius of Arles* (Washington 1960), supports the position of Lambot.

[J. J. GAVIGAN]

AUGUSTINIAN NUNS

This term, in its widest sense, could include all orders or congregations of women who follow the Rule of St. *Augustine. These groups, however, are discussed under their more proper titles, e.g., *Canonesses Regular of St. Augustine, *Bridgettines, *Dominicans, *Visitation Nuns. Considered here will be only (1) the Augustinian nuns founded by or jurisdictionally dependent on the first order of the *Augustinians, (2) those who today partake of that first order's privileges, and (3) the hospital sisters of the Hôtel-Dieu and Malestroit.

Augustinians. The second order of St. Augustine began in Germany (1264) when the cloistered nuns (*moniales*) of Oberndorf am Neckar were placed "under the obedience and protection, the guidance and help" of the German province of Augustinian friars. In 1266 the first cardinal protector, Richard Annibaldi, gave this province the right to affiliate nunneries, to accept their spiritual direction, and to exercise canonical *visitation. In 1289 the prior general, Clement of Osimo, accepted jurisdiction over the newly founded convent of the Holy Cross in Montefalco, which produced St. *Clare of Montefalco. Simon Fidati of Cascia established two important convents in Florence *c.* 1325 (his constitutions for them are extant).

At first the Augustinians wanted only cloistered (second order) nuns, as the general chapter of Paris stated in 1329. But during the *Western Schism third order regulars came to be favored, and on Nov. 7, 1401, the Augustinians, like the Dominicans and Franciscans, received the privilege of accepting *mantellatae* or *pinzocherae* (literally, ladies dressed in a grey mantle) as individuals or in communities. The first known group of sisters was formed *c.* 1431 in Rome by Sister Maria Thomaei under the direction of Father Cesario Orsini. Within these groups were often found *reclusoria,* but it is not certain whether this word refers to recluses or to strictly cloistered nuns. The latter is more probable because *mantellatae* and *moniales* had become interchangeable terms. Fathers Augustine Cazuli and Philip of Bergamo of the reform congregation of Lombardy were prime movers in establishing new sisterhoods; Maria Bianca Visconti, wife of Francis Sforza, took a special interest in the convent of St. Martha at Milan, where Bl. Veronica of Binasco was the central figure. Monte Varese with Bl. Catherine of Pallanzia and especially Bl. Giuliana of Busto Arsizio was another spiritual center. The most famous Augustinian nun of the 15th century was St. *Rita of Cascia.

Every Augustinian nunnery was an independent *priory or abbey, except for the congregation of Pavia founded in 1408 by the sisters Michaelinda and Margarita Gundini, which fostered a strictly observant life. Before 1515 there were 23 Augustinian convents in Germany, 2 in France, 81 in Italy, and 9 in Spain, totaling 115.

After the Council of *Trent diocesan bishops gained greater control over all sisterhoods (*see* EXEMPTION), and even the mendicant orders lost the full jurisdiction given to them in the *Mare magnum* of Pope *Sixtus IV. Reformed groups of the Augustinian friars, however, retained a real concern for second order Augustinian nuns. In Spain Abp. Juan de Ribera established the discalced Augustinian (*see* DISCALCED ORDERS) nuns (1599) who produced Bl. Inés of Beniganim. The Spanish reformers (*see* AUGUSTINIAN RECOLLECTS) cultivated the educational work of sisters and successfully introduced them abroad. Archbishop Alexius Meneses established a convent in Goa. By 1631 the Incarnacion convent in Lima, Peru, numbered almost 800 persons. In 1965 28 second order houses in Italy, 46 in Spain, and 9 in other lands are affiliated with the Augustinian first order.

Modern Congregations. In the post-Tridentine era Augustinian *third order members, or tertiaries, came more to the foreground. These could be either lay people or sisters living in communities, such as the Sisters of St. Thomas Villanova, founded by A. Proust (d. 1690) in Angers, a hospital order surviving today. Under Prior General E. Esteban (1925–31) more than 56 congregations following the Rule of St. Augustine entered into a spiritual aggregation and now partake of the privileges and graces of the first order. Several new groups of third order regular Augustinian sisters were established during the 20th century, e.g., the St. Rita Sisters in Germany and the Augustinesses in Holland. Furthermore, a reorganization of the cloistered second order followed the apostolic constitution ***Sponsa Christi* of 1951; e.g., all houses in Italy held a general chapter in Rome in 1953 for the first time and decided on a common direction and novitiate. The three Spanish groups followed suit in 1955.

Hospital Sisters of Hôtel-Dieu and Malestroit. The *Hôtel-Dieu in Paris was staffed by a group of sisters who followed the Rule of St. *Augustine and took the fourth vow of serving the sick poor. Their origins may be as old as the Hôtel-Dieu itself, but the first document relating to them dates from *c.* 1217. These hospital sisters were allowed to continue their work even through the French Revolution (although wearing their habit was forbidden), but in 1907 these Augustinians of the Hôtel-Dieu were expelled from both the Hôtel-Dieu and their second hospital, Saint-Louis. The refugees subsequently founded the present Asile et Hôpital N.-D. de Bon-Secours. In 1938 they annexed to themselves the Hôtel-Dieus of Étampes and Orléans, and today they are a group with about 14 institutions in 6 dioceses.

The Augustinians of Malestroit had a Hôtel-Dieu in Dieppe, France, in the 9th century. In the 15th century they founded another at Vannes (later moved to Malestroit). A product of their 17th-century expansion was the Hôtel-Dieu du Précieux Sang at Quebec (1639). Today the Malestroit federation of Augustinian nuns is made up of 29 houses (excluding those in Canada).

Bibliography: T. Herrera, *Alphabetum augustinianum,* 2 v. (Madrid 1644). Heimbucher 1:565–571. M. T. Disdier, DHGE 5:595–601. G. Bernoville, *Les Religieuses de saint Thomas de Villeneuve* (Paris 1953). W. Hümpfner, LexThK[2] 1:1087–89. D. Gutiérrez, DictSpirAscMyst 4.1:989–990. *Catalogus fratrum totius ordinis sancti Augustini* (Rome 1963).

[F. ROTH]

AUGUSTINIAN RECOLLECTS

The Order of the Augustinian Recollects (OAR) was not a reform of the *Augustinians, for, at least in Spain, the latter had not fallen into any notable decline. The presence of men such as (St.) *Thomas of Villanova and Luis de *León, contemporaries of the Recollect movement, testified to the Augustinian spiritual vitality of the time. Nevertheless, there did exist among the Spanish Augustinians of the 16th century a desire for stricter observance and a realization of the eremitical ideals of solitude and contemplation.

In 1588, the Augustinian Province of Castile decided to favor the movement. It designated the monastery at Talavera de la Reina for the Recollects, and directed Luis de León to devise constitutions for their government. Except for this constitutional change and a stricter observance of the Augustinian rule, Talavera did not differ from, and was not independent of, the province's other houses. Two years later the Recollects possessed a second monastery, and by 1600 they had four houses and a representative among the provincial counselors. A modified habit was soon adopted, sandals were substituted for shoes, and the movement became strictly contemplative. That same year the Holy See published norms governing relations between the Recollects and the Augustinian Order. On Sept. 19, 1600, the Province of Castile renounced its rights to the four Recollect houses, yielding their government to the monasteries themselves. On Feb. 11, 1602, Clement VIII issued the brief *Apostolici muneris,* elevating the monasteries into a province directly subject to the prior general of the Augustinians.

In 1605 the Recollects entered the mission field, a decision due, probably, to the influence of the crown. Philip III had appointed Juan de San Jerónimo, first provincial of the Recollects, to the bishopric of Chiapa in New Spain (Mexico) in 1604. Juan declined, but offered to lead a band of missionaries to the Indies. The King, accepting the exchange, appointed the friars to the Philippine Islands, April 3, 1605. Gregory XV raised the Recollect province to the status of a congregation in 1621. Its many houses were soon divided into four provinces, three in Spain and one in the Philippines. For 200 years the Spanish provinces served almost exclusively as sources of vocations for the missions in the Philippine Archipelago. Missions were attempted in Japan but were abandoned in 1634 when the last Recollect was martyred in Nagasaki. Much later, in 1923, the friars began a new Far Eastern mission when the Holy See entrusted the Chinese territory of Kweiteh, Honan, to the Province of the Philippines.

In 1835 an edict of the Spanish government suppressing religious communities caused the destruction of the three Spanish provinces. Fortunately, the province in the Philippines was exempted from this decree. Attached to that province, since 1827, was a monastery in Monteagudo in Spain. Until the end of the 19th century the history of the Recollects was confined to Monteagudo and the Philippines. Recovery began in 1888 with the revival of the Colombian Province that had been begun in the early 17th century, but was suppressed in 1860. After the Spanish American War the friars lost extensive mission properties in the Orient when the Philippines were acquired by the U.S. By 1901 the personnel displaced from the Philippines had been reassigned to Latin America and Spain, where in time new provinces developed. The Recollects finally became completely separated from the Augustinian Order when, in 1912, Pius X, by the brief *Religiosas familias,* established them as an independent order.

In 1917 Abp. Jeremiah Harty, of Omaha, Nebr., invited the friars to establish a parish within the diocese. Three members of the Colombian province were sent to Omaha to staff this parish, which, dedicated to the Holy Ghost, became the nucleus of Recollect development in the U.S. In 1935 a novitiate was opened in Kansas City, Kans., and in 1943 the houses in the U.S., Puerto Rico, and the Dominican Republic formed the new Province of St. Augustine. The members of this province, which numbered about 90 priests in 1964, are engaged mainly in parish work among Spanish-speaking people. They administer extensive parishes, not only in the U.S., but also in the Dominican Republic and Mexico. Since 1960 a retreat house has been operated in conjunction with the theological seminary at Suffern, N.Y., and a preparatory college in Norfolk, Conn.

The order in 1964 comprised 7 provinces in 14 nations, with 1,580 priests, lay brothers, and professed religious. The Recollects now engage in teaching in high schools and colleges, as well as conducting parishes and missions.

Bibliography: M. T. Disdier, DHGE, 5:581–587, bibliog. 593–595. P. Corro, *El Orden de Agustinos Recoletos* (Granada 1930). I. Fernández, *De figura iuridica Ordinis Recollectorum S. Augustini* (Rome 1938).

[G. LA MOUNTAIN]

AUGUSTINIAN SPIRITUALITY

A school of spirituality common to those whose religious life is based on the teachings and example of St. Augustine as expressed in his writings, and especially in his Rule (*see* AUGUSTINE, RULE OF ST.). The word school is used here in a very wide sense for two reasons: (1) Augustine did not write an organized treatise of spiritual doctrine with a well-defined method of prayer, and (2) just as the term *Augustinianism may be used in several ways, so also the term Augustinian spirituality may be applied to any of the several schools of theological thought that are called Augustinian. In this article the term is used to designate the teachings and traditions common to the Augustinian Order, regarded historically as the principal inheritor of the spiritual and monastic ideals of Augustine. Even though the historical continuity between the Augustinians of the 13th century and their "Father" Augustine of the 5th century is at best tenuous, it is historically certain that the Augustinian friars, from the time of their corporate union in 1256, made persistent, conscious efforts to model their life on the teachings and example of Augustine.

Sources. In addition to the sources common to all schools of Christian spirituality, the following are the particular sources from which Augustinian spirituality is drawn. The works of Augustine, first of all, both authentic and spurious, were constantly employed. Among these works, those that provide the chief guide to life and practice, as distinguished from the more speculative and theological aspects of spirituality, are Augustine's Rule, his *De opere monachorum,* his sermons and letters, and the *vita* by St. *Possidius. One of the earliest and most widely used guides to the spiritual and monastic teachings of Augustine was the *Liber vitasfratrum* (1357) of *Jordan of Quedlinburg (Saxony). Jordan's work was not a systematic treatise, however, and he drew his material from many sources other than the works of Augustine. The *Milleloquium S. Augustini* (Lyons 1555) of Bartholomew of Urbino (d. 1350) was, on the other hand, a veritable thesaurus of Augustine's doctrine, theological and philosophical, as well as spiritual. The most familiar text was naturally Augustine's Rule. Numerous commentaries were written, both by Augustinians and by other religious who follow the same Rule. Among those composed by Augustinians, that of Bl. Alfonso de *Orozco (d. 1591) went through numerous editions and translations. The most recent commentaries are those of L. Cilleruelo, *El monacato de S. Agustín y su Regla* (Valladolid 1947); A. Zumkeller, *Die Regel des heiligen Augustinus* (Würzburg 1956); and C. Vaca, *La vida religiosa en S. Agustín,* 4 v. (Madrid 1955–64).

The Holy Trinity and St. Augustine reading his Rule to monks and nuns, in a Missal of the Hermits of Saint Augustine, 1362 (Bibl. mun. Toulouse MS 91, fol. 121).

In the history of Augustinian spirituality Biblical studies are particularly prominent. In the period from the 13th to the 16th centuries there were 85 known Augustinian Biblical commentators; 13 of these wrote on the Canticle of Canticles, and an even greater number commented on the life of Christ. Best known among the last-mentioned is *Thomas of Jesus (de Andrada), author of *Trabalhos de Jesús* (written between 1578 and 1582). Eminent writers and preachers on Biblical spirituality in the 16th century were: Dionisio Vázquez (d. 1539), St. *Thomas of Villanova (d. 1555), Girolamo *Seripando (d. 1563), and Luis de *León (d. 1591).

The constitutions of the order—the oldest extant text is that of Ratisbon (1290)—are another source of Augustinian spirituality, for they spelled out the purpose of the religious life; the practices of asceticism; and the harmonious blending of worship, studies, and apostolate (especially preaching). Further sources of the spirituality of the order are the teachings of Augustinian theologians and the example of the saints and blessed. (Concerning the canonized and beatified members of the order, *see* AUGUSTINIANS.) The theologians are represented most typically by men like Seripando, and by certain later figures, such as Henry *Noris (d. 1704), Fulgenzio Bellelli (d. 1742), and Giovanni L. *Berti (d. 1766). The theses that they developed, however, were already present in the writings of *Giles of Rome (d. 1316), who, though he was essentially a Thomist, took certain characteristically Augustinian positions that have a bearing on the spiritual life and its growth.

Characteristics. The following are, briefly, some of the characteristic notes of Augustinian spirituality: the defining of theology as an affective science, with the tendency to unite doctrine and piety, making use of expressions that are more patristic and Biblical than scholastic; the defense of the primacy of grace, while safeguarding essential human freedom and insisting on the importance of prayer and ascetical practices; and the emphasizing of the centrality of Christ and His Mystical Body in the order of salvation. From this last point there developed in the Augustinian tradition: emphasis on the role of Christ in justification; defense of the vicar of Christ, especially by early 14th-century Augustinian writers [Giles of Rome, *James of Viterbo, *Augustine (Triumphus) of Ancona, and others]; and the counsel that the preferred life of seclusion, prayer, and study is to be sacrificed for the service of the Church.

In an effort to identify the one, key characteristic of Augustinian spirituality, several opinions have been put forth. These may be reduced to an option between alternatives, depending on one's preference for a more speculative or a more practical approach. According to the one alternative, the fundamental note is interiorness, that is, the pursuit of wisdom through retirement from the world and dedication to the interior life, especially in the loving contemplation of the Holy Trinity. According to the other, it is perfect common life, a holy community of love, epitomized in Augustine's maxim: *anima una et cor unum in Deo.* [For a discussion of these viewpoints, see A. Manrique and L. Cilleruelo, "Diálogo fraterno," *Revista agustiniana de espiritualidad,* v.3 (1962), 355–362, and v.4 (1963), 123–131.] In spite of the diversity of opinion there is among those who have discussed the point a certain unanimity insofar as most agree that it is charity that ultimately lies at the heart of Augustinian spirituality. Augustine himself is often depicted holding in his hand a flaming heart, the symbol of charity; and the spirit of his rule is clearly one of paternal, filial, and fraternal love.

The veneration of the Mother of God is also a part of Augustinian spirituality. Of the several traditional titles under which Mary has been honored, the two most popular originated in the 15th century—*Our Lady of Good Counsel and Mother of Consolation. The two Augustinian writers who are best remembered for their contributions to Mariology are Thomas of Villanova and Bartolomé de los Rios, author of *Hierarchia mariana* (Antwerp 1641).

Bibliography: D. Gutiérrez, DictSpirAscMyst 4:983–1018, contains extensive bibliog. *Sanctus Augustinus vitae spiritualis magister,* 2 v. (Rome 1959). Jordan of Quedlinburg, *Liber vitasfratrum,* ed. R. Arbesmann and W. Hümpfner (New York 1943). A. Zumkeller, *Das Mönchtum des hl. Augustinus* (Würzburg 1950). A. Orozco, *The Rule of Saint Augustine: Commentary,* tr. T. A. Hand (Westminster, Md. 1956). A. Manrique, *La vida monástica en S. Agustín* (Salamanca 1959); *Teología agustiniana de la vida religiosa* (El Escorial, Spain 1964). Tomé de Jesús, *The Sufferings of Our Lord Jesus Christ,* ed. E. Gallagher (Westminster, Md. 1960). T. A. Hand, *St. Augustine on Prayer* (Westminster, Md. 1963). J. Morán, *El equilibrio ideal de la vida monástica en S. Agustín* (Valladolid 1964). A. Sage, "La Doctrine et le culte de Marie dans la famille augustinienne," H. Du Manoir, ed., *Maria: Études sur la Sainte Vierge,* v.2 (Paris 1952) 679–712; *La Règle de saint Augustin, commentée par ses écrits* (Paris 1961). *Revista agustiniana de espiritualidad* (Calahorra, Spain 1960–), contains bibliog. RevÉtAug. **Illustration credit:** Bibliothèque Municipale, Toulouse.

[A. J. ENNIS]

AUGUSTINIANISM

The particular philosophical and theological doctrines identified with the Order of St. Augustine, as well as the entire intellectual tradition stemming from Augustine and continuing, in various forms, to the 20th century. This article outlines the history of Augustinianism, discussing its doctrinal origins with St. Augustine, its development in the Middle Ages, and its status in the modern and contemporary periods.

General Doctrines

For its founder, St. *Augustine, Augustinianism represented an attempt to reach an ever fuller understanding of revealed truth through supernatural graces and gifts, aided by the principles of philosophical inquiry. The various doctrines presented in this section express the more characteristic features of Augustinianism.

The Primacy of Faith. The esteem of Augustine for the role of *understanding (*intellectum valde ama—Epist.* 120.3.13; PL 33:458–459) was to exercise a decisive influence not only on the destiny of Augustinianism but also on the whole intellectual history of the West. The roles of faith and reason, as distinct but inseparable sources of learning, constitute a point of departure already clearly formulated in the earliest of Augustine's works (cf. *C. acad.* 3.20.43). The basis for faith is the supreme authority of Christ; for reason, the philosophy of *Plato and *Plotinus, but only to the extent that it is not at variance with revealed truth. The emphasis on the primacy of faith and on the necessary function of reason permanently determined the Augustinian view of philosophy, which appears to exclude the possibility of a philosophy autonomous in its own right or completely independent of theology. Accordingly, Augustine anticipated by some 5 centuries the celebrated formula of Anselm of Canterbury, *credo ut intelligam.* Intimately connected with this relation between faith and reason is the entire Augustinian anthropology, which, neglecting a purely abstract or purely natural view of man, considers him in his full historical situation—a creature destined to share in the life of God, redeemed after his fall by Christ, who thereby becomes the central and unifying factor in any "philosophy" of history. This constant and compelling consciousness of God imparts to Augustinianism its preeminently theocentric character and leads Augustine to view God as the source of man's total life (*causa, subsistendi, ratio, cognoscendi, ordo vivendi—Civ.* 8.4).

The Soul. Again, because speculation is so strongly focused on God, knowledge of the soul takes on a unique importance for Augustine and his successors (*see* SOUL, HUMAN). In two of his earliest works, composed before his baptism in April 387, he had declared God and the soul the two principal objects of philosophic inquiry (*Ordine* 2.18.47; *Soliloq.* 1.15.27). But to know the soul is, in some measure, to know God, since no other creature approaches Him so closely in perfection (*nihil . . . Deo esse propinquus—Quant. anim.* 34.77). Here is the basis for the important doctrine of image, termed "the cornerstone of Augustinian anthropology," which underlies and inspires the psychological doctrine of the *Trinity as well as the discovery of its manifold analogies in the soul. Such concentration on the soul also gives Augustinianism its character of "interiority," which stems from Augustine's conviction that it is within the soul itself that man must search for truth and certitude (*in interiore homine habitat veritas—Vera relig.* 39.72). Deserving of special mention here is Augustine's refutation of universal doubt by the compelling and infallible fact of personal existence implied in acts of the thinking subject (*scio me cogitare—Soliloq.* 2.1.1; *si fallor, sum—Civ.* 11.26), which anticipates the Cartesian "cogito" and leads further to the soul's direct knowledge of itself (*semetipsam per semetipsam novit—Trin.* 9.3.3), which was a controversial doctrine for the Augustinians of the 13th century.

Divine Illumination. The doctrine of divine *illumination is so central as to be almost identified with the very substance and spirit of Augustinianism. By reason of its spiritual nature, the soul enjoys a continuous and connatural union with the world of intelligible reality, which it is able to perceive in a kind of incorporeal light akin to its own nature (*in quadam luce sui generis incorporea—Trin.* 12.15.24). The soul, however, is not the source of its light but is a derived light (*lumen quod illuminatur*) participating in the light of God (*Deus intelligibilis lux*). It is the Truth itself, present within, that alone instructs man (*Mag.* 11.38), so as to exclude learning by any mere human agency (*nusquam igitur discere—ibid.* 12.40). From the presence of truth in the soul Augustine develops his most characteristic proof for the existence of God as "the unchangeable Truth containing all those things that are unchangeably true" (*Lib. arb.* 2.12.33). Truth is not so much an object of intellectual contemplation for man as it is a good conferring joy and happiness (*gaudium de veritate—Conf.* 10.23.33). This doctrine was to oppose the *intellectualism of the Aristotelian-Thomistic position in the 13th century. From the primacy of love Augustine distinguished between what must be loved (*fruenda*) and what should merely be used (*utenda*); he concluded that God alone, as man's true end, is to be loved for His own sake, whereas creatures are to be used only as means toward this good (cf. *Doctr. christ.* 1.3–5); hence, too, the Augustinian notion of virtue as the right ordering of love (*ordo amoris, Civ.* 15.22).

Seminal Reasons. Augustine's teaching on the *seminal reasons (*rationes seminales*), sometimes regarded as a forerunner of modern evolutionary theory, is, essentially, an attempt to reconcile the simultaneity and uniqueness of God's creative act with the progressive appearance of new living things throughout the course of time. According to Augustine's notion of a virtual creation, newly emerging forms of life were already present from the moment of creation, not in their actual state but in a seminal, potential, and causal condition (*invisibiliter, potentialiter, causaliter—Gen. ad litt.* 5.23.45). Although it would be an exaggeration to deny Augustine a notion of efficient causality in physical nature, it is undeniable that in the Augustinian universe the role of secondary causes is reduced to a relatively minimal status.

Grace. In the realm of moral activity the Augustinian conception of God's sovereignty and man's dependence finds its most profound and perennial expression in the saint's teaching on *grace. His doctrines on *original sin and on the necessity and gratuity of grace, developed during his extended polemic with Pelagianism and *Semi-Pelagianism, have dominated the whole theology of grace (*see* PELAGIUS AND PELAGIANISM). In a letter to Vitalis of Carthage, *c.* 427, Augustine formulates in 12 propositions his entire anti-Pelagian teaching on grace and *free will, assuring Vitalis that these doctrines "belong to the right and Catholic rule of faith" (*Epist.* 217.5.16–17). However, Augustine's treatment of certain aspects of these doctrines and his views on predestination seem to have influenced later Augustinians to exalt divine action and minimize the role of created causality.

Origins and Transmission to 13th Century

Although Augustine founded no school or system, properly speaking, even before his death the influence of his thought had won him a position of eminence and authority that remained unique and unchallenged for more than 800 years. In tracing the course of Augustinianism to the 13th century, a review is here made of writers, or compilers, whose familiarity with the Augustinian corpus made them influential vehicles of his thought, and this not only in theology but also in the apostolate of preaching and in the foundation and development of the first Christian schools in the West. Next, mention must be made of several important controversies in which recourse to St. Augustine served to transmit and formalize his teaching.

Compilers. Paul *Orosius was a friend of Augustine and author of the *Liber apologeticus contra Pelagium de arbitrii libertate,* written in defense of his own orthodoxy, in which he presented the saint's teaching on the necessity of grace for every salutary and meritorious act. He also composed, at Augustine's suggestion, a compendium of universal history in seven books, *Historiarum adversus paganos,* which resumed a central thesis of Augustine's *City of God,* viz, that temporal calamities had afflicted the world long before the advent of Christianity.

Prosper of Aquitaine defended Augustine against attacks by John *Cassian and the Semi-Pelagians and composed the *Book of 392 Sentences,* excerpted from works of Augustine. Prosper is important as a faithful exponent of Augustine's teaching. By way of exception, he mitigated Augustine's view on the predestination of reprobates by substituting the notion of a condemnation subsequent to God's foreknowledge of their sins (*post praevisa demerita*).

Cesarius of Arles (470–542) played a dominant role in the condemnation of Semi-Pelagianism by the Council of Orange (529) and in the vindication of Augustine's essential teaching on original sin and on the necessity and absolute gratuity of grace. Besides his treatise *De gratia,* he composed a rule for monastic foundations that follows closely Augustine's ideas and even his expressions.

*Fulgentius of Ruspe was known in the Middle Ages as *Augustinus breviatus* because of his brief and concise presentations of Augustine's doctrine. His Manual, modeled after Augustine's *Enchiridion,* contains an excellent summary of the principal beliefs of faith. He has been called "Augustine of the strict observance" (F. Cayré) because of his rigid interpretations of Augustine's teaching on predestination. He composed three works against Semi-Pelagianism, including one against *Faustus of Riez. In imitation of Augustine's "abecedary" poem against the Donatists (*Psalmus contra partem Donati*), Fulgentius wrote a *Psalmus abecedarius* against the Arians.

The unfinished *Complexio in psalmos* of *Cassiodorus is patterned after Augustine's *Ennarationes in* *psalmos.* Cassiodorus is best known for his celebrated *Institutiones,* a detailed program of studies for Christian schools, inspired in large part by Augustine's *De doctrina christiana* and later developed by *Alcuin and *Rabanus Maurus.

St. *Isidore of Seville wrote *Tres libri sententiarum,* the forerunner of similar works in the 12th century, drawn for the most part from Augustine and Gregory the Great. He reproduced, in substance, the prevailing Augustinian theology of the period.

St. *Anselm of Canterbury was one of the most authentic and influential representatives of Augustinianism in the early Middle Ages. He defended such basic Augustinian tenets as ontological truth, divine exemplarism, and divine illumination and preferred the Platonic-Augustinian argument for God's existence from the diverse levels of perfection in nature. In his effort to reconcile divine foreknowledge, predestination, and grace with free will, he emphasized the absolute mastery and sovereignty of God.

*Hugh of Saint-Victor was a representative of the school of Saint-Victor, "the school perhaps most directly and intimately inspired by St. Augustine's thought" (Marrou). In keeping with Augustine's principle of interiority, outlined in the *Soliloquies,* Hugh stressed the necessity of inner experience, not only as the ground of certitude for personal existence but also as valid evidence for the spiritual nature of the soul. He composed an important commentary on the Rule of St. Augustine.

*Peter Lombard, also of the school of Saint-Victor, wrote four books of the *Sentences,* drawn mainly from the teachings of Augustine, which reproduced copious passages from his works in a systematized presentation. Commentaries on the *Sentences* continued to appear until the end of the 16th century.

Controversies. The controversies that recurred intermittently within the Church from the 10th to the 12th centuries dealt with the validity of simoniacal ordinations and the related problem of the lawfulness of reordaining, and with the politicotheological doctrines underlying the conflicts between the Church and civil authority. Regarding ordinations, the anti-Donatist writings of Augustine provided the principal source of arguments for defenders of the orthodox position. The validity of the Sacraments, for Augustine, did not depend on the faith of the minister (vs. *Cyprian) or on his moral dispositions (vs. *Donatism). Augustine's views gradually prevailed and, with their acceptance by the theologians of the 13th century, secured a permanent place in sacramental theology. Similarly, from various interpretations of such notions as peace, justice, and kingdom, drawn from Augustine's *City of God,* political theories were formulated for the new Christian society and for resolving the conflicts between papal and imperial claims. It remained, however, for theologians of the Augustinian school, such as Giles of Rome and Augustine of Ancona, to expound a politicotheological theory in support of a theocratic view of papal authority.

Medieval and Scholastic Augustinianism

Although the intellectual influence of Augustine dominated the West until the 13th century, it must be acknowledged, with F. van Steenberghen that "the synthesis achieved by the Bishop of Hippo was wholly theological in character." On the other hand, this theological synthesis had assimilated much of the prevailing *Neoplatonism of his age and, quite possibly, in an already Christianized form. Because many 13th-century theologians viewed with alarm an *Aristotelianism that was clearly incompatible with a number of revealed truths, a new Augustinian synthesis began to emerge, containing, besides its theological component, philosophical notions taken from St. Augustine or, at least, reputed to be Augustinian in origin. This resulting doctrinal amalgam, championed mainly within the Franciscan Order, is what has come to be known as medieval or scholastic Augustinianism.

Characteristic Theses. The following summary embodies the more characteristic theses of this intellectual movement: (1) No strict formal distinction between rational and revealed truths, with a denial, at least implicit, of an autonomous philosophy completely independent of theology. (2) A primacy of the will and of the affective powers over the intellectual. (3) A real identity between the essence of the soul and its powers. (4) The soul as a complete substance, composed of spiritual matter and form and therefore individuated by its own principles without reference to the body. (5) Necessity of divine illumination, together with the complementary notion of *exemplarism, which makes the divine ideas the guarantee of certitude for the mind. (6) Direct and immediate knowledge of the soul's nature by the soul itself. (7) A universal *hylomorphism, embracing all created reality. (8) The doctrine of *seminal reasons. (9) A pluralism allowing for several substantial forms in the concrete structure of every created composite (*see* FORMS, UNICITY AND PLURALITY OF). (10) The impossibility of creation *ab aeterno.*

Opinions concerning the authenticity of this doctrinal corpus attributed to St. Augustine range from the view that all these theses have a foundation in Augustine (Mariani) to the opposite position, which denies their Augustinian authenticity *in toto* (Boyer). Accordingly, some historians have rejected the term medieval Augustinianism, preferring instead to describe the movement as early scholasticism, pre-Thomistic school (De Wulf), or eclectic Aristotelianism (Van Steenberghen).

Dominican and Franciscan Proponents. Opposition on the part of medieval Augustinians to Aristotelianism, culminating in the ecclesiastical condemnation of 1277, came from Dominican as well as Franciscan theologians. The Dominicans included Peter of Tarentaise (later *Innocent V), who denied the possibility of creation *ab aeterno* and defended the doctrine of seminal reasons, and *Richard Fishacre, who subscribed to such notions as seminal reasons, illumination, and universal hylomorphism. Since the Franciscans were far more numerous, it is convenient to identify them according to the following doctrinal schema:

1. Primacy of will: *John Peckham, *Roger Marston, *Richard of Middleton, and *William of Ware
2. Identity of soul with its powers: *Alexander of Hales, *John of La Rochelle, John Peckham, and William of Ware
3. Illumination: Alexander of Hales, John of La Rochelle, *Bonaventure, *Thomas of York, *Matthew of Aquasparta, John Peckham, and Roger Marston
4. Universal hylomorphism: Alexander of Hales, Bonaventure, Thomas of York, John Peckham, *William de la Mare, Roger Marston, and Richard of Middleton (except for four elements)

5. Seminal reasons: Bonaventure, Thomas of York, Matthew of Aquasparta, and Roger Marston
6. Pluralism (substantial): Thomas of York, William de la Mare, and Roger Marston
7. Impossibility of eternal creation: Bonaventure, Thomas of York, Matthew of Aquasparta, John Peckham, William de la Mare, Roger Marston, and Richard of Middleton

The condemnation of 1277, which included several theses of Thomas Aquinas, was followed by a gradual adaptation and fusion of Augustinianism with the main body of *scholasticism, both Thomistic and non-Thomistic. Such a doctrinal assimilation was possible because of the eclectic character of these schools and the influence of Aristotelian notions present within the Augustinian synthesis itself.

Within the Augustinian Order. The origin of the Augustinian school is commonly identified with the decree of the general chapter of 1287, which made the works of Giles of Rome, present and future (*scripta et scribenda*), mandatory upon all members of his order (*see* AUGUSTINIANS). Liberal interpretations of the decree were promoted by Giles himself, founder of the school, for whom "our intellect has been made subject, not to the service of man, but to Christ" (*De gradibus formarum* 2.6). The spirit of independence and adaptation within the school is evident in its relation to Augustinianism and is exemplified by its founder, himself an immediate disciple of Thomas Aquinas.

Foundations and Development. *Giles of Rome followed, in general, the basic metaphysical positions of Aquinas, although he occasionally blended them with Augustinian elements. Thus, while accepting the peripatetic notion of matter and form as a "more complete" explanation for the origin of new substances, he also insisted that the doctrine of seminal reasons is complementary to the hylomorphic thesis rather than opposed to it. The seminal reasons are described as "certain capacities implanted in nature which produce things like themselves" (*In 2 sent.* 18.2). At first a defender of the plurality of substantial forms, he gradually accepted the Thomistic view of the unicity of the substantial form, even going so far as to brand his former position as contrary to Catholic teaching. In political philosophy he passed from the Aristotelian-Thomistic view of society and civil authority to a doctrine of papal theocracy, based on an interpretation of notions drawn from Augustine's *City of God*. He retained the Augustinian teaching on the primacy of the will against the intellectualism of St. Thomas, arguing that the "good" is more excellent than the "true" (*see* VOLUNTARISM).

*James of Viterbo also accepted the voluntarist teaching because, for him, the notion of the "good" derives immediately from the "one" and, being prior to the "true," is thereby superior to it. He assigned to seminal reasons an intermediate place between primary matter —which is pure *potency, excluding forms, even in potency—and substantial form itself. He equated seminal reasons with the forms present in potency.

*Augustine of Ancona indirectly influenced the wider acceptance of Augustine's teachings within the order by his *Milleloquium S. Augustini,* the first concordance of the saint's works, which was completed by his pupil Bartholomew of Urbino.

The politicotheological views of Augustine of Ancona are reflected in his famous treatise on papal authority, *Summa de potestate ecclesiastica.* He went beyond Giles in formulating a strict theocratic conception of the papacy. Alexander of St. Elpidio (d. 1326) also wrote political treatises in defense of papal authority, notably his *De potestate ecclesiastica ad Joannem XXII.* *Bartholomew of Urbino defended political teachings of the Augustinian school against *Marsilius of Padua and *William of Ockham.

*Thomas of Strassburg upheld the primacy of the will, adducing, in addition to St. Augustine, the authority of Anselm and Bernard. Alphonsus Vargas maintained a voluntarist position and used the Augustinian argument for God's existence from diverse grades of perfections manifested in the world.

*Gregory of Rimini, despite nominalist tendencies in philosophy, remained faithful to the main body of the theological doctrine of his school. Because of his success in reproducing the theology of Augustine in the language of his own time, he has been called "the true author of Augustinianism in the 14th century."

Council of Trent. The order was represented among the fathers of the Council of *Trent by four bishops and two generals, assisted by some 50 theologians. Besides Girolamo *Seripando, who was present successively as prior general, cardinal president, and papal legate, the fathers included Christopher of Padua (1500–69), prior general, and Bps. John Barba of Teramo (d. 1564), Gaspar of Coimbra (1512–84), Juan Suárez of Portugal (d. 1572), and Juan de Muñatones of Segarbe (d. 1571). Seripando was unquestionably the principal spokesman of the Augustinians at Trent; according to H. Jedin, his name is "inseparable from the story of the Decree on original sin and justification."

To understand properly Seripando's teaching on original sin and justification, it is necessary to examine his view on *concupiscence, which he describes as the sum total of forces of the lower appetite opposed to the law of God; consequently, something displeasing in His sight and therefore somehow sinful (*aliquam pecati rationem*). The impact of this view of concupiscence upon the notion of justification is clear. First, Baptism of itself is insufficient for justification and must be joined with faith in the death and Resurrection of Christ. But concupiscence remains in the baptized and continues somehow to be sinful, not merely as the penal consequence of original sin but also as a dynamic source of personal sins and a positive obstacle to the perfect observation of God's law. Accordingly, the Augustinians tried unsuccessfully to have removed from the decree on justification statements that Baptism removes "whatever has the true and proper character of sin," that in the baptized the "old man is put off," and that "God finds nothing hateful in the reborn."

The same view of concupiscence underlies Seripando's doctrine of "double justice," a critical thesis within his description of the total process of *justification (*see* JUSTICE, DOUBLE). In relating double justice to the *Mystical Body of Christ, Seripando was convinced that he was following faithfully the teaching of Augustine himself. And although the Council did not accept his views, his influence was positive as well as negative, since his theory "furnished the occasion for reexamining the fundamental problems of the dogma with unprecedented care" (Jedin, 391).

Modern and Contemporary Augustinianism

This section discusses the revival within the Augustinian school during the 17th and 18th centuries occasioned by controversies growing out of the Protestant and Jansenist theologies, including the theology of grace and its most outstanding representatives of this period, and the later influence of Augustinianism in the 20th century.

17th and 18th Centuries. This period is characterized by (1) a gradual lessening of Thomistic influence; (2) the appearance of numerous tracts composed "ad mentem Aegidii"; and (3) the adaptation and interpretations of St. Augustine's teaching on grace in a manner already delineated by *Gregory of Rimini.

Lesser Figures. Before an outlining of the theology of grace of the so-called Augustinians, viz, Noris, Bellelli, and Berti, mention should be made of the following representatives of the period.

Federico Gavardi (1640–1715), teacher of Henry Noris, was the principal influence in the revival of the Augustinian school. He wrote a voluminous tract, *Theologia exantiquata juxta B. Augustini doctrinam ab Aegidio Columna expositam.* A compendium of this work, *Hecatombe theologica,* was written by Anselm Hormannseder (d. 1740). Nicholas Straforelli composed in 1679 a compendium, *Theoremata theologica Aegidianae scholae conformia.* Agostina Arpe (d. 1704) wrote a manual, *Summa totus Aegidii Columnae . . . ex doctrina eiusdem collecta.* Benignus Sichrowski (d. 1737) was a disciple of Gavardi and author of the manual *Theologia scholastica Aegidio-Augustiniana.* Pedro Manso (d. 1736) wrote philosophical and theological works marked by a return to the teaching of Giles of Rome and Gregory of Rimini. A staunch defender of Noris, he wrote tracts against Jansenist interpretations of St. Augustine, including a masterful treatise, *Augustinus sui interpres.*

Theology of Grace. Of more significance than the foregoing are those Augustinians of the period who gave distinctive interpretations of St. Augustine's doctrines on grace. Since their teachings evidence a basic doctrinal continuity with the earlier Augustinian school, it is inaccurate to represent them as having founded a "new" school. Their teachings, in fact, occupy an important place in the history of Augustinianism.

The writings of Henry *Noris aim at refuting the Protestant and Jansenistic interpretations of Augustine by an authentic presentation of his teaching accommodated to the doctrinal demands of the period. They include *Historia Pelagiana, Dissertati de Synodo V Oecumenica,* and *Vindiciae Augustinianae.* Later, Fulgentius Bellelli (1675–1742), a general of the order, wrote two important polemical works against *Baius and *Jansen, dealing with the states of man before and after the *Fall respectively: *Mens Augustini de statu naturae rationalis ante peceatum . . .* and *Mens Augustini de modo reparationis humanae naturae Post lapsum.* Finally, Lorenzo *Berti composed a theological compendium in 6 volumes, *De theologicis disciplinis,* described by M. Grabmann as "the best manual of the school."

The more characteristic doctrines of these theologians may be reduced to the following: First, the entire economy of grace rests on a concrete and historical conception of man before and after the Fall rather than on any purely metaphysical or abstract consideration of man's nature. In fact, the denial of a state of pure nature is a capital and decisive doctrine in this theology of grace. Having distinguished between God's absolute and ordered power, they maintain that while such a state of pure nature is possible according to God's absolute power, it is impossible by reason of His ordered power, i.e., viewed in the light of His goodness or wisdom, or from a certain fittingness on His part (*ex decentia Creatoris*). Consequently, the gifts of immortality, knowledge, and even sanctifying grace itself were conferred on Adam not as strictly owing to his nature, but as called for by God's goodness (*ex decentia bonitatis suae*). Hence, man's fallen state is envisaged as the loss of all those qualities given him *ex decentia Creatoris,* leaving him, as Noris put it, "despoiled of the gratuitous gifts and impaired in his natural endowments" (*expoliatus gratuitis et laesus insuper in naturalibus*). The latter privation accounts for concupiscence, which, for these theologians, is meaningless apart from original sin. Again, the distinction between the "innocent" and "fallen" states explains the two kinds of grace conferred respectively, namely, "indifferent grace" (*gratia versatilis*) and "efficacious grace" (*gratia efficax*). In the state of innocence, man's will was able to determine itself either for good or evil, whereas, since the Fall, it lacks sufficient power to do the good and must be determined by efficacious grace. Similarly, before the Fall, predestination to glory (and reprobation) was subsequent to God's foreknowledge of man's merits (*post praevisa merita*). To explain the nature of efficacious grace, Augustinians adduced the notion of a *delectatio victrix,* a doctrine developed by St. Augustine that had been interpreted by Jansenists to support their theology of grace. For Noris and his followers, the role of this *delectatio* is described as follows: the human will is beset by two opposing forces, or attractions, grace (charity) and cupidity. Since, in his fallen state, man's will follows the stronger attraction, it is only when grace is the more powerful that it efficaciously produces its effect. Yet as Berti insists, the will responds to this attraction not from necessity, but with complete freedom (*liberima voluntate*). Otherwise, grace remains inefficacious and, as Augustine had pointed out, leaves the will weak, *parva,* and feeble, *invalida* (*Grat. et lib. arb.* 17). Again, though admitting the salvific will of God, Augustinians claimed that sufficient grace is not bestowed on all, as evidenced, e.g., in infants who die without Baptism and pagans unenlightened by the Christian revelation.

A final feature of this theology of grace is its somewhat rigorous teaching on the role of charity in human acts. Since the precept to love God obliges at all times (*semper et pro semper*), these theologians maintain that man's every act must be directed to God, either actually or, at least, by a virtual intention. Further, man is bound to love God above all things not only *appretiative,* i.e., in preference to everything else, but also *intensive,* with a maximum intensity of love.

Contemporary Influence. Although Augustine founded no school, properly speaking, he remains in the 20th century a source and inspiration for many and diversified currents of thought. In general, these represent reactions to earlier mechanistic and materialistic systems, as well as to schools of rationalism and idealism. Contemporary thinkers whose orientation reveals certain affinities to, or dependence on, the doctrines and spirit of Augustine include Bergson, Scheler, Lavelle, Sciacca, Carlini, Kierkegaard, and Jaspers.

Bergson. The insistence of Henri *Bergson on the primacy of a concrete apprehension of reality, his preference for intuitive cognition and the method of "interiority," and his theory of intuition of duration reveal striking analogies with corresponding doctrines in Augustine. However, in view of Bergson's disavowal of any conscious Augustinian influence, such similarities can, at best, be ascribed to a common source, viz, Plotinianism, with which Bergson was well acquainted.

Scheler. No philosopher of the 20th century has professed so great a dependence on Augustine as Max *Scheler, who regarded Augustine as the true founder and sole representative of Christian philosophy. Augustine alone produced, though only tentatively, a philosophy directly inspired by the Christian "living-experience" (*Erlebnis*). In Scheler's view, other thinkers, e.g., Aquinas, merely gave a Christian coloring to preexisting forms of Greek philosophy. Scheler undertook to correct Augustine's imperfect realization of this ideal by the complete removal of all Neoplatonic vestiges, with the help of later Augustinians such as N. *Malebranche, B. *Pascal, J. H. *Newman, and A. *Gratry. The primacy of love, prior even to the will, is the focal point in Scheler's attempt to reconstruct Augustine's thought, replacing Neoplatonism with modern *phenomenology and its *Wesenerfarung*. However, Scheler's highly personal interpretations of Augustine, as well as his later tendency toward pantheism, have raised serious doubts concerning the validity of his professed Augustinianism.

Lavelle. The spiritualistic philosophy of Louis *Lavelle reflects certain characteristic positions of Augustine, although the influence is mainly indirect, stemming from the writings of Malebranche. The influence of Augustine is discernible in Lavelle's point of departure, his basic scope of philosophy, and his analysis of time. His notions of *présence total* and *expérience métaphysique fondamentale,* as primordial intuitions, recall the twofold object of speculation, God and the soul, outlined in Augustine's early dialogue *On Order* and the *Soliloquies.* In Augustinian fashion, Lavelle attempts to elaborate his whole philosophy by the "dialectic of *participation"; but whereas Augustine is always careful to safeguard the divine *transcendence, Lavelle's language, if not his thought, lends itself possibly to pantheistic interpretations.

Sciacca. M. F. Sciacca (1908–) is an exponent of the Italian "philosophy of the spirit." For him, Augustine's doctrine of divine illumination is the central problem of metaphysics, revealing the essential dependence of man's spiritual nature on God, whose transcendent and necessary existence is the absolute source of certitude. Consequently, the certitude of personal existence follows from the intuition of truth ultimately identified with God in a manner reminiscent of Augustine's dictum: "I could more easily doubt my own existence than that Truth exists" (*Conf.* 7.10.6). *See* SPIRIT, MODERN PHILOSOPHIES OF.

Carlini. Armando Carlini (1878–1959), also of the Italian spiritualist school, evidences even more of Augustine's influence. For Carlini, the central and crucial problem for philosophy is the nature and destiny of the human *person; any solution must follow Augustine's method of introspection and interiority. But since philosophy can do no more than discover and formulate this problem, man must turn to faith, specifically the Catholic faith, which alone can satisfy the demands of reason.

Kierkegaard. Since existentialist philosophers recognize the influence of S. A. *Kierkegaard in the development of their movement, it is important to consider Augustine's influence on him. He possessed the complete works of Augustine and regarded him as the one writer who used the "dialectic of existence" to solve the problem of human existence by recourse to faith rather than to reason. The conflict between the abstract religion of reason and that of faith and the eventual triumph of the latter have, according to Kierkegaard, been dramatically portrayed in the *Confessions,* in the case of Augustine himself, and in *The City of God,* with respect to the human race as a whole.

Jaspers. While existentialists such as M. Heidegger, G. Marcel, and J. P. Sartre show a certain affinity with Augustinianism by their concentration on the problem of human existence, only K. Jaspers (1883–) reveals any real dependence on Augustine (*see* EXISTENTIALISM). His insistence, for example, on the necessity of faith to discover reality itself, including one's personal existence and God, since reason cannot reach beyond phenomena, derives from his understanding of Augustine's injunction *credo ut intelligam.* And though he calls Augustine the founder of true philosophy, Jaspers contends that this philosophy, being specifically Christian and tentative, must be transformed and perfected by an inner and "fundamental revelation" to achieve a philosophy of absolute validity and value.

Bibliography: Doctrines and origins. E. PORTALIÉ, DTC 1: 2501–61. DTC, Tables générales 1:314–324. É. H. GILSON, *The Christian Philosophy of St. Augustine,* tr. L. E. M. LYNCH (New York 1960); *Spirit of Medieval Philosophy* (New York 1950). Gilson HistChrPhil. H. I. MARROU, *St. Augustine and His Influence through the Ages,* tr. P. HEPBURNE-SCOTT (Torchbks; New York 1958). E. PORTALIÉ, *A Guide to the Thought of Saint Augustine* (Chicago 1960). F. CAYRÉ, "The Great Augustinism," TheolDig 2 (1954) 169–173; *Patrologie et histoire de théologie,* v.3 (2d ed. Paris 1950). M. GRABMANN, *Die Geschichte der scholastichen Methode,* 2 v. (Freiburg 1909–11). G. A. LEFF, *Medieval Thought: St. Augustine to Ockham* (Chicago 1960).

Medieval and Scholastic. F. EHRLE, "Der Augustinimus und der Aristotelismus in der Scholastik gegen Ende des Jhs.," Denifle-Ehrle Arch 5:605–635. "L'Agostinismo e L'Aristotelismo nella scholastica del sec. XIII," *Xenia Thomistica* 3 (1925) 517–588. A. FOREST et al., *Le Mouvement doctrinal du XIe au XIVe siècle* (Fliche-Martin 13; 1951) 179–305. L. DE SIMONE, "S. Agostino e l'agostinianismo medievale," *Sapientia* 8 (1955) 5–17. F. J. THONNARD, "Augustinisme et Aristotélisme au XIIIe siècle," *L'Année théologique augustinienne* 5 (1944) 442–466. F. VAN STEENBERGHEN, *The Philosophical Movement in the 13th Century* (Edinburgh 1955). K. WERNER, *Der Augustinimus des späteren Mittelalters* (Vienna 1833). D. A. PERINI, *Bibliographia Augustiniana: Scriptores Itali,* 4 v. (Florence 1929–38). L. FERNENDEZ, *Trajectoria Historica de la Escuela Agustiniana* (Bogotá 1963). G. LEFF, *Gregory of Rimini* (New York 1961). J. L. SHANNON, *Good Works and Predestination according to Thomas of Strassburg* (Westminster, Md. 1940). R. KUITERS, "The Development of the Theological School of Aegidius Romanus . . .," *Augustiniana* 4 (1954) 157–177. D. TRAPP, "Augustinian Theology of the 14th Century," *ibid.* 6 (1956) 146–274. A. ZUMKELLER, "Die Augustinerschule des Mittelalters," *Analecta Augustiniana* 27 (1964) 167–262. M. WILKS, *The Problem of Sovereignty in the Later Middle Ages: The Papal Monarchy with Augustinus Triumphus and the Publicists* (Cambridge, Mass. 1963). H. JEDIN, *Papal Legate at the Council of Trent: Cardinal Seripando,* tr. F. C. ECKHOFF (St. Louis 1947). Jedin Trent. E. STAKEMEIER, *Der Kampf um Augustinus: Augustinus und die Augustiner auf dem Tridentinum* (Paderborn 1937). D. GUTTIÉRREZ, "Los Agostinos en el Concilio de Trento," *La Ciudad de Dios* 158 (1946) 385–491.

Modern and contemporary. F. ROJO, "Ensaya bibliográphica de Noris, Bellelli y Berti," *Analecta Augustiniana* 26 (1963) 294–363. A. TRAPÈ, "De gratuitate ordinis supernaturalis apud theologos Augustinienses," *ibid.* 21 (1950) 217–265. L. RENWART, *Augustiniens du XVIIIe siècle et "Nature Pure"* (Paris 1948). H. DE LUBAC, *Surnaturel: Études historiques* (Paris 1946). B. HWANG, "The Nature and Destiny of Man according to F. Bellelli," *Augustiniana* 3 (1953) 224–259. *S. Agostino e le grandi correnti della filosofia contemporanea* (Atti del Congresso Ital. di Filos. agostiniana; Rome 1954). F. THONNARD, "Saint Augustin et les grands courants de la philosophie contemporaine," *Revue des Études Augustiniennes* 1.1 (1955) 69–80. J. GUITTON, *The Modernity of St. Augustine,* tr. A. V. LITTLEDALE (Baltimore 1959). *Augustinus Magister,* 3 v. (Études Augustiniennes; Paris 1955), *passim.*

[R. P. RUSSELL]

AUGUSTINIANISM, THEOLOGICAL SCHOOL OF

The school arose toward the end of the 13th century and includes theologians of the Order of Hermits of St. Augustine (*see* AUGUSTINIANS), beginning with *Giles of Rome (Aegidius Romanus, *c.* 1243–1316), its foremost representative. At the general chapter of Florence in 1287, Giles's teachings were made mandatory upon all the members of the order. That the decree came to be liberally interpreted, despite its rigid formulation, is largely due to Giles's own conviction that freedom should be enjoyed wherever there is no danger to faith, since man's intellect is subject only to Christ (cf. *De gradibus formarum* 2.6).

For convenience, the history of the school may be divided into two periods: the early period, from Giles to the end of the 16th century; and the later period, comprising the 17th and 18th centuries. Members of the school in the later period are described in theological literature as the *Augustinenses.* That the theologians of the later period do not constitute a new or distinct school will be seen from an examination of their most characteristic teachings, which reflect a clear dependence upon those of their predecessors.

Early Period. Besides Giles, the most important representatives include the following: *James of Viterbo (d. 1307 or 1308), Alexander of San Elpidio (d. *c.* 1326), *Augustine (Triumphus) of Ancona (d. 1328), Gerard of Siena (d. 1336), Michael de Massa (d. 1337), *Henry of Friemar (d. 1340), *Bartholomew of Urbino (d. 1350), *William of Cremona (d. 1356), *Thomas of Strassburg (d. 1357), Alfonsus of Toledo (d. 1366), *Gregory of Rimini (d. 1358), *Ugolino of Orvieto (d. 1373), *John Klenkok (d. 1374), Augustine Favaroni (d. 1443), John Hiltalinger (d. 1392), *Giles of Viterbo (d. 1532), Gerolamo *Seripando (d. 1563), and Luis de León (d. 1591).

Representative Doctrine. Allowing for occasional differences, the following doctrinal summary may be taken as representative of this period, as well as of the Augustinian school in general.

(1) It is characterized by an eclecticism based on fundamental Thomistic doctrines and Augustinian teachings wherein the latter are given interpretations proper to this school. After Giles, however, and beginning with Gregory of Rimini, there is a gradual lessening of Thomistic influence and a corresponding stronger emphasis on St. Augustine in developing a more positive theology.

(2) There is an insistence upon the primacy of the will over the intellect, together with the corollary that beatitude is essentially and primarily achieved through love rather than knowledge. This pivotal position is reflected in several teachings of the school, particularly on grace and the kind of obligation attached to the precept of charity.

(3) Inspired by Augustine's familiar dictum, ". . . our heart is restless until it rests in Thee" (*Conf.* 1.1), as well as by the Augustinian notion of image, which accounts for the soul's radical capacity for possessing God (*Trin.* 14.8.11), the school defends man's natural *desire to see God. Against the objection of a disproportion between natural powers and *beatific vision, Augustinians reply with Gerard of Siena that, while the tendency is natural, the actual attainment requires *grace (*In 1 sent.* 3.2.).

(4) The end of *theology, according to the school, is neither speculative nor practical, but affective, since this science directs man to beatitude that consists essentially in love. Similarly, the central consideration in theology is not God in Himself, *sub ratione deitatis,* or in His infinity but, as Giles teaches, God as the source of glory and beatitude, *Deus glorificator et beatificator* (*In 2 sent.* 1.1.1.).

(5) The school holds the impossibility of a state of *pure nature for man, not from any strict exigency on the part of his nature but by reason of the divine wisdom and goodness and a fittingness on the part of the Creator (*ex quadam decentia Creatoris*). This notion, already found in Giles, will receive further development and importance with the Augustinian theologians of the 17th and 18th centuries.

(6) It stresses the necessity for medicinal grace (*gratia sanans*) consequent upon original sin, by which man is deprived not only of *supernatural goods but also suffers impairment in his natural endowments (*vulneratus in naturalibus*), with the further result that he is incapable without this grace of observing the natural law or of performing acts possessed of a natural morality (Giles, *In 2 sent.* 28.1.2).

(7) The school emphasizes the primacy of grace over free will in salutary and meritorious works [". . . magis agimur quam agamus" (Giles, *In 2 sent.* 38.1.3)] as further reflected in the Augustinian teaching on the nature of predestination. Consequent upon original sin, *predestination to glory is absolutely gratuitous and is antecedent to God's foreknowledge of man's merits (*ante praevisa merita*); *reprobation (negative), on the other hand, an effect of God's justice, and likewise consequent upon original sin, is the lot of those left unrescued from what Augustine had called the "massa perditionis" (*Persev.* 19.35). In explaining the efficacy of grace Augustinians of the period introduce the notion of an attraction to good ["non movetur voluntas . . . nisi per amorem" (Giles, *In 2 sent.* 41.1.2)]. This notion of a *delectatio victrix,* already formulated by St. Augustine (cf. *Pecc. merit.* 2.19), will be more fully developed by the Augustinians of Salamanca during the celebrated controversy *de auxiliis* and, even to a greater degree, by theologians of the so-called school of Noris.

(8) A strict theocratic position is held by the Augustinian school on the nature and scope of papal authority. The position is inspired by an interpretation of Augustine's notion of the state (*res publica*) and its foundation upon "justice," namely, that "true justice is not to be found except in that commonwealth [*res publica*] whose founder and ruler is Christ" (*Civ.* 2.21). First enunciated by Giles, this theory of direct power (*potestas directa*) in the temporal order is mitigated by James of Viterbo under the influence of Aristotle's teaching on the natural origin of the state. From man's social nature the state comes to an "inchoative" existence ("inchoa-

tive habet esse"), whereas in its full and formal condition ("perfective autem et formaliter") it exists for the spiritual power in somewhat the same way that grace does not destroy nature but perfects it. The *De regimine christiano* of James has been called the earliest treatise on the Church. The most extreme proponent of the Augustinian theory, Augustine of Ancona, holds that both powers, spiritual and temporal, reside solely in the pope, through whom ("mediante ipso") all others, clerical and lay, receive their authority (*see* CHURCH AND STATE).

Beginning with Gregory of Rimini and extending to the 16th century, the Augustinian school takes on a somewhat new direction characterized by the following trends: an increasing dependence upon the teachings and authority of St. Augustine, a vigorous anti-Pelagian polemic occasioned by the nominalist influence, and the development of a more positive theology based upon an extensive study of the Fathers of the Church, particularly St. Augustine.

During the Tridentine period the Augustinian theologians naturally focused their attention upon doctrines relative to the controversies of the times, such as original sin, concupiscence, and the nature of justification.

Gerolamo Seripando. Since Cardinal Seripando, onetime president of the Council, is unquestionably the most important representative of the period, a summary of his teachings will serve to outline the broad doctrinal positions of the Augustinian theologians of the 16th century.

Seripando's entire notion of *justification is developed from his definitive teaching on *concupiscence, understood as the cumulative impact of man's lower appetite in conflict with God's law. Concupiscence, being displeasing to God, is thereby somehow sinful in His sight. Following Baptism, which requires the complement of faith, personal or at least vicarious, concupiscence, while no longer imputed, remains an active source of personal sins, a hindrance to the perfect observance of God's law. It is therefore denominated as sinful. This understanding of concupiscence is essential to Seripando's theory of the double *justice, the culminating point in his theory of justification, which includes the following steps: (1) first grace, or call to faith (*gratia praeveniens*), (2) an additional grace (*adjutorium*) to accept the former, enabling man to abandon sin through penance, (3) incorporation into the Mystical Body by faith and trust in Christ, resulting in the remission of sin, (4) infusion of charity and the gifts of the Holy Spirit, whereby man is able to observe the commandments, and (5) the justice of Christ, which must still be applied to His members, since, owing to the active and sinful influence of concupiscence, man's justice remains otherwise incomplete and cannot merit eternal life.

Further Development. Related doctrines on original justice, grace, predestination, and the law of charity were later developed and systematized by the Augustinians of the 17th and 18th centuries. For a complete list of Augustinians, fathers and theologians, at Trent, see D. Gutiérrez, *Analecta augustiniana* 22 (1949) 55–157.

Finally, toward the end of this earlier period, there was a notable resurgence of interest in Giles, as evidenced by a number of systematic summaries of his teaching. Most important were F. Gavardi (d. 1715), *Theologica exantiquata juxta b. Augustini doctrinam ab Aegidio expositam,* in six volumes, and A. Hormannseder (d. 1740), *Hecatombe theologica,* a compendium in two volumes of Gavardi's work. P. Manso (d. 1736), author of a *Cursus philosophicus ad mentem Aegidii Romani* and an important treatise on Augustine's teaching on grace, *Augustinus sui interpres,* was a link between the early and later periods of Augustinianism. A pioneer in adapting Augustinianism to the doctrinal exigencies of the period, against *Jansenism, he was also a defender of Cardinal Henry *Noris.

Later Period. Augustinianism of the later period is sometimes known as the school of Noris, after its most important representative; the theologians of this school are also known as the *Augustinenses* in various theological tracts and histories. They attempt to remove the authority of St. Augustine from the teachings of Calvin, *Baius, and *Jansen on grace and to present a new synthesis of the saint's theology on grace conformable to Catholic teaching and accommodated to the doctrinal exigencies of the time. Principal theologians of the period are: Cardinal Henry Noris (1631–1704), whose more important works include *Historia pelagiana, Dissertatio de synodo V oecumenica,* and *Vindiciae augustinianae;* Fulgenzio Bellelli (1675–1742), general of his order and author of two works against doctrines of Baius and Jansen, namely, *Mens Augustini de statu naturae rationalis ante peccatum* and *Mens Augustini de modo reparationis humanae naturae post lapsum;* Giovanni Lorenzo Berti (1696–1766), author of *De theologicis disciplinis,* a systematic, six-volume synthesis of St. Augustine's theology, particularly on grace and free will. A compendium of the work by Buzio appeared in 1767. For a complete listing of works by these theologians, see D. Perini, OSA, *Bibliographia augustiniana: Scriptores itali* (Florence 1929–38).

Representative Doctrine. Undoubtedly, the central and controlling doctrine underlying the Augustinian theology of this period is that of man's natural desire to see God in beatific vision and its corollary of the impossibility of a state of pure nature for man. Continuing St. Augustine's doctrine of image, already elaborated in the earlier period, the later theologians of the school conclude that without the beatific vision man's state would be one of utmost misery. Similarly, since the soul, by reason of its inborn tendency to inform the body, would be in a violent state unless permanently united with the body, in which, in turn, concupiscence is an active force to sin, immortality and immunity from concupiscence are qualities eminently suited to man's true nature. Consequently, while these gifts are in no manner strictly due to man's nature itself and are, therefore, gratuitous, they are due to it by reason of God's goodness and wisdom, i.e., by a kind of fittingness on the part of God Himself (*ex decentia Creatoris*). Hence the conclusion that, though a state of pure nature is possible from God's absolute power, it is impossible from His ordered power—whence comes the insistence upon the necessity of a medicinal grace (*gratia sanans*) or, better, upon the medicinal aspect of grace to remedy man's nature following the loss of gifts due him by God's goodness and wisdom. Concupiscence, consequent upon the loss of this integrity, remains inconceivable, therefore, apart from original sin and constitutes its material element.

In explaining the divine economy of grace, Augustinians proceed historically and concretely in distinguishing the two states of man, that of innocence and fallen nature. To the former, God granted an indifferent grace (*gratia versatilis*), giving the will the power (*posse*) to do good, which Adam could resist, but not the grace of actual volition (*velle*) and of the performance (*perficere*) of the good. After the Fall man has need of efficacious grace, which infallibly produces its effect without detriment to man's freedom. Similarly, in the state of innocence predestination and reprobation were subsequent upon God's foreknowledge of man's merits (*post praevisa merita*), while after the Fall predestination to glory is absolutely gratuitous and previous to any merit (*ante praevisa merita*); reprobation (negative), consequent upon original sin, is the lot of those comprising the "massa perditionis," in keeping with God's "just judgment," as Augustine had expressed it (*Persev.* 19.35).

To explain the nature of efficacious grace, Augustinians develop the notion already adumbrated in Giles of the *delectatio victrix,* the most crucial and controversial point in their theology of grace. According to Noris, for example, man's will is beset by two opposing forces or attractions: concupiscence (*cupiditas mali*) and grace (*caritas—cupiditas boni*). Since, in his fallen state, man's will follows the stronger attraction, it is only when grace is the more powerful that it efficaciously produces its effect; however, as Berti points out, the will responds to this attraction not from necessity but with complete freedom (*liberrima voluntate*). Otherwise grace remains inefficacious or sufficient, bestowing the power (*posse*) but not the actual accomplishment of good since it fails to overcome the stronger attraction of evil. These graces differ in degree rather than in kind, so that the efficacy of grace is not absolute but relative, i.e., measured by the intensity of the evil attraction to be overcome and the moral condition of the individual subject. In other words, a grace efficacious for one may be inefficacious for another.

Finally, reacting in part against the laxism of the period, Augustinians propose a strict interpretation of the divine precept of charity and of the role of love in human acts. Since the commandment obliges man to love God always, he must, at least frequently and in particular instances, do so actually; at all other times, by a virtual disposition of soul. Furthermore, in the performance of acts morally good in every respect, he must refer them to God by at least a virtual intention. Finally, even in the Sacrament of Penance, fear alone of punishment does not justify the sinner unless there is present a kind of initial love.

Opposition. The teachings of Noris and his followers were violently attacked because of their alleged affinity or even identity with the errors of Baius and Jansen, e.g., by the Franciscans Neusser in Germany and F. de Macedo in Italy, by the Jesuit J. Hardouin in France, and by the Benedictine Navarro in Spain. Although Noris's works were favorably reviewed by the Roman Inquisition, his *Historia pelagiana* was placed on the Index of the Spanish Inquisition in 1742. In a brief of July 31, 1748, Benedict XIV protested this action (Denz 2564) and, in a later brief, of Feb. 19, 1749, ordered the book removed from the Index. In the first brief, the Pope significantly granted the same status to the Augustinian system as that enjoyed by Bañezianism (*see* BÁÑEZ AND BAÑEZIANISM) and *Molinism on the question of grace and free will. Favorable judgment was also passed upon the teachings of Berti by a papal commission appointed by Benedict XIV.

See also AUGUSTINIANISM; AUGUSTINE, ST.; THEOLOGY, HISTORY OF.

Bibliography: E. PORTALIÉ, DTC 1.2:2485–2561. L. HÖDL, LexThK[2] 1:1089–92. W. BOCXE, *Introduction to the Teaching of the Italian Augustinians of the 18th Century on the Nature of Actual Grace* (Héverlé-Louvain 1958). L. FERNANDEZ, *Trayectoria historica de la escuela agustiniana* (Bogotà 1963). H. JEDIN, *Papal Legate at the Council of Trent: Cardinal Seripando,* tr. F. C. ECKHOFF (St. Louis 1947). G. LEFF, *Gregory of Rimini* (New York 1961). L. RENWART, *Augustiniens du XVIIIe siècle et "nature pure"* (Paris 1945). J. L. SHANNON, *Good Works and Predestination according to Thomas of Strassburg* (Westminster, Md. 1940). M. WILKS, *The Problem of Sovereignty in the Later Middle Ages: The Papal Monarchy with Augustinus Triumphus and the Publicists* (Cambridge, Eng. 1963). D. GUTIÉRREZ, "Los agustinos en el concilio de Trento," *La Ciudad de Dios* 158 (1946) 385–491. B. HWANG, "The Nature and Destiny of Man according to F. Bellelli," *Augustiniana* 3 (1953) 224–259. R. KUITERS, "The Development of the Theological School of Aegidius Romanus in the Order of St. Augustine," *ibid.* 4 (1954) 157–177. F. ROJO, "Ensayo bibliográfico de Noris, Bellelli y Berti," *Analecta Augustiniana* 26 (1963) 294–383. D. TRAPP, "Augustinian Theology of the 14th Century," *Augustiniana* 6 (1956) 146–222. A. ZUMKELLER, "Die Augustinerschule des Mittelalters," *Analecta Augustiniana* 27 (1964) 167–262.

[R. P. RUSSELL]

AUGUSTINIANS

The Order of Hermits of St. Augustine (OSA)—commonly known as Augustinians or Austin Friars—is a *mendicant order that traces its spiritual lineage back to St. *Augustine (354–430), Bishop of Hippo and Doctor of the Church. The word "hermits" is simply a historical vestige from the 13th century when the order began canonically. The order's history can be understood only in terms of Augustine's monastic teaching and example, for even though a historical continuity between Augustine and the hermitic groups of the 13th century has never been established, the Augustinians have always regarded themselves as sons of their "Father" Augustine, a usage sanctioned by centuries of tradition and expressly acknowledged in pontifical documents from John XXII to Pius XII.

The monastic ideal that has permeated the entire history of the Augustinians is found in the writings of Augustine and can be summarized in the following brief formula: Unity of heart and mind in God, and life in common without personal possessions. As he related in his *Confessions,* Augustine wished to live a community life even before his conversion. Upon his return to Tagaste in North Africa he organized a monastic group after the fashion of the primitive apostolic community in Jerusalem. After his ordination at Hippo, he established a monastery there within the church confines. Later, when he was consecrated bishop (396), Augustine had to leave this monastery, but he continued to live the monastic life together with his clerics in the episcopal residence. Out of this twofold development of lay and clerical monasticism there came, according to *Possidius, Augustine's biographer, a rich heritage for the North African Church, for Augustine left an ample clergy and many monasteries for both men and women. Some of his followers—Gaudiosus, *Donatus, Eugenius, *Fulgentius of Ruspe, and others—became in turn monastic founders and extended Augustine's influence even beyond Africa into Italy, Spain, and the Mediterranean islands. Because of his widespread and perduring influence, Augustine has been called the Father of Monasticism in Africa.

There is no need to go into the intricate question of Augustine's Rule (*see* AUGUSTINE, RULE OF ST.). The Augustinian friars have traditionally followed the opinion that the rule is authentic and that it was first composed in its masculine form. Regardless of the literary problem alluded to here, it is a fact that the rule has always been regarded by Augustinians as the chief embodiment of the monastic spirit of their spiritual father Augustine. Numerous commentaries have been composed through the centuries, and today the rule is still read weekly in the monastery refectory.

Canonical Foundation—The "Great Union" of 1256. In the 11th and 12th centuries when the *Canons Regular were adopting the rule of Augustine, a different development was taking place in Italy. A number of semieremitic or penitent communities dedicated to a life of prayer and solitude began to appear in Tuscany, Lombardy, the Romagna, and The Marches of Ancona. Some of these used Augustine's rule as the basis for their life, and a few of them sent out colonies to Spain, Germany, and southern France early in the 13th century. Because these and other similar groups lacked organization and direction, the Church began to intervene in order to centralize religious life and to guide it toward meeting more effectively the needs of the time. From 1215 onward it became impossible to found an order unless it had an approved rule, a central government, organization, and, lastly, the approbation of the Apostolic See. The hermits of Tuscany, complying with the desire of the Church, requested the pope to unite them into an order under a fixed rule. In 1243 Innocent IV prescribed the Rule of St. Augustine and charged Cardinal Annibaldi to undertake the task of unification.

After this "Little Union" (1244) of the Tuscan Order of the Hermits of St. Augustine, Pope Alexander IV in 1255 directed the unification of the following groups: the Order of St. William, the orders of St. Augustine, the followers of Friar John Bonus, the brethren of Favali, and the hermits of Brettino. The first group, followers of St. William of Maleval (d. 1157), subsequently withdrew from the union, as did the brethren of Favali, who dated their papal approbation from 1224. The orders of St. Augustine consisted principally of the abovementioned hermits of Tuscany and numbered some 70 monasteries, including houses in Spain, Germany, France, and England. The followers of Bl. John Bonus (d. 1249) were concentrated in Lombardy and the Romagna, with about 26 houses, while the hermits of Brettino were settled mostly in The Marches of Ancona and possessed approximately 45 houses. The bull *Licet Ecclesiae* of April 9, 1256, confirmed the work of the first general chapter held at Rome. This meeting, referred to as the "Great Union," consolidated the several groups into one Order of Hermits of St. Augustine, bound to regular observance under one prior general canonically constituted. The vow of absolute poverty originally agreed upon was mitigated by the Pope (1257) to permit goods to be held in the name of the community when it was deemed necessary. There remained the question of evolving constitutions and of accelerating the orderly transfer from rural hermitages into the more active life of the cities where the needs of the Church could be better served.

Santa Maria del Popolo, Rome. Scene of the "Great Union" of the Augustinians in 1256.

In the bull of union the matter of constitutions was passed over, probably in order to emphasize unity rather than the diversity of customs peculiar to each group. Since the original constitutions are no longer extant, the earliest edition is that prepared by Bl. Clement of St. Elpidio and Bl. *Augustine Novellus and promulgated at the general chapter of Ratisbon in 1290. These constitutions were made in the form of the new mendicant orders: one superior ruling over a general curia in Rome for the entire order, which in turn was distributed into provinces, each under one major superior (provincial) subject to the prior general, and one local superior (prior) in each house. All except the local superiors were elected. Legislative power rested in the general chapters and executive power in the superiors within the limits of their jurisdiction. The constitutions went through several revisions (1551, 1581, 1686, 1895, 1926) and in 1964 were in the process of a thorough revision at Rome. The Augustinians of the 13th century thus took the form and direction of the other mendicant orders; they enjoyed exemption from episcopal jurisdiction and were dedicated to the works of the active apostolate. Like the other mendicants they came to be known as friars rather than hermits. Still, the contemplative and even the solitary aspect of their tradition were never lost. Inspired by Augustine's ideal and guided by his rule, the Augustinians, within the framework of their constitutions, pursued both the contemplative and the active aspects of the monastic life.

Internal Development. The characteristic note in the early constitutions and acts of the general chapters was the impelling concern for the finest education for the youth of the order. Though funds were scarce, great efforts were made to defray the expenses of the young friars at the major study houses at Paris, Oxford, Bologna, Naples, Padua, Rome, and later, at Salamanca, Cambridge, and Cologne. In these intellectual pursuits the order found its greatest inspiration in the study and imitation of St. Augustine.

Lanfranc Septala (d. 1264), the first prior general, established a *studium generale* at Paris in 1259, and sent to it *Giles of Rome, who was to become the greatest theologian of the order, a contemporary and successor of Thomas Aquinas, and the founder of the *schola aegidiana.* Giles, as master at Paris and later as prior general, guided much of the early development of Augustinian religious and intellectual life. His school of thought was primarily Thomistic, although Giles of Rome adhered to certain characteristically Augustinian theses. His Augustinianism, however, needs to be distinguished both from certain other schools of thought contemporary with his own and from later developments among the theologians of his own order, even though it can be said that by reason of his great influence Giles was the forerunner of these later theologians. (*See* AUGUSTINIANISM; AUGUSTINIANISM, THEOLOGICAL SCHOOL OF.)

The spiritual life of Augustinians was based on Sacred Scripture, the teaching of the Church, and the doctrine of the saints, especially that of Augustine (*see* AUGUSTINIAN SPIRITUALITY). The first constitutions established the spiritual framework by regulating the daily life in harmony with studies, apostolic work, and contemplative life. The mandate to study the Scriptures assiduously produced about 84 recognized exegetes in the first 3 centuries. The cooperation of man with God by a generous obedience and docility to His grace was the common heritage of Augustinian writers. But in insisting on the primacy of grace they did not neglect the necessity and importance of penance, prayer, and good works. Devotion to the Mother of God also had its due place: Augustinians from the 13th century have invoked the protection of Our Lady under the title of Mother of Grace, and from the 15th century as Mother of Good Counsel, of Consolation, and of Help (*see* OUR LADY OF GOOD COUNSEL). Among the persons prominent for holiness in the early period were St. *Nicholas of Tolentino and St. *Clare of Montefalco.

Growth and Influence. After the Great Union the order began to expand into new provinces. By the beginning of the 14th century there were: a province in England and Ireland with about 27 foundations and 500 religious, including monasteries at Oxford, London, York, Cambridge, Lincoln, Clare, and Canterbury; a province in France with 22 houses, including Paris, Narbonne, Toulouse, Montpelier, and Bordeaux; 4 provinces in Germany with houses in the Low Countries, Switzerland, Austria, Moravia, and Poland, with possibly 83 houses; 2 provinces in Spain; and one each in Hungary, Portugal, and the Holy Land. Together with the Italian provinces, the Augustinians aggregated some 350 houses in 22 provinces with about 8,000 members. A century later France had evolved into 4 provinces with an additional 39 houses; Germany added 47 houses; Italy, 22; and England, 17. This was true despite the Black Death that had taken the lives of 5,084 Augustinians.

In their unwavering devotion to the Holy See the Augustinians of the 14th century made some of their finest contributions. To dissipate doubts on the validity of the election of Boniface VIII arising from the question as to whether his predecessor Celestine V could legitimately resign, Giles of Rome composed his *De renunciatione papae tractatus*. Against the caesaropapistic arrogance of Philip the Fair came the *De ecclesiastica potestate* of Giles, and the *De regimine christiano* of Bl. *James of Viterbo, the author of the first treatise on the Church. In answer to Marsiglio of Padua's *Defensor Pacis,* *Augustine Triumphus of Ancona wrote his *Summa de ecclesiastica potestate,* and *William of Cremona his *Refutatio errorum*. Against Lewis of Bavaria, Alexander of St. Elpidio (d. 1326) indited his *De ecclesiastica potestate* and *De jurisdictione imperii*. *Thomas of Strassburg wrote against *William of Ockham and the antipope Nicholas V (Pietro Rainalluci).

Among the Italian friars of the 14th century there were professors of theology and philosophy who were considered to be among the best of the time; the Augustinians, moreover, were then the only masters of theology in Hungary. Besides those already mentioned, the following are noteworthy Augustinians of this period: Bl. Simon Fidati of Cascia (d. 1348), *Herman of Schildesche, John of Lana (d. 1350), *Gregory of Rimini, Hugolinus of Orvieto (d. 1373), John of Basle (d. 1392), and William *Flete. The first historians of the order, *Henry of Friemar and *Jordan of Quedlinburg, appeared at about the same time. Since 1352 the Augustinians have held the office of papal sacristan; the incumbent in 1964 was Bp. Peter Canisius van Lierde. In the 15th century there were about 340 Augustinian members of the hierarchy. It was the age of St. *Rita of Cascia; St. John of *Sahagún; Ambrogio *Calepino, the lexicographer; and Ambrose of Cori (d. 1485), historian and humanist. Among the English Austin Friars was John *Capgrave, author of the *Chronicle of England*.

Reformation Period. The 15th century was characterized generally by religious decline, caused in part by such tragedies as the Black Death and the Western Schism. In reaction to the decline in monastic discipline there sprang up in all the mendicant orders observantine congregations dedicated to the restoration of pristine observance. These congregations were ordinarily governed by their own vicar, subject directly to the prior general. In the Augustinian order were the following groups: Lecceto (1387–1782); Carbonara (1421–1947); Saxony (1419–1525); Spain (1431–1505); Monte Ortone (1436–1810); Perugia (1436–1770); Lombardy (1439–1815); Genoa (1473–1822); Apulia (1487–1667); Calabria (1501–1667); Dalmatia (1511–1786); Colloreto in Calabria (1546–1751). Some fruit was forthcoming from these reform groups, but at the same time they often exhibited an unruly pride and spirit of independence, so that the general's control over them fluctuated widely.

The observantine Congregation of Saxony caused special concern. The third vicar general, Andreas Proles, in his excessive zeal to spread reform, introduced the pernicious principle that secular princes had the right and even the duty to prosecute reform. Deposed by the prior general, he was later reinstated. His successor, Johann von *Staupitz, attempted in 1510 to bring the whole province of Saxony under the observantine rule. This drive for reform was quite in accord with the efforts of *Giles of Viterbo who, during his term as general from 1507 to 1517 (when he was elevated to the cardinalate), devoted himself wholeheartedly to the reintroduction of the *vita communis*. In order to achieve this he undertook a thorough visitation of the whole order, including that sector residing in Germany. Through one of the quirks of history Martin *Luther, as a representative of seven monasteries of the observantine group, objected to the inclusion of all the monasteries of the Saxon province into the congregation lest thereby the reforming principles be diluted. Unsuccessful in this pilgrimage to Rome (1511) to appeal this decision, he returned to Germany, where he later turned against the observantine group and began to evolve his own ideas of reform, which led to heresy and catastrophe.

At this critical juncture (1517) the generalate was changing hands in Rome from Giles of Viterbo to Gabriel of Venice (d. 1537), and in the interim Luther began his reform in Germany. These events are recounted elsewhere, but so far as the Augustinians were concerned, it may be noted that, while some of Luther's fellow religious followed him, others were among his strongest opponents—Bartholomaeus *Arnoldi von Usingen, one of Luther's former professors at Erfurt; Konrad Treger (d. 1543), and Johannes Hoffmeister (d. 1547). How many Augustinians joined Luther in his heresy is unknown. In the history of the period relatively few Augustinians are mentioned as heretics, and some of those named as Augustinian defectors had not in fact been members of the order.

Although the Saxon congregation disappeared, there was not an internal collapse of the order. Some monasteries, however, were confiscated outright by hostile authorities. In other cases removal of the means of sustenance and prohibition against the reception of novices gradually reduced the monasteries. The destruction attending the Peasants' War also contributed to the disappearance of the friars. Despite all this, the Augustinian Order survived in Germany, and in the rest of the world, with the exception of England, it increased. The friars were fortunate in having as prior general, from 1539 to 1551, a man of rare ability, Girolamo *Seripando, who labored vigorously through able legislation and by a personal 2-year visitation to assist his order and the Church through this difficult time.

Post-Reformation. By 1540 the entire English province of some 34 houses and 400 friars was lost, but the order still possessed: in Italy (including Dalmatia) 13 provinces with 345 monasteries, and 9 congregations with 171 monasteries; 5 provinces in France with 95 houses, Paris alone counting 200 friars and Toulouse 120; 5 provinces in Spain, Portugal, and Sardinia with 101 houses; 3 provinces in Germany, including the Low Countries, Austria, and Poland. A century later, the 17th, the order aggregated more than 1,000 monasteries and about 20,000 friars.

Much of this growth was the result of extensive missionary activity in the New World, the Far East, and Africa. The missions begun in this period were those of: Mexico (1533), Peru (1550), the Philippines (1565), India (1572), Colombia (1575), Chile (1595), China (1575—reestablished in 1680), Angola and the Congo (1578), Malacca (1587), Arabia (1596), Kenya (1598), Japan (1602), Persia (1602), Ceylon (1606), and Iraq (1623). This was the age, too, of St. *Thomas of Villanova, Bl. Alfonso of *Orozco, *Thomas of Jesus (de Andrada), and Luis de *León in Spain. In the Americas, Andrés de *Urdaneta completed and made practical Magellan's work by charting a return course from the Philippines back to Mexico in 1565, and Alonso de la *Vera Cruz was a prime contributor to the religious and academic apostolate of Mexico.

The renewed activity, both in the mission apostolate and in studies, continued into the 17th century. Augustinians made distinguished progress especially in historiography and theology. The principal works published in history were: N. Crusenius, *Monasticon augustinianum* (Munich 1623); L. Empoli, *Bullarium* (Rome 1628); T. Herrera, *Alphabetum augustinianum* (Madrid 1644); A. Torelli, *Secoli agostiniani* (8 v., Bologna 1659–86); and A. Lubin, *Orbis augustinianus* (Paris 1662). In the field of history Enrique *Flórez achieved notable fame. The theologians, Agustín *Antolínez, Juan Márquez (d. 1621), and Basilio Ponce de León (d. 1629), shone at the University of Salamanca, and at Rome Angelo *Rocca was one of the most learned ecclesiastics. About a century later the Augustinian school of theology was represented by Cardinal Henry *Noris, Fulgencio Bellelli (1675–1742), and Giovanni *Berti.

From 1767 to 1870 suppressions by the civil powers, the French Revolution, and the subsequent 19th-century confiscations and secularizations wrought havoc with the Augustinians, as with the Church at large. Eleven provinces were suppressed: Italy alone lost more than 540 monasteries, while in France the order succumbed entirely. The period from 1870 to the present has been one of rebuilding and expansion. The monastery of Valladolid was the springboard for the restoration in Spain and the numerous Spanish missions. Pius Keller led the rejuvenation in Germany; while Belgium, Holland, and Ireland not only emerged as major provinces, but also undertook extensive missionary activities. It was in the 19th century that Gregor Johann *Mendel carried on his experiments in plant hybridization at Brno.

American Province. While revolution and secularization were decimating the Augustinian order in Europe, its history in the U.S. followed a different path. The Irish province sent John Rosseter (d. 1812) in 1794 and 2 years later Thomas Matthew *Carr to assist Bp. John *Carroll in evangelizing the new nation. The center of their initial activity was St. Mary's Church in Philadelphia, Pa. In 1796 their petition to Rome to establish a new province was granted, and plans were undertaken to erect St. Augustine's Church in Philadelphia. The new church was opened in 1801 and, next to it, St. Augustine's Academy in 1811. Other recruits were sent from Ireland, including Nicholas O'Donnell (d. 1863), who became editor of the *Catholic Herald* (1833) of Philadelphia and later, rector of St. Paul's in Brooklyn, N.Y. Michael *Hurley was the first American novice (*c.*

Thomas M. Carr.

1797). Progress was slow, however, and after almost 50 years of existence there were only five priests of the order serving in the U.S.

Two events marked a turning point in the 1840s. The Rudolph farm outside Philadelphia was purchased in 1841 and Villanova College opened its doors there in 1843 (*see* VILLANOVA, UNIVERSITY OF). The other event was the brutal burning of St. Augustine's Church, rectory, school, and library in Philadelphia on May 8, 1844, during the Nativist riots. Within 4 years a new and larger church was built and from that point forward progress was made.

The need for parishes and schools demanded paramount attention in America, and it was to this activity that the Augustinians devoted their full efforts. St. Denis's in Ardmore, Pa., was put in the care of the friars in 1853, and Our Mother of Consolation Church in Chestnut Hill, Pa., in 1855. In the Archdiocese of Boston, Mass., St. Mary's in Lawrence came under their direction in 1848, and from there missions were inaugurated in Andover, Methuen, Ballardvale, Wilmington, and Tewksbury. In 1964 the Augustinians administered seven churches in Lawrence and one in Andover. During the same period the friars were invited to assume charge of parishes in North Troy (1858), Waterford (1858), Cambridge (1862), Hoosick Falls (1862), and Greenwich (1880) in the Diocese of Albany, N.Y., and Carthage (1874) in the Diocese of Ogdensburg, N.Y.

In 1874, when the American province was juridically established, Thomas *Galberry was elected the first provincial. Two years later he became the fourth bishop of Hartford, Conn. William A. *Jones, who in 1899 had gone to Cuba in charge of St. Augustine's Church in Havana, was elevated to the bishopric in San Juan, P.R., in 1907.

The opening of the 20th century found the Augustinians in New York City with a parish in Tompkinsville, Staten Island. A new parish and school were commenced in the Bronx, N.Y., in 1905, the predecessors of the present magnificent church, high school, rectory, and convent of St. Nicholas of Tolentine. In the same year the friars were called to Chicago, Ill., to establish a new parish and school (St. Rita) and later the church of St. Clare of Montefalco (1909). Some years later they founded three parishes in the Diocese of Detroit, Mich.: St. Augustine's in Detroit, St. Matthew's in Flint, and St. Clare's in Grosse Pointe. Four preparatory schools were opened about the same time: Malvern, Pa. (1922), St. Augustine's in San Diego (1923), Villanova Preparatory in Ojai, Calif. (1924), and Cascia Hall in Tulsa, Okla. (1924). Meanwhile, a new house of theology, Augustinian College, was erected in Washington, D.C. (1920), a preparatory seminary at Mt. St. Rita, Staten Island (1924), a new novitiate at New Hamburg, N.Y. (1925), while St. Mary's Hall at Villanova had already (since 1912) served as a separate house of philosophy for the young friars.

Present Status. Today the Augustinian Friars in the U.S. staff two provinces and three vice-provinces. The Province of St. Thomas of Villanova serves 33 parishes in the Sees of Philadelphia, Pa.; Camden, N.J.; St. Augustine, Fla.; New York, Brooklyn, Albany, and Ogdensburg, N.Y.; Boston, Mass.; and Havana in Cuba. Besides Villanova (now a university), there are the colleges of Merrimack (Mass.) and Biscayne (Fla.). The Universidad Católica de Santo Tomás de Villanueva in Havana, Cuba, was closed by the Castro government. In addition to the high schools already mentioned, the Augustinians administer Archbishop Carroll High School in Washington, D.C., Monsignor Bonner High School in Philadelphia, and Austin High School in Reading, Mass. Both American provinces have sent missionaries to Japan, where they tend missions in Nagasaki, Nagoya, Fukuoka, and Hatano.

The Province of Our Mother of Good Counsel in Chicago was raised to full status in 1941. Serving parishes in several midwestern states, the province maintains a preparatory seminary at Holland, Mich.; a novitiate at Oconomowoc, Wis.; a major seminary at Olympia Fields, Ill.; and a mission band headquarters at Fort Wayne, Ind. Besides the schools mentioned earlier, the province staffs Mendel High School in Chicago and Austin High school in Detroit.

The vice-province of California has parishes and schools in the Sees of San Diego and Los Angeles. The Italian vice-province in East Vineland, N.J., serves parishes there and in Philadelphia as well as Dobbs Ferry, N.Y., and maintains a minor seminary and high school at Richland, N.J. The German vice-province, with houses in Racine and Kenosha, Wis., Riverdale, N.Y., and five houses in Canada, has its minor seminary and novitiate at Monastery, Nova Scotia.

In the world at large the Augustinian Order aggregates (1964) 4,287 friars with another 2,406 candidates distributed among 24 provinces and 8 vice-provinces, including 400 monasteries. The provinces are located as follows: 7 in Italy; 1 in Malta with houses in North Africa; 4 in Spain (including one province for the Philippines) with houses in Brazil, Puerto Rico, Dominican Republic, U.S., Venezuela, and Uruguay; 1 in Ireland; a vice-province in England and Scotland; 1 province in Holland with two houses in Paris; a commissariate of Bohemia with houses in Austria and Germany; 1 province in Germany with houses in Switzerland; 2 in Mexico; 1 each in Belgium, Ecuador, Chile, and Australia; vice-provinces in Brazil, Argentina, Peru, Colombia, and Bolivia. Missions are maintained in Nigeria, Belgian Congo, Ethiopia, Dutch New Guinea, Peru, and Japan. St. Monica's International College at Rome is the order's main study house.

Besides the nuns belonging to the Second Order of St. Augustine, there are about 52 congregations of sisters aggregated to the order in Italy, Spain, Germany, Belgium, and France (*see* AUGUSTINIAN NUNS). There is also a Third Order Secular, besides the many congregations that are affiliated with the order. The Augustinians sponsor a number of religious societies: The Archconfraternity of the Cincture of Our Mother of Consolation, St. Augustine, and St. Monica; the Pious Union and the White Scapular of Our Mother of Good Counsel; the Sodality of Christian Mothers; the Sodality of St. Rita and St. Clare; and the Pious Union of St. Nicholas for the Holy Souls. With respect to the habit, the Augustinians wear a tunic, a black leather cincture, and a capuche. The habit may be white or black, but in the U.S. white is worn by clerics only during the novitiate year, black at all other times. With the white habit a long scapular is worn.

Bibliography: D. GUTIÉRREZ, DictSpirAscMyst 4.2:983–1018, esp. bibliography. W. HÜMPFNER, LexThK[2] 1:1084–88. HENRY OF FRIEMAR, *Treatise on the Origin and Development of the*

Order of Hermit Friars and Its True and Real Title (1334), ed. R. ARBESMANN, *Augustiniana,* 6 (1956) 37–145. T. HERRERA, *Alphabetum augustinianum,* 2 v. (Madrid 1644). JORDAN OF SAXONY (von Quedlinburg), *Liber Vitasfratrum* (1357), ed. R. ARBESMANN and W. HÜMPFNER (New York 1943). A. GWYNN, *The English Austin Friars in The Time of Wyclif* (London 1940). H. JEDIN, *Papal Legate at the Council of Trent: Cardinal Seripando,* tr. F. C. ECKHOFF (St. Louis 1947). F. ROTH, "Cardinal Richard Annibaldi, First Protector of the Augustinian Order, 1243–1276," *Augustiniana* 2 (1952) 26–60, 108–149, 230–247; 3 (1953) 21–34, 238–313; 4 (1954) 5–24. F. TOURSCHER, *Old Saint Augustine's in Philadelphia, with Some Records of the Work of the Austin Friars in the United States* (Philadelphia 1937). G. DE SANTIAGO VELA, *Ensayo de una biblioteca iberoamericana de la orden de San Agustín,* 7 v. in 8 (Madrid 1913–31). *Analecta Augustiniana* (Rome 1905–). *Augustiniana* (Louvain 1951–). *Augustinianum* (Rome 1961–). *Archivo histórico hispano-agustiniano* (Madrid 1914–), superseded by *Archivo Agustiniano* (Madrid 1928–). **Illustration credit:** Fig. 1. Alinari-Art Reference Bureau.

[A. C. SHANNON]

AUGUSTINIS, AEMILIO DE, theologian, educator; b. Naples, Italy, Dec. 28, 1829; d. Rome, Jan. 17, 1899. Service in the army interrupted his legal studies at the Royal University in Naples. After briefly resuming the study of law, he entered the novitiate of the Society of Jesus at Conocchia, near Naples, Jan. 24, 1855. Garibaldi's revolution disrupted his theological studies, and he was transferred to the theologate at Laval, France, where he remained until his ordination, 1861. Two years later he left to spend a year in the Jesuit province of Champagne, France, after which he returned to Laval, where he served as professor of dogma, prefect of studies, and director of the library. In 1869 De Augustinis joined the faculty of the Jesuits' new scholasticate in Woodstock, Md., as professor of Sacred Scripture and librarian. During his tenure at Woodstock he served also as professor of ethics and dogma, and was one of the founders and editors of the *Woodstock Letters,* a news publication for Jesuits. In 1885 De Augustinis, who had been cited by Leo XIII for his contributions as a theologian, was assigned to the commission revising Jesuit theological studies. When the commission completed its work, he succeeded his former Woodstock colleague, Cardinal Camillo Mazzella, as professor of dogma at the Gregorian University in Rome. De Augustinis served also as rector of the Gregorian University from September 1891 to October 1895. In October 1897 he became ill and was forced to give up teaching, but he held certain minor positions until his death.

Bibliography: P. J. DOOLEY, *Woodstock and Its Makers* (Woodstock, Md. 1927). "Two of Woodstock's Founders," *Woodstock Letters* 29 (1900) 309–315.

[F. G. MC MANAMIN]

AUGUSTINUS, a posthumous work by Cornelius *Jansen, Bishop of Ypres, published in Louvain, Belgium, in October 1640, which is the source of the Jansenist controversies. The work was finished just before the author's premature death on May 6, 1638. In his will Jansen had entrusted its publication to his friends and disciples Henri Calenus and Liber Froidmont and at the same time had submitted the work to the judgment of the Holy See. Despite the precautions taken by Jansen, his project became known, especially by the Jesuits, who endeavored to prevent the publication of the work. At their intervention Stravius, the internuncio of Brussels, opposed the publishers with the decrees of Paul V (1611) and Urban VIII, which forbade any publication on the subject of grace. But these decrees had never been officially served at the University of Louvain, which consequently attached no importance to them. Since they had already gone to considerable expense in the printing, Calenus and Froidmont used this as an argument to obtain permission in September 1640 to put the work up for sale. However, in view of the difficulties that they had encountered, they did not include at the beginning of the work the dedicatory letter to Urban VIII that Jansen had composed. Despite its considerable bulk—nearly 1,300 folio pages in two columns of close printing—copies of *Augustinus* were disseminated rapidly across Europe, especially in France. In 1641 it was reprinted in Paris with the approval of six Parisian doctors; other editions followed in Rouen in 1642 and 1643. The French editions added to *Augustinus* an austere treatise by the Franciscan F. Conrius that condemned to hell children who died without Baptism. There were no further editions, a fact that shows only too well that the controversy had left *Augustinus* behind it.

See also JANSENISM.

Bibliography: L. CEYSSENS, *Sources relatives aux débuts du jansénisme et de l'antijansénisme* (Louvain 1957).

[L. J. COGNET]

AUGUSTUS II (THE STRONG), KING OF POLAND, Sept. 15, 1697, to Feb. 1, 1733, Elector of Saxony (Augustus I); b. Dresden, May 12, 1670; d. Warsaw. As the second son of John George III, Elector of Saxony, he was educated principally at his father's court. After joining the anti-French forces in the War of the League of Augsburg, he succeeded his brother, John George IV, as Elector of Saxony in 1694. On the death of *John III Sobieski, in 1696, he entered the contest for the Polish throne, in which cause he hastily espoused Catholicism. In the election that followed, he secured the support of a minority of the Polish nobility, who elected him king in opposition to F. L. de Bourbon, Prince of Conti, the majority candidate. The latter's delay in departing for *Poland enabled Augustus to occupy Cracow and to secure his own coronation. The manner of his ascent to the throne and his attempts to impose a despotic rule on Poland caused a cleavage to develop between himself and the Polish nobility, especially after it became known that he was secretly negotiating to partition Poland among those of his neighbors who would assist him in crushing the power of the nobility. At the end of the War with the Turks (1699) he allied Poland with Denmark and Russia in the Great Northern War against Charles XII of Sweden, whose possessions he and his allies hoped to partition. He marched against Livonia without the support of the Poles and was promptly defeated by Charles XII at Klissow in 1702. His continued alienation of large segments of the Polish nobility led to the election of Stanislas Leszczynski, a strong partisan of Charles XII, as antiking, in 1704. The renewal of his alliance with Russia led Charles XII in 1706 to invade Saxony, where Augustus was defeated again and forced to sign the humiliating Treaty of Altranstaedt, in which he recognized Leszczynski as King of Poland and abandoned his alliance with Russia. He supported the imperial cause during the War of the Spanish Succession, but reentered the war with Sweden after the battle of

Poltava (1709). In 1719 the Treaty of Stockholm restored peace between Poland and Sweden and recognized Augustus as King of Poland. Thereafter he followed a more conservative foreign policy.

From the time of Poltava onward, Augustus became involved in serious disputes with the Polish and Saxon nobility; with the former, because of his attempts to turn Poland into a hereditary monarchy; with the latter, because of his attempts to spread Catholicism within Saxony. Though his rule in Saxony saw the embellishment of Dresden, his rule in Poland marks one of the bleakest periods in Polish history. In fact, the growth of Russian influence in Polish affairs dates from this period, as does the decline of Poland that eventually culminated in her partition. Augustus left one son, Frederick Augustus, who succeeded him, and a large number of illegitimate children.

Bibliography: C. GURLITT, *August der Starke,* 2 v. (2d ed. Dresden 1924). P. HAAKE, *August der Starke* (Berlin 1927). K. EDER, LexThK[2] 1:1083.

[E. KUSIELEWICZ]

AUGUSTUS, ROMAN EMPEROR, founder of the principate; b. Sept. 23, 63 B.C.; d. Nola, Aug. 19, A.D. 14. He was the son of Gaius Octavius and Atia, niece of Julius Caesar. When Caesar adopted him, his name became Gaius Iulius Caesar Octavianus. Although only 18 at Caesar's death, he immediately showed unusual political ability and courage, and could not be set aside, as both Cicero and Marc Antony had hoped—if for different motives. With the efficient help of men like Maecenas, the famous patron of *Vergil and Horace, and the great general, M. Agrippa, he gradually made himself supreme in Italy, and in 31 B.C. won a decisive victory over the combined fleets of Antony and Cleopatra at the Battle of Actium.

Head of a statue of Augustus in the Museo delle Terme.

He was hailed as the bringer of peace, given the religious title of Augustus, and urged to restore a world torn by strife for nearly a century. He carried through a complete political, social, and religious organization of the Roman State and Empire. The old governmental machinery was retained as far as possible, but new elements were added. Administration of the city of Rome and of the provinces was reorganized; a professional army was recruited for the adequate defense of the frontiers; and emphasis was placed on the restoration of old Roman traditions and institutions, especially in the field of religion and morals. Writers and artists were encouraged to glorify Rome, her traditions, and her mission. The imperial cult (*see* RULER-CULT) was developed as a means of fostering loyalty and unity in the empire. The government established by Augustus was in theory a magistracy, in which the head of the state, as *princeps,* "first citizen," shared authority with the Senate. But the *princeps,* as *imperator* or "commander-in-chief" of the armies of the state, was the dominant ruler from the first. The principate in practice was a military dictatorship. In spite of certain inherent weaknesses in his system, Augustus created a government that was destined to last for centuries, and one under which Rome was to make her greatest and most influential contributions to civilization.

See also ROMAN EMPIRE.

Bibliography: A. MOMIGLIANO, OxClDict 122–124. M. P. CHARLESWORTH et al., CAH 10: ch. 1–18, bibliography 893–959.
Illustration credit: Alinari-Art Reference Bureau.

[M. R. P. MCGUIRE]

AULARD, FRANÇOIS ALPHONSE, historian of the French Revolution; b. Montbron (Charente), France, July 19, 1849; d. Paris, Oct. 23, 1928. After completing his studies at the École Normale Supérieure, he taught history at the Universities of Aix, Montpellier, and Poitiers before going to the University of Paris as the first incumbent of the chair of the history of the French Revolution; he taught there until 1922. In 1888 he founded the Société de l'histoire de la révolution française, as well as a review called *La Révolution française.* His *Histoire politique de la révolution française: Origines et développement de la démocratie et de la république: 1789–1804* (1901), later translated into English, established his leadership of the school that portrayed the republican movement of *Danton as the authentic French Revolution. The book maintained also that revolutionary religious policy was a by-product of war conditions rather than the result of deeply held convictions. His principal work on the religious history of the Revolution was *Le Christianisme et la Révolution française* (1925; Eng. tr. 1927). Although his views were narrowly political, Aulard's archival research and his use of the most advanced techniques of historical methodology constituted a major contribution to the study of the French Revolution.

Bibliography: A. MATHIEZ, "Aulard, historien et professeur," *Révolution française* 55 (1908). J. W. THOMPSON and B. J. HOLM, *History of Historical Writing . . .,* 2 v. (New York 1942) 2:275–277. A. MARTIN, DictBiogFranc 4:583–585.

[M. H. QUINLAN]

AULNE-SUR-SAMBRE, ABBEY OF, former Cistercian monastery, on the Sambre River, former Diocese of Liège, present Diocese of Tournai, Belgium (also Alna, Alne, Aune). Founded as a *Benedictine abbey in the 7th century, it came briefly under the Rule of St. *Augustine in 1144, but in 1147 became a *Cistercian abbey, daughterhouse of *Clairvaux. It continued as a flourishing monastery until it was burned by the French revolutionary armies in 1794. Its extensive ruins include the church (13th- and 16th-century Gothic) and several monastic buildings dating from the

Ruins of the 16th-century church of Aulne-sur-Sambre.

18th century when the entire monastery was restored in the baroque manner, except for the earlier church. Hagiography records several names from Aulne: Bl. Walter and Bl. Wéry (d. 1217), priors; Bl. Simon (d. 1229), a conversus. Jean de Gesves (d. 1420) was an effective reformer of monks and nuns. Outstanding in the intellectual sphere was Reginald de la Buissière (d. after 1400), master at Paris, Heidelberg, and Cologne. The abbey library, before it was burned, was especially noteworthy. In 1629, Aulne erected a university college in Louvain which in 1857 became the American College for clergy from the U.S.

Bibliography: *Statuta capitulorum generalium ordinis cisterciensis,* ed. J. M. Canivez, 8 v. (Louvain 1933–41), *passim.* L. Janauschek, *Origines cistercienses,* v.1 (Vienna 1877) 108. U. Berlière, *Monasticon belge* (Bruges 1890–) 1:329–342. E. Reusens, "Collège de l'abbaye d'Alne," *Analectes pour servir à l'histoire ecclésiastique de la Belgique* 23 (1892) 106–124. G. Boulmont, *Les Fastes de l'abbaye d'Aulne* (Ghent n.d., *c.* 1907). P. Clemen and C. Gurlitt, *Die Klosterbauten der Cistercienser in Belgien* (Berlin 1916). J. M. Canivez, *L'Ordre de Cîteaux en Belgique* (Forges-lez-Chimay, Belg. 1926) 94–103; DHGE 5:667–669. Cottineau 1:202–203. **Illustration credit:** Copyright, A.C.L., Brussels.

[M. STANDAERT]

AUNARIUS (AUNACHARIUS) OF AUXERRE, ST., bishop of Auxerre; b. Orléanais, date unknown; d. Auxerre, Sept. 25, 601. As a youth of noble birth, Aunarius was sent to the royal court of Burgundy, which he soon left in order to become a priest. Trained by Syagrius, Bishop of Autun, he was later elected and consecrated bishop of Auxerre (July 31, 561), participating in the Councils of Paris (573) and Mâcon (583, 585). He is famous for the 45 canons of a diocesan synod of Auxerre (578?, 588?), some of which discuss marriage and superstitions. Concerned for the cult of the saints, Aunarius arranged for a transcription of the martyrology attributed to St. *Jerome (592), and from that MS all extant copies are derived. He also provided vitae of his predecessors, *Amator (390–418) and *Germain (418–448), and organized liturgical prayer in the diocese. He received two letters from Pope *Pelagius II announcing the sending of relics. Aunarius was buried in the abbatial church of Saint-Germain. His relics, transferred to the crypt in 859 and stolen by the Calvinists in 1567, were recovered and are recognized as authentic.

Bibliography: ActSS Sept. 7:79–102. Hericus, *De gestis episcoporum Antissiodorensium,* PL 138:231–236. MGConc 1.1: 178–184. J. Lebeuf, *Mémoires concernant l'histoire civile et ecclésiastique d'Auxerre,* ed. A. Challe and M. Quantin, 4 v. (Auxerre 1848–55) v.1. G. Le Bras, "L'Organisation du diocèse d'Auxerre à l'époque mérovingienne," *Études de sociologie religieuse* (Paris 1950–) 1:27–38.

[P. COUSIN]

AUNEMUND OF LYONS, ST., bishop; d. Mâcon, France, Sept. 28, 658 (feast, Sept. 28). He was reared at the court of Dagobert I and Clovis II and probably held an official position there before his appointment to the archbishopric of *Lyons. According to *Bede (*Eccl. Hist.* 5.19), in 653 *Benedict Biscop and *Wilfrid stopped at Lyons during their journey to Rome and were hospitably received by Aunemund, who is called Dalfinus in Bede's narrative. The archbishop of Lyons was so favorably impressed by Wilfrid that he offered him "the government of a large part of France" (*ibid.*) and his niece as wife. Determined upon a different course of life, Wilfrid declined and went on to Rome, but after his visit there he returned to Lyons and remained for 3 years, received the *tonsure from Aunemund, and was present when Queen *Bathildis, a second Jezebel in the opinion of Wilfrid's biographer Stephen Eddi, sent soldiers and "commanded that the bishop be put to death" (*ibid.*). Most modern scholars, however, put the blame for Aunemund's murder on Ebroin (d. 681), Mayor of the Palace of Neustria. His body was returned to Lyons, and his name appears in the martyrologies of that city at the beginning of the 9th century.

Bibliography: MGSrerMer 6:197, 199–200. ActSS Sept. 7:673–698. Baudot-Chaussin 9:579–581. A. M. Zimmermann, LexThK[2] 1:1106. H. Leclercq, DACL 10.1:219–226. C. Lefebvre, Bibl Sanct 1:1311. R. Aigrain, *Catholicisme* 1:1064–65.

[H. DRESSLER]

AURAEUS, ST., 5th-century bishop of Mainz (feast, June 16). *Rabanus Maurus and the oldest sources link Auraeus and his sister, (St.) Justina, as martyrs in the time of Attila (*c.* 451). P. *Gams places Auraeus's martyrdom at the time of the destruction of Mainz by the Vandals (406). The monk Sigehard (13th century) wrote of SS. Auraeus and Justinus as the patron saints of Heiligenstadt. Justinus is called a deacon in a Heiligenstadt MS printed by the Bollandists, and he is sometimes called a subdeacon. Some would recognize in Justina and Justinus two persons, but such a coincidence of names in the circumstances of our information on Auraeus is unlikely.

Bibliography: ActSS June 4:37–79. Gams 289. H. Leclercq, DACL 11.1:26.

[W. A. JURGENS]

AUREA OF CÓRDOBA, ST., martyr; b. Córdoba or Seville, *c.* 810; d. Córdoba, July 19, 856 (feast: July 19). An Arab of noble descent, Aurea lived as a Christian with her mother Artemia in the monastery of Cuteclara for more than 30 years after the martyrdom of her brothers Adulfus and John in Córdoba. When her own relatives from Seville brought her before the cadi, also related to her, Aurea agreed to abandon Christianity but immediately returned to the practice of her faith. Persecuted a second time, she denied that her previous lapse had been genuine and, constant in her faith, was imprisoned and executed by decree of the emir. Her body was thrown into the Guadalquivir with the bodies of thieves and was never recovered. She was included in the Roman martyrology in 1583.

Bibliography: Source. EULOGIUS, *Memoriale sanctorum,* PL 115:815–818. Literature. A. LAMBERT, DHGE 5:706–707. E. P. COLBERT, *The Martyrs of Córdoba, 850–859* (Washington 1962) 263–264.

[E. P. COLBERT]

AURELIAN OF ARLES, ST., archbishop; d. Lyons, France, June 16, 551 (feast, June 16). He was elected to the See of *Arles to succeed Auxanius in 546. Pope *Vigilius wrote four letters to him between 546 and 550, the first of which (Aug. 23, 546) named him papal vicar for Gaul, i.e., for the kingdom of Childebert I (d. 558), son of *Clovis, and granted him the *pallium. On Oct. 28, 549, Aurelian signed the *acta* of the Fifth Synod of Orléans; his signature appears in the second place, immediately after that of the archbishop of Lyons. In its first canon the synod condemned *Eutyches and *Nestorius; it discussed further the matter of the *Three Chapters. This problem concerned three bishops, *Theodore of Mopsuestia, Ibas of Edessa, and *Theodoret of Cyr, whom the *Monophysites particularly detested and whom Emperor *Justinian I felt should be condemned by papal approval of the Three Chapters. Consulted on this subject by Aurelian, Vigilius, who was not disposed to give in to the Emperor and anxious to avoid weakening the authority of the Council of *Chalcedon of 451, replied in vague terms on April 29, 558. He made a special point of begging the bishop of Arles to use his influence with Childebert to prevent Totila, the Arian King of the Ostrogoths, who had captured Rome, from harming the Catholics living there. Showered with endowments by Childebert, Aurelian founded at Arles a monastery and a convent. His rule for the former, consisting of a prologue, 55 chapters, and an appendix, was based on that of St. *Benedict and of his predecessor *Caesarius of Arles; it later entered the collection of *Benedict of Aniane. Aurelian wished the monks to be educated, imposed a strict *cloister, and went beyond the Benedictine rule in prescribing additional *Psalms for the hours. The rule for the nuns of Saint Mary of Arles, in 40 articles, was, with variations, modeled on the rule for the monks. The archbishop was interred in the basilica of the Holy Apostles (Saint-Nizier), where his epitaph was discovered in 1308.

Bibliography: Sources. *Regula,* PL 68:385–408. MGEp 3:124–126, letter to Théodebert. ActSS June 4:91–94. Literature. Gall Christ 1:537–539. HistLittFranc 3:252–256. Ceillier[2] 11:198–201. Jaffé K 1:119–122. Hefele-Leclercq 3.1:157–164, synod of Orléans of 549. L. ROYER, DHGE 4:231–243, esp. 235–236, 242. S. BOSQ, *ibid.* 5:741. H. FUHRMANN, LexThK[2] 1:1107.

[J. DAOUST]

AURELIAN OF RÉOMÉ, first theorist of *Gregorian chant, flourished in mid-9th-century France. His importance rests upon his treatise *Musica disciplina* (*c.* 830; repr. in GerbScriptEccl 1:27–63). In the introduction he mentions his name and that of his monastery and Bernard to whom the treatise is dedicated (*Bernardo, futuro nostro Archiepiscopo*). No other facts about his life can be ascertained. His treatise is divided into two parts: ch. 1 to 7, which transmit the theories of music inherited from Greek authors through Boethius, Cassiodorus, and Isidore; and ch. 8 to 20, which deal with the chant repertory of his day. In the second part he reveals his familiarity with the practical performance of chant, treating at great length how antiphons are to be intercalated into psalm singing, both at Mass and at Office. In this context he speaks for the first time of modes, using the terminology *protus, deuterus, tritus,* and *tetrardus* in authentic and plagal forms. Several passages show his knowledge of a primitive notation and chironomy. The treatise is thus a juxaposition of ancient theory and contemporary practice without achieving a synthesis of the two.

Bibliography: A. GASTOUÉ, DACL 1.2:3150–51. H. HÜSCHEN, MusGG 1:858–859. J. P. PONTE, *The 'Musica disciplina' of Aurelianus Reomensis,* 3 v. (Unpub. doctoral diss., Brandeis U. 1961), a rev. text, tr. and commentary.

[R. G. WEAKLAND]

AURELIUS OF ARMENIA, ST., bishop in Armenia; d. Milan, 475 (feast, Nov. 9; formerly Sept. 13). Nothing is known of his early life. He is said to have brought from Cappadocia to Milan the relics of St. *Dionysius, Bishop of Milan (355), who had died in exile, and to have been buried in Milan beside him. In 830 Bp. Noting of Vercelli removed his body to *Hirsau, where he founded a church of which Aurelius is patron. The earliest vita, now lost, was written in the 9th century, probably at *Reichenau. The extant life is an 11th-century revision by Abbot Williram of Ebersberg.

Bibliography: ActSS Nov. 4:128–142. BHL 1:819–822. F. LUTZ, *Württemberger Vierteljahrbücher,* NS 33 (1939) 29–72. M. MILLER, LexThK[2] 1:1108.

[R. BROWNING]

AURELIUS AND SABIGOTONA, SS., martyrs; b. Córdoba, *c.* 820; d. Córdoba, July 27, 852 (feast, July 27). From Christian-Moslem homes, they lived as Christians in secret before and after their marriage. When the persecution of Christians began in 851, they devoted themselves to asceticism and chastity. They placed their two young daughters in the care of a monastery, and with their relatives Felix and Liliosa, let their faith be known publicly. Both couples were tried before the cadi and imprisoned before execution. At the same time George, a monk from Jerusalem, was slain for his denunciation of the prophet Mohammed. The relics of the five martyrs were buried in and near Córdoba. In 858 *Usuard and Odilard translated relics of Aurelius, Sabigotona, and George to Paris. Usuard included the five martyrs in his martyrology on August 27.

Bibliography: EULOGIUS, *Memoriale sanctorum* 2.10, and Aimoin, *Translatio* in PL 115:772–792, 939–960. E. P. COLBERT, *The Martyrs of Córdoba, 850–859* (Washington 1962).

[E. P. COLBERT]

AUREOLE (NIMBUS)

Latin, *aureolus* (of gold, golden), one of a number of symbols or devices used in pagan and Christian art and archeology to suggest or represent divinity, holiness, or eminence in the person portrayed. Closely related are the halo, *mandorla,* and glory. Such symbols antedate the Christian era; in Greek and Roman art the heads of gods, heroes, and distinguished citizens

Fig. 1. Christ surrounded by an aureole, detail of a 12th-century mosaic in the Cappella Reale at Palermo.

Fig. 3. Pope John VII with a square halo, 8th-century mosaic in the Grotto of St. Peter's Basilica, Rome.

were often portrayed with a circle of light or a rayed fillet about the head.

In Christian art the aureole is the symbol of divinity and has therefore been reserved for representing the Holy Trinity and Christ. It has been extended only to representations of the Virgin Mary. The aureole consists essentially in a radiant field of light that appears to surround the whole body of the person represented and to emerge from it. The rays of light may be attached directly to the body, or they may be separated from it. If the rays are not attached directly to the body, they give the impression of emerging from a central point, such as the head. The rays of light depicted in the aureole terminate in pointed flames, which may be white in color, or may be tinted with the colors of the rainbow. Early examples of the aureole are usually white, but in Renaissance art gold and blue are often used.

The Italian name for the aureole is *mandorla,* since the symbol was often enclosed in an almond-shaped framework. In some instances, instead of a framework, seven doves are used to frame the *mandorla,* denoting the seven gifts of the Holy Spirit. Other examples show a group of angels as a framework, although this form is less frequent. The *mandorla* is often used to depict certain mysteries of the life of Christ and the Blessed Virgin Mary, such as the Last Judgment or the Assumption into heaven.

The distinction between an aureole and a halo is somewhat vague, but the word halo refers most often to the symbol of divinity or holiness, which is placed about the head of the one represented, and which is enclosed in a geometrical figure. The shape and the form of the halo differ according to the degree of divinity, holiness, or eminence of the person depicted. The type of geometrical figure used to enclose the halo suggests also the degree of eminence in the person for whom it is used. The triangle, for example, is used exclusively for representations of the Holy Trinity, and particularly for the Father, the three sides of the triangle suggesting the Trinity. The halo used to portray Christ, the Blessed Virgin Mary, and the saints is circular. The cross within the circle is used only for Christ, and suggests the redemption through the cross. To indicate her eminence

Fig. 2. The Virgin surrounded by an aureole, detail of an Italian painting of the 15th century.

among the saints, the halo of the Virgin is elaborately decorated, while those of the saints are less ornate.

The square halo is used to distinguish eminent persons from canonized saints, and often for persons who may still be living. Thus for example, a square halo may be used to depict a living person such as the founder of a religious order, or of a great monastery, or a great benefactor. Since the square is thought to be a less perfect geometrical figure than the circle, it suggests the earth, while the circle suggests heaven. Polygons are also used, the hexagon being preferred; the sides of the polygon suggest the virtues or have some other allegorical meaning. The glory is merely a luminous glow that combines the halo surrounding the head and the aureole surrounding the whole body. This combination is used to suggest the most exalted state of being, and therefore is reserved for God as the lord of heaven, or for Christ as the judge of mankind, or for some other function associated closely with divinity.

See also HALO.

Bibliography: J. H. EMMINGHAUS, LexThK² 7:1004–05, with bibliog. H. LECLERCQ, DACL 12.1:1272–1312, with list of illus. E. ZOCCA, "Mandorla," EncCatt 7:1950–51. E. JOSI and A. P. FRUTAZ, EncCatt 8:1884–88. K. KEYSSNER, Pauly-Wiss RE 17.1 (1936) 591–624. M. COLLINET-GUÉRIN, *Histoire du nimbe* (Paris 1961). Réau IAC 1:423–425. Künstle Ikonog 1:25–29. **Illustration credits:** Figs. 1 and 3, Alinari-Art Reference Bureau. Fig. 2, Samuel H. Kress Collection, Philbrook Art Center, Tulsa, Okla.

[E. E. MALONE]

AURILLAC, ABBEY OF, former Benedictine monastery of Saint-Pierre (later Saint-Géraud), founded *c.* 890 by Count *Gerald of Aurillac in a valley where the present town of Aurillac was later to develop. Very early an integral part of the Cluniac Reform, the abbey flourished in the 10th century, numbering among its monks Gerbert, the future Pope *Sylvester II. Aurillac remained a powerful *Benedictine abbey to the end of the 16th century, holding as many as 74 dependent priories scattered over various provinces of France. But decline set in with the practice of *commendation and culminated in the secularization of 1561, which transformed the abbey into a collegiate church of secular priests. It was ruined during the *Wars of Religion (1569), and the church was not restored until 1642. Since the suppression of its college of priests in 1790 during the French Revolution, the church, which has undergone modifications, has been the main church of Aurillac in the Diocese of Saint-Flour.

Bibliography: G. SITWELL, ed. and tr., *St. Odo of Cluny . . . St. Gerald of Aurillac* (New York 1958). GallChrist 2:438–447. G. M. BOUANGE, *Histoire de l'abbaye d'Aurillac,* 2 v. (Paris 1899). P. FONTAINE, DHGE 5:757–760.

[L. GAILLARD]

AURISPA, GIOVANNI, humanist, collector and translator of Greek manuscripts; b. probably in Noto, Sicily, *c.* 1369; d. Ferrara, Italy, 1459. Nothing is known about his early life. He may have studied in Naples. From 1414 to 1419 he had a school in Savona. He taught Greek literature in Bologna in 1424 and in Florence from 1425 until 1427. The marquis of *Este appointed him tutor to his son Meliaduce in 1427, and Aurispa moved to Ferrara. He was an emissary of the Este to Rome and to the Council of *Basel in 1433. Until 1443 he was a curial secretary; thereafter Aurispa spent the remainder of his life in the service of the Este, and became famous for his discovery of a large number of Greek MSS. From his trips to Greece (*c.* 1413 and from 1421 to 1423) he brought back to Italy more than 200 MSS, including the *Iliad* and works of Aristophanes, Xenophon, Sophocles, Aeschylus, Plato, and Plutarch. Many of these MSS were copied, sold, or translated, thus further diffusing the knowledge of Greek classics in the West. While attending the Council of Basel, he discovered in Germany the Latin commentary on Terence by Donatus.

Bibliography: *Carteggio di Giovanni Aurispa,* ed. R. SABBADINI (Rome 1931). R. SABBADINI, *Biografia documentata di G. A.* (Noto, Sicily 1890); "G. A., scopritore di testi antichi," *Historia* 1 (Milan 1927) 77–84. P. F. PALUMBO, EncCatt 2:413. W. L. GRANT, "On G. A.'s Name," PhilolQ 32 (1953) 219–223.

[E. G. GLEASON]

AURORA IAM SPARGIT POLUM, a hymn once ascribed to St. Ambrose, but now generally considered to be the work either of Pope Gregory the Great (Blume) or of an anonymous author as late as the 8th century (Szövérffy). Its four "Ambrosian" strophes are in octosyllabic iambic dimeter (*see* HYMNOLOGY). In vigorous but rather obscure language, the hymn greets the dawn and prays for the shadows of night and evil to disappear so that its singers may be fit to welcome both this and the last day. Appearing in the 9th-century "Later Hymnal" (which *Blume considers Irish in origin, though Wilmart and others call it "Old Benedictine"), it spread widely throughout Carolingian Europe as a hymn for Lauds on Saturdays. Closely following earlier usage, the Roman *Breviary (1632) assigns it to the Saturday office from the Octave of Epiphany to the first Sunday in Lent, and from the Octave of Corpus Christi to the first Sunday of Advent. The Mozarabic Breviary (*see* MOZARABIC RITE) of 1775 assigns it to Matins for Saturdays in Lent. Among its English translators are E. Caswall ("The dawn is sprinkling in the East," *Lyra Catholica,* 1849) and R. Campbell ("The morn has spread its crimson rays," *St. Andrew's Hymnal,* 1850).

Bibliography: B. STÄBLEIN, ed., *Monumenta monodica medii aevi* (Kassel-Basel 1956–) 1.1:665. AnalHymn 51:xiii–xxi, 34. C. BLUME, *Unsere liturgischen Lieder* (Regensburg 1932) 149–152. M. BRITT, ed., *The Hymns of the Breviary and Missal* (new ed. New York 1948). Connelly Hymns. A. WILMART, "Le Psautier de la reine," RevBén 28 (1911) 341–376. Julian DictHym 93–94. A. S. WALPOLE, ed., *Early Latin Hymns* (Cambridge, Eng. 1922) 279–280. Raby ChrLP 36–40. Szövérffy AnnLatHymn 1:142, 214–216.

[J. DU Q. ADAMS]

AURORA LUCIS RUTILAT, an Easter hymn consisting of eleven 4-line strophes of somewhat loose iambic dimeter, unusually rich in end-rhyme and internal alliteration, which is strikingly exemplified in the first strophe. The theme is one of joy at the Lord's triumphant Resurrection, successive incidents of which banish fear among His disciples. Vivid and extremely visual in development despite a simple vocabulary, this hymn may be a stylistic ancestor of late Carolingian rhythms and Easter *tropes. It was admired by Abelard. Once attributed to St. *Ambrose, it is now thought to be of Gallican origin (Wilmart); it was composed sometime between the 6th and the early 8th century (Bulst, Szövérffy). Besides St. Ambrose's authentic works, this and *Christe, qui lux es et dies* are the only pieces common to the two hymnal traditions most widespread before the Carolingian liturgical reforms (Blume, Raby, Walpole).

The hymn is generally sung at Matins or Lauds daily from Low Sunday to the Ascension—although the Mozarabic Breviary (*see* MOZARABIC RITE) of 1502 assigns it to Prime in Paschaltide. It was divided and drastically altered by the compilers of the Roman *Breviary of 1632. Lines 1 to 16, scarcely recognizable as *Aurora caelum purpurat,* were left at Lauds between Low Sunday and Ascension (and in the Dominican rite, at Matins during Paschaltide); lines 17 to 32 (*Tristes erant Apostoli*) were assigned to Vespers and Matins of Apostles and Evangelists during Paschaltide; and lines 32 to 44 (*Paschale mundo gaudium,* originally *Claro paschali gaudio*), to Lauds of that Office. Pope *Pius V was responsible for the division at line 32 and for the association with the Common of Apostles. The best known English translations of both versions of this hymn, whole and divided, are those by E. Caswall (1849) and J. M. Neale (1852 and later).

Bibliography: B. STÄBLEIN, ed., *Monumenta monodica medii aevi* (Kassel-Basel 1956–) 1.1:665, melodies. AnalHymn 51: 89–90. M. BRITT, ed., *The Hymns of the Breviary and Missal* (new ed. New York 1948). C. BLUME, *Unsere liturgischen Lieder* (Regensburg 1932) 53–59, 188–190. A. BYRNES, ed., *Hymns of the Dominican Missal and Breviary* (St. Louis 1943), nos. 27, 28. W. BULST, ed., *Hymni Latini antiquissimi LXXV* (Heidelberg 1956) 114–115. Connelly Hymns, No. 59. A. WILMART, "Le Psautier de la reine," RevBén 28 (1911) 341–376. Julian Dict Hym 94–96. A. S. WALPOLE, ed., *Early Latin Hymns* (Cambridge, Eng. 1922) xi–xx, 356–359. Raby ChrLP 36–40. Szövérffy AnnLatHymn 1:163, 214–216.

[J. DU Q. ADAMS]

AUSCULTA FILI, a bull of Pope *Boniface VIII indicting King *Philip IV the Fair of France and announcing a synod for the reform of the Church in France. It was written Dec. 5, 1301. It is the most striking example in practice of Boniface's theory of the direct power of the papacy over the secular order (*see* CHURCH AND STATE). "Wherefore, dearest son," Boniface wrote, "let no one persuade you that you have not a superior or that you are not subordinate to the head of the ecclesiastical hierarchy. For he is a fool who so thinks, and whosoever pertinaciously affirms it brands himself an unbeliever." Philip burned the letter publicly in Paris. He circulated an emended version, together with a pretended answer to Boniface that started "your great fatuousness . . . in temporalities we are subject to no one." There followed 2 years of bitter controversy culminating at Anagni, in September 1303. Though the original bull was burned, copies are extant in Boniface's *Register* in the Vatican Archives. The register copy is mutilated, since *Clement V had the more forceful passages erased. See *Les Registres de Boniface VIII,* ed. G. Digard (Paris, 1921), 3, 328–335.

Bibliography: J. RIVIÈRE, DHGE 5:767–768; *Le Problème de l'Église et de l'État au temps de Philippe le Bel* (Paris 1926). T. S. R. BOASE, *Boniface VIII* (London 1933).

[L. E. BOYLE]

AUSONIUS, DECIMUS MAGNUS, rhetorician and poet; b. Bordeaux, *c.* 310; d. *c.* 394. At the age of 30 he began to teach as a *grammaticus,* then became rhetor at Bordeaux, where he had St. *Paulinus of Nola as a student. The Roman Emperor *Valentinian I appointed him tutor to his son Gratian in 365, and he held a number of high offices including the consulship (379). After the death of Gratian in 383, Ausonius apparently retired to Bordeaux. His poetry is of a purely factitious inspiration and shows little influence of the Christian faith that he seems to have professed during his association with the Emperor Valentinian (364–375). His *opuscula* include an *Ephemeris,* short poems on the business of a typical day; *Parentalia,* commemorative verses on 32 deceased members of his family; and *Commemoratio Professorum Burdigalensium,* on famous professors connected with Bordeaux. Romantic critics speak highly of his *Mosella,* a description of the Moselle River and its valley. He wrote a *Versus paschales* or paschal prayer in 31 hexameters with a Nicene confession of the Trinity for the Emperor and an *Oratio versibus rhopalicis,* so called because the verses begin with words of one syllable that are followed by a regular increase in the number of syllables, giving the poem the shape of a club (*rhopalicus*). Three of his 25 verse letters are addressed to St. Paulinus of Nola.

Bibliography: MGAuctAnt 5.2; 1883, ed. C. SCHENKL; Loeb ClLib; 1919–21, tr. H. G. E. WHITE; *The Mosella,* ed. and tr., E. H. BLAKENEY (London 1933). F. MARX, Pauly-Wiss RE 2.2 (1896) 2562–80. P. DE LABRIOLLE, DHGE 5:773–779. Altaner 478–479.

[M. P. CUNNINGHAM]

AUSTIN, JOHN, controversialist and hymnodist; b. Walpole, Norfolk, 1613; d. London, 1669. Austin (pseudonym, William Birchley) was educated at St. John's College, Cambridge, where he was contemporary with John *Sergeant. He became a Catholic *c.* 1640 and left the university for Lincoln's Inn. For some time he was tutor to Walter Fowler of St. Thomas's, Staffordshire, a noted recusant literary center. He probably visited the English Hospice at Rome in 1640 and 1646. During the Interregnum Austin belonged to the group of Catholics (White, Sergeant, Holden, Belson, Keightley) who advocated allegiance to the Cromwellian government and hoped for a degree of toleration and sympathy from the Independents. Austin's *Christian Moderator* (1651–53) advocated toleration for recusants from an Independent viewpoint and was quick to use T. Hobbes's *Leviathan* (1651) in support of its arguments. When the question of toleration arose again at the Restoration, Austin published *Reflexions upon the Oathes of Supremacy and Allegiance* (1661). He published also *Devotions in the Ancient Way of Offices* (1668), a version of the primer with original hymn versions, which ran through several editions. There had been several recusant primer versions before this, but Austin's was adapted for non-Catholic use by Theophilus Dorrington (*Reform'd Devotions,* 1686) and Susanna Hopton (*Devotions in the Ancient Way of Offices,* ed. G. Hickes, 1700); both these works were often reedited. The hymns in Austin's book also found their way separately into other non-Catholic collections, most notably S. Speed's *Prison Pietie* (1677), John Wesley's *Collection of Psalms and Hymns* (Charlestown 1737), and Roundell Palmer's *Book of Praise* (1862).

Bibliography: O. SHIPLEY, *Annus Sanctus* (New York 1884). Julian DictHym. E. HOSKINS, *Horae Beatae Mariae Virginis* (London 1901). DictEngCath 1:87–90.

[T. A. BIRRELL]

AUSTIN, DIOCESE OF (AUSTINIENSIS), suffragan of the metropolitan See of *San Antonio. When erected in 1948, the diocese consisted of 7 counties separated from the Archdiocese of San Antonio; 19, from the Diocese of Galveston (later *Galveston-Houston); and 4, from the Diocese of *Dallas, all in Texas. In 1961 Austin was reduced in size when three of its counties were taken for the new Diocese of San Angelo. Catholicity in the area dates from the Spanish colonization in the 18th century. Missions San Francisco de los Neches, Nuestra Señora de la Purísima Concepción, and San José de los Nazonis were established in Travis County around 1730. The San Xavier Missions in Williamson County followed: San Francisco Xavier (1746), San Ildefonso (1748), and Nuestra Señora de la Candelaria (1749). The missionaries who served in the area included Father Aponte y Lis, first pastor of a permanent mission; Bartolomé García, author of the first Ritual for the administering of Sacraments to the Texas Indians; and José Francisco Ganzabal, martyred at Mission Candelaria. State historical markers designate the sites of these missions, which were totally destroyed by Indians.

The history of parishes within the diocese began in 1836 with the building of a church at Frelsburg and the erection of a parish there in 1847. John Mary *Odin, who became the first bishop of Galveston in 1847, celebrated the first Mass in Austin, the capital of the Republic of Texas, in 1840. The first church in Austin, St. Patrick's, was dedicated in 1855; its name was changed to St. Mary's of the Immaculate Conception in 1866. A new St. Mary's was built in 1875 and became the cathedral in 1948, at which time the Diocese of Austin was placed under the patronage of the Immaculate Conception. Louis Joseph Reicher, who had served for 30 years as chancellor of the Diocese of Galveston, was named first bishop of Austin and consecrated at St. Mary's Cathedral, Galveston, April 14, 1948. Under his direction the diocese sponsored a building program to care for the needs of a growing population. In 1963

St. Mary's Cathedral, Austin, Texas.

Catholics numbered about 125,340 in a total population of 728,850, and were organized in 74 parishes and 31 missions. They were served by 147 priests, of whom 57 were religious, including Claretians, Holy Cross Fathers, Paulists, Oblates of Mary Immaculate, Dominicans, Franciscans, and Divine Word Missionaries. There were 159 brothers and 255 sisters, representing 18 communities of religious women, helping to staff the diocese's 6 high and 34 elementary schools, 6 general hospitals, and 1 home for the aged. St. Edward's University (1876), Austin, enrolled nearly 600 men students.

Bibliography: C. E. CASTAÑEDA, *Our Catholic Heritage in Texas, 1519–1936,* 7 v. (Austin 1936–58).

[M. C. DEASON]

AUSTRALIA

The world's smallest continent and largest island (roughly the size of the U.S.), it is 3 million square miles in area and is situated in the western Pacific in latitudes south of the Equator corresponding to the latitudes of Mexico north of the Equator. Geologically the most ancient of the continents, it has the largest desert in the southern hemisphere (600,000 square miles). Forty per cent of its land mass lies within the tropics. The bulk of the population lives in the temperate southeastern quarter of the continent. Politically, Australia is a sovereign state, a parliamentary democracy within the British Commonwealth of Nations. Like the U.S., it has a federal government with a written constitution; it also elects six state governments corresponding to the six original British colonies—New South Wales, Victoria, South Australia, Tasmania, Queensland, and Western Australia—which formed a federal union in 1900. Socially, Australia is a "welfare state" and a highly urbanized pluralist society, in which Church and State, constitutionally separate, cooperate for the public welfare. The total white population in 1961 was 10,508,000, of whom 9,274,000 described themselves as Christians. Of these, 2,620,000 were Catholics.

DISCOVERY AND SETTLEMENT

Despite an ancient belief in a Great South Land (*Terra Australis Incognita*) and successive Hindu, Chinese, and Moslem migrations and colonizations in the island world of the western Pacific, Australia remained a mystery until comparatively recent times.

Discovery. It was left for European explorers and colonial traders to unveil the hidden continent. Spanish and Portuguese mariners, based on Peru, came close to discovering it in the 16th and early 17th centuries. One of them, Pedro Fernandez de Quiros, inspired by religious idealism and missionary fervor, believed himself providentially chosen to discover the elusive land for Christ. In preparation, he made a pilgrimage to Rome and received the blessing of Pope Clement VIII on his venture. In December 1605 he set out from Callao, sailing due west until he reached a harbor that in the first flush of discovery he named "Austrialia del Espiritu Santo." But through errors in measuring longitude, he had reached not the Australian coast, but the islands we know today as the New Hebrides. In the 17th century, Dutch seamen, sponsored by the Dutch East India Company, discovered the Australian coast in their voyages out of Batavia for gold, spices, and trade. They named the land New Holland, but finding

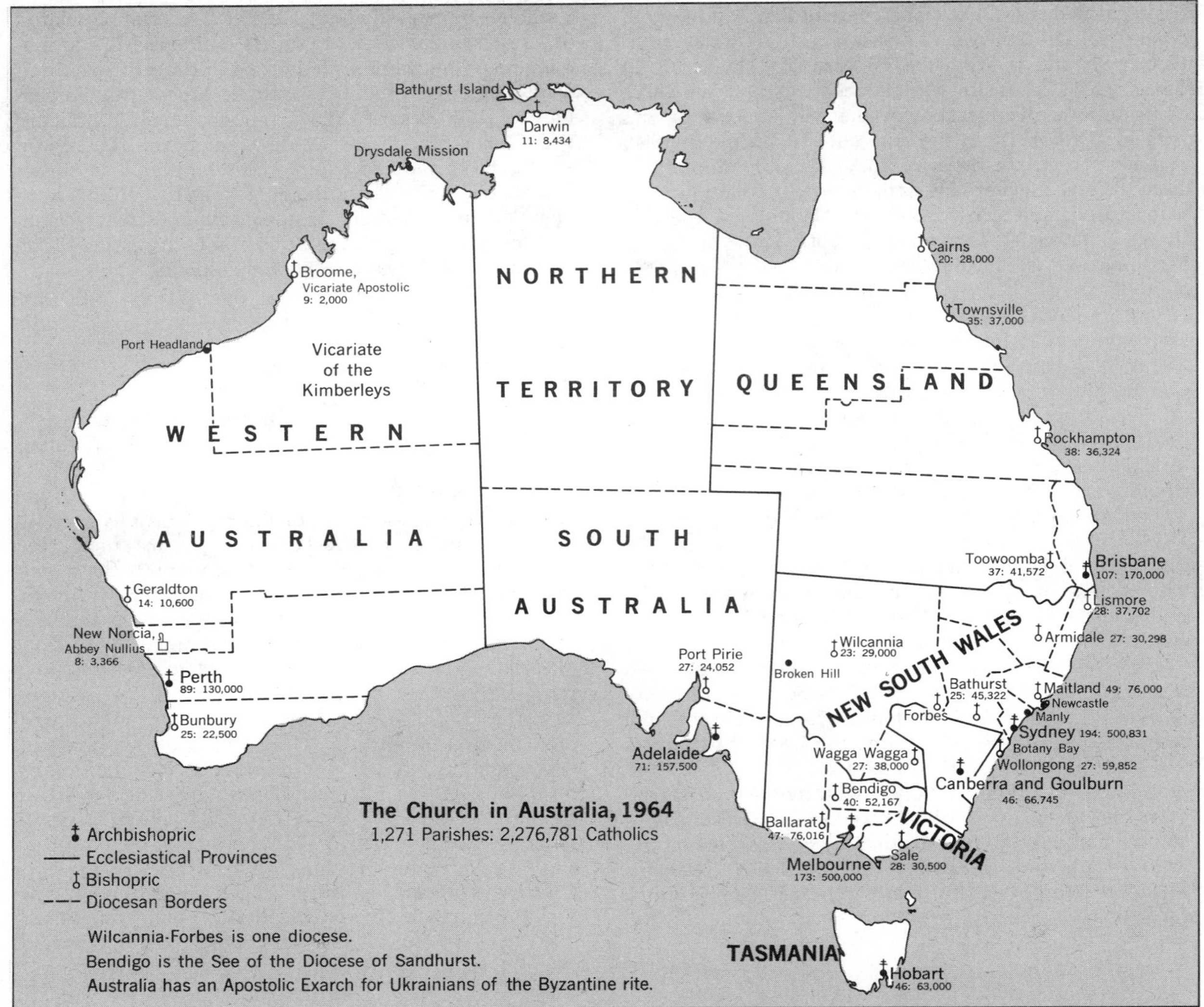

Fig. 1. Ecclesiastical provinces coincide with civil states, except Canberra and Goulburn include part of New South Wales and Australian Capital Territory; Northern Territory and South Australia form the province of Adelaide.

only the dry and barren western coast, they were not interested in colonizing it. In the end, the English navigator Captain James Cook discovered by chance the rich east coast of the continent, landed at Botany Bay, and claimed the country for the British crown (April 1770).

Settlement. The American War of Independence led to the first white settlement. In the early 18th century, the British government began sending convicts to her North American colonies, where they were sold by shipping contractors to plantation owners. But Washington's victory closed the transatlantic colonies to the traffic, and England's criminals soon overcrowded the prisons and overflowed into the hulks on the Thames. A member of Captain Cook's crew had proposed a settlement at Botany Bay as a haven for American loyalists "to atone in time for the loss of our American colonies." But the Pitt ministry seized upon the idea to relieve the cluttered British jails. On Jan. 26, 1788, a thousand souls, of whom over 700 (estimates vary) were prisoners of the crown, landed at a little cove and named the spot Sydney, after the British secretary of state. In due course New Holland was renamed New South Wales.

The colony failed as a penal institution and as a small farm settlement, but succeeded as a land of vast estates, growing wool for English mills. A unique system of colonial slavery evolved, with a master class of sheep ranchers exploiting free convict labor. But the abuses of the system, the growth of liberal and humanitarian ideas, and free immigration led to its suppression. During the period 1788 to 1850, some 187,000 free settlers migrated, and 146,000 convicts were transported to Australia.

The convicts comprised four main groups: urban law breakers from the towns, rural workers led by poverty to offend against property and gaming laws, educated felons of the lower middle class, and social reformers and political agitators. Although lawbreakers formed by far the largest portion, the majority were transported for crimes that would be regarded as trivial today. The social and political reformers were in general condemned for crimes that are today regarded as virtues. In the early years the largest group came from

Ireland, following the Irish Rebellion of 1798. Between 1795 and 1804 nearly 6,000 Irishmen were transported to New South Wales. They included many of considerable education and ability, inspired by the normal idealism associated with a struggle for national freedom.

The early settlers, both bond and free, brought with them three different world views—the Protestant, the Catholic, and that of the *Enlightenment. Main themes in the history of Christian civilization in Australia are the decline of Protestant groups, through compromise and alliance with secular liberalism; the efforts of the Catholic Church to protect its members from secular influences, especially in education; and the rise of a labor movement, influenced by Protestant, Catholic, and secular ideas on social justice.

Catholic Origins

The religious welfare of the convicts was apparently an afterthought on the part of the colonial office. The first official instructions contained no reference to religion. Nevertheless an Anglican chaplain accompanied the First Fleet. Later *Instructions,* however, directed the governor "to enforce a due observance of religion" and "take steps for the celebrations of public worship as circumstances permit." The religion to be observed was that of the Church of England.

No provision was made for the religious needs of Catholics, even though two Irish priests who attended Catholics in Newgate prison and on the hulks applied more than once for the "privilege" of accompanying the "First Fleet," even offering to pay their own fares.

Attendance at Anglican religious service was compulsory for all convicts, whatever their religion, under penalty of reduced rations, the stocks, or the lash. For Catholics, this violation of conscience and religious rights lasted for 32 years, save for two short periods of toleration.

When the flood tide of Irish rebel transportation began to ebb, the Irish formed a quarter of the population. Among them were three priests, convicted for alleged complicity in the '98 Rebellion. They were Fathers Peter O'Neill (or O'Neil), James Dixon, and James Harold. They eventually returned to Ireland; O'Neill in 1803, Dixon in 1808, and Harold in 1810.

Father Dixon. Dixon alone left his mark on the religious history of the colony. He was officially emancipated and authorized to exercise his priestly ministry (April, 1803). Dixon offered the first public Mass in the settlement (May 15, 1803). There was no altar stone, an Irish convict made a small chalice of tin, and some old damask curtains served as vestments. The official government *Gazette* (May 22) reported briefly that "on Sunday last the Roman Catholic congregation asembled for the first time in Sydney."

But Father Dixon's Masses, which "had the most salutary effect on Irish Catholics," according to the governor's report, lasted less than 12 months. When a foolhardy insurrection of some 400 United Irishmen took place outside Sydney (April 1804), the governor concluded that the Irish leaders had used the Mass gatherings to stir up the revolt and held Dixon personally responsible. His permission to celebrate Mass and his salary were withdrawn. He remained another 4 years in Sydney, ministering privately to Catholics, with several Protestants contributing to his support.

During the following decade, the Catholics of Sydney were without the services of a priest, and they were virtually forgotten by the English vicars apostolic and the Irish bishops. The period has been called the "catacomb era" of the Church in Australia. The faith was kept alive by laymen alone.

Father O'Flynn. In August 1816, a petition to the Vatican on behalf of the Catholics of New South Wales

Fig. 2. Ruins of the old convict settlement at Port Arthur, Tasmania, founded in 1830.

pleaded for a priest. Within a month, Father Jeremiah O'Flynn, a former Cistercian monk who had become a secular priest, was appointed prefect apostolic. Although neither the colonial office nor the vicar apostolic of London would endorse his appointment, O'Flynn paid his own passage out, hoping that authorization would eventually follow, and crashed the barriers of the penal colony. When he arrived in Sydney (November 1817), the governor told him that no "Popish missionary" would be allowed to work in the colony. He also prohibited him from saying Mass in public, but allowed him to remain temporarily, since O'Flynn claimed that his credentials were on the way. When they failed to arrive, a warrant for O'Flynn's deportation was served (Dec. 12, 1817). But O'Flynn determined to evade the authorities and spar for time. He eluded them for 6 months, meanwhile carrying on a busy underground apostolate. Eventually he was arrested, lodged in a common jail, and put aboard a ship for London (May 20, 1818).

O'Flynn's apostolic escapade had an unexpected sequel. The matter of his deportation from Sydney was raised in the House of Commons, and a newspaper campaign aroused public opinion against the intolerant treatment of Catholics in Australia. The most forthright and effective writing came from the pen of Father John *England, parish priest of Bandon (who was destined to become one of the foremost bishops in the U.S.). When chaplain to Cork jail, he had volunteered for New South Wales and had helped O'Flynn before his departure for Sydney. Father England published a vigorous appeal to the authorities in the form of an open letter (Jan. 5, 1819) to the vicars apostolic and government of England, demanding legal status for the Catholic Church in Australia. As a result, almost 10 years before Catholic emancipation in England, freedom of conscience was allowed, and a Catholic mission was established and subsidized in Australia. O'Flynn, therefore, emerged as the unwitting reformer of British social policy in New South Wales. He spent his last years in Philadelphia (U.S.), where he died in 1831.

Foundation. The Church was officially founded in Australia when Dom Edward Slater, OSB, was appointed vicar apostolic of the Cape of Good Hope with jurisdiction over Madagascar, Mauritius and New Holland with the adjacent islands, and two volunteer Irish priests, John Joseph *Therry and Philip Conolly, landed in Sydney (May 1820).

Despite their official status, their presence was resented. Anglicanism was regarded by the governor as the established religion, *de facto,* if not *de jure,* and the priests were given official instructions forbidding them to receive converts, to perform mixed marriages, or to attend Catholic children in state institutions. After 2 years in Sydney, Conolly went to Tasmania to minister to the convicts, while Therry carried on a tireless apostolate on the mainland.

Development Since 1820

The coming of Catholic *Emancipation in Britain in 1829 was soon felt in the antipodes. An 1828 census gave a total population of 36,600, of whom 24,250 were Protestants and 11,230 Catholics. In February 1833, a remarkable young English Benedictine, William *Ullathorne, arrived in Sydney as vicar-general. Although only 27 years of age, he provided vigorous leadership for the struggling Catholics, closely studied the social effects of the convict system, and during a visit to England campaigned brilliantly for its suppression. Ullathorne recommended to the Holy See that the Australian mission be separated from Mauritius. In May 1834 New Holland became a vicariate in its own right, and in September 1835, Ullathorne's friend and teacher at *Downside Abbey, John Bede *Polding, arrived as Australia's first bishop. Meanwhile a new policy resulted in the passing of a church act (1836), which placed all religious groups in the colony on an equal footing. In 1841, when convict transportation to eastern Australia officially ended, the total population was 211,000, of whom 40,000 were Catholics. There were 15 churches, several chapels, 31 schools, 24 priests, and a community of nuns. In 1842 two new sees were erected, the hierarchy was established, and Dr. Polding became an archbishop.

In the 1850s Australia was virtually rediscovered. Gold, found in fabulous quantities, attracted waves of immigrants from all parts of the world. Population trebled in a decade. Between 1841 and 1891 the Catholic population increased from 40,000 to 713,800. When the colonies federated as the Commonwealth of Australia (1901), Catholics numbered 856,000 in a total population of 3,782,000. During the second half of the 19th century, the present ecclesiastical provinces and most of the archdioceses and their suffragan sees were established.

The 20th century has witnessed a remarkable numerical increase in the Catholic population. By the variety and activity of its charitable works, organizations, and missions to the aborigines, the Church has proved energetically apostolic. It has also met the challenge of communism and provided its own solution to the problem of providing a Catholic educational system.

Missions to the Aborigines. When Australia was colonized, it was already occupied by a race of dark-skinned peoples of extremely primitive life and culture. Ethnologists have found so many differences between this native race and other great divisions of mankind that the Australian aboriginal is now classified as a special group, the Australoid. Authorities differ on how many aborigines occupied mainland Australia at the time of the first European settlement. A common estimate is approximately 300,000. The occupation of their tribal domains, the brutality of settlers, and contact with the white man and his vices led to the steady decline of the natives. The aboriginal population (full-blood and half-caste) in 1954 totaled only 70,680, scattered over the whole continent, but mostly in Western Australia, Queensland, and the Northern Territory.

A Catholic mission to the aborigines was attempted as early as 1843. But the nomadic nature of the aboriginal did not lend itself to traditional missionary methods. Results were disappointing. The most successful was at Bathurst Island under Father Francis Xavier Gzell, MSC, administrator (1906) and first bishop of Darwin (1938). For his work among the aborigines, Bishop Gzell was awarded The Order of the British Empire and the French Legion of Honor. The diocese of Darwin, staffed by *Sacred Heart Missionaries, and the vicariate of the Kimberleys, staffed by *Pallottines, both situated in northwestern Australia

Fig. 3. "Aboriginal Madonna," painting by Karel Kupka in the War Memorial Cathedral, Darwin, Australia.

and together covering an area of 642,000 square miles, conduct the main missions to aborigines. Other mission settlements are at *New Norcia and Drysdale River (West Australia) Palm and Fantome Islands (Queensland) and Bowraville and Wilcannia (New South Wales).

Communism and the Church. When World War II ended, every major trade union in Australia except one was either controlled by Communists or in the process of falling under their control. The National Secretariat of *Catholic Action, acutely aware of the situation and its dangers to the nation, organized groups of Catholics in various cities, particularly in Melbourne and Sydney, in a social studies movement, which became known as "The Movement," to counter Communist infiltration in the unions. Members of The Movement cooperated with the Australian Labor party in industrial groups; this cooperation had spectacular success against the Communists in the years 1948 to 1953. But their success in the industrial field had repercussions in the political field; this success was followed by a split in the Labor party and the formation of a splinter Democratic Labor party. This party had the support of The Movement and has attracted a large Catholic vote in subsequent national elections.

Catholic Action. Since these developments could be traced, directly or indirectly, to the National Secretariat of Catholic Action (NSCA) and its director, B. A. Santamaria, the question of the nature and aims of Catholic Action and the complex question of the relationship between religion and politics became subjects of national debate. There was even a division of opinion among Catholics, including the bishops themselves, on the best way to counter communism in terms of Catholic Action theory and practice. This raised the question whether or not The Movement was Catholic Action in the strict sense. The problem was submitted to the Holy See. The decision was in effect a compromise: on the one hand The Movement, which began as a social studies movement, should restrict itself to the religious and moral formation of the laity; on the other, the laity should be free, and indeed feel themselves obliged, to act in the trade union and political fields in the struggle against communism. As a result Movement groups were reconstructed for exclusively adult educational purposes under the direct control of each bishop in his own diocese. But to carry on the work in the temporal sphere, Movement leaders created a strictly civic organization to continue their active fight against communism. This was founded in December 1957 as the National Civil Council.

The NSCA functioned from 1938 to 1954, when the Young Christian Workers (YCW), National Catholic Girls Movement (NCGM), Young Christian Students Movement (YCSM), and the National Catholic Rural Movement (NCRM) became autonomous. The Institute of Social Order (ISO) carries on sociological research and publishes social study programs and periodicals for the lay apostolate and social movement. The ISO also sponsors an annual Christian Social Week at Melbourne University in the form of a symposium of Catholic and non-Catholic scholars on some problem of national or international concern.

One of the most widely known activities of the NSCA was the publication of social justice statements authorized by the Australian bishops. Inaugurated in 1940 with a bishops' statement on social justice, these annual pronouncements drew inspiration from papal social encyclicals and endeavored to apply them to the major social and economic problems of the country. The series ended in 1962 with a pastoral letter of the hierarchy on Vatican Council II.

Fig. 4. View of Bourke Street, Melbourne, with St. Patrick's Cathedral in the background.

Fig. 5. St. Mary's Cathedral, Sydney, designed by the Australian architect William Wardell, begun in 1866.

Catholic Organizations. Adult education is provided by a variety of lay apostolate organizations. All capital cities have central Catholic libraries, where lunch-hour lectures, evening classes, or discussion groups are available. During the 1930s Melbourne's library became the center of a vigorous lay movement of university graduates and undergraduates called the Campion Society. With the encouragement of Archbishop *Mannix, this movement, which spread to other cities, led to the establishment of the NSCA. Lay leaders inaugurated a general social studies movement and developed four specialized movements of Catholic Action: the YCW, NCGM, YCS, and NCRM. Some years later the League of St. Thomas More was established for business and professional men. In each movement, the emphasis in training programs and discussion groups was on the social and moral problems peculiar to the environment of each group. The YCW and NCGM amalgamated to form the largest Christian youth movement in Australia. Established in 20 dioceses, its membership approximated 10,000 boys and girls. It contacts another 26,000 young people through services it sponsors, such as *Cana conferences, housing cooperatives, and sporting activities. Organized competitive sport under Church auspices is common throughout the country. Tennis and basketball courts are regarded as essential equipment of fully developed parishes. Over 150 members of the YCW have served for a year or two as lay missionaries in New Guinea. Over 50 former members have been ordained to the priesthood, and 130 are at present studying in seminaries.

The NCRM, established in 20 dioceses, is an organization of farmers concerning itself with the establishment of cooperatives, credit unions, and land settlement schemes.

Catholic Charities. Australian Catholics maintain a comprehensive system of individual social service and institutional charity. The lay apostolate in the field of charity is carried on by societies such as the *St. Vincent de Paul Society and the *Legion of Mary, while Catholic family welfare bureaus, established in the main capital cities and staffed by trained priests and laity, provide professional marriage counseling, child guidance, and adoption services. This work has been coordinated by a National Catholic Welfare Committee. In 1965 there were 80 Catholic hospitals, 53 children's homes and orphanages, and 105 other charitable institutions such as homes for the aged, schools for the blind, deaf, and mentally retarded, and a variety of residential hostels for men and women in the cities.

Synods and Congresses. There have been six synods of Australian bishops—two provincial synods, in Sydney (1844) and in Melbourne (1859), and four plenary synods in Sydney (1885, 1895, 1905, and 1937). In 1900 a series of Catholic congresses, planned to be held every 4 years, was inaugurated in Sydney. The second was held in Melbourne (1904) and the third in Sydney (1909). World War I interrupted the series. They never resumed in the original form. In 1928 the 29th International Eucharistic Congress was held in Sydney, followed by a National Eucharistic Congress in Melbourne (1934) and another in Sydney (1953), an All-Australian Education Congress in Adelaide (1936), the Fourth Plenary Council of the Australian Hierarchy (1937), and a Regional Missionary Congress at Newcastle (1938) attended by delegates from Indonesia and the South Seas Islands.

Immigration. Australia's population reached 11 million in 1963. Up to World War II, 90 per cent of the inhabitants were of British stock. Since 1945, however, immigrants have come in vast numbers from a great variety of European countries. This migration has contributed almost 60 per cent of Australia's total postwar population increase of 3.6 million. The largest single migrant group is the British (957,400 in June 1963), followed by Italians (257,550), Dutch (131,700), Greek (98,900), German (94,000), Polish (79,000), Yugoslav (41,600), plus others. Almost every European nationality is represented, though in smaller groups.

A Federal Catholic Immigration Committee provides for the spiritual and social welfare of Catholic migrants. Some 140 ethnic priests, representing 18 nationalities, work under the committee's direction. National parishes have not been erected, nor have the bishops sought the erection of territorial parishes in which migrant chaplains care for souls. Mass centers, however, have been set up, mainly in metropolitan areas, where foreign nationals, at regular periods and fixed hours, may assist at Mass and hear sermons in their respective languages. The Federal Catholic Immigration authorities estimate that postwar migration has increased the Catholic population by about 50 per cent.

Religious Practice. According to official census figures, Australia is a predominantly Christian country. The accompanying table was compiled from the 1961 census. Despite these figures, however, large numbers of Australians have little more than nominal affiliation

CHURCH MEMBERSHIP IN AUSTRALIA

Denomination	Membership	Percentage of population
Church of England	3,669,000	34.9
Catholic	2,620,000	24.9
Methodist	1,076,000	10.3
Presbyterian	977,000	9.3
Lutheran	160,000	1.5
Greek Orthodox	155,000	1.5
Other Christians and non-Christians	748,000	7.1
No reply	1,103,000	10.5
Total	10,508,000	100

with the religious denomination set down in their census returns. Gallup polls on religious worship, held regularly since 1947, reveal that as churchgoers, Australians divide into three groups: only 3 in 10 go to church every week; 4 in 10 go irregularly; 3 in 10 rarely or never go. Catholics have by far the highest rating in church attendance, followed by Baptists, Methodists, Presbyterians, and Anglicans. In a 1958 poll, Catholics replied as follows: attend Mass regularly, 64 per cent; occasionally, 19; never, 17.

A survey of nine parishes in Melbourne made by a Jesuit sociologist substantially bears out the Gallup poll findings, and notes that in some industrial parishes the attendance figure would not reach 64 per cent, but in many middle-class and country parishes it would exceed 70 per cent. The survey indicated a fairly healthy state of basic religious practice in Australia, in terms of reception of the Sacraments, meetings of parish confraternities, attendance at missions, lay retreats, public novenas, and other special devotions. All this, plus the buoyant rate of vocations, the growth of the liturgical movement, the great financial sacrifices to maintain Catholic education and charitable institutions, and contributions to the Pontifical Missions Aid Societies—after the U.S. Australia makes the second highest per capita contribution in the world—suggests that the religious practice of a majority of Australian Catholics springs from a sound conviction of the truth and value of their faith.

Convert Apostolate. This work is carried on by a national Catholic Enquiry Center, by the Catholic Evidence Guild, by the Legion of Mary, and by radio and television. The best-known radio session is the "Question Box," conducted by Rev. Dr. Rumble MSC, on Sydney's Catholic radio station (2SM). Established in 1928, on the occasion of the 29th International Eucharistic Congress, to explain Catholic doctrine to non-Catholics, the session's replies to letters of enquiry are printed in the Catholic press and have been published throughout the English-speaking world. Dr. Rumble's radio replies have had 70 printings and a circulation of 6 million in the U.S. The Catholic Evidence Guild engages in street-corner speaking in Sydney and Melbourne, organizes lectures for non-Catholics, and sponsors advertisements in public transport. The Legion of Mary arranges "Enquiry Days" for non-Catholics and conducts classes for converts. The national Catholic Enquiry Center, founded by the bishops in 1959, advertises the Church in daily newspapers and sends a postal course of religious instruction free and in confidence to any non-Catholic who requests it. Up to mid-1963, some 11,600 non-Catholics had enrolled for the course throughout Australia.

Numerical Growth. The percentage growth of Catholics in the total population over the past quarter of a century is illustrated in the following figures: in 1933 Catholics were 17.5 per cent of the population; in 1947, 20.7; in 1954, 22.9; in 1961, 24.9; in 1963, at least 25.5.

Current Statistics. In 1965, there were 7 archdioceses, 18 suffragan dioceses, one vicariate apostolic (Kimberleys), one abbey *nullius* (New Norcia), and one *sui juris* mission territory (Drysdale River). The seats of the archdioceses are in the capital cities. *Sydney, *Melbourne, *Adelaide, *Perth, and *Brisbane are metropolitan sees; *Canberra and *Hobart are immediately subject to the Holy See. The Church is under the direction of the Congregation for the Propagation of the Faith and has an apostolic delegation, which was established in 1914.

Although the first priests in Australia were Irish missionaries, the first bishop, Polding, an English Benedictine, hoped to consolidate the work of the archdiocese of Sydney within the framework of an Anglo-Benedictine community. However, his coadjutor and successor, Roger Bede *Vaughan, also a Benedictine, recognized that the rapidly expanding and predominantly Irish-Australian population called for a conventional diocesan structure and the recruitment of many more Irish priests. The Benedictine priests were therefore dispersed among the parishes, and the English Benedictine foundation in New South Wales came to an end.

The first major step to provide for the education of a native-born clergy was taken when Cardinal *Moran founded St. Patrick's College, Manly (1885). Dedicated in 1888, this seminary trained priests for the whole of Australia until the 1920s, when establishment of provincial seminaries began in all the mainland states of the commonwealth, in Victoria (1923), Queensland (1941), South Australia (1942) and Western Australia (1942). Missionary priests from Irish seminaries continued coming to Australia but by 1965 the vast majority of Australian priests were native-born. There were then 2,338 diocesan priests, 1,313 parishes, and 2,918 churches.

The 32 religious orders or congregations had another 1,342 priests. All these institutes were branches of overseas foundations, with the exception of the Confraternity of Christ the King, founded in North Queensland in 1955. Most of these priests have been trained in Australia at national houses of studies.

There were 40 ecclesiastical colleges, which train priests for the dioceses, religious orders and foreign missions, with a total of 1,463 seminarians. The ratio of priests to Catholic laity in Australia is 1 to 650. In the mission fields, Australian Columban, Capuchin, Divine Word, Dominican, Franciscan, Jesuit, Marist, Redemptorist, and Sacred Heart Fathers are working in New Guinea and other islands of Oceania and in India, Singapore, the Phillipines, Japan, and South America (Peru).

There were five institutes of brothers with a total membership of 1,937 trained in Australia and mostly engaged in education.

SUMMARY OF ECCLESIASTICAL STATISTICS, 1965

Province	DIOCESE	Parishes	Churches	Diocesan Priests	Religious Priests	Religious Brothers	Religious Sisters	Hospitals	Orphanages	Charitable Institutions	Catholic Population
Sydney	SYDNEY	199	249	420	313	644	2,976	16	13	20	634,320
	Armidale	28	89	55	3	22	210	—	1	1	30,515
	Bathurst	33	130	60	12	17	409	1	2	1	50,145
	Lismore	28	91	51	16	20	328	1	1	2	44,710
	Maitland	51	163	111	17	34	625	2	2	5	76,756
	Wagga Wagga	29	77	56	4	26	220	2	1	2	41,000
	Wilcannia-Forbes	24	54	44	3	15	201	1	1	2	36,907
	Wollongong	28	60	41	49	40	246	—	—	2	59,852
	State of New South Wales	420	913	838	417	818	5,215	23	21	35	974,205
	CANBERRA & GOULBURN	51	161	112	48	75	592	3	2	3	72,736
Melbourne	MELBOURNE	183	302	381	349	372	2,219	12	7	13	583,968
	Ballarat	50	189	96	39	69	505	2	2	1	74,016
	Sale	28	75	42	5	20	158	—	—	—	42,489
	Sandhurst	40	129	70	26	22	296	1	1	2	47,130
	State of Victoria	301	695	589	419	483	3,178	15	10	16	747,603
	HOBART—*Tasmania*	46	122	70	43	38	350	2	2	3	63,987
Adelaide	ADELAIDE	72	167	94	98	64	716	1	4	6	158,500
	Port Pirie	27	66	41	7	7	85	—	1	2	24,052
	Darwin	5	14	—	23	15	54	5	1	—	10,000
	State of South Australia	104	247	135	128	86	855	6	6	8	192,552
Perth	PERTH	97	130	120	83	104	1,100	7	5	10	130,000
	Bunbury	26	56	37	3	13	142	2	—	1	25,778
	Geraldton	13	35	16	2	24	123	1	—	3	10,800
	Kimberleys	5	9	—	12	7	40	5	—	9	2,250
	New Norcia	8	25	8	23	21	40	1	2	—	2,783
	Mission Sui Juris Drysdale River	1	1	—	2	2	3	1	2	—	250
	State of Western Aust.	150	256	181	125	171	1,448	17	9	23	171,861
Brisbane	BRISBANE	109	214	184	108	131	1,336	7	2	6	202,500
	Cairns	22	48	27	10	19	145	1	—	—	30,562
	Rockhampton	38	93	76	7	35	333	3	1	3	46,000
	Toowoomba	37	93	73	23	38	232	2	—	1	47,900
	Townsville	35	76	53	14	43	216	1	—	7	42,900
	State of Queensland	241	524	413	162	266	2,262	14	3	17	369,862
	Australia	1,313	2,918	2,338	1,342	1,937	13,900	80	53	105	2,592,806

SOURCE: *The Official Year Book of the Catholic Church of Australasia* (Sydney 1965–66).

The 72 religious congregations of women (including two secular institutes) had a total membership of 13,900. Most are branches of overseas foundations that have their own novitiates in Australia. The following twelve congregations are original Australian foundations: Sisters of the Good Samaritan (1857), Sisters of St. Joseph of the Sacred Heart (1866), Sisters of St. Joseph (Bathurst Diocese 1872), Sisters of Perpetual Adoration (1874), Sisters of St. Joseph (Goulburn 1882), Sisters of St. Joseph (Lochinvar 1883), Our Lady's Nurses for the Poor (1913), Companions of Our Lady of the Blessed Sacrament (1930), Sisters of Our Lady Help of Christians (1931), Home Missionary Sisters of Our Lady (1944), Sisters of Reparation (1949), Ver Sacrum Mariae Lay Institute (1957).

CATHOLIC EDUCATION

The most significant achievement of the Church in Australia is its comprehensive education system. Built and maintained without direct aid from public revenues, it covers all levels from kindergarten to university, and provides for 70 per cent of the Catholic student population. It is a recognized part of a "dual system" of government and nongovernment schools. The two systems work harmoniously side by side and are integrated into the general educational structure of each state. By far the largest sector of the nongovernment or independent school system is conducted by the Catholic Church (over 80 per cent).

Growth. Catholic education began in Australia with the arrival of Father Therry in 1820. Forbidden access to Catholic children in state schools and orphanages, he opened two Catholic schools, taught by lay teachers. A system of denominational education developed, which left teaching to the churches. The government cooperated with grants of land and financial assistance for the construction of buildings. The state also paid part of the teachers' salaries and supplied books and school requisites. The foundation of Catholic primary education was laid during this period, which lasted until 1870.

During the period 1870 to 1880, the governments of the Australian colonies withdrew state support for church schools and established a system of "free, secular and compulsory" education. Reasons for the change were complex. Existing schools were inefficient and failed to provide for the whole population. To make education universal, governments decided to make it a state responsibility. Theories of secular education, propounded by the American educationalist William *Harris, found favor among theorists in the newly created departments of education. Finally, "fear of Rome" and sectarian prejudice against Catholics, who had the greatest number of church schools, played a large part in the destruction of the denominational system.

Confronted with a crisis, the Australian bishops called on Catholics to establish their own education system. The Catholic community proved itself capable, at immense sacrifice, of shouldering the burden. A tradition grew that a parish begins by building a school that serves as a church on Sundays. Eighty per cent of Catholic children were in parochial schools by 1950. The "School-Church" period of Australian parishes forged close links between priests and people, created genuine Catholic communities and loyalties, and established a national tradition that no sacrifice is too great in the cause of Catholic education.

When state aid was withdrawn in the 1870s, it was found impossible to continue paying the salaries of lay teachers, and religious teaching orders gradually took over. Since existing orders were not sufficiently numerous, Australian bishops visited Europe. As a result, between 1870 and 1890, 10 more religious orders entered Australian Catholic education. Their membership by mid-20th century was predominantly Australian.

Organization. The general administration of the Catholic school system is on a diocesan basis under the direction of the bishop, who appoints a priest director of Catholic education and who selects also the inspecting staff. The diocesan education office maintains contact with the state education department and other public authorities. For the most part, Catholic schools follow the syllabuses in secular subjects issued under the authority of the state education departments and universities, and the students take the public examinations. Besides the supervision exercised by the Church over its own schools, inspections are also carried out by the government authorities, varying in degree from state to state. Religious orders conduct 13 institutes for training their personnel, who are then registered as teachers by the Council for Public Education.

Up to World War II, about 90 per cent of the teachers in Catholic schools were sisters, brothers, and priests. After 1945, however, an increase in the Australian birthrate, a huge influx of Catholic migrants from Europe, and a steady increase in the numbers seeking high education confronted the Church with a new crisis—an "education explosion"—which also confronted the government school system and all non-Catholic independent schools.

In mid-20th century existing Catholic schools and teachers had become inadequate to cope with the rapid increase both at the primary and secondary levels, and increasing numbers had to attend government schools. A major effort was being made to train lay teachers in greater numbers to work with the religious teachers in the schools. In more than one diocese a school's provident fund was established to borrow money from Catholics at current interest rates, so that advances might be made to parishes that had to build or add to their schools. In the Melbourne Archdiocese alone, Catholics had invested 12 million dollars in the fund. Lay catechists were also being trained to teach Christian doctrine, during released time in public schools, to children who could not be taken at Catholic schools. A new catechism for primary grades, incorporating the latest theological and catechical trends and methods, was approved and prescribed by the Australian bishops. The first text for the 10 to 12 age group was published in 1962; a second text for the 13 and 14 age group was published in 1963. Four texts for children aged 6 to 10 years were published in 1964.

State Aid. Meanwhile the Catholic community and its leaders continued to protest, as they had for 80 years, against double taxation, that is, payment out of their own taxes for the secular education imparted in their own schools, and to agitate for state aid. After World War II, public opinion gradually favored some kind of assistance to all independent schools. As a result Church schools received indirect aid, varying from state to state, in the form of scholarships, bursaries, free transport, free books, etc. At the national level, the government granted income tax deductions for each child attending an independent school and also deductions for contributions to school building funds. In the Federal Capital Territory (Australia's "District of Columbia") it also provided an interest subsidy of over 5 per cent for 20 years on loans for new buildings for nonresidential independent schools. In the national election of 1963, the Conservative Coalition party, led by Sir Robert Menzies, was returned to power with a large majority. Its policy included a grant to provide science teaching facilities in all secondary schools, including church schools, and a fund available to the states for the building and equipment of technical schools, both state and independent. This meant that the principle of direct federal aid to church schools was conceded by the Australian people—for Catholics a historic breakthrough in the long campaign for educational justice carried on since the 1870s.

Statistics. In 1964, Australia's 1,545 Catholic primary schools and 494 secondary schools had 471,600 students. Specialized secondary education was also given in various centers along technical, agricultural, and commercial lines. Although there were no Catholic

SUMMARY OF CATHOLIC EDUCATIONAL STATISTICS, 1964

Province	Diocese	Ecclesiastical Colleges	Seminarists	University Colleges	Secondary Schools Boys	Secondary Schools Girls	Primary Schools	Pupils As of August 1964: Secondary	Primary	Total
Sydney	SYDNEY	10	473	2	46	54	272	33,359	76,183	109,542
	Armidale	1	4	—	3	4	36	1,656	4,663	6,319
	Bathurst	—	—	—	4	5	50	2,575	7,163	9,738
	Lismore	—	—	—	2	2	37	2,203	6,003	8,206
	Maitland	—	—	—	3	10	58	3,855	9,920	13,775
	Wagga Wagga	—	—	—	4	4	32	2,006	5,631	7,637
	Wilcannia-Forbes	—	—	—	1	14	27	1,080	4,247	5,327
	Wollongong	3	45	—	4	7	30	2,861	7,880	10,741
	State of New South Wales	14	522	2	67	100	542	49,595	121,690	171,285
	CANBERRA & GOULBURN	3	68	—	5	5	60	7,477	10,447	17,924
Melbourne	MELBOURNE	14	519	2	26	39	217	30,597	75,457	106,054
	Ballarat	2	79	—	5	18	74	5,548	12,793	18,341
	Sale	—	—	—	3	5	26	2,159	6,496	8,655
	Sandhurst	—	—	—	4	13	41	3,123	8,952	12,075
	State of Victoria	16	598	2	38	75	358	41,427	103,698	145,125
	HOBART—*Tasmania*	—	—	1	7	10	33	3,381	6,848	10,229
Adelaide	ADELAIDE	2	95	1	10	16	102	5,889	17,627	23,516
	Port Pirie	—	—	—	2	7	22	477	2,707	3,184
	Darwin	—	—	—	1	2	13	87	1,529	1,616
	State of South Australia	2	95	1	13	25	137	6,453	21,863	28,316
Perth	PERTH	1	46	1	15	20	97	6,202	16,430	22,632
	Bunbury	—	—	—	3	7	25	734	2,633	3,367
	Geraldton	—	—	—	1	4	22	443	1,755	2,198
	Kimberleys	—	—	—	—	—	—	—	655	655
	New Norcia	1	8	—	2	1	8	245	407	652
	Mission Sui Juris Drysdale River	—	—	—	—	—	1	—	55	55
	State of Western Australia	2	54	1	21	32	153	7,624	21,935	29,559
Brisbane	BRISBANE	3	126	2	4	29	124	11,500	29,591	41,091
	Cairns	—	—	—	2	3	19	958	3,120	4,078
	Rockhampton	—	—	—	5	8	47	1,886	6,337	8,223
	Toowoomba	—	—	—	16	14	35	1,851	6,671	8,522
	Townsville	—	—	—	7	8	37	1,728	5,539	7,267
	State of Queensland	3	126	2	34	62	262	17,923	51,258	69,181
	Australia	40	1,463	9	185	309	1,545	133,880	337,739	471,619

SOURCE: *The Official Year Book of the Catholic Church of Australasia* (Sydney 1964).

universities, the Church maintained nine residential colleges for men and women within the various state universities. In addition to normal tutorials, these colleges offered courses in scholastic philosophy. The *Newman Apostolate, aided nonresidential undergraduates and promoted social and cultural activities for Catholic students. A Universities Catholic Federation of Australia for both graduates and undergraduates holds annual conventions in the various capital cities.

See also AUSTRALIAN LITERATURE; CATHOLIC PRESS, WORLD SURVEY, 4.

Bibliography: C. M. H. CLARK, *A History of Australia* (New York 1963) v.1 to 1829. J. G. MURTAGH, *Australia: The Catholic Chapter* (New York 1946; rev. ed. Sydney 1959). R. FOGARTY, *Catholic Education in Australia, 1806–1950,* 2 v. (Melbourne 1959). E. M. O'BRIEN, *Life and Letters of Archpriest John Therry: The Foundation of Catholicism in Australia,* 2 v. (Sydney 1922); *The Dawn of Catholicism in Australia,* 2 v. (Sydney 1928). H. N. BIRT, *Benedictine Pioneers in Australia,* 2 v. (London 1911). P. F. MORAN, *History of the Catholic Church in Australasia* (Sydney 1897). *The Official Year Book of the Catholic Church of Australasia* (Sydney). C. M. H. CLARK, *A Short History of Australia* (Mentor Bks; New York 1963). **Illustration credits:** Figs. 2, 4, and 5, Australian News and Information Bureau.

[J. G. MURTAGH]

AUSTRALIAN LITERATURE

The settlement of Australia by European colonists began in 1788; the literature of the continent properly dates from a year later, with the publication in London of *The Voyage of Governor Phillip to Botany Bay.* In the first century of the colony's existence, the writings—mainly factual prose, along with popular verse and fiction—are of value to the historian rather than the student of literature. Thereafter, though one finds a steady advance in the quality of the poems and novels, it is only toward the beginning of the 20th century that writers appear who demand sustained critical attention. After 1925, the rise in the number and skill of poets and novelists was remarkable, though the drama still lagged. The best of the contemporary writers, such as A. D. Hope and Patrick White, can sustain comparison with literature in any language.

Development of Poetry. In poetry, apart from the winner of a Cambridge prize for a poem on Australasia,

Fig. 1. Christopher Brennan.

William Charles Wentworth (1792–1872), the first names to note are those of Charles Harpur (1813–68), Henry Kendall (1839–62), and Adam Lindsay Gordon (1833–70). Harpur and Kendall, despite some original elements of Australian matter and idiom, wrote, in general, typical minor Victorian verse; Gordon had more vigor, that of the swashbuckling amateur. He wrote many ballads; this form of verse, indeed, had a considerable vogue between about 1880 and World War I; other well-known balladists were A. B. ("Banjo") Paterson (1864–1941) and Henry *Lawson. Their ballads were about the rough pioneering life of the back country; though mainly literary in origin, they are the closest Australia has come to folk poetry.

Much more sophisticated verse was written by Christopher *Brennan, who long enjoyed the reputation of being Australia's finest poet. His poems have been reassessed, and it may well be that critics will find them wanting, as with the previously well-regarded verse of Hugh McCrae (1876–1958), a neopagan lyrist; Bernard O'Dowd (1866–1953), a voluminous publicist who turned from Catholicism to a prophetic secularism; and William Baylebridge (1883–1942), a sententious imitator. The poetry of this period that best retains appeal is that of Shaw Neilson (1872–1942), author of many deceptively simple lyrics, similar to (and fit to be compared with) those of Blake.

The remarkable rise in poetic achievement after World War I is first seen in the highly skillful work of Kenneth Slessor (1901–), who progressed from a youthful hedonism to mature reflection. Slessor's early poems are set in the pagan, medieval or exotic Eastern past, described with sensuous richness; the later verse is sparer and more contemplative, especially in the very fine *Five Bells,* a meditation on time and the sea. A similar reflective quality is found in the poems of Robert D. FitzGerald (1902–), another postwar poet: the title of his best-known work, *Essay on Memory* (1938), in a sense describes all his verse, for he constantly reviews the past in a semiphilosophical, semicolloquial idiom.

If Slessor and FitzGerald were later less admired than they had been between the wars, the reason is the rise of three later poets of major eminence. Judith Wright (1915–) has published several graceful volumes that rank her among the best women poets writing in English. At their best her short lyrics perfectly marry thought and expression, and several of the handful of really memorable Australian poems would include hers. She writes mostly of the land itself and its history—as she had done in a distinguished memoir of her family, *The Generations of Men* (1959)—but also of the universal themes of love, birth, and death as felt by a woman.

These themes permeate as well the work of a very different poet; he is probably Australia's finest, Alec Derwent Hope (1907–). Labeled a satirist for his pungent commentaries on Australian mores, Hope is also a very moving lyric poet, as in his excellent *The Death of the Bird* and his elegy on W. B. Yeats. Hope's verse, fortified by a wide-ranging and richly stocked mind, expresses passion (both moral and physical) with a justness of diction and a technical control previously unattained in Australian poetry; and the same can be said of the work of James McAuley (1917–). A convert to Catholicism, and deeply instructed in the various movements of the Church's contemporary renewal, McAuley has written poetry of extreme lucidity, grace, and control, although it somewhat lacks power. The world view that informs it is clearly expressed in his book *The End of Modernity* (1959).

Of younger poets, mention should be made of Vincent Buckley (1925–), an articulate Catholic layman, whose two volumes *The World's Flesh* (1954) and *Masters in Israel* (1961) offer poetry of range and power, marred only by some obscurity. Two other younger poets who, like Buckley, wrote in the Yeatsian mode are Christopher Wallace-Crabbe (1934–) and Evan Jones (1931–).

Fig. 2. Alec Derwent Hope.

Rise of the Novel. The first Australian novel is *Quintus Servinton* (1830–31), by Henry Savery (1792–1842). Four other early novels worth noting are *The Recollections of Geoffry Hamlyn* (1859) by Henry Kingsley (1830–76), a tale of the colonial gentry;

Robbery Under Arms (1882–83) by "Rolf Boldrewood" (T. A. Browne, 1826–1915), about bushrangers and the gold fields; and two convict stories, the picaresque *Ralph Rashleigh* (1844–45) by James Tucker

Fig. 3. Patrick White.

(1808–66), and *For the Term of His Natural Life* (1870–71), a Dickensian indictment by Marcus Clarke (1846–81).

The better fiction of the later 19th century is found in the short story, much encouraged by the Sydney magazine, the *Bulletin;* of this genre Henry Lawson was the master. After 1900 the novel regained supremacy, particularly with Joseph *Furphy and Henry Handel *Richardson. Realism, prominent in these writers, continued to dominate Australian fiction, in quantity if not in quality. Of later years, only rarely has it reached the standard of Xavier Herbert's *Capricornia* (1938), which excels conventional realism by a rich gift of ironic comedy. History, too, has been a recurrent theme, notably in the novels of Eleanor Dark (1901–) and Martin Boyd (1893–); the latter is widely read outside Australia.

The continent's best-known novelist is clearly Patrick White (1915–), whose five novels, though far from completely successful, represent an attempt to give the Australian experience epic dimensions, resulting in fictional art of a previously unknown seriousness and depth, particularly in *Voss* (1957).

History, Criticism, Drama. The vast bulk of nonfictional prose has little literary distinction except in his-

Fig. 4. Ray Lawler.

tory—notably in the work of Sir Keith Hancock (1898–) and R. M. Crawford (1906–)—and in literary criticism, where two men of note are A. J. A. Waldock (1898–1950), known particularly for his *Paradise Lost and its Critics* (1947); and Vincent Buckley, author of *Poetry and Morality* (1959).

Until the success of *The Summer of the Seventeenth Doll* (1957), by Ray Lawler (1921–), the only Australian drama of quality was a series of poetic dramas for radio by Douglas Stewart (1913–), of which the best is *The Fire on the Snow* (1944); Stewart is also an important poet and critic.

It is not very rewarding to seek a specifically Catholic contribution to Australian literature until later years; where once poets like Brennan and O'Dowd forsook their faith in adulthood, later poets like McAuley and Buckley were deeply informed by it; and the flourishing life of periodicals such as the two Melbourne journals *Twentieth Century* and *Prospect* augured well for the future.

Bibliography: H. M. GREEN, *A History of Australian Literature, Pure and Applied,* 2 v. (Sidney 1961). G. DUTTON, ed., *The Literature of Australia* (Baltimore 1965). G. K. W. JOHNSTON, ed., *Australian Literary Criticism* (Melbourne 1963). V. BUCKLEY, *Essays in Poetry, Mainly Australian* (Melbourne 1957). **Illustration credits:** Australian News and Information Bureau.

[G. K. W. JOHNSTON]

AUSTREBERTA, ST., Benedictine abbess; b. Thérouanne, France *c.* 635; d. Abbey of Pavilly, France, Feb. 10, 704 (feast, Feb. 10). Her father, Badefridus, was apparently a member of the Merovingian royal family; her mother, Framehilda (d. *c.* 680), of German royal blood, was later honored as a saint and had a feast celebrated on May 17, at the Abbey of Sainte-Austreberta at Montreuil-sur-Mer. While Austreberta was still a young girl, her parents contracted her marriage, but she secretly took the veil in 655–656 under the spiritual direction of *Omer, Bishop of Thérouanne. Shortly thereafter, with parental permission, she entered the abbey of Port-le-Grand in Ponthieu. She was prioress there for 14 years until *Philibert, founder of *Jumièges, persuaded her to become abbess of his foundation at Pavilly. Her relics were transferred to Montreuil-sur-Mer in the 9th century and were venerated also at the cathedral of Saint-Omer, but they were burned in 1793.

Bibliography: Mabillon AS 3:23–38. BHL 1:831–838. L. VAN DER ESSEN, DHGE 5:790–792. AnalBoll 54 (1936) 9. A. M. ZIMMERMANN, LexThK² 1:1122. Zimmermann KalBen 1:194–197. R. AIGRAIN, *Catholicisme* 1:1077–78.

[P. BLECKER]

AUSTREGISILUS (OUTRIL), ST., abbot and bishop; b. Bourges, France, Nov. 29, 551; d. May 20, 624 (feast, May 20). It seems that he was born of noble but not very wealthy parents; and when he was about 24, he was sent to live at the court of King Guntram (d. 593). There, according to his vita, he was falsely accused of forging an authorization for one of the courtiers and was ordered to fight a duel to prove his innocence. By divine intervention, it is reported, his traducer was kicked to death by his horse on the morning of the day appointed for the *ordeal. Austregisilus then left the court, became a priest, and was appointed abbot of St. Nicetius. He was consecrated bishop of Bourges on Feb. 13, 612. In October 614 he attended a synod that met at Paris, and his name appears eighth in the list of 79 bishops who signed the decrees (MGConc 1:191). He is reported to have granted a hermitage at Bourges to *Amandus, later the apostle of Belgium.

Bibliography: BHL 1:835–843. ActSS May 5:60–69. MGSrer Mer 4:188–200. L. BOURNET, DHGE 5:792–793. Zimmermann KalBen 2:207. R. AIGRAIN, *Catholicisme* 1:1078. H. PLATELLE, BiblSanct 2:630. A. ZIMMERMANN, LexThK[2] 1:1122.

[H. DRESSLER]

AUSTRIA

This article summarizes the origin and historical development of the Catholic Church in Austria. This country, 32,366 square miles in area, had a population of 7,073,807 in 1961. Bordering it are *Czechoslovakia, *Hungary, *Yugoslavia, *Italy, *Switzerland, and *Germany.

CHRISTIANITY TO 1500

The Christianization of Austria was an irregular process that developed in three phases stretching over several centuries. Christian origins date from Roman times and produced several martyrs. St. Florian, who lived in the district of Cetium (St. Pölten) and held a high administrative post in the Danubian province of Noricum, hastened to Lauriacum (Lorch, near Enns), the capital of the province during Diocletian's persecution and there suffered a martyr's death (304). St. *Severin, the apostle of Noricum, died at Favianis (Mautern, near Krems) on Jan. 8, 482, after working among the Roman population, which was suffering from the invasion of the Germanic Rugieri. Ecclesiastical organization developed early. Bishoprics existed at Lauriacum, Virunum (Zollfeld near Klagenfurt), Teurnia (St. Peter im Holz near Spittal on the Drau), and Aguntum (near Lienz in eastern Tyrol). Excavations have uncovered about 20 churches from this period and discovered a well-preserved mosaic floor in the cemetery church in Teurnia. Toward the end of this period a bishopric was established in Sabiona (Säben, in southern Tyrol), which was a forerunner of the medieval bishopric of Brixen (Bressanone). St. *Ingenuin was bishop there *c.* 590.

The second period of Christianization coincides with the conversion of the Bavarians who settled in the Alpine Foreland in the 6th century. St. *Columban and his disciples SS. *Gall and *Eustace were active among the Alamannians in the district of Bregenz on the Lake of Constance *c.* 600. A century later St. *Rupert founded the bishopric of *Salzburg. Rupert (Hrodbert), a descendant of Rhenish-Franconian counts related to the *Carolingians, was probably bishop of Worms. He came to Bavaria *c.* 700 as part of the missionary expansion attendant upon the growth of the Frankish Empire. On the site of the ancient Roman Juvavum he founded the Abbey of *Sankt Peter, the oldest monastery still existing in Austria. He founded also the Abbey of *Nonnberg and installed his niece St. Erentrude as abbess. When St. *Boniface organized the Church in *Bavaria, Salzburg became a diocese with St. *Virgilius as bishop. During his episcopate Salzburg established itself as the principal see in Bavaria. Virgilius was a prominent exemplar of Irish-Scottish *monasticism on the Continent in contrast to Boniface, who introduced the Anglo-Saxon *Benedictines into the Frankish Church. In 774 Virgilius consecrated the cathedral of St. Rupert. Bishop Modestus evangelized in Carinthia. The monastery of Maria Saal was founded to serve the mission to the Slavonians. Among the other new foundations were the monasteries of Mondsee (748), *Kremsmünster (777), and the collegiate monastery of Innichen (San Candido 769).

The third period of Christianization began with *Charlemagne's establishment of an empire and his expansion eastward. After the fall of Duke Tassilo III, Bp. Arno became Charlemagne's trusted adviser for ecclesiastical matters in the east. At the King's command he received the *pallium from Pope Leo III (798). Salzburg thereupon became the head of the ecclesiastical province of Bavaria until its secularization (1803). After the defeat of the *Avars the area between the Drau, Raab, and Danube Rivers was placed under Salzburg's jurisdiction. Salzburg, followed by Passau and *Regensburg, extended its mission activity eastward to Moravia, where it encountered the apostles of the Slavs, SS. *Cyril (Constantine) and Methodius, who had come westward from Constantinople. The development of parishes in Bavarian dioceses followed. Charlemagne's foundations in the Diocese of Chur in Vorarlberg, along the lower part of the River Inn, and around the episcopal town of Salzburg were mostly *proprietary churches. They were more numerous in the old Bavarian settlements of the Diocese of Passau between the Rivers Inn and Enns, and to the east as far as the Vienna Woods. In the early Carolingian period the monastery of *Sankt Florian was established in Lorch; and St. Pölten was established as a daughter-house of the Bavarian monastery of *Tegernsee.

Medieval Growth. The victory of *Otto I over the Magyars on the Lechfeld (955) and the erection of a fortified frontier along the Danube made the Church more secure against invasions from the east. The frontier district was entrusted in 976 to the counts of Babenberg; it was called Ostarrichi (Österreich) in 996. About that time Bp. *Pilgrim of Passau (971–991) undertook a mission to the Hungarians. His name is immortalized in the **Nibelungenlied,* one of the greatest medieval epics. His activity led to the conversion of Grand Duke Geza and to the baptism of his son St. *Stephen I. He failed to secure metropolitan jurisdiction over Moravia and Hungary for the See of Passau, though he forged charters to support his claim that Passau should be independent of Salzburg (Falsification of Lorch). He kept enlarging the limits of his diocese until it became one of the largest in Germany, extending to the Hungarian frontier. Numerous churches along the Danube testify to the vigorous missionary activity of the Austrian bishops. Their work was crowned by the consecration of St. Stephen's Cathedral in Vienna by Bishop Reginbert, who died in the Second Crusade (1147). The Bavarian Dioceses of Salzburg, Freising, *Bamberg, and Regensburg shared with Passau in the spiritual development of medieval Austria; so did *Niederaltaich and other monasteries.

The most eminent bishop of Passau was St. *Altmann (1065–91), a firm supporter of the popes during the *investiture struggle. He founded St. Nikola in Passau and other houses for canons and also the Benedictine Abbey of *Göttweig (1094). He also reformed the monasteries of St. Florian and St. Pölten. Archbishops *Gebhard (1060–88) and Thiemo (1090–1101) of Salzburg were faithful adherents of the popes. Con-

Fig. 1. Austria, showing places of ecclesiastical interest.

rad I (1106–47), a leading reform bishop, made 14 foundations of canons in his diocese and introduced their reforms into his own chapter. His most influential collaborators were Bp. Roman of Gurk and Provost *Gerhoh of Reichersberg, whose writings defended the rights of the Church during the contest of Pope *Alexander III with Emperor *Frederick I Barbarossa.

Monastic Life. Benedictine foundations and reforms were characterized by the spirit of monastic renewal emanating from *Gorze and *Cluny. *Lambach Abbey, established (1056) by Adalbero of Würzburg on his family estate, was first to be affected by the Gorze reform. Next was Kremsmünster, where Bp. Altmann installed the monk Theodorich de Gorze as a reforming abbot. After that came *Melk, where Abbot Sigibold organized a monastic community (1089). Melk, located on Babenberg property, was richly endowed by Margrave Leopold III and placed under papal protection (1110). St. *Coloman, Austria's first patron saint (before St. *Leopold III), has been interred at Melk since 1014. The *Cluniac reform came to Austria through the Abbeys of *Sankt Blasien, Siegburg, near Cologne, and *Hirsau in Swabia. In 1094 Bp. Udalrich of Passau brought some Benedictines to Göttweig from Sankt Blasien in the Black Forest. Hartmann, Göttweig's first abbot, sent monks to Garsten (1107) and *Seitenstetten (1112) and reformed *Sankt Lambrecht. Garsten belonged to the counts of Traungau, who were margraves of Steyr. *Berthold (1111–42), the first abbot of Garsten, is venerated as a saint. Sankt Lambrecht was established before 1076 by the Carinthian ducal family of Eppensteiner. Bishop Kuno of Regensburg, formerly abbot in Siegburg, introduced the reform of that monastery into Mondsee, which belonged to Regensburg. From Hirsau monks went to *Sankt Paul in Carinthia (1091), a foundation of the Spanheims, who succeeded the Eppensteiners as dukes in 1122. The main support for Hirsau reform in Austria, however, was *Admont Abbey in the Styrian Valley of the Enns River. The abbey was built in 1074 by Gebhard on the property of Bl. *Hemma of Gurk (d. 1045) and peopled with monks from Sankt Peter. Under the reforming abbots Wolfhold (1115–37) and Gottfried (1137–65) it influenced most religious houses in Bavaria and Austria. The first monasteries in Styria and Carinthia were Göss, near Leoben, founded for nuns by Count Palatine Aribo (before 1020), Sankt Georgen on Längsee (1022–23), and Gurk, founded by Bl. Hemma (before 1043). During the 11th century the Benedictines established Sankt Lambrecht, Sankt Paul, Ossiach (before 1028), and Millstatt (*c.* 1070).

The Margrave St. Leopold III (1095–1136), patron saint of Austria, transformed a frontier district into a territorial duchy. He gave his residence of *Klosterneuburg near Vienna to Canons Regular of St. Augustine. He also brought *Cistercians from *Morimond to *Heiligenkreuz, where his son *Otto, later bishop of Freising, had become a monk. From Heiligenkreuz St. Bernard's monks went to *Zwettl (1138), Baumgartenberg (1142), and *Lilienfeld (1202). Cistercian monasteries arose also in *Viktring (Carinthia, 1142), and *Wilhering in Upper Austria (1146). The Schottenkloster in Vienna (founded 1155 by Henry Jasomirgott) is a reminder that Austria was transformed into a dukedom by Margrave Henry II, Leopold's son. The monasteries of the old orders, joined by the *mendicant orders (*Dominicans in 1217 at Friesach, *Franciscans in 1230 in Vienna), established in Austria a firm structure that lasted until the dissolution of religious houses by Emperor Joseph II. In the 14th century the House of *Hapsburg favored the *Augustinians and *Carthusians.

Austria's frontier position prevented the creation of a regular bishopric. Some unsuccessful attempts in this direction were made later by the dukes of Babenberg, the Bohemian King Přemysl Ottokar, and Duke Rudolph IV. The last-named founded the University of Vienna (1365) and a collegiate chapter at St. Stephen's Cathedral (*see* VIENNA, UNIVERSITY OF). It was Emperor Frederic III who established *Vienna (1469) and Wiener Neustadt as bishoprics. Within the Diocese of Salzburg private bishoprics appeared at Gurk (1072), Seckau (1218), and Lavant (1225). Among the prominent bishops of Brixen where St. *Albuin (975–1005 or 1006), who transferred his seat from Säben to Brixen; Poppo who became Pope *Damasus II (1048); Reginbert, who, before 1138, brought *Praemonstratensians to Wilten, near Innsbruck, and Benedictines to St. Georgenberg (transferred in 1706 to Fiecht); and Hartmann (1140–64), who sent Augustinian Canons from Klosterneuburg to Neustift, near Brixen. Together with the bishops of *Trent, the bishops of Brixen exercised sovereign rights in Tyrol until the local counts of Andechs-Meranien, Tyrol, and Görz contested these rights.

During the *Western Schism and the reforming councils it evoked, the University of Vienna advocated moderate *nominalism and *Conciliarism. This was the university's golden age. Among its most prominent professors were *Henry Heinbuche of Langenstein and *Henry of Oyta (both former professors in Paris), the Dominicans Francis of Retz and John Nider, *Nicholas of Dinkelsbühl, Peter of Pulkau, and Thomas Ebendorfer of Haselbach. The Melk reform movement under Abbot Nicholas Seyringer and the priors Peter of Rosenheim and John Schlitpacher of Weilheim, and also the reform of Raudnitz effected a monastic revival. The two outstanding Austrian churchmen of the 15th century were Cardinals *Nicholas of Cusa, who as bishop of Brixen came into sharp conflict with Duke Sigismund of Tyrol, and St. *John Capistran, who introduced the Franciscan strict observance into Austria and collaborated effectively in the victory over the Turks at Belgrade (1456).

The best known churches in Romanesque style are the cathedral of Gurk, with its crypt of 100 columns and remarkable frescoes in the western gallery, and the collegiate churches of Seckau and St. Paul. The development from Romanesque to Gothic appears in the Cistercian churches of Heiligenkreuz, Lilienfeld, and Zwettl. Surpassing all these is St. Stephen's Cathedral in Vienna with it matchless spire. Among the examples of early medieval art are the Tassilo chalice at Kremsmünster and Carolingian and Romanesque illuminations. The Verdun altar in the monastery of Klosterneuburg (1181) is a masterpiece of enamel painting. The richness and religious fervor of late Gothic are most impressively shown by Michael *Pacher's winged altar in St. Wolfgang's parish church and in the altar at Kefermarkt.

Fig. 2. (a) Exterior view of the cathedral of Gurk, Carinthia, Austria, and (b) one of its famed Romanesque murals.

1500 TO 1848

The crises of the Protestant revolt and the energetic policies of Catholic reform led the Church in Austria into its Baroque age, when it displayed a distinctive piety in its devotional practices and its religious art forms. In the subsequent period of *Josephinism it experienced the good and evil effects of the *Enlightenment, surrendering under force much of its internal government to state controls.

Reformation and Counter Reformation. Rivalry for power between the Hapsburg rulers and their subject nobles was a prominent factor in the rise of Protestantism within Austria. Thus the growth of Protestantism was promoted by the nobles, who as lords of their estates could encroach upon the administration of parishes, confiscate Church property, and replace Catholic pastors with Evangelical preachers. The towns and marketplaces were influenced by the example of the nobles, so that at the time of its widest spread, the *Reformation would claim three quarters of the Austrian population. The alliance between the nobles and *Lutheranism was favored also by the latent danger from the Turks. The enormous expenses for the protection of the frontier against the Turkish advance could not be met by the contributions of the churches and monasteries alone. The Emperor relied upon taxes within the states of the Empire, which were often granted to him at the price of religious concessions. Furthermore, the condition of the clergy did not provide a strong weapon of defense against the spread of Protestantism. Vienna, for example, had two eminent bishops, Johannes *Faber (1530–41) and Friedrich *Nausea (Grau, 1541–52), who rank with Johann *Eck and Johannes *Cochlaeus (Johann Dobeneck) as Luther's most outstanding literary adversaries, but who failed to achieve effective reform in their small bishopric. Spiritual indifference and moral breakdown continued to increase. The Bishop of Salzburg, Cardinal Matthäus *Lang (1519–40), was more successful despite his unclerical private life. As sovereign and bishop, he was able to prevent the uprisings of the peasants on his lands and thus hinder the victory of Lutheranism. Protestantism was likewise aided by the favor of Maximilian II (1564–76), who throughout his reign remained in sympathy with creedal innovation and allowed his lords to accept the Confession of *Augsburg, until finally, for dynastic reasons, he withstood the power of the Protestant states. His son Rudolph II (1576–1612) pursued a policy of Catholic support.

Jesuits and Capuchins. Of particular importance in withstanding Lutheranism in Austria were the *Jesuits, who were invited by King Ferdinand I (emperor 1556–64). Peter *Canisius arrived in Vienna in 1552, where he taught theology in the newly founded Jesuit college, preached in the cathedral of St. Stephen, and administered to many of the abandoned parishes of Lower Austria. However, he refused Ferdinand's offer of the bishopric of Vienna through his own disinclination and the resistance of Ignatius of Loyola. Other Jesuits lectured at the universities, served as confessors and advisers of Hapsburg princes, founded colleges and spiritual gymnasia at Innsbruck (1562) and Graz (1573), and later at Hall in the Tyrol, Leoben, Linz, Klagenfurt, Krems, Judenburg, and Steyr. They were joined by the Capuchins *c.* 1600. St. *Lawrence of Brindisi was active as an army chaplain with the imperial troops in Hungary, and he founded Capuchin convents in Vienna and Graz.

Melchior Klesl. The year 1580 marks the beginning of substantial Catholic recovery in Vienna and Lower Austria. Archduke Ernest governed Upper and Lower Austria for his brother Emperor Rudolph II, while the latter resided in Prague. Ernest was aided by the gifted Cardinal Melchior *Klesl, who had been converted from Protestantism by the Jesuit court chaplain George Scherer, and began early to assume the role of leader of the *Counter Reformation. He became the provost of St. Stephen's Cathedral and chancellor of the University of Vienna (1579), councilor of the bishop of Passau in Lower Austria (1580), imperial councilor of Rudolph

Fig. 3. Austria: (a) A cloister of the Abbey of Seckau, Styria. (b) The abbey church of the Abbey of Sankt Lambrecht, Styria. (c) The Angel Chapel of the monastery of Seckau, with frescoes executed in 1963 by H. Boeckel. (d) The famed enamel altar executed in 1811 by Nicholas of Verdun in a chapel of the abbey church at Klosterneuburg.

II (1585), court chaplain and administrator of the Diocese of Wiener Neustadt (1588), and bishop of Vienna (1598). His diplomatic skill and firm belief in Catholicism fitted him for the political and religious problems of the period. With much personal risk he won back the cities of Baden, Krems, and Stein and restored organization to the dioceses under his control.

Styria and Carinthia. The champion of reform in these provinces was Archduke Charles, who married into the House of Bavaria, then the main support of the Catholic cause in Germany. Charles was aided in his reform schemes by the capable bishops Martin Brenner of Seckau and George Stobäus of Lavant.

Tyrol. In the Tyrol and neighboring territories, not so touched by Evangelicalism, Archduke Ferdinand, husband of Philippa Welser, and his successor, Archduke Maximilian, carried out comprehensive policies of reform. Maximilian, made Grandmaster of the Teutonic Order by Paul V, encouraged the regular visitations of parishes enacted by the reform synod of 1603, built a school for the Jesuits at Innsbruck, established the Capuchins in a convent at Meran (1616), and aided in the foundation of another at Neumarkt in the valley of the Adige. The court provided good example by the conduct of its household and the foundation of a house at Hall for gentlewomen interested in works of charity. There five archduchesses resided, including the saintly second wife of Ferdinand of Tyrol, Anna Caterina de Medici, who established convents for the Servites at Innsbruck and later became a Servite Tertiary under the name of Anna Juliana. From 1621 the Servites of Innsbruck spread over most of the crown lands of the Hapsburgs as far as the Rhine.

Salzburg. In the Archdiocese of Salzburg, Catholic restoration dates from the provincial synod of 1569, the work of the Dominican Feliciano *Ninguarda, who as papal commissioner implemented the reform decrees of the Council of Trent in Salzburg and southern Germany. His work was continued by the three archbishops who made Salzburg a cultural center: Wolfdietrich (Wolfgang Theodorich) of Reitenau (1587–1612), Mark Sittich of Hohenems (1612–19), who was descended from relatives of Charles Borromeo, and Paris, Count of Lodron (1619–53), whose wise politics kept his archbishopric free from the troubles of the *Thirty Years' War. Under Archbishop Leopold Anton *Firmian (1724–44) the Lutherans in the territory of Salzburg formed into a league that grew strong. Firmian published an edict (Oct. 31, 1731) demanding their recantation or emigration. Within 10 years more than 30,000 emigrated to East Prussia, Hanover, and North American colonies (Georgia).

Ferdinand II. The main strength of Protestantism in Austria was concentrated in the land along the Enns River. It was there that the hard-fought struggle of the Protestant states for religious liberty took place. The principal combatants were the noble families of Jörger and Starhemberg, and especially George Erasmus of Tschernemble, who abandoned Lutheranism for Calvinism. The fraternal discord within the House of Hapsburg aided Protestantism and kept it a threat in Upper Austria. Burckhard Furtenbacher (d. 1598) at Lambach, Alexander of Lacu (d. 1612) at Wilhering, Anthony Wolfrat (d. 1639) at Kremsmünster, and other prelates continued the work of Church renovation. Wolfrat succeeded Klesl as bishop of Vienna (1631–39). In the Diocese of Passau the Archduke-bishops Leopold (1597–1626) and Leopold Wilhelm (1626–62) kept Catholicism strong. In *Ferdinand II of Inner Austria (emperor 1619–37), the Counter Reformation had its most sincere and consistent leader. His Catholicism alienated the Bohemians, who rebelled in 1618 and chose as ruler Frederick V, ruler of the Palatinate and leader of the Protestant Union. Their forceful ejection of the imperial emissaries in the defenestration of Prague occasioned the Thirty Years' War. This event terminated the irresolute policy of Ferdinand's predecessor, Matthias (1612–19), who had adopted at the counsel of Klesl an attitude of compromise regarding the Bohemians. Ferdinand's forceful reign drove the nobles of Upper Austria into open revolt and into alliance with the Calvinists. The victory of the Catholic League in the battle of the White Mountain (Nov. 8, 1620) decided the fate of Protestantism in Austria by forcing the rebellious nobles to accept Catholicism or emigrate.

The Baroque Age. As a result of the Counter Reformation, Austria remained Catholic and the Hapsburgs became Catholicism's chief defenders in the Thirty Years' War and in the struggle to repulse the Turkish assault against Western Christendom that ended with the defeat of the Turks before the walls of Vienna (Sept. 12, 1683). This heroic period in Austria's history was characterized by a strong religious stamp.

Revived Faith. It was a time of enthusiasm for the renewed ancient faith, when Church and State joined in close union against the dangers of the Crescent. The baroque piety that florished (*pietas Austriaca*) affected the devotion to the Trinity, the Eucharist, and the veneration of the cross, Our Lady, and the saints (*see* BAROQUE, THE; BAROQUE ART; BAROQUE THEOLOGY). The Forty Hours devotion, general Communions, formation of pious confraternities and congregations, processions and *pilgrimages became popular. Besides visiting places of pilgrimage such as the Sonntagsberg, near Waidhofen on Ybbs, and Stadlpaura, near Lambach, Austrians covered the land with Calvaries, Ways of the Cross, columns in honor of the Trinity and Mary, wayside chapels and memorials, and statues of St. John of Nepomuc erected on bridges. They listened with pleasure to impressive musical services and to ornate baroque sermons, best represented by the Discalced Augustinian friar *Abraham of Sancta Clara (Ulrich Megerle) in Vienna.

Marian Devotion. Although SS. Joseph, Charles Borromeo, Teresa of Avila, Ignatius of Loyola, Francis Xavier, Leopold, and John of Nepomuc had a wide popularity, this was preeminently Mary's century. The Jesuits and various Marian congregations cultivated her devotion and sought her intercession in times of danger from plague or Turk. The numerous sanctuaries to the *Mater dolorosa,* called *Mariahilf,* recall these times of distressed Christianity. The oldest of the Marian *shrines, at Mariazell, had attracted pilgrims since the late Middle Ages. There were sanctuaries also at Maria-Taferl and Maria-Dreieichen. In the environs of Vienna were erected the shrines of Mariabrunn, Maria-Lanzendorf, and Maria-Enzersdorf; in Upper Austria, Pöstlingberg near Linz; in Styria, Maria-Trost, near Graz; in Salzburg, Maria-Plain and Maria-Kirchental; in Carinthia, Maria-Saal, Maria-Wörth, and

Fig. 4. Vested statue of the Virgin and Child in the basilica at Mariazell, the oldest Marian shrine in Austria.

the baroque sanctuaries of Maria-Rain, Maria-Loretto (St. Andrä), and Maria-Luggau.

Church Art. The revival of religious life and monastic discipline introduced a lustrous period of church ornamentation, in which a display of outward pomp was joined to the practice of the monastic ideal. There arose a group of baroque prelates, such as Godfrey of Bessel, Abbot of Göttweig (1714–49), a noted historian, and Abbot Berthold Dietmayr of Melk (1700–39), who patronized the best artists and selected them to erect and adorn their churches and convents. The baroque church followed a pattern of an amply articulate façade, double spire, and cupola; its uniform, spacious interior was well lighted, richly decorated with frescoes on ceiling and dome, and pompously ornamented. The most representative baroque church in Austria is the cathedral of Salzburg, combining the beautiful elements of the Renaissance with the later baroque forms. Erected after the plans of the Italian architects Vincenzo Scamossi (d. 1616) and Santino Solari (d. 1646), it became the most noted sacred building north of the Alps in the 17th century. Other churches built in Salzburg during the time of the high baroque elevated the "German Rome" to its artistic peak.

Baroque Artists. The most illustrious Austrian baroque architects were Johann Bernhard Fischer of Erlach (1656–1723), whose masterpiece is the Charles's Church in Vienna, begun on behalf of Emperor Charles VI; Lucas of Hildebrand (1668–1745), who created the Vienna Belvedere; and Jakob Prandtauer (1660–1726), who designed the church at Melk and the shrine on Sonntagsberg. Prandtauer changed the courtly style of Fischer and Lucas into a rural and popular form, and by conforming the architectural totality of his work to site and environs, he created unique and monumental effects. Among the baroque architects of monasteries were: Carlo Antonio Carlone (d. 1708), whose spirit breathes in the Upper Austrian monasteries of St. Florian, Garsten, Kremsmünster, and Schlierbach; Donato Felice d'Allio (d. 1761), creator of the huge monastic building of Klosterneuburg; and Joseph Mungenast (d. 1741), who erected or completed several monasteries in Lower Austria (Herzogenburg, Dürnstein, *Seitenstetten, *Altenburg, Zwettl, and Geras). The chief baroque painters who ornamented these buildings were Daniel Gran della Torre (d. 1757), Paul Troger (d. 1762), Bartolomeo Altomonte (d. 1783), Johann Michael Rottmayer (d. 1730), Franz Anton Maulpertsch (d. 1796), and Martin Johann Schmidt (d. 1796), who left more than 1,000 altarpieces. In sculpture no one in Austria surpassed Georg Raphael Donner (d. 1740).

Fig. 5. Nave of the church of the Abbey of Heiligenkreuz.

Josephinism. The Hapsburgs had rescued the Church from Protestantism and the threats of Turkish invasion, but their role of protection grew gradually into an attempted control of ecclesiastical government. When the Empire turned into a centralized, utilitarian, and materialistic state under the influence of enlightened absolutism, it could not tolerate the Church as an equal, much less as a superior partner. As a result it took measures to subordinate the Church and fit it into its own apparatus of jurisdiction. During the reign of *Maria Theresa (1740–80), Prince Wenzel Anton von *Kaunitz took the preliminary steps toward the system of Church-State relations that came to be known as *Josephinism and that brought hardship to the Church.

Isolation from Rome. Josephinism represented a mixture of *Jansenism and the principles of the Enlightenment matured in the soil of Austrian Catholicism. Emperor *Joseph II (1765–90) aimed at isolating the Austrian Church from Rome and subjecting it to his own far-reaching control. The Clerical Court Commission became the state office for Church affairs. Its exponents were Barons Franz Kressel-Gautenberg and Franz Joseph *Heinke, the Emperor's privy councillor. The Josephinist decrees *in publico-ecclesiasticis* have been estimated to total 6,000. Cutting deeply into the clerical sphere was the marriage decree (Jan. 17, 1783), which regarded marriage as a civil contract whose privileges and obligations depended entirely for their force upon civil law. In 1783 episcopal and monastic schools for training the clergy were abolished and replaced by general seminaries at Vienna, Louvain, Budapest, Pavia, Graz, Olmütz, Innsbruck, Freiburg, Pressburg (Bratislava), and Prague. By the Patent of Tolerance (Oct. 13, 1784) Lutherans and Calvinists were permitted the private practice of their religion. Of special concern was the dissolution of all monasteries and convents that were not engaged in pastoral, educational, or social activities. The sums realized from the sale of this confiscated property were placed into the Religious Fund to create new parishes and to provide salaries for the clergy.

Diocesan and Parochial Reorganization. The attempt to conform diocesan boundaries with those of the provinces of Austria resulted in several changes. In 1785 the Diocese of Wiener Neustadt was incorporated into the Archdiocese of Vienna. The newly instituted Dioceses of St. Pöltin (S. Hippolyti) and Linz became suffragans to Vienna. The archbishopric of Salzburg gained as suffragans the enlarged Dioceses of Seckau-Graz and Gurk-Klagenfurt. The Upper Styrian Diocese of Leoben, with its seat at Göss, was united to Sechau. Several bishoprics were incorporated in the Diocese of Lavant, including the district of Völkermarkt in Carinthia, which was detatched and given to Gurk in 1859; Lavant itself was transferred in 1859 to the South Styrian bishopric of Marburg (Maribor). The Vicariate of Feldkirch (Vorarlberg) was established for the Diocese of Brixen. In addition, 600 new parishes were founded.

Curricular Reforms in Education. A firm state control of schools and educational method also was set up in Josephinist Austria. In 1774 there appeared the Theresan school regulations, which were the work of Abbot Johann Ignaz von *Felbiger of Sagan (Silesia), the noted reformer of elementary schools and the originator of a systematic method of religious instruction. After the suppression of the Society of Jesus (1773), Jesuits departed the faculty of the University of Vienna. Thereupon a new curriculum was organized by a disciple of *Febronianism, Abbot Franz Stephan von *Rautenstrauch of Braunau (Bohemia). Though it was viewed with suspicion because of its shortened courses in dogmatic theology, it brought progress by its new stress upon Biblical and patristic study, Church history, pastoral theology, and catechetics.

Church Opposition. During the struggle to halt the encroachments of the state in ecclesiastical jurisdiction, Christoph Anton *Migazzi, Archbishop of Vienna (1757–1803), and the papal nuncios Giuseppe *Garampi and Giovanni Battista *Caprara worked to prevent an open rupture between Emperor Joseph II and *Pius VI, who journeyed to Vienna in the spring of 1782 in a vain attempt at conciliation. Josephinism was a more stubborn problem than Lutheranism, which disappeared from Austria almost completely during the renewed religious enthusiasm of the baroque period. After the death of Joseph II, Josephinism declined slowly during the reign of Francis I (1804–35), who declared himself hereditary emperor of Austria (1804) and abdicated (1806) the crown of the Holy Roman Empire that he had assumed as Francis II in 1792. Civil functionaries attempted to keep the Church in subordination and suppressed any movement toward clerical liberty. Meanwhile there developed a type of Josephinist cleric, who was a civil officer and spiritual bureaucrat, performing his service in the office, school, and church. During the Napoleonic era and the ensuing Restoration period after the Congress of *Vienna (1814–15), Josephinism weakened. Much of the decline can be ascribed to the revival of Catholic life in Austria brought about by the Redemptorist St. Clement *Hofbauer, the "Apostle of Vienna," and his disciples, Anton *Günther, Johann Emmanuel Veith (1787–1876), and Cardinal Joseph Othmar von *Rauscher, Archbishop of Vienna (1853–75).

Since 1848

The period since mid-19th century is divided by World War I.

1848-1918. The Revolution of 1848 brought liberty to the Church but also abolished the privileged position Catholicism had enjoyed as the state religion. After long negotiations carried on by Archbishop Rauscher, Count Leo Thun, the Austrian minister of worship and public instruction, and Archbishop Viale-Prelá, the papal nuncio, a concordat was concluded (1855), which marked the culmination of the movement for renewal. The concordat benefited the Church even though it was infected with a new type of state absolutism that did not collapse until the Austrian military defeats of Solferino and Königgrätz. Contemporary *liberalism opposed the concordat as a purely clerical solution of Church-State questions and even as an abdication of the State's power in the face of the Church. Count Antony Alexander of Auersperg (Anastase Grün), a liberal member of Parliament, called the concordat a printed canossa in which 19th-century Austria atoned in sackcloth and ashes for 18th-century Josephinism. Liberal opposition to the concordat assumed massive proportions after the constitution of February 1861 was promulgated. With the rise of parliamentary government, the concordat was doomed. The Fundamental Law of the State (1867) was a strongly liberal code. The May Laws (1868) placed marriages and education completely under state control. By unilateral action in 1870 Austria abrogated the concordat on the pretext that *Vatican Council I had altered essentially the nature of the papacy by its decrees on papal primacy and infallibility. Under the leadership of Franz *Rudigier, Bishop of Linz, and Joseph *Fessler, Bishop of St. Pölten and general secretary at Vatican Council I, the Austrian hierarchy vigorously opposed the May Laws and sought to mobilize Catholics. Legislation in 1874 that attempted to regulate Church-State relations led almost to a rupture with Rome and to the excommunication of Emperor Francis Joseph. An open breach was averted only by the monarch's refusal to sign the legislation (*see* KULTURKAMPF).

During this period the Austrian Church was forced for the first time to struggle alone and fight for its rights. Aware of the growing importance of social problems, some Catholics initiated in 1870 a movement for Christian social reform and a program of social legislation. The pioneer leader in these ventures was Baron Karl von *Vogelsang (*see* SOCIAL MOVEMENTS, CATHOLIC, 3). Unfortunately the Church did not at first grasp all the intimations of Austria's rapid industrialization and consequent labor problems. This failure was not catastrophic because the Catholic conservative movement, supported by the nobility, successfully advocated social legislation earlier than in other countries. Through the influence of Vogelsang and the Count of Kufstein, Austria played a significant role in efforts preceding the issuance of Leo XIII's encyclical **Rerum novarum*. However, the tardiness in adapting pastoral outlooks and methods to the needs of a changing environment resulted in large-scale defections of the proletariat from the Church. A Christian social movement under the political leadership of Dr. Karl *Lueger (d. 1910) defeated the liberal regime in Vienna. Under Franz Schindler (d. 1922) and the conservative Prince Alois of Liechtenstein, the Christian Social party ultimately became the main support of the Catholic ideal in Austria. This was effected only after painful adjustments during which the conservatives, supported by the bishops, tried to secure a papal censure of the Christian Social movement. Fortunately the zealous Joseph Scheicher (d. 1924) won over the younger clergy. In 1907 the conservatives fused with the Christian Social party; their publications were combined in 1911 (*see* POLITICAL PARTIES, CATHOLIC).

Catholics tried to influence public life by organizing unions and associations. The Catholic Union, later styled the Severin Union, originated in 1848. St. Michael's Union, whose original purpose was the defense of the papacy, concerned itself more and more with bringing Catholic interests to public notice. By 1870 popular Catholic associations of patriotic character (Casinos) and associations of journeymen developed. Christian labor unions encountered great opposition from Socialists in the 1890's. Leopold Kunschak and Anton Orel were outstanding in their efforts to aid the young workers. The Catholic Popular Union originated in 1909 as a nonpolitical central organization of Austrian Catholics. Until 1938 it embraced all Catholic organizations and unions in the various dioceses. To some extent it exercised the functions carried out since 1945 by *Catholic Action.

Sebastian *Brunner, the Austrian Görres, inaugurated the Austrian Catholic press in 1848 with his newspaper *Wiener Kirchen-Zeitung,* which continued to appear until 1873. The conservative *Vaterland* began in 1860. The Christian Social daily, *Reichspost,* founded in 1892 and published until 1938, was a model Christian newspaper. Several dioceses had Catholic press associations that published minor local weeklies (*see* CATHOLIC PRESS, WORLD SURVEY, 4).

The revival of Catholic intellectual life was most evident in the five Catholic congresses held between 1877 and 1905. Each one centered around a specific theme. Thus education was the main topic in 1877, social problems in 1889, the press in 1892, agrarian reform in 1896, and Catholic organizations in 1905. Crowning these gatherings was the International *Eucharistic Congress (1913).

This period witnessed the estrangement from the Church of a large portion of the educated classes, as well as the proletariat. The *Los-von-Rom early in the 20th century cost the Church many members. On the other hand, there was a great increase in the number of vocations to religious congregations of women. The development of sodalities and the retreat movement strengthened Catholic life. Henry Abel, SJ, promoted an apostolate among men. The Leo-Gesellschaft, founded in 1892, fostered Catholic scientific activities. The Catholic Associations of Academicians, especially the Austrian Cartel Unions, stove to overcome the spirit of nationalistic liberalism in universities and academies. The emergence of a more energetic clergy and the training of Catholic lay elite helped to reinvigorate Catholicism.

Since 1918. The overthrow of the Empire of Austria-Hungary and the creation of the Austrian Republic after World War I involved a thorough reorientation. Catholics recalled the glories of the old monarchy more vividly than its shortcomings and grieved at its passing; but they quickly returned to the harsh realities of catastrophic economic conditions in the postwar years. Between 1918 and 1932 the Church was preoccupied with strong opposition from the Socialists. Once the throne was overturned, hostile attention was focused on the altar. In its search for a new "secular arm" to support it, the Church discovered the Christian Social party, whose leader was Ignaz *Seipel. The Socialist party, called the Social Democrats, had power and numbers. Moreover, Austrian Marxism was radical, atheistic, and class-conscious. As early as 1911 the Socialists had defeated the Christian Social party by allying with anticlerical capitalistic liberals. The Social Democrats increased their strength by profiting from the disturbed conditions after 1918. Their aim was complete separation of Church and State and the abolition of any public recognition of the Church's legal character. Religion to them was a private matter, opium for the people. They attacked the Church continually as an enemy of the working class and an accomplice of capitalism. Defections from the Church resulted. There were about 23,000 defections in 1922 and another 30,000 in 1927 and in 1928 after the July *coup-de-main.* Jewish publications joined in the attack.

In this troubled period, Cardinal *Piffl of Vienna stood out as a resolute and far-sighted leader of the clergy. A second outstanding Catholic was Ignaz Seipel, a Christian diplomat of European stature, a planner, and a statesman, whose efforts as head of the government saved Austria from economic collapse, revolution, and Communist rule. He based his state policies on fundamental Christian principles and esteemed sound souls above sound currency. Among the evidences of spiritual vitality were the establishment of the Canisiuswerk für Priesterberufe, a society to promote priestly vocations, and the charitable association known as Caritas Socialis. New Catholic newspapers included *Wiener Kirchenblatt,* started in Vienna by Monsignor Mörzinger, and the *Reichspost,* published by Frederic Funder. Among the new Catholic periodicals were *Neues Reich,* edited by Joseph Eberle, and *Schönere Zukunft,* edited by Johannes Messner. Canon Handlos and Monsignor Rudolf opened an institute for pastoral theology. The liturgical writings of Pius *Parsch circulated widely; several of them were translated into English.

Engelbert *Dollfuss, leader of the Christian Social party, became chancellor in 1932. During his short term in power previous to his assassination by Nazi agitators in 1934, he ratified a concordat with the Holy See. His social program was much influenced by the Catholic social thought of Karl Sonnenschein (d. 1929) and Ignaz Seipel. As chancellor, Dollfuss tried to end class conflicts by putting into effect the corporative state advocated by Pius XI in the encyclical **Quadragesimo anno.* Despite the opposition of his own party, the chancellor put into practice the new corporative constitution, which went contrary to the traditional concept of parliamentary representation and gave much autonomy to the federated states. In order to effect his lofty aims amid growing agitation by the advocates of *National Socialism, Dollfuss used authoritarian methods.

Once the Nazis seized power in 1938, the corporative state and the concordat came to an end. Blame was laid on the Church for the defects of the former system. Oppression of the Church began without delay. Some 1,400 establishments under clerical control were closed. All Catholic societies and youth organizations were disbanded. Numerous charitable and Church institutions were seized. More than 200 convents were suppressed. The government systematically hindered pastoral work and religious instruction and curbed clerical training. About 300,000 withdrew from the

Church rather than make the requested contributions to it. Of the 724 priests arrested, 110 were sent to concentration camps, where 27 of them died and 15 others were executed. This persecution had a positive as well as a negative side, because it led many to return to their faith. Since all activity in associations was forbidden, young persons joined their priests in parish groups. Since 1939 financial contributions have been based on lists that included all parishioners. One effect of persecution has been to silence discontent over this practice.

Since 1945 the Church has been free of bondage, but it has had to confront the prevailing worldliness. Since all Catholic associations had been destroyed, Catholic Action was organized under episcopal control; it soon became an important element in public life. Church and clergy retired from active politics, but the struggle of political parties over the respective philosophies of life continued. The Church has been represented by her bishops rather than by clerical politicians. It has been financially independent of the state, with which it associates on congenial terms. The concordat of 1934 was recognized by the new federal government. Arrangements were made with the Holy See about the Religious Fund, the school problem, and the creation of the Dioceses of Eisenstadt and Innsbruck.

Statistics. Austria is divided ecclesiastically into two provinces. The Archdiocese of Salzburg has as suffragans Innsbruck (with the Vicariate of Feldkirch), Graz, and Klagenfurt. Suffragan to the Archdiocese of Vienna are Eisenstadt, Linz, and Sankt Pölten. *Wettingen-Mehrerau is an abbey *nullius*. Parishes total about 3,000.

In 1963 there were 4,240 secular and 2,225 religious priests. Pastoral work occupied 4,220 priests, with one priest per 1,500 faithful. There were 600 seminarians in 1960. Religious men numbered about 4,000, and religious women 17,600.

According to the 1951 census Austria's population was 7,073,087. Of this total there were 6,170,084 Catholics, 429,493 Protestants, 32,919 *Old Catholics, 15,000 Orthodox, 11,224 Jews, and 264,000 without religious affiliation. Religious liberty is accorded to all beliefs. In 1961, when the population was 7,074,000 Catholics totaled 6,260,000. Of these, 46.5 per cent made their Easter duty and 34.5 per cent attended Sunday Mass regularly. The annual excess of defections over conversions is about 3,300. Almost all children of Catholic families are baptized and sent to religious instruction, although only 83 per cent of the Catholics are married before a priest. The birthrate is one of the lowest in the world. Population increases have been due to refugee immigrants. The 293 Catholic schools in 1956 enrolled about 40,000 students.

Bibliography: General. E. TOMEK, *Kirchengeschichte Österreichs,* 3 v. (Innsbruck 1935–59). J. WODKA, *Kirche in Österreich* (Vienna 1959), W. LORENZ, *Du bist doch in unserer Mitte. Wege der Kirche in Österreich* (Vienna 1962). History of dioceses. E. TOMEK and K. AMON, *Geschichte der Diözese Seckau,* v.1 (Graz 1918); v.3.1 (Graz 1960). M. HEUWIESER, *Geschichte des Bistums Passau,* v.1 (Passau 1939). J. WODKA, *Das Bistum St. Pölten* (St. Pölten 1950). A. MAIER, *Kirchengeschichte von Kärnten,* 3 v. (Klagenfurt 1951–56). A. SPARBER, *Kirchengeschichte Tirols* (Innsbruck 1957). *Erläuterungen zum Historischen Atlas der österreichischen Alpenländer,* 2. Abteilung: *Kirchen- und Grafschaftskarte,* pt. 1–8 (Vienna 1940–58). Special periods. R. NOLL, *Frühes Christentum in Österreich* (Vienna 1954). I. ZIBERMAYR, *Noricum, Baiern und Österreich* (2d ed. Horn 1956). K. OETTINGER, *Das Werden Wiens* (Vienna 1951). H. VON SRBIK, *Die Beziehungen von Staat und Kirche in Österreich während des Mittelalters* (Innsbruck 1904; repr. Leipzig 1938). S. R. VON LAMA, *Am tiefsten Quell,* 3 v. (Vienna 1963–64), v.1 *Der Aufbau des christlichen Österreich;* v.2 *Im Zeitalter des Kampfes um die Glaubenserneuerung;* v.3 *Überwindung der Aufklärung.* Austrian saints, mystics since the Middle Ages. F. KLOSTERMANN et al., *Die Kirche in Österreich . . .* (Vienna 1966). W. BUCHOWIECKI, *Die gotischen Kirchen Österreichs* (Vienna 1952). K. EDER, *Studien zur Reformationsgeschichte Oberösterreichs,* 2 v. (Linz 1933–36). G. MECENSEFFY, *Geschichte des Protestantismus in Österreich* (Graz 1956). A. CORETH, *Pietas Austriaca. Ursprung und Entwicklung barocker Frömmigkeit in Österreich* (Munich 1960). F. MAASS, *Der Josephinismus,* 5 v. (Vienna 1951–61). F. ENGEL-JANOSI, *Österreich und der Vatikan,* 2 v. (Graz 1958–60). E. WEINZIERL-FISCHER, *Die österreichischen Konkordate von 1855 und 1933* (Vienna 1961). F. FUNDER, *Vom Gestern ins Heute* (Vienna 1955); *Als Österreich den Sturm bestand* (Vienna 1957). A. DIAMANT, *Austrian Catholics and the First Republic: Democracy, Capitalism and the Social Order, 1918–1934* (Princeton 1960). A. HUDAL, *Der Katholizismus in Österreich* (Innsbruck 1931). K. RUDOLF, *Aufbau im Widerstand* (Salzburg 1947). L. LENTNER, "Custos quid de nocte?", *Festschrift Michael Pfliegler* (Vienna 1961). E. BODZENTA, *Die Katholiken in Österreich: Ein religions-soziologischer Überblick* (Vienna 1962). J. WODKA, LexThK^2 7:1279–84. *Bilan du Monde* 2:109–118. Latourette Christ19th–20thCent v.1, 4. F. ENGEL-JANOSI, *Die politische Korrespondenz der Päpste mit den österreichischen Kaisern, 1804–1918* (Vienna 1964). AnnPont has annual data on all dioceses. **Illustration credits:** Figs. 2, 3, and 4, Austrian Information Service, New York. Fig. 5, P. Ledermann, Vienna.

[J. WODKA]

AUSTRIAN LITERATURE

Austria belongs linguistically and culturally to the German-speaking world, but the Catholic religion, as well as the multinational character and geopolitical situation of the hereditary Empire of Austria (1804–1918), have kept its intellectual and cultural history singularly distinct and independent. Vienna, as the one-time capital of a system of kingdoms and countries, as a center of music, as one of the most important places in Germany from a political and social point of view, and, since 1800, as the single real metropolis, has always played a leading role in the intellectual life of Austria and maintains its importance as a meeting place for the intellectual currents of East and West, North and South; yet among the states and state capitals of Austria, Vienna can claim leadership today only in the realm of the theater.

The intellectual exchange between Austria and Germany has, at every era, enriched the literature of both countries (*see* GERMAN LITERATURE). Austria did not experience the break with tradition caused by the *Reformation; the unity of culture created by the *baroque era postponed or weakened the influence of German movements, especially of German *idealism and the *Enlightenment. The blossoming of Romanticism and classicism bore fruit in Austria only at a later date; between 1809 and 1815 Vienna was a Romantic center (*see* ROMANTICISM, LITERARY; NEOCLASSICISM). Conversely, the polished style of Austria's administration and legislation, of her free professions and social life, had its effect on German men of letters.

Austrian writers, unlike those of Germany, stand quite naturally within the framework of their society, although they often lived surprisingly lonely lives (e.g., Stifter, Grillparzer, Anzengruber, F. v. Saar, Marie v. Ebner-Eschenbach, Kafka, H. v. Hofmannsthal, and Rilke). Many of them combine, in a striking way, closeness to soil and people with a highly developed artistic

Fig. 1. The Burgtheater at Vienna. The spire of the cathedral of St. Stephen can be seen in the middle background.

sensibility. Because of the still evident ecclesiastical origin of their intellectual culture and the still valid social distinctions of nobility, peasantry, and rather small middle class (toward which German literature is predominantly oriented), Austrian authors develop a particular awareness of primal states, of the natural structure of the social order, of natural intellectual worth, of organic growth rather than formless abstractions (Austria has had, for example, no share in the construction and development of philosophical systems). The population evidences a highly lyrical musical talent, a strongly realistic character, and a predilection for jest. Even in the treatment of deeply serious matters, Austria's artists are capable of lightness (e.g., Mozart, Haydn, Raimund, Nestroy, Rosegger, Max Mell, and F. K. Ginzkey) and are characterized by a naïve dedication to art as the natural expression of a life that is both melancholy and serene. In contrast to the new Germany with its amazingly rapid development away from the old way of life, Austria is, in every respect, a land of greater closeness to nature and is possessed of a gentle, highly attractive intellectual climate.

Austrian literature in a broad sense begins in the early Middle Ages; in a specific sense it begins with the period 1804–06, when the Hapsburg dynasty renounced the title of "German Emperor" and assumed that of "Austrian Emperor," thereby beginning to foster national consciousness without sacrificing Austria's role as the center of the Occident. Not to be overlooked, however, is the significant and unique development of Austrian baroque drama, especially in the schools of the Jesuits and other orders, a heritage whose directive force determined artistic literary practice for centuries (*see* JESUIT DRAMA). Humanistic traditions and ancient Latinity, the bases of baroque culture, have conferred upon Austrian literature a uniform and steady flow of development, in which those sudden outbursts and upheavals that might have engendered "movements" have been absent. In the lineal and conservative course of political and intellectual development, literary individualists have appeared but rarely. It was not until the dissolution of the old Austria (1918) that intellectually "emancipated" authors made their appearance. As literary epochs, one may distinguish the literature of the pre-March era (Vormärz), the literature under Franz Josef (1848–1916), and the literature of the 20th century.

PRE-MARCH ERA

During the *Metternich regime there arose an artistic literature that compensated for the modest achievement of the 18th century, when the chief representative had been Joseph von Sonnenfels (1733–1817). The struggle against foreign domination by the French reached its peak in the uprising of the Tyrolean peasantry in 1809, which nourished national consciousness and was itself both fostered and used by literature. Because of the changed intellectual atmosphere and the resultant attacks upon it, the basis of the unified culture created by the baroque began to give way, thus preparing favorable conditions for the literary efforts that culminated in Grillparzer and Stifter. The Young Germany movement had no noticeable repercussions in Austria; German classicism and Romanticism likewise gained few followers. The basis of Austrian *Biedermeier,* in which the whole of society was for the last time consciously united in a uniform way of life, was the contrast between ideal and reality; it contributed to one-sidedness by its resignation. The *Biedermeier* attitude toward life after the Congress of *Vienna was ruptured politically by both the ideological storm of 1789 and the romantic belief in the nation; it was shaken philosophically by the influence of a concentrated Enlightenment. There was an astounding mixture of backwardness and radical modernity in the literature, which had been struggling mightily upward since 1800, especially in Vienna, Prague, Graz, the army, and officialdom.

The Drama. Because of the highly developed theatrical tradition (the Vienna *Burgtheater* was made Court and National Theater in 1776, and general "freedom of the theater" was proclaimed) and because of the struggling mode of existence in the pre-March era, achievements in drama surpassed those in other literary genres. Franz *Grillparzer and Ferdinand *Raimund brought the baroque music drama to the full development of literary spoken drama. The perfecter and conqueror of the Viennese theatrical tradition was Johann Nepomuk Nestroy (1801–62), often referred to as the "Viennese Aristophanes." Gifted with unusual psychological perception and distinguished by a ruthless love of truth,

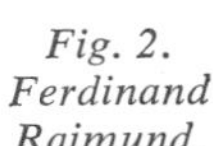

Fig. 2. Ferdinand Raimund.

to which, however, he never sacrificed his Viennese sense of humor, he pointed mercilessly, by jest, wit, comedy, trick, and obscenity, to the wounds and crassness under Vienna's outer finery. His Mephistophelean

Fig. 3. Johann Nepomuk Nestroy.

intellect charmed the Vienna *Vorstadttheater* away from sentimentality and the world of fairies; his sober realism surpasses that of Karl Georg Büchner (1813–37) in its use of irony and humorous scepticism. Most important of his 83 plays, which are mainly concerned with social criticism, are *Der böse Geist des Lumpazivagabundus,* or *Das liederliche Kleeblatt* (1833); his still successful *Zu ebener Erde und im ersten Stock* (1835), which depicts a farcical reconciliation between poverty and riches; *Das Haus der Temperamente* (1837), a technical masterpiece; *Die Zerrissene* (1844), which portrays the typical sophisticated rich man whom nothing pleases because he can attain effortlessly all the pleasures of life; *Einen Jux will er sich machen* (1842); *Judith und Holofernes* (1849), a parody of Friedrich Hebbel (1813–63). Besides their theatrical value, Nestroy's plays have inestimable significance as documents of the actual life of the people in the then capital and introduce many newly created local types. Like Nestroy, Eduard von Bauernfeld (1802–90), the most successful playwright of the period, was committed to the middle-class world. He was master par excellence of the pleasant conversational tone of well-bred society and offered primarily entertainment. A predilection for the unusual with scant action and little pure nature characterized the plays of Friedrich Halm (pseudonym of Eligius F. J. von Münch-Bellinghausen, 1806–71). With these important authors should be mentioned J. A. Gleich (1772–1841), Karl Meisl (1775–1853), and Adolf Bäuerle (1786–1859), whose abundant productions are revealing portraits of the cultural history of Vienna.

Prose. In the field of narrative prose Adalbert *Stifter achieved a monumental art that was unique in the 19th century. Charles Sealsfield (pseudonym of Karl Postl, 1793–1864) appropriated the subject matter of his models (Cooper, Chateaubriand, Scott) in German and English narratives drawn from the turbulent world of farmers, adventurers, merchants, scouts, and Indians. In his homeland, after abandoning his vocation at the Kreuzherrenstift, he had been active on baroque palace stages, had fled to America in 1823, and there found quick success as speculator, political agent, and writer. Although an American citizen, he emigrated to Switzerland in 1831 and after a life filled with many changes and journeys, which sometimes took him again to America, he was buried at Yverdon (Switzerland). Sealsfield founded the exotic realistic novel, which was further developed by F. Gerstäcker (1816–72), T. Mügge (1806–61), and others. He worked out a politicosociological type of novel, alive with dramatic impulses, that anticipated the technique of the "novel of juxtaposition," far more forcefully than did K. F. Gutzkow (1811–78), and the American novel of more recent times, e.g., Hemingway, Steinbeck, Faulkner. His principal works are *Die Legitime und die Republikaner* (1833; the improved German edition of *Tokeah or The White Rose,* 1828), *Der Virey und die Aristokraten* (1834), *Lebensbilder aus der westlichen Hemisphäre* (1834–37), *Deutsch-Amerikanische Wahlverwandtschaften* (1839–40), *Das Kajütenbuch* (1841), and *Süden und Norden* (1842). His later works especially, confront the romantic, fantastic distortion of German America-enthusiasts with a picture that, though prosaic and harsh, yet conveyed all the grandeur of the America the author actually experienced. Sealsfield shared the view of the liberals: "A glance toward America is a glance toward the future."

To the number of lesser writers, who imitated Wieland, Tieck, E. T. A. Hoffmann, W. Scott, and the *novelle*-writers of the Italian Renaissance, belong Friedrich Halm (1806–71); Karoline Pichler (1769–1843); her imitator Joseph von Hammer-Purgstall (1774–1856); Andreas Schuhmacher; J. N. Vogl (1802–66); S. Brunner (1814–93); the Prince Bishop of Salzburg, Friedrich Schwarzenberg (1809–85), who represented an intelligent and courageous conservatism and whose little-known work shows strong understanding of the national character; and Adolf von Tschabuschnigg, who, in his novel *Die Industriellen* (2 pts., 1854), made one of the first attempts to give artistic formulation to a theme drawn from the sociologically

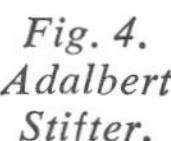

Fig. 4. Adalbert Stifter.

changed era. Johann Ladislaus Pyrker (1772–1842), a Hungarian bishop of Tyrolean origin, presented an obsolete, mythologizing Renaissance art in his *Versepik.* The Viennese priests Sebastian Brunner and Ferdinand

Sauter (1804–54) dedicated themselves to satire and parody in the mood of *Abraham of Sancta Clara.

Poetry. In the lyric, Nikolaus *Lenau achieved a high level. The first to raise their voices against the ruling system as representatives of the Young Germany group were Anastasius Grün (pseudonym of Count Anton Alexander Auersperg, 1806–76), who later showed more moderation, and J. C. von Zedlitz (1790–1862). They were soon joined by the youth of the provinces: Karl Isidor Beck (1817–79) and the "Lark of Freedom," Hermann von Gilm (1812–64). *Biedermeier* poets were Johann Nepomuk Vogl (1802–66), Johann Gabriel Seidl (1804–75), and others, including writers in dialect. With his discovery of the Innviertel peasants, Franz Stelzhamer (1802–74), brilliant offspring of the Austrian peasantry, gave powerful impulse, in verses full of natural rhythm, to literature in dialect, a genre that had previously been cultivated largely by priests and that continues to flourish.

Era of Franz Josef

After the unsuccessful Revolution of 1848 political and social conditions remained unaltered; only the industrial revolution made new progress in Vienna, Prague, Brünn, and Reichenberg, creating a conflict between the half-feudal political structure and the needs of modern economic development. In 1866 the Hapsburgs surrendered to Prussia the leadership of Germany, thus eliminating Austria from German political life. The liberal middle class took over the intellectual leadership; its struggle for national ascendancy, in a state in which the German-speaking population numbered only a fourth of the total, kindled those national antagonisms that led to the dissolution of the monarchy in 1918.

The literature reflected the increasing ills of the political, national, and moral spheres. The cultural decline ran parallel to the ideological uncertainty, which, for its part, explained the rejection of drama after the pre-March era. Under H. Laube (1806–84) the *Burgtheater* entered the service of the liberal *bourgeoisie*. The Viennese theater, however, was beginning to forfeit its supremacy; its control lessened, thereby emancipating epic and lyric forces through which the countries whose capitals had won increased political weight in consequence of the Parliament could compete with Vienna on equal terms.

Beginnings of Realism. The predilection for historicity and eclecticism, represented especially by Robert Hamerling (1830–89), brought the people no new aesthetic culture. The realists, at first not accepted by the public, finally gained recognition through the middle-class youth of the nineties, whose revolutionary temper and positivistic, socialistic, and impressionistic attitudes were at variance with the liberalism of their fathers. Ludwig Anzengruber (1839–89), first realist of the Austrian stage, hoped, by his somewhat didactic and tendentious dramas of peasant life, to renew the Austrian (especially Viennese) popular play, which was bound to the operations of the highly capitalized entertainment theater. Following Raimund and Nestroy, he did not achieve their stature; many of his couplets seem outmoded and out of place, and have neither Nestroy's wit nor Raimund's charm. The tragedy *Der Pfarrer von Kirchfeld* (1870) is a plea for civil marriage and marriage of the clergy as well as for an enlightened priesthood; like the comedy *Die Kreuzelschreiber* (1872), it is an echo of the intellectual struggle that arose throughout Europe as a result of *Vatican Council I, the proclamation of the dogma of *infallibility, and the *Old Catholic movement in Germany. *Der Meineidbauer* (1872), a tragedy, was intended to "illumine the dark nature of religion with the torch of reason," but was in fact more concerned with peasant avarice. *Der G'wissenswurm* (1874), a comedy, shows the conflict between joy in the world and renunciation of it. *Das vierte Gebot* (1878) reveals the frightening backgrounds of the changing Viennese atmosphere; it is the tragedy of the sins of the fathers, which bear fruit a hundredfold in the crimes of the children. Anzengruber supported the view that genuine humanity is to be found only among the peasantry. A better storyteller than playwright, he wrote "stories which showed how life is," thus approaching naturalism. His novels are masterpieces of realistic technique: *Der Schandfleck* (1876) and, his best achievement, *Der Sternsteinhof* (1884).

The best picture of the era of Franz Josef between 1848 and 1900 is afforded by the works of Ferdinand von Saar (1833–1906), whose technique, though stronger and harsher, is not unlike that of Theodor *Storm. With his first *novella, Innocens, ein Lebensbild* (1866), Von Saar reached his zenith; in form and content the volume *Herbstreigen* (1897) is characteristic of his whole art. In his dramas he showed himself a fine and deep psychologist whose plays, though the action is often heavy, are nonetheless marked by clear exposition, excellent characterization, and suspenseful endings. His best drama is *Kaiser Heinrich* (2 pts.: *Hildebrandt* and *Heinrichs Tod,* 1865–67). As lyricist (*Gedichte,* 1882, 1888, 1904), Von Saar gives melancholy expression to the transitoriness and vanity of things. Peter Rosegger (1845–1918) composed models of genuine popular narratives, especially in *Schriften des Waldschulmeisters* (1875) and *Waldheimat* (1877), which couple true feeling for nature with didactic intention and basically peasant sensibilities with acquired but sincere liberalism, at the same time bearing witness to his belief in life. Born of poor peasant stock, Rosegger furthered his own education. He is the direct successor of Stifter and Sealsfield.

Maria von Ebner-Eschenbach (1830–1916), born into a noble Bohemian family as Countess Dubsky, is closely related to Theodor Fontane (1819–98), among others, both in choice of material and in theme and style. In her father's palace she learned to know the Moravian peasantry; and in Vienna, the nobles of the court and the petty bourgeoisie. In her works she pictures both without flourish but with understanding. Her femininity is evidenced by her kindly serenity and inner balance. The novel *Das Gemeindekind* (1887) and the volume *Aus Spätherbsttagen* (1901) are considered her best achievements. Her epigrams and aphorisms combine mature wisdom and artistic form. Ferdinand Kürnberger (1823–79), outstanding literary critic of the realistic school, is known only for his novel about Lenau, *Der Amerikamüde* (1855), in which he exposed the contemporary capitalistic way of life in America. By his penetrating historical presentations of the life of Polish Jews (4 v. *Das Vermächtnis Kains,* 1870–77), Leopold von Sacher-Masoch (1836–95) associated himself with the realists; later he also pictured sexual aberrations (masochism). Karl Emil Franzos (1848–1904) represented the democratic tradition of 1848. He came from the ghetto of East Galicia, a world that fills his sketches, *Aus Halbasien* (1876), and his collection of *novelle, Die Juden von Barnow* (1877), and gives substance to his novel *Ein Kampf ums Recht* (1882). He was "ardently concerned to give artistic formulation to truth." Besides his writing, he won literary merit as the rediscoverer of Georg Büchner (1813–37), whose hitherto unknown MS for *Wozzek* he found. To the group of realistic writers belong also Jakob Julius David (1859–1906), Ada Christian (1844–1901), Franz Michael Felder (1839–69), and Wilhelm Fischer (1846–1932), who, as artist, strove to establish a synthesis between nature and culture. In form Fischer excelled P. Rosegger, but, because of his aristocratic reserve, he had less popular appeal.

Among the literary successors of Anzengruber and Rosegger the long-cultivated genre of *Heimatdichtung* (regional literature) attained new heights as light literature with a free-from-Vienna (*Los-von-Wien*) tendency; it quickly absorbed the techniques of naturalism and Impressionism, then formed close ties with the new Romanticism. Its chief representatives are Emil Ertl (1860–1935), Karl Schönherr (1867–1943). Rudolf H. Bartsch (1873–1952), Otto Stoessl (1875–1936), Friedrich von Gagern (1882–1947), and Sebastian Riegel (pseud. Reimmichel; 1867–1953).

Naturalism. To the ranks of naturalism belong, among others, Ferdinand Bronner (pseud. Franz Adamus, 1867–1948); Felix Salten (pseud. of Siegmund Salzmann, 1869–1945), author of the well known *Bambi* books; Franz Nabl (1883–), whose novel *Oedhof* (1911) is a worthy companionpiece to Stifter's *Nachsommer* and who was also active as playwright; Gottlieb A. Crüwell (1866–1931); and Anton Wildgans (1881–1932). In his dramas Wildgans dealt with daring and striking themes, becoming more and more expressionistic; as a lyricist skilled in word and verse, he attempted to make a place for himself in the lyric of naturalism. At the turn of the century the rejection of naturalism and an ultrarefinement of spirit and sense gave rise to a decadent literature, whose chief representatives—Peter Altenberg (1862?–1919), Arthur *Schnitzler, Richard Beer-Hofmann (1866–1945), Jakob Wassermann (1873–1934), Hugo von Hofmannsthal (1874–1929), Richard von Schaukal, Leopold von Andrian, the young *Rilke, and Stefan *Zweig—as aesthetes of the so-called Vienna Circle (*Wiener Kreis*), gave expression to Vienna's overrefined culture. They brought the literature of the Franz Josef era through the school of new Romanticism into the 20th century and, after some changes, assumed an important position there. As critical leaders and opponents, Hermann Bahr and Karl *Kraus exercised an important influence, but they too completed their task only in the following era. The remarkable synthesis of naturalism, new Romanticism, and psychological Impressionism provided fertile soil for the teachings of Sigmund *Freud, the founder of psychoanalysis (*see* NATURALISM, LITERARY).

Fig. 5. Karl Kraus.

Catholic Revival. With the publication of *Steht die katholische Belletristik auf der Höhe der Zeit?* in 1898, the German Carl *Muth inaugurated the so-called Catholic Literary Strife (*see* LITERARY REVIVAL, CATHOLIC). He demanded the renewal of literature by recourse to religious sources and the broadening of Catholic literature in the spirit of the times. The Catholic elite united around his periodical, *Hochland* (1903–). In Austria, Catholic and near-Catholic literature was so imbued with liberalism and so "modern" that it required not a broadening but a return to fundamentals (the unity of life and faith in the Middle Ages and the baroque period). The convert Richard von Kralik (1852–1934) wrote unproducible dramas in this vein; in 1905 he united the Catholic writers of Vienna in the *Gralbund,* whose program aspired to a Catholic Romantic literature in the spirit of the Hofbauer circle in Vienna and the Görres circle in Munich. Their periodical, *Der Gral,* which began to appear in 1906, was later transferred to Germany by the German Jesuit Friedrich Muckermann (1883–1946), where it won high esteem even among non-Catholics.

THE 20TH-CENTURY LITERATURE

As the literature of acknowledged masters (the Vienna Circle), Austrian literature was at its zenith when the monarchy collapsed. Both as a writer and as a brilliant critic of literature and art, Hermann Bahr (1863–1934) exerted a special influence on the modern era. From 1892 to 1912 he was dramatic critic at the *Burgtheater;* besides theatrical pieces, novels, and critical studies, he published, after 1800, the periodical *Moderne Dichtung.* Through him and through Arthur Schnitzler, the chief representative of literary Impressionism in drama and narrative literature (he has been called the engineer of the soul), Austrian literature once more established contact with modern German literature. A warning against corruption of language, the surest sign of approaching cultural disintegration, was voiced by Karl Kraus. In his much-admired and much-despised journal *Die Fackel* (1899–1937), he presented essays that were absolute masterpieces of form and substance, and which appeared in collected volumes (e.g., *Untergang der Welt durch schwarze Magie,* 1922). Kraus, a sharp critic and keen observer of modern society, saw clearly that "progress" aroused only ruthless striving after profit, power, riches, and fame and led to dissipation and loss of culture, of which he saw the concentrated expression, if not the origin, in the press. In his poems and dramas, he gave evidence of structural power; his colossal drama (219 scenes in 5 acts), *Die letzten Tage der Menschheit* (1919; first produced in the *Theater an der Wien,* 1964, with 42 scenes), raised a devastating complaint against those who waged wars. In satire and form he can be compared with Jonathan

Swift. Inspired by the *Fackel,* Ludwig von Focker's *Der Brenner* (1910–32) made its appearance in Innsbruck as an autonomous, culturally conservative, yet highly radical, Catholic periodical.

Fig. 6. Max Mell.

Symbolism and Neo-Romanticism. In the period around 1900 the terms symbolism and new Romanticism were used to designate a movement that was in danger of turning aside from the presentation of the real problems of life and fleeing into the mystically comprehended inner renewal and self-absorption of individualism, with its one-sided and exaggerated appreciation of the formal side of art (*see* SYMBOLISM, LITERARY). In Austria forces that kept themselves apart from this movement produced such outstanding figures of modern German and world literature as Hugo von Hofmannsthal and Rainer Maria Rilke, and later, Robert *Musil and Franz *Kafka. With his novel *Der Mann ohne Eigenschaften* (v.1 1931; v.2 1933; compl. ed. 1952) Musil took his place beside such novelists as *Proust and *Joyce, winning recognition as the most important novelist of the first half of the 20th century. Expressionism appeared not only in the works of Franz Kafka but also in those of Paul Adler (1878–1946), who to some extent paved the way for Kafka; of Max Brod (1884–), the custodian of Kafka's works; of Gustav Meyrink (1887–1914), whose pamphlets had prepared for an understanding of Kafka's work; and of Robert Michel (1876–1957). To these novelists should be added the lyric poets of expressionism: Theodor Däubler (1876–1934), Georg *Trakl, and Franz *Werfel, who was important also as a novelist.

Stefan Zweig absorbed the overrefined culture of Vienna in the period of Impressionism around 1900. As playwright and author of *novelle,* he was an imitator; his chief accomplishment lay in his fictionalized and somewhat controversial monographs of world figures of literature and history, in which his treatment of contemporary issues and problems of human nature revealed his liberal and cosmopolitan humanism. His best work is *Die Welt von gestern: Erinnerungen eines Europäers* (1942).

New Cultural Currents. The rise of the worker into intellectual life was documented by, among others, Alfons Petzold (1882–1923) in his writings about the working class. For the younger generation, who came principally from the provinces, the break with the past after 1919 was complete. As a German buffer state, the new Austria enjoyed but briefly the free play of democracy; after the catastrophe of the Third Reich it faced, both politically and intellectually, a new beginning. The concerns of the new generation were rural, whereas those of the older generation were linked with the problems of the cosmopolitan city of Vienna and its decadence. From the world of yesterday comes the inspiration of Felix Braun (1885–) in the novel *Agnes Altkirchner* (1927; repub. 1957 as *Herbst des Reiches*), Joseph Roth (1894–1939) in *Radetzkymarsch* (1932), Alexander Lernet-Holenia (1897–) in *Die Standarte* (1934), Franz Karl Ginzkey (1871–1963), whose *Prinz Tunors* (1934) is a Köpenich-saga about the Salzburg of 1804, Ernst Weiss (1884–1940), Albert Paris Gütersloh (1887–), and many others. Like Kafka and Musil, Hermann *Broch portrayed the end of an era in his preoccupation with the problem of the destruction of value (*Schlafwandler,* 1931–32); his most famous work, *Der Tod des Vergil* (1947), is permeated with mysticism in search of salvation. A significant narrative talent reveals itself also in the works of Heimito von Doderer (1896–), whose universal picture of deterioration is masterful in structure and plastically exact, sometimes baroque in language.

Themes of a Catholic regional literature appear in the lyrics, novels, and dramas of Max Mell (1882–); he combines humanistic traditions with a theatrical art that is popular and rooted in the soil, e.g., *Apostelspiel* (1923) and *Das Nachfolge-Christi-Spiel* (1927). Inspired by her Catholic experience of faith, Baroness Enrica von Handel-Mazzetti (1871–1955) shaped historical materials from the Danube Valley into epic narratives, whose style, form, and mood reflect the antithetical world of the baroque *Counter Reformation. Her best work is *Meinrad Helmpergers denkwürdiges Jahr* (1900); in 1906 appeared *Jesse und Maria;* in 1912–14, *Stephana Schwertner;* and later, some biographical novels.

Midcentury Trends. Disregarding the achievements of modern technical science, Karl Heinrich Waggerl (1897–) attempts somewhat less pretentious fictional accounts of peasant life in his novels *Brot* (1930), *Schweres Blut* (1931), *Mütter* (1935), and others; he is, besides, a master of the short story. From a more earthbound spirit, one that believes now in God, now in natural myth, Richard Billinger (1893–1964) com-

Fig. 7. Karl Heinrich Waggerl.

posed tales, poems, and dramas (in part, peasant plays in the baroque manner) that regard man's life as a spectacle before God and the adversary. In stirring dramas, rich in thought and imagery and often ecstatic in language, Franz Theodor Csokor (1885–) exercises his desire for self-expression. The dramatist Arnolt Bronnen (1895–1959) misdirected his course through political extremism. Franz Tumler (1912–) writes lyrics and tales; Herbert Eisenreich (1925–), lyrics, tales and, more recently, dramas. In lyric poetry mention should be made of Theodor Kramer (1897–1958) and, in particular, of Josef Weinheber (1892–1945), who sought a way out of chaos and found his goal in "form." With his odes in ancient meters he continued the traditions of baroque and Renaissance poetry and glorified the heroic and the tragic, as well as the metaphysical powers. Among the more recent lyricists Christine Busta (1915–), Christine Lavant (1915–), and the very laudable Ingeborg Bachmann (1926–) are outstanding; this strong participation of women in the most recent Austrian literature receives considerable increase from the prose works of Gertrud Fussenegger (1912–) and Ilse Aichinger (1921–).

Fig. 8. Josef Weinheber.

Bibliography: J. W. NAGL et al., eds., *Deutsch-österreichische Literaturgeschichte,* 4 v. (Vienna 1899–1937). J. NADLER, *Literaturgeschichte Österreichs* (2d ed. Salzburg 1951). E. J. GÖRLICH, *Einführung in die Geschichte der österreichischen Literatur* (3d ed. Vienna 1948). E. ALKER, *Die deutsche Literatur im 19. Jahrhundert: 1832–1914* (2d ed. Stuttgart 1962), esp. "Die österreichische Dichtung im Vormärz," 127–217; "Das österreichische Schrifttum in der Zeit Franz Josephs I.," 597–659; 660–926. J. KÖRNER, *Bibliographisches Handbuch des deutschen Schrifttums* (3d ed. Bern 1949), index s.v. "Österreich." A. SCHMIDT, *Dichtung und Dichter Österreichs im 19. und 20. Jahrhundert,* 2 v. (Salzburg-Stuttgart 1964).

H. KINDERMANN, *Wegweiser durch die moderne Literatur in Österreich* (Innsbruck 1954). F. HEER, "Perspektiven österreichischer Gegenwartsdichtung," in *Deutsche Literatur in unserer Zeit,* ed. W. KAYSER et al. (2d ed. Göttingen 1959). O. BASIL et al., *Das grosse Erbe: Aufsätze zur österreichischen Literatur* (Vienna 1962). W. BRECHT, "Österreichische Geistesform und österreichische Dichtung," *Deutsche Vierteljahrsschrift für Literaturwissenschaft und Geistesgeschichte* 9 (1931) 607–627. F. KOCH, "Zur Literatur- und Geistesgeschichte Österreichs," *ibid.* 745–770. W. BIETAK, *Das Lebensgefühl des "Biedermeier" in der österreichischen Dichtung* (Vienna 1931). R. A. KANN, *A Study in Austrian Intellectual History: From Baroque to Romanticism* (New York 1960). F. HEER, *Land im Strom der Zeit: Österreich gestern, heute, morgen* (Vienna 1958). H. WEIGEL, *Flucht vor der Grösse: Beiträge zur Erkenntnis und Selbsterkenntnis Österreichs* (Vienna 1960). H. OLLES, "Gibt es eine österreichische Literatur? Ein Versuch zu ihrer Wesensbestimmung," *Wort und Wahrheit* 12 (1957) 115–134. **Illustration credit**: Fig. 4, Library of Congress. Figs. 1–3, 5–8, Austrian Information Service, New York City.

[L. SPULER]

AUTHORITY

A moral power that exercises an essential function as a cause of united action. Using a twofold analysis, one negative and the other positive, this article considers respectively the disrepute into which authority has fallen, the kind of case briefed by antiauthoritarian philosophies, what is meant by the essential function of authority, and various views of its source.

Disrepute of Authority. In a century devoted to excessive egalitarianism, authority is held in considerable disrepute. Some writers have gone so far as to suggest that one ought to talk about what authority "was" and not what it "is" (e.g., H. Arendt). Long before the current disrepute, G. W. F. *Hegel suggested that the leading thought of his day was the principle of "interiority," which regards both externality and authority as impertinent and lifeless.

Generally speaking, social philosophers rarely question the fact that social happiness depends on a felicitous combination of authority and freedom. No matter how well-defined they are, however, the terms authority and freedom imply, even on the level of ordinary understanding, a kind of opposition and a kind of complementary quality. The opposition arises because authority suggests coerciveness, and coerciveness at once is considered antinomical to freedom. And indeed, even ordinary analysis suggests that unless authority is balanced by freedom, tyranny is almost inevitable. But if freedom is taken as an absolute and if it be not balanced by some kind of authority, then it leads to chaos or degenerates inevitably into abusive license. An excess of the one or the other, of freedom or of authority, leads to mutual self-destruction.

A more critical analysis of the suspicion against authority has been furnished by Yves *Simon. Persons in authority enjoy positions of privilege and have access to goods and honors not available to the majority of men; thus it seems that authority is in "conflict with justice." And because vitality is evidenced by immanence and spontaneity, it may appear that the core of freedom is weakened by authority, which is in "conflict with life." Sometimes authority seems to be in "conflict with truth," since lovers of truth see all too often that authority is a kind of tool used to keep people in a state of ignorance favoring the *status quo*. Even more, many think that law can take the place of authority, that law is stable and orderly, free from the contingencies of the exercise of authority; thus they envision authority as in "conflict with order." Despite all of these suspicions that continue to undermine authority in the 20th century, however, every *community manifests an undeniable form of authority. It must be cautioned that there is no necessary connection between authority and any specific form in which it is embodied. But embodied it must be, if any community is to continue in existence.

Philosophers have long claimed that it is natural for man to live in *society, to unite with others. Society in this sense implies only reasonable members, not in any superficial connotation of acting reasonably, but as human beings who belong together by nature and exist together by reason of their common end. Natural sociability is not like membership in a club or union, into which one enters at will or from which he may withdraw arbitrarily. *Aristotle states this truth most powerfully: "He who is unable to live in society, or who has no need because he is sufficient for himself, must be either a beast or a god" (*Pol.* 1253a 28). It is because society is natural to man, whether it be the society of the family or of the state, that authority is necessary. For authority has a necessary function to perform in attaining the goal of any society.

Antiauthoritarian Philosophies. Some antiauthority theorists assert that authority is necessary only on a provisional basis because of the "insufficiency" of its members, as in the case of children, the illiterate, and the primitive. The implication of this position is that once (and if) the deficiency is removed, authority is no longer necessary. A subtle justification of sterilization and euthanasia has sometimes found its roots in such a theory. The basis of the deficiency theory of authority springs from the myth that there is a direct proportion between social progress and the progress of personal freedom. The next logical step in the theory is to equate social development and personal freedom with the inevitable or proportionate decay of authority.

The Comtian ideal of a society based on enlightened reason is summarized in the famous formula "Savoir pour prévoir pour pouvoir." Although covert antiauthority theories of society originating in some sociological circles have not been fully developed in technical fashion, they tend to imply constructs such as Edward Shils's "consensual collectivity," in which a so-called process of illumination is thought to modify individuals and finally result in collective self-transformations. The theory of enlightened reason is expressed by Shils thus: ". . . the very difference between the states of mind induced by attachment to or repulsion from authority and the detached and dispassionate states of mind induced by the exercise of sociological analysis means that different images of man, the world, and the authoritative self will almost inevitably persist."

The function of authority extends beyond the work of merely supplying for deficiency or waiting for the dawn of enlightened reason. The natural sociability of man demands association not for material needs alone, and not merely for defense against animal life, hunger, and disease. Man needs man for the furtherance of knowledge, for reciprocal spiritual profundity, for the enrichment of the "otherness" that underlies *friendship in a profoundly existential sense. The endless quest for totality is proper to man. This totality is one and the same for the single individual and for the collection of individuals; it is the totality that is, in fact, what was meant initially by the term *common good. The glory of human society goes beyond the glory of the individual it is meant to serve, a collective glory to which each individual brings himself as a proper gift and contributor. The human community so understood is a good itself that stands to serve mankind and every individual. It is this kind of good that demands a kind of common life wherein authority is properly necessary.

It is, of course, conceivable that some communities will attain their end without authority. In such instances, it merely happens that the good of one member coincides with that of another; here it is sufficient that an arbitrary contract effect the desired end. In these cases, the collective action can be achieved by a "consensual collectivity," since what is desired is not a proper common good but the interdependence of private goods. Even in these instances, however, if bad faith or some unforeseen circumstance intervene, authority may have to be invoked to achieve the end sought through the contract. The authority of the courts would then be invoked to achieve a judgment in line with the laws governing contractual relationships. An unrealistic view of society might lead one to suggest that all of human society could be composed of such simple partnerships. Were this possible, authority would not be necessary save for accidental reasons.

It may be noted here, however, that there is an authentic substitutional function to authority in the society of the *family. In this case, parental authority is necessary for survival and for education of offspring. Children go through periods of insufficiency in which the authority proper to the home is provisionally indispensable. In case of parental deficiency in this matter or in case of death, society takes over the exercise of such a parental function. Authority on this level aims at its own disappearance. In fact, the postponement of the period of self-determination is a genuine deficiency in any theory of parental control and child training.

Essential Function of Authority. A more realistic view of human societies suggests that few if any societies can survive for any length of time unless there is a firm and stable principle at work to assure, by unified action, the achievement of their common end. A multiplicity of practical judgments is inevitable in every nontheoretical situation. The weakness of every social theory of the "consensual collectivity" type is its inability to assure uniformity of action in such a way that it can extend to all the concrete particulars of a social situation. Unanimity cannot be such a principle since it overlooks the obvious differences existing among humans, such as those traceable to ignorance, ill will, selfishness, vested interests, and the like. All judgments made for an action are surrounded with contingencies that make it impossible to demonstrate the necessity of any given prudential judgment. It is true that certain circumstances may generate a kind of spontaneity, such as that which takes place in times of emergency—e.g., an unjust attack or a natural disaster. Even here, however, society has to fight against plunder and treachery, factors that make unanimity highly improbable. Simon states that "unanimity is a precarious principle of united action whenever the common good can be attained in more than one way."

The main thesis of this article, then, is that authority is a moral power exercising an essential function as a cause of united action. The basis of this proposition is that the rich plurality of means for achieving the common good of any society demands the election of one from among many. The power to make such a choice lies in authority, which is a moral power residing in the regulator of the society. The desired unified action that is indispensable for the attainment of the common end comes from compliance with rules that bind all the members of the society in question. Therefore, except for the cases mentioned above, authority must exercise a vital function to guarantee consistent unified action.

It must be pointed out, however, that the need for authority in society and the need for any given form of governing personnel are quite distinct; the confusion of the two leads to multiple confusions. The power to issue commands for the sake of a common action neither implies nor excludes the actual use of coercion or persuasion. It is commonly held that the actual use of coercion or persuasion implies a failure of authority. The basis of this position is that persons who hold positions of authority and those who are said to be under authority must recognize that they are not equals; but persuasion ought to exist only among equals; therefore persuasion in society implies a contradiction. But if authority lacks the power to enforce the rules it makes for common action, then it is inefficacious. Thus the right to influence opinion by persuasion belongs to authority as a fitting instrument, just as the right to use coercion belongs to it, and both for the sake of the common good. It goes without saying that both persuasion and coercion are valid instruments only insofar as they respect the intrinsic dignity of the human *person.

Source of Authority. The position stated above stands in direct opposition to that of J. J. *Rousseau, whose dialectic of authority led to the *social contract. In the latter analysis, one is led to the myth of the general will, in which the individual human will is annihilated by an initial voluntary act; this theory terminates in a general formality making authority a power that resides in a multitude, i.e., as an attribute of multitude itself. Such power, then, could emerge without authority and makes possible the usurpation of power by the *state. The 20th century has already provided many examples of such a rise to power without authority.

It is generally held among Catholics that civil authority is of God, not by any specifically divine institution, but by the fact that God is the author of nature and nature demands authority. In this general position, submission to authority is enjoined. The designation theory holds that the power proper to authority comes from God but that human beings designate the ruling person by cultural conventions. This is a modification of the divine-right theory, which holds that power is from God and that the person in whom it is vested also is designated by God. The transmission theory holds that civil authority is proper to the civil multitude; that the multitude not only designates the ruling person but also transmits to him the authority originally given them by God. Both the designation and the transmission theories guard the integrity of the individual while enjoining obedience to authority. The position of T. *Hobbes and that of Rousseau, on the other hand, ascribe the source of authority to the multitude alone, who yield all powers to the state (Leviathan), thereby destroying the freedoms of the individual.

Teaching Authority. Sometimes authority is used in reference to a pedagogical process. In such a case, authority is, once again, properly substitutional and is necessary only as long as the learner fails to observe the relations between mind and object. In *science, properly speaking, there can be no authority, since *demonstration begets the kind of authentic objectivity that alone can necessitate the mind to its assent.

Totalitarianism. A persistent tendency in the 20th century would identify authority with *totalitarianism. This tendency is rooted in the confusing of authority with *tyranny. A proper authority ultimately rests on *law, whereas every form of tyranny springs from the subjective interests of the tyrant. Power in totalitarianism rests on sources external to the political structure itself; these are unlike the legitimate sources of power in a properly democratic government or society. In all circles, familial, political, and ecclesiastical, authority does, indeed, imply *obedience, but an obedience that is consonant with a proper freedom. If one fails to see that the source of authority transcends not only power but also those who are in power, then he has little hope of escaping a deepening suspicion of every kind of authority. Continuing aversion to authority springs from apodictic and authoritarian statements concerning its nature.

Conclusion. Reduced to its essence, then, authority is indispensable for the achievement of the common welfare of any society. It is not necessary as a contract, nor is it established by convention or force, nor is it the result of sin. It is necessary because the nature of society demands it. The moment the connection between authority and the common good is severed, the community begins to weaken and finds itself preparing the way for the kind of *anarchism espoused by L. N. *Tolstoi. If and when authority is abused and issues into arbitrariness, such an issue is traceable only to accidental causes and is not proper to authority as such. Justice and a proper political friendship are the cement of society and are assumed in any reasonable theory of authority. It should be noted that the common good here mentioned, referring as it does to any and all natural societies, is not the absolute end of the person. Authority on the human level, whether familial or political, is thus indirectly related to the absolutely ultimate end of man, viz, eternal life. Therefore authority in the political community ought to look with equity and justice toward the possibility of each person's achieving his ultimate destiny. In the overall view, this demands that there be an authority that is proportionate to the natural and supernatural destiny of man (*see* AUTHORITY, CIVIL; AUTHORITY, ECCLESIASTICAL).

See also POLITICAL PHILOSOPHY; SOCIETY.

Bibliography: Y. SIMON, *A General Theory of Authority* (Notre Dame, Ind. 1962); *The Nature and Function of Authority* (Aquinas Lecture; Milwaukee 1940); *Philosophy of Democratic Government* (Chicago 1951). J. MARITAIN, "Democracy and Authority" in his *Scholasticism and Politics* (New York 1940). H. ARENDT, "What Is Authority?" in her *Between Past and Future: Six Exercises in Political Thought* (New York 1961). G. J. LYNAM, *The Good Political Ruler According to St. Thomas* (Washington 1953). J. WRIGHT, "Reflections on Conscience and Authority," *Critic* 22 (April–May 1964) 11–15, 18–28. M. WEBER, "The Types of Authority" in *Theories of Society*, ed. T. PARSONS et al., 2 v. (New York 1961) 1:626–632. C. BERNARD, "The Theory of Authority," *ibid.* 1:632–641. E. SHILS, "The Calling of Sociology," *ibid.* 2:1405–48. R. MICHELS, Enc SocSc 1:319–321.

[G. J. MC MORROW]

AUTHORITY, CIVIL

The duty of respect for lawful civil authority, even when this was exercised by non-Christian rulers, was too plainly spelled out in the NT to be reasonably questioned by anyone professing to accept the Christian revelation. Christ Himself had acknowledged a duty to Caesar (Mt 22.21; Mk 12.17; Lk 20.25). Christians were admonished to accept civil authority as coming from God (Rom 13.1–7; Ti 3.1; 1 Tm 2.2), to regard those vested with it as sent by God (Rom 13.16; 1 Pt 2.14), to be subject to them for the Lord's sake (1 Pt 2.13), to give them their due (Rome 13.7), to look upon resistance to them as resistance to the ordinance of God (Rom 13.2).

In the early Church these plain statements of Christian duty were enough to forestall any tendency to civil anarchy or disobedience that might have arisen among Christians in consequence of the severity with which they were treated in times of persecution. But if they did not deny the rights of civil authority, the recognition they accorded it was limited by the distinction, inadmissible in the Roman state, that they drew between civil and religious authority. Christianity professed no essential antagonism to the secular claims of the state, for Christianity was not a political theory and offered no political program, but was merely a doctrine and a way of salvation. My kingdom, Christ had said, is not of the world (Jn 18.36). But if the rights of the civil ruler within his own legitimate sphere of authority were not to be questioned, there could be no compromise with the religious pretensions of the Roman state. Nevertheless, apart from this, the Christian was as willing to cooperate civilly with the government as any other citizen of the Empire. His faith did not free him from his obligation to obey or set him apart from the social community or the order of justice. On the contrary, it provided him with a new motive for submission by making him see the civil ruler as the minister of God's justice. Moreover, the virtues inculcated by Christianity, such as charity, justice, piety, and temperance, tended to make him a better and more reliable citizen.

Origin. St. Paul's insistence on the coercive function of the civil ruler made it possible for most of the Fathers to think that civil government had no other purpose and that it existed simply as a remedy to disorders arising from sin. This was the view taken by St. Augustine, who held that, had men continued in a state of innocence, no man would have been master of his fellows and neither slavery nor civil subjection would have existed (*Civ.* 19.15). Gregory the Great and Isidore of Seville held the same opinion. There is some superficial resemblance between this position and the political idealism of Seneca, Rousseau, and others who dreamed of a lost Eden in which men were free. Through the schoolmen, however, the influence of Aristotle prevented this from becoming the dominant view of Catholic theologians. According to Aristotle, political organization and government are conditions necessary for civilized life and indispensable means for bringing man to the full development of his powers. This opinion was adopted by St. Thomas Aquinas (ST 1a, 96.3–4), and has been commonly accepted by theologians since the 13th century.

The NT makes it clear that civil authority is from God, but this does not mean that God establishes it apart from the agency of secondary causes. By the 13th century theologians explicitly recognized that authority was derived from the people as a whole. Civil obedience is not submission to force, however benign, but a free acceptance of government. Some theologians, such as Suárez, have held that the people themselves first possess this power collectively, and then transmit it to the individuals they choose to govern them. In this view authority comes from God through the people. Others have thought that God immediately vests the ruler with authority, the intervention of the people being confined to the designation of the person or persons upon whom God confers it.

Limitations. The first and major limitation of the authority of the civil ruler, as this has been understood in Christian thought, arises from the distinction between civil and religious authority. The Christian sees himself, in effect, as a citizen of two cities, one temporal and the other spiritual, existing side by side and institutionally distinct, each autonomous in its own sphere. The doctrine of the two authorities, recognized in practice from the beginning of the Church, was expressly formulated by Pope *Gelasius I in a letter to the Emperor Anastasius in 494 (see Denz 347), and is known as the Gelasian doctrine, or the doctrine of the two swords. It holds that human society is subject to dual organization and control, based on the difference in kind of the values that need to be secured: spiritual interests and salvation are the concern of the Church; secular interests, on the other hand, such as the maintenance of peace, order, and justice, are the concern of civil government. Thus the authority of the civil ruler is restricted to the temporal and secular order; moreover, the ruler himself, if he is a Christian, is subject to the Church in spiritual matters, as St. Ambrose declared to the Emperor Valentinian (*Ep.* 21.4).

Other limitations took longer to be distinctly recognized. The doctrine that the ruler's authority comes from God, together with the notion that God has given men rulers as a remedy for sin—which was understood to mean that God may give men evil rulers to punish them for sin—tended to make some of the Fathers hesitate to question the legitimacy of *de facto* authority or of authority used wickedly or tyrannously (e.g., see Irenaeus, *Adv. Haer.,* 5.24; Augustine, *Civ.,* 5.19; Isidore of Seville, *Sententiae,* 3.48; St. Gregory the Great, *Regulae pastoralis lib.,* 3.4). Instead of concluding that there can be a wicked authority that does not come from God, they were disposed rather to think of the ruler as the representative of God regardless of how he came by his authority or how he conducted himself in its use.

In the changed political climate of later times, Christian philosophers and theologians from John of Salisbury onward were more forthrightly critical of bad government, and came to assert other limitations. These depended on considerations of natural and positive law determining the nature and purpose of civil authority and the conditions of its rightful establishment and exercise. Great stress was laid on legitimacy—authority must be legitimate or at least legitimized; otherwise the ruler is such in name only and possesses no real authority. In the exercise of his office the ruler may make no demands that exceed the powers vested in him, nor may he impose useless or unjust burdens on his subjects. Indeed, unjust laws or ordinances are not, from the moral point of view, binding at all, and thus the obedience owed by subjects is always conditioned by the rightful exercise of authority (see, for example, St. Thomas Aquinas, ST 1a2ae, 96.1–6; 2a2ae, 42.2 ad 3; 104.5–6; *De reg. princ.* 3.10–12).

See also OBEDIENCE; CIVIL LAW, MORAL OBLIGATION OF; CHURCH AND STATE.

Bibliography: THOMAS AQUINAS, *Selected Political Writings,* ed. A. PASSERIN D'ENTRÈVES, tr. J. G. DAWSON (Oxford 1948). T. GILBY, *The Political Thought of Thomas Aquinas* (Chicago 1958). R. W. and A. J. CARLYLE, *A History of Mediaeval Political Theory in the West,* 6 v. (New York 1903–36). A. MESSINEO, EncCatt 2:475–486.

[P. K. MEAGHER]

AUTHORITY, ECCLESIASTICAL

Authority in the Church, or ecclesiastical authority, will verify, though in its own way, the concept already developed in the general treatment of the term *authority. If the Church is a true *society of human beings, a group seeking a common end through concerted action, it is inevitable that there is need of control, some power to determine ways and means, to allot functions, to redress grievances—in a word, to protect against the centrifugal tendencies that jeopardize communal action. Men in the *supernatural order still display the diversity of viewpoint that makes authority necessary wherever life is to be lived within community structures.

Early Church. From the beginning the Church was conscious of this need for persons who could decide points of conflict, administer community goods, preside over community assemblies; and the Church recognized that those so empowered owed their selection and their rights not to any decision by the community, but to Christ's own determination.

As the Gospels testify to the preparation of the *Twelve as surrogates of Christ, so the Acts of the Apostles and the Pauline Epistles testify that the Twelve and *Paul (as one later raised to the same dignity and functions) directed community life. In ch. 6 of Acts St. Luke describes the first major rift in community relations, the outburst of the Hellenist group against the Hebrews on the grounds that the Hellenist widows were being slighted in the distribution of community alms. He makes it clear that the plaintiffs instinctively brought their grievances to the *Apostles for adjudication. He makes it clear too that the Twelve without hesitation acknowledged its competence to apply a remedy by setting up a subordinate commission.

Within the Pauline communities the same picture emerges and nowhere more clearly than in 1 Corinthians, where Paul rules on the exclusion from the community of the incestuous man (5.1–5), on the handling of quarrels among the brethren (6.1–8), on the liceity of eating flesh of animals sacrificed in pagan rites (ch. 8–10, esp. 10.23–30), on the attire of women at religious services (11.2–16), on the conduct to be observed at the Lord's Supper (11.17–34), on the discipline to be observed in the exercise of charisms (ch. 12–14, esp. 14.26–40), and on the manner of gathering alms for the relief of the brethren in Jerusalem (16.1–4). The pastorals, too, whether from the hand of Paul or in the spirit of Paul, are filled with instructions that cover nearly every aspect of community life and chart for Titus and Timothy the course they are to follow in arranging ecclesiastical life in Crete and at Ephesus. This claim to direct is always based on the mandate from the Lord, who entrusted them in His place with powers of *binding and loosing (Mt 18.18) and of teaching the baptized to observe whatever He had commanded (Mt 28.20). And as He will be with them constantly till the end of time, this claim will be reiterated by those who succeed the original Apostles, who are as such "not from men nor by man, but by Jesus Christ and God the Father" (Gal 1.1).

A description of ecclesiastical authority would be inadequate and misleading if it were confined to the area of external Church order. For the competence of the Apostles is also a doctrinal one; i.e., they are commissioned to propose the message of *salvation, and in such a way that their presentation is not that of simple messengers. From the start it was to the "teaching of the apostles" as well as to "communion of the breaking of the bread and prayers" (Acts 2.42) that the community devoted itself. The gospel is that "which also you received, wherein also you stand, through which also you are being saved, if you hold it fast, as I preached it to you" (1 Cor 15.1–2). And Paul is always ready to explain further and authoritatively the sense in which he and the other Apostles had preached it. He did not deliver the message of salvation once for all; he constantly renewed and deepened their intelligence, so that he could claim not only that he delivered the gospel but that through the gospel he had begotten them in Christ Jesus (1 Cor 4.15). The gospel is in St. Paul not something merely to be brought externally to the attention of others, but a principle of fecundity by which he generates offspring in Christ and assumes the direction incumbent on a parent: to develop and train those whom he has procreated.

Adequate Concept. Real and pervasive as this authority is in the Catholic understanding, it need not operate to smother the activity of those who are subject to it. The Christian life is not to be thought a mechanical execution of impulses externally received; those begotten in the gospel are the human children of God and must develop internal principles too of *supernatural life by which they continually grow. The very need for authority arises in part from the need of pruning the exuberance of Christian activity and from the need of maintaining free from aberration doctrines not passively received sometime in the past but doctrines constantly pondered and daily being reduced to principles of action. Authority is not to hinder fructification, but through its divine-human action to prune every branch that does bear fruit that it may bear more fruit (Jn 15.2).

Though by reason of the constitution of the Church as a perfect society its authority is frequently compared with that which exists in the perfect civil society, it is not to be forgotten that ecclesiastical authority has close analogies also with familial authority. As this latter flows from the natural procreative act and the ensuing relationship, so Church authority is grounded in the sacramental action by which the Church brings forth children to God (*see* SACRAMENT OF THE CHURCH). In both the family and the Church the procreative role issues in a role of training and direction whose exercise, even when it imposes obligations and penalties, is structured within a framework of solicitude and love that distinguishes it from the role of authority and the manner of its exercise in civil society.

See also DISCIPLINE, ECCLESIASTICAL; HIERARCHY; JURISDICTION, POWER OF; KEYS, POWER OF; OFFICE, ECCLESIASTICAL; SOCIETY (IN THEOLOGY); TEACHING AUTHORITY OF THE CHURCH (MAGISTERIUM); CHURCH, ARTICLES ON.

Bibliography: E. DUBLANCHY, DTC 4.2:2175–2207. DTC, Tables générales 1:1125–26. K. MÖRSDORF, LexThK[2] 6:218–221. J. GEWIESS and O. KARRER, Fries HbThGrdbgr 1:31–49. S. GRUNDMANN, RGG[3] 3:1434–35. L. BOUYER, *The Word, Church and Sacraments in Protestantism and Catholicism,* tr. A. V. LITTLEDALE (New York 1961). T. D. ROBERTS, *Black Popes: Authority, Its Use and Abuse* (New York 1954).

[S. E. DONLON]

AUTO-DA-FÉ, the Portuguese term (Spanish, *auto de fé;* Latin, *actus fidei*) for the public ceremonies surrounding the proclamation of sentences that terminated *Inquisition trials, especially in Spain. *Autos* never included burning at the stake. The first was at Seville (1481); the last, in Mexico (1850). The Spanish solemnities, derived from the medieval Inquisition's *sermo generalis,* acquired a harsh, show-trial atmosphere, to impress and instruct the populace. Increasingly elaborate and expensive, *autos* were staged in the city plaza; a concourse of people surrounded two platforms, one of prisoners and the other of inquisitors with dignitaries. These cautionary exercises usually included a lengthy procession (prisoners wore penitential *sambenito* gowns with miter), a sermon, oaths, interminable reading of sentences, abjurations, reconciliations, and "relaxation" of the obdurate to the secular authorities.

An early *auto* (Toledo 1486) lasted 6 hours for 750 prisoners; later *autos* could take all day. The presence of Charles V at Valencia (1528) set the precedent for the attendance of rulers at these spectacles. After 1515, *autos* could be held only where an inquisitorial court functioned. Victims were usually apostate former Jews and former Moslems, then *alumbrados* and some Protestants, and occasionally bigamists, sorcerers, etc. Barcelona had 30 *autos* between 1488 and 1498; Saragossa had 61 between 1484 and 1502. The major Protestant *autos* were in 1559 at Valladolid (14 "relaxed") and Seville (55). Of all the Spanish possessions, the Netherlands suffered the most, 2,000 dying within 50 years. After 1600, *autos* became ever less frequent and gradually assumed the tone of popular fetes. *Autos* often included no death penalties and never involved executions. If a death sentence was given, it was executed later, usually outside the town.

Bibliography: J. GUIRAUD, *Histoire de l'inquisition au moyen âge,* 2 v. (Paris 1935–38). B. LLORCA, *La Inquisición en España* (3d ed. Barcelona 1954). **Illustration credit:** Spanish Embassy, Washington, D.C.

[R. I. BURNS]

AUTOCEPHALI, in Greek, αὐτός (self) and κεφαλή (head), self-governing or independent, a term in common usage among the Orthodox, was introduced by Greek canonists to distinguish independent metropolitans or exarchs from patriarchs. Historically, it denoted an ecclesiastical independence within the framework of Church organization and, legally, meant a juridical exemption from any subordination to such established authority on a *praeter legem* basis. For Catholics it assumed the theological meaning of schismatic, or dissident; it was applied to those who held different tenets or who, imbued with a national and self-governing spirit, claimed the right to choose their own heads. Some of these Churches existed entirely within the boundaries of one state (ethnarch), others within a political framework comprising various nationalities, in accordance with former metropolitan provinces and their dioceses, whose bishops met regularly in synod and elected their own primate. Their relative rank was determined by a kind of hierarchy of honor, with the ecumenical patriarch of Constantinople at its head. Among the Oriental patriarchates of Alexandria, Antioch, and Jerusalem, the order of precedence was fixed at the Council of Chalcedon, and, later, the Patriarchate of Moscow (established in 1589) assumed fifth place. Other autocephalous Churches were assigned rank in accordance

Auto-da-fé in Madrid, painting of the last quarter of the 17th century, during the reign of Charles II.

with the date of their achieving ecclesiastical independence—the Church of Cyprus (431), the Archbishopric of Sinai (6th century), the Bulgarian Church (927), the Serbian Church (1220), the Church of Georgia, under its own Catholicos, the Church of Greece (1833), the Czechoslovak Orthodox Church (1923), the Church of Finland (1923), the Polish Orthodox Church (1924), the Albanian Church (1937), and certain emigré Churches in West Europe and the Americas separated from their mother Churches mainly for political reasons. As for the Church of Georgia, its original autocephalous status dated from the 5th century. In 1817 this status was abolished, and it was annexed to the Russian Church and governed by a Russian exarch. In 1917 it recovered its autocephalous status, which was recognized by the patriarch of Moscow in 1943. Occasionally the adjective autocephalous also came to be applied to members of the clergy dissenting from patriarchal or metropolitan jurisdiction.

Bibliography: D. Attwater, *The Christian Churches of the East,* 2 v. (Milwaukee 1946–47). J. Hackett, *A History of the Orthodox Church of Cyprus* (London 1901). J. Meyendorff, *The Orthodox Church,* tr. J. Chapin (New York 1962). S. H. Scott, *The Eastern Churches and the Papacy* (London 1928).

[L. NEMEC]

AUTOMATION

A term adopted in the 1950s to designate the self-regulating production systems that were being adopted by industry. In the 1960s it is sometimes given broader meanings, being equated in some instances with total achievement in the art of mechanization, of which automation in the narrow sense is a subdivision, and in others with total achievement in industrial technology (advances in energy development and utilization, in transportation, in chemistry and metallurgy, etc.) of which mechanization is a division.

Concept of Automation. Although it is a new word, automation is not a new concept. The transfer to machines of functions formerly performed by man had been going on at a rapid rate since the industrial revolution and at a constantly accelerating rate since early 20th century. What is new about automation is the complexity of its technology and the widened range of its actual and potential application. Descriptions of automation in the narrow sense usually emphasize one or both of the following characteristics—the integration of production processes and the application of the feedback concept, with or without the use of electronic computational mechanisms, in the control of production systems.

Transfer machines, typical of what has been called the Detroit-type of automation, are examples of the integration, or linking up, of production operations. The component parts of complex products, of automobiles, for example, go through many operations in the course of their conversion from raw materials to finished parts. The transfer of these parts from one operation to the next and the positioning and securing of them for machining require a great amount of production time and labor effort. Machines now have been built that move materials through hundreds of operations without any direct human intervention. One such machine, 350 feet long and performing 555 operations on a cylinder head, built for the automobile industry in the 1940s, is operated by a crew of three men. Such achievements in mechanization are now regarded as crude examples of the current potential of automation.

Dr. A. V. Astin, Director of the U.S. Bureau of Standards, has defined feedback as a concept of control that uses the results of measurements at one stage of a production system to adjust the operation of the system at some earlier stage. Simple examples are the float valve, known to the ancient Romans and still used today, and the thermostat. In the case of the former a rising or falling water level in a tank causes a float to rise or fall and through a lever attached to close or open an intake valve. In the case of the latter a rising or falling temperature causes a metal strip to expand or contract and to open or close an electric circuit that controls the operation of a furnace. Feedback control may be open-loop or closed-loop control. It is open-loop control if the results of the measurement are reported to a human operator who makes the adjustments in the control system. It is closed-loop control if the results of the measurement are used to actuate automatic control devices.

There are three elements in a feedback system of control: a sensing device that makes a measurement; a communication system that reports the measurement to a control station; and a control element that uses the results of the measurement to alter the operation of the system. During and since World War II achievements in the fields of electronics, communications, and high-speed electronic computational techniques have produced a variety of amazingly accurate sensing and measuring instruments, reporting devices, and decision-making and controlling mechanisms that have given rise to a new era in mechanization. Machines are constructed that constantly monitor themselves, report deviations from predetermined tolerances, and use these reports to make needed corrections in their own operations.

The Computer. The recent development of electronic computational mechanisms has given a wholly new dimension to automatic control processes. Because these computers can store detailed instructions and make highly complicated computations almost instantaneously, they permit control systems to make choices that are based on constantly changing data from a number of sources. Car-arresting systems in railroad classification yards, for example, measure the speed of a car as it approaches the arresting device, its weight, and its rolling characteristics; they measure also the distance that the car must roll before it makes contact with cars already on the classification track. These data, together with predetermined information about the decelerating characteristics of the tracks over which the car must roll, are instantaneously analyzed by a computational device to determine the speed at which the car should leave the arrester; and the results of these computations are used to select the proper braking force to be applied to the car and to actuate the braking system. Systems similar in principle but vastly different in detail automatically control the operations of entire establishments such as petroleum refineries and chemical plants, and the range of their actual and possible application is constantly being extended. How vast that range may ultimately become is suggested by a few considerations. Computers may be programmed to play games such as checkers, and in such play to profit from experience, that is, before making an offensive or defensive move to scan in a fraction of a second the results of prior moves. Moreover, the content of a computer's memory or experience can be automatically transferred to other computers.

Social Effects. Automation obviously has far-reaching social consequences. However, as already indicated, it is but one aspect of the art of mechanization, and the latter is but one dimension of an industrial technology that has been undergoing rapid change throughout its whole range. The social effects of automation merge with and are practically indistinguishable from the social effects of this wider technological change, and for this reason are discussed elsewhere (*see* TECHNOLOGY, HISTORY OF; TECHNOLOGY, SOCIAL EFFECTS OF).

Bibliography: U.S. Congress, Joint Committee on Economic Report, *Automation and Technological Change Hearings before the Subcommittee on Economic Stabilization* (Washington 1955). U.S. Congress, Senate, Committee on Labor and Public Welfare, *Nation's Manpower Revolution, Hearings before the Subcommittee on Employment and Manpower of the Committee on Labor and Public Welfare* (Washington 1963). G. B. BALDWIN and G. P. SCHULTZ, "Automation: A New Dimension to Old Problems," *Proceedings of the Seventh Annual Meeting of the Industrial Relations Research Association* (Madison 1955) 114–178. J. DIEBOLD, *Automation: Its Impact on Business and Labor* (Washington 1959). W. BUCKINGHAM, *Automation: Its Impact on Business and People* (New York 1961). E. CLAGUE and L. GREENBERG, "Employment" in *Automation and Technological Change,* ed. J. T. DUNLOP (Spectrum Bk. Englewood Cliffs, N.J. 1962) 114–131. G. P. SCHULTZ and T. L. WHISLER, eds., *Management Organization and the Computer* (New York 1960).

[L. C. BROWN]

AUTOMATION (THEOLOGICAL ASPECT)

The Church has constantly confronted ambivalent attitudes toward earthly realities. A tendency in man (observable also in pre-Christian times) to equate his personal experience of a body-spirit tension with the moral good-evil tension led some Christians to suspect material values and to emphasize Christ's mandate to "seek first the kingdom of God and his justice" (Mt 6.33). An equally strong conviction of the true value of earthly endeavors led others to emphasize the role of man in redeeming material creatures by reestablishing all things in Christ (Eph 1.3–14).

One extreme position became heretical, constraining St. John in the prologue to his Gospel to seek to stifle incipient Gnostic doctrine, which denied the reality of the Incarnation and, hence, this elevation of material realities (Jn 1.3, 14). Nevertheless, even Origen eventually fell victim to Gnostic exaggerations (Περὶ ἀρχῶν 1.6, 8, PG 11:165–182, and *passim*). The first Council of Nicaea reasserted that God created all things both visible and invisible (Denz 125).

St. Augustine encouraged cenobitic life, but he opposed a purely eschatological attitude toward work (*Op. monach.,* PL 40:547–582). In this he was followed by St. Benedict, who, in the establishment of his monastic rule, espoused the positive values in work [*Rule of St. Benedict,* ed. and tr. O. H. Blair (Ft. Augustus, Scotland 1934) 129]. The Council of Ephesus ratified the decrees of the Synod of Sidon, which rejected the Messalian aversion to manual work [J. De Guibert, *Documenta ecclesiastica Christianae perfectionis studium spectantia* (Rome 1931) 83].

In medieval times, when St. Albert the Great condemned the Brothers of the Free Spirit for similar reasons (*ibid.* 219), his pupil, St. Thomas Aquinas, effected a remarkable synthesis of the sacral and mundane orders in his Christian view of all reality (ST 1a, 65.2). In the 19th century, Vatican Council I, viewing the work of the industrial revolution, reiterated the principle that the Church encourages technical progress (Denz 3019); and in the 20th century Pius XII praised the progress of science and technology and suggested that it should bring man to worship his Creator more perfectly [ActApS 46 (1954) 7–8].

Automation enables man better to subdue the earth and rule over it (Gn 1.28). The invention of self-operating machines is an analogous sharing in the creative work of God, who made the universe, preserves it in existence, but does not have to interfere with its operation (Ps 8.6–7; Sir 17.1–8). Christ Himself gave the example, for He was a τέκτων (Mk 6.3; cf. Mt 13.55), which is commonly interpreted to mean a maker of wooden things, but can also be understood as an iron or bronze worker. In any case, He used the tools of His day.

Automated machinery enables man to serve the needs of his neighbor through increased productivity, to distribute more effectively the necessities of life in economically underdeveloped areas [*Mater et magistra,* ActApS 53 (1961) 440–442], to provide the means for the solution of social problems (*ibid.* 445–448), to liberate himself from burdensome work for the purpose of constructive leisure (*ibid.* 459). It also renders more possible the observance of the Sabbath rest (cf. Ex 20.8–11), so that man can reduce his anxious care and thus commune more readily with God (Lk 10.38–42). The reduction of working hours consequent on automation gives man more time for a Christian home life (Eph 5.21–6.4) and personal service to the needy (Mt 25.31–46).

But the Christian must dedicate himself to the world without becoming of the world (Jn 17.14–16). Technological success can be an occasion of pride; pride, of godlessness; godlessness, of immorality (Rom 1.20–32).

Exclusive concentration on the material encourages a materialistic outlook which ignores God and the value of the human person [Pius XII, ActApS 46 (1954) 8–12]. Overinvolvement can blind man to the primacy of the spirit. A falsely scientific mentality closes man's openness to genuine philosophical and theological investigation.

Nor may the Christian hold himself aloof from a consideration of the economic effects of automation. Failure to act can surrender automation to the designs of the devil. The Christian should alert his community to the fact that the displacement of workers places an obligation first on responsible individuals and then on government to retrain and relocate them [*Rerum novarum;* ActSSed 23 (1891) 657–659]. The human right to suitable work is inviolable.

Religious, educational, and civic leaders, moreover, have an obligation to look ahead, to explore, discover, suggest, and program ways by which those who come into increased amounts of leisure may progress spiritually and culturally during the added time at their disposal.

The opportunities of automation allow man to extend Christ's Redemption by enabling material creation to glorify God in a new way [*Pacem in terris,* ActApS 55 (1963) 257–259]. Automation can hasten the day for which all nature groans, when material creation will be transformed (Rom 8.19–22) and the People of God will enter the Sabbath rest of the new earth and the new heaven (Heb 4.9–10; Ap 21.1–27).

See also INCARNATIONAL THEOLOGY; INCARNATIONISM; JESUS CHRIST, III, 12; LEISURE; WORK, THEOLOGY OF; RECAPITULATION IN CHRIST; TEMPORAL VALUES, THEOLOGY OF.

Bibliography: T. MAYER-MALY, LexThK[2] 1:1130. P. RIGA, *Catholic Thought in Crisis* (Milwaukee 1963). F. X. QUINN, *The Ethical Aftermath of Automation* (Westminster, Md. 1962) bibliog. 261–266. R. P. MOHAN, ed., *Technology and Christian Culture* (Washington 1960).

[A. C. HUGHES]

AUTOS SACRAMENTALES

The literal meaning, from the Latin *actus sacramentales,* is "sacramental plays." Though variant types exist, an *auto* (as it was often called in abbreviation) may be defined as a one-act play presenting, with personified abstractions as characters, an allegorical action about ideas closely or loosely related to the Holy Eucharist, and, from the 16th to the 18th century, performed in Castilian Spanish during the Octave of Corpus Christi before outdoor audiences.

The institution of the Feast of *Corpus Christi by Urban IV in 1264 gave Christendom a new holy day, rooted in dogma and conducive of joy. It was early characterized by street processions in which the Host, attended by the clergy, was borne from the sanctuary for public adoration. In Spain the procession also featured less solemn marchers—giants, dancers, figures of fantastic animals. Floats carried statues representing Biblical or allegorical scenes; in time the statues were replaced by men, who gradually relaxed their frozen postures, and performed slight choreographic movements. Eventually, at the stations, or stopping places, of the procession, the masqueraders acted, first in dumb show and then with improvised speech, the scenes they had portrayed as *tableaux vivants.* Drama had entered the procession, and from this stage to the presentation of written sacramental plays was but a short step.

By the end of the 15th century, Spain, unlike other European countries, was still producing only simple liturgical dramas based on the *Officium pastorum* (*see* DRAMA, MEDIEVAL, 1). But she progressed rapidly in the 16th century. Out of these primitive works emerged piece by piece the great secular and religious theater of the golden age (*see* SPANISH LITERATURE, 2). The *autos sacramentales* were but one of several lines of development. The *Officium pastorum* plays had three parts: the appearance of the shepherds, the angel's announcement of the birth of Christ, and the adoration of the shepherds. In the plays that anticipate the *autos* the angel is replaced by a hermit or a friar, who answers the questions of the simple shepherds. The next step was to substitute for the learned informant a personification of Faith. Meanwhile, the shepherds had themselves become individuated, and made to represent some idea. The plays became wholly allegorized.

By the 17th century it was customary, in the capital and other large cities, to erect trestle stages in the plazas. Huge wagons, on which elaborate scenery had been constructed, were drawn up around the stage. After each performance the wagons, bearing the props and actors, would move to the next plaza. Performances of as many as four plays might be given each day in four locations. The city commissioned poets to write *autos* and bore the cost of the entire production. Intercity rivalry led to lavish expenditures. The actors, men and women, were professionals from the secular theater, attracted to the *autos* by their devotion and the financial rewards. In addition to the fees, the municipality offered a substantial prize to the best troupe. Dignitaries sat near the stage; the citizenry was free to stand and watch. The poetry was often lost in the hubbub, and action and spectacle were thus almost as important as the words. The *autos* were the main contribution of the civic authorities to the religious feast.

Allegory was the proper form for a Eucharistic play. A Sacrament, says St. Thomas, is *signum rei sacrae,* and a sign serves *per nota ad ignota pervenire.* The *autos* played their part in helping man to grasp the unknown through analogy with the known. During the 16th century the allegorization process continued in the works of Diego Sánchez (before 1550), the 100 anonymous plays of the *Códice de autos viejos* (*c.* 1575), and the *autos* written or edited by Juan de Timoneda (d. 1583). The genre approached its maturity in the works of Lope de *Vega and José de Valdivielso (1560?–1638). These dramatists wrote essentially penitential *autos,* designed to move spectators to compunction, Confession, and Communion. Their *autos* were not yet great intellectual constructions illuminating with poetic intuitions the mysteries of theology.

It was left to *Calderón to raise the *autos* to these heights. Interpreting the Eucharist as an all-embracing Sacrament, Calderón explored, in daring allegories, a wide range of dogmatic themes. An abundance of allegorical personifications—Judaism, Nature, Grace, Thought, Beauty, Night—carry the profound religious action. His art was best described by the poet himself: "Sermons set in verse, problems of Sacred Theology set in representable ideas, which my words cannot explain or comprehend, inclining man to joyfulness on this Corpus Christi day." With Calderón's enormous production—some 80 *autos*—the sacramental play reached its perfection.

Rationalists in the 18th century found the *autos* incomprehensible and irreverent, and in 1765 Carlos III banned their performance. Since that time *autos* have been produced in Spain only as archaic curiosities. Occasionally a modern poet (Rafael Alberti, Miguel Hernández) writes an *auto* as a tour de force, but with little Eucharistic significance. *Autos* were performed in Spanish-speaking areas abroad, and among other Latin American authors, Sister *Juana Inés de la Cruz is known to have written them. In isolated pockets of the New World the custom of writing and performing primitive *autos* is reported to survive.

Bibliography: E. GONZÁLEZ PEDROSO, ed., *Autos sacramentales* (Biblioteca de Autores Españoles 58; Madrid 1865). P. CALDERÓN DE LA BARCA, *Autos sacramentales,* ed. A. VALBUENA PRAT, 2 v. (Clásicos Castellanos 69 and 74; Madrid 1926–27); "The Great Theatre of the World," tr. M. H. SINGLETON in *Masterpieces of the Spanish Golden Age,* ed. A. FLORES (pa. New York 1957) 368–395. B. W. WARDROPPER, *Introducción al teatro religioso del Siglo de Oro* (*La evolución del auto sacramental: 1500–1648*) (Madrid 1953). A. A. PARKER, *The Allegorical Drama of Calderón* (New York 1943).

[B. W. WARDROPPER]

AUTPERT, AMBROSE, Benedictine preacher and writer; b. southern Gaul, early 8th century; d. Italy, Jan. 30, 784. He entered the monastery of St. Vincent on the Volturno near Benevento in 754 and after ordination devoted himself especially to preaching. He soon acquired a reputation for learning and holiness and in 777 was elected abbot by the Frankish monks of the monastery; a rival group of Lombard monks elected another abbot. Although in the conflict Autpert resigned, Charlemagne ordered the matter to be submitted to the Pope. On the way to Rome Autpert died. The Benedictine chronicler calls him "sanctissimus" because of his great virtue, and the Bollandists gave him the title "saint" with a feast observed July 19. Autpert was one of the most outstanding men of his time, far in advance of his contemporaries in learning, culture, and spiritual insight. Though a prolific writer, he remained comparatively unknown for many centuries, and his writings were ascribed to famous men of preceding ages, including SS. Augustine, Ambrose, Gregory the Great, Leo the Great, and Isidore of Seville. Recent scholarship has reestablished much of Autpert's literary heritage. Among his works are a long commentary on the Apocalypse [*Speculum parvulorum* in *Maxima Bibliotheca vet. Patrum* (v. 13 Lyons 1677) 403–657]; an ascetical treatise very widely read in the Middle Ages under the name of other authors, *Conflictus vitiorum atque virtutum* (PL 83:1131–44); the lives of several saints; and a number of sermons and homilies.

Bibliography: J. WINANDY, *Ambroise Autpert: Moine et théologien* (Paris 1953); "L'Oeuvre littéraire d' A. A.," RevBén 60 (1950) 93–119. U. BERLIÈRE, DHGE 2:1115–16. I. CECCHETTI, EncCatt 2:499–500. L. BERGERON, DictSpirAscMyst 1:429.

[M. J. BARRY]

AUTUN

City, and diocese containing the entire area of Saône-et-Loire in southern France, about 60 miles southwest of Dijon. Christianity came to Autun (*Augustodunum*) from Lyons at the beginning of the 3d century. The famous 3d-century Christian epitaph (in Greek) of *Pectorius was discovered (1830) in the cemetery of St. Peter l'Estrier, a few miles from Autun. Sacked by the warriors of Tetricus in 269, Autun became an independent city (*c.* 300); and tradition designates St. Amator as its first bishop (*c.* 250). But the first recorded bishop was St. Reticius, who assisted at a council in Rome in 313 (Eusebius, *Hist. eccl.,* 5.5). In 542 Bishop Nectarius brought the relics of St. Nazarius from Milan for his cathedral; St. Syagrius was the first bishop of Autun to receive the pallium. SS. Léger and Ansbert restored the monuments of the city (7th century) and founded the diocesan legacy. Under the Merovingians a number of monasteries were founded, including St. Symphorian (5th century), St. Martin (*c.* 589) by Brunhilde, and St. Andochius (restored in the 8th century).

In the 11th century the monks of Cluny effected a reform that was destined to spread to the Church at large and to constitute a powerful aid to the papacy. Bishops Valterius (975–1024) and Stephen of Bâgé (1112–36) favored the reform, and Norgaud (1098–1112) opposed it in favor of episcopal rights. The great Abbey of *Cluny was located in Autun; Romanesque, it was completed early in the 12th century and until the erection of the basilica of St. Peter in Rome was

The cathedral of Saint-Lazare, Autun, built between the 11th and the 15th century.

the largest ecclesiastical building in Europe. For many centuries the library of Cluny was one of the richest and most important in France and the storehouse of a vast number of valuable MSS. The conclave that elected Pope *Callistus II (1119–24) was held at Cluny. The main structure of the cathedral of Saint-Lazare dates from the 11th and 12th centuries, though the Gothic central towers and the chapels were added in the 15th century by Nicolas Rolin, chancellor of Burgundy, who was born in Autun.

The first council at Autun was held in 589. A second council took place during the episcopate of Bishop Léger (659–678); it acknowledged the Rule of St. Benedict as the normal monastic rule. Another council in 1065 reconciled Robert, Duke of Burgundy, with the bishop of Autun. In 1077 Pope Gregory VII convened a council in Autun that deposed Manasses, Archbishop of Reims, for simony and usurpation of the see. In 1094 Hugues, Archbishop of Lyons, renewed the excommunications of Henry IV of Germany and of Guibert, the antipope. Autun was sacked by the Protestant adherents of Coligny in 1570; but the Counter Reformation was inaugurated by Bp. Peter IV Saulnier (1588–1612), who installed the Capuchins (1606), Minims, and Jesuits. Bishop Claude de Ragny (1621–25) renewed the diocesan clergy and with the aid of St. Vincent de Paul reformed the local monasteries. The seminary was founded by Bp. Gabriel de Raquette and entrusted to the Sulpicians; and he introduced the daughters of charity at Paray-le-Monial, where St. Margaret Mary (d. 1690) had the apparitions of the Sacred Heart. In

1964 the Diocese of Autun had 541 parishes or quasi-parochial churches, 527 diocesan priests, 49 seminarians, 10 newly ordained priests, 13 houses for male religious, and 123 convents.

Bibliography: Mansi 19:1039–40; 20:489–492. H. GLASER, LexThK[2] 1:1137. E. JARRY, *Catholicisme* 1:1095–97. V. TERRET, DHGE 5:896–925. H. LECLERCQ, DACL 1.2:3189–3203; 13.2: 2884–98. É. GRIFFE, *La Gaule chrétienne à l'époque romaine* (Paris 1947–) 1:48–50. A. DE CHARMASSE, ed., *Cartulaire de l'église d'Autun,* 3 pts. in 2 v. (Autun 1865–1900). **Illustration credit:** Archives Photographiques, Paris.

[D. KELLEHER]

AUTUN, COUNCILS OF, a number of Church councils held at the diocesan seat of *Autun, France, near Lyons and *Cluny.

In 589 a council under St. Syagrius, Bishop of Autun, restored order in the monastery of Sainte-Radegonde at Poitiers by excommunicating the two nuns who were in rebellion against their abbess.

A council, *c.* 670, under Bp. *Leodegar of Autun, promulgated a number of disciplinary canons including one requiring priests to know the Apostles' and Athanasian Creeds and one demanding monastic stability and the strict observance of the *Benedictine Rule. Sacramental communion by all Christians was required at Christmas, Easter, and Pentecost. Priests were to be punished for celebrating Mass unworthily.

In 1065 the archbishops of Lyons and Besançon and the bishops of Chalon-sur-Sâone, Mâcon, and Autun met to consider the misrule of Duke Robert I of Burgundy whom Abbot *Hugh of Cluny is said to have then brought to repentance.

In 1077 a council promoting Pope *Gregory VII's reforms was held by the papal legate *Hugh of Die. It had to restore order after the violence of the late Duke Robert. It promulgated the law forbidding lay *investiture, a subject raised when the council regularized the position of *Gerard, Bishop of Cambrai. The council found Abp. *Manasses of Reims guilty of simony and suspended him. Manasses then became an open supporter of Emperor *Henry IV and the antipope *Guibert of Ravenna.

On Oct. 15, 1094, another council under Hugh of Die renewed the excommunications of Henry IV and Guibert. Eudes I of Burgundy returned some Church property. In 1100 famine forced the council scheduled for Autun to be held instead at *Valence.

Bibliography: Hefele-Leclercq 3:307–308; 4:1233–34; 5:387–388. V. TERRET, DHGE 5:922–925.

[A. CONDIT]

AUXERRE

City of 33,000 (1962) on the left bank of the Yonne River, in Yonne department, Archdiocese of *Sens, central France. The See of Auxerre (4th–18th century) lost its territory at various times to Sens, *Orléans, and *Nevers (detached from Auxerre *c.* 500); Auxerre's history reflects its position between Sens, the Loire Valley, and Burgundy.

The Roman *Autissiodorum* was constituted in the late 3d century near the Gallic *Autricum.* By 400 it was one of the seven cities of the civil province *Lugdunensis IV*. It was in Frankish hands when its bishop Theodosius signed the acts of the Council of Orléans in 511. From the 10th century there was a hereditary county of Auxerre, which John IV conveyed to Charles V of France (1370). The territory passed to the Duke of Burgundy (1435) but was reannexed to the French crown after the death of Charles the Bold (1477).

Local tradition records the martyrdom of Priscus (Bris) and his companions in flight from *Besançon during the reign of Emperor Aurelian (270–275). Peregrinus, who heads the episcopal list, may have been an itinerant evangelist. From Marcellian (306?–335?) can be traced a true succession, which includes *Amator (388?–418); *Germain (418–448), who was active in Britain (Bede, *Hist. Eccl.* 1:17–21); *Aunarius (561–605), under whom a diocesan synod assembled; and Wala (872–79), in whose pontificate the *Gesta pontificum Autissiodorensium* (PL 138:219–394) was inaugurated. The episcopal domain, established by 700 and confiscated by Pepin the Short (751–768), was restored under Bps. Herbert I (971–995) and Hugh (999–1039). Later bishops were as much feudal lords as prelates, and the diocese was rent by the Hundred Years War and the Wars of Religion. Jansenism was strong, especially under Bp. Charles G. de Caylus (1704–54). The 106th prelate, J. B. M. Champion de Cicé (1760–90; d. 1805), saw the diocese suppressed in 1790 and the territory assigned to Sens. The *Concordat of 1801 gave the area to *Troyes, but the restoration of Sens as an archdiocese (1822) brought about Sens's jurisdiction over all Yonne, except the commune of *Pontigny (since 1954). In 1823 the archbishop of Sens added Auxerre to his title.

Auxerre produced famous philosophers: *Heiric (d. 876), *Remigius (d. 908), *William (d. *c.* 1237), and Lambert (*c.* 1250). The artistic worth of the city's three parishes is considerable. The former cathedral of St. Étienne, with stained glass of the 13th and 16th centuries, has a crypt (11th century) and an upper church

The former cathedral of St. Etienne at Auxerre.

with an elegant Gothic choir (13th century) and nave (14th–15th century). The Church of St. Eusèbe (12th–16th century) is graced with a Romanesque nave. The Gothic St. Pierre (16th–17th century) boasts a late Renaissance façade. Significant too are the remnants of the 12th-century episcopal palace incorporated into the Prefecture, and the abbey church of St. Germain, founded in the early 6th century, with 9th-century crypts (Carolingian frescoes) and an upper church (13th-century choir and 15th-century nave).

Bibliography: GallChrist 12 (1770) 260–482. P. R. BARBIER, *Auxerre et l'Auxerrois, pays d'art et d'histoire* (Paris 1936). G. LEBRAS, *S. Germain d'Auxerre et son temps* (Auxerre 1950). R. LOUIS, *Les Églises d'Auxerre des origines au XIe siècle* (Paris 1952). *Congrès archéologique de France: 116e session: Auxerre* (Paris 1959). E. JARRY, *Catholicisme* 1:1100–03. E. CHARTRAINE, DHGE 5:939–958. **Illustration credit:** Archives Photographiques, Paris.

[H. G. J. BECK]

AUXILIUS OF NAPLES, Frankish priest, polemicist; date and place of birth and death unknown. He was ordained in Rome by Pope *Formosus (891–896), and may have either established himself as a grammarian near Naples, or entered *Monte Cassino, where a necrology mentions an "Auxilius" as author of a commentary on Genesis. When *Sergius III (904–911) reenacted the decrees of the "cadaveric synod," which had declared all actions of Pope Formosus invalid and threatened with excommunication those who exercised Holy Orders conferred by him unless they were reordained, Auxilius and *Eugenius Vulgarius became spokesmen of the position. In several pamphlets they defended the legality of the election of Formosus and the validity of the Holy Orders conferred by him. According to Auxilius, the validity of Orders did not depend on the personal worthiness of the bishop and, therefore, he opposed *reordination. Despite the prerogatives of the Apostolic See, Auxilius believed a council was necessary to vindicate Formosus, and to judge Sergius. His pamphlets included *De ordinationibus a Formoso papa factis* (PL 129:1059–74, completed in Dümmler, 107–116); *Infensor et defensor,* (PL 129: 1073–1102); *In defensionem sacrae ordinationis papae Formosi,* (Dümmler, 59–95); *In defensionem Stephani episcopi et prefatae ordinationis,* (Dümmler, 96–105).

Bibliography: E. DÜMMLER, ed., *Auxilius und Vulgarius* (Leipzig 1866). L. SALTET, *Les Réordinations: Étude sur le sacrament de l'ordre* (Paris 1907) 143–145, 152–163. Manitius 1:437–439, 2:805. D. POP, *La Défense du pape Formose* (Paris 1933). J. POZZI, "Le Manuscrit Tomus XVIIIus de la Vallicelliana et le Libelle 'De Episcoporum Transmigratione'" *Apollinaris* 31 (1958) 313–350. S. LINDEMANS, "Auxilius et le Manuscrit Vallicellan Tome XVIII," RHE 57 (1962) 470–484.

[S. P. LINDEMANS]

AVARICE

A vice, and one of the capital *sins, consisting in excessive appetite for wealth; it is directly opposed, by defect, to the virtue of liberality, which controls desire for possessions, and is indirectly subversive of many other virtues. While earthly wealth in itself can be considered a good thing and even a blessing from God, it is also a dangerous thing, and the inordinate desire of it or excessive preoccupation with acquiring it is dangerous. Christ condemned avarice "because a man's life does not consist in the abundance of his possessions" (Lk 12.15). If a man lives primarily for riches, he will have no part in the kingdom of heaven (Mt 19.24) "for you cannot serve God and Mammon" (Mt 6.24; Lk 16.13). Avarice in its extreme form would occur in the case of an individual who attaches such value to wealth and possessions that he makes the accumulation and retention of them the major goal of his life, to which he subordinates all else. Such a perversion of values would obviously be mortally sinful and totally disruptive of the moral life. However, so basically disordered a desire for wealth is probably a rare thing, occurring only in the true miser, whose preoccupation with money is so manifestly foolish that it must be explained in terms of some deep distortion of the psyche. But an individual's unreasonable pursuit of riches does not not necessarily mean that he makes an ultimate goal of them. He may seek wealth for what he gets by means of it. Money can buy gratification of many kinds—pleasures, fame, power, the envy of others, etc.—and those immoderately dedicated to gathering riches may also be lavish in their expenditures, which indicates that the wealth is sought as a means rather than an end. But this can also involve a perversion of values more or less seriously sinful depending on the objectives that are sought through wealth or the good things that are sacrificed in its pursuit. Evidently, too, avarice can be seriously sinful when it is so uncontrolled as to cause one to sin gravely against other virtues, such as justice or charity.

The error of attaching too great an importance to wealth is generally committed in the practical rather than the theoretical order. St. Thomas Aquinas called it an error of common (*vulgares*) men, but the "common" is to be understood in distinction to philosophers and not as implying that the fault is more prevalent among rude and uncultured folk. Indeed, primitive peoples, and generally those whose culture is unsophisticated, tend to be more content with their relative indigence, and even to lack something of the *auri sacra fames* (the accursed love of gold) of which Vergil spoke (*Aeneid* 3.57). In a more complex society, particularly one based economically on the principle of individual competition, men feel the need of reassurance against their fears of hostility, failure, and insecurity, and too often it is sought in an intensified quest for possessions [see K. Horney, *The Neurotic Personality of Our Time* (New York 1937) ch. 10].

In earlier times avarice was considered a more reprehensible moral fault than prodigality, which is its opposite extreme (St. Thomas Aquinas, ST 2a2ae, 19.3). The latter was deemed to stand nearer to, or to have more affinity with, the mean, which is liberality, than the former, as is apparent in the terms themselves: one who gives too freely has a greater likeness to the ideally liberal man than another who gives too sparingly. In later times when bourgeois thinking had dignified trade and moneymaking with ethical or near-ethical values, the virtuous mean shifted in popular thought from a position nearer the extreme of prodigality to one more closely approaching avarice. The older term liberality accordingly became less appropriate and was largely replaced in popular use by thrift and frugality. But in the more recent stage of the economic development of society the encouragement of consumption is seen as desirable for the stimulation of industry and production. Thrift and frugality have therefore lost something of the respectability they formerly enjoyed. Nevertheless this does not appear to have resulted in a new shift in the mean popularly considered desirable between avarice and prodigality, so much as in a change in the relative values assigned to different kinds of possessions an individual will desire—for example, consumer goods, such as homes, cars, appliances, which give comfort and status to the possessor, as compared with money.

St. Thomas noted that the inclination to avarice tends to grow stronger in the aged. Because their strength and prospects are diminishing, it may seem more urgent to them to compensate for this deficiency by storing up external goods and holding onto them more tenaciously.

See also POVERTY, RELIGIOUS.

Bibliography: THOMAS AQUINAS, ST 2a2ae, 118.1–8. A. BEUGNET, DTC 1.2:2623–27. R. H. TAWNEY, *Religion and the Rise of Capitalism* (pa. Baltimore 1947; New York 1958). G. VANN, "Money," *Furrow* 13 (1962) 151–159.

[P. K. MEAGHER]

AVARS, Mongol nomads who formed a central European state from *c.* A.D. 559 to 796. They closely resembled the Huns in appearance, way of life, and warfare. They came into contact with Justinian in 558, and under Khan Baian swept across southern Russia to the Frankish borders where they were checked in 561 and 566. With Lombard aid they conquered the Hungarian plain (Pannonia) from the Gepids and, after the Lombards' departure in 568, established themselves there. They gained ascendancy over the more numerous Slavs, assumed leadership of the Slavs' southward migration, probably their most significant achievement, and indirectly contributed to the separation of the West and South Slavs. The combined horde of Avars and Slavs took Singidunum and Sirmium *c.* 582 and by 597 reached Thessalonika. Driven back across the Danube by 601, they destroyed the Antes in Bessarabia in 602. In 617 they ravaged the Balkans and reached Constantinople. In 622 the West Slavs revolted from the Avars, and in 626 the South Slavs, after an Avar defeat at Constantinople, did the same with Bulgar help. The Avars thereafter remained confined in Hungary until Charlemagne's campaign of 791 to 796 ended their history, although uprisings against the Franks occurred until 803. After 805 the Avars became Christian. Many of them were absorbed by the Bulgars.

Bibliography: F. DVORNIK, *The Slavs: Their Early History and Civilization* (Boston 1956). G. OSTROGORSKY, *History of the Byzantine State,* tr. J. HUSSEY (New Brunswick, N.J. 1957). E. KLEBEL, LexThK[2] 1:1139–40.

[R. H. SCHMANDT]

AVE MARIA (ANTIPHON). That the text of *Ave Maria* is composed of three segments—Lk 1.28, Lk 1.42, and a prayer appended in the 15th century (*see* HAIL MARY)—is reflected in its musical settings. The Antiphonary of Hartker, for example, a 10th-century source from St. Gall (*see* SANKT GALLEN) (PalMus, Ser. 2, 2), contains an antiphon that sets only the first segment followed by "Alleluia" (also in *Antiphonale monasticum* 228 and, in slightly different form, in *Liber usualis* 1416). Essentially the same melody is given in the 12th-century Codex Worcester F. 160 (PalMus 12: 301). The text is also used twice as an *Offertory antiphon—once with only the text previously mentioned and a modern melody (*Liber usualis* 1318) and once, with Lk 1.42 added and with a medieval melody (*Liber usualis* 355, found in various early MSS, among them the Codex Montpellier H. 159, PalMus 8:283, where it has two verses beginning "Quomodo in me" and "Ideo quod nascetur"). An even shorter segment of the text, ending with the words "Dominus tecum," is used as an invitatory antiphon in the Codex Worcester; it appears there with two different melodies. None of these four different medieval melodies sets the complete prayer in use today.

Renaissance polyphonists only rarely quoted any of these medieval melodies in setting the *Ave Maria.* The most celebrated early monument of music printing, *Harmonice Musices Odhecaton A* (*Petrucci, 1501) begins with an *Ave Maria* by Marbriano de Orto (d. 1529) in which the melody of the first antiphon is only briefly quoted (if at all), and the text ends "Dominus tecum." *Vittoria set the text twice without referring to the chant melodies. However, Josquin *Desprez's setting opens with a figure very much like that beginning the antiphon, and continues with figures derived from the chant as the basis for sections in polyphonic style on the words "gratia plena," "Dominus tecum," and "benedicta tu"; but from there on his setting seems to be unrelated to the chant. His text includes Lk 1.28 and 1.42 and appends a few more lines, not part of the modern prayer, that replace the section beginning "Sancta Maria." Similarly, the text set for four voices by *Palestrina is almost entirely different from the usual text after the words "Sancta Maria." Giacomo Fogliano (1473–1548), however, provided a simple four-part setting for the complete modern text. The best-known of Renaissance settings of the *Ave Maria,* that attributed to *Arcadelt, is really a 19th-century adaptation of the music of a secular song by Arcadelt, *Nous voyons que les hommes,* to the sacred text. *Ave Maria* has been set by many composers since the Renaissance—*Schubert's setting is particularly well known—and contemporary composers, including Stravinsky, have continued to write music for it.

Bibliography: Reese MusR. H. LECLERCQ, DACL 10.2:2043–62.

[R. STEINER]

AVE MARIS STELLA, the first verse of an unrhymed accentual hymn in honor of Our Lady. There are seven strophes of four lines each, written in trochaic dimeter brachycatalectic with three trochees to each line. It was first recorded in the Codex Sangallensis 95, found in the Abbey of *Sankt Gallen, dating from the 9th century. The hymn has been attributed to various authors: St. *Bernard of Clairvaux, *Paul the Deacon, and Venantius *Fortunatus are the most frequently mentioned, although the MS date makes it obvious that it could not have been the work of Bernard. It was one of the most popular hymns used for *Marian feasts in the Middle Ages and has been retained in the Roman *Breviary as the *Vespers hymn for the Common of feasts of the Blessed Virgin Mary as well as for the Saturday Office and the *Little Office of Our Lady. The title by which Mary's intercession is sought, *maris stella,* is similar to those used in the *Litany of Loreto. In the first strophe Mary is referred to as the gate of heaven, *caeli porta,* while the second stanza contrasts Mary's place in the work of redemption with *Eve's responsibility for the Fall. The third stanza appeals for help and enlightenment, and in the fourth Mary is asked to use a mother's influence with her Son on our behalf. The fifth strophe recognizes the virtues we should follow if we are to reach the salvation described in the sixth stanza, *ut videntes Iesum.* The last stanza is a brief *doxology. The poem, with great beauty and moving simplicity, has been translated many times, most notably by E. Caswall. The complete text with notes has been edited by C. Blume [AnalHymn 51 (1908) 140–142], and the text with three musical variations may be found in the Liber usualis edited by the Benedictines of *Solesmes (New York 1959) 1259–63.

Bibliography: F. J. MONE, ed., *Lateinische Hymnen des Mittelalters,* 3 v. (Freiburg 1853–55) 2:216–229. F. B. PLAINE, "Hymni Marialis *Ave Maris Stella* Expositio," *Studien und Mitteilungen aus dem Benedictiner- und Cistercienser Orden* 14 (1893) 244–255. G. M. DREVES, "Der Hymnus vom Meerestern," *Stimmen aus Maria Laach* 50 (1896) 558–569. P. WAGNER, "Le due melodie dell'inno *Ave Maris Stella,*" *Rassegna Gregoriana* 1 (1902) 73–75. G. BAS, *Rhythme Grégorien* (Rome 1906) 15–19. E. COSTANZI, "Quando invaluerit disciplina genuflectendi ad I stroph. Hymni *Ave Maris Stella,*" EphemLiturg 42 (1928) 322–326. M. BRITT, ed., *The Hymns of the Breviary and Missal* (new ed. New York 1948) 347–349. A. DAL ZOTTO, "Ricerche sull'autore dell' *Ave Maris Stella,*" *Aevum* 25 (1951) 494–503. J. CARCIA and E. R. PANYAGUA, "Estudios de *Ave Maris Stella,*" *Helmantica* 8 (1959) 421–475. A. MOLIEN, *Catholicisme* 1:1111–12. H. LAUSBERG, LexThK[2] 1:1141–42. Cross ODCC 113. Szövérffy AnnLatHymn 1:219–220.

[B. J. COMASKEY]

AVE REGINA CAELORUM. One of the four Marian antiphons, *Ave Regina caelorum* is sung at the end of Compline from February 2 (Candlemas Day) until Wednesday in Holy Week. Its original role in the liturgy, however, seems to have been to precede and follow the chanting of a psalm. Peter Wagner found it assigned to None on the Feast of the Assumption in a 12th-century source (Wagner GregMel 141). The more elaborate of the two melodies for this antiphon in the *Liber usualis* is apparently the older. The structure of the text, consisting of two pairs of similar phrases followed by an unmatched pair, is reflected in the musical form, which may be outlined as: *a a', b c, b' c, d' e.* The chant was apparently a special favorite of the composer *Dufay (*c.* 1400–74), who composed a Mass in which the chant melody appears in all the movements. A four-part setting of the text by Dufay uses the chant theme (embellished) in the tenor; the text is troped with such personal expressions as *Miserere tui labentis Dufay,* and the composer expressed in his will a desire to have this piece sung as he died. Other Renaissance composers setting this text include *Palestrina (four settings, all quoting the chant melody) and *Victoria, who composed a version for eight voices and organ and later based a Mass on the eight-part work. *Gesualdo, noted for his use of chromatic progressions, also set this text, his work being in five parts.

Bibliography: Reese MusR. Apel GregCh. Wagner GregMel. B. STÄBLEIN, "Antiphon," MusGG 1:523–545.

[R. STEINER]

AVE VERUM CORPUS, short Eucharistic hymn, no longer in liturgical use. Although regarded as a *sequence, it was actually sung during the *Elevation of the Mass, a part of the Mass introduced only in the 12th century. The hymn has been ascribed to Pope Innocent VI (1352–62), but this is improbable since the text is found in MSS from the late 13th or early 14th centuries. This hymn excels the many similar texts written during the 14th and 15th centuries (e.g., the MS of the *Orationale Augiense* contains some 26 pieces of similar character). At one time it was more popular than the **Adoro te devote.* It originated probably in northern Italy, and it is written in trochaic tetrameter, rhyming at the caesura and at the end of lines. The last two lines reverse the roles Christ and Mary play in the famous **Salve regina (mater) misericordiae.* Of the many musical compositions composed for this text, *Mozart's motet is particularly appropriate to its spirit.

Bibliography: I. CECCHETTI, EncCatt 2:535. G. MARSOT, *Catholicisme* 1.1112–13. Szövérffy AnnLatHymns 2:298–299. Connelly Hymns 130. AnalHymn 54:257.

[J. SZÖVÉRFFY]

AVELLANA COLLECTIO, a canonical collection of the letters of emperors and popes, beginning with a rescript of Valentinian I, dated 368, and ending with a letter of Pope *Vigilius to Justinian, dated May 14, 553. Evidence available indicates that the collection was prepared shortly after A.D. 553. The collection reproduces in succession: letters of the emperors (from Valentinian to Honorius) interspersed with a few letters addressed to the emperors, letters of the popes from Innocent I to Vigilius, and letters and acts from the pontificate of Pope St. *Hormisdas. (The best edition is the work of O. Günther in CSEL 35.) The interest of the collection lies above all in the compiler's intention of providing texts not included in collections then in existence, and of seeking them directly in the archival deposits, e.g., a reference to the use of the *gesta* after Hormisdas' letter. But the author also collected apocryphal writings, e.g., the correspondence of Peter of Antioch relating to monophysitism. The collection was not widely disseminated because the Gelasian Collections had summarized ancient law, and the legislative activity of the papacy suffered as a result of political crises. However, through the *Avellana Collectio* we know a good portion of the letters of Vigilius and certain imperial letters.

Bibliography: Fournier-LeBras 1:35–41. Maassen 787–792. O. Günther, "Avellana-Studien," SBWien 134.5 (1896). R. NAZ, DDC 1:1491.

[J. GAUDEMET]

AVELLINO, ANDREW, ST., preacher and reformer; b. Castronuovo, Naples, 1521; d. Naples, Nov. 10, 1608 (feast, Nov. 10). His parents, who were of the nobility, named him Lancelot at Baptism. He pursued his studies in various cities and in 1537 became a cleric. After ordination in 1545, he undertook the study of Canon and civil law at Naples in 1547. In 1548 he made the spiritual exercises under the Jesuit, James Laynez. This experience, as well as his remorse at the recollection of a lie he had told in pleading a legal case led to his determination to devote himself completely to the care of souls. He was badly beaten by men who resented his effort to reform a convent in Baiano, and was taken to the Theatine house of St. Paul in Naples where he recovered. In 1556 he joined the Theatines and took the name Andrew. He evidenced qualities suitable for a spiritual director and promoter of ecclesiastical discipline, and in 1567 became superior of his community in Naples. At the request of Charles Borromeo he founded a Theatine house in Milan in 1570, and the next year went to Piacenza where he directed the diocesan seminary and a house of penitent women. Three times he acted as visitor of the Theatine houses in Lombardy. In 1582 he returned to Naples. In 1590 he officially visited the Theatine houses of the Roman and Neapolitan provinces, and successfully pleaded that he be excused from elevation to the hierarchy. An articulate and cultivated man, he left about 3,000 letters of spiritual direction, a little more than a 1,000 of which were published in Naples (1731–32). Other works also, including conferences, were published in Naples (1733–34). He was canonized in 1712. Naples and Sicily honor him as a patron.

Bibliography: ActSS Nov. 4:609–622. G. M. MAGENIS, *Vita di S. Andrea Avellino* (Venice 1714). A. PALMIERI, DHGE 2: 1635–37, bibliog.

[W. BANGERT]

AVEMPACE (IBN BĀJJAḤ, ABŪ BAKR MUḤAMMAD IBN YAḤYĀ), Arab philosopher who flourished in Spain; b. Saragossa (date unknown) and went to Seville in 1118; d. at the Almoravid court at Fez, 1138. He wrote works on medicine and mathematics, and commented on Aristotle's *Physica, Meteorologica, De generatione et corruptione, De generatione animalium,* and *De partibus animalium.* His main philosophical writings include treatises on logic, the *Regime* or *Guide of the Solitary, On the Contact of the Intellect with Man,* a treatise on the soul, and a letter of farewell. The last three were cited by *Averroës in his *Commentarium magnum* on Aristotle's *De anima.*

In the *Regime of the Solitary,* according to a synopsis given by a 14th-century Jewish writer, Moses of Narbonne, Avempace tries to show how man can achieve union with the Agent Intellect. By seeking not merely forms of material things but also universal spiritual forms or ideas, the human intellect can gradually work up to a level where it grasps ideas of ideas. Thus, by its own power, it can come to know separated substances. In other works, too, Avempace holds that through a progressive abstraction of quiddities man's intellect can reach a *quiddity that has no further quiddities, i.e., the quiddity of a separated substance. Averroës reports these views and notes their author's abiding concern with the question of how man's intellect can achieve its end: union with the separated Agent Intellect. That question, says Averroës, never left the thought of Avempace, "not even for the space of time it takes to blink an eye" (*Comm. de anim.* 3.36, 487 Med. Acad. ed.). Aquinas restates Avempace's views and criticizes them as "frivolous" (*C. gent.* 3.41).

Avempace's commentary on the *Physica* seems to have been influential in the formulation of Galileo's law of falling bodies.

See also ARABIAN PHILOSOPHY; INTELLECT, UNITY OF; SCIENCE (IN THE MIDDLE AGES).

Bibliography: AVEMPACE, "Ibn Bājjah's Tadbīru'l-Mutawaḥḥīd (Rule of the Solitary)," ed. and tr. D. M. DUNLOP, JRoyAsSoc (1945) 61–81, partial text in Arabic and Eng. S. MUNK, *Mélanges de philosophie juive et arabe* (new ed. Paris 1955). M. CLAGGET, *The Science of Mechanics in the Middle Ages* (Madison, Wis. 1959). E. A. MOODY, "Galileo and Avempace: The Dynamics of the Leaning Tower Experiment," JHistIdeas 12 (1951) 163–193, 375–422.

[B. H. ZEDLER]

AVENDAÑO, DIEGO DE, Jesuit specialist in law for the Indies; b. Segovia, Spain, Sept. 29, 1596; d. Lima, Peru, Aug. 30, 1688. After studying philosophy at Seville, he went to Lima in 1610, and while a student at its Colegio de San Martín, he entered the Society of Jesus on April 21, 1612. He completed his studies at the Jesuit college in Lima and taught philosophy in Cuzco, where he became rector in 1628. He made his profession on May 24, 1629. He was professor of theology in the Jesuit University of Chuquisaca (today Sucre, Bolivia), rector of the major seminary of Lima during two periods (1651, 1667), and provincial from 1663 to 1666. In his great work *Thesaurus indicus* he formulated, discussed, and resolved a varied range of legal topics, no doubt submitted to him for study, as an expert in canon, civil, and moral law, by the episcopal tribunals and the Spanish-American courts. In it he showed his fine speculative talent, his rigidly scholastic education, his eclecticism, and his extensive and up-to-date reading. He was an illustrious example of 17th-century education in Lima. He neither tried to be nor was original, but he was useful for the correct administration of justice. His intrinsic value lay in having adapted the traditional doctrine of both bodies of law to the Indian environment and to its particular problems.

Bibliography: M. DE MENDIBURU, *Diccionario histórico-biográfico del Perú,* 11 v. (2d ed. Lima 1931–34) 2:291–294. J. E. DE URIARTE and M. LECINA, *Biblioteca de escritores de la Compañía de Jesús . . . ,* 2 v. (Madrid 1925–30).

[A. DE EGAÑA]

AVENTINUS (JOHANNES THURMAYR), humanist and historian; b. Abensberg, Bavaria, July 4, 1477; d. Regensburg, Jan. 9, 1534. He was educated at Ingolstadt, Vienna, Cracow, and Paris. At Ingolstadt and Vienna he came under the influence of the humanist Conrad *Celtis, who inspired him to write German history. At Paris he felt the influence of *Lefèvre d'Étaples and his circle, and he took his master's degree there (1504). He served the dukes of Bavaria as tutor (1509–17), then as historiographer. Commissioned to write a Bavarian history, he collected important original documents, and produced *Annales ducum Boiariae* (German epitome, 1522; first ed., purged of the worst anticlerical passages, 1544) and *Bayerische Chronik* (1533; pub. 1556). The delay in publication of his chief works, as well as a brief arrest in 1528, resulted from his bitter anticlericalism. Though a friend of Philipp *Melanchthon and other Protestant leaders, Aventinus was essentially an anticlerical and nationalist humanist (sentiments expressed in his works); but he never left the Church.

Bibliography: *Sämtliche Werke,* 6 v. in 7 (Munich 1881–1908). G. STRAUSS, *Historian in an Age of Crisis: The Life and Work of Johannes Aventinus, 1477–1534* (Cambridge, Mass. 1963), excellent bibliographical essay. T. WIEDEMANN, *Johann Turmair, genannt Aventinus, Geschichtschreiber des bayerischen Volkes* (Freising 1850). H. RALL, LexThK² 1:1142–43.

[C. G. NAUERT, JR.]

AVERROËS (IBN RUSHD)

Moslem philosopher whose writings influenced medieval Christian thinkers; b. Córdoba, Spain, 1126; d. Morocco, 1198. Averroës came from a distinguished family of judges. He studied law, medicine, theology, and philosophy and served in high positions under two Almohad rulers: Ya'qūb Yusūf and his successor, Yusūf Ya'qūb al-Manṣur. When the latter persecuted the philosophers in 1196–97, Averroës was banished from Córdoba, but he was later restored to favor.

Averroës wrote a general work on medicine, *Kullīyāt*—known to the Latins as *Colliget* and used as a textbook in medieval universities. His main philosophical works include *Sermo de substantia orbis; Faṣl al-maqāl* (*On the Harmony of Religion and Philosophy*); *Tahāfut al-Tahāfut* (or, in the Latin version, *Destructio destructionis philosophiae Algazelis*); commentaries on many works of Aristotle including the *Metaphysics, Physics, De generatione et corruptione, Nicomachean Ethics, De anima, De caelo et mundo, Posterior Analytics;* and a paraphrase of Plato's *Republic.*

Teaching. The Aristotelian commentaries, written at the request of Ya'qūb Yusūf, were of three types. The great commentary reproduced in the order of the original text each paragraph of Aristotle's work and explained it in a detailed way. The middle commentary cited only the first words of each of Aristotle's paragraphs before proceeding to some exposition. The paraphrase was a summary that followed the order that seemed most suitable to Averroës; this was not necessarily the order of the book he was explaining. The commentaries reflected Averroës's great admiration for *Aristotle. Though he was influenced also by *Plato, Aristotle, for him, was the Master, the "exemplar that Nature found to show forth the highest human perfection" [*Comm. mag. in Arist. de anim. lib.* 3.14 (Mediaeval Academy ed. 433)].

Notion of Intellect. In his commentary on the *De anima* Averroës discussed a problem that had arisen from a text in book 3: Does each man have his own intellect or is there one intellect for all men? Some of the Arabs, among them *Avicenna (980–1037), had thought that although each man has his own possible intellect, the active, or agent, intellect is a separated substance and one for all men. Averroës held that the possible, or "material," intellect, as well as the agent intellect, was a separated substance and one for all men. In his view the individual man has no spiritual intellect; but because man's imagination, memory, and cogitative power supply and prepare sensory data for the use of the separated intellect, he thought man shared in the latter's knowledge. For Averroës, the separated agent intellect actuates the intelligible species potentially present in man's phantasms and thus enables the separated possible intellect to become the subject in which knowledge exists (*Comm. mag.* 3.4, 383–385; 3.5, 388–389, 412; 3.18, 439–440; 3.19, 441; 3.33, 476). St. *Thomas Aquinas was to point out that to say man provides the objects of knowledge for a separated intellect is not to explain how the individual man knows; and to deny to the individual man a spiritual power of knowing is to destroy the philosophical basis for the personal immortality of the soul (*De unit. intell.* proem.; 3). Averroës himself was not content with his own explanation, but tried to keep the intellect separate from matter to ensure its function of knowing *universals (*Comm. mag.* 3.4, 383–384; 3.5, 388–389; 3.19, 441; 3.36, 502). He had no awareness of a spiritual intellective soul that could be the form of the body without being immersed in matter.

Concept of Being. In metaphysics Averroës found the clue to the meaning of being in the book of his Master. Aristotle had seemed to identify being with substance and substance with "what" a thing is (*Meta.* 1028a 13–14). Averroës taught that being is eminently substance and that substance is eminently form [*In 7 meta.* 1 (Venice 1574)]. He criticized Avicenna for teaching that existence is an accident of essence. "Avicenna sinned much," he said, "in this that he thought that 'one' and 'being' signify dispositions added to the essence of a thing" (*In 4 meta.* 2, fol. 67r–v). For Averroës "to be" is in no way an addition to essence: "This name *ens* that is imposed from the 'to be' of a thing, signifies the same reality as the name that is imposed from its essence" (*In 4 meta.* 2, fol. 67r). Being means nothing else than "that which is." To him it seemed that Avicenna had mixed up theological teachings with metaphysics.

Averroës also rejected Avicenna's version of emanation, which provided a cosmological framework for showing that existence is something that "happens" to a possible essence [*Tahāfut al-Tahāfut* 3 (tr. S. Van den Bergh 118–119)]. It is wrong, Averroës thought, to insist that from the one only one can proceed. In Averroës's cosmology this principle applies more evidently to the lower world—made up of beings composed of matter and form—than it does to the realm of Intelligences. Rather, the first effect possesses plurality, a plurality that depends on unity (*ibid.* 3.107–109, 148–149, 154).

God and the World. Averroës agreed with Avicenna that there are many Intelligences and that their number and their rank are determined by the number and physical rank (i.e., the size and speed) of the celestial bodies they move. But this hierarchy of rank is not a sequence of production. Though some are subordinate to others in rank, the whole hierarchy of Intelligences is related to God as its formal and final cause. God is the First Principle, "the principle of all these principles" (*ibid.* 3.111–115; 138).

In Averroës's context the heavens, motion, time, and primary matter are all eternal. The world must be eternal, he thought; to deny its eternity would be to imply that something could prevent God's act from being eternally connected with His existence. But such a constraint upon His activity would point to an inadmissible lack of power and perfection in God (*ibid.* 1.56). The assumption that an eternal effect must necessarily result from God's eternal action was later opposed by St. Thomas Aquinas (*C. gent.* 2.35; ST 1a, 46.1 ad 10).

Averroës's God was the productive cause of the things of the sublunary world. As such, He made sensible things to be by bringing into actual existence forms that existed potentially in eternal matter. Although this God might seem to a Christian to be only a First Mover and not a Creator, Averroës called Him a cause of existence, since to his way of thinking, "the bestower of the conjunction of matter and form is the bestower of existence" (*Tahāfut* 3.108).

Religion. This and other conclusions of Averroës seemed incompatible with traditional teachings of the religion of Islam, which he also accepted. Did he then teach a doctrine of double truth, as some later interpreters claimed? The answer is negative. In his *Faṣl al-maqāl* (*On the Harmony of Religion and Philosophy*) he tried to show that religion points through symbolic representations to the same truths that philosophical knowledge attains. For most people, he held, the religious approach is best (*Faṣl al-maqāl,* ch. 2, 3; *Tahāfut* About the Natural Sciences 1, 4). But by implying that

Averroës, detail of a 14th-century fresco by Taddeo Gaddi in the Cappella degli Spagnoli of the Chiòstro di Santa Maria Novella at Florence.

only the philosopher, and not the believer, sees truth as it is, Averroës seemed to accept the speculative primacy of reason.

Influence. The thought of Averroës did not have much influence in his own Moslem world, but many of his works were preserved in Hebrew and Latin translations. As "The Commentator," he was used by Christians as an aid in reading Aristotle and became the source of a new movement of thought that opposed, on some points, the teachings of faith. This Latin Averroism of 13th-century Paris was succeeded by a second Averroism in 14th-, 15th-, and 16th-century Italy, especially at Padua. Petrarch declared that for some thinkers, Aristotle held the place of Christ, and Averroës that of St. Peter [quoted by J. R. Charbonnel, *La Pensée italienne au XIVe siècle* (Paris 1919) 178].

See also AVERROISM, LATIN; DOUBLE TRUTH, THEORY OF; INTELLECT, UNITY OF; ARABIAN PHILOSOPHY; SCHOLASTICISM.

Bibliography: Works. *Commentarium magnum in Aristotelis De anima libros,* ed. F. S. CRAWFORD (Cambridge, Mass. 1953), and other Mediaeval Academy eds. of his commentaries; *Commentarium in Aristotelis Metaphysicorum libros,* in ARISTOTLE, *Opera cum Averrois commentariis,* 9 v. in 11 and 3 suppl. (Venice 1562–74; repr. Frankfurt a. M. 1962); *Commentary on Plato's Republic,* ed. and tr. E. I. J. ROSENTHAL (Cambridge, Eng. 1956); *On the Harmony of Religion and Philosophy,* tr. G. F. HOURANI (London 1961); *Tahāfut al-Tahāfut* (*The Incoherence of the Incoherence*), tr. S. VAN DEN BERGH, 2 v. (London 1954); *Destructio destructionum philosophiae Algazelis in the Latin Version of Calo Calonymos,* ed. B. H. ZEDLER (Milwaukee 1961).

Literature. M. ALLARD, *Le Rationalisme d'Averroès d'après une étude sur la création* (Paris 1955). L. GAUTHIER, *Ibn Rochd (Averroès)* (Paris 1948). É. H. GILSON, *Being and Some Philosophers* (2d ed. Toronto 1952). Gilson HistChrPhil. E. RENAN, *Oeuvres philosophiques: Averroès et l'averroïsme . . .,* v.3 of *Oeuvres complètes* (Paris 1949). H. A. WOLFSON, "Revised Plan for the Publication of a *Corpus commentariorum Averrois in Aristotelem,*" *Speculum* 38 (1963) 88–98. **Illustration credit:** Alinari-Art Reference Bureau.

[B. H. ZEDLER]

AVERROISM, LATIN

A philosophical movement originating in the 13th century among masters of the faculty of arts in the University of Paris; also called integral, radical, and heterodox *Aristotelianism. Its main source was the philosophy of *Aristotle as interpreted by *Averroës.

Origins. In the early Middle Ages Aristotle's philosophy was known in western Europe chiefly through Latin translations of his minor logical works. In the second half of the 12th and the first half of the 13th century, the rest of his works were translated, decisively influencing the development of philosophy and theology. Along with the *corpus aristotelicum* a rich and varied Arabic philosophical and scientific literature, including some of the works of *Avicenna and Averroës, was also translated into Latin. Averroës's commentaries on Aristotle were so highly regarded that he was called the Commentator.

The portion of Avicenna's works known in the Christian West was translated in the 12th century, and its influence was felt in the first decades of the 13th century. The impact of Averroës's works came shortly afterward. They were translated between 1220 and 1235 and were first quoted in the 1230s and 1240s by theologians such as *William of Auvergne, *Philip the Chancellor, and St. *Albert the Great. At this time the scholastics used Averroës's works without suspecting how dangerous they could be to Christian thought. There is no indication of a Christian following of Averroës at this early date.

On March 16, 1255, a statute of the faculty of arts at Paris prescribed the teaching of the works of Aristotle (ChartUnParis 1:277). This date marks the official reception of Aristotelianism into the university. Since Aristotle's works were usually read along with Averroës's commentaries on them, it was to be expected that Averroës's influence would grow with Aristotle's.

The first criticisms of the errors of Averroës appeared shortly afterward. In 1256 St. Albert wrote his *De unitate intellectus contra Averroem* at the request of Pope Alexander IV. A few years later St. *Thomas Aquinas refuted Averroës's doctrine of the oneness of the intellect in his *Summa contra Gentiles* (2.73–76). These works were directed against Averroës's own teachings. They give no hint that he was acquiring a following among the philosophers at Paris. In 1270, however, St. Thomas directed his *De unitate intellectus contra Averroistas* against Parisian Averroists, especially Siger of Brabant. In the first chapter he says that "for some time now the error concerning the intellect has been implanted in many minds, originating in the statements of Averroës." The criticism by St. *Bonaventure of the heterodox Parisian masters of arts in 1267 and the official condemnation of the Averroists in 1270 by the bishop of Paris are conclusive evidence of the existence at this time of a Latin Averroist movement.

Principal Proponents. Not all the medieval philosophers and theologians who used and admired Averroës's commentaries can be called Averroists. Masters of arts such as *Adam of Buckfield, *Roger Bacon, and

John Sackville used them when lecturing on Aristotle; and theologians such as St. Albert and St. Thomas found the works of Averroës helpful, though they did not subscribe to his heterodox positions. The true Averroists were those who, like Averroës, tended to identify Aristotle's philosophy with philosophy itself, and generally accepted the Averroist interpretation of Aristotle. Like Averroës, they also advocated the freedom of philosophy from the influence of religion. The doctrine of Averroës that most clearly identified a scholastic as an Averroist was the oneness of the possible intellect in all men.

The leading Averroist in the 13th century was *Siger of Brabant, a master of arts at Paris from about 1260 to 1273. Writing in 1492, A. *Nifo, himself an Averroist in his youth, called Siger the originator of the Averroist school. Siger taught an Aristotelianism strongly influenced by Averroës and to a lesser extent by the *Neoplatonism of Avicenna. Another leading figure in the movement was *Boethius of Sweden (Dacia). From his few works that have survived and have been edited, he is known to have been an important logician and exponent of an Aristotelianism on some points contrary to the faith. One of the oldest manuscripts containing the heterodox propositions condemned by the bishop of Paris in 1277 names him as their principal exponent. While striving to find a *modus vivendi* for philosophy and theology, he advocated their strict separation. He also stressed the freedom of the philosopher to teach, even if his conclusions run counter to the faith. Other names associated with the condemnation of Averroism in the 13th century are Bernier of Nivelles and Goswin of La Chapelle. Nothing is known of their doctrine.

Unedited manuscripts, some anonymous, attest to the widespread influence of heterodox Aristotelianism in the late 13th and the early 14th century. A group of commentaries on Aristotle's *Nicomachean Ethics* reveals a naturalism in ethics opposed to Christian morality. James of Douai probably wrote one of these commentaries about 1275; another was written by Giles of Orléans in the beginning of the 14th century. Both were influenced by the ethical writings of Siger of Brabant and Boethius of Sweden. James of Douai was a man of moderate views, and in his Questions on the *De anima* he argued against the Averroistic doctrine of the oneness of the intellect.

Main Teachings. In the late Middle Ages and in the Renaissance the Averroists were conscious of forming a distinct school of philosophy. Averroism in the 13th century had not reached this stage of self-awareness but its characteristic spirit and general positions were already apparent.

The Averroists taught that the world and all species are eternal, and consequently that there was no first man. They adopted the Greek cyclical view of history, according to which all events, ideas, and religions eternally recur. For Siger and Boethius, this was a necessary conclusion of the philosophy of nature. God acts only indirectly on the world; hence miracles are unintelligible. God, the primary efficient cause, produced the world through intermediary separate substances, according to Siger of Brabant, reflecting the views of Avicenna; or God is only the final cause of the world, according to John of Jandun, following Averroës. God and all other celestial causes act on the world with necessity; contingency and indetermination are found only in the sublunar world, owing to the presence of matter. God's knowledge does not directly extend to contingent events.

Perhaps the most distinctive Averroistic tenet was the oneness of the possible intellect for the whole human race. This distinguishes Averroism from Avicennism, according to which the agent intellect is one for all men but each man possesses his own possible intellect. For the Averroists, the possible intellect is a separate substance that uses the sense faculties of individual men, and they can be said to understand insofar as their powers cooperate in the act of knowing. Since the individual does not possess his own intellective soul, human reason cannot demonstrate personal immortality. The ultimate end of man, or happiness, is in the present life. The highest felicity of man consists in philosophical contemplation.

The Latin Averroists did not deny their Christian faith, even though they taught doctrines contrary to it in their philosophy. In their view, the faith is true because it rests on the supernatural light of revelation. The conclusions of reason are less certain, being known by the inferior light of the human intellect. Hence a conclusion can be probable, or even necessary, in philosophy, while contradicting a revealed truth. To the theologians this was tantamount to a double truth, one for philosophy and another contradictory one for faith. The Latin Averroists themselves carefully avoided proposing a double truth. In cases of conflict between reason and faith, they invariably placed truth on the side of faith. It is difficult, if not impossible, to know whether this was done sincerely or as a cloak for unbelief. (*See* DOUBLE TRUTH, THEORY OF.)

Theological Reaction. Latin Averroism was immediately opposed by the theologians. The Franciscan school, headed by St. Bonaventure, took the lead in attacking the Aristotelians who, mainly under the influence of Averroës, taught doctrines contrary to the faith. In his commentary on the *Sentences* (*c.* 1250), St. Bonaventure had argued against Aristotelian doctrines such as the eternity of the world. Later, in his *Collationes de decem praeceptis* (1267), he criticized Parisian masters who erroneously taught that the world is eternal, that there is only one intellect in all men, and that a mortal being cannot attain immortality. The following year, in his *De donis Spiritus Sancti,* he opposed an even longer list of errors taught by the philosophers at Paris. His most vigorous polemic against Aristotle and his medieval followers is in the *Collationes in Hexaemeron* (1273). The threat of Greek and Arabian philosophy to the faith was clearly growing stronger at this time.

In 1270 St. Thomas wrote the *De unitate intellectus contra Averroistas* in opposition to the masters in the Parisian faculty of arts who taught the Averroistic doctrine of the unity of the intellect. This treatise seems to have been the first to use the term Averroists. In the next few centuries the term was widely used. St. Thomas wrote his own commentaries on Aristotle, using the new and more accurate translations of his works by *William of Moerbeke, to make available an Aristotelianism unadulterated by Arabian interpretations.

In 1270 *Giles of Rome exposed the errors of Aristotle, Avicenna, Averroës, and other non-Christian philosophers in his *De erroribus philosophorum,* and in his *De plurificatione intellectus possibilis* (*c.* 1272–75) he launched a direct attack on Averroism, based mainly on St. Thomas. About the same time *Giles of Lessines sent St. Albert in Cologne a list of 15 propositions "taught by the most eminent masters in the schools of Paris." St. Albert replied in a treatise entitled *De quindecim problematibus,* criticizing the teaching of the Aristotelian masters at Paris as contrary not only to theology but also to sound philosophy.

Ecclesiastical Condemnations. The ecclesiastical authorities also tried to stem the rising tide of Aristotelian naturalism and Averroism. In 1270 the Bishop of Paris, Étienne *Tempier, condemned 13 propositions traceable to Aristotle as interpreted by Averroës and his followers at Paris, and he excommunicated those who knowingly taught them. The condemned errors included the oneness of the intellect, the eternity of the world and the human species, the mortality of the human soul, the denial of providence and free will, and the necessitating influence of the heavenly bodies on the sublunar world.

On Jan. 18, 1277, Pope John XXI asked Tempier to inform him of the errors taught at Paris and of the names of the masters who taught them. No report of the bishop to the Pope is extant. On March 7, 1277, the bishop, seemingly on his own authority, condemned 219 propositions, all of which were linked with philosophical naturalism and Aristotelianism. Among the condemned propositions were some upheld by St. Thomas. No written source has been discovered for some of the proscribed theses, e.g., that the Christian religion hinders education, that this religion like others contains errors, and that theology rests on myths. Other theses exalt philosophy at the expense of faith, e.g., that there is no state superior to that of the philosopher. This was taught by Boethius of Sweden. Some propositions denied the Christian moral life and ultimate end of man. In the prologue to the condemnation the bishop censured those "who say that these things are true according to philosophy but not according to the Catholic faith, as though there were two contrary truths . . ." (ChartUnParis 1:543). On March 18, 1277, *Robert Kilwardby, Archbishop of Canterbury, condemned a similar list of 30 propositions.

Later Averroism. After the condemnations, Averroism continued to be attacked by theologians, such as Raymond *Lull, who wrote several treatises against Averroës and his followers. Despite these criticisms, Averroism remained alive at Paris and spread to England and Italy.

The outstanding Averroist in Paris in the early 14th century was *John of Jandun, the self-styled "ape of Averroës." Jandun praised Averroës as the "most perfect and glorious friend and defender of philosophical truth." Associated with him at Paris was *Marsilius of Padua. Both Marsilius and John of Jandun were adversaries of the Pope and, with *William of Ockham, took refuge with the Emperor Louis of Bavaria. Marsilius's *Defensor pacis* is an example of political Averroism, advocating the separation of Church and State and the subordination of the former to the latter.

The Englishman *John Baconthorp was called "the prince of the Averroists" during the Renaissance, though in fact he accepted none of the heterodox teachings of Averroës. He wrote outstanding and somewhat benign commentaries on Aristotle and Averroës that won him the acclaim of Renaissance Averroists. Another 14th-century Englishman, *Thomas of Wilton, was more favorable to Averroism. A master of arts and theology at Paris and chancellor of St. Paul's in London, Thomas believed that human reason left to itself cannot refute the doctrine of Averroës.

Through *Petrarch, a violent anti-Averroist, it is known that Averroism reached Italy in the early 14th century, accompanied by skepticism in religion. Among the radical Italian Averroists was Anthony of Parma, a master of arts and famous doctor and philosopher of nature. Averroistic Aristotelianism was represented at Bologna by Thaddaeus of Parma and Angelo of Arezzo. Angelo's Averroism is evident even in his logical treatises. A. Maier has recently added two more names to the list of Bolognese Averroists, Matthew of Gubbio and Anselm of Como.

From Bologna Averroism made its way to Padua and Venice, where its main representatives were Paolo *Veneto, Gaetano da Thiene (*see* CAJETAN, ST.), Alexander Achillini (1463–1512), and Nicoletto Vernia (1420–99). Pietro *Pomponazzi was a product of Paduan Averroism. Though he sharply criticized the Averroist doctrine of the soul in his *De immortalitate animae,* the spirit of Averroism is reflected in his naturalism and in his separation of faith and reason.

Appreciation. Latin Averroism was a serious danger to the Church because it set reason in conflict with faith. According to Christian tradition, as expressed by the Fathers of the Church and the great scholastic theologians, natural knowledge cannot be contrary to divine revelation because God is the source of both (see St. Thomas, *C. gent.* 1.7). Although the Latin Averroists wished to exalt reason and philosophy, in fact they degraded them by opposing them to the truth of faith. They misunderstood the nature of philosophy, making it an inquiry into the thought of the great philosophers of the past, especially Aristotle, rather than an investigation of reality. Centered as it was on the texts of Aristotle and his commentators, Latin Averroism was one of the most pedantic and unprogressive philosophical movements in the Middle Ages. It disappeared with the eclipse of Aristotelianism in the 16th and 17th centuries.

See also ARABIAN PHILOSOPHY.

Bibliography: E. RENAN, *Averroès et l'averroïsme* (2d ed. Paris 1860). P. F. MANDONNET, *Siger de Brabant et l'averroïsme latin au XIIIe siècle,* 2 v. (Les Philosophes belges 6–7; 2d ed. Louvain 1908–11). F. VAN STEENBERGHEN, *Siger de Brabant d'après ses oeuvres inédites,* 2 v. (*ibid.* 12–13; Louvain 1931–42); *Aristotle in the West,* tr. L. JOHNSTON (Louvain 1955). M. GRABMANN, *Der lateinische Averroismus des 13. Jahrhunderts und seine Stellung zur christlichen Weltanschauung* (Munich 1931); *Mittelalterliches Geistesleben,* v.2 (Munich 1936). R. DE VAUX, "La première entrée d'Averroès chez les Latins," RevScPhilTh 22 (1933) 193–245. R. A. GAUTHIER, "Trois commentaires averroistes sur l'Ethique à Nicomaque," ArchHistDoctLitMA 22–23 (1947–48) 187–336. A. MAIER, *An der Grenze von Scholastik und Naturwissenschaft* (Essen 1943; 2d ed. Rome 1952); *Die Vorläufer Galileis im 14. Jahrhundert* (Rome 1949). B. NARDI, *Sigieri di Brabante nel pensiero del Rinascimento italiano* (Rome 1945); *Saggi sull'Aristotelismo Padovano dal secolo XIV al XVI* (Florence 1958). Gilson HistChrPhil. H. LEY, *Studie zur Geschichte des Materialismus im Mittelalter* (Berlin 1957).

[A. MAURER]

AVERSA, RAPHAEL, Theatine theologian; b. Sanseverino, Italy, 1588; d. Rome, June 10, 1657. He served five times as superior general of the Clerks Regular Minor and was greatly respected for his learning and his ability as a theologian. He twice refused the episcopacy offered him by Innocent X and Alexander VII. His most notable work was a complete treatment of scholastic theology, *Theologia scholastica universa ad mentem s. Thomae,* divided into six parts and published in nine volumes appearing at various times and under various titles at Rome, Venice, Genoa, and Bologna between 1631 and 1642. He also wrote *Logica* (Rome 1623) and *Philosophia* (2 v. Rome 1625–27).

Bibliography: Hurter Nomencl 3:934–935. G. FUSSENEGGER, LexThK² 1:1146–47.

[J. C. WILLKE]

AVESTA, the sacred book of the Parsees, the modern Persian followers of the ancient religion of *Zoroaster. Its oldest part, the **Gāthās,* dates back probably to Zoroaster himself. Its most recent parts may be as late as the Sassanian period (3d cent.–7th cent. A.D.). The Avesta is composed in two different dialects of a very archaic language, probably of equal antiquity with Vedic Sanskrit. This language was already obsolete in Sassanian times, when it became necessary to furnish the text with a paraphrase and commentary in the vernacular Pahlavi, or language of the Sassanians. Because such commentaries were called *zand,* the Avesta has been mistakenly designated as the *Zand-Avesta* or *Zend-Avesta.* A summary of the contents of the Avesta surviving in Pahlavi shows that the Sassanian Avesta was about four times longer than the extant form. It contained 21 books, but only one has been preserved intact, the *Videvdat* or "Code against the Demons." The rest of the extant Avesta is made up of fragments of the other 20 books, arranged for liturgical purposes.

The first part of the Avesta is the *Yasna* or "Sacrifice," a text recited during the performance of the chief ceremony of the Zoroastrian ritual, a sacrifice—faintly suggestive of the Catholic Mass—of sacred liquor and water before an ever-burning fire. In the *Yasna* are embedded the *Gāthās,* metrical discourses and revelations of Zoroaster. The *Visprat,* or "All the patrons," is a collection of additions to the *Yasna,* recited in more solemn circumstances.

The second part of the Avesta is a series of 21 *Yashts* or "Hymns" to as many divinities, including ancient gods whom Zoroaster had ignored or combated, but whose cult had crept again into Zoroastrianism. The chief divinities are Mithra, the goddess Anahita, the star-god Tishtrya, and others. There are also hymns to the spirits of the deceased, to the *Fravashis, to the Xvarnah or Royal Fortune, etc. The third part is the *Videvdat,* cited above. In addition there are several minor sections.

Although the Avesta is valuable to the historian of religion, only the *Gāthās* and parts of the *Yashts* have any literary value.

Bibliography: R. C. ZAEHNER, *The Dawn and Twilight of Zoroastrianism* (New York 1961). J. DUCHESNE-GUILLEMIN, *La Religion de l'Iran ancien* (Paris 1962).

[J. DUCHESNE-GUILLEMIN]

AVICEBRON (IBN GABIROL, SOLOMON BEN JUDAH)

Jewish philosopher and poet; b. Malaga, Spain, *c.* 1021; d. Valencia, Spain, *c.* 1058. He has two distinct careers in history. As Ibn Gabirol (Shĕlōmōh ben Yĕhūdāh) he stood in the first rank of medieval Hebrew poets; as Avicebron (Avicembron, Avicenbrol, Avencebrol) he was an Arabian philosopher whose work was translated into Latin *c.* 1150 by *Dominic Gundisalvi and *John of Spain under the title of *Fons Vitae* (Fountain of Life) and became a subject of scholastic controversy. Not until 1846 was the identification of the philosopher with the poet effected. Avicebron's philosophical work evoked little interest in medieval Spain; severely criticized by one of the earliest of the Spanish Aristotelians, Abraham ibn Daoud (Avendauth, *c.* 1110–80), it was ignored by Moses *Maimonides and thus dismissed from the tradition. The true philosophical home of Avicebron is in the *Zohar and in the speculative sections of the *Cabala.

Avicebron's universe displays the usual Neoplatonic "chain of being." At the summit is God, a being in pure act. Through His agent, Will—a being that is identified with God and that plays a role analogous to that of the Logos of *Philo Judaeus—God confers His gift of being through the descending ranks of His creation: spiritual essences, the celestial bodies, the corporeal sublunary world. Though this is similar to Plotinus's *emanationism, the crucial and, for the theologians of the University of Paris, disturbing point was that Avicebron taught that the *entire* created universe was composed of matter and form—everything but the Will itself. Since, for him, all forms are modified and not limitless, the limiting principle (matter) extends into the realm of simple substances. When there is substance there must be composition, he argued, because form demands the support of matter.

The scholastic opposition to, and defense of, Avicebron took place in a context larger than that of the controversy over the *Fons Vitae.* The Spanish Jew's position actually echoed one held by the Franciscan adherents of St. *Augustine at Paris, such as *Alexander of Hales and St. *Bonaventure. The attack against it by St. *Thomas Aquinas, answered by *Duns Scotus and others, thus involved issues at question among contemporary theologians: the nature of spiritual substances, the existence of "spiritual matter," and, indeed, the nature of matter itself.

The other works of Ibn Gabirol circulated solely in Jewish circles in Spain. The *Improvement of Moral Qualities,* an ethical treatise written in Arabic and later translated into Hebrew, ultimately derives from the peripatetic ethical tradition but bears a distinctly Jewish character. Similarly, the *Choice of Pearls,* which is probably Ibn Gabirol's, addresses to the common reader a selection of moral aphorisms. Ibn Gabirol continues to be read and studied as the author of the *Kingly Crown,* a collection of religious poems in Hebrew that has gone through frequent editions and translations and that still forms part of the Sephardic ritual for Yom kippūr.

See also NEOPLATONISM; SCHOLASTICISM; FORMS, UNICITY AND PLURALITY OF.

Bibliography: Works. *Fons Vitae,* Latin tr. C. BAEUMKER, BeitrGeschPhiMA 1.2–4 (1892–95); Heb. paraphrase, ed. and tr. S. MUNK, *Mélanges de philosophie juive et arabe,* (new ed. Paris 1955), Heb. text in appendix; Eng. *Fountain of Life,* tr. A. B. JACOB (Philadelphia 1954); tr. H. E. WEDICK (New York 1962), from Baeumker's Latin text; *The Improvement of Moral Qualities,* tr. S. S. WISE (Columbia U. Oriental Studies 1; New York 1902); *Solomon Ibn Gabirol's Choice of Pearls,* tr. A. COHEN (New York 1925); *Selected Religious Poems of Ibn Gabirol,* tr. I. ZANGWILL (Philadelphia 1923), Eng. and Heb.; *Kether Malkuth,* ed. J. SEIDMAN (Jerusalem 1950); Eng. *Solo-*

mon Ibn Gabirol: The Kingly Crown,* tr. B. LEWIS (London 1961).

Studies. Bibliog. in J. SCHIRMANN and J. KLAUSNER, Enc Judaica 7:10–11, 23–24. Also in G. VAJDA, *Jüdische Philosophie* (Bern 1950) 14–16; *Introduction à la pensée juive du moyen âge* (Paris 1947) 75–83. S. MUNK, *op. cit.* 151–306. I. HUSIK, *A History of Medieval Jewish Philosophy* (2d ed. New York 1959) 59–79. Gilson HistChrPhil. M. WITTMANN, "Die Stellung des Hl. Thomas von Aquin zu Avencebrol," BeitrGeschPhilMA 3.3 (1900). J. GOHEEN, *The Problem of Matter and Form in the 'De Ente et Essentia' of Thomas Aquinas* (Cambridge, Mass. 1940).

[F. E. PETERS]

AVICENNA (IBN SĪNĀ, ABŪ 'ALĪ AL-ḤUSAYN)

Arab physician, scholar, and philosopher, one of the greatest names in Arabian-Iranian Moslem culture; b. Afshana, near Bukhārā, in 370 of the Hegira (A.D. 980); d. Hamadhān, 428 H. (A.D. 1037).

Life. Avicenna wrote an autobiography, completed by his pupil and secretary Jūzajāni after his death. He writes that he had an astonishing precociousness. Having surpassed all his teachers in the study of the Mohammedan religious sciences, logic, geometry, and astronomy, he pursued his work alone, notably in medicine and philosophy. Among the Arabian translations of Greek science, he encountered the works of *Aristotle. After reading the *Metaphysics* 40 times without understanding it, he found help in the Arabian commentary of his predecessor *Alfarabi. For this help he gave thanks at the mosque and distributed generous alms among the poor.

He was not yet 20 years old when he healed the Sultan of Bukhārā, who, through gratitude, invited him to use his rich library. Within a few years, Avicenna acquired as complete a culture as possible for that time. He started to write on his own when he was about 21. An orphan and master of his fortune at 22, he led an agitated and dangerous life. The favorite and vizier (prime minister) of the Emir of Hamadhān, then of the Emir of Ispahān, he spent some time in prison. While he was engaged in military expeditions under the latter Emir, his books were pillaged, and some of his MSS disappeared. In the course of such an expedition, an illness, long before contracted as a result of "excesses of every sort," became worse. He died after freeing his slaves, distributing his goods among the poor, and reciting the entire Koran.

Works. Avicenna's bibliography, thoroughly examined by G. C. Anawati (in Arabic) and Yahra Mahdavi (in Persian), is immense. His great medical treatise is *Qānūn fi l-Ṭibb*. His best known philosophical writings are the *Summa* of the *Shifā'* (Healing) and the compendium of the *Najāt* (Salvation). He left several small "treatises" (*rasā'il*) exhibiting occasional gnostic characteristics. One of the treatises, *al-Risāla al-aḍḥawiyya,* teaches that the bodily resurrection professed in the Moslem faith has only symbolic value. His last great work, *al-Ishārāt wa l-tanbīhāt* (Directives and Remarks), goes beyond the Aristotelian structures of the *Shifā'*. The works of the last part of his life refer to an Oriental Philosophy (or Wisdom), *al-Ḥikma almashriqiyya,* left incomplete (or lost). What remains of this work are his logic and certain chapters included in the *Ishārāt,* as well as preliminary small treatises from other sources. Another work, the *Insāf,* refuted the Baghdad commentators on Aristotle; only a rough draft of this work survived a pillage. Then there are three commentaries extant only in rough drafts, namely, on Book Λ of the *Metaphysics,* the *De anima,* and especially the spurious *Theology of Aristotle;* the latter, comprising extracts from the *Enneads* of Plotinus, for many centuries was falsely attributed to the Stagirite.

Teaching. Avicenna is representative of the so-called school of the *falāsifa* (philosophers), namely, Moslem Hellenistic philosophers who were nourished with the thought of Plato and Aristotle (the latter called "the Prime Teacher") and wrote in Arabic and Persian. Others of this school are al-*Kindī, Alfarabi, *Avempace, *Averroës, and Abū-Bakr *Ibn-Ṭufail. Official *Islam took a stand against the *falāsifa* in the East during the second half of the 11th century and the beginning of the 12th. *Algazel, an orthodox thinker—deemed an Aristotelian because of a misinterpretation of the Latin Middle Ages—tried to refute Alfarabi and Avicenna in his famous *Tahāfut al-falāsifa* (The Collapse of the Philosophers). A century later, Averroës gave his answer in his *Tahāfut al-Tahāfut* (The Collapse of the Collapse), where he took his great predecessor to task and made certain "errors" of Avicenna responsible for Algazel's criticisms. Despite such explanations, however, the *falāsifa* never fully recovered from the attacks of the Moslems, and the teaching of the great mosques manifests a solid distrust toward them to this day.

Religion and Philosophy. Avicenna presents himself as a believing Moslem, but he places his philosophy and the "revealed law" (*shar'*) expressed in the Koran on the same level. He thought that he succeeded in reconciling the two because of his theory about prophetism, which was in turn dependent upon his theory of knowledge. All the *falāsifa* held that the human spirit rises to intellectual knowledge only by illumination received from a single, separated Agent Intellect. For Avicenna, philosophy, like prophecy, receives illumination from the universal Intellect, the summation of separated Intellects. Yet prophecy alone receives, in its imaginative power, added lights from the Souls of the Heavenly Bodies, and these lights enable it to adapt purely intelligible truths to the masses, under a veil of symbols and allegories. This explains how religious beliefs are formed. Moreover, this influx of the heavenly Souls enables prophecy to know and teach religious practices that most aptly guarantee the fidelity of hearts. On the basis of these postulates, the "philosopher" does not hesitate to "interpret" the scriptural texts in accord with his own view of the world.

Because his era was completely imbued with influences of Shiïte Islam and esoteric and gnostic tendencies and there was no living teaching authority, one can conclude that Avicenna was sincere in claiming his "accord" between religion and philosophy. Yet one can also understand why Algazel later stated that such notorious theses as those about the temporal eternity of the created world, God's ignorance about the singular as such, and the allegorical interpretation anent bodily resurrection are "tarnished with impiety."

Being and Emanation. Avicenna's highly constructed view of the world is hardly consonant with the creationism and divine voluntarism of the Koran. His cosmogony is related with the conceptions of time—the arranged tiers of eight or ten heavenly spheres, in successive triads of separated Intellects, Souls, and Heavenly Bodies, terminating in the Active Intellect of the sublunary world, in the multiplicity of individuated human souls, each having a passive intellect, and in the "world of generation and corruption." In this system, creation seems to be a necessary and voluntary emanation from the First Being, a necessary and voluntary participation of being and light, traversed by a returning movement of natural, necessitated love of the part for the Whole. Thus a universal determinism corresponds to the necessary participation; in Avicenna's universe, there is no place for existential contingency. Yet the notion of contingency is found on the level of essence, since Avicenna's "transunivocity" of being does not destroy a certain inferior analogy between the First Being and "possible" beings, in which not only is the essence really distinct from the existence, but the existence is, in some way, an accident of the essence. Finally, according to him, the human soul is the "form" of its body, but the body remains a mere instrument of the soul; a "form of corporeity" is joined with the soul, the subsistent form. Freed from the body through death, the soul "returns" to the world of the intelligibles to which it naturally belongs.

These ideas are based on notions contained in the works of Aristotle, Plato, and Plotinus, reexamined and coordinated according to Avicenna's own dialectic. In general, Avicenna's thought is more Plotinian than Aristotelian. Abetted by influences and myths from ancient Iran, his thought is decisively Plotinian in his aforementioned Oriental Philosophy (or Wisdom).

Influence. The most illustrious aspect of Avicenna's great and immediate renown is probably a result of his studies in chemistry, astronomy, and medicine. But his philosophical work was the most durable and had a profound influence even on Moslem thought, especially in Shiïte Islam. His adversaries in Sunnite Islam attacked it, but they became imbued with it, and many Islam "theologians" followed them. Later *Sufism (Moslem mysticism) derived its great theses on the *monism of being from him. During the 12th and 13th centuries, Latin translations were made of the *Shifā'* (Lat. *Sufficientia*), the *Qānūn fi l-Ṭibb* (Lat. *Canon*), and various commentaries or treatises, in Spain and Italy. Avicenna's thought made a deep impression on certain currents in medieval Christian *scholasticism. *Thomas Aquinas made use of Avicenna's philosophical structures, even though he criticized them. But possibly the most profound influence of Avicenna in the West was on John *Duns Scotus.

See also ARABIAN PHILOSOPHY; EMANATIONISM; FORMS, UNICITY AND PLURALITY OF.

Bibliography: Eng. selections in R. LERNER and M. MAHDI, *Medieval Political Philosophy: A Sourcebook* (Glencoe, Ill. 1963). *Avicenna's Psychology,* tr. and ed. F. RAHMAN (New York 1952). Gilson HistChrPhil. A. M. GOIÇHON, EncFil 1:525–535; *La Philosophie d'Avicenne et son influence en Europe médiévale* (2d ed. Paris 1951). M. M. ANAWATI, *Mu' allafāt Ibn Sīnā* (Cairo 1950); "La Tradition manuscrite orientale de l'oeuvre d'Avicenne," RevThom 51 (1951) 407–440. Y. MAHDAVI, *Bibliographie d'Ibn Sina* (Tehran 1954). L. GARDET, *La Pensée religieuse d'Avicenne* (*Ibn Sīnā*) (Paris 1951). M. CRUZ HERNÁNDEZ, *La metafisica de Avicenna* (Granada 1949). B. H. ZEDLER, "Saint Thomas and Avicenna in the 'De potentia Dei,'" *Traditio* 6 (1948) 105–159.

[L. GARDET]

AVIGNON

Capital of Vaucluse department, on the left bank of the Rhone River in southeast France. The Archdiocese of Avignon (*Avenionensis*), a metropolitan see since 1475, was 1,382 square miles in area and had 175 parishes, 154 secular and 35 religious priests, 70 men in 46 religious houses, 630 women in 46 convents, and 313,000 Catholics (1960). Its four suffragans, which had 1,330 parishes, 1,523 secular and 253 religious priests, 2,541 sisters, and 1,265,000 Catholics, were: *Montpellier (1536 sucessor to the 3d-century See of Maguelonne and site of a university), *Nimes, Valence (4th century), and Viviers (3d century).

Originally under nearby *Marseilles and in the 1st century a Roman colony, with its first known bishop (Nectarius) in 439, Avignon became a commune in the 12th century under the suzerainty of the Counts of *Toulouse and Provence; in 1251 it went to France and the House of *Anjou. In 1309 Clement V (1305–14) installed the Holy See in Avignon, his successors remaining there until 1376: John XXII (1316–34), Benedict XII (1334–42), Clement VI (1342–52), Innocent VI (1352–62), Urban V (1362–70), and Gregory XI (1370–78). Clement VII (1378–94) and Benedict XIII (1394–1411) resided there during the Western Schism.

Benedict XII's purchase of Avignon from the Countess of Provence (1348) extended the *States of the Church to France, where the popes had held the adjoining county of *Venaissin since the end of the Albigensian war. The first stay of the popes in Avignon, part of the Holy Roman Empire, was justified by the impossibility of their staying in their Italian states, which were in constant revolt. But the nearness of the kings of France to the popes, who were French, has given the impression that the kings ran the affairs of the Church. Italians call the period the Babylonian Captivity. From this stay in Avignon, when the popes required money to live, build their palace, and maintain a court, dates the development of papal taxation and centralization (*see* AVIGNON PAPACY).

The 14th-century palace at Avignon, the "Palace of the Popes," built during the papal residence.

After the popes departed, Avignon as papal territory was governed by a cardinal legate until 1693 and thereafter by a congregation in Rome through a vice-legate. Both legate and vice-legate had the spiritual powers of a *legate in the provinces of *Vienne, *Arles, *Aix, Embrun, and *Narbonne. Seized several times by French kings in dispute with the Holy See (1663, 1668, 1768–74), the Avignon papal states were occupied by Revolutionaries (1790) and annexed to France (1791). This annexation influenced the general policy of the popes toward the French Revolution. As the capital of Vaucluse, Avignon soon lost importance in Church history.

The Cathedral of Notre-Dames-des-Doms (12th century) was there before the popes, who built the walls and a Gothic palace (161,400 square feet in area) that is also a fortress. The Old Palace (1334–42) adjoins the New Palace (1342–52). There are rooms for the supreme pontiff and his servants, spacious halls for business (Tribunal, Consistory, Conclave, Treasury), chapels, kitchens, etc. The Abbot of Saint-Ruf (1039–1793) became head of an Augustinian order, presiding over 20 men's and 20 women's communities (350 women *c.* 1750).

Avignon had many penitent confraternities: grays (1226), blacks (1448), whites (1527), blues (16th century), violets (1622), reds (1700), each with its chapel; some still survive. The university established by Boniface VIII (1303) flourished with seven colleges to 1791. The colleges of the Jesuits (1564) and of the Brothers of Christian Schools (1703) were noteworthy. Charitable establishments included hospitals, hospices, two orphanages, and two houses of repentant girls (14th and 18th centuries).

Many councils (and diocesan synods) were held in Avignon: 1060, 1080, 1209 (excommunication of the Count of Toulouse, who favored *Albigenses), 1260, 1279, 1282, 1326, 1327 (John XXII condemned antipope *Nicholas V), 1337, 1457 (canons of the Council of Basel confirmed), 1594 (canons of the Council of Trent applied), and 1725. Of 57 known synodal statutes, 14 date from the 70-year period of the Avignon papacy.

Sixtus IV made Avignon a metropolitan see (1475) so that his nephew (the future Julius II), recently created bishop, would not be under the Archbishop of Arles; the suffragans (Carpentras, Cavaillon, and Vaison) were all in papal territory. The *Concordat of 1801 made Avignon a vast bishopric (Vaucluse and Gard departments) under Aix. In 1822, when Nîmes (Gard) was restored, Avignon became a metropolitan again with its present suffragans.

Bishop Geoffrey (1143–68) developed the domain of the Church; Zoen Tencarari (1240–61) fought heresy, installed mendicant orders, and was several times papal legate; Cardinal Georges d'*Armagnac was bishop (1577–85). César de *Bus (1544–1607), a missionary in the Protestant areas of Cévennes, founded the Fathers of Christian Doctrine and, with Jean-Baptiste Romillon (1553–1622), introduced the Ursulines in France.

Several former cathedrals are in the diocese: Apt (11th–12th century), Carpentras in flamboyant Gothic (15th century), Cavaillon in Romanesque (enlarged 14th–18th century), *Orange with a Provençal Romanesque interior, and Vaison with its cloister (6th, 11th–13th century). The Cistercian Abbey of Sénanque (1148) was restored in 1854.

Bibliography: J. Girard, DHGE 5:1121–53. J. Sautel et al., *Vaucluse. Essai d'histoire locale* (Avignon 1944). G. Mollat, *Les Papes d'Avignon* (9th ed. rev.; Paris 1949), Eng. tr. J. Love (New York 1963); *Catholicisme* 1:1129–30. Y. Renouard, *La Papauté à Avignon* (Paris 1954). AnnPont (1964) 45. B. Guillemain, *La Cour pontificale d'Avignon (1309–76): Étude d'une société* (Paris 1962). **Illustration credit:** National Council of Catholic Men.

[E. JARRY]

AVIGNON, SCHOOL OF.

AVIGNON, SCHOOL OF. During the 14th century the residence of the popes in Avignon made the city an important artistic center. The Sienese painter Simone *Martini spent his last years there (1339?–44), and Italian artists continued to dominate 14th-century painting in the city. The intricate, massive Palace of the Popes contains many frescoes, including cycles devoted to SS. Martial, John the Baptist, and John the Evangelist, done in the 1340s and 1350s under the direction of Matteo Giovanetti; the style is close to that of Siena. Especially interesting are the charming frescoes with tapestrylike scenes of woodland sport, by an unknown painter, in the palace *garderobe*.

In the period of the Great Schism there was little artistic activity in Avignon, but with the revival of prosperity in the region during the mid-15th century, a major school took form. Its greatest representatives are the unidentified painter of the famous "Avignon Pietà" (Louvre; see illustration) and Enguerrand *Charonton (Quarton), painter of a sumptuous "Coronation of the Virgin" (1453–54, Musée de l'Hospice, Villeneuve-les-Avignon) and a "Madonna of Mercy" (1452, Musée Condé, Chantilly). These works are characterized by a profound dignity and bold, sharply defined forms. Aix-en-Provence, also an important center of the period, is associated with two major works: an altarpiece of "The Annunciation," by an unidentified hand (*c.* 1445; central panel: Église de la Madeleine, Aix-en-Provence; fragments in Rotterdam, Amsterdam, and Brussels), and an altarpiece by Nicolas Froment (active 1450–90) showing "The Virgin Mary in the Burning Bush" (1476, Saint-Sauveur Cathedral, Aix-en-Provence).

See also GOTHIC ART.

Bibliography: L. H. Labande, *Le Palais des papes et les monuments d'Avignon au XIVe siècle,* 2 v. (Marseilles 1925); *Les Primitifs français,* 2 v. (Marseilles 1932). G. Ring, *A Century of French Painting, 1400–1500* (New York 1949), *passim.* M. Laclotte, *L'École d'Avignon: La Peinture en Provence aux XIVe et XVe siècles* (Paris 1960), with bibliog. **Illustration credit:** Alinari-Art Reference Bureau.

[D. DENNY]

AVIGNON PAPACY

The name given to the papacy (1308–78) because of its residence for some 70 years at *Avignon instead of at Rome.

Reasons for Residence at Avignon. The popes took up residence at Avignon for reasons that were partly historical, partly personal, and partly political. The papacy was still suffering from the shattering effects of the pontificate of *Boniface VIII, which had created external enemies and which had also internally split the College of Cardinals (*see* CARDINAL, 1). The brief pontificate of *Benedict XI did not help matters. The cardinals were anxious to elect a pontiff who had been

Southern French Master, "The Avignon Pietà," c. 1455, panel, 64 by 86 inches, in The Louvre, Paris.

connected in no way with any previous papal measures and who could be seen as a "neutral" both in external and internal affairs. The long vacancy after Benedict's death testifies to the serious efforts made by the cardinals to find a man who fulfilled the requirements. After several abortive ballots in conclave—one of the candidates was the English Dominican provincial, Walter Winterbourne—the choice fell on Abp. Bertrand de Got of Bordeaux (*Clement V).

Clement had not been a member of the Curia, was politically a subject of the English King, but culturally thoroughly French, and seemed to be exactly the man to steer the papacy through difficult times. Although he intended to go to Rome after his election, Clement was prevented by a number of circumstances, chiefly by the posthumous trial of Boniface VIII. Clement considered it more prudent to be near the French King to dissuade him from resuming the trial against the dead pope, to convene the General Council at *Vienne, and to direct affairs arising from *Philip IV's sudden arrest of the *Templars. Moreover, the absence of the Curia from Rome since the death of Benedict had made Rome and Italy more insecure than ever, especially as the peninsula was seething with the strife between *Guelfs and Ghibellines, and as the new Luxembourg Emperor, *Henry VII, pursued a policy in Italy diametrically opposed to that of the papacy.

In 1308 the papal court came to reside at Avignon, which provided easy communication with both France and Italy. Avignon belonged to vassals of the Roman Church and was not then on French soil (*see* VENAISSIN). It was intended merely as a temporary abode until the questions between the French King and the papacy were solved and the Council of Vienne had finished its work. The Council ended May 6, 1312, but the state of Clement's health did not permit the arduous move back to Rome; he seems to have suffered from cancer and died 2 years later. Although the situation in Italy had meanwhile deteriorated, *John XXII nevertheless planned to return to Italy and to reside at *Bologna. But that city was as unruly and insecure as any other place in Italy, and soon the plan was dropped.

Each succeeding pope entertained the idea of moving back to Italy, and *Urban V did in fact return to Rome. But he found himself confronted by the hostility of the Roman populace, even though the papal emissary, Cardinal *Albornoz, had shortly before established some sort of order in the *States of the Church. Realizing also that if he were nearer the French King he might hope to mediate the struggle between England and France, Urban V resumed residence at Avignon. Under his successor, *Gregory XI, the papacy finally effected a return to Rome. A further motive for the prolonged residence at Avignon was the perhaps illusory plan of a crusade, continuously entertained by virtually all the Avignon popes. A crusading appeal, it was thought, would find a readier response, if the war between England and France were brought to a speedy end.

Assessment. The Avignonese papacy has prompted many adverse judgments. One of the most frequently voiced criticisms is that it came entirely under French influence and was in fact an appendix of French policy. This is a highly colored view rising, on the one hand, from the hostility of contemporary English sources, which understandably linked the papacy with French political designs, and on the other hand from contemporary German sources, which also were colored by the antagonism between the Emperor, *Louis IV, and the papacy. The one-sided judgments of *Petrarch, St. *Catherine of Siena, and St. *Bridget of Sweden also added to the pejorative bias that has ever since distorted the view of the Avignon papacy.

On balance, however, the constant peace efforts of the Avignon popes showed that they stood above the turmoil of regal rivalries. Moreover, so far from being in the tow of France, they frequently pursued policies, particularly in regard to Italy, that would be quite inexplicable had the popes been mere tools of the French kings. A proper assessment of the Avignon papacy must never lose sight of the somewhat artificial situation in which the popes found themselves. This situation, which the popes had done nothing to bring about and of which they had become the victims, bred in them a sense of insecurity that may explain the restlessness and impetuosity of papal measures initiated at Avignon. Torn though they were from their natural abode, the popes of Avignon accelerated the process of bringing principles of government to their logical conclusion and theoretical perfection.

It is perhaps a paradox that the full *élan* and vigor of papal principles of government were to be witnessed on "foreign" soil and in a period not unjustifiably called the waning of the Middle Ages. But one thing is clear, the papacy itself introduced no new principles while at Avignon. What it did was to create a highly advanced system out of what had so far grown in an unsystematic manner. The administrative and organizational measures of the Avignon papacy were designed to create the machinery that was to serve the perfected system of government. And some of these measures continued to be practiced long after the return to Rome.

Measures Adopted at Avignon. The administration was thoroughly overhauled, mainly during John XXII's pontificate. There were four main departments that constituted the hub of the papal government at work.

*Apostolic *Camera.* This was the supreme financial office, exercising supervision and control over all papal tax collectors operating in distant lands and over all financial transactions within and without the Curia itself. The papal exchequer also controlled the papal mint. Attached to it was the secretariat, which conducted the secret correspondence of the pope through specially appointed *secretarii,* as well as all diplomatic correspondence not of a routine nature. The chamberlain, the head of the apostolic chamber, was the pope's most trusted adviser.

At Avignon ecclesiastical *finance was perfected. It was precisely because of demands made by a stringent financial system that numerous categories of taxes, fees, and profits were rigorously collected. By contemporary standards, the expenditures of the Roman Church at Avignon reached astronomical figures. Rigorous tax collection caused understandable opposition, especially in the ranks of the lower clergy. Large expenditure was caused also by many undertakings financed by the papacy, such as the wars in Italy, the missions to distant lands, the support of universities, and the financing of inquisitorial machinery for the suppression of heresy. But it is also true that the Curia at Avignon had become the most splendidly equipped in Europe. Cardinals and other members of the Curia displayed an amount of luxury and pomp that was both unnecessary and inadvisable in view of the current demand that the Church return to apostolic poverty.

The Chancery. Also highly developed at Avignon, the *Chancery was the nerve center of the pope's government in practice. It was concerned with the drafting, registration, and dispatch of papal administrative acts, letters, and decrees, and was headed by the vice-chancellor. All routine business went through the chancery.

Judicial Department. This department dealt with all litigations and contentious matters not primarily of a financial nature. It was subdivided into several branches, of which the most important was the consistory, headed by the pope himself assisted by the cardinals. The consistory dealt with major issues and was also the supreme court of appeal. Subsidiaries of the consistory were the *audientia sacri palatii* and the *audientia litterarum contradictarum,* both consisting of trained lawyers. The former, also called the *Rota, was concerned primarily with purely ecclesiastical matters, such as collation of *benefices, *provisions, reservations, and immunities; the latter dealt with proper litigations.

Arms of Clement VI, portal, Palace of the Popes, Avignon.

Apostolic *Penitentiary. This department handled matters concerning *interdict, *excommunication, and other ecclesiastical censures, as well as the removal of canonical matrimonial impediments. The head was a cardinal who functioned as grand penitentiary.

Organization and Reform. The proliferation of offices and departments at Avignon should not lead to the view that the papacy was nothing but a gigantic administrative machine. It was a highly complicated organization which, if it were to function properly, had to be effectively controlled. For this purpose central offices and departments were a necessity. It was precisely through its first-class organization that the Avignon papacy was enabled to continue old policies and to initiate new ones. Most notable among the former were the reform measures concerning the state of the clergy and above all the religious orders, especially the *Friars. Among the latter must be mentioned the initiation of missionary enterprises on a scale much larger than hitherto envisaged. [*See* MISSIONS, HISTORY OF (MEDIEVAL).]

The missions to Asia, as far as China and Persia, India and Turkestan, testify to the earnestness of the Avignon papacy to spread Christianity in regions that offered nothing but risks and unimaginable hazards. What needs special emphasis is the promotion by the Avignon papacy of educational work, notably in the universities, and the establishment of new fields of study, such as Arabic.

On the other hand, the variegated nature of the Avignon papacy at work brought about noteworthy constitutional practices, virtually dictated by governmental exigencies. The cardinals began *de facto* to assume powers which amounted, in practice, to an oligarchic form of government; the pope was virtually bound to take counsel from the cardinals in charge of special departments. It was a symptom of the increased power of the cardinals that they hit upon the device of the so-called papal electoral pacts (*see* CAPITULATIONS) first recorded in 1352, according to which the pope was to be severely restricted in the exercise of his monarchic powers. The outbreak of the *Western Schism, soon after the Pope's return to Rome, was to no small extent the result of the assumption of cardinalitial power. The peculiarities and achievements of the Avignon papacy can be understood only when viewed against the historical background.

Bibliography: Sources. É. BALUZE, *Vitae paparum Avenionensium,* ed. G. MOLLAT, 4 v. (Paris 1914–27). Bibliothèque des Écoles françaises d'Athènes et de Rome, *Lettres des papes d'Avignon se rapportant à la France* (Paris 1899–). F. BOCK, *Einführung in das Registerwesen des avignonesischen Papsttums,* 2 v. (Rome 1941). O. BERTHOLD, ed. and tr., *Kaiser, Volk, und Avignon: Ausgewählte Quellen zur antikurialen Bewegung in Deutschland in der ersten Hälfte des 14. Jahrhunderts* (Berlin 1960). Literature. G. MOLLAT, *The Popes at Avignon, 1305–1378,* tr. J. LOVE (London 1963). E. KRAACK, *Rom oder Avignon? Die römische Frage unter den Päpsten Clemens V. und Johann XXII* (Marburg 1929). E. DUPRÉ THESEIDER, *Problemi del papato avignonese* (Bologna 1961). B. GUILLEMAIN, *La Cour pontificale d'Avignon (1309–76): Étude d'une société* (Paris 1962). **Illustration credit:** National Council of Catholic Men.

[W. ULLMANN]

ÁVILA, FRANCISCO DE, Quechua scholar and crusader against Indian idolatry; b. Cuzco, Peru, 1573; d. Lima, Sept. 17, 1647. He was a foundling and took his name from Beatriz de Ávila, wife of Cristóbal Rodríguez, who cared for him as a child. He began his studies in Cuzco and was ordained in 1591. He studied civil and Canon Law in the University of San Marcos in Lima and received a doctorate in 1606. In 1597 he became pastor of San Damián (Huarochirí) and began his campaign to wipe out Indian idolatry and superstition. He was accused of exceeding his authority in this matter, but Abp. Toribio de *Mogrovejo exonerated him during his visitation, and this was ratified by the visitor general of the archdiocese in 1600–01. Using his knowledge of Quechua, Ávila continued his work against idolatry. In 1608, in his zeal he held an *auto-da-fé* in which a number of idols were burned and the Indian Hernando Paucar was scourged for idolatry and for being a friend of the devil. Ávila subsequently spent some time in prison, but he was absolved in 1609. The chronicler *Huamán Poma de Ayala criticized Ávila for depriving the Indians of their idols and other objects of worship. Archbishop Lobo de Guerrero appointed Ávila the first Visitador de Idolatrías, but in the course of his duties he became ill and had to return to Lima. His writings are extensive. In 1608 he wrote *Tratado y relación de los errores, falsos dioses y otras supersticiones y ritos diabólicos en que vivían antiguamente los indios de las provincias de Huarochirí, Mama y Chaclla y hoy también viven engañados con gran perdición de sus almas* (published in 1942). His *Oratio habita in ecclesia cathedrali limensi* was printed in 1610. The next year he wrote a *Memoria* on a visit to the towns in the Province of Huarochirí, later published by Medina as *Cura de Huánacu.* In 1646 he wrote his most literary book, *Tratado de los evangelios.* The second volume of this was published posthumously as was a collection of sermons in Quechua and Spanish entitled *De los misterios de nuestra santa fe.* The work of Ávila, along with that of Hernando de Avendaño, is considered to represent the transition from the Quechua of evangelism to the Quechua of literature.

Bibliography: F. DE ÁVILA, *Dämonen und Zauber im Inkareich,* ed. and tr. H. TRIMBORN (Leipzig 1939). H. TRIMBORN, "Francisco de Ávila," *Ciencias* 3 (1936) 163–174. J. T. POLO, "Un Quechuista," *Revista histórica del Instituto histórico del Perú* 1 (1906) 24–38.

[C. D. VALCÁRCEL]

ÁVILA, JOSÉ CECILIO, professor and rector of the University of Caracas; b. Pedernales, Güigüe, Venezuela, Nov. 22, 1786; d. Caracas, Oct. 24, 1833. He received a humanistic education in the Royal Pontifical University of Caracas, where he obtained the highest academic degrees in philosophy, theology, and civil and Canon Law. He was ordained on Aug. 10, 1811. At 27 he was a university professor of Canon Law. His prudence and talent later obtained for him the positions of prebendary, fiscal of the ecclesiastical tribunal, and, for many years, secretary of the archiepiscopal government. The gentleness and firmness of his character were proverbial. Ávila's administrative talents and his devotion to intellectual activities were demonstrated when the University of Caracas, after the war of independence, suffered a serious economic crisis and was in imminent danger of being closed. Ávila, named rector for a 2-year period (1825–27), devoted all of his zeal to saving the life of the institution. While he contrived immediate sources of aid, he wrote a moving letter to Bolívar for help. When the Liberator went to Caracas in

1827 he decreed new revenues. The University had been saved thanks to the diligence of Ávila. He also induced José Vargas to come to fill the professorship of anatomy. The rector himself then persuaded the first group of students to enroll in that subject. The first centennial of the University was solemnly commemorated in 1825 during Ávila's rectorship. As a professor he was a steadfast exponent of Catholic doctrine in the face of heterodox influences. As a preacher, he enjoyed great prestige. His disciple and biographer, Juan V. González, wrote: "Ávila's talent, virtues, and activity secured for him an authority in the moral and ecclesiastical field which no one surpassed in his day in his country."

Bibliography: J. V. González, *Tres biografías* (Caracas 1941). N. E. Navarro, "El centenario de la muerte del Pbro. Ávila," *Boletín de la Academia Nacional de la Historia* 17 (Caracas 1934) 1–6, memorial.

[P. P. BARNOLA]

ÁVILA Y ZÚÑIGA, LUIS DE, Spanish historian, general, and diplomat; b. Plasencia in Estramadura, 1500; d. 1564. He was a member of the court of Charles I, and was entrusted by the King with diplomatic missions to Paul IV and Pius IV in preparation for the Council of Trent. He was in Charles's entourage during the religious wars in Germany and acted as commander in chief of the imperial cavalry at the siege of Metz (1552). He spent his last years in Plasencia, whence he frequently visited Emperor Charles in his retirement at the monastery of Yuste. In direct imitation of the *Commentaries* of Caesar, he wrote the *Commentario de la guerra de Alemania hecha por Carlos V, Maximo Emperador Romano, Rey de España* (1548). Although the *Commentario* is panegyric in character, it is of great value as a source for the reign of Charles because of Ávila's direct acquaintance with important events and eminent statesmen of the century. It reflects many of the views of Charles I and has been translated into Italian, Latin, French, and German. The best edition is found in the *Biblioteca de Autores Españoles,* in which the title is changed to *Crónica de la guerra de Alemania* (Madrid 1852).

Bibliography: J. Lenzenweger, LexThK[2] 1:1154. Espasa 6: 1297–98. J. Coignet, DHGE 5:1192–94, bibliog.

[S. J. T. MILLER]

AVILA COLLEGE. A liberal arts college for women conducted in Kansas City, Mo., by the Sisters of St. Joseph of Carondelet. Its history goes back to 1866, to a time when there were no private institutions for young women in Kansas City. Six Sisters of St. Joseph came from St. Louis, Mo., to establish an academy. From this early institution, a junior college, St. Teresa's, was chartered in 1916. The 4-year liberal arts college, founded in 1940, was known as the College of St. Teresa until January 1963 when it was renamed Avila College, from the full title of its patroness, St. Teresa of Avila. The College moved to a 48-acre campus in the southern section of Kansas City, leaving the campus it had shared with St. Teresa's Academy since 1916. In September 1963, Avila opened its first classes on the separate campus.

In 1946 the College received full accreditation enabling it to grant the baccalaureate degree. In 1951, a coeducational evening program of credit courses was offered to the community, followed 2 years later by a noncredit program of adult education, making Avila a pioneer in adult education within Kansas City. A 10-year development plan was initiated in 1962 to obtain financial support from the Kansas City community and from national foundations.

Avila College is administered by a board of trustees composed of the mother provincial of the Sisters of St. Joseph of Carondelet, St. Louis Province; two members of her council; the president of the college; and the local superior of the house. Officers of the College are the president, an academic dean, the registrar, and the treasurer.

In 1964 the administrative and teaching staff consisted of 36 full-time and 20 part-time members. Distributed among the faculty were 14 doctoral, 1 professional, and 28 master's degrees. Full-time enrollment numbered 278 students; part-time, 209. The 1963 summer session registered 513. The College library housed approximately 40,000 volumes and received 260 periodicals.

Avila combines the liberal and fine arts with the professional arts. Majors are offered in fine arts, liberal arts, natural sciences, business and economics, elementary and secondary education, education of the mentally retarded, mathematics, medical record library science, nursing, speech and drama, and sociology. The College confers the B.A. degree and the B.S. degree in nursing. It offers a 2-year business certificate program. Evening and summer divisions at Avila are coeducational.

The College is accredited by the state, the Association of American Colleges, the North Central Association of Colleges and Secondary Schools, and the American Medical Association. It is affiliated with the National Catholic Educational Association, the American Council on Education, the Catholic Library Association, the American Association of Colleges for Teacher Education, and the Council on Medical Education. It also holds memberships in various national and regional educational associations including the Missouri College Union.

[M. R. ANDERSON]

AVITUS, ST., abbot of Micy; b. Auvergne, France, mid-5th century; d. Châteaudun, France, June 17, *c.* 530 (feast, June 17). He entered religious life between 485 and 490 at the abbey of Ménat near Clermont. Desiring to embrace the life of a *hermit, he left Ménat and journeyed with *Carileffus through the Loire Valley, finally settling at the abbey of *Micy. Maximinus, who had been abbot there since *c.* 508, permitted him to lead a solitary existence nearby, but when Maximinus died in 520 the monks of the community sought out Avitus and made him their abbot. *Gregory of Tours relates (MGSrerMer 1:113, 810) that the abbot pleaded unsuccessfully with King Clodimir, the son of *Clovis I, to spare the lives of *Sigismund of Burgundy and his family who had been captured in war. Avitus was buried in the church of Saint-Georges at *Orléans. His oldest biography dates from the 9th century and some modern scholars conjecture that the vita confuses two monks named Avitus, one who was abbot of Micy and the other, a monk at Ménat.

Bibliography: MGSrerMer 3:380–385. ActSS June 4:282–291. BHL 879–883. A. Poncelet, AnalBoll 24 (1905) 5–97. C. Belmon, DHGE 5:1204–05. Butler Th Attw 2:564–565.

[B. J. COMASKEY]

AVITUS OF VIENNE, ST., 5th-century bishop; b. probably Vienne, *c.* 450; d. Vienne, *c.* 519 (feast, Feb. 5). Alcimus Ecdicius Avitus succeeded his father, St. Hesychius (Isicius) in the See of Vienne (*c.* 490) and became a leader of the Gallo-Roman episcopate. Prominent at several synods, especially Epaon (517), he persuaded the Burgundian King Gundobad, though an Arian, to extend protection to the Catholic faith. Gundobad's son and successor, Sigismund, was converted by Avitus and made him his adviser in ecclesiastical matters. Avitus contended against heresy in his diocese, especially *Arianism, and was an ardent defender of the primacy of Rome. Ennodius of Pavia, Gregory of Tours, Isidore of Seville, and Fortunatus praised his charity, learning, and literary achievement. Some 80 historically valuable letters have been preserved together with 3 complete sermons and fragments of possibly 30 others, the *De spiritualis historiae gestis* (a series of 5 poems inspired by Genesis), and a poem in praise of virginity.

Bibliography: *Opera,* ed. R. Peiper (MGAuctAnt 6.2; 1883); *Oeuvres complètes,* ed. U. Chevalier (Lyon 1890). ActSS Feb. 1:666–675. Bardenhewer 5:337–345. G. Bardy, *Catholicisme* 1:1134–35. H. Leclercq, DACL 15.2:3061–63. J. H. Fischer, LexThK² 1:1154–55.

[G. M. COOK]

AVIZ, ORDER OF, Portuguese military religious order, known originally as the Order of Evora. In 1166 the fortress of Evora, in the province of Alemtejo, was taken from the Moors. Ten years later the king ceded various properties to the master and knights of Evora, *promovendis ordinem sancti Benedicti.* This is the first authentic document concerning the order. Whether it began as an independent community or as a branch of the Castilian Order of *Calatrava is debatable. Considering that properties given to the Order of Evora are listed among Calatrava's possessions in 1187, an affiliation of the two orders before that date seems certain. This is implied in *Innocent III's bull of 1201 granting the privileges of Calatrava to the knights of Evora, *professis ordinem de Calatrava.* As a result of Afonso II's donation of Aviz in 1211, the knights transferred their headquarters to that fortress. Henceforth the order was known as Aviz. The visitation of Aviz in 1238 by the master of Calatrava reveals that Aviz was affiliated to Calatrava just as Calatrava was affiliated to the Cistercian abbey of *Morimond. In 1385 the master of Aviz was elected King João I of Portugal; his dynasty came to be known as Aviz. He attempted to free the order from any dependency on Calatrava; in the 15th century the administration of the order was entrusted to royal princes. In 1551 Pope *Julius III annexed the mastership to the crown in perpetuity.

Bibliography: A. L. Javierre Mur, "La Orden de Calatrava en Portugal," BolRealAcHist 130 (1952) 323–376. M. de Oliveira, "A milicia de Évora e a Ordem de Calatrava," *Lusitania Sacra* 1 (1956) 51–67.

[J. F. O'CALLAGHAN]

AVOGADRO, AMEDEO, Italian chemist and physicist; b. Turin, Aug. 9, 1776; d. there, July 9, 1856. Avogadro was educated in the legal profession, receiving his baccalaureate degree in jurisprudence at 16 and his doctorate in ecclesiastical law at 20. After practicing law for 3 years, he turned to the study of chemistry, physics, mathematics, and philosophy. In 1809 he was appointed professor of physics at the Royal College at Vercelli. Two years later he published his famous paper, *Essay on a Way of Determining the Relative Masses of Elementary Molecules of Bodies and the Proportions*

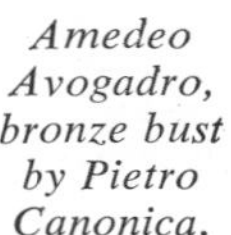

Amedeo Avogadro, bronze bust by Pietro Canonica.

in Which They Enter into These Compounds, enunciating what is now known as Avogadro's law: "Equal volumes of all gases under the same conditions of temperature and pressure contain the same number of molecules." This simple statement resolved a conflict between Dalton's atomic theory and Gay-Lussac's law of combining volumes of gases and laid the foundation for the correct understanding of atomic and molecular weights, gas behavior, and reactions between gases. No scientists commented on this paper at the time, and it was forgotten for almost 50 years. In 1860 at the Congress of Karlsruhe, Avogadro's countryman Stanislao *Cannizzaro publicized and explained its great importance.

Avogadro's theory explained the reason why gases behave uniformly with changing temperature, why they combine in simple ratios by volume (Gay-Lussac's law), and why certain elementary gases such as oxygen, hydrogen, nitrogen, and chlorine consist normally of two atoms each to the molecule instead of one as Dalton and the rest of the world had supposed. This theory was later experimentally verified by R. A. Millikan of the U.S., J. Perrin of France, and others, and the actual number of molecules in a mole of any gas was found to be 6.02×10^{23}. This is known as the Avogadro Number.

In 1820 Avogadro became the first occupant of the chair of mathematical physics at the University of Turin. Avogadro took an active part in the life of his community and held offices dealing with education, weights and measures, meteorology, and national statistics. He retired at 74 to spend the last 6 years of his life in study and meditation.

Bibliography: B. Jaffe, *Crucibles: The Lives and Achievements of Great Chemists* (New York 1934). T. M. Lowry, *Historical Introduction to Chemistry* (rev. ed. London 1936). J. R. Partington, *A Short History of Chemistry* (3d ed. London 1957). **Illustration credit:** Library of Congress.

[B. JAFFE]

AVRANCHES, COUNCIL OF, famous Church council held at the former diocesan seat of Avranches, Normandy, to confirm the peace between the Church and King *Henry II of England after the murder of Thomas *Becket. An initial meeting of Henry, papal legates, and bishops bore fruit; and on May 21, 1172, at St. Andrew's Cathedral in Avranches, Henry, in the presence of Pope *Alexander III's legates and the bishops, was solemnly reconciled with the Church, swearing innocence of the murder. He vowed to obey the Pope, to permit appeals to Rome, to make restitution, and to support the *Crusade. It was at Avranches, Sept. 27–28, that same year, that Henry convoked a council of his bishops. This council, which was attended by the papal legates, promulgated 12 disciplinary canons. It forbade granting children rights to benefices that had the care of souls; it forbade also the giving to priests' children their fathers' churches. It urged priests of large churches to take assistants; it prohibited the ordaining of a priest without a definite title or source of income; it barred married persons ordinarily from entering religion during the spouse's lifetime. The Council also commended fasting during Advent and forbade priests to participate in civil tribunals.

Bibliography: Hefele-Leclercq 5.2:1054–57. J. C. ROBERTSON, ed., *Materials for the History of Thomas Becket,* 7 v. (RollsS 67; 1875–85) 7:513–523. Mansi 22:135–140. Duchesne FÉ 2: 222–225.

[A. CONDIT]

AVRIL, PHILIPPE, Jesuit missionary; b. Angoulême, France, July 21, 1654; d. 1698. While teaching mathematics and philosophy in Paris (1684), he was assigned to find an overland route to China independent of the Portuguese. Avril went by Aleppo to Kurdistan and Armenia. Detained at Astrakhan, he turned north by the Volga to Moscow, but was expelled from Russia. After a long stay in Warsaw he returned to France by Constantinople in 1690. His *Voyages* (1692), an account of his travels, was translated into many languages, including English in 1693. A promised history of Muscovy did not appear. On his second attempt to reach the Far East he was lost at sea.

Bibliography: E. LAMALLE, DHGE 5:1251. J. BALTEAU, Dict BiogFranc 4:905. J. SEBES, *The Jesuits and the Sino-Russian Treaty of Nerchinsk, 1689* (Rome 1961).

[B. LAHIFF]

AVVAKUM, Russian archpriest and author; b. Grigorovo, Province of Nijni Novgorod, 1620; d. Pustozersk, April 24 (N.S.; April 14, O.S.), 1682. The son of a village priest, he received a wide ecclesiastical and secular education. He was involved early in a movement for church reform, and first as pastor in a small town and later as archpriest of Iourevets on the Volga, he ruled his flocks with a vigorous hand. After exile because of his reforming zeal, he went to Moscow to serve as archpriest at Notre Dame of Kazan; he was a member of the Friends of God, a group protected by Czar Alexis and his confessor Stephen. When Nikon was elected patriarch (1652) and reoriented the reform toward adopting the customs of the Greek Church, the group refused to follow him (*see* NIKON, PATRIARCH OF MOSCOW).

The conflict grew worse under the violence of Nikon. Avvakum was exiled to Siberia in 1653 as assistant to the Pashkov expedition, organized to gain control of regions along the Sakhalin River. For protesting this shameless adventure, he suffered the knout and several times narrowly escaped death. Nikon was deposed in 1662 and Avvakum was recalled to Moscow, only to be exiled again (to Mezen) for denouncing the growing abuses of the official church. He was repatriated and again exiled by the Synod of Moscow (1666) to Pustozersk on the Arctic Ocean. Though confined (1670) in an underground prison, he stayed in contact with the Old Believers throughout Russia: he was their spiritual director from afar, their consoler, and their prophet. In 1672 he wrote his *Life,* which, particularly because of its deep and pure religious inspiration, is a masterpiece of 17th-century Russian literature. Under the harsh decrees against the Old Believers passed by the council of 1682, Avvakum was burned to death in Pustozersk Square. His memory has remained sacred to the Old Believers and his works were collected and hand-copied until the end of the 19th century.

Bibliography: Collected Works. *Russkaîa istoricheskaîa biblioteka,* 39 v. (Leningrad 1927); *Zhitie protopopa Avvakuma, im samim napisannoe i drugie ego sochineniîa,* ed. N. K. GUDZIÎA (Moscow 1960). Autobiography. *The Life of the Archpriest Avvakum by Himself,* tr. J. HARRISON and H. MIRRLEES (London 1924); *La Vie de l'archiprêtre Avvakum,* tr. P. PASCAL (Paris 1961); *Vita dell'arciprete Avvakum,* tr. L. RADOYCE (Turin 1962). Literature. P. PASCAL, *Avvakum et les débuts du Raskol.* (new ed. The Hague-Paris 1964).

[P. PASCAL]

AXIOLOGY, term in modern philosophy generally used to designate theory of value. It is taken from the Greek ἄξιος, value or worth, and λόγος, study of or science of. As a general synonym for value theory, axiology was first used extensively by Paul Lapie (*Logique de la volonté,* 1902) and Eduard von *Hartmann (*Grundriss der Axiologie,* 1908). Among English speaking philosophers the term received popularization through the numerous books and articles written by Wilbur Marshall Urban, the most notable of which is *Valuation* (1909).

There is no universal agreement among philosophers that the term axiology is completely satisfactory. Those who defend its usage, such as Urban and Nicolai *Hartmann, point out that the term properly emphasizes the necessity of a metaphysical investigation into the nature and status of values as a prelude to further ethical, epistemological, and psychological studies. The term value theory is of sufficient significance in sociology, anthropology, and economics that confusions might easily be avoided if philosophy had its own term to designate its approach to problems of value. Others, such as Louis *Lavelle (*Traité des Valeurs,* 1951), judge that value theory is a more suitable term since it is not so pedantic and thus conveys immediately to all the fact that there are many ramifications of value study and value problems. The current tendency is generally to favor the usage of value theory over axiology.

In those areas where value is especially relevant, especially metaphysics and ethics, scholastic philosophers have preferred to speak in terms of *good in its various senses. Complete understanding between scholastics and other axiologists is hampered by the lack of adequate translation of their vocabularies.

See also VALUE, PHILOSOPHY OF; VALUE JUDGMENT.

Bibliography: EncFil 1:536. W. M. URBAN, "Value, Theory of," EncBrit 22 (1965) 961–963.

[R. R. KLINE]

AXIOMATIC SYSTEM

A type of deductive theory, such as those used in mathematics, of which Euclid's *Elements* is one of the early forms. Long a model for scientific theorizing, the axiomatic system has been studied intensively only since the end of the 19th century, and this in conjunction with the development of mathematical, or symbolic, logic in research on the foundations of logic and of mathematics (*see* LOGIC, SYMBOLIC). In its earlier sense the axiomatic system was considered as having a meaning content, whereas more recently it has been understood in a purely formal sense—as practically synonymous, in fact, with the formal system (*see* FORMALISM). According to H. B. Curry, the notion of formal system is more restricted than that of axiomatic system, whereas for other authors the formal system is more general since it lacks the conditions of effectiveness that should characterize the axiomatic system.

General Characterization. A scientific theory is made up of propositions that are in turn composed of terms. One can establish the validity of a *proposition by deducing it from other propositions, but it is impossible to proceed in this way to infinity. In the same manner, one can explain the sense of a *term by defining it through the use of other terms, but again it is impossible to proceed to infinity. To build a theory it is therefore necessary to start from terms that are accepted without *definition and from propositions that are considered as valid without *demonstration. To these primitive elements are then added rules of definition, with whose help it is possible to define new terms from the undefined primitive terms or from terms already defined, and rules of deduction, with whose help it is possible to obtain new propositions from the primitive propositions or from propositions already deduced. The primitive propositions are called the axioms of the theory. The propositions that can be deduced by means of the rules of deduction are said to be proved or demonstrated. The axioms and the proved propositions are the theorems of the theory.

According to the earlier view, an axiomatic system expresses a certain order of *truth. A deductive *science is based on postulates or *first principles that express self-evident truths or on propositions demonstrated by a superior science. The whole order of demonstrative knowledge is thus founded on self-evident propositions. The primitive terms are taken with their natural meaning, while the rules of deduction are those of ordinary logic and are not considered to be part of the theory.

According to the modern view, however, an axiomatic system is considered simply as expressing an order of possible deductions. The axioms are not considered to be true, but only as propositions provisionally accepted as valid. An axiomatic system is thus nothing but a hypotheticodeductive system. The undefined terms are not understood with regard to their intuitive meaning, but are understood in terms of what is asserted about them in the axioms. On the other hand, the logic that is used is explicitly incorporated into the system. This complete formalization of the deductive process is what is referred to as formal axiomatic method.

Interpretation. A formal axiomatic system must be considered as a pure system of deduction. Such a system, however, has interest only to the extent that it can be used to investigate the properties of theories having a factual content, i.e., to the extent that there are relationships between this system and "contensive statements," to use Curry's terminology. A contensive statement is a statement that pertains to some factual domain and is such that its truth or falsity can be established by appropriate methods that take account of the facts such statements concern; these may be mathematical or empirical in nature. An interpretation of an axiomatic system is a many-to-one correspondence between some propositions of the system and some contensive statements belonging to a given field. An interpretation is valid if every contensive statement corresponding to a theorem is true.

The advantage of the formal axiomatic method is that it offers the possibility of studying in a synthetic manner the properties of all theories having the same form, such as those of the different empirical domains of the physical sciences. The construction of such theories raises the problem of the choice of the appropriate axioms, which itself is related to the problem of *induction. Such theories must also be located with reference to empirical facts by way of interpretation, and this is connected with the problem of *verification.

Abstract Characterization. Curry refers to axiomatic systems as deductive theories, themselves a particular type of theory. A *theory is defined as a class of statements belonging to a certain definite class of statements that are previously postulated. (A statement must be distinguished from a sentence, which is a linguistic expression designating a statement.) A class is said to be definite if some effective process exists that makes it possible to determine whether a given object is a member of the class or not. The statements that belong to a theory are called its theorems. A theory is said to be deductive when it constitutes an inductive class of statements. An inductive class is a class whose elements are generated from certain initial elements (forming a definite class) by means of certain specified modes of combination that have an "effective character"—in the sense that some effective method exists that makes it possible to determine whether a given element has been actually produced from given elements of the class. (It should be noted that an inductive class is not necessarily definite.) The initial statements of a deductive theory form a definite class of statements; they are called the axioms of the theory. The modes of combination of a deductive theory are its rules of deduction; when applied to an appropriate number of theorems, such a rule produces a new theorem. Every construction of a theorem from given theorems by means of the rules of deduction is called a demonstration. The theorems of the deductive theory are then the statements for which demonstrations exist.

Formal System. When it is specified that the statements assert that certain formal objects have particular properties or stand in particular relation to each other, a theory is called a *system* or, more explicitly, a formal system. To describe such a system, one identifies a particular class of objects, called formal objects, and a particular class of predicates, called basic predicates. The statements of the system are formed by applying a basic predicate to an appropriate number of formal objects.

Types. There are two types of systems: syntactical systems and ob systems. In a syntactical system, the formal objects are taken as the expressions of a particular language. In an ob system, the formal objects form a monotectonic inductive class—monotectonic in the sense that, for every element, there exists only one construction that produces it. The elements of this class are called obs; its initial elements, atoms; and the modes of combination, operations.

Epitheory. When a system is constituted, it can be studied as a given object; such a study is then referred to as an epitheory. The main epitheoretical questions pertaining to an axiomatic system concern its consistency (the impossibility of deducing within the system both a proposition and its negation), its independence (the impossibility of deducing any axiom from the others), and its completeness (every proposition formulable in the terms of the system is provable or refutable, in which case its negation is provable, within the system). Also of interest is the decision problem, which is concerned with formulating an effective method that makes it possible to determine, for every proposition formulable in the terms of the system, whether the proposition is provable in the system. One of the most famous epitheoretical theorems is the incompleteness theorem of K. Gödel: in every consistent system that is sufficient to formalize ordinary arithmetic there are undecidable propositions, i.e., propositions that are neither provable nor refutable.

Bibliography: A. TARSKI, *Introduction to Logic and to the Methodology of Deductive Sciences* (New York 1941), first pub. in Polish 1936. H. B. CURRY, *Foundations of Mathematical Logic* (New York 1963). J. A. LADRIÈRE, *Les Limitations internes des formalismes* (Louvain 1957).

[J. A. LADRIÈRE]

AYALA, MANUEL JOSÉ DE, Spanish jurist; b. Panama, March 26, 1728; d. Madrid, March 8, 1805. Educated in Panama, Ayala held the post of fiscal in the ecclesiastical court and in the royal *audiencia.* In 1753 he went to Spain and, after graduating in Seville as a canon lawyer, was appointed archivist in the Secretariat of State and in the Council of the Indies (1763). His career developed in this secretariat, of which he rose to be first officer. He finally became councilor of the Indies. A driving, ambitious man, he presented many petitions to the crown, received many material benefits, and was made a knight of the Order of Charles III in 1785. Only a small part of his extensive writings has ever been published, but his *Yndice del diccionario del gobierno y legislación de Indias y España* (Madrid 1792) noted that his works consisted of "225 volumes of manuscripts up to the present." The most important are *Notas a la Recopilación de Indias,* which contains a history of each law dealing with the Indies and his recommendations for reform; the *Diccionario* mentioned above, the *Colección de cédulas y consultas,* and the *Miscelánea.* All of them formed part of his plan for the utilization and modification of legislation dealing with the Indies. His suggestions were not used by his contemporaries, but were at least responsible for his appointment to one of the committees formed in the 18th century to reform the *Recopilación de Indias* of 1680.

Bibliography: M. J. DE AYALA, *Notas a la Recopilación de Indias,* ed. J. MANZANO, 2 v. (Madrid 1945–46). J. M. OTS CAPDEQUÍ, "Don Manuel Josef de Ayala y la historia de nuestra legislación de Indias," *Hispanic American Historical Review* 3 (1920) 281–286.

[J. MALAGÓN-BARCELÓ]

AYMARD, BL., third abbot of Cluny; d. Cluny, Oct. 5, 965 (feast, Sept. 12; Oct. 5 in Benedictine calendar). He was elected between April 21 and June 13, 942, to succeed St. *Odo of Cluny, whose work in the *Cluniac Reform he continued. During his short administration the possessions of *Cluny increased considerably. In 948 Pope Agapetus II confirmed the direct dependence of Cluny and its dependencies on the Apostolic See. Because he had become blind, Aymard resigned his office in 948, having provided for the election of *Majolus of Cluny as fourth abbot. In 1063 *Peter Damian collected the oral testimony of Aymard's patience, simplicity, and humility.

Bibliography: Mabillon AS 7:316–323. M. MARRIER and A. DUCHESNE, *Bibliotheca cluniacensis* (Paris 1614; repr. Mâcon 1915). PETER DAMIAN, *Op. 33,* PL 145:570–572. A. BRUEL, *Recueil des chartes de l'abbaye de Cluny,* 6 v. (Paris 1876–1903) v.1–2. E. SACKUR, *Die Cluniacenser,* 2 v. (Halle 1892–94) *passim.* P. SCHMITZ, *Histoire de l'Ordre de Saint-Benoît,* 7 v. (Maredsous, Bel. 1942–56) 1:132–133.

[R. GRÉGOIRE]

AYMER DE LUSIGNAN, bishop of Winchester, one of King Henry III's Poitevin favorites; d. Paris, Dec. 4, 1260. He was the younger son of Isabella, widow of King John, by Hugh X, Count of La Marche, and thus a half-brother of Henry III. Aymer went to England in 1247 and studied at Oxford. In 1250 *Henry III secured his election to the bishopric of *Winchester, whose revenues he is said to have spent extravagantly. He was consecrated in Rome by Alexander IV, May 1260. On a few occasions he spoke in favor of ecclesiastical reform, as in 1253, when, ironically, he pressed the King to allow free episcopal elections. But Aymer, unlike Bishop *Walter of Cantelupe, opposed the political reform outlined in the Provisions of Oxford in 1258, and he and his brothers were forced by the barons to leave the country. The barons' document, which justified this action to the Pope was notable: it maintained that the Lusignan brothers by their irresponsibility had harmed the crown and that the *communitas* would never tolerate their return.

Bibliography: W. HUNT, DNB 1:758–760. Emden 2:1179–80. F. M. POWICKE, *King Henry III and the Lord Edward,* 2 v. (Oxford 1947). H. S. SNELLGROVE, *The Lusignans in England, 1247–1258* (Albuquerque, N.Mex. 1950).

[H. MAYR-HARTING]

AYMER DE LA CHEVALERIE, HENRIETTE, cofoundress of the *Picpus Sisters; b. at the

Henriette Aymer de la Chevalerie.

de la Chevalerie chateau in Poitou, France, Aug. 11, 1767; d. Paris, Nov. 23, 1834. She was of noble birth and was imprisoned, along with her mother, during the French Revolution for giving asylum to two priests

(1794). When released she joined a pious association of laywomen in Poitiers devoted to charitable works and perpetual adoration of the Blessed Sacrament. Abbé *Coudrin, their spiritual director, persuaded her to act as cofoundress of the Sisters of the Sacred Hearts and Perpetual Adoration. The congregation had its beginnings in Poitiers when a residence was purchased in 1797. Henriette acted as superior of a few former members of the association. The small group received local ecclesiastical approval and pronounced religious vows (1800). Papal approval came in 1817. In 1804 headquarters were moved to Rue Picpus in Paris. Henriette remained as superior general during life and saw the institute grow to 18 houses in France and its apostolate extend to the religious education of children, along with perpetual adoration.

Bibliography: *Mère Henriette and Her Work,* tr. from Fr. (St. Louis 1926). F. TROCHU, *La Servante de Dieu, Henriette Aymer de la Chevalerie* (Lyons 1950). H. CHOMON, *DictBiogFranc* 4:947–948.

[P. HERAN]

AZARA, FÉLIX DE, Spanish naturalist and geographer; b. Barbuñales, Spain, May 18, 1746; d. there, Oct. 20, 1821. He studied philosophy at the University of Huesca and later enrolled in the military academy of Barcelona. As a lieutenant he participated in and was wounded in the Argel campaign. In 1781 he received orders to embark at Lisbon for America, in order to establish the boundaries of the Spanish and Portuguese possessions according to the treaty of 1771. During his travels Azara devoted himself to the study of Paraguay, and after 13 years of work he produced his geographical chart. He undertook the classification of the fauna and wrote detailed descriptions that gave him worldwide fame. His book, *Viajes por la América Meridional,* aroused the interest of the men of the May Revolution, for they interpreted it as being critical of the government of the metropolis. He was entrusted with the development of the colonies on the frontiers of Brazil; this required him to travel very frequently. He founded the town of San Gabriel de Batoví and provided for the defense of 70 leagues of coastline. In 1801 he returned to Spain, where he was appointed a navy captain. Afterward he was reunited with his brother Nicolas, Ambassador of Spain in France. In Paris he continued his studies of natural sciences until his death. His works as an expert naturalist and geographer were numerous, and he left a large number of manuscripts.

Félix de Azara.

Bibliography: J. C. GONZÁLEZ, *Memoria histórica* (Buenos Aires 1954). F. MARQUEZ MIRANDA, "Lo que debemos a Azara desde el punto de vista de las ciencias del hombre," *Ciencia e Investigación* 2 (1946) 328–339. **Illustration credit:** Library of Congress.

[V. O. CUTOLO]

AZARIA, KING OF JUDA, *c.* 783 to *c.* 742 B.C., son and successor of *Amasia. Besides his name Azaria [Heb. *'ăzaryāh(û),* Yahweh has helped], he was known also as Ozia or Uzziah [Heb. *'uzzîyāh(û),* My strength is Yahweh]; probably the latter was his *throne name (cf. Is 1.1; 6.1; Os 1.1; Am 1.1.; etc.). The account of his reign in 4 Kgs 15.1–7 tells only of his piety and of his leprosy, on account of which his son Joatham and successor as king (*c.* 750–*c.* 735) had to act as regent for him, probably for about 8 years. The more detailed account in 2 Chr 26.1–23, however, not only ascribes his leprosy to divine retribution for his attempt to usurp the priestly function of burning incense in the Temple, but also tells of his successful wars against various neighboring peoples, his restoration of the port of Elath or *Asiongaber (Eziongeber) at the head of what is now called the Gulf of Aqaba, his building activities in Jerusalem and elsewhere, and some of his other beneficial measures, particularly in agriculture. He was a contemporary of the great *Jeroboam II of Israel (*c.* 786–*c.* 746) in a time of extraordinary prosperity for both the Northern and the Southern Kingdom. In 743 B.C. Azaria refused to pay tribute to *Tiglath-Pileser (Theglath-Phalasar) III [Pritchard

Inscription from the tomb of Azaria, King of Juda. From the language and script it can be dated from the time of the end of the Second Temple and was thus probably carved during a reinterment of the bones of the King.

ANET² 282b–283a; see W. H. Hallo, BiblArchaeol 23 (1960) 47].

Bibliography: G. STANO, EncCatt 9:490. EncDictBibl 179–180. **Illustration credit:** From *Bulletin of the American Schools of Oriental Research* 44 (1932) 9.

[B. MC GRATH]

AZAZEL, demon of the desert into whose power the *scapegoat, laden with the impurities and sins of the people, was sent on the annual Day of *Atonement (Yom Kippur). Of the two goats presented before the Meeting Tent, one was designated for Yahweh, the other "for Azazel" (Lv 16.8, 10, 26). Most modern commentators, following the Syriac and Aramaic versions of the OT and the apocryphal Book of Henoch (6.8; 8.1; 10.4–9), see in Azazel a supernatural being, i.e., a demon. An alternate view suggests that the term, at least originally, was a place name, meaning "rugged rocks, precipice" (Heb. *'zz,* Arab. *'azâzun,* "rough ground") and thus referred to the destination of the sin-laden goat; only later, with the original meaning lost, would it have taken on a personal meaning. Arguments against this latter view center on the parallelism of persons suggested by context: a goat for Yahweh, and one "for Azazel." The desert was considered the usual haunt of evil spirits (Is 34.14; Mt 12.43). A faulty translation of the Hebrew phrase "for Azazel" in the Vulgate, following the Greek Septuagint τράγος ἀποπομπαῖος (goat sent out), as *caper emissarius* or emissary goat has given rise to the English word scapegoat, i.e., escaping goat.

Bibliography: InterDictBibl 1:325–326. De Vaux AncIsr 508–509. J. G. FRAZER, *The Golden Bough,* 12 v. (3d ed. London 1911–15) 9:210. S. LYONNET, "De munere sacrificali sanguinis" with app. "De ritu capri emissarii," VerbDom 39 (1961) 18–38. G. R. DRIVER, "Three Technical Terms in the Pentateuch," JSemitSt 1 (1956) 97–98.

[R. J. FALEY]

AZEGLIO, MASSIMO TAPARELLI D', statesman, writer, painter; b. Turin, Oct. 24, 1798; d. Turin, Jan. 15, 1866. Massimo, the son of a distinguished noble family, attended the University of Turin for a time. He then spent several years in Rome where he developed his exceptional artistic talents. An unfortunate love affair caused him to leave Rome and wander aimlessly through Italy for a while. Meanwhile, he published the *Sagra di San Michele* (1829), a historical tourist guide. In 1831 he visited Milan where he married the daughter of *Manzoni, Giulia, who died in 1834. His second marriage to his aunt, Luisa Blondel, was most unhappy. In Milan he resumed painting, eventually holding exhibits at Brera and Paris.

Massimo Taparelli d'Azeglio.

In 1845, upon invitation from the liberals of the *States of the Church, he studied the political situation in the Romagna region, and published *Degli ultimi casi di Romagna* (1846). Convinced that Italy could not be united through the secret societies, he espoused the cause of a united Italy under the leadership of the House of Savoy. At the request of the papal government, he was banished from Turin and Tuscany. However, following Pius IX's election (1846), D'Azeglio returned to Rome, where he organized the Concordia, a moderate, progressive, liberal party that upheld social and political morality, and the triumph of legality. He expounded these views in *Proposta di un programma per l'opinione nazionale italiana* (1847). He protested strongly against Austrian brutality in Milan, in *I lutti di Lombardia* (1848). He was wounded fighting against Austria in 1848. After the defeat at Novara (May 1849), he acted as premier of the kingdom of Sardinia (1849–52) with dignity, strength of character, and shrewdness. Later he served as envoy to Rome, minister plenipotentiary to Paris and London, commissioner in Romagna (1859), and governor of Milan (1860). His autobiography, *I miei ricordi* (1867), has been frequently republished. Outstanding among his other works are: *Timori e Speranze* (1848) and two historical novels, *Ettore Fieramosca: Disfida di Barletta* (1833) and *Niccolo de' Lapi* (1841).

Bibliography: N. VACCALLUZZO, *Massimo D'Azeglio* (2d ed. Rome 1930). EncCatt 2:571–574. W. MATURI, DizBiogItal 4: 746–752.

[H. R. MARRARO]

AZEVEDO, IGNACIO DE, BL., missionary, martyr; b. Oporto, Portugal, 1527; martyred off the Canary Islands, July 15, 1570 (feast, July 15). Ignacio became a Jesuit in 1548, and was named rector of the College of St. Anthony in Lisbon in 1553. Eight years later he became rector of the new college established at Braga by the saintly Dominican, Archbishop Bartholomew of the Martyrs. As a superior, Ignacio was distinguished for his thoughtful concern for his subjects and his heroic service to the poor and sick of the area. His desire to serve God on the foreign missions was fulfilled in 1566 when the general, Francis Borgia, appointed him visitor of the Jesuit Missions in Brazil. Azevedo, finding the missions flourishing but severely short of manpower, received permission to return to Europe to recruit volunteers. His infectious zeal inspired 69 young Europeans to volunteer for the Brazilian mission. They sailed in two groups on June 5, 1570. The *Santiago* on which Ignatius and 39 companions embarked was captured by five Huguenot privateers commanded by Jacques Sourie, on Saturday, July 15, 1570. Though the others aboard were spared, Ignacio and 39 companions were brutally slaughtered and thrown into the sea. Pope Pius IX beatified these martyrs on May 11, 1854.

Bibliography: F. J. CORLEY and R. J. WILLMES, *Wings of Eagles: The Jesuit Saints and Blessed* (Milwaukee 1941). E. LAMALLE, EncCatt 2:575. M. G. DA COSTA, *Inácio de Azevedo* (Braga, Port. 1946).

[F. A. SMALL]

AZEVEDO, LUIZ DE, missionary in India and Ethiopia; b. Carrazzedo, Montenegro, Portugal, 1573; d. Dambea, Ethiopia, Feb. 22, 1634. After entering the Society of Jesus (1588), he spent the first years of his priesthood in India (1592–1604), where he was successively master of novices at Goa and rector of the college at Thana. In 1605 he began his fruitful labors of 28 years as a missionary in Ethiopia, particularly among the Agaus, many of whom left the schismatic Church of Ethiopia for the Catholic Church. Later, however, his converts were forced to return to schism, and his fellow missionaries were expelled from the country. Too infirm to accompany them, he remained and died in Ethiopia. To assist his fellow missionaries and to aid his converts, Azevedo prepared an Ethiopic grammar and translated into Ethiopic the New Testament, a catechism, and instructions on the Apostles' Creed. His letters were published in Lisbon (1609) and Lyons (1625).

Bibliography: Sommervogel 1:735–737. DHGE 5:1352. Hurter Nomencl 3:800.

[L. F. HARTMAN]

AZOR, JUAN, Jesuit moral theologian; b. Lorca, Spain, 1535, or more probably 1536; d. Rome, Feb. 19, 1603. Besides teaching extensively in Spain and Rome, Azor served from 1584 on the committee that drafted the *Ratio Studiorum, the program of studies for Jesuit institutions. Since the Ratio required, in addition to a course explaining the *Summa*, another course on "cases of conscience," Azor wrote his *Institutiones morales* (3 v., Rome 1600–11), a new type of moral treatise in which the basic division followed that of the Commandments, not the virtues. This was intended to supplant the smaller *Summae confessorum* and is rightly considered the forerunner of the modern manuals of moral theology.

Bibliography: J. E. DE URIARTE and M. LECINA, *Biblioteca de escritores de la Compañía de Jesús* (Madrid 1925–30) 1:394–399. E. MOORE, *La moral en el siglo XVI y primera mitad del XVII* (Granada 1956) 78–79. B. HÄRING, *The Law of Christ,* tr. E. G. KAISER, 3 v. (Westminster, Md. 1961–) 1:18–20.

[R. A. COUTURE]

AZORES, mountainous archipelago consisting of nine islands and several islets with a total land area of 890 square miles, located in the North Atlantic Ocean about 750 miles west of Portugal. Politically the three widely separated island groups form three districts of *Portugal and are an integral part of it. Portuguese is the official language. Most of the 337,000 inhabitants (1960 census) were Portuguese in origin, with marked strains of Moorish and Flemish blood. The population numbered also many English, Scottish, Irish, Negro, and mulatto immigrants. The entire population, except for 1,100, was Catholic.

The Azores were uninhabited at the time of their discovery by the Portuguese *c.* 1427. Christianity entered with Portuguese settlement a few years later. Ecclesiastical jurisdiction over the Azores, as over other Portuguese overseas territories, was given to the *Order of Christ. In 1514 the Azores became part of the newly created Diocese of Funchal in the *Madeira Islands. The Diocese of Angra do Heroísmo on Terceira Island, created in 1534 as a suffragan to Funchal, comprised and still comprises the entire archipelago. Since *c.* 1550 the see has been suffragan to *Lisbon.

In 1963 the Diocese of Angra do Heroísmo had 168 parishes, 303 secular and 10 religious priests, 81 seminarians, 24 brothers, 115 sisters, and 950 students in Catholic schools. Church-State relations were regulated by the Portuguese concordat of 1940 with the Holy See.

Bibliography: F. DE ALMEIDA, *História da Igreja em Portugal,* 4 v. (Coimbra 1910–22); "Angra do Heroismo," DHGE 3:257–258, with list of bishops to 1914. M. A. DE OLIVEIRA, *História eclesiástica de Portugal* (3d ed. Lisbon 1958). C. DERVENN, *The Azores* (London 1956). AnnPont (1964) 32.

[T. P. JOYCE]

AZOTUS (ASHDOD)

Ancient city of Palestine. The mound of ancient Ashdod lies on the Via Maris, the great maritime highway connecting Egypt with Syria and Mesopotamia, about 10 miles northeast of Ashkelon, and 2½ miles inland from the Mediterranean coast. Archeological excavations in 1962–63 supplied significant data relating to the successive cities of Ashdod. Combined with information from the Bible and other ancient sources, they yield the following general picture: there are approximately 19 strata or levels of occupation ranging from *c.* 1600 B.C. (the transition period to the Late Bronze Age) to Byzantine (*c.* A.D. 600), with some stray sherds of still earlier times (Early and Middle Bronze).

The earliest stratified remains belong to a Canaanite city of the 16th century B.C., built apparently by the Egyptians as a military and commercial center to consolidate their hold on Palestine following the expulsion of the Hyksos. Several phases of the Canaanite city have been identified, and dated by imported pottery from Greece and the islands of the Mediterranean. An interesting sidelight is provided by a commercial tablet from Ugarit (14th century B.C.) containing the oldest known reference to Ashdod, which mentions a shipment of linen from the Palestinian city.

The last Canaanite city was violently destroyed in the latter half of the 13th century B.C., and apparently not reoccupied until the Philistine settlement in the 2d quarter of the 12th century. Ashdod is mentioned ambiguously in the boundary lists of Joshua and in connection with the tribal conquests of Judges 1. A satisfactory synthesis of archeological and Biblical data has not been worked out, but the possibility of early Israelite penetration to the coastal plain must be considered. There is ample evidence of the Philistine occupation during the 12th and 11th centuries B.C., including the remains of a great fortresslike structure, which contained fine examples of characteristic decorated pottery. Ashdod figures prominently in Biblical narratives concerning the *Philistines, especially in connection with the capture of the ark of the covenant (1 Sm 5).

Ashdod's heyday coincided with the rise of the monarchy in Israel and Judah (from the 10th to the 8th centuries B.C.). Population boomed and spread out from the upper city over the slopes of the mound and into the plain, filling a lower city of perhaps 70 to 80 acres, to be added to the upper city of 17 to 18 acres, thus constituting the largest known city of Iron-Age Palestine. In this period it is mentioned in the historical books and prophecies of the OT, as well as the Assyrian records. It was overrun by *Azaria, King of Juda (2 Chr 26.6) before 750 B.C., and conquered by *Sargon II, King of Assyria (712–711 B.C.), an event mentioned in the Bible (Is 20.1) and described in detail in Assyrian inscriptions. Three fragments of a monumental cuneiform inscription were found at Ashdod in the summer of 1963, linking the site directly to Sargon II and his invasion.

During the 7th century B.C. the city was rebuilt, but on a smaller scale; it suffered another devastation, perhaps at the hands of *Nabuchodonosor (Nebuchadrezzar) at the turn of the century. It was restored during the Persian period and served as the provincial capital. Occupation levels have been much disturbed, but rich finds belonging to this period confirm the existence and importance of the city. Among them is an ostracon in the Aramaic script of the 5th century B.C.

The city flourished in the Greco-Roman period under the name Azotus. The ruins of a large public building have been uncovered, along with impressive quantities of pottery, coins, lamps, and other artifacts. Contemporary literary sources add information about the fortunes and fate of the city. Jonathan, the brother of Judas Machabee, invaded the territory of Azotus and destroyed the famous temple of Dagon (1 Sm 5–7). Later on, Alexander Jannaeus incorporated it into his kingdom. During the later Roman period it declined in importance, and by Byzantine times it had been eclipsed by its sister city on the coast, Azotus Paralius. An Arab village, preserving the ancient name (Isdud), occupied an adjacent mound until 1948.

[D. N. FREEDMAN]

AZTEC RELIGION

The Aztec Empire constituted one of the important civilizations of the New World at the time of Spanish conquest. Although the heart of the Empire was concentrated in the Valley of Mexico, its influence and control spread over a large part of Mexico. Aztec religion was a result of a mixture of its own tribal concepts of the supernatural world and that of the other cultures with which it came into contact. As a result, its mythology, world view, and religious organization were unusually complex. Of extreme importance for the continuance of daily life was the propitiation of the many gods.

One of the most important of these was Huitzilopochtli, war god and symbol of the sun. In order for life to continue, Huitzilopochtli had to be well nourished, vigorous, and healthy. Since his major source of sustenance was human blood, human sacrifice was a necessary part of religious rites and the securing of victims through warfare an important function of the Empire.

According to the Aztecs, the creation of the world was achieved in four ages ruled over by four different gods and called: (1) Four Ocelot, ruled by Tezcatlipoca; (2) Four Wind, ruled by Quetzalcoatl; (3) Four Rain, ruled by Tlaloc; and (4) Four Sun, ruled by Chalchihuitlicue. The present age, the fifth, is to be extinguished by earthquakes. The basic cosmic principle uniting the multiplicity of gods was that of duality or the opposition of male and female, darkness and light, life and death, which were personified by the struggle of Quetzalcoatl and Tezcatlipoca or by Quetzalcoatl and the Death God. The world was divided in two ways, vertically and horizontally, into areas of religious significance. The horizontal universe recognized five directions—four cardinal points and the center. The vertical world was divided into heavens and hells that had little moral significance. Each of the deities was thought to consist of four forms, each corresponding to one of the four horizontal directions and associated with a particular color.

The God Quetzalcoatl, Plumed Serpent, sculpture, carved in gray volcanic stone, from the Aztec Period (1350–1500).

The priestly order consisted of: (1) two high priests of equal rank—one was the high priest of the cult of Huitzilopochtli, the second was the high priest of the cult of Tlaloc; (2) a priest in charge of the tribal religious school for the sons of the nobility; (3) priests, junior priests, and initiates concerned with the cult of each important god. According to some, the priests had great control over the actions of ordinary people. Religious ceremonies were intimately connected with the calendar and recurred every month (20 days). These required feasts, dances and songs, individual confessions and penances, prayers, torture, and sacrifice.

Bibliography: BERNARDINO DE SAHAGUN, *General History of the Things of New Spain,* tr. from the *Nahuatl,* J. O. ANDERSON and E. DIBBLE (Santa Fé 1950). C. C. VAILLANT, *The Aztecs of Mexico* (Penguin Bks; Baltimore 1956) 168–181. A. CASO, *The Aztecs: People of the Sun* (Norman, Okla. 1958). F. HAMPL, "Mexico," König Christus 2:751–769. P. HONIGSHEIM, RGG[3] 4:923–925 with good bibliog. W. VON KRICKEBERG, "Die Religionen der Kulturvölker Mesoamerikas," *Religionen der Menschheit,* ed. C. M. SCHRÖDER (Stuttgart 1961) 7:1–89. **Illustration credit:** Courtesy, The Cleveland Museum of Art.

[J. RUBIN]